CLASSIFIED LIBRARY OF CONGRESS SUBJECT HEADINGS

Volume 2.   ALPHABETIC LIST

BOOKS IN
LIBRARY AND INFORMATION SCIENCE

A Series of Monographs and Textbooks

EDITOR
ALLEN KENT

Director, Office of Communications Programs
University of Pittsburgh
Pittsburgh, Pennsylvania

Volume 1. CLASSIFIED LIBRARY OF CONGRESS SUBJECT HEADINGS, Volume 1—CLASSIFIED LIST, edited by James G. Williams, Martha L. Manheimer, and Jay E. Daily.

Volume 2. CLASSIFIED LIBRARY OF CONGRESS SUBJECT HEADINGS, Volume 2—ALPHABETIC LIST, edited by James G. Williams, Martha L. Manheimer, and Jay E. Daily.

Volume 3. ORGANIZING NONPRINT MATERIALS by Jay E. Daily

Volume 4. COMPUTER-BASED CHEMICAL INFORMATION, edited by Edward McC. Arnett and Allen Kent.

Volume 5. STYLE MANUAL: A GUIDE FOR THE PREPARATION OF REPORTS AND DISSERTATIONS by Martha L. Manheimer.

Volume 6. THE ANATOMY OF CENSORSHIP by Jay E. Daily.

Volumes in Preparation

Volume 7. INFORMATION SCIENCE: SEARCH FOR UNITY, edited by Anthony Debons.

Volume 8. RESOURCE SHARING IN LIBRARIES, edited by Allen Kent.

Volume 9. CATALOGING AND CLASSIFICATION: A WORKBOOK by Martha L. Manheimer.

Additional volumes in preparation

CLASSIFIED LIBRARY OF CONGRESS SUBJECT HEADINGS

Volume 2
ALPHABETIC LIST

Edited by

James G. Williams

College of Librarianship
University of South Carolina
Columbia, South Carolina

Martha L. Manheimer   Jay E. Daily

Graduate School of Library
* and Information Sciences*
University of Pittsburgh
Pittsburgh, Pennsylvania

MARCEL DEKKER, INC., New York   1972

PREFACE

The purpose of this volume of *Classified Library of Congress Subject Headings* will be apparent to the cataloger who has read the three essays that appear in Volume I. There are certain features that must be explained, not for the purpose of excusing them, but rather as an indication of what further volumes are being considered. The authors have elected me to explain that we are bound by the work done at the Library of Congress in classifying subject headings, and by the errors found in the computer tape that served as the basis for all our work. Many lengthy discussions, all of them so pleasant as to encourage further work, brought to light shortcomings in our effort that we could do nothing about.

Our work is based on the computer tape provided by the Library of Congress. The basic data on the tape comprise the headings in the seventh edition and additions and changes made during the eighteen months following its publication. No attempt has been made to revise what appears on the computer tape.

We decided that we would include only the headings with class references and the *see* references to these headings, even though this omits a sizable number of subject headings found in the Library of Congress list. Inclusion of the *see* references in the alphabetic list is important because, 1) they provide additional points of access to the classified array in Volume 1; and 2) they are notoriously often as good as the legal heading, and some libraries may prefer using the *see* reference rather than the legal heading in their catalogs. To include the unclassified headings would simply reprint what can be found in the published list without in any way making them more useful than they are now. We attempted a shortcut method of suggesting classification numbers only to discover that while these would be reasonably accurate for science and technology (Classes Q and T) and to some extent for the infrequently used classification for medicine (Class R) they would be far out of line for most of the rest of the classification. To attempt classification manually would involve the gross inaccuracies of student assistants and other novices or the endless deliberation of specialists and would, in any case, delay the publication of a volume that is essential if the full advantage of a classified list is to be realized.

Second, we decided to arrange the headings in this volume in alphabetic order and to precede them with the suggested class number. The user must read down the alphabetic list and look to the left to see what the suggested classification number is. This again was a compromise. The Library of Congress may suggest several numbers for a subject heading, so that the semantic area of the classification serves to identify the headings in a way that nothing else duplicates. There seemed to be no way of showing the classification number except by placing it first, as we did not wish to bury it among other references when our whole purpose is to bring the suggested classification numbers to the prominence they deserve.

Finally, we corrected errors in the tapes when these were obvious and did not involve a methodical search and a monumental amount of proofreading. What we found in our spot-checking annoys us; but in the choice between lengthy delays and immediate usefulness we decided to settle for the latter, no matter how much it displeases us. We cannot assert that we are taking a perfect tool of subject analysis to begin with, because the list, although a marvel of editing and accuracy, still bears the marks of human fallibility. The list is not sufficient for the task of subject analysis that must be performed every day in every library, first by the cataloger and then by those who use the catalog. This volume is especially directed toward the latter group. The cataloger will find that the classified arrangement of subject headings in Volume 1 will reduce his work measurably and save him much frustration. He will find this volume especially useful in providing additional subject headings which do not occupy the same subject area of the classification as provided in the subject heading that relates most directly to the classification number chosen or is most explanatory of the subject approach to the work at hand.

The essay that follows is meant for the researcher, whether reference librarian, specialist, or student, a group that includes everyone who has occasion to use a library in which the Library of Congress classification and subject headings are employed. The cataloger is begged to excuse the explanation that may seem superfluous if his professional education has resulted in a clear understanding of subject headings and how they are listed and used. If this has been the case, he is most unusual because Dr. Manheimer and I agree that it has been all but impossible, heretofore, to teach subject headings in our courses for professional catalogers.

There is no need to reiterate the indebtedness that all the authors feel to their colleagues in the Graduate School of Library and Information Science at the University of Pittsburgh, especially to Professor Allen Kent who swiftly perceived the usefulness of what is offered here. I am especially indebted to Dr. Williams, without whose ability the programming problems of the Library of Congress computer tape could never have been solved, and to Dr. Manheimer, without whose thoroughness the development of the list would still await someone whose talent for patient effort matches her own. I am bound to say that I played what I am assured is an essential part in the production of this work. Modesty forbids me to expound on my own role, but honesty requires me to say that it doesn't seem like much.

Jay E. Daily
Pittsburgh, Pennsylvania
June 17, 1972

CONTENTS

v

CLASSIFIED LIBRARY OF CONGRESS SUBJECT HEADINGS

Volume 2.   ALPHABETIC LIST

SECTION ONE

ALPHABETIC INDEX TO
THE CLASSIFIED
LIBRARY OF CONGRESS
SUBJECT HEADINGS

INTRODUCTION

A library user accustomed to a classified catalog will find the dictionary catalog much less to his liking. The dictionary catalog contains authors, titles, and subjects in one alphabet and therefore serves as a convenient tool, especially for relatively small collections. As the collection grows, several problems develop that work against the effectiveness of this arrangement. Subject headings rely on natural language, and English is particularly unsuited to the assumptions that were made about subject analysis before a consistent theory of language had been developed. The user finds that subject headings are ambiguous and can be understood only when read in combination with the titles of the books to which they provide access. The customary arrangement of adjectives and nouns has been tampered with to such an extent that it is impossible to find a consistent pattern in the way the language has been manipulated for the purposes of a subject heading list. The increase in the number of headings inevitably makes the instances of apparently irrational choice more numerous and more frustrating. The increasing number of cards to be found with the same heading makes searching a slow and inconclusive task; and worst of all, there is no way of knowing whether the heading sought will provide the information desired or whether it is the best heading that can be used.

The great libraries in the United States would face a future incomparably bleak if the only choice available were between recataloging the library—regardless of its size—and continually increasing the annoyance of users as the collection grows. There is a middle way that can begin to solve these problems, and it is offered here in two volumes.

The first volume includes all the subject headings in classified order, arranged according to the numbers suggested by the Library of Congress. While a significant number of headings have not been supplied with classification numbers, the majority have been and in such a way as to make the unclassified headings less of a problem of omission than they might be. For one thing, many of the classified headings are followed by strings of unclassified headings that represent a distinction of terminology not reflected in the classification itself. A classified heading will lead the user to an area of the classification which does not make the distinctions established in the list of subject headings. This is particularly true of music subject headings in which the precise instrumentation of small groups such as octets is exactly defined in the subject heading list but is omitted from the classification. This serves the Library of Congress better than other libraries, and it does nothing for a library that employs another method to arrange a large collection of music scores for which the headings are meaningful. A user seeking a book on octets is not concerned with just which eight instruments comprise this kind of group.

Another feature of the Library of Congress list reduces the deficiency that unclassified headings would otherwise represent. Many of the unclassified main headings are followed by classified subdivisions, so that the subject heading including the dash is classified, while the portion without the subdivision has no classification number. This means that a user can reach the area of the classification that is of interest to him without further effort. The Library of Congress classification includes in each section provision for forms of material, such as early works. juvenile literature, and works within a certain period. Although some of these subdivisions may lead away from the classification area of the subject heading, almost all of them refer to the area where the main heading would be classified if the Library of Congress ever made the effort to classify all headings.

Not all the areas of the classification had been developed when the major work of classifying subject headings was completed. The K classification for law was published only a few years ago, and the headings that would ordinarily be found in this classification either have no suggested numbers at all or at best refer only to the most general area, K for Law. A number of subject headings that are not classified are of such highly specialized semantic distinction as to be of little interest to anyone who would not know the heading in advance. Notwithstanding this, there are many subject headings that could very easily be classified and it remains a mystery why this has not been done.

Even so, the authors felt justified in omitting from the list all those headings that have not been provided with a suggested Library of Congress classification number. This is, after all, a Classified List, and the unclassified headings do not belong in such a work if the title is to have any meaning at all. Giving all the subject headings where possible in classified order at least provides a key to the classification not hitherto available, and it provides the cataloger with a means of relating the subject heading to the classification number in a way that will make subject analysis using the Library of Congress scheme at once more useful and more rational.

Any classified list must have an index. This volume provides that and something more. As an index to the classified arrangement of subject headings, both the heading as given in the first volume and all the *see* references are included. This means that *see* references and subject headings are listed in one alphabet and that the classification numbers given by the Library of Congress are included for all these headings—both the preferred headings and the unused headings (the *see* references). Such an alphabetic list enables the user to find a reference to the classification (and the classified list) independently of the subject catalog, and to proceed directly from the terminology he employs to the classification itself and the collection. This is particularly important in those instances in which the cataloger has interfered with natural language and the grammar of English to create a heading that would escape any but the most sophisticated user of the subject heading list.

All the *see* references and the preferred headings are listed in one alphabet with the suggested classification number shown to the left. This is necessary because all the *see* references are followed by the main heading to which they refer in the list. Putting the classification number after this reference would tend to lose it when our chief purpose is to make it readily available. Many of the subject headings are provided with several classification numbers, so the Library of Congress found it necessary to include the class name to show the semantic area of the subject heading in addition to the classification number. Here again, the number would tend to be obscured by the explanation rather than revealed by the arrangement. In one alphabet, then, the user of this volume will find all the subject headings for which the Library of Congress has provided suggested classification numbers, with the semantic area of the subject heading shown in lower case italics following a slash mark (/), and all the *see* references, in capital italics, followed by the used heading to which they refer. Under ordinary circumstances, only the headings shown in Roman type will be found in the card catalog.

It must have occurred to those librarians who are familiar with the Library of Congress classification that this volume is something more than an index to the classified arrangement of subject headings. The nonprofessional user of this volume will find it an improvement over the original list on which it is based, because much of the internal mechanism of an alphabetic list has been omitted. There are no *see also* references in this volume because none are needed. The classified arrangement obviates any need for a syndetic structure, which has the general effect of clogging the list with references without making it more usable. Legal headings, those that the user will find in the card catalog, and *see* references when supplied with classification numbers arrange the headings in the order of the classification and provide a key that has so far never been supplied despite the obvious need. The *see* references do not appear in the classified arrangement, but the legal heading in Roman type is obviously the more important, for it is under this term that the cards in the catalog are arranged. No catalog card can ever take the place of a book, and the user can employ this volume as the key not only to the card catalog but also to the classification itself. This volume comes as close to being a general index to the classification as has ever been provided. It usually comes as quite a shock to the average person that the Library of Congress classification in all its multivolume complexity has been without a general index since its inception. Immroth's study* showed that this index could not be made by combining the indexes to the separate volumes, and that the subject heading list as given by the Library of Congress does not make up either for the deficiency of a general index or for the lack of relationship between the headings as shown in the classification, which may differ from those shown in the index to that area of the classification. A combined index composed of terms from the classification schedules would not supply a means of relating the subject headings to the classification without extensive and futile word games.

A general index to the Library of Congress classification has been suggested, and some small efforts have been proposed toward achieving this highly desirable feature of a classification. This volume does not complete the task, however much it remedies the situation. Only a complete reworking of the whole classification, providing subject headings where none may now be found, classifying the headings that would fill a gap, and utilizing the work so far accomplished can make up for the diffuse method that the Library of Congress classification and subject headings have imposed on those who must rely on the subject analysis of large collections.

With this index to the classified list of subject headings, the searcher who has access to the shelf-list of a library can employ it as if it were a classified catalog. Indeed, those library administrators who would like to supply a classified catalog to their patrons but can see no way of doing this without indexing the whole classification, can employ this volume as a stopgap measure infinitely superior to the unusable *Subject Headings Used in the Dictionary Catalog of the Library of Congress*. That this is not the complete answer, the authors are first not only to admit but to proclaim, but it is much closer to what is needed than anything now provided. Those libraries that do not permit the user to have access to the shelves should at once consider making the shelf-list available in some form, because that monumental tool of cataloging, in combination with this index, is equivalent to a classified catalog for any library using the Library of Congress classification. The present technological advances in printing would seem to eliminate most of the problems of turning the shelf-list into a book catalog that all the users of the library would greatly appreciate. With this index, the only reason to delay such a service other than financial is overcome.

The user of a classified catalog will find that this index provides a reasonably accurate key to the classification and that all the customary advantages of a classified catalog can be realized, granting that some flexibility guides the search. This index puts one in the right ball park, although it may not be able to get the user to home plate by direct and obvious means. Until subsequent effort and subsequent volumes —concluding with a general index to the classified list of subject headings as repre-

*Immroth John Phillip, *An Analysis of Vocabulary Control in Library of Congress Classification and Subject Headings*. Libraries Unlimited, Inc., 1970.

sented by the Library of Congress classification—can bring the method of subject analysis into conformity with what is known as the most efficient and productive procedure for both cataloger and searcher, this volume will serve quite well.

The problem for the searcher using the shelf-list as a classified catalog is in locating the area of the classification where the books he is searching for can be found. If he has a natural language key, then he can try out a term to see if its listing gives him a classification number to go to. If the term is not listed, he can try out synonyms, those broader in semantic coverage and those narrower, until he finds the part of the classification he should investigate. The numerical arrangement and shelf-listing by the Library of Congress classification provides that geographic subdivisions always follow the main subject area, except in a few instances, so that the term sought should be topical rather than the name of a place. The names of persons are generally omitted from this list except for the Library of Congress examples, any of which will provide a key to the classified arrangement. The name of a person, place, or event can be found in the dictionary catalog more readily than any other kind of subject heading.

This alphabetic list omits such puzzling features as indications of direct or indirect subdivision, scope notes, and the whole complicated structure of *see also* references. There might be some reason for including scope notes, which are in any case still available in the original list, but there are no rational explanations to be found for the designation of "indirect" with some subject headings and "direct" with others, especially when this can change, and with the understanding that only indirect subdivision is truly distinctive. Lacking this designation, any subject heading may be subdivided directly by place, so that one goes from the topic, such as "Laundries," to the place, such as "Chicago," rather than through the larger geographical areas as would be necessary for indirectly subdivided headings.

The result of omitting all these parts does not diminish, but rather increases, the usefulness of this alphabetic index. Subject headings are an imperfect product of library tradition rather than the ideal means of subject analysis. The ideal has yet to be defined, let alone found, and the fallacies that have attended much subject-heading work are still affirmed as prevailing and guiding catalogers, when in fact catalogers find this the most difficult and least rewarding part of subject cataloging. The user who has had to do extensive searching in a card catalog can appreciate the difficulties of the cataloger, however hard they may be to accept when the result is not a clear guide to the subject content of a collection but an opprobrious mishmash of terms, only a few of which seem to have been chosen with the user in mind.

Using the alphabetic listing of terms, the user can see that a pattern exists and an effort has been made to accommodate his needs; and with any imagination and effort, he can realize much more success with this volume than with other methods. Some sophisticated searchers have found that relating a subject heading to a classification number will lead them to the part of the collection that interests them. This index at least eliminates the need for guesswork and gives the user an approximation of the terminology he has in mind, whether the term is a *see* reference or a legal heading.

Each line is complete, except for "runovers" where the complete entry requires an additional line of type. There is only one alphabet, somewhat different from the al-phabetic arrangement of the original list, but nonetheless usable and as logical as the computer's mathematical approach to language will permit. A slight familiarity with the method of classification will aid the searcher, and some study both of this index and of the classification will prove most advantageous.

The authors have been guided by two principles: on the one hand they wish to preserve the great effort made for the past three-quarters of a century to provide adequate subject analysis of a vast collection in many libraries all using the same scheme, and on the other hand they wish to provide a tool that will make this scheme fully usable despite the deficiencies obvious to anyone who must employ it. An ideal system, if any could be demonstrated, would have the monumental disadvantage of requiring that all the work done to date be done over again. It is to prevent this that the authors have labored.

JAMES WILLIAMS

MARTHA MANHEIMER

JAY E. DAILY

SECTION TWO

EXPLANATORY NOTES

1. Volume 2 is an alphabetic index to Volume 1 of *The Classified List of Library of Congress Subject Headings.*

2. All the main headings with classification numbers, including those with subdivisions are listed. All the **SEE** references to main headings are listed in alphabetic order, to the right of the classification number.

3. Main headings are in Roman capital letters; subdivisions include a dash; **SEE** references are in capital italics.

4. The classification numbers are shown at the left of the list of headings.

5. A main heading may have several classification numbers. When the areas are identified by the Library of Congress, these are shown in lower case italics following a slash mark (/).

6. No attempt has been made to correct certain peculiarities of the Library of Congress list, so that not all the headings are included in this index—only those with suggested classification numbers are listed.

7. At the top of each page, the alphabetic range contained on that page is indicated; for example, Acids—Administration.

8. Each entry contains Classification number, space, heading or **SEE** reference, subdivision, if any, and then slash mark and area of classification.

TL685.3	*A-36 (FIGHTER-BOMBER PLANES)* **SEE** MUSTANG (FIGHTER PLANES)
QL737.E2	AARDVARK
QA75	ABACUS
QL430.5.H3	ABALONES
QE809.A	ABALONES, FOSSIL
HV701-1420	*ABANDONED CHILDREN* **SEE** CHILD WELFARE
HV835-847	*ABANDONED CHILDREN* **SEE** FOUNDLINGS
HV959-1420	*ABANDONED CHILDREN* **SEE** ORPHANS AND ORPHAN-ASYLUMS
HE961-971	*ABANDONMENT (MARINE INSURANCE)* **SEE** INSURANCE, MARINE
HQ805	*ABANDONMENT OF FAMILY* **SEE** DESERTION AND NON-SUPPORT / *marriage law*
TS1960-1967	*ABATTOIRS* **SEE** SLAUGHTERING AND SLAUGHTER-HOUSES / *butchering*
HD9410.9	*ABATTOIRS* **SEE** SLAUGHTERING AND SLAUGHTER-HOUSES / *inspection*
RA578.A6	*ABATTOIRS* **SEE** SLAUGHTERING AND SLAUGHTER-HOUSES / *public health*
PK9201.A2	ABAZIN LANGUAGE
DS234-8	ABBASIDS
NA4800-6113	ABBEYS / *architecture*
BX2501-2749	ABBEYS / *church history*
D-F	ABBEYS / *local history*
BX1939.A	ABBOTS (CANON LAW)
RD668	ABDOMEN — CANCER
RC280.A2	ABDOMEN — CANCER
RC944	ABDOMEN — DISEASES
RD540-547	ABDOMEN — SURGERY
RD668	ABDOMEN — TUMORS
RC280.A2	ABDOMEN — TUMORS
RD131	ABDOMEN — WOUNDS AND INJURIES
QM543	ABDOMEN / *regional anatomy*
HV6571-4	ABDUCTION
QA215	*ABELIAN EQUATIONS* **SEE** EQUATIONS, ABELIAN
QA345	*ABELIAN FUNCTIONS* **SEE** FUNCTIONS, ABELIAN
QA171	ABELIAN GROUPS
SF199.A14	ABERDEEN-ANGUS CATTLE
SF193.A14	ABERDEEN-ANGUS CATTLE
QB163	ABERRATION / *astronomy*
QC671	ABERRATION / *physics*
QC385	*ABERRATION, CHROMATIC AND SPHERICAL* **SEE** ACHROMATISM
QB85-135	*ABERRATION, CHROMATIC AND SPHERICAL* **SEE** LENSES / *astronomical instruments*
RE961-2	*ABERRATION, CHROMATIC AND SPHERICAL* **SEE** LENSES / *ophthalmology*
QC385	*ABERRATION, CHROMATIC AND SPHERICAL* **SEE** LENSES / *optics*
NK8440	*ABERRATION, CHROMATIC AND SPHERICAL* **SEE** MIRRORS / *art*
QC385	*ABERRATION, CHROMATIC AND SPHERICAL* **SEE** MIRRORS / *optics*
TP867	*ABERRATION, CHROMATIC AND SPHERICAL* **SEE** MIRRORS / *technology*
RE73	*ABERRATION, CHROMATIC AND SPHERICAL* **SEE** OPTICAL INSTRUMENTS / *examination of eye*
QC371-6	*ABERRATION, CHROMATIC AND SPHERICAL* **SEE** OPTICAL INSTRUMENTS / *optics*
DS432.A	*ABHIRAS* **SEE** AHIRS
QD341.A2	ABIETIC ACID
PL8576.N4	*ABIGAR LANGUAGE* **SEE** NUER LANGUAGE
BF431	ABILITY — TESTING
LB3061	ABILITY GROUPING IN EDUCATION
BF431	*ABILITY TESTS* **SEE** ABILITY — TESTING
HF5500	*ABILITY, EXECUTIVE* **SEE** EXECUTIVE ABILITY
QH325	*ABIOGENESIS* **SEE** LIFE — ORIGIN
QH325	*ABIOGENESIS* **SEE** SPONTANEOUS GENERATION
QH331	*ABIOSIS* **SEE** CRYPTOBIOSIS
F2230.2	ABIPONE INDIANS
PM5301	ABIPONE LANGUAGE
E99.A12	ABITIBI INDIANS
E99.A12	*ABITTIBI INDIANS* **SEE** ABITIBI INDIANS
DK34.A	*ABKHASIANS* **SEE** ABKHAZIANS
PK9201.A3	ABKHAZIAN LANGUAGE
PK9201.A2	ABKHAZIAN PHILOLOGY
PK9201.A37	ABKHAZIAN POETRY / *collections*
PK9201.A35	ABKHAZIAN POETRY / *history*
DK34.A	ABKHAZIANS

E99.A1	*ABNAKI CALENDAR* **SEE** CALENDAR, ABNAKI
E99.A13	ABNAKI INDIANS — TREATIES
E99.A13	ABNAKI INDIANS
E99.A1	*ABNAKI INDIANS-CALENDAR* **SEE** CALENDAR, ABNAKI
PM551	ABNAKI LANGUAGE
QC973	*ABNORMAL E (IONOSPHERE)* **SEE** SPORADIC E (IONOSPHERE)
QC879	*ABNORMAL E (IONOSPHERE)* **SEE** SPORADIC E (IONOSPHERE) / *exploration*
BF173	*ABNORMAL PSYCHOLOGY* **SEE** PSYCHOLOGY, PATHOLOGICAL
QL991	ABNORMALITIES (ANIMALS)
QK664	ABNORMALITIES (PLANTS)
QM691-9	*ABNORMALITIES* **SEE** DEFORMITIES / *human anatomy*
GN68-69.8	*ABNORMALITIES* **SEE** DEFORMITIES / *somatic anthropology*
QL991	*ABNORMALITIES* **SEE** MONSTERS / *animals*
GR825-830	*ABNORMALITIES* **SEE** MONSTERS / *folk-lore*
QM691-9	*ABNORMALITIES* **SEE** MONSTERS / *human anatomy*
HT851-1445	*ABOLITION OF SLAVERY* **SEE** SLAVERY
GN	*ABORIGINES* **SEE** ETHNOLOGY
JV305-317	*ABORIGINES* **SEE** NATIVE RACES / *colonization*
HV3176-7	*ABORIGINES* **SEE** NATIVE RACES / *protection*
DS485.A86	ABORS
SF871	ABORTION IN ANIMALS
HQ767	ABORTION
RA1067	ABORTION / *medical jurisprudence*
RG734	ABORTION / *obstetrical operations*
RG648	ABORTION / *obstetrics*
DC226.N5	*ABOUKIR, BATTLE OF, 1798* **SEE** NILE, BATTLE OF THE, 1798
DC226.A3	*ABOUKIR, BATTLE OF, 1801* **SEE** ALEXANDRIA, BATTLE OF, 1801
TJ1296	ABRASIVES / *mechanical engineering*
TN936	ABRASIVES / *mineral resources*
PN6013.5	*ABRIDGED BOOKS* **SEE** BOOKS, CONDENSED
E99.C92	*ABSAHROKEE INDIANS* **SEE** CROW INDIANS
E99.C92	*ABSAROKA INDIANS* **SEE** CROW INDIANS
RD641	ABSCESS
QK763	ABSCISSION (BOTANY)
BX1939	ABSENCE AND PRESUMPTION OF DEATH (CANON LAW)
LC142-5	*ABSENCE FROM SCHOOL* **SEE** SCHOOL ATTENDANCE / *limitation*
LB3081	*ABSENCE FROM SCHOOL* **SEE** SCHOOL ATTENDANCE / *truancy*
RZ400-406	*ABSENT TREATMENT* **SEE** MENTAL HEALING
JF1033	*ABSENT VOTING* **SEE** VOTING, ABSENT
JF1033	*ABSENTEE VOTING* **SEE** VOTING, ABSENT
HD5115	ABSENTEEISM (LABOR)
QA433	*ABSOLUTE DIFFERENTIAL CALCULUS* **SEE** CALCULUS OF TENSORS
JC571-609	*ABSOLUTE RIGHTS* **SEE** NATURAL LAW
BD416	ABSOLUTE, THE
BX1939.A	ABSOLUTION (CANON LAW)
JC375-392	*ABSOLUTISM* **SEE** DESPOTISM
QC331-8	*ABSORPTION (HEAT)* **SEE** HEAT — RADIATION AND ABSORPTION
QP88	ABSORPTION (PHYSIOLOGY)
S594	*ABSORPTION IN SOILS* **SEE** SOIL ABSORPTION
QC182	*ABSORPTION OF GASES* **SEE** GASES — ABSORPTION AND ADSORPTION
QC437	ABSORPTION OF LIGHT
QC233	ABSORPTION OF SOUND
QC437	ABSORPTION SPECTRA
QB531	*ABSORPTION, ATMOSPHERIC* **SEE** SOLAR RADIATION / *astronomy*
QC911	*ABSORPTION, ATMOSPHERIC* **SEE** SOLAR RADIATION / *meteorology*
RM226-8	*ABSTINENCE* **SEE** FASTING
BV5055	*ABSTINENCE* **SEE** FASTING / *asceticism*
HV5001-5720	*ABSTINENCE* **SEE** TEMPERANCE
QA266	*ABSTRACT ALGEBRA* **SEE** ALGEBRA, ABSTRACT
N6490	*ABSTRACT ART* **SEE** ART, ABSTRACT
QA613	*ABSTRACT METRICS* **SEE** DISTANCE GEOMETRY
N6490	*ABSTRACT PAINTINGS* **SEE** ART, ABSTRACT
PE1477	*ABSTRACT WRITING* **SEE** PRECIS WRITING / *english language*
JN435.P7	*ABSTRACT WRITING* **SEE** PRECIS WRITING / *gt. brit.*

JK717	*ABSTRACT WRITING* **SEE** PRECIS WRITING / *u.s.*
DC226.A3	*ABUKIR, BATTLE OF, 1801* **SEE** ALEXANDRIA, BATTLE OF, 1801
PR1111.I65	*ABUSE* **SEE** INVECTIVE / *english literature*
JC375-392	*ABUSE OF POWER* **SEE** DESPOTISM
BX140-149	*ABYSSINIAN CHURCH* **SEE** ETHIOPIC CHURCH
DT387.3	*ABYSSINO-ITALIAN WAR, 1895-1896* **SEE** ITALO-ETHIOPIAN WAR, 1895-1896
TP978	*ACACIA (GUM)* **SEE** GUM ARABIC
LB2389	ACADEMIC COSTUME
LB2381-2391	*ACADEMIC DECORATIONS OF HONOR* **SEE** DECORATIONS OF HONOR, ACADEMIC
LB2381-2391	*ACADEMIC DEGREES* **SEE** DEGREES, ACADEMIC
LB2369	*ACADEMIC DISSERTATIONS* **SEE** DISSERTATIONS, ACADEMIC / *preparation*
LB2389	*ACADEMIC DRESS* **SEE** ACADEMIC COSTUME
LB2332	*ACADEMIC FREEDOM* **SEE** TEACHING, FREEDOM OF
LC148	*ACADEMIC PROBATION* **SEE** COLLEGE ATTENDANCE
AS	*ACADEMIES (LEARNED SOCIETIES)* **SEE** LEARNED INSTITUTIONS AND SOCIETIES
AS	*ACADEMIES (LEARNED SOCIETIES)* **SEE** SOCIETIES / *academies and learned societies*
HS	*ACADEMIES (LEARNED SOCIETIES)* **SEE** SOCIETIES / *etc.*
E99.J	*ACAGCHEMIN INDIANS* **SEE** JUANENO INDIANS
QL391.A2	ACANTHOCEPHALA
QL458.A2	*ACARI* **SEE** MITES
QL458.A2	*ACARIDA* **SEE** MITES
QL458.A2	*ACARIDEA* **SEE** MITES
QL458.A2	*ACARINA* **SEE** MITES
F1219	ACAXEE INDIANS
DS72	*ACCADIANS (SUMERIANS)* **SEE** SUMERIANS
PM5308	ACCAWAI LANGUAGE
RC685.W6	*ACCELERATED CONDUCTION* **SEE** WOLFF-PARKINSON-WHITE SYNDROME
LB1050.5	*ACCELERATED READING* **SEE** DEVELOPMENTAL READING
LB1050.5	*ACCELERATED READING* **SEE** RAPID READING
QC786	*ACCELERATORS, ELECTRON* **SEE** PARTICLE ACCELERATORS
TL589.2.A3	ACCELEROMETERS
VM880-881	*ACCEPTANCE TRIALS OF SHIPS* **SEE** SHIP TRIALS
Z711	*ACCESS TO BOOKS IN LIBRARIES* **SEE** OPEN AND CLOSED SHELVES
TT560	*ACCESSORIES (DRESS)* **SEE** DRESS ACCESSORIES
HG9301-9343	*ACCIDENT INSURANCE* **SEE** INSURANCE, ACCIDENT
HD7101-2	*ACCIDENT INSURANCE* **SEE** INSURANCE, ACCIDENT / *industrial*
HV675-7	*ACCIDENT PREVENTION* **SEE** ACCIDENTS — PREVENTION
HV675-7	ACCIDENTS — PREVENTION
TL553.5	*ACCIDENTS, AIRCRAFT* **SEE** AERONAUTICS — ACCIDENTS
TX150	*ACCIDENTS, HOME* **SEE** HOME ACCIDENTS
LB3407	*ACCIDENTS, SCHOOL* **SEE** SCHOOL ACCIDENTS
HE5614	*ACCIDENTS, TRAFFIC* **SEE** TRAFFIC ACCIDENTS
QK913	ACCLIMATIZATION (PLANTS)
SB109	ACCLIMATIZATION (PLANTS)
QH543	ACCLIMATIZATION
SF87	ACCLIMATIZATION / *animal industry*
MT239	*ACCOMPANIMENT, MUSICAL* **SEE** MUSICAL ACCOMPANIMENT / *etc.*
MT68	*ACCOMPANIMENT, MUSICAL* **SEE** MUSICAL ACCOMPANIMENT / *instruction*
MT190	*ACCOMPANIMENT, MUSICAL* **SEE** MUSICAL ACCOMPANIMENT / *organ*
BX1939.A25	ACCOMPLICES (CANON LAW)
ML990.A4	*ACCORDEON* **SEE** ACCORDION / *history and construction*
ML990.A4	ACCORDION — CONSTRUCTION
MT680	ACCORDION — INSTRUCTION AND STUDY
M298	ACCORDION AND GUITAR MUSIC
M284.A3	ACCORDION AND PIANO MUSIC
M285.A3	ACCORDION AND PIANO MUSIC
MT680	ACCORDION MUSIC — TEACHING PIECES
M175.A4	ACCORDION MUSIC (JAZZ)
M175.A4	ACCORDION MUSIC
M1039.4.A3	ACCORDION WITH ORCHESTRA
M1360	ACCORDION WITH PLECTRAL ENSEMBLE
M1105-6	ACCORDION WITH STRING ORCHESTRA
ML990.A4	ACCORDION / *history and construction*
MT680	*ACCORDION-SELF-INSTRUCTION* **SEE** ACCORDION — METHODS — — SELF-INSTRUCTION
MT801.A3	ACCORDION — METHODS — — JUVENILE
MT680	ACCORDION — METHODS — — SELF-INSTRUCTION
HF5371	*ACCOUNTING -FORMS, BLANKS, ETC.* **SEE** BUSINESS — FORMS, BLANKS, ETC.
HF5629	ACCOUNTING AS A PROFESSION
HF5688	ACCOUNTING MACHINES / *machines*
TK4100-4101	ACCOUNTING MACHINES / *manufacture*
HF5629	ACCOUNTING MACHINES / *use*
HF5601-5689	ACCOUNTING
HF5679	*ACCOUNTING-MACHINE METHODS* **SEE** MACHINE ACCOUNTING
HF5568	*ACCOUNTS RECEIVABLE FINANCE COMPANIES* **SEE** INSTALMENT PLAN
HF5681.A3	ACCOUNTS RECEIVABLE
HF5556-9	*ACCOUNTS, COLLECTING OF* **SEE** COLLECTING OF ACCOUNTS
PL8191	*ACCRA LANGUAGE* **SEE** GA LANGUAGE
RA971	*ACCREDITATION OF HOSPITALS* **SEE** HOSPITALS — ACCREDITATION
RA971	*ACCREDITING OF HOSPITALS* **SEE** HOSPITALS — ACCREDITATION
HJ4653.U46	*ACCUMULATED EARNINGS TAX* **SEE** UNDISTRIBUTED PROFITS TAX / *u.s.*
QC605	*ACCUMULATORS* **SEE** STORAGE BATTERIES
TL272	*ACCUMULATORS* **SEE** STORAGE BATTERIES / *automobile*
TK2891	*ACCUMULATORS* **SEE** STORAGE BATTERIES / *central stations*
TK5378	*ACCUMULATORS* **SEE** STORAGE BATTERIES / *telegraph*
TK6278	*ACCUMULATORS* **SEE** STORAGE BATTERIES / *telephone*
QL430.6-7	*ACEPHALA* **SEE** LAMELLIBRANCHIATA
QD341.A8	ACETANILID / *chemistry*
RM666.A2	ACETANILID / *therapeutics*
TS1688	*ACETATE SILK* **SEE** RAYON
TP248.A18	ACETIC ACID / *chemical technology*
QD305.A2	ACETIC ACID / *chemistry*
QD305.K2	ACETONE
RB145	ACETONEMIA
RJ416.A	ACETONEMIA / *diseases of children*
TP951	*ACETYLENE BLACK* **SEE** CARBON-BLACK
QD305.H8	ACETYLENE COMPOUNDS
TP769	ACETYLENE GENERATORS
TP765-770	ACETYLENE / *chemical technology*
QD305.H8	ACETYLENE / *chemistry*
DF236-7	ACHAEAN LEAGUE
DF135	ACHAEANS
DF236-7	*ACHAIAN LEAGUE* **SEE** ACHAEAN LEAGUE
E99.S65	*ACHAOTINNE INDIANS* **SEE** SLAVE INDIANS
E99.S65	*ACHEOTENNE INDIANS* **SEE** SLAVE INDIANS
E99.S65	*ACHETOETINNE INDIANS* **SEE** SLAVE INDIANS
LB1065	ACHIEVEMENT MOTIVATION
CR41.A	ACHIEVEMENTS (HERALDRY)
QM141	*ACHILLES, TENDON OF* **SEE** TENDON OF ACHILLES
PL5191-4	ACHINESE LANGUAGE
PL8041	*ACHOLI LANGUAGE* **SEE** ACOLI LANGUAGE
E99.A15	ACHOMAWI INDIANS
PM561	ACHOMAWI LANGUAGE
QC385	ACHROMATISM
RM640.P5	*ACID PROTEINASE* **SEE** PEPSIN
S593.5	*ACIDITY OF SOILS* **SEE** SOIL ACIDITY
RB147	ACIDOSIS
QP905-917	ACIDS — PHYSIOLOGICAL EFFECT
TP213	ACIDS / *technology*
QD305.A2	ACIDS, FATTY
QD167	ACIDS, INORGANIC / *chemistry*
TP213-217	ACIDS, INORGANIC / *technology*
QD305.A2	ACIDS, ORGANIC / *chemistry*
QD341.A2	ACIDS, ORGANIC / *chemistry*
TP247.2	ACIDS, ORGANIC / *technology*
F347.A25	ACKIA, BATTLE OF, 1736
RL131	ACNE
F1221.T	*ACOLHUA INDIANS* **SEE** TEZCUCAN INDIANS
PL8041	ACOLI LANGUAGE
BX1972	*ACOLYTES* **SEE** ALTAR BOYS / *catholic church*
E99.A16	ACOMA INDIANS

RS165.A   ACONITE / pharmacy
RM666.A   ACONITE / therapeutics
PL8041   ACOOLI LANGUAGE SEE ACOLI LANGUAGE
TA365   ACOUSTIC ENGINEERING SEE ACOUSTICAL
                 ENGINEERING
NA2800   ACOUSTIC VASES SEE VASES, ACOUSTIC
TA365   ACOUSTICAL ENGINEERING
NA2800   ACOUSTICS SEE ARCHITECTURAL ACOUSTICS
GN275   ACOUSTICS SEE HEARING / anthropology
QP461-9   ACOUSTICS SEE HEARING / physiology
BF251   ACOUSTICS SEE HEARING / psychology
ML3805-3817   ACOUSTICS SEE MUSIC — ACOUSTICS AND PHYSICS
QC220-246   ACOUSTICS SEE SOUND
QC225   ACOUSTICS SEE UNDERWATER ACOUSTICS
JX4088   ACQUISITION OF TERRITORY
PL8191   ACRA LANGUAGE SEE GA LANGUAGE
DC226.A   ACRE, ISRAEL — SIEGE, 1799
GV551-3   ACROBATICS SEE ACROBATS AND ACROBATISM
GV551-3   ACROBATS AND ACROBATISM
QK505-635   ACROGENS SEE CRYPTOGAMS
QK520-532   ACROGENS SEE FERNS
SB429   ACROGENS SEE FERNS / culture
QK534-549   ACROGENS SEE MOSSES
PN6369-6377   ACROSTICS
M1510-1518   ACT-TUNE SEE ENTR'ACTE MUSIC
ML2000   ACT-TUNE SEE ENTR'ACTE MUSIC / history
GT500-2370   ACTING-COSTUME SEE COSTUME / manners and
                 customs
PN2068   ACTING-MAKE-UP SEE MAKE-UP, THEATRICAL
QL377.C7   ACTINIARIA SEE SEA-ANEMONES
QD172.A3   ACTINIDE ELEMENTS
QD172.A3   ACTINIDE SERIES SEE ACTINIDE ELEMENTS
QD172.A3   ACTINIDES SEE ACTINIDE ELEMENTS
QC912   ACTINOMETER
RC120   ACTINOMYCOSIS / practice of medicine
SF784   ACTINOMYCOSIS / veterinary medicine
RM835-844   ACTINOTHERAPY SEE PHOTOTHERAPY
QL377.C5-7   ACTINOZOA SEE ANTHOZOA
NC785   ACTION IN ART
M1993   ACTION SONGS SEE GAMES WITH MUSIC
BX2348   ACTION, CATHOLIC SEE CATHOLIC ACTION
DG269   ACTIUM, BATTLE OF, 31 B.C.
LB3605   ACTIVITIES, STUDENT SEE STUDENT ACTIVITIES
QD501   ACTIVITY COEFFICIENTS / chemistry
QD561   ACTIVITY COEFFICIENTS / electrochemistry
QD541-3   ACTIVITY COEFFICIENTS / solution
LB1027   ACTIVITY PROGRAMS IN EDUCATION
LB1027   ACTIVITY SCHOOLS SEE ACTIVITY PROGRAMS IN
                 EDUCATION
QD501   ACTIVITY THEORY SEE ACTIVITY COEFFICIENTS
                 / chemistry
QD561   ACTIVITY THEORY SEE ACTIVITY COEFFICIENTS
                 / electrochemistry
QD541-3   ACTIVITY THEORY SEE ACTIVITY COEFFICIENTS
                 / solution
PN2042-5   ACTORS — LEGAL STATUS, LAWS, ETC.
PN2205-2217   ACTORS
PN2286   ACTORS, NEGRO SEE NEGRO ACTORS / u.s.
PN2056   ACTORS, PROFESSIONAL ETHICS FOR
PN2056   ACTORS' ETHICS SEE ACTORS, PROFESSIONAL
                 ETHICS FOR
PN2205-2217   ACTORS-BIOGRAPHY SEE ACTORS
PN2205-2217   ACTRESSES
PN2205-2217   ACTRESSES-BIOGRAPHY SEE ACTRESSES
BV4618   ACTS, HUMAN SEE HUMAN ACTS
HG8781-2   ACTUARIAL SCIENCE SEE INSURANCE —
                 MATHEMATICS
HG8781-8793   ACTUARIAL SCIENCE SEE INSURANCE, LIFE —
                 MATHEMATICS
HG8751-9200   ACTUARIAL SCIENCE SEE INSURANCE, LIFE
QL568.F7   ACULEATA SEE ANTS
SF521-538   ACULEATA SEE BEES / beekeeping
QL568.A6   ACULEATA SEE BEES / entomology
QL568.V5   ACULEATA SEE WASPS
RM184   ACUPUNCTURE
HJ6603-7380   AD VALOREM TARIFF SEE TARIFF
                 / administration
HF1761-2580   AD VALOREM TARIFF SEE TARIFF / other countries
HJ6041-6464   AD VALOREM TARIFF SEE TARIFF / schedules
HF1701-2701   AD VALOREM TARIFF SEE TARIFF / theory and history

HF1750-1759   AD VALOREM TARIFF SEE TARIFF / u.s.
PN6299-6308   ADAGES SEE MAXIMS
PN6400-6525   ADAGES SEE PROVERBS
PJ2421   ADAIEL LANGUAGE SEE AFAR LANGUAGE
DS51.A2   ADANA, TURKEY (CITY) — MASSACRE, 1909
BF335   ADAPTABILITY (PSYCHOLOGY)
QH546   ADAPTATION (BIOLOGY)
QK915-924   ADAPTATION (BIOLOGY) / plants
PN1997.85   ADAPTATIONS, FILM SEE FILM ADAPTATIONS
PJ9293   ADARI LANGUAGE SEE HARARI LANGUAGE
HF5688-9   ADDING-MACHINES SEE CALCULATING-MACHINES
                 / bookkeeping
QA75   ADDING-MACHINES SEE CALCULATING-MACHINES
                 / mechanical devices
RC659   ADDISON'S DISEASE — PSYCHOSOMATIC ASPECTS
RC659   ADDISON'S DISEASE
QA115   ADDITION
TX553.A3   ADDITIVE COMPOUNDS SEE FOOD ADDITIVES
TX553.A3   ADDITIVES, FOOD SEE FOOD ADDITIVES
CR3499-4420   ADDRESS, FORMS OF SEE FORMS OF ADDRESS
CR3499-4420   ADDRESS, TITLES OF SEE FORMS OF ADDRESS
CR3499-4420   ADDRESS, TITLES OF SEE TITLES OF HONOR AND
                 NOBILITY
BV4255   ADDRESSES SEE BACCALAUREATE ADDRESSES
PN4193.L4   ADDRESSES SEE LECTURES AND LECTURING
LC6501-6560   ADDRESSES SEE LECTURES AND LECTURING
                 / lyceum and lecture courses
PN6121-9   ADDRESSES SEE ORATIONS / collections
PN4012-4061   ADDRESSES SEE ORATIONS / history and criticism
PS660-668   ADDRESSES SEE SPEECHES, ADDRESSES, ETC.
                 / american
PR1321-9   ADDRESSES SEE SPEECHES, ADDRESSES, ETC.
                 / english
PN6121-9   ADDRESSES SEE SPEECHES, ADDRESSES, ETC.
                 / general collections
PN4199-4355   ADDRESSES SEE SPEECHES, ADDRESSES, ETC.
                 / general collections
BT1417   ADELPHIANS SEE MESSALIANS
RG301   ADENOMYOSIS SEE ENDOMETRIOSIS
QC183   ADHESION
TP967-970   ADHESIVES
BT32   ADIAPHORA
PK9201.A4   ADIGHE LANGUAGE SEE ADYGHE LANGUAGE
QM565   ADIPOSE TISSUES
DS485.A86   ADIS SEE ABORS
PL8091   ADIYAH LANGUAGE SEE BUBE LANGUAGE
P273   ADJECTIVE SEE GRAMMAR, COMPARATIVE AND
                 GENERAL — ADJECTIVE
P273   ADJECTIVE SEE GRAMMAR, COMPARATIVE AND
                 GENERAL — ADJECTIVE
HG9323.A3   ADJUSTMENT OF CLAIMS SEE INSURANCE,
                 ACCIDENT — ADJUSTMENT OF CLAIMS
HG9721-7   ADJUSTMENT OF CLAIMS SEE INSURANCE, FIRE —
                 ADJUSTMENT OF CLAIMS
JF1571   ADMINISTRATION SEE ADMINISTRATIVE LAW
JK-JQ   ADMINISTRATION SEE ADMINISTRATIVE LAW / by
                 country
JF1321-1671   ADMINISTRATION SEE CIVIL SERVICE
JV443-5   ADMINISTRATION SEE CIVIL SERVICE / colonial
JS148-163   ADMINISTRATION SEE CIVIL SERVICE / municipal
JN-JQ   ADMINISTRATION SEE CIVIL SERVICE / other
                 countries
HD8011-8023   ADMINISTRATION SEE CIVIL SERVICE / state labor
JK631-901   ADMINISTRATION SEE CIVIL SERVICE / u.s.
HD31-37   ADMINISTRATION SEE MANAGEMENT
B65   ADMINISTRATION SEE POLITICAL SCIENCE / j
                 political science and philosophy
HM33   ADMINISTRATION SEE POLITICAL SCIENCE
                 / political science and sociology
JC   ADMINISTRATION SEE STATE, THE
JK-JQ   ADMINISTRATION OF JUSTICE SEE JUSTICE,
                 ADMINISTRATION OF / by country
JF701-721   ADMINISTRATION OF JUSTICE SEE JUSTICE,
                 ADMINISTRATION OF / departments general
S484   ADMINISTRATION, AGRICULTURAL SEE
                 AGRICULTURAL ADMINISTRATION
HF5500   ADMINISTRATIVE ABILITY SEE EXECUTIVE ABILITY
JF1571   ADMINISTRATIVE LAW
JK-JQ   ADMINISTRATIVE LAW / by country

JF1621	ADMINISTRATIVE RESPONSIBILITY
BX1939.A3	ADMINISTRATORS APOSTOLIC
HJ5797	*ADMISSIONS, TAXATION OF* **SEE** AMUSEMENTS — TAXATION
HQ35	ADOLESCENCE
LB1135	ADOLESCENCE */ child study*
RJ550	ADOLESCENCE */ diseases*
GN63	ADOLESCENCE */ somatology*
HS417.A3	*ADONHIRAMITE MASONRY* **SEE** FREEMASONS, ADONHIRAMITE
BT1320	*ADOPTIANISM* **SEE** ADOPTIONISM
HV875	ADOPTION
BT1320	ADOPTIONISM
PL8045	*ADOUMA LANGUAGE* **SEE** ADUMA LANGUAGE
QP951	ADRENALIN */ physiological effect*
RM292	ADRENALIN */ therapeutics*
DF559	ADRIANOPLE, BATTLE OF, 378
QC182	*ADSORPTION OF GASES* **SEE** GASES — ABSORPTION AND ADSORPTION
LC5201-6660	*ADULT EDUCATION* **SEE** EDUCATION OF ADULTS
HQ806-8	ADULTERY
BF724.5	ADULTHOOD
PL8045	ADUMA LANGUAGE
B132.A3	ADVAITA
U190-195	*ADVANCE GUARDS* **SEE** GUARD DUTY
BV40	ADVENT SERMONS
BX6101-6193	ADVENTISTS
G525-530	ADVENTURE AND ADVENTURERS
F2936	ADVENTURE AND BEAGLE EXPEDITION, 1826-1830
G525-530	*ADVENTURERS* **SEE** ADVENTURE AND ADVENTURERS
NC997	*ADVERTISING ART* **SEE** COMMERCIAL ART
HF5851	ADVERTISING CARDS
TT360	ADVERTISING CARDS */ card and sign writing*
HF5817-5819	ADVERTISING LAWS
TR690	*ADVERTISING PHOTOGRAPHY* **SEE** PHOTOGRAPHY, ADVERTISING
HF5801-6191	ADVERTISING
NC997	*ADVERTISING, ART IN* **SEE** COMMERCIAL ART
HF5839	*ADVERTISING, COLOR IN* **SEE** COLOR IN ADVERTISING
HF5801-6191	*ADVERTISING, CONSUMER* **SEE** ADVERTISING
TR690	*ADVERTISING, PHOTOGRAPHY IN* **SEE** PHOTOGRAPHY, ADVERTISING
NC997	*ADVERTISING, PICTORIAL* **SEE** COMMERCIAL ART
NC1800-1850	*ADVERTISING, PICTORIAL* **SEE** POSTERS
HF5843	*ADVERTISING, PICTORIAL* **SEE** POSTERS */ advertising*
HF6146.P75	*ADVERTISING, PRIZE CONTESTS IN* **SEE** PRIZE CONTESTS IN ADVERTISING
HF6146.R3	*ADVERTISING, RADIO* **SEE** RADIO ADVERTISING
HF5801-6191	*ADVERTISING, RETAIL* **SEE** ADVERTISING
HF5851	*ADVERTISING, TRANSPORTATION* **SEE** ADVERTISING CARDS
TT360	*ADVERTISING, TRANSPORTATION* **SEE** ADVERTISING CARDS */ card and sign writing*
HF5817-5819	*ADVERTISING-LAW* **SEE** ADVERTISING LAWS
HF5801-6191	*ADVERTISING-RETAIL TRADE* **SEE** ADVERTISING
LC220	*ADVISORY COMMITTEES IN EDUCATION* **SEE** CITIZENS' ADVISORY COMMITTEES IN EDUCATION
PK9201.A4	ADYGHE LANGUAGE
BV168.A	ADZES (IN RELIGION, FOLK-LORE, ETC.)
GN447.A3	ADZES */ anthropology*
TS5618	ADZES */ carpenter's tools*
ML1005-6	AEOLIAN HARP
ML1050-1055	*AEOLIAN PIPE-ORGAN* **SEE** PLAYER-ORGAN
MT150	*AEOLIAN PIPE-ORGAN* **SEE** PLAYER-ORGAN */ analytical guides*
MT700	*AEOLIAN PIPE-ORGAN* **SEE** PLAYER-ORGAN */ instruction*
ML1055.A3	AEOLIAN-VOCALION
BX1759.5.P	*AEQUIPROBABILISM* **SEE** PROBABILISM
TD458	*AERATION OF WATER* **SEE** WATER — AERATION
UF767	*AERIAL BOMBS* **SEE** PROJECTILES, AERIAL
G142	*AERIAL GEOGRAPHY* **SEE** GEOGRAPHY, AERIAL
JX5771	*AERIAL LAW* **SEE** AERONAUTICS — LAWS AND REGULATIONS */ international law*
HE9915-9925	*AERIAL LAW* **SEE** AERONAUTICS — LAWS AND REGULATIONS */ transportation and communication*
TL586-9	*AERIAL NAVIGATION* **SEE** NAVIGATION (AERONAUTICS)

UG630-670	*AERIAL OBSERVATION* **SEE** AERONAUTICS, MILITARY — OBSERVATIONS
TA593	AERIAL PHOTOGRAMMETRY
UG476	*AERIAL PHOTOGRAPH READING* **SEE** PHOTOGRAPHIC INTERPRETATION (MILITARY SCIENCE)
TA593	*AERIAL PHOTOGRAPHIC SURVEYING* **SEE** AERIAL PHOTOGRAMMETRY
TR810	*AERIAL PHOTOGRAPHY* **SEE** PHOTOGRAPHY, AERIAL
UF767	*AERIAL PROJECTILES* **SEE** PROJECTILES, AERIAL
TL705-8	*AERIAL PROPELLERS* **SEE** PROPELLERS, AERIAL
TF692	*AERIAL RAILROADS* **SEE** RAILROADS, ATMOSPHERIC
UG630-670	*AERIAL RECONNAISSANCE* **SEE** AERONAUTICS, MILITARY — OBSERVATIONS
UF767	*AERIAL ROCKETS* **SEE** PROJECTILES, AERIAL
TL780-783	*AERIAL ROCKETS* **SEE** ROCKETS (AERONAUTICS)
UF767	*AERIAL ROCKETS* **SEE** ROCKETS (ORDNANCE)
RA640	*AERIAL SPRAYING* **SEE** AERONAUTICS IN MOSQUITO CONTROL
UG630	*AERIAL STRATEGY* **SEE** AIR WARFARE
UG630	*AERIAL TACTICS* **SEE** AIR WARFARE
UG630	*AERIAL WARFARE* **SEE** AIR WARFARE
TL711.S8	*AEROBATIC FLYING* **SEE** STUNT FLYING
TL711.S8	*AEROBATICS* **SEE** STUNT FLYING
TL725-6	*AERODROMES* **SEE** AIRPORTS
TL574.C6	*AERODYNAMIC CONTROL OF AEROPLANES* **SEE** AEROPLANES — CONTROL SURFACES */ theory*
TL676	*AERODYNAMIC CONTROL OF AEROPLANES* **SEE** AEROPLANES — CONTROL SURFACES */ technology*
TL574.P7	*AERODYNAMIC FORCES* **SEE** AERODYNAMIC LOAD
TL574.P7	AERODYNAMIC LOAD
TL573	AERODYNAMIC MEASUREMENTS
TL566-8	*AERODYNAMICAL LABORATORIES* **SEE** AERONAUTICAL LABORATORIES
TL571.5	*AERODYNAMICS OF HYPERSONIC FLIGHT* **SEE** AERODYNAMICS, HYPERSONIC
TL570-574	AERODYNAMICS
QA930	AERODYNAMICS
TL571.5	AERODYNAMICS, HYPERSONIC
QA930	*AERODYNAMICS, SUBSONIC* **SEE** AERODYNAMICS
TL570-574	*AERODYNAMICS, SUBSONIC* **SEE** AERODYNAMICS
TL570	AEROELASTICITY
TJ267.C3	*AEROFOILS IN CASCADE* **SEE** CASCADES (FLUID DYNAMICS)
TL574.A4	AEROFOILS
TL574.M6	*AEROFOILS-ROLLING* **SEE** ROLLING (AERODYNAMICS)
QK635	*AEROGASTRES* **SEE** MYXOMYCETES
QB755	*AEROLITES* **SEE** METEORITES */ astronomy*
QE395	*AEROLITES* **SEE** METEORITES */ mineralogy*
TL588	*AEROLOGATION* **SEE** PRESSURE PATTERN FLYING
QC822	*AEROMAGNETIC MAPS* **SEE** MAGNETISM, TERRESTRIAL — MAPS
TL553.5	*AERONAUTICAL ACCIDENTS* **SEE** AERONAUTICS — ACCIDENTS
TL589	AERONAUTICAL INSTRUMENTS
TL566-8	AERONAUTICAL LABORATORIES
Z675.A5	AERONAUTICAL LIBRARIES
TL506	AERONAUTICAL MUSEUMS
TL586-9	*AERONAUTICAL NAVIGATION* **SEE** NAVIGATION (AERONAUTICS)
TL513	*AERONAUTICAL PATENTS* **SEE** AERONAUTICS — PATENTS
TL695	AERONAUTICAL RADIO STATIONS
TL500-504	AERONAUTICAL SOCIETIES
GV750-770	AERONAUTICAL SPORTS
TL692	*AERONAUTICAL TELECOMMUNICATION SERVICES* **SEE** AERONAUTICS — COMMUNICATION SYSTEMS
TL509	AERONAUTICS — ABBREVIATIONS
TL553.5	AERONAUTICS — ACCIDENTS
TL537	AERONAUTICS — AWARDS
TL539-540	AERONAUTICS — BIOGRAPHY
TL692	AERONAUTICS — COMMUNICATION SYSTEMS
TL554	AERONAUTICS — DRAMA
TL721	AERONAUTICS — FLIGHTS
TL551	AERONAUTICS — HANDBOOKS, MANUALS, ETC.
TL515-532	AERONAUTICS — HISTORY
TL554.5	AERONAUTICS — HUMOR, CARICATURES, ETC.
TL547	AERONAUTICS — JUVENILE LITERATURE
JX5771	AERONAUTICS — LAWS AND REGULATIONS */ international law*

HE9915-9925	AERONAUTICS — LAWS AND REGULATIONS / transportation and communication
TL513	AERONAUTICS — PATENTS
TL549	AERONAUTICS — PICTORIAL WORKS
TL554	AERONAUTICS — POETRY
TL560	AERONAUTICS — PROBLEMS, EXERCISES, ETC.
TL722.8	AERONAUTICS — RELIEF SERVICE
TL553.5	AERONAUTICS — SAFETY MEASURES
TL697.S3	AERONAUTICS — SAFETY MEASURES
RA615.2	AERONAUTICS — SANITARY ASPECTS
M1977.A	AERONAUTICS — SONGS AND MUSIC
M1978.A	AERONAUTICS — SONGS AND MUSIC
ML3780	AERONAUTICS — SONGS AND MUSIC / history and criticism
TL521-530	AERONAUTICS — STATISTICS
LB1594.5	AERONAUTICS — STUDY AND TEACHING (ELEMENTARY)
TL551	AERONAUTICS — TABLES
TL509	AERONAUTICS — TERMINOLOGY
HE9915-9925	AERONAUTICS AND STATE
TL561	AERONAUTICS AS A PROFESSION
TL722.1	AERONAUTICS IN AGRICULTURE
N8217.A4	AERONAUTICS IN ART
TL722.3	AERONAUTICS IN FORESTRY
RA640	*AERONAUTICS IN INSECT CONTROL* **SEE** AERONAUTICS IN MOSQUITO CONTROL
TL554	AERONAUTICS IN LITERATURE
QC879	AERONAUTICS IN METEOROLOGY
RA640	AERONAUTICS IN MOSQUITO CONTROL
M1977.A	*AERONAUTICS IN MUSIC* **SEE** AERONAUTICS — SONGS AND MUSIC
ML3780	*AERONAUTICS IN MUSIC* **SEE** AERONAUTICS — SONGS AND MUSIC / history and criticism
M1978.A	*AERONAUTICS IN MUSIC* **SEE** AERONAUTICS — SONGS AND MUSIC
JX5771	AERONAUTICS / international law
TL500-830	AERONAUTICS / technology
HE9911-9925	AERONAUTICS / transportation and communication
TL720.7	AERONAUTICS, COMMERCIAL — FREIGHT
TL720.3	AERONAUTICS, COMMERCIAL — PASSENGER TRAFFIC
TL552	AERONAUTICS, COMMERCIAL — STATISTICS
TL553	AERONAUTICS, COMMERCIAL — TAXATION
TL552	AERONAUTICS, COMMERCIAL
TL515-532	AERONAUTICS, COMMERCIAL
TL720.2	*AERONAUTICS, COMMERCIAL-ACCOUNTING* **SEE** AIR LINES — ACCOUNTING
TL720.2	*AERONAUTICS, COMMERCIAL-FARES* **SEE** AIR LINES — RATES
TL547	*AERONAUTICS, COMMERCIAL-JUVENILE LITERATURE* **SEE** AERONAUTICS — JUVENILE LITERATURE
TL720.2	*AERONAUTICS, COMMERCIAL-RATES* **SEE** AIR LINES — RATES
TL695	*AERONAUTICS, ELECTRONICS IN* **SEE** ELECTRONICS IN AERONAUTICS
TL551.5	*AERONAUTICS, HIGH-SPEED* **SEE** HIGH-SPEED AERONAUTICS
UG630-670	AERONAUTICS, MILITARY — OBSERVATIONS
UG630-670	AERONAUTICS, MILITARY
JX5124	AERONAUTICS, MILITARY / international law
UG630-670	*AERONAUTICS, NAVAL* **SEE** AERONAUTICS, MILITARY
JX5124	*AERONAUTICS, NAVAL* **SEE** AERONAUTICS, MILITARY / international law
TL693-6	*AERONAUTICS, RADIO IN* **SEE** RADIO IN AERONAUTICS
RA615.2	*AERONAUTICS-HYGIENIC ASPECTS* **SEE** AERONAUTICS — SANITARY ASPECTS
HG9970.A7	*AERONAUTICS-INSURANCE* **SEE** INSURANCE, AVIATION
RC1050-1099	*AERONAUTICS-MEDICAL ASPECTS* **SEE** AVIATION MEDICINE
TL722.8	*AERONAUTICS-MEDICAL SERVICE* **SEE** AERONAUTICS — RELIEF SERVICE
M1977.A	*AERONAUTICS-MUSIC* **SEE** AERONAUTICS — SONGS AND MUSIC
M1978.A	*AERONAUTICS-MUSIC* **SEE** AERONAUTICS — SONGS AND MUSIC
ML3780	*AERONAUTICS-MUSIC* **SEE** AERONAUTICS — SONGS AND MUSIC / history and criticism
TL586-9	*AERONAUTICS-NAVIGATION* **SEE** NAVIGATION (AERONAUTICS)
TL721	*AERONAUTICS-VOYAGES* **SEE** AERONAUTICS — FLIGHTS
RC840	*AEROPHAGIA* **SEE** AEROPHAGY
RC840	AEROPHAGY
TL553.5	*AEROPLANE ACCIDENTS* **SEE** AERONAUTICS — ACCIDENTS
TL722.8	AEROPLANE AMBULANCES
TL683.B7	*AEROPLANE BRAKES* **SEE** AEROPLANES — BRAKES
TL725.8	AEROPLANE CARRIERS / aeronautics
V895	AEROPLANE CARRIERS / naval science
TL676	*AEROPLANE CONTROL SURFACES* **SEE** AEROPLANES — CONTROL SURFACES / technology
TL574.C6	*AEROPLANE CONTROL SURFACES* **SEE** AEROPLANES — CONTROL SURFACES / theory
TL699.F2	*AEROPLANE FABRICS* **SEE** AEROPLANES — FABRICS
TL704.7	*AEROPLANE FUEL* **SEE** AEROPLANES — FUEL
TL724.1.F5	AEROPLANE INDUSTRY AND TRADE — FINANCE
TL724.1.S78	AEROPLANE INDUSTRY AND TRADE — SUBCONTRACTING
TL724	AEROPLANE INDUSTRY AND TRADE / technology
GV759	AEROPLANE RACING
TL685.5.S4	*AEROPLANE SEATS* **SEE** AEROPLANES — SEATS
TL671.1	AEROPLANES — AIRWORTHINESS
TL688	AEROPLANES — APPARATUS AND SUPPLIES
TL683.B7	AEROPLANES — BRAKES
TL686	AEROPLANES — CATALOGS
TL681.C6	AEROPLANES — COCKPITS
TL676	AEROPLANES — CONTROL SURFACES / technology
TL574.C6	AEROPLANES — CONTROL SURFACES / theory
TL678	AEROPLANES — CONTROLS
TL671.2	AEROPLANES — DESIGN AND CONSTRUCTION
TL555	AEROPLANES — DISINFECTION
TL725.3.D4	AEROPLANES — DISPATCHING
TL690-691	AEROPLANES — ELECTRIC EQUIPMENT
TL691.W5	AEROPLANES — ELECTRIC WIRING
TL693	AEROPLANES — ELECTRONIC EQUIPMENT
TL699.F2	AEROPLANES — FABRICS
TL681.C6	AEROPLANES — FIELD OF VIEW
TL697.F5	AEROPLANES — FIRES AND FIRE PREVENTION
TL702.F8	AEROPLANES — FUEL TANKS
TL704.7	AEROPLANES — FUEL
TL680-681	AEROPLANES — FUSELAGE
TL671.4	AEROPLANES — HANDLING CHARACTERISTICS
TL697.H9	AEROPLANES — HYDRAULIC EQUIPMENT
TL557.I3	AEROPLANES — ICE PREVENTION
TL603	AEROPLANES — IDENTIFICATION MARKS
TL694.I	AEROPLANES — IFF EQUIPMENT
TL671.7	AEROPLANES — INSPECTION
TL682.3	AEROPLANES — LANDING GEAR
TL711.L3	AEROPLANES — LANDING
TL691	AEROPLANES — LIGHTING
TL671.9	AEROPLANES — MAINTENANCE AND REPAIR
TL688	AEROPLANES — MATERIALS
TL698-9	AEROPLANES — MATERIALS
TL770-777	AEROPLANES — MODELS
TL701-4	AEROPLANES — MOTORS
TL681.5	AEROPLANES — NACELLES
TL708	AEROPLANES — NUCLEAR POWER PLANTS
TL697.O8	AEROPLANES — OXYGEN EQUIPMENT
TL513	AEROPLANES — PATENTS
TL671.4	AEROPLANES — PERFORMANCE
TL710	AEROPLANES — PILOTING
TL696.2	AEROPLANES — RADAR EQUIPMENT
TL702.R3	AEROPLANES — RADIATORS
TL694.A6	AEROPLANES — RADIO ANTENNAS
TL711.R4	AEROPLANES — REFUELING
TL512	AEROPLANES — REGISTERS
TL671.5	AEROPLANES — RIGGING
TL685.5.S4	AEROPLANES — SEATS
TL683.S6	AEROPLANES — SKIS
TL671.1	AEROPLANES — SPECIFICATIONS
TL671.1	AEROPLANES — STANDARDS
TL677.T3	AEROPLANES — TAIL SURFACES
TL711.T3	AEROPLANES — TAKE-OFF
TL671.7	AEROPLANES — TESTING
TL671.5	AEROPLANES — WELDING
TL675	AEROPLANES — WINGS
TL672-3	AEROPLANES — WINGS
TL673.C7	AEROPLANES — WINGS, CRUCIFORM

TL673.R4	AEROPLANES — WINGS, RECTANGULAR
TL673.S9	AEROPLANES — WINGS, SWEPT-BACK
TL673.T7	AEROPLANES — WINGS, TRIANGULAR
TL722.1	*AEROPLANES IN AGRICULTURE* **SEE** AERONAUTICS IN AGRICULTURE
TL722.3	*AEROPLANES IN FORESTRY* **SEE** AERONAUTICS IN FORESTRY
RA640	*AEROPLANES IN MOSQUITO CONTROL* **SEE** AERONAUTICS IN MOSQUITO CONTROL
TL670-688	AEROPLANES
TL722.8	*AEROPLANES, AMBULANCE* **SEE** AEROPLANE AMBULANCES
TL685.3	*AEROPLANES, GOVERNMENT* **SEE** AEROPLANES, MILITARY
TL723	*AEROPLANES, GOVERNMENT* **SEE** GOVERNMENT AIRCRAFT
QC849	*AEROPLANES, MAGNETISM OF* **SEE** MAGNETISM OF AIRCRAFT
UG630-635	AEROPLANES, MILITARY — TURRETS */ general and army*
VG90-95	AEROPLANES, MILITARY — TURRETS */ navy*
TL685.3	AEROPLANES, MILITARY
TL553.5	*AEROPLANES-ACCIDENTS* **SEE** AERONAUTICS — ACCIDENTS
TL677.A5	*AEROPLANES-AILERONS* **SEE** AILERONS
TL708	*AEROPLANES-ATOMIC POWER* **SEE** AEROPLANES — NUCLEAR POWER PLANTS
TL720.7	*AEROPLANES-CARGO* **SEE** AERONAUTICS, COMMERCIAL — FREIGHT
TL725.8	*AEROPLANES-CARRIERS* **SEE** AEROPLANE CARRIERS */ aeronautics*
V895	*AEROPLANES-CARRIERS* **SEE** AEROPLANE CARRIERS */ naval science*
TL553.5	*AEROPLANES-COLLISIONS WITH BIRDS* **SEE** AERONAUTICS — ACCIDENTS
TL557.C7	*AEROPLANES-CONDENSATION TRAILS* **SEE** CONDENSATION TRAILS
TL702.C6	*AEROPLANES-COWLINGS* **SEE** AEROPLANES — MOTORS — — COWLINGS
TL696.D65	*AEROPLANES-DISTANCE MEASURING EQUIPMENT* **SEE** DISTANCE MEASURING EQUIPMENT (AIRCRAFT TO GROUND STATION)
TL699.F2	*AEROPLANES-DOPES AND DOPING* **SEE** AEROPLANES — FABRICS
TL671.25	*AEROPLANES-DRAFTING* **SEE** AIRCRAFT DRAFTING
TL673.F6	*AEROPLANES-FLAPS* **SEE** FLAPS (AEROPLANES)
TL671.4	*AEROPLANES-FLYING QUALITIES* **SEE** AEROPLANES — HANDLING CHARACTERISTICS
TL720.7	*AEROPLANES-FREIGHT* **SEE** AERONAUTICS, COMMERCIAL — FREIGHT
TL557.I3	*AEROPLANES-ICE FORMATION* **SEE** AEROPLANES — ICE PREVENTION
TL589	*AEROPLANES-INSTRUMENTS* **SEE** AERONAUTICAL INSTRUMENTS
HG9970.A7	*AEROPLANES-INSURANCE* **SEE** INSURANCE, AVIATION
TL547.S7	*AEROPLANES-LATERAL STABILITY* **SEE** STABILITY OF AEROPLANES, LATERAL
TL574.S7	*AEROPLANES-LONGITUDINAL STABILITY* **SEE** STABILITY OF AEROPLANES, LONGITUDINAL
QC849	*AEROPLANES-MAGNETIC FIELDS* **SEE** MAGNETISM OF AIRCRAFT
TL710	*AEROPLANES-OPERATION* **SEE** AEROPLANES — PILOTING
TL712	*AEROPLANES-PILOTS* **SEE** AIR PILOTS */ training*
TL554	*AEROPLANES-POETRY* **SEE** AERONAUTICS — POETRY
TL705-8	*AEROPLANES-PROPELLERS* **SEE** PROPELLERS, AERIAL
GV759	*AEROPLANES-RACING* **SEE** AEROPLANE RACING
TL681.C6	*AEROPLANES-RANGE OF VISION* **SEE** AEROPLANES — FIELD OF VIEW
TL671.5	*AEROPLANES-RIVETS AND RIVETING* **SEE** RIVETS AND RIVETING, AIRCRAFT
TL574.M6	*AEROPLANES-ROLLING* **SEE** ROLLING (AERODYNAMICS)
TL574.S7	*AEROPLANES-STABILITY* **SEE** STABILITY OF AEROPLANES
TL699.S8	*AEROPLANES-STEEL* **SEE** AIRCRAFT STEEL
TL673.S9	*AEROPLANES-SWEEPBACK* **SEE** AEROPLANES — WINGS, SWEPT-BACK

TL682.3	*AEROPLANES-WHEELS* **SEE** AEROPLANES — LANDING GEAR
TL673.T7	*AEROPLANES-WINGS, DELTA* **SEE** AEROPLANES — WINGS, TRIANGULAR
TL673.S9	*AEROPLANES-WINGS, OBLIQUE* **SEE** AEROPLANES — WINGS, SWEPT-BACK
TL574.M6	*AEROPLANES-YAWING* **SEE** YAWING (AERODYNAMICS)
TL693	AEROPLANES — ELECTRONIC EQUIPMENT — — COOLING
TL777	AEROPLANES — MODELS — — MOTORS
TL770	AEROPLANES — MODELS — — RADIO CONTROL
TL702.C3	AEROPLANES — MOTORS — — CARBURETORS
TL702.R3	AEROPLANES — MOTORS — — COOLING
TL702.C6	AEROPLANES — MOTORS — — COWLINGS
TL704.6	AEROPLANES — MOTORS — — MODELS
TL702.M8	AEROPLANES — MOTORS — — MUFFLERS
TL701.7	AEROPLANES — MOTORS — — SPECIFICATIONS
TL702.S8	AEROPLANES — MOTORS — — SUPERCHARGERS
TL709.5.I5	AEROPLANES — RAMJET ENGINES — — AIR INTAKES
TL709.5.I5	AEROPLANES — TURBOJET ENGINES — — AIR INTAKES
TL709	AEROPLANES — TURBOJET ENGINES — — BLADES
TL694.T35	*AEROSPACE TELEMETER* **SEE** AEROSPACE TELEMETRY
TL694.T35	AEROSPACE TELEMETRY
QC168	AEROSTATICS
TL578	AEROSTATICS
JX5771	*AEROSTATION* **SEE** AERONAUTICS */ international law*
TL500-830	*AEROSTATION* **SEE** AERONAUTICS */ technology*
HE9911-9925	*AEROSTATION* **SEE** AERONAUTICS */ transportation and communication*
RM824-9	*AEROTHERAPEUTICS* **SEE** AEROTHERAPY
RM824-9	AEROTHERAPY
BH301.F6	*AESTHETIC FORM* **SEE** FORM (AESTHETICS)
N62-65	AESTHETICS — EARLY WORKS TO 1800
BH91-188	AESTHETICS — EARLY WORKS TO 1800
N61-79	AESTHETICS */ art*
BH	AESTHETICS */ philosophy*
BH108-9	AESTHETICS, GREEK
QD305.E7	*AETHER* **SEE** ETHER
RB151	*AETIOLOGY* **SEE** DISEASES — CAUSES AND THEORIES OF CAUSATION
DF236-7	AETOLIAN LEAGUE
PJ2421	AFAR LANGUAGE
BJ1533.F8	*AFFECTION* **SEE** FRIENDSHIP
BJ1533.K5	*AFFECTION* **SEE** KINDNESS
GR460	*AFFECTION* **SEE** LOVE */ folk-lore*
HQ61	*AFFECTION* **SEE** LOVE */ love and religion*
GT2600-2640	*AFFECTION* **SEE** LOVE */ manners and customs*
BD436	*AFFECTION* **SEE** LOVE */ philosophy*
BF575.L8	*AFFECTION* **SEE** LOVE */ psychology*
QD501	*AFFINITY, CHEMICAL* **SEE** CHEMICAL AFFINITY
SD409	AFFORESTATION
HE2242	*AFFREIGHTMENT* **SEE** BILLS OF LADING
HE596	*AFFREIGHTMENT* **SEE** CHARTER-PARTIES */ water transport*
HE2301-2500	*AFFREIGHTMENT* **SEE** FREIGHT AND FREIGHTAGE */ railroads*
HE593-7	*AFFREIGHTMENT* **SEE** FREIGHT AND FREIGHTAGE */ shipping*
SF429.A4	AFGHAN HOUNDS
PK6701-6799	*AFGHAN LANGUAGE* **SEE** PUSHTO LANGUAGE
DT160-177	AFRICA, NORTH — HISTORY
DT730-995	AFRICA, SOUTH — HISTORY
DT930-939	*AFRICA, SOUTH-HISTORY-SOUTH AFRICAN WAR, 1899-1902* **SEE** SOUTH AFRICAN WAR, 1899-1902
DT773	AFRICA, SOUTH — HISTORY — — GREAT TREK, 1836-1840
DT773	AFRICA, SOUTH — HISTORY — — TO 1836
QL737.U5	*AFRICAN CAPE BUFFALO* **SEE** BUFFALOES
QK495.C	*AFRICAN DAISY* **SEE** GERBERA */ botany*
SB413.G	*AFRICAN DAISY* **SEE** GERBERA */ floriculture*
PL8010	AFRICAN LITERATURE
SB299.P3	*AFRICAN OIL-PALM* **SEE** OIL-PALM
SB235	*AFRICAN SUGAR-CANE* **SEE** SORGHUM
TP405	*AFRICAN SUGAR-CANE* **SEE** SORGHUM */ chemical technology*
QK495.G4	AFRICAN VIOLETS */ botany*

SB413.A4	AFRICAN VIOLETS / *culture*
SF199.A3	AFRICANDER CATTLE
DT888-944	*AFRICANDERS* **SEE** BOERS
DT888-944	*AFRIKAANDERS* **SEE** BOERS
PT6565	AFRIKAANS DRAMA / *collections*
PT6520	AFRIKAANS DRAMA / *history*
PT6570	AFRIKAANS FICTION / *collections*
PT6525	AFRIKAANS FICTION / *history*
PF861-884	AFRIKAANS LANGUAGE
PT6500-6590	AFRIKAANS LITERATURE
PT6560	AFRIKAANS POETRY / *collections*
PT6545	AFRIKAANS POETRY / *folk literature*
PT6515	AFRIKAANS POETRY / *history*
PT6570	AFRIKAANS PROSE LITERATURE / *collections*
PT6525	AFRIKAANS PROSE LITERATURE / *history*
PN6222.A	AFRIKAANS WIT AND HUMOR
SF199.A3	*AFRIKANDER CATTLE* **SEE** AFRICANDER CATTLE
PF861-884	*AFRIKANDER LANGUAGE* **SEE** AFRIKAANS LANGUAGE
DT888-944	*AFRIKANDERS* **SEE** BOERS
GN630.A18	*AFSAR (TURKISH TRIBE)* **SEE** AFSHAR (TURKISH TRIBE)
GN630.A18	AFSHAR (TURKISH TRIBE)
BF241	*AFTEREFFECTS, FIGURAL* **SEE** FIGURAL AFTEREFFECTS
DS432.A	AGARIAS
DS432.A	*AGARIYAS* **SEE** AGARIAS
DS422.C3	AGARWALS
PJ2425	AGAU LANGUAGE
SB317.A2	AGAVE
PJ2425	*AGAW LANGUAGE* **SEE** AGAU LANGUAGE
LB775.A4125	AGAZZI METHOD OF TEACHING
HV6163	*AGE AND CRIME* **SEE** CRIME AND AGE
QE508	*AGE OF ROCKS* **SEE** GEOLOGICAL TIME
QE651-699	*AGE OF ROCKS* **SEE** GEOLOGY, STRATIGRAPHIC
NA7195.A4	AGED — DWELLINGS
TR680	AGED — PORTRAITS
GV184	AGED — RECREATION
BV4580	AGED — RELIGIOUS LIFE
BV4316.A4	AGED — SERMONS
HV1451-1493	AGED
HD5861-6000	*AGENCIES, EMPLOYMENT* **SEE** EMPLOYMENT AGENCIES
P632	AGENT-NOUNS / *aryans*
PE1205	AGENT-NOUNS / *english*
PF3201	AGENT-NOUNS / *german*
JX1896	*AGENTS OF FOREIGN PRINCIPALS IN THE U.S.* **SEE** FOREIGN PROPAGANDISTS IN THE U.S.
TP967-970	*AGGLUTINANTS* **SEE** ADHESIVES
QR185	AGGLUTINATION
QR185	AGGLUTININS
QA248	AGGREGATES
LB1117	AGGRESSIVENESS (PSYCHOLOGY) / *child study*
DC101.5.A2	AGINCOURT, BATTLE OF, 1415
TP156.M5	*AGITATORS (MACHINERY)* **SEE** MIXING MACHINERY
PM21	AGLEMIUT DIALECT
PM21	*AGLEMUTE DIALECT* **SEE** AGLEMIUT DIALECT
GN655.A	AGNI (AFRICAN TRIBE)
DT545	AGNI (AFRICAN TRIBE) / *ivory coast*
RC382	AGNOSIA
B808	AGNOSTICISM / *philosophic agnosticism*
BL2700-2790	AGNOSTICISM / *religion*
B837	AGNOSTICISM / *skepticism*
B1917	AGNOSTICISM / *skepticism in france*
BD150-232	AGNOSTICISM / *theory of knowledge*
BX2310.A	AGNUS DEI (SACRAMENTAL)
E99.I7	*AGONEASEAH INDIANS* **SEE** IROQUOIS INDIANS
BT1365	*AGONISTS* **SEE** CIRCUMCELLIONS
RC640	AGRANULOCYTOSIS
HD101-1395	*AGRARIAN QUESTION* **SEE** LAND TENURE
DS422.C3	*AGRAWALS* **SEE** AGARWALS
HF1253-5	*AGREEMENTS* **SEE** CONTRACTS / *commercial law*
HD2381-5	*AGREEMENTS* **SEE** CONTRACTS / *subcontracting*
JK2441	*AGREEMENTS, INTERSTATE* **SEE** INTERSTATE AGREEMENTS
S484	AGRICULTURAL ADMINISTRATION
QR51	*AGRICULTURAL BACTERIOLOGY* **SEE** BACTERIOLOGY, AGRICULTURAL
QR111	*AGRICULTURAL BACTERIOLOGY* **SEE** BACTERIOLOGY, AGRICULTURAL / *bacteria in soil*

QR351	*AGRICULTURAL BACTERIOLOGY* **SEE** BACTERIOLOGY, AGRICULTURAL / *bacteria of plant diseases*
HG2041-2051	*AGRICULTURAL BANKS* **SEE** AGRICULTURAL CREDIT / *banking*
HD1439-1440	*AGRICULTURAL BANKS* **SEE** AGRICULTURAL CREDIT / *theory*
HG1501-3540	*AGRICULTURAL BANKS* **SEE** BANKS AND BANKING
HG2041-2051	*AGRICULTURAL BANKS* **SEE** MORTGAGE BANKS
HD1439-1440	*AGRICULTURAL BANKS* **SEE** MORTGAGE BANKS / *theory*
SB107-9	*AGRICULTURAL BOTANY* **SEE** BOTANY, ECONOMIC
S583-8	AGRICULTURAL CHEMISTRY
S600	*AGRICULTURAL CLIMATOLOGY* **SEE** CROPS AND CLIMATE
HD1516	AGRICULTURAL COLONIES
S-SB	*AGRICULTURAL COMMODITIES* **SEE** FARM PRODUCE / *agriculture*
HD9000-9019	*AGRICULTURAL COMMODITIES* **SEE** FARM PRODUCE / *economics*
HD1491	*AGRICULTURAL COOPERATION* **SEE** AGRICULTURE, COOPERATIVE
HD1483-6	*AGRICULTURAL COOPERATION* **SEE** AGRICULTURE, COOPERATIVE
HG2041-2051	AGRICULTURAL COOPERATIVE CREDIT ASSOCIATIONS
HG2041-2051	AGRICULTURAL CREDIT / *banking*
HD1439-1440	AGRICULTURAL CREDIT / *theory*
S531.5	AGRICULTURAL EDUCATION — AUDIO-VISUAL AIDS
S671-760	AGRICULTURAL ENGINEERING
S551-9	AGRICULTURAL EXHIBITIONS
S541-3	AGRICULTURAL EXPERIMENT STATIONS
S541-3	*AGRICULTURAL EXPERIMENTATION* **SEE** AGRICULTURAL EXPERIMENT STATIONS
S531.5	*AGRICULTURAL EXTENSION WORK - AUDIO-VISUAL AIDS* **SEE** AGRICULTURAL EDUCATION — AUDIO-VISUAL AIDS
S544	AGRICULTURAL EXTENSION WORK
S531.5	*AGRICULTURAL EXTENSION WORK-AUDIO-VISUAL AIDS* **SEE** AGRICULTURAL EDUCATION — AUDIO-VISUAL AIDS
S551-9	*AGRICULTURAL FAIRS* **SEE** AGRICULTURAL EXHIBITIONS
S676	AGRICULTURAL IMPLEMENTS
HG9966-9	*AGRICULTURAL INSURANCE* **SEE** INSURANCE, AGRICULTURAL
PN4784.A3	*AGRICULTURAL JOURNALISM* **SEE** JOURNALISM, AGRICULTURAL
HD7269.A29	AGRICULTURAL LABORERS — DISEASES AND HYGIENE
HD1521-1539	AGRICULTURAL LABORERS
HD109	AGRICULTURAL LAWS AND LEGISLATION / *general*
HD301-1130	AGRICULTURAL LAWS AND LEGISLATION / *other countries*
HD185-6	AGRICULTURAL LAWS AND LEGISLATION / *u.s.*
Z675.A8	AGRICULTURAL LIBRARIES
S678	AGRICULTURAL MACHINERY — TESTING
HD9486	AGRICULTURAL MACHINERY — TRADE AND MANUFACTURE
S671-760	AGRICULTURAL MACHINERY
S565	*AGRICULTURAL MACHINERY-SAFETY MEASURES* **SEE** AGRICULTURE — SAFETY MEASURES
S566	AGRICULTURAL MATHEMATICS
S600	*AGRICULTURAL METEOROLOGY* **SEE** METEOROLOGY, AGRICULTURAL / *crops and climate*
S549	AGRICULTURAL MUSEUMS
SB599-999	AGRICULTURAL PESTS
S589-600	AGRICULTURAL PHYSICS
S698	AGRICULTURAL PROCESSING
S-SB	*AGRICULTURAL PRODUCTS* **SEE** FARM PRODUCE / *agriculture*
HD9000-9019	*AGRICULTURAL PRODUCTS* **SEE** FARM PRODUCE / *economics*
HD9000-9019	*AGRICULTURAL PRODUCTS* **SEE** PRODUCE TRADE
S675	*AGRICULTURAL SUPPLIES* **SEE** FARM EQUIPMENT
S676	*AGRICULTURAL TOOLS* **SEE** AGRICULTURAL IMPLEMENTS
HG2041-2051	*AGRICULTURAL WARRANTS* **SEE** AGRICULTURAL CREDIT / *banking*
HD1439-1440	*AGRICULTURAL WARRANTS* **SEE** AGRICULTURAL CREDIT / *theory*
S532	*AGRICULTURAL WORK OF MISSIONS* **SEE** MISSIONS — AGRICULTURAL WORK

HD1521-1539	*AGRICULTURAL WORKERS* **SEE** AGRICULTURAL LABORERS
HD7269.A52	AGRICULTURE — ACCIDENTS
S567-9	AGRICULTURE — ACCOUNTING
S567	AGRICULTURE — COSTS
S565	AGRICULTURE — SAFETY MEASURES
S531-9	AGRICULTURE — STUDY AND TEACHING
S413	AGRICULTURE — TABLES AND READY-RECKONERS
S566	*AGRICULTURE - MATHEMATICS* **SEE** AGRICULTURAL MATHEMATICS
HD1483-6	AGRICULTURE, COOPERATIVE
HD1491	AGRICULTURE, COOPERATIVE
GR895	*AGRICULTURE, FOLK-LORE OF* **SEE** FOLK-LORE OF AGRICULTURE
GN424-6	AGRICULTURE, PRIMITIVE
S551-9	*AGRICULTURE-EXHIBITIONS* **SEE** AGRICULTURAL EXHIBITIONS
HD109	*AGRICULTURE-LAWS AND LEGISLATION* **SEE** AGRICULTURAL LAWS AND LEGISLATION / *general*
HD301-1130	*AGRICULTURE-LAWS AND LEGISLATION* **SEE** AGRICULTURAL LAWS AND LEGISLATION / *other countries*
HD185-6	*AGRICULTURE-LAWS AND LEGISLATION* **SEE** AGRICULTURAL LAWS AND LEGISLATION / *u.s.*
S566	*AGRICULTURE-MATHEMATICS* **SEE** AGRICULTURAL MATHEMATICS
S549	*AGRICULTURE-MUSEUMS* **SEE** AGRICULTURAL MUSEUMS
QK495.G74	*AGROSTOLOGY* **SEE** GRASSES / *botany*
SB197-201	*AGROSTOLOGY* **SEE** GRASSES / *culture*
PL5550	AGTA LANGUAGE
PM5337.A5	AGUARUNA DIALECT
RC156-166	*AGUE* **SEE** MALARIAL FEVER
QM201.M2	*AGUE* **SEE** MALARIAL FEVER / *bacteriology*
PK9201.A6	AGUL LANGUAGE
DS432.A	AHIRS
PL4251.A4	AHOM LANGUAGE
E99.N85	*AHT INDIANS* **SEE** NOOTKA INDIANS
PM2031	*AHT LANGUAGE* **SEE** NOOTKA LANGUAGE
E99.A28	AHTENA INDIANS
E99.A28	*AHTINNE INDIANS* **SEE** AHTENA INDIANS
VK1150-1246	AIDS TO NAVIGATION — LISTS
VK1000-1249	AIDS TO NAVIGATION / *lighthouse service*
VK381-397	AIDS TO NAVIGATION / *signaling*
GV1111	AIKIDO
SF459	AILANTHUS MOTH / *sericulture*
QL561.S2	AILANTHUS MOTH / *zoology*
SF459	*AILANTHUS SILKWORM* **SEE** AILANTHUS MOTH / *sericulture*
QL561.S2	*AILANTHUS SILKWORM* **SEE** AILANTHUS MOTH / *zoology*
TL677.A5	AILERONS
F2520.1.B76	*AIMORES* **SEE** BOTOCUDO INDIANS
PL495	*AINO LANGUAGE* **SEE** AINU LANGUAGE
BL2370.A5	AINU — RELIGION
PL495	AINU LANGUAGE
QD121	AIR — ANALYSIS
NC915.A35	*AIR BRUSH ART* **SEE** AIRBRUSH ART
TL720.7	*AIR CARGO* **SEE** AERONAUTICS, COMMERCIAL — FREIGHT
TL711.D7	*AIR CARGO DROPPING* **SEE** AIRDROP
UC330-335	*AIR CARGO DROPPING* **SEE** AIRDROP / *military*
TH7687	AIR CONDITIONING — CLIMATIC FACTORS
TH7687	*AIR CONDITIONING AND CLIMATE* **SEE** AIR CONDITIONING — CLIMATIC FACTORS
TH7687	*AIR CONDITIONING AND WEATHER* **SEE** AIR CONDITIONING — CLIMATIC FACTORS
TH7687	AIR CONDITIONING
TH7683.D8	*AIR CONDITIONING-DUCTS* **SEE** AIR DUCTS
UF625	AIR DEFENSES, MILITARY / *anti-aircraft guns*
UG630-635	AIR DEFENSES, MILITARY / *military aeronautics*
TH7683.D8	AIR DUCTS
TH7683.A3	AIR FILTERS
TJ1025	AIR FLOW
TL720.7	*AIR FREIGHT* **SEE** AERONAUTICS, COMMERCIAL — FREIGHT
HD6073	*AIR HOSTESSES* **SEE** AIR LINES — HOSTESSES
TL709.5.I5	*AIR INLETS (JET PLANES)* **SEE** AEROPLANES — RAMJET ENGINES — — AIR INTAKES
TL709.5.I5	*AIR INTAKES (JET PLANES)* **SEE** AEROPLANES — RAMJET ENGINES — — AIR INTAKES
TL709.5.I5	*AIR INTAKES (JET PLANES)* **SEE** AEROPLANES — TURBOJET ENGINES — — AIR INTAKES
TJ1030	AIR JETS
JX5771	*AIR LAW* **SEE** AERONAUTICS — LAWS AND REGULATIONS / *international law*
HE9915-9925	*AIR LAW* **SEE** AERONAUTICS — LAWS AND REGULATIONS / *transportation and communication*
TL720.2	AIR LINES — ACCOUNTING
TL720.2	AIR LINES — COST OF OPERATION
TL720	AIR LINES — FINANCE
HD6073	AIR LINES — HOSTESSES
TL720.2	AIR LINES — RATES
TL552	AIR LINES
TL720	AIR LINES
TL726	AIR LINES, LOCAL SERVICE
TL720.2	*AIR LINES-FARES* **SEE** AIR LINES — RATES
TL539-540	AIR LINES — HOSTESSES — — CORRESPONDENCE, REMINISCENCES, ETC.
HE6238	AIR MAIL SERVICE / *general*
HE6496	AIR MAIL SERVICE / *u.s.*
JX5771	*AIR NAVIGATION* **SEE** AERONAUTICS / *international law*
TL500-830	*AIR NAVIGATION* **SEE** AERONAUTICS / *technology*
HE9911-9925	*AIR NAVIGATION* **SEE** AERONAUTICS / *transportation and communication*
TL586-9	*AIR NAVIGATION* **SEE** NAVIGATION (AERONAUTICS)
TL712	AIR PILOTS / *training*
TH7683.D8	*AIR PIPES* **SEE** AIR DUCTS
QK922	*AIR PLANTS* **SEE** EPIPHYTES
TL725-6	*AIR PORTS* **SEE** AIRPORTS
TL705-8	*AIR PROPELLERS* **SEE** PROPELLERS, AERIAL
TL553.8	*AIR RESCUE SERVICE* **SEE** SEARCH AND RESCUE OPERATIONS / *aeronautics*
TL711.D7	*AIR RESUPPLY* **SEE** AIRDROP
UC330-335	*AIR RESUPPLY* **SEE** AIRDROP / *military*
JX5771	*AIR SPACE (INTERNATIONAL LAW)* **SEE** AIRSPACE (INTERNATIONAL LAW)
HD6073	*AIR STEWARDESSES* **SEE** AIR LINES — HOSTESSES
UG630	*AIR STRATEGY* **SEE** AIR WARFARE
TL711.D7	*AIR SUPPLY* **SEE** AIRDROP
UC330-335	*AIR SUPPLY* **SEE** AIRDROP / *military*
UG630	*AIR TACTICS* **SEE** AIR WARFARE
TL725.3.T7	AIR TRAFFIC CONTROL — EQUIPMENT AND SUPPLIES
TL725.3.T	AIR TRAFFIC CONTROL
TL552	*AIR TRANSPORT* **SEE** AERONAUTICS, COMMERCIAL
TL515-532	*AIR TRANSPORT* **SEE** AERONAUTICS, COMMERCIAL
TL554.5	AIR TRAVEL — ANECDOTES, FACETIAE, SATIRE, ETC.
UG630	AIR WARFARE
G142	*AIR-AGE GEOGRAPHY* **SEE** GEOGRAPHY, AERIAL
TA352	*AIR-BEARING LIFT* **SEE** GROUND-CUSHION PHENOMENON
TL574.G7	*AIR-BEARING LIFT* **SEE** GROUND-CUSHION PHENOMENON / *aeronautics*
QL855	AIR-BLADDER (IN FISHES)
TF420-430	AIR-BRAKES
TJ990-992	AIR-COMPRESSORS
HD6073	*AIR-LINE HOSTESSES* **SEE** AIR LINES — HOSTESSES
QL845-855	*AIR-PASSAGES* **SEE** RESPIRATORY ORGANS / *comparative anatomy*
QM251-261	*AIR-PASSAGES* **SEE** RESPIRATORY ORGANS / *human anatomy*
QP121	*AIR-PASSAGES* **SEE** RESPIRATORY ORGANS / *physiology*
TL726	AIR-PILOT GUIDES
QC166	AIR-PUMP / *physics*
TJ955	AIR-PUMP / *pneumatic machinery*
QL855	AIR-SACS (OF BIRDS)
TL553.8	*AIR-SEA RESCUE* **SEE** SEARCH AND RESCUE OPERATIONS / *aeronautics*
TL666	*AIR-SHIP GASES* **SEE** BALLOON GASES
TL660	AIR-SHIPS — DESIGN AND CONSTRUCTION
TL701-4	AIR-SHIPS — MOTORS
TL663	AIR-SHIPS — PILOTING
TL650-668	AIR-SHIPS
HG9970.A7	*AIR-SHIPS-INSURANCE* **SEE** INSURANCE, AVIATION
TL554	*AIR-SHIPS-POETRY* **SEE** AERONAUTICS — POETRY
TL589.2.A5	AIR-SPEED INDICATORS

TJ981-1009	AIR, COMPRESSED **SEE** COMPRESSED AIR / technology
QD535	AIR, LIQUID **SEE** LIQUID AIR
QC915-917	AIR, MOISTURE OF **SEE** HUMIDITY
RM824-9	AIR, RAREFIED-THERAPEUTICS **SEE** AEROTHERAPY
TL693	AIRBORNE ELECTRONIC EQUIPMENT **SEE** AEROPLANES — ELECTRONIC EQUIPMENT
TR696	AIRBORNE PROFILE RECORDER
NC915.A35	AIRBRUSH ART
TL553.5	AIRCRAFT ACCIDENTS **SEE** AERONAUTICS — ACCIDENTS
TL694.A6	AIRCRAFT ANTENNAS **SEE** AEROPLANES — RADIO ANTENNAS
TL702.C3	AIRCRAFT CARBURETORS **SEE** AEROPLANES — MOTORS — — CARBURETORS
TL725.8	AIRCRAFT CARRIERS **SEE** AEROPLANE CARRIERS / aeronautics
V895	AIRCRAFT CARRIERS **SEE** AEROPLANE CARRIERS / naval science
TL671.25	AIRCRAFT DRAFTING
TL671.25	AIRCRAFT DRAWING **SEE** AIRCRAFT DRAFTING
TL701-4	AIRCRAFT ENGINES **SEE** AEROPLANES — MOTORS
TL724.1.F5	AIRCRAFT FINANCING **SEE** AEROPLANE INDUSTRY AND TRADE — FINANCE
VG93	AIRCRAFT HANDLING GROUP **SEE** U.S. — AVIATION BOATSWAIN'S MATES
TL697.H9	AIRCRAFT HYDRAULIC EQUIPMENT **SEE** AEROPLANES — HYDRAULIC EQUIPMENT
TL694.I	AIRCRAFT IFF EQUIPMENT **SEE** AEROPLANES — IFF EQUIPMENT
TL589	AIRCRAFT INSTRUMENTS **SEE** AERONAUTICAL INSTRUMENTS
TL725.3.L2	AIRCRAFT LANDING AIDS **SEE** LANDING AIDS (AERONAUTICS)
TL724	AIRCRAFT PRODUCTION **SEE** AEROPLANE INDUSTRY AND TRADE / technology
TL695	AIRCRAFT RADIO STATIONS **SEE** AERONAUTICAL RADIO STATIONS
TL671.5	AIRCRAFT RIVETING **SEE** RIVETS AND RIVETING, AIRCRAFT
TL685.5.S4	AIRCRAFT SEATS **SEE** AEROPLANES — SEATS
TL699.S8	AIRCRAFT STEEL
UG630-635	AIRCRAFT TURRETS **SEE** AEROPLANES, MILITARY — TURRETS / general and army
VG90-95	AIRCRAFT TURRETS **SEE** AEROPLANES, MILITARY — TURRETS / navy
TL671.5	AIRCRAFT WELDING **SEE** AEROPLANES — WELDING
TL685.3	AIRCRAFT, GOVERNMENT **SEE** AEROPLANES, MILITARY
TL723	AIRCRAFT, GOVERNMENT **SEE** GOVERNMENT AIRCRAFT
TL725-6	AIRDROMES **SEE** AIRPORTS
TL711.D7	AIRDROP
UC330-335	AIRDROP / military
SF429.A6	AIREDALE TERRIERS
TL574.A4	AIRFOILS **SEE** AEROFOILS
TL670-688	AIRFRAME **SEE** AEROPLANES
TL685.7	AIRLINERS **SEE** TRANSPORT PLANES
TL720	AIRLINES **SEE** AIR LINES
TL552	AIRLINES **SEE** AIR LINES
TL670-688	AIRPLANES **SEE** AEROPLANES
TL725.3.D7	AIRPORT DRAINAGE
TL725.3.L3	AIRPORT LANDING FEES **SEE** AIRPORTS — LANDING FEES
TL725.3.M2	AIRPORT MANAGEMENT **SEE** AIRPORTS — MANAGEMENT
TL725.3.N6	AIRPORT NOISE
TL725.3.P5	AIRPORT PLANNING **SEE** AIRPORTS — PLANNING
TL695	AIRPORT RADIO STATIONS **SEE** AERONAUTICAL RADIO STATIONS
TL725.2	AIRPORTS — CONTRACTS AND SPECIFICATIONS
TL725.3.E6	AIRPORTS — EQUIPMENT AND SUPPLIES
TL725.3.F5	AIRPORTS — FINANCE
TL730.1	AIRPORTS — FIRES AND FIRE PREVENTION
TL725.3.L3	AIRPORTS — LANDING FEES
TL725.3.L5	AIRPORTS — LIGHTING
TL725.3.L6	AIRPORTS — LOCATION
TL725.3.M2	AIRPORTS — MANAGEMENT
TL725.3.P5	AIRPORTS — PLANNING
TL725.3.R8	AIRPORTS — RUNWAYS

TL557.V5	AIRPORTS — VISIBILITY
TL726.15	AIRPORTS OF ENTRY **SEE** INTERNATIONAL AIRPORTS
TL725-6	AIRPORTS
TL725.7	AIRPORTS, FLOATING
TL725.3.D7	AIRPORTS-DRAINAGE **SEE** AIRPORT DRAINAGE
TL725.3.L2	AIRPORTS-LANDING AIDS **SEE** LANDING AIDS (AERONAUTICS)
TL725.3.N6	AIRPORTS-NOISE **SEE** AIRPORT NOISE
TL725.2	AIRPORTS-SPECIFICATIONS **SEE** AIRPORTS — CONTRACTS AND SPECIFICATIONS
TL725.3.P5	AIRPORTS — PLANNING — — MATHEMATICAL MODELS
TL725.3.R8	AIRPORTS — RUNWAYS — — MATHEMATICAL MODELS
JX5771	AIRSPACE (INTERNATIONAL LAW)
RA640	AIRSPRAYING **SEE** AERONAUTICS IN MOSQUITO CONTROL
TL725.3.R8	AIRSTRIPS **SEE** AIRPORTS — RUNWAYS
TL725.3	AIRWAYS — FINANCE
TL725.3.L5	AIRWAYS — LIGHTING
TL725-733	AIRWAYS
TL671.1	AIRWORTHINESS REQUIREMENTS **SEE** AEROPLANES — AIRWORTHINESS
DA545.A5	AISNE, BATTLE OF THE, 1914
D545.A5	AISNE, BATTLE OF THE, 1917-AILETTE
DA545.A5	AISNE, BATTLE OF THE, 1918
D276.A3	AIX-LA-CHAPELLE, PEACE OF, 1668
D294	AIX-LA-CHAPELLE, PEACE OF, 1748
BL2020.A4	AJIVIKAS
PL8046.A6	AKA LANGUAGE **SEE** AKAN LANGUAGE
PL8046.A6	AKAN LANGUAGE
BL2480.A	AKANS (AFRICAN PEOPLE) — RELIGION
DT511	AKANS (AFRICAN PEOPLE)
PL8046.A7	AKARIMOJONG LANGUAGE
DS432.A44	AKAS
PJ3101-3595	AKKADIAN (EAST SEMITIC) LANGUAGE **SEE** ASSYRO-BABYLONIAN LANGUAGE
DS72	AKKADIANS (SUMERIANS) **SEE** SUMERIANS
SD397.14	AKOMU **SEE** ILOMBA
PM7183	AKONIKEN LANGUAGE **SEE** TZONECA LANGUAGE
PL8191	AKRA LANGUAGE **SEE** GA LANGUAGE
PL8821-4	AKU LANGUAGE **SEE** YORUBA LANGUAGE
F1221.A4	AKWA'ALA INDIANS
BP186.45	AL-'ID AL-SAGHIR **SEE** 'ID AL-FITR
BP186.38	AL-BARA'AH, LAYLAT **SEE** LAYLAT AL-BARA'AH
BP195.J3-32	AL-JAHMIYAH
DS232	AL-KHANDAQ, BATTLE OF, 627 **SEE** DITCH, BATTLE OF THE, 627
BP195.M	AL-MU'ATTILAH
ML3086	ALABADOS
F321-355	ALABAMA — HISTORY
JX238.A4-7	ALABAMA CLAIMS
E99.A4	ALABAMA INDIANS **SEE** ALIBAMU INDIANS
E83.836	ALABAMA-HISTORY-CREEK WAR, 1836 **SEE** CREEK WAR, 1836
E495	ALABAMA — HISTORY — — CIVIL WAR
E551	ALABAMA — HISTORY — — CIVIL WAR / confederate
QD181.A15	ALABAMINE
TN989.A3	ALABASTER
F2823.A4	ALACALUF INDIANS
PM5378	ALACALUF LANGUAGE
F2823.A4	ALAKALUF INDIANS **SEE** ALACALUF INDIANS
D766.9	ALAM EL HALFA, BATTLE OF, 1942 **SEE** ALAM HALFA, BATTLE OF, 1942
D766.9	ALAM HALFA, BATTLE OF, 1942
DD78.A5	ALAMANNI **SEE** ALEMANNI
D766.9	ALAMEIN, BATTLE OF, 1942 **SEE** EL ALAMEIN, BATTLE OF, 1942
DK465.A4	ALAND QUESTION
P959	ALARODIAN LANGUAGE **SEE** VANNIC LANGUAGE
QL696.P2	ALAUDIDAE **SEE** LARKS
PG9501-9599	ALBANIAN LANGUAGE
PG9601-9678	ALBANIAN LITERATURE
DR701.S49-85	ALBANIANS
DF747.A3	ALBANIANS / greece
QL696.P6	ALBATROSSES
BX4873-4893	ALBIGENSES
GN199	ALBINISM **SEE** ALBINOS AND ALBINISM / anthropology
QL767	ALBINISM **SEE** ALBINOS AND ALBINISM / zoology

TN775	ALUMINUM — ELECTROMETALLURGY
TS555	*ALUMINUM ALLOY FORGINGS* **SEE** ALUMINUM FORGINGS
TS555	*ALUMINUM ALLOY PLATES* **SEE** PLATES, ALUMINUM / *manufacture*
TA492.P7	*ALUMINUM ALLOY PLATES* **SEE** PLATES, ALUMINUM / *testing*
TS555	ALUMINUM ALLOYS / *manufacture*
TN775	ALUMINUM ALLOYS / *metallurgy*
TS650	ALUMINUM BRONZE
TK2798	ALUMINUM CELL
TS555	ALUMINUM FORGINGS
TS555	ALUMINUM FOUNDING
TS555	*ALUMINUM FOUNDRY PRACTICE* **SEE** ALUMINUM FOUNDING
QP535.A4	ALUMINUM IN THE BODY
HD9539.A6	ALUMINUM INDUSTRY AND TRADE
TS555	*ALUMINUM PLATES (STRUCTURAL)* **SEE** PLATES, ALUMINUM / *manufacture*
TA492.P7	*ALUMINUM PLATES (STRUCTURAL)* **SEE** PLATES, ALUMINUM / *testing*
QD181.S6	ALUMINUM SILICATES
QD181.A4	ALUMINUM / *chemistry*
TN775	ALUMINUM / *production*
TA480.A6	ALUMINUM, STRUCTURAL
TA480.A6	*ALUMINUM-CREEP* **SEE** CREEP OF ALUMINUM
HD1481	*AMALGAMATION OF LAND* **SEE** CONSOLIDATION OF LAND HOLDINGS / *economics*
K	*AMALGAMATION OF LAND* **SEE** CONSOLIDATION OF LAND HOLDINGS / *law*
TN763	AMALGAMATION
QD181.H65	AMALGAMS / *chemistry*
TS650	AMALGAMS / *technology*
BT1325	AMALRICIANS
PL8597	*AMANAYA LANGUAGE* **SEE** NZIMA LANGUAGE
P943	*AMARDIC LANGUAGE* **SEE** ELAMITE LANGUAGE
PJ9201-9250	*AMARIGNA LANGUAGE* **SEE** AMHARIC LANGUAGE
PN4825-4830	AMATEUR JOURNALISM
TK9956	AMATEUR RADIO STATIONS
PN3151-3191	AMATEUR THEATRICALS
GV733	*AMATEURISM IN SPORTS* **SEE** PROFESSIONALISM IN SPORTS
BT1325	*AMAURIANI* **SEE** AMALRICIANS
RE91	*AMAUROSIS* **SEE** BLINDNESS
HQ1139	AMAZONS
SB261.A	*AMBARI HEMP* **SEE** AMBARY HEMP / *culture*
TS1544.A	*AMBARI HEMP* **SEE** AMBARY HEMP / *fiber*
SB261.A	AMBARY HEMP / *culture*
TS1544.A	AMBARY HEMP / *fiber*
JX1621-1894	AMBASSADORS
QE391.A5	AMBER
NK6000	AMBER / *carving*
BJ1533.A4	AMBITION
PL5206-9	AMBOINESE LANGUAGES
TR370	AMBROTYPE
RC86-88	*AMBULANCE DRILL* **SEE** FIRST AID IN ILLNESS AND INJURY
RA995-6	AMBULANCES
U167	AMBUSHES AND SURPRISES
Z1201-1939	AMERICA — BIBLIOGRAPHY
E18	AMERICA — HISTORY
PM8077	AMERICAN (ARTIFICIAL LANGUAGE)
PN4001-4321	*AMERICAN (FRENCH, GREEK, ETC.)ORATORS* **SEE** ORATORY
E77-99	*AMERICAN ABORIGINES* **SEE** INDIANS OF NORTH AMERICA
F2229-2230	*AMERICAN ABORIGINES* **SEE** INDIANS OF SOUTH AMERICA
E51-99	*AMERICAN ABORIGINES* **SEE** INDIANS
PS583-619	AMERICAN BALLADS AND SONGS / *collections*
PS309-324	AMERICAN BALLADS AND SONGS / *history*
Z479	AMERICAN BOOKS ABROAD
SF429.T3	*AMERICAN BULLTERRIERS* **SEE** STAFFORDSHIRE TERRIERS
SF455	AMERICAN CHECKERED GIANT RABBITS
E456-655	*AMERICAN CIVIL WAR* **SEE** UNITED STATES — HISTORY — — CIVIL WAR
PS669	AMERICAN DIARIES / *collections*
PS409	AMERICAN DIARIES / *history*
PS336.C7	AMERICAN DRAMA (COMEDY) / *history*
PS336.T7	AMERICAN DRAMA (TRAGEDY) / *history*
PS623-635	AMERICAN DRAMA / *collections*
PS330-351	AMERICAN DRAMA / *history*
LB3562	AMERICAN EDUCATION WEEK
PS680-688	AMERICAN ESSAYS / *collections*
PS420-428	AMERICAN ESSAYS / *history*
PZ1	AMERICAN FICTION / *collections*
PS371-9	AMERICAN FICTION / *history*
E77-99	*AMERICAN INDIANS* **SEE** INDIANS OF NORTH AMERICA
F2229-2230	*AMERICAN INDIANS* **SEE** INDIANS OF SOUTH AMERICA
E51-99	*AMERICAN INDIANS* **SEE** INDIANS
PS670-678	AMERICAN LETTERS / *collections*
PS410-418	AMERICAN LETTERS / *history*
Z1225-1231	AMERICAN LITERATURE — BIBLIOGRAPHY
PS591.C3	AMERICAN LITERATURE — CATHOLIC AUTHORS / *collections of poetry*
PS508.C3	AMERICAN LITERATURE — CATHOLIC AUTHORS / *collections*
PS185-191	AMERICAN LITERATURE — COLONIAL PERIOD
PS208	AMERICAN LITERATURE — EARLY 19TH CENTURY
PS508.N3	AMERICAN LITERATURE — NEGRO AUTHORS / *collections*
PS193	AMERICAN LITERATURE — REVOLUTIONARY PERIOD ;'
PS201-214	AMERICAN LITERATURE — 19TH CENTURY
PS221-8	AMERICAN LITERATURE — 20TH CENTURY
PG5050-5069	*AMERICAN LITERATURE (CZECH)* **SEE** CZECH-AMERICAN LITERATURE
PQ3920-3939	AMERICAN LITERATURE (FRENCH)
PS595.I	AMERICAN LITERATURE (IRISH) / *collected poems*
PS508.I	AMERICAN LITERATURE (IRISH) / *collections*
PS153.I	AMERICAN LITERATURE (IRISH) / *history*
PS504-688	AMERICAN LITERATURE / *collections*
PS1-478	AMERICAN LITERATURE / *history*
Z1231.F5	AMERICAN LITERATURE — BIBLIOGRAPHY — — FIRST EDITIONS
E277	AMERICAN LOYALISTS
PN4884-5	AMERICAN NEWSPAPERS — FOREIGN LANGUAGE PRESS
Z6953.5	AMERICAN NEWSPAPERS — FOREIGN LANGUAGE PRESS / *directories*
PN4840-4899	AMERICAN NEWSPAPERS / *etc.*
PS660-668	AMERICAN ORATIONS / *collections*
PS400-408	AMERICAN ORATIONS / *history*
JK2341	AMERICAN PARTY
PN4840-4900	AMERICAN PERIODICALS / *etc.*
PS312	AMERICAN POETRY — COLONIAL PERIOD
PS319	AMERICAN POETRY — EARLY 19TH CENTURY
PS314	AMERICAN POETRY — REVOLUTIONARY PERIOD
PS316-321	AMERICAN POETRY — 19TH CENTURY
PS324	AMERICAN POETRY — 20TH CENTURY
PQ3914	AMERICAN POETRY (FRENCH)
PQ3910	AMERICAN POETRY (FRENCH)
PT9986	*AMERICAN POETRY (SWEDISH)* **SEE** SWEDISH-AMERICAN POETRY / *history*
PT9991	*AMERICAN POETRY (SWEDISH)* **SEE** SWEDISH-AMERICAN POETRY / *collections*
PS	AMERICAN POETRY
PS591.C3	*AMERICAN POETRY-CATHOLIC AUTHORS* **SEE** AMERICAN LITERATURE — CATHOLIC AUTHORS / *collections of poetry*
PS508.C3	*AMERICAN POETRY-CATHOLIC AUTHORS* **SEE** AMERICAN LITERATURE — CATHOLIC AUTHORS / *collections*
PS591.N4	*AMERICAN POETRY-NEGRO AUTHORS* **SEE** NEGRO POETRY (AMERICAN)
PS651	AMERICAN PROSE LITERATURE — COLONIAL PERIOD
PS643-659	AMERICAN PROSE LITERATURE / *collections*
PS362-379	AMERICAN PROSE LITERATURE / *history*
HD5325. R121894C5	*AMERICAN RAILWAY UNION STRIKE, 1894* **SEE** CHICAGO STRIKE, 1894
E201-298	*AMERICAN REVOLUTION* **SEE** UNITED STATES — HISTORY — — REVOLUTION
SF293.A	AMERICAN SADDLE HORSE
PN6157-6162	AMERICAN WIT AND HUMOR / *collections*
PS430-438	AMERICAN WIT AND HUMOR / *history*
NC1420-1429	AMERICAN WIT AND HUMOR, PICTORIAL
RS165.C35	*AMERICAN WORMSEED-OIL* **SEE** CHENOPODIUM OIL

RM666.C38	*AMERICAN WORMSEED-OIL* **SEE** CHENOPODIUM OIL
E714-735	*AMERICAN-SPANISH WAR, 1898* **SEE** UNITED STATES — HISTORY — — WAR OF 1898
BX1407.A5	AMERICANISM (CATHOLIC CONTROVERSY)
PE2801-3101	AMERICANISMS
JK1758	AMERICANIZATION / *citizenship*
LC3731-3	AMERICANIZATION / *education*
Z1207	AMERICA — BIBLIOGRAPHY — — CATALOGS
Z1202-3	AMERICA — BIBLIOGRAPHY — — EARLY
QD181.A5	AMERICIUM
E51-99	*AMERINDS* **SEE** INDIANS
QD394.A6	AMETHYSTS / *mineralogy*
RE925-939	*AMETROPIA* **SEE** EYE — ACCOMMODATION AND REFRACTION / *pathology*
QP476	*AMETROPIA* **SEE** EYE — ACCOMMODATION AND REFRACTION / *physiology*
PJ9201-9250	AMHARIC LANGUAGE
PJ9262	AMHARIC POETRY
PJ9266	AMHARIC POETRY
QD305.A7	AMIC ACIDS
QD341.A7	AMIC ACIDS
QD341.A7	AMIDES
QD305.A7	AMIDES
QD341.A7	AMIDINES
TP914	*AMIDO-BENZENE* **SEE** ANILINE
QD341.A8	*AMIDO-BENZENE* **SEE** ANILINE
DC309.A5	AMIENS, BATTLE OF, 1870
D545.A56	AMIENS, BATTLE OF, 1918
D756.5.A	AMIENS, BATTLE OF, 1940
DC222.5	AMIENS, TREATY OF, 1802
PM610.A6	AMIKWA LANGUAGE
QD281.A6	AMINATION
QD305.A8	AMINES
QD341.A8	AMINES
QP801.A5	AMINO ACID METABOLISM
QD341.A7	AMINO ACIDS
QD305.A7	AMINO ACIDS
QP801.A5	AMINO ACIDS / *physiology*
TP986.A	*AMINO RESINS* **SEE** AMINOPLASTICS
TP986.A	*AMINO-FORMALDEHYDE RESINS* **SEE** AMINOPLASTICS
TP986.A	AMINOPLASTICS
TP986.A	*AMINOPLASTS* **SEE** AMINOPLASTICS
E99.P	*AMISCOGGING INDIANS* **SEE** PEQUAWKET INDIANS
E83.7	*AMISCOGGING INDIANS* **SEE** PEQUAWKET INDIANS / *wars*
BX8101-8143	*AMISH* **SEE** MENNONITES
BX8101-8143	*AMISH MENNONITES* **SEE** MENNONITES
PM3516	AMISHGO LANGUAGE
QC544.A5	AMMETER
QP913.N15	AMMONIA — PHYSIOLOGICAL EFFECT
QD181.N15	AMMONIA / *chemistry*
TP223	AMMONIA / *manufacture*
RM666.A5	AMMONIA / *therapeutics*
QE807.A5	*AMMONITES* **SEE** AMMONOIDEA
QD181.C6	*AMMONIUM COBALT BASES* **SEE** COBALT-AMMONIUM COMPOUNDS
QE807.A5	AMMONOIDEA
UF700-780	AMMUNITION
RC394.A5	AMNESIA
QL975	AMNION / *embryology*
QM611	AMNION / *human embryology*
QL975	AMNIOTIC LIQUID / *embryology*
QM611	AMNIOTIC LIQUID / *human embryology*
QL368.A5	AMOEBA
DS72.5	AMORITES
HG8793	*AMORTIZATION TABLES* **SEE** ANNUITIES — TABLES
HG1626-1638	*AMORTIZATION TABLES* **SEE** INTEREST AND USURY — TABLES, ETC.
HG1626-1638	*AMORTIZATION-TABLES, ETC.* **SEE** INTEREST AND USURY — TABLES, ETC.
QL696.P2	*AMPELIDAE* **SEE** WAXWINGS
QC536	AMPERES
QD115	*AMPEROMETRIC ANALYSIS* **SEE** CONDUCTOMETRIC ANALYSIS
QL641-669	*AMPHIBIA* **SEE** BATRACHIA
QL641-669	*AMPHIBIA* **SEE** REPTILES
GR740	*AMPHIBIA* **SEE** REPTILES / *folk-lore*
V880	*AMPHIBIOUS MOTOR VEHICLES* **SEE** MOTOR VEHICLES, AMPHIBIOUS / *naval science*

QE399	AMPHIBOLITE
DF85	AMPHICTYONIC LEAGUE
QH471-489	*AMPHIMIXIS* **SEE** REPRODUCTION
QP251-281	*AMPHIMIXIS* **SEE** REPRODUCTION / *animals*
QL430.1	AMPHINEURA
QL444.A5	AMPHIPODA
NK4620-4657	*AMPHORAE* **SEE** VASES / *ceramics*
NK7220	*AMPHORAE* **SEE** VASES / *gold*
NK4623-4	*AMPHORAE* **SEE** VASES / *museums collections*
NK7230	*AMPHORAE* **SEE** VASES / *silver*
TK7872.A5	AMPLIFIERS (ELECTRONICS)
TK2851	*AMPLIFIERS, MAGNETIC* **SEE** MAGNETIC AMPLIFIERS
TK7872.M3	*AMPLIFIERS, MAGNETIC* **SEE** MAGNETIC AMPLIFIERS / *electronics*
TK7872.A5	*AMPLIFIERS, PARAMETRIC* **SEE** PARAMETRIC AMPLIFIERS
TK2699	*AMPLIFIERS, ROTATING* **SEE** ROTATING AMPLIFIERS
QC544.V3	AMPLIFIERS, VACUUM-TUBE
CR4480	AMPULLAS, CORONATION
RD553	AMPUTATION
RD557	AMPUTATIONS OF ARM
RD560	AMPUTATIONS OF LEG
PM6358	*AMUEIXA LANGUAGE* **SEE** LORENZAN LANGUAGE
PM6358	*AMUESA LANGUAGE* **SEE** LORENZAN LANGUAGE
GR600	AMULETS
GV1835	AMUSEMENT PARKS
GV1851-5	AMUSEMENT PARKS
BV4597	AMUSEMENTS — MORAL AND RELIGIOUS ASPECTS
HJ5797	AMUSEMENTS — TAXATION
GV1231	*AMUSEMENTS FOR INVALIDS* **SEE** INVALIDS — RECREATION
PM3516	*AMUZGO LANGUAGE* **SEE** AMISHGO LANGUAGE
QK896	*AMYLASE* **SEE** DIASTASE / *botany*
QP601	*AMYLASE* **SEE** DIASTASE / *physiological chemistry*
QP321	*AMYOTROPHY* **SEE** ATROPHY, MUSCULAR / *physiology*
RD688	*AMYOTROPHY* **SEE** ATROPHY, MUSCULAR / *surgery*
QD419	AMYRIN
PN6259-6268	*ANA* **SEE** ANECDOTES / *collections*
D10	*ANA* **SEE** ANECDOTES / *historical*
PN6299-6308	*ANA* **SEE** APHORISMS AND APOTHEGMS
PN6269-6278	*ANA* **SEE** APHORISMS AND APOTHEGMS
PN6299-6308	*ANA* **SEE** MAXIMS
PN6400-6525	*ANA* **SEE** PROVERBS
PN6259-6268	*ANA* **SEE** TABLE-TALK
BX4929-4946	ANABAPTISTS
QH331	*ANABIOSIS* **SEE** CRYPTOBIOSIS
QH521	*ANABOLISM* **SEE** METABOLISM / *biology*
QH631	*ANABOLISM* **SEE** METABOLISM / *cytology*
QP171	*ANABOLISM* **SEE** METABOLISM / *physiology*
PN6231.B8	*ANACHRONISMS, LITERARY* **SEE** ERRORS AND BLUNDERS, LITERARY
DS432.Y	*ANADIS* **SEE** YANADIS
RC641	*ANAEMIA* **SEE** ANEMIA
QR84	*ANAEROBIC BACTERIA* **SEE** BACTERIA, ANAEROBIC
RD79-87	*ANAESTHESIA* **SEE** ANESTHESIA
RD79-87	*ANAESTHETICS* **SEE** ANESTHETICS
PN6369-6377	ANAGRAMS / *collections*
PN1525	ANAGRAMS / *poetry*
PL6217	*ANAITEUM LANGUAGE* **SEE** ANEITYUM LANGUAGE
QE391.A55	*ANALCIM* **SEE** ANALCITE
QE391.A55	ANALCITE
QA76	*ANALOG CALCULATING-MACHINES* **SEE** ELECTRONIC ANALOG COMPUTERS
TK7872.M8	ANALOG MULTIPLIERS
BT1100-1101	ANALOGY (RELIGION) / *apologetics*
BL210	ANALOGY (RELIGION) / *natural theology*
BD190	ANALOGY
TN550-580	*ANALYSIS (CHEMISTRY)* **SEE** ASSAYING
HG325-9	*ANALYSIS (CHEMISTRY)* **SEE** ASSAYING / *mints*
QD87	*ANALYSIS (CHEMISTRY)* **SEE** BLOWPIPE
QD71-142	*ANALYSIS (CHEMISTRY)* **SEE** CHEMISTRY, ANALYTIC
QA300-316	*ANALYSIS (MATHEMATICS)* **SEE** CALCULUS
QA331-351	*ANALYSIS (MATHEMATICS)* **SEE** FUNCTIONS
QA401-411	*ANALYSIS (MATHEMATICS)* **SEE** HARMONIC ANALYSIS
B808.5	ANALYSIS (PHILOSOPHY)
QP91-95	*ANALYSIS OF BLOOD* **SEE** BLOOD — ANALYSIS AND CHEMISTRY / *physiology*

RB145	*ANALYSIS OF BLOOD* **SEE** BLOOD — ANALYSIS AND CHEMISTRY / *pathology*
QC495	*ANALYSIS OF COLORS* **SEE** COLORS — ANALYSIS
P93	*ANALYSIS OF CONTENT (COMMUNICATION)* **SEE** CONTENT ANALYSIS (COMMUNICATION)
TX541-5	*ANALYSIS OF FOOD* **SEE** FOOD — ANALYSIS
HD9000.9	*ANALYSIS OF FOOD* **SEE** FOOD ADULTERATION AND INSPECTION / *economics*
TX501-595	*ANALYSIS OF FOOD* **SEE** FOOD ADULTERATION AND INSPECTION / *technical works*
TP671	*ANALYSIS OF OIL* **SEE** OIL ANALYSIS
S593	*ANALYSIS OF SOILS* **SEE** SOILS — ANALYSIS
QA276	*ANALYSIS OF TIME SERIES* **SEE** TIME-SERIES ANALYSIS
QA611	*ANALYSIS SITUS* **SEE** TOPOLOGY / *geometry*
QD115	*ANALYSIS, ELECTROCHEMICAL* **SEE** ELECTROCHEMICAL ANALYSIS
QD115	*ANALYSIS, ELECTROLYTIC* **SEE** ELECTROCHEMICAL ANALYSIS
HF5549.5.J6	*ANALYSIS, JOB* **SEE** JOB ANALYSIS
B808.5	*ANALYSIS, LINGUISTIC* **SEE** ANALYSIS (PHILOSOPHY)
B808.5	*ANALYSIS, LOGICAL* **SEE** ANALYSIS (PHILOSOPHY)
TN565	*ANALYSIS, METALLURGICAL* **SEE** METALLURGICAL ANALYSIS / *assaying*
QD133	*ANALYSIS, METALLURGICAL* **SEE** METALLURGICAL ANALYSIS / *chemistry*
TN690-693	*ANALYSIS, MICROSCOPIC* **SEE** METALLOGRAPHY
QH201-277	*ANALYSIS, MICROSCOPIC* **SEE** MICROSCOPE AND MICROSCOPY
B808.5	*ANALYSIS, PHILOSOPHICAL* **SEE** ANALYSIS (PHILOSOPHY)
QC451-467	*ANALYSIS, SPECTRUM* **SEE** SPECTRUM ANALYSIS
QD95	*ANALYSIS, SPECTRUM* **SEE** SPECTRUM ANALYSIS / *chemical analysis*
QD111	*ANALYSIS, VOLUMETRIC* **SEE** VOLUMETRIC ANALYSIS
QD71-142	*ANALYTICAL CHEMISTRY* **SEE** CHEMISTRY, ANALYTIC
QA551-581	*ANALYTICAL GEOMETRY* **SEE** GEOMETRY, ANALYTIC
QA801-935	*ANALYTICAL MECHANICS* **SEE** MECHANICS, ANALYTIC
B808.5	*ANALYTICAL PHILOSOPHY* **SEE** ANALYSIS (PHILOSOPHY)
QR185	ANAPHYLAXIS
SF967.A	ANAPLASMOSIS
HX821-970	ANARCHISM AND ANARCHISTS
E99.P9	*ANASAZI CULTURE* **SEE** PUEBLO INDIANS
BX2275	*ANATHEMA* **SEE** EXCOMMUNICATION / *catholic church*
QM41	ANATOMICAL LABORATORIES
QM51	ANATOMICAL MUSEUMS
QL814	ANATOMICAL MUSEUMS
QL814	ANATOMICAL SPECIMENS
QM16	ANATOMISTS
QK641-707	*ANATOMY OF PLANTS* **SEE** BOTANY — ANATOMY
NC760	ANATOMY, ARTISTIC
QL812	ANATOMY, COMPARATIVE — LABORATORY MANUALS
QL801-950	ANATOMY, COMPARATIVE
QL858	*ANATOMY, DENTAL* **SEE** TEETH / *comparative anatomy*
QM311	*ANATOMY, DENTAL* **SEE** TEETH / *human anatomy*
GN209	*ANATOMY, DENTAL* **SEE** TEETH / *somatology*
QM25	ANATOMY, HUMAN — ATLASES
QM33	ANATOMY, HUMAN — CHARTS, DIAGRAMS, ETC.
QM21	ANATOMY, HUMAN — EARLY WORKS TO 1800
QM32	ANATOMY, HUMAN — EXAMINATIONS, QUESTIONS, ETC.
QM34-39	ANATOMY, HUMAN — LABORATORY MANUALS
QM81	ANATOMY, HUMAN — TERMINOLOGY
QM	ANATOMY, HUMAN
QM550-575	*ANATOMY, MICROSCOPIC* **SEE** HISTOLOGY
RB24-57	*ANATOMY, MORBID* **SEE** ANATOMY, PATHOLOGICAL
RB24-57	ANATOMY, PATHOLOGICAL
QM531-549	*ANATOMY, REGIONAL* **SEE** ANATOMY, SURGICAL AND TOPOGRAPHICAL
QM531-549	ANATOMY, SURGICAL AND TOPOGRAPHICAL
QK641-707	*ANATOMY, VEGETABLE* **SEE** BOTANY — ANATOMY
SF761-7	*ANATOMY, VETERINARY* **SEE** VETERINARY ANATOMY
QM41	*ANATOMY-LABORATORIES* **SEE** ANATOMICAL LABORATORIES
BL467	ANCESTOR-WORSHIP
CS	*ANCESTRY* **SEE** GENEALOGY
QH431	*ANCESTRY* **SEE** HEREDITY / *biology*
HQ753	*ANCESTRY* **SEE** HEREDITY / *eugenics*
HV5133	*ANCESTRY* **SEE** HEREDITY / *heredity and alcoholism*
RJ91	*ANCESTRY* **SEE** HEREDITY / *heredity and child culture*
HV6121-5	*ANCESTRY* **SEE** HEREDITY / *heredity and crime*
BF418	*ANCESTRY* **SEE** HEREDITY / *heredity and genius*
BF341-6	*ANCESTRY* **SEE** HEREDITY / *psychology*
HM121	*ANCESTRY* **SEE** HEREDITY / *sociology*
VM831	*ANCHOR DAVITS* **SEE** DAVITS
VM801	*ANCHOR DAVITS* **SEE** DAVITS / *boat lowering*
CT9990-9991	*ANCHORITES* **SEE** HERMITS / *biography*
BX2845-7	*ANCHORITES* **SEE** HERMITS / *monasticism*
VM791	ANCHORS
N5315-5899	*ANCIENT ART* **SEE** ART, ANCIENT
PL2241-5	*ANCIENT CHINESE LANGUAGE* **SEE** CHINESE LANGUAGE — ARCHAIC CHINESE
G82-88	*ANCIENT GEOGRAPHY* **SEE** GEOGRAPHY, ANCIENT
D51-90	*ANCIENT HISTORY* **SEE** HISTORY, ANCIENT
F3097.3	ANCON, TREATY OF, 1883
SF489.A6	ANCONAS (POULTRY)
F2270.2.A	*ANDAKI INDIANS* **SEE** ANDAQUI INDIANS
SF489.A65	ANDALUSIANS (POULTRY)
F2270.2.A	ANDAQUI INDIANS
F3430.1.C3	*ANDE INDIANS* **SEE** CAMPA INDIANS
PM5716	*ANDE LANGUAGE* **SEE** CAMPA LANGUAGE
PL4771-9	*ANDHRA LANGUAGE* **SEE** TELUGU LANGUAGE
DT429	*ANDOROBO* **SEE** DOROBO (AFRICAN PEOPLE)
E473.55	*ANDREWS' RAID, 1862* **SEE** CHATTANOOGA RAILROAD EXPEDITION, 1862
E473.55	*ANDREWS' RAILROAD RAID* **SEE** CHATTANOOGA RAILROAD EXPEDITION, 1862
PN6259-6268	ANECDOTES / *collections*
D10	ANECDOTES / *historical*
PN6231.L4	*ANECDOTES, LEGAL* **SEE** LAW — ANECDOTES, FACETIAE, SATIRE, ETC. / *wit and humor*
PN6268.L4	*ANECDOTES, LEGAL* **SEE** LAW — ANECDOTES, FACETIAE, SATIRE, ETC. / *anecdotes*
R705	*ANECDOTES, MEDICAL* **SEE** MEDICINE — ANECDOTES, FACETIAE, SATIRE, ETC.
PN6231.M4	*ANECDOTES, MEDICAL* **SEE** MEDICINE — ANECDOTES, FACETIAE, SATIRE, ETC.
ML65	*ANECDOTES, MUSICAL* **SEE** MUSIC — ANECDOTES, FACETIAE, SATIRE, ETC.
PL6217	ANEITYUM LANGUAGE
QC191	*ANELASTICITY* **SEE** INTERNAL FRICTION
RC641	ANEMIA
QC932	ANEMOMETER
QC896	ANEROID BAROMETER
RD86.E4	*ANESTHESIA (ELECTRIC)* **SEE** ELECTRIC ANESTHESIA
RD139	*ANESTHESIA IN CHILDHOOD* **SEE** PEDIATRIC ANESTHESIA
RK510	ANESTHESIA IN DENTISTRY
RG732	ANESTHESIA IN OBSTETRICS
RE82	ANESTHESIA IN OPHTHALMOLOGY
RD79-87	ANESTHESIA
RD85.I	*ANESTHESIA, ENDOTRACHEAL* **SEE** INTRATRACHEAL ANESTHESIA
RD85.I	*ANESTHESIA, INTRATRACHEAL* **SEE** INTRATRACHEAL ANESTHESIA
RD85.I	*ANESTHESIA, INTRAVENOUS* **SEE** INTRAVENOUS ANESTHESIA
RD84	*ANESTHESIA, LOCAL* **SEE** LOCAL ANESTHESIA
RD85.P	*ANESTHESIA, PARAVERTEBRAL* **SEE** PARAVERTEBRAL ANESTHESIA
RD85.S7	*ANESTHESIA, SPINAL* **SEE** SPINAL ANESTHESIA
RK510	*ANESTHETICS IN DENTISTRY* **SEE** ANESTHESIA IN DENTISTRY
RG732	*ANESTHETICS IN OBSTETRICS* **SEE** ANESTHESIA IN OBSTETRICS
RE82	*ANESTHETICS IN OPHTHALMOLOGY* **SEE** ANESTHESIA IN OPHTHALMOLOGY
RD79-87	ANESTHETICS
RD84	*ANESTHETICS, LOCAL* **SEE** LOCAL ANESTHESIA
RC693	*ANEURISMS* **SEE** ANEURYSMS
RC693	ANEURYSMS
RC693	*ANEURYSMS, AORTIC* **SEE** AORTIC ANEURYSMS
F2846	ANGACO, BATTLE OF, 1841
DS432.N3	*ANGAMI NAGAS* **SEE** NAGAS
PL8047	ANGAS LANGUAGE
PL8047	*ANGASS LANGUAGE* **SEE** ANGAS LANGUAGE

RS165.A5	ANGELICA
BL477	*ANGELOLOGY* **SEE** ANGELS / *comparative religion*
BT965-8	*ANGELOLOGY* **SEE** ANGELS / *theology*
N8090	ANGELS — ART
BP166.89	ANGELS (ISLAM)
BM645.A6	ANGELS (JUDAISM)
BL477	ANGELS / *comparative religion*
BT965-8	ANGELS / *theology*
BJ1535.A6	ANGER / *ethics*
BF575.A5	ANGER / *psychology*
RD641-2	*ANGINA LUDOVICI* **SEE** NECK — ABSCESS
RC685.A6	ANGINA PECTORIS
QK495.A	ANGIOSPERMS
QA468	*ANGLE TRISECTION* **SEE** TRISECTION OF ANGLE
QA482	ANGLE
QL638.L75	ANGLER-FISHES
BX5011-5199	*ANGLICAN CHURCH* **SEE** CHURCH OF ENGLAND
NA4821.A	*ANGLICAN CHURCHES* **SEE** CHURCHES, ANGLICAN
BX5008	ANGLICAN COMMUNION — SERMONS
BX5003-9	ANGLICAN COMMUNION
BX5969	*ANGLICAN COMMUNION-PARISH MISSIONS* **SEE** PARISH MISSIONS — ANGLICAN COMMUNION / *protestant episcopal*
BX5197-9	*ANGLICAN CONVERTS* **SEE** CONVERTS, ANGLICAN / *church of england*
BX5990-5995	*ANGLICAN CONVERTS* **SEE** CONVERTS, ANGLICAN / *protestant episcopal church*
BX5178	ANGLICAN ORDERS
SH401-691	*ANGLING* **SEE** FISHING
BX5121	ANGLO-CATHOLICISM
DJ193	ANGLO-DUTCH WAR, 1652-1654
DJ180-182	ANGLO-DUTCH WAR, 1664-1667
D277-8	*ANGLO-DUTCH WAR, 1672-1674* **SEE** DUTCH WAR, 1672-1678
DJ205-6	ANGLO-DUTCH WAR, 1780-1784
DA337	ANGLO-FRENCH WAR, 1512-1513
DC108	ANGLO-FRENCH WAR, 1512-1513
D274.5-6	ANGLO-FRENCH WAR, 1666-1667
DA448	ANGLO-FRENCH WAR, 1666-1667 / *english history*
DC127.3-8	ANGLO-FRENCH WAR, 1666-1667 / *french history*
E196	*ANGLO-FRENCH WAR, 1689-1697* **SEE** UNITED STATES — HISTORY — — KING WILLIAM'S WAR, 1689-1697
DC133	ANGLO-FRENCH WAR, 1755-1763
DA500-510	ANGLO-FRENCH WAR, 1755-1763
DD409-412	ANGLO-FRENCH WAR, 1755-1763
DC136	ANGLO-FRENCH WAR, 1778-1783
DA510	ANGLO-FRENCH WAR, 1778-1783
DA520	ANGLO-FRENCH WAR, 1793-1802
DC220-222	ANGLO-FRENCH WAR, 1793-1802
PR9735-9	ANGLO-INDIAN FICTION / *history*
PR9700-9799	ANGLO-INDIAN LITERATURE
PR9755-9769	ANGLO-INDIAN POETRY / *collections*
PR9726-9732	ANGLO-INDIAN POETRY / *history*
DS432.A	ANGLO-INDIANS
DS131	ANGLO-ISRAELISM
PC2941-8	ANGLO-NORMAN DIALECT
PR1344	ANGLO-NORMAN LETTERS / *collections*
PR913	ANGLO-NORMAN LETTERS / *history*
PR1119-1120	ANGLO-NORMAN LITERATURE / *collections*
PR1119-1120	ANGLO-NORMAN LITERATURE / *collections*
PR251-369	ANGLO-NORMAN LITERATURE / *history*
PR251-369	ANGLO-NORMAN LITERATURE / *history*
PR1203	ANGLO-NORMAN POETRY / *collections*
PR311-369	ANGLO-NORMAN POETRY / *history*
D749.5.A	ANGLO-RUSSIAN TREATY, 1942
PE101-299	ANGLO-SAXON LANGUAGE
PR1490-1508	ANGLO-SAXON LITERATURE / *collections*
PR171-236	ANGLO-SAXON LITERATURE / *history*
PR1490-1508	ANGLO-SAXON POETRY / *collections*
PR201-217	ANGLO-SAXON POETRY / *history*
CB216-220	ANGLO-SAXON RACE
DA150-162	ANGLO-SAXONS
D749.5.A	*ANGLO-SOVIET TREATY, 1942* **SEE** ANGLO-RUSSIAN TREATY, 1942
DA498-9	ANGLO-SPANISH WAR, 1718-1720
DP194	ANGLO-SPANISH WAR, 1718-1720
DA505-512	ANGLO-SPANISH WAR, 1762-1763
DP199	ANGLO-SPANISH WAR, 1762-1763
DP199	ANGLO-SPANISH WAR, 1779-1783
DA505-512	ANGLO-SPANISH WAR, 1779-1783
PL8381	*ANGOLA LANGUAGE* **SEE** KIMBUNDU LANGUAGE
SF449	ANGORA CAT
SF385	ANGORA GOAT
SF455	ANGORA RABBITS
RS165.A6	ANGOSTURA BARK
SF193.A14	*ANGUS CATTLE* **SEE** ABERDEEN-ANGUS CATTLE
SF199.A14	*ANGUS CATTLE* **SEE** ABERDEEN-ANGUS CATTLE
RS165.A6	*ANGUSTURA BARK* **SEE** ANGOSTURA BARK
QK495.C11	*ANHALONIUM* **SEE** PEYOTE / *cactus*
RS165.A7	*ANHALONIUM* **SEE** PEYOTE / *vegetable drugs*
QD341.A2	ANHYDRIDES
QD305.A2	ANHYDRIDES
QD181.N15	*ANHYDROUS AMMONIA* **SEE** AMMONIA / *chemistry*
TP223	*ANHYDROUS AMMONIA* **SEE** AMMONIA / *manufacture*
RM666.A5	*ANHYDROUS AMMONIA* **SEE** AMMONIA / *therapeutics*
TP918.A5	ANILINE BLACK
TP914	*ANILINE COLORS* **SEE** COAL-TAR COLORS
Z252.5.F6	*ANILINE PRINTING* **SEE** FLEXOGRAPHY
TP914	ANILINE
QD341.A8	ANILINE
GV1107	*ANIMAL BAITING* **SEE** BULL-FIGHTS
SF503	*ANIMAL BAITING* **SEE** COCK-FIGHTING
GV1109	*ANIMAL BAITING* **SEE** DOG-FIGHTING
QL750-785	*ANIMAL BEHAVIOR* **SEE** ANIMALS, HABITS AND BEHAVIOR OF
TP378	*ANIMAL BLACK* **SEE** ANIMAL CHARCOAL / *sugar manufacture*
SF757	*ANIMAL BODIES, DISPOSAL OF* **SEE** DEAD ANIMALS, REMOVAL AND DISPOSAL OF
TP378	ANIMAL CHARCOAL / *sugar manufacture*
QL767	*ANIMAL COLORATION* **SEE** COLOR OF ANIMALS
ND1380	*ANIMAL DRAWING* **SEE** ANIMAL PAINTING AND ILLUSTRATION / *painting*
NC780	*ANIMAL DRAWING* **SEE** ANIMAL PAINTING AND ILLUSTRATION / *drawing*
QP341-8	*ANIMAL ELECTRICITY* **SEE** ELECTROPHYSIOLOGY
QP951	ANIMAL EXTRACTS / *pharmacology*
RM283-298	ANIMAL EXTRACTS / *therapeutics*
TS1545	ANIMAL FIBERS
GV1107	*ANIMAL FIGHTING* **SEE** BULL-FIGHTS
SF503	*ANIMAL FIGHTING* **SEE** COCK-FIGHTING
GV1109	*ANIMAL FIGHTING* **SEE** DOG-FIGHTING
QP88	*ANIMAL FLUIDS AND HUMORS* **SEE** BODY FLUIDS
TX371-389	ANIMAL FOOD
NK1555	*ANIMAL FORMS IN DESIGN* **SEE** DESIGN, DECORATIVE — ANIMAL FORMS
QP135	ANIMAL HEAT
QL756	*ANIMAL HOMES* **SEE** ANIMALS, HABITATIONS OF
HD9410-9429	ANIMAL INDUSTRY / *economics*
BF685	*ANIMAL INSTINCT* **SEE** INSTINCT / *psychology*
QL781	*ANIMAL INSTINCT* **SEE** INSTINCT / *zoology*
QL785	ANIMAL INTELLIGENCE
QL	*ANIMAL KINGDOM* **SEE** ZOOLOGY
QL765	*ANIMAL LANGUAGE* **SEE** SOUND PRODUCTION BY ANIMALS
QH641	*ANIMAL LIGHT* **SEE** PHOSPHORESCENCE / *cytology*
QC478	*ANIMAL LIGHT* **SEE** PHOSPHORESCENCE / *optics*
QP301	ANIMAL LOCOMOTION
GR820-830	ANIMAL LORE
QL89	ANIMAL LORE
BF1111-1156	ANIMAL MAGNETISM / *psychical research*
RZ430	ANIMAL MAGNETISM / *therapeutics*
QP303	ANIMAL MECHANICS
QL754	ANIMAL MIGRATION
QP141-185	*ANIMAL NUTRITION* **SEE** NUTRITION
TP670-695	*ANIMAL OILS* **SEE** OILS AND FATS
NC780	ANIMAL PAINTING AND ILLUSTRATION / *drawing*
ND1380	ANIMAL PAINTING AND ILLUSTRATION / *painting*
QL757	*ANIMAL PARASITES* **SEE** PARASITES / *animal*
QK918	*ANIMAL PARASITES* **SEE** PARASITES / *plant*
SF810	*ANIMAL PARASITES* **SEE** PARASITES / *veterinary medicine*
QH245	*ANIMAL PHOTOGRAPHY* **SEE** PHOTOGRAPHY OF ANIMALS
SF76	ANIMAL PICTURES / *animal culture*

N7660	ANIMAL PICTURES / art
QP235	ANIMAL POISONS **SEE** VENOM / secretion
BF660-678	ANIMAL PSYCHOLOGY **SEE** PSYCHOLOGY, COMPARATIVE
QL791-5	ANIMAL STORIES **SEE** ANIMALS, LEGENDS AND STORIES OF
PZ	ANIMAL STORIES **SEE** ANIMALS, LEGENDS AND STORIES OF
GV1829-1831	ANIMAL TRAINING **SEE** ANIMALS, TRAINING OF
GT6715	ANIMAL TRIALS AND PUNISHMENT **SEE** ANIMALS, PROSECUTION AND PUNISHMENT OF
QL940-943	ANIMAL WEAPONS
BL439-443	ANIMAL-WORSHIP
QL365	ANIMALCULES
M1977.A5	ANIMALS — SONGS AND MUSIC
M1978.A5	ANIMALS — SONGS AND MUSIC
BF723.A45	ANIMALS AND CHILDREN **SEE** CHILDREN AND ANIMALS
QL85	ANIMALS AND CIVILIZATION
QL785	ANIMALS AS ARTISTS
QL89	ANIMALS IN FOLK-LORE **SEE** ANIMAL LORE
GR820-830	ANIMALS IN FOLK-LORE **SEE** ANIMAL LORE
QL991	ANIMALS, ABNORMALITIES OF **SEE** ABNORMALITIES (ANIMALS)
QH96-99	ANIMALS, AQUATIC **SEE** FRESH-WATER FAUNA / natural history
QL121-138	ANIMALS, AQUATIC **SEE** MARINE FAUNA
QL767	ANIMALS, COLOR OF **SEE** COLOR OF ANIMALS
HV4701-4959	ANIMALS, CRUELTY TO **SEE** ANIMALS, TREATMENT OF
SF600-998	ANIMALS, DISEASES OF **SEE** VETERINARY MEDICINE
SF	ANIMALS, DOMESTIC **SEE** DOMESTIC ANIMALS / animal industry
GN426	ANIMALS, DOMESTIC **SEE** DOMESTIC ANIMALS / ethnology
GT5870-5895	ANIMALS, DOMESTIC **SEE** DOMESTIC ANIMALS / manners and customs
S494	ANIMALS, DOMESTICATION OF **SEE** DOMESTICATION
SB123	ANIMALS, DOMESTICATION OF **SEE** DOMESTICATION
SF41	ANIMALS, DOMESTICATION OF **SEE** DOMESTICATION / agriculture
GT5870-5899	ANIMALS, DOMESTICATION OF **SEE** DOMESTICATION / manners and customs
QL55	ANIMALS, EXPERIMENTAL **SEE** LABORATORY ANIMALS
SF77	ANIMALS, EXPERIMENTAL **SEE** LABORATORY ANIMALS
QL88	ANIMALS, EXTINCT **SEE** EXTINCT ANIMALS
GR820-830	ANIMALS, FICTITIOUS **SEE** ANIMALS, MYTHICAL
QL756	ANIMALS, FOOD HABITS OF
QE701-996	ANIMALS, FOSSIL **SEE** PALEONTOLOGY
QL756	ANIMALS, HABITATIONS OF
QL750-785	ANIMALS, HABITS AND BEHAVIOR OF
GR820-830	ANIMALS, IMAGINARY **SEE** ANIMALS, MYTHICAL
QH647	ANIMALS, IRRITABILITY OF **SEE** IRRITABILITY / cells
PZ	ANIMALS, LEGENDS AND STORIES OF
QL791-5	ANIMALS, LEGENDS AND STORIES OF
QL754	ANIMALS, MIGRATION OF **SEE** ANIMAL MIGRATION
QP301	ANIMALS, MOVEMENTS OF **SEE** ANIMAL LOCOMOTION
QP303	ANIMALS, MOVEMENTS OF **SEE** ANIMAL MECHANICS
QH647	ANIMALS, MOVEMENTS OF **SEE** IRRITABILITY / cells
GR820-830	ANIMALS, MYTHICAL
QP443	ANIMALS, ORIENTATION OF **SEE** ORIENTATION
QH487	ANIMALS, PARTHENOGENESIS IN **SEE** PARTHENOGENESIS (ANIMALS)
QH245	ANIMALS, PHOTOGRAPHY OF **SEE** PHOTOGRAPHY OF ANIMALS
QP941	ANIMALS, POISONOUS **SEE** POISONOUS ANIMALS
GT6715	ANIMALS, PROSECUTION AND PUNISHMENT OF
HV4701-4959	ANIMALS, PROTECTION OF **SEE** ANIMALS, TREATMENT OF
QL88	ANIMALS, RARE **SEE** RARE ANIMALS
QP121	ANIMALS, RESPIRATION OF **SEE** RESPIRATION
HV4701-4959	ANIMALS, RESTRAINT OF **SEE** ANIMALS, TREATMENT OF
QL121-138	ANIMALS, SEA **SEE** MARINE FAUNA
QL765	ANIMALS, SOUND PRODUCTION BY **SEE** SOUND PRODUCTION BY ANIMALS
CB475	ANIMALS, SYMBOLIC **SEE** SYMBOLISM / civilization
BL600-620	ANIMALS, SYMBOLIC **SEE** SYMBOLISM / comparative religion
BF1623.S9	ANIMALS, SYMBOLIC **SEE** SYMBOLISM / occult sciences
BF458	ANIMALS, SYMBOLIC **SEE** SYMBOLISM / psychology
GV1829-1831	ANIMALS, TRAINING OF
QL89	ANIMALS, TRANSMUTATION OF **SEE** TRANSMUTATION OF ANIMALS
HV4701-4959	ANIMALS, TREATMENT OF
UH87-100	ANIMALS, WAR USE OF
BL439-443	ANIMALS, WORSHIP OF **SEE** ANIMAL-WORSHIP
QL791-5	ANIMALS-LEGENDS AND STORIES **SEE** ANIMALS, LEGENDS AND STORIES OF
PZ	ANIMALS-LEGENDS AND STORIES **SEE** ANIMALS, LEGENDS AND STORIES OF
NC1765	ANIMATED CARTOONS **SEE** MOVING-PICTURE CARTOONS / drawing
PN1997.5	ANIMATED CARTOONS **SEE** MOVING-PICTURE CARTOONS / scenarios
GN471	ANIMISM
QD553	ANIONS
QM131	ANKLE
RD562	ANKLE-EXCISION **SEE** EXCISION OF ANKLE
RC199.95	ANKYLOSTOMIA **SEE** HOOKWORMS
RC199.95	ANKYLOSTOMIASIS **SEE** HOOKWORM DISEASE
D11	ANNALS **SEE** CHRONOLOGY, HISTORICAL
JX1253	ANNALS **SEE** HISTORY / d history and international law
PN50	ANNALS **SEE** HISTORY / history and literature
B61	ANNALS **SEE** HISTORY / history and philosophy
JA78	ANNALS **SEE** HISTORY / history and political science
HM36	ANNALS **SEE** HISTORY / history and sociology
BX1950	ANNATES
QL391.A6	ANNELIDA
JS344.A5	ANNEXATION (MUNICIPAL GOVERNMENT) / u.s.
BT930	ANNIHILATION **SEE** ANNIHILATIONISM
BT930	ANNIHILATIONISM
AS7	ANNIVERSARIES
PN4784.A5	ANNIVERSARY EDITIONS OF NEWSPAPERS **SEE** NEWSPAPERS — ANNIVERSARY EDITIONS
BX961.H6	ANNO SANTO **SEE** HOLY YEAR
QB813	ANNUAL PARALLAX **SEE** PARALLAX — STARS
QB167	ANNUAL PARALLAX **SEE** PARALLAX — STARS / correction of observations
HD4928.A	ANNUAL WAGE PLANS **SEE** WAGES — ANNUAL WAGE
AY	ANNUALS **SEE** ALMANACS
QB8	ANNUALS **SEE** ALMANACS / nautical
QC999	ANNUALS **SEE** ALMANACS / weather
CE91	ANNUALS **SEE** CALENDARS
D11.5	ANNUALS **SEE** CALENDARS
AY10-19	ANNUALS **SEE** GIFT-BOOKS (ANNUALS, ETC.)
AY	ANNUALS **SEE** YEARBOOKS
HG8793	ANNUITIES — TABLES
HG8790-8793	ANNUITIES / life insurance
HJ4631	ANNUITIES / taxation
HQ822	ANNULMENT OF MARRIAGE **SEE** MARRIAGE — ANNULMENT
HQ1024	ANNULMENT OF MARRIAGE **SEE** MARRIAGE — ANNULMENT / canon law
BT610	ANNUNCIATION OF THE VIRGIN MARY **SEE** MARY, VIRGIN — ANNUNCIATION
BX2203	ANOINTINGS **SEE** UNCTION / catholic sacraments
BV4337	ANOINTINGS **SEE** UNCTION / pastoral theology
BV875	ANOINTINGS **SEE** UNCTION / sacramentals
BV800	ANOINTINGS **SEE** UNCTION / sacraments
BV860	ANOINTINGS **SEE** UNCTION / unction of the sick
BT1350	ANOMAEANS **SEE** EUNOMIANISM / arianism
NA203	ANONYMOUS ARCHITECTURE **SEE** ARCHITECTURE, ANONYMOUS
Z1041-1115	ANONYMS AND PSEUDONYMS
QL503.A6	ANOPLURA
QE461	ANORTHOSITE
BP195.N7	ANSARII **SEE** NOSAIRIANS
AG195-6	ANSWERS TO QUESTIONS **SEE** QUESTIONS AND ANSWERS

QL568.F7	*ANT* **SEE** ANTS
QL737.E2	ANT BEAR
QL513.M	ANT LIONS
PL5379	ANTAISAKA DIALECT
DF231.55	ANTALCIDAS, PEACE OF, 387 B.C.
G850-890	*ANTARCTIC EXPEDITIONS* **SEE** ANTARCTIC REGIONS
QK474	*ANTARCTIC EXPEDITIONS* **SEE** ANTARCTIC REGIONS / *botany*
QC994.9	*ANTARCTIC EXPEDITIONS* **SEE** ANTARCTIC REGIONS / *meteorology*
QH84.2	*ANTARCTIC EXPEDITIONS* **SEE** ANTARCTIC REGIONS / *natural history*
QC825.9	*ANTARCTIC EXPEDITIONS* **SEE** ANTARCTIC REGIONS / *terrestrial magnetism*
QL106	*ANTARCTIC EXPEDITIONS* **SEE** ANTARCTIC REGIONS / *zoology*
G850-890	ANTARCTIC REGIONS
QK474	ANTARCTIC REGIONS / *botany*
QC994.9	ANTARCTIC REGIONS / *meteorology*
QH84.2	ANTARCTIC REGIONS / *natural history*
QC825.9	ANTARCTIC REGIONS / *terrestrial magnetism*
QL106	ANTARCTIC REGIONS / *zoology*
QL737.E2	*ANTEATER, GREAT* **SEE** ANT BEAR
QE701-996	*ANTEDILUVIAN ANIMALS* **SEE** PALEONTOLOGY
QL737.U5	ANTELOPES
QE882.U3	ANTELOPES, FOSSIL
TK7872.A6	ANTENNAS (ELECTRONICS)
TK6565.A6	*ANTENNAS, RADIO* **SEE** RADIO — ANTENNAS
RC180-181	*ANTERIOR SPINAL PARALYSIS* **SEE** POLIOMYELITIS
PL5379	*ANTESAKA DIALECT* **SEE** ANTAISAKA DIALECT
RM635	ANTHELMINTICS
QK898.A6	ANTHOCYANIN
PN6014	ANTHOLOGIES
QL568.A6	*ANTHOPHORA* **SEE** MASON-BEES
QL377.C5-7	ANTHOZOA
QD393	ANTHRACENE
HD5325. M63 1887	ANTHRACITE COAL STRIKE, 1887-1888
HD5325. M63 1902	ANTHRACITE COAL STRIKE, 1902
HD5325. M63 1922	ANTHRACITE COAL STRIKE, 1922
HD5325. M63 1925	ANTHRACITE COAL STRIKE, 1925-1926
TN820-823	ANTHRACITE COAL
HD9450 9559	ANTHRACITE COAL
SB741.A55	ANTHRACNOSE
RC774	*ANTHRACOSIS* **SEE** LUNGS — DUST DISEASES
HD7264	*ANTHRACOSIS* **SEE** LUNGS — DUST DISEASES / *labor*
QD401	ANTHRANIL
QD305.K2	ANTHRAQUINONES
RM755	ANTHRAX — PREVENTIVE INOCULATION
RC121.A6	ANTHRAX
QR201.A6	ANTHRAX / *bacteriology*
SF787	ANTHRAX, SYMPTOMATIC / *veterinary medicine*
GF37	ANTHROPO-GEOGRAPHY — JUVENILE LITERATURE
GF	ANTHROPO-GEOGRAPHY
GN2	ANTHROPOLOGICAL INSTITUTES
GN35-41	ANTHROPOLOGICAL MUSEUMS AND COLLECTIONS
GN20-21	ANTHROPOLOGISTS
GN34	ANTHROPOLOGY — CLASSIFICATION
GN31.5	ANTHROPOLOGY — JUVENILE LITERATURE
Z286.A5	ANTHROPOLOGY PUBLISHING
GN	ANTHROPOLOGY
BS661	*ANTHROPOLOGY, BIBLICAL* **SEE** MAN (THEOLOGY) / *bible*
BT700-745	*ANTHROPOLOGY, BIBLICAL* **SEE** MAN (THEOLOGY) / *doctrinal theology*
BL256	*ANTHROPOLOGY, BIBLICAL* **SEE** MAN (THEOLOGY) / *religion*
HV6001-6197	*ANTHROPOLOGY, CRIMINAL* **SEE** CRIMINAL ANTHROPOLOGY
BS661	*ANTHROPOLOGY, DOCTRINAL* **SEE** MAN (THEOLOGY) / *bible*
BT700-745	*ANTHROPOLOGY, DOCTRINAL* **SEE** MAN (THEOLOGY) / *doctrinal theology*
BL256	*ANTHROPOLOGY, DOCTRINAL* **SEE** MAN (THEOLOGY) / *religion*
GN51-211	*ANTHROPOLOGY, PHYSICAL* **SEE** SOMATOLOGY
BS661	*ANTHROPOLOGY, THEOLOGICAL* **SEE** MAN (THEOLOGY) / *bible*
BT700-745	*ANTHROPOLOGY, THEOLOGICAL* **SEE** MAN (THEOLOGY) / *doctrinal theology*
BL256	*ANTHROPOLOGY, THEOLOGICAL* **SEE** MAN (THEOLOGY) / *religion*
Z286.A5	*ANTHROPOLOGY-PUBLISHING* **SEE** ANTHROPOLOGY PUBLISHING
GN53	ANTHROPOMETRY — INSTRUMENTS
GN51-59	ANTHROPOMETRY
GV435	ANTHROPOMETRY
BL215	ANTHROPOMORPHISM
GN409	*ANTHROPOPHAGY* **SEE** CANNIBALISM
BP595	ANTHROPOSOPHY
F3430.1.C3	*ANTI INDIANS* **SEE** CAMPA INDIANS
PM5716	*ANTI LANGUAGE* **SEE** CAMPA LANGUAGE
TL697.P7	*ANTI-ACCELERATION SUITS* **SEE** PRESSURE SUITS
UF625	ANTI-AIRCRAFT GUNS
TL697.P7	*ANTI-BLACKOUT SUITS* **SEE** PRESSURE SUITS
D749.5.A	ANTI-COMINTERN PACT
D749.5.A	*ANTI-COMMUNIST PACT* **SEE** ANTI-COMINTERN PACT
TA467	*ANTI-CORROSIVE PAINT* **SEE** CORROSION AND ANTI-CORROSIVES
TA462	*ANTI-CORROSIVE PAINT* **SEE** CORROSION AND ANTI-CORROSIVES
HD7819	*ANTI-INJUNCTION LAW* **SEE** INJUNCTIONS / *labor law*
JF721	*ANTI-INJUNCTION LAW* **SEE** INJUNCTIONS / *theory*
JK1542	*ANTI-INJUNCTION LAW* **SEE** INJUNCTIONS / *u.s. judiciary*
TP692.2	*ANTI-KNOCK COMPOUNDS* **SEE** GASOLINE — ANTI-KNOCK AND ANTI-KNOCK MIXTURES
DD256.3	ANTI-NAZI MOVEMENT
BR430	*ANTI-REFORMATION* **SEE** COUNTER-REFORMATION / *church history*
DD176-189	*ANTI-REFORMATION* **SEE** COUNTER-REFORMATION / *germany*
D220-271	*ANTI-REFORMATION* **SEE** COUNTER-REFORMATION / *history general*
HD199	ANTI-RENT TROUBLES, NEW YORK, 1839-1846
QP45	*ANTI-VIVISECTION* **SEE** VIVISECTION
HV4905-4959	*ANTI-VIVISECTION* **SEE** VIVISECTION / *antivivisection*
PM8080	ANTIBABELE (ARTIFICIAL LANGUAGE)
RS161	ANTIBIOTICS / *pharmacy*
RM265-7	ANTIBIOTICS / *therapeutics*
BT985	ANTICHRIST
TL691	*ANTICOLLISION LIGHTS, AIRCRAFT* **SEE** AEROPLANES — LIGHTING
RA1195-1260	*ANTIDOTES* **SEE** POISONS
E474.61	*ANTIETAM CAMPAIGN* **SEE** MARYLAND CAMPAIGN, 1862
E474.65	ANTIETAM, BATTLE OF, 1862
QD341.A8	*ANTIFEBRIN* **SEE** ACETANILID / *chemistry*
RM666.A2	*ANTIFEBRIN* **SEE** ACETANILID / *therapeutics*
HS525-7	ANTIMASONIC PARTY
E381-390	ANTIMASONIC PARTY
F123	ANTIMASONIC PARTY
QP801.A	ANTIMETABOLITES
UA10	*ANTIMILITARISM* **SEE** MILITARISM
JX1937-1964	*ANTIMILITARISM* **SEE** MILITARISM
U21	*ANTIMILITARISM* **SEE** MILITARISM
RM666.A55	ANTIMONY — THERAPEUTIC USE
TN490.A6	ANTIMONY ORES
QD181.S3	ANTIMONY / *chemistry*
TN799.A6	ANTIMONY / *metallurgy*
TN490.A6	ANTIMONY / *mining*
B2799.A6	ANTINOMY / *kant*
BF575.P9	*ANTIPATHIES* **SEE** PREJUDICES AND ANTIPATHIES
RM321	ANTIPHLOGISTICS
RM321	ANTIPYRETICS / *therapeutics*
RM666.A56	ANTIPYRIN / *therapeutics*
AM200-501	*ANTIQUES* **SEE** COLLECTORS AND COLLECTING
GN539	*ANTIQUITIES, ARYAN* **SEE** ARYAN ANTIQUITIES
BS620	*ANTIQUITIES, BIBLICAL* **SEE** BIBLE — ANTIQUITIES
BR130-133	*ANTIQUITIES, CHRISTIAN* **SEE** CHRISTIAN ANTIQUITIES
DE	*ANTIQUITIES, CLASSICAL* **SEE** CLASSICAL ANTIQUITIES

DG	*ANTIQUITIES, CLASSICAL* **SEE** CLASSICAL ANTIQUITIES / *rome*
BR130-133	*ANTIQUITIES, ECCLESIASTICAL* **SEE** CHRISTIAN ANTIQUITIES
CC140	*ANTIQUITIES, FORGERY OF* **SEE** FORGERY OF ANTIQUITIES
DD51-55	*ANTIQUITIES, GERMANIC* **SEE** GERMANIC ANTIQUITIES
DE	*ANTIQUITIES, GRECIAN* **SEE** CLASSICAL ANTIQUITIES
DF	*ANTIQUITIES, GRECIAN* **SEE** CLASSICAL ANTIQUITIES / *greece*
DG	*ANTIQUITIES, GRECIAN* **SEE** CLASSICAL ANTIQUITIES / *rome*
DS56	*ANTIQUITIES, ORIENTAL* **SEE** ORIENTAL ANTIQUITIES / *ancient orient*
N5343-5	*ANTIQUITIES, ORIENTAL* **SEE** ORIENTAL ANTIQUITIES / *art*
DS11	*ANTIQUITIES, ORIENTAL* **SEE** ORIENTAL ANTIQUITIES / *asia*
CC	*ANTIQUITIES, PREHISTORIC* **SEE** ARCHAEOLOGY
GT	*ANTIQUITIES, PREHISTORIC* **SEE** ARCHAEOLOGY / *manners and customs general*
DA-DU	*ANTIQUITIES, PREHISTORIC* **SEE** ARCHAEOLOGY / *national antiquities other than american*
E-F	*ANTIQUITIES, PREHISTORIC* **SEE** ARCHAEOLOGY / *n indian and other american antiquities*
GN	*ANTIQUITIES, PREHISTORIC* **SEE** ARCHAEOLOGY / *prehistoric antiquities*
GN700-875	*ANTIQUITIES, PREHISTORIC* **SEE** MAN, PREHISTORIC
DE	*ANTIQUITIES, ROMAN* **SEE** CLASSICAL ANTIQUITIES
DF	*ANTIQUITIES, ROMAN* **SEE** CLASSICAL ANTIQUITIES / *greece*
DG	*ANTIQUITIES, ROMAN* **SEE** CLASSICAL ANTIQUITIES / *rome*
QH361-371	*ANTIQUITY OF MAN* **SEE** MAN — ORIGIN
DS145	ANTISEMITISM
RM647-8	ANTISEPTIC MEDICATION
RD91-96	*ANTISEPTIC SURGERY* **SEE** SURGERY, ASEPTIC AND ANTISEPTIC
RG730	ANTISEPTICS IN OBSTETRICS
RD91	ANTISEPTICS / *surgery*
RM400	ANTISEPTICS / *therapeutics*
HT851-1445	*ANTISLAVERY* **SEE** SLAVERY
TP690.6	*ANTISTATIC COMPOUNDS* **SEE** PETROLEUM PRODUCTS — ANTISTATIC ADDITIVES
UF628	ANTITANK GUNS
BL325.P7	*ANTITHESES (IN RELIGION, FOLK-LORE, ETC.)* **SEE** POLARITY (IN RELIGION, FOLK-LORE, ETC.)
RA401	*ANTITOXINS* **SEE** TOXINS AND ANTITOXINS / *etc.*
QP941	*ANTITOXINS* **SEE** TOXINS AND ANTITOXINS / *experimental pharmacology*
QP631	*ANTITOXINS* **SEE** TOXINS AND ANTITOXINS / *physiological chemistry*
HD2750-2752	*ANTITRUST LAWS* **SEE** TRUSTS, INDUSTRIAL — LAW
HD2777-2781	*ANTITRUST LAWS* **SEE** TRUSTS, INDUSTRIAL — LAW / *u.s.*
QL942	ANTLERS
BX9998.A6	ANTOINISM
PZ10.3	ANTS — LEGENDS AND STORIES / *juvenile*
QL795.A65	ANTS — LEGENDS AND STORIES / *zoology*
QL568.F7	ANTS
QE832.H9	ANTS, FOSSIL
DH652	ANTWERP — SIEGE, 1832
D542.A6	ANTWERP — SIEGE, 1914
PL6240	*ANUDHA LANGUAGE* **SEE** FLORIDA LANGUAGE
QL668.E2	ANURA
RC864-6	ANUS — DISEASES
RD672	ANUS — SURGERY
RD544	ANUS — SURGERY
P943	*ANZANIC LANGUAGE* **SEE** ELAMITE LANGUAGE
PL4001.A7	AO LANGUAGE
F2823.05	*AONAS* **SEE** ONA INDIANS
PM6691	*AONIK LANGUAGE* **SEE** ONA LANGUAGE
RC691	AORTA — DISEASES
QM191	AORTA
QL835	AORTA
RC693	AORTIC ANEURYSMS
RC685.V2	*AORTIC REGURGITATION* **SEE** HEART — VALVES — — DISEASES
PL8089	*AOWIN LANGUAGE* **SEE** BRISSA LANGUAGE
PK1421-9	APABHRAMSA LANGUAGES
PK1428	APABHRAMSA LITERATURE
E83.88	APACHE INDIANS — WARS, 1883-1886
E99.A6	APACHE INDIANS
PM631	APACHE LANGUAGE
E99.Y	*APACHE MOHAVE INDIANS* **SEE** YAVAPAI INDIANS
PM633	APALACHEE LANGUAGE
E99.A63	APALACHICOLA INDIANS
F2520.1.A62	APALAI INDIANS
F2520.1.A	APALAKIRI INDIANS
F2520.1.A62	*APARAI INDIANS* **SEE** APALAI INDIANS
HF5686.A	APARTMENT HOUSES — ACCOUNTING
NA7860	APARTMENT HOUSES / *architecture*
TX957-8	APARTMENT HOUSES / *service*
TN948.A7	APATITE / *mineral resources*
QE391.A6	APATITE / *mineralogy*
DS666.I7	*APAYAO* **SEE** ISNEG
GR730.A6	APES (IN RELIGION, FOLK-LORE, ETC.)
QL785	*APES AS ARTISTS* **SEE** ANIMALS AS ARTISTS
QL737.P9	APES
RC425	APHASIA
SB945.P64	*APHIDIDAE* **SEE** PLANT-LICE / *insect pests*
QL523.A6	*APHIDIDAE* **SEE** PLANT-LICE / *zoology*
SB945.P64	*APHIDS* **SEE** PLANT-LICE / *insect pests*
QL523.A6	*APHIDS* **SEE** PLANT-LICE / *zoology*
PN6269-6278	APHORISMS AND APOTHEGMS
PN6299-6308	APHORISMS AND APOTHEGMS
HQ12	APHRODISIACS / *sex relations*
RC815	*APHTHAE* **SEE** THRUSH (MOUTH DISEASE)
RJ463	*APHTHAE* **SEE** THRUSH (MOUTH DISEASE) / *children*
SF521-539	*APICULTURE* **SEE** BEE CULTURE
F2520.1.A65	APINAGE INDIANS
F2520.1.A65	*APINAYE INDIANS* **SEE** APINAGE INDIANS
QL430.1	*APLACOPHORA* **SEE** SOLENOGASTRES
BS1705	APOCALYPTIC LITERATURE
BS646	APOCALYPTIC LITERATURE
BX9901-9996	*APOCATASTASIS* **SEE** RESTORATIONISM / *universalism*
RM666.A6	APOCYNUM / *therapeutics*
QL638.A55	*APODAL FISHES* **SEE** EELS
QL638.A55	*APODES* **SEE** EELS
QK826	APOGAMY
ML1015-1018	*APOLLO LYRE* **SEE** LYRE-GUITAR
BT1115-1116	APOLOGETICS — EARLY CHURCH
BT1100	APOLOGETICS — MIDDLE AGES
BT1100	APOLOGETICS — 17TH CENTURY
BT1100	APOLOGETICS — 18TH CENTURY
BT1101-5	APOLOGETICS — 19TH CENTURY
BT1101-5	APOLOGETICS — 20TH CENTURY
BT1095-1255	APOLOGETICS
BP170	*APOLOGETICS, ISLAMIC* **SEE** ISLAM — APOLOGETIC WORKS
BM648	*APOLOGETICS, JEWISH* **SEE** JUDAISM — APOLOGETIC WORKS
BV2063)	APOLOGETICS, MISSIONARY
BP170	*APOLOGETICS, MUSLIM* **SEE** ISLAM — APOLOGETIC WORKS
PL8675	*APONO LANGUAGE* **SEE** SHIRA LANGUAGE
RC394.A7	APOPLEXY
BM720.H5	APOSTASY (JUDAISM)
BS2440	APOSTLES
BT992-3	APOSTLES' CREED
BX2348	*APOSTOLATE, LAY* **SEE** CATHOLIC ACTION
BX1970	*APOSTOLATE, LITURGICAL* **SEE** LITURGICAL MOVEMENT — CATHOLIC CHURCH
BX1939.A3	*APOSTOLIC ADMINISTRATORS* **SEE** ADMINISTRATORS APOSTOLIC
BR160-240	*APOSTOLIC CHURCH* **SEE** CHURCH HISTORY — PRIMITIVE AND EARLY CHURCH
BR1705	APOSTOLIC FATHERS / *collective biography*
BR60-67	APOSTOLIC FATHERS / *patrology*
BX1910	*APOSTOLIC PREFECTS* **SEE** VICARS APOSTOLIC
BV665	APOSTOLIC SUCCESSION
BX1910	*APOSTOLIC VICARS* **SEE** VICARS APOSTOLIC
RS	*APOTHECARIES* **SEE** PHARMACISTS
GT6380	*APOTHECARIES* **SEE** PHARMACISTS / *manners and customs*
PN6299-6308	*APOTHEGMS* **SEE** APHORISMS AND APOTHEGMS
PN6269-6278	*APOTHEGMS* **SEE** APHORISMS AND APOTHEGMS

BL465	APOTHEOSIS
DS666.I7	*APOYAO* **SEE** ISNEG
ML1015-1018	*APPALACHIAN DULCIMER* **SEE** DULCIMER
PM633	*APPALACHIAN LANGUAGE* **SEE** APALACHEE LANGUAGE
E99.A63	*APPALACHICOLA INDIANS* **SEE** APALACHICOLA INDIANS
HV1701	*APPARATUS FOR THE BLIND* **SEE** BLIND, APPARATUS FOR THE
QD53	*APPARATUS, CHEMICAL* **SEE** CHEMICAL APPARATUS
TK	*APPARATUS, ELECTRIC* **SEE** ELECTRIC APPARATUS AND APPLIANCES / *electric industries*
RM889	*APPARATUS, ELECTRIC* **SEE** ELECTRIC APPARATUS AND APPLIANCES / *medical apparatus*
QC543-4	*APPARATUS, ELECTRIC* **SEE** ELECTRIC APPARATUS AND APPLIANCES / *scientific apparatus*
RE	*APPARATUS, OPHTHALMOLOGICAL* **SEE** EYE, INSTRUMENTS AND APPARATUS FOR
RD755-7	*APPARATUS, ORTHOPEDIC* **SEE** ORTHOPEDIC APPARATUS
QP55	*APPARATUS, PHYSIOLOGICAL* **SEE** PHYSIOLOGICAL APPARATUS
Q184-5	*APPARATUS, SCIENTIFIC* **SEE** SCIENTIFIC APPARATUS AND INSTRUMENTS
RD71-78	*APPARATUS, SURGICAL* **SEE** SURGICAL INSTRUMENTS AND APPARATUS
QC104	*APPARATUS, VOLUMETRIC* **SEE** VOLUMETRIC APPARATUS / *physics*
BF1445-1486	APPARITIONS
BX1939.A6	APPELLATE PROCEDURE (CANON LAW)
RD542	APPENDICITIS
QL863	APPENDIX (ANATOMY) / *comparative anatomy*
QM345	APPENDIX (ANATOMY) / *human anatomy*
QL863	*APPENDIX VERMIFORMIS* **SEE** APPENDIX (ANATOMY) / *comparative anatomy*
QM345	*APPENDIX VERMIFORMIS* **SEE** APPENDIX (ANATOMY) / *human anatomy*
BF433.A6	APPERCEPTION — TESTING
BF321	APPERCEPTION
LB1067	APPERCEPTION / *educational psychology*
BF575.D4	*APPETENCY* **SEE** DESIRE
TX819	*APPETIZERS* **SEE** COOKERY (RELISHES)
PN2091.A7	*APPLAUSE IN THEATERS* **SEE** THEATER — APPLAUSE, DEMONSTRATIONS, ETC.
SB608.A6	APPLE — DISEASES AND PESTS
SB608.A6	APPLE BLUE MOLD
SB945.E	*APPLE-TREE TENT CATERPILLAR* **SEE** EASTERN TENT CATERPILLAR
SB363	APPLE
QC543-4	*APPLIANCES, ELECTRIC* **SEE** ELECTRIC APPARATUS AND APPLIANCES / *scientific apparatus*
RM889	*APPLIANCES, ELECTRIC* **SEE** ELECTRIC APPARATUS AND APPLIANCES / *medical apparatus*
TK	*APPLIANCES, ELECTRIC* **SEE** ELECTRIC APPARATUS AND APPLIANCES / *electric industries*
HF5383	APPLICATIONS FOR POSITIONS
NK	*APPLIED ART* **SEE** ART INDUSTRIES AND TRADE
TA350	*APPLIED MECHANICS* **SEE** MECHANICS, APPLIED
TS245	*APPLIED POWDER METALLURGY* **SEE** POWDER METAL PROCESSES
BF67	*APPLIED PSYCHOLOGY* **SEE** PSYCHOLOGY, APPLIED
BF636	*APPLIED PSYCHOLOGY* **SEE** PSYCHOLOGY, APPLIED
T-TX	*APPLIED SCIENCE* **SEE** TECHNOLOGY
NK9100-9199	APPLIQUE
E477.67	APPOMATTOX CAMPAIGN, 1865
HJ3241	*APPRAISAL* **SEE** ASSESSMENT
HF5681.V3	*APPRAISAL* **SEE** VALUATION / *accounting*
HG4028.V3	*APPRAISAL* **SEE** VALUATION / *corporation finance*
HJ6670	*APPRAISAL* **SEE** VALUATION / *customs administration*
TA178	*APPRAISAL* **SEE** VALUATION / *engineering*
HD2765	*APPRAISAL* **SEE** VALUATION / *public service corporations*
HD1387	*APPRAISAL* **SEE** VALUATION / *real estate*
Z1035	*APPRAISAL OF BOOKS* **SEE** BIBLIOGRAPHY — BEST BOOKS
Z1003	*APPRAISAL OF BOOKS* **SEE** BOOKS AND READING
BH39-41	*APPRAISAL OF BOOKS* **SEE** CRITICISM / *aesthetics*
PN75-99	*APPRAISAL OF BOOKS* **SEE** CRITICISM / *literary criticism*
PN441-595	*APPRAISAL OF BOOKS* **SEE** LITERATURE — HISTORY AND CRITICISM / *history*
PN75-99	*APPRAISAL OF BOOKS* **SEE** LITERATURE — HISTORY AND CRITICISM / *criticism*
N61-79	*APPRECIATION OF ART* **SEE** AESTHETICS / *art*
BH	*APPRECIATION OF ART* **SEE** AESTHETICS / *philosophy*
N7435-6	*APPRECIATION OF ART* **SEE** ART CRITICISM
N8370-8375	*APPRECIATION OF ART* **SEE** ART CRITICISM / *art critics*
ND	*APPRECIATION OF ART* **SEE** PAINTING
N350-375	*APPRECIATION OF ART* **SEE** PICTURES / *art study in schools*
ND1142-6	*APPRECIATION OF ART* **SEE** PICTURES / *popular works*
MT6	*APPRECIATION OF MUSIC* **SEE** MUSIC — ANALYSIS, APPRECIATION
BF311	*APPREHENSION* **SEE** PERCEPTION
HD4881-5	APPRENTICES
Z122.5	APPRENTICES / *printers' apprentices*
E91-93	*APPROPRIATIONS, INDIAN* **SEE** INDIANS OF NORTH AMERICA — APPROPRIATIONS
QA221	APPROXIMATE COMPUTATION
SB379.A7	APRICOT
QL503.T6	*APTERA* **SEE** THYSANURA
BF431	*APTITUDE TESTS* **SEE** ABILITY — TESTING
QL78-79	AQUARIUMS
QH68	AQUARIUMS
QH96-99	*AQUATIC ANIMALS* **SEE** FRESH-WATER FAUNA / *natural history*
QL121-138	*AQUATIC ANIMALS* **SEE** MARINE FAUNA
QL671-698	*AQUATIC BIRDS* **SEE** WATER-BIRDS
SK351-579	*AQUATIC BIRDS* **SEE** WATER-BIRDS / *game preservation*
SK331-3	*AQUATIC BIRDS* **SEE** WATER-BIRDS / *hunting*
QL496	*AQUATIC INSECTS* **SEE** INSECTS, AQUATIC
SB423	AQUATIC PLANTS·
GV771-840	AQUATIC SPORTS
NE1820	AQUATINT
TD398	AQUEDUCTS
QL949	AQUEOUS HUMOR / *animals*
QM511	AQUEOUS HUMOR / *man*
NA380-388	*ARAB ARCHITECTURE* **SEE** ARCHITECTURE, ISLAMIC
N6260-6271	*ARAB ART* **SEE** ART, ISLAMIC
DS215	*ARAB CIVILIZATION* **SEE** CIVILIZATION, ARAB
B740-753	*ARAB PHILOSOPHY* **SEE** PHILOSOPHY, ARAB / *medieval*
DS126	*ARAB RIOTS, 1929* **SEE** PALESTINE — HISTORY — — ARAB RIOTS, 1929
DS126.9-99	*ARAB-ISRAEL WAR, 1948-1949* **SEE** ISRAEL-ARAB WAR, 1948-1949
NK1575	ARABESQUES
SF293.A8	ARABIAN HORSE
PJ6123	ARABIC ALPHABET
PJ6001-7134	ARABIC LANGUAGE
PJ6123	*ARABIC LANGUAGE-ALPHABET* **SEE** ARABIC ALPHABET
PJ1623-6	*ARABIC LANGUAGE-WRITING* **SEE** WRITING, ARABIC
Z675.A82	ARABIC LIBRARIES
PJ7501-8518	ARABIC LITERATURE
QA27.A	*ARABIC MATHEMATICS* **SEE** MATHEMATICS, ARABIC
PN5449.A	ARABIC PERIODICALS
PJ6001-6071	ARABIC PHILOLOGY
B740-753	*ARABIC PHILOSOPHY* **SEE** PHILOSOPHY, ARAB / *medieval*
B163	*ARABIC PHILOSOPHY* **SEE** PHILOSOPHY, ISLAMIC
B740-753	*ARABIC PHILOSOPHY* **SEE** PHILOSOPHY, ISLAMIC / *medieval*
PJ7631-7661	ARABIC POETRY / *collections*
PJ7541-7561	ARABIC POETRY / *history*
PN6222.A	ARABIC WIT AND HUMOR
PQ6056	*ARABIC-SPANISH POETRY* **SEE** MOZARABIC POETRY
DP98-123	ARABS IN SPAIN
DS218-219	ARABS
QL451-9	ARACHNIDA
PJ5201-5329	ARAMAIC LANGUAGE
PJ5201-5329	*ARAMEAN LANGUAGE* **SEE** ARAMAIC LANGUAGE
DS59.A7	ARAMEANS
PL7101.A6	ARANDA LANGUAGE
DU122.A	ARANDA TRIBE

GN666	ARANDA TRIBE / *anthropology*
QL451-9	*ARANEIDA* **SEE** SPIDERS
GR755	*ARANEIDA* **SEE** SPIDERS / *folk-lore*
F1929.B7	ARANJUEZ, TREATY OF, 1777
PL7101.A6	*ARANTA LANGUAGE* **SEE** ARANDA LANGUAGE
DU122.A	*ARANTA TRIBE* **SEE** ARANDA TRIBE
GN666	*ARANTA TRIBE* **SEE** ARANDA TRIBE / *anthropology*
E99.A7	ARAPAHO INDIANS
PM635	ARAPAHO LANGUAGE
PL6621.A7	ARAPESH LANGUAGE
GN671.N5	ARAPESH TRIBE / *new guinea*
PJ9293	*ARARGE LANGUAGE* **SEE** HARARI LANGUAGE
F3126	ARAUCANIAN INDIANS
PM5461-9	ARAUCANIAN LANGUAGE
PM5468	ARAUCANIAN LITERATURE
F3126	*ARAUCANOS* **SEE** ARAUCANIAN INDIANS
PM5476	ARAWAK LANGUAGE
F2230.2.A	ARAWAKAN INDIANS
PM5476	ARAWAKAN LANGUAGES
DQ98	ARBEDO, BATTLE OF, 1422
HD5481-5630	ARBITRATION, INDUSTRIAL
JX1901-1991	ARBITRATION, INTERNATIONAL
SD363	ARBOR DAY
QK479	ARBORETUMS
TK4321-4335	*ARC LAMPS* **SEE** ELECTRIC LAMPS, ARC
TK4311-4335	*ARC LIGHT* **SEE** ELECTRIC LIGHTING, ARC
QB291	ARC MEASURES
TK4660	*ARC WELDING* **SEE** ELECTRIC WELDING
QC705	*ARC, ELECTRIC* **SEE** ELECTRIC ARC
TG327-340	*ARCH* **SEE** ARCHES
QE653	*ARCHAEAN PERIOD* **SEE** GEOLOGY, STRATIGRAPHIC — ARCHAEAN
CC105	ARCHAEOLOGICAL EXPEDITIONS
CC100	ARCHAEOLOGICAL EXPEDITIONS
CC73-75	ARCHAEOLOGICAL SURVEYING
CC130	ARCHAEOLOGY — LAW AND LEGISLATION
CC73-75	ARCHAEOLOGY — METHODOLOGY
CC	ARCHAEOLOGY
GT	ARCHAEOLOGY / *manners and customs general*
DA-DU	ARCHAEOLOGY / *national antiquities other than american*
E-F	ARCHAEOLOGY / *n indian and other american antiquities*
GN	ARCHAEOLOGY / *prehistoric antiquities*
BS620	*ARCHAEOLOGY, BIBLICAL* **SEE** BIBLE — ANTIQUITIES
BR130-133	*ARCHAEOLOGY, CHRISTIAN* **SEE** CHRISTIAN ANTIQUITIES
DE	*ARCHAEOLOGY, CLASSICAL* **SEE** CLASSICAL ANTIQUITIES
DF	*ARCHAEOLOGY, CLASSICAL* **SEE** CLASSICAL ANTIQUITIES / *greece*
DG	*ARCHAEOLOGY, CLASSICAL* **SEE** CLASSICAL ANTIQUITIES / *rome*
QE653	*ARCHAEOZOIC PERIOD* **SEE** GEOLOGY, STRATIGRAPHIC — ARCHAEAN
PL2241-5	*ARCHAIC CHINESE LANGUAGE* **SEE** CHINESE LANGUAGE — ARCHAIC CHINESE
BX1911	ARCHDEACONS / *catholic church*
BX5179	ARCHDEACONS / *church of england*
QE653	*ARCHEAN PERIOD* **SEE** GEOLOGY, STRATIGRAPHIC — ARCHAEAN
QH325	*ARCHEBIOSIS* **SEE** SPONTANEOUS GENERATION
QH325	*ARCHEGENESIS* **SEE** SPONTANEOUS GENERATION
CC	*ARCHEOLOGY* **SEE** ARCHAEOLOGY
GT	*ARCHEOLOGY* **SEE** ARCHAEOLOGY / *manners and customs general*
DA-DU	*ARCHEOLOGY* **SEE** ARCHAEOLOGY / *national antiquities other than american*
E-F	*ARCHEOLOGY* **SEE** ARCHAEOLOGY / *n indian and other american antiquities*
GN	*ARCHEOLOGY* **SEE** ARCHAEOLOGY / *prehistoric antiquities*
QE653	*ARCHEOZOIC PERIOD* **SEE** GEOLOGY, STRATIGRAPHIC — ARCHAEAN
GV1185-9	ARCHERY
TG327-340	ARCHES
TG410	ARCHES, METAL
TG329	ARCHES, OBLIQUE
NA9360-9380	ARCHES, TRIUMPHAL

ML653-5	ARCHICEMBALO
TP925.L7	*ARCHIL* **SEE** ORCHIL
TJ901	ARCHIMEDEAN SCREW
NA2570	ARCHITECTS — FEES
NA	ARCHITECTS
NA1997	*ARCHITECTS, WOMEN* **SEE** WOMEN AS ARCHITECTS
NA2800	ARCHITECTURAL ACOUSTICS
NA3310-3950	*ARCHITECTURAL DECORATION AND ORNAMENT* **SEE** DECORATION AND ORNAMENT, ARCHITECTURAL
NA2835-3060	*ARCHITECTURAL DESIGN* **SEE** ARCHITECTURE — DETAILS
NA3310-3950	*ARCHITECTURAL DESIGN* **SEE** DECORATION AND ORNAMENT, ARCHITECTURAL
NA2600-2635	*ARCHITECTURAL DESIGNS* **SEE** ARCHITECTURE — DESIGNS AND PLANS
NA2835-3060	*ARCHITECTURAL DETAILS* **SEE** ARCHITECTURE — DETAILS
NA2700-2780	ARCHITECTURAL DRAWING
TH	*ARCHITECTURAL ENGINEERING* **SEE** BUILDING
TA684-5	*ARCHITECTURAL ENGINEERING* **SEE** BUILDING, IRON AND STEEL / *engineering*
TH1610-1621	*ARCHITECTURAL ENGINEERING* **SEE** BUILDING, IRON AND STEEL / *building*
TH845-891	*ARCHITECTURAL ENGINEERING* **SEE** STRAINS AND STRESSES / *architectural engineering*
TG265-7	*ARCHITECTURAL ENGINEERING* **SEE** STRAINS AND STRESSES / *bridge and roof engineering*
QA931-5	*ARCHITECTURAL ENGINEERING* **SEE** STRAINS AND STRESSES / *elasticity*
TA405	*ARCHITECTURAL ENGINEERING* **SEE** STRENGTH OF MATERIALS
TA410-417	*ARCHITECTURAL ENGINEERING* **SEE** STRENGTH OF MATERIALS / *testing*
TG260	*ARCHITECTURAL ENGINEERING* **SEE** STRUCTURES, THEORY OF
NA4050.I5	ARCHITECTURAL INSCRIPTIONS
NA3950	ARCHITECTURAL IRONWORK
TH1651-5	ARCHITECTURAL IRONWORK
TH219-255	*ARCHITECTURAL LAW AND LEGISLATION* **SEE** BUILDING LAWS
TA221-324	*ARCHITECTURAL LAW AND LEGISLATION* **SEE** ENGINEERING LAW
NA4050.I5	*ARCHITECTURAL LETTERING* **SEE** ARCHITECTURAL INSCRIPTIONS
Z675.A83	ARCHITECTURAL LIBRARIES
TH7703	*ARCHITECTURAL LIGHTING* **SEE** LIGHTING, ARCHITECTURAL AND DECORATIVE
TA685	ARCHITECTURAL METAL-WORK
TH1651-5	ARCHITECTURAL METAL-WORK
NA2790	ARCHITECTURAL MODELS
NA2810-2817	*ARCHITECTURAL ORDERS* **SEE** ARCHITECTURE — ORDERS
NC749-750	*ARCHITECTURAL PERSPECTIVE* **SEE** PERSPECTIVE
QA515	*ARCHITECTURAL PERSPECTIVE* **SEE** PERSPECTIVE / *geometry*
T369	*ARCHITECTURAL PERSPECTIVE* **SEE** PERSPECTIVE / *mechanical drawing*
TR630	*ARCHITECTURAL PHOTOGRAPHY* **SEE** PHOTOGRAPHY, ARCHITECTURAL
NA2795	*ARCHITECTURAL POLYCHROMY* **SEE** COLOR IN ARCHITECTURE
NA2335-2360	ARCHITECTURE — COMPETITIONS
NA2760	ARCHITECTURE — COMPOSITION, PROPORTION, ETC.
NA2600-2635	ARCHITECTURE — DESIGNS AND PLANS
NA2835-3060	ARCHITECTURE — DETAILS
NA2515-2517	ARCHITECTURE — EARLY WORKS TO 1800
NA2430-2460	ARCHITECTURE — EXHIBITIONS
NA2555	ARCHITECTURE — JUVENILE LITERATURE
NA2810-2817	ARCHITECTURE — ORDERS
ML3849	*ARCHITECTURE AND MUSIC* **SEE** MUSIC AND ARCHITECTURE
NA1995	ARCHITECTURE AS A PROFESSION
PN56.A	ARCHITECTURE IN LITERATURE
PR149.A	ARCHITECTURE IN LITERATURE / *english literature*
NA	ARCHITECTURE
NA210-340	ARCHITECTURE, ANCIENT
NA203	ARCHITECTURE, ANONYMOUS
NA380-388	*ARCHITECTURE, ARAB* **SEE** ARCHITECTURE, ISLAMIC
NA220-221	ARCHITECTURE, ASSYRO-BABYLONIAN

NA590	ARCHITECTURE, BAROQUE
NA370-373	ARCHITECTURE, BYZANTINE
NA8455	*ARCHITECTURE, CAVE* **SEE** CAVE ARCHITECTURE
NA4790-6113	*ARCHITECTURE, CHURCH* **SEE** CHURCH ARCHITECTURE
NA4820	ARCHITECTURE, CISTERCIAN
NA707	ARCHITECTURE, COLONIAL
NA7127-7135	ARCHITECTURE, DOMESTIC — DESIGNS AND PLANS
NA7100-7786	ARCHITECTURE, DOMESTIC
NA4790-6113	*ARCHITECTURE, ECCLESIASTICAL* **SEE** CHURCH ARCHITECTURE
NA1581-5	ARCHITECTURE, EGYPTIAN
NA215-216	ARCHITECTURE, EGYPTIAN / *ancient*
NA966	ARCHITECTURE, GEORGIAN
NA707	ARCHITECTURE, GEORGIAN
NA640	ARCHITECTURE, GEORGIAN
NA1061-1088	ARCHITECTURE, GERMANIC
NA440-489	ARCHITECTURE, GOTHIC
NA270-285	ARCHITECTURE, GREEK
NA8455	*ARCHITECTURE, GROTTO* **SEE** CAVE ARCHITECTURE
NA380-388	ARCHITECTURE, ISLAMIC
NA4820	ARCHITECTURE, JESUIT
NA1325	ARCHITECTURE, MANUELINE
NA350-497	ARCHITECTURE, MEDIEVAL
NA490-497	*ARCHITECTURE, MILITARY* **SEE** MILITARY ARCHITECTURE / *architecture*
UG460	*ARCHITECTURE, MILITARY* **SEE** MILITARY ARCHITECTURE / *military science*
NA680	ARCHITECTURE, MODERN — 20TH CENTURY
NA500-680	ARCHITECTURE, MODERN
NA380-388	*ARCHITECTURE, MOORISH* **SEE** ARCHITECTURE, ISLAMIC
NA380-388	*ARCHITECTURE, MUSLIM* **SEE** ARCHITECTURE, ISLAMIC
VM	*ARCHITECTURE, NAVAL* **SEE** NAVAL ARCHITECTURE
VM	*ARCHITECTURE, NAVAL* **SEE** SHIP-BUILDING
NA423-9	ARCHITECTURE, NORMAN
NA1460-1579	ARCHITECTURE, ORIENTAL
NA205-7	ARCHITECTURE, PRIMITIVE
GN414	ARCHITECTURE, PRIMITIVE / *anthropology*
HV8805-8829	*ARCHITECTURE, PRISON* **SEE** PRISONS — CONSTRUCTION
NA510-575	ARCHITECTURE, RENAISSANCE
NA590	ARCHITECTURE, ROCOCO
NA310-340	ARCHITECTURE, ROMAN
NA390-419	ARCHITECTURE, ROMANESQUE
NA7100-7786	*ARCHITECTURE, RURAL* **SEE** ARCHITECTURE, DOMESTIC
NA7571-2	*ARCHITECTURE, RURAL* **SEE** BUNGALOWS
NA7551-5	*ARCHITECTURE, RURAL* **SEE** COTTAGES
NA8200-8260	*ARCHITECTURE, RURAL* **SEE** FARM BUILDINGS / *architecture*
NA380-388	*ARCHITECTURE, SARACENIC* **SEE** ARCHITECTURE, ISLAMIC
NA1301-1313	ARCHITECTURE, SPANISH
NA3310-3950	*ARCHITECTURE-DECORATION AND ORNAMENT* **SEE** DECORATION AND ORNAMENT, ARCHITECTURAL
TH219-255	*ARCHITECTURE-LAW AND LEGISLATION* **SEE** BUILDING LAWS
TA221-324	*ARCHITECTURE-LAW AND LEGISLATION* **SEE** ENGINEERING LAW
TH860	*ARCHITECTURE-MODULAR DESIGN* **SEE** MODULAR COORDINATION (ARCHITECTURE) / *building*
NA2760	*ARCHITECTURE-MODULAR DESIGN* **SEE** MODULAR COORDINATION (ARCHITECTURE) / *design*
NA2700	*ARCHITECTURE-MODULAR DESIGN* **SEE** MODULAR COORDINATION (ARCHITECTURE) / *drafting*
NA2600-2635	*ARCHITECTURE-PLANS* **SEE** ARCHITECTURE — DESIGNS AND PLANS
NA2760	*ARCHITECTURE-PROPORTION* **SEE** ARCHITECTURE — COMPOSITION, PROPORTION, ETC.
CD981	ARCHIVE BUILDINGS
Z695.2	*ARCHIVES - CATALOGING* **SEE** CATALOGING OF ARCHIVAL MATERIAL
CD931-4279	ARCHIVES
CD941	ARCHIVES / *directories*
CD950-965	ARCHIVES / *handbooks*
Z695.2	*ARCHIVES-CATALOGING* **SEE** CATALOGING OF ARCHIVAL MATERIAL
DF83	ARCHONS

DF277-285	ARCHONS / *athens*
G600-830	*ARCTIC EXPEDITIONS* **SEE** ARCTIC REGIONS
QK474	*ARCTIC EXPEDITIONS* **SEE** ARCTIC REGIONS / *botany*
QC994.8	*ARCTIC EXPEDITIONS* **SEE** ARCTIC REGIONS / *meteorology*
QH84.1	*ARCTIC EXPEDITIONS* **SEE** ARCTIC REGIONS / *natural history*
QC825.8	*ARCTIC EXPEDITIONS* **SEE** ARCTIC REGIONS / *terrestrial magnetism*
QL105	*ARCTIC EXPEDITIONS* **SEE** ARCTIC REGIONS / *zoology*
GN673	ARCTIC RACES
G630	ARCTIC REGIONS — AMERICAN (CANADIAN, RUSSIAN, ETC.) EXPLORATION
G600-830	ARCTIC REGIONS
QK474	ARCTIC REGIONS / *botany*
QC994.8	ARCTIC REGIONS / *meteorology*
QH84.1	ARCTIC REGIONS / *natural history*
QC825.8	ARCTIC REGIONS / *terrestrial magnetism*
QL105	ARCTIC REGIONS / *zoology*
TD940-949	*ARCTIC SANITARY ENGINEERING* **SEE** SANITARY ENGINEERING, LOW TEMPERATURE
QB805.A7	ARCTURUS
QL696.A7	*ARDEIDAE* **SEE** HERODIONES
QL696.A7	*ARDEIDAE* **SEE** HERONS
D756.5.A7	ARDENNES, BATTLE OF THE, 1944-1945
GA23	AREA MEASUREMENT / *mathematical geography*
D16.25	*AREA RESEARCH* **SEE** AREA STUDIES
D16.25	AREA STUDIES
TH3000	*AREAS (BUILDING)* **SEE** AREAWAYS
TH3000	AREAWAYS
QK495.P	*ARECA NUT* **SEE** BETEL NUT / *botany*
RS165.B	*ARECA NUT* **SEE** BETEL NUT / *pharmacy*
SB295.B	*ARECA NUT* **SEE** BETEL NUT / *plant culture and horticulture*
QM563	*AREOLAR TISSUE* **SEE** CONNECTIVE TISSUES
QC111	*AREOMETER* **SEE** HYDROMETER
PQ7760-7761	ARGENTINE BALLADS AND SONGS / *collections*
PQ7680	ARGENTINE BALLADS AND SONGS / *history*
PQ7764-7770	ARGENTINE DRAMA / *collections*
PQ7683-7695	ARGENTINE DRAMA / *history*
PQ7600-7799	ARGENTINE LITERATURE
PN5001-5010	ARGENTINE NEWSPAPERS / *etc.*
PN5001-5010	ARGENTINE PERIODICALS / *etc.*
PQ7749-7763	ARGENTINE POETRY / *collections*
PQ7661-7681	ARGENTINE POETRY / *history*
F2801-3021	ARGENTINE REPUBLIC — HISTORY
F2684	*ARGENTINE REPUBLIC-HISTORY-GUARANI WAR, 1754-1756* **SEE** SEVEN REDUCTIONS, WAR OF THE, 1754-1756
F2849	ARGENTINE REPUBLIC — HISTORY — — 1943-
GV1295.C2	*ARGENTINE RUMMY* **SEE** CANASTA (GAME)
F2726	ARGENTINE-BRAZILIAN WAR, 1825-1828
QD181.A6	ARGON
D545.A6	ARGONNE, BATTLE OF THE, 1915
D545.A63	ARGONNE, BATTLE OF THE, 1918
PE3726	*ARGOT* **SEE** CANT / *english*
P409	*ARGOT* **SEE** SLANG
PE3701-3729	*ARGOT* **SEE** SLANG / *english*
PC3721-3761	*ARGOT* **SEE** SLANG / *french*
PN4181-4191	*ARGUMENTATION* **SEE** DEBATES AND DEBATING
BC	*ARGUMENTATION* **SEE** LOGIC
PN4001-4321	*ARGUMENTATION* **SEE** ORATORY / *general works*
BC177	*ARGUMENTATION* **SEE** REASONING / *argumentation in logic*
BC	*ARGUMENTATION* **SEE** REASONING / *logic*
BC185	*ARGUMENTATION* **SEE** SYLLOGISM / *logic*
RA1231.S5	ARGYRIA
RA1231.S5	*ARGYRIASIS* **SEE** ARGYRIA
RA1231.S5	*ARGYRISM* **SEE** ARGYRIA
QL451-2	*ARGYRONETA AQUATICA* **SEE** WATER-SPIDERS
SB205.P5	*ARHAR* **SEE** PIGEON-PEA
F2270.2.A67	ARHUACO INDIANS
RC685.A65	*ARHYTHMIA* **SEE** ARRHYTHMIA
BT1350	ARIANISM
RC299.A	ARIBOFLAVINOSIS
E99.A8	*ARICKARA INDIANS* **SEE** ARIKARA INDIANS
E99.A8	*ARICKAREE INDIANS* **SEE** ARIKARA INDIANS
E99.A8	ARIKARA INDIANS
PM636.A7	ARIKARA LANGUAGE

JC411-417	ARISTOCRACY / *political science*
HT647	ARISTOCRACY / *social classes*
TR395	ARISTOTYPE
QA139	ARITHMETIC — EXAMINATIONS, QUESTIONS, ETC.
QA248	ARITHMETIC — FOUNDATIONS
QA135	ARITHMETIC — REMEDIAL TEACHING
QA101-145	ARITHMETIC
GN476.1	ARITHMETIC / *primitive*
HF5688-9	*ARITHMETIC, MECHANICAL* **SEE** CALCULATING-MACHINES / *bookkeeping*
QA75	*ARITHMETIC, MECHANICAL* **SEE** CALCULATING-MACHINES / *mechanical devices*
BM657.A85	ARK OF THE LAW
BM657.A85	*ARK, HOLY* **SEE** ARK OF THE LAW
BS658	*ARK, NOAH'S* **SEE** NOAH'S ARK
BL325.D4	*ARK, NOAH'S* **SEE** NOAH'S ARK
F406-420	ARKANSAS — HISTORY
E496	ARKANSAS — HISTORY — — CIVIL WAR
E553	ARKANSAS — HISTORY — — CIVIL WAR / *confederate*
RD551-7	ARM — SURGERY
QL950.7	ARM / *comparative anatomy general*
QM165	ARM / *human anatomy muscles*
QL831	ARM / *muscles*
QL821	ARM / *skeleton*
QM117	ARM / *skeleton*
QM548	ARM / *surgical and topographical anatomy*
RD756	*ARM-PROSTHESIS* **SEE** ARTIFICIAL ARMS
DA360	ARMADA, 1588
QL737.E2	ARMADILLOS
TK2477	ARMATURES
U750	ARMED FORCES — MASCOTS
U43.U	ARMED FORCES DAY
JX5383	*ARMED NEUTRALITY, 1780 AND 1800* **SEE** NEUTRALITY, ARMED / *international law*
D295	*ARMED NEUTRALITY, 1780 AND 1800* **SEE** NEUTRALITY, ARMED / *armed neutrality of 1780*
PK8537-8	ARMENIAN DRAMA / *collections*
PK8521	ARMENIAN DRAMA / *history*
PK8001-8454	ARMENIAN LANGUAGE
PK8500-8958	ARMENIAN LITERATURE
DS194-5	ARMENIAN QUESTION
DS161-199	ARMENIANS
UC700-780	ARMIES — COMMISSARIAT
UC460-465	ARMIES — EQUIPMENT
UC530-535	ARMIES — INSIGNIA
UB410-415	ARMIES — OFFICERS
UB220-225	ARMIES — STAFFS
UA17	ARMIES, COST OF
UB790-795	*ARMIES-DISCIPLINE* **SEE** MILITARY DISCIPLINE
U250-255	*ARMIES-MANEUVERS* **SEE** MILITARY MANEUVERS
UD460-465	*ARMIES-MANEUVERS* **SEE** MILITARY MANEUVERS / *infantry*
UC340-345	*ARMIES-MOTORIZATION* **SEE** MOTORIZATION, MILITARY
M1270	*ARMIES-MUSIC* **SEE** MILITARY MUSIC
UH40-45	*ARMIES-MUSIC* **SEE** MUSIC IN THE ARMY / *military science*
UC600-620	*ARMIES-REMOUNT SERVICE* **SEE** REMOUNT SERVICE
UC700-780	*ARMIES-SUPPLIES* **SEE** ARMIES — COMMISSARIAT
UC260-267	*ARMIES-SUPPLIES* **SEE** MILITARY SUPPLIES
BX6195-7	ARMINIANISM
BX6195-7	ARMINIANS
DP219.2	ARMINON, BATTLE OF, 1837
JX5173	ARMISTICES
U800-825	*ARMOR* **SEE** ARMS AND ARMOR
NK6600-6699	*ARMOR* **SEE** ARMS AND ARMOR / *art*
HD9743	*ARMOR* **SEE** ARMS AND ARMOR / *industry*
V900-925	ARMOR-PLATE
UG446.5	*ARMORED CARS (TANKS)* **SEE** TANKS (MILITARY SCIENCE)
UG345	ARMORED TRAINS
V799-800	ARMORED VESSELS
Z993-6	*ARMORIAL BOOK-PLATES* **SEE** BOOK-PLATES
PB2800-2849	*ARMORIC LANGUAGE* **SEE** BRETON LANGUAGE
PB2856-2931	*ARMORIC LITERATURE* **SEE** BRETON LITERATURE
UA	ARMORIES
U800-825	ARMS AND ARMOR
NK6600-6699	ARMS AND ARMOR / *art*
HD9743	ARMS AND ARMOR / *industry*

GN498	ARMS AND ARMOR, PRIMITIVE
RD756	*ARMS, ARTIFICIAL* **SEE** ARTIFICIAL ARMS
CR67-69	*ARMS, COATS OF* **SEE** DEVICES / *heraldry*
JC345	*ARMS, COATS OF* **SEE** HERALDRY / *national theory*
CR	*ARMS, COATS OF* **SEE** HERALDRY / *national*
UB147	*ARMS, PROFESSION OF* **SEE** MILITARY SERVICE AS A PROFESSION
U	*ARMY* **SEE** MILITARY ART AND SCIENCE
U104	*ARMY* **SEE** STANDING ARMY
U43.U	*ARMY DAY* **SEE** ARMED FORCES DAY
UC340-345	*ARMY MOTORIZATION* **SEE** MOTORIZATION, MILITARY
UB410-415	*ARMY OFFICERS* **SEE** ARMIES — OFFICERS
UA26	*ARMY POSTS* **SEE** MILITARY POSTS / *u.s.*
U400-714	*ARMY SCHOOLS* **SEE** MILITARY EDUCATION
UC700-780	*ARMY SUPPLIES* **SEE** ARMIES — COMMISSARIAT
UC260-267	*ARMY SUPPLIES* **SEE** MILITARY SUPPLIES
U750-773	ARMY WIVES
UB23	*ARMY-MCCARTHY CONTROVERSY, 1954* **SEE** MCCARTHY-ARMY CONTROVERSY, 1954
SB945.A8	ARMY-WORMS
D763.N4	ARNHEM, BATTLE OF, 1944
TP958	*AROMATIC PLANT PRODUCTS* **SEE** ESSENCES AND ESSENTIAL OILS / *chemical technology*
QD416	*AROMATIC PLANT PRODUCTS* **SEE** ESSENCES AND ESSENTIAL OILS / *chemistry*
DR27.A8	AROMUNES
BM657.A85	*ARON HA-KODESH* **SEE** ARK OF THE LAW
E398	AROOSTOOK WAR, 1839
PL6245	*ARORAI LANGUAGE* **SEE** GILBERTESE LANGUAGE
D756.5.A	ARRAS, BATTLE OF, 1917
DC102.535	ARRAS, TREATY OF, 1485
DA60	*ARRAY, COMMISSIONS OF* **SEE** COMMISSIONS OF ARRAY / *english military history*
QB723.A7	ARREST'S COMET
RC685.A65	ARRHYTHMIA
GN498.B78	ARROW-HEADS
U877-8	*ARROWS* **SEE** BOW AND ARROW
GN498.B78	*ARROWS* **SEE** BOW AND ARROW / *primitive*
DS329.P2	ARSACIDAE / *parthia*
DS285	ARSACIDAE / *parthian empire*
UF540-545	ARSENALS
SB951-3	*ARSENATE OF LEAD* **SEE** LEAD ARSENATE / *insecticides*
TN245.A8	*ARSENATE OF LEAD* **SEE** LEAD ARSENATE / *technology*
RA1231.A7	*ARSENIASIS* **SEE** ARSENIC POISONING
QP913.A7	ARSENIC — PHYSIOLOGICAL EFFECT
RM666.A7	ARSENIC — THERAPEUTIC USE
RA1231.A7	ARSENIC POISONING
QD181.A7	ARSENIC / *chemistry*
QP913.A7	ARSENIC / *pharmacology*
RA1231.A7	*ARSENIC-TOXICOLOGY* **SEE** ARSENIC POISONING
RA1231.A7	*ARSENICISM* **SEE** ARSENIC POISONING
HV6638	ARSON
RM666.A77	ARSPHENAMINE
N7460-7470	ART — ANECDOTES, FACETIAE, SATIRE, ETC.
N400-490	ART — GALLERIES AND MUSEUMS
N8370	ART — HISTORIOGRAPHY
N5300-7415	ART — HISTORY
N7440	ART — JUVENILE LITERATURE
N460	ART — LIGHTING
N5210-5297	ART — PRIVATE COLLECTIONS
N70	ART — PSYCHOLOGY
PN6084.A8	ART — QUOTATIONS, MAXIMS, ETC.
N347	ART — SCHOLARSHIPS, FELLOWSHIPS, ETC.
N7430-7433	ART — TECHNIQUE
N33	ART — TERMINOLOGY
N8770	*ART - TARIFF* **SEE** TARIFF ON WORKS OF ART
GT529.A7	*ART AND FASHION* **SEE** FASHION AND ART
N71.5	*ART AND INSANITY* **SEE** ART AND MENTAL ILLNESS / *art*
RC455	*ART AND INSANITY* **SEE** ART AND MENTAL ILLNESS / *medicine*
N72	ART AND LITERATURE / *art*
PR149.A	ART AND LITERATURE / *english literature*
PT112	ART AND LITERATURE / *german literature*
PN53	ART AND LITERATURE / *literature*
N8223	*ART AND MEDICINE* **SEE** MEDICINE AND ART
N71.5	ART AND MENTAL ILLNESS / *art*
RC455	ART AND MENTAL ILLNESS / *medicine*

N70-72	ART AND MORALS
N7760	ART AND MYTHOLOGY
BH301.N3	*ART AND NATURE* **SEE** NATURE (AESTHETICS)
N72	ART AND SOCIETY
N72	*ART AND SOCIOLOGY* **SEE** ART AND SOCIETY
N72	*ART AND SOCIOLOGY* **SEE** ART AND SOCIETY
N8700-8850	ART AND STATE
N8252	*ART AND THEATER* **SEE** THEATER IN ART
NA6820-6845	*ART AND THEATER* **SEE** THEATERS — DECORATION
PN2091.S8	*ART AND THEATER* **SEE** THEATERS — STAGE-SETTING AND SCENERY
N61-79	*ART APPRECIATION* **SEE** AESTHETICS / *art*
BH	*ART APPRECIATION* **SEE** AESTHETICS / *philosophy*
N7435-6	*ART APPRECIATION* **SEE** ART CRITICISM
N8370-8375	*ART APPRECIATION* **SEE** ART CRITICISM / *art critics*
ND	*ART APPRECIATION* **SEE** PAINTING
N350-375	*ART APPRECIATION* **SEE** PICTURES / *art study in schools*
ND1142-6	*ART APPRECIATION* **SEE** PICTURES / *popular works*
NK1125-1130	*ART COLLECTORS* **SEE** ART OBJECTS — COLLECTORS AND COLLECTING
N7435-6	ART CRITICISM
N8370-8375	ART CRITICISM / *art critics*
N8610-8660	ART DEALERS
N347	*ART FELLOWSHIPS* **SEE** ART — SCHOLARSHIPS, FELLOWSHIPS, ETC.
N8790	*ART FORGERIES* **SEE** FORGERY OF WORKS OF ART
N400-490	*ART GALLERIES* **SEE** ART — GALLERIES AND MUSEUMS
NC997	*ART IN ADVERTISING* **SEE** COMMERCIAL ART
PN56.A	ART IN LITERATURE
PN682.A7	ART IN LITERATURE / *medieval literature*
NK	ART INDUSTRIES AND TRADE
NK720-725	ART INDUSTRIES AND TRADE, ISLAMIC
NK720-725	*ART INDUSTRIES AND TRADE, MUSLIM* **SEE** ART INDUSTRIES AND TRADE, ISLAMIC
T179-183	*ART INDUSTRIES AND TRADE-MUSEUMS* **SEE** INDUSTRIAL MUSEUMS
HG9970.A	*ART INSURANCE* **SEE** INSURANCE, ART
Z675.A85	ART LIBRARIES
NK6400-8450	ART METAL-WORK
TT	ART METAL-WORK
TS	ART METAL-WORK
NK6473	ART METAL-WORK, ISLAMIC
NK6473	*ART METAL-WORK, MUSLIM* **SEE** ART METAL-WORK, ISLAMIC
NK6472	ART METAL-WORK, ORIENTAL
N400-490	*ART MUSEUMS* **SEE** ART — GALLERIES AND MUSEUMS
NK1125-1130	ART OBJECTS — COLLECTORS AND COLLECTING
N8560	ART OBJECTS — CONSERVATION AND RESTORATION
NK510-520	ART OBJECTS — EXHIBITIONS
N8750	ART OBJECTS — FIRES AND FIRE PREVENTION
NK530-570	ART OBJECTS — PRIVATE COLLECTIONS
NK	ART OBJECTS
NK665-680	ART OBJECTS, CLASSICAL
N8790	*ART OBJECTS, FORGERY OF* **SEE** FORGERY OF WORKS OF ART
NK1037	ART OBJECTS, ORIENTAL
N8410	ART PATRONAGE
QL785	*ART PRODUCTION BY ANIMALS* **SEE** ANIMALS AS ARTISTS
N347	*ART SCHOLARSHIPS* **SEE** ART — SCHOLARSHIPS, FELLOWSHIPS, ETC.
RC489.A	ART THERAPY
N8750	ART TREASURES IN WAR
N6491	ART TREASURES IN WAR / *european war*
Z50.2	ART TYPING
N	ART
N6490	ART, ABSTRACT
N5315-5899	ART, ANCIENT
NK	*ART, APPLIED* **SEE** ART INDUSTRIES AND TRADE
N6260-6271	*ART, ARAB* **SEE** ART, ISLAMIC
N7810-8185	*ART, CHRISTIAN* **SEE** CHRISTIAN ART AND SYMBOLISM
BV150-168	*ART, CHRISTIAN* **SEE** CHRISTIAN ART AND SYMBOLISM / *theology*
NC997	*ART, COMMERCIAL* **SEE** COMMERCIAL ART
NK	ART, DECORATIVE
N7832	ART, EARLY CHRISTIAN
BV150-168	*ART, ECCLESIASTICAL* **SEE** CHRISTIAN ART AND SYMBOLISM / *theology*
N7810-8185	*ART, ECCLESIASTICAL* **SEE** CHRISTIAN ART AND SYMBOLISM
RC489.A	*ART, EFFECT OF* **SEE** ART THERAPY
NK801-1094	*ART, FOLK* **SEE** FOLK ART
N9201-9211	*ART, FOLK* **SEE** FOLK ART
E59.A7	*ART, INDIAN* **SEE** INDIANS — ART
F1434.2.A	*ART, INDIAN* **SEE** INDIANS OF CENTRAL AMERICA — ART
F1219.3.A7	*ART, INDIAN* **SEE** INDIANS OF MEXICO — ART
E98.A7	*ART, INDIAN* **SEE** INDIANS OF NORTH AMERICA — ART
N6260-6271	ART, ISLAMIC
N5940-6311	ART, MEDIEVAL
N6243	ART, MEROVINGIAN
N6490	ART, MODERN 20TH CENTURY
N6490	*ART, MODERNIST* **SEE** MODERNISM (ART)
N6260-6271	*ART, MOORISH* **SEE** ART, ISLAMIC
NA9000-9425	ART, MUNICIPAL / *aesthetics of cities*
N8700-8850	ART, MUNICIPAL / *public art*
N6260-6271	*ART, MUSLIM* **SEE** ART, ISLAMIC
E185.82	*ART, NEGRO* **SEE** NEGRO ART / *u.s.*
N6538.N5	*ART, NEGRO* **SEE** NEGRO ART / *u.s.*
N6490	*ART, NON-OBJECTIVE* **SEE** ART, ABSTRACT
N7260	ART, ORIENTAL
NK	*ART, POPULAR* **SEE** ART INDUSTRIES AND TRADE
N9201-9211	*ART, POPULAR* **SEE** FOLK ART
NK801-1094	*ART, POPULAR* **SEE** FOLK ART
N5310	*ART, PREHISTORIC* **SEE** ART, PRIMITIVE
N5310	ART, PRIMITIVE
N7428	ART, REGIONAL
N6370	ART, RENAISSANCE
N6410	ART, ROCOCO
N6280	ART, ROMANESQUE
N6260-6271	*ART, SARACENIC* **SEE** ART, ISLAMIC
N8217.E6	*ART, SEX IN* **SEE** SEX IN ART / *erotica*
N6242	ART, VISIGOTHIC
BH	*ART-ANALYSIS, INTERPRETATION, APPRECIATION* **SEE** AESTHETICS / *philosophy*
N61-79	*ART-ANALYSIS, INTERPRETATION, APPRECIATION* **SEE** AESTHETICS / *art*
N8370-8375	*ART-ANALYSIS, INTERPRETATION, APPRECIATION* **SEE** ART CRITICISM / *art critics*
N7435-6	*ART-ANALYSIS, INTERPRETATION, APPRECIATION* **SEE** ART CRITICISM
ND	*ART-ANALYSIS, INTERPRETATION, APPRECIATION* **SEE** PAINTING
ND1142-6	*ART-ANALYSIS, INTERPRETATION, APPRECIATION* **SEE** PICTURES / *popular works*
N350-375	*ART-ANALYSIS, INTERPRETATION, APPRECIATION* **SEE** PICTURES / *art study in schools*
N7430	*ART-COMPOSITION* **SEE** COMPOSITION (ART)
N8560	*ART-CONSERVATION AND RESTORATION* **SEE** ART OBJECTS — CONSERVATION AND RESTORATION
Z654	*ART-COPYRIGHT* **SEE** COPYRIGHT — ART
N7435-6	*ART-CRITICISM* **SEE** ART CRITICISM
N8370-8375	*ART-CRITICISM* **SEE** ART CRITICISM / *art critics*
N347	*ART-FELLOWSHIPS* **SEE** ART — SCHOLARSHIPS, FELLOWSHIPS, ETC.
N8790	*ART-FORGERIES* **SEE** FORGERY OF WORKS OF ART
N400-490	*ART-MUSEUMS* **SEE** ART — GALLERIES AND MUSEUMS
E185.82	*ART-NEGROES* **SEE** NEGRO ART / *u.s.*
N6538.N5	*ART-NEGROES* **SEE** NEGRO ART / *u.s.*
N76	*ART-RHYTHM* **SEE** PROPORTION (ART)
NC745	*ART-RHYTHM* **SEE** PROPORTION (ART) / *design*
N8770	*ART-TARIFF* **SEE** TARIFF ON WORKS OF ART
RC489.A	*ART-THERAPEUTIC USE* **SEE** ART THERAPY
NK	*ART-TRADE* **SEE** ART INDUSTRIES AND TRADE
RC691	ARTERIES — DISEASES
RD598	ARTERIES — LIGATURE
QM191	ARTERIES
QL835	ARTERIES
RC691	ARTERIOSCLEROSIS
TD410	ARTESIAN WELLS
RC933	ARTHRITIS DEFORMANS
RD686	ARTHRODESIS
RD686	*ARTHROPATHY* **SEE** JOINTS — DISEASES

RD686	ARTHROPLASTY
QL434-599	ARTHROPODA
QE815-832	ARTHROPODA, FOSSIL
RC933	*ARTHROSIS DEFORMANS* **SEE** ARTHRITIS DEFORMANS
QL444.A7	ARTHROSTRACA
SB351.A8	ARTICHOKES
P277	*ARTICLE* **SEE** GRAMMAR, COMPARATIVE AND GENERAL — ARTICLE
P277	*ARTICLE* **SEE** GRAMMAR, COMPARATIVE AND GENERAL — ARTICLE
UB461-736	*ARTICLES OF WAR* **SEE** MILITARY LAW
TJ608	*ARTICULATED LOCOMOTIVES* **SEE** LOCOMOTIVES, ARTICULATED
LB2350	ARTICULATION (EDUCATION)
QL825	*ARTICULATIONS* **SEE** JOINTS / *comparative anatomy*
QM131	*ARTICULATIONS* **SEE** JOINTS / *human anatomy*
RD756	ARTIFICIAL ARMS
QP101	*ARTIFICIAL BLOOD CIRCULATION* **SEE** BLOOD — CIRCULATION, ARTIFICIAL
Q327	*ARTIFICIAL CONSCIOUSNESS* **SEE** CONSCIOUS AUTOMATA
QM691-9	*ARTIFICIAL DEFORMITIES* **SEE** DEFORMITIES / *human anatomy*
GN68-69.8	*ARTIFICIAL DEFORMITIES* **SEE** DEFORMITIES / *somatic anthropology*
TP873.5.D5	*ARTIFICIAL DIAMONDS* **SEE** DIAMONDS, ARTIFICIAL
RE986	*ARTIFICIAL EYES* **SEE** EYES, ARTIFICIAL
RM223-4	ARTIFICIAL FEEDING
RM868	*ARTIFICIAL FEVER* **SEE** FEVER THERAPY
SH451-5	*ARTIFICIAL FLIES* **SEE** FLIES, ARTIFICIAL
TT890-894	ARTIFICIAL FLOWERS
TX357	*ARTIFICIAL FOOD* **SEE** FOOD, ARTIFICIAL
RM258-261	*ARTIFICIAL FOOD* **SEE** FOOD, ARTIFICIAL / *diet*
QP55	*ARTIFICIAL HEART* **SEE** PERFUSION PUMP (HEART)
VK584.H	*ARTIFICIAL HORIZONS* **SEE** HORIZONS, ARTIFICIAL
SF105.5	*ARTIFICIAL IMPREGNATION* **SEE** ARTIFICIAL INSEMINATION
SF105.5	ARTIFICIAL INSEMINATION
BX1759.5.A7	ARTIFICIAL INSEMINATION, HUMAN / *catholic moral theology*
RG134	ARTIFICIAL INSEMINATION, HUMAN / *obstetrics*
RC901.7.A7	ARTIFICIAL KIDNEY
PM8001-9021	*ARTIFICIAL LANGUAGES* **SEE** LANGUAGES, ARTIFICIAL
TS1045-7	*ARTIFICIAL LEATHER* **SEE** LEATHER, ARTIFICIAL
RD756	ARTIFICIAL LIMBS — RESEARCH
RD756	ARTIFICIAL LIMBS
RM676	*ARTIFICIAL MINERAL WATERS* **SEE** MINERAL WATERS, ARTIFICIAL / *therapeutics*
TP625	*ARTIFICIAL MINERAL WATERS* **SEE** MINERAL WATERS, ARTIFICIAL
QC929.R1	*ARTIFICIAL MODIFICATION OF CLOUDS* **SEE** RAIN-MAKING
RM825	*ARTIFICIAL PNEUMOPERITONEUM* **SEE** PNEUMOPERITONEUM, ARTIFICIAL
TP977-8	*ARTIFICIAL RESINS* **SEE** GUMS AND RESINS, SYNTHETIC
TP986	*ARTIFICIAL RESINS* **SEE** GUMS AND RESINS, SYNTHETIC / *plastics*
RC87	ARTIFICIAL RESPIRATION
TL796.8	ARTIFICIAL SATELLITES — OBSERVERS' MANUALS
TL796.6.S	ARTIFICIAL SATELLITES — SUN
TL796	ARTIFICIAL SATELLITES
TL796.5.R	ARTIFICIAL SATELLITES, RUSSIAN
TS1688	*ARTIFICIAL SILK* **SEE** RAYON
TP871	*ARTIFICIAL STONE* **SEE** STONE, ARTIFICIAL
TP248.S3	*ARTIFICIAL SWEETENERS* **SEE** SACCHARIN / *chemical technology*
QP981.S2	*ARTIFICIAL SWEETENERS* **SEE** SACCHARIN / *physiological effects*
QC928	*ARTIFICIAL WEATHER CONTROL* **SEE** WEATHER CONTROL
TS1635	*ARTIFICIAL WOOL* **SEE** WOOL, ARTIFICIAL
UF157-302	ARTILLERY DRILL AND TACTICS
U300-305	*ARTILLERY RANGES* **SEE** BOMBING AND GUNNERY RANGES
UF	ARTILLERY
UF450-455	ARTILLERY, COAST
UF400-445	ARTILLERY, FIELD AND MOUNTAIN
U13	*ARTILLERY-MUSEUMS* **SEE** MILITARY MUSEUMS
NC760	*ARTISTIC ANATOMY* **SEE** ANATOMY, ARTISTIC
TR650-682	*ARTISTIC PHOTOGRAPHY* **SEE** PHOTOGRAPHY, ARTISTIC
TR183	*ARTISTIC PHOTOGRAPHY* **SEE** PHOTOGRAPHY, ARTISTIC / *aesthetics*
N40	ARTISTS
N71.3	*ARTISTS, HANDICAPPED* **SEE** ARTISTS, PHYSICALLY HANDICAPPED
N71.5	*ARTISTS, INSANE* **SEE** ART AND MENTAL ILLNESS / *art*
RC455	*ARTISTS, INSANE* **SEE** ART AND MENTAL ILLNESS / *medicine*
N6538.N5	*ARTISTS, NEGRO* **SEE** NEGRO ARTISTS / *u.s.*
N71.3	ARTISTS, PHYSICALLY HANDICAPPED
ND38	ARTISTS, WOMEN
N43	ARTISTS, WOMEN
N45	ARTISTS' MARKS
N7434	*ARTISTS' MODELS* **SEE** MODELS, ARTISTS'
N7460-7470	*ARTISTS-ANECDOTES, FACETIAE, SATIRE, ETC.* **SEE** ART — ANECDOTES, FACETIAE, SATIRE, ETC.
TK5811	*ARTOM SYSTEM OF WIRELESS TELEGRAPHY* **SEE** TELEGRAPH, WIRELESS — ARTOM SYSTEM
NK1135-1149	ARTS AND CRAFTS MOVEMENT
LB2383	*ARTS, BACHELOR OF* **SEE** BACHELOR OF ARTS DEGREE
NK	*ARTS, DECORATIVE* **SEE** ART INDUSTRIES AND TRADE
NK	*ARTS, DECORATIVE* **SEE** ART, DECORATIVE
NK1135-1149	*ARTS, DECORATIVE* **SEE** ARTS AND CRAFTS MOVEMENT
NK1160-1590	*ARTS, DECORATIVE* **SEE** DECORATION AND ORNAMENT
NK1160-1590	*ARTS, DECORATIVE* **SEE** DESIGN, DECORATIVE
NK1700-3505	*ARTS, DECORATIVE* **SEE** INTERIOR DECORATION / *art*
TX311-317	*ARTS, DECORATIVE* **SEE** INTERIOR DECORATION / *home economics*
LB2385	*ARTS, MASTER OF* **SEE** MASTER OF ARTS DEGREE
T-TX	*ARTS, USEFUL* **SEE** INDUSTRIAL ARTS
T-TX	*ARTS, USEFUL* **SEE** TECHNOLOGY
N6410	ART — HISTORY — — 17TH-18TH CENTURIES
N6450-6460	ART — HISTORY — — 19TH CENTURY
N6490-6493	ART — HISTORY — — 20TH CENTURY
PM8085	ARULO (ARTIFICIAL LANGUAGE)
DU122.A	*ARUNNDTA TRIBE* **SEE** ARANDA TRIBE
GN666	*ARUNNDTA TRIBE* **SEE** ARANDA TRIBE / *anthropology*
PL7101.A6	*ARUNTA LANGUAGE* **SEE** ARANDA LANGUAGE
DU122.A	*ARUNTA TRIBE* **SEE** ARANDA TRIBE
GN666	*ARUNTA TRIBE* **SEE** ARANDA TRIBE / *anthropology*
GN539	ARYAN ANTIQUITIES
GN539	*ARYAN CIVILIZATION* **SEE** CIVILIZATION, ARYAN
CB201-231	*ARYAN CIVILIZATION* **SEE** CIVILIZATION, ARYAN
P501-769	ARYAN LANGUAGES
P501-769	ARYAN PHILOLOGY
GN539	ARYANS
DS15	ARYANS
CJ937	AS (COIN)
PL8675	*ASANGO LANGUAGE* **SEE** SHIRA LANGUAGE
TN930	ASBESTOS
BV57	ASCENSION DAY
BT500	*ASCENSION OF CHRIST* **SEE** JESUS CHRIST — ASCENSION
BV57	*ASCENSION, FEAST OF THE* **SEE** ASCENSION DAY
BL625	*ASCETICAL THEOLOGY* **SEE** ASCETICISM
BV5021-5068	*ASCETICAL THEOLOGY* **SEE** ASCETICISM / *christian*
BJ1491	*ASCETICAL THEOLOGY* **SEE** ASCETICISM / *ethics*
BL625	ASCETICISM
BV5021-5068	ASCETICISM / *christian*
BJ1491	ASCETICISM / *ethics*
QK649	ASCIDIA (BOTANY)
QL613	*ASCIDIANS* **SEE** TUNICATA
QK623	ASCOMYCETES
VK388	*ASDIC* **SEE** SONAR
VK560	*ASDIC* **SEE** SONAR / *navigation*
RD91-96	*ASEPTIC SURGERY* **SEE** SURGERY, ASEPTIC AND ANTISEPTIC
RM666.A8	ASEPTOLIN
QH475-9	*ASEXUAL REPRODUCTION* **SEE** REPRODUCTION, ASEXUAL

TJ1410	ASH DISPOSAL / *conveying machinery*
PL8675	*ASHANGO LANGUAGE* **SEE** SHIRA LANGUAGE
PL8751	*ASHANTI LANGUAGE* **SEE** TSHI LANGUAGE
DT507	ASHANTI WAR, 1822-1831
DT507	ASHANTI WAR, 1873-1874
DT507	ASHANTIS
TJ1410	*ASHES, REMOVAL OF* **SEE** ASH DISPOSAL / *conveying machinery*
PL8675	*ASHIRA LANGUAGE* **SEE** SHIRA LANGUAGE
F2230.2.A	ASHLUSLAY INDIANS
PJ	*ASIA-LANGUAGES* **SEE** ORIENTAL LANGUAGES
RC150	ASIAN FLU
SB945.A	ASIATIC BEETLE
RC126-134	*ASIATIC CHOLERA* **SEE** CHOLERA, ASIATIC
PM94	*ASIATIC ESKIMO LANGUAGE* **SEE** YUIT LANGUAGE
RC150	*ASIATIC FLU* **SEE** ASIAN FLU
PL8675	*ASIRA LANGUAGE* **SEE** SHIRA LANGUAGE
QP921.A7	ASPARAGIN
SB608.A8	ASPARAGUS — DISEASES AND PESTS
SB325	ASPARAGUS
SD397.A7	ASPEN
DC234.6	ASPERN, BATTLE OF, 1809
TN853	ASPHALT
RJ256	ASPHYXIA / *diseases of newly born*
RC87-88	ASPHYXIA / *first aid*
RA1071	ASPHYXIA / *legal medicine*
RJ256	*ASPHYXIATING GASES* **SEE** ASPHYXIA / *diseases of newly born*
RC87-88	*ASPHYXIATING GASES* **SEE** ASPHYXIA / *first aid*
RA1071	*ASPHYXIATING GASES* **SEE** ASPHYXIA / *legal medicine*
RA577	*ASPHYXIATING GASES* **SEE** GASES, ASPHYXIATING AND POISONOUS / *public health*
RA1245-7	*ASPHYXIATING GASES* **SEE** GASES, ASPHYXIATING AND POISONOUS / *toxicology*
QP921.A75	ASPIDOSPERMIN
RM666.A82	ASPIRIN / *therapeutics*
HD9675.A73	ASPIRIN / *trade*
PK1550-1599	ASSAMESE LANGUAGE
PK1560-1588	ASSAMESE LITERATURE
PK1550	ASSAMESE PHILOLOGY
HV6499-6535	ASSASSINATION
HV6278	ASSASSINATION / *political*
BP195.A8	ASSASSINS (ISMAILITES)
E99.A83	ASSATEAGUE INDIANS
HV6558-6569	*ASSAULT, CRIMINAL* **SEE** RAPE
TN550	ASSAYERS / *assaying*
TN139-140	ASSAYERS / *biography*
TN575	ASSAYING APPARATUS
TN550-580	ASSAYING
HG325-9	ASSAYING / *mints*
JC607	ASSEMBLY, RIGHT OF
LB3015-3031	*ASSEMBLY, SCHOOL* **SEE** SCHOOLS — EXERCISES AND RECREATIONS
GR730	ASSES AND MULES (IN RELIGION, FOLK-LORE, ETC.)
SF361	ASSES AND MULES
HG9201-9245	*ASSESSMENT INSURANCE* **SEE** INSURANCE, ASSESSMENT
HG8826	*ASSESSMENT INSURANCE* **SEE** INSURANCE, ASSESSMENT
HJ3241	ASSESSMENT
JK1991-7	*ASSESSMENTS, POLITICAL* **SEE** CAMPAIGN FUNDS / *u.s.*
E99.A83	*ASSETEAGUE INDIANS* **SEE** ASSATEAGUE INDIANS
HG174	*ASSETS, FROZEN* **SEE** LIQUIDITY (ECONOMICS)
HG174	*ASSETS, LIQUID* **SEE** LIQUIDITY (ECONOMICS)
D293.5.A8	ASSIETTA, BATTLE OF, 1747
HG978.2	ASSIGNATS
T58	*ASSIGNMENT SPECIFICATIONS* **SEE** JOB DESCRIPTIONS / *industrial management*
HF5382	*ASSIGNMENT SPECIFICATIONS* **SEE** JOB DESCRIPTIONS / *occupational descriptions (collective)*
E99.A84	ASSINIBOIN INDIANS
LB2844.1.A	*ASSISTANT TEACHERS* **SEE** TEACHERS' ASSISTANTS
BX8999.A7	ASSOCIATE REFORMED CHURCH OF NORTH AMERICA
HM131	*ASSOCIATION* **SEE** SOCIAL GROUPS
GV943	*ASSOCIATION FOOTBALL* **SEE** SOCCER
BF365-7	ASSOCIATION OF IDEAS
JC607	*ASSOCIATION, FREEDOM OF* **SEE** FREEDOM OF ASSOCIATION
JK-JQ	*ASSOCIATION, FREEDOM OF* **SEE** FREEDOM OF ASSOCIATION
JK-JQ	*ASSOCIATION, RIGHT OF* **SEE** FREEDOM OF ASSOCIATION
JC607	*ASSOCIATION, RIGHT OF* **SEE** FREEDOM OF ASSOCIATION
HD6350-6940	*ASSOCIATIONS, EMPLOYERS'* **SEE** EMPLOYERS' ASSOCIATIONS
BC183	*ASSUMPTION* **SEE** HYPOTHESIS / *logic*
BV50.A7	ASSUMPTION OF THE BLESSED VIRGIN MARY, FEAST OF THE
HG8011-9970	*ASSURANCE (INSURANCE)* **SEE** INSURANCE
BT785	ASSURANCE (THEOLOGY)
NA220-221	*ASSYRO-BABYLONIAN ARCHITECTURE* **SEE** ARCHITECTURE, ASSYRO-BABYLONIAN
QB19	*ASSYRO-BABYLONIAN ASTRONOMY* **SEE** ASTRONOMY, ASSYRO-BABYLONIAN
CE33	*ASSYRO-BABYLONIAN CALENDAR* **SEE** CALENDAR, ASSYRO-BABYLONIAN
CE33	*ASSYRO-BABYLONIAN CHRONOLOGY* **SEE** CHRONOLOGY, ASSYRO-BABYLONIAN
DS70.7	*ASSYRO-BABYLONIAN CIVILIZATION* **SEE** CIVILIZATION, ASSYRO-BABYLONIAN
CN	*ASSYRO-BABYLONIAN INSCRIPTIONS* **SEE** CUNEIFORM INSCRIPTIONS
PK	*ASSYRO-BABYLONIAN INSCRIPTIONS* **SEE** CUNEIFORM INSCRIPTIONS
PJ	*ASSYRO-BABYLONIAN INSCRIPTIONS* **SEE** CUNEIFORM INSCRIPTIONS
PJ3101-3595	ASSYRO-BABYLONIAN LANGUAGE
PJ5801-9	*ASSYRO-BABYLONIAN LANGUAGE, MODERN* **SEE** SYRIAC LANGUAGE, MODERN
PJ3601-3959	ASSYRO-BABYLONIAN LITERATURE
BF1591	*ASSYRO-BABYLONIAN MAGIC* **SEE** MAGIC, ASSYRO-BABYLONIAN
PJ3785	ASSYRO-BABYLONIAN PRAYERS
BL1620-1625	ASSYRO-BABYLONIAN RELIGION
QD181.A8	ASTATINE
QD941	ASTERISM (CRYSTALLOGRAPHY)
QL384.A8	*ASTEROIDEA* **SEE** STARFISHES
QB651	*ASTEROIDS* **SEE** PLANETS, MINOR / *descriptive astronomy*
QB516	*ASTEROIDS* **SEE** PLANETS, MINOR / *observations for solar parallax*
QB377-8	*ASTEROIDS* **SEE** PLANETS, MINOR / *planetary theory*
QK495.A84	ASTERS / *botany*
SB413.A7	ASTERS / *culture*
RC591	ASTHMA
RE932	ASTIGMATISM
BF575.S8	*ASTONISHMENT* **SEE** SURPRISE
BF1389.A7	ASTRAL PROJECTION
RM392	ASTRINGENTS
BF1718	*ASTRODIAGNOSIS* **SEE** MEDICAL ASTROLOGY
TL1050	ASTRODYNAMICS
TL1065	*ASTROGATION* **SEE** NAVIGATION (ASTRONAUTICS)
QB6	ASTROGRAPHIC CATALOG AND CHART
QB85	ASTROLABES
BF1713	ASTROLOGY — CONTROVERSIAL LITERATURE
QB25-26	ASTROLOGY
BF1651-1729	ASTROLOGY
QB807	ASTROMETRY
TL1070	ASTRONAUTICAL CHARTS
TL793	ASTRONAUTICS — JUVENILE LITERATURE
TL793.3	ASTRONAUTICS — PICTORIAL WORKS
BJ60	ASTRONAUTICS AND ETHICS
TL850	ASTRONAUTICS AS A PROFESSION
QC879.5	ASTRONAUTICS IN METEOROLOGY
VK	ASTRONAUTICS IN NAVIGATION
TL787-799	ASTRONAUTICS
TL1070	*ASTRONAUTICS-CHARTS, DIAGRAMS, ETC.* **SEE** ASTRONAUTICAL CHARTS
TL850	*ASTRONAUTICS-VOCATIONAL GUIDANCE* **SEE** ASTRONAUTICS AS A PROFESSION
TL856	ASTRONAUTS — MEDICAL EXAMINATIONS
TL1065	*ASTRONAVIGATION* **SEE** NAVIGATION (ASTRONAUTICS)
QB35-36	ASTRONOMERS
QB6	*ASTRONOMICAL CHARTS* **SEE** ASTROGRAPHIC CATALOG AND CHART

QB107	ASTRONOMICAL CLOCKS
QB631-8	ASTRONOMICAL GEOGRAPHY
QB85-137	ASTRONOMICAL INSTRUMENTS
QB67	ASTRONOMICAL MODELS
QB2	ASTRONOMICAL MUSEUMS
QB4	*ASTRONOMICAL OBSERVATIONS* **SEE** ASTRONOMY — OBSERVATIONS
QB81-84	ASTRONOMICAL OBSERVATORIES
QB121	ASTRONOMICAL PHOTOGRAPHY
QB815	*ASTRONOMICAL PHOTOMETRY* **SEE** PHOTOMETRY, ASTRONOMICAL */ stellar magnitudes*
QB135	*ASTRONOMICAL PHOTOMETRY* **SEE** PHOTOMETRY, ASTRONOMICAL
QB461	*ASTRONOMICAL PHYSICS* **SEE** ASTROPHYSICS
QB155-6	*ASTRONOMICAL REFRACTION* **SEE** REFRACTION, ASTRONOMICAL
QB461	*ASTRONOMICAL SPECTROSCOPY* **SEE** ASTROPHYSICS
QC451-467	*ASTRONOMICAL SPECTROSCOPY* **SEE** SPECTRUM ANALYSIS
QD95	*ASTRONOMICAL SPECTROSCOPY* **SEE** SPECTRUM ANALYSIS */ chemical analysis*
QB65	ASTRONOMY — CHARTS, DIAGRAMS, ETC.
QB1	ASTRONOMY — CONGRESSES
QB52	ASTRONOMY — CURIOSA AND MISCELLANY
QB41-42	ASTRONOMY — EARLY WORKS TO 1800
QB33	ASTRONOMY — HISTORY
QB46	ASTRONOMY — JUVENILE LITERATURE
QB62	ASTRONOMY — LABORATORY MANUALS
QB4	ASTRONOMY — OBSERVATIONS
QB62-64	ASTRONOMY — OBSERVERS' MANUALS
QB68	ASTRONOMY — PICTORIAL WORKS
QB62.5	ASTRONOMY — PROBLEMS, EXERCISES, ETC.
QB11-12	ASTRONOMY — TABLES, ETC.
QB51.5	ASTRONOMY AS A PROFESSION
QB	ASTRONOMY
QB16	ASTRONOMY, ANCIENT
QB19	ASTRONOMY, ASSYRO-BABYLONIAN
QB23	*ASTRONOMY, CAMBODIAN* **SEE** ASTRONOMY, KHMER
QB34	*ASTRONOMY, HEBREW* **SEE** ASTRONOMY, JEWISH
QB34	ASTRONOMY, JEWISH
QB23	ASTRONOMY, KHMER
VK549-587	*ASTRONOMY, NAUTICAL* **SEE** NAUTICAL ASTRONOMY
QB145-237	ASTRONOMY, SPHERICAL AND PRACTICAL
QB149	*ASTRONOMY, STATISTICAL* **SEE** STATISTICAL ASTRONOMY
QB6	*ASTRONOMY-ATLASES* **SEE** ASTROGRAPHIC CATALOG AND CHART
QB65	*ASTRONOMY-ATLASES* **SEE** ASTRONOMY — CHARTS, DIAGRAMS, ETC.
QB65	*ASTRONOMY-ATLASES* **SEE** STARS — ATLASES
QB7-9	*ASTRONOMY-EPHEMERIDES* **SEE** EPHEMERIDES
QB8	*ASTRONOMY-EPHEMERIDES* **SEE** NAUTICAL ALMANACS
QB81-84	*ASTRONOMY-OBSERVATORIES* **SEE** ASTRONOMICAL OBSERVATORIES
QB461	ASTROPHYSICS
DS432	ASURS
JX4275-4399	ASYLUM, RIGHT OF
HV8652-4	ASYLUM, RIGHT OF
QA559	ASYMPTOTES
QA565	ASYMPTOTES
TK2785	*ASYNCHRONOUS ELECTRIC MOTORS* **SEE** ELECTRIC MOTORS, INDUCTION
F3070.1.A7	*ATACAMAS* **SEE** ATACAMENO INDIANS
PM5521	ATACAMENIAN LANGUAGE
F3070.1.A7	ATACAMENO INDIANS
D280.A8	ATH, BELGIUM — SIEGE, 1697
F1060.9	ATHABASCA AND PEACE RIVER TREATY EXPEDITION, 1889
PM641	*ATHABASCAN LANGUAGES* **SEE** ATHAPASCAN LANGUAGES
BT995	ATHANASIAN CREED
BT995	ATHANASIANISM
PM641	ATHAPASCAN LANGUAGES
BL2700-2790	ATHEISM
DF277	*ATHENIAN STRATEGI* **SEE** STRATEGI, ATHENIAN
RC691	*ATHEROSCLEROSIS* **SEE** ARTERIOSCLEROSIS
RA781	ATHLETES — HYGIENE
TX361.A8	ATHLETES — NUTRITION
GV697	ATHLETES
GV436	*ATHLETES-ABILITY TESTING* **SEE** ATHLETIC ABILITY
GV436	ATHLETIC ABILITY
GV563	ATHLETIC CLUBS
GV411-413	ATHLETIC FIELDS
GV743-7	*ATHLETIC GOODS* **SEE** SPORTING GOODS
GV561-751	ATHLETICS
GV563	*ATHLETICS-SOCIETIES, ETC.* **SEE** ATHLETIC CLUBS
PM2451	*ATIMUCA LANGUAGE* **SEE** TIMUCUA LANGUAGE
E476.7	ATLANTA CAMPAIGN, 1864
HE7725	*ATLANTIC CABLE* **SEE** CABLES, SUBMARINE — ATLANTIC */ economics*
TK5611	*ATLANTIC CABLE* **SEE** CABLES, SUBMARINE — ATLANTIC */ technology*
GN543	*ATLANTO-MEDITERRANEAN RACE* **SEE** MEDITERRANEAN RACE
CB224	*ATLANTO-MEDITERRANEAN RACE* **SEE** MEDITERRANEAN RACE */ civilization*
QB6	*ATLASES, ASTRONOMICAL* **SEE** ASTROGRAPHIC CATALOG AND CHART
QB65	*ATLASES, ASTRONOMICAL* **SEE** ASTRONOMY — CHARTS, DIAGRAMS, ETC.
QB65	*ATLASES, ASTRONOMICAL* **SEE** STARS — ATLASES
GA205-213	*ATLASES, HISTORICAL* **SEE** GEOGRAPHY, ANCIENT — MAPS
G1033	*ATLASES, HISTORICAL* **SEE** GEOGRAPHY, ANCIENT — MAPS
QC366	*ATLASES, OPTICAL* **SEE** OPTICS — ATLASES
GN498.T5	*ATLATL* **SEE** THROWING-STICKS
QC851-999	ATMOSPHERE
QC931	ATMOSPHERE */ circulation*
QC880	ATMOSPHERE */ mechanics and thermodynamics*
QC879	ATMOSPHERE, UPPER — ROCKET OBSERVATIONS
QC879	ATMOSPHERE, UPPER
QB531	*ATMOSPHERIC ABSORPTION OF SOLAR RADIATION* **SEE** SOLAR RADIATION */ astronomy*
QC911	*ATMOSPHERIC ABSORPTION OF SOLAR RADIATION* **SEE** SOLAR RADIATION */ meteorology*
QC961-972	ATMOSPHERIC ELECTRICITY
QC915-917	*ATMOSPHERIC HUMIDITY* **SEE** HUMIDITY
QC918	ATMOSPHERIC NUCLEATION
QP82	ATMOSPHERIC PRESSURE — PHYSIOLOGICAL EFFECT
QC885-896	ATMOSPHERIC PRESSURE
TF692	*ATMOSPHERIC RAILROADS* **SEE** RAILROADS, ATMOSPHERIC
QC901-6	ATMOSPHERIC TEMPERATURE
QC976.T7	ATMOSPHERIC TRANSPARENCY
E99.A28	*ATNAH INDIANS* **SEE** AHTENA INDIANS
E99.A28	*ATNATANA INDIANS* **SEE** AHTENA INDIANS
QE565	*ATOLLS* **SEE** CORAL REEFS AND ISLANDS
JX1974.7	*ATOMIC BOMB AND DISARMAMENT* **SEE** ATOMIC WEAPONS AND DISARMAMENT
BR115.A85	*ATOMIC BOMB-MORAL AND RELIGIOUS ASPECTS* **SEE** ATOMIC WARFARE — MORAL AND RELIGIOUS ASPECTS
Z5160	ATOMIC ENERGY — MICROCARD CATALOGS
BR115.A83	ATOMIC ENERGY — MORAL AND RELIGIOUS ASPECTS
HD	ATOMIC ENERGY INDUSTRIES */ economics*
TK9001-9401	ATOMIC ENERGY INDUSTRIES */ technology*
TK9360	*ATOMIC FUEL* **SEE** NUCLEAR FUELS
VM451	ATOMIC ICEBREAKERS
HD	*ATOMIC INDUSTRIES* **SEE** ATOMIC ENERGY INDUSTRIES */ economics*
TK9001-9401	*ATOMIC INDUSTRIES* **SEE** ATOMIC ENERGY INDUSTRIES */ technology*
TJ623	ATOMIC LOCOMOTIVES
QD466	ATOMIC MASS */ chemistry*
QC173	ATOMIC MASS */ physics*
RC91	ATOMIC MEDICINE
VM776	ATOMIC MERCHANT SHIPS — SAFETY MEASURES
QC173	*ATOMIC NUCLEI* **SEE** NUCLEAR PHYSICS
QC786	*ATOMIC PILES* **SEE** NUCLEAR REACTORS */ physics*
TK9202	*ATOMIC PILES* **SEE** NUCLEAR REACTORS */ technology*
TK9153	ATOMIC POWER — PSYCHOLOGICAL ASPECTS
TK9001-9401	*ATOMIC POWER ENGINEERING* **SEE** NUCLEAR ENGINEERING
HD9698	ATOMIC POWER INDUSTRY */ economics*
TK9001-9401	ATOMIC POWER INDUSTRY */ technology*

VM774.3	*ATOMIC SHIP PROPULSION* **SEE** MARINE NUCLEAR REACTOR PLANTS
VM317	ATOMIC SHIPS
QD461	ATOMIC THEORY
BR115.A85	ATOMIC WARFARE — MORAL AND RELIGIOUS ASPECTS
UF767	ATOMIC WEAPONS — TESTING
JX1974.7	ATOMIC WEAPONS AND DISARMAMENT
QD463-4	ATOMIC WEIGHTS
TK9230	*ATOMIC-POWERED VEHICLES* **SEE** NUCLEAR PROPULSION
BD646	ATOMISM / *cosmology*
B193	ATOMISM / *greek philosophy*
TC173	ATOMIZATION
QC173	ATOMS
QC721	ATOMS / *disintegration*
QC173	*ATOMS, NUCLEI OF* **SEE** NUCLEAR PHYSICS
QD481	*ATOMS-SPACE ARRANGEMENT* **SEE** STEREOCHEMISTRY
ML3811	*ATONALITY* **SEE** TONALITY
BT264-5	ATONEMENT
BM695.A8	*ATONEMENT, DAY OF* **SEE** YOM KIPPUR
BM675.A8	*ATONEMENT, DAY OF* **SEE** YOM KIPPUR / *liturgical forms*
QP321	ATROPHY, MUSCULAR / *physiology*
RD688	ATROPHY, MUSCULAR / *surgery*
RA1238.A8	ATROPINE — TOXICOLOGY
RE991	ATROPINE / *ophthalmology*
QP921.A8	ATROPINE / *pharmacology*
RN666.A85	ATROPINE / *therapeutics*
E99.A87	ATSINA INDIANS
PM653	ATSINA LANGUAGE
E99.A875	ATSUGEWI INDIANS
PM655	ATSUGEWI LANGUAGE
E99.A88	ATTACAPA INDIANS
PM661	ATTACAPA LANGUAGE
UG443-9	ATTACK AND DEFENSE (MILITARY SCIENCE)
TN948.F9	*ATTAPULGITE* **SEE** FULLER'S EARTH
TN948.F9	*ATTAPULGUS CLAY* **SEE** FULLER'S EARTH
BV652	*ATTENDANCE, CHURCH* **SEE** CHURCH ATTENDANCE
BV4523	*ATTENDANCE, CHURCH* **SEE** CHURCH ATTENDANCE
LC142-5	*ATTENDANCE, SCHOOL* **SEE** SCHOOL ATTENDANCE / *limitation*
LB3081	*ATTENDANCE, SCHOOL* **SEE** SCHOOL ATTENDANCE / *truancy*
LB1065	ATTENTION / *educational*
BF321	ATTENTION / *psychology*
TH3000	ATTICS
LB1117	ATTITUDE (PSYCHOLOGY) / *child study*
BF175	ATTITUDE (PSYCHOLOGY) / *psychoanalysis*
HM251-291	ATTITUDE (PSYCHOLOGY) / *sociology*
GN231	*ATTITUDE AND POSTURE OF MAN* **SEE** MAN — ATTITUDE AND MOVEMENT
E99.N	*ATTIWENDARONK INDIANS* **SEE** NEUTRAL NATION INDIANS
QA827	ATTRACTIONS OF ELLIPSOIDS
QA825-7	ATTRACTIONS
BL205	*ATTRIBUTES OF GOD* **SEE** GOD — ATTRIBUTES / *comparative religion*
BT130-153	*ATTRIBUTES OF GOD* **SEE** GOD — ATTRIBUTES / *doctrinal theology*
BV840	*ATTRITION* **SEE** PENANCE
BX2260	*ATTRITION* **SEE** PENANCE / *catholic church*
BT800	*ATTRITION* **SEE** REPENTANCE
F3126	*AUCA INDIANS* **SEE** ARAUCANIAN INDIANS
GV1282	AUCTION BRIDGE
GV1295.A8	AUCTION PIQUET
HF5476	AUCTIONS
LB1043-1044.9	AUDIO-VISUAL EDUCATION
TS2301.A7	AUDIO-VISUAL EQUIPMENT — CATALOGS
TS2301.A7	AUDIO-VISUAL EQUIPMENT
Z717	AUDIO-VISUAL LIBRARY SERVICE
Z695.64	*AUDIO-VISUAL MATERIALS (CATALOGING)* **SEE** CATALOGING OF AUDIO-VISUAL MATERIALS
GN275	*AUDIOLOGY* **SEE** HEARING / *anthropology*
QP461-9	*AUDIOLOGY* **SEE** HEARING / *physiology*
BF251	*AUDIOLOGY* **SEE** HEARING / *psychology*
HF5667	AUDITING
TK7882.T5	AUDITORIUMS — ELECTRONIC SOUND CONTROL
NA6815	AUDITORIUMS
QL671	AUDUBON SOCIETIES
QC721	AUGER EFFECT
BX8069	AUGSBURG CONFESSION
BL613	*AUGURY* **SEE** DIVINATION / *comparative religion*
BF1745-1779	*AUGURY* **SEE** DIVINATION / *occult sciences*
DG83.A7	AUGUSTALES
BX4265-8	AUGUSTINIAN CANONESSES
BX2830	AUGUSTINIAN CANONS
BX3980	*AUGUSTINIAN RECOLLETS* **SEE** RECOLLETS (AUGUSTINIAN)
BV2245	AUGUSTINIANS — MISSIONS
BX2901-2955	AUGUSTINIANS
BX4265-8	AUGUSTINIANS / *women*
QP77	AURA / *physiology*
BF1389.A8	AURA / *spiritism*
BP573.A8	AURA / *theosophy*
RE3	*AURAL HOSPITALS* **SEE** HOSPITALS, OPHTHALMIC AND AURAL
RF6	*AURAL HOSPITALS* **SEE** HOSPITALS, OPHTHALMIC AND AURAL / *nose and throat*
RS165.A	AUREOMYCIN / *pharmacy*
RM666.A	AUREOMYCIN / *therapeutics*
BV845-7	*AURICULAR CONFESSION* **SEE** CONFESSION
BX2262-7	*AURICULAR CONFESSION* **SEE** CONFESSION / *catholic church*
BX5149.C6	*AURICULAR CONFESSION* **SEE** CONFESSION / *church of england*
BX5949.C6	*AURICULAR CONFESSION* **SEE** CONFESSION / *protestant episcopal church*
GN775	AURIGNACIAN CULTURE
QC971-2	*AURORA AUSTRALIS* **SEE** AURORAS
QC971-2	*AURORA BOREALIS* **SEE** AURORAS
QC971-2	AURORAS
DG225.A	AURUNCI
QP111	*AUSCULTATION OF THE HEART* **SEE** HEART — SOUNDS
RC76.3	AUSCULTATION
QA259	AUSDEHNUNGSLEHRE
DG225.A	*AUSONES* **SEE** AURUNCI
TN731	AUSTENITE
DC227.5.A8	AUSTERLITZ, BATTLE OF, 1805
TL215.A9	AUSTIN AUTOMOBILE
BX2901-2955	*AUSTIN FRIARS* **SEE** AUGUSTINIANS
BX4265-8	*AUSTIN FRIARS* **SEE** AUGUSTINIANS / *women*
PR9560	AUSTRALIAN BALLADS AND SONGS / *collections*
PR9480	AUSTRALIAN BALLADS AND SONGS / *history*
JF1111	AUSTRALIAN BALLOT
JK2215	AUSTRALIAN BALLOT / *u.s.*
PR9583	AUSTRALIAN ESSAYS / *collections*
PR9513	AUSTRALIAN ESSAYS / *history*
PR9497-9507	AUSTRALIAN FICTION / *history*
GV947	AUSTRALIAN FOOTBALL
PL7001-7101	AUSTRALIAN LANGUAGES
PR9400-9597	AUSTRALIAN LITERATURE
SF473.B	*AUSTRALIAN LOVEBIRD* **SEE** BUDGERIGARS
PN5510-5590	AUSTRALIAN NEWSPAPERS / *etc.*
PN5510-5590	AUSTRALIAN PERIODICALS / *etc.*
PR9531-9563	AUSTRALIAN POETRY / *collections*
PR9461-9481	AUSTRALIAN POETRY / *history*
NC1760	AUSTRALIAN WIT AND HUMOR, PICTORIAL
DB	AUSTRIA — HISTORY
DD436-440	*AUSTRIA-HISTORY-AUSTRO-PRUSSIAN WAR, 1866* **SEE** AUSTRO-PRUSSIAN WAR, 1866
PT1185	*AUSTRIAN BALLADS AND SONGS* **SEE** GERMAN BALLADS AND SONGS / *collections*
PT1199-1232	*AUSTRIAN BALLADS AND SONGS* **SEE** GERMAN BALLADS AND SONGS / *collections*
PT507	*AUSTRIAN BALLADS AND SONGS* **SEE** GERMAN BALLADS AND SONGS / *history*
HB101	*AUSTRIAN ECONOMISTS* **SEE** AUSTRIAN SCHOOL OF ECONOMISTS
PT3822	AUSTRIAN FICTION (GERMAN)
PT3826	AUSTRIAN FICTION (GERMAN)
PT3823-9	*AUSTRIAN LITERATURE (GERMAN)* **SEE** GERMAN LITERATURE — AUSTRIAN AUTHORS / *collections*
PT3810-3822	*AUSTRIAN LITERATURE (GERMAN)* **SEE** GERMAN LITERATURE — AUSTRIAN AUTHORS / *history*
PN5161-9	AUSTRIAN NEWSPAPERS / *etc.*
PN5161-5170	AUSTRIAN PERIODICALS / *etc.*

HB101	AUSTRIAN SCHOOL OF ECONOMISTS
D291-4	AUSTRIAN SUCCESSION, WAR OF, 1740-1748
DB72	AUSTRIAN SUCCESSION, WAR OF, 1740-1748 / *austria*
D802.A9	AUSTRIA — HISTORY — — ALLIED OCCUPATION, 1945-1955
DD436-440	*AUSTRO-GERMAN WAR, 1866* **SEE** AUSTRO-PRUSSIAN WAR, 1866
DG553	*AUSTRO-ITALIAN WAR, 1848-1849* **SEE** AUSTRO-SARDINIAN WAR, 1848-1849
DG558	AUSTRO-ITALIAN WAR, 1866
DD436-440	AUSTRO-PRUSSIAN WAR, 1866
DG553	AUSTRO-SARDINIAN WAR, 1848-1849
DR545	AUSTRO-TURKISH WAR, 1716-1718
PL5021-6571	*AUSTRONESIAN LANGUAGES* **SEE** MALAY-POLYNESIAN LANGUAGES
HD82-85	AUTARCHY
Z696-7	*AUTHOR NOTATION* **SEE** SHELF-LISTING (LIBRARY SCIENCE)
HD3850	AUTHORITIES, PUBLIC **SEE** CORPORATIONS, GOVERNMENT
HD4001-4420	*AUTHORITIES, PUBLIC* **SEE** CORPORATIONS, GOVERNMENT / *other countries*
HD3881-8	*AUTHORITIES, PUBLIC* **SEE** CORPORATIONS, GOVERNMENT / *u.s.*
BP165.7	AUTHORITY (ISLAM)
BT88-92	AUTHORITY (RELIGION)
BD209	AUTHORITY / *epistemology*
JC571	AUTHORITY / *political theory*
HM271	AUTHORITY / *social psychology*
Z41-42	AUTHORS — AUTOGRAPHS
GV1483	AUTHORS (GAME)
PN147	*AUTHORS AND PRINTERS* **SEE** AUTHORSHIP — HANDBOOKS, MANUALS, ETC.
Z253	*AUTHORS AND PRINTERS* **SEE** PRINTING, PRACTICAL — STYLE MANUALS
PN	AUTHORS / *general*
Z1231.F5	*AUTHORS, AMERICAN-FIRST EDITIONS* **SEE** AMERICAN LITERATURE — BIBLIOGRAPHY — — FIRST EDITIONS
Z2014.F5	*AUTHORS, ENGLISH-FIRST EDITIONS* **SEE** ENGLISH LITERATURE — BIBLIOGRAPHY — — FIRST EDITIONS
PN471-9	*AUTHORS, FEMALE* **SEE** AUTHORS, WOMEN
PS147-151	*AUTHORS, FEMALE* **SEE** AUTHORS, WOMEN / *american*
PR111-115	*AUTHORS, FEMALE* **SEE** AUTHORS, WOMEN / *english*
PQ149	*AUTHORS, FEMALE* **SEE** AUTHORS, WOMEN / *french*
PN471-9	*AUTHORS, FEMALE* **SEE** WOMEN AS AUTHORS
Z2174.F5	*AUTHORS, FRENCH-FIRST EDITIONS* **SEE** FRENCH LITERATURE — BIBLIOGRAPHY — — FIRST EDITIONS
PN661-694	AUTHORS, MEDIEVAL
PS153.N5	*AUTHORS, NEGRO* **SEE** NEGRO AUTHORS / *u.s.*
PN471-9	AUTHORS, WOMEN
PS147-151	AUTHORS, WOMEN / *american*
PR111-115	AUTHORS, WOMEN / *english*
PQ149	AUTHORS, WOMEN / *french*
PN164	*AUTHORS-HOMES AND HAUNTS* **SEE** LITERARY LANDMARKS
PN165	AUTHORSHIP — ANECDOTES, FACETIAE, SATIRE, ETC.
PN147	AUTHORSHIP — HANDBOOKS, MANUALS, ETC.
PN101-249	AUTHORSHIP
RB152	AUTO-INTOXICATION
PN3448.A8	*AUTOBIOGRAPHIC FICTION* **SEE** FICTION, AUTOBIOGRAPHIC
PR830.A8	*AUTOBIOGRAPHIC FICTION* **SEE** FICTION, AUTOBIOGRAPHIC / *english*
PT747.A8	*AUTOBIOGRAPHIC FICTION* **SEE** FICTION, AUTOBIOGRAPHIC / *german*
CT101	AUTOBIOGRAPHIES / *collections in english*
CT25	AUTOBIOGRAPHY
TP159.A8	AUTOCLAVES
TS227	*AUTOGENOUS WELDING* **SEE** WELDING / *machine*
TT211	*AUTOGENOUS WELDING* **SEE** WELDING / *manual*
TL715	AUTOGIROS
TL554	*AUTOGIROS-POETRY* **SEE** AERONAUTICS — POETRY
Z48	*AUTOGRAPHIC PROCESSES* **SEE** COPYING PROCESSES
Z42	AUTOGRAPHS — COLLECTIONS
Z41-42	AUTOGRAPHS
Z42	*AUTOGRAPHS-CATALOGS* **SEE** AUTOGRAPHS — COLLECTIONS
M175.A8	AUTOHARP MUSIC
ML1015	AUTOHARP
TJ215	AUTOMATA
ML1055.A8	AUTOMATA
LB1029.A85	*AUTOMATED INSTRUCTION* **SEE** TEACHING MACHINES
TA165	AUTOMATIC CONTROL
TJ213-215	*AUTOMATIC MACHINERY* **SEE** MACHINERY AUTOMATIC
TL589.5	AUTOMATIC PILOT (AEROPLANES)
TS2301.P3	*AUTOMATIC RECORD CHANGERS* **SEE** RECORD CHANGERS
TH9336	*AUTOMATIC SPRINKLERS* **SEE** FIRE SPRINKLERS
LB1029.A85	*AUTOMATIC TEACHING* **SEE** TEACHING MACHINES
TK6397	*AUTOMATIC TELEPHONE* **SEE** TELEPHONE, AUTOMATIC
TJ214.T5	AUTOMATIC TIMERS
TF638	*AUTOMATIC TRAIN CONTROL* **SEE** RAILROADS — AUTOMATIC TRAIN CONTROL
TL260	*AUTOMATIC TRANSMISSIONS, AUTOMOBILE* **SEE** AUTOMOBILES — TRANSMISSION DEVICES, AUTOMATIC
LB1029.A85	*AUTOMATION OF INSTRUCTION* **SEE** TEACHING MACHINES
HE5614	*AUTOMOBILE ACCIDENTS* **SEE** TRAFFIC ACCIDENTS
TL272	*AUTOMOBILE BATTERIES* **SEE** AUTOMOBILES — BATTERIES
TL255	*AUTOMOBILE BODIES* **SEE** AUTOMOBILES — BODIES
TL275	*AUTOMOBILE BRAKES* **SEE** AUTOMOBILES — BRAKES
TL212	*AUTOMOBILE CARBURETORS* **SEE** AUTOMOBILES — MOTORS — — CARBURETORS
TL152	AUTOMOBILE DRIVERS — JUVENILE LITERATURE
TL152	AUTOMOBILE DRIVERS
TL152	*AUTOMOBILE DRIVING* **SEE** AUTOMOBILE DRIVERS
TL158	AUTOMOBILE ENGINEERING RESEARCH
QD121	AUTOMOBILE EXHAUST GAS — ANALYSIS
TL275	*AUTOMOBILE FENDERS* **SEE** AUTOMOBILES — FENDERS
TL153	*AUTOMOBILE FILLING STATIONS* **SEE** AUTOMOBILES — SERVICE STATIONS
TL154	*AUTOMOBILE GASOLINE CONSUMPTION* **SEE** AUTOMOBILES — FUEL CONSUMPTION
GV1024-5	*AUTOMOBILE GUIDES* **SEE** AUTOMOBILES — ROAD GUIDES
TL240	AUTOMOBILE INDUSTRY AND TRADE — AUTOMATION
HD9710	*AUTOMOBILE INDUSTRY AND TRADE-USED CARS* **SEE** USED CAR TRADE
TL285	*AUTOMOBILE INSPECTION* **SEE** AUTOMOBILES — INSPECTION
HG9970.A4-68	*AUTOMOBILE INSURANCE* **SEE** INSURANCE, AUTOMOBILE
HE5619-5720	*AUTOMOBILE LAW* **SEE** AUTOMOBILES — LAWS AND REGULATIONS
TL154	AUTOMOBILE PARKING
GV1029	AUTOMOBILE RACING
TL158	*AUTOMOBILE RESEARCH* **SEE** AUTOMOBILE ENGINEERING RESEARCH
TL159	*AUTOMOBILE SAFETY BELTS* **SEE** AUTOMOBILE SEAT BELTS
TL159	AUTOMOBILE SEAT BELTS
TL153	*AUTOMOBILE SERVICE STATIONS* **SEE** AUTOMOBILES — SERVICE STATIONS
TA472	*AUTOMOBILE STEEL* **SEE** STEEL, AUTOMOBILE
TL270	*AUTOMOBILE TIRES* **SEE** AUTOMOBILES — TIRES
TL297	*AUTOMOBILE TRAILERS* **SEE** AUTOMOBILES — TRAILERS
TL235	AUTOMOBILE TRAINS
TL260	*AUTOMOBILE TRANSMISSION* **SEE** AUTOMOBILES — TRANSMISSION DEVICES
TL230	*AUTOMOBILE TRUCKS* **SEE** MOTOR-TRUCKS
TL275	*AUTOMOBILE WINDOWS* **SEE** AUTOMOBILES — WINDOWS AND WINDSHIELDS
TL275	*AUTOMOBILE WINDSHIELDS* **SEE** AUTOMOBILES — WINDOWS AND WINDSHIELDS
TL272	*AUTOMOBILE WIRING* **SEE** AUTOMOBILES — ELECTRIC WIRING
TL245	AUTOMOBILES — AERODYNAMICS

TL272	AUTOMOBILES — BATTERIES
TL255	AUTOMOBILES — BODIES
TL275	AUTOMOBILES — BRAKES
TL240	AUTOMOBILES — DESIGN AND CONSTRUCTION
TL240	AUTOMOBILES — DRAWINGS
TL272	AUTOMOBILES — ELECTRIC EQUIPMENT
TL272	AUTOMOBILES — ELECTRIC WIRING
TL272.5	AUTOMOBILES — ELECTRONIC EQUIPMENT
TL275	AUTOMOBILES — FENDERS
TL154	AUTOMOBILES — FUEL CONSUMPTION
TL229.G3	AUTOMOBILES — GAS-PRODUCERS
TL275	AUTOMOBILES — HORNS
TL285	AUTOMOBILES — INSPECTION
HE5619-5720	AUTOMOBILES — LAWS AND REGULATIONS
TL272	AUTOMOBILES — LIGHTING / *electric equipment*
TL153.5	AUTOMOBILES — LUBRICATION
TL154	AUTOMOBILES — MATERIALS
TL237	AUTOMOBILES — MODELS
TL229.G3	AUTOMOBILES — MOTORS (COMPRESSED-GAS)
TL210	AUTOMOBILES — MOTORS
TL154	AUTOMOBILES — PAINTING
TL280	AUTOMOBILES — PATENTS
TL275	AUTOMOBILES — RADIATORS
HE5621-5720	AUTOMOBILES — REGISTRATION
GV1024-5	AUTOMOBILES — ROAD GUIDES
TL153	AUTOMOBILES — SERVICE STATIONS
TL272	AUTOMOBILES — STARTING DEVICES
TL260	AUTOMOBILES — STEERING-GEAR
HD9710	AUTOMOBILES — TAXATION
TL285-295	AUTOMOBILES — TESTING
TL270	AUTOMOBILES — TIRES
GV1021-5	AUTOMOBILES — TOURING
TL297	AUTOMOBILES — TRAILERS
TL260	AUTOMOBILES — TRANSMISSION DEVICES
TL260	AUTOMOBILES — TRANSMISSION DEVICES, AUTOMATIC
TL270	AUTOMOBILES — WHEELS
TL275	AUTOMOBILES — WINDOWS AND WINDSHIELDS
TL1-445	AUTOMOBILES / *history*
HD9710	AUTOMOBILES / *industry and statistics*
GV1021-1030	AUTOMOBILES / *sports and amusements*
HE5601-5720	AUTOMOBILES / *transportation*
TL229.G3	*AUTOMOBILES, COMPRESSED-GAS* **SEE** AUTOMOBILES — MOTORS (COMPRESSED-GAS)
TL220	AUTOMOBILES, ELECTRIC
TL229.G3	*AUTOMOBILES, GAS-GENERATOR* **SEE** AUTOMOBILES — GAS-PRODUCERS
TL1-445	*AUTOMOBILES, GASOLINE* **SEE** AUTOMOBILES / *history*
HD9710	*AUTOMOBILES, GASOLINE* **SEE** AUTOMOBILES / *industry and statistics*
GV1021-1030	*AUTOMOBILES, GASOLINE* **SEE** AUTOMOBILES / *sports and amusements*
HE5601-5720	*AUTOMOBILES, GASOLINE* **SEE** AUTOMOBILES / *transportation*
TL236.5	*AUTOMOBILES, MIDGET* **SEE** KARTS (MIDGET CARS)
UC340-345	AUTOMOBILES, MILITARY — COLD WEATHER OPERATION
UC340-345	AUTOMOBILES, MILITARY — HEATING AND VENTILATION
UG680-685	AUTOMOBILES, MILITARY
TL210	AUTOMOBILES, RACING — MOTORS
TL236	AUTOMOBILES, RACING
TL200	AUTOMOBILES, STEAM
HE5614	*AUTOMOBILES-ACCIDENTS* **SEE** TRAFFIC ACCIDENTS
TL229.G3	*AUTOMOBILES-BOTTLED-GAS MOTORS* **SEE** AUTOMOBILES — MOTORS (COMPRESSED-GAS)
TL212	*AUTOMOBILES-CARBURETORS* **SEE** AUTOMOBILES — MOTORS — — CARBURETORS
TL253	*AUTOMOBILES-DRAFTING* **SEE** AUTOMOTIVE DRAFTING
TL240	*AUTOMOBILES-DRAWING* **SEE** AUTOMOBILES — DRAWINGS
TL152	*AUTOMOBILES-DRIVING* **SEE** AUTOMOBILE DRIVERS
TL229.G3	*AUTOMOBILES-GAS ENGINES* **SEE** AUTOMOBILES — MOTORS (COMPRESSED-GAS)
TL260	*AUTOMOBILES-GEARING* **SEE** AUTOMOBILES — STEERING-GEAR
TL260	*AUTOMOBILES-GEARING* **SEE** AUTOMOBILES — TRANSMISSION DEVICES
GV1024-5	*AUTOMOBILES-GUIDES* **SEE** AUTOMOBILES — ROAD GUIDES
TL272	*AUTOMOBILES-HEADLIGHTS* **SEE** AUTOMOBILES — LIGHTING / *electric equipment*
HG9970.A4-68	*AUTOMOBILES-INSURANCE* **SEE** INSURANCE, AUTOMOBILE
HE5621-5720	*AUTOMOBILES-LICENSES* **SEE** AUTOMOBILES — REGISTRATION
HD9710	*AUTOMOBILES-LICENSES* **SEE** AUTOMOBILES — TAXATION
TL214.05	*AUTOMOBILES-OIL FILTERS* **SEE** AUTOMOBILES — MOTORS — — OIL FILTERS
TL154	*AUTOMOBILES-PARKING* **SEE** AUTOMOBILE PARKING
TL158	*AUTOMOBILES-RESEARCH* **SEE** AUTOMOBILE ENGINEERING RESEARCH
TL159	*AUTOMOBILES-SEAT BELTS* **SEE** AUTOMOBILE SEAT BELTS
TL152	*AUTOMOBILES-SIGNALS* **SEE** SIGNALS AND SIGNALING, AUTOMOBILE / *motoring*
HE369-370	*AUTOMOBILES-SIGNALS* **SEE** SIGNALS AND SIGNALING, AUTOMOBILE / *street signs*
HE5615	*AUTOMOBILES-SIGNALS* **SEE** SIGNALS AND SIGNALING, AUTOMOBILE / *regulations*
TL154	*AUTOMOBILES-USED CARS* **SEE** USED CARS
TL212	AUTOMOBILES — MOTORS — — CARBURETORS
TL214.05	AUTOMOBILES — MOTORS — — OIL FILTERS
TL1-445	*AUTOMOBILING* **SEE** AUTOMOBILES / *history*
HD9710	*AUTOMOBILING* **SEE** AUTOMOBILES / *industry and statistics*
GV1021-1030	*AUTOMOBILING* **SEE** AUTOMOBILES / *sports and amusements*
HE5601-5720	*AUTOMOBILING* **SEE** AUTOMOBILES / *transportation*
QA351	*AUTOMORPHIC FUNCTIONS* **SEE** FUNCTIONS, AUTOMORPHIC
TL253	AUTOMOTIVE DRAFTING
TL253	*AUTOMOTIVE DRAWING* **SEE** AUTOMOTIVE DRAFTING
TL158	*AUTOMOTIVE ENGINEERING RESEARCH* **SEE** AUTOMOBILE ENGINEERING RESEARCH
TP343	*AUTOMOTIVE FUELS* **SEE** MOTOR FUELS
HE5601-5720	*AUTOMOTIVE TRANSPORTATION* **SEE** TRANSPORTATION, AUTOMOTIVE
TL	*AUTOMOTIVE VEHICLES* **SEE** MOTOR VEHICLES
QP368	*AUTONOMIC NERVOUS SYSTEM* **SEE** NERVOUS SYSTEM, AUTONOMIC / *physiology*
QM471	*AUTONOMIC NERVOUS SYSTEM* **SEE** NERVOUS SYSTEM, AUTONOMIC / *human anatomy*
QL939	*AUTONOMIC NERVOUS SYSTEM* **SEE** NERVOUS SYSTEM, AUTONOMIC / *comparative anatomy*
TL589.5	*AUTOPILOT* **SEE** AUTOMATIC PILOT (AEROPLANES)
RA1058	AUTOPSY / *medical jurisprudence*
RB57	AUTOPSY / *pathology*
BF1111-1156	*AUTOSUGGESTION* **SEE** HYPNOTISM
HV6110	*AUTOSUGGESTION* **SEE** HYPNOTISM / *hypnotism and crime*
RC490-499	*AUTOSUGGESTION* **SEE** HYPNOTISM / *psychiatry*
BF1111-1156	*AUTOSUGGESTION* **SEE** MENTAL SUGGESTION
RB152	*AUTOTOXAEMIA* **SEE** AUTO-INTOXICATION
RC743	*AUTUMNAL CATARRH* **SEE** HAY-FEVER
PK9201.A9	*AVAR LANGUAGE* **SEE** AVARIC LANGUAGE
PK9201.A9	AVARIC LANGUAGE
BJ1535.A8	AVARICE
HE970	AVERAGE (MARITIME LAW)
HF5696	AVERAGE OF ACCOUNTS
RD86.A9	AVERTIN / *anesthetics*
QD981.A9	AVERTIN / *experimental pharmacy*
PK6101-9	AVESTA LANGUAGE
PK6111-6119	AVESTA / *etc.*
BL1515	AVESTA / *zoroastrianism*
SF995	*AVIAN MALARIA* **SEE** MALARIAL FEVER IN BIRDS
QL677.8	AVIARIES
JX5771	*AVIATION* **SEE** AERONAUTICS / *international law*
TL500-830	*AVIATION* **SEE** AERONAUTICS / *technology*
HE9911-9925	*AVIATION* **SEE** AERONAUTICS / *transportation and communication*
TL553.5	*AVIATION ACCIDENTS* **SEE** AERONAUTICS — ACCIDENTS

VG93	*AVIATION BOATSWAIN'S MATES* **SEE** U.S. — AVIATION BOATSWAIN'S MATES
TL692	*AVIATION COMMUNICATIONS* **SEE** AERONAUTICS — COMMUNICATION SYSTEMS
TL704.7	*AVIATION GASOLINE* **SEE** AEROPLANES — FUEL
RA615.2	*AVIATION HYGIENE* **SEE** AERONAUTICS — SANITARY ASPECTS
HG9970.A7	*AVIATION INSURANCE* **SEE** INSURANCE, AVIATION
JX5771	*AVIATION LAW* **SEE** AERONAUTICS — LAWS AND REGULATIONS / *international law*
HE9915-9925	*AVIATION LAW* **SEE** AERONAUTICS — LAWS AND REGULATIONS / *transportation and communication*
RC1058	AVIATION MEDICINE — RESEARCH
RC1050-1099	AVIATION MEDICINE
RC1075	*AVIATION PHYSIOLOGY* **SEE** FLIGHT — PHYSIOLOGICAL ASPECTS
TL712	*AVIATORS* **SEE** AIR PILOTS / *training*
TL586-9	*AVIGATION* **SEE** NAVIGATION (AERONAUTICS)
RC620-632	*AVITAMINOSIS* **SEE** DEFICIENCY DISEASES
SB379.A9	AVOCADO
GV1201	*AVOCATIONS* **SEE** HOBBIES
GN630.A18	*AVSAR (TURKISH TRIBE)* **SEE** AFSHAR (TURKISH TRIBE)
PK2001-7	AWADHI DIALECT
BR520	*AWAKENING, GREAT* **SEE** GREAT AWAKENING
BF575.A	AWE
TJ990-992	*AXIAL FLOW COMPRESSORS* **SEE** COMPRESSORS
BD232	*AXIOLOGY* **SEE** WORTH / *metaphysics*
BD430-435	*AXIOLOGY* **SEE** WORTH / *philosophy of life*
BF778	*AXIOLOGY* **SEE** WORTH / *psychology*
QA681	AXIOMS / *geometry*
QA481	AXIOMS / *geometry*
QL668.C2	AXOLOTLS
PM6714	*AYANA LANGUAGE* **SEE** OYANA LANGUAGE
F2230.2.A9	AYMARA INDIANS
PM5571-9	AYMARA LANGUAGE
PM4011	*AYOOK LANGUAGE* **SEE** MIXE LANGUAGE
SF199.A9	AYRSHIRE CATTLE
DT132	AZANDE
PL311-314	AZERBAIJANI LANGUAGE
PL311-314	*AZERI LANGUAGE* **SEE** AZERBAIJANI LANGUAGE
QB207	AZIMUTH
VK563	AZIMUTH / *navigation*
TA597	AZIMUTH / *surveying*
QD341.A9	AZO COMPOUNDS
TP918	AZO DYES
QD401	*AZOLE* **SEE** PYRROL
F1219.3.A6	*AZTEC ARCHITECTURE* **SEE** INDIANS OF MEXICO — ARCHITECTURE
F1219.3.C2	*AZTEC CALENDAR* **SEE** CALENDAR, MEXICAN
PM4061-9	AZTEC LANGUAGE
PM4068	AZTEC LITERATURE
E77	AZTECO-TANOAN INDIANS
F1219	AZTECS
BL1671	BAAL (DEITY)
PJ2395.B2	BAAMARANI DIALECT
SB299.P3	BABASSU PALM
BF723.I6	*BABIES* **SEE** INFANTS / *psychology*
HQ769-785	*BABIES* **SEE** INFANTS / *social groups*
DT570	BABINGAS
QE391.B2	BABINGTONITE
QL737.U5	BABIRUSSA
BP340	BABISM
QL737.P9	BABOONS
QB19	*BABYLONIAN ASTRONOMY* **SEE** ASTRONOMY, ASSYRO-BABYLONIAN
CE33	*BABYLONIAN CALENDAR* **SEE** CALENDAR, ASSYRO-BABYLONIAN
DS70.7	*BABYLONIAN CIVILIZATION* **SEE** CIVILIZATION, ASSYRO-BABYLONIAN
PJ	*BABYLONIAN INSCRIPTIONS* **SEE** CUNEIFORM INSCRIPTIONS
PK	*BABYLONIAN INSCRIPTIONS* **SEE** CUNEIFORM INSCRIPTIONS
CN	*BABYLONIAN INSCRIPTIONS* **SEE** CUNEIFORM INSCRIPTIONS
PJ3101-3595	*BABYLONIAN LANGUAGE* **SEE** ASSYRO-BABYLONIAN LANGUAGE
PJ3601-3959	*BABYLONIAN LITERATURE* **SEE** ASSYRO-BABYLONIAN LITERATURE

DS682.B2	BACALOD, BATTLE OF, 1903
BV4255	BACCALAUREATE ADDRESSES
GV1295.B3	BACCARAT
LB2383	BACHELOR OF ARTS DEGREE
HJ5580-5582	BACHELORS — TAXATION
HQ800	BACHELORS
RM666.B2	BACITRACIN
QL821	*BACKBONE* **SEE** SPINE / *comparative anatomy*
QM111	*BACKBONE* **SEE** SPINE / *human anatomy*
GV951.3	BACKFIELD PLAY (FOOTBALL)
TH6523	*BACKFLOW CONNECTIONS* **SEE** CROSS-CONNECTIONS (PLUMBING)
LC4661-4700	*BACKWARD CHILDREN* **SEE** SLOW LEARNING CHILDREN
PR2941-6	*BACON-SHAKESPEARE CONTROVERSY* **SEE** SHAKESPEARE, WILLIAM, 1564-1616 — AUTHORSHIP — — BACONIAN THEORY
F229	BACON'S REBELLION, 1676
QR75-84	BACTERIA
QR84	BACTERIA, ANAEROBIC
QR84	BACTERIA, CHROMOGENIC
QR105	BACTERIA, DENITRIFYING
QR111	BACTERIA, DENITRIFYING
QR105	BACTERIA, NITRIFYING
QR111	BACTERIA, NITRIFYING
RC112	*BACTERIA, PATHOGENIC* **SEE** SPIRILLOSIS
QR175-241	BACTERIA, PATHOGENIC
UG447.8	*BACTERIA, PATHOGENIC-WAR USE* **SEE** BIOLOGICAL WARFARE
QR351	BACTERIA, PHYTOPATHOGENIC
QR84	BACTERIA, THERMOPHILIC
UG447.8	*BACTERIAL WARFARE* **SEE** BIOLOGICAL WARFARE
SF995	*BACTERIAL WHITE DIARRHEA* **SEE** PULLORUM DISEASE
QR63-71	BACTERIOLOGICAL LABORATORIES
UG447.8	*BACTERIOLOGICAL WARFARE* **SEE** BIOLOGICAL WARFARE
QR71	BACTERIOLOGY — APPARATUS AND SUPPLIES
QR81	BACTERIOLOGY — CLASSIFICATION
QR63	BACTERIOLOGY — LABORATORY MANUALS
QR65 69	BACTERIOLOGY — TECHNIQUE
QR	BACTERIOLOGY
QR51	BACTERIOLOGY, AGRICULTURAL
QR111	BACTERIOLOGY, AGRICULTURAL / *bacteria in soil*
QR351	BACTERIOLOGY, AGRICULTURAL / *bacteria of plant diseases*
QR47	*BACTERIOLOGY, DENTAL* **SEE** MOUTH — BACTERIOLOGY
QR46	BACTERIOLOGY, MEDICAL
QR47	*BACTERIOLOGY, ORAL* **SEE** MOUTH — BACTERIOLOGY
QR46	*BACTERIOLOGY, SANITARY* **SEE** SANITARY MICROBIOLOGY
QR49	*BACTERIOLOGY, VETERINARY* **SEE** VETERINARY BACTERIOLOGY
QR185	BACTERIOLYSIS
PK6101-9	*BACTRIAN LANGUAGE (OLD BACTRIAN)* **SEE** AVESTA LANGUAGE
PL4641-9	BADAGA DIALECT
GT2695.J4	*BADCHANIM* **SEE** BADHANIM
PL8421	*BADEN LANGUAGE* **SEE** KUNAMA LANGUAGE
D283.5	BADEN, TREATY OF, 1714
SF429.D25	*BADGER-DOGS, GERMAN* **SEE** DACHSHUND
QL737.C2	BADGERS
QL795.B2	BADGERS / *legends and stories*
CR4501-6305	*BADGES OF HONOR* **SEE** DECORATIONS OF HONOR
UB430-435	*BADGES OF HONOR* **SEE** DECORATIONS OF HONOR / *military*
NK7400-7419	*BADGES OF HONOR* **SEE** INSIGNIA / *jeweled*
UC530-535	*BADGES OF HONOR* **SEE** INSIGNIA / *military*
VC345	*BADGES OF HONOR* **SEE** INSIGNIA / *naval*
CR4480	*BADGES OF HONOR* **SEE** INSIGNIA / *royalty*
HS159-160	*BADGES OF HONOR* **SEE** INSIGNIA / *secret societies*
CJ5501-6651	*BADGES OF HONOR* **SEE** MEDALS
CR67-69	BADGES / *heraldry*
TS761	BADGES / *manufacture*
GT2695.J4	BADHANIM
GV1007	BADMINTON (GAME)
GN635.J3	*BADOEINEN* **SEE** BADOEJ (JAVANESE PEOPLE)
GN635.J3	BADOEJ (JAVANESE PEOPLE)

GN635.J3	*BADOEWI* **SEE** BADOEJ (JAVANESE PEOPLE)
GN635.J3	*BADUJS (JAVANESE PEOPLE)* **SEE** BADOEJ (JAVANESE PEOPLE)
GN635.J3	*BADUWI (JAVANESE PEOPLE)* **SEE** BADOEJ (JAVANESE PEOPLE)
DT570	BAFIA (AFRICAN TRIBE)
GV1139	BAG PUNCHING
E235	*BAGADUCE EXPEDITION, 1779* **SEE** PENOBSCOT EXPEDITION, 1779
GV1469.B	BAGATELLE
TS2301.L	*BAGGAGE* **SEE** LUGGAGE
TF656	*BAGGAGE, RAILROAD* **SEE** RAILROADS — BAGGAGE
HE2556	*BAGGAGE, RAILROAD* **SEE** RAILROADS — BAGGAGE / economics
DT132	BAGGARA (AFRICAN TRIBE)
PL5551-4	BAGOBO LANGUAGE
M298	BAGPIPE AND DRUM MUSIC
M288-9	BAGPIPE MUSIC (2 BAGPIPES)
M145	BAGPIPE MUSIC
ML980	BAGPIPE
BP300-395	BAHAISM
PL5071-9	*BAHASA INDONESIA* **SEE** INDONESIAN LANGUAGE
PL3801.B2	BAHING DIALECT
PL4311-4314	BAHNAR LANGUAGE
DT584.B35	*BAIA (AFRICAN TRIBE)* **SEE** BAYA (AFRICAN TRIBE)
DS432	BAIGAS
DC233.B3	BAILEN, BATTLE OF, 1808
TG418	*BAILEY BRIDGES* **SEE** BRIDGES, PREFABRICATED
HV7983	BAILIFFS
HF1249	BAILMENTS / u.s.
BP186.45	*BAIRAM* **SEE** 'ID AL-FITR
SH459	BAIT-CASTING
SH459	BAIT
DT584.B35	*BAJA (AFRICAN TRIBE)* **SEE** BAYA (AFRICAN TRIBE)
F2520.1.B	BAKAIRI INDIANS
PM5581	BAKAIRI LANGUAGE
DT797.K	*BAKALAHADI* **SEE** KGALAGADI (AFRICAN PEOPLE)
PL8377	*BAKELE LANGUAGE* **SEE** KELE LANGUAGE
TX761-778	BAKERS AND BAKERIES
HD8039.B2	BAKERS AND BAKERIES / bakers
HD9057	BAKERS AND BAKERIES / industry
DT797.K	*BAKGALAGADI* **SEE** KGALAGADI (AFRICAN PEOPLE)
DS269.B3	BAKHTIARI
TX409	BAKING-POWDER
HD9330	BAKING-POWDER
TX761-778	BAKING
DT570	BAKOKO (AFRICAN TRIBE)
QL737.C4	*BALAENOPTERA* **SEE** WHALES
DS485.C6	BALAHIS
DK215.3	BALAKLAVA, BATTLE OF, 1854
DT797.K	*BALALA* **SEE** KGALAGADI (AFRICAN PEOPLE)
M282-3	BALALAIKA AND PIANO MUSIC
M142.B2	BALALAIKA MUSIC
M1037.4.B3	BALALAIKA WITH CHAMBER ORCHESTRA
M1015-1018	BALALAIKA
PL8725	*BALALI LANGUAGE* **SEE** TEKE LANGUAGE
DT955	*BALAMBA* **SEE** LAMBAS
N76	*BALANCE (ART)* **SEE** PROPORTION (ART)
NC745	*BALANCE (ART)* **SEE** PROPORTION (ART) / design
QP471	*BALANCE (PHYSIOLOGY)* **SEE** EQUILIBRIUM (PHYSIOLOGY)
QH540-541	*BALANCE OF NATURE* **SEE** ECOLOGY
D217	BALANCE OF POWER
JX1318	BALANCE OF POWER / international law
HF1014	BALANCE OF TRADE
HF5681.B2	*BALANCE SHEETS* **SEE** FINANCIAL STATEMENTS / balance sheet
QC107	BALANCE / weights and measures
GV551-3	*BALANCING (GYMNASTICS)* **SEE** ACROBATS AND ACROBATISM
TJ153	BALANCING OF MACHINERY
TJ153	*BALANCING-MACHINES* **SEE** BALANCING OF MACHINERY
RC122.B3	BALANTIDIUM COLI
NA3070	BALCONIES
RL91	BALDNESS
TJ625.B2-45	BALDWIN LOCOMOTIVES
ML579	BALDWIN ORGAN
SH385	*BALEEN* **SEE** WHALEBONE
PL8380.K5	*BALEGA LANGUAGE* **SEE** KILEGA LANGUAGE
GN654	*BALEGGAS* **SEE** WAREGAS / anthropology
DT650	*BALEGGAS* **SEE** WAREGAS / history
PL5221	BALINESE DRAMA
PL5221-4	BALINESE LANGUAGE
PL5224	BALINESE LITERATURE
SB252	*BALING OF COTTON* **SEE** COTTON BALING
DR46	BALKAN PENINSULA — HISTORY — — WAR OF 1912-1913
D461-9	*BALKAN QUESTION* **SEE** EASTERN QUESTION (BALKAN) / history
D374-7	*BALKAN QUESTION* **SEE** EASTERN QUESTION (BALKAN) / history
JX1319	*BALKAN QUESTION* **SEE** EASTERN QUESTION (BALKAN) / international law
DK34.B	BALKARIANS
GV861	BALL GAMES
GV1751	*BALL ROOM DANCING* **SEE** BALLROOM DANCING
TJ1071-3	BALL-BEARINGS
E472.63	BALL'S BLUFF, BATTLE OF, 1861
ML1950	BALLAD OPERA / history
M1500-1503.5	BALLAD OPERAS
PN1471	BALLADE / history and criticism
PR1194	BALLADES / english literature
PN1376	BALLADS / history and criticism
M1627	BALLADS / music
ML3545	BALLADS / music literature
VK237	BALLAST (SHIPS)
GV1795	BALLET — ANECDOTES, FACETIAE, SATIRE, ETC.
GT1740-1745	BALLET — COSTUME
GV1787.5	BALLET — JUVENILE LITERATURE
GV1779	BALLET IN MOVING-PICTURES, TELEVISION, ETC.
GV1779	*BALLET IN TELEVISION* **SEE** BALLET IN MOVING-PICTURES, TELEVISION, ETC.
GV1782	*BALLET PRODUCTION* **SEE** DANCE PRODUCTION
GV1787	BALLET / dancing
ML3460	BALLET / music
GV1782	*BALLET-PRODUCTION AND DIRECTION* **SEE** DANCE PRODUCTION
M1523	BALLETS — PIANO SCORES
M1520	BALLETS — SCORES (REDUCED) AND PARTS
M1520	BALLETS — SCORES
MT95-100	BALLETS — STORIES, PLOTS, ETC.
M1524	*BALLETS - SCORES (REDUCED) AND PARTS -- EXCERPTS* **SEE** BALLETS — EXCERPTS — — SCORES (REDUCED) AND PARTS
M1524-5	*BALLETS - SCORES -- EXCERPTS* **SEE** BALLETS — EXCERPTS — — SCORES
M243-4	BALLETS ARRANGED FOR FLUTE AND PIANO
M1523	BALLETS ARRANGED FOR PIANO (2 PIANOS)
M33	BALLETS / instrumental
M208	BALLETS / instrumental
M1520-1526	BALLETS / vocal
M1524	*BALLETS-SCORES (REDUCED) AND PARTS-EXCERPTS* **SEE** BALLETS — EXCERPTS — — SCORES (REDUCED) AND PARTS
M1524-5	*BALLETS-SCORES-EXCERPTS* **SEE** BALLETS — EXCERPTS — — SCORES
M1524	BALLETS — EXCERPTS — — SCORES (REDUCED) AND PARTS
M1524-5	BALLETS — EXCERPTS — — SCORES
U875	BALLISTA
UF830-857	BALLISTIC INSTRUMENTS
UF840	*BALLISTIC PHOTOGRAPHY* **SEE** PHOTOGRAPHY, BALLISTIC
VF550	*BALLISTIC TABLES* **SEE** BALLISTICS — TABLES, CALCULATIONS, ETC.
UF820	*BALLISTIC TABLES* **SEE** BALLISTICS — TABLES, CALCULATIONS, ETC.
UF820	BALLISTICS — TABLES, CALCULATIONS, ETC.
VF550	BALLISTICS — TABLES, CALCULATIONS, ETC.
UF820-840	BALLISTICS
HV8077	*BALLISTICS, FORENSIC* **SEE** FORENSIC BALLISTICS
TL620	BALLOON ASCENSIONS
TL554	*BALLOON ASCENSIONS-POETRY* **SEE** AERONAUTICS — POETRY
TL699	*BALLOON FABRICS* **SEE** BALLOONS — MATERIALS
TL665	*BALLOON FABRICS* **SEE** BALLOONS — MATERIALS
TL666	BALLOON GASES
TR810	*BALLOON PHOTOGRAPHY* **SEE** PHOTOGRAPHY, AERIAL

GV763	*BALLOON RACES* **SEE** BALLOON RACING
GV763	BALLOON RACING
TL665	BALLOONS — MATERIALS
TL699	BALLOONS — MATERIALS
TL609-639	BALLOONS
TL634-7	BALLOONS, CAPTIVE
TL650-668	*BALLOONS, DIRIGIBLE* **SEE** AIR-SHIPS
TL635	BALLOONS, KITE
TL631	BALLOONS, SOUNDING
TL554	*BALLOONS-POETRY* **SEE** AERONAUTICS — POETRY
JK2217	BALLOT-BOX / *u.s.*
JF1091-1177	BALLOT
JK2215-2217	BALLOT / *u.s.*
JF1111	*BALLOT, AUSTRALIAN* **SEE** AUSTRALIAN BALLOT
JK2215	*BALLOT, AUSTRALIAN* **SEE** AUSTRALIAN BALLOT / *u.s.*
JK2217	*BALLOT, COUPON* **SEE** COUPON BALLOT
JF1071-5	*BALLOT, PREFERENTIAL* **SEE** PREFERENTIAL BALLOT
JK2217	*BALLOT, PREFERENTIAL* **SEE** PREFERENTIAL BALLOT / *u.s.*
GV1751	BALLROOM DANCING
GV1757	BALLS (PARTIES)
GV1746-1750	BALLS (PARTIES)
PK6851-9	*BALOCHI LANGUAGE* **SEE** BALUCHI LANGUAGE
DT650	*BALOLO (BANTU TRIBE)* **SEE** MONGO (BANTU TRIBE)
DK511.B3	BALTIC ENTENTE, 1934-
QL696.P2	*BALTIMORE ORIOLE* **SEE** ORIOLES
E356.B2	BALTIMORE, BATTLE OF, 1814
PG1-9198	*BALTO-SLAVIC LANGUAGES* **SEE** SLAVIC LANGUAGES
PG1-41	*BALTO-SLAVIC PHILOLOGY* **SEE** SLAVIC PHILOLOGY
PK6851-9	BALUCHI LANGUAGE
PL8049.B3	*BAMANA LANGUAGE* **SEE** BAMBARA LANGUAGE
PL8049.B3	BAMBARA LANGUAGE
SB317.B2	BAMBOO
PL8441	*BAMONGO* **SEE** MONGO LANGUAGE
DT570	*BAMOUN (AFRICAN TRIBE)* **SEE** BAMUN (AFRICAN TRIBE)
DT570	*BAMUM (AFRICAN TRIBE)* **SEE** BAMUN (AFRICAN TRIBE)
DT570	BAMUN (AFRICAN TRIBE)
SB608.B16	BANANA — DISEASES AND PESTS
SB608.B16	BANANA BLACK-END DISEASE
QK495.M98	BANANA / *botany*
SB379.B2	BANANA / *culture*
PL4311-4314	*BANAR LANGUAGE* **SEE** BAHNAR LANGUAGE
MT125	BAND MUSIC — ANALYSIS, APPRECIATION
MT130	BAND MUSIC — ANALYSIS, APPRECIATION
M1200-1268	BAND MUSIC
M1420	BAND MUSIC, JUVENILE
RD113	BANDAGES AND BANDAGING
F2528	BANDEIRAS
PL8204	*BANDI LANGUAGE* **SEE** GBANDI LANGUAGE
QL677.5	*BANDING OF BIRDS* **SEE** BIRD-BANDING
HV6441-6453	*BANDITS* **SEE** BRIGANDS AND ROBBERS
HV6441-6453	*BANDITTI* **SEE** BRIGANDS AND ROBBERS
ML419	*BANDMASTERS* **SEE** BANDSMEN
ML399	*BANDMASTERS* **SEE** BANDSMEN
ML402	*BANDMASTERS* **SEE** CONDUCTORS (MUSIC) / *biography collective*
ML422	*BANDMASTERS* **SEE** CONDUCTORS (MUSIC) / *individual*
U43	*BANDMASTERS* **SEE** U.S. — BANDMASTERS
ML399	*BANDMEN* **SEE** BANDSMEN
ML419	*BANDMEN* **SEE** BANDSMEN
ML990	*BANDONEON* **SEE** BANDONION
M175.B2	BANDONION MUSIC
ML990	BANDONION
ML1300-1354	BANDS (MUSIC)
MT733	BANDS (MUSIC)
HV5287.B2-25	BANDS OF HOPE
ML419	BANDSMEN
ML399	BANDSMEN
ML1015-1018	BANDURRIA
SF871	*BANG'S DISEASE* **SEE** BRUCELLOSIS IN CATTLE
PL8055	BANGALA LANGUAGE
DT584.B3	BANGANGTE
PK1940	BANGARU DIALECT
MT562	BANJO — METHODS
M1360	*BANJO BAND* **SEE** PLECTRAL ENSEMBLES
M120-122	BANJO MUSIC

ML1015-1018	BANJO
MT568	*BANJO-SELF-INSTRUCTION* **SEE** BANJO — METHODS — — SELF-INSTRUCTION
MT568	BANJO — METHODS — — SELF-INSTRUCTION
NA6240-6243	BANK BUILDINGS
HG1662	*BANK DEPOSIT INSURANCE* **SEE** INSURANCE, DEPOSIT
HG1651-4	*BANK DISCOUNT* **SEE** DISCOUNT / *banking*
HF5553	*BANK DISCOUNT* **SEE** DISCOUNT / *business*
K	*BANK DISCOUNT* **SEE** DISCOUNT / *law*
HF1215.D7	*BANK DRAFTS* **SEE** DRAFTS
HF1277-1400	*BANK DRAFTS* **SEE** DRAFTS / *other countries*
HF1259	*BANK DRAFTS* **SEE** DRAFTS / *u.s.*
HG1997.16	BANK FOR INTERNATIONAL SETTLEMENTS
HG1641	BANK LOANS
HG2994-6	BANK OF ENGLAND
HG1706-8	*BANK STATEMENTS* **SEE** BANKS AND BANKING — ACCOUNTING
HG651-1490	BANK-NOTES / *other countries*
HG348-353	BANK-NOTES / *paper money*
HG607-610	BANK-NOTES / *u.s. bank-notes*
HG621-7	BANK-NOTES / *u.s. local*
HG1552	BANKERS / *general*
HG2701	BANKERS / *other countries*
HG2463	BANKERS / *u.s.*
HG1501-3540	*BANKING* **SEE** BANKS AND BANKING
HG1731-1756	BANKING LAW / *general*
HG2701	BANKING LAW / *other countries*
HG2421-6	BANKING LAW / *u.s.*
BX1939.B3	BANKRUPTCY (CANON LAW)
HG3760-3773	BANKRUPTCY
HJ8061	*BANKRUPTCY, NATIONAL* **SEE** STATE BANKRUPTCY
HG1706-8	BANKS AND BANKING — ACCOUNTING
HG1781-2	BANKS AND BANKING — GOVERNMENT GUARANTY OF DEPOSITS
HG1766-8	BANKS AND BANKING — TAXATION
HG1501-3540	BANKS AND BANKING
HG2035-2051	BANKS AND BANKING, COOPERATIVE
HG2052-2069	*BANKS AND BANKING, INDUSTRIAL* **SEE** LOANS, PERSONAL
HG1731-1756	*BANKS AND BANKING-LAWS AND LEGISLATION* **SEE** BANKING LAW / *general*
HG2701	*BANKS AND BANKING-LAWS AND LEGISLATION* **SEE** BANKING LAW / *other countries*
HG2421-6	*BANKS AND BANKING-LAWS AND LEGISLATION* **SEE** BANKING LAW / *u.s.*
HG4301-4480	*BANKS AND BANKING-TRUST DEPARTMENTS* **SEE** TRUST COMPANIES
HG1781-2	*BANKS AND BANKING-U.S.-GOVERNMENT GUARANTY OF DEPOSITS* **SEE** BANKS AND BANKING — GOVERNMENT GUARANTY OF DEPOSITS
NK4698	*BANKS, COIN* **SEE** COIN BANKS
JC345-7	*BANNERS* **SEE** FLAGS / *emblems of state*
CR101-115	*BANNERS* **SEE** FLAGS / *heraldry*
VK385	*BANNERS* **SEE** FLAGS / *merchant marine signaling*
UC590-595	*BANNERS* **SEE** FLAGS / *military science*
U360-365	*BANNERS* **SEE** FLAGS / *military science*
V300-305	*BANNERS* **SEE** FLAGS / *naval science*
E99.B33	BANNOCK INDIANS
DA783.41	BANNOCKBURN, BATTLE OF, 1314
HG1997.16	*BANQUE DES REGLEMENTS* **SEE** BANK FOR INTERNATIONAL SETTLEMENTS
TX737	*BANQUETS* **SEE** DINNERS AND DINING
SF489.B2	BANTAMS
PL8025	BANTU LANGUAGES
DT16.B2	BANTUS
GN657.B2	BANTUS / *ethnology*
DT764.B2	BANTUS / *south africa*
DS234-8	*BANU 'UMAJJA* **SEE** OMAYYADS
BX1939.B3	BAPTISM (CANON LAW)
BV820	BAPTISM AND CHURCH MEMBERSHIP
BV814	BAPTISM FOR THE DEAD
BV806-814	BAPTISM
NA5070	*BAPTISMAL FONTS* **SEE** FONTS
BX2307.3	BAPTISMAL WATER / *catholic church*
NA4821.B	*BAPTIST CHURCHES* **SEE** CHURCHES, BAPTIST
NA4910	BAPTISTERIES
NA5201-6113	BAPTISTERIES / *local*
BX3645	BAPTISTS — CLERGY
BX6201-6495	BAPTISTS

BX6440-6460	*BAPTISTS, COLORED* **SEE** BAPTISTS, NEGRO
BX6247.A-Z	BAPTISTS, DANISH, (GERMAN, ETC.) / u.s.
BX6440-6460	BAPTISTS, NEGRO
QD421	*BAPTITOXINE* **SEE** CYTISINE / chemistry
QP921.C	*BAPTITOXINE* **SEE** CYTISINE / physiological effect
GV485	BAR-BELLS
GV527	*BAR, HORIZONTAL* **SEE** HORIZONTAL BAR
PL5379	BARA DIALECT (MADAGASCAR)
PL4001.B3	BARA LANGUAGE
BP190.5.B3	*BARAKA* **SEE** BARAKAH
BP190.5.B3	BARAKAH
SF293.B3	*BARB* **SEE** BARBARY HORSE
DG500-514	BARBARIAN INVASIONS OF ROME
G535-7	*BARBARY CORSAIRS* **SEE** PIRATES
JX4444.6	*BARBARY CORSAIRS* **SEE** PIRATES / international law
SF293.B3	BARBARY HORSE
DT160-329	BARBARY STATES — HISTORY
TX840.B3	BARBECUE COOKERY
UG407	*BARBED-WIRE ENTANGLEMENTS* **SEE** WIRE OBSTACLES / military engineering
SH691.B	BARBEL (FISH) / fishing
QL638.C94	BARBEL (FISH) / zoology
SB386.B2	BARBERRIES
TT979	BARBERS' SUPPLIES
QK495.C	*BARBERTON DAISY* **SEE** GERBERA / botany
SB413.G	*BARBERTON DAISY* **SEE** GERBERA / floriculture
RM325	BARBITURATES
ND547	BARBIZON SCHOOL
SH691.M	*BARBUS MOSAL* **SEE** MAHSEER / fishing
QL638.C94	*BARBUS MOSAL* **SEE** MAHSEER / zoology
D283.B3	BARCELONA — SIEGE, 1713-1714
QE391.B3	BARCENITE
ML3653-6	BARDS AND BARDISM
ML287-9	BARDS AND BARDISM
PL8062	*BAREA LANGUAGE* **SEE** BARIA LANGUAGE
PL5231-4	BAREE DIALECT
BX3680.H8	*BARETTINI* **SEE** HUMILIATI
PL8061	BARI LANGUAGE
PL8062	BARIA LANGUAGE
TP245.S7	BARILLA
QE391.B35	BARITE
MT496	BARITONE (MUSICAL INSTRUMENT) — ORCHESTRA STUDIES
MT496	BARITONE (MUSICAL INSTRUMENT) — STUDIES AND EXERCISES
ML975-8	BARITONE (MUSICAL INSTRUMENT) / history and construction
M288-9	BARITONE AND CORNET MUSIC
M262-3	BARITONE AND PIANO MUSIC
QD181.B2	BARIUM COMPOUNDS
QD181.B2	BARIUM / chemistry
TN948.B18	BARIUM / mineral industries
GN432	*BARK CLOTH* **SEE** TAPA / primitive fabrics
SB945.B3	BARK-BEETLES
SB761	BARK-WEEVIL
BP190.5.B3	*BARKAH* **SEE** BARAKAH
SB608.B2	BARLEY — DISEASES AND PESTS
QK495.H75	BARLEY / botany
SB191.B2	BARLEY / culture
HD9049.B3-4	BARLEY / trade
RJ399.S3	*BARLOW'S DISEASE* **SEE** SCURVY, INFANTILE
TX950-951	*BARMAIDS* **SEE** BARTENDERS
HD6350.H8	*BARMAIDS* **SEE** BARTENDERS / trade-unions
BX2960.B6	BARNABITES
QL444.C5	*BARNACLES* **SEE** CIRRIPEDIA
NA8230	BARNS
S655	*BARNYARD MANURE* **SEE** FARM MANURE
QC886	BAROMETER
QC896	*BAROMETER, ANEROID* **SEE** ANEROID BAROMETER
QC895	BAROMETRIC HYPSOMETRY
HT647	*BARONAGE* **SEE** PEERAGE
CS421-3	*BARONAGE* **SEE** PEERAGE / gt. brit.
DA227.5	BARONS' WAR, 1263-1267
NA590	*BAROQUE ARCHITECTURE* **SEE** ARCHITECTURE, BAROQUE
NK1345	*BAROQUE DECORATION AND ORNAMENT* **SEE** DECORATION AND ORNAMENT, BAROQUE
NK2365	*BAROQUE FURNITURE* **SEE** FURNITURE, BAROQUE
NB193	*BAROQUE SCULPTURE* **SEE** SCULPTURE, BAROQUE
UC400-405	BARRACKS
TC540-555	BARRAGES
F59.B15	BARRE, VT. — FLOOD, 1927
TH2416	*BARREL-SHELL ROOFS* **SEE** ROOFS, SHELL
TS890	BARRELS
BT378.B2	BARREN FIG TREE (PARABLE)
DA490	BARRIER TREATY, 1709
D282	BARRIER TREATY, 1709
D282	BARRIER TREATY, 1715
DA499	BARRIER TREATY, 1715
UG375	*BARRIERS (MILITARY SCIENCE)* **SEE** OBSTACLES (MILITARY SCIENCE)
GN795-6	*BARROWS* **SEE** MOUNDS
TC209	*BARS (SAND)* **SEE** SAND-BARS / harbors and coasts
TC409	*BARS (SAND)* **SEE** SAND-BARS / rivers
TS320	*BARS, STEEL* **SEE** STEEL BARS
TX950-951	BARTENDERS
HD6350.H8	BARTENDERS / trade-unions
BT78	*BARTHIANISM* **SEE** DIALECTICAL THEOLOGY
DC118	*BARTHOLOMEW, ST., MASSACRE OF* **SEE** ST. BARTHOLOMEW'S DAY, MASSACRE OF, 1572
DT443	BARUNDI
QE391.B35	*BARYTES* **SEE** BARITE
M59	BARYTON MUSIC
ML760	BARYTON
NB1280-1291	BAS-RELIEF
PL8065	BASA LANGUAGE
NK4340.B5	*BASALTES POTTERY* **SEE** BLACK BASALTES
PL5571	*BASCO LANGUAGE* **SEE** BATAN LANGUAGE
QB303	*BASE APPARATUS* **SEE** BASE MEASURING
QB303	BASE MEASURING
GV862-881	*BASE-BALL* **SEE** BASEBALL
TP156.I6	*BASE-EXCHANGE* **SEE** ION EXCHANGE / chemical engineering
QD561	*BASE-EXCHANGE* **SEE** ION EXCHANGE / chemistry
TS350	*BASE-PLATES* **SEE** PLATES, IRON AND STEEL
TA492.P7	*BASE-PLATES* **SEE** PLATES, IRON AND STEEL / testing
GV873	BASEBALL — ANECDOTES, FACETIAE, SATIRE, ETC.
GV880	BASEBALL — ECONOMIC ASPECTS
M1977.S713	BASEBALL — SONGS AND MUSIC
M1978.S713	BASEBALL — SONGS AND MUSIC
GV876	BASEBALL — UMPIRING
GV880	*BASEBALL AND RADIO* **SEE** RADIO AND BASEBALL
GV880	*BASEBALL AND TELEVISION* **SEE** TELEVISION AND BASEBALL
GV875.A1	BASEBALL CLUBS
GV875.A1	*BASEBALL CLUBS, PROFESSIONAL* **SEE** BASEBALL CLUBS
GV862-881	BASEBALL
GV875.A1	*BASEBALL-SOCIETIES, ETC.* **SEE** BASEBALL CLUBS
RC656	*BASEDOW'S DISEASE* **SEE** GRAVES' DISEASE
BX830 1431	BASEL, COUNCIL OF, 1431-1449
DC222.B3	BASEL, TREATY OF, 1795
PK7055.B3	BASHGALI LANGUAGE
PL65.B3	BASHKIR LANGUAGE
PL65.B3	BASHKIR PHILOLOGY
PE1073.5	BASIC ENGLISH
QK626-9	BASIDIOMYCETES
NA4150	BASILICAS
LB1543	BASKET MAKING / elementary education
GN431	BASKET MAKING / ethnology
TS910	BASKET MAKING / manufacture
GV1295.C2	*BASKET RUMMY* **SEE** CANASTA (GAME)
SD397.O82	*BASKET WILLOWS* **SEE** OSIERS
GV885	*BASKET-BALL* **SEE** BASKETBALL
E99.B37	BASKET-MAKER INDIANS
GV886	BASKETBALL FOR WOMEN
GV885	BASKETBALL
PH5001-5259	BASQUE LANGUAGE
PH5280-5490	BASQUE LITERATURE
GN549.B3	BASQUES / ethnology
DC611.B31-322	BASQUES / french history
DP302.B46	BASQUES / spanish history
ML1035	*BASS DRUM* **SEE** DRUM
GN467.D8	*BASS DRUM* **SEE** DRUM / primitive
SH681	BASS FISHING
ML970-973	*BASS HORN* **SEE** TUBA

ML920-925	*BASS VIOL* **SEE** DOUBLE BASS
ML760	*BASS VIOL* **SEE** VIOLA DA GAMBA
QL638.C3	BASS
SH351.B	BASS / fish-culture
QL638.S2	*BASS, OTSEGO* **SEE** WHITEFISHES
ML990.B35	BASSET HORN
M271.B4	BASSET-HORN AND PIANO MUSIC
M270.B4	BASSET-HORN AND PIANO MUSIC
M110.B35	BASSET-HORN MUSIC
SF429.B2	BASSET-HOUNDS
ML442	*BASSO CONTINUO* **SEE** THOROUGH BASS / history
MT49	*BASSO CONTINUO* **SEE** THOROUGH BASS / instruction and study
ML448	*BASSO OSTINATO* **SEE** GROUND BASS
MT406	BASSOON — ORCHESTRA STUDIES
MT405	BASSOON — STUDIES AND EXERCISES
M1040-1041	BASSOON AND CLARINET WITH ORCHESTRA
M1106	BASSOON AND CLARINET WITH STRING ORCHESTRA — SOLOS WITH PIANO
M1105-6	BASSOON AND CLARINET WITH STRING ORCHESTRA
M290-291	BASSOON AND DOUBLE-BASS MUSIC
M288-9	BASSOON AND FLUTE MUSIC
M253-4	BASSOON AND HARPSICHORD MUSIC
M288-9	BASSOON AND OBOE MUSIC
M1040-1041	BASSOON AND OBOE WITH ORCHESTRA
M1105-6	BASSOON AND OBOE WITH STRING ORCHESTRA
M253-4	BASSOON AND PIANO MUSIC
M253-4	BASSOON AND PIANO MUSIC, ARRANGED
M288-9	BASSOON AND RECORDER MUSIC
M1105-6	BASSOON AND RECORDER WITH STRING ORCHESTRA
M288-9	BASSOON AND TRUMPET MUSIC
M1105-6	BASSOON AND TRUMPET WITH STRING ORCHESTRA
M290-291	BASSOON AND VIOLIN MUSIC
M290-291	BASSOON AND VIOLONCELLO MUSIC
M455-7	*BASSOON MUSIC (4 BASSOONS)* **SEE** WIND QUARTETS (4 BASSOONS)
M288-9	BASSOON MUSIC (2 BASSOONS)
M288-9	BASSOON MUSIC (2 BASSOONS), ARRANGED
M455-7	*BASSOON MUSIC (4 BASSOONS)* **SEE** WIND QUARTETS (4 BASSOONS)
M75-77	BASSOON MUSIC
M1027	BASSOON WITH CHAMBER ORCHESTRA — SOLO WITH PIANO
M1026-7	BASSOON WITH CHAMBER ORCHESTRA
M1027	BASSOON WITH ORCHESTRA — SOLO WITH PIANO
M1026-7	BASSOON WITH ORCHESTRA
M1027	BASSOON WITH ORCHESTRA, ARRANGED — SOLO WITH PIANO
M1026-7	BASSOON WITH ORCHESTRA, ARRANGED
M1106	BASSOON WITH STRING ORCHESTRA — SOLO WITH PIANO
M1105-6	BASSOON WITH STRING ORCHESTRA
ML953	BASSOON / history
M1105-6	BASSOON, CLARINET, FLUTE WITH STRING ORCHESTRA
M1040-1041	BASSOON, CLARINET, FLUTE, HORN, OBOE WITH CHAMBER ORCHESTRA
M1040	BASSOON, CLARINET, FLUTE, HORN, OBOE WITH CHAMBER ORCHESTRA — SCORES
M1040-1041	BASSOON, CLARINET, FLUTE, HORN, OBOE WITH ORCHESTRA
M1105-6	BASSOON, CLARINET, FLUTE, HORN, VIOLONCELLO WITH STRING ORCHESTRA
M1040-1041	BASSOON, CLARINET, FLUTE, OBOE WITH CHAMBER ORCHESTRA
M1040-1041	BASSOON, CLARINET, FLUTE, OBOE, HARP WITH ORCHESTRA
M1105	BASSOON, CLARINET, FLUTE, OBOE, 2 VIOLINS, VIOLA, VIOLONCELLO WITH STRING ORCHESTRA — SCORES
M1105-6	BASSOON, CLARINET, FLUTE, OBOE, 2 VIOLINS, VIOLA, VIOLONCELLO WITH STRING ORCHESTRA
M1105-6	BASSOON, CLARINET, FLUTE, TRUMPET WITH STRING ORCHESTRA
M1105	BASSOON, CLARINET, FLUTE, TRUMPET WITH STRING ORCHESTRA — SCORES
M1040-1041	BASSOON, CLARINET, HORN, OBOE WITH ORCHESTRA
M1105-6	BASSOON, CLARINET, HORN, OBOE WITH STRING ORCHESTRA
M1105-6	BASSOON, CLARINET, OBOE WITH STRING ORCHESTRA
M1040-1041	BASSOON, CLARINET, TRUMPET WITH ORCHESTRA
M1040-1041	BASSOON, FLUTE, HORN, OBOE WITH ORCHESTRA
M1105	BASSOON, FLUTE, HORN, OBOE WITH STRING ORCHESTRA — SCORES
M1105-6	BASSOON, FLUTE, HORN, OBOE WITH STRING ORCHESTRA
M1040-1041	BASSOON, HORN, TRUMPET, DOUBLE BASS WITH ORCHESTRA
M1040	BASSOON, HORN, TRUMPET, DOUBLE BASS WITH ORCHESTRA — SCORES
M1105-6	BASSOON, OBOE, TRUMPET WITH STRING ORCHESTRA
M1040	BASSOON, OBOE, VIOLIN, VIOLONCELLO WITH CHAMBER ORCHESTRA — SCORES
M1040-1041	BASSOON, OBOE, VIOLIN, VIOLONCELLO WITH CHAMBER ORCHESTRA
M1040-1041	BASSOON, OBOE, VIOLIN, VIOLONCELLO WITH ORCHESTRA
M1041	BASSOON, OBOE, VIOLIN, VIOLONCELLO WITH ORCHESTRA — TO 1800 — — SOLOS WITH PIANO
DT764.G	*BASTAARDS* **SEE** GRIQUAS
HQ998-9	*BASTARDY* **SEE** ILLEGITIMACY
HB903.I6	*BASTARDY* **SEE** ILLEGITIMACY / statistics
D756.5.A7	*BASTOGNE, BATTLE OF, 1944-1945* **SEE** ARDENNES, BATTLE OF THE, 1944-1945
QL737.C5	*BAT* **SEE** BATS
PL5241-4	BATAK LANGUAGE
F2688.5	*BATALLA DE BOQUERON, 1932* **SEE** BOQUERON, BATTLE OF, 1932
E2324	*BATALLA DE NIQUITAO, 1813* **SEE** NIQUITAO, BATTLE OF, 1813
PL5571	BATAN LANGUAGE
PL5571	*BATANESE LANGUAGE* **SEE** BATAN LANGUAGE
SF247	*BATES LABORATORY ASPIRATOR* **SEE** SEPARATORS (MACHINES) / dairy machinery
TN515	*BATES LABORATORY ASPIRATOR* **SEE** SEPARATORS (MACHINES) / mining
TJ1540	*BATES LABORATORY ASPIRATOR* **SEE** SEPARATORS (MACHINES) / screening
PN1059.B	BATHETIC POETRY
PR1175	BATHETIC POETRY / english collections
GT2845	BATHING CUSTOMS
QE461	BATHOLITHS
PN203	BATHOS
TH6485-6496	BATHROOMS / building
NK2117	BATHROOMS / interior decoration
RM801-822	BATHS
LB3461	BATHS / school hygiene
RM822.C6	BATHS, COLD
RM885	BATHS, ELECTRIC
RM820	BATHS, FINNISH
RM865-7	BATHS, HOT-AIR
RM822.V2	BATHS, MEDICATED
RM822.M9	BATHS, MOOR AND MUD
RM822.M9	*BATHS, MUD* **SEE** BATHS, MOOR AND MUD
RM822.P3	BATHS, PARTIAL
TH4761	BATHS, PUBLIC / building
RA605	BATHS, PUBLIC / public hygiene
RM820	BATHS, RUSSIAN
RM819	BATHS, SEA
RM821	BATHS, TURKISH
RM822.V2	BATHS, VAPOR
RM822.W2	BATHS, WARM
NK9503	BATIK
MT733.6	BATON TWIRLING
QL669	BATRACHIA — ANATOMY
QL641-669	BATRACHIA
QE867-8	BATRACHIA, FOSSIL
PK9201.T8	*BATS LANGUAGE* **SEE** TSOVA-TUSH LANGUAGE
QL737.C5	BATS
PL5241-4	*BATTA LANGUAGE (SUMATRA)* **SEE** BATAK LANGUAGE
TT800-805	BATTENBERG LACE
QC603-5	*BATTERIES, ELECTRIC* **SEE** ELECTRIC BATTERIES
QC605	*BATTERIES, ELECTRIC* **SEE** STORAGE BATTERIES
TL272	*BATTERIES, ELECTRIC* **SEE** STORAGE BATTERIES / automobile
TK2891	*BATTERIES, ELECTRIC* **SEE** STORAGE BATTERIES / central stations
TK5378	*BATTERIES, ELECTRIC* **SEE** STORAGE BATTERIES / telegraph

QC605	*BATTERY ADDITIVES* **SEE** STORAGE BATTERIES — ADDITIVES
TK6564.P6	*BATTERY RADIOS* **SEE** PORTABLE RADIOS
D756.5.B	BATTICE, BATTLE OF, 1940
GV869	BATTING (BASEBALL)
V810	*BATTLE DAMAGE REPAIR (WARSHIPS)* **SEE** DAMAGE CONTROL (WARSHIPS)
BX6510.B3	BATTLE-AXES (SECT)
GV1017.B33	BATTLE-BALL
CR79	BATTLE-CRIES / *heraldry*
CR4565	*BATTLE, WAGER OF* **SEE** WAGER OF BATTLE
TG416	*BATTLEDECK FLOOR BRIDGES* **SEE** BRIDGES, STEEL PLATE DECK
N8260	BATTLES IN ART
D25	BATTLES
D27	*BATTLES, NAVAL* **SEE** NAVAL BATTLES
PM1171	*BATUCO LANGUAGE* **SEE** EUDEVE LANGUAGE
DT443	*BATUSSI* **SEE** BATUTSI
DT443	BATUTSI
PL4001.L2	*BAUNGSHE DIALECT* **SEE** LAI LANGUAGE
RZ410	BAUNSCHEIDTISM
PM5606	BAURE LANGUAGE
DC236.7.B3	BAUTZEN, BATTLE OF, 1813
TN948.B2	BAUXITE / *mineral industries*
QE391.B4	BAUXITE / *mineralogy*
DD801.B31-55	BAVARIA — HISTORY
DD801.B376	BAVARIAN SUCCESSION, WAR OF, 1778-1779
DD801.B34-348	BAVARIANS
GN657.B3	BAVENDA / *anthropology*
DT764.B	BAVENDA / *south africa*
GN654	BAVILI TRIBE
E474.9	BAXTER SPRINGS, KAN., BATTLE OF, 1863
DT584.B35	BAYA (AFRICAN TRIBE)
PL8725	*BAYAKA LANGUAGE* **SEE** TEKE LANGUAGE
NK3049.B3	BAYEUX TAPESTRY
DC233.B3	*BAYLEN, BATTLE OF, 1808* **SEE** BAILEN, BATTLE OF, 1808
UD400	BAYONETS
PL8421	*BAZA LANGUAGE* **SEE** KUNAMA LANGUAGE
HV544	BAZAARS, CHARITABLE
HV544	*BAZARS, CHARITABLE* **SEE** BAZAARS, CHARITABLE
PL8421	*BAZEN LANGUAGE* **SEE** KUNAMA LANGUAGE
ML3561	*BE BOP MUSIC* **SEE** JAZZ MUSIC
QL444.A5	BEACH-FLEA
PM7895.B4	BEACH-LA-MAR JARGON
GB454.B3	BEACHES
DA86.8	BEACHY HEAD, BATTLE OF, 1690
VK1000-1246	BEACONS
NK3650	BEADS / *art industries*
TS2301.B4	BEADS / *technology*
NK3650	BEADWORK / *art industries*
TT860	BEADWORK / *technology*
QH11	BEAGLE EXPEDITION, 1831-1836
SF429.B3	BEAGLES (DOGS)
TG350-360	*BEAMS* **SEE** GIRDERS
TA891	*BEAMS* **SEE** GIRDERS / *riveting*
SB945.M59	*BEAN BEETLE* **SEE** MEXICAN BEAN BEETLE
SB945.M59	*BEAN LADYBIRD* **SEE** MEXICAN BEAN BEETLE
TP684.S6	*BEAN OIL* **SEE** SOY-BEAN OIL
SB608.B3	BEANS — DISEASES AND PESTS
QK495.L52	BEANS / *botany*
SB327	BEANS / *culture*
SK295	BEAR HUNTING
QL447.T2	*BEAR-ANIMALCULES* **SEE** TARDIGRADA
QL737.R6	*BEAR-MICE* **SEE** MARMOTS
GT2320	BEARD
RL91	BEARD / *dermatology*
TJ1061-1073	BEARINGS (MACHINERY)
TJ1073.5	*BEARINGS, GAS-LUBRICATED* **SEE** GAS-LUBRICATED BEARINGS
PC3427.B	BEARNAIS DIALECT
QL795.B4	BEARS — LEGENDS AND STORIES
QL737.C2	BEARS
GV1105	BEARS / *bear-baiting*
SK295	BEARS / *hunting*
QE882.C1	BEARS, FOSSIL
SF	*BEASTS* **SEE** DOMESTIC ANIMALS / *animal industry*
GN426	*BEASTS* **SEE** DOMESTIC ANIMALS / *ethnology*
GT5870-5895	*BEASTS* **SEE** DOMESTIC ANIMALS / *manners and customs*
BT382	BEATITUDES — STORIES
BT382	BEATITUDES
DC309.B4	BEAUNE-LA-ROLANDE, BATTLE OF, 1870
N61-79	*BEAUTIFUL, THE* **SEE** AESTHETICS / *art*
BH	*BEAUTIFUL, THE* **SEE** AESTHETICS / *philosophy*
N61-79	*BEAUTY* **SEE** AESTHETICS / *art*
BH	*BEAUTY* **SEE** AESTHETICS / *philosophy*
RA778	*BEAUTY* **SEE** BEAUTY, PERSONAL
TT950-979	BEAUTY CULTURE
RA778	BEAUTY, PERSONAL
NK3049.B4	BEAUVAIS TAPESTRY
CT9985-6	*BEAUX* **SEE** DANDIES / *biography*
E356.B3	BEAVER DAMS, BATTLE OF, 1813
E99.T77	*BEAVER INDIANS (ATHAPASCAN TRIBE)* **SEE** TSATTINE INDIANS
QL737.R6	BEAVERS
QL795.B5	BEAVERS / *legends and stories*
QE882.R6	BEAVERS, FOSSIL
ML3561	*BEBOP MUSIC* **SEE** JAZZ MUSIC
PM7895.B4	*BECHE-DE-MER JARGON* **SEE** BEACH-LA-MAR JARGON
DT797	*BECHUANA* **SEE** TSWANA (BANTU TRIBE)
DT797	*BECHWANA* **SEE** TSWANA (BANTU TRIBE)
QC721	BECQUEREL RAYS
RD629	BED-SORES
RC918.U5	*BED-WETTING* **SEE** URINE — INCONTINENCE
QL523.C6	BEDBUGS
TX325	BEDBUGS / *household pests*
SB451-466	*BEDDING (HORTICULTURE)* **SEE** GARDENING
GN635.J3	*BEDOEWI* **SEE** BADOEJ (JAVANESE PEOPLE)
DS219.B4	BEDOUINS
TT197.5.B4	BEDROOM FURNITURE / *cabinet work*
NK2117	BEDROOM FURNITURE / *interior decoration*
TS880	BEDROOM FURNITURE / *manufacture*
NK9100-9199	*BEDSPREADS* **SEE** COVERLETS / *art*
TT835	*BEDSPREADS* **SEE** COVERLETS / *technology*
DS219.B4	*BEDUINS* **SEE** BEDOUINS
SF521-538	*BEE* **SEE** BEES / *beekeeping*
QL568.A6	*BEE* **SEE** BEES / *entomology*
SF532-3	BEE CULTURE — EQUIPMENT AND SUPPLIES
N7660	*BEE CULTURE IN ART* **SEE** BEES IN ART
SF521-539	BEE CULTURE
SF537	BEE HUNTING
SF537	*BEE TREES* **SEE** BEE HUNTING
SF521	BEE-KEEPERS' SOCIETIES
QL561.P9	BEE-MOTH
QK495.B56	BEECH / *botany*
SD397.B4	BEECH / *forestry*
E83.868	BEECHER ISLAND, BATTLE OF, 1868
SF207	BEEF CATTLE
HD9410-9429	BEEF PACKERS / *industry*
TS1950-1975	BEEF PACKERS / *technology*
HD2769.P3	BEEF PACKERS / *u.s.*
TX556.B4	BEEF
HD9559.C68-7	*BEEHIVE COKE INDUSTRY* **SEE** COKE INDUSTRY
SF532-3	*BEEHIVES* **SEE** BEE CULTURE — EQUIPMENT AND SUPPLIES
SF521-539	*BEEKEEPING* **SEE** BEE CULTURE
HD9397	BEER / *industry*
TP569-587	BEER / *technology*
SF538	BEES — DISEASES
N7660	BEES IN ART
SF521-538	BEES / *beekeeping*
QL568.A6	BEES / *entomology*
GR750	*BEES, FOLK-LORE OF* **SEE** FOLK-LORE OF BEES
QL568.M	*BEES, STINGLESS* **SEE** STINGLESS BEES
TP678	BEESWAX
SB219-221	*BEET* **SEE** BEETS AND BEET SUGAR / *culture*
SB329	*BEET* **SEE** BEETS AND BEET SUGAR / *culture*
HD9100-9119	*BEET* **SEE** BEETS AND BEET SUGAR / *industry*
TP390-391	*BEET* **SEE** BEETS AND BEET SUGAR / *technology*
SB608.B4	BEET PESTS
QL571-597	BEETLES
QE832.C6	BEETLES, FOSSIL
SB219-221	BEETS AND BEET SUGAR / *culture*
SB329	BEETS AND BEET SUGAR / *culture*
HD9100-9119	BEETS AND BEET SUGAR / *industry*
TP390-391	BEETS AND BEET SUGAR / *technology*

N8217.B4	BEGGARS IN ART
DH187-193	*BEGGARS, THE* **SEE** GUEUX
HV4480-4630	BEGGING
HV6174	BEGGING / *pauperism and crime*
BX2975.B5	BEGHARDS
SB413.B4	BEGONIAS
BX4270.B5	BEGUINES
PK1801-1831	*BEHARI LANGUAGE* **SEE** BIHARI LANGUAGE
QL750-785	*BEHAVIOR (PSYCHOLOGY)* **SEE** ANIMALS, HABITS AND BEHAVIOR OF
BJ1545-1695	*BEHAVIOR* **SEE** CONDUCT OF LIFE
BJ1801-2193	*BEHAVIOR* **SEE** ETIQUETTE
BF455	*BEHAVIOR, VERBAL* **SEE** VERBAL BEHAVIOR
BF39	*BEHAVIORAL MODELS* **SEE** HUMAN BEHAVIOR — MATHEMATICAL MODELS
BF199	BEHAVIORISM (PSYCHOLOGY)
PK	*BEHISTUN INSCRIPTIONS* **SEE** CUNEIFORM INSCRIPTIONS
PJ	*BEHISTUN INSCRIPTIONS* **SEE** CUNEIFORM INSCRIPTIONS
CN	*BEHISTUN INSCRIPTIONS* **SEE** CUNEIFORM INSCRIPTIONS
PK6128	*BEHISTUN INSCRIPTIONS* **SEE** OLD PERSIAN INSCRIPTIONS
QE391.B	BEIDELLITE
BD300-444	*BEING* **SEE** ONTOLOGY
BP175.D4	BEKTASHI
BP175.D4	*BEKTASHITES* **SEE** BEKTASHI
BL1671	*BEL* **SEE** BAAL (DEITY)
MT845	BEL CANTO
QE807.B4	BELEMNITES
DC305.22	BELFORT, BATTLE OF, 1871
DC305.92	BELFORT, FRANCE — SIEGE, 1870-1871
NA2930	*BELFRIES* **SEE** TOWERS / *architecture*
SF293.B4	BELGIAN DRAFT HORSE
PQ3848	BELGIAN FICTION (FRENCH) / *collections*
PQ3832	BELGIAN FICTION (FRENCH) / *history*
SF455	BELGIAN HARE
PT6215-6397	*BELGIAN LITERATURE (FLEMISH)* **SEE** FLEMISH LITERATURE / *collections*
PT6000-6199	*BELGIAN LITERATURE (FLEMISH)* **SEE** FLEMISH LITERATURE / *etc.*
PC3048	*BELGIAN LITERATURE (WALLOON)* **SEE** WALLOON LITERATURE
PN5261-9	BELGIAN NEWSPAPERS / *etc.*
PN5261-5270	BELGIAN PERIODICALS / *etc.*
PT6330-6340	*BELGIAN POETRY (FLEMISH)* **SEE** FLEMISH POETRY / *collections*
PT6140	*BELGIAN POETRY (FLEMISH)* **SEE** FLEMISH POETRY / *etc.*
PC3048	*BELGIAN POETRY (WALLOON)* **SEE** WALLOON POETRY
PN6222.B4	BELGIAN WIT AND HUMOR
G850	*BELGICA EXPEDITION* **SEE** EXPEDITION ANTARCTIQUE BELGE, 1897-1899
DH401-811	BELGIUM — HISTORY
D623.B4	BELGIUM — HISTORY — — GERMAN OCCUPATION, 1914-1918
DH682	BELGIUM — HISTORY — — GERMAN OCCUPATION, 1914-1918
DH631	BELGIUM — HISTORY — — PEASANTS' WAR, 1798
DR386	BELGRAD, BOMBARDMENT OF, 1862
DR548	BELGRAD, PEACE OF, 1739
F1449.B7	*BELICE QUESTION* **SEE** BRITISH HONDURAS QUESTION
BD215	BELIEF AND DOUBT / *philosophy*
BF773	BELIEF AND DOUBT / *psychology*
SB351.P4	*BELL PEPPERS* **SEE** PEPPERS
MT710	*BELL RINGING* **SEE** CHANGE RINGING
MT710	*BELL RINGING* **SEE** HANDBELL RINGING
VK1000-1246	*BELL-BUOYS* **SEE** BUOYS
CC200-250	BELL-FOUNDERS / *antiquities*
TS583-9	BELL-FOUNDERS / *technology*
ML1040	*BELL-LYRA* **SEE** GLOCKENSPIEL / *history*
E99.B	BELLABELLA INDIANS
RM666.B4	BELLADONNA
TL588	*BELLAMY SYSTEM* **SEE** PRESSURE PATTERN FLYING
GV1017.B4	BELLE COQUETTE (GAME)
DC241-4	*BELLE-ALLIANCE, BATTLE OF, 1815* **SEE** WATERLOO, BATTLE OF, 1815

PN45	*BELLES-LETTRES* **SEE** LITERATURE
PN500-519	*BELLES-LETTRES* **SEE** LITERATURE
JX4571-5187	BELLIGERENCY
JX4093	*BELLIGERENT OCCUPATION* **SEE** MILITARY OCCUPATION
JX5003	*BELLIGERENT OCCUPATION* **SEE** MILITARY OCCUPATION
DQ98	*BELLINZONE, BATTLE OF, 1422* **SEE** ARBEDO, BATTLE OF, 1422
CC200-250	BELLS — INSCRIPTIONS
CC200-250	BELLS / *antiquities*
TS583-9	BELLS / *technology*
M1105-6	BELLS, XYLOPHONE, STRING QUARTET WITH STRING ORCHESTRA
M1105	BELLS, XYLOPHONE, STRING QUARTET WITH STRING ORCHESTRA — SCORES
GV1295.B4	BELOTE (GAME)
PK6851-9	*BELOUTCHI LANGUAGE* **SEE** BALUCHI LANGUAGE
TJ1385-1418	*BELT CONVEYORS* **SEE** CONVEYING MACHINERY
TJ1350-1353	*BELT CONVEYORS* **SEE** CONVEYING MACHINERY
TS2301.B5	*BELT INDUSTRY* **SEE** BELTS (CLOTHING) — TRADE AND MANUFACTURE
TJ1100-1119	*BELT INDUSTRY* **SEE** BELTS AND BELTING
TS2301.B5	BELTS (CLOTHING) — TRADE AND MANUFACTURE
TJ1100-1119	BELTS AND BELTING
E98.C8	*BELTS, INDIAN* **SEE** WAMPUM BELTS
QL737.C4	*BELUGA (WHALE)* **SEE** WHITE WHALE
DT963	BEMBA (AFRICAN TRIBE)
PL8069.7	BEMBA POETRY
E241.S2	*BEMIS'S HEIGHTS, BATTLE OF, 1777* **SEE** SARATOGA CAMPAIGN, 1777
PJ2453	*BEN AMIR LANGUAGE* **SEE** BENI AMER LANGUAGE
DT443	*BENA (AFRICAN PEOPLE)* **SEE** WABENA
TA610	BENCH-MARKS
PL8771	*BENDA LANGUAGE (BANTU)* **SEE** VENDA LANGUAGE
BF204.B4	BENDER GESTALT TEST
QC621	BENEDICKS EFFECT
BV2250	BENEDICTINES — MISSIONS
BX3001-3055	BENEDICTINES
BX4275-8	BENEDICTINES / *women*
BX3460-3470	*BENEDICTINES, CLUNIAC* **SEE** CLUNIACS
BV197.B5	BENEDICTION
BX2048.B5	BENEDICTION / *catholic church*
BX1939.B4	BENEFICES, ECCLESIASTICAL (CANON LAW)
BV775	BENEFICES, ECCLESIASTICAL
BX1955	BENEFICES, ECCLESIASTICAL / *catholic church*
HS1501-1510	*BENEFIT SOCIETIES* **SEE** FRIENDLY SOCIETIES
HG9201-9245	*BENEFIT SOCIETIES* **SEE** FRIENDLY SOCIETIES / *fraternal insurance*
VF620.B4	*BENET-MERCIE GUN* **SEE** BENET-MERCIE MACHINE-GUN
VF620.B4	*BENET-MERCIE MACHINE RIFLE* **SEE** BENET-MERCIE MACHINE-GUN
VF620.B4	BENET-MERCIE MACHINE-GUN
HV1-4959	*BENEVOLENT INSTITUTIONS* **SEE**
HV61	*BENEVOLENT INSTITUTIONS* **SEE** ALMSHOUSES
HV85-527	*BENEVOLENT INSTITUTIONS* **SEE** ALMSHOUSES
RA960-996	*BENEVOLENT INSTITUTIONS* **SEE** HOSPITALS
HV1-4959	*BENEVOLENT SOCIETIES* **SEE** CHARITABLE SOCIETIES
PL8071-4	BENGA LANGUAGE
PK1716	BENGALI BALLADS AND SONGS / *collections*
PK1712	BENGALI BALLADS AND SONGS / *history*
PK1715	BENGALI DRAMA / *collections*
PK1711	BENGALI DRAMA / *history*
PK1651-1695	BENGALI LANGUAGE
PK1700-1788	BENGALI LITERATURE
PN5378.B4-5	BENGALI NEWSPAPERS
PK1714	BENGALI POETRY / *collections*
PK1710	BENGALI POETRY / *history*
PL8755	*BENGUELA LANGUAGE* **SEE** UMBUNDU LANGUAGE
PL5731-4	*BENGUETANO LANGUAGE* **SEE** IGOROT LANGUAGE
PJ2453	BENI AMER LANGUAGE
DT319	BENI MARIN DYNASTY
PL8077	*BENIN LANGUAGE* **SEE** BINI LANGUAGE
QE391.B5	BENITOITE
DS113.5.B	BENJAMIN (TRIBE OF ISRAEL)
E241.B4	BENNINGTON, BATTLE OF, 1777
TN948.B4	BENTONITE
QD341.A6	BENZALDEHYDE
QP981.B	BENZENE — PHYSIOLOGICAL EFFECT

TP359.B4	BENZENE AS FUEL
QP801.B5	BENZENE IN THE BODY
QD341.H9	BENZENE
TP914	*BENZENE, AMIDO-* **SEE** ANILINE
QD341.A8	*BENZENE, AMIDO-* **SEE** ANILINE
QD341.K2	BENZOIN
QD341.H9	*BENZOL* **SEE** BENZENE
E99.B4	*BEOTHIKAN INDIANS* **SEE** BEOTHUK INDIANS
E99.B4	BEOTHUK INDIANS
PM695	BEOTHUK LANGUAGE
E99.B4	*BEOTHUKAN INDIANS* **SEE** BEOTHUK INDIANS
PM695	*BEOTHUKAN LANGUAGES* **SEE** BEOTHUK LANGUAGE
HB715	*BEQUESTS* **SEE** INHERITANCE AND SUCCESSION / *economics*
BP186.38	*BERAT GECESI* **SEE** LAYLAT AL-BARA'AH
QE391.B	BERAUNITE
PJ2340-2349	BERBER LANGUAGES
PJ2369-2399	BERBER LANGUAGES
DT193	BERBERS
GN649	BERBERS
BV4330	*BEREAVED, CHURCH WORK WITH THE* **SEE** CHURCH WORK WITH THE BEREAVED
GT2110	BERETS
UF620.B45	BERETTA SUBMACHINE GUN
D267.B3	BERGEN-OP-ZOOM — SIEGE, 1622
RC624	BERI-BERI
G296.B4	BERING'S EXPEDITION, 1ST, 1725-1730
G296.B4	BERING'S EXPEDITION, 2D, 1733-1743
D757.9	BERLIN, BATTLE OF, 1945
D375.3	BERLIN, TREATY OF, 1878
D757.9	*BERLIN-SIEGE, 1945* **SEE** BERLIN, BATTLE OF, 1945
DD879-880	BERLIN — HISTORY — — 1918-1945
QA246	BERNOULLIAN NUMBERS
PL4621-4	*BEROUHI LANGUAGE* **SEE** BRAHUI LANGUAGE
SB381-6	BERRIES / *culture*
DL65	BERSERKERS
HV6068	BERTILLON SYSTEM
RA1231.B4	BERYLLIUM — TOXICOLOGY
QD181.B4	BERYLLIUM
DR27.P4	*BESENYOK* **SEE** PETCHENEGS
QA76.8.B4	*BESM (COMPUTER)* **SEE** BESM COMPUTER
TK7889.B	*BESM (COMPUTER)* **SEE** BESM COMPUTER / *technology*
QA76.8.B4	BESM COMPUTER — PROGRAMMING
QA76.8.B4	BESM COMPUTER
TK7889.B	BESM COMPUTER / *technology*
QA408	*BESSEL'S FUNCTIONS (THIRD KIND)* **SEE** HANKEL FUNCTIONS
QA408	BESSEL'S FUNCTIONS
TN736-8	*BESSEMER FURNACE* **SEE** BESSEMER PROCESS
TN736-8	BESSEMER PROCESS
Z1035	*BEST BOOKS* **SEE** BIBLIOGRAPHY — BEST BOOKS
QC787.B	BETATRON
SF473.B	*BETCHERRYGAH* **SEE** BUDGERIGARS
QK495.P	BETEL NUT / *botany*
RS165.B	BETEL NUT / *pharmacy*
SB295.B	BETEL NUT / *plant culture and horticulture*
E472.14	*BETHEL, BATTLE OF, 1861* **SEE** BIG BETHEL, BATTLE OF, 1861
TA439-446	*BETON* **SEE** CONCRETE
BX1939.B	BETROTHAL (CANON LAW)
GT2650	BETROTHAL
DT469.M264	BETSIMISARAKA
HJ4175	*BETTERMENT TAX* **SEE** SPECIAL ASSESSMENTS
HV6708-6722	*BETTING* **SEE** GAMBLING
GV1245	*BETTING* **SEE** GAMBLING / *ethics of*
TJ193-6	*BEVEL-GEARING* **SEE** GEARING, BEVEL
TX951	BEVERAGES / *bartenders' manuals*
TX815-817	BEVERAGES / *home economics*
TP500-659	BEVERAGES / *technology*
RM238-257	BEVERAGES / *therapeutics*
GV1295.B5	BEZIQUE
BL1215.B5	*BHAKTI-MARGA* **SEE** BHAKTI
BL1215.B5	BHAKTI
BL2015.F2	*BHIKSHU* **SEE** FAKIRS
PK1800	BHILI LANGUAGE
DS432.B	BHILS
PK1825-1830	BHOJPURI LANGUAGE
DS485.O6	*BHONDAS* **SEE** BONDOS
PL3601-3651	*BHOTANTA LANGUAGE* **SEE** TIBETAN LANGUAGE

PL3651.D2	*BHOTIA OF SIKKIM LANGUAGE* **SEE** DANJONG-KA LANGUAGE
DS485.O6	*BHUINHARS* **SEE** BHUIYAS
DS485.O6	BHUIYAS
DS432	*BHUMIA BAIGAS* **SEE** BAIGAS
DS485.O6	*BHUMIAS* **SEE** BHUIYAS
PL3601-3651	*BHUTAN LANGUAGE* **SEE** TIBETAN LANGUAGE
DS485.O6	*BHUYAS* **SEE** BHUIYAS
BS540	BIBLE — ADDRESSES, ESSAYS, LECTURES
BS620	BIBLE — ANTIQUITIES
BS538	BIBLE — APPRECIATION
BS655	BIBLE — ASTRONOMY
Z7770-7772	BIBLE — BIBLIOGRAPHY
BS570-580	BIBLE — BIOGRAPHY
BS465	BIBLE — CANON
BS470	BIBLE — CANON, CATHOLIC VS. PROTESTANT
BS465	BIBLE — CANON, CATHOLIC VS. PROTESTANT
BS612	BIBLE — CATECHISMS, QUESTION-BOOKS
BS637	BIBLE — CHRONOLOGY
BS413-415	BIBLE — COLLECTED WORKS
BS482-498	BIBLE — COMMENTARIES
BS420-429	BIBLE — CONCORDANCES
BS500-534	BIBLE — CRITICISM, INTERPRETATION, ETC.
BS471	BIBLE — CRITICISM, TEXTUAL
BS440-443	BIBLE — DICTIONARIES
BS670	BIBLE — ECONOMICS
BS680.E	BIBLE — ETHICS
BS661	BIBLE — ETHNOLOGY
BS480	BIBLE — EVIDENCES, AUTHORITY, ETC.
BS612	BIBLE — EXAMINATIONS, QUESTIONS, ETC.
BS569	BIBLE — GENEALOGY
BS630-633	BIBLE — GEOGRAPHY
DS44-110	BIBLE — GEOGRAPHY / *asia*
BS417	BIBLE — HANDBOOKS, MANUALS, ETC.
BS481	BIBLE — HARMONIES
BS476	BIBLE — HERMENEUTICS
BS635	BIBLE — HISTORY OF BIBLICAL EVENTS
BS635	BIBLE — HISTORY OF CONTEMPORARY EVENTS, ETC.
BS2410	BIBLE — HISTORY OF CONTEMPORARY EVENTS, ETC. / *new testament*
BS1197	BIBLE — HISTORY OF CONTEMPORARY EVENTS, ETC. / *old testament*
BS1180	BIBLE — HISTORY OF CONTEMPORARY EVENTS, ETC. / *old testament*
BS445-460	BIBLE — HISTORY
BS432	BIBLE — INDEXES, TOPICAL
BS472	BIBLE — INFLUENCE
BS480	BIBLE — INSPIRATION
BS474-5	BIBLE — INTRODUCTIONS
BS539	BIBLE — JUVENILE LITERATURE
BS537	BIBLE — LANGUAGE, STYLE
R135.5	BIBLE — MEDICINE, HYGIENE, ETC.
BS483.5	BIBLE — MEDITATIONS
BS667	BIBLE — MINERALOGY
BS534	BIBLE — MISCELLANEA
ML166	BIBLE — MUSIC
BS660-667	BIBLE — NATURAL HISTORY
CJ255	BIBLE — NUMISMATICS
BS680.P3	BIBLE — PARABLES
BS410	BIBLE — PERIODICALS
BS645	BIBLE — PHILOSOPHY
BS560	BIBLE — PICTURE BIBLES
N8020-8037	BIBLE — PICTURE BIBLES
ND3355	BIBLE — PICTURE BIBLES / *illuminated manuscripts*
N8020-8185	BIBLE — PICTURES, ILLUSTRATIONS, ETC.
BS560	BIBLE — PICTURES, ILLUSTRATIONS, ETC. / *juvenile*
BV228-235	BIBLE — PRAYERS
BS647-9	BIBLE — PROPHECIES
D524	BIBLE — PROPHECIES / *european war*
BS2827	BIBLE — PROPHECIES / *new testament*
BS1198	BIBLE — PROPHECIES / *old testament*
BS645	BIBLE — PSYCHOLOGY
BV2369	BIBLE — PUBLICATION AND DISTRIBUTION
BS617	BIBLE — READING
BS585-613	BIBLE — STUDY
BS543	BIBLE — THEOLOGY
BS450-460	BIBLE — VERSIONS
BS470	BIBLE — VERSIONS, CATHOLIC VS. PROTESTANT
BS453	BIBLE — VERSIONS, CATHOLIC
BS657	BIBLE AND GEOLOGY

Z1033.L6	BIBLIOGRAPHY — LIBRARY EDITIONS
Z1033.M6	BIBLIOGRAPHY — MICROSCOPIC AND MINIATURE EDITIONS
Z1033.P3	BIBLIOGRAPHY — PAPERBACK EDITIONS
Z1008	BIBLIOGRAPHY — SOCIETIES, ETC.
Z1006	BIBLIOGRAPHY — TERMINOLOGY
Z1011-1012	BIBLIOGRAPHY — UNIVERSAL CATALOGS
Z1001-9000	BIBLIOGRAPHY
Z1035	*BIBLIOGRAPHY, CRITICAL* **SEE** BIBLIOGRAPHY — BEST BOOKS
Z1003	*BIBLIOGRAPHY, CRITICAL* **SEE** BOOKS AND READING
BH39-41	*BIBLIOGRAPHY, CRITICAL* **SEE** CRITICISM */ aesthetics*
PN75-99	*BIBLIOGRAPHY, CRITICAL* **SEE** CRITICISM */ literary criticism*
PN441-595	*BIBLIOGRAPHY, CRITICAL* **SEE** LITERATURE — HISTORY AND CRITICISM */ history*
PN75-99	*BIBLIOGRAPHY, CRITICAL* **SEE** LITERATURE — HISTORY AND CRITICISM */ criticism*
Z1033.L6	*BIBLIOGRAPHY-BOOKS IN LIBRARY BINDINGS* **SEE** BIBLIOGRAPHY — LIBRARY EDITIONS
Z240-241	*BIBLIOGRAPHY-EARLY PRINTED BOOKS 15TH CENTURY* **SEE** INCUNABULA
Z121	*BIBLIOGRAPHY-EXHIBITIONS* **SEE** BIBLIOGRAPHICAL EXHIBITIONS
Z1033.P3	*BIBLIOGRAPHY-PAPER-BOUND EDITIONS* **SEE** BIBLIOGRAPHY — PAPERBACK EDITIONS
Z1033.L6	*BIBLIOGRAPHY-PUBLISHERS' LIBRARY EDITIONS* **SEE** BIBLIOGRAPHY — LIBRARY EDITIONS
Z711	*BIBLIOGRAPHY-REFERENCE BOOKS* **SEE** REFERENCE BOOKS
Z1030	*BIBLIOGRAPHY-VELLUM PRINTED BOOKS* **SEE** VELLUM PRINTED BOOKS
Z241.3	BIBLIOGRAPHY — EARLY PRINTED BOOKS 16TH CENTURY — FACSIMILES
Z992	BIBLIOMANIA
Z992	*BIBLIOPHILY* **SEE** BIBLIOMANIA
Z987-997	*BIBLIOPHILY* **SEE** BOOK COLLECTING
JF501-637	*BICAMERALISM* **SEE** LEGISLATIVE BODIES
ML597	BICHROMATIC HARMONIUM
QL696.P2	BICKNELL'S THRUSH
PL5581-4	*BICOL LANGUAGE* **SEE** BIKOL LANGUAGE
PL5581-4	*BICOLANO LANGUAGE* **SEE** BIKOL LANGUAGE
GV1059	BICYCLE POLO
GV1049	BICYCLE RACING
TL437	BICYCLES AND TRICYCLES — PATENTS
TL430	BICYCLES AND TRICYCLES — REPAIRING
TL425	BICYCLES AND TRICYCLES — TIRES
GV1041-1059	BICYCLES AND TRICYCLES */ sports and amusements*
TL400-445	BICYCLES AND TRICYCLES */ technology*
HD9999.B4-43	BICYCLES AND TRICYCLES */ trade*
UH30-35	*BICYCLES, MILITARY* **SEE** MILITARY CYCLING
GV1041-1059	*BICYCLING* **SEE** CYCLING
DT671.B58	*BIDJAGO* **SEE** BISSAGOS
DT671.B58	*BIDJUGOS* **SEE** BISSAGOS
DT671.B58	*BIDYOGO* **SEE** BISSAGOS
BF698	*BIEDMA TEST* **SEE** WARTEGG-BIEDMA TEST
QB723.B5	BIELA'S COMET
E472.14	BIG BETHEL, BATTLE OF, 1861
E477.16	BIG BLUE, BATTLE OF THE, 1864
QK495.L88	*BIG TREFOIL (LOTUS ULGINOSUS)* **SEE** LOTUS
BR1610	*BIGOTRY* **SEE** TOLERATION
E235	*BIGUYDUCE EXPEDITION, 1779* **SEE** PENOBSCOT EXPEDITION, 1779
PK1801-1831	BIHARI LANGUAGE
PL5581-4	BIKOL LANGUAGE
QP197	BILE PIGMENTS
QL867	BILE-DUCTS */ comparative anatomy*
RC849	BILE-DUCTS */ diseases*
QM351	BILE-DUCTS */ human anatomy*
RD546-7	BILE-DUCTS */ surgical treatment*
QP197	BILE
PJ2430	*BILEN LANGUAGE* **SEE** BILIN LANGUAGE
RC122.B5	*BILHARZIASIS* **SEE** SCHISTOSOMIASIS
RC122.B5	*BILHARZIOSIS* **SEE** SCHISTOSOMIASIS
RC850	*BILIARY CALCULI* **SEE** CALCULI, BILIARY
RD547	*BILIARY CALCULI* **SEE** CALCULI, BILIARY
PJ2430	BILIN LANGUAGE
LB1131	BILINGUALISM */ mental tests*
RC799-853	BILIOUS DISEASES AND BILIOUSNESS

QL697	BILL (ANATOMY) */ birds*
JF525	BILL DRAFTING
JN608	BILL DRAFTING */ gt. brit.*
JK1106	BILL DRAFTING */ u.s.*
HF5843.5	BILL-POSTING — LAWS AND REGULATIONS
HF5843	BILL-POSTING
UC410	*BILLETING OF SOLDIERS* **SEE** SOLDIERS — BILLETING
NE965	BILLHEADS
GV891	BILLIARDS
GV891-9	*BILLIARDS, POCKET* **SEE** POOL (GAME)
JX6288-9	*BILLS AND NOTES* **SEE** NEGOTIABLE INSTRUMENTS */ international law*
HF1259	*BILLS AND NOTES* **SEE** NEGOTIABLE INSTRUMENTS */ u.s.*
HG3745	*BILLS OF CREDIT* **SEE** LETTERS OF CREDIT
JX6288-9	*BILLS OF CREDIT* **SEE** NEGOTIABLE INSTRUMENTS */ international law*
HF1259	*BILLS OF CREDIT* **SEE** NEGOTIABLE INSTRUMENTS */ u.s.*
JX6289.B5	BILLS OF EXCHANGE (INTERNATIONAL LAW)
TX727-8	*BILLS OF FARE* **SEE** MENUS
HE2242	BILLS OF LADING
E99.B5	BILOXI INDIANS
PM702	BILOXI LANGUAGE
PK6851-9	*BILUCHI LANGUAGE* **SEE** BALUCHI LANGUAGE
PL5440	BIMANESE LANGUAGE
HG401-423	BIMETALLISM */ international*
HG651	BIMETALLISM */ other countries*
HG561-2	BIMETALLISM */ u.s.*
SB261.A	*BIMLIPATUM JUTE* **SEE** AMBARY HEMP */ culture*
TS1544.A	*BIMLIPATUM JUTE* **SEE** AMBARY HEMP */ fiber*
ML338	*BIN* **SEE** VINA */ music of india*
ML1015	*BIN* **SEE** VINA */ musical instruments*
DU740	BINANDELI (PAPUAN PEOPLE)
GN671.N5	BINANDELI (PAPUAN PEOPLE) */ anthropology*
TJ780	*BINARY ENGINES* **SEE** WASTE-HEAT ENGINES
QB821-9	*BINARY STARS* **SEE** STARS, DOUBLE
QB903	*BINARY STARS* **SEE** STARS, DOUBLE */ spectra*
QB421	*BINARY STARS* **SEE** STARS, DOUBLE */ theory*
TJ403	*BINARY VAPOR SYSTEMS* **SEE** STEAM POWER-PLANTS — BINARY VAPOR SYSTEMS
Z266-275	*BINDING OF BOOKS* **SEE** BOOKBINDING
TS1795	*BINDING TWINE* **SEE** TWINE
SB615.B5	BINDWEED
LB1131	BINET-SIMON TEST
PL8077	BINI LANGUAGE
QP487	BINOCULAR VISION
QC373.F5	*BINOCULARS* **SEE** FIELD-GLASSES
UF845	*BINOCULARS* **SEE** FIELD-GLASSES */ military*
QA245	*BINOMIAL EQUATIONS* **SEE** EQUATIONS, BINOMIAL
QA161	BINOMIAL THEOREM
TH4498	BINS
Z1010	BIO-BIBLIOGRAPHY
GF	*BIO-GEOGRAPHY* **SEE** ANTHROPO-GEOGRAPHY
QH84	*BIO-GEOGRAPHY* **SEE** GEOGRAPHICAL DISTRIBUTION OF ANIMALS AND PLANTS
GB2405	*BIO-GEOGRAPHY* **SEE** SNOW-LINE
RZ422	*BIOCHEMIC MEDICINE* **SEE** MEDICINE, BIOCHEMIC
QD415-431	*BIOCHEMISTRY* **SEE** BIOLOGICAL CHEMISTRY
QP501-801	*BIOCHEMISTRY* **SEE** BIOLOGICAL CHEMISTRY
QH345	*BIOCHEMISTRY* **SEE** BIOLOGICAL CHEMISTRY
RZ422	*BIOCHEMISTRY* **SEE** MEDICINE, BIOCHEMIC
QP501-801	*BIOCHEMISTRY* **SEE** PHYSIOLOGICAL CHEMISTRY
QH659	BIOCHEMORPHOLOGY
QH543	*BIOCLIMATICS* **SEE** BIOCLIMATOLOGY
QH543	BIOCLIMATOLOGY
QD549	BIOCOLLOIDS */ chemistry*
QP525	BIOCOLLOIDS */ physiology*
Q327	*BIOCOMPUTERS* **SEE** CONSCIOUS AUTOMATA
QH325	*BIOGENESIS* **SEE** LIFE — ORIGIN
CT21	BIOGRAPHY (AS A LITERARY FORM)
CT	BIOGRAPHY
CT21	*BIOGRAPHY, WRITING OF* **SEE** BIOGRAPHY (AS A LITERARY FORM)
CT21	*BIOGRAPHY-TECHNIQUE* **SEE** BIOGRAPHY (AS A LITERARY FORM)
QH324	BIOLOGICAL APPARATUS AND SUPPLIES
QH324	BIOLOGICAL CHEMISTRY — LABORATORY MANUALS
QP501-801	BIOLOGICAL CHEMISTRY
QD415-431	BIOLOGICAL CHEMISTRY

QH345	BIOLOGICAL CHEMISTRY
RB150-151	*BIOLOGICAL CONSTITUTION OF MAN* **SEE** MAN — CONSTITUTION / *theories of disease*
BF818	*BIOLOGICAL CONSTITUTION OF MAN* **SEE** MAN — CONSTITUTION / *character*
GN60	*BIOLOGICAL CONSTITUTION OF MAN* **SEE** MAN — CONSTITUTION / *anthropology*
BF698	*BIOLOGICAL CONSTITUTION OF MAN* **SEE** MAN — CONSTITUTION / *personality*
BF795-811	*BIOLOGICAL CONSTITUTION OF MAN* **SEE** MAN — CONSTITUTION / *temperament*
SB975	*BIOLOGICAL CONTROL OF INSECTS* **SEE** INSECTS, INJURIOUS AND BENEFICIAL — BIOLOGICAL CONTROL
QH321	BIOLOGICAL LABORATQRIES
QP177	*BIOLOGICAL OXIDATION* **SEE** OXIDATION, PHYSIOLOGICAL
QH245	*BIOLOGICAL PHOTOGRAPHY* **SEE** PHOTOGRAPHY, BIOLOGICAL
QH505	BIOLOGICAL PHYSICS — RESEARCH
RA401	BIOLOGICAL PRODUCTS / *public health*
RM270-282	BIOLOGICAL PRODUCTS / *therapeutics*
QH505	*BIOLOGICAL RHEOLOGY* **SEE** RHEOLOGY (BIOLOGY)
QH301	BIOLOGICAL SOCIETIES
UG447.8	BIOLOGICAL WARFARE
QH26	BIOLOGISTS
QH83	BIOLOGY — CLASSIFICATION
QH306	BIOLOGY — EARLY WORKS TO 1800
QH48	BIOLOGY — JUVENILE LITERATURE
QH324	BIOLOGY — LABORATORY MANUALS
QH331	BIOLOGY — PHILOSOPHY
QH310	BIOLOGY — TABLES, ETC.
QH314	BIOLOGY AS A PROFESSION
QH301-705	BIOLOGY
QH324	*BIOLOGY-APPARATUS AND SUPPLIES* **SEE** BIOLOGICAL APPARATUS AND SUPPLIES
QH540-541	*BIOLOGY-ECOLOGY* **SEE** ECOLOGY
QH321	*BIOLOGY-LABORATORIES* **SEE** BIOLOGICAL LABORATORIES
QH314	*BIOLOGY-VOCATIONAL GUIDANCE* **SEE** BIOLOGY AS A PROFESSION
QH324	BIOMATHEMATICS
QP303	*BIOMECHANICS* **SEE** ANIMAL MECHANICS
GN51-59	BIOMETRY / *anthropology*
QH401-5	BIOMETRY / *variation*
QH540-541	*BIONOMICS* **SEE** ECOLOGY
QH505	*BIOPHYSICAL RESEARCH* **SEE** BIOLOGICAL PHYSICS — RESEARCH
QH505	*BIORHEOLOGY* **SEE** RHEOLOGY (BIOLOGY)
TR890	*BIOSCOPE* **SEE** MOVING-PICTURE PROJECTION
TN933	*BIOTITE* **SEE** MICA
TN933	*BIOTITE-GRANITE* **SEE** MICA
QA215	*BIQUADRATIC EQUATIONS* **SEE** EQUATIONS, BIQUADRATIC
D766.93	*BIR HACHEIM, BATTLE OF, 1942* **SEE** BIR HAKEIM, BATTLE OF, 1942
D766.93	BIR HAKEIM, BATTLE OF, 1942
QL696.G2	*BIRCH PARTRIDGES* **SEE** RUFFED GROUSE
SK325.G7	*BIRCH PARTRIDGES* **SEE** RUFFED GROUSE
GN440.2	*BIRCH-BARK CANOES* **SEE** CANOES AND CANOEING / *ethnology*
GV781-5	*BIRCH-BARK CANOES* **SEE** CANOES AND CANOEING / *sport*
E98.C2	*BIRCH-BARK CANOES* **SEE** INDIANS OF NORTH AMERICA — BOATS
SB945.R	*BIRCH-LEAF SKELETONIZER* **SEE** RIBBED-COCOON-MAKER / *insect pests*
QL561.T7	*BIRCH-LEAF SKELETONIZER* **SEE** RIBBED-COCOON-MAKER / *zoology*
QK495.B56	BIRCH / *botany*
SD397.B5	BIRCH / *forestry*
SK311-333	*BIRD HUNTING* **SEE** FOWLING
SF995	*BIRD MALARIA* **SEE** MALARIAL FEVER IN BIRDS
QL677	*BIRD NAMES, POPULAR* **SEE** BIRDS — NOMENCLATURE (POPULAR)
QH245	*BIRD PHOTOGRAPHY* **SEE** PHOTOGRAPHY OF BIRDS
QL677.5	BIRD-BANDING
QL676.5	BIRD-HOUSES
QL503.M2	BIRD-LICE
QL698	BIRD-SONG
QK495.L88	*BIRD'S FOOT TREFOIL* **SEE** LOTUS

QL697	BIRDS — ANATOMY
QL677	BIRDS — CATALOGS AND COLLECTIONS
QL677	BIRDS — CLASSIFICATION
QL677.7	BIRDS — COLLECTION AND PRESERVATION
SF995	BIRDS — DISEASES
QL675	BIRDS — EGGS AND NESTS
QL698	BIRDS — FOOD
QL678-695	BIRDS — GEOGRAPHICAL DISTRIBUTION
QL676	BIRDS — JUVENILE LITERATURE
QL795.B57	BIRDS — LEGENDS AND STORIES
QL698	BIRDS — MIGRATION
QL677	BIRDS — NOMENCLATURE (POPULAR)
QL677	BIRDS — NOMENCLATURE
QL698	BIRDS — PHYSIOLOGY
QL674	BIRDS — PICTORIAL WORKS
RA641.B	BIRDS AS CARRIERS OF DISEASE
N7665	BIRDS IN ART
PN6110.B6	BIRDS IN LITERATURE / *poetry*
PN6110.B6	*BIRDS IN POETRY* **SEE** BIRDS IN LITERATURE / *poetry*
QL696.P2	BIRDS OF PARADISE
QL696.A2	BIRDS OF PREY
QL671-699	BIRDS
QL671-698	*BIRDS, AQUATIC* **SEE** WATER-BIRDS
SK351-579	*BIRDS, AQUATIC* **SEE** WATER-BIRDS / *game preservation*
SK331-3	*BIRDS, AQUATIC* **SEE** WATER-BIRDS / *hunting*
QL677.5	*BIRDS, BANDING OF* **SEE** BIRD-BANDING
QL698	*BIRDS, COLOR OF* **SEE** COLOR OF BIRDS
GR735	*BIRDS, FOLK-LORE OF* **SEE** FOLK-LORE OF BIRDS
QE875	BIRDS, FOSSIL — EGGS
QE871-5	BIRDS, FOSSIL
SB995	BIRDS, INJURIOUS AND BENEFICIAL
QL677.5	*BIRDS, MARKING OF* **SEE** BIRD-BANDING
QH245	*BIRDS, PHOTOGRAPHY OF* **SEE** PHOTOGRAPHY OF BIRDS
QL671	BIRDS, PROTECTION OF / *etc.*
SK351-579	BIRDS, PROTECTION OF / *game-laws*
QL675	*BIRDS' NESTS* **SEE** BIRDS — EGGS AND NESTS
TL553.5	*BIRDS-COLLISIONS WITH AEROPLANES* **SEE** AERONAUTICS — ACCIDENTS
SB995	*BIRDS-ECONOMIC ASPECTS* **SEE** BIRDS, INJURIOUS AND BENEFICIAL
QL698	*BIRDS-FLIGHT* **SEE** FLIGHT / *bird flight*
TL570-578	*BIRDS-FLIGHT* **SEE** FLIGHT / *mechanics of flight*
QL675	*BIRDS-NESTS* **SEE** BIRDS — EGGS AND NESTS
QK495.L88	*BIRDSFOOT TREFOIL* **SEE** LOTUS
BX4285-8	BIRGITTINES
DA415	BIRMINGHAM, BATTLE OF, 1643
PL4621-4	*BIROHI LANGUAGE* **SEE** BRAHUI LANGUAGE
GR450	BIRTH (IN RELIGION, FOLK-LORE, ETC.)
BD443	BIRTH (PHILOSOPHY)
HQ763-6	BIRTH CONTROL
HA38-39	*BIRTH RECORDS* **SEE** REGISTERS OF BIRTHS, ETC.
HB849-875	*BIRTH-RATE* **SEE** POPULATION
JV6205	*BIRTH-RATE* **SEE** POPULATION / *population and immigration*
GR805	BIRTH-STONES
RG696	BIRTH, MULTIPLE
RJ250	*BIRTH, PREMATURE* **SEE** INFANTS (PREMATURE)
M1978.B56	BIRTHDAYS — SONGS AND MUSIC
M1977.B56	BIRTHDAYS — SONGS AND MUSIC
BF1729.B5	BIRTHPLACES / *astrology*
HA38-39	*BIRTHS, REGISTERS OF* **SEE** REGISTERS OF BIRTHS, ETC.
PL4621-4	*BIRUHI LANGUAGE* **SEE** BRAHUI LANGUAGE
PL5621-9	BISAYA LANGUAGE
DS666.B	*BISAYANS (PHILIPPINE TRIBE)* **SEE** BISAYAS (PHILIPPINE TRIBE)
DS666.B	BISAYAS (PHILIPPINE TRIBE)
GN549.B3	*BISCAYANS* **SEE** BASQUES / *ethnology*
DC611.B31-322	*BISCAYANS* **SEE** BASQUES / *french history*
DP302.B46	*BISCAYANS* **SEE** BASQUES / *spanish history*
TX769	BISCUITS
TX772	*BISCUITS, ENGLISH* **SEE** COOKIES
BX1939.B5	BISHOPS (CANON LAW)
BX2304	*BISHOPS-CONSECRATION* **SEE** CONSECRATION OF BISHOPS / *catholic church*
RM666.B	BISMUTH — THERAPEUTIC USE
TN490.B6	BISMUTH ORES

QD181.B5	BISMUTH
QL737.U5	BISON
SK297	BISON / hunting
QE882.U3	BISON, FOSSIL
DT671.B58	BISSAGOS
DR27.P4	*BISSENI* **SEE** PETCHENEGS
QP941	*BITES, VENOMOUS* **SEE** VENOM — PHYSIOLOGICAL EFFECT
SF309	*BITS (BRIDLES)* **SEE** BRIDLE
QK495.S7	BITTERSWEET
TN850	BITUMEN — GEOLOGY
TN850	BITUMEN
TP325-6	BITUMINOUS COAL / fuel
TN825	BITUMINOUS COAL / mining
TE221	BITUMINOUS MATERIALS
TE270	*BITUMINOUS PAVEMENTS* **SEE** PAVEMENTS, BITUMINOUS
QD305.A7	BIURET REACTION
QL430.6-7	*BIVALVES* **SEE** LAMELLIBRANCHIATA
DK264 1905	BJORKO, TREATY OF, 1905
BF1563-1584	*BLACK ART* **SEE** WITCHCRAFT
GR530	*BLACK ART* **SEE** WITCHCRAFT / folk-lore
NK4340.B5	BLACK BASALTES
SH681	BLACK BASS
QC484	*BLACK BODY RADIATION* **SEE** BLACKBODY RADIATION
TX325	BLACK CARPET BEETLE
SB608.W5	BLACK CHAFF OF WHEAT
RC171	BLACK DEATH
SF968	*BLACK DISEASE OF SHEEP* **SEE** BRAXY
S598	*BLACK EARTH* **SEE** CHERNOZEM SOILS
BX3501-3555	*BLACK FRIARS* **SEE** DOMINICANS
BX4341-4	*BLACK FRIARS* **SEE** DOMINICANS / women
SB945.B48	BLACK GRAIN-STEM SAWFLY
E83.83	BLACK HAWK WAR, 1832
GV1295.B	*BLACK JACK (GAME)* **SEE** BLACKJACK (GAME)
BL480	*BLACK MASS* **SEE** SATANISM / comparative religion
BF1546-1550	*BLACK MASS* **SEE** SATANISM / occult sciences
BX3001-3055	*BLACK MONKS* **SEE** BENEDICTINES
BX4275-8	*BLACK MONKS* **SEE** BENEDICTINES / women
E185.61	BLACK MUSLIMS / race question
BP221-3	BLACK MUSLIMS / religion
QK495.Q4	BLACK OAK / botany
SD397.O12	BLACK OAK / forestry
NK4340.B5	*BLACK POTTERY* **SEE** BLACK BASALTES
SF787	*BLACK QUARTER* **SEE** ANTHRAX, SYMPTOMATIC / veterinary medicine
SB741.B6	BLACK ROT
SB608.P8	*BLACK SCAB* **SEE** POTATO WART
NK4340.B5	*BLACK WARE* **SEE** BLACK BASALTES
QL696.L3	BLACK-HEADED GULLS
TN845	*BLACK-LEAD* **SEE** GRAPHITE
TP261.G7	*BLACK-LEAD* **SEE** GRAPHITE / artificial
QD441	BLACK
TP913	BLACK
SB386.B6	BLACKBERRIES
QL696.P2	BLACKBIRDS
NC865	BLACKBOARD DRAWING
LB1187	BLACKBOARD DRAWING / kindergarten
QC484	BLACKBODY RADIATION
E99.S53	*BLACKFOOT INDIANS (DAKOTA)* **SEE** SIHASAPA INDIANS
E99.S54	*BLACKFOOT INDIANS* **SEE** SIKSIKA INDIANS
PM2341-4	*BLACKFOOT LANGUAGE* **SEE** SIKSIKA LANGUAGE
GV1295.B	BLACKJACK (GAME)
SF787	*BLACKLEG* **SEE** ANTHRAX, SYMPTOMATIC / veterinary medicine
TT218-223	BLACKSMITHING
SF805	*BLACKWATER (DISEASE OF CATTLE)* **SEE** TEXAS FEVER
RC919-923	BLADDER — DISEASES
RG484-8	BLADDER — DISEASES / gynecology
RD581	BLADDER — DISPLACEMENT
RC920	BLADDER — EXPLORATION
RC919	BLADDER — INFLAMMATION
RD581	BLADDER — PERFORATION
RD581	BLADDER — PUNCTURE AND ASPIRATION
RC919	BLADDER — SACCULATION
RD581	BLADDER — SURGERY
RD670	BLADDER — TUMORS

RC242	*BLADDER-WORM* **SEE** HYDATIDS
QL872	BLADDER / comparative anatomy
QM411	BLADDER / human anatomy
RC921.V4	*BLADDER-CALCULUS* **SEE** CALCULI, URINARY
RD581	*BLADDER-CALCULUS* **SEE** CALCULI, URINARY
RD581	*BLADDER-PROLAPSUS* **SEE** BLADDER — DISPLACEMENT
RL301	*BLADDERY FEVER* **SEE** PEMPHIGUS
E356.B5	BLADENSBURG, BATTLE OF, 1814
TJ267.B5	BLADES
TP894	*BLANCHING* **SEE** BLEACHING
P311	BLANK VERSE
PE5115	BLANK VERSE / english
BP167.3	BLASPHEMY (ISLAM)
BV763.B6	BLASPHEMY / church law
BJ1535.P95	BLASPHEMY / ethics
BV4627.B6	BLASPHEMY / moral theology
TN677	BLAST-FURNACES
TN713-718	BLAST-FURNACES / cast-iron
TP285	*BLASTING OIL* **SEE** NITROGLYCERIN
TN279	BLASTING
TC191-2	BLASTING, SUBMARINE
TP297-9	*BLASTING-LAW AND LEGISLATION* **SEE** EXPLOSIVES — LAW AND LEGISLATION
RC123.B6	*BLASTOMYCETIC DERMATITIS* **SEE** BLASTOMYCOSIS
RC123.B6	BLASTOMYCOSIS
QL508.B6	*BLATTARIAE* **SEE** COCKROACHES
QL508.B6	*BLATTIDAE* **SEE** COCKROACHES
QL508.B6	*BLATTOIDEA* **SEE** COCKROACHES
JC345	*BLAZONRY* **SEE** HERALDRY / national theory
CR	*BLAZONRY* **SEE** HERALDRY / national
TP894	BLEACHING
RM182	*BLEEDING* **SEE** BLOODLETTING
RD33.3	*BLEEDING* **SEE** HEMORRHAGE
RB144	*BLEEDING* **SEE** HEMORRHAGE
D283.B6	BLENHEIM, BATTLE OF, 1704
RE121-155	*BLEPHAROSPASM* **SEE** EYELIDS — DISEASES
BX2307	*BLESSED WATER* **SEE** HOLY WATER / catholic church
BV885	*BLESSED WATER* **SEE** HOLY WATER / practical theology
BV283.G7	*BLESSINGS, TABLE* **SEE** GRACE AT MEALS
HV1623-4	BLIND — BIOGRAPHY
HV1652-8	BLIND — EMPLOYMENT
HV1666-1698	BLIND — PRINTING AND WRITING SYSTEMS
TL711.B6	*BLIND FLYING* **SEE** INSTRUMENT FLYING
TL696.L33	*BLIND LANDING* **SEE** GROUND CONTROLLED APPROACH
TL696.L33	*BLIND LANDING* **SEE** INSTRUMENT LANDING SYSTEMS
ML385	*BLIND MUSICIANS* **SEE** MUSICIANS, BLIND
GV1511.J4	BLIND PILGRIMS (GAME)
HV1571-2349	BLIND / charities
HV1701	BLIND, APPARATUS FOR THE
Z695.72	*BLIND, BOOKS FOR THE-CATALOGING* **SEE** CATALOGING OF BOOKS FOR THE BLIND
HV1721-1756	BLIND, LIBRARIES FOR THE
Z675.B6	BLIND, LIBRARIES FOR THE
MT38	BLIND, MUSIC FOR THE
HV1695	BLIND, MUSIC FOR THE
HV1767	BLIND, PHYSICAL EDUCATION FOR THE
HV1767	*BLIND, SPORTS FOR THE* **SEE** BLIND, PHYSICAL EDUCATION FOR THE
HV1666-1698	*BLIND-EDUCATION-READING* **SEE** BLIND — PRINTING AND WRITING SYSTEMS
RE91	BLINDNESS
RA1146	BLINDNESS, FEIGNED
TH2276	BLINDS
SB608.A6	BLISTER SPOT
LB1139.C7	BLOCK BUILDING (EDUCATION)
ML935-6	*BLOCK FLUTE* **SEE** RECORDER (MUSICAL INSTRUMENT)
LB1139.C7	*BLOCK PLAY* **SEE** BLOCK BUILDING (EDUCATION)
Z240-241	BLOCK-BOOKS
NE1330	*BLOCK-PRINTING, LINOLEUM* **SEE** LINOLEUM BLOCK-PRINTING
TF630	*BLOCK-SIGNAL SYSTEMS* **SEE** RAILROADS — SIGNALING — — BLOCK SYSTEM
JX5225	BLOCKADE
JX4494	BLOCKADE, PACIFIC

QR185	BLOOD — AGGLUTINATION / immunology
QP91	BLOOD — AGGLUTINATION / physiology
RB145	BLOOD — ANALYSIS AND CHEMISTRY / pathology
QP91-95	BLOOD — ANALYSIS AND CHEMISTRY / physiology
QP91	BLOOD — BUFFY COAT
QP101	BLOOD — CIRCULATION
QP101	BLOOD — CIRCULATION, ARTIFICIAL
RC636	BLOOD — CIRCULATION, DISORDERS OF
QP91	BLOOD — COAGULATION
QP91-95	BLOOD — CORPUSCLES AND PLATELETS
RC636-643	BLOOD — DISEASES
RB145	BLOOD — EXAMINATION
RC226-248	BLOOD — PARASITES / parasitic diseases
QR251	BLOOD — PARASITES / pathogenic protozoa
QP91	BLOOD — PIGMENTS
RB145	BLOOD — PIGMENTS
RM171	BLOOD — TRANSFUSION
RM172	BLOOD — TRANSPORTATION
BL600	BLOOD (IN RELIGION, FOLK-LORE, ETC.) / comparative religion
BL570	BLOOD (IN RELIGION, FOLK-LORE, ETC.) / comparative religion
GR489	BLOOD (IN RELIGION, FOLK-LORE, ETC.) / folk-lore
BM717	BLOOD ACCUSATION
QP801.A3	BLOOD ALCOHOL LEVEL SEE ALCOHOL IN THE BODY
GN491.5	BLOOD BROTHERHOOD
QP91-95	BLOOD CELLS SEE BLOOD — CORPUSCLES AND PLATELETS
HV6441-6453	BLOOD FEUDS SEE VENDETTA
GN495	BLOOD FEUDS SEE VENDETTA / primitive
QP91	BLOOD GROUPS
E99.K15	BLOOD INDIANS SEE KAINAH INDIANS
BM717	BLOOD LIBEL SEE BLOOD ACCUSATION
BX2159.P7	BLOOD OF JESUS, DEVOTION TO SEE PRECIOUS BLOOD, DEVOTION TO
RC691-700	BLOOD-VESSELS — DISEASES
RD598	BLOOD-VESSELS — SURGERY
QL835	BLOOD-VESSELS / comparative anatomy
QM191	BLOOD-VESSELS / human anatomy
QP91-95	BLOOD
QP91	BLOOD, GASES IN
BT465	BLOOD, RELICS OF THE PRECIOUS SEE PRECIOUS BLOOD, RELICS OF THE
RB145	BLOOD-COLOR AND COLORING MATTER SEE BLOOD — PIGMENTS
QP91	BLOOD-COLOR AND COLORING MATTER SEE BLOOD — PIGMENTS
RC901.7.A7	BLOOD-DIALYSIS SEE ARTIFICIAL KIDNEY
QP91	BLOOD-GROUPS SEE BLOOD GROUPS
RB145	BLOOD-SEMIOLOGY SEE BLOOD — EXAMINATION
SF429.B6	BLOODHOUNDS
RM182	BLOODLETTING
QK495.S18	BLOODROOT / botany
RS165.S2	BLOODROOT / materia medica
E83.67	BLOODY BROOK, BATTLE OF, 1675
SF805	BLOODY MURRAIN SEE TEXAS FEVER
E99.A63	BLOUNT INDIANS SEE APALACHICOLA INDIANS
QL537.M7	BLOW-FLIES SEE BLOWFLIES
TJ990-992	BLOWERS SEE COMPRESSORS
QL537.M7	BLOWFLIES
QD87	BLOWPIPE
E475.58	BLUE AND GRAY REUNION, 1938 SEE GETTYSBURG REUNION, 1938
QL444.D3	BLUE CRABS
QL696.A5	BLUE GOOSE
SB201.B5	BLUE GRAMA GRASS
PM8101-9	BLUE LANGUAGE SEE BOLAK
HD5114	BLUE LAWS SEE SUNDAY LEGISLATION / labor
HE6497.S8	BLUE LAWS SEE SUNDAY LEGISLATION / mails
HE6239.S8	BLUE LAWS SEE SUNDAY LEGISLATION / mails
BV133	BLUE LAWS SEE SUNDAY LEGISLATION / religious aspects
HE1825	BLUE LAWS SEE SUNDAY LEGISLATION / trains
F454	BLUE LICKS, BATTLE OF THE, 1782
SB608.A6	BLUE MOLD DISEASE OF APPLES SEE APPLE BLUE MOLD
SB608.T	BLUE MOLD OF TOBACCO SEE TOBACCO BLUE MOLD
HG4651-5990	BLUE SKY LAWS SEE SECURITIES
RM835-844	BLUE-GLASS CURE SEE LIGHT, COLORED / therapeutics
RM835-844	BLUE-GLASS CURE SEE PHOTOTHERAPY
TR415	BLUE-PRINTING
TR921	BLUE-PRINTING / industrial reproduction
T379	BLUE-PRINTS / mechanical drawing
QL696.A5	BLUE-WINGED TEALS
SB386.B7	BLUEBERRIES
QL696.P2	BLUEBIRDS
T379	BLUEPRINTS SEE BLUE-PRINTS / mechanical drawing
PN6231.B8	BLUNDERS SEE BULLS, COLLOQUIAL
PN6231.B8	BLUNDERS SEE ERRORS AND BLUNDERS, LITERARY
AZ999	BLUNDERS SEE ERRORS, POPULAR
E99.A63	BLUNT INDIANS SEE APALACHICOLA INDIANS
QP401	BLUSHING
QL666.O6	BOA-CONSTRICTORS
SK305.W5	BOAR HUNTING SEE WILD BOAR / hunting
SK305.W5	BOAR, WILD SEE WILD BOAR / hunting
GV1312	BOARD GAMES
NA7800-7850	BOARDING-HOUSES SEE HOTELS, TAVERNS, ETC. / architecture
GT3770-3899	BOARDING-HOUSES SEE HOTELS, TAVERNS, ETC. / manners and customs
K	BOARDS OF DIRECTORS SEE DIRECTORS OF CORPORATIONS
HD2745	BOARDS OF DIRECTORS SEE DIRECTORS OF CORPORATIONS
LB2831	BOARDS OF EDUCATION SEE SCHOOL BOARDS
RA5	BOARDS OF HEALTH SEE HEALTH BOARDS
RA11-388	BOARDS OF HEALTH SEE HEALTH BOARDS / reports
K	BOARDS OF SUPERVISION (CORPORATION LAW) SEE DIRECTORS OF CORPORATIONS
HD2745	BOARDS OF SUPERVISION (CORPORATION LAW) SEE DIRECTORS OF CORPORATIONS
HF294	BOARDS OF TRADE
HF295-343	BOARDS OF TRADE / etc.
VM831	BOAT DAVITS SEE DAVITS
VM801	BOAT DAVITS SEE DAVITS / boat lowering
GV771-836	BOAT HANDLING SEE BOATS AND BOATING
VM320-361	BOAT-BUILDING
NA6920	BOAT-HOUSES
GV835	BOAT-RACING SEE MOTOR-BOAT RACING
GV791-809	BOAT-RACING SEE ROWING
GV826.5-832	BOAT-RACING SEE YACHT RACING
VK200	BOATS AND BOATING — SAFETY MEASURES
GV771-836	BOATS AND BOATING
V858-9	BOATS, SUBMARINE SEE SUBMARINE BOATS / by country
VM365	BOATS, SUBMARINE SEE SUBMARINE BOATS / construction
V210	BOATS, SUBMARINE SEE SUBMARINE BOATS / use in war
VG953	BOATSWAIN'S MATES SEE U.S. — BOATSWAINS
VG93	BOATSWAIN'S MATES, AVIATION SEE U.S. — AVIATION BOATSWAIN'S MATES
VG953	BOATSWAINS SEE U.S. — BOATSWAINS
QL696.G2	BOB-WHITES SEE QUAILS
SF510.Q2	BOB-WHITES SEE QUAILS / breeding
SK325.Q2	BOB-WHITES SEE QUAILS / hunting
TS1580	BOBBINET
TP290.B7	BOBBINITE
QL696.P2	BOBOLINKS
GV855	BOBSLEDDING SEE COASTING
QL696.G2	BOBWHITES SEE QUAILS
SF510.Q2	BOBWHITES SEE QUAILS / breeding
SK325.Q2	BOBWHITES SEE QUAILS / hunting
BL1475.B6	BODDHISATTVAS
HB93	BODENREFORM SEE PHYSIOCRATS
HD1311-1313	BODENREFORM SEE SINGLE TAX
HD1315	BODENREFORM SEE UNEARNED INCREMENT
PL3871-4	BODO LANGUAGES
RA790	BODY AND MIND SEE MIND AND BODY / rz400 mental hygiene
BF150-171	BODY AND MIND SEE MIND AND BODY / psychology
RA790	BODY AND SOUL (PHILOSOPHY) SEE MIND AND BODY / rz400 mental hygiene

BS661	BODY AND SOUL (THEOLOGY) SEE MAN (THEOLOGY) / bible
BT700-745	BODY AND SOUL (THEOLOGY) SEE MAN (THEOLOGY) / doctrinal theology
BL256	BODY AND SOUL (THEOLOGY) SEE MAN (THEOLOGY) / religion
QP88	BODY FLUIDS
GN231	BODY MECHANICS SEE POSTURE / anthropology
RA781	BODY MECHANICS SEE POSTURE / personal hygiene
GV341	BODY MECHANICS SEE POSTURE / physical training
GV443	BODY MECHANICS SEE POSTURE / physical training
QP301	BODY MECHANICS SEE POSTURE / physiology
LB3427	BODY MECHANICS SEE POSTURE / school hygiene
RC75	BODY TEMPERATURE / diagnosis
QP135	BODY TEMPERATURE / physiology
GN418	BODY-MARKING
ML935-7	BOEHM FLUTE SEE FLUTE / history
DT930-939	BOER WAR, 1899-1902 SEE SOUTH AFRICAN WAR, 1899-1902
PL5281	BOEROE LANGUAGE SEE BURU LANGUAGE
DT888-944	BOERS
TN827	BOGHEAD COAL SEE TORBANITE
BX6510.B7	BOGOMILES
DB191-215	BOHEMIA — HISTORY
BX4920-4921	BOHEMIAN BRETHREN
PG4771	BOHEMIAN LANGUAGE SEE CZECH LANGUAGE
PN5168	BOHEMIAN NEWSPAPERS SEE CZECH NEWSPAPERS / etc.
DB191-217	BOHEMIANS SEE CZECHS
DB47-48	BOHEMIANS SEE CZECHS
DB214	BOHEMIA — HISTORY — REVOLUTION, 1848
QK100	BOHON-UPAS SEE UPAS
D70	BOII
TH6565	BOILER EXPLOSIONS SEE KITCHEN-BOILER EXPLOSIONS
TJ299-301	BOILER EXPLOSIONS SEE STEAM-BOILER EXPLOSIONS
HG9963.B5-8	BOILER INSURANCE SEE INSURANCE, BOILER
TJ375-387	BOILER WATER SEE FEED-WATER
TJ290-291	BOILER-PLATES
TJ390-392	BOILER-SCALE SEE STEAM-BOILERS — INCRUSTATIONS
TH7470-7476	BOILERS / heating of buildings
TH7538	BOILERS / hot water heating
TH7588	BOILERS / steam-heating
TK9203.B6	BOILING REACTORS SEE BOILING WATER REACTORS
TK9203.B6	BOILING WATER REACTORS
QD518	BOILING-POINTS
D70	BOJI SEE BOII
D70	BOJI SEE BOII
PL5291.Z9B	BOLAANG MONGONDO LANGUAGE
PM8101-9	BOLAK
M1249	BOLEROS (BAND)
M1266	BOLEROS (BAND)
M276-7	BOLEROS (GUITAR AND PIANO)
M1060	BOLEROS (ORCHESTRA)
M1049	BOLEROS (ORCHESTRA)
M233	BOLEROS (VIOLONCELLO AND PIANO)
M230	BOLEROS (VIOLONCELLO AND PIANO)
F3321-4	BOLIVIA — HISTORY
GV1295.B6	BOLIVIA (GAME)
F3097	BOLIVIA-HISTORY-WAR WITH CHILE, 1879-1884 SEE WAR OF THE PACIFIC, 1879-1884
PQ7812	BOLIVIAN FICTION / history
PQ7801-7819	BOLIVIAN LITERATURE
PN5011-5015	BOLIVIAN NEWSPAPERS / etc.
PN5011-5015	BOLIVIAN PERIODICALS / etc.
PQ7814	BOLIVIAN POETRY / collections
PQ7810	BOLIVIAN POETRY / history
SB945.C8	BOLL-WEEVIL
BX4662	BOLLANDISTS
SB945.C82	BOLLWORM
DG571	BOLOGNA — RIOT, NOV. 21, 1920
QC338	BOLOMETER
HX626-795	BOLSHEVISM SEE COMMUNISM
TJ1330	BOLTS AND NUTS
QC175.2	BOLTZMANN TRANSPORT EQUATION SEE TRANSPORT THEORY

TH1097	BOMB-PROOF BUILDING SEE BUILDING, BOMBPROOF
TH1097	BOMB-PROOF CONSTRUCTION SEE BUILDING, BOMBPROOF
JX5117	BOMBARDMENT
ML970-973	BOMBARDON SEE TUBA
U300-305	BOMBING AND GUNNERY RANGES
TH1097	BOMBPROOF BUILDING SEE BUILDING, BOMBPROOF
TH1097	BOMBPROOF CONSTRUCTION SEE BUILDING, BOMBPROOF
UF767	BOMBS, AERIAL SEE PROJECTILES, AERIAL
DT834	BOMVANA (AFRICAN TRIBE)
PL8081	BONDEI LANGUAGE
HG9970.S4-8	BONDING OF EMPLOYEES SEE INSURANCE, SURETY AND FIDELITY / economics
K	BONDING OF EMPLOYEES SEE INSURANCE, SURETY AND FIDELITY / law
DS485.06	BONDOS
HG4651	BONDS
HG9970.S4-8	BONDS, FIDELITY SEE INSURANCE, SURETY AND FIDELITY / economics
K	BONDS, FIDELITY SEE INSURANCE, SURETY AND FIDELITY / law
HG4726	BONDS, MUNICIPAL SEE MUNICIPAL BONDS
HG5151-5890	BONDS, MUNICIPAL SEE MUNICIPAL BONDS / other countries
HG4951-3	BONDS, MUNICIPAL SEE MUNICIPAL BONDS / u.s.
HG9970.S4-8	BONDS, SURETY SEE INSURANCE, SURETY AND FIDELITY / economics
K	BONDS, SURETY SEE INSURANCE, SURETY AND FIDELITY / law
HG4537	BONDS-TABLES, ETC. SEE INVESTMENTS — TABLES, ETC.
HJ5901-5919	BONDS-TAXATION SEE TAXATION OF BONDS, SECURITIES, ETC.
RD123	BONE BANKS
TP378	BONE BLACK SEE ANIMAL CHARCOAL / sugar manufacture
NK6020	BONE CARVING
QM569	BONE MARROW SEE MARROW
GN477.R	BONE RATTLE SEE NOTCHED RATTLE
RD123	BONE-GRAFTING
SF99	BONE-MEAL / feed
S659	BONE-MEAL / fertilizer
TP995	BONE-MEAL / utilization of wastes
QM569	BONE / histology of bony tissue
RD761-789	BONES — ABNORMITIES AND DEFORMITIES
RD684	BONES — DISEASES
RD684	BONES — SURGERY
RC312.5.B	BONES — TUBERCULOSIS
RC280.B	BONES — TUMORS
ML1040	BONES (MUSICAL INSTRUMENT)
QL821	BONES / animal
QM101-117	BONES / human
ML1035	BONGO
MT662	BONGO — METHODS — — SELF-INSTRUCTION
PL6621.B7	BONGU LANGUAGE
Q115	BONITE EXPEDITION, 1836-1837
BX7577.F3	BONJOURS, LES FRERES SEE FAREINISTES
PL8276	BONNY LANGUAGE SEE IJO LANGUAGE
PN6147-6231	BONS MOTS SEE WIT AND HUMOR
F199	BONUS EXPEDITIONARY FORCE, 1932
F199	BONUS EXPEDITIONARY FORCE, 1933
HD4928.B6	BONUS SYSTEM
UG490	BOOBY TRAPS (MILITARY SCIENCE) SEE MINES, MILITARY
M20-32	BOOGIE-WOOGIE MUSIC SEE PIANO MUSIC (BOOGIE WOOGIE)
HF5456.B7	BOOK AGENTS SEE BOOKSELLERS AND BOOKSELLING — COLPORTAGE, SUBSCRIPTION TRADE, ETC.
Z685	BOOK CASES SEE SHELVING (FOR BOOKS)
Z1008	BOOK CLUBS
Z549	BOOK CLUBS
Z987-997	BOOK COLLECTING
Z989	BOOK COLLECTORS
PN171.D4	BOOK DEDICATIONS SEE DEDICATIONS (IN BOOKS)
Z116.A3	BOOK DESIGN
PN6013.5	BOOK DIGESTS SEE BOOKS, CONDENSED

M31	BOURREES (HARPSICHORD)
M1048	BOURREES (ORCHESTRA)
PL3601-3651	*BOUTAN LANGUAGE* **SEE** TIBETAN LANGUAGE
DC90	BOUVINES, BATTLE OF, 1214
SF871	*BOVINE BRUCELLOSIS* **SEE** BRUCELLOSIS IN CATTLE
SF805	*BOVINE FEVER* **SEE** TEXAS FEVER
SF805	*BOVINE MALARIA* **SEE** TEXAS FEVER
SF967.E	*BOVINE THEILERIASIS* **SEE** EAST COAST FEVER
U877-8	BOW AND ARROW
GN498.B78	BOW AND ARROW / *primitive*
NK4399.B7	BOW PORCELAIN
QL696.P2	*BOWER-BIRDS* **SEE** BOWERBIRDS
QL696.P2	BOWERBIRDS
GV910	BOWLING GREENS
GV909	BOWLING ON THE GREEN
GV901-9	BOWLING
GV909	*BOWLS (GAME)* **SEE** BOWLING ON THE GREEN
SB608.B	BOX — DISEASES AND PESTS
TS900	BOX MAKING
HF5716.B6	BOX MAKING / *etc.*
QK495.B9	BOX / *botany*
SB435	BOX / *culture*
SD397.14	*BOXBOARD (TREE)* **SEE** ILOMBA
DS771.5	BOXERS — INDEMNITIES
SF429.B75	BOXERS (DOGS)
DS770-772	BOXERS
HD9999.B7	BOXES / *trade*
GV1116	BOXING — LAWS AND REGULATIONS
GV1135	BOXING — MORAL AND RELIGIOUS ASPECTS
GV1135	BOXING STORIES
GV1115-1137	BOXING
MT915	*BOY CHOIR TRAINING* **SEE** CHOIRBOY TRAINING
HS3313.B5-9	BOY SCOUTS
BV50.H6	BOY-BISHOP
HD5461	BOYCOTT
DA945	BOYNE, BATTLE OF THE, 1690
BJ1641-8	BOYS — CONDUCT OF LIFE
HS3301-3325	BOYS — SOCIETIES AND CLUBS
HV878	BOYS — SOCIETIES AND CLUBS
BS576-8	*BOYS IN THE BIBLE* **SEE** CHILDREN IN THE BIBLE
BS2446	*BOYS IN THE BIBLE* **SEE** CHILDREN IN THE BIBLE / *new testament*
HQ775	BOYS / *care*
BJ1641-8	BOYS / *ethics*
HV877	BOYS / *protection*
HS3301-3325	*BOYS' CLUBS* **SEE** BOYS — SOCIETIES AND CLUBS
HV878	*BOYS' CLUBS* **SEE** BOYS — SOCIETIES AND CLUBS
HD6228-6250	*BOYS-EMPLOYMENT* **SEE** CHILDREN — EMPLOYMENT
HD6270	*BOYS-EMPLOYMENT* **SEE** YOUTH — EMPLOYMENT
QM471	BRACHIAL PLEXUS / *anatomy*
QL395-9	BRACHIOPODA
QE796-7	BRACHIOPODA, FOSSIL
GN71	BRACHYCEPHALY
GN131	BRACHYCEPHALY
Z53-100	*BRACHYGRAPHY* **SEE** SHORTHAND
Z54-57	*BRACHYGRAPHY* **SEE** SHORTHAND / *english*
QL444.D3	*BRACHYURA* **SEE** CRABS
QH91-95	*BRACKISH WATER BIOLOGY* **SEE** MARINE BIOLOGY / *natural history*
QL121-138	*BRACKISH WATER FAUNA* **SEE** MARINE FAUNA
QK103	*BRACKISH WATER FLORA* **SEE** MARINE FLORA
NK7157-7161	BRACTEATES (ORNAMENTS)
E199	BRADDOCK'S CAMPAIGN, 1755
SF968	*BRADSOT* **SEE** BRAXY
E83.76	BRADSTREET'S EXPEDITION, 1764
PK119	*BRAHMA ALPHABET* **SEE** BRAHMI ALPHABET
BL1260-1265	BRAHMA-SAMAJ
QL737.U5	*BRAHMAN CATTLE* **SEE** ZEBUS
SF213	*BRAHMAN CATTLE* **SEE** ZEBUS / *animal industries*
PK3000-3581	*BRAHMAN MYTHOLOGY* **SEE** VEDAS
BL1115	*BRAHMAN MYTHOLOGY* **SEE** VEDAS / *hinduism*
PK3021	BRAHMANAS
PK3002	BRAHMANAS
PK3421	BRAHMANAS
PK3321	BRAHMANAS
BL1100-1245	BRAHMANISM
QL737.U5	*BRAHMANS (CATTLE)* **SEE** ZEBUS
SF213	*BRAHMANS (CATTLE)* **SEE** ZEBUS / *animal industries*
BL1215.B7	BRAHMANS
SF489.B8	BRAHMAS (POULTRY)
BL1260-1265	*BRAHMASABBA* **SEE** BRAHMA-SAMAJ
PK119	BRAHMI ALPHABET
BL1215.B7	*BRAHMINS* **SEE** BRAHMANS
BL1260-1265	*BRAHMIYASAMAJ* **SEE** BRAHMA-SAMAJ
BL1260-1265	*BRAHMOSOMAJ* **SEE** BRAHMA-SAMAJ
PL4621-4	BRAHUI LANGUAGE
TT850	*BRAIDED RUGS* **SEE** RUGS, BRAIDED
BF1111-1156	*BRAIDISM* **SEE** HYPNOTISM
HV6110	*BRAIDISM* **SEE** HYPNOTISM / *hypnotism and crime*
RC490-499	*BRAIDISM* **SEE** HYPNOTISM / *psychiatry*
MT38	BRAILLE MUSIC-NOTATION
HV1666-1698	*BRAILLE SYSTEM* **SEE** BLIND — PRINTING AND WRITING SYSTEMS
QL991	BRAIN — ABNORMALITIES AND DEFORMITIES
QM691	BRAIN — ABNORMALITIES AND DEFORMITIES / *teratology*
RC394.A	BRAIN — ABSCESS
RC394.A5	BRAIN — ANEMIA
RC280.B7	BRAIN — CANCER
RC394.C7	BRAIN — CONCUSSION
RC386-394	BRAIN — DISEASES
QP385	BRAIN — LOCALIZATION OF FUNCTIONS
RD594	BRAIN — SURGERY
RD663	BRAIN — TUMORS
GN181	BRAIN — WEIGHT / *anthropology*
QL933-7	BRAIN — WEIGHT / *comparative anatomy*
QM455	BRAIN — WEIGHT / *human anatomy*
RD594	BRAIN — WOUNDS AND INJURIES
BF633	BRAIN-WASHING
GN181-190	BRAIN / *anthropology*
QL933-7	BRAIN / *comparative anatomy*
QM455	BRAIN / *human anatomy*
QP376-425	BRAIN / *physiology*
QM691	*BRAIN-HERNIA* **SEE** ENCEPHALOCELE
BF633	*BRAINWASHING* **SEE** BRAIN-WASHING
RC386.5	BRAIN — DISEASES — — DIAGNOSIS
RX281-301	BRAIN — DISEASES — — HOMEOPATHIC TREATMENT
PK1941-9	*BRAJ BHAKHA* **SEE** BRAJ LANGUAGE
PK1941-9	*BRAJ BHASHA* **SEE** BRAJ LANGUAGE
PK1941-9	BRAJ LANGUAGE
QK671	*BRANCH DIMORPHISM* **SEE** DIMORPHISM (PLANTS)
Z686	*BRANCH LIBRARIES* **SEE** LIBRARIES — BRANCHES, DELIVERY STATIONS, ETC.
HF5468	*BRANCH STORES* **SEE** CHAIN STORES
QL444.B8	BRANCHIOPODA
T325	*BRAND NAMES* **SEE** TRADE-MARKS
T221-323	*BRAND NAMES* **SEE** TRADE-MARKS / *by country*
DD491.B81-95	BRANDENBURG — HISTORY
T325	*BRANDS (COMMERCE)* **SEE** TRADE-MARKS
T221-323	*BRANDS (COMMERCE)* **SEE** TRADE-MARKS / *by country*
E475.51	BRANDY STATION, BATTLE OF, 1863
HD9393	BRANDY / *industry*
TP599	BRANDY / *technology*
E241.B8	BRANDYWINE, BATTLE OF, 1777
TS565	BRASS FOUNDING
TS564-5	BRASS INDUSTRY AND TRADE
HD9539.B7	BRASS INDUSTRY AND TRADE
ML930-980	*BRASS INSTRUMENTS* **SEE** WIND INSTRUMENTS / *history and construction*
TS692.B	BRASS PLATING
TS564-5	BRASS
NK7800-7899	BRASSES / *art objects*
NB1840-1846	BRASSES / *sepulchral monuments*
BJ1533.C8	*BRAVERY* **SEE** COURAGE
SF968	BRAXY
F2521-2538	BRAZIL — HISTORY
SB401	BRAZIL NUT
F2684	*BRAZIL-HISTORY-GUARANI WAR, 1754-1756* **SEE** SEVEN REDUCTIONS, WAR OF THE, 1754-1756
PQ9660	BRAZILIAN BALLADS AND SONGS / *collections*
PQ9580	BRAZILIAN BALLADS AND SONGS / *history*
SB205.A4	*BRAZILIAN CLOVER* **SEE** ALFALFA
PQ9675-6	BRAZILIAN FICTION / *collections*
PQ9597-9607	BRAZILIAN FICTION / *history*
PQ9500-9699	BRAZILIAN LITERATURE
PN5021-9	BRAZILIAN NEWSPAPERS / *etc.*
PN5021-5030	BRAZILIAN PERIODICALS / *etc.*
PQ9649-9663	BRAZILIAN POETRY / *collections*

PQ9561-9581	BRAZILIAN POETRY / *history*
PQ9672-9687	BRAZILIAN PROSE LITERATURE / *collections*
PQ9597-9617	BRAZILIAN PROSE LITERATURE / *history*
PN6227.B7	BRAZILIAN WIT AND HUMOR
F2726	*BRAZILIAN-ARGENTINE WAR, 1825-1828* **SEE** ARGENTINE-BRAZILIAN WAR, 1825-1828
F2537	BRAZIL — HISTORY — — 1889-1930
F2538	BRAZIL — HISTORY — — 1930-1954
TT267	BRAZING
HQ804	BREACH OF PROMISE
QR119	BREAD — BACTERIOLOGY
TX769	BREAD / *bread making*
HD9057	BREAD / *industry*
SB379.B8	BREADFRUIT
TX595.F6	*BREADSTUFFS* **SEE** FLOUR / *adulteration*
TX393	*BREADSTUFFS* **SEE** FLOUR / *food supply*
TX558.W5	*BREADSTUFFS* **SEE** FLOUR / *food values*
TS2120-2159	*BREADSTUFFS* **SEE** FLOUR / *manufacture*
SB189-191	*BREADSTUFFS* **SEE** GRAIN / *culture*
SB191.W5	*BREADSTUFFS* **SEE** WHEAT
GT5899.W5	*BREADSTUFFS* **SEE** WHEAT / *manners and customs*
GC211	*BREAKERS* **SEE** OCEAN WAVES
TX395	*BREAKFAST FOODS* **SEE** CEREALS, PREPARED
TX557	*BREAKFAST FOODS* **SEE** CEREALS, PREPARED
TX733	BREAKFASTS
TC333	BREAKWATERS
RG499	BREAST — ABNORMITIES AND DEFORMITIES
RC280.B8	BREAST — CANCER
RG491-9	BREAST — DISEASES
RG861	BREAST — DISEASES / *puerperal state*
RC312.5.B7	BREAST — TUBERCULOSIS
RC280.B8	BREAST — TUMORS
N8217.B75	BREAST IN ART
RG866	BREAST-PUMP
QM495	BREAST
QL821	*BREASTBONE* **SEE** STERNUM / *comparative anatomy*
QM113	*BREASTBONE* **SEE** STERNUM / *human anatomy*
BM657.B2	BREASTPLATE OF THE HIGH PRIEST
QP121	*BREATHING* **SEE** RESPIRATION
HD7275	*BREATHING APPARATUS* **SEE** RESPIRATORS
UF620.B	BREDA MACHINE-GUN
D274.6	BREDA, TREATY OF, 1667
E241.B9	*BREED'S HILL, BATTLE OF, 1775* **SEE** BUNKER HILL, BATTLE OF, 1775
S494	BREEDING
SF191-9	*BREEDS OF CATTLE* **SEE** CATTLE BREEDS
D267.L3	*BREITENFELD, BATTLE OF, 1631* **SEE** LEIPZIG, BATTLE OF, 1631
UF620.B57	BREN MACHINE-GUN
DA86.8 1694	BREST EXPEDITION, 1694
BT313	*BRETHREN OF JESUS* **SEE** JESUS CHRIST — BRETHREN
BX3070	*BRETHREN OF THE COMMON LIFE* **SEE** BROTHERS OF THE COMMON LIFE
BX8551-8593	*BRETHREN, UNITED* **SEE** MORAVIANS
DC99.5.B7	BRETIGNY, TREATY OF, 1360
DC178	*BRETON CLUB* **SEE** JACOBINS
PB2800-2849	BRETON LANGUAGE
PB2856-2931	BRETON LITERATURE
PB2887	BRETON POETRY / *collections*
PB2858	BRETON POETRY / *history*
DC611. B814-915	BRETONS
NA6420	BREWERIES / *architecture*
TP569-587	BREWERIES / *technology*
HF5686.B5	BREWING INDUSTRY — ACCOUNTING
HD9397	BREWING INDUSTRY / *economics*
TP569-587	BREWING INDUSTRY / *technology*
TP569-587	BREWING
HV6301-6321	BRIBERY
HV6306	BRIBERY / *officials*
HV6314	BRIBERY / *voters*
PM3541	BRIBRI DIALECT
NK	*BRIC-A-BRAC* **SEE** ART OBJECTS
TG330	*BRICK BRIDGES* **SEE** BRIDGES, BRICK
TH1301	*BRICK BUILDING* **SEE** BUILDING, BRICK
NA7150	BRICK HOUSES
TE255	*BRICK PAVEMENTS* **SEE** PAVEMENTS, BRICK
TE255	*BRICK ROADS* **SEE** ROADS, BRICK
HD9605	BRICK TRADE / *economics*

TP785	BRICK TRADE / *periodicals and societies*
TP827-842	BRICK TRADE / *technology*
TH2243	BRICK WALLS
TH5501	BRICKLAYING
TP829	BRICKMAKING MACHINERY
TP827-833	BRICKMAKING
TP827	BRICKS / *technology*
TA432-3	BRICKS / *testing*
GT2660-2800	*BRIDAL CUSTOMS* **SEE** MARRIAGE CUSTOMS AND RITES
GN480.1	BRIDE PRICE
GN480.1	*BRIDE PURCHASE* **SEE** BRIDE PRICE
GV1281	*BRIDGE (GAME)* **SEE** BRIDGE WHIST
GV1282.9.T7	*BRIDGE FOR THREE PLAYERS* **SEE** THREE-HANDED BRIDGE
VK1247-9	BRIDGE LIGHTS (NAVIGATION)
GV1281	BRIDGE WHIST
TG470	BRIDGES — ACCIDENTS
TG326	BRIDGES — BEARINGS
TG157	BRIDGES — CATALOGS
TG300-301	BRIDGES — DESIGN
TG144	BRIDGES — EARLY WORKS TO 1800
TG313	BRIDGES — ESTIMATES
TG320	BRIDGES — FOUNDATIONS AND PIERS
TG153	BRIDGES — MODELS
TG310	BRIDGES — SPECIFICATIONS
TG151	BRIDGES — TABLES, CALCULATIONS, ETC.
TG305	BRIDGES — TESTING
TG	BRIDGES
TG327-340	BRIDGES, ARCHED
TG410	BRIDGES, ARCHED
TG330	BRIDGES, BRICK
TG385	BRIDGES, CANTILEVER
TG335-340	BRIDGES, CONCRETE
TG435	*BRIDGES, FERRY* **SEE** FERRY-BRIDGES
TG330	BRIDGES, MASONRY
UG335	*BRIDGES, MILITARY* **SEE** MILITARY BRIDGES
TG420	BRIDGES, MOVABLE
UG335	*BRIDGES, PONTOON* **SEE** PONTOON-BRIDGES
TG418	BRIDGES, PREFABRICATED
TG416	BRIDGES, STEEL PLATE DECK
TG330	BRIDGES, STONE
TG400	BRIDGES, SUSPENSION
TG390	BRIDGES, TUBULAR
TG365	BRIDGES, WOODEN
TG375	BRIDGES, WOODEN
TG418	*BRIDGES-BAILEY CONSTRUCTION* **SEE** BRIDGES, PREFABRICATED
TG365-370	*BRIDGES-TRESTLES* **SEE** TRESTLES
BX4285-8	*BRIDGETTINES* **SEE** BIRGITTINES
E356.L9	*BRIDGEWATER, BATTLE OF, 1814* **SEE** LUNDY'S LANE, BATTLE OF, 1814
SF309	BRIDLE
Z53-100	*BRIEFHAND* **SEE** SHORTHAND
Z54-57	*BRIEFHAND* **SEE** SHORTHAND / *english*
HV6441-6453	BRIGANDS AND ROBBERS
LC3991-4000	*BRIGHT CHILDREN* **SEE** GIFTED CHILDREN
RX356.B8	BRIGHT'S DISEASE — HOMEOPATHIC TREATMENT
RC907	BRIGHT'S DISEASE
RC199	*BRILL'S DISEASE* **SEE** TYPHUS FEVER
QR201.T95	*BRILL'S DISEASE* **SEE** TYPHUS FEVER / *bacteriology*
QD939	BRILLOUIN ZONES / *crystallography*
QC176	BRILLOUIN ZONES / *physics*
SF95	*BRINE* **SEE** SALT / *feeding and feeds*
GT2870	*BRINE* **SEE** SALT / *manners and customs*
TN900-909	*BRINE* **SEE** SALT / *mineral industries*
HD9213	*BRINE* **SEE** SALT / *trade*
TA407	*BRINELL NUMBER* **SEE** BRINELL TEST
TA407	BRINELL TEST
TP327	BRIQUETS (FUEL)
TP323	BRIQUETS (FUEL)
TP156.B7	BRIQUETS
GV1511.B8	BRISK (GAME)
PL8089	BRISSA LANGUAGE
GV1099	BRIST (GAME)
QL503.T6	*BRISTLE-TAILS* **SEE** THYSANURA
E475.75	BRISTOE STATION, BATTLE OF, 1863
NK4399.B75	BRISTOL PORCELAIN
NK4088.B8	BRISTOL POTTERY

DA690.B8	BRISTOL, ENG. — RIOTS, 1831
F2361-2391	BRITISH GUIANA — HISTORY
F1449.B7	BRITISH HONDURAS QUESTION
F1449.B7	*BRITISH HONDURAS-GUATEMALA DISPUTE* **SEE** BRITISH HONDURAS QUESTION
PR1101-1149	*BRITISH LITERATURE* **SEE** ENGLISH LITERATURE / collections
PB1306-1449	*BRITISH LITERATURE* **SEE** IRISH LITERATURE
PR8631-8644	*BRITISH LITERATURE* **SEE** SCOTTISH LITERATURE / collections
PR8510-8553	*BRITISH LITERATURE* **SEE** SCOTTISH LITERATURE / history
PB2206-2499	*BRITISH LITERATURE* **SEE** WELSH LITERATURE
BV2200	*BRITISH MISSIONS* **SEE** MISSIONS, BRITISH / catholic
BV2420	*BRITISH MISSIONS* **SEE** MISSIONS, BRITISH / protestant
PN5111-5129	*BRITISH NEWSPAPERS* **SEE** ENGLISH NEWSPAPERS / history
PN5141-9	*BRITISH NEWSPAPERS* **SEE** IRISH NEWSPAPERS / history
PN5131-9	*BRITISH NEWSPAPERS* **SEE** SCOTTISH NEWSPAPERS / history
PN5111-5130	*BRITISH PERIODICALS* **SEE** ENGLISH PERIODICALS / etc.
PN5141-5150	*BRITISH PERIODICALS* **SEE** IRISH PERIODICALS / history
PN5131-5140	*BRITISH PERIODICALS* **SEE** SCOTTISH PERIODICALS / history
PN5127.W	*BRITISH PERIODICALS* **SEE** WELSH PERIODICALS / gt. brit.
PN4885.W	*BRITISH PERIODICALS* **SEE** WELSH PERIODICALS / u.s.
PR1171-1227	*BRITISH POETRY* **SEE** ENGLISH POETRY / collections
PR500-609	*BRITISH POETRY* **SEE** ENGLISH POETRY / history
PB1331-3	*BRITISH POETRY* **SEE** IRISH POETRY / history
PR8649-8661	*BRITISH POETRY* **SEE** SCOTTISH POETRY / collections
PR8561-8581	*BRITISH POETRY* **SEE** SCOTTISH POETRY / history
PB2248	*BRITISH POETRY* **SEE** WELSH POETRY / collections
PB2281	*BRITISH POETRY* **SEE** WELSH POETRY / collections
PB2289	*BRITISH POETRY* **SEE** WELSH POETRY / collections
PB2227-2231	*BRITISH POETRY* **SEE** WELSH POETRY / history
PN6173-5	*BRITISH WIT AND HUMOR* **SEE** ENGLISH WIT AND HUMOR / collections
PR931-7	*BRITISH WIT AND HUMOR* **SEE** ENGLISH WIT AND HUMOR / history
D749.5.A	*BRITISH-SOVIET TREATY, 1942* **SEE** ANGLO-RUSSIAN TREATY, 1942
TJ1250	*BROACHES (MACHINERY)* **SEE** BROACHING MACHINES
TJ1250	BROACHING MACHINES
TK6570.B7	*BROADCASTING* **SEE** RADIO BROADCASTING
Z240.4	BROADSIDES — 15TH AND 16TH CENTURIES
GV1469.B7	BROADWAY CHECKERS
NK8900-8999	BROCADE / art
SB351.B7	BROCCOLI
BX3070	*BROEDERS DES GEMEENEN LEVENS* **SEE** BROTHERS OF THE COMMON LIFE
PL4621-4	*BROHKI LANGUAGE* **SEE** BRAHUI LANGUAGE
TX687	BROILING
HF5686.B65	BROKERS — ACCOUNTING
HF5421	BROKERS
HG4621	BROKERS / stockbrokers
SB201.B8	BROME-GRASS / culture
TP217.B	BROMIC ACID / chemical technology
QD181.B7	BROMIC ACID / chemistry
QP535.B7	BROMIDES IN THE BODY
QP281.B7	BROMINATION
QD181.B7	BROMINE
QD305.H6	BROMOFORM / chemistry
QP915.B7	BROMOFORM / physiological effects
RM666.B	BROMOFORM / therapeutics
DL703	BROMSEBRO, TREATY OF, 1541
DL190	BROMSEBRO, TREATY OF, 1645
RC280.B	BRONCHI — CANCER
RC778	BRONCHI — DISEASES
QM257	BRONCHI
QL854	BRONCHI
QM257	*BRONCHIA* **SEE** BRONCHI
QL854	*BRONCHIA* **SEE** BRONCHI
RC778	BRONCHITIS
RC656	*BRONCHOCELE* **SEE** GOITER
RC778	BRONCHOPULMONARY SPIROCHAETOSIS
RC778	BRONCHOSCOPE AND BRONCHOSCOPY
RC778	*BRONCHOSPIROCHAETOSIS* **SEE** BRONCHOPULMONARY SPIROCHAETOSIS
QD133	BRONZE — ANALYSIS
GN777-8	BRONZE AGE
SB945.B	BRONZE BIRCH BORER
TS570	BRONZE / manufacture
RC659	*BRONZED SKIN* **SEE** ADDISON'S DISEASE
NK7900-7999	BRONZES / art
TS570	BRONZES / technology
TS715	BRONZING
TT380	BRONZING
SF495-7	*BROODERS* **SEE** INCUBATORS
SF495	*BROODING* **SEE** EGGS — INCUBATION
HX656.B8	BROOK FARM
B905	BROOK FARM / american philosophy
QB723.B7	BROOKS' COMET
HD9999.B8	BROOM AND BRUSH INDUSTRY / economics
HD9999.B84	BROOM AND BRUSH INDUSTRY / economics
TS2301	BROOM AND BRUSH INDUSTRY / technology
SB317.B8	BROOM-CORN
SB317.S	*BROOM, SPANISH* **SEE** SPANISH BROOM
TS2301.B8	BROOMS AND BRUSHES
QB723.B8	BRORSEN'S COMET (I)
HQ101-440	*BROTHELS* **SEE** PROSTITUTION
BV950-970	*BROTHERHOOD* **SEE** BROTHERHOODS
BV4647.B7	*BROTHERHOOD* **SEE** BROTHERLINESS
BV950-970	BROTHERHOODS
BV4647.B7	BROTHERLINESS
BX2835	BROTHERS (IN RELIGIOUS ORDERS, CONGREGATIONS, ETC.)
BT313	*BROTHERS OF JESUS* **SEE** JESUS CHRIST — BRETHREN
BX4190.X3	*BROTHERS OF ST. FRANCIS XAVIER* **SEE** XAVERIAN BROTHERS
BX3070	BROTHERS OF THE COMMON LIFE
BX2835	*BROTHERS, LAY* **SEE** LAY BROTHERS
R733.B9	BROUSSAISISM
HD9559.L4	*BROWN COAL* **SEE** LIGNITE / economics
TP329	*BROWN COAL* **SEE** LIGNITE / fuel
TN831-4	*BROWN COAL* **SEE** LIGNITE / mining
SB261.A	*BROWN INDIAN HEMP* **SEE** AMBARY HEMP / culture
TS1544.A	*BROWN INDIAN HEMP* **SEE** AMBARY HEMP / fiber
SB495.B9	BROWN-TAIL MOTH
QC183	BROWNIAN MOVEMENTS
UD395.B8	BROWNING AUTOMATIC RIFLE
UF620.B	BROWNING MACHINE-GUN
E356.B6	BROWNSTOWN, MICH., BATTLE OF, AUG. 5, 1812
E356.M	*BROWNSTOWN, MICH., BATTLE OF, AUG. 9, 1812* **SEE** MONGUAGON, MICH., BATTLE OF, AUG. 9, 1812
UB323.A4	BROWNSVILLE, TEX. — RIOT, 1906
RC123.B7	*BRUCELLIASIS* **SEE** UNDULANT FEVER
SF871	BRUCELLOSIS IN CATTLE
RC123.B7	*BRUCELLOSIS IN MAN* **SEE** UNDULANT FEVER
SF971	BRUCELLOSIS IN SWINE
QE391.B	BRUCITE
BX3070	*BRUDER DES GEMEINSAMEN LEBENS* **SEE** BROTHERS OF THE COMMON LIFE
E99.B8	BRULE INDIANS
DA154.1	BRUNANBURH, BATTLE OF, 937
F1545.2.B6	*BRUNCA INDIANS* **SEE** BORUCA INDIANS
F1545.2.B6	*BRUNKA INDIANS* **SEE** BORUCA INDIANS
QL863	BRUNNER'S GLANDS
QM345	BRUNNER'S GLANDS
TK4329.B	BRUSH ARC-LIGHT SYSTEM
ND2460	BRUSH DRAWING
HD9999.B8	*BRUSH INDUSTRY* **SEE** BROOM AND BRUSH INDUSTRY / economics
HD9999.B84	*BRUSH INDUSTRY* **SEE** BROOM AND BRUSH INDUSTRY / economics

TS2301.B8	*BRUSHES* **SEE** BROOMS AND BRUSHES
TK2484	BRUSHES, CARBON
TK2484	BRUSHES, ELECTRIC
DC123.5	BRUSOL, TREATY OF, 1610
BJ1535.C	*BRUTALITY* **SEE** CRUELTY
F454	BRYAN STATION, KY. — SIEGE, 1782
QK533	*BRYOPHYTA* **SEE** BRYOPHYTES
QK533	BRYOPHYTES
QL396-9	*BRYOZOA* **SEE** POLYZOA
D552.B7	BRZEZINY, BATTLE OF, 1914
D276.B8	BRZNN — SIEGE, 1645
TP159.P6	*BUBBLE-CAP PLATE TOWERS* **SEE** PLATE TOWERS
PL8091	BUBE LANGUAGE
PL8091	*BUBI LANGUAGE* **SEE** BUBE LANGUAGE
RC201	BUBOES
RC171-9	*BUBONIC PLAGUE* **SEE** PLAGUE
QL696.S8	*BUBONIDAE* **SEE** OWLS
RD621-6	*BUBONOCELE* **SEE** HERNIA
F2161	BUCCANEERS
G535-7	BUCCANEERS
BX6510.B9	BUCHANITES
DR46.95	BUCHAREST, TREATY OF, 1913
D614.B8	BUCHAREST, TREATY OF, 1918
BV4915	*BUCHMANISM* **SEE** OXFORD GROUP
HG6001-6051	*BUCKET-SHOPS* **SEE** SPECULATION
QA935	BUCKLING (MECHANICS) / *mathematics*
TA410	BUCKLING (MECHANICS) / *strength of materials*
TG265	BUCKLING (MECHANICS) / *theory of structures*
F153	BUCKSHOT WAR, 1838
SB191.B9	BUCKWHEAT / *culture*
HD9049.B7-8	BUCKWHEAT / *trade*
PN1421	*BUCOLIC POETRY* **SEE** PASTORAL POETRY
PN6110.P4	*BUCOLIC POETRY* **SEE** PASTORAL POETRY
SB125	*BUD-GRAFTING* **SEE** BUDDING
D765.562.B8	BUDAPEST — SIEGE, 1945
BL1478.9	BUDDHA AND BUDDHISM — MISSIONS
BL1475.P7	BUDDHA AND BUDDHISM — PSYCHOLOGY
BL1458	BUDDHA AND BUDDHISM — RELATIONS
PK4501-4681	BUDDHA AND BUDDHISM — SACRED BOOKS / *pali literature*
BL1400-1485	BUDDHA AND BUDDHISM
BL1477.3	*BUDDHA AND BUDDHISM-HYMNS* **SEE** BUDDHIST HYMNS
BL1480	*BUDDHA AND BUDDHISM-SECTS* **SEE** BUDDHIST SECTS
BL1421.1	BUDDHA AND BUDDHISM — HISTORY — — TO CA. 100 A.D.
BL1400-1485	*BUDDHISM* **SEE** BUDDHA AND BUDDHISM
BR128.B8	*BUDDHISM AND CHRISTIANITY* **SEE** CHRISTIANITY AND OTHER RELIGIONS — BUDDHISM
BL1435.S35	BUDDHISM AND SCIENCE
BL1478.93-95	BUDDHIST CONVERTS
BL1422.A1	BUDDHIST COUNCILS AND SYNODS
BL1475.D4	*BUDDHIST DEMONOLOGY* **SEE** DEMONOLOGY, BUDDHIST
BL1477.3	BUDDHIST HYMNS
BC25-26	BUDDHIST LOGIC
BL1478.9	*BUDDHIST MISSIONS* **SEE** BUDDHA AND BUDDHISM — MISSIONS
B123	*BUDDHIST PHILOSOPHY* **SEE** PHILOSOPHY, BUDDHIST
BL1475.P7	*BUDDHIST PSYCHOLOGY* **SEE** BUDDHA AND BUDDHISM — PSYCHOLOGY
BL1480	BUDDHIST SECTS
BL1422.A1	*BUDDHIST SYNODS* **SEE** BUDDHIST COUNCILS AND SYNODS
BL1495.T3	*BUDDHIST TANTRISM* **SEE** TANTRISM, BUDDHIST
NA5960	*BUDDHIST TEMPLES* **SEE** TEMPLES, BUDDHIST
BL1478.9	*BUDDHISTS-MISSIONS* **SEE** BUDDHA AND BUDDHISM — MISSIONS
SB125	BUDDING
SF473.B	BUDGERIGARS
HJ2005-2199	BUDGET
TX326	*BUDGETS, FAMILY* **SEE** HOME ECONOMICS — ACCOUNTING
HF5686.H8	*BUDGETS, FAMILY* **SEE** HOME ECONOMICS — ACCOUNTING / *finance*
TX326	*BUDGETS, HOUSEHOLD* **SEE** HOME ECONOMICS — ACCOUNTING

SF473.B	*BUDGIE BIRDS* **SEE** BUDGERIGARS
SF473.B	*BUDGIES* **SEE** BUDGERIGARS
SF473.B	*BUDJEREGAR* **SEE** BUDGERIGARS
E406.B9	BUENA VISTA, BATTLE OF, 1847
F1234	*BUFA, CERRO DE LA, BATTLE OF, 1872* **SEE** ZACATECAS, BATTLE OF, 1872
QL795.B	BUFFALOES — LEGENDS AND STORIES
QL737.U5	BUFFALOES
TJ1280-1298	*BUFFING* **SEE** GRINDING AND POLISHING
QP91	*BUFFY COAT* **SEE** BLOOD — BUFFY COAT
VM311.B8	BUGEYES (BOATS)
PL5271	*BUGI LANGUAGE* **SEE** BUGINESE LANGUAGE
PL5271	BUGINESE LANGUAGE
M1270	BUGLE AND DRUM MUSIC
ML960-961	BUGLE
QL89	BUGONIA / *animal lore*
PL6225	BUGOTU LANGUAGE
SB951	*BUHACH* **SEE** PYRETHRUM / *insecticides*
TH443	BUILDING — ACCIDENTS
TH148	BUILDING — AMATEURS' MANUALS
TH425	BUILDING — CONTRACTS AND SPECIFICATIONS
TH2031-3000	BUILDING — DETAILS
TH434-7	BUILDING — ESTIMATES
TH438	BUILDING — SUPERINTENDENCE
TH151	BUILDING — TABLES, CALCULATIONS, ETC.
HF5686.B8	BUILDING AND LOAN ASSOCIATIONS — ACCOUNTING
HG2131-5	BUILDING AND LOAN ASSOCIATIONS — LAW
HG2129	BUILDING AND LOAN ASSOCIATIONS — TABLES, ETC.
HG2121-2156	BUILDING AND LOAN ASSOCIATIONS
TH1715	*BUILDING BOARD* **SEE** WALL BOARD
TH2055	BUILDING FITTINGS / *catalogs*
TH455	BUILDING FITTINGS / *catalogs*
TH8901	BUILDING FITTINGS / *maintenance*
HV8290	*BUILDING GUARDS* **SEE** WATCHMEN
NA4050.I5	*BUILDING INSCRIPTIONS* **SEE** ARCHITECTURAL INSCRIPTIONS
TH439	BUILDING INSPECTION
TH219-255	BUILDING LAWS
TH900	BUILDING MACHINERY
TA401-492	BUILDING MATERIALS — TESTING
TA401-492	BUILDING MATERIALS
TH425	*BUILDING MATERIALS-SPECIFICATIONS* **SEE** BUILDING — CONTRACTS AND SPECIFICATIONS
HG2121-2156	*BUILDING SOCIETIES* **SEE** BUILDING AND LOAN ASSOCIATIONS
TA368	*BUILDING STANDARDS* **SEE** STANDARDS, ENGINEERING
TA427	BUILDING STONES — TESTING
TA426-8	BUILDING STONES
TN950-973	BUILDING STONES
TH438	*BUILDING SUPERINTENDENCE* **SEE** BUILDING — SUPERINTENDENCE
TX339	*BUILDING SUPERINTENDENTS* **SEE** JANITORS
HD9715	BUILDING TRADES / *economics*
TH	BUILDING TRADES / *technology*
TH	BUILDING
TH1097	BUILDING, BOMBPROOF
TH1301	BUILDING, BRICK
TA680-683	*BUILDING, CONCRETE* **SEE** CONCRETE CONSTRUCTION
TH1461-1501	*BUILDING, CONCRETE* **SEE** CONCRETE CONSTRUCTION / *building*
TH1095	*BUILDING, EARTHQUAKE-PROOF* **SEE** EARTHQUAKES AND BUILDING
TH1061-1093	BUILDING, FIREPROOF
TH1431	BUILDING, ICE AND SNOW
TH1610-1621	BUILDING, IRON AND STEEL / *building*
TA684-5	BUILDING, IRON AND STEEL / *engineering*
TH1421	*BUILDING, PISE* **SEE** PISE / *building construction*
TH1421	*BUILDING, RAMMED EARTH* **SEE** PISE / *building construction*
TH1201	BUILDING, STONE
TA712	*BUILDING, UNDERGROUND* **SEE** UNDERGROUND CONSTRUCTION
TA684	*BUILDING, WELDED STEEL* **SEE** WELDED STEEL STRUCTURES
TH434-7	*BUILDING-COSTS* **SEE** BUILDING — ESTIMATES
TH439	*BUILDING-INSPECTION* **SEE** BUILDING INSPECTION
TH219-255	*BUILDING-LAWS AND REGULATIONS* **SEE** BUILDING LAWS

TA401-492	*BUILDING-MATERIALS* **SEE** BUILDING MATERIALS
TH860	*BUILDING-MODULAR COORDINATION* **SEE** MODULAR COORDINATION (ARCHITECTURE) / *building*
NA2700	*BUILDING-MODULAR COORDINATION* **SEE** MODULAR COORDINATION (ARCHITECTURE) / *drafting*
NA2760	*BUILDING-MODULAR COORDINATION* **SEE** MODULAR COORDINATION (ARCHITECTURE) / *design*
TH434-7	*BUILDING-PRICE BOOKS* **SEE** BUILDING — ESTIMATES
TH425	*BUILDING-SPECIFICATIONS* **SEE** BUILDING — CONTRACTS AND SPECIFICATIONS
CD981	*BUILDINGS, ARCHIVE* **SEE** ARCHIVE BUILDINGS
NA6210-6280	*BUILDINGS, COMMERCIAL* **SEE** MERCANTILE BUILDINGS
NA6230-6233	*BUILDINGS, COMMERCIAL* **SEE** OFFICE BUILDINGS
TH9031	*BUILDINGS, DAMPNESS IN* **SEE** DAMPNESS IN BUILDINGS
NA8480	*BUILDINGS, DEMOUNTABLE* **SEE** BUILDINGS, PREFABRICATED / *architecture*
TH1098	*BUILDINGS, DEMOUNTABLE* **SEE** BUILDINGS, PREFABRICATED / *building*
NA6598	*BUILDINGS, EMPLOYEES'* **SEE** EMPLOYEES' BUILDINGS AND FACILITIES
NA8200-8260	*BUILDINGS, FARM* **SEE** FARM BUILDINGS / *architecture*
NA7175	*BUILDINGS, HALF-TIMBERED* **SEE** HALF-TIMBERED HOUSES
NA6400-6581	*BUILDINGS, INDUSTRIAL* **SEE** INDUSTRIAL BUILDINGS
Z679	*BUILDINGS, LIBRARY* **SEE** LIBRARY ARCHITECTURE
NA6210-6280	*BUILDINGS, MERCANTILE* **SEE** MERCANTILE BUILDINGS
TH153	*BUILDINGS, MOVING OF* **SEE** MOVING OF BUILDINGS, BRIDGES, ETC. / *building*
JS201-8	*BUILDINGS, MUNICIPAL* **SEE** MUNICIPAL BUILDINGS
NA4430-4437	*BUILDINGS, MUNICIPAL* **SEE** MUNICIPAL BUILDINGS / *architecture*
NA4160	BUILDINGS, OCTAGONAL
NA6230-6233	*BUILDINGS, OFFICE* **SEE** OFFICE BUILDINGS
NA8480	*BUILDINGS, PACKAGED* **SEE** BUILDINGS, PREFABRICATED / *architecture*
TH1098	*BUILDINGS, PACKAGED* **SEE** BUILDINGS, PREFABRICATED / *building*
NA8480	BUILDINGS, PORTABLE / *architecture*
TH1098	BUILDINGS, PORTABLE / *building*
NA8480	BUILDINGS, PREFABRICATED / *architecture*
TH1098	BUILDINGS, PREFABRICATED / *building*
NA4170-4510	*BUILDINGS, PUBLIC* **SEE** PUBLIC BUILDINGS / *architecture*
JN855-9	*BUILDINGS, PUBLIC* **SEE** PUBLIC BUILDINGS / *other countries*
JK1651	*BUILDINGS, PUBLIC* **SEE** PUBLIC BUILDINGS / *state*
JK1613-1649	*BUILDINGS, PUBLIC* **SEE** PUBLIC BUILDINGS / *u.s. national*
LB3205-3295	*BUILDINGS, SCHOOL* **SEE** SCHOOL-HOUSES
LB3221	*BUILDINGS, SCHOOL* **SEE** SCHOOL-HOUSES / *plans*
NA4890	*BUILDINGS, SUNDAY-SCHOOL* **SEE** SUNDAY-SCHOOL BUILDINGS
NA2835-3060	*BUILDINGS-DETAILS* **SEE** ARCHITECTURE — DETAILS
TH2031-3000	*BUILDINGS-DETAILS* **SEE** BUILDING — DETAILS
TH455	*BUILDINGS-FITTINGS* **SEE** BUILDING FITTINGS / *catalogs*
TH2055	*BUILDINGS-FITTINGS* **SEE** BUILDING FITTINGS / *catalogs*
TH8901	*BUILDINGS-FITTINGS* **SEE** BUILDING FITTINGS / *maintenance*
TA401-492	*BUILDINGS-MATERIALS* **SEE** BUILDING MATERIALS
NA2790	*BUILDINGS-MODELS* **SEE** ARCHITECTURAL MODELS
TH2031	BUILDING — DETAILS — — DRAWINGS
TT197.5.B8	BUILT-IN FURNITURE / *cabinet work*
NK2712	BUILT-IN FURNITURE / *design*
SB425	*BULBOUS AND TUBEROUS ROOTED PLANTS* **SEE** BULBS
SB425	BULBS
PG1010	BULGARIAN BALLADS AND SONGS / *collections*
PG1021	BULGARIAN BALLADS AND SONGS / *folk poetry*
PG601-698	*BULGARIAN CHURCH SLAVIC LANGUAGE* **SEE** CHURCH SLAVIC LANGUAGE
PG1022	BULGARIAN DRAMA (COMEDY) / *collections*
PG1011	BULGARIAN DRAMA (COMEDY) / *history*
PG771-799	BULGARIAN LANGUAGE — MIDDLE BULGARIAN
PG801-993	BULGARIAN LANGUAGE
PG601-698	*BULGARIAN LANGUAGE-OLD BULGARIAN* **SEE** CHURCH SLAVIC LANGUAGE
PG1000-1158	BULGARIAN LITERATURE
PN5355.B8	BULGARIAN NEWSPAPERS / *etc.*
PN5355.B8	BULGARIAN PERIODICALS / *etc.*
PG1014	BULGARIAN POETRY / *collections*
PG1021	BULGARIAN POETRY / *collections*
PG1010	BULGARIAN POETRY / *history*
D374-7	*BULGARIAN QUESTION* **SEE** EASTERN QUESTION (BALKAN) / *history*
D461-9	*BULGARIAN QUESTION* **SEE** EASTERN QUESTION (BALKAN) / *history*
JX1319	*BULGARIAN QUESTION* **SEE** EASTERN QUESTION (BALKAN) / *international law*
PG1023	BULGARIAN WIT AND HUMOR / *collections*
PG1012	BULGARIAN WIT AND HUMOR / *history*
DR354	*BULGARIAN-SERBIAN WAR, 1885* **SEE** SERBO-BULGARIAN WAR, 1885
DR64	BULGARIANS / *ethnography*
D756.5.A7	*BULGE, BATTLE OF THE* **SEE** ARDENNES, BATTLE OF THE, 1944-1945
VM469	BULKHEADS (NAVAL ARCHITECTURE)
BL443.B8	BULL (IN RELIGION, FOLK-LORE, ETC.) / *religion*
E123	*BULL OF DEMARCATION* **SEE** DEMARCATION LINE OF ALEXANDER VI
E472.18	BULL RUN, 1ST BATTLE, 1861
E473.77	BULL RUN, 2D BATTLE, 1862
GV1108	BULL-FIGHTERS
N8250	BULL-FIGHTS IN ART
GV1107	BULL-FIGHTS
GV1107	*BULL-FIGHTS-SPAIN* **SEE** BULL-FIGHTS
SF429.B8	BULL-TERRIERS
JN3270.G8	*BULL, GOLDEN* **SEE** GOLDEN BULL, 1356
E241.B87	BULL'S FERRY, N.J., ENGAGEMENT AT, 1780
SF429.B85	BULLDOGS
TE223	BULLDOZERS / *road machinery*
UF750-770	*BULLETS* **SEE** PROJECTILES / *military*
VF480-500	*BULLETS* **SEE** PROJECTILES / *naval*
HG261-313	*BULLION* **SEE** PRECIOUS METALS / *finance*
TN410-439	*BULLION* **SEE** PRECIOUS METALS / *mining*
PL8093	BULLOM LANGUAGE
HG4551-4595	*BULLS AND BEARS* **SEE** STOCK-EXCHANGE
PN6231.B8	BULLS, COLLOQUIAL
PN6231.B8	*BULLS, IRISH* **SEE** BULLS, COLLOQUIAL
PN6178.I6	*BULLS, IRISH* **SEE** IRISH WIT AND HUMOR
PL8093	*BULOM LANGUAGE* **SEE** BULLOM LANGUAGE
QL568.A6	BUMBLEBEES
PL1841	*BUN-SIO DIALECT* **SEE** CHINESE LANGUAGE — DIALECTS — — HAINAN
PL8381	*BUNDA LANGUAGE* **SEE** KIMBUNDU LANGUAGE
DS485.O6	*BUNDAS* **SEE** BONDOS
PK1968	BUNDELI DIALECT
PK1968	*BUNDELKHANDI DIALECT* **SEE** BUNDELI DIALECT
GT2651	BUNDLING
DD174.4	BUNDSCHUH INSURRECTIONS, 1493-1517
NA7571-2	BUNGALOWS
E241.B9	BUNKER HILL, BATTLE OF, 1775
V240	*BUNKERING STATIONS* **SEE** COALING-STATIONS
SB608.W5	BUNT (DISEASE OF WHEAT)
TS1630	BUNTING (CLOTH)
VK1000-1246	BUOYS
QK495.L52	BUR CLOVER
SB205.B	BUR CLOVER
QK495.A	BURDOCK / *arctium*
SB615.B	BURDOCK / *weeds*
Q183	*BUREAUS, SCIENTIFIC* **SEE** SCIENTIFIC BUREAUS
QC104	BURETTES
JS261-7	*BURGHS* **SEE** BOROUGHS
TK7251	BURGLAR-ALARMS
HG9970.B8	*BURGLARY INSURANCE* **SEE** INSURANCE, BURGLARY
HV6646-6665	BURGLARY
E233	BURGOYNE'S INVASION, 1777
PD1301	BURGUNDIAN LANGUAGE
DC611.B771-9	BURGUNDIANS
D149	BURGUNDIANS / *migrations*
HG9466-9479	*BURIAL CLUBS* **SEE** INSURANCE, BURIAL
GN486	*BURIAL CUSTOMS* **SEE** FUNERAL RITES AND CEREMONIES / *ethnology*

HG9466-9479	*BURIAL INSURANCE* **SEE** INSURANCE, BURIAL
BX1939.B8	BURIAL LAWS (CANON LAW)
BV199.F8	*BURIAL SERVICE* **SEE** FUNERAL SERVICE
HB1321-1530	*BURIAL STATISTICS* **SEE** MORTALITY / statistics
HG8783-7	*BURIAL STATISTICS* **SEE** MORTALITY / tables
HA38-39	*BURIAL STATISTICS* **SEE** REGISTERS OF BIRTHS, ETC.
HB881-3700	*BURIAL STATISTICS* **SEE** VITAL STATISTICS
GN486	BURIAL / ethnology
GT3150-3390	BURIAL / manners and customs
RA625	BURIAL / public health
RA1063	BURIAL, PREMATURE
PL428	BURIAT DRAMA
PL427	BURIAT LANGUAGE
PL428	BURIAT LITERATURE
PL428	BURIAT POETRY
DK759.B	BURIATS
PL7501.B8	*BURISHKI LANGUAGE* **SEE** BURUSHASKI LANGUAGE
DU102	BURKE AND WILLS EXPEDITION, 1860-1861
TS1735	BURLAP
PN6149.B8	BURLESQUE (LITERATURE)
PN1940-1949	BURLESQUE (THEATER)
PN6231.B84	BURLESQUES
PL3921-3969	*BURMAN LANGUAGE* **SEE** BURMESE LANGUAGE
PL3971	BURMESE DRAMA
PL3921-3969	BURMESE LANGUAGE
PL3971-3999	BURMESE LITERATURE
DS475.7	BURMESE WAR, 1824-1826
DS477.65	BURMESE WAR, 1852
RA631-7	*BURNING THE DEAD* **SEE** CREMATION
GT3330	*BURNING THE DEAD* **SEE** CREMATION / manners and customs
RD131	BURNS AND SCALDS
RC87	BURNS AND SCALDS / popular medicine
E473.3	BURNSIDE'S EXPEDITION TO NORTH CAROLINA, 1862
BL570	*BURNT OFFERING* **SEE** SACRIFICE
BL1215.S2	*BURNT OFFERING* **SEE** SACRIFICE / brahmanism
E334	BURR CONSPIRACY, 1805-1807
SF361	*BURRO* **SEE** ASSES AND MULES
QL697	BURSA FABRICII
QM367	BURSA OMENTALIS
QL864	BURSA OMENTALIS
QM331	*BURSA PHARYNGEA* **SEE** PHARYNGEAL BURSA
QM485	BURSAE MUCOSAE
RD688	BURSAE OF HIP / diseases
RC935.B8	BURSAE OF HIP / diseases
QM141	BURSAE OF HIP / human anatomy
QM485	*BURSAL SYNOVIAE* **SEE** BURSAE MUCOSAE
LB2338-9	*BURSARIES* **SEE** SCHOLARSHIPS / college and university
LB2848-9	*BURSARIES* **SEE** SCHOLARSHIPS / school
RC935.B8	BURSITIS
PL5281	BURU LANGUAGE
PL7501.B8	BURUSHASKI LANGUAGE
DS485.H8	BURUSHO
GN486	*BURYING-GROUNDS* **SEE** BURIAL / ethnology
GT3150-3390	*BURYING-GROUNDS* **SEE** BURIAL / manners and customs
RA625	*BURYING-GROUNDS* **SEE** BURIAL / public health
RA626-630	*BURYING-GROUNDS* **SEE** CEMETERIES
GT3320	*BURYING-GROUNDS* **SEE** CEMETERIES / manners and customs
TK2821	*BUS BARS* **SEE** BUS CONDUCTORS (ELECTRICITY)
TK2821	*BUS CHANNELS* **SEE** BUS CONDUCTORS (ELECTRICITY)
TK2821	BUS CONDUCTORS (ELECTRICITY)
HE5601-5720	*BUS LINES* **SEE** MOTOR BUS LINES
TK2821	*BUS TUBES (ELECTRICITY)* **SEE** BUS CONDUCTORS (ELECTRICITY)
DC233.B8	BUSACO, BATTLE OF, 1810
DP802.B8	BUSACO, BATTLE OF, 1810 / local history
TK2821	*BUSBARS* **SEE** BUS CONDUCTORS (ELECTRICITY)
TL232	*BUSES* **SEE** MOTOR BUSES
HE5601-5720	*BUSES* **SEE** OMNIBUSES
HV6453.A73	BUSH-RANGERS / australia
TJ1061-1073	*BUSHINGS* **SEE** BEARINGS (MACHINERY)
TK3331-3441	*BUSHINGS* **SEE** ELECTRIC INSULATORS AND INSULATION / engineering
QC611	*BUSHINGS* **SEE** ELECTRIC INSULATORS AND INSULATION / physics
TJ415-444	*BUSHINGS* **SEE** PIPE-FITTINGS
PL8101-4	BUSHMAN LANGUAGES
GN660.B8	BUSHMEN / anthropology
GR360.B9	BUSHMEN / folk-lore
DT763-4	BUSHMEN / south africa
DT650	BUSHONGO
D25.5	*BUSHWHACKERS* **SEE** GUERRILLAS
E83.76	BUSHY RUN, BATTLE OF, 1763
HF5028	BUSINESS — CALENDARS
HF5371	BUSINESS — FORMS, BLANKS, ETC.
HA31	BUSINESS — GRAPHIC METHODS
HF5001-6201	*BUSINESS ADMINISTRATION* **SEE** BUSINESS
HF5548	*BUSINESS AUTOCODES* **SEE** PROGRAMMING LANGUAGES (ELECTRONIC COMPUTERS) — BUSINESS
HF5851	*BUSINESS CARDS* **SEE** ADVERTISING CARDS
TT360	*BUSINESS CARDS* **SEE** ADVERTISING CARDS / card and sign writing
HG4001-4280	*BUSINESS CORPORATIONS* **SEE** CORPORATIONS / finance
HD2709-2930	*BUSINESS CORPORATIONS* **SEE** CORPORATIONS / theory and policy
HF5721-5733	*BUSINESS CORRESPONDENCE* **SEE** COMMERCIAL CORRESPONDENCE
HB3711-3840	BUSINESS CYCLES
HF1101-1181	BUSINESS EDUCATION
PE1115	*BUSINESS ENGLISH* **SEE** ENGLISH LANGUAGE — BUSINESS ENGLISH
HF5386	BUSINESS ETHICS
HF5391	BUSINESS ETHICS
HG3760-3773	*BUSINESS FAILURES* **SEE** BANKRUPTCY
HG8937	*BUSINESS INSURANCE* **SEE** INSURANCE, BUSINESS LIFE / economics
K	*BUSINESS INSURANCE* **SEE** INSURANCE, BUSINESS LIFE / law
HG9970.B85	*BUSINESS INTERRUPTION INSURANCE* **SEE** INSURANCE, BUSINESS INTERRUPTION
HF5721-5733	*BUSINESS LETTERS* **SEE** COMMERCIAL CORRESPONDENCE
K	*BUSINESS LIFE INSURANCE* **SEE** INSURANCE, BUSINESS LIFE / law
HG8937	*BUSINESS LIFE INSURANCE* **SEE** INSURANCE, BUSINESS LIFE / economics
HF5548	*BUSINESS MACHINES* **SEE** OFFICE EQUIPMENT AND SUPPLIES
S566	*BUSINESS MATHEMATICS-AGRICULTURE* **SEE** AGRICULTURAL MATHEMATICS
PG2120.C6	*BUSINESS RUSSIAN* **SEE** RUSSIAN LANGUAGE — BUSINESS RUSSIAN
PC4120.C6	*BUSINESS SPANISH* **SEE** SPANISH LANGUAGE — BUSINESS SPANISH
HB3730	*BUSINESS STABILIZATION* **SEE** ECONOMIC STABILIZATION
HF5001-6201	BUSINESS
HF5548	*BUSINESS-PROGRAMMING LANGUAGES* **SEE** PROGRAMMING LANGUAGES (ELECTRONIC COMPUTERS) — BUSINESS
HD58	*BUSINESS-REMOVAL* **SEE** INDUSTRIES, LOCATION OF
HF1101-1181	*BUSINESS-STUDY AND TEACHING* **SEE** BUSINESS EDUCATION
QL696.G8	BUSTARDS
NB1300	BUSTS
TK2821	*BUSWAYS (ELECTRICITY)* **SEE** BUS CONDUCTORS (ELECTRICITY)
LB1537	*BUSY WORK* **SEE** CREATIVE ACTIVITIES AND SEAT WORK
TP765-770	*BUTADIINE* **SEE** ACETYLENE / chemical technology
QD305.H8	*BUTADIINE* **SEE** ACETYLENE / chemistry
HD9410-9429	*BUTCHER SHOPS* **SEE** BUTCHERS
TS1960-1967	*BUTCHERING* **SEE** SLAUGHTERING AND SLAUGHTER-HOUSES / butchering
HD9410.9	*BUTCHERING* **SEE** SLAUGHTERING AND SLAUGHTER-HOUSES / inspection
RA578.A6	*BUTCHERING* **SEE** SLAUGHTERING AND SLAUGHTER-HOUSES / public health
HD9410-9429	BUTCHERS
SF265	BUTTER — ANALYSIS AND EXAMINATION
SF263	BUTTER — EARLY WORKS TO 1800
SF263	BUTTER — PRESERVATION
SF266	*BUTTER FACTORIES* **SEE** CREAMERIES
SF263-9	BUTTER / butter making

HD9278	BUTTER / *trade*
SF268	*BUTTER, ARTIFICIAL* **SEE** OLEOMARGARINE
HD9441	*BUTTER, ARTIFICIAL* **SEE** OLEOMARGARINE / *trade*
QK465	BUTTERFLIES — COLLECTION AND PRESERVATION
QL543	BUTTERFLIES — PICTORIAL WORKS
QL541-562	BUTTERFLIES
QE832.L5	BUTTERFLIES, FOSSIL
TH2416	*BUTTERFLY-SHELL ROOFS* **SEE** ROOFS, SHELL
SF275.B8	BUTTERMILK / *dairying*
NK3670	BUTTONS — COLLECTORS AND COLLECTING
UC487	BUTTONS / *military science*
TS2301.B9	BUTTONS / *technology*
HD9969.B9	BUTTONS / *trade*
RM666.B9	BUTYL-CHLORAL
TX335	*BUYERS' GUIDES* **SEE** CONSUMER EDUCATION
TX356	*BUYERS' GUIDES* **SEE** MARKETING (HOME ECONOMICS)
TX335	*BUYERS' GUIDES* **SEE** SHOPPING
HF5437	*BUYING* **SEE** PURCHASING
QL696.A2	BUZZARDS
BL2465	BWITI SECT
TK9203.B6	*BWR* **SEE** BOILING WATER REACTORS
HD9559.C68-7	*BY-PRODUCT COKE INDUSTRY* **SEE** COKE INDUSTRY
TP995	*BY-PRODUCTS* **SEE** WASTE PRODUCTS
DS432	*BYGAS* **SEE** BAIGAS
G850 1928	BYRD ANTARCTIC EXPEDITION, 1ST, 1928-1930
G850 1933	BYRD ANTARCTIC EXPEDITION, 2D, 1933-1935
RC774	*BYSSINOSIS* **SEE** LUNGS — DUST DISEASES
HD7264	*BYSSINOSIS* **SEE** LUNGS — DUST DISEASES / *labor*
NA370-373	*BYZANTINE ARCHITECTURE* **SEE** ARCHITECTURE, BYZANTINE
NK1265	*BYZANTINE DECORATION AND ORNAMENT* **SEE** DECORATION AND ORNAMENT, BYZANTINE
PA5160	BYZANTINE DRAMA
DF506	BYZANTINE EMPERORS
DF501-649	BYZANTINE EMPIRE
PA5170-5198	BYZANTINE LITERATURE / *collections*
PA5101-5167	BYZANTINE LITERATURE / *history*
PA5180-5189	BYZANTINE POETRY / *collections*
PA5150-5155	BYZANTINE POETRY / *history*
DF501-649	BYZANTINE STUDIES
D765.2.B	BZURA RIVER, BATTLE OF, 1939
BM525	CABALA / *jewish religion*
BF1585-1623	CABALA / *occult sciences*
PK9201.K3	*CABARDAN BALLADS AND SONGS* **SEE** KABARDIAN BALLADS AND SONGS
PK9201.K3	*CABARDAN LANGUAGE* **SEE** KABARDIAN LANGUAGE
PN1960-1969	*CABARETS* **SEE** MUSIC-HALLS (VARIETY-THEATERS, CABARETS, ETC.)
SB608.C14	CABBAGE — DISEASES AND PESTS
SB945.C	CABBAGE LOOPER
SB608.C14	CABBAGE MAGGOT
SB608.C14	*CABBAGE-ROOT MAGGOT* **SEE** CABBAGE MAGGOT
SB331	CABBAGE
BM525	*CABBALA* **SEE** CABALA / *jewish religion*
BF1585-1623	*CABBALA* **SEE** CABALA / *occult sciences*
JF331-341	*CABINET GOVERNMENT* **SEE** CABINET SYSTEM
JK610-616	CABINET OFFICERS / *u.s.*
ML597	*CABINET ORGAN* **SEE** REED-ORGAN
JF331-341	CABINET SYSTEM
TT197	CABINET-WORK
HD9773	CABINET-WORKERS / *industry*
NA8470	*CABINS* **SEE** LOG CABINS
BL313	CABIRI
HE7669-7679	*CABLE CODES* **SEE** CIPHER AND TELEGRAPH CODES
HE7676-7	*CABLE CODES* **SEE** CIPHER AND TELEGRAPH CODES / *commercial codes*
HE7678	*CABLE CODES* **SEE** CIPHER AND TELEGRAPH CODES / *foreign languages*
HE7710	*CABLE DIRECTORIES* **SEE** CABLES, SUBMARINE — DIRECTORIES
TF835	*CABLE RAILROADS* **SEE** RAILROADS, CABLE
TS1784-7	CABLES / *manufacture*
VM791	CABLES / *marine engineering*
HE7709-7741	*CABLES, ELECTRIC* **SEE** CABLES, SUBMARINE / *economics*
UG607	*CABLES, ELECTRIC* **SEE** CABLES, SUBMARINE / *military art and science*
TK5605-5681	*CABLES, ELECTRIC* **SEE** CABLES, SUBMARINE / *technology*
TK3301-3351	*CABLES, ELECTRIC* **SEE** ELECTRIC CABLES
TK5481	*CABLES, ELECTRIC* **SEE** TELEGRAPH CABLES
TK6381	*CABLES, ELECTRIC* **SEE** TELEPHONE CABLES
HE7725	CABLES, SUBMARINE — ATLANTIC / *economics*
TK5611	CABLES, SUBMARINE — ATLANTIC / *technology*
HE7710	CABLES, SUBMARINE — DIRECTORIES
HE7715	CABLES, SUBMARINE — LAWS AND REGULATIONS / *international law*
HE7731	CABLES, SUBMARINE — PACIFIC / *economics*
TK5613	CABLES, SUBMARINE — PACIFIC / *technology*
HE7709-7741	CABLES, SUBMARINE / *economics*
UG607	CABLES, SUBMARINE / *military art and science*
TK5605-5681	CABLES, SUBMARINE / *technology*
HE5601-5720	*CABS* **SEE** TAXICABS
PM6366	*CACANE LANGUAGE* **SEE** LULE LANGUAGE
SB608.C17	CACAO — DISEASES AND PESTS
TP684.C2	CACAO-BUTTER
F1465.2.K5	*CACCHI INDIANS* **SEE** KEKCHI INDIANS
PM3913	*CACCHI LANGUAGE* **SEE** KEKCHI LANGUAGE
PL4001.B3	*CACHARI LANGUAGE* **SEE** BARA LANGUAGE
HE6181-5	*CACHETS (PHILATELY)* **SEE** POSTMARKS
PM3576	*CACHIQUEL LANGUAGE* **SEE** CAKCHIKEL LANGUAGE
QL737.C2	CACOMITL CAT
QK495.C11	CACTUS
SF99	CACTUS / *cattle food*
SB317.C2	CACTUS / *culture*
SB413.C12	CACTUS / *culture*
HD301-1130	*CADASTRAL SURVEYS* **SEE** REAL PROPERTY / *other countries*
HD251-279	*CADASTRAL SURVEYS* **SEE** REAL PROPERTY / *u.s.*
HD251-279	*CADASTRAL SURVEYS* **SEE** REAL PROPERTY / *u.s.*
GV977	*CADDIES* **SEE** CADDYING
QL516-519	CADDIS-FLIES
E99.C12	CADDO INDIANS
PM721	CADDO LANGUAGE
E99.C13	CADDOAN INDIANS
PM721	CADDOAN LANGUAGES
GV977	CADDYING
DA257	CADE'S REBELLION, 1450
MT50	CADENCE (MUSIC) / *harmony*
ML444	CADENCE (MUSIC) / *harmony*
M1497	*CADENZAS, VOCAL* **SEE** VOCAL MUSIC — CADENZAS
F2520.1.C	*CADIHEOS* **SEE** CADIOEO INDIANS
F2520.1.C	CADIOEO INDIANS
F2520.1.C	*CADIQUES* **SEE** CADIOEO INDIANS
DP402.C29	CADIZ EXPEDITION, 1587
DP402.C29	CADIZ EXPEDITION, 1596
DP402.C29	CADIZ EXPEDITION, 1625
DA86.8 1656	CADIZ, BATTLE OF, 1656
TN799.C2	CADMIUM — METALLURGY
TK4381	*CADMIUM-VAPOR ELECTRIC LIGHTING* **SEE** ELECTRIC LIGHTING, CADMIUM VAPOR
QD181.C3	CADMIUM / *chemistry*
TN490.C2	CADMIUM / *mining*
DC193.4	CADOUDAL-PICHEGRU CONSPIRACY, 1803-1804
BL457.C3	CADUCEUS
QE690-699	*CAENOZOIC PERIOD* **SEE** GEOLOGY, STRATIGRAPHIC — CENOZOIC
QE925-931	*CAENOZOIC PERIOD* **SEE** PALEOBOTANY — CENOZOIC
QE735-741	*CAENOZOIC PERIOD* **SEE** PALEONTOLOGY — CENOZOIC
RG761	*CAESAREAN SECTION* **SEE** CESAREAN SECTION
DG270-365	*CAESARS* **SEE** ROMAN EMPERORS
DG124	*CAESARS* **SEE** ROMAN EMPERORS / *cult*
QD181.C8	*CAESIUM* **SEE** CESIUM / *chemistry*
NA7800-7850	*CAFES* **SEE** HOTELS, TAVERNS, ETC. / *architecture*
GT3770-3899	*CAFES* **SEE** HOTELS, TAVERNS, ETC. / *manners and customs*
TX945	*CAFES* **SEE** RESTAURANTS, LUNCH ROOMS, ETC.
TX945	*CAFETERIAS* **SEE** RESTAURANTS, LUNCH ROOMS, ETC.
QP921.C3	CAFFEIN — PHYSIOLOGICAL EFFECT
RM666.C2	CAFFEIN — PHYSIOLOGICAL EFFECT / *therapeutics*
QD421	CAFFEIN / *chemistry*
DT764.K2	*CAFFRES* **SEE** KAFIRS (AFRICAN PEOPLE)
GN657.K2	*CAFFRES* **SEE** KAFIRS (AFRICAN PEOPLE) / *anthropology*

DT777	*CAFFRES* **SEE** KAFIRS (AFRICAN PEOPLE) / *kafir wars*	QA304-6	CALCULUS, DIFFERENTIAL
DS374.K2	*CAFIRS* **SEE** KAFIRS (KAFIRISTAN)	QA308-311	CALCULUS, INTEGRAL
DT764.K2	*CAFRES* **SEE** KAFIRS (AFRICAN PEOPLE)	QA432	CALCULUS, OPERATIONAL
GN657.K2	*CAFRES* **SEE** KAFIRS (AFRICAN PEOPLE) / *anthropology*	DR504	CALDERAN, BATTLE OF, 1514
		DR504	*CALDIRAN, BATTLE OF, 1514* **SEE** CALDERAN, BATTLE OF, 1514
DT777	*CAFRES* **SEE** KAFIRS (AFRICAN PEOPLE) / *kafir wars*	F1219.3.C2	*CALENDAR STONE OF MEXICO* **SEE** CALENDAR, MEXICAN
F2726	CAGANCHA, BATTLE OF, 1839		
SF461	CAGE-BIRDS	CE73	CALENDAR
E99.C	*CAGHNAWAGA INDIANS* **SEE** CAUGHNAWAGA INDIANS	E99.A1	CALENDAR, ABNAKI
		CE33	CALENDAR, ASSYRO-BABYLONIAN
CB353	CAGOTS	F1219.3.C2	*CALENDAR, AZTEC* **SEE** CALENDAR, MEXICAN
F1221.C3	CAHITA INDIANS	CE81-83	*CALENDAR, ECCLESIASTICAL* **SEE** CHURCH CALENDAR
E99.K27	*CAHUILLA INDIANS* **SEE** KAWIA INDIANS		
F2684	CAIBATE, BATTLE OF, 1756	CE61.G3	CALENDAR, GERMANIC
F2230.2.C	*CAIGUA INDIANS* **SEE** CAINGUA INDIANS	CE76	CALENDAR, GREGORIAN
RC563	CAIN COMPLEX	CE35	*CALENDAR, HEBREW* **SEE** CALENDAR, JEWISH
F2823.K3	*CAINGANGUE INDIANS* **SEE** KAINGANGUE INDIANS / *argentine republic*	CE59	CALENDAR, ISLAMIC
		CE35	CALENDAR, JEWISH
F2520.1.K	*CAINGANGUE INDIANS* **SEE** KAINGANGUE INDIANS / *brazil*	CE75	CALENDAR, JULIAN
		F1435.3.C14	CALENDAR, MAYA
PM6276	*CAINGANGUE LANGUAGE* **SEE** KAINGANGUE LANGUAGE	F1219.3.C2	CALENDAR, MEXICAN
		CE59	*CALENDAR, MUSLIM* **SEE** CALENDAR, ISLAMIC
F2230.2.C	CAINGUA INDIANS	CE91-92	CALENDAR, PERPETUAL
SF429.C3	CAIRN TERRIERS	CE77	CALENDAR, REPUBLICAN
RC103.C3	CAISSON-DISEASE	CE61.G3	*CALENDAR, SCANDINAVIAN* **SEE** CALENDAR, GERMANIC
TC199	CAISSONS		
F2230.2.C	*CAIUAS* **SEE** CAINGUA INDIANS	F1219.3.C2	CALENDAR, TARASCAN
F1465.2.K5	*CAKCHI INDIANS* **SEE** KEKCHI INDIANS	F1435.3.C14	CALENDAR, TZELTAL
PM3913	*CAKCHI LANGUAGE* **SEE** KEKCHI LANGUAGE	F1219.3.C2	CALENDAR, ZAPOTEC
PM3576	CAKCHIKEL LANGUAGE	Z695.5	*CALENDARING OF MANUSCRIPTS* **SEE** CATALOGING OF MANUSCRIPTS
TX771	CAKE DECORATING		
TX771	CAKE	CE91	CALENDARS
RS165.C	CALABAR BEAN	D11.5	CALENDARS
PQ4222.S7	*CALABRESE* **SEE** STRAMBOTTO / *collections*	PD2014	CALENDARS, RUNIC
PQ4128.S7	*CALABRESE* **SEE** STRAMBOTTO / *history and criticism*	SF205	*CALF* **SEE** CALVES
		TP930	*CALICO ENGRAVING* **SEE** CALICO-PRINTING
DC98.5.C2	CALAIS — SIEGE, 1346	TP930	CALICO-PRINTING
D756.5.C	CALAIS, BATTLE OF, 1940	F865	CALIFORNIA — GOLD DISCOVERIES
PL5841	*CALAMIAN LANGUAGE* **SEE** KALAMIAN LANGUAGE	F856-870	CALIFORNIA — HISTORY
PL5841	*CALAMIANO LANGUAGE* **SEE** KALAMIAN LANGUAGE	HD5325. R12 1894C	CALIFORNIA RAILROAD STRIKE, 1894
E99.K	*CALAPOOYAN INDIANS* **SEE** KALAPUYAN INDIANS	QL696.P5	CALIFORNIA WOODPECKER
F2823.C3	CALCHAQUI INDIANS	F497	CALIFORNIA — HISTORY — — CIVIL WAR
TH8161	CALCIMINING	QE391.V55	*CALIFORNITE* **SEE** VESUVIANITE
QE391.C2	CALCITE	DS234-8	*CALIFS* **SEE** CALIPHS / *arabian*
QP913.C2	CALCIUM — PHYSIOLOGICAL EFFECT	TJ1313	CALIPERS
RM666.C24	CALCIUM — PHYSIOLOGICAL EFFECT / *therapeutics*	DS234-8	CALIPHS / *arabian*
		GV481-508	*CALISTHENICS* **SEE** CALLISTHENICS
TP770	CALCIUM CARBIDE	SB413.C15	*CALLA-LILY* **SEE** CALLA
QP535.C2	CALCIUM IN THE BODY	SB413.C15	CALLA
QB551	*CALCIUM VAPOR IN THE SUN* **SEE** SUN — FLOCCULI	F3447	CALLAO — BOMBARDMENT, 1866
QD181.C2	CALCIUM / *chemistry*	Z43-45	CALLIGRAPHY
QP535.C2	CALCIUM / *physiological chemistry*	M175.C3	CALLIOPE MUSIC
TK3141	*CALCULATING BOARDS, NETWORK* **SEE** ELECTRIC NETWORK ANALYZERS / *alternating current*	ML597	CALLIOPE
		GV481-508	CALLISTHENICS
TK3111	*CALCULATING BOARDS, NETWORK* **SEE** ELECTRIC NETWORK ANALYZERS / *direct current*	TR400	*CALLITYPE* **SEE** KALLITYPE
		M1270	*CALLS, MILITARY* **SEE** MILITARY CALLS
TK3001	*CALCULATING BOARDS, NETWORK* **SEE** ELECTRIC NETWORK ANALYZERS	UH40-45	*CALLS, MILITARY* **SEE** MILITARY CALLS
		QK769	CALLUS (BOTANY)
HF5688-9	CALCULATING-MACHINES / *bookkeeping*	QM569	CALLUS
QA75	CALCULATING-MACHINES / *mechanical devices*	DL710	*CALMAR WAR, 1611-1613* **SEE** KALMAR WAR, 1611-1613
HF5688-9	*CALCULATORS* **SEE** CALCULATING-MACHINES / *bookkeeping*	DL179	*CALMAR, UNION OF, 1397* **SEE** KALMAR, UNION OF, 1397 / *denmark*
QA75	*CALCULATORS* **SEE** CALCULATING-MACHINES / *mechanical devices*	DL485	*CALMAR, UNION OF, 1397* **SEE** KALMAR, UNION OF, 1397 / *norway*
QA111	*CALCULATORS* **SEE** READY-RECKONERS / *arithmetic*	DL694	*CALMAR, UNION OF, 1397* **SEE** KALMAR, UNION OF, 1397 / *sweden*
HF5697-5702	*CALCULATORS* **SEE** READY-RECKONERS / *business arithmetic*	VK547	*CALMING OF WAVES* **SEE** WAVES, CALMING OF
		PL429	*CALMUCK LANGUAGE* **SEE** KALMUCK LANGUAGE
RC850	CALCULI, BILIARY	PL430	*CALMUCK LITERATURE* **SEE** KALMUCK LITERATURE
RD547	CALCULI, BILIARY	DK34.K14	*CALMUCKS* **SEE** KALMUCKS
RC921.V4	CALCULI, URINARY	RM666.M5	CALOMEL
RD581	CALCULI, URINARY	QP135	*CALOR ANIMALIS* **SEE** ANIMAL HEAT
QA431	*CALCULUS OF DIFFERENCES* **SEE** DIFFERENCE EQUATIONS	TJ765	CALORIC ENGINES
		QC291-7	CALORIMETERS AND CALORIMETRY
QA253	CALCULUS OF OPERATIONS	TR395	CALOTYPE
QA433	*CALCULUS OF SPINORS* **SEE** SPINOR ANALYSIS	DS451	*CALUKYAS* **SEE** CHALUKYAS
QA433	CALCULUS OF TENSORS	SF961-7	CALVES — DISEASES
QA315-316	CALCULUS OF VARIATIONS		
QA300-316	CALCULUS		
QA433	*CALCULUS, ABSOLUTE DIFFERENTIAL* **SEE** CALCULUS OF TENSORS		

SF205	CALVES
BX9401-9595	CALVINISM
JX5485.C2	*CALVO CLAUSE* **SEE** CALVO DOCTRINE AND CLAUSE
JX5485.C2	CALVO DOCTRINE AND CLAUSE
GV1295.C	CALYPSO (GAME)
DS560	*CAM* **SEE** CHAMS
PL4491	*CAM LANGUAGE* **SEE** CHAM LANGUAGE
BX3085.C	*CAMALDOLESE* **SEE** CAMALDOLITES
BX4290.C	*CAMALDOLESE* **SEE** CAMALDOLITES
BX3085.C	CAMALDOLITES
BX4290.C	CAMALDOLITES
BX4290.C	*CAMALDULIANS* **SEE** CAMALDOLITES
BX3085.C	*CAMALDULIANS* **SEE** CAMALDOLITES
E99.C85	*CAMANCHE INDIANS* **SEE** COMANCHE INDIANS
PL3801.C4	*CAMBA LAHULI DIALECT* **SEE** CHAMBA LAHULI DIALECT
QL444.D3	*CAMBARUS* **SEE** CRAYFISH
HG3811-4000	*CAMBISTRY* **SEE** FOREIGN EXCHANGE
HG219	*CAMBISTRY* **SEE** MONEY — TABLES, ETC.
QC81-119	*CAMBISTRY* **SEE** WEIGHTS AND MEASURES
RS57	*CAMBISTRY* **SEE** WEIGHTS AND MEASURES */ pharmaceutical*
QK725	CAMBIUM
QK707	CAMBIUM
QB23	*CAMBODIAN ASTRONOMY* **SEE** ASTRONOMY, KHMER
PL4328	*CAMBODIAN LITERATURE* **SEE** KHMER LITERATURE
DG678.26	CAMBRAI, LEAGUE OF, 1508
DC113.5	CAMBRAI, TREATY OF, 1529
QE656	*CAMBRIAN PERIOD* **SEE** GEOLOGY, STRATIGRAPHIC — CAMBRIAN
QE916	*CAMBRIAN PERIOD* **SEE** PALEOBOTANY — CAMBRIAN
QE726	*CAMBRIAN PERIOD* **SEE** PALEONTOLOGY — CAMBRIAN
B1133.C2	CAMBRIDGE PLATONISTS
DS416-419	*CAMDELLA DYNASTY* **SEE** CHANDELA DYNASTY */ antiquities*
DS451	*CAMDELLA DYNASTY* **SEE** CHANDELA DYNASTY */ history of india*
E241.C17	CAMDEN, S.C., BATTLE OF, 1780
SB413.C18	CAMELLIA */ culture*
SF979.C2	CAMELS — DISEASES
QL737.U5	CAMELS
SF249	CAMELS */ animal industries*
NK5720	CAMEOS
TR250-265	CAMERAS
DC127.C3	CAMISARDS
HV6453.I8	CAMORRA
UG449	CAMOUFLAGE (MILITARY SCIENCE)
V215	CAMOUFLAGE (MILITARY SCIENCE)
GV198.A4	*CAMP ADMINISTRATION* **SEE** CAMPS — ADMINISTRATION
TX823	*CAMP COOKERY* **SEE** OUTDOOR COOKERY
GV198.C6	CAMP COUNSELORS
HS3353.C3	CAMP FIRE GIRLS
GV198.L3	*CAMP LAYOUTS* **SEE** CAMP SITES, FACILITIES, ETC.
Z675.W2	*CAMP LIBRARIES* **SEE** EUROPEAN WAR, 1914-1918 — LIBRARIES (IN CAMPS, ETC.)
Z675.W2	*CAMP LIBRARIES* **SEE** WAR LIBRARIES
GV198.L3	*CAMP MAINTENANCE* **SEE** CAMP SITES, FACILITIES, ETC.
GV198.A4	*CAMP MANAGEMENT* **SEE** CAMPS — ADMINISTRATION
GV198.L3	CAMP SITES, FACILITIES, ETC.
BV460	*CAMP-MEETING HYMNS* **SEE** REVIVALS — HYMNS
BV3798-9	CAMP-MEETINGS
BX8475-6	CAMP-MEETINGS */ methodist*
F3430.1.C3	CAMPA INDIANS
PM5716	CAMPA LANGUAGE
CJ5806	*CAMPAIGN BUTTONS* **SEE** CAMPAIGN INSIGNIA
JK1991-7	CAMPAIGN FUNDS */ u.s.*
CJ5806	CAMPAIGN INSIGNIA
JK2251-2391	CAMPAIGN LITERATURE
CJ5806	*CAMPAIGN PINS* **SEE** CAMPAIGN INSIGNIA
M1660-1665	CAMPAIGN SONGS */ music*
E	CAMPAIGN SONGS */ u.s. history*
JK524-9	*CAMPAIGNS, PRESIDENTIAL* **SEE** PRESIDENTS — U.S. — — ELECTION
JK1967-8	*CAMPAIGNS, PRESIDENTIAL* **SEE** PRESIDENTS — U.S. — — ELECTION
E356.C2	CAMPBELL'S ISLAND, BATTLE OF, 1814
BX7301-7343	*CAMPBELLITES* **SEE** DISCIPLES OF CHRIST
DA87.51797	CAMPERDOWN, BATTLE OF, 1797
QP917.C2	CAMPHOR — PHYSIOLOGICAL EFFECT
HD9675.C24	CAMPHOR INDUSTRY AND TRADE
QD416	CAMPHOR
RM666.C25	CAMPHOR */ therapeutics*
QP917.C2	CAMPHORIC ACID — PHYSIOLOGICAL EFFECT
QD341.A2	CAMPHORIC ACID
SF489.C2	CAMPINES
SK601-602	CAMPING — ANECDOTES, FACETIAE, SATIRE, ETC.
M1977.C3	CAMPING — SONGS AND MUSIC
M1978.C3	CAMPING — SONGS AND MUSIC
SK601	CAMPING
BV3798-9	*CAMPMEETINGS* **SEE** CAMP-MEETINGS
BX8475-6	*CAMPMEETINGS* **SEE** CAMP-MEETINGS */ methodist*
F2687	CAMPO GRANDE, BATTLE OF, 1869
DC222.C3	CAMPO-FORMIO, PEACE OF, 1797
GV198.A4	CAMPS — ADMINISTRATION
BV1650	*CAMPS (CHURCH)* **SEE** CHURCH CAMPS
BX7830	*CAMPS (CHURCH)* **SEE** CHURCH CAMPS */ church of the brethren*
U180-185	CAMPS (MILITARY)
UC400-405	CAMPS (MILITARY)
UG365	CAMPS (MILITARY) */ camp making*
GV197.H3	CAMPS FOR THE HANDICAPPED
U290-295	*CAMPS OF INSTRUCTION* **SEE** MILITARY TRAINING CAMPS
GV192-8	CAMPS
TX820	*CAMPS-COOKERY* **SEE** COOKERY FOR INSTITUTIONS, ETC.
GV198.C6	*CAMPS-COUNSELORS* **SEE** CAMP COUNSELORS
GV771-840	*CAMPS-WATER PROGRAMS* **SEE** AQUATIC SPORTS
LB3253	CAMPUS PARKING
TJ206	CAMS
DS121.4	CANAANITES
F1001-1035	CANADA — HISTORY
E351-364	*CANADA - HISTORY -- WAR OF 1812* **SEE** UNITED STATES — HISTORY — — WAR OF 1812
QL696.A5	CANADA GOOSE
F1063	*CANADA-HISTORY-REBELLION, 1869-1870* **SEE** RED RIVER REBELLION, 1869-1870
F1060.9	*CANADA-HISTORY-REBELLION, 1885* **SEE** RIEL REBELLION, 1885
E351-364	*CANADA-HISTORY-WAR OF 1812* **SEE** UNITED STATES — HISTORY — — WAR OF 1812
F1033	CANADA — HISTORY — — 1867-1914
F1034	CANADA — HISTORY — — 1914-
PR9260	CANADIAN BALLADS AND SONGS */ collections*
PR9180	CANADIAN BALLADS AND SONGS */ history*
PR9264-9270	CANADIAN DRAMA */ collections*
PR9183-9195	CANADIAN DRAMA */ history*
PR9275-6	CANADIAN FICTION */ collections*
PR9197-9207	CANADIAN FICTION */ history*
GV948	CANADIAN FOOTBALL
E231	CANADIAN INVASION, 1775-1776
PR9231-9293	CANADIAN LITERATURE */ collections*
PR9100-9221	CANADIAN LITERATURE */ etc.*
PR9291-3	CANADIAN LITERATURE */ etc.*
PN4901-4919	CANADIAN NEWSPAPERS */ etc.*
PR9279	CANADIAN ORATIONS */ collections*
PR9209	CANADIAN ORATIONS */ history*
PN4901-4920	CANADIAN PERIODICALS */ etc.*
PR9249-9263	CANADIAN POETRY */ collections*
PR9161-9181	CANADIAN POETRY */ etc.*
PR9272-3	CANADIAN PROSE LITERATURE */ collections*
PR9197-9207	CANADIAN PROSE LITERATURE */ history*
SB315.C3	CANAIGRE
TC764	CANAL AQUEDUCTS
QC711	CANAL RAYS
TC769	CANAL-BOATS — ELECTRIC TRACTION
TC769	CANAL-BOATS — MECHANICAL TRACTION
TC765	CANAL-BOATS
TC763	CANALS — INCLINED PLANES
TC763	CANALS — LIFTS
TC769	CANALS — STEAM-NAVIGATION
HE526	CANALS */ economics general*
TC601-791	CANALS */ technology*
HE395-6	CANALS */ u.s.*
JX1398-1403	CANALS, INTEROCEANIC */ diplomatic history*

HE528-545	CANALS, INTEROCEANIC / economics	M1245	CANONS, FUGUES, ETC. (BAND)
TC601-791	CANALS, INTEROCEANIC / technology	M1258	CANONS, FUGUES, ETC. (BAND), ARRANGED
TC761	CANALS-LOCKS SEE LOCKS (HYDRAULIC	M658-9	CANONS, FUGUES, ETC. (BARITONE, 2 CORNETS,
	ENGINEERING)		HORN, TROMBONE, TUBA), ARRANGED
TX819	CANAPES SEE COOKERY (RELISHES)	M655-7	CANONS, FUGUES, ETC. (BARITONE, 2 CORNETS,
PL4641-9	CANARESE LANGUAGE SEE KANNADA LANGUAGE		HORN, TROMBONE, TUBA)
PJ2371	CANARIAN LANGUAGE SEE GUANCHE LANGUAGE	M555-7	CANONS, FUGUES, ETC. (BASSOON, CLARINET, FLUTE,
PM5718.C5	CANARIAN LANGUAGE		HORN, OBOE)
SF463	CANARIES	M558-9	CANONS, FUGUES, ETC. (BASSOON, CLARINET, FLUTE,
SF473.B	CANARY PARROT SEE BUDGERIGARS		HORN, OBOE), ARRANGED
GV1295.C2	CANASTA (GAME)	M455-7	CANONS, FUGUES, ETC. (BASSOON, CLARINET, FLUTE,
PL5865	CANCANAI DIALECT SEE KANKANAY DIALECT		OBOE)
M1060	CANCANS (ORCHESTRA) — SCORES	M458-9	CANONS, FUGUES, ETC. (BASSOON, CLARINET, FLUTE,
M1048	CANCANS (ORCHESTRA) — SCORES		OBOE), ARRANGED
M1040	CANCANS (ORCHESTRA)	M355-7	CANONS, FUGUES, ETC. (BASSOON, CLARINET, OBOE)
M1060	CANCANS (ORCHESTRA)	M455-7	CANONS, FUGUES, ETC. (BASSOON, CLARINET, OBOE,
Z242.C2	CANCELS (PRINTING) SEE PRINTING — CANCELS		PICCOLO)
RC266	CANCER NURSING	M1045	CANONS, FUGUES, ETC. (CHAMBER ORCHESTRA) —
RC261	CANCER		SCORES
QL668.C2	CANDATA SEE URODELA	M1045	CANONS, FUGUES, ETC. (CHAMBER ORCHESTRA)
NK8360	CANDELABRA	M1060	CANONS, FUGUES, ETC. (CHAMBER ORCHESTRA),
DS416-419	CANDELLA DYNASTY SEE CHANDELA DYNASTY		ARRANGED
	/ antiquities	M288-9	CANONS, FUGUES, ETC. (CLARINET AND FLUTE)
DS451	CANDELLA DYNASTY SEE CHANDELA DYNASTY	M560-562	CANONS, FUGUES, ETC. (CLARINET, 2 VIOLINS, VIOLA,
	/ history of india		VIOLONCELLO)
DR534.3-4	CANDIA — SIEGE, 1667-1669	M455-7	CANONS, FUGUES, ETC. (CORNET, 3 TROMBONES)
M2078.C2	CANDLEMAS MUSIC	M458-9	CANONS, FUGUES, ETC. (CORNET, 3 TROMBONES),
BV50.C3	CANDLEMAS		ARRANGED
BV196.C3	CANDLES AND LIGHTS	M240-242	CANONS, FUGUES, ETC. (FLUTE AND PIANO)
BX2308	CANDLES AND LIGHTS / catholic church	M1105-6	CANONS, FUGUES, ETC. (FLUTE WITH STRING
BM657.C3	CANDLES AND LIGHTS / judaism		ORCHESTRA)
TP993	CANDLES	M165	CANONS, FUGUES, ETC. (GLASS HARMONICA)
BV196.C3	CANDLES, LITURGICAL SEE CANDLES AND LIGHTS	M25	CANONS, FUGUES, ETC. (HARPSICHORD)
BX2308	CANDLES, LITURGICAL SEE CANDLES AND LIGHTS	M820-822	CANONS, FUGUES, ETC. (HARPSICHORD, FLUTE, 2
	/ catholic church		VIOLINS, 2 VIOLAS, 2 VIOLONCELLOS)
BM657.C3	CANDLES, LITURGICAL SEE CANDLES AND LIGHTS	M510-512	CANONS, FUGUES, ETC. (HARPSICHORD, 3 VIOLINS,
	/ judaism		VIOLA DA GAMBA)
BL2590.U5	CANDOMBLE (CULTUS) SEE UMBANDA (CULTUS)	M140-141	CANONS, FUGUES, ETC. (LUTE)
DS416-419	CANDRELLA DYNASTY SEE CHANDELA DYNASTY	M1105-6	CANONS, FUGUES, ETC. (OBOE WITH STRING
	/ antiquities		ORCHESTRA)
DS451	CANDRELLA DYNASTY SEE CHANDELA DYNASTY	M1060	CANONS, FUGUES, ETC. (ORCHESTRA)
	/ history of india	M1045	CANONS, FUGUES, ETC. (ORCHESTRA)
TX783-799	CANDY SEE CONFECTIONERY / candy-making	M1060	CANONS, FUGUES, ETC. (ORCHESTRA), ARRANGED —
HD9999.C72	CANDY SEE CONFECTIONERY / industry		SCORES
F2520.1.C	CANELLA INDIANS	M10	CANONS, FUGUES, ETC. (ORGAN)
PM5719	CANELLA LANGUAGE	M12-13	CANONS, FUGUES, ETC. (ORGAN), ARRANGED
NB169	CANEPHORES	M500-502	CANONS, FUGUES, ETC. (ORGAN, BARITONE, 2
GT2220	CANES SEE STAFFS (STICKS, CANES, ETC.)		CORNETS, TROMBONE)
PM5723	CANICHANA LANGUAGE	M300-302	CANONS, FUGUES, ETC. (ORGAN, VIOLIN, VIOLA DA
E99.M8	CANIENGA INDIANS SEE MOHAWK INDIANS		GAMBA)
SF991	CANINE DISTEMPER SEE DISTEMPER	M400-402	CANONS, FUGUES, ETC. (ORGAN, 2 VIOLINS, VIOLA DA
TT199	CANING OF CHAIRS SEE CHAIR CANING		GAMBA)
SB945.C33	CANKER-WORMS	M410-412	CANONS, FUGUES, ETC. (PIANO QUARTET)
RC371.C2	CANNABIS INDICA / intoxications	M1010-1011	CANONS, FUGUES, ETC. (PIANO WITH ORCHESTRA)
RM666.C26	CANNABIS INDICA / therapeutics	M20-22	CANONS, FUGUES, ETC. (PIANO)
DG247.3	CANNAE, BATTLE OF, 216 B.C.	M25	CANONS, FUGUES, ETC. (PIANO)
TX552	CANNED FOODS SEE FOOD, CANNED	M835	CANONS, FUGUES, ETC. (PIANO, BELLS, CYMBALS, 2
TN827	CANNEL COAL		DRUMS, KETTLEDRUMS, TRIANGLE, XYLOPHONE)
QL756	CANNIBALISM (ANIMALS)	M26.2	CANONS, FUGUES, ETC. (PIANO, 1 HAND)
GN409	CANNIBALISM	M26	CANONS, FUGUES, ETC. (PIANO, 1 HAND)
TX599-613	CANNING AND PRESERVING	M310-311	CANONS, FUGUES, ETC. (PIANO, 2 VIOLINS)
UF520-630	CANNON SEE ORDNANCE	M312.4	CANONS, FUGUES, ETC. (PIANO, 2 VIOLINS)
GN440.2	CANOE TRIPS SEE CANOES AND CANOEING	M510-512	CANONS, FUGUES, ETC. (PIANO, 3 VIOLINS,
	/ ethnology		VIOLONCELLO)
GV781-5	CANOE TRIPS SEE CANOES AND CANOEING / sport	M200-201	CANONS, FUGUES, ETC. (PIANO, 4 HANDS)
GN440.2	CANOEING SEE CANOES AND CANOEING	M204	CANONS, FUGUES, ETC. (PIANO, 4 HANDS)
	/ ethnology	M240-242	CANONS, FUGUES, ETC. (RECORDER AND PIANO)
GV781-5	CANOEING SEE CANOES AND CANOEING / sport	M243-4	CANONS, FUGUES, ETC. (RECORDER AND PIANO),
GN440.2	CANOES AND CANOEING / ethnology		ARRANGED
GV781-5	CANOES AND CANOEING / sport	M950-952	CANONS, FUGUES, ETC. (STRING ENSEMBLE)
ML448	CANON (MUSIC) / history	M1145	CANONS, FUGUES, ETC. (STRING ORCHESTRA)
MT59	CANON (MUSIC) / instruction	M1160	CANONS, FUGUES, ETC. (STRING ORCHESTRA),
BV761	CANON LAW — EARLY CHURCH		ARRANGED
BX4235-4250	CANONESSES / catholic church	M450-452	CANONS, FUGUES, ETC. (STRING QUARTET)
BX1939.F3	CANONICAL FACULTIES SEE FACULTIES (CANON	M453-4	CANONS, FUGUES, ETC. (STRING QUARTET),
	LAW)		ARRANGED
BX2330	CANONIZATION / catholic church	M349-351	CANONS, FUGUES, ETC. (STRING TRIO)
BX576	CANONIZATION / greek church	M352-3	CANONS, FUGUES, ETC. (STRING TRIO), ARRANGED
M175.A4	CANONS, FUGUES, ETC. (ACCORDION)	M47	CANONS, FUGUES, ETC. (VIOLA)
M175.A4	CANONS, FUGUES, ETC. (ACCORDION), ARRANGED	M221	CANONS, FUGUES, ETC. (VIOLIN AND HARPSICHORD)

M217-218	CANONS, FUGUES, ETC. (VIOLIN AND HARPSICHORD)
M349-351	CANONS, FUGUES, ETC. (VIOLIN, VIOLA, VIOLA DA GAMBA)
M229-230	CANONS, FUGUES, ETC. (VIOLONCELLO AND PIANO)
M233	CANONS, FUGUES, ETC. (VIOLONCELLO AND PIANO)
M1105	CANONS, FUGUES, ETC. (2 FLUTES WITH STRING ORCHESTRA) — SCORES
M1105-6	CANONS, FUGUES, ETC. (2 FLUTES WITH STRING ORCHESTRA)
M288-9	CANONS, FUGUES, ETC. (2 FLUTES)
M214	CANONS, FUGUES, ETC. (2 PIANOS)
M215	CANONS, FUGUES, ETC. (2 PIANOS), ARRANGED
M455-7	CANONS, FUGUES, ETC. (2 TROMBONES, 2 TRUMPETS)
M458-9	CANONS, FUGUES, ETC. (2 TROMBONES, 2 TRUMPETS), ARRANGED
M550-552	CANONS, FUGUES, ETC. (2 VIOLINS, VIOLA, VIOLONCELLO, DOUBLE BASS)
M550-552	CANONS, FUGUES, ETC. (2 VIOLINS, 2 VIOLAS, VIOLONCELLO)
M355-7	CANONS, FUGUES, ETC. (3 CLARINETS)
M358-9	CANONS, FUGUES, ETC. (3 RECORDERS), ARRANGED
M355-7	CANONS, FUGUES, ETC. (3 SAXOPHONES)
M349-351	CANONS, FUGUES, ETC. (3 VIOLINS)
M349-351	CANONS, FUGUES, ETC. (3 VIOLS)
M455-7	CANONS, FUGUES, ETC. (4 BASSOONS)
M455-7	CANONS, FUGUES, ETC. (4 CLARINETS)
M458-9	CANONS, FUGUES, ETC. (4 CLARINETS), ARRANGED
M455-7	CANONS, FUGUES, ETC. (4 SAXOPHONES)
M550-552	CANONS, FUGUES, ETC. (5 VIOLS)
DC226.A3	*CANOPUS, BATTLE OF, 1801* **SEE** ALEXANDRIA, BATTLE OF, 1801
DT62.S8	*CANOPUS, DECREE OF* **SEE** DECREE OF CANOPUS
PJ1531.C	*CANOPUS, DECREE OF* **SEE** DECREE OF CANOPUS
TS2301.C8	*CANS* **SEE** CONTAINERS
PE3726	CANT / *english*
SB339	*CANTALOUPS* **SEE** MELONS
ML1500-1554	CANTATA
ML3260	CANTATA
ML2400	CANTATA
M1996	CANTATAS, JUVENILE
M2190	CANTATAS, JUVENILE
M2023	CANTATAS, SACRED — VOCAL SCORES WITH 2 PIANOS
M2101.5	CANTATAS, SACRED (UNISON)
M2033-6	CANTATAS, SACRED (WOMEN'S VOICES)
M2020-2036	CANTATAS, SACRED
M2027-8	*CANTATAS, SACRED-VOCAL SCORES WITH PIANO-EXCERPTS* **SEE** CANTATAS, SACRED — EXCERPTS — — VOCAL SCORES WITH PIANO
M2027-8	CANTATAS, SACRED — EXCERPTS — — VOCAL SCORES WITH PIANO
M1609	CANTATAS, SECULAR (UNISON)
M1543-6	CANTATAS, SECULAR (WOMEN'S VOICES)
M1530-1546	CANTATAS, SECULAR
M1534	*CANTATAS, SECULAR-TO 1800-SCORES-EXCERPTS* **SEE** CANTATAS, SECULAR — TO 1800 — — EXCERPTS — — — SCORES
M1530	CANTATAS, SECULAR — TO 1800 — — SCORES
M1533	CANTATAS, SECULAR — TO 1800 — — VOCAL SCORES WITH PIANO
M1534	CANTATAS, SECULAR — TO 1800 — — EXCERPTS — — — SCORES
PQ7001.A6	*CANTE FLAMENCO* **SEE** CANTE HONDO
ML3712	*CANTE FLAMENCO* **SEE** CANTE HONDO
PQ7001.A6	CANTE HONDO
ML3712	CANTE HONDO
ML3712	*CANTE JONDO* **SEE** CANTE HONDO
PQ7001.A6	*CANTE JONDO* **SEE** CANTE HONDO
UC755.G7	CANTEEN (BRITISH ARMY)
VC395.G7	CANTEEN (BRITISH NAVY)
UC755.C2	CANTEEN (CANADIAN ARMY)
RM666.C27	CANTHARIDES
D545.C	CANTIGNY, BATTLE OF, 1918
TG385	*CANTILEVER BRIDGES* **SEE** BRIDGES, CANTILEVER
MT860	CANTILLATION — INSTRUCTION AND STUDY
DS135.R9	CANTONISTS
BM652	CANTORS, JEWISH
HF5446-5456	CANVASSING
PT1241.C3	CANZONE / *german*

PQ4128.C6	CANZONE / *italian*
SB291	*CAOUTCHOUC* **SEE** RUBBER / *culture*
QC587	*CAPACITORS* **SEE** CONDENSERS (ELECTRICITY)
PF861-884	*CAPE DUTCH* **SEE** AFRIKAANS LANGUAGE
E99.M19	*CAPE INDIANS* **SEE** MAKAH INDIANS
D775.5.M	*CAPE MATAPAN, BATTLE OF, 1941* **SEE** MATAPAN, BATTLE OF, 1941
QM191	CAPILLARIES
QP101	CAPILLARIES
QL835	CAPILLARIES
QC183	CAPILLARITY
HD6961	*CAPITAL AND LABOR* **SEE** INDUSTRIAL RELATIONS
HG3811-4000	*CAPITAL EXPORTS* **SEE** FOREIGN EXCHANGE
HG4538	*CAPITAL EXPORTS* **SEE** INVESTMENTS, FOREIGN
HJ4639	CAPITAL GAINS TAX / *general*
HJ4653.C3	CAPITAL GAINS TAX / *u.s.*
HG3811-4000	*CAPITAL IMPORTS* **SEE** FOREIGN EXCHANGE
HG4538	*CAPITAL IMPORTS* **SEE** INVESTMENTS, FOREIGN
HG4028.C4	CAPITAL INVESTMENTS
HJ4132-3	CAPITAL LEVY
HV8694-9	CAPITAL PUNISHMENT
BV4626-7	*CAPITAL SINS* **SEE** DEADLY SINS
HB501	CAPITAL / *theory*
HJ4132-3	*CAPITAL-TAXATION* **SEE** CAPITAL LEVY
PN51	CAPITALISM AND LITERATURE
HB501	CAPITALISM
HG4001-4280	*CAPITALIZATION (FINANCE)* **SEE** CORPORATIONS — FINANCE
HE2231-2261	*CAPITALIZATION (FINANCE)* **SEE** RAILROADS — FINANCE
HG4761-4771	*CAPITALIZATION (FINANCE)* **SEE** RAILROADS — FINANCE / *securities*
HE1071-6	*CAPITALIZATION (FINANCE)* **SEE** RAILROADS — VALUATION
HG4651-5990	*CAPITALIZATION (FINANCE)* **SEE** SECURITIES
HF5681.V3	*CAPITALIZATION (FINANCE)* **SEE** VALUATION / *accounting*
HG4028.V3	*CAPITALIZATION (FINANCE)* **SEE** VALUATION / *corporation finance*
HJ6670	*CAPITALIZATION (FINANCE)* **SEE** VALUATION / *customs administration*
TA178	*CAPITALIZATION (FINANCE)* **SEE** VALUATION / *engineering*
HD2765	*CAPITALIZATION (FINANCE)* **SEE** VALUATION / *public service corporations*
HD1387	*CAPITALIZATION (FINANCE)* **SEE** VALUATION / *real estate*
NA2870	CAPITALS (ARCHITECTURE)
G140	CAPITALS (CITIES)
JF1900	CAPITALS (CITIES) / *political science*
E159	CAPITALS (CITIES) / *u.s.*
NA4410-4417	CAPITOLS / *architecture*
BX1939.V52	*CAPITULAR VICARS* **SEE** VICARS CAPITULAR / *canon law*
JX	CAPITULATIONS
SF499	CAPONS AND CAPONIZING
E99.C	CAPOTE INDIANS
P1003	CAPPADOCIAN LANGUAGE
SB365	*CAPRIFIG* **SEE** FIG-INSECT / *fig culture*
SB365	*CAPRIFIG* **SEE** FIG
TS1688	*CAPRON* **SEE** NYLON
LB2389	*CAPS AND GOWNS* **SEE** ACADEMIC COSTUME
VM811	CAPSTAN
RS201.C	CAPSULES (PHARMACY)
TL634-7	*CAPTIVE BALLOONS* **SEE** BALLOONS, CAPTIVE
JX5228	CAPTURE AT SEA
JX5295-5313	*CAPTURED PROPERTY* **SEE** BOOTY (INTERNATIONAL LAW)
JX5228	*CAPTURED PROPERTY* **SEE** CAPTURE AT SEA
BV2255	CAPUCHINS — MISSIONS
BX3101-3155	CAPUCHINS
BX4301-4	CAPUCHINS / *women*
TF386	CAR AXLES
TF947	CAR FENDERS
TF445-9	*CAR HEATING* **SEE** RAILROADS — CARS — — HEATING AND VENTILATION
TF445-9	*CAR LIGHTING* **SEE** RAILROADS — CARS — — LIGHTING
HE1826	*CAR SERVICE (FREIGHT)* **SEE** DEMURRAGE (CAR SERVICE)

HE2331-3	*CAR SERVICE (FREIGHT)* **SEE** RAILROADS — FREIGHT-CARS / *car service*
TF600-606	*CAR SERVICE (FREIGHT)* **SEE** RAILROADS — FREIGHT-CARS / *operation*
TF470-481	*CAR SERVICE (FREIGHT)* **SEE** RAILROADS — FREIGHT-CARS
TF662-7	*CAR SERVICE (FREIGHT)* **SEE** RAILROADS — FREIGHT
HE2301-2550	*CAR SERVICE (FREIGHT)* **SEE** RAILROADS — FREIGHT / *economics*
TF380	CAR TRUCKS (RAILROADS)
HG4971-7	CAR TRUSTS / *finance*
HE1828	CAR TRUSTS / *railroads*
HE2236	CAR TRUSTS / *railroads*
TF445-9	*CAR VENTILATION* **SEE** RAILROADS — CARS — — HEATING AND VENTILATION
HD8039.R12	*CAR WORKERS* **SEE** RAILROADS — EMPLOYEES / *labor*
HE1741-1759	*CAR WORKERS* **SEE** RAILROADS — EMPLOYEES / *railway management*
TF520-522	*CAR WORKERS* **SEE** RAILROADS — EMPLOYEES / *service rules*
HD6350.R1-45	*CAR WORKERS* **SEE** RAILROADS — EMPLOYEES / *trade-union periodicals*
TF518	*CAR WORKERS* **SEE** RAILROADS — EMPLOYEES / *training*
TF410	CAR-COUPLINGS
TF391	CAR-SPRINGS
TF383	CAR-WHEELS — MAINTENANCE AND REPAIR
TF383	CAR-WHEELS
RL775	*CARAATE* **SEE** PINTA
F2324	CARABOBO, BATTLE OF, 1821
F2001	*CARAIB INDIANS* **SEE** CARIB INDIANS
PM5756-9	*CARAIB LANGUAGE* **SEE** CARIB LANGUAGE
F2520.1.C	CARAJA INDIANS
PM5741	CARAJA LANGUAGE
TP380	CARAMEL
E99.K26	*CARANCAHUA INDIANS* **SEE** KARANKAWA INDIANS
QC106	CARAT (UNIT OF WEIGHT)
TL297	*CARAVANS (AUTOMOBILE TRAILERS)* **SEE** AUTOMOBILES — TRAILERS
F2520.1.C	*CARAYAS INDIANS* **SEE** CARAJA INDIANS
TP770	CARBIDES / *manufacture*
UD390-395	*CARBINES* **SEE** RIFLES / *army*
SK274	*CARBINES* **SEE** RIFLES / *hunting*
VD370	*CARBINES* **SEE** RIFLES / *navy*
QP701	CARBOHYDRATE METABOLISM
QP701	CARBOHYDRATES IN THE BODY
QD321	CARBOHYDRATES / *organic chemistry*
QP701	CARBOHYDRATES / *physiological chemistry*
QP917.C	CARBOLIC ACID — PHYSIOLOGICAL EFFECT
RM666.C33	CARBOLIC ACID — THERAPEUTIC USE
RA1242.C2	CARBOLIC ACID — TOXICOLOGY
QD341.P5	CARBOLIC ACID
QD466.5.C1	CARBON — ISOTOPES
TK7725	CARBON — MANUFACTURE
QD181.C1	*CARBON BISULPHIDE* **SEE** CARBON DISULPHIDE
HD7265.C3	*CARBON BISULPHIDE* **SEE** CARBON DISULPHIDE / *labor hygiene*
TK2484	*CARBON BRUSHES* **SEE** BRUSHES, CARBON
QD248-449	CARBON COMPOUNDS
QP913.C1	CARBON DIOXIDE — PHYSIOLOGICAL EFFECT
RM666.C35	CARBON DIOXIDE — THERAPEUTIC USE
QD181.C1	CARBON DIOXIDE / *chemistry*
TP244.C1	CARBON DIOXIDE / *manufacture*
TP492.8	*CARBON DIOXIDE, SOLID* **SEE** DRY ICE
QD181.C1	CARBON DISULPHIDE
HD7265.C3	CARBON DISULPHIDE / *labor hygiene*
TK7725	*CARBON ELECTRODES* **SEE** ELECTRODES, CARBON
QP535.C1	CARBON IN THE BODY
QD466.5.C1	*CARBON ISOTOPES* **SEE** CARBON — ISOTOPES
QD181.C1	CARBON MONOXIDE
QP913.C1	CARBON MONOXIDE / *physiology*
RA1247.C17	CARBON MONOXIDE / *toxicology*
QD181.C1	CARBON TETRACHLORIDE
TP951	CARBON-BLACK
TP245.C4	CARBON / *chemical technology*
QD181.C1	CARBON / *chemistry*
DG551-2	CARBONARI
HS2394.C4	CARBONARI
TP628-636	CARBONATED BEVERAGES
TP628-636	*CARBONATED DRINKS* **SEE** CARBONATED BEVERAGES
TP628-636	*CARBONATED WATERS* **SEE** CARBONATED BEVERAGES
TN923-9	*CARBONATED WATERS* **SEE** MINERAL WATERS
RA793-954	*CARBONATED WATERS* **SEE** MINERAL WATERS / *health resorts*
RM674-6	*CARBONATED WATERS* **SEE** MINERAL WATERS / *therapeutics*
QD181.C1	*CARBONIC ACID* **SEE** CARBON DIOXIDE / *chemistry*
TP244.C1	*CARBONIC ACID* **SEE** CARBON DIOXIDE / *manufacture*
TP492.8	*CARBONIC ACID, REFRIGERATING* **SEE** DRY ICE
QD181.C1	*CARBONIC OXIDE* **SEE** CARBON MONOXIDE
QP913.C1	*CARBONIC OXIDE* **SEE** CARBON MONOXIDE / *physiology*
RA1247.C17	*CARBONIC OXIDE* **SEE** CARBON MONOXIDE / *toxicology*
QE671-3	*CARBONIFEROUS PERIOD* **SEE** GEOLOGY, STRATIGRAPHIC — CARBONIFEROUS
QE919	*CARBONIFEROUS PERIOD* **SEE** PALEOBOTANY — CARBONIFEROUS
QE729	*CARBONIFEROUS PERIOD* **SEE** PALEONTOLOGY — CARBONIFEROUS
TP156.C3	CARBONIZATION / *chemical technology*
TK7725	*CARBONS (ELECTRIC LIGHT)* **SEE** ELECTRIC LIGHT CARBONS / *manufacture*
TK4335	*CARBONS (ELECTRIC LIGHT)* **SEE** ELECTRIC LIGHT CARBONS / *use*
RL221	CARBUNCLE
TJ787	*CARBURETERS* **SEE** CARBURETORS
TJ787	CARBURETORS
TJ787	*CARBURETTORS* **SEE** CARBURETORS
RC261	*CARCINOMA* **SEE** CANCER
RC254-272	*CARCINOMA* **SEE** TUMORS
RD651-678	*CARCINOMA* **SEE** TUMORS
GV1233-1299	*CARD GAMES* **SEE** CARDS
M1985	*CARD GAMES* **SEE** MUSICAL CARD GAMES
GV1247	*CARD SHARPING* **SEE** CARDSHARPING
HF5736-5746	CARD SYSTEM IN BUSINESS
GV1549	CARD TRICKS
TT848	CARD WEAVING
QK495.Z	CARDAMOMS / *botany*
SB307.C3	CARDAMOMS / *culture*
RM666.C	CARDAMOMS / *therapeutics*
SD397.14	*CARDBOARD (TREE)* **SEE** ILOMBA
RC682	*CARDIAC ARREST* **SEE** HEART FAILURE
RC666-687	*CARDIAC DISEASES* **SEE** HEART — DISEASES
G108.C3	CARDINAL POINTS
BV4645	CARDINAL VIRTUES
QL696.P2	CARDINAL-BIRDS
Z7838.C	CARDINALS — BIO-BIBLIOGRAPHY
BX4663-5	CARDINALS — PORTRAITS
TS1487	CARDING-MACHINES
TS1485	CARDING
QA567	CARDIOD
RC683	CARDIOGRAPHY
RC666-701	CARDIOVASCULAR SYSTEM — DISEASES
RD598	CARDIOVASCULAR SYSTEM — SURGERY
QL835-841	CARDIOVASCULAR SYSTEM / *comparative anatomy*
QM178-197	CARDIOVASCULAR SYSTEM / *human anatomy*
SB351.C	CARDOON
GV1233-1299	CARDS
HF5851	*CARDS, ADVERTISING* **SEE** ADVERTISING CARDS
TT360	*CARDS, ADVERTISING* **SEE** ADVERTISING CARDS / *card and sign writing*
NC1860	*CARDS, GREETING* **SEE** GREETING CARDS / *art*
BJ2095.G7	*CARDS, GREETING* **SEE** GREETING CARDS / *etiquette*
BJ2081-8	*CARDS, VISITING* **SEE** VISITING-CARDS / *etiquette*
GV1549	*CARDS-TRICKS* **SEE** CARD TRICKS
GV1247	CARDSHARPING
BV4012.2	*CARE OF SOULS* **SEE** PASTORAL COUNSELING
BV4000-4396	*CARE OF SOULS* **SEE** PASTORAL THEOLOGY
PH501-9	*CARELIAN LANGUAGE* **SEE**. KARELIAN LANGUAGE
DP219.2	*CARGA DE ARMINON* **SEE** ARMINON, BATTLE OF 1837
VK235	*CARGO* **SEE** CARGO HANDLING

TL711.D7	*CARGO DROPPING (AEROPLANE)* **SEE** AIRDROP
UC330-335	*CARGO DROPPING (AEROPLANE)* **SEE** AIRDROP / military
VK235	CARGO HANDLING
TL685.7	*CARGO PLANES* **SEE** TRANSPORT PLANES
F2001	CARIB INDIANS
PM5756-9	CARIB LANGUAGE
PM5756-9	CARIBAN LANGUAGES
QL737.U5	CARIBOU
NC1300-1763	CARICATURE
NC1300-1763	CARICATURES AND CARTOONS
RK301-450	*CARIES, DENTAL* **SEE** TEETH — DISEASES
M172	CARILLON MUSIC
F2520.1.K	*CARIRI INDIANS* **SEE** KARIRI INDIANS / brazil
PM6286-9	*CARIRI LANGUAGE* **SEE** KARIRI LANGUAGE
E232	CARLETON'S INVASION, 1776
DC70-81	*CARLOVINGIANS* / france
DD129-134	*CARLOVINGIANS* / germany
DQ85-87	*CARLOVINGIANS* / switzerland
DB63 1699	CARLOWITZ, PEACE OF, 1699
BP195.K3	*CARMATHIANS* **SEE** KARMATHIANS
Z7840.C2	CARMELITES — BIO-BIBLIOGRAPHY
BX3201-3255	CARMELITES
BX4321-4	CARMELITES / women
PL4641-9	*CARNATACA LANGUAGE* **SEE** KANNADA LANGUAGE
SB413.C3	CARNATIONS
GV1796.C	CARNAVALITO (DANCE)
PT963.C3	CARNIVAL PLAYS / german literature
PQ4222.C4	CARNIVAL SONGS / italian literature
GT4180-4299	CARNIVAL
GV1851-5	*CARNIVALS (CIRCUS)* **SEE** AMUSEMENT PARKS
GV1835	*CARNIVALS (CIRCUS)* **SEE** AMUSEMENT PARKS
QL737.C2	CARNIVORA
QE882.C1-4	CARNIVORA, FOSSIL
QK917	*CARNIVOROUS PLANTS* **SEE** INSECTIVOROUS PLANTS
TN948.R3	CARNOTITE
DC70-81	*CAROLINGIANS* **SEE** CARLOVINGIANS / france
DD129-134	*CAROLINGIANS* **SEE** CARLOVINGIANS / germany
DQ85-87	*CAROLINGIANS* **SEE** CARLOVINGIANS / switzerland
QK898.C	*CAROTENE* **SEE** CAROTIN
QP671	*CAROTENOIDS* **SEE** CAROTINOIDS
RD598	CAROTID ARTERY — EXCISION
QM191	CAROTID ARTERY
QL835	CAROTID ARTERY
QM105	CAROTID CANAL
QL821	CAROTID CANAL
QM371	CAROTID GLAND / human anatomy
QP187	CAROTID GLAND / physiology
QK898.C	CAROTIN
QP671	CAROTINOIDS
QL638.C94	CARP
SH167.C3	CARP / culture
QK659	CARPEL
TH5619	CARPENTERS' SQUARE
TH5614-5615	CARPENTRY — ESTIMATES
TH5608	CARPENTRY — TABLES, CALCULATIONS, ETC.
TH5618	CARPENTRY — TOOLS
HD9773	CARPENTRY / economics
TH5601-5691	CARPENTRY / technology
HD9937	*CARPET AND RUG INDUSTRY* **SEE** RUG AND CARPET INDUSTRY
HD9937	*CARPET INDUSTRY* **SEE** RUG AND CARPET INDUSTRY
NK2775-2896	*CARPET MANUFACTURE* **SEE** CARPETS / art
TS1772-6	*CARPET MANUFACTURE* **SEE** CARPETS / technology
TP931.C2	CARPET-PRINTING
E668	*CARPETBAG RULE* **SEE** RECONSTRUCTION / u.s.
NK2790	CARPETS — PRIVATE COLLECTIONS
NK2775-2896	CARPETS / art
TS1772-6	CARPETS / technology
HF5686.C15	CARRIAGE AND WAGON MAKING — ACCOUNTING
TS2001-2035	CARRIAGE AND WAGON MAKING
TS2030-2032	CARRIAGE AND WAGON PAINTING
HD9999.C3	CARRIAGE INDUSTRY / economics
TS2001-2035	CARRIAGE INDUSTRY / technology
E99.T17	*CARRIER INDIANS* **SEE** TAKULLI INDIANS
PM2411	*CARRIER LANGUAGE* **SEE** TAKULLI LANGUAGE
SF469	*CARRIER PIGEONS* **SEE** HOMING PIGEONS / animal culture
UH90	*CARRIER PIGEONS* **SEE** HOMING PIGEONS / military art and science
TL725.8	*CARRIERS, AEROPLANE* **SEE** AEROPLANE CARRIERS / aeronautics
V895	*CARRIERS, AEROPLANE* **SEE** AEROPLANE CARRIERS / naval science
HE1831-2220	*CARRIERS-RATES* **SEE** TRANSPORTATION — RATES / railroads
HE593-601	*CARRIERS-RATES* **SEE** TRANSPORTATION — RATES / waterways
E159	*CARRIES* **SEE** PORTAGES / u.s.
SB608.C	CARROTS — DISEASES AND PESTS
SB211.C3	CARROTS
T55.3.L5	*CARRYING WEIGHTS* **SEE** LIFTING AND CARRYING
TL1-445	*CARS (AUTOMOBILES)* **SEE** AUTOMOBILES / history
HD9710	*CARS (AUTOMOBILES)* **SEE** AUTOMOBILES / industry and statistics
GV1021-1030	*CARS (AUTOMOBILES)* **SEE** AUTOMOBILES / sports and amusements
HE5601-5720	*CARS (AUTOMOBILES)* **SEE** AUTOMOBILES / transportation
TF371-497	*CARS AND CAR BUILDING* **SEE** RAILROADS — CARS
HE1830	*CARS AND CAR BUILDING* **SEE** RAILROADS — CARS / car service
TF600-606	*CARS AND CAR BUILDING* **SEE** RAILROADS — CARS / operation
UG446.5	*CARS, ARMORED (TANKS)* **SEE** TANKS (MILITARY SCIENCE)
TF371-497	*CARS, RAILROAD* **SEE** RAILROADS — CARS
HE1830	*CARS, RAILROAD* **SEE** RAILROADS — CARS / car service
TF600-606	*CARS, RAILROAD* **SEE** RAILROADS — CARS / operation
F2272	CARTAGENA, COLOMBIA — SIEGE, 1697
F2272.5	CARTAGENA, COLOMBIA — SIEGE, 1741
E611-616	*CARTEL FOR EXCHANGE OF PRISONERS, 1862-1864* **SEE** UNITED STATES — HISTORY — — CIVIL WAR — — — PRISONERS, EXCHANGE OF
HD2709-2930	*CARTELS* **SEE** TRUSTS, INDUSTRIAL
HD2801-2930	*CARTELS* **SEE** TRUSTS, INDUSTRIAL / other countries
HD2771-2798	*CARTELS* **SEE** TRUSTS, INDUSTRIAL / u.s.
DT168-9	*CARTHAGE* — HISTORY
BX3301-3355	CARTHUSIANS
QM567	CARTILAGE
GA473-1773	CARTOGRAPHERS / other countries
GA407	CARTOGRAPHERS / u.s.
GA23	CARTOGRAPHY — CONVERSION TABLES
GA101-1999	CARTOGRAPHY
GN476.5	CARTOGRAPHY, PRIMITIVE
HF5770	CARTONS / commerce
TS1200	CARTONS / manufacture
NC1300-1763	*CARTOONS* **SEE** CARICATURES AND CARTOONS
UF740-745	CARTRIDGES
RS165.C	CARVACROL
TX885	CARVING (MEAT, ETC.)
NA3683	CARYATIDS
QH605	*CARYOCINESIS* **SEE** KARYOKINESIS
D569.C	CARZANO, BATTLE OF, 1917
DT324	CASABLANCA MASSACRE, 1907
TK2797	CASCADE CONVERTERS
TJ267.C3	*CASCADE THEORY (DYNAMICS)* **SEE** CASCADES (FLUID DYNAMICS)
TJ267.C3	CASCADES (FLUID DYNAMICS)
RM663.C37	CASCARA
P253	*CASE* **SEE** GRAMMAR, COMPARATIVE AND GENERAL — CASE
P253	*CASE* **SEE** GRAMMAR, COMPARATIVE AND GENERAL — CASE
ND2490	CASEIN PAINTING
TP248.C4	CASEIN / chemical technology
SF253	CASEIN / chemistry of milk
TP986.C2	CASEIN / plastics
F2846	CASEROS, BATTLE OF, 1852
BX1757-9	*CASES OF CONSCIENCE* **SEE** CASUISTRY / catholic church
BJ1440-1448	*CASES OF CONSCIENCE* **SEE** CASUISTRY / ethics
HF5531	CASH REGISTERS
SB401	CASHEW NUT
PM6290.K3	*CASHINAUA LANGUAGE* **SEE** KASHINAUA LANGUAGE

PG7901-5	*CASHUBIAN LANGUAGE* **SEE** KASHUBIAN LANGUAGE
TS2301.U5	*CASKETS (COFFINS)* **SEE** COFFINS / manufacture
NK2725	*CASKETS* **SEE** CHESTS / art
TT197	*CASKETS* **SEE** CHESTS / cabinet-work
DP131.6	CASPE DECLARATION, 1412
SB211.C3	CASSAVA
DH801.F465	CASSEL, FRANCE, BATTLE OF, 1328
D278.C	CASSEL, FRANCE, BATTLE OF, 1677
TX693	CASSEROLE RECEIPTS
RS165.S4	CASSIA
QK495.C	CASSIA
TN793	CASSITERITE / metallurgy
TN470-479	CASSITERITE / tin ores
QL696.C3	CASSOWARIES
TP871	*CAST STONE* **SEE** STONE, CAST
QD133	CAST-IRON — ANALYSIS
TA475	CAST-IRON — TESTING
TA474-5	CAST-IRON / materials of engineering
TN710	CAST-IRON / metallurgy
MT720	CASTANETS
TL553.7	*CASTAWAYS* **SEE** SURVIVAL (AFTER AEROPLANE ACCIDENTS, SHIPWRECKS, ETC.) / aeronautics
BL1215.C3	CASTE — RELIGIOUS ASPECTS / hinduism
GN492.4	CASTE / anthropology
DS422.C3	CASTE / india
HT713-725	CASTE / social classes
RC778	*CASTELLANI'S BRONCHITIS* **SEE** BRONCHOPULMONARY SPIROCHAETOSIS
HV8626	*CASTIGATORY* **SEE** CUCKING STOOL
PC4001-4977	*CASTILIAN LANGUAGE* **SEE** SPANISH LANGUAGE
TS229-240	*CASTING* **SEE** FOUNDING
TS229-240	*CASTING* **SEE** IRON-FOUNDING
NB1190	*CASTING* **SEE** PLASTER CASTS
TP986.5	*CASTING* **SEE** PLASTICS — MOLDING
GV1469.C3	CASTLE-GAMMON (GAME)
NA7710-7786	CASTLES / architecture
DA660-664	CASTLES / england
DC20	CASTLES / france
DC801	CASTLES / france
DD20	CASTLES / germany
DG420	CASTLES / italy
DP22	CASTLES / spain
SB299.C3	*CASTOR SEED* **SEE** CASTOR-BEAN
SB299.C3	CASTOR-BEAN
SB299.C3	CASTOR-OIL PLANT
TP684.C3	CASTOR-OIL / chemical technology
RM666.C375	CASTOR-OIL / therapeutics
UC400-405	*CASTRAMETATION* **SEE** CAMPS (MILITARY)
U180-185	*CASTRAMETATION* **SEE** CAMPS (MILITARY)
UG365	*CASTRAMETATION* **SEE** CAMPS (MILITARY) / camp making
ML1460	CASTRATI / history of vocal technique
MT821	CASTRATI / voice culture
QP251-5	CASTRATION / physiology
HV4989	CASTRATION / social pathology
RD571	CASTRATION / surgery
SF889	CASTRATION / veterinary medicine
HD5855-6	CASUAL LABOR
HG9956-9970	*CASUALTY INSURANCE* **SEE** INSURANCE, CASUALTY
SD397.C	CASUARINA
BX1757-9	CASUISTRY / catholic church
BJ1440-1448	CASUISTRY / ethics
SF441-9	*CAT* **SEE** CATS
QL795.C	*CAT* **SEE** CATS / stories and anecdotes
QL737.C2	*CAT* **SEE** CATS / zoology
BL443.C3	*CAT-WORSHIP* **SEE** CATS (IN RELIGION, FOLK-LORE, ETC.) / religion
GR725	*CAT-WORSHIP* **SEE** CATS (IN RELIGION, FOLK-LORE, ETC.) / folk-lore
GN455.S9	*CAT'S CRADLE* **SEE** STRING-FIGURES / primitive
BX4929-4946	*CATABAPTISTS* **SEE** ANABAPTISTS
QH521	*CATABOLISM* **SEE** METABOLISM / biology
QH631	*CATABOLISM* **SEE** METABOLISM / cytology
QP171	*CATABOLISM* **SEE** METABOLISM / physiology
DG807.4	CATACOMBS / rome
PC3929	CATALAN BALLADS AND SONGS / collections
PC3913	CATALAN BALLADS AND SONGS / history
PC3915	CATALAN DRAMA
PC3929.5	CATALAN DRAMA
PC3801-3899	CATALAN LANGUAGE
PC3930.L4	CATALAN LETTERS
PC3901-3975	CATALAN LITERATURE
PN5311-5319	CATALAN NEWSPAPERS
PC3930.07	CATALAN ORATIONS
PN5311-5320	CATALAN PERIODICALS
PC3801-3899	CATALAN PHILOLOGY
PC3929	CATALAN POETRY
PC3913	CATALAN POETRY
QK896	CATALASE / botany
QP601	CATALASE / physiological chemistry
Z711.3	*CATALOG USE* **SEE** LIBRARY CATALOGS AND READERS
Z695.2	CATALOGING OF ARCHIVAL MATERIAL
Z695.64	CATALOGING OF AUDIO-VISUAL MATERIALS
Z695.72	CATALOGING OF BOOKS FOR THE BLIND
Z695.72	*CATALOGING OF BOOKS IN RAISED CHARACTERS* **SEE** CATALOGING OF BOOKS FOR THE BLIND
Z695.1.T3	CATALOGING OF CATHOLIC LITERATURE
Z695.1.C5	CATALOGING OF CHEMICAL LITERATURE
Z695	CATALOGING OF CHILDREN'S LITERATURE
Z695.1.07	CATALOGING OF CHINESE LITERATURE
Z695.8	*CATALOGING OF CORPORATE ENTRIES* **SEE** CORPORATE ENTRY (CATALOGING)
Z695.1.G7	*CATALOGING OF DOCUMENTS* **SEE** CATALOGING OF GOVERNMENT PUBLICATIONS
Z695.64	CATALOGING OF FILMSTRIPS
Z695.1.G7	CATALOGING OF GOVERNMENT PUBLICATIONS
Z695.3	CATALOGING OF INCUNABULA
Z695.1.L3	*CATALOGING OF LAW BOOKS* **SEE** CATALOGING OF LEGAL LITERATURE
Z695.1.L3	CATALOGING OF LEGAL LITERATURE
Z695.1.H6	CATALOGING OF LOCAL HISTORY
Z695.5	CATALOGING OF MANUSCRIPTS
Z695.6	CATALOGING OF MAPS
Z695.1.M48	CATALOGING OF MEDICAL LITERATURE
Z695.1.L6	CATALOGING OF MODERN LITERATURE
Z691.5.T3	CATALOGING OF MORMON LITERATURE
Z695.64	CATALOGING OF MOVING-PICTURES
ML111	CATALOGING OF MUSIC
Z695.1.07	CATALOGING OF ORIENTAL LITERATURE
Z695.7	*CATALOGING OF PERIODICALS* **SEE** CATALOGING OF SERIAL PUBLICATIONS
Z695.7	*CATALOGING OF PERIODICALS* **SEE** CATALOGING OF SERIAL PUBLICATIONS
Z695.1.P4	*CATALOGING OF PERSONAL NAMES* **SEE** NAMES, PERSONAL (CATALOGING)
Z695.715	*CATALOGING OF PHONOGRAPH RECORDS* **SEE** CATALOGING OF PHONORECORDS
Z695.715	CATALOGING OF PHONORECORDS
Z695.74	CATALOGING OF RARE BOOKS
Z695.7	CATALOGING OF SERIAL PUBLICATIONS
Z695.7	*CATALOGING OF SERIALS* **SEE** CATALOGING OF SERIAL PUBLICATIONS
Z695.7	*CATALOGING OF SERIALS* **SEE** CATALOGING OF SERIAL PUBLICATIONS
Z695.8	CATALOGING OF SOCIETY PUBLICATIONS
Z695.1.S3	CATALOGING OF TECHNICAL LITERATURE
Z695.1.T3	CATALOGING OF THE BIBLE
Z695	CATALOGING
Z695	CATALOGING, COOPERATIVE
Z695.87	CATALOGS — PRINTING
Z1036	CATALOGS, BOOKSELLERS'
Z999	CATALOGS, BOOKSELLERS' / second-hand books
HF5861-2	CATALOGS, COMMERCIAL
Z710	*CATALOGS, LIBRARY* **SEE** LIBRARY CATALOGS
Z695	CATALOGS, SHEAF
QB6	*CATALOGS, STAR* **SEE** STARS — CATALOGS
Z695	CATALOGS, SUBJECT
Z695.83	CATALOGS, UNION
Z1011-1012	*CATALOGS, UNIVERSAL* **SEE** BIBLIOGRAPHY — UNIVERSAL CATALOGS
Z695	*CATALOGUING* **SEE** CATALOGING
QK495.C35	CATALPA / botany
SD397.C35	CATALPA / forestry
QD501	CATALYSIS
QD501	CATALYSTS
TP159.C3	CATALYSTS / technology
QD501	*CATALYTIC AGENTS* **SEE** CATALYSTS

VM311.C3	CATAMARANS
QL737.C2	*CATAMOUNTS* **SEE** PUMAS
U875	CATAPULT
TL732	CATAPULTS (AERONAUTICS)
RE451	CATARACT
E356.L9	*CATARACT, BATTLE OF THE, 1814* **SEE** LUNDY'S LANE, BATTLE OF, 1814
GB1401-1597	*CATARACTS* **SEE** WATERFALLS
RX326.C2	CATARRH — HOMEOPATHIC TREATMENT
RC741	CATARRH
RC743	*CATARRH, AUTUMNAL* **SEE** HAY-FEVER
HD301-1130	*CATASTRAL SURVEYS* **SEE** REAL PROPERTY / *other countries*
HD251-279	*CATASTRAL SURVEYS* **SEE** REAL PROPERTY / *u.s.*
HD251-279	*CATASTRAL SURVEYS* **SEE** REAL PROPERTY / *u.s.*
QE506	CATASTROPHES (GEOLOGY)
BD375	CATASTROPHICAL, THE
E99.C24	CATAWBA INDIANS
PM751	CATAWBA LANGUAGE
GV872	CATCHING (BASEBALL)
DC114	CATEAU-CAMBRESIS, TREATY OF, 1559
BV4224-4230	*CATECHETICAL ILLUSTRATIONS* **SEE** HOMILETICAL ILLUSTRATIONS
BX1939.C3	CATECHETICS (CANON LAW)
BV1474-5	CATECHETICS
BX1968	CATECHETICS / *catholic church*
BX8070	CATECHETICS / *lutheran church*
BT1030-1039	CATECHISMS / *general*
BX	CATECHISMS / *particular denominations*
RS165.C	CATECHU / *materia medica*
BC172	CATEGORIES (PHILOSOPHY) / *logic*
BD331-346	CATEGORIES (PHILOSOPHY) / *ontology*
BS	CATENAE / *bible commentaries*
BR63	CATENAE / *patristics*
QA835	CATENARY
RA601	CATERERS AND CATERING — HYGIENIC ASPECTS
TX901-921	CATERERS AND CATERING
QL638.S6	CATFISHES
RD73.S8	CATGUT SUTURES
BX4873-4893	*CATHARI* **SEE** ALBIGENSES
BX4873-4893	*CATHARISTS* **SEE** ALBIGENSES
RM357	*CATHARTICS* **SEE** PURGATIVES
NA4830	CATHEDRALS / *architecture*
NA5201-6113	CATHEDRALS / *architecture*
RC923	CATHETERS
QC102	CATHETOMETERS
PM753	CATHLAMET DIALECT
TK7872	CATHODE RAY OSCILLOGRAPH / *electronics*
TK6565.C4	CATHODE RAY OSCILLOGRAPH / *radio*
TK6655.P5	*CATHODE RAY PICTURE TUBES* **SEE** TELEVISION PICTURE TUBES
TK7895.C3	CATHODE RAY TUBE MEMORY SYSTEMS
QC544.C3	CATHODE RAY TUBES
QC711	CATHODE RAYS
BX2348	CATHOLIC ACTION
BS453	*CATHOLIC BIBLES* **SEE** BIBLE — VERSIONS, CATHOLIC
BX1750-1755	CATHOLIC CHURCH — APOLOGETIC WORKS
BX1780	CATHOLIC CHURCH — APOLOGETIC WORKS
Z7837-7840	CATHOLIC CHURCH — BIBLIOGRAPHY
BX4650-4705	CATHOLIC CHURCH — BIOGRAPHY
BX1958-1968	CATHOLIC CHURCH — CATECHISMS AND CREEDS
BX1969	CATHOLIC CHURCH — CEREMONIES AND PRACTICES
HV530	CATHOLIC CHURCH — CHARITIES
BX1912	CATHOLIC CHURCH — CLERGY
BX890	CATHOLIC CHURCH — COLLECTED WORKS
BX841	CATHOLIC CHURCH — DICTIONARIES
BX841	CATHOLIC CHURCH — DICTIONARIES, JUVENILE
BX1417-1691	CATHOLIC CHURCH — DIOCESES
JX1801-2	CATHOLIC CHURCH — DIPLOMATIC SERVICE
BX845	CATHOLIC CHURCH — DIRECTORIES
BX1749-1755	CATHOLIC CHURCH — DOCTRINAL AND CONTROVERSIAL WORKS
LC461-510	CATHOLIC CHURCH — EDUCATION
LC107-120	CATHOLIC CHURCH — EDUCATION / *church and school*
LC493	CATHOLIC CHURCH — EDUCATION / *jesuit*
LB375	CATHOLIC CHURCH — EDUCATION / *jesuit*
BX840	CATHOLIC CHURCH — EXHIBITIONS AND MUSEUMS
BX1950	CATHOLIC CHURCH — FINANCE
BX1800-1915	CATHOLIC CHURCH — GOVERNMENT
BX940-1749	CATHOLIC CHURCH — HISTORY
BV360	CATHOLIC CHURCH — HYMNS
BV467-510	CATHOLIC CHURCH — HYMNS
BT88	CATHOLIC CHURCH — INFALLIBILITY
BV2130-2300	CATHOLIC CHURCH — MISSIONS
BX1753	CATHOLIC CHURCH — NAME
BX4710-4715	CATHOLIC CHURCH — ORIENTAL RITES
BX874	CATHOLIC CHURCH — PASTORAL LETTERS AND CHARGES
BX801-6	CATHOLIC CHURCH — PERIODICALS
BX2000-2198	CATHOLIC CHURCH — PRAYER-BOOKS AND DEVOTIONS
BX1790-1793	CATHOLIC CHURCH — RELATIONS (DIPLOMATIC)
BX850-1691	CATHOLIC CHURCH — RELATIONS (DIPLOMATIC) / *history*
JX1552	CATHOLIC CHURCH — RELATIONS (DIPLOMATIC) / *international law*
BX1908	CATHOLIC CHURCH — RELATIONS (DIPLOMATIC) / *nuncios*
BX1781-8	CATHOLIC CHURCH — RELATIONS
BX1756	CATHOLIC CHURCH — SERMONS
BX808-817	CATHOLIC CHURCH — SOCIETIES, ETC.
BX845	CATHOLIC CHURCH — YEARBOOKS
HS495	*CATHOLIC CHURCH AND FREEMASONRY* **SEE** FREEMASONS AND CATHOLIC CHURCH
HD6338	*CATHOLIC CHURCH AND LABOR* **SEE** CHURCH AND LABOR
BT755	*CATHOLIC CHURCH AND SALVATION* **SEE** SALVATION OUTSIDE THE CATHOLIC CHURCH
HS614	*CATHOLIC CHURCH AND SECRET SOCIETIES* **SEE** SECRET SOCIETIES AND CATHOLIC CHURCH
HX536	*CATHOLIC CHURCH AND SOCIALISM* **SEE** SOCIALISM AND CATHOLIC CHURCH
BX1790-1793	*CATHOLIC CHURCH AND STATE* **SEE** CHURCH AND STATE — CATHOLIC CHURCH
BX808-817	*CATHOLIC CHURCH IN THE U.S.-SOCIETIES, ETC.* **SEE** CATHOLIC CHURCH — SOCIETIES, ETC.
BX1971	CATHOLIC CHURCH. — RUBRICS
BX801-4715	CATHOLIC CHURCH
BX1417-1691	*CATHOLIC CHURCH-ARCHDIOCESES* **SEE** CATHOLIC CHURCH — DIOCESES
BV775	*CATHOLIC CHURCH-BENEFICES* **SEE** BENEFICES, ECCLESIASTICAL
BX1955	*CATHOLIC CHURCH-BENEFICES* **SEE** BENEFICES, ECCLESIASTICAL / *catholic church*
BX4668	*CATHOLIC CHURCH-CONVERTS* **SEE** CONVERTS, CATHOLIC
JX1552	*CATHOLIC CHURCH-DIPLOMATIC RELATIONS* **SEE** CATHOLIC CHURCH — RELATIONS (DIPLOMATIC) / *international law*
BX1908	*CATHOLIC CHURCH-DIPLOMATIC RELATIONS* **SEE** CATHOLIC CHURCH — RELATIONS (DIPLOMATIC) / *nuncios*
BX1790-1793	*CATHOLIC CHURCH-DIPLOMATIC RELATIONS* **SEE** CATHOLIC CHURCH — RELATIONS (DIPLOMATIC)
BX850-1691	*CATHOLIC CHURCH-DIPLOMATIC RELATIONS* **SEE** CATHOLIC CHURCH — RELATIONS (DIPLOMATIC) / *history*
BX841	*CATHOLIC CHURCH-ENCYCLOPEDIAS* **SEE** CATHOLIC CHURCH — DICTIONARIES
JX1552	*CATHOLIC CHURCH-FOREIGN RELATIONS* **SEE** CATHOLIC CHURCH — RELATIONS (DIPLOMATIC) / *international law*
BX850-1691	*CATHOLIC CHURCH-FOREIGN RELATIONS* **SEE** CATHOLIC CHURCH — RELATIONS (DIPLOMATIC) / *history*
BX1790-1793	*CATHOLIC CHURCH-FOREIGN RELATIONS* **SEE** CATHOLIC CHURCH — RELATIONS (DIPLOMATIC)
BX1908	*CATHOLIC CHURCH-FOREIGN RELATIONS* **SEE** CATHOLIC CHURCH — RELATIONS (DIPLOMATIC) / *nuncios*
BR160-240	*CATHOLIC CHURCH-HISTORY-EARLY PERIOD* **SEE** CHURCH HISTORY — PRIMITIVE AND EARLY CHURCH
BR160-270	*CATHOLIC CHURCH-HISTORY-MIDDLE AGES* **SEE** CHURCH HISTORY — MIDDLE AGES
BX1970	*CATHOLIC CHURCH-LITURGICAL MOVEMENT* **SEE** LITURGICAL MOVEMENT — CATHOLIC CHURCH
BX2250	*CATHOLIC CHURCH-MARRIAGE* **SEE** MARRIAGE — CATHOLIC CHURCH

BX840	*CATHOLIC CHURCH-MUSEUMS* **SEE** CATHOLIC CHURCH — EXHIBITIONS AND MUSEUMS
CR5547-5577	*CATHOLIC CHURCH-NOBILITY* **SEE** NOBILITY, PAPAL / etc.
BX1790-1793	*CATHOLIC CHURCH-RELATION TO THE STATE* **SEE** CHURCH AND STATE — CATHOLIC CHURCH
BX1781-8	*CATHOLIC CHURCH-RELATIONS (ECCLESIASTICAL)* **SEE** CATHOLIC CHURCH — RELATIONS
BX2390.Y7	*CATHOLIC CHURCH-WORK WITH YOUTH* **SEE** CHURCH WORK WITH YOUTH — CATHOLIC CHURCH
BX2390.Y7	*CATHOLIC CHURCH-YOUTH, WORK WITH* **SEE** CHURCH WORK WITH YOUTH — CATHOLIC CHURCH
NA4820	*CATHOLIC CHURCHES* **SEE** CHURCHES, CATHOLIC
NA5200-6113	*CATHOLIC CHURCHES* **SEE** CHURCHES, CATHOLIC / architecture
BX1760-1779	CATHOLIC CHURCH — DOCTRINAL AND CONTROVERSIAL WORKS — — PROTESTANT AUTHORS
BX1779	CATHOLIC CHURCH — DOCTRINAL AND CONTROVERSIAL WORKS — — DEBATES, ETC.
BX1780	CATHOLIC CHURCH — DOCTRINAL AND CONTROVERSIAL WORKS — — CATHOLIC AUTHORS
BX1749-1755	CATHOLIC CHURCH — DOCTRINAL AND CONTROVERSIAL WORKS — — CATHOLIC AUTHORS
BX938	CATHOLIC CHURCH — HISTORY — — HISTORIOGRAPHY
BX948	CATHOLIC CHURCH — HISTORY — — JUVENILE LITERATURE
BX850-873	CATHOLIC CHURCH — HISTORY — — SOURCES
BV2160	CATHOLIC CHURCH — MISSIONS — — CONGRESSES
BX324.3	CATHOLIC CHURCH — RELATIONS — — ORTHODOX EASTERN CHURCH
JX1552	CATHOLIC CHURCH — RELATIONS (DIPLOMATIC) — — TREATIES / international law
BX850-1691	CATHOLIC CHURCH — RELATIONS (DIPLOMATIC) — — TREATIES
BX4668	*CATHOLIC CONVERTS* **SEE** CONVERTS, CATHOLIC
BX1492	CATHOLIC EMANCIPATION
DA950.3	CATHOLIC EMANCIPATION / act
BX938-9	CATHOLIC HISTORIANS
PN4888.R4	*CATHOLIC JOURNALISM* **SEE** JOURNALISM, RELIGIOUS
BX961.I5	CATHOLIC LEARNING AND SCHOLARSHIP
Z695.1.T3	*CATHOLIC LITERATURE-CATALOGING* **SEE** CATALOGING OF CATHOLIC LITERATURE
BX5121	*CATHOLIC MOVEMENT (ANGLICAN COMMUNION)* **SEE** ANGLO-CATHOLICISM
DA499	*CATHOLIC NONJURORS, ENGLISH* **SEE** NONJURORS, ENGLISH CATHOLIC / 18th century
BX801-6	*CATHOLIC PERIODICALS* **SEE** CATHOLIC CHURCH — PERIODICALS
BX808-817	*CATHOLIC SOCIETIES* **SEE** CATHOLIC CHURCH — SOCIETIES, ETC.
BX8-9	*CATHOLICISM* **SEE** CATHOLICITY
BX4751-4793	*CATHOLICISM, OLD* **SEE** OLD CATHOLICISM
BX8-9	CATHOLICITY
BX961.I5	CATHOLICS — INTELLECTUAL LIFE
BX1407.I5	CATHOLICS — INTELLECTUAL LIFE / u.s.
BX1407.N4	*CATHOLICS, COLORED* **SEE** CATHOLICS, NEGRO / u.s.
BX1407.N4	CATHOLICS, NEGRO / u.s.
BX961.I5	*CATHOLICS-LEARNING AND SCHOLARSHIP* **SEE** CATHOLIC LEARNING AND SCHOLARSHIP
BX808-817	*CATHOLICS-SOCIETIES, ETC.* **SEE** CATHOLIC CHURCH — SOCIETIES, ETC.
PM5778	CATIO LANGUAGE
QD553	CATIONS
BF1331	CATOPTROMANCY
F2520.1.C	CATOQUINA INDIANS
SF985	CATS — DISEASES
PN6071.C3	CATS — LEGENDS AND STORIES / general literature
PN6110.C3	CATS — LEGENDS AND STORIES / general literature
PZ10.3	CATS — LEGENDS AND STORIES / juvenile literature
QL795.C2	CATS — LEGENDS AND STORIES / zoology
N7660	CATS — PICTURES, ILLUSTRATIONS, ETC.
SF446	CATS — PICTURES, ILLUSTRATIONS, ETC.
SF443	CATS — STUD-BOOKS
GR725	CATS (IN RELIGION, FOLK-LORE, ETC.)`/ folk-lore
BL443.C3	CATS (IN RELIGION, FOLK-LORE, ETC.) / religion
SF441-9	CATS
QL795.C	CATS / stories and anecdotes
QL737.C2	CATS / zoology
QE882.C1	CATS, FOSSIL
SF961-7	CATTLE — DISEASES
SF192-3	CATTLE — HERD-BOOKS
HE2321.L7	CATTLE — TRANSPORTATION / railroads
HE595.L7	CATTLE — TRANSPORTATION / ships
SF101-3	CATTLE BRANDS
SF191.5	CATTLE BREEDERS — DIRECTORIES
SF191.5	*CATTLE BREEDERS' DIRECTORIES* **SEE** CATTLE BREEDERS — DIRECTORIES
SF191	CATTLE BREEDERS' SOCIETIES
SF191-9	CATTLE BREEDS
QL537.O3	*CATTLE GRUBS* **SEE** WARBLE-FLIES
SF967.W3	*CATTLE GRUBS* **SEE** WARBLE-FLIES / cattle pests
HG9968.L5-8	*CATTLE INSURANCE* **SEE** INSURANCE, AGRICULTURAL — LIVE STOCK
TS1970-1971	*CATTLE MARKETS* **SEE** STOCK-YARDS
HD9410-9441	*CATTLE MARKETS* **SEE** STOCK-YARDS / economics
SF966	*CATTLE PLAGUE (RINDERPEST)* **SEE** RINDERPEST
SF85	*CATTLE RANGES* **SEE** STOCK-RANGES
HV6646-6665	CATTLE STEALING
HF5716.C2	CATTLE TRADE — TABLES AND READY-RECKONERS
HD9433	CATTLE TRADE
SF805	*CATTLE-TICK FEVER* **SEE** TEXAS FEVER
SF593.T5	CATTLE-TICK
SF191-219	CATTLE
SF207	*CATTLE, BEEF* **SEE** BEEF CATTLE
SF191-9	*CATTLE-BREEDS* **SEE** CATTLE BREEDS
SF912	*CATTLE-DEHORNING* **SEE** DEHORNING
HD9433	*CATTLE-MARKETING* **SEE** CATTLE TRADE
F2520.1.C	*CATUQUINARU INDIANS* **SEE** CATOQUINA INDIANS
PK9001-9201	CAUCASIAN LANGUAGES
PK9040	CAUCASIAN LITERATURE / collections
PK9030	CAUCASIAN LITERATURE / history
JF2085	CAUCUS
NK4399.C	CAUGHLEY PORCELAIN
E99.C	CAUGHNAWAGA INDIANS
SB333	CAULIFLOWER / culture
E356.C3	CAULK'S FIELD, BATTLE OF, 1814
BD530-595	*CAUSALITY* **SEE** CAUSATION
BD530-595	CAUSATION
BD530-595	*CAUSE AND EFFECT* **SEE** CAUSATION
QE399.8	CAUSTOBIOLITHS
UE460	CAVALRY — REMOUNTS
UE157-302	CAVALRY DRILL AND TACTICS
UE490	CAVALRY PIONEER TROOPS
UE	CAVALRY
NA8455	CAVE ARCHITECTURE
NA4910	CAVE CHURCHES
NA5201-6113	CAVE CHURCHES
QL117	CAVE FAUNA
QK938.C3	CAVE FLORA
NA4640-4641	CAVE TEMPLES
N5310	CAVE-DRAWINGS
GN783-4	CAVE-DWELLERS
GN783-4	CAVE-DWELLINGS
RF421	CAVERNOUS SINUS / diseases
QM505	CAVERNOUS SINUS / human anatomy
GB601-8	*CAVERNS* **SEE** CAVES / physical geography
GN783-4	*CAVERNS* **SEE** CAVES / prehistoric archaeology
GR665	CAVES (IN RELIGION, FOLK-LORE, ETC.)
GB601-8	CAVES / physical geography
GN783-4	CAVES / prehistoric archaeology
PM7088	*CAVINA LANGUAGE* **SEE** TACANAN LANGUAGE
PM7088	*CAVINENA LANGUAGE* **SEE** TACANAN LANGUAGE
E717.7	*CAVITE, BATTLE OF, 1898* **SEE** MANILA BAY, BATTLE OF, 1898
DS486.C3	CAWNPORE — RIOTS, 1931
DS478	CAWNPORE — SIEGE, 1857
PM6290.K3	*CAXINAUA LANGUAGE* **SEE** KASHINAUA LANGUAGE
GN440.2	*CAYAKS* **SEE** CANOES AND CANOEING / ethnology
GV781-5	*CAYAKS* **SEE** CANOES AND CANOEING / sport
F3722.1.C3	CAYAPA INDIANS
F2520.1.C3	CAYAPO INDIANS
PM5791	CAYAPO LANGUAGE
F2684	*CAYBATE, BATTLE OF, 1756* **SEE** CAIBATE, BATTLE OF, 1756
F2230.2.C	*CAYUA INDIANS* **SEE** CAINGUA INDIANS

E99.C3	CAYUGA INDIANS
E99.C	CAYUSE INDIANS
F1655	*CEBOYNAS* **SEE** LUCAYAN INDIANS
PL5649	CEBU DIALECT
PL5649	CEBU LITERATURE
PL5649	*CEBUANO (BISAYA DIALECT)* **SEE** CEBU DIALECT
SB767	*CECIDOLOGY* **SEE** GALLS (BOTANY)
E477.33	CEDAR CREEK, BATTLE OF, 1864
E473.76	CEDAR MOUNTAIN, BATTLE OF, 1862
SD397.C4	CEDAR / *forestry*
PM1058	*CEGIHA LANGUAGE* **SEE** DHEGIHA LANGUAGE
NA2950	CEILINGS / *architecture*
TH2531	CEILINGS / *building*
NK2119	CEILINGS / *decoration*
QC923	CEILOMETER
F1391.C3	CELAYA, BATTLE OF, 1915
PM4461	*CELDAL LANGUAGE* **SEE** TZELTAL LANGUAGE
SB351.C	*CELERY CABBAGE* **SEE** CHINESE CABBAGE
SB335	CELERY / *culture*
M284.C4	CELESTA AND HARPSICHORD MUSIC
M285.C4	CELESTA AND HARPSICHORD MUSIC
M298	*CELESTA AND PERCUSSION MUSIC* **SEE** PERCUSSION AND CELESTA MUSIC
M298	*CELESTA AND PERCUSSION MUSIC* **SEE** PERCUSSION AND CELESTA MUSIC
M20-32	CELESTA MUSIC
QB351-421	*CELESTIAL MECHANICS* **SEE** MECHANICS, CELESTIAL
HQ800	CELIBACY
BV4390	CELIBACY / *clergy*
QH605	CELL DIVISION (BIOLOGY)
QH595	CELL NUCLEI
QH595	*CELL NUCLEUS* **SEE** CELL NUCLEI
QC603-5	*CELL, VOLTAIC* **SEE** ELECTRIC BATTERIES
DC132	CELLAMARE CONSPIRACY, 1718
ML910-915	*CELLO* **SEE** VIOLONCELLO
TP986.C4	CELLOPHANE
QH581-671	CELLS
RB25	*CELLULAR PATHOLOGY* **SEE** PATHOLOGY, CELLULAR
RM287	CELLULAR THERAPY
QM563	*CELLULAR TISSUE* **SEE** CONNECTIVE TISSUES
TP986.C5	CELLULOID
QR160	CELLULOSE — MICROBIOLOGY
QR160	CELLULOSE / *bacteriology*
QK898.C35	CELLULOSE / *botany*
QD321	CELLULOSE / *chemistry*
TS1145	CELLULOSE / *technology*
DP95	CELTIBERI
CJ3194	CELTIBERIAN ALPHABET
CN	CELTIBERIAN ALPHABET
DP95	*CELTIBERIANS* **SEE** CELTIBERI
BR748-9	CELTIC CHURCH
BR794	CELTIC CHURCH
PB1001-1095	CELTIC LANGUAGES
PB1096-1100	CELTIC LITERATURE / *celtic languages*
PR8490-8499	CELTIC LITERATURE / *english language*
PB1001-1095	CELTIC PHILOLOGY
PR8496	CELTIC POETRY (ENGLISH)
PR8491	CELTIC POETRY (ENGLISH)
PB	CELTIC POETRY
D70	CELTS
GN549.C3	CELTS
DA140-143	CELTS / *england*
DC62-63	CELTS / *france*
ML1015-1018	*CEMBALO* **SEE** DULCIMER
ML650-697	*CEMBALO* **SEE** HARPSICHORD / *history and construction*
TA435	CEMENT — TESTING
TP881	CEMENT CLINKERS
TA446	CEMENT GUN
TP875-885	CEMENT INDUSTRIES
TP881	CEMENT KILNS
TP885.P5	CEMENT PIPE AND TILE
TH4541	CEMENT PLANTS — DESIGN AND CONSTRUCTION
TH1461-1501	CEMENT / *building*
HD9622	CEMENT / *economics*
TA680-683	CEMENT / *engineering*
TA434-5	CEMENT / *etc.*
TP875-885	CEMENT / *manufacture*
TN945	CEMENT / *mineral resources*
TP884.M2	*CEMENT, MAGNESIA* **SEE** MAGNESIA CEMENT

TN734	CEMENTATION (METALLURGY)
TN756	CEMENTITE
TP967-8	CEMENTS, ADHESIVE
BV880	CEMETERIES — CONSECRATION
RA626-630	CEMETERIES
GT3320	CEMETERIES / *manners and customs*
BV823-8	*CENA, ULTIMA* **SEE** LORD'S SUPPER
BX2215	*CENA, ULTIMA* **SEE** LORD'S SUPPER / *catholic church*
BX5149.C5	*CENA, ULTIMA* **SEE** LORD'S SUPPER / *church of england*
BV823-8	*CENACOLO* **SEE** LORD'S SUPPER
BX2215	*CENACOLO* **SEE** LORD'S SUPPER / *catholic church*
BX5149.C5	*CENACOLO* **SEE** LORD'S SUPPER / *church of england*
QE391.C	CENOSITE
QE690-699	*CENOZOIC PERIOD* **SEE** GEOLOGY, STRATIGRAPHIC — CENOZOIC
QE925-931	*CENOZOIC PERIOD* **SEE** PALEOBOTANY — CENOZOIC
QE735-741	*CENOZOIC PERIOD* **SEE** PALEONTOLOGY — CENOZOIC
BV196.C	CENSERS
DG83.5.C4	CENSORS, ROMAN
Z657-9	*CENSORSHIP OF THE PRESS* **SEE** LIBERTY OF THE PRESS
PN4735-4748	*CENSORSHIP OF THE PRESS* **SEE** PRESS LAW
PN2042-5	*CENSORSHIP OF THE STAGE* **SEE** THEATER — CENSORSHIP
BX1939.C5	CENSURES, ECCLESIASTICAL
HA175-4010	CENSUS / *by country*
HA37	CENSUS / *organization*
LC130	*CENSUS, SCHOOL* **SEE** SCHOOL CENSUS
CJ1836	CENT / *u.s.*
BL820.C	CENTAURS
QA839	*CENTER OF GRAVITY* **SEE** CENTER OF MASS
QA839	CENTER OF MASS
TH5591	CENTERING OF ARCHES
QL449	CENTIPEDES
PN1475	CENTOS
F1436-8	CENTRAL AMERICA — HISTORY
PQ7471-7539	CENTRAL AMERICAN LITERATURE
D378	*CENTRAL ASIAN QUESTION* **SEE** EASTERN QUESTION (CENTRAL ASIA)
TH7641	*CENTRAL HEATING PLANTS* **SEE** HEATING FROM CENTRAL STATIONS
TH7641	*CENTRAL STATION HEATING* **SEE** HEATING FROM CENTRAL STATIONS
Z678	*CENTRALIZATION OF LIBRARIES* **SEE** LIBRARIES — CENTRALIZATION
Z678	*CENTRALIZATION OF LIBRARIES* **SEE** LIBRARIES — CENTRALIZATION
LB2861	*CENTRALIZATION OF SCHOOLS* **SEE** SCHOOLS — CENTRALIZATION / *rural*
TF639	*CENTRALIZED TRAFFIC CONTROL (RAILROADS)* **SEE** RAILROADS — SIGNALING — — CENTRALIZED TRAFFIC CONTROL
TJ990-992	*CENTRIFUGAL COMPRESSORS* **SEE** COMPRESSORS
QC73	CENTRIFUGAL FORCE
TJ919	CENTRIFUGAL PUMPS
TJ1055	*CENTRIFUGAL REGULATORS* **SEE** GOVERNORS (MACHINERY)
QD54.C4	CENTRIFUGES / *chemistry*
QH597	CENTROSOMES
F2861	CEPEDA, BATTLE OF, 1859
RD661	CEPHALAEMATOMA
QP801.C	CEPHALIN
QL430.2	CEPHALOPODA
QE806-7	CEPHALOPODA, FOSSIL
QB837	CEPHEIDS
TP815	CERAMICS — DRYING
RK655	*CERAMICS, DENTAL* **SEE** DENTISTRY — CERAMICS
DS451	*CERAS* **SEE** CHERAS
GV1017.C4	CERCLE (GAME)
SB189-191	*CEREALS* **SEE** GRAIN / *culture*
TX557	CEREALS AS FOOD
TX393	CEREALS AS FOOD
TX395	CEREALS, PREPARED
TX557	CEREALS, PREPARED
RC394.A	CEREBELLUM — ABSCESS
QM455	CEREBELLUM
QP379	CEREBELLUM
QL937	CEREBELLUM

RC394.C7	*CEREBRAL CONCUSSION* **SEE** BRAIN — CONCUSSION
RC394.A7	*CEREBRAL HEMORRHAGE* **SEE** APOPLEXY
QP385	*CEREBRAL LOCALIZATION* **SEE** BRAIN — LOCALIZATION OF FUNCTIONS
RC388	CEREBRAL PALSY
RC388	*CEREBRAL PARALYSIS* **SEE** CEREBRAL PALSY
QP801.C4	CEREBRIN
QP375	*CEREBRORACHIDIAN FLUID* **SEE** CEREBROSPINAL FLUID
RC124	*CEREBROSPINAL FEVER* **SEE** MENINGITIS, CEREBROSPINAL
QP375	CEREBROSPINAL FLUID
RC124	*CEREBROSPINAL MENINGITIS* **SEE** MENINGITIS, CEREBROSPINAL
BJ1801-2193	*CEREMONIES* **SEE** ETIQUETTE
GT	*CEREMONIES* **SEE** MANNERS AND CUSTOMS
BV170-199	*CEREMONIES* **SEE** RITES AND CEREMONIES / christian
BL600-619	*CEREMONIES* **SEE** RITES AND CEREMONIES / comparative religion
GT	*CEREMONIES* **SEE** RITES AND CEREMONIES / manners and customs
GN473	*CEREMONIES* **SEE** RITES AND CEREMONIES / primitive religion
TP695	CERESIN
TN857	CERESIN
F1221.S43	*CERI INDIANS* **SEE** SERI INDIANS
QL377.C7	CERIANTHIDEA
QD172.R2	CERIUM GROUP
QD181.C4	CERIUM
NK9580	*CEROPLASTIC* **SEE** WAX-MODELING
F1234	*CERRO DE LA BUFA, BATTLE OF, 1872* **SEE** ZACATECAS, BATTLE OF, 1872
BD215	*CERTAINTY* **SEE** BELIEF AND DOUBT / philosophy
BF773	*CERTAINTY* **SEE** BELIEF AND DOUBT / psychology
QA273-7	*CERTAINTY* **SEE** PROBABILITIES
HG8781-2	*CERTAINTY* **SEE** PROBABILITIES / life insurance
BC141	*CERTAINTY* **SEE** PROBABILITIES / logic
BT50	*CERTAINTY* **SEE** TRUTH / doctrinal theology
BC171	*CERTAINTY* **SEE** TRUTH / logic
BD150-171	*CERTAINTY* **SEE** TRUTH / metaphysics
QL696.P2	*CERTHIIDAE* **SEE** CREEPERS
QL696.P2	*CERTHIOMORPHAE* **SEE** CREEPERS
QL696.P2	*CERTHIOMORPHAE* **SEE** NUTHATCHES
HJ6617	CERTIFICATES OF ORIGIN
RA405	*CERTIFICATION OF DEATH* **SEE** DEATH — PROOF AND CERTIFICATION / state medicine
Z677	*CERTIFICATION OF LIBRARIANS* **SEE** LIBRARIANS — CERTIFICATION
LB1771	*CERTIFICATION OF TEACHERS* **SEE** TEACHERS — CERTIFICATION
BT50	*CERTITUDE* **SEE** TRUTH / doctrinal theology
BC171	*CERTITUDE* **SEE** TRUTH / logic
BD150-171	*CERTITUDE* **SEE** TRUTH / metaphysics
TP918.C	CERULEIN
TN450-459	CERUSSITE / lead ores
QE391.C	CERUSSITE / mineralogy
QL821	*CERVICAL VERTEBRAE* **SEE** VERTEBRAE, CERVICAL
QM111	*CERVICAL VERTEBRAE* **SEE** VERTEBRAE, CERVICAL
QL737.U5	*CERVIDAE* **SEE** DEER
RG761	CESAREAN SECTION
PM8125	CESGES DE DAMIS (ARTIFICIAL LANGUAGE)
QD181.C8	CESIUM / chemistry
DR553	CESME, BATTLE OF, 1770
HG3760-3773	*CESSIO BONORUM* **SEE** BANKRUPTCY
TD775	CESSPOOLS
QL391.C4	CESTODA / zoology
DE61.C35	CESTUS
QL737.C4	CETACEA
QE882.C5	CETACEA, FOSSIL
QL737.C4	*CETE* **SEE** CETACEA
QL737.C4	*CETOMORPHA* **SEE** CETACEA
ML1015-1018	*CETRA* **SEE** ENGLISH GUITAR
PL8110.C5	*CEWA DIALECT* **SEE** CHEWA DIALECT
DS918.2.C4	CH'ONGCH'ON-GANG, BATTLE OF, 1950
DS731.C	CH'IANG PEOPLE
ML1015-1018	CH'IN (MUSICAL INSTRUMENT)
GT2910	*CHA-NO-YU* **SEE** JAPANESE TEA CEREMONY

DA346.C	CHAAMBA
PM8128	CHABE (ARTIFICIAL LANGUAGE)
F3094	CHACABUCO, BATTLE OF, 1817
GV1796.C	CHACARERA (DANCE)
F2688.5	*CHACO BOREAL WAR, 1932-1935* **SEE** CHACO WAR, 1932-1935
F2688.5	*CHACO DISPUTE* **SEE** CHACO WAR, 1932-1935
F2688.5	CHACO WAR, 1932-1935
M555-7	CHACONNES (BASSOON, CLARINET, FLUTE, HORN, OBOE)
M415-417	CHACONNES (HARPSICHORD, 3 RECORDERS)
M11	CHACONNES (ORGAN)
M6-7	CHACONNES (ORGAN)
M25	CHACONNES (PIANO)
M1145	CHACONNES (STRING ORCHESTRA)
M264-5	CHACONNES (TUBA AND PIANO)
M224-6	CHACONNES (VIOLA AND PIANO)
M217-218	CHACONNES (VIOLIN AND HARPSICHORD)
M221	CHACONNES (VIOLIN AND HARPSICHORD)
M182-4	CHACONNES (VIOLIN AND ORGAN)
M185-6	CHACONNES (VIOLIN AND ORGAN), ARRANGED
M217-218	CHACONNES (VIOLIN AND PIANO)
M221	CHACONNES (VIOLIN AND PIANO)
M1105-6	CHACONNES (VIOLIN WITH STRING ORCHESTRA)
M1105	CHACONNES (VIOLIN WITH STRING ORCHESTRA), ARRANGED — SCORES
M1105-6	CHACONNES (VIOLIN WITH STRING ORCHESTRA), ARRANGED
M40-42	CHACONNES (VIOLIN)
M233-6	CHACONNES (VIOLONCELLO AND PIANO)
M229-230	CHACONNES (VIOLONCELLO AND PIANO)
M355-7	CHACONNES (3 CLARINETS)
QL391.C7	CHAETOPODA
TX825	CHAFING-DISH RECEIPTS
TX825	CHAFING-DISH
PL8110.C3	CHAGA LANGUAGE
PL55.J3	*CHAGATAI LANGUAGE* **SEE** JAGATAIC LANGUAGE
PL8110.C3	*CHAGGA LANGUAGE* **SEE** CHAGA LANGUAGE
GN659.W2	*CHAGGAS* **SEE** WACHAGA / ethnology
DT449.K4	*CHAGGAS* **SEE** WACHAGA / kilimanjaro region
DS451.8	CHAHAMANAS
PM871-4	*CHAHTA LANGUAGE* **SEE** CHOCTAW LANGUAGE
QC786	*CHAIN REACTION PILES* **SEE** NUCLEAR REACTORS / physics
TK9202	*CHAIN REACTION PILES* **SEE** NUCLEAR REACTORS / technology
HF5468	CHAIN STORES
TJ1100-1119	*CHAIN-BELTING* **SEE** BELTS AND BELTING
TJ1119	*CHAIN-BELTING* **SEE** LINK-BELTING
TS440	CHAINS
TA492.C6	CHAINS / testing
QA835	*CHAINS, EQUILIBRIUM OF* **SEE** EQUILIBRIUM OF CHAINS
TT199	CHAIR CANING
BX1786	CHAIR OF UNITY OCTAVE
DG79	CHAIRS (SELLA)
NK2715	CHAIRS / art industries
TS880	CHAIRS / technology
BP573.C5	CHAKRAS (THEOSOPHY)
BR225	CHALCEDON, COUNCIL OF, 451
F1219	CHALCHIHUITL
F1219	*CHALCHUITE* **SEE** CHALCHIHUITL
QE391.C35	CHALCOCITE
QE391.C	CHALCODITE
TN440-449	CHALCOPYRITE / copper ores
PJ5201-5329	*CHALDAIC LANGUAGE* **SEE** ARAMAIC LANGUAGE
QB19	*CHALDEAN ASTRONOMY* **SEE** ASTRONOMY, ASSYRO-BABYLONIAN
BX150-159	*CHALDEAN CHURCH* **SEE** NESTORIAN CHURCH
PJ5201-5329	*CHALDEAN LANGUAGE* **SEE** ARAMAIC LANGUAGE
PJ5201-5329	*CHALDEE LANGUAGE* **SEE** ARAMAIC LANGUAGE
P959	*CHALDIAN LANGUAGE* **SEE** CUNEIFORM INSCRIPTIONS, VANNIC
P959	*CHALDIAN LANGUAGE* **SEE** VANNIC LANGUAGE
NK7215-7230	CHALICES / gold and silver plate
RC774	*CHALICOSIS* **SEE** LUNGS — DUST DISEASES
HD7264	*CHALICOSIS* **SEE** LUNGS — DUST DISEASES / labor
BM720.H3	*CHALIZA* **SEE** HALITSAH
NC865	*CHALK DRAWING* **SEE** BLACKBOARD DRAWING

NE2280	*CHALK ENGRAVING* **SEE** GRAPHOTYPING
CC710	*CHALK FIGURES* **SEE** HILL FIGURES
NC865	CHALK-TALKS
BV4227	CHALK-TALKS / *pastoral theology*
BV1535	CHALK-TALKS / *sunday-schools*
TP245.C3	CHALK / *chemical technology*
HD9999.C36	CHALK / *economics*
QH471	CHALK / *geology*
TN948.C5	CHALK / *mineral resources*
TL694.I	*CHALLENGE-REPLY SYSTEMS (RADAR)* **SEE** AEROPLANES — IFF EQUIPMENT
TL696.D65	*CHALLENGE-REPLY SYSTEMS (RADAR)* **SEE** DISTANCE MEASURING EQUIPMENT (AIRCRAFT TO GROUND STATION)
G420.C4	CHALLENGER EXPEDITION, 1872-1876
QH11	CHALLENGER EXPEDITION, 1872-1876 / *natural history*
Q115	CHALLENGER EXPEDITION, 1872-1876 / *science*
DS451	CHALUKYAS
PL4491	CHAM LANGUAGE
DS560	*CHAM TRIBE* **SEE** CHAMS
F2230.2.C5	CHAMACOCO INDIANS
PK9201.C	CHAMALAL LANGUAGE
DS422.C3	CHAMARS
PL3801.C4	CHAMBA LAHULI DIALECT
DA346.C	*CHAMBAS* **SEE** CHAAMBA
MT145	CHAMBER MUSIC — ANALYTICAL GUIDES
MT140	CHAMBER MUSIC — ANALYTICAL GUIDES
ML102	CHAMBER MUSIC — DICTIONARIES
ML156.4.C4	CHAMBER MUSIC — DISCOGRAPHY
ML1100-1165	CHAMBER MUSIC — HISTORY AND CRITICISM
M177-9	CHAMBER MUSIC
ML1200-1251	CHAMBER ORCHESTRA
M1000-1049	CHAMBER-ORCHESTRA MUSIC
M1060-1075	CHAMBER-ORCHESTRA MUSIC, ARRANGED
HF294	*CHAMBERS OF COMMERCE* **SEE** BOARDS OF TRADE
HF295-343	*CHAMBERS OF COMMERCE* **SEE** BOARDS OF TRADE / *etc.*
E476.66	CHAMBERSBURG, PA., BURNING OF, 1864
QL666.L2	CHAMELEONS
QL737.U5	CHAMOIS
PL5295	CHAMORRO LANGUAGE
TP555	CHAMPAGNE (WINE)
D545.C37	CHAMPAGNE, BATTLES OF, 1914-1917
DS560	*CHAMPAS* **SEE** CHAMS
QK617	*CHAMPIGNONS* **SEE** MUSHROOMS
E475.26	CHAMPION'S HILL, BATTLE OF, 1863
F1031.1	CHAMPLAIN TERCENTENARY CELEBRATIONS
E356.C	CHAMPLAIN, LAKE, BATTLE OF, 1814
DS560	CHAMS
F1221.T	*CHAMULA INDIANS* **SEE** TZOTZIL INDIANS
PM4466	*CHAMULA LANGUAGE* **SEE** TZOTZIL LANGUAGE
PM3601	CHANABAL LANGUAGE
PM3601	*CHANABLE LANGUAGE* **SEE** CHANABAL LANGUAGE
F3430.1.C	CHANCA INDIANS
BD595	CHANCE / *cosmology*
BC141	CHANCE / *logic*
QA273	CHANCE / *mathematics*
E475.35	CHANCELLORSVILLE, BATTLE OF, 1863
RC203.C5	CHANCROID
DA346.C	*CHANDA* **SEE** CHAAMBA
DS416-419	CHANDELA DYNASTY / *antiquities*
DS451	CHANDELA DYNASTY / *history of india*
NK8360	CHANDELIERS / *art*
TH7960-7970	CHANDELIERS / *technology*
DS416-419	*CHANDELLAS* **SEE** CHANDELA DYNASTY / *antiquities*
DS451	*CHANDELLAS* **SEE** CHANDELA DYNASTY / *history of india*
PH1401-1409	*CHANDI LANGUAGE* **SEE** OSTIAK LANGUAGE
PM3601	*CHANEABAL LANGUAGE* **SEE** CHANABAL LANGUAGE
F3430.1.C	*CHANGA INDIANS* **SEE** CHANCA INDIANS
DS784	*CHANGCHIH INCIDENT, 1938* **SEE** CHANGKUFENG INCIDENT, 1938
QC301-310	CHANGE OF STATE (PHYSICS)
MT710	CHANGE RINGING
BD373	CHANGE / *ontology*
HM101	*CHANGE, SOCIAL* **SEE** SOCIAL CHANGE
DS784	*CHANGKAOFENG INCIDENT, 1938* **SEE** CHANGKUFENG INCIDENT, 1938
DS784	*CHANGKU FENG INCIDENT, 1938* **SEE** CHANGKUFENG INCIDENT, 1938
DS784	CHANGKUFENG INCIDENT, 1938
QL430.5.T85	CHANK
F3430.1.C	*CHANKA INDIANS* **SEE** CHANCA INDIANS
PQ445	*CHANSONS* **SEE** FRENCH BALLADS AND SONGS
PQ1189	*CHANSONS* **SEE** FRENCH BALLADS AND SONGS / *collections*
PQ1310	CHANSONS DE GESTE / *collections*
PQ201-3	CHANSONS DE GESTE / *history*
PN6110.S4	*CHANTEYS* **SEE** SAILORS' SONGS / *literature*
M1977.S2	*CHANTEYS* **SEE** SAILORS' SONGS / *music*
M1978.S2	*CHANTEYS* **SEE** SAILORS' SONGS / *music*
ML3780	*CHANTEYS* **SEE** WORK-SONGS
M1977.L3	*CHANTEYS* **SEE** WORK-SONGS
MT860	CHANTS (ANGLICAN) — INSTRUCTION AND STUDY
ML3195	CHANTS (JEWISH) — HISTORY AND CRITICISM
MT860	CHANTS (JEWISH) — INSTRUCTION AND STUDY
MT190	CHANTS (PLAIN, GREGORIAN, ETC.) — ACCOMPANIMENT
M14	CHANTS (PLAIN, GREGORIAN, ETC.) — ACCOMPANIMENT
ML3082	CHANTS (PLAIN, GREGORIAN, ETC.) — HISTORY AND CRITICISM
MT860	CHANTS (PLAIN, GREGORIAN, ETC.) — INSTRUCTION AND STUDY
PN6110.S4	*CHANTYS* **SEE** SAILORS' SONGS / *literature*
M1978.S2	*CHANTYS* **SEE** SAILORS' SONGS / *music*
M1977.S2	*CHANTYS* **SEE** SAILORS' SONGS / *music*
ML3780	*CHANTYS* **SEE** WORK-SONGS
M1977.L3	*CHANTYS* **SEE** WORK-SONGS
PR972-5	CHAP-BOOKS / *english*
PN970	CHAP-BOOKS / *general*
F1221.C5	*CHAPANEC INDIANS* **SEE** CHIAPANEC INDIANS
PM3618	*CHAPANEC LANGUAGE* **SEE** CHIAPANEC LANGUAGE
QK149	CHAPARRAL / *botany*
SD397.C47	CHAPARRAL / *forestry*
BV26	*CHAPEL EXERCISES* **SEE** UNIVERSITIES AND COLLEGES — CHAPEL EXERCISES
NA5200-6113	*CHAPELS ROYAL* **SEE** CHAPELS, COURT
NA4870	*CHAPELS ROYAL* **SEE** CHAPELS, COURT
NA4870	CHAPELS
NA4870	CHAPELS, COURT
NA5200-6113	CHAPELS, COURT
BV2695.W6	CHAPLAINS, INDUSTRIAL
BV280	*CHAPLAINS' PRAYERS* **SEE** LEGISLATIVE BODIES — CHAPLAINS' PRAYERS
RD631	CHAPPA
LC251-318	*CHARACTER EDUCATION* **SEE** MORAL EDUCATION
LC2751	*CHARACTER EDUCATION* **SEE** MORAL EDUCATION / *negro*
BF818-839	CHARACTER TESTS
LC251-301	CHARACTER / *character building*
BJ1518-1535	CHARACTER / *ethics*
BF818-839	CHARACTER / *psychology*
BF818-839	*CHARACTERISTICS* **SEE** CHARACTERS AND CHARACTERISTICS
CB195-7	*CHARACTERISTICS* **SEE** NATIONAL CHARACTERISTICS
CB203	*CHARACTERISTICS* **SEE** NATIONAL CHARACTERISTICS / *europe*
PN218	CHARACTERS AND CHARACTERISTICS IN LITERATURE
PN1689	CHARACTERS AND CHARACTERISTICS IN LITERATURE / *drama*
BF818-839	CHARACTERS AND CHARACTERISTICS IN LITERATURE / *psychology*
BF818-839	CHARACTERS AND CHARACTERISTICS
PN6369-6377	CHARADES
NC850	CHARCOAL-DRAWING
TP331	CHARCOAL / *fuel*
TH7423	CHARCOAL / *heating*
TP378	*CHARCOAL, ANIMAL* **SEE** ANIMAL CHARCOAL / *sugar manufacture*
DK215.3	*CHARGE OF THE LIGHT BRIGADE* **SEE** BALAKLAVA, BATTLE OF, 1854
QC786	*CHARGED PARTICLE ACCELERATORS* **SEE** PARTICLE ACCELERATORS
Z714	CHARGING SYSTEMS (LIBRARIES)
F2001	*CHARIBBS* **SEE** CARIB INDIANS
GV33	CHARIOTS / *chariot-racing*
BT769	*CHARISMATA* **SEE** GIFTS, SPIRITUAL

HV1-4959	*CHARITABLE INSTITUTIONS* **SEE** CHARITIES
HV61	*CHARITABLE INSTITUTIONS* **SEE** ALMSHOUSES
HV85-527	*CHARITABLE INSTITUTIONS* **SEE** ALMSHOUSES
HV959-1420	*CHARITABLE INSTITUTIONS* **SEE** ORPHANS AND ORPHAN-ASYLUMS
HV1-4959	CHARITABLE SOCIETIES
HF5686.C2-3	CHARITIES — ACCOUNTING
HV1-4959	CHARITIES
HV680-685	*CHARITIES, LEGAL* **SEE** LEGAL AID SOCIETIES
HV3000-3003	CHARITIES, MEDICAL
HV687-694	CHARITIES, MEDICAL
RA960-996	CHARITIES, MEDICAL / *hospitals*
HV75-83	CHARITY LAWS AND LEGISLATION
HV40-69	CHARITY ORGANIZATION
LC4096.G7	CHARITY-SCHOOLS / *gt. brit.*
BV4639	CHARITY / *moral theology*
BX4452-4470	*CHARITY, SISTERS OF* **SEE** SISTERS OF CHARITY
HV6751-6761	*CHARLATANS* **SEE** IMPOSTORS AND IMPOSTURE / *criminal*
R730	*CHARLATANS* **SEE** QUACKS AND QUACKERY
GV1796.C4	CHARLESTON (DANCE)
E241.C4	CHARLESTON, S.C. — SIEGE, 1780
E475.62	CHARLESTON, S.C. — SIEGE, 1863
BJ1609-1610	CHARM
GR600	CHARMS / *folk-lore*
F2230.2.C54	CHARRUA INDIANS
PM5808.C5	CHARRUA LANGUAGE
HE596	CHARTER-PARTIES / *water transport*
HE596	*CHARTERING OF SHIPS* **SEE** CHARTER-PARTIES / *water transport*
HD8396	CHARTISM / *economics*
DA559.7	CHARTISM / *english history*
GA101-1999	*CHARTOGRAPHY* **SEE** CARTOGRAPHY
BX3301-3355	*CHARTREUX, ORDRE DES* **SEE** CARTHUSIANS
TL1070	*CHARTS, ASTRONAUTICAL* **SEE** ASTRONAUTICAL CHARTS
QB6	*CHARTS, ASTRONOMICAL* **SEE** ASTROGRAPHIC CATALOG AND CHART
QB65	*CHARTS, ASTRONOMICAL* **SEE** ASTRONOMY — CHARTS, DIAGRAMS, ETC.
GC235	*CHARTS, BOTTLE* **SEE** BOTTLE-CHARTS
D11	*CHARTS, HISTORICAL* **SEE** CHRONOLOGY, HISTORICAL — CHARTS
SK	*CHASE, THE* **SEE** HUNTING / *hunting sports*
GT5810-5899	*CHASE, THE* **SEE** HUNTING / *manners and customs*
BM198	*CHASIDISM* **SEE** HASIDISM
E99.C48	CHASTA INDIANS
PM761	CHASTACOSTA LANGUAGE
GT2810	CHASTITY BELTS
BJ1533.C4	CHASTITY / *ethics*
GT2810	CHASTITY / *girdles of chastity*
HQ	CHASTITY / *sociology*
BV4647.C5	CHASTITY / *theology*
D545.C4	CHATEAU-THIERRY, BATTLE OF, 1918
DC309.C4	CHATEAUDUN, FRANCE — SIEGE, 1870
NA7710-7786	*CHATEAUX* **SEE** CASTLES / *architecture*
DA660-664	*CHATEAUX* **SEE** CASTLES / *england*
DC20	*CHATEAUX* **SEE** CASTLES / *france*
DC801	*CHATEAUX* **SEE** CASTLES / *france*
DD20	*CHATEAUX* **SEE** CASTLES / *germany*
DG420	*CHATEAUX* **SEE** CASTLES / *italy*
DP22	*CHATEAUX* **SEE** CASTLES / *spain*
PM3616	CHATINO LANGUAGE
E473.55	CHATTANOOGA RAILROAD EXPEDITION, 1862
E475.97	CHATTANOOGA, BATTLE OF, 1863
JX6564	*CHATTELS* **SEE** PERSONAL PROPERTY / *private international law*
HF1263	*CHATTELS* **SEE** PERSONAL PROPERTY / *u.s.*
DS66	*CHATTI* **SEE** HITTITES
QP915.C45	CHAULMUGRA OIL / *physiological effects*
RM666.C38	CHAULMUGRA OIL / *therapeutics*
LC6301.C4-6	CHAUTAUQUAS
F2520.1.C5	CHAVANTE INDIANS
PM5809	CHAVANTE LANGUAGE
SB351.C4	CHAYOTE
BM652	*CHAZANIM* **SEE** CANTORS, JEWISH
BM652	*CHAZZANIM* **SEE** CANTORS, JEWISH
SB201.B8	*CHEAT GRASS* **SEE** BROME-GRASS / *culture*
GV1247	*CHEATING AT CARDS* **SEE** CARDSHARPING
QA404.5	CHEBYSHEV POLYNOMIALS
PK9201.C3	CHECHEN LANGUAGE
DK34.C	CHECHEN
GV1295.P6	CHECK PINOCHLE (GAME)
HV4751	CHECK-REIN
GV1469.C5	CHECKER POOL
SF455	*CHECKERED GIANT RABBITS* **SEE** AMERICAN CHECKERED GIANT RABBITS
GV1461-3	CHECKERS
GV1450.3	CHECKMATE (CHESS)
JX6289.C5	CHECKS (INTERNATIONAL LAW)
HG1691-1700	CHECKS
HF1259	CHECKS / *law*
HD4932.C5	CHECKWEIGHING
QM105	CHEEK-BONE
QM535	CHEEK
BJ1533.C5	CHEERFULNESS
BJ1477-1486	CHEERFULNESS / *ethics*
PN6071.O7	CHEERFULNESS / *literary extracts*
LB3635	*CHEERLEADERS* **SEE** CHEERLEADING
LB3635	CHEERLEADING
LB3635	CHEERS / *school life*
QR121	CHEESE — BACTERIOLOGY
TS1580	CHEESE-CLOTH
SF271-3	CHEESE
QL737.C2	CHEETAHS
QL737.C2	*CHEETAS* **SEE** CHEETAHS
E99.C49	CHEHALIS INDIANS
BF908-935	*CHEIROGNOMY* **SEE** PALMISTRY
BF908-935	*CHEIROMANCY* **SEE** PALMISTRY
QL737.C5	*CHEIROPTERA* **SEE** BATS
BF908-935	*CHEIROSOPHY* **SEE** PALMISTRY
NK4399.C5	CHELSEA PORCELAIN
TX553.A3	*CHEMICAL ADDITIVES IN FOOD* **SEE** FOOD ADDITIVES
QD501	CHEMICAL AFFINITY
QD71-142	*CHEMICAL ANALYSIS* **SEE** CHEMISTRY, ANALYTIC
QC495	*CHEMICAL ANALYSIS OF COLORS* **SEE** COLORS — ANALYSIS
QK865	*CHEMICAL ANALYSIS OF FRUIT* **SEE** FRUIT — CHEMICAL COMPOSITION
QD53	CHEMICAL APPARATUS
QK865	*CHEMICAL COMPOSITION OF FRUIT* **SEE** FRUIT — CHEMICAL COMPOSITION
QE515	*CHEMICAL COMPOSITION OF THE EARTH* **SEE** GEOCHEMISTRY
QE581	CHEMICAL DENUDATION
QD466-7	CHEMICAL ELEMENTS
TP157-9	CHEMICAL ENGINEERING — APPARATUS AND SUPPLIES
TP168	CHEMICAL ENGINEERING — PROBLEMS, EXERCISES, ETC.
TP186	CHEMICAL ENGINEERING AS A PROFESSION
TP155	CHEMICAL ENGINEERING
TP186	*CHEMICAL ENGINEERING-VOCATIONAL GUIDANCE* **SEE** CHEMICAL ENGINEERING AS A PROFESSION
TP139	CHEMICAL ENGINEERS
QD501	CHEMICAL EQUILIBRIUM
QD7	*CHEMICAL FORMULAE* **SEE** CHEMISTRY — NOTATION
QE515	*CHEMICAL GEOLOGY* **SEE** GEOCHEMISTRY
QE364	*CHEMICAL GEOLOGY* **SEE** MINERALOGICAL CHEMISTRY
QE367-9	*CHEMICAL GEOLOGY* **SEE** MINERALOGY, DETERMINATIVE
QE434	*CHEMICAL GEOLOGY* **SEE** ROCKS — ANALYSIS
QE438	*CHEMICAL GEOLOGY* **SEE** ROCKS — ANALYSIS
ML1055	*CHEMICAL HARMONICON* **SEE** PYROPHONE
HD9650-9660	CHEMICAL INDUSTRIES
QD53	*CHEMICAL INSTRUMENTS* **SEE** CHEMICAL APPARATUS
QD501	*CHEMICAL KINETICS* **SEE** CHEMICAL REACTION, RATE OF
QD51	CHEMICAL LABORATORIES
Z675.C	CHEMICAL LIBRARIES
Z699.5.C5	*CHEMICAL LITERATURE SEARCHING* **SEE** INFORMATION STORAGE AND RETRIEVAL SYSTEMS — CHEMISTRY
QD61	*CHEMICAL MANIPULATION* **SEE** CHEMISTRY — MANIPULATION
QD7	*CHEMICAL NOMENCLATURE* **SEE** CHEMISTRY — NOMENCLATURE
TP155.5	CHEMICAL PLANTS

TA467	*CHEMICAL POLISHING OF METALS* **SEE** METALS — PICKLING
QD501	*CHEMICAL REACTION, KINETICS OF* **SEE** CHEMICAL REACTION, RATE OF
QD501	CHEMICAL REACTION, RATE OF
QD501	CHEMICAL REACTION-CONDITIONS AND LAWS
QD73	CHEMICAL REACTIONS
QD77	*CHEMICAL REAGENTS* **SEE** CHEMICAL TESTS AND REAGENTS
QD63.R4	*CHEMICAL REDUCTION* **SEE** REDUCTION, CHEMICAL
QD281.R4	*CHEMICAL REDUCTION* **SEE** REDUCTION, CHEMICAL / organic
QD63.R4	*CHEMICAL REDUCTION* **SEE** REDUCTION, ELECTROLYTIC
QD281.R4	*CHEMICAL REDUCTION* **SEE** REDUCTION, ELECTROLYTIC / organic
QD40	CHEMICAL RESEARCH
QD1	CHEMICAL SOCIETIES
QD7	*CHEMICAL SYMBOLS* **SEE** CHEMISTRY — NOMENCLATURE
QD7	*CHEMICAL SYMBOLS* **SEE** CHEMISTRY — NOTATION
TP	*CHEMICAL TECHNOLOGY* **SEE** CHEMISTRY, TECHNICAL
QD77	CHEMICAL TESTS AND REAGENTS
UG447	CHEMICAL WARFARE
TP155.5	*CHEMICAL WORKS* **SEE** CHEMICAL PLANTS
HD9650-9660	CHEMICALS — MANUFACTURE AND INDUSTRY / economics
TP200-248	CHEMICALS — MANUFACTURE AND INDUSTRY / technology
TP210	CHEMICALS — PATENTS
TP149	CHEMICALS — SAFETY MEASURES
TR212	*CHEMICALS, PHOTOGRAPHIC* **SEE** PHOTOGRAPHIC CHEMICALS
QD9	CHEMISTRY — ABSTRACTING AND INDEXING
Z5521-6	CHEMISTRY — BIBLIOGRAPHY
QD467	CHEMISTRY — CLASSIFICATION
QD27	CHEMISTRY — EARLY WORKS TO 1800
QD42	CHEMISTRY — EXAMINATIONS, QUESTIONS, ETC.
QD43	CHEMISTRY — EXPERIMENTS
QD40	CHEMISTRY — FILM CATALOGS
QD11-18	CHEMISTRY — HISTORY
QD35	CHEMISTRY — JUVENILE LITERATURE
QD45	CHEMISTRY — LABORATORY BLANKS
QD45	CHEMISTRY — LABORATORY MANUALS
QD61	CHEMISTRY — MANIPULATION
QD7	CHEMISTRY — NOMENCLATURE
QD7	CHEMISTRY — NOTATION
QD14	CHEMISTRY — PHLOGISTON
QD27	CHEMISTRY — PHLOGISTON
QD42	CHEMISTRY — PROBLEMS, EXERCISES, ETC.
QD40-45	CHEMISTRY — STUDY AND TEACHING
QD65	CHEMISTRY — TABLES, ETC.
UG447	*CHEMISTRY IN WARFARE* **SEE** CHEMICAL WARFARE
TX541-5	*CHEMISTRY OF FOOD* **SEE** FOOD — ANALYSIS
QD	CHEMISTRY
S583-8	*CHEMISTRY, AGRICULTURAL* **SEE** AGRICULTURAL CHEMISTRY
QD81-95	CHEMISTRY, ANALYTIC — QUALITATIVE
QD101-142	CHEMISTRY, ANALYTIC — QUANTITATIVE
QD71-142	CHEMISTRY, ANALYTIC
QP501-801	*CHEMISTRY, ANIMAL* **SEE** PHYSIOLOGICAL CHEMISTRY
QH345	*CHEMISTRY, BIOLOGICAL* **SEE** BIOLOGICAL CHEMISTRY
QD415-431	*CHEMISTRY, BIOLOGICAL* **SEE** BIOLOGICAL CHEMISTRY
QP501-801	*CHEMISTRY, BIOLOGICAL* **SEE** BIOLOGICAL CHEMISTRY
QK861-6	*CHEMISTRY, BOTANICAL* **SEE** BOTANICAL CHEMISTRY
QR121	*CHEMISTRY, DAIRY* **SEE** DAIRY BACTERIOLOGY
RK290	*CHEMISTRY, DENTAL* **SEE** DENTAL CHEMISTRY
HV8073	CHEMISTRY, FORENSIC
RA1057	CHEMISTRY, FORENSIC / medical jurisprudence
QD133	*CHEMISTRY, FOUNDRY* **SEE** FOUNDRY CHEMISTRY
TP155	*CHEMISTRY, INDUSTRIAL* **SEE** CHEMICAL ENGINEERING
TP	*CHEMISTRY, INDUSTRIAL* **SEE** CHEMISTRY, TECHNICAL
QD45	CHEMISTRY, INORGANIC — LABORATORY MANUALS
QD151-199	CHEMISTRY, INORGANIC
HV8073	*CHEMISTRY, LEGAL* **SEE** CHEMISTRY, FORENSIC
RA1057	*CHEMISTRY, LEGAL* **SEE** CHEMISTRY, FORENSIC / medical jurisprudence
RS407	CHEMISTRY, MEDICAL AND PHARMACEUTICAL — LABORATORY MANUALS
RS402-431	CHEMISTRY, MEDICAL AND PHARMACEUTICAL
QD133	CHEMISTRY, METALLURGIC
QE364	*CHEMISTRY, MINERALOGICAL* **SEE** MINERALOGICAL CHEMISTRY
QD261	CHEMISTRY, ORGANIC — EXPERIMENTS
QD261	CHEMISTRY, ORGANIC — LABORATORY MANUALS
QD262	CHEMISTRY, ORGANIC — SYNTHESIS
QD291	CHEMISTRY, ORGANIC — TABLES, ETC.
QD248-449	CHEMISTRY, ORGANIC
RS402-431	*CHEMISTRY, PATHOLOGICAL* **SEE** CHEMISTRY, MEDICAL AND PHARMACEUTICAL
QP501-801	*CHEMISTRY, PATHOLOGICAL* **SEE** PHYSIOLOGICAL CHEMISTRY
RS402-431	*CHEMISTRY, PHARMACEUTICAL* **SEE** CHEMISTRY, MEDICAL AND PHARMACEUTICAL
TR210	*CHEMISTRY, PHOTOGRAPHIC* **SEE** PHOTOGRAPHIC CHEMISTRY
QD457	CHEMISTRY, PHYSICAL AND THEORETICAL — LABORATORY MANUALS
QD453-651	CHEMISTRY, PHYSICAL AND THEORETICAL
QD476	CHEMISTRY, PHYSICAL ORGANIC
QP501-801	*CHEMISTRY, PHYSIOLOGICAL* **SEE** PHYSIOLOGICAL CHEMISTRY
TX149	*CHEMISTRY, SANITARY* **SEE** SANITARY CHEMISTRY / home economics
QD506	*CHEMISTRY, SURFACE* **SEE** SURFACE CHEMISTRY
QD262	*CHEMISTRY, SYNTHETIC* **SEE** CHEMISTRY, ORGANIC — SYNTHESIS
TP151	CHEMISTRY, TECHNICAL — FORMULAE, RECEIPTS, PRESCRIPTIONS
TP165	CHEMISTRY, TECHNICAL — RESEARCH
TP151	CHEMISTRY, TECHNICAL — TABLES, ETC.
TP	CHEMISTRY, TECHNICAL
TX1449	*CHEMISTRY, TEXTILE* **SEE** TEXTILE CHEMISTRY
QD453-651	*CHEMISTRY, THEORETICAL* **SEE** CHEMISTRY, PHYSICAL AND THEORETICAL
QD53	*CHEMISTRY-APPARATUS* **SEE** CHEMICAL APPARATUS
Z695.1.C5	*CHEMISTRY-CATALOGING* **SEE** CATALOGING OF CHEMICAL LITERATURE
QD51	*CHEMISTRY-LABORATORIES* **SEE** CHEMICAL LABORATORIES
QD43	*CHEMISTRY-LECTURE EXPERIMENTS* **SEE** CHEMISTRY — EXPERIMENTS
QD40	*CHEMISTRY-RESEARCH* **SEE** CHEMICAL RESEARCH
QD21-22	CHEMISTS
RM663	CHEMOTHERAPY
TP149	*CHEMURGICS* **SEE** CHEMURGY
TP149	CHEMURGY
QL696.A5	*CHEN CAERULESCENS (LINNAEUS)* **SEE** BLUE GOOSE
RS165.C35	CHENOPODIUM OIL
RM666.C38	CHENOPODIUM OIL
E99.C59	*CHEPEWYAN INDIANS* **SEE** CHIPEWYAN INDIANS
DS451	CHERAS
E99.C	CHERAW INDIANS
PH801-9	*CHEREMIS LANGUAGE* **SEE** CHEREMISSIAN LANGUAGE
DK34.C5	CHEREMISSES
PH801-9	CHEREMISSIAN LANGUAGE
PH808-9	CHEREMISSIAN LITERATURE
PH824	CHEREMISSIAN POETRY / collections
PH812	CHEREMISSIAN POETRY / history
D766.84	CHEREN, BATTLE OF, 1941
QC490	*CHERENKOV LIGHT* **SEE** CHERENKOV RADIATION
QC490	*CHERENKOV RADIATION* **SEE** CHERENKOV RADIATION
QC490	CHERENKOV RADIATION
DS644	CHERIBON AGREEMENT, 1946
DS39	*CHERIFS* **SEE** SHERIFS
DA417	CHERITON, ENG., BATTLE OF, 1644
PK9201.C5	*CHERKESS LANGUAGE* **SEE** CIRCASSIAN LANGUAGE
S598	CHERNOZEM SOILS
E83.759	CHEROKEE INDIANS — WARS, 1759-1761
E99.C5	CHEROKEE INDIANS

PM781-4	CHEROKEE LANGUAGE
SB608.C43	CHERRY — DISEASES AND PESTS
SB945.C45	CHERRY LEAF-BEETLE
SB379.C5	CHERRY
SB435	*CHERRY, JAPANESE* **SEE** JAPANESE FLOWERING CHERRY
QE391.C4	CHERT
BL477	*CHERUBIM* **SEE** ANGELS / *comparative religion*
BT965-8	*CHERUBIM* **SEE** ANGELS / *theology*
VM311.B8	*CHESAPEAKE BAY BUGEYES* **SEE** BUGEYES (BOATS)
SF429.C4	*CHESAPEAKE BAY DOGS* **SEE** CHESAPEAKE BAY RETRIEVERS
SF429.C4	CHESAPEAKE BAY RETRIEVERS
E357.3	CHESAPEAKE-LEOPARD AFFAIR, 1807
GV1469	CHESICA
GV1446	CHESS — JUVENILE LITERATURE
GV1458	CHESS — VARIANTS
SB201.B8	*CHESS (GRASS)* **SEE** BROME-GRASS / *culture*
NK9990.C4	*CHESS MEN* **SEE** CHESSMEN
GV1313-1457	CHESS
NK9990.C4	CHESSMEN
RD766	CHEST — ABNORMITIES AND DEFORMITIES
RC941	CHEST — DISEASES
RD536	CHEST — PARACENTESIS
RD536	CHEST — SURGERY
RC280.C	CHEST — TUMORS
RD667	CHEST — TUMORS
RD536	CHEST — WOUNDS AND INJURIES
GV515	CHEST WEIGHTS
RC941	*CHEST-EXPLORATION* **SEE** CHEST — DISEASES — — DIAGNOSIS
SF393.C5	CHESTER WHITE SWINE
SB608.C45	CHESTNUT — DISEASES AND PESTS
E241.C52	CHESTNUT HILL, BATTLE OF, 1777
SD397.O12	CHESTNUT OAK
SB608.C45	CHESTNUT-BLIGHT
SB608.C45	CHESTNUT-BORER
SB608.C45	CHESTNUT-WEEVIL
SD397.C5	CHESTNUT
NK2725	CHESTS / *art*
TT197	CHESTS / *cabinet-work*
RC941	CHEST — DISEASES — — DIAGNOSIS
RV293	CHEST — DISEASES — — ECLECTIC TREATMENT
RX360	CHEST — DISEASES — — HOMEOPATHIC TREATMENT
QL737.C2	*CHETAHS* **SEE** CHEETAHS
QL737.C2	*CHETAS* **SEE** CHEETAHS
E99.C526	CHETCO INDIANS
E99.C526	*CHETKOE INDIANS* **SEE** CHETCO INDIANS
SF375	CHEVIOT SHEEP
TL215.C5	CHEVROLET AUTOMOBILE
UC530-535	CHEVRONS
DA783.53	*CHEVY CHASE, BATTLE OF, 1388* **SEE** OTTERBURN, BATTLE OF, 1388
PL8110.C5	CHEWA DIALECT
E83.863	CHEYENNE INDIANS — WARS, 1864
E83.866	CHEYENNE INDIANS — WARS, 1876
E99.C53	CHEYENNE INDIANS
PM795	CHEYENNE LANGUAGE
PL8751	*CHI LANGUAGE* **SEE** TSHI LANGUAGE
PL8740	*CHI-TONGA LANGUAGE* **SEE** TONGA LANGUAGE (NYASA)
DS560	*CHIAM TRIBE* **SEE** CHAMS
F2230.2.C5	*CHIAMACOCO INDIANS* **SEE** CHAMACOCO INDIANS
TP559.I8	CHIANTI WINE
F1221.C5	CHIAPANEC INDIANS
PM3618	CHIAPANEC LANGUAGE
F1221.C5	*CHIAPAS INDIANS* **SEE** CHIAPANEC INDIANS
NC755	CHIAROSCURO
F2270.2.C4	CHIBCHA INDIANS
PM5811	CHIBCHA LANGUAGE
PM5811	CHIBCHAN LANGUAGES
E99.C55	*CHICACHAS INDIANS* **SEE** CHICKASAW INDIANS
HX846.C4	CHICAGO — HAYMARKET SQUARE RIOT, 1886
F548	CHICAGO — HISTORY
E356.C53	CHICAGO — MASSACRE, 1812
HD5325. R12 1894C5	CHICAGO STRIKE, 1894
F548.4	CHICAGO — HISTORY — — CIVIL WAR
E99.C55	*CHICASA INDIANS* **SEE** CHICKASAW INDIANS
E99.C55	*CHICHACHA INDIANS* **SEE** CHICKASAW INDIANS

F1221.C53	CHICHIMECA-JONAZ INDIANS
F1219	CHICHIMECS
QL696.P2	CHICKADEES
E475.81	CHICKAMAUGA, BATTLE OF, 1863
E83.739	CHICKASAW INDIANS — WARS, 1739-1740
E99.C55	CHICKASAW INDIANS
SF995	CHICKEN CHOLERA
S486	*CHICKEN COOPS* **SEE** POULTRY HOUSES AND EQUIPMENT
SF995	CHICKEN-MITE
SF995	CHICKEN-POX IN POULTRY
RJ406.C4	CHICKEN-POX
TX375	*CHICKENS* **SEE** POULTRY
SF481-507	*CHICKENS* **SEE** POULTRY
TX556.P9	*CHICKENS* **SEE** POULTRY
E99.C55	*CHICKESAW INDIANS* **SEE** CHICKASAW INDIANS
SB289-291	CHICLE-GUM
SB211.C5	CHICORY / *agriculture*
SB351.C5	CHICORY / *vegetables*
JF700-721	*CHIEF JUSTICES* **SEE** JUDGES
JK1507-1599	*CHIEF JUSTICES* **SEE** JUDGES
QL503.A7	*CHIGGA* **SEE** CHIGOE / *fleas*
QL458.A2	*CHIGGA* **SEE** CHIGOE / *mites*
QL458.A2	CHIGGERS (MITES)
PM73	*CHIGLIT LANGUAGE* **SEE** KOPAGMIUT LANGUAGE
QL503.A7	CHIGOE / *fleas*
QL458.A2	CHIGOE / *mites*
PL8208	*CHIGOGO LANGUAGE* **SEE** GOGO LANGUAGE
SF429.C45	CHIHUAHUA DOGS
E405.2	*CHIHUAHUA EXPEDITION, 1846-1847* **SEE** DONIPHAN'S EXPEDITION, 1846-1847
E99.C55	*CHIKASAW INDIANS* **SEE** CHICKASAW INDIANS
PM803	*CHIL-WAY-UK DIALECT* **SEE** CHILLIWACK DIALECT
RL271	CHILBLAINS
E99.T78	*CHILCOTIN INDIANS* **SEE** TSILKOTIN INDIANS
HV697-700	*CHILD ENDOWMENT* **SEE** FAMILY ALLOWANCES / *social welfare*
HD4925	*CHILD ENDOWMENT* **SEE** FAMILY ALLOWANCES / *wages and social insurance*
HG9271-7	*CHILD INSURANCE* **SEE** INSURANCE, CHILD
HD6228-6250	*CHILD LABOR* **SEE** CHILDREN — EMPLOYMENT
HD6270	*CHILD LABOR* **SEE** YOUTH — EMPLOYMENT
HV875	*CHILD PLACING* **SEE** ADOPTION
HV875	*CHILD PLACING* **SEE** FOSTER HOME CARE
RJ499	CHILD PSYCHIATRY
LB1101-1139	*CHILD PSYCHOLOGY* **SEE** CHILD STUDY
HQ771-785	*CHILD PSYCHOLOGY* **SEE** CHILD STUDY / *child in the family*
HQ781-5	*CHILD PSYCHOLOGY* **SEE** CHILD STUDY / *child life*
BF721	*CHILD PSYCHOLOGY* **SEE** CHILD STUDY / *child psychology*
GN63	*CHILD PSYCHOLOGY* **SEE** CHILD STUDY / *somatology*
HQ768.8	*CHILD RESEARCH* **SEE** CHILDREN — RESEARCH
LB1101-1139	CHILD STUDY
HQ771-785	CHILD STUDY / *child in the family*
HQ781-5	CHILD STUDY / *child life*
BF721	CHILD STUDY / *child psychology*
GN63	CHILD STUDY / *somatology*
HV701-1420	CHILD WELFARE
HV721-739	*CHILD WELFARE-LAW AND LEGISLATION* **SEE** CHILDREN — LAW
RG661	CHILDBIRTH — PSYCHOLOGY
RG661	*CHILDBIRTH, NATURAL* **SEE** CHILDBIRTH — PSYCHOLOGY
BV50.H6	*CHILDERMAS* **SEE** HOLY INNOCENTS, FEAST OF THE
PN6328.C5	CHILDREN — ANECDOTES AND SAYINGS
CT107	CHILDREN — BIOGRAPHY
CT145	CHILDREN — BIOGRAPHY
RJ101	CHILDREN — CARE AND HYGIENE
RJ61	CHILDREN — CARE AND HYGIENE
BJ1631-8	CHILDREN — CONDUCT OF LIFE
GT1730	CHILDREN — COSTUME
BV4907	CHILDREN — DEATH AND FUTURE STATE
RJ	CHILDREN — DISEASES
HD6228-6250	CHILDREN — EMPLOYMENT
RJ131	CHILDREN — GROWTH
RJ27-28	CHILDREN — HOSPITALS
LB1139.L3	CHILDREN — LANGUAGE
HV721-739	CHILDREN — LAW

HQ769-780	CHILDREN — MANAGEMENT
HB1323.C5	CHILDREN — MORTALITY
RJ206	CHILDREN — NUTRITION
N7640-7649	CHILDREN — PORTRAITS
BV4870	CHILDREN — PRAYER-BOOKS AND DEVOTIONS
BV4560-4579	CHILDREN — RELIGIOUS LIFE
BV4925-6	CHILDREN — RELIGIOUS LIFE / conversion
HQ768.8	CHILDREN — RESEARCH
RD137	CHILDREN — SURGERY
LB1139.W	CHILDREN — WRITING
BF723.A45	CHILDREN AND ANIMALS
GR43.C4	CHILDREN AND FOLK-LORE SEE FOLK-LORE AND CHILDREN
HQ784.N4	CHILDREN AND NEWSPAPERS SEE NEWSPAPERS AND CHILDREN
PN3157	CHILDREN AS ACTORS
PN3171	CHILDREN AS ACTORS
PN2071.C	CHILDREN AS ACTORS
N352	CHILDREN AS ARTISTS
BF723.A8	CHILDREN AS AUTHORS / child study
PN171.C5	CHILDREN AS AUTHORS / literature
ML83	CHILDREN AS MUSICIANS
BF723.A8	CHILDREN AS POETS SEE CHILDREN AS AUTHORS / child study
PN171.C5	CHILDREN AS POETS SEE CHILDREN AS AUTHORS / literature
N7640-7649	CHILDREN IN ART
HT206	CHILDREN IN CITIES SEE CITY CHILDREN
DE61.C4	CHILDREN IN CLASSICAL ANTIQUITY
G570	CHILDREN IN FOREIGN COUNTRIES
PN6110.C4	CHILDREN IN POETRY
BS576-8	CHILDREN IN THE BIBLE
BS2446	CHILDREN IN THE BIBLE / new testament
LC5151-3	CHILDREN OF MIGRANT LABORERS — EDUCATION
BF723.F3	CHILDREN SEPARATED FROM THEIR FATHERS SEE FATHER-SEPARATED CHILDREN
HQ750-789	CHILDREN
LC4661-4700	CHILDREN, BACKWARD SEE SLOW LEARNING CHILDREN
HQ754.F5	CHILDREN, FIRST-BORN
GR475-487	CHILDREN, FOLK-LORE OF SEE FOLK-LORE OF CHILDREN
G570	CHILDREN, FOREIGN SEE CHILDREN IN FOREIGN COUNTRIES
E185.89.C3	CHILDREN, NEGRO SEE NEGRO CHILDREN
TR680	CHILDREN, PHOTOGRAPHY OF SEE PHOTOGRAPHY OF CHILDREN
TR575	CHILDREN, PHOTOGRAPHY OF SEE PHOTOGRAPHY OF CHILDREN
LC4661-4700	CHILDREN, RETARDED SEE SLOW LEARNING CHILDREN
AY81.J8	CHILDREN'S ALMANACS SEE ALMANACS, CHILDREN'S
PZ5-90	CHILDREN'S BOOKS SEE CHILDREN'S LITERATURE
M1996	CHILDREN'S CANTATAS SEE CANTATAS, JUVENILE
M2190	CHILDREN'S CANTATAS SEE CANTATAS, JUVENILE
TT635	CHILDREN'S CLOTHING
HV9088-9096	CHILDREN'S COURTS SEE JUVENILE COURTS
D169	CHILDREN'S CRUSADE, 1212
GV1799	CHILDREN'S DANCES SEE DANCING — CHILDREN'S DANCES
RJ	CHILDREN'S DISEASES SEE CHILDREN — DISEASES
AG1-91	CHILDREN'S ENCYCLOPEDIAS AND DICTIONARIES
SB457	CHILDREN'S GARDENS
RJ27-28	CHILDREN'S HOSPITALS SEE CHILDREN — HOSPITALS
Z718.1	CHILDREN'S LIBRARIES SEE LIBRARIES, CHILDREN'S
Z675.S3	CHILDREN'S LIBRARIES SEE SCHOOL LIBRARIES
Z1037	CHILDREN'S LITERATURE — BIBLIOGRAPHY
PN1009	CHILDREN'S LITERATURE — HISTORY AND CRITICISM
Z695	CHILDREN'S LITERATURE - CATALOGING SEE CATALOGING OF CHILDRREN'S LITERATURE
PZ5-90	CHILDREN'S LITERATURE
Z695	CHILDREN'S LITERATURE-CATALOGING SEE CATALOGING OF CHILDREN'S LITERATURE
BX2015.A55	CHILDREN'S MISSALS / catholic
AM8	CHILDREN'S MUSEUMS
M1378-1380	CHILDREN'S MUSIC (PIANO) SEE PIANO MUSIC, JUVENILE
GV1203	CHILDREN'S PARTIES
PN4835	CHILDREN'S PERIODICALS / history
PN3157	CHILDREN'S PLAYS — PRESENTATION, ETC.
PN6120.A4-5	CHILDREN'S PLAYS
PZ8.3	CHILDREN'S POETRY
PN6110.C4	CHILDREN'S POETRY
N7640-7649	CHILDREN'S PORTRAITS SEE CHILDREN — PORTRAITS
PN6328.C5	CHILDREN'S SAYINGS SEE CHILDREN — ANECDOTES AND SAYINGS
BV4315	CHILDREN'S SERMONS
BM743	CHILDREN'S SERMONS, JEWISH
M1990-1998	CHILDREN'S SONGS / music
GV1215	CHILDREN'S SONGS / singing games
PZ5-90	CHILDREN'S STORIES / collections
PN3157	CHILDREN'S THEATER SEE CHILDREN'S PLAYS — PRESENTATION, ETC.
BS2446	CHILDREN-BIBLICAL TEACHING SEE CHILDREN IN THE BIBLE / new testament
BS576-8	CHILDREN-BIBLICAL TEACHING SEE CHILDREN IN THE BIBLE
HV701-1420	CHILDREN-CHARITIES SEE CHILD WELFARE
TT635	CHILDREN-CLOTHING SEE CHILDREN'S CLOTHING
HQ748.C	CHILDREN-CRYING SEE CRYING
RJ101	CHILDREN-HEALTH SEE CHILDREN — CARE AND HYGIENE
RJ61	CHILDREN-HEALTH SEE CHILDREN — CARE AND HYGIENE
HD5106-5250	CHILDREN-HOURS OF LABOR SEE HOURS OF LABOR
RJ101	CHILDREN-HYGIENE SEE CHILDREN — CARE AND HYGIENE
RJ61	CHILDREN-HYGIENE SEE CHILDREN — CARE AND HYGIENE
TR575	CHILDREN-PHOTOGRAPHY SEE PHOTOGRAPHY OF CHILDREN
TR680	CHILDREN-PHOTOGRAPHY SEE PHOTOGRAPHY OF CHILDREN
BV4870	CHILDREN-PRAYER-BOOKS AND DEVOTIONS-ENGLISH SEE CHILDREN — PRAYER-BOOKS AND DEVOTIONS
HV701-1420	CHILDREN-PROTECTION SEE CHILD WELFARE
LB1537	CHILDREN-RECREATION SEE CREATIVE ACTIVITIES AND SEAT WORK
GV1200-1511	CHILDREN-RECREATION SEE GAMES
LB1137	CHILDREN-RECREATION SEE GAMES / educational
GN454-6	CHILDREN-RECREATION SEE GAMES / ethnology
GR480-485	CHILDREN-RECREATION SEE GAMES / folk-lore
LB1177	CHILDREN-RECREATION SEE GAMES / kindergarten
BF717	CHILDREN-RECREATION SEE GAMES / psychology of play
LB3031	CHILDREN-RECREATION SEE GAMES / school management
HQ769-780	CHILDREN-TRAINING SEE CHILDREN — MANAGEMENT
LB2864	CHILDREN-TRANSPORTATION SEE SCHOOL CHILDREN — TRANSPORTATION
LB1139.L3	CHILDREN-VOCABULARY SEE CHILDREN — LANGUAGE
RJ50	CHILDREN — DISEASES — — DIAGNOSIS
RV375-7	CHILDREN — DISEASES — — ECLECTIC TREATMENT
RX501-531	CHILDREN — DISEASES — — HOMEOPATHIC TREATMENT
F3081-3098	CHILE — HISTORY
F3097	CHILE-HISTORY-WAR WITH BOLIVIA, 1879-1884 SEE WAR OF THE PACIFIC, 1879-1884
F3097	CHILE-HISTORY-WAR WITH PERU, 1879-1884 SEE WAR OF THE PACIFIC, 1879-1884
PQ8060-8061	CHILEAN BALLADS AND SONGS / collections
PQ7979-7980	CHILEAN BALLADS AND SONGS / history
SB205.A4	CHILEAN CLOVER SEE ALFALFA
PQ8064-8070	CHILEAN DRAMA / collections
PQ7997-8007	CHILEAN DRAMA / history
PQ8075-6	CHILEAN FICTION / collections
PQ7997-8007	CHILEAN FICTION / history
PQ8081	CHILEAN LETTERS / collections
PQ8011	CHILEAN LETTERS / history
PQ7900-8099	CHILEAN LITERATURE
PN5041-9	CHILEAN NEWSPAPERS / etc.
PN5041-5050	CHILEAN PERIODICALS / etc.

PQ8049-8063	CHILEAN POETRY / *collections*
PQ7961-7981	CHILEAN POETRY / *history*
PN6222.C	CHILEAN WIT AND HUMOR
BT890-891	*CHILIASM* **SEE** MILLENNIUM
QB214	*CHILINDRE* **SEE** CYLINDER (TIMEPIECE)
E99.C552	CHILKAT INDIANS
PM803	CHILLIWACK DIALECT
RC156-166	*CHILLS AND FEVER* **SEE** MALARIAL FEVER
QM201.M2	*CHILLS AND FEVER* **SEE** MALARIAL FEVER / *bacteriology*
PM803	*CHILLWAYUK DIALECT* **SEE** CHILLIWACK DIALECT
QL449	*CHILOPODA* **SEE** CENTIPEDES
E99.C553	CHILULA INDIANS
PM805	CHILULA LANGUAGE
E99.C56	CHIMARIKO INDIANS
PM821	CHIMARIKO LANGUAGE
QH406	CHIMERAS (BOTANY)
MT710	*CHIMING* **SEE** CHANGE RINGING
E99.C	CHIMMESYAN INDIANS
PM831	CHIMMESYAN LANGUAGES
HJ2612	*CHIMNEY-MONEY* **SEE** HEARTH-MONEY / *english tax*
QL696.C9	*CHIMNEY-SWALLOWS* **SEE** SWIFTS
HD8039.C49	CHIMNEY-SWEEPS
NA3050-3055	*CHIMNEYPIECES* **SEE** FIREPLACES / *architecture*
TH7421-7434	*CHIMNEYPIECES* **SEE** FIREPLACES / *heating*
NA3050-3055	*CHIMNEYPIECES* **SEE** MANTELS / *architecture*
TH2288	*CHIMNEYPIECES* **SEE** MANTELS / *construction*
TH2281-4	CHIMNEYS
NA3040	CHIMNEYS / *architecture*
TH4591	CHIMNEYS / *power-plants*
QL737.P9	CHIMPANZEES
PM831	*CHIMSYAN LANGUAGES* **SEE** CHIMMESYAN LANGUAGES
F3430.1.C	CHIMU INDIANS
PM5813	CHIMU LANGUAGE
PL3891-4	CHIN LANGUAGES
QM535	CHIN
DS701-796	CHINA — HISTORY
TP822	*CHINA (PORCELAIN)* **SEE** PORCELAIN
NK4370-4584	*CHINA (PORCELAIN)* **SEE** PORCELAIN
NK4605	CHINA PAINTING
DS770-772	CHINA RELIEF EXPEDITION, 1900-1901
TP684.T8	*CHINA WOOD-OIL* **SEE** TUNG-OIL
SB299.T8	*CHINA WOOD-OIL TREE* **SEE** TUNG TREE
TN941-3	*CHINA-CLAY* **SEE** KAOLIN / *mineral resources*
QE391.K	*CHINA-CLAY* **SEE** KAOLIN / *mineralogy*
TP811	*CHINA-CLAY* **SEE** KAOLIN / *pottery*
DS765-7	*CHINA-JAPAN WAR, 1894-1895* **SEE** CHINESE-JAPANESE WAR, 1894-1895
DS765-7	*CHINA-HISTORY-WAR WITH JAPAN, 1894-1895* **SEE** CHINESE-JAPANESE WAR, 1894-1895
SB87.M6	CHINAMPAS / *mexican horticulture*
F1221.C56	CHINANTEC INDIANS
PM3630	CHINANTEC LANGUAGE
NK4370-4584	*CHINAWARE* **SEE** PORCELAIN
TP822	*CHINAWARE* **SEE** PORCELAIN
NK3700-4695	*CHINAWARE* **SEE** POTTERY / *ceramics*
TP785-825	*CHINAWARE* **SEE** POTTERY / *chemical technology*
HD9610-9620	*CHINAWARE* **SEE** POTTERY / *trade*
DS748	CHINA — HISTORY — — HAN DYNASTY, 202 B.C.-220 A.D.
DS751	CHINA — HISTORY — — LIAO DYNASTY, 907-1125
DS748.6	CHINA — HISTORY — — NORTHERN WEI DYNASTY, 386-636
DS748.2	CHINA — HISTORY — — THREE KINGDOMS, 220-265
DS747.2	CHINA — HISTORY — — WARRING STATES, 403-221 B.C.
SB945.C5	CHINCH-BUGS
PM5814.C3	CHINCHASUYU DIALECT
SF455	CHINCHILLA RABBITS
QL737.R6	CHINCHILLAS
QK495.C57	*CHINCHONA* **SEE** CINCHONA / *botany*
SB295.C5	*CHINCHONA* **SEE** CINCHONA / *culture*
RS165.C3	*CHINCHONA* **SEE** CINCHONA / *pharmacy*
RM666.C53	*CHINCHONA* **SEE** CINCHONA / *therapeutics*
PL8110.C	CHINDAU LANGUAGE
GN635.C5	CHINESE — ORIGIN
SB351.C	CHINESE CABBAGE
GV1458.C5	CHINESE CHESS
PL2934-5	CHINESE DRAMA / *history*
PN2870-2878	CHINESE DRAMA / *theater*
PL3277.E5	CHINESE DRAMA / *translations*
PL2936-2940	CHINESE FICTION / *history*
PL3277.E8	CHINESE FICTION / *translations*
VM101	*CHINESE JUNKS* **SEE** JUNKS
PL2241-5	CHINESE LANGUAGE — ARCHAIC CHINESE
PL1001-2239	CHINESE LANGUAGE
PL1841	CHINESE LANGUAGE — DIALECTS — — HAINAN
PL2501-3299	CHINESE LITERATURE
Z695.1.O7	*CHINESE LITERATURE-CATALOGING* **SEE** CATALOGING OF CHINESE LITERATURE
ML1015-1018	*CHINESE LUTE* **SEE** P'I P'A
PN5361-9	CHINESE NEWSPAPERS / *etc.*
SB299.T8	*CHINESE OIL TREE* **SEE** TUNG TREE
PN5361-5370	CHINESE PERIODICALS
PL2956-2967	CHINESE POETRY
PL3277.E3	CHINESE POETRY / *translations*
DS701-796	*CHINESE QUESTION* **SEE** CHINA — HISTORY
DS515-519	*CHINESE QUESTION* **SEE** EASTERN QUESTION (FAR EAST) / *history*
JX1321	*CHINESE QUESTION* **SEE** EASTERN QUESTION (FAR EAST) / *international law*
PN6120.S5	*CHINESE SHADOWS* **SEE** SHADOW PANTOMIMES AND PLAYS / *texts*
PN1979.S5	*CHINESE SHADOWS* **SEE** SHADOW PANTOMIMES AND PLAYS / *texts*
PL1001-1095	CHINESE STUDIES (SINOLOGY)
SB235	*CHINESE SUGAR-CANE* **SEE** SORGHUM
TP405	*CHINESE SUGAR-CANE* **SEE** SORGHUM / *chemical technology*
PN6222.C5	CHINESE WIT AND HUMOR
SB299.T8	*CHINESE WOOD-OIL TREE* **SEE** TUNG TREE
DS549	CHINESE-FRENCH WAR, 1884-1885
DS480.85	*CHINESE-INDIAN BORDER DISPUTE, 1957-* **SEE** SINO-INDIAN BORDER DISPUTE, 1957-
UH302 1894	CHINESE-JAPANESE WAR, 1894-1895 — MEDICAL AND SANITARY AFFAIRS
DS765-7	CHINESE-JAPANESE WAR, 1894-1895
PL4001.K3	*CHINGPAW LANGUAGE* **SEE** KACHIN LANGUAGE
DS485.B85	*CHINGPAWS* **SEE** KACHIN TRIBES / *burma*
QD421	*CHINIOIDINA* **SEE** QUINOIDINE / *chemistry*
QP921.Q5	*CHINIOIDINA* **SEE** QUINOIDINE / *physiological effect*
DS549	*CHINO-FRENCH WAR, 1884-1885* **SEE** CHINESE-FRENCH WAR, 1884-1885
DS765-7	*CHINO-JAPANESE WAR, 1894-1895* **SEE** CHINESE-JAPANESE WAR, 1894-1895
QD421	*CHINOIDINE* **SEE** QUINOIDINE / *chemistry*
QP921.Q5	*CHINOIDINE* **SEE** QUINOIDINE / *physiological effect*
QD341.K2	*CHINONE* **SEE** QUINONE
E99.C57	CHINOOK INDIANS
PM846-9	CHINOOK JARGON
PM841-4	CHINOOK LANGUAGE
PM841-4	CHINOOKAN LANGUAGES
NK8800-8899	CHINTZ / *art*
PL8593	*CHINYANJA LANGUAGE* **SEE** NYANJA LANGUAGE
DR534.5.C5	CHIOS, BATTLE OF, 1657
DR539	CHIOS, BATTLE OF, 1694
E99.C59	CHIPEWYAN INDIANS
PM850.C2	CHIPEWYAN LANGUAGE
PZ10.3	CHIPMUNKS — LEGENDS AND STORIES / *juvenile*
QL795.C	CHIPMUNKS — LEGENDS AND STORIES / *zoology*
QL737.R6	CHIPMUNKS
E83.895	CHIPPEWA INDIANS — WARS, 1898
E99.C6	CHIPPEWA INDIANS
PM851-4	CHIPPEWA LANGUAGE
E356.C55	CHIPPEWA, BATTLE OF, 1814
E99.C6	*CHIPPEWAY INDIANS* **SEE** CHIPPEWA INDIANS
PM850.C2	*CHIPPEWYAN LANGUAGE* **SEE** CHIPEWYAN LANGUAGE
F3320.2.C	CHIQUITO INDIANS
PM5816	CHIQUITO LANGUAGE
E99.A6	*CHIRICAHUA INDIANS* **SEE** APACHE INDIANS
F3320.2.C4	CHIRIGUANO INDIANS
PM5817.C2	CHIRIGUANO LANGUAGE
BF908-935	*CHIROGNOMY* **SEE** PALMISTRY

Z40-115	*CHIROGRAPHY* **SEE** WRITING
BF908-935	*CHIROMANCY* **SEE** PALMISTRY
MT221	CHIROPLAST
RD563	CHIROPODY
RM730	CHIROPRACTIC
QL737.C5	*CHIROPTERA* **SEE** BATS
BF908-935	*CHIROSOPHY* **SEE** PALMISTRY
RM721	*CHIROTHERAPY* **SEE** MASSAGE
E99.C7	CHITIMACHA INDIANS
PM861	CHITIMACHA LANGUAGE
E99.C7	*CHITIMACHAN INDIANS* **SEE** CHITIMACHA INDIANS
QD321	CHITIN / *chemistry*
QP701	CHITIN / *physiological chemistry*
QL737.C2	*CHITTAHS* **SEE** CHEETAHS
GV1017.C5	CHIVALRIE (GAME)
CR	CHIVALRY
PR2064-5	*CHIVALRY-ROMANCES* **SEE** ROMANCES / *english*
PR321-347	*CHIVALRY-ROMANCES* **SEE** ROMANCES / *english*
PQ1411-1545	*CHIVALRY-ROMANCES* **SEE** ROMANCES / *french*
PQ201-221	*CHIVALRY-ROMANCES* **SEE** ROMANCES / *french*
PN692-3	*CHIVALRY-ROMANCES* **SEE** ROMANCES / *medieval*
PN688-690	*CHIVALRY-ROMANCES* **SEE** ROMANCES / *medieval*
QL737.E2	*CHLAMYDOPHORIDAE* **SEE** ARMADILLOS
QD305.A2	*CHLORACETIC ACIDS* **SEE** CHLOROACETIC ACIDS
HV5813	CHLORAL HABIT
RM666.C4	*CHLORAL-HYDRATE* **SEE** CHLORAL / *therapeutics*
RM666.C4	CHLORAL / *therapeutics*
QD181.C5	CHLORATES
SB952.C4	CHLORDAN
SB952.C4	*CHLORDANE* **SEE** CHLORDAN
QP913.C5	CHLORIDES — PHYSIOLOGICAL EFFECT
RM666.C5	CHLORIDES — THERAPEUTIC USE
QP535.C5	CHLORIDES IN THE BODY
QD181.C5	CHLORIDES / *chemistry*
RE766.C4-5	CHLORIDES / *disinfectants*
QD535.C5	CHLORIDES / *physiological chemistry*
TS1892	*CHLORINATED RUBBER* **SEE** RUBBER, CHLORINATED
TD468	*CHLORINATION OF WATER* **SEE** WATER — PURIFICATION — — CHLORINATION
QD281.C5	CHLORINATION / *chemistry*
TN765	CHLORINATION / *metallurgy*
RA766.C4	CHLORINE AND DERIVATIVES AS DISINFECTANTS
TP245.C5	CHLORINE INDUSTRY / *chemical technology*
HD9660.C	CHLORINE INDUSTRY / *trade*
QD281.C5	*CHLORINE PROCESS* **SEE** CHLORINATION / *chemistry*
TN765	*CHLORINE PROCESS* **SEE** CHLORINATION / *metallurgy*
QD181.C5	CHLORINE
QD181.C5	CHLORITES
QE389.62	CHLORITES / *mineralogy*
QD305.A2	CHLOROACETIC ACIDS
QP915.C6	CHLOROFORM — PHYSIOLOGICAL EFFECT
RD86.C5	CHLOROFORM / *anesthetics*
QD305.H6	CHLOROFORM / *chemistry*
RC643	*CHLOROLEUKEMIA* **SEE** CHLOROMA
RC643	CHLOROMA
QK898.C5	CHLOROPHYLL
QL767	*CHLOROPLASTIDS* **SEE** CHROMATOPHORES
QL767	*CHLOROPLASTS* **SEE** CHROMATOPHORES
QD181.P8	CHLOROPLATINIC ACID
RC643	*CHLOROSARCOMA* **SEE** CHLOROMA
RC641	CHLOROSIS
PM3641	CHOCHO LANGUAGE
PM5817.C4	CHOCO LANGUAGE
HD9999.C	CHOCOLATE INDUSTRY / *economics*
TP640	CHOCOLATE INDUSTRY / *technology*
TP638-640	CHOCOLATE / *chemical technology*
RM241	CHOCOLATE / *therapeutics*
HD9200	CHOCOLATE / *trade*
E99.C8	CHOCTAW INDIANS
PM871-4	CHOCTAW LANGUAGE
BF1779.L6	CHOICE BY LOT
Z1035	*CHOICE OF BOOKS* **SEE** BIBLIOGRAPHY — BEST BOOKS
Z689	*CHOICE OF BOOKS* **SEE** BOOK SELECTION
Z1035.A1	*CHOICE OF BOOKS* **SEE** BOOK SELECTION
Z1003	*CHOICE OF BOOKS* **SEE** BOOKS AND READING
LB2350.5	*CHOICE OF COLLEGE* **SEE** COLLEGE, CHOICE OF
MT915	*CHOIR BOY TRAINING* **SEE** CHOIRBOY TRAINING
NA5080	*CHOIR-SCREENS* **SEE** SCREENS (CHURCH DECORATION)
NA5075	CHOIR-STALLS
MT915	CHOIRBOY TRAINING — MANUALS, TEXT-BOOKS, ETC.
MT915	CHOIRBOY TRAINING
MT88	CHOIRS (MUSIC) / *instruction*
PL8113	CHOKWE LANGUAGE
PM3649	*CHOL LANGUAGE* **SEE** CHOLTI LANGUAGE
RC849-853	*CHOLECYSTITIS* **SEE** GALL-BLADDER — DISEASES
QD416	*CHOLEIN* **SEE** CHOLINE / *chemistry*
QP801.C55	*CHOLEIN* **SEE** CHOLINE / *physiological chemistry*
RC850	*CHOLELITHIASIS* **SEE** CALCULI, BILIARY
RD547	*CHOLELITHIASIS* **SEE** CALCULI, BILIARY
RJ456.C	CHOLERA INFANTUM
RC809	CHOLERA MORBUS
QR201.C5	CHOLERA SPIRILLUM
RX226.C5	CHOLERA, ASIATIC — HOMEOPATHIC TREATMENT
RA644.C3	CHOLERA, ASIATIC — PREVENTION
RM761	CHOLERA, ASIATIC — PREVENTIVE INOCULATION
RC126-134	CHOLERA, ASIATIC
QD416	*CHOLESTERIN* **SEE** CHOLESTEROL / *chemistry*
QP801.C5	*CHOLESTERIN* **SEE** CHOLESTEROL / *physiological chemistry*
QP801.C5	CHOLESTEROL METABOLISM
QD416	CHOLESTEROL / *chemistry*
QP801.C5	CHOLESTEROL / *physiological chemistry*
QD416	CHOLINE / *chemistry*
QP801.C55	CHOLINE / *physiological chemistry*
PM5817.C4	*CHOLO LANGUAGE* **SEE** CHOCO LANGUAGE
PM3649	CHOLTI LANGUAGE
PM3943	*CHOLUTECA LANGUAGE* **SEE** MANGUE LANGUAGE
PM3651	*CHONDAL LANGUAGE* **SEE** CHONTAL LANGUAGE
QE391.C6	CHONDRODITE
F2936	*CHONEK INDIANS* **SEE** TZONECA INDIANS / *patagonia*
F2986	CHONO INDIANS
F2986	*CHONOAN INDIANS* **SEE** CHONO INDIANS
F1221.C	CHONTAL INDIANS
PM3651	CHONTAL LANGUAGE
PM5818	*CHONTAQUIRO LANGUAGE* **SEE** CHUNTAQUIRO LANGUAGE
PL8115	CHOPI LANGUAGE
E99.N5	*CHOPUNNISH INDIANS* **SEE** NEZ PERCE INDIANS
PM3711	*CHORA LANGUAGE* **SEE** CORA LANGUAGE
ML457	*CHORAL CONDUCTING* **SEE** CONDUCTING, CHORAL / *history*
MT85	*CHORAL CONDUCTING* **SEE** CONDUCTING, CHORAL / *instruction*
ML1500-1554	CHORAL MUSIC / *history general*
ML2900-3275	CHORAL MUSIC / *sacred*
ML2400-2770	CHORAL MUSIC / *secular*
PN4193.C5	*CHORAL READING* **SEE** CHORAL SPEAKING
PN4305.C4	CHORAL RECITATIONS
MT875	CHORAL SINGING — DICTION
MT898-945	CHORAL SINGING — INSTRUCTION AND STUDY
MT875	CHORAL SINGING — INTERPRETATION (PHRASING, DYNAMICS, ETC.)
MT875	CHORAL SINGING
MT898-945	CHORAL SINGING, JUVENILE
MT88	CHORAL SOCIETIES
ML25-28	CHORAL SOCIETIES
ML26-28	CHORAL SOCIETIES, GERMAN
PN4193.C5	CHORAL SPEAKING
M1258	CHORALE PRELUDES (BAND)
M1245	CHORALE PRELUDES (BAND)
M182-6	CHORALE PRELUDES (OBOE AND ORGAN)
M1060	CHORALE PRELUDES (ORCHESTRA)
M1045	CHORALE PRELUDES (ORCHESTRA)
M600-602	CHORALE PRELUDES (ORGAN, 2 HORNS, TROMBONE, 2 TRUMPETS)
M182-6	CHORALE PRELUDES (PIANO AND ORGAN)
M1160	CHORALE PRELUDES (STRING ORCHESTRA) — SCORES AND PARTS
M1145	CHORALE PRELUDES (STRING ORCHESTRA) — SCORES AND PARTS
M1160	CHORALE PRELUDES (STRING ORCHESTRA)
M1145	CHORALE PRELUDES (STRING ORCHESTRA)
M182-6	CHORALE PRELUDES (TRUMPET AND ORGAN)
M217-218	CHORALE PRELUDES (VIOLIN AND PIANO)

M221-3	CHORALE PRELUDES (VIOLIN AND PIANO)
M229-230	CHORALE PRELUDES (VIOLONCELLO AND PIANO)
M233-6	CHORALE PRELUDES (VIOLONCELLO AND PIANO)
M214-215	CHORALE PRELUDES (2 PIANOS)
M455-7	CHORALE PRELUDES (2 TROMBONES, 2 TRUMPETS)
ML3084	CHORALE / *catholic*
ML3265	CHORALE / *nondenominational*
ML3184	CHORALE / *protestant*
QL605-7	CHORDATA
RC389	CHOREA
RC389	CHOREA, EPIDEMIC
BX1939.R8	CHOREPISCOPI
RG591	CHORION — TUMORS
QM611	CHORION
QL977	CHORION
RE551-661	CHOROID — DISEASES
QM455	CHOROID PLEXUS
QL937	CHOROID PLEXUS
QL949	CHOROID
QM511	CHOROID
RE551-661	*CHOROIDITIS* **SEE** CHOROID — DISEASES
F1434.3.M	*CHOROTEGA INDIANS* **SEE** MANGUE INDIANS / *central america*
PM3943	*CHOROTEGA LANGUAGE* **SEE** MANGUE LANGUAGE
F1434.3.M	*CHOROTEGANS* **SEE** MANGUE INDIANS / *central america*
F3320.2.C	*CHOROTES INDIANS* **SEE** CHOROTI INDIANS
F3320.2.C	CHOROTI INDIANS
PM5817.C7	CHOROTI LANGUAGE
F1465.2.C5	CHORTI INDIANS
PM3661	CHORTI LANGUAGE
PA3136	*CHORUS (DRAMA)* **SEE** DRAMA — CHORUS (GREEK DRAMA)
M1495	CHORUSES (EQUAL VOICES)
M1495	CHORUSES (MEN'S VOICES) WITH PIANO
M1495	CHORUSES (MEN'S VOICES)
M1495	CHORUSES (MEN'S VOICES), UNACCOMPANIED
M1495	CHORUSES (MEN'S VOICES, 3 PTS.) WITH PIANO
M1495	CHORUSES (MEN'S VOICES, 4 PTS.) WITH PIANO
M1495	CHORUSES (MEN'S VOICES, 4 PTS.)
M1495	CHORUSES (MEN'S VOICES, 4 PTS.), UNACCOMPANIED
M1495	CHORUSES (MIXED VOICES) WITH PIANO
M1495	CHORUSES (MIXED VOICES)
M1495	CHORUSES (MIXED VOICES), UNACCOMPANIED
M1495	CHORUSES (MIXED VOICES, 3 PTS.) WITH PIANO
M1495	CHORUSES (MIXED VOICES, 3 PTS.)
M1495	CHORUSES (MIXED VOICES, 4 PTS.) WITH PIANO
M1495	CHORUSES (MIXED VOICES, 4 PTS.)
M1495	CHORUSES (MIXED VOICES, 4 PTS.), UNACCOMPANIED
M1495	CHORUSES (UNISON) WITH PIANO
M1495	CHORUSES (UNISON)
M1495	CHORUSES (WOMEN'S VOICES) WITH PIANO
M1495	CHORUSES (WOMEN'S VOICES)
M1495	CHORUSES (WOMEN'S VOICES), UNACCOMPANIED
M1495	CHORUSES (WOMEN'S VOICES, 2 PTS.) WITH PIANO
M1495	CHORUSES (WOMEN'S VOICES, 3 PTS.) WITH PIANO
M1495	CHORUSES WITH PIANO
M1495	CHORUSES WITH PIANO, 4 HANDS
M1495	CHORUSES
M2060	CHORUSES, SACRED (EQUAL VOICES)
M2084	CHORUSES, SACRED (EQUAL VOICES), UNACCOMPANIED
M2021	CHORUSES, SACRED (EQUAL VOICES, 2 PTS.) WITH INSTR. ENSEMBLE
M2064.2	CHORUSES, SACRED (EQUAL VOICES, 2 PTS.) WITH ORGAN
M2074.2	CHORUSES, SACRED (EQUAL VOICES, 2 PTS.) WITH ORGAN
M2064.2	CHORUSES, SACRED (EQUAL VOICES, 2 PTS.) WITH PIANO
M2074.2	CHORUSES, SACRED (EQUAL VOICES, 2 PTS.) WITH PIANO
M2074.2	CHORUSES, SACRED (EQUAL VOICES, 2 PTS.) WITH 2 TRUMPETS
M2064.2	CHORUSES, SACRED (EQUAL VOICES, 2 PTS.) WITH 2 TRUMPETS
M2074.3	CHORUSES, SACRED (EQUAL VOICES, 3 PTS.) WITH ORGAN
M2064.3	CHORUSES, SACRED (EQUAL VOICES, 3 PTS.) WITH ORGAN
M2064.3	CHORUSES, SACRED (EQUAL VOICES, 3 PTS.) WITH PIANO
M2074.3	CHORUSES, SACRED (EQUAL VOICES, 3 PTS.) WITH PIANO
M2060	CHORUSES, SACRED (EQUAL VOICES, 3 PTS.)
M2084.3	CHORUSES, SACRED (EQUAL VOICES, 3 PTS.), UNACCOMPANIED
M2094.3	CHORUSES, SACRED (EQUAL VOICES, 3 PTS.), UNACCOMPANIED
M2029	CHORUSES, SACRED (MEN'S VOICES) WITH INSTR. ENSEMBLE
M2073	CHORUSES, SACRED (MEN'S VOICES) WITH ORGAN
M2063	CHORUSES, SACRED (MEN'S VOICES) WITH ORGAN
M2060	CHORUSES, SACRED (MEN'S VOICES)
M2083	CHORUSES, SACRED (MEN'S VOICES), UNACCOMPANIED
M2029	CHORUSES, SACRED (MEN'S VOICES, 12 PTS.) WITH ORCHESTRA — SCORES
M2063.2	CHORUSES, SACRED (MEN'S VOICES, 2 PTS.) WITH ORGAN
M2073.2	CHORUSES, SACRED (MEN'S VOICES, 2 PTS.) WITH ORGAN
M2029	CHORUSES, SACRED (MEN'S VOICES, 3 PTS.) WITH INSTR. ENSEMBLE
M2029	CHORUSES, SACRED (MEN'S VOICES, 3 PTS.) WITH ORCHESTRA — SCORES
M2029-2032	CHORUSES, SACRED (MEN'S VOICES, 3 PTS.) WITH ORCHESTRA
M2083.3	CHORUSES, SACRED (MEN'S VOICES, 3 PTS.), UNACCOMPANIED
M2093.3	CHORUSES, SACRED (MEN'S VOICES, 3 PTS.), UNACCOMPANIED
M2029	CHORUSES, SACRED (MEN'S VOICES, 4 PTS.) WITH BAND — PARTS
M2029	CHORUSES, SACRED (MEN'S VOICES, 4 PTS.) WITH INSTR. ENSEMBLE
M2030	CHORUSES, SACRED (MEN'S VOICES, 4 PTS.) WITH ORCHESTRA — VOCAL SCORES WITH ORGAN
M2063.4	CHORUSES, SACRED (MEN'S VOICES, 4 PTS.) WITH ORGAN
M2073.4	CHORUSES, SACRED (MEN'S VOICES, 4 PTS.) WITH ORGAN
M2063.4	CHORUSES, SACRED (MEN'S VOICES, 4 PTS.) WITH PIANO, 4 HANDS
M2073.4	CHORUSES, SACRED (MEN'S VOICES, 4 PTS.) WITH PIANO, 4 HANDS
M2063.4	CHORUSES, SACRED (MEN'S VOICES, 4 PTS.) WITH PIANO
M2073.4	CHORUSES, SACRED (MEN'S VOICES, 4 PTS.) WITH PIANO
M2060	CHORUSES, SACRED (MEN'S VOICES, 4 PTS.)
M2093.4	CHORUSES, SACRED (MEN'S VOICES, 4 PTS.), UNACCOMPANIED
M2083.4	CHORUSES, SACRED (MEN'S VOICES, 4 PTS.), UNACCOMPANIED
M2029	CHORUSES, SACRED (MEN'S VOICES, 6 PTS.) WITH ORCHESTRA — SCORES
M2029	CHORUSES, SACRED (MEN'S VOICES, 6 PTS.) WITH ORCHESTRA
M2030	CHORUSES, SACRED (MEN'S VOICES, 7 PTS.) WITH ORCHESTRA — VOCAL SCORES WITH PIANO
M2063.6	CHORUSES, SACRED (MEN'S VOICES, 7 PTS.) WITH PIANO
M2073.6	CHORUSES, SACRED (MEN'S VOICES, 7 PTS.) WITH PIANO
M2021	CHORUSES, SACRED (MIXED VOICES) WITH INSTR. ENSEMBLE
M2020	CHORUSES, SACRED (MIXED VOICES) WITH ORCHESTRA — TO 1800 — — SCORES
M2023	CHORUSES, SACRED (MIXED VOICES) WITH ORCHESTRA — TO 1800 — — VOCAL SCORES WITH ORGAN
M2023	CHORUSES, SACRED (MIXED VOICES) WITH ORCHESTRA — TO 1800 — — VOCAL SCORES WITH PIANO
M2062	CHORUSES, SACRED (MIXED VOICES) WITH ORGAN
M2062	CHORUSES, SACRED (MIXED VOICES) WITH PIANO
M2021	CHORUSES, SACRED (MIXED VOICES) WITH STRING ORCHESTRA — TO 1800 — — SCORES

M2060	CHORUSES, SACRED (MIXED VOICES) WITH VARIOUS ACC.
M2060	CHORUSES, SACRED (MIXED VOICES)
M2082	CHORUSES, SACRED (MIXED VOICES), UNACCOMPANIED
M2020-2023	CHORUSES, SACRED (MIXED VOICES, 10 PTS.) WITH ORCHESTRA
M2020	CHORUSES, SACRED (MIXED VOICES, 10 PTS.) WITH ORCHESTRA — SCORES
M2072.6	CHORUSES, SACRED (MIXED VOICES, 10 PTS.) WITH ORGAN
M2062.6	CHORUSES, SACRED (MIXED VOICES, 10 PTS.) WITH ORGAN
M2082.6	CHORUSES, SACRED (MIXED VOICES, 12 PTS.), UNACCOMPANIED
M2092.6	CHORUSES, SACRED (MIXED VOICES, 12 PTS.), UNACCOMPANIED
M2021	CHORUSES, SACRED (MIXED VOICES, 13 PTS.) WITH INSTR. ENSEMBLE
M2021	CHORUSES, SACRED (MIXED VOICES, 14 PTS.) WITH INSTR. ENSEMBLE
M2021	CHORUSES, SACRED (MIXED VOICES, 16 PTS.) WITH INSTR. ENSEMBLE
M2023	CHORUSES, SACRED (MIXED VOICES, 16 PTS.) WITH ORCHESTRA — VOCAL SCORES WITH PIANO
M2062.6	CHORUSES, SACRED (MIXED VOICES, 16 PTS.) WITH PIANO
M2072.6	CHORUSES, SACRED (MIXED VOICES, 16 PTS.) WITH PIANO
M2092.6	CHORUSES, SACRED (MIXED VOICES, 16 PTS.), UNACCOMPANIED
M2082.6	CHORUSES, SACRED (MIXED VOICES, 16 PTS.), UNACCOMPANIED
M2072.2	CHORUSES, SACRED (MIXED VOICES, 2 PTS.) WITH ORGAN
M2062.2	CHORUSES, SACRED (MIXED VOICES, 2 PTS.) WITH ORGAN
M2062.6	CHORUSES, SACRED (MIXED VOICES, 24 PTS.) WITH ORGAN
M2072.6	CHORUSES, SACRED (MIXED VOICES, 24 PTS.) WITH ORGAN
M2103.3	CHORUSES, SACRED (MIXED VOICES, 3 PTS.) WITH BAND — SCORES
M2072.3	CHORUSES, SACRED (MIXED VOICES, 3 PTS.) WITH HARPSICHORD
M2062.3	CHORUSES, SACRED (MIXED VOICES, 3 PTS.) WITH HARPSICHORD
M2021	CHORUSES, SACRED (MIXED VOICES, 3 PTS.) WITH INSTR. ENSEMBLE
M2020	CHORUSES, SACRED (MIXED VOICES, 3 PTS.) WITH ORCHESTRA — TO 1800 — — SCORES
M2020	CHORUSES, SACRED (MIXED VOICES, 3 PTS.) WITH ORCHESTRA — SCORES
M2072.3	CHORUSES, SACRED (MIXED VOICES, 3 PTS.) WITH ORGAN
M2062.3	CHORUSES, SACRED (MIXED VOICES, 3 PTS.) WITH ORGAN
M2062.3	CHORUSES, SACRED (MIXED VOICES, 3 PTS.) WITH PIANO
M2072.3	CHORUSES, SACRED (MIXED VOICES, 3 PTS.) WITH PIANO
M2060	CHORUSES, SACRED (MIXED VOICES, 3 PTS.)
M2092.3	CHORUSES, SACRED (MIXED VOICES, 3 PTS.), UNACCOMPANIED
M2082.3	CHORUSES, SACRED (MIXED VOICES, 3 PTS.), UNACCOMPANIED
M2023	CHORUSES, SACRED (MIXED VOICES, 4 PTS.) WITH BAND — VOCAL SCORES WITH ORGAN
M2021	CHORUSES, SACRED (MIXED VOICES, 4 PTS.) WITH BAND — SCORES (REDUCED) AND PARTS
M2021	CHORUSES, SACRED (MIXED VOICES, 4 PTS.) WITH BAND — SCORES (REDUCED) AND PARTS (INSTRUMENTAL)
M2023	CHORUSES, SACRED (MIXED VOICES, 4 PTS.) WITH CHAMBER ORCHESTRA — VOCAL SCORES WITH PIANO
M2021	CHORUSES, SACRED (MIXED VOICES, 4 PTS.) WITH CHAMBER ORCHESTRA — SCORES
M2021	CHORUSES, SACRED (MIXED VOICES, 4 PTS.) WITH INSTR. ENSEMBLE
M2020	CHORUSES, SACRED (MIXED VOICES, 4 PTS.) WITH ORCHESTRA — TO 1800 — — SCORES
M2023	CHORUSES, SACRED (MIXED VOICES, 4 PTS.) WITH ORCHESTRA — VOCAL SCORES WITH ORGAN
M2023	CHORUSES, SACRED (MIXED VOICES, 4 PTS.) WITH ORCHESTRA — TO 1800 — — VOCAL SCORES WITH PIANO
M2023	CHORUSES, SACRED (MIXED VOICES, 4 PTS.) WITH ORCHESTRA AND PIANO — VOCAL SCORES WITH PIANO
M2023	CHORUSES, SACRED (MIXED VOICES, 4 PTS.) WITH ORCHESTRA — VOCAL SCORES WITH PIANO
M2023	CHORUSES, SACRED (MIXED VOICES, 4 PTS.) WITH ORCHESTRA AND ORGAN — VOCAL SCORES WITH PIANO
M2020	CHORUSES, SACRED (MIXED VOICES, 4 PTS.) WITH ORCHESTRA — SCORES
M2072.4	CHORUSES, SACRED (MIXED VOICES, 4 PTS.) WITH ORGAN
M2062.4	CHORUSES, SACRED (MIXED VOICES, 4 PTS.) WITH ORGAN
M2072.4	CHORUSES, SACRED (MIXED VOICES, 4 PTS.) WITH PIANO AND ORGAN
M2062.4	CHORUSES, SACRED (MIXED VOICES, 4 PTS.) WITH PIANO AND ORGAN
M2062.4	CHORUSES, SACRED (MIXED VOICES, 4 PTS.) WITH PIANO
M2072.4	CHORUSES, SACRED (MIXED VOICES, 4 PTS.) WITH PIANO
M2021	CHORUSES, SACRED (MIXED VOICES, 4 PTS.) WITH STRING ORCHESTRA AND ORGAN — SCORES
M2023	CHORUSES, SACRED (MIXED VOICES, 4 PTS.) WITH STRING ORCHESTRA — TO 1800 — — VOCAL SCORES WITH ORGAN
M2023	CHORUSES, SACRED (MIXED VOICES, 4 PTS.) WITH STRING ORCHESTRA — VOCAL SCORES WITH PIANO
M2082.4	CHORUSES, SACRED (MIXED VOICES, 4 PTS.), UNACCOMPANIED
M2092.4	CHORUSES, SACRED (MIXED VOICES, 4 PTS.), UNACCOMPANIED
M2021	CHORUSES, SACRED (MIXED VOICES, 5 PTS.) WITH CHAMBER ORCHESTRA
M2021	CHORUSES, SACRED (MIXED VOICES, 5 PTS.) WITH INSTR. ENSEMBLE
M2020	CHORUSES, SACRED (MIXED VOICES, 5 PTS.) WITH ORCHESTRA — TO 1800 — — SCORES
M2023	CHORUSES, SACRED (MIXED VOICES, 5 PTS.) WITH ORCHESTRA — VOCAL SCORES WITH PIANO
M2072.5	CHORUSES, SACRED (MIXED VOICES, 5 PTS.) WITH ORGAN
M2062.5	CHORUSES, SACRED (MIXED VOICES, 5 PTS.) WITH ORGAN
M2062.5	CHORUSES, SACRED (MIXED VOICES, 5 PTS.) WITH PIANO
M2072.5	CHORUSES, SACRED (MIXED VOICES, 5 PTS.) WITH PIANO
M2021	CHORUSES, SACRED (MIXED VOICES, 5 PTS.) WITH STRING ORCHESTRA
M2092.5	CHORUSES, SACRED (MIXED VOICES, 5 PTS.), UNACCOMPANIED
M2082.5	CHORUSES, SACRED (MIXED VOICES, 5 PTS.), UNACCOMPANIED
M2021	CHORUSES, SACRED (MIXED VOICES, 6 PTS.) WITH BAND — SCORES AND PARTS
M2021	CHORUSES, SACRED (MIXED VOICES, 6 PTS.) WITH INSTR. ENSEMBLE
M2023	CHORUSES, SACRED (MIXED VOICES, 6 PTS.) WITH ORCHESTRA — VOCAL SCORES WITH 2 PIANOS
M2020	CHORUSES, SACRED (MIXED VOICES, 6 PTS.) WITH ORCHESTRA — SCORES (REDUCED) AND PARTS
M2023	CHORUSES, SACRED (MIXED VOICES, 6 PTS.) WITH ORCHESTRA — VOCAL SCORES WITH ORGAN
M2023	CHORUSES, SACRED (MIXED VOICES, 6 PTS.) WITH ORCHESTRA — VOCAL SCORES WITH PIANO
M2020	CHORUSES, SACRED (MIXED VOICES, 6 PTS.) WITH ORCHESTRA — SCORES (REDUCED)
M2062.6	CHORUSES, SACRED (MIXED VOICES, 6 PTS.) WITH ORGAN
M2072.6	CHORUSES, SACRED (MIXED VOICES, 6 PTS.) WITH ORGAN

M2072.6	CHORUSES, SACRED (MIXED VOICES, 6 PTS.) WITH PIANO
M2062.6	CHORUSES, SACRED (MIXED VOICES, 6 PTS.) WITH PIANO
M2072.6	CHORUSES, SACRED (MIXED VOICES, 6 PTS.) WITH 2 PIANOS
M2062.6	CHORUSES, SACRED (MIXED VOICES, 6 PTS.) WITH 2 PIANOS
M2082.6	CHORUSES, SACRED (MIXED VOICES, 6 PTS.), UNACCOMPANIED
M2092.6	CHORUSES, SACRED (MIXED VOICES, 6 PTS.), UNACCOMPANIED
M2023	CHORUSES, SACRED (MIXED VOICES, 7 PTS.) WITH BAND — VOCAL SCORES WITH PIANO
M2021	CHORUSES, SACRED (MIXED VOICES, 7 PTS.) WITH BAND
M2023	CHORUSES, SACRED (MIXED VOICES, 7 PTS.) WITH CHAMBER ORCHESTRA — VOCAL SCORES WITH PIANO
M2023	CHORUSES, SACRED (MIXED VOICES, 7 PTS.) WITH ORCHESTRA — VOCAL SCORES WITH PIANO
M2062.6	CHORUSES, SACRED (MIXED VOICES, 7 PTS.) WITH ORGAN
M2072.6	CHORUSES, SACRED (MIXED VOICES, 7 PTS.) WITH ORGAN
M2062.6	CHORUSES, SACRED (MIXED VOICES, 7 PTS.) WITH PIANO
M2072.6	CHORUSES, SACRED (MIXED VOICES, 7 PTS.) WITH PIANO
M2082.6	CHORUSES, SACRED (MIXED VOICES, 7 PTS.), UNACCOMPANIED
M2092.6	CHORUSES, SACRED (MIXED VOICES, 7 PTS.), UNACCOMPANIED
M2021	CHORUSES, SACRED (MIXED VOICES, 8 PTS.) WITH BAND — SCORES (REDUCED) AND PARTS
M2023	CHORUSES, SACRED (MIXED VOICES, 8 PTS.) WITH CHAMBER ORCHESTRA — VOCAL SCORES WITH PIANO
M2021	CHORUSES, SACRED (MIXED VOICES, 8 PTS.) WITH INSTR. ENSEMBLE
M2023	CHORUSES, SACRED (MIXED VOICES, 8 PTS.) WITH ORCHESTRA — VOCAL SCORES WITH PIANO
M2022	CHORUSES, SACRED (MIXED VOICES, 8 PTS.) WITH ORCHESTRA — VOCAL SCORES
M2020	CHORUSES, SACRED (MIXED VOICES, 8 PTS.) WITH ORCHESTRA — SCORES
M2020	CHORUSES, SACRED (MIXED VOICES, 8 PTS.) WITH ORCHESTRA — TO 1800 — — SCORES
M2023	CHORUSES, SACRED (MIXED VOICES, 8 PTS.) WITH ORCHESTRA — VOCAL SCORES WITH 2 PIANOS
M2020	CHORUSES, SACRED (MIXED VOICES, 8 PTS.) WITH ORCHESTRA — SCORES (REDUCED) AND PARTS
M2023	CHORUSES, SACRED (MIXED VOICES, 8 PTS.) WITH ORCHESTRA AND ORGAN — VOCAL SCORES WITH PIANO
M2020	CHORUSES, SACRED (MIXED VOICES, 8 PTS.) WITH ORCHESTRA AND ORGAN
M2062.6	CHORUSES, SACRED (MIXED VOICES, 8 PTS.) WITH ORGAN
M2072.6	CHORUSES, SACRED (MIXED VOICES, 8 PTS.) WITH ORGAN
M2072.6	CHORUSES, SACRED (MIXED VOICES, 8 PTS.) WITH PIANO, 4 HANDS
M2062.6	CHORUSES, SACRED (MIXED VOICES, 8 PTS.) WITH PIANO, 4 HANDS
M2072.6	CHORUSES, SACRED (MIXED VOICES, 8 PTS.) WITH PIANO
M2062.6	CHORUSES, SACRED (MIXED VOICES, 8 PTS.) WITH PIANO
M2021	CHORUSES, SACRED (MIXED VOICES, 8 PTS.) WITH STRING ORCHESTRA — SCORES
M2023	CHORUSES, SACRED (MIXED VOICES, 8 PTS.) WITH STRING ORCHESTRA AND ORGAN — VOCAL SCORES WITH PIANO
M2062.6	CHORUSES, SACRED (MIXED VOICES, 8 PTS.) WITH 2 PIANOS
M2072.6	CHORUSES, SACRED (MIXED VOICES, 8 PTS.) WITH 2 PIANOS
M2082.6	CHORUSES, SACRED (MIXED VOICES, 8 PTS.), UNACCOMPANIED
M2092.6	CHORUSES, SACRED (MIXED VOICES, 8 PTS.), UNACCOMPANIED
M2023	CHORUSES, SACRED (MIXED VOICES, 9 PTS.) WITH ORCHESTRA — VOCAL SCORES WITH PIANO
M2062.6	CHORUSES, SACRED (MIXED VOICES, 9 PTS.) WITH PIANO
M2072.6	CHORUSES, SACRED (MIXED VOICES, 9 PTS.) WITH PIANO
M2082.6	CHORUSES, SACRED (MIXED VOICES, 9 PTS.), UNACCOMPANIED
M2092.6	CHORUSES, SACRED (MIXED VOICES, 9 PTS.), UNACCOMPANIED
M2101.5	CHORUSES, SACRED (UNISON) WITH INSTR. ENSEMBLE
M2101.5	CHORUSES, SACRED (UNISON) WITH OBOE AND ORGAN
M2101.5	CHORUSES, SACRED (UNISON) WITH ORCHESTRA — SCORES
M2101.5	CHORUSES, SACRED (UNISON) WITH ORGAN
M2101.5	CHORUSES, SACRED (UNISON) WITH PIANO
M2101.5	CHORUSES, SACRED (UNISON) WITH STRING ENSEMBLE
M2101.5	CHORUSES, SACRED (UNISON) WITH STRING ORCHESTRA — VOCAL SCORES WITH PIANO
M2101.5	CHORUSES, SACRED (UNISON)
M2033	CHORUSES, SACRED (WOMEN'S VOICES) WITH INSTR. ENSEMBLE
M2064	CHORUSES, SACRED (WOMEN'S VOICES) WITH ORGAN
M2064	CHORUSES, SACRED (WOMEN'S VOICES) WITH PIANO
M2060	CHORUSES, SACRED (WOMEN'S VOICES)
M2084	CHORUSES, SACRED (WOMEN'S VOICES), UNACCOMPANIED
M2034	CHORUSES, SACRED (WOMEN'S VOICES, 2 PTS.) WITH ORCHESTRA — TO 1800 — — VOCAL SCORES WITH ORGAN
M2074.2	CHORUSES, SACRED (WOMEN'S VOICES, 2 PTS.) WITH ORGAN
M2064.2	CHORUSES, SACRED (WOMEN'S VOICES, 2 PTS.) WITH ORGAN
M2074.2	CHORUSES, SACRED (WOMEN'S VOICES, 2 PTS.) WITH PIANO
M2064.2	CHORUSES, SACRED (WOMEN'S VOICES, 2 PTS.) WITH PIANO
M2034	CHORUSES, SACRED (WOMEN'S VOICES, 2 PTS.) WITH STRING ORCHESTRA — VOCAL SCORES WITH PIANO
M2033	CHORUSES, SACRED (WOMEN'S VOICES, 2 PTS.) WITH STRING ORCHESTRA — SCORES
M2094.2	CHORUSES, SACRED (WOMEN'S VOICES, 2 PTS.), UNACCOMPANIED
M2084.2	CHORUSES, SACRED (WOMEN'S VOICES, 2 PTS.), UNACCOMPANIED
M2074.3	CHORUSES, SACRED (WOMEN'S VOICES, 3 PTS.) WITH FLUTE AND PIANO
M2064.3	CHORUSES, SACRED (WOMEN'S VOICES, 3 PTS.) WITH FLUTE AND PIANO
M2064.3	CHORUSES, SACRED (WOMEN'S VOICES, 3 PTS.) WITH HARP
M2074.3	CHORUSES, SACRED (WOMEN'S VOICES, 3 PTS.) WITH HARP
M2033	CHORUSES, SACRED (WOMEN'S VOICES, 3 PTS.) WITH INSTR. ENSEMBLE
M2034	CHORUSES, SACRED (WOMEN'S VOICES, 3 PTS.) WITH ORCHESTRA — VOCAL SCORES
M2033	CHORUSES, SACRED (WOMEN'S VOICES, 3 PTS.) WITH ORCHESTRA — SCORES
M2074.3	CHORUSES, SACRED (WOMEN'S VOICES, 3 PTS.) WITH ORGAN
M2064.3	CHORUSES, SACRED (WOMEN'S VOICES, 3 PTS.) WITH ORGAN
M2074.3	CHORUSES, SACRED (WOMEN'S VOICES, 3 PTS.) WITH PIANO
M2064.3	CHORUSES, SACRED (WOMEN'S VOICES, 3 PTS.) WITH PIANO
M2033	CHORUSES, SACRED (WOMEN'S VOICES, 3 PTS.) WITH STRING ORCHESTRA — SCORES
M2060	CHORUSES, SACRED (WOMEN'S VOICES, 3 PTS.)
M2084.3	CHORUSES, SACRED (WOMEN'S VOICES, 3 PTS.), UNACCOMPANIED
M2094.3	CHORUSES, SACRED (WOMEN'S VOICES, 3 PTS.), UNACCOMPANIED
M2033	CHORUSES, SACRED (WOMEN'S VOICES, 4 PTS.) WITH INSTR. ENSEMBLE

M2033	CHORUSES, SACRED (WOMEN'S VOICES, 4 PTS.) WITH ORCHESTRA — TO 1800 — — SCORES
M2074.4	CHORUSES, SACRED (WOMEN'S VOICES, 4 PTS.) WITH ORGAN
M2064.4	CHORUSES, SACRED (WOMEN'S VOICES, 4 PTS.) WITH ORGAN
M2064.4	CHORUSES, SACRED (WOMEN'S VOICES, 4 PTS.) WITH PIANO
M2074.4	CHORUSES, SACRED (WOMEN'S VOICES, 4 PTS.) WITH PIANO
M2033	CHORUSES, SACRED (WOMEN'S VOICES, 4 PTS.) WITH STRING ORCHESTRA — SCORES
M2034	CHORUSES, SACRED (WOMEN'S VOICES, 4 PTS.) WITH STRING ORCHESTRA — VOCAL SCORES
M2060	CHORUSES, SACRED (WOMEN'S VOICES, 4 PTS.)
M2094.4	CHORUSES, SACRED (WOMEN'S VOICES, 4 PTS.), UNACCOMPANIED
M2084.4	CHORUSES, SACRED (WOMEN'S VOICES, 4 PTS.), UNACCOMPANIED
M2094.5	CHORUSES, SACRED (WOMEN'S VOICES, 5 PTS.), UNACCOMPANIED
M2084.5	CHORUSES, SACRED (WOMEN'S VOICES, 5 PTS.), UNACCOMPANIED
M2033	CHORUSES, SACRED (WOMEN'S VOICES, 6 PTS.) WITH ORCHESTRA — SCORES
M2064.6	CHORUSES, SACRED (WOMEN'S VOICES, 6 PTS.) WITH PIANO
M2074.6	CHORUSES, SACRED (WOMEN'S VOICES, 6 PTS.) WITH PIANO
M2094.6	CHORUSES, SACRED (WOMEN'S VOICES, 8 PTS.), UNACCOMPANIED
M2084.6	CHORUSES, SACRED (WOMEN'S VOICES, 8 PTS.), UNACCOMPANIED
M2060	CHORUSES, SACRED
M2081	CHORUSES, SACRED, UNACCOMPANIED
M2061	CHORUSES, SACRED, WITH ORGAN
M2061	CHORUSES, SACRED, WITH PIANO
M1581	CHORUSES, SECULAR (EQUAL VOICES), UNACCOMPANIED
M1551.2	CHORUSES, SECULAR (EQUAL VOICES, 2 PTS.) WITH PIANO
M1572	CHORUSES, SECULAR (EQUAL VOICES, 2 PTS.) WITH PIANO
M1544	CHORUSES, SECULAR (EQUAL VOICES, 3 PTS.) WITH ORCHESTRA — VOCAL SCORES WITH PIANO
M1543-6	CHORUSES, SECULAR (EQUAL VOICES, 3 PTS.) WITH ORCHESTRA
M1603	CHORUSES, SECULAR (EQUAL VOICES, 3 PTS.), UNACCOMPANIED
M1581.3	CHORUSES, SECULAR (EQUAL VOICES, 3 PTS.), UNACCOMPANIED
M1550	CHORUSES, SECULAR (MEN'S VOICES) WITH ACCORDION
M1539	CHORUSES, SECULAR (MEN'S VOICES) WITH BAND
M1550	CHORUSES, SECULAR (MEN'S VOICES) WITH PIANO
M1550	CHORUSES, SECULAR (MEN'S VOICES) WITH PIANO, 4 HANDS
M1547	CHORUSES, SECULAR (MEN'S VOICES)
M1580	CHORUSES, SECULAR (MEN'S VOICES), UNACCOMPANIED
M1540	CHORUSES, SECULAR (MEN'S VOICES, 2 PTS.) WITH ORCHESTRA — VOCAL SCORES WITH PIANO
M1562	CHORUSES, SECULAR (MEN'S VOICES, 2 PTS.) WITH PIANO
M1550.2	CHORUSES, SECULAR (MEN'S VOICES, 2 PTS.) WITH PIANO
M1540	CHORUSES, SECULAR (MEN'S VOICES, 3 PTS.) WITH BAND — VOCAL SCORES WITH PIANO
M1563	CHORUSES, SECULAR (MEN'S VOICES, 3 PTS.) WITH PIANO
M1550.3	CHORUSES, SECULAR (MEN'S VOICES, 3 PTS.) WITH PIANO
M1593	CHORUSES, SECULAR (MEN'S VOICES, 3 PTS.), UNACCOMPANIED
M1580.3	CHORUSES, SECULAR (MEN'S VOICES, 3 PTS.), UNACCOMPANIED
M1540	CHORUSES, SECULAR (MEN'S VOICES, 4 PTS.) WITH BAND — VOCAL SCORES WITH PIANO
M1539	CHORUSES, SECULAR (MEN'S VOICES, 4 PTS.) WITH BAND — SCORES (REDUCED) AND PARTS
M1539	CHORUSES, SECULAR (MEN'S VOICES, 4 PTS.) WITH INSTR. ENSEMBLE
M1540	CHORUSES, SECULAR (MEN'S VOICES, 4 PTS.) WITH ORCHESTRA — VOCAL SCORES WITH PIANO
M1540	CHORUSES, SECULAR (MEN'S VOICES, 4 PTS.) WITH ORCHESTRA — PARTS (VOCAL)
M1538	CHORUSES, SECULAR (MEN'S VOICES, 4 PTS.) WITH ORCHESTRA — SCORES (REDUCED) AND PARTS
M1539	CHORUSES, SECULAR (MEN'S VOICES, 4 PTS.) WITH PERCUSSION INSTRUMENTS
M1564	CHORUSES, SECULAR (MEN'S VOICES, 4 PTS.) WITH PIANO
M1564	CHORUSES, SECULAR (MEN'S VOICES, 4 PTS.) WITH PIANO, 4 HANDS
M1550.4	CHORUSES, SECULAR (MEN'S VOICES, 4 PTS.) WITH PIANO
M1550.4	CHORUSES, SECULAR (MEN'S VOICES, 4 PTS.) WITH PIANO, 4 HANDS
M1540	CHORUSES, SECULAR (MEN'S VOICES, 4 PTS.) WITH STRING ORCHESTRA — VOCAL SCORES WITH PIANO
M1550.4	CHORUSES, SECULAR (MEN'S VOICES, 4 PTS.) WITH 2 PIANOS
M1564	CHORUSES, SECULAR (MEN'S VOICES, 4 PTS.) WITH 2 PIANOS
M1547	CHORUSES, SECULAR (MEN'S VOICES, 4 PTS.)
M1580.4	CHORUSES, SECULAR (MEN'S VOICES, 4 PTS.), UNACCOMPANIED
M1594	CHORUSES, SECULAR (MEN'S VOICES, 4 PTS.), UNACCOMPANIED
M1539	CHORUSES, SECULAR (MEN'S VOICES, 6 PTS.) WITH BAND — SCORES
M1596	CHORUSES, SECULAR (MEN'S VOICES, 6 PTS.), UNACCOMPANIED
M1580.6	CHORUSES, SECULAR (MEN'S VOICES, 6 PTS.), UNACCOMPANIED
M1539	CHORUSES, SECULAR (MEN'S VOICES, 8 PTS.) WITH INSTR. ENSEMBLE
M1538-1542	CHORUSES, SECULAR (MEN'S VOICES, 8 PTS.) WITH ORCHESTRA
M1540	CHORUSES, SECULAR (MEN'S VOICES, 8 PTS.) WITH ORCHESTRA — VOCAL SCORES WITH PIANO
M1566	CHORUSES, SECULAR (MEN'S VOICES, 8 PTS.) WITH PIANO
M1550.6	CHORUSES, SECULAR (MEN'S VOICES, 8 PTS.) WITH PIANO
M1540	CHORUSES, SECULAR (MEN'S VOICES, 8 PTS.) WITH STRING ORCHESTRA — VOCAL SCORES WITH PIANO
M1596	CHORUSES, SECULAR (MEN'S VOICES, 8 PTS.), UNACCOMPANIED
M1580.6	CHORUSES, SECULAR (MEN'S VOICES, 8 PTS.), UNACCOMPANIED
M1531	CHORUSES, SECULAR (MIXED VOICES) WITH INSTR. ENSEMBLE
M1530	CHORUSES, SECULAR (MIXED VOICES) WITH ORCHESTRA
M1549	CHORUSES, SECULAR (MIXED VOICES) WITH PIANO
M1547	CHORUSES, SECULAR (MIXED VOICES)
M1579	CHORUSES, SECULAR (MIXED VOICES), UNACCOMPANIED
M1530	CHORUSES, SECULAR (MIXED VOICES, 10 PTS.) WITH ORCHESTRA — SCORES (REDUCED)
M1586	CHORUSES, SECULAR (MIXED VOICES, 10 PTS.), UNACCOMPANIED
M1579.6	CHORUSES, SECULAR (MIXED VOICES, 10 PTS.), UNACCOMPANIED
M1556	CHORUSES, SECULAR (MIXED VOICES, 11 PTS.) WITH PIANO
M1549.6	CHORUSES, SECULAR (MIXED VOICES, 11 PTS.) WITH PIANO
M1533	CHORUSES, SECULAR (MIXED VOICES, 12 PTS.) WITH ORCHESTRA — VOCAL SCORES WITH PIANO
M1556	CHORUSES, SECULAR (MIXED VOICES, 12 PTS.) WITH PIANO
M1549.6	CHORUSES, SECULAR (MIXED VOICES, 12 PTS.) WITH PIANO
M1586	CHORUSES, SECULAR (MIXED VOICES, 12 PTS.), UNACCOMPANIED
M1579.6	CHORUSES, SECULAR (MIXED VOICES, 12 PTS.), UNACCOMPANIED

M1549.2	CHORUSES, SECULAR (MIXED VOICES, 2 PTS.) WITH PIANO
M1552	CHORUSES, SECULAR (MIXED VOICES, 2 PTS.) WITH PIANO
M1530	CHORUSES, SECULAR (MIXED VOICES, 20 PTS.) WITH ORCHESTRA — SCORES
M1530-1537	CHORUSES, SECULAR (MIXED VOICES, 20 PTS.) WITH ORCHESTRA
M1531	CHORUSES, SECULAR (MIXED VOICES, 24 PTS.) WITH INSTR. ENSEMBLE
M1531	CHORUSES, SECULAR (MIXED VOICES, 28 PTS.) WITH INSTR. ENSEMBLE
M1531	CHORUSES, SECULAR (MIXED VOICES, 3 PTS.) WITH INSTR. ENSEMBLE
M1533	CHORUSES, SECULAR (MIXED VOICES, 3 PTS.) WITH ORCHESTRA — VOCAL SCORES WITH PIANO
M1530	CHORUSES, SECULAR (MIXED VOICES, 3 PTS.) WITH ORCHESTRA — SCORES
M1549.3	CHORUSES, SECULAR (MIXED VOICES, 3 PTS.) WITH PIANO, 4 HANDS
M1553	CHORUSES, SECULAR (MIXED VOICES, 3 PTS.) WITH PIANO
M1549.3	CHORUSES, SECULAR (MIXED VOICES, 3 PTS.) WITH PIANO
M1553	CHORUSES, SECULAR (MIXED VOICES, 3 PTS.) WITH PIANO, 4 HANDS
M1531	CHORUSES, SECULAR (MIXED VOICES, 3 PTS.) WITH STRING ORCHESTRA — SCORES
M1579.3	CHORUSES, SECULAR (MIXED VOICES, 3 PTS.), UNACCOMPANIED
M1583	CHORUSES, SECULAR (MIXED VOICES, 3 PTS.), UNACCOMPANIED
M1531	CHORUSES, SECULAR (MIXED VOICES, 32 PTS.) WITH PERCUSSION INSTRUMENTS
M1533	CHORUSES, SECULAR (MIXED VOICES, 4 PTS.) WITH BAND — VOCAL SCORES WITH PIANO
M1531	CHORUSES, SECULAR (MIXED VOICES, 4 PTS.) WITH BAND — SCORES (REDUCED) AND PARTS
M1533	CHORUSES, SECULAR (MIXED VOICES, 4 PTS.) WITH CHAMBER ORCHESTRA — VOCAL SCORES WITH PIANO
M1554	CHORUSES, SECULAR (MIXED VOICES, 4 PTS.) WITH GUITAR
M1549.4	CHORUSES, SECULAR (MIXED VOICES, 4 PTS.) WITH GUITAR
M1531	CHORUSES, SECULAR (MIXED VOICES, 4 PTS.) WITH INSTR. ENSEMBLE
M1533	CHORUSES, SECULAR (MIXED VOICES, 4 PTS.) WITH ORCHESTRA — VOCAL SCORES WITH PIANO AND PARTS (INSTRUMENTAL)
M1530	CHORUSES, SECULAR (MIXED VOICES, 4 PTS.) WITH ORCHESTRA — SCORES (REDUCED) AND PARTS
M1530	CHORUSES, SECULAR (MIXED VOICES, 4 PTS.) WITH ORCHESTRA — SCORES
M1533	CHORUSES, SECULAR (MIXED VOICES, 4 PTS.) WITH ORCHESTRA — VOCAL SCORES WITH PIANO
M1532	CHORUSES, SECULAR (MIXED VOICES, 4 PTS.) WITH ORCHESTRA — VOCAL SCORES
M1530	CHORUSES, SECULAR (MIXED VOICES, 4 PTS.) WITH ORCHESTRA — SCORES AND PARTS
M1530	CHORUSES, SECULAR (MIXED VOICES, 4 PTS.) WITH ORCHESTRA — SCORES (REDUCED) AND PARTS (INSTRUMENTAL)
M1549.4	CHORUSES, SECULAR (MIXED VOICES, 4 PTS.) WITH ORGAN
M1554	CHORUSES, SECULAR (MIXED VOICES, 4 PTS.) WITH ORGAN
M1531	CHORUSES, SECULAR (MIXED VOICES, 4 PTS.) WITH PERCUSSION INSTRUMENTS
M1554	CHORUSES, SECULAR (MIXED VOICES, 4 PTS.) WITH PIANO
M1554	CHORUSES, SECULAR (MIXED VOICES, 4 PTS.) WITH PIANO, 4 HANDS
M1549.4	CHORUSES, SECULAR (MIXED VOICES, 4 PTS.) WITH PIANO, 4 HANDS
M1549.4	CHORUSES, SECULAR (MIXED VOICES, 4 PTS.) WITH PIANO
M1531	CHORUSES, SECULAR (MIXED VOICES, 4 PTS.) WITH STRING ORCHESTRA — SCORES
M1533	CHORUSES, SECULAR (MIXED VOICES, 4 PTS.) WITH STRING ORCHESTRA — VOCAL SCORES WITH PIANO
M1549.4	CHORUSES, SECULAR (MIXED VOICES, 4 PTS.) WITH 2 PIANOS
M1554	CHORUSES, SECULAR (MIXED VOICES, 4 PTS.) WITH 2 PIANOS
M1547	CHORUSES, SECULAR (MIXED VOICES, 4 PTS.)
M1584	CHORUSES, SECULAR (MIXED VOICES, 4 PTS.), UNACCOMPANIED
M1579.4	CHORUSES, SECULAR (MIXED VOICES, 4 PTS.), UNACCOMPANIED
M1533	CHORUSES, SECULAR (MIXED VOICES, 5 PTS.) WITH CHAMBER ORCHESTRA — VOCAL SCORES WITH PIANO
M1531	CHORUSES, SECULAR (MIXED VOICES, 5 PTS.) WITH DANCE ORCHESTRA
M1531	CHORUSES, SECULAR (MIXED VOICES, 5 PTS.) WITH DANCE ORCHESTRA — SCORES (REDUCED)
M1555	CHORUSES, SECULAR (MIXED VOICES, 5 PTS.) WITH FLUTE
M1549.5	CHORUSES, SECULAR (MIXED VOICES, 5 PTS.) WITH FLUTE
M1531	CHORUSES, SECULAR (MIXED VOICES, 5 PTS.) WITH INSTR. ENSEMBLE
M1533	CHORUSES, SECULAR (MIXED VOICES, 5 PTS.) WITH ORCHESTRA — VOCAL SCORES WITH PIANO AND TRUMPETS
M1533	CHORUSES, SECULAR (MIXED VOICES, 5 PTS.) WITH ORCHESTRA — VOCAL SCORES WITH PIANO (4 HANDS)
M1530	CHORUSES, SECULAR (MIXED VOICES, 5 PTS.) WITH ORCHESTRA — SCORES
M1533	CHORUSES, SECULAR (MIXED VOICES, 5 PTS.) WITH ORCHESTRA — VOCAL SCORES WITH PIANO
M1555	CHORUSES, SECULAR (MIXED VOICES, 5 PTS.) WITH PIANO
M1549.5	CHORUSES, SECULAR (MIXED VOICES, 5 PTS.) WITH PIANO
M1555	CHORUSES, SECULAR (MIXED VOICES, 5 PTS.) WITH PIANO, 4 HANDS
M1549.5	CHORUSES, SECULAR (MIXED VOICES, 5 PTS.) WITH PIANO AND TRUMPETS
M1555	CHORUSES, SECULAR (MIXED VOICES, 5 PTS.) WITH PIANO AND TRUMPETS
M1549.5	CHORUSES, SECULAR (MIXED VOICES, 5 PTS.) WITH PIANO, 4 HANDS
M1531	CHORUSES, SECULAR (MIXED VOICES, 5 PTS.) WITH STRING ORCHESTRA — VOCAL SCORES
M1579.5	CHORUSES, SECULAR (MIXED VOICES, 5 PTS.), UNACCOMPANIED
M1585	CHORUSES, SECULAR (MIXED VOICES, 5 PTS.), UNACCOMPANIED
M1533	CHORUSES, SECULAR (MIXED VOICES, 6 PTS.) WITH BAND — VOCAL SCORES WITH PIANO
M1531	CHORUSES, SECULAR (MIXED VOICES, 6 PTS.) WITH CHAMBER ORCHESTRA — SCORES
M1531	CHORUSES, SECULAR (MIXED VOICES, 6 PTS.) WITH INSTR. ENSEMBLE
M1533	CHORUSES, SECULAR (MIXED VOICES, 6 PTS.) WITH ORCHESTRA — VOCAL SCORES WITH PIANO
M1530	CHORUSES, SECULAR (MIXED VOICES, 6 PTS.) WITH ORCHESTRA — SCORES
M1556	CHORUSES, SECULAR (MIXED VOICES, 6 PTS.) WITH ORGAN
M1549.6	CHORUSES, SECULAR (MIXED VOICES, 6 PTS.) WITH ORGAN
M1531	CHORUSES, SECULAR (MIXED VOICES, 6 PTS.) WITH PERCUSSION INSTRUMENTS
M1549.6	CHORUSES, SECULAR (MIXED VOICES, 6 PTS.) WITH PIANO
M1556	CHORUSES, SECULAR (MIXED VOICES, 6 PTS.) WITH PIANO, 4 HANDS
M1556	CHORUSES, SECULAR (MIXED VOICES, 6 PTS.) WITH PIANO
M1549.6	CHORUSES, SECULAR (MIXED VOICES, 6 PTS.) WITH PIANO, 4 HANDS
M1586	CHORUSES, SECULAR (MIXED VOICES, 6 PTS.), UNACCOMPANIED
M1579.6	CHORUSES, SECULAR (MIXED VOICES, 6 PTS.), UNACCOMPANIED
M1531	CHORUSES, SECULAR (MIXED VOICES, 7 PTS.) WITH INSTR. ENSEMBLE

M1549.6	CHORUSES, SECULAR (MIXED VOICES, 7 PTS.) WITH PIANO
M1556	CHORUSES, SECULAR (MIXED VOICES, 7 PTS.) WITH PIANO
M1586	CHORUSES, SECULAR (MIXED VOICES, 7 PTS.), UNACCOMPANIED
M1579.6	CHORUSES, SECULAR (MIXED VOICES, 7 PTS.), UNACCOMPANIED
M1531	CHORUSES, SECULAR (MIXED VOICES, 8 PTS.) WITH BAND — SCORES (REDUCED) AND PARTS (INSTRUMENTAL)
M1533	CHORUSES, SECULAR (MIXED VOICES, 8 PTS.) WITH CHAMBER ORCHESTRA — VOCAL SCORES WITH PIANO
M1533	CHORUSES, SECULAR (MIXED VOICES, 8 PTS.) WITH CHAMBER ORCHESTRA — VOCAL SCORES WITH 2 PIANOS
M1556	CHORUSES, SECULAR (MIXED VOICES, 8 PTS.) WITH HARP
M1549.6	CHORUSES, SECULAR (MIXED VOICES, 8 PTS.) WITH HARP
M1556	CHORUSES, SECULAR (MIXED VOICES, 8 PTS.) WITH HORN
M1549.6	CHORUSES, SECULAR (MIXED VOICES, 8 PTS.) WITH HORN
M1531	CHORUSES, SECULAR (MIXED VOICES, 8 PTS.) WITH INSTR. ENSEMBLE
M1532	CHORUSES, SECULAR (MIXED VOICES, 8 PTS.) WITH ORCHESTRA — VOCAL SCORES
M1530	CHORUSES, SECULAR (MIXED VOICES, 8 PTS.) WITH ORCHESTRA — SCORES
M1533	CHORUSES, SECULAR (MIXED VOICES, 8 PTS.) WITH ORCHESTRA — VOCAL SCORES WITH PIANO
M1530	CHORUSES, SECULAR (MIXED VOICES, 8 PTS.) WITH ORCHESTRA — SCORES AND PARTS (INSTRUMENTAL)
M1533	CHORUSES, SECULAR (MIXED VOICES, 8 PTS.) WITH ORCHESTRA — VOCAL SCORES WITH 2 PIANOS
M1531	CHORUSES, SECULAR (MIXED VOICES, 8 PTS.) WITH PERCUSSION INSTRUMENTS
M1556	CHORUSES, SECULAR (MIXED VOICES, 8 PTS.) WITH PIANO
M1556	CHORUSES, SECULAR (MIXED VOICES, 8 PTS.) WITH PIANO, 4 HANDS
M1549.6	CHORUSES, SECULAR (MIXED VOICES, 8 PTS.) WITH PIANO
M1549.6	CHORUSES, SECULAR (MIXED VOICES, 8 PTS.) WITH PIANO, 4 HANDS
M1531	CHORUSES, SECULAR (MIXED VOICES, 8 PTS.) WITH STRING ORCHESTRA
M1533	CHORUSES, SECULAR (MIXED VOICES, 8 PTS.) WITH STRING ORCHESTRA — VOCAL SCORES WITH PIANO
M1586	CHORUSES, SECULAR (MIXED VOICES, 8 PTS.), UNACCOMPANIED
M1579.6	CHORUSES, SECULAR (MIXED VOICES, 8 PTS.), UNACCOMPANIED
M1531	CHORUSES, SECULAR (MIXED VOICES, 9 PTS.) WITH INSTR. ENSEMBLE
M1530	CHORUSES, SECULAR (MIXED VOICES, 9 PTS.) WITH ORCHESTRA — SCORES (REDUCED)
M1530	CHORUSES, SECULAR (MIXED VOICES, 9 PTS.) WITH ORCHESTRA — SCORES
M1549.6	CHORUSES, SECULAR (MIXED VOICES, 9 PTS.) WITH ORGAN
M1556	CHORUSES, SECULAR (MIXED VOICES, 9 PTS.) WITH ORGAN
M1586	CHORUSES, SECULAR (MIXED VOICES, 9 PTS.), UNACCOMPANIED
M1579.6	CHORUSES, SECULAR (MIXED VOICES, 9 PTS.), UNACCOMPANIED
M1609	CHORUSES, SECULAR (UNISON) WITH BAND — VOCAL SCORES WITH PIANO
M1609	CHORUSES, SECULAR (UNISON) WITH INSTR. ENSEMBLE
M1609	CHORUSES, SECULAR (UNISON) WITH ORCHESTRA — PARTS (VOCAL)
M1609	CHORUSES, SECULAR (UNISON) WITH ORCHESTRA — VOCAL SCORES WITH PIANO
M1609	CHORUSES, SECULAR (UNISON) WITH PIANO
M1609	CHORUSES, SECULAR (UNISON) WITH STRING ORCHESTRA — VOCAL SCORES WITH PIANO
M1609	CHORUSES, SECULAR (UNISON)

M1543	CHORUSES, SECULAR (WOMEN'S VOICES) WITH CHAMBER ORCHESTRA — SCORES
M1543-6	CHORUSES, SECULAR (WOMEN'S VOICES) WITH CHAMBER ORCHESTRA
M1551	CHORUSES, SECULAR (WOMEN'S VOICES) WITH PIANO
M1544	CHORUSES, SECULAR (WOMEN'S VOICES) WITH STRING ORCHESTRA — VOCAL SCORES WITH PIANO
M1547	CHORUSES, SECULAR (WOMEN'S VOICES)
M1581	CHORUSES, SECULAR (WOMEN'S VOICES), UNACCOMPANIED
M1543.5	CHORUSES, SECULAR (WOMEN'S VOICES, 2 PTS.) WITH CHAMBER ORCHESTRA
M1544	CHORUSES, SECULAR (WOMEN'S VOICES, 2 PTS.) WITH CHAMBER ORCHESTRA — VOCAL SCORES WITH PIANO
M1543.5	CHORUSES, SECULAR (WOMEN'S VOICES, 2 PTS.) WITH INSTR. ENSEMBLE
M1543	CHORUSES, SECULAR (WOMEN'S VOICES, 2 PTS.) WITH ORCHESTRA — SCORES
M1544	CHORUSES, SECULAR (WOMEN'S VOICES, 2 PTS.) WITH ORCHESTRA — VOCAL SCORES WITH PIANO
M1572	CHORUSES, SECULAR (WOMEN'S VOICES, 2 PTS.) WITH PIANO
M1551.2	CHORUSES, SECULAR (WOMEN'S VOICES, 2 PTS.) WITH PIANO
M1543.5	CHORUSES, SECULAR (WOMEN'S VOICES, 2 PTS.) WITH STRING ORCHESTRA — SCORES
M1581.2	CHORUSES, SECULAR (WOMEN'S VOICES, 2 PTS.), UNACCOMPANIED
M1602	CHORUSES, SECULAR (WOMEN'S VOICES, 2 PTS.), UNACCOMPANIED
M1543.5	CHORUSES, SECULAR (WOMEN'S VOICES, 3 PTS.) WITH BAND — SCORES AND PARTS (INSTRUMENTAL)
M1543.5	CHORUSES, SECULAR (WOMEN'S VOICES, 3 PTS.) WITH BAND
M1543.5	CHORUSES, SECULAR (WOMEN'S VOICES, 3 PTS.) WITH CHAMBER ORCHESTRA — SCORES
M1551.3	CHORUSES, SECULAR (WOMEN'S VOICES, 3 PTS.) WITH HARP
M1573	CHORUSES, SECULAR (WOMEN'S VOICES, 3 PTS.) WITH HARP
M1543.5	CHORUSES, SECULAR (WOMEN'S VOICES, 3 PTS.) WITH INSTR. ENSEMBLE
M1544	CHORUSES, SECULAR (WOMEN'S VOICES, 3 PTS.) WITH ORCHESTRA — VOCAL SCORES WITH PIANO
M1551.3	CHORUSES, SECULAR (WOMEN'S VOICES, 3 PTS.) WITH PIANO
M1551.3	CHORUSES, SECULAR (WOMEN'S VOICES, 3 PTS.) WITH PIANO, 4 HANDS
M1573	CHORUSES, SECULAR (WOMEN'S VOICES, 3 PTS.) WITH PIANO, 4 HANDS
M1573	CHORUSES, SECULAR (WOMEN'S VOICES, 3 PTS.) WITH PIANO
M1544	CHORUSES, SECULAR (WOMEN'S VOICES, 3 PTS.) WITH STRING ORCHESTRA — VOCAL SCORES WITH PIANO
M1603	CHORUSES, SECULAR (WOMEN'S VOICES, 3 PTS.), UNACCOMPANIED
M1581.3	CHORUSES, SECULAR (WOMEN'S VOICES, 3 PTS.), UNACCOMPANIED
M1544	CHORUSES, SECULAR (WOMEN'S VOICES, 4 PTS.) WITH CHAMBER ORCHESTRA — VOCAL SCORES WITH PIANO
M1544	CHORUSES, SECULAR (WOMEN'S VOICES, 4 PTS.) WITH CHAMBER ORCHESTRA — VOCAL SCORES WITH ORGAN
M1543.5	CHORUSES, SECULAR (WOMEN'S VOICES, 4 PTS.) WITH INSTR. ENSEMBLE
M1543	CHORUSES, SECULAR (WOMEN'S VOICES, 4 PTS.) WITH ORCHESTRA — SCORES AND PARTS (INSTRUMENTAL)
M1551.4	CHORUSES, SECULAR (WOMEN'S VOICES, 4 PTS.) WITH ORGAN
M1543	CHORUSES, SECULAR (WOMEN'S VOICES, 4 PTS.) WITH ORCHESTRA — SCORES AND PARTS
M1574	CHORUSES, SECULAR (WOMEN'S VOICES, 4 PTS.) WITH ORGAN
M1544	CHORUSES, SECULAR (WOMEN'S VOICES, 4 PTS.) WITH ORCHESTRA — VOCAL SCORES WITH PIANO

M1551.4	CHORUSES, SECULAR (WOMEN'S VOICES, 4 PTS.) WITH PIANO
M1544	CHORUSES, SECULAR (WOMEN'S VOICES, 4 PTS.) WITH STRING ORCHESTRA — VOCAL SCORES WITH PIANO
M1543.5	CHORUSES, SECULAR (WOMEN'S VOICES, 4 PTS.) WITH 4 HORNS
M1581.4	CHORUSES, SECULAR (WOMEN'S VOICES, 4 PTS.), UNACCOMPANIED
M1604	CHORUSES, SECULAR (WOMEN'S VOICES, 4 PTS.), UNACCOMPANIED
M1551.5	CHORUSES, SECULAR (WOMEN'S VOICES, 5 PTS.) WITH PIANO
M1575	CHORUSES, SECULAR (WOMEN'S VOICES, 5 PTS.) WITH PIANO
M1581.5	CHORUSES, SECULAR (WOMEN'S VOICES, 5 PTS.), UNACCOMPANIED
M1605	CHORUSES, SECULAR (WOMEN'S VOICES, 5 PTS.), UNACCOMPANIED
M1544	CHORUSES, SECULAR (WOMEN'S VOICES, 6 PTS.) WITH ORCHESTRA — VOCAL SCORES WITH PIANO
M1576	CHORUSES, SECULAR (WOMEN'S VOICES, 6 PTS.) WITH PIANO
M1551.6	CHORUSES, SECULAR (WOMEN'S VOICES, 6 PTS.) WITH PIANO
M1581.6	CHORUSES, SECULAR (WOMEN'S VOICES, 6 PTS.), UNACCOMPANIED
M1606	CHORUSES, SECULAR (WOMEN'S VOICES, 6 PTS.), UNACCOMPANIED
M1544	CHORUSES, SECULAR (WOMEN'S VOICES, 8 PTS.) WITH ORCHESTRA — VOCAL SCORES
M1544	CHORUSES, SECULAR (WOMEN'S VOICES, 8 PTS.) WITH ORCHESTRA — VOCAL SCORES WITH PIANO
M1576	CHORUSES, SECULAR (WOMEN'S VOICES, 8 PTS.) WITH PIANO
M1551.6	CHORUSES, SECULAR (WOMEN'S VOICES, 8 PTS.) WITH PIANO
M1547	CHORUSES, SECULAR
M1578	CHORUSES, SECULAR, UNACCOMPANIED
M1548	CHORUSES, SECULAR, WITH ACCORDION
M1531	CHORUSES, SECULAR, WITH BAND — SCORES AND PARTS
M1531	CHORUSES, SECULAR, WITH BAND
M1548	CHORUSES, SECULAR, WITH PIANO
M1548	CHORUSES, SECULAR, WITH PIANO, 4 HANDS
M1495	CHORUSES, UNACCOMPANIED
BM613	*CHOSEN PEOPLE (JEWS)* **SEE** JEWS — ELECTION, DOCTRINE OF
JX6564	*CHOSES* **SEE** PERSONAL PROPERTY / *private international law*
HF1263	*CHOSES* **SEE** PERSONAL PROPERTY / *u.s.*
DC218.5	CHOUANS
SF429.C5	CHOW CHOWS (DOGS)
PN6014	*CHRESTOMATHIES* **SEE** ANTHOLOGIES
PE1117-1130	*CHRESTOMATHIES* **SEE** READERS AND SPEAKERS / *english*
PN4199-4321	*CHRESTOMATHIES* **SEE** READERS AND SPEAKERS / *recitations*
PE1417	*CHRESTOMATHIES* **SEE** READERS AND SPEAKERS / *rhetoric*
BT198-590	*CHRIST* **SEE** JESUS CHRIST
BV64.J4	*CHRIST THE KING, FEAST OF* **SEE** JESUS CHRIST THE KING, FEAST OF
BV806-814	*CHRISTENING* **SEE** BAPTISM
B631	*CHRISTIAN ALEXANDRIAN SCHOOL* **SEE** ALEXANDRIAN SCHOOL, CHRISTIAN
BR130-133	CHRISTIAN ANTIQUITIES
BR130-133	*CHRISTIAN ARCHAEOLOGY* **SEE** CHRISTIAN ANTIQUITIES
BX1939	CHRISTIAN ART AND SYMBOLISM (CANON LAW)
N7810-8185	CHRISTIAN ART AND SYMBOLISM
BV150-168	CHRISTIAN ART AND SYMBOLISM / *theology*
BR1690-1725	CHRISTIAN BIOGRAPHY
BX4751-4793	*CHRISTIAN CATHOLICISM* **SEE** OLD CATHOLICISM
BR115.C5	*CHRISTIAN CIVILIZATION* **SEE** CIVILIZATION, CHRISTIAN
BV4319	*CHRISTIAN COMMUNICATION* **SEE** COMMUNICATION (THEOLOGY)
BV4930-4935	*CHRISTIAN CONVERTS* **SEE** CONVERTS

BV4800-4895	*CHRISTIAN DEVOTIONAL LITERATURE* **SEE** DEVOTIONAL LITERATURE
BX2177-2198	*CHRISTIAN DEVOTIONAL LITERATURE* **SEE** DEVOTIONAL LITERATURE / *catholic church*
BV1460-1615	*CHRISTIAN EDUCATION* **SEE** RELIGIOUS EDUCATION
BJ1212	CHRISTIAN ETHICS — EARLY CHURCH
BJ1200	CHRISTIAN ETHICS — METHODOLOGY
BJ1217	CHRISTIAN ETHICS — MIDDLE AGES
BJ1190-1278	CHRISTIAN ETHICS
BJ1190-1278	*CHRISTIAN ETHICS-MODERN PERIOD* **SEE** CHRISTIAN ETHICS
BJ2018-2019	*CHRISTIAN ETIQUETTE* **SEE** CHURCH ETIQUETTE
BT1095-1255	*CHRISTIAN EVIDENCES* **SEE** APOLOGETICS
BV168.F5	*CHRISTIAN FLAGS* **SEE** CHURCH PENNANTS / *christian art and symbolism*
BV772	CHRISTIAN GIVING
BV301-525	*CHRISTIAN HYMNS* **SEE** HYMNS
M2115-2145	*CHRISTIAN HYMNS* **SEE** HYMNS / *hymns with music*
E99.M9	*CHRISTIAN INDIANS (MORAVIAN)* **SEE** MORAVIAN INDIANS
BV652.1	CHRISTIAN LEADERSHIP
BV4515	CHRISTIAN LIFE — PICTURES, ILLUSTRATIONS, ETC.
BV4513	CHRISTIAN LIFE — QUOTATIONS, MAXIMS, ETC.
BV4515	CHRISTIAN LIFE — STORIES
BV4500-4595	CHRISTIAN LIFE
BR1690-1725	*CHRISTIAN LIFE-BIOGRAPHY* **SEE** CHRISTIAN BIOGRAPHY
BV4610-4612	*CHRISTIAN LIFE-QUESTIONS AND ANSWERS* **SEE** QUESTIONS AND ANSWERS — CHRISTIAN LIFE
CS2300-2389	*CHRISTIAN NAMES* **SEE** NAMES, PERSONAL
BT766	*CHRISTIAN PERFECTION* **SEE** PERFECTION / *theology*
PA6124	CHRISTIAN POETRY, EARLY / *latin*
BX6953	CHRISTIAN SCIENCE — LEGAL ASPECTS
BX6901-6997	CHRISTIAN SCIENCE
BM729.J4	*CHRISTIAN SCIENCE, JEWISH* **SEE** JEWISH SCIENCE
HX51-54	*CHRISTIAN SOCIALISM* **SEE** SOCIALISM, CHRISTIAN
BT738	*CHRISTIAN SOCIOLOGY* **SEE** SOCIOLOGY, CHRISTIAN
BV772	*CHRISTIAN STEWARDSHIP* **SEE** STEWARDSHIP, CHRISTIAN
N7810-8185	*CHRISTIAN SYMBOLISM* **SEE** CHRISTIAN ART AND SYMBOLISM
BV150-168	*CHRISTIAN SYMBOLISM* **SEE** CHRISTIAN ART AND SYMBOLISM / *theology*
BX1-9	CHRISTIAN UNION
BV30	*CHRISTIAN YEAR* **SEE** CHURCH YEAR
E450	CHRISTIANA, PA. — RIOT, 1851
BL2700-2790	CHRISTIANITY — CONTROVERSIAL LITERATURE
BR165	CHRISTIANITY — EARLY CHURCH
BS2410-2413	CHRISTIANITY — EARLY CHURCH
BR120-123	CHRISTIANITY — ESSENCE, GENIUS, NATURE
BR125.5	CHRISTIANITY — JUVENILE LITERATURE
BR250-275	CHRISTIANITY — MIDDLE AGES
BR100	CHRISTIANITY — PHILOSOPHY
BR100	CHRISTIANITY — PSYCHOLOGY
BR129	CHRISTIANITY — SOURCES
BR280	CHRISTIANITY — 16TH CENTURY
BR440	CHRISTIANITY — 17TH CENTURY
BR120	CHRISTIANITY — 17TH CENTURY
BR470	CHRISTIANITY — 18TH CENTURY
BR120	CHRISTIANITY — 18TH CENTURY
BR121-5	CHRISTIANITY — 19TH CENTURY
BR477	CHRISTIANITY — 19TH CENTURY
BR121-5	CHRISTIANITY — 20TH CENTURY
BR479	CHRISTIANITY — 20TH CENTURY
BV4319	*CHRISTIANITY AND COMMUNICATION* **SEE** COMMUNICATION (THEOLOGY)
BX1396.4	*CHRISTIANITY AND COMMUNISM* **SEE** COMMUNISM AND RELIGION / *catholic church*
HX536	*CHRISTIANITY AND COMMUNISM* **SEE** COMMUNISM AND RELIGION
BR115.E3	CHRISTIANITY AND ECONOMICS
BS670	*CHRISTIANITY AND ECONOMICS-BIBLICAL TEACHING* **SEE** BIBLE — ECONOMICS
BR115.I7	CHRISTIANITY AND INTERNATIONAL AFFAIRS
BL65.L33	*CHRISTIANITY AND LAW* **SEE** RELIGION AND LAW
RC89	*CHRISTIANITY AND MEDICINE* **SEE** MEDICINE AND RELIGION / *pastoral medicine*
BL65.M4	*CHRISTIANITY AND MEDICINE* **SEE** MEDICINE AND RELIGION

BR128.B8	CHRISTIANITY AND OTHER RELIGIONS — BUDDHISM
BR128.H5	CHRISTIANITY AND OTHER RELIGIONS — HINDUISM
BP172	CHRISTIANITY AND OTHER RELIGIONS — ISLAM
BM535	CHRISTIANITY AND OTHER RELIGIONS — JUDAISM
BR127	CHRISTIANITY AND OTHER RELIGIONS / general
BR115.P7	CHRISTIANITY AND POLITICS
BL239-265	CHRISTIANITY AND SCIENCE SEE RELIGION AND SCIENCE
BL65.W2	CHRISTIANITY AND WAR SEE WAR AND RELIGION
BR115.W2	CHRISTIANITY AND WAR SEE WAR AND RELIGION / christianity
PN49	CHRISTIANITY IN LITERATURE
BR1-129	CHRISTIANITY
BT1095-1255	CHRISTIANITY-APOLOGETIC WORKS SEE APOLOGETICS
BT1095-1255	CHRISTIANITY-EVIDENCES SEE APOLOGETICS
BR	CHRISTIANITY-HISTORY SEE CHURCH HISTORY
PN6110.R4	CHRISTIANITY-POETRY SEE RELIGIOUS POETRY / general collections
BR96	CHRISTIANITY-QUESTIONS AND ANSWERS SEE QUESTIONS AND ANSWERS — THEOLOGY
BX1-9	CHRISTIANITY-UNION BETWEEN CHURCHES SEE CHRISTIAN UNION
CB353	CHRISTIANOS SEE CAGOTS
BT1405	CHRISTIANS OF ST. JOHN SEE MANDAEANS
BR158	CHRISTIANS, JEWISH SEE JEWISH CHRISTIANS
PN6110.C5	CHRISTMAS — POETRY
PN6120.C5	CHRISTMAS BOOKS SEE CHRISTMAS PLAYS
PN6071.C6	CHRISTMAS BOOKS SEE CHRISTMAS STORIES
GT4985	CHRISTMAS BOOKS SEE CHRISTMAS
AY10-19	CHRISTMAS BOOKS SEE GIFT-BOOKS (ANNUALS, ETC.)
NC1860	CHRISTMAS CARDS
PN6120.C5	CHRISTMAS PLAYS
PN2159.C	CHRISTMAS PLAYS, MEDIEVAL
NC1280	CHRISTMAS SEALS SEE SEALS (CHRISTMAS, ETC.)
BV4257	CHRISTMAS SERMONS
PN6071.C6	CHRISTMAS STORIES
GT4985	CHRISTMAS TREES
GT4985	CHRISTMAS
PN6120.C5	CHRISTMAS DRAMA SEE CHRISTMAS PLAYS
BT198-590	CHRISTOLOGY SEE JESUS CHRIST
QC385	CHROMATIC ABERRATION (OPTICS) SEE ACHROMATISM
QB85-135	CHROMATIC ABERRATION (OPTICS) SEE LENSES / astronomical instruments
RE961-2	CHROMATIC ABERRATION (OPTICS) SEE LENSES / ophthalmology
QC385	CHROMATIC ABERRATION (OPTICS) SEE LENSES / optics
ML173	CHROMATIC ALTERATION (MUSIC)
ND1279-1286	CHROMATICS SEE COLOR / art
QC495	CHROMATICS SEE COLOR / physics
QH599	CHROMATIN
QL767	CHROMATOPHORES
TN757.C5	CHROME STEEL / metallurgy
TA479.C5	CHROME STEEL / testing
TA479	CHROME-VANADIUM STEEL / construction
TN575	CHROME VANADIUM STEEL / metallurgy
TP936	CHROME-YELLOW
QD181.C7	CHROMICYANIDES
TN490.C4	CHROMITE
TA490	CHROMIUM ALLOYS
TN490.C4	CHROMIUM ORES
TS692.C4	CHROMIUM-PLATING
QD181.C7	CHROMIUM
QK899	CHROMOGEN
NE2520-2529	CHROMOLITHOGRAPHS
NE2500-2529	CHROMOLITHOGRAPHY
MT50	CHROMOPHONE SEE HARMONY — MECHANICAL AIDS
TR510-525	CHROMOPHOTOGRAPHY SEE COLOR PHOTOGRAPHY
QL767	CHROMOPLASTIDS SEE CHROMATOPHORES
QH605	CHROMOSOME THEORY SEE CHROMOSOMES
QH605	CHROMOSOMES
NE1850-1879	CHROMOXYLOGRAPHY SEE COLOR PRINTS
RB156	CHRONIC DISEASES / pathology
RA973.5	CHRONIC DISEASES / public health
PN1870-1879	CHRONICLE HISTORY (DRAMA) SEE HISTORICAL DRAMA / history and criticism
PN1870-1879	CHRONICLE PLAY SEE HISTORICAL DRAMA / history and criticism
Z1121	CHRONOGRAMS
QB107	CHRONOGRAPH / astronomical instruments
UF830-840	CHRONOGRAPH / ballistic instruments
CE	CHRONOLOGY
CE33	CHRONOLOGY, ASSYRO-BABYLONIAN
BS637	CHRONOLOGY, BIBLICAL SEE BIBLE — CHRONOLOGY
CE81	CHRONOLOGY, ECCLESIASTICAL
CE42	CHRONOLOGY, GREEK — TABLES
CE42	CHRONOLOGY, GREEK
D11	CHRONOLOGY, HISTORICAL — CHARTS
D11	CHRONOLOGY, HISTORICAL — TABLES
D11	CHRONOLOGY, HISTORICAL
F1435	CHRONOLOGY, MAYA
CE46	CHRONOLOGY, ROMAN
CE61.S	CHRONOLOGY, SPANISH
CE33	CHRONOLOGY, SUMERIAN SEE CHRONOLOGY, ASSYRO-BABYLONIAN
F1435	CHRONOLOGY, YUCATECAN SEE CHRONOLOGY, MAYA
ML1080	CHRONOMETER (MUSIC) SEE METRONOME
QB107	CHRONOMETER
QP445	CHRONOMETRY, MENTAL SEE TIME PERCEPTION
TR845-899	CHRONOPHOTOGRAPHY SEE CINEMATOGRAPHY
RZ414	CHRONOTHERMAL MEDICINE SEE MEDICINE, CHRONOTHERMAL
RZ414	CHRONOTHERMALISM SEE MEDICINE, CHRONOTHERMAL
SB413.C55	CHRYSANTHEMUMS
RS165.C	CHRYSAROBIN
NB69	CHRYSELEPHANTINE SCULPTURE SEE SCULPTURE, CHRYSELEPHANTINE
QE391.C	CHRYSOLITE
QE391.S47	CHRYSOTILE SEE SERPENTINE / mineralogy
QE475	CHRYSOTILE SEE SERPENTINE / petrology
PL8651	CHUANA LANGUAGE SEE SECHUANA LANGUAGE
PM3641	CHUCHONA LANGUAGE SEE CHOCHO LANGUAGE
RS165.C28	CHUCHUHUASHA
TJ1219	CHUCKS
DK121	CHUDNOF, RUSSIA, BATTLE OF, 1660
PK6996.K	CHUF DIALECT SEE KHUF DIALECT
F915	CHUGACH ESKIMOS
PM41-44	CHUKCHI LANGUAGE
DK759.C	CHUKCHI
F1435.1.C	CHULTUNES
E99.C	CHUMASH INDIANS SEE CHUMASHAN INDIANS
PM891	CHUMASH LANGUAGE SEE CHUMASHAN LANGUAGE
E99.C	CHUMASHAN INDIANS
PM891	CHUMASHAN LANGUAGE
PL4001.A7	CHUNGLI DIALECT SEE AO LANGUAGE
PM5818	CHUNTAQUIRO LANGUAGE
BT91	CHURCH — AUTHORITY
BX1746	CHURCH — PAPAL DOCUMENTS
PE1599.C	CHURCH (THE WORD)
LA	CHURCH AND COLLEGE IN GREAT BRITAIN, (INDIA, THE U.S., ETC.) / history of education
LC321-629	CHURCH AND COLLEGE IN GREAT BRITAIN, (INDIA, THE U.S., ETC.) / religion and education
LC383	CHURCH AND COLLEGE
LC351-629	CHURCH AND EDUCATION / church education
LA91-131	CHURCH AND EDUCATION / history of education
LC107-120	CHURCH AND EDUCATION / separation of church and schools
BV628	CHURCH AND INDUSTRY
BR115.I7	CHURCH AND INTERNATIONAL AFFAIRS SEE CHRISTIANITY AND INTERNATIONAL AFFAIRS
HD6338	CHURCH AND LABOR
HT910-921	CHURCH AND SLAVERY SEE SLAVERY AND THE CHURCH
HN30-39	CHURCH AND SOCIAL PROBLEMS
BX1790-1793	CHURCH AND STATE — CATHOLIC CHURCH
BX5157	CHURCH AND STATE — CHURCH OF ENGLAND
BR740-759	CHURCH AND STATE IN ENGLAND SEE CHURCH AND STATE IN GREAT BRITAIN / church history
BX5157	CHURCH AND STATE IN ENGLAND SEE CHURCH AND STATE IN GREAT BRITAIN / church of england
BR846	CHURCH AND STATE IN FRANCE — 20TH CENTURY
BR840-849	CHURCH AND STATE IN FRANCE / church history
BR856	CHURCH AND STATE IN GERMANY — 1933-1945

BX5139	CHURCH OF ENGLAND — CATECHISMS AND CREEDS
BX5175-5180	CHURCH OF ENGLAND — CLERGY
BX5106-7	CHURCH OF ENGLAND — DIOCESES
BX5150-5155	CHURCH OF ENGLAND — DISCIPLINE
BX5130-5132	CHURCH OF ENGLAND — DOCTRINAL AND CONTROVERSIAL WORKS
LC582-3	CHURCH OF ENGLAND — EDUCATION
BX5157	CHURCH OF ENGLAND — ESTABLISHMENT AND DISESTABLISHMENT
BX5157-5165	CHURCH OF ENGLAND — FINANCE
BX5150-5182	CHURCH OF ENGLAND — GOVERNMENT
BX5051-5101	CHURCH OF ENGLAND — HISTORY
BV370	CHURCH OF ENGLAND — HYMNS
BV2500	CHURCH OF ENGLAND — MISSIONS
BX5115-5126	CHURCH OF ENGLAND — PARTIES AND MOVEMENTS
BX5034	CHURCH OF ENGLAND — PASTORAL LETTERS AND CHARGES
BX5133	CHURCH OF ENGLAND — SERMONS
BX5881	CHURCH OF ENGLAND IN AMERICA
BX5410-5595	*CHURCH OF ENGLAND IN IRELAND* **SEE** CHURCH OF IRELAND
BX5210-5393	*CHURCH OF ENGLAND IN SCOTLAND* **SEE** EPISCOPAL CHURCH IN SCOTLAND
BX5011-5199	*CHURCH OF ENGLAND*
BX5150-5182	*CHURCH OF ENGLAND-CONSTITUTION* **SEE** CHURCH OF ENGLAND — GOVERNMENT
BX5197-9	*CHURCH OF ENGLAND-CONVERTS* **SEE** CONVERTS, ANGLICAN */ church of england*
BX5990-5995	*CHURCH OF ENGLAND-CONVERTS* **SEE** CONVERTS, ANGLICAN */ protestant episcopal church*
BX5034	*CHURCH OF ENGLAND-EPISCOPAL CHARGES* **SEE** CHURCH OF ENGLAND — PASTORAL LETTERS AND CHARGES
BX5125	*CHURCH OF ENGLAND-EVANGELICAL PARTY* **SEE** EVANGELICALISM — CHURCH OF ENGLAND
BX5149.M2	*CHURCH OF ENGLAND-MARRIAGE* **SEE** MARRIAGE — CHURCH OF ENGLAND
BX5126	*CHURCH OF ENGLAND-MODERNISM* **SEE** MODERNISM — CHURCH OF ENGLAND
BX5115-5126	*CHURCH OF ENGLAND-MOVEMENTS* **SEE** CHURCH OF ENGLAND — PARTIES AND MOVEMENTS
BX5969	*CHURCH OF ENGLAND-PARISH MISSIONS* **SEE** PARISH MISSIONS — ANGLICAN COMMUNION */ protestant episcopal*
BX5157	*CHURCH OF ENGLAND-RELATION TO THE STATE* **SEE** CHURCH AND STATE — CHURCH OF ENGLAND
BX5176	CHURCH OF ENGLAND — BISHOPS — — TEMPORAL POWER
BX140-149	*CHURCH OF ETHIOPIA* **SEE** ETHIOPIC CHURCH
BX7020	CHURCH OF GOD
BX5550	CHURCH OF IRELAND — ESTABLISHMENT AND DISESTABLISHMENT
BX5410-5595	CHURCH OF IRELAND
BX8601-8695	CHURCH OF JESUS CHRIST OF LATTER-DAY SAINTS
BX9078	CHURCH OF SCOTLAND — ESTABLISHMENT AND DISESTABLISHMENT
BX9075-9	CHURCH OF SCOTLAND
BX7801-7843	CHURCH OF THE BRETHREN
BX8701-8749	*CHURCH OF THE NEW JERUSALEM* **SEE** NEW JERUSALEM CHURCH
BV705	CHURCH OFFICERS
BV761.A1-5	CHURCH ORDERS, ANCIENT
NA5000	*CHURCH ORNAMENT* **SEE** CHURCH DECORATION AND ORNAMENT
NK2190	*CHURCH ORNAMENT* **SEE** CHURCH DECORATION AND ORNAMENT
BV168.F5	CHURCH PENNANTS */ christian art and symbolism*
NK7100-7215	CHURCH PLATE
NK7112	CHURCH PLATE, AMERICAN
NK7215	CHURCH PLATE, AMERICAN
BV648	CHURCH POLITY — EARLY CHURCH
BV646-651	CHURCH POLITY
BV4720	*CHURCH PRECEPTS* **SEE** COMMANDMENTS OF THE CHURCH
BX1939.C66	CHURCH PROPERTY (CANON LAW)
BV775-7	CHURCH PROPERTY
BX5165	CHURCH RATES */ church of england*
HA38-39	*CHURCH REGISTERS* **SEE** REGISTERS OF BIRTHS, ETC.
BX1939.S35	CHURCH SCHOOLS (CANON LAW)

LC427-629	CHURCH SCHOOLS
BV1580-1583	*CHURCH SCHOOLS, WEEK-DAY* **SEE** WEEK-DAY CHURCH SCHOOLS
HV4175-4320	*CHURCH SETTLEMENTS* **SEE** SOCIAL SETTLEMENTS
PG601-698	CHURCH SLAVIC LANGUAGE
PG701-5	CHURCH SLAVIC LITERATURE
BV1620-1643	*CHURCH SOCIABLES* **SEE** CHURCH ENTERTAINMENTS
BX1939.C	CHURCH SOCIETIES (CANON LAW)
BV900-1450	CHURCH SOCIETIES
BV705	*CHURCH STAFF* **SEE** CHURCH OFFICERS
HF5035.C3	CHURCH SUPPLIES
TS2301.C5	CHURCH SUPPLIES
NA2930	*CHURCH TOWERS* **SEE** TOWERS */ architecture*
BX1-9	*CHURCH UNITY* **SEE** CHRISTIAN UNION
BX1786	*CHURCH UNITY OCTAVE* **SEE** CHAIR OF UNITY OCTAVE
BV705	CHURCH USHERS
BV1585	*CHURCH VACATION SCHOOLS* **SEE** VACATION SCHOOLS, RELIGIOUS
BV167	CHURCH VESTMENTS
BX1925	CHURCH VESTMENTS */ catholic church*
BX5180	CHURCH VESTMENTS */ church of england*
BX2790	CHURCH VESTMENTS */ monastic*
BX1947	CHURCH WORK — FORMS, BLANKS, ETC. */ catholic church*
BV773	CHURCH WORK — FORMS, BLANKS, ETC. */ church finance*
BV707	CHURCH WORK — FORMS, BLANKS, ETC. */ ministry*
BV683	CHURCH WORK AS A PROFESSION
BV4400-4470	*CHURCH WORK WITH ADULTS* **SEE** CHURCH WORK
BV639.C4	*CHURCH WORK WITH BOYS* **SEE** CHURCH WORK WITH CHILDREN
BV639.C4	CHURCH WORK WITH CHILDREN
BV4438	CHURCH WORK WITH FAMILIES
BV639.I4	CHURCH WORK WITH FOREIGNERS */ immigrants*
BV639.C4	*CHURCH WORK WITH GIRLS* **SEE** CHURCH WORK WITH CHILDREN
BV4464.5	CHURCH WORK WITH JUVENILE DELINQUENTS
BV4464	CHURCH WORK WITH PROBLEM CHILDREN
BV639.S5	CHURCH WORK WITH SINGLE PEOPLE
BV1610	CHURCH WORK WITH STUDENTS
BV4435	CHURCH WORK WITH THE AGED
BV4330	CHURCH WORK WITH THE BEREAVED
BV4463	CHURCH WORK WITH THE DEAF
BV4335	CHURCH WORK WITH THE SICK
BV4460	CHURCH WORK WITH THE SICK
BX2390.S5	CHURCH WORK WITH THE SICK */ catholic church*
BV4446	CHURCH WORK WITH YOUNG ADULTS
BV4446	*CHURCH WORK WITH YOUNG MARRIED COUPLES* **SEE** CHURCH WORK WITH YOUNG ADULTS
BX2390.Y7	CHURCH WORK WITH YOUTH — CATHOLIC CHURCH
BV4447	CHURCH WORK WITH YOUTH
BV4400-4470	CHURCH WORK
BV638	*CHURCH WORK, RURAL* **SEE** RURAL CHURCHES
BV683	*CHURCH WORK-VOCATIONAL GUIDANCE* **SEE** CHURCH WORK AS A PROFESSION
BX2170.C55	CHURCH YEAR — MEDITATIONS */ catholic*
BV30	CHURCH YEAR
BV652	*CHURCH-GOING* **SEE** CHURCH ATTENDANCE
BV4523	*CHURCH-GOING* **SEE** CHURCH ATTENDANCE
BV28	CHURCH-NIGHT SERVICES
BV590-640	CHURCH
BR160-240	*CHURCH, APOSTOLIC* **SEE** CHURCH HISTORY — PRIMITIVE AND EARLY CHURCH
BX1939.C	CHURCHES (CANON LAW)
NA4790-6113	CHURCHES */ architecture*
NA4821.A	CHURCHES, ANGLICAN
NA4821.B	CHURCHES, BAPTIST
NA4820	CHURCHES, CATHOLIC
NA5200-6113	CHURCHES, CATHOLIC */ architecture*
BV637	*CHURCHES, CITY* **SEE** CITY CHURCHES
BV636	*CHURCHES, COMMUNITY* **SEE** COMMUNITY CHURCHES
BV638	*CHURCHES, COUNTRY* **SEE** RURAL CHURCHES
NA4821.A	*CHURCHES, EPISCOPAL* **SEE** CHURCHES, ANGLICAN
BV636	*CHURCHES, FEDERATED* **SEE** FEDERATED CHURCHES
NA4821.A	*CHURCHES, PROTESTANT EPISCOPAL* **SEE** CHURCHES, ANGLICAN

NA5200-6113	CHURCHES, PROTESTANT / architecture
BV638	CHURCHES, RURAL SEE RURAL CHURCHES
BV637.7	CHURCHES, SUBURBAN SEE SUBURBAN CHURCHES
BX1407.S8	CHURCHES, SUBURBAN SEE SUBURBAN CHURCHES / catholic
BV637	CHURCHES, TOWN SEE CITY CHURCHES
BV636	CHURCHES, UNDENOMINATIONAL SEE COMMUNITY CHURCHES
BV636	CHURCHES, UNITED SEE COMMUNITY CHURCHES
BV637	CHURCHES, URBAN SEE CITY CHURCHES
CS436	CHURCHWARDENS' ACCOUNTS
DA690	CHURCHWARDENS' ACCOUNTS
RA626-630	CHURCHYARDS SEE CEMETERIES
GT3320	CHURCHYARDS SEE CEMETERIES / manners and customs
E406.C5	CHURUBUSCO, BATTLE OF, 1847
PL4001.C7	CHUTIYA LANGUAGE
PL381-4	CHUVAK LANGUAGE SEE CHUVASHIAN LANGUAGE
DK34.C	CHUVASHES
PL381-4	CHUVASHIAN LANGUAGE
PL8651	CHWANA LANGUAGE SEE SECHUANA LANGUAGE
PL8751	CHWEE LANGUAGE SEE TSHI LANGUAGE
QP91	CHYLE / blood-making
QP165	CHYLE / digestion
QP601	CHYMOSIN SEE RENNET
QP601	CHYMOTRYPSIN
PL8741	CI-TONGA LANGUAGE SEE TONGA LANGUAGE (ZAMBESI)
PL8771	CI-VENDA LANGUAGE SEE VENDA LANGUAGE
PL8113	CIBOKWE LANGUAGE SEE CHOKWE LANGUAGE
F1769	CIBONEY INDIANS
QL523.C5	CICADA
RL621	CICATRICES
Z81	CICERONIAN NOTES SEE TIRONIAN NOTES
PA6346	CICERONIANISM
PQ4222.S7	CICILIANA SEE STRAMBOTTO / collections
PQ4128.S7	CICILIANA SEE STRAMBOTTO / history and criticism
HD9398	CIDER / economics
TP563	CIDER / technology
TS2280	CIGAR LIGHTERS
HD9149.C48-5	CIGAR MANUFACTURE AND TRADE / economics
TS2260	CIGAR MANUFACTURE AND TRADE / technology
NE965	CIGARETTE CARDS — COLLECTORS AND COLLECTING
NE965	CIGARETTE CARDS
HV5740-5745	CIGARETTE HABIT
TS2280	CIGARETTE LIGHTERS SEE CIGAR LIGHTERS
HD9149.C39-42	CIGARETTE MANUFACTURE AND TRADE / economics
TS2260	CIGARETTE MANUFACTURE AND TRADE / technology
HV5740-5745	CIGARETTES SEE CIGARETTE HABIT
HD9149.C39-42	CIGARETTES SEE CIGARETTE MANUFACTURE AND TRADE / economics
TS2260	CIGARETTES SEE CIGARETTE MANUFACTURE AND TRADE / technology
TS2260	CIGARS
QP311	CILIA AND CILIARY MOTION
QL852	CILIA AND CILIARY MOTION
QL368.C5	CILIATA
M283.C5	CIMBALOM AND PIANO MUSIC
M282.C5	CIMBALOM AND PIANO MUSIC
M142.C	CIMBALOM MUSIC
ML1015-1018	CIMBALOM
DG255.5	CIMBRI
F1221.C56	CINANTEC INDIANS SEE CHINANTEC INDIANS
PM3630	CINANTEC LANGUAGE SEE CHINANTEC LANGUAGE
PM3630	CINATENC LANGUAGE SEE CHINANTEC LANGUAGE
GV1295.P3	CINCH (GAME) SEE PEDRO (GAME)
QK495.C57	CINCHONA / botany
SB295.C5	CINCHONA / culture
RS165.C3	CINCHONA / pharmacy
RM666.C53	CINCHONA / therapeutics
QD421	CINCHONIDINE / chemistry
RM666.C54	CINCHONIDINE / therapeutics
QL696.P2	CINCLIDAE SEE DIPPERS (BIRDS)
F1233	CINCO DE MAYO, BATTLE OF, 1862
PL8110.C	CINDAU LANGUAGE SEE CHINDAU LANGUAGE
TH1491	CINDER BLOCKS / building
TH1491	CINDER CONCRETE BLOCKS SEE CINDER BLOCKS / building
TR855	CINEMASCOPE SEE WIDE-SCREEN PROCESSES (CINEMATOGRAPHY)
TR893	CINEMATOGRAPHY — SCIENTIFIC APPLICATIONS
TR852	CINEMATOGRAPHY — STUDY AND TEACHING
TR845-899	CINEMATOGRAPHY
TR855	CINEMATOGRAPHY, WIDE-SCREEN SEE WIDE-SCREEN PROCESSES (CINEMATOGRAPHY)
TR855	CINERAMA SEE WIDE-SCREEN PROCESSES (CINEMATOGRAPHY)
NK3700-4657	CINERARY URNS SEE URNS / ceramics
DS489.2	CINGALESE SEE SINHALESE
TN490.M	CINNABAR / mineral industries
QE391.C	CINNABAR / mineralogy
TX407.C	CINNAMON
SB307.C	CINNAMON
GV1295.05	CINQUILLE (GAME) SEE QUINTILLE (GAME) / ombre
RD525	CIONORRHAPHY SEE PALATE — SURGERY
QC872	CIPHER AND TELEGRAPH CODES — METEOROLOGY
HE7669-7679	CIPHER AND TELEGRAPH CODES
HE7676-7	CIPHER AND TELEGRAPH CODES / commercial codes
HE7678	CIPHER AND TELEGRAPH CODES / foreign languages
NK3640	CIPHERS (LETTERING) SEE MONOGRAMS
NE2710	CIPHERS (LETTERING) SEE MONOGRAMS / engraving
Z103-4	CIPHERS
PK9201.C5	CIRCASSIAN LANGUAGE
QA467	CIRCLE-SQUARING
QA557	CIRCLE / analytic geometry
QA484	CIRCLE / plane geometry
QB103	CIRCLE, VERTICAL SEE VERTICAL CIRCLE
QA557	CIRCLES OF THE TRIANGLE SEE TRIANGLE / analytic geometry
QA482	CIRCLES OF THE TRIANGLE SEE TRIANGLE / plane geometry
BV664	CIRCUIT RIDING SEE ITINERANCY (CHURCH POLITY)
TK2842	CIRCUIT-BREAKERS, ELECTRIC SEE ELECTRIC CIRCUIT-BREAKERS
QC601	CIRCUITS, ELECTRIC SEE ELECTRIC CIRCUITS
TK3001-3226	CIRCUITS, ELECTRIC SEE ELECTRIC CIRCUITS / electric engineering
QA55	CIRCULAR FUNCTIONS SEE TRIGONOMETRICAL FUNCTIONS / tables
QA342	CIRCULAR FUNCTIONS SEE TRIGONOMETRICAL FUNCTIONS / theory of functions
QA531-8	CIRCULAR FUNCTIONS SEE TRIGONOMETRICAL FUNCTIONS / trigonometry
QP101	CIRCULATION OF THE BLOOD SEE BLOOD — CIRCULATION
QL835-841	CIRCULATORY SYSTEM SEE CARDIOVASCULAR SYSTEM / comparative anatomy
QM178-197	CIRCULATORY SYSTEM SEE CARDIOVASCULAR SYSTEM / human anatomy
BT1365	CIRCUMCELLIANS SEE CIRCUMCELLIONS
BT1365	CIRCUMCELLIONS
GN484	CIRCUMCISION / ethnology
RD590	CIRCUMCISION / surgery
G420-440	CIRCUMNAVIGATION SEE VOYAGES AROUND THE WORLD
GV1801-1837	CIRCUS
TR263.C	CIRO-FLEX CAMERA
QL444.C5	CIRRHIPEDIA SEE CIRRIPEDIA
RC848.C5	CIRRHOSIS HEPATIS SEE LIVER — CIRRHOSIS
RC848.C5	CIRRHOSIS OF THE LIVER SEE LIVER — CIRRHOSIS
QL444.C5	CIRRIPEDIA
NA4820	CISTERCIAN ARCHITECTURE SEE ARCHITECTURE, CISTERCIAN
BX3401-3455	CISTERCIANS
ML760	CITARA SEE CITHARA
ML760	CITHARA
M142.C5	CITHERN MUSIC
ML760	CITHERN
JS93-99	CITIES AND TOWNS — CIVIC IMPROVEMENT
JS302-3	CITIES AND TOWNS — CIVIC IMPROVEMENT / societies u.s.
HT371	CITIES AND TOWNS — GROWTH / city problem
HB2161-2370	CITIES AND TOWNS — GROWTH / statistics
NA9000-9284	CITIES AND TOWNS — PLANNING
PN56.C	CITIES AND TOWNS IN LITERATURE
PS374.C5	CITIES AND TOWNS IN LITERATURE / american fiction
PR830.C	CITIES AND TOWNS IN LITERATURE / english fiction

PN3448.C5	CITIES AND TOWNS IN LITERATURE / fiction
HT101-381	CITIES AND TOWNS
HV6177	CITIES AND TOWNS / influence on crime
JS	CITIES AND TOWNS / local government
D134	CITIES AND TOWNS, MEDIEVAL
HT371	CITIES AND TOWNS, MOVEMENT TO SEE CITIES AND TOWNS — GROWTH / city problem
HB2161-2370	CITIES AND TOWNS, MOVEMENT TO SEE CITIES AND TOWNS — GROWTH / statistics
JS	CITIES AND TOWNS-LAW AND LEGISLATION SEE MUNICIPAL CORPORATIONS
TP741	CITIES AND TOWNS-LIGHTING SEE STREET-LIGHTING
TK4188	CITIES AND TOWNS-LIGHTING SEE STREET-LIGHTING / electric
TA501-625	CITIES AND TOWNS-SURVEYING SEE SURVEYING
NA9050	CITIES AND TOWNS — PLANNING — — HYGIENIC ASPECTS
NA9013	CITIES AND TOWNS — PLANNING — — VOCATIONAL GUIDANCE
G100	CITIES, IMAGINARY SEE GEOGRAPHICAL MYTHS
GR650-690	CITIES, IMAGINARY SEE GEOGRAPHICAL MYTHS / folk-lore
LC220	CITIZENS' ADVISORY COMMITTEES IN EDUCATION
LC220	CITIZENS' COMMITTEES IN EDUCATION SEE CITIZENS' ADVISORY COMMITTEES IN EDUCATION
JK1759	CITIZENSHIP — JUVENILE LITERATURE / u.s.
JF800-823	CITIZENSHIP
LC1091	CITIZENSHIP / education for
JK1751-1788	CITIZENSHIP / u.s.
TL215.C	CITROEN AUTOMOBILE
SB369	CITRON
SB945.B45	CITRUS BLACK FLY
SB741.C5	CITRUS CANKER
SB369	CITRUS FRUIT BY-PRODUCTS SEE CITRUS FRUITS — BY-PRODUCTS
TP506	CITRUS FRUIT BY-PRODUCTS SEE CITRUS FRUITS — BY-PRODUCTS
TP506	CITRUS FRUITS — BY-PRODUCTS
SB369	CITRUS FRUITS — BY-PRODUCTS
SB608.C5	CITRUS FRUITS — DISEASES AND PESTS
SB369	CITRUS FRUITS / culture
SB369	CITRUS PRODUCTS SEE CITRUS FRUITS — BY-PRODUCTS
TP506	CITRUS PRODUCTS SEE CITRUS FRUITS — BY-PRODUCTS
SB945.C	CITRUS RUST MITE
SB608.C5	CITRUS THRIPS
JS348-9	CITY AND STATE, RELATION OF SEE MUNICIPAL HOME RULE / u.s.
JS3131-7	CITY AND STATE, RELATION OF SEE MUNICIPAL HOME RULE / gt. brit.
JS113	CITY AND STATE, RELATION OF SEE MUNICIPAL HOME RULE
HT151-3	CITY AND TOWN LIFE
HT361	CITY AND TOWN LIFE
HT206	CITY CHILDREN
BV637	CITY CHURCHES
BV637.5	CITY CLERGY
JS	CITY GOVERNMENT SEE MUNICIPAL GOVERNMENT
HT361	CITY LIFE SEE CITY AND TOWN LIFE
HT151-3	CITY LIFE SEE CITY AND TOWN LIFE
JS344.C5	CITY MANAGER SEE MUNICIPAL GOVERNMENT BY CITY MANAGER / u.s.
NA9000-9284	CITY PLANNING SEE CITIES AND TOWNS — PLANNING
TA501-625	CITY SURVEYING SEE SURVEYING
NA9000-9425	CIVIC ART SEE ART, MUNICIPAL / aesthetics of cities
N8700-8850	CIVIC ART SEE ART, MUNICIPAL / public art
JS93-99	CIVIC IMPROVEMENT SEE CITIES AND TOWNS — CIVIC IMPROVEMENT
JS302-3	CIVIC IMPROVEMENT SEE CITIES AND TOWNS — CIVIC IMPROVEMENT / societies u.s.
PN2268	CIVIC THEATER SEE THEATER, MUNICIPAL
UA926-9	CIVIL DEFENSE
JC328	CIVIL DISOBEDIENCE SEE GOVERNMENT, RESISTANCE TO
TA144	CIVIL ENGINEERING — EARLY WORKS TO 1850
TA151	CIVIL ENGINEERING — PROBLEMS, EXERCISES, ETC.
TA157	CIVIL ENGINEERING AS A PROFESSION SEE ENGINEERING AS A PROFESSION

TA	CIVIL ENGINEERING
TA183	CIVIL ENGINEERING-ESTIMATES AND COSTS SEE ENGINEERING — ESTIMATES AND COSTS
TA190	CIVIL ENGINEERING-MANAGEMENT SEE ENGINEERING — MANAGEMENT
T61-173	CIVIL ENGINEERING-STUDY AND TEACHING SEE ENGINEERING — STUDY AND TEACHING
B65	CIVIL GOVERNMENT SEE POLITICAL SCIENCE / j political science and philosophy
HM33	CIVIL GOVERNMENT SEE POLITICAL SCIENCE / political science and sociology
JC585-599	CIVIL LIBERTY SEE LIBERTY / political theory
HM271	CIVIL LIBERTY SEE LIBERTY / sociology
HQ1006	CIVIL MARRIAGE
JC328	CIVIL OBEDIENCE SEE GOVERNMENT, RESISTANCE TO
BX1939.C664	CIVIL PROCEDURE (CANON LAW)
JX6601-6625	CIVIL PROCEDURE (INTERNATIONAL LAW)
JK716	CIVIL SERVICE — EXAMINATIONS / u.s.
JK716	CIVIL SERVICE EXAMINATIONS SEE CIVIL SERVICE — EXAMINATIONS / u.s.
JF1671	CIVIL SERVICE PENSIONS
JK791	CIVIL SERVICE PENSIONS / u.s.
JK681-699	CIVIL SERVICE REFORM / u.s.
JF1321-1671	CIVIL SERVICE
JV443-5	CIVIL SERVICE / colonial
JS148-163	CIVIL SERVICE / municipal
JN-JQ	CIVIL SERVICE / other countries
HD8011-8023	CIVIL SERVICE / state labor
JK631-901	CIVIL SERVICE / u.s.
JX1995	CIVIL SERVICE, INTERNATIONAL SEE INTERNATIONAL OFFICIALS AND EMPLOYEES
HV8007	CIVIL UNIFORMS SEE UNIFORMS, CIVIL / police
JX4541	CIVIL WAR / international law
E456-655	CIVIL WAR-U.S. SEE UNITED STATES — HISTORY — — CIVIL WAR
UA926-9	CIVILIAN DEFENSE SEE CIVIL DEFENSE
CB19	CIVILIZATION — PHILOSOPHY
CB478	CIVILIZATION AND MACHINERY SEE TECHNOLOGY AND CIVILIZATION / history
HM221	CIVILIZATION AND MACHINERY SEE TECHNOLOGY AND CIVILIZATION / sociology
CB151	CIVILIZATION AND SCIENCE SEE SCIENCE AND CIVILIZATION
HM221	CIVILIZATION AND TECHNOLOGY SEE TECHNOLOGY AND CIVILIZATION / sociology
CB478	CIVILIZATION AND TECHNOLOGY SEE TECHNOLOGY AND CIVILIZATION / history
CB481	CIVILIZATION AND WAR SEE WAR AND CIVILIZATION
CB	CIVILIZATION
HM101	CIVILIZATION
E59.C95	CIVILIZATION, AMERICAN SEE INDIANS — CULTURE
E162-8	CIVILIZATION, AMERICAN SEE UNITED STATES — CIVILIZATION / early periods
E169.1	CIVILIZATION, AMERICAN SEE UNITED STATES — CIVILIZATION
CB311	CIVILIZATION, ANCIENT
DS215	CIVILIZATION, ARAB
CB201-231	CIVILIZATION, ARYAN
GN539	CIVILIZATION, ARYAN
DS70.7	CIVILIZATION, ASSYRO-BABYLONIAN
DS70.7	CIVILIZATION, BABYLONIAN SEE CIVILIZATION, ASSYRO-BABYLONIAN
BR115.C5	CIVILIZATION, CHRISTIAN
DS425	CIVILIZATION, DRAVIDIAN
CB213-214	CIVILIZATION, GERMANIC
DF75-129	CIVILIZATION, GREEK
DS423-5	CIVILIZATION, HINDU
CB226	CIVILIZATION, HISPANIC
PA4037	CIVILIZATION, HOMERIC
E59.C95	CIVILIZATION, INDIAN SEE INDIANS — CULTURE
D199.3	CIVILIZATION, ISLAMIC
DS427	CIVILIZATION, ISLAMIC / india
DS112-113	CIVILIZATION, JEWISH SEE JEWS — CIVILIZATION
CB351-5	CIVILIZATION, MEDIEVAL
CB411	CIVILIZATION, MODERN — 18TH CENTURY
CB415-417	CIVILIZATION, MODERN — 19TH CENTURY
CB425-7	CIVILIZATION, MODERN — 20TH CENTURY
CB357-425	CIVILIZATION, MODERN
D199.3	CIVILIZATION, MUSLIM SEE CIVILIZATION, ISLAMIC

DS427	*CIVILIZATION, MUSLIM* **SEE** CIVILIZATION, ISLAMIC / *india*
CB245	CIVILIZATION, OCCIDENTAL
CB251	*CIVILIZATION, OCCIDENTAL-ORIENTAL INFLUENCES* **SEE** EAST AND WEST
CB253	CIVILIZATION, ORIENTAL
CB251	*CIVILIZATION, ORIENTAL-OCCIDENTAL INFLUENCES* **SEE** EAST AND WEST
CB151	CIVILIZATION, PAGAN
E59.C95	*CIVILIZATION, PRE-COLUMBIAN* **SEE** INDIANS — CULTURE
CB241	CIVILIZATION, SEMITIC
CB226	*CIVILIZATION, SPANISH* **SEE** CIVILIZATION, HISPANIC
DS72	*CIVILIZATION, SUMERIAN* **SEE** SUMERIANS
DS423-5	*CIVILIZATION, VEDIC* **SEE** CIVILIZATION, HINDU
CB245	*CIVILIZATION, WESTERN* **SEE** CIVILIZATION, OCCIDENTAL
QL444.C6	CLADOCERA
E99.C83	*CLAIAKWAT INDIANS* **SEE** CLAYOQUOT INDIANS
HD226	*CLAIM ASSOCIATIONS* **SEE** LAND CLAIM ASSOCIATIONS
HJ8903-8963	CLAIMS
JX238	CLAIMS / *international law*
HG9323.A3	*CLAIMS, ADJUSTMENT OF* **SEE** INSURANCE, ACCIDENT — ADJUSTMENT OF CLAIMS
HG9721-7	*CLAIMS, ADJUSTMENT OF* **SEE** INSURANCE, FIRE — ADJUSTMENT OF CLAIMS
HE1795	*CLAIMS, FREIGHT* **SEE** FREIGHT AND FREIGHTAGE — CLAIMS
BF1338	CLAIRAUDIENCE
NC755	*CLAIROBSCUR* **SEE** CHIAROSCURO
BF1325	CLAIRVOYANCE
QD319	CLAISEN CONDENSATION
E99.C82	CLALLAM INDIANS
PM895	CLALLAM LANGUAGE
E99.K26	*CLAMCOET INDIANS* **SEE** KARANKAWA INDIANS
JC20-45	CLANS AND CLAN SYSTEM
GN492	CLANS AND CLAN SYSTEM / *ethnology*
BX4361-4	*CLARES, POOR* **SEE** POOR CLARES
TP548-559	CLARET
TP156.C	*CLARIFICATION OF LIQUIDS* **SEE** LIQUIDS — CLARIFICATION
MT382	CLARINET — METHODS (JAZZ)
MT382	CLARINET — METHODS
MT386	CLARINET — ORCHESTRA STUDIES
MT385	CLARINET — STUDIES AND EXERCISES
M288-9	CLARINET AND FLUTE MUSIC
M1040-1041	CLARINET AND FLUTE WITH CHAMBER ORCHESTRA
M1105	CLARINET AND FLUTE WITH STRING ORCHESTRA — SCORES
M1105-6	CLARINET AND FLUTE WITH STRING ORCHESTRA
M296-7	CLARINET AND GUITAR MUSIC
M296-7	CLARINET AND HARP MUSIC
M1105-6	CLARINET AND HARP WITH STRING ORCHESTRA
M288-9	CLARINET AND HORN MUSIC
M288-9	CLARINET AND OBOE MUSIC
M248-252	CLARINET AND PIANO MUSIC (JAZZ)
M248-250	CLARINET AND PIANO MUSIC
M248-252	*CLARINET AND PIANO MUSIC, ARRANGED (JAZZ)* **SEE** CLARINET AND PIANO MUSIC (JAZZ)
M251-2	CLARINET AND PIANO MUSIC, ARRANGED
M290-291	CLARINET AND VIOLIN MUSIC
M1105	CLARINET AND VIOLIN WITH STRING ORCHESTRA — SCORES
M1105-6	CLARINET AND VIOLIN WITH STRING ORCHESTRA
M288-9	CLARINET MUSIC (2 CLARINETS)
M288-9	CLARINET MUSIC (2 CLARINETS), ARRANGED
M355-7	*CLARINET MUSIC (3 CLARINETS)* **SEE** WIND TRIOS (3 CLARINETS)
M355-7	*CLARINET MUSIC (3 CLARINETS)* **SEE** WIND TRIOS (3 CLARINETS)
M455-7	*CLARINET MUSIC (4 CLARINETS)* **SEE** WIND QUARTETS (4 CLARINETS)
M455-7	*CLARINET MUSIC (4 CLARINETS)* **SEE** WIND QUARTETS (4 CLARINETS)
M655-7	*CLARINET MUSIC (6 CLARINETS)* **SEE** WIND SEXTETS (6 CLARINETS)
M655-7	*CLARINET MUSIC (6 CLARINETS)* **SEE** WIND SEXTETS (6 CLARINETS)

M855-7	*CLARINET MUSIC (8 CLARINETS)* **SEE** WIND OCTETS (8 CLARINETS)
M70-72	CLARINET MUSIC
M73-74	CLARINET MUSIC, ARRANGED
M1205	CLARINET WITH BAND
M1025	CLARINET WITH CHAMBER ORCHESTRA — SOLO WITH PIANO
M1025	CLARINET WITH ORCHESTRA — SOLO WITH PIANO
M1024-5	CLARINET WITH ORCHESTRA
M1106	CLARINET WITH STRING ORCHESTRA — SOLO WITH PIANO
M1105-6	CLARINET WITH STRING ORCHESTRA
ML945-8	CLARINET / *history and construction*
M1105	CLARINET, FLUTE, OBOE WITH STRING ORCHESTRA — SCORES
M1105-6	CLARINET, FLUTE, OBOE WITH STRING ORCHESTRA
M1105-6	CLARINET, FLUTE, TRUMPET WITH STRING ORCHESTRA
M1105-6	CLARINET, TROMBONE, TRUMPET WITH STRING ORCHESTRA
MT388	*CLARINET-SELF-INSTRUCTION* **SEE** CLARINET — METHODS — — SELF-INSTRUCTION
M1105	CLARINETS (3) WITH STRING ORCHESTRA — SCORES
M1105-6	CLARINETS (3) WITH STRING ORCHESTRA
M1105	CLARINETS (4) WITH STRING ORCHESTRA — SCORES
M1105-6	CLARINETS (4) WITH STRING ORCHESTRA
MT388	CLARINET — METHODS — — SELF-INSTRUCTION
ML945-8	*CLARIONET* **SEE** CLARINET / *history and construction*
BX4361-4	*CLARISSES* **SEE** POOR CLARES
E237	CLARK'S EXPEDITION AGAINST DETROIT, 1781
E234	CLARK'S EXPEDITION TO THE ILLINOIS, 1778-1779
BX8346	CLASS MEETINGS, METHODIST
LB3013	CLASS SIZE
E99.M19	*CLASSET INDIANS* **SEE** MAKAH INDIANS
DE	CLASSICAL ANTIQUITIES
DF	CLASSICAL ANTIQUITIES / *greece*
DG	CLASSICAL ANTIQUITIES / *rome*
DE5	*CLASSICAL ANTIQUITIES-DICTIONARIES* **SEE** CLASSICAL DICTIONARIES
DE	*CLASSICAL ARCHAEOLOGY* **SEE** CLASSICAL ANTIQUITIES
DF	*CLASSICAL ARCHAEOLOGY* **SEE** CLASSICAL ANTIQUITIES / *greece*
DG	*CLASSICAL ARCHAEOLOGY* **SEE** CLASSICAL ANTIQUITIES / *rome*
DE23-31	*CLASSICAL ATLASES* **SEE** CLASSICAL GEOGRAPHY
G87	*CLASSICAL ATLASES* **SEE** CLASSICAL GEOGRAPHY
DE7	CLASSICAL BIOGRAPHY
GV1783	*CLASSICAL DANCING* **SEE** MODERN DANCE
DE5	CLASSICAL DICTIONARIES
PA3461-6	CLASSICAL DRAMA / *collections*
PA3024-9	CLASSICAL DRAMA / *history and criticism*
LC1001-1021	CLASSICAL EDUCATION
G87	CLASSICAL GEOGRAPHY
DE23-31	CLASSICAL GEOGRAPHY
PA3013	CLASSICAL LITERATURE — APPRECIATION
PA3301-3671	CLASSICAL LITERATURE / *collections*
PA3001-3045	CLASSICAL LITERATURE / *history and criticism*
PA1-199	CLASSICAL PHILOLOGY
PA3431-3459	CLASSICAL POETRY / *collections*
PA3019-3022	CLASSICAL POETRY / *history and criticism*
PN56.C6	CLASSICISM
Z696-7	CLASSIFICATION — BOOKS
HF5736	CLASSIFICATION — CORRESPONDENCE / *business*
Z697.D	CLASSIFICATION — DRAWINGS
Z697.M	CLASSIFICATION — MANUSCRIPTS
Z6621	CLASSIFICATION — MANUSCRIPTS / *catalogs*
Z697.M	CLASSIFICATION — MAPS
ML111	CLASSIFICATION — MUSIC
Z697.P	CLASSIFICATION — PHONORECORDS
Z697.P	CLASSIFICATION — PHOTOGRAPHS
HG9687	*CLASSIFICATION OF RISKS* **SEE** INSURANCE, FIRE — CLASSIFICATION OF RISKS
LB3061	*CLASSIFICATION OF SCHOOL CHILDREN* **SEE** ABILITY GROUPING IN EDUCATION
Q177	CLASSIFICATION OF SCIENCES
BD240-241	CLASSIFICATION OF SCIENCES / *methodology*
TF590	*CLASSIFICATION YARDS* **SEE** RAILROADS — YARDS
Z696	CLASSIFICATION
Z696	CLASSIFICATION, DECIMAL
Z696	CLASSIFICATION, DUPLEX-NUMERIC

Z696	CLASSIFICATION, EXPANSIVE
Z696	CLASSIFICATION, LIBRARY OF CONGRESS
QK91-95	*CLASSIFICATION-BOTANY* **SEE** BOTANY — CLASSIFICATION
QE388	*CLASSIFICATION-MINERALS* **SEE** MINERALOGY — CLASSIFICATION
QH83	*CLASSIFICATION-NATURAL HISTORY* **SEE** NATURAL HISTORY — CLASSIFICATION
QK91-95	*CLASSIFICATION-PLANTS* **SEE** BOTANY — CLASSIFICATION
BL350	*CLASSIFICATION-RELIGIONS* **SEE** RELIGIONS — CLASSIFICATION
QE425	*CLASSIFICATION-ROCKS* **SEE** ROCKS — CLASSIFICATION AND NOMENCLATURE
QB881	*CLASSIFICATION-STARS* **SEE** STARS — CLASSIFICATION
LB3011	CLASSROOM MANAGEMENT
LB1731	CLASSROOM SIMULATORS
E99.M19	*CLATSET INDIANS* **SEE** MAKAH INDIANS
MT50	*CLAUSULA* **SEE** CADENCE (MUSIC) / *harmony*
ML444	*CLAUSULA* **SEE** CADENCE (MUSIC) / *harmony*
RD96.C	CLAVACIN
ML650-697	*CLAVECIN* **SEE** HARPSICHORD / *history and construction*
ML650-697	*CLAVICEMBALO* **SEE** HARPSICHORD / *history and construction*
MT252	CLAVICHORD — INSTRUCTION AND STUDY
ML651	CLAVICHORD MAKERS
ML700-742	CLAVICHORD MUSIC — HISTORY AND CRITICISM
M20-39	CLAVICHORD MUSIC
M32.8-38.5	CLAVICHORD MUSIC, ARRANGED
ML651	CLAVICHORD
MT165	CLAVICHORD / *tuning*
RD684	CLAVICLE — ABNORMITIES AND DEFORMITIES
RD101	CLAVICLE — FRACTURE
QM101	CLAVICLE
QL821	CLAVICLE
ML1055	CLAVICYLINDER
HD9590-9600	CLAY INDUSTRIES / *economics*
TN941.3	CLAY INDUSTRIES / *mineral resources*
TP785-842	CLAY INDUSTRIES / *technology*
NB1180-1185	*CLAY MODELING* **SEE** MODELING / *sculpture*
QE471	CLAY / *geology*
TN941-3	CLAY / *mineral resources*
TP811	CLAY / *technology*
E99.C83	CLAYOQUOT INDIANS
F1438	CLAYTON-BULWER TREATY, 1850
TP932	CLEANING AND DYEING INDUSTRY / *garment cleaning*
TP909	CLEANING AND DYEING INDUSTRY / *garment dyeing*
TP932	CLEANING COMPOUNDS
TP932	*CLEANING INDUSTRY* **SEE** CLEANING AND DYEING INDUSTRY / *garment cleaning*
TP909	*CLEANING INDUSTRY* **SEE** CLEANING AND DYEING INDUSTRY / *garment dyeing*
TP932	CLEANING MACHINERY AND APPLIANCES
TP932	*CLEANING PREPARATIONS* **SEE** CLEANING COMPOUNDS
TP932	CLEANING
TP895	CLEANING
TP909	CLEANING / *garments*
RM801-822	*CLEANLINESS* **SEE** BATHS
LB3461	*CLEANLINESS* **SEE** BATHS / *school hygiene*
RA771	*CLEANLINESS* **SEE** HYGIENE / *domestic*
BJ1695	*CLEANLINESS* **SEE** HYGIENE / *ethical aspects*
RA773-790	*CLEANLINESS* **SEE** HYGIENE / *personal*
TP932	*CLEANSERS (COMPOUNDS)* **SEE** CLEANING COMPOUNDS
RA766.W3	*CLEANSERS* **SEE** WASHING POWDERS / *disinfectants*
TP991	*CLEANSERS* **SEE** WASHING POWDERS / *technology*
S607	CLEARING OF LAND
QE605	*CLEAVAGE OF ROCKS* **SEE** ROCKS — CLEAVAGE
RD524	*CLEFT LIP* **SEE** HARELIP
QK495.C62	CLEMATIS / *botany*
SB413.C6	CLEMATIS / *culture*
BF173	*CLEPTOMANIA* **SEE** KLEPTOMANIA
BV4012	CLERGY — APPOINTMENT, CALL, AND ELECTION
BV4012	CLERGY — ETIQUETTE
BV4165	CLERGY — POST-ORDINATION TRAINING
BV4382	CLERGY — RETIREMENT
BV4380-4382	CLERGY — SALARIES, PENSIONS, ETC.
BX1950	CLERGY — SALARIES, PENSIONS, ETC. / *catholic*
BX1939.C665	CLERGY (CANON LAW)
BX1939.C69	CLERGY CONFERENCES (CANON LAW)
PR151.C7	CLERGY IN LITERATURE / *english literature*
PT151.C7	CLERGY IN LITERATURE / *german literature*
BV659-685	CLERGY
BV637.5	*CLERGY, CITY* **SEE** CITY CLERGY
BV664	*CLERGY, ITINERANT* **SEE** ITINERANCY (CHURCH POLITY)
BV637.5	*CLERGY, URBAN* **SEE** CITY CLERGY
BV4396	*CLERGY-FAMILIES* **SEE** CLERGYMEN'S FAMILIES
BV4290	*CLERGY-INSTALLATION* **SEE** INSTALLATION (CLERGY)
Z987-997	*CLERGY-LIBRARIES* **SEE** LIBRARIES, PRIVATE
BV659-685	*CLERGY-MAJOR ORDERS* **SEE** CLERGY
BV4012	*CLERGY-VOCATION* **SEE** CLERGY — APPOINTMENT, CALL, AND ELECTION
PN171.C	CLERGYMEN AS AUTHORS
PR120.C	CLERGYMEN AS AUTHORS
BV4396	CLERGYMEN'S FAMILIES
BV4395	CLERGYMEN'S WIVES
HQ800	*CLERICAL CELIBACY* **SEE** CELIBACY
BV4390	*CLERICAL CELIBACY* **SEE** CELIBACY / *clergy*
HF5501	*CLERICAL EMPLOYEES* **SEE** CLERKS
HV3165-3173	*CLERICAL EMPLOYEES* **SEE** CLERKS / *aid to*
HD8039.M4	*CLERICAL EMPLOYEES* **SEE** CLERKS / *mercantile clerks*
BV4012	*CLERICAL ETIQUETTE* **SEE** CLERGY — ETIQUETTE
RC89	*CLERICAL MEDICINE* **SEE** PASTORAL MEDICINE
BT732	*CLERICAL MEDICINE* **SEE** PASTORAL MEDICINE / *theology*
BV4012	*CLERICAL PSYCHOLOGY* **SEE** PASTORAL PSYCHOLOGY
HF5549	CLERKS — SALARIES, PENSIONS, ETC.
HF5501	CLERKS
HV3165-3173	CLERKS / *aid to*
HD8039.M4	CLERKS / *mercantile clerks*
D161	CLERMONT, COUNCIL OF, 1095 / *first crusade*
E99.P9	CLIFF-DWELLERS
E61	CLIFF-DWELLINGS / *america*
E78.S7	CLIFF-DWELLINGS / *southwest*
QC981-999	*CLIMATE* **SEE** CLIMATOLOGY
GF71	*CLIMATE, INFLUENCE OF* **SEE** MAN — INFLUENCE OF CLIMATE
QC981-999	CLIMATOLOGY
S600	*CLIMATOLOGY, AGRICULTURAL* **SEE** CROPS AND CLIMATE
RA791-954	CLIMATOLOGY, MEDICAL
QH544	*CLIMATOLOGY, PHENOLOGICAL* **SEE** PHENOLOGY
QK773	CLIMBING PLANTS / *botany*
SB427	CLIMBING PLANTS / *culture*
RC61-69	*CLINICAL MEDICINE* **SEE** MEDICINE, CLINICAL
RB113	*CLINICAL PHYSIOLOGY* **SEE** PHYSIOLOGY, PATHOLOGICAL
RC75	*CLINICAL THERMOMETERS* **SEE** THERMOMETERS AND THERMOMETRY, MEDICAL
RK3	*CLINICS, DENTAL* **SEE** DENTAL CLINICS
TP832.C5	CLINKER BRICK
TA579	CLINOMETER
QK771	CLINOSTAT
VM	CLIPPER-SHIPS
VK	CLIPPER-SHIPS
AG500-551	CLIPPING BUREAUS
Z691	CLIPPINGS (BOOKS, NEWSPAPERS, ETC.)
Z697.C6	CLIPPINGS (BOOKS, NEWSPAPERS, ETC.)
QL871	CLOACA (ZOOLOGY)
TT530	CLOAKS / *dressmaking*
HD9940	CLOAKS / *economics*
GV1295.B4	*CLOB-E-OSH (GAME)* **SEE** BELOTE (GAME)
SB127	CLOCHE GARDENING
NK7486-7497	CLOCK AND WATCH MAKERS / *art*
TS542-3	CLOCK AND WATCH MAKERS / *technology*
TS546	CLOCK AND WATCH MAKING — MACHINERY
HD9999.C6	CLOCK AND WATCH MAKING / *economics*
TS540-549	CLOCK AND WATCH MAKING / *technology*
NA2930	*CLOCK-TOWERS* **SEE** TOWERS / *architecture*
TS545	CLOCKS AND WATCHES — ESCAPEMENTS
NK7483	CLOCKS AND WATCHES — PRIVATE COLLECTIONS
TS547	CLOCKS AND WATCHES — REPAIRING AND ADJUSTING

N8217.C4	CLOCKS AND WATCHES IN ART
NK7480-7499	CLOCKS AND WATCHES / art
HD9999.C6	CLOCKS AND WATCHES / economics
TS540-549	CLOCKS AND WATCHES / technology
TS547	*CLOCKS AND WATCHES-ADJUSTING* **SEE** CLOCKS AND WATCHES — REPAIRING AND ADJUSTING
TS547	*CLOCKS AND WATCHES-REGULATION* **SEE** CLOCKS AND WATCHES — REPAIRING AND ADJUSTING
QB107	*CLOCKS, ASTRONOMICAL* **SEE** ASTRONOMICAL CLOCKS
TS544	CLOCKS, ELECTRIC
CE89	CLOG-ALMANACS
GV1793	CLOG-DANCING
NK5010-5015	CLOISONNE
BX4200-4560	*CLOISTERS* **SEE** CONVENTS AND NUNNERIES / catholic church
NA4850	*CLOISTERS* **SEE** MONASTERIES / architecture
NA5201-6113	*CLOISTERS* **SEE** MONASTERIES / architecture
BX2460-2749	*CLOISTERS* **SEE** MONASTERIES / catholic church
RC139	CLONORCHIASIS
DA932.6	CLONTARF, BATTLE OF, 1014
BV820	CLOSE AND OPEN COMMUNION
BV820	*CLOSE COMMUNION* **SEE** CLOSE AND OPEN COMMUNION
D580	*CLOSED SEA (MARE CLAUSUM)* **SEE** FREEDOM OF THE SEAS / european war
JX4423-5	*CLOSED SEA (MARE CLAUSUM)* **SEE** FREEDOM OF THE SEAS / international law
JX5203-5268	*CLOSED SEA (MARE CLAUSUM)* **SEE** FREEDOM OF THE SEAS / maritime war international law
Z711	*CLOSED SHELVES IN LIBRARIES* **SEE** OPEN AND CLOSED SHELVES
HD6488	*CLOSED SHOP* **SEE** OPEN AND CLOSED SHOP
Z711	*CLOSED STACKS IN LIBRARIES* **SEE** OPEN AND CLOSED SHELVES
TK6680	CLOSED-CIRCUIT TELEVISION
TH6498	*CLOSETS* **SEE** WATER-CLOSETS
NK8800-8999	*CLOTH* **SEE** TEXTILE INDUSTRY AND FABRICS / art industries
TS1300-1781	*CLOTH* **SEE** TEXTILE INDUSTRY AND FABRICS / manufacture
HD9850-9869	*CLOTH* **SEE** TEXTILE INDUSTRY AND FABRICS / trade
HD9940	*CLOTHIERS* **SEE** CLOTHING TRADE / economics
TT490-695	*CLOTHIERS* **SEE** CLOTHING TRADE / manufacture
GT521	CLOTHING AND DRESS — PSYCHOLOGY
TT720-730	CLOTHING AND DRESS — REPAIRING
GT500-2350	CLOTHING AND DRESS
TT507	CLOTHING AND DRESS / design
TX340	CLOTHING AND DRESS / domestic economy
GN418-419	CLOTHING AND DRESS / ethnology
RA779	CLOTHING AND DRESS / hygiene
GT527-8	*CLOTHING AND DRESS-LAWS AND REGULATIONS* **SEE** SUMPTUARY LAWS / dress
HB845	*CLOTHING AND DRESS-LAWS AND REGULATIONS* **SEE** SUMPTUARY LAWS
HD9940	CLOTHING TRADE / economics
TT490-695	CLOTHING TRADE / manufacture
TT525	*CLOTHING, FUR* **SEE** FUR GARMENTS
HD7395.C5	CLOTHING, PROTECTIVE
QC928	*CLOUD MODIFICATION* **SEE** WEATHER CONTROL
QC921.5	CLOUD PHYSICS
QC929.R1	*CLOUD SEEDING* **SEE** RAIN-MAKING
QL737.C2	CLOUDED LEOPARD
QL737.C2	*CLOUDED TIGER* **SEE** CLOUDED LEOPARD
QC921-3	CLOUDS
SB608.C55	CLOVER — DISEASES AND PESTS
SB205.C64	CLOVER
GV1811	*CLOWNING* **SEE** CLOWNS / circus clowns
PN1955	*CLOWNING* **SEE** CLOWNS / drama
GV1811	CLOWNS / circus clowns
PN1955	CLOWNS / drama
NA7910-7970	CLUB-HOUSES
QK524.L9	CLUB-MOSSES
SB733	CLUBROOT
HF5686.C45	CLUBS — ACCOUNTING
JF2101	CLUBS / political
HS2501-3200	CLUBS / social
HG9466-9479	*CLUBS, BURIAL* **SEE** INSURANCE, BURIAL
ML25-28	*CLUBS, MUSICAL* **SEE** MUSICAL SOCIETIES

BX3460-3470	*CLUGNIACS* **SEE** CLUNIACS
BX3460-3470	CLUNIACS
BX3460-3470	*CLUNY, ORDER OF* **SEE** CLUNIACS
QK495.P66	CLUSTER-PINE / botany
SD397.P	CLUSTER-PINE / forestry
TJ1074	CLUTCHES (MACHINERY)
SF293.C	CLYDESDALE HORSE
SF429.D3	*COACH DOGS* **SEE** DALMATIAN DOGS
SF305-7	*COACHES* **SEE** COACHING
GV711	COACHING (ATHLETICS)
SF305-7	COACHING
E99.K27	*COAHUILA INDIANS* **SEE** KAWIA INDIANS
PM3681	*COAHUILTECAN LANGUAGES* **SEE** COAHUILTECO LANGUAGE
PM4158	*COAHUILTECAN LANGUAGES* **SEE** PAKAWAN LANGUAGES
PM3681	COAHUILTECO LANGUAGE
TP325-9	COAL — ANALYSIS
HD9540.8	COAL — TAXATION
HD9551.6	COAL — TAXATION
TP325-9	COAL — TESTING
HE2321.C6	COAL — TRANSPORTATION
HE595.C6	COAL — TRANSPORTATION
TP759	COAL GASIFICATION
TP759	COAL GASIFICATION, UNDERGROUND
HD9540-9559	*COAL LANDS* **SEE** COAL / economics
TN800-834	*COAL LANDS* **SEE** COAL / mining
TN311-319	COAL MINES AND MINING — ACCIDENTS
HF5686.M6	COAL MINES AND MINING — ACCOUNTING
TN803	COAL MINES AND MINING — EXPLOSIVES
TN295	COAL MINES AND MINING — SAFETY MEASURES
TN803	COAL MINES AND MINING — VALUATION
TN800-834	COAL MINES AND MINING
DA140	COAL MONEY / celtic antiquities
DA670.D7	COAL MONEY / dorset
TN816	COAL PREPARATION
HD9540.8	*COAL TAXATION* **SEE** COAL — TAXATION
HD9551.6	*COAL TAXATION* **SEE** COAL — TAXATION
HF5686.C48	COAL TRADE — ACCOUNTING
HF5716.C4	COAL TRADE — TABLES AND READY-RECKONERS
HD9540-9559	COAL TRADE
HD9551.6	*COAL TRADE-TAXATION* **SEE** COAL — TAXATION
HD9540.8	*COAL TRADE-TAXATION* **SEE** COAL — TAXATION
HE595.C6	*COAL TRANSPORTATION* **SEE** COAL — TRANSPORTATION
HE2321.C6	*COAL TRANSPORTATION* **SEE** COAL — TRANSPORTATION
TN816	COAL WASHING
VM401	COAL-CARRYING VESSELS
TP751-764	*COAL-GAS* **SEE** GAS
TP700	*COAL-GAS* **SEE** GAS
TJ1405	COAL-HANDLING MACHINERY
TH4471	COAL-HANDLING
RC964-5	COAL-MINERS — DISEASES AND HYGIENE / diseases
RA787	COAL-MINERS — DISEASES AND HYGIENE / hygiene
HD7269.M6	COAL-MINERS — DISEASES AND HYGIENE / labor hygiene
HD8039.M62	COAL-MINERS
TN813-814	COAL-MINING MACHINERY
TP692.4.K4	*COAL-OIL* **SEE** KEROSENE
TN860-879	*COAL-OIL* **SEE** PETROLEUM / production
TP690-692	*COAL-OIL* **SEE** PETROLEUM / refining
TP953	COAL-TAR — TESTING
QP971	COAL-TAR COLORS — PHYSIOLOGICAL EFFECT
RA1242.C7	COAL-TAR COLORS — TOXICOLOGY
TP914	COAL-TAR COLORS
HD9660.C6-63	COAL-TAR INDUSTRY
TP953	COAL-TAR PRODUCTS — TESTING
TP953	COAL-TAR PRODUCTS
TP953	COAL-TAR
TN817	COAL-WEATHERING
HD9540-9559	COAL / economics
TN800-834	COAL / mining
TP328	COAL, PULVERIZED
QD516	*COAL-COMBUSTION* **SEE** COMBUSTION
TP759	*COAL-GASIFICATION* **SEE** COAL GASIFICATION
TN817	*COAL-WEATHERING* **SEE** COAL-WEATHERING
V240	COALING-STATIONS
JX5244.C5	COALING / international law

VK361	COALING / navigation
NK4399.C	COALPORT PORCELAIN
UF450-455	*COAST ARTILLERY* **SEE** ARTILLERY, COAST
TC330-345	COAST CHANGES / hydraulic engineering
GB451-460	COAST CHANGES / physical geography
UG410-448	COAST DEFENSES
TC330-339	*COAST PROTECTIVE WORKS* **SEE** SHORE PROTECTION
VK397	*COAST RADIO STATIONS* **SEE** MARINE RADIO STATIONS
HJ6897	COAST-GUARD (GT. BRIT.)
VG55.G7	COAST-GUARD (GT. BRIT.) / naval science
VK798-995	*COAST-PILOT GUIDES* **SEE** PILOT GUIDES
HE9723-9737	*COASTAL SIGNALS* **SEE** SIGNALS AND SIGNALING
UG570-582	*COASTAL SIGNALS* **SEE** SIGNALS AND SIGNALING / military
V280-285	*COASTAL SIGNALS* **SEE** SIGNALS AND SIGNALING / naval
VK381-397	*COASTAL SIGNALS* **SEE** SIGNALS AND SIGNALING / navigation
GV855	COASTING
GB451-460	COASTS / physical geography
HE751-3	COASTWISE NAVIGATION / u.s.
BT587.C6-7	*COAT, HOLY* **SEE** HOLY COAT
TS1109	*COATED PAPER* **SEE** PAPER COATINGS
TP935	*COATING COMPOSITIONS* **SEE** PROTECTIVE COATINGS
TP935	*COATINGS, PROTECTIVE* **SEE** PROTECTIVE COATINGS
CR67-69	*COATS OF ARMS* **SEE** DEVICES / heraldry
JC345	*COATS OF ARMS* **SEE** HERALDRY / national theory
CR	*COATS OF ARMS* **SEE** HERALDRY / national
TT530-535	COATS
TT595-600	COATS
TH1421	COB (BUILDING MATERIAL)
QD181.C6	*COBALT AMINES* **SEE** COBALT-AMMONIUM COMPOUNDS
TN490.C6	COBALT MINES AND MINING
QD181.C6	COBALT-AMMONIUM COMPOUNDS
QD181.C6	COBALT / chemistry
QL638.C94	*COBITIDAE* **SEE** LOACHES
HF5548.5.C2	COBOL (COMPUTER PROGRAM LANGUAGE)
PM3686	COCA LANGUAGE
RM666.C	COCA / therapeutics
RA1238.C7	COCAINE — TOXICOLOGY
HV5810	COCAINE HABIT
RD86.C6	COCAINE / anesthetics
QP921.C7	COCAINE / physiological effect
F3430.1.C	COCAMA INDIANS / peru
PM5823	COCAMA LANGUAGE
QL523.C7	*COCCIDAE* **SEE** SCALE-INSECTS
SB939	*COCCIDAE* **SEE** SCALE-INSECTS / economic entomology
SF967.C6	COCCIDIOSIS / cattle diseases
SF792	COCCIDIOSIS / veterinary medicine
QL596.C65	*COCCINELLIDAE* **SEE** LADYBIRDS
RS165.P65	*COCCULIN* **SEE** PICROTOXIN / pharmacy
QP981.P5	*COCCULIN* **SEE** PICROTOXIN / physiological effects
RD672	COCCYGEAL GLAND — DISEASES / tumors
QM371	COCCYGEAL GLAND / human anatomy
QP187	COCCYGEAL GLAND / physiology
QM111	COCCYX
RD672	*COCCYX-TUMORS* **SEE** SACROCOCCYGEAL REGION — TUMORS
QL696.C5	*COCCYZUS* **SEE** CUCKOOS
SF489.C	COCHIN BANTAMS
SF561	COCHINEAL
E99.C84	COCHITI INDIANS
SF503	COCK-FIGHTING
SF473.C	COCKATEELS / animal culture
QL696.P7	COCKATEELS / zoology
SF473.C	*COCKATIELS* **SEE** COCKATEELS / animal culture
QL696.P7	*COCKATIELS* **SEE** COCKATEELS / zoology
QL596.S3	COCKCHAFERS
SF429.S7	*COCKER SPANIELS* **SEE** SPANIELS
RC641.C6	COCKROACHES AS CARRIERS OF DISEASE
QL508.B6	COCKROACHES
QE832.O7	COCKROACHES, FOSSIL
QK495.G74	*COCKSFOOT GRASS* **SEE** ORCHARD GRASS / botany
SB201.O6	*COCKSFOOT GRASS* **SEE** ORCHARD GRASS / culture
TX951	COCKTAILS
TX817.C5	COCOA / beverages
TP640	COCOA / manufacture
TX415	COCOA / sources
RM241	COCOA / therapeutics
HD9200	COCOA / trade
SD397.C6	COCOBOLO
E99.M	*COCOMARICOPA INDIANS* **SEE** MARICOPA INDIANS
SB608.C58	COCONUT-PALM — DISEASES AND PESTS
SB401	COCONUT-PALM
SB401	COCONUT / culture
HD9259.C6	COCONUT / economics
TP684.C7	COCONUT / oils
E99.C	COCOPA INDIANS
TP684.R7	*COD OIL* **SEE** ROSIN-OIL
SH351.C5	COD-FISHERIES
RM666.C6	COD-LIVER OIL
PM8129	CODE ARI (ARTIFICIAL LANGUAGE)
RS165.C6	CODEINE
HE7669-7679	*CODES, TELEGRAPH* **SEE** CIPHER AND TELEGRAPH CODES
HE7676-7	*CODES, TELEGRAPH* **SEE** CIPHER AND TELEGRAPH CODES / commercial codes
HE7678	*CODES, TELEGRAPH* **SEE** CIPHER AND TELEGRAPH CODES / foreign languages
HD5650-5659	*CODETERMINATION (INDUSTRIAL RELATIONS)* **SEE** EMPLOYEES' REPRESENTATION IN MANAGEMENT
QL638.G2	CODFISH
SH351.C5	CODFISH / fisheries
SB945.C7	CODLING-MOTH
LC1601	COEDUCATION
QC281-6	*COEFFICIENT OF EXPANSION* **SEE** EXPANSION (HEAT)
QC284	*COEFFICIENT OF EXPANSION* **SEE** EXPANSION OF LIQUIDS
QC282	*COEFFICIENT OF EXPANSION* **SEE** EXPANSION OF SOLIDS
TP242-4	*COEFFICIENT OF EXPANSION* **SEE** GASES / chemical technology
QC241	*COEFFICIENT OF EXPANSION* **SEE** GASES / etc.
QC286	*COEFFICIENT OF EXPANSION* **SEE** GASES / expansion
QD531	*COEFFICIENT OF EXPANSION* **SEE** GASES / manipulation
QC161-8	*COEFFICIENT OF EXPANSION* **SEE** GASES / mechanics
QC297	*COEFFICIENT OF EXPANSION* **SEE** GASES / specific heats
QL378	COELENTERATA — ANATOMY
QL375-9	COELENTERATA
QE777-9	COELENTERATA / fossil
QE777	COELENTERATA, FOSSIL
M2079.2.L19	*COELI ENARRANT (MUSIC)* **SEE** PSALMS (MUSIC) — 19TH PSALM
M2099.2.L19	*COELI ENARRANT (MUSIC)* **SEE** PSALMS (MUSIC) — 19TH PSALM
QB97	COELOSTAT
QK565	COENOBIC PLANTS / algae
TP918.C	*COERULEIN* **SEE** CERULEIN
E99.S63	*COEUR D'ALENE INDIANS* **SEE** SKITSWISH INDIANS
HD5325.	
M81899.4	COEUR D'ALENE STRIKE, 1899
SB608.C6	COFFEE — DISEASES AND PESTS
HF5716.C5	COFFEE — TABLES, ETC.
HD9199	COFFEE — TAXATION
SB608.C6	COFFEE BERRY BORER
HD5112	*COFFEE BREAKS* **SEE** REST PERIODS / labor
K	*COFFEE BREAKS* **SEE** REST PERIODS / law
HD9199	COFFEE TRADE
HD9195	COFFEE TRADE
TD899	COFFEE WASTE / trade waste
TX901-910	COFFEE-HOUSES
TX583	COFFEE / adulteration
TP645	COFFEE / chemical technology
SB269	COFFEE / culture
GT2910	COFFEE / manners and customs
TX415	COFFEE / sources
RM246	COFFEE / therapeutics
TC198	COFFER-DAMS
NK2725	*COFFERS* **SEE** CHESTS / art

TT197	*COFFERS* **SEE** CHESTS / *cabinet-work*
TS2301.U5	COFFINS / *manufacture*
TF684	*COG RAILROADS* **SEE** RACK-RAILROADS
TJ184-204	*COG-WHEELS* **SEE** GEARING
HD9393	*COGNAC* **SEE** BRANDY / *industry*
TP599	*COGNAC* **SEE** BRANDY / *technology*
BF311	COGNITION
QC665	COHERER / *physics*
TK5863	COHERER / *technology*
QC183	COHESION
QA611	*COHOMOLOGY THEORY* **SEE** HOMOLOGY THEORY
TK2391	*COILS, ELECTRIC* **SEE** ELECTRIC COILS / *electric engineering*
QC544.C7	*COILS, ELECTRIC* **SEE** ELECTRIC COILS / *physics*
TK6565.C6	*COILS, ELECTRIC* **SEE** ELECTRIC COILS / *radio*
NK4698	COIN BANKS
TJ1560	*COIN OPERATED MACHINES* **SEE** VENDING MACHINES
HG532	COIN REDEMPTION FUND / *etc.*
GV1559	COIN TRICKS
P331-361	*COINAGE OF WORDS* **SEE** WORDS, NEW / *comparative lexicography*
HG261-315	COINAGE / *general*
HG651-1490	COINAGE / *other countries*
HG551-566	COINAGE / *u.s.*
HG381-395	COINAGE, INTERNATIONAL
HG335-341	*COINING, ILLICIT* **SEE** COUNTERFEITS AND COUNTERFEITING
HG641-5	*COINING, ILLICIT* **SEE** COUNTERFEITS AND COUNTERFEITING / *u.s.*
CJ255	*COINS OF THE BIBLE* **SEE** BIBLE — NUMISMATICS
CJ	COINS
CJ201-1397	COINS, ANCIENT
CJ1601-1715	COINS, MEDIEVAL
CJ3430-3890	COINS, ORIENTAL
CJ1301-1397	COINS, ORIENTAL / *ancient*
CJ2928.P3	COINS, PAPAL
TP336	COKE INDUSTRY — EQUIPMENT AND SUPPLIES
HD9559.C68-7	COKE INDUSTRY
TP336	COKE-OVENS
HD9559.C68	COKE / *economics*
TP336	COKE / *technology*
PL8113	*COKWE LANGUAGE* **SEE** CHOKWE LANGUAGE
RS165.C64	*COLA* **SEE** COLA-NUT / *pharmacy*
RS165.C64	COLA-NUT / *pharmacy*
DA415	COLCHESTER, ENG. — SIEGE, 1648
QP82	COLD — PHYSIOLOGICAL EFFECT
RM863	COLD — THERAPEUTIC USE
RX326.C6	COLD (DISEASE) — HOMEOPATHIC TREATMENT
RF361	COLD (DISEASE)
TK7872.C3	*COLD CATHODE COUNTER TUBES* **SEE** COLD CATHODE TUBES
TK7872.C3	*COLD CATHODE COUNTERS* **SEE** COLD CATHODE TUBES
TK7872.C3	COLD CATHODE TUBES
TA460	*COLD FLOW* **SEE** CREEP OF METALS
E476.52	COLD HARBOR, BATTLE OF, 1864
TP493	COLD STORAGE — INSULATION
VM485	COLD STORAGE ON SHIPBOARD
TP493	COLD STORAGE
U167.5.W5	*COLD WEATHER OPERATIONS (MILITARY)* **SEE** WINTER WARFARE
TS462	*COLD WORKING OF METALS* **SEE** METALS — COLD WORKING
SB415	COLD-FRAMES / *flower culture*
SB352	COLD-FRAMES / *vegetable culture*
TP493.5	COLD-STORAGE LOCKERS
QE391.C	COLEMANITE
TN948.C7	COLEMANITE
QL571-597	*COLEOPTERA* **SEE** BEETLES
HT731	*COLIBERTI* **SEE** COLLIBERTS
RC809	COLIC
RJ456.C	COLIC / *diseases of children*
QL696.G2	*COLINAE* **SEE** QUAILS
SF510.Q2	*COLINAE* **SEE** QUAILS / *breeding*
SK325.Q2	*COLINAE* **SEE** QUAILS / *hunting*
RC862.C6	COLITIS
F3430.1.C6	COLLA INDIANS / *peru*
HV6275	*COLLABORATIONISTS* **SEE** TREASON
JC328	*COLLABORATIONISTS* **SEE** TREASON / *political theory*
F3430.1.C6	*COLLAGUA INDIANS* **SEE** COLLA INDIANS / *peru*
CR41.C5	COLLAR (IN HERALDRY)
QL821	*COLLARBONE* **SEE** CLAVICLE
QM101	*COLLARBONE* **SEE** CLAVICLE
HG2071-2106	*COLLATERAL LOANS* **SEE** PAWNBROKING
AM200-501	*COLLECTING* **SEE** COLLECTORS AND COLLECTING
HF5556-9	COLLECTING OF ACCOUNTS
HF5556-9	COLLECTION LAWS
HF5556-9	*COLLECTION LETTERS* **SEE** COLLECTING OF ACCOUNTS
HF5556-9	*COLLECTION OF ACCOUNTS* **SEE** COLLECTING OF ACCOUNTS
LB1029.C5	COLLECTIVE EDUCATION
RC488	*COLLECTIVE PSYCHOTHERAPY* **SEE** GROUP PSYCHOTHERAPY
JX1901-1995	*COLLECTIVE SECURITY* **SEE** SECURITY, INTERNATIONAL
HX	COLLECTIVISM
AM200-501	COLLECTORS AND COLLECTING
N8380	*COLLECTORS AND COLLECTING-MARKS* **SEE** COLLECTORS' MARKS
N8380	COLLECTORS' MARKS
LC383	*COLLEGE AND CHURCH* **SEE** CHURCH AND COLLEGE
LC237	*COLLEGE AND COMMUNITY* **SEE** COMMUNITY AND COLLEGE
PN3175-3191	COLLEGE AND SCHOOL DRAMA / *history and criticism*
LB3621	COLLEGE AND SCHOOL JOURNALISM
PN4825-4830	COLLEGE AND SCHOOL JOURNALISM / *amateur journalism*
LB3621	*COLLEGE ANNUALS* **SEE** SCHOOL YEARBOOKS
GV561-751	*COLLEGE ATHLETICS* **SEE** ATHLETICS
GV561-751	*COLLEGE ATHLETICS* **SEE** TRACK-ATHLETICS
GV1061-1099	*COLLEGE ATHLETICS* **SEE** TRACK-ATHLETICS / *special*
LC148	COLLEGE ATTENDANCE
NA6600-6603	*COLLEGE BUILDINGS* **SEE** UNIVERSITIES AND COLLEGES — BUILDINGS
LB3635	*COLLEGE CHEERS* **SEE** CHEERS / *school life*
LB3630	*COLLEGE COLORS* **SEE** SCHOOL COLORS
LB3640	*COLLEGE COMMUNITY CENTERS* **SEE** STUDENT UNIONS
LB2331.5	*COLLEGE COOPERATION* **SEE** UNIVERSITY COOPERATION
LB2342	COLLEGE COSTS
LB2381-2391	*COLLEGE DEGREES* **SEE** DEGREES, ACADEMIC
PN3175-3191	*COLLEGE DRAMA* **SEE** COLLEGE AND SCHOOL DRAMA / *history and criticism*
LB2342	*COLLEGE EDUCATION COSTS* **SEE** COLLEGE COSTS
LB2351-2360	*COLLEGE ENTRANCE REQUIREMENTS* **SEE** UNIVERSITIES AND COLLEGES — ENTRANCE REQUIREMENTS
BJ1857.S75	*COLLEGE ETIQUETTE* **SEE** STUDENT ETIQUETTE / *american*
LJ	*COLLEGE FRATERNITIES* **SEE** GREEK LETTER SOCIETIES
LB3602	*COLLEGE FRATERNITIES* **SEE** STUDENTS' SOCIETIES
LB2389	*COLLEGE GOWNS* **SEE** ACADEMIC COSTUME
LB2411	*COLLEGE GRADUATES* **SEE** UNIVERSITIES AND COLLEGES — ALUMNI
LB3621	*COLLEGE JOURNALISM* **SEE** COLLEGE AND SCHOOL JOURNALISM
PN4825-4830	*COLLEGE JOURNALISM* **SEE** COLLEGE AND SCHOOL JOURNALISM / *amateur journalism*
Z675.U5	*COLLEGE LIBRARIES* **SEE** LIBRARIES, UNIVERSITY AND COLLEGE
LB2397	*COLLEGE LIFE* **SEE** STUDENTS / *reminiscences*
LB3602-3635	*COLLEGE LIFE* **SEE** STUDENTS / *student life*
M1504	COLLEGE OPERAS, REVUES, ETC.
PS663.C7	COLLEGE ORATIONS / *u.s.*
PN3175-3191	*COLLEGE PLAYS* **SEE** COLLEGE AND SCHOOL DRAMA / *history and criticism*
PN6110.C7	*COLLEGE POETRY* **SEE** COLLEGE VERSE
Z231.5.U6	*COLLEGE PRESSES* **SEE** UNIVERSITY PRESSES
LB2341	COLLEGE REGISTRARS
M1504	*COLLEGE REVUES* **SEE** COLLEGE OPERAS, REVUES, ETC.
BV4310	*COLLEGE SERMONS* **SEE** UNIVERSITIES AND COLLEGES — SERMONS
HV4175-4320	*COLLEGE SETTLEMENTS* **SEE** SOCIAL SETTLEMENTS

LB3220	*COLLEGE SITES* **SEE** SCHOOL SITES
M1940-1973	*COLLEGE SONGS* **SEE** STUDENTS' SONGS / music
PN6110.C7	*COLLEGE SONGS* **SEE** STUDENTS' SONGS / poetry
GV706	*COLLEGE SPORTS-PHILOSOPHY* **SEE** SPORTS — PHILOSOPHY
PZ1-7	COLLEGE STORIES
LB2397	*COLLEGE STUDENTS* **SEE** STUDENTS / reminiscences
LB3602-3635	*COLLEGE STUDENTS* **SEE** STUDENTS / student life
LB2334	COLLEGE TEACHERS — SALARIES, PENSIONS, ETC.
LB2331	COLLEGE TEACHERS — WORK LOAD
LB1778	COLLEGE TEACHERS
LB2331	COLLEGE TEACHING
PN3175-3191	*COLLEGE THEATRICALS* **SEE** COLLEGE AND SCHOOL DRAMA / history and criticism
LB2341	COLLEGE TRUSTEES
LB3640	*COLLEGE UNIONS* **SEE** STUDENT UNIONS
PN6110.C7	COLLEGE VERSE
LB3621	*COLLEGE YEARBOOKS* **SEE** SCHOOL YEARBOOKS
LB2350.5	COLLEGE, CHOICE OF
LB2300-2411	*COLLEGES* **SEE** UNIVERSITIES AND COLLEGES
LD-LG	*COLLEGES* **SEE** UNIVERSITIES AND COLLEGES / individual institutions
LA410-2270	*COLLEGES* **SEE** UNIVERSITIES AND COLLEGES / other countries
LA225-8	*COLLEGES* **SEE** UNIVERSITIES AND COLLEGES / u.s.
LB2327	*COLLEGES, SMALL* **SEE** SMALL COLLEGES
M1504	*COLLEGIATE SHOWS* **SEE** COLLEGE OPERAS, REVUES, ETC.
QL503.C6	COLLEMBOLA
HT731	COLLIBERTS
SF429.C6	COLLIES
QA601	COLLINEATION
HE2930.M2	COLLINS EXPEDITION, 1878-1879
VK371-8	COLLISIONS AT SEA — PREVENTION
JX4434	COLLISIONS AT SEA / international law
TL553.5	*COLLISIONS, AIRCRAFT* **SEE** AERONAUTICS — ACCIDENTS
HE5614	*COLLISIONS, AUTOMOBILE* **SEE** TRAFFIC ACCIDENTS
HE1779-1795	*COLLISIONS, RAILROAD* **SEE** RAILROADS — ACCIDENTS
TS1145	COLLODION
TP360	*COLLOIDAL FUEL* **SEE** FUEL, COLLOIDAL
QD549	COLLOIDS / chemistry
QP525	COLLOIDS / physiology
PN6231.B8	*COLLOQUIAL BULLS* **SEE** BULLS, COLLOQUIAL
BR355.R2	*COLLOQUY OF RATISBON, 1541* **SEE** RATISBON, COLLOQUY OF, 1541
BR355.R3	*COLLOQUY OF RATISBON, 1546* **SEE** RATISBON, COLLOQUY OF, 1546
TR930	COLLOTYPE
QL449	COLOBOGNATHA / millepeds
F2251-2277	COLOMBIA — HISTORY
PQ8176.F3	COLOMBIAN FICTION / collections
PQ8172	COLOMBIAN FICTION / history
PQ8160-8179	COLOMBIAN LITERATURE
PN5051-5	COLOMBIAN NEWSPAPERS / etc.
PN5051-5	COLOMBIAN PERIODICALS / etc.
PQ8174	COLOMBIAN POETRY / collections
PQ8170	COLOMBIAN POETRY / history
PQ8176	COLOMBIAN PROSE LITERATURE / collections
PQ8172	COLOMBIAN PROSE LITERATURE / history
F2276.5	COLOMBIA — HISTORY — — REVOLUTION, 1899-1903
F2276.5	COLOMBIA — HISTORY — — 1886-1903
F2277	COLOMBIA — HISTORY — — 1903-1946
F2278	COLOMBIA — HISTORY — — 1946-
RC280.C	COLON (ANATOMY) — CANCER
RC860	COLON (ANATOMY) — DISEASES
QL863	COLON (ANATOMY)
QM345	COLON (ANATOMY)
RC862.C6	*COLON (ANATOMY)-INFLAMMATION* **SEE** COLITIS
HD139.C7	COLONATE
NA707	*COLONIAL ARCHITECTURE* **SEE** ARCHITECTURE, COLONIAL
HF481-491	COLONIAL COMPANIES
E186-199	*COLONIAL WARS* **SEE** UNITED STATES — HISTORY — — COLONIAL PERIOD
E186-199	*COLONIAL WARS* **SEE** UNITED STATES — HISTORY — — COLONIAL PERIOD

RM163	*COLONIC IRRIGATION* **SEE** ENEMA
JV412-485	COLONIES — ADMINISTRATION
HJ240	COLONIES — FINANCE
HJ2025	COLONIES — FINANCE / budgets
HJ8043-5	COLONIES — FINANCE / debts
HF1723	COLONIES — FINANCE / tariffs
QH549	COLONIES (BIOLOGY)
JX4027	COLONIES (INTERNATIONAL LAW)
JV	COLONIES
JX4027	*COLONIES-INTERNATIONAL LAW* **SEE** COLONIES (INTERNATIONAL LAW)
RC862.C6	*COLONITIS* **SEE** COLITIS
E448	*COLONIZATION OF NEGROES* **SEE** NEGROES — COLONIZATION
HD301-1130	COLONIZATION / other countries
HD171-279	COLONIZATION / u.s.
BX8128.C	*COLONIZATION, MENNONITE* **SEE** MENNONITES — COLONIZATION
Z110.C6	COLOPHONS OF MANUSCRIPTS
Z242.C7	COLOPHONS
BF789.C7	COLOR — PSYCHOLOGY
BF241	COLOR — PSYCHOLOGY / psychology of vision
ML3840	*COLOR AND MUSIC* **SEE** MUSIC AND COLOR
TR853	COLOR CINEMATOGRAPHY
RE921	*COLOR DISCRIMINATION* **SEE** COLOR-BLINDNESS
QP481	*COLOR DISCRIMINATION* **SEE** COLOR-SENSE
NE1850-1879	*COLOR ETCHINGS* **SEE** COLOR PRINTS
HF5839	COLOR IN ADVERTISING
NA2795	COLOR IN ARCHITECTURE
NA2795	*COLOR IN BUILDING* **SEE** COLOR IN ARCHITECTURE
NB93	*COLOR IN SCULPTURE* **SEE** POLYCHROMY / sculpture
NB1275	*COLOR IN SCULPTURE* **SEE** POLYCHROMY / sculpture
TS1475	COLOR IN THE TEXTILE INDUSTRIES / design
TP892	COLOR IN THE TEXTILE INDUSTRIES / dyeing
QL767	COLOR OF ANIMALS
QL698	COLOR OF BIRDS
QL639	COLOR OF FISHES
QK926	COLOR OF FLOWERS / ecology
QK669	COLOR OF FLOWERS / nomenclature
QK899	COLOR OF FRUIT
QL496	COLOR OF INSECTS
GN197	COLOR OF MAN
QK899	COLOR OF PLANTS
QL699	COLOR OF REPTILES
QB816	*COLOR OF STARS* **SEE** STARS — COLOR
QB829	*COLOR OF STARS* **SEE** STARS — COLOR
TR510	COLOR PHOTOGRAPHY — AUTOCHROME PROCESS
TR525	COLOR PHOTOGRAPHY — LIPPMANN PROCESS
TR520	COLOR PHOTOGRAPHY — THREE-COLOR PROCESS
TR510-525	COLOR PHOTOGRAPHY
NE1850-1879	COLOR PRINTS
ND1595	*COLOR SLIDES* **SEE** LANTERN SLIDES / painting
TR730	*COLOR SLIDES* **SEE** LANTERN SLIDES / photography
TK6670	COLOR TELEVISION — REPAIRING
TK6670	COLOR TELEVISION
RE921	COLOR-BLINDNESS
BF497	COLOR-HEARING
ML3840	*COLOR-MUSIC* **SEE** MUSIC AND COLOR
Z258	COLOR-PRINTING
QP481	COLOR-SENSE
QH401-8	COLOR-VARIATION (BIOLOGY)
ND1279-1286	COLOR / art
QC495	COLOR / physics
F771-781	COLORADO — HISTORY
SB608.P8	*COLORADO BEETLE* **SEE** POTATO-BEETLE / pests
QL596.C5	*COLORADO BEETLE* **SEE** POTATO-BEETLE / zoology
F3722.1.C	COLORADO INDIANS (ECUADOR)
E498	COLORADO — HISTORY — — CIVIL WAR
BX6440-6460	*COLORED BAPTISTS* **SEE** BAPTISTS, NEGRO
BX1407.N4	*COLORED CATHOLICS* **SEE** CATHOLICS, NEGRO / u.s.
BX8060.N5	*COLORED LUTHERANS* **SEE** LUTHERANS, NEGRO
BX8460-8469	COLORED METHODIST EPISCOPAL CHURCH
BX8435-8473	*COLORED METHODISTS* **SEE** METHODISTS, NEGRO
E185	*COLORED PEOPLE (AMERICA)* **SEE** NEGROES
E441-453	*COLORED PEOPLE (AMERICA)* **SEE** NEGROES / slavery and anti-slavery movement

QC495	COLORIMETRY
QD113	COLORIMETRY / *chemical analysis*
ND2399	*COLORING BOOKS* **SEE** PAINTING BOOKS
LB1187-8	COLORING FOR CHILDREN
TX571.C7	COLORING MATTER IN FOOD
TP910-925	COLORING MATTER / *dyes*
TP936	COLORING MATTER / *etc.*
TS710	*COLORING OF METALS* **SEE** METALS — COLORING
TR485	*COLORING OF PHOTOGRAPHS* **SEE** PHOTOGRAPHS — COLORING
TP910-925	*COLORINGS* **SEE** COLORING MATTER / *dyes*
TP936	*COLORINGS* **SEE** COLORING MATTER / *etc.*
QC495	COLORS — ANALYSIS
JC345-7	*COLORS (FLAGS)* **SEE** FLAGS / *emblems of state*
CR101-115	*COLORS (FLAGS)* **SEE** FLAGS / *heraldry*
VK385	*COLORS (FLAGS)* **SEE** FLAGS / *merchant marine signaling*
U360-365	*COLORS (FLAGS)* **SEE** FLAGS / *military science*
UC590-595	*COLORS (FLAGS)* **SEE** FLAGS / *military science*
V300-305	*COLORS (FLAGS)* **SEE** FLAGS / *naval science*
BS680.C55	COLORS IN THE BIBLE
ND1510	COLORS / *artists' pigments*
ND1279-1286	COLORS / *color in painting*
TT310-324	COLORS / *industrial painting*
QC495	COLORS / *physics*
BV165	COLORS, LITURGICAL
LB3630	*COLORS, SCHOOL* **SEE** SCHOOL COLORS
QP246	COLOSTRUM
F3446	COLPAHUAICO, BATTLE OF, 1824
BV2369	*COLPORTAGE* **SEE** BIBLE — PUBLICATION AND DISTRIBUTION
HF5456.B7	*COLPORTAGE* **SEE** BOOKSELLERS AND BOOKSELLING — COLPORTAGE, SUBSCRIPTION TRADE, ETC.
UF620.C6	COLT AUTOMATIC MACHINE-GUN
QL696.C6	*COLUMBAE* **SEE** PIGEONS
SF465-472	*COLUMBAE* **SEE** PIGEONS / *breeding*
HE6239.P	*COLUMBAE* **SEE** PIGEONS / *carrier pigeons*
UH90	*COLUMBAE* **SEE** PIGEONS / *military communications*
E477.75	COLUMBIA, S.C., BURNING OF, 1865
QL696.C6	*COLUMBIDAE* **SEE** PIGEONS
SF465-472	*COLUMBIDAE* **SEE** PIGEONS / *breeding*
HE6239.P	*COLUMBIDAE* **SEE** PIGEONS / *carrier pigeons*
UH90	*COLUMBIDAE* **SEE** PIGEONS / *military communications*
E120	COLUMBUS DAY
QM507	COLUMELLA AURIS
QL948	COLUMELLA AURIS
TH2252-3	COLUMNS / *building*
TA492.C7	COLUMNS / *testing*
TA681-3	COLUMNS, CONCRETE
TA439-445	COLUMNS, CONCRETE / *testing*
NA2860	COLUMNS, CORINTHIAN
NA2860	COLUMNS, DORIC
NA2860	COLUMNS, IONIC
TH1610-1625	COLUMNS, IRON AND STEEL / *building*
TA492.C7	COLUMNS, IRON AND STEEL / *testing*
TP159.P3	*COLUMNS, PACKED* **SEE** PACKED TOWERS
TP159.P6	*COLUMNS, PLATE* **SEE** PLATE TOWERS
TH2252-3	COLUMNS, WOODEN
E99.C	COLVILLE INDIANS
QL696.P9	*COLYMBIDAE* **SEE** DIVERS (BIRDS)
TP684.R3	*COLZA-OIL* **SEE** RAPE-OIL
RC383.C6	COMA
PL318	*COMAN LANGUAGE* **SEE** KIPCHAK LANGUAGE
E99.C85	COMANCHE INDIANS
PM921	COMANCHE LANGUAGE
QB723.C	COMAS SOLA'S COMET
UG623	*COMBAT TELEVISION* **SEE** MILITARY TELEVISION
CR4565	*COMBAT, TRIAL BY* **SEE** WAGER OF BATTLE
DP219.2	*COMBATE DE ARMINON* **SEE** ARMINON, BATTLE OF, 1837
BF723.F5	*COMBATIVENESS* **SEE** FIGHTING (PSYCHOLOGY) / *child study*
HD2709-2930	*COMBINATIONS IN RESTRAINT OF TRADE* **SEE** MONOPOLIES
HD2801-2930	*COMBINATIONS IN RESTRAINT OF TRADE* **SEE** TRUSTS, INDUSTRIAL / *other countries*
HD2771-2798	*COMBINATIONS IN RESTRAINT OF TRADE* **SEE** TRUSTS, INDUSTRIAL / *u.s.*

HD5306-5450	*COMBINATIONS OF LABOR* **SEE** STRIKES AND LOCKOUTS
QA165	COMBINATIONS / *mathematics*
HD2709-2930	*COMBINATIONS, INDUSTRIAL* **SEE** TRUSTS, INDUSTRIAL
HD2801-2930	*COMBINATIONS, INDUSTRIAL* **SEE** TRUSTS, INDUSTRIAL / *other countries*
HD2771-2798	*COMBINATIONS, INDUSTRIAL* **SEE** TRUSTS, INDUSTRIAL / *u.s.*
U260	*COMBINED OPERATIONS (MILITARY SCIENCE)* **SEE** UNIFIED OPERATIONS (MILITARY SCIENCE)
S699	COMBINES (AGRICULTURAL MACHINERY)
HD9999.C7	COMBS
HD3623-4	*COMBUSTIBLE LIQUIDS* **SEE** INFLAMMABLE LIQUIDS / *dangerous industries*
QD516	COMBUSTION — TABLES, ETC.
QD516	COMBUSTION
RA1171	COMBUSTION, SPONTANEOUS HUMAN
TN817	COMBUSTION, SPONTANEOUS / *coal storage*
TH9198	COMBUSTION, SPONTANEOUS / *fire prevention*
TN313-315	COMBUSTION, SPONTANEOUS / *mine accidents*
QD516	COMBUSTION, THEORY OF
F2823.C	COMECHINGONE INDIANS / *argentine republic*
PN6147-9	COMEDY / *collections*
PN1920-1929	COMEDY / *history*
TL686.D4	COMET (JET TRANSPORTS)
TL686.D4	*COMET JET LINER* **SEE** COMET (JET TRANSPORTS)
QB357	COMETS — ORBITS
QB721-732	COMETS
E99.K18	*COMEYA INDIANS* **SEE** KAMIA INDIANS
NA7020	*COMFORT STATIONS* **SEE** PUBLIC COMFORT STATIONS / *architecture*
RA607	*COMFORT STATIONS* **SEE** PUBLIC COMFORT STATIONS / *hygiene*
HD6977-7080	*COMFORT, STANDARD OF* **SEE** COST AND STANDARD OF LIVING
PN6149.B8	*COMIC LITERATURE* **SEE** BURLESQUE (LITERATURE)
PN6147-9	*COMIC LITERATURE* **SEE** COMEDY / *collections*
PN1920-1929	*COMIC LITERATURE* **SEE** COMEDY / *history*
PQ4236-8	*COMIC LITERATURE* **SEE** COMMEDIA DELL' ARTE / *collections*
PQ4155-9	*COMIC LITERATURE* **SEE** COMMEDIA DELL' ARTE / *history*
PN1940-1949	*COMIC LITERATURE* **SEE** FARCE
PN6149.P3	*COMIC LITERATURE* **SEE** PARODY
PN6231.S2	*COMIC LITERATURE* **SEE** SATIRE / *collections*
PN6149.S2	*COMIC LITERATURE* **SEE** SATIRE / *history*
ML3858	*COMIC OPERA* **SEE** OPERA / *aesthetics*
ML1700-2110	*COMIC OPERA* **SEE** OPERA / *history and criticism*
ML1900	*COMIC OPERA* **SEE** OPERETTA
ML1950	*COMIC OPERA* **SEE** ZARZUELA
BH301.C7	COMIC, THE
JX4081	COMITY OF NATIONS
E99.C85	*COMMANCHE INDIANS* **SEE** COMANCHE INDIANS
BV4720	COMMANDMENTS OF THE CHURCH
BM646	COMMANDMENTS, SIX HUNDRED AND THIRTEEN
BV4656	COMMANDMENTS, TEN — JUVENILE LITERATURE
BV4655-4710	COMMANDMENTS, TEN / *moral theology*
BS1281-5	COMMANDMENTS, TEN / *texts*
BV4714	*COMMANDMENTS, TEN-SUMMARY* **SEE** SUMMARY OF THE LAW (THEOLOGY)
PQ4236-8	COMMEDIA DELL' ARTE / *collections*
PQ4155-9	COMMEDIA DELL' ARTE / *history*
BV194.C6	*COMMEMORATION OF SAINTS* **SEE** SAINTS — COMMEMORATION
BV194.C6	*COMMEMORATION OF THE FAITHFUL DEPARTED* **SEE** SAINTS — COMMEMORATION
AS7	*COMMEMORATIONS* **SEE** ANNIVERSARIES
BV4255	*COMMENCEMENT ADDRESSES* **SEE** BACCALAUREATE ADDRESSES
QH548	*COMMENSALISM* **SEE** SYMBIOSIS / *biology*
QK918	*COMMENSALISM* **SEE** SYMBIOSIS / *botany*
BS482-498	*COMMENTARIES, BIBLICAL* **SEE** BIBLE — COMMENTARIES
PN4841-5650	*COMMENTATORS* **SEE** JOURNALISTS
PN4820-4823	*COMMENTATORS* **SEE** JOURNALISTS
PN5122-3	*COMMENTATORS* **SEE** JOURNALISTS / *gt. brit.*
PN4871-4	*COMMENTATORS* **SEE** JOURNALISTS / *u.s.*
HF1002	COMMERCE — TERMINOLOGY

HE2710-2712	*COMMERCE CLAUSE (U.S. CONSTITUTION)* **SEE** INTERSTATE COMMERCE / *law and cases*
HE1853	*COMMERCE CLAUSE (U.S. CONSTITUTION)* **SEE** INTERSTATE COMMERCE / *rates*
HE2757	*COMMERCE CLAUSE (U.S. CONSTITUTION)* **SEE** INTERSTATE COMMERCE / *discussion*
HE1843	*COMMERCE CLAUSE (U.S. CONSTITUTION)* **SEE** INTERSTATE COMMERCE / *rates*
HE2708	*COMMERCE CLAUSE (U.S. CONSTITUTION)* **SEE** INTERSTATE COMMERCE / *commission reports*
HF	COMMERCE
GT6010-6050	COMMERCE / *commercial customs*
GN436-440	COMMERCE / *primitive*
HF3211-4040	*COMMERCE-STATISTICS* **SEE** COMMERCIAL STATISTICS / *other countries*
HF91-293	*COMMERCE-STATISTICS* **SEE** COMMERCIAL STATISTICS / *serial documents*
HF1016-1017	*COMMERCE-STATISTICS* **SEE** COMMERCIAL STATISTICS / *theory and method*
HF3001-6	*COMMERCE-STATISTICS* **SEE** COMMERCIAL STATISTICS / *u.s.*
TL552	*COMMERCIAL AERONAUTICS* **SEE** AERONAUTICS, COMMERCIAL
TL515-532	*COMMERCIAL AERONAUTICS* **SEE** AERONAUTICS, COMMERCIAL
NC997	COMMERCIAL ART
HF294-343	COMMERCIAL ASSOCIATIONS
NA6210-6280	*COMMERCIAL BUILDINGS* **SEE** MERCANTILE BUILDINGS
NA6230-6233	*COMMERCIAL BUILDINGS* **SEE** OFFICE BUILDINGS
HF5861-2	*COMMERCIAL CATALOGS* **SEE** CATALOGS, COMMERCIAL
HF481-491	*COMMERCIAL COMPANIES* **SEE** COLONIAL COMPANIES
HD2709-2930	*COMMERCIAL CORNERS* **SEE** MONOPOLIES
HG6001-6051	*COMMERCIAL CORNERS* **SEE** SPECULATION
HG4551-4595	*COMMERCIAL CORNERS* **SEE** STOCK-EXCHANGE
HD2709-2930	*COMMERCIAL CORNERS* **SEE** TRUSTS, INDUSTRIAL
HD2801-2930	*COMMERCIAL CORNERS* **SEE** TRUSTS, INDUSTRIAL / *other countries*
HD2771-2798	*COMMERCIAL CORNERS* **SEE** TRUSTS, INDUSTRIAL / *u.s.*
HF5721-5733	COMMERCIAL CORRESPONDENCE
Z48	*COMMERCIAL CORRESPONDENCE-COPYING PROCESSES* **SEE** COPYING PROCESSES
HF5565-5585	*COMMERCIAL CREDIT* **SEE** CREDIT / *practice*
HG3701-3781	*COMMERCIAL CREDIT* **SEE** CREDIT / *theory*
HF5568	*COMMERCIAL CREDIT COMPANIES* **SEE** INSTALMENT PLAN
HB3711-3840	*COMMERCIAL CRISES* **SEE** DEPRESSIONS
NC997	*COMMERCIAL DESIGN* **SEE** COMMERCIAL ART
HF1101-1181	*COMMERCIAL EDUCATION* **SEE** BUSINESS EDUCATION
HF5501	*COMMERCIAL EMPLOYEES* **SEE** CLERKS
HV3165-3173	*COMMERCIAL EMPLOYEES* **SEE** CLERKS / *aid to*
HD8039.M4	*COMMERCIAL EMPLOYEES* **SEE** CLERKS / *mercantile clerks*
HF5386	*COMMERCIAL ETHICS* **SEE** BUSINESS ETHICS
HF5391	*COMMERCIAL ETHICS* **SEE** BUSINESS ETHICS
HF1021-9	*COMMERCIAL GEOGRAPHY* **SEE** GEOGRAPHY, COMMERCIAL
PN4784.C7	*COMMERCIAL JOURNALISM* **SEE** JOURNALISM, COMMERCIAL
HF1201-1400	COMMERCIAL LAW
Z675.C7	COMMERCIAL LIBRARIES
HF61	COMMERCIAL MUSEUMS
HF294-343	*COMMERCIAL ORGANIZATIONS* **SEE** COMMERCIAL ASSOCIATIONS
JX6288-9	*COMMERCIAL PAPER* **SEE** NEGOTIABLE INSTRUMENTS / *international law*
HF1259	*COMMERCIAL PAPER* **SEE** NEGOTIABLE INSTRUMENTS / *u.s.*
TR690	*COMMERCIAL PHOTOGRAPHY* **SEE** PHOTOGRAPHY, COMMERCIAL
HF1401-1650	COMMERCIAL POLICY
HF1041-1051	COMMERCIAL PRODUCTS
HF5571-8	*COMMERCIAL RATINGS* **SEE** CREDIT GUIDES
HE323-8	*COMMERCIAL ROUTES* **SEE** TRADE ROUTES
HF1101-1181	*COMMERCIAL SCHOOLS* **SEE** BUSINESS EDUCATION
HF3211-4040	COMMERCIAL STATISTICS / *other countries*
HF91-293	COMMERCIAL STATISTICS / *serial documents*
HF1016-1017	COMMERCIAL STATISTICS / *theory and method*
HF3001-6	COMMERCIAL STATISTICS / *u.s.*
HF5441-4	COMMERCIAL TRAVELERS
HF1721-1733	COMMERCIAL TREATIES
HD2709-2930	*COMMERCIAL TRUSTS* **SEE** TRUSTS, INDUSTRIAL
HD2801-2930	*COMMERCIAL TRUSTS* **SEE** TRUSTS, INDUSTRIAL / *other countries*
HD2771-2798	*COMMERCIAL TRUSTS* **SEE** TRUSTS, INDUSTRIAL / *u.s.*
HF6146.R3	*COMMERCIALS, RADIO* **SEE** RADIO ADVERTISING
UC700-780	*COMMISSARIAT* **SEE** ARMIES — COMMISSARIAT
UC703	*COMMISSARIAT* **SEE** U.S. — COMMISSARIAT
UC40-44	*COMMISSARIAT* **SEE** U.S. — COMMISSARIAT
JS342-3	*COMMISSION GOVERNMENT* **SEE** MUNICIPAL GOVERNMENT BY COMMISSION / *u.s.*
JS344.C5	*COMMISSION GOVERNMENT WITH CITY MANAGER* **SEE** MUNICIPAL GOVERNMENT BY CITY MANAGER / *u.s.*
HF5421-6	COMMISSION MERCHANTS
DA60	COMMISSIONS OF ARRAY / *english military history*
JX1971	COMMISSIONS OF INQUIRY, INTERNATIONAL
Z716	*COMMISSIONS, LIBRARY* **SEE** LIBRARY COMMISSIONS
Z732	*COMMISSIONS, LIBRARY* **SEE** LIBRARY COMMISSIONS / *state library commission reports*
HD2763-8	*COMMISSIONS, PUBLIC SERVICE* **SEE** PUBLIC SERVICE COMMISSIONS
HG6046	COMMODITY EXCHANGES
HF5548	*COMMON BUSINESS LANGUAGES* **SEE** PROGRAMMING LANGUAGES (ELECTRONIC COMPUTERS) — BUSINESS
HF5548.5.C2	*COMMON BUSINESS ORIENTED LANGUAGE* **SEE** COBOL (COMPUTER PROGRAM LANGUAGE)
HD1286-9	*COMMON LANDS* **SEE** COMMONS
L-LC	*COMMON SCHOOLS* **SEE** PUBLIC SCHOOLS
PN6245-6	COMMONPLACE-BOOKS
PN245	COMMONPLACE-BOOKS / *authors' aids*
HD4801-8942	*COMMONS (SOCIAL ORDER)* **SEE** LABOR AND LABORING CLASSES
HT680-690	*COMMONS (SOCIAL ORDER)* **SEE** MIDDLE CLASSES
DG83.3	*COMMONS (SOCIAL ORDER)* **SEE** PLEBS (ROME)
HD4801-4854	*COMMONS (SOCIAL ORDER)* **SEE** PROLETARIAT
HD1286-9	COMMONS
LB3640	*COMMONS, STUDENT* **SEE** STUDENT UNIONS
B65	*COMMONWEALTH, THE* **SEE** POLITICAL SCIENCE / *j political science and philosophy*
HM33	*COMMONWEALTH, THE* **SEE** POLITICAL SCIENCE / *political science and sociology*
JC421-458	*COMMONWEALTH, THE* **SEE** REPUBLICS / *theory*
JC	*COMMONWEALTH, THE* **SEE** STATE, THE
RA769	COMMUNICABLE DISEASES / *miscellaneous preventive measures*
RC111-216	COMMUNICABLE DISEASES / *practice of medicine*
RA643-4	COMMUNICABLE DISEASES / *public hygiene*
BV4319	COMMUNICATION (THEOLOGY)
HE	COMMUNICATION AND TRAFFIC
GN38	COMMUNICATION AND TRAFFIC / *primitive*
R118	COMMUNICATION IN MEDICINE
Q223	*COMMUNICATION IN RESEARCH* **SEE** COMMUNICATION IN SCIENCE
Q223	COMMUNICATION IN SCIENCE
P90	COMMUNICATION
P93	*COMMUNICATION-CONTENT ANALYSIS* **SEE** CONTENT ANALYSIS (COMMUNICATION)
UA940-945	COMMUNICATIONS, MILITARY
UA940-945	*COMMUNICATIONS, NAVAL* **SEE** COMMUNICATIONS, MILITARY
HV7936.C8	*COMMUNICATIONS, POLICE* **SEE** POLICE COMMUNICATION SYSTEMS
BV823-8	*COMMUNION* **SEE** LORD'S SUPPER
BX2215	*COMMUNION* **SEE** LORD'S SUPPER / *catholic church*
BX5149.C5	*COMMUNION* **SEE** LORD'S SUPPER / *church of england*
BT972	COMMUNION OF SAINTS
NK7100-7215	*COMMUNION PLATE* **SEE** CHURCH PLATE
BV4257.5	COMMUNION SERMONS
CJ5407-5415	*COMMUNION TOKENS* **SEE** TOKENS, COMMUNION

M2017.2	COMMUNION-SERVICE MUSIC
M2017	COMMUNION-SERVICE MUSIC
M2016.5	COMMUNION-SERVICE MUSIC
BV820	*COMMUNION, CLOSE* **SEE** CLOSE AND OPEN COMMUNION
BX2217	*COMMUNION, FIRST* **SEE** FIRST COMMUNION
BV828	*COMMUNION, INFANT* **SEE** INFANT COMMUNION
BV820	*COMMUNION, OPEN* **SEE** CLOSE AND OPEN COMMUNION
HX87	COMMUNISM — MISCELLANEOUS
BX1396.4	*COMMUNISM AND CATHOLIC CHURCH* **SEE** COMMUNISM AND RELIGION / catholic church
HX536	*COMMUNISM AND CATHOLIC CHURCH* **SEE** COMMUNISM AND RELIGION
BX1396.4	*COMMUNISM AND CHRISTIANITY* **SEE** COMMUNISM AND RELIGION / catholic church
HX536	*COMMUNISM AND CHRISTIANITY* **SEE** COMMUNISM AND RELIGION
HX536	COMMUNISM AND RELIGION
BX1396.4	COMMUNISM AND RELIGION / catholic church
HX626-795	COMMUNISM
D847	COMMUNIST COUNTRIES
BJ1390	COMMUNIST ETHICS
LC237	COMMUNITY AND COLLEGE
LC215	COMMUNITY AND SCHOOL
NA6598	*COMMUNITY CENTERS FOR EMPLOYEES* **SEE** EMPLOYEES' BUILDINGS AND FACILITIES
HV97	*COMMUNITY CHESTS* **SEE** FEDERATIONS, FINANCIAL (SOCIAL SERVICE) / national
HV99	*COMMUNITY CHESTS* **SEE** FEDERATIONS, FINANCIAL (SOCIAL SERVICE) / u.s. local
HV40-41	*COMMUNITY CHESTS* **SEE** FEDERATIONS, FINANCIAL (SOCIAL SERVICE)
BV636	COMMUNITY CHURCHES
LB2329	*COMMUNITY COLLEGES* **SEE** MUNICIPAL UNIVERSITIES AND COLLEGES
SD561-668	COMMUNITY FORESTS
HM131	COMMUNITY LIFE
M1997.C5	COMMUNITY MUSIC
ML2500-2770	COMMUNITY MUSIC / history and criticism
MT875	COMMUNITY MUSIC / instruction
PN3203-5	COMMUNITY PLAYS, ETC.
M1977.C5	*COMMUNITY SONG-BOOKS* **SEE** SONG-BOOKS
HN29	*COMMUNITY SURVEYS* **SEE** SOCIAL SURVEYS
PN2267	*COMMUNITY THEATER* **SEE** THEATER — LITTLE THEATER MOVEMENT / u.s.
HE1959-1960	*COMMUTATION RATES (RAILROADS)* **SEE** RAILROADS — FARES — — SPECIAL RATES
QA171	*COMMUTATIVE GROUPS* **SEE** ABELIAN GROUPS
QL430.6-7	*COMOPODA* **SEE** LAMELLIBRANCHIATA
JK2441	*COMPACTS, INTERSTATE* **SEE** INTERSTATE AGREEMENTS
BX4060	*COMPAGNIE DE SAINT-SULPICE* **SEE** SULPICIANS
HD6464-6	COMPAGNONNAGES
HG4001-4280	*COMPANIES* **SEE** CORPORATIONS / finance
HD2709-2930	*COMPANIES* **SEE** CORPORATIONS / theory and policy
HF1261	*COMPANIES* **SEE** PARTNERSHIP
HF481-491	*COMPANIES, COLONIAL* **SEE** COLONIAL COMPANIES
HD2709-2930	*COMPANIES, STOCK* **SEE** STOCK COMPANIES / corporations
HG4001-4480	*COMPANIES, STOCK* **SEE** STOCK COMPANIES / finance
HG4301-4480	*COMPANIES, TRUST* **SEE** TRUST COMPANIES
S603.5	COMPANION CROPS
HQ803	*COMPANIONATE MARRIAGE* **SEE** MARRIAGE, COMPANIONATE
HV8081-9	*COMPANY POLICE* **SEE** POLICE, PRIVATE
HD6490.C6	COMPANY UNIONS
HD5261	*COMPANY VACATIONS* **SEE** VACATIONS, EMPLOYEE
QL801-950	*COMPARATIVE ANATOMY* **SEE** ANATOMY, COMPARATIVE
LA126-133	COMPARATIVE EDUCATION
P151-295	*COMPARATIVE GRAMMAR* **SEE** GRAMMAR, COMPARATIVE AND GENERAL
P151-295	*COMPARATIVE LINGUISTICS* **SEE** GRAMMAR, COMPARATIVE AND GENERAL
P1-409	*COMPARATIVE LINGUISTICS* **SEE** LANGUAGE AND LANGUAGES
PN851-883	*COMPARATIVE LITERATURE* **SEE** LITERATURE, COMPARATIVE

PQ-PT	*COMPARATIVE LITERATURE* **SEE** LITERATURE, COMPARATIVE / by country
QL801-950	*COMPARATIVE MORPHOLOGY* **SEE** ANATOMY, COMPARATIVE
QH351	*COMPARATIVE MORPHOLOGY* **SEE** MORPHOLOGY / general biology
RB114	*COMPARATIVE PATHOLOGY* **SEE** PATHOLOGY, COMPARATIVE
B799	*COMPARATIVE PHILOSOPHY* **SEE** PHILOSOPHY, COMPARATIVE
QP31-33	*COMPARATIVE PHYSIOLOGY* **SEE** PHYSIOLOGY, COMPARATIVE
BF660-678	*COMPARATIVE PSYCHOLOGY* **SEE** PSYCHOLOGY, COMPARATIVE
BL74-98	*COMPARATIVE RELIGION* **SEE** RELIGIONS
BT990	*COMPARATIVE SYMBOLICS* **SEE** CREEDS — COMPARATIVE STUDIES
BF441	COMPARISON (PSYCHOLOGY)
G108.C3	*COMPASS CARD* **SEE** CARDINAL POINTS
G108.C3	*COMPASS ROSE* **SEE** CARDINAL POINTS
VK577	COMPASS
QC849	COMPASS / deviation
VK577	*COMPASS, GYROSCOPIC* **SEE** GYRO COMPASS
TL589.C6	*COMPASS, GYROSCOPIC* **SEE** GYRO COMPASS
QA862.G9	*COMPASS, GYROSCOPIC* **SEE** GYRO COMPASS
VK577	*COMPASS, RADIO* **SEE** RADIO COMPASS
TL696.C7	*COMPASS, RADIO* **SEE** RADIO COMPASS / aeronautics
QB105	*COMPASS, SOLAR* **SEE** SOLAR COMPASS
TA563	*COMPASS, SURVEYOR'S* **SEE** SURVEYOR'S COMPASS
TP290.C7	COMPENSATING-POWDER
JF1671	*COMPENSATION* **SEE** PENSIONS / civil service
HJ7491	*COMPENSATION* **SEE** PENSIONS / public fiinance
LB2842-4	*COMPENSATION* **SEE** PENSIONS / teachers
HD4906-5100	*COMPENSATION* **SEE** WAGES
HB301	*COMPENSATION* **SEE** WAGES / theory
HD6977-7080	*COMPENSATION* **SEE** WAGES / wages and cost of living
HV8688-8691	*COMPENSATION FOR VICTIMS OF CRIME* **SEE** REPARATION
HD4928.D5	*COMPENSATION, DISMISSAL* **SEE** WAGES — DISMISSAL WAGE
QH647	*COMPENSATORY MOTION* **SEE** IRRITABILITY / cells
HF1436	COMPETITION / commercial
HD41	COMPETITION / industrial
HD3625-6	COMPETITION, UNFAIR
LB3068-9	*COMPETITIONS* **SEE** SCHOOL CONTESTS
QP801.A	*COMPETITIVE ANTAGONISTS (METABOLISM)* **SEE** ANTIMETABOLITES
JK716	*COMPETITIVE EXAMINATIONS* **SEE** CIVIL SERVICE — EXAMINATIONS / u.s.
LB2353	*COMPETITIVE EXAMINATIONS* **SEE** EXAMINATIONS / college
QR185	*COMPLEMENT DEFLECTION* **SEE** COMPLEMENT FIXATION
QR185	*COMPLEMENT DEVIATION* **SEE** COMPLEMENT FIXATION
QR185	COMPLEMENT FIXATION
QR185	COMPLEMENTS (IMMUNITY)
QA255	COMPLEX NUMBERS **SEE** NUMBERS, COMPLEX
RC563	*COMPLEXES (PSYCHOLOGY)* **SEE** CAIN COMPLEX
QA608	COMPLEXES
RA778	*COMPLEXION* **SEE** BEAUTY, PERSONAL
GN197	*COMPLEXION* **SEE** COLOR OF MAN
GT2340	*COMPLEXION* **SEE** COSMETICS / manners and customs
TP983	*COMPLEXION* **SEE** COSMETICS / manufacture
RA778	*COMPLEXION* **SEE** COSMETICS / toilet
NA8480	*COMPONENTS CONSTRUCTION* **SEE** BUILDINGS, PREFABRICATED / architecture
TH1098	*COMPONENTS CONSTRUCTION* **SEE** BUILDINGS, PREFABRICATED / building
ML93-98	COMPOSERS — AUTOGRAPHS
ML87-88	COMPOSERS — PORTRAITS
ML390	COMPOSERS / biography collective
ML410	COMPOSERS / individual
ML390	COMPOSERS, WOMEN
ML385-429	*COMPOSERS-DICTIONARIES* **SEE** MUSIC — BIO-BIBLIOGRAPHY / history and criticism

Z253	*COMPOSING-MACHINES* **SEE** TYPE-SETTING MACHINES
TR685	*COMPOSITE PHOTOGRAPHY* **SEE** PHOTOGRAPHY, COMPOSITE
N7430	COMPOSITION (ART)
ML430-455	COMPOSITION (MUSIC) / history
MT40-67	COMPOSITION (MUSIC) / instruction
TR179	COMPOSITION (PHOTOGRAPHY)
PE1481-1497	*COMPOSITION (RHETORIC)* **SEE** LETTER-WRITING / english rhetoric
BJ2100-2115	*COMPOSITION (RHETORIC)* **SEE** LETTER-WRITING / etiquette
PN173-229	*COMPOSITION (RHETORIC)* **SEE** RHETORIC
PE1402-1497	*COMPOSITION (RHETORIC)* **SEE** RHETORIC / english
QD305	COMPOUNDS, UNSATURATED
QD341	COMPOUNDS, UNSATURATED
BF325	COMPREHENSION
RM827	COMPRESSED AIR — THERAPEUTIC USE
TJ981-1009	COMPRESSED AIR / technology
TP761.C65	*COMPRESSED GAS* **SEE** GASES, COMPRESSED
TS837	*COMPRESSED WOOD* **SEE** WOOD, COMPRESSED
RC103.C3	*COMPRESSED-AIR DISEASE* **SEE** CAISSON-DISEASE
TF838	*COMPRESSED-AIR RAILROADS* **SEE** RAILROADS, COMPRESSED-AIR
TL229.G3	*COMPRESSED-GAS AUTOMOBILES* **SEE** AUTOMOBILES — MOTORS (COMPRESSED-GAS)
QC284	COMPRESSIBILITY / liquids
TJ990-992	*COMPRESSING MACHINERY* **SEE** COMPRESSORS
TS837	*COMPRESSION OF WOOD* **SEE** WOOD, COMPRESSED
TS1449	COMPRESSOMETERS / textile testing
TJ267.5.C5	COMPRESSORS — AERODYNAMICS
TJ990	COMPRESSORS — BLADES
TJ990-992	COMPRESSORS
TJ990-992	*COMPRESSORS, AIR* **SEE** AIR-COMPRESSORS
TJ267.5.C6	*COMPRESSORS, SUPERSONIC* **SEE** SUPERSONIC COMPRESSORS
BJ1430-1438	COMPROMISE (ETHICS)
E423	COMPROMISE OF 1850
DP131.6	*COMPROMISO DE CASPE* **SEE** CASPE DECLARATION, 1412
QA75	COMPTOMETERS
HF5550	*COMPTROLLERSHIP* **SEE** CONTROLLERSHIP
LC129-139	*COMPULSORY EDUCATION* **SEE** EDUCATION, COMPULSORY
HJ8047	*COMPULSORY LOANS* **SEE** FORCED LOANS
UB340-355	*COMPULSORY MILITARY SERVICE* **SEE** MILITARY SERVICE, COMPULSORY
HD4905.5	*COMPULSORY NON-MILITARY SERVICE* **SEE** SERVICE, COMPULSORY NON-MILITARY / in wartime
HD4871-5	*COMPULSORY NON-MILITARY SERVICE* **SEE** SERVICE, COMPULSORY NON-MILITARY
LC129-139	*COMPULSORY SCHOOL ATTENDANCE* **SEE** EDUCATION, COMPULSORY
LB2503-2797	*COMPULSORY SCHOOL ATTENDANCE* **SEE** EDUCATIONAL LAW AND LEGISLATION
LC142-5	*COMPULSORY SCHOOL ATTENDANCE* **SEE** SCHOOL ATTENDANCE / limitation
LB3081	*COMPULSORY SCHOOL ATTENDANCE* **SEE** SCHOOL ATTENDANCE / truancy
JF1031	*COMPULSORY VOTING* **SEE** VOTING, COMPULSORY
QA248.5	*COMPUTABILITY THEORY* **SEE** RECURSIVE FUNCTIONS
QA248.5	*COMPUTABLE FUNCTIONS* **SEE** RECURSIVE FUNCTIONS
QA74	COMPUTATION LABORATORIES
TK7885	*COMPUTER CIRCUITS* **SEE** ELECTRONIC CALCULATING-MACHINES — CIRCUITS
QA74	*COMPUTER LABORATORIES* **SEE** COMPUTATION LABORATORIES
P307-310	*COMPUTER TRANSLATING* **SEE** MACHINE TRANSLATING
TL557.D4	*COMPUTERS, DENSITY ALTITUDE* **SEE** DENSITY ALTITUDE COMPUTERS
QA76	*COMPUTERS, ELECTRONIC* **SEE** ELECTRONIC CALCULATING-MACHINES
QA76	*COMPUTERS, ELECTRONIC ANALOG* **SEE** ELECTRONIC ANALOG COMPUTERS
QA74	*COMPUTING LABORATORIES* **SEE** COMPUTATION LABORATORIES
HF5688-9	*COMPUTING MACHINES* **SEE** CALCULATING-MACHINES / bookkeeping
QA75	*COMPUTING MACHINES* **SEE** CALCULATING-MACHINES / mechanical devices
QA111	*COMPUTING TABLES* **SEE** READY-RECKONERS / arithmetic
HF5697-5702	*COMPUTING TABLES* **SEE** READY-RECKONERS / business arithmetic
CE81-83	*COMPUTUS ECCLESIASTICUS* **SEE** CHURCH CALENDAR
BJ1533.C56	COMRADESHIP
PK2231-7	*CONCANI LANGUAGE* **SEE** KONKANI LANGUAGE
Z104.5	*CONCEALED WRITING* **SEE** WRITING, INVISIBLE
BX2231.5	CONCELEBRATION / catholic church
LB1065	*CONCENTRATION* **SEE** ATTENTION / educational
BF321	*CONCENTRATION* **SEE** ATTENTION / psychology
QD568	CONCENTRATION CELLS / electrochemistry
QC603	CONCENTRATION CELLS / physics
LB2861	*CONCENTRATION OF SCHOOLS* **SEE** SCHOOLS — CENTRALIZATION / rural
RG136	CONCEPTION — PREVENTION
HQ763-6	CONCEPTION — PREVENTION / limitation of offspring
HB875	CONCEPTION — PREVENTION / neo-malthusianism
LB1139	*CONCEPTION OF GEOMETRY* **SEE** GEOMETRY CONCEPT
RG136	CONCEPTION / gynecology
QP251-281	CONCEPTION / reproduction
B731	CONCEPTUALISM
NA6820-6840	*CONCERT HALLS* **SEE** MUSIC-HALLS / architecture
MT130	CONCERTI GROSSI — ANALYTICAL GUIDES
MT125	CONCERTI GROSSI — ANALYTICAL GUIDES
M1106	CONCERTI GROSSI — SOLOS WITH PIANO
M1041	CONCERTI GROSSI — SOLOS WITH PIANO
M1257	CONCERTI GROSSI ARRANGED FOR BAND
M12-13	CONCERTI GROSSI ARRANGED FOR ORGAN
M215	CONCERTI GROSSI ARRANGED FOR PIANO (2 PIANOS)
M210	CONCERTI GROSSI ARRANGED FOR PIANO (4 HANDS)
M1040-1041	CONCERTI GROSSI
M1040-1041	CONCERTI GROSSI, ARRANGED
M154	CONCERTINA MUSIC
ML1055.C6	CONCERTINA
ML1263	CONCERTO (ORGAN)
ML1263	CONCERTO (PIANO)
ML1263	CONCERTO (VIOLIN)
ML1263	CONCERTO (VIOLONCELLO)
ML1263	CONCERTO / history
M1360	CONCERTOS (ACCORDION WITH PLECTRAL ENSEMBLE) — SCORES
M1360	CONCERTOS (ACCORDION WITH PLECTRAL ENSEMBLE)
M1105	CONCERTOS (ACCORDION WITH STRING ORCHESTRA) — SCORES
M1040-1041	CONCERTOS (ACCORDION WITH STRING ORCHESTRA)
M1039.4.A3	CONCERTOS (ACCORDION) — SOLO WITH PIANO
M1037.4.B3	CONCERTOS (BALALAIKA WITH CHAMBER ORCHESTRA) — SCORES
M1037.4.B3	CONCERTOS (BALALAIKA WITH CHAMBER ORCHESTRA)
M1105-6	CONCERTOS (BASSOON AND CLARINET WITH STRING ORCHESTRA)
M1041	CONCERTOS (BASSOON AND CLARINET) — SOLOS WITH PIANO
M1040-1041	CONCERTOS (BASSOON AND CLARINET)
M1105-6	CONCERTOS (BASSOON AND OBOE WITH STRING ORCHESTRA)
M1106	CONCERTOS (BASSOON AND OBOE WITH STRING ORCHESTRA) — SOLOS WITH PIANO
M1040-1041	CONCERTOS (BASSOON AND OBOE)
M1105-6	CONCERTOS (BASSOON AND RECORDER WITH STRING ORCHESTRA)
M1105-6	CONCERTOS (BASSOON AND TRUMPET WITH STRING ORCHESTRA)
M1106	CONCERTOS (BASSOON AND TRUMPET WITH STRING ORCHESTRA) — SOLOS WITH PIANO
M1026-7	CONCERTOS (BASSOON WITH CHAMBER ORCHESTRA)
M1106	CONCERTOS (BASSOON WITH STRING ORCHESTRA) — SOLO WITH PIANO
M1105-6	CONCERTOS (BASSOON WITH STRING ORCHESTRA)

M1106	CONCERTOS (BASSOON WITH STRING ORCHESTRA), ARRANGED — SOLO WITH PIANO
M1105-6	CONCERTOS (BASSOON WITH STRING ORCHESTRA), ARRANGED
M1026.5	CONCERTOS (BASSOON) — CADENZAS
M1004.7	CONCERTOS (BASSOON) — CADENZAS
M1027	CONCERTOS (BASSOON) — SOLO WITH PIANO
M1026-7	CONCERTOS (BASSOON)
M1105-6	CONCERTOS (BASSOON, CLARINET, FLUTE WITH STRING ORCHESTRA)
M1040-1041	CONCERTOS (BASSOON, CLARINET, FLUTE, HORN, OBOE WITH CHAMBER ORCHESTRA)
M1040	CONCERTOS (BASSOON, CLARINET, FLUTE, HORN, OBOE) — SCORES
M1040-1041	CONCERTOS (BASSOON, CLARINET, FLUTE, HORN, OBOE)
M1105-6	CONCERTOS (BASSOON, CLARINET, FLUTE, HORN, VIOLONCELLO WITH STRING ORCHESTRA)
M1040-1041	CONCERTOS (BASSOON, CLARINET, FLUTE, OBOE WITH CHAMBER ORCHESTRA)
M1040	CONCERTOS (BASSOON, CLARINET, FLUTE, OBOE, HARP) — SCORES
M1040-1041	CONCERTOS (BASSOON, CLARINET, FLUTE, OBOE, HARP)
M1105-6	CONCERTOS (BASSOON, CLARINET, FLUTE, OBOE, 2 VIOLINS, VIOLA, VIOLONCELLO WITH STRING ORCHESTRA)
M1105-6	CONCERTOS (BASSOON, CLARINET, FLUTE, TRUMPET WITH STRING ORCHESTRA)
M1105-6	CONCERTOS (BASSOON, CLARINET, HORN, OBOE WITH STRING ORCHESTRA) — SCORES
M1105-6	CONCERTOS (BASSOON, CLARINET, HORN, OBOE WITH STRING ORCHESTRA)
M1040-1041	CONCERTOS (BASSOON, CLARINET, HORN, OBOE)
M1041	CONCERTOS (BASSOON, CLARINET, HORN, OBOE) — TO 1800 — — SOLOS WITH PIANO
M1040	CONCERTOS (BASSOON, CLARINET, HORN, OBOE) — TO 1800 — — SCORES
M1105-6	CONCERTOS (BASSOON, CLARINET, OBOE WITH STRING ORCHESTRA)
M1040	CONCERTOS (BASSOON, CLARINET, TRUMPET) — SCORES
M1040-1041	CONCERTOS (BASSOON, CLARINET, TRUMPET)
M1040-1041	CONCERTOS (BASSOON, FLUTE, HORN, OBOE WITH CHAMBER ORCHESTRA)
M1105-6	CONCERTOS (BASSOON, FLUTE, HORN, OBOE WITH STRING ORCHESTRA)
M1041	CONCERTOS (BASSOON, FLUTE, HORN, OBOE) — SOLOS WITH PIANO
M1040-1041	CONCERTOS (BASSOON, FLUTE, HORN, OBOE)
M1040-1041	CONCERTOS (BASSOON, HORN, TRUMPET, DOUBLE BASS)
M1105-6	CONCERTOS (BASSOON, OBOE, TRUMPET WITH STRING ORCHESTRA)
M1040-1041	CONCERTOS (BASSOON, OBOE, VIOLIN, VIOLONCELLO WITH CHAMBER ORCHESTRA)
M1040-1041	CONCERTOS (BASSOON, OBOE, VIOLIN, VIOLONCELLO)
M1040-1041	CONCERTOS (CLARINET AND FLUTE WITH CHAMBER ORCHESTRA)
M1105-6	CONCERTOS (CLARINET AND HARP WITH STRING ORCHESTRA)
M1105-6	CONCERTOS (CLARINET AND VIOLIN WITH STRING ORCHESTRA)
M1205	CONCERTOS (CLARINET WITH BAND) — SOLO WITH PIANO
M1205	CONCERTOS (CLARINET WITH BAND)
M1025	CONCERTOS (CLARINET WITH CHAMBER ORCHESTRA) — SOLO WITH PIANO
M1024-5	CONCERTOS (CLARINET WITH CHAMBER ORCHESTRA)
M1106	CONCERTOS (CLARINET WITH STRING ORCHESTRA) — SOLO WITH PIANO
M1105-6	CONCERTOS (CLARINET WITH STRING ORCHESTRA)
M1105-6	CONCERTOS (CLARINET WITH STRING ORCHESTRA), ARRANGED
M1106	CONCERTOS (CLARINET WITH STRING ORCHESTRA), ARRANGED — SOLO WITH PIANO
M1025	CONCERTOS (CLARINET) — SOLO WITH PIANO
M1024-5	CONCERTOS (CLARINET)
M1105-6	CONCERTOS (CLARINET, ENGLISH HORN, FLUTE, OBOE WITH STRING ORCHESTRA)
M1105-6	CONCERTOS (CLARINET, FLUTE, OBOE WITH STRING ORCHESTRA)
M1105-6	CONCERTOS (CLARINET, FLUTE, TRUMPET WITH STRING ORCHESTRA)
M1105	CONCERTOS (CLARINET, TROMBONE, TRUMPET WITH STRING ORCHESTRA) — SCORES
M1105-6	CONCERTOS (CLARINET, TROMBONE, TRUMPET WITH STRING ORCHESTRA)
M1205	CONCERTOS (CORNET WITH BAND)
M1030-1031	CONCERTOS (CORNET)
M1037.4.D64	CONCERTOS (DOMRA WITH CHAMBER ORCHESTRA) — SOLO WITH PIANO
M1037.4.D64	CONCERTOS (DOMRA WITH CHAMBER ORCHESTRA)
M1037.4.D64	CONCERTOS (DOMRA) — SOLO WITH PIANO
M1037.4.D64	CONCERTOS (DOMRA)
M1018	CONCERTOS (DOUBLE BASS WITH CHAMBER ORCHESTRA)
M1106	CONCERTOS (DOUBLE BASS WITH STRING ORCHESTRA) — SOLO WITH PIANO
M1105-6	CONCERTOS (DOUBLE BASS WITH STRING ORCHESTRA)
M1018	CONCERTOS (DOUBLE BASS) — SOLO WITH PIANO
M1018	CONCERTOS (DOUBLE BASS)
M1018	CONCERTOS (DOUBLE BASS), ARRANGED — SOLO WITH PIANO
M1018	CONCERTOS (DOUBLE BASS), ARRANGED
M1106	CONCERTOS (ENGLISH HORN AND FLUTE WITH STRING ORCHESTRA) — SOLOS WITH PIANO
M1105-6	CONCERTOS (ENGLISH HORN AND FLUTE WITH STRING ORCHESTRA)
M1105-6	CONCERTOS (ENGLISH HORN AND HARP WITH STRING ORCHESTRA)
M1105-6	CONCERTOS (ENGLISH HORN AND OBOE WITH STRING ORCHESTRA)
M1105-6	CONCERTOS (ENGLISH HORN AND TRUMPET WITH STRING ORCHESTRA)
M1034	CONCERTOS (ENGLISH HORN WITH CHAMBER ORCHESTRA) — SCORES
M1034-5	CONCERTOS (ENGLISH HORN WITH CHAMBER ORCHESTRA)
M1105	CONCERTOS (ENGLISH HORN WITH STRING ORCHESTRA) — SCORES
M1106	CONCERTOS (ENGLISH HORN WITH STRING ORCHESTRA) — SOLO WITH PIANO
M1105-6	CONCERTOS (ENGLISH HORN WITH STRING ORCHESTRA)
M1034.E5	CONCERTOS (ENGLISH HORN)
M1035.E5	CONCERTOS (ENGLISH HORN)
M1105-6	CONCERTOS (FLUTE AND HARP WITH STRING ORCHESTRA)
M1040-1041	CONCERTOS (FLUTE AND HARP)
M1041	CONCERTOS (FLUTE AND HARP) — TO 1800 — — SOLOS WITH PIANO
M1105	CONCERTOS (FLUTE AND HARPSICHORD WITH STRING ORCHESTRA) — SCORES
M1105-6	CONCERTOS (FLUTE AND HARPSICHORD WITH STRING ORCHESTRA)
M1106	CONCERTOS (FLUTE AND HORN WITH STRING ORCHESTRA) — SOLOS WITH PIANO
M1105-6	CONCERTOS (FLUTE AND HORN WITH STRING ORCHESTRA)
M1105-6	CONCERTOS (FLUTE AND OBOE WITH STRING ORCHESTRA)
M1040-1041	CONCERTOS (FLUTE AND OBOE)
M1105-6	CONCERTOS (FLUTE AND PIANO WITH STRING ORCHESTRA)
M1105-6	CONCERTOS (FLUTE AND RECORDER WITH STRING ORCHESTRA)
M1105-6	CONCERTOS (FLUTE AND VIOLA D'AMORE WITH STRING ORCHESTRA), ARRANGED
M1106	CONCERTOS (FLUTE AND VIOLA D'AMORE WITH STRING ORCHESTRA), ARRANGED — SOLOS WITH PIANO
M1105-6	CONCERTOS (FLUTE AND VIOLA D'AMORE WITH STRING ORCHESTRA)
M1105-6	CONCERTOS (FLUTE AND VIOLIN WITH STRING ORCHESTRA)
M1041	CONCERTOS (FLUTE AND VIOLIN) — SOLOS WITH PIANO
M1040-1041	CONCERTOS (FLUTE AND VIOLIN)

M1105-6	CONCERTOS (FLUTE AND VIOLONCELLO WITH STRING ORCHESTRA)
M1021	CONCERTOS (FLUTE WITH CHAMBER ORCHESTRA) — SOLO WITH PIANO
M1020-1021	CONCERTOS (FLUTE WITH CHAMBER ORCHESTRA)
M1106	CONCERTOS (FLUTE WITH STRING ORCHESTRA) — SOLO WITH PIANO
M1105-6	CONCERTOS (FLUTE WITH STRING ORCHESTRA)
M1106	CONCERTOS (FLUTE WITH STRING ORCHESTRA), ARRANGED — SOLO WITH PIANO
M1105-6	CONCERTOS (FLUTE WITH STRING ORCHESTRA), ARRANGED
M1106	CONCERTOS (FLUTE WITH STRING ORCHESTRA), ARRANGED — TO 1800 — — SOLO WITH PIANO
M1106	CONCERTOS (FLUTE WITH STRING ORCHESTRA) — TO 1800 — — SOLO WITH PIANO
M955-7	CONCERTOS (FLUTE WITH WIND ENSEMBLE)
M1004.7	CONCERTOS (FLUTE) — CADENZAS
M1020.5	CONCERTOS (FLUTE) — CADENZAS
M1021	CONCERTOS (FLUTE) — SOLO WITH PIANO
M1020-1021	CONCERTOS (FLUTE)
M1105-6	CONCERTO (FLUTE, HORN, HARP WITH STRING ORCHESTRA)
M1105	CONCERTOS (FLUTE, HORN, HARP WITH STRING ORCHESTRA) — SCORES
M1105-6	CONCERTOS (FLUTE, OBOE D'AMORE, VIOLA D'AMORE WITH STRING ORCHESTRA)
M1105-6	CONCERTOS (FLUTE, OBOE, TRUMPET WITH STRING ORCHESTRA)
M1105-6	CONCERTOS (FLUTE, OBOE, VIOLIN, VIOLONCELLO)
M1105	CONCERTOS (FLUTE, VIOLA, VIOLONCELLO WITH STRING ORCHESTRA) — SCORES
M1105-6	CONCERTOS (FLUTE, VIOLA, VIOLONCELLO WITH STRING ORCHESTRA)
M1105	CONCERTOS (GLOCKENSPIEL WITH STRING ORCHESTRA) — SCORES
M1105-6	CONCERTOS (GLOCKENSPIEL WITH STRING ORCHESTRA)
M1037.4.G8	CONCERTOS (GUITAR WITH CHAMBER ORCHESTRA) — SOLO WITH PIANO
M1037.4.G8	CONCERTOS (GUITAR WITH CHAMBER ORCHESTRA)
M1105-6	CONCERTOS (GUITAR WITH STRING ORCHESTRA)
M1037.4.G8	CONCERTOS (GUITAR) — SOLO WITH PIANO
M1037.4.G8	CONCERTOS (GUITAR)
M1037.4.G8	CONCERTOS (GUITAR), ARRANGED
M1105-6	CONCERTOS (HARP AND ORGAN WITH STRING ORCHESTRA)
M1105-6	CONCERTOS (HARP AND PERCUSSION WITH STRING ORCHESTRA)
M1036-7	CONCERTOS (HARP WITH CHAMBER ORCHESTRA)
M1105-6	CONCERTOS (HARP WITH STRING ORCHESTRA)
M1037	CONCERTOS (HARP) — SOLO WITH PIANO
M1036-7	CONCERTOS (HARP)
M1036-7	CONCERTOS (HARP), ARRANGED
M1105-6	CONCERTOS (HARP, HARPSICHORD, PIANO WITH STRING ORCHESTRA)
M1040-1041	CONCERTOS (HARP, VIOLIN, VIOLONCELLO)
M1105-6	CONCERTOS (HARPISCHORD, FLUTE, HARP WITH STRING ORCHESTRA)
M1010-1011	CONCERTOS (HARPSICHORD AND PIANO)
M1010	CONCERTOS (HARPSICHORD WITH CHAMBER ORCHESTRA) — SCORES
M1010-1011	CONCERTOS (HARPSICHORD WITH CHAMBER ORCHESTRA)
M1105-6	CONCERTOS (HARPSICHORD WITH STRING ORCHESTRA)
M1106	CONCERTOS (HARPSICHORD WITH STRING ORCHESTRA) — TO 1800 — — 2-PIANO SCORES
M1010-1011	CONCERTOS (HARPSICHORD)
M1011	*CONCERTOS (HARPSICHORD)-TO 1800 2-HARPSICHORD SCORES* **SEE** CONCERTOS (HARPSICHORD) — TO 1800 — — 2-PIANO SCORES
M1011	CONCERTOS (HARPSICHORD) — TO 1800 — — 2-PIANO SCORES
M1105-6	CONCERTOS (HARPSICHORD, FLUTE, OBOE WITH STRING ORCHESTRA)
M1105	CONCERTOS (HARPSICHORD, FLUTE, VIOLIN WITH STRING ORCHESTRA) — TO 1800 — — SCORES
M1105-6	CONCERTOS (HARPSICHORD, FLUTE, VIOLIN WITH STRING ORCHESTRA)

M1105-6	CONCERTOS (HARPSICHORD, 2 FLUTES WITH STRING ORCHESTRA)
M1205	CONCERTOS (HORN WITH BAND) — SCORES
M1205	CONCERTOS (HORN WITH BAND)
M1257	CONCERTOS (HORN WITH BAND), ARRANGED — SCORES
M1257	CONCERTOS (HORN WITH BAND), ARRANGED
M1105	CONCERTOS (HORN WITH STRING ORCHESTRA) — SCORES
M1106	CONCERTOS (HORN WITH STRING ORCHESTRA) — SOLO WITH PIANO
M1105-6	CONCERTOS (HORN WITH STRING ORCHESTRA)
M1105	CONCERTOS (HORN WITH STRING ORCHESTRA), ARRANGED — SCORES
M1105-6	CONCERTOS (HORN WITH STRING ORCHESTRA), ARRANGED
M1106	CONCERTOS (HORN WITH STRING ORCHESTRA) — TO 1800 — — SOLO WITH PIANO
M1029	CONCERTOS (HORN) — SOLO WITH PIANO
M1028-9	CONCERTOS (HORN)
M1040-1041	CONCERTOS (JAZZ ENSEMBLE WITH CHAMBER ORCHESTRA)
M1040-1041	CONCERTOS (JAZZ QUARTET)
M1205	CONCERTOS (KETTLEDRUMS WITH BAND)
M1039	CONCERTOS (KETTLEDRUMS) — SOLO WITH PIANO
M1038-9	CONCERTOS (KETTLEDRUMS)
M1037.4.K68	CONCERTOS (KOTO) — SCORES
M1037.4.K68	CONCERTOS (KOTO)
M1105-6	CONCERTOS (LUTE WITH STRING ORCHESTRA)
M1105-6	CONCERTOS (MANDOLIN WITH STRING ORCHESTRA)
M1105	CONCERTOS (MANDOLIN WITH STRING ORCHESTRA) — TO 1800 — — SCORES
M1037.4.M3	CONCERTOS (MANDOLIN) — SOLO WITH PIANO
M1037.4.M3	CONCERTOS (MANDOLIN)
M1037.4.M3	CONCERTOS (MANDOLIN), ARRANGED
M1039.4	CONCERTOS (MARIMBA) — SOLO WITH PIANO
M1039.4.M3	CONCERTOS (MARIMBA)
M1039.4.M6	CONCERTOS (MOUTH-ORGAN WITH CHAMBER ORCHESTRA) — SCORES
M1039.4.M6	CONCERTOS (MOUTH-ORGAN WITH CHAMBER ORCHESTRA)
M1039.4.M6	CONCERTOS (MOUTH-ORGAN) — SOLO WITH PIANO
M1039.4.M6	CONCERTOS (MOUTH-ORGAN)
M1105-6	CONCERTOS (OBOE AND HARP WITH STRING ORCHESTRA)
M1105-6	CONCERTOS (OBOE AND HARPSICHORD WITH STRING ORCHESTRA)
M1105	CONCERTOS (OBOE AND HARPSICHORD WITH STRING ORCHESTRA), ARRANGED — SCORES
M1105-6	CONCERTOS (OBOE AND HARPSICHORD WITH STRING ORCHESTRA), ARRANGED
M1105-6	CONCERTOS (OBOE AND RECORDER WITH STRING ORCHESTRA)
M1105	CONCERTOS (OBOE AND VIOLA WITH STRING ORCHESTRA) — SCORES
M1105-6	CONCERTOS (OBOE AND VIOLA WITH STRING ORCHESTRA)
M1105-6	CONCERTOS (OBOE AND VIOLIN WITH STRING ORCHESTRA)
M1105-6	CONCERTOS (OBOE AND VIOLIN WITH STRING ORCHESTRA), ARRANGED
M1040-1041	CONCERTOS (OBOE AND VIOLIN)
M1040-1041	CONCERTOS (OBOE AND VIOLIN), ARRANGED
M1105-6	CONCERTOS (OBOE D'AMORE WITH STRING ORCHESTRA)
M1105-6	CONCERTOS (OBOE D'AMORE WITH STRING ORCHESTRA), ARRANGED
M1023	CONCERTOS (OBOE WITH CHAMBER ORCHESTRA) — SOLO WITH PIANO
M1022-3	CONCERTOS (OBOE WITH CHAMBER ORCHESTRA)
M1106	CONCERTOS (OBOE WITH STRING ORCHESTRA) — SOLO WITH PIANO
M1105-6	CONCERTOS (OBOE WITH STRING ORCHESTRA)
M1105	CONCERTOS (OBOE WITH STRING ORCHESTRA), ARRANGED — SCORES
M1105-6	CONCERTOS (OBOE WITH STRING ORCHESTRA), ARRANGED
M1023	CONCERTOS (OBOE) — SOLO WITH PIANO
M1022-3	CONCERTOS (OBOE)
M1023	CONCERTOS (OBOE), ARRANGED — SOLO WITH PIANO

M1022-3	CONCERTOS (OBOE), ARRANGED	M1105-6	CONCERTOS (PIANO, OBOE, TRUMPET, VIOLIN, DOUBLE BASS WITH STRING ORCHESTRA)
M1105-6	CONCERTOS (OBOE, VIOLIN, VIOLONCELLO WITH STRING ORCHESTRA)	M1040-1041	CONCERTOS (PIANO, TRUMPET, VIOLA)
M1106	CONCERTOS (ONDES MARTENOT WITH STRING ORCHESTRA) — SOLO WITH PIANO	M1011	CONCERTOS (PIANO, 1 HAND) — 2-PIANO SCORES
		M1010-1011	CONCERTOS (PIANO, 1 HAND)
M1105-6	CONCERTOS (ONDES MARTENOT WITH STRING ORCHESTRA)	M1105-6	CONCERTOS (PIANO, 2 VIOLINS WITH STRING ORCHESTRA)
M1039.4.05	CONCERTOS (ONDES MARTENOT) — SCORES	M1105-6	CONCERTOS (PICCOLO WITH STRING ORCHESTRA)
M1039.4.05	CONCERTOS (ONDES MARTENOT)	M1105-6	CONCERTOS (PICCOLO WITH STRING ORCHESTRA), ARRANGED
M1205	CONCERTOS (ORGAN WITH BAND)	M1106	CONCERTOS (PICCOLO WITH STRING ORCHESTRA), ARRANGED — SOLO WITH PIANO
M1005-6	CONCERTOS (ORGAN WITH CHAMBER ORCHESTRA)		
M1106	CONCERTOS (ORGAN WITH STRING ORCHESTRA) — SOLO WITH PIANO	M1106	CONCERTOS (RECORDER AND VIOLA DA GAMBA WITH STRING ORCHESTRA) — TO 1800 — — SOLOS WITH PIANO
M1105-6	CONCERTOS (ORGAN WITH STRING ORCHESTRA)		
M1105-6	CONCERTOS (ORGAN WITH STRING ORCHESTRA), ARRANGED	M1105-6	CONCERTOS (RECORDER AND VIOLA DA GAMBA WITH STRING ORCHESTRA)
M1005	CONCERTOS (ORGAN) — PARTS (SOLO)	M1105-6	CONCERTOS (RECORDER AND VIOLIN WITH STRING ORCHESTRA)
M1005	CONCERTOS (ORGAN) — PARTS	M1106	CONCERTOS (RECORDER AND VIOLIN WITH STRING ORCHESTRA) — TO 1800 — — SOLOS WITH PIANO
M1006	CONCERTOS (ORGAN) — SOLO WITH PIANO		
M1105-6	CONCERTOS (ORGAN)	M1105-6	CONCERTOS (RECORDER WITH STRING ORCHESTRA)
M1105	CONCERTOS (ORGAN, HARP, KETTLEDRUMS WITH STRING ORCHESTRA) — SCORES	M1105-6	CONCERTOS (RECORDER WITH STRING ORCHESTRA), ARRANGED
M1105-6	CONCERTOS (ORGAN, HARP, KETTLEDRUMS WITH STRING ORCHESTRA)	M1106	CONCERTOS (RECORDER WITH STRING ORCHESTRA) — TO 1800 — — SOLO WITH PIANO
M1105-6	CONCERTOS (PERCUSSION AND ORGAN WITH STRING ORCHESTRA)	M1020-1021	CONCERTOS (RECORDER)
		M1020-1021	CONCERTOS (RECORDER), ARRANGED
M1105-6	CONCERTOS (PERCUSSION AND PIANO WITH STRING ORCHESTRA)	M1040	CONCERTOS (SAXOPHONE AND PIANO) — SCORES
		M1040-1041	CONCERTOS (SAXOPHONE AND PIANO)
M1039	CONCERTOS (PERCUSSION AND PIANO WITH STRING ORCHESTRA) — SOLOS WITH PIANO	M1034-5	CONCERTOS (SAXOPHONE WITH CHAMBER ORCHESTRA)
M1105-6	CONCERTOS (PERCUSSION WITH STRING ORCHESTRA)	M1353	CONCERTOS (SAXOPHONE WITH DANCE ORCHESTRA)
M1039	CONCERTOS (PERCUSSION) — SOLO WITH PIANO	M1106	CONCERTOS (SAXOPHONE WITH STRING ORCHESTRA) — SOLO WITH PIANO
M1038-9	CONCERTOS (PERCUSSION)		
M1105	CONCERTOS (PIANO TRIO WITH STRING ORCHESTRA) — SCORES	M1105-6	CONCERTOS (SAXOPHONE WITH STRING ORCHESTRA)
		M1035	CONCERTOS (SAXOPHONE) — SOLO WITH PIANO
M1105-6	CONCERTOS (PIANO TRIO WITH STRING ORCHESTRA)	M1034-5	CONCERTOS (SAXOPHONE)
M1040	CONCERTOS (PIANO TRIO) — SCORES	M1035	*CONCERTOS (SAXOPHONE)-SOLO WITH PIANO-EXCERPTS* **SEE** CONCERTOS (SAXOPHONE) — EXCERPTS — — SOLO WITH PIANO
M1040-1041	CONCERTOS (PIANO TRIO)		
M1205	CONCERTOS (PIANO WITH BAND) — 2-PIANO SCORES	M1035	CONCERTOS (SAXOPHONE) — EXCERPTS — — SOLO WITH PIANO
M1205	CONCERTOS (PIANO WITH BAND)		
M1257	CONCERTOS (PIANO WITH BAND), ARRANGED	M1205	CONCERTOS (STRING QUARTET WITH BAND) — SCORES
M1011	CONCERTOS (PIANO WITH CHAMBER ORCHESTRA) — 2-PIANO SCORES	M1205-6	CONCERTOS (STRING QUARTET WITH BAND)
		M1040	CONCERTOS (STRING QUARTET WITH CHAMBER ORCHESTRA) — SCORES
M1010-1011	CONCERTOS (PIANO WITH CHAMBER ORCHESTRA)		
M1353	CONCERTOS (PIANO WITH DANCE ORCHESTRA) — SCORES	M1040-1041	CONCERTOS (STRING QUARTET WITH CHAMBER ORCHESTRA)
M1353	CONCERTOS (PIANO WITH DANCE ORCHESTRA)	M1105-6	CONCERTOS (STRING QUARTET WITH STRING ORCHESTRA)
M1353	CONCERTOS (PIANO WITH SALON ORCHESTRA)	M1040-1041	CONCERTOS (STRING QUARTET)
M1106	CONCERTOS (PIANO WITH STRING ORCHESTRA) — 2-PIANO SCORES	M1041	CONCERTOS (STRING QUARTET), ARRANGED — SOLOS WITH PIANO
M1105-6	CONCERTOS (PIANO WITH STRING ORCHESTRA)	M1040-1041	CONCERTOS (STRING QUARTET), ARRANGED
M1106	CONCERTOS (PIANO WITH STRING ORCHESTRA), ARRANGED — 2-PIANO SCORES	M040-1041	CONCERTOS (STRING TRIO)
		M1037.4.T3	CONCERTOS (TAR) — SOLO WITH PIANO
M1105-6	CONCERTOS (PIANO WITH STRING ORCHESTRA), ARRANGED	M1037.4.T3	CONCERTOS (TAR)
M1106	CONCERTOS (PIANO WITH STRING ORCHESTRA) — TO 1800 — — 2-PIANO SCORES	M1039.4.T	CONCERTOS (TRAUTONIUM)
		M1105-6	CONCERTOS (TROMBONE AND KETTLEDRUMS WITH STRING ORCHESTRA)
M1105	CONCERTOS (PIANO WITH STRING ORCHESTRA) — TO 1800 — — SCORES AND PARTS	M1205-6	CONCERTOS (TROMBONE AND TRUMPET WITH BAND)
M1010.5	CONCERTOS (PIANO) — CADENZAS	M1105-6	CONCERTOS (TROMBONE AND TRUMPET WITH STRING ORCHESTRA)
M1004.7	CONCERTOS (PIANO) — CADENZAS		
M1010	CONCERTOS (PIANO) — PARTS (SOLO)	M1106	CONCERTOS (TROMBONE AND TRUMPET WITH STRING ORCHESTRA) — SOLOS WITH PIANO
M1011	CONCERTOS (PIANO) — 2-PIANO SCORES		
M1010-1011	CONCERTOS (PIANO)	M1205	CONCERTOS (TROMBONE WITH BAND) — SCORES AND PARTS
M1010-1011	CONCERTOS (PIANO), ARRANGED		
M1011	*CONCERTOS (PIANO)-TO 1800 2-PIANO SCORES-EXCERPTS* **SEE** CONCERTOS (PIANO) — TO 1800 — — EXCERPTS — — — 2-PIANO SCORES	M1206	CONCERTOS (TROMBONE WITH BAND) — SOLO WITH PIANO
		M1205	CONCERTOS (TROMBONE WITH BAND)
M1011	*CONCERTOS (PIANO) 2-PIANO SCORES-EXCERPTS* **SEE** CONCERTOS (PIANO) — EXCERPTS — — 2-PIANO SCORES	M1105	CONCERTOS (TROMBONE WITH STRING ORCHESTRA) — SCORES
		M1106	CONCERTOS (TROMBONE WITH STRING ORCHESTRA) — SOLO WITH PIANO
M1011	CONCERTOS (PIANO) — EXCERPTS — — 2-PIANO SCORES		
M1011	CONCERTOS (PIANO) — TO 1800 — — 2-PIANO SCORES	M1105-6	CONCERTOS (TROMBONE WITH STRING ORCHESTRA)
		M1033	CONCERTOS (TROMBONE) — SOLO WITH PIANO
M1011	CONCERTOS (PIANO) — TO 1800 — — EXCERPTS — — — 2-PIANO SCORES	M1032-3	CONCERTOS (TROMBONE)
M1105-6	CONCERTOS (PIANO, FLUTE, VIOLIN WITH STRING ORCHESTRA)		

M1040-1041	CONCERTOS (TRUMPET AND PIANO)
M1205	CONCERTOS (TRUMPET WITH BAND)
M1257	CONCERTOS (TRUMPET WITH BAND), ARRANGED
M1030	CONCERTOS (TRUMPET WITH CHAMBER ORCHESTRA) — SCORES
M1030-1031	CONCERTOS (TRUMPET WITH CHAMBER ORCHESTRA)
M1353	CONCERTOS (TRUMPET WITH DANCE ORCHESTRA)
M1106	CONCERTOS (TRUMPET WITH STRING ORCHESTRA) — SOLO WITH PIANO
M1105-6	CONCERTOS (TRUMPET WITH STRING ORCHESTRA)
M1031	CONCERTOS (TRUMPET) — SOLO WITH PIANO
M1030-1031	CONCERTOS (TRUMPET)
M1030-1031	CONCERTOS (TRUMPET), ARRANGED
M1031	CONCERTOS (TRUMPET) — TO 1800 — — SOLO WITH PIANO
M1205	CONCERTOS (TUBA WITH BAND)
M1035	CONCERTOS (TUBA) — SOLO WITH PIANO
M1034-5	CONCERTOS (TUBA)
M1205	CONCERTOS (VIOLA AND PIANO WITH BAND) — SCORES
M1205-6	CONCERTOS (VIOLA AND PIANO WITH BAND)
M1105-6	CONCERTOS (VIOLA AND PIANO WITH STRING ORCHESTRA)
M1040	CONCERTOS (VIOLA AND PIANO) — SCORES
M1040-1041	CONCERTOS (VIOLA AND PIANO)
M1105-6	CONCERTOS (VIOLA D'AMORE AND LUTE WITH STRING ORCHESTRA)
M1019	CONCERTOS (VIOLA D'AMORE WITH CHAMBER ORCHESTRA)
M1105-6	CONCERTOS (VIOLA D'AMORE WITH STRING ORCHESTRA)
M1106	CONCERTOS (VIOLA D'AMORE WITH STRING ORCHESTRA) — TO 1800 — — SOLO WITH PIANO
M1019	CONCERTOS (VIOLA D'AMORE)
M1019	CONCERTOS (VIOLA D'AMORE) — TO 1800 — — SOLO WITH PIANO
M1105-6	CONCERTOS (VIOLA DA GAMBA WITH STRING ORCHESTRA)
M1105	CONCERTOS (VIOLA DA GAMBA WITH STRING ORCHESTRA) — TO 1800 — — SCORES
M1019	CONCERTOS (VIOLA DA GAMBA)
M1205-6	CONCERTOS (VIOLA WITH BAND)
M1015	CONCERTOS (VIOLA WITH CHAMBER ORCHESTRA) — SOLO WITH PIANO
M1014-1015	CONCERTOS (VIOLA WITH CHAMBER ORCHESTRA)
M1105-6	CONCERTOS (VIOLA WITH STRING ORCHESTRA)
M1106	CONCERTOS (VIOLA WITH STRING ORCHESTRA), ARRANGED — SOLO WITH PIANO
M1105-6	CONCERTOS (VIOLA WITH STRING ORCHESTRA), ARRANGED
M1105	CONCERTOS (VIOLA WITH STRING ORCHESTRA) — TO 1800 — — SCORES AND PARTS
M1015	CONCERTOS (VIOLA) — SOLO WITH PIANO
M1014-1015	CONCERTOS (VIOLA)
M1015	CONCERTOS (VIOLA), ARRANGED — SOLO WITH PIANO
M1014-1015	CONCERTOS (VIOLA), ARRANGED
M1015	CONCERTOS (VIOLA) — TO 1800 — — SOLO WITH PIANO
M1040-1041	CONCERTOS (VIOLIN AND HARP)
M1105-6	CONCERTOS (VIOLIN AND HARPSICHORD WITH STRING ORCHESTRA)
M1105	CONCERTOS (VIOLIN AND HARPSICHORD WITH STRING ORCHESTRA) — SCORES
M1040-1041	CONCERTOS (VIOLIN AND HARPSICHORD)
M1040	CONCERTOS (VIOLIN AND PIANO WITH CHAMBER ORCHESTRA) — SCORES
M1041	CONCERTOS (VIOLIN AND PIANO WITH CHAMBER ORCHESTRA) — SOLOS WITH PIANO
M1040-1041	CONCERTOS (VIOLIN AND PIANO WITH CHAMBER ORCHESTRA)
M1106	CONCERTOS (VIOLIN AND PIANO WITH STRING ORCHESTRA) — SOLOS WITH PIANO
M1105-6	CONCERTOS (VIOLIN AND PIANO WITH STRING ORCHESTRA)
M1040-1041	CONCERTOS (VIOLIN AND PIANO)
M1041	CONCERTOS (VIOLIN AND VIOLA WITH CHAMBER ORCHESTRA) — SOLOS WITH PIANO
M1040-1041	CONCERTOS (VIOLIN AND VIOLA WITH CHAMBER ORCHESTRA)
M1040-1041	CONCERTOS (VIOLIN AND VIOLA)
M985	CONCERTOS (VIOLIN AND VIOLONCELLO WITH INSTR. ENSEMBLE)
M1105-6	CONCERTOS (VIOLIN AND VIOLONCELLO WITH STRING ORCHESTRA)
M1041	CONCERTOS (VIOLIN AND VIOLONCELLO) — SOLOS WITH PIANO
M1040-1041	CONCERTOS (VIOLIN AND VIOLONCELLO)
M1205-6	CONCERTOS (VIOLIN WITH BAND)
M1013	CONCERTOS (VIOLIN WITH CHAMBER ORCHESTRA) — SOLO WITH PIANO
M1012-1013	CONCERTOS (VIOLIN WITH CHAMBER ORCHESTRA)
M1106	CONCERTOS (VIOLIN WITH STRING ORCHESTRA) — SOLO WITH PIANO
M1105-6	CONCERTOS (VIOLIN WITH STRING ORCHESTRA)
M1105-6	CONCERTOS (VIOLIN WITH STRING ORCHESTRA), ARRANGED
M1106	CONCERTOS (VIOLIN WITH STRING ORCHESTRA), ARRANGED — SOLO WITH PIANO
M1012.5	CONCERTOS (VIOLIN) — CADENZAS
M1004.7	CONCERTOS (VIOLIN) — CADENZAS
M1013	CONCERTOS (VIOLIN) — SOLO WITH PIANO
M1012-1013	CONCERTOS (VIOLIN)
M1013	CONCERTOS (VIOLIN), ARRANGED — SOLO WITH PIANO
M1012-1013	CONCERTOS (VIOLIN), ARRANGED
M1013	CONCERTOS (VIOLIN) — EXCERPTS — — SOLO WITH PIANO
M1013	CONCERTOS (VIOLIN) — TO 1800 — — SOLO WITH PIANO
M1105-6	CONCERTOS (VIOLONCELLO AND HARP WITH STRING ORCHESTRA)
M1105-6	CONCERTOS (VIOLONCELLO PICCOLO WITH STRING ORCHESTRA)
M1105	CONCERTOS (VIOLONCELLO PICCOLO WITH STRING ORCHESTRA) — TO 1800 — — SCORES
M1205	CONCERTOS (VIOLONCELLO WITH BAND) — SCORES
M1205-6	CONCERTOS (VIOLONCELLO WITH BAND)
M1017	CONCERTOS (VIOLONCELLO WITH CHAMBER ORCHESTRA) — SOLO WITH PIANO
M1016-1017	CONCERTOS (VIOLONCELLO WITH CHAMBER ORCHESTRA)
M1106	CONCERTOS (VIOLONCELLO WITH STRING ORCHESTRA) — SOLO WITH PIANO
M1105-6	CONCERTOS (VIOLONCELLO WITH STRING ORCHESTRA)
M1105-6	CONCERTOS (VIOLONCELLO WITH STRING ORCHESTRA), ARRANGED
M1106	CONCERTOS (VIOLONCELLO WITH STRING ORCHESTRA), ARRANGED — SOLO WITH PIANO
M1017	CONCERTOS (VIOLONCELLO) — SOLO WITH PIANO
M1016-1017	CONCERTOS (VIOLONCELLO)
M1017	CONCERTOS (VIOLONCELLO), ARRANGED — SOLO WITH PIANO
M1016-1017	CONCERTOS (VIOLONCELLO), ARRANGED
M1017	*CONCERTOS (VIOLONCELLO)-SOLO WITH PIANO-EXCERPTS* **SEE** CONCERTOS (VIOLONCELLO) — EXCERPTS — — SOLO WITH PIANO
M1017	CONCERTOS (VIOLONCELLO) — EXCERPTS — — SOLO WITH PIANO
M1020-1021	CONCERTOS (2 FLUTES WITH CHAMBER ORCHESTRA)
M1020-1021	CONCERTOS (2 FLUTES WITH CHAMBER ORCHESTRA), ARRANGED
M1020-1021	CONCERTOS (2 FLUTES WITH CHAMBER ORCHESTRA), ARRANGED — PARTS
M1105-6	CONCERTOS (2 FLUTES WITH STRING ORCHESTRA)
M1105	CONCERTOS (2 FLUTES) — SCORES
M1020-1021	CONCERTOS (2 FLUTES)
M1020	CONCERTOS (2 FLUTES) — TO 1800 — — SCORES
M1021	CONCERTOS (2 FLUTES) — TO 1800 — — SOLOS WITH PIANO
M1105	CONCERTOS (2 FLUTES, GLOCKENSPIEL WITH STRING ORCHESTRA) — SCORES
M1105-6	CONCERTOS (2 FLUTES, GLOCKENSPIEL WITH STRING ORCHESTRA)
M1105-6	CONCERTOS (2 FLUTES, MARIMBA WITH STRING ORCHESTRA)
M1037.4.G8	CONCERTOS (2 GUITARS WITH CHAMBER ORCHESTRA)
M1037.4.G8	CONCERTOS (2 GUITARS WITH CHAMBER ORCHESTRA), ARRANGED

ML457	CONDUCTING / history
MT85	CONDUCTING / instruction
ML457	CONDUCTING, CHORAL / history
MT85	CONDUCTING, CHORAL / instruction
RD84	CONDUCTION ANESTHESIA SEE LOCAL ANESTHESIA
QC321-3	CONDUCTION OF HEAT SEE HEAT — CONDUCTION
QD565	CONDUCTIVITY OF ELECTROLYTES SEE ELECTROLYTES — CONDUCTIVITY
QC607-611	CONDUCTIVITY, ELECTRIC SEE ELECTRIC CONDUCTIVITY
QD115	CONDUCTOMETRIC ANALYSIS
ML402	CONDUCTORS (MUSIC) / biography collective
ML422	CONDUCTORS (MUSIC) / individual
TK3301-3351	CONDUCTORS, ELECTRIC SEE ELECTRIC CONDUCTORS / engineering
QC611	CONDUCTORS, ELECTRIC SEE ELECTRIC CONDUCTORS / physics
HE1811	CONDUCTORS, RAILROAD SEE RAILROAD CONDUCTORS
TD398	CONDUITS SEE AQUEDUCTS
TK3261	CONDUITS SEE ELECTRIC CONDUITS
RS165.C67	CONDURANGO SEE CUNDURANGO
QA491	CONE
QA521	CONE
QA561	CONE
E99.C87	CONESTOGA INDIANS
HD9999.C72	CONFECTIONERS / economics
TX793	CONFECTIONERY — APPLIANCES, UTENSILS, ETC.
TX783-799	CONFECTIONERY / candy-making
HD9999.C72	CONFECTIONERY / industry
E645	CONFEDERATE MEMORIAL DAY SEE MEMORIAL DAY, CONFEDERATE
E467	CONFEDERATE STATES OF AMERICA — BIOGRAPHY
HJ8943	CONFEDERATE STATES OF AMERICA — CLAIMS
HF3027.6	CONFEDERATE STATES OF AMERICA — COMMERCE
HF3153	CONFEDERATE STATES OF AMERICA — COMMERCE
UA580-585	CONFEDERATE STATES OF AMERICA — DEFENSES
E487	CONFEDERATE STATES OF AMERICA — ECONOMIC CONDITIONS
JK9720-9770	CONFEDERATE STATES OF AMERICA — EXECUTIVE DEPARTMENTS
E487	CONFEDERATE STATES OF AMERICA — FOREIGN POPULATION
E487-8	CONFEDERATE STATES OF AMERICA — FOREIGN RELATIONS
E469	CONFEDERATE STATES OF AMERICA — FOREIGN RELATIONS
E487-8	CONFEDERATE STATES OF AMERICA — HISTORY
E545	CONFEDERATE STATES OF AMERICA — HISTORY, MILITARY
E470	CONFEDERATE STATES OF AMERICA — HISTORY, MILITARY
E591-600	CONFEDERATE STATES OF AMERICA — HISTORY, NAVAL
E621-5	CONFEDERATE STATES OF AMERICA — HOSPITALS, CHARITIES, ETC.
HC105.6	CONFEDERATE STATES OF AMERICA — INDUSTRIES
JK9661-9993	CONFEDERATE STATES OF AMERICA — POLITICS AND GOVERNMENT
JK9663	CONFEDERATE STATES OF AMERICA — REGISTERS
E650	CONFEDERATE STATES OF AMERICA — RELIGION
BR535	CONFEDERATE STATES OF AMERICA — RELIGION
CD5610	CONFEDERATE STATES OF AMERICA — SEAL
E487	CONFEDERATE STATES OF AMERICA — SOCIAL CONDITIONS
E487	CONFEDERATE STATES OF AMERICA — SOCIAL LIFE AND CUSTOMS
UB414.5	CONFEDERATE STATES OF AMERICA. — APPOINTMENTS AND RETIREMENTS
UA583.5	CONFEDERATE STATES OF AMERICA. — APPROPRIATIONS AND EXPENDITURES
E546.7	CONFEDERATE STATES OF AMERICA. — CHAPLAINS
UC85-86	CONFEDERATE STATES OF AMERICA. — COMMISSARIAT
UD160.5	CONFEDERATE STATES OF AMERICA. — DRILL AND TACTICS
UE160.5	CONFEDERATE STATES OF AMERICA. — DRILL AND TACTICS
UF160.5	CONFEDERATE STATES OF AMERICA. — DRILL AND TACTICS
U173.5	CONFEDERATE STATES OF AMERICA. — FIELD SERVICE
UD383.5	CONFEDERATE STATES OF AMERICA. — FIREARMS
U193.5	CONFEDERATE STATES OF AMERICA. — GUARD DUTY
U113.5	CONFEDERATE STATES OF AMERICA. — HANDBOOKS, MANUALS, ETC.
E591-600	CONFEDERATE STATES OF AMERICA. — HISTORY
UB433.5	CONFEDERATE STATES OF AMERICA. — MEDALS, BADGES, DECORATIONS, ETC.
E585.N3	CONFEDERATE STATES OF AMERICA. — NEGRO TROOPS
VF23.5	CONFEDERATE STATES OF AMERICA. — ORDNANCE AND ORDNANCE STORES
UF23.5	CONFEDERATE STATES OF AMERICA. — ORDNANCE AND ORDNANCE STORES
UF153.5	CONFEDERATE STATES OF AMERICA. — ORDNANCE AND ORDNANCE STORES
UC87	CONFEDERATE STATES OF AMERICA. — PAY, ALLOWANCES, ETC.
E611-612	CONFEDERATE STATES OF AMERICA. — PRISONS
UB414.5	CONFEDERATE STATES OF AMERICA. — PROMOTIONS
UB343.5	CONFEDERATE STATES OF AMERICA. — RECRUITING, ENLISTMENT, ETC.
V11.C8	CONFEDERATE STATES OF AMERICA. — REGISTERS
E548	CONFEDERATE STATES OF AMERICA. — REGISTERS
UB504.5	CONFEDERATE STATES OF AMERICA. — REGULATIONS
VB369.5	CONFEDERATE STATES OF AMERICA. — REGULATIONS
UH224	CONFEDERATE STATES OF AMERICA. — SANITARY AFFAIRS
UC85-88	CONFEDERATE STATES OF AMERICA. — SUPPLIES AND STORES
UC86	CONFEDERATE STATES OF AMERICA. — TRANSPORTATION
UC483.5	CONFEDERATE STATES OF AMERICA. — UNIFORMS
E491-3	CONFEDERATE STATES OF AMERICA-REGIMENTAL HISTORIES SEE UNITED STATES — HISTORY — — CIVIL WAR — — — REGIMENTAL HISTORIES
E551-582	CONFEDERATE STATES OF AMERICA-REGIMENTAL HISTORIES SEE UNITED STATES — HISTORY — — CIVIL WAR — — — REGIMENTAL HISTORIES
E545-7	CONFEDERATE STATES OF AMERICA-REGIMENTAL HISTORIES SEE UNITED STATES — HISTORY — — CIVIL WAR — — — REGIMENTAL HISTORIES
E495-537	CONFEDERATE STATES OF AMERICA-REGIMENTAL HISTORIES SEE UNITED STATES — HISTORY — — CIVIL WAR — — — REGIMENTAL HISTORIES
E482	CONFEDERATE STATES OF AMERICA — HISTORY — — PERIODICALS
E483	CONFEDERATE STATES OF AMERICA — HISTORY — — SOCIETIES, ETC.
E484	CONFEDERATE STATES OF AMERICA — HISTORY — — SOURCES
E467.1	CONFEDERATE STATES OF AMERICA — HISTORY — — SOURCES
HE745-940	CONFERENCE LINES SEE SHIPPING CONFERENCES
BR355.R2	CONFERENCE OF RATISBON, 1541 SEE RATISBON, COLLOQUY OF, 1541
BR355.R3	CONFERENCE OF RATISBON, 1546 SEE RATISBON, COLLOQUY OF, 1546
AS	CONFERENCES SEE CONGRESSES AND CONVENTIONS
LC6501-6560	CONFERENCES SEE FORUMS (DISCUSSION AND DEBATE)
PN4177-4191	CONFERENCES SEE FORUMS (DISCUSSION AND DEBATE) / debating
BM723.7	CONFESSION — JUDAISM
BV845-7	CONFESSION
BX2262-7	CONFESSION / catholic church
BX5149.C6	CONFESSION / church of england
BX5949.C6	CONFESSION / protestant episcopal church
BV845-7	CONFESSION-CATHOLIC CHURCH SEE CONFESSION
BX2262-7	CONFESSION-CATHOLIC CHURCH SEE CONFESSION / catholic church
BX5149.C6	CONFESSION-CATHOLIC CHURCH SEE CONFESSION / church of england
BX5949.C6	CONFESSION-CATHOLIC CHURCH SEE CONFESSION / protestant episcopal church
NA5095.C	CONFESSIONALS (ARCHITECTURE)
BX	CONFESSIONS OF FAITH SEE CREEDS / by denomination
BT990-999	CONFESSIONS OF FAITH SEE CREEDS / general

BX1939.C7	CONFESSORS (CANON LAW)
BX2262-7	CONFESSORS
BV845	CONFESSORS
BJ1533.C6	CONFIDENCE
BF203	*CONFIGURATION (PSYCHOLOGY)* **SEE** GESTALT PSYCHOLOGY
QA607	CONFIGURATIONS
BX1939.C72	CONFIRMATION (CANON LAW)
BM707	CONFIRMATION (JEWISH RITE)
BV4257.7	CONFIRMATION SERMONS
BV815	CONFIRMATION
BX	CONFIRMATION */ by denomination*
TH9448-9	*CONFLAGRATIONS* **SEE** FIRES
BF740	*CONFLICT OF CULTURES* **SEE** CULTURE CONFLICT
QA360	CONFORMAL MAPPING
QA646	CONFORMAL MAPPING
QA360	*CONFORMAL REPRESENTATION OF SURFACES* **SEE** CONFORMAL MAPPING
QA646	*CONFORMAL REPRESENTATION OF SURFACES* **SEE** CONFORMAL MAPPING
QA646	*CONFORMAL REPRESENTATION OF SURFACES* **SEE** SURFACES, REPRESENTATION OF
BX808-9	CONFRATERNITIES */ catholic church*
BL1830-1870	CONFUCIUS AND CONFUCIANISM
B128.C6-8	CONFUCIUS AND CONFUCIANISM */ philosophy*
P101	CONFUSION OF TONGUES
GV1796.C	CONGA (DANCE)
RC776	*CONGESTION OF THE LUNGS* **SEE** LUNGS — CONGESTION
QE471	CONGLOMERATE
PL8401-4	CONGO LANGUAGE
BX7101-7260	CONGREGATIONAL CHURCHES
BX7101-7260	CONGREGATIONALISM
AS	CONGRESSES AND CONVENTIONS
UB433	*CONGRESSIONAL MEDAL OF HONOR* **SEE** MEDAL OF HONOR
VB333	*CONGRESSIONAL MEDAL OF HONOR* **SEE** MEDAL OF HONOR
QA608	CONGRUENCES (GEOMETRY)
QA242-4	CONGRUENCES AND RESIDUES
QA559	CONIC SECTIONS */ analytic geometry*
QA485	CONIC SECTIONS */ plane geometry*
QA561	CONICS, SPHERICAL
QK601	CONIDIA */ fungi*
SB608.C7	CONIFERAE — DISEASES AND PESTS
QK495.C75	CONIFERAE */ botany*
QE977	CONIFERAE */ fossil*
SD397.C7	CONIFERAE */ sylviculture*
RM666.C	*CONIINE* **SEE** CONINE
RM666.C	CONINE
RS165.C	CONIUM */ pharmacy*
RM666.C	CONIUM */ therapeutics*
RE310-326	CONJUNCTIVA — DISEASES
QM511	CONJUNCTIVA
QL949	CONJUNCTIVA
RE321	CONJUNCTIVITIS
RJ296	CONJUNCTIVITIS, INFANTILE
GV1546	CONJURING — EARLY WORKS TO 1800
GV1548	CONJURING — JUVENILE LITERATURE
GV1541-1561	CONJURING
GV1561	CONJURING — APPARATUS AND SUPPLIES — — CATALOGS
M14.8	*CONN ORGAN MUSIC* **SEE** ELECTRONIC ORGAN MUSIC (CONN REGISTRATION)
M14.85	*CONN ORGAN MUSIC* **SEE** ELECTRONIC ORGAN MUSIC (CONN REGISTRATION)
F91-100	CONNECTICUT — HISTORY
E499	CONNECTICUT — HISTORY — — CIVIL WAR
E199	CONNECTICUT — HISTORY — — FRENCH AND INDIAN WAR, 1755-1763
E263.C5	CONNECTICUT — HISTORY — — REVOLUTION
E359.5.C7	CONNECTICUT — HISTORY — — WAR OF 1812
QM563	CONNECTIVE TISSUES
QA608	CONNEXES
M14.8	*CONNSONATA ORGAN MUSIC* **SEE** ELECTRONIC ORGAN MUSIC (CONN REGISTRATION)
M14.85	*CONNSONATA ORGAN MUSIC* **SEE** ELECTRONIC ORGAN MUSIC (CONN REGISTRATION)
QE899	CONODONTS
E99.C873	CONOY INDIANS
GV1295.C6	*CONQUIEN* **SEE** COONCAN
HQ1026	CONSANGUINITY */ consanguineous marriages*
HV4981	CONSANGUINITY */ degeneration*
HB1113.R38	CONSANGUINITY */ statistics*
BS2545.C58	CONSCIENCE — BIBLICAL TEACHING
BJ1471	CONSCIENCE */ ethics*
BV4615	CONSCIENCE */ theology*
BX2377	CONSCIENCE, EXAMINATION OF
UB341-2	CONSCIENTIOUS OBJECTORS
Q327	CONSCIOUS AUTOMATA
QP411	CONSCIOUSNESS */ physiology*
BF311-315	CONSCIOUSNESS */ psychology*
RC554-574	*CONSCIOUSNESS, MULTIPLE* **SEE** PERSONALITY, DISORDERS OF
HD4871-5	*CONSCRIPT LABOR* **SEE** CONTRACT LABOR
HD4905.5	*CONSCRIPT LABOR* **SEE** SERVICE, COMPULSORY NON-MILITARY */ in wartime*
HD4871-5	*CONSCRIPT LABOR* **SEE** SERVICE, COMPULSORY NON-MILITARY '
UB340-355	*CONSCRIPTION, MILITARY* **SEE** MILITARY SERVICE, COMPULSORY
BX2304	CONSECRATION OF BISHOPS */ catholic church*
BV880	*CONSECRATION OF CEMETERIES* **SEE** CEMETERIES — CONSECRATION
BV880	*CONSECRATION OF CHURCHES* **SEE** CHURCH DEDICATION
BX2302	*CONSECRATION OF CHURCHES* **SEE** CHURCH DEDICATION */ catholic church*
BX2305	CONSECRATION OF VIRGINS
BV199.D4	*CONSECRATION PROGRAMS* **SEE** DEDICATION SERVICES
BV199.D4	*CONSECRATION SERVICES* **SEE** DEDICATION SERVICES
BV4501	CONSECRATION */ christian life*
N8560	*CONSERVATION OF ART OBJECTS* **SEE** ART OBJECTS — CONSERVATION AND RESTORATION
Z700-701	*CONSERVATION OF BOOKS* **SEE** BOOKS — CONSERVATION AND RESTORATION
QC73	*CONSERVATION OF ENERGY* **SEE** FORCE AND ENERGY
NE380	*CONSERVATION OF ENGRAVINGS* **SEE** ENGRAVINGS — CONSERVATION AND RESTORATION
TX357	*CONSERVATION OF FOOD* **SEE** FOOD CONSERVATION
SB411-428	*CONSERVATION OF FORESTS* **SEE** FOREST CONSERVATION
N8850	*CONSERVATION OF MONUMENTS* **SEE** MONUMENTS — PRESERVATION */ art*
CC135	*CONSERVATION OF MONUMENTS* **SEE** MONUMENTS — PRESERVATION
QH75-77	*CONSERVATION OF NATURAL MONUMENTS* **SEE** NATURAL MONUMENTS
HC	*CONSERVATION OF NATURAL RESOURCES* **SEE** NATURAL RESOURCES
ND1640-1650	*CONSERVATION OF PAINTINGS* **SEE** PAINTINGS — CONSERVATION AND RESTORATION
TR465	*CONSERVATION OF PHOTOGRAPHS* **SEE** PHOTOGRAPHS — CONSERVATION AND RESTORATION
NE380	*CONSERVATION OF PRINTS* **SEE** PRINTS — CONSERVATION AND RESTORATION
NB1199	*CONSERVATION OF SCULPTURE* **SEE** SCULPTURE — CONSERVATION AND RESTORATION
S623	*CONSERVATION OF THE SOIL* **SEE** SOIL CONSERVATION
ND1640-1650	*CONSERVATION OF WATER-COLORS* **SEE** PAINTINGS — CONSERVATION AND RESTORATION
BM197.5	CONSERVATIVE JUDAISM
JN1129.C7	CONSERVATIVE PARTY (GT. BRIT.)
SB415-416	*CONSERVATORIES* **SEE** GREENHOUSES
ML3795	CONSERVATORIES OF MUSIC
BV4900-4908	CONSOLATION
HD1481	CONSOLIDATION OF LAND HOLDINGS */ economics*
K	CONSOLIDATION OF LAND HOLDINGS */ law*
LB2861	*CONSOLIDATION OF SCHOOLS* **SEE** SCHOOLS — CENTRALIZATION */ rural*
HV6275	CONSPIRACIES
E83.76	*CONSPIRACY OF PONTIAC* **SEE** PONTIAC'S CONSPIRACY, 1763-1765
HV7981	CONSTABLES
BX8301414	CONSTANCE, COUNCIL OF, 1414-1418
DD149.7	CONSTANCE, TREATY OF, 1183

BJ1533.C67	CONSTANCY
BX875.D6-7	CONSTANTINE, DONATION OF SEE DONATION OF CONSTANTINE
BR215	CONSTANTINOPLE, COUNCIL OF, 1ST, 381
BR230	CONSTANTINOPLE, COUNCIL OF, 2D, 553
BT1003.C6	CONSTANTINOPOLITAN CREED
QC100-105	CONSTANTS SEE UNITS / weights and measures
QB802	CONSTELLATIONS
QB63	CONSTELLATIONS / popular works
RX336.C	CONSTIPATION — HOMEOPATHIC TREATMENT
RC861	CONSTIPATION
QC173	CONSTITUTION OF MATTER SEE MATTER — CONSTITUTION
GN60	CONSTITUTION, HUMAN SEE MAN — CONSTITUTION / anthropology
BF818	CONSTITUTION, HUMAN SEE MAN — CONSTITUTION / character
BF698	CONSTITUTION, HUMAN SEE MAN — CONSTITUTION / personality
BF795-811	CONSTITUTION, HUMAN SEE MAN — CONSTITUTION / temperament
RB150-151	CONSTITUTION, HUMAN SEE MAN — CONSTITUTION / theories of disease
JF71-99	CONSTITUTIONAL CONVENTIONS / general
JK301	CONSTITUTIONAL CONVENTIONS / u.s.
RC251-320	CONSTITUTIONAL DISEASES
RJ390-399	CONSTITUTIONAL DISEASES / diseases of children
J-JQ	CONSTITUTIONAL HISTORY
J-JQ	CONSTITUTIONAL HISTORY, MODERN SEE CONSTITUTIONAL HISTORY
J-JQ	CONSTITUTIONAL LAW
J-JQ	CONSTITUTIONAL LAW-HISTORY SEE CONSTITUTIONAL HISTORY
J-JQ	CONSTITUTIONAL LIMITATIONS SEE CONSTITUTIONAL LAW
J-JQ	CONSTITUTIONS
JK2413-2428	CONSTITUTIONS, STATE
JK18-19	CONSTITUTIONS, STATE
NA	CONSTRUCTION SEE ARCHITECTURE
TH	CONSTRUCTION SEE BUILDING
TA	CONSTRUCTION SEE ENGINEERING
HD9680-9712	CONSTRUCTION SEE ENGINEERING / economics
HD7290	CONSTRUCTION CAMPS SEE LABOR CAMPS
TH900	CONSTRUCTION EQUIPMENT SEE BUILDING MACHINERY
TH443	CONSTRUCTION INDUSTRY-ACCIDENTS SEE BUILDING — ACCIDENTS
TH425	CONSTRUCTION INDUSTRY-CONTRACTS AND SPECIFICATIONS SEE BUILDING — CONTRACTS AND SPECIFICATIONS
TH434-7	CONSTRUCTION INDUSTRY-ESTIMATES SEE BUILDING — ESTIMATES
TA680-683	CONSTRUCTION, CONCRETE SEE CONCRETE CONSTRUCTION
TH1461-1501	CONSTRUCTION, CONCRETE SEE CONCRETE CONSTRUCTION / building
TA663	CONSTRUCTION, LIGHTWEIGHT SEE LIGHTWEIGHT CONSTRUCTION
TA684	CONSTRUCTION, WELDED STEEL SEE WELDED STEEL STRUCTURES
BV823-8	CONSUBSTANTIATION SEE LORD'S SUPPER — REAL PRESENCE
BX8073	CONSUBSTANTIATION SEE LORD'S SUPPER — REAL PRESENCE / lutheran
BX5149.C5	CONSUBSTANTIATION SEE LORD'S SUPPER — REAL PRESENCE / church of england
HF5773.C7	CONSULAR DOCUMENTS
JX1698	CONSULAR JURISDICTION
JX1625-1894	CONSULAR LAW
HC1-8	CONSULAR REPORTS
JX1621-1894	CONSULAR SERVICE SEE DIPLOMATIC AND CONSULAR SERVICE
JX1621-1894	CONSULATES SEE DIPLOMATIC AND CONSULAR SERVICE
JX1625-1894	CONSULS
DG83.5.C7	CONSULS, ROMAN
BX1939.C73	CONSULTORS, DIOCESAN / canon law
HF5801-6191	CONSUMER ADVERTISING SEE ADVERTISING
TX335	CONSUMER EDUCATION
HG2052-2069	CONSUMER LOANS SEE LOANS, PERSONAL
HF5415	CONSUMER RATIONING SEE RATIONING, CONSUMER
TS	CONSUMERS' GOODS SEE MANUFACTURES
HD9720-9739	CONSUMERS' GOODS SEE MANUFACTURES / economics
HD3271-3570	CONSUMERS' LEAGUES / cooperation
HD6951-7	CONSUMERS' LEAGUES / labor
HB801-845	CONSUMPTION (ECONOMICS)
HJ5711-5721	CONSUMPTION (ECONOMICS)-TAXATION SEE TAXATION OF ARTICLES OF CONSUMPTION
RC306-320	CONSUMPTION SEE TUBERCULOSIS
QR201.T6	CONSUMPTION SEE TUBERCULOSIS / bacteriology
RA644.T7	CONSUMPTION SEE TUBERCULOSIS / public health
RC592	CONTACT DERMATITIS
RE977.C6	CONTACT LENSES
T379	CONTACT PRINTS SEE BLUE-PRINTS / mechanical drawing
NE2685	CONTACT PRINTS SEE LUMIPRINTS
QA385	CONTACT TRANSFORMATIONS
PM7801-7895	CONTACT VERNACULARS SEE LANGUAGES, MIXED
TK2821	CONTACTORS, ELECTRIC SEE ELECTRIC CONTACTORS
RA769	CONTAGION AND CONTAGIOUS DISEASES SEE COMMUNICABLE DISEASES / miscellaneous preventive measures
RA643-4	CONTAGION AND CONTAGIOUS DISEASES SEE COMMUNICABLE DISEASES / public hygiene
RC111-216	CONTAGION AND CONTAGIOUS DISEASES SEE COMMUNICABLE DISEASES / practice of medicine
SF871	CONTAGIOUS ABORTION SEE BRUCELLOSIS IN CATTLE
RA769	CONTAGIOUS DISEASES SEE COMMUNICABLE DISEASES / miscellaneous preventive measures
RC111-216	CONTAGIOUS DISEASES SEE COMMUNICABLE DISEASES / practice of medicine
RA643-4	CONTAGIOUS DISEASES SEE COMMUNICABLE DISEASES / public hygiene
SB415	CONTAINER GARDENING SEE PLANTS, POTTED / greenhouse plants
TS2301.C8	CONTAINERS
BV5091.C7	CONTEMPLATION
BX2810	CONTEMPLATIVE ORDERS / men
BX4230	CONTEMPLATIVE ORDERS / women
JK1543	CONTEMPT OF COURT / u.s.
P93	CONTENT ANALYSIS (COMMUNICATION)
BV4627.Q	CONTENTIOUSNESS SEE QUARRELING
BJ1533.C7	CONTENTMENT / ethics
BV4647.C7	CONTENTMENT / theology
JF1083	CONTESTED ELECTIONS
HF6146.P75	CONTESTS, PRIZE, IN ADVERTISING SEE PRIZE CONTESTS IN ADVERTISING
GB423	CONTINENTAL DRIFT SEE CONTINENTS
JX4143	CONTINENTAL SHELF / international law
HF1532	CONTINENTAL SYSTEM OF NAPOLEON
HF1543	CONTINENTAL SYSTEM OF NAPOLEON
GB423	CONTINENTS
LC5501-5560	CONTINUATION SCHOOLS SEE EVENING AND CONTINUATION SCHOOLS
QA295	CONTINUED FRACTIONS SEE FRACTIONS, CONTINUED
QA9	CONTINUITY / mathematics
B105.C5	CONTINUITY / philosophy
QC6	CONTINUITY / physics
TG355	CONTINUOUS GIRDERS SEE GIRDERS, CONTINUOUS
QA385	CONTINUOUS GROUPS SEE GROUPS, CONTINUOUS
TF262	CONTINUOUS RAILS (RAILROADS) SEE RAILROADS — CONTINUOUS RAILS
JX5234	CONTINUOUS VOYAGES (INTERNATIONAL LAW)
QA9	CONTINUUM SEE CONTINUITY / mathematics
B105.C5	CONTINUUM SEE CONTINUITY / philosophy
QC6	CONTINUUM SEE CONTINUITY / physics
CJ5665	CONTORNIATES
GV551-3	CONTORTION SEE ACROBATS AND ACROBATISM
JX5231-2	CONTRABAND OF WAR
HJ6750-7380	CONTRABAND TRADE SEE SMUGGLING / other countries
HJ6690-6720	CONTRABAND TRADE SEE SMUGGLING / u.s.
HQ763-6	CONTRACEPTION SEE BIRTH CONTROL
RG136	CONTRACEPTION SEE CONCEPTION — PREVENTION

HB875	*CONTRACEPTION* **SEE** CONCEPTION — PREVENTION / *neo-malthusianism*
GV1282.3	CONTRACT BRIDGE
HD4871-5	CONTRACT LABOR
GV1295.P6	CONTRACT PENUCHLE
HD20	*CONTRACT RESEARCH* **SEE** RESEARCH, INDUSTRIAL / *economics*
T175-8	*CONTRACT RESEARCH* **SEE** RESEARCH, INDUSTRIAL / *technology*
VM880-881	*CONTRACT-ACCEPTANCE TRIALS OF SHIPS* **SEE** SHIP TRIALS
Z103-4	*CONTRACTIONS* **SEE** CIPHERS
Z105-115	*CONTRACTIONS* **SEE** PALEOGRAPHY
TA12-13	CONTRACTORS
T12	CONTRACTORS
TH12-13	CONTRACTORS
TA201-210	CONTRACTORS' OPERATIONS
HF1253-5	CONTRACTS / *commercial law*
HD2381-5	CONTRACTS / *subcontracting*
HD2365	CONTRACTS, LETTING OF / *competitive system*
HD3858-3860	CONTRACTS, LETTING OF / *public contracts*
HF1253-5	*CONTRACTUAL LIMITATIONS* **SEE** CONTRACTS / *commercial law*
HD2381-5	*CONTRACTUAL LIMITATIONS* **SEE** CONTRACTS / *subcontracting*
GV1763	*CONTRADANCE* **SEE** COUNTRY-DANCE
QA611	*CONTRAHOMOLOGY THEORY* **SEE** HOMOLOGY THEORY
TL557.C7	*CONTRAILS* **SEE** CONDENSATION TRAILS
BL325.P7	*CONTRARIETY (IN RELIGION, FOLK-LORE, ETC.)* **SEE** POLARITY (IN RELIGION, FOLK-LORE, ETC.)
BC199.O6	*CONTRARIETY* **SEE** OPPOSITION, THEORY OF / *logic*
BF455	*CONTRARIETY* **SEE** OPPOSITION, THEORY OF / *psychology*
ML927.V63	*CONTRE-BASS DE VIOL* **SEE** VIOLONE
JX5321	*CONTRIBUTIONS, MILITARY* **SEE** REQUISITIONS, MILITARY / *international law*
UC15	*CONTRIBUTIONS, MILITARY* **SEE** REQUISITIONS, MILITARY / *military science*
BV840	*CONTRITION* **SEE** PENANCE
BX2260	*CONTRITION* **SEE** PENANCE / *catholic church*
BT800	*CONTRITION* **SEE** REPENTANCE
TA165	*CONTROL ENGINEERING* **SEE** AUTOMATIC CONTROL
TA165	*CONTROL EQUIPMENT* **SEE** AUTOMATIC CONTROL
TL678	*CONTROL SYSTEMS OF AEROPLANES* **SEE** AEROPLANES — CONTROLS
QA402.3	CONTROL THEORY
TP242	*CONTROLLED ATMOSPHERES (INDUSTRIAL PROCESSES)* **SEE** PROTECTIVE ATMOSPHERES
LB1050.5	*CONTROLLED READING* **SEE** DEVELOPMENTAL READING
TK2851	*CONTROLLERS, ELECTRIC* **SEE** ELECTRIC CONTROLLERS
TF930	*CONTROLLERS, ELECTRIC* **SEE** ELECTRIC CONTROLLERS / *electric railroads*
HF5550	CONTROLLERSHIP
PN6366-6377	*CONUNDRUMS* **SEE** RIDDLES
GR975	*CONUNDRUMS* **SEE** RIDDLES / *folk literature*
GV1231	CONVALESCENCE / *amusements*
SB413.L71	*CONVALLARIA* **SEE** LILIES-OF-THE-VALLEY
QC327	*CONVECTION OF HEAT* **SEE** HEAT — CONVECTION
E233	*CONVENTION TROOPS* **SEE** BURGOYNE'S INVASION, 1777
AS	*CONVENTIONS (CONGRESSES)* **SEE** CONGRESSES AND CONVENTIONS
JX4161-4171	*CONVENTIONS (TREATIES)* **SEE** TREATIES
JX1985-9	*CONVENTIONS (TREATIES)* **SEE** TREATIES / *arbitration*
JX120-191	*CONVENTIONS (TREATIES)* **SEE** TREATIES / *collections*
JX235-6	*CONVENTIONS (TREATIES)* **SEE** TREATIES / *collections*
JX351-1195	*CONVENTIONS (TREATIES)* **SEE** TREATIES / *collections*
HF1721-1733	*CONVENTIONS (TREATIES)* **SEE** TREATIES / *commercial*
HE6281	*CONVENTIONS (TREATIES)* **SEE** TREATIES / *postal*
JF71-99	*CONVENTIONS, CONSTITUTIONAL* **SEE** CONSTITUTIONAL CONVENTIONS / *general*
JK2251-6	*CONVENTIONS, POLITICAL* **SEE** POLITICAL CONVENTIONS / *u.s.*
HE6251-6281	*CONVENTIONS, POSTAL* **SEE** POSTAL CONVENTIONS / *international and other*
HE6307	*CONVENTIONS, POSTAL* **SEE** POSTAL CONVENTIONS / *u.s.*
HF5438	*CONVENTIONS, SALES* **SEE** SALES MEETINGS
BX4200-4560	CONVENTS AND NUNNERIES / *catholic church*
QA295	CONVERGENCE / *mathematical series*
BJ2120-2128	CONVERSATION
BV4912-4950	CONVERSION / *general*
BR110	CONVERSION / *psychology*
BT780	CONVERSION / *theology*
BV3750-3799	*CONVERT MAKING* **SEE** EVANGELISTIC WORK
TK2797	*CONVERTERS, ELECTRIC* **SEE** CASCADE CONVERTERS
TK2796	*CONVERTERS, ELECTRIC* **SEE** ELECTRIC CURRENT CONVERTERS
TK2796	*CONVERTERS, ELECTRIC* **SEE** ROTARY CONVERTERS
TK2796	*CONVERTERS, SYNCHRONOUS* **SEE** ROTARY CONVERTERS
TL685	*CONVERTIBLE AIRCRAFT* **SEE** CONVERTIPLANES
TL685	CONVERTIPLANES
BP170.5	*CONVERTS FROM CHRISTIANITY TO ISLAM* **SEE** MUSLIM CONVERTS FROM CHRISTIANITY
BV2626.3-4	CONVERTS FROM ISLAM
BV2619-2623	CONVERTS FROM JUDAISM
BL1478.93-95	*CONVERTS TO BUDDHISM* **SEE** BUDDHIST CONVERTS
BV4930-4935	*CONVERTS TO CHRISTIANITY* **SEE** CONVERTS
BV2626.3-4	*CONVERTS TO CHRISTIANITY FROM ISLAM* **SEE** CONVERTS FROM ISLAM
BV2619-2623	*CONVERTS TO CHRISTIANITY FROM JUDAISM* **SEE** CONVERTS FROM JUDAISM
BP170.5	*CONVERTS TO ISLAM* **SEE** MUSLIM CONVERTS
BM729.P7	*CONVERTS TO JUDAISM* **SEE** PROSELYTES AND PROSELYTING, JEWISH
BV4930-4935	CONVERTS
BX5197-9	CONVERTS, ANGLICAN / *church of england*
BX5990-5995	CONVERTS, ANGLICAN / *protestant episcopal church*
BL1478.93-95	*CONVERTS, BUDDHIST* **SEE** BUDDHIST CONVERTS
BX4668	CONVERTS, CATHOLIC
BP170.5	*CONVERTS, ISLAMIC* **SEE** MUSLIM CONVERTS
BX8141	CONVERTS, MENNONITE
BP170.5	*CONVERTS, MUSLIM* **SEE** MUSLIM CONVERTS
HF1243	CONVEYANCING / *forms*
TJ1350	CONVEYING MACHINERY — TERMINOLOGY
TJ1350-1353	CONVEYING MACHINERY
TJ1385-1418	CONVEYING MACHINERY
TJ1385-1418	*CONVEYORS* **SEE** CONVEYING MACHINERY
TJ1350-1353	*CONVEYORS* **SEE** CONVEYING MACHINERY
HV8888-8931	CONVICT LABOR
BD215	*CONVICTION* **SEE** BELIEF AND DOUBT / *philosophy*
BF773	*CONVICTION* **SEE** BELIEF AND DOUBT / *psychology*
BT50	*CONVICTION* **SEE** TRUTH / *doctrinal theology*
BC171	*CONVICTION* **SEE** TRUTH / *logic*
BD150-171	*CONVICTION* **SEE** TRUTH / *metaphysics*
RS165.J	*CONVOLVULIN* **SEE** JALAP / *pharmacy*
RM666.J	*CONVOLVULIN* **SEE** JALAP / *therapeutics*
JX5268	CONVOY
BX4732	CONVULSIONARIES
BX4732	*CONVULSIONISTS* **SEE** CONVULSIONARIES
RX301.C7	CONVULSIONS — HOMEOPATHIC TREATMENT
SB615.Q3	*COOCH-GRASS* **SEE** QUITCH-GRASS
E241.C73	COOCH'S BRIDGE, SKIRMISH OF, 1777
TX645-840	*COOK-BOOKS* **SEE** COOKERY
E356.C74	COOK'S MILLS, BATTLE OF, 1814
TX645-840	*COOKBOOKS* **SEE** COOKERY
TX831	*COOKERS, FIRELESS* **SEE** FIRELESS COOKERS
TX727	COOKERY — EARLY WORKS TO 1800
TX703-713	COOKERY — EARLY WORKS TO 1800
TX346	COOKERY — EXHIBITIONS
TX652.5	COOKERY — JUVENILE LITERATURE
TX663	COOKERY — LABORATORY MANUALS
TX813.A6	COOKERY (APPLES)
TX740	COOKERY (BABY FOODS)
TX726.3	COOKERY (BEER)
TX803.B	COOKERY (BRUSSELS SPROUTS)
TX759	*COOKERY (BUTTERMILK)* **SEE** COOKERY (SOUR CREAM AND MILK)

TX821	COOKERY (CANNED FOODS)
TX808-9	COOKERY (CEREALS)
TX759	COOKERY (CHEESE)
TX813.C5	COOKERY (CITRUS FRUITS)
TX819.C6	COOKERY (COFFEE)
TX809.M2	*COOKERY (CORN)* **SEE** COOKERY (MAIZE)
TX809.C8	COOKERY (COTTONSEED MEAL)
TX813.C7	COOKERY (CRANBERRIES)
TX749	COOKERY (CURRY)
TX759	COOKERY (DAIRY PRODUCTS)
TX813.D5	COOKERY (DATES)
TX745	*COOKERY (DRIED EGGS)* **SEE** COOKERY (EGGS)
TX747	COOKERY (EELS)
TX745	COOKERY (EGGS)
TX740	COOKERY (ENTREES)
TX813.F5	COOKERY (FIGS)
TX747	COOKERY (FISH)
TX749	COOKERY (FROGS)
TX811-813	COOKERY (FRUIT)
TX652	COOKERY (GARNISHES)
TX560.H7	COOKERY (HONEY)
TX726	COOKERY (LIQUORS)
TX809.M	COOKERY (MACARONI)
TX809.M2	COOKERY (MAIZE)
TX749	COOKERY (MEAT)
TX804	COOKERY (MUSHROOMS)
TX809.M	*COOKERY (NOODLES)* **SEE** COOKERY (MACARONI)
TX814	COOKERY (NUTS)
TX813.O	COOKERY (OLIVES)
TX813.O6	COOKERY (ORANGES)
TX753	COOKERY (OYSTERS)
TX803.P35	COOKERY (PEANUTS)
TX803.P4	COOKERY (PEAS)
TX814	COOKERY (PECANS)
TX749	COOKERY (PORK)
TX803.P8	COOKERY (POTATOES)
TX749	COOKERY (POULTRY)
TX749	COOKERY (RABBITS)
TX819	COOKERY (RELISHES)
TX809.R5	COOKERY (RICE)
TX753	COOKERY (SHELLFISH)
TX753	COOKERY (SHRIMP)
TX759	COOKERY (SOUR CREAM AND MILK)
TX759	*COOKERY (SOUR MILK)* **SEE** COOKERY (SOUR CREAM AND MILK)
TX809.M	*COOKERY (SPAGHETTI)* **SEE** COOKERY (MACARONI)
TX726	*COOKERY (SPIRITS, ALCOHOLIC)* **SEE** COOKERY (LIQUORS)
TX813.S9	COOKERY (STRAWBERRIES)
TX801-3	COOKERY (VEGETABLES)
TX809.M	*COOKERY (VERMICELLI)* **SEE** COOKERY (MACARONI)
TX726	COOKERY (WINE)
TX820	*COOKERY FOR CAMPS* **SEE** COOKERY FOR INSTITUTIONS, ETC.
TX820	COOKERY FOR INSTITUTIONS, ETC.
RM219	COOKERY FOR THE SICK
VC370-375	*COOKERY ON SHIPS* **SEE** COOKERY, MARINE
VK224	*COOKERY ON SHIPS* **SEE** COOKERY, MARINE
TX645-840	COOKERY
TX715	COOKERY, AMERICAN
TX703	COOKERY, AMERICAN */ before 1801*
TX725	COOKERY, BALKAN
TX840.B3	*COOKERY, BARBECUE* **SEE** BARBECUE COOKERY
TX823	*COOKERY, CAMP* **SEE** OUTDOOR COOKERY
TX831	*COOKERY, FIRELESS* **SEE** FIRELESS COOKERS
TX725	COOKERY, INTERNATIONAL
VC370-375	COOKERY, MARINE
VK224	COOKERY, MARINE
UC720-735	COOKERY, MILITARY
VC370-375	*COOKERY, NAVAL* **SEE** COOKERY, MARINE
VK224	*COOKERY, NAVAL* **SEE** COOKERY, MARINE
TX823	*COOKERY, OUTDOOR* **SEE** OUTDOOR COOKERY
TX725	COOKERY, PHILIPPINE
TX725	COOKERY, TAGALOG
TX713	COOKERY, TROPICAL */ before 1800*
TX725	COOKERY, TROPICAL */ before 1800*
TX652	*COOKERY-GARNISHES AND GARNISHING* **SEE** COOKERY (GARNISHES)
TX772	COOKIES
TX661-9	COOKING SCHOOLS

TX656-8	*COOKING UTENSILS* **SEE** KITCHEN UTENSILS
TP490-497	*COOLING APPLIANCES* **SEE** REFRIGERATION AND REFRIGERATING MACHINERY
TL702.R3	*COOLING OF AIRCRAFT ENGINES* **SEE** AEROPLANES — MOTORS — — COOLING
TJ563	COOLING TOWERS
QC331	COOLING
SK341.C6	COON HUNTING
GV1295.C6	COONCAN
TS840	*COOPERAGE* **SEE** COOPERS AND COOPERAGE
TS890	*COOPERAGE* **SEE** COOPERS AND COOPERAGE
HD9750-9769	*COOPERAGE* **SEE** COOPERS AND COOPERAGE / trade
HD4966.C82	*COOPERAGE* **SEE** COOPERS AND COOPERAGE / wages
HD2951-3570	COOPERATION
HF5431-6	COOPERATION / cooperative business
HD1491	*COOPERATION, AGRICULTURAL* **SEE** AGRICULTURE, COOPERATIVE
HD1483-6	*COOPERATION, AGRICULTURAL* **SEE** AGRICULTURE, COOPERATIVE
AS4	*COOPERATION, INTELLECTUAL* **SEE** INTELLECTUAL COOPERATION
JC362	*COOPERATION, INTELLECTUAL* **SEE** INTELLECTUAL COOPERATION / political theory
JX1975	*COOPERATION, INTELLECTUAL* **SEE** INTELLECTUAL COOPERATION / league of nations
BV625	*COOPERATION, INTERCHURCH* **SEE** INTERDENOMINATIONAL COOPERATION
BV625	*COOPERATION, INTERDENOMINATIONAL* **SEE** INTERDENOMINATIONAL COOPERATION
JC362	*COOPERATION, INTERNATIONAL* **SEE** INTERNATIONAL COOPERATION
JX1995	*COOPERATION, INTERNATIONAL* **SEE** INTERNATIONAL COOPERATION / etc.
JK2441	*COOPERATION, INTERSTATE* **SEE** INTERSTATE AGREEMENTS
HD1491	*COOPERATIVE AGRICULTURE* **SEE** AGRICULTURE, COOPERATIVE
HD1483-6	*COOPERATIVE AGRICULTURE* **SEE** AGRICULTURE, COOPERATIVE
HG2035-2051	*COOPERATIVE BANKS* **SEE** BANKS AND BANKING, COOPERATIVE
HG2121-2156	*COOPERATIVE BUILDING ASSOCIATIONS* **SEE** BUILDING AND LOAN ASSOCIATIONS
Z695	*COOPERATIVE CATALOGING* **SEE** CATALOGING, COOPERATIVE
HG2041-2051	*COOPERATIVE CREDIT ASSOCIATIONS, AGRICULTURAL* **SEE** AGRICULTURAL COOPERATIVE CREDIT ASSOCIATIONS
HD2951-3570	*COOPERATIVE DISTRIBUTION* **SEE** COOPERATION
HF5431-6	*COOPERATIVE DISTRIBUTION* **SEE** COOPERATION / cooperative business
LB1029.C	*COOPERATIVE EDUCATION* **SEE** EDUCATION, COOPERATIVE
HD7287.7	*COOPERATIVE HOUSING* **SEE** HOUSING, COOPERATIVE
LB1140	COOPERATIVE NURSERY SCHOOLS
HD2951-3570	*COOPERATIVE PRODUCTION* **SEE** COOPERATION
HF5431-6	*COOPERATIVE PRODUCTION* **SEE** COOPERATION / cooperative business
HD1483-6	*COOPERATIVE SOCIETIES, AGRICULTURAL* **SEE** AGRICULTURE, COOPERATIVE
HD1491	*COOPERATIVE SOCIETIES, AGRICULTURAL* **SEE** AGRICULTURE, COOPERATIVE
TS840	COOPERS AND COOPERAGE
TS890	COOPERS AND COOPERAGE
HD9750-9769	COOPERS AND COOPERAGE / trade
HD4966.C82	COOPERS AND COOPERAGE / wages
QA556	COORDINATES / analytic geometry
QB147	COORDINATES / spherical astronomy
QA556	COORDINATES, POLAR
PL4671	*COORG LANGUAGE* **SEE** KODAGU LANGUAGE
E99.C874	COOS INDIANS
PM1611	COOS LANGUAGE
E99.K85	*COOTENAI INDIANS* **SEE** KUTENAI INDIANS
PM1631	*COOTENAI LANGUAGE* **SEE** KUTENAI LANGUAGE
QL696.G8	COOTS
QP981.C7	COPAIBA — PHYSIOLOGICAL EFFECT
RS165.C8	COPAIBA

TP996.C6	CORNCOBS
RE336	CORNEA — DISEASES
QL949	CORNEA
QM511	CORNEA
ML980	*CORNEMUSE* **SEE** BAGPIPE
HD2709-2930	*CORNERS, COMMERCIAL* **SEE** MONOPOLIES
HG6001-6051	*CORNERS, COMMERCIAL* **SEE** SPECULATION
HG4551-4595	*CORNERS, COMMERCIAL* **SEE** STOCK-EXCHANGE
HD2709-2930	*CORNERS, COMMERCIAL* **SEE** TRUSTS, INDUSTRIAL
HD2801-2930	*CORNERS, COMMERCIAL* **SEE** TRUSTS, INDUSTRIAL / *other countries*
HD2771-2798	*CORNERS, COMMERCIAL* **SEE** TRUSTS, INDUSTRIAL / *u.s.*
MT446	CORNET — ORCHESTRA STUDIES
MT445	CORNET — STUDIES AND EXERCISES
M288-9	*CORNET AND BARITONE MUSIC* **SEE** BARITONE AND CORNET MUSIC
M260-261	CORNET AND PIANO MUSIC (JAZZ)
M260-261	CORNET AND PIANO MUSIC
M260-261	CORNET AND PIANO MUSIC, ARRANGED
M288-9	CORNET AND TRUMPET MUSIC
M1040-1041	CORNET AND TRUMPET WITH ORCHESTRA
M1040-1041	CORNET AND TRUMPET WITH ORCHESTRA, ARRANGED
M85-89	CORNET MUSIC (JAZZ)
M288-9	CORNET MUSIC (2 CORNETS)
M455-7	*CORNET MUSIC (4 CORNETS)* **SEE** WIND QUARTETS (4 CORNETS)
M455-7	*CORNET MUSIC (4 CORNETS)* **SEE** WIND QUARTETS (4 CORNETS)
M85-89	CORNET MUSIC
M85-89	*CORNET MUSIC, ARRANGED (JAZZ)* **SEE** CORNET MUSIC (JAZZ)
M1205	CORNET WITH BAND — SOLO WITH PIANO
M1205	CORNET WITH BAND
M1030-1031	CORNET WITH ORCHESTRA
M1030-1031	CORNET WITH ORCHESTRA, ARRANGED
ML960-961	CORNET / *history and construction*
TH2482	CORNICE WORK
NA2960	CORNICES / *architecture*
TH2482	CORNICES / *building*
PB2569	CORNISH DRAMA / *collections*
PB2552	CORNISH DRAMA / *history and criticism*
SF489.C6	CORNISH FOWL
PB2501-2549	CORNISH LANGUAGE
PB2563-2621	CORNISH LITERATURE / *collections*
PB2551-4	CORNISH LITERATURE / *history and criticism*
TP966.C7	*CORNSTALKS* **SEE** CORN-STALKS
RL427	*CORNUA CUTANEA* **SEE** HORNS, CUTANEOUS
QC643	CORONA (ELECTRICITY)
QB529	*CORONA, SOLAR* **SEE** SUN — CORONA
RC685.C6	CORONARY HEART DISEASE
CR4480	*CORONATION AMPULLAS* **SEE** AMPULLAS, CORONATION
CR4480	*CORONATION STONE* **SEE** STONE OF SCONE
DA111-112	CORONATIONS / *england*
DC33	CORONATIONS / *france*
DD61.8	CORONATIONS / *germany*
JC391	CORONATIONS / *institutional history*
DG441-450	CORONATIONS / *italy*
GT5050	CORONATIONS / *manners and customs*
D127	CORONATIONS / *medieval*
DK32	CORONATIONS / *russia*
DA773	CORONATIONS / *scotland*
DP48	CORONATIONS / *spain*
D582.F2	CORONEL, BATTLE OF, 1914
HV8609	CORPORAL PUNISHMENT / *penology*
LB3025	CORPORAL PUNISHMENT / *schools*
BV4647.M4	CORPORAL WORKS OF MERCY
HG4028.D3	CORPORATE DEBT
Z695.8	CORPORATE ENTRY (CATALOGING)
HG4001-4280	*CORPORATE FINANCE* **SEE** CORPORATIONS — FINANCE
HD3611-3616	CORPORATE STATE / *economic history*
JC481	CORPORATE STATE / *fascism*
HF5686.C7	*CORPORATION ACCOUNTING* **SEE** CORPORATIONS — ACCOUNTING
HG4001-4280	*CORPORATION FINANCE* **SEE** CORPORATIONS — FINANCE
HD2753	*CORPORATION INCOME TAX* **SEE** CORPORATIONS — TAXATION
HD2753	*CORPORATION TAX* **SEE** CORPORATIONS — TAXATION
HF5686.C7	CORPORATIONS — ACCOUNTING
HG4001-4280	CORPORATIONS — FINANCE
HD2753	CORPORATIONS — TAXATION
HD2781	CORPORATIONS — VALUATION / *u.s.*
HD3611-3616	*CORPORATIONS (CORPORATE STATE)* **SEE** CORPORATE STATE / *economic history*
JC481	*CORPORATIONS (CORPORATE STATE)* **SEE** CORPORATE STATE / *fascism*
HD6350-6940	*CORPORATIONS (CORPORATE STATE)* **SEE** TRADE AND PROFESSIONAL ASSOCIATIONS / *trade-unions*
HD2421-9	*CORPORATIONS (CORPORATE STATE)* **SEE** TRADE AND PROFESSIONAL ASSOCIATIONS / *trade associations*
HG4001-4280	CORPORATIONS / *finance*
HD2709-2930	CORPORATIONS / *theory and policy*
HG4001-4280	*CORPORATIONS, BUSINESS* **SEE** CORPORATIONS / *finance*
HD2709-2930	*CORPORATIONS, BUSINESS* **SEE** CORPORATIONS / *theory and policy*
BV765	*CORPORATIONS, ECCLESIASTICAL* **SEE** CORPORATIONS, RELIGIOUS
HD3850	CORPORATIONS, GOVERNMENT
HD4001-4420	CORPORATIONS, GOVERNMENT / *other countries*
HD3881-8	CORPORATIONS, GOVERNMENT / *u.s.*
BX1939.C75	CORPORATIONS, RELIGIOUS (CANON LAW)
BV765	CORPORATIONS, RELIGIOUS
HD3611-3616	*CORPORATISM* **SEE** CORPORATE STATE / *economic history*
JC481	*CORPORATISM* **SEE** CORPORATE STATE / *fascism*
HD3611-3616	*CORPORATIVE STATE* **SEE** CORPORATE STATE / *economic history*
JC481	*CORPORATIVE STATE* **SEE** CORPORATE STATE / *fascism*
HD3611-3616	*CORPORATIVISM* **SEE** CORPORATE STATE / *economic history*
JC481	*CORPORATIVISM* **SEE** CORPORATE STATE / *fascism*
RC628	CORPULENCE
BV63	CORPUS CHRISTI FESTIVAL
F2841	CORPUS CHRISTI, ARGENTINE REPUBLIC, BATTLE OF, 1536
QM421	CORPUS LUTEUM
QP261	CORPUS LUTEUM
QL881	CORPUS LUTEUM
QC402	*CORPUSCULAR THEORY OF LIGHT* **SEE** LIGHT, CORPUSCULAR THEORY OF
QC721	*CORPUSCULAR THEORY OF MATTER* **SEE** ELECTRONS
QC173	*CORPUSCULAR THEORY OF MATTER* **SEE** MATTER — CONSTITUTION
QA273-281	CORRELATION (STATISTICS) / *mathematics*
HA33	CORRELATION (STATISTICS) / *statistics*
QC73	*CORRELATION OF FORCES* **SEE** FORCE AND ENERGY
BV652	*CORRESPONDENCE* **SEE** CHURCH CORRESPONDENCE
HF5721-5733	*CORRESPONDENCE* **SEE** COMMERCIAL CORRESPONDENCE
LB3614	*CORRESPONDENCE* **SEE** INTERNATIONAL CORRESPONDENCE / *students*
PE1481-1497	*CORRESPONDENCE* **SEE** LETTER-WRITING / *english rhetoric*
BJ2100-2115	*CORRESPONDENCE* **SEE** LETTER-WRITING / *etiquette*
PN6131-6140	*CORRESPONDENCE* **SEE** LETTERS / *collections*
PN4400	*CORRESPONDENCE* **SEE** LETTERS / *history and criticism*
HQ801.3-5	*CORRESPONDENCE* **SEE** LOVE-LETTERS
PS673.L6-7	*CORRESPONDENCE* **SEE** LOVE-LETTERS / *american literature*
R1349.L8	*CORRESPONDENCE* **SEE** LOVE-LETTERS / *english literature*
PN6140.L7	*CORRESPONDENCE* **SEE** LOVE-LETTERS / *general literature*
LC5901-6101	CORRESPONDENCE SCHOOLS AND COURSES
HF1133	CORRESPONDENCE SCHOOLS AND COURSES / *business schools*

T172	CORRESPONDENCE SCHOOLS AND COURSES / technology
BX8727	CORRESPONDENCES, DOCTRINE OF
SF373.C	CORRIEDALE SHEEP
TA467	CORROSION AND ANTI-CORROSIVES
TA462	CORROSION AND ANTI-CORROSIVES
TD491	*CORROSION, ELECTROLYTIC* **SEE** ELECTROLYTIC CORROSION / etc.
TF912	*CORROSION, ELECTROLYTIC* **SEE** ELECTROLYTIC CORROSION / electric railroads
TK3255	*CORROSION, ELECTROLYTIC* **SEE** ELECTROLYTIC CORROSION / electric engineering
RA1231.M5	*CORROSIVE SUBLIMATE-TOXICOLOGY* **SEE** MERCURY — TOXICOLOGY
JF1081	CORRUPTION (IN POLITICS)
JK-JQ	CORRUPTION (IN POLITICS) / by country
JS	CORRUPTION (IN POLITICS) / etc.
G535-7	*CORSAIRS* **SEE** PIRATES
JX4444.6	*CORSAIRS* **SEE** PIRATES / international law
JX5241	*CORSAIRS* **SEE** PRIVATEERING
GT2075	CORSET / costume
RA779	CORSET / hygiene
TT677	CORSET / manufacture
DC611.C8-839	CORSICA — HISTORY
PC1796-9	CORSICAN LITERATURE / italian dialects
DC611.C8-839	CORSICANS
QP187	CORTIN
DC233.C7	CORUNA, BATTLE OF, 1809
TN948.C8	CORUNDUM / mineral resources
QE391.C9	CORUNDUM / mineralogy
HJ5951-7	CORVEE
TL215.C	CORVETTE AUTOMOBILE
F1376	CORWITH EXPEDITION, 1895
E99.K77	*COSHATTA INDIANS* **SEE** KOASATI INDIANS
GT2340	COSMETICS / manners and customs
TP983	COSMETICS / manufacture
RA778	COSMETICS / toilet
TT950-979	*COSMETOLOGY* **SEE** BEAUTY CULTURE
QC809.E55	COSMIC ELECTRODYNAMICS
QB461	COSMIC ELECTRODYNAMICS / astrophysics
BD645	*COSMIC HARMONY* **SEE** HARMONY OF THE SPHERES
QC801-8	COSMIC PHYSICS
QC883	COSMIC PHYSICS / meteorology
QC485	COSMIC RAYS
QB981	COSMOGONY
QE506	COSMOGONY / geological
BS651	*COSMOGONY, BIBLICAL* **SEE** CREATION / bible
BL224-5	*COSMOGONY, BIBLICAL* **SEE** CREATION / comparative religion
BD701	COSMOLOGY — CURIOSA AND MISCELLANY
BD493-708	COSMOLOGY
BS651	*COSMOLOGY, BIBLICAL* **SEE** CREATION / bible
BL224-5	*COSMOLOGY, BIBLICAL* **SEE** CREATION / comparative religion
B745.C6	COSMOLOGY, ISLAMIC
B745.C6	*COSMOLOGY, MUSLIM* **SEE** COSMOLOGY, ISLAMIC
JC361	*COSMOPOLITANISM* **SEE** INTERNATIONALISM
DK35	COSSACKS / ethnography
DK35.3	*COSSACKS, DNIEPERIAN* **SEE** ZAPOROGIANS
HF5686.C8	COST ACCOUNTING
HD6977-7080	COST AND STANDARD OF LIVING
UA17	*COST OF ARMIES* **SEE** ARMIES, COST OF
VA20-25	*COST OF NAVIES* **SEE** NAVIES, COST OF
VA60-750	*COST OF NAVIES* **SEE** NAVIES, COST OF / particular countries
UA17	*COST OF WAR* **SEE** WAR, COST OF
HB199	COST
HB3719	COST / crises
HF5686.C8	*COST-ACCOUNTING* **SEE** COST ACCOUNTING
F1541-1557	COSTA RICA — HISTORY
PQ7480-7489	COSTA RICAN LITERATURE
PQ7486	COSTA RICAN POETRY / collections
PQ7482	COSTA RICAN POETRY / history
PM971	COSTANOAN LANGUAGE
TT507	COSTUME DESIGN
GT500-2370	COSTUME / manners and customs
GT530-560	*COSTUME, ANCIENT* **SEE** COSTUME — HISTORY — — ANCIENT
GT540	COSTUME, JEWISH
UC480-485	*COSTUME, MILITARY* **SEE** UNIFORMS, MILITARY
GT500-2370	*COSTUME, THEATRICAL* **SEE** COSTUME / manners and customs
HB845	*COSTUME-LAWS AND REGULATIONS* **SEE** SUMPTUARY LAWS
GT527-8	*COSTUME-LAWS AND REGULATIONS* **SEE** SUMPTUARY LAWS / dress
GT530-560	COSTUME — HISTORY — — ANCIENT
GT575	COSTUME — HISTORY — — MEDIEVAL
GT585	COSTUME — HISTORY — — 16TH CENTURY
GT585	COSTUME — HISTORY — — 17TH CENTURY
GT585	COSTUME — HISTORY — — 18TH CENTURY
GT595	COSTUME — HISTORY — — 19TH CENTURY
GT596	COSTUME — HISTORY — — 20TH CENTURY
GV1757	*COTILLION* **SEE** GERMAN (DANCE)
GV1763-7	*COTILLION* **SEE** QUADRILLE (DANCE)
M30	COTILLIONS (PIANO)
NA7551-5	COTTAGES
TH4835	*COTTAGES, SUMMER* **SEE** SUMMER HOMES
SB608.C8	COTTON — DISEASES AND PESTS
TS1542	COTTON — GRADING
HD9070-9089	COTTON — GRADING / economics
HF5716.C6	COTTON — TABLES, ETC.
HD9070.8	COTTON — TAXATION
HD9076	COTTON — WEIGHTS AND MEASURES / u.s.
SB252	COTTON BALING
SB945.C8	*COTTON BOLL-WEEVII* **SEE** BOLL-WEEVIL
SB945.C82	*COTTON BOLLWORM* **SEE** BOLLWORM
SB249	COTTON BREEDING
TS1578	COTTON CARDING
TS1578	COTTON COMBING
TP930	*COTTON DYEING* **SEE** DYES AND DYEING — COTTON
HD9881.5	COTTON FAMINE, 1861-1864 / gt. brit.
TS1580	COTTON FINISHING
SB252	*COTTON GINNING* **SEE** COTTON GINS AND GINNING
TS1585	*COTTON GINNING* **SEE** COTTON GINS AND GINNING
TS1585	COTTON GINS AND GINNING
SB252	COTTON GINS AND GINNING
SB245-252	COTTON GROWING / agriculture
HD9070-9089	COTTON GROWING / economics
TT681	*COTTON HOSIERY* **SEE** HOSIERY, COTTON
SB608.C	COTTON LEAF CURL
TS1583	COTTON MACHINERY — SAFETY APPLIANCES
TS1583	COTTON MACHINERY
TS1550-1590	COTTON MANUFACTURE
TS1550-1590	*COTTON MILLS* **SEE** COTTON MANUFACTURE
TH4521	*COTTON MILLS* **SEE** TEXTILE FACTORIES / building
SB608.C8	*COTTON PESTS* **SEE** COTTON — DISEASES AND PESTS
TS1580	COTTON SIZING
HD7269.C7	COTTON SPINNING — SAFETY MEASURES / labor
TS1577	COTTON SPINNING — SAFETY MEASURES / manufacture
TS1577	COTTON SPINNING — TABLES, CALCULATIONS, ETC.
TS1577	COTTON SPINNING
SB945.C	COTTON STALK-BORER
HF5716.C7	COTTON TRADE — TABLES AND READY-RECKONERS
HD9870-9889	COTTON TRADE / cloth
HD9070-9089	COTTON TRADE / raw cotton
HF2651.C85	COTTON TRADE / tariff
TS1580	COTTON WEAVING — SAFETY MEASURES
TS1579	COTTON WEAVING
TS1577	COTTON YARN
HD9093	*COTTON-SEED* **SEE** COTTONSEED
SB252	COTTON-TIES
HF2651.C91	COTTON-TIES / tariff
TS1587	COTTON-WASTE
HD4966.C88	COTTON-WASTE / wages
SB945.C85	COTTON-WORM
SB245-252	COTTON / agriculture
TS1542	COTTON / fibers
HF5716.C8	COTTONSEED — TABLES AND READY-RECKONERS
SF99	COTTONSEED MEAL / animal feeds
TX558.C8	COTTONSEED MEAL / human food
TP681.5	COTTONSEED OIL — TABLES AND READY-RECKONERS / chemical technology
HF5716.C85	COTTONSEED OIL — TABLES AND READY-RECKONERS / commerce
TP681	COTTONSEED OIL

HD9093	COTTONSEED		M217-218	COUNTRY-DANCES (VIOLIN AND HARPSICHORD)
SB945.C	COTTONWOOD BEETLE		M221-3	COUNTRY-DANCES (VIOLIN AND PIANO)
SB945.C86	COTTONWOOD BORER		M217-218	COUNTRY-DANCES (VIOLIN AND PIANO)
SD397.C8	COTTONWOOD		M40-44	COUNTRY-DANCES (VIOLIN)
QL973	*COTYLEDON (ANATOMY)* **SEE** PLACENTA */ embryology*		M655-7	COUNTRY-DANCES (2 BASSOONS, 2 HORNS, 2 OBOES)
QM611	*COTYLEDON (ANATOMY)* **SEE** PLACENTA */ human embryology*		M286-7	COUNTRY-DANCES (2 VIOLINS)
			M349-353	COUNTRY-DANCES (2 VIOLINS, VIOLONCELLO)
RG664	*COTYLEDON (ANATOMY)* **SEE** PLACENTA */ obstetrics*		M349-353	COUNTRY-DANCES (3 VIOLINS)
			M455-9	COUNTRY-DANCES (4 CLARINETS)
QP281	*COTYLEDON (ANATOMY)* **SEE** PLACENTA */ physiology*		S533-4	*COUNTY AGENTS* **SEE** COUNTY AGRICULTURAL AGENTS
SB615.Q3	*COUCH-GRASS* **SEE** QUITCH-GRASS		S533-4	COUNTY AGRICULTURAL AGENTS
QL737.C2	*COUGARS* **SEE** PUMAS		LB2329	*COUNTY COLLEGES (ENGLISH)* **SEE** MUNICIPAL UNIVERSITIES AND COLLEGES
DC309.C7	COULMIERS, BATTLE OF, 1870			
TK331	*COULOMETER* **SEE** VOLTAMETER		JS261-7	COUNTY GOVERNMENT */ general*
QC615	*COULOMETER* **SEE** VOLTAMETER */ physics*		JS3260	COUNTY GOVERNMENT */ gt. brit.*
SB307.T6	*COUMARA NUT* **SEE** TONKA BEAN		JS411-414	COUNTY GOVERNMENT */ u.s.*
QD341.A2	COUMARINS		JS451	COUNTY GOVERNMENT */ u.s.*
BR225	*COUNCIL OF CHALCEDON, 451* **SEE** CHALCEDON, COUNCIL OF, 451		Z675.C8	*COUNTY LIBRARIES* **SEE** LIBRARIES, COUNTY
			LB2813	COUNTY SCHOOL SYSTEMS
D161	*COUNCIL OF CLERMONT, 1095* **SEE** CLERMONT, COUNCIL OF, 1095 */ first crusade*		QA831	*COUPLES (MECHANICS)* **SEE** FORCES AND COUPLES
			QA823	*COUPLES (MECHANICS)* **SEE** FORCES AND COUPLES
BX8301414	*COUNCIL OF CONSTANCE, 1414-1418* **SEE** CONSTANCE, COUNCIL OF, 1414-1418		TJ183	COUPLINGS */ machinery*
			JK2217	COUPON BALLOT
BR210	*COUNCIL OF NICAEA, 325* **SEE** NICAEA, COUNCIL OF, 325		JC494	COUPS D'ETAT
			BJ1533.C8	COURAGE
BX830 1545	*COUNCIL OF TRENT, 1545-1563* **SEE** TRENT, COUNCIL OF, 1545-1563		M455-9	COURANTES (BASSOON, CLARINET, FLUTE, OBOE)
			GT3600	*COURS D'AMOUR* **SEE** COURTS OF LOVE
BX1939.C78	COUNCILS AND SYNODS (CANON LAW)		DC611.P961	*COURS D'AMOUR* **SEE** COURTS OF LOVE */ provence*
BV710	COUNCILS AND SYNODS */ general*			
BL1422.A1	*COUNCILS AND SYNODS, BUDDHIST* **SEE** BUDDHIST COUNCILS AND SYNODS		TL696.C8	*COURSE COMPUTERS* **SEE** COURSE-LINE COMPUTERS
			TL696.C8	*COURSE INDICATORS* **SEE** COURSE-LINE COMPUTERS
HD3611	*COUNCILS, ECONOMIC* **SEE** ECONOMIC COUNCILS		TL696.C8	COURSE-LINE COMPUTERS
BV4012.2	*COUNSELING, PASTORAL* **SEE** PASTORAL COUNSELING		LB2361-5	*COURSES OF STUDY* **SEE** EDUCATION — CURRICULA */ colleges and universities*
BM652.5	*COUNSELING, RABBINICAL* **SEE** PASTORAL COUNSELING (JUDAISM)		LB1570-1571	*COURSES OF STUDY* **SEE** EDUCATION — CURRICULA */ elementary schools*
GV198.C6	*COUNSELORS, CAMP* **SEE** CAMP COUNSELORS		LB1628-9	*COURSES OF STUDY* **SEE** EDUCATION — CURRICULA */ secondary schools*
TK7872.C3	*COUNTER TUBES* **SEE** COLD CATHODE TUBES		SK291	COURSING
BR430	COUNTER-REFORMATION */ church history*		NA4870	*COURT CHAPELS (BUILDINGS)* **SEE** CHAPELS, COURT
DD176-189	COUNTER-REFORMATION */ germany*		NA5200-6113	*COURT CHAPELS (BUILDINGS)* **SEE** CHAPELS, COURT
D220-271	COUNTER-REFORMATION */ history general*		PT203	COURT EPIC, GERMAN
HG335-341	COUNTERFEITS AND COUNTERFEITING		D107.7	*COURT FAVORITES* **SEE** FAVORITES, ROYAL
HG641-5	COUNTERFEITS AND COUNTERFEITING */ u.s.*		GT3670	*COURT FOOLS* **SEE** FOOLS AND JESTERS
QC976.C7	COUNTERGLOW		VB800-815	*COURT MARTIAL* **SEE** COURTS-MARTIAL AND COURTS OF INQUIRY */ naval*
ML446	COUNTERPOINT */ history*			
MT55	COUNTERPOINT */ instruction*		UB850-867	*COURT MARTIAL* **SEE** COURTS-MARTIAL AND COURTS OF INQUIRY */ military*
JF341	*COUNTERSIGNATURE (CONSTITUTIONAL LAW)* **SEE** MINISTERIAL RESPONSIBILITY		TH7392.C	COURT-HOUSES — HEATING AND VENTILATION
			TH7684.C8	COURT-HOUSES — HEATING AND VENTILATION
QA141	*COUNTING* **SEE** NUMERATION		NA4470-4477	COURT-HOUSES */ architecture*
GR485	*COUNTING RHYMES* **SEE** COUNTING-OUT RHYMES		JK1543	*COURT, CONTEMPT OF* **SEE** CONTEMPT OF COURT */ u.s.*
TK7872.C3	*COUNTING TUBES* **SEE** COLD CATHODE TUBES			
QC476	*COUNTING TUBES* **SEE** GEIGER-MÜLLER COUNTERS		JX4081	*COURTESY OF NATIONS* **SEE** COMITY OF NATIONS
GR485	COUNTING-OUT RHYMES		BJ1533.C9	COURTESY
BV638	*COUNTRY CHURCHES* **SEE** RURAL CHURCHES		BJ1520-1688	COURTESY */ conduct of life*
S521	COUNTRY LIFE — PICTORIAL WORKS		GT3510-3530	*COURTIERS* **SEE** COURTS AND COURTIERS */ court life*
PN6110.C8	COUNTRY LIFE — POETRY		GT2650	*COURTING* **SEE** COURTSHIP */ manners and customs*
S521	COUNTRY LIFE		HQ801	*COURTING* **SEE** COURTSHIP */ sociology*
GT3470	COUNTRY LIFE */ manners and customs*		GT2620	COURTLY LOVE
HT401-485	COUNTRY LIFE */ social groups*		GT3510-3530	COURTS AND COURTIERS */ court life*
LB1567	*COUNTRY SCHOOLS* **SEE** RURAL SCHOOLS		UB880	COURTS OF HONOR */ k military*
GV1763	COUNTRY-DANCE		UB850-867	*COURTS OF INQUIRY* **SEE** COURTS-MARTIAL AND COURTS OF INQUIRY */ military*
M1362	COUNTRY-DANCES (ACCORDION ENSEMBLE)			
M1248	COUNTRY-DANCES (BAND) — SCORES AND PARTS		VB800-815	*COURTS OF INQUIRY* **SEE** COURTS-MARTIAL AND COURTS OF INQUIRY */ naval*
M1248	COUNTRY-DANCES (BAND)		GT3600	COURTS OF LOVE
M455-9	COUNTRY-DANCES (BASSOON, CLARINET, FLUTE, OBOE)		DC611.P961	COURTS OF LOVE */ provence*
			UB850-867	COURTS-MARTIAL AND COURTS OF INQUIRY */ military*
M1048	COUNTRY-DANCES (CHAMBER ORCHESTRA)			
M1060	COUNTRY-DANCES (CHAMBER ORCHESTRA)		VB800-815	COURTS-MARTIAL AND COURTS OF INQUIRY */ naval*
M31	COUNTRY-DANCES (HARPSICHORD)		JF700-723	COURTS
M32.8	COUNTRY-DANCES (HARPSICHORD)		JK-JQ	COURTS */ by country*
M1048	COUNTRY-DANCES (ORCHESTRA)		JV471	COURTS */ colonial*
M1060	COUNTRY-DANCES (ORCHESTRA)		PN56.L6	*COURTSHIP IN LITERATURE* **SEE** LOVE IN LITERATURE
M32.8	COUNTRY-DANCES (PIANO)			
M31	COUNTRY-DANCES (PIANO)		GT2650	COURTSHIP */ manners and customs*
M315-319	COUNTRY-DANCES (PIANO, 2 RECORDERS)		HQ801	COURTSHIP */ sociology*
M1145	COUNTRY-DANCES (STRING ORCHESTRA)			
M1160	COUNTRY-DANCES (STRING ORCHESTRA)			
M221-3	COUNTRY-DANCES (VIOLIN AND HARPSICHORD)			

E99.K77	COUSHATTA INDIANS SEE KOASATI INDIANS
GT2460	COUVADE
TN440-449	COVELLIN / copper ores
TN780	COVELLIN / metallurgy
BT155	COVENANT OF GRACE SEE COVENANTS (THEOLOGY)
BT155	COVENANT OF WORKS SEE COVENANTS (THEOLOGY)
BT155	COVENANT THEOLOGY SEE COVENANTS (THEOLOGY)
E184.C8	COVENANTERS IN THE U.S.
BX9081-2	COVENANTERS
BX9081-2	COVENANTS (CHURCH HISTORY) SEE COVENANTERS
BX9081	COVENANTS (CHURCH HISTORY) SEE SOLEMN LEAGUE AND COVENANT
BX7235-6	COVENANTS (CHURCH POLITY) / congregational
BT1010	COVENANTS (CHURCH POLITY) / general
BX9183	COVENANTS (CHURCH POLITY) / presbyterian
BL617	COVENANTS (RELIGION)
BT155	COVENANTS (THEOLOGY)
SB432	COVER PLANTS SEE GROUND COVER PLANTS
NK9100-9199	COVERLETS / art
TT835	COVERLETS / technology
BJ1535.A8	COVETOUSNESS SEE AVARICE
SF191-219	COW SEE COWS
NA8230	COW BARNS SEE DAIRY BARNS / architecture
TH4930	COW BARNS SEE DAIRY BARNS / building
E99.U45	COW CREEK INDIANS SEE UMPQUA INDIANS
CC260	COW-BELLS
QL696.P2	COW-BIRDS SEE COWBIRDS
SB945.C	COW-PEA CURCULIO
SB945.C	COW-PEA WEEVIL
SB205.C8	COW-PEAS
QL696.P2	COWBIRDS
PE3727.C6	COWBOY SLANG SEE COWBOYS — LANGUAGE (NEW WORDS, SLANG, ETC.)
PE3727.C6	COWBOYS — LANGUAGE (NEW WORDS, SLANG, ETC.)
PS595.C6	COWBOYS — POETRY / american
PS595.C6	COWBOYS — SONGS AND MUSIC / literature
M1629-1630	COWBOYS — SONGS AND MUSIC / music
F596	COWBOYS
E99.C875	COWICHAN INDIANS
TL702.C6	COWL FLAPS SEE AEROPLANES — MOTORS — — COWLINGS
TL702.C6	COWLINGS (AEROPLANES) SEE AEROPLANES — MOTORS — — COWLINGS
E241.C9	COWPENS, BATTLE OF, 1781
QL876-881	COWPER'S GLANDS / comparative anatomy
QM416-421	COWPER'S GLANDS / human anatomy
QP265	COWPER'S GLANDS / physiology
QP257	COWPER'S GLANDS / physiology
RM276	COWPOX SEE VACCINIA
GN436.2	COWRIES / ethnology
QL430.5.C77	COWRIES / mollusca
SF191-219	COWS
RD772	COXALGIA SEE HIP JOINT — DISEASES
QL737.C2	COYOTES
DK35	COZACKS SEE COSSACKS / ethnography
SB363	CRAB APPLE SEE APPLE
SH380	CRAB FISHERIES
QL444.D3	CRABS
QE817.D3	CRABS, FOSSIL
TP692.2	CRACKING PROCESS / gasoline
GN415.C8	CRADLES / ethnology
TT	CRAFTS (HANDICRAFTS) SEE HANDICRAFT
NK	CRAFTS (HANDICRAFTS) SEE HANDICRAFT / artistic crafts
GV1796.C	CRAMIGNONS
LB1049	CRAMMING SEE STUDY, METHOD OF
LC63	CRAMMING SEE STUDY, METHOD OF / examinations
R133	CRAMP-RINGS
RC429	CRAMP, TELEGRAPHERS' SEE TELEGRAPHERS' CRAMP
RC429	CRAMP, WRITERS' SEE WRITERS' CRAMP
SB608.C87	CRANBERRIES — DISEASES AND PESTS
SB383	CRANBERRIES
SB608.C87	CRANBERRY FIRE-WORM
QL537.T6	CRANE-FLIES
QL696.G8	CRANES (BIRDS)
TJ1363-5	CRANES, DERRICKS, ETC.
E356.C8	CRANEY ISLAND, BATTLE OF, 1813
RJ546.C	CRANIAL OSTEOPOROSIS SEE CRANIOTABES
GN131	CRANIAL SUTURES / anthropology
QL821	CRANIAL SUTURES / comparative anatomy
QM105	CRANIAL SUTURES / human anatomy
GN71-131	CRANIOLOGY
GN130.J4	CRANIOLOGY-JEWS SEE JEWS — CRANIOLOGY
GN130.N3	CRANIOLOGY-NEGROES SEE NEGROES — CRANIOLOGY
GN71-131	CRANIOMETRY
GN72	CRANIOPHORE
RJ546.C	CRANIOTABES
RG781	CRANIOTOMY
GN71-131	CRANIUM SEE CRANIOLOGY
GN71-131	CRANIUM SEE CRANIOMETRY
GN71-131	CRANIUM SEE SKULL / anthropology
QL821-3	CRANIUM SEE SKULL / comparative anatomy
QM105	CRANIUM SEE SKULL / human anatomy
CT9990-9991	CRANKS SEE ECCENTRICS AND ECCENTRICITIES / biography
GV1295.R9	CRAPETTE (GAME) SEE RUSSIAN BANK (GAME)
GV1303	CRAPS (GAME)
TS900	CRATES
GT2120	CRAVATS
E238	CRAWFORD'S INDIAN CAMPAIGN, 1782
QL444.D3	CRAYFISH
NC855-875	CRAYON DRAWING
NC855-875	CRAYON DRAWINGS
NE1795	CRAYON MANNER SEE STIPPLE ENGRAVING
SB401	CREAM NUT SEE BRAZIL NUT
TX409	CREAM OF TARTAR / etc.
RM666.C	CREAM OF TARTAR / therapeutics
SF247	CREAM-SEPARATORS
SF251-262	CREAM
SF247	CREAMERIES — APPARATUS AND SUPPLIES
SF266	CREAMERIES
QP801.C8	CREATINE
QP801.C8	CREATININE
N8180	CREATION — ART
BL325.C7	CREATION — COMPARATIVE STUDIES
BL224	CREATION — EARLY WORKS TO 1800
BF408	CREATION (LITERARY, ARTISTIC, ETC.)
BS651	CREATION / bible
BL224-5	CREATION / comparative religion
Z7204.C8	CREATIVE ABILITY — TESTING / bibliography
LB1537	CREATIVE ACTIVITIES AND SEAT WORK
LB1062	CREATIVE THINKING (EDUCATION) / educational psychology
BF408	CREATIVE THINKING (EDUCATION) / psychology
BF408	CREATIVENESS SEE CREATION (LITERARY, ARTISTIC, ETC.)
BF408	CREATIVITY (EDUCATION) SEE CREATIVE THINKING (EDUCATION) / psychology
LB1062	CREATIVITY (EDUCATION) SEE CREATIVE THINKING (EDUCATION) / educational psychology
BF408	CREATIVITY SEE CREATION (LITERARY, ARTISTIC, ETC.)
HV851-861	CRECHES SEE DAY NURSERIES
DC98.5.C8	CRECY, BATTLE OF, 1346
HF5568	CREDIT COMPANIES SEE INSTALMENT PLAN
HG2035-2051	CREDIT COOPERATIVES SEE BANKS AND BANKING, COOPERATIVE
HG2041-2051	CREDIT FONCIER SEE AGRICULTURAL CREDIT / banking
HD1439-1440	CREDIT FONCIER SEE AGRICULTURAL CREDIT / theory
HF5571-8	CREDIT GUIDES
HG9970.C6-89	CREDIT INSURANCE SEE INSURANCE, CREDIT
HG2035-2051	CREDIT UNIONS SEE BANKS AND BANKING, COOPERATIVE
HF5565-5585	CREDIT / practice
HG3701-3781	CREDIT / theory
HG2041-2051	CREDIT, AGRICULTURAL SEE AGRICULTURAL CREDIT / banking
HD1439-1440	CREDIT, AGRICULTURAL SEE AGRICULTURAL CREDIT / theory
HG3745	CREDIT, LETTERS OF SEE LETTERS OF CREDIT

HG355-9	CREDIT, SOCIAL **SEE** SOCIAL CREDIT
M2079.L3	CREDO (MUSIC)
M2099.L3	CREDO (MUSIC)
BF773	CREDULITY
E99.C88	CREE INDIANS
PM986-9	CREE LANGUAGE
BT990	CREEDS — COMPARATIVE STUDIES
BX	CREEDS / by denomination
BT990-999	CREEDS / general
BT990	CREEDS, ECUMENICAL
E99.C9	CREEK INDIANS
PM991	CREEK LANGUAGE
E83.813	CREEK WAR, 1813-1814
E83.836	CREEK WAR, 1836
TA480.A6	CREEP OF ALUMINUM
TA480.C7	CREEP OF COPPER
TL480.L	CREEP OF LEAD
TA480.M	CREEP OF MAGNESIUM
TA407	CREEP OF MATERIALS
TA460	CREEP OF METALS
TA480.M	CREEP OF MOLYBDENUM
TA455.P5	CREEP OF PLASTICS
TA480.T	CREEP OF TITANIUM
TA420	CREEP OF WOOD
QL696.P2	CREEPERS
RA631-7	CREMATION
GT3330	CREMATION / manners and customs
RA631-7	CREMATORIES **SEE** CREMATION
GT3330	CREMATORIES **SEE** CREMATION / manners and customs
QA602	CREMONA TRANSFORMATIONS
PM7831-7875	CREOLE DIALECTS
F380.C9	CREOLES / louisiana
RA766.C9	CREOLIN
TP248.C	CREOSOTE / chemical technology
RM666.C8	CREOSOTE / therapeutics
TS1109	CREPE PAPER
QB155	CREPUSCULE **SEE** TWILIGHT / astronomy
QC976.T9	CREPUSCULE **SEE** TWILIGHT / meteorological optics
TP248.C67	CRESOL / chemical technology
QD341.P5	CRESOL / chemistry
CR55-57	CRESTS
QE685-8	CRETACEOUS PERIOD **SEE** GEOLOGY, STRATIGRAPHIC — CRETACEOUS
QE924	CRETACEOUS PERIOD **SEE** PALEOBOTANY — CRETACEOUS
QE734	CRETACEOUS PERIOD **SEE** PALEONTOLOGY — CRETACEOUS
DF261.C8	CRETE — HISTORY / ancient
DF901.C78-89	CRETE — HISTORY / modern
RC657	CRETINISM
N8180	CRIB IN CHRISTIAN ART AND TRADITION / art
GV1295.C9	CRIBBAGE
QM505	CRIBRIFORM PLATE
TC197	CRIBWORK
F2519-2520. .1.C	CRICHANA INDIANS
GV927	CRICKET GROUNDS
GV911-925	CRICKET
GV911-925	CRICKET-ENGLAND **SEE** CRICKET
GV911-925	CRICKET-GT. BRIT. **SEE** CRICKET
QL508.G8	CRICKETS
GT3450	CRIES
HV6163	CRIME AND AGE
HV5053-5	CRIME AND ALCOHOLISM **SEE** ALCOHOLISM AND CRIME
HV6245-8	CRIME AND CRIMINALS — BIOGRAPHY
HV6945	CRIME AND CRIMINALS — BIOGRAPHY / gt. brit.
HV6785	CRIME AND CRIMINALS — BIOGRAPHY / u.s.
HV6065-6079	CRIME AND CRIMINALS — IDENTIFICATION
M1977.C7	CRIME AND CRIMINALS — SONGS AND MUSIC
M1978.C7	CRIME AND CRIMINALS — SONGS AND MUSIC
HV6001-9920	CRIME AND CRIMINALS
GT6550-6715	CRIME AND CRIMINALS / manners and customs
PE3726	CRIME AND CRIMINALS-LANGUAGE **SEE** CANT / english
HV6166	CRIME AND EDUCATION **SEE** EDUCATION AND CRIME
HV8741-2	CRIME AND INSANITY **SEE** INSANE, CRIMINAL AND DANGEROUS / prisons
HV6133	CRIME AND INSANITY **SEE** INSANE, CRIMINAL AND DANGEROUS / insanity and crime
HV6189	CRIME AND WAR **SEE** WAR AND CRIME
K	CRIME D'AMOUR **SEE** CRIME PASSIONNEL
HV6053	CRIME D'AMOUR **SEE** CRIME PASSIONNEL
HV8073	CRIME DETECTION **SEE** CRIMINAL INVESTIGATION
HV6249	CRIME IN LITERATURE
HV6053	CRIME OF PASSION **SEE** CRIME PASSIONNEL
K	CRIME OF PASSION **SEE** CRIME PASSIONNEL
HV6053	CRIME PASSIONNEL
K	CRIME PASSIONNEL
TR830	CRIME PHOTOGRAPHY **SEE** PHOTOGRAPHY, LEGAL
HV6071	CRIME PHOTOGRAPHY **SEE** PHOTOGRAPHY, LEGAL / social pathology
HV8077	CRIME PHOTOGRAPHY **SEE** PHOTOGRAPHY, LEGAL / social pathology
DK214-215	CRIMEAN WAR, 1853-1856 / russia
DR567	CRIMEAN WAR, 1853-1856 / turkey
VB850-880	CRIMES, NAVAL **SEE** NAVAL OFFENSES
K	CRIMES, NAVAL **SEE** NAVAL OFFENSES
HV6254-6321	CRIMES, POLITICAL **SEE** POLITICAL CRIMES AND OFFENSES
HV6001-6197	CRIMINAL ANTHROPOLOGY
GN51-59	CRIMINAL ANTHROPOMETRY **SEE** ANTHROPOMETRY
GV435	CRIMINAL ANTHROPOMETRY **SEE** ANTHROPOMETRY
HV6068	CRIMINAL ANTHROPOMETRY **SEE** BERTILLON SYSTEM
HV6001-6197	CRIMINAL ANTHROPOMETRY **SEE** CRIMINAL ANTHROPOLOGY
HV6558-6569	CRIMINAL ASSAULT **SEE** RAPE
HV6133	CRIMINAL INSANE **SEE** INSANE, CRIMINAL AND DANGEROUS / insanity and crime
HV8741-2	CRIMINAL INSANE **SEE** INSANE, CRIMINAL AND DANGEROUS / prisons
HV8073	CRIMINAL INVESTIGATION
HV6080-6113	CRIMINAL PSYCHOLOGY
HV6208	CRIMINAL STATISTICS / criminal classes
HV7245-7400	CRIMINAL STATISTICS / documents
HV7415	CRIMINAL STATISTICS / monographs
HV6001-9920	CRIMINALS **SEE** CRIME AND CRIMINALS
GT6550-6715	CRIMINALS **SEE** CRIME AND CRIMINALS / manners and customs
HV6001-9920	CRIMINOLOGY **SEE** CRIME AND CRIMINALS
GT6550-6715	CRIMINOLOGY **SEE** CRIME AND CRIMINALS / manners and customs
QL384.C8	CRINOIDEA
QE782	CRINOIDEA, FOSSIL
GT2075	CRINOLINE
TP986.P	CRINOTHENE **SEE** POLYETHYLENE
SF293.C	CRIOLLO HORSE
HD5325	CRIPPLE CREEK STRIKE, 1893
HD5325. M8 1903.	CRIPPLE CREEK STRIKE, 1903-1904
UB360-366	CRIPPLES, WAR **SEE** VETERANS, DISABLED
PM986-9	CRIS LANGUAGE **SEE** CREE LANGUAGE
RB153	CRISES AND CRITICAL DAYS (PATHOLOGY)
HB3711-3840	CRISES, COMMERCIAL **SEE** DEPRESSIONS
BT78	CRISIS THEOLOGY **SEE** DIALECTICAL THEOLOGY
QC307	CRITICAL POINT
B809.3	CRITICISM (PHILOSOPHY)
BH39-41	CRITICISM / aesthetics
PN75-99	CRITICISM / literary criticism
P47	CRITICISM, TEXTUAL
PA47	CRITICISM, TEXTUAL
E99.C91	CROATAN INDIANS
DB378	CROATIA-SLAVONIA — HISTORY — — UPRISING OF 1573
DB378	CROATIA-HISTORY-UPRISING OF 1573 **SEE** CROATIA-SLAVONIA — HISTORY — — UPRISING OF 1573
PG1464	CROATIAN BALLADS AND SONGS
PG1615	CROATIAN DRAMA / collections
PG1611	CROATIAN DRAMA / history
PG1616	CROATIAN FICTION / collections
PG1612	CROATIAN FICTION / history
PG1224-1399	CROATIAN LANGUAGE **SEE** SERBO-CROATIAN LANGUAGE
PG1600-1798	CROATIAN LITERATURE
PG1614	CROATIAN POETRY / collections
PG1610	CROATIAN POETRY / history

PG1616	CROATIAN PROSE LITERATURE / *collections*
PG1612	CROATIAN PROSE LITERATURE / *history*
DB33-34	*CROATIANS* **SEE** CROATS / *austria*
DB361-379	*CROATIANS* **SEE** CROATS / *croatia*
DR364-7	*CROATIANS* **SEE** CROATS / *yugoslavia*
DB33-34	CROATS / *austria*
DB361-379	CROATS / *croatia*
DR364-7	CROATS / *yugoslavia*
TT685	CROCHETING MACHINES
TT820-825	CROCHETING
NK3700-4695	*CROCKERY* **SEE** POTTERY / *ceramics*
TP785-825	*CROCKERY* **SEE** POTTERY / *chemical technology*
HD9610-9620	*CROCKERY* **SEE** POTTERY / *trade*
QL666.C9	CROCODILES
QE862.C8	CROCODILES, FOSSIL
HD1511.G66	CROFTERS
UB435.F	CROIX DE GUERRE (FRANCE)
GN790-792	CROMLECHS
E241.C94	CROOKED BILLET, BATTLE OF THE, 1778
HG9968.C6-8	*CROP INSURANCE* **SEE** INSURANCE, AGRICULTURAL — CROPS
S603	*CROP ROTATION* **SEE** ROTATION OF CROPS
S439	CROP ZONES
SB183-317	*CROPS* **SEE** FIELD CROPS
SB	*CROPS* **SEE** PLANTS, CULTIVATED
GT5897-9	*CROPS* **SEE** PLANTS, CULTIVATED / *manners and customs*
S600	CROPS AND CLIMATE
S603	*CROPS, ROTATION OF* **SEE** ROTATION OF CROPS
GV931-5	CROQUET
BV168.S7	*CROSIER* **SEE** STAFF, PASTORAL
BT465	*CROSS* **SEE** HOLY CROSS
TH6523	CROSS-CONNECTIONS (PLUMBING)
GV1061-9	*CROSS-COUNTRY RUNNING* **SEE** RUNNING
TK2699	*CROSS-FIELD GENERATORS* **SEE** ROTATING AMPLIFIERS
TT771	CROSS-STITCH
GV1507.C7	*CROSS-WORD PUZZLES* **SEE** CROSSWORD PUZZLES
BV197.S5	CROSS, SIGN OF THE
BX2048.S5	CROSS, SIGN OF THE / *catholic church*
QL696.P2	CROSSBILLS
U878	CROSSBOW
BX2310.C7	CROSSES — CULTUS
CR41.C7	CROSSES (IN HERALDRY)
CC300-350	CROSSES / *antiquities*
BV160	CROSSES / *christian art and symbolism*
BL640.C7	CROSSES / *comparative religion*
BT465	CROSSES / *etc.*
BT453	CROSSES / *theology*
TF263	*CROSSINGS, RAILROAD* **SEE** RAILROADS — CROSSINGS
HE1617-1619	*CROSSINGS, RAILROAD* **SEE** RAILROADS — CROSSINGS / *economics*
GV1507.C7	CROSSWORD PUZZLES
QL666.O6	*CROTALINAE* **SEE** PIT-VIPERS
RS163.C	CROTALUS (MATERIA MEDICA)
RX615.C	CROTALUS (MATERIA MEDICA) / *homeopathy*
QL666.O6	*CROTALUS* **SEE** RATTLESNAKES
QP941	CROTIN
RM666.C9	CROTON TIGLIUM
RM666.B9	*CROTON-CHLORAL* **SEE** BUTYL-CHLORAL
QD305.A2	CROTONIC ACID
RC746	CROUP
E99.C92	CROW INDIANS
ML1015-1018	CROWD (MUSICAL INSTRUMENT)
HM281-3	CROWDS
CJ2485	CROWN (COIN) / *silver*
NK7400-7419	CROWN JEWELS
CR5511	*CROWN OF ITALY, ORDER OF THE* **SEE** ORDER OF THE CROWN OF ITALY
E199	CROWN POINT EXPEDITION, 1755
SB741.C9	CROWN-GALL DISEASE
CR4480	CROWNS
QL696.P2	CROWS
BV168.S7	*CROZIER* **SEE** STAFF, PASTORAL
TP159.C	CRUCIBLES
TN677	CRUCIBLES
QD54.C	CRUCIBLES
BT450-455	*CRUCIFIXION OF CHRIST* **SEE** JESUS CHRIST — CRUCIFIXION

HV8569	CRUCIFIXION
TL673.C7	*CRUCIFORM WINGS (AEROPLANES)* **SEE** AEROPLANES — WINGS, CRUCIFORM
BJ1535.C	CRUELTY
D168	CRUSADES — EIGHTH, 1270
D165	CRUSADES — FIFTH, 1218-1221
D161	CRUSADES — FIRST, 1096-1099
D164	CRUSADES — FOURTH, 1202-1204
D157-160	CRUSADES — INFLUENCE
D158	CRUSADES — JUVENILE LITERATURE
D171-2	CRUSADES — LATER, 13TH, 14TH, AND 15TH CENTURIES
D162	CRUSADES — SECOND, 1147-1149
D167	CRUSADES — SEVENTH, 1248-1250
D166	CRUSADES — SIXTH, 1228-1229
D163	CRUSADES — THIRD, 1189-1192
D151-173	CRUSADES
TE235-9	*CRUSHED STONE* **SEE** STONE, CRUSHED / *road material*
TJ1345	CRUSHING MACHINERY
QL445	CRUSTACEA — ANATOMY
SH175	CRUSTACEA — DISEASES AND PESTS
QL445	CRUSTACEA — PHYSIOLOGY
QL435-445	CRUSTACEA
QE816-817	CRUSTACEA, FOSSIL
RD756	*CRUTCH WALKING* **SEE** CRUTCHES
RD756	CRUTCHES
ML1015-1018	*CRWTH* **SEE** CROWD (MUSICAL INSTRUMENT)
HQ748.C	CRYING
QC278	*CRYOGENICS* **SEE** LOW TEMPERATURE RESEARCH
QD515	*CRYOGENICS* **SEE** LOW TEMPERATURES / *chemistry*
QC278	*CRYOGENICS* **SEE** LOW TEMPERATURES / *physics*
TP490-497	*CRYOGENICS* **SEE** REFRIGERATION AND REFRIGERATING MACHINERY
TN948.C	CRYOLITE
QC303	CRYOPHORUS
QD545	CRYOSCOPY
QC278	CRYOSTAT
RM863	*CRYOTHERAPY* **SEE** COLD — THERAPEUTIC USE
Z103-4	*CRYPTANALYSIS* **SEE** CRYPTOGRAPHY
QH331	CRYPTOBIOSIS
RC186.T7	*CRYPTOCOCCOSIS* **SEE** TORULOSIS
QK505-635	CRYPTOGAMS
QK520-532	*CRYPTOGAMS, VASCULAR* **SEE** PTERIDOPHYTA
Z103-4	CRYPTOGRAPHY
Z103-4	*CRYPTOLOGY* **SEE** CRYPTOGRAPHY
RC898	*CRYPTORCHIS* **SEE** TESTICLE — ABNORMITIES AND DEFORMITIES
NA2880	CRYPTS / *architecture*
TH2150-2160	CRYPTS / *building*
QL696.T4	*CRYPTURI* **SEE** TINAMIFORMES
QD921	*CRYSTAL GROWTH* **SEE** CRYSTALS — GROWTH
QD941	CRYSTAL OPTICS
BF1331	CRYSTAL-GAZING
BF1331	*CRYSTAL-VISION* **SEE** CRYSTAL-GAZING
QE475	*CRYSTALLINE AND METAMORPHIC ROCKS* **SEE** ROCKS, CRYSTALLINE AND METAMORPHIC
QL949	CRYSTALLINE LENS / *comparative anatomy*
RE401-461	CRYSTALLINE LENS / *diseases*
QM511	CRYSTALLINE LENS / *human anatomy*
QD901-999	CRYSTALLIZATION
QD548	CRYSTALLIZATION / *supersaturated solutions*
QD951	CRYSTALLIZATION, WATER OF
QD903.5-6	CRYSTALLOGRAPHERS
QD904	CRYSTALLOGRAPHY — EARLY WORKS TO 1800
QD901-999	CRYSTALLOGRAPHY
QD911-915	CRYSTALLOGRAPHY, MATHEMATICAL
QK899	CRYSTALLOIDS (BOTANY)
QD911-915	*CRYSTALLOMETRY* **SEE** CRYSTALLOGRAPHY, MATHEMATICAL
QD921	CRYSTALS — GROWTH
QD945	*CRYSTALS, DISLOCATIONS IN* **SEE** DISLOCATIONS IN CRYSTALS
QD921	*CRYSTALS, LIQUID* **SEE** LIQUID CRYSTALS
QD941	*CRYSTALS-OPTICAL PROPERTIES* **SEE** CRYSTAL OPTICS
TF639	*CTC SYSTEM (RAILROADS)* **SEE** RAILROADS — SIGNALING — — CENTRALIZED TRAFFIC CONTROL
QL377.C8	CTENOPHORA (COELENTERATA)

QL398.C8	CTENOSTOMATA
D568.5	CTESIPHON, BATTLE OF, 1915.
GV1796.C	CUANDO (DANCE)
PL8417	*CUANHAMA LANGUAGE* **SEE** KUANYAMA LANGUAGE
F1751-1849	CUBA — HISTORY
PQ7386.D7	CUBAN DRAMA / *collections*
PQ7381	CUBAN DRAMA / *history*
PQ7386.E	CUBAN ESSAYS / *collections*
PQ7382	CUBAN ESSAYS / *history*
PQ7386.F	CUBAN FICTION / *collections*
PQ7382	CUBAN FICTION / *history*
PQ7383	CUBAN LITERATURE — 20TH CENTURY / *collections*
PQ7378	CUBAN LITERATURE — 20TH CENTURY / *history*
PQ7370-7389	CUBAN LITERATURE
PN4931-9	CUBAN NEWSPAPERS / *etc.*
PQ7386.O	CUBAN ORATIONS / *collections*
PQ7382	CUBAN ORATIONS / *history*
PN4931-4940	CUBAN PERIODICALS / *etc.*
PQ7384	CUBAN POETRY — 20TH CENTURY / *collections*
PQ7380	CUBAN POETRY — 20TH CENTURY / *history*
PQ7384	CUBAN POETRY / *collections*
PQ7380	CUBAN POETRY / *history*
PQ7386.P7	CUBAN PROSE LITERATURE / *collections*
PQ7382	CUBAN PROSE LITERATURE / *history*
F1783-5	CUBAN QUESTION-TO 1895
F1786	CUBAN QUESTION 1895-1898
E721	CUBAN QUESTION 1895-1898 / *u.s. political history*
PN6222.C8	CUBAN WIT AND HUMOR
QA119	CUBE ROOT
QA49	CUBE ROOT / *tables*
QA469	CUBE, DUPLICATION OF
RS165.C9	CUBEBS
QA215	*CUBIC EQUATIONS* **SEE** EQUATIONS, CUBIC
QA465	*CUBIC MEASUREMENT* **SEE** VOLUME (MATHEMATICS) / *mathematics*
QC104	*CUBIC MEASUREMENT* **SEE** VOLUME (MATHEMATICS) / *weights and measures*
TN911	*CUBIC SALTPETER* **SEE** SALTPETER, CHILE
QA573	*CUBIC SURFACES* **SEE** SURFACES, CUBIC
ND1265	CUBISM
E99.Y94	*CUCHAN INDIANS* **SEE** YUMA INDIANS
HV8626	CUCKING STOOL
QL696.C5	CUCKOOS
QL696.C5	*CUCULIDAE* **SEE** CUCKOOS
SB337	CUCUMBERS
GV1796.C	CUECA (DANCE)
PM3731	CUICATEC LANGUAGE
F1219	*CUITLATECOS* **SEE** TECO INDIANS
BR747	CULDEES
DA814.5	CULLODEN, BATTLE OF, 1746
BL600	CULT
PQ6066	*CULTERANISMO* **SEE** GONGORISM
PQ6066	*CULTISM* **SEE** GONGORISM
SB	*CULTIVATED PLANTS* **SEE** PLANTS, CULTIVATED
GT5897-9	*CULTIVATED PLANTS* **SEE** PLANTS, CULTIVATED / *manners and customs*
S603	*CULTIVATION OF SOILS* **SEE** TILLAGE
HD1519	*CULTIVATION OF VACANT LOTS* **SEE** WORKING-MEN'S GARDENS
TJ1482	CULTIVATORS / *mechanical engineering and machinery*
GN	*CULTURAL ANTHROPOLOGY* **SEE** ETHNOLOGY
HM101	*CULTURAL CHANGE* **SEE** SOCIAL CHANGE
HM101	*CULTURAL EVOLUTION* **SEE** SOCIAL CHANGE
HM101	CULTURAL LAG
BF740	CULTURE CONFLICT
HM101	*CULTURE LAG* **SEE** CULTURAL LAG
CB	CULTURE
GN400-406	CULTURE / *primitive*
HM101	CULTURE / *sociology*
BL550-620	CULTUS
BL2443	CULTUS, ALEXANDRIAN
HQ1031	*CULTUS, DISPARITY OF* **SEE** MARRIAGE, MIXED
DF122	CULTUS, GREEK
BM	CULTUS, JEWISH
DG123-4	CULTUS, ROMAN / *history*
BL800-820	CULTUS, ROMAN / *religion*
DS72	*CULTUS, SUMERIAN* **SEE** SUMERIANS
TE213	CULVERTS
TF282	CULVERTS
QL444.C9	CUMACEA
PL318	*CUMAN LANGUAGE* **SEE** KIPCHAK LANGUAGE
F2319	CUMANA INDIANS
PM5876	CUMANA LANGUAGE
F2319	*CUMANAGOTO INDIANS* **SEE** CUMANA INDIANS
QD341.A2	*CUMARINS* **SEE** COUMARINS
RC121.A6	*CUMBERLAND DISEASE* **SEE** ANTHRAX
QR201.A6	*CUMBERLAND DISEASE* **SEE** ANTHRAX / *bacteriology*
E473.52	CUMBERLAND GAP, BATTLE OF, 1862
QD305.A4	CUMENOL
QD341.P5	CUMOL
F1565.2.C8	CUNA INDIANS
PM3743	CUNA LANGUAGE
PL8421	*CUNAMA LANGUAGE* **SEE** KUNAMA LANGUAGE
DT393.5	*CUNAMAS* **SEE** KUNAMAS
RS165.C67	CUNDURANGO
PJ	CUNEIFORM INSCRIPTIONS
CN	CUNEIFORM INSCRIPTIONS
PK	CUNEIFORM INSCRIPTIONS
P943	CUNEIFORM INSCRIPTIONS, ELAMITE
PK6128	*CUNEIFORM INSCRIPTIONS, PERSIAN* **SEE** OLD PERSIAN INSCRIPTIONS
PJ4051-4075	CUNEIFORM INSCRIPTIONS, SUMERIAN
P959	CUNEIFORM INSCRIPTIONS, VANNIC
PJ3191-3225	CUNEIFORM WRITING
PM5521	*CUNZA LANGUAGE* **SEE** ATACAMENIAN LANGUAGE
QK623.D6	*CUP FUNGI* **SEE** DISCOMYCETES
NK5440.C8	CUP PLATES / *glassware*
NK2725	CUPBOARDS / *art*
TT197	CUPBOARDS / *cabinet-making*
N7760	CUPID — ART
BL820.C	CUPID
F3430.1.C8	CUPISNIQUE INDIANS
TS231	CUPOLA-FURNACES
NA2890	*CUPOLAS* **SEE** DOMES / *architecture*
TH2170	*CUPOLAS* **SEE** DOMES / *building*
RM184	CUPPING
TS1688	*CUPRAMMONIUM SILK* **SEE** RAYON
QD181.C9	CUPROUS CHLORIDE
TP822	*CUPS AND SAUCERS* **SEE** PORCELAIN
NK4370-4584	*CUPS AND SAUCERS* **SEE** PORCELAIN
NK3700-4695	*CUPS AND SAUCERS* **SEE** POTTERY / *ceramics*
TP785-825	*CUPS AND SAUCERS* **SEE** POTTERY / *chemical technology*
HD9610-9620	*CUPS AND SAUCERS* **SEE** POTTERY / *trade*
QP921.C8	*CURARA* **SEE** CURARE / *pharmacology*
RM666.C94	*CURARA* **SEE** CURARE / *therapeutics*
QP921.C8	CURARE / *pharmacology*
RM666.C94	CURARE / *therapeutics*
QP921.C8	*CURARI* **SEE** CURARE / *pharmacology*
RM666.C94	*CURARI* **SEE** CURARE / *therapeutics*
SF309	CURB-BIT
BV4012.2	*CURE OF SOULS* **SEE** PASTORAL COUNSELING
BV4000-4396	*CURE OF SOULS* **SEE** PASTORAL THEOLOGY
BL820.C7	CURETES
RG109.C8	CURETTE
AG241-3	CURIOSITIES
BF323.C8	CURIOSITY
QD181.C55	CURIUM
SB608.G6	CURLEW BUG
QL696.L7	CURLEWS
GV845	CURLING
SB608.B4	CURLY-TOP / *beet diseases*
SB399	CURRANT GRAPES
SB386.C9	CURRANTS
HG201-1490	*CURRENCY* **SEE** MONEY
GN436.2	*CURRENCY* **SEE** MONEY / *primitive*
HG534	CURRENCY ACT OF MARCH 14, 1900 / *speeches in congress*
HG651-1490	*CURRENCY DEVALUATION* **SEE** CURRENCY QUESTION / *other countries*
HG501-538	*CURRENCY DEVALUATION* **SEE** CURRENCY QUESTION / *u.s.*
HG651-1490	CURRENCY QUESTION / *other countries*
HG501-538	CURRENCY QUESTION / *u.s.*

TK1141-1168	*CURRENTS, ALTERNATING* **SEE** ELECTRIC CURRENTS, ALTERNATING / *engineering*
QC641	*CURRENTS, ALTERNATING* **SEE** ELECTRIC CURRENTS, ALTERNATING / *theory*
QC601-641	*CURRENTS, ELECTRIC* **SEE** ELECTRIC CURRENTS
GC231-296	*CURRENTS, OCEANIC* **SEE** OCEAN CURRENTS
LB1628-9	*CURRICULA (COURSES OF STUDY)* **SEE** EDUCATION — CURRICULA / *secondary schools*
LB2361-5	*CURRICULA (COURSES OF STUDY)* **SEE** EDUCATION — CURRICULA / *colleges and universities*
LB1570-1571	*CURRICULA (COURSES OF STUDY)* **SEE** EDUCATION — CURRICULA / *elementary schools*
DR516	*CURSOLARI, BATTLE OF, 1571* **SEE** LEPANTO, BATTLE OF, 1571
TH2231	CURTAIN WALLS
TT390	*CURTAINS* **SEE** DRAPERY
NK3195	*CURTAINS* **SEE** DRAPERY / *upholstery*
HF5849.D6	*CURTAINS* **SEE** DRAPERY / *window displays*
ML953	*CURTALL* **SEE** BASSOON / *history*
F2687	CURUPAITY, BATTLE OF, 1866
QL821	*CURVE, LUMBAR* **SEE** LUMBAR CURVE / *comparative anatomy*
QM111	*CURVE, LUMBAR* **SEE** LUMBAR CURVE / *human anatomy*
QA571-3	*CURVED SURFACES* **SEE** SURFACES / *analytic geometry*
QA641-9	*CURVED SURFACES* **SEE** SURFACES / *differential geometry*
QA631-8	*CURVED SURFACES* **SEE** SURFACES / *infinitesimal geometry*
QA626	CURVES — RECTIFICATION AND QUADRATURE
TF216-217	CURVES IN ENGINEERING / *railroads*
TE153	CURVES IN ENGINEERING / *roads*
QA581	CURVES OF DOUBLE CURVATURE
QA643	CURVES ON SURFACES
QA581	*CURVES, KNOTTED* **SEE** CURVES OF DOUBLE CURVATURE
QA567	CURVES, ORTHOGONAL
QA565-7	CURVES, QUARTIC
QA565-7	CURVES, QUINTIC
QA628	CURVES, TRANSCENDENTAL
GN545	CUSHITES
PJ2401-2413	CUSHITIC LANGUAGES
DC309.C8	CUSSEY, BATTLE OF, 1870
TX339	*CUSTODIAN-ENGINEERS* **SEE** JANITORS
TX339	*CUSTODIANS* **SEE** JANITORS
HJ6603-7380	*CUSTOM-HOUSE* **SEE** CUSTOMS ADMINISTRATION
BX1939.C85	CUSTOMARY LAW (CANON LAW)
HJ6603-7380	*CUSTOMS (TARIFF)* **SEE** TARIFF / *administration*
HF1761-2580	*CUSTOMS (TARIFF)* **SEE** TARIFF / *other countries*
HJ6041-6464	*CUSTOMS (TARIFF)* **SEE** TARIFF / *schedules*
HF1701-2701	*CUSTOMS (TARIFF)* **SEE** TARIFF / *theory and history*
HF1750-1759	*CUSTOMS (TARIFF)* **SEE** TARIFF / *u.s.*
HF1761-2580	CUSTOMS ADMINISTRATION
HJ6603-7380	*CUSTOMS DUTIES* **SEE** TARIFF / *administration*
HF1761-2580	*CUSTOMS DUTIES* **SEE** TARIFF / *other countries*
HJ6041-6464	*CUSTOMS DUTIES* **SEE** TARIFF / *schedules*
HF1701-2701	*CUSTOMS DUTIES* **SEE** TARIFF / *theory and history*
HF1750-1759	*CUSTOMS DUTIES* **SEE** TARIFF / *u.s.*
HJ9120	*CUSTOMS DUTIES, INTERNAL* **SEE** OCTROI
HF1713	CUSTOMS UNIONS
E59.S	*CUSTOMS, SOCIAL* **SEE** INDIANS — SOCIAL LIFE AND CUSTOMS
DS112-113	*CUSTOMS, SOCIAL* **SEE** JEWS — SOCIAL LIFE AND CUSTOMS
GT	*CUSTOMS, SOCIAL* **SEE** MANNERS AND CUSTOMS
DG553.5.C8	CUSTOZZA, BATTLE OF, 1848
DG558	CUSTOZZA, BATTLE OF, 1866
TP861	CUT GLASS
TK2846	*CUT-OUTS, ELECTRIC* **SEE** ELECTRIC CUT-OUTS
RL	*CUTANEOUS DISEASES* **SEE** SKIN — DISEASES
QM491	CUTANEOUS GLANDS
QL943	CUTANEOUS GLANDS
QP221	CUTANEOUS GLANDS
RL427	*CUTANEOUS HORNS* **SEE** HORNS, CUTANEOUS
SB615.Q3	*CUTCH-GRASS* **SEE** QUITCH-GRASS
GN191-9	*CUTIS* **SEE** SKIN / *anthropology*
QL941	*CUTIS* **SEE** SKIN / *comparative anatomy*
QM481-4	*CUTIS* **SEE** SKIN / *human anatomy*
HD6461.C9	CUTLERS / *england*
TS380	CUTLERY
Z696	*CUTTER CLASSIFICATION* **SEE** CLASSIFICATION, EXPANSIVE
TT500-560	*CUTTING* **SEE** DRESSMAKING
HD9942	*CUTTING* **SEE** DRESSMAKING / *economics*
TT500-678	*CUTTING* **SEE** GARMENT CUTTING
TT570-630	*CUTTING* **SEE** TAILORING
TJ1230	CUTTING MACHINES
TJ1215-1240	*CUTTING OF METALS* **SEE** METAL-CUTTING / *machine-tools*
Z697.C6	*CUTTINGS* **SEE** CLIPPINGS (BOOKS, NEWSPAPERS, ETC.)
Z691	*CUTTINGS* **SEE** CLIPPINGS (BOOKS, NEWSPAPERS, ETC.)
SB945.C92	CUTWORMS
QD305.E7	CYANACETIC ETHER
S651	CYANAMID
TN767	CYANIDE PROCESS
RA1242.H9	CYANIDES — TOXICOLOGY
QD181.C15	CYANIDES / *chemistry*
TP248.C9	CYANIDES / *manufacture*
TN948.C95	CYANITE
QL696.P2	*CYANOCITTA* **SEE** JAYS
QD181.C15	CYANOGEN COMPOUNDS
RC669	CYANOSIS
TR415	*CYANOTYPE* **SEE** BLUE-PRINTING
TR921	*CYANOTYPE* **SEE** BLUE-PRINTING / *industrial reproduction*
QE973	CYCADOFILICES
SB945.M65	CYCLAMEN MITE
QK495.C	CYCLAMEN / *botany*
SB413.C	CYCLAMEN / *culture*
TL399	CYCLE-CARS
TL440-445	*CYCLES, MOTOR* **SEE** MOTORCYCLES
QA603	CYCLIDE
GV1041-1059	CYCLING
GV1041-1059	CYCLISTS
QA623	CYCLODES
QA623	CYCLOIDS
QD400-409	*CYCLOIDS, MIXED (CHEMISTRY)* **SEE** HETEROCYCLIC COMPOUNDS
TJ1540	*CYCLONES (CHEMICAL TECHNOLOGY)* **SEE** SEPARATORS (MACHINES) / *screening*
TN515	*CYCLONES (CHEMICAL TECHNOLOGY)* **SEE** SEPARATORS (MACHINES) / *mining*
SF247	*CYCLONES (CHEMICAL TECHNOLOGY)* **SEE** SEPARATORS (MACHINES) / *dairy machinery*
SF247	*CYCLONES (MACHINES)* **SEE** SEPARATORS (MACHINES) / *dairy machinery*
TN515	*CYCLONES (MACHINES)* **SEE** SEPARATORS (MACHINES) / *mining*
TJ1540	*CYCLONES (MACHINES)* **SEE** SEPARATORS (MACHINES) / *screening*
QC941-951	CYCLONES
QC951	CYCLONOMETER
GN791-2	*CYCLOPEAN REMAINS* **SEE** MEGALITHIC MONUMENTS
AE	*CYCLOPEDIAS* **SEE** ENCYCLOPEDIAS AND DICTIONARIES
AG	*CYCLOPEDIAS* **SEE** ENCYCLOPEDIAS AND DICTIONARIES
QM691	*CYCLOPIA* **SEE** EYE — ABNORMITIES AND DEFORMITIES
ND2880	CYCLORAMAS
QA245	CYCLOTOMY
QC544	CYCLOTRON
QA491	CYLINDER (MATHEMATICS)
QB214	CYLINDER (TIMEPIECE)
CD5344	CYLINDER SEALS
TL702.C9	CYLINDERS / *aircraft engines*
TL210	CYLINDERS / *automobile motors*
TP243	CYLINDERS / *compressed gases*
TA492.C9	CYLINDERS / *strength and testing*
QA408	*CYLINDRICAL HARMONICS* **SEE** BESSEL'S FUNCTIONS
CD5344	*CYLINDRICAL SEALS* **SEE** CYLINDER SEALS
TH2416	*CYLINDRICAL SHELL ROOFS* **SEE** ROOFS, SHELL
QA841	CYLINDROID
ML1015-1018	*CYMBALOM* **SEE** CIMBALOM

ML1040	CYMBALS
QD341.H9	CYMENE
DA700-730	*CYMRI* **SEE** WELSH
PB2101-2199	*CYMRIC LANGUAGE* **SEE** WELSH LANGUAGE
DA700-730	*CYMRY* **SEE** WELSH
RC746	*CYNANCHE TRACHEALIS* **SEE** CROUP
B508	CYNICISM
QL568.C9	*CYNIPIDAE* **SEE** GALL-FLIES
SF459	*CYNTHIA SILK MOTH* **SEE** AILANTHUS MOTH / sericulture
QL561.S2	*CYNTHIA SILK MOTH* **SEE** AILANTHUS MOTH / zoology
QP801.C9	CYNURENIC ACID / physiological chemistry
QK495.C97	CYPRESS / botany
TA419	CYPRESS / building materials
SD397.C9	CYPRESS / forestry
SB608.C9	CYPRESS / plant pathology
BL444	CYPRESS / religion
DR515-516	CYPRIAN WAR, 1570-1571
QL638.C95	CYPRINODONTES
PA567.S3	CYPRIOTE SYLLABARY
QL696.C9	*CYPSELIDAE* **SEE** SWIFTS
PG92	CYRILLIC ALPHABET
QK569.R4	CYSTOCARP
RC920	*CYSTOSCOPY* **SEE** BLADDER — EXPLORATION
RD581	*CYSTOTOMY* **SEE** BLADDER — SURGERY
RD676-7	CYSTS
QD421	CYTISINE / chemistry
QP921.C	CYTISINE / physiological effect
QH605	*CYTOKINESIS* **SEE** KARYOKINESIS
RB25	*CYTOPATHOLOGY* **SEE** PATHOLOGY, CELLULAR
QH591	*CYTOPLASM* **SEE** PROTOPLASM
M240-242	CZAKAN AND PIANO MUSIC
M1248	CZARDAS (BAND)
M1264	CZARDAS (BAND)
M1060	CZARDAS (ORCHESTRA) — SCORES
M1048	CZARDAS (ORCHESTRA) — SCORES
M1048	CZARDAS (ORCHESTRA)
M1060	CZARDAS (ORCHESTRA)
PG5008	CZECH BALLADS AND SONGS
PG5025	CZECH BALLADS AND SONGS
PG5015	CZECH BALLADS AND SONGS
PG5029	CZECH FICTION / collections
PG5011	CZECH FICTION / history
PG4771	CZECH LANGUAGE
PG5000-5198	CZECH LITERATURE
PN5168	CZECH NEWSPAPERS / etc.
PN5168	CZECH PERIODICALS / etc.
PG4001-4771	CZECH PHILOLOGY
PT3836	*CZECH POETRY (GERMAN)* **SEE** GERMAN POETRY — CZECH AUTHORS
PG5025	CZECH POETRY / collections
PG5008	CZECH POETRY / history
PG5029	CZECH PROSE LITERATURE / collections
PG5010	CZECH PROSE LITERATURE / history
PG5050-5069	CZECH-AMERICAN LITERATURE
PN4885	CZECH-AMERICAN NEWSPAPERS
DB47-48	CZECHS
DB191-217	CZECHS
SF429.D25	DACHSHUND
HV6453.I6	DACOITS
GN192	*DACTYLOGRAPHY* **SEE** FINGERPRINTS / anthropology
HV6074	*DACTYLOGRAPHY* **SEE** FINGERPRINTS / criminology
HV2471-2500	*DACTYLOLOGY* **SEE** DEAF — MEANS OF COMMUNICATION
GN192	*DACTYLOSCOPY* **SEE** FINGERPRINTS / anthropology
HV6074	*DACTYLOSCOPY* **SEE** FINGERPRINTS / criminology
E83.835	DADE'S BATTLE, 1835
SB413.D12	DAFFODILS
PL4001.D2	DAFLA LANGUAGE
RC568.C2	*DAGGA* **SEE** HASHISH / intoxications
RS165.H3	*DAGGA* **SEE** HASHISH / materia medica
DT346.D	DAGGATUNS
NK6805	DAGGERS / art
PK9051	DAGHESTAN LITERATURE
PK9051	DAGHESTAN POETRY

DS416-419	*DAGOBAS* **SEE** TOPES (MONUMENTS) / antiquities
NA6001	*DAGOBAS* **SEE** TOPES (MONUMENTS) / architecture
TR365	DAGUERREOTYPE
PL431.D3	DAGUR LANGUAGE
E476.27	*DAHLGREN'S RAID* **SEE** KILPATRICK-DAHLGREN RAID, 1864
SB413.D13	DAHLIAS
PL431.D3	*DAHUR LANGUAGE* **SEE** DAGUR LANGUAGE
BV4810-4812	*DAILY READINGS (SPIRITUAL EXERCISES)* **SEE** DEVOTIONAL CALENDARS
BV1585	*DAILY VACATION BIBLE SCHOOLS* **SEE** VACATION SCHOOLS, RELIGIOUS
SF247	*DAIRIES* **SEE** DAIRY PLANTS
SF221-275	*DAIRIES* **SEE** DAIRYING
SF247	*DAIRY* **SEE** DAIRY PLANTS
SF221-275	*DAIRY* **SEE** DAIRYING
QR121	DAIRY BACTERIOLOGY
NA8230	DAIRY BARNS / architecture
TH4930	DAIRY BARNS / building
SF253	*DAIRY CHEMISTRY* **SEE** DAIRY PRODUCTS — ANALYSIS AND EXAMINATION
SF255	DAIRY INSPECTION
PN4784.A3	*DAIRY JOURNALISM* **SEE** JOURNALISM, AGRICULTURAL
HD9000.9	DAIRY LAWS
HD9275	DAIRY LAWS
SF247	DAIRY PLANTS
SF253	DAIRY PRODUCTS — ANALYSIS AND EXAMINATION
SF261	DAIRY PRODUCTS — MARKETING / dairy industry
HD9275	DAIRY PRODUCTS — MARKETING / economics
SF247	*DAIRY PRODUCTS PLANTS* **SEE** DAIRY PLANTS
HD9275	DAIRY PRODUCTS
SF253	*DAIRY PRODUCTS-COMPOSITION* **SEE** DAIRY PRODUCTS — ANALYSIS AND EXAMINATION
SF253	*DAIRY PRODUCTS-TESTING* **SEE** DAIRY PRODUCTS — ANALYSIS AND EXAMINATION
SF241-5	DAIRY SCHOOLS
SF261	DAIRYING — ACCOUNTING
SF247	DAIRYING — APPARATUS AND SUPPLIES
SF253	DAIRYING — LABORATORY MANUALS
SF240	DAIRYING — TABLES AND READY-RECKONERS
SF221-275	DAIRYING
HD9000.9	*DAIRYING-LAWS AND LEGISLATION* **SEE** DAIRY LAWS
HD9275	*DAIRYING-LAWS AND LEGISLATION* **SEE** DAIRY LAWS
SB413.D	DAISIES
PL5301-4	*DAJAK LANGUAGE* **SEE** DYAK LANGUAGE
DS685	DAJO, MOUNT, BATTLE OF, 1906
PK1975-1987	*DAKHINI HINDUSTANI* **SEE** URDU LANGUAGE
GT3350	*DAKHMAS* **SEE** DOKHMAS
HV6453.I6	*DAKOITS* **SEE** DACOITS
E83.86	DAKOTA INDIANS — WARS, 1862-1865
E83.876	DAKOTA INDIANS — WARS, 1876
E83.89	DAKOTA INDIANS — WARS, 1890-1891
E99.D1	DAKOTA INDIANS
PM1021-4	DAKOTA LANGUAGE
GV1011	*DAKYU* **SEE** POLO, JAPANESE
SF429.D3	DALMATIAN DOGS
PC890	DALMATIAN LANGUAGE (ROMANCE)
PG1224-1399	*DALMATIAN LANGUAGE (SLAVIC)* **SEE** SERBO-CROATIAN LANGUAGE
PG1640-1658	DALMATIAN LITERATURE / croatian
PG1654	DALMATIAN POETRY / collections
PG1650	DALMATIAN POETRY / history
PC890	*DALMATICO LANGUAGE* **SEE** DALMATIAN LANGUAGE (ROMANCE)
LB1029.L3	DALTON LABORATORY PLAN
LB1029.L3	*DALTON PLAN* **SEE** DALTON LABORATORY PLAN
V810	DAMAGE CONTROL (WARSHIPS)
DT709	*DAMARAS* **SEE** HEREROS
GN657.H	*DAMARAS* **SEE** HEREROS
DT709	*DAMARAS* **SEE** HILL DAMARAS
NK6676	*DAMASCENE WORK* **SEE** DAMASCENING
NK6676	DAMASCENING
DS99.D3	DAMASCUS — SIEGE, 633
GV1461-3	*DAMEN (GAME)* **SEE** CHECKERS
D165	DAMIETTA — SIEGE, 1218-1219
TA355	DAMPING (MECHANICS) / engineering
QA935	DAMPING (MECHANICS) / mathematics

JX4574	*DE FACTO DOCTRINE (INTERNATIONAL LAW)* **SEE** RECOGNITION (INTERNATIONAL LAW) / *belligerency*
JX4574	*DE FACTO GOVERNMENT* **SEE** RECOGNITION (INTERNATIONAL LAW) / *belligerency*
JX4044	*DE FACTO GOVERNMENT* **SEE** RECOGNITION (INTERNATIONAL LAW) / *sovereignty*
TL686.D4	*DE HAVILLAND COMET* **SEE** COMET (JET TRANSPORTS)
TL557.I3	*DE-ICING OF AEROPLANES* **SEE** AEROPLANES — ICE PREVENTION
PL3651.D2	*DE-JONG KE LANGUAGE* **SEE** DANJONG-KA LANGUAGE
BV4423-5	DEACONESSES
BV680	DEACONS
BX1912	DEACONS / *catholic church*
RA1055	DEAD — IDENTIFICATION
BL470	DEAD (IN RELIGION, FOLK-LORE, ETC.) / *comparative religion*
BL2443	DEAD (IN RELIGION, FOLK-LORE, ETC.) / *egyptian religion*
GR455	DEAD (IN RELIGION, FOLK-LORE, ETC.) / *folk-lore*
SF757	*DEAD ANIMALS, DISPOSAL OF* **SEE** DEAD ANIMALS, REMOVAL AND DISPOSAL OF
SF757	DEAD ANIMALS, REMOVAL AND DISPOSAL OF
RA619-640	DEAD / *disposition of*
GR455	DEAD / *folk-lore*
GT3150-3390	DEAD / *manners and customs*
BV814	*DEAD, BAPTISM FOR THE* **SEE** BAPTISM FOR THE DEAD
NB1420	*DEAD, LANTERNS OF THE* **SEE** LANTERNS OF THE DEAD
BL467	*DEAD, WORSHIP OF THE* **SEE** ANCESTOR-WORSHIP
BV194.C6	*DEAD-COMMEMORATION* **SEE** SAINTS — COMMEMORATION
BV4626-7	DEADLY SINS
HQ1040	DEAF — MARRIAGE
HV2471-2500	DEAF — MEANS OF COMMUNICATION
RF320	*DEAF AND DUMB* **SEE** DEAF
HV2350-2990	*DEAF AND DUMB* **SEE** DEAF / *charities*
PN171.D	DEAF AS AUTHORS
GR950.D	DEAF IN FOLK-LORE
RF320	*DEAF-MUTES* **SEE** DEAF
HV2350-2990	*DEAF-MUTES* **SEE** DEAF / *charities*
RF320	DEAF
HV2350-2990	DEAF / *charities*
Z1039.D4	DEAF, BOOKS FOR THE / *bibliography*
HV2471-2500	*DEAF-EDUCATION-SPEECH* **SEE** DEAF — MEANS OF COMMUNICATION
HV2471-2500	*DEAF-SIGN LANGUAGE* **SEE** DEAF — MEANS OF COMMUNICATION
RF290-310	DEAFNESS
RF300-310	*DEAFNESS, INSTRUMENTS FOR* **SEE** HEARING AIDS, MECHANICAL
BV4381	*DEANERIES (BUILDINGS)* **SEE** PARSONAGES
LC1567	DEANS (IN SCHOOLS) / *education of women*
LB2341	DEANS (IN SCHOOLS) / *higher education*
BX1939.R8	*DEANS, RURAL* **SEE** RURAL DEANS / *canon law*
BX1911	*DEANS, RURAL* **SEE** RURAL DEANS / *catholic church*
BX5179	*DEANS, RURAL* **SEE** RURAL DEANS / *church of england*
N8217.D5	DEATH — ART
RA1063	DEATH — CAUSES / *medical jurisprudence*
BT825	DEATH — MEDITATIONS
BX1939	DEATH — PROOF AND CERTIFICATION (CANON LAW)
RA405	DEATH — PROOF AND CERTIFICATION / *state medicine*
QH559	DEATH (BIOLOGY)
N8217.D5	*DEATH IN ART* **SEE** DEATH — ART
PN56.D	DEATH IN LITERATURE
PR149.D	DEATH IN LITERATURE / *english literature*
BV4907	*DEATH OF CHILDREN* **SEE** CHILDREN — DEATH AND FUTURE STATE
HV8694-9	*DEATH PENALTY* **SEE** CAPITAL PUNISHMENT
HB1321-1530	*DEATH RATE* **SEE** MORTALITY / *statistics*
HG8783-7	*DEATH RATE* **SEE** MORTALITY / *tables*
HB881-3700	*DEATH RATE* **SEE** VITAL STATISTICS
HJ5801-5819	*DEATH-DUTIES* **SEE** INHERITANCE AND TRANSFER TAX
NB1310	*DEATH-MASKS* **SEE** MASKS (SCULPTURE)
QH671	DEATH / *cytology*
GR455	DEATH / *folk-lore*
HG8896	DEATH / *in life insurance*
GT3150-3390	DEATH / *manners and customs*
RA1063	DEATH / *medical jurisprudence*
BD444	DEATH / *philosophy*
QP87	DEATH / *physiology*
HB1321-1530	DEATH / *statistics*
BT825	DEATH / *theology*
RC87-88	DEATH, APPARENT / *first aid*
RA1063	DEATH, APPARENT / *medical jurisprudence*
RJ255	DEATH, APPARENT / *new-born infants*
N7720	*DEATH, DANCE OF* **SEE** DANCE OF DEATH
Z241.D17	*DEATH, DANCE OF* **SEE** DANCE OF DEATH / *block-books*
BJ1469	*DEATH, POWER OVER* **SEE** LIFE AND DEATH, POWER OVER
HA38-39	*DEATHS, REGISTERS OF* **SEE** REGISTERS OF BIRTHS, ETC.
PN4181-4191	DEBATES AND DEBATING
HG4651	*DEBENTURES* **SEE** BONDS
HV8650-8651	DEBT, IMPRISONMENT FOR
HD4871-5	*DEBT, SERVITUDE FOR* **SEE** PEONAGE
HJ8003-8897	DEBTS, PUBLIC
TK7872.C3	*DECADE COUNTER TUBES* **SEE** COLD CATHODE TUBES
QH556	*DECADENCE* **SEE** DEGENERATION / *biology*
HV4961-4998	*DECADENCE* **SEE** DEGENERATION / *criminology*
HM111	*DECADENCE* **SEE** DEGENERATION / *sociology*
NK9510	DECALCOMANIA
BV4655-4710	*DECALOGUE* **SEE** COMMANDMENTS, TEN / *moral theology*
BS1281-5	*DECALOGUE* **SEE** COMMANDMENTS, TEN / *texts*
QL444.D3	DECAPODA (CRUSTACEA)
QE817.D3	DECAPODA (CRUSTACEA), FOSSIL
GV1060.7	DECATHLON
VK560	DECCA NAVIGATION
SB261.A	*DECCAN HEMP* **SEE** AMBARY HEMP / *culture*
TS1544.A	*DECCAN HEMP* **SEE** AMBARY HEMP / *fiber*
HQ1028	*DECEASED WIFE'S SISTER, MARRIAGE WITH* **SEE** MARRIAGE WITH DECEASED WIFE'S SISTER
HV6691-9	*DECEIT* **SEE** FRAUD
DS775	DECEMBER NINTH MOVEMENT
DG270-365	*DECENNALIA* **SEE** ROMAN EMPERORS
DG124	*DECENNALIA* **SEE** ROMAN EMPERORS / *cult*
TK381	DECIBELS
Z696	*DECIMAL CLASSIFICATION* **SEE** CLASSIFICATION, DECIMAL
QA242	*DECIMAL FRACTIONS* **SEE** FRACTIONS, DECIMAL / *theory of numbers*
HG393	DECIMAL SYSTEM / *international coinage*
QC91-94	DECIMAL SYSTEM / *weights and measures*
PQ6209	DECIMAS / *collections*
PQ6096	DECIMAS / *history*
BJ1468.5	*DECISION (ETHICS)* **SEE** DECISION-MAKING (ETHICS)
BJ1468.5	DECISION-MAKING (ETHICS)
VM781	DECK MACHINERY
VK235-7	*DECK-CARGO* **SEE** SHIPS — CARGO
TH4970	DECKS (ARCHITECTURE, DOMESTIC)
PN4071-4197	*DECLAMATION* **SEE** ELOCUTION
PN6121-9	*DECLAMATION* **SEE** ORATIONS / *collections*
PN4012-4061	*DECLAMATION* **SEE** ORATIONS / *history and criticism*
PE1117-1130	*DECLAMATION* **SEE** READERS AND SPEAKERS / *english*
PN4199-4321	*DECLAMATION* **SEE** READERS AND SPEAKERS / *recitations*
PE1417	*DECLAMATION* **SEE** READERS AND SPEAKERS / *rhetoric*
M1625-6	*DECLAMATION, MUSICAL* **SEE** MONOLOGUES WITH MUSIC
JX5203 1909	*DECLARATION OF LONDON, 1909* **SEE** LONDON, DECLARATION OF, 1909
JX1367	*DECLARATION OF PARIS, 1856* **SEE** PARIS, DECLARATION OF, 1856
JX4552-4564	*DECLARATION OF WAR* **SEE** WAR, DECLARATION OF
JF256	*DECLARATION OF WAR* **SEE** WAR, DECLARATION OF / *constitutional law*
NK1370	DECORATION AND ORNAMENT — EMPIRE STYLE
NK1350	DECORATION AND ORNAMENT — LOUIS XIV STYLE
NK1355	DECORATION AND ORNAMENT — LOUIS XV STYLE

NK1360	DECORATION AND ORNAMENT — LOUIS XVI STYLE
NK1160-1590	DECORATION AND ORNAMENT
NK1180-1250	DECORATION AND ORNAMENT, ANCIENT
NA3310-3950	DECORATION AND ORNAMENT, ARCHITECTURAL
NK1345	DECORATION AND ORNAMENT, BAROQUE
NK1265	DECORATION AND ORNAMENT, BYZANTINE
NK1295	DECORATION AND ORNAMENT, GOTHIC
NK1270-1275	DECORATION AND ORNAMENT, ISLAMIC
NK1443	DECORATION AND ORNAMENT, JACOBEAN
NK1260-1295	DECORATION AND ORNAMENT, MEDIEVAL
NK1270-1275	*DECORATION AND ORNAMENT, MUSLIM* **SEE** DECORATION AND ORNAMENT, ISLAMIC
NK1177	DECORATION AND ORNAMENT, PRIMITIVE
NK1330-1339	DECORATION AND ORNAMENT, RENAISSANCE
NK1355	DECORATION AND ORNAMENT, ROCOCO
NK1285	DECORATION AND ORNAMENT, ROMANESQUE
E642	*DECORATION DAY* **SEE** MEMORIAL DAY
TX652	*DECORATION OF FOOD* **SEE** COOKERY (GARNISHES)
ND2370	*DECORATION, FORE-EDGE* **SEE** FORE-EDGE PAINTING
NK1700-3505	*DECORATION, INTERIOR* **SEE** INTERIOR DECORATION / art
TX311-317	*DECORATION, INTERIOR* **SEE** INTERIOR DECORATION / home economics
CR4501-6305	DECORATIONS OF HONOR
UB430-435	DECORATIONS OF HONOR / military
LB2381-2391	DECORATIONS OF HONOR, ACADEMIC
CR5547-5577	DECORATIONS OF HONOR, PAPAL
NK	*DECORATIVE ART* **SEE** ART, DECORATIVE
NK	*DECORATIVE ARTS* **SEE** ART INDUSTRIES AND TRADE
NK	*DECORATIVE ARTS* **SEE** ART, DECORATIVE
NK1135-1149	*DECORATIVE ARTS* **SEE** ARTS AND CRAFTS MOVEMENT
NK1160-1590	*DECORATIVE ARTS* **SEE** DECORATION AND ORNAMENT
NK1160-1590	*DECORATIVE ARTS* **SEE** DESIGN, DECORATIVE
NK1700-3505	*DECORATIVE ARTS* **SEE** INTERIOR DECORATION / art
TX311-317	*DECORATIVE ARTS* **SEE** INTERIOR DECORATION / home economics
NK1160-1590	*DECORATIVE DESIGN* **SEE** DESIGN, DECORATIVE
TH7703	*DECORATIVE LIGHTING* **SEE** LIGHTING, ARCHITECTURAL AND DECORATIVE
TS	*DECORATIVE METAL-WORK* **SEE** ART METAL-WORK
NK6400-8450	*DECORATIVE METAL-WORK* **SEE** ART METAL-WORK
TT	*DECORATIVE METAL-WORK* **SEE** ART METAL-WORK
SK335	DECOYS (HUNTING)
PJ1531.C	DECREE OF CANOPUS
DT62.S8	DECREE OF CANOPUS
QL544.D4	DECREMETER
RD629	*DECUBITUS* **SEE** BED-SORES
BV880	*DEDICATION OF CHURCHES* **SEE** CHURCH DEDICATION
BX2302	*DEDICATION OF CHURCHES* **SEE** CHURCH DEDICATION / catholic church
BV199.D4	*DEDICATION PROGRAMS* **SEE** DEDICATION SERVICES
BV199.D4	DEDICATION SERVICES
BM695.H3	*DEDICATION, FEAST OF* **SEE** HANUKKAH (FEAST OF LIGHTS)
PN171.D4	DEDICATIONS (IN BOOKS)
BC	*DEDUCTION (LOGIC)* **SEE** LOGIC
TS250	DEEP DRAWING (METAL-WORK)
VM453	*DEEP-OCEAN DRILLING SHIPS* **SEE** DEEP-SEA DRILLING SHIPS
GC380-399	*DEEP-SEA DEPOSITS* **SEE** MARINE SEDIMENTS
VM453	DEEP-SEA DRILLING SHIPS
GC75-78	*DEEP-SEA EXPLORATION* **SEE** DEEP-SEA SOUNDING
QH91-95	*DEEP-SEA EXPLORATION* **SEE** MARINE BIOLOGY / natural history
QL121-138	*DEEP-SEA EXPLORATION* **SEE** MARINE FAUNA
QK103	*DEEP-SEA EXPLORATION* **SEE** MARINE FLORA
GC75-78	DEEP-SEA SOUNDING
GC161-177	DEEP-SEA TEMPERATURE
TN871.3	*DEEP-WATER DRILLING (PETROLEUM)* **SEE** OIL WELL DRILLING, SUBMARINE
TC193	*DEEP-WATER DRILLING* **SEE** UNDERWATER DRILLING
BL1213.D5	*DEEPAVALI* **SEE** DIVALI
SK301	DEER HUNTING
SF429.D4	DEER-HOUNDS
QL737.U5	DEER
QE882.U3	DEER, FOSSIL

HV6675-6685	*DEFALCATION* **SEE** EMBEZZLEMENT
QP156	DEFECATION
RC423-7	*DEFECTIVE SPEECH* **SEE** SPEECH, DISORDERS OF
GV1469.D3	DEFENCE (GAME)
UG443-9	*DEFENSE (MILITARY SCIENCE)* **SEE** ATTACK AND DEFENSE (MILITARY SCIENCE)
UA926-9	*DEFENSE, CIVIL* **SEE** CIVIL DEFENSE
UA18	*DEFENSES* **SEE** INDUSTRIAL MOBILIZATION
UG410-448	*DEFENSES, COAST* **SEE** COAST DEFENSES
GV951.1	*DEFENSIVE FOOTBALL* **SEE** FOOTBALL — DEFENSE
BJ1533.R4	*DEFERENCE* **SEE** RESPECT
HE594	*DEFERRED REBATES* **SEE** SHIPPING — RATES
HE597	*DEFERRED REBATES* **SEE** SHIPPING — RATES / by countries
HJ10	*DEFICIENCY APPROPRIATION BILLS* **SEE** UNITED STATES — APPROPRIATIONS AND EXPENDITURES
HJ2050-2052	*DEFICIENCY APPROPRIATION BILLS* **SEE** UNITED STATES — APPROPRIATIONS AND EXPENDITURES
SF780.5	DEFICIENCY DISEASES IN DOMESTIC ANIMALS
SB742-3	DEFICIENCY DISEASES IN PLANTS
RC620-632	DEFICIENCY DISEASES
BC199.D4	*DEFINABILITY* **SEE** DEFINITION (LOGIC)
BC199.D4	DEFINITION (LOGIC)
GN479	DEFLORATION
QK763	DEFOLIATION
QA648	*DEFORMATION OF SURFACES* **SEE** SURFACES, DEFORMATION OF
TG265	DEFORMATIONS (MECHANICS) / strains and stresses
QA611	*DEFORMATIONS, CONTINUOUS* **SEE** HOMOTOPY THEORY
QM691-9	DEFORMITIES / human anatomy
GN68-69.8	DEFORMITIES / somatic anthropology
GN477.6	DEFORMITIES, ARTIFICIAL / ethnology
RD701-795	*DEFORMITIES, CURE OF* **SEE** ORTHOPEDIA
VM479	DEGAUSSING
QH556	DEGENERATION / biology
HV4961-4998	DEGENERATION / criminology
HM111	DEGENERATION / sociology
RC394.H4	*DEGENERATION, HEPATOLENTICULAR* **SEE** HEPATOLENTICULAR DEGENERATION
QP311	DEGLUTITION
TH7225	DEGREE DAYS / heating
HD9566	DEGREE DAYS / petroleum trade
LB2388	*DEGREE MILLS* **SEE** DIPLOMA MILLS
QB281-341	*DEGREES OF LATITUDE AND LONGITUDE* **SEE** GEODESY
QB231-5	*DEGREES OF LATITUDE AND LONGITUDE* **SEE** LATITUDE
VK565	*DEGREES OF LATITUDE AND LONGITUDE* **SEE** LATITUDE / navigation
QB225-9	*DEGREES OF LATITUDE AND LONGITUDE* **SEE** LONGITUDE / astronomy
VK565-7	*DEGREES OF LATITUDE AND LONGITUDE* **SEE** LONGITUDE / navigation
LB2381-2391	DEGREES, ACADEMIC
SF912	DEHORNING
TX609	*DEHYDRATED FOODS* **SEE** FOOD, DRIED
SF259	*DEHYDRATED MILK* **SEE** MILK, DRIED
TP493.5	*DEHYDROFROZEN FOOD* **SEE** FOOD, FROZEN
BL465	*DEIFICATION* **SEE** APOTHEOSIS
DS98-99	DEIR EL-QAMAR, MASSACRE OF, 1860
BL2700-2790	DEISM
BL473	*DEITIES* **SEE** GODS
BF173	*DEJECTION* **SEE** DEPRESSION, MENTAL
QB723.D	DELAVAN'S COMET
F161-175	DELAWARE — HISTORY
E99.D2	DELAWARE INDIANS
PM1031-4	DELAWARE LANGUAGE
E500	DELAWARE — HISTORY — — CIVIL WAR
E263.D3	DELAWARE — HISTORY — — REVOLUTION
E359.5.D3	DELAWARE — HISTORY — — WAR OF 1812
HE1826	*DELAYAGE (CAR SERVICE)* **SEE** DEMURRAGE (CAR SERVICE)
JK-JQ	DELEGATION OF POWERS
JF225	DELEGATION OF POWERS
NK4295	DELFT WARE
DS478	DELHI — SIEGE, 1857
RL331	DELHI BOIL
DF227.5	DELIAN LEAGUE, FIRST, 5TH CENTURY, B.C.
DF231.2	DELIAN LEAGUE, SECOND, 4TH CENTURY, B.C.

QA469	*DELIAN PROBLEM* **SEE** CUBE, DUPLICATION OF
HV9051-9230	*DELINQUENCY, JUVENILE* **SEE** JUVENILE DELINQUENCY
HV6046	DELINQUENT WOMEN
RC368	DELIRIUM TREMENS
RC48	DELIRIUM
RC106	DELIRIUM
RC610	DELIRIUM
HF5761-5780	DELIVERY OF GOODS
PR1219	DELLA CRUSCANS (ENGLISH WRITERS)
DF261.D35	DELPHIAN ORACLE
DF261.D35	*DELPHIC ORACLE* **SEE** DELPHIAN ORACLE
QL737.C4	*DELPHINIDAE* **SEE** DOLPHINS
PN4157	DELSARTE SYSTEM
GV463	DELSARTE SYSTEM
QC721	DELTA RAYS
TL673.T7	*DELTA WINGS (AEROPLANES)* **SEE** AEROPLANES — WINGS, TRIANGULAR
GB1205	DELTAS
BS658	DELUGE / *bible*
QE507	DELUGE / *geology*
RC520	*DELUSIONAL INSANITY* **SEE** PARANOIA
AZ999	*DELUSIONS* **SEE** ERRORS, POPULAR
BF1048-1063	*DELUSIONS* **SEE** HALLUCINATIONS AND ILLUSIONS
RC534	*DELUSIONS* **SEE** HALLUCINATIONS AND ILLUSIONS / *psychiatry and psychopathology*
BF491-3	*DELUSIONS* **SEE** HALLUCINATIONS AND ILLUSIONS / *psychology*
HV6751-6761	*DELUSIONS* **SEE** IMPOSTORS AND IMPOSTURE / *criminal*
R133	*DELUSIONS* **SEE** MEDICAL DELUSIONS
QL89	*DELUSIONS* **SEE** SEA SERPENT
BF1001-1999	*DELUSIONS* **SEE** SUPERSTITION / *occult sciences*
AZ999	*DELUSIONS* **SEE** SUPERSTITION / *popular delusions*
BL490	*DELUSIONS* **SEE** SUPERSTITION / *religion*
HV6691-9	*DELUSIONS* **SEE** SWINDLERS AND SWINDLING
BF1563-1584	*DELUSIONS* **SEE** WITCHCRAFT
GR530	*DELUSIONS* **SEE** WITCHCRAFT / *folk-lore*
HB201-5	*DEMAND AND SUPPLY* **SEE** SUPPLY AND DEMAND / *value*
E123	DEMARCATION LINE OF ALEXANDER VI
JC75.D	DEME / *ancient greece*
RC514	*DEMENTIA PRAECOX* **SEE** SCHIZOPHRENIA
QL865	*DEMILUNES OF HEIDENHAIN* **SEE** SALIVARY GLANDS / *comparative anatomy*
QM325	*DEMILUNES OF HEIDENHAIN* **SEE** SALIVARY GLANDS / *human anatomy*
QP191	*DEMILUNES OF HEIDENHAIN* **SEE** SALIVARY GLANDS / *physiology*
LB3021	*DEMOCRACY IN EDUCATION* **SEE** SELF-GOVERNMENT (IN EDUCATION) / *student honor*
LB3092-5	*DEMOCRACY IN EDUCATION* **SEE** SELF-GOVERNMENT (IN EDUCATION)
JC421-458	DEMOCRACY
JK2311-2319	DEMOCRATIC PARTY
HB881-3700	DEMOGRAPHY
UG370	DEMOLITION, MILITARY
BS2545.D5	DEMONIAC POSSESSION / *new testament*
BF1555	DEMONIAC POSSESSION / *occult sciences*
BL480	DEMONOLOGY / *comparative religion*
GR525-540	DEMONOLOGY / *folk-lore*
BF1501-1561	DEMONOLOGY / *occult sciences*
BT975	DEMONOLOGY / *theology*
BL1475.D4	DEMONOLOGY, BUDDHIST
BL480	*DEMONOLOGY, CHRISTIAN* **SEE** DEMONOLOGY / *comparative religion*
GR525-540	*DEMONOLOGY, CHRISTIAN* **SEE** DEMONOLOGY / *folk-lore*
BF1501-1561	*DEMONOLOGY, CHRISTIAN* **SEE** DEMONOLOGY / *occult sciences*
BT975	*DEMONOLOGY, CHRISTIAN* **SEE** DEMONOLOGY / *theology*
BP166.89	DEMONOLOGY, ISLAMIC
BP166.89	*DEMONOLOGY, MUSLIM* **SEE** DEMONOLOGY, ISLAMIC
BL480	*DEMONOLOGY-COMPARATIVE STUDIES* **SEE** DEMONOLOGY / *comparative religion*
GR525-540	*DEMONOLOGY-COMPARATIVE STUDIES* **SEE** DEMONOLOGY / *folk-lore*
BF1501-1561	*DEMONOLOGY-COMPARATIVE STUDIES* **SEE** DEMONOLOGY / *occult sciences*

BT975	*DEMONOLOGY-COMPARATIVE STUDIES* **SEE** DEMONOLOGY / *theology*
RC616	DEMONOMANIA
RC616	*DEMONOPATHY* **SEE** DEMONOMANIA
LB2153-5	*DEMONSTRATION SCHOOLS* **SEE** LABORATORY SCHOOLS
PJ1501-1819	*DEMOTIC INSCRIPTIONS* **SEE** EGYPTIAN LANGUAGE — INSCRIPTIONS
PJ1809-1921	*DEMOTIC WRITING* **SEE** EGYPTIAN LANGUAGE — PAPYRI, DEMOTIC
PJ1107	*DEMOTIC WRITING* **SEE** EGYPTIAN LANGUAGE — WRITING, DEMOTIC
NA8480	*DEMOUNTABLE BUILDINGS* **SEE** BUILDINGS, PREFABRICATED / *architecture*
TH1098	*DEMOUNTABLE BUILDINGS* **SEE** BUILDINGS, PREFABRICATED / *building*
HE1826	DEMURRAGE (CAR SERVICE)
BS2378	DEMYTHOLOGIZATION
BX1950	*DENARIUS SANCTI PETRI* **SEE** PETER'S PENCE
TP593	*DENATURED ALCOHOL* **SEE** ALCOHOL, DENATURED / *technology*
HD9399	*DENATURED ALCOHOL* **SEE** ALCOHOL, DENATURED / *trade*
D802.G3	DENAZIFICATION
PL8131	*DENCA LANGUAGE* **SEE** DINKA LANGUAGE
QC883	DENDROCHRONOLOGY
QC883	*DENDROCLIMATOLOGY* **SEE** DENDROCHRONOLOGY
QK475-494	*DENDROLOGY* **SEE** TREES / *botany*
GR785	*DENDROLOGY* **SEE** TREES / *folk-lore*
GT5150	*DENDROLOGY* **SEE** TREES / *manners and customs*
SB435-7	*DENDROLOGY* **SEE** TREES / *ornamental*
SD391-535	*DENDROLOGY* **SEE** TREES / *sylviculture*
SD555	DENDROMETER
E99.T56	*DENE INDIANS* **SEE** TINNE INDIANS
DK856	*DENGHIL TEPE-SIEGE, 1880-1881* **SEE** GEOK-TEPE — SIEGE, 1880-1881
RC137	DENGUE
JX4263.D45	DENIAL OF JUSTICE / *k international law*
TS1580	DENIM
S651-2	*DENITRIFICATION* **SEE** NITRIFICATION / *agriculture*
TD433	*DENITRIFICATION* **SEE** NITRIFICATION / *water-supply*
PL3651.D2	*DENJONG-KE LANGUAGE* **SEE** DANJONG-KA LANGUAGE
PL8131	*DENKA LANGUAGE* **SEE** DINKA LANGUAGE
DL101-291	DENMARK — HISTORY
DL192	*DENMARK-HISTORY-DANO-SWEDISH WARS, 1643-1660* **SEE** DANO-SWEDISH WARS, 1657-1660
DL190	*DENMARK-HISTORY-DANO-SWEDISH WARS, 1643-1660* **SEE** DANO-SWEDISH WARS, 1643-1645
DL188.5	*DENMARK-HISTORY-NORTHERN SEVEN YEARS' WAR, 1563-1570* **SEE** NORTHERN SEVEN YEARS' WAR, 1563-1570 / *denmark*
QB723.D4	DENNING'S COMET
LC427-629	*DENOMINATIONAL SCHOOLS* **SEE** CHURCH SCHOOLS
BL74-98	*DENOMINATIONS, RELIGIOUS* **SEE** RELIGIONS
BR157	*DENOMINATIONS, RELIGIOUS* **SEE** SECTS
TS837	*DENSIFIED WOOD* **SEE** WOOD, COMPRESSED
QC111-114	*DENSITY* **SEE** SPECIFIC GRAVITY
TL557.D4	DENSITY ALTITUDE COMPUTERS
QC581	*DENSITY, ELECTRIC* **SEE** ELECTRIC CHARGE AND DISTRIBUTION
QL858	*DENTAL ANATOMY* **SEE** TEETH / *comparative anatomy*
QM311	*DENTAL ANATOMY* **SEE** TEETH / *human anatomy*
GN209	*DENTAL ANATOMY* **SEE** TEETH / *somatology*
RK510	*DENTAL ANESTHESIA* **SEE** ANESTHESIA IN DENTISTRY
QR47	*DENTAL BACTERIOLOGY* **SEE** MOUTH — BACTERIOLOGY
RK655	*DENTAL CERAMICS* **SEE** DENTISTRY — CERAMICS
RK290	DENTAL CHEMISTRY
RK3	DENTAL CLINICS
RK61	*DENTAL HYGIENE* **SEE** TEETH — CARE AND HYGIENE
RK681-6	DENTAL INSTRUMENTS AND APPARATUS
RK1062	DENTAL JURISPRUDENCE
RK4-15	DENTAL LAWS AND LEGISLATION
Z675.D3	DENTAL LIBRARIES

PN6120.M9	DETECTIVE AND MYSTERY PLAYS / collections
PN3383.D4	DETECTIVE AND MYSTERY STORIES — TECHNIQUE
PZ1-3	DETECTIVE AND MYSTERY STORIES / collections
PN3448.D4	DETECTIVE AND MYSTERY STORIES / history
HV7551-8077	DETECTIVES / police
HV8081-8099	DETECTIVES / private
TP932	DETERGENTS **SEE** CLEANING COMPOUNDS
QA191	DETERMINANTS
QE367-9	DETERMINATIVE MINERALOGY **SEE** MINERALOGY, DETERMINATIVE
BJ1460-1468	DETERMINISM AND INDETERMINISM **SEE** FREE WILL AND DETERMINISM / ethics
BF620-628	DETERMINISM AND INDETERMINISM **SEE** FREE WILL AND DETERMINISM / psychology
U162.6	DETERRENCE (STRATEGY)
E197	DETROIT — SIEGE, 1712
E83.76	DETROIT — SIEGE, 1763
E356.D4	DETROIT — SURRENDER TO THE BRITISH, 1812
HD1519	DETROIT PLAN **SEE** WORKING-MEN'S GARDENS
QD181.H1	DEUTERIUM OXIDE
QD181.H1	DEUTERIUM
QC721	DEUTERON SCATTERING **SEE** DEUTERONS — SCATTERING
QC721	DEUTERONS — SCATTERING
BX4740	DEUTSCHKATHOLIZISMUS **SEE** GERMAN CATHOLICISM
HG651-1490	DEVALUATION OF CURRENCY **SEE** CURRENCY QUESTION / other countries
HG501-538	DEVALUATION OF CURRENCY **SEE** CURRENCY QUESTION / u.s.
PK119	DEVANAGARI ALPHABET
QL951-973	DEVELOPMENT **SEE** EMBRYOLOGY
QH361-371	DEVELOPMENT **SEE** EVOLUTION
QE721	DEVELOPMENT **SEE** EVOLUTION / paleontology
B818	DEVELOPMENT **SEE** EVOLUTION / philosophy
QH511	DEVELOPMENT **SEE** GROWTH / biology
QP84	DEVELOPMENT **SEE** GROWTH / physiology
HG4517	DEVELOPMENT BANKS
HJ4175	DEVELOPMENT CHARGES **SEE** SPECIAL ASSESSMENTS
LB1050.5	DEVELOPMENT READING **SEE** DEVELOPMENTAL READING
BF701-724.8	DEVELOPMENTAL PSYCHOLOGY **SEE** GENETIC PSYCHOLOGY
LB1050.5	DEVELOPMENTAL READING
DH199.D4	DEVENTER, SURRENDER OF, 1587
VK577	DEVIATION OF THE COMPASS **SEE** COMPASS
QC849	DEVIATION OF THE COMPASS **SEE** COMPASS / deviation
CR67-69	DEVICES / heraldry
N8140	DEVIL — ART
BS1199.D	DEVIL — BIBLICAL TEACHING / old testament
GV1641.B6	DEVIL DANCE
PN57.D4	DEVIL IN LITERATURE
BL480	DEVIL-WORSHIP / comparative religion
BF1546-1550	DEVIL-WORSHIP / demonology
BL480	DEVIL / comparative religion
BF1546-1561	DEVIL / demonology
BT980-981	DEVIL / theology
QL430.3.O2	DEVILFISH **SEE** OCTOPUS
D275-6	DEVOLUTION, WAR OF, 1667-1668
SF199.D5	DEVON CATTLE
SF193.D5	DEVON CATTLE / herd-books
QE665	DEVONIAN PERIOD **SEE** GEOLOGY, STRATIGRAPHIC — DEVONIAN
QE918	DEVONIAN PERIOD **SEE** PALEOBOTANY — DEVONIAN
QE728	DEVONIAN PERIOD **SEE** PALEONTOLOGY — DEVONIAN
BR270	DEVOTIO MODERNA
BX2159.H75	DEVOTION TO THE HOLY NAME **SEE** HOLY NAME, DEVOTION TO
BV4815	DEVOTION
BV4810-4812	DEVOTIONAL CALENDARS
BV4810-4812	DEVOTIONAL EXERCISES (DAILY READINGS) **SEE** DEVOTIONAL CALENDARS
BV4800-4870	DEVOTIONAL EXERCISES
BX	DEVOTIONAL EXERCISES / by denomination
BV4800-4895	DEVOTIONAL LITERATURE
BX2177-2198	DEVOTIONAL LITERATURE / catholic church
BP188.2	DEVOTIONAL LITERATURE, ISLAMIC **SEE** ISLAMIC DEVOTIONAL LITERATURE
BP188.2	DEVOTIONAL LITERATURE, MUSLIM **SEE** ISLAMIC DEVOTIONAL LITERATURE
BV4515	DEVOTIONAL STORIES **SEE** CHRISTIAN LIFE — STORIES
BV4800-4870	DEVOTIONAL THEOLOGY **SEE** DEVOTIONAL EXERCISES
BX	DEVOTIONAL THEOLOGY **SEE** DEVOTIONAL EXERCISES / by denomination
BV4800-4895	DEVOTIONAL THEOLOGY **SEE** DEVOTIONAL LITERATURE
BX2177-2198	DEVOTIONAL THEOLOGY **SEE** DEVOTIONAL LITERATURE / catholic church
BV4800-4870	DEVOTIONAL THEOLOGY **SEE** MEDITATIONS
BX2177-2198	DEVOTIONAL THEOLOGY **SEE** MEDITATIONS / catholic church
BV228-283	DEVOTIONAL THEOLOGY **SEE** PRAYERS
BL560	DEVOTIONAL THEOLOGY **SEE** PRAYERS / comparative religion
BV4810-4812	DEVOTIONAL YEARBOOKS **SEE** DEVOTIONAL CALENDARS
BV4800-4870	DEVOTIONS **SEE** DEVOTIONAL EXERCISES
BX	DEVOTIONS **SEE** DEVOTIONAL EXERCISES / by denomination
TD395	DEW-PONDS
QC929.D5	DEW
BL1213.D5	DEWALI **SEE** DIVALI
QD535	DEWAR FLASKS
F128.5	DEWEY CELEBRATION, NEW YORK, SEPT. 28-30, 1899
Z696	DEWEY DECIMAL CLASSIFICATION **SEE** CLASSIFICATION, DECIMAL
QD321	DEXTRINE / chemistry
TP417	DEXTRINE / manufacture
QD321	DEXTROSE / chemistry
TP414	DEXTROSE / manufacture
RM666.D45	DEXTROSE / therapeutics
B132.D5	DHARMA
DS422.C3	DHEDS
E99.D	DHEGIHA INDIANS
PM1058	DHEGIHA LANGUAGE
PL3801.D5	DHIMAL DIALECT
VM371	DHOWS
PL8377	DI-KELE LANGUAGE **SEE** KELE LANGUAGE
F1418	DIA DE LAS AMERICAS **SEE** PAN AMERICAN DAY
QE391.D	DIABANTITE
QE461	DIABASE
RC658.5	DIABETES
RC660-662	DIABETES
GV1216	DIABLO (GAME)
BV680	DIACONATE **SEE** DEACONS
BX1912	DIACONATE **SEE** DEACONS / catholic church
RB37-55	DIAGNOSIS / laboratory methods
RC71-78	DIAGNOSIS / practice of medicine
RC71.5	DIAGNOSIS, DIFFERENTIAL
RC78	DIAGNOSIS, RADIOSCOPIC
RD35	DIAGNOSIS, SURGICAL
SF773	DIAGNOSIS, URINARY **SEE** URINE — ANALYSIS AND PATHOLOGY / veterinary medicine
RB53	DIAGNOSIS, URINARY **SEE** URINE — ANALYSIS AND PATHOLOGY
SF771-4	DIAGNOSIS, VETERINARY **SEE** VETERINARY MEDICINE — DIAGNOSIS
HA48	DIAGRAMS, STATISTICAL **SEE** STATISTICS — CHARTS, TABLES, ETC.
HA31	DIAGRAMS, STATISTICAL **SEE** STATISTICS — GRAPHIC METHODS
F2823.D5	DIAGUITA INDIANS
BC	DIALECTIC (LOGIC) **SEE** LOGIC
BT78	DIALECTIC (RELIGION) **SEE** DIALECTICAL THEOLOGY
BL325.P7	DIALECTIC (RELIGION) **SEE** POLARITY (IN RELIGION, FOLK-LORE, ETC.)
B809.8	DIALECTICAL MATERIALISM / philosophy
HX55	DIALECTICAL MATERIALISM / socialism
BT78	DIALECTICAL THEOLOGY
PM7831-7875	DIALECTS **SEE** CREOLE DIALECTS
PC3081-3148	DIALECTS **SEE** FRANCO-PROVENCAL DIALECTS
PC1851-1874	DIALECTS **SEE** GALLO-ITALIAN DIALECTS

P151-295	*DIALECTS* **SEE** GRAMMAR, COMPARATIVE AND GENERAL
PA2420-2550	*DIALECTS* **SEE** ITALIC LANGUAGES AND DIALECTS
PM7801-7895	*DIALECTS* **SEE** LANGUAGES, MIXED
QB215	DIALING
QB215	*DIALLING* **SEE** DIALING
PN1551	DIALOGUE
PR618	DIALOGUE / *english literature*
PN4290-4291	DIALOGUES
QC771	DIAMAGNETISM
TN281	*DIAMOND DRILLING* **SEE** BORING / *mining*
TA745-7	*DIAMOND DRILLING* **SEE** ROCK-DRILLS
TN279-281	*DIAMOND DRILLING* **SEE** ROCK-DRILLS / *use in mines*
TN281	*DIAMOND DRILLING* **SEE** SULLIVAN DIAMOND DRILL
E233	DIAMOND ISLAND, LAKE GEORGE, SKIRMISH AT, 1777
TN990-994	DIAMOND MINES AND MINING
DC137.15	DIAMOND NECKLACE AFFAIR
TJ1193	*DIAMOND TOOLS* **SEE** DIAMONDS, INDUSTRIAL / *tools*
SB945.D	DIAMOND-BACK MOTH
NK7660	DIAMONDS / *art*
QE393	DIAMONDS / *mineralogy*
TS753	DIAMONDS / *technology*
TP873.5.D5	DIAMONDS, ARTIFICIAL
TJ1193	DIAMONDS, INDUSTRIAL / *tools*
SB413.P55	*DIANTHUS* **SEE** PINKS
RM551	DIAPHORESIS AND DIAPHORETICS
RD621	DIAPHRAGM — HERNIA
QL851	DIAPHRAGM / *comparative anatomy*
QM265	DIAPHRAGM / *human anatomy*
QP121	DIAPHRAGM / *physiology*
CT9999	DIARIES (BLANK-BOOKS)
PN4390	DIARIES
PR1330	DIARIES / *english literature*
PR908	DIARIES / *english literature*
RC811	DIARRHEA
RJ456.D5	DIARRHEA / *children's diseases*
RX336.D5	DIARRHEA / *homeopathic treatment*
QL523.C7	*DIASPINAE* **SEE** SCALE-INSECTS
SB939	*DIASPINAE* **SEE** SCALE-INSECTS / *economic entomology*
QK896	DIASTASE / *botany*
QP601	DIASTASE / *physiological chemistry*
RM874	DIATHERMY
RB151	DIATHESIS
RC251	DIATHESIS
TN948.D5	DIATOMACEOUS EARTH
TN948.D5	*DIATOMITE* **SEE** DIATOMACEOUS EARTH
QD305.A9	DIAZO COMPOUNDS
QD341.A9	DIAZO COMPOUNDS
QD305.A9	DIAZOAMIDS
QD341.A9	DIAZOAMIDS
QL430.2	DIBRANCHIATA
GV1303	DICE
QC446.D	DICHROISM
TN948.C75	*DICHROITE* **SEE** CORDIERITE
QC373.D	DICHROSCOPE
QE391.D	DICKITE
QK671	DICOTYLEDONS / *plant anatomy*
QE983	DICOTYLEDONS, FOSSIL
QL737.U5	*DICOTYLES* **SEE** PECCARIES
HF5548	*DICTAGRAPH* **SEE** DICTOGRAPH
HF5548	*DICTAPHONE* **SEE** DICTATING MACHINES
HF5548	DICTATING MACHINES
LB1029.D5	DICTATION (EDUCATIONAL METHOD)
JC495	DICTATORS
Z51	*DICTATYPY* **SEE** STENOTYPY
PN173-5	DICTION
AE	*DICTIONARIES* **SEE** ENCYCLOPEDIAS AND DICTIONARIES
AG	*DICTIONARIES* **SEE** ENCYCLOPEDIAS AND DICTIONARIES
DE5	*DICTIONARIES, CLASSICAL* **SEE** CLASSICAL DICTIONARIES
P361	DICTIONARIES, POLYGLOT
HF5548	DICTOGRAPH
PN605.D6	DIDACTIC LITERATURE
PN1401	DIDACTIC POETRY / *etc.*
LB	*DIDACTICS* **SEE** TEACHING
LB1775-1785	*DIDACTICS* **SEE** TEACHING / *teaching as a profession*
QL737.M3	*DIDELPHYIDAE* **SEE** OPOSSUMS
QD181.N4	DIDYMIUM
TS239	DIE-CASTING
E99.D5	DIEGUENO INDIANS
PM1071	DIEGUENO LANGUAGE
QC585	DIELECTRICS
D756.5.D	DIEPPE RAID, 1942
TS253	DIES (METAL-WORKING)
TJ1335	*DIES (SCREW-CUTTING)* **SEE** TAPS AND DIES
TJ1335	*DIES AND TAPS* **SEE** TAPS AND DIES
TJ1255-7	*DIES, BLANKING AND PIERCING* **SEE** PUNCHING MACHINERY
TJ795	*DIESEL ENGINE* **SEE** DIESEL MOTOR
TP343	DIESEL FUELS
TJ669.C6	DIESEL LOCOMOTIVES — COMPRESSORS
TJ619	DIESEL LOCOMOTIVES — INSPECTION
TJ619	DIESEL LOCOMOTIVES
TJ795	DIESEL MOTOR — MODELS
TJ795	DIESEL MOTOR
TP343	*DIESEL MOTOR-FUEL* **SEE** DIESEL FUELS
TP343	*DIESEL OIL* **SEE** DIESEL FUELS
TJ619	*DIESEL-ELECTRIC LOCOMOTIVES* **SEE** DIESEL LOCOMOTIVES
TJ795	*DIESEL-ELECTRIC MOTOR* **SEE** DIESEL MOTOR
RM215	DIET — EARLY WORKS TO 1800
TX645-840	*DIET* **SEE** COOKERY
RM214-259	DIET IN DISEASE
DD184	*DIET OF RATISBON, 1532* **SEE** RATISBON, DIET OF, 1532
BR355.S7	*DIET OF SPIRES, 1529* **SEE** SPIRES, DIET OF, 1529
BR353	*DIET OF WORMS, 1521* **SEE** WORMS, DIET OF, 1521
HV694	DIET-KITCHENS
TX551-560	DIET / *food values*
QP141	DIET / *nutrition*
RM214-259	DIET / *therapeutics*
TX551-560	DIETARIES / *food values*
RM214-261	DIETARIES / *therapeutics*
RA975.5.D5	*DIETARY DEPARTMENTS OF HOSPITALS, ETC.* **SEE** HOSPITALS — FOOD SERVICE
BM710	*DIETARY LAWS, JEWISH* **SEE** JEWS — DIETARY LAWS
RM214-218	*DIETISTS* **SEE** DIETITIANS
RM214-218	DIETITIANS
BF697	DIFFERENCE (PSYCHOLOGY)
QA431	DIFFERENCE EQUATIONS
QA373	*DIFFERENCE-DIFFERENTIAL EQUATIONS* **SEE** DIFFERENTIAL-DIFFERENCE EQUATIONS
QA431	*DIFFERENCES, CALCULUS OF* **SEE** DIFFERENCE EQUATIONS
QA612	*DIFFERENTIABLE MANIFOLDS* **SEE** DIFFERENTIAL TOPOLOGY
QA76	*DIFFERENTIAL ANALYZERS, ELECTRONIC* **SEE** ELECTRONIC DIFFERENTIAL ANALYZERS / *mathematics*
QA304-6	*DIFFERENTIAL CALCULUS* **SEE** CALCULUS, DIFFERENTIAL
RC71.5	*DIFFERENTIAL DIAGNOSIS* **SEE** DIAGNOSIS, DIFFERENTIAL
QA371-7	DIFFERENTIAL EQUATIONS — PROBLEMS, EXERCISES, ETC.
QA371-7	DIFFERENTIAL EQUATIONS
QA372-7	DIFFERENTIAL EQUATIONS, LINEAR
QA374-7	DIFFERENTIAL EQUATIONS, PARTIAL
QA381	DIFFERENTIAL FORMS
QA641-9	*DIFFERENTIAL GEOMETRY* **SEE** GEOMETRY, DIFFERENTIAL
QA381	DIFFERENTIAL INVARIANTS
QA612	DIFFERENTIAL TOPOLOGY
QA373	DIFFERENTIAL-DIFFERENCE EQUATIONS
QC415	DIFFRACTION
QD543	DIFFUSION / *chemistry*
QC185	DIFFUSION / *physics*
QC321-3	*DIFFUSIVITY, THERMAL* **SEE** THERMAL DIFFUSIVITY
PL4001.T35	*DIGARU LANGUAGE* **SEE** TARAON LANGUAGE
TP159.A8	*DIGESTERS (CHEMICAL ENGINEERING)* **SEE** AUTOCLAVES
QP145-156	DIGESTION / *physiology*
QR171	DIGESTIVE ORGANS — BACTERIOLOGY
RC280.D	DIGESTIVE ORGANS — CANCER
RC799-869	DIGESTIVE ORGANS — DISEASES
RD540	DIGESTIVE ORGANS — SURGERY

RD547	DIGESTIVE ORGANS — SURGERY
QL856-867	DIGESTIVE ORGANS / comparative anatomy
QM301-353	DIGESTIVE ORGANS / human anatomy
RC803-4	DIGESTIVE ORGANS — DISEASES — — DIAGNOSIS
PN6013.5	DIGESTS OF BOOKS SEE BOOKS, CONDENSED
DA405	DIGGERS SEE LEVELLERS
TA735-747	DIGGING MACHINES SEE EXCAVATING MACHINERY
TK7888.3	DIGITAL COMPUTER CIRCUITS SEE ELECTRONIC DIGITAL COMPUTERS — CIRCUITS
QA76	DIGITAL DIFFERENTIAL ANALYZERS, ELECTRONIC SEE ELECTRONIC DIFFERENTIAL ANALYZERS / mathematics
RS165.D5	DIGITALIS / pharmacy
RM666.D5	DIGITALIS / therapeutics
BV4647.D	DIGNITY
DC305.7	DIJON — SIEGE, 1870-1871
TC337	DIKES (ENGINEERING)
QE611	DIKES (GEOLOGY)
QD341.K2	DIKETONES SEE KETONES
QD305.K2	DIKETONES SEE KETONES
QC281-6	DILATOMETER
QC100.5-111	DILATOMETER
BC185	DILEMMA
QA351	DILOGARITHMS
PM8161-4	DILPOK LANGUAGE
PS374.D5	DIME NOVELS
QD305.H6	DIMETHYL SEE ETHANES
QK671	DIMORPHISM (PLANTS)
PK2461-9	DINGAL LANGUAGE
HF1755-6	DINGLEY BILL SEE DINGLEY TARIFF / discussion
HJ6085	DINGLEY BILL SEE DINGLEY TARIFF / schedules
HF1755-6	DINGLEY TARIFF / discussion
HJ6085	DINGLEY TARIFF / schedules
TX737	DINING SEE DINNERS AND DINING
TF668	DINING CARS SEE RAILROADS — DINING-CAR SERVICE
BJ2041	DINING ETIQUETTE SEE TABLE ETIQUETTE
BJ2041	DINING ROOM ETIQUETTE SEE TABLE ETIQUETTE
TT197.5.D5	DINING ROOM FURNITURE / cabinet work
NK2117	DINING ROOM FURNITURE / interior decoration
TS880	DINING ROOM FURNITURE / manufacture
TX855-9	DINING ROOMS / domestic science
NK2117	DINING ROOMS / house decoration
PL8131	DINKA LANGUAGE
TX645-840	DINNERS AND DINING SEE COOKERY
TX737	DINNERS AND DINING
QE882.U8	DINOCERATA
QE862.D5	DINOSAURIA
E477.67	DINWIDDIE, BATTLE OF, 1865
BX1939.C73	DIOCESAN CONSULTORS SEE CONSULTORS, DIOCESAN / canon law
LC427-629	DIOCESAN SCHOOLS SEE CHURCH SCHOOLS
BX1939.D55	DIOCESES (CANON LAW)
PL8134	DIOLA LANGUAGE
QL696.P6	DIOMEDEIDAE SEE ALBATROSSES
BL820.B2	DIONYSIA
DF123	DIONYSIA / greek antiquities
PA3203	DIONYSIA / greek drama
QA242	DIOPHANTINE ANALYSIS
QC385	DIOPTRICS SEE REFRACTION / geometrical
QC425	DIOPTRICS SEE REFRACTION / physical
ND2880	DIORAMA / painting
QE461	DIORITE
QD543	DIOSMOSIS
PL8143	DIOUR LANGUAGE SEE DYUR LANGUAGE
VK572	DIP OF THE HORIZON SEE HORIZON, DIP OF
BL1213.D5	DIPAVALI SEE DIVALI
QR201.D5	DIPHTHERIA — BACTERIOLOGY
RC138	DIPHTHERIA — BIOCHEMIC TREATMENT
RX226.D6	DIPHTHERIA — HOMEOPATHIC TREATMENT
RC138	DIPHTHERIA — HOSPITALS
RA644.D6	DIPHTHERIA — PREVENTION
RC138	DIPHTHERIA
QB213	DIPLEIDOSCOPE
LB2388	DIPLOMA FACTORIES SEE DIPLOMA MILLS
LB2388	DIPLOMA MILLS
JX1677	DIPLOMACY — LANGUAGE
JX1621-1894	DIPLOMACY
JX1705-1894	DIPLOMATIC AND CONSULAR SERVICE — REGISTERS, LISTS, ETC.
JX1621-1894	DIPLOMATIC AND CONSULAR SERVICE
JX1671-2	DIPLOMATIC IMMUNITIES SEE DIPLOMATIC PRIVILEGES AND IMMUNITIES
JX1705-1894	DIPLOMATIC LISTS SEE DIPLOMATIC AND CONSULAR SERVICE — REGISTERS, LISTS, ETC.
JX4473	DIPLOMATIC NEGOTIATIONS IN INTERNATIONAL DISPUTES
JX1671-2	DIPLOMATIC PRIVILEGES AND IMMUNITIES
JX4263.P7-8	DIPLOMATIC PROTECTION
CD	DIPLOMATICS
Z6601-6625	DIPLOMATICS / catalogs of manuscripts
Z105-115	DIPLOMATICS / paleography
JX1621-1894	DIPLOMATS
QL449	DIPLOPODA SEE MILLEPEDS
QL696.P2	DIPPERS (BIRDS)
SF918.D5	DIPPING FLUIDS
QC819	DIPPING-NEEDLE
RC565	DIPSOMANIA SEE ALCOHOLISM / disease
HV5001-5720	DIPSOMANIA SEE ALCOHOLISM / temperance
QL531-8	DIPTERA
QE832.D6	DIPTERA, FOSSIL
HD5306	DIRECT ACTION / strikes
TK2661-5	DIRECT CURRENT MACHINERY SEE DYNAMOS — DIRECT CURRENT
TK2611-2699	DIRECT CURRENT MACHINERY SEE ELECTRIC MACHINERY — DIRECT CURRENT
TK2681	DIRECT CURRENT MACHINERY SEE ELECTRIC MOTORS, DIRECT CURRENT
TK3111	DIRECT CURRENT POWER DISTRIBUTION SEE ELECTRIC POWER DISTRIBUTION — DIRECT CURRENT
TK2896	DIRECT ENERGY CONVERSION
TK2896	DIRECT GENERATION OF ELECTRICITY SEE DIRECT ENERGY CONVERSION
JF491-7	DIRECT LEGISLATION SEE REFERENDUM
JF2081	DIRECT PRIMARIES SEE PRIMARIES
JK2071-7	DIRECT PRIMARIES SEE PRIMARIES / u.s.
HJ4621-4831	DIRECT TAXATION SEE INCOME TAX
HJ4651-5	DIRECT TAXATION SEE INCOME TAX / u.s.
HJ2240-7395	DIRECT TAXATION SEE TAXATION
LB1047.5	DIRECTED STUDY SEE SUPERVISED STUDY
TK6565.D5	DIRECTION FINDERS, RADIO SEE RADIO DIRECTION FINDERS / radio
TL696.D5	DIRECTION FINDERS, RADIO SEE RADIO DIRECTION FINDERS / aeronautics
TK6592.M6	DIRECTION FINDING BY SIMULTANEOUS LOBING SEE MONOPULSE RADAR
QP443	DIRECTION, SENSE OF SEE ORIENTATION
BV5053	DIRECTION, SPIRITUAL SEE SPIRITUAL DIRECTION
BX2350.7	DIRECTION, SPIRITUAL SEE SPIRITUAL DIRECTION / catholic
BX2348	DIRECTION, SPIRITUAL SEE SPIRITUAL DIRECTION / monastic
BX382.5	DIRECTION, SPIRITUAL SEE SPIRITUAL DIRECTION / orthodox eastern
AY2001	DIRECTORIES
HD2745	DIRECTORS OF CORPORATIONS
K	DIRECTORS OF CORPORATIONS
BV1531	DIRECTORS OF RELIGIOUS EDUCATION
QA295	DIRICHLET'S SERIES SEE SERIES, DIRICHLET'S
TL650-668	DIRIGIBLE BALLOONS SEE AIR-SHIPS
TE230	DIRT ROADS SEE ROADS, EARTH
DA950.3	DISABILITIES, POLITICAL (GT. BRIT.) SEE CATHOLIC EMANCIPATION / act
BX1492	DISABILITIES, POLITICAL (GT. BRIT.) SEE CATHOLIC EMANCIPATION
BX5200-5207	DISABILITIES, POLITICAL (GT. BRIT.) SEE DISSENTERS, RELIGIOUS — ENGLAND
BR757	DISABILITIES, POLITICAL (GT. BRIT.) SEE TEST ACT, 1673
UB360-366	DISABLED SAILORS SEE VETERANS, DISABLED
UB360-366	DISABLED SOLDIERS SEE VETERANS, DISABLED
UB360-366	DISABLED VETERANS SEE VETERANS, DISABLED
UA12.5	DISARMAMENT — INSPECTION
JX1974.7	DISARMAMENT AND ATOMIC WEAPONS SEE ATOMIC WEAPONS AND DISARMAMENT
JX1974	DISARMAMENT
UA12.5	DISARMAMENT-CONTROL AND INSPECTION SEE DISARMAMENT — INSPECTION
RT108	DISASTER NURSING
HV553-5	DISASTER RELIEF

BF789.D5	DISASTERS — PSYCHOLOGICAL ASPECTS
BF723.D5	DISASTERS — PSYCHOLOGICAL ASPECTS / *child study*
BV5083	DISCERNMENT OF SPIRITS
HD4928.D5	*DISCHARGE BENEFITS* **SEE** WAGES — DISMISSAL WAGE
HV8887	*DISCHARGE GRATUITIES, PRISON* **SEE** PRISON RELEASE GRATUITIES
BV397	DISCIPLES OF CHRIST — HYMNS
BV2532	DISCIPLES OF CHRIST — MISSIONS
BX7301-7343	DISCIPLES OF CHRIST
BT1405	*DISCIPLES OF ST. JOHN* **SEE** MANDAEANS
BS2440	*DISCIPLES, TWELVE* **SEE** APOSTLES
BF632	*DISCIPLINE, MENTAL* **SEE** MENTAL DISCIPLINE / *psychology*
UB790-795	*DISCIPLINE, MILITARY* **SEE** MILITARY DISCIPLINE
LB3011-3095	*DISCIPLINE, SCHOOL* **SEE** SCHOOL DISCIPLINE
QK623.D6	DISCOMYCETES
QA351	*DISCONTINUOUS FUNCTIONS* **SEE** FUNCTIONS, DISCONTINUOUS
QL377.S4	DISCOPHORA (COELENTERATA)
HG1654	DISCOUNT — TABLES, ETC.
HF5551	*DISCOUNT (REBATE)* **SEE** REBATES / *business*
K	*DISCOUNT (REBATE)* **SEE** REBATES / *law*
HG1651-4	DISCOUNT / *banking*
HF5553	DISCOUNT / *business*
K	DISCOUNT / *law*
PN4193.L4	*DISCOURSES* **SEE** LECTURES AND LECTURING
LC6501-6560	*DISCOURSES* **SEE** LECTURES AND LECTURING / *lyceum and lecture courses*
PN6121-9	*DISCOURSES* **SEE** ORATIONS / *collections*
PN4012-4061	*DISCOURSES* **SEE** ORATIONS / *history and criticism*
PS660-668	*DISCOURSES* **SEE** SPEECHES, ADDRESSES, ETC. / *american*
PR1321-9	*DISCOURSES* **SEE** SPEECHES, ADDRESSES, ETC. / *english*
PN4199-4355	*DISCOURSES* **SEE** SPEECHES, ADDRESSES, ETC. / *general collections*
PN6121-9	*DISCOURSES* **SEE** SPEECHES, ADDRESSES, ETC. / *general collections*
TL796.5.U6D	DISCOVERER (ARTIFICIAL SATELLITE)
G220-420	*DISCOVERERS* **SEE** DISCOVERIES (IN GEOGRAPHY)
G80-99	*DISCOVERERS* **SEE** DISCOVERIES (IN GEOGRAPHY)
G575-890	*DISCOVERERS* **SEE** DISCOVERIES (IN GEOGRAPHY) / *polar regions*
G80-890	*DISCOVERERS* **SEE** EXPLORERS
G80-99	DISCOVERIES (IN GEOGRAPHY)
G220-420	DISCOVERIES (IN GEOGRAPHY)
G575-890	DISCOVERIES (IN GEOGRAPHY) / *polar regions*
T-TX	*DISCOVERIES (IN SCIENCE)* **SEE** INDUSTRIAL ARTS
T15-35	*DISCOVERIES (IN SCIENCE)* **SEE** INVENTIONS / *history*
T201-339	*DISCOVERIES (IN SCIENCE)* **SEE** INVENTIONS / *patents*
T201-339	*DISCOVERIES (IN SCIENCE)* **SEE** PATENTS
Q	*DISCOVERIES (IN SCIENCE)* **SEE** SCIENCE
G575-890	*DISCOVERIES, MARITIME* **SEE** DISCOVERIES (IN GEOGRAPHY) / *polar regions*
G80-99	*DISCOVERIES, MARITIME* **SEE** DISCOVERIES (IN GEOGRAPHY)
G220-420	*DISCOVERIES, MARITIME* **SEE** DISCOVERIES (IN GEOGRAPHY)
HD4903	DISCRIMINATION IN EMPLOYMENT
TS2301.P3	*DISCS* **SEE** PHONORECORDS / *manufacture*
GV1093	*DISCUS THROWING* **SEE** WEIGHT THROWING
RB	*DISEASE (PATHOLOGY)* **SEE** PATHOLOGY
QR175-241	*DISEASE GERMS* **SEE** BACTERIA, PATHOGENIC
RB214	*DISEASE GERMS* **SEE** GERM THEORY OF DISEASE
UG447.8	*DISEASE WARFARE* **SEE** BIOLOGICAL WARFARE
RM214-259	*DISEASE, DIET IN* **SEE** DIET IN DISEASE
RB148	*DISEASE, PERIODIC* **SEE** PERIODIC DISEASE
RB151	DISEASES — CAUSES AND THEORIES OF CAUSATION
RB127	DISEASES — COMPLICATIONS AND SEQUELAE
SF600-998	*DISEASES OF ANIMALS* **SEE** VETERINARY MEDICINE
RJ	*DISEASES OF CHILDREN* **SEE** CHILDREN — DISEASES
RJ	*DISEASES OF CHILDREN* **SEE** INFANTS — DISEASES
SB599-791	*DISEASES OF PLANTS* **SEE** PLANT DISEASES
RG	*DISEASES OF WOMEN* **SEE** WOMAN — DISEASES
RB156	*DISEASES, CHRONIC* **SEE** CHRONIC DISEASES / *pathology*
RA769	*DISEASES, COMMUNICABLE* **SEE** COMMUNICABLE DISEASES / *miscellaneous preventive measures*
RC111-216	*DISEASES, COMMUNICABLE* **SEE** COMMUNICABLE DISEASES / *practice of medicine*
RA643-4	*DISEASES, COMMUNICABLE* **SEE** COMMUNICABLE DISEASES / *public hygiene*
RJ390-399	*DISEASES, CONSTITUTIONAL* **SEE** CONSTITUTIONAL DISEASES / *diseases of children*
RC251-320	*DISEASES, CONSTITUTIONAL* **SEE** CONSTITUTIONAL DISEASES
RA769	*DISEASES, CONTAGIOUS* **SEE** COMMUNICABLE DISEASES / *miscellaneous preventive measures*
RC111-216	*DISEASES, CONTAGIOUS* **SEE** COMMUNICABLE DISEASES / *practice of medicine*
RA643-4	*DISEASES, CONTAGIOUS* **SEE** COMMUNICABLE DISEASES / *public hygiene*
RC620-632	*DISEASES, DEFICIENCY* **SEE** DEFICIENCY DISEASES
RA1146	*DISEASES, FEIGNED* **SEE** BLINDNESS, FEIGNED
RA1146	*DISEASES, FEIGNED* **SEE** MALINGERING
RC633	*DISEASES, HEMORRHAGIC* **SEE** HEMORRHAGIC DISEASES
RB155	*DISEASES, HEREDITARY* **SEE** HEREDITY OF DISEASE
RC90	*DISEASES, IATROGENIC* **SEE** IATROGENIC DISEASES
RA769	*DISEASES, INFECTIOUS* **SEE** COMMUNICABLE DISEASES / *miscellaneous preventive measures*
RC111-216	*DISEASES, INFECTIOUS* **SEE** COMMUNICABLE DISEASES / *practice of medicine*
RA643-4	*DISEASES, INFECTIOUS* **SEE** COMMUNICABLE DISEASES / *public hygiene*
BF173	*DISEASES, MENTAL* **SEE** PSYCHOLOGY, PATHOLOGICAL
RC512-528	*DISEASES, MENTAL* **SEE** PSYCHOSES
RC811	*DISEASES, SUMMER* **SEE** SUMMER DISEASES
UH611	*DISEASES, TROPICAL* **SEE** TROPICS — DISEASES AND HYGIENE / *military hygiene*
RC960-962	*DISEASES, TROPICAL* **SEE** TROPICS — DISEASES AND HYGIENE / *tropical medicine*
VG471	*DISEASES, TROPICAL* **SEE** TROPICS — DISEASES AND HYGIENE / *naval hygiene*
RA789	*DISEASES, TROPICAL* **SEE** TROPICS — DISEASES AND HYGIENE / *hygiene*
RC96	*DISEASES-CLASSIFICATION* **SEE** NOSOLOGY
RB127	*DISEASES-SEQUELAE* **SEE** DISEASES — COMPLICATIONS AND SEQUELAE
SB419	*DISH GARDENING* **SEE** GARDENS, MINIATURE
BF723.H7	*DISHONESTY* **SEE** HONESTY / *child psychology*
BJ1533.H7	*DISHONESTY* **SEE** HONESTY / *ethics*
TX657.D6	*DISHWASHERS* **SEE** DISHWASHING MACHINES
TX657.D6	DISHWASHING MACHINES
RA761-6	DISINFECTION AND DISINFECTANTS
RA637	*DISINTERMENT* **SEE** EXHUMATION
TA492.P7	*DISKS (MECHANICS)* **SEE** PLATES (ENGINEERING)
QD945	*DISLOCATION THEORY* **SEE** DISLOCATIONS IN CRYSTALS
TN690	*DISLOCATION THEORY* **SEE** DISLOCATIONS IN METALS
QD945	*DISLOCATIONS (CRYSTALS)* **SEE** DISLOCATIONS IN CRYSTALS
TN690	*DISLOCATIONS (METALS)* **SEE** DISLOCATIONS IN METALS
QD945	DISLOCATIONS IN CRYSTALS
TN690	DISLOCATIONS IN METALS
RD106	DISLOCATIONS
HD7813	*DISMISSAL OF EMPLOYEES* **SEE** EMPLOYEES, DISMISSAL OF
HD4928.D5	*DISMISSAL WAGE* **SEE** WAGES — DISMISSAL WAGE
QP303	*DISORDERS OF LOCOMOTION* **SEE** LOCOMOTION, DISORDERED / *physiology*
RD680	*DISORDERS OF LOCOMOTION* **SEE** LOCOMOTION, DISORDERED / *pathology*
RC554-574	*DISORDERS OF PERSONALITY* **SEE** PERSONALITY, DISORDERS OF
RC423-7	*DISORDERS OF SPEECH* **SEE** SPEECH, DISORDERS OF
HQ1031	*DISPARITY OF CULTUS* **SEE** MARRIAGE, MIXED
RA960-993	DISPENSARIES
RX6	*DISPENSARIES, HOMEOPATHIC* **SEE** HOMEOPATHY — HOSPITALS AND DISPENSARIES
RE3	DISPENSARIES, OPHTHALMIC AND AURAL
BT157	*DISPENSATIONAL THEOLOGY* **SEE** DISPENSATIONALISM

BT157	DISPENSATIONALISM
BX1939.D6	DISPENSATIONS (CANON LAW)
RS151	DISPENSATORIES
RV431	DISPENSATORIES, ECLECTIC
QC431-5	DISPERSION
QD549	*DISPERSOIDS* **SEE** COLLOIDS / *chemistry*
QP525	*DISPERSOIDS* **SEE** COLLOIDS / *physiology*
D808	*DISPLACED PERSONS (WORLD WAR, 1939-1945)* **SEE** WORLD WAR, 1939-1945 — DISPLACED PERSONS
VM157	DISPLACEMENT (SHIPS)
HD6073.M7	*DISPLAY FIGURES* **SEE** MODELS, FASHION
HF5845-9	DISPLAY OF MERCHANDISE
AM151-3	*DISPLAY TECHNIQUES* **SEE** MUSEUM TECHNIQUES
Z250	*DISPLAY TYPE* **SEE** PRINTING — SPECIMENS
SF757	*DISPOSAL OF DEAD ANIMALS* **SEE** DEAD ANIMALS, REMOVAL AND DISPOSAL OF
TD791-870	*DISPOSAL OF REFUSE* **SEE** REFUSE AND REFUSE DISPOSAL
BV4627.Q	*DISPUTING* **SEE** QUARRELING
QL812	DISSECTION / *comparative anatomy*
BX5200-5207	DISSENTERS, RELIGIOUS — ENGLAND
LB2369	DISSERTATIONS, ACADEMIC / *preparation*
RC554-574	*DISSOCIATION OF PERSONALITY* **SEE** PERSONALITY, DISORDERS OF
QD517	DISSOCIATION
QD561	DISSOCIATION / *electrolysis*
QA613	DISTANCE GEOMETRY
TL696.D65	DISTANCE MEASURING EQUIPMENT (AIRCRAFT TO GROUND STATION)
QC102	DISTANCES — MEASUREMENT / *physics*
TA601	DISTANCES — MEASUREMENT / *surveying*
TL551	DISTANCES — TABLES, ETC. / *aeronautics*
GV1024-5	DISTANCES — TABLES, ETC. / *automobiling*
G109-110	DISTANCES — TABLES, ETC. / *geography*
VF550	DISTANCES — TABLES, ETC. / *naval ordnance*
VK799	DISTANCES — TABLES, ETC. / *navigation*
UF857	DISTANCES — TABLES, ETC. / *ordnance*
SF991	DISTEMPER
QD63.D6	DISTILLATION
TP156.D5	DISTILLATION
QD526	DISTILLATION, FRACTIONAL
QD181.H1	*DISTILLED WATER* **SEE** WATER, DISTILLED
VM505	*DISTILLED WATER* **SEE** WATER, DISTILLED / *sea-water*
HJ5020	DISTILLERY WAREHOUSES / *u.s.*
HD9390-9395	DISTILLING INDUSTRIES / *economics*
TP589-618	DISTILLING INDUSTRIES / *technology*
HD9350.8	*DISTILLING INDUSTRIES-TAXATION* **SEE** LIQUOR TRAFFIC — TAXATION
HJ5021	DISTILLING, ILLICIT / *u.s.*
RC139	DISTOMATOSIS
RC139	*DISTOMIASIS* **SEE** DISTOMATOSIS
HF	*DISTRIBUTION (ECONOMICS)* **SEE** COMMERCE
GT6010-6050	*DISTRIBUTION (ECONOMICS)* **SEE** COMMERCE / *commercial customs*
GN436-440	*DISTRIBUTION (ECONOMICS)* **SEE** COMMERCE / *primitive*
HF5415	*DISTRIBUTION (ECONOMICS)* **SEE** MARKETING
QA273	DISTRIBUTION (PROBABILITY THEORY)
QA273	*DISTRIBUTION FUNCTIONS* **SEE** DISTRIBUTION (PROBABILITY THEORY)
S21.Z2-8	*DISTRIBUTION OF SEED BY THE GOVERNMENT* **SEE** SEED DISTRIBUTION / *congressional committee hearings*
S21.S2	*DISTRIBUTION OF SEED BY THE GOVERNMENT* **SEE** SEED DISTRIBUTION / *dept. of agriculture publications*
HB821	*DISTRIBUTION OF WEALTH* **SEE** WEALTH / *distribution*
HB251	*DISTRIBUTION OF WEALTH* **SEE** WEALTH / *theory*
HB831-8	*DISTRIBUTION OF WEALTH* **SEE** WEALTH / *use*
HD2951-3570	*DISTRIBUTION, COOPERATIVE* **SEE** COOPERATION
HF5431-6	*DISTRIBUTION, COOPERATIVE* **SEE** COOPERATION / *cooperative business*
HF5415	DISTRIBUTIVE EDUCATION
TH7641	*DISTRICT HEATING* **SEE** HEATING FROM CENTRAL STATIONS
RT	*DISTRICT NURSES* **SEE** NURSES AND NURSING
UH490-495	*DISTRICT NURSES* **SEE** NURSES AND NURSING / *army*
VG350-355	*DISTRICT NURSES* **SEE** NURSES AND NURSING / *navy*
F191-205	*DISTRICT OF COLUMBIA-HISTORY* **SEE** WASHINGTON, D.C. — HISTORY
DS232	DITCH, BATTLE OF THE, 627
S621	DITCHES / *agriculture*
TC970	DITCHES / *land drainage*
QD181.S1	DITHIONATES
PA3118.D5	DITHYRAMB / *greek poetry*
DS485.D5	DIU, INDIA — SIEGE, 1539 AND 1545
PL8143	*DIUR LANGUAGE* **SEE** DYUR LANGUAGE
RM375-7	DIURETICS AND DIURESIS
RM666.D6	DIURETIN
QC831	*DIURNAL VARIATION (TERRESTRIAL MAGNETISM)* **SEE** MAGNETISM, TERRESTRIAL — DIURNAL VARIATION
BL1213.D5	DIVALI
QA295	*DIVERGENT SERIES* **SEE** SERIES, DIVERGENT
QL696.P9	DIVERS (BIRDS)
BT378.D5	DIVES AND LAZARUS (PARABLE)
HG4537	*DIVIDENDS-TABLES, ETC.* **SEE** STOCKS — TABLES, ETC.
BL613	DIVINATION / *comparative religion*
BF1745-1779	DIVINATION / *occult sciences*
BT180.G6	*DIVINE GLORY* **SEE** GLORY OF GOD
BX6901-6997	*DIVINE HEALING* **SEE** CHRISTIAN SCIENCE
BT732.5	*DIVINE HEALING* **SEE** FAITH-CURE
RZ400-401	*DIVINE HEALING* **SEE** FAITH-CURE / *medical aspects*
BT97	*DIVINE HEALING* **SEE** MIRACLES
BS2545.M5	*DIVINE HEALING* **SEE** MIRACLES / *new testament*
BS1199.M5	*DIVINE HEALING* **SEE** MIRACLES / *old testament*
BT124	*DIVINE IMMANENCE* **SEE** IMMANENCE OF GOD
JC389	DIVINE RIGHT OF KINGS
VM987	DIVING-BELLS
GV837	DIVING / *aquatic sports*
VM981	DIVING, SUBMARINE — SAFETY MEASURES
VM981-9	DIVING, SUBMARINE
TC183	DIVING, SUBMARINE / *submarine construction*
BF1628	DIVINING-ROD
BT214-215	*DIVINITY OF CHRIST* **SEE** JESUS CHRIST — DIVINITY
QA49	DIVISION — TABLES
HD51	DIVISION OF LABOR
JC355	*DIVISION OF POWERS* **SEE** FEDERAL GOVERNMENT
JF751-786	*DIVISION OF POWERS* **SEE** FEDERAL GOVERNMENT / *federal and state relations*
JF229	*DIVISION OF POWERS* **SEE** SEPARATION OF POWERS
JL-JQ	*DIVISION OF POWERS* **SEE** SEPARATION OF POWERS / *other countries*
JK305	*DIVISION OF POWERS* **SEE** SEPARATION OF POWERS / *u.s.*
QA115	DIVISION / *arithmetic*
HQ824	DIVORCE — BIBLICAL TEACHING
HQ1024	DIVORCE (CANON LAW)
HQ811-960	DIVORCE
BL1213.D5	*DIWALI* **SEE** DIVALI
D542.Y8	*DIXMUDE, BATTLE OF, 1914* **SEE** YSER, BATTLE OF THE, 1914
PL8110.C3	*DJAGA LANGUAGE* **SEE** CHAGA LANGUAGE
BP195.J3-32	*DJAHMIYYA* **SEE** AL-JAHMIYAH
PL8164.Z9	*DJEDJI DIALECT* **SEE** FON DIALECT
PL8276	*DJO LANGUAGE* **SEE** IJO LANGUAGE
F2431.N3	DJUKA TRIBE
TL696.D65	*DME* **SEE** DISTANCE MEASURING EQUIPMENT (AIRCRAFT TO GROUND STATION)
D764	*DNIEPER RIVER CAMPAIGN, 1943* **SEE** WORLD WAR, 1939-1945 — CAMPAIGNS — — DNIEPER RIVER
PL8077	*DO LANGUAGE* **SEE** BINI LANGUAGE
SF429.P5	DOBERMANN PINSCHERS
CJ3188	*DOBLONS* **SEE** DOUBLOONS
RA1065	DOCIMASIA PULMONUM
SB945.D7	DOCK FALSE-WORM
TC553	*DOCK GATES* **SEE** SLUICE GATES
HD8039.L8-82	*DOCK HANDS* **SEE** LONGSHOREMEN
TC355-365	DOCKS / *construction*
VK361-5	DOCKS / *docking facilities*
HE951-3	DOCKS / *etc.*
HE551-9	DOCKS / *transportation and communication*
V220-240	*DOCKYARDS* **SEE** NAVY-YARDS AND NAVAL STATIONS

LB2386	DOCTOR OF PHILOSOPHY DEGREE
GT6330-6370	*DOCTORS* **SEE** PHYSICIANS / *manners and customs*
UH221-324	*DOCTORS* **SEE** PHYSICIANS / *military*
UH400	*DOCTORS* **SEE** PHYSICIANS / *military*
VG100-224	*DOCTORS* **SEE** PHYSICIANS / *naval*
N8223	*DOCTORS IN ART* **SEE** MEDICINE AND ART
BX4669	DOCTORS OF THE CHURCH
LB2381-2391	*DOCTORS' DEGREES* **SEE** DEGREES, ACADEMIC
BS661	*DOCTRINAL ANTHROPOLOGY* **SEE** MAN (THEOLOGY) / *bible*
BT700-745	*DOCTRINAL ANTHROPOLOGY* **SEE** MAN (THEOLOGY) / *doctrinal theology*
BL256	*DOCTRINAL ANTHROPOLOGY* **SEE** MAN (THEOLOGY) / *religion*
BX8727	*DOCTRINE OF CORRESPONDENCES* **SEE** CORRESPONDENCES, DOCTRINE OF
BT19-33	*DOCTRINES* **SEE** DOGMA
TR825	*DOCUMENT COPYING* **SEE** PHOTOCOPYING PROCESSES
HF5736-5746	*DOCUMENT FILES* **SEE** FILES AND FILING (DOCUMENTS) — LIBRARY RECORDS
CD931-4279	*DOCUMENTS* **SEE** ARCHIVES
CD941	*DOCUMENTS* **SEE** ARCHIVES / *directories*
CD950-965	*DOCUMENTS* **SEE** ARCHIVES / *handbooks*
CD	*DOCUMENTS* **SEE** DIPLOMATICS
Z6601-6625	*DOCUMENTS* **SEE** DIPLOMATICS / *catalogs of manuscripts*
Z105-115	*DOCUMENTS* **SEE** DIPLOMATICS / *paleography*
Z265	DOCUMENTS ON MICROFILM
HV8074	*DOCUMENTS, IDENTIFICATION OF* **SEE** LEGAL DOCUMENTS — IDENTIFICATION
QK495.C98	DODDER
QE872.C7	DODO
SF421-439	*DOG* **SEE** DOGS
GR720	*DOG* **SEE** DOGS / *folk-lore*
GT5890	*DOG* **SEE** DOGS / *manners and customs*
QL737.C2	*DOG* **SEE** DOGS / *zoology*
SF421	DOG BREEDERS' SOCIETIES
HJ5791-2	*DOG LICENSES* **SEE** DOGS — TAXATION
BX2015.5.H	DOG MASS
SF440	DOG RACING
QL795.D6	*DOG STORIES* **SEE** DOGS — LEGENDS AND STORIES
GV1109	DOG-FIGHTING
SF425	DOG-SHOWS
D582.D6	DOGGER BANK, BATTLE OF THE, 1915
BT19-33	DOGMA
SF991	DOGS — DISEASES
SF437-9	DOGS — LAWS AND LEGISLATION
QL795.D6	DOGS — LEGENDS AND STORIES
QP	DOGS — PHYSIOLOGY
SF430	DOGS — PICTURES, ILLUSTRATIONS, ETC.
N7660	DOGS — PICTURES, ILLUSTRATIONS, ETC.
PN6110.D	DOGS — POETRY
SF423	DOGS — STUD-BOOKS
HJ5791-2	DOGS — TAXATION
SF431	DOGS — TRAINING
GR720	DOGS (IN RELIGION, FOLK-LORE, ETC.) / *folk-lore*
BL325.A6	DOGS (IN RELIGION, FOLK-LORE, ETC.) / *religion*
SF421-439	DOGS
GR720	DOGS / *folk-lore*
GT5890	DOGS / *manners and customs*
QL737.C2	DOGS / *zoology*
QE882.C1	DOGS, FOSSIL
UH100	DOGS, WAR USE OF
SF425	*DOGS-EXHIBITIONS* **SEE** DOG-SHOWS
QK495.C785	DOGWOOD / *botany*
RS165.C85	DOGWOOD / *materia medica*
SB618.P	*DOGWOOD, POISON* **SEE** POISON-SUMAC
PM1171	*DOHEMA LANGUAGE* **SEE** EUDEVE LANGUAGE
PM1171	*DOHME LANGUAGE* **SEE** EUDEVE LANGUAGE
TT775	DOILIES
TT825	DOILIES
TT751	DOILIES
GT3350	DOKHMAS
PQ4094-9	*DOLCE STIL NUOVO* **SEE** ITALIAN POETRY — EARLY TO 1400
GN71-72	DOLICHOCEPHALY
TT200	*DOLL FURNITURE* **SEE** FURNITURE — MODELS
GV1219	DOLL-HOUSES
NK495	DOLL-HOUSES / *art museums*

TS2301.T7	DOLL-HOUSES / *toy manufacture*
HG	DOLLAR
CJ	DOLLAR
GV1219	DOLLS
NK495	DOLLS / *art museums*
TS2301.T7	DOLLS / *manufacture*
GN790-792	DOLMENS
TN967	DOLOMITE / *building stones*
QE391.D6	DOLOMITE / *minerals*
QE471	DOLOMITE / *petrology*
BX2161.5.S	*DOLORS OF OUR LADY, DEVOTION TO* **SEE** SORROWS OF THE BLESSED VIRGIN MARY, DEVOTION TO
QL737.C4	DOLPHINS
QE882.C5	DOLPHINS, FOSSIL
HD1261-5	*DOMAIN, EMINENT* **SEE** EMINENT DOMAIN
HD3865-6	*DOMAIN, EMINENT* **SEE** EMINENT DOMAIN / *public works*
ML1015-1018	*DOMBRA* **SEE** DOMRA
NA2890	DOMES / *architecture*
TH2170	DOMES / *building*
QB84	*DOMES, OBSERVATORY* **SEE** OBSERVATORY DOMES
DA190	DOMESDAY BOOK
SF869	DOMESTIC ANIMALS — AGE
SF998	DOMESTIC ANIMALS — TRANSPORTATION / *quarantine*
SF	DOMESTIC ANIMALS / *animal industry*
GN426	DOMESTIC ANIMALS / *ethnology*
GT5870-5895	DOMESTIC ANIMALS / *manners and customs*
SF757.8	DOMESTIC ANIMALS, EFFECT OF RADIATION ON
SF761-7	*DOMESTIC ANIMALS-ANATOMY* **SEE** VETERINARY ANATOMY
SF600-998	*DOMESTIC ANIMALS-DISEASES* **SEE** VETERINARY MEDICINE
SF757.8	*DOMESTIC ANIMALS-RADIATION EFFECTS* **SEE** DOMESTIC ANIMALS, EFFECT OF RADIATION ON
NA7100-7786	*DOMESTIC ARCHITECTURE* **SEE** ARCHITECTURE, DOMESTIC
TX	*DOMESTIC ECONOMY* **SEE** HOME ECONOMICS
LC37	DOMESTIC EDUCATION
TX298	DOMESTIC ENGINEERING
TH	DOMESTIC ENGINEERING
TD	DOMESTIC ENGINEERING
TX	*DOMESTIC SCIENCE* **SEE** HOME ECONOMICS
TX331-3	*DOMESTIC SERVICE* **SEE** SERVANTS / *home economics*
HD8039.D5-52	*DOMESTIC SERVICE* **SEE** SERVANTS / *labor*
S494	DOMESTICATION
SB123	DOMESTICATION
SF41	DOMESTICATION / *agriculture*
GT5870-5899	DOMESTICATION / *manners and customs*
TX331-3	*DOMESTICS* **SEE** SERVANTS / *home economics*
HD8039.D5-52	*DOMESTICS* **SEE** SERVANTS / *labor*
BX1939.D65	DOMICILE (CANON LAW)
JX4241	DOMICILE / *international law*
E271	DOMINICA, BATTLE OF, 1782
CE85	DOMINICAL LETTERS
PQ7406	DOMINICAN BALLADS AND SONGS / *collections*
PQ7402	DOMINICAN BALLADS AND SONGS / *history*
PQ7400-7409	DOMINICAN LITERATURE
PQ7406	DOMINICAN POETRY / *collections*
PQ7402	DOMINICAN POETRY / *history*
F1938.45	DOMINICAN REPUBLIC — HISTORY — — AMERICAN OCCUPATION, 1916-1924
F1938.3	DOMINICAN REPUBLIC — HISTORY — — TO 1844
F1938.4	DOMINICAN REPUBLIC — HISTORY — — 1844-1930
F1938.5	DOMINICAN REPUBLIC — HISTORY — — 1930-
Z7840.D7	DOMINICANS — BIO-BIBLIOGRAPHY
BX3501-3555	DOMINICANS
BX4341-4	DOMINICANS / *women*
JX4408-4449	*DOMINION OF THE SEA* **SEE** MARITIME LAW / *international law*
JX63	*DOMINION OF THE SEA* **SEE** MARITIME LAW / *private*
GV1468	DOMINO BRIDGE
GV1467	DOMINOES
BX7801-7843	*DOMPELAERS* **SEE** CHURCH OF THE BRETHREN
MT643.3	DOMRA — STUDIES AND EXERCISES
M282-3	DOMRA AND PIANO MUSIC
M282-3	DOMRA AND PIANO MUSIC, ARRANGED
M142.D6	DOMRA MUSIC

M1037.4.D64	DOMRA WITH CHAMBER ORCHESTRA
M1037.4.D64	DOMRA WITH ORCHESTRA
ML1015-1018	DOMRA
MT643	DOMRA — METHODS — — SELF-INSTRUCTION
QB723.D	DONATI'S COMET
BX875.D6-7	DONATION OF CONSTANTINE
DD126.5	DONATION OF PEPIN
HV16-25	*DONATIONS* **SEE** ENDOWMENTS / *charities*
LB2336-7	*DONATIONS* **SEE** ENDOWMENTS / *higher education*
GT3050	*DONATIONS* **SEE** GIFTS / *manners and customs*
BT1370	DONATISTS
E472.97	DONELSON, FORT, BATTLE OF, 1862
E405.2	DONIPHAN'S EXPEDITION, 1846-1847
SF361	*DONKEYS* **SEE** ASSES AND MULES
F868.N5	DONNER PARTY
RC203.G	*DONOVANOSIS* **SEE** GRANULOMA VENEREUM
BT880-881	*DOOMSDAY* **SEE** JUDGMENT DAY
DA190	*DOOMSDAY BOOK* **SEE** DOMESDAY BOOK
TH2279	DOOR FITTINGS
HF5446-5456	*DOOR-TO-DOOR SELLING* **SEE** CANVASSING
HF5458-9	*DOOR-TO-DOOR SELLING* **SEE** PEDDLERS AND PEDDLING
HF5716.D	DOORS — TABLES AND READY-RECKONERS
TH2278	DOORS / *building*
NA3010	DOORWAYS
QL596.S3	*DOR-BUG* **SEE** COCKCHAFERS
PM3753	DORASKEAN LANGUAGES
DF251	DORIANS
NA2860	*DORIC COLUMNS* **SEE** COLUMNS, DORIC
SF489.D7	DORKINGS
NA6602.D6	DORMITORIES — DESIGNS AND PLANS
TH9445.D6	DORMITORIES — FIRES AND FIRE PREVENTION
LB3227	DORMITORIES
DQ107.S8	DORNACH, BATTLE OF, 1499
DT429	DOROBO (AFRICAN PEOPLE)
F83.4	DORR REBELLION, 1842
QL638.Z4	DORY (FISH)
HQ1017	*DOS* **SEE** DOWRY
RZ416	*DOSIMETRIC MEDICINE* **SEE** MEDICINE, DOSIMETRIC
NE440	DOTTED PRINTS (ENGRAVINGS)
MT331	DOUBLE BASS — ORCHESTRA STUDIES
MT330	DOUBLE BASS — STUDIES AND EXERCISES
M1018	DOUBLE BASS WITH CHAMBER ORCHESTRA
M1018	DOUBLE BASS WITH ORCHESTRA — SOLO WITH PIANO
M1018	DOUBLE BASS WITH ORCHESTRA
M1105-6	DOUBLE BASS WITH STRING ORCHESTRA
ML920-925	DOUBLE BASS
RC554-574	*DOUBLE CONSCIOUSNESS* **SEE** PERSONALITY, DISORDERS OF
QA581	*DOUBLE CURVATURE, CURVES OF* **SEE** CURVES OF DOUBLE CURVATURE
QA311	*DOUBLE INTEGRALS* **SEE** INTEGRALS, MULTIPLE
JX4231.D7	*DOUBLE NATIONALITY* **SEE** DUAL NATIONALITY
GV1295.P6	DOUBLE PENUCHLE
M850-852	*DOUBLE QUARTETS* **SEE** STRING OCTETS (4 VIOLINS, 2 VIOLAS, 2 VIOLONCELLOS)
QC425	*DOUBLE REFRACTION* **SEE** REFRACTION, DOUBLE
QD191	*DOUBLE SALTS* **SEE** SALTS, DOUBLE
QB821-9	*DOUBLE STARS* **SEE** STARS, DOUBLE
QB903	*DOUBLE STARS* **SEE** STARS, DOUBLE / *spectra*
QB421	*DOUBLE STARS* **SEE** STARS, DOUBLE / *theory*
HJ2341-3	*DOUBLE TAXATION* **SEE** TAXATION, DOUBLE
M290-291	*DOUBLE-BASS AND BASSOON MUSIC* **SEE** BASSOON AND DOUBLE-BASS MUSIC
M290-291	*DOUBLE-BASS AND BASSOON MUSIC* **SEE** BASSOON AND DOUBLE-BASS MUSIC
M237-8	DOUBLE-BASS AND PIANO MUSIC
M237-8	DOUBLE-BASS AND PIANO MUSIC, ARRANGED
M286-7	*DOUBLE-BASS AND VIOLA D'AMORE MUSIC* **SEE** VIOLA D'AMORE AND DOUBLE-BASS MUSIC
M55-57	DOUBLE-BASS MUSIC
ML398	*DOUBLE-BASS PLAYERS* **SEE** VIOLINISTS, VIOLONCELLISTS, ETC. / *biography collective*
ML418	*DOUBLE-BASS PLAYERS* **SEE** VIOLINISTS, VIOLONCELLISTS, ETC. / *individual*
ML927.V63	*DOUBLE-BASS VIOL* **SEE** VIOLONE
GV1507.D65	DOUBLE-CROSTICS
CJ3188	DOUBLOONS
BD215	*DOUBT* **SEE** BELIEF AND DOUBT / *philosophy*
BF773	*DOUBT* **SEE** BELIEF AND DOUBT / *psychology*
TX769	DOUGH
SB608.F4	DOUGLAS FIR PITCH MOTH
TA419-420	DOUGLAS FIR / *building materials*
SD397.D7	DOUGLAS FIR / *forestry*
TL686.D65	DOUGLAS TRANSPORT PLANES
BX7433	*DOUKHOBORS* **SEE** DUKHOBORS
PL8045	*DOUMA LANGUAGE* **SEE** ADUMA LANGUAGE
SF959.D6	DOURINE
BV168.D6	DOVE (IN RELIGION, FOLK-LORE, ETC.) / *religion*
NA8370	DOVE-COTES
BV168.D6	*DOVES* **SEE** DOVE (IN RELIGION, FOLK-LORE, ETC.) / *religion*
QL696.C6	*DOVES* **SEE** PIGEONS
SF465-472	*DOVES* **SEE** PIGEONS / *breeding*
HE6239.P	*DOVES* **SEE** PIGEONS / *carrier pigeons*
UH90	*DOVES* **SEE** PIGEONS / *military communications*
QL697	*DOWN* **SEE** FEATHERS
DH206.D6	DOWNS, BATTLE OF THE, 1639
TL574.D6	DOWNWASH (AERODYNAMICS)
BX1939.D	DOWRY (CANON LAW)
HG9281-7	*DOWRY INSURANCE* **SEE** INSURANCE, MARRIAGE ENDOWMENT
HQ1017	DOWRY
BV194.D	DOXOLOGY
QA141.5	*DOZEN SYSTEM* **SEE** DUODECIMAL SYSTEM
SF78	DRAFT ANIMALS
SF311	DRAFT HORSES
F128.44	DRAFT RIOT, 1863
TF413	DRAFT-GEAR / *railroad cars*
TJ335	*DRAFT, MECHANICAL* **SEE** MECHANICAL DRAFT
UB340-355	*DRAFT, MILITARY* **SEE** MILITARY SERVICE, COMPULSORY
JF525	*DRAFTING OF BILLS* **SEE** BILL DRAFTING
JN608	*DRAFTING OF BILLS* **SEE** BILL DRAFTING / *gt. brit.*
JK1106	*DRAFTING OF BILLS* **SEE** BILL DRAFTING / *u.s.*
TJ227	*DRAFTING-ROOM PRACTICE* **SEE** DRAWING-ROOM PRACTICE / *mechanical engineering*
T352	*DRAFTING-ROOM PRACTICE* **SEE** DRAWING-ROOM PRACTICE / *mechanical drawing*
TL671.25	*DRAFTING, AIRCRAFT* **SEE** AIRCRAFT DRAFTING
TL253	*DRAFTING, AUTOMOTIVE* **SEE** AUTOMOTIVE DRAFTING
T351-377	*DRAFTING, MECHANICAL* **SEE** MECHANICAL DRAWING
HF1215.D7	DRAFTS
HF1277-1400	DRAFTS / *other countries*
HF1259	DRAFTS / *u.s.*
VG913	*DRAFTSMEN, NAVAL* **SEE** U.S. — DRAFTSMEN
JX1393.D8	DRAGO DOCTRINE / *international relations*
RS165.D7	DRAGON'S BLOOD / *pharmacy*
TP936	DRAGON'S BLOOD / *pigments*
DC127	DRAGONNADES
GR830.D7	DRAGONS
VK594	DRAGS (HYDROGRAPHY)
S594	DRAIN-GAGES
TP839	DRAIN-TILES
TA447	DRAIN-TILES / *testing*
HD1681-3	DRAINAGE LAWS
TN321-5	*DRAINAGE OF MINES* **SEE** MINE DRAINAGE
S621	DRAINAGE / *agriculture*
HD1681-3	DRAINAGE / *economics*
TC970-978	DRAINAGE / *engineering*
GB906	DRAINAGE / *physical geography*
TD913	DRAINAGE, HOUSE
TH6571-6675	DRAINAGE, HOUSE / *plumbing*
TD929	DRAINAGE, HOUSE / *rural sanitation*
TE215	*DRAINAGE, ROAD* **SEE** ROAD DRAINAGE
PN1621-3	DRAMA — ADDRESSES, ESSAYS, LECTURES
Z5781-5	DRAMA — BIO-BIBLIOGRAPHY
PA3136	DRAMA — CHORUS (GREEK DRAMA)
PN6110.5-6120	DRAMA — COLLECTIONS
PN1625	DRAMA — DICTIONARIES
PN1720-1861	DRAMA — HISTORY AND CRITICISM
PN1731	DRAMA — OUTLINES, SYLLABI, ETC.
PN1600-1609	DRAMA — PERIODICALS
PN1611-1619	DRAMA — SOCIETIES, ETC.
PN1701	DRAMA — STUDY AND TEACHING
PN1660-1691	DRAMA — TECHNIQUE
PN1831	DRAMA — 17TH CENTURY
PN1841	DRAMA — 18TH CENTURY

PN1851	DRAMA — 19TH CENTURY
PN1861	DRAMA — 20TH CENTURY
PN3171	DRAMA IN EDUCATION
PN1600-1861	DRAMA
PN3175-3191	*DRAMA, ACADEMIC* **SEE** COLLEGE AND SCHOOL DRAMA / *history and criticism*
PA3461-6	*DRAMA, CLASSICAL* **SEE** CLASSICAL DRAMA / *collections*
PA3024-9	*DRAMA, CLASSICAL* **SEE** CLASSICAL DRAMA / *history and criticism*
PN1870-1879	*DRAMA, HISTORICAL* **SEE** HISTORICAL DRAMA / *history and criticism*
PN1751	DRAMA, MEDIEVAL
PN1831	*DRAMA, MODERN* **SEE** DRAMA — 17TH CENTURY
PN1841	*DRAMA, MODERN* **SEE** DRAMA — 18TH CENTURY
PN1851	*DRAMA, MODERN* **SEE** DRAMA — 19TH CENTURY
PN1861	*DRAMA, MODERN* **SEE** DRAMA — 20TH CENTURY
PN1600-1861	*DRAMA, MODERN* **SEE** DRAMA
PJ371	*DRAMA, ORIENTAL* **SEE** ORIENTAL DRAMA / *collections*
PJ334	*DRAMA, ORIENTAL* **SEE** ORIENTAL DRAMA / *history*
PJ431-3	*DRAMA, ORIENTAL* **SEE** ORIENTAL DRAMA / *translations*
PJ464	*DRAMA, ORIENTAL* **SEE** ORIENTAL DRAMA / *translations*
PN1880	*DRAMA, RELIGIOUS* **SEE** RELIGIOUS DRAMA
PN6120.R4	*DRAMA, RELIGIOUS* **SEE** RELIGIOUS DRAMA / *collections*
PN1720-1861	*DRAMA-BIOGRAPHY* **SEE** DRAMATISTS
Z652.D7	*DRAMA-COPYRIGHT* **SEE** COPYRIGHT — DRAMA
PN44	*DRAMA-PLOT* **SEE** PLOTS (DRAMA, NOVEL, ETC.)
PN145	*DRAMA-PLOT* **SEE** PLOTS (DRAMA, NOVEL, ETC.)
PN1683	*DRAMA-PLOT* **SEE** PLOTS (DRAMA, NOVEL, ETC.) / *drama*
PN3378	*DRAMA-PLOT* **SEE** PLOTS (DRAMA, NOVEL, ETC.) / *fiction*
PN3373	*DRAMA-PLOT* **SEE** PLOTS (DRAMA, NOVEL, ETC.) / *short story*
PN6110.5-6120	*DRAMA-SELECTIONS* **SEE** DRAMA — COLLECTIONS
PN1707	DRAMATIC CRITICISM
ML1950	*DRAMATIC MUSIC* **SEE** BALLAD OPERA / *history*
ML3860	*DRAMATIC MUSIC* **SEE** MUSIC, INCIDENTAL / *aesthetics*
ML2000	*DRAMATIC MUSIC* **SEE** MUSIC, INCIDENTAL / *history*
ML3858	*DRAMATIC MUSIC* **SEE** OPERA / *aesthetics*
ML1700-2110	*DRAMATIC MUSIC* **SEE** OPERA / *history and criticism*
ML1900	*DRAMATIC MUSIC* **SEE** OPERETTA
ML1950	*DRAMATIC MUSIC* **SEE** SINGSPIEL
ML1950	*DRAMATIC MUSIC* **SEE** ZARZUELA
PN145	*DRAMATIC PLOTS* **SEE** PLOTS (DRAMA, NOVEL, ETC.)
PN44	*DRAMATIC PLOTS* **SEE** PLOTS (DRAMA, NOVEL, ETC.)
PN1683	*DRAMATIC PLOTS* **SEE** PLOTS (DRAMA, NOVEL, ETC.) / *drama*
PN3378	*DRAMATIC PLOTS* **SEE** PLOTS (DRAMA, NOVEL, ETC.) / *fiction*
PN3373	*DRAMATIC PLOTS* **SEE** PLOTS (DRAMA, NOVEL, ETC.) / *short story*
PN1720-1861	DRAMATISTS
NA7800-7850	*DRAMSHOPS* **SEE** HOTELS, TAVERNS, ETC. / *architecture*
GT3770-3899	*DRAMSHOPS* **SEE** HOTELS, TAVERNS, ETC. / *manners and customs*
HD9350-9399	*DRAMSHOPS* **SEE** LIQUOR TRAFFIC
HV5001-5720	*DRAMSHOPS* **SEE** LIQUOR TRAFFIC
DD119.2	DRANG NACH OSTEN
NC775	DRAPERY IN ART
TT390	DRAPERY
NK3195	DRAPERY / *upholstery*
HF5849.D6	DRAPERY / *window displays*
SF78	*DRAUGHT ANIMALS* **SEE** DRAFT ANIMALS
TJ335	*DRAUGHT, MECHANICAL* **SEE** MECHANICAL DRAFT
GV1461-3	*DRAUGHTS* **SEE** CHECKERS
DS425	*DRAVIDIAN CIVILIZATION* **SEE** CIVILIZATION, DRAVIDIAN
PL4601-4794	DRAVIDIAN LANGUAGES
PL4906	DRAVIDIAN POETRY / *collections*
PL4902	DRAVIDIAN POETRY / *history*
GV1251-3	*DRAW-POKER* **SEE** POKER
HF1715-1718	DRAWBACKS

TG420	DRAWBRIDGES
NC390-670	DRAWING — INSTRUCTION
NC610-635	DRAWING — INSTRUCTION / *public schools*
N8530-8540	DRAWING INSTRUMENTS
T375-7	DRAWING INSTRUMENTS / *mechanical drawing*
N8540	DRAWING MATERIALS — CATALOGS
T377	DRAWING MATERIALS — CATALOGS / *mechanical drawing*
T352	DRAWING-ROOM PRACTICE / *mechanical drawing*
TJ227	DRAWING-ROOM PRACTICE / *mechanical engineering*
NC	DRAWING
TL671.25	*DRAWING, AIRCRAFT* **SEE** AIRCRAFT DRAFTING
NA2700-2780	*DRAWING, ARCHITECTURAL* **SEE** ARCHITECTURAL DRAWING
TL253	*DRAWING, AUTOMOTIVE* **SEE** AUTOMOTIVE DRAFTING
BF456.D7	DRAWING, PSYCHOLOGY OF
BF723.D7	DRAWING, PSYCHOLOGY OF / *child study*
T355	*DRAWING, STRUCTURAL* . **SEE** STRUCTURAL DRAWING
NC390-670	*DRAWING-STUDY AND TEACHING* **SEE** DRAWING — INSTRUCTION
NC610-635	*DRAWING-STUDY AND TEACHING* **SEE** DRAWING — INSTRUCTION / *public schools*
NC390-670	*DRAWING-TECHNIQUE* **SEE** DRAWING — INSTRUCTION
NC610-635	*DRAWING-TECHNIQUE* **SEE** DRAWING — INSTRUCTION / *public schools*
NC37-38	DRAWINGS — CATALOGS
NC15	DRAWINGS — EXHIBITIONS
NC30-33	DRAWINGS — PRIVATE COLLECTIONS
NC	DRAWINGS
NC855-875	*DRAWINGS, CRAYON* **SEE** CRAYON DRAWINGS
Z697.D	*DRAWINGS-CLASSIFICATION* **SEE** CLASSIFICATION — DRAWINGS
TT785-791	DRAWN-WORK — PATTERNS
TT785-791	DRAWN-WORK
BF1074-1099	DREAMS
QH61-63	DREDGING (BIOLOGY)
TN422	*DREDGING (GOLD MINING)* **SEE** GOLD DREDGING
TC188	DREDGING MACHINERY
TC187-8	DREDGING
D397	*DREIKAISERBUND, 1881* **SEE** THREE EMPERORS' LEAGUE, 1881
NK4380	DRESDEN PORCELAIN
DC236.7.D8	DRESDEN, BATTLE OF, 1813
DD407.5	DRESDEN, PEACE OF, 1745
GT500-2350	*DRESS* **SEE** CLOTHING AND DRESS
TT507	*DRESS* **SEE** CLOTHING AND DRESS / *design*
TX340	*DRESS* **SEE** CLOTHING AND DRESS / *domestic economy*
GN418-419	*DRESS* **SEE** CLOTHING AND DRESS / *ethnology*
RA779	*DRESS* **SEE** CLOTHING AND DRESS / *hygiene*
TT560	DRESS ACCESSORIES
TT507	*DRESS DESIGN* **SEE** COSTUME DESIGN
TN500-535	*DRESSING OF ORES* **SEE** ORE-DRESSING
TS1962	*DRESSING OF POULTRY* **SEE** POULTRY, DRESSING OF
RD113	*DRESSINGS (SURGERY)* **SEE** BANDAGES AND BANDAGING
RD113	*DRESSINGS (SURGERY)* **SEE** SPLINTS (SURGERY)
HF5686.D	DRESSMAKING — ACCOUNTING
TT500-560	DRESSMAKING
HD9942	DRESSMAKING / *economics*
UF620.D	DREYSE MACHINE-GUN
TX609	*DRIED FOODS* **SEE** FOOD, DRIED
SF259	*DRIED MILK* **SEE** MILK, DRIED
TP937.7	DRIERS
GB2401-2598	*DRIFT OF SEA ICE* **SEE** SEA ICE DRIFT
QE697	DRIFT
GB423	*DRIFT, CONTINENTAL* **SEE** CONTINENTS
S687-9	DRILL (AGRICULTURAL IMPLEMENT)
GV1797	DRILL (NOT MILITARY)
TJ1260	DRILL PRESSES
TJ1260-1270	DRILLING AND BORING MACHINERY / *machine tools*
TJ1160	DRILLING AND BORING / *machine-shop practice*
GN447.D7	DRILLING AND BORING / *primitive man*
VM453	*DRILLING PLATFORMS* **SEE** DEEP-SEA DRILLING SHIPS
TN871.5	*DRILLING RIGS, OIL WELL* **SEE** OIL WELL DRILLING RIGS

HV5001-5720	DRINK QUESTION SEE LIQUOR PROBLEM
RA642	DRINKING CUPS — HYGIENIC ASPECTS
NK4895	DRINKING CUPS / art objects
NK7100-7230	DRINKING CUPS / gold and silver plate
GT2940-2947	DRINKING CUPS / manners and customs
GT2850-2930	DRINKING CUSTOMS
NA9420	DRINKING FOUNTAINS
RA642	DRINKING FOUNTAINS / hygiene
NK4895	DRINKING HORNS SEE DRINKING VESSELS
PN6237	DRINKING SONGS
NK4895	DRINKING VESSELS
TX951	DRINKS SEE BEVERAGES / bartenders' manuals
TX815-817	DRINKS SEE BEVERAGES / home economics
TP500-659	DRINKS SEE BEVERAGES / technology
RM238-257	DRINKS SEE BEVERAGES / therapeutics
TP589-618	DRINKS SEE LIQUORS
GV1291.D7	DRIVE WHIST
TL152	DRIVER EDUCATION SEE AUTOMOBILE DRIVERS
TL152	DRIVERS, AUTOMOBILE SEE AUTOMOBILE DRIVERS
SF305	DRIVING
TL152	DRIVING, AUTOMOBILE SEE AUTOMOBILE DRIVERS
DA943	DROGHEDA — SIEGE, 1641-1642
JN1409-1410	DROGHEDA, STATUTE OF SEE POYNINGS' LAW
JX6505	DROIT D'AUBAINE
PR1251	DROLLS / english drama
QL696.C3	DROMAEIDAE SEE EMUS
QL696.T4	DROMAEOGNATHAE SEE TINAMIFORMES
QL737.U5	DROMEDARIES SEE CAMELS
SF249	DROMEDARIES SEE CAMELS / animal industries
E475.76	DROOP MOUNTAIN, BATTLE OF, 1863
QD98	DROP TESTS (CHEMISTRY) SEE SPOT TESTS (CHEMISTRY)
TS225	DROP-FORGING SEE FORGING / manufacture
TT215-240	DROP-FORGING SEE FORGING / shop work
LC142-8	DROP-OUTS SEE DROPOUTS
LC142-8	DROPOUTS
QD571	DROPPING MERCURY ELECTRODES SEE ELECTRODES, DROPPING MERCURY
QC183	DROPS
RB144	DROPSY
QC929.D8	DROUGHTS
RA1076	DROWNING / legal medicine
RC88	DROWNING, RESTORATION FROM
RC566	DRUG ADDICTIONS SEE NARCOTIC HABIT
HV5800-5840	DRUG ADDICTIONS SEE NARCOTIC HABIT / economics
RC566	DRUG HABIT SEE NARCOTIC HABIT
HV5800-5840	DRUG HABIT SEE NARCOTIC HABIT / economics
RS122	DRUG RESEARCH SEE PHARMACEUTICAL RESEARCH
HF6201.D4-6	DRUG TRADE / business
HD9665-9675	DRUG TRADE / economics
HD9000.9	DRUG TRADE-LAW AND LEGISLATION SEE DRUGS — LAWS AND LEGISLATION / food and drug laws
HD9665.7	DRUG TRADE-LAW AND LEGISLATION SEE DRUGS — LAWS AND LEGISLATION
RS4-17	DRUG TRADE-LAW AND LEGISLATION SEE PHARMACY — LAWS AND LEGISLATION
RS	DRUGGISTS SEE PHARMACISTS
GT6380	DRUGGISTS SEE PHARMACISTS / manners and customs
RS421-431	DRUGS — ADULTERATION AND ANALYSIS / pharmaceutical chemistry
RS355-6	DRUGS — CATALOGS
HD9665.7	DRUGS — LAWS AND LEGISLATION
HD9000.9	DRUGS — LAWS AND LEGISLATION / food and drug laws
RS159	DRUGS — PRESERVATION
HD9665-9675	DRUGS — PRICES AND SALE
RS189	DRUGS — STANDARDS
QP905-981	DRUGS / pharmacology
RS	DRUGS / pharmacy
RM	DRUGS / therapeutics
RS122	DRUGS-RESEARCH SEE PHARMACEUTICAL RESEARCH
BL910	DRUIDS AND DRUIDISM
M298	DRUM AND BAGPIPE MUSIC SEE BAGPIPE AND DRUM MUSIC
M1270	DRUM AND BUGLE MUSIC SEE BUGLE AND DRUM MUSIC
M1270	DRUM AND BUGLE-CALLS SEE MILITARY CALLS

UH40-45	DRUM AND BUGLE-CALLS SEE MILITARY CALLS
M1270	DRUM AND FIFE MUSIC SEE FIFE AND DRUM MUSIC
M298	DRUM AND GUITAR MUSIC SEE GUITAR AND DRUM MUSIC
M298	DRUM AND GUITAR MUSIC SEE GUITAR AND DRUM MUSIC
M298	DRUM AND TRUMPET MUSIC SEE TRUMPET AND DRUM MUSIC
M298	DRUM AND TRUMPET MUSIC SEE TRUMPET AND DRUM MUSIC
MT733.5	DRUM MAJORS
M146	DRUM MUSIC SEE PERCUSSION MUSIC
ML1035	DRUM
GN467.D8	DRUM / primitive
QE697	DRUMLINS
HF5441-4	DRUMMERS SEE COMMERCIAL TRAVELERS
RC565	DRUNKENNESS SEE ALCOHOLISM / disease
HV5001-5720	DRUNKENNESS SEE ALCOHOLISM / temperance
HV5001-5720	DRUNKENNESS SEE LIQUOR PROBLEM
HV5001-5720	DRUNKENNESS SEE TEMPERANCE
QP801.A3	DRUNKENNESS TESTING SEE ALCOHOL IN THE BODY
DS94.8.D8	DRUSES
BL1695	DRUSES
DS94.8.D8	DRUZES SEE DRUSES
BL1695	DRUZES SEE DRUSES
TP932	DRY CLEANING SEE CLEANING AND DYEING INDUSTRY / garment cleaning
TP909	DRY CLEANING SEE CLEANING AND DYEING INDUSTRY / garment dyeing
TP932	DRY CLEANING SEE CLEANING
TP895	DRY CLEANING SEE CLEANING
TP909	DRY CLEANING SEE CLEANING / garments
SB110	DRY FARMING
TP492.8	DRY ICE
TC361	DRY-DOCKS
HF5686.D	DRY-GOODS — ACCOUNTING
HF5716.D8	DRY-GOODS — TABLES, ETC.
HD9950-9969	DRY-GOODS / economics
TS1760-1768	DRY-GOODS / manufacture
NE2220-2225	DRY-POINT
TA422	DRY-ROT
BL820.D	DRYADS
TX609	DRYING APPARATUS — FOOD
TP363	DRYING APPARATUS
TX609	DRYING OF FRUIT SEE FRUIT — EVAPORATION
TP937.7	DRYING OILS
PL8110.C3	DSCHAGGA LANGUAGE SEE CHAGA LANGUAGE
GN659.W2	DSCHAGGAS SEE WACHAGA / ethnology
DT449.K4	DSCHAGGAS SEE WACHAGA / kilimanjaro region
JX4231.D7	DUAL ALLEGIANCE SEE DUAL NATIONALITY
JX4231.D7	DUAL CITIZENSHIP SEE DUAL NATIONALITY
JX4231.D7	DUAL NATIONALITY
PL8141	DUALA LANGUAGE
B812	DUALISM
BD331	DUALISM / ontology
B851-4695	DUALISM / systems
PL8141	DUALLA LANGUAGE SEE DUALA LANGUAGE
TS1580	DUCK (TEXTILE)
SK333.D8	DUCK HUNTING SEE DUCK SHOOTING
SK333.D8	DUCK SHOOTING
QL737.M7	DUCKBILLS
HV8626	DUCKING STOOL SEE CUCKING STOOL
QL696.A5	DUCKS
SF505	DUCKS / breeding
QL868	DUCTLESS GLANDS SEE GLANDS, DUCTLESS / comparative anatomy
QM371	DUCTLESS GLANDS SEE GLANDS, DUCTLESS / human anatomy
QP187	DUCTLESS GLANDS SEE GLANDS, DUCTLESS / physiology
TH7683.D8	DUCTS, AIR SEE AIR DUCTS
QL867	DUCTS, BILE SEE BILE-DUCTS / comparative anatomy
RC849	DUCTS, BILE SEE BILE-DUCTS / diseases
QM351	DUCTS, BILE SEE BILE-DUCTS / human anatomy
RD546-7	DUCTS, BILE SEE BILE-DUCTS / surgical treatment
M145	DUDA MUSIC
ML980	DUDA
SK601	DUDE RANCHES
CT9985-6	DUDES SEE DANDIES / biography

E99.D8	DUDLEY INDIANS
E356.D8	DUDLEY'S DEFEAT, 1813
JL-JQ	DUE PROCESS OF LAW / u.s.
JK1548.D	DUE PROCESS OF LAW / u.s.
K	DUE PROCESS OF LAW / u.s.
CR4571-4595	DUELING / code
CR4571-4595	*DUELS* **SEE** DUELING / code
TL215.D8	DUESENBERG AUTOMOBILE
M253-4	*DUETS* **SEE** BASSOON AND PIANO MUSIC
M288-9	*DUETS* **SEE** FLUTE MUSIC (2 FLUTES)
M146	*DUETS* **SEE** PERCUSSION MUSIC
M204	*DUETS* **SEE** PIANO MUSIC (4 HANDS)
M200-201	*DUETS* **SEE** PIANO MUSIC (4 HANDS)
BX7433	DUKHOBORS
E98.R2	*DUKWALLI* **SEE** WOLF RITUAL
QK495.S7	*DULCAMARA* **SEE** BITTERSWEET
M142.D8	DULCIMER MUSIC
ML1015-1018	DULCIMER
PL4001.L8	*DULIEN LANGUAGE* **SEE** LUSHEI LANGUAGE
PL8045	*DUMA LANGUAGE* **SEE** ADUMA LANGUAGE
PK1837	DUMAKI LANGUAGE
RF320	*DUMB (DEAF-MUTES)* **SEE** DEAF
HV2350-2990	*DUMB (DEAF-MUTES)* **SEE** DEAF / charities
GV487	DUMB-BELLS
E83.72	*DUMMER'S WAR* **SEE** EASTERN INDIANS, WARS WITH, 1722-1726
TL230	DUMP TRUCKS
TL230	*DUMPERS (MOTOR TRUCKS)* **SEE** DUMP TRUCKS
HF1425	DUMPING (COMMERCIAL POLICY)
TJ1418	DUMPING APPLIANCES
GB631-8	*DUNES* **SEE** SAND-DUNES
DC124.45	DUNES, BATTLE OF THE, 1658
PL801.D9	DUNGAN LANGUAGE
HV8301-9920	*DUNGEONS* **SEE** PRISONS
QE461	DUNITE
BX7801-7843	*DUNKARDS* **SEE** CHURCH OF THE BRETHREN
BX7801-7843	*DUNKERS* **SEE** CHURCH OF THE BRETHREN
DS220.5	DUNKIRK, FRANCE — SIEGE, 1793
DC124.45	*DUNKIRK, FRANCE, BATTLE OF, 1658* **SEE** DUNES, BATTLE OF THE, 1658
D756.5.D8	DUNKIRK, FRANCE, BATTLE OF, 1940
E83.77	DUNMORE'S EXPEDITION, 1774
QA141.5	DUODECIMAL SYSTEM
RC804.R6	DUODENUM — RADIOGRAPHY
QL863	DUODENUM / comparative anatomy
QM345	DUODENUM / human anatomy
QP156	DUODENUM / physiology
Z696	*DUPLEX-NUMERIC CLASSIFICATION* **SEE** CLASSIFICATION, DUPLEX-NUMERIC
GV1282	DUPLICATE AUCTION BRIDGE
GV1282.3	DUPLICATE CONTRACT BRIDGE
GV1283	DUPLICATE WHIST
Z689	DUPLICATES IN LIBRARIES
Z48	*DUPLICATING PROCESSES* **SEE** COPYING PROCESSES
QA469	*DUPLICATION OF THE CUBE* **SEE** CUBE, DUPLICATION OF
TL699.D9	DURALUMIN / aeronautics
TA480.A6	DURALUMIN / materials of construction general
QP445	*DURATION, INTUITION OF* **SEE** TIME PERCEPTION
D589.U6	DURAZZO, BATTLE OF, 1918 / u.s. navy
DG266	DURAZZO, BATTLE OF, 48 B.C.
DS480.3	DURBARS
DS422	DURBARS
DS480	DURBARS
SF193.D9	*DURHAM CATTLE* **SEE** POLLED DURHAM CATTLE / herd-books
SF199.S56	*DURHAM CATTLE* **SEE** SHORTHORN CATTLE
SF193.S5	*DURHAM CATTLE* **SEE** SHORTHORN CATTLE / herd-books
SF393.D9	DUROC JERSEY SWINE
SB191.W5	*DURUM WHEAT* **SEE** WHEAT
GT5899.W5	*DURUM WHEAT* **SEE** WHEAT / manners and customs
BL1213.D	*DUSSERA* **SEE** DASARA
QR101	DUST — BACTERIOLOGY
TE221	DUST — PREVENTION
TH7692-8	DUST — REMOVAL
RC774	*DUST DISEASES* **SEE** LUNGS — DUST DISEASES
HD7264	*DUST DISEASES* **SEE** LUNGS — DUST DISEASES / labor

HD7262	DUST EXPLOSION
TH7692-8	*DUST EXTRACTION* **SEE** DUST — REMOVAL
QC929.S5	*DUST SHOWERS* **SEE** DUST-FALL
QC958	DUST STORMS
QC929.S5	DUST-FALL
QC882	DUST / atmosphere
HD7264	DUST / labor hygiene
HD7262	*DUST-EXPLOSIONS* **SEE** DUST EXPLOSION
DS646.33	DUSUNS
PT5480	DUTCH BALLADS AND SONGS / collections
PT5239	DUTCH BALLADS AND SONGS / history
PT5490-5515	DUTCH DRAMA / collections
PT5250-5295	DUTCH DRAMA / etc.
SB608.E	DUTCH ELM DISEASE
PT5539	DUTCH ESSAYS
PT5520-5530	DUTCH FICTION / collections
PT5320-5336	DUTCH FICTION / etc.
PF771-8	DUTCH LANGUAGE — EARLY TO 1500
PF1-979	DUTCH LANGUAGE
PT5121-5137	DUTCH LITERATURE — EARLY TO 1500
PT5141-5165	DUTCH LITERATURE — 1500-1800
PT5170-5175	DUTCH LITERATURE — 19TH CENTURY
PT5180-5185	DUTCH LITERATURE — 20TH CENTURY
PT5400-5547	DUTCH LITERATURE / collections
PT5001-5395	DUTCH LITERATURE / etc.
PN5251-9	DUTCH NEWSPAPERS / etc.
PT5535	DUTCH ORATIONS / collections
PT5340	DUTCH ORATIONS / history
PN5251-5260	DUTCH PERIODICALS / etc.
PF1-979	DUTCH PHILOLOGY
PT5425-5435	DUTCH POETRY — EARLY TO 1500 / collections
PT5131-4	DUTCH POETRY — EARLY TO 1500 / history
PT5477	DUTCH POETRY — 1500-1800 / collections
PT5215-5222	DUTCH POETRY — 1500-1800 / history
PT5478	DUTCH POETRY — 19TH CENTURY / collections
PT5225-7	DUTCH POETRY — 19TH CENTURY / history
PT5478	DUTCH POETRY — 20TH CENTURY / collections
PT5230-5232	DUTCH POETRY — 20TH CENTURY / history
PT5470-5488	DUTCH POETRY / collections
PT5201-5245	DUTCH POETRY / etc.
TP382	*DUTCH STANDARD (SUGAR TESTING)* **SEE** SUGAR — ANALYSIS AND TESTING
D277-8	DUTCH WAR, 1672-1678
PT5346	DUTCH WIT AND HUMOR
PT5541	DUTCH WIT AND HUMOR
PN6222.D8	DUTCH WIT AND HUMOR / minor collections
DL192	*DUTCH-SWEDISH WAR, 1658-1659* **SEE** SWEDISH-DUTCH WAR, 1658-1659
HJ9120	*DUTIES* **SEE** OCTROI
HJ6603-7380	*DUTIES* **SEE** TARIFF / administration
HF1761-2580	*DUTIES* **SEE** TARIFF / other countries
HJ6041-6464	*DUTIES* **SEE** TARIFF / schedules
HF1701-2701	*DUTIES* **SEE** TARIFF / theory and history
HF1750-1759	*DUTIES* **SEE** TARIFF / u.s.
HJ2240-7395	*DUTIES* **SEE** TAXATION
BJ1450-1458	DUTY
PK3811	*DVAITA (SANKHYA)* **SEE** SANKHYA / philology
B132.S3	*DVAITA (SANKHYA)* **SEE** SANKHYA / philosophy
E99.D9	DWAMISH INDIANS
SB357.5	DWARF FRUIT TREES
SB357.5	*DWARF TREES* **SEE** DWARF FRUIT TREES
GN681	DWARFS / ethnography
GR555	DWARFS / folk-lore
GN69.3-5	DWARFS / somatology
TH9445.D9	DWELLINGS — FIRES AND FIRE PREVENTION
TH4811	DWELLINGS — TESTING
NA7100-7566	DWELLINGS / architecture
TH148	DWELLINGS / building popular works
TH8901	DWELLINGS / building maintenance
TX301-339	DWELLINGS / domestic economy
HD1341	DWELLINGS / economics
GR490	DWELLINGS / folk-lore
GT170-384	DWELLINGS / manners and customs
PL5301-4	DYAK LANGUAGE
DS646.3	DYAKS
SB285-7	DYE PLANTS
HD9999.D8-9	*DYEING* **SEE** DYES AND DYEING / economics

TP897-929	*DYEING* **SEE** DYES AND DYEING / *technology*
TP909	*DYEING INDUSTRY* **SEE** CLEANING AND DYEING INDUSTRY / *garment dyeing*
TP932	*DYEING INDUSTRY* **SEE** CLEANING AND DYEING INDUSTRY / *garment cleaning*
TP893	*DYEING MACHINERY* **SEE** DYES AND DYEING — APPARATUS
QK495.Q4	*DYERS' OAK* **SEE** BLACK OAK / *botany*
SD397.O12	*DYERS' OAK* **SEE** BLACK OAK / *forestry*
TP893	DYES AND DYEING — APPARATUS
TP893	DYES AND DYEING — CHEMISTRY
TP930	DYES AND DYEING — COTTON
TS1109	DYES AND DYEING — PAPER
TP901	DYES AND DYEING — SILK
TP899	DYES AND DYEING — WOOL
HD9999.D8-9	DYES AND DYEING / *economics*
TP897-929	DYES AND DYEING / *technology*
TP909	DYES AND DYEING, DOMESTIC
TX571.C7	*DYES AND DYEING-FOOD* **SEE** COLORING MATTER IN FOOD
TS1061	*DYES AND DYEING-FUR* **SEE** FUR — DRESSING AND DYEING
TT973	*DYES AND DYEING-HAIR* **SEE** HAIR — DYEING AND BLEACHING
TP893	*DYESTUFFS* **SEE** DYES AND DYEING — CHEMISTRY
TC337	*DYKES* **SEE** DIKES (ENGINEERING)
QE611	*DYKES* **SEE** DIKES (GEOLOGY)
HF5548	*DYNAMIC MODELS (COMPUTER PROGRAM LANGUAGE)* **SEE** DYNAMO (COMPUTER PROGRAM LANGUAGE)
QA264	*DYNAMIC PROGRAMMING* **SEE** PROGRAMMING (MATHEMATICS)
QA851-5	DYNAMICS OF A PARTICLE
QA845-871	DYNAMICS
QC173	*DYNAMICS, MOLECULAR* **SEE** MOLECULAR DYNAMICS
QC183	*DYNAMICS, MOLECULAR* **SEE** MOLECULAR DYNAMICS / *capillarity*
QA861-3	DYNAMICS, RIGID
QA611.5	*DYNAMICS, TOPOLOGICAL* **SEE** TOPOLOGICAL DYNAMICS
TP285	DYNAMITE
HF5548	DYNAMO (COMPUTER PROGRAM LANGUAGE)
TK2184	DYNAMO TENDERS' MANUALS
TJ1053	DYNAMOMETER
TK2761-5	DYNAMOS — ALTERNATING CURRENT
TK9911	DYNAMOS — AMATEURS' MANUALS
TK2435	DYNAMOS — DESIGN AND CONSTRUCTION
TK2661-5	DYNAMOS — DIRECT CURRENT
TK2475	DYNAMOS — FIELD COILS
TK2433	DYNAMOS — TESTING
TK2411-2491	DYNAMOS
PL8134	*DYOLA LANGUAGE* **SEE** DIOLA LANGUAGE
QA76.8.S4	*DYSEAC COMPUTER* **SEE** SEAC COMPUTER
TK7889.S4	*DYSEAC COMPUTER* **SEE** SEAC COMPUTER / *engineering*
RC140	DYSENTERY
RJ320.D9	DYSOSTOSIS
RX336.D9	DYSPEPSIA — HOMEOPATHIC TREATMENT
RC829	DYSPEPSIA
RB149	DYSTROPHY
PL8143	DYUR LANGUAGE
PL8475	*DZEMA LANGUAGE* **SEE** MABA LANGUAGE
PL8061	*DZILIO LANGUAGE* **SEE** BARI LANGUAGE
PL8276	*DZO LANGUAGE* **SEE** IJO LANGUAGE
DC227.5.D8	DÜRNSTEIN, BATTLE OF, 1805
PL8143	*DZUR LANGUAGE* **SEE** DYUR LANGUAGE
PJ7121-4	*E KILI LANGUAGE* **SEE** SHAURI LANGUAGE
CR4480	*EAGLE (AMPULLA)* **SEE** AMPULLAS, CORONATION
CR41.E2	EAGLE (IN HERALDRY)
CR542	EAGLE (IN HERALDRY) / *france*
BL325.E3	EAGLE (IN RELIGION, FOLK-LORE, ETC.) / *mythology*
E98.D2	EAGLE DANCE
QL696.A2	EAGLES
RF135	EAR — CARE AND HYGIENE
RF1-320	EAR — DISEASES
RF190	EAR — FUNGI
RF126	EAR — SURGERY
RC280.E2	EAR — TUMORS
MT35	EAR TRAINING
NK7300-7399	EAR-RINGS / *art*
TS740-759	EAR-RINGS / *manufacture*
QL430.5.H3	*EAR-SHELLS* **SEE** ABALONES
QP471	*EAR-STONES* **SEE** OTOLITHS / *physiology*
QL948	*EAR-STONES* **SEE** OTOLITHS / *zoology*
QL948	EAR / *comparative anatomy*
QM507	EAR / *human anatomy*
QP461-471	EAR / *physiology*
N7832	*EARLY CHRISTIAN ART* **SEE** ART, EARLY CHRISTIAN
BV185	*EARLY CHRISTIAN LITURGIES* **SEE** LITURGIES, EARLY CHRISTIAN
PA6124	*EARLY CHRISTIAN POETRY* **SEE** CHRISTIAN POETRY, EARLY / *latin*
BV236	*EARLY CHRISTIAN PRAYERS* **SEE** PRAYERS, EARLY CHRISTIAN
BR60-63	*EARLY CHRISTIAN SERMONS* **SEE** SERMONS, EARLY CHRISTIAN
Z1014	*EARLY PRINTED BOOKS* **SEE** BIBLIOGRAPHY — EARLY PRINTED BOOKS 16TH CENTURY
Z240-241	*EARLY PRINTED BOOKS* **SEE** INCUNABULA
E476.66	*EARLY'S INVASION OF MARYLAND AND PENNSYLVANIA, 1864* **SEE** MARYLAND CAMPAIGN, JUNE-AUG., 1864
QE508	EARTH — AGE
QB638	EARTH — CURIOSA AND MISCELLANY
QB341	EARTH — DENSITY
QB281-3	EARTH — FIGURE
QE509	EARTH — INTERNAL STRUCTURE
QB633	EARTH — ROTATION
QE511	EARTH — SURFACE
GR655	EARTH (IN RELIGION, FOLK-LORE, ETC.) / *folk-lore*
BL435	EARTH (IN RELIGION, FOLK-LORE, ETC.) / *nature-worship*
TC543	EARTH DAMS
GN783	EARTH HOUSES
GN783	*EARTH LODGES* **SEE** EARTH HOUSES
TH1094	EARTH MOVEMENTS AND BUILDING
GB481-8	EARTH MOVEMENTS
TA725	*EARTH MOVING MACHINERY* **SEE** EARTHMOVING MACHINERY
TA765	EARTH PRESSURE
TE230	*EARTH ROADS* **SEE** ROADS, EARTH
TL796	*EARTH SATELLITES* **SEE** ARTIFICIAL SATELLITES
QC907	EARTH TEMPERATURE
BL435	*EARTH-WORSHIP* **SEE** EARTH (IN RELIGION, FOLK-LORE, ETC.) / *nature-worship*
GR655	*EARTH-WORSHIP* **SEE** EARTH (IN RELIGION, FOLK-LORE, ETC.) / *folk-lore*
QB631	EARTH / *earth as planet*
QE501	EARTH / *physical history*
RD96.E2	*EARTH, MEDICAL AND SURGICAL USES OF* **SEE** EARTHS, MEDICAL AND SURGICAL USES OF / *antiseptics*
TH1421	*EARTH, RAMMED* **SEE** PISE / *building construction*
QE515	*EARTH-CHEMICAL COMPOSITION* **SEE** GEOCHEMISTRY
QC811-849	*EARTH-MAGNETISM* **SEE** MAGNETISM, TERRESTRIAL
GN783	*EARTHEN HOUSES* **SEE** EARTH HOUSES
NK3700-4695	*EARTHENWARE* **SEE** POTTERY / *ceramics*
TP785-825	*EARTHENWARE* **SEE** POTTERY / *chemical technology*
HD9610-9620	*EARTHENWARE* **SEE** POTTERY / *trade*
NK4670	*EARTHENWARE STOVES* **SEE** STOVES, EARTHENWARE / *art*
TA725	*EARTHMOVERS* **SEE** EARTHMOVING MACHINERY
TA725	EARTHMOVING MACHINERY
HG9970.E3	*EARTHQUAKE INSURANCE* **SEE** INSURANCE, EARTHQUAKE
TH1095	EARTHQUAKES AND BUILDING
TC181	EARTHQUAKES AND HYDRAULIC STRUCTURES
QE531-541	EARTHQUAKES
QC843	EARTHQUAKES / *magnetic effects*
QE541	*EARTHQUAKES-MEASUREMENT* **SEE** SEISMOMETRY
RD96.E2	EARTHS, MEDICAL AND SURGICAL USES OF / *antiseptics*
QD172.R2	EARTHS, RARE
TA721	EARTHWORK — TABLES, CALCULATIONS, ETC.
TA715-770	EARTHWORK
GN789	EARTHWORKS (ARCHAEOLOGY)
QL391.O4	EARTHWORMS
QL510	*EARWIGS* **SEE** DERMAPTERA
RF123	EAR — DISEASES — — DIAGNOSIS

RX441-6	EAR — DISEASES — — HOMEOPATHIC TREATMENT
JX4068.S5	*EASEMENTS* **SEE** SERVITUDES
	/ international law
DS501-519	EAST (FAR EAST)
SF967.E	*EAST AFRICAN COAST FEVER* **SEE** EAST COAST FEVER
CB251	EAST AND WEST
PR8451-4	EAST ARMENIAN LANGUAGE
SF967.E	EAST COAST FEVER
D137-8	*EAST GOTHS* **SEE** GOTHS */ migrations*
BP130-133	*EAST INDIAN PHILOSOPHY* **SEE** PHILOSOPHY, INDIC
BX150-159	*EAST SYRIAN CHURCH* **SEE** NESTORIAN CHURCH
PN6120.E2	EASTER — DRAMA
PN6110.E2	EASTER — POETRY
BV4259	EASTER — SERMONS
NC1280	*EASTER SEALS* **SEE** SEALS (CHRISTMAS, ETC.)
BV55	EASTER
CE83	EASTER */ church calendar*
GT4935	EASTER */ manners and customs*
BX100-189	EASTERN CHURCHES
DF501-649	*EASTERN EMPIRE* **SEE** BYZANTINE EMPIRE
E83.72	EASTERN INDIANS, WARS WITH, 1722-1726
BX200-750	*EASTERN ORTHODOX CHURCH* **SEE** ORTHODOX EASTERN CHURCH
D461-9	EASTERN QUESTION (BALKAN) */ history*
D374-7	EASTERN QUESTION (BALKAN) */ history*
JX1319	EASTERN QUESTION (BALKAN) */ international law*
D378	EASTERN QUESTION (CENTRAL ASIA)
DS515-519	EASTERN QUESTION (FAR EAST) */ history*
JX1321	EASTERN QUESTION (FAR EAST) */ international law*
D371-3	EASTERN QUESTION */ general history*
D374-5	EASTERN QUESTION */ 19th century*
D461-9	EASTERN QUESTION */ 20th century*
BX303	*EASTERN SCHISM* **SEE** SCHISM — EASTERN AND WESTERN CHURCH
SB945.E	EASTERN TENT CATERPILLAR
TX737	*EATING* **SEE** DINNERS AND DINING
TX631-641	*EATING* **SEE** GASTRONOMY
TX871-9	*EATING* **SEE** TABLE
BT1375	EBIONISM
BT1375	*EBIONITES* **SEE** EBIONISM
PL6255	*EBON LANGUAGE* **SEE** MARSHALL LANGUAGE
SB291	*EBONITE* **SEE** RUBBER */ culture*
QC304	EBULLITION
GV1295.E3	ECARTE (GAME)
TK6421	*ECCARD TELEPHONE* **SEE** TELEPHONE — ECCARD SYSTEM
CT9990-9991	*ECCENTRICITIES* **SEE** ECCENTRICS AND ECCENTRICITIES */ biography*
TJ543	ECCENTRICS (MACHINERY)
CT9990-9991	ECCENTRICS AND ECCENTRICITIES */ biography*
BR130-133	*ECCLESIASTICAL ANTIQUITIES* **SEE** CHRISTIAN ANTIQUITIES
NA4790-6113	*ECCLESIASTICAL ARCHITECTURE* **SEE** CHURCH ARCHITECTURE
N7810-8185	*ECCLESIASTICAL ART* **SEE** CHRISTIAN ART AND SYMBOLISM
BV150-168	*ECCLESIASTICAL ART* **SEE** CHRISTIAN ART AND SYMBOLISM */ theology*
BV775	*ECCLESIASTICAL BENEFICES* **SEE** BENEFICES, ECCLESIASTICAL
BX1955	*ECCLESIASTICAL BENEFICES* **SEE** BENEFICES, ECCLESIASTICAL */ catholic church*
BR1690-1725	*ECCLESIASTICAL BIOGRAPHY* **SEE** CHRISTIAN BIOGRAPHY
CE81-83	*ECCLESIASTICAL CALENDAR* **SEE** CHURCH CALENDAR
CE81	*ECCLESIASTICAL CHRONOLOGY* **SEE** CHRONOLOGY, ECCLESIASTICAL
BV765	*ECCLESIASTICAL CORPORATIONS* **SEE** CORPORATIONS, RELIGIOUS
BV167	*ECCLESIASTICAL COSTUME* **SEE** CHURCH VESTMENTS
BX1925	*ECCLESIASTICAL COSTUME* **SEE** CHURCH VESTMENTS */ catholic church*
BX5180	*ECCLESIASTICAL COSTUME* **SEE** CHURCH VESTMENTS */ church of england*
BX2790	*ECCLESIASTICAL COSTUME* **SEE** CHURCH VESTMENTS */ monastic*
BX4223	*ECCLESIASTICAL COSTUME* **SEE** MONASTICISM AND RELIGIOUS ORDERS — HABIT */ sisterhoods*
BX2790	*ECCLESIASTICAL COSTUME* **SEE** MONASTICISM AND RELIGIOUS ORDERS — HABIT
NA5000	*ECCLESIASTICAL DECORATION AND ORNAMENT* **SEE** CHURCH DECORATION AND ORNAMENT
NK2190	*ECCLESIASTICAL DECORATION AND ORNAMENT* **SEE** CHURCH DECORATION AND ORNAMENT
BR97-99	*ECCLESIASTICAL DIVISIONS* **SEE** ECCLESIASTICAL GEOGRAPHY
CE81	*ECCLESIASTICAL FASTS AND FEASTS* **SEE** FASTS AND FEASTS */ church calendar*
BL590	*ECCLESIASTICAL FASTS AND FEASTS* **SEE** FASTS AND FEASTS */ comparative religion*
BV30-135	*ECCLESIASTICAL FASTS AND FEASTS* **SEE** FASTS AND FEASTS */ christianity*
GT3930-4995	*ECCLESIASTICAL FASTS AND FEASTS* **SEE** FASTS AND FEASTS */ manners and customs*
NA5050-5090	*ECCLESIASTICAL FURNITURE* **SEE** CHURCH FURNITURE
BR98	ECCLESIASTICAL GEOGRAPHY — MAPS
BR97-99	ECCLESIASTICAL GEOGRAPHY
BR	*ECCLESIASTICAL HISTORY* **SEE** CHURCH HISTORY
BV759-763	ECCLESIASTICAL LAW
BV4380-4382	*ECCLESIASTICAL PENSIONS* **SEE** CLERGY — SALARIES, PENSIONS, ETC.
BX1950	*ECCLESIASTICAL PENSIONS* **SEE** CLERGY — SALARIES, PENSIONS, ETC. */ catholic*
BV646-651	*ECCLESIASTICAL POLITY* **SEE** CHURCH POLITY
BV170-199	*ECCLESIASTICAL RITES AND CEREMONIES* **SEE** LITURGIES
BX	*ECCLESIASTICAL RITES AND CEREMONIES* **SEE** LITURGIES */ particular denominations*
GT	*ECCLESIASTICAL RITES AND CEREMONIES* **SEE** RITES AND CEREMONIES */ manners and customs*
BV170-199	*ECCLESIASTICAL RITES AND CEREMONIES* **SEE** RITES AND CEREMONIES */ christian*
GN473	*ECCLESIASTICAL RITES AND CEREMONIES* **SEE** RITES AND CEREMONIES */ primitive religion*
BL600-619	*ECCLESIASTICAL RITES AND CEREMONIES* **SEE** RITES AND CEREMONIES */ comparative religion*
BV800-873	*ECCLESIASTICAL RITES AND CEREMONIES* **SEE** SACRAMENTS
BX	*ECCLESIASTICAL RITES AND CEREMONIES* **SEE** SACRAMENTS */ by denomination*
TS2301.C5	*ECCLESIASTICAL SUPPLIES* **SEE** CHURCH SUPPLIES
HF5035.C3	*ECCLESIASTICAL SUPPLIES* **SEE** CHURCH SUPPLIES
BV590-640	*ECCLESIASTICAL THEOLOGY* **SEE** CHURCH
BV167	*ECCLESIASTICAL VESTMENTS* **SEE** CHURCH VESTMENTS
BX1925	*ECCLESIASTICAL VESTMENTS* **SEE** CHURCH VESTMENTS */ catholic church*
BX5180	*ECCLESIASTICAL VESTMENTS* **SEE** CHURCH VESTMENTS */ church of england*
BX2790	*ECCLESIASTICAL VESTMENTS* **SEE** CHURCH VESTMENTS */ monastic*
BV4011.4	*ECCLESIASTICAL VOCATION* **SEE** VOCATION, ECCLESIASTICAL */ pastoral theology*
BV4740	*ECCLESIASTICAL VOCATION* **SEE** VOCATION, ECCLESIASTICAL
BX2380	*ECCLESIASTICAL VOCATION* **SEE** VOCATION, ECCLESIASTICAL */ catholic church*
BV30	*ECCLESIASTICAL YEAR* **SEE** CHURCH YEAR
NA2800	*ECHEA* **SEE** VASES, ACOUSTIC
NA2800	*ECHEIA* **SEE** VASES, ACOUSTIC
RC242	*ECHINOCOCCUS* **SEE** HYDATIDS
QL391.C4	*ECHINOCOCCUS* **SEE** TAPEWORMS
RC184.T5-6	*ECHINOCOCCUS* **SEE** TAPEWORMS */ parasitic diseases*
QL381-5	ECHINODERMATA
QE781-3	ECHINODERMATA, FOSSIL
QL384.E2	*ECHINOIDEA* **SEE** SEA-URCHINS
QL391.G5	ECHIUROIDEA
VK388	*ECHO RANGING* **SEE** SONAR
VK560	*ECHO RANGING* **SEE** SONAR */ navigation*
VK584	*ECHO SOUNDERS* **SEE** ECHO SOUNDING */ navigation*
GC78.E	*ECHO SOUNDERS* **SEE** ECHO SOUNDING */ oceanography*
VK584	ECHO SOUNDING */ navigation*

GC78.E	ECHO SOUNDING / oceanography
QC233	ECHO
RG831	ECLAMPSIA PUERPERALIS SEE PUERPERAL CONVULSIONS
RV431	ECLECTIC DISPENSATORIES SEE DISPENSATORIES, ECLECTIC
RV	ECLECTIC MEDICINE SEE MEDICINE, ECLECTIC
RV365	ECLECTIC OBSTETRICS SEE OBSTETRICS, ECLECTIC
RV301-311	ECLECTIC SURGERY SEE SURGERY, ECLECTIC
QB175	ECLIPSES / calculation and prediction
QB579	ECLIPSES, LUNAR
QB541-551	ECLIPSES, SOLAR
QB171	ECLIPTIC
QE461	ECLOGITE
PN1421	ECLOGUES SEE PASTORAL POETRY
PN6110.P4	ECLOGUES SEE PASTORAL POETRY
QH540-541	ECOLOGY
SB107-9	ECONOMIC BOTANY SEE BOTANY, ECONOMIC
HD3611	ECONOMIC COUNCILS
HB3711-3840	ECONOMIC CYCLES SEE BUSINESS CYCLES
HB3711-3840	ECONOMIC DEPRESSIONS SEE DEPRESSIONS
SB821-945	ECONOMIC ENTOMOLOGY SEE INSECTS, INJURIOUS AND BENEFICIAL
HD	ECONOMIC GEOGRAPHY SEE GEOGRAPHY, ECONOMIC
HC	ECONOMIC GEOGRAPHY SEE GEOGRAPHY, ECONOMIC
TN260	ECONOMIC GEOLOGY SEE GEOLOGY, ECONOMIC
HD82-85	ECONOMIC NATIONALISM SEE ECONOMIC POLICY
HD	ECONOMIC NATIONALISM SEE ECONOMIC POLICY / by industry
HF1401-2580	ECONOMIC NATIONALISM SEE ECONOMIC POLICY / hc
SB995	ECONOMIC ORNITHOLOGY SEE BIRDS, INJURIOUS AND BENEFICIAL
HD82-85	ECONOMIC PLANNING SEE ECONOMIC POLICY
HD	ECONOMIC PLANNING SEE ECONOMIC POLICY / by industry
HF1401-2580	ECONOMIC PLANNING SEE ECONOMIC POLICY / hc
SB951	ECONOMIC POISONS SEE PESTICIDES
HD82-85	ECONOMIC POLICY
HD	ECONOMIC POLICY / by industry
HF1401-2580	ECONOMIC POLICY / hc
HD82-85	ECONOMIC SELF-SUFFICIENCY SEE AUTARCHY
HB3730	ECONOMIC STABILIZATION
HA	ECONOMIC STATISTICS SEE STATISTICS
HB71	ECONOMICS — GRAPHIC METHODS
HB75-125	ECONOMICS — HISTORY
HB171.7	ECONOMICS — JUVENILE LITERATURE
HB71	ECONOMICS — METHODOLOGY
BR115.E3	ECONOMICS AND CHRISTIANITY SEE CHRISTIANITY AND ECONOMICS
BP173.75	ECONOMICS AND ISLAM SEE ISLAM AND ECONOMICS
HB195	ECONOMICS OF WAR SEE WAR — ECONOMIC ASPECTS
UA17	ECONOMICS OF WAR SEE WAR, COST OF
HB	ECONOMICS
HB	ECONOMICS, MATHEMATICAL
R728	ECONOMICS, MEDICAL SEE MEDICAL ECONOMICS
RA410-415	ECONOMICS, MEDICAL SEE MEDICAL ECONOMICS
GN489	ECONOMICS, PRIMITIVE
HB77-83	ECONOMICS — HISTORY — — TO 1800
HB85	ECONOMICS — HISTORY — — 19TH CENTURY
HB87	ECONOMICS — HISTORY — — 20TH CENTURY
HG7920-7933	ECONOMY SEE SAVING AND THRIFT
BJ1533.E2	ECONOMY SEE SAVING AND THRIFT / ethics
BV5091.E3	ECSTASY / christianity
BL626	ECSTASY / comparative religion
BF1321	ECSTASY / spiritualism
QL503.T6	ECTOGNATHA SEE THYSANURA
RD581	ECTOPIA VESICAE SEE BLADDER — DISPLACEMENT
QL503.T6	ECTOTROPHI SEE THYSANURA
F3701-3799	ECUADOR — HISTORY
PQ8200-8219	ECUADORIAN LITERATURE
PN5066-9	ECUADORIAN NEWSPAPERS / etc.
PQ8216.0	ECUADORIAN ORATIONS
PN5066-5070	ECUADORIAN PERIODICALS / etc.
PQ8214	ECUADORIAN POETRY / collections
PQ8210	ECUADORIAN POETRY / history

RL251	ECZEMA
PT7233-7241	EDDAS / elder edda
PT7312-7314	EDDAS / younger edda
TK2271	EDDY CURRENTS (ELECTRIC)
RB144	EDEMA
RJ268	EDEMA / infantile
BS1237	EDEN
QL737.E2	EDENTATA
QE882.E2	EDENTATA, FOSSIL
QK617	EDIBLE FUNGI SEE MUSHROOMS, EDIBLE
QK617	EDIBLE MUSHROOMS SEE MUSHROOMS, EDIBLE
QK98.5	EDIBLE PLANTS SEE PLANTS, EDIBLE
BR180	EDICT OF MILAN, 313
BR845	EDICT OF NANTES
D267.E3	EDICT OF RESTITUTION, 1629
DR46.9	EDIRNE, TURKEY (CITY) — SIEGE, 1912-1913
PN162	EDITING
Z6514.F5	EDITIONS, FIRST SEE LITERATURE — BIBLIOGRAPHY — — FIRST EDITIONS
PL8091	EDIYA LANGUAGE SEE BUBE LANGUAGE
PL8077	EDO LANGUAGE SEE BINI LANGUAGE
DS110.E	EDOMITES
LB41	EDUCATION — AIMS AND OBJECTIVES / essays
Z5811-5819	EDUCATION — BIBLIOGRAPHY
LB2361-5	EDUCATION — CURRICULA / colleges and universities
LB1570-1571	EDUCATION — CURRICULA / elementary schools
LB1628-9	EDUCATION — CURRICULA / secondary schools
LB1026-7	EDUCATION — EXPERIMENTAL METHODS
LB2824-2830	EDUCATION — FINANCE
LB2846	EDUCATION — GRAPHIC METHODS
LB125-875	EDUCATION — PHILOSOPHY
L111-791	EDUCATION — STATISTICS / serial documents
LB2846	EDUCATION — STATISTICS / theory
LB15	EDUCATION — TERMINOLOGY
LC383	EDUCATION AND CHURCH SEE CHURCH AND COLLEGE
LC351-629	EDUCATION AND CHURCH SEE CHURCH AND EDUCATION / church education
LA91-131	EDUCATION AND CHURCH SEE CHURCH AND EDUCATION / history of education
LC107-120	EDUCATION AND CHURCH SEE CHURCH AND EDUCATION / separation of church and schools
HV6166	EDUCATION AND CRIME
LB1044.9.F6	EDUCATION AND FOLK-LORE SEE FOLK-LORE AND EDUCATION
LC201	EDUCATION AND HEREDITY
LC71	EDUCATION AND NATIONALISM SEE NATIONALISM AND EDUCATION
LC351-629	EDUCATION AND RELIGION SEE CHURCH AND EDUCATION / church education
LA91-131	EDUCATION AND RELIGION SEE CHURCH AND EDUCATION / history of education
LC107-120	EDUCATION AND RELIGION SEE CHURCH AND EDUCATION / separation of church and schools
HX526	EDUCATION AND SOCIALISM SEE SOCIALISM AND EDUCATION
LC71-245	EDUCATION AND SOCIOLOGY SEE EDUCATIONAL SOCIOLOGY
LC71-188	EDUCATION AND STATE
LC6681	EDUCATION AND TRAVEL SEE STUDENT TRAVEL
PN56.E	EDUCATION IN LITERATURE
PS169.S4	EDUCATION IN LITERATURE / schools in american literature
PN3448.S4	EDUCATION IN LITERATURE / schools in fiction
LC5201-6660	EDUCATION OF ADULTS
LC5219	EDUCATION OF ADULTS-PERSONNEL SERVICE SEE PERSONNEL SERVICE IN ADULT EDUCATION
HV8875-8883	EDUCATION OF CRIMINALS SEE EDUCATION OF PRISONERS
LC1401-2571	EDUCATION OF GIRLS SEE EDUCATION OF WOMEN
LC4929-4949	EDUCATION OF PRINCES
JC393	EDUCATION OF PRINCES / political theory
HV8875-8883	EDUCATION OF PRISONERS
UB356-9	EDUCATION OF VETERANS SEE VETERANS — EDUCATION
LC1401-2571	EDUCATION OF WOMEN
LC1707	EDUCATION OF WOMEN, MEDIEVAL
LB3562	EDUCATION WEEK SEE AMERICAN EDUCATION WEEK
L	EDUCATION
HF1101-1181	EDUCATION, BUSINESS SEE BUSINESS EDUCATION

LC251-318	EDUCATION, CHARACTER **SEE** MORAL EDUCATION
LC2751	EDUCATION, CHARACTER **SEE** MORAL EDUCATION / negro
BV1460-1615	EDUCATION, CHRISTIAN **SEE** RELIGIOUS EDUCATION
LC1001-1021	EDUCATION, CLASSICAL **SEE** CLASSICAL EDUCATION
LA126-133	EDUCATION, COMPARATIVE **SEE** COMPARATIVE EDUCATION
LC142-5	EDUCATION, COMPULSORY **SEE** SCHOOL ATTENDANCE / limitation
LB3081	EDUCATION, COMPULSORY **SEE** SCHOOL ATTENDANCE / truancy
LC129-139	EDUCATION, COMPULSORY
LB1029.C	EDUCATION, COOPERATIVE
HF5415	EDUCATION, DISTRIBUTIVE **SEE** DISTRIBUTIVE EDUCATION
LB1555-1601	EDUCATION, ELEMENTARY
LB1027.5	EDUCATION, ELEMENTARY-PERSONNEL SERVICE **SEE** PERSONNEL SERVICE IN ELEMENTARY EDUCATION
LC251-318	EDUCATION, ETHICAL **SEE** MORAL EDUCATION
LC2751	EDUCATION, ETHICAL **SEE** MORAL EDUCATION / negro
BV1460-1615	EDUCATION, ETHICAL **SEE** RELIGIOUS EDUCATION
LA75	EDUCATION, GREEK
LB2300-2397	EDUCATION, HIGHER / general
LA410	EDUCATION, HIGHER / other countries
LA225-8	EDUCATION, HIGHER / u.s.
LB2343	EDUCATION, HIGHER-PERSONNEL SERVICE **SEE** PERSONNEL SERVICE IN HIGHER EDUCATION
LC1001-1021	EDUCATION, HUMANISTIC
LA106-8	EDUCATION, HUMANISTIC / renaissance
LB1595-9	EDUCATION, INDUSTRIAL **SEE** MANUAL TRAINING / education
TT161-9	EDUCATION, INDUSTRIAL **SEE** MANUAL TRAINING / technology
T61-173	EDUCATION, INDUSTRIAL **SEE** TECHNICAL EDUCATION
LC1081	EDUCATION, INDUSTRIAL **SEE** TECHNICAL EDUCATION / theory
LC1041-7	EDUCATION, INDUSTRIAL **SEE** TECHNICAL EDUCATION / vocational education
CB199	EDUCATION, INTERCULTURAL **SEE** INTERCULTURAL EDUCATION
LC901-915	EDUCATION, ISLAMIC **SEE** ISLAM — EDUCATION
LC1001-1021	EDUCATION, LIBERAL **SEE** EDUCATION, HUMANISTIC
LA106-8	EDUCATION, LIBERAL **SEE** EDUCATION, HUMANISTIC / renaissance
LA85-98	EDUCATION, MEDIEVAL
U400-714	EDUCATION, MILITARY **SEE** MILITARY EDUCATION
TN165-213	EDUCATION, MINING **SEE** MINING SCHOOLS AND EDUCATION
LC251-318	EDUCATION, MORAL **SEE** MORAL EDUCATION
LC2751	EDUCATION, MORAL **SEE** MORAL EDUCATION / negro
MT	EDUCATION, MUSICAL **SEE** MUSIC — INSTRUCTION AND STUDY
LC901-915	EDUCATION, MUSLIM **SEE** ISLAM — EDUCATION
V400-695	EDUCATION, NAVAL **SEE** NAVAL EDUCATION
LB1047	EDUCATION, OUTDOOR **SEE** OUTDOOR EDUCATION
GV201-547	EDUCATION, PHYSICAL **SEE** PHYSICAL EDUCATION AND TRAINING
RM721	EDUCATION, PHYSICAL **SEE** PHYSICAL EDUCATION AND TRAINING / physical culture and therapeutics
RA781	EDUCATION, PHYSICAL **SEE** PHYSICAL EDUCATION AND TRAINING / physical culture and hygiene
R838	EDUCATION, PREMEDICAL **SEE** PREMEDICAL EDUCATION
LB1140	EDUCATION, PRESCHOOL
LB1501-1547	EDUCATION, PRIMARY
GN488.5	EDUCATION, PRIMITIVE
LC1051-1071	EDUCATION, PROFESSIONAL **SEE** PROFESSIONAL EDUCATION
BV1460-1615	EDUCATION, RELIGIOUS **SEE** RELIGIOUS EDUCATION
LC5146-8	EDUCATION, RURAL
Q181	EDUCATION, SCIENTIFIC **SEE** SCIENCE — STUDY AND TEACHING
LB1603-1694	EDUCATION, SECONDARY
LA410	EDUCATION, SECONDARY / other countries

LA222	EDUCATION, SECONDARY / u.s.
LB1620.5	EDUCATION, SECONDARY-PERSONNEL SERVICE **SEE** PERSONNEL SERVICE IN SECONDARY EDUCATION
T61-173	EDUCATION, TECHNICAL **SEE** TECHNICAL EDUCATION
LC1081	EDUCATION, TECHNICAL **SEE** TECHNICAL EDUCATION / theory
LC1041-7	EDUCATION, TECHNICAL **SEE** TECHNICAL EDUCATION / vocational education
BV1460-1615	EDUCATION, THEOLOGICAL **SEE** RELIGIOUS EDUCATION
BV4019-4160	EDUCATION, THEOLOGICAL **SEE** THEOLOGY — STUDY AND TEACHING
LC5101-5143	EDUCATION, URBAN
LB1043.5	EDUCATION, VISUAL **SEE** VISUAL EDUCATION
LC1041-7	EDUCATION, VOCATIONAL **SEE** VOCATIONAL EDUCATION
LB2825	EDUCATION-FEDERAL AID **SEE** FEDERAL AID TO EDUCATION
LA75	EDUCATION-GREECE, ANCIENT **SEE** EDUCATION, GREEK
LA85-98	EDUCATION-HISTORY-MEDIEVAL **SEE** EDUCATION, MEDIEVAL
LC5219	EDUCATION-PERSONNEL SERVICE **SEE** PERSONNEL SERVICE IN ADULT EDUCATION
LB2343	EDUCATION-PERSONNEL SERVICE **SEE** PERSONNEL SERVICE IN HIGHER EDUCATION
LB1620.5	EDUCATION-PERSONNEL SERVICE **SEE** PERSONNEL SERVICE IN SECONDARY EDUCATION
LB1027.5	EDUCATION-PERSONNEL SERVICE **SEE** PERSONNEL SERVICE IN EDUCATION / application
LB1027.5	EDUCATION-PERSONNEL SERVICE **SEE** PERSONNEL SERVICE IN ELEMENTARY EDUCATION
LB3046-9	EDUCATION-PERSONNEL SERVICE **SEE** PERSONNEL SERVICE IN EDUCATION / organization
LB1051-1091	EDUCATION-PSYCHOLOGY **SEE** EDUCATIONAL PSYCHOLOGY
Z286.E	EDUCATION-PUBLISHING **SEE** EDUCATIONAL PUBLISHING
LB2342	EDUCATION-PUNCHED CARD SYSTEMS **SEE** PUNCHED CARD SYSTEMS — EDUCATION / colleges
LB2830	EDUCATION-PUNCHED CARD SYSTEMS **SEE** PUNCHED CARD SYSTEMS — EDUCATION / schools
LB1028	EDUCATION-RESEARCH **SEE** EDUCATIONAL RESEARCH
LB3062	EDUCATION-SEGREGATION **SEE** SEGREGATION IN EDUCATION
LC2601-5	EDUCATION-STATES, NEW **SEE** STATES, NEW — EDUCATION
LB2801-2997	EDUCATIONAL ADMINISTRATION **SEE** SCHOOL MANAGEMENT AND ORGANIZATION / organization and supervision
LB3011-3095	EDUCATIONAL ADMINISTRATION **SEE** SCHOOL MANAGEMENT AND ORGANIZATION / management and discipline
LB2341	EDUCATIONAL ADMINISTRATION **SEE** UNIVERSITIES AND COLLEGES — ADMINISTRATION
L10-97	EDUCATIONAL ASSOCIATIONS
LB2331.5	EDUCATIONAL COOPERATION **SEE** UNIVERSITY COOPERATION
LB2336-7	EDUCATIONAL ENDOWMENTS **SEE** ENDOWMENT OF RESEARCH
Q181	EDUCATIONAL ENDOWMENTS **SEE** ENDOWMENT OF RESEARCH
HV16-25	EDUCATIONAL ENDOWMENTS **SEE** ENDOWMENTS / charities
LB2336-7	EDUCATIONAL ENDOWMENTS **SEE** ENDOWMENTS / higher education
LB2283-5	EDUCATIONAL EXCHANGES
LC6691	EDUCATIONAL EXHIBITS, TRAVELING
GV1480	EDUCATIONAL GAMES
LB1027.5	EDUCATIONAL GUIDANCE **SEE** PERSONNEL SERVICE IN EDUCATION / application
LB3046-9	EDUCATIONAL GUIDANCE **SEE** PERSONNEL SERVICE IN EDUCATION / organization
LB2827	EDUCATIONAL LAND USE **SEE** SCHOOL LANDS
LB2503-2797	EDUCATIONAL LAW AND LEGISLATION
Z675.P3	EDUCATIONAL LIBRARIES **SEE** PEDAGOGICAL LIBRARIES

LB3051	*EDUCATIONAL MEASUREMENTS* **SEE** EDUCATIONAL TESTS AND MEASUREMENTS
BV2630	*EDUCATIONAL MISSIONS* **SEE** MISSIONS — EDUCATIONAL WORK
LB1051-1091	EDUCATIONAL PSYCHOLOGY
LB2846	*EDUCATIONAL PUBLICITY* **SEE** SCHOOL PUBLICITY
Z286.E	EDUCATIONAL PUBLISHING
LB1028	EDUCATIONAL RESEARCH
LB2844.4	*EDUCATIONAL SECRETARIES* **SEE** SCHOOL SECRETARIES
L10-97	*EDUCATIONAL SOCIETIES* **SEE** EDUCATIONAL ASSOCIATIONS
LC71-245	EDUCATIONAL SOCIOLOGY
LB2846	EDUCATIONAL STATISTICS
LB2823	EDUCATIONAL SURVEYS
LB3051	EDUCATIONAL TESTS AND MEASUREMENTS
LA2301-2397	EDUCATORS / *biography*
LB51-875	EDUCATORS / *theories and systems*
TJ901	*EDUCTORS (PUMPS)* **SEE** EJECTOR PUMPS
QL638.A55	EELS
QL638.G9	*EELS, ELECTRIC* **SEE** ELECTRIC EEL
QL391.N4	*EELWORMS* **SEE** NEMATODA
PL6231	EFATE LANGUAGE
BD530-595	*EFFECT AND CAUSE* **SEE** CAUSATION
T60.R	*EFFICIENCY RATING* **SEE** EMPLOYEES, RATING OF
T58	EFFICIENCY, INDUSTRIAL
HF5386	*EFFICIENCY, PERSONAL* **SEE** SUCCESS / *business*
BJ1611-1618	*EFFICIENCY, PERSONAL* **SEE** SUCCESS / *ethics*
NB1800-1885	*EFFIGIES, SEPULCHRAL* **SEE** SEPULCHRAL MONUMENTS / *sculpture*
BD437	*EFFORT* **SEE** STRUGGLE
PL8147	EFIK LANGUAGE
QL951-973	*EGG (BIOLOGY)* **SEE** EMBRYOLOGY
E241.L7	*EGG HARBOR, N.J., SKIRMISH OF, 1778* **SEE** LITTLE EGG HARBOR, N.J., SKIRMISH OF, 1778
NK9990.E5	*EGG-CUPS* **SEE** EGGCUPS / *art*
SB608.E2	EGG-PLANT — DISEASES AND PESTS
SB608.E2	EGG-PLANT LACE-BUG
SB608.E2	EGG-PLANT TORTOISE BEETLE
SB351.E5	EGG-PLANT
NK9990.E5	EGGCUPS / *art*
SF495	EGGS — INCUBATION
SF501	EGGS — PRESERVATION
SF487-8	EGGS — PRODUCTION
GR735	EGGS (IN RELIGION, FOLK-LORE, ETC.)
SF490	EGGS
HD9284	EGGS / *egg trade*
QE875	*EGGS, FOSSIL* **SEE** BIRDS, FOSSIL — EGGS
SF495	*EGGS-HATCHING* **SEE** EGGS — INCUBATION
BJ1474	EGOISM
QL696.A7	*EGRETS* **SEE** HERONS
DT43-154	EGYPT — HISTORY
NA1581-5	*EGYPTIAN ARCHITECTURE* **SEE** ARCHITECTURE, EGYPTIAN
NA215-216	*EGYPTIAN ARCHITECTURE* **SEE** ARCHITECTURE, EGYPTIAN / *ancient*
PJ1487	EGYPTIAN BALLADS AND SONGS
PJ1945	EGYPTIAN BALLADS AND SONGS / *translations*
PJ1571	EGYPTIAN DRAMA
PJ1947	EGYPTIAN DRAMA / *translations*
PJ1487	EGYPTIAN FICTION
PJ1949	EGYPTIAN FICTION / *translations*
PJ1091-7	*EGYPTIAN HIEROGLYPHICS* **SEE** EGYPTIAN LANGUAGE — WRITING, HIEROGLYPHIC
PJ1501-1819	EGYPTIAN LANGUAGE — INSCRIPTIONS
PJ1501-1921	EGYPTIAN LANGUAGE — PAPYRI
PJ1809-1921	EGYPTIAN LANGUAGE — PAPYRI, DEMOTIC
PJ1051-1109	EGYPTIAN LANGUAGE — WRITING
PJ1107	EGYPTIAN LANGUAGE — WRITING, DEMOTIC
PJ1105	EGYPTIAN LANGUAGE — WRITING, HIERATIC
PJ1091-7	EGYPTIAN LANGUAGE — WRITING, HIEROGLYPHIC
PJ1001-1479	EGYPTIAN LANGUAGE
PJ1487	EGYPTIAN LETTERS
PJ1947	EGYPTIAN LETTERS / *translations*
PJ1501-1989	EGYPTIAN LITERATURE / *collections*
PJ1481-8	EGYPTIAN LITERATURE / *history*
BF1591	*EGYPTIAN MAGIC* **SEE** MAGIC, EGYPTIAN
RE310-326	*EGYPTIAN OPHTHALMIA* **SEE** CONJUNCTIVA — DISEASES
PN5499.E4	EGYPTIAN PERIODICALS / *etc.*
DT57-154	*EGYPTIAN STUDIES* **SEE** EGYPTOLOGY / *archaeology and history*
PJ1001-1989	*EGYPTIAN STUDIES* **SEE** EGYPTOLOGY / *language and literature*
DS97.5	*EGYPTIAN-TURKISH CONFLICT, 1831-1840* **SEE** TURCO-EGYPTIAN CONFLICT, 1831-1840
DT71	EGYPTIANS
DT61	EGYPTIANS
DT57-154	*EGYPTOLOGISTS* **SEE** EGYPTOLOGY / *archaeology and history*
PJ1001-1989	*EGYPTOLOGISTS* **SEE** EGYPTOLOGY / *language and literature*
DT57-154	EGYPTOLOGY / *archaeology and history*
PJ1001-1989	EGYPTOLOGY / *language and literature*
DT107.83	EGYPT — HISTORY — — 1952-
BF367	EIDETIC IMAGERY
HD5106-5250	EIGHT-HOUR MOVEMENT
LB1026	EIGHT-YEAR STUDY
GV1299.H3	*EIGHTY-EIGHT (GAME)* **SEE** HACHI-JU-HACHI (GAME)
N7956	*EIKONS* **SEE** ICONS / *russian art*
QC6.5	*EINSTEIN UNIFIED FIELD THEORY* **SEE** UNIFIED FIELD THEORIES
BF311	EJECTION (PSYCHOLOGY)
TJ901	EJECTOR PUMPS
TJ901	*EJECTORS (PUMPS)* **SEE** EJECTOR PUMPS
PL8276	*EJO LANGUAGE* **SEE** IJO LANGUAGE
QE461	*EKLOGITE* **SEE** ECLOGITE
GN653	EKOI
D766.9	EL ALAMEIN, BATTLE OF, 1942
E717.1	EL CANEY, BATTLE OF, 1898
E121	EL DORADO
F1234	EL EBANO, BATTLE OF, 1915
TP684.T8	*ELAEOCOCCA OIL* **SEE** TUNG-OIL
P943	ELAMITE LANGUAGE
QL737.U5	ELANDS
QE882.U3	ELANDS, FOSSIL
QL638.7-9	ELASMOBRANCHII
QA935	ELASTIC PLATES AND SHELLS
QA935	ELASTIC RODS AND WIRES
QA935	*ELASTIC SHELLS* **SEE** ELASTIC PLATES AND SHELLS
QC191	ELASTIC SOLIDS — MODELS
QA935	ELASTIC SOLIDS
QC191	ELASTIC SOLIDS
TG265	ELASTIC SOLIDS
QA933	*ELASTIC SOLIDS-THERMAL PROPERTIES* **SEE** THERMOELASTICITY
QM563	ELASTIC TISSUE
QA935	ELASTIC WAVES
QC809.E5	ELASTIC WAVES / *geophysics*
QE539	ELASTIC WAVES / *seismology*
QC191	ELASTIC WAVES / *solids*
QA931-5	ELASTICITY / *mathematical theory*
QC191	ELASTICITY / *physics*
BF575.E	ELATION
HV57	ELBERFELD SYSTEM
GN799.E	ELBOW-STONES
QM131	ELBOW
RD558	*ELBOW-EXCISION* **SEE** EXCISION OF ELBOW
DC227.5.E6	ELCHINGEN, BATTLE OF, 1805
HQ754.F5	*ELDEST CHILD* **SEE** CHILDREN, FIRST-BORN
B196	ELEATICS
BT810	ELECTION (THEOLOGY)
BX1930.E4	ELECTION LAW (CANON LAW)
JF825-831	ELECTION LAW
JK1961-3	ELECTION LAW / *u.s.*
JK2241-6	*ELECTION LAW-CRIMINAL PROVISIONS* **SEE** ELECTIONS — CORRUPT PRACTICES
JK1994-7	*ELECTION LAW-CRIMINAL PROVISIONS* **SEE** ELECTIONS — CORRUPT PRACTICES
JN1081-1097	*ELECTION LAW-CRIMINAL PROVISIONS* **SEE** ELECTIONS — CORRUPT PRACTICES / *gt. brit.*
JF1081-5	*ELECTION LAW-CRIMINAL PROVISIONS* **SEE** ELECTIONS — CORRUPT PRACTICES
BM613	*ELECTION OF ISRAEL* **SEE** JEWS — ELECTION, DOCTRINE OF
BV4260	ELECTION SERMONS
JK2241-6	ELECTIONS — CORRUPT PRACTICES
JK1994-7	ELECTIONS — CORRUPT PRACTICES
JF1081-5	ELECTIONS — CORRUPT PRACTICES

S723	ELECTRIC FENCES / *agricultural engineering*
QC661	ELECTRIC FILTERS
TK6565.F5	ELECTRIC FILTERS / *radio*
QP348	*ELECTRIC FISHES* **SEE** ELECTRIC ORGANS IN FISHES
QD277	ELECTRIC FURNACES / *chemistry*
QD157	ELECTRIC FURNACES / *chemistry*
TK4661	ELECTRIC FURNACES / *electric engineering*
TN681-7	ELECTRIC FURNACES / *metallurgy*
TN706	ELECTRIC FURNACES / *metallurgy of iron and steel*
TK3511	ELECTRIC FUSES
TK2846	ELECTRIC FUSES / *switchboards*
TK2411-2491	*ELECTRIC GENERATORS* **SEE** DYNAMOS
TK4601-4661	ELECTRIC HEATING
HD9697	*ELECTRIC HOUSEHOLD APPLIANCES* **SEE** HOUSEHOLD APPLIANCES, ELECTRIC / *economics*
TK7018-7301	*ELECTRIC HOUSEHOLD APPLIANCES* **SEE** HOUSEHOLD APPLIANCES, ELECTRIC / *technology*
TK7291	*ELECTRIC IGNITION OF GAS* **SEE** GAS — ELECTRIC IGNITION
HF5686.E3	ELECTRIC INDUSTRIES — ACCOUNTING
TK6	ELECTRIC INDUSTRIES — EXHIBITIONS
HG4029.E4	ELECTRIC INDUSTRIES — FINANCE
HD9685-9697	ELECTRIC INDUSTRIES / *economics*
TK	ELECTRIC INDUSTRIES / *technology*
TK3431	ELECTRIC INSULATORS AND INSULATION — TESTING
TK3331-3441	ELECTRIC INSULATORS AND INSULATION / *engineering*
QC611	ELECTRIC INSULATORS AND INSULATION / *physics*
TP841	ELECTRIC KILNS
TK411-415	ELECTRIC LABORATORIES / *engineering*
QC541	ELECTRIC LABORATORIES / *physics*
TK9921	ELECTRIC LAMPS — AMATEURS' MANUALS
TK4310-4399	ELECTRIC LAMPS
TK4321-4335	ELECTRIC LAMPS, ARC
TK4386	*ELECTRIC LAMPS, FLUORESCENT* **SEE** FLUORESCENT LAMPS
TK4365	ELECTRIC LAMPS, INCANDESCENT — FILAMENTS
TK4367	ELECTRIC LAMPS, INCANDESCENT — TESTING
TK4351-4367	ELECTRIC LAMPS, INCANDESCENT
TN307	ELECTRIC LAMPS, PORTABLE / *mining*
QC702	ELECTRIC LEAKAGE
TK4131-4399	*ELECTRIC LIGHT* **SEE** ELECTRIC LIGHTING
QC391	*ELECTRIC LIGHT* **SEE** PHOTOMETRY
TK4175	*ELECTRIC LIGHT* **SEE** PHOTOMETRY / *electric light general*
TP754	*ELECTRIC LIGHT* **SEE** PHOTOMETRY / *gas testing*
TK4367	*ELECTRIC LIGHT* **SEE** PHOTOMETRY / *incandescent*
RM835-844	*ELECTRIC LIGHT* **SEE** PHOTOTHERAPY
HD9685	*ELECTRIC LIGHT AND POWER INDUSTRY* **SEE** ELECTRIC UTILITIES
TK7725	ELECTRIC LIGHT CARBONS / *manufacture*
TK4335	ELECTRIC LIGHT CARBONS / *use*
TH7960-7967	ELECTRIC LIGHT FIXTURES
TR600	*ELECTRIC LIGHT IN PHOTOGRAPHY* **SEE** PHOTOGRAPHY — ARTIFICIAL LIGHT
TR573	*ELECTRIC LIGHT IN PHOTOGRAPHY* **SEE** PHOTOGRAPHY — PORTRAITS — — LIGHTING AND POSING
TK4181	ELECTRIC LIGHT PLANTS — CONTRACTS AND SPECIFICATIONS
TK4201-4238	ELECTRIC LIGHT PLANTS
TK4175	ELECTRIC LIGHT, CANDLE POWER OF
TK9921	ELECTRIC LIGHTING — AMATEURS' MANUALS
TK4181	ELECTRIC LIGHTING — CONTRACTS AND SPECIFICATIONS
TK4160	ELECTRIC LIGHTING — EARLY WORKS TO 1870
TK4255	ELECTRIC LIGHTING — INSTALLATION
TK3275	ELECTRIC LIGHTING — INSURANCE REQUIREMENTS
TK4241	ELECTRIC LIGHTING — MACHINERY
TK152	ELECTRIC LIGHTING — SAFETY MEASURES
TK4255	ELECTRIC LIGHTING — WIRING
VM493	ELECTRIC LIGHTING OF SHIPS
TK4131-4399	ELECTRIC LIGHTING
TK4311-4335	ELECTRIC LIGHTING, ARC
TK4381	ELECTRIC LIGHTING, CADMIUM VAPOR
TK4386	*ELECTRIC LIGHTING, FLUORESCENT* **SEE** FLUORESCENT LIGHTING
TK4341-4367	ELECTRIC LIGHTING, INCANDESCENT
TK4381	ELECTRIC LIGHTING, MERCURY VAPOR

TK4381	ELECTRIC LIGHTING, SODIUM VAPOR
TK3226	ELECTRIC LINES — MODELS
TK3231-3248	ELECTRIC LINES — OVERHEAD
TK3242-3	ELECTRIC LINES — POLES
TK3207	ELECTRIC LINES — TESTING
TK3307	ELECTRIC LINES — TESTING
TK3251-3261	ELECTRIC LINES — UNDERGROUND
TK3201-3261	ELECTRIC LINES
TF975	ELECTRIC LOCOMOTIVES
TN871.35	*ELECTRIC LOGGING (OIL WELLS)* **SEE** OIL WELL LOGGING, ELECTRIC
TK2711-2799	ELECTRIC MACHINERY — ALTERNATING CURRENT
TK2189	ELECTRIC MACHINERY — COOLING
TK2331	ELECTRIC MACHINERY — DESIGN AND CONSTRUCTION
TK2611-2699	ELECTRIC MACHINERY — DIRECT CURRENT
TK2325	ELECTRIC MACHINERY — DRAWING
TK2189	ELECTRIC MACHINERY — MAINTENANCE AND REPAIR
TK2081	ELECTRIC MACHINERY — MOTIVE POWER
TK257	ELECTRIC MACHINERY — PATENTS
TK2745	ELECTRIC MACHINERY — POLYPHASE
TK2851	ELECTRIC MACHINERY — REGULATION
TK2311	ELECTRIC MACHINERY — STANDARDS
TK401	ELECTRIC MACHINERY — TESTING
TK2316	ELECTRIC MACHINERY — TESTING
TK2000-2799	ELECTRIC MACHINERY
TK2731	ELECTRIC MACHINERY, SYNCHRONOUS
QC573	ELECTRIC MACHINES
TK275-399	ELECTRIC MEASUREMENTS / *electric engineering*
QC535	ELECTRIC MEASUREMENTS / *physics*
TK301-399	ELECTRIC METERS
TK393	ELECTRIC METERS, RECORDING
TK9911	ELECTRIC MOTORS — AMATEURS' MANUALS
TK2435	ELECTRIC MOTORS — DESIGN AND CONSTRUCTION
TK4057	ELECTRIC MOTORS — REPAIRING
TF935	ELECTRIC MOTORS — REPAIRING / *electric railways*
TK2541	ELECTRIC MOTORS — STARTING DEVICES
TK2433	ELECTRIC MOTORS — TESTING
TK2511-2541	ELECTRIC MOTORS
TK2781-9	ELECTRIC MOTORS / *alternating current*
TK2681	ELECTRIC MOTORS / *direct current*
TK4055-8	ELECTRIC MOTORS / *use*
TK2781-9	ELECTRIC MOTORS, ALTERNATING CURRENT
TK2785	*ELECTRIC MOTORS, ASYNCHRONOUS* **SEE** ELECTRIC MOTORS, INDUCTION
TK2681	ELECTRIC MOTORS, DIRECT CURRENT
TK2537	ELECTRIC MOTORS, FRACTIONAL HORSEPOWER
TK2785	ELECTRIC MOTORS, INDUCTION
TK2785	ELECTRIC MOTORS, POLYPHASE
TK2789	ELECTRIC MOTORS, REPULSION
TK2787	ELECTRIC MOTORS, SYNCHRONOUS
TK3001	ELECTRIC NETWORK ANALYZERS
TK3141	ELECTRIC NETWORK ANALYZERS / *alternating current*
TK3111	ELECTRIC NETWORK ANALYZERS / *direct current*
TK3226	ELECTRIC NETWORKS
QP348	ELECTRIC ORGANS IN FISHES
QP348	ELECTRIC ORGANS IN INSECTS
TK6565.07	*ELECTRIC OSCILLATORS* **SEE** OSCILLATORS, ELECTRIC / *radio*
QC601-641	*ELECTRIC POTENTIAL* **SEE** ELECTRIC CURRENTS
QC618	*ELECTRIC POTENTIAL* **SEE** ELECTROMOTIVE FORCE
QD561	*ELECTRIC POTENTIAL* **SEE** ELECTROMOTIVE FORCE / *electrolysis*
QC571-595	*ELECTRIC POTENTIAL* **SEE** ELECTROSTATICS
QA825	*ELECTRIC POTENTIAL* **SEE** POTENTIAL, THEORY OF
TK3141-3171	ELECTRIC POWER DISTRIBUTION — ALTERNATING CURRENT
TK3091	ELECTRIC POWER DISTRIBUTION — COMMUNICATION SYSTEMS
TK3111	ELECTRIC POWER DISTRIBUTION — DIRECT CURRENT
TK3144	ELECTRIC POWER DISTRIBUTION — HIGH TENSION
TK3158	ELECTRIC POWER DISTRIBUTION — MULTIPHASE
TK3159	ELECTRIC POWER DISTRIBUTION — POLYCYCLIC
TK3001-3511	ELECTRIC POWER DISTRIBUTION
TK3227	*ELECTRIC POWER DISTRIBUTION-GROUNDING* **SEE** ELECTRIC CURRENTS — GROUNDING
TK3141	*ELECTRIC POWER DISTRIBUTION-NETWORK ANALYZERS* **SEE** ELECTRIC NETWORK ANALYZERS / *alternating current*
TK3001	*ELECTRIC POWER DISTRIBUTION-NETWORK ANALYZERS* **SEE** ELECTRIC NETWORK ANALYZERS

TK3111	*ELECTRIC POWER DISTRIBUTION-NETWORK ANALYZERS* **SEE** ELECTRIC NETWORK ANALYZERS / *direct current*
TN343	*ELECTRIC POWER IN MINING* **SEE** ELECTRICITY IN MINING
HD9685	*ELECTRIC POWER INDUSTRY* **SEE** ELECTRIC UTILITIES
TK2901	ELECTRIC POWER PRODUCTION FROM CHEMICAL ACTION
TK1001-1831	ELECTRIC POWER PRODUCTION
TK3201-3261	*ELECTRIC POWER TRANSMISSION* **SEE** ELECTRIC LINES
TK3001-3511	*ELECTRIC POWER TRANSMISSION* **SEE** ELECTRIC POWER DISTRIBUTION
TK1001-1831	*ELECTRIC POWER TRANSMISSION* **SEE** ELECTRIC POWER PRODUCTION
TK1191	ELECTRIC POWER-PLANTS — CONTRACTS AND SPECIFICATIONS
TH9445.E4	ELECTRIC POWER-PLANTS — FIRES AND FIRE PREVENTION
TK1811	ELECTRIC POWER-PLANTS — MANAGEMENT
TK1831	ELECTRIC POWER-PLANTS — TESTING
TK1191-1831	ELECTRIC POWER-PLANTS
TK3001-3511	ELECTRIC POWER / *distribution*
TK2000-2941	ELECTRIC POWER / *machinery*
TK1001-1831	ELECTRIC POWER / *production*
TK4001-9971	ELECTRIC POWER / *uses*
TP156.P7	*ELECTRIC PRECIPITATION* **SEE** ELECTROSTATIC PRECIPITATION
QC483	ELECTRIC RADIATION
HE4351	ELECTRIC RAILROADS — ACCOUNTING
TF949.B7	ELECTRIC RAILROADS — BRAKES
TF920-949	ELECTRIC RAILROADS — CARS
TF863-900	ELECTRIC RAILROADS — CONSTRUCTION
TF857	ELECTRIC RAILROADS — CONTRACTS AND SPECIFICATIONS
TF857	ELECTRIC RAILROADS — COST OF CONSTRUCTION
HE4311	ELECTRIC RAILROADS — EMPLOYEES / *street-railroads*
HD6350.S8	ELECTRIC RAILROADS — EMPLOYEES / *trade-union periodicals*
TF920-952	ELECTRIC RAILROADS — EQUIPMENT AND SUPPLIES
HE4351	ELECTRIC RAILROADS — FINANCE
TF970	ELECTRIC RAILROADS — FREIGHT
TF960-962	ELECTRIC RAILROADS — MANAGEMENT
TF197	ELECTRIC RAILROADS — MODELS
TF965	ELECTRIC RAILROADS — MOTORMEN'S MANUALS
TF872	ELECTRIC RAILROADS — RAILS
TF863	ELECTRIC RAILROADS — SUBSTATIONS
TF857	ELECTRIC RAILROADS — TESTING
TF890	ELECTRIC RAILROADS — THIRD RAIL
TF885	ELECTRIC RAILROADS — TROLLEY-WHEELS
TF880-900	ELECTRIC RAILROADS — WIRES AND WIRING
TF855-1124	ELECTRIC RAILROADS
HE5351-5600	ELECTRIC RAILROADS / *interurban*
HE4201-5300	ELECTRIC RAILROADS / *street-railroads*
TF857	ELECTRIC RAILROADS, MINIATURE
TF935	*ELECTRIC RAILROADS-MOTORS* **SEE** ELECTRIC RAILWAY MOTORS
TF952	ELECTRIC RAILROADS — EQUIPMENT AND SUPPLIES — — CATALOGS
TF935	ELECTRIC RAILWAY MOTORS
TT967	*ELECTRIC RAZORS* **SEE** ELECTRIC SHAVERS
TK2851	ELECTRIC REACTORS
QC611	ELECTRIC RESISTANCE
TK2851	ELECTRIC RESISTORS / *electric machinery*
TK6565.R	ELECTRIC RESISTORS / *radio*
QC655	ELECTRIC RESONATORS / *electric waves*
TK6565.R43	ELECTRIC RESONATORS / *radio*
TK2851	ELECTRIC RHEOSTATS
TL783.5	ELECTRIC ROCKET ENGINES
TL783.5	*ELECTRIC ROCKET PROPULSION* **SEE** ELECTRIC ROCKET ENGINES
TT967	ELECTRIC SHAVERS
VM773	*ELECTRIC SHIP PROPULSION* **SEE** SHIP PROPULSION, ELECTRIC
TK4399.S6	ELECTRIC SIGNS
TK4660.5	*ELECTRIC SPARK CUTTING* **SEE** ELECTRIC CUTTING MACHINERY
QC703	ELECTRIC SPARK
QC537	ELECTRIC STANDARDS
TK4631	*ELECTRIC STOVES* **SEE** STOVES, ELECTRIC / *for heating*
TX657.S5	*ELECTRIC STOVES* **SEE** STOVES, ELECTRIC / *home economics*
TF855-1124	*ELECTRIC STREET-RAILROADS* **SEE** ELECTRIC RAILROADS
HE5351-5600	*ELECTRIC STREET-RAILROADS* **SEE** ELECTRIC RAILROADS / *interurban*
HE4201-5300	*ELECTRIC STREET-RAILROADS* **SEE** ELECTRIC RAILROADS / *street-railroads*
TF701-1124	*ELECTRIC STREET-RAILROADS* **SEE** STREET-RAILROADS
HE4201-5300	*ELECTRIC STREET-RAILROADS* **SEE** STREET-RAILROADS / *economics*
HE4251	*ELECTRIC STREET-RAILROADS* **SEE** STREET-RAILROADS / *taxation*
TK1751	ELECTRIC SUBSTATIONS
TK3226	*ELECTRIC SURGE* **SEE** TRANSIENTS (ELECTRICITY)
TK2821-2846	*ELECTRIC SWITCHES* **SEE** ELECTRIC SWITCHGEAR
TK2821-2846	ELECTRIC SWITCHGEAR
HE7601-8630	*ELECTRIC TELEGRAPH* **SEE** TELEGRAPH / *economics*
TK5105-5865	*ELECTRIC TELEGRAPH* **SEE** TELEGRAPH / *technology*
TK401	ELECTRIC TESTING
QC271-8	*ELECTRIC THERMOMETRY* **SEE** THERMOMETERS AND THERMOMETRY
TK9971	ELECTRIC TOYS
TC769	*ELECTRIC TRACTION CANAL-BOATS* **SEE** CANAL-BOATS — ELECTRIC TRACTION
TK2551	ELECTRIC TRANSFORMERS — TESTING
TK2551	ELECTRIC TRANSFORMERS
TK3226	*ELECTRIC TRANSIENT PHENOMENA* **SEE** TRANSIENTS (ELECTRICITY)
QC536	ELECTRIC UNITS
HD9685	ELECTRIC UTILITIES
TK215-255	*ELECTRIC UTILITIES-LAW* **SEE** ELECTRIC ENGINEERING — LAWS AND LEGISLATION
TK2798	*ELECTRIC VALVES* **SEE** ELECTRIC CURRENT RECTIFIERS
QC661	*ELECTRIC WAVE FILTERS* **SEE** ELECTRIC FILTERS
TK6565.F5	*ELECTRIC WAVE FILTERS* **SEE** ELECTRIC FILTERS / *radio*
QC665	ELECTRIC WAVES — DAMPING
QC661-5	ELECTRIC WAVES
TK4660	ELECTRIC WELDING
HD7269.W	*ELECTRIC WELDING-HYGIENIC ASPECTS* **SEE** WELDING — HYGIENIC ASPECTS
TN871.35	*ELECTRIC WELL LOGGING* **SEE** OIL WELL LOGGING, ELECTRIC
TK3307	ELECTRIC WIRE — STANDARDS
TK3307	ELECTRIC WIRE — TESTING
TK3301-3351	ELECTRIC WIRE
TK3335	ELECTRIC WIRE, INSULATED — TESTING
TK3331-3351	ELECTRIC WIRE, INSULATED
TK3205	ELECTRIC WIRING — DIAGRAMS
TK435	ELECTRIC WIRING — ESTIMATES
TK3275	ELECTRIC WIRING — INSURANCE REQUIREMENTS
TK152	ELECTRIC WIRING — SAFETY MEASURES
TK3275	ELECTRIC WIRING — SAFETY MEASURES / *indoor wiring*
TK3205	ELECTRIC WIRING — TABLES, CALCULATIONS, ETC.
TK3201-3285	ELECTRIC WIRING
TK3285	ELECTRIC WIRING, INTERIOR — DIAGRAMS
TK3271-3285	ELECTRIC WIRING, INTERIOR
ML1092	*ELECTRICAL MUSICAL INSTRUMENTS* **SEE** MUSICAL INSTRUMENTS, ELECTRONIC
QC703	*ELECTRICALLY EXPLODED WIRES* **SEE** EXPLODING WIRE PHENOMENA
QC514-515	ELECTRICIANS / *physics*
TK139-140	ELECTRICIANS / *technology*
Z5831-5	ELECTRICITY — BIBLIOGRAPHY
QC516-517	ELECTRICITY — EARLY WORKS TO 1850
QC527	ELECTRICITY — EXPERIMENTS / *popular works*
QC533-4	ELECTRICITY — EXPERIMENTS / *study and teaching*
QC523	ELECTRICITY — JUVENILE LITERATURE
QC534	ELECTRICITY — LABORATORY MANUALS
QC532	ELECTRICITY — PROBLEMS, EXERCISES, ETC.
QC529	ELECTRICITY — TABLES, ETC.
TL690-691	ELECTRICITY IN AERONAUTICS

TK4018	ELECTRICITY IN AGRICULTURE
SB139	*ELECTRICITY IN HORTICULTURE* **SEE** ELECTROHORTICULTURE
RM869-890	*ELECTRICITY IN MEDICINE* **SEE** ELECTROTHERAPEUTICS
UG480	ELECTRICITY IN MILITARY ENGINEERING
TN343	ELECTRICITY IN MINING
RD33.5	*ELECTRICITY IN SURGERY* **SEE** ELECTROSURGERY
VM471-9	ELECTRICITY ON SHIPS
QC501-721	ELECTRICITY
QP341-8	*ELECTRICITY, ANIMAL* **SEE** ELECTROPHYSIOLOGY
QC961-972	*ELECTRICITY, ATMOSPHERIC* **SEE** ATMOSPHERIC ELECTRICITY
RA1091	ELECTRICITY, INJURIES FROM / *medical jurisprudence*
RD96.5	ELECTRICITY, INJURIES FROM / *treatment*
RM869-890	*ELECTRICITY, MEDICAL* **SEE** ELECTROTHERAPEUTICS
QC595	*ELECTRICITY, PIEZO-* **SEE** PYRO- AND PIEZO-ELECTRICITY
QC595	*ELECTRICITY, PYRO-* **SEE** PYRO- AND PIEZO-ELECTRICITY
QC573	*ELECTRICITY, STATIC* **SEE** ELECTRIC MACHINES
QC571-595	*ELECTRICITY, STATIC* **SEE** ELECTROSTATICS
RA1091	*ELECTRICITY-ACCIDENTS* **SEE** ELECTRICITY, INJURIES FROM / *medical jurisprudence*
RD96.5	*ELECTRICITY-ACCIDENTS* **SEE** ELECTRICITY, INJURIES FROM / *treatment*
TK	*ELECTRICITY-APPARATUS AND APPLIANCES* **SEE** ELECTRIC APPARATUS AND APPLIANCES / *electric industries*
RM889	*ELECTRICITY-APPARATUS AND APPLIANCES* **SEE** ELECTRIC APPARATUS AND APPLIANCES / *medical apparatus*
QC543-4	*ELECTRICITY-APPARATUS AND APPLIANCES* **SEE** ELECTRIC APPARATUS AND APPLIANCES / *scientific apparatus*
QC543-4	*ELECTRICITY-CATALOGS OF SUPPLIES, ETC.* **SEE** ELECTRIC APPARATUS AND APPLIANCES — CATALOGS / *scientific apparatus*
TK455	*ELECTRICITY-CATALOGS OF SUPPLIES, ETC.* **SEE** ELECTRIC APPARATUS AND APPLIANCES — CATALOGS / *electric industries*
QC701-715	*ELECTRICITY-DISCHARGES* **SEE** ELECTRIC DISCHARGES
QC711	*ELECTRICITY-DISCHARGES THROUGH GASES* **SEE** ELECTRIC DISCHARGES THROUGH GASES
TK3201-3261	*ELECTRICITY-DISTRIBUTION* **SEE** ELECTRIC LINES
TK3001-3511	*ELECTRICITY-DISTRIBUTION* **SEE** ELECTRIC POWER DISTRIBUTION
TK6	*ELECTRICITY-EXHIBITIONS* **SEE** ELECTRIC INDUSTRIES — EXHIBITIONS
TK411-415	*ELECTRICITY-LABORATORIES* **SEE** ELECTRIC LABORATORIES / *engineering*
QC541	*ELECTRICITY-LABORATORIES* **SEE** ELECTRIC LABORATORIES / *physics*
TK215-255	*ELECTRICITY-LAWS AND LEGISLATION* **SEE** ELECTRIC ENGINEERING — LAWS AND LEGISLATION
TK	*ELECTRICITY-TRANSMISSION* **SEE** ELECTRIC ENGINEERING
TK3201-3261	*ELECTRICITY-TRANSMISSION* **SEE** ELECTRIC LINES
TK3001-3511	*ELECTRICITY-TRANSMISSION* **SEE** ELECTRIC POWER DISTRIBUTION
TK1001-1831	*ELECTRICITY-TRANSMISSION* **SEE** ELECTRIC POWER PRODUCTION
TF858-9	*ELECTRIFICATION OF RAILROADS* **SEE** RAILROADS — ELECTRIFICATION
TK4018	*ELECTRIFICATION, RURAL* **SEE** RURAL ELECTRIFICATION
HD9688	*ELECTRIFICATION, RURAL* **SEE** RURAL ELECTRIFICATION
TK5981	ELECTRO-ACOUSTICS
QC463	*ELECTRO-OPTICAL SHUTTERS* **SEE** KERR CELL SHUTTERS
QP341-8	*ELECTROBIOLOGY* **SEE** ELECTROPHYSIOLOGY
QC577	ELECTROCAPILLARY PHENOMENA
RC683.5.E5	ELECTROCARDIOGRAPHY / *medicine*
QD115	ELECTROCHEMICAL ANALYSIS
TK3255	*ELECTROCHEMICAL CORROSION* **SEE** ELECTROLYTIC CORROSION / *electric engineering*
TF912	*ELECTROCHEMICAL CORROSION* **SEE** ELECTROLYTIC CORROSION / *electric railroads*
TD491	*ELECTROCHEMICAL CORROSION* **SEE** ELECTROLYTIC CORROSION / *etc.*
TK2920	*ELECTROCHEMICAL DEVICES* **SEE** FUEL CELLS
QD557	ELECTROCHEMISTRY — LABORATORY MANUALS
QD65	ELECTROCHEMISTRY — TABLES, ETC.
QD273	ELECTROCHEMISTRY / *organic chemistry*
QD553-585	ELECTROCHEMISTRY / *physical and theoretical chemistry*
TP250-261	ELECTROCHEMISTRY, INDUSTRIAL
HV8696	ELECTROCUTION
TS693	*ELECTRODEPOSITION OF ALLOYS* **SEE** ALLOY PLATING
TS670-692	*ELECTRODEPOSITION OF METALS* **SEE** ELECTROPLATING
TK7725	ELECTRODES, CARBON
QD571	ELECTRODES, DROPPING MERCURY
QD561	ELECTRODES, GLASS / *electrochemistry*
RC77	ELECTRODIAGNOSIS
QC631-645	ELECTRODYNAMICS
QC680	*ELECTRODYNAMICS, QUANTUM* **SEE** QUANTUM ELECTRODYNAMICS
QC544.E3	ELECTRODYNAMOMETER
RM891	ELECTROHOMEOPATHY
SB139	ELECTROHORTICULTURE
RM886	ELECTROLYSIS IN MEDICINE
RD33.5	ELECTROLYSIS IN SURGERY
TP259	*ELECTROLYSIS OF WATER* **SEE** WATER — ELECTROLYSIS
QD553-585	ELECTROLYTES
QD565	ELECTROLYTES — CONDUCTIVITY
QD599	ELECTROLYTES / *colloids*
QD553-585	ELECTROLYTES / *electrolysis*
QD541-3	ELECTROLYTES / *solutions*
QD115	*ELECTROLYTIC ANALYSIS* **SEE** ELECTROCHEMICAL ANALYSIS
QC587	*ELECTROLYTIC CAPACITORS* **SEE** CONDENSERS (ELECTRICITY)
QC587	*ELECTROLYTIC CONDENSERS* **SEE** CONDENSERS (ELECTRICITY)
TK3255	ELECTROLYTIC CORROSION / *electric engineering*
TF912	ELECTROLYTIC CORROSION / *electric railroads*
TD491	ELECTROLYTIC CORROSION / *etc.*
TA467	*ELECTROLYTIC PICKLING OF METALS* **SEE** METALS — PICKLING
QD63.R4	*ELECTROLYTIC REDUCTION* **SEE** REDUCTION, ELECTROLYTIC
QD281.R4	*ELECTROLYTIC REDUCTION* **SEE** REDUCTION, ELECTROLYTIC / *organic*
TK9909	*ELECTROMAGNETIC MACHINES* **SEE** MAGNETO-ELECTRIC MACHINES / *amateurs' manuals*
QC661-675	ELECTROMAGNETIC THEORY
QC661-5	*ELECTROMAGNETIC WAVES* **SEE** ELECTRIC WAVES
RZ422	ELECTROMAGNETISM IN MEDICINE
QC760	ELECTROMAGNETISM
QC760	ELECTROMAGNETS
TN681-7	ELECTROMETALLURGY
QC544.E4	ELECTROMETER
QC618	ELECTROMOTIVE FORCE
QD561	ELECTROMOTIVE FORCE / *electrolysis*
QC721	*ELECTRON DIFFRACTION* **SEE** ELECTRONS — DIFFRACTION
TK7872.I6	*ELECTRON IMAGE CONVERTER TUBES* **SEE** IMAGE CONVERTERS
TK7872.E5	*ELECTRON MULTIPLIERS* **SEE** PHOTOELECTRIC MULTIPLIERS
QC447	ELECTRON OPTICS
QC721	*ELECTRON SCATTERING* **SEE** ELECTRONS — SCATTERING
TK7872.V3	ELECTRON TUBES — MATERIALS
QC176	*ELECTRON-HOLE PAIR THEORY* **SEE** EXCITON THEORY
TK7872.A5	*ELECTRONIC AMPLIFIERS* **SEE** AMPLIFIERS (ELECTRONICS)
TK7888	ELECTRONIC ANALOG COMPUTERS — DESIGN AND CONSTRUCTION
QA76	ELECTRONIC ANALOG COMPUTERS
TK7870	ELECTRONIC APPARATUS AND APPLIANCES — CATALOGS
TK7870	ELECTRONIC APPARATUS AND APPLIANCES — CLEANING

TK7870	ELECTRONIC APPARATUS AND APPLIANCES
Q327	*ELECTRONIC BRAINS* **SEE** CONSCIOUS AUTOMATA
QA76	*ELECTRONIC BRAINS* **SEE** ELECTRONIC CALCULATING-MACHINES
TK7885	ELECTRONIC CALCULATING-MACHINES — CIRCUITS
TK7887.5	ELECTRONIC CALCULATING-MACHINES — INPUT-OUTPUT EQUIPMENT
TK7895.06	ELECTRONIC CALCULATING-MACHINES — OPTICAL EQUIPMENT
QA76	ELECTRONIC CALCULATING-MACHINES
QA76	*ELECTRONIC CALCULATING-MACHINES-PROGRAMMING* **SEE** PROGRAMMING (ELECTRONIC COMPUTERS)
QA76	*ELECTRONIC COMPUTER PROGRAMMING* **SEE** PROGRAMMING (ELECTRONIC COMPUTERS)
QA76	*ELECTRONIC COMPUTERS* **SEE** ELECTRONIC CALCULATING-MACHINES
QA76	ELECTRONIC DIFFERENTIAL ANALYZERS / *mathematics*
TK7888.3	ELECTRONIC DIGITAL COMPUTERS — CIRCUITS
QA76.5	ELECTRONIC DIGITAL COMPUTERS — PROGRAMMING
TK7870	*ELECTRONIC EQUIPMENT, MINIATURE* **SEE** MINIATURE ELECTRONIC EQUIPMENT
TK7870	ELECTRONIC INDUSTRIES — AUTOMATION
TK7870	ELECTRONIC INSTRUMENTS
TK7882.M	ELECTRONIC MEASUREMENTS / *electronics*
QC535	ELECTRONIC MEASUREMENTS / *physics*
ML1092	*ELECTRONIC MUSICAL INSTRUMENTS* **SEE** MUSICAL INSTRUMENTS, ELECTRONIC
VK560	*ELECTRONIC NAVIGATION* **SEE** ELECTRONICS IN NAVIGATION
QC447	*ELECTRONIC OPTICS* **SEE** ELECTRON OPTICS
ML597	ELECTRONIC ORGAN — CONSTRUCTION
MT192	ELECTRONIC ORGAN — REGISTRATION
ML597	ELECTRONIC ORGAN — REPAIRING
M14.8	ELECTRONIC ORGAN MUSIC (CONN REGISTRATION)
M14.85	ELECTRONIC ORGAN MUSIC (CONN REGISTRATION)
M14.85	ELECTRONIC ORGAN MUSIC (HAMMOND REGISTRATION)
M14.8	ELECTRONIC ORGAN MUSIC (HAMMOND REGISTRATION)
M14.8	ELECTRONIC ORGAN MUSIC (SILVERTONE REGISTRATION)
M14.85	ELECTRONIC ORGAN MUSIC (SILVERTONE REGISTRATION)
M14.8	ELECTRONIC ORGAN MUSIC
M14.85	ELECTRONIC ORGAN MUSIC
ML597	ELECTRONIC ORGAN
MT250	ELECTRONIC PIANO — INSTRUCTION AND STUDY
ML697	ELECTRONIC PIANO
QB301	*ELECTRONIC SURVEYING* **SEE** ELECTRONICS IN SURVEYING / *geodetic surveying*
TA595	*ELECTRONIC SURVEYING* **SEE** ELECTRONICS IN SURVEYING / *plane surveying*
TK7872.T	ELECTRONIC TRANSFORMERS
P307-310	*ELECTRONIC TRANSLATING* **SEE** MACHINE TRANSLATING
TK7825	ELECTRONICS — GRAPHIC METHODS
TK7835	ELECTRONICS — MATERIALS
TK7855	ELECTRONICS — RESEARCH
TK7845	ELECTRONICS AS A PROFESSION
TL695	ELECTRONICS IN AERONAUTICS
TA595	*ELECTRONICS IN GEODESY* **SEE** ELECTRONICS IN SURVEYING / *plane surveying*
QB301	*ELECTRONICS IN GEODESY* **SEE** ELECTRONICS IN SURVEYING / *geodetic surveying*
R895	*ELECTRONICS IN MEDICINE* **SEE** MEDICAL ELECTRONICS
UG485	ELECTRONICS IN MILITARY ENGINEERING
VK560	ELECTRONICS IN NAVIGATION
TL784.E4	ELECTRONICS IN ROCKETRY
QB301	ELECTRONICS IN SURVEYING / *geodetic surveying*
TA595	ELECTRONICS IN SURVEYING / *plane surveying*
Z699.5.E5	*ELECTRONICS LITERATURE SEARCHING* **SEE** INFORMATION STORAGE AND RETRIEVAL SYSTEMS — ELECTRONICS
VM325	ELECTRONICS ON BOATS
TK7800-7882	ELECTRONICS
TK7870	*ELECTRONICS-APPARATUS AND APPLIANCES* **SEE** ELECTRONIC APPARATUS AND APPLIANCES
QC721	ELECTRONS — DIFFRACTION
QC721	ELECTRONS — SCATTERING
QC721	ELECTRONS
ML1092	*ELECTROPHONIC MUSICAL INSTRUMENTS* **SEE** MUSICAL INSTRUMENTS, ELECTRONIC
QC544.E6	ELECTROPHORUS
QK845	ELECTROPHYSIOLOGY OF PLANTS
QP341-8	ELECTROPHYSIOLOGY
TS670-692	ELECTROPLATING
TP156.P7	ELECTROSTATIC PRECIPITATION
TL783.63	*ELECTROSTATIC PROPULSION SYSTEMS* **SEE** ION ROCKETS
TP156.E5	*ELECTROSTATIC SEPARATION* **SEE** ELECTROSTATIC SEPARATORS
TP156.E5	ELECTROSTATIC SEPARATORS
TK7872.S7	*ELECTROSTATIC STORAGE TUBES* **SEE** STORAGE TUBES
QC571-595	ELECTROSTATICS
RD33.5	ELECTROSURGERY
RM889	ELECTROTHERAPEUTICS — APPARATUS AND INSTRUMENTS
RM873	ELECTROTHERAPEUTICS — LABORATORY MANUALS
RM869-890	ELECTROTHERAPEUTICS
Z252	ELECTROTYPING
PN1389	ELEGIAC POETRY
PN1389	*ELEGIES* **SEE** ELEGIAC POETRY
QL862	ELEIDIN / *comparative anatomy of stomach*
QM561	ELEIDIN / *histology*
DU740	ELEMA (PAPUAN PEOPLE)
LB1555-1601	*ELEMENTARY EDUCATION* **SEE** EDUCATION, ELEMENTARY
LB2822.5	ELEMENTARY SCHOOL ADMINISTRATION
LB2822.5	ELEMENTARY SCHOOL PRINCIPALS
QD466-7	*ELEMENTS, CHEMICAL* **SEE** CHEMICAL ELEMENTS
CR41.E6	ELEPHANT (IN HERALDRY)
SK305.E3	ELEPHANT HUNTING
RC142.5	ELEPHANTIASIS
QL795.E4	ELEPHANTS — LEGENDS AND STORIES
QL737.U8	ELEPHANTS
QE882.U7	ELEPHANTS, FOSSIL
QE882.U7	*ELEPHAS PRIMIGENIUS* **SEE** MAMMOTH
BL795.E5	ELEUSINIAN MYSTERIES
PM31-34	*ELEUTH LANGUAGE* **SEE** ALEUT LANGUAGE
TF840	*ELEVATED RAILROADS* **SEE** RAILROADS, ELEVATED
HE4201-5300	*ELEVATED RAILROADS* **SEE** RAILROADS, ELEVATED / *economics*
QC276	*ELEVATED TEMPERATURES* **SEE** HIGH TEMPERATURES
GB491-8	*ELEVATIONS* **SEE** ALTITUDES
TL677.E6	ELEVATORS (AEROPLANES)
TJ1370-1380	ELEVATORS
TH4461	*ELEVATORS, GRAIN* **SEE** GRAIN ELEVATORS
TJ1374	ELEVATORS, PRIVATE RESIDENCE
DT434.E	ELGEYO (AFRICAN TRIBE)
DT429	ELGEYO (AFRICAN TRIBE) / *ethnography*
NB92	ELGIN MARBLES
QA192	ELIMINATION
GR605	ELIXIR OF LIFE
RS201.E4	ELIXIRS
E473.3	ELIZABETH CITY, N.C. — CAPTURE, 1862
E241.E39	ELIZABETH, N.J., BATTLE OF, 1780
E241.E4	ELIZABETHTOWN, N.C., BATTLE OF, 1781
QL737.U5	ELK
SF429.N	*ELKHOUNDS* **SEE** NORWEGIAN ELKHOUNDS
PL6431	ELLICE LANGUAGE
QA485	ELLIPSE
QA559	ELLIPSE
QA561	ELLIPSOID / *analytic geometry*
QA827	ELLIPSOID / *attractions and potential*
QA409	*ELLIPSOIDAL HARMONICS* **SEE** LAME'S FUNCTIONS
QA827	*ELLIPSOIDS, ATTRACTIONS OF* **SEE** ATTRACTIONS OF ELLIPSOIDS
QA343	*ELLIPTIC FUNCTIONS* **SEE** FUNCTIONS, ELLIPTIC
QA343	*ELLIPTIC FUNCTIONS* **SEE** FUNCTIONS, MODULAR
SB608.E5	ELM — DISEASES AND PESTS
SB608.E	*ELM BLIGHT* **SEE** DUTCH ELM DISEASE
SB608.E5	ELM LEAF-BEETLE
QK495.U4	ELM / *botany*
GN659.M3	*ELMORAN* **SEE** MASAI / *anthropology*
DT429	*ELMORAN* **SEE** MASAI / *history*
DT434.E2	*ELMORAN* **SEE** MASAI / *history*

DT434.E2	*ELMORAN* **SEE** MASAI / *kenya*
PN4071-4197	ELOCUTION
PN4059	ELOCUTIONISTS
PN4001-4173	ELOQUENCE
DP635	ELVAS, LINHAS DE, BATTLE OF, 1659
GR550	*ELVES* **SEE** FAIRIES / *folk-lore*
BF552	*ELVES* **SEE** FAIRIES / *occultism*
BL795.E6	*ELYSIAN FIELDS* **SEE** ELYSIUM / *greek mythology*
BL795.E6	ELYSIUM / *greek mythology*
RC814	*EMACIATION* **SEE** LEANNESS
QD181.R2	*EMANATION (RADIOACTIVE SUBSTANCES)* **SEE** RADON
E453	*EMANCIPATION OF SLAVES* **SEE** 'EMANCIPATION PROCLAMATION
HT1025-1037	*EMANCIPATION OF SLAVES* **SEE** SLAVERY — EMANCIPATION
E453	*EMANCIPATION OF SLAVES* **SEE** SLAVERY IN THE U.S. — EMANCIPATION
HQ1456-1870	*EMANCIPATION OF WOMEN* **SEE** WOMAN — RIGHTS OF WOMEN / *other countries*
HQ1423-6	*EMANCIPATION OF WOMEN* **SEE** WOMAN — RIGHTS OF WOMEN / *u.s.*
E453	EMANCIPATION PROCLAMATION
BX1492	*EMANCIPATION, CATHOLIC* **SEE** CATHOLIC EMANCIPATION
DA950.3	*EMANCIPATION, CATHOLIC* **SEE** CATHOLIC EMANCIPATION / *act*
QD181.R2	*EMANON* **SEE** RADON
QP251-5	*EMASCULATION* **SEE** CASTRATION / *physiology*
HV4989	*EMASCULATION* **SEE** CASTRATION / *social pathology*
RD571	*EMASCULATION* **SEE** CASTRATION / *surgery*
SF889	*EMASCULATION* **SEE** CASTRATION / *veterinary medicine*
RA622-3	EMBALMING
GT3340	EMBALMING / *manners and customs*
TA760-770	EMBANKMENTS
TC759	EMBANKMENTS / *canals*
TC337	EMBANKMENTS / *coasts*
TC533	EMBANKMENTS / *rivers*
JX4491	EMBARGO / *international law*
HF3027.1	EMBARGO, 1807-1809
E336.5	EMBARGO, 1807-1809
JX1621-1894	*EMBASSIES* **SEE** AMBASSADORS
JX1621-1894	*EMBASSIES* **SEE** DIPLOMATIC AND CONSULAR SERVICE
MT80	EMBELLISHMENT (MUSIC)
MT80	EMBELLISHMENT (VOCAL MUSIC)
TX739	*EMBER-DAY MENUS* **SEE** LENTEN MENUS
TX837	*EMBER-DAY MENUS* **SEE** LENTEN MENUS / *with recipes*
HV6675-6685	EMBEZZLEMENT
QL638.E5	*EMBIOTOCIDAE* **SEE** SURF-FISHES
N7740	EMBLEMS
BV150-155	EMBLEMS / *christianity*
BL603	EMBLEMS / *comparative religion*
CR	EMBLEMS / *heraldry*
PN6349-6358	EMBLEMS / *literature*
RC691	EMBOLISM
PL8401-4	*EMBOMMA LANGUAGE* **SEE** CONGO LANGUAGE
Z256	EMBOSSING (TYPOGRAPHY)
TP863	*EMBOSSING OF GLASS* **SEE** GLASS EMBOSSING
TT770-773	EMBROIDERY — PATTERNS
TT753-5	EMBROIDERY — PATTERNS
NK9200-9310	EMBROIDERY / *art*
TS1783	EMBROIDERY / *manufacture*
TT770-777	EMBROIDERY / *needlework*
HD9935	EMBROIDERY / *trade*
E98.E5	*EMBROIDERY, INDIAN* **SEE** INDIANS OF NORTH AMERICA — EMBROIDERY
TS1783	EMBROIDERY, MACHINE
NK9272-9285	EMBROIDERY, ORIENTAL
QL951-973	*EMBRYOGENY* **SEE** EMBRYOLOGY
QL957	EMBRYOLOGY — LABORATORY MANUALS
QK665	*EMBRYOLOGY (BOTANY)* **SEE** BOTANY — EMBRYOLOGY
QL951-973	EMBRYOLOGY
QL961	EMBRYOLOGY, EXPERIMENTAL
QM601-611	EMBRYOLOGY, HUMAN
QK665	*EMBRYOLOGY, VEGETABLE* **SEE** BOTANY — EMBRYOLOGY
SF761	*EMBRYOLOGY, VETERINARY* **SEE** VETERINARY EMBRYOLOGY
SF887	*EMBRYOTOMY, VETERINARY* **SEE** VETERINARY OBSTETRICS
TN997.E5	EMERALD MINES AND MINING
QE394.E	EMERALDS / *mineralogy*
TS755.E5	EMERALDS / *technology*
RC86-88	*EMERGENCIES* **SEE** FIRST AID IN ILLNESS AND INJURY
RC86-88	*EMERGENCIES, MEDICAL* **SEE** FIRST AID IN ILLNESS AND INJURY
TX946	EMERGENCY MASS FEEDING
RA645.5-7	*EMERGENCY MEDICAL CARE* **SEE** EMERGENCY MEDICAL SERVICES
RA645.5-7	EMERGENCY MEDICAL SERVICES
RT108	*EMERGENCY NURSING* **SEE** DISASTER NURSING
JF251-314	*EMERGENCY POWERS* **SEE** EXECUTIVE POWER
JN-JQ	*EMERGENCY POWERS* **SEE** EXECUTIVE POWER / *other countries*
JK501-901	*EMERGENCY POWERS* **SEE** EXECUTIVE POWER / *u.s.*
JF256	*EMERGENCY POWERS* **SEE** WAR AND EMERGENCY POWERS
JK339	*EMERGENCY POWERS* **SEE** WAR AND EMERGENCY POWERS / *u.s. government*
JK560	*EMERGENCY POWERS* **SEE** WAR AND EMERGENCY POWERS / *u.s. president*
HV553-5	*EMERGENCY RELIEF* **SEE** DISASTER RELIEF
TJ1290	EMERY-WHEELS
TN936	EMERY
RM359	EMETICS
RM666.E5	EMETINE
RK701	EMETINE / *dentistry*
JV6001-9500	EMIGRATION AND IMMIGRATION
DC158.1-17	EMIGRES
JX598.E7	EMILIO RONDANINI (SHIP)
HD1261-5	EMINENT DOMAIN
HD3865-6	EMINENT DOMAIN / *public works*
RZ400	EMMANUEL MOVEMENT
RM521	EMMENAGOGUES
LB1139.E	EMOTIONAL PROBLEMS OF CHILDREN
BF511-593	EMOTIONS
BF575.E55	EMPATHY
BL465	EMPEROR WORSHIP
DG124	EMPEROR WORSHIP, ROMAN
D107	EMPERORS
RC776	EMPHYSEMA, PULMONARY
DA18	EMPIRE DAY
BT98-101	*EMPIRICAL ARGUMENT* **SEE** GOD — PROOF, EMPIRICAL
B816	EMPIRICISM
HD5115	*EMPLOYEE ABSENTEEISM* **SEE** ABSENTEEISM (LABOR)
HD2970-3110	EMPLOYEE OWNERSHIP / *profit-sharing*
HD2781.S7	EMPLOYEE OWNERSHIP / *stockholders*
HD7395.R4	*EMPLOYEE RECREATION* **SEE** INDUSTRIAL RECREATION
HF5549	*EMPLOYEE SENIORITY* **SEE** SENIORITY, EMPLOYEE
HF5549	*EMPLOYEE TURNOVER* **SEE** LABOR TURNOVER
HD5261	*EMPLOYEE VACATIONS* **SEE** VACATIONS, EMPLOYEE
HD6961	*EMPLOYEE-EMPLOYER RELATIONS* **SEE** INDUSTRIAL RELATIONS
HF5501	*EMPLOYEES, CLERICAL* **SEE** CLERKS
HV3165-3173	*EMPLOYEES, CLERICAL* **SEE** CLERKS / *aid to*
HD8039.M4	*EMPLOYEES, CLERICAL* **SEE** CLERKS / *mercantile clerks*
HD7813	EMPLOYEES, DISMISSAL OF
T60.R	EMPLOYEES, RATING OF
T58	EMPLOYEES, TRAINING OF
HF5549.5.T7	EMPLOYEES, TRAINING OF
NA6598	EMPLOYEES' BUILDINGS AND FACILITIES
HD5650-5659	EMPLOYEES' REPRESENTATION IN MANAGEMENT
NA6598	*EMPLOYEES' SERVICE BUILDINGS* **SEE** EMPLOYEES' BUILDINGS AND FACILITIES
HD5261	*EMPLOYEES' VACATIONS* **SEE** VACATIONS, EMPLOYEE
HD6961	*EMPLOYER-EMPLOYEE RELATIONS* **SEE** INDUSTRIAL RELATIONS
HD6350-6940	EMPLOYERS' ASSOCIATIONS
HG9964.E4-7	*EMPLOYERS' LIABILITY INSURANCE* **SEE** INSURANCE, EMPLOYERS' LIABILITY

HD7814-7816	EMPLOYERS' LIABILITY
HB301	EMPLOYMENT (ECONOMIC THEORY)
HD5861-6000	EMPLOYMENT AGENCIES
HD4903	*EMPLOYMENT DISCRIMINATION* **SEE** DISCRIMINATION IN EMPLOYMENT
HD5861-6000	*EMPLOYMENT EXCHANGES* **SEE** EMPLOYMENT AGENCIES
HF5549.5.I6	EMPLOYMENT INTERVIEWING
T56-58	*EMPLOYMENT MANAGEMENT* **SEE** PERSONNEL MANAGEMENT
HF5549	*EMPLOYMENT MANAGEMENT* **SEE** PERSONNEL MANAGEMENT
HD6228-6250	*EMPLOYMENT OF CHILDREN* **SEE** CHILDREN — EMPLOYMENT
HV9288	*EMPLOYMENT OF EX-CONVICTS* **SEE** EX-CONVICTS, EMPLOYMENT OF
LB3611	*EMPLOYMENT OF STUDENTS* **SEE** STUDENT EMPLOYMENT
HV1652-8	*EMPLOYMENT OF THE BLIND* **SEE** BLIND — EMPLOYMENT
UB356-9	*EMPLOYMENT OF VETERANS* **SEE** VETERANS — EMPLOYMENT
HD6050-6220	*EMPLOYMENT OF WOMEN* **SEE** WOMAN — EMPLOYMENT
HD6270	*EMPLOYMENT OF YOUTH* **SEE** YOUTH — EMPLOYMENT
HD5861-6000	*EMPLOYMENT OFFICES* **SEE** EMPLOYMENT AGENCIES
HD4903	*EMPLOYMENT, FREE CHOICE OF* **SEE** FREE CHOICE OF EMPLOYMENT
HF5549	*EMPLOYMENT, SENIORITY IN* **SEE** SENIORITY, EMPLOYEE
RC742	EMPYEMA
RJ436.E5	EMPYEMA / *children's diseases*
QP601	EMULSIN
TP156.E6	EMULSIONS / *chemical engineering*
RS201.E5	EMULSIONS / *pharmacy*
QC183	EMULSIONS / *physics*
QL696.C3	EMUS
NK5000-5015	ENAMEL AND ENAMELING / *art*
TP812	ENAMEL AND ENAMELING / *pottery*
TP934-7	*ENAMEL PAINTS* **SEE** PAINT / *manufacture*
TT300-380	*ENAMEL PAINTS* **SEE** PAINTING, INDUSTRIAL
TP938	*ENAMEL PAINTS* **SEE** VARNISH AND VARNISHING / *varnish*
TT340	*ENAMEL PAINTS* **SEE** VARNISH AND VARNISHING / *varnishing*
TS700-705	ENAMELED WARE
NK5000-5015	*ENAMELS* **SEE** ENAMEL AND ENAMELING / *art*
TP812	*ENAMELS* **SEE** ENAMEL AND ENAMELING / *pottery*
TN780	ENARGITE
ND2480	ENCAUSTIC PAINTING
QM691	ENCEPHALOCELE
RC386.5	ENCEPHALOGRAPHY
QB723.E3	ENCKE'S COMET
TH2231	*ENCLOSURE WALLS* **SEE** CURTAIN WALLS
HD594.6	*ENCLOSURES* **SEE** INCLOSURES / *gt. brit.*
HD464	ENCOMIENDAS (LATIN AMERICA)
F1411	ENCOMIENDAS (LATIN AMERICA)
BX860	ENCYCLICALS, PAPAL / *collections*
AE	ENCYCLOPEDIAS AND DICTIONARIES
AG	ENCYCLOPEDIAS AND DICTIONARIES
B1911	ENCYCLOPEDISTS
QL369	ENCYSTMENT (ZOOLOGY) / *protozoa*
BT875-6	END OF THE WORLD
GV951.25	END PLAY (FOOTBALL)
BD437	*ENDEAVOR* **SEE** STRUGGLE
RM151	ENDERMIC MEDICATION
RM151	*ENDERMIC METHOD* **SEE** ENDERMIC MEDICATION
RM151	*ENDERMOSIS* **SEE** ENDERMIC MEDICATION
BT834-8	*ENDLESS PUNISHMENT* **SEE** FUTURE PUNISHMENT
BL1475.H5	*ENDLESS PUNISHMENT* **SEE** HELL / *buddhism*
BL735	*ENDLESS PUNISHMENT* **SEE** HELL / *classical mythology*
BL545	*ENDLESS PUNISHMENT* **SEE** HELL / *comparative religion*
BT834-8	*ENDLESS PUNISHMENT* **SEE** HELL / *theology*
QE391.E5	ENDLICHITE
RC685.E5	ENDOCARDITIS
QM371	*ENDOCRINE GLANDS* **SEE** GLANDS, DUCTLESS / *human anatomy*
QP187	*ENDOCRINE GLANDS* **SEE** GLANDS, DUCTLESS / *physiology*
RC648-665	*ENDOCRINE THERAPY* **SEE** ENDOCRINOLOGY / *medicine*
QP187	*ENDOCRINE THERAPY* **SEE** ENDOCRINOLOGY / *physiology*
RC648-665	*ENDOCRINES* **SEE** ENDOCRINOLOGY / *medicine*
QP187	*ENDOCRINES* **SEE** ENDOCRINOLOGY / *physiology*
RC648-665	ENDOCRINOLOGY / *medicine*
QP187	ENDOCRINOLOGY / *physiology*
RC648-665	*ENDOCRINOTHERAPY* **SEE** ENDOCRINOLOGY / *medicine*
QP187	*ENDOCRINOTHERAPY* **SEE** ENDOCRINOLOGY / *physiology*
RK351	*ENDODONTIA* **SEE** ENDODONTICS
RK351	ENDODONTICS
GN480.3	ENDOGAMY AND EXOGAMY
RF270	*ENDOLYMPHATIC HYDROPS* **SEE** MENIERE'S DISEASE
RG301	ENDOMETRIOSIS
RG301	*ENDOMETRIUM-INFLAMMATION* **SEE** ENDOMETRIOSIS
RF476	ENDOSCOPE AND ENDOSCOPY
RF514	ENDOSCOPE AND ENDOSCOPY
RC872	ENDOSCOPE AND ENDOSCOPY / *special*
RC864	ENDOSCOPE AND ENDOSCOPY / *special*
RC786	ENDOSCOPE AND ENDOSCOPY / *special*
QM562	ENDOTHELIUM
RD85.I	*ENDOTRACHEAL ANESTHESIA* **SEE** INTRATRACHEAL ANESTHESIA
HV1-4959	*ENDOWED CHARITIES* **SEE**
HV16-25	*ENDOWED CHARITIES* **SEE** ENDOWMENTS / *charities*
LB2336-7	*ENDOWED CHARITIES* **SEE** ENDOWMENTS / *higher education*
HG8818	*ENDOWMENT INSURANCE* **SEE** INSURANCE, LIFE — ENDOWMENT POLICIES
Q181	ENDOWMENT OF RESEARCH
LB2336-7	ENDOWMENT OF RESEARCH
HV16-25	ENDOWMENTS / *charities*
LB2336-7	ENDOWMENTS / *higher education*
RM163	ENEMA
JV6001-9500	*ENEMY ALIENS* **SEE** ALIENS / *emigration and immigration*
D570.8.A6	*ENEMY ALIENS* **SEE** ALIENS / *european war u.s.*
JX4203-4270	*ENEMY ALIENS* **SEE** ALIENS / *nationality and alienage*
D801	*ENEMY ALIENS* **SEE** ALIENS / *other countries*
D636.A3-Z	*ENEMY ALIENS* **SEE** ALIENS / *other countries*
D769.8.A6	*ENEMY ALIENS* **SEE** ALIENS / *world war u.s.*
QC73	*ENERGY* **SEE** FORCE AND ENERGY
TK2896	*ENERGY CONVERSION, DIRECT* **SEE** DIRECT ENERGY CONVERSION
QC310	*ENERGY OF IMMERSION* **SEE** HEAT OF WETTING
QH341	*ENERGY, VITAL* **SEE** VITAL FORCE
UD395.E	ENFIELD RIFLE
JX1246	*ENFORCEMENT MEASURES (INTERNATIONAL LAW)* **SEE** SANCTIONS (INTERNATIONAL LAW)
JX1975.6	*ENFORCEMENT MEASURES (INTERNATIONAL LAW)* **SEE** SANCTIONS (INTERNATIONAL LAW) / *league of nations*
GT2650	*ENGAGEMENT* **SEE** BETROTHAL
TL681.5	*ENGINE NACELLES (AEROPLANE)* **SEE** AEROPLANES — NACELLES
TA185	ENGINEERING — ACCOUNTING
TA5	ENGINEERING — CONGRESSES
TA180-182	ENGINEERING — CONTRACTS AND SPECIFICATIONS
TA183	ENGINEERING — ESTIMATES AND COSTS
TA159	ENGINEERING — EXAMINATIONS, QUESTIONS, ETC.
TA6	ENGINEERING — EXHIBITIONS
Z5851	ENGINEERING — INDEXES
TA190	ENGINEERING — MANAGEMENT
TA11	ENGINEERING — NOTATION
T65.5.P7	ENGINEERING — PROGRAMMED INSTRUCTION
T61-173	ENGINEERING — STUDY AND TEACHING
T12-13	ENGINEERING — SUPPLIES
TA151	ENGINEERING — TABLES, CALCULATIONS, ETC.
TA213-215	ENGINEERING — TOOLS AND IMPLEMENTS
TA157	ENGINEERING AS A PROFESSION
T351-377	*ENGINEERING DRAWING* **SEE** MECHANICAL DRAWING

TA157	ENGINEERING ETHICS
TA416-417	ENGINEERING EXPERIMENT STATIONS
TA705	ENGINEERING GEOLOGY / *engineering*
QE33	ENGINEERING GEOLOGY / *geology*
TN260	ENGINEERING GEOLOGY / *mining engineering*
TA190	ENGINEERING INSPECTION
TA165	ENGINEERING INSTRUMENTS
TA416-417	ENGINEERING LABORATORIES
TA221-324	ENGINEERING LAW
Z675.E6	ENGINEERING LIBRARIES
TA197	ENGINEERING METEOROLOGY
TA177	ENGINEERING MODELS
TA1-4	ENGINEERING SOCIETIES
TA368	*ENGINEERING STANDARDS* **SEE** STANDARDS, ENGINEERING
TA11	*ENGINEERING SYMBOLS* **SEE** ENGINEERING — NOTATION
TA368	*ENGINEERING TOLERANCES* **SEE** TOLERANCE (ENGINEERING)
TA	ENGINEERING
HD9680-9712	ENGINEERING / *economics*
S671-760	*ENGINEERING, AGRICULTURAL* **SEE** AGRICULTURAL ENGINEERING
TH	*ENGINEERING, ARCHITECTURAL* **SEE** BUILDING
TA684-5	*ENGINEERING, ARCHITECTURAL* **SEE** BUILDING, IRON AND STEEL / *engineering*
TH1610-1621	*ENGINEERING, ARCHITECTURAL* **SEE** BUILDING, IRON AND STEEL / *building*
TH845-891	*ENGINEERING, ARCHITECTURAL* **SEE** STRAINS AND STRESSES / *architectural engineering*
QA931-5	*ENGINEERING, ARCHITECTURAL* **SEE** STRAINS AND STRESSES / *elasticity*
TG265-7	*ENGINEERING, ARCHITECTURAL* **SEE** STRAINS AND STRESSES / *bridge and roof engineering*
TA410-417	*ENGINEERING, ARCHITECTURAL* **SEE** STRENGTH OF MATERIALS / *testing*
TA405	*ENGINEERING, ARCHITECTURAL* **SEE** STRENGTH OF MATERIALS
TG260	*ENGINEERING, ARCHITECTURAL* **SEE** STRUCTURES, THEORY OF
TP155	*ENGINEERING, CHEMICAL* **SEE** CHEMICAL ENGINEERING
TA	*ENGINEERING, CIVIL* **SEE** CIVIL ENGINEERING
TK	*ENGINEERING, ELECTRICAL* **SEE** ELECTRIC ENGINEERING
TC	*ENGINEERING, HYDRAULIC* **SEE** HYDRAULIC ENGINEERING
VM600-989	*ENGINEERING, MARINE* **SEE** MARINE ENGINEERING
TJ	*ENGINEERING, MECHANICAL* **SEE** MECHANICAL ENGINEERING
TA350	*ENGINEERING, MECHANICAL* **SEE** MECHANICS, APPLIED
UG	*ENGINEERING, MILITARY* **SEE** MILITARY ENGINEERING
TN	*ENGINEERING, MINING* **SEE** MINING ENGINEERING
TD	*ENGINEERING, MUNICIPAL* **SEE** MUNICIPAL ENGINEERING
TF	*ENGINEERING, RAILROAD* **SEE** RAILROAD ENGINEERING
TD	*ENGINEERING, SANITARY* **SEE** SANITARY ENGINEERING
TJ268-740	*ENGINEERING, STEAM* **SEE** STEAM ENGINEERING
TH1610-1621	*ENGINEERING, STRUCTURAL* **SEE** BUILDING, IRON AND STEEL / *building*
TA684-5	*ENGINEERING, STRUCTURAL* **SEE** BUILDING, IRON AND STEEL / *engineering*
TH845-891	*ENGINEERING, STRUCTURAL* **SEE** STRAINS AND STRESSES / *architectural engineering*
TG265-7	*ENGINEERING, STRUCTURAL* **SEE** STRAINS AND STRESSES / *bridge and roof engineering*
QA931-5	*ENGINEERING, STRUCTURAL* **SEE** STRAINS AND STRESSES / *elasticity*
TA405	*ENGINEERING, STRUCTURAL* **SEE** STRENGTH OF MATERIALS
TA410-417	*ENGINEERING, STRUCTURAL* **SEE** STRENGTH OF MATERIALS / *testing*
TG260	*ENGINEERING, STRUCTURAL* **SEE** STRUCTURES, THEORY OF
TC404-555	*ENGINEERING, WATER-SUPPLY* **SEE** WATER-SUPPLY ENGINEERING

TD201-500	*ENGINEERING, WATER-SUPPLY* **SEE** WATER-SUPPLY ENGINEERING / *municipal*
TA705	*ENGINEERING-GEOLOGY* **SEE** ENGINEERING GEOLOGY / *engineering*
QE33	*ENGINEERING-GEOLOGY* **SEE** ENGINEERING GEOLOGY / *geology*
TN260	*ENGINEERING-GEOLOGY* **SEE** ENGINEERING GEOLOGY / *mining engineering*
TA221-324	*ENGINEERING-LAW AND LEGISLATION* **SEE** ENGINEERING LAW
TA177	*ENGINEERING-MODELS* **SEE** ENGINEERING MODELS
TA139-140	ENGINEERS / *biography*
TJ250-255	ENGINES
PN56	ENGLAND IN LITERATURE
BX5011-5199	*ENGLAND, CHURCH OF* **SEE** CHURCH OF ENGLAND
DA	*ENGLAND-HISTORY* **SEE** GREAT BRITAIN — HISTORY
PR1181-8	ENGLISH BALLADS AND SONGS / *collections*
PR507	ENGLISH BALLADS AND SONGS / *history*
DA499	*ENGLISH CATHOLIC NONJURORS* **SEE** NONJURORS, ENGLISH CATHOLIC / *18th century*
PR8880	ENGLISH DIARIES — IRISH AUTHORS / *collections*
PR8810	ENGLISH DIARIES — IRISH AUTHORS / *history*
PR8680	ENGLISH DIARIES — SCOTTISH AUTHORS / *collections*
PR8610	ENGLISH DIARIES — SCOTTISH AUTHORS / *history*
PR1330	ENGLISH DIARIES / *collections*
PR908	ENGLISH DIARIES / *history*
PR627	ENGLISH DRAMA — ADDRESSES, ESSAYS, LECTURES
Z2014.D7	ENGLISH DRAMA — BIO-BIBLIOGRAPHY
PR623	ENGLISH DRAMA — DICTIONARIES
PR1262-3	ENGLISH DRAMA — EARLY MODERN AND ELIZABETHAN / *collections*
PR646-658	ENGLISH DRAMA — EARLY MODERN AND ELIZABETHAN / *history*
PR621-739	ENGLISH DRAMA — HISTORY AND CRITICISM
PR8864-8870	ENGLISH DRAMA — IRISH AUTHORS / *collections*
PR8783-8795	ENGLISH DRAMA — IRISH AUTHORS / *history*
PR1260	ENGLISH DRAMA — MEDIEVAL / *collections*
PR641-4	ENGLISH DRAMA — MEDIEVAL / *history*
PR1265-6	ENGLISH DRAMA — RESTORATION / *collections*
PR691-8	ENGLISH DRAMA — RESTORATION / *history*
PR8664-8670	ENGLISH DRAMA — SCOTTISH AUTHORS / *collections*
PR8583-8595	ENGLISH DRAMA — SCOTTISH AUTHORS / *history*
PR625	ENGLISH DRAMA — SOURCES
PR635.P5	ENGLISH DRAMA — STORIES, PLOTS, ETC.
PR8970-8976	ENGLISH DRAMA — WELSH AUTHORS / *collections*
PR8933-4	ENGLISH DRAMA — WELSH AUTHORS / *history*
PR1269	ENGLISH DRAMA — 18TH CENTURY / *collections*
PR701-719	ENGLISH DRAMA — 18TH CENTURY / *history*
PR1271	ENGLISH DRAMA — 19TH CENTURY / *collections*
PR721-734	ENGLISH DRAMA — 19TH CENTURY / *history*
PR1272	ENGLISH DRAMA — 20TH CENTURY / *collections*
PR736-9	ENGLISH DRAMA — 20TH CENTURY / *history*
PR1248	ENGLISH DRAMA (COMEDY) / *collections*
PR631	ENGLISH DRAMA (COMEDY) / *history*
PR1257	ENGLISH DRAMA (TRAGEDY) / *collections*
PR633	ENGLISH DRAMA (TRAGEDY) / *history*
PR1241-1273	ENGLISH DRAMA / *collections*
PR87	*ENGLISH DRAMA-EXAMINATIONS, QUESTIONS, ETC.* **SEE** ENGLISH LITERATURE — EXAMINATIONS, QUESTIONS, ETC.
PR87	*ENGLISH DRAMA-OUTLINES, SYLLABI, ETC.* **SEE** ENGLISH LITERATURE — OUTLINES, SYLLABI, ETC.
PS9992.P4	*ENGLISH DRAMA-PHILIPPINE ISLANDS* **SEE** PHILIPPINE DRAMA (ENGLISH)
PR31-55	*ENGLISH DRAMA-STUDY AND TEACHING* **SEE** ENGLISH LITERATURE — STUDY AND TEACHING
PR1361-9	ENGLISH ESSAYS / *collections*
PR921-7	ENGLISH ESSAYS / *history*
PR824	ENGLISH FICTION — ADDRESSES, ESSAYS, LECTURES
Z2010	ENGLISH FICTION — BIO-BIBLIOGRAPHY
PR1293-5	ENGLISH FICTION — EARLY MODERN (TO 1700) / *collections*

PR767-9	ENGLISH FICTION — EARLY MODERN (TO 1700) / history
PR821-888	ENGLISH FICTION — HISTORY AND CRITICISM
PR8875-6	ENGLISH FICTION — IRISH AUTHORS / collections
PR8797-8807	ENGLISH FICTION — IRISH AUTHORS / history
PR1119-1120	ENGLISH FICTION — MIDDLE ENGLISH (1100-1500) / collections
PR251-297	ENGLISH FICTION — MIDDLE ENGLISH (1100-1500) / history
PR8675-6	ENGLISH FICTION — SCOTTISH AUTHORS / collections
PR8597-8607	ENGLISH FICTION — SCOTTISH AUTHORS / history
PR1297	ENGLISH FICTION — 18TH CENTURY / collections
PR769	ENGLISH FICTION — 18TH CENTURY / history
PR1301-4	ENGLISH FICTION — 19TH CENTURY / collections
PR771-789	ENGLISH FICTION — 19TH CENTURY / history
PR881-8	ENGLISH FICTION — 20TH CENTURY / history
PZ1	ENGLISH FICTION / collections
PZ1	*ENGLISH FICTION-NEW ZEALAND* **SEE** NEW ZEALAND FICTION / collections
PR9635-9	*ENGLISH FICTION-NEW ZEALAND* **SEE** NEW ZEALAND FICTION / history
M142.E5	ENGLISH GUITAR MUSIC
ML1015-1018	ENGLISH GUITAR
MT376	ENGLISH HORN — ORCHESTRA STUDIES
MT376	ENGLISH HORN — STUDIES AND EXERCISES
M288-9	ENGLISH HORN AND FLUTE MUSIC
M1105-6	ENGLISH HORN AND FLUTE WITH STRING ORCHESTRA
M296-7	ENGLISH HORN AND HARP MUSIC
M1105	ENGLISH HORN AND HARP WITH STRING ORCHESTRA — SCORES AND PARTS
M1105-6	ENGLISH HORN AND HARP WITH STRING ORCHESTRA
M288-9	ENGLISH HORN AND OBOE MUSIC
M1105	ENGLISH HORN AND OBOE WITH STRING ORCHESTRA — SCORES
M1105-6	ENGLISH HORN AND OBOE WITH STRING ORCHESTRA
M182-4	ENGLISH HORN AND ORGAN MUSIC
M246.2	ENGLISH HORN AND PIANO MUSIC
M246.2	ENGLISH HORN AND PIANO MUSIC, ARRANGED
M288-9	ENGLISH HORN AND TRUMPET MUSIC
M1106	ENGLISH HORN AND TRUMPET WITH STRING ORCHESTRA — SOLOS WITH PIANO
M1105-6	ENGLISH HORN AND TRUMPET WITH STRING ORCHESTRA
M1034-5	ENGLISH HORN WITH CHAMBER ORCHESTRA
M1034.E	ENGLISH HORN WITH ORCHESTRA — SCORES AND PARTS
M1034.E5	ENGLISH HORN WITH ORCHESTRA
M1035.E5	ENGLISH HORN WITH ORCHESTRA
M1105-6	ENGLISH HORN WITH STRING ORCHESTRA
ML940-941	ENGLISH HORN
PE1115	ENGLISH LANGUAGE — BUSINESS ENGLISH
PE1079-1081	ENGLISH LANGUAGE — EARLY MODERN (1500-1700)
PE501-685	ENGLISH LANGUAGE — MIDDLE ENGLISH (1100-1500)
LB1576	ENGLISH LANGUAGE — STUDY AND TEACHING (ELEMENTARY)
LB1524-8	ENGLISH LANGUAGE — STUDY AND TEACHING (PRIMARY)
LB1631	ENGLISH LANGUAGE — STUDY AND TEACHING (SECONDARY)
PE1591	ENGLISH LANGUAGE — SYNONYMS AND ANTONYMS
PE1083	ENGLISH LANGUAGE — 18TH CENTURY
Z2015	*ENGLISH LANGUAGE - BIBLIOGRAPHY* **SEE** ENGLISH PHILOLOGY — BIBLIOGRAPHY
PE2751	ENGLISH LANGUAGE IN FOREIGN COUNTRIES
PE1001-3729	ENGLISH LANGUAGE
PE2801-3101	*ENGLISH LANGUAGE-AMERICANISMS* **SEE** AMERICANISMS
PE1591	*ENGLISH LANGUAGE-ANTONYMS* **SEE** ENGLISH LANGUAGE — SYNONYMS AND ANTONYMS
Z2015	*ENGLISH LANGUAGE-BIBLIOGRAPHY* **SEE** ENGLISH PHILOLOGY — BIBLIOGRAPHY
PN4199-4321	*ENGLISH LANGUAGE-CHRESTOMATHIES AND READERS* **SEE** READERS AND SPEAKERS / recitations
PE1117-1130	*ENGLISH LANGUAGE-CHRESTOMATHIES AND READERS* **SEE** READERS AND SPEAKERS / english

PE1417	*ENGLISH LANGUAGE-CHRESTOMATHIES AND READERS* **SEE** READERS AND SPEAKERS / rhetoric
PM7871-4	*ENGLISH LANGUAGE-DIALECTS-NEGRO* **SEE** NEGRO-ENGLISH DIALECTS
PE1447	*ENGLISH LANGUAGE-EPITHETS* **SEE** EPITHETS
PN227-8	*ENGLISH LANGUAGE-FIGURES OF SPEECH* **SEE** FIGURES OF SPEECH
BX1970	*ENGLISH LANGUAGE-LITURGICAL USE* **SEE** LITURGICAL LANGUAGE — ENGLISH / catholic
PE101-299	*ENGLISH LANGUAGE-OLD ENGLISH* **SEE** ANGLO-SAXON LANGUAGE
PE1119	*ENGLISH LANGUAGE-PRIMERS* **SEE** PRIMERS
PN4199-4321	*ENGLISH LANGUAGE-READERS AND SPEAKERS* **SEE** READERS AND SPEAKERS / recitations
PE1417	*ENGLISH LANGUAGE-READERS AND SPEAKERS* **SEE** READERS AND SPEAKERS / rhetoric
PE1117-1130	*ENGLISH LANGUAGE-READERS AND SPEAKERS* **SEE** READERS AND SPEAKERS / english
PE1144-6	*ENGLISH LANGUAGE-SPELLERS* **SEE** SPELLERS
PE1147-1153	*ENGLISH LANGUAGE-SPELLING REFORM* **SEE** SPELLING REFORM / english
PR1341-9	ENGLISH LETTERS / collections
PR911-91	ENGLISH LETTERS / history
PR99-101	ENGLISH LITERATURE — ADDRESSES, ESSAYS, LECTURES
Z2001-2029	ENGLISH LITERATURE — BIBLIOGRAPHY
Z2010-2014	ENGLISH LITERATURE — BIO-BIBLIOGRAPHY
PR1110.C3	ENGLISH LITERATURE — CATHOLIC AUTHORS / collections
PR1195.C4	ENGLISH LITERATURE — CATHOLIC AUTHORS / collections of poetry
PR19	ENGLISH LITERATURE — DICTIONARIES
PR1119-1131	ENGLISH LITERATURE — EARLY MODERN (TO 1700) / collections
PR401-439	ENGLISH LITERATURE — EARLY MODERN (TO 1700) / history
PR87	ENGLISH LITERATURE — EXAMINATIONS, QUESTIONS, ETC.
PR1-978	ENGLISH LITERATURE — HISTORY AND CRITICISM
PR9700-9799	ENGLISH LITERATURE — INDIC AUTHORS
PR8831-8893	ENGLISH LITERATURE — IRISH AUTHORS / collections
PR8700-8821	ENGLISH LITERATURE — IRISH AUTHORS / history
PR9900.J	ENGLISH LITERATURE — JAPANESE AUTHORS
PR251-369	ENGLISH LITERATURE — MIDDLE ENGLISH (1100-1500) / history
PR1119-1121	ENGLISH LITERATURE — MIDDLE ENGLISH (1100-1500) / collections
PR87	ENGLISH LITERATURE — OUTLINES, SYLLABI, ETC.
PR8631-8693	ENGLISH LITERATURE — SCOTTISH AUTHORS / collections
PR8500-8621	ENGLISH LITERATURE — SCOTTISH AUTHORS / history
PR31-55	ENGLISH LITERATURE — STUDY AND TEACHING
PR1134-9	ENGLISH LITERATURE — 18TH CENTURY / collections
PR441-9	ENGLISH LITERATURE — 18TH CENTURY / history
PR1143-5	ENGLISH LITERATURE — 19TH CENTURY / collections
PR451-469	ENGLISH LITERATURE — 19TH CENTURY / history
PR1149	ENGLISH LITERATURE — 20TH CENTURY / collections
PR471-9	ENGLISH LITERATURE — 20TH CENTURY / history
PR1101-1149	ENGLISH LITERATURE / collections
PR9400-9597	*ENGLISH LITERATURE-AUSTRALIA* **SEE** AUSTRALIAN LITERATURE
PR9231-9293	*ENGLISH LITERATURE-CANADA* **SEE** CANADIAN LITERATURE / collections
PR9291-3	*ENGLISH LITERATURE-CANADA* **SEE** CANADIAN LITERATURE / etc.
PR9100-9221	*ENGLISH LITERATURE-CANADA* **SEE** CANADIAN LITERATURE / etc.
PR9600-9699	*ENGLISH LITERATURE-NEW ZEALAND* **SEE** NEW ZEALAND LITERATURE
PR1490-1508	*ENGLISH LITERATURE-OLD ENGLISH* **SEE** ANGLO-SAXON LITERATURE / collections
PR171-236	*ENGLISH LITERATURE-OLD ENGLISH* **SEE** ANGLO-SAXON LITERATURE / history
PR9797.P6	*ENGLISH LITERATURE-PHILIPPINE ISLANDS* **SEE** PHILIPPINE LITERATURE (ENGLISH)

MT728	ENSEMBLE PLAYING
QA248	*ENSEMBLES (MATHEMATICS)* **SEE** AGGREGATES
M900-949	*ENSEMBLES (MUSIC)* **SEE** INSTRUMENTAL ENSEMBLES
M960-985	*ENSEMBLES (MUSIC)* **SEE** INSTRUMENTAL ENSEMBLES
M900-949	*ENSEMBLES (MUSIC)* **SEE** JAZZ ENSEMBLES
M960-985	*ENSEMBLES (MUSIC)* **SEE** JAZZ ENSEMBLES
M950-952	*ENSEMBLES (MUSIC)* **SEE** STRING ENSEMBLES
M955-7	*ENSEMBLES (MUSIC)* **SEE** WIND ENSEMBLES
JC345-7	*ENSIGNS* **SEE** FLAGS / *emblems of state*
CR101-115	*ENSIGNS* **SEE** FLAGS / *heraldry*
VK385	*ENSIGNS* **SEE** FLAGS / *merchant marine signaling*
UC590-595	*ENSIGNS* **SEE** FLAGS / *military science*
U360-365	*ENSIGNS* **SEE** FLAGS / *military science*
V300-305	*ENSIGNS* **SEE** FLAGS / *naval science*
SB195	ENSILAGE
QE391.E6	ENSTATITE
DK511.B3	*ENTENTE, BALTIC, 1934-* **SEE** BALTIC ENTENTE, 1934-
D460	*ENTENTE, LITTLE, 1920-1939* **SEE** LITTLE ENTENTE, 1920-1939
D511	*ENTENTE, TRIPLE, 1907* **SEE** TRIPLE ENTENTE, 1907
D443	*ENTENTE, TRIPLE, 1907* **SEE** TRIPLE ENTENTE, 1907
RC187-197	*ENTERIC FEVER* **SEE** TYPHOID FEVER
QR201.T9	*ENTERIC FEVER* **SEE** TYPHOID FEVER / *bacteriology*
RA644.T8	*ENTERIC FEVER* **SEE** TYPHOID FEVER / *public health measures*
RC860-862	*ENTERITIS* **SEE** INTESTINES — DISEASES
QL612	ENTEROPNEUSTA
RC862	ENTEROPTOSIS
GV1472.5	ENTERTAINERS
GV1470-1561	ENTERTAINING / *amusements*
TX851-885	ENTERTAINING / *dining-room service*
TX731-9	ENTERTAINING / *etc.*
BJ2021-2038	ENTERTAINING / *etiquette*
BV1620-1643	*ENTERTAINMENTS* **SEE** CHURCH ENTERTAINMENTS
BF575.E6	ENTHUSIASM / *psychology*
BR112	ENTHUSIASM / *religion*
BT1417	*ENTHUSIASTS (MESSALIANS)* **SEE** MESSALIANS
QA351	*ENTIRE FUNCTIONS* **SEE** FUNCTIONS, ENTIRE
QL26-31	ENTOMOLOGISTS
Z5856	ENTOMOLOGISTS / *bibliography*
SB821-945	*ENTOMOLOGY, ECONOMIC* **SEE** INSECTS, INJURIOUS AND BENEFICIAL
QL444.E6	ENTOMOSTRACA
QL757	*ENTOZOA* **SEE** PARASITES / *animal*
QK918	*ENTOZOA* **SEE** PARASITES / *plant*
SF810	*ENTOZOA* **SEE** PARASITES / *veterinary medicine*
M1510-1518	ENTR'ACTE MUSIC
ML2000	ENTR'ACTE MUSIC / *history*
LB2353	*ENTRANCE EXAMINATIONS* **SEE** UNIVERSITIES AND COLLEGES — EXAMINATIONS / *entrance*
LB2367	*ENTRANCE EXAMINATIONS* **SEE** UNIVERSITIES AND COLLEGES — EXAMINATIONS / *term*
TX740	*ENTREES* **SEE** COOKERY (ENTREES)
PQ6127.E6	ENTREMES
PQ6127.E6	*ENTREMETS* **SEE** ENTREMES
UG403	*ENTRENCHMENTS* **SEE** INTRENCHMENTS / *field fortification*
UG446	*ENTRENCHMENTS* **SEE** INTRENCHMENTS / *trenches and trench warfare*
HB601	ENTREPRENEUR
RC918.U5	*ENURESIS* **SEE** URINE — INCONTINENCE
QA621	ENVELOPES (GEOMETRY)
QH543	*ENVIRONMENT* **SEE** ACCLIMATIZATION
SF87	*ENVIRONMENT* **SEE** ACCLIMATIZATION / *animal industry*
QH546	*ENVIRONMENT* **SEE** ADAPTATION (BIOLOGY)
QK915-924	*ENVIRONMENT* **SEE** ADAPTATION (BIOLOGY) / *plants*
GF	*ENVIRONMENT* **SEE** ANTHROPO-GEOGRAPHY
HN64	*ENVIRONMENT* **SEE** EUTHENICS
GN320	*ENVIRONMENT* **SEE** MAN — INFLUENCE OF ENVIRONMENT / *ethnography*
BF353	*ENVIRONMENT* **SEE** MAN — INFLUENCE OF ENVIRONMENT / *psychology*

HM206-8	*ENVIRONMENT* **SEE** MAN — INFLUENCE OF ENVIRONMENT / *sociology*
BF575.E6	ENVY
D278.E6	ENZHEIM, BATTLE OF, 1674
QP601	ENZYMES
QE692	*EOCENE PERIOD* **SEE** GEOLOGY, STRATIGRAPHIC — EOCENE
QE927	*EOCENE PERIOD* **SEE** PALEOBOTANY — EOCENE
QE737	*EOCENE PERIOD* **SEE** PALEONTOLOGY — EOCENE
ML1005-6	*EOLIAN HARP* **SEE** AEOLIAN HARP
GN775-6	*EOLITHIC PERIOD* **SEE** STONE AGE
GN775-6	EOLITHS
QD441	EOSIN
RB145	EOSINOPHILES / *hematology*
QP95	EOSINOPHILES / *physiology of the blood*
PM5817.C4	*EPERA SPEECH* **SEE** CHOCO LANGUAGE
DF95	EPHEBIA
QD421	EPHEDRINE
SF967.T47	*EPHEMERAL FEVER* **SEE** THREE-DAY SICKNESS OF CATTLE
Z6944.E6	*EPHEMERAL PERIODICALS* **SEE** PERIODICALS, EPHEMERAL
QL513.E7	*EPHEMERIDAE* **SEE** MAY-FLIES
QB7-9	EPHEMERIDES
BR220	EPHESUS, COUNCIL OF, 431
BM657.E7	EPHOD
F159.E6	EPHRATA COMMUNITY
PN6110.E6	EPIC POETRY / *collections*
PN1301-1333	EPIC POETRY / *history*
PN689-690	EPIC POETRY / *history*
PL8594.N3	EPIC POETRY, NYANKOLE
QA623	EPICYCLOIDS AND HYPOCYCLOIDS
RC389	*EPIDEMIC CHOREA* **SEE** CHOREA, EPIDEMIC
RC532	*EPIDEMIC HYSTERIA* **SEE** HYSTERIA, EPIDEMIC
RA649-653	EPIDEMICS
RC532	*EPIDEMICS, MENTAL* **SEE** HYSTERIA, EPIDEMIC
RA651	EPIDEMIOLOGY
QL941	EPIDERMIS / *comparative anatomy*
QM561	EPIDERMIS / *histology*
QM484	EPIDERMIS / *human anatomy*
QP88	EPIDERMIS / *physiology*
QE391.E8	EPIDOTE
QH301-705	*EPIGENESIS* **SEE** BIOLOGY
QL951-973	*EPIGENESIS* **SEE** EMBRYOLOGY
QH361-371	*EPIGENESIS* **SEE** EVOLUTION
QE721	*EPIGENESIS* **SEE** EVOLUTION / *paleontology*
B818	*EPIGENESIS* **SEE** EVOLUTION / *philosophy*
QH325	*EPIGENESIS* **SEE** LIFE — ORIGIN
QL853	EPIGLOTTIS / *comparative anatomy*
QM255	EPIGLOTTIS / *human anatomy*
PN6279-6288	EPIGRAMS
PN1441	EPIGRAMS / *poetry*
CN	*EPIGRAPHY* **SEE** INSCRIPTIONS
RC372-4	EPILEPSY
PN171.P8	*EPILOGUES* **SEE** PROLOGUES AND EPILOGUES
PR1195.P7	*EPILOGUES* **SEE** PROLOGUES AND EPILOGUES / *english literature*
DC309.E8	EPINAL, BATTLE OF, 1870
QP951	*EPINEPHRIN* **SEE** ADRENALIN / *physiological effect*
RM292	*EPINEPHRIN* **SEE** ADRENALIN / *therapeutics*
B817	EPIPHANISM
BV50.E7	EPIPHANY
QM569	EPIPHYSIS / *human anatomy*
QL821	EPIPHYSIS / *zoology*
QK922	EPIPHYTES
BV669-670	EPISCOPACY
BX5176	EPISCOPACY / *church of england*
BX5011-5199	*EPISCOPAL CHURCH* **SEE** CHURCH OF ENGLAND
BX5410-5595	*EPISCOPAL CHURCH* **SEE** CHURCH OF IRELAND
BX5210-5393	*EPISCOPAL CHURCH* **SEE** EPISCOPAL CHURCH IN SCOTLAND
BX5800-5995	*EPISCOPAL CHURCH* **SEE** PROTESTANT EPISCOPAL CHURCH IN THE U.S.A.
BX5210-5393	EPISCOPAL CHURCH IN SCOTLAND
NA4821.A	*EPISCOPAL CHURCHES* **SEE** CHURCHES, ANGLICAN
BX5800-5997	EPISCOPALIANS
BX5979-5980	EPISCOPALIANS, NEGRO
BD150-241	*EPISTEMOLOGY* **SEE** KNOWLEDGE, THEORY OF
PN3448.E6	EPISTOLARY FICTION

CN	EPITAPHS / f greek and latin
PN6288.5-6298	EPITAPHS / general collections
CS	EPITAPHS / other
PN1441	EPITAPHS / poetry
PR1195.E6	EPITHALAMIA / english
QM561	EPITHELIUM
PE1447	EPITHETS
QL757	EPIZOA SEE PARASITES / animal
QK918	EPIZOA SEE PARASITES / plant
SF810	EPIZOA SEE PARASITES / veterinary medicine
SF809.E	EPIZOOTIC LYMPHANGITIS
QL881	EPOOPHORON SEE PAROVARIUM / comparative anatomy
QM421	EPOOPHORON SEE PAROVARIUM / human anatomy
TP986.E6	EPOXY RESINS
JC578	EQUALITY BEFORE THE LAW
JK1001	EQUALITY BEFORE THE LAW / u.s.
K	EQUALITY BEFORE THE LAW / u.s.
JX4003	EQUALITY OF STATES
JC575-8	EQUALITY / political science
HM146	EQUALITY / sociology
HF5696	EQUATION OF PAYMENTS SEE AVERAGE OF ACCOUNTS
QB217	EQUATION OF TIME SEE TIME, EQUATION OF
QA218	EQUATIONS — NUMERICAL SOLUTIONS
QA211-218	EQUATIONS
QA215	EQUATIONS, ABELIAN
QA245	EQUATIONS, BINOMIAL
QA215	EQUATIONS, BIQUADRATIC
QA215	EQUATIONS, CUBIC
QA245	EQUATIONS, CYCLOTOMIC SEE CYCLOTOMY
QA431	EQUATIONS, DIFFERENCE SEE DIFFERENCE EQUATIONS
QA371-7	EQUATIONS, DIFFERENTIAL SEE DIFFERENTIAL EQUATIONS
QA431	EQUATIONS, FUNCTIONAL SEE FUNCTIONAL EQUATIONS
QA242	EQUATIONS, INDETERMINATE SEE DIOPHANTINE ANALYSIS
QA431	EQUATIONS, INTEGRAL SEE INTEGRAL EQUATIONS
QA161	EQUATIONS, QUADRATIC
QA215	EQUATIONS, QUARTIC
QA215	EQUATIONS, QUINTIC
QA212	EQUATIONS, ROOTS OF
QA215	EQUATIONS, SEXTIC
QA195	EQUATIONS, SIMULTANEOUS
QA211-218	EQUATIONS, THEORY OF
GR910	EQUATOR (IN RELIGION, FOLK-LORE, ETC.) SEE SHELLBACKS
DG83.3	EQUESTRIAN ORDER (ROME)
NB	EQUESTRIAN STATUES SEE STATUES
SF309	EQUESTRIANISM SEE HORSEMANSHIP
UE470-475	EQUESTRIANISM SEE HORSEMANSHIP / cavalry
QP471	EQUILIBRIUM (PHYSIOLOGY)
QA835	EQUILIBRIUM OF CHAINS
QA835	EQUILIBRIUM OF FLEXIBLE SURFACES
GC301-376	EQUILIBRIUM THEORY OF TIDES SEE TIDES
QB414-419	EQUILIBRIUM THEORY OF TIDES SEE TIDES / astronomy
QA821-835	EQUILIBRIUM / analytical mechanics
QC131	EQUILIBRIUM / physics
QD501	EQUILIBRIUM, CHEMICAL SEE CHEMICAL EQUILIBRIUM
QC251-338	EQUILIBRIUM, THERMAL SEE HEAT
QC311-319	EQUILIBRIUM, THERMAL SEE THERMODYNAMICS
TJ265	EQUILIBRIUM, THERMAL SEE THERMODYNAMICS / mechanical engineering
TP492.5	EQUILIBRIUM, THERMAL SEE THERMODYNAMICS / refrigeration
QA556.5	EQUIPOLLENCE, MATHEMATICAL
BX1759.5.P	EQUIPROBABILISM SEE PROBABILISM
SF309	EQUITATION SEE HORSEMANSHIP
UE470-475	EQUITATION SEE HORSEMANSHIP / cavalry
DG83.3	EQUITES (ROME) SEE EQUESTRIAN ORDER (ROME)
PK6001-6996	ERANIAN LANGUAGES SEE IRANIAN LANGUAGES
PK6001-6996	ERANIAN LITERATURE SEE IRANIAN LITERATURE
PK6001-6996	ERANIAN PHILOLOGY SEE IRANIAN PHILOLOGY
CE	ERAS SEE CHRONOLOGY
QD181.E6	ERBIUM
BX2901-2955	EREMITES SEE AUGUSTINIANS
BX4265-8	EREMITES SEE AUGUSTINIANS / women
BX3085.C	EREMITES SEE CAMALDOLITES
BX4290.C	EREMITES SEE CAMALDOLITES
BX3301-3355	EREMITES SEE CARTHUSIANS
CT9990-9991	EREMITES SEE HERMITS / biography
BX2845-7	EREMITES SEE HERMITS / monasticism
QP601	EREPSIN
QA614	ERGODIC THEORY
QA614	ERGODIC TRANSFORMATIONS SEE ERGODIC THEORY
QP321	ERGOGRAPH
TJ1053	ERGOMETER SEE DYNAMOMETER
QP921.E6	ERGOT / experimental pharmacology
RS165.E7	ERGOT / pharmacy
RM666.E8	ERGOT / therapeutics
SF459	ERIA SILK MOTH SEE AILANTHUS MOTH / sericulture
QL561.S2	ERIA SILK MOTH SEE AILANTHUS MOTH / zoology
SF459	ERIA SILKWORM SEE AILANTHUS MOTH / sericulture
QL561.S2	ERIA SILKWORM SEE AILANTHUS MOTH / zoology
E99.E5	ERIE INDIANS
E356.E5	ERIE, FORT — SIEGE, 1814
E356.E6	ERIE, LAKE, BATTLE OF, 1813
QC373.E	ERIOMETER / optics
QL737.C2	ERMINES SEE WEASELS
PL6271	EROMANGA LANGUAGE
S623	EROSION CONTROL SEE SOIL CONSERVATION
TA460	EROSION OF METALS
QE571-597	EROSION
HQ450-471	EROTIC LITERATURE
PL6271	ERROMANGA LANGUAGE SEE EROMANGA LANGUAGE
BD171	ERROR
PN6231.B8	ERRORS AND BLUNDERS, LITERARY
BC175	ERRORS, LOGICAL SEE FALLACIES (LOGIC)
AZ999	ERRORS, POPULAR
QA275	ERRORS, THEORY OF
PB1501-1599	ERSE SEE GAELIC LANGUAGE
PB1201-1299	ERSE SEE IRISH LANGUAGE
AZ	ERUDITION SEE LEARNING AND SCHOLARSHIP / etc.
RC106	ERUPTIVE FEVER SEE EXANTHEMATA
QE461	ERUPTIVE ROCKS SEE ROCKS, IGNEOUS
RC142	ERYSIPELAS
QC973	ES (IONOSPHERE) SEE SPORADIC E (IONOSPHERE)
QC879	ES (IONOSPHERE) SEE SPORADIC E (IONOSPHERE) / exploration
TJ1376	ESCALATORS
TS545	ESCAPEMENTS SEE CLOCKS AND WATCHES — ESCAPEMENTS
HV8657-8	ESCAPES / prisons
BT820	ESCHATOLOGY — EARLY WORKS TO 1800 / doctrinal theology
BL500-547	ESCHATOLOGY / comparative religion
BT819-890	ESCHATOLOGY / theology
BP166.8	ESCHATOLOGY, ISLAMIC
BP166.8	ESCHATOLOGY, MUSLIM SEE ESCHATOLOGY, ISLAMIC
JC116.S4	ESCUAGE SEE SCUTAGE
CR91-93	ESCUTCHEONS
PL8675	ESIRA LANGUAGE SEE SHIRA LANGUAGE
QE578	ESKAR
QE578	ESKER SEE ESKAR
E99.E7	ESKIMAUAN INDIANS SEE ESKIMOS
SF429.E8	ESKIMO DOGS
PM61-64	ESKIMO LANGUAGE
PM94	ESKIMO LANGUAGE, ASIATIC SEE YUIT LANGUAGE
ML3560	ESKIMO MUSIC SEE ESKIMOS — MUSIC
PM64	ESKIMO POETRY
E99.E7	ESKIMOS — EDUCATION
ML3560	ESKIMOS — MUSIC
E99.E7	ESKIMOS
RC280	ESOPHAGUS — CANCER
RC815.7	ESOPHAGUS — DISEASES
RC815.7	ESOPHAGUS — DIVERTICULA
RC476	ESOPHAGUS — EXPLORATION
RF545	ESOPHAGUS — FOREIGN BODIES
RD516	ESOPHAGUS — SURGERY
QL861	ESOPHAGUS / comparative anatomy
QM331	ESOPHAGUS / human anatomy
QP146	ESOPHAGUS / physiology

E83.655	ESOPUS INDIANS — WARS, 1655-1660	HD9391	*ETHANOL* **SEE** ALCOHOL / *trade*
E83.663	ESOPUS INDIANS — WARS, 1663-1664	RD86.E8	ETHER (ANESTHETIC) — PHYSIOLOGICAL EFFECT
E99.E8	ESOPUS INDIANS	RD79-86	ETHER (ANESTHETIC)
PM1961	*ESOPUS LANGUAGE* **SEE** MUNSEE LANGUAGE	QC177	ETHER (OF SPACE)
QK495.G74	ESPARTO / *grasses*	QD305.E7	ETHER
TS1109	ESPARTO / *paper making*	QD281.E8	ETHERIFICATION
PM8201-8298	ESPERANTO	QD305.E7	ETHERS
E99.E7	*ESQUIMAUX* **SEE** ESKIMOS	QD341.E7	ETHERS
PN4500	ESSAY	BJ10.E8	ETHICAL CULTURE MOVEMENT
PN6141-5	ESSAYS	LC251-318	*ETHICAL EDUCATION* **SEE** MORAL EDUCATION
PM1137	*ESSELENE LANGUAGE* **SEE** ESSELENIAN LANGUAGE	LC2751	*ETHICAL EDUCATION* **SEE** MORAL EDUCATION / *negro*
PM1137	ESSELENIAN LANGUAGE	BV1460-1615	*ETHICAL EDUCATION* **SEE** RELIGIOUS EDUCATION
TP958	ESSENCES AND ESSENTIAL OILS / *chemical technology*	PR3007	*ETHICAL IDEAS, MORAL IDEAS* **SEE** SHAKESPEARE, WILLIAM, 1564-1616 — RELIGION AND ETHICS
QD416	ESSENCES AND ESSENTIAL OILS / *chemistry*	BJ1190-1278	*ETHICAL THEOLOGY* **SEE** CHRISTIAN ETHICS
BM175.E8	ESSENES	BJ1286.W59-6	*ETHICAL WILLS* **SEE** WILLS, ETHICAL
QD416	*ESSENTIAL OILS* **SEE** ESSENCES AND ESSENTIAL OILS / *chemistry*	BJ71-1185	ETHICS — HISTORY
TP958	*ESSENTIAL OILS* **SEE** ESSENCES AND ESSENTIAL OILS / *chemical technology*	BJ60	*ETHICS AND ASTRONAUTICS* **SEE** ASTRONAUTICS AND ETHICS
SF393.E7	ESSEX SWINE	BJ1468.5	*ETHICS OF DECISION-MAKING* **SEE** DECISION-MAKING (ETHICS)
DC234.6	*ESSLING, BATTLE OF, 1809* **SEE** ASPERN, BATTLE OF, 1809	HB835	*ETHICS OF WEALTH* **SEE** WEALTH, ETHICS OF
DC234.6	*ESSLINGEN, BATTLE OF, 1809* **SEE** ASPERN, BATTLE OF, 1809	BJ	ETHICS
BX5410-5595	*ESTABLISHED CHURCH OF IRELAND* **SEE** CHURCH OF IRELAND	BJ1190-1278	*ETHICS, CHRISTIAN* **SEE** CHRISTIAN ETHICS
BV633	ESTABLISHED CHURCHES / *ecclesiastical aspects*	HF5386	*ETHICS, COMMERCIAL* **SEE** BUSINESS ETHICS
HJ5801-5819	*ESTATE TAX* **SEE** INHERITANCE AND TRANSFER TAX	HF5391	*ETHICS, COMMERCIAL* **SEE** BUSINESS ETHICS
CS23	ESTATES, UNCLAIMED	BJ1390	*ETHICS, COMMUNIST* **SEE** COMMUNIST ETHICS
QD305.A2	ESTERIFICATION	TA157	*ETHICS, ENGINEERING* **SEE** ENGINEERING ETHICS
QD341.A2	ESTERIFICATION	BJ1298-1335	ETHICS, EVOLUTIONARY
QD341.A2	ESTERS	BJ1360	*ETHICS, HUMANISTIC* **SEE** HUMANISTIC ETHICS
QD305.A2	ESTERS	BJ1291	*ETHICS, ISLAMIC* **SEE** ISLAMIC ETHICS
BM695.P8	*ESTHER, FEAST OF* **SEE** PURIM (FEAST OF ESTHER)	BJ1290	*ETHICS, JAINA* **SEE** JAINA ETHICS
N61-79	*ESTHETICS* **SEE** AESTHETICS / *art*	PN154	*ETHICS, LITERARY* **SEE** LITERARY ETHICS
BH	*ESTHETICS* **SEE** AESTHETICS / *philosophy*	R724-5	*ETHICS, MEDICAL* **SEE** MEDICAL ETHICS
F454	ESTILL'S DEFEAT, 1782	BJ1291	*ETHICS, MUSLIM* **SEE** ISLAMIC ETHICS
PH651	ESTONIAN BALLADS AND SONGS	BJ1298-1335	*ETHICS, NATURALISTIC* **SEE** ETHICS, EVOLUTIONARY
PH663	ESTONIAN BALLADS AND SONGS	HV7924	*ETHICS, POLICE* **SEE** POLICE ETHICS
PH641	ESTONIAN BALLADS AND SONGS	JK1751-1788	*ETHICS, POLITICAL* **SEE** POLITICAL ETHICS / *citizenship*
PH663	ESTONIAN DRAMA / *collections*	JA79	*ETHICS, POLITICAL* **SEE** POLITICAL ETHICS / *political science and ethics*
PH632	ESTONIAN DRAMA / *history*	BJ1365-1385	ETHICS, POSITIVIST
PH601-629	ESTONIAN LANGUAGE	BJ1545-1695	*ETHICS, PRACTICAL* **SEE** CONDUCT OF LIFE
PH631-688	ESTONIAN LITERATURE	BJ	*ETHICS, PRACTICAL* **SEE** ETHICS
PN5355.E8	ESTONIAN NEWSPAPERS	BJ1188	*ETHICS, RELIGIOUS* **SEE** RELIGIOUS ETHICS
PN5355.E8	ESTONIAN PERIODICALS	HQ31	*ETHICS, SEXUAL* **SEE** SEXUAL ETHICS
DK511.E4-8	ESTONIANS	HM216	*ETHICS, SOCIAL* **SEE** SOCIAL ETHICS
GN103.E8	ESTONIANS / *craniology*	BJ1388	*ETHICS, SOCIALIST* **SEE** SOCIALIST ETHICS
JX4044	*ESTRADA DOCTRINE* **SEE** RECOGNITION (INTERNATIONAL LAW) / *sovereignty*	BJ1392	*ETHICS, TOTALITARIAN* **SEE** TOTALITARIAN ETHICS
JX4574	*ESTRADA DOCTRINE* **SEE** RECOGNITION (INTERNATIONAL LAW) / *belligerency*	PJ8991-9	ETHIOPIAN LANGUAGES
SF56-59	*ESTRAYS* **SEE** POUNDS / *domestic animals*	DT387.3	*ETHIOPIAN-ITALIAN WAR, 1895-1896* **SEE** ITALO-ETHIOPIAN WAR, 1895-1896
QD281.O9	ETARD'S REACTION	DT387.8	*ETHIOPIAN-ITALIAN WAR, 1935-1936* **SEE** ITALO-ETHIOPIAN WAR, 1935-1936
E99.S65	*ETCHAOTTINE INDIANS* **SEE** SLAVE INDIANS	DT380	ETHIOPIANS
E99.S65	*ETCHAREOTTINE INDIANS* **SEE** SLAVE INDIANS	DT383	ETHIOPIA — HISTORY — — TO 1490
PM1341	*ETCHEETEE LANGUAGE* **SEE** HITCHITI LANGUAGE	DT384-6	ETHIOPIA — HISTORY — — 1490-1889
E99.M195	*ETCHEMIN INDIANS* **SEE** MALECITE INDIANS	DT387	ETHIOPIA — HISTORY — — 1889-
PM1695	*ETCHEMIN LANGUAGE* **SEE** MALECITE LANGUAGE	BX140-149	ETHIOPIC CHURCH
NE2110-2115	ETCHERS	PJ9001-9085	ETHIOPIC LANGUAGE
NE2120-2130	ETCHING — TECHNIQUE	PJ9090-9101	ETHIOPIC LITERATURE
NE1940-2210	ETCHING	JX4115-4181	ETHNIC BARRIERS
NE1950-1955	ETCHINGS — EXHIBITIONS	BF730-738	*ETHNIC PSYCHOLOGY* **SEE** ETHNOPSYCHOLOGY
NE1945	ETCHINGS — PRIVATE COLLECTIONS	GN	ETHNIC TYPES
NE1940-2210	ETCHINGS	GN	*ETHNOGRAPHY* **SEE** ETHNOLOGY
PM1341	*ETCHITA LANGUAGE* **SEE** HITCHITI LANGUAGE	GN35-41	ETHNOLOGICAL MUSEUMS AND COLLECTIONS
BL535-547	*ETERNAL LIFE* **SEE** FUTURE LIFE / *comparative religion*	GN406	ETHNOLOGY — JUVENILE LITERATURE
BT899-904	*ETERNAL LIFE* **SEE** FUTURE LIFE / *theology*	GN31	ETHNOLOGY — JUVENILE LITERATURE
BT834-8	*ETERNAL PUNISHMENT* **SEE** FUTURE PUNISHMENT	GN330	ETHNOLOGY — JUVENILE LITERATURE
BL1475.H5	*ETERNAL PUNISHMENT* **SEE** HELL / *buddhism*	GN	ETHNOLOGY
BL735	*ETERNAL PUNISHMENT* **SEE** HELL / *classical mythology*	GN673	*ETHNOLOGY-ARCTIC REGIONS* **SEE** ARCTIC RACES
BL545	*ETERNAL PUNISHMENT* **SEE** HELL / *comparative religion*	ML3797	ETHNOMUSICOLOGY
BT834-8	*ETERNAL PUNISHMENT* **SEE** HELL / *theology*	BF730-738	ETHNOPSYCHOLOGY
BT910-911	ETERNITY	LC251-301	*ETHOLOGY* **SEE** CHARACTER / *character building*
QD305.H6	ETHANES	BJ1518-1535	*ETHOLOGY* **SEE** CHARACTER / *ethics*
QD305.A4	*ETHANOL* **SEE** ALCOHOL / *chemistry*	BF818-839	*ETHOLOGY* **SEE** CHARACTER / *psychology*
TP593	*ETHANOL* **SEE** ALCOHOL / *technology*	BJ	*ETHOLOGY* **SEE** ETHICS
		SB369	*ETHROG* **SEE** CITRON
		QD305.A4	*ETHYL ALCOHOL* **SEE** ALCOHOL / *chemistry*

TP593	*ETHYL ALCOHOL* **SEE** ALCOHOL / *technology*
HD9391	*ETHYL ALCOHOL* **SEE** ALCOHOL / *trade*
RD86.E85	ETHYL BROMIDE / *anesthetics*
RM666.B8	ETHYL BROMIDE / *therapeutics*
RA1247.E68	ETHYL BROMIDE / *toxicology*
RD86.E86	ETHYL CHLORIDE
QD341.A2	ETHYL TANNATE
QD305.A4	*ETHYLENE ALCOHOL* **SEE** GLYCOLS
QD305.A4	*ETHYLENE GLYCOL* **SEE** GLYCOLS
QK757	ETIOLATION
RB151	*ETIOLOGY* **SEE** DISEASES — CAUSES AND THEORIES OF CAUSATION
PN6231.E8	ETIQUETTE — ANECDOTES, FACETIAE, SATIRE, ETC.
BJ2081-2095	ETIQUETTE — STATIONERY
BJ1855	ETIQUETTE FOR MEN / *american*
BJ1856	ETIQUETTE FOR WOMEN / *american*
BJ1801-2193	ETIQUETTE
BJ2018-2019	*ETIQUETTE, CHRISTIAN* **SEE** CHURCH ETIQUETTE
BJ2018-2019	*ETIQUETTE, CHURCH* **SEE** CHURCH ETIQUETTE
BV4012	*ETIQUETTE, CLERICAL* **SEE** CLERGY — ETIQUETTE
BJ1921	ETIQUETTE, MEDIEVAL (TO 1600)
BJ1821	ETIQUETTE, MEDIEVAL (TO 1600)
BJ1981	ETIQUETTE, MEDIEVAL (TO 1600)
BJ1871	ETIQUETTE, MEDIEVAL (TO 1600)
BJ2193	*ETIQUETTE, TELEPHONE* **SEE** TELEPHONE ETIQUETTE
NC1280	*ETIQUETTES* **SEE** LABELS
SB369	*ETROG* **SEE** CITRON
DG223	ETRURIANS — ORIGIN
GN85.I8	ETRURIANS / *craniology*
DG223-4	ETRURIANS / *history*
PA2400-2409	ETRUSCAN LANGUAGE
NA300	*ETRUSCAN TEMPLES* **SEE** TEMPLES, ETRUSCAN
NK3845	*ETRUSCAN URNS* **SEE** URNS, ETRUSCAN / *ceramics*
NB110	*ETRUSCAN URNS* **SEE** URNS, ETRUSCAN / *sculpture*
GN85.I8	*ETRUSCANS* **SEE** ETRURIANS / *craniology*
DG223-4	*ETRUSCANS* **SEE** ETRURIANS / *history*
E99.S65	*ETTCHAOTTINE INDIANS* **SEE** SLAVE INDIANS
P321	*ETYMOLOGY* **SEE** LANGUAGE AND LANGUAGES — ETYMOLOGY
QK495.E86	EUCALYPTUS / *botany*
SD397.E8	EUCALYPTUS / *culture*
BV823-8	*EUCHARIST* **SEE** LORD'S SUPPER
BX2215	*EUCHARIST* **SEE** LORD'S SUPPER / *catholic church*
BX5149.C5	*EUCHARIST* **SEE** LORD'S SUPPER / *church of england*
BT1417	*EUCHITES* **SEE** MESSALIANS
GV1249	EUCHRE
QA451	EUCLID'S ELEMENTS
BJ1491	*EUDEMONISM* **SEE** HEDONISM / *ethics*
B279	*EUDEMONISM* **SEE** HEDONISM / *greek philosophy*
PM1171	EUDEVE LANGUAGE
HQ750-799	EUGENICS
PA2461	EUGUBINE TABLES
BL42	EUHEMERISM / *religions*
QA246	EULER'S NUMBERS
QE461	EULYSITE
BT1350	EUNOMIANISM / *arianism*
BT1350	*EUNOMIANS* **SEE** EUNOMIANISM / *arianism*
HQ449	EUNUCHS
QC271	EUPATHEOSCOPE
ML1055	*EUPHONIUM (CHLADNI'S)* **SEE** CLAVICYLINDER
M90-92	EUPHONIUM MUSIC
ML965-8	EUPHONIUM
PR427	EUPHUISM
PR2659.L9	EUPHUISM / *lyly*
PR2955.L8	EUPHUISM / *shakespeare*
DS430	EURASIANS / *india*
D101-725	EUROPE — HISTORY
SB945.E75	EUROPEAN CORN BORER
SB608.M2	EUROPEAN CORN BORER / *maize pests*
SB945.E	EUROPEAN SPRUCE SAWFLY
D523-5	EUROPEAN WAR, 1914-1918 — ADDRESSES, SERMONS, ETC.
D600-607	EUROPEAN WAR, 1914-1918 — AERIAL OPERATIONS
D570.9	EUROPEAN WAR, 1914-1918 — ANECDOTES
D640	EUROPEAN WAR, 1914-1918 — ANECDOTES
D526	EUROPEAN WAR, 1914-1918 — ANECDOTES
D641	EUROPEAN WAR, 1914-1918 — ARMISTICES
N6491	EUROPEAN WAR, 1914-1918 — ART AND THE WAR
D625-6	EUROPEAN WAR, 1914-1918 — ATROCITIES
D503	EUROPEAN WAR, 1914-1918 — AUTOGRAPHS
D528	EUROPEAN WAR, 1914-1918 — BATTLE-FIELDS
D507	EUROPEAN WAR, 1914-1918 — BIOGRAPHY / *collections*
D580-581	EUROPEAN WAR, 1914-1918 — BLOCKADES
D529-569	EUROPEAN WAR, 1914-1918 — CAMPAIGNS
D609	EUROPEAN WAR, 1914-1918 — CASUALTIES (STATISTICS, ETC.)
D622	EUROPEAN WAR, 1914-1918 — CATHOLIC CHURCH
D511-520	EUROPEAN WAR, 1914-1918 — CAUSES
D529.4	EUROPEAN WAR, 1914-1918 — CAVALRY OPERATIONS
D631-3	EUROPEAN WAR, 1914-1918 — CENSORSHIP
D639.S2	EUROPEAN WAR, 1914-1918 — CHEMISTRY
D639.C4	EUROPEAN WAR, 1914-1918 — CHILDREN
D522.5	EUROPEAN WAR, 1914-1918 — CHRONOLOGY
JX5326	EUROPEAN WAR, 1914-1918 — CLAIMS
JX5295-5313	EUROPEAN WAR, 1914-1918 — CONFISCATIONS AND CONTRIBUTIONS
D504	EUROPEAN WAR, 1914-1918 — CONGRESSES, CONFERENCES, ETC.
D639.D5	EUROPEAN WAR, 1914-1918 — DEPORTATIONS FROM BELGIUM
D639.D5	EUROPEAN WAR, 1914-1918 — DEPORTATIONS FROM FRANCE
D639.D5	EUROPEAN WAR, 1914-1918 — DEPORTATIONS FROM LITHUANIA
D639.D5	EUROPEAN WAR, 1914-1918 — DEPORTATIONS FROM TURKEY AND THE NEAR EAST
D639.D5	EUROPEAN WAR, 1914-1918 — DEPORTATIONS OF ARMENIANS
D510	EUROPEAN WAR, 1914-1918 — DICTIONARIES
D505	EUROPEAN WAR, 1914-1918 — DIPLOMATIC HISTORY
D610-621	EUROPEAN WAR, 1914-1918 — DIPLOMATIC HISTORY
D635	EUROPEAN WAR, 1914-1918 — ECONOMIC ASPECTS
HC56	EUROPEAN WAR, 1914-1918 — ECONOMIC ASPECTS
HC106.2	EUROPEAN WAR, 1914-1918 — ECONOMIC ASPECTS / *u.s.*
D529.7	EUROPEAN WAR, 1914-1918 — ENGINEERING AND CONSTRUCTION
HJ236	EUROPEAN WAR, 1914-1918 — FINANCE
D635	EUROPEAN WAR, 1914-1918 — FINANCE
HJ257	EUROPEAN WAR, 1914-1918 — FINANCE / *u.s.*
HD9000.6	EUROPEAN WAR, 1914-1918 — FOOD QUESTION
HD9006	EUROPEAN WAR, 1914-1918 — FOOD QUESTION / *u.s.*
D522.42	EUROPEAN WAR, 1914-1918 — HISTORIOGRAPHY
D628-9	EUROPEAN WAR, 1914-1918 — HOSPITALS, CHARITIES, ETC.
D637-8	EUROPEAN WAR, 1914-1918 — HOSPITALS, CHARITIES, ETC.
D526	EUROPEAN WAR, 1914-1918 — HUMOR, CARICATURES, ETC.
D503	EUROPEAN WAR, 1914-1918 — ICONOGRAPHY
CJ6170	EUROPEAN WAR, 1914-1918 — ICONOGRAPHY / *german medals*
D512-520	EUROPEAN WAR, 1914-1918 — INFLUENCE AND RESULTS
D639.J4	EUROPEAN WAR, 1914-1918 — JEWS
D631-3	EUROPEAN WAR, 1914-1918 — JOURNALISTS
D522.7	EUROPEAN WAR, 1914-1918 — JUVENILE LITERATURE
PE3727.S7	EUROPEAN WAR, 1914-1918 — LANGUAGE (NEW WORDS, SLANG, ETC.)
PC3747.S7	EUROPEAN WAR, 1914-1918 — LANGUAGE (NEW WORDS, SLANG, ETC.)
D523	EUROPEAN WAR, 1914-1918 — LANGUAGE (NEW WORDS, SLANG, ETC.)
D635	EUROPEAN WAR, 1914-1918 — LAW AND LEGISLATION
D505	EUROPEAN WAR, 1914-1918 — LAW AND LEGISLATION
Z675.W2	EUROPEAN WAR, 1914-1918 — LIBRARIES (IN CAMPS, ETC.)
D525	EUROPEAN WAR, 1914-1918 — MISCELLANEA
D640	EUROPEAN WAR, 1914-1918 — MISCELLANEA
D524	EUROPEAN WAR, 1914-1918 — MORAL ASPECTS
D639.S3	EUROPEAN WAR, 1914-1918 — MORAL ASPECTS

D639.M6	EUROPEAN WAR, 1914-1918 — MORAL ASPECTS
D503	EUROPEAN WAR, 1914-1918 — MUSEUMS
D580-589	EUROPEAN WAR, 1914-1918 — NAVAL OPERATIONS
D639.N4	EUROPEAN WAR, 1914-1918 — NEGROES
CJ	EUROPEAN WAR, 1914-1918 — NUMISMATICS
D522.5	EUROPEAN WAR, 1914-1918 — OUTLINES, SYLLABI, ETC.
D613	EUROPEAN WAR, 1914-1918 — PEACE
D501	EUROPEAN WAR, 1914-1918 — PERIODICALS
D640	EUROPEAN WAR, 1914-1918 — PERSONAL NARRATIVES
D527	EUROPEAN WAR, 1914-1918 — PICTORIAL WORKS
D522	EUROPEAN WAR, 1914-1918 — PICTORIAL WORKS
D507	EUROPEAN WAR, 1914-1918 — PORTRAITS
D635	EUROPEAN WAR, 1914-1918 — POSTAL SERVICE
D627	EUROPEAN WAR, 1914-1918 — PRISONERS AND PRISONS
JX5245-5266	EUROPEAN WAR, 1914-1918 — PRIZES, ETC.
D639.P6-7	EUROPEAN WAR, 1914-1918 — PROPAGANDA
D619.3	EUROPEAN WAR, 1914-1918 — PROPAGANDA
D524	EUROPEAN WAR, 1914-1918 — PROPHECIES
D637-8	EUROPEAN WAR, 1914-1918 — REFUGEES
D609	EUROPEAN WAR, 1914-1918 — REGISTERS OF DEAD
D609	EUROPEAN WAR, 1914-1918 — REGISTERS, LISTS, ETC.
D639.R4	EUROPEAN WAR, 1914-1918 — RELIGIOUS ASPECTS
D524	EUROPEAN WAR, 1914-1918 — RELIGIOUS ASPECTS
D648-9	EUROPEAN WAR, 1914-1918 — REPARATIONS
D639.S2	EUROPEAN WAR, 1914-1918 — SCIENCE
D639.S7	EUROPEAN WAR, 1914-1918 — SECRET SERVICE
D502	EUROPEAN WAR, 1914-1918 — SOCIETIES, ETC.
D570.A1	EUROPEAN WAR, 1914-1918 — SOCIETIES, ETC. / u.s.
M1646	EUROPEAN WAR, 1914-1918 — SONGS AND MUSIC
D505	EUROPEAN WAR, 1914-1918 — SOURCES
D639.S9	EUROPEAN WAR, 1914-1918 — SUPPLIES
D639.S2	EUROPEAN WAR, 1914-1918 — TECHNOLOGY
D650.T4	EUROPEAN WAR, 1914-1918 — TERRITORIAL QUESTIONS
D651	EUROPEAN WAR, 1914-1918 — TERRITORIAL QUESTIONS
D639.T	EUROPEAN WAR, 1914-1918 — THEATER AND THE WAR
PN2220-3035	EUROPEAN WAR, 1914-1918 — THEATER AND THE WAR / by country
D639.T8	EUROPEAN WAR, 1914-1918 — TRANSPORTATION
D570.72-3	EUROPEAN WAR, 1914-1918 — TRANSPORTATION / u.s.
D610-614	EUROPEAN WAR, 1914-1918 — TREATIES
D642-651	EUROPEAN WAR, 1914-1918 — TREATIES
UH650-655	EUROPEAN WAR, 1914-1918 — VETERINARY SERVICE
D637-9	EUROPEAN WAR, 1914-1918 — WAR WORK
D639.W7	EUROPEAN WAR, 1914-1918 — WOMEN'S WORK
D501-680	EUROPEAN WAR, 1914-1918
D568.3	*EUROPEAN WAR, 1914-1918-CAMPAIGNS-DARDANELLES* **SEE** EUROPEAN WAR, 1914-1918 — CAMPAIGNS — — TURKEY AND THE NEAR EAST — — — GALLIPOLI
D541-2	*EUROPEAN WAR, 1914-1918-CAMPAIGNS-FLANDERS* **SEE** EUROPEAN WAR, 1914-1918 — CAMPAIGNS — — BELGIUM
D561-2	*EUROPEAN WAR, 1914-1918-CAMPAIGNS-MACEDONIA* **SEE** EUROPEAN WAR, 1914-1918 — CAMPAIGNS — — SERBIA
D560-565	*EUROPEAN WAR, 1914-1918-CAMPAIGNS-MACEDONIA* **SEE** EUROPEAN WAR, 1914-1918 — CAMPAIGNS — — BALKAN PENINSULA
D526	*EUROPEAN WAR, 1914-1918-CARTOONS* **SEE** EUROPEAN WAR, 1914-1918 — HUMOR, CARICATURES, ETC.
D503	*EUROPEAN WAR, 1914-1918-CARTOONS* **SEE** EUROPEAN WAR, 1914-1918 — ICONOGRAPHY
CJ6170	*EUROPEAN WAR, 1914-1918-CARTOONS* **SEE** EUROPEAN WAR, 1914-1918 — ICONOGRAPHY / german medals
D637-8	*EUROPEAN WAR, 1914-1918-CHARITIES* **SEE** EUROPEAN WAR, 1914-1918 — HOSPITALS, CHARITIES, ETC.
D628-9	*EUROPEAN WAR, 1914-1918-CHARITIES* **SEE** EUROPEAN WAR, 1914-1918 — HOSPITALS, CHARITIES, ETC.
HV560-583	*EUROPEAN WAR, 1914-1918-CHARITIES* **SEE** RED CROSS
UH535-7	*EUROPEAN WAR, 1914-1918-CHARITIES* **SEE** RED CROSS / army
D628-630	*EUROPEAN WAR, 1914-1918-CHARITIES* **SEE** RED CROSS / european war
VG457	*EUROPEAN WAR, 1914-1918-CHARITIES* **SEE** RED CROSS / navy
HC106.2	*EUROPEAN WAR, 1914-1918-COMMERCE* **SEE** EUROPEAN WAR, 1914-1918 — ECONOMIC ASPECTS / u.s.
D635	*EUROPEAN WAR, 1914-1918-COMMERCE* **SEE** EUROPEAN WAR, 1914-1918 — ECONOMIC ASPECTS
HC56	*EUROPEAN WAR, 1914-1918-COMMERCE* **SEE** EUROPEAN WAR, 1914-1918 — ECONOMIC ASPECTS
JX5268	*EUROPEAN WAR, 1914-1918-COMMERCE* **SEE** SEARCH, RIGHT OF / international law
D529.7	*EUROPEAN WAR, 1914-1918-CONSTRUCTION* **SEE** EUROPEAN WAR, 1914-1918 — ENGINEERING AND CONSTRUCTION
JX5231-2	*EUROPEAN WAR, 1914-1918-CONTRABAND OF WAR* **SEE** CONTRABAND OF WAR
D631-3	*EUROPEAN WAR, 1914-1918-CORRESPONDENTS* **SEE** EUROPEAN WAR, 1914-1918 — JOURNALISTS
JX4491	*EUROPEAN WAR, 1914-1918-EMBARGOES* **SEE** EMBARGO / international law
HC106.2	*EUROPEAN WAR, 1914-1918-EMBARGOES* **SEE** EUROPEAN WAR, 1914-1918 — ECONOMIC ASPECTS / u.s.
HC56	*EUROPEAN WAR, 1914-1918-EMBARGOES* **SEE** EUROPEAN WAR, 1914-1918 — ECONOMIC ASPECTS
D635	*EUROPEAN WAR, 1914-1918-EMBARGOES* **SEE** EUROPEAN WAR, 1914-1918 — ECONOMIC ASPECTS
UG447	*EUROPEAN WAR, 1914-1918-GAS WARFARE* **SEE** GASES, ASPHYXIATING AND POISONOUS — WAR USE
D528	*EUROPEAN WAR, 1914-1918-GUIDE-BOOKS* **SEE** EUROPEAN WAR, 1914-1918 — BATTLE-FIELDS — — GUIDE-BOOKS
D627	*EUROPEAN WAR, 1914-1918-INTERNMENT CAMPS* **SEE** EUROPEAN WAR, 1914-1918 — PRISONERS AND PRISONS
T15-35	*EUROPEAN WAR, 1914-1918-INVENTIONS* **SEE** INVENTIONS / history
T201-339	*EUROPEAN WAR, 1914-1918-INVENTIONS* **SEE** INVENTIONS / patents
CJ6170	*EUROPEAN WAR, 1914-1918-MEDALS, BADGES, DECORATIONS, ETC.* **SEE** EUROPEAN WAR, 1914-1918 — ICONOGRAPHY / german medals
D503	*EUROPEAN WAR, 1914-1918-MEDALS, BADGES, DECORATIONS, ETC.* **SEE** EUROPEAN WAR, 1914-1918 — ICONOGRAPHY
D639.S9	*EUROPEAN WAR, 1914-1918-MILITARY SUPPLIES* **SEE** EUROPEAN WAR, 1914-1918 — SUPPLIES
D590-595	*EUROPEAN WAR, 1914-1918-MINES, SUBMARINE* **SEE** EUROPEAN WAR, 1914-1918 — NAVAL OPERATIONS — — SUBMARINE
M1646	*EUROPEAN WAR, 1914-1918-MUSIC* **SEE** EUROPEAN WAR, 1914-1918 — SONGS AND MUSIC
JX1416	*EUROPEAN WAR, 1914-1918-NEUTRALITY OF THE U.S.* **SEE** UNITED STATES — NEUTRALITY / international law
D619	*EUROPEAN WAR, 1914-1918-NEUTRALITY OF THE U.S.* **SEE** UNITED STATES — NEUTRALITY / european war before entrance of the u.s.
D628-9	*EUROPEAN WAR, 1914-1918-NURSES AND NURSING* **SEE** EUROPEAN WAR, 1914-1918 — HOSPITALS, CHARITIES, ETC.
D639.W7	*EUROPEAN WAR, 1914-1918-NURSES AND NURSING* **SEE** EUROPEAN WAR, 1914-1918 — WOMEN'S WORK
D637-8	*EUROPEAN WAR, 1914-1918-NURSES AND NURSING* **SEE** EUROPEAN WAR, 1914-1918 — HOSPITALS, CHARITIES, ETC.
VB280-285	*EUROPEAN WAR, 1914-1918-PENSIONS* **SEE** PENSIONS, MILITARY / navy
UB400-405	*EUROPEAN WAR, 1914-1918-PENSIONS* **SEE** PENSIONS, MILITARY / army
E255	*EUROPEAN WAR, 1914-1918-PENSIONS* **SEE** PENSIONS, MILITARY / pension rolls

VB340-345	EUROPEAN WAR, 1914-1918-PENSIONS **SEE** PENSIONS, MILITARY / navy
D512-520	EUROPEAN WAR, 1914-1918-POLITICS, PSYCHOLOGY, ETC. **SEE** EUROPEAN WAR, 1914-1918 — INFLUENCE AND RESULTS
D639.T8	EUROPEAN WAR, 1914-1918-RAILROADS **SEE** EUROPEAN WAR, 1914-1918 — TRANSPORTATION
D570.72-3	EUROPEAN WAR, 1914-1918-RAILROADS **SEE** EUROPEAN WAR, 1914-1918 — TRANSPORTATION / u.s.
D653-9	EUROPEAN WAR, 1914-1918-RECONSTRUCTION **SEE** RECONSTRUCTION (1914-1939)
D639.D4	EUROPEAN WAR, 1914-1918-SOLDIERS' BODIES, DISPOSITION OF **SEE** SOLDIERS' BODIES, DISPOSITION OF / european war
D810.D4	EUROPEAN WAR, 1914-1918-SOLDIERS' BODIES, DISPOSITION OF **SEE** SOLDIERS' BODIES, DISPOSITION OF / world war
D609	EUROPEAN WAR, 1914-1918-STATISTICS OF DEAD, WOUNDED, ETC. **SEE** EUROPEAN WAR, 1914-1918 — REGISTERS OF DEAD
D609	EUROPEAN WAR, 1914-1918-STATISTICS OF DEAD, WOUNDED, ETC. **SEE** EUROPEAN WAR, 1914-1918 — REGISTERS, LISTS, ETC.
D609	EUROPEAN WAR, 1914-1918-STATISTICS OF DEAD, WOUNDED, ETC. **SEE** EUROPEAN WAR, 1914-1918 — CASUALTIES (STATISTICS, ETC.)
D590-595	EUROPEAN WAR, 1914-1918-SUBMARINE OPERATIONS **SEE** EUROPEAN WAR, 1914-1918 — NAVAL OPERATIONS — — SUBMARINE
D529-569	EUROPEAN WAR, 1914-1918-TACTICAL HISTORY **SEE** EUROPEAN WAR, 1914-1918 — CAMPAIGNS
D522	EUROPEAN WAR, 1914-1918-VIEWS **SEE** EUROPEAN WAR, 1914-1918 — PICTORIAL WORKS
CJ6170	EUROPEAN WAR, 1914-1918-VIEWS **SEE** EUROPEAN WAR, 1914-1918 — ICONOGRAPHY / german medals
D527	EUROPEAN WAR, 1914-1918-VIEWS **SEE** EUROPEAN WAR, 1914-1918 — PICTORIAL WORKS
D503	EUROPEAN WAR, 1914-1918-VIEWS **SEE** EUROPEAN WAR, 1914-1918 — ICONOGRAPHY
D639.S9	EUROPEAN WAR, 1914-1918-WAR MATERIALS **SEE** EUROPEAN WAR, 1914-1918 — SUPPLIES
D639.E2-6	EUROPEAN WAR, 1914-1918-WAR WORK-COLLEGES **SEE** EUROPEAN WAR, 1914-1918 — WAR WORK — — SCHOOLS
M1646	EUROPEAN WAR, 1914-1918-WAR-SONGS **SEE** EUROPEAN WAR, 1914-1918 — SONGS AND MUSIC
D528	EUROPEAN WAR, 1914-1918 — BATTLE-FIELDS — — GUIDE-BOOKS
DT779.5	EUROPEAN WAR, 1914-1918 — CAMPAIGNS — — AFRICA
D575-6	EUROPEAN WAR, 1914-1918 — CAMPAIGNS — — AFRICA
D545.A55	EUROPEAN WAR, 1914-1918 — CAMPAIGNS — — ALSACE
D560-565	EUROPEAN WAR, 1914-1918 — CAMPAIGNS — — BALKAN PENINSULA
D541-2	EUROPEAN WAR, 1914-1918 — CAMPAIGNS — — BELGIUM
D550-558	EUROPEAN WAR, 1914-1918 — CAMPAIGNS — — EASTERN
D520.08	EUROPEAN WAR, 1914-1918 — CAMPAIGNS — — FAR EAST
D544-5	EUROPEAN WAR, 1914-1918 — CAMPAIGNS — — FRANCE
D548	EUROPEAN WAR, 1914-1918 — CAMPAIGNS — — FRANCE
D569	EUROPEAN WAR, 1914-1918 — CAMPAIGNS — — ITALO-AUSTRIAN
D545.L	EUROPEAN WAR, 1914-1918 — CAMPAIGNS — — LORRAINE
D578.N4	EUROPEAN WAR, 1914-1918 — CAMPAIGNS — — NEW GUINEA, GERMAN
D551-2	EUROPEAN WAR, 1914-1918 — CAMPAIGNS — — POLAND
D565	EUROPEAN WAR, 1914-1918 — CAMPAIGNS — — RUMANIA
D561-2	EUROPEAN WAR, 1914-1918 — CAMPAIGNS — — SERBIA
D576.C3	EUROPEAN WAR, 1914-1918 — CAMPAIGNS — — AFRICA — — — CAMEROONS
D576.G3	EUROPEAN WAR, 1914-1918 — CAMPAIGNS — — AFRICA — — — GERMAN EAST
D576.G5	EUROPEAN WAR, 1914-1918 — CAMPAIGNS — — AFRICA — — — GERMAN SOUTHWEST
D576.T7	EUROPEAN WAR, 1914-1918 — CAMPAIGNS — — AFRICA — — — TOGOLAND
D567.C3	EUROPEAN WAR, 1914-1918 — CAMPAIGNS — — TURKEY AND THE NEAR EAST — — — CAUCASUS
D568.3	EUROPEAN WAR, 1914-1918 — CAMPAIGNS — — TURKEY AND THE NEAR EAST — — — GALLIPOLI
D568.7	EUROPEAN WAR, 1914-1918 — CAMPAIGNS — — TURKEY AND THE NEAR EAST — — — PALESTINE
D568.5	EUROPEAN WAR, 1914-1918 — CAMPAIGNS — — TURKEY AND THE NEAR EAST — — — MESOPOTAMIA
D568.8	EUROPEAN WAR, 1914-1918 — CAMPAIGNS — — TURKEY AND THE NEAR EAST — — — IRAN
D568.2	EUROPEAN WAR, 1914-1918 — CAMPAIGNS — — TURKEY AND THE NEAR EAST — — — EGYPT
D590-595	EUROPEAN WAR, 1914-1918 — NAVAL OPERATIONS — — SUBMARINE
D639.B	EUROPEAN WAR, 1914-1918 — WAR WORK — — BOY SCOUTS
D547.B7	EUROPEAN WAR, 1914-1918 — WAR WORK — — BOY SCOUTS / gt. brit.
D639.C5	EUROPEAN WAR, 1914-1918 — WAR WORK — — CHRISTIAN SCIENTISTS
D639.F9	EUROPEAN WAR, 1914-1918 — WAR WORK — — FRIENDS, SOCIETY OF
D637.8	EUROPEAN WAR, 1914-1918 — WAR WORK — — FRIENDS, SOCIETY OF
BX7747	EUROPEAN WAR, 1914-1918 — WAR WORK — — FRIENDS, SOCIETY OF
D622	EUROPEAN WAR, 1914-1918 — WAR WORK — — KNIGHTS OF COLUMBUS
BX8116	EUROPEAN WAR, 1914-1918 — WAR WORK — — MENNONITES
D639.M	EUROPEAN WAR, 1914-1918 — WAR WORK — — MENNONITES
D639.S15	EUROPEAN WAR, 1914-1918 — WAR WORK — — SALVATION ARMY
D639.E2-6	EUROPEAN WAR, 1914-1918 — WAR WORK — — SCHOOLS
BX6154	EUROPEAN WAR, 1914-1918 — WAR WORK — — SEVENTH-DAY ADVENTISTS
D639.S	EUROPEAN WAR, 1914-1918 — WAR WORK — — SEVENTH-DAY ADVENTISTS
D639.Y7	EUROPEAN WAR, 1914-1918 — WAR WORK — — Y.M.C.A.
D639.Y7	EUROPEAN WAR, 1914-1918 — WAR WORK — — Y.W.C.A.
D731-838	EUROPEAN WAR, 1939-1945 **SEE** WORLD WAR, 1939-1945
SB608.W5	EUROPEAN WHEAT SAWFLY **SEE** EUROPEAN WHEAT-STEM SAWFLY
SB608.W5	EUROPEAN WHEAT-STEM SAWFLY
QD181.E8	EUROPIUM
QE823.E8	EURYPTERIDA
PH5001-5259	EUSKARA LANGUAGE **SEE** BASQUE LANGUAGE
QL948	EUSTACHIAN TUBE / comparative anatomy
QM507	EUSTACHIAN TUBE / human anatomy
QP461	EUSTACHIAN TUBE / physiology
E241.E	EUTAW SPRINGS, BATTLE OF, 1781
R726	EUTHANASIA
HN64	EUTHENICS
BT1380	EUTYCHIANS
QE391.E	EUXENITE
E239	EVACUATION DAY, NOV. 25, 1783
Z1035	EVALUATION OF LITERATURE **SEE** BIBLIOGRAPHY — BEST BOOKS
Z1003	EVALUATION OF LITERATURE **SEE** BOOKS AND READING
BH39-41	EVALUATION OF LITERATURE **SEE** CRITICISM / aesthetics
PN75-99	EVALUATION OF LITERATURE **SEE** CRITICISM / literary criticism
PN75-99	EVALUATION OF LITERATURE **SEE** LITERATURE — HISTORY AND CRITICISM / criticism

LB2823	*EVALUATION OF SCHOOLS* **SEE** EDUCATIONAL SURVEYS
HF5549.5.J62	*EVALUATION, JOB* **SEE** JOB EVALUATION
BR758	EVANGELICAL REVIVAL / *gt. brit.*
BX5125	EVANGELICALISM — CHURCH OF ENGLAND
BX5925	EVANGELICALISM — PROTESTANT EPISCOPAL CHURCH IN THE U.S.A.
BV3797	EVANGELISTIC SERMONS
BV3750-3799	EVANGELISTIC WORK
BV3780-3785	EVANGELISTS
QE391.E9	EVANSITE
TP363	EVAPORATING APPLIANCES
QC915-917	EVAPORATION (METEOROLOGY)
QC915-917	*EVAPORATION MEASUREMENTS* **SEE** EVAPORATION (METEOROLOGY)
TX609	*EVAPORATION OF FRUIT* **SEE** FRUIT — EVAPORATION
QC304	EVAPORATION / *physics*
QC304	EVAPORATION, LATENT HEAT OF
QC915-917	*EVAPOTRANSPIRATION* **SEE** EVAPORATION (METEOROLOGY)
QK873	*EVAPOTRANSPIRATION* **SEE** PLANTS — TRANSPIRATION
HJ2348.5	*EVASION, FISCAL* **SEE** TAX EVASION
HJ4653.E75	*EVASION, FISCAL* **SEE** TAX EVASION / *k income tax*
PL461.L3	*EVEN LANGUAGE* **SEE** LAMUT LANGUAGE
LC5501-5560	EVENING AND CONTINUATION SCHOOLS
LC5501-5560	*EVENING COLLEGES* **SEE** EVENING AND CONTINUATION SCHOOLS
LC5501-5560	*EVENING SCHOOLS* **SEE** EVENING AND CONTINUATION SCHOOLS
DK759.T9	*EVENKI* **SEE** TUNGUSES
PL451-9	*EVENKI LANGUAGE* **SEE** TUNGUS LANGUAGE
SB435	EVERGREENS / *culture*
SB447	EVERLASTING FLOWERS
BT834-8	*EVERLASTING PUNISHMENT* **SEE** FUTURE PUNISHMENT
BL1475.H5	*EVERLASTING PUNISHMENT* **SEE** HELL / *buddhism*
BL735	*EVERLASTING PUNISHMENT* **SEE** HELL / *classical mythology*
BL545	*EVERLASTING PUNISHMENT* **SEE** HELL / *comparative religion*
BT834-8	*EVERLASTING PUNISHMENT* **SEE** HELL / *theology*
BC171-3	EVIDENCE / *logic*
BF761-8	EVIDENCE / *psychology*
BT1095-1255	*EVIDENCES OF CHRISTIANITY* **SEE** APOLOGETICS
BS480	*EVIDENCES OF THE BIBLE* **SEE** BIBLE — EVIDENCES, AUTHORITY, ETC.
BT1095-1255	*EVIDENCES, CHRISTIAN* **SEE** APOLOGETICS
BJ1400-1408	*EVIL* **SEE** GOOD AND EVIL
BF1553	EVIL EYE
GR590	EVIL EYE / *folk-lore*
BL480	*EVIL SPIRITS* **SEE** DEMONOLOGY / *comparative religion*
GR525-540	*EVIL SPIRITS* **SEE** DEMONOLOGY / *folk-lore*
BF1501-1561	*EVIL SPIRITS* **SEE** DEMONOLOGY / *occult sciences*
BT975	*EVIL SPIRITS* **SEE** DEMONOLOGY / *theology*
BR115.W2	EVIL, NON-RESISTANCE TO / *religion*
HV8686	EVIL, NON-RESISTANCE TO / *social pathology*
HM278	EVIL, NON-RESISTANCE TO / *sociology*
QH361-371	EVOLUTION
QE721	EVOLUTION / *paleontology*
B818	EVOLUTION / *philosophy*
BJ1298-1335	*EVOLUTIONARY ETHICS* **SEE** ETHICS, EVOLUTIONARY
DT582	EWE (AFRICAN PEOPLE)
DT511	EWE (AFRICAN PEOPLE)
DT500	EWE (AFRICAN PEOPLE)
PL8161-4	EWE LANGUAGE
QC703	*EWP* **SEE** EXPLODING WIRE PHENOMENA
Z993-6	*EX LIBRIS* **SEE** BOOK-PLATES
HV9288	EX-CONVICTS, EMPLOYMENT OF
UB356-9	*EX-SERVICE MEN* **SEE** VETERANS / *military science*
BX2377	*EXAMINATION OF CONSCIENCE* **SEE** CONSCIENCE, EXAMINATION OF
TN272	*EXAMINATION OF MINES* **SEE** MINE EXAMINATION
QP91-95	*EXAMINATION OF THE BLOOD* **SEE** BLOOD — ANALYSIS AND CHEMISTRY / *physiology*
RB145	*EXAMINATION OF THE BLOOD* **SEE** BLOOD — ANALYSIS AND CHEMISTRY / *pathology*
RB145	*EXAMINATION OF THE BLOOD* **SEE** BLOOD — EXAMINATION

LB2367	EXAMINATIONS / *college*
LB2353	EXAMINATIONS / *college*
LC1070-1071	EXAMINATIONS / *professional courses*
LB3051-3060	EXAMINATIONS / *school*
RB37-55	*EXAMINATIONS, MEDICAL* **SEE** DIAGNOSIS / *laboratory methods*
RC71-78	*EXAMINATIONS, MEDICAL* **SEE** DIAGNOSIS / *practice of medicine*
HG8886-8891	*EXAMINATIONS, MEDICAL* **SEE** INSURANCE, ACCIDENT — MEDICAL EXAMINATIONS
HG8886-8891	*EXAMINATIONS, MEDICAL* **SEE** INSURANCE, HEALTH — MEDICAL EXAMINATIONS
HG8886-8891	*EXAMINATIONS, MEDICAL* **SEE** INSURANCE, LIFE — MEDICAL EXAMINATIONS
RC990-991	*EXAMINATIONS, MEDICAL* **SEE** PENSIONS, MEDICAL EXAMINATIONS FOR
HQ1018.M4	*EXAMINATIONS, MEDICAL* **SEE** PREMARITAL EXAMINATIONS
LB1049	*EXAMINATIONS, PREPARATION FOR* **SEE** STUDY, METHOD OF
LC63	*EXAMINATIONS, PREPARATION FOR* **SEE** STUDY, METHOD OF / *examinations*
RC106	EXANTHEMATA
BX1939.E	EXCARDINATION (CANON LAW)
TA735-747	EXCAVATING MACHINERY
TA721	EXCAVATION — TABLES, CALCULATIONS, ETC.
TH5101	EXCAVATION / *building*
TA730-747	EXCAVATION / *engineering*
CC75	EXCAVATIONS (ARCHAEOLOGY)
CC165	EXCAVATIONS (ARCHAEOLOGY)
LC3951-3990	EXCEPTIONAL CHILDREN — EDUCATION
HJ4631	EXCESS PROFITS TAX
HJ4653.E8	EXCESS PROFITS TAX / *u.s.*
TP156.I6	*EXCHANGE ADSORPTION* **SEE** ION EXCHANGE / *chemical engineering*
QD561	*EXCHANGE ADSORPTION* **SEE** ION EXCHANGE / *chemistry*
JX5141	*EXCHANGE OF PRISONERS OF WAR* **SEE** PRISONERS OF WAR / *international law*
HG3811-4000	*EXCHANGE, FOREIGN* **SEE** FOREIGN EXCHANGE
HG6046	*EXCHANGES, COMMODITY* **SEE** COMMODITY EXCHANGES
LB2283-5	*EXCHANGES, EDUCATIONAL* **SEE** EDUCATIONAL EXCHANGES
Z690	EXCHANGES, LITERARY AND SCIENTIFIC
HG6046	*EXCHANGES, PRODUCE* **SEE** COMMODITY EXCHANGES
HG4551-4595	*EXCHANGES, STOCK* **SEE** STOCK-EXCHANGE
HJ3251	*EXCISE* **SEE** INTERNAL REVENUE LAW / *u.s.*
HJ5001-5231	*EXCISE* **SEE** INTERNAL REVENUE
HJ5711-5721	*EXCISE* **SEE** TAXATION OF ARTICLES OF CONSUMPTION
RD553	EXCISION (SURGERY)
RD562	EXCISION OF ANKLE
RD558	EXCISION OF ELBOW
RD549	EXCISION OF HIP
RD526	*EXCISION OF JAWS* **SEE** JAWS — SURGERY
RD561	EXCISION OF KNEE
QC176	EXCITON THEORY
QC176	*EXCITONS, THEORY OF* **SEE** EXCITON THEORY
BX1805	EXCLUSION, RIGHT OF
BX1805	*EXCLUSIVA* **SEE** EXCLUSION, RIGHT OF
BX1939.E8	EXCOMMUNICATION (CANON LAW)
BM720.E9	EXCOMMUNICATION (JEWISH LAW)
BX2275	EXCOMMUNICATION / *catholic church*
QP159	EXCRETION
QP211	EXCRETION
QL872	EXCRETORY ORGANS
E88.813	*EXECUTION OF TENNESSEE MILITIAMEN, 1815* **SEE** TENNESSEE MILITIAMEN, EXECUTION OF, 1815
BV4262	EXECUTION SERMONS
HV8551-3	EXECUTIONS AND EXECUTIONERS
HF5500	EXECUTIVE ABILITY
JF251-314	EXECUTIVE POWER
JN-JQ	EXECUTIVE POWER / *other countries*
JK501-901	EXECUTIVE POWER / *u.s.*
HF5686.E9	EXECUTORS AND ADMINISTRATORS — ACCOUNTING
BV4224	EXEMPLA
BX1939.E	EXEMPTION (CANON LAW)

HJ2336-7	*EXEMPTION FROM TAXATION* **SEE** TAXATION, EXEMPTION FROM
GV461-547	EXERCISE
RA781	EXERCISE / *hygiene*
QP301	EXERCISE / *physiology*
RM721	EXERCISE / *therapeutics*
BV4800-4870	*EXERCISES, DEVOTIONAL* **SEE** DEVOTIONAL EXERCISES
BX	*EXERCISES, DEVOTIONAL* **SEE** DEVOTIONAL EXERCISES / *by denomination*
QD121	*EXHAUST GAS ANALYSIS* **SEE** AUTOMOBILE EXHAUST GAS — ANALYSIS
TJ789	*EXHAUST MUFFLERS* **SEE** GAS AND OIL ENGINES — MUFFLERS
TJ960	EXHAUST SYSTEMS
TJ990-992	*EXHAUSTERS* **SEE** COMPRESSORS
LB3431	*EXHAUSTION* **SEE** FATIGUE / *educational hygiene*
LB1075	*EXHAUSTION* **SEE** FATIGUE / *educational psychology*
QP321	*EXHAUSTION* **SEE** FATIGUE / *muscle*
BF481	*EXHAUSTION* **SEE** FATIGUE / *psychology*
NA6750	EXHIBITION BUILDINGS
HQ79	EXHIBITIONISM / *social pathology*
T396-7	EXHIBITIONS — CLASSIFICATION OF EXHIBITS
T391-999	EXHIBITIONS
S551-9	*EXHIBITIONS, AGRICULTURAL* **SEE** AGRICULTURAL EXHIBITIONS
TK6	*EXHIBITIONS, ELECTRICAL* **SEE** ELECTRIC INDUSTRIES — EXHIBITIONS
TA6	*EXHIBITIONS, ENGINEERING* **SEE** ENGINEERING — EXHIBITIONS
SF114-121	*EXHIBITIONS, LIVE STOCK* **SEE** LIVE STOCK EXHIBITIONS
T391-999	*EXHIBITS* **SEE** EXHIBITIONS
RA637	EXHUMATION
CT105	EXILES / *biography*
JX4261	EXILES / *international law*
QA311	EXISTENCE THEOREMS
B819	EXISTENTIALISM / *modern philosophy*
B819	*EXISTENZPHILOSOPHIE* **SEE** EXISTENTIALISM / *modern philosophy*
QL638.E9	*EXOCOETUS* **SEE** FLYING-FISH
GN480.3	*EXOGAMY* **SEE** ENDOGAMY AND EXOGAMY
RC656	*EXOPHTHALMIC GOITER* **SEE** GRAVES' DISEASE
RE715.E9	EXOPHTHALMOS
BF1559	EXORCISM
GR540	EXORCISM / *folk-lore*
BX2340	EXORCISM / *religion*
RD608	EXOSTOSIS
TL940	EXPANDABLE SPACE STRUCTURES
GV1299.E9	EXPANSION (GAME)
TA405.5	*EXPANSION (HEAT)* **SEE** THERMAL STRESSES
QC281-6	EXPANSION (HEAT)
JN276	*EXPANSION (U.S. POLITICS)* **SEE** IMPERIALISM / *constitutional history gt. brit.*
JC359	*EXPANSION (U.S. POLITICS)* **SEE** IMPERIALISM / *political theory*
JK304	*EXPANSION (U.S. POLITICS)* **SEE** IMPERIALISM / *u.s.*
E713	*EXPANSION (U.S. POLITICS)* **SEE** IMPERIALISM / *u.s.*
E713	*EXPANSION (U.S. POLITICS)* **SEE** UNITED STATES — COLONIAL QUESTION
E179.5	*EXPANSION (U.S. POLITICS)* **SEE** UNITED STATES — TERRITORIAL EXPANSION
TP242-4	*EXPANSION OF GASES* **SEE** GASES / *chemical technology*
QC241	*EXPANSION OF GASES* **SEE** GASES / *etc.*
QC286	*EXPANSION OF GASES* **SEE** GASES / *expansion*
QD531	*EXPANSION OF GASES* **SEE** GASES / *manipulation*
QC161-8	*EXPANSION OF GASES* **SEE** GASES / *mechanics*
QC297	*EXPANSION OF GASES* **SEE** GASES / *specific heats*
QC284	EXPANSION OF LIQUIDS
TA405.5	*EXPANSION OF SOLIDS* **SEE** THERMAL STRESSES
QC282	EXPANSION OF SOLIDS
Z696	*EXPANSIVE CLASSIFICATION* **SEE** CLASSIFICATION, EXPANSIVE
JX4226	EXPATRIATION
BV775	*EXPECTATIVE GRACES* **SEE** BENEFICES, ECCLESIASTICAL
BX1955	*EXPECTATIVE GRACES* **SEE** BENEFICES, ECCLESIASTICAL / *catholic church*
RM390	EXPECTORANTS
G850	EXPEDITION ANTARCTIQUE BELGE, 1897-1899
G850-890	*EXPEDITIONS, ANTARCTIC* **SEE** ANTARCTIC REGIONS
QK474	*EXPEDITIONS, ANTARCTIC* **SEE** ANTARCTIC REGIONS / *botany*
QC994.9	*EXPEDITIONS, ANTARCTIC* **SEE** ANTARCTIC REGIONS / *meteorology*
QH84.2	*EXPEDITIONS, ANTARCTIC* **SEE** ANTARCTIC REGIONS / *natural history*
QC825.9	*EXPEDITIONS, ANTARCTIC* **SEE** ANTARCTIC REGIONS / *terrestrial magnetism*
QL106	*EXPEDITIONS, ANTARCTIC* **SEE** ANTARCTIC REGIONS / *zoology*
CC105	*EXPEDITIONS, ARCHAEOLOGICAL* **SEE** ARCHAEOLOGICAL EXPEDITIONS
CC100	*EXPEDITIONS, ARCHAEOLOGICAL* **SEE** ARCHAEOLOGICAL EXPEDITIONS
G600-830	*EXPEDITIONS, ARCTIC* **SEE** ARCTIC REGIONS
QK474	*EXPEDITIONS, ARCTIC* **SEE** ARCTIC REGIONS / *botany*
QC994.8	*EXPEDITIONS, ARCTIC* **SEE** ARCTIC REGIONS / *meteorology*
QH84.1	*EXPEDITIONS, ARCTIC* **SEE** ARCTIC REGIONS / *natural history*
QC825.8	*EXPEDITIONS, ARCTIC* **SEE** ARCTIC REGIONS / *terrestrial magnetism*
QL105	*EXPEDITIONS, ARCTIC* **SEE** ARCTIC REGIONS / *zoology*
BX2375	*EXPEDITIONS, SACRED* **SEE** PARISH MISSIONS
Q115	*EXPEDITIONS, SCIENTIFIC* **SEE** SCIENTIFIC EXPEDITIONS
BV4912-4915	EXPERIENCE (RELIGION) / *conversion*
BR110	EXPERIENCE (RELIGION) / *philosophy and christianity*
BL53	EXPERIENCE (RELIGION) / *psychology of religion*
SF77	*EXPERIMENTAL ANIMALS* **SEE** LABORATORY ANIMALS
QL55	*EXPERIMENTAL ANIMALS* **SEE** LABORATORY ANIMALS
QL961	*EXPERIMENTAL EMBRYOLOGY* **SEE** EMBRYOLOGY, EXPERIMENTAL
S541-3	*EXPERIMENTAL FARMS* **SEE** AGRICULTURAL EXPERIMENT STATIONS
R850-854	*EXPERIMENTAL MEDICINE* **SEE** MEDICINE, EXPERIMENTAL
RB125	*EXPERIMENTAL PATHOLOGY* **SEE** PATHOLOGY, EXPERIMENTAL
QP351-499	*EXPERIMENTAL PSYCHOLOGY* **SEE** PSYCHOLOGY, PHYSIOLOGICAL
TE191	*EXPERIMENTAL ROADS* **SEE** ROADS, EXPERIMENTAL
RD61	*EXPERIMENTAL SURGERY* **SEE** SURGERY, EXPERIMENTAL
RM111	*EXPERIMENTAL THERAPEUTICS* **SEE** THERAPEUTICS, EXPERIMENTAL
QC703	*EXPLODED WIRE PHENOMENA* **SEE** EXPLODING WIRE PHENOMENA
QC703	EXPLODING WIRE PHENOMENA
GC75-78	*EXPLORATION OF THE DEEP-SEA* **SEE** DEEP-SEA SOUNDING
QH91-95	*EXPLORATION OF THE DEEP-SEA* **SEE** MARINE BIOLOGY / *natural history*
QL121-138	*EXPLORATION OF THE DEEP-SEA* **SEE** MARINE FAUNA
QK103	*EXPLORATION OF THE DEEP-SEA* **SEE** MARINE FLORA
G80-890	EXPLORERS
TN313	*EXPLOSIONS IN MINES* **SEE** MINE EXPLOSIONS
QD516	EXPLOSIONS / *chemistry*
HD7262	*EXPLOSIONS, DUST* **SEE** DUST EXPLOSION
TP297-9	EXPLOSIVES — LAW AND LEGISLATION
TP297	EXPLOSIVES — SAFETY MEASURES
TP271	EXPLOSIVES — TESTING
HE2321.E8	EXPLOSIVES — TRANSPORTATION / *railroads*
S679	EXPLOSIVES IN AGRICULTURE
HD9663	EXPLOSIVES / *economics*
TP268-299	EXPLOSIVES / *technology*
TP268-299	EXPLOSIVES, MILITARY
TP297-9	*EXPLOSIVES-SAFETY REGULATIONS* **SEE** EXPLOSIVES — LAW AND LEGISLATION
QA342	*EXPONENTIAL FUNCTIONS* **SEE** FUNCTIONS, EXPONENTIAL

HG9903	EXPORT INSURANCE SEE INSURANCE, INLAND MARINE
HF2701	EXPORT PREMIUMS
HF	EXPORTS SEE COMMERCE
GT6010-6050	EXPORTS SEE COMMERCE / commercial customs
GN436-440	EXPORTS SEE COMMERCE / primitive
HJ6603-7380	EXPORTS SEE TARIFF / administration
HF1761-2580	EXPORTS SEE TARIFF / other countries
HJ6041-6464	EXPORTS SEE TARIFF / schedules
HF1701-2701	EXPORTS SEE TARIFF / theory and history
HF1750-1759	EXPORTS SEE TARIFF / u.s.
PE1429	EXPOSITION (RHETORIC) / english
NA6750	EXPOSITION BUILDINGS SEE EXHIBITION BUILDINGS
T391-999	EXPOSITIONS SEE EXHIBITIONS .
GT3350	EXPOSURE OF THE DEAD SEE DOKHMAS
GT3350	EXPOSURE OF THE DEAD SEE SCAFFOLD BURIAL
HE5880-5990	EXPRESS SERVICE
BF585-593	EXPRESSION / emotions
PN4155-4165	EXPRESSION / oratory
ND1265	EXPRESSIONISM (ART)
BH301.E9	EXPRESSIONISM / aesthetics
HD1261-5	EXPROPRIATION SEE EMINENT DOMAIN
HD3865-6	EXPROPRIATION SEE EMINENT DOMAIN / public works
JX4261	EXPULSION SEE DEPORTATION / international law
D639.D5	EXPULSION SEE EUROPEAN WAR, 1914-1918 — DEPORTATIONS FROM BELGIUM
D639.D5	EXPULSION SEE EUROPEAN WAR, 1914-1918 — DEPORTATIONS FROM FRANCE
JV373	EXPULSION SEE PENAL COLONIES / colonization
HV8935-8962	EXPULSION SEE PENAL COLONIES / penology
JV6403-7127	EXPULSION SEE UNITED STATES — EMIGRATION AND IMMIGRATION
D810.D5	EXPULSION SEE WORLD WAR, 1939-1945 — DEPORTATIONS FROM LATVIA
E384.7	EXPUNGING RESOLUTIONS, 1834-1837
Z1019-1020	EXPURGATED BOOKS
BV4235.E8	EXTEMPORANEOUS PREACHING SEE PREACHING, EXTEMPORANEOUS
MT68	EXTEMPORIZATION (MUSIC) SEE IMPROVISATION (MUSIC)
S544	EXTENSION WORK, AGRICULTURAL SEE AGRICULTURAL EXTENSION WORK
TA413	EXTENSOMETER
JX1671-2	EXTERRITORIALITY
JX4175	EXTERRITORIALITY
QL88	EXTINCT ANIMALS
BF319	EXTINCTION (PSYCHOLOGY)
TH9362	EXTINGUISHERS, FIRE SEE FIRE EXTINGUISHERS
LB3605	EXTRA-CURRICULAR ACTIVITIES SEE STUDENT ACTIVITIES
QP101	EXTRACORPOREAL CIRCULATION SEE BLOOD — CIRCULATION, ARTIFICIAL
TP156.E8	EXTRACTION (CHEMISTRY)
RS201.E9	EXTRACTS / pharmacy
JX4275-4399	EXTRADITION / international
JF781	EXTRADITION / interstate
JX1671-2	EXTRATERRITORIALITY SEE EXTERRITORIALITY
JX4175	EXTRATERRITORIALITY SEE EXTERRITORIALITY
BX2290	EXTREME UNCTION
RD101	EXTREMITIES (ANATOMY) — FRACTURES
QL950.7	EXTREMITIES (ANATOMY) / comparative anatomy general
QM548-9	EXTREMITIES (ANATOMY) / human anatomy general
QL831	EXTREMITIES (ANATOMY) / muscles
QM165	EXTREMITIES (ANATOMY) / muscles
QM117	EXTREMITIES (ANATOMY) / skeleton
QL821	EXTREMITIES (ANATOMY) / skeleton
RD781-9	EXTREMITIES, LOWER — ABNORMITIES AND DEFORMITIES
RC951	EXTREMITIES, LOWER — DISEASES
QL950.7	EXTREMITIES, LOWER
QM549	EXTREMITIES, LOWER
RD557-9	EXTREMITIES, UPPER — SURGERY
TS255	EXTRUSION (METALS)
TJ1450	EXTRUSION PROCESS
QM691	EYE — ABNORMITIES AND DEFORMITIES

QP476	EYE — ACCOMMODATION AND REFRACTION / physiology
QR171	EYE — BACTERIOLOGY
RE51	EYE — CARE AND HYGIENE
RE	EYE — DISEASES AND DEFECTS
RE75-79	EYE — EXAMINATION
RE835	EYE — FOREIGN BODIES
RE96	EYE — INFLAMMATION
RE731	EYE — MOVEMENTS / pathology
QP476	EYE — MOVEMENTS / physiology
RE731	EYE — MUSCLES / diseases
RE760	EYE — PARALYSIS
RE80-87	EYE — SURGERY
RE201.7.E9	EYE — SYPHILIS
RC280.E9	EYE — TUMORS
RE831	EYE — WOUNDS AND INJURIES
RE48	EYE FATIGUE SEE EYESTRAIN
RE51	EYE FATIGUE SEE EYESTRAIN
N8217.E9	EYE IN ART
PN56.E9	EYE IN LITERATURE
TS350	EYE-BARS / manufacture
TA492.E	EYE-BARS / materials of engineering
GN131	EYE-SOCKETS
QL949	EYE / comparative anatomy
QM511	EYE / human anatomy
QP475-495	EYE / physiology
RE	EYE, INSTRUMENTS AND APPARATUS FOR
QL949	EYE, PARIETAL
RE3	EYE-HOSPITALS SEE HOSPITALS, OPHTHALMIC AND AURAL
RF6	EYE-HOSPITALS SEE HOSPITALS, OPHTHALMIC AND AURAL / nose and throat
RE940-981	EYEGLASSES
GT2370	EYEGLASSES / costume
QM488	EYELASHES
RE121-155	EYELIDS — DISEASES
QL949	EYELIDS / comparative anatomy
QM511	EYELIDS / human anatomy
QL949	EYES SEE EYE / comparative anatomy
QM511	EYES SEE EYE / human anatomy
QP475-495	EYES SEE EYE / physiology
RE986	EYES, ARTIFICIAL
RE51	EYESTRAIN
RE48	EYESTRAIN
RE41	EYE — DISEASES AND DEFECTS — — EARLY WORKS TO 1800
RX401-431	EYE — DISEASES AND DEFECTS — — HOMEOPATHIC TREATMENT
RE906	EYE — MUSCLES — — ANOMALIES
DC230.E8	EYLAU, BATTLE OF, 1807 SEE PREUSSISCH-EYLAU, BATTLE OF, 1807
PL8821-4	EYO LANGUAGE SEE YORUBA LANGUAGE
QL737.C2	EYRA
TL685.3	F-51 (FIGHTER PLANES) SEE MUSTANG (FIGHTER PLANES)
PZ8.2	FABLES
PN980-994	FABLES
PZ14.2	FABLES
NK9315	FABRIC PICTURES
TS1781	FABRICS, NONWOVEN SEE NONWOVEN FABRICS
TS1688	FABRICS, SYNTHETIC SEE SYNTHETIC FABRICS
TS1520	FABRICS, WATERPROOFING OF SEE WATERPROOFING OF FABRICS
NA2840-2841	FACADES
RD763	FACE — ABNORMITIES AND DEFORMITIES
RD523-7	FACE — SURGERY
RD523	FACE — WOUNDS AND INJURIES
NK3700-4657	FACE URNS SEE URNS / ceramics
QL950.5	FACE / comparative anatomy
RL87	FACE / dermatology
NC770	FACE / drawing
QM535	FACE / human anatomy
PN6147-6231	FACETIAE SEE WIT AND HUMOR
RC412	FACIAL NEURALGIA SEE NEURALGIA, FACIAL
RC418	FACIAL PARALYSIS SEE PARALYSIS, FACIAL
TK6710	FACSIMILE TRANSMISSION
TK6600	FACSIMILE, RADIO SEE RADIO FACSIMILE
QA51	FACTOR TABLES
HF5686.M3	FACTORIES — ACCOUNTING
TH7684.F2	FACTORIES — AIR CONDITIONING

TS155	FACTORIES — COST OF OPERATION
TS155	FACTORIES — DESIGN AND CONSTRUCTION
TH4511	FACTORIES — DESIGN AND CONSTRUCTION
TH4511	FACTORIES — EQUIPMENT AND SUPPLIES
TH9445	FACTORIES — FIRES AND FIRE PREVENTION
TH7392.M6	FACTORIES — HEATING AND VENTILATION
TH7684.F2	FACTORIES — HEATING AND VENTILATION
TH7975.F2	FACTORIES — LIGHTING
TK4399.F2	FACTORIES — LIGHTING / electric lighting
T56	FACTORIES — LOCATION
TS155	FACTORIES — MAINTENANCE AND REPAIR
HD7273	FACTORIES — SAFETY APPLIANCES
TH4511	FACTORIES — VALUATION
NA6400-6510	FACTORIES / architecture
TH4511-4541	FACTORIES / building
HD6270	FACTORIES / junior labor
HD7406-7510	FACTORIES / model
HD6974	FACTORIES / social conditions
HD6068	FACTORIES / women in
TH4518	*FACTORIES, UNDERGROUND* **SEE** UNDERGROUND FACTORIES / construction
HD3656-3790	*FACTORIES-INSPECTION* **SEE** FACTORY INSPECTION
HD3621-7	*FACTORIES-LAW AND LEGISLATION* **SEE** FACTORY LAWS AND LEGISLATION
TH4511	*FACTORIES-LAYOUT* **SEE** FACTORIES — DESIGN AND CONSTRUCTION
TS155	*FACTORIES-LAYOUT* **SEE** FACTORIES — DESIGN AND CONSTRUCTION
TS155	*FACTORIES-MANAGEMENT* **SEE** FACTORY MANAGEMENT
TD895	*FACTORIES-SANITATION* **SEE** FACTORY SANITATION
TH7684.F2	*FACTORIES-VENTILATION* **SEE** FACTORIES — HEATING AND VENTILATION
TH7392.M6	*FACTORIES-VENTILATION* **SEE** FACTORIES — HEATING AND VENTILATION
HF5681.A3	*FACTORING (FINANCE)* **SEE** ACCOUNTS RECEIVABLE
QA161	FACTORS (ALGEBRA) / algebraic expressions
QA242	FACTORS (ALGEBRA) / numbers
HF5421-6	*FACTORS* **SEE** COMMISSION MERCHANTS
TD897-9	FACTORY AND TRADE WASTE
NA6400-6510	*FACTORY BUILDINGS* **SEE** FACTORIES / architecture
TH4511-4541	*FACTORY BUILDINGS* **SEE** FACTORIES / building
HD6270	*FACTORY BUILDINGS* **SEE** FACTORIES / junior labor
HD7406-7510	*FACTORY BUILDINGS* **SEE** FACTORIES / model
HD6974	*FACTORY BUILDINGS* **SEE** FACTORIES / social conditions
HD6068	*FACTORY BUILDINGS* **SEE** FACTORIES / women in
TS155	*FACTORY CONSTRUCTION* **SEE** FACTORIES — DESIGN AND CONSTRUCTION
TH4511	*FACTORY CONSTRUCTION* **SEE** FACTORIES — DESIGN AND CONSTRUCTION
HF5686.M3	*FACTORY COSTS* **SEE** MANUFACTURES — COSTS
TH4511	*FACTORY DESIGN* **SEE** FACTORIES — DESIGN AND CONSTRUCTION
TS155	*FACTORY DESIGN* **SEE** FACTORIES — DESIGN AND CONSTRUCTION
HD3656-3790	FACTORY INSPECTION
HD3621-7	FACTORY LAWS AND LEGISLATION
TS155	*FACTORY LAYOUT* **SEE** FACTORIES — DESIGN AND CONSTRUCTION
TH4511	*FACTORY LAYOUT* **SEE** FACTORIES — DESIGN AND CONSTRUCTION
Z675.F3	FACTORY LIBRARIES
TS155	FACTORY MANAGEMENT
TD895	FACTORY SANITATION
LC5501-5560	*FACTORY SCHOOLS* **SEE** EVENING AND CONTINUATION SCHOOLS
HD2351-6	FACTORY SYSTEM
TD897-9	*FACTORY WASTE* **SEE** FACTORY AND TRADE WASTE
BX1939.F3	FACULTIES (CANON LAW)
BX1939.F3	*FACULTIES, CANONICAL* **SEE** FACULTIES (CANON LAW)
LB1778	*FACULTY (EDUCATION)* **SEE** COLLEGE TEACHERS
LA2301-2397	*FACULTY (EDUCATION)* **SEE** EDUCATORS / biography
LB51-875	*FACULTY (EDUCATION)* **SEE** EDUCATORS / theories and systems
LA2301-2397	*FACULTY (EDUCATION)* **SEE** TEACHERS / biography
LB2331	*FACULTY WORK LOAD* **SEE** COLLEGE TEACHERS — WORK LOAD
M1781-2	FADOS
NK3700-4695	*FAIENCE* **SEE** POTTERY / ceramics
TP785-825	*FAIENCE* **SEE** POTTERY / chemical technology
HD9610-9620	*FAIENCE* **SEE** POTTERY / trade
HG3760-3773	*FAILURE (IN BUSINESS)* **SEE** BANKRUPTCY
NA6750	*FAIR BUILDINGS* **SEE** EXHIBITION BUILDINGS
HD4903	*FAIR EMPLOYMENT PRACTICE* **SEE** DISCRIMINATION IN EMPLOYMENT
E473.65	FAIR OAKS, BATTLE OF, 1862
HF1701-2701	*FAIR TRADE (TARIFF)* **SEE** FREE TRADE AND PROTECTION
HF1721-1733	*FAIR TRADE (TARIFF)* **SEE** RECIPROCITY / tariff
HD3625-6	*FAIR TRADE* **SEE** COMPETITION, UNFAIR
HF5417	*FAIR TRADE* **SEE** PRICE MAINTENANCE
GR550	FAIRIES / folk-lore
BF552	FAIRIES / occultism
BJ1533.F2	FAIRNESS
HV544	FAIRS / charity fairs
GT4580-4699	FAIRS / manners and customs
HF5470-5475	FAIRS / markets
HF5481	FAIRS / street fairs
PN6120.A4-5	FAIRY PLAYS / juvenile
PN6110.F3	FAIRY POETRY
GR550	FAIRY TALES — CLASSIFICATION
Z5983.F17	FAIRY TALES — CLASSIFICATION
GR550	FAIRY TALES — DICTIONARIES
GR550	FAIRY TALES / folk-lore
PN3437	FAIRY TALES / history and criticism
PZ14	FAIRY TALES / juvenile works
PZ8	FAIRY TALES / juvenile works
PZ24	FAIRY TALES / juvenile works
BF1552	FAIRY TALES / occultism
Z5983.F17	*FAIRY TALES-THEMES, MOTIVES* **SEE** FAIRY TALES — CLASSIFICATION
GR550	*FAIRY TALES-THEMES, MOTIVES* **SEE** FAIRY TALES — CLASSIFICATION
Z5983.F17	*FAIRY TALES-TYPES* **SEE** FAIRY TALES — CLASSIFICATION
GR550	*FAIRY TALES-TYPES* **SEE** FAIRY TALES — CLASSIFICATION
BP177	FAITH (ISLAM)
BT763-4	*FAITH AND JUSTIFICATION* **SEE** JUSTIFICATION
BT50	FAITH AND REASON
BT732.5	*FAITH HEALING* **SEE** FAITH-CURE
RZ400-401	*FAITH HEALING* **SEE** FAITH-CURE / medical aspects
BT732.5	FAITH-CURE
RZ400-401	FAITH-CURE / medical aspects
BV4637	FAITH / moral theology
BT770-772	FAITH / theology
BX	*FAITH, CONFESSIONS OF* **SEE** CREEDS / by denomination
BT990-999	*FAITH, CONFESSIONS OF* **SEE** CREEDS / general
BT88	*FAITH, RULE OF* **SEE** RULE OF FAITH
BL2015.F2	FAKIRS
DT380	FALASHAS / ethiopia
DS135.E75	FALASHAS / jews
SK321	FALCONRY
QL696.A2	FALCONS
D582.F2	FALKLAND ISLANDS, BATTLE OF THE, 1914
SB945.A8	FALL ARMY-WORMS
BT710	FALL OF MAN
E99.P	*FALL RIVER INDIANS* **SEE** POCASSET INDIANS
BC175	FALLACIES (LOGIC)
QB741-755	*FALLING-STARS* **SEE** METEORS
QL881	FALLOPIAN TUBES / comparative anatomy
RG421-433	FALLOPIAN TUBES / gynecology
QM421	FALLOPIAN TUBES / human anatomy
E83.67	FALLS FIGHT, 1676
TA407	*FALSE BRINELLING* **SEE** FRETTING CORROSION
BM752	*FALSE MESSIAHS* **SEE** PSEUDO-MESSIAHS
HV6326	*FALSE SWEARING* **SEE** PERJURY
HV6326	*FALSE TESTIMONY* **SEE** PERJURY
SB945.F	FALSE WIREWORM
BJ1420-1428	*FALSEHOOD* **SEE** TRUTHFULNESS AND FALSEHOOD / ethics
PL318	*FALVEN LANGUAGE* **SEE** KIPCHAK LANGUAGE
DS54.7	FAMAGUSTA, CYPRUS — SIEGE, 1571

CS55	*FAMILIES OF ROYAL DESCENT* **SEE** ROYAL DESCENT, FAMILIES OF / *u.s.*
CS418	*FAMILIES OF ROYAL DESCENT* **SEE** ROYAL DESCENT, FAMILIES OF / *gt. brit.*
CS586	*FAMILIES OF ROYAL DESCENT* **SEE** ROYAL DESCENT, FAMILIES OF / *france*
BX7575	FAMILISTS
BS680.F3	FAMILY — BIBLICAL TEACHING
BX2351	FAMILY — PAPAL DOCUMENTS
BV255-9	FAMILY — PRAYER-BOOKS AND DEVOTIONS
BX2170.F3	FAMILY — PRAYER-BOOKS AND DEVOTIONS / *catholic*
BP188.3.F3	FAMILY — RELIGIOUS LIFE (ISLAM)
BV4526	FAMILY — RELIGIOUS LIFE
HV697-700	FAMILY ALLOWANCES / *social welfare*
HD4925	FAMILY ALLOWANCES / *wages and social insurance*
TX326	*FAMILY BUDGETS* **SEE** HOME ECONOMICS — ACCOUNTING
HF5686.H8	*FAMILY BUDGETS* **SEE** HOME ECONOMICS — ACCOUNTING / *finance*
HV9088-9096	*FAMILY COURTS* **SEE** JUVENILE COURTS
BV255-9	*FAMILY DEVOTIONS* **SEE** FAMILY — PRAYER-BOOKS AND DEVOTIONS
BX2170.F3	*FAMILY DEVOTIONS* **SEE** FAMILY — PRAYER-BOOKS AND DEVOTIONS / *catholic*
HV697-700	*FAMILY ENDOWMENT* **SEE** FAMILY ALLOWANCES / *social welfare*
HD4925	*FAMILY ENDOWMENT* **SEE** FAMILY ALLOWANCES / *wages and social insurance*
GV182.8	*FAMILY FUN* **SEE** FAMILY RECREATION
BX7575	*FAMILY OF LOVE (RELIGIOUS SECT)* **SEE** FAMILISTS
BV255-9	*FAMILY PRAYERS* **SEE** FAMILY — PRAYER-BOOKS AND DEVOTIONS
BX2170.F3	*FAMILY PRAYERS* **SEE** FAMILY — PRAYER-BOOKS AND DEVOTIONS / *catholic*
HQ747	FAMILY RECORDS / *etc.*
CS24	FAMILY RECORDS / *genealogical forms*
GV182.8	FAMILY RECREATION
HV697-700	*FAMILY WAGES* **SEE** FAMILY ALLOWANCES / *social welfare*
HD4925	*FAMILY WAGES* **SEE** FAMILY ALLOWANCES / *wages and social insurance*
BV4526	*FAMILY WORSHIP* **SEE** FAMILY — RELIGIOUS LIFE
HQ	FAMILY
GT2420	FAMILY / *manners and customs*
GN478-486	FAMILY / *primitive*
BT313	*FAMILY, HOLY* **SEE** JESUS CHRIST — FAMILY
GV182.8	*FAMILY-RECREATION* **SEE** FAMILY RECREATION
BV4526	FAMILY — RELIGIOUS LIFE — — SERMONS — — — OUTLINES
HC275	FAMINE COMPACT, 1765
HC95-695	FAMINES / *by country*
HC63	FAMINES / *general*
HV630	FAMINES / *relief agencies*
QA466-9	*FAMOUS PROBLEMS (IN GEOMETRY)* **SEE** GEOMETRY — PROBLEMS, FAMOUS
BL2480.F	FAN (AFRICAN PEOPLE) — RELIGION
GN655.F3	FAN (AFRICAN PEOPLE) / *ethnology*
PL8167.F3	FAN LANGUAGE
DR241	*FANARIOTS* **SEE** PHANARIOTS
BF575.F16	FANATICISM / *psychology*
BR114	FANATICISM / *religion*
GT500-2370	*FANCY DRESS* **SEE** COSTUME / *manners and customs*
TT740-897	FANCY WORK
M1270	FANFARES
GN655.F3	*FANG (AFRICAN PEOPLE)* **SEE** FAN (AFRICAN PEOPLE) / *ethnology*
S699	FANNING-MILLS
NK4870	FANS / *art*
GT2150	FANS / *manners and customs*
ML448	FANTASIA
PL8167.F4	*FANTE LANGUAGE* **SEE** FANTI LANGUAGE
PL8167.F4	FANTI LANGUAGE
GN655.F	FANTIS
DT511	FANTIS
PL8167.F4	*FANTSI LANGUAGE* **SEE** FANTI LANGUAGE
BL2015.F2	*FAQIRS* **SEE** FAKIRS
DS501-519	*FAR EAST* **SEE** EAST (FAR EAST)
JX1321	*FAR EASTERN QUESTION* **SEE** EASTERN QUESTION (FAR EAST) / *international law*
QC536	*FARAD* **SEE** ELECTRIC UNITS
RM869-890	*FARADIZATION* **SEE** ELECTROTHERAPEUTICS
PN1940-1949	FARCE
PN6120.F3	FARCES / *collections*
SF796	*FARCY (GLANDERS)* **SEE** GLANDERS
RC146	*FARCY (GLANDERS)* **SEE** GLANDERS / *human*
SF809.E	*FARCY (LYMPHANGITIS)* **SEE** EPIZOOTIC LYMPHANGITIS
TX727-8	*FARE, BILLS OF* **SEE** MENUS
BX7577.F3	FAREINISTES
TP415	*FARINACEOUS PRODUCTS* **SEE** STARCH / *chemical technology*
QD321	*FARINACEOUS PRODUCTS* **SEE** STARCH / *organic chemistry*
QK887	*FARINACEOUS PRODUCTS* **SEE** STARCH / *plant physiology*
SF	*FARM ANIMALS* **SEE** DOMESTIC ANIMALS / *animal industry*
GN426	*FARM ANIMALS* **SEE** DOMESTIC ANIMALS / *ethnology*
GT5870-5895	*FARM ANIMALS* **SEE** DOMESTIC ANIMALS / *manners and customs*
SF1-121	*FARM ANIMALS* **SEE** STOCK AND STOCK-BREEDING
TH7392.F	FARM BUILDINGS — HEATING AND VENTILATION
HD1393	FARM BUILDINGS — VALUATION
NA8200-8260	FARM BUILDINGS / *architecture*
TH7392.F	*FARM BUILDINGS-VENTILATION* **SEE** FARM BUILDINGS — HEATING AND VENTILATION
SB183-317	*FARM CROPS* **SEE** FIELD CROPS
TJ712	FARM ENGINES
S675	FARM EQUIPMENT
NA8210	*FARM HOUSES* **SEE** FARMHOUSES / *architecture*
TH4920	*FARM HOUSES* **SEE** FARMHOUSES / *building*
S676	*FARM IMPLEMENTS* **SEE** AGRICULTURAL IMPLEMENTS
HD1521-1539	*FARM LABORERS* **SEE** AGRICULTURAL LABORERS
HD185-6	FARM LAW / *u.s.*
PN6231.C65	FARM LIFE — ANECDOTES, FACETIAE, SATIRE, ETC.
S521	FARM LIFE / *popular works*
HT421	FARM LIFE / *sociology*
S671-760	*FARM MACHINERY* **SEE** AGRICULTURAL MACHINERY
S560-575	FARM MANAGEMENT
S655	FARM MANURE
S671-760	*FARM MECHANICS* **SEE** AGRICULTURAL ENGINEERING
S560-575	*FARM ORGANIZATION* **SEE** FARM MANAGEMENT
S571	FARM PRODUCE — MARKETING
HD9000.6	FARM PRODUCE — MARKETING / *economics*
HD9006	FARM PRODUCE — MARKETING / *economics*
SB129	FARM PRODUCE — STORAGE
HD9000.9	FARM PRODUCE — STORAGE / *economics*
HD9000.8-9019	FARM PRODUCE — TAXATION
S571	FARM PRODUCE — TRANSPORTATION
S-SB	FARM PRODUCE / *agriculture*
HD9000-9019	FARM PRODUCE / *economics*
S698	*FARM PRODUCE-PROCESSING* **SEE** AGRICULTURAL PROCESSING
TS155	*FARM SHOPS* **SEE** WORKSHOPS / *factory management*
S675	*FARM SUPPLIES* **SEE** FARM EQUIPMENT
HD1511	FARM TENANCY — ECONOMIC ASPECTS
S676	*FARM TOOLS* **SEE** AGRICULTURAL IMPLEMENTS
HD1521-1539	*FARM WORKERS* **SEE** AGRICULTURAL LABORERS
HG2041-2051	*FARMERS' COOPERATIVES* **SEE** AGRICULTURAL COOPERATIVE CREDIT ASSOCIATIONS
HD1483-6	*FARMERS' COOPERATIVES* **SEE** AGRICULTURE, COOPERATIVE
HD1491	*FARMERS' COOPERATIVES* **SEE** AGRICULTURE, COOPERATIVE
NA8210	FARMHOUSES / *architecture*
TH4920	FARMHOUSES / *building*
HJ3247	*FARMING OF TAXES* **SEE** TAXES, FARMING OF
HD1478	*FARMING ON SHARES* **SEE** METAYER SYSTEM
HD1478	*FARMING ON SHARES* **SEE** SHARE-CROPPING
SB110	*FARMING, DRY* **SEE** DRY FARMING
HD1393	FARMS — VALUATION

S560-575	FARMS
HD1471	FARMS / large
HD1476	FARMS / small
S541-3	*FARMS, EXPERIMENTAL* **SEE** AGRICULTURAL EXPERIMENT STATIONS
S567-9	*FARMS-ACCOUNTING* **SEE** AGRICULTURE — ACCOUNTING
E477.67	FARMVILLE, VA., BATTLE OF, 1865
S655	*FARMYARD MANURE* **SEE** FARM MANURE
PT7594	FAROESE BALLADS AND SONGS / collections
PT7590	FAROESE BALLADS AND SONGS / history
PD2483	FAROESE DIALECT — TEXTS
PD2483	FAROESE DIALECT
PT7581-7599	FAROESE LITERATURE
PT7594	FAROESE POETRY / collections
PT7590	FAROESE POETRY / history
QL737.U6	*FARRIERY* **SEE** HORSES
HV4749-4755	*FARRIERY* **SEE** HORSES / cruelty to horses
GR715	*FARRIERY* **SEE** HORSES / folk-lore
SF277-359	*FARRIERY* **SEE** HORSES / horse raising
HD9434	*FARRIERY* **SEE** HORSES / horse raising
GT5885	*FARRIERY* **SEE** HORSES / manners and customs
UC600-695	*FARRIERY* **SEE** HORSES / military service
UE460-475	*FARRIERY* **SEE** HORSES / military service
UF370	*FARRIERY* **SEE** HORSES / military service
SF907	*FARRIERY* **SEE** HORSESHOEING
UC640-645	*FARRIERY* **SEE** HORSESHOEING / military service
SF600-998	*FARRIERY* **SEE** VETERINARY MEDICINE
SF911-913	*FARRIERY* **SEE** VETERINARY SURGERY
GT2075	*FARTHINGALE* **SEE** CRINOLINE
QM563	FASCIAE (ANATOMY)
QK664	*FASCIATIONS* **SEE** ABNORMALITIES (PLANTS)
JC481	FASCISM
DG571	FASCISM / italy
GT529.A7	FASHION AND ART
TT507	FASHION AS A PROFESSION
TT509	FASHION DRAWING
HD6073.M7	*FASHION MODELS* **SEE** MODELS, FASHION
TT502	FASHION SHOWS
GT500-2370	FASHION
TT500-645	FASHION
BV30-135	*FAST DAYS* **SEE** FASTS AND FEASTS / christianity
CE81	*FAST DAYS* **SEE** FASTS AND FEASTS / church calendar
BL590	*FAST DAYS* **SEE** FASTS AND FEASTS / comparative religion
GT3930-4995	*FAST DAYS* **SEE** FASTS AND FEASTS / manners and customs
TX739	*FAST-DAY MENUS* **SEE** LENTEN MENUS
TX837	*FAST-DAY MENUS* **SEE** LENTEN MENUS / with recipes
BV4270	FAST-DAY SERMONS
HD9999.F3-33	*FASTENERS* **SEE** FASTENINGS / trade
HD9999.F3-33	FASTENINGS / trade
LB1050.5	*FASTER READING* **SEE** RAPID READING
BX2225	FASTING — DISPENSATIONS / catholic eucharist
BX1939.F35	FASTING (CANON LAW)
BP179	FASTING (ISLAM)
RM226-8	FASTING
BV5055	FASTING / asceticism
PT963.C3	*FASTNACHTSPIELE* **SEE** CARNIVAL PLAYS / german literature
BL1212	FASTS AND FEASTS — HINDUISM
BP186	FASTS AND FEASTS — ISLAM
BV30-135	FASTS AND FEASTS / christianity
CE81	FASTS AND FEASTS / church calendar
BL590	FASTS AND FEASTS / comparative religion
GT3930-4995	FASTS AND FEASTS / manners and customs
BL1212	*FASTS AND FEASTS, HINDU* **SEE** FASTS AND FEASTS — HINDUISM
BP186	*FASTS AND FEASTS, ISLAMIC* **SEE** FASTS AND FEASTS — ISLAM
BP186	*FASTS AND FEASTS, MUSLIM* **SEE** FASTS AND FEASTS — ISLAM
QP751	FAT METABOLISM
RB149	FAT NECROSIS
QM565	*FAT TISSUE* **SEE** ADIPOSE TISSUES
QP751	FAT / physiological chemistry
BP166.3	FATE AND FATALISM (ISLAM)

BJ1460-1468	FATE AND FATALISM / ethics
BD411	FATE AND FATALISM / philosophy
BL235	FATE AND FATALISM / religion
PL6231	*FATE LANGUAGE* **SEE** EFATE LANGUAGE
PN57.F25	FATHER-SEARCH IN LITERATURE
BF723.F3	FATHER-SEPARATED CHILDREN
HQ756	FATHER'S DAY
BS579.F3	FATHERS IN THE BIBLE
Z7791	FATHERS OF THE CHURCH — BIO-BIBLIOGRAPHY
BR1705	FATHERS OF THE CHURCH / collective biography
BR60-67	FATHERS OF THE CHURCH / patrology
HQ756	FATHERS / eugenics
BR1705	*FATHERS, APOSTOLIC* **SEE** APOSTOLIC FATHERS / collective biography
BR60-67	*FATHERS, APOSTOLIC* **SEE** APOSTOLIC FATHERS / patrology
BS579.F3	*FATHERS-BIBLICAL TEACHING* **SEE** FATHERS IN THE BIBLE
TA460	*FATIGUE OF METALS* **SEE** METALS ⎦ FATIGUE
TA413	*FATIGUE TESTING* **SEE** FATIGUE TESTING MACHINES
TA413	FATIGUE TESTING MACHINES
LB3431	FATIGUE / educational hygiene
LB1075	FATIGUE / educational psychology
QP321	FATIGUE / muscle
BF481	FATIGUE / psychology
RA788	FATIGUE, MENTAL / mental hygiene
QP421	FATIGUE, MENTAL / physiology
RC351	FATIGUE, MENTAL / popular works
BF481	FATIGUE, MENTAL / psychology
DT173	FATIMITES
QP751	*FATS* **SEE** FAT / physiological chemistry
TP670-695	*FATS* **SEE** OILS AND FATS
QD305.A2	*FATTY ACIDS* **SEE** ACIDS, FATTY
SF811	*FATTY HEART* **SEE** HEART, FATTY
RC685.F	*FATTY HEART* **SEE** HEART, FATTY
QM565	*FATTY TISSUE* **SEE** ADIPOSE TISSUES
BJ1535.F3	FAULTFINDING
QE606	FAULTS (GEOLOGY)
QL117	*FAUNA* **SEE** CAVE FAUNA
QL116	*FAUNA* **SEE** DESERT FAUNA
QL112	*FAUNA* **SEE** FOREST FAUNA
QH96-99	*FAUNA* **SEE** FRESH-WATER FAUNA / natural history
QL121-138	*FAUNA* **SEE** MARINE FAUNA
QE701-996	*FAUNA, PREHISTORIC* **SEE** PALEONTOLOGY
HF1721-1733	FAVORED NATION CLAUSE
D107.7	FAVORITES, ROYAL
RL770	FAVUS
TK6710	*FAX* **SEE** FACSIMILE TRANSMISSION
QB723.F2	FAYE'S COMET
NK3700-4695	*FAYENCE* **SEE** POTTERY / ceramics
TP785-825	*FAYENCE* **SEE** POTTERY / chemical technology
HD9610-9620	*FAYENCE* **SEE** POTTERY / trade
BF723.F4	FEAR / child study
BF575.F2	FEAR / psychology
BM695.H3	*FEAST OF DEDICATION* **SEE** HANUKKAH (FEAST OF LIGHTS)
BM695.P8	*FEAST OF ESTHER* **SEE** PURIM (FEAST OF ESTHER)
GT4995.F6	*FEAST OF FOOLS* **SEE** FOOLS, FEAST OF
BV64.J4	*FEAST OF JESUS CHRIST THE KING* **SEE** JESUS CHRIST THE KING, FEAST OF
BM695.H3	*FEAST OF LIGHTS* **SEE** HANUKKAH (FEAST OF LIGHTS)
BM695.S	*FEAST OF REJOICING OVER THE LAW* **SEE** SIMHAT TORAH
BM695.S	*FEAST OF TABERNACLES* **SEE** SUKKOTH
BV50.A7	*FEAST OF THE ASSUMPTION OF THE BLESSED VIRGIN MARY* **SEE** ASSUMPTION OF THE BLESSED VIRGIN MARY, FEAST OF THE
BV50.H6	*FEAST OF THE HOLY INNOCENTS* **SEE** HOLY INNOCENTS, FEAST OF THE
BV50.I6	*FEAST OF THE IMMACULATE CONCEPTION* **SEE** IMMACULATE CONCEPTION, FEAST OF THE
BM695.H3	*FEAST OF THE MACCABEES* **SEE** HANUKKAH (FEAST OF LIGHTS)
BV50.C3	*FEAST OF THE PRESENTATION OF JESUS CHRIST* **SEE** CANDLEMAS
BV50.P7	*FEAST OF THE PRESENTATION OF THE BLESSED VIRGIN MARY* **SEE** PRESENTATION OF THE BLESSED VIRGIN MARY, FEAST OF THE

BM695.S5	FEAST OF WEEKS **SEE** SHAVU'OTH (FEAST OF WEEKS)
BV30-135	FEASTS **SEE** FASTS AND FEASTS / christianity
CE81	FEASTS **SEE** FASTS AND FEASTS / church calendar
BL590	FEASTS **SEE** FASTS AND FEASTS / comparative religion
GT3930-4995	FEASTS **SEE** FASTS AND FEASTS / manners and customs
QL697	FEATHERS
RB49	FECES — ANALYSIS
QR171	FECES — BACTERIOLOGY
QP159	FECES
BF237	FECHNER'S LAW / psychology
QP273	FECUNDITY **SEE** FERTILITY / physiology
LB2825	FEDERAL AID TO EDUCATION
HD2753	FEDERAL CORPORATION TAX **SEE** CORPORATIONS — TAXATION
JC355	FEDERAL GOVERNMENT
JF751-786	FEDERAL GOVERNMENT / federal and state relations
LB2825	FEDERAL GRANTS FOR EDUCATION **SEE** FEDERAL AID TO EDUCATION
HG3729.U4-5	FEDERAL HOME LOAN BANKS
HG2051.U5	FEDERAL LAND BANKS
JK2300-2309	FEDERAL PARTY
HG2559-2565	FEDERAL RESERVE BANKS
BT155	FEDERAL THEOLOGY **SEE** COVENANTS (THEOLOGY)
JC355	FEDERAL-STATE RELATIONS **SEE** FEDERAL GOVERNMENT
JF751-786	FEDERAL-STATE RELATIONS **SEE** FEDERAL GOVERNMENT / federal and state relations
JC355	FEDERALISM **SEE** FEDERAL GOVERNMENT
JF751-786	FEDERALISM **SEE** FEDERAL GOVERNMENT / federal and state relations
JK2300-2309	FEDERALISTS (U.S.) **SEE** FEDERAL PARTY
BV636	FEDERATED CHURCHES
JN276	FEDERATION, IMPERIAL **SEE** IMPERIAL FEDERATION
DA18	FEDERATION, IMPERIAL **SEE** IMPERIAL FEDERATION / history
HV99	FEDERATIONS FOR CHARITY AND PHILANTHROPY **SEE** FEDERATIONS, FINANCIAL (SOCIAL SERVICE) / u.s. local
HV97	FEDERATIONS FOR CHARITY AND PHILANTHROPY **SEE** FEDERATIONS, FINANCIAL (SOCIAL SERVICE) / national
HV40-41	FEDERATIONS FOR CHARITY AND PHILANTHROPY **SEE** FEDERATIONS, FINANCIAL (SOCIAL SERVICE)
HV40-41	FEDERATIONS, FINANCIAL (SOCIAL SERVICE)
HV97	FEDERATIONS, FINANCIAL (SOCIAL SERVICE) / national
HV99	FEDERATIONS, FINANCIAL (SOCIAL SERVICE) / u.s. local
BV626	FEDERATIONS, LOCAL CHURCH **SEE** LOCAL CHURCH COUNCILS
HD2961	FEDRITIVE MOVEMENT
HJ5001-5231	FEE SYSTEM (TAXATION) **SEE** INTERNAL REVENUE
HJ5301-5515	FEE SYSTEM (TAXATION) **SEE** STAMP-DUTIES
HJ5321-5374	FEE SYSTEM (TAXATION) **SEE** STAMP-DUTIES / u.s.
HJ2240-7395	FEE SYSTEM (TAXATION) **SEE** TAXATION
HD9056	FEED INDUSTRY AND TRADE **SEE** FLOUR AND FEED TRADE
HF2651.F6	FEED INDUSTRY AND TRADE **SEE** FLOUR AND FEED TRADE / tariff
HD2769.M58	FEED INDUSTRY AND TRADE **SEE** FLOUR AND FEED TRADE / trusts
TS2158	FEED MILLS
HD9056	FEED TRADE **SEE** FLOUR AND FEED TRADE
HF2651.F6	FEED TRADE **SEE** FLOUR AND FEED TRADE / tariff
HD2769.M58	FEED TRADE **SEE** FLOUR AND FEED TRADE / trusts
S709	FEED-GRINDERS
TJ381-3	FEED-WATER HEATERS
TJ379	FEED-WATER PURIFICATION
TJ375-387	FEED-WATER
TK7835	FEEDBACK (ELECTRONICS)
TJ216	FEEDBACK CONTROL SYSTEMS
TL726	FEEDER AIR LINES **SEE** AIR LINES, LOCAL SERVICE
RM223-4	FEEDING, ARTIFICIAL **SEE** ARTIFICIAL FEEDING
SF97	FEEDS — ANALYSIS
RA761	FEEDS — DISINFECTION
BF311	FEELING **SEE** PERCEPTION
QP451	FEELING **SEE** TOUCH / physiology

BF275	FEELING **SEE** TOUCH / psychology
BF511-593	FEELINGS **SEE** EMOTIONS
BX1939.F	FEES, ECCLESIASTICAL / canon law
QL950.7	FEET **SEE** FOOT
QM549	FEET **SEE** FOOT
BV873.F7	FEET WASHING **SEE** FOOT WASHING (RITE)
BV873.F7	FEET, WASHING OF **SEE** FOOT WASHING (RITE)
QD321	FEHLING'S SOLUTION
TP382	FEHLING'S SOLUTION
DL190	FEHMARN, BATTLE OF, 1644
JN3269	FEHMIC COURTS
DD394.3	FEHRBELLIN, BATTLE OF, 1675
RA1146	FEIGNED DISEASES **SEE** BLINDNESS, FEIGNED
RA1146	FEIGNED DISEASES **SEE** MALINGERING
GN652.F9	FELATA **SEE** FULAHS
QE391.F3	FELDSPAR
QL737.C2	FELIS MARMORATA **SEE** MARBLED CAT
QL737.C2	FELIS NEBULOSA **SEE** CLOUDED LEOPARD
GN652.F9	FELLANS **SEE** FULAHS
LB2338-9	FELLOWSHIPS **SEE** SCHOLARSHIPS / college and university
LB2848-9	FELLOWSHIPS **SEE** SCHOLARSHIPS / school
TS1825	FELT BOOTS **SEE** BOOTS AND SHOES, FELT
TS1825	FELT
GN	FEMALE **SEE** WOMAN / anthropology
GT1720	FEMALE **SEE** WOMAN / costumes
GT2520-2540	FEMALE **SEE** WOMAN / customs
GR470	FEMALE **SEE** WOMAN / folk-lore
GN481	FEMALE **SEE** WOMAN / primitive society
HQ1101-2030	FEMALE **SEE** WOMAN / sociology
HV6046	FEMALE OFFENDERS **SEE** DELINQUENT WOMEN
GN	FEMINISM **SEE** WOMAN / anthropology
GT1720	FEMINISM **SEE** WOMAN / costumes
GT2520-2540	FEMINISM **SEE** WOMAN / customs
GR470	FEMINISM **SEE** WOMAN / folk-lore
GN481	FEMINISM **SEE** WOMAN / primitive society
HQ1101-2030	FEMINISM **SEE** WOMAN / sociology
QL835	FEMORAL VEIN / comparative
QM191	FEMORAL VEIN / human
RD101	FEMUR — FRACTURE
QL821	FEMUR / comparative
QM117	FEMUR / human
NA8390-8392	FENCES
S723-5	FENCES / agriculture
U860-863	FENCING
TL275	FENDERS FOR AUTOMOBILES **SEE** AUTOMOBILES — FENDERS
TF947	FENDERS FOR STREET-CARS **SEE** CAR FENDERS
TL275	FENDERS, AUTOMOBILE **SEE** AUTOMOBILES — FENDERS
QP461	FENESTRA ROTUNDA
QL948	FENESTRA ROTUNDA
QM507	FENESTRA ROTUNDA
BF1779.F4	FENG-SHUI
DA954	FENIANS
DT380	FENJAS **SEE** FALASHAS / ethiopia
DS135.E75	FENJAS **SEE** FALASHAS / jews
DA670.F33	FENS / england
QE391.F4	FERBERITE
QA244	FERMAT'S THEOREM
QR66	FERMENTATION TUBE
TP500-618	FERMENTATION / fermentation industries
QR151	FERMENTATION / micro-organisms
QP601	FERMENTATION / physiological chemistry
QK896	FERMENTATION / plant physiology
QP601	FERMENTS **SEE** ENZYMES
TP500-618	FERMENTS **SEE** FERMENTATION / fermentation industries
QR151	FERMENTS **SEE** FERMENTATION / micro-organisms
QP601	FERMENTS **SEE** FERMENTATION / physiological chemistry
QK896	FERMENTS **SEE** FERMENTATION / plant physiology
QC176	FERMI SURFACES
QK520-532	FERN ALLIES **SEE** PTERIDOPHYTA
PL8091	FERNANDIAN LANGUAGE **SEE** BUBE LANGUAGE
QK521	FERNS — ANATOMY
QK520-532	FERNS
SB429	FERNS / culture
QE961	FERNS, FOSSIL

QA76.8.P4	*FERRANT PEGASUS COMPUTER* **SEE** PEGASUS COMPUTER
BX830 1438	FERRARA-FLORENCE, COUNCIL OF, 1438-1439
SB994.R2	FERRETS / *rat-catching*
QL737.C2	FERRETS / *zoology*
QD181.F4	*FERRIC HYDRATES* **SEE** FERRIC HYDROXIDES
QD181.F4	FERRIC HYDROXIDES
QD181.F4	FERRIC NITRATE
QD181.F4	FERRIC SALTS
QE391.F45	FERRIERITE
HE5751-5870	FERRIES
TN693.I7	FERRITE / *metallography*
QC595	*FERROELECTRIC EFFECT* **SEE** FERROELECTRICITY
QC595	FERROELECTRICITY
QC595	*FERROELECTRICS* **SEE** FERROELECTRICITY
TN757.F3	FERROMANGANESE
TN757.F4	FERROSILICON
TR375	*FERROTYPE* **SEE** TINTYPE
HD9510-9529	*FERROUS METAL INDUSTRIES* **SEE** IRON INDUSTRY AND TRADE
HD9510-9529	*FERROUS METAL INDUSTRIES* **SEE** STEEL INDUSTRY AND TRADE
QD181.F4	FERROUS SALTS
QD181.F4	FERROUS SULPHATE
TG435	FERRY-BRIDGES
QP273	FERTILITY / *physiology*
GN241	FERTILITY, HUMAN / *physiological anthropology*
QP273	FERTILITY, HUMAN / *physiology*
HB903.F4	FERTILITY, HUMAN / *statistics*
QH485	FERTILIZATION (BIOLOGY)
QK926	FERTILIZATION OF PLANTS / *pollination*
QK827	FERTILIZATION OF PLANTS / *sexual reproduction*
S639	FERTILIZERS AND MANURES — ANALYSIS
S635	FERTILIZERS AND MANURES — DISINFECTION
S635	FERTILIZERS AND MANURES — PRESERVATION AND STORAGE
HF5716.F3	FERTILIZERS AND MANURES — TABLES AND READY-RECKONERS
SD408	*FERTILIZERS AND MANURES IN FORESTRY* **SEE** FOREST SOILS — FERTILIZATION
S631-667	FERTILIZERS AND MANURES / *agriculture*
TP963	FERTILIZERS AND MANURES / *manufacture*
HD9483	FERTILIZERS AND MANURES / *trade*
BM695.H3	*FESTIVAL OF HANUKKAH* **SEE** HANUKKAH (FEAST OF LIGHTS)
BV4254.3	FESTIVAL-DAY SERMONS
LB3560-3575	FESTIVALS / *educational*
GT3930-4995	FESTIVALS / *manners and customs*
SB191.S7	FETERITA / *culture*
TX558.S6	FETERITA / *food values*
JX2025	FETIALES
GN472	*FETICHISM* **SEE** FETISHISM / *ethnology*
HQ767	*FETICIDE* **SEE** ABORTION
RA1067	*FETICIDE* **SEE** ABORTION / *medical jurisprudence*
RG734	*FETICIDE* **SEE** ABORTION / *obstetrical operations*
RG648	*FETICIDE* **SEE** ABORTION / *obstetrics*
GN472	FETISHISM / *ethnology*
RG626-9	FETUS — DISEASES
RG600	FETUS — RESPIRATION AND CRY
RG600	FETUS / *physiology*
RG631	FETUS, DEATH OF
NA7710-7786	*FEUDAL CASTLES* **SEE** CASTLES / *architecture*
DA660-664	*FEUDAL CASTLES* **SEE** CASTLES / *england*
DC801	*FEUDAL CASTLES* **SEE** CASTLES / *france*
DC20	*FEUDAL CASTLES* **SEE** CASTLES / *france*
DD20	*FEUDAL CASTLES* **SEE** CASTLES / *germany*
DG420	*FEUDAL CASTLES* **SEE** CASTLES / *italy*
DP22	*FEUDAL CASTLES* **SEE** CASTLES / *spain*
D131	*FEUDAL TENURE* **SEE** FEUDALISM
JC109-116	*FEUDAL TENURE* **SEE** FEUDALISM / *feudal state*
HD101-1395	*FEUDAL TENURE* **SEE** LAND TENURE
D131	FEUDALISM
JC109-116	FEUDALISM / *feudal state*
HV6441-6453	*FEUDS* **SEE** VENDETTA
GN495	*FEUDS* **SEE** VENDETTA / *primitive*
RV211	FEVER — ECLECTIC TREATMENT
RX211	FEVER — HOMEOPATHIC TREATMENT
RM868	FEVER THERAPY
SF593.T5	*FEVER-TICK* **SEE** CATTLE-TICK
RC106	FEVER
RM868	*FEVER, ARTIFICIAL* **SEE** FEVER THERAPY
RC187-197	*FEVER, ENTERIC* **SEE** TYPHOID FEVER
QR201.T9	*FEVER, ENTERIC* **SEE** TYPHOID FEVER / *bacteriology*
RA644.T8	*FEVER, ENTERIC* **SEE** TYPHOID FEVER / *public health measures*
RC106	*FEVER, ERUPTIVE* **SEE** EXANTHEMATA
RG811	*FEVER, PUERPERAL* **SEE** PUERPERAL SEPTICEMIA
RM868	*FEVER, THERAPEUTIC* **SEE** FEVER THERAPY
RC106	*FEVER, TRAUMATIC* **SEE** TRAUMATIC FEVER
HB233.A3	FIARS PRICES / *agricultural prices*
TL215.F	FIAT AUTOMOBILE
UF620.F	FIAT MACHINE-GUN
HG651-1490	*FIAT MONEY* **SEE** CURRENCY QUESTION / *other countries*
HG501-538	*FIAT MONEY* **SEE** CURRENCY QUESTION / *u.s.*
HG361-3	*FIAT MONEY* **SEE** LEGAL TENDER
HG348-353	*FIAT MONEY* **SEE** PAPER MONEY
HG651-1490	*FIAT MONEY* **SEE** PAPER MONEY / *other countries*
HG571-627	*FIAT MONEY* **SEE** PAPER MONEY / *u.s.*
SB241-261	*FIBER PLANTS* **SEE** FIBERS / *fiber plants culture*
HD9155-6	*FIBER PLANTS* **SEE** FIBERS / *industry*
TS1540-1549	*FIBER PLANTS* **SEE** FIBERS / *textile fibers*
SB241-261	FIBERS / *fiber plants culture*
HD9155-6	FIBERS / *industry*
TS1540-1549	FIBERS / *textile fibers*
QP91	FIBRIN
QP91	FIBRINOGEN
QE391.S	*FIBROLITE* **SEE** SILLIMANITE
QM691	FIBULA — ABNORMITIES AND DEFORMITIES
CC400	FIBULA (ARCHAEOLOGY)
NK7306-8	FIBULA (ARCHAEOLOGY) / *art*
PZ1	FICTION — COLLECTIONS / *fiction in english*
PN41-44	FICTION — DICTIONARIES
PN3329-3503	FICTION — HISTORY AND CRITICISM
PN3347	FICTION — MORAL AND RELIGIOUS ASPECTS
PN3351	FICTION — MORAL AND RELIGIOUS ASPECTS
PN3355-3383	FICTION — TECHNIQUE
Z711.5	FICTION IN LIBRARIES
PN3311-3503	FICTION
PN3448.A8	FICTION, AUTOBIOGRAPHIC
PR830.A8	FICTION, AUTOBIOGRAPHIC / *english*
PT747.A8	FICTION, AUTOBIOGRAPHIC / *german*
PN3441	*FICTION, HISTORICAL* **SEE** HISTORICAL FICTION
PN44	*FICTION-PLOTS* **SEE** PLOTS (DRAMA, NOVEL, ETC.)
PN145	*FICTION-PLOTS* **SEE** PLOTS (DRAMA, NOVEL, ETC.)
PN1683	*FICTION-PLOTS* **SEE** PLOTS (DRAMA, NOVEL, ETC.) / *drama*
PN3378	*FICTION-PLOTS* **SEE** PLOTS (DRAMA, NOVEL, ETC.) / *fiction*
PN3373	*FICTION-PLOTS* **SEE** PLOTS (DRAMA, NOVEL, ETC.) / *short story*
B1574.B	FICTIONS, THEORY OF / *bentham*
BC199.F5	FICTIONS, THEORY OF / *logic*
BL51	FICTIONS, THEORY OF / *philosophy and religion*
B3354.V	FICTIONS, THEORY OF / *vaihinger*
GR820-830	*FICTITIOUS ANIMALS* **SEE** ANIMALS, MYTHICAL
Z1041-1115	*FICTITIOUS NAMES* **SEE** ANONYMS AND PSEUDONYMS
Z1024	*FICTITIOUS TITLES OF BOOKS* **SEE** IMAGINARY BOOKS AND LIBRARIES
ML800-897	*FIDDLE* **SEE** VIOLIN
QL444.D3	FIDDLER-CRABS
HD1236-9	FIDEICOMMISSUM
HG9970.S4-8	*FIDELITY BONDS* **SEE** INSURANCE, SURETY AND FIDELITY / *economics*
K	*FIDELITY BONDS* **SEE** INSURANCE, SURETY AND FIDELITY / *law*
K	*FIDELITY INSURANCE* **SEE** INSURANCE, SURETY AND FIDELITY / *law*
HG9970.S4-8	*FIDELITY INSURANCE* **SEE** INSURANCE, SURETY AND FIDELITY / *economics*
D131	*FIEFS* **SEE** FEUDALISM
JC109-116	*FIEFS* **SEE** FEUDALISM / *feudal state*
HD101-1395	*FIEFS* **SEE** LAND TENURE
UF400-445	*FIELD ARTILLERY* **SEE** ARTILLERY, FIELD AND MOUNTAIN

GV561-751	*FIELD ATHLETICS* **SEE** TRACK-ATHLETICS
GV1061-1099	*FIELD ATHLETICS* **SEE** TRACK-ATHLETICS / *special*
SB183-317	FIELD CROPS
UG403	*FIELD FORTIFICATION* **SEE** FORTIFICATION, FIELD
QE45	*FIELD GEOLOGY* **SEE** GEOLOGY — FIELD WORK
GV1017.H7	FIELD HOCKEY
UH460-485	*FIELD HOSPITALS* **SEE** HOSPITALS, MILITARY
RC970-971	*FIELD HOSPITALS* **SEE** MEDICINE, MILITARY / *medical practice*
UH	*FIELD HOSPITALS* **SEE** MEDICINE, MILITARY / *military science*
HV560-583	*FIELD HOSPITALS* **SEE** RED CROSS
UH535-7	*FIELD HOSPITALS* **SEE** RED CROSS / *army*
D628-630	*FIELD HOSPITALS* **SEE** RED CROSS / *european war*
VG457	*FIELD HOSPITALS* **SEE** RED CROSS / *navy*
UH201-551	*FIELD HOSPITALS* **SEE** WAR — RELIEF OF SICK AND WOUNDED / *medical and sanitary service*
GV405	FIELD HOUSES
SB994.F5	FIELD MICE / *agricultural pests*
QL737.R6	FIELD MICE / *zoology*
TL681.C6	*FIELD OF VIEW FROM AEROPLANES* **SEE** AEROPLANES — FIELD OF VIEW
RE79.P4	*FIELD OF VISION, MEASUREMENT OF* **SEE** PERIMETRY
VB255	*FIELD ORDERS* **SEE** ORDERS, PREPARATION OF (MILITARY SCIENCE) / *naval*
UB280-285	*FIELD ORDERS* **SEE** ORDERS, PREPARATION OF (MILITARY SCIENCE) / *military*
U170-175	FIELD SERVICE (MILITARY SCIENCE)
SK	*FIELD SPORTS* **SEE** HUNTING / *hunting sports*
GT5810-5899	*FIELD SPORTS* **SEE** HUNTING / *manners and customs*
GV	*FIELD SPORTS* **SEE** SPORTS
GN457	*FIELD SPORTS* **SEE** SPORTS / *primitive*
UG590-610	*FIELD TELEGRAPH* **SEE** MILITARY TELEGRAPH
QC6.5	*FIELD THEORIES, UNIFIED* **SEE** UNIFIED FIELD THEORIES
QC174.45	*FIELD THEORY, QUANTIZED* **SEE** QUANTUM FIELD THEORY
LB2394	FIELD WORK (EDUCATIONAL METHOD)
QE45	*FIELD WORK (GEOLOGY)* **SEE** GEOLOGY — FIELD WORK
GB25	*FIELD WORK (PHYSICAL GEOGRAPHY)* **SEE** PHYSICAL GEOGRAPHY — FIELD WORK
QC373.F5	FIELD-GLASSES
UF845	FIELD-GLASSES / *military*
QA247	FIELDS, ALGEBRAIC
M1270	FIFE AND DRUM MUSIC
M288-9	FIFE MUSIC (2 FIFES)
M60-62	FIFE MUSIC
ML935	FIFE / *history*
GV1511.F4	FIFTEEN PUZZLE
DA420-429	FIFTH MONARCHY MEN
SB608.F35	FIG — DISEASES AND PESTS
BT378.B2	*FIG TREE, BARREN* **SEE** BARREN FIG TREE (PARABLE)
SB365	FIG-INSECT / *fig culture*
SB608.F35	FIG-MOTH
SB365	FIG
TL685.3	FIGHTER PLANES
BF723.F5	FIGHTING (PSYCHOLOGY) / *child study*
D25	*FIGHTING* **SEE** BATTLES
GV1115-1137	*FIGHTING* **SEE** BOXING
GV1107	*FIGHTING* **SEE** BULL-FIGHTS
SF503	*FIGHTING* **SEE** COCK-FIGHTING
GV1109	*FIGHTING* **SEE** DOG-FIGHTING
CR4571-4595	*FIGHTING* **SEE** DUELING / *code*
U860-863	*FIGHTING* **SEE** FENCING
GV1111	*FIGHTING* **SEE** FIGHTING, HAND-TO-HAND
DG95	*FIGHTING* **SEE** GLADIATORS
GV35	*FIGHTING* **SEE** GLADIATORS
U	*FIGHTING* **SEE** MILITARY ART AND SCIENCE
V	*FIGHTING* **SEE** NAVAL ART AND SCIENCE
U167	*FIGHTING* **SEE** NIGHT FIGHTING (MILITARY SCIENCE)
U860	*FIGHTING* **SEE** SWORDPLAY
CR4553-7	*FIGHTING* **SEE** TOURNAMENTS / *heraldry*
GV1191	*FIGHTING* **SEE** TOURNAMENTS / *sports*
GN497-9	*FIGHTING* **SEE** WAR / *v primitive*
GV1111	FIGHTING, HAND-TO-HAND
BF241	FIGURAL AFTEREFFECTS
QB281-3	*FIGURE OF THE EARTH* **SEE** EARTH — FIGURE
ND1290	FIGURE PAINTING
GV849	*FIGURE SKATING* **SEE** SKATING
ML442	*FIGURED BASS* **SEE** THOROUGH BASS / *history*
MT49	*FIGURED BASS* **SEE** THOROUGH BASS / *instruction and study*
VM308	FIGUREHEADS OF SHIPS
PN227-8	FIGURES OF SPEECH
NK7900-7999	*FIGURINES* **SEE** BRONZES / *art*
TS570	*FIGURINES* **SEE** BRONZES / *technology*
GV1219	*FIGURINES* **SEE** DOLLS
NK495	*FIGURINES* **SEE** DOLLS / *art museums*
TS2301.T7	*FIGURINES* **SEE** DOLLS / *manufacture*
NK5800-5998	*FIGURINES* **SEE** IVORIES / *art industries*
TS1050	*FIGURINES* **SEE** IVORIES / *manufacture*
NK5750	*FIGURINES* **SEE** JADE / *art industries*
QE391.J2	*FIGURINES* **SEE** JADE / *mineralogy*
NK4165	*FIGURINES* **SEE** MING CH'I / *chinese art objects*
GT3283	*FIGURINES* **SEE** MING CH'I / *chinese burial customs*
NB145-159	*FIGURINES* **SEE** TERRA-COTTAS / *statuettes*
NB157	*FIGURINES* **SEE** TERRA-COTTAS / *tanagra figurines*
DT62.T6	*FIGURINES* **SEE** USHABTI
PL6235	FIJIAN LANGUAGE
PL6235.Z77	FIJIAN POETRY / *texts*
PL6235.Z95	FIJIAN POETRY / *translations*
DU600	FIJIANS
TK4365	*FILAMENTS FOR ELECTRIC LAMPS* **SEE** ELECTRIC LAMPS, INCANDESCENT — FILAMENTS
RC142.5	FILARIA AND FILARIASIS
SB401	FILBERT
HF5736-5746	FILES AND FILING (DOCUMENTS) — LIBRARY RECORDS
HF5736-5746	FILES AND FILING (DOCUMENTS)
TJ1285-7	FILES AND RASPS
PB1321	FILI (IRISH POETS)
G535-7	*FILIBUSTERS (WEST INDIAN BUCCANEERS)* **SEE** BUCCANEERS
F2161	*FILIBUSTERS (WEST INDIAN BUCCANEERS)* **SEE** BUCCANEERS
G539	FILIBUSTERS
QK520-532	*FILICINEAE* **SEE** FERNS
SB429	*FILICINEAE* **SEE** FERNS / *culture*
Z237	*FILIGRAINS* **SEE** WATER-MARKS / *early printed books*
TS1115	*FILIGRAINS* **SEE** WATER-MARKS / *paper manufacture*
NK3625.F	FILIGREE LETTERING
HF5736-5746	*FILING SYSTEMS* **SEE** FILES AND FILING (DOCUMENTS)
F1392.F	FILIPINOS IN MEXICO, (THE U.S., ETC.) / *mexico*
E184.F	FILIPINOS IN MEXICO, (THE U.S., ETC.) / *u.s.*
JV6891.F5-59	FILIPINOS IN MEXICO, (THE U.S., ETC.) / *u.s. immigration*
TN948.F45	FILLERS (IN PAPER, PAINT, ETC.)
TL153	*FILLING STATIONS* **SEE** AUTOMOBILES — SERVICE STATIONS
TD795	*FILLS, SANITARY* **SEE** SANITARY LANDFILLS
PN1997.85	FILM ADAPTATIONS
PN1996-7	*FILM AUTHORSHIP* **SEE** MOVING-PICTURE PLAYS
ML2075	*FILM MUSIC* **SEE** MOVING-PICTURE MUSIC
PN1997.85	*FILMED BOOKS* **SEE** FILM ADAPTATIONS
TR283	*FILMS* **SEE** PHOTOGRAPHY — FILMS
PN1997.85	*FILMS FROM BOOKS* **SEE** FILM ADAPTATIONS
TN690	*FILMS, METALLIC* **SEE** METALLIC FILMS / *metallography*
Z695.64	*FILMSTRIPS-CATALOGING* **SEE** CATALOGING OF FILMSTRIPS
TJ1470-1475	FILTER-PRESSES
TP156.F5	FILTERS AND FILTRATION / *chemical technology*
QD63.F5	FILTERS AND FILTRATION / *chemistry*
TD441-9	FILTERS AND FILTRATION / *water-supply*
QC373.L5	*FILTERS, LIGHT* **SEE** LIGHT FILTERS
BD530-595	*FINAL CAUSE* **SEE** CAUSATION
BD530-595	*FINAL CAUSE* **SEE** TELEOLOGY
HD201-5	*FINAL UTILITY* **SEE** MARGINAL UTILITY
HF5568	*FINANCE COMPANIES, COMMERCIAL* **SEE** INSTALMENT PLAN
BV770-777	*FINANCE, CHURCH* **SEE** CHURCH FINANCE
UA17	*FINANCE, MILITARY* **SEE** WAR, COST OF
HJ9000-9697	*FINANCE, MUNICIPAL* **SEE** MUNICIPAL FINANCE
HG179	FINANCE, PERSONAL
GN489	*FINANCE, PRIMITIVE* **SEE** ECONOMICS, PRIMITIVE
HJ9701-9995	FINANCE, PUBLIC — ACCOUNTING
HJ233	FINANCE, PUBLIC — ISLAMIC COUNTRIES
HJ135	*FINANCE, WAR* **SEE** WAR FINANCE

HV97	*FINANCIAL FEDERATIONS* **SEE** FEDERATIONS, FINANCIAL (SOCIAL SERVICE) / *national*
HV99	*FINANCIAL FEDERATIONS* **SEE** FEDERATIONS, FINANCIAL (SOCIAL SERVICE) / *u.s. local*
PN4784.C7	*FINANCIAL JOURNALISM* **SEE** JOURNALISM, COMMERCIAL
Z675.F5	FINANCIAL LIBRARIES
PN4784.F5	*FINANCIAL NEWS* **SEE** NEWSPAPERS — SECTIONS, COLUMNS, ETC. — — FINANCE
HF5681.B2	FINANCIAL STATEMENTS / *balance sheet*
QL696.P2	FINCHES
Z710	*FINDING LISTS* **SEE** LIBRARY CATALOGS
DA25	FINE-ROLLS
HV2471-2500	*FINGER ALPHABET* **SEE** DEAF — MEANS OF COMMUNICATION
GV1218.F5	*FINGER GAMES* **SEE** FINGER PLAY
GN192	*FINGER MARKS* **SEE** FINGERPRINTS / *anthropology*
HV6074	*FINGER MARKS* **SEE** FINGERPRINTS / *criminology*
GV1218.F5	FINGER PLAY
GN192	*FINGER PRINTS* **SEE** FINGERPRINTS / *anthropology*
HV6074	*FINGER PRINTS* **SEE** FINGERPRINTS / *criminology*
NK7440-7459	*FINGER RINGS* **SEE** RINGS / *art*
GT2270	*FINGER RINGS* **SEE** RINGS / *costume*
TS720-770	*FINGER RINGS* **SEE** RINGS / *manufacture*
HQ784.N3	*FINGERNAIL BITING* **SEE** NAIL-BITING
GN192	FINGERPRINTS / *anthropology*
HV6074	FINGERPRINTS / *criminology*
RD776	FINGERS — ABNORMITIES AND DEFORMITIES / *surgery*
QM691	FINGERS — ABNORMITIES AND DEFORMITIES / *teratology*
QM548	FINGERS
TH2495	FINIALS
TP934-944	FINISHES AND FINISHING / *finishes*
TT300-345	FINISHES AND FINISHING / *finishing*
TP934-944	*FINISHING* **SEE** FINISHES AND FINISHING / *finishes*
TT300-345	*FINISHING* **SEE** FINISHES AND FINISHING / *finishing*
TP934-944	*FINISHING MATERIALS* **SEE** FINISHES AND FINISHING / *finishes*
TT300-345	*FINISHING MATERIALS* **SEE** FINISHES AND FINISHING / *finishing*
QA9	*FINITE* **SEE** INFINITE / *mathematics*
BD411	*FINITE* **SEE** INFINITE / *metaphysics*
QA431	*FINITE DIFFERENCES* **SEE** DIFFERENCE EQUATIONS
DK445-465	FINLAND — HISTORY
DK459.45	FINLAND — HISTORY — — 1939-
PH319	FINNISH BALLADS AND SONGS / *collections*
PH315	FINNISH BALLADS AND SONGS / *history*
RM820	*FINNISH BATHS* **SEE** BATHS, FINNISH
PH347	FINNISH DRAMA / *collections*
PH311	FINNISH DRAMA / *history*
PH101-293	FINNISH LANGUAGE
PH101-1109	FINNISH LANGUAGES
PH300-498	FINNISH LITERATURE
PN5355.F5	FINNISH PERIODICALS / *etc.*
PH345-6	FINNISH POETRY / *collections*
PH310	FINNISH POETRY / *history*
PH101-1109	*FINNO-BALTIC LANGUAGES* **SEE** FINNISH LANGUAGES
PH	*FINNO-HUNGARIAN LANGUAGES* **SEE** FINNO-UGRIAN LANGUAGES
DK459.5	*FINNO-RUSSIAN WAR, 1939-1940* **SEE** RUSSO-FINNISH WAR, 1939-1940
PH	FINNO-UGRIAN LANGUAGES
PH	FINNO-UGRIAN PHILOLOGY
QL639	FINS
RM835-844	*FINSEN RAYS* **SEE** PHOTOTHERAPY
RM835-844	*FINSEN THERAPY* **SEE** PHOTOTHERAPY
QA689	*FINSLER SPACE* **SEE** SPACES, GENERALIZED
GB454.F5	*FIORDS* **SEE** FJORDS
PL8401-4	*FIOTI LANGUAGE* **SEE** CONGO LANGUAGE
QK495.A14	FIR
SD397.F	FIR / *sylviculture*

GR495	FIRE (IN RELIGION, FOLK-LORE, ETC.) / *folk-lore*
E98.F6	FIRE (IN RELIGION, FOLK-LORE, ETC.) / *folk-lore of the indians*
BL1590.F5	FIRE (IN RELIGION, FOLK-LORE, ETC.) / *zoroastrianism*
QB741-755	*FIRE BALLS* **SEE** METEORS
TH9500-9599	*FIRE COMPANIES* **SEE** FIRE-DEPARTMENTS
UF849	FIRE CONTROL (GUNNERY) — OPTICAL EQUIPMENT
UF848	FIRE CONTROL (GUNNERY)
VF530	FIRE CONTROL (NAVAL GUNNERY) — RADAR EQUIPMENT
VF520	FIRE CONTROL (NAVAL GUNNERY)
UF849	*FIRE CONTROL OPTICS* **SEE** FIRE CONTROL (GUNNERY) — OPTICAL EQUIPMENT
VF530	*FIRE CONTROL RADAR* **SEE** FIRE CONTROL (NAVAL GUNNERY) — RADAR EQUIPMENT
SF429.D3	*FIRE DOGS* **SEE** DALMATIAN DOGS
NK8600-8605	*FIRE ETCHING* **SEE** PYROGRAPHY
TH9338	FIRE EXTINCTION — CHEMICAL SYSTEMS
TH9339	FIRE EXTINCTION — EXPLOSION SYSTEMS
TH9311-9334	FIRE EXTINCTION — WATER-SUPPLY
TH9111-9599	FIRE EXTINCTION
TH9362	FIRE EXTINGUISHERS
TH9111-9599	*FIRE FIGHTING* **SEE** FIRE EXTINCTION
N8217.F5	FIRE IN ART
HG9651-9899	*FIRE INSURANCE* **SEE** INSURANCE, FIRE
TH9180	FIRE INVESTIGATION
TH9448-9	*FIRE LOSSES* **SEE** FIRES
HG9651-9899	*FIRE LOSSES* **SEE** INSURANCE, FIRE
TH9176	FIRE PREVENTION — INSPECTION
TH9120	FIRE PREVENTION — RESEARCH
TH9111-9599	FIRE PREVENTION
TH1061-1093	*FIRE PROOFING* **SEE** FIREPROOFING / *building*
TP267	*FIRE PROOFING* **SEE** FIREPROOFING / *fabrics*
TJ900-925	*FIRE PUMPS* **SEE** PUMPING MACHINERY
TH9120	*FIRE RESEARCH* **SEE** FIRE PREVENTION — RESEARCH
TH9336	FIRE SPRINKLERS
TH9323	FIRE STREAMS
TK7271	FIRE-ALARMS
TH9391	*FIRE-BOATS* **SEE** FIREBOATS
TJ646	*FIRE-BOXES* **SEE** LOCOMOTIVES — FIRE-BOXES
TP832.F5	FIRE-BRICK
TN941-3	FIRE-CLAY / *mineral resources*
TP838	FIRE-CLAY / *technology*
TA455.F5	FIRE-CLAY / *testing*
TN305	FIRE-DAMP
TH9361-9383	FIRE-DEPARTMENTS — EQUIPMENT AND SUPPLIES
TH9500-9599	FIRE-DEPARTMENTS
GV1559	FIRE-EATING
TH9371-6	FIRE-ENGINES
TH9338	FIRE-ENGINES / *chemical engines*
TH2274	FIRE-ESCAPES
GN416-417	FIRE-MAKING / *ethnology*
HG9799	FIRE-MARKS / *british insurance*
HG9799	*FIRE-PLATES* **SEE** FIRE-MARKS / *british insurance*
TH1091-1098	FIRE-TESTING
BL453	FIRE-WORSHIPERS
BL1590.F5	FIRE-WORSHIPERS / *zoroastrianism*
TP265	FIRE / *chemistry*
GN416-417	FIRE / *ethnology*
GR495	FIRE / *folk-lore*
TP268-9	*FIRE, GREEK* **SEE** GREEK FIRE / *ancient*
TP300	*FIRE, GREEK* **SEE** GREEK FIRE / *modern*
HV8077	FIREARMS — IDENTIFICATION
TS535	FIREARMS — LOCKS
TS535	FIREARMS — MAINTENANCE AND REPAIR
TS535	FIREARMS — PATENTS
TS535	FIREARMS — SIGHTS
UF854	FIREARMS — SIGHTS / *artillery*
UD390	FIREARMS — SIGHTS / *military rifles*
HD9743	FIREARMS INDUSTRY AND TRADE
TS535-7	FIREARMS / *manufacture*
V	FIREARMS / *u naval science*
TH9391	FIREBOATS
QL596.M2	FIREFLIES
TX831	FIRELESS COOKERS
TH9151	FIREMEN'S MANUALS
NA3050-3055	FIREPLACES / *architecture*
TH7421-7434	FIREPLACES / *heating*
TH1061-1093	*FIREPROOF BUILDING* **SEE** BUILDING, FIREPROOF

HV8613-8621	*FLAGELLATION* **SEE** FLAGELLANTS AND FLAGELLATION
M240-242	FLAGEOLET AND PIANO MUSIC
M1405	FLAGEOLET AND PIANO MUSIC, JUVENILE
M290	FLAGEOLET AND VIOLIN MUSIC
M290	FLAGEOLET AND VIOLIN MUSIC, ARRANGED
M288-9	FLAGEOLET MUSIC (2 FLAGEOLETS)
M288-9	FLAGEOLET MUSIC (2 FLAGEOLETS), ARRANGED
M60-62	FLAGEOLET MUSIC
M63-64	FLAGEOLET MUSIC, ARRANGED
ML935-6	FLAGEOLET
JC345-7	FLAGS / *emblems of state*
CR101-115	FLAGS / *heraldry*
VK385	FLAGS / *merchant marine signaling*
U360-365	FLAGS / *military science*
UC590-595	FLAGS / *military science*
V300-305	FLAGS / *naval science*
TN752.F	FLAME HARDENING
UG447	FLAME THROWERS
QD516	FLAME / *chemistry*
QC241	FLAME / *sound*
GV1796.F	FLAMENCO
TH1061-1093	*FLAMEPROOFING* **SEE** FIREPROOFING / *building*
TP267	*FLAMEPROOFING* **SEE** FIREPROOFING / *fabrics*
QL696.P45	FLAMINGOS
TA407	*FLAMMABLE MATERIALS* **SEE** INFLAMMABLE MATERIALS
E99.S22	*FLANDREAU INDIANS* **SEE** SANTEE INDIANS
TA492.F5	FLANGES
TS1580	FLANNELLET
TH9446.F6	FLANNELLET / *fire protection*
TL673.F6	FLAPS (AEROPLANES)
TR605	*FLASH-LIGHT PHOTOGRAPHY* **SEE** PHOTOGRAPHY, FLASH-LIGHT
SB205.F	FLAT PEA
QL638.P7	FLATFISHES
E99.S2	*FLATHEAD INDIANS* **SEE** SALISH INDIANS
NA7860	*FLATS* **SEE** APARTMENT HOUSES / *architecture*
TX957-8	*FLATS* **SEE** APARTMENT HOUSES / *service*
QL391.P7	*FLATWORMS* **SEE** PLATYHELMINTHES
TP450-453	FLAVORING ESSENCES
SB253	FLAX / *culture*
TS1700-1731	FLAX / *technology*
HD9155	FLAX / *trade*
HE7677.F55	FLAX / *trade*
HF5716.F4	FLAX / *trade*
SB299.F6	FLAXSEED / *culture*
HF5716.F5	FLAXSEED / *trade*
HD9155	FLAXSEED / *trade*
QL596.C5	FLEA-BEETLES
SB608	FLEA-BEETLES
SB945	FLEA-BEETLES / *pests*
RA641.F5	FLEAS AS CARRIERS OF DISEASE
QL503.A7	FLEAS
SF371-9	*FLEECE* **SEE** WOOL / *sheep raising*
TS1547	*FLEECE* **SEE** WOOL / *textile fibers*
V990-995	FLEET BALLISTIC MISSILE WEAPONS SYSTEMS
E475.51	*FLEETWOOD, BATTLE OF, 1863* **SEE** BRANDY STATION, BATTLE OF, 1863
DH491	FLEMINGS
DA122.F6	FLEMINGS / *england*
PT6330-40	FLEMISH BALLADS AND SONGS / *collections*
PT6140	FLEMISH BALLADS AND SONGS / *history*
PF1001-1199	FLEMISH LANGUAGE
PT6215-6397	FLEMISH LITERATURE / *collections*
PT6000-6199	FLEMISH LITERATURE / *etc.*
DH491	FLEMISH MOVEMENT
PN5261-9	FLEMISH NEWSPAPERS / *etc.*
PN5261-5270	FLEMISH PERIODICALS / *etc.*
PT6330-6340	FLEMISH POETRY / *collections*
PT6140	FLEMISH POETRY / *etc.*
PN6222.B4	FLEMISH WIT AND HUMOR
CR41.F6	FLEUR-DE-LIS
D280.F6	FLEURUS, BATTLE OF, 1690
DC222.F6	FLEURUS, BATTLE OF, 1794
TJ1057	FLEXIBLE SHAFTING
QA835	*FLEXIBLE SURFACES, EQUILIBRIUM OF* **SEE** EQUILIBRIUM OF FLEXIBLE SURFACES
Z252.5.F6	FLEXOGRAPHY
TS1449	FLEXOMETER / *textile testing*
QB154	FLEXURE / *astronomical adjustments*
TG265	FLEXURE / *beams*
ML975-7	*FLICORNO* **SEE** FLUEGELHORN
RA641.F6	FLIES AS CARRIERS OF DISEASE
QL531-8	FLIES
SH451-5	FLIES, ARTIFICIAL
RC1075	FLIES / *physiological aspects*
RC1050-1099	*FLIGHT CREWS-DISEASES AND HYGIENE* **SEE** AVIATION MEDICINE
TL710-713	*FLIGHT INSTRUCTION* **SEE** FLIGHT TRAINING
BP315	*FLIGHT INTO EGYPT* **SEE** JESUS CHRIST — FLIGHT INTO EGYPT
TL799.M3	*FLIGHT TO MARS* **SEE** SPACE FLIGHT TO MARS
TL799.M6	*FLIGHT TO THE MOON* **SEE** SPACE FLIGHT TO THE MOON
TL4030	*FLIGHT TRACKING* **SEE** SPACE VEHICLES — TRACKING
TL710-713	FLIGHT TRAINING
QL698	FLIGHT / *bird flight*
TL570-578	FLIGHT / *mechanics of flight*
TL760	*FLIGHT, UNPOWERED* **SEE** GLIDING AND SOARING
GV764-6	*FLIGHT, UNPOWERED* **SEE** GLIDING AND SOARING / *sport*
RC1050-1099	*FLIGHT-MEDICAL ASPECTS* **SEE** AVIATION MEDICINE
G445	FLIGHTS AROUND THE WORLD
GN446.1	*FLINT IMPLEMENTS* **SEE** STONE IMPLEMENTS / *primitive*
HD9585.F4	FLINT / *economics*
TN948.F5	FLINT / *mineral industries*
QE391.F5	FLINT / *mineralogy*
V890	FLOATING BATTERIES
QC147	FLOATING BODIES
QA907	FLOATING BODIES
TJ1363	FLOATING CRANES
GC41	*FLOATING INSTRUMENT PLATFORMS* **SEE** OCEANOGRAPHIC BUOYS
QC183	FLOCCULATION
QB551	*FLOCCULI* **SEE** SUN — FLOCCULI
DA784.6	FLODDEN, BATTLE OF, 1513
HV8609	*FLOGGING* **SEE** CORPORAL PUNISHMENT / *penology*
LB3025	*FLOGGING* **SEE** CORPORAL PUNISHMENT / *schools*
HV8613-8621	*FLOGGING* **SEE** FLAGELLANTS AND FLAGELLATION
TC530	FLOOD DAMS AND RESERVOIRS
TC540-555	FLOOD DAMS AND RESERVOIRS / *dams*
TC167	FLOOD DAMS AND RESERVOIRS / *hydraulics*
BS658	*FLOOD, BIBLICAL* **SEE** DELUGE / *bible*
QE507	*FLOOD, BIBLICAL* **SEE** DELUGE / *geology*
TC553	*FLOODGATES* **SEE** SLUICE GATES
TC404-535	FLOODS / *engineering*
SD425	FLOODS / *floods and forests*
GB1201-1397	FLOODS / *physical geography*
HV610	FLOODS / *relief work*
HD9937	FLOOR COVERINGS
NA2970	FLOORS / *architecture*
TH2521	FLOORS / *building*
TH2521.T	FLOORS, CONCRETE
NA3850.T	*FLOORS, TERRAZZO* **SEE** TERRAZZO
HD7288	*FLOPHOUSES* **SEE** LODGING-HOUSES / *laboring classes*
QK937	*FLORA* **SEE** ALPINE FLORA / *botany*
QK331	*FLORA* **SEE** ALPINE FLORA / *botany*
SB421	*FLORA* **SEE** ALPINE FLORA / *culture*
QK	*FLORA* **SEE** BOTANY
QK938.C3	*FLORA* **SEE** CAVE FLORA
QK922	*FLORA* **SEE** DESERT FLORA
QK938.D4	*FLORA* **SEE** DESERT FLORA
QK105	*FLORA* **SEE** FRESH-WATER FLORA / *botany*
QK916	*FLORA* **SEE** FRESH-WATER FLORA / *ecology*
QH96-99	*FLORA* **SEE** FRESH-WATER FLORA / *natural history*
QK103	*FLORA* **SEE** MARINE FLORA
SB445-9	*FLORAL DECORATION* **SEE** FLOWER ARRANGEMENT
NK1560-1565	*FLORAL DESIGN* **SEE** DESIGN, DECORATIVE — PLANT FORMS
DC801.T725	FLORAL GAMES / *toulouse*
DA87.5 1591	FLORES, BATTLE OF, 1591
SB403-450	FLORICULTURE
SB441	*FLORICULTURE-EXHIBITIONS* **SEE** FLOWER SHOWS
F306-320	FLORIDA — HISTORY

QA76.8.S4	FLORIDA AUTOMATIC COMPUTER **SEE** SEAC COMPUTER
TK7889.S4	FLORIDA AUTOMATIC COMPUTER **SEE** SEAC COMPUTER / engineering
SB945.F6	FLORIDA FERN CATERPILLAR
PL6240	FLORIDA LANGUAGE
SB205.B3	FLORIDA VELVET BEAN
E83.835	FLORIDA WAR, 1835-1842 **SEE** SEMINOLE WAR, 2D, 1835-1842
E83.817	FLORIDA-HISTORY-SEMINOLE WARS **SEE** SEMINOLE WAR, 1ST, 1817-1818
E83.835	FLORIDA-HISTORY-SEMINOLE WARS **SEE** SEMINOLE WAR, 2D, 1835-1842
E83.855	FLORIDA-HISTORY-SEMINOLE WARS **SEE** SEMINOLE WAR, 3D, 1855-1858
E558	FLORIDA — HISTORY —— CIVIL WAR
HF5585.F6	FLORISTS — CREDIT GUIDES
SB404	FLORISTS — DIRECTORIES
SB443	FLORISTS
TN523	FLOTATION
QL638.P7	FLOUNDERS
SH351.F	FLOUNDERS / fisheries
HG3875.F6	FLOUR AND FEED TRADE — TABLES AND READY-RECKONERS / exchange tables
HD9056	FLOUR AND FEED TRADE
HF2651.F6	FLOUR AND FEED TRADE / tariff
HD2769.M58	FLOUR AND FEED TRADE / trusts
TS2120-2159	FLOUR-MILLS
TX595.F6	FLOUR / adulteration
TX393	FLOUR / food supply
TX558.W5	FLOUR / food values
TS2120-2159	FLOUR / manufacture
TC177	FLOW MEASUREMENT **SEE** FLOW METERS
TC177	FLOW METERS
TC160-179	FLOW OF WATER **SEE** HYDRAULICS
SB449.5.C4	FLOWER ARRANGEMENT IN CHURCHES
SB445-9	FLOWER ARRANGEMENT
QK84	FLOWER LANGUAGE
SB441	FLOWER SHOWS
QK692-8	FLOWERS — ANATOMY
QK653-9	FLOWERS — ANATOMY
QK653-9	FLOWERS — MORPHOLOGY
QK98	FLOWERS — PICTORIAL WORKS
PN6110.F6	FLOWERS IN POETRY
QK	FLOWERS / botany
SB403-450	FLOWERS / culture
GT5160	FLOWERS / manners and customs
TT890-894	FLOWERS, ARTIFICIAL **SEE** ARTIFICIAL FLOWERS
SB447	FLOWERS, EVERLASTING **SEE** EVERLASTING FLOWERS
SB127	FLOWERS, FORCING OF **SEE** FORCING (PLANTS)
QK84	FLOWERS, LANGUAGE OF **SEE** FLOWER LANGUAGE
QK85	FLOWERS, NATIONAL **SEE** NATIONAL FLOWERS
QK86	FLOWERS, PROTECTION OF **SEE** PLANTS, PROTECTION OF
SB599-999	FLOWERS, PROTECTION OF **SEE** PLANTS, PROTECTION OF / diseases and pests
QK85	FLOWERS, STATE **SEE** STATE FLOWERS
QK84	FLOWERS, SYMBOLISM OF **SEE** SYMBOLISM OF FLOWERS
TT894	FLOWERS, WAX **SEE** WAX FLOWERS
SB447	FLOWERS, WAX **SEE** WAX FLOWERS / reproduction of flowers
SB445-9	FLOWERS-ARRANGEMENT **SEE** FLOWER ARRANGEMENT
TC177	FLOWMETERS **SEE** FLOW METERS
ML975-7	FLUEGELHORN
TH2281	FLUES
TP156.F65	FLUID BED PROCESSES **SEE** FLUIDIZATION
Z48	FLUID COPYING PROCESSES
TK9203.F5	FLUID FUEL REACTORS
TC177	FLUID METERS **SEE** FLOW METERS
RM170	FLUID THERAPY
TP156.F65	FLUIDIZATION
TP156.F65	FLUIDIZED SYSTEMS **SEE** FLUIDIZATION
QP88	FLUIDS AND HUMORS, ANIMAL **SEE** BODY FLUIDS
QA901-930	FLUIDS / analytical mechanics
QC141-168	FLUIDS / physics
RM170	FLUIDS-THERAPEUTIC USE **SEE** FLUID THERAPY
SF968	FLUKE **SEE** LIVER-FLUKE / diseases of sheep

QL391.T7	FLUKE **SEE** LIVER-FLUKE / zoology
TC175	FLUMES / hydraulics
TC933	FLUMES / irrigation
TJ847	FLUMES / water-power
QD441	FLUORESCEIN / chemistry
QC477	FLUORESCENCE
TK4386	FLUORESCENT LAMPS
TK4386	FLUORESCENT LIGHTING
QD181.F1	FLUORIDES
QD181.F1	FLUORINE
TN948.F6	FLUORITE **SEE** FLUORSPAR / mineral resources
QE391.F6	FLUORITE **SEE** FLUORSPAR / mineralogy
TN948.F6	FLUORSPAR / mineral resources
QE391.F6	FLUORSPAR / mineralogy
SB951	FLUOSILICATES / insecticides
RD86.H3	FLUOTHANE **SEE** HALOTHANE
ML936	FLUTE — CONSTRUCTION
MT15	FLUTE — FINGERING CHARTS
ML935-6	FLUTE — HISTORY ·
MT346	FLUTE — ORCHESTRA STUDIES
MT345	FLUTE — STUDIES AND EXERCISES
M288-9	FLUTE AND BASSOON MUSIC **SEE** BASSOON AND FLUTE MUSIC
M288-9	FLUTE AND CLARINET MUSIC **SEE** CLARINET AND FLUTE MUSIC
M288-9	FLUTE AND ENGLISH-HORN MUSIC **SEE** ENGLISH HORN AND FLUTE MUSIC
M296-7	FLUTE AND GUITAR MUSIC
M296-7	FLUTE AND GUITAR MUSIC, ARRANGED
M296-7	FLUTE AND HARP MUSIC
M1040-1041	FLUTE AND HARP WITH ORCHESTRA
M1105-6	FLUTE AND HARP WITH STRING ORCHESTRA
M240-242	FLUTE AND HARPSICHORD MUSIC
M1105	FLUTE AND HARPSICHORD WITH STRING ORCHESTRA — SCORES
M1105-6	FLUTE AND HARPSICHORD WITH STRING ORCHESTRA
M288-9	FLUTE AND HORN MUSIC
M1105-6	FLUTE AND HORN WITH STRING ORCHESTRA
M296-7	FLUTE AND KOTO MUSIC
M288-9	FLUTE AND OBOE MUSIC
M1040-1041	FLUTE AND OBOE WITH ORCHESTRA
M1105	FLUTE AND OBOE WITH STRING ORCHESTRA — SCORES
M1105-6	FLUTE AND OBOE WITH STRING ORCHESTRA
MT182-4	FLUTE AND ORGAN MUSIC
M240-242	FLUTE AND PIANO MUSIC
M243-4	FLUTE AND PIANO MUSIC, ARRANGED
M1405	FLUTE AND PIANO MUSIC, JUVENILE
M1105	FLUTE AND PIANO WITH STRING ORCHESTRA — SCORES
M1105-6	FLUTE AND PIANO WITH STRING ORCHESTRA
M288-9	FLUTE AND RECORDER MUSIC
M1105-6	FLUTE AND RECORDER WITH STRING ORCHESTRA
M290-291	FLUTE AND VIOLA D'AMORE MUSIC
M1105-6	FLUTE AND VIOLA D'AMORE WITH STRING ORCHESTRA
M290-291	FLUTE AND VIOLA MUSIC
M290-291	FLUTE AND VIOLIN MUSIC
M1041	FLUTE AND VIOLIN WITH ORCHESTRA — SOLOS WITH PIANO
M1040-1041	FLUTE AND VIOLIN WITH ORCHESTRA
M1105-6	FLUTE AND VIOLIN WITH STRING ORCHESTRA
M290-291	FLUTE AND VIOLONCELLO MUSIC
M1105	FLUTE AND VIOLONCELLO WITH STRING ORCHESTRA — SCORES
M1105-6	FLUTE AND VIOLONCELLO WITH STRING ORCHESTRA
MT140	FLUTE MUSIC — INTERPRETATION (PHRASING, DYNAMICS, ETC.)
MT145	FLUTE MUSIC — INTERPRETATION (PHRASING, DYNAMICS, ETC.)
M288-9	FLUTE MUSIC (2 FLUTES)
M288-9	FLUTE MUSIC (2 FLUTES), ARRANGED
M355-7	FLUTE MUSIC (3 FLUTES) **SEE** WIND TRIOS (3 FLUTES)
M355-7	FLUTE MUSIC (3 FLUTES) **SEE** WIND TRIOS (3 FLUTES)
M455-7	FLUTE MUSIC (4 FLUTES) **SEE** WIND QUARTETS (4 FLUTES)
M455-7	FLUTE MUSIC (4 FLUTES) **SEE** WIND QUARTETS (4 FLUTES)

M555-7	*FLUTE MUSIC (5 FLUTES)* **SEE** WIND QUINTETS (5 FLUTES)
M60-62	FLUTE MUSIC
M63-64	FLUTE MUSIC, ARRANGED
M1021	FLUTE WITH CHAMBER ORCHESTRA — SOLO WITH PIANO
M1020-1021	FLUTE WITH CHAMBER ORCHESTRA
M1020-1021	FLUTE WITH CHAMBER ORCHESTRA, ARRANGED
M1021	FLUTE WITH ORCHESTRA — SOLO WITH PIANO
M1020-1021	FLUTE WITH ORCHESTRA
M1020	FLUTE WITH ORCHESTRA, ARRANGED — SCORES
M1020-1021	FLUTE WITH ORCHESTRA, ARRANGED
M1021	FLUTE WITH ORCHESTRA — TO 1800 — — SOLO WITH PIANO
M1106	FLUTE WITH STRING ORCHESTRA — SOLO WITH PIANO
M1105-6	FLUTE WITH STRING ORCHESTRA
M1105-6	FLUTE WITH STRING ORCHESTRA, ARRANGED
M955-7	FLUTE WITH WIND ENSEMBLE
ML937	FLUTE-PLAYERS
ML1055.A8	*FLUTE-PLAYERS, MECHANICAL* **SEE** AUTOMATA
TJ215	*FLUTE-PLAYERS, MECHANICAL* **SEE** AUTOMATA
ML935-7	*FLUTE / history*
M1105-6	FLUTE, HORN, HARP WITH STRING ORCHESTRA
M1105-6	FLUTE, KETTLEDRUMS, VIOLIN WITH STRING ORCHESTRA
M1105-6	FLUTE, OBOE D'AMORE, VIOLA D'AMORE WITH STRING ORCHESTRA
M1105-6	FLUTE, OBOE, TRUMPET WITH STRING ORCHESTRA
M1040-1041	FLUTE, OBOE, VIOLIN, VIOLONCELLO WITH ORCHESTRA
M1105-6	FLUTE, VIOLA, VIOLONCELLO WITH STRING ORCHESTRA
M1020-1021	FLUTES (2) WITH CHAMBER ORCHESTRA
M1020-1021	FLUTES (2) WITH ORCHESTRA
M1105-6	FLUTES (2) WITH STRING ORCHESTRA
M1105-6	FLUTES (2), GLOCKENSPIEL WITH STRING ORCHESTRA
M1105	FLUTES (2), MARIMBA WITH STRING ORCHESTRA — SCORES
M1105-6	FLUTES (2), MARIMBA WITH STRING ORCHESTRA
M1105-6	FLUTES (3) WITH STRING ORCHESTRA
ML937	*FLUTISTS* **SEE** FLUTE-PLAYERS
TL574.F6	FLUTTER (AERODYNAMICS)
QA300-316	*FLUXIONS* **SEE** CALCULUS
QL531-8	*FLY* **SEE** FLIES
RC186.T82	*FLY DISEASE* **SEE** TRYPANOSOMIASIS
SF807	*FLY DISEASE* **SEE** TRYPANOSOMIASIS / veterinary medicine
SH456	FLY-CASTING
SH456	*FLY-FISHING* **SEE** FLY-CASTING
TJ541	FLY-WHEELS
QL696.P2	FLYCATCHERS / birds
QL698	*FLYING* **SEE** FLIGHT / bird flight
TL570-578	*FLYING* **SEE** FLIGHT / mechanics of flight
TL684	*FLYING BOATS* **SEE** SEAPLANES
TL710-713	*FLYING CLASSES* **SEE** FLIGHT TRAINING
SB994.F6	FLYING FOXES / noxious animals
QL737.C5	FLYING FOXES / zoology
QL737.M3	FLYING PHALANGERS
TL671.4	*FLYING QUALITIES OF AIRCRAFT* **SEE** AEROPLANES — HANDLING CHARACTERISTICS
TL716	*FLYING QUALITIES OF HELICOPTERS* **SEE** HELICOPTERS — HANDLING CHARACTERISTICS
QL638.E9	FLYING-FISH
TL670-724	FLYING-MACHINES
TL554	*FLYING-MACHINES-POETRY* **SEE** AERONAUTICS — POETRY
TK6553	*FM RADIO* **SEE** RADIO FREQUENCY MODULATION
PL8164.Z9	*FO DIALECT* **SEE** FON DIALECT
TR263.F	FOCA CAMERA
SB211.M27	*FODDER BEET* **SEE** MANGEL-WURZEL
RG600	*FOETUS* **SEE** FETUS / physiology
VK383	FOG-BELLS
VK383	FOG-SIGNALS
RA575	FOG / hygiene of atmosphere
QC929.F7	FOG / meteorology
DT380	*FOGGARA* **SEE** FALASHAS / ethiopia
DS135.E75	*FOGGARA* **SEE** FALASHAS / jews
GN783-4	*FOGOUS* **SEE** CAVE-DWELLINGS
QC939.F6	FOHN
Z261	FOLDING-MACHINES
QE606	FOLDS (GEOLOGY)

QK689	*FOLIAGE* **SEE** LEAVES
QK649	*FOLIAGE* **SEE** LEAVES
SB431	FOLIAGE PLANTS
S662.5	FOLIAR FEEDING
S662.5	*FOLIAR FERTILIZATION* **SEE** FOLIAR FEEDING
N9201-9211	FOLK ART
NK801-1094	FOLK ART
M1627	FOLK DANCE MUSIC
GV1580-1799	FOLK DANCING
PN57.A1	FOLK LITERATURE — THEMES, MOTIVES
PN905-1008	FOLK LITERATURE
PN1008.D7	FOLK-DRAMA / history
Z5981-5	FOLK-LORE — BIO-BIBLIOGRAPHY
Z5981-5	FOLK-LORE — CLASSIFICATION
GR40	FOLK-LORE — CLASSIFICATION
GR35	FOLK-LORE — DICTIONARIES
BL303	FOLK-LORE — DICTIONARIES / mythology
GR40	FOLK-LORE — THEORY, METHODS, ETC.
GR43.C4	FOLK-LORE AND CHILDREN
LB1044.9.F6	FOLK-LORE AND EDUCATION
GR43.C4	*FOLK-LORE AND YOUTH* **SEE** FOLK-LORE AND CHILDREN
BV168.A	*FOLK-LORE OF ADZES* **SEE** ADZES (IN RELIGION, FOLK-LORE, ETC.)
GR895	FOLK-LORE OF AGRICULTURE
GR820-830	*FOLK-LORE OF ANIMALS* **SEE** ANIMAL LORE
QL89	*FOLK-LORE OF ANIMALS* **SEE** ANIMAL LORE
GR730.A6	*FOLK-LORE OF APES* **SEE** APES (IN RELIGION, FOLK-LORE, ETC.)
GR730	*FOLK-LORE OF ASSES* **SEE** ASSES AND MULES (IN RELIGION, FOLK-LORE, ETC.)
GR750	FOLK-LORE OF BEES
GR735	FOLK-LORE OF BIRDS
GR450	*FOLK-LORE OF BIRTH* **SEE** BIRTH (IN RELIGION, FOLK-LORE, ETC.)
BL600	*FOLK-LORE OF BLOOD* **SEE** BLOOD (IN RELIGION, FOLK-LORE, ETC.) / comparative religion
BL570	*FOLK-LORE OF BLOOD* **SEE** BLOOD (IN RELIGION, FOLK-LORE, ETC.) / comparative religion
GR489	*FOLK-LORE OF BLOOD* **SEE** BLOOD (IN RELIGION, FOLK-LORE, ETC.) / folk-lore
BL443.B8	*FOLK-LORE OF BULLS* **SEE** BULL (IN RELIGION, FOLK-LORE, ETC.) / religion
BL443.C3	*FOLK-LORE OF CATS* **SEE** CATS (IN RELIGION, FOLK-LORE, ETC.) / religion
GR725	*FOLK-LORE OF CATS* **SEE** CATS (IN RELIGION, FOLK-LORE, ETC.) / folk-lore
GR665	*FOLK-LORE OF CAVES* **SEE** CAVES (IN RELIGION, FOLK-LORE, ETC.)
GR475-487	FOLK-LORE OF CHILDREN
G100	*FOLK-LORE OF COUNTRIES* **SEE** GEOGRAPHICAL MYTHS
GR650-690	*FOLK-LORE OF COUNTRIES* **SEE** GEOGRAPHICAL MYTHS / folk-lore
BL605	*FOLK-LORE OF DANCING* **SEE** DANCING (IN RELIGION, FOLK-LORE, ETC.)
GR930	*FOLK-LORE OF DAWN* **SEE** DAWN (IN RELIGION, FOLK-LORE, ETC.) / folk-lore
BL325.D	*FOLK-LORE OF DAWN* **SEE** DAWN (IN RELIGION, FOLK-LORE, ETC.) / mythology
BL1215.D3	*FOLK-LORE OF DAWN* **SEE** DAWN (IN RELIGION, FOLK-LORE, ETC.) / hinduism
GR930	*FOLK-LORE OF DAYS* **SEE** DAYS / folk-lore
GR720	*FOLK-LORE OF DOGS* **SEE** DOGS (IN RELIGION, FOLK-LORE, ETC.) / folk-lore
BL325.A6	*FOLK-LORE OF DOGS* **SEE** DOGS (IN RELIGION, FOLK-LORE, ETC.) / religion
BV168.D6	*FOLK-LORE OF DOVES* **SEE** DOVE (IN RELIGION, FOLK-LORE, ETC.) / religion
BL325.E3	*FOLK-LORE OF EAGLES* **SEE** EAGLE (IN RELIGION, FOLK-LORE, ETC.) / mythology
GR735	*FOLK-LORE OF EGGS* **SEE** EGGS (IN RELIGION, FOLK-LORE, ETC.)
GR495	*FOLK-LORE OF FIRE* **SEE** FIRE (IN RELIGION, FOLK-LORE, ETC.) / folk-lore
E98.F6	*FOLK-LORE OF FIRE* **SEE** FIRE (IN RELIGION, FOLK-LORE, ETC.) / folk-lore of the indians
BL1590.F5	*FOLK-LORE OF FIRE* **SEE** FIRE (IN RELIGION, FOLK-LORE, ETC.) / zoroastrianism

GN423	*FOLK-LORE OF FISHING* **SEE** FISHING (IN RELIGION, FOLK-LORE, ETC.)
GR805	*FOLK-LORE OF GEMS* **SEE** GEMS (IN RELIGION, FOLK-LORE, ETC.)
BL325.H	*FOLK-LORE OF HARES* **SEE** HARES (IN RELIGION, FOLK-LORE, ETC.) / *religion*
GR730.H	*FOLK-LORE OF HARES* **SEE** HARES (IN RELIGION, FOLK-LORE, ETC.) / *folk-lore*
GR895	*FOLK-LORE OF HARVESTING* **SEE** FOLK-LORE OF AGRICULTURE
GR715	*FOLK-LORE OF HORSES* **SEE** HORSES (IN RELIGION, FOLK-LORE, ETC.) / *folk-lore*
BL443.H	*FOLK-LORE OF HORSES* **SEE** HORSES (IN RELIGION, FOLK-LORE, ETC.) / *religion*
GN422	*FOLK-LORE OF HUNTING* **SEE** HUNTING (IN RELIGION, FOLK-LORE, ETC.)
BL325.I5	*FOLK-LORE OF INCUBATION* **SEE** INCUBATION (IN RELIGION, FOLK-LORE, ETC.)
BL615	*FOLK-LORE OF INITIATIONS* **SEE** INITIATIONS (IN RELIGION, FOLK-LORE, ETC.)
GR750	FOLK-LORE OF INSECTS
BL325.K5	*FOLK-LORE OF KINGS AND RULERS* **SEE** KINGS AND RULERS (IN RELIGION, FOLK-LORE, ETC.)
JC374	*FOLK-LORE OF KINGS AND RULERS* **SEE** KINGS AND RULERS (IN RELIGION, FOLK-LORE, ETC.)
GT2640	*FOLK-LORE OF KISSING* **SEE** KISSING (IN RELIGION, FOLK-LORE, ETC.)
BL443.L6	*FOLK-LORE OF LLAMAS* **SEE** LLAMAS (IN RELIGION, FOLK-LORE, ETC.)
BL457.M4	*FOLK-LORE OF METAL-WORK* **SEE** METALS (IN RELIGION, FOLK-LORE, ETC.)
BL457.M4	*FOLK-LORE OF METALLURGY* **SEE** METALS (IN RELIGION, FOLK-LORE, ETC.)
BL457.M4	*FOLK-LORE OF METALS* **SEE** METALS (IN RELIGION, FOLK-LORE, ETC.)
BL325.M4	*FOLK-LORE OF METAMORPHOSIS* **SEE** METAMORPHOSIS (IN RELIGION, FOLK-LORE, ETC.)
GR730.M	*FOLK-LORE OF MICE* **SEE** MICE (IN RELIGION, FOLK-LORE, ETC.) / *folk-lore*
BL325.M5	*FOLK-LORE OF MICE* **SEE** MICE (IN RELIGION, FOLK-LORE, ETC.) / *mythology*
GR950.M	*FOLK-LORE OF MILK* **SEE** MILK (IN RELIGION, FOLK-LORE, ETC.) / *folk-lore*
BL730	*FOLK-LORE OF MILK* **SEE** MILK (IN RELIGION, FOLK-LORE, ETC.) / *greek and roman cults*
GR900	FOLK-LORE OF MINES
BL457.M4	*FOLK-LORE OF MINING* **SEE** METALS (IN RELIGION, FOLK-LORE, ETC.)
BL447	*FOLK-LORE OF MOUNTAINS* **SEE** MOUNTAINS (IN RELIGION, FOLK-LORE, ETC.) / *religion*
GR660	*FOLK-LORE OF MOUNTAINS* **SEE** MOUNTAINS (IN RELIGION, FOLK-LORE, ETC.) / *folk-lore*
GR730	*FOLK-LORE OF MULES* **SEE** ASSES AND MULES (IN RELIGION, FOLK-LORE, ETC.)
BL2450.N	*FOLK-LORE OF NAVELS* **SEE** NAVEL (IN RELIGION, FOLK-LORE, ETC.) / *egyptian religion*
GR485	*FOLK-LORE OF NUMBERS* **SEE** COUNTING-OUT RHYMES
BL619.P3	*FOLK-LORE OF PAPER* **SEE** PAPER (IN RELIGION, FOLK-LORE, ETC.) / *religion*
GR785	*FOLK-LORE OF PLANTS* **SEE** FOLK-LORE OF TREES
QK83	*FOLK-LORE OF PLANTS* **SEE** PLANT LORE
BL325.P7	*FOLK-LORE OF POLARITY* **SEE** POLARITY (IN RELIGION, FOLK-LORE, ETC.)
GR730.H	*FOLK-LORE OF RABBITS* **SEE** HARES (IN RELIGION, FOLK-LORE, ETC.) / *folk-lore*
BL325.H	*FOLK-LORE OF RABBITS* **SEE** HARES (IN RELIGION, FOLK-LORE, ETC.) / *religion*
GR920.R3	FOLK-LORE OF RAILROADS
GR690	*FOLK-LORE OF SPRINGS* **SEE** SPRINGS (IN RELIGION, FOLK-LORE, ETC.) / *folk-lore*
BL450	*FOLK-LORE OF SPRINGS* **SEE** SPRINGS (IN RELIGION, FOLK-LORE, ETC.) / *religion*
GR625	*FOLK-LORE OF STARS* **SEE** STARS (IN RELIGION, FOLK-LORE, ETC.)
GR800	FOLK-LORE OF STONES
BL325.T	*FOLK-LORE OF TEETH* **SEE** TEETH (IN RELIGION, FOLK-LORE, ETC.) / *religion*
GR489	*FOLK-LORE OF TEETH* **SEE** TEETH (IN RELIGION, FOLK-LORE, ETC.) / *folk-lore*
GR455	*FOLK-LORE OF THE DEAD* **SEE** DEAD (IN RELIGION, FOLK-LORE, ETC.) / *folk-lore*
BL470	*FOLK-LORE OF THE DEAD* **SEE** DEAD (IN RELIGION, FOLK-LORE, ETC.) / *comparative religion*
BL2443	*FOLK-LORE OF THE DEAD* **SEE** DEAD (IN RELIGION, FOLK-LORE, ETC.) / *egyptian religion*
GR950.D	*FOLK-LORE OF THE DEAF* **SEE** DEAF IN FOLK-LORE
GR655	*FOLK-LORE OF THE EARTH* **SEE** EARTH (IN RELIGION, FOLK-LORE, ETC.) / *folk-lore*
BL435	*FOLK-LORE OF THE EARTH* **SEE** EARTH (IN RELIGION, FOLK-LORE, ETC.) / *nature-worship*
GR910	*FOLK-LORE OF THE EQUATOR* **SEE** SHELLBACKS
BL325.H25	*FOLK-LORE OF THE HEAD* **SEE** HEAD (IN RELIGION, FOLK-LORE, ETC.) / *religion*
GR489	*FOLK-LORE OF THE HEAD* **SEE** HEAD (IN RELIGION, FOLK-LORE, ETC.) / *folk-lore*
BL443	*FOLK-LORE OF THE HIPPOPOTAMUS* **SEE** HIPPOPOTAMUS (IN RELIGION, FOLK-LORE, ETC.)
BL2450.H5	*FOLK-LORE OF THE HIPPOPOTAMUS* **SEE** HIPPOPOTAMUS (IN RELIGION, FOLK-LORE, ETC.)
GR910	FOLK-LORE OF THE SEA
GR620	FOLK-LORE OF THE SKY
BL325.S	*FOLK-LORE OF THE SWAN* **SEE** SWAN (IN RELIGION, FOLK-LORE, ETC.) / *mythology*
GR735	*FOLK-LORE OF THE SWAN* **SEE** SWAN (IN RELIGION, FOLK-LORE, ETC.) / *folk-lore*
PN687.S8	*FOLK-LORE OF THE SWAN* **SEE** SWAN (IN RELIGION, FOLK-LORE, ETC.) / *medieval legends*
BL820.T6	*FOLK-LORE OF THE TIBER RIVER* **SEE** TIBER RIVER (IN RELIGION, FOLK-LORE, ETC.)
GR785	FOLK-LORE OF TREES
BL604.T7	*FOLK-LORE OF TRIANGLES* **SEE** TRIANGLE (IN RELIGION, FOLK-LORE, ETC.)
GR830	*FOLK-LORE OF VAMPIRES* **SEE** VAMPIRES / *folk-lore*
BF1556	*FOLK-LORE OF VAMPIRES* **SEE** VAMPIRES / *occult sciences*
BL1475.W4	*FOLK-LORE OF WHEELS* **SEE** WHEELS (IN RELIGION, FOLK-LORE, ETC.)
GR635	*FOLK-LORE OF WINDS* **SEE** WINDS (IN RELIGION, FOLK-LORE, ETC.)
GR470	FOLK-LORE OF WOMAN
BF1779.W7	*FOLK-LORE OF WRITING* **SEE** WRITING (IN RELIGION, FOLK-LORE, ETC.)
GR	FOLK-LORE
DX157	FOLK-LORE, GIPSY
E98.F6	FOLK-LORE, INDIAN
GR350	FOLK-LORE, NEGRO / *africa*
GR103	FOLK-LORE, NEGRO / *u.s.*
GR40	*FOLK-LORE-METHODOLOGY* **SEE** FOLK-LORE — THEORY, METHODS, ETC.
GR40	*FOLK-LORE-THEMES, MOTIVES* **SEE** FOLK-LORE — CLASSIFICATION
Z5981-5	*FOLK-LORE-THEMES, MOTIVES* **SEE** FOLK-LORE — CLASSIFICATION
PN1008.D7	*FOLK-PLAYS* **SEE** FOLK-DRAMA / *history*
BF730-738	*FOLK-PSYCHOLOGY* **SEE** ETHNOPSYCHOLOGY
PN1341-5	FOLK-SONGS / *folk poetry*
M1627	FOLK-SONGS / *music*
ML3545	FOLK-SONGS / *music literature*
M1838.A5	FOLK-SONGS, ANGOLAN
M1838.C67	FOLK-SONGS, BAMBUTE
M1832.L85	FOLK-SONGS, LUNDA
M1831.L85	FOLK-SONGS, LUNDA
ML3556	*FOLK-SONGS, NEGRO (AMERICAN)* **SEE** NEGRO SONGS / *history*
M1670-1671	*FOLK-SONGS, NEGRO (AMERICAN)* **SEE** NEGRO SONGS / *music*
ML3556	*FOLK-SONGS, NEGRO* **SEE** NEGRO SONGS / *history*
M1670-1671	*FOLK-SONGS, NEGRO* **SEE** NEGRO SONGS / *music*
M1766.S4	FOLK-SONGS, SIBERIAN
M1767.S4	FOLK-SONGS, SIBERIAN
M1766.U95	FOLK-SONGS, UZBEK
M1767.U95	FOLK-SONGS, UZBEK
PN905-1008	*FOLK-TALES* **SEE** FOLK LITERATURE
GR	*FOLK-TALES* **SEE** FOLK-LORE
PN683-7	*FOLK-TALES* **SEE** LEGENDS
N7760	*FOLK-TALES* **SEE** LEGENDS / *iconography*
PZ8.1	*FOLK-TALES* **SEE** LEGENDS / *juvenile*

GR	*FOLKLORE* **SEE** FOLK-LORE
GR50	FOLKLORISTS
GT	*FOLKWAYS* **SEE** MANNERS AND CUSTOMS
NA8460	FOLLIES
NA8460	*FOLLY (ARCHITECTURE)* **SEE** FOLLIES
E98.I4	FOLSOM POINTS
PL8164.Z9	FON DIALECT
GN71-131	*FONTANEL* **SEE** SKULL / *anthropology*
QL821-3	*FONTANEL* **SEE** SKULL / *comparative anatomy*
QM105	*FONTANEL* **SEE** SKULL / *human anatomy*
GN71-131	*FONTANELLE* **SEE** SKULL / *anthropology*
QL821-3	*FONTANELLE* **SEE** SKULL / *comparative anatomy*
QM105	*FONTANELLE* **SEE** SKULL / *human anatomy*
D293.7.F6	FONTENOY, BATTLE OF, 1745
NA5070	FONTS
TX541-5	FOOD — ANALYSIS
QR115-129	FOOD — BACTERIOLOGY
TX351	FOOD — EARLY WORKS TO 1800
TX355	FOOD — JUVENILE LITERATURE
TX599-613	FOOD — PRESERVATION
TX645-840	*FOOD* **SEE** COOKERY
TX553.A3	FOOD ADDITIVES
HD9000.9	FOOD ADULTERATION AND INSPECTION / *economics*
TX501-595	FOOD ADULTERATION AND INSPECTION / *technical works*
RC596	FOOD ALLERGY
TX541-5	*FOOD CHEMISTRY* **SEE** FOOD — ANALYSIS
TX357	FOOD CONSERVATION
HD9000-9019	*FOOD CONTROL* **SEE** FOOD SUPPLY / *economics*
TX652	*FOOD DECORATION* **SEE** COOKERY (GARNISHES)
RM219	*FOOD FOR INVALIDS* **SEE** COOKERY FOR THE SICK
LB3473-9	*FOOD FOR SCHOOL CHILDREN* **SEE** SCHOOL CHILDREN — FOOD
QL756	*FOOD HABITS OF ANIMALS* **SEE** ANIMALS, FOOD HABITS OF
TX357	FOOD HABITS
GT2860	FOOD HABITS
TX537	FOOD HANDLING
TP370	FOOD INDUSTRY AND TRADE — SANITATION
HD9000.7-9	*FOOD INDUSTRY AND TRADE-LAW AND LEGISLATION* **SEE** FOOD LAW AND LEGISLATION
TX501-595	*FOOD INSPECTION* **SEE** FOOD ADULTERATION AND INSPECTION / *technical works*
HD9000.9	*FOOD INSPECTION* **SEE** FOOD ADULTERATION AND INSPECTION / *economics*
HD9000.7-9	FOOD LAW AND LEGISLATION
QK98.5	*FOOD PLANTS* **SEE** PLANTS, EDIBLE
RC143	FOOD POISONING
TX599-613	*FOOD PRESERVATION* **SEE** FOOD — PRESERVATION
QP981.P8	FOOD PRESERVATIVES — PHYSIOLOGICAL EFFECT
TX607-8	FOOD PRESERVATIVES
HV696.F6	FOOD RELIEF
TX341	FOOD RESEARCH
TX537	*FOOD SANITATION* **SEE** FOOD HANDLING
HV696.F6	*FOOD STAMP PLAN* **SEE** FOOD RELIEF
TX357	FOOD SUBSTITUTES
HC286.2	FOOD SUBSTITUTES / *european war*
HD9000-9019	FOOD SUPPLY / *economics*
S571	*FOOD TRADE* **SEE** FARM PRODUCE — MARKETING
HD9006	*FOOD TRADE* **SEE** FARM PRODUCE — MARKETING / *economics*
HD9000.6	*FOOD TRADE* **SEE** FARM PRODUCE — MARKETING / *economics*
HD9000-9019	*FOOD TRADE* **SEE** PRODUCE TRADE
TP370	*FOOD-PLANT SANITATION* **SEE** FOOD INDUSTRY AND TRADE — SANITATION
QH521	FOOD / *biology*
TP370-465	FOOD / *chemical technology*
RM214-261	FOOD / *diet*
TX341-641	FOOD / *home economics*
GT2860	FOOD / *manners and customs*
RA601-2	FOOD / *public health*
HD9000-9490	FOOD / *trade*
TX357	FOOD, ARTIFICIAL
RM258-261	FOOD, ARTIFICIAL / *diet*
TX552	FOOD, CANNED
TX541-5	*FOOD, CHEMISTRY OF* **SEE** FOOD — ANALYSIS
HD6977-7080	*FOOD, COST OF* **SEE** COST AND STANDARD OF LIVING

TX609	*FOOD, DEHYDRATED* **SEE** FOOD, DRIED
TP493.5	*FOOD, DEHYDROFROZEN* **SEE** FOOD, FROZEN
TX609	FOOD, DRIED
TP493.5	FOOD, FROZEN
HD9000.9	*FOOD, PURE* **SEE** FOOD ADULTERATION AND INSPECTION / *economics*
TX501-595	*FOOD, PURE* **SEE** FOOD ADULTERATION AND INSPECTION / *technical works*
HD9000.7-9	*FOOD, PURE* **SEE** FOOD LAW AND LEGISLATION
TX392	FOOD, RAW
TX541-5	*FOOD-CHEMISTRY* **SEE** FOOD — ANALYSIS
TX357	*FOOD-CONSERVATION* **SEE** FOOD CONSERVATION
TX501-595	*FOOD-INSPECTION* **SEE** FOOD ADULTERATION AND INSPECTION / *technical works*
HD9000.9	*FOOD-INSPECTION* **SEE** FOOD ADULTERATION AND INSPECTION / *economics*
HD9000.7-9	*FOOD-LAW AND LEGISLATION* **SEE** FOOD LAW AND LEGISLATION
TX341	*FOOD-RESEARCH* **SEE** FOOD RESEARCH
GT3670	FOOLS AND JESTERS
GT4995.F6	FOOLS, FEAST OF
QM691	FOOT — ABNORMITIES AND DEFORMITIES
RD781-9	FOOT — ABNORMITIES AND DEFORMITIES / *surgical treatment*
GN477.6	FOOT — ARTIFICIAL DEFORMITIES
RC951	FOOT — DISEASES
RD551-3	FOOT — SURGERY
GV1061-9	*FOOT RACING* **SEE** RUNNING
SF968	FOOT ROT IN SHEEP
UD	*FOOT SOLDIERS* **SEE** INFANTRY
BV873.F7	FOOT WASHING (RITE)
SF793	FOOT-AND-MOUTH DISEASE
GV939-959	*FOOT-BALL* **SEE** FOOTBALL
QM549	FOOT
QL950.7	FOOT
BV873.F7	*FOOT, WASHING OF* **SEE** FOOT WASHING (RITE)
E381	FOOT'S RESOLUTION, 1829
GV951.1	FOOTBALL — DEFENSE
GV955	FOOTBALL — RULES
M1977.S718	FOOTBALL — SONGS AND MUSIC
M1978.S718	FOOTBALL — SONGS AND MUSIC
GV959	FOOTBALL SCOUTING
GV939-959	FOOTBALL
QE845	FOOTPRINTS, FOSSIL
GT2130	*FOOTWEAR* **SEE** BOOTS AND SHOES / *manners and customs*
SB193-207	FORAGE PLANTS
SF95-99	FORAGE / *animal culture*
UC660-665	FORAGE / *military science*
QL368.F6	FORAMINIFERA
QE772	FORAMINIFERA, FOSSIL
E199	FORBES EXPEDITION AGAINST FORT DUQUESNE, 1758
QC73	FORCE AND ENERGY
TJ900-925	*FORCE PUMPS* **SEE** PUMPING MACHINERY
QC73	*FORCE, CENTRIFUGAL* **SEE** CENTRIFUGAL FORCE
QC618	*FORCE, ELECTROMOTIVE* **SEE** ELECTROMOTIVE FORCE
QD561	*FORCE, ELECTROMOTIVE* **SEE** ELECTROMOTIVE FORCE / *electrolysis*
QH341	*FORCE, VITAL* **SEE** VITAL FORCE
HJ8047	FORCED LOANS
RD73.F7	FORCEPS
RG739	FORCEPS, OBSTETRIC
QA823	FORCES AND COUPLES
QA831	FORCES AND COUPLES
SB127	FORCING (PLANTS)
TL215.F7	FORD AUTOMOBILE
ND2370	FORE-EDGE PAINTING
QC995	*FORECASTING, WEATHER* **SEE** WEATHER FORECASTING
JX1896	*FOREIGN AGENTS IN THE U.S.* **SEE** FOREIGN PROPAGANDISTS IN THE U.S.
D16.25	*FOREIGN AREA STUDIES* **SEE** AREA STUDIES
HG3811-4000	FOREIGN EXCHANGE
HG219	*FOREIGN EXCHANGE-TABLES, ETC.* **SEE** MONEY — TABLES, ETC.
HG4538	*FOREIGN INVESTMENTS* **SEE** INVESTMENTS, FOREIGN
JX6607	*FOREIGN JUDGMENTS* **SEE** JUDGMENTS, FOREIGN
BV2000-3705	*FOREIGN MISSIONS* **SEE** MISSIONS, FOREIGN

JV6001-9500	*FOREIGN POPULATION* **SEE** EMIGRATION AND IMMIGRATION
Z711.8	*FOREIGN POPULATION* **SEE** LIBRARIES AND FOREIGN POPULATION
JX1896	FOREIGN PROPAGANDISTS IN THE U.S.
JX4263.P6	*FOREIGN PROPERTY* **SEE** ALIEN PROPERTY
HF	*FOREIGN TRADE* **SEE** COMMERCE
GT6010-6050	*FOREIGN TRADE* **SEE** COMMERCE / *commercial customs*
GN436-440	*FOREIGN TRADE* **SEE** COMMERCE / *primitive*
HF1418	*FOREIGN TRADE ZONES* **SEE** FREE PORTS AND ZONES
JV6001-9500	*FOREIGNERS* **SEE** ALIENS / *emigration and immigration*
D570.8.A6	*FOREIGNERS* **SEE** ALIENS / *european war u.s.*
JX4203-4270	*FOREIGNERS* **SEE** ALIENS / *nationality and alienage*
D636.A3-Z	*FOREIGNERS* **SEE** ALIENS / *other countries*
D801	*FOREIGNERS* **SEE** ALIENS / *other countries*
D769.8.A6	*FOREIGNERS* **SEE** ALIENS / *world war u.s.*
JX4216	*FOREIGNERS* **SEE** NATURALIZATION / *international law*
JF811	*FOREIGNERS* **SEE** NATURALIZATION / *theory*
JK1800-1836	*FOREIGNERS* **SEE** NATURALIZATION / *u.s.*
BV639.I4	*FOREIGNERS, CHURCH WORK WITH* **SEE** CHURCH WORK WITH FOREIGNERS / *immigrants*
HF5549	FOREMEN / *business management*
T56	FOREMEN / *technology*
TS155	FOREMEN / *technology*
HD6490.F6	FOREMEN'S UNIONS
CS2300-2389	*FORENAMES* **SEE** NAMES, PERSONAL
HV8077	FORENSIC BALLISTICS
HV8073	*FORENSIC CHEMISTRY* **SEE** CHEMISTRY, FORENSIC
RA1057	*FORENSIC CHEMISTRY* **SEE** CHEMISTRY, FORENSIC / *medical jurisprudence*
RK1062	*FORENSIC DENTISTRY* **SEE** DENTAL JURISPRUDENCE
RA1001-1171	*FORENSIC MEDICINE* **SEE** MEDICAL JURISPRUDENCE
RA1147	FORENSIC NEUROLOGY
RA1147	*FORENSIC NEUROPATHOLOGY* **SEE** FORENSIC NEUROLOGY
TR830	*FORENSIC PHOTOGRAPHY* **SEE** PHOTOGRAPHY, LEGAL
HV6071	*FORENSIC PHOTOGRAPHY* **SEE** PHOTOGRAPHY, LEGAL / *social pathology*
HV8077	*FORENSIC PHOTOGRAPHY* **SEE** PHOTOGRAPHY, LEGAL / *social pathology*
RA1151	FORENSIC PSYCHIATRY
BT810	*FOREORDINATION* **SEE** PREDESTINATION
SB411-428	FOREST CONSERVATION
SD	*FOREST ECONOMICS* **SEE** FORESTS AND FORESTRY — ECONOMIC ASPECTS
SB761	*FOREST ENTOMOLOGY* **SEE** FOREST INSECTS
QL112	FOREST FAUNA
SD408	*FOREST FERTILIZATION* **SEE** FOREST SOILS — FERTILIZATION
SD421	*FOREST FIRE CONTROL* **SEE** FOREST FIRES — PREVENTION AND CONTROL
SD421	*FOREST FIRE FIGHTING* **SEE** FOREST FIRES — PREVENTION AND CONTROL
HG9970.F	*FOREST FIRE INSURANCE* **SEE** INSURANCE, FOREST
SD421	FOREST FIRES — PREVENTION AND CONTROL
SD421	FOREST FIRES
SD421	*FOREST FIRES-CONTROL* **SEE** FOREST FIRES — PREVENTION AND CONTROL
SD421	*FOREST FIRES-EXTINCTION* **SEE** FOREST FIRES — PREVENTION AND CONTROL
SD	*FOREST FLORA* **SEE** FORESTS AND FORESTRY
HJ3805	*FOREST FLORA* **SEE** FORESTS AND FORESTRY / *income from state forests*
HJ4167	*FOREST FLORA* **SEE** FORESTS AND FORESTRY / *taxation*
SD425	FOREST INFLUENCES
SB761	FOREST INSECTS
HG9970.F	*FOREST INSURANCE* **SEE** INSURANCE, FOREST
SD561-668	*FOREST LAW* **SEE** FORESTRY LAW AND LEGISLATION
SD551-7	*FOREST MENSURATION* **SEE** FORESTS AND FORESTRY — MENSURATION
SD401	FOREST NURSERIES
SD409	*FOREST PLANTING* **SEE** AFFORESTATION
SD	*FOREST PLANTING* **SEE** FORESTS AND FORESTRY

HJ4167	*FOREST PLANTING* **SEE** FORESTS AND FORESTRY / *taxation*
SD561-668	FOREST POLICY
HD9750-9769	FOREST PRODUCTS / *economics*
SD	FOREST PRODUCTS / *forestry*
SD561-668	*FOREST PROTECTION-LAW AND LEGISLATION* **SEE** FORESTRY LAW AND LEGISLATION
SD426-8	FOREST RESERVES
SD408	FOREST SOILS — FERTILIZATION
SD396.5	FOREST THINNING
SD551-7	*FOREST VALUATION* **SEE** FORESTS AND FORESTRY — VALUATION
HD2709-2930	*FORESTALLING* **SEE** MONOPOLIES
SD409	*FORESTATION* **SEE** AFFORESTATION
SD	*FORESTATION* **SEE** FORESTS AND FORESTRY
HJ3805	*FORESTATION* **SEE** FORESTS AND FORESTRY / *income from state forests*
HJ4167	*FORESTATION* **SEE** FORESTS AND FORESTRY / *taxation*
SD409	*FORESTATION* **SEE** REFORESTATION
SD127	FORESTERS
SD561-668	*FORESTRY AND STATE* **SEE** FOREST POLICY
SD251-356	*FORESTRY EDUCATION* **SEE** FORESTRY SCHOOLS AND EDUCATION
SD388	FORESTRY ENGINEERING
SD561-668	FORESTRY LAW AND LEGISLATION
SD251-356	FORESTRY SCHOOLS AND EDUCATION
SD1	FORESTRY SOCIETIES
SD425	*FORESTS AND CLIMATE* **SEE** FOREST INFLUENCES
SD425	*FORESTS AND FLOODS* **SEE** FOREST INFLUENCES
SD118	FORESTS AND FORESTRY — CONGRESSES
SD	FORESTS AND FORESTRY — ECONOMIC ASPECTS
SD359	FORESTS AND FORESTRY — EXPERIMENTAL AREAS
SD551-7	FORESTS AND FORESTRY — MENSURATION
SD411	FORESTS AND FORESTRY — SAFETY MEASURES
SD551-7	FORESTS AND FORESTRY — VALUATION
SD	FORESTS AND FORESTRY
HJ3805	FORESTS AND FORESTRY / *income from state forests*
HJ4167	FORESTS AND FORESTRY / *taxation*
SD388	*FORESTS AND FORESTRY-ENGINEERING* **SEE** FORESTRY ENGINEERING
SD	*FORESTS AND FORESTRY-FINANCE* **SEE** FORESTS AND FORESTRY — ECONOMIC ASPECTS
SD561-668	*FORESTS AND FORESTRY-LAW* **SEE** FORESTRY LAW AND LEGISLATION
SD251-356	*FORESTS AND FORESTRY-STUDY AND TEACHING* **SEE** FORESTRY SCHOOLS AND EDUCATION
SD396.5	*FORESTS AND FORESTRY-THINNING* **SEE** FOREST THINNING
SD425	*FORESTS AND RAINFALL* **SEE** FOREST INFLUENCES
SD425	*FORESTS AND WATER-SUPPLY* **SEE** FOREST INFLUENCES
SD426-8	*FORESTS, NATIONAL* **SEE** FOREST RESERVES
QE991	*FORESTS, PETRIFIED* **SEE** PETRIFIED FORESTS
GB481-8	FORESTS, SUBMERGED
TS225	FORGE SHOPS
TS555	*FORGED ALUMINUM* **SEE** ALUMINUM FORGINGS
CC140	FORGERY OF ANTIQUITIES
Z41	FORGERY OF MANUSCRIPTS / *autographs*
BX875	FORGERY OF MANUSCRIPTS / *church history*
PN171.F6-7	FORGERY OF MANUSCRIPTS / *literature*
N8790	FORGERY OF WORKS OF ART
HV6675-6685	FORGERY
Z41	FORGERY / *autographs*
HG1696-8	FORGERY / *checks*
TS225	*FORGES* **SEE** FORGE SHOPS
SB413	FORGET-ME-NOTS / *culture*
LB1063	*FORGETFULNESS* **SEE** MEMORY / *educational*
BF370-385	*FORGETFULNESS* **SEE** MEMORY / *psychology*
TS225	FORGING / *manufacture*
TT215-240	FORGING / *shop work*
BP134.F6	FORGIVENESS OF SIN (ISLAM) / *koran*
BT795	FORGIVENESS OF SIN
TX298-9	FORKS / *household utensils*
NK7230-7240	FORKS / *silver*
BH301.F6	FORM (AESTHETICS)
BD648	*FORM AND MATTER* **SEE** HYLOMORPHISM
BF203	*FORM PSYCHOLOGY* **SEE** GESTALT PSYCHOLOGY
ML448	*FORM, MUSICAL* **SEE** MUSICAL FORM / *history*

SB451-466	*FORMAL GARDENS* **SEE** GARDENS
RA1242.F6	FORMALDEHYDE — TOXICOLOGY
TP248.F6	FORMALDEHYDE / *chemical technology*
QD305.A6	FORMALDEHYDE / *chemistry*
RA766.F6	FORMALDEHYDE / *disinfectants*
TP248.F6	*FORMALIN* **SEE** FORMALDEHYDE / *chemical technology*
QD305.A6	*FORMALIN* **SEE** FORMALDEHYDE / *chemistry*
RA766.F6	*FORMALIN* **SEE** FORMALDEHYDE / *disinfectants*
QD305.A2	FORMIC ACID / *chemistry*
RM666.F6	FORMIC ACID / *therapeutics*
QL568.F7	*FORMICIDAE* **SEE** ANTS
PL5321	FORMOSAN LANGUAGES
HF5371	*FORMS (BUSINESS)* **SEE** BUSINESS — FORMS, BLANKS, ETC.
BX1939.F6	FORMS (CANON LAW)
TA681	*FORMS (CONCRETE CONSTRUCTION)* **SEE** CONCRETE CONSTRUCTION — FORMWORK
HF1243	FORMS (LAW) / *commercial law u.s.*
QA201	FORMS (MATHEMATICS)
QA243-4	FORMS (MATHEMATICS)
CR3499-4420	FORMS OF ADDRESS
QA381	*FORMS, DIFFERENTIAL* **SEE** DIFFERENTIAL FORMS
QA201	FORMS, QUADRILINEAR
CD80	FORMULARIES (DIPLOMATICS)
RS125-7	*FORMULARIES, MEDICAL* **SEE** MEDICINE — FORMULAE, RECEIPTS, PRESCRIPTIONS
QA41	*FORMULAS (MATHEMATICS)* **SEE** MATHEMATICS — FORMULAE
DG541	FORNOVO, BATTLE OF, 1495
E477.63	*FORT FISHER EXPEDITIONS* **SEE** FISHER, FORT — EXPEDITIONS, 1864-1865
E356.B2	*FORT MCHENRY, MD., BOMBARDMENT OF* **SEE** BALTIMORE, BATTLE OF, 1814
E476.17	FORT PILLOW, BATTLE OF, 1864
E476.66	FORT STEVENS, D.C., BATTLE OF, 1864
UG400	FORTIFICATION — EARLY WORKS TO 1800
UG400-409	FORTIFICATION
UG403	FORTIFICATION, FIELD
GN789	FORTIFICATION, PRIMITIVE
UG443-9	*FORTIFICATIONS, ATTACK AND DEFENSE OF* **SEE** ATTACK AND DEFENSE (MILITARY SCIENCE)
F2688.5	*FORTIN BOQUERON, BATTLE OF, 1932* **SEE** BOQUERON, BATTLE OF, 1932
BV4647.F6	FORTITUDE
UG443-9	*FORTRESS WARFARE* **SEE** ATTACK AND DEFENSE (MILITARY SCIENCE)
UG400-409	*FORTS* **SEE** FORTIFICATION
BF1891.F6	FORTUNE-TELLING BY DICE
BF1850-1891	FORTUNE-TELLING
G539	*FORTUNE, SOLDIERS OF* **SEE** SOLDIERS OF FORTUNE
HC	*FORTUNES* **SEE** INCOME / *national income*
HB601	*FORTUNES* **SEE** INCOME / *theory*
HB821	*FORTUNES* **SEE** WEALTH / *distribution*
HB251	*FORTUNES* **SEE** WEALTH / *theory*
HB831-8	*FORTUNES* **SEE** WEALTH / *use*
BX2169	FORTY HOURS' DEVOTION
GV1295.F7	FORTY-FIVE (GAME)
LC6501-6560	*FORUM, OPEN* **SEE** FORUMS (DISCUSSION AND DEBATE)
PN4177-4191	*FORUM, OPEN* **SEE** FORUMS (DISCUSSION AND DEBATE) / *debating*
LC6501-6560	FORUMS (DISCUSSION AND DEBATE)
PN4177-4191	FORUMS (DISCUSSION AND DEBATE) / *debating*
QE832.C6	*FOSSIL BEETLES* **SEE** BEETLES, FOSSIL
QE871-5	*FOSSIL BIRDS* **SEE** BIRDS, FOSSIL
QE901-996	*FOSSIL BOTANY* **SEE** PALEOBOTANY
QE832.L5	*FOSSIL BUTTERFLIES* **SEE** BUTTERFLIES, FOSSIL
TN948.D5	*FOSSIL DUST* **SEE** DIATOMACEOUS EARTH
QE875	*FOSSIL EGGS* **SEE** BIRDS, FOSSIL — EGGS
QE845	*FOSSIL FOOTPRINTS* **SEE** FOOTPRINTS, FOSSIL
QE901-996	*FOSSIL PLANTS* **SEE** PALEOBOTANY
QE845	*FOSSIL TRACKS* **SEE** FOOTPRINTS, FOSSIL
QE991	*FOSSIL WOOD* **SEE** TREES, FOSSIL
QE701-996	*FOSSILS* **SEE** PALEONTOLOGY
HV875	*FOSTER CARE, HOME* **SEE** FOSTER HOME CARE
HV875	*FOSTER FAMILY CARE* **SEE** FOSTER HOME CARE
HV875	FOSTER HOME CARE
QB633	FOUCAULT'S PENDULUM

GN652.F9	*FOULAHS* **SEE** FULAHS
HV16-25	*FOUNDATIONS (ENDOWMENTS)* **SEE** ENDOWMENTS / *charities*
LB2336-7	*FOUNDATIONS (ENDOWMENTS)* **SEE** ENDOWMENTS / *higher education*
QA248	*FOUNDATIONS OF ARITHMETIC* **SEE** ARITHMETIC — FOUNDATIONS
QA681	*FOUNDATIONS OF GEOMETRY* **SEE** GEOMETRY — FOUNDATIONS
TH5201	FOUNDATIONS / *building construction*
TH2101	FOUNDATIONS / *building design*
TA775-787	FOUNDATIONS / *engineering*
TC197	FOUNDATIONS / *hydraulic engineering*
HF5686.F65	FOUNDING — ACCOUNTING
TS233	FOUNDING — SAFETY MEASURES
TS235	FOUNDING — TABLES, CALCULATIONS, ETC.
TS229-240	FOUNDING
HV835-847	FOUNDLINGS
TS233	FOUNDRIES — AUTOMATION
TS238	FOUNDRIES — MANAGEMENT
TS236	FOUNDRIES — SAFETY MEASURES
TS229-238	FOUNDRIES
QD133	FOUNDRY CHEMISTRY
TS229-240	*FOUNDRY PRACTICE* **SEE** FOUNDING
TS243.5	*FOUNDRY SAND* **SEE** SAND, FOUNDRY
NA9400-9425	FOUNTAINS
M1105-6	*FOUR CLARINETS WITH STRING ORCHESTRA* **SEE** CLARINETS (4) WITH STRING ORCHESTRA
M1105-6	*FOUR HARPSICHORDS WITH STRING ORCHESTRA* **SEE** HARPSICHORDS (4) WITH STRING ORCHESTRA
M1028-9	*FOUR HORNS WITH ORCHESTRA* **SEE** HORNS (4) WITH ORCHESTRA
QA404	*FOURIER INTEGRALS* **SEE** FOURIER SERIES
QA404	FOURIER SERIES
QA699	FOURTH DIMENSION
RC182.R8	*FOURTH DISEASE* **SEE** RUBELLA
M1629.3.F6	FOURTH OF JULY — SONGS AND MUSIC
E286	FOURTH OF JULY CELEBRATIONS
PN4305.H7	FOURTH OF JULY CELEBRATIONS / *recitations*
E286	FOURTH OF JULY ORATIONS
SF995	*FOWL POX* **SEE** CHICKEN-POX IN POULTRY
SF995	FOWL TYPHOID
SK311-333	FOWLING
TX556.P9	*FOWLS* **SEE** POULTRY
SF481-507	*FOWLS* **SEE** POULTRY
TX375	*FOWLS* **SEE** POULTRY
QL795.F8	*FOX* **SEE** FOXES / *stories and anecdotes*
QL737.C2	*FOX* **SEE** FOXES / *zoology*
E99.F7	FOX INDIANS
PM1195	FOX LANGUAGE
GV1796.F6	FOX TROT
M1264	FOX TROTS (BAND)
M1248	FOX TROTS (BAND)
SB994.F6	*FOX-BATS* **SEE** FLYING FOXES / *noxious animals*
QL737.C5	*FOX-BATS* **SEE** FLYING FOXES / *zoology*
SK284-7	FOX-HUNTING
SF429.F5	FOX-TERRIERS
QL795.F8	FOXES / *stories and anecdotes*
QL737.C2	FOXES / *zoology*
UG403	*FOXHOLES* **SEE** INTRENCHMENTS / *field fortification*
UG446	*FOXHOLES* **SEE** INTRENCHMENTS / *trenches and trench warfare*
SF429.F6	FOXHOUNDS
SB201.F	FOXTAIL / *agriculture*
QK495.G74	FOXTAIL / *botany*
SB608.F7	FOXTAIL / *diseases and pests*
QD526	*FRACTIONAL DISTILLATION* **SEE** DISTILLATION, FRACTIONAL
TK2537	*FRACTIONAL HORSEPOWER ELECTRIC MOTORS* **SEE** ELECTRIC MOTORS, FRACTIONAL HORSEPOWER
QA117	FRACTIONS — TABLES, ETC.
QA117	FRACTIONS
QA137	FRACTIONS / *methods of teaching*
QA295	FRACTIONS, CONTINUED
QA242	FRACTIONS, DECIMAL / *theory of numbers*
RD101	FRACTURES
RD101	FRACTURES, SPONTANEOUS
Z1033.U6	*FRAGMENTARY BOOKS* **SEE** UNFINISHED BOOKS
G7002 1893	FRAM EXPEDITION, 1ST, 1893-1896
G6702 1898	FRAM EXPEDITION, 2D, 1898-1902

RC205	*FRAMBOESIA* **SEE** YAWS
PN3383.F7	FRAME-STORIES
TG260	*FRAMED STRUCTURES* **SEE** STRUCTURAL FRAMES
TG260	*FRAMES (STRUCTURES)* **SEE** STRUCTURAL FRAMES
TG260	*FRAMEWORKS (STRUCTURES)* **SEE** STRUCTURAL FRAMES
TH2301	FRAMING (BUILDING)
N8550-8553	*FRAMING OF PICTURES* **SEE** PICTURE FRAMES AND FRAMING
N8550-8553	*FRAMING OF PICTURES* **SEE** PICTURE FRAMES AND FRAMING
DC	FRANCE — HISTORY
PN56.F	FRANCE IN LITERATURE
DR567	*FRANCE-HISTORY-CRIMEAN WAR, 1853-1856* **SEE** CRIMEAN WAR, 1853-1856 / *turkey*
DK214-215	*FRANCE-HISTORY-CRIMEAN WAR, 1853-1856* **SEE** CRIMEAN WAR, 1853-1856 / *russia*
DC281-326	*FRANCE-HISTORY-FRANCO-GERMAN WAR, 1870-1871* **SEE** FRANCO-GERMAN WAR, 1870-1871
DC397	FRANCE — HISTORY — — GERMAN OCCUPATION, 1940-1945
DC139-195	FRANCE — HISTORY — — REVOLUTION
JF1001-1191	*FRANCHISE* **SEE** ELECTIONS
JK1951-2246	*FRANCHISE* **SEE** ELECTIONS / *u.s.*
JK2700-9595	*FRANCHISE* **SEE** ELECTIONS / *u.s.*
JF825-1191	*FRANCHISE* **SEE** SUFFRAGE
JC75.S8	*FRANCHISE* **SEE** SUFFRAGE / *ancient greece*
JC85.S8	*FRANCHISE* **SEE** SUFFRAGE / *ancient rome*
JS393	*FRANCHISE* **SEE** SUFFRAGE / *municipal js215 u.s.*
JS1700	*FRANCHISE* **SEE** SUFFRAGE / *other countries*
JK1846-1936	*FRANCHISE* **SEE** SUFFRAGE / *u.s.*
HD2763-8	*FRANCHISES, MUNICIPAL* **SEE** MUNICIPAL FRANCHISES
HD2753	*FRANCHISES-TAXATION* **SEE** CORPORATIONS — TAXATION
BX3980	*FRANCISCAN RECOLLETS* **SEE** RECOLLETS (FRANCISCAN)
Z7840.F8	FRANCISCANS — BIO-BIBLIOGRAPHY
BV2280	FRANCISCANS — MISSIONS
BX4361-4	*FRANCISCANS. SECOND ORDER* **SEE** POOR CLARES
BX3601-3655	FRANCISCANS
BX4361-4	FRANCISCANS / *women*
DS549	*FRANCO-CHINESE WAR, 1884-1885* **SEE** CHINESE-FRENCH WAR, 1884-1885
E199	*FRANCO-ENGLISH WAR, 1755-1763* **SEE** UNITED STATES — HISTORY — — FRENCH AND INDIAN WAR, 1755-1763
DC300	FRANCO-GERMAN WAR, 1870-1871 — ARMISTICE
DC281-326	FRANCO-GERMAN WAR, 1870-1871
PC3081-3148	FRANCO-PROVENCAL DIALECTS
DC281-326	*FRANCO-PRUSSIAN WAR, 1870-1871* **SEE** FRANCO-GERMAN WAR, 1870-1871
D397	FRANCO-RUSSIAN ALLIANCE
DC124.45	FRANCO-SPANISH WAR, 1635-1659
D275-6	*FRANCO-SPANISH WAR, 1667-1668* **SEE** DEVOLUTION, WAR OF, 1667-1668
D25.5	*FRANCS-TIREURS* **SEE** GUERRILLAS
QP981.F	FRANGULA / *experimental pharmacology*
RM666.F	FRANGULA / *therapeutics*
NK4399.F8	FRANKENTHAL PORCELAIN
DC300	FRANKFURT AM MAIN, PEACE OF, 1871
HE6148	FRANKING PRIVILEGE
HE6448	FRANKING PRIVILEGE / *u.s.*
E477.52	FRANKLIN, TENN., BATTLE OF, 1864
DC64-81	FRANKS
DH576	FRANKS / *belgium*
DD127-134	FRANKS / *germany*
DG515	FRANKS / *italy*
DH151	FRANKS / *netherlands*
HS1501-1510	*FRATERNAL BENEFIT SOCIETIES* **SEE** FRIENDLY SOCIETIES
HG9201-9245	*FRATERNAL BENEFIT SOCIETIES* **SEE** FRIENDLY SOCIETIES / *fraternal insurance*
J	*FRATERNITIES* **SEE** GREEK LETTER SOCIETIES
HD4889	*FRATERNITIES* **SEE** INITIATIONS (INTO TRADES, SOCIETIES, ETC.) / *labor*
HS	*FRATERNITIES* **SEE** SECRET SOCIETIES
GN495.2	*FRATERNITIES* **SEE** SECRET SOCIETIES / *primitive*
B3602	*FRATERNITIES* **SEE** STUDENTS' SOCIETIES
M1960	FRATERNITY SONGS
BX3602	FRATICELLI
HE6323	*FRAUD ORDERS* **SEE** POSTAL SERVICE — U.S. — — LAWS AND REGULATIONS
HV6691-9	FRAUD
PN171.F6-7	*FRAUDS, LITERARY* **SEE** LITERARY FORGERIES AND MYSTIFICATIONS
QM691-9	*FREAKS* **SEE** DEFORMITIES / *human anatomy*
GN68-69.8	*FREAKS* **SEE** DEFORMITIES / *somatic anthropology*
QL991	*FREAKS* **SEE** MONSTERS / *animals*
GR825-830	*FREAKS* **SEE** MONSTERS / *folk-lore*
QM691-9	*FREAKS* **SEE** MONSTERS / *human anatomy*
E474.85	FREDERICKSBURG, BATTLE OF, 1862
QA431	*FREDHOLM'S EQUATION* **SEE** INTEGRAL EQUATIONS
F389	FREDONIAN INSURRECTION, 1826-1827 / *texas*
BJ1460-1468	*FREE AGENCY* **SEE** FREE WILL AND DETERMINISM / *ethics*
BF620-628	*FREE AGENCY* **SEE** FREE WILL AND DETERMINISM / *psychology*
HG2471-8	FREE BANKING / *u.s.*
HD4903	FREE CHOICE OF EMPLOYMENT
BX9084	FREE CHURCH OF SCOTLAND
JX4068.I6	*FREE CITIES* **SEE** INTERNATIONALIZED TERRITORIES
HG651-1490	*FREE COINAGE* **SEE** CURRENCY QUESTION / *other countries*
HG501-538	*FREE COINAGE* **SEE** CURRENCY QUESTION / *u.s.*
HG527-538	*FREE COINAGE* **SEE** SILVER QUESTION
HB95	*FREE ENTERPRISE* **SEE** LAISSEZ-FAIRE
HF1418	*FREE HARBORS* **SEE** FREE PORTS AND ZONES
HQ961-7	FREE LOVE
HX546	FREE LOVE / *socialism and free love*
TJ779	FREE PISTON ENGINES
HF1418	FREE PORTS AND ZONES
L-LC	*FREE SCHOOLS* **SEE** PUBLIC SCHOOLS
S21.Z2-8	*FREE SEED DISTRIBUTION* **SEE** SEED DISTRIBUTION / *congressional committee hearings*
S21.S2	*FREE SEED DISTRIBUTION* **SEE** SEED DISTRIBUTION / *dept. of agriculture publications*
JC591	*FREE SPEECH* **SEE** LIBERTY OF SPEECH
BL2700-2790	FREE THOUGHT
HF1701-2580	FREE TRADE AND PROTECTION — FREE TRADE
HF1701-2580	FREE TRADE AND PROTECTION — PROTECTION
HF1701-2701	FREE TRADE AND PROTECTION
PN1059.F	FREE VERSE
BP166.3	FREE WILL AND DETERMINISM (ISLAM)
BJ1460-1468	FREE WILL AND DETERMINISM / *ethics*
BF620-628	FREE WILL AND DETERMINISM / *psychology*
HF1418	*FREE ZONES* **SEE** FREE PORTS AND ZONES
JK2336	FREE-SOIL PARTY
VK237	*FREEBOARD, TABLES OF* **SEE** LOAD-LINE
VM155	*FREEBOARD, TABLES OF* **SEE** SHIPS — MEASUREMENT
G535-7	*FREEBOOTERS* **SEE** BUCCANEERS
F2161	*FREEBOOTERS* **SEE** BUCCANEERS
G539	*FREEBOOTERS* **SEE** FILIBUSTERS
G535-7	*FREEBOOTERS* **SEE** PIRATES
JX4444.6	*FREEBOOTERS* **SEE** PIRATES / *international law*
HT731	FREEDMEN
E185.2	FREEDMEN / *u.s.*
JC585-599	*FREEDOM* **SEE** LIBERTY / *political theory*
HM271	*FREEDOM* **SEE** LIBERTY / *sociology*
HT851-1445	*FREEDOM* **SEE** SLAVERY
JC607	FREEDOM OF ASSOCIATION
JK-JQ	FREEDOM OF ASSOCIATION
BJ1468.5	*FREEDOM OF DECISION (ETHICS)* **SEE** DECISION-MAKING (ETHICS)
HD4903	*FREEDOM OF EMPLOYMENT* **SEE** FREE CHOICE OF EMPLOYMENT
HD4903	*FREEDOM OF OCCUPATION* **SEE** FREE CHOICE OF EMPLOYMENT
BV741	*FREEDOM OF RELIGION* **SEE** RELIGIOUS LIBERTY
JC591	*FREEDOM OF SPEECH* **SEE** LIBERTY OF SPEECH
BV740	*FREEDOM OF SPEECH IN THE CHURCH* **SEE** LIBERTY OF SPEECH IN THE CHURCH
LB2332	*FREEDOM OF TEACHING* **SEE** TEACHING, FREEDOM OF
JX5771	*FREEDOM OF THE AIR* **SEE** AIRSPACE (INTERNATIONAL LAW)

D580	FREEDOM OF THE SEAS / *european war*
JX4423-5	FREEDOM OF THE SEAS / *international law*
JX5203-5268	FREEDOM OF THE SEAS / *maritime war international law*
BJ1460-1468	*FREEDOM OF THE WILL* **SEE** FREE WILL AND DETERMINISM / *ethics*
BF620-628	*FREEDOM OF THE WILL* **SEE** FREE WILL AND DETERMINISM / *psychology*
BV741	*FREEDOM OF WORSHIP* **SEE** RELIGIOUS LIBERTY
JK4	FREEDOM TRAIN
HD101-1395	*FREEHOLD* **SEE** LAND TENURE
HD301-1130	*FREEHOLD* **SEE** REAL PROPERTY / *other countries*
HD251-279	*FREEHOLD* **SEE** REAL PROPERTY / *u. s.*
HD251-279	*FREEHOLD* **SEE** REAL PROPERTY / *u.s.*
E241.S2	*FREEMAN'S FARM, BATTLE OF, 1777* **SEE** SARATOGA CAMPAIGN, 1777
HS351-929	*FREEMASONRY* **SEE** FREEMASONS
HS551-680	*FREEMASONRY* **SEE** FREEMASONS / *other countries*
HS505-539	*FREEMASONRY* **SEE** FREEMASONS / *u.s.*
HS397	FREEMASONS — ADDRESSES, ESSAYS, LECTURES
HS399-400	FREEMASONS — BIOGRAPHY
HS471	FREEMASONS — CHARITIES
HS463-5	FREEMASONS — COSTUMES, SUPPLIES, ETC.
HS375	FREEMASONS — DICTIONARIES
HS381	FREEMASONS — DIRECTORIES
HS390	FREEMASONS — DIRECTORIES / *other countries*
HS383-7	FREEMASONS — DIRECTORIES / *u.s.*
HS435	FREEMASONS — FICTION
HS403-418	FREEMASONS — HISTORY
HS440-447	FREEMASONS — LAWS, DECISIONS, ETC.
HS396	FREEMASONS — LODGE MANAGEMENT
HS433	FREEMASONS — MEDALS
HS351-9	FREEMASONS — PERIODICALS
HS431	FREEMASONS — POETRY
HS455-9	FREEMASONS — RITUALS
HS453-4	FREEMASONS — SONGS AND MUSIC
M1900-1901	FREEMASONS — SONGS AND MUSIC
HS425	FREEMASONS — SYMBOLISM
HS365	FREEMASONS — YEARBOOKS
HS495	FREEMASONS AND CATHOLIC CHURCH
HS351-929	FREEMASONS
HS551-680	FREEMASONS / *other countries*
HS505-539	FREEMASONS / *u.s.*
HS417.A3	FREEMASONS, ADONHIRAMITE
HS875-891	FREEMASONS, NEGRO
HS455-9	*FREEMASONS-MONITORS* **SEE** FREEMASONS — RITUALS
QC929.H6	*FREEZING* **SEE** FROST
GB2401-2597	*FREEZING* **SEE** ICE
TP490-497	*FREEZING* **SEE** REFRIGERATION AND REFRIGERATING MACHINERY
TA713	*FREEZING* **SEE** SOIL FREEZING
GB1201-1397	*FREEZING AND OPENING OF RIVERS, LAKES, ETC.* **SEE** ICE ON RIVERS, LAKES, ETC. (INDIRECT) / *rivers*
GB1601-1797	*FREEZING AND OPENING OF RIVERS, LAKES, ETC.* **SEE** ICE ON RIVERS, LAKES, ETC. (INDIRECT) / *lakes*
QD545	*FREEZING POINTS OF SOLUTIONS* **SEE** CRYOSCOPY
QD545	*FREEZING POINTS OF SOLUTIONS* **SEE** MOLECULAR WEIGHTS
QD545	FREEZING POINTS
TA713	*FREEZING PROCESS (CIVIL ENGINEERING)* **SEE** SOIL FREEZING
QL696.S6	*FREGATIDAE* **SEE** FRIGATE-BIRDS
D267.F85	FREIBURG I. B., BATTLE OF, 1644
HE1795	FREIGHT AND FREIGHTAGE — CLAIMS
TF664	FREIGHT AND FREIGHTAGE — TABLES AND READY-RECKONERS
HE2301-2500	FREIGHT AND FREIGHTAGE / *railroads*
HE593-7	FREIGHT AND FREIGHTAGE / *shipping*
HE2301-2500	*FREIGHT HANDLING* **SEE** FREIGHT AND FREIGHTAGE / *railroads*
HE593-7	*FREIGHT HANDLING* **SEE** FREIGHT AND FREIGHTAGE / *shipping*
TF662-7	*FREIGHT HANDLING* **SEE** RAILROADS — FREIGHT
HE2301-2550	*FREIGHT HANDLING* **SEE** RAILROADS — FREIGHT / *economics*
TL685.7	*FREIGHT PLANES* **SEE** TRANSPORT PLANES
HE2301-2500	*FREIGHT RATES* **SEE** FREIGHT AND FREIGHTAGE / *railroads*
HE1826	*FREIGHT-CAR SERVICE* **SEE** DEMURRAGE (CAR SERVICE)
TF470-481	*FREIGHT-CAR SERVICE* **SEE** RAILROADS — FREIGHT-CARS
HE2331-3	*FREIGHT-CAR SERVICE* **SEE** RAILROADS — FREIGHT-CARS / *car service*
TF600-606	*FREIGHT-CAR SERVICE* **SEE** RAILROADS — FREIGHT-CARS / *operation*
TF662-7	*FREIGHT-CAR SERVICE* **SEE** RAILROADS — FREIGHT
HE2301-2550	*FREIGHT-CAR SERVICE* **SEE** RAILROADS — FREIGHT / *economics*
TF470-481	*FREIGHT-CARS* **SEE** RAILROADS — FREIGHT-CARS
HE2331-3	*FREIGHT-CARS* **SEE** RAILROADS — FREIGHT-CARS / *car service*
TF600-606	*FREIGHT-CARS* **SEE** RAILROADS — FREIGHT-CARS / *operation*
E199	*FRENCH AND INDIAN WAR* **SEE** UNITED STATES — HISTORY — — FRENCH AND INDIAN WAR, 1755-1763
PQ445	FRENCH BALLADS AND SONGS
PQ1189	FRENCH BALLADS AND SONGS / *collections*
S429.F8	FRENCH BULLDOGS
SB205.A4	*FRENCH CLOVER* **SEE** ALFALFA
PQ1284	FRENCH DIARIES / *collections*
PQ3846	FRENCH DRAMA — BELGIAN AUTHORS / *collections*
PQ3830	FRENCH DRAMA — BELGIAN AUTHORS / *history*
PQ1341-1385	FRENCH DRAMA — MEDIEVAL / *collections*
PQ511-515	FRENCH DRAMA — MEDIEVAL / *history*
PQ1219	FRENCH DRAMA — 16TH CENTURY / *collections*
PQ521-3	FRENCH DRAMA — 16TH CENTURY / *history*
PQ1220	FRENCH DRAMA — 17TH CENTURY / *collections*
PQ1220	FRENCH DRAMA — 17TH CENTURY / *collections*
PQ526-8	FRENCH DRAMA — 17TH CENTURY / *history*
PQ526-8	FRENCH DRAMA — 17TH CENTURY / *history*
PQ1221	FRENCH DRAMA — 18TH CENTURY / *collections*
PQ536-8	FRENCH DRAMA — 18TH CENTURY / *history*
PQ1222	FRENCH DRAMA — 19TH CENTURY / *collections*
PQ541-553	FRENCH DRAMA — 19TH CENTURY / *history*
PQ1223	FRENCH DRAMA — 20TH CENTURY / *collections*
PQ556-8	FRENCH DRAMA — 20TH CENTURY / *history*
PQ1229-1231	FRENCH DRAMA (COMEDY) / *collections*
PQ566-8	FRENCH DRAMA (COMEDY) / *history*
PQ1227	FRENCH DRAMA (TRAGEDY) / *collections*
PQ561-3	FRENCH DRAMA (TRAGEDY) / *history*
PQ1211-1241	FRENCH DRAMA / *collections*
PQ500-591	FRENCH DRAMA / *history*
PQ1290-1291	FRENCH ESSAYS / *collections*
PQ731	FRENCH ESSAYS / *history*
PQ1237.F2	FRENCH FARCES / *collections*
PQ584	FRENCH FARCES / *history*
PQ3848	FRENCH FICTION — BELGIAN AUTHORS / *collections*
PQ3842	FRENCH FICTION — BELGIAN AUTHORS / *history*
PQ1391	FRENCH FICTION — OLD FRENCH / *collections*
PQ221	FRENCH FICTION — OLD FRENCH / *history*
PQ1266	FRENCH FICTION — 16TH CENTURY / *collections*
PQ643	FRENCH FICTION — 16TH CENTURY / *history*
PQ1267	FRENCH FICTION — 17TH CENTURY / *collections*
PQ645	FRENCH FICTION — 17TH CENTURY / *history*
PQ1268	FRENCH FICTION — 18TH CENTURY / *collections*
PQ648	FRENCH FICTION — 18TH CENTURY / *history*
PQ1269	FRENCH FICTION — 19TH CENTURY / *collections*
PQ651-661	FRENCH FICTION — 19TH CENTURY / *history*
PQ1271	FRENCH FICTION — 20TH CENTURY / *collections*
PQ671	FRENCH FICTION — 20TH CENTURY / *history*
PQ1261-1279	FRENCH FICTION / *collections*
PQ631-671	FRENCH FICTION / *history*
ML955-8	*FRENCH HORN* **SEE** HORN (MUSICAL INSTRUMENT)
PC2120.C6	FRENCH LANGUAGE — BUSINESS FRENCH

BX3601-3655	*FRIARS MINOR* **SEE** FRANCISCANS
BX4361-4	*FRIARS MINOR* **SEE** FRANCISCANS / *women*
BX3501-3555	*FRIARS PREACHERS* **SEE** DOMINICANS
BX4341-4	*FRIARS PREACHERS* **SEE** DOMINICANS / *women*
BX2820	FRIARS
BX3501-3555	*FRIARS, BLACK* **SEE** DOMINICANS
BX4341-4	*FRIARS, BLACK* **SEE** DOMINICANS / *women*
BX3601-3655	*FRIARS, GRAY* **SEE** FRANCISCANS
BX4361-4	*FRIARS, GRAY* **SEE** FRANCISCANS / *women*
TJ1074	*FRICTION CLUTCHES* **SEE** CLUTCHES (MACHINERY)
TA407	*FRICTION OXIDATION* **SEE** FRETTING CORROSION
QC197	FRICTION
TX739	*FRIDAY MENUS* **SEE** LENTEN MENUS
TX837	*FRIDAY MENUS* **SEE** LENTEN MENUS / *with recipes*
QD501	FRIEDEL-CRAFTS REACTION
QD341.A2	FRIEDEL-CRAFTS REACTION / *aromatic anhydrides*
BJ1533.F8	*FRIENDLINESS* **SEE** FRIENDSHIP
HF5686.F	FRIENDLY SOCIETIES — ACCOUNTING
HS1501-1510	FRIENDLY SOCIETIES
HG9201-9245	FRIENDLY SOCIETIES / *fraternal insurance*
HV43	FRIENDLY VISITING
BV5070.F73	FRIENDS OF GOD ("GOTTESFREUNDE")
Z7845.F8	FRIENDS, SOCIETY OF — BIO-BIBLIOGRAPHY
BX7790-7795	FRIENDS, SOCIETY OF — BIOGRAPHY
BX7740-7746	FRIENDS, SOCIETY OF — DISCIPLINE
BX7730-7732	FRIENDS, SOCIETY OF — DOCTRINAL AND CONTROVERSIAL WORKS
LC570-571	FRIENDS, SOCIETY OF — EDUCATION
BX7630-7728	FRIENDS, SOCIETY OF — HISTORY
BV2535	FRIENDS, SOCIETY OF — MISSIONS
BX7751-2	FRIENDS, SOCIETY OF (HICKSITE)
BX7601-7795	FRIENDS, SOCIETY OF
LB3614	*FRIENDSHIP LETTERS* **SEE** INTERNATIONAL CORRESPONDENCE / *students*
BJ1533.F8	FRIENDSHIP
E326	FRIES REBELLION, 1798-1799
SF199.H75	*FRIESIAN CATTLE* **SEE** HOLSTEIN-FRIESIAN CATTLE
SF193.H7	*FRIESIAN CATTLE* **SEE** HOLSTEIN-FRIESIAN CATTLE / *herd-books*
PF1401-1497	FRIESIAN LANGUAGE
PF1501-1558	FRIESIAN LITERATURE
PF1513	FRIESIAN POETRY / *collections*
DJ401.F5-59	FRIESIANS
NA2965	FRIEZES
NK2120	FRIEZES / *decoration*
QL696.S6	FRIGATE-BIRDS
BM657.F7	FRINGES (JEWISH CULTUS)
QL696.P2	*FRINGILLIDAE* **SEE** FINCHES
QL696.P2	*FRINGILLIDAE* **SEE** GROSBEAKS
QL696.P2	*FRINGILLIDAE* **SEE** SPARROWS
PF1401-1497	*FRISIAN LANGUAGE* **SEE** FRIESIAN LANGUAGE
PF1501-1558	*FRISIAN LITERATURE* **SEE** FRIESIAN LITERATURE
SB608.G6	FRIT-FLIES
LB1141-1499	*FROEBEL SYSTEM OF EDUCATION* **SEE** KINDERGARTEN
HV1643	*FROEBEL SYSTEM OF EDUCATION* **SEE** KINDERGARTEN / *blind*
HV2443	*FROEBEL SYSTEM OF EDUCATION* **SEE** KINDERGARTEN / *deaf*
DC302.5	*FROESCHWILLER, BATTLE OF, 1870* **SEE** WORTH, BATTLE OF, 1870
SH185	FROG-CULTURE
SH185	*FROG-RAISING* **SEE** FROG-CULTURE
QL668.E2	FROGS / *zoology*
DC124.4	FRONDE
RF421-5	FRONTAL SINUS — DISEASES
RF421	FRONTAL SINUS — SURGERY
QL947	FRONTAL SINUS / *comparative anatomy*
QM505	FRONTAL SINUS / *human anatomy*
E199	FRONTENAC, FORT — CAPTURE, 1758
E179	FRONTIER AND PIONEER LIFE / *u.s.*
JX4111-4145	*FRONTIERS* **SEE** BOUNDARIES / *international law*
JC323	*FRONTIERS* **SEE** BOUNDARIES / *theory of the state*
Z242	FRONTISPIECE
NA2920	*FRONTONS* **SEE** PEDIMENTS
QC929.H6	FROST
HG174	*FROZEN ASSETS* **SEE** LIQUIDITY (ECONOMICS)
TP493.5	*FROZEN FOOD* **SEE** FOOD, FROZEN
TP493.5	*FROZEN FRUIT* **SEE** FRUIT, FROZEN

TP493.5	*FROZEN VEGETABLES* **SEE** VEGETABLES, FROZEN
TP493.5	*FROZEN-FOOD LOCKERS* **SEE** COLD-STORAGE LOCKERS
QD321	FRUCTOSANS
QP701	FRUCTOSE METABOLISM
QD321	FRUCTOSE
QK660	FRUIT — ANATOMY
QK699	FRUIT — ANATOMY
QK865	FRUIT — CHEMICAL COMPOSITION
SB608.F8	FRUIT — DISEASES AND PESTS
TX609	FRUIT — EVAPORATION
SB360	FRUIT — MARKETING
QK660	FRUIT — MORPHOLOGY
SB361	FRUIT — PICTORIAL WORKS
SB354-399	FRUIT — RIPENING
SB360	FRUIT — STORAGE
TP562	FRUIT JUICES
SB945.F	FRUIT LECANIUM
SB608.F8	*FRUIT PESTS* **SEE** FRUIT — DISEASES AND PESTS
HF5716.F9	FRUIT TRADE — TABLES AND READY-RECKONERS
HD9240-9259	FRUIT TRADE
HF2651.F8	FRUIT TRADE / *tariff*
HE7677.F9	FRUIT TRADE / *telegraph codes*
HD2769.F7	FRUIT TRADE / *trusts*
TP561	FRUIT WINES
SB354-399	FRUIT-CULTURE
SB994.F6	*FRUIT-EATING BATS* **SEE** FLYING FOXES / *noxious animals*
QL737.C5	*FRUIT-EATING BATS* **SEE** FLYING FOXES / *zoology*
SB945.F8	FRUIT-FLIES / *fruit pests*
QL537.M6	FRUIT-FLIES / *zoology*
SB354-399	FRUIT / *culture*
HD9240-9259	FRUIT / *trade*
SB127	*FRUIT, FORCING OF* **SEE** FORCING (PLANTS)
QE995	FRUIT, FOSSIL
TP493.5	FRUIT, FROZEN
SB359	*FRUIT, TROPICAL* **SEE** TROPICAL FRUIT
QK899	*FRUIT-COLOR* **SEE** COLOR OF FRUIT
TX609	*FRUIT-DRYING* **SEE** FRUIT — EVAPORATION
SB608.F8	*FRUIT-PESTS* **SEE** FRUIT — DISEASES AND PESTS
BF575.F7	FRUSTRATION
QE391.F	FUCHSITE
F2986	FUEGIANS
TP321	FUEL — ANALYSIS
TP321-2	FUEL — TESTING
TK2920	FUEL CELLS
TP355	*FUEL OIL* **SEE** PETROLEUM AS FUEL
TJ619	*FUEL OIL* **SEE** PETROLEUM AS FUEL / *locomotives*
TH7466.O6	*FUEL OIL BURNERS* **SEE** OIL BURNERS / *heating of buildings*
HD9540-9559	FUEL TRADE
TP315-360	FUEL / *technology*
TP360	FUEL, COLLOIDAL
TP343	*FUEL, LIQUID* **SEE** LIQUID FUELS
BL815.R	*FUGALIA* **SEE** REGIFUGIUM
E450	*FUGITIVE SLAVES IN THE U.S.* **SEE** SLAVERY IN THE U.S. — FUGITIVE SLAVES
MT59	FUGUE
ML448	FUGUE
PL8181-4	*FUL LANGUAGE* **SEE** FULAH LANGUAGE
PL8181-4	FULAH LANGUAGE
GN652.F9	FULAHS
GN652.F9	*FULANI* **SEE** FULAHS
GN652.F9	*FULBE* **SEE** FULAHS
PL8181-4	*FULBE LANGUAGE* **SEE** FULAH LANGUAGE
PL8181-4	*FULDE LANGUAGE* **SEE** FULAH LANGUAGE
GN652.F9	*FULFULDE* **SEE** FULAHS
PL8181-4	*FULFULDE LANGUAGE* **SEE** FULAH LANGUAGE
TN948.F9	FULLER'S EARTH
TS1510	*FULLING (TEXTILES)* **SEE** TEXTILE FINISHING
QD305.A2	FUMARIC ACID
SB955	FUMIGATION / *plant culture*
PL6431	*FUNAFUTI LANGUAGE* **SEE** ELLICE LANGUAGE
BF323.S4	*FUNCTION, SECONDARY* **SEE** SECONDARY FUNCTION (PSYCHOLOGY)
QA320	FUNCTIONAL ANALYSIS
QA320	*FUNCTIONAL CALCULUS* **SEE** FUNCTIONAL ANALYSIS
QA431	FUNCTIONAL EQUATIONS
JF1057-9	FUNCTIONAL REPRESENTATION

QA320	*FUNCTIONALS* **SEE** FUNCTIONAL ANALYSIS
QA331	FUNCTIONS OF COMPLEX VARIABLES
QA331.5	FUNCTIONS OF REAL VARIABLES
QA331-351	FUNCTIONS
QA345	FUNCTIONS, ABELIAN
QA341	FUNCTIONS, ALGEBRAIC
QA351	FUNCTIONS, AUTOMORPHIC
QA246	*FUNCTIONS, BERNOULLI'S* **SEE** BERNOULLIAN NUMBERS
QA408	*FUNCTIONS, BESSELIAN* **SEE** BESSEL'S FUNCTIONS
QA404.5	*FUNCTIONS, CHEBYSHEV'S* **SEE** CHEBYSHEV POLYNOMIALS
QA55	*FUNCTIONS, CIRCULAR* **SEE** TRIGONOMETRICAL FUNCTIONS / *tables*
QA342	*FUNCTIONS, CIRCULAR* **SEE** TRIGONOMETRICAL FUNCTIONS / *theory of functions*
QA531-8	*FUNCTIONS, CIRCULAR* **SEE** TRIGONOMETRICAL FUNCTIONS / *trigonometry*
QA351	FUNCTIONS, DISCONTINUOUS
QA343	FUNCTIONS, ELLIPTIC
QA351	FUNCTIONS, ENTIRE
QA342	FUNCTIONS, EXPONENTIAL
QA351	FUNCTIONS, GAMMA
QA405	*FUNCTIONS, HARMONIC* **SEE** HARMONIC FUNCTIONS
QA342	*FUNCTIONS, HYPERBOLIC* **SEE** FUNCTIONS, EXPONENTIAL
QA351	FUNCTIONS, HYPERGEOMETRIC
QA351	*FUNCTIONS, INTEGRAL* **SEE** FUNCTIONS, ENTIRE
QA409	*FUNCTIONS, LAME'S* **SEE** LAME'S FUNCTIONS
QA405	*FUNCTIONS, MATHIEU* **SEE** MATHIEU FUNCTIONS
QA331	FUNCTIONS, MEROMORPHIC
QA343	FUNCTIONS, MODULAR
QA246	*FUNCTIONS, NUMERICAL* **SEE** NUMERICAL FUNCTIONS
QA404.5	FUNCTIONS, ORTHOGONAL
QA374-7	*FUNCTIONS, POTENTIAL* **SEE** DIFFERENTIAL EQUATIONS, PARTIAL
QA401-411	*FUNCTIONS, POTENTIAL* **SEE** HARMONIC ANALYSIS
QA825	*FUNCTIONS, POTENTIAL* **SEE** POTENTIAL, THEORY OF
QA406	*FUNCTIONS, POTENTIAL* **SEE** SPHERICAL HARMONICS
QA248.5	*FUNCTIONS, RECURSIVE* **SEE** RECURSIVE FUNCTIONS
QA212	*FUNCTIONS, SYMMETRIC* **SEE** SYMMETRIC FUNCTIONS
QA345	FUNCTIONS, THETA
QA411	*FUNCTIONS, TOROIDAL* **SEE** TOROIDAL HARMONICS
QA351	FUNCTIONS, TRANSCENDENTAL
QA342	*FUNCTIONS, TRIGONOMETRICAL* **SEE** TRIGONOMETRICAL FUNCTIONS / *theory of functions*
QA531-8	*FUNCTIONS, TRIGONOMETRICAL* **SEE** TRIGONOMETRICAL FUNCTIONS / *trigonometry*
QA55	*FUNCTIONS, TRIGONOMETRICAL* **SEE** TRIGONOMETRICAL FUNCTIONS / *tables*
QA351	FUNCTIONS, ZETA
HG174	FUND RAISING
HV40-41	FUND RAISING / *charity organization*
BT1095-1255	*FUNDAMENTAL THEOLOGY* **SEE** APOLOGETICS
BT82.2	FUNDAMENTALISM
RA622-3	*FUNERAL DIRECTORS* **SEE** UNDERTAKERS AND UNDERTAKING
TS2301.U5	*FUNERAL DIRECTORS* **SEE** UNDERTAKERS AND UNDERTAKING / *supplies*
PA3264	FUNERAL ORATIONS / *greek*
PA3482	FUNERAL ORATIONS / *greek*
N8180	FUNERAL RITES AND CEREMONIES — ART
GN486	FUNERAL RITES AND CEREMONIES / *ethnology*
GT3150-3390	FUNERAL RITES AND CEREMONIES / *manners and customs*
BV4275	FUNERAL SERMONS / *collections*
BV199.F8	FUNERAL SERVICE
QK601	FUNGI — ANATOMY
QK601	FUNGI — PHYSIOLOGY
SB733	FUNGI IN AGRICULTURE / *fungus diseases*
QK600-635	FUNGI
QK617	*FUNGI, EDIBLE* **SEE** MUSHROOMS, EDIBLE
QE958	FUNGI, FOSSIL
QR145	FUNGI, PATHOGENIC
QK617	FUNGI, POISONOUS
SB951	FUNGICIDES
RC117	*FUNGOUS DISEASES* **SEE** MEDICAL MYCOLOGY
DT132	FUNGS'
TF835	*FUNICULAR RAILROADS* **SEE** RAILROADS, CABLE
TS1061	FUR — DRESSING AND DYEING
TT525	*FUR COATS* **SEE** FUR GARMENTS
TS1061	*FUR DRESSING* **SEE** FUR — DRESSING AND DYEING
TS1061	*FUR DYEING* **SEE** FUR — DRESSING AND DYEING
SF402-5	FUR FARMING
TT525	FUR GARMENTS
SH361-3	*FUR SEAL* **SEE** SEALING
HD9944	FUR TRADE
SF403-5	FUR-BEARING ANIMALS / *animal culture*
SK283	FUR-BEARING ANIMALS / *trapping*
QL942	FUR / *anatomy*
TS1060-1067	FUR / *technology*
BL820.F8	FURIES
TH7623-4	FURNACES — CATALOGS
TH7609	FURNACES — CONSTRUCTION
TJ322-4	FURNACES — GRATES / *steam-boilers*
TS887	FURNITURE — CATALOGS
NK2265	FURNITURE — CATALOGS
NK2240	FURNITURE — COLLECTORS AND COLLECTING
TT200	FURNITURE — MODELS
NK2220	FURNITURE — PRIVATE COLLECTIONS
TT199	FURNITURE — REPAIRING
HF5686.F8	FURNITURE INDUSTRY AND TRADE — ACCOUNTING
TS840-887	FURNITURE INDUSTRY AND TRADE
HD9773	FURNITURE INDUSTRY AND TRADE
TT200	*FURNITURE MODELS* **SEE** FURNITURE — MODELS
NK2200-2740	FURNITURE / *art*
GT450	FURNITURE / *manners and customs*
TS880-887	FURNITURE / *technology*
NK2365	FURNITURE, BAROQUE
TT197.5.B8	*FURNITURE, BUILT-IN* **SEE** BUILT-IN FURNITURE / *cabinet work*
NK2712	*FURNITURE, BUILT-IN* **SEE** BUILT-IN FURNITURE / *design*
TT525	*FURRIERY* **SEE** FUR GARMENTS
TT525	*FURS (CLOTHING)* **SEE** FUR GARMENTS
NC850	*FUSAIN (ART)* **SEE** CHARCOAL-DRAWING
SB741.F9	*FUSARIUM NIVALE* **SEE** SNOW MOLD
TP593	FUSEL-OIL / *alcohol*
TK3511	*FUSES, ELECTRIC* **SEE** ELECTRIC FUSES
TK2846	*FUSES, ELECTRIC* **SEE** ELECTRIC FUSES / *switchboards*
QC303	FUSION
QC303	FUSION, LATENT HEAT OF
QC791	*FUSION, NUCLEAR* **SEE** NUCLEAR FUSION
DT515	*FUTA TORO* **SEE** TOUCOULEURS
DT515	*FUTANKOBE* **SEE** TOUCOULEURS
BF575.F7	*FUTILITY* **SEE** FRUSTRATION
PL6435	FUTUNA LANGUAGE
BP166.8	FUTURE LIFE (ISLAM)
BL535-547	FUTURE LIFE / *comparative religion*
BT899-904	FUTURE LIFE / *theology*
BP166.88	FUTURE PUNISHMENT (ISLAM)
BT834-8	FUTURE PUNISHMENT
HG6046	*FUTURES* **SEE** COMMODITY EXCHANGES
HG6001-6051	*FUTURES* **SEE** SPECULATION
ND1265	FUTURISM (ART)
PN56.F8	FUTURISM / *literature*
GN671.N5	*FUYUGE* **SEE** MAFULUS / *anthropology*
DU740	*FUYUGE* **SEE** MAFULUS / *history*
PL6621.F8	FUYUGE LANGUAGE
BL604.S8	*FYLFOT* **SEE** SWASTIKA
NK1177	*FYLFOT* **SEE** SWASTIKA / *art*
PL8401-4	*FYOTI LANGUAGE* **SEE** CONGO LANGUAGE
DD407.F8	FÜSSEN, TREATY OF, 1745
DT511	GA (AFRICAN PEOPLE)
PL8191	GA LANGUAGE
PM8360.G2	GAB (ARTIFICIAL LANGUAGE)
QE461	GABBRO
HD9213	*GABEL* **SEE** SALT — TAXATION
NA2920	GABLES
E99.G15	GABRIELENO INDIANS
PM1201	GABRIELENO LANGUAGE
D432.G	GADABAS
QL537.T2	*GADFLIES* **SEE** HORSEFLIES
GN446-7	*GADGETS* **SEE** IMPLEMENTS, UTENSILS, ETC. / *primitive*
QE391.G	GADOLINITE

QD181.G4	GADOLINIUM EARTHS
F786	GADSDEN PURCHASE
F786	GADSDEN TREATY, 1853
PB1607	GAELIC BALLADS AND SONGS
PB1648	GAELIC BALLADS AND SONGS
PB1633	GAELIC BALLADS AND SONGS
PB1201-1299	*GAELIC LANGUAGE (IRISH)* **SEE** IRISH LANGUAGE
PB1501-1599	GAELIC LANGUAGE
PB1605-1709	GAELIC LITERATURE
PB1648	GAELIC POETRY
PB1631-4	GAELIC POETRY
PB1605-7	GAELIC POETRY
D70	*GAELS* **SEE** CELTS
GN549.C3	*GAELS* **SEE** CELTS
DA140-143	*GAELS* **SEE** CELTS / *england*
DC62-63	*GAELS* **SEE** CELTS / *france*
DG554.5.G2	GAETA, ITALY — SIEGE, 1860-1861
PJ9285	GAFAT LANGUAGE
QL638.A75	GAFF-TOPSAILS (FISHES)
TJ1166	GAGE BLOCKS
TF244	*GAGES (RAILROADS)* **SEE** RAILROADS — GAGES
TJ1166	GAGES
HF5716.L4	GAGING — TABLES AND READY-RECKONERS
TP609	GAGING
DK508.7	*GAIDAMAKS* **SEE** HAIDAMAKS
GV1299.G2	GAIGLE (GAME)
QL696.A3	*GAIRFOWL* **SEE** GREAT AUK
ML980	GAITA
PL8055	*GALA LANGUAGE* **SEE** BANGALA LANGUAGE
QD321	GALACTOSE
QB819	*GALAXY (MILKY WAY)* **SEE** MILKY WAY
PL5323	*GALELA LANGUAGE* **SEE** GALELARESE LANGUAGE
PL5323	GALELARESE LANGUAGE
QC941-959	*GALES* **SEE** STORMS
QC931-940	*GALES* **SEE** WINDS
DK34.I	*GALGA* **SEE** INGUSH
PK9201.C3	*GALGA LANGUAGE* **SEE** CHECHEN LANGUAGE
F2460	GALIBI INDIANS
PM5976	GALIBI LANGUAGE
PC5411-5414	*GALICIAN DIALECT* **SEE** GALLEGAN DIALECT
DP302.G11-12	*GALICIANS (SPANISH)* **SEE** GALLEGANS
F1789.G3	*GALICIANS (SPANISH)* **SEE** GALLEGANS / *cuba*
MT20	GALIN-PARIS-CHEVE METHOD (MUSIC)
QP197	*GALL* **SEE** BILE
QL568.C	*GALL MIDGES* **SEE** GALL-GNATS
SF967.A	*GALL SICKNESS* **SEE** ANAPLASMOSIS
RC849-853	GALL-BLADDER — DISEASES
RC849	GALL-BLADDER — RADIOGRAPHY
QL867	GALL-BLADDER / *comparative anatomy*
QM351	GALL-BLADDER / *human anatomy*
QP197	GALL-BLADDER / *physiology*
RC850	*GALL-BLADDER-CALCULI* **SEE** CALCULI, BILIARY
RD547	*GALL-BLADDER-CALCULI* **SEE** CALCULI, BILIARY
QL867	*GALL-DUCTS* **SEE** BILE-DUCTS / *comparative anatomy*
RC849	*GALL-DUCTS* **SEE** BILE-DUCTS / *diseases*
QM351	*GALL-DUCTS* **SEE** BILE-DUCTS / *human anatomy*
RD546-7	*GALL-DUCTS* **SEE** BILE-DUCTS / *surgical treatment*
QL568.C9	GALL-FLIES
QL568.C	GALL-GNATS
RD547	*GALL-STONES* **SEE** CALCULI, BILIARY
RC850	*GALL-STONES* **SEE** CALCULI, BILIARY
PJ2471-9	GALLA LANGUAGE
PN6120.S5	*GALLANTY-SHOWS* **SEE** SHADOW PANTOMIMES AND PLAYS / *texts*
PN1979.S5	*GALLANTY-SHOWS* **SEE** SHADOW PANTOMIMES AND PLAYS / *texts*
DT390.G2	GALLAS
PQ9464-5	GALLEGAN BALLADS AND SONGS / *collections*
PQ9460	GALLEGAN BALLADS AND SONGS / *history*
PC5411-5414	GALLEGAN DIALECT
PQ9463-8	GALLEGAN LITERATURE / *collections*
PQ9450-9462	GALLEGAN LITERATURE / *history*
PQ9464	GALLEGAN POETRY
PQ9460	GALLEGAN POETRY
DP302.G11-12	GALLEGANS
F1789.G3	GALLEGANS / *cuba*
DP302.G11-12	*GALLEGOS* **SEE** GALLEGANS
F1789.G3	*GALLEGOS* **SEE** GALLEGANS / *cuba*
QD441	GALLEIN
N400-490	*GALLERIES (ART)* **SEE** ART — GALLERIES AND MUSEUMS
VM15-17	GALLEYS
PA2337.G	GALLIAMBIC
PA416.G	GALLIAMBIC
PA188.G	GALLIAMBIC
M125-9	GALLIARDS (GUITAR)
QD341.A2	GALLIC ACID / *chemistry*
RM666.G	GALLIC ACID / *therapeutics*
PB3001-3029	*GALLIC LANGUAGE* **SEE** GAULISH LANGUAGE
PB307	GALLICISMS
QL696.G2	GALLINAE
D568.3	*GALLIPOLI CAMPAIGN, 1915* **SEE** EUROPEAN WAR, 1914-1918 — CAMPAIGNS — — TURKEY AND THE NEAR EAST — — — GALLIPOLI
QD181.G2	GALLIUM
PC1851-1874	GALLO-ITALIAN DIALECTS
DA933-7	*GALLOGLAIGH* **SEE** GALLOGLASSES / *ireland*
DA933-7	GALLOGLASSES / *ireland*
SF199.G	GALLOWAY CATTLE
SF193.G2	GALLOWAY CATTLE
DA933-7	*GALLOWGLASSES* **SEE** GALLOGLASSES / *ireland*
SB767	GALLS (BOTANY)
QA211	GALOIS THEORY / *equations*
QA214	GALOIS THEORY / *equations*
QA171	GALOIS THEORY / *groups*
M1264	GALOPS (BAND)
M1248	GALOPS (BAND)
M1060	GALOPS (CHAMBER ORCHESTRA)
M1048	GALOPS (CHAMBER ORCHESTRA)
M1060	GALOPS (ORCHESTRA)
M1048	GALOPS (ORCHESTRA)
M31	GALOPS (PIANO)
M32.8	GALOPS (PIANO)
M298	GALOUBET AND TAMBOURIN MUSIC
ML935-7	GALOUBET
QC603-5	*GALVANIC BATTERIES* **SEE** ELECTRIC BATTERIES
TF912	*GALVANIC CORROSION* **SEE** ELECTROLYTIC CORROSION / *electric railroads*
TK3255	*GALVANIC CORROSION* **SEE** ELECTROLYTIC CORROSION / *electric engineering*
TD491	*GALVANIC CORROSION* **SEE** ELECTROLYTIC CORROSION / *etc.*
QC501-721	*GALVANISM* **SEE** ELECTRICITY
TS660	*GALVANIZED IRON* **SEE** IRON, GALVANIZED
TS660	*GALVANIZED STEEL* **SEE** STEEL, GALVANIZED
TA473	*GALVANIZED STEEL* **SEE** STEEL, GALVANIZED / *testing*
TS660	GALVANIZING
QC544.G2	GALVANOMETER
Z252	*GALVANOPLASTIC PROCESS* **SEE** ELECTROTYPING
TN681-7	*GALVANOPLASTY* **SEE** ELECTROMETALLURGY
TS670-692	*GALVANOPLASTY* **SEE** ELECTROPLATING
Z252	*GALVANOPLASTY* **SEE** ELECTROTYPING
RD33.5	*GALVANOSURGERY* **SEE** ELECTROSURGERY
F394.G2	GALVESTON — STORM, 1900
PJ2438	*GAMANT LANGUAGE* **SEE** KEMANT LANGUAGE
QA273	*GAMBLING PROBLEM (MATHEMATICS)* **SEE** GAMES OF CHANCE (MATHEMATICS)
HV6708-6722	GAMBLING
GV1245	GAMBLING / *ethics of*
SB261.A	*GAMBO HEMP* **SEE** AMBARY HEMP / *culture*
TS1544.A	*GAMBO HEMP* **SEE** AMBARY HEMP / *fiber*
SK	GAME AND GAME-BIRDS / *hunting*
QL696.G2	GAME AND GAME-BIRDS / *ornithology*
SK351-579	GAME PROTECTION
SK355-579	*GAME PROTECTION-LAW AND LEGISLATION* **SEE** GAME-LAWS
QA269	GAME THEORY
SK351-579	*GAME WARDENS* **SEE** GAME PROTECTION
SK355-579	GAME-LAWS
SK357	GAME-PRESERVES
SK357	GAME-PRESERVES
ML1251	GAMELAN
ML1251	*GAMELANG* **SEE** GAMELAN
GV1227	GAMES — EARLY WORKS TO 1800
GV1206	GAMES FOR TRAVELERS
GV1202.T	GAMES FOR TWO
QA273	GAMES OF CHANCE (MATHEMATICS)
QA270	GAMES OF STRATEGY (MATHEMATICS)

M1993	GAMES WITH MUSIC
QA270	*GAMES WITH RATIONAL PAY-OFF (MATHEMATICS)* **SEE** GAMES OF STRATEGY (MATHEMATICS)
GV1200-1511	GAMES
LB1137	GAMES / *educational*
GN454-6	GAMES / *ethnology*
GR480-485	GAMES / *folk-lore*
LB1177	GAMES / *kindergarten*
BF717	GAMES / *psychology of play*
LB3031	GAMES / *school management*
DC801.T725	*GAMES, FLORAL* **SEE** FLORAL GAMES / *toulouse*
GV23	*GAMES, OLYMPIC* **SEE** OLYMPIC GAMES
GN454-7	GAMES, PRIMITIVE
M1993	*GAMES, RHYTHMIC* **SEE** GAMES WITH MUSIC
DG95	*GAMES, SECULAR* **SEE** SECULAR GAMES / *roman antiquities*
QA269	*GAMES, THEORY OF* **SEE** GAME THEORY
HV6708-6722	*GAMING* **SEE** GAMBLING
GV1245	*GAMING* **SEE** GAMBLING / *ethics of*
QA351	*GAMMA FUNCTIONS* **SEE** FUNCTIONS, GAMMA
QC490	GAMMA RAYS
QK495.G	GAMOPETALAE
PL8201	GANDA LANGUAGE
PL8041	*GANG LANGUAGE* **SEE** ACOLI LANGUAGE
QM575	*GANGLIA, NERVOUS* **SEE** NERVES / *histology*
QP331	*GANGLIA, NERVOUS* **SEE** NERVES / *physiology*
QL939	*GANGLIA, NERVOUS* **SEE** NERVOUS SYSTEM, SYMPATHETIC / *comparative anatomy*
QM471	*GANGLIA, NERVOUS* **SEE** NERVOUS SYSTEM, SYMPATHETIC / *human anatomy*
QP368	*GANGLIA, NERVOUS* **SEE** NERVOUS SYSTEM, SYMPATHETIC / *physiology*
QP368	*GANGLIONIC NERVOUS SYSTEM* **SEE** NERVOUS SYSTEM, SYMPATHETIC / *physiology*
QL939	*GANGLIONIC NERVOUS SYSTEM* **SEE** NERVOUS SYSTEM, SYMPATHETIC / *comparative anatomy*
QM471	*GANGLIONIC NERVOUS SYSTEM* **SEE** NERVOUS SYSTEM, SYMPATHETIC / *human anatomy*
RD153	GANGRENE / *military surgery*
RD628	GANGRENE / *pathology*
HV6437-9	GANGS
HV6774-7220	GANGS / *by country*
HV6437-9	*GANGSTERS* **SEE** GANGS
HV6774-7220	*GANGSTERS* **SEE** GANGS / *by country*
PL8202	GANGUELA LANGUAGE
BD396	*GANZHEIT (PHILOSOPHY)* **SEE** WHOLE AND PARTS (PHILOSOPHY)
BF202	*GANZHEIT (PSYCHOLOGY)* **SEE** WHOLE AND PARTS (PSYCHOLOGY)
HV8301-9920	*GAOLS* **SEE** PRISONS
NA8348	GARAGES
TD791-870	*GARBAGE* **SEE** REFUSE AND REFUSE DISPOSAL
NA7100-7786	*GARDEN ARCHITECTURE* **SEE** ARCHITECTURE, DOMESTIC
SB469-479	*GARDEN ARCHITECTURE* **SEE** LANDSCAPE GARDENING
HD7526-7630	GARDEN CITIES
HT161-5	GARDEN CITIES
SB476	GARDEN LIGHTING
QK495.C	*GARDEN ORACH* **SEE** ORACH / *botany*
SB351.O	*GARDEN ORACH* **SEE** ORACH / *vegetables*
SB423	*GARDEN PONDS* **SEE** WATER GARDENS
SB423	*GARDEN POOLS* **SEE** WATER GARDENS
SB133	*GARDEN SUPPLIES* **SEE** GARDENING — EQUIPMENT AND SUPPLIES
SB92	GARDENING — EARLY WORKS TO 1800
SB97	GARDENING — EARLY WORKS TO 1800
SB99	GARDENING — EARLY WORKS TO 1800
SB133	GARDENING — EQUIPMENT AND SUPPLIES
SB55	GARDENING — JUVENILE LITERATURE
SB455-7	GARDENING — JUVENILE LITERATURE
SB51	*GARDENING AS A PROFESSION* **SEE** HORTICULTURE AS A PROFESSION
SB451-466	GARDENING
SB465-6	GARDENS — PICTORIAL WORKS
PN6110.G2	GARDENS — POETRY
SB451-466	GARDENS
SB419	GARDENS, MINIATURE
VF410.G2-24	GARDNER MACHINE-GUN / *naval*
QL696.A3	*GAREFOWL* **SEE** GREAT AUK
QL638.5	*GARFISHES* **SEE** GARPIKES
QL696.A3	*GARFOWL* **SEE** GREAT AUK
RM666.G	GARLIC — THERAPEUTIC USE
TT500-678	GARMENT CUTTING
TN997.G3	GARNET
TX652	*GARNISHES IN COOKERY* **SEE** COOKERY (GARNISHES)
PL4001.G2	GARO LANGUAGE
DS485.A84-88	GAROS
GN635.I4	GAROS / *ethnology*
QL638.5	GARPIKES
QL638.5	*GARPIPES* **SEE** GARPIKES
TH3000	*GARRETS* **SEE** ATTICS
U370-375	GARRISONS
HV8696	GARROTE
PL4001.G2	*GARROW LANGUAGE* **SEE** GARO LANGUAGE
QL666.O6	GARTER SNAKES
DS785	GARTOK EXPEDITION, 1904-1905
TK7291	GAS — ELECTRIC IGNITION
TH7453-7	GAS — HEATING AND COOKING / *gas-stoves*
TP754	GAS — TESTING
RA1247.G2	GAS — TOXICOLOGY
TJ789	GAS AND OIL ENGINES — COOLING
TJ787	GAS AND OIL ENGINES — IGNITION
TJ789	GAS AND OIL ENGINES — MUFFLERS
TJ758	GAS AND OIL ENGINES — PATENTS
TJ751-805	GAS AND OIL ENGINES
TJ787	*GAS AND OIL ENGINES-CARBURETORS* **SEE** CARBURETORS
TJ787	*GAS AND OIL ENGINES-SUPERCHARGERS* **SEE** SUPERCHARGERS
TP758	*GAS APPARATUS AND APPLIANCES* **SEE** GAS APPLIANCES
TP758	GAS APPLIANCES
TP345-350	GAS AS FUEL
TJ1073.5	*GAS BEARINGS* **SEE** GAS-LUBRICATED BEARINGS
QL855	*GAS BLADDER* **SEE** AIR-BLADDER (IN FISHES)
HF5686.G3	GAS COMPANIES — ACCOUNTING
HF6161.G2	GAS COMPANIES / *advertising*
HG4029.G2	GAS COMPANIES / *finance*
HG4841.G2	GAS COMPANIES / *securities*
TP764	GAS CONDENSERS
TP753	GAS DISTRIBUTION — TABLES, CALCULATIONS, ETC.
TP757	GAS DISTRIBUTION
TJ751-805	*GAS ENGINES* **SEE** GAS AND OIL ENGINES
TL229.G3	*GAS ENGINES, AUTOMOTIVE* **SEE** AUTOMOBILES — MOTORS (COMPRESSED-GAS)
TP758	*GAS EQUIPMENT AND APPLIANCES* **SEE** GAS APPLIANCES
UG447	*GAS IN WAR* **SEE** GASES, ASPHYXIATING AND POISONOUS — WAR USE
TP751.1	GAS INDUSTRY — SAFETY MEASURES
TP751-764	GAS INDUSTRY
TP755	GAS MANUFACTURE AND WORKS — BY-PRODUCTS
HG4029.G2	GAS MANUFACTURE AND WORKS — FINANCE
TP751.3	GAS MANUFACTURE AND WORKS — FINANCE / *business management*
TP700-764	GAS MANUFACTURE AND WORKS
HD4486-4495	GAS MANUFACTURE AND WORKS / *public ownership*
HD7275	GAS MASKS / *labor hygiene*
UG447	GAS MASKS / *military science*
TN297	GAS MASKS / *mining*
TJ768	GAS POWER-PLANTS
TX657.S6	*GAS RANGES* **SEE** STOVES, GAS / *for cooking*
TH7454-7	*GAS RANGES* **SEE** STOVES, GAS / *for heating*
TL153	*GAS STATIONS* **SEE** AUTOMOBILES — SERVICE STATIONS
TX657.S6	*GAS STOVES* **SEE** STOVES, GAS / *for cooking*
TH7454-7	*GAS STOVES* **SEE** STOVES, GAS / *for heating*
TP757	GAS TUBING
UG447	*GAS WARFARE* **SEE** GASES, ASPHYXIATING AND POISONOUS — WAR USE
TS227	*GAS WELDING* **SEE** OXYACETYLENE WELDING AND CUTTING
TN880-883	GAS WELLS
TH7950	GAS-BURNERS
HD7264	GAS-DETECTORS
TH7920-7930	GAS-FITTING
TH7960-7967	GAS-FIXTURES
TH7945	GAS-GOVERNORS

TH7700-7975	*GAS-LIGHTING* **SEE** LIGHTING
GT440-445	*GAS-LIGHTING* **SEE** LIGHTING / *manners and customs*
TH7910-7970	GAS-LIGHTING
TJ1073.5	GAS-LUBRICATED BEARINGS
TP764	GAS-MACHINES
TH7940	GAS-METERS
TP751.1	GAS-PIPES — CLEANING
TP757	GAS-PIPES
TP751.1	*GAS-PIPES-PURGING* **SEE** GAS-PIPES — CLEANING
TP762	GAS-PRODUCERS
TH7945	*GAS-REGULATORS* **SEE** GAS-GOVERNORS
TP764	GAS-RETORTS
TJ778	GAS-TURBINE DISKS
TJ778	*GAS-TURBINE MATERIALS* **SEE** GAS-TURBINES — MATERIALS
TJ778	*GAS-TURBINE WHEELS* **SEE** GAS-TURBINE DISKS
TJ778	GAS-TURBINES — MATERIALS
TJ778	GAS-TURBINES
TJ778	*GAS-TURBINES-DISKS* **SEE** GAS-TURBINE DISKS
TP700	GAS
TP751-764	GAS
TN880	GAS, NATURAL — TRANSPORTATION
HD9580	GAS, NATURAL — TRANSPORTATION
TP350	GAS, NATURAL / *fuel*
HD242.5	GAS, NATURAL / *gas lands*
TN880	GAS, NATURAL / *mineral industries*
HF6161.G2	*GAS, NATURAL-COMPANIES* **SEE** GAS COMPANIES / *advertising*
HG4029.G2	*GAS, NATURAL-COMPANIES* **SEE** GAS COMPANIES / *finance*
HG4841.G2	*GAS, NATURAL-COMPANIES* **SEE** GAS COMPANIES / *securities*
QD121	*GAS-ANALYSIS* **SEE** GASES — ANALYSIS
TP754	*GAS-ANALYSIS* **SEE** GASES — ANALYSIS / *illuminating gas*
UG447	*GAS-WAR USE* **SEE** GASES, ASPHYXIATING AND POISONOUS — WAR USE
PC3428	GASCON BALLADS AND SONGS
PC3421-8	GASCON DIALECT
PC3428	GASCON LITERATURE
PC3428	GASCON POETRY
QC711	*GASEOUS DISCHARGE* **SEE** PLASMA (IONIZED GASES)
QC809.P5	*GASEOUS DISCHARGE* **SEE** PLASMA (IONIZED GASES) / *cosmic physics*
QC175	*GASEOUS DISCHARGE* **SEE** PLASMA (IONIZED GASES) / *kinetic theory of gases*
QC711	*GASEOUS PLASMA* **SEE** PLASMA (IONIZED GASES)
QC809.P5	*GASEOUS PLASMA* **SEE** PLASMA (IONIZED GASES) / *cosmic physics*
QC175	*GASEOUS PLASMA* **SEE** PLASMA (IONIZED GASES) / *kinetic theory of gases*
QC182	GASES — ABSORPTION AND ADSORPTION
QD121	GASES — ANALYSIS
TP754	GASES — ANALYSIS / *illuminating gas*
QD535	GASES — LIQUEFACTION
QC182	GASES — OCCLUSION
RA576	GASES — PHYSIOLOGICAL EFFECT / *air pollution*
RA1245-7	GASES — PHYSIOLOGICAL EFFECT / *toxicology*
QC454	GASES — SPECTRA
RM666.G2	GASES — THERAPEUTIC USE
TN305-6	*GASES IN MINES* **SEE** MINE GASES
QK875	*GASES IN PLANTS* **SEE** PLANTS, GASES IN
QE511	GASES IN ROCKS
QP91	*GASES IN THE BLOOD* **SEE** BLOOD, GASES IN
TP242-4	GASES / *chemical technology*
QC241	GASES / *etc.*
QC286	GASES / *expansion*
QD531	GASES / *manipulation*
QC161-8	GASES / *mechanics*
QC297	GASES / *specific heats*
RA1245	GASES, ASPHYXIATING AND POISONOUS — LAWS AND LEGISLATION
RA1245	GASES, ASPHYXIATING AND POISONOUS — TOXICOLOGY
UG447	GASES, ASPHYXIATING AND POISONOUS — WAR USE
RA577	GASES, ASPHYXIATING AND POISONOUS / *public health*
TP761.C65	GASES, COMPRESSED
QC711	*GASES, ELECTRIC DISCHARGES THROUGH* **SEE** ELECTRIC DISCHARGES THROUGH GASES
QC702-721	*GASES, IONIZATION OF* **SEE** IONIZATION OF GASES
QC918	*GASES, IONIZATION OF* **SEE** IONIZATION OF GASES / *atmosphere*
RA577	*GASES, IRRESPIRABLE, OFFENSIVE, AND POISONOUS* **SEE** GASES, ASPHYXIATING AND POISONOUS / *public health*
RA1245-7	*GASES, IRRESPIRABLE, OFFENSIVE, AND POISONOUS* **SEE** GASES, ASPHYXIATING AND POISONOUS / *toxicology*
QC175	GASES, KINETIC THEORY OF
TP243	*GASES, LIQUEFIED* **SEE** LIQUEFIED GASES
QD543	*GASES-DIFFUSION* **SEE** DIFFUSION / *chemistry*
QC185	*GASES-DIFFUSION* **SEE** DIFFUSION / *physics*
QC702-721	*GASES-IONIZATION* **SEE** IONIZATION OF GASES
QC918	*GASES-IONIZATION* **SEE** IONIZATION OF GASES / *atmosphere*
QC189	*GASES-VISCOSITY* **SEE** VISCOSITY
TP759	*GASIFICATION OF COAL* **SEE** COAL GASIFICATION
TP759	*GASIFICATION OF COAL, UNDERGROUND* **SEE** COAL GASIFICATION, UNDERGROUND
TP692.2	GASOLINE — ANTI-KNOCK AND ANTI-KNOCK MIXTURES
HD9579.G3-5	GASOLINE — TAXATION
TP692.2	GASOLINE — TRANSPORTATION
TL1-445	*GASOLINE AUTOMOBILES* **SEE** AUTOMOBILES / *history*
HD9710	*GASOLINE AUTOMOBILES* **SEE** AUTOMOBILES / *industry and statistics*
GV1021-1030	*GASOLINE AUTOMOBILES* **SEE** AUTOMOBILES / *sports and amusements*
HE5601-5720	*GASOLINE AUTOMOBILES* **SEE** AUTOMOBILES / *transportation*
TL154	*GASOLINE CONSUMPTION OF AUTOMOBILES* **SEE** AUTOMOBILES — FUEL CONSUMPTION
TJ751-805	*GASOLINE ENGINES* **SEE** GAS AND OIL ENGINES
HD9560.9	*GASOLINE INSPECTION* **SEE** OIL INSPECTION / *state reports*
TP691	*GASOLINE INSPECTION* **SEE** OIL INSPECTION / *technology*
TN338	GASOLINE LOCOMOTIVES / *mining*
TJ751-805	*GASOLINE MOTORS* **SEE** GAS AND OIL ENGINES
TL153	*GASOLINE STATIONS* **SEE** AUTOMOBILES — SERVICE STATIONS
TX657.S7	*GASOLINE STOVES* **SEE** STOVES, GASOLINE
TP692.2	GASOLINE
QK629.G2	GASTEROMYCETES
QL430.4-5	GASTEROPODA
QE808-9	GASTEROPODA, FOSSIL
RD540.5	*GASTRECTOMY* **SEE** STOMACH — SURGERY
QP193	GASTRIC JUICE
RD540.5	*GASTRIC RESECTION* **SEE** STOMACH — SURGERY
RC840.G3	GASTROENTERITIS
TX631-641	GASTRONOMY — EARLY WORKS TO 1800
TX645-840	*GASTRONOMY* **SEE** COOKERY
TX631-641	GASTRONOMY
QL430.4-5	*GASTROPODA* **SEE** GASTEROPODA
RC804.G3	GASTROSCOPE AND GASTROSCOPY
RD540.5	*GASTROSTOMY* **SEE** STOMACH — SURGERY
RD540.5	*GASTROTOMY* **SEE** STOMACH — SURGERY
QL391.G2	GASTROTRICHA
HV8887	*GATE MONEY (PRISONS)* **SEE** PRISON RELEASE GRATUITIES
HJ5797	*GATE RECEIPTS-TAXATION* **SEE** AMUSEMENTS — TAXATION
S723	GATES / *agriculture*
NA8385-8392	GATES / *architecture*
NA493-5	GATES / *military architecture*
UF630	GATHMANN TORPEDO GUN
UF620.G3	GATLING GUNS
VF410.G3-34	GATLING GUNS / *naval*
GV1796.G	GATO (DANCE)
F2809	GAUCHOS / *argentine republic*
PK1501-2845	*GAUDIAN LANGUAGES* **SEE** INDO-ARYAN LANGUAGES, MODERN
TJ1166	*GAUGES* **SEE** GAGES
TP609	*GAUGING* **SEE** GAGING
DC21	GAUL — HISTORY

DC62	GAUL — HISTORY
PB3001-3029	GAULISH LANGUAGE
DC62-63	GAULS
QL737.U5	*GAUR* **SEE** BUFFALOES
Q380	*GAUSSIAN NOISE* **SEE** RANDOM NOISE THEORY
TK5101	*GAUSSIAN NOISE* **SEE** RANDOM NOISE THEORY / *telecommunication*
D775.5.M	*GAVDO (ISLAND), BATTLE OF, 1941* **SEE** MATAPAN, BATTLE OF, 1941
M1362	GAVOTTES (ACCORDION ENSEMBLE)
M1264	GAVOTTES (BAND)
M1248	GAVOTTES (BAND)
M355-9	GAVOTTES (BASSOON, CLARINET, OBOE)
M355-9	GAVOTTES (CLARINET, 2 FLUTES)
M125-9	GAVOTTES (GUITAR)
M315-319	GAVOTTES (HARPSICHORD, 2 RECORDERS)
M1060	GAVOTTES (ORCHESTRA)
M1048	GAVOTTES (ORCHESTRA)
M31	GAVOTTES (PIANO)
M32.8	GAVOTTES (PIANO)
M315-319	GAVOTTES (PIANO, 2 RECORDERS)
M1145	GAVOTTES (STRING ORCHESTRA)
M1160	GAVOTTES (STRING ORCHESTRA)
M955-7	GAVOTTES (WIND ENSEMBLE)
M214-215	GAVOTTES (2 PIANOS)
M349-353	GAVOTTES (3 VIOLINS)
M455-9	GAVOTTES (4 CLARINETS)
F74.G25	GAY HEAD INDIANS
D568.7	GAZA, BATTLES OF, 1917
PN1361	GAZEL (POETRY)
PT581.G3	GAZEL (POETRY) / *german*
PK6420.G3	GAZEL (POETRY) / *persian*
QL737.U5	GAZELLES
G101-8	*GAZETTEERS* **SEE** GEOGRAPHY — DICTIONARIES
PL8204	GBANDI LANGUAGE
TL696.L33	*GCA* **SEE** GROUND CONTROLLED APPROACH
PL8221	*GDEBO LANGUAGE* **SEE** GREBO LANGUAGE
PL8164.Z9	*GE DIALECT* **SEE** MINA DIALECT
TJ917	GEAR PUMPS
TJ187	GEAR-CUTTING MACHINES
TJ187	GEAR-SHAPING MACHINES
TJ185	GEARING — TABLES, CALCULATIONS, ETC.
TJ184	GEARING — TESTING
TJ184-204	GEARING
TJ193-6	GEARING, BEVEL
TJ192	*GEARING, HELICAL* **SEE** GEARING, SPIRAL
TJ189	*GEARING, INVOLUTE* **SEE** GEARING, SPUR
TJ192	GEARING, SPIRAL
TJ189	GEARING, SPUR
TJ200	GEARING, WORM
QB723.G	GEDDES' COMET
PL8221	*GEDEBO LANGUAGE* **SEE** GREBO LANGUAGE
QL696.A5	GEESE
SF505	GEESE / *breeding*
SK333.G	GEESE / *hunting*
PJ9001-9085	*GEEZ LANGUAGE* **SEE** ETHIOPIC LANGUAGE
QC976.C7	*GEGENSCHEIN* **SEE** COUNTERGLOW
QC476	*GEIGER COUNTERS* **SEE** GEIGER-MÜLLER COUNTERS
QC476	GEIGER-MÜLLER COUNTERS
PL6240	*GELA LANGUAGE* **SEE** FLORIDA LANGUAGE
QP935.G5	GELATIN — PHYSIOLOGICAL EFFECT
RM666.G3	GELSEMIUM / *therapeutics*
BS1187	GEMATRIA
BS2390	GEMATRIA
BM525	GEMATRIA
D756.5.G	GEMBLOUX, BATTLE OF, 1940
QK825-7	*GEMMATION (BOTANY)* **SEE** PLANTS — REPRODUCTION
QH475-9	*GEMMATION (ZOOLOGY)* **SEE** REPRODUCTION, ASEXUAL
NK5530	GEMS — COLLECTORS AND COLLECTING
NK5515	GEMS — PRIVATE COLLECTIONS
GR805	GEMS (IN RELIGION, FOLK-LORE, ETC.)
PN6110.G3	GEMS IN LITERATURE
GV1299.G3	GEMS OF ART (GAME)
NK7650-7690	GEMS / *art industries*
NK5505-5735	GEMS / *glyptics*
GT2250-2280	GEMS / *manners and customs*
TS750-757	GEMS / *manufacture*

RE991	*GENATROPIN* **SEE** ATROPINE / *ophthalmology*
QP921.A8	*GENATROPIN* **SEE** ATROPINE / *pharmacology*
RN666.A85	*GENATROPIN* **SEE** ATROPINE / *therapeutics*
HV7551-8280	*GENDARMES* **SEE** POLICE
HV7965-7985	*GENDARMES* **SEE** POLICE, RURAL
P271	*GENDER* **SEE** GRAMMAR, COMPARATIVE AND GENERAL — GENDER
P271	*GENDER* **SEE** GRAMMAR, COMPARATIVE AND GENERAL — GENDER
CS8	GENEALOGISTS
CS24	GENEALOGY — FORMS, BLANKS, ETC.
CS	GENEALOGY
HE970	*GENERAL AVERAGE* **SEE** AVERAGE (MARITIME LAW)
BT880-881	*GENERAL JUDGMENT* **SEE** JUDGMENT DAY
HJ4101-4129	*GENERAL PROPERTY TAX* **SEE** PROPERTY TAX
B820	GENERAL SEMANTICS
UB220-225	*GENERAL STAFFS* **SEE** ARMIES — STAFFS
HD5307	GENERAL STRIKE
HD6477	GENERAL STRIKE / *direct action*
HD5366	GENERAL STRIKE, GREAT BRITAIN, 1926
BX1910	*GENERAL VICARS* **SEE** VICARS-GENERAL
BX1939.V5	*GENERAL VICARS* **SEE** VICARS-GENERAL / *canon law*
DS150.G4-6	GENERAL ZIONISM
QA689	*GENERALIZED SPACES* **SEE** SPACES, GENERALIZED
D507	GENERALS / *european war*
U51-54	GENERALS / *military biography*
QH471-489	*GENERATION* **SEE** REPRODUCTION
QP251-281	*GENERATION* **SEE** REPRODUCTION / *animals*
QH325	*GENERATION, SPONTANEOUS* **SEE** SPONTANEOUS GENERATION
QH489	GENERATIONS, ALTERNATING
RG211-215	GENERATIVE ORGANS — ABNORMITIES AND DEFORMITIES / *female*
QM691	GENERATIVE ORGANS — ABNORMITIES AND DEFORMITIES
QR171	GENERATIVE ORGANS — BACTERIOLOGY
QP90	GENERATIVE ORGANS — TRANSPLANTATION
QP251	GENERATIVE ORGANS — TRANSPLANTATION
QL876-881	GENERATIVE ORGANS / *comparative anatomy*
QM416-421	GENERATIVE ORGANS / *human anatomy*
QP251-281	GENERATIVE ORGANS / *physiology*
QL881	GENERATIVE ORGANS, FEMALE / *comparative anatomy*
QM421	GENERATIVE ORGANS, FEMALE / *human anatomy*
QP261-281	GENERATIVE ORGANS, FEMALE / *physiology*
QL878	GENERATIVE ORGANS, MALE / *comparative anatomy*
QM416	GENERATIVE ORGANS, MALE / *human anatomy*
QP255-7	GENERATIVE ORGANS, MALE / *physiology*
TK2411-2491	*GENERATORS, ELECTRIC* **SEE** DYNAMOS
BJ1533.G4	GENEROSITY
QH431	*GENES* **SEE** HEREDITY / *biology*
HQ753	*GENES* **SEE** HEREDITY / *eugenics*
HV5133	*GENES* **SEE** HEREDITY / *heredity and alcoholism*
RJ91	*GENES* **SEE** HEREDITY / *heredity and child culture*
HV6121-5	*GENES* **SEE** HEREDITY / *heredity and crime*
BF418	*GENES* **SEE** HEREDITY / *heredity and genius*
BF341-6	*GENES* **SEE** HEREDITY / *psychology*
HM121	*GENES* **SEE** HEREDITY / *sociology*
BF701-724.8	GENETIC PSYCHOLOGY
JX238.A4-7	*GENEVA AWARD* **SEE** ALABAMA CLAIMS
QM401-421	GENITO-URINARY ORGANS — ABNORMITIES AND DEFORMITIES / *human anatomy*
QM691	GENITO-URINARY ORGANS — ABNORMITIES AND DEFORMITIES / *human anatomy*
QL991	GENITO-URINARY ORGANS — ABNORMITIES AND DEFORMITIES / *comparative anatomy*
QL871-881	GENITO-URINARY ORGANS — ABNORMITIES AND DEFORMITIES / *comparative anatomy*
QR171	GENITO-URINARY ORGANS — BACTERIOLOGY
RC870-923	GENITO-URINARY ORGANS — DISEASES
RJ466-476	GENITO-URINARY ORGANS — DISEASES / *children*
RG	GENITO-URINARY ORGANS — DISEASES / *female*
RD571-590	GENITO-URINARY ORGANS — SURGERY
RC312.5.G4-5	GENITO-URINARY ORGANS — TUBERCULOSIS
RC280.G4-5	GENITO-URINARY ORGANS — TUMORS
RC874	GENITO-URINARY ORGANS — DISEASES — — DIAGNOSIS
RV281-6	GENITO-URINARY ORGANS — DISEASES — — ECLECTIC TREATMENT
BF412-426	*GENIUS AND INSANITY* **SEE** GENIUS

BF426	*GENIUS AND INSANITY* **SEE** GENIUS / *genius and degeneration*
BF418	*GENIUS AND INSANITY* **SEE** GENIUS / *genius and heredity*
BF423	*GENIUS AND INSANITY* **SEE** GENIUS / *genius and insanity*
HV6133	*GENIUS AND INSANITY* **SEE** INSANITY / *insanity and crime*
HV4977	*GENIUS AND INSANITY* **SEE** INSANITY / *insanity and degeneration*
BF423	*GENIUS AND INSANITY* **SEE** INSANITY / *insanity and genius*
BF412-426	GENIUS
HV5141	GENIUS / *genius and alcoholism*
BF426	GENIUS / *genius and degeneration*
BF418	GENIUS / *genius and heredity*
BF423	GENIUS / *genius and insanity*
DC224.G4	GENOA — SIEGE, 1800
ND1450	GENRE PAINTING
ND2350	GENRE PAINTING / *water-color*
SB413.G3	GENTIANS / *flower culture*
PL4771-9	*GENTOO LANGUAGE* **SEE** TELUGU LANGUAGE
TN270	GEOCHEMICAL PROSPECTING
QE515	GEOCHEMISTRY
QE508	*GEOCHRONOLOGY* **SEE** GEOLOGICAL TIME
QE508	*GEOCHRONY* **SEE** GEOLOGICAL TIME
QE495	GEODES
QB321	GEODESY — PROBLEMS, EXERCISES, ETC.
QB321	GEODESY — TABLES, ETC.
QB281-341	GEODESY
TL798.G4	GEODETIC SATELLITES
QB281-341	*GEODETICS* **SEE** GEODESY
QE500-505	GEODYNAMICS
QE	*GEOGNOSY* **SEE** GEOLOGY
G67-69	GEOGRAPHERS
G87	GEOGRAPHERS / *ancient*
G87	*GEOGRAPHERS, GREEK* **SEE** GREEK GEOGRAPHERS
G101-8	*GEOGRAPHICAL DICTIONARIES* **SEE** GEOGRAPHY — DICTIONARIES
QH84	GEOGRAPHICAL DISTRIBUTION OF ANIMALS AND PLANTS
GF	*GEOGRAPHICAL DISTRIBUTION OF MAN* **SEE** ANTHROPO-GEOGRAPHY
GN	*GEOGRAPHICAL DISTRIBUTION OF MAN* **SEE** ETHNOLOGY
GN370	*GEOGRAPHICAL DISTRIBUTION OF MAN* **SEE** MAN — MIGRATIONS / *ethnology*
GF101	*GEOGRAPHICAL DISTRIBUTION OF MAN* **SEE** MAN — MIGRATIONS / *anthropo-geography*
QH84	*GEOGRAPHICAL DISTRIBUTION OF PLANTS AND ANIMALS* **SEE** GEOGRAPHICAL DISTRIBUTION OF ANIMALS AND PLANTS
G100	GEOGRAPHICAL MYTHS
GR650-690	GEOGRAPHICAL MYTHS / *folk-lore*
G104-8	*GEOGRAPHICAL NAMES* **SEE** NAMES, GEOGRAPHICAL
RA791-954	*GEOGRAPHICAL PATHOLOGY* **SEE** MEDICAL GEOGRAPHY
G109-110	GEOGRAPHICAL POSITIONS
QB201-237	GEOGRAPHICAL POSITIONS / *determination of*
GV1485	GEOGRAPHICAL RECREATIONS
G2-56	GEOGRAPHICAL SOCIETIES
Z6001-6028	GEOGRAPHY — BIO-BIBLIOGRAPHY
G101-8	GEOGRAPHY — DICTIONARIES
G131	GEOGRAPHY — EXAMINATIONS, QUESTIONS, ETC.
G80-99	GEOGRAPHY — HISTORY
G133	GEOGRAPHY — JUVENILE LITERATURE
G129	GEOGRAPHY — LABORATORY MANUALS
G136-9	GEOGRAPHY — PICTORIAL WORKS
G72-76	GEOGRAPHY — STUDY AND TEACHING
G109-110	GEOGRAPHY — TABLES, ETC.
G104-8	GEOGRAPHY — TERMINOLOGY
G125-7	GEOGRAPHY — TEXT-BOOKS
G113	GEOGRAPHY — 15TH-16TH CENTURIES
G114	GEOGRAPHY — 17TH-18TH CENTURIES
G120-121	GEOGRAPHY — 17TH-18TH CENTURIES
G142	*GEOGRAPHY AND AVIATION* **SEE** GEOGRAPHY, AERIAL
BL65.G	*GEOGRAPHY AND RELIGION* **SEE** RELIGION AND GEOGRAPHY
G-GF	GEOGRAPHY
GN476.4	GEOGRAPHY / *ethnology*
G142	GEOGRAPHY, AERIAL
G101-3	GEOGRAPHY, ANCIENT — DICTIONARIES
DE25	GEOGRAPHY, ANCIENT — DICTIONARIES
D54	GEOGRAPHY, ANCIENT — DICTIONARIES
G1033	GEOGRAPHY, ANCIENT — MAPS
GA205-213	GEOGRAPHY, ANCIENT — MAPS
G82-88	GEOGRAPHY, ANCIENT
QB631-8	*GEOGRAPHY, ASTRONOMICAL* **SEE** ASTRONOMICAL GEOGRAPHY
BS630-633	*GEOGRAPHY, BIBLICAL* **SEE** BIBLE — GEOGRAPHY
DS44-110	*GEOGRAPHY, BIBLICAL* **SEE** BIBLE — GEOGRAPHY / *asia*
DE23-31	*GEOGRAPHY, CLASSICAL* **SEE** CLASSICAL GEOGRAPHY
G87	*GEOGRAPHY, CLASSICAL* **SEE** CLASSICAL GEOGRAPHY
HF1021-9	GEOGRAPHY, COMMERCIAL
BR97-99	*GEOGRAPHY, ECCLESIASTICAL* **SEE** ECCLESIASTICAL GEOGRAPHY
HC	GEOGRAPHY, ECONOMIC
HD	GEOGRAPHY, ECONOMIC
G141	GEOGRAPHY, HISTORICAL
D-F	GEOGRAPHY, HISTORICAL
P375-381	*GEOGRAPHY, LINGUISTIC* **SEE** LINGUISTIC GEOGRAPHY
GA4	GEOGRAPHY, MATHEMATICAL — TABLES, ETC.
GA	GEOGRAPHY, MATHEMATICAL
RA791-954	*GEOGRAPHY, MEDICAL* **SEE** MEDICAL GEOGRAPHY
G89-95	GEOGRAPHY, MEDIEVAL
UA985-997	*GEOGRAPHY, MILITARY* **SEE** MILITARY GEOGRAPHY
GB	*GEOGRAPHY, PHYSICAL* **SEE** PHYSICAL GEOGRAPHY
GF	*GEOGRAPHY, SOCIAL* **SEE** ANTHROPO-GEOGRAPHY
DS425	*GEOGRAPHY, VEDIC* **SEE** VEDAS — GEOGRAPHY
G87	*GEOGRAPHY-EARLY WORKS* **SEE** CLASSICAL GEOGRAPHY
DE23-31	*GEOGRAPHY-EARLY WORKS* **SEE** CLASSICAL GEOGRAPHY
G113	*GEOGRAPHY-EARLY WORKS* **SEE** GEOGRAPHY — 15TH-16TH CENTURIES
G114	*GEOGRAPHY-EARLY WORKS* **SEE** GEOGRAPHY — 17TH-18TH CENTURIES
G120-121	*GEOGRAPHY-EARLY WORKS* **SEE** GEOGRAPHY — 17TH-18TH CENTURIES
G82-88	*GEOGRAPHY-EARLY WORKS* **SEE** GEOGRAPHY, ANCIENT
G89-95	*GEOGRAPHY-EARLY WORKS* **SEE** GEOGRAPHY, MEDIEVAL
GV1485	*GEOGRAPHY-GAMES* **SEE** GEOGRAPHICAL RECREATIONS
G101-8	*GEOGRAPHY-GAZETTEERS* **SEE** GEOGRAPHY — DICTIONARIES
G104-8	*GEOGRAPHY-NOMENCLATURE* **SEE** GEOGRAPHY — TERMINOLOGY
G109-110	*GEOGRAPHY-STATISTICS* **SEE** GEOGRAPHY — TABLES, ETC.
G82-88	*GEOGRAPHY-TO 400 A.D.* **SEE** GEOGRAPHY, ANCIENT
G136-9	*GEOGRAPHY-VIEWS* **SEE** GEOGRAPHY — PICTORIAL WORKS
G136-9	*GEOGRAPHY-VIEWS* **SEE** VIEWS
G89-95	*GEOGRAPHY 400-1400* **SEE** GEOGRAPHY, MEDIEVAL
G125	GEOGRAPHY — TEXT-BOOKS — — BEFORE 1800
G125	GEOGRAPHY — TEXT-BOOKS — — 1800-1870
G126-7	GEOGRAPHY — TEXT-BOOKS — — 1870-1945
DK856	GEOK-TEPE — SIEGE, 1880-1881
QE515	*GEOLOGICAL CHEMISTRY* **SEE** GEOCHEMISTRY
QE33	*GEOLOGICAL MAPS* **SEE** GEOLOGY — MAPS
QE43	GEOLOGICAL MODELING
QE51	GEOLOGICAL MUSEUMS
QE500-501	*GEOLOGICAL PHYSICS* **SEE** GEOPHYSICS
QC806	*GEOLOGICAL PHYSICS* **SEE** GEOPHYSICS
QE1	GEOLOGICAL SOCIETIES
QE50	GEOLOGICAL SPECIMENS-COLLECTION AND PRESERVATION
QE61-350	GEOLOGICAL SURVEYS
QE508	GEOLOGICAL TIME
QE21-22	GEOLOGISTS

E359.5.G4	GEORGIA — HISTORY — — WAR OF 1812
QE601-611	*GEOTECTONICS* **SEE** GEOLOGY, STRUCTURAL
QH511	GEOTROPISM / *biology*
QK776	GEOTROPISM / *botany*
QL391.G5	*GEPHYRA* **SEE** GEPHYREA
QL391.G5	GEPHYREA
DD78.G5	GEPIDAE
SB413.G35	GERANIUMS
QK495.C	GERBERA / *botany*
SB413.G	GERBERA / *floriculture*
RD145	GERIATRIC ANESTHESIA
RC954	GERIATRIC NURSING
RC952-954	GERIATRICS
QH325	*GERM THEORY* **SEE** LIFE — ORIGIN
QH325	*GERM THEORY* **SEE** SPONTANEOUS GENERATION
RB214	GERM THEORY OF DISEASE
UG447.8	*GERM WARFARE* **SEE** BIOLOGICAL WARFARE
GV1757	GERMAN (DANCE)
PT3874	GERMAN BALLADS AND SONGS — SWISS AUTHORS / *collections*
PT3870	GERMAN BALLADS AND SONGS — SWISS AUTHORS / *history*
PT1199-1232	GERMAN BALLADS AND SONGS / *collections*
PT1185	GERMAN BALLADS AND SONGS / *collections*
PT507	GERMAN BALLADS AND SONGS / *history*
BX7801-7843	*GERMAN BAPTIST BRETHREN* **SEE** CHURCH OF THE BRETHREN
BX4740	GERMAN CATHOLICISM
PT203	*GERMAN COURT EPIC* **SEE** COURT EPIC, GERMAN
PT3826.D8	GERMAN DRAMA — AUSTRIAN AUTHORS / *collections*
PT3821	GERMAN DRAMA — AUSTRIAN AUTHORS / *history*
PT1263-4	GERMAN DRAMA — EARLY MODERN (TO 1700) / *collections*
PT636-8	GERMAN DRAMA — EARLY MODERN (TO 1700) / *history*
PT631-3	GERMAN DRAMA — EARLY MODERN (TO 1700) / *history*
PT1435-1477	GERMAN DRAMA — MEDIEVAL / *collections*
PT621	GERMAN DRAMA — MEDIEVAL / *history*
PT626	GERMAN DRAMA — STORIES, PLOTS, ETC.
PT1265	GERMAN DRAMA — 18TH CENTURY / *collections*
PT636-643	GERMAN DRAMA — 18TH CENTURY / *history*
PT1266	GERMAN DRAMA — 19TH CENTURY / *collections*
PT651-663	GERMAN DRAMA — 19TH CENTURY / *history*
PT1268	GERMAN DRAMA — 20TH CENTURY / *collections*
PT666-8	GERMAN DRAMA — 20TH CENTURY / *history*
PT1275-7	GERMAN DRAMA (COMEDY) / *collections*
PT676	GERMAN DRAMA (COMEDY) / *history*
PT1271-3	GERMAN DRAMA (TRAGEDY) / *collections*
PT671	GERMAN DRAMA (TRAGEDY) / *history*
PT1251-1299	GERMAN DRAMA / *collections*
PT605-709	GERMAN DRAMA / *history*
PT1354	GERMAN ESSAYS / *collections*
PT831	GERMAN ESSAYS / *history*
DS771.5	GERMAN EXPEDITION TO CHINA, 1900-1901
PT1283.F2	GERMAN FARCES / *collections*
PT696	GERMAN FARCES / *history*
PT3826	GERMAN FICTION — AUSTRIAN AUTHORS / *collections*
PT3822	GERMAN FICTION — AUSTRIAN AUTHORS / *history*
PT1313-1314	GERMAN FICTION — EARLY MODERN (TO 1700) / *collections*
PT753-6	GERMAN FICTION — EARLY MODERN (TO 1700) / *history*
PT230	GERMAN FICTION — MIDDLE HIGH GERMAN
PT1315	GERMAN FICTION — 18TH CENTURY / *collections*
PT759	GERMAN FICTION — 18TH CENTURY / *history*
PT1332	GERMAN FICTION — 19TH CENTURY / *collections*
PT763-771	GERMAN FICTION — 19TH CENTURY / *history*
PT1334	GERMAN FICTION — 20TH CENTURY / *collections*
PT772	GERMAN FICTION — 20TH CENTURY / *history*
PT1321-1340	GERMAN FICTION / *collections*
PT741-772	GERMAN FICTION / *history*

PJ5111-5119	*GERMAN HEBREW* **SEE** YIDDISH LANGUAGE
PF3120.C7	GERMAN LANGUAGE — BUSINESS GERMAN
HF5728.G3	GERMAN LANGUAGE — BUSINESS GERMAN / *correspondence*
PF4501-4596	GERMAN LANGUAGE — EARLY MODERN (TO 1700)
PF4043-4350	GERMAN LANGUAGE — MIDDLE HIGH GERMAN
PF3801-3991	GERMAN LANGUAGE — OLD HIGH GERMAN
PF3001-5999	GERMAN LANGUAGE
PT1348-1352	GERMAN LETTERS / *collections*
PT811	GERMAN LETTERS / *history*
PT3823-9	GERMAN LITERATURE — AUSTRIAN AUTHORS / *collections*
PT3810-3822	GERMAN LITERATURE — AUSTRIAN AUTHORS / *history*
Z2221-2249	GERMAN LITERATURE — BIBLIOGRAPHY
Z2230-2234	GERMAN LITERATURE — BIO-BIBLIOGRAPHY
PT1109.C3	GERMAN LITERATURE — CATHOLIC AUTHORS
PT89	GERMAN LITERATURE — CATHOLIC AUTHORS
PT1121-6	GERMAN LITERATURE — EARLY MODERN (TO 1700) / *collections*
PT238-281	GERMAN LITERATURE — EARLY MODERN (TO 1700) / *history*
PT1375-1479	GERMAN LITERATURE — MIDDLE HIGH GERMAN / *collections*
PT175-230	GERMAN LITERATURE — MIDDLE HIGH GERMAN / *history*
PF3985-3991	GERMAN LITERATURE — OLD HIGH GERMAN / *collections*
PT183	GERMAN LITERATURE — OLD HIGH GERMAN / *history*
PT3873-6	GERMAN LITERATURE — SWISS AUTHORS / *collections*
PT3860-3872	GERMAN LITERATURE — SWISS AUTHORS / *history*
PT1131	GERMAN LITERATURE — 18TH CENTURY / *collections*
PT1136	GERMAN LITERATURE — 19TH CENTURY / *collections*
PT1141	GERMAN LITERATURE — 20TH CENTURY / *collections*
PT401-3	GERMAN LITERATURE — 20TH CENTURY / *history*
PT3808-9	GERMAN LITERATURE IN FOREIGN COUNTRIES
PT1100-1485	GERMAN LITERATURE / *collections*
PT1-951	GERMAN LITERATURE / *history*
Z2222	GERMAN LITERATURE — BIBLIOGRAPHY — — EARLY
Z2232	GERMAN LITERATURE — BIBLIOGRAPHY — — EARLY
Z2234.F5	GERMAN LITERATURE — BIBLIOGRAPHY — — FIRST EDITIONS
PT285-321	GERMAN LITERATURE — 18TH CENTURY — — HISTORY AND CRITICISM
PT341-395	GERMAN LITERATURE — 19TH CENTURY — — HISTORY AND CRITICISM
RC182.R8	*GERMAN MEASLES* **SEE** RUBELLA
DD102.7	GERMAN MERCENARIES
Z6956.G3	GERMAN NEWSPAPERS — DIRECTORIES
PN5201-5219	GERMAN NEWSPAPERS / *history*
DL532	*GERMAN OCCUPATION OF NORWAY, 1940-1945* **SEE** NORWAY — HISTORY — — GERMAN OCCUPATION, 1940-1945
PT1344-5	GERMAN ORATIONS / *collections*
PT801	GERMAN ORATIONS / *history*
Z6956.G3	GERMAN PERIODICALS — DIRECTORIES
PN5201-5220	GERMAN PERIODICALS / *history*
PF3001-3095	GERMAN PHILOLOGY
PT3824	GERMAN POETRY — AUSTRIAN AUTHORS / *collections*
PT3820	GERMAN POETRY — AUSTRIAN AUTHORS / *history*
PT3836	GERMAN POETRY — CZECH AUTHORS
PT1163-5	GERMAN POETRY — EARLY MODERN (TO 1700) / *collections*
PT525-531	GERMAN POETRY — EARLY MODERN (TO 1700) / *history*
PT1391-1429	GERMAN POETRY — MIDDLE HIGH GERMAN / *collections*
PT175-227	GERMAN POETRY — MIDDLE HIGH GERMAN / *history*
PT3874	GERMAN POETRY — SWISS AUTHORS / *collections*
PT3870	GERMAN POETRY — SWISS AUTHORS / *history*
PT1167-9	GERMAN POETRY — 18TH CENTURY / *collections*

BT769	GIFTS, SPIRITUAL
PL6245	GILBERTESE LANGUAGE
BX3670	GILBERTINES
HD6479	GILD SOCIALISM
TT380	GILDING / mechanical trades
TS715	GILDING / metal manufactures
HD6451-6473	GILDS / history
HD2341-6	GILDS / modern
HV4175-4320	GILDS, NEIGHBORHOOD SEE SOCIAL SETTLEMENTS
PM67	GILIAK LANGUAGE SEE GILYAK LANGUAGE
QL846	GILLS / anatomy
QE391.G	GILSONITE
PM67	GILYAK LANGUAGE
GN635.S2	GILYAKS / sakhalin island
TS1585	GIN (COTTON MACHINERY) SEE COTTON GINS AND GINNING
SB252	GIN (COTTON MACHINERY) SEE COTTON GINS AND GINNING
GV1295.R8	GIN RUMMY SEE RUMMY (GAME)
TP607.G4	GIN
TX771	GINGERBREAD SEE CAKE
RK401-410	GINGIVITIS SEE GUMS — DISEASES
QK495.G48	GINKGO
SB295.G5	GINSENG
DX161	GIPSIES — LANGUAGE
DX101-301	GIPSIES
GN685-6	GIPSIES / ethnography
DX157	GIPSY FOLK-LORE SEE FOLK-LORE, GIPSY
DX161	GIPSY POETRY
PQ7001.A6	GIPSY SEGUIDILLA SEE CANTE HONDO
ML3712	GIPSY SEGUIDILLA SEE CANTE HONDO
SB945.G9	GIPSY-MOTH
QL737.U5	GIRAFFES
QE882.U3	GIRAFFES, FOSSIL
TG350-360	GIRDERS
TA891	GIRDERS / riveting
TG355	GIRDERS, CONTINUOUS
QL821	GIRDLE, SHOULDER SEE SHOULDER GIRDLE / comparative anatomy
QM101	GIRDLE, SHOULDER SEE SHOULDER GIRDLE / human anatomy
GT2810	GIRDLES OF CHASTITY SEE CHASTITY BELTS
HS3353.G5	GIRL SCOUTS
CT3205	GIRLS — BIOGRAPHY
BJ1631-8	GIRLS — CONDUCT OF LIFE
HS3341-3365	GIRLS — SOCIETIES AND CLUBS
HV879	GIRLS — SOCIETIES AND CLUBS
BS576-8	GIRLS IN THE BIBLE SEE CHILDREN IN THE BIBLE
BS2446	GIRLS IN THE BIBLE SEE CHILDREN IN THE BIBLE / new testament
HV879-887	GIRLS / aids and homes for
HQ777	GIRLS / care of
BJ1651-8	GIRLS / ethics
GT2540	GIRLS / manners and customs
GV886	GIRLS' BASKETBALL SEE BASKETBALL FOR WOMEN
HV879	GIRLS' CLUBS SEE GIRLS — SOCIETIES AND CLUBS
HS3341-3365	GIRLS' CLUBS SEE GIRLS — SOCIETIES AND CLUBS
LC1601	GIRLS-EDUCATION SEE COEDUCATION
LC1401-2571	GIRLS-EDUCATION SEE EDUCATION OF WOMEN
HD6228-6250	GIRLS-EMPLOYMENT SEE CHILDREN — EMPLOYMENT
HD6050-6220	GIRLS-EMPLOYMENT SEE WOMAN — EMPLOYMENT
HD6270	GIRLS-EMPLOYMENT SEE YOUTH — EMPLOYMENT
PL8675	GISIRA LANGUAGE SEE SHIRA LANGUAGE
PL8739	GITONGA LANGUAGE SEE TONGA LANGUAGE (INHAMBANE)
PL8143	GIUR LANGUAGE SEE DYUR LANGUAGE
F3722.1.J5	GIVARO INDIANS SEE JIVARO INDIANS
BV772	GIVING, CHRISTIAN SEE CHRISTIAN GIVING
QL862	GIZZARD
QE697	GLACIAL DRIFT SEE DRIFT
QE697-8	GLACIAL EPOCH
QE575-6	GLACIERS
DG95	GLADIATORS
GV35	GLADIATORS
SB413.G5	GLADIOLUS
BJ1533.C5	GLADNESS SEE CHEERFULNESS
BJ1477-1486	GLADNESS SEE CHEERFULNESS / ethics
PN6071.O7	GLADNESS SEE CHEERFULNESS / literary extracts
BJ1533.C7	GLADNESS SEE CONTENTMENT / ethics

BV4647.C7	GLADNESS SEE CONTENTMENT / theology
BJ1480-1486	GLADNESS SEE HAPPINESS
PG91	GLAGOLITIC ALPHABET
PG91	GLAGOLITIC LITERATURE / alphabet
QM371	GLAND OF LUSCHKA SEE COCCYGEAL GLAND / human anatomy
QP187	GLAND OF LUSCHKA SEE COCCYGEAL GLAND / physiology
SF796	GLANDERS
RC146	GLANDERS / human
RC633	GLANDS — DISEASES
RC648-659	GLANDS — DISEASES
QK650	GLANDS (BOTANY)
QK703	GLANDS (BOTANY)
QL863	GLANDS OF BRUNNER SEE BRUNNER'S GLANDS
QM345	GLANDS OF BRUNNER SEE BRUNNER'S GLANDS
QL865-8	GLANDS / comparative anatomy
QM325-371	GLANDS / human anatomy
QP190-246	GLANDS / physiology
QP221	GLANDS, CUTANEOUS SEE CUTANEOUS GLANDS
QM491	GLANDS, CUTANEOUS SEE CUTANEOUS GLANDS
QL943	GLANDS, CUTANEOUS SEE CUTANEOUS GLANDS
QL868	GLANDS, DUCTLESS / comparative anatomy
QM371	GLANDS, DUCTLESS / human anatomy
QP187	GLANDS, DUCTLESS / physiology
QL949	GLANDS, LACRIMAL SEE LACRIMAL ORGANS / comparative anatomy
QM511	GLANDS, LACRIMAL SEE LACRIMAL ORGANS / human anatomy
QP231	GLANDS, LACRIMAL SEE LACRIMAL ORGANS / physiology
QL944	GLANDS, MAMMARY SEE MAMMARY GLANDS / comparative anatomy
QM495	GLANDS, MAMMARY SEE MAMMARY GLANDS / human anatomy
QP246	GLANDS, MAMMARY SEE MAMMARY GLANDS / physiology
QL943	GLANDS, ODORIFEROUS
QL494-6	GLANDS, ODORIFEROUS / insects
QL865	GLANDS, SALIVARY SEE SALIVARY GLANDS / comparative anatomy
QM325	GLANDS, SALIVARY SEE SALIVARY GLANDS / human anatomy
QP191	GLANDS, SALIVARY SEE SALIVARY GLANDS / physiology
QL943	GLANDS, SEBACEOUS SEE SEBACEOUS GLANDS / comparative anatomy
QM491	GLANDS, SEBACEOUS SEE SEBACEOUS GLANDS / human anatomy
QL697	GLANDULA UROPYGALIS SEE UROPYGIAL GLAND
RB145	GLANDULAR FEVER SEE MONONUCLEOSIS
NA4140	GLASS AS STRUCTURAL MATERIAL SEE GLASS CONSTRUCTION / architecture
TP859	GLASS BLOWING AND WORKING
NA4140	GLASS CONSTRUCTION / architecture
QD561	GLASS ELECTRODES SEE ELECTRODES, GLASS / electrochemistry
TP863	GLASS EMBOSSING
MT670	GLASS HARMONICA — INSTRUCTION AND STUDY
ML1055	GLASS HARMONICA
TP845-869	GLASS INDUSTRY SEE GLASS MANUFACTURE
HD9623	GLASS INDUSTRY SEE GLASS TRADE
HF2651.G5	GLASS INDUSTRY SEE GLASS TRADE / tariff
QD139.G5	GLASS MANUFACTURE — CHEMISTRY
TP856	GLASS MANUFACTURE — EARLY WORKS TO 1800
TP845-869	GLASS MANUFACTURE
NK5300-5410	GLASS PAINTERS AND STAINERS SEE GLASS PAINTING AND STAINING
NK5300-5410	GLASS PAINTING AND STAINING
TN939	GLASS SAND SEE SAND, GLASS / mineral industries
HF5716.G4	GLASS TRADE — TABLES AND READY-RECKONERS
HD9623	GLASS TRADE
HF2651.G5	GLASS TRADE / tariff
CJ3413	GLASS WEIGHTS
QL444.D3	GLASS-CRABS
M298	GLASS-HARMONICA AND LUTE MUSIC
M285.G6	GLASS-HARMONICA AND PIANO MUSIC
M284.G6	GLASS-HARMONICA AND PIANO MUSIC
M165	GLASS-HARMONICA MUSIC

BT107	GOD — JUVENILE LITERATURE
BT140	GOD — LOVE
BT153.M4	GOD — MERCY
BT153.M6	GOD — MOTHERHOOD
BT180.N2	GOD — NAME
BT133	GOD — OMNIPOTENCE
BT132	GOD — OMNIPRESENCE
BT131	GOD — OMNISCIENCE
BT180.P7	GOD — PROMISES
BT98-101	GOD — PROOF, EMPIRICAL
BT98-101	GOD — PROOF, ONTOLOGICAL
BT98-101	GOD — PROOF, TELEOLOGICAL
BT145	GOD — RIGHTEOUSNESS
BT150	GOD — WISDOM
BV4817	GOD — WORSHIP AND LOVE
BL1200-1225	*GOD (BRAHMANISM)* **SEE** GOD (HINDUISM)
BL1800-1810	GOD (CHINESE RELIGION)
BL795.G6	GOD (GREEK RELIGION)
B398.G6	GOD (GREEK RELIGION)
BL1200-1225	GOD (HINDUISM)
BP166.2	GOD (ISLAM)
BM610	GOD (JUDAISM)
BT98-101	GOD (THEORY OF KNOWLEDGE)
BT769	*GOD AND MAN, MYSTICAL UNION OF* **SEE** MYSTICAL UNION
BT98-180	GOD
BM610	GOD / *judaism*
BT180.G6	*GOD, GLORY OF* **SEE** GLORY OF GOD
BT124	*GOD, IMMANENCE OF* **SEE** IMMANENCE OF GOD
BT95-96	*GOD, PROVIDENCE AND GOVERNMENT OF* **SEE** PROVIDENCE AND GOVERNMENT OF GOD / *government of god*
BT135	*GOD, PROVIDENCE AND GOVERNMENT OF* **SEE** PROVIDENCE AND GOVERNMENT OF GOD / *providence*
DC56	*GOD'S TRUCE* **SEE** TRUCE OF GOD / *france*
BT180.G6	*GOD-GLORY* **SEE** GLORY OF GOD
BT124	*GOD-IMMANENCE* **SEE** IMMANENCE OF GOD
BT95-96	*GOD-PROVIDENCE AND GOVERNMENT* **SEE** PROVIDENCE AND GOVERNMENT OF GOD / *government of god*
BT135	*GOD-PROVIDENCE AND GOVERNMENT* **SEE** PROVIDENCE AND GOVERNMENT OF GOD / *providence*
BT135	*GOD-SOVEREIGNTY* **SEE** PROVIDENCE AND GOVERNMENT OF GOD / *providence*
BT95-96	*GOD-SOVEREIGNTY* **SEE** PROVIDENCE AND GOVERNMENT OF GOD / *government of god*
BL325.M	*GODDESSES, MOTHER* **SEE** MOTHER-GODDESSES
P141	GODS — LANGUAGE
BL473	GODS
BL325.H4	*GODS, HEALING* **SEE** HEALING GODS
BL1216-1225	GODS, VEDIC
BL303	*GODS-DICTIONARIES* **SEE** MYTHOLOGY — DICTIONARIES
TJ1530	GOFFERING-MACHINES
PL8208	GOGO LANGUAGE
V46	*GOGSTAD SHIP* **SEE** VIKING SHIPS
ML3086	GOIGS
RC656	GOITER
RC656	*GOITER, EXOPHTHALMIC* **SEE** GRAVES' DISEASE
V46	*GOKSTAD SHIP* **SEE** VIKING SHIPS
PL8211	GOLA LANGUAGES
TN580.G6	GOLD — ASSAYING
TN768	GOLD — ELECTROMETALLURGY
TN760-769	GOLD — METALLURGY
TN762	GOLD — MILLING
HG321	GOLD — MINTING
HD9747	GOLD — STANDARDS OF FINENESS
RM666.G7	GOLD — THERAPEUTIC USE
TS729	GOLD ALLOYS
RK653	GOLD ALLOYS / *dentistry*
NB69	*GOLD AND IVORY SCULPTURE* **SEE** SCULPTURE, CHRYSELEPHANTINE
QD412.A9	GOLD COMPOUNDS
TN422	GOLD DREDGING
HG297	*GOLD EXCHANGE STANDARD* **SEE** GOLD STANDARD
TN760-769	*GOLD METALLURGY* **SEE** GOLD — METALLURGY
HD9536	GOLD MINES AND MINING / *economics*
TN410-429	GOLD MINES AND MINING / *mineral industries*

NK7100-7695	*GOLD PLATE* **SEE** PLATE / *gold and silver*
HG297	GOLD STANDARD
QL638.H5	GOLD-EYE
TS260	GOLD-LEAF
TS670	GOLD-PLATING
QD181.A9	GOLD / *chemistry*
HG289-297	GOLD / *finance*
HG551	GOLD / *finance*
TN410-429	GOLD / *mineral resources*
JN3270.G8	GOLDEN BULL, 1356
DS22.7	GOLDEN HORDE
QL696.P2	*GOLDEN ROBIN* **SEE** ORIOLES
BL85	GOLDEN RULE / *comparative religion*
BV4715	GOLDEN RULE / *moral theology*
QA466	GOLDEN SECTION
QK495.S	GOLDENROD / *solidago*
HD5325. M8 1907.G	GOLDFIELD STRIKE, 1907
SH167.G6	GOLDFISH / *fish-culture*
QL638.C25	GOLDFISH / *zoology*
QL638.C94	GOLDFISH / *zoology*
PL461.G	GOLDIAN DIALECT
E474.52	GOLDSBORO, N.C., BATTLE OF, 1862
NK7100-7695	GOLDSMITHING / *art industries*
TS720-761	GOLDSMITHING / *manufactures*
QC711	*GOLDSTEIN RAYS* **SEE** CANAL RAYS
DT262	GOLETTA, TUNIS — SIEGE, 1573
GV967	GOLF — ANECDOTES, FACETIAE, SATIRE, ETC.
GV971	GOLF — RULES
GV966	GOLF FOR WOMEN
GV1017.G	GOLF-CROQUET
GV975	GOLF-LINKS — CONSTRUCTION AND CARE
GV975	GOLF-LINKS
GV961-987	GOLF
GV987	GOLF, MINIATURE
F390	GOLIAD, TEX. — MASSACRE, 1836
PA8065.S8	GOLIARDS / *latin verse*
PL8211	GOLO LANGUAGE
PL4631-4	*GOND LANGUAGE* **SEE** GONDI LANGUAGE
PL4631-4	GONDI LANGUAGE
PL4634	GONDI POETRY / *texts*
DS432.G6	GONDS
MT720	*GONG* **SEE** TAMTAM
ML1040	*GONG* **SEE** TAMTAM
PQ6066	GONGORISM
QC103	GONIOMETRY
RE79.G	GONIOSCOPY
RC202	GONORRHEA
BJ1400-1405	GOOD AND EVIL (ISLAM)
BJ1400-1408	GOOD AND EVIL
BV95	GOOD FRIDAY SERMONS
BV95	GOOD FRIDAY
JX4475	*GOOD OFFICES* **SEE** MEDIATION, INTERNATIONAL
BT378.G6	GOOD SAMARITAN (PARABLE)
HF5353	GOOD-WILL (IN BUSINESS, ETC.)
HF5035.C3	*GOODS, ECCLESIASTICAL* **SEE** CHURCH SUPPLIES
TS2301.C5	*GOODS, ECCLESIASTICAL* **SEE** CHURCH SUPPLIES
PL8222	*GOOR LANGUAGES* **SEE** GUR LANGUAGES
DS485.N4	*GOORKHAS* **SEE** GURKHAS
GV1469.G	GOOSE (GAME)
QL696.A5	*GOOSE* **SEE** GEESE
SF505	*GOOSE* **SEE** GEESE / *breeding*
SK333.G	*GOOSE* **SEE** GEESE / *hunting*
SB386.G6	GOOSEBERRIES
QL737.R6	GOPHERS
PL8211	*GORA LANGUAGE* **SEE** GOLA LANGUAGES
DA510	GORDON RIOTS, 1780
QL377.C6	GORGONACEA
QL377.C6	*GORGONARIA* **SEE** GORGONACEA
QL377.C6	*GORGONIACEAE* **SEE** GORGONACEA
BL820.G7	GORGONS
QL737.P9	GORILLAS
D569.G7	GORIZIA, BATTLE OF, 1916
PK2595-9	*GORKHALI LANGUAGE* **SEE** NEPALI LANGUAGE
DS485.N4	*GORKHAS* **SEE** GURKHAS
D557.G6	GORLICE-TARNOW, BATTLE OF, 1915
HS247.G6	GORMOGONS
GV903	GORODKI (GAME)
DT764.K6	*GORONA* **SEE** KORANA (AFRICAN PEOPLE)
PL5327	GORONTALO LANGUAGE

E99.G67	*GOSHUTE INDIANS* **SEE** GOSIUTE INDIANS
E99.G67	GOSIUTE INDIANS
BT85	*GOSPEL AND LAW* **SEE** LAW AND GOSPEL
BJ1535.G6	GOSSIP
QD401	*GOSSYPEIN* **SEE** GOSSYPOL
SF99	*GOSSYPEIN* **SEE** GOSSYPOL / *cottonseed feeds*
TP681	*GOSSYPEIN* **SEE** GOSSYPOL / *cottonseed oil*
QD401	GOSSYPOL
SF99	GOSSYPOL / *cottonseed feeds*
TP681	GOSSYPOL / *cottonseed oil*
HV5092-5	GOTHENBURG SYSTEM
NA440-489	*GOTHIC ARCHITECTURE* **SEE** ARCHITECTURE, GOTHIC
NK1295	*GOTHIC DECORATION AND ORNAMENT* **SEE** DECORATION AND ORNAMENT, GOTHIC
PD1101-1211	GOTHIC LANGUAGE
NB180	*GOTHIC SCULPTURE* **SEE** SCULPTURE, GOTHIC
PD1117	*GOTHIC WRITING* **SEE** WRITING, GOTHIC
DG506-9	GOTHS IN ITALY
D137-8	GOTHS / *migrations*
DD901.H27	GOTTORF, TREATY OF, MAY 27, 1768 / *hamburg*
PJ9288	*GOURAGE LANGUAGE* **SEE** GURAGE LANGUAGE
SH167.G64	GOURAMI / *fish-culture*
SB413.G6	GOURDS
RC291	GOUT
LC41	GOVERNESSES
B65	*GOVERNMENT* **SEE** POLITICAL SCIENCE / *j political science and philosophy*
HM33	*GOVERNMENT* **SEE** POLITICAL SCIENCE / *political science and sociology*
HJ9701-9995	*GOVERNMENT ACCOUNTING* **SEE** FINANCE, PUBLIC — ACCOUNTING
TL685.3	*GOVERNMENT AEROPLANES* **SEE** AEROPLANES, MILITARY
TL723	*GOVERNMENT AEROPLANES* **SEE** GOVERNMENT AIRCRAFT
TL723	GOVERNMENT AIRCRAFT
HG1951-6	*GOVERNMENT BANKING* **SEE** POSTAL SAVINGS-BANKS
NA4170-4510	*GOVERNMENT BUILDINGS* **SEE** PUBLIC BUILDINGS / *architecture*
JN855-9	*GOVERNMENT BUILDINGS* **SEE** PUBLIC BUILDINGS / *other countries*
JK1651	*GOVERNMENT BUILDINGS* **SEE** PUBLIC BUILDINGS / *state*
JK1613-1649	*GOVERNMENT BUILDINGS* **SEE** PUBLIC BUILDINGS / *u.s. national*
JS342-3	*GOVERNMENT BY COMMISSION* **SEE** MUNICIPAL GOVERNMENT BY COMMISSION / *u.s.*
HD4001-4420	*GOVERNMENT CORPORATIONS* **SEE** CORPORATIONS, GOVERNMENT / *other countries*
HD3881-8	*GOVERNMENT CORPORATIONS* **SEE** CORPORATIONS, GOVERNMENT / *u.s.*
HD3850	*GOVERNMENT CORPORATIONS* **SEE** CORPORATIONS, GOVERNMENT
JF1321-1671	*GOVERNMENT EMPLOYEES* **SEE** CIVIL SERVICE
JV443-5	*GOVERNMENT EMPLOYEES* **SEE** CIVIL SERVICE / *colonial*
JS148-163	*GOVERNMENT EMPLOYEES* **SEE** CIVIL SERVICE / *municipal*
JN-JQ	*GOVERNMENT EMPLOYEES* **SEE** CIVIL SERVICE / *other countries*
HD8011-8023	*GOVERNMENT EMPLOYEES* **SEE** CIVIL SERVICE / *state labor*
JK631-901	*GOVERNMENT EMPLOYEES* **SEE** CIVIL SERVICE / *u.s.*
JK-JQ	GOVERNMENT LIABILITY
JF1621	GOVERNMENT LIABILITY
Z675.G7	*GOVERNMENT LIBRARIES* **SEE** LIBRARIES, GOVERNMENTAL, ADMINISTRATIVE, ETC.
HD3853-6	GOVERNMENT MONOPOLIES
HD9506-9559	*GOVERNMENT OWNERSHIP OF MINES* **SEE** MINES AND MINERAL RESOURCES — GOVERNMENT OWNERSHIP
HE2757	*GOVERNMENT OWNERSHIP OF RAILROADS* **SEE** RAILROADS AND STATE / *u.s.*
HE1051-1081	*GOVERNMENT OWNERSHIP OF RAILROADS* **SEE** RAILROADS AND STATE
HD3840-4420	GOVERNMENT OWNERSHIP
HB236	*GOVERNMENT PRICE CONTROL* **SEE** PRICE REGULATION
HB236	*GOVERNMENT PRICE REGULATION* **SEE** PRICE REGULATION
Z695.1.G7	*GOVERNMENT PUBLICATIONS-CATALOGING* **SEE** CATALOGING OF GOVERNMENT PUBLICATIONS
HF1401-1650	*GOVERNMENT REGULATION OF COMMERCE* **SEE** COMMERCIAL POLICY
HD3621-7	*GOVERNMENT REGULATION OF COMMERCE* **SEE** INDUSTRIAL LAWS AND LEGISLATION
HD3611-3790	*GOVERNMENT REGULATION OF COMMERCE* **SEE** INDUSTRY AND STATE
HE2708	*GOVERNMENT REGULATION OF COMMERCE* **SEE** INTERSTATE COMMERCE / *commission reports*
HE1853	*GOVERNMENT REGULATION OF COMMERCE* **SEE** INTERSTATE COMMERCE / *rates*
HE2710-2712	*GOVERNMENT REGULATION OF COMMERCE* **SEE** INTERSTATE COMMERCE / *law and cases*
HE2757	*GOVERNMENT REGULATION OF COMMERCE* **SEE** INTERSTATE COMMERCE / *discussion*
HE1843	*GOVERNMENT REGULATION OF COMMERCE* **SEE** INTERSTATE COMMERCE / *rates*
HE2710-2712	*GOVERNMENT REGULATION OF RAILROADS* **SEE** INTERSTATE COMMERCE / *law and cases*
HE1843	*GOVERNMENT REGULATION OF RAILROADS* **SEE** INTERSTATE COMMERCE / *rates*
HE1853	*GOVERNMENT REGULATION OF RAILROADS* **SEE** INTERSTATE COMMERCE / *rates*
HE2757	*GOVERNMENT REGULATION OF RAILROADS* **SEE** INTERSTATE COMMERCE / *discussion*
HE2708	*GOVERNMENT REGULATION OF RAILROADS* **SEE** INTERSTATE COMMERCE / *commission reports*
HE2710-2712	*GOVERNMENT REGULATION OF RAILROADS* **SEE** RAILROAD LAW / *u.s.*
HE1053-9	*GOVERNMENT REGULATION OF RAILROADS* **SEE** RAILROAD LAW
HE2801- 3600	*GOVERNMENT REGULATION OF RAILROADS* **SEE** RAILROAD LAW / *other countries*
HE1051-1081	*GOVERNMENT REGULATION OF RAILROADS* **SEE** RAILROADS AND STATE
HE2757	*GOVERNMENT REGULATION OF RAILROADS* **SEE** RAILROADS AND STATE / *u.s.*
JF1621	*GOVERNMENT RESPONSIBILITY* **SEE** GOVERNMENT LIABILITY
JK-JQ	*GOVERNMENT RESPONSIBILITY* **SEE** GOVERNMENT LIABILITY
HG8059.G6	*GOVERNMENT RISKS INSURANCE* **SEE** INSURANCE, GOVERNMENT RISKS
JC518-519	*GOVERNMENT SUPPORT OF SCIENCE, LITERATURE, AND ART* **SEE** STATE ENCOURAGEMENT OF SCIENCE, LITERATURE, AND ART / *political science*
N8750	*GOVERNMENT SUPPORT OF SCIENCE, LITERATURE, AND ART* **SEE** STATE ENCOURAGEMENT OF SCIENCE, LITERATURE, AND ART / *art*
Q181	*GOVERNMENT SUPPORT OF SCIENCE, LITERATURE, AND ART* **SEE** STATE ENCOURAGEMENT OF SCIENCE, LITERATURE, AND ART / *science*
GA51-87	*GOVERNMENT SURVEYS* **SEE** SURVEYS
QB296	*GOVERNMENT SURVEYS* **SEE** SURVEYS / *by country*
QB301-325	*GOVERNMENT SURVEYS* **SEE** SURVEYS / *geodetic surveying*
QE61-350	*GOVERNMENT SURVEYS* **SEE** SURVEYS / *geological*
QH101-199	*GOVERNMENT SURVEYS* **SEE** SURVEYS / *natural history*
TL685.3	*GOVERNMENT-OWNED AIRCRAFT* **SEE** AEROPLANES, MILITARY
TL723	*GOVERNMENT-OWNED AIRCRAFT* **SEE** GOVERNMENT AIRCRAFT
HD4001-4420	*GOVERNMENT-OWNED CORPORATIONS* **SEE** CORPORATIONS, GOVERNMENT / *other countries*
HD3881-8	*GOVERNMENT-OWNED CORPORATIONS* **SEE** CORPORATIONS, GOVERNMENT / *u.s.*
HD3850	*GOVERNMENT-OWNED CORPORATIONS* **SEE** CORPORATIONS, GOVERNMENT
GN490	GOVERNMENT, PRIMITIVE
JC328	GOVERNMENT, RESISTANCE TO
E198	*GOVERNOR SHIRLEY'S WAR* **SEE** UNITED STATES — HISTORY — — KING GEORGE'S WAR, 1744-1748
TJ1055	GOVERNORS (MACHINERY)
TJ550-551	GOVERNORS (STEAM-ENGINE)

JK2447-2458	GOVERNORS — U.S. — — POWERS AND DUTIES
LB2389	*GOWNS, COLLEGE* **SEE** ACADEMIC COSTUME
DA789	GOWRIE CONSPIRACY, 1600
QM611	GRAAFIAN FOLLICLE
QL965	GRAAFIAN FOLLICLE
PN57.G7	*GRAAL* **SEE** GRAIL / *literature*
BT760-761	GRACE (THEOLOGY)
BV283.G7	GRACE AT MEALS
BT769	*GRACE, GIFTS OF* **SEE** GIFTS, SPIRITUAL
BV775	*GRACES, EXPECTATIVE* **SEE** BENEFICES, ECCLESIASTICAL
BX1955	*GRACES, EXPECTATIVE* **SEE** BENEFICES, ECCLESIASTICAL / *catholic church*
PN57.G6	GRACES, THE / *literature*
BL820.G8	GRACES, THE / *mythology*
QL696.P2	*GRACKLES* **SEE** BLACKBIRDS
TF263	*GRADE CROSSINGS* **SEE** RAILROADS — CROSSINGS
HE1617-1619	*GRADE CROSSINGS* **SEE** RAILROADS — CROSSINGS / *economics*
NC1280	*GRADE LABELING* **SEE** LABELS
LB3061	*GRADED SCHOOLS* **SEE** ABILITY GROUPING IN EDUCATION
LB3051-3063	*GRADED SCHOOLS* **SEE** GRADING AND MARKING (STUDENTS)
DL170.8	GRADEHEDE, BATTLE OF, 1157
LB2846	*GRADING AND MARKING (STUDENTS)* **SEE** SCHOOL REPORTS
LB3051-3063	GRADING AND MARKING (STUDENTS)
M2079.L416	GRADUALS (MUSIC)
M2099.L416	GRADUALS (MUSIC)
M2149	GRADUALS (MUSIC)
LB2371	*GRADUATE WORK* **SEE** UNIVERSITIES AND COLLEGES — GRADUATE WORK
HJ2326-7	*GRADUATED TAXATION* **SEE** TAXATION, PROGRESSIVE
BV4255	*GRADUATION SERMONS* **SEE** BACCALAUREATE ADDRESSES
GV1299.G7	GRAFT (GAME)
JF1081	*GRAFT (IN POLITICS)* **SEE** CORRUPTION (IN POLITICS)
JK-JQ	*GRAFT (IN POLITICS)* **SEE** CORRUPTION (IN POLITICS) / *by country*
JS	*GRAFT (IN POLITICS)* **SEE** CORRUPTION (IN POLITICS) / *etc.*
RD121	*GRAFTING OF SKIN* **SEE** SKIN-GRAFTING
SB125	GRAFTING
S691-3	GRAFTING / *implements*
TX558.W5	GRAHAM FLOUR / *food values*
TS2149	GRAHAM FLOUR / *milling*
TN885	GRAHAMITE
TX392	GRAHAMITES
BP605.B4)	GRAIL MOVEMENT (BERNHARDT)
PN57.G7	GRAIL / *literature*
SB608.G6	GRAIN — DISEASES AND PESTS
HE2321.G7	GRAIN — TRANSPORTATION / *railroads*
HF5716.G7	GRAIN — WEIGHTS AND MEASURES
QC89	GRAIN — WEIGHTS AND MEASURES
NA8240	*GRAIN BINS* **SEE** GRANARIES
TH9445.G	GRAIN ELEVATORS — FIRES AND FIRE PREVENTION
TH4461	GRAIN ELEVATORS
SB608.G6	*GRAIN PESTS* **SEE** GRAIN — DISEASES AND PESTS
SB191.R5	*GRAIN RESEARCH* **SEE** RICE RESEARCH
HF5686.G5	GRAIN TRADE — ACCOUNTING
HF5716.G7	GRAIN TRADE — TABLES AND READY-RECKONERS
HG3875.G7	GRAIN TRADE — TABLES AND READY-RECKONERS / *foreign exchange*
HD9030-9049	GRAIN TRADE
HF2651.G8	GRAIN TRADE / *tariff*
SB945.G7	*GRAIN-APHIS* **SEE** GRAIN-LOUSE
QL523.A6	*GRAIN-APHIS* **SEE** GRAIN-LOUSE / *zoology*
SB945.G7	GRAIN-LOUSE
QL523.A6	GRAIN-LOUSE / *zoology*
SB189-191	GRAIN / *culture*
HG3875.G7	*GRAIN-TABLES AND READY-RECKONERS* **SEE** GRAIN TRADE — TABLES AND READY-RECKONERS / *foreign exchange*
HF5716.G7	*GRAIN-TABLES AND READY-RECKONERS* **SEE** GRAIN TRADE — TABLES AND READY-RECKONERS
NA8240	*GRAINERIES* **SEE** GRANARIES
TT330	GRAINING

PN57.G7	*GRAL* **SEE** GRAIL / *literature*
SB201.B5	*GRAMA GRASS, BLUE* **SEE** BLUE GRAMA GRASS
P151-295	*GRAMMAR* **SEE** GRAMMAR, COMPARATIVE AND GENERAL
P207	*GRAMMAR* **SEE** LANGUAGE AND LANGUAGES — GRAMMARS
L-LC	*GRAMMAR SCHOOLS* **SEE** PUBLIC SCHOOLS
P273	GRAMMAR, COMPARATIVE AND GENERAL — ADJECTIVE
P277	GRAMMAR, COMPARATIVE AND GENERAL — ARTICLE
P253	GRAMMAR, COMPARATIVE AND GENERAL — CASE
P271	GRAMMAR, COMPARATIVE AND GENERAL — GENDER
P251-9	GRAMMAR, COMPARATIVE AND GENERAL — INFLECTION
P275	GRAMMAR, COMPARATIVE AND GENERAL — NUMERALS
P215-240	GRAMMAR, COMPARATIVE AND GENERAL — PHONOLOGY
P285	GRAMMAR, COMPARATIVE AND GENERAL — PREPOSITIONS
P279	GRAMMAR, COMPARATIVE AND GENERAL — PRONOUN
P245	GRAMMAR, COMPARATIVE AND GENERAL — REDUPLICATION
P236	GRAMMAR, COMPARATIVE AND GENERAL — SYLLABLE
P291-5	GRAMMAR, COMPARATIVE AND GENERAL — SYNTAX
P152	GRAMMAR, COMPARATIVE AND GENERAL — TERMINOLOGY
P281	GRAMMAR, COMPARATIVE AND GENERAL — VERB
P259	GRAMMAR, COMPARATIVE AND GENERAL — VERB
P281	GRAMMAR, COMPARATIVE AND GENERAL — VOICE
P245	GRAMMAR, COMPARATIVE AND GENERAL — WORD FORMATION
P151-295	GRAMMAR, COMPARATIVE AND GENERAL
P215-240	*GRAMMAR, COMPARATIVE AND GENERAL-CONSONANTS* **SEE** GRAMMAR, COMPARATIVE AND GENERAL — PHONOLOGY
P215-240	*GRAMMAR, COMPARATIVE AND GENERAL-VOWELS* **SEE** GRAMMAR, COMPARATIVE AND GENERAL — PHONOLOGY
P151-295	*GRAMMAR, PHILOSOPHICAL* **SEE** GRAMMAR, COMPARATIVE AND GENERAL
P207	*GRAMMAR, POLYGLOT* **SEE** LANGUAGE AND LANGUAGES — GRAMMARS
P151-295	*GRAMMAR, UNIVERSAL* **SEE** GRAMMAR, COMPARATIVE AND GENERAL
TK2441	GRAMME DYNAMOS
MT150	*GRAMOPHONE* **SEE** PHONOGRAPH / *instruction*
TS2301.P3	*GRAMOPHONE* **SEE** PHONOGRAPH / *manufacture*
ML1055	*GRAMOPHONE* **SEE** PHONOGRAPH / *music history*
DP164	GRANADA (CITY) — SIEGE, 1491-1492
DP115-118	GRANADA (KINGDOM) — HISTORY
DP121-3	GRANADA (KINGDOM) — HISTORY — — SPANISH CONQUEST, 1476-1492
NA8240	GRANARIES
D279-280	GRAND ALLIANCE, WAR OF THE, 1689-1697
DA397	GRAND REMONSTRANCE, 1641
HD1485.P2-55	*GRANGE* **SEE** PATRONS OF HUSBANDRY
TN970	GRANITE / *building stones*
QE462.G2	GRANITE / *petrology*
QE461	GRANODIORITE
GV1469.G3	GRANT'S LINE (GAME)
RC203.G	*GRANULOMA INGUINALE* **SEE** GRANULOMA VENEREUM
RC203.G	GRANULOMA VENEREUM
QK495.V84	*GRAPE* **SEE** GRAPES / *botany*
SB387-399	*GRAPE* **SEE** GRAPES / *culture*
HD9259.G68-7	*GRAPE* **SEE** GRAPES / *trade*
SB387-399	*GRAPE CULTURE* **SEE** VITICULTURE
SB945.G58	GRAPE LEAF-FOLDER
SB945.G6	GRAPE LEAF-HOPPER
SB608.G7	*GRAPE PESTS* **SEE** GRAPES — DISEASES AND PESTS
SB945.G	GRAPE-LEAF SKELETONIZER
SB945.G	GRAPE-SCALE
SB945.G	GRAPE-VINE APHIS
SB608.G7	GRAPE-VINE ROOT-WORM
SB370.G7	GRAPEFRUIT
SB608.G7	GRAPES — DISEASES AND PESTS
QK495.V84	GRAPES / *botany*

SB387-399	GRAPES / *culture*
HD9259.G68-7	GRAPES / *trade*
QA90	GRAPHIC METHODS
QA277	GRAPHIC METHODS / *discussion of observations*
TG270	GRAPHIC STATICS
TJ235	GRAPHIC STATICS / *machinery*
TN845	GRAPHITE
TP261.G7	GRAPHITE / *artificial*
BF889-905	GRAPHOLOGY
MT150	*GRAPHOPHONE* **SEE** PHONOGRAPH / *instruction*
TS2301.P3	*GRAPHOPHONE* **SEE** PHONOGRAPH / *manufacture*
ML1055	*GRAPHOPHONE* **SEE** PHONOGRAPH / *music history*
NE2280	GRAPHOTYPING
QA90	*GRAPHS* **SEE** GRAPHIC METHODS
QA277	*GRAPHS* **SEE** GRAPHIC METHODS / *discussion of observations*
QE779	GRAPTOLITES
SF473.B	*GRASS PARAKEET* **SEE** BUDGERIGARS
SF967.G7	*GRASS STAGGERS* **SEE** GRASS TETANY
SF967.G7	GRASS TETANY
TH7458.G7	*GRASS-BURNER* **SEE** MENNONITE GRASS-BURNER
SB608.G8	GRASSES — DISEASES AND PESTS
QK495.G74	GRASSES / *botany*
SB197-201	GRASSES / *culture*
QL508.A2	*GRASSHOPPERS* **SEE** LOCUSTS
SB945.L7	*GRASSHOPPERS* **SEE** LOCUSTS / *economic entomology*
QA259	*GRASSMANN'S THEORY OF EXTENSION* **SEE** AUSDEHNUNGSLEHRE
SB945.A8	*GRASSWORM* **SEE** FALL ARMY-WORMS
BJ1533.G8	*GRATEFULNESS* **SEE** GRATITUDE / *ethics*
BV4647.G8	*GRATEFULNESS* **SEE** GRATITUDE / *theology*
NA3050-3055	*GRATES* **SEE** FIREPLACES / *architecture*
TH7421-7434	*GRATES* **SEE** FIREPLACES / *heating*
BV4647.G8	GRATITUDE — JUVENILE LITERATURE
BJ1533.G8	GRATITUDE / *ethics*
BV4647.G8	GRATITUDE / *theology*
RC921.V4	*GRAVEL (PATHOLOGY)* **SEE** CALCULI, URINARY
RD581	*GRAVEL (PATHOLOGY)* **SEE** CALCULI, URINARY
TE233	*GRAVEL ROADS* **SEE** ROADS, GRAVEL
TN939	GRAVEL
DC127.6	GRAVELINES, FRANCE — SIEGE, 1644
E477.67	GRAVELLY RUN, VA., BATTLE OF, 1865
DC303.4	GRAVELOTTE, BATTLE OF, 1870
GN486	*GRAVES* **SEE** BURIAL / *ethnology*
GT3150-3390	*GRAVES* **SEE** BURIAL / *manners and customs*
RA625	*GRAVES* **SEE** BURIAL / *public health*
RA626-630	*GRAVES* **SEE** CEMETERIES
GT3320	*GRAVES* **SEE** CEMETERIES / *manners and customs*
CN	*GRAVES* **SEE** EPITAPHS / *f greek and latin*
PN6288.5-6298	*GRAVES* **SEE** EPITAPHS / *general collections*
CS	*GRAVES* **SEE** EPITAPHS / *other*
PN1441	*GRAVES* **SEE** EPITAPHS / *poetry*
GN486	*GRAVES* **SEE** FUNERAL RITES AND CEREMONIES / *ethnology*
GT3150-3390	*GRAVES* **SEE** FUNERAL RITES AND CEREMONIES / *manners and customs*
GN795-6	*GRAVES* **SEE** MOUNDS
NB1800-1885	*GRAVES* **SEE** SEPULCHRAL MONUMENTS / *sculpture*
NA6120-6199	*GRAVES* **SEE** TOMBS / *architecture*
D639.D4	*GRAVES, MILITARY* **SEE** SOLDIERS' BODIES, DISPOSITION OF / *european war*
D810.D4	*GRAVES, MILITARY* **SEE** SOLDIERS' BODIES, DISPOSITION OF / *world war*
RC656	GRAVES' DISEASE
NB1800-1885	*GRAVESTONES* **SEE** SEPULCHRAL MONUMENTS / *sculpture*
RA626-630	*GRAVEYARDS* **SEE** CEMETERIES
GT3320	*GRAVEYARDS* **SEE** CEMETERIES / *manners and customs*
QB331	GRAVIMETER (GEOPHYSICAL INSTRUMENT)
QD101-142	*GRAVIMETRIC ANALYSIS* **SEE** CHEMISTRY, ANALYTIC — QUANTITATIVE
TC361	*GRAVING-DOCKS* **SEE** DRY-DOCKS
QB341	GRAVITATION / *constant of*
QC178	GRAVITATION / *theories of*
QP82	GRAVITY — PHYSIOLOGICAL EFFECT
QH657	GRAVITY — PHYSIOLOGICAL EFFECT
QB331	GRAVITY — TABLES, ETC.
QB331	*GRAVITY BALANCE* **SEE** GRAVIMETER (GEOPHYSICAL INSTRUMENT)
QB331	*GRAVITY METER* **SEE** GRAVIMETER (GEOPHYSICAL INSTRUMENT)
TF686	*GRAVITY RAILROADS* **SEE** RAILROADS, GRAVITY
QA927	GRAVITY WAVES / *mathematics*
QB331-9	GRAVITY
QA839	*GRAVITY, CENTER OF* **SEE** CENTER OF MASS
QB338	*GRAVITY, LOCAL DISTURBANCE OF* **SEE** PLUMB-LINE DEFLECTIONS
QC111-114	*GRAVITY, SPECIFIC* **SEE** SPECIFIC GRAVITY
PJ7121-4	*GRAWI LANGUAGE* **SEE** SHAURI LANGUAGE
BX3601-3655	*GRAY FRIARS* **SEE** FRANCISCANS
BX4361-4	*GRAY FRIARS* **SEE** FRANCISCANS / *women*
QL638.M	GRAY MULLETS
SH351.G	GRAY MULLETS / *fish-culture*
SD397.P575	*GRAY PINE* **SEE** JACK-PINE
QL696.P2	*GRAY-CHEEKED THRUSH, BICKNELL'S* **SEE** BICKNELL'S THRUSH
SH691.G	GRAYLING FISHING
QL638.S2	GRAYLING
SH167.G8	GRAYLING / *culture*
SD427.G8	GRAZING / *forests*
HD241	GRAZING / *public lands*
PN57.G7	*GREAL* **SEE** GRAIL / *literature*
TJ1075-1081	*GREASE* **SEE** LUBRICATION AND LUBRICANTS
TP670-695	*GREASE* **SEE** OILS AND FATS
QL737.E2	*GREAT ANTEATER* **SEE** ANT BEAR
QL696.A3	GREAT AUK
BR520	GREAT AWAKENING
LC6601-6660	*GREAT BOOKS PROGRAM* **SEE** GROUP READING
E241.G	GREAT BRIDGE, VA., BATTLE OF, 1775
DA	GREAT BRITAIN — HISTORY
SF429.G7	GREAT DANES
E199	*GREAT MEADOWS, BATTLE OF, 1754* **SEE** NECESSITY, FORT, BATTLE OF, 1754
BL604.Y5	*GREAT MONAD (SYMBOL)* **SEE** YIN YANG SYMBOL
DL733-743	*GREAT NORTHERN WAR, 1700-1721* **SEE** NORTHERN WAR, 1700-1721 / *sweden*
SF429.G75	GREAT PYRENEES (DOGS)
BX303	*GREAT SCHISM* **SEE** SCHISM — EASTERN AND WESTERN CHURCH
BX1301	*GREAT SCHISM* **SEE** SCHISM, THE GREAT WESTERN, 1378-1417
DT773	*GREAT TREK* **SEE** AFRICA, SOUTH — HISTORY — — GREAT TREK, 1836-1840
BX1301	*GREAT WESTERN SCHISM* **SEE** SCHISM, THE GREAT WESTERN, 1378-1417
VK571	GREAT-CIRCLE SAILING
BL1483	*GREATER VEHICLE* **SEE** MAHAYANA BUDDHISM
BF412-426	*GREATNESS* **SEE** GENIUS
HV5141	*GREATNESS* **SEE** GENIUS / *genius and alcoholism*
BF426	*GREATNESS* **SEE** GENIUS / *genius and degeneration*
BF418	*GREATNESS* **SEE** GENIUS / *genius and heredity*
BF423	*GREATNESS* **SEE** GENIUS / *genius and insanity*
QL696.P9	GREBES
PL8221	GREBO LANGUAGE
TP268-9	*GRECIAN FIRE* **SEE** GREEK FIRE / *ancient*
TP300	*GRECIAN FIRE* **SEE** GREEK FIRE / *modern*
BX303	*GRECO-ROMAN SCHISM* **SEE** SCHISM — EASTERN AND WESTERN CHURCH
DF827	GRECO-TURKISH WAR, 1897
DR575	GRECO-TURKISH WAR, 1897 / *period in turkey*
DF1-951	GREECE — HISTORY
DE	GREECE — HISTORY / *classical antiquity*
DF501-649	GREECE, MEDIEVAL — HISTORY
DF701-951	GREECE, MODERN — HISTORY
DF827	*GREECE, MODERN-HISTORY-WAR WITH TURKEY, 1897* **SEE** GRECO-TURKISH WAR, 1897
DR575	*GREECE, MODERN-HISTORY-WAR WITH TURKEY, 1897* **SEE** GRECO-TURKISH WAR, 1897 / *period in turkey*
DF75-129	*GREECE-CIVILIZATION* **SEE** CIVILIZATION, GREEK
BJ1535.A8	*GREED* **SEE** AVARICE
BH108-9	*GREEK AESTHETICS* **SEE** AESTHETICS, GREEK
NA270-285	*GREEK ARCHITECTURE* **SEE** ARCHITECTURE, GREEK
PA3445	GREEK BALLADS AND SONGS / *ancient*
PA5255	GREEK BALLADS AND SONGS / *modern*
PA5285	GREEK BALLADS AND SONGS / *modern*

CE42	*GREEK CHRONOLOGY* **SEE** CHRONOLOGY, GREEK
BX200-750	*GREEK CHURCH* **SEE** ORTHODOX EASTERN CHURCH
DF75-129	*GREEK CIVILIZATION* **SEE** CIVILIZATION, GREEK
BR128.G8	*GREEK CIVILIZATION* **SEE** HELLENISM / christianity
DF77	*GREEK CIVILIZATION* **SEE** HELLENISM / history
BM176	*GREEK CIVILIZATION* **SEE** HELLENISM / judaism
BM536.G7	*GREEK CIVILIZATION* **SEE** HELLENISM / judaism
PN56.H4	*GREEK CIVILIZATION* **SEE** HELLENISM / literature
DF122	*GREEK CULTUS* **SEE** CULTUS, GREEK
PA3238	GREEK DRAMA — PRESENTATION, MODERN
PA3465-6	GREEK DRAMA (COMEDY) / collections
PA3161-3199	GREEK DRAMA (COMEDY) / history
PA3464	GREEK DRAMA (SATYR PLAY)
PA3160	GREEK DRAMA (SATYR PLAY)
PA3461-3	GREEK DRAMA (TRAGEDY) / collections
PA3131-3159	GREEK DRAMA (TRAGEDY) / history
PA3461-8	GREEK DRAMA / collections
PA3131-3239	GREEK DRAMA / history
PA3136	*GREEK DRAMA-CHORUS* **SEE** DRAMA — CHORUS (GREEK DRAMA)
LA75	*GREEK EDUCATION* **SEE** EDUCATION, GREEK
PA3487.E7	GREEK FICTION / collections
PA3267	GREEK FICTION / history
TP268-9	GREEK FIRE / ancient
TP300	GREEK FIRE / modern
G87	GREEK GEOGRAPHERS
DF211-212	GREEK HISTORIANS / historiography
PA600-691	*GREEK LANGUAGE (KOINE)* **SEE** GREEK LANGUAGE, HELLENISTIC (300 B.C.-600 A.D.)
PA201-1179	GREEK LANGUAGE
PA695-895	GREEK LANGUAGE, BIBLICAL
PA1001-1179	*GREEK LANGUAGE, BYZANTINE* **SEE** GREEK LANGUAGE, MEDIEVAL AND LATE
PA600-691	GREEK LANGUAGE, HELLENISTIC (300 B.C.-600 A.D.)
PA1001-1179	GREEK LANGUAGE, MEDIEVAL AND LATE
PA1001-1179	GREEK LANGUAGE, MODERN
LJ	GREEK LETTER SOCIETIES
PA3487.E4	GREEK LETTERS / collections
PA3042	GREEK LETTERS / history
PA3403.E6	GREEK LETTERS / teubner collections
PA3601-3671	GREEK LETTERS / translations
PA3421.G8	GREEK LITERATURE — JEWISH AUTHORS
PA3050-4500	GREEK LITERATURE
PA5650-5665	GREEK LITERATURE, MODERN
PA5201-5298	GREEK LITERATURE, MODERN
QA22	*GREEK MATHEMATICS* **SEE** MATHEMATICS, GREEK
DF89	GREEK MERCENARIES
PN5231-9	GREEK NEWSPAPERS / history
DF125	*GREEK ORACLES* **SEE** ORACLES, GREEK
PA3479-3482	GREEK ORATIONS / collections
PA3263-4	GREEK ORATIONS / history
PN5231-5240	GREEK PERIODICALS / history
PA1-99	GREEK PHILOLOGY
B108-708	*GREEK PHILOSOPHY* **SEE** PHILOSOPHY, ANCIENT
PA3431-3459	GREEK POETRY / collections
PA3092-3129	GREEK POETRY / history
PA5280-5289	GREEK POETRY, MODERN / collections
PA5250-5255	GREEK POETRY, MODERN / history
PA3473-3515	GREEK PROSE LITERATURE / collections
PA3255-3281	GREEK PROSE LITERATURE / history
PA5295	GREEK PROSE LITERATURE, MODERN / collections
PA5265	GREEK PROSE LITERATURE, MODERN / history
PA3265	*GREEK RHETORIC* **SEE** RHETORIC, ANCIENT
NA281-5	*GREEK TEMPLES* **SEE** TEMPLES, GREEK
NA275	*GREEK TEMPLES* **SEE** TEMPLES, GREEK
DF251	GREEK TRIBES
PA3469.W5	GREEK WIT AND HUMOR / collections
PA3249	GREEK WIT AND HUMOR / history
DF	GREEKS
SB945.G7	*GREEN BUG* **SEE** GRAIN-LOUSE
QL523.A6	*GREEN BUG* **SEE** GRAIN-LOUSE / zoology
RC643	*GREEN CANCER* **SEE** CHLOROMA
S661	GREEN MANURING
SB945	GREEN PEACH APHID
QL696.L7	*GREEN PLOVERS* **SEE** LAPWINGS
SB945.G	GREEN SOLDIER-BUG
QL537.M7	GREEN-BOTTLE FLIES
QA825	*GREEN'S OPERATORS* **SEE** POTENTIAL, THEORY OF
QA825	*GREEN'S THEOREM* **SEE** POTENTIAL, THEORY OF
HG604-5	*GREENBACK PARTY* **SEE** NATIONAL GREENBACK PARTY
HG604-5	*GREENBACKERS* **SEE** NATIONAL GREENBACK PARTY
HG604-5	GREENBACKS
SH351.B3	*GREENHEAD* **SEE** STRIPED BASS
SB415	*GREENHOUSE CROPS* **SEE** GREENHOUSE PLANTS
SB415	*GREENHOUSE CULTURE* **SEE** GREENHOUSE MANAGEMENT
SB415	*GREENHOUSE GARDENING* **SEE** GREENHOUSE MANAGEMENT
SB415	GREENHOUSE MANAGEMENT
SB392	GREENHOUSE PLANTS — DISEASES AND PESTS
SB415	GREENHOUSE PLANTS
SB945.T	GREENHOUSE THRIPS
SB416	GREENHOUSES — HEATING AND VENTILATION
SB415-416	GREENHOUSES
SB415	*GREENHOUSES-MANAGEMENT* **SEE** GREENHOUSE MANAGEMENT
GV975	*GREENKEEPING* **SEE** GOLF-LINKS — CONSTRUCTION AND CARE
PM61-64	*GREENLANDIC LANGUAGE* **SEE** ESKIMO LANGUAGE
S643	GREENSAND / fertilizers
QE471	GREENSAND / geology
QE685	GREENSAND / geology
RC641	*GREENSICKNESS* **SEE** CHLOROSIS
E83.794	GREENVILLE, TREATY OF, 1795
NC1860	GREETING CARDS / art
BJ2095.G7	GREETING CARDS / etiquette
GT3050	*GREETINGS* **SEE** SALUTATIONS
CE76	*GREGORIAN CALENDAR* **SEE** CALENDAR, GREGORIAN
E271	GRENADA, BATTLE OF, 1779
UF765	GRENADES
HG225	GRESHAM'S LAW
BX3601-3655	*GREY FRIARS* **SEE** FRANCISCANS
BX4361-4	*GREY FRIARS* **SEE** FRANCISCANS / women
SF429.G8	GREYHOUNDS
BJ1480-1487	*GRIEF* **SEE** JOY AND SORROW
E475.23	GRIERSON'S CAVALRY RAID, 1863
QD77	*GRIGNARD REACTION* **SEE** GRIGNARD REAGENTS
QD77	GRIGNARD REAGENTS
PK3357	GRIHYASUTRAS
PK3157	GRIHYASUTRAS
PK3457	GRIHYASUTRAS
PK3257	GRIHYASUTRAS
PK3057	GRIHYASUTRAS
NA3030	GRILLES
TJ1280-1298	GRINDING AND POLISHING
G665 1850	GRINNEL EXPEDITION, 1ST, 1850-1851
G665 1853	GRINNEL EXPEDITION, 2D, 1853-1855
RC150	*GRIPPE* **SEE** INFLUENZA
DT764.G	GRIQUAS
DL658.8	GRISBADA QUESTION
DL658.8	*GRISEBAA QUESTION* **SEE** GRISBADA QUESTION
TS2120-2159	*GRIST-MILLS* **SEE** FLOUR-MILLS
QM567	*GRISTLE* **SEE** CARTILAGE
RD560	*GRITTI'S AMPUTATION* **SEE** AMPUTATIONS OF LEG
HD9320-9330	GROCERIES / economics
TX341-357	GROCERIES / home economics
HD9320-9330	GROCERS / economics
TX341-357	GROCERS / home economics
HF5686.G8	GROCERY TRADE — ACCOUNTING
HF6161.G8	GROCERY TRADE / advertising
HF6201.G73	GROCERY TRADE / business
HD9320-9330	GROCERY TRADE / economics
HF5716.G8	GROCERY TRADE / etc.
HF5849.G8	GROCERY TRADE / window displays
QM543	GROIN
QM161	GROIN / muscles
E99.A87	*GROS VENTRES OF MONTANA* **SEE** ATSINA INDIANS
E99.H6	*GROS VENTRES OF THE MISSOURI* **SEE** HIDATSA INDIANS
E99.A87	*GROS VENTRES OF THE PRAIRIE* **SEE** ATSINA INDIANS
QL696.P2	GROSBEAKS
PM653	*GROSVENTRE LANGUAGE* **SEE** ATSINA LANGUAGE
PM1331	*GROSVENTRE LANGUAGE* **SEE** HIDATSA LANGUAGE
E99.H6	*GROSVENTRES OF THE MISSOURI* **SEE** HIDATSA INDIANS

E99.A87	*GROSVENTRES OF THE PRAIRIE* **SEE** ATSINA INDIANS
BH301.G74	GROTESQUE / *aesthetics*
NA8460	GROTESQUE / *architecture*
E241.G8	GROTON HEIGHTS, BATTLE OF, 1781
NA8455	*GROTTO ARCHITECTURE* **SEE** CAVE ARCHITECTURE
GB601-8	*GROTTOES* **SEE** CAVES / *physical geography*
GN783-4	*GROTTOES* **SEE** CAVES / *prehistoric archaeology*
ML448	GROUND BASS
TL696.L33	GROUND CONTROLLED APPROACH
SB432	GROUND COVER PLANTS
TL574.G7	*GROUND EFFECT (AERODYNAMICS)* **SEE** GROUND-CUSHION PHENOMENON / *aeronautics*
TA352	*GROUND EFFECT (AERODYNAMICS)* **SEE** GROUND-CUSHION PHENOMENON
TA352	*GROUND PRESSURE (AERODYNAMICS)* **SEE** GROUND-CUSHION PHENOMENON
TL574.G7	*GROUND PRESSURE (AERODYNAMICS)* **SEE** GROUND-CUSHION PHENOMENON / *aeronautics*
QC907	GROUND TEMPERATURE **SEE** EARTH TEMPERATURE
GB1001-1197	*GROUND WATER* **SEE** WATER, UNDERGROUND
TA352	GROUND-CUSHION PHENOMENON
TL574.G7	GROUND-CUSHION PHENOMENON / *aeronautics*
QL737.R6	*GROUND-HOGS* **SEE** MARMOTS
SB351.P3	*GROUND-NUTS* **SEE** PEANUTS
HB401	*GROUND-RENT* **SEE** RENT (ECONOMIC THEORY)
HB401	*GROUND-RENT* **SEE** RENT / *economic theory*
HJ4631	*GROUND-RENT* **SEE** RENT / *taxation*
RA641.G7	GROUND-SQUIRRELS AS CARRIERS OF DISEASE
QL737.R6	GROUND-SQUIRRELS
TK3227	*GROUNDING (ELECTRICITY)* **SEE** ELECTRIC CURRENTS — GROUNDING
LC6501-6560	*GROUP DISCUSSION* **SEE** FORUMS (DISCUSSION AND DEBATE)
PN4177-4191	*GROUP DISCUSSION* **SEE** FORUMS (DISCUSSION AND DEBATE) / *debating*
HM131	*GROUP DYNAMICS* **SEE** SOCIAL GROUPS
HG8059.G7	*GROUP INSURANCE* **SEE** INSURANCE, GROUP
HG8830	*GROUP INSURANCE* **SEE** INSURANCE, GROUP / *life*
BV287	*GROUP PRAYER* **SEE** PRAYER GROUPS
RC488	GROUP PSYCHOTHERAPY
LC6601-6660	GROUP READING
LB3061	*GROUPING BY ABILITY* **SEE** ABILITY GROUPING IN EDUCATION
LB3061	*GROUPING, HOMOGENEOUS* **SEE** ABILITY GROUPING IN EDUCATION
QA603	GROUPS OF POINTS
QA385	GROUPS, CONTINUOUS
HM131	*GROUPS, SOCIAL* **SEE** SOCIAL GROUPS
QA171	GROUPS, THEORY OF
SK325.G	GROUSE / *hunting*
QL696.G2	GROUSE / *zoology*
QL696.G2	*GROUSE, RUFFED* **SEE** RUFFED GROUSE
SK325.G7	*GROUSE, RUFFED* **SEE** RUFFED GROUSE
BL583	*GROVES, SACRED* **SEE** SACRED GROVES
E473.77	*GROVETON, BATTLE OF, 1862* **SEE** BULL RUN, 2D BATTLE, 1862
QK731-769	GROWTH (PLANTS)
QK731	GROWTH PROMOTING SUBSTANCES
QK731	*GROWTH SUBSTANCES* **SEE** GROWTH PROMOTING SUBSTANCES
QH511	GROWTH / *biology*
QP84	GROWTH / *physiology*
QR201.T9	*GRUBER-WIDAL REACTION* **SEE** TYPHOID FEVER — DIAGNOSIS — — AGGLUTINATION REACTION
BR986	GRUNDTVIGIANISM
BR986	*GRUNDTVIGIANS* **SEE** GRUNDTVIGIANISM
PK9160-9178	*GRUSIAN LITERATURE* **SEE** GEORGIAN LITERATURE
DK511.G36	*GRUSINIANS* **SEE** GEORGIANS
GR820-830	*GRYPHONS* **SEE** ANIMALS, MYTHICAL
JC345	*GRYPHONS* **SEE** HERALDRY / *national theory*
CR	*GRYPHONS* **SEE** HERALDRY / *national*
U549.2	GT. BRIT. — BOYS' UNITS
DK214-215	*GT. BRIT.-HISTORY-CRIMEAN WAR, 1853-1856* **SEE** CRIMEAN WAR, 1853-1856 / *russia*
DR567	*GT. BRIT.-HISTORY-CRIMEAN WAR, 1853-1856* **SEE** CRIMEAN WAR, 1853-1856 / *turkey*
DA235	*GT. BRIT.-HISTORY-PEASANTS' REVOLT, 1381* **SEE** TYLER'S INSURRECTION, 1381
U549.2	*GT. BRIT. ARMY-BOYS* **SEE** GT. BRIT. — BOYS' UNITS
F1219	GUACHICHILE INDIANS
DP269.2.G	GUADALAJARA, BATTLE OF, 1937
E408	GUADALUPE HIDALGO, TREATY OF, 1848
PM6116	*GUAICURUAN LANGUAGES* **SEE** GUAYCURUAN LANGUAGES
F2520.1.G	GUAJAJARA INDIANS / *brazil*
F2270.2.G6	*GUAJIRO INDIANS* **SEE** GOAJIRO INDIANS
F2230.2.G	GUANA INDIANS
PM6051	GUANA LANGUAGE
SF401.H	*GUANACO* **SEE** HUANACO / *animal culture*
QL737.U5	*GUANACO* **SEE** HUANACO / *zoology*
PJ2371	GUANCHE LANGUAGE
DP302.C36-51	GUANCHES / *canary islands*
GN661.C2	GUANCHES / *ethnology*
S649	GUANO
HD9484.G9	GUANO / *trade*
F2230.2.G72	GUARANI INDIANS
PM7171-9	GUARANI LANGUAGE
HD4928.A	*GUARANTEED ANNUAL WAGE* **SEE** WAGES — ANNUAL WAGE
HD4928.A	*GUARANTEED WAGES* **SEE** WAGES — ANNUAL WAGE
HG9970.S4-8	*GUARANTY INSURANCE* **SEE** INSURANCE, SURETY AND FIDELITY / *economics*
K	*GUARANTY INSURANCE* **SEE** INSURANCE, SURETY AND FIDELITY / *law*
HG1781-2	*GUARANTY OF BANK DEPOSITS* **SEE** BANKS AND BANKING — GOVERNMENT GUARANTY OF DEPOSITS
JX4171.G8	GUARANTY, TREATIES OF
F2420	*GUARAO* **SEE** WARRAU INDIANS
PM6091	GUARAUNA LANGUAGE
F2420	*GUARAUNO INDIANS* **SEE** WARRAU INDIANS
PM6096	GUARAYO LANGUAGE
U190-195	GUARD DUTY
UA749.5	*GUARDS, PAPAL* **SEE** PAPAL GUARDS
F2823.G	GUARPE INDIANS
PM5386	*GUARPE LANGUAGE* **SEE** ALLENTIAC LANGUAGE
F1221.H	*GUASTEC INDIANS* **SEE** HUASTEC INDIANS
PM3831	*GUASTEC LANGUAGE* **SEE** HUASTEC LANGUAGE
F1461-1477	GUATEMALA — HISTORY
F1449.B7	*GUATEMALA-BRITISH HONDURAS DISPUTE* **SEE** BRITISH HONDURAS QUESTION
PQ7490-7499	GUATEMALAN LITERATURE
PN4989.G	GUATEMALAN PERIODICALS
PQ7496	GUATEMALAN POETRY / *collections*
PQ7492	GUATEMALAN POETRY / *history*
F2520.1.G	GUATO INDIANS
F2679	*GUAYAKI INDIANS* **SEE** GUAYAQUI INDIANS
F2230.2.G75	GUAYANA INDIANS
F2679	GUAYAQUI INDIANS
F2235.36	GUAYAQUIL MEETING, 1822
F2230.2.G78	GUAYCURU INDIANS
PM6116	GUAYCURUAN LANGUAGES
PM6485	*GUAYCURURU LANGUAGE* **SEE** MBAYA LANGUAGE
F1434	GUAYMI INDIANS
PM3806	GUAYMI LANGUAGE
SB608.G	GUAYULE — DISEASES AND PESTS
DG522-3	GUELFS AND GHIBELLINES
DD147	GUELFS AND GHIBELLINES / *germany*
DG522-3	*GUELPHS* **SEE** GUELFS AND GHIBELLINES
DD147	*GUELPHS* **SEE** GUELFS AND GHIBELLINES / *germany*
D25.5	*GUERILLAS* **SEE** GUERRILLAS
SF199.G8	GUERNSEY CATTLE
SF193.G9	GUERNSEY CATTLE / *herd-books*
F3097	*GUERRA DEL PACIFICO, 1879-1884* **SEE** WAR OF THE PACIFIC, 1879-1884
ML1727.33	GUERRE DES BOUFFONS
U240	GUERRILLA WARFARE
JX5123	GUERRILLAS (INTERNATIONAL LAW)
D25.5	GUERRILLAS
PL8411	*GUERZE LANGUAGE* **SEE** KPELLE LANGUAGE
GV1295.G9	GUEST (GAME)
GV1470-1561	*GUESTS* **SEE** ENTERTAINING / *amusements*
TX851-885	*GUESTS* **SEE** ENTERTAINING / *dining-room service*
TX731-9	*GUESTS* **SEE** ENTERTAINING / *etc.*
BJ2021-2038	*GUESTS* **SEE** ENTERTAINING / *etiquette*
BJ1801-2193	*GUESTS* **SEE** ETIQUETTE
BJ2021-8	*GUESTS* **SEE** HOSPITALITY
PT5484	GUEUX — SONGS AND MUSIC
DH187-193	GUEUX
PM3841	*GUICHOLA LANGUAGE* **SEE** HUICHOL LANGUAGE
TL589.4	GUIDANCE SYSTEMS (FLIGHT)

DA392	GUNPOWDER PLOT, 1605
TP272	GUNPOWDER / chemical technology
HD9663	GUNPOWDER / industry
TP273	GUNPOWDER, SMOKELESS
TS535-7	GUNS SEE FIREARMS / manufacture
V	GUNS SEE FIREARMS / u naval science
UF520-630	GUNS SEE ORDNANCE
UD390-395	GUNS SEE RIFLES / army
SK274	GUNS SEE RIFLES / hunting
VD370	GUNS SEE RIFLES / navy
SK274	GUNS SEE SHOT-GUNS / hunting
TS535	GUNS SEE SHOT-GUNS / manufacture
UF440-445	GUNS, MOUNTAIN SEE MOUNTAIN GUNS
RD156	GUNSHOT WOUNDS
TS535	GUNSMITHING
QA73	GUNTER'S LINE SEE SLIDE-RULE
TH5613	GUNTER'S LINE SEE SLIDE-RULE / carpentry
SH167.G	GUPPIES / culture
PL8222	GUR LANGUAGES
PL8211	GURA LANGUAGE SEE GOLA LANGUAGES
PJ9288	GURAGE LANGUAGE
PL5327	GURANTALA LANGUAGE SEE GORONTALO LANGUAGE
PK9132	GURIAN DIALECT
PK9132	GURIC DIALECT SEE GURIAN DIALECT
PK9132	GURISH DIALECT SEE GURIAN DIALECT
DS451.8	GURJARA-PRATIHARA DYNASTY
DS485.N4	GURKHAS
ML1015.G8	GUSLI / russian
SB291.I5	GUTTA-PERCHA / culture
TS1930	GUTTA-PERCHA / manufacture
HD9161	GUTTA-PERCHA / trade
TH2493	GUTTERS
PL8287	GWEABO LANGUAGE SEE JABO LANGUAGE
PL3651.G9	GYARUNG LANGUAGE
GV407-410	GYMNASIUMS — APPARATUS AND EQUIPMENT
GV403-5	GYMNASIUMS
GV461-475	GYMNASTICS
RA781	GYMNASTICS, MEDICAL
RM719-721	GYMNASTICS, MEDICAL
QL430.4	GYMNOBRANCHIATA SEE NUDIBRANCHIATA
QL430.4	GYMNOSOMATA
QK495.G9	GYMNOSPERMS
QK683.G9	GYMNOSPERMS / anatomy
QK643.G99	GYMNOSPERMS / morphology
GN480.4	GYNECOCRACY SEE MATRIARCHY
RG106	GYNECOLOGY — CASES, CLINICAL REPORTS, STATISTICS
RG	GYNECOLOGY
RG104	GYNECOLOGY, OPERATIVE
RZ386	GYNECOLOGY, OSTEOPATHIC
RJ466	GYNECOLOGY, PEDIATRIC SEE PEDIATRIC GYNECOLOGY
RG12-16	GYNECOLOGY-HOSPITALS SEE HOSPITALS, GYNECOLOGIC AND OBSTETRIC
DX101-301	GYPSIES SEE GIPSIES
GN685-6	GYPSIES SEE GIPSIES / ethnography
TN946	GYPSUM
DX161	GYPSY LANGUAGE SEE GIPSIES — LANGUAGE
SB945.G9	GYPSY-MOTH SEE GIPSY-MOTH
TL589.C6	GYRO COMPASS
VK577	GYRO COMPASS
QA862.G9	GYRO COMPASS
TL589.5	GYRO PILOT SEE AUTOMATIC PILOT (AEROPLANES)
TL589.C6	GYROCOMPASS SEE GYRO COMPASS
VK577	GYROCOMPASS SEE GYRO COMPASS
QA862.G9	GYROCOMPASS SEE GYRO COMPASS
TL589.5	GYROPILOT SEE AUTOMATIC PILOT (AEROPLANES)
TL715	GYROPLANES SEE AUTOGIROS
QA862.G9	GYROSCOPE
QA862.G9	GYROSTAT SEE GYROSCOPE
TL589.C6	GYROSTATIC COMPASS SEE GYRO COMPASS
QA862.G9	GYROSTATIC COMPASS SEE GYRO COMPASS
VK577	GYROSTATIC COMPASS SEE GYRO COMPASS
PM6126	GÜENOA LANGUAGE
DH206.H	HAARLEM — SIEGE, 1572-1573
TT572-630	HABERDASHERY SEE MEN'S FURNISHING GOODS
BF335-7	HABIT
BX4223	HABIT, MONASTIC SEE MONASTICISM AND RELIGIOUS ORDERS — HABIT / sisterhoods

BL1458	HABIT, MONASTIC SEE MONASTICISM AND RELIGIOUS ORDERS, BUDDHIST — HABIT
BX2790	HABIT, MONASTIC SEE MONASTICISM AND RELIGIOUS ORDERS — HABIT
QL750-785	HABITS OF ANIMALS SEE ANIMALS, HABITS AND BEHAVIOR OF
HV6049	HABITUAL CRIMINALS SEE RECIDIVISTS
GV1299.H3	HACHI-HACHI SEE HACHI-JU-HACHI (GAME)
GV1299.H3	HACHI-JU-HACHI (GAME)
TJ1233	HACK SAWS SEE HACKSAWS
QK495.C	HACKBERRY / celtis
E99.H15	HACKENSACK INDIANS
SF293.H2	HACKNEY HORSE
TJ1233	HACKSAWS
QL638.G2	HADDOCK
SH351.H18	HADDOCK / fisheries
PJ2457	HADENDOA LANGUAGE
BL535-547	HADES SEE FUTURE LIFE / comparative religion
BT899-904	HADES SEE FUTURE LIFE / theology
BL1475.H5	HADES SEE HELL / buddhism
BL735	HADES SEE HELL / classical mythology
BL545	HADES SEE HELL / comparative religion
BT834-8	HADES SEE HELL / theology
PJ6971	HADHRAMI INSCRIPTIONS SEE INSCRIPTIONS, HADRAMI
PL8223	HADIA LANGUAGE
BP136.46-48	HADITH — AUTHORITIES
BP135	HADITH — CRITICISM, INTERPRETATION, ETC.
BP135	HADITH
BP135	HADITH-COMMENTARIES SEE HADITH — CRITICISM, INTERPRETATION, ETC.
PJ6971	HADRAMI INSCRIPTIONS SEE INSCRIPTIONS, HADRAMI
DT443	HADZAPI (AFRICAN PEOPLE) SEE TINDIGA (AFRICAN PEOPLE)
PM1321	HAELTZUK LANGUAGE SEE HEILTSUK LANGUAGE
QD181.H5	HAFNIUM
DT199	HAFSIDES
DT199	HAFSITE DYNASTY SEE HAFSIDES
QL638.1	HAGFISH
BX4662	HAGIOGRAPHY
BX4662	HAGIOLOGY SEE HAGIOGRAPHY
D283.5	HAGUE, TREATY OF, 1717
E99.H2	HAIDA INDIANS
PM1271-4	HAIDA LANGUAGE
DK508.7	HAIDAMAKS
HG9968.H2-5	HAIL INSURANCE SEE INSURANCE, HAIL
QC929.H1	HAIL
PL1841	HAILAM DIALECT SEE CHINESE LANGUAGE — DIALECTS — — HAINAN
PM1321	HAILTSA LANGUAGE SEE HEILTSUK LANGUAGE
PM1321	HAILTSUK LANGUAGE SEE HEILTSUK LANGUAGE
QM488	HAIR — ABNORMITIES
QL942	HAIR — ABNORMITIES
RL91	HAIR — CARE AND HYGIENE
RL91	HAIR — DISEASES
TT973	HAIR — DYEING AND BLEACHING
QK650	HAIR (BOTANY) SEE TRICHOMES
SF851	HAIR-BALLS / veterinary medicine
TT975-6	HAIR-WORK
GN193	HAIR / anthropology
QL942	HAIR / comparative
QM488	HAIR / human
RL115	HAIR, REMOVAL OF / by electricity
SB741.H3	HAIRY-ROOT DISEASE
E99.H23	HAISLA INDIANS
F1901-1939	HAITI — HISTORY
PQ3940-3949	HAITIAN LITERATURE (FRENCH)
PQ3946	HAITIAN POETRY (FRENCH) / collections
PQ3942	HAITIAN POETRY (FRENCH) / history
F1938.3	HAITIAN REVOLUTION, 1843 SEE HAITI — HISTORY — — REVOLUTION, 1843
F1927	HAITI — HISTORY — — AMERICAN OCCUPATION, 1915-1934
F1938.3	HAITI — HISTORY — — REVOLUTION, 1843
F1926	HAITI — HISTORY — — 1844-1915
F1928	HAITI — HISTORY — — 1934-
PL4001.L2	HAKA DIALECT SEE LAI LANGUAGE
DS432.H	HAKAS (TRIBE)
SH351.H185	HAKE FISHERIES

QL638.M	HAKE / zoology
PJ7121-4	HAKILI LANGUAGE SEE SHAURI LANGUAGE
BM500-509	HALACHA SEE TALMUD
BM500-509	HALAKHA SEE TALMUD
PL5699	HALAYA DIALECT
CJ1836	HALF-CENT
CJ1835	HALF-DIME
CJ1835	HALF-DOLLAR / u.s.
NA7175	HALF-TIMBER WORK SEE HALF-TIMBERED HOUSES
NA7175	HALF-TIMBERED HOUSES
TR975	HALF-TONE PROCESS SEE PHOTOENGRAVING — HALFTONE PROCESS
BX7235-6	HALF-WAY COVENANT SEE COVENANTS (CHURCH POLITY) / congregational
BT1010	HALF-WAY COVENANT SEE COVENANTS (CHURCH POLITY) / general
BX9183	HALF-WAY COVENANT SEE COVENANTS (CHURCH POLITY) / presbyterian
QL638.H5	HALFBEAKS
TR975	HALFTONE PROCESS SEE PHOTOENGRAVING — HALFTONE PROCESS
SH351.H2	HALIBUT FISHERIES
QD165	HALIDES
SF95	HALITE SEE SALT / feeding and feeds
GT2870	HALITE SEE SALT / manners and customs
TN900-909	HALITE SEE SALT / mineral industries
HD9213	HALITE SEE SALT / trade
BM720.H3	HALITSAH
QC611	HALL EFFECT
NK7210	HALL-MARKS
QB723.H2	HALLEY'S COMET
GT4965	HALLOW-EVE SEE HALLOWEEN
GT4965	HALLOWEEN
LB3227	HALLS OF RESIDENCE SEE DORMITORIES
GN779-780	HALLSTATT PERIOD
BF1048-1063	HALLUCINATIONS AND ILLUSIONS
RC534	HALLUCINATIONS AND ILLUSIONS / psychiatry and psychopathology
BF491-3	HALLUCINATIONS AND ILLUSIONS / psychology
RD563	HALLUX VALGUS SEE TOES — ABNORMITIES AND DEFORMITIES
PL7511.H3	HALMAHERAN LANGUAGES
N8160	HALO - ART SEE NIMBUS — ART
SB608.O2	HALO-BLIGHT
N8160	HALO-ART SEE NIMBUS — ART
QD441	HALOCHROMISM
QD281.H3	HALOGENATION
QD165	HALOGENS
QC976.H1	HALOS (METEOROLOGY)
RD86.H3	HALOTHANE
TX373	HAM / food supply
TX556.H	HAM / food values
TS1962	HAM / meat industry
SF489.H2	HAMBURGS (POULTRY)
DS76	HAMDANIDS
D267.H2	HAMELN — SIEGE, 1633
GN545	HAMITES / anthropology
HT1581-9	HAMITES / races
PJ2301-2551	HAMITIC LANGUAGES
PJ991-5	HAMITO-SEMITIC LANGUAGES
GV1093	HAMMER THROWING SEE WEIGHT THROWING
RD563	HAMMER TOE SEE TOES — ABNORMITIES AND DEFORMITIES
ML750-925	HAMMERED STRINGED INSTRUMENTS SEE STRINGED INSTRUMENTS
ML1000-1018	HAMMERED STRINGED INSTRUMENTS SEE STRINGED INSTRUMENTS
TJ1201.H3	HAMMERS
TJ1305	HAMMERS / power tool
GN415.H	HAMMOCKS / ethnology
TS1781	HAMMOCKS / manufacture
ML597	HAMMOND ELECTRIC ORGAN SEE HAMMOND ORGAN
M14.85	HAMMOND ORGAN MUSIC SEE ELECTRONIC ORGAN MUSIC (HAMMOND REGISTRATION)
M14.8	HAMMOND ORGAN MUSIC SEE ELECTRONIC ORGAN MUSIC (HAMMOND REGISTRATION)
ML597	HAMMOND ORGAN
SF393.H3	HAMPSHIRE SWINE
QD535	HAMPSON LIQUEFIER

E473.2	HAMPTON ROADS, BATTLE OF, 1862
DS748	HAN DYNASTY SEE CHINA — HISTORY — — HAN DYNASTY, 202 B.C.-220 A.D.
GV1299.H3	HANA SEE HACHI-JU-HACHI (GAME)
GV1299.H3	HANA-KARUTA SEE HACHI-JU-HACHI (GAME)
QM691	HAND — ABNORMITIES AND DEFORMITIES
RD776	HAND — ABNORMITIES AND DEFORMITIES / surgery
RC951	HAND — DISEASES
MT710	HAND BELL RINGING SEE HANDBELL RINGING
N8217.H3	HAND IN ART
BF205.H3	HAND TEST
UF765	HAND-GRENADES SEE GRENADES
TH5675-7	HAND-RAILING
GV1111	HAND-TO-HAND FIGHTING SEE FIGHTING, HAND-TO-HAND
QM548	HAND / anatomy
NC774	HAND / art
MT221	HAND / piano
BF908-940	HAND / psychology
GV1017.H2	HANDBALL
M147	HANDBELL MUSIC
MT710	HANDBELL RINGING
AG103-191	HANDBOOKS, VADE-MECUMS, ETC.
PH1401-1409	HANDE-HUI LANGUAGE SEE OSTIAK LANGUAGE
GN233	HANDEDNESS SEE LEFT- AND RIGHT-HANDEDNESS / anthropology
QP385	HANDEDNESS SEE LEFT- AND RIGHT-HANDEDNESS / physiological psychology
N71.3	HANDICAPPED ARTISTS SEE ARTISTS, PHYSICALLY HANDICAPPED
LC4001-4100	HANDICAPPED CHILDREN — EDUCATION
SF331	HANDICAPPING SEE HORSE RACE BETTING
TT	HANDICRAFT
NK	HANDICRAFT / artistic crafts
TS1725	HANDKERCHIEFS / manufacture
HD9930	HANDKERCHIEFS / trade
TX537	HANDLING OF FOOD SEE FOOD HANDLING
BV873.L3	HANDS, IMPOSITION OF SEE IMPOSITION OF HANDS / christian sacraments
BM715	HANDS, IMPOSITION OF SEE IMPOSITION OF HANDS / jewish sacrifices
BV873.L3	HANDS, LAYING ON OF SEE IMPOSITION OF HANDS / christian sacraments
BM715	HANDS, LAYING ON OF SEE IMPOSITION OF HANDS / jewish sacrifices
Z41-42	HANDWRITING SEE AUTOGRAPHS
BF889-905	HANDWRITING SEE GRAPHOLOGY
Z105-115	HANDWRITING SEE PALEOGRAPHY
Z40-115	HANDWRITING SEE WRITING
TL730	HANGARS
TH2417	HANGING ROOFS SEE ROOFS, SUSPENSION
HV8579-8581	HANGING
QL696.P2	HANGNEST SEE ORIOLES
DL743.H	HANGO, BATTLE OF, 1714
QA408	HANKEL FUNCTIONS
DG247.2	HANNIBAL-CROSSING OF THE ALPS, 218 B.C.
E475.51	HANOVER, PA., BATTLE OF, 1863
D287.7	HANOVER, TREATY OF, 1725
DA500	HANOVERIAN MERCENARIES
DA503	HANOVERIAN MERCENARIES
DD801.H17-25	HANSEATIC LEAGUE
HF455-463	HANSEATIC LEAGUE / commerce
RC154	HANSEN'S DISEASE SEE LEPROSY
QR201.L5	HANSEN'S DISEASE SEE LEPROSY / bacteriology
BM695.H3	HANUKKAH (FEAST OF LIGHTS)
BM657.H3	HANUKKAH LAMP
BJ1480-1486	HAPPINESS
QP451	HAPTICS SEE TOUCH / physiology
BF275	HAPTICS SEE TOUCH / psychology
PJ9293	HARARI LANGUAGE
DT443	HARARIS / tanganyika
PL5701	HARAYA DIALECT
UG410-448	HARBOR DEFENSES SEE COAST DEFENSES
HE951-3	HARBORS — PORT CHARGES
HE951-3	HARBORS — REGULATIONS
VK369-369.8	HARBORS OF REFUGE
TC203-324	HARBORS / engineering
JX4138	HARBORS / international law
HE551-560	HARBORS / transportation

TS227	HARD-FACING
TS227	*HARD-SURFACING* **SEE** HARD-FACING
ML760	HARDANGER FIDDLE
TT787	HARDANGER NEEDLEWORK
M59	HARDANGER-FIDDLE MUSIC
ML760	*HARDANGERFELE* **SEE** HARDANGER FIDDLE
QK754	*HARDINESS OF PLANTS* **SEE** PLANTS — HARDINESS
ML760	*HARDINGFELE* **SEE** HARDANGER FIDDLE
TA407	HARDNESS / *engineering tests*
HF5686.H3	HARDWARE — ACCOUNTING
TS405	HARDWARE — CATALOGS
HF5585.H3	HARDWARE — CREDIT GUIDES
HF5716.H3	HARDWARE — TABLES, ETC.
TS400-455	HARDWARE / *manufacture*
HD9745	HARDWARE / *trade*
GV1063	HARE AND HOUNDS / *games*
E477.61	*HARE'S HILL, VA., BATTLE OF, 1865* **SEE** STEDMAN, FORT, BATTLE OF, 1865
RD524	HARELIP
DT192	HAREM / *barbary states*
DT70	HAREM / *egypt*
DR432	HAREM / *turkey*
HQ1707	HAREM / *turkey*
HQ1170	HAREM / *women in the orient*
GR730.H	HARES (IN RELIGION, FOLK-LORE, ETC.) / *folk-lore*
BL325.H	HARES (IN RELIGION, FOLK-LORE, ETC.) / *religion*
QL737.R6	HARES
SF451-5	HARES / *breeding*
SK341.H3	HARES / *hunting*
QE882.R6	HARES, FOSSIL
DS422.C3	*HARIJANS* **SEE** UNTOUCHABLES
E241.H2	HARLEM HEIGHTS, BATTLE OF, 1776
PN1988.H3	HARLEQUIN
E83.79	HARMAR'S EXPEDITION, 1790
QA401-411	HARMONIC ANALYSIS
QA405	HARMONIC FUNCTIONS
ML1055	*HARMONICA, GLASS* **SEE** GLASS HARMONICA
ML1050-1053	*HARMONICA, MOUTH* **SEE** MOUTH-ORGAN
ML1055	*HARMONICON, CHEMICAL* **SEE** PYROPHONE
ML597	*HARMONIUM* **SEE** REED-ORGAN
ML597	*HARMONIUM, BICHROMATIC* **SEE** BICHROMATIC HARMONIUM
MT50	HARMONY — MECHANICAL AIDS
BH301.H3	HARMONY (AESTHETICS)
BD645	*HARMONY (COSMOLOGY)* **SEE** HARMONY OF THE SPHERES
BD645	HARMONY OF THE SPHERES
ML3815	HARMONY / *acoustics*
ML3852	HARMONY / *aesthetics*
ML444	HARMONY / *history*
MT50	HARMONY / *instruction*
ML3836	HARMONY / *psychology*
MT224	HARMONY, KEYBOARD
TS1032	HARNESS — REPAIRING
TS1030-1035	HARNESS MAKING AND TRADE / *manufacture*
HD9780	HARNESS MAKING AND TRADE / *trade*
S720-721	HARNESS / *farm implements*
GT5888	HARNESS / *manners and customs*
MT540-548	HARP — INSTRUCTION AND STUDY
MT546	HARP — ORCHESTRA STUDIES
M296-7	*HARP AND CLARINET MUSIC* **SEE** CLARINET AND HARP MUSIC
M1105-6	*HARP AND CLARINET WITH STRING ORCHESTRA* **SEE** CLARINET AND HARP WITH STRING ORCHESTRA
M296-7	*HARP AND ENGLISH HORN MUSIC* **SEE** ENGLISH HORN AND HARP MUSIC
M296-7	*HARP AND FLUTE MUSIC* **SEE** FLUTE AND HARP MUSIC
M1105-6	*HARP AND FLUTE WITH STRING ORCHESTRA* **SEE** FLUTE AND HARP WITH STRING ORCHESTRA
M182-4	HARP AND ORGAN MUSIC
M1105-6	HARP AND ORGAN WITH STRING ORCHESTRA
M298	HARP AND PERCUSSION MUSIC
M1105	HARP AND PERCUSSION WITH STRING ORCHESTRA — SCORES
M1105-6	HARP AND PERCUSSION WITH STRING ORCHESTRA
M272-3	HARP AND PIANO MUSIC
M294-5	HARP AND VIOLA MUSIC
M294-5	*HARP AND VIOLIN MUSIC* **SEE** VIOLIN AND HARP MUSIC
M294-5	*HARP AND VIOLONCELLO MUSIC* **SEE** VIOLONCELLO AND HARP MUSIC
ML128.H3	HARP MUSIC — BIBLIOGRAPHY
MT545	HARP MUSIC — TEACHING PIECES
M465-7	*HARP MUSIC (4 HARPS)* **SEE** QUARTETS (4 HARPS)
M292-3	HARP MUSIC (2 HARPS)
M465-7	*HARP MUSIC (4 HARPS)* **SEE** QUARTETS (4 HARPS)
M115-117	HARP MUSIC
M118-119	HARP MUSIC, ARRANGED
ML132.H3	*HARP MUSIC-GRADED LISTS* **SEE** HARP MUSIC — BIBLIOGRAPHY — — GRADED LISTS
ML132.H3	HARP MUSIC — BIBLIOGRAPHY — — GRADED LISTS
M1036-7	HARP WITH CHAMBER ORCHESTRA
M1036	HARP WITH CHAMBER ORCHESTRA, ARRANGED — SCORES
M1036-7	HARP WITH CHAMBER ORCHESTRA, ARRANGED
M1037	HARP WITH ORCHESTRA — SOLO WITH PIANO
M1036-7	HARP WITH ORCHESTRA
M1106	HARP WITH STRING ORCHESTRA — SOLO WITH PIANO
M1105-6	HARP WITH STRING ORCHESTRA
M1105-6	HARP WITH STRING ORCHESTRA, ARRANGED
M142.H2	HARP-LUTE GUITAR MUSIC
ML1015-1018	HARP-LUTE GUITAR
ML1005-6 .	HARP / *history and construction*
M1105-6	HARP, HARPSICHORD, PIANO WITH STRING ORCHESTRA
M1040	HARP, VIOLIN, VIOLONCELLO WITH ORCHESTRA — SCORES
M1040-1041	HARP, VIOLIN, VIOLONCELLO WITH ORCHESTRA
E451	HARPERS FERRY, W. VA. — JOHN BROWN RAID, 1859
ML399	HARPISTS / *biography collective*
ML419	HARPISTS / *individual*
SH387	HARPOONS
GN447.H29	HARPOONS / *primitive*
M1105-6	HARPS (2) WITH STRING ORCHESTRA
M253-4	*HARPSICHORD AND BASSOON MUSIC* **SEE** BASSOON AND HARPSICHORD MUSIC
M285.C4	*HARPSICHORD AND CELESTA MUSIC* **SEE** CELESTA AND HARPSICHORD MUSIC
M284.C4	*HARPSICHORD AND CELESTA MUSIC* **SEE** CELESTA AND HARPSICHORD MUSIC
M240-242	*HARPSICHORD AND FLUTE MUSIC* **SEE** FLUTE AND HARPSICHORD MUSIC
M278-9	*HARPSICHORD AND MANDOLIN MUSIC* **SEE** MANDOLIN AND HARPSICHORD MUSIC
M245-6	*HARPSICHORD AND OBOE MUSIC* **SEE** OBOE AND HARPSICHORD MUSIC
M182-4	HARPSICHORD AND ORGAN MUSIC
M185-6	HARPSICHORD AND ORGAN MUSIC, ARRANGED
M214	HARPSICHORD AND PIANO MUSIC
M1010-1011	HARPSICHORD AND PIANO WITH ORCHESTRA
M915-917	HARPSICHORD AND PIANO WITH WIND ENSEMBLE
M240-242	*HARPSICHORD AND RECORDER MUSIC* **SEE** RECORDER AND HARPSICHORD MUSIC
M239	*HARPSICHORD AND VIOLA D'AMORE MUSIC* **SEE** VIOLA D'AMORE AND HARPSICHORD MUSIC
M239	*HARPSICHORD AND VIOLA DA GAMBA MUSIC* **SEE** VIOLA DA GAMBA AND HARPSICHORD MUSIC
M224-6	*HARPSICHORD AND VIOLA MUSIC* **SEE** VIOLA AND HARPSICHORD MUSIC
M239	*HARPSICHORD AND VIOLA POMPOSA MUSIC* **SEE** VIOLA POMPOSA AND HARPSICHORD MUSIC
M221	*HARPSICHORD AND VIOLIN MUSIC* **SEE** VIOLIN AND HARPSICHORD MUSIC
M217-218	*HARPSICHORD AND VIOLIN MUSIC* **SEE** VIOLIN AND HARPSICHORD MUSIC
M233	*HARPSICHORD AND VIOLONCELLO MUSIC* **SEE** VIOLONCELLO AND HARPSICHORD MUSIC
M229-230	*HARPSICHORD AND VIOLONCELLO MUSIC* **SEE** VIOLONCELLO AND HARPSICHORD MUSIC
ML651	HARPSICHORD MAKERS
ML700-742	HARPSICHORD MUSIC — HISTORY AND CRITICISM
MT245-7	HARPSICHORD MUSIC — INSTRUCTIVE EDITIONS
M214	HARPSICHORD MUSIC (2 HARPSICHORDS)
M215	HARPSICHORD MUSIC (2 HARPSICHORDS), ARRANGED
M216	HARPSICHORD MUSIC (3 HARPSICHORDS)
M216	HARPSICHORD MUSIC (4 HARPSICHORDS)
M20-39	HARPSICHORD MUSIC
M216	*HARPSICHORD QUARTETS (4 HARPSICHORDS)* **SEE** HARPSICHORD MUSIC (4 HARPSICHORDS)

M216	*HARPSICHORD QUARTETS (4 HARPSICHORDS)* **SEE** HARPSICHORD MUSIC (4 HARPSICHORDS)
M36.5	*HARPSICHORD REALIZATIONS OF THOROUGH BASS* **SEE** THOROUGH BASS — REALIZATIONS
M216	*HARPSICHORD TRIOS (3 HARPSICHORDS)* **SEE** HARPSICHORD MUSIC (3 HARPSICHORDS)
M216	*HARPSICHORD TRIOS (3 HARPSICHORDS)* **SEE** HARPSICHORD MUSIC (3 HARPSICHORDS)
M1010-1011	HARPSICHORD WITH CHAMBER ORCHESTRA
M1010-1011	HARPSICHORD WITH ORCHESTRA
M1105-6	HARPSICHORD WITH STRING ORCHESTRA
ML650-697	HARPSICHORD / *history and construction*
M1105-6	HARPSICHORD, FLUTE, HARP WITH STRING ORCHESTRA
M1105-6	HARPSICHORD, FLUTE, OBOE WITH STRING ORCHESTRA — SCORES
M1105-6	HARPSICHORD, FLUTE, OBOE WITH STRING ORCHESTRA
M1105-6	HARPSICHORD, FLUTE, VIOLIN WITH STRING ORCHESTRA
M1105-6	HARPSICHORD, 2 FLUTES WITH STRING ORCHESTRA
M1010-1011	HARPSICHORDS (2) WITH ORCHESTRA
M1105-6	HARPSICHORDS (2) WITH STRING ORCHESTRA
M1105-6	HARPSICHORDS (3) WITH STRING ORCHESTRA
M1105-6	HARPSICHORDS (4) WITH STRING ORCHESTRA
BL1635	HARRANIANS
PJ9293	*HARRARJIE LANGUAGE* **SEE** HARARI LANGUAGE
QL696.A2	HARRIERS
F153	*HARRISBURG INSURRECTION, 1838* **SEE** BUCKSHOT WAR, 1838
E356.H3	HARRISON, FORT, BATTLE OF, 1812
E477.21	HARRISON, FORT, CAPTURE OF, 1864
TJ1482	HARROWS / *mechanical engineering and machinery*
GT4380-4499	HARVEST FESTIVALS
S695-7	*HARVESTERS* **SEE** HARVESTING MACHINERY
HD9486	*HARVESTERS* **SEE** HARVESTING MACHINERY / *industry*
S695-7	HARVESTING MACHINERY
HD9486	HARVESTING MACHINERY / *industry*
SB129	HARVESTING / *agriculture*
GT4380-4499	HARVESTING / *manners and customs*
DS784	*HASANG INCIDENT, 1938* **SEE** CHANGKUFENG INCIDENT, 1938
RC568.C2	*HASHEESH* **SEE** HASHISH / *intoxications*
RS165.H3	*HASHEESH* **SEE** HASHISH / *materia medica*
RC568.C2	HASHISH / *intoxications*
RS165.H3	HASHISH / *materia medica*
BM198	HASIDISM
DA196	HASTINGS, BATTLE OF, 1066
HD9948	HAT TRADE
VM831	*HATCH DAVITS* **SEE** DAVITS
VM801	*HATCH DAVITS* **SEE** DAVITS / *boat lowering*
QE391.H	HATCHETTIN
SF495	*HATCHING OF EGGS* **SEE** EGGS — INCUBATION
BF575.H	HATE
PL4001.A7	*HATIGORRIA LANGUAGE* **SEE** AO LANGUAGE
GT2110	HATS / *manners and customs*
TS2180-2193	HATS / *manufacture*
DS784	*HATSANG INCIDENT, 1938* **SEE** CHANGKUFENG INCIDENT, 1938
E99.C91	*HATTERAS INDIANS* **SEE** CROATAN INDIANS
TE450	HAULING TESTS
BF1445-1486	*HAUNTED HOUSES* **SEE** GHOSTS
GR580	*HAUNTED HOUSES* **SEE** GHOSTS / *folk-lore*
PL8231-4	HAUSA LANGUAGE
DT518.H3	HAUSAS
GN653	HAUSAS
DT518.H3	*HAUSSAS* **SEE** HAUSAS
GN653	*HAUSSAS* **SEE** HAUSAS
F1781	HAVANA — SIEGE, 1762
E99.H3	HAVASUPAI INDIANS
PM1311	HAVASUPAI LANGUAGE
DL464	HAVSFJORD, BATTLE OF, 872
DU620-629	HAWAII — HISTORY
SB608.B4	HAWAIIAN BEET WEB-WORM
MT590	HAWAIIAN GUITAR — INSTRUCTION AND STUDY
ML1015	HAWAIIAN GUITAR
PL6441-9	HAWAIIAN LANGUAGE
PN5621-9	HAWAIIAN NEWSPAPERS
PL6448.5	HAWAIIAN POETRY

M1360	*HAWAIIAN-GUITAR BAND* **SEE** PLECTRAL ENSEMBLES
MT590.5	HAWAIIAN-GUITAR MUSIC — TEACHING PIECES
M142.H3	HAWAIIAN-GUITAR MUSIC
HF5458-9	*HAWKERS AND HAWKING* **SEE** PEDDLERS AND PEDDLING
SK321	*HAWKING* **SEE** FALCONRY
QL696.A2	HAWKS
BL457.H3	HAWTHORN (IN RELIGION, FOLK-LORE, ETC.)
QK495.C8	HAWTHORN
HF5716.H4	HAY TRADE — TABLES AND READY-RECKONERS
HD9030-9049	HAY TRADE
TX831	*HAY-BOXES* **SEE** FIRELESS COOKERS
RX326.H3	HAY-FEVER — HOMEOPATHIC TREATMENT
QK100.U6	HAY-FEVER PLANTS
RC743	HAY-FEVER
JX1398.7	HAY-PAUNCEFOTE TREATY, 1901
SB198	HAY
PL8834	*HAYA LANGUAGE* **SEE** ZIBA LANGUAGE
DK508.7	*HAYDAMAKS* **SEE** HAIDAMAKS
HX846.C4	*HAYMARKET SQUARE RIOT, 1886* **SEE** CHICAGO — HAYMARKET SQUARE RIOT, 1886
PL3801.V2	HAYU DIALECT
DS784	*HAZAN INCIDENT, 1938* **SEE** CHANGKUFENG INCIDENT, 1938
BM652	*HAZANIM* **SEE** CANTORS, JEWISH
QK495.C	HAZEL
V415.E9	HAZING / *annapolis*
LB3604-3615	HAZING / *student life*
U410.E9	HAZING / *west point*
BM652	*HAZZANIM* **SEE** CANTORS, JEWISH
QL991	HEAD — ABNORMITIES AND DEFORMITIES
QM691	HEAD — ABNORMITIES AND DEFORMITIES
RD763	HEAD — ABNORMITIES AND DEFORMITIES / *surgical treatment*
RC936	HEAD — DISEASES
RD521-9	HEAD — SURGERY
RD763	HEAD — SURGERY / *orthopedic*
RC280.H	HEAD — TUMORS
RD661-3	HEAD — TUMORS
RD131	HEAD — WOUNDS AND INJURIES
GR489	HEAD (IN RELIGION, FOLK-LORE, ETC.) / *folk-lore*
BL325.H25	HEAD (IN RELIGION, FOLK-LORE, ETC.) / *religion*
N8217.H5	HEAD IN ART
HJ4911-4939	*HEAD TAX* **SEE** POLL-TAX
GN419.1	HEAD-GEAR / *anthropology*
GT2110	HEAD-GEAR / *manners and customs*
NC770-773	HEAD / *artistic*
QM535	HEAD / *human*
RX301.H5	HEADACHE — HOMEOPATHIC TREATMENT
RB128	HEADACHE
RC392	HEADACHE / *migraine*
GN419.1	*HEADDRESS* **SEE** HEAD-GEAR / *anthropology*
GT2110	*HEADDRESS* **SEE** HEAD-GEAR / *manners and customs*
Z695	*HEADINGS, SUBJECT* **SEE** SUBJECT HEADINGS
TL272	*HEADLIGHTS* **SEE** AUTOMOBILES — LIGHTING / *electric equipment*
TJ668	*HEADLIGHTS* **SEE** LOCOMOTIVES — HEADLIGHTS
PN4784.H4	*HEADLINE WRITING* **SEE** NEWSPAPERS — HEADLINES
D-F	HEADS OF STATE
JF251	HEADS OF STATE
RX637	HEAD — DISEASES — — HOMEOPATHIC TREATMENT
BL325.H4	HEALING GODS
RZ400-406	*HEALING, MENTAL* **SEE** MENTAL HEALING
RA771	*HEALTH* **SEE** HYGIENE / *domestic*
BJ1695	*HEALTH* **SEE** HYGIENE / *ethical aspects*
RA773-790	*HEALTH* **SEE** HYGIENE / *personal*
RA5	HEALTH BOARDS
RA11-388	HEALTH BOARDS / *reports*
R118	*HEALTH COMMUNICATION* **SEE** COMMUNICATION IN MEDICINE
HG9383-9399	*HEALTH INSURANCE* **SEE** INSURANCE, HEALTH
HD7101-2	*HEALTH INSURANCE* **SEE** INSURANCE, HEALTH / *industrial*
R133	*HEALTH MISCONCEPTIONS* **SEE** MEDICAL DELUSIONS
RJ101	*HEALTH OF CHILDREN* **SEE** CHILDREN — CARE AND HYGIENE
RJ61	*HEALTH OF CHILDREN* **SEE** CHILDREN — CARE AND HYGIENE

RJ61	*HEALTH OF INFANTS* **SEE** INFANTS — CARE AND HYGIENE
RJ101	*HEALTH OF INFANTS* **SEE** INFANTS — CARE AND HYGIENE
RG121	*HEALTH OF WOMEN* **SEE** WOMAN — HEALTH AND HYGIENE
RA778	*HEALTH OF WOMEN* **SEE** WOMAN — HEALTH AND HYGIENE / *hygiene*
HD7260-7780	*HEALTH OF WORKERS* **SEE** INDUSTRIAL HYGIENE
RA791-954	HEALTH RESORTS, WATERING-PLACES, ETC.
RA795	HEALTH RESORTS, WATERING-PLACES, ETC., ANCIENT
RZ400-406	*HEALTH THOUGHTS* **SEE** MENTAL HEALING
RA440.8	HEALTH-OFFICERS
RA5	HEALTH-OFFICERS
GT2850-2930	*HEALTHS, DRINKING OF* **SEE** DRINKING CUSTOMS
PN6340-6348	*HEALTHS, DRINKING OF* **SEE** TOASTS
RF300-310	HEARING AIDS, MECHANICAL
GN275	HEARING / *anthropology*
QP461-9	HEARING / *physiology*
BF251	HEARING / *psychology*
RC666-687	HEART — DISEASES
RC685.H9	HEART — HYPERTROPHY AND DILATATION
RC685.I6	HEART — INFARCTION
QM181	HEART — MEASUREMENT / *human anatomy*
RC685.P2	HEART — PALPITATION
RC685.R9	HEART — RUPTURE
QP111	HEART — SOUNDS
RC682	HEART FAILURE
BX2157-8	*HEART OF JESUS, DEVOTION TO* **SEE** SACRED HEART, DEVOTION TO
QL838	HEART / *comparative anatomy*
QM181	HEART / *human anatomy*
QP101-111	HEART / *physiology*
QP55	*HEART, ARTIFICIAL* **SEE** PERFUSION PUMP (HEART)
SF811	HEART, FATTY
RC685.F	HEART, FATTY
RC685.H9	*HEART-DILATATION* **SEE** HEART — HYPERTROPHY AND DILATATION
HJ2612	HEARTH-MONEY / *english tax*
GV1295.H4	HEARTS (GAME)
RC683	HEART — DISEASES — — DIAGNOSIS
RX311-316	HEART — DISEASES — — HOMEOPATHIC TREATMENT
RC685.V2	HEART — VALVES — — DISEASES
QC321-3	HEAT — CONDUCTION
QC327	HEAT — CONVECTION
QC263	HEAT — LABORATORY MANUALS
QH653	HEAT — PHYSIOLOGICAL EFFECT / *cells*
QP82	HEAT — PHYSIOLOGICAL EFFECT / *physiology*
QC331-8	HEAT — RADIATION AND ABSORPTION
QC320-338	HEAT — TRANSMISSION
QC331-8	*HEAT ABSORPTION* **SEE** HEAT — RADIATION AND ABSORPTION
RA766.H4	HEAT AS A DISINFECTANT
QC276	*HEAT BARRIER* **SEE** HIGH TEMPERATURES
TP363	HEAT EXCHANGERS
QC310	*HEAT OF DILUTION* **SEE** HEAT OF SOLUTION
QC310	*HEAT OF IMMERSION* **SEE** HEAT OF WETTING
QC310	HEAT OF SOLUTION
QC310	HEAT OF WETTING
QK755	*HEAT PRODUCTION IN PLANTS* **SEE** PLANTS, HEAT PRODUCTION IN
TJ266	HEAT PUMPS
TN700	HEAT RESISTANT ALLOYS
QC320-338	*HEAT TRANSFER* **SEE** HEAT — TRANSMISSION
TJ255-265	HEAT-ENGINES / *mechanical engineering*
QC251-338	HEAT
QC312	·HEAT, MECHANICAL EQUIVALENT OF
QC291-7	*HEAT, SPECIFIC* **SEE** SPECIFIC HEAT
QC331-8	*HEAT-ABSORPTION* **SEE** HEAT — RADIATION AND ABSORPTION
QK495.E68	*HEATH (BOTANY)* **SEE** HEATHER
QK495.E68	HEATHER
GB621-8	*HEATHS* **SEE** MOORS AND HEATHS
HD1665-1683	*HEATHS* **SEE** MOORS AND HEATHS / *agriculture*
S621	*HEATHS* **SEE** MOORS AND HEATHS / *agriculture*
TH7335-7	HEATING — ESTIMATES
TH7466.5	HEATING — REGULATORS
TH7325	HEATING — SPECIFICATIONS

TH7225	HEATING — TABLES, CALCULATIONS, ETC.
TH7641	HEATING FROM CENTRAL STATIONS
TH7461	HEATING PLANTS
TJ395	HEATING PLANTS
TH7478	HEATING-PIPES
TH7010-7641	HEATING
GT420	HEATING / *manners and customs*
TP363	*HEATING, INFRA-RED* **SEE** INFRA-RED HEATING / *chemical engineering*
TK4635	*HEATING, INFRA-RED* **SEE** INFRA-RED HEATING / *electric engineering*
QC304	*HEATS OF VAPORIZATION* **SEE** VAPORIZATION, HEATS OF
BP166.87	*HEAVEN (ISLAM)* **SEE** PARADISE (ISLAM)
BT844-9	HEAVEN
N8150	HEAVEN / *art*
BT847	HEAVENLY RECOGNITION
QD181.H1	*HEAVY WATER* **SEE** DEUTERIUM OXIDE
TK9203.H4	*HEAVY WATER PILES* **SEE** HEAVY WATER REACTORS
TK9203.H4	HEAVY WATER REACTORS
QP187	HEBIN
QB34	*HEBREW ASTRONOMY* **SEE** ASTRONOMY, JEWISH
CE35	*HEBREW CALENDAR* **SEE** CALENDAR, JEWISH
PJ4603	HEBREW LANGUAGE — ROOT
PJ4501-5089	HEBREW LANGUAGE
PJ5001-5041	*HEBREW LANGUAGE, MISHNAIC* **SEE** HEBREW LANGUAGE, TALMUDIC
PJ5001-5041	HEBREW LANGUAGE, POST-BIBLICAL
PJ5001-5041	*HEBREW LANGUAGE, RABBINIC* **SEE** HEBREW LANGUAGE, POST-BIBLICAL
PJ5001-5041	HEBREW LANGUAGE, TALMUDIC
Z675.J4	*HEBREW LIBRARIES* **SEE** JEWISH LIBRARIES
Z7070	HEBREW LITERATURE — BIO-BIBLIOGRAPHY
PJ5001-5060	HEBREW LITERATURE
PJ5038	HEBREW LITERATURE, MODERN / *collections*
PJ5017-5021	HEBREW LITERATURE, MODERN / *history*
PN5650	HEBREW NEWSPAPERS
PN5650	HEBREW PERIODICALS
PJ4501-4541	HEBREW PHILOLOGY
PJ5039-5042	HEBREW POETRY / *collections*
PJ5022-5	HEBREW POETRY / *history*
PN3035	*HEBREW THEATER* **SEE** THEATER — JEWS
DS101-151	*HEBREWS* **SEE** JEWS
GN547	*HEBREWS* **SEE** JEWS / *anthropology*
TL704.7	HECTER FUEL
Z48	HECTOGRAPH
QL737.I5	HEDGEHOGS
SB437	HEDGES
QP981.H5	HEDONAL / *physiology*
RM666.H	HEDONAL / *therapeutics*
BJ1491	HEDONISM / *ethics*
B279	HEDONISM / *greek philosophy*
QL537.O3	*HEEL FLIES* **SEE** WARBLE-FLIES
SF967.W3	*HEEL FLIES* **SEE** WARBLE-FLIES / *cattle pests*
D763.N62	HEGRA — SIEGE, 1940
PM1171	*HEGUE LANGUAGE* **SEE** EUDEVE LANGUAGE
GB491-8	*HEIGHTS* **SEE** ALTITUDES
D267.H3	HEILBRONN, UNION OF, 1633
PM1321	HEILTSUK LANGUAGE
HB715	*HEIRS* **SEE** INHERITANCE AND SUCCESSION / *economics*
PT204-212	HELDENSAGE
PN684	HELDENSAGE
E474.9	HELENA, ARK., BATTLE OF, 1863
QK495.C74	*HELENIUM* **SEE** SNEEZEWEED / *botany*
SB618.S7	*HELENIUM* **SEE** SNEEZEWEED / *weeds*
D582.H	HELGOLAND, BATTLE OF, 1914
ML970-973	*HELICON BASS* **SEE** TUBA
TL716	HELICOPTERS — HANDLING CHARACTERISTICS
TL716.5	HELICOPTERS — PILOTING
TL716	HELICOPTERS
TL716	*HELICOPTERS-FLYING QUALITIES* **SEE** HELICOPTERS — HANDLING CHARACTERISTICS
TL554	*HELICOPTERS-POETRY* **SEE** AERONAUTICS — POETRY
TL716	*HELICOPTERS-STABILITY* **SEE** STABILITY OF HELICOPTERS
TR510-525	*HELIOCHROMY* **SEE** COLOR PHOTOGRAPHY
QC912	HELIODON
UG582.H4	HELIOGRAPH

TR980	*HELIOGRAVURE* **SEE** PHOTOGRAVURE
QB97	HELIOMETER
QB97	HELIOMICROMETER
QC373.H5	HELIOSTAT / *optical*
QB97	HELIOSTAT / *sun observations*
RM843	*HELIOTHERAPY* **SEE** SUN-BATHS
QH651	*HELIOTROPISM* **SEE** PHOTOTROPISM
QK776	*HELIOTROPISM* **SEE** PHOTOTROPISM / *botany*
TR937	HELIOTYPE
QL368.H5	HELIOZOA
TL725.5	HELIPORTS
TL666	HELIUM / *aeronautics*
TP245.H4	HELIUM / *chemical technology*
QD181.H4	HELIUM / *chemistry*
N8150	HELL — ART
BL545	HELL — COMPARATIVE STUDIES
BL735	HELL — COMPARATIVE STUDIES / *classical mythology*
BT837	HELL — CONTROVERSIAL LITERATURE
BL1475.H5	HELL (BUDDHISM)
BP166.88	HELL (ISLAM)
BL1475.H5	HELL / *buddhism*
BL735	HELL / *classical mythology*
BL545	HELL / *comparative religion*
BT834-8	HELL / *theology*
BR128.G8	HELLENISM / *christianity*
DF77	HELLENISM / *history*
BM176	HELLENISM / *judaism*
BM536.G7	HELLENISM / *judaism*
PN56.H4	HELLENISM / *literature*
PA600-691	*HELLENISTIC GREEK* **SEE** GREEK LANGUAGE, HELLENISTIC (300 B.C.-600 A.D.)
N6600-6699	HELMETS / *art*
U825	HELMETS / *military science*
QL386-394	HELMINTHOLOGY
DL743.H3	HELSINGBORG, BATTLE OF, 1710
RB145	HEMACYTOMETER
QR185	*HEMAGGLUTINATION* **SEE** BLOOD — AGGLUTINATION / *immunology*
QP91	*HEMAGGLUTINATION* **SEE** BLOOD — AGGLUTINATION / *physiology*
QP91	HEMAGGLUTININ / *blood*
QR185	HEMAGGLUTININ / *immunity*
QP91	HEMATIN
RC918.H4	HEMATOCHYLURIA
RC642	*HEMATOPHILIA* **SEE** HEMOPHILIA
QP671	HEMATOPORPHYRIN
RC918.H4	HEMATURIA
SF961	HEMATURIA
RE94	HEMIANOPSIA
QK865	HEMICELLULOSE
QL612	HEMICHORDATA
RJ496.P2	*HEMIPLEGIA* **SEE** PARALYSIS / *children's diseases*
RJ301	*HEMIPLEGIA* **SEE** PARALYSIS / *newborn infants*
QL521-4	HEMIPTERA
RS165.C	*HEMLOCK (MATERIA MEDICA)* **SEE** CONIUM / *pharmacy*
RM666.C	*HEMLOCK (MATERIA MEDICA)* **SEE** CONIUM / *therapeutics*
QP951	HEMOGLOBIN — PHYSIOLOGICAL EFFECT
QP91	HEMOGLOBIN
QP91	*HEMOGLOBULIN* **SEE** HEMOGLOBIN
QL841	HEMOLYMPH GLANDS
QL91	HEMOLYMPH
QR185	HEMOLYSIS AND HEMOLYSINS
RC642	HEMOPHILIA
RB144	*HEMOPTYSIS* **SEE** HEMORRHAGE
RD33.3	*HEMOPTYSIS* **SEE** HEMORRHAGE
RD33.3	HEMORRHAGE
RB144	HEMORRHAGE
RC394.A7	*HEMORRHAGE, CEREBRAL* **SEE** APOPLEXY
RG711	HEMORRHAGE, UTERINE / *labor*
RG573	HEMORRHAGE, UTERINE / *pregnancy*
RG821	HEMORRHAGE, UTERINE / *puerperal state*
RC778	*HEMORRHAGIC BRONCHITIS* **SEE** BRONCHOPULMONARY SPIROCHAETOSIS
RC642	*HEMORRHAGIC DIATHESIS* **SEE** HEMOPHILIA
RC633	HEMORRHAGIC DISEASES
RC633	*HEMORRHAGIC DISORDERS* **SEE** HEMORRHAGIC DISEASES
SF967.H	HEMORRHAGIC SEPTICEMIA OF CATTLE
RX343	HEMORRHOIDS — HOMEOPATHIC TREATMENT
RC865	HEMORRHOIDS
QP551	HEMOSIDERIN
RZ999	HEMOSPASIA
RZ999	*HEMOSPASIS* **SEE** HEMOSPASIA
RD33.3	*HEMOSTASIS* **SEE** HEMORRHAGE
RB144	*HEMOSTASIS* **SEE** HEMORRHAGE
RD33.3	HEMOSTATICS
SB255	HEMP / *culture*
TS1733	HEMP / *technology*
HD9155	HEMP / *trade*
RC371.C2	*HEMP, INDIAN* **SEE** CANNABIS INDICA / *intoxications*
RM666.C26	*HEMP, INDIAN* **SEE** CANNABIS INDICA / *therapeutics*
RC568.C2	*HEMP, INDIAN* **SEE** HASHISH / *intoxications*
RS165.H3	*HEMP, INDIAN* **SEE** HASHISH / *materia medica*
SB261.S4	*HENEQUEN* **SEE** SISAL HEMP / *culture*
TS1747.S5	*HENEQUEN* **SEE** SISAL HEMP / *manufacture*
HD9156.S6-8	*HENEQUEN* **SEE** SISAL HEMP / *trade*
E472.96	HENRY, FORT, BATTLE OF, 1862
TX375	*HENS* **SEE** POULTRY
SF481-507	*HENS* **SEE** POULTRY
TX556.P9	*HENS* **SEE** POULTRY
QL696.P2	HENSLOW'S SPARROW
CE81-83	*HEORTOLOGY* **SEE** CHURCH CALENDAR
BV30	*HEORTOLOGY* **SEE** CHURCH YEAR
BV30-135	*HEORTOLOGY* **SEE** FASTS AND FEASTS / *christianity*
CE81	*HEORTOLOGY* **SEE** FASTS AND FEASTS / *church calendar*
BL590	*HEORTOLOGY* **SEE** FASTS AND FEASTS / *comparative religion*
GT3930-4995	*HEORTOLOGY* **SEE** FASTS AND FEASTS / *manners and customs*
QK551-563	*HEPATICAE* **SEE** LIVERWORTS
RC394.H4	HEPATOLENTICULAR DEGENERATION
RJ456.G	*HEPATONEPHROMEGALIA GLYCOGENICA* **SEE** GLYCOGENOSIS
RC846	*HEPATOPTOSIS* **SEE** LIVER — DISPLACEMENT
CN397.H4	HERACLEAN TABLETS
Z993-6	*HERALDIC BOOK-PLATES* **SEE** BOOK-PLATES
CS410-497	*HERALDIC VISITATIONS* **SEE** VISITATIONS, HERALDIC
JC345	HERALDRY / *national theory*
CR	HERALDRY / *national*
CR1101-1131	*HERALDRY, ECCLESIASTICAL* **SEE** HERALDRY, SACRED
CR29-69	HERALDRY, ORNAMENTAL
CR1101-1131	HERALDRY, SACRED
CR183-5	HERALDS
GT5020	HERALDS / *manners and customs*
QK495.G74	*HERBAGE* **SEE** GRASSES / *botany*
SB197-201	*HERBAGE* **SEE** GRASSES / *culture*
QK41	*HERBALS* **SEE** BOTANY — PRE-LINNEAN WORKS
RS164-5	*HERBALS* **SEE** MATERIA MEDICA, VEGETABLE
R128	*HERBALS* **SEE** MEDICINE, MEDIEVAL
QK75-77	HERBARIA
RS164-5	*HERBS-THERAPEUTIC USE* **SEE** MATERIA MEDICA, VEGETABLE
R128	*HERBS-THERAPEUTIC USE* **SEE** MEDICINE, MEDIEVAL
QB851-3	*HERCULES (CONSTELLATION)* **SEE** STARS — CLUSTERS
SF192-3	*HERD BOOKS* **SEE** CATTLE — HERD-BOOKS
SF393	*HERD-BOOKS* **SEE** SWINE — HERD-BOOKS
HB715	*HEREDITARY SUCCESSION* **SEE** INHERITANCE AND SUCCESSION / *economics*
QH431	*HEREDITY IN MAN* **SEE** HEREDITY, HUMAN
HQ753	*HEREDITY IN MAN* **SEE** HEREDITY, HUMAN
RB155	HEREDITY OF DISEASE
QH431	HEREDITY / *biology*
HQ753	HEREDITY / *eugenics*
HV5133	HEREDITY / *heredity and alcoholism*
RJ91	HEREDITY / *heredity and child culture*
HV6121-5	HEREDITY / *heredity and crime*
BF418	HEREDITY / *heredity and genius*
BF341-6	HEREDITY / *psychology*
HM121	HEREDITY / *sociology*
QH431	HEREDITY, HUMAN
HQ753	HEREDITY, HUMAN
SF199.H4	HEREFORD CATTLE

SF193.H5	HEREFORD CATTLE / herd-books
BM720.E9	HEREM SEE EXCOMMUNICATION (JEWISH LAW)
PL8241	HERERO LANGUAGE
DT709	HEREROS
GN657.H	HEREROS
BT1313-1470	HERESIES AND HERETICS — EARLY CHURCH
BT1313-1490	HERESIES AND HERETICS
BP167.5	HERESIES AND HERETICS, ISLAMIC
BP167.5	HERESIES AND HERETICS, MUSLIM SEE HERESIES AND HERETICS, ISLAMIC
BR250-270	HERESIES AND HERETICS-MIDDLE AGES SEE SECTS, MEDIEVAL
BR157	HERESIES AND HERETICS-MODERN PERIOD SEE SECTS
BX1939.H4	HERESY (CANON LAW)
BT1313-1490	HERESY
RC883	HERMAPHRODITISM
PA49	HERMENEUTICS / classics
BD240-241	HERMENEUTICS / methodology
BS476	HERMENEUTICS, BIBLICAL SEE BIBLE — HERMENEUTICS
QD24-26.5	HERMETIC ART AND PHILOSOPHY SEE ALCHEMY
QD13	HERMETIC ART AND PHILOSOPHY SEE ALCHEMY / history
QB25-26	HERMETIC ART AND PHILOSOPHY SEE ASTROLOGY
BF1651-1729	HERMETIC ART AND PHILOSOPHY SEE ASTROLOGY
GN475	HERMETIC ART AND PHILOSOPHY SEE MAGIC / ethnology
BF1585-1623	HERMETIC ART AND PHILOSOPHY SEE MAGIC / occult sciences
BF1405-1999	HERMETIC ART AND PHILOSOPHY SEE OCCULT SCIENCES
QD24-26.5	HERMETIC MEDICINES SEE ALCHEMY
QD13	HERMETIC MEDICINES SEE ALCHEMY / history
DA87.7	HERMIONE MUTINY, 1797
QL696.P2	HERMIT THRUSH SEE THRUSHES
QL444.D3	HERMIT-CRABS
CT9990-9991	HERMITAGES SEE HERMITS / biography
BX2845-7	HERMITAGES SEE HERMITS / monasticism
NA4850	HERMITAGES SEE MONASTERIES / architecture
NA5201-6113	HERMITAGES SEE MONASTERIES / architecture
BX2460-2749	HERMITAGES SEE MONASTERIES / catholic church
CT9990-9991	HERMITS / biography
BX2845-7	HERMITS / monasticism
RS165.H5	HERMODACTYL / drugs
RD621	HERNIA — HOSPITALS
RD705	HERNIA — HOSPITALS
RD621-6	HERNIA
RD621-6	HERNIOTOMY SEE HERNIA
QL696.A7	HERODIONES
PN6071.H4	HEROES IN LITERATURE
PE1515	HEROIC COUPLET SEE HEROIC VERSE, ENGLISH
PN6110.E6	HEROIC POETRY SEE EPIC POETRY / collections
PN689-690	HEROIC POETRY SEE EPIC POETRY / history
PN1301-1333	HEROIC POETRY SEE EPIC POETRY / history
PT204-212	HEROIC SAGA SEE HELDENSAGE
PN684	HEROIC SAGA SEE HELDENSAGE
PE1515	HEROIC VERSE, ENGLISH
PN1415	HEROID
PT581.H5	HEROID / german
PT581.H5	HEROIDS / german poetry
PN1415	HEROIDS / poetry
HV5822.H4	HEROIN
CT3200-3830	HEROINES SEE WOMAN — BIOGRAPHY
HQ1123	HEROINES SEE WOMAN — BIOGRAPHY / feminism
HQ1455-1870	HEROINES SEE WOMAN — BIOGRAPHY / other countries
HQ1412-1413	HEROINES SEE WOMAN — BIOGRAPHY / reformers u.s.
PN56.W6	HEROINES SEE WOMEN IN LITERATURE
HQ1386	HEROINES SEE WOMEN IN LITERATURE
BS575	HEROINES SEE WOMEN IN THE BIBLE
BJ1533.C8	HEROISM SEE COURAGE
QL696.A7	HERONS
RC147.H6	HERPES SIMPLEX
RC147.H6	HERPES ZOSTER
RL281	HERPES
GN657.H	HERREROS SEE HEREROS
DT709	HERREROS SEE HEREROS
SH351.H5	HERRING-FISHERIES
QL696.L3	HERRING-GULL
QL638.C64	HERRING
SH167.H5	HERRING / fish-culture
BX4920-4921	HERRNHUTER SEE BOHEMIAN BRETHREN
BX8551-8593	HERRNHUTER SEE MORAVIANS
QC661-5	HERTZIAN WAVES SEE ELECTRIC WAVES
DD801.H5-69	HESSE — HISTORY
SB945.H3	HESSIAN FLIES
E268	HESSIANS IN THE AMERICAN REVOLUTION SEE UNITED STATES — HISTORY — — REVOLUTION — — — GERMAN MERCENARIES
BT1392	HESYCHASM
QL541-562	HETEROCERA SEE MOTHS
QD400-409	HETEROCYCLIC COMPOUNDS
QH489	HETEROGENESIS SEE GENERATIONS, ALTERNATING
QH325	HETEROGENESIS SEE LIFE — ORIGIN
QH325	HETEROGENESIS SEE SPONTANEOUS GENERATION
RE776	HETEROPHORIA
QL430.4	HETEROPODA / mollusks
QL523.H6	HETEROPTERA
SF105	HETEROSIS / animal breeding
QH421	HETEROSIS / biology
S494	HETEROSIS / breeding
SB123	HETEROSIS / plant breeding
QK926	HETEROSTYLISM
RE771	HETEROTROPIA SEE STRABISMUS
QH21-5	HETEROZYGOSIS / biology
SB123	HETEROZYGOSIS / plant breeding
RM666.H	HETOL
QE391.H55	HEULANDITE
PM1171	HEVE LANGUAGE SEE EUDEVE LANGUAGE
SB291.H	HEVEA
QL373.H6	HEXACTINELLIDA
P311	HEXAMETER
PE1531.H6	HEXAMETER / english
PA416.H6	HEXAMETER / greek
PA2337.H6	HEXAMETER / latin
QL461-599	HEXAPODA SEE INSECTS
GR750	HEXAPODA SEE INSECTS / folk-lore
TK7882.H5	HI-FI SYSTEMS SEE HIGH-FIDELITY SOUND SYSTEMS
E99.Y3	HIAQUI INDIANS SEE YAQUI INDIANS
QL755	HIBERNATION
E277	HICKEY PLOT, 1776
SD397.H6	HICKORY / forestry
BX7751-2	HICKSITES SEE FRIENDS, SOCIETY OF (HICKSITE)
HJ4337	HIDAGE / taxation gt. brit.
E99.H6	HIDATSA INDIANS — LEGENDS
E99.H6	HIDATSA INDIANS
PM1331	HIDATSA LANGUAGE
TS985	HIDE POWDER
RA761	HIDES AND SKINS — DISINFECTION
TS967	HIDES AND SKINS / manufactures
HD9778	HIDES AND SKINS / trade
DA380	HIDING-PLACES (SECRET CHAMBERS, ETC.) / england
PJ1501-1819	HIERATIC INSCRIPTIONS SEE EGYPTIAN LANGUAGE — INSCRIPTIONS
PJ1105	HIERATIC WRITING SEE EGYPTIAN LANGUAGE — WRITING, HIERATIC
BS560	HIEROGLYPHIC BIBLES
PJ1091-7	HIEROGLYPHICS / egyptian
PJ1091-7	HIEROGLYPHICS, EGYPTIAN SEE EGYPTIAN LANGUAGE — WRITING, HIEROGLYPHIC
BX3680.H5	HIERONYMITES IN SPAIN
BX3680.H5	HIERONYMITES
QC879	HIGH ALTITUDE ROCKET RESEARCH SEE ATMOSPHERE, UPPER — ROCKET OBSERVATIONS
TS256	HIGH ENERGY FORMING
TS256	HIGH ENERGY RATE METAL FORMING SEE HIGH ENERGY FORMING
GV1295.P3	HIGH FIVE (GAME) SEE PEDRO (GAME)
BM693.H5	HIGH HOLIDAYS SEE HIGH HOLY DAYS
BM693.H5	HIGH HOLY DAYS
GV529	HIGH JUMPING SEE JUMPING
HV5084-7	HIGH LICENSE SEE LICENSE SYSTEM
HV5074-5080	HIGH LICENSE SEE LIQUOR LAWS
HV5001-5720	HIGH LICENSE SEE LIQUOR PROBLEM

QC281	HIGH PRESSURE (SCIENCE)
LB2822	*HIGH SCHOOL ADMINISTRATION* **SEE** HIGH SCHOOLS — ADMINISTRATION
LC146	*HIGH SCHOOL ATTENDANCE* **SEE** SCHOOL ATTENDANCE — HIGH SCHOOL
LB1627.7	HIGH SCHOOL EQUIVALENCY CERTIFICATES
Z675.S3	*HIGH SCHOOL LIBRARIES* **SEE** SCHOOL LIBRARIES (HIGH SCHOOL)
LB3621	*HIGH SCHOOL YEARBOOKS* **SEE** SCHOOL YEARBOOKS
LB2822	HIGH SCHOOLS — ADMINISTRATION
LB1627	HIGH SCHOOLS — ENTRANCE REQUIREMENTS
LB1695	HIGH SCHOOLS — POSTGRADUATE WORK
LB1603-1694	HIGH SCHOOLS
LB1623	*HIGH SCHOOLS, JUNIOR* **SEE** JUNIOR HIGH SCHOOLS
LB1567	*HIGH SCHOOLS, RURAL* **SEE** RURAL SCHOOLS
LB2830	*HIGH SCHOOLS-ACCOUNTING* **SEE** SCHOOLS — ACCOUNTING
LB1695	*HIGH SCHOOLS-GRADUATE WORK* **SEE** HIGH SCHOOLS — POSTGRADUATE WORK
JX4408-4449	*HIGH SEAS, JURISDICTION OVER* **SEE** MARITIME LAW / international law
JX63	*HIGH SEAS, JURISDICTION OVER* **SEE** MARITIME LAW / private
JX5203-5268	*HIGH SEAS, JURISDICTION OVER* **SEE** WAR, MARITIME (INTERNATIONAL LAW)
TN700	*HIGH TEMPERATURE METALS* **SEE** HEAT RESISTANT ALLOYS
QC276	HIGH TEMPERATURES
QC277	*HIGH TEMPERATURES-MEASUREMENT* **SEE** PYROMETERS AND PYROMETRY
HV6275	*HIGH TREASON* **SEE** TREASON
JC328	*HIGH TREASON* **SEE** TREASON / political theory
QC166	*HIGH VACUUM TECHNIQUE* **SEE** VACUUM
TS256	*HIGH VELOCITY FORMING* **SEE** HIGH ENERGY FORMING
TL697.P7	*HIGH-ALTITUDE SUITS* **SEE** PRESSURE SUITS
TK7882.H5	*HIGH-FIDELITY AUDIO EQUIPMENT* **SEE** HIGH-FIDELITY SOUND SYSTEMS
TK7882.H5	HIGH-FIDELITY SOUND SYSTEMS
TK4601	*HIGH-FREQUENCY INDUCTION HEATING* **SEE** INDUCTION HEATING
TK6553	*HIGH-FREQUENCY RADIO* **SEE** RADIO, SHORT WAVE
TL673.F6	*HIGH-LIFT DEVICES* **SEE** FLAPS (AEROPLANES)
TP692.2	*HIGH-OCTANE GASOLINE* **SEE** GASOLINE — ANTI-KNOCK AND ANTI-KNOCK MIXTURES
TJ279	*HIGH-PRESSURE STEAM* **SEE** STEAM, HIGH-PRESSURE
TL551.5	HIGH-SPEED AERONAUTICS
TL551.5	*HIGH-SPEED FLIGHT* **SEE** HIGH-SPEED AERONAUTICS
TK3144	*HIGH-TENSION POWER DISTRIBUTION* **SEE** ELECTRIC POWER DISTRIBUTION — HIGH TENSION
LB2300-2397	*HIGHER EDUCATION* **SEE** EDUCATION, HIGHER / general
LA410	*HIGHER EDUCATION* **SEE** EDUCATION, HIGHER / other countries
LA225-8	*HIGHER EDUCATION* **SEE** EDUCATION, HIGHER / u.s.
LC171-182	HIGHER EDUCATION AND STATE
JC389	*HIGHER LAW* **SEE** DIVINE RIGHT OF KINGS
JC328	*HIGHER LAW* **SEE** GOVERNMENT, RESISTANCE TO
JC20-45	*HIGHLAND CLANS* **SEE** CLANS AND CLAN SYSTEM
GN492	*HIGHLAND CLANS* **SEE** CLANS AND CLAN SYSTEM / ethnology
DA880.H76	*HIGHLAND COSTUME* **SEE** TARTANS
GV1796.H	HIGHLAND FLING (DANCE)
HE5614	*HIGHWAY ACCIDENTS* **SEE** TRAFFIC ACCIDENTS
TE175	*HIGHWAY DESIGN* **SEE** ROADS — DESIGN
TE215	*HIGHWAY DRAINAGE* **SEE** ROAD DRAINAGE
TE	*HIGHWAY ENGINEERING* **SEE** ROADS / etc.
HE331-368	*HIGHWAY ENGINEERING* **SEE** ROADS / transportation
TE315-424	HIGHWAY LAW
HD9710	*HIGHWAY TAX* **SEE** AUTOMOBILES — TAXATION
HD9579.G4	*HIGHWAY TAX* **SEE** MOTOR FUELS — TAXATION / gasoline
HE5601-5720	*HIGHWAY TRANSPORTATION* **SEE** TRANSPORTATION, AUTOMOTIVE
HV6441-6453	*HIGHWAYMEN* **SEE** BRIGANDS AND ROBBERS
TE315-424	*HIGHWAYS* **SEE** HIGHWAY LAW
TE	*HIGHWAYS* **SEE** ROADS / etc.
HE331-368	*HIGHWAYS* **SEE** ROADS / transportation
PK9201.C	*HIHATL LANGUAGE* **SEE** CHAMALAL LANGUAGE
G504	HIKING
QA691	HILBERT SPACE
PL5711	HILIGAINA DIALECT
DT709	HILL DAMARAS
CC710	HILL FIGURES
TL215.H	HILLMAN MINX AUTOMOBILE
TR510	HILLOTYPE
CC710	*HILLSIDE FIGURES* **SEE** HILL FIGURES
PL3551-4001	*HIMALAYAN LANGUAGES* **SEE** TIBETO-BURMAN LANGUAGES
BL1480	HINAYANA BUDDHISM
QD481	*HINDERED ROTATION THEORY* **SEE** MOLECULAR ROTATION
PK1991-7	HINDI LANGUAGE
PK1931-7	*HINDI LANGUAGE, EASTERN* **SEE** HINDUSTANI LANGUAGE
PK1931-7	*HINDI LANGUAGE, WESTERN* **SEE** HINDUSTANI LANGUAGE
PN5371-5380	HINDI PERIODICALS / etc.
DS421-3	*HINDOOS* **SEE** HINDUS / civilization
GN635.I4	*HINDOOS* **SEE** HINDUS / ethnology
DS423-5	*HINDU CIVILIZATION* **SEE** CIVILIZATION, HINDU
BL1212	*HINDU FASTS AND FEASTS* **SEE** FASTS AND FEASTS — HINDUISM
RA776	*HINDU HYGIENE* **SEE** HYGIENE, HINDU
RA529	*HINDU HYGIENE* **SEE** HYGIENE, HINDU
BL1226.3	HINDU HYMNS
BL1215.P3	*HINDU PARABLES* **SEE** PARABLES, HINDU
BL1215.P8	*HINDU PSYCHOLOGY* **SEE** HINDUISM — PSYCHOLOGY
BL2003	*HINDU SAINTS* **SEE** SAINTS, HINDU
BL1245.A1	HINDU SECTS
BL1227	*HINDU TEMPLES* **SEE** TEMPLES, HINDU
BL1215.P8	HINDUISM — PSYCHOLOGY
BR128.H5	*HINDUISM AND CHRISTIANITY* **SEE** CHRISTIANITY AND OTHER RELIGIONS — HINDUISM
BL1100-1270	HINDUISM
BL2000-2030	HINDUISM / india
B130-133	HINDUISM / philosophy
BL1226.3	*HINDUISM-HYMNS* **SEE** HINDU HYMNS
BL1245.A1	*HINDUISM-SECTS* **SEE** HINDU SECTS
DS421-3	HINDUS / civilization
GN635.I4	HINDUS / ethnology
PK2071	HINDUSTANI DRAMA / collections
PK2041	HINDUSTANI DRAMA / history
PK1931-7	HINDUSTANI LANGUAGE
PK2030-2158	HINDUSTANI LITERATURE
PN5371-5380	HINDUSTANI PERIODICALS / etc.
PK2057-9	HINDUSTANI POETRY / collections
PK2040	HINDUSTANI POETRY / history
TS400	HINGES
RD772	HIP JOINT — DISEASES
RD101	HIP JOINT — DISLOCATION
QM131	HIP JOINT
RD549	*HIP-EXCISION* **SEE** EXCISION OF HIP
QL737.U6	*HIPPOLOGY* **SEE** HORSES
HV4749-4755	*HIPPOLOGY* **SEE** HORSES / cruelty to horses
GR715	*HIPPOLOGY* **SEE** HORSES / folk-lore
HD9434	*HIPPOLOGY* **SEE** HORSES / horse raising
SF279-359	*HIPPOLOGY* **SEE** HORSES / horse raising
GT5885	*HIPPOLOGY* **SEE** HORSES / manners and customs
UF370	*HIPPOLOGY* **SEE** HORSES / military service
UE460-475	*HIPPOLOGY* **SEE** HORSES / military service
UC600-695	*HIPPOLOGY* **SEE** HORSES / military service
TX556.H8	*HIPPOPHAGY* **SEE** HORSE MEAT / foods
BL2450.H5	HIPPOPOTAMUS (IN RELIGION, FOLK-LORE, ETC.)
BL443	HIPPOPOTAMUS (IN RELIGION, FOLK-LORE, ETC.)
QL737.U5	HIPPOPOTAMUS
QP211	HIPPURIC ACID
BX1939.H	HIRE (CANON LAW)
HF5568	*HIRE-PURCHASE PLAN* **SEE** INSTALMENT PLAN
QL391.H6	*HIRUDINIDAE* **SEE** LEECHES
RM182	*HIRUDINIDAE* **SEE** LEECHES / blood-letting
QL696.P2	*HIRUNDINIDAE* **SEE** SWALLOWS
CB226	*HISPANIC CIVILIZATION* **SEE** CIVILIZATION, HISPANIC
E714-735	*HISPANO-AMERICAN WAR, 1898* **SEE** UNITED STATES — HISTORY — — WAR OF 1898

PN2091.A7	*HISSING* **SEE** THEATER — APPLAUSE, DEMONSTRATIONS, ETC.
QH611	HISTOCHEMISTRY
QM553	HISTOLOGY — EXAMINATIONS, QUESTIONS, ETC.
QM555	HISTOLOGY — LABORATORY MANUALS
QM550-575	HISTOLOGY
RB24-35	HISTOLOGY, PATHOLOGICAL
QK641-707	*HISTOLOGY, VEGETABLE* **SEE** BOTANY — ANATOMY
SF761	*HISTOLOGY, VETERINARY* **SEE** VETERINARY HISTOLOGY
D13-15	HISTORIANS
BX938-9	*HISTORIANS, CATHOLIC* **SEE** CATHOLIC HISTORIANS
BR139	*HISTORIANS, CHURCH* **SEE** CHURCH HISTORIANS
DF211-212	*HISTORIANS, GREEK* **SEE** GREEK HISTORIANS / historiography
DG205-6	*HISTORIANS, LATIN* **SEE** LATIN HISTORIANS
DG205-6	*HISTORIANS, ROMAN* **SEE** LATIN HISTORIANS
JX4122-4141	*HISTORIC BAYS (INTERNATIONAL LAW)* **SEE** TERRITORIAL WATERS
TH9445.H5	HISTORIC HOUSES, ETC. — FIRES AND FIRE PREVENTION
NA7205	HISTORIC HOUSES, ETC. / architecture
NA7123	HISTORIC HOUSES, ETC. / architecture
JX4122-4141	*HISTORIC WATERS (INTERNATIONAL LAW)* **SEE** TERRITORIAL WATERS
GA205-213	*HISTORICAL ATLASES* **SEE** GEOGRAPHY, ANCIENT — MAPS
G1033	*HISTORICAL ATLASES* **SEE** GEOGRAPHY, ANCIENT — MAPS
D11	*HISTORICAL CHARTS* **SEE** CHRONOLOGY, HISTORICAL — CHARTS
D11	*HISTORICAL CHRONOLOGY* **SEE** CHRONOLOGY, HISTORICAL
D13-15	*HISTORICAL CRITICISM* **SEE** HISTORIOGRAPHY
D9	*HISTORICAL DICTIONARIES* **SEE** HISTORY — DICTIONARIES
D9	*HISTORICAL DICTIONARIES* **SEE** HISTORY — DICTIONARIES
PN1870-1879	HISTORICAL DRAMA / history and criticism
PN3441	HISTORICAL FICTION
G141	*HISTORICAL GEOGRAPHY* **SEE** GEOGRAPHY, HISTORICAL
D-F	*HISTORICAL GEOGRAPHY* **SEE** GEOGRAPHY, HISTORICAL
QE651-699	*HISTORICAL GEOLOGY* **SEE** GEOLOGY, STRATIGRAPHIC
Z675.H5	HISTORICAL LIBRARIES
B809.8	*HISTORICAL MATERIALISM* **SEE** DIALECTICAL MATERIALISM / philosophy
HX55	*HISTORICAL MATERIALISM* **SEE** DIALECTICAL MATERIALISM / socialism
CD931-4279	*HISTORICAL RECORDS-PRESERVATION* **SEE** ARCHIVES
CD941	*HISTORICAL RECORDS-PRESERVATION* **SEE** ARCHIVES / directories
CD950-965	*HISTORICAL RECORDS-PRESERVATION* **SEE** ARCHIVES / handbooks
D1	HISTORICAL SOCIETIES
HM104	HISTORICAL SOCIOLOGY
Z286	*HISTORICAL SOURCES, PUBLISHING OF* **SEE** HISTORY — SOURCES — — PUBLISHING
D13-15	HISTORIOGRAPHY
Z6201-9	HISTORY — BIO-BIBLIOGRAPHY
D10	HISTORY — CURIOSA AND MISCELLANY
D9	HISTORY — DICTIONARIES
D10	HISTORY — ERRORS, INVENTIONS, ETC.
D21	HISTORY — EXAMINATIONS, QUESTIONS, ETC.
D16	HISTORY — METHODOLOGY
D16.7-9	HISTORY — PHILOSOPHY
PN6110.H3	HISTORY — POETRY
D5	HISTORY — SOURCES
D17-18	*HISTORY - EARLY WORKS TO 1800* **SEE** WORLD HISTORY — EARLY WORKS TO 1800
D21.1	*HISTORY - PICTORIAL WORKS* **SEE** WORLD HISTORY — PICTORIAL WORKS
PN50	*HISTORY AND LITERATURE* **SEE** LITERATURE AND HISTORY
CB151	*HISTORY AND SCIENCE* **SEE** SCIENCE AND CIVILIZATION
JX1253	HISTORY / d history and international law
PN50	HISTORY / history and literature
B61	HISTORY / history and philosophy
JA78	HISTORY / history and political science
HM36	HISTORY / history and sociology
D54.5	HISTORY, ANCIENT — CHRONOLOGY
D59	HISTORY, ANCIENT — JUVENILE LITERATURE
D51-90	HISTORY, ANCIENT
BS635	*HISTORY, BIBLICAL* **SEE** BIBLE — HISTORY OF BIBLICAL EVENTS
BR	*HISTORY, CHURCH* **SEE** CHURCH HISTORY
J-JQ	*HISTORY, CONSTITUTIONAL* **SEE** CONSTITUTIONAL HISTORY
BR	*HISTORY, ECCLESIASTICAL* **SEE** CHURCH HISTORY
D21	*HISTORY, JUVENILE* **SEE** WORLD HISTORY — JUVENILE LITERATURE
Z695.1.H6	*HISTORY, LOCAL (CATALOGING)* **SEE** CATALOGING OF LOCAL HISTORY
D111-203	*HISTORY, MEDIEVAL* **SEE** MIDDLE AGES — HISTORY
D25	*HISTORY, MILITARY* **SEE** MILITARY HISTORY
U27-43	*HISTORY, MILITARY* **SEE** MILITARY HISTORY / military science
D210	HISTORY, MODERN — CURIOSA AND MISCELLANY
D220-234	HISTORY, MODERN — 16TH CENTURY
D242-280	HISTORY, MODERN — 17TH CENTURY
D284-309	HISTORY, MODERN — 18TH CENTURY
D351-400	HISTORY, MODERN — 19TH CENTURY
D410-725	HISTORY, MODERN — 20TH CENTURY
D204-725	HISTORY, MODERN
D210	*HISTORY, MODERN-ANECDOTES* **SEE** HISTORY, MODERN — CURIOSA AND MISCELLANY
D11	*HISTORY, MODERN-CHRONOLOGY* **SEE** CHRONOLOGY, HISTORICAL
D16.7-9	*HISTORY, MODERN-PHILOSOPHY* **SEE** HISTORY — PHILOSOPHY
QH	*HISTORY, NATURAL* **SEE** NATURAL HISTORY
D27	*HISTORY, NAVAL* **SEE** NAVAL HISTORY
D-F	*HISTORY, NAVAL* **SEE** NAVAL HISTORY / and battles of particular countries
D16.7-9	*HISTORY, PHILOSOPHY OF* **SEE** HISTORY — PHILOSOPHY
D17-24	*HISTORY, UNIVERSAL* **SEE** WORLD HISTORY
D10	*HISTORY-ANECDOTES* **SEE** HISTORY — CURIOSA AND MISCELLANY
GA205-213	*HISTORY-ATLASES* **SEE** GEOGRAPHY, ANCIENT — MAPS
G1033	*HISTORY-ATLASES* **SEE** GEOGRAPHY, ANCIENT — MAPS
D11	*HISTORY-CHRONOLOGY* **SEE** CHRONOLOGY, HISTORICAL
D13-15	*HISTORY-CRITICISM* **SEE** HISTORIOGRAPHY
D17-18	*HISTORY-EARLY WORKS TO 1800* **SEE** WORLD HISTORY — EARLY WORKS TO 1800
D13-15	*HISTORY-HISTORIOGRAPHY* **SEE** HISTORIOGRAPHY
D21.1	*HISTORY-PICTORIAL WORKS* **SEE** WORLD HISTORY — PICTORIAL WORKS
Z286	HISTORY — SOURCES — — PUBLISHING
PN2000-3299	*HISTRIONICS* **SEE** THEATER
PM1341	HITCHITI LANGUAGE
D184.8	HITTIN, BATTLE OF, 1187
P945	HITTITE LANGUAGE
P945	HITTITE LITERATURE
BL2370.H5	HITTITES — RELIGION
DS66	HITTITES
PL8452	*HLE DIALECT* **SEE** LELE DIALECT
PL8115	*HLENGWE LANGUAGE* **SEE** CHOPI LANGUAGE
DS432.H6	*HO (MUNDA TRIBE)* **SEE** HOS
QL696.G2	HOACTZIN
GV1201	HOBBIES
E241.H	HOBKIRK'S HILL, BATTLE OF, 1781
M1978.H6	HOBO SONGS
M1977.H6	HOBO SONGS
HV4480-4630	*HOBOES* **SEE** TRAMPS
TP559.G3	*HOCHHEIMER WINE* **SEE** HOCK (WINE)
DD412.6.H7	HOCHKIRCH, BATTLE OF, 1758
D283.B6	*HOCHSTADT, BATTLE OF, 1704* **SEE** BLENHEIM, BATTLE OF, 1704
TP559.G3	HOCK (WINE)
GV848	HOCKEY CLUBS
GV847	HOCKEY
RC644	HODGKIN'S DISEASE
QA841	HODOGRAPH

TH842.H7	HOFFMANN KILN
SF973	HOG CHOLERA
PE3729.U	*HOG LATIN* **SEE** PIG LATIN
QL737.U5	*HOGS* **SEE** SWINE
SF391.7	*HOGS* **SEE** SWINE / *animal industries*
D280.H6	HOGUE, LA, BATTLE OF, 1692
DD407.H7	HOHENFRIEDBERG, BATTLE OF, 1745
TJ1367	HOISTING MACHINERY — RIGGING
TJ1350-1383	HOISTING MACHINERY
HD2771-2798	HOLDING COMPANIES / *corporations u.s.*
HD2709-2930	HOLDING COMPANIES / *corporations*
HG4001-4280	HOLDING COMPANIES / *finance*
HD5261	*HOLIDAYS WITH PAY* **SEE** VACATIONS, EMPLOYEE
HV3167	HOLIDAYS / *for shop workers*
GT3930-4995	HOLIDAYS / *manners and customs*
JK1761	HOLIDAYS / *national u.s.*
PN4305.H7	HOLIDAYS / *recitations*
BT767	HOLINESS
B818	HOLISM
TH1083	*HOLLOW TILE CONSTRUCTION* **SEE** TILE CONSTRUCTION
QK495.I3	HOLLY
QB723.H7	HOLMES' COMET
RE997.H7	HOLOCAIN
PL5327	*HOLONTALO LANGUAGE* **SEE** GORONTALO LANGUAGE
TC379	HOLOPHOTE
QL384.H7	HOLOTHURIANS
QE783.H7	HOLOTHURIANS, FOSSIL
QL384.H7	*HOLOTHURIOIDEA* **SEE** HOLOTHURIANS
QE783.H7	*HOLOTHURIOIDEA, FOSSIL* **SEE** HOLOTHURIANS, FOSSIL
SF293.H7	HOLSTEIN HORSE
SF199.H75	HOLSTEIN-FRIESIAN CATTLE
SF193.H7	HOLSTEIN-FRIESIAN CATTLE / *herd-books*
JX1349	HOLY ALLIANCE
D383	HOLY ALLIANCE
BM657.A85	*HOLY ARK* **SEE** ARK OF THE LAW
BT587.C6-7	HOLY COAT
BT465	HOLY CROSS
BT313	*HOLY FAMILY* **SEE** JESUS CHRIST — FAMILY
BT120-123	*HOLY GHOST* **SEE** HOLY SPIRIT
PN57.G7	*HOLY GRAIL* **SEE** GRAIL / *literature*
BX2159.H7	HOLY HOUR
BV50.H6	HOLY INNOCENTS, FEAST OF THE
BS2545.H	HOLY INNOCENTS, MASSACRE OF THE
DR515-516	*HOLY LEAGUE (VENICE, SPAIN, AND THE POPE) 1570-1571* **SEE** CYPRIAN WAR, 1570-1571
DG541	HOLY LEAGUE AGAINST FRANCE, 1511-1513
DR536	HOLY LEAGUE AGAINST THE TURKS, 1684
DC120	HOLY LEAGUE, 1576-1593
BX2159.H75	HOLY NAME, DEVOTION TO
BX1700-1745	*HOLY OFFICE* **SEE** INQUISITION
BX200-750	*HOLY ORTHODOX EASTERN CATHOLIC AND APOSTOLIC CHURCH* **SEE** ORTHODOX EASTERN CHURCH
DD125-198.7	HOLY ROMAN EMPIRE — HISTORY
BX950-960	*HOLY SEE* **SEE** PAPACY
BX1805-1810	*HOLY SEE* **SEE** POPES
BX1001-1378	*HOLY SEE* **SEE** POPES / *individual popes*
DS109.4	HOLY SEPULCHER
BT587.S4	HOLY SHROUD
N8055	HOLY SPIRIT — ART
BT120-123	HOLY SPIRIT
BV94	*HOLY THURSDAY* **SEE** MAUNDY THURSDAY
BP182	*HOLY WAR (ISLAM)* **SEE** JIHAD
BX2307	HOLY WATER / *catholic church*
BV885	HOLY WATER / *practical theology*
BV90	HOLY WEEK / *ceremonial*
BT414	HOLY WEEK / *events*
GR690	HOLY WELLS
BX961.H6	HOLY YEAR
BV90	HOLY-WEEK SERMONS
PM8370	HOM-IDYOMO (ARTIFICIAL LANGUAGE)
RE997.H8	HOMATROPIN
TX150	HOME ACCIDENTS — PREVENTION
TX150	HOME ACCIDENTS
LC225	HOME AND SCHOOL
TH	*HOME BUILDING* **SEE** BUILDING
NA7100-7566	*HOME BUILDING* **SEE** DWELLINGS / *architecture*
TH148	*HOME BUILDING* **SEE** DWELLINGS / *building popular works*
TH8901	*HOME BUILDING* **SEE** DWELLINGS / *building maintenance*
TX301-339	*HOME BUILDING* **SEE** DWELLINGS / *domestic economy*
HD1341	*HOME BUILDING* **SEE** DWELLINGS / *economics*
GR490	*HOME BUILDING* **SEE** DWELLINGS / *folk-lore*
GT170-384	*HOME BUILDING* **SEE** DWELLINGS / *manners and customs*
NK1700-3505	*HOME DECORATION* **SEE** INTERIOR DECORATION / *art*
TX311-317	*HOME DECORATION* **SEE** INTERIOR DECORATION / *home economics*
TX326	HOME ECONOMICS — ACCOUNTING
HF5686.H8	HOME ECONOMICS — ACCOUNTING / *finance*
TX144	HOME ECONOMICS — EARLY WORKS TO 1800
TX298-9	HOME ECONOMICS — EQUIPMENT AND SUPPLIES
TX645-840	*HOME ECONOMICS* **SEE** COOKERY
TX165	HOME ECONOMICS AS A PROFESSION
TX	HOME ECONOMICS
TX298-9	*HOME ECONOMICS, RURAL-EQUIPMENT AND SUPPLIES* **SEE** HOME ECONOMICS — EQUIPMENT AND SUPPLIES
LC5901-6101	*HOME EDUCATION* **SEE** CORRESPONDENCE SCHOOLS AND COURSES
HF1133	*HOME EDUCATION* **SEE** CORRESPONDENCE SCHOOLS AND COURSES / *business schools*
T172	*HOME EDUCATION* **SEE** CORRESPONDENCE SCHOOLS AND COURSES / *technology*
HF1116	*HOME EDUCATION* **SEE** CORRESPONDENCE SCHOOLS AND COURSES / *business schools*
LC37	*HOME EDUCATION* **SEE** DOMESTIC EDUCATION
LC25-31	*HOME EDUCATION* **SEE** SELF-CULTURE
GV1221-9	*HOME GAMES* **SEE** INDOOR GAMES
HD2331-6	HOME LABOR
HG3729.U4-5	*HOME LOAN BANKS* **SEE** FEDERAL HOME LOAN BANKS
BV2650	*HOME MISSIONS* **SEE** MISSIONS, HOME
BV2750-3697	*HOME MISSIONS* **SEE** MISSIONS, HOME / *by country*
BV2495-2595	*HOME MISSIONS* **SEE** MISSIONS, HOME / *by denomination*
RT61	HOME NURSING
HD7287	HOME OWNERSHIP
LB1620.7	HOME ROOM GUIDANCE
DA947-962	HOME RULE (IRELAND)
DA765	HOME RULE (SCOTLAND)
JS113	*HOME RULE FOR CITIES* **SEE** MUNICIPAL HOME RULE
JS3131-7	*HOME RULE FOR CITIES* **SEE** MUNICIPAL HOME RULE / *gt. brit.*
JS348-9	*HOME RULE FOR CITIES* **SEE** MUNICIPAL HOME RULE / *u.s.*
HF1116	*HOME STUDY COURSES* **SEE** CORRESPONDENCE SCHOOLS AND COURSES / *business schools*
T172	*HOME STUDY COURSES* **SEE** CORRESPONDENCE SCHOOLS AND COURSES / *technology*
HF1133	*HOME STUDY COURSES* **SEE** CORRESPONDENCE SCHOOLS AND COURSES / *business schools*
LC5901-6101	*HOME STUDY COURSES* **SEE** CORRESPONDENCE SCHOOLS AND COURSES
LC25-31	*HOME STUDY COURSES* **SEE** SELF-CULTURE
MT893	*HOME STUDY COURSES* **SEE** SINGING — METHODS — — SELF-INSTRUCTION
TS155	*HOME WORKSHOPS* **SEE** WORKSHOPS / *factory management*
HQ503-743	HOME
GT2420	HOME / *manners and customs*
RX6	*HOMEOPATHIC HOSPITALS* **SEE** HOMEOPATHY — HOSPITALS AND DISPENSARIES
RX671-5	*HOMEOPATHIC PHARMACY* **SEE** PHARMACY, HOMEOPATHIC
RX61-66	*HOMEOPATHIC PHYSICIANS* **SEE** PHYSICIANS, HOMEOPATHIC
RX81	HOMEOPATHY — ATTENUATIONS, DILUTIONS, AND POTENCIES
RX61-66	HOMEOPATHY — BIOGRAPHY
RX6	HOMEOPATHY — HOSPITALS AND DISPENSARIES
RX601-675	HOMEOPATHY — MATERIA MEDICA AND THERAPEUTICS
RX76	HOMEOPATHY — POPULAR WORKS

RX71-75	HOMEOPATHY — PRACTICE
RX	HOMEOPATHY
RX601-675	*HOMEOPATHY-THERAPEUTICS* **SEE** HOMEOPATHY — MATERIA MEDICA AND THERAPEUTICS
PA4037	*HOMERIC CIVILIZATION* **SEE** CIVILIZATION, HOMERIC
LB1620.7	*HOMEROOM GUIDANCE* **SEE** HOME ROOM GUIDANCE
HV1-4959	*HOMES (INSTITUTIONS)* **SEE**
HV85-527	*HOMES (INSTITUTIONS)* **SEE** ALMSHOUSES
HV61	*HOMES (INSTITUTIONS)* **SEE** ALMSHOUSES
HV1451-1493	*HOMES (INSTITUTIONS)* **SEE** OLD AGE HOMES
HV959-1420	*HOMES (INSTITUTIONS)* **SEE** ORPHANS AND ORPHAN-ASYLUMS
UB380-385	*HOMES (INSTITUTIONS)* **SEE** SOLDIERS' HOMES
HV1451-1493	*HOMES FOR THE AGED* **SEE** OLD AGE HOMES
BF575.N6	*HOMESICKNESS* **SEE** NOSTALGIA
HD1337	HOMESTEAD LAW / *homestead and exemption*
HD197-205	HOMESTEAD LAW / *land law*
HD5325. 15 1892.H	HOMESTEAD STRIKE, 1892
LB1048	HOMEWORK
HV6499-6535	HOMICIDE
HQ750-799	*HOMICULTURE* **SEE** EUGENICS
BV4224-4230	HOMILETICAL ILLUSTRATIONS
BV4307.S7	*HOMILETICAL STORIES* **SEE** SERMON STORIES
BV4200-4235	*HOMILETICS* **SEE** PREACHING
BV4240-4316	*HOMILIES* **SEE** SERMONS
BX	*HOMILIES* **SEE** SERMONS / *by denomination*
SF469	HOMING PIGEONS / *animal culture*
UH90	HOMING PIGEONS / *military art and science*
ML760	*HOMMEL* **SEE** NOORDSCHE BALK
RX	*HOMOEOPATHY* **SEE** HOMEOPATHY
LB3061	*HOMOGENEOUS GROUPING* **SEE** ABILITY GROUPING IN EDUCATION
SF259	*HOMOGENIZED MILK* **SEE** MILK, HOMOGENIZED
QA611	*HOMOLOGICAL ALGEBRA* **SEE** HOMOLOGY THEORY
QA611	HOMOLOGY THEORY
QL523.H7	HOMOPTERA
RA1141	HOMOSEXUALITY / *medical jurisprudence*
RC558	HOMOSEXUALITY / *neuropsychiatry*
HQ76	HOMOSEXUALITY / *social pathology*
QA611	HOMOTOPY THEORY
DC220.5	HONDSCHOOTE, BATTLE OF, 1793
PQ7500-7509	HONDURAN LITERATURE
F1507	HONDURAS — HISTORY — — TO 1838
F1507.5	HONDURAS — HISTORY — — 1838-1933
F1508	HONDURAS — HISTORY — — 1933-
BF723.H7	HONESTY / *child psychology*
BJ1533.H7	HONESTY / *ethics*
TX560.H7	*HONEY COOKERY* **SEE** COOKERY (HONEY)
E477.44	HONEY HILL, S.C., BATTLE OF, 1864
SB397	HONEY LOCUST
SF535	HONEY PLANTS
QL568.F7	HONEY-ANTS
SF535	*HONEY-BEARING PLANTS* **SEE** HONEY PLANTS
QL696.P2	HONEY-CREEPERS
QL696.P2	HONEY-EATERS / *birds*
SF539	HONEY
TX560.H7	HONEY / *foods*
SF521-538	*HONEYBEES* **SEE** BEES / *beekeeping*
QL568.A6	*HONEYBEES* **SEE** BEES / *entomology*
LB3092-5	*HONOR SYSTEM* **SEE** SELF-GOVERNMENT (IN EDUCATION)
LB3021	*HONOR SYSTEM* **SEE** SELF-GOVERNMENT (IN EDUCATION) / *student honor*
BJ1533.H8	HONOR / *ethics*
JB880	*HONOR, COURTS OF* **SEE** COURTS OF HONOR / *k military*
CR4501-6305	*HONOR, DECORATIONS OF* **SEE** DECORATIONS OF HONOR
JB430-435	*HONOR, DECORATIONS OF* **SEE** DECORATIONS OF HONOR / *military*
B2381-2391	*HONORARY DEGREES* **SEE** DEGREES, ACADEMIC
CR3499-4420	*HONORARY TITLES* **SEE** TITLES OF HONOR AND NOBILITY
B2364	*HONORS COURSES IN COLLEGES* **SEE** UNIVERSITIES AND COLLEGES — HONORS COURSES
B2364	*HONORS WORK IN COLLEGES* **SEE** UNIVERSITIES AND COLLEGES — HONORS COURSES
GT4985	HOODEN HORSE
LB2389	*HOODS* **SEE** ACADEMIC COSTUME
QL942	HOOFS
TJ183	HOOKE'S COUPLING
TS2301.H	HOOKS AND EYES / *manufacture*
HD9969.H5-53	HOOKS AND EYES / *trade*
TS440-445	HOOKS
TA492.H6	HOOKS / *strength of materials*
RC199.95	HOOKWORM DISEASE
RC199.95	HOOKWORMS
GV490	HOOP EXERCISES
E99.H8	*HOOPAH INDIANS* **SEE** HUPA INDIANS
QL696.C7	HOOPOES
GV490	*HOOPS* **SEE** HOOP EXERCISES
F257	HOOSIER (NICKNAME)
DB350.7	*HOOTZOOLS* **SEE** HUCULS
QL942	*HOOVES* **SEE** HOOFS
SB608.H8	HOP FLEA-BEETLE
TP585	*HOP INDUSTRY AND TRADE* **SEE** HOPS / *brewing*
SB295.H8	*HOP INDUSTRY AND TRADE* **SEE** HOPS / *culture*
SB608.H8	HOP-APHIS
BV4638	HOPE / *moral theology*
BD216	HOPE / *philosophy*
E99.H7	HOPI INDIANS
PM1351	HOPI LANGUAGE
TL210	*HOPPED-UP MOTORS* **SEE** AUTOMOBILES, RACING — MOTORS
SB608.H8	HOPS — DISEASES AND PESTS
TP585	HOPS / *brewing*
SB295.H8	HOPS / *culture*
GV1218.H	HOPSCOTCH
ND3363	*HORAE (BOOKS OF HOURS)* **SEE** HOURS, BOOKS OF / *art*
BX2080	*HORAE (BOOKS OF HOURS)* **SEE** HOURS, BOOKS OF / *catholic church*
VK572	HORIZON, DIP OF
VK584.H	HORIZONS, ARTIFICIAL
GV527	HORIZONTAL BAR
RM283-298	HORMONE THERAPY
QK731	HORMONES (PLANTS)
QP187	HORMONES
RM283-298	*HORMONES-THERAPEUTIC USE* **SEE** HORMONE THERAPY
MT426	HORN (MUSICAL INSTRUMENT) — ORCHESTRA STUDIES
MT425	HORN (MUSICAL INSTRUMENT) — STUDIES AND EXERCISES
ML955-8	HORN (MUSICAL INSTRUMENT)
M288-9	*HORN AND CLARINET MUSIC* **SEE** CLARINET AND HORN MUSIC
M288-9	*HORN AND CLARINET MUSIC* **SEE** CLARINET AND HORN MUSIC
M288-9	*HORN AND FLUTE MUSIC* **SEE** FLUTE AND HORN MUSIC
M296-7	HORN AND GUITAR MUSIC
M296-7	HORN AND GUITAR MUSIC, ARRANGED
M255-7	HORN AND PIANO MUSIC
M258-9	HORN AND PIANO MUSIC, ARRANGED
NK6020	HORN CARVING
SF810.H6	HORN FLY / *agriculture*
QL537.M7	HORN FLY / *zoology*
M288-9	HORN MUSIC (2 HORNS)
M355-7	*HORN MUSIC (3 HORNS)* **SEE** WIND TRIOS (3 HORNS)
M355-7	*HORN MUSIC (3 HORNS)* **SEE** WIND TRIOS (3 HORNS)
M455-7	*HORN MUSIC (4 HORNS)* **SEE** WIND QUARTETS (4 HORNS)
M455-7	*HORN MUSIC (4 HORNS)* **SEE** WIND QUARTETS (4 HORNS)
M80-84	HORN MUSIC
ML419	HORN PLAYERS
ML399	HORN PLAYERS
M1205	HORN WITH BAND
M1257	HORN WITH BAND, ARRANGED — SCORES
M1257	HORN WITH BAND, ARRANGED
M1029	HORN WITH ORCHESTRA — SOLO WITH PIANO
M1028-9	HORN WITH ORCHESTRA
M1028-9	HORN WITH ORCHESTRA, ARRANGED
M1105-6	HORN WITH STRING ORCHESTRA

M1105-6	HORN WITH STRING ORCHESTRA, ARRANGED
QL674	HORNBILLS
QL696.C7	HORNBILLS
QE391.H	HORNBLENDE
Z1033.H8	HORNBOOKS
QL668.E2	*HORNED FROGS* **SEE** HORNED TOADS
QL696.P2	*HORNED LARKS* **SEE** LARKS
QL668.E2	HORNED TOADS
M1048	HORNPIPES (ORCHESTRA)
M1060	HORNPIPES (ORCHESTRA)
M217-218	HORNPIPES (VIOLIN AND PIANO)
M211-213	HORNPIPES (VIOLIN AND PIANO)
M1028-9	HORNS (2) WITH ORCHESTRA
M1028-9	HORNS (3) WITH ORCHESTRA
M1028	HORNS (4) WITH ORCHESTRA — SCORES
M1028-9	HORNS (4) WITH ORCHESTRA
QL942	HORNS
RL427	HORNS, CUTANEOUS
SF912	*HORNS, REMOVAL OF* **SEE** DEHORNING
QE391.C4	*HORNSTONE* **SEE** CHERT
TS540-549	HOROLOGY
QB25-26	*HOROSCOPE* **SEE** ASTROLOGY
BF1651-1729	*HOROSCOPE* **SEE** ASTROLOGY
TX819	*HORS D'OEUVRES* **SEE** COOKERY (RELISHES)
QL737.U6	*HORSE* **SEE** HORSES
HV4749-4755	*HORSE* **SEE** HORSES / cruelty to horses
GR715	*HORSE* **SEE** HORSES / folk-lore
HD9434	*HORSE* **SEE** HORSES / horse raising
SF277-359	*HORSE* **SEE** HORSES / horse raising
GT5885	*HORSE* **SEE** HORSES / manners and customs
UC600-695	*HORSE* **SEE** HORSES / military service
UE460-475	*HORSE* **SEE** HORSES / military service
UF370	*HORSE* **SEE** HORSES / military service
SF277	HORSE BREEDERS' SOCIETIES
SF277-318	HORSE BREEDING
HD9434	HORSE BREEDING
TX556.H8	HORSE MEAT / foods
SF331	HORSE RACE BETTING
E83.813	HORSE SHOE, BATTLE OF THE, 1814
HV6646-6665	HORSE STEALING
SF287	*HORSE-BREAKING* **SEE** HORSE-TRAINING / animal culture
GV1831.H8	*HORSE-BREAKING* **SEE** HORSE-TRAINING / trained animals
QK495.A	HORSE-CHESTNUT
SF335	HORSE-RACING SOCIETIES
SF321-359	HORSE-RACING
HV6718	HORSE-RACING / gambling
SB608.H82	HORSE-RADISH WEB-WORM
SB307.H	HORSE-RADISH
TF701-1124	*HORSE-RAILROADS* **SEE** STREET-RAILROADS
HE4201-5300	*HORSE-RAILROADS* **SEE** STREET-RAILROADS / economics
HE4251	*HORSE-RAILROADS* **SEE** STREET-RAILROADS / taxation
SF295-7	HORSE-SHOWS
SF287	HORSE-TRAINING / animal culture
GV1831.H8	HORSE-TRAINING / trained animals
GV517	*HORSE, VAULTING* **SEE** VAULTING-HORSE
QL537.T2	HORSEFLIES
TS1747.H6	HORSEHAIR / manufactures
SF309	HORSEMANSHIP
UE470-475	HORSEMANSHIP / cavalry
SF336	HORSEMEN — CORRESPONDENCE, REMINISCENCES, ETC.
SF31	HORSEMEN
QK495.M	HORSEMINT
TJ173	HORSEPOWER (MECHANICS) / machinery
TJ475-8	HORSEPOWER (MECHANICS) / steam-engines
SB307.H	*HORSERADISH* **SEE** HORSE-RADISH
SF869	HORSES — AGE
SF765	HORSES — ANATOMY
SF951-9	HORSES — DISEASES
SF197	HORSES — JUDGING
PZ10.3	HORSES — LEGENDS AND STORIES
QL795.H7	HORSES — LEGENDS AND STORIES
SF289	HORSES — PACES, GAITS, ETC.
SF337	HORSES — PICTURES, ILLUSTRATIONS, ETC. / animal culture
N7660	HORSES — PICTURES, ILLUSTRATIONS, ETC. / art
SF293	HORSES — STUD-BOOKS
UC680-695	HORSES — TRANSPORTATION / military service
GR715	HORSES (IN RELIGION, FOLK-LORE, ETC.) / folk-lore
BL443.H	HORSES (IN RELIGION, FOLK-LORE, ETC.) / religion
N7660	HORSES IN ART
QL737.U6	HORSES
HV4749-4755	HORSES / cruelty to horses
GR715	HORSES / folk-lore
HD9434	HORSES / horse raising
SF277-359	HORSES / horse raising
GT5885	HORSES / manners and customs
UE460-475	HORSES / military service
UF370	HORSES / military service
UC600-695	HORSES / military service
QE882.U6	HORSES, FOSSIL
HD9434	*HORSES-BREEDING* **SEE** HORSE BREEDING
SF277-318	*HORSES-BREEDING* **SEE** HORSE BREEDING
SF295-7	*HORSES-EXHIBITIONS* **SEE** HORSE-SHOWS
SF287	*HORSES-TRAINING* **SEE** HORSE-TRAINING / animal culture
GV1831.H8	*HORSES-TRAINING* **SEE** HORSE-TRAINING / trained animals
GV1095	*HORSESHOE PITCHING* **SEE** QUOITS
SF907	HORSESHOEING
UC640-645	HORSESHOEING / military service
SF31	*HORSEWOMEN* **SEE** HORSEMEN
SB59.5	HORTICULTURAL EXHIBITIONS
SB1-13	HORTICULTURAL SOCIETIES
SB51	HORTICULTURE AS A PROFESSION
SB61-63	*HORTICULTURE-BIOGRAPHY* **SEE** HORTICULTURISTS
SB1-13	*HORTICULTURE-SOCIETIES, ETC.* **SEE** HORTICULTURAL SOCIETIES
SB61-63	HORTICULTURISTS
DS432.H6	HOS
TH9380	HOSE — TESTING
TS2301.H7	HOSE — TESTING
TS2301.H7	HOSE-COUPLINGS
TH9380	HOSE-COUPLINGS
TS2301.H7	HOSE
TH9380	HOSE / fire hose
HD9969.H6-8	HOSIERY INDUSTRY / industry
TT679-695	HOSIERY INDUSTRY / manufacture
TT679-695	HOSIERY / manufacture
TT681	HOSIERY, COTTON
TT681	HOSIERY, NYLON
TT681	HOSIERY, SILK
RA971	*HOSPITAL ACCREDITATION* **SEE** HOSPITALS — ACCREDITATION
RA972.5	HOSPITAL ADMINISTRATORS
RA972	*HOSPITAL ATTENDANTS* **SEE** HOSPITALS — STAFF
RA975.5.D5	*HOSPITAL DIETARY DEPARTMENT* **SEE** HOSPITALS — FOOD SERVICE
HV16-25	*HOSPITAL ENDOWMENTS* **SEE** ENDOWMENTS / charities
LB2336-7	*HOSPITAL ENDOWMENTS* **SEE** ENDOWMENTS / higher education
RA975.5.H6	HOSPITAL HOUSEKEEPING
RA972	*HOSPITAL INTERNS* **SEE** INTERNS (MEDICINE)
RA969	*HOSPITAL LAUNDRIES* **SEE** LAUNDRIES, HOSPITAL
Z675.H7	HOSPITAL LIBRARIES
RA975.5.P5	HOSPITAL PHARMACIES
VG450	*HOSPITAL SERVICE (WAR)* **SEE** HOSPITAL-SHIPS / naval medicine
UH460-485	*HOSPITAL SERVICE (WAR)* **SEE** HOSPITALS, MILITARY
RA975	*HOSPITAL SERVICE (WAR)* **SEE** HOSPITALS, NAVAL AND MARINE / marine
VG410-450	*HOSPITAL SERVICE (WAR)* **SEE** HOSPITALS, NAVAL AND MARINE / naval
RA980-993	*HOSPITAL SERVICE (WAR)* **SEE** HOSPITALS, NAVAL AND MARINE / marine
HV560-583	*HOSPITAL SERVICE (WAR)* **SEE** RED CROSS
UH535-7	*HOSPITAL SERVICE (WAR)* **SEE** RED CROSS / army
D628-630	*HOSPITAL SERVICE (WAR)* **SEE** RED CROSS / european war
VG457	*HOSPITAL SERVICE (WAR)* **SEE** RED CROSS / navy
UH201-551	*HOSPITAL SERVICE (WAR)* **SEE** WAR — RELIEF OF SICK AND WOUNDED / medical and sanitary service

VG450	HOSPITAL-SHIPS / *naval medicine*
BX2825	HOSPITALERS
BJ2021-8	HOSPITALITY
BX2825	*HOSPITALLERS* **SEE** HOSPITALERS
HF5686.H7	HOSPITALS — ACCOUNTING
RA971	HOSPITALS — ACCREDITATION
RA967	HOSPITALS — CONSTRUCTION
TH9445.H7	HOSPITALS — FIRES AND FIRE PREVENTION
RA975.5.D5	HOSPITALS — FOOD SERVICE
RA968	HOSPITALS — FURNITURE, EQUIPMENT, ETC.
RA969	HOSPITALS — HEATING AND VENTILATION
RA969	HOSPITALS — HYGIENE
RA971	HOSPITALS — INSPECTION
RA965	HOSPITALS — JUVENILE LITERATURE
RA974	HOSPITALS — LAWS AND LEGISLATION
RA967.7	HOSPITALS — LOCATION
RA974	HOSPITALS — OUTPATIENT SERVICES
RA967.5	HOSPITALS — SPECIFICATIONS
RA972	HOSPITALS — STAFF
RA960-996	HOSPITALS
RA973	HOSPITALS, CONVALESCENT
UH460-485	*HOSPITALS, FIELD* **SEE** HOSPITALS, MILITARY
RC970-971	*HOSPITALS, FIELD* **SEE** MEDICINE, MILITARY / *medical practice*
UH	*HOSPITALS, FIELD* **SEE** MEDICINE, MILITARY / *military science*
UH201-551	*HOSPITALS, FIELD* **SEE** WAR — RELIEF OF SICK AND WOUNDED / *medical and sanitary service*
RG12-16	HOSPITALS, GYNECOLOGIC AND OBSTETRIC
RX6	*HOSPITALS, HOMEOPATHIC* **SEE** HOMEOPATHY — HOSPITALS AND DISPENSARIES
RA981.A35	*HOSPITALS, INDIAN* **SEE** INDIANS OF NORTH AMERICA — HOSPITALS
RG12-16	*HOSPITALS, MATERNITY* **SEE** HOSPITALS, GYNECOLOGIC AND OBSTETRIC
RA964	HOSPITALS, MEDIEVAL
UH460-485	HOSPITALS, MILITARY
RA980-993	HOSPITALS, NAVAL AND MARINE / *marine*
RA975	HOSPITALS, NAVAL AND MARINE / *marine*
VG410-450	HOSPITALS, NAVAL AND MARINE / *naval*
RE3	HOSPITALS, OPHTHALMIC AND AURAL
RF6	HOSPITALS, OPHTHALMIC AND AURAL / *nose and throat*
RA975	HOSPITALS, RURAL
RA972	*HOSPITALS-ATTENDANTS* **SEE** HOSPITALS — STAFF
RA972	*HOSPITALS-EMPLOYEES* **SEE** HOSPITALS — STAFF
RA972	*HOSPITALS-NURSES* **SEE** HOSPITALS — STAFF
RT	*HOSPITALS-NURSES* **SEE** NURSES AND NURSING
UH490-495	*HOSPITALS-NURSES* **SEE** NURSES AND NURSING / *army*
VG350-355	*HOSPITALS-NURSES* **SEE** NURSES AND NURSING / *navy*
JX5143	HOSTAGES / *law of war*
JX4505-5326	*HOSTILITIES* **SEE** WAR (INTERNATIONAL LAW)
GN497-9	*HOSTILITIES* **SEE** WAR / *v primitive*
JX4552-4564	*HOSTILITIES* **SEE** WAR, DECLARATION OF
JF256	*HOSTILITIES* **SEE** WAR, DECLARATION OF / *constitutional law*
JX5203-5268	*HOSTILITIES* **SEE** WAR, MARITIME (INTERNATIONAL LAW)
TL210	*HOT MOTORS* **SEE** AUTOMOBILES, RACING — MOTORS
QE528	*HOT SPRINGS* **SEE** GEYSERS
GB1001-1197	*HOT SPRINGS* **SEE** SPRINGS
GR690	*HOT SPRINGS* **SEE** SPRINGS / *folk-lore*
RM253	HOT WATER-THERAPEUTIC USE
RM865-7	*HOT-AIR BATHS* **SEE** BATHS, HOT-AIR
TJ765	*HOT-AIR ENGINES* **SEE** CALORIC ENGINES
TH7601-7635	HOT-AIR HEATING
TH7683.D8	*HOT-AIR HEATING-DUCTS* **SEE** AIR DUCTS
RM865-8	*HOT-AIR TREATMENT* **SEE** THERMOTHERAPY
SB415-416	*HOT-HOUSES* **SEE** GREENHOUSES
TH7541	HOT-WATER HEATING — REGULATORS
TH7511-7549	HOT-WATER HEATING
TH6551-6568	HOT-WATER SUPPLY
JF620.H8	HOTCHKISS MACHINE-GUN
JF620.H8	HOTCHKISS REVOLVING CANNON
TX912	HOTEL HOUSEKEEPING
TX911.5	HOTEL LAUNDRY SERVICE
HF5686.H75	HOTELS, TAVERNS, ETC. — ACCOUNTING

TX930	HOTELS, TAVERNS, ETC. — EMPLOYEES
TX911	HOTELS, TAVERNS, ETC. — EMPLOYEES
TH9445.H	HOTELS, TAVERNS, ETC. — FIRES AND FIRE PREVENTION
TX912	HOTELS, TAVERNS, ETC. — FURNITURE, EQUIPMENT, ETC.
NA7800-7850	HOTELS, TAVERNS, ETC. / *architecture*
GT3770-3899	HOTELS, TAVERNS, ETC. / *manners and customs*
PL8251-4	HOTTENTOT LANGUAGE
GN660.H6	HOTTENTOTS / *ethnography*
DT764.H6	HOTTENTOTS / *south africa*
QL696.L7	HOUBARA
SF489.H7	HOUDANS (POULTRY)
SF429.H6	HOUNDS
QB214	HOUR-GLASSES
CE	*HOURS (TIME)* **SEE** CHRONOLOGY
GR930	*HOURS (TIME)* **SEE** DAYS / *folk-lore*
TS540-549	*HOURS (TIME)* **SEE** HOROLOGY
QB215	*HOURS (TIME)* **SEE** SUN-DIALS
QB209-224	*HOURS (TIME)* **SEE** TIME
BF467-475	*HOURS (TIME)* **SEE** TIME / *psychology*
BD638	*HOURS (TIME)* **SEE** TIME / *speculative philosophy*
HD5106-5250	HOURS OF LABOR
ND3363	HOURS, BOOKS OF / *art*
BX2080	HOURS, BOOKS OF / *catholic church*
E99.S8	*HOUSATONIC INDIANS* **SEE** STOCKBRIDGE INDIANS
E99.S8	*HOUSATUNNUK INDIANS* **SEE** STOCKBRIDGE INDIANS
TH7692-8	HOUSE CLEANING / *etc.*
NK1700-3505	*HOUSE DECORATION* **SEE** INTERIOR DECORATION / *art*
TX311-317	*HOUSE DECORATION* **SEE** INTERIOR DECORATION / *home economics*
TD913	*HOUSE DRAINAGE* **SEE** DRAINAGE, HOUSE
TH6571-6675	*HOUSE DRAINAGE* **SEE** DRAINAGE, HOUSE / *plumbing*
TD929	*HOUSE DRAINAGE* **SEE** DRAINAGE, HOUSE / *rural sanitation*
TH6101-6691	*HOUSE DRAINAGE* **SEE** PLUMBING
TD511-780	*HOUSE DRAINAGE* **SEE** SEWERAGE
TH2055	*HOUSE FITTINGS* **SEE** BUILDING FITTINGS / *catalogs*
TH455	*HOUSE FITTINGS* **SEE** BUILDING FITTINGS / *catalogs*
TH8901	*HOUSE FITTINGS* **SEE** BUILDING FITTINGS / *maintenance*
TH2301-2398	HOUSE FRAMING
TH153	*HOUSE MOVING* **SEE** MOVING OF BUILDINGS, BRIDGES, ETC. / *building*
HF6121.H6	HOUSE ORGANS
TT320	HOUSE PAINTING — AMATEURS' MANUALS
TT320	HOUSE PAINTING — CONTRACTS AND SPECIFICATIONS
TT320	HOUSE PAINTING — ESTIMATES
TT320-324	HOUSE PAINTING
NA7127-7135	*HOUSE PLANS* **SEE** ARCHITECTURE, DOMESTIC — DESIGNS AND PLANS
SB419	HOUSE PLANTS
TH6021-7696	*HOUSE SANITATION* **SEE** SANITATION, HOUSEHOLD / *building*
TD905-935	*HOUSE SANITATION* **SEE** SANITATION, HOUSEHOLD / *sanitary engineering*
GV836	HOUSE-BOATS / *boating*
VM335	HOUSE-BOATS / *naval architecture*
QL531-8	*HOUSE-FLIES* **SEE** FLIES
QL396.P2	HOUSE-MARTIN
GV836	*HOUSEBOATS* **SEE** HOUSE-BOATS / *boating*
VM335	*HOUSEBOATS* **SEE** HOUSE-BOATS / *naval architecture*
TK9901	HOUSEHOLD APPLIANCES, ELECTRIC — MAINTENANCE AND REPAIR / *amateurs' manuals*
TK7018	HOUSEHOLD APPLIANCES, ELECTRIC — MAINTENANCE AND REPAIR
HD9697	HOUSEHOLD APPLIANCES, ELECTRIC / *economics*
TK7018-7301	HOUSEHOLD APPLIANCES, ELECTRIC / *technology*
TX326	*HOUSEHOLD BUDGETS* **SEE** HOME ECONOMICS — ACCOUNTING
HF5686.H8	*HOUSEHOLD BUDGETS* **SEE** HOME ECONOMICS — ACCOUNTING / *finance*
HD6977-7080	*HOUSEHOLD EXPENSES* **SEE** COST AND STANDARD OF LIVING

HF5686.H8	*HOUSEHOLD EXPENSES* **SEE** HOME ECONOMICS — ACCOUNTING / *finance*
TX656-8	*HOUSEHOLD GOODS* **SEE** KITCHEN UTENSILS
HE5601-5999	*HOUSEHOLD GOODS CARRIERS* **SEE** STORAGE AND MOVING TRADE / *transportation*
HF5484-5495	*HOUSEHOLD GOODS CARRIERS* **SEE** STORAGE AND MOVING TRADE / *storage*
TX	*HOUSEHOLD MANAGEMENT* **SEE** HOME ECONOMICS
TX325	HOUSEHOLD PESTS
TX150	*HOUSEHOLD SAFETY* **SEE** HOME ACCIDENTS — PREVENTION
TH6021-7696	*HOUSEHOLD SANITATION* **SEE** SANITATION, HOUSEHOLD / *building*
TD905-935	*HOUSEHOLD SANITATION* **SEE** SANITATION, HOUSEHOLD / *sanitary engineering*
TX	*HOUSEHOLD SCIENCE* **SEE** HOME ECONOMICS
GN446-7	*HOUSEHOLD UTENSILS* **SEE** IMPLEMENTS, UTENSILS, ETC. / *primitive*
TX656-8	*HOUSEHOLD UTENSILS* **SEE** KITCHEN UTENSILS
TX	*HOUSEKEEPING* **SEE** HOME ECONOMICS
TX331-3	*HOUSEMAIDS* **SEE** SERVANTS / *home economics*
HD8039.D5-52	*HOUSEMAIDS* **SEE** SERVANTS / *labor*
NA7100-7786	*HOUSES* **SEE** ARCHITECTURE, DOMESTIC
NA7100-7566	*HOUSES* **SEE** DWELLINGS / *architecture*
TH148	*HOUSES* **SEE** DWELLINGS / *building popular works*
TH8901	*HOUSES* **SEE** DWELLINGS / *building maintenance*
TX301-339	*HOUSES* **SEE** DWELLINGS / *domestic economy*
HD1341	*HOUSES* **SEE** DWELLINGS / *economics*
GR490	*HOUSES* **SEE** DWELLINGS / *folk-lore*
GT170-384	*HOUSES* **SEE** DWELLINGS / *manners and customs*
NA7860	*HOUSES, APARTMENT* **SEE** APARTMENT HOUSES / *architecture*
TX957-8	*HOUSES, APARTMENT* **SEE** APARTMENT HOUSES / *service*
NA7150	*HOUSES, BRICK* **SEE** BRICK HOUSES
NA7160	*HOUSES, CONCRETE* **SEE** CONCRETE HOUSES
NA8480	*HOUSES, DEMOUNTABLE* **SEE** BUILDINGS, PREFABRICATED / *architecture*
TH1098	*HOUSES, DEMOUNTABLE* **SEE** BUILDINGS, PREFABRICATED / *building*
NA7175	*HOUSES, HALF-TIMBERED* **SEE** HALF-TIMBERED HOUSES
NA7123	*HOUSES, HISTORIC* **SEE** HISTORIC HOUSES, ETC. / *architecture*
NA7205	*HOUSES, HISTORIC* **SEE** HISTORIC HOUSES, ETC. / *architecture*
NA8480	*HOUSES, PORTABLE* **SEE** BUILDINGS, PORTABLE / *architecture*
TH1098	*HOUSES, PORTABLE* **SEE** BUILDINGS, PORTABLE / *building*
NA8480	*HOUSES, PREFABRICATED* **SEE** BUILDINGS, PREFABRICATED / *architecture*
TH1098	*HOUSES, PREFABRICATED* **SEE** BUILDINGS, PREFABRICATED / *building*
NA7170	*HOUSES, STONE* **SEE** STONE HOUSES / *architecture*
TH1201	*HOUSES, STONE* **SEE** STONE HOUSES / *building*
NA7195.A4	*HOUSING FOR THE AGED* **SEE** AGED — DWELLINGS
TX960	HOUSING MANAGEMENT
HD7286-7390	HOUSING
HD7287.7	HOUSING, COOPERATIVE
VC423	*HOUSING, NAVAL* **SEE** U.S. — BARRACKS AND QUARTERS
E185.89.H6	*HOUSING, NEGRO* **SEE** NEGROES — HOUSING
TX960	*HOUSING-MANAGEMENT* **SEE** HOUSING MANAGEMENT
E99.S8	*HOUSSATONNOC INDIANS* **SEE** STOCKBRIDGE INDIANS
PL5379	*HOVA DIALECT* **SEE** MERINA DIALECT
UF560-565	HOWITZERS
UF470-475	HOWITZERS
VF390-395	HOWITZERS / *naval*
QE391.H	HOWLITE
PL3801.S5	*HSI-HSIA LANGUAGE* **SEE** SI-HIA LANGUAGE
GV1458.C5	*HSIANG CHI (GAME)* **SEE** CHINESE CHESS
M175.H8	HU CH'IN MUSIC
ML531	HU CH'IN
F1221.H	*HUABI INDIANS* **SEE** HUAVE INDIANS
PM3836	*HUABI LANGUAGE* **SEE** HUAVE LANGUAGE
F1565	HUACAS / *panaman antiquities*
F3429	HUACAS / *peruvian antiquities*
SF401.H	HUANACO / *animal culture*
QL737.U5	HUANACO / *zoology*
F3430.1.H	HUANCA INDIANS
F2823.G	*HUARPE INDIANS* **SEE** GUARPE INDIANS
F1221.H	HUASTEC INDIANS
PM3831	HUASTEC LANGUAGE
F1221.H	HUAVE INDIANS
PM3836	HUAVE LANGUAGE
F1221.H	*HUAXTEC INDIANS* **SEE** HUASTEC INDIANS
PM3831	*HUAXTEC LANGUAGE* **SEE** HUASTEC LANGUAGE
QL696.L7	*HUBARA* **SEE** HOUBARA
E241.H8	*HUBBARDSTON, BATTLE OF, 1777* **SEE** HUBBARDTON, BATTLE OF, 1777
E241.H8	HUBBARDTON, BATTLE OF, 1777
TS1580	HUCKABACK
SB386.H	HUCKLEBERRIES
HF5458-9	*HUCKSTERS* **SEE** PEDDLERS AND PEDDLING
DB350.7	HUCULS
F127.H8	HUDSON-FULTON CELEBRATION, 1909
BX9450-9459	HUGUENOTS IN FRANCE
DC111-130	HUGUENOTS IN FRANCE / *history*
BX9450-9459	HUGUENOTS
E99.H78	HUICHOL INDIANS
F1221.H	HUICHOL INDIANS / *mexico*
PM3841	HUICHOL LANGUAGE
SB945.H	HUISACHE GIRDLER / *insect pests*
PM7254	*HUITOTO LANGUAGE* **SEE** WITOTO LANGUAGE
GV1726.H	HULA (DANCE)
VM	HULLS (NAVAL ARCHITECTURE)
F219	*HULMECAS* **SEE** OLMECS
BV4618	HUMAN ACTS
QM	*HUMAN ANATOMY* **SEE** ANATOMY, HUMAN
BF39	HUMAN BEHAVIOR — MATHEMATICAL MODELS
QM601-611	*HUMAN EMBRYOLOGY* **SEE** EMBRYOLOGY, HUMAN
N7570-7649	HUMAN FIGURE IN ART
NK1550	HUMAN FIGURE IN ART / *design*
NC760-775	HUMAN FIGURE IN ART / *drawing*
ND1290-1337	HUMAN FIGURE IN ART / *painting*
NB1930	HUMAN FIGURE IN ART / *sculpture*
PN56.H	HUMAN FIGURE IN LITERATURE
GF	*HUMAN GEOGRAPHY* **SEE** ANTHROPO-GEOGRAPHY
HM291	*HUMAN INTERACTION* **SEE** SOCIAL INTERACTION
GN495.2	*HUMAN LEOPARDS* **SEE** LEOPARD MEN
BF636	*HUMAN RELATIONS* **SEE** INTERPERSONAL RELATIONS
DS422.S2	*HUMAN SACRIFICE* **SEE** SACRIFICE, HUMAN / *india*
BP595	*HUMAN SCIENCE* **SEE** ANTHROPOSOPHY
HV1-4959	*HUMANE SOCIETIES* **SEE** CHARITABLE SOCIETIES
HV701-1420	*HUMANE SOCIETIES* **SEE** CHILD WELFARE
B821	HUMANISM — 20TH CENTURY
B778	HUMANISM
B821	HUMANISM / *modern*
BJ1360	*HUMANIST ETHICS* **SEE** HUMANISTIC ETHICS
LC1001-1021	*HUMANISTIC EDUCATION* **SEE** EDUCATION, HUMANISTIC
LA106-8	*HUMANISTIC EDUCATION* **SEE** EDUCATION, HUMANISTIC / *renaissance*
BJ1360	HUMANISTIC ETHICS
PA83-85	HUMANISTS
BT1350	*HUMANITARIANISM (RELIGION)* **SEE** ARIANISM
B821	*HUMANITARIANISM (RELIGION)* **SEE** HUMANISM — 20TH CENTURY
BT214-215	*HUMANITARIANISM (RELIGION)* **SEE** JESUS CHRIST — DIVINITY
B831	*HUMANITARIANISM (RELIGION)* **SEE** POSITIVISM
B2200-2249	*HUMANITARIANISM (RELIGION)* **SEE** POSITIVISM / *comte*
BT1480	*HUMANITARIANISM (RELIGION)* **SEE** SOCINIANISM
BT110-115	*HUMANITARIANISM (RELIGION)* **SEE** TRINITY
BX9801-9869	*HUMANITARIANISM (RELIGION)* **SEE** UNITARIANISM
AZ361	*HUMANITIES AND SCIENCE* **SEE** SCIENCE AND THE HUMANITIES
BJ1533.H	HUMANITY / *virtues*
B831	*HUMANITY, RELIGION OF* **SEE** POSITIVISM
B2200-2249	*HUMANITY, RELIGION OF* **SEE** POSITIVISM / *comte*
QL568.A6	*HUMBLEBEES* **SEE** BUMBLEBEES
HV6751-6761	*HUMBUG* **SEE** IMPOSTORS AND IMPOSTURE / *criminal*
HV6691-9	*HUMBUG* **SEE** SWINDLERS AND SWINDLING
RD557	HUMERUS — FRACTURE

QL821	HUMERUS / *comparative anatomy*
QM117	HUMERUS / *human anatomy*
RD557	*HUMERUS-DISLOCATION* **SEE** SHOULDER JOINT — DISLOCATION
QD341.A2	HUMIC ACID
QC915-917	HUMIDITY
BX3680.H8	HUMILIATI
BV4647.H8	HUMILITY
S598	HUMIN
ML760	*HUMMEL* **SEE** NOORDSCHE BALK
QL696.T6	HUMMING-BIRDS
PN6147-6231	*HUMOR* **SEE** WIT AND HUMOR
BS2545.W5	*HUMOR AND RELIGION* **SEE** RELIGION AND HUMOR / *new testament*
BX4661	*HUMOR AND RELIGION* **SEE** RELIGION AND HUMOR / *saints*
PN6147	HUMORISTS
NC1300-1763	*HUMOROUS ILLUSTRATIONS* **SEE** CARICATURES AND CARTOONS
NC1300-1765	*HUMOROUS ILLUSTRATIONS* **SEE** WIT AND HUMOR, PICTORIAL
S598	HUMUS
DC96-105	HUNDRED YEARS' WAR, 1339-1453
PH3125	HUNGARIAN BALLADS AND SONGS
PH3165-3171	HUNGARIAN DRAMA / *collections*
PH3084-3096	HUNGARIAN DRAMA / *history*
PH2001-2800	HUNGARIAN LANGUAGE
PH3141	HUNGARIAN LITERATURE — EARLY TO 1800 / *collections*
PH3036	HUNGARIAN LITERATURE — EARLY TO 1800 / *history*
PH3132-3188	HUNGARIAN LITERATURE / *collections*
PH3001-3123	HUNGARIAN LITERATURE / *history*
PN5168.H8	HUNGARIAN NEWSPAPERS / *history*
PN5168.H8	HUNGARIAN PERIODICALS / *history*
PH3151-3164	HUNGARIAN POETRY / *collections*
PH3062-3082	HUNGARIAN POETRY / *history*
DB901-975	HUNGARY — HISTORY
QP141	HUNGER
E99.H795	HUNKPAPA INDIANS
F3341.T6	*HUNO INDIANS* **SEE** PUQUINA INDIANS / *bolivia*
F2230.2.P	*HUNO INDIANS* **SEE** PUQUINA INDIANS / *south america*
D141-3	HUNS
SK36	HUNTING — ACCIDENTS
SK273-5	HUNTING — IMPLEMENTS AND APPLIANCES
SK271	HUNTING — PICTORIAL WORKS
GN422	HUNTING (IN RELIGION, FOLK-LORE, ETC.)
SK36	*HUNTING ACCIDENTS* **SEE** HUNTING — ACCIDENTS
SH403	HUNTING AND FISHING CLUBS
SK1	HUNTING AND FISHING CLUBS
SH1	HUNTING AND FISHING CLUBS
GT5810-5850	HUNTING CUSTOMS
SF428.5	HUNTING DOGS
N8250	HUNTING IN ART
PN56.H	HUNTING IN LITERATURE
SK355-579	*HUNTING LAW* **SEE** GAME-LAWS
ML3780	HUNTING MUSIC — HISTORY AND CRITICISM
M1977.H8	HUNTING SONGS
PR1195.H9	HUNTING SONGS / *english poetry*
ML3780	HUNTING SONGS / *etc.*
SK36	HUNTING WITH BOW AND ARROW
QL737.C2	*HUNTING-LEOPARDS* **SEE** CHEETAHS
SK	HUNTING / *hunting sports*
GT5810-5899	HUNTING / *manners and customs*
N422	HUNTING, PRIMITIVE
S485.H8	*HUNZUKUTS* **SEE** BURUSHO
99.H8	HUPA INDIANS
M1361-4	HUPA LANGUAGE
V1067	HURDLE-RACING
M286-7	HURDY-GURDY MUSIC (2 HURDY-GURDIES)
M59	HURDY-GURDY MUSIC
ML760	HURDY-GURDY
GV1017.H8	HURLING (GAME)
E99.H9	HURON INDIANS
PM1366	HURON LANGUAGE
DS59.H	*HURRI* **SEE** HURRIANS
P951	*HURRIAN LANGUAGE* **SEE** MITANNIAN LANGUAGE
P951	*HURRIAN LANGUAGE* **SEE** MITANNIAN LANGUAGE
DS59.H	HURRIANS

GC225-6	*HURRICANE WAVES* **SEE** STORM SURGES
QC941-959	HURRICANES
HD1485.P2-55	*HUSBANDRY, PATRONS OF* **SEE** PATRONS OF HUSBANDRY
SF429.5	*HUSKIES, SIBERIAN* **SEE** SIBERIAN HUSKIES
SF429.5	*HUSKY, SIBERIAN* **SEE** SIBERIAN HUSKIES
BX4913-4918	HUSSITES
DB350.7	*HUZULS* **SEE** HUCULS
PK6141-6181	*HUZVARESH* **SEE** PAHLAVI LANGUAGE
SB413.H9	HYACINTHS
QL737.C2	*HYAENAS* **SEE** HYENAS
QH421-5	*HYBRIDISM* **SEE** HYBRIDIZATION
GN237	*HYBRIDITY OF RACES* **SEE** MISCEGENATION
E185.62	*HYBRIDITY OF RACES* **SEE** MISCEGENATION / *negroes in the u.s.*
QH421-5	HYBRIDIZATION
QH423	HYBRIDIZATION, VEGETABLE
RC242	HYDATIDS
TH9365	HYDRANTS / *fire prevention*
QD181.H1	HYDRATES
QD63.H	HYDRATION
TH1461-1501	*HYDRAULIC CEMENT* **SEE** CEMENT / *building*
HD9622	*HYDRAULIC CEMENT* **SEE** CEMENT / *economics*
TA680-683	*HYDRAULIC CEMENT* **SEE** CEMENT / *engineering*
TA434-5	*HYDRAULIC CEMENT* **SEE** CEMENT / *etc.*
TP875-885	*HYDRAULIC CEMENT* **SEE** CEMENT / *manufacture*
TN945	*HYDRAULIC CEMENT* **SEE** CEMENT / *mineral resources*
TJ1370-1380	*HYDRAULIC ELEVATORS* **SEE** ELEVATORS
TC144	HYDRAULIC ENGINEERING — EARLY WORKS TO 1800
TC177	HYDRAULIC ENGINEERING — INSTRUMENTS
TC151	HYDRAULIC ENGINEERING — TABLES, CALCULATIONS, ETC.
TC158	*HYDRAULIC ENGINEERING LABORATORIES* **SEE** HYDRAULIC LABORATORIES
TC	HYDRAULIC ENGINEERING
TC543	*HYDRAULIC FILL DAMS* **SEE** EARTH DAMS
TJ844	HYDRAULIC FLUIDS
TJ1435	HYDRAULIC JACKS
TC175	HYDRAULIC JUMP
TC158	HYDRAULIC LABORATORIES
TJ840-890	HYDRAULIC MACHINERY
TN421	HYDRAULIC MINING / *gold*
TC163	HYDRAULIC MODELS
TJ855-7	HYDRAULIC MOTORS
ML553	HYDRAULIC ORGAN
TK1421-1524	*HYDRAULIC POWER PLANTS* **SEE** WATER-POWER ELECTRIC PLANTS / *by plant*
TK1081	*HYDRAULIC POWER PLANTS* **SEE** WATER-POWER ELECTRIC PLANTS
TC415-524	*HYDRAULIC POWER PLANTS* **SEE** WATER-POWER / *by place*
TC147	*HYDRAULIC POWER PLANTS* **SEE** WATER-POWER / *hydraulic engineering*
TJ840-890	*HYDRAULIC POWER PLANTS* **SEE** WATER-POWER / *machinery*
TJ1460	HYDRAULIC PRESSES
TJ905	HYDRAULIC RAMS
TJ857	HYDRAULIC SERVOMECHANISMS
TJ843	*HYDRAULIC TRANSMISSION* **SEE** OIL HYDRAULIC MACHINERY
TJ870-875	HYDRAULIC TURBINES
TC179	HYDRAULICS — TABLES, CALCULATIONS, ETC.
TC160-179	HYDRAULICS
ML553	*HYDRAULUS* **SEE** HYDRAULIC ORGAN
QD181.N15	HYDRAZINE
QD341.A8	HYDRAZINES
QD305.A8	HYDRAZINES
QD181.N1	*HYDRAZOIC ACID* **SEE** HYDRONITRIC ACID
QD181.I1	HYDRIODIC ACID
TL684	*HYDRO-AEROPLANES* **SEE** SEAPLANES
TK1081	*HYDRO-ELECTRIC PLANTS* **SEE** WATER-POWER ELECTRIC PLANTS
TK1421-1524	*HYDRO-ELECTRIC PLANTS* **SEE** WATER-POWER ELECTRIC PLANTS / *by plant*
QH91-95	*HYDROBIOLOGY* **SEE** MARINE BIOLOGY / *natural history*
QD181.B7	HYDROBROMIC ACID

QC463.H9	HYDROCARBONS — SPECTRA
QD305.H5-8	HYDROCARBONS
QD341.H9	HYDROCARBONS
RC898	HYDROCELE
RC391	HYDROCEPHALUS
TP217.H8	HYDROCHLORIC ACID / *chemical technology*
QD181.C5	HYDROCHLORIC ACID / *chemistry*
QP913.C15	HYDROCYANIC ACID — PHYSIOLOGICAL EFFECT
RM666.H8	HYDROCYANIC ACID — THERAPEUTIC USE
RA1242.H9	HYDROCYANIC ACID — TOXICOLOGY
QD181.C15	HYDROCYANIC ACID / *chemistry*
RA766.H8	HYDROCYANIC ACID / *disinfectants*
QA911-929	HYDRODYNAMICS
QD181.F1	HYDROFLUORIC ACID
VM362	HYDROFOIL BOATS
VM362	*HYDROFOILS (VESSELS)* **SEE** HYDROFOIL BOATS
TL684.2	*HYDROFOILS* **SEE** PLANING HULLS / *aeronautics*
VM341-9	*HYDROFOILS* **SEE** PLANING HULLS / *naval architecture*
TN707	*HYDROGEN IN IRON* **SEE** IRON — HYDROGEN CONTENT
TN799.T5	*HYDROGEN IN TITANIUM* **SEE** TITANIUM — HYDROGEN CONTENT
QC173	*HYDROGEN NUCLEUS* **SEE** PROTONS
QC711	*HYDROGEN NUCLEUS* **SEE** PROTONS / *electric discharges*
QD181.H1	HYDROGEN PEROXIDE / *chemistry*
RA766.H9	HYDROGEN PEROXIDE / *disinfectants*
RM648.H	HYDROGEN PEROXIDE / *therapeutics*
QD181.S1	HYDROGEN SULPHIDE
QD561	HYDROGEN-ION CONCENTRATION
TP245.H9	HYDROGEN / *chemical technology*
QD181.H1	HYDROGEN / *chemistry*
QD281.H8	HYDROGENATION
VK591-7	HYDROGRAPHIC SURVEYING
VK593.5	HYDROGRAPHY — OBSERVERS' MANUALS
GB651-2597	HYDROGRAPHY
VK	HYDROGRAPHY / *marine*
QL377.H9	*HYDROIDEA* **SEE** HYDROMEDUSAE
QL377.H9	*HYDROIDEA* **SEE** HYDROZOA
QD501	HYDROLYSIS
QD281.H	HYDROLYSIS / *organic chemistry*
QL377.H9	HYDROMEDUSAE
GT2920	HYDROMEL
TN688	HYDROMETALLURGY
QC111	HYDROMETER
QD181.N1	HYDRONITRIC ACID
RM801-822	*HYDROPATHY* **SEE** HYDROTHERAPY
QK564-580	*HYDROPHYTES* **SEE** ALGAE
QK105	*HYDROPHYTES* **SEE** FRESH-WATER FLORA / *botany*
QK916	*HYDROPHYTES* **SEE** FRESH-WATER FLORA / *ecology*
QH96-99	*HYDROPHYTES* **SEE** FRESH-WATER FLORA / *natural history*
QK103	*HYDROPHYTES* **SEE** MARINE FLORA
VM341-9	HYDROPLANES
QA905-7	HYDROSTATICS / *analytic*
QC147	HYDROSTATICS / *experimental*
RM810	HYDROTHERAPY — EARLY WORKS TO 1800
RM801-822	HYDROTHERAPY
RM276	HYDROTHORAX
QD305.A8	HYDROXYLAMINE
QD181.N15	HYDROXYLAMINE
QL377.H9	HYDROZOA
RM671	HYDROZONE
SF995	HYDRURIA
SF871	HYDRURIA
QL737.C2	HYENAS
RA775	HYGIENE — EARLY WORKS TO 1800
QP36-38	HYGIENE — JUVENILE LITERATURE
RA423	HYGIENE — TERMINOLOGY
RA771	HYGIENE / *domestic*
BJ1695	HYGIENE / *ethical aspects*
RA773-790	HYGIENE / *personal*
RK61	*HYGIENE, DENTAL* **SEE** TEETH — CARE AND HYGIENE
RA529	HYGIENE, HINDU
RA776	HYGIENE, HINDU
HD7260-7780	*HYGIENE, INDUSTRIAL* **SEE** INDUSTRIAL HYGIENE
RA561	HYGIENE, JEWISH

F1435.M4	HYGIENE, MAYA
RA790	*HYGIENE, MENTAL* **SEE** MENTAL HYGIENE
UH600-625	*HYGIENE, MILITARY* **SEE** MILITARY HYGIENE
VG470-475	*HYGIENE, NAVAL* **SEE** NAVAL HYGIENE
RA422	HYGIENE, PUBLIC — CONGRESSES
RA438	HYGIENE, PUBLIC — EXHIBITIONS
RA	HYGIENE, PUBLIC
RA425	HYGIENE, PUBLIC / *comprehensive treatises*
RA11-388	HYGIENE, PUBLIC / *general documents*
RA440.9	*HYGIENE, PUBLIC-VOCATIONAL GUIDANCE* **SEE** PUBLIC HEALTH AS A PROFESSION
RA771	HYGIENE, RURAL
RA427	HYGIENE, RURAL
HQ31-58	HYGIENE, SEXUAL
RC881	HYGIENE, SEXUAL / *men*
RG121	HYGIENE, SEXUAL / *women*
RA771	*HYGIENE, SOCIAL* **SEE** HYGIENE / *domestic*
BJ1695	*HYGIENE, SOCIAL* **SEE** HYGIENE / *ethical aspects*
RA773-790	*HYGIENE, SOCIAL* **SEE** HYGIENE / *personal*
RA	*HYGIENE, SOCIAL* **SEE** HYGIENE, PUBLIC
RA425	*HYGIENE, SOCIAL* **SEE** HYGIENE, PUBLIC / *comprehensive treatises*
RA11-388	*HYGIENE, SOCIAL* **SEE** HYGIENE, PUBLIC / *general documents*
HQ31-58	*HYGIENE, SOCIAL* **SEE** HYGIENE, SEXUAL
RC881	*HYGIENE, SOCIAL* **SEE** HYGIENE, SEXUAL / *men*
RG121	*HYGIENE, SOCIAL* **SEE** HYGIENE, SEXUAL / *women*
HQ101-440	*HYGIENE, SOCIAL* **SEE** PROSTITUTION
RC200-203	*HYGIENE, SOCIAL* **SEE** VENEREAL DISEASES
RC960-962	*HYGIENE, TROPICAL* **SEE** TROPICS — DISEASES AND HYGIENE / *tropical medicine*
VG471	*HYGIENE, TROPICAL* **SEE** TROPICS — DISEASES AND HYGIENE / *naval hygiene*
UH611	*HYGIENE, TROPICAL* **SEE** TROPICS — DISEASES AND HYGIENE / *military hygiene*
RA789	*HYGIENE, TROPICAL* **SEE** TROPICS — DISEASES AND HYGIENE / *hygiene*
SF757	*HYGIENE, VETERINARY* **SEE** VETERINARY HYGIENE
QC917	HYGROMETRY — TABLES, ETC.
QC915-917	HYGROMETRY
DT86	HYKSOS
BD648	*HYLEMORPHISM* **SEE** HYLOMORPHISM
BD648	HYLOMORPHISM
QM421	HYMEN (GYNECOLOGY) / *anatomy*
RG519	HYMEN (GYNECOLOGY) / *obstetrics*
QK629.H9	HYMENOMYCETES
QL563-9	HYMENOPTERA
QE832.H9	HYMENOPTERA, FOSSIL
BV341	HYMN FESTIVALS
MT240	*HYMN PLAYING* **SEE** HYMNS — ACCOMPANIMENT
BV325	HYMN WRITERS
BV325	*HYMNISTS* **SEE** HYMN WRITERS
BV301-525	*HYMNOLOGY* **SEE** HYMNS
M2115-2145	*HYMNOLOGY* **SEE** HYMNS / *hymns with music*
MT240	HYMNS — ACCOMPANIMENT
ML102	HYMNS — DICTIONARIES
ML156.4.R4	HYMNS — DISCOGRAPHY
BV310-340	HYMNS — HISTORY AND CRITICISM
ML3186	HYMNS — HISTORY AND CRITICISM / *music*
ML3086	HYMNS — HISTORY AND CRITICISM / *music*
BV301-525	HYMNS
M2115-2145	HYMNS / *hymns with music*
BL1477.3	*HYMNS, BUDDHIST* **SEE** BUDDHIST HYMNS
BL1226.3	*HYMNS, HINDU* **SEE** HINDU HYMNS
BP183.5	*HYMNS, ISLAMIC* **SEE** ISLAMIC HYMNS
BM679	*HYMNS, JEWISH* **SEE** JEWS — HYMNS
BP183.5	*HYMNS, MUSLIM* **SEE** ISLAMIC HYMNS
BP183.5	*HYMNS, RAMADAN* **SEE** RAMADAN HYMNS
BV460	*HYMNS, REVIVAL* **SEE** REVIVALS — HYMNS
QA559	HYPERBOLA / *analytical geometry*
QA485	HYPERBOLA / *plane geometry*
QA342	*HYPERBOLIC FUNCTIONS* **SEE** FUNCTIONS, EXPONENTIAL
QA685	*HYPERBOLIC GEOMETRY* **SEE** GEOMETRY, HYPERBOLIC
VK560	HYPERBOLIC NAVIGATION
QA561	HYPERBOLOID
PM1-95	HYPERBOREAN LANGUAGES
GN673	*HYPERBOREANS* **SEE** ARCTIC RACES
GN71	HYPERBRACHYCEPHALY

QD471	HYPERCONJUGATION
BT645	*HYPERDULIA* **SEE** MARY, VIRGIN — CULTUS
RB145	HYPEREMIA
RM184	HYPEREMIA, ARTIFICIAL
QA351	*HYPERGEOMETRIC FUNCTIONS* **SEE** FUNCTIONS, HYPERGEOMETRIC
TL571.5	*HYPERSONIC AERODYNAMICS* **SEE** AERODYNAMICS, HYPERSONIC
TL571.5	*HYPERSONIC SPEEDS* **SEE** AERODYNAMICS, HYPERSONIC
TL571.5	*HYPERSONICS* **SEE** AERODYNAMICS, HYPERSONIC
QA691	HYPERSPACE
RC645	HYPERSPLENISM
QR185	*HYPERSUSCEPTIBILITY* **SEE** ANAPHYLAXIS
RG580.H9	HYPERTENSION IN PREGNANCY
RL431	HYPERTRICHOSIS
RB140	HYPERTROPHY
QK625	HYPHOMYCETES
RM325	HYPNOTICS
BX1759.5.H8	HYPNOTISM — MORAL AND RELIGIOUS ASPECTS / *catholic church*
RD85.H9	HYPNOTISM IN SURGERY
BF1111-1156	HYPNOTISM
HV6110	HYPNOTISM / *hypnotism and crime*
RC490-499	HYPNOTISM / *psychiatry*
RC552.H8	HYPOCHONDRIA
RC552.H8	*HYPOCHONDRIASIS* **SEE** HYPOCHONDRIA
QK623.P9	HYPOCREALES
BJ1535.H8	HYPOCRISY / *ethics*
BV4627.H8	HYPOCRISY / *theology*
QA623	*HYPOCYCLOIDS* **SEE** EPICYCLOIDS AND HYPOCYCLOIDS
RM169	*HYPODERMIC INJECTIONS* **SEE** INJECTIONS, HYPODERMIC
QD305.A2	HYPOGAEIC ACID
QK866.P3	HYPOGAEIC ACID / *botanical chemistry*
RC857	HYPOGLYCEMIA / *disease*
RC857	*HYPOGLYCEMOSIS* **SEE** HYPOGLYCEMIA / *disease*
RC640	*HYPOLEUCEMIA* **SEE** LEUCOPENIA
RC640	*HYPOLEUCIA* **SEE** LEUCOPENIA
RC640	*HYPOLEUCOCYTOSIS* **SEE** LEUCOPENIA
RM666.H9	HYPOPHOSPHITES / *therapeutics*
QL868	*HYPOPHYSIS CEREBRI* **SEE** PITUITARY BODY / *comparative anatomy*
QM371	*HYPOPHYSIS CEREBRI* **SEE** PITUITARY BODY / *human anatomy*
QP187	*HYPOPHYSIS CEREBRI* **SEE** PITUITARY BODY / *physiology*
BT205	HYPOSTATIC UNION
QD181.S1	HYPOSULPHITES
QM455	HYPOTHALAMUS
HD1443	*HYPOTHECATION* **SEE** MORTGAGES / *farm economics*
HG5095	*HYPOTHECATION* **SEE** MORTGAGES / *investments*
HG4655	*HYPOTHECATION* **SEE** MORTGAGES / *investments*
BC183	HYPOTHESIS / *logic*
QC895	*HYPSOMETRY* **SEE** ALTITUDES — MEASUREMENT / *meteorology*
TA606-9	*HYPSOMETRY* **SEE** ALTITUDES — MEASUREMENT / *surveying*
QC895	*HYPSOMETRY, BAROMETRIC* **SEE** BAROMETRIC HYPSOMETRY
QL737.U7	HYRACOIDEA
BX1759.5.H9	HYSTERECTOMY — MORAL AND RELIGIOUS ASPECTS
QC761	HYSTERESIS
RC532	HYSTERIA
RC532	HYSTERIA, EPIDEMIC
PA2394	*IAPYGIAN LANGUAGE* **SEE** MESSAPIAN LANGUAGE
RC90	IATROGENIC DISEASES
R148	*IATROMATHEMATICAL SCHOOL* **SEE** IATROPHYSICAL SCHOOL
R148	IATROPHYSICAL SCHOOL
PL5721	IBANAG LANGUAGE
PL5571	*IBATAN LANGUAGE* **SEE** BATAN LANGUAGE
P1081	IBERIAN LANGUAGE
DP53.I2	IBERIANS
DK511.G36	*IBERNIANS* **SEE** GEORGIANS
GN543	*IBERO-INSULAR RACE* **SEE** MEDITERRANEAN RACE

CB224	*IBERO-INSULAR RACE* **SEE** MEDITERRANEAN RACE / *civilization*
QL737.U5	*IBEX* **SEE** BOUQUETIN / *zoology*
DT515	IBIBIOS / *nigeria*
QL696.A7	IBIS
QA76.8.I	IBM 1401 (COMPUTER) — PROGRAMMING
HF5548	IBM 1401 (COMPUTER) — PROGRAMMING / *business*
PL8261	IBO LANGUAGE
DT515	IBO TRIBE
QR107	ICE — BACTERIOLOGY
RA599	ICE — HYGIENIC ASPECTS
TP490-495	ICE — MANUFACTURE
QE697-8	*ICE AGE* **SEE** GLACIAL EPOCH
TH1431	*ICE AND SNOW BUILDING* **SEE** BUILDING, ICE AND SNOW
GV841-857	*ICE CARNIVALS* **SEE** WINTER SPORTS
NK6030	ICE CARVING
GB602	ICE CAVES
TX795	ICE CREAM, ICES, ETC.
GB2401-2598	*ICE DRIFT* **SEE** SEA ICE DRIFT
GB2401-2598	*ICE FIELD DRIFT* **SEE** SEA ICE DRIFT
SH459	ICE FISHING
GV847	*ICE HOCKEY* **SEE** HOCKEY
HF5686.I4	ICE INDUSTRY — ACCOUNTING
TP498	ICE INDUSTRY / *storage*
HD9481	ICE INDUSTRY / *trade*
TP490-495	*ICE MAKING* **SEE** ICE — MANUFACTURE
TL557.I3	*ICE ON AEROPLANES* **SEE** AEROPLANES — ICE PREVENTION
GB1601-1797	ICE ON RIVERS, LAKES, ETC. (INDIRECT) / *lakes*
GB1201-1397	ICE ON RIVERS, LAKES, ETC. (INDIRECT) / *rivers*
NA6890	ICE PALACES
GV852	*ICE RINKS* **SEE** SKATING RINKS
TE245	*ICE ROADS* **SEE** ROADS, ICE
GV849	*ICE SKATING* **SEE** SKATING
GV841-857	*ICE SPORTS* **SEE** WINTER SPORTS
GV843	ICE-BOATS
VM451	ICE-BREAKING VESSELS
NA6360	ICE-HOUSES / *commercial*
NA8350	ICE-HOUSES / *private*
TP490-495	*ICE-MACHINERY* **SEE** ICE — MANUFACTURE
TP490-497	*ICE-MACHINERY* **SEE** REFRIGERATION AND REFRIGERATING MACHINERY
GB2401-2597	ICE
GB2401-2597	ICEBERGS
VK1299	ICEBERGS / *navigation*
VM451	*ICEBREAKERS, ATOMIC* **SEE** ATOMIC ICEBREAKERS
QE391.I	ICELAND SPAR
PD2201-2392	ICELANDIC AND OLD NORSE LANGUAGES
PT7220-7262	ICELANDIC AND OLD NORSE LITERATURE / *collections*
PT7101-7211	ICELANDIC AND OLD NORSE LITERATURE / *history*
PT7230-7252	ICELANDIC AND OLD NORSE POETRY / *collections*
PT7170-7174	ICELANDIC AND OLD NORSE POETRY / *history*
PT7470-7477	ICELANDIC DRAMA / *collections*
PT7411	ICELANDIC DRAMA / *history*
PT7485-7	ICELANDIC FICTION / *collections*
PT7413	ICELANDIC FICTION / *history*
PD2201-2392	*ICELANDIC LANGUAGE* **SEE** ICELANDIC AND OLD NORSE LANGUAGES
PD2401-2447	*ICELANDIC LANGUAGE* **SEE** ICELANDIC LANGUAGE, MODERN
PD2401-2447	ICELANDIC LANGUAGE, MODERN
PT7101-7211	*ICELANDIC LITERATURE* **SEE** ICELANDIC AND OLD NORSE LITERATURE / *history*
PT7220-7262	*ICELANDIC LITERATURE* **SEE** ICELANDIC AND OLD NORSE LITERATURE / *collections*
PT7451-7495	*ICELANDIC LITERATURE* **SEE** ICELANDIC LITERATURE, MODERN / *collections*
PT7351-7438	*ICELANDIC LITERATURE* **SEE** ICELANDIC LITERATURE, MODERN / *history*
PT7451-7495	ICELANDIC LITERATURE, MODERN / *collections*
PT7351-7438	ICELANDIC LITERATURE, MODERN / *history*
PN5355.I3	ICELANDIC NEWSPAPERS
PN5355.I3	ICELANDIC PERIODICALS
PT7465-7	ICELANDIC POETRY — EARLY MODERN (TO CA. 1700) / *collections*

PT7465-7	ICELANDIC POETRY, MODERN / collections
PT7410	ICELANDIC POETRY, MODERN / history
PT7480-7495	ICELANDIC PROSE, MODERN / collections
PT7412-7419	ICELANDIC PROSE, MODERN / history
PT7526-7545	ICELANDIC-AMERICAN LITERATURE
TX795	ICES SEE ICE CREAM, ICES, ETC.
PM1341	ICHITI LANGUAGE SEE HITCHITI LANGUAGE
QE845	ICHNOLOGY SEE FOOTPRINTS, FOSSIL
QP915.I2	ICHTHYOL / physiological effect
RM666.I2	ICHTHYOL / therapeutics
QL668.C2	ICHTHYOMORPHA SEE URODELA
QE862.I2	ICHTHYOSAURIA
RL435	ICHTHYOSIS FOLLICULARIS SEE KERATOSIS
TL557.I3	ICING OF AEROPLANES SEE AEROPLANES — ICE PREVENTION
BR238	ICONOCLASM / 8th century
N7810-8185	ICONOGRAPHY SEE CHRISTIAN ART AND SYMBOLISM
BV150-168	ICONOGRAPHY SEE CHRISTIAN ART AND SYMBOLISM / theology
NB960-1113	ICONOGRAPHY SEE IDOLS AND IMAGES / art
N7575-7649	ICONOGRAPHY SEE PORTRAITS
N7956	ICONS / russian art
QA491	ICOSAHEDRA
QL696.P2	ICTERUS (ORNITHOLOGY) SEE ORIOLES
RC851	ICTERUS (PATHOLOGY) SEE JAUNDICE
RJ276	ICTERUS (PATHOLOGY) SEE JAUNDICE / infants
BP183.66	IDAL-ADHA SERMONS
BP183.645	IDAL-FITR SERMONS
BP186.45	IDAL-FITR
BP186,45	IDAL-SADAQ AH SEE IDAL-FITR
QE391.I	IDDINGSITE
B398.I3	IDEA (PHILOSOPHY) / plato
HX806-811	IDEAL STATES SEE UTOPIAS
N61-79	IDEALISM IN ART
PN56.I4	IDEALISM IN LITERATURE
B823	IDEALISM
B851-4695	IDEALISM / by country
B941	IDEALISM / u.s.
QA247	IDEALS (ALGEBRA)
B398.I3	IDEAS (PHILOSOPHY) SEE IDEA (PHILOSOPHY) / plato
BF365-7	IDEAS, ASSOCIATION OF SEE ASSOCIATION OF IDEAS
BF365	IDEAS, REPRODUCTION OF SEE REPRODUCTION (PSYCHOLOGY)
B398.I3	IDEAS, THEORY OF SEE IDEA (PHILOSOPHY) / plato
BV4509.5	IDENTIFICATION (RELIGION)
HV6065-6079	IDENTIFICATION OF CRIMINALS SEE CRIME AND CRIMINALS — IDENTIFICATION
HV8074	IDENTIFICATION OF DOCUMENTS SEE LEGAL DOCUMENTS — IDENTIFICATION
HV8077	IDENTIFICATION OF FIREARMS SEE FIREARMS — IDENTIFICATION
HV8074-6	IDENTIFICATION OF HANDWRITING SEE WRITING — IDENTIFICATION
RA1055	IDENTIFICATION OF THE DEAD SEE DEAD — IDENTIFICATION
HV8075	IDENTIFICATION OF TYPEWRITING SEE TYPEWRITING — IDENTIFICATION
GN192	IDENTIFICATION / anthropology
RA1055	IDENTIFICATION / medical jurisprudence
HV8073	IDENTIFICATION / penology
TL694.I	IDENTIFICATION, FRIEND OR FOE (ELECTRONIC EQUIPMENT) SEE AEROPLANES — IFF EQUIPMENT
BV4509.5	IDENTITY (RELIGION) SEE IDENTIFICATION (RELIGION)
BC199.I4	IDENTITY / logic
BD236	IDENTITY / theory of knowledge
BD331	IDENTITY, PERSONAL SEE PERSONALITY / ontology
BF698	IDENTITY, PERSONAL SEE PERSONALITY / psychology
PJ1091-7	IDEOGRAPHY SEE HIEROGLYPHICS / egyptian
Z102	IDEOGRAPHY SEE PASIGRAPHY
RC571	IDIOCY
HV3004-8	IDIOCY / charities
HV891-901	IDIOCY / children
HV3004-8	IDIOT ASYLUMS
RC571	IDIOTS SEE IDIOCY
HV3004-8	IDIOTS SEE IDIOCY / charities
HV891-901	IDIOTS SEE IDIOCY / children
PL8276	IDO (AFRICAN LANGUAGE) SEE IJO LANGUAGE
PM8391-4	IDO
QE391.V55	IDOCRASE SEE VESUVIANITE
BL485	IDOLATRY SEE IDOLS AND IMAGES — WORSHIP
BL485	IDOLS AND IMAGES — WORSHIP
NB960-1113	IDOLS AND IMAGES / art
PL8263	IDOMA LANGUAGE
PN6110.P4	IDYLLIC POETRY SEE PASTORAL POETRY
PN1421	IDYLLIC POETRY SEE PASTORAL POETRY
PL8811	IDZEBU LANGUAGE SEE YEBU LANGUAGE
PL8276	IDZO LANGUAGE SEE IJO LANGUAGE
TL694.I	IFF SYSTEMS SEE AEROPLANES — IFF EQUIPMENT
DS666.I15	IFUGAOS
PL8261	IGBO LANGUAGE SEE IBO LANGUAGE
TP986.I	IGELITES
QE461	IGNEOUS ROCKS SEE ROCKS, IGNEOUS
QE461	IGNIMBRITE SEE VOLCANIC ASH, TUFF, ETC.
TJ787	IGNITION DEVICES SEE GAS AND OIL ENGINES — IGNITION
TL213	IGNITION DEVICES SEE MAGNETO / automobiles
TJ787	IGNITION DEVICES SEE MAGNETO / oil and gasoline engines
TJ787	IGNITION DEVICES SEE SPARK-PLUGS
GV1469.G7	IGO (GAME) SEE GO (GAME)
PL5731-4	IGOROT LANGUAGE
DS666.I2	IGOROT
PL5731-4	IGORROTE LANGUAGE SEE IGOROT LANGUAGE
DS666.I2	IGORROTES SEE IGOROT
PL8276	IJAW LANGUAGE SEE IJO LANGUAGE
F2270.2.I5	IJCA INDIANS
PL8276	IJO LANGUAGE
PL8276	IJOH LANGUAGE SEE IJO LANGUAGE
PL8538	IKI-KUKWE LANGUAGE SEE MWAMBA LANGUAGE
PL8549	IKINYI-KIUSA LANGUAGE SEE NGONDE LANGUAGE
ML3730	IKLIG
TR263	IKOFLEX CAMERA
N7956	IKONS SEE ICONS / russian art
TR263.I3	IKONTA CAMERA
PL8281	ILA LANGUAGE
PL8725	ILALI LANGUAGE SEE TEKE LANGUAGE
E99.C83	ILAOQUATSH INDIANS SEE CLAYOQUOT INDIANS
HD5311	ILLEGAL STRIKES SEE WILDCAT STRIKES
HQ998-9	ILLEGITIMACY
HB903.I6	ILLEGITIMACY / statistics
QA76.8.I5	ILLIAC (COMPUTER) SEE ILLIAC COMPUTER
TK7889.I5	ILLIAC (COMPUTER) SEE ILLIAC COMPUTER / engineering
QA76.8.I5	ILLIAC COMPUTER — PROGRAMMING
QA76.8.I5	ILLIAC COMPUTER
TK7889.I5	ILLIAC COMPUTER / engineering
HG641-5	ILLICIT COINING SEE COUNTERFEITS AND COUNTERFEITING / u.s.
HG335-341	ILLICIT COINING SEE COUNTERFEITS AND COUNTERFEITING
HJ5021	ILLICIT DISTILLING SEE DISTILLING, ILLICIT / u.s.
F536-550	ILLINOIS — HISTORY
QA76.8.I5	ILLINOIS AUTOMATIC COMPUTER SEE ILLIAC COMPUTER
TK7889.I5	ILLINOIS AUTOMATIC COMPUTER SEE ILLIAC COMPUTER / engineering
F542	ILLINOIS INDIANS — LAND TRANSFERS
E99.I2	ILLINOIS INDIANS — MISSIONS
E99.I2	ILLINOIS INDIANS
PM1371	ILLINOIS LANGUAGE
E83.83	ILLINOIS-HISTORY-BLACK HAWK WAR, 1832 SEE BLACK HAWK WAR, 1832
E505	ILLINOIS — HISTORY — — CIVIL WAR
LC149-160	ILLITERACY
HS142	ILLUMINATI
TP700	ILLUMINATING GAS SEE GAS
TP751-764	ILLUMINATING GAS SEE GAS
TH7700-7975	ILLUMINATION SEE LIGHTING
GT440-445	ILLUMINATION SEE LIGHTING / manners and customs
ND2895-9	ILLUMINATION OF BOOKS AND MANUSCRIPTS — CATALOGS
ND2893	ILLUMINATION OF BOOKS AND MANUSCRIPTS — EXHIBITIONS

ND2890-3416	ILLUMINATION OF BOOKS AND MANUSCRIPTS
ND2955	ILLUMINATION OF BOOKS AND MANUSCRIPTS, ISLAMIC
ND2955	*ILLUMINATION OF BOOKS AND MANUSCRIPTS, MUSLIM* **SEE** ILLUMINATION OF BOOKS AND MANUSCRIPTS, ISLAMIC
BF1048-1063	*ILLUSIONS* **SEE** HALLUCINATIONS AND ILLUSIONS
RC534	*ILLUSIONS* **SEE** HALLUCINATIONS AND ILLUSIONS / *psychiatry and psychopathology*
BF491-3	*ILLUSIONS* **SEE** HALLUCINATIONS AND ILLUSIONS / *psychology*
QP495	*ILLUSIONS, OPTICAL* **SEE** OPTICAL ILLUSIONS
Z1023	ILLUSTRATED BOOKS
NC15	ILLUSTRATION OF BOOKS — EXHIBITIONS
NC960-996	ILLUSTRATION OF BOOKS
NC975-995	ILLUSTRATION OF BOOKS / *by country*
R836	*ILLUSTRATION, MEDICAL* **SEE** MEDICAL ILLUSTRATION
BV4224-4230	*ILLUSTRATIONS, HOMILETICAL* **SEE** HOMILETICAL ILLUSTRATIONS
NC1300-1763	*ILLUSTRATIONS, HUMOROUS* **SEE** CARICATURES AND CARTOONS
NC1300-1765	*ILLUSTRATIONS, HUMOROUS* **SEE** WIT AND HUMOR, PICTORIAL
NC	ILLUSTRATORS
PG1224-1399	*ILLYRIAN LANGUAGE (SLAVIC)* **SEE** SERBO-CROATIAN LANGUAGE
PA2393	ILLYRIAN LANGUAGES
DB370.5	*ILLYRIAN MOVEMENT* **SEE** ILLYRISM
DG246	ILLYRIAN WARS
D90.I3	ILLYRIANS
DB370.5	ILLYRISM
PJ2471-9	*ILMORNA LANGUAGE* **SEE** GALLA LANGUAGE
PL5751-4	*ILOCANO LANGUAGE* **SEE** ILOKO LANGUAGE
DS666.I6	*ILOCANOS* **SEE** ILOKANOS
PL5751-4	*ILOCO LANGUAGE* **SEE** ILOKO LANGUAGE
DS666.I6	ILOKANOS
PL5751-4	ILOKO LANGUAGE
PL5751	ILOKO LITERATURE
SD397.14	ILOMBA
DS666.I4	ILONGOT (PHILIPPINE TRIBE)
TL696.L33	*ILS* **SEE** INSTRUMENT LANDING SYSTEMS
TK7872.I6	IMAGE CONVERTERS
TR882	IMAGE ICONOSCOPE
TK7872.I6	*IMAGE TUBES* **SEE** IMAGE CONVERTERS
BF367	*IMAGERY, EIDETIC* **SEE** EIDETIC IMAGERY
NB960-1113	*IMAGES AND IDOLS* **SEE** IDOLS AND IMAGES / *art*
GR820-830	*IMAGINARY ANIMALS* **SEE** ANIMAL LORE
QL89	*IMAGINARY ANIMALS* **SEE** ANIMAL LORE
GR820-830	*IMAGINARY ANIMALS* **SEE** ANIMALS, MYTHICAL
U313	*IMAGINARY BATTLES* **SEE** IMAGINARY WARS AND BATTLES
UA	*IMAGINARY BATTLES* **SEE** IMAGINARY WARS AND BATTLES / *military situation in special countries*
V253	*IMAGINARY BATTLES* **SEE** IMAGINARY WARS AND BATTLES / *naval*
JX1964	*IMAGINARY BATTLES* **SEE** IMAGINARY WARS AND BATTLES / *peace literature*
D445	*IMAGINARY BATTLES* **SEE** IMAGINARY WARS AND BATTLES / *world politics*
Z995.5	*IMAGINARY BOOK-PLATES* **SEE** BOOK-PLATES, IMAGINARY
Z1024	IMAGINARY BOOKS AND LIBRARIES
G100	*IMAGINARY CITIES* **SEE** GEOGRAPHICAL MYTHS
GR650-690	*IMAGINARY CITIES* **SEE** GEOGRAPHICAL MYTHS / *folk-lore*
G100	*IMAGINARY ISLANDS* **SEE** GEOGRAPHICAL MYTHS
GR650-690	*IMAGINARY ISLANDS* **SEE** GEOGRAPHICAL MYTHS / *folk-lore*
Z1024	*IMAGINARY LIBRARIES* **SEE** IMAGINARY BOOKS AND LIBRARIES
QA255	*IMAGINARY QUANTITIES* **SEE** NUMBERS, COMPLEX
G560	*IMAGINARY TRAVELS* **SEE** VOYAGES, IMAGINARY
G560	*IMAGINARY VOYAGES* **SEE** VOYAGES, IMAGINARY
U313	IMAGINARY WARS AND BATTLES
UA	IMAGINARY WARS AND BATTLES / *military situation in special countries*
V253	IMAGINARY WARS AND BATTLES / *naval*
JX1964	IMAGINARY WARS AND BATTLES / *peace literature*
D445	IMAGINARY WARS AND BATTLES / *world politics*
BF408	IMAGINATION
N61-79	IMAGINATION / *artistic*
BP166.94	IMAMATE
BP193	*IMAMITES* **SEE** SHIITES
PL5379	*IMERINA DIALECT* **SEE** MERINA DIALECT
QD305.I6	IMIDOESTERS
PN166	IMITATION (IN LITERATURE)
ML430	IMITATION (IN MUSIC)
BF357	IMITATION
BT620	IMMACULATE CONCEPTION
BV50.I6	IMMACULATE CONCEPTION, FEAST OF THE
N8070	*IMMACULATE CONCEPTION-ART* **SEE** MARY, VIRGIN — ART
BT124	IMMANENCE OF GOD
BV806-814	*IMMERSION, BAPTISMAL* **SEE** BAPTISM
QC310	*IMMERSION, HEAT OF* **SEE** HEAT OF WETTING
JV6001-9500	*IMMIGRANTS* **SEE** EMIGRATION AND IMMIGRATION
JV6001-9500	*IMMIGRATION* **SEE** EMIGRATION AND IMMIGRATION
HQ471	*IMMORAL LITERATURE* **SEE** LITERATURE, IMMORAL
Z659	*IMMORAL LITERATURE* **SEE** LITERATURE, IMMORAL / *copyright*
PN49	*IMMORAL LITERATURE* **SEE** LITERATURE, IMMORAL / *literature and ethics*
HV6727	*IMMORAL LITERATURE* **SEE** LITERATURE, IMMORAL / *social pathology*
BL530	IMMORTALITY / *comparative religion*
BL2450.I5	IMMORTALITY / *egyptian religion*
BT919-925	IMMORTALITY / *theology*
BT930	*IMMORTALITY, CONDITIONAL* **SEE** ANNIHILATIONISM
SB447	*IMMORTELLE* **SEE** EVERLASTING FLOWERS
JC116.I3	IMMUNITY (FEUDALISM)
QR181-5	IMMUNITY
QC131	IMPACT
QA935	IMPACT
JF295	IMPEACHMENTS / *executive*
JK446	IMPEACHMENTS / *impeachable offenses*
JK1595	IMPEACHMENTS / *judiciary*
JK1268	IMPEACHMENTS / *powers and procedure of congress*
JK1079	IMPEACHMENTS / *powers and procedure of congress*
JK593-5	IMPEACHMENTS / *president*
JF475	IMPEACHMENTS / *procedure*
JK2700-9599	IMPEACHMENTS / *states*
JK751-2	IMPEACHMENTS / *u.s. civil service*
TJ267.I6	IMPELLERS
QL696.S5	*IMPENNES* **SEE** PENGUINS
DG83.5.I6	IMPERATOR (ROMAN TITLE)
JN276	IMPERIAL FEDERATION
DA18	IMPERIAL FEDERATION / *history*
G850 1914	IMPERIAL TRANS-ANTARCTIC EXPEDITION, 1914-1917
JN276	IMPERIALISM / *constitutional history gt. brit.*
JC359	IMPERIALISM / *political theory*
JK304	IMPERIALISM / *u.s.*
E713	IMPERIALISM / *u.s.*
BC181	*IMPERSONAL JUDGMENT* **SEE** JUDGMENT (LOGIC)
RL283	IMPETIGO
SB235	*IMPHEE* **SEE** SORGHUM
TP405	*IMPHEE* **SEE** SORGHUM / *chemical technology*
GN446-7	IMPLEMENTS, UTENSILS, ETC. / *primitive*
HF1401-1650	*IMPORT CONTROLS* **SEE** IMPORT QUOTAS
HJ6603-7380	*IMPORT CONTROLS* **SEE** TARIFF / *administration*
HF1761-2580	*IMPORT CONTROLS* **SEE** TARIFF / *other countries*
HJ6041-6464	*IMPORT CONTROLS* **SEE** TARIFF / *schedules*
HF1701-2701	*IMPORT CONTROLS* **SEE** TARIFF / *theory and history*
HF1750-1759	*IMPORT CONTROLS* **SEE** TARIFF / *u.s.*
HF1401-1650	*IMPORT LICENSES* **SEE** IMPORT QUOTAS
HF1401-1650	IMPORT QUOTAS
HF	*IMPORTS* **SEE** COMMERCE
GT6010-6050	*IMPORTS* **SEE** COMMERCE / *commercial customs*
GN436-440	*IMPORTS* **SEE** COMMERCE / *primitive*
HJ6603-7380	*IMPORTS* **SEE** TARIFF / *administration*
HF1761-2580	*IMPORTS* **SEE** TARIFF / *other countries*
HJ6041-6464	*IMPORTS* **SEE** TARIFF / *schedules*
HF1701-2701	*IMPORTS* **SEE** TARIFF / *theory and history*
HF1750-1759	*IMPORTS* **SEE** TARIFF / *u.s.*
BT378.U4	*IMPORTUNATE WIDOW (PARABLE)* **SEE** UNJUST JUDGE (PARABLE)
Z255	*IMPOSITION (TYPOGRAPHY)* **SEE** PRINTING, PRACTICAL — IMPOSITION, ETC.
BV873.L3	IMPOSITION OF HANDS / *christian sacraments*
BM715	IMPOSITION OF HANDS / *jewish sacrifices*

HV6751-6761	IMPOSTORS AND IMPOSTURE / *criminal*
RC889	IMPOTENCE
SF105.5	*IMPREGNATION, ARTIFICIAL* **SEE** ARTIFICIAL INSEMINATION
ML429	IMPRESARIOS
ND1265	IMPRESSIONISM (ART)
ML197	IMPRESSIONISM (MUSIC)
BH301.I6	IMPRESSIONISM / *aesthetics*
NE440	*IMPRESSIONS IN PASTE* **SEE** PRINTS IN PASTE
E357.2-3	IMPRESSMENT / *war of 1812*
Z242.I3	IMPRINTS (IN BOOKS)
HV8650-8651	*IMPRISONMENT FOR DEBT* **SEE** DEBT, IMPRISONMENT FOR
PN2071.I5	*IMPROMPTU THEATER* **SEE** IMPROVISATION (ACTING)
PN2071.I5	IMPROVISATION (ACTING)
MT68	IMPROVISATION (MUSIC)
BF695	IMPULSE / *instinct*
T58	*IN-SERVICE TRAINING* **SEE** EMPLOYEES, TRAINING OF
HF5549.5.T7	*IN-SERVICE TRAINING* **SEE** EMPLOYEES, TRAINING OF
QC244	*INAUDIBLE SOUND* **SEE** ULTRASONICS / *acoustics*
JK536-550	INAUGURATION DAY
SF105	INBREEDING / *animal breeding*
HV4981	INBREEDING / *inbreeding and degeneration*
S494	INBREEDING / *principles of breeding*
ML3575	*INCA MUSIC* **SEE** INCAS — MUSIC
PM6301-9	*INCAN LANGUAGE* **SEE** KECHUA LANGUAGE
TK4341-4367	*INCANDESCENT ELECTRIC LIGHTING* **SEE** ELECTRIC LIGHTING, INCANDESCENT
TH7953-5	INCANDESCENT GAS-LIGHTING — FIXTURES
TH7953-5	INCANDESCENT GAS-LIGHTING
TK4351-4367	*INCANDESCENT LAMPS* **SEE** ELECTRIC LAMPS, INCANDESCENT
TK4341-4367	*INCANDESCENT LIGHTING* **SEE** ELECTRIC LIGHTING, INCANDESCENT
TH7953-5	*INCANDESCENT MANTLES* **SEE** INCANDESCENT GAS-LIGHTING
GR540	INCANTATIONS
BF1558	INCANTATIONS
BX1939.I44	INCARDINATION (CANON LAW)
BL510	INCARNATION
BT220	INCARNATION / *christology*
F3429.3.A7	INCAS — ART
F3429.3.L	INCAS — LEGENDS
ML3575	INCAS — MUSIC
F3429.3.R38	INCAS — RELIGION AND MYTHOLOGY
F3429	INCAS
F3442	INCAS
HV6638	*INCENDIARISM* **SEE** ARSON
BV197.I6	INCENSE / *christian worship*
LB3025	*INCENTIVES IN EDUCATION* **SEE** REWARDS AND PUNISHMENTS IN EDUCATION
PN56.I55	INCEST IN LITERATURE
GN480.3	INCEST / *anthropology*
HQ71	INCEST / *sociology*
ML3860	*INCIDENTAL MUSIC* **SEE** MUSIC, INCIDENTAL / *aesthetics*
ML2000	*INCIDENTAL MUSIC* **SEE** MUSIC, INCIDENTAL / *history*
RA631-7	*INCINERATION* **SEE** CREMATION
GT3330	*INCINERATION* **SEE** CREMATION / *manners and customs*
TJ1374	*INCLINED PASSENGER LIFTS* **SEE** ELEVATORS, PRIVATE RESIDENCE
TL89	INCLINOMETER / *aeronautical instruments*
HD594.6	INCLOSURES / *gt. brit.*
HJ4621-4831	INCOME TAX
HJ4651-5	INCOME TAX / *u.s.*
HC	INCOME / *national income*
HB601	INCOME / *theory*
BX4737	*INCOMMUNICANTS* **SEE** LOUISETS
RM143	INCOMPATIBLES (PHARMACY)
Z1033.U6	*INCOMPLETE BOOKS* **SEE** UNFINISHED BOOKS
PL8191	*INCRAN LANGUAGE* **SEE** GA LANGUAGE
HD1315	*INCREMENT, UNEARNED* **SEE** UNEARNED INCREMENT
BL325.I5	INCUBATION (IN RELIGION, FOLK-LORE, ETC.)
SF495	*INCUBATION OF EGGS* **SEE** EGGS — INCUBATION
SF497	INCUBATORS — CATALOGS
SF495-7	INCUBATORS

Z240-241	INCUNABULA — BIBLIOGRAPHY
Z241	INCUNABULA — FACSIMILES
ML112	INCUNABULA — MUSIC
Z695.3	*INCUNABULA - CATALOGING* **SEE** CATALOGING OF INCUNABULA
Z240-241	INCUNABULA
Z695.3	*INCUNABULA-CATALOGING* **SEE** CATALOGING OF INCUNABULA
Z240	INCUNABULA — BIBLIOGRAPHY — — CATALOGS
HV3000-3003	INCURABLES — HOSPITALS AND ASYLUMS
HV8715	*INDEFINITE SENTENCE* **SEE** INDETERMINATE SENTENCE
HG9964.E	*INDEMNITY INSURANCE* **SEE** INSURANCE, LIABILITY / *employers' liability*
JX5326	INDEMNITY
HD4871-5	INDENTURED SERVANTS
HD4875.U5	INDENTURED SERVANTS / *u.s.*
BX7101-7260	*INDEPENDENCY (CHURCH POLITY)* **SEE** CONGREGATIONALISM
HD8395	INDEPENDENT LABOUR PARTY (GT. BRIT.)
HS951-1179	*INDEPENDENT ORDER OF ODD-FELLOWS* **SEE** ODD-FELLOWS, INDEPENDENT ORDER OF
HG604-5	*INDEPENDENT PARTY* **SEE** NATIONAL GREENBACK PARTY
LC47-57	*INDEPENDENT SCHOOLS* **SEE** PRIVATE SCHOOLS
HG2539	INDEPENDENT TREASURY — SPEECHES IN CONGRESS
HG2535-9	INDEPENDENT TREASURY / *u.s.*
QA242	*INDETERMINATE ANALYSIS* **SEE** DIOPHANTINE ANALYSIS
HV8715	INDETERMINATE SENTENCE
BJ1460-1468	*INDETERMINISM* **SEE** FREE WILL AND DETERMINISM / *ethics*
BF620-628	*INDETERMINISM* **SEE** FREE WILL AND DETERMINISM / *psychology*
Z1020	*INDEX EXPURGATORIUS* **SEE** INDEX LIBRORUM PROHIBITORUM
Z1020	INDEX LIBRORUM PROHIBITORUM
HB225	INDEX NUMBERS (ECONOMICS)
AI	INDEXES
HF5736-5746	*INDEXES, CARD* **SEE** CARD SYSTEM IN BUSINESS
HF5736-5746	*INDEXES, CARD* **SEE** FILES AND FILING (DOCUMENTS)
TJ1167	INDEXING (MACHINE-SHOP PRACTICE)
Z695.9	INDEXING
HF5735-5746	INDEXING / *business filing and indexing*
DS401-498	INDIA — HISTORY
TP948.I6	INDIA INK
SB291	*INDIA-RUBBER* **SEE** RUBBER / *culture*
TS1870-1920	*INDIA-RUBBER INDUSTRY* **SEE** RUBBER INDUSTRY AND TRADE / *technology*
HD9161	*INDIA-RUBBER INDUSTRY* **SEE** RUBBER INDUSTRY AND TRADE / *economics*
DS475.7	*INDIA-HISTORY-BURMESE WARS* **SEE** BURMESE WAR, 1824-1826
DS477.65	*INDIA-HISTORY-BURMESE WARS* **SEE** BURMESE WAR, 1852
DS473	*INDIA-HISTORY-ROHILLA WAR, 1774* **SEE** ROHILLA WAR, 1774
DS477.1	*INDIA-HISTORY-SIKH WARS* **SEE** SIKH WAR, 1845-1846
DS477.63	*INDIA-HISTORY-SIKH WARS* **SEE** SIKH WAR, 1848 1849
DS477.8	*INDIA-HISTORY-SIKKIM EXPEDITION, 1861* **SEE** SIKKIM EXPEDITION, 1861
DS479.7	*INDIA-HISTORY-SIKKIM EXPEDITION, 1888* **SEE** SIKKIM EXPEDITION, 1888
E91-93	*INDIAN APPROPRIATIONS* **SEE** INDIANS OF NORTH AMERICA — APPROPRIATIONS
E98.B3	*INDIAN BASKETS* **SEE** INDIANS OF NORTH AMERICA — BASKET MAKING
F2230.1.B	*INDIAN BASKETS* **SEE** INDIANS OF SOUTH AMERICA — BASKET MAKING
E98.C8	*INDIAN BELTS* **SEE** WAMPUM BELTS
E59.T35	*INDIAN BLANKETS* **SEE** INDIANS — TEXTILE INDUSTRY AND FABRICS
E98.T35	*INDIAN BLANKETS* **SEE** INDIANS OF NORTH AMERICA — TEXTILE INDUSTRY AND FABRICS
F2230.1.T3	*INDIAN BLANKETS* **SEE** INDIANS OF SOUTH AMERICA — TEXTILE INDUSTRY AND FABRICS
E59.C95	*INDIAN CIVILIZATION* **SEE** INDIANS — CULTURE

GV491-3	INDIAN CLUBS / exercises
SB191.M2	INDIAN CORN SEE MAIZE / culture
HD9049.C8	INDIAN CORN SEE MAIZE / grain trade
RC371.C2	INDIAN HEMP SEE CANNABIS INDICA / intoxications
RM666.C26	INDIAN HEMP SEE CANNABIS INDICA / therapeutics
RA981.A35	INDIAN HOSPITALS SEE INDIANS OF NORTH AMERICA — HOSPITALS
PM1-7356	INDIAN LANGUAGES SEE INDIANS — LANGUAGES
PM3001-4566	INDIAN LANGUAGES SEE INDIANS OF MEXICO — LANGUAGES
PM1-7356	INDIAN LANGUAGES SEE INDIANS OF NORTH AMERICA — LANGUAGES
E59.L7	INDIAN LITERATURE (AMERICAN INDIAN) SEE INDIANS — LITERATURE
E59.M9	INDIAN MUSIC (AMERICAN INDIAN) SEE INDIANS — MUSIC
ML3547	INDIAN MUSIC (AMERICAN INDIAN) SEE INDIANS — MUSIC
E59.R38	INDIAN MYTHOLOGY (AMERICAN INDIAN) SEE INDIANS — RELIGION AND MYTHOLOGY
E98.O7	INDIAN ORATIONS SEE INDIANS OF NORTH AMERICA — ORATORY
SF315	INDIAN PONIES / animal culture
E98.H55	INDIAN PONIES / indians of north america
E78	INDIAN RESERVATIONS SEE INDIANS OF NORTH AMERICA — RESERVATIONS
E99	INDIAN RESERVATIONS SEE INDIANS OF NORTH AMERICA — RESERVATIONS
E91-93	INDIAN RESERVATIONS SEE INDIANS OF NORTH AMERICA — RESERVATIONS
SB191.I5	INDIAN RICE / culture
E98.F7	INDIAN RICE / indian food
E98.C7	INDIAN TRADE FACTORIES SEE INDIANS OF NORTH AMERICA — TRADING POSTS
E98.T7	INDIAN TRAILS
U240	INDIAN WARFARE
E98.W2	INDIAN WARFARE
DS480.85	INDIAN-CHINESE BORDER DISPUTE, 1957- SEE SINO-INDIAN BORDER DISPUTE, 1957-
TS1109	INDIAN-CORN PAPER SEE PAPER, MAIZE
F521-535	INDIANA — HISTORY
E506	INDIANA — HISTORY — — CIVIL WAR
E409.5.I7	INDIANA — HISTORY — — WAR WITH MEXICO, 1845-1848
E59.A	INDIANS — AGRICULTURE
E59.A63	INDIANS — ANTIQUITIES
E58	INDIANS — ANTIQUITIES
E61	INDIANS — ANTIQUITIES
E59.A7	INDIANS — ART
E59.C2	INDIANS — BOATS
E59.C	INDIANS — COLOR
E98.C8	INDIANS — COSTUME AND ADORNMENT
E59.C95	INDIANS — CULTURE
E59.D9	INDIANS — DWELLINGS
E59.E	INDIANS — ECONOMIC CONDITIONS
E57.E4	INDIANS — EDUCATION
E59.F	INDIANS — FOOD
E59.G3	INDIANS — GAMES
E59.G	INDIANS — GOVERNMENT RELATIONS
E58	INDIANS — HISTORY
E59.I4	INDIANS — IMPLEMENTS
PM1-7356	INDIANS — LANGUAGES
E59.F6	INDIANS — LEGENDS
E59.L7	INDIANS — LITERATURE
E59.M65	INDIANS — MISSIONS
E59.M7	INDIANS — MONEY
E59.M8	INDIANS — MORTUARY CUSTOMS
ML3547	INDIANS — MUSIC
E59.M9	INDIANS — MUSIC
E59.N	INDIANS — NAMES
E61	INDIANS — ORIGIN
E59.P53	INDIANS — PHYSICAL CHARACTERISTICS
E59.P7	INDIANS — POETRY
E59.P8	INDIANS — POTTERY
E59.R38	INDIANS — RELIGION AND MYTHOLOGY
E59.S	INDIANS — SOCIAL LIFE AND CUSTOMS
E59.S7	INDIANS — STATISTICS
E59.T35	INDIANS — TEXTILE INDUSTRY AND FABRICS

E59.W9	INDIANS — WRITING
E77-99	INDIANS - ETHNOLOGY SEE INDIANS OF NORTH AMERICA
E77	INDIANS IN ART SEE INDIANS OF NORTH AMERICA — PICTURES, ILLUSTRATIONS, ETC.
PN56.I	INDIANS IN LITERATURE
PS173.I6	INDIANS IN LITERATURE / american literature
F1434.A55	INDIANS OF CENTRAL AMERICA — ANTHROPOMETRY
F1434.2.A	INDIANS OF CENTRAL AMERICA — ANTHROPOMETRY
F1434	INDIANS OF CENTRAL AMERICA — ANTIQUITIES
F1434.2.A	INDIANS OF CENTRAL AMERICA — ARCHITECTURE
F1434.2.A	INDIANS OF CENTRAL AMERICA — ART
F1434.2.C	INDIANS OF CENTRAL AMERICA — COSTUME AND ADORNMENT
PM3001-4566	INDIANS OF CENTRAL AMERICA — LANGUAGES
F1434.2.F6	INDIANS OF CENTRAL AMERICA — LEGENDS
F1435.3.F6	INDIANS OF CENTRAL AMERICA — LEGENDS / mayas
F1434.2.M6	INDIANS OF CENTRAL AMERICA — MISSIONS
ML3572	INDIANS OF CENTRAL AMERICA — MUSIC
F1434.2.P6	INDIANS OF CENTRAL AMERICA — POTTERY
F1434.2.R3	INDIANS OF CENTRAL AMERICA — RELIGION AND MYTHOLOGY
F1434-5	INDIANS OF CENTRAL AMERICA
F1434-5	INDIANS OF CENTRAL AMERICA-ETHNOLOGY SEE INDIANS OF CENTRAL AMERICA
F1219.3.A	INDIANS OF MEXICO — AGRICULTURE
F1219.3.A	INDIANS OF MEXICO — ANTHROPOMETRY
F1219	INDIANS OF MEXICO — ANTIQUITIES
F1219.3.A6	INDIANS OF MEXICO — ARCHITECTURE
F1219.3.A	INDIANS OF MEXICO — ARMS AND ARMOR
F1219.3.A7	INDIANS OF MEXICO — ART
F1219.3.C	INDIANS OF MEXICO — COSTUME AND ADORNMENT
F1219.3.C8	INDIANS OF MEXICO — CRANIOLOGY
F1219-1220	INDIANS OF MEXICO — CULTURE
F1219.3.D2	INDIANS OF MEXICO — DANCES
F1219	INDIANS OF MEXICO — HISTORY
PM3001-4566	INDIANS OF MEXICO — LANGUAGES
F1219.3.M4	INDIANS OF MEXICO — MASKS
F1219.3.M5	INDIANS OF MEXICO — MEDICINE
F1219.3.M	INDIANS OF MEXICO — MORTUARY CUSTOMS
F1219.3.M	INDIANS OF MEXICO — MUSIC
ML3570	INDIANS OF MEXICO — MUSIC
F1219.3.P3	INDIANS OF MEXICO — PAPER MAKING AND TRADE
F1219.3.P5	INDIANS OF MEXICO — PHILOSOPHY
F1219.3.P8	INDIANS OF MEXICO — POTTERY
F1219.3.R38	INDIANS OF MEXICO — RELIGION AND MYTHOLOGY
F1219	INDIANS OF MEXICO — SOCIAL LIFE AND CUSTOMS
F1219.3.T	INDIANS OF MEXICO — TAXATION
F1219.3.T35	INDIANS OF MEXICO — TEXTILE INDUSTRY AND FABRICS
F1219.3.W	INDIANS OF MEXICO — WOMEN
F1219.3.W94	INDIANS OF MEXICO — WRITING
E98.F6	INDIANS OF MEXICO (NORTH AMERICA, SOUTH AMERICA, ETC.)-FOLK-LORE SEE FOLK-LORE, INDIAN
E61	INDIANS OF MEXICO (NORTH AMERICA, SOUTH AMERICA, ETC.)-ORIGIN SEE INDIANS — ORIGIN
F1219-1220	INDIANS OF MEXICO
E98.P6	INDIANS OF MEXICO, (NORTH AMERICA, SOUTH AMERICA, ETC.)-PICTURE-WRITING SEE PICTURE-WRITING, INDIAN
F1219-1220	INDIANS OF MEXICO-ETHNOLOGY SEE INDIANS OF MEXICO
E98.A6	INDIANS OF NORTH AMERICA — ANTIQUITIES
E91-93	INDIANS OF NORTH AMERICA — APPROPRIATIONS
E98.A65	INDIANS OF NORTH AMERICA — ARCHITECTURE
E98.A65	INDIANS OF NORTH AMERICA — ARMS AND ARMOR
E98.A7	INDIANS OF NORTH AMERICA — ART
E98.B3	INDIANS OF NORTH AMERICA — BASKET MAKING
Z1209-1210	INDIANS OF NORTH AMERICA — BIBLIOGRAPHY
E89-90	INDIANS OF NORTH AMERICA — BIOGRAPHY
E98.C2	INDIANS OF NORTH AMERICA — BOATS
E98.C14	INDIANS OF NORTH AMERICA — CALENDAR
E85-87	INDIANS OF NORTH AMERICA — CAPTIVITIES
E98.C3	INDIANS OF NORTH AMERICA — CENSUS
E98.C5	INDIANS OF NORTH AMERICA — CHILDREN
E91-93	INDIANS OF NORTH AMERICA — CITIZENSHIP
E98.C62	INDIANS OF NORTH AMERICA — CLAIMS (AGAINST THE INDIANS)
E98.C6	INDIANS OF NORTH AMERICA — CLAIMS
E98.C7	INDIANS OF NORTH AMERICA — COMMERCE

E98.G2	INDIANS OF NORTH AMERICA-SPORTS SEE INDIANS OF NORTH AMERICA — GAMES
E98.T7	INDIANS OF NORTH AMERICA-TRAILS SEE INDIAN TRAILS
E540.I3	INDIANS OF NORTH AMERICA — HISTORY — — CIVIL WAR
E77	INDIANS OF NORTH AMERICA — HISTORY — — COLONIAL PERIOD
E82	INDIANS OF NORTH AMERICA — WARS — — 1600-1750
E81	INDIANS OF NORTH AMERICA — WARS — — 1750-1815
E83.775	INDIANS OF NORTH AMERICA — WARS — — 1775-1783
E83.79	INDIANS OF NORTH AMERICA — WARS — — 1790-1794
E83.812	INDIANS OF NORTH AMERICA — WARS — — 1812-1815
E81	INDIANS OF NORTH AMERICA — WARS — — 1815-1875
E83.863	INDIANS OF NORTH AMERICA — WARS — — 1862-1865
E83.866	INDIANS OF NORTH AMERICA — WARS — — 1866-1895
E83.866	INDIANS OF NORTH AMERICA — WARS — — 1868-1869
F2230.1.A3	INDIANS OF SOUTH AMERICA — AGRICULTURE
F2230.1.A	INDIANS OF SOUTH AMERICA — ANTHROPOMETRY
F2229	INDIANS OF SOUTH AMERICA — ANTIQUITIES
F2230.1.A	INDIANS OF SOUTH AMERICA — ARCHITECTURE
F2230.1.A7	INDIANS OF SOUTH AMERICA — ART
F2230.1.B	INDIANS OF SOUTH AMERICA — BASKET MAKING
F2230.1.C2	INDIANS OF SOUTH AMERICA — CALENDAR
F2230.1.C5	INDIANS OF SOUTH AMERICA — CHILDREN
F2230.1.C8	INDIANS OF SOUTH AMERICA — COSTUME AND ADORNMENT
F2230.1.C85	INDIANS OF SOUTH AMERICA — CRANIOLOGY
LC2658-2679	INDIANS OF SOUTH AMERICA — EDUCATION
F2230.1.F	INDIANS OF SOUTH AMERICA — FOOD
F2230.1.G2	INDIANS OF SOUTH AMERICA — GAMES
F2230.1.I4	INDIANS OF SOUTH AMERICA — IMPLEMENTS
PM5001-7356	INDIANS OF SOUTH AMERICA — LANGUAGES
F2230.1.F6	INDIANS OF SOUTH AMERICA — LEGENDS
F2230.1.M3	INDIANS OF SOUTH AMERICA — MAGIC
F2230.1.M4	INDIANS OF SOUTH AMERICA — MEDICINE
F2230-3799	INDIANS OF SOUTH AMERICA — MISSIONS
F2230.1.M	INDIANS OF SOUTH AMERICA — MIXED BLOODS
F2230.1.M	INDIANS OF SOUTH AMERICA — MORTUARY CUSTOMS
ML3575	INDIANS OF SOUTH AMERICA — MUSIC
F2230.1.M9	INDIANS OF SOUTH AMERICA — MUSIC
F2230.1.N	INDIANS OF SOUTH AMERICA — NAMES
F2230.1.P8	INDIANS OF SOUTH AMERICA — POTTERY
F2230.1.R3	INDIANS OF SOUTH AMERICA — RELIGION AND MYTHOLOGY
F2230.1.S7	INDIANS OF SOUTH AMERICA — SOCIAL LIFE AND CUSTOMS
F2230.1.T3	INDIANS OF SOUTH AMERICA — TEXTILE INDUSTRY AND FABRICS
F2301.W	INDIANS OF SOUTH AMERICA — WRITING
F2229-2230	INDIANS OF SOUTH AMERICA
F2230.1.G2	INDIANS OF SOUTH AMERICA-AMUSEMENTS SEE INDIANS OF SOUTH AMERICA — GAMES
F2230.1.S7	INDIANS OF SOUTH AMERICA-AMUSEMENTS SEE INDIANS OF SOUTH AMERICA — SOCIAL LIFE AND CUSTOMS
F2230.1.T3	INDIANS OF SOUTH AMERICA-BLANKETS SEE INDIANS OF SOUTH AMERICA — TEXTILE INDUSTRY AND FABRICS
F2230.1.S7	INDIANS OF SOUTH AMERICA-CUSTOMS SEE INDIANS OF SOUTH AMERICA — SOCIAL LIFE AND CUSTOMS
F2229-2230	INDIANS OF SOUTH AMERICA-ETHNOLOGY SEE INDIANS OF SOUTH AMERICA
F2230.1.G2	INDIANS OF SOUTH AMERICA-RECREATIONS SEE INDIANS OF SOUTH AMERICA — GAMES
F2230.1.G2	INDIANS OF SOUTH AMERICA-SPORTS SEE INDIANS OF SOUTH AMERICA — GAMES
F2230.1.I4	INDIANS OF SOUTH AMERICA-STONE IMPLEMENTS SEE INDIANS OF SOUTH AMERICA — IMPLEMENTS
E77-99	INDIANS OF THE U.S. SEE INDIANS OF NORTH AMERICA
F1619	INDIANS OF THE WEST INDIES — ANTHROPOMETRY
PM5071-9	INDIANS OF THE WEST INDIES — LANGUAGES
F1619	INDIANS OF THE WEST INDIES — RELIGION AND MYTHOLOGY
F1619	INDIANS OF THE WEST INDIES
E51-99	INDIANS
F1411	INDIANS, TREATMENT OF / spanish america
E98.B3	INDIANS-BASKET MAKING SEE INDIANS OF NORTH AMERICA — BASKET MAKING
F2230.1.B	INDIANS-BASKET MAKING SEE INDIANS OF SOUTH AMERICA — BASKET MAKING
E59.C95	INDIANS-CIVILIZATION SEE INDIANS — CULTURE
F2229-2230	INDIANS-ETHNOLOGY SEE INDIANS OF SOUTH AMERICA
E51-99	INDIANS-ETHNOLOGY SEE INDIANS
E98.F6	INDIANS-FOLK-LORE SEE FOLK-LORE, INDIAN
E59.R38	INDIANS-MYTHOLOGY SEE INDIANS — RELIGION AND MYTHOLOGY
E98.P6	INDIANS-PICTURE-WRITING SEE PICTURE-WRITING, INDIAN
PM102	INDIANS — LANGUAGES — — TEXTS
DS478	INDIA — HISTORY — — SEPOY REBELLION, 1857-1858 — — — ATROCITIES
PK5437-8	INDIC DRAMA / modern collections
PK5421	INDIC DRAMA / modern history
PK101-119	INDIC PHILOLOGY SEE INDO-ARYAN PHILOLOGY
BP130-133	INDIC PHILOSOPHY SEE PHILOSOPHY, INDIC
PK11	INDIC STUDIES
QP801.I4	INDICAN / physiological chemistry
QP211	INDICAN / secretions
SF771	INDICAN / veterinary medicine
TK393	INDICATING INSTRUMENTS SEE RECORDING INSTRUMENTS / electric engineering
QC53	INDICATING INSTRUMENTS SEE RECORDING INSTRUMENTS / physics
QD77	INDICATORS AND TEST-PAPERS / analytic chemistry
TJ759	INDICATORS FOR GAS AND OIL ENGINES
TJ478	INDICATORS FOR STEAM-ENGINES
AI	INDICES SEE INDEXES
BT33	INDIFFERENCE, RELIGIOUS SEE INDIFFERENTISM (RELIGION)
BJ1535.I	INDIFFERENTISM (ETHICS)
BT33	INDIFFERENTISM (RELIGION)
RC829	INDIGESTION SEE DYSPEPSIA
BJ1535.A6	INDIGNATION SEE ANGER / ethics
BF575.A5	INDIGNATION SEE ANGER / psychology
SB287.I4	INDIGO / agriculture
HD9019.I	INDIGO / economics
TP923-4	INDIGO / technology
HJ5001-5231	INDIRECT TAXATION SEE INTERNAL REVENUE
HJ6603-7380	INDIRECT TAXATION SEE TARIFF / administration
HF1761-2580	INDIRECT TAXATION SEE TARIFF / other countries
HJ6041-6464	INDIRECT TAXATION SEE TARIFF / schedules
HF1701-2701	INDIRECT TAXATION SEE TARIFF / theory and history
HF1750-1759	INDIRECT TAXATION SEE TARIFF / u.s.
HJ2240-7395	INDIRECT TAXATION SEE TAXATION
QD181.I5	INDIUM / chemistry
GV708	INDIVIDUAL SPORTS SEE SPORTS FOR INDIVIDUALS
B824	INDIVIDUALISM / philosophy
JC571	INDIVIDUALISM / political theory
HM136	INDIVIDUALISM / sociology
BF697	INDIVIDUALITY
PK101-2899	INDO-ARYAN LANGUAGES
PK1501-2845	INDO-ARYAN LANGUAGES, MODERN
PK101-119	INDO-ARYAN PHILOLOGY
P501-769	INDO-EUROPEAN LANGUAGES SEE ARYAN LANGUAGES
P501-769	INDO-EUROPEAN PHILOLOGY SEE ARYAN PHILOLOGY
GN539	INDO-EUROPEANS SEE ARYANS
DS15	INDO-EUROPEANS SEE ARYANS
P501-769	INDO-GERMANIC LANGUAGES SEE ARYAN LANGUAGES
DS15	INDO-GERMANIC PEOPLES SEE ARYANS
GN539	INDO-GERMANIC PEOPLES SEE ARYANS
PK1-9201	INDO-IRANIAN LANGUAGES
PK1-17	INDO-IRANIAN PHILOLOGY

PL3521-9	INDOCHINESE LANGUAGES
PL5071-9	INDONESIAN LANGUAGE
PL5021-6571	*INDONESIAN LANGUAGES* **SEE** MALAY-POLYNESIAN LANGUAGES
PL5051-9	*INDONESIAN LANGUAGES* **SEE** MALAYAN LANGUAGES
DS643.5	INDONESIA — HISTORY — — JAPANESE OCCUPATION, 1942-1945
DS641	INDONESIA — HISTORY — — TO 1478
DS642	INDONESIA — HISTORY — — 1478-1798
DS643	INDONESIA — HISTORY — — 1798-1942
GV881	INDOOR BASEBALL
GV1221-9	INDOOR GAMES
QC638	INDUCTANCE
QC631-8	INDUCTION (ELECTRICITY) / *electromagnetic*
QC581	INDUCTION (ELECTRICITY) / *electrostatic*
BC	*INDUCTION (LOGIC)* **SEE** LOGIC
QC761	*INDUCTION (MAGNETISM)* **SEE** MAGNETIC INDUCTION
QC787.B	*INDUCTION ACCELERATOR* **SEE** BETATRON
QC645	INDUCTION COILS
TN752.I5	INDUCTION HARDENING
TN672	INDUCTION HARDENING
TK4601	INDUCTION HEATING
TK2785	*INDUCTION MOTORS* **SEE** ELECTRIC MOTORS, INDUCTION
BX1939.I45	INDULGENCES (CANON LAW)
BX2279-2283	INDULGENCES
T55	*INDUSTRIAL ACCIDENTS-PREVENTION* **SEE** INDUSTRIAL SAFETY
TP593	*INDUSTRIAL ALCOHOL* **SEE** ALCOHOL, DENATURED / *technology*
HD9399	*INDUSTRIAL ALCOHOL* **SEE** ALCOHOL, DENATURED / *trade*
HD5481-5630	*INDUSTRIAL ARBITRATION* **SEE** ARBITRATION, INDUSTRIAL
Z675.T3	INDUSTRIAL ART LIBRARIES
Z7911-7916	INDUSTRIAL ARTS — BIBLIOGRAPHY
T39-40	INDUSTRIAL ARTS — BIOGRAPHY
T15-35	INDUSTRIAL ARTS — HISTORY
T9-10	INDUSTRIAL ARTS — TERMINOLOGY
T-TX	INDUSTRIAL ARTS
T391-999	*INDUSTRIAL ARTS-EXHIBITIONS* **SEE** EXHIBITIONS
T179-183	*INDUSTRIAL ARTS-MUSEUMS* **SEE** INDUSTRIAL MUSEUMS
HG2052-2069	*INDUSTRIAL BANKING* **SEE** LOANS, PERSONAL
NA6400-6581	INDUSTRIAL BUILDINGS
BV2695.W6	*INDUSTRIAL CHAPLAINS* **SEE** CHAPLAINS, INDUSTRIAL
TP155	*INDUSTRIAL CHEMISTRY* **SEE** CHEMICAL ENGINEERING
TP	*INDUSTRIAL CHEMISTRY* **SEE** CHEMISTRY, TECHNICAL
HD2709-2930	*INDUSTRIAL COMBINATIONS* **SEE** TRUSTS, INDUSTRIAL
HD2801-2930	*INDUSTRIAL COMBINATIONS* **SEE** TRUSTS, INDUSTRIAL / *other countries*
HD2771-2798	*INDUSTRIAL COMBINATIONS* **SEE** TRUSTS, INDUSTRIAL / *u.s.*
HD5650-5660	*INDUSTRIAL COUNCILS* **SEE** WORKS COUNCILS
T351-377	*INDUSTRIAL DRAWING* **SEE** MECHANICAL DRAWING
LB1595-9	*INDUSTRIAL EDUCATION* **SEE** MANUAL TRAINING / *education*
TT161-9	*INDUSTRIAL EDUCATION* **SEE** MANUAL TRAINING / *technology*
T61-173	*INDUSTRIAL EDUCATION* **SEE** TECHNICAL EDUCATION
LC1081	*INDUSTRIAL EDUCATION* **SEE** TECHNICAL EDUCATION / *theory*
LC1041-7	*INDUSTRIAL EDUCATION* **SEE** TECHNICAL EDUCATION / *vocational education*
T58	*INDUSTRIAL EFFICIENCY* **SEE** EFFICIENCY, INDUSTRIAL
TP250-261	*INDUSTRIAL ELECTROCHEMISTRY* **SEE** ELECTROCHEMISTRY, INDUSTRIAL
T391-999	*INDUSTRIAL EXHIBITIONS* **SEE** EXHIBITIONS
HD7260-7780	*INDUSTRIAL HEALTH ENGINEERING* **SEE** INDUSTRIAL HYGIENE
HD7260-7780	INDUSTRIAL HYGIENE
HD7090-7250	*INDUSTRIAL INSURANCE* **SEE** INSURANCE, INDUSTRIAL / *labor*
HD3621-7	INDUSTRIAL LAWS AND LEGISLATION
T60.G7	INDUSTRIAL MANAGEMENT — GRAPHIC METHODS
RC963-9	*INDUSTRIAL MEDICINE* **SEE** MEDICINE, INDUSTRIAL
QR53	INDUSTRIAL MICROBIOLOGY
UA18	INDUSTRIAL MOBILIZATION
T179-183	INDUSTRIAL MUSEUMS
RC966	INDUSTRIAL NURSING
TT300-380	*INDUSTRIAL PAINTING* **SEE** PAINTING, INDUSTRIAL
NA6400-6510	*INDUSTRIAL PLANTS* **SEE** FACTORIES / *architecture*
TH4511-4541	*INDUSTRIAL PLANTS* **SEE** FACTORIES / *building*
HD6270	*INDUSTRIAL PLANTS* **SEE** FACTORIES / *junior labor*
HD7406-7510	*INDUSTRIAL PLANTS* **SEE** FACTORIES / *model*
HD6974	*INDUSTRIAL PLANTS* **SEE** FACTORIES / *social conditions*
HD6068	*INDUSTRIAL PLANTS* **SEE** FACTORIES / *women in*
RC963.5	*INDUSTRIAL POISONS* **SEE** INDUSTRIAL TOXICOLOGY
HV8081-9	*INDUSTRIAL POLICE* **SEE** POLICE, PRIVATE
TL296	INDUSTRIAL POWER TRUCKS / *manufacture*
TS155	INDUSTRIAL POWER TRUCKS / *material handling*
HD3611-3616	*INDUSTRIAL PRIORITIES* **SEE** PRIORITIES, INDUSTRIAL
TP249	*INDUSTRIAL RADIOCHEMISTRY* **SEE** RADIOCHEMISTRY — INDUSTRIAL APPLICATIONS
TF677	*INDUSTRIAL RAILROADS* **SEE** RAILROADS, INDUSTRIAL
HE3601-4050	*INDUSTRIAL RAILROADS* **SEE** RAILROADS, INDUSTRIAL / *economics*
HD7395.R4	INDUSTRIAL RECREATION
HD5650-5660	*INDUSTRIAL RELATIONS COUNCILS* **SEE** WORKS COUNCILS
HD6961	INDUSTRIAL RELATIONS
HD20	*INDUSTRIAL RESEARCH* **SEE** RESEARCH, INDUSTRIAL / *economics*
T175-8	*INDUSTRIAL RESEARCH* **SEE** RESEARCH, INDUSTRIAL / *technology*
HD2321	*INDUSTRIAL REVOLUTION* **SEE** INDUSTRY — HISTORY
T55	INDUSTRIAL SAFETY
LB1595-9	*INDUSTRIAL SCHOOLS* **SEE** MANUAL TRAINING / *education*
TT161-9	*INDUSTRIAL SCHOOLS* **SEE** MANUAL TRAINING / *technology*
HV9051-9230	*INDUSTRIAL SCHOOLS* **SEE** REFORMATORIES
UB249	*INDUSTRIAL SECURITY MEASURES* **SEE** INDUSTRY — SECURITY MEASURES
HD6971-4	INDUSTRIAL SOCIOLOGY
HC	INDUSTRIAL STATISTICS
HD9000-9999	INDUSTRIAL STATISTICS / *special industries*
HA40.I6	INDUSTRIAL STATISTICS / *theory*
HC28	INDUSTRIAL SURVEYS
TA158	*INDUSTRIAL TECHNICIANS* **SEE** TECHNICIANS IN INDUSTRY
RC963.5	INDUSTRIAL TOXICOLOGY
TL296	*INDUSTRIAL TRACTORS* **SEE** INDUSTRIAL POWER TRUCKS / *manufacture*
TS155	*INDUSTRIAL TRACTORS* **SEE** INDUSTRIAL POWER TRUCKS / *material handling*
HF5761-5780	*INDUSTRIAL TRAFFIC MANAGEMENT* **SEE** SHIPMENT OF GOODS
TL296	*INDUSTRIAL TRUCKS* **SEE** INDUSTRIAL POWER TRUCKS / *manufacture*
TS155	*INDUSTRIAL TRUCKS* **SEE** INDUSTRIAL POWER TRUCKS / *material handling*
HD2709-2930	*INDUSTRIAL TRUSTS* **SEE** TRUSTS, INDUSTRIAL
HD2801-2930	*INDUSTRIAL TRUSTS* **SEE** TRUSTS, INDUSTRIAL / *other countries*
HD2771-2798	*INDUSTRIAL TRUSTS* **SEE** TRUSTS, INDUSTRIAL / *u.s.*
HD6350-6940	*INDUSTRIAL UNIONS* **SEE** TRADE-UNIONS
TJ940	*INDUSTRIAL VACUUM* **SEE** VACUUM TECHNOLOGY
TD897-9	*INDUSTRIAL WASTES* **SEE** FACTORY AND TRADE WASTE
TP995	*INDUSTRIAL WASTES* **SEE** WASTE PRODUCTS
HD7260-7780	*INDUSTRIAL WELFARE WORK* **SEE** WELFARE WORK IN INDUSTRY
T-TX	*INDUSTRIES* **SEE** INDUSTRIAL ARTS
UA18	*INDUSTRIES* **SEE** INDUSTRIAL MOBILIZATION
HD	*INDUSTRIES* **SEE** INDUSTRY
HC	*INDUSTRIES* **SEE** INDUSTRY
HD9650-9660	*INDUSTRIES, CHEMICAL* **SEE** CHEMICAL INDUSTRIES

TK	INDUSTRIES, ELECTRIC **SEE** ELECTRIC INDUSTRIES / technology
HD2331-6	INDUSTRIES, HOME **SEE** HOME LABOR
HD58	INDUSTRIES, LOCATION OF
GN429-434	INDUSTRIES, PRIMITIVE
HD2321	INDUSTRY — HISTORY
UB249	INDUSTRY — SECURITY MEASURES
BJ1498	INDUSTRY (PSYCHOLOGY) **SEE** WORK / ethics
BF481	INDUSTRY (PSYCHOLOGY) **SEE** WORK / psychology
HD3611-3790	INDUSTRY AND STATE
BV628	INDUSTRY AND THE CHURCH **SEE** CHURCH AND INDUSTRY
HB195	INDUSTRY AND WAR **SEE** WAR — ECONOMIC ASPECTS
N8218	INDUSTRY IN ART
PN56.I	INDUSTRY IN LITERATURE
HD	INDUSTRY
HC	INDUSTRY
HC	INDUSTRY-STATISTICS **SEE** INDUSTRIAL STATISTICS
HD9000-9999	INDUSTRY-STATISTICS **SEE** INDUSTRIAL STATISTICS / special industries
HA40.I6	INDUSTRY-STATISTICS **SEE** INDUSTRIAL STATISTICS / theory
HC28	INDUSTRY-SURVEYS **SEE** INDUSTRIAL SURVEYS
RC565	INEBRIETY **SEE** ALCOHOLISM / disease
HV5001-5720	INEBRIETY **SEE** ALCOHOLISM / temperance
BF435-7	INEFFICIENCY, INTELLECTUAL
QA295	INEQUALITIES (MATHEMATICS)
JC575-8	INEQUALITY **SEE** EQUALITY / political science
HM146	INEQUALITY **SEE** EQUALITY / sociology
QA839	INERTIA, MOMENTS OF **SEE** MOMENTS OF INERTIA / analytic mechanics
TG265-7	INERTIA, MOMENTS OF **SEE** MOMENTS OF INERTIA / engineering
QA839	INERTIA, PRODUCTS OF **SEE** MOMENTS OF INERTIA / analytic mechanics
TG265-7	INERTIA, PRODUCTS OF **SEE** MOMENTS OF INERTIA / engineering
TL588.5	INERTIAL NAVIGATION (AERONAUTICS)
BT88	INFALLIBILITY OF THE CHURCH **SEE** CATHOLIC CHURCH — INFALLIBILITY
BX1806	INFALLIBILITY OF THE POPE **SEE** POPES — INFALLIBILITY
BV813	INFANT BAPTISM
BV828	INFANT COMMUNION
LB1140	INFANT EDUCATION **SEE** EDUCATION, PRESCHOOL
HB1323.C5	INFANT MORTALITY **SEE** CHILDREN — MORTALITY
RJ598	INFANT MORTALITY **SEE** INFANTS — MORTALITY / public health
RJ59	INFANT MORTALITY **SEE** INFANTS — MORTALITY / public health
HB1323.I4	INFANT MORTALITY **SEE** INFANTS — MORTALITY / vital statistics
BT758	INFANT SALVATION
HV697-700	INFANT WELFARE **SEE** MATERNAL AND INFANT WELFARE
HV6537-6541	INFANTICIDE
RJ296	INFANTILE CONJUNCTIVITIS **SEE** CONJUNCTIVITIS, INFANTILE
RC180-181	INFANTILE PARALYSIS **SEE** POLIOMYELITIS
RJ399.S3	INFANTILE SCURVY **SEE** SCURVY, INFANTILE
RJ135	INFANTILISM
UD370-375	INFANTRY — EQUIPMENT
UD157-302	INFANTRY DRILL AND TACTICS
UD	INFANTRY
RJ61	INFANTS — CARE AND HYGIENE
RJ101	INFANTS — CARE AND HYGIENE
TT635-645	INFANTS — CLOTHING
RJ	INFANTS — DISEASES
RJ131	INFANTS — GROWTH
RJ59	INFANTS — MORTALITY / public health
RJ598	INFANTS — MORTALITY / public health
HB1323.I4	INFANTS — MORTALITY / vital statistics
RJ216	INFANTS — NUTRITION
RJ216	INFANTS — WEANING
GN63	INFANTS — WEIGHT
RJ251-325	INFANTS (NEW-BORN)
RJ250	INFANTS (PREMATURE)
RG631	INFANTS (STILL-BORN) **SEE** STILL-BIRTH

BF723.I6	INFANTS / psychology
HQ769-785	INFANTS / social groups
RJ216	INFANTS, FOOD FOR **SEE** INFANTS — NUTRITION
HV697-700	INFANTS-CHARITIES, PROTECTION, ETC. **SEE** MATERNAL AND INFANT WELFARE
HQ748.C	INFANTS-CRYING **SEE** CRYING
HG9271-7	INFANTS-INSURANCE **SEE** INSURANCE, CHILD
HV721-739	INFANTS-LAW **SEE** CHILDREN — LAW
RJ50	INFANTS — DISEASES — — DIAGNOSIS
RX501-531	INFANTS — DISEASES — — HOMEOPATHIC TREATMENT
RB144	INFARCTION
SF871	INFECTIOUS ABORTION **SEE** BRUCELLOSIS IN CATTLE
RA769	INFECTIOUS DISEASES **SEE** COMMUNICABLE DISEASES / miscellaneous preventive measures
RC111-216	INFECTIOUS DISEASES **SEE** COMMUNICABLE DISEASES / practice of medicine
RA643-4	INFECTIOUS DISEASES **SEE** COMMUNICABLE DISEASES / public hygiene
SF968	INFECTIOUS NECROTIC HEPATITIS **SEE** BRAXY
QA295	INFINITE PROCESSES **SEE** PROCESSES, INFINITE
QA295	INFINITE PRODUCTS **SEE** PRODUCTS, INFINITE
QA295	INFINITE SERIES **SEE** SERIES, INFINITE
QA9	INFINITE / mathematics
BD411	INFINITE / metaphysics
QA300-316	INFINITESIMAL CALCULUS **SEE** CALCULUS
QA615-639	INFINITESIMAL GEOMETRY **SEE** GEOMETRY, INFINITESIMAL
QA385	INFINITESIMAL TRANSFORMATIONS **SEE** TRANSFORMATIONS, INFINITESIMAL
QA9	INFINITY **SEE** INFINITE / mathematics
BD411	INFINITY **SEE** INFINITE / metaphysics
RA960-996	INFIRMARIES **SEE** HOSPITALS
HD3623-4	INFLAMMABLE LIQUIDS / dangerous industries
TA407	INFLAMMABLE MATERIALS
RB131	INFLAMMATION / pathology
RC104	INFLAMMATION / treatment
TL940	INFLATABLE SPACE STRUCTURES **SEE** EXPANDABLE SPACE STRUCTURES
P251-9	INFLECTION **SEE** GRAMMAR, COMPARATIVE AND GENERAL — INFLECTION
P251-9	INFLECTION **SEE** GRAMMAR, COMPARATIVE AND GENERAL — INFLECTION
PB101	INFLECTION **SEE** LANGUAGES, MODERN — INFLECTION
QK691	INFLORESCENCE
QK652	INFLORESCENCE
TG270	INFLUENCE LINES
QC573	INFLUENCE MACHINES **SEE** ELECTRIC MACHINES
QR201.I6	INFLUENZA — BACTERIOLOGY
RX326.I	INFLUENZA — HOMEOPATHIC TREATMENT
RC150	INFLUENZA RESEARCH
RC150	INFLUENZA
RC150	INFLUENZA-RESEARCH **SEE** INFLUENZA RESEARCH
AG500-551	INFORMATION CENTERS **SEE** INFORMATION SERVICES
Z675.G7	INFORMATION LIBRARIES **SEE** LIBRARIES, GOVERNMENTAL, ADMINISTRATIVE, ETC.
Z675.G7	INFORMATION LIBRARIES
AG500-551	INFORMATION SERVICES
Z699.5.C5	INFORMATION STORAGE AND RETRIEVAL SYSTEMS — CHEMISTRY
Z699.5.E5	INFORMATION STORAGE AND RETRIEVAL SYSTEMS — ELECTRONICS
Z699.5.M4	INFORMATION STORAGE AND RETRIEVAL SYSTEMS — METALLURGY
Z699.5.S3	INFORMATION STORAGE AND RETRIEVAL SYSTEMS — SCIENCE
Z699.5.W3	INFORMATION STORAGE AND RETRIEVAL SYSTEMS — WATER-SUPPLY
TX687	INFRA-RED BROILING **SEE** BROILING
TP363	INFRA-RED DRYING APPARATUS
TP363	INFRA-RED HEATING / chemical engineering
TK4635	INFRA-RED HEATING / electric engineering
TR755	INFRA-RED PHOTOGRAPHY **SEE** PHOTOGRAPHY, INFRA-RED
QC457	INFRA-RED SPECTRUM **SEE** SPECTRUM, INFRA-RED
QL368-9	INFUSORIA
QL365	INFUSORIA / early works
TN948.D5	INFUSORIAL EARTH **SEE** DIATOMACEOUS EARTH

E99.I5	INGALIK INDIANS
PM1373	INGALIK LANGUAGE
F3324	INGAVI, BATTLE OF, 1841
F229	*INGRAM'S REBELLION (VIRGINIA)* **SEE** BACON'S REBELLION, 1676
RD563	*INGROWING NAILS* **SEE** NAILS, INGROWING
PK9201.C3	*INGUSH LANGUAGE* **SEE** CHECHEN LANGUAGE
DK34.I	INGUSH
RA1245	*INHALATION TOXICOLOGY* **SEE** GASES, ASPHYXIATING AND POISONOUS — TOXICOLOGY
QH431	*INHERITANCE (BIOLOGY)* **SEE** HEREDITY / *biology*
HQ753	*INHERITANCE (BIOLOGY)* **SEE** HEREDITY / *eugenics*
HV5133	*INHERITANCE (BIOLOGY)* **SEE** HEREDITY / *heredity and alcoholism*
RJ91	*INHERITANCE (BIOLOGY)* **SEE** HEREDITY / *heredity and child culture*
HV6121-5	*INHERITANCE (BIOLOGY)* **SEE** HEREDITY / *heredity and crime*
BF418	*INHERITANCE (BIOLOGY)* **SEE** HEREDITY / *heredity and genius*
BF341-6	*INHERITANCE (BIOLOGY)* **SEE** HEREDITY / *psychology*
HM121	*INHERITANCE (BIOLOGY)* **SEE** HEREDITY / *sociology*
BX1939.I	INHERITANCE AND SUCCESSION (CANON LAW)
HB715	INHERITANCE AND SUCCESSION / *economics*
HJ5801-5819	INHERITANCE AND TRANSFER TAX
BF335-7	INHIBITION / *psychology*
QL737.C4	*INIA* **SEE** DOLPHINS
NK3600-3640	INITIALS
ND3335	INITIALS / *illumination*
BL615	INITIATIONS (IN RELIGION, FOLK-LORE, ETC.)
HD4889	INITIATIONS (INTO TRADES, SOCIETIES, ETC.) / *labor*
JF491-7	*INITIATIVE AND REFERENDUM* **SEE** REFERENDUM
RM163-176	INJECTIONS / *therapeutics*
QH324	INJECTIONS, ANATOMICAL / *biology*
QL812	INJECTIONS, ANATOMICAL / *comparative anatomy*
QM39	INJECTIONS, ANATOMICAL / *human anatomy*
RM169	INJECTIONS, HYPODERMIC
RM180	INJECTIONS, INTRAPERITONEAL
RM170	INJECTIONS, INTRAVENOUS
RM178	INJECTIONS, SALINE
RM169	*INJECTIONS, SUBCUTANEOUS* **SEE** INJECTIONS, HYPODERMIC
TJ387	INJECTORS / *steam-boilers*
HD7819	INJUNCTIONS / *labor law*
JF721	INJUNCTIONS / *theory*
JK1542	INJUNCTIONS / *u.s. judiciary*
HD7814-7816	*INJURIES (LAW)* **SEE** EMPLOYERS' LIABILITY
RA1001-1171	*INJURIES (LAW)* **SEE** MEDICAL JURISPRUDENCE
RC86-88	*INJURIES* **SEE** FIRST AID IN ILLNESS AND INJURY
RC87	*INJURIES* **SEE** WOUNDS / *first aid*
RA1121	*INJURIES* **SEE** WOUNDS / *medical jurisprudence*
RD58	*INJURIES* **SEE** WOUNDS / *reparative processes*
RD93-96.6	*INJURIES* **SEE** WOUNDS / *surgery*
RD96.5	*INJURIES FROM ELECTRICITY* **SEE** ELECTRICITY, INJURIES FROM / *treatment*
RA1091	*INJURIES FROM ELECTRICITY* **SEE** ELECTRICITY, INJURIES FROM / *medical jurisprudence*
RD131	*INJURIES FROM SPORTS* **SEE** SPORTS — ACCIDENTS AND INJURIES
SB821-945	*INJURIOUS INSECTS* **SEE** INSECTS, INJURIOUS AND BENFFICIAL
HD7262	*INJURIOUS OCCUPATIONS* **SEE** OCCUPATIONS, DANGEROUS
HD3623-4	*INJURIOUS OCCUPATIONS* **SEE** OCCUPATIONS, DANGEROUS / *legislation*
T54	*INJURIOUS OCCUPATIONS* **SEE** OCCUPATIONS, DANGEROUS / *technology*
ND2460	*INK BRUSHWORK* **SEE** BRUSH DRAWING
NC905	*INK DRAWING* **SEE** PEN DRAWING
Z260	*INK DRYING* **SEE** PRINTING-INK — DRYING
TP948.I6	*INK SLABS* **SEE** INK-STONES
TP948.I6	INK-STONES
Z112	INK / *paleography*
TP946-950	INK / *technology*

E99.I5	*INKALIK INDIANS* **SEE** INGALIK INDIANS
PM1373	*INKALIK LANGUAGE* **SEE** INGALIK LANGUAGE
DK215.5	INKERMANN, BATTLE OF, 1854
HG9903	*INLAND MARINE INSURANCE* **SEE** INSURANCE, INLAND MARINE
HE586-7	INLAND NAVIGATION — LAWS AND REGULATIONS
TC601-791	INLAND NAVIGATION / *engineering*
HE617-720	INLAND NAVIGATION / *transportation*
HJ5001-5231	*INLAND REVENUE* **SEE** INTERNAL REVENUE
HE586-7	*INLAND RULES OF THE ROAD* **SEE** INLAND NAVIGATION — LAWS AND REGULATIONS
HG9903	*INLAND TRANSPORTATION INSURANCE* **SEE** INSURANCE, INLAND MARINE
NK9920	*INLAYING IN WOOD* **SEE** MARQUETRY
NK2710	*INLAYING IN WOOD* **SEE** MARQUETRY / *inlaid furniture*
PL5801	*INMEAS DIALECT* **SEE** ISINAI DIALECT
BX7748.I6	INNER LIGHT
BV2950	INNER MISSIONS / *germany*
BV50.H6	*INNOCENTS, FEAST OF THE HOLY* **SEE** HOLY INNOCENTS, FEAST OF THE
BS2545.H	*INNOCENTS, MASSACRE OF THE HOLY* **SEE** HOLY INNOCENTS, MASSACRE OF THE
BV50.H6	*INNOCENTS' DAY* **SEE** HOLY INNOCENTS, FEAST OF THE
NA7800-7850	*INNS* **SEE** HOTELS, TAVERNS, ETC. / *architecture*
GT3770-3899	*INNS* **SEE** HOTELS, TAVERNS, ETC. / *manners and customs*
E99.E7	*INNUIT* **SEE** ESKIMOS
S652	*INOCULATION OF SOILS* **SEE** SOIL INOCULATION
QK623.D6	*INOPERCULATES* **SEE** DISCOMYCETES
QD151-199	*INORGANIC CHEMISTRY* **SEE** CHEMISTRY, INORGANIC
QD321	INOSITE
TK7887.5	*INPUT EQUIPMENT (ELECTRONIC COMPUTERS)* **SEE** ELECTRONIC CALCULATING-MACHINES — INPUT-OUTPUT EQUIPMENT
QA265	*INPUT-OUTPUT ANALYSIS* **SEE** LINEAR PROGRAMMING
TK7887.5	*INPUT-OUTPUT EQUIPMENT (ELECTRONIC COMPUTERS)* **SEE** ELECTRONIC CALCULATING-MACHINES — INPUT-OUTPUT EQUIPMENT
UB850-867	*INQUIRY, COURTS OF* **SEE** COURTS-MARTIAL AND COURTS OF INQUIRY / *military*
VB800-815	*INQUIRY, COURTS OF* **SEE** COURTS-MARTIAL AND COURTS OF INQUIRY / *naval*
BX1700-1745	INQUISITION
DA670	INQUISITIONES POST MORTEM / *english counties*
CS434-6	INQUISITIONES POST MORTEM / *english genealogical records*
DA25	INQUISITIONES POST MORTEM / *english records*
BF323.C8	*INQUISITIVENESS* **SEE** CURIOSITY
HV6133	INSANE, CRIMINAL AND DANGEROUS / *insanity and crime*
HV8741-2	INSANE, CRIMINAL AND DANGEROUS / *prisons*
RC435-576	*INSANE-CARE AND TREATMENT* **SEE** MENTALLY ILL — CARE AND TREATMENT
RA1151	*INSANE-LEGAL STATUS, LAWS, ETC.* **SEE** INSANITY — JURISPRUDENCE
RA1151	INSANITY — JURISPRUDENCE
E185.88	*INSANITY - NEGROES* **SEE** NEGROES — INSANITY
N71.5	*INSANITY AND ART* **SEE** ART AND MENTAL ILLNESS / *art*
RC455	*INSANITY AND ART* **SEE** ART AND MENTAL ILLNESS / *medicine*
HV8741-2	*INSANITY AND CRIME* **SEE** INSANE, CRIMINAL AND DANGEROUS / *prisons*
HV6133	*INSANITY AND CRIME* **SEE** INSANE, CRIMINAL AND DANGEROUS / *insanity and crime*
BF412-426	*INSANITY AND GENIUS* **SEE** GENIUS
HV5141	*INSANITY AND GENIUS* **SEE** GENIUS / *genius and alcoholism*
BF426	*INSANITY AND GENIUS* **SEE** GENIUS / *genius and degeneration*
BF418	*INSANITY AND GENIUS* **SEE** GENIUS / *genius and heredity*
BF423	*INSANITY AND GENIUS* **SEE** GENIUS / *genius and insanity*

HV4977	INSANITY AND GENIUS SEE INSANITY / insanity and degeneration
BF423	INSANITY AND GENIUS SEE INSANITY / insanity and genius
PR658.I5	INSANITY IN LITERATURE / elizabethan era
PR3065	INSANITY IN LITERATURE / shakespeare
HV6133	INSANITY / insanity and crime
HV4977	INSANITY / insanity and degeneration
BF423	INSANITY / insanity and genius
RC520	INSANITY, DELUSIONAL SEE PARANOIA
RC532	INSANITY, HYSTERICAL SEE HYSTERIA
E185.88	INSANITY-NEGROES SEE NEGROES — INSANITY
CC200-250	INSCRIPTIONS ON BELLS SEE BELLS — INSCRIPTIONS
CN	INSCRIPTIONS
NA4050.I5	INSCRIPTIONS, ARCHITECTURAL SEE ARCHITECTURAL INSCRIPTIONS
CN	INSCRIPTIONS, ASSYRIAN SEE CUNEIFORM INSCRIPTIONS
PK	INSCRIPTIONS, ASSYRIAN SEE CUNEIFORM INSCRIPTIONS
PJ	INSCRIPTIONS, ASSYRIAN SEE CUNEIFORM INSCRIPTIONS
PJ	INSCRIPTIONS, BABYLONIAN SEE CUNEIFORM INSCRIPTIONS
CN	INSCRIPTIONS, BABYLONIAN SEE CUNEIFORM INSCRIPTIONS
PK	INSCRIPTIONS, BABYLONIAN SEE CUNEIFORM INSCRIPTIONS
PK	INSCRIPTIONS, BEHISTUN SEE CUNEIFORM INSCRIPTIONS
PJ	INSCRIPTIONS, BEHISTUN SEE CUNEIFORM INSCRIPTIONS
CN	INSCRIPTIONS, BEHISTUN SEE CUNEIFORM INSCRIPTIONS
PK6128	INSCRIPTIONS, BEHISTUN SEE OLD PERSIAN INSCRIPTIONS
PK	INSCRIPTIONS, CUNEIFORM SEE CUNEIFORM INSCRIPTIONS
PJ	INSCRIPTIONS, CUNEIFORM SEE CUNEIFORM INSCRIPTIONS
CN	INSCRIPTIONS, CUNEIFORM SEE CUNEIFORM INSCRIPTIONS
PJ1501-1819	INSCRIPTIONS, DEMOTIC SEE EGYPTIAN LANGUAGE — INSCRIPTIONS
PJ1501-1819	INSCRIPTIONS, EGYPTIAN SEE EGYPTIAN LANGUAGE — INSCRIPTIONS
P943	INSCRIPTIONS, ELAMITE SEE CUNEIFORM INSCRIPTIONS, ELAMITE
PJ6971	INSCRIPTIONS, HADRAMI
PJ1501-1819	INSCRIPTIONS, HIERATIC SEE EGYPTIAN LANGUAGE — INSCRIPTIONS
CN1153	INSCRIPTIONS, ISLAMIC
PJ4149	INSCRIPTIONS, MOABITIC SEE MOABITE STONE
CN1153	INSCRIPTIONS, MUSLIM SEE INSCRIPTIONS, ISLAMIC
PJ5239	INSCRIPTIONS, NABATAEAN
PK6128	INSCRIPTIONS, PERSIAN (OLD) SEE OLD PERSIAN INSCRIPTIONS
PJ6971	INSCRIPTIONS, SOUTH ARABIAN SEE INSCRIPTIONS, HADRAMI
CN350	INSCRIPTIONS, STOICHEDON SEE STOICHEDON INSCRIPTIONS
P959	INSCRIPTIONS, VANNIC SEE CUNEIFORM INSCRIPTIONS, VANNIC
SB951	INSECT ATTRACTANTS SEE INSECT BAITS AND REPELLENTS
SB951	INSECT BAITS AND REPELLENTS
SB767	INSECT GALLS SEE GALLS (BOTANY)
SB951	INSECT REPELLENTS SEE INSECT BAITS AND REPELLENTS
SB959	INSECT TRAPS
SB292	INSECTICIDAL PLANTS SEE PLANTS, INSECTICIDAL
SB951	INSECTICIDES
QL737.I5	INSECTIVORA
QE882.I5	INSECTIVORA, FOSSIL
QK917	INSECTIVOROUS PLANTS
QL494	INSECTS — ANATOMY
QL496	INSECTS — BIOLOGY
QL468	INSECTS — CATALOGS AND COLLECTIONS
QL468	INSECTS — CLASSIFICATION

QL465	INSECTS — COLLECTION AND PRESERVATION
QL496	INSECTS — DEVELOPMENT
QL469-491	INSECTS — GEOGRAPHICAL DISTRIBUTION
QL467	INSECTS — JUVENILE LITERATURE
QL464	INSECTS — LABORATORY MANUALS
QL496	INSECTS — MIGRATION
QL355	INSECTS — NOMENCLATURE (POPULAR)
QL353-4	INSECTS — NOMENCLATURE
QL495	INSECTS — PHYSIOLOGY
QL466	INSECTS — PICTORIAL WORKS
SB931	INSECTS AND PLANT DISEASES SEE INSECTS AS CARRIERS OF PLANT DISEASES
RA639-641	INSECTS AS CARRIERS OF DISEASE
SB931	INSECTS AS CARRIERS OF PLANT DISEASES
QL461-599	INSECTS
GR750	INSECTS / folk-lore
QL496	INSECTS, AQUATIC
QL496	INSECTS, COLOR OF SEE COLOR OF INSECTS
SB821-945	INSECTS, DESTRUCTIVE AND USEFUL SEE INSECTS, INJURIOUS AND BENEFICIAL
QE831-2	INSECTS, FOSSIL
SB975	INSECTS, INJURIOUS AND BENEFICIAL — BIOLOGICAL CONTROL
SB821-945	INSECTS, INJURIOUS AND BENEFICIAL
SB975	INSECTS-BIOLOGICAL CONTROL SEE INSECTS, INJURIOUS AND BENEFICIAL — BIOLOGICAL CONTROL
QL496	INSECTS-COLOR SEE COLOR OF INSECTS
QL496	INSECTS-METAMORPHOSIS SEE INSECTS — DEVELOPMENT
SF105.5	INSEMINATION, ARTIFICIAL SEE ARTIFICIAL INSEMINATION
NK7400-7419	INSIGNIA / jeweled
UC530-535	INSIGNIA / military
VC345	INSIGNIA / naval
CR4480	INSIGNIA / royalty
HS159-160	INSIGNIA / secret societies
HG3760-3773	INSOLVENCY SEE BANKRUPTCY
RC548	INSOMNIA
UA12.5	INSPECTION FOR DISARMAMENT SEE DISARMAMENT — INSPECTION
TH439	INSPECTION OF BUILDINGS SEE BUILDING INSPECTION
UA12.5	INSPECTION OF DISARMAMENT SEE DISARMAMENT — INSPECTION
HD3656-3790	INSPECTION OF FACTORIES SEE FACTORY INSPECTION
HD9000.9	INSPECTION OF FOOD SEE FOOD ADULTERATION AND INSPECTION / economics
TX501-595	INSPECTION OF FOOD SEE FOOD ADULTERATION AND INSPECTION / technical works
HD9410.9	INSPECTION OF MEAT SEE MEAT INSPECTION / legislation
TS1975	INSPECTION OF MEAT SEE MEAT INSPECTION / practice
HD9560.9	INSPECTION OF OIL SEE OIL INSPECTION / state reports
TP691	INSPECTION OF OIL SEE OIL INSPECTION / technology
LB2801-2997	INSPECTION OF SCHOOLS SEE SCHOOL MANAGEMENT AND ORGANIZATION / organization and supervision
LB3011-3095	INSPECTION OF SCHOOLS SEE SCHOOL MANAGEMENT AND ORGANIZATION / management and discipline
TJ298-308	INSPECTION OF STEAM-BOILERS SEE STEAM-BOILER INSPECTION
SF998	INSPECTION OF STOCK SEE STOCK INSPECTION
SF621-723	INSPECTION OF STOCK SEE STOCK INSPECTION / by country
BF410	INSPIRATION / psychology
BT125	INSPIRATION / theology
HX656.A4	INSPIRATIONISTS
BV4290	INSTALLATION (CLERGY) — ANNIVERSARY SERMONS
BV4290	INSTALLATION (CLERGY)
BV4290	INSTALLATION SERMONS
BV199.I5	INSTALLATION SERVICE (CHURCH OFFICERS)
HF5568	INSTALMENT CREDIT COMPANIES SEE INSTALMENT PLAN
HF5568	INSTALMENT PLAN

BF685	INSTINCT / psychology
QL781	INSTINCT / zoology
GN2	INSTITUTES, ANTHROPOLOGICAL SEE ANTHROPOLOGICAL INSTITUTES
LB1823-2151	INSTITUTES, TEACHERS' SEE TEACHERS' INSTITUTES
LB1751-5	INSTITUTES, TEACHERS' SEE TEACHERS' INSTITUTES
Z675.I6	INSTITUTION LIBRARIES
HV40	INSTITUTION MANAGEMENT / charities
TX147	INSTITUTION MANAGEMENT / home economics
BV4400-4470	INSTITUTIONAL CHURCH SEE CHURCH WORK
BV2000-3705	INSTITUTIONAL MISSIONS
HV1-4959	INSTITUTIONS, CHARITABLE AND PHILANTHROPIC SEE CHARITIES
JC362	INSTITUTIONS, INTERNATIONAL SEE INTERNATIONAL COOPERATION
JX1995	INSTITUTIONS, INTERNATIONAL SEE INTERNATIONAL COOPERATION / etc.
RA793	INSTITUTIONS, OPEN-AIR SEE OPEN-AIR INSTITUTIONS / hygiene
L	INSTRUCTION SEE EDUCATION
MT	INSTRUCTION SEE MUSIC — INSTRUCTION AND STUDY
LB	INSTRUCTION SEE TEACHING
LB1775-1785	INSTRUCTION SEE TEACHING / teaching as a profession
U290-295	INSTRUCTION, CAMPS OF SEE MILITARY TRAINING CAMPS
LB2801-2822	INSTRUCTIONAL SUPERVISION SEE SCHOOL SUPERVISION
GV1480	INSTRUCTIVE GAMES SEE EDUCATIONAL GAMES
LB1778	INSTRUCTORS SEE COLLEGE TEACHERS
TL696.L33	INSTRUMENT APPROACH SYSTEMS SEE INSTRUMENT LANDING SYSTEMS
TL711.B6	INSTRUMENT FLIGHT SEE INSTRUMENT FLYING
TL711.B6	INSTRUMENT FLYING
TL696.L33	INSTRUMENT LANDING SYSTEMS
TS500	INSTRUMENT MANUFACTURE
GC41	INSTRUMENT PLATFORMS, FLOATING SEE OCEANOGRAPHIC BUOYS
TS500	INSTRUMENT-MAKING SEE INSTRUMENT MANUFACTURE
QD73	INSTRUMENTAL ANALYSIS
M900-949	INSTRUMENTAL ENSEMBLES
M960-985	INSTRUMENTAL ENSEMBLES
M14.3	INSTRUMENTAL MASSES SEE ORGAN MASSES
ML460-547	INSTRUMENTAL MUSIC — HISTORY AND CRITICISM
MT170	INSTRUMENTAL MUSIC — INSTRUCTION AND STUDY
MT170	INSTRUMENTAL MUSIC — STUDIES AND EXERCISES (JAZZ)
MT170	INSTRUMENTAL MUSIC — STUDIES AND EXERCISES
ML128.I65	INSTRUMENTAL MUSIC — THEMATIC CATALOGS
M5-1459	INSTRUMENTAL MUSIC
ML132.I5	INSTRUMENTAL MUSIC-GRADED LISTS SEE INSTRUMENTAL MUSIC — BIBLIOGRAPHY — — GRADED LISTS
ML132.I5	INSTRUMENTAL MUSIC — BIBLIOGRAPHY — — GRADED LISTS
ML156.4.I5	INSTRUMENTAL MUSIC — TO 1800 — — DISCOGRAPHY
ML455	INSTRUMENTATION AND ORCHESTRATION (BAND)
MT73	INSTRUMENTATION AND ORCHESTRATION (BAND)
MT86	INSTRUMENTATION AND ORCHESTRATION (DANCE ORCHESTRA)
ML455	INSTRUMENTATION AND ORCHESTRATION / history
MT70	INSTRUMENTATION AND ORCHESTRATION / instruction
HD9743	INSTRUMENTS OF WAR SEE MUNITIONS / economics
JX5390	INSTRUMENTS OF WAR SEE MUNITIONS / international law
UF530-537	INSTRUMENTS OF WAR SEE MUNITIONS / manufacture
TL589	INSTRUMENTS, AERONAUTICAL SEE AERONAUTICAL INSTRUMENTS
QB85-137	INSTRUMENTS, ASTRONOMICAL SEE ASTRONOMICAL INSTRUMENTS
UF830-857	INSTRUMENTS, BALLISTIC SEE BALLISTIC INSTRUMENTS
RK681-6	INSTRUMENTS, DENTAL SEE DENTAL INSTRUMENTS AND APPARATUS
N8530-8540	INSTRUMENTS, DRAWING SEE DRAWING INSTRUMENTS
T375-7	INSTRUMENTS, DRAWING SEE DRAWING INSTRUMENTS / mechanical drawing
TK	INSTRUMENTS, ELECTRIC SEE ELECTRIC APPARATUS AND APPLIANCES / electric industries
QC543-4	INSTRUMENTS, ELECTRIC SEE ELECTRIC APPARATUS AND APPLIANCES / scientific apparatus
RM889	INSTRUMENTS, ELECTRIC SEE ELECTRIC APPARATUS AND APPLIANCES / medical apparatus
TK7870	INSTRUMENTS, ELECTRONIC SEE ELECTRONIC INSTRUMENTS
TA165	INSTRUMENTS, ENGINEERING SEE ENGINEERING INSTRUMENTS
QC819	INSTRUMENTS, MAGNETIC SEE MAGNETIC INSTRUMENTS / terrestrial magnetism
VK573-585	INSTRUMENTS, MARINE SEE NAUTICAL INSTRUMENTS
QA71-85	INSTRUMENTS, MATHEMATICAL SEE MATHEMATICAL INSTRUMENTS
TJ1313	INSTRUMENTS, MEASURING SEE MEASURING INSTRUMENTS / machine-shop practice
QC100.5	INSTRUMENTS, MEASURING SEE MEASURING INSTRUMENTS / physical instruments
QC876	INSTRUMENTS, METEOROLOGICAL SEE METEOROLOGICAL INSTRUMENTS
ML462	INSTRUMENTS, MUSICAL SEE MUSICAL INSTRUMENTS / exhibitions
ML460-1055	INSTRUMENTS, MUSICAL SEE MUSICAL INSTRUMENTS / history
HD9999.M8	INSTRUMENTS, MUSICAL SEE MUSICAL INSTRUMENTS / industry
MT170-805	INSTRUMENTS, MUSICAL SEE MUSICAL INSTRUMENTS / instruction
VK573-585	INSTRUMENTS, NAUTICAL SEE NAUTICAL INSTRUMENTS
JX6288-9	INSTRUMENTS, NEGOTIABLE SEE NEGOTIABLE INSTRUMENTS / international law
HF1259	INSTRUMENTS, NEGOTIABLE SEE NEGOTIABLE INSTRUMENTS / u.s.
GC41	INSTRUMENTS, OCEANOGRAPHIC SEE OCEANOGRAPHIC INSTRUMENTS
RE	INSTRUMENTS, OPHTHALMOLOGICAL SEE EYE, INSTRUMENTS AND APPARATUS FOR
RE73	INSTRUMENTS, OPTICAL SEE OPTICAL INSTRUMENTS / examination of eye
QC371-6	INSTRUMENTS, OPTICAL SEE OPTICAL INSTRUMENTS / optics
ML1030-1040	INSTRUMENTS, PERCUSSION SEE PERCUSSION INSTRUMENTS / history and criticism
QC53	INSTRUMENTS, PHYSICAL SEE PHYSICAL INSTRUMENTS
Q184-5	INSTRUMENTS, SCIENTIFIC SEE SCIENTIFIC APPARATUS AND INSTRUMENTS
RD71-78	INSTRUMENTS, SURGICAL SEE SURGICAL INSTRUMENTS AND APPARATUS
TA562-581	INSTRUMENTS, SURVEYING SEE SURVEYING — INSTRUMENTS
UB789	INSUBORDINATION / military
VB880	INSUBORDINATION / naval
TK3441.05	INSULATING OILS
TK3331-3441	INSULATION (ELECTRIC) SEE ELECTRIC INSULATORS AND INSULATION / engineering
QC611	INSULATION (ELECTRIC) SEE ELECTRIC INSULATORS AND INSULATION / physics
TH1715	INSULATION (HEAT)
TH1725	INSULATION (SOUND) SEE SOUNDPROOFING
QP951	INSULIN
HG8077	INSURANCE — ACCOUNTING
HG8091-8102	INSURANCE — AGENTS
PN6231.I6	INSURANCE — ANECDOTES, FACETIAE, SATIRE, ETC.
HG8025	INSURANCE — DICTIONARIES
HG8021	INSURANCE — DIRECTORIES
HG8076-8	INSURANCE — FINANCE
HG8027-8039	INSURANCE — HISTORY
HG8781-2	INSURANCE — MATHEMATICS
HG8011-8015	INSURANCE — PERIODICALS
HG8051	INSURANCE — PLANS
HG8065-7	INSURANCE — RATES AND TABLES
HG8522	INSURANCE — SOCIETIES, ETC. / by country

HG8016	INSURANCE — SOCIETIES, ETC. / etc. international
HG8111-8117	INSURANCE — STATE SUPERVISION
HG8045	INSURANCE — STATISTICS
HG8119-8123	INSURANCE — TAXATION
HG8055	INSURANCE — WAR RISKS
HG8019	INSURANCE — YEARBOOKS
HG8091-8102	*INSURANCE AGENTS* **SEE** INSURANCE — AGENTS
HG8111-8117	*INSURANCE AND STATE* **SEE** INSURANCE — STATE SUPERVISION
HG9739	*INSURANCE AND STATE* **SEE** INSURANCE, FIRE — STATE SUPERVISION
HG8916-8919	*INSURANCE AND STATE* **SEE** INSURANCE, LIFE — STATE SUPERVISION
HG8077	*INSURANCE COMPANIES-ACCOUNTING* **SEE** INSURANCE — ACCOUNTING
HG8021	*INSURANCE COMPANIES-DIRECTORIES* **SEE** INSURANCE — DIRECTORIES
HG8758	*INSURANCE COMPANIES-DIRECTORIES* **SEE** INSURANCE, LIFE — DIRECTORIES
HG8119-8123	*INSURANCE COMPANIES-TAXATION* **SEE** INSURANCE — TAXATION
HG8910-8914	*INSURANCE COMPANIES-TAXATION* **SEE** INSURANCE, LIFE — TAXATION
TH9201-9237	INSURANCE ENGINEERING
HG8115	INSURANCE LAW
HG9471	INSURANCE LAW / etc. burial
HG9734	INSURANCE LAW / fire
HG9393	INSURANCE LAW / health
HG8906-9	INSURANCE LAW / life
Z675.I7	INSURANCE LIBRARIES
HG8011-9970	INSURANCE
HG9323.A3	INSURANCE, ACCIDENT — ADJUSTMENT OF CLAIMS
HG8886-8891	INSURANCE, ACCIDENT — MEDICAL EXAMINATIONS
HG9323.R3	INSURANCE, ACCIDENT — RATES AND TABLES
HG9310	INSURANCE, ACCIDENT — STATISTICS
HG9301-9343	INSURANCE, ACCIDENT
HD7101-2	INSURANCE, ACCIDENT / industrial
HG9970.A7	*INSURANCE, AERONAUTICAL* **SEE** INSURANCE, AVIATION
HG9968.C6-8	INSURANCE, AGRICULTURAL — CROPS
HG9968.L5-8	INSURANCE, AGRICULTURAL — LIVE STOCK
HG9966-9	INSURANCE, AGRICULTURAL
HG9968.H2-5	*INSURANCE, AGRICULTURAL-HAIL* **SEE** INSURANCE, HAIL
HG9968.T5-7	*INSURANCE, AGRICULTURAL-TORNADO* **SEE** INSURANCE, TORNADO
HG9970.A	INSURANCE, ART
HG9221.R3	INSURANCE, ASSESSMENT — RATES AND TABLES
HG9201-9245	INSURANCE, ASSESSMENT
HG8826	INSURANCE, ASSESSMENT
HG9970.A4-68	INSURANCE, AUTOMOBILE
HG9970.A7	INSURANCE, AVIATION
HG1662	*INSURANCE, BANK DEPOSIT* **SEE** INSURANCE, DEPOSIT
HG9963.B5-8	INSURANCE, BOILER
HG9970.B8	INSURANCE, BURGLARY
HG9466-9479	INSURANCE, BURIAL
HG9970.B85	INSURANCE, BUSINESS INTERRUPTION
HG8937	INSURANCE, BUSINESS LIFE / economics
K	INSURANCE, BUSINESS LIFE / law
HG9956	INSURANCE, CASUALTY — ADJUSTMENT OF CLAIMS
HG9956-9970	INSURANCE, CASUALTY
HG9271-7	INSURANCE, CHILD
HG9970.C6-89	*INSURANCE, CONSUMER CREDIT* **SEE** INSURANCE, CREDIT
HG9970.C6-89	INSURANCE, CREDIT
HG9968.C6-8	*INSURANCE, CROP* **SEE** INSURANCE, AGRICULTURAL — CROPS
HG1662	INSURANCE, DEPOSIT
HG9281-7	*INSURANCE, DOWRY* **SEE** INSURANCE, MARRIAGE ENDOWMENT
HG9970.E3	INSURANCE, EARTHQUAKE
HG9964.E4-7	INSURANCE, EMPLOYERS' LIABILITY
HG8886-8891	*INSURANCE, EMPLOYERS' LIABILITY-MEDICAL EXAMINATIONS* **SEE** INSURANCE, ACCIDENT — MEDICAL EXAMINATIONS
HG8818	*INSURANCE, ENDOWMENT* **SEE** INSURANCE, LIFE — ENDOWMENT POLICIES
HG9903	*INSURANCE, EXPORT* **SEE** INSURANCE, INLAND MARINE
HG9970.C6-89	*INSURANCE, EXPORT CREDIT* **SEE** INSURANCE, CREDIT
K	*INSURANCE, FIDELITY* **SEE** INSURANCE, SURETY AND FIDELITY / law
HG9970.S4-8	*INSURANCE, FIDELITY* **SEE** INSURANCE, SURETY AND FIDELITY / economics
HG9678-9	INSURANCE, FIRE — ACCOUNTING
HG9721-7	INSURANCE, FIRE — ADJUSTMENT OF CLAIMS
HG9706-9	INSURANCE, FIRE — AGENTS
HG9687	INSURANCE, FIRE — CLASSIFICATION OF RISKS
HG9665	INSURANCE, FIRE — DICTIONARIES
HG9674-9	INSURANCE, FIRE — FINANCE
HG9660	INSURANCE, FIRE — HISTORY
HG9711-9717	INSURANCE, FIRE — INSPECTORS
HG9771	INSURANCE, FIRE — MAPS AND SURVEYS
HG9651	INSURANCE, FIRE — PERIODICALS
HG9882	INSURANCE, FIRE — PLANS
HG9665	INSURANCE, FIRE — PLANS
HG9695-9	INSURANCE, FIRE — POLICIES
HG9685-9691	INSURANCE, FIRE — RATES AND TABLES
HG9731.A-Z	INSURANCE, FIRE — RISKS
HG9753	INSURANCE, FIRE — SOCIETIES, ETC. / by country
HG9653	INSURANCE, FIRE — SOCIETIES, ETC. / international
HG9739	INSURANCE, FIRE — STATE SUPERVISION
HG9663	INSURANCE, FIRE — STATISTICS
HG9735	INSURANCE, FIRE — TAXATION
HG9731.W3	INSURANCE, FIRE — WAR RISKS
HG9655	INSURANCE, FIRE — YEARBOOKS
HG9651-9899	INSURANCE, FIRE
HG9799	*INSURANCE, FIRE-OFFICE MARKS* **SEE** FIRE-MARKS / british insurance
HG9685-9691	*INSURANCE, FIRE-PREMIUMS* **SEE** INSURANCE, FIRE — RATES AND TABLES
HG9771	*INSURANCE, FIRE-SURVEYS* **SEE** INSURANCE, FIRE — MAPS AND SURVEYS
HG9970.F	INSURANCE, FOREST
HG8059.G6	INSURANCE, GOVERNMENT RISKS
HG8059.G7	INSURANCE, GROUP
HG8830	INSURANCE, GROUP / life
HG9970.S4-8	*INSURANCE, GUARANTY* **SEE** INSURANCE, SURETY AND FIDELITY / economics
K	*INSURANCE, GUARANTY* **SEE** INSURANCE, SURETY AND FIDELITY / law
HG9968.H2-5	INSURANCE, HAIL
HG8886-8891	INSURANCE, HEALTH — MEDICAL EXAMINATIONS
HG9389.R3	INSURANCE, HEALTH — RATES AND TABLES
HG9383-9399	INSURANCE, HEALTH
HD7101-2	INSURANCE, HEALTH / industrial
HG9964.E	*INSURANCE, INDEMNITY* **SEE** INSURANCE, LIABILITY / employers' liability
HG9257.A3	INSURANCE, INDUSTRIAL — ADJUSTMENT OF CLAIMS
HG9255	INSURANCE, INDUSTRIAL — AGENTS
HG9257.R3	INSURANCE, INDUSTRIAL — RATES AND TABLES
HG9251-9262	INSURANCE, INDUSTRIAL / finance
HD7090-7250	INSURANCE, INDUSTRIAL / labor
HG9271-7	*INSURANCE, INFANT* **SEE** INSURANCE, CHILD
HG9903	INSURANCE, INLAND MARINE
HG4538	INSURANCE, INVESTMENT GUARANTY
HG9970.L6	*INSURANCE, LEGAL COSTS* **SEE** INSURANCE, LITIGATION
HG9964.E	INSURANCE, LIABILITY / employers' liability
HG8848	INSURANCE, LIFE — ACCOUNTING
HG8876-8883	INSURANCE, LIFE — AGENTS
HG8755	INSURANCE, LIFE — CONGRESSES
HG8758	INSURANCE, LIFE — DIRECTORIES
HG8811.D6	INSURANCE, LIFE — DISABILITY BENEFITS
HG8818	INSURANCE, LIFE — ENDOWMENT POLICIES
HG8844-8850	INSURANCE, LIFE — FINANCE
HG8761	INSURANCE, LIFE — HISTORY
HG8781-8793	INSURANCE, LIFE — MATHEMATICS
HG8886-8891	INSURANCE, LIFE — MEDICAL EXAMINATIONS
HG8751	INSURANCE, LIFE — PERIODICALS
HG8816-8830	INSURANCE, LIFE — PLANS
HG8861-6	INSURANCE, LIFE — POLICIES
HG8851-3	INSURANCE, LIFE — RATES AND TABLES
HG8941	INSURANCE, LIFE — SOCIETIES, ETC. / by country
HG8754	INSURANCE, LIFE — SOCIETIES, ETC. / etc. international
HG8916-8919	INSURANCE, LIFE — STATE SUPERVISION

HG8766	INSURANCE, LIFE — STATISTICS
HG8910-8914	INSURANCE, LIFE — TAXATION
HG8817	INSURANCE, LIFE — TONTINE POLICIES
HG8811.W2	INSURANCE, LIFE — WAR RISKS
HG8756	INSURANCE, LIFE — YEARBOOKS
HG8751-9200	INSURANCE, LIFE
HG8851-3	*INSURANCE, LIFE-PREMIUMS* **SEE** INSURANCE, LIFE — RATES AND TABLES
HG9970.L6	INSURANCE, LITIGATION
HG9968.L5-8	*INSURANCE, LIVE STOCK* **SEE** INSURANCE, AGRICULTURAL — LIVE STOCK
HG9970.C6-89	*INSURANCE, LOAN* **SEE** INSURANCE, CREDIT
HG9963.M	INSURANCE, MACHINERY
HE967	INSURANCE, MARINE — ACCOUNTING
HE965-7	INSURANCE, MARINE — ADJUSTMENT OF CLAIMS
HE964	INSURANCE, MARINE — HISTORY
HE967	INSURANCE, MARINE — POLICIES
HE966	INSURANCE, MARINE — WAR RISKS
HE961-971	INSURANCE, MARINE
HG9281-7	INSURANCE, MARRIAGE ENDOWMENT
HG9291-5	INSURANCE, MATERNITY
UB370-375	*INSURANCE, MILITARY* **SEE** INSURANCE, WAR RISK
HG9970.M6	INSURANCE, MORTGAGE GUARANTY
HG8011-9970	*INSURANCE, MUTUAL* **SEE** INSURANCE
HG8937	*INSURANCE, PARTNERSHIP* **SEE** INSURANCE, BUSINESS LIFE / *economics*
K ·	*INSURANCE, PARTNERSHIP* **SEE** INSURANCE, BUSINESS LIFE / *law*
HG9963.P6	INSURANCE, PLATE-GLASS
HG8751-9200	*INSURANCE, POSTAL LIFE* **SEE** INSURANCE, LIFE
HG9970.B85	*INSURANCE, PROFITS* **SEE** INSURANCE, BUSINESS INTERRUPTION
HG9970.B8	*INSURANCE, ROBBERY* **SEE** INSURANCE, BURGLARY
HG1662	*INSURANCE, SAVINGS* **SEE** INSURANCE, DEPOSIT
VM299.5-7	INSURANCE, SHIP MORTGAGE
HG9383-9399	*INSURANCE, SICKNESS* **SEE** INSURANCE, HEALTH
HD7101-2	*INSURANCE, SICKNESS* **SEE** INSURANCE, HEALTH / *industrial*
HD7090-7250	INSURANCE, SOCIAL
HD7090-7250	*INSURANCE, STATE AND COMPULSORY* **SEE** INSURANCE, SOCIAL
HG9964.S6	INSURANCE, STRIKE
HG9970.S4-8	INSURANCE, SURETY AND FIDELITY / *economics*
K	INSURANCE, SURETY AND FIDELITY / *law*
HG9970.B8	*INSURANCE, THEFT* **SEE** INSURANCE, BURGLARY
HG9970.F	*INSURANCE, TIMBER* **SEE** INSURANCE, FOREST
HG9970.T4-68	INSURANCE, TITLE
HG9968.T5-7	INSURANCE, TORNADO
HG9970.A7	*INSURANCE, TRANSPORTATION* **SEE** INSURANCE, AVIATION
HG9903	*INSURANCE, TRANSPORTATION* **SEE** INSURANCE, INLAND MARINE
HE961-971	*INSURANCE, TRANSPORTATION* **SEE** INSURANCE, MARINE
HD7095-6	INSURANCE, UNEMPLOYMENT
HG9970.B85	*INSURANCE, USE AND OCCUPANCY* **SEE** INSURANCE, BUSINESS INTERRUPTION
HG8055	*INSURANCE, WAR* **SEE** INSURANCE — WAR RISKS
HG8811.W2	*INSURANCE, WAR* **SEE** INSURANCE, LIFE — WAR RISKS
HE966	*INSURANCE, WAR* **SEE** INSURANCE, MARINE — WAR RISKS
UB370-375	*INSURANCE, WAR* **SEE** INSURANCE, WAR RISK
UB370-375	INSURANCE, WAR RISK
HD7090-7250	*INSURANCE, WORKING-MEN'S* **SEE** INSURANCE, SOCIAL
HG8021	*INSURANCE-AGENTS-DIRECTORIES* **SEE** INSURANCE — DIRECTORIES
HG8065-7	*INSURANCE-PREMIUMS* **SEE** INSURANCE — RATES AND TABLES
HG8091-8102	*INSURANCE-SALESMANSHIP* **SEE** INSURANCE — AGENTS
HM281-3	*INSURRECTIONS* **SEE** REVOLUTIONS / *psychology of*
JC491	*INSURRECTIONS* **SEE** REVOLUTIONS / *theory*
E447	*INSURRECTIONS* **SEE** SLAVERY IN THE U.S. — INSURRECTIONS, ETC.
NK5730	INTAGLIOS
NK9920	*INTARSIA* **SEE** MARQUETRY
NK2710	*INTARSIA* **SEE** MARQUETRY / *inlaid furniture*

QA308-311	*INTEGRAL CALCULUS* **SEE** CALCULUS, INTEGRAL
QA431	INTEGRAL EQUATIONS
QA351	*INTEGRAL FUNCTIONS* **SEE** FUNCTIONS, ENTIRE
QA308-311	INTEGRALS
QA345	*INTEGRALS, ABELIAN* **SEE** FUNCTIONS, ABELIAN
QA311	INTEGRALS, DEFINITE
QA311	*INTEGRALS, DOUBLE* **SEE** INTEGRALS, MULTIPLE
QA343	*INTEGRALS, ELLIPTIC* **SEE** FUNCTIONS, ELLIPTIC
QA312	INTEGRALS, GENERALIZED
QA311	INTEGRALS, MULTIPLE
LB2350	*INTEGRATION IN EDUCATION* **SEE** ARTICULATION (EDUCATION)
LB3062	*INTEGRATION IN EDUCATION* **SEE** SEGREGATION IN EDUCATION
HT1501-1595	*INTEGRATION, RACIAL* **SEE** RACE PROBLEMS
QA75	INTEGRATORS
BJ1533.S3	*INTEGRITY* **SEE** SELF-RESPECT
BC	*INTELLECT* **SEE** LOGIC
BF	INTELLECT / *psychology*
AS4	INTELLECTUAL COOPERATION
JX1975	INTELLECTUAL COOPERATION / *league of nations*
JC362	INTELLECTUAL COOPERATION / *political theory*
BF435-7	*INTELLECTUAL INEFFICIENCY* **SEE** INEFFICIENCY, INTELLECTUAL
Z551-656	*INTELLECTUAL PROPERTY* **SEE** COPYRIGHT
T15-35	*INTELLECTUAL PROPERTY* **SEE** INVENTIONS / *history*
T201-339	*INTELLECTUAL PROPERTY* **SEE** INVENTIONS / *patents*
T201-339	*INTELLECTUAL PROPERTY* **SEE** PATENTS
HM213	INTELLECTUALS
BF	*INTELLIGENCE* **SEE** INTELLECT / *psychology*
LB1131	*INTELLIGENCE LEVELS-TESTING* **SEE** MENTAL TESTS
BF431	*INTELLIGENCE LEVELS-TESTING* **SEE** MENTAL TESTS / *psychology*
QL785	*INTELLIGENCE OF ANIMALS* **SEE** ANIMAL INTELLIGENCE
BF685	*INTELLIGENCE OF ANIMALS* **SEE** INSTINCT / *psychology*
QL781	*INTELLIGENCE OF ANIMALS* **SEE** INSTINCT / *zoology*
BF660-678	*INTELLIGENCE OF ANIMALS* **SEE** PSYCHOLOGY, COMPARATIVE
Q327	*INTELLIGENT MACHINES* **SEE** CONSCIOUS AUTOMATA
QA76	*INTELLIGENT MACHINES* **SEE** ELECTRONIC CALCULATING-MACHINES
BC137-8	*INTELLIGENT MACHINES* **SEE** LOGIC MACHINES
RC565	*INTEMPERANCE* **SEE** ALCOHOLISM / *disease*
HV5001-5720	*INTEMPERANCE* **SEE** ALCOHOLISM / *temperance*
HV5001-5720	*INTEMPERANCE* **SEE** LIQUOR PROBLEM
HV5001-5720	*INTEMPERANCE* **SEE** TEMPERANCE
JS4843.I6	INTENDANTS / *intendants de province*
BC199.I5	INTENTION (LOGIC)
LB2331.5	*INTER-COLLEGE COOPERATION* **SEE** UNIVERSITY COOPERATION
Z713	INTER-LIBRARY LOANS
HM291	*INTERACTION, SOCIAL* **SEE** SOCIAL INTERACTION
BP166.825	INTERCESSION (ISLAM)
Z672	*INTERCHANGE OF LIBRARIANS* **SEE** LIBRARIANS, INTERCHANGE OF / *international cooperation*
Z669.8	*INTERCHANGE OF LIBRARIANS* **SEE** LIBRARIANS, INTERCHANGE OF
LB2376	*INTERCHANGE OF STUDENTS* **SEE** STUDENTS, INTERCHANGE OF
LB2283-5	*INTERCHANGE OF TEACHERS* **SEE** TEACHERS, INTERCHANGE OF
TJ1180	INTERCHANGEABLE MECHANISMS
TJ233	INTERCHANGEABLE MECHANISMS
BV625	*INTERCHURCH COOPERATION* **SEE** INTERDENOMINATIONAL COOPERATION
HE751	INTERCOASTAL SHIPPING
BX9.5.I5	INTERCOMMUNION
TH6523	*INTERCONNECTION (PLUMBING)* **SEE** CROSS-CONNECTIONS (PLUMBING)
S603.5	*INTERCROPPING* **SEE** COMPANION CROPS
CB199	INTERCULTURAL EDUCATION
BV625	INTERDENOMINATIONAL COOPERATION
BX1939.I5	INTERDICT (CANON LAW)
BF321	INTEREST (PSYCHOLOGY)

HG1626-1638	INTEREST AND USURY — TABLES, ETC.
HG1621-3	INTEREST AND USURY / banking practice
HB521-539	INTEREST AND USURY / theory of interest
LB1027.5	INTEREST INVENTORIES
LB1027.5	INTEREST MEASURES SEE INTEREST INVENTORIES
QD506	INTERFACES, CHEMISTRY OF SEE SURFACE CHEMISTRY
QC411	INTERFERENCE (LIGHT)
QC233	INTERFERENCE (SOUND)
QC411	INTERFEROMETER
PM8398	INTERGLOSSA (ARTIFICIAL LANGUAGE)
NK2116	INTERIOR DECORATION AS A PROFESSION
NK1700-3505	INTERIOR DECORATION / art
TX311-317	INTERIOR DECORATION / home economics
TC601-791	INTERIOR NAVIGATION SEE INLAND NAVIGATION / engineering
HE617-720	INTERIOR NAVIGATION SEE INLAND NAVIGATION / transportation
TF635	INTERLOCKING SIGNALS SEE RAILROADS — SIGNALING — — INTERLOCKING SYSTEMS
PN1934	INTERLUDES / drama
HQ1026	INTERMARRIAGE SEE CONSANGUINITY / consanguineous marriages
HV4981	INTERMARRIAGE SEE CONSANGUINITY / degeneration
HB1113.R38	INTERMARRIAGE SEE CONSANGUINITY / statistics
HQ1031	INTERMARRIAGE SEE MARRIAGE, MIXED
GN237	INTERMARRIAGE SEE MISCEGENATION
E185.62	INTERMARRIAGE SEE MISCEGENATION / negroes in the u.s.
QL821	INTERMAXILLARY BONES / comparative anatomy
QM105	INTERMAXILLARY BONES / human anatomy
BP166.82	INTERMEDIATE STATE (ISLAM)
BT830	INTERMEDIATE STATE
GN486	INTERMENT SEE BURIAL / ethnology
GT3150-3390	INTERMENT SEE BURIAL / manners and customs
RA625	INTERMENT SEE BURIAL / public health
RC156-166	INTERMITTENT FEVER SEE MALARIAL FEVER
QM201.M2	INTERMITTENT FEVER SEE MALARIAL FEVER / bacteriology
TJ800	INTERNAL COMBUSTION ENGINES SEE ALCOHOL MOTORS
TJ751-805	INTERNAL COMBUSTION ENGINES SEE GAS AND OIL ENGINES
QC189	INTERNAL FRICTION (LIQUIDS) SEE VISCOSITY
QC191	INTERNAL FRICTION
HD3840-4420	INTERNAL IMPROVEMENT MOVEMENT SEE PUBLIC WORKS / economics
TA21-124	INTERNAL IMPROVEMENT MOVEMENT SEE PUBLIC WORKS / national
TD21-124	INTERNAL IMPROVEMENT MOVEMENT SEE PUBLIC WORKS / u.s. municipal
HB1951-2580	INTERNAL MIGRATION SEE MIGRATION, INTERNAL
HJ3251	INTERNAL REVENUE LAW / u.s.
HJ5315	INTERNAL REVENUE STAMPS SEE REVENUE-STAMPS
HJ5321-5515	INTERNAL REVENUE STAMPS SEE REVENUE-STAMPS / by country
HJ5001-5231	INTERNAL REVENUE
QD481	INTERNAL ROTATION (MOLECULAR) SEE MOLECULAR ROTATION
BR115.I7	INTERNATIONAL AFFAIRS AND CHRISTIANITY SEE CHRISTIANITY AND INTERNATIONAL AFFAIRS
JX4171.03	INTERNATIONAL AGREEMENTS SEE INTERNATIONAL OBLIGATIONS
JX4161-4171	INTERNATIONAL AGREEMENTS SEE TREATIES
JX1985-9	INTERNATIONAL AGREEMENTS SEE TREATIES / arbitration
JX351-1195	INTERNATIONAL AGREEMENTS SEE TREATIES / collections
JX120-191	INTERNATIONAL AGREEMENTS SEE TREATIES / collections
JX235-6	INTERNATIONAL AGREEMENTS SEE TREATIES / collections
HF1721-1733	INTERNATIONAL AGREEMENTS SEE TREATIES / commercial
HE6281	INTERNATIONAL AGREEMENTS SEE TREATIES / postal
TL726.15	INTERNATIONAL AIRPORTS
P227	INTERNATIONAL ALPHABET SEE PHONETIC ALPHABET / international
P226	INTERNATIONAL ALPHABET SEE TRANSLITERATION
JX1248	INTERNATIONAL AND MUNICIPAL LAW
JK-JQ	INTERNATIONAL AND MUNICIPAL LAW
Q115	INTERNATIONAL ANTARCTIC EXPEDITION, 1901-1903 / scientific results
JX1901-1991	INTERNATIONAL ARBITRATION SEE ARBITRATION, INTERNATIONAL
HG401-423	INTERNATIONAL BIMETALLISM SEE BIMETALLISM / international
HG651	INTERNATIONAL BIMETALLISM SEE BIMETALLISM / other countries
HG561-2	INTERNATIONAL BIMETALLISM SEE BIMETALLISM / u.s.
JX1995	INTERNATIONAL CIVIL SERVICE SEE INTERNATIONAL OFFICIALS AND EMPLOYEES
HG381-395	INTERNATIONAL COINAGE SEE COINAGE, INTERNATIONAL
JX1971	INTERNATIONAL COMMISSIONS OF INQUIRY SEE COMMISSIONS OF INQUIRY, INTERNATIONAL
JX4475	INTERNATIONAL CONCILIATION SEE MEDIATION, INTERNATIONAL
AS	INTERNATIONAL CONFERENCES, CONGRESSES AND CONVENTIONS SEE CONGRESSES AND CONVENTIONS
TX725	INTERNATIONAL COOKERY SEE COOKERY, INTERNATIONAL
LB2283-5	INTERNATIONAL COOPERATION IN EDUCATION SEE EDUCATIONAL EXCHANGES
JC362	INTERNATIONAL COOPERATION
JX1995	INTERNATIONAL COOPERATION / etc.
Z552	INTERNATIONAL COPYRIGHT SEE COPYRIGHT, INTERNATIONAL
LB3614	INTERNATIONAL CORRESPONDENCE / students
JX4081	INTERNATIONAL COURTESY SEE COMITY OF NATIONS
LB2283-5	INTERNATIONAL EDUCATIONAL EXCHANGES SEE EDUCATIONAL EXCHANGES
HG3811-4000	INTERNATIONAL EXCHANGE SEE FOREIGN EXCHANGE
Z669.8	INTERNATIONAL EXCHANGE OF LIBRARIANS SEE LIBRARIANS, INTERCHANGE OF
Z672	INTERNATIONAL EXCHANGE OF LIBRARIANS SEE LIBRARIANS, INTERCHANGE OF / international cooperation
LB2376	INTERNATIONAL EXCHANGE OF STUDENTS SEE STUDENTS, INTERCHANGE OF
LB2283-5	INTERNATIONAL EXCHANGE OF TEACHERS SEE TEACHERS, INTERCHANGE OF
Z690	INTERNATIONAL EXCHANGES, LITERARY AND SCIENTIFIC SEE EXCHANGES, LITERARY AND SCIENTIFIC
T391-999	INTERNATIONAL EXHIBITIONS SEE EXHIBITIONS
QC801.3	INTERNATIONAL GEOPHYSICAL YEAR, 1957-1958
JC362	INTERNATIONAL INSTITUTIONS SEE INTERNATIONAL COOPERATION
JX1995	INTERNATIONAL INSTITUTIONS SEE INTERNATIONAL COOPERATION / etc.
HD7791	INTERNATIONAL LABOR DAY SEE MAY DAY (LABOR HOLIDAY)
HD7801-9	INTERNATIONAL LABOR LAWS AND LEGISLATION SEE LABOR LAWS AND LEGISLATION, INTERNATIONAL
JX1677	INTERNATIONAL LANGUAGE SEE DIPLOMACY — LANGUAGE
PM8008	INTERNATIONAL LANGUAGE SEE LANGUAGE, UNIVERSAL
JX63-91	INTERNATIONAL LAW — CASES
JX1261-1283	INTERNATIONAL LAW — CODIFICATION
JX63-91	INTERNATIONAL LAW — SOURCES
JX1226	INTERNATIONAL LAW — TERMINOLOGY
GV999	INTERNATIONAL LAWN TENNIS CHAMPIONSHIP SEE DAVIS CUP
JX4475	INTERNATIONAL MEDIATION SEE MEDIATION, INTERNATIONAL
HG381-395	INTERNATIONAL MONEY SEE COINAGE, INTERNATIONAL
AM	INTERNATIONAL MUSEUMS
JX4171.03	INTERNATIONAL OBLIGATIONS
JX1995	INTERNATIONAL OFFICIALS AND EMPLOYEES

G670	INTERNATIONAL POLAR EXPEDITION, 1882-1883
JX1981.P7	INTERNATIONAL POLICE
JX4150	INTERNATIONAL RIVERS
JX1901-1995	*INTERNATIONAL SECURITY* **SEE** SECURITY, INTERNATIONAL
HG1997.16	*INTERNATIONAL SETTLEMENTS, BANK FOR* **SEE** BANK FOR INTERNATIONAL SETTLEMENTS
JX4068.I6	*INTERNATIONAL TERRITORIES* **SEE** INTERNATIONALIZED TERRITORIES
JX1974	*INTERNATIONAL TREATY FOR THE LIMITATION AND REDUCTION OF NAVAL ARMAMENT, LONDON, 1930* **SEE** LONDON NAVAL TREATY, 1930
JC361	INTERNATIONALISM
JX4068.I6	INTERNATIONALIZED TERRITORIES
RA972	INTERNS (MEDICINE)
JX1398-1403	*INTEROCEANIC CANALS* **SEE** CANALS, INTEROCEANIC / *diplomatic history*
HE528-545	*INTEROCEANIC CANALS* **SEE** CANALS, INTEROCEANIC / *economics*
TC601-791	*INTEROCEANIC CANALS* **SEE** CANALS, INTEROCEANIC / *technology*
TC771	*INTEROCEANIC SHIP-RAILROADS* **SEE** SHIP-RAILROADS
BF636	INTERPERSONAL RELATIONS
TL789-790	INTERPLANETARY VOYAGES
QA281	INTERPOLATION — TABLES, ETC.
QA281	INTERPOLATION
PA49	*INTERPRETATION* **SEE** HERMENEUTICS / *classics*
BD240-241	*INTERPRETATION* **SEE** HERMENEUTICS / *methodology*
BS500-534	*INTERPRETATION, BIBLICAL* **SEE** BIBLE — CRITICISM, INTERPRETATION, ETC.
PN4145	*INTERPRETATIVE READING* **SEE** ORAL INTERPRETATION
PN4145	*INTERPRETATIVE SPEECH* **SEE** ORAL INTERPRETATION
GV1783	*INTERPRETIVE DANCING* **SEE** MODERN DANCE
LB1027	*INTERROGATION* **SEE** QUESTIONING
TL694.I	*INTERROGATOR-TRANSPONDOR SYSTEMS* **SEE** AEROPLANES — IFF EQUIPMENT
TL696.D65	*INTERROGATOR-TRANSPONDOR SYSTEMS* **SEE** DISTANCE MEASURING EQUIPMENT (AIRCRAFT TO GROUND STATION)
RC883	*INTERSEXUALITY* **SEE** HERMAPHRODITISM
JK2441	INTERSTATE AGREEMENTS
HE2708	INTERSTATE COMMERCE / *commission reports*
HE2757	INTERSTATE COMMERCE / *discussion*
HE2710-2712	INTERSTATE COMMERCE / *law and cases*
HE1853	INTERSTATE COMMERCE / *rates*
HE1843	INTERSTATE COMMERCE / *rates*
JK2441	*INTERSTATE COMPACTS* **SEE** INTERSTATE AGREEMENTS
JK2441	*INTERSTATE COOPERATION* **SEE** INTERSTATE AGREEMENTS
QB500	INTERSTELLAR MATTER
TL789-790	*INTERSTELLAR VOYAGES* **SEE** INTERPLANETARY VOYAGES
TF701-1124	*INTERURBAN RAILROADS* **SEE** STREET-RAILROADS
HE4201-5300	*INTERURBAN RAILROADS* **SEE** STREET-RAILROADS / *economics*
HE4251	*INTERURBAN RAILROADS* **SEE** STREET-RAILROADS / *taxation*
ML3809	*INTERVALS (MUSIC)* **SEE** MUSICAL INTERVALS AND SCALES
JX4481	INTERVENTION (INTERNATIONAL LAW)
PN4784.I6	INTERVIEWING (JOURNALISM)
HV43	INTERVIEWING / *charities*
BF761-8	INTERVIEWING / *evidence*
HB715	*INTESTACY* **SEE** INHERITANCE AND SUCCESSION / *economics*
HB715	*INTESTATE SUCCESSION* **SEE** INHERITANCE AND SUCCESSION / *economics*
RM163	*INTESTINAL IRRIGATION* **SEE** ENEMA
QR171	INTESTINES — BACTERIOLOGY
RC860-862	INTESTINES — DISEASES
QR155-171	INTESTINES — MICRO-ORGANISMS
RD540-544	INTESTINES — SURGERY
RC312.5.T7	INTESTINES — TUBERCULOSIS
QL863	INTESTINES / *comparative anatomy*
QM345	INTESTINES / *human anatomy*
QP156	INTESTINES / *physiology*
RC803-5	INTESTINES — DISEASES — — DIAGNOSIS
QP921.C8	*INTOCOSTRIN* **SEE** CURARE / *pharmacology*
RM666.C94	*INTOCOSTRIN* **SEE** CURARE / *therapeutics*
BF575.F16	*INTOLERANCE* **SEE** FANATICISM / *psychology*
BR114	*INTOLERANCE* **SEE** FANATICISM / *religion*
BV741	*INTOLERANCE* **SEE** LIBERTY OF CONSCIENCE
BV741	*INTOLERANCE* **SEE** RELIGIOUS LIBERTY
BR1610	*INTOLERANCE* **SEE** TOLERATION
ML3082	*INTONARIUM* **SEE** TONARIUS
ML171-4	*INTONARIUM* **SEE** TONARIUS / *history*
QD305.A4	*INTOXICANTS* **SEE** ALCOHOL / *chemistry*
TP593	*INTOXICANTS* **SEE** ALCOHOL / *technology*
HD9391	*INTOXICANTS* **SEE** ALCOHOL / *trade*
TP589-618	*INTOXICANTS* **SEE** LIQUORS
RM332	*INTOXICANTS* **SEE** STIMULANTS / *therapeutics*
RC565	*INTOXICATION* **SEE** ALCOHOLISM / *disease*
HV5001-5720	*INTOXICATION* **SEE** ALCOHOLISM / *temperance*
HV5001-5720	*INTOXICATION* **SEE** LIQUOR PROBLEM
RC566	*INTOXICATION* **SEE** NARCOTIC HABIT
HV5800-5840	*INTOXICATION* **SEE** NARCOTIC HABIT / *economics*
HV5001-5720	*INTOXICATION* **SEE** TEMPERANCE
TC623.4-624	*INTRACOASTAL NAVIGATION* **SEE** INTRACOASTAL WATERWAYS / *u.s.*
TC623.4-624	INTRACOASTAL WATERWAYS / *u.s.*
RC693	INTRACRANIAL ANEURYSMS
QB607	*INTRAMERCURIAL PLANETS* **SEE** PLANETS, INTRAMERCURIAL
GV710	INTRAMURAL SPORTS
RM180	*INTRAPERITONEAL INJECTIONS* **SEE** INJECTIONS, INTRAPERITONEAL.
RD85.I	INTRATRACHEAL ANESTHESIA
RD85.I	INTRAVENOUS ANESTHESIA
UG380	INTRENCHING TOOLS
UG403	INTRENCHMENTS / *field fortification*
UG446	INTRENCHMENTS / *trenches and trench warfare*
BF175	INTROVERSION
BF311	INTUITION (PSYCHOLOGY)
QP445	*INTUITION OF DURATION* **SEE** TIME PERCEPTION
BD181	INTUITION
BD181	*INTUITIONALISM* **SEE** INTUITION
SB732	INTUMESCENCES (BOTANY) / *plant pathology*
E99.E7	*INUIT* **SEE** ESKIMOS
QK896	INULASE / *plant physiology*
QD321	INULIN
TC404-535	*INUNDATIONS* **SEE** FLOODS / *engineering*
SD425	*INUNDATIONS* **SEE** FLOODS / *floods and forests*
GB1201-1397	*INUNDATIONS* **SEE** FLOODS / *physical geography*
HV610	*INUNDATIONS* **SEE** FLOODS / *relief work*
RM219	*INVALID COOKERY* **SEE** COOKERY FOR THE SICK
GV1231	*INVALID SEAMEN-OCCUPATIONS* **SEE** INVALIDS — RECREATION
GV1231	*INVALID SOLDIERS-OCCUPATIONS* **SEE** INVALIDS — RECREATION
GV1231	INVALIDS — RECREATION
QA431	INVARIANT IMBEDDING
QA201	INVARIANTS
QA244	INVARIANTS / *theory of numbers*
QA381	*INVARIANTS, DIFFERENTIAL* **SEE** DIFFERENTIAL INVARIANTS
DG500-514	*INVASIONS OF ROME, BARBARIAN* **SEE** BARBARIAN INVASIONS OF ROME
PR1111.I65	INVECTIVE / *english literature*
PN45	*INVENTION (RHETORIC)* **SEE** ORIGINALITY (IN LITERATURE)
T15-35	INVENTIONS / *history*
T201-339	INVENTIONS / *patents*
HF5681.S8	INVENTORIES
T39-40	INVENTORS
E185.8	*INVENTORS, NEGRO* **SEE** NEGRO INVENTORS
HF5495	*INVENTORY CONTROL* **SEE** STORES OR STOCK-ROOM KEEPING
TS160	*INVENTORY CONTROL* **SEE** STORES OR STOCK-ROOM KEEPING / *factory*
DA89	INVERGORDON MUTINY, 1931
QA473	*INVERSION GEOMETRY* **SEE** INVERSIONS (GEOMETRY)
QD321	*INVERSION OF SUGAR* **SEE** SUGAR — INVERSION / *chemistry*

QP535.F4	IRON IN THE BODY
HF5716.I8	IRON INDUSTRY AND TRADE — TABLES AND READY-RECKONERS
HD9510-9529	IRON INDUSTRY AND TRADE
TN295	IRON MINES AND MINING — SAFETY MEASURES
TN400-409	IRON MINES AND MINING / mining
HD4966.F8	IRON MOLDERS / founders' wages
HD6350.I7	IRON MOLDERS / trade-union periodicals
QD133	IRON ORES — ANALYSIS
TN400-409	IRON ORES
QD181.F4	IRON OXIDES
TH2457	IRON ROOFING SEE ROOFING, IRON AND STEEL
QD181.F4	IRON SALTS
QD181.F4	IRON SULPHATE SEE FERROUS SULPHATE
TA479.A4	IRON-ALUMINUM ALLOYS
V799-800	IRON-CLAD VESSELS SEE ARMORED VESSELS
TS229-240	IRON-FOUNDING
TN757.N	IRON-NICKEL ALLOYS / metallurgy
TA479.N	IRON-NICKEL ALLOYS / testing
TA479.S5	IRON-SILICON ALLOYS
TS300-360	IRON-WORKS
QD181.F4	IRON / chemistry
TA464-479	IRON / etc.
TS300-445	IRON / manufactures
TN693.I7	IRON / metallography
TS660	IRON, GALVANIZED
TN707	IRON, HYDROGEN IN SEE IRON — HYDROGEN CONTENT
RM666.I8	IRON, PHOSPHORIC SALTS OF
TA685	IRON, STRUCTURAL — TABLES, CALCULATIONS, ETC.
TA684-5	IRON, STRUCTURAL / engineering
TS350	IRON, STRUCTURAL / manufacture
TA469-470	IRON, WROUGHT SEE WROUGHT-IRON / etc.
TS300-360	IRON, WROUGHT SEE WROUGHT-IRON / manufacture
TN693.I7	IRON, WROUGHT SEE WROUGHT-IRON / metallography
TN720-725	IRON, WROUGHT SEE WROUGHT-IRON / metallurgy
TA684-5	IRON, WROUGHT SEE WROUGHT-IRON / structural engineering
V799-800	IRONCLADS SEE ARMORED VESSELS
TT980-999	IRONING SEE LAUNDRY
TA890-891	IRONWORK / engineering construction
TT215-240	IRONWORK / mechanic trades
NK8200-8299	IRONWORK / ornamental ironwork
BH301.I7	IRONY / aesthetics
PN1680	IRONY / drama
E99.I69	IROQUOIAN INDIANS
PM1381-4	IROQUOIAN LANGUAGES
E99.I7	IROQUOIS INDIANS
PM1381-4	IROQUOIS LANGUAGE
QA247.5	IRRATIONAL NUMBERS SEE NUMBERS, IRRATIONAL
SB112	IRRIGATION AGRICULTURE SEE IRRIGATION FARMING
TC930-933	IRRIGATION CANALS AND FLUMES
SB112	IRRIGATION FARMING
HD1741	IRRIGATION LAWS / other countries
HD1727-9	IRRIGATION LAWS / u.s.
S613-615	IRRIGATION / agriculture
HD1711-1741	IRRIGATION / economic history
TC801-937	IRRIGATION / irrigation engineering
TD760	IRRIGATION, SEWAGE SEE SEWAGE IRRIGATION
QH647	IRRITABILITY / cells
PL5571	ISAMURANG LANGUAGE SEE BATAN LANGUAGE
SB287.W8	ISATIS TINCTORIA SEE WOAD
F3430.1.I	ISCAYCINCA INDIANS
DT313	ISEKSAWAN SEE SEKSAWA (BERBER TRIBE)
PK6996.I7	ISHKASHMI DIALECT
PL8321-4	ISI-XOSA SEE KAFIR LANGUAGE (BANTU)
PL5801	ISINAI DIALECT
TS2301.I8	ISINGLASS
F1799.I8	ISLA DE PINOS, BATTLE OF, 1596
BP170	ISLAM — APOLOGETIC WORKS
BP163	ISLAM — APPRECIATION
BP70-80	ISLAM — BIOGRAPHY
BP169	ISLAM — CONTROVERSIAL LITERATURE
BP160	ISLAM — EARLY WORKS TO 1800
LC901-915	ISLAM — EDUCATION
BP185	ISLAM — FUNCTIONARIES
BP49	ISLAM — HISTORIOGRAPHY

BP170.3	ISLAM — MISSIONS
BP55	ISLAM — ORIGIN
BP183.3	ISLAM — PRAYER-BOOKS AND DEVOTIONS
BP171	ISLAM — RELATIONS
BP163	ISLAM — 20TH CENTURY
BP173.75	ISLAM AND ECONOMICS
BP166.72	ISLAM AND MEDICINE SEE MEDICINE AND ISLAM
BP173.7	ISLAM AND POLITICS
BP190.5.S	ISLAM AND SCIENCE
HN40.I	ISLAM AND SOCIAL PROBLEMS
HX550.I8	ISLAM AND SOCIALISM SEE SOCIALISM AND ISLAM
BP173.6	ISLAM AND STATE
BP185	ISLAM-CLERGY SEE ISLAM — FUNCTIONARIES
BP176	ISLAM-FIVE PILLARS SEE PILLARS OF ISLAM
BP183.5	ISLAM-HYMNS SEE ISLAMIC HYMNS
HQ525.M6	ISLAM-MARRIAGE SEE MARRIAGE — ISLAM
BP176	ISLAM-PILLARS SEE PILLARS OF ISLAM
BP166.89	ISLAMIC ANGELOLOGY SEE ANGELS (ISLAM)
BP170	ISLAMIC APOLOGETICS SEE ISLAM — APOLOGETIC WORKS
NA380-388	ISLAMIC ARCHITECTURE SEE ARCHITECTURE, ISLAMIC
N6260-6271	ISLAMIC ART SEE ART, ISLAMIC
NK720-725	ISLAMIC ART INDUSTRIES AND TRADE SEE ART INDUSTRIES AND TRADE, ISLAMIC
NK6473	ISLAMIC ART METAL-WORK SEE ART METAL-WORK, ISLAMIC
BP70-80	ISLAMIC BIOGRAPHY SEE ISLAM — BIOGRAPHY
CE59	ISLAMIC CALENDAR SEE CALENDAR, ISLAMIC
D199.3	ISLAMIC CIVILIZATION SEE CIVILIZATION, ISLAMIC
DS427	ISLAMIC CIVILIZATION SEE CIVILIZATION, ISLAMIC / india
BP170.5	ISLAMIC CONVERTS SEE MUSLIM CONVERTS
BV2626.3-4	ISLAMIC CONVERTS TO CHRISTIANITY SEE CONVERTS FROM ISLAM
B745.C6	ISLAMIC COSMOLOGY SEE COSMOLOGY, ISLAMIC
DS36-40	ISLAMIC COUNTRIES
NK1270-1275	ISLAMIC DECORATION AND ORNAMENT SEE DECORATION AND ORNAMENT, ISLAMIC
BP166.89	ISLAMIC DEMONOLOGY SEE DEMONOLOGY, ISLAMIC
BP188.2	ISLAMIC DEVOTIONAL LITERATURE
LC901-915	ISLAMIC EDUCATION SEE ISLAM — EDUCATION
BP166.8	ISLAMIC ESCHATOLOGY SEE ESCHATOLOGY, ISLAMIC
BJ1291	ISLAMIC ETHICS — EARLY WORKS TO 1800
BJ1291	ISLAMIC ETHICS — QUOTATIONS, MAXIMS, ETC.
BJ1291	ISLAMIC ETHICS
BP186	ISLAMIC FASTS AND FEASTS SEE FASTS AND FEASTS — ISLAM
BP167.5	ISLAMIC HERESIES AND HERETICS SEE HERESIES AND HERETICS, ISLAMIC
BP182	ISLAMIC HOLY WAR SEE JIHAD
BP184.25	ISLAMIC HOMILETICS SEE PREACHING, ISLAMIC
BP183.5	ISLAMIC HYMNS
ND2955	ISLAMIC ILLUMINATION OF BOOKS AND MANUSCRIPTS SEE ILLUMINATION OF BOOKS AND MANUSCRIPTS, ISLAMIC
CN1153	ISLAMIC INSCRIPTIONS SEE INSCRIPTIONS, ISLAMIC
BP137-7.5	ISLAMIC LEGENDS SEE LEGENDS, ISLAMIC
BP87-89	ISLAMIC LITERATURE
BP170.3	ISLAMIC MISSIONS SEE ISLAM — MISSIONS
BP189.2-7	ISLAMIC MONASTICISM AND RELIGIOUS ORDERS SEE MONASTICISM AND RELIGIOUS ORDERS, ISLAMIC
BP189	ISLAMIC MYSTICISM SEE MYSTICISM — ISLAM
ND198	ISLAMIC PAINTING SEE PAINTING, ISLAMIC
ND198	ISLAMIC PAINTINGS SEE PAINTINGS, ISLAMIC
BP184	ISLAMIC PASTORAL THEOLOGY SEE PASTORAL THEOLOGY (ISLAM)
B163	ISLAMIC PHILOSOPHY SEE PHILOSOPHY, ISLAMIC
B740-753	ISLAMIC PHILOSOPHY SEE PHILOSOPHY, ISLAMIC / medieval
NK3880	ISLAMIC POTTERY SEE POTTERY, ISLAMIC
BP183.3	ISLAMIC PRAYERS
BP184.25	ISLAMIC PREACHING SEE PREACHING, ISLAMIC
HJ233	ISLAMIC PUBLIC FINANCE SEE FINANCE, PUBLIC — ISLAMIC COUNTRIES
BP42-48	ISLAMIC RELIGIOUS EDUCATION SEE RELIGIOUS EDUCATION, ISLAMIC
BP185	ISLAMIC RELIGIOUS FUNCTIONARIES SEE ISLAM — FUNCTIONARIES

BP174	ISLAMIC RELIGIOUS PRACTICE
BP189.3-5	*ISLAMIC SAINTS* SEE SAINTS, MUSLIM
BP191-223	ISLAMIC SECTS
BP183.6	ISLAMIC SERMONS
BP183.6	ISLAMIC SERMONS, ARABIC, (INDONESIAN, TURKISH, ETC.)
HN40.M6	*ISLAMIC SOCIOLOGY* SEE SOCIOLOGY, ISLAMIC
BP166.7	*ISLAMIC THEOLOGICAL ANTHROPOLOGY* SEE MAN (ISLAM)
BP166	ISLAMIC THEOLOGY
HQ1170	*ISLAMIC WOMEN* SEE WOMEN, MUSLIM
BP172	ISLAM — RELATIONS — — CHRISTIANITY
BP172.5.C6	ISLAM — RELATIONS — — COPTIC CHURCH
QL866	*ISLANDS OF LANGERHANS* SEE PANCREAS / comparative anatomy
QM353	*ISLANDS OF LANGERHANS* SEE PANCREAS / human anatomy
GB471-8	ISLANDS
GR675	ISLANDS / folk-lore
G555	ISLANDS / lost islands
G100	*ISLANDS, IMAGINARY* SEE GEOGRAPHICAL MYTHS
GR650-690	*ISLANDS, IMAGINARY* SEE GEOGRAPHICAL MYTHS / folk-lore
E99.I8	ISLETA INDIANS
PM1387	ISLETA LANGUAGE
DR555.7	ISMAIL, RUSSIA — SIEGE, 1790
BP195.I8	*ISMAILI* SEE ISMAILITES
PJ891.I55	ISMAILI LITERATURE
BP195.I8	*ISMAILIANS* SEE ISMAILITES
BP195.I8	ISMAILITES
DS666.I7	ISNEG
QR185	*ISOAGGLUTINATION* SEE BLOOD — AGGLUTINATION / immunology
QP91	*ISOAGGLUTINATION* SEE BLOOD — AGGLUTINATION / physiology
QC885-896	*ISOBARS* SEE ATMOSPHERIC PRESSURE
GN71	*ISOCEPHALY (CRANIOLOGY)* SEE BRACHYCEPHALY
GN131	*ISOCEPHALY (CRANIOLOGY)* SEE BRACHYCEPHALY
TR453	*ISOCHROMATIC PHOTOGRAPHY* SEE PHOTOGRAPHY, ORTHOCHROMATIC
QC811-849	*ISOGONIC LINES* SEE MAGNETISM, TERRESTRIAL
QR185	*ISOHEMAGGLUTINATION* SEE BLOOD — AGGLUTINATION / immunology
QP91	*ISOHEMAGGLUTINATION* SEE BLOOD — AGGLUTINATION / physiology
QD471	ISOMERISM
QA505	*ISOMETRIC DRAWING* SEE ISOMETRIC PROJECTION / mathematics
T365	*ISOMETRIC DRAWING* SEE ISOMETRIC PROJECTION / mechanical drawing
QA505	ISOMETRIC PROJECTION / mathematics
T365	ISOMETRIC PROJECTION / mechanical drawing
D569.I7	ISONZO, BATTLES OF THE, 1915-1917
QA315-316	*ISOPERIMETRICAL PROBLEMS* SEE CALCULUS OF VARIATIONS
QL444.I8	ISOPODA
QL513.T3	*ISOPTERA* SEE TERMITES
QL638.I	ISOSPONDYLI
QB283	ISOSTASY
QE511	ISOSTASY / geology
QB331	ISOSTASY / gravity
QA649	*ISOTHERMIC SURFACES* SEE SURFACES, ISOTHERMIC
QC901-6	*ISOTHERMS* SEE ATMOSPHERIC TEMPERATURE
QD466	*ISOTOPE ENRICHMENT* SEE ISOTOPE SEPARATION
TK9350	*ISOTOPE ENRICHMENT* SEE ISOTOPE SEPARATION / engineering
QD466	ISOTOPE SEPARATION
TK9350	ISOTOPE SEPARATION / engineering
TP202	ISOTOPES — CATALOGS
QD466	ISOTOPES
QD466.5.C1	*ISOTOPIC CARBON* SEE CARBON — ISOTOPES
TP245.U7	*ISOTOPIC URANIUM* SEE URANIUM — ISOTOPES / chemical technology
QD464.5.U	*ISOTOPIC URANIUM* SEE URANIUM — ISOTOPES / chemistry
PM8999	ISOTYPE (PICTURE LANGUAGE)
DS126.9-99	ISRAEL-ARAB WAR, 1948-1949
BM613	*ISRAEL, ELECTION OF* SEE JEWS — ELECTION, DOCTRINE OF

D164	ISTANBUL — SIEGE, 1203-1204
DF645-9	ISTANBUL — SIEGE, 1453
PQ4217-4219	ITALIAN BALLADS AND SONGS / collections
PQ4119-4123	ITALIAN BALLADS AND SONGS / history
PQ4137-9	ITALIAN DRAMA — EARLY TO 1700
PQ4141	ITALIAN DRAMA — 18TH CENTURY
PQ4143	ITALIAN DRAMA — 19TH CENTURY
PQ4145	ITALIAN DRAMA — 20TH CENTURY
PQ4149	ITALIAN DRAMA (COMEDY)
PQ4147	ITALIAN DRAMA (TRAGEDY)
PQ4227-4245	ITALIAN DRAMA / collections
PQ4133-4160	ITALIAN DRAMA / history
PQ4260	ITALIAN ESSAYS / collections
PQ4183.E8	ITALIAN ESSAYS / history
PQ4236-8	ITALIAN FARCES / collections
PQ4155-9	ITALIAN FARCES / history
PQ4171	ITALIAN FICTION — EARLY TO 1400
PQ4171-2	ITALIAN FICTION — 15TH CENTURY
PQ4172	ITALIAN FICTION —·16TH CENTURY
PQ4172	ITALIAN FICTION — 17TH CENTURY
PQ4173	ITALIAN FICTION — 18TH CENTURY
PQ4173	ITALIAN FICTION — 19TH CENTURY
PQ4174	ITALIAN FICTION — 20TH CENTURY
PQ4251-7	ITALIAN FICTION / collections
PQ4169-4181	ITALIAN FICTION / history
PC1715	ITALIAN LANGUAGE — EARLY TO 1300
PC1001-1977	ITALIAN LANGUAGE
PQ4259	ITALIAN LETTERS / collections
PQ4183.L4	ITALIAN LETTERS / history
Z2341-2369	ITALIAN LITERATURE — BIBLIOGRAPHY
Z2350-2354	ITALIAN LITERATURE — BIO-BIBLIOGRAPHY
PQ4064-4073	ITALIAN LITERATURE — EARLY TO 1400
PQ4075	ITALIAN LITERATURE — 15TH CENTURY
PQ4079-4080	ITALIAN LITERATURE — 16TH CENTURY
PQ4081-2	ITALIAN LITERATURE — 17TH CENTURY
PQ4083-4	ITALIAN LITERATURE — 18TH CENTURY
PQ4085-6	ITALIAN LITERATURE — 19TH CENTURY
PQ4087	ITALIAN LITERATURE — 20TH CENTURY
PQ4201-4263	ITALIAN LITERATURE / collections
PQ4001-4199	ITALIAN LITERATURE / history
Z2342	ITALIAN LITERATURE — BIBLIOGRAPHY — — EARLY
Z2352	ITALIAN LITERATURE — BIBLIOGRAPHY — — EARLY
PN5241-9	ITALIAN NEWSPAPERS / history
TS2157	*ITALIAN PASTE* SEE MACARONI / manufacture
PN5241-5250	ITALIAN PERIODICALS / history
PC1001-1977	ITALIAN PHILOLOGY
PQ4094-9	ITALIAN POETRY — EARLY TO 1400
PQ4101	ITALIAN POETRY — 15TH CENTURY
PQ4103	ITALIAN POETRY — 16TH CENTURY
PQ4105	ITALIAN POETRY — 17TH CENTURY
PQ4107	ITALIAN POETRY — 18TH CENTURY
PQ4109	ITALIAN POETRY — 19TH CENTURY
PQ4113	ITALIAN POETRY — 20TH CENTURY
PQ4207-4225	ITALIAN POETRY / collections
PQ4091-4131	ITALIAN POETRY / history
PQ4247-4263	ITALIAN PROSE LITERATURE / collections
PQ4161-4185	ITALIAN PROSE LITERATURE / history
DG497-8	ITALIAN QUESTION, 1848-1870
DG552-4	ITALIAN QUESTION, 1848-1870
PN6203-5	ITALIAN WIT AND HUMOR
PN1885.I	ITALIAN-AMERICAN NEWSPAPERS / history
PN1885.I	ITALIAN-AMERICAN PERIODICALS / history
PA2420-2550	ITALIC LANGUAGES AND DIALECTS
Z43	*ITALIC WRITING* SEE WRITING, ITALIC
DT387.3	ITALO-ETHIOPIAN WAR, 1895-1896
DT387.8	ITALO-ETHIOPIAN WAR, 1935-1936
DT234	*ITALO-TURKISH WAR, 1911-1912* SEE TURCO-ITALIAN WAR, 1911-1912 / tripoli
DR586	*ITALO-TURKISH WAR, 1911-1912* SEE TURCO-ITALIAN WAR, 1911-1912 / turkey
DG	ITALY — HISTORY
PN56.I	ITALY IN LITERATURE
PR129.I8	ITALY IN LITERATURE / english literature
DG558	*ITALY-HISTORY-AUSTRO-ITALIAN WAR, 1866* SEE AUSTRO-ITALIAN WAR, 1866
DT387.3	*ITALY-HISTORY-WAR WITH ETHIOPIA, 1895-1896* SEE ITALO-ETHIOPIAN WAR, 1895-1896
DT387.8	*ITALY-HISTORY-WAR WITH ETHIOPIA, 1935-1936* SEE ITALO-ETHIOPIAN WAR, 1935-1936

DT234	*ITALY-HISTORY-WAR WITH TURKEY, 1911-1912* **SEE** TURCO-ITALIAN WAR, 1911-1912 / *tripoli*
PL5571	*ITBAYAT LANGUAGE* **SEE** BATAN LANGUAGE
RC182.S17	*ITCH (DISEASE)* **SEE** SCABIES
PM70	*ITELMES LANGUAGE* **SEE** KAMCHADAL LANGUAGE
PL8726	*ITESO LANGUAGE* **SEE** TESO LANGUAGE
BX8345	ITINERANCY (CHURCH POLITY) — METHODIST CHURCH
BV664	ITINERANCY (CHURCH POLITY)
BV664	*ITINERANT CLERGY* **SEE** ITINERANCY (CHURCH POLITY)
PL8725	*ITIO LANGUAGE* **SEE** TEKE LANGUAGE
PM6241	ITONAMA LANGUAGE
F2726	ITUZAINGO, BATTLE OF, 1827
E474.42	IUKA, MISS., BATTLE OF, 1862
PL5571	*IVATAN LANGUAGE* **SEE** BATAN LANGUAGE
NK5815	IVORIES — PRIVATE COLLECTIONS
NK5800-5998	IVORIES / *art industries*
TS1050	IVORIES / *manufacture*
NK5800-5998	IVORY CARVING
SB317.I	IVORY-NUT / *vegetable ivory*
HD9999.I7	IVORY / *trade*
TT345	*IVORY-STAINING* **SEE** STAINS AND STAINING / *wood-staining*
D767.99.I9	IWO JIMA, BATTLE OF, 1945
PM3881	IXIL LANGUAGE
QL458.A2	*IXODIDAE* **SEE** TICKS
PL8276	*IYO LANGUAGE* **SEE** IJO LANGUAGE
PL6251	*JABEM LANGUAGE* **SEE** JABIM LANGUAGE
PL6251	JABIM LANGUAGE
DT630.5.J3	JABO (AFRICAN PEOPLE)
PL8287	JABO LANGUAGE
RS165.J2	JABORANDI / *pharmacy*
RM666.J15	JABORANDI / *therapeutics*
F1465.2.J3	JACALTECA INDIANS / *guatemala*
F1221.J3	JACALTECA INDIANS / *mexico*
PM3889	JACALTECA LANGUAGE
DA257	*JACK CADE'S REBELLION* **SEE** CADE'S REBELLION, 1450
SD397.P575	JACK-PINE
QL737.R6	JACK-RABBITS
QL737.C2	JACKALS
TT595-600	*JACKETS* **SEE** COATS
TT530-535	*JACKETS* **SEE** COATS
TJ1425-1435	*JACKS* **SEE** LIFTING-JACKS
TJ1435	*JACKS, HYDRAULIC* **SEE** HYDRAULIC JACKS
E184.J	JACKSON WHITES
GV1511.J3	JACKSTRAWS (GAME)
NK1443	*JACOBEAN DECORATION AND ORNAMENT* **SEE** DECORATION AND ORNAMENT, JACOBEAN
QA404.5	*JACOBI POLYNOMIALS* **SEE** FUNCTIONS, ORTHOGONAL
BX3501-3555	*JACOBINS (DOMINICANS)* **SEE** DOMINICANS
BX4341-4	*JACOBINS (DOMINICANS)* **SEE** DOMINICANS / *women*
DC178	JACOBINS
PR8661.J3	*JACOBITE BALLADS AND SONGS* **SEE** JACOBITES — POETRY / *scottish poetry*
PR1195.H5	*JACOBITE BALLADS AND SONGS* **SEE** JACOBITES — POETRY / *english poetry*
DA814.2	JACOBITE EXPEDITION, 1707
DA814.3	JACOBITE REBELLION, 1715
DA814.4	JACOBITE REBELLION, 1719
DA814.5	JACOBITE REBELLION, 1745-1746
PR1195.H5	JACOBITES — POETRY / *english poetry*
PR8661.J3	JACOBITES — POETRY / *scottish poetry*
DA813-814	JACOBITES
QL947	JACOBSON'S ORGAN
TS1500	JACQUARD WEAVING
DC99.3	JACQUERIE, 1358
NK5750	JADE / *art industries*
QE391.J2	JADE / *mineralogy*
DS126	JAFFA RIOT, 1921
PM7266	*JAGANE LANGUAGE* **SEE** YAHGAN LANGUAGE
PL55.J3	JAGATAIC LANGUAGE
PL8110.C3	*JAGGA LANGUAGE* **SEE** CHAGA LANGUAGE
GN659.W2	*JAGGAS* **SEE** WACHAGA / *ethnology*
DT449.K4	*JAGGAS* **SEE** WACHAGA / *kilimanjaro region*
TL215.J	JAGUAR AUTOMOBILE
QL737.C2	JAGUARS
BP182	*JAHAD* **SEE** JIHAD
GV1017.P4	*JAI ALAI* **SEE** PELOTA (GAME)
RC199	*JAIL-FEVER* **SEE** TYPHUS FEVER
QR201.T95	*JAIL-FEVER* **SEE** TYPHUS FEVER / *bacteriology*
HV8301-9920	*JAILS* **SEE** PRISONS
BJ1290	JAINA ETHICS
BL1305-1365	JAINA LITERATURE
B162.5	JAINA LOGIC
BC25-26	JAINA LOGIC / *ancient*
B162.5	*JAINA PHILOSOPHY* **SEE** PHILOSOPHY, JAINA
BL1300-1365	*JAINAS* **SEE** JAINS
BL1300-1365	JAINISM
BL1300-1365	JAINS
PL361-4	*JAKUT LANGUAGE* **SEE** YAKUT LANGUAGE
RS165.J	JALAP / *pharmacy*
RM666.J	JALAP / *therapeutics*
RS165.J	*JALAPIN* **SEE** JALAP / *pharmacy*
RM666.J	*JALAPIN* **SEE** JALAP / *therapeutics*
PL8785	*JALOOF LANGUAGE* **SEE** WOLOF LANGUAGE
TX612.J3	JAM
F1861-1895	JAMAICA — HISTORY
DT929	JAMESON'S RAID, 1895-1896
RS165.D2	*JAMESTOWN WEED* **SEE** DATURA / *pharmacy*
RM666.D3	*JAMESTOWN WEED* **SEE** DATURA / *therapeutics*
TK6553	*JAMMING (RADIO)* **SEE** RADIO — INTERFERENCE
F2520.1.U3	*JAMUNDA INDIANS* **SEE** UABOI INDIANS
PL4001.T4	*JANGSTEN LANGUAGE* **SEE** THADO LANGUAGE
DR46.8	JANINA — SIEGE, 1912-1913
UA816	*JANISSARIES* **SEE** JANIZARIES / *turkish army*
DR448	*JANISSARIES* **SEE** JANIZARIES / *turkish history*
TX339	JANITORS
UA816	JANIZARIES / *turkish army*
DR448	JANIZARIES / *turkish history*
D267.J	JANKAU, BATTLE OF, 1645
BX4720-4735	JANSENISTS
BX7990.J3	JANSONISTS
DS801-897	JAPAN — HISTORY
GC296.K85	*JAPAN CURRENT* **SEE** KUROSHIO
DS809	*JAPAN EXPEDITION OF THE AMERICAN SQUADRON, 1852-1854* **SEE** UNITED STATES NAVAL EXPEDITION TO JAPAN, 1852-1854
TP937.7	JAPAN GOLD-SIZE
DS765-7	*JAPAN-HISTORY-WAR WITH CHINA, 1894-1895* **SEE** CHINESE-JAPANESE WAR, 1894-1895
U735	*JAPAN-HISTORY-WAR WITH RUSSIA, 1904-1905* **SEE** RUSSO-JAPANESE WAR, 1904-1905 / *military observations*
V713	*JAPAN-HISTORY-WAR WITH RUSSIA, 1904-1905* **SEE** RUSSO-JAPANESE WAR, 1904-1905 / *naval observations*
DS516-517	*JAPAN-HISTORY-WAR WITH RUSSIA, 1904-1905* **SEE** RUSSO-JAPANESE WAR, 1904-1905
JX1393	*JAPAN-HISTORY-WAR WITH RUSSIA, 1904-1905* **SEE** RUSSO-JAPANESE WAR, 1904-1905 / *diplomatic history*
QL596.S3	JAPANESE BEETLE
SB945.J3	JAPANESE BEETLE / *insect pests*
SB435	*JAPANESE CHERRY* **SEE** JAPANESE FLOWERING CHERRY
GV1458.C5	*JAPANESE CHESS* **SEE** CHINESE CHESS
PL887-8	JAPANESE DRAMA / *collections in european languages*
PL871	JAPANESE DRAMA / *history in european languages*
PL734-5	JAPANESE DRAMA / *japanese*
PL771-7	JAPANESE DRAMA / *japanese*
PL890	JAPANESE FICTION / *collections in european languages*
PL873	JAPANESE FICTION / *history in european languages*
PL781-2	JAPANESE FICTION / *japanese*
PL736-740	JAPANESE FICTION / *japanese*
SB435	JAPANESE FLOWERING CHERRY
PL501-700	JAPANESE LANGUAGE
PR9900.J	JAPANESE LITERATURE (ENGLISH)
PL701-898	JAPANESE LITERATURE
PN5401-9	JAPANESE NEWSPAPERS
TT870	*JAPANESE PAPER FOLDING* **SEE** ORIGAMI
PN5401-5410	JAPANESE PERIODICALS
PL501-699	JAPANESE PHILOLOGY
PL884-6	JAPANESE POETRY / *collections in european languages*
PL867-870	JAPANESE POETRY / *history in european languages*
PL717-720	JAPANESE POETRY / *japanese*

PL756-770	JAPANESE POETRY / *japanese*
GV1011	*JAPANESE POLO* **SEE** POLO, JAPANESE
RC186.T83	*JAPANESE RIVER FEVER* **SEE** TSUTSUGAMUSHI DISEASE
GT2910	JAPANESE TEA CEREMONY
GV1197	*JAPANESE WRESTLING* **SEE** SUMO
DS765-7	*JAPANESE-CHINESE WAR, 1894-1895* **SEE** CHINESE-JAPANESE WAR, 1894-1895
DS784	*JAPANESE-RUSSIAN BORDER CONFLICTS, 1932-1941* **SEE** RUSSO-JAPANESE BORDER CONFLICTS, 1932-1941
V713	*JAPANESE-RUSSIAN WAR, 1904-1905* **SEE** RUSSO-JAPANESE WAR, 1904-1905 / *naval observations*
DS516-517	*JAPANESE-RUSSIAN WAR, 1904-1905* **SEE** RUSSO-JAPANESE WAR, 1904-1905
U735	*JAPANESE-RUSSIAN WAR, 1904-1905* **SEE** RUSSO-JAPANESE WAR, 1904-1905 / *military observations*
JX1393	*JAPANESE-RUSSIAN WAR, 1904-1905* **SEE** RUSSO-JAPANESE WAR, 1904-1905 / *diplomatic history*
DS830	JAPANESE
TP942	JAPANNING
GV1796.J	JARABE (DANCE)
GV1796.J	*JARAVE (DANCE)* **SEE** JARABE (DANCE)
PM7801-7895	*JARGONS* **SEE** LANGUAGES, MIXED
QE391.J	JASPER
GV1295.J3	JASS (GAME)
PK2261-2270	*JATKI LANGUAGE* **SEE** LAHNDI LANGUAGE
RC851	JAUNDICE
RJ276	JAUNDICE / *infants*
RC184.S5	*JAUNDICE, SPIROCHAETAL* **SEE** WEIL'S DISEASE
D774.J	JAVA SEA, BATTLE OF THE, 1942
PL5177	JAVANESE DRAMA / *collections*
PL5173	JAVANESE DRAMA / *history*
PL5161-9	JAVANESE LANGUAGE
PL5151-9	*JAVANESE LANGUAGE-OLD JAVANESE* **SEE** KAWI LANGUAGE
PL5170-5189	JAVANESE LITERATURE
PN5449.J3	JAVANESE NEWSPAPERS
GV1093	JAVELIN THROWING
ML1040	JAW BONE, MUSICAL
RK280	*JAW JOINT* **SEE** TEMPOROMANDIBULAR JOINT
PL5052	JAWI ALPHABET
RD763	JAWS — ABNORMITIES AND DEFORMITIES
RC936	JAWS — DISEASES
RD526	JAWS — FRACTURE
RA1231.P5	JAWS — NECROSIS / *phosphorus poisoning*
RD526	JAWS — SURGERY
RD661	JAWS — TUMORS
RC280.J	JAWS — TUMORS
QL821	JAWS / *comparative anatomy*
QM105	JAWS / *human anatomy*
QP311	JAWS / *physiology*
E314	JAY'S TREATY, 1794
GR830	JAYHAWK
QL696.P2	JAYS
MT733	*JAZZ BAND* **SEE** DANCE ORCHESTRA
ML1200	*JAZZ BAND* **SEE** DANCE ORCHESTRA
M1040	JAZZ ENSEMBLE WITH CHAMBER ORCHESTRA — SCORES
M1040-1041	JAZZ ENSEMBLE WITH CHAMBER ORCHESTRA
M960-985	JAZZ ENSEMBLES
M900-949	JAZZ ENSEMBLES
ML3930	JAZZ MUSIC — JUVENILE LITERATURE
ML108	JAZZ MUSIC — TERMINOLOGY
ML3561	JAZZ MUSIC
ML87-88	*JAZZ MUSICIANS-PORTRAITS* **SEE** MUSICIANS — PORTRAITS
MT733	*JAZZ ORCHESTRA* **SEE** DANCE ORCHESTRA
ML1200	*JAZZ ORCHESTRA* **SEE** DANCE ORCHESTRA
M1040-1041	JAZZ QUARTET WITH ORCHESTRA
BF575.J4	JEALOUSY / *psychology*
D568.6	JEBEL MUSA, SYRIA, DEFENSE OF, 1915
TL1-445	*JEEPS* **SEE** AUTOMOBILES / *history*
HD9710	*JEEPS* **SEE** AUTOMOBILES / *industry and statistics*
GV1021-1030	*JEEPS* **SEE** AUTOMOBILES / *sports and amusements*
HE5601-5720	*JEEPS* **SEE** AUTOMOBILES / *transportation*
UG680-685	*JEEPS* **SEE** AUTOMOBILES, MILITARY

TL230	*JEEPS* **SEE** MOTOR-TRUCKS
BP182	*JEHAD* **SEE** JIHAD
BS1199.D3	*JEHOVAH, DAY OF* **SEE** DAY OF JEHOVAH
PL8164.Z9	*JEJI DIALECT* **SEE** FON DIALECT
TX612.J4	JELLY
QL375-9	*JELLYFISH* **SEE** MEDUSAE
E99.J4	JEMEZ INDIANS
DC222.J3	JEMMAPES, BATTLE OF, 1792
QC375	JENA GLASS
LB1029.J	JENA PLAN
DC230.J4	JENA, BATTLE OF, 1806
RS165.J	JEQUIRITY / *pharmacy*
RH666.J	JEQUIRITY / *therapeutics*
QL737.R6	JERBOAS
SF199.J5	JERSEY CATTLE
SF193.J5	JERSEY CATTLE / *herd-books*
SD397.P615	*JERSEY PINE* **SEE** SCRUB-PINE
DS122.8	JERUSALEM — SIEGE, 70 A.D.
SB211.J	JERUSALEM ARTICHOKE
BM518.J4	JERUSALEM IN THE MIDRASH
D175-195	JERUSALEM — HISTORY — — LATIN KINGDOM, 1099-1244
PR972-5	*JEST-BOOKS* **SEE** CHAP-BOOKS / *english*
PN970	*JEST-BOOKS* **SEE** CHAP-BOOKS / *general*
PN6147-6231	*JEST-BOOKS* **SEE** WIT AND HUMOR
GT3670	*JESTERS* **SEE** FOOLS AND JESTERS
PN6147-6231	*JESTS* **SEE** WIT AND HUMOR
BX3760.J	JESUATS
NA4820	*JESUIT ARCHITECTURE* **SEE** ARCHITECTURE, JESUIT
F2684	*JESUIT WAR, 1754-1756 (SOUTH AMERICA)* **SEE** SEVEN REDUCTIONS, WAR OF THE, 1754-1756
Z7840.J5	JESUITS — BIO-BIBLIOGRAPHY
BX3755	JESUITS — BIOGRAPHY
LC493	JESUITS — EDUCATION
BX3706-3749	JESUITS — HISTORY
BV2290	JESUITS — MISSIONS
BX3714.P4-5	JESUITS IN PARAGUAY
F2684	JESUITS IN PARAGUAY
BX3701-3755	JESUITS
BX4371-4	JESUITS / *women*
QK495.C57	*JESUITS' BARK* **SEE** CINCHONA / *botany*
SB295.C5	*JESUITS' BARK* **SEE** CINCHONA / *culture*
RS165.C3	*JESUITS' BARK* **SEE** CINCHONA / *pharmacy*
RM666.C53	*JESUITS' BARK* **SEE** CINCHONA / *therapeutics*
BT580	JESUS CHRIST — APPARITIONS AND MIRACLES (MODERN)
BT490	JESUS CHRIST — APPEARANCES
N8050-8054	JESUS CHRIST — ART
BT500	JESUS CHRIST — ASCENSION
BT590.W6	JESUS CHRIST — ATTITUDE TOWARDS WOMEN
BT350	JESUS CHRIST — BAPTISM
BT298-500	JESUS CHRIST — BIOGRAPHY
BT313	JESUS CHRIST — BRETHREN
BT460	JESUS CHRIST — BURIAL
BT304	JESUS CHRIST — CHARACTER
BT320-325	JESUS CHRIST — CHILDHOOD
BT303	JESUS CHRIST — CHRONOLOGY
BT303	JESUS CHRIST — CONFLICTS
BT450-455	JESUS CHRIST — CRUCIFIXION
BT470	JESUS CHRIST — DESCENT INTO HELL
BT214-215	JESUS CHRIST — DIVINITY
BT555	JESUS CHRIST — DRAMA
BT330	JESUS CHRIST — EDUCATION
BT415	JESUS CHRIST — ENTRY INTO JERUSALEM
BS2417.E8	JESUS CHRIST — ETHICS
BT590.E8	JESUS CHRIST — EVANGELISTIC METHODS
BT200-201	JESUS CHRIST — EXALTATION
BT275	JESUS CHRIST — EXAMPLE
BT313	JESUS CHRIST — FAMILY
BT560	JESUS CHRIST — FICTION
BP315	JESUS CHRIST — FLIGHT INTO EGYPT
BT485	JESUS CHRIST — FORTY DAYS
BS2430-2520	JESUS CHRIST — FRIENDS AND ASSOCIATES
BT314	JESUS CHRIST — GENEALOGY
BT303	JESUS CHRIST — HISTORICITY
BT198	JESUS CHRIST — HISTORY OF DOCTRINES
BT218	JESUS CHRIST — HUMANITY
BT220	JESUS CHRIST — HUMILIATION
BT590.I	JESUS CHRIST — ICONOGRAPHY

BT303	JESUS CHRIST — INFLUENCE
BT590.I6	JESUS CHRIST — INTELLECTUAL LIFE
BT255	JESUS CHRIST — INTERCESSION
BP172	JESUS CHRIST — ISLAMIC INTERPRETATIONS
BM620	JESUS CHRIST — JEWISH INTERPRETATIONS
BT590.J7	JESUS CHRIST — JOURNEYS
BT94	JESUS CHRIST — KINGDOM
BT590.L3	JESUS CHRIST — LANGUAGE
BT230-240	JESUS CHRIST — MESSIAHSHIP
BT364-5	JESUS CHRIST — MIRACLES
BT295	JESUS CHRIST — MISCELLANEA
BT308	JESUS CHRIST — MISCELLANEA / occult
BT590.N2	JESUS CHRIST — NAME
BT315	JESUS CHRIST — NATIVITY
BT304.92	JESUS CHRIST — NEW THOUGHT INTERPRETATIONS
BT304.94	JESUS CHRIST — ORIENTAL INTERPRETATIONS
BT373-8	JESUS CHRIST — PARABLES
BT430-465	JESUS CHRIST — PASSION
BT304	JESUS CHRIST — PERSON AND OFFICES
BT200-201	JESUS CHRIST — PERSON AND OFFICES
BT550	JESUS CHRIST — POETRY
BV229-234	JESUS CHRIST — PRAYERS
BT200-201	JESUS CHRIST — PRE-EXISTENCE
BT590.P7	JESUS CHRIST — PREACHING
BT260	JESUS CHRIST — PRIESTHOOD
BT114	JESUS CHRIST — PROCESSION
BT370	JESUS CHRIST — PROPHECIES
BT590.P8	JESUS CHRIST — PSYCHIATRY
BT590.P9	JESUS CHRIST — PSYCHOLOGY
BT304.95	JESUS CHRIST — RATIONALISTIC INTERPRETATIONS
BT465	JESUS CHRIST — RELICS OF THE PASSION
BT480-490	JESUS CHRIST — RESURRECTION
BF1623.R7	JESUS CHRIST — ROSICRUCIAN INTERPRETATIONS
BT270	JESUS CHRIST — ROYAL OFFICE
BT455-6	JESUS CHRIST — SEVEN LAST WORDS
BT590.S5	JESUS CHRIST — SIMILITUDES
BT304.96	JESUS CHRIST — SPIRITUALISTIC INTERPRETATIONS
BT590.T5	JESUS CHRIST — TEACHING METHODS
BS2415-2417	JESUS CHRIST — TEACHINGS
BT355	JESUS CHRIST — TEMPTATION
BT304.97	JESUS CHRIST — THEOSOPHICAL INTERPRETATIONS
BT410	JESUS CHRIST — TRANSFIGURATION
BT440-445	JESUS CHRIST — TRIAL
BT306	JESUS CHRIST — WORDS
N8050-8054	*JESUS CHRIST IN ART* **SEE** JESUS CHRIST — ART
BP172	*JESUS CHRIST IN ISLAM* **SEE** JESUS CHRIST — ISLAMIC INTERPRETATIONS
BT540-560	JESUS CHRIST IN LITERATURE
BT550	*JESUS CHRIST IN POETRY* **SEE** JESUS CHRIST — POETRY
BV64.J4	JESUS CHRIST THE KING, FEAST OF
BT198-590	JESUS CHRIST
BT264-5	*JESUS CHRIST-ATONEMENT* **SEE** ATONEMENT
BT382	*JESUS CHRIST-BEATITUDES* **SEE** BEATITUDES
BT555	*JESUS CHRIST-BIOGRAPHY-DRAMA* **SEE** JESUS CHRIST — DRAMA
BT315	*JESUS CHRIST-BIRTH* **SEE** JESUS CHRIST — NATIVITY
BT317	*JESUS CHRIST-BIRTH* **SEE** VIRGIN BIRTH
BT313	*JESUS CHRIST-BROTHERS* **SEE** JESUS CHRIST — BRETHREN
BV4714	*JESUS CHRIST-COMMANDMENTS* **SEE** SUMMARY OF THE LAW (THEOLOGY)
BT460	*JESUS CHRIST-DESCENT FROM THE CROSS* **SEE** JESUS CHRIST — BURIAL
BT355	*JESUS CHRIST-FORTY DAYS IN THE WILDERNESS* **SEE** JESUS CHRIST — TEMPTATION
BT587.C6-7	*JESUS CHRIST-HOLY COAT* **SEE** HOLY COAT
BT587.S4	*JESUS CHRIST-HOLY SHROUD* **SEE** HOLY SHROUD
BL510	*JESUS CHRIST-INCARNATION* **SEE** INCARNATION
BT220	*JESUS CHRIST-INCARNATION* **SEE** INCARNATION / christology
BP172	*JESUS CHRIST-INTERPRETATIONS, ISLAMIC* **SEE** JESUS CHRIST — ISLAMIC INTERPRETATIONS
BT270	*JESUS CHRIST-KINGSHIP* **SEE** JESUS CHRIST — ROYAL OFFICE
BT455-6	*JESUS CHRIST-LAST WORDS* **SEE** JESUS CHRIST — SEVEN LAST WORDS
BT298-500	*JESUS CHRIST-LIFE* **SEE** JESUS CHRIST — BIOGRAPHY
BT210	*JESUS CHRIST-LOGOS DOCTRINE* **SEE** LOGOS
BV230-233	*JESUS CHRIST-LORD'S PRAYER* **SEE** LORD'S PRAYER
BV823-8	*JESUS CHRIST-LORD'S SUPPER* **SEE** LORD'S SUPPER
BX2215	*JESUS CHRIST-LORD'S SUPPER* **SEE** LORD'S SUPPER / catholic church
BX5149.C5	*JESUS CHRIST-LORD'S SUPPER* **SEE** LORD'S SUPPER / church of england
BP172	*JESUS CHRIST-MUSLIM INTERPRETATIONS* **SEE** JESUS CHRIST — ISLAMIC INTERPRETATIONS
N8050-8054	*JESUS CHRIST-NATIVITY-ART* **SEE** JESUS CHRIST — ART
BT555	*JESUS CHRIST-NATIVITY-DRAMA* **SEE** JESUS CHRIST — DRAMA
BV4257	*JESUS CHRIST-NATIVITY-SERMONS* **SEE** CHRISTMAS SERMONS
N8050-8054	*JESUS CHRIST-PASSION-ART* **SEE** JESUS CHRIST — ART
BT555	*JESUS CHRIST-PASSION-DRAMA* **SEE** JESUS CHRIST — DRAMA
PN3203-3299	*JESUS CHRIST-PASSION-DRAMA* **SEE** PASSION-PLAYS
BT304	*JESUS CHRIST-PERSONALITY* **SEE** JESUS CHRIST — CHARACTER
N8180	*JESUS CHRIST-PICTURES, ILLUSTRATIONS, ETC.* **SEE** JESUS CHRIST — PARABLES — — PICTURES, ILLUSTRATIONS, ETC.
N8050-8054	*JESUS CHRIST-PICTURES, ILLUSTRATIONS, ETC.* **SEE** JESUS CHRIST — ART
BT465	*JESUS CHRIST-PRECIOUS BLOOD* **SEE** PRECIOUS BLOOD, RELICS OF THE
BX2157-8	*JESUS CHRIST-SACRED HEART, DEVOTION TO* **SEE** SACRED HEART, DEVOTION TO
BT306	*JESUS CHRIST-SAYINGS* **SEE** JESUS CHRIST — WORDS
BT885	*JESUS CHRIST-SECOND ADVENT* **SEE** SECOND ADVENT
BT380	*JESUS CHRIST-SERMON ON THE MOUNT* **SEE** SERMON ON THE MOUNT
BV4714	*JESUS CHRIST-SUMMARY OF THE LAW* **SEE** SUMMARY OF THE LAW (THEOLOGY)
BT590.N2	*JESUS CHRIST-TITLES* **SEE** JESUS CHRIST — NAME
DS109.4	*JESUS CHRIST-TOMB* **SEE** HOLY SEPULCHER
BS478	*JESUS CHRIST-TYPOLOGY* **SEE** TYPOLOGY (THEOLOGY) / bible
BT225	*JESUS CHRIST-TYPOLOGY* **SEE** TYPOLOGY (THEOLOGY) / jesus christ
BT520	JESUS CHRIST — BIOGRAPHY — — APOCRYPHAL AND LEGENDARY LITERATURE
BT306.28-5	JESUS CHRIST — BIOGRAPHY — — DEVOTIONAL LITERATURE
BT310-330	JESUS CHRIST — BIOGRAPHY — — EARLY LIFE
BT300	JESUS CHRIST — BIOGRAPHY — — EARLY WORKS TO 1800
BT303	JESUS CHRIST — BIOGRAPHY — — HISTORY AND CRITICISM
BT302	JESUS CHRIST — BIOGRAPHY — — JUVENILE LITERATURE
BT414	JESUS CHRIST — BIOGRAPHY — — PASSION WEEK
BT340-500	JESUS CHRIST — BIOGRAPHY — — PUBLIC LIFE
BT305	JESUS CHRIST — BIOGRAPHY — — SOURCES
BT298-9	JESUS CHRIST — BIOGRAPHY — — SOURCES, BIBLICAL
BT305	JESUS CHRIST — BIOGRAPHY — — SOURCES, JEWISH
N8180	JESUS CHRIST — PARABLES — — PICTURES, ILLUSTRATIONS, ETC.
BT481	JESUS CHRIST — RESURRECTION — — MEDITATIONS
BX3701-3755	*JESUS, SOCIETY OF* **SEE** JESUITS
BX4371-4	*JESUS, SOCIETY OF* **SEE** JESUITS / women
QA911	*JET FLOW* **SEE** JETS — FLUID DYNAMICS
TL681.5	*JET NACELLES (AEROPLANE)* **SEE** AEROPLANES — NACELLES
TL709.5.T5	JET PLANES — THRUST REVERSERS
TJ901	JET PUMPS
QC935	JET STREAM
TL685.7	JET TRANSPORTS
NK5755	JET / art objects
TL685.7	*JETLINERS* **SEE** JET TRANSPORTS
CJ5450	*JETONS* **SEE** JETTONS
QA911	JETS — FLUID DYNAMICS
TC173	JETS / hydraulic engineering
BF1553	*JETTATURA* **SEE** EVIL EYE
GR590	*JETTATURA* **SEE** EVIL EYE / folk-lore

E184.J5	*JEWS IN THE U.S.-SOCIETIES, ETC.* **SEE** JEWS — SOCIETIES, ETC. / *u.s.*
DS101-151	JEWS
GN547	JEWS / *anthropology*
DS135.A-Z	*JEWS, SEPHARDIC* **SEE** SEPHARDIM
BM648	*JEWS-APOLOGETIC WORKS* **SEE** JUDAISM — APOLOGETIC WORKS
BM525	*JEWS-CABALA* **SEE** CABALA / *jewish religion*
BF1585-1623	*JEWS-CABALA* **SEE** CABALA / *occult sciences*
BM613	*JEWS-CHOSEN PEOPLE* **SEE** JEWS — ELECTION, DOCTRINE OF
BV2619-2623	*JEWS-CONVERTS TO CHRISTIANITY* **SEE** CONVERTS FROM JUDAISM
DS112-113	*JEWS-CUSTOMS* **SEE** JEWS — SOCIAL LIFE AND CUSTOMS
BM613	*JEWS-DOCTRINE OF ELECTION* **SEE** JEWS — ELECTION, DOCTRINE OF
RA561	*JEWS-HYGIENE* **SEE** HYGIENE, JEWISH
DS113	*JEWS-LEARNING AND SCHOLARSHIP* **SEE** JEWISH LEARNING AND SCHOLARSHIP
PJ5001-5060	*JEWS-LITERATURE* **SEE** HEBREW LITERATURE
DS131	*JEWS-LOST TRIBES* **SEE** LOST TRIBES OF ISRAEL
HQ507	*JEWS-MARRIAGE* **SEE** MARRIAGE — JEWS
BM613	*JEWS-MISSION* **SEE** JEWS — ELECTION, DOCTRINE OF
BM729.P7	*JEWS-MISSIONS* **SEE** PROSELYTES AND PROSELYTING, JEWISH
ML166	*JEWS-MUSIC* **SEE** MUSIC — JEWS / *history and criticism*
ML3195	*JEWS-MUSIC* **SEE** MUSIC — JEWS / *vocal music*
BM652	*JEWS-PRIESTS* **SEE** PRIESTS, JEWISH
DS112-113	*JEWS-RITUAL* **SEE** JEWS — SOCIAL LIFE AND CUSTOMS
BM175	*JEWS-SECTS* **SEE** JEWISH SECTS
DS111-135	*JEWS-SOCIAL CONDITIONS* **SEE** JEWS — POLITICAL AND SOCIAL CONDITIONS
HC35	*JEWS-SOCIAL CONDITIONS* **SEE** JEWS — POLITICAL AND SOCIAL CONDITIONS / *early economic conditions*
HN10.H4	*JEWS-SOCIAL CONDITIONS* **SEE** JEWS — POLITICAL AND SOCIAL CONDITIONS / *early social conditions*
DS131	*JEWS-TEN LOST TRIBES* **SEE** LOST TRIBES OF ISRAEL
HQ1172	*JEWS-WOMEN* **SEE** WOMEN, JEWISH
DS149	*JEWS-ZIONISM* **SEE** ZIONISM
DS124	JEWS — HISTORY — — 70-1789
DS121	JEWS — HISTORY — — 953-586 B.C.
BL1595	*JEZIDES* **SEE** YEZIDIS
F1505.2.X	*JICAQUE INDIANS* **SEE** XICAQUE INDIANS
E99.J	JICARILLA INDIANS
PM1389	JICARILLA LANGUAGE
GV1796.J5	JIG (DANCE)
QL503.A7	*JIGGER* **SEE** CHIGOE / *fleas*
QL458.A2	*JIGGER* **SEE** CHIGOE / *mites*
QL458.A2	*JIGGERS (MITES)* **SEE** CHIGGERS (MITES)
TN500-535	*JIGGING* **SEE** ORE-DRESSING
TJ1185	*JIGS (MECHANICAL DEVICES)* **SEE** JIGS AND FIXTURES
M1048	JIGS (ORCHESTRA) — SCORES
M1048	JIGS (ORCHESTRA)
M32	JIGS (PIANO)
M1145	JIGS (STRING ORCHESTRA)
M1160	JIGS (STRING ORCHESTRA)
M1105-6	JIGS (VIOLIN WITH STRING ORCHESTRA)
TJ1185	JIGS AND FIXTURES
BP182	JIHAD
RS165.D2	*JIMSON WEED* **SEE** DATURA / *pharmacy*
RM666.D3	*JIMSON WEED* **SEE** DATURA / *therapeutics*
PL4001.K3	*JINGHPAW LANGUAGE* **SEE** KACHIN LANGUAGE
TL232	*JITNEY BUSES* **SEE** MOTOR BUSES
GV1796.J	JITTERBUG DANCING
GV475	JIU-JITSU
PM6273	JIVARAN LANGUAGES
F3722.1.J5	JIVARO INDIANS
GV1295.J6	JO-JOTTE (GAME)
HF5549.5.J6	JOB ANALYSIS
T58	JOB DESCRIPTIONS / *industrial management*
HF5382	JOB DESCRIPTIONS / *occupational descriptions (collective)*
HD4903	*JOB DISCRIMINATION* **SEE** DISCRIMINATION IN EMPLOYMENT
HF5549.5.J62	JOB EVALUATION

HF5549.5.J62	*JOB RATING* **SEE** JOB EVALUATION
BL1442.S5	*JODO-SHIN-SHU* **SEE** SHIN (SECT)
E451	*JOHN BROWN RAID, 1859* **SEE** HARPERS FERRY, W. VA. — JOHN BROWN RAID, 1859
E302.6.M4	JOHN MARSHALL DAY
BV70.J	JOHN THE BAPTIST'S DAY
QL638.Z4	*JOHN-DORY* **SEE** DORY (FISH)
SF810.J6	JOHNE'S DISEASE
SB201.J5	JOHNSON GRASS
TH5662-3	JOINERY
U260	*JOINT OPERATIONS (MILITARY SCIENCE)* **SEE** UNIFIED OPERATIONS (MILITARY SCIENCE)
HD5650-5660	*JOINT PRODUCTION COMMITTEES* **SEE** WORKS COUNCILS
TH6295	JOINT WIPING / *plumbing*
HD2709-2930	*JOINT-STOCK COMPANIES* **SEE** STOCK COMPANIES / *corporations*
HG4001-4480	*JOINT-STOCK COMPANIES* **SEE** STOCK COMPANIES / *finance*
TF262	*JOINTLESS RAILS (RAILROADS)* **SEE** RAILROADS — CONTINUOUS RAILS
RD686	JOINTS — DISEASES
RD684	JOINTS — SURGERY
RD551	JOINTS — SURGERY
RD686	JOINTS — SURGERY
RC312.5.J	JOINTS — TUBERCULOSIS
QE605	JOINTS (GEOLOGY)
QL825	JOINTS / *comparative anatomy*
QM131	JOINTS / *human anatomy*
RD106	*JOINTS-DISLOCATION* **SEE** DISLOCATIONS
PL8113	JOK LANGUAGE **SEE** CHOKWE LANGUAGE
PN6147-6231	*JOKES* **SEE** WIT AND HUMOR
PL6041-4	*JOLOANO LANGUAGE* **SEE** SULU LANGUAGE
PL8785	*JOLOF LANGUAGE* **SEE** WOLOF LANGUAGE
F1221.C53	*JONAZ-CHICHIMECA INDIANS* **SEE** CHICHIMECA-JONAZ INDIANS
GV1541-1561	*JONGLEURS* **SEE** JUGGLERS AND JUGGLING
GT3650	*JONGLEURS* **SEE** MINSTRELS / *manners and customs*
ML182-4	*JONGLEURS* **SEE** MINSTRELS / *musical history*
PC3304-3330	*JONGLEURS* **SEE** TROUBADOURS
GT3650	*JONGLEURS* **SEE** TROUBADOURS / *manners and customs*
ML182	*JONGLEURS* **SEE** TROUBADOURS / *music*
PQ3841	*JONGLEURS* **SEE** TROUVERES / *belgian literature*
PQ3824	*JONGLEURS* **SEE** TROUVERES / *belgian literature*
PQ199	*JONGLEURS* **SEE** TROUVERES / *french literature*
PQ1300-1308	*JONGLEURS* **SEE** TROUVERES / *french literature*
ML182	*JONGLEURS* **SEE** TROUVERES / *music*
GV1796.J7	JOROPO (DANCE)
BR815	JOSEPHINISM
BR815	*JOSEPHISM* **SEE** JOSEPHINISM
GV1796.J	JOTA / *dancing*
ML3447	JOTA / *musical history*
M1049	JOTAS (ORCHESTRA)
PN4838	JOURNALISM — ANECDOTES, FACETIAE, SATIRE, ETC.
PN4798	JOURNALISM — COMPETITIONS
PN4731	JOURNALISM — PHILOSOPHY
PN4751	JOURNALISM — POLITICAL ASPECTS
PN4749	JOURNALISM — SOCIAL ASPECTS
PN4797	JOURNALISM AS A PROFESSION
PN4700-5650	JOURNALISM
PN4784.A3	JOURNALISM, AGRICULTURAL
PN4784.C7	JOURNALISM, COMMERCIAL
PN4784.A3	*JOURNALISM, DAIRY* **SEE** JOURNALISM, AGRICULTURAL
PN4784.T3	*JOURNALISM, INDUSTRIAL* **SEE** JOURNALISM, TECHNICAL
PN4784.M4	JOURNALISM, MEDICAL
PN4888.R4	JOURNALISM, RELIGIOUS
PN4888.S	JOURNALISM, SCIENTIFIC
PN4784.T3	JOURNALISM, TECHNICAL
PN4784.A3	*JOURNALISM-AGRICULTURE* **SEE** JOURNALISM, AGRICULTURAL
PN4841-5650	*JOURNALISM-BIOGRAPHY* **SEE** JOURNALISTS
PN4820-4823	*JOURNALISM-BIOGRAPHY* **SEE** JOURNALISTS
PN5122-3	*JOURNALISM-BIOGRAPHY* **SEE** JOURNALISTS / *gt. brit.*
PN4871-4	*JOURNALISM-BIOGRAPHY* **SEE** JOURNALISTS / *u.s.*
PN4784.C7	*JOURNALISM-COMMERCE* **SEE** JOURNALISM, COMMERCIAL

PN4784.M4	*JOURNALISM-MEDICINE* **SEE** JOURNALISM, MEDICAL		JK1736	*JUDGMENTS BY PEERS* **SEE** JURY / *u.s.*
PN4888.R4	*JOURNALISM-RELIGION* **SEE** JOURNALISM, RELIGIOUS		JX6607	JUDGMENTS, FOREIGN
PN4784.S6	*JOURNALISM-SPORTS* **SEE** SPORTS JOURNALISM		JK1533	*JUDICIAL DECISIONS, RECALL OF* **SEE** RECALL OF
PN4756	JOURNALISTIC ETHICS			JUDICIAL DECISIONS
Z675.N4	*JOURNALISTIC LIBRARIES* **SEE** NEWSPAPER OFFICE		JF265	JUDICIAL POWER
	LIBRARIES		JF700-723	JUDICIAL POWER
TR820	*JOURNALISTIC PHOTOGRAPHY* **SEE** PHOTOGRAPHY,		JK-JQ	JUDICIAL POWER
	JOURNALISTIC		JF711	JUDICIAL REVIEW
PN4820-4823	JOURNALISTS — CORRESPONDENCE, REMINSCENCES,		JK1541	JUDICIAL REVIEW / *u.s.*
	ETC.		JF700-723	*JUDICIARY* **SEE** COURTS
PN4841-5650	JOURNALISTS — CORRESPONDENCE, REMINSCENCES,		JK-JQ	*JUDICIARY* **SEE** COURTS / *by country*
	ETC.		JV471	*JUDICIARY* **SEE** COURTS / *colonial*
PN4820-4823	JOURNALISTS		JF700-723	*JUDICIARY* **SEE** JUDICIAL POWER
PN4841-5650	JOURNALISTS		JK-JQ	*JUDICIARY* **SEE** JUDICIAL POWER
PN5122-3	JOURNALISTS / *gt. brit.*		JF265	*JUDICIARY* **SEE** JUDICIAL POWER
PN4871-4	JOURNALISTS / *u.s.*		GV475	JUDO
PN4820-4823	*JOURNALISTS-BIOGRAPHY* **SEE** JOURNALISTS		GV1541-1561	JUGGLERS AND JUGGLING
PN4841-5650	*JOURNALISTS-BIOGRAPHY* **SEE** JOURNALISTS		D465	*JUGOSLAVS* **SEE** YUGOSLAVS
PN5122-3	*JOURNALISTS-BIOGRAPHY* **SEE** JOURNALISTS / *gt.*		DB48	*JUGOSLAVS* **SEE** YUGOSLAVS / *austria*
	brit.		DR366	*JUGOSLAVS* **SEE** YUGOSLAVS / *yugoslavia*
PN4871-4	*JOURNALISTS-BIOGRAPHY* **SEE** JOURNALISTS / *u.s.*		DG255	JUGURTHINE WAR, 111-105 B.C.
TJ1061-1073	*JOURNALS (MACHINERY)* **SEE** BEARINGS		GV475	*JUJITSU* **SEE** JIU-JITSU
	(MACHINERY)		SB379.J8	JUJUBE (PLANT)
G149-890	*JOURNEYS* **SEE** VOYAGES AND TRAVELS		PM95	*JUKAGHIR LANGUAGE* **SEE** YUKAGHIR LANGUAGE
G420-440	*JOURNEYS* **SEE** VOYAGES AROUND THE WORLD		CE75	*JULIAN CALENDAR* **SEE** CALENDAR, JULIAN
BJ1480-1487	JOY AND SORROW		E99.J9	JUMANO INDIANS
E99.J	JUANENO INDIANS		GV498	*JUMP ROPE* **SEE** ROPE SKIPPING
BX2279-2283	*JUBILEE INDULGENCES* **SEE** INDULGENCES		QL523.P8	JUMPING PLANT-LICE
ML400	JUBILEE SINGERS		GV529	JUMPING
BX961.H6	*JUBILEE YEAR* **SEE** HOLY YEAR		TK7872.T73	JUNCTION TRANSISTORS
PJ5111-5119	*JUDAEO-GERMAN* **SEE** YIDDISH LANGUAGE		BX2157-8	*JUNE DEVOTIONS* **SEE** SACRED HEART, DEVOTION
DS101-151	*JUDAICA* **SEE** JEWS			TO
GN547	*JUDAICA* **SEE** JEWS / *anthropology*		U167.5.J	JUNGLE WARFARE
BM648	JUDAISM — APOLOGETIC WORKS		F3446	JUNIN, BATTLE OF, 1824
BM585	JUDAISM — CONTROVERSIAL LITERATURE		LB2328	JUNIOR COLLEGES
BT1120	JUDAISM — CONTROVERSIAL LITERATURE		LB1623	JUNIOR HIGH SCHOOLS
	/ *christian apologetics*		HV876	JUNIOR REPUBLICS
BT173.J8	JUDAISM — CONTROVERSIAL LITERATURE		QK495.J9	JUNIPER
	/ *mohammedan apologetics*		TP995	*JUNK* **SEE** WASTE PRODUCTS
BM652	JUDAISM — FUNCTIONARIES		VM101	JUNKS
BM535	*JUDAISM AND CHRISTIANITY* **SEE** CHRISTIANITY AND		QB384	JUPITER (PLANET) — TABLES
	OTHER RELIGIONS — JUDAISM		QB661	JUPITER (PLANET) / *descriptive astronomy*
HN40.J5	JUDAISM AND SOCIAL PROBLEMS		QB384	JUPITER (PLANET) / *theoretical astronomy*
BM538.S7	JUDAISM AND STATE		PL8143	*JUR LANGUAGE* **SEE** DYUR LANGUAGE
BM197.5	*JUDAISM, CONSERVATIVE* **SEE** CONSERVATIVE		PL16.Y8	*JURAK LANGUAGE* **SEE** YURAK LANGUAGE
	JUDAISM		QE681-3	*JURASSIC PERIOD* **SEE** GEOLOGY, STRATIGRAPHIC —
BM652	*JUDAISM-CLERGY* **SEE** JUDAISM — FUNCTIONARIES			JURASSIC
BM665-9	*JUDAISM-DEVOTIONAL EXERCISES* **SEE** JEWS —		QE923	*JURASSIC PERIOD* **SEE** PALEOBOTANY — JURASSIC
	PRAYER-BOOKS AND DEVOTIONS / *prayer and service*		QE733	*JURASSIC PERIOD* **SEE** PALEONTOLOGY — JURASSIC
	books		BX1939.J85	JURISDICTION (CANON LAW)
BM724	*JUDAISM-DEVOTIONAL EXERCISES* **SEE** JEWS —		JX4173-4195	JURISDICTION
	PRAYER-BOOKS AND DEVOTIONS / *devotional works*		JX1698	*JURISDICTION, CONSULAR* **SEE** CONSULAR
BM165	*JUDAISM-HISTORY-BIBLICAL PERIOD* **SEE** JUDAISM —			JURISDICTION
	HISTORY — — ANCIENT PERIOD		JX4175	*JURISDICTION, EXTERRITORIAL* **SEE**
BM176	*JUDAISM-HISTORY-GRECO-ROMAN PERIOD* **SEE**			EXTERRITORIALITY
	JUDAISM — HISTORY — — POST-EXILIC PERIOD		JX1671-2	*JURISDICTION, EXTERRITORIAL* **SEE**
BM176	*JUDAISM-HISTORY-INTER-TESTAMENTAL PERIOD* **SEE**			EXTERRITORIALITY
	JUDAISM — HISTORY — — POST-EXILIC PERIOD		RK1062	*JURISPRUDENCE, DENTAL* **SEE** DENTAL
BM176	*JUDAISM-HISTORY-PRE-TALMUDIC PERIOD* **SEE**			JURISPRUDENCE
	JUDAISM — HISTORY — — POST-EXILIC PERIOD		RA1001-1171	*JURISPRUDENCE, MEDICAL* **SEE** MEDICAL
BM165	JUDAISM — HISTORY — — ANCIENT PERIOD			JURISPRUDENCE
BM190	JUDAISM — HISTORY — — MODERN PERIOD		SF780	*JURISPRUDENCE, VETERINARY* **SEE** VETERINARY
BM176	JUDAISM — HISTORY — — POST-EXILIC PERIOD			JURISPRUDENCE
BM177	JUDAISM — HISTORY — — TALMUDIC PERIOD		JX4000-4081	*JURISTIC PERSONS (INTERNATIONAL LAW)* **SEE**
PC4813	*JUDEO-SPANISH LANGUAGE* **SEE** LADINO LANGUAGE			PERSONS (INTERNATIONAL LAW)
PC4813	*JUDESMO* **SEE** LADINO LANGUAGE		F2520.1.J	JURUNA INDIANS
GT6230-6280	JUDGES — COSTUME		JF723	JURY
JK1507-1599	JUDGES		JN923	JURY / *england*
JF700-721	JUDGES		JK1736	JURY / *u.s.*
GV735	*JUDGING (SPORTS)* **SEE** SPORTS OFFICIATING		BX1805	*JUS EXCLUSIVAE* **SEE** EXCLUSION, RIGHT OF
BC177	*JUDGMENT (LOGIC)* **SEE** REASONING		BV4647.J	JUSTICE (VIRTUE)
	/ *argumentation in logic*		JC578	JUSTICE / *political theory*
BC	*JUDGMENT (LOGIC)* **SEE** REASONING / *logic*		GN493	JUSTICE / *primitive*
BC181	JUDGMENT (LOGIC)		JK-JQ	JUSTICE, ADMINISTRATION OF / *by country*
N8120	JUDGMENT DAY — ART		JF701-721	JUSTICE, ADMINISTRATION OF / *departments general*
BT880-881	JUDGMENT DAY		JX4263.D45	*JUSTICE, DENIAL OF* **SEE** DENIAL OF JUSTICE / *k*
BT880-881	*JUDGMENT, LAST* **SEE** JUDGMENT DAY			*international law*
BX1939.J8	JUDGMENTS (CANON LAW)		BT763-4	JUSTIFICATION
JF723	*JUDGMENTS BY PEERS* **SEE** JURY		HB221-236	*JUSTUM PRETIUM* **SEE** PRICES / *economic theory*
JN923	*JUDGMENTS BY PEERS* **SEE** JURY / *england*		HG229	*JUSTUM PRETIUM* **SEE** PRICES / *prices and money*

HD6978-7080	*JUSTUM PRETIUM* **SEE** PRICES / *prices and wages*
SB257	JUTE / *culture*
HD9156.J8	JUTE / *industry*
TS1735	JUTE / *manufacture*
D582.J8	JUTLAND, BATTLE OF, 1916
DA122.J8	JUTLAND, BATTLE OF, 1916 / *english history*
M2190	*JUVENILE CANTATAS* **SEE** CANTATAS, JUVENILE
M1996	*JUVENILE CANTATAS* **SEE** CANTATAS, JUVENILE
HV9088-9096	JUVENILE COURTS
HV9051-9230	JUVENILE DELINQUENCY
AG1-91	*JUVENILE DICTIONARIES* **SEE** CHILDREN'S ENCYCLOPEDIAS AND DICTIONARIES
AG1-91	*JUVENILE ENCYCLOPEDIAS* **SEE** CHILDREN'S ENCYCLOPEDIAS AND DICTIONARIES
PZ5-90	*JUVENILE LITERATURE* **SEE** CHILDREN'S LITERATURE
BX4657	*JUVENILE SAINTS* **SEE** SAINTS, JUVENILE
G570	*JUVENILE VOYAGES AND TRAVELS* **SEE** VOYAGES AND TRAVELS, JUVENILE
G175	*JUVENILE VOYAGES AND TRAVELS* **SEE** VOYAGES AND TRAVELS, JUVENILE
GV1295.B4	*KA-LA-BRE-OSH (GAME)* **SEE** BELOTE (GAME)
DS539.K	*KA-TU* **SEE** KHA TAHOI
DT298.K2	*KABAIL* **SEE** KABYLES
PJ2373	*KABAIL LANGUAGE* **SEE** KABYLE LANGUAGE
PK9201.K3	KABARDIAN BALLADS AND SONGS
PK9201.K3	KABARDIAN LANGUAGE
PK9201.K3	KABARDIAN PHILOLOGY
DK34.K	KABARDIANS
BM525	*KABBALA* **SEE** CABALA / *jewish religion*
BF1585-1623	*KABBALA* **SEE** CABALA / *occult sciences*
GN667.Q8	KABI TRIBE / *anthropology*
DU274	KABI TRIBE / *history*
PL736	*KABUKI KYOGEN PLAYS* **SEE** KYOGEN PLAYS
PL766	*KABUKI KYOGEN PLAYS* **SEE** KYOGEN PLAYS / *collections*
PL737	KABUKI PLAYS
PL767	KABUKI PLAYS / *collections*
PN2924.5.K3	KABUKI
PJ2373	KABYLE LANGUAGE
DT298.K2	KABYLES
PM3576	*KACCHIQUEL LANGUAGE* **SEE** CAKCHIKEL LANGUAGE
PL4001.B3	*KACHARI LANGUAGE* **SEE** BARA LANGUAGE
DS432.K15	KACHARIS
PL55.K3	*KACHGAR LANGUAGE* **SEE** KASHGAR LANGUAGE
PL3901-4	KACHIN DIALECTS
PL4001.K3	KACHIN LANGUAGE
DS485.B85	KACHIN TRIBES / *burma*
E99.K	*KACHINAS* **SEE** KATCINAS
DS485.K17	KADAMBAS
DS432.K	KADARS
DT88	KADESH, BATTLE OF, 1300 B.C.( )
E99.E7	*KADIAK (ESKIMO TRIBE)* **SEE** KANIAGMIUT (ESKIMO TRIBE)
F2520.1.C	*KADIEUEU INDIANS* **SEE** CADIOEO INDIANS
PJ2507	KAFFA LANGUAGE
DT380	KAFFA
PL8321-4	*KAFFIR LANGUAGE (BANTU)* **SEE** KAFIR LANGUAGE (BANTU)
DT764.K2	*KAFFIRS* **SEE** KAFIRS (AFRICAN PEOPLE)
GN657.K2	*KAFFIRS* **SEE** KAFIRS (AFRICAN PEOPLE) / *anthropology*
DT777	*KAFFIRS* **SEE** KAFIRS (AFRICAN PEOPLE) / *kafir wars*
DS374.K2	*KAFFIRS* **SEE** KAFIRS (KAFIRISTAN)
SB191.K3	KAFIR CORN
PL8321-4	KAFIR LANGUAGE (BANTU)
PK7001-7070	*KAFIR LANGUAGES (KAFIRISTAN)* **SEE** PISACHA LANGUAGES
DT764.K2	KAFIRS (AFRICAN PEOPLE)
GN657.K2	KAFIRS (AFRICAN PEOPLE) / *anthropology*
DT777	KAFIRS (AFRICAN PEOPLE) / *kafir wars*
DS374.K2	KAFIRS (KAFIRISTAN)
PL8341	KAGURU LANGUAGE
DU740	*KAI (TRIBE)* **SEE** KAIA-KAIAS
DU740	KAIA-KAIAS
PM5791	*KAIAPO LANGUAGE* **SEE** CAYAPO LANGUAGE
PL45.K6	*KAIBALIAN LANGUAGE* **SEE** KOIBALIAN LANGUAGE
F2684	*KAIBATE, BATTLE OF, 1756* **SEE** CAIBATE, BATTLE OF, 1756
E99.S	*KAIKOMAS* **SEE** SINKYONE INDIANS
DT380	*KAILA* **SEE** FALASHAS / *ethiopia*
DS135.E75	*KAILA* **SEE** FALASHAS / *jews*
E99.K15	KAINAH INDIANS
F2823.K3	KAINGANGUE INDIANS / *argentine republic*
F2520.1.K	KAINGANGUE INDIANS / *brazil*
PM6276	KAINGANGUE LANGUAGE
F2230.2.C	*KAINGUA INDIANS* **SEE** CAINGUA INDIANS
PN687.K3	KAISERAGE
DU740	*KAJA-KAJAS* **SEE** KAIA-KAIAS
DS646.3	*KAJANS* **SEE** KAYANS / *borneo*
RC624	*KAKKE* **SEE** BERI-BERI
RC236	KALA-AZAR
PJ2491-2515	*KALACCO LANGUAGE* **SEE** SIDAMA LANGUAGE
BP166	*KALAM* **SEE** ISLAMIC THEOLOGY
PL5841	KALAMIAN LANGUAGE
F2520.1.A	*KALAPALO INDIANS* **SEE** APALAKIRI INDIANS
E99.K	*KALAPOOIAN INDIANS* **SEE** KALAPUYAN INDIANS
E99.K	KALAPUYAN INDIANS
PM1421	KALAPUYAN LANGUAGE
SB351.K3	KALE
QC373.K3	KALEIDOSCOPE
D764	KALININ, BATTLE OF, 1941
E99.K·	KALISPEL INDIANS
PM1431	KALISPEL LANGUAGE
PL421	*KALKA LANGUAGE* **SEE** KHALKHA LANGUAGE
DS793.M7	*KALKAS* **SEE** KHALKHAS / *mongolia*
TR400	KALLITYPE
DL710	KALMAR WAR, 1611-1613
DL179	KALMAR, UNION OF, 1397 / *denmark*
DL485	KALMAR, UNION OF, 1397 / *norway*
DL694	KALMAR, UNION OF, 1397 / *sweden*
PL429	KALMUCK LANGUAGE
PL430	KALMUCK LITERATURE
DK34.K14	KALMUCKS
TH8161	*KALSOMINING* **SEE** CALCIMINING
PJ2438	*KAMANT LANGUAGE* **SEE** KEMANT LANGUAGE
PL16.K3	KAMASSIN LANGUAGE
PL8351	KAMBA LANGUAGE
GN657.B2	KAMBA TRIBE
PM70	KAMCHADAL LANGUAGE
QE578	*KAMES* **SEE** ESKAR
PL4351.K6	*KAMHMU LANGUAGE* **SEE** KHMU' LANGUAGE
PH1051-9	*KAMI LANGUAGE* **SEE** SYRYENIAN LANGUAGE
E99.K18	KAMIA INDIANS
QE391.S8	*KAMMERERITE* **SEE** STICHTITE
QC912	KAMPOMETER
PL4641-9	*KANADA LANGUAGE* **SEE** KANNADA LANGUAGE
PL4641-9	*KANARESE LANGUAGE* **SEE** KANNADA LANGUAGE
PL3801.K3	KANAURI LANGUAGE
PL3801.K3	*KANAWARI LANGUAGE* **SEE** KANAURI LANGUAGE
PL4695	*KANDH LANGUAGE* **SEE** KUI LANGUAGE
DS432.K17	KANDHS
QL737.R6	KANGAROO RATS
QL737.M3	KANGAROOS
E99.E7	KANIAGMIUT (ESKIMO TRIBE)
PM72	KANIAGMIUT LANGUAGE
PM5723	*KANICHANA LANGUAGE* **SEE** CANICHANA LANGUAGE
DS432.K	*KANIKARS* **SEE** KANIS
DS432.K	KANIS
PL5865	KANKANAY DIALECT
PL4641-9	KANNADA LANGUAGE
PL4650-4659	KANNADA LITERATURE
PL8493	*KANOP LANGUAGE* **SEE** MANDJAK LANGUAGE
E99.K2	KANSA INDIANS — LAND TRANSFERS
E99.K2	KANSA INDIANS
F676-690	KANSAS — HISTORY
E433	KANSAS-NEBRASKA BILL
E508	KANSAS — HISTORY — — CIVIL WAR
ML509	KANTELE (MUSICAL INSTRUMENT) / *finnish*
PL8361	KANURI LANGUAGE
TN941-3	KAOLIN / *mineral resources*
QE391.K	KAOLIN / *mineralogy*
TP811	KAOLIN / *pottery*
QE391.K	KAOLINITE
GN432	*KAPA* **SEE** TAPA / *primitive fabrics*
PL6252.K	KAPINGAMARANGI LANGUAGE
PL8375	*KAPIRONDO LANGUAGE* **SEE** KAVIRONDO LANGUAGE
SB261.K3	KAPOK / *culture*
TS1688	*KAPRON* **SEE** NYLON

GB601-8	KAR FORMATION
PL55.K	KARA-KALPAK LANGUAGE
DK855.4	KARA-KALPAKS
DK34.K	KARACHAEVS
PL45.K3	KARAGASSIAN LANGUAGE
PL65.K3	*KARAIM DIALECTS* **SEE** KARAITIC DIALECTS
BM185.K3	KARAITES
PL65.K3	KARAITIC DIALECTS
BM175.K3	KARAITIC LITERATURE
F2520.1.C	*KARAJA INDIANS* **SEE** CARAJA INDIANS
SF375	KARAKUL SHEEP
PL8047	*KARAN LANGUAGE* **SEE** ANGAS LANGUAGE
E99.K26	KARANKAWA INDIANS
E99.K26	*KARANKAWAN INDIANS* **SEE** KARANKAWA INDIANS
TR263.K	KARAT CAMERA
GV476	KARATE
PH501-9	KARELIAN LANGUAGE
PH508.5-9	KARELIAN LITERATURE / *collections*
PH508	KARELIAN LITERATURE / *history*
DK511.O1	KARELIANS
DK34.K3	KARELIANS
PL4051-4	KAREN LANGUAGE
DS432.K2	KARENS
BP195.K4-42	*KARIGITES* **SEE** KHARIJITES
F2520.1.K	KARIRI INDIANS / *brazil*
PM6286-9	KARIRI LANGUAGE
RK858.K2	KARLSBAD SALT
BL2015.K3	KARMA
BP195.K3	KARMATHIANS
PL5244.Z9K	*KARO DIALECT (SUMATRA)* **SEE** KARO-BATAK DIALECT
PL5244.Z9K	KARO-BATAK DIALECT
E99.K25	KAROK INDIANS
PM1461	KAROK LANGUAGE
GB601-8	KARST
GV1029.5	*KART RACING* **SEE** KARTING
DK511.G36	*KARTHVELI* **SEE** GEORGIANS
GV1029.5	KARTING
TL236.5	KARTS (MIDGET CARS)
PK9160-9178	*KARTVELIAN LITERATURE* **SEE** GEORGIAN LITERATURE
QH605	KARYOKINESIS
PL8055	*KASANDSI LANGUAGE* **SEE** BANGALA LANGUAGE
BM710	*KASHER FOOD* **SEE** JEWS — DIETARY LAWS
PL55.K3	KASHGAR LANGUAGE
PM6290.K3	KASHINAUA LANGUAGE
PK7021-9	KASHMIRI LANGUAGE
PK7031-7	KASHMIRI LITERATURE
BM710	*KASHRUTH, LAWS OF* **SEE** JEWS — DIETARY LAWS
DD491.P748	KASHUBES / *pomerania*
PG7901-5	KASHUBIAN LANGUAGE
E99.K	KASKA INDIANS
E99.K264	KASKASKIA INDIANS
DS73.4	KASSITES
DP614	KASSR-EL-KEBIR, BATTLE OF, 1578
DT322	KASSR-EL-KEBIR, BATTLE OF, 1578
DD491.P748	*KASSUBES* **SEE** KASHUBES / *pomerania*
PG7901-5	*KASUBE LANGUAGE* **SEE** KASHUBIAN LANGUAGE
E99.C24	*KATABA INDIANS* **SEE** CATAWBA INDIANS
E99.K52	*KATAKA INDIANS* **SEE** KIOWA APACHE INDIANS
RC122.B5	*KATAYAMA DISEASE* **SEE** SCHISTOSOMIASIS
PL8113	*KATCHOKUE LANGUAGE* **SEE** CHOKWE LANGUAGE
E99.K	KATCINAS
GV1693	KATHAKALI
PM753	*KATHLAMET DIALECT* **SEE** CATHLAMET DIALECT
PM5778	*KATIO LANGUAGE* **SEE** CATIO LANGUAGE
E99.K	KATO INDIANS
PM1481	KATO LANGUAGE
F1435	*KATUN* **SEE** CHRONOLOGY, MAYA
QL508.L8	KATYDIDS
BL1245.K3	KAULAS
BL1245.K3	*KAULIKAS* **SEE** KAULAS
RS165.K2	KAURI GUM / *pharmacy*
PM1611	*KAUS LANGUAGE* **SEE** COOS LANGUAGE
PL5151-9	*KAVI LANGUAGE* **SEE** KAWI LANGUAGE
DT429	KAVIRONDO (AFRICAN PEOPLE)
DT434.E2	KAVIRONDO (AFRICAN PEOPLE) / *east africa protectorate*
PL8375	KAVIRONDO LANGUAGE

E99.K2	*KAW INDIANS* **SEE** KANSA INDIANS
PM1487	KAWAIISU LANGUAGE
PL5151-9	KAWI LANGUAGE
E99.K27	KAWIA INDIANS
GN440.2	*KAYAKS* **SEE** CANOES AND CANOEING / *ethnology*
GV781-5	*KAYAKS* **SEE** CANOES AND CANOEING / *sport*
DS646.3	KAYANS / *borneo*
PM5791	*KAYAPO LANGUAGE* **SEE** CAYAPO LANGUAGE
PM1531	*KAYOWE LANGUAGE* **SEE** KIOWA LANGUAGE
F2230.2.C	*KAYUA INDIANS* **SEE** CAINGUA INDIANS
PL65.K4-44	*KAZAK-KIRGHIZ LANGUAGE* **SEE** KAZAKH LANGUAGE
PL65.K4-44	KAZAKH LANGUAGE
PL65.K46-48	KAZAKH LITERATURE / *collections*
PL65.K45	KAZAKH LITERATURE / *history*
PL65.K47	KAZAKH POETRY / *collections*
PL65.K45	KAZAKH POETRY / *history*
DK861.K	*KAZAKHS* **SEE** KAZAKS
DK861.K	KAZAKS
PK9201.L3	*KAZI-KUMUKH LANGUAGE* **SEE** LAK LANGUAGE
E405.2	KEARNY'S EXPEDITION, 1846
F2230.2.K4	KECHUA INDIANS
PM6301-9	KECHUA LANGUAGE
PM6308	KECHUA LITERATURE
PM6308	KECHUA POETRY
E99.K	KEECHE INDIANS
TJ220	KEELY MOTOR
AY10-19	*KEEPSAKES (BOOKS)* **SEE** GIFT-BOOKS (ANNUALS, ETC.)
SF429.K4	KEESHONDS
F1465.2.K5	KEKCHI INDIANS
PM3913	KEKCHI LANGUAGE
PL8377	KELE LANGUAGE
SB945.B7	KELEP / *boll-weevil control*
QL568.F7	KELEP / *zoology*
E475.3	KELLY'S FORD, VA., BATTLE OF, 1863
RD621-6	*KELOTOMY* **SEE** HERNIA
QK569.L2	KELP
ML1040.K4	KEMANAK
PJ2438	KEMANT LANGUAGE
SB261.A	*KENAF* **SEE** AMBARY HEMP / *culture*
TS1544.A	*KENAF* **SEE** AMBARY HEMP / *fiber*
PM1561	*KENAI LANGUAGE* **SEE** KNAIAKHOTANA LANGUAGE
DS646.3	*KENJAS* **SEE** KENYAS / *borneo*
F27.K3	*KENNEBEC CLAIMS* **SEE** KENNEBEC PATENT
E99.A13	*KENNEBEC INDIANS* **SEE** ABNAKI INDIANS
E78.M4	*KENNEBEC INDIANS* **SEE** NORRIDGEWOCK INDIANS
E99.N	*KENNEBEC INDIANS* **SEE** NORRIDGEWOCK INDIANS
F27.K3	KENNEBEC PATENT
SF428	KENNELS
E476.7	KENNESAW MOUNTAIN, BATTLE OF, 1864
BL510	*KENOSIS (THEOLOGY)* **SEE** INCARNATION
BT220	*KENOSIS (THEOLOGY)* **SEE** INCARNATION / *christology*
F446-460	KENTUCKY — HISTORY
E328	KENTUCKY AND VIRGINIA RESOLUTIONS OF 1798
JK176	KENTUCKY AND VIRGINIA RESOLUTIONS OF 1798 / *constitutional history*
E328	*KENTUCKY-HISTORY-RESOLUTIONS OF 1798* **SEE** KENTUCKY AND VIRGINIA RESOLUTIONS OF 1798
JK176	*KENTUCKY-HISTORY-RESOLUTIONS OF 1798* **SEE** KENTUCKY AND VIRGINIA RESOLUTIONS OF 1798 / *constitutional history*
E564	KENTUCKY — HISTORY — — CIVIL WAR
E509	KENTUCKY — HISTORY — — CIVIL WAR
E263.K	KENTUCKY — HISTORY — — REVOLUTION
E726.K37	KENTUCKY — HISTORY — — WAR OF 1898
E409.5.K	KENTUCKY — HISTORY — — WAR WITH MEXICO, 1845-1848
DS646.3	KENYAS / *borneo*
TP565	KEPHIR / *beverages*
RM257.K4	KEPHIR / *therapeutics*
QB355-7	*KEPLER'S EQUATION* **SEE** ORBITS / *theoretical astronomy*
QB355-7	*KEPLER'S LAWS* **SEE** ORBITS / *theoretical astronomy*
DS451	*KERALAS* **SEE** CHERAS
QL942	KERATIN
RE201	KERATOCONJUNCTIVITIS SICCA
RE336	*KERATOMALACIA* **SEE** CORNEA — DISEASES
RL435	KERATOSIS

D766.84	*KEREN, BATTLE OF, 1941* **SEE** CHEREN, BATTLE OF, 1941
PM1511	KERES LANGUAGE
E99.K39	KERESAN INDIANS
E473.72	KERNSTOWN, BATTLE OF, 1862
TP692.4.K4	KEROSENE
QC463	KERR CELL SHUTTERS
QC463	KERR EFFECT
QC463	*KERR ELECTRO-OPTICAL EFFECT* **SEE** KERR EFFECT
SF429.K4	KERRY BLUE TERRIERS
QE461	KERSANTITE
PM6301-9	*KESHUA LANGUAGE* **SEE** KECHUA LANGUAGE
DD407.K4	KESSELSDORF, BATTLE OF, 1745
PM6301-9	*KESWA LANGUAGE* **SEE** KECHUA LANGUAGE
BV4487.K5	KESWICK MOVEMENT
DA345	*KET'S REBELLION, 1549* **SEE** KETT'S REBELLION, 1549
QD305.K2	KETINE
RB145	*KETONEMIA* **SEE** ACETONEMIA
RJ416.A	*KETONEMIA* **SEE** ACETONEMIA / *diseases of children*
QD305.K2	KETONES
QD341.K2	KETONES
RB145	*KETOSIS* **SEE** ACETONEMIA
RJ416.A	*KETOSIS* **SEE** ACETONEMIA / *diseases of children*
DK759.K	KETS
DA345	KETT'S REBELLION, 1549
M146	*KETTLEDRUM MUSIC* **SEE** PERCUSSION MUSIC
ML1035	KETTLEDRUM / *history*
M1038-9	KETTLEDRUMS WITH ORCHESTRA
TX657.K4	KETTLES
MT224	*KEYBOARD HARMONY* **SEE** HARMONY, KEYBOARD
ML549-697	KEYBOARDS
TA472	*KEYS (STEELWORK)* **SEE** KEYS AND KEYWAYS (STEELWORK) / *specifications*
TS519-530	*KEYS* **SEE** LOCKS AND KEYS
TA472	KEYS AND KEYWAYS (STEELWORK) / *specifications*
DT797.K	KGALAGADI (AFRICAN PEOPLE)
DS539.M6	*KHA (SOUTHEAST-ASIATIC PEOPLE)* **SEE** MOI (SOUTHEAST-ASIATIC PEOPLE)
DS539.K	KHA TAHOI
PL7501.B8	*KHAJUNA LANGUAGE* **SEE** BURUSHASKI LANGUAGE
PL391-4	KHAKASS LANGUAGE
PL394.A2	KHAKASS LITERATURE / *collections*
PL393.5	KHAKASS LITERATURE / *history*
DK759.K	KHAKASSIANS
TP907	KHAKI
P959	*KHALDIAN LANGUAGE* **SEE** VANNIC LANGUAGE
DS234-8	*KHALIFS* **SEE** CALIPHS / *arabian*
PL421	KHALKHA LANGUAGE
DS793.M7	KHALKHAS / *mongolia*
PL4351.K6	*KHAMOU LANGUAGE* **SEE** KHMU' LANGUAGE
PL4351.K6	*KHAMUK LANGUAGE* **SEE** KHMU' LANGUAGE
PL4695	*KHAND LANGUAGE* **SEE** KUI LANGUAGE
PH1401-1409	*KHANTE LANGUAGE* **SEE** OSTIAK LANGUAGE
DK759.O8	*KHANTY* **SEE** OSTIAKS
BP195.K4-42	*KHAREJITES* **SEE** KHARIJITES
PL4579	KHARIA LANGUAGE
DS432.K48	KHARIAS
BP195.K4-42	KHARIJITES
D764	KHARKOV, BATTLE OF, 1943
PK119	KHAROSTHI ALPHABET
DS59.H	*KHARRI* **SEE** HURRIANS
DS432.K48	*KHARRIAS* **SEE** KHARIAS
PK2595-9	*KHAS LANGUAGE* **SEE** NEPALI LANGUAGE
DS784	*KHASAN INCIDENT, 1938* **SEE** CHANGKUFENG INCIDENT, 1938
PL4451	KHASI LANGUAGE
DS432.K5	KHASIS
PL4451	*KHASSI LANGUAGE* **SEE** KHASI LANGUAGE
BP195.K4-42	*KHAWARIJS* **SEE** KHARIJITES
PL4511-4519	KHERWARI LANGUAGE
DS66	*KHETA* **SEE** HITTITES
F2230.2.K4	*KHETSCHUA INDIANS* **SEE** KECHUA INDIANS
PM6301-9	*KHETSCHUA LANGUAGE* **SEE** KECHUA LANGUAGE
PM6308	*KHETSCHUA LITERATURE* **SEE** KECHUA LITERATURE
PK9201.K51	KHINALUGH LANGUAGE
F3429.3.Q6	*KHIPU* **SEE** QUIPU
DS66	*KHITA* **SEE** HITTITES
QB23	*KHMER ASTRONOMY* **SEE** ASTRONOMY, KHMER
PL4321-9	KHMER LANGUAGE
PL4328	KHMER LITERATURE
GN630.K4	KHMERS / *anthropology*
DS557.C25	KHMERS / *cambodian antiquities*
PL4351.K6	*KHMOU LANGUAGE* **SEE** KHMU' LANGUAGE
PL4351.K6	KHMU' LANGUAGE
BP195.K45	KHOJAHS
PL4695	*KHOND LANGUAGE* **SEE** KUI LANGUAGE
DS432.K17	*KHONDS* **SEE** KANDHS
DT764.K6	*KHORA* **SEE** KORANA (AFRICAN PEOPLE)
P918	KHOREZMI LANGUAGE
P911	*KHOTAN-SAKA LANGUAGE* **SEE** KHOTANESE LANGUAGE
P911	KHOTANESE LANGUAGE
P911	*KHOTANI LANGUAGE* **SEE** KHOTANESE LANGUAGE
P911	*KHOTANSAKA LANGUAGE* **SEE** KHOTANESE LANGUAGE
PK7070	KHOWAR LANGUAGE
PK6996.K	KHUF DIALECT
PL4001.N8	*KHUNUNG LANGUAGE* **SEE** NUNG LANGUAGE
DS59.H	*KHURRIANS* **SEE** HURRIANS
DT786	KHWAKHWA (AFRICAN PEOPLE)
PJ2439	*KHWARA LANGUAGE* **SEE** QUARA LANGUAGE
PL4001.K6	KHYANG LANGUAGE
PL4001.K6	*KHYENG LANGUAGE* **SEE** KHYANG LANGUAGE
PL8401-4	*KI-KONGO LANGUAGE* **SEE** CONGO LANGUAGE
PL8774	*KI-VILI LANGUAGE* **SEE** VILI LANGUAGE
PL8774	*KI-VUMBU LANGUAGE* **SEE** VILI LANGUAGE
PM4231	*KICHE LANGUAGE* **SEE** QUICHE LANGUAGE
F2230.2.K4	*KICHUA INDIANS* **SEE** KECHUA INDIANS
PM6301-9	*KICHUA LANGUAGE* **SEE** KECHUA LANGUAGE
PM6308	*KICHUA LITERATURE* **SEE** KECHUA LITERATURE
E99.K4	KICKAPOO INDIANS
PM1526	KICKAPOO LANGUAGE
GV951.7	KICKING (FOOTBALL)
HV6595-6604	KIDNAPPING
RC901.7.A7	*KIDNEY, ARTIFICIAL* **SEE** ARTIFICIAL KIDNEY
RC280.K5	KIDNEYS — CANCER
RC902-918	KIDNEYS — DISEASES
RC184.T6	KIDNEYS — HYDATIDS
RD575	KIDNEYS — SURGERY
RC312.5.K5	KIDNEYS — TUBERCULOSIS
RC280.K5	KIDNEYS — TUMORS
QL872	KIDNEYS / *comparative anatomy*
QM404	KIDNEYS / *human anatomy*
QP211	KIDNEYS / *physiology*
RC918.M8	KIDNEYS, MOVABLE
RX351-6	KIDNEYS — DISEASES — — HOMEOPATHIC TREATMENT
GV827	KIEL REGATTA, 1907
GV827	KIEL REGATTA, 1914
DL500-501	KIEL, TREATY OF, 1814
TN948.D5	*KIESELGUHR* **SEE** DIATOMACEOUS EARTH
TR263.K	KIEV CAMERA
D764	*KIEV, BATTLE OF, 1943* **SEE** WORLD WAR, 1939-1945 — CAMPAIGNS — — DNIEPER RIVER
PL8401-4	*KIFIOTI LANGUAGE* **SEE** CONGO LANGUAGE
E99.K4	*KIKAPOO INDIANS* **SEE** KICKAPOO INDIANS
PL8379	KIKUYU LANGUAGE
DT429	KIKUYU TRIBE
DT434.E2	KIKUYU TRIBE
PL8380.K5	KILEGA LANGUAGE
DA943	*KILKENNY CONFEDERATION* **SEE** IRISH CONFEDERATION, 1642-1648
TP841-2	KILNS
TP841	*KILNS, ELECTRIC* **SEE** ELECTRIC KILNS
TP841-2	KILNS, ROTARY
TP881	KILNS, ROTARY / *cement*
QC105	*KILOGRAM* **SEE** STANDARDS OF MASS
E476.27	KILPATRICK-DAHLGREN RAID, 1864
E476.27	*KILPATRICK'S RAID* **SEE** KILPATRICK-DAHLGREN RAID, 1864
DT934.K5	KIMBERLEY — SIEGE, 1899-1900
PL8381	KIMBUNDU LANGUAGE
PL8625	*KIMEGI LANGUAGE* **SEE** SAGARA LANGUAGE
GT1560	KIMONOS
LB1169-1188	KINDERGARTEN — METHODS AND MANUALS
M1990	KINDERGARTEN — MUSIC
MT920-925	KINDERGARTEN — MUSIC / *instruction and study*
LB1141-1499	KINDERGARTEN

HV1643	KINDERGARTEN / blind
HV2443	KINDERGARTEN / deaf
LB1169-1188	*KINDERGARTEN-GIFTS* **SEE** KINDERGARTEN — METHODS AND MANUALS
LB1141-1499	KINDERGARTENS
DT443	*KINDIGA (AFRICAN PEOPLE)* **SEE** TINDIGA (AFRICAN PEOPLE)
HV4701-4959	*KINDNESS TO ANIMALS* **SEE** ANIMALS, TREATMENT OF
BJ1533.K5	KINDNESS
QA623	KINEMATIC GEOMETRY
TJ175	*KINEMATICS OF MACHINERY* **SEE** MACHINERY, KINEMATICS OF
QA841	KINEMATICS
QA913	KINEMATICS / fluids
QC231	KINEMATICS / vibrations
BF285	*KINESTHESIA* **SEE** MUSCULAR SENSE
QC175	*KINETIC THEORY OF GASES* **SEE** GASES, KINETIC THEORY OF
QC175.3	*KINETIC THEORY OF LIQUIDS* **SEE** LIQUIDS, KINETIC THEORY OF
QA845-871	*KINETICS* **SEE** DYNAMICS
QA801-935	*KINETICS* **SEE** MECHANICS, ANALYTIC
QA801-935	*KINETICS* **SEE** MOTION / analytic mechanics
QC122-168	*KINETICS* **SEE** MOTION / physics
TR885	KINETO-PHONOGRAPH
TR885	KINETOGRAPH
PN1995.7	*KINETOPHONE* **SEE** MOVING-PICTURES, TALKING
TR870	KINETOSCOPE
E198	*KING GEORGE'S WAR, 1744-1748* **SEE** UNITED STATES — HISTORY — — KING GEORGE'S WAR, 1744-1748
E83.67	KING PHILIP'S WAR, 1675-1676
QL666.O6	KING SNAKES
E196	*KING WILLIAM'S WAR, 1689-1697* **SEE** UNITED STATES — HISTORY — — KING WILLIAM'S WAR, 1689-1697
RC311.1	*KING'S EVIL* **SEE** SCROFULA
BT378.M3	*KING'S SON, MARRIAGE OF THE* **SEE** MARRIAGE OF THE KING'S SON (PARABLE)
BT94	KINGDOM OF GOD
QL696.H3	KINGFISHERS
JC381	KINGS AND RULERS — DUTIES
CS27	KINGS AND RULERS — GENEALOGY
N7575-7639	KINGS AND RULERS — PORTRAITS
JN351-7	KINGS AND RULERS — SUCCESSION
JF285	KINGS AND RULERS — SUCCESSION
JC374	KINGS AND RULERS (IN RELIGION, FOLK-LORE, ETC.)
BL325.K5	KINGS AND RULERS (IN RELIGION, FOLK-LORE, ETC.)
D107	KINGS AND RULERS / biography comprehensive
JF253	KINGS AND RULERS / comparative government
JC374-408	KINGS AND RULERS / political theory
D352.1	KINGS AND RULERS / 19th century
D399.7	KINGS AND RULERS / 19th century
D412.7	KINGS AND RULERS / 20th century
D107	*KINGS AND RULERS, MODERN* **SEE** KINGS AND RULERS / biography comprehensive
JF253	*KINGS AND RULERS, MODERN* **SEE** KINGS AND RULERS / comparative government
JC374-408	*KINGS AND RULERS, MODERN* **SEE** KINGS AND RULERS / political theory
D399.7	*KINGS AND RULERS, MODERN* **SEE** KINGS AND RULERS / 19th century
D352.1	*KINGS AND RULERS, MODERN* **SEE** KINGS AND RULERS / 19th century
D412.7	*KINGS AND RULERS, MODERN* **SEE** KINGS AND RULERS / 20th century
GN495.5	KINGS AND RULERS, PRIMITIVE
BL325.K5	*KINGS AND RULERS-CULTUS* **SEE** KINGS AND RULERS (IN RELIGION, FOLK-LORE, ETC.)
JC374	*KINGS AND RULERS-CULTUS* **SEE** KINGS AND RULERS (IN RELIGION, FOLK-LORE, ETC.)
BL325.K5	*KINGS AND RULERS-DIVINITY* **SEE** KINGS AND RULERS (IN RELIGION, FOLK-LORE, ETC.)
JC374	*KINGS AND RULERS-DIVINITY* **SEE** KINGS AND RULERS (IN RELIGION, FOLK-LORE, ETC.)
JC393	*KINGS AND RULERS-EDUCATION* **SEE** EDUCATION OF PRINCES / political theory
LC4929-4949	*KINGS AND RULERS-EDUCATION* **SEE** EDUCATION OF PRINCES
E241.K5	KINGS MOUNTAIN, BATTLE OF, 1780
JC389	*KINGS, DIVINE RIGHT OF* **SEE** DIVINE RIGHT OF KINGS
PL8387	KINGWANA LANGUAGE
PL8593	*KINIASSA LANGUAGE* **SEE** NYANJA LANGUAGE
RS165.K5	KINO / pharmacy
RM666.K	KINO / therapeutics
GN480	KINSHIP
E474.52	KINSTON, N.C., BATTLE OF, 1862
PL8608	*KINYARUANDA LANGUAGE* **SEE** RUANDA LANGUAGE
PL8113	*KIOKWE LANGUAGE* **SEE** CHOKWE LANGUAGE
PL8815	*KIOMBE LANGUAGE* **SEE** YOMBE LANGUAGE
NA8450	*KIOSKS* **SEE** PAVILIONS
NA8450	*KIOSQUES* **SEE** PAVILIONS
E99.K52	KIOWA APACHE INDIANS
E99.K5	KIOWA INDIANS
PM1531	KIOWA LANGUAGE
E99.K5	*KIOWAN INDIANS* **SEE** KIOWA INDIANS
DS22.7	*KIPCHAK (KHANATE)* **SEE** GOLDEN HORDE
PL318	KIPCHAK LANGUAGE
GN659.K5	KIPSIGIS
DS22.7	*KIPTCHAK (KHANATE)* **SEE** GOLDEN HORDE
PL318	*KIPTCHAK LANGUAGE* **SEE** KIPCHAK LANGUAGE
F3429.3.Q6	*KIPU* **SEE** QUIPU
DS432.K	*KIRANTI (TRIBE)* **SEE** KIRATI (TRIBE)
DS432.K	KIRATI (TRIBE)
PL65.K5	KIRGHIZ PHILOLOGY
PL65.K4-44	*KIRGHIZ-KAISSAK LANGUAGE* **SEE** KAZAKH LANGUAGE
DK861.K	*KIRGHIZ-KAZAKS* **SEE** KAZAKS
F2520.1.K	*KIRIRI INDIANS* **SEE** KARIRI INDIANS / brazil
PM6286-9	*KIRIRI LANGUAGE* **SEE** KARIRI LANGUAGE
PL6252.K5	KIRIWINIAN LANGUAGE
PL4583	*KIRKU LANGUAGE* **SEE** KURKU LANGUAGE
PL8666	*KISHAMBALA LANGUAGE* **SEE** SHAMBALA LANGUAGE
DS135.R9	KISHINEV MASSACRE, 1903
PL8425	*KISOGO LANGUAGE* **SEE** KWAFI LANGUAGE
PN6084.K5	KISSING — QUOTATIONS, MAXIMS, ETC.
GT2640	KISSING (IN RELIGION, FOLK-LORE, ETC.)
QL523.R	KISSING-BUG
GT2640	KISSING
BP187.4	KISWAH
ML760	*KIT (MUSICAL INSTRUMENT)* **SEE** POCHETTE
PL8391	KITABWA LANGUAGE
E99.H23	*KITAMAT INDIANS* **SEE** HAISLA INDIANS
TX656-8	KITCHEN UTENSILS
TH6565	KITCHEN-BOILER EXPLOSIONS
SB320-353	*KITCHEN-GARDENS* **SEE** VEGETABLE GARDENING
GN787-8	KITCHEN-MIDDENS
NA8330	KITCHENS / architecture
TX653-5	KITCHENS / etc.
TL635	*KITE BALLOONS* **SEE** BALLOONS, KITE
PL8725	*KITEKE LANGUAGE* **SEE** TEKE LANGUAGE
QC879	KITES (METEOROLOGY)
UG670	KITES (MILITARY AND NAVAL RECONNAISSANCE)
TL800-830	KITES
ML760	*KITHARA* **SEE** CITHARA
E99.H23	*KITIMAT INDIANS* **SEE** HAISLA INDIANS
E99.H23	*KITLOPE INDIANS* **SEE** HAISLA INDIANS
PM1631	*KITONAQA LANGUAGE* **SEE** KUTENAI LANGUAGE
E99.K85	*KITUNAHAN INDIANS* **SEE** KUTENAI INDIANS
PM1631	*KITUNAHAN LANGUAGES* **SEE** KUTENAI LANGUAGE
PL8549	*KIUSA LANGUAGE* **SEE** NGONDE LANGUAGE
PL8774	*KIVILI LANGUAGE* **SEE** VILI LANGUAGE
PL8774	*KIVUMBU LANGUAGE* **SEE** VILI LANGUAGE
DU740	KIWAI (PAPUAN PEOPLE)
PL6621.K5	KIWAI LANGUAGES
QL696.A6	KIWIS
PL8815	*KIYOMBE LANGUAGE* **SEE** YOMBE LANGUAGE
E99.K59	KIYUKSA INDIANS
E99.G15	*KIZH INDIANS* **SEE** GABRIELENO INDIANS
PK9201.L3	*KIZI-KUMUK LANGUAGE* **SEE** LAK LANGUAGE
SF293.K	KLADRUB HORSE
E99.C83	*KLAHOQUAHT INDIANS* **SEE** CLAYOQUOT INDIANS
E99.C82	*KLALLAM INDIANS* **SEE** CLALLAM INDIANS
E99.K7	KLAMATH INDIANS
PM1551	KLAMATH LANGUAGE
N6887	*KLEINMEISTER* **SEE** LITTLE MASTERS (ARTISTS)
DF801	KLEPHTS

BF173	KLEPTOMANIA
E99.K76	KLIKITAT INDIANS
E98.R2	*KLUKWALLE* **SEE** WOLF RITUAL
E98.R2	*KLUKWANA* **SEE** WOLF RITUAL
PM1561	KNAIAKHOTANA LANGUAGE
TP156.M5	*KNEADING MACHINERY* **SEE** MIXING MACHINERY
QP372	*KNEE JERK* **SEE** REFLEXES
QL825	KNEE / *comparative anatomy*
QM131	KNEE / *human anatomy*
RD560	*KNEE-AMPUTATION* **SEE** AMPUTATIONS OF LEG
RD561	*KNEE-EXCISION* **SEE** EXCISION OF KNEE
QL821	*KNEECAP* **SEE** PATELLA / *comparative anatomy*
QM117	*KNEECAP* **SEE** PATELLA / *human anatomy*
QP372	*KNEECAP* **SEE** PATELLA / *reflexes*
RM801-822	*KNEIPP CURE* **SEE** HYDROTHERAPY
CR5109	*KNIGHT'S CROSS (GERMANY)* **SEE** RITTERKREUZ (GERMANY)
CR	*KNIGHTHOOD* **SEE** KNIGHTS AND KNIGHTHOOD
CR4701-4775	*KNIGHTHOOD, ORDERS OF* **SEE** MILITARY RELIGIOUS ORDERS
CR4501-6305	*KNIGHTHOOD, ORDERS OF* **SEE** ORDERS OF KNIGHTHOOD AND CHIVALRY
CR	KNIGHTS AND KNIGHTHOOD
CR4735-4755	*KNIGHTS TEMPLARS (MONASTIC AND MILITARY ORDER)* **SEE** TEMPLARS
DG83.3	*KNIGHTS, ROMAN* **SEE** EQUESTRIAN ORDER (ROME)
PM986-9	*KNISTENAUX LANGUAGE* **SEE** CREE LANGUAGE
PM986-9	*KNISTENEUX LANGUAGE* **SEE** CREE LANGUAGE
TT679-695	KNIT GOODS
TT685-7	KNITTING-MACHINES
TT820-829	KNITTING
TT679-695	KNITTING, MACHINE
TS380	KNIVES / *manufacture*
HD9745	KNIVES / *trade*
VM533	KNOTS AND SPLICES
QA581	*KNOTTED CURVES* **SEE** CURVES OF DOUBLE CURVATURE
VM533	*KNOTTING AND SPLICING* **SEE** KNOTS AND SPLICES
JK2341	*KNOW-NOTHING PARTY* **SEE** AMERICAN PARTY
AG	*KNOWLEDGE, BOOKS OF* **SEE** ENCYCLOPEDIAS AND DICTIONARIES
AE	*KNOWLEDGE, BOOKS OF* **SEE** ENCYCLOPEDIAS AND DICTIONARIES
Q177	*KNOWLEDGE, CLASSIFICATION OF* **SEE** CLASSIFICATION OF SCIENCES
BD240-241	*KNOWLEDGE, CLASSIFICATION OF* **SEE** CLASSIFICATION OF SCIENCES / *methodology*
Z696	*KNOWLEDGE, CLASSIFICATION OF* **SEE** CLASSIFICATION
BD175	KNOWLEDGE, SOCIOLOGY OF
BL51	KNOWLEDGE, THEORY OF (RELIGION)
BD175	*KNOWLEDGE, THEORY OF (SOCIOLOGY)* **SEE** KNOWLEDGE, SOCIOLOGY OF
BD150-241	KNOWLEDGE, THEORY OF
E475.94	KNOXVILLE, TENN. — SIEGE, 1863
QL737.M3	KOALAS
E99.K77	KOASATI INDIANS
ML1015.K6	*KOBSA* **SEE** KOBZA
M142.K55	KOBZA MUSIC
ML1015.K6	KOBZA
RM796	*KOCH'S LYMPH* **SEE** TUBERCULIN
PL4671	KODAGU LANGUAGE
E99.K85	*KOETENAY INDIANS* **SEE** KUTENAI INDIANS
PM1631	*KOETENAY LANGUAGE* **SEE** KUTENAI LANGUAGE
PL7101.K6	KOGAI LANGUAGE
DU274	KOGAI TRIBES / *queensland*
SB317.K	*KOHEMP* **SEE** KUDZU
PL4559	*KOHL LANGUAGE* **SEE** MUNDARI LANGUAGE
PL4351.S6	*KOHO LANGUAGE* **SEE** SRE LANGUAGE
PL45.K6	KOIBALIAN LANGUAGE
SB291.K	KOK-SAGHYZ / *culture*
PL31	*KOK-TURK LANGUAGE* **SEE** OLD TURKISH LANGUAGE
F3430.1.C	*KOKAMA INDIANS* **SEE** COCAMA INDIANS / *peru*
PL4559	*KOL LANGUAGE* **SEE** MUNDARI LANGUAGE
RS165.C64	*KOLA-NUT* **SEE** COLA-NUT / *pharmacy*
PL4681	KOLAMI LANGUAGE
PL4501-9	*KOLARIAN LANGUAGES* **SEE** MUNDA LANGUAGES
PL8062	*KOLKOTTA LANGUAGE* **SEE** BARIA LANGUAGE
F3430.1.C6	*KOLLA INDIANS* **SEE** COLLA INDIANS / *peru*
M1048	KOLOS (ORCHESTRA)

DS432.M8	*KOLS* **SEE** MUNDAS
E99.T6	*KOLUSCHAN INDIANS* **SEE** TLINGIT INDIANS
PM2455	*KOLUSCHAN LANGUAGE* **SEE** TLINGIT LANGUAGE
PJ2438	*KOMANT LANGUAGE* **SEE** KEMANT LANGUAGE
PL8396	KOMBE LANGUAGE
PH1051-9	*KOMI LANGUAGE* **SEE** SYRYENIAN LANGUAGE
PH1071-9	*KOMI-PERMYAK DIALECT* **SEE** PERMYAK DIALECT
DK34.S9	*KOMIS* **SEE** SYRYENIANS
PK2231-7	*KOMKANI LANGUAGE* **SEE** KONKANI LANGUAGE
JN6598	KOMMUNISTICHESKAIA PARTIIA SOVETSKOGO SOIUZA — ELECTIONS
M42.K58	KOMUNKO MUSIC
ML1015-1018	KOMUNKO
PL8432.M8	*KONDE LANGUAGE* **SEE** MAKONDE LANGUAGE
PL8549	*KONDE LANGUAGE* **SEE** NGONDE LANGUAGE
GN659.N45	*KONDE TRIBES* **SEE** NGONDE (AFRICAN TRIBE)
E99.E7	*KONIAGI INDIANS* **SEE** KANIAGMIUT (ESKIMO TRIBE)
DT530	KONIAGUI (AFRICAN PEOPLE)
DD439.K7	KONIGGRATZ, BATTLE OF, 1866
D764	KONIGSBERG, BATTLE OF, 1945
E99.E7	*KONJAGEN INDIANS* **SEE** KANIAGMIUT (ESKIMO TRIBE)
PK2231-7	KONKANI LANGUAGE
BL2222.K6	KONKO (SECT)
DT582	KONKOMBA (AFRICAN TRIBE)
BL2480.K	KONO (AFRICAN TRIBE) — RELIGION
DT516	KONO (AFRICAN TRIBE)
PL8406	KONO LANGUAGE
PM1585	KONOMIHU LANGUAGE
QL737.M3	*KOOLAH* **SEE** KOALAS
TP565	*KOOMIS* **SEE** KUMISS / *manufacture*
RM257.K8	*KOOMIS* **SEE** KUMISS / *therapeutics*
E99.K85	*KOOTENAI INDIANS* **SEE** KUTENAI INDIANS
PM1631	*KOOTENAI LANGUAGE* **SEE** KUTENAI LANGUAGE
PM73	KOPAGMIUT LANGUAGE
RC794	*KOPP'S ASTHMA* **SEE** LARYNGISMUS STRIDULUS
PL8407	*KORA LANGUAGE* **SEE** KORANA LANGUAGE
BP130.3	KORAN — ABROGATOR AND ABROGATED VERSES
BP134.E84	KORAN — ETHICS
BP130.2	KORAN — HERMENEUTICS
BP131.5	KORAN — READINGS
BP134.B4	KORAN — RELATION TO THE BIBLE
BP134.S6	KORAN — SOCIOLOGY
BP132	KORAN — THEOLOGY
BP131.8	KORAN AS LITERATURE
BP130.58	KORAN STORIES
BP100-130	KORAN
BP130.2	*KORAN-CRITICISM, INTERPRETATION, ETC.-THEORY, METHODS, ETC.* **SEE** KORAN — HERMENEUTICS
BP130.2	*KORAN-EXEGESIS* **SEE** KORAN — HERMENEUTICS
BP130.2	*KORAN-INTERPRETATION* **SEE** KORAN — HERMENEUTICS
BP131.5	*KORAN-QIRA'AT* **SEE** KORAN — READINGS
DT764.K6	KORANA (AFRICAN PEOPLE)
PL8407	KORANA LANGUAGE
DS432.K6	KORAVAS
DS918	*KOREA-HISTORY-WAR AND INTERVENTION, 1950-1953* **SEE** KOREAN WAR, 1950-1953
PL901-949	KOREAN LANGUAGE
PL950-988	KOREAN LITERATURE
DS921.3	KOREAN WAR, 1950-1953 — CIVILIAN RELIEF
DS921.5.D4	KOREAN WAR, 1950-1953 — DESTRUCTION AND PILLAGE
DS920.6	KOREAN WAR, 1950-1953 — REGISTERS OF DEAD
DS918.A2-55	KOREAN WAR, 1950-1953 — SOURCES
DS918	KOREAN WAR, 1950-1953
E84.K	KOREANS IN THE U.S.
TR263.K	KORELLE CAMERA
PL4583	*KORKU LANGUAGE* **SEE** KURKU LANGUAGE
D764	KORSUN'-SHEVCHENKOVSKIY, BATTLE OF, 1944
PM75	KORYAK LANGUAGE
DK759.K	KORYAKS
BM710	*KOSHER FOOD* **SEE** JEWS — DIETARY LAWS
DR337	KOSOVO, BATTLE OF, 1389
DR498	KOSOVO, BATTLE OF, 1448
PL4691	KOTA LANGUAGE
M296-7	*KOTO AND FLUTE MUSIC* **SEE** FLUTE AND KOTO MUSIC
M296-7	*KOTO AND FLUTE MUSIC* **SEE** FLUTE AND KOTO MUSIC

M142.K6	KOTO MUSIC
M1037.4.K68	KOTO WITH ORCHESTRA
ML1015-1018	KOTO
DB86.7	KOTOR MUTINY, 1918
PL4351.K8	*KOUI LANGUAGE* **SEE** KUI LANGUAGE (MON-KHMER)
TP565	*KOUMYS* **SEE** KUMISS / *manufacture*
RM257.K8	*KOUMYS* **SEE** KUMISS / *therapeutics*
DS432.K8	*KOUROUMBS* **SEE** KURUMBAS
PL8411	KPELLE LANGUAGE
DT630.5.K	KPELLE
PL8411	*KPWELE LANGUAGE* **SEE** KPELLE LANGUAGE
UD395.K9	KRAG-JORGENSEN RIFLE
RS165.R3	*KRAMERIA* **SEE** RATANY / *pharmacy*
RM666.R3	*KRAMERIA* **SEE** RATANY / *therapeutics*
QP801.C8	*KREATINE* **SEE** CREATINE
PL8221	*KREBO LANGUAGE* **SEE** GREBO LANGUAGE
PL8413	KREJ LANGUAGE
TP248.C	*KREOSOTE* **SEE** CREOSOTE / *chemical technology*
RM666.C8	*KREOSOTE* **SEE** CREOSOTE / *therapeutics*
TP248.C67	*KRESOL* **SEE** CRESOL / *chemical technology*
QD341.P5	*KRESOL* **SEE** CRESOL / *chemistry*
U310	*KRIEGSSPIEL* **SEE** WAR GAMES
V250	*KRIEGSSPIEL* **SEE** WAR GAMES / *naval*
NK6805	*KRISES* **SEE** DAGGERS / *art*
DK265.8.K	KRONSTADT, RUSSIA — HISTORY —— REVOLT, 1921
QD181.K6	KRYPTON
PM1631	*KSANKA LANGUAGE* **SEE** KUTENAI LANGUAGE
DS432.K7	*KSATRIYAS* **SEE** KSHATRIYAS
DS432.K7	KSHATRIYAS
HS2330.K6-63	KU KLUX KLAN (1915-)
E668	KU-KLUX KLAN
PL8417	KUANYAMA LANGUAGE
P911.T	*KUCHEAN LANGUAGE* **SEE** TOKHARIAN LANGUAGE
DR553	KUCHUK KAINARJI, TREATY OF, 1774
DR553	*KUCUKKAYNARCA, TREATY OF, 1774* **SEE** KUCHUK KAINARJI, TREATY OF, 1774
HF5381.5	KUDER PREFERENCE RECORD
SB317.K	KUDZU
SF199.K9	KUHLAND CATTLE
PL4351.K8	KUI LANGUAGE (MON-KHMER)
PL4695	KUI LANGUAGE
E99.K	KUITSH INDIANS
PM1598	KUITSH LANGUAGE
PL3891-4	KUKI-CHIN LANGUAGES
DS432.K8	KUKIS / *india*
E99.P65	*KULANAPAN INDIANS* **SEE** POMO INDIANS
BL1245.K3	*KULINAS* **SEE** KAULAS
DD118	KULTURKAMPF
PK2610.K8	*KULU LANGUAGE* **SEE** KULUI LANGUAGE
PK2610.K8	*KULUHI LANGUAGE* **SEE** KULUI LANGUAGE
PK2610.K8	KULUI LANGUAGE
ML1015-1018	*KUM* **SEE** KOMUNKO
PL318	*KUMAN LANGUAGE* **SEE** KIPCHAK LANGUAGE
PL7101.G8	*KUMBAINGGERI LANGUAGE* **SEE** GUMBAINGAR LANGUAGE
TP565	KUMISS / *manufacture*
RM257.K8	KUMISS / *therapeutics*
PL65.K	KUMYK LANGUAGE
DK34.K	KUMYKS
PL8421	KUNAMA LANGUAGE
DT393.5	KUNAMAS
DD412.6.K8	KUNERSDORF, BATTLE OF, 1759
JS775	KUO MIN TANG
JS219	*KURAISH (ARAB TRIBE)* **SEE** QURAYSH (ARAB TRIBE)
DS432.K6	*KURAVERS* **SEE** KORAVAS
PK6901-9	KURDISH LANGUAGE
PK6908	KURDISH LITERATURE
PK6908	KURDISH POETRY
DS51.K7	KURDS
PL4671	*KURG LANGUAGE* **SEE** KODAGU LANGUAGE
PK9201.K8	KURI LANGUAGE
PL4583	KURKU LANGUAGE
PK6901-9	*KURMANJI LANGUAGE* **SEE** KURDISH LANGUAGE
DU122.K	KURNAI TRIBE
GC296.K85	*KURO SIWO* **SEE** KUROSHIO
GC296.K85	KUROSHIO
BL2222.K8	KUROZUMI (SECT)
DK412	KURPIE
DK412	*KURPS* **SEE** KURPIE
PL8475	*KURSA LANGUAGE* **SEE** MABA LANGUAGE
PL4701-4	KURUKH LANGUAGE
PL4704	KURUKH POETRY
DS432.K8	KURUMBAS
PL8423	*KUSA LANGUAGE* **SEE** KUSSASSI LANGUAGE
PL6252.K8	KUSAIE LANGUAGE
E99.C874	*KUSAN INDIANS* **SEE** COOS INDIANS
PM1611	KUSAN LANGUAGES
PL8423	*KUSASI LANGUAGE* **SEE** KUSSASSI LANGUAGE
PL8423	KUSSASSI LANGUAGE
D568.5	KUT EL AMARA — SIEGE, 1915-1916
PM1615	KUTCHAKUTCHIN LANGUAGE
E99.K	KUTCHIN INDIANS
PM1621	KUTCHIN LANGUAGES
E99.K85	KUTENAI INDIANS
PM1631	KUTENAI LANGUAGE
DR27.A8	*KUTZO-VLAKHS* **SEE** AROMUNES
PL4706	KUVI LANGUAGE
PL4351.K8	*KUY LANGUAGE* **SEE** KUI LANGUAGE (MON-KHMER)
PL8425	KWAFI LANGUAGE
E99.K9	KWAKIUTL INDIANS
PM1641	KWAKIUTL LANGUAGE
PL8417	*KWANYAMA LANGUAGE* **SEE** KUANYAMA LANGUAGE
PL8425	*KWAPI LANGUAGE* **SEE** KWAFI LANGUAGE
PJ2439	*KWARA LANGUAGE* **SEE** QUARA LANGUAGE
RJ399.K9	KWASHIORKOR
PL8425	*KWAVI LANGUAGE* **SEE** KWAFI LANGUAGE
E99.Y94	*KWICHAN INDIANS* **SEE** YUMA INDIANS
E99.Q6	*KWINAIUTL INDIANS* **SEE** QUINAIELT INDIANS
PM1611	*KWOKWOOS LANGUAGE* **SEE** COOS LANGUAGE
TA422-4	*KYANIZING* **SEE** WOOD — PRESERVATION
PL736	KYOGEN PLAYS
PL766	KYOGEN PLAYS / *collections*
RD768	*KYPHOSIS* **SEE** SPINE — ABNORMALITIES AND DEFORMITIES
PK9201.K8	*KYURINISCH LANGUAGE* **SEE** KURI LANGUAGE
BX4737	*LA PETITE EGLISE* **SEE** LOUISETS
DC117	LA ROCHE-L'ABEILLE, BATTLE OF, 1569
DC117.L3	LA ROCHELLE — SIEGE, 1573
DC123.3	LA ROCHELLE — SIEGE, 1627-1628
GN779-780	LA TENE PERIOD
BX7990.L2	LABADISTS IN MARYLAND
BX7990.L2	LABADISTS
TP659	LABELING-MACHINES / *bottling*
HD6489	*LABELS (TRADE-UNION)* **SEE** UNION LABEL
NC1280	LABELS
RG651-791	LABOR (OBSTETRICS)
HD5115	*LABOR ABSENTEEISM* **SEE** ABSENTEEISM (LABOR)
HD6961	*LABOR AND CAPITAL* **SEE** INDUSTRIAL RELATIONS
HD4813	LABOR AND LABORING CLASSES — CONGRESSES
LC5001-5060	LABOR AND LABORING CLASSES — EDUCATION
RC963	LABOR AND LABORING CLASSES — MEDICAL CARE
HD7261	LABOR AND LABORING CLASSES — MEDICAL EXAMINATIONS
M1977.L3	LABOR AND LABORING CLASSES — SONGS AND MUSIC / *collections*
ML3780	LABOR AND LABORING CLASSES — SONGS AND MUSIC / *history and criticism*
M1664-5.L3	LABOR AND LABORING CLASSES — SONGS AND MUSIC / *political songs*
M1978.L3	LABOR AND LABORING CLASSES — SONGS AND MUSIC / *single songs*
N8219.L	LABOR AND LABORING CLASSES IN ART
HD4801-8942	LABOR AND LABORING CLASSES
HD6228-6250	*LABOR AND LABORING CLASSES-CHILD LABOR* **SEE** CHILDREN — EMPLOYMENT
HD7095-6	*LABOR AND LABORING CLASSES-INSURANCE* **SEE** INSURANCE, UNEMPLOYMENT
HD7101-2	*LABOR AND LABORING CLASSES-INSURANCE* **SEE** INSURANCE, ACCIDENT / *industrial*
HG9301-9343	*LABOR AND LABORING CLASSES-INSURANCE* **SEE** INSURANCE, ACCIDENT
HG9383-9399	*LABOR AND LABORING CLASSES-INSURANCE* **SEE** INSURANCE, HEALTH
HD7101-2	*LABOR AND LABORING CLASSES-INSURANCE* **SEE** INSURANCE, HEALTH / *industrial*
HG9426-9446	*LABOR AND LABORING CLASSES-INSURANCE* **SEE** OLD AGE PENSIONS / *age insurance*
HD7105-6	*LABOR AND LABORING CLASSES-INSURANCE* **SEE** OLD AGE PENSIONS / *working-men's insurance*

HD4906-5100	*LABOR AND LABORING CLASSES-WAGES* **SEE** WAGES
HB301	*LABOR AND LABORING CLASSES-WAGES* **SEE** WAGES / *theory*
HD6977-7080	*LABOR AND LABORING CLASSES-WAGES* **SEE** WAGES / *wages and cost of living*
HD8072	LABOR AND LABORING CLASSES — U.S. — — 1914-
HD6338	*LABOR AND THE CHURCH* **SEE** CHURCH AND LABOR
HD4831-5	LABOR BUREAUS
HD7290	LABOR CAMPS
HD1516	*LABOR COLONIES* **SEE** AGRICULTURAL COLONIES
HD4813	*LABOR CONGRESSES* **SEE** LABOR AND LABORING CLASSES — CONGRESSES
HD4905.5	*LABOR CONSCRIPTION* **SEE** SERVICE, COMPULSORY NON-MILITARY / *in wartime*
HD4871-5	*LABOR CONSCRIPTION* **SEE** SERVICE, COMPULSORY NON-MILITARY
HD7811-7813	LABOR CONTRACT
HD4929	LABOR CONTRACT
BX2015.9.J6	LABOR DAY MASS
HD7791	LABOR DAY
HD4831-5	*LABOR DEPARTMENTS* **SEE** LABOR BUREAUS
HD5861-6000	*LABOR EXCHANGES* **SEE** EMPLOYMENT AGENCIES
HD5701-5851	*LABOR FORCE* **SEE** LABOR SUPPLY
HD7801-7960	LABOR LAWS AND LEGISLATION
HD7801-9	LABOR LAWS AND LEGISLATION, INTERNATIONAL
HD5701-5851	*LABOR MARKET* **SEE** LABOR SUPPLY
HD4831-5	*LABOR MINISTRIES* **SEE** LABOR BUREAUS
HD6451-6473	*LABOR ORGANIZATIONS* **SEE** GILDS / *history*
HD2341-6	*LABOR ORGANIZATIONS* **SEE** GILDS / *modern*
HD6350-6940	*LABOR ORGANIZATIONS* **SEE** TRADE-UNIONS
HD6961	*LABOR RELATIONS* **SEE** INDUSTRIAL RELATIONS
HD5650-5659	*LABOR REPRESENTATION IN REGULATION OF INDUSTRY* **SEE** EMPLOYEES' REPRESENTATION IN MANAGEMENT
HD5701-5851	LABOR SUPPLY
HF5549	LABOR TURNOVER
HD6961	*LABOR-MANAGEMENT RELATIONS* **SEE** INDUSTRIAL RELATIONS
HD6350-6940	*LABOR-UNIONS* **SEE** TRADE-UNIONS
HD5855-6	*LABOR, CASUAL* **SEE** CASUAL LABOR
RG701-721	LABOR, COMPLICATED
HD4871-5	*LABOR, CONSCRIPTION OF* **SEE** SERVICE, COMPULSORY NON-MILITARY
HD4905.5	*LABOR, CONSCRIPTION OF* **SEE** SERVICE, COMPULSORY NON-MILITARY / *in wartime*
HD51	*LABOR, DIVISION OF* **SEE** DIVISION OF LABOR
HD5106-5250	*LABOR, HOURS OF* **SEE** HOURS OF LABOR
HD5855-6	*LABOR, MIGRANT* **SEE** MIGRANT LABOR
HD6350-6940	*LABOR, ORGANIZED* **SEE** TRADE-UNIONS
HD4903	*LABOR, RIGHT TO* **SEE** RIGHT TO LABOR
Q185	LABORATORIES — APPARATUS AND SUPPLIES
Q183	LABORATORIES — FURNITURE, EQUIPMENT, ETC.
Q183	LABORATORIES
TL566-8	*LABORATORIES, AERODYNAMICAL* **SEE** AERONAUTICAL LABORATORIES
TL566-8	*LABORATORIES, AERONAUTICAL* **SEE** AERONAUTICAL LABORATORIES
QM41	*LABORATORIES, ANATOMICAL* **SEE** ANATOMICAL LABORATORIES
QR63-71	*LABORATORIES, BACTERIOLOGICAL* **SEE** BACTERIOLOGICAL LABORATORIES
QH321	*LABORATORIES, BIOLOGICAL* **SEE** BIOLOGICAL LABORATORIES
QK78	*LABORATORIES, BOTANICAL* **SEE** BOTANICAL LABORATORIES
QD51	*LABORATORIES, CHEMICAL* **SEE** CHEMICAL LABORATORIES
TK411-415	*LABORATORIES, ELECTRIC* **SEE** ELECTRIC LABORATORIES / *engineering*
QC541	*LABORATORIES, ELECTRIC* **SEE** ELECTRIC LABORATORIES / *physics*
TA416-417	*LABORATORIES, ENGINEERING* **SEE** ENGINEERING LABORATORIES
TA416-417	*LABORATORIES, MECHANICAL* **SEE** ENGINEERING LABORATORIES
TN570-571	*LABORATORIES, METALLURGICAL* **SEE** METALLURGICAL LABORATORIES
RB37	*LABORATORIES, PATHOLOGICAL* **SEE** PATHOLOGICAL LABORATORIES / *methods*
QP51-53	*LABORATORIES, PHYSIOLOGICAL* **SEE** PHYSIOLOGICAL LABORATORIES
TA416-417	*LABORATORIES, TESTING* **SEE** TESTING LABORATORIES
QL55	LABORATORY ANIMALS
SF77	LABORATORY ANIMALS
LB2153-5	LABORATORY SCHOOLS
HD4801-8942	*LABORERS* **SEE** LABOR AND LABORING CLASSES
BT378.P	LABORERS IN THE VINEYARD (PARABLE)
SF429.L3	LABRADOR DOGS
SF429.L3	*LABRADOR RETRIEVERS* **SEE** LABRADOR DOGS
GN419.L	LABRETS
QD421	*LABURNINE* **SEE** CYTISINE / *chemistry*
QP921.C	*LABURNINE* **SEE** CYTISINE / *physiological effect*
QL948	LABYRINTH (EAR) / *comparative anatomy*
QM507	LABYRINTH (EAR) / *human anatomy*
QP461	LABYRINTH (EAR) / *physiology*
RF270	*LABYRINTHINE HYDROPS* **SEE** MENIERE'S DISEASE
QL523.C7	LAC-INSECTS
SF561	LAC / *animal culture*
TP938	LAC / *etc.*
HD9769.L3-33	LAC / *trade*
F1465.2.L2	LACANDON INDIANS / *guatemala*
F1221.L2	LACANDON INDIANS / *mexico*
SF561	LACCOL / *animal culture*
HD9679.L3-33	LACCOL / *trade*
QE611	LACCOLITHS
NK9400-9499	LACE AND LACE MAKING / *fine arts*
TS1782	LACE AND LACE MAKING / *manufacture*
TT800-805	LACE AND LACE MAKING / *needlework*
HD9933	LACE AND LACE MAKING / *trade*
QL523.T	LACE-BUGS
QL666.L2	*LACERTILIA* **SEE** LIZARDS
QH513.H	LACEWING FLIES
QL949	*LACHRYMAL ORGANS* **SEE** LACRIMAL ORGANS / *comparative anatomy*
QM511	*LACHRYMAL ORGANS* **SEE** LACRIMAL ORGANS / *human anatomy*
QP231	*LACHRYMAL ORGANS* **SEE** LACRIMAL ORGANS / *physiology*
TP939	LACQUER AND LACQUERING / *chemical technology*
NK9900	LACQUER AND LACQUERING / *fine arts*
TS710	LACQUER AND LACQUERING / *lacquering of metals*
QL949	*LACRIMAL CANAL* **SEE** LACRIMAL ORGANS / *comparative anatomy*
QM511	*LACRIMAL CANAL* **SEE** LACRIMAL ORGANS / *human anatomy*
QP231	*LACRIMAL CANAL* **SEE** LACRIMAL ORGANS / *physiology*
RD643	*LACRIMAL FISTULA* **SEE** FISTULA, LACRIMAL
RE201-216	LACRIMAL ORGANS — DISEASES
QL949	LACRIMAL ORGANS / *comparative anatomy*
QM511	LACRIMAL ORGANS / *human anatomy*
QP231	LACRIMAL ORGANS / *physiology*
GV989	LACROSSE
QL949	*LACRYMAL ORGANS* **SEE** LACRIMAL ORGANS / *comparative anatomy*
QM511	*LACRYMAL ORGANS* **SEE** LACRIMAL ORGANS / *human anatomy*
QP231	*LACRYMAL ORGANS* **SEE** LACRIMAL ORGANS / *physiology*
RJ231	LACTATED FOOD
RJ216	LACTATION
QP246	LACTATION / *physiology*
QP915.L2	LACTIC ACID — PHYSIOLOGICAL EFFECT
QR121	LACTIC ACID BACTERIA
QD305.A2	LACTIC ACID / *chemistry*
RM666.L18	LACTIC ACID / *therapeutics*
QP801.V5	*LACTOFLAVIN* **SEE** RIBOFLAVIN
QD305.A2	LACTONES
QP701	LACTOSE IN THE BODY
QD321	LACTOSE
RM666.L2	LACTOSE / *therapeutics*
RM666.L	LACTUCARIUM
TH2258	LADDERS — STANDARDS / *fixed ladders*
TS903	LADDERS — STANDARDS / *wood ladders*
TS903	LADDERS
PL3651.L3	*LADHAKI LANGUAGE* **SEE** TIBETAN LANGUAGE — DIALECTS — — LADAK
DC113.5	*LADIES' PEACE* **SEE** CAMBRAI, TREATY OF, 1529

PC901-949	*LADIN LANGUAGE* **SEE** RAETO-ROMANCE LANGUAGE
HE2242	*LADING, BILLS OF* **SEE** BILLS OF LADING
PC4813	LADINO LANGUAGE
QL596.C65	*LADY-BEETLES* **SEE** LADYBIRDS
QL596.C65	LADYBIRDS
QL596.C65	*LADYBUGS* **SEE** LADYBIRDS
DT934.L2	LADYSMITH, NATAL — SIEGE, 1899
QD321	*LAEVULOSE* **SEE** LEVULOSE
HM101	*LAG, CULTURAL* **SEE** CULTURAL LAG
GB2201-2397	LAGOONS
QA845-871	*LAGRANGE'S EQUATIONS* **SEE** DYNAMICS
QA306	*LAGRANGE'S SERIES (MATHEMATICS)* **SEE** SERIES, LAGRANGE'S
E99.L2	LAGUNA INDIANS
PM1645	LAGUNA LANGUAGE
PK2261-2270	LAHNDI LANGUAGE
PL4001.L2	LAI LANGUAGE
HB95	LAISSEZ-FAIRE
BX1920	LAITY — CATHOLIC CHURCH
BV687	LAITY
PK9201.L3	LAK LANGUAGE
F1031.1	*LAKE CHAMPLAIN TERCENTENARY CELEBRATION, 1909* **SEE** CHAMPLAIN TERCENTENARY CELEBRATIONS
F1030	LAKE OF THE WOODS MASSACRE, 1736
PR590	LAKE POETS
PR590	*LAKE SCHOOL* **SEE** LAKE POETS
GN785-6	LAKE-DWELLERS AND LAKE-DWELLINGS
QC909	LAKES — TEMPERATURE
GB1601-1797	LAKES
TD392	LAKES / *water-supply*
GB1201-1397	*LAKES, FREEZING AND OPENING OF* **SEE** ICE ON RIVERS, LAKES, ETC. T (INDIRECT) / *rivers*
GB1601-1797	*LAKES, FREEZING AND OPENING OF* **SEE** ICE ON RIVERS, LAKES, ETC. T (INDIRECT) / *lakes*
DS485.A86	LAKHERS
PR590	*LAKISTS* **SEE** LAKE POETS
PL8431	*LALA LANGUAGE* **SEE** LAMBA LANGUAGE
PL8725	*LALI LANGUAGE* **SEE** TEKE LANGUAGE
BL1485	LAMAISM
PL8431	LAMBA LANGUAGE
DT955	LAMBAS
QA409	LAME'S FUNCTIONS
QL430.6-7	LAMELLIBRANCHIATA
QE811-812	LAMELLIBRANCHIATA, FOSSIL
PN1389	*LAMENTATIONS* **SEE** ELEGIAC POETRY
DF235.5	LAMIAN WAR, 323-322 B.C.
TL574.L	LAMINAR FLOW / *aerodynamics*
QA929	LAMINAR FLOW / *theory*
TP862	*LAMINATED GLASS* **SEE** GLASS, SAFETY
TA403	LAMINATED MATERIALS
TS870	*LAMINATED WOOD* **SEE** PLYWOOD
SF959.L	LAMINITIS
TP868	LAMP-CHIMNEYS, GLOBES, ETC.
TP951	LAMPBLACK
BT1417	*LAMPETIANS* **SEE** MESSALIANS
QL638.1	LAMPREYS
QE461	LAMPROPHYRES
TP746	LAMPS
GR950.L3	LAMPS / *folk-lore*
GT445	LAMPS / *manners and customs*
PL461.L3	LAMUT LANGUAGE
PL5884	LANAO MORO DIALECT
DA461	LANCASHIRE PLOT, 1689-1694
LB1029.M7	*LANCASTERIAN SYSTEM* **SEE** MONITORIAL SYSTEM OF EDUCATION
U872	LANCES
HD105	LAND — CONGRESSES
HD226	LAND CLAIM ASSOCIATIONS
S607	*LAND CLEARING* **SEE** CLEARING OF LAND
HD1481	*LAND CONSOLIDATION* **SEE** CONSOLIDATION OF LAND HOLDINGS / *economics*
K	*LAND CONSOLIDATION* **SEE** CONSOLIDATION OF LAND HOLDINGS / *law*
HG2041-2051	*LAND CREDIT* **SEE** AGRICULTURAL CREDIT / *banking*
HD1439-1440	*LAND CREDIT* **SEE** AGRICULTURAL CREDIT / *theory*
S621	*LAND DRAINAGE* **SEE** DRAINAGE / *agriculture*
HD1681-3	*LAND DRAINAGE* **SEE** DRAINAGE / *economics*
TC970-978	*LAND DRAINAGE* **SEE** DRAINAGE / *engineering*
GB906	*LAND DRAINAGE* **SEE** DRAINAGE / *physical geography*
GB423-445	*LAND FORMS* **SEE** LANDFORMS
LB2827	*LAND GRANTS FOR EDUCATION* **SEE** SCHOOL LANDS
HD625	*LAND LEAGUE, IRISH* **SEE** IRISH LAND LEAGUE / *economic history*
DA951	*LAND LEAGUE, IRISH* **SEE** IRISH LAND LEAGUE / *history of ireland*
HD101-1395	*LAND QUESTION* **SEE** LAND TENURE
TC343-5	*LAND RECLAMATION* **SEE** RECLAMATION OF LAND / *coast works*
TC970-978	*LAND RECLAMATION* **SEE** RECLAMATION OF LAND / *etc.*
S605-623	*LAND RECLAMATION* **SEE** RECLAMATION OF LAND / *farm lands*
TC801-937	*LAND RECLAMATION* **SEE** RECLAMATION OF LAND / *irrigation*
QE599	*LAND SLIDES* **SEE** LANDSLIDES
TA501-625	*LAND SURVEYING* **SEE** SURVEYING
HD1141-1239	LAND TENURE — LAW
HD101-1395	LAND TENURE
HD1188-1208	LAND TITLES — REGISTRATION AND TRANSFER
HD1181-1211	LAND TITLES
HD1188-1208	*LAND TRANSFER* **SEE** LAND TITLES — REGISTRATION AND TRANSFER
HD101-1395	*LAND USE* **SEE** LAND
HD101-243	*LAND USE* **SEE** LAND / *land and agriculture*
NA9000-9284	*LAND USE* **SEE** REGIONAL PLANNING
HD101-1395	*LAND UTILIZATION* **SEE** LAND
HD101-243	*LAND UTILIZATION* **SEE** LAND / *land and agriculture*
HD1393	*LAND VALUATION* **SEE** FARMS — VALUATION
LB2329.5	*LAND-GRANT COLLEGES* **SEE** STATE UNIVERSITIES AND COLLEGES
HD1181-1211	*LAND-WARRANTS* **SEE** LAND TITLES
HD101-1395	LAND
HD101-243	LAND / *land and agriculture*
HD1519	*LAND, ALLOTMENT OF* **SEE** ALLOTMENT OF LAND
HD1261-5	*LAND, CONDEMNATION OF* **SEE** EMINENT DOMAIN
HD3865-6	*LAND, CONDEMNATION OF* **SEE** EMINENT DOMAIN / *public works*
HD1301-1315	LAND, NATIONALIZATION OF
TC343-5	*LAND, RECLAMATION OF* **SEE** RECLAMATION OF LAND / *coast works*
TC970-978	*LAND, RECLAMATION OF* **SEE** RECLAMATION OF LAND / *etc.*
S605-623	*LAND, RECLAMATION OF* **SEE** RECLAMATION OF LAND / *farm lands*
TC801-937	*LAND, RECLAMATION OF* **SEE** RECLAMATION OF LAND / *irrigation*
HD1481	*LAND-CONSOLIDATION* **SEE** CONSOLIDATION OF LAND HOLDINGS / *economics*
K	*LAND-CONSOLIDATION* **SEE** CONSOLIDATION OF LAND HOLDINGS / *law*
HD1393	*LAND-VALUATION* **SEE** FARMS — VALUATION
TD795	*LANDFILLS, SANITARY* **SEE** SANITARY LANDFILLS
GB423-445	LANDFORMS
JN3259	LANDFRIEDE
DD137.5	LANDFRIEDE / *german history*
DD165.5	LANDFRIEDE / *german history*
TL725.3.L2	LANDING AIDS (AERONAUTICS)
TL725.3.L3	*LANDING FEES (AIRPORTS)* **SEE** AIRPORTS — LANDING FEES
TL691	*LANDING LIGHTS, AIRCRAFT* **SEE** AEROPLANES — LIGHTING
TL696.L33	*LANDING PATH* **SEE** GLIDE PATH SYSTEMS
TL725.3.R8	*LANDING STRIPS* **SEE** AIRPORTS — RUNWAYS
M175.A4	LANDLER (ACCORDION)
M240-244	LANDLER (CZAKAN AND PIANO)
M125-9	LANDLER (GUITAR)
M470-474	LANDLER (GUITAR, 2 VIOLINS, VIOLONCELLO)
M1105-6	LANDLER (HARP WITH STRING ORCHESTRA)
M1060	LANDLER (ORCHESTRA)
M1049	LANDLER (ORCHESTRA)
M20-22	LANDLER (PIANO)
M32	LANDLER (PIANO)
M32.8	LANDLER (PIANO)
M40-44	LANDLER (VIOLIN)
M286-7	LANDLER (2 VIOLINS)
M349-353	LANDLER (2 VIOLINS, VIOLONCELLO)
M349-353	LANDLER (3 VIOLINS)

PN164	*LANDMARKS, LITERARY* **SEE** LITERARY LANDMARKS
QH75-77	*LANDMARKS, PRESERVATION OF* **SEE** NATURAL MONUMENTS
JN3259	*LANDPEACE* **SEE** LANDFRIEDE
DD165.5	*LANDPEACE* **SEE** LANDFRIEDE / *german history*
DD137.5	*LANDPEACE* **SEE** LANDFRIEDE / *german history*
DC309.L2	LANDRECIES, FRANCE — SIEGE, 1871
NC790-800	LANDSCAPE DRAWING
SB469-479	LANDSCAPE GARDENING
PN48	*LANDSCAPE IN LITERATURE* **SEE** NATURE IN LITERATURE
PS163	*LANDSCAPE IN LITERATURE* **SEE** NATURE IN LITERATURE / *american literature*
PR143	*LANDSCAPE IN LITERATURE* **SEE** NATURE IN LITERATURE / *english literature*
PQ145.3	*LANDSCAPE IN LITERATURE* **SEE** NATURE IN LITERATURE / *french literature*
PN6071.N3	*LANDSCAPE IN LITERATURE* **SEE** NATURE IN LITERATURE / *general collections*
PT139	*LANDSCAPE IN LITERATURE* **SEE** NATURE IN LITERATURE / *german literature*
PN1065	*LANDSCAPE IN POETRY* **SEE** NATURE IN POETRY
PS310.N3	*LANDSCAPE IN POETRY* **SEE** NATURE IN POETRY / *american literature*
PR508.N3	*LANDSCAPE IN POETRY* **SEE** NATURE IN POETRY / *english literature*
PQ413.N3	*LANDSCAPE IN POETRY* **SEE** NATURE IN POETRY / *french literature*
PN6110.N2	*LANDSCAPE IN POETRY* **SEE** NATURE IN POETRY / *general collections*
PT509.N3	*LANDSCAPE IN POETRY* **SEE** NATURE IN POETRY / *german literature*
ND1340-1367	LANDSCAPE PAINTERS
ND1340-1342	LANDSCAPE PAINTING — TECHNIQUE
ND1340-1367	LANDSCAPE PAINTING
TR660	*LANDSCAPE PHOTOGRAPHY* **SEE** PHOTOGRAPHY — LANDSCAPES
BH301.L3	LANDSCAPE / *aesthetics*
QH75	LANDSCAPE / *natural history*
DD102.7	*LANDSKNECHTE* **SEE** GERMAN MERCENARIES
QE599	LANDSLIDES
PD2900-2999	*LANDSMAAL* **SEE** NORWEGIAN LANGUAGE (NYNORSK)
D542.L	LANGEMARCK, BATTLE OF, 1914
QL866	*LANGERHANS, ISLANDS OF* **SEE** PANCREAS / *comparative anatomy*
QM353	*LANGERHANS, ISLANDS OF* **SEE** PANCREAS / *human anatomy*
ML760	*LANGLEIK* **SEE** NOORDSCHE BALK
GN659.L3	LANGO (AFRICAN TRIBE) / *anthropology*
DT434.U2	LANGO (AFRICAN TRIBE) / *uganda*
PL8451	LANGO LANGUAGE
D145	*LANGOBARDS* **SEE** LOMBARDS
DG511-514	*LANGOBARDS* **SEE** LOMBARDS / *italy*
DG657.2	*LANGOBARDS* **SEE** LOMBARDS / *lombardy*
P203	LANGUAGE AND LANGUAGES — CLASSIFICATION
P321	LANGUAGE AND LANGUAGES — ETYMOLOGY
P331-347	LANGUAGE AND LANGUAGES — GLOSSARIES, VOCABULARIES, ETC.
P207	LANGUAGE AND LANGUAGES — GRAMMARS
P124	LANGUAGE AND LANGUAGES — JUVENILE LITERATURE
P51-59	LANGUAGE AND LANGUAGES — STUDY AND TEACHING
P301	LANGUAGE AND LANGUAGES — STYLE
P251-9	*LANGUAGE AND LANGUAGES - INFLECTION* **SEE** GRAMMAR,COMPARATIVE AND GENERAL — INFLECTION
P236	*LANGUAGE AND LANGUAGES - SYLLABLE* **SEE** GRAMMAR, COMPARATIVE AND GENERAL — SYLLABLE
P1-409	LANGUAGE AND LANGUAGES
P151-295	*LANGUAGE AND LANGUAGES-GRAMMAR, COMPARATIVE* **SEE** GRAMMAR, COMPARATIVE AND GENERAL
P251-9	*LANGUAGE AND LANGUAGES-INFLECTION* **SEE** GRAMMAR, COMPARATIVE AND GENERAL — INFLECTION
PB101	*LANGUAGE AND LANGUAGES-INFLECTION* **SEE** LANGUAGES, MODERN — INFLECTION
JF195.L3	*LANGUAGE AND LANGUAGES-POLITICAL ASPECTS* **SEE** LANGUAGES — POLITICAL ASPECTS
Z253	*LANGUAGE AND LANGUAGES-PRINTING* **SEE** PRINTING, PRACTICAL — STYLE MANUALS
P101-5	*LANGUAGE AND LANGUAGES-PSYCHOLOGY* **SEE** LANGUAGES — PSYCHOLOGY
BX1970	*LANGUAGE AND LANGUAGES-RELIGIOUS ASPECTS* **SEE** LITURGICAL LANGUAGE / *catholic*
P236	*LANGUAGE AND LANGUAGES-SYLLABLE* **SEE** GRAMMAR, COMPARATIVE AND GENERAL — SYLLABLE
P291-5	*LANGUAGE AND LANGUAGES-SYNTAX* **SEE** GRAMMAR, COMPARATIVE AND GENERAL — SYNTAX
P351-7	*LANGUAGE AND LANGUAGES-TEXTS* **SEE** POLYGLOT TEXTS, SELECTIONS, QUOTATIONS, ETC.
PB213	*LANGUAGE AND LANGUAGES-WORD ORDER* **SEE** LANGUAGES, MODERN — WORD ORDER
B824.6	*LANGUAGE AND LOGIC* **SEE** LOGICAL POSITIVISM
P90	*LANGUAGE ARTS* **SEE** COMMUNICATION
PE1001-3729	*LANGUAGE ARTS* **SEE** ENGLISH LANGUAGE
PN59-72	*LANGUAGE ARTS* **SEE** LITERATURE — STUDY AND TEACHING
PN83	*LANGUAGE ARTS* **SEE** READING / *literature*
PN4145·	*LANGUAGE ARTS* **SEE** READING / *oratory*
LB1050	*LANGUAGE ARTS* **SEE** READING / *teaching*
QP306	*LANGUAGE ARTS* **SEE** SPEECH / *physiology*
BF455	*LANGUAGE ARTS* **SEE** SPEECH / *psychology*
LB1139.L3	*LANGUAGE ARTS* **SEE** SPEECH / *speech development of children*
P375-381	*LANGUAGE GEOGRAPHY* **SEE** LINGUISTIC GEOGRAPHY
QK84	*LANGUAGE OF FLOWERS* **SEE** FLOWER LANGUAGE
JX1677	*LANGUAGE, INTERNATIONAL* **SEE** DIPLOMACY — LANGUAGE
PM8008	*LANGUAGE, INTERNATIONAL* **SEE** LANGUAGE, UNIVERSAL
BX1970	*LANGUAGE, LITURGICAL* **SEE** LITURGICAL LANGUAGE / *catholic*
P101-5	*LANGUAGE, PHILOSOPHY OF* **SEE** LANGUAGES — PHILOSOPHY
P101-5	*LANGUAGE, PSYCHOLOGY OF* **SEE** LANGUAGES — PSYCHOLOGY
PM8008	LANGUAGE, UNIVERSAL
PM8008	*LANGUAGE, WORLD* **SEE** LANGUAGE, UNIVERSAL
P101-5	LANGUAGES — PHILOSOPHY
JF195.L3	LANGUAGES — POLITICAL ASPECTS
P101-5	LANGUAGES — PSYCHOLOGY
PM8001-9021	LANGUAGES, ARTIFICIAL
P501-769	*LANGUAGES, ARYAN* **SEE** ARYAN LANGUAGES
P501-769	*LANGUAGES, ARYAN* **SEE** ARYAN PHILOLOGY
PJ2301-2551	*LANGUAGES, HAMITIC* **SEE** HAMITIC LANGUAGES
PM7801-7895	LANGUAGES, MIXED
PB73	LANGUAGES, MODERN — CONVERSATION AND PHRASE BOOKS
PB325-349	LANGUAGES, MODERN — DICTIONARIES
PB324	LANGUAGES, MODERN — GLOSSARIES, VOCABULARIES, ETC.
PB260	LANGUAGES, MODERN — IDIOMS, CORRECTIONS, ERRORS
PB101	LANGUAGES, MODERN — INFLECTION
PB77	LANGUAGES, MODERN — PHONETICS
PB76-82	LANGUAGES, MODERN — PHONOLOGY
PB79	LANGUAGES, MODERN — PRONUNCIATION
PB35-39	LANGUAGES, MODERN — STUDY AND TEACHING
PB201-225	LANGUAGES, MODERN — SYNTAX
PB213	LANGUAGES, MODERN — WORD ORDER
PB1-431	LANGUAGES, MODERN
JF195.L3	*LANGUAGES, NATIONAL* **SEE** LANGUAGES — POLITICAL ASPECTS
PB1-431	*LANGUAGES, OCCIDENTAL* **SEE** LANGUAGES, MODERN
JF195.L3	*LANGUAGES, OFFICIAL* **SEE** LANGUAGES — POLITICAL ASPECTS
PJ	*LANGUAGES, ORIENTAL* **SEE** ORIENTAL LANGUAGES
PM9001-9021	LANGUAGES, SECRET
PJ3001-9278	*LANGUAGES, SEMITIC* **SEE** SEMITIC LANGUAGES
PB1-431	*LANGUAGES, WESTERN* **SEE** LANGUAGES, MODERN
P375-381	*LANGUAGES-GEOGRAPHY* **SEE** LINGUISTIC GEOGRAPHY
P101-5	*LANGUAGES-PSYCHOANALYSIS* **SEE** LANGUAGES — PSYCHOLOGY

PM8101-9	*LANGUE BLEUE (ARTIFICIAL LANGUAGE)* **SEE** BOLAK
PC3201-3299	*LANGUE D'OC* **SEE** PROVENCAL LANGUAGE
PC2001-3761	*LANGUE D'OIL* **SEE** FRENCH LANGUAGE
PM8128	*LANGUE INTERNATIONALE NATURELLE* **SEE** CHABE (ARTIFICIAL LANGUAGE)
PM8457	LANGUE INTERNATIONALE NEO-LATINE (ARTIFICIAL LANGUAGE)
TP676	LANOLIN
Q186	LANTERN PROJECTION
ND1595	LANTERN SLIDES / *painting*
TR730	LANTERN SLIDES / *photography*
QL638.M8	LANTERN-FISHES
NB1420	LANTERNS OF THE DEAD
GR950.L4	LANTERNS / *folk-lore*
GT445	LANTERNS / *manners and customs*
QD181.L2	LANTHANUM
DS560	*LAO* **SEE** LAOS (TAI PEOPLE) / *indochina*
PL4251.L3	LAO LANGUAGE
DS560	LAOS (TAI PEOPLE) / *indochina*
PL4251.L3	*LAOS LANGUAGE* **SEE** LAO LANGUAGE
PL4251.L3	*LAOTIAN LANGUAGE* **SEE** LAO LANGUAGE
DS560	*LAOTIANS* **SEE** LAOS (TAI PEOPLE) / *indochina*
TL159	*LAP BELTS, AUTOMOBILE* **SEE** AUTOMOBILE SEAT BELTS
PN682.L	LAPIDARIES (MEDIEVAL LITERATURE)
PQ1327.L3	LAPIDARIES (MEDIEVAL LITERATURE) / *old french*
QA432	LAPLACE TRANSFORMATION
QA405	*LAPLACE'S EQUATIONS* **SEE** HARMONIC FUNCTIONS
TJ1280-1298	*LAPPING* **SEE** GRINDING AND POLISHING
PH701-729	LAPPISH LANGUAGE
DL971.L2	LAPPS
GN585.L2	LAPPS / *anthropology*
QL696.L7	LAPWINGS
QE685-8	*LARAMIE FORMATION* **SEE** GEOLOGY, STRATIGRAPHIC — CRETACEOUS
QE924	*LARAMIE FORMATION* **SEE** PALEOBOTANY — CRETACEOUS
QE734	*LARAMIE FORMATION* **SEE** PALEONTOLOGY — CRETACEOUS
SB608.L3	LARCH LEAF-ROLLER
QK495.L32	LARCH / *botany*
SD397.L3	LARCH / *sylviculture*
TP676	LARD-OIL
HD9441	LARD / *economics*
TS1980	LARD / *technology*
QL391.N4	*LARDWORM* **SEE** SWINE KIDNEY WORM / *zoology*
BV638.4	LARGER PARISHES
PL8725	*LARI LANGUAGE* **SEE** TEKE LANGUAGE
DS432.H6	*LARKA KOLS* **SEE** HOS
QL696.P2	LARKS
QP366	LARYNGEAL NERVE
QM471	LARYNGEAL NERVE
QL939	LARYNGEAL NERVE
RC794	LARYNGISMUS STRIDULUS
RC786	LARYNGOSCOPE AND LARYNGOSCOPY
RC280.L	LARYNX — CANCER
RF510-547	LARYNX — DISEASES
RF476	LARYNX — EXPLORATION
RF514	LARYNX — EXPLORATION
RD533	LARYNX — FRACTURE
RF517	LARYNX — INTUBATION
RF516-517	LARYNX — SURGERY
RF516	LARYNX — TUMORS
RC280.T	LARYNX — TUMORS
QL853	LARYNX / *comparative anatomy*
QM255	LARYNX / *human anatomy*
QP306	LARYNX / *physiology*
RX456	LARYNX — DISEASES — — HOMEOPATHIC TREATMENT
F3442	LAS SALINAS, BATTLE OF, 1538
F596	LASSO / *cowboys*
GV1559	LASSO / *sports and games*
BT880-881	*LAST JUDGMENT* **SEE** JUDGMENT DAY
BV823-8	*LAST SUPPER* **SEE** LORD'S SUPPER
BX2215	*LAST SUPPER* **SEE** LORD'S SUPPER / *catholic church*
BX5149.C5	*LAST SUPPER* **SEE** LORD'S SUPPER / *church of england*
GT2130	*LASTS (SHOES)* **SEE** BOOTS AND SHOES / *manners and customs*
VM371	*LATEENS* **SEE** DHOWS
QC304	*LATENT HEAT OF EVAPORATION* **SEE** EVAPORATION, LATENT HEAT OF
QC303	*LATENT HEAT OF FUSION* **SEE** FUSION, LATENT HEAT OF
QH331	*LATENT LIFE* **SEE** CRYPTOBIOSIS
TL547.S7	*LATERAL STABILITY OF AEROPLANES* **SEE** STABILITY OF AEROPLANES, LATERAL
BX830 1215	LATERAN COUNCIL, 4TH, 1215
BX830 1512	LATERAN COUNCIL, 5TH, 1512-1517
QE475	LATERITE
TS1890	LATEX
TJ1218-1222	*LATHE WORK* **SEE** LATHES
TS546	*LATHE WORK* **SEE** LATHES / *watchmakers' lathes*
TT201-3	*LATHE WORK* **SEE** TURNING
TT207	*LATHE WORK* **SEE** TURNING / *metal*
TJ1218-1222	LATHES
TS546	LATHES / *watchmakers' lathes*
TH1675	LATHING / *metal*
TH8132	LATHING / *plastering*
TH1675	*LATHS* **SEE** LATHING / *metal*
TH8132	*LATHS* **SEE** LATHING / *plastering*
F1409.6-1419	LATIN AMERICA — HISTORY
PA6121	LATIN BALLADS AND SONGS / *collections ancient*
PA6047	LATIN BALLADS AND SONGS / *history ancient*
PA8050-8052	LATIN BALLADS AND SONGS / *medieval and modern*
PA8122-3	LATIN BALLADS AND SONGS / *medieval and modern*
PA6069	LATIN DRAMA (COMEDY)
PA6068	LATIN DRAMA (TRAGEDY)
PA6137	LATIN DRAMA / *collections*
PA6067-6071	LATIN DRAMA / *history*
PA8135-8140	LATIN DRAMA, MEDIEVAL AND MODERN / *collections*
PA8073-9	LATIN DRAMA, MEDIEVAL AND MODERN / *history*
DF610-629	LATIN EMPIRE, 1204-1261
PA6091	LATIN FICTION / *ancient*
PA8150-8155	LATIN FICTION / *medieval and modern*
PA8145	LATIN FICTION / *medieval and modern*
PA8091	LATIN FICTION / *medieval and modern*
DG205-6	LATIN HISTORIANS
D175-195	*LATIN KINGDOM OF JERUSALEM* **SEE** JERUSALEM — HISTORY — — LATIN KINGDOM, 1099-1244
PA2001-2995	LATIN LANGUAGE
PA2801-2915	LATIN LANGUAGE, MEDIEVAL AND MODERN
PA2600-2748	*LATIN LANGUAGE, POPULAR* **SEE** LATIN LANGUAGE, VULGAR
PA2300-2309	LATIN LANGUAGE, POSTCLASSICAL
PA2510-2519	LATIN LANGUAGE, PRECLASSICAL TO CA. 100 B.C.
PA2600-2748	LATIN LANGUAGE, VULGAR
BX1970	*LATIN LANGUAGE-LITURGICAL USE* **SEE** LITURGICAL LANGUAGE — LATIN / *catholic*
PA2337.S2	*LATIN LANGUAGE-SATURNIAN VERSE* **SEE** SATURNIAN VERSE
PA6139.E7	LATIN LETTERS / *collections*
PA6089	LATIN LETTERS / *history*
PA6101-6139	LATIN LITERATURE / *collections*
PA6001-6098	LATIN LITERATURE / *history*
PA8001-8595	LATIN LITERATURE, MEDIEVAL AND MODERN
HG207-9	LATIN MONETARY UNION
PA6138	LATIN ORATIONS / *collections*
PA6083	LATIN ORATIONS / *history*
D175-195	LATIN ORIENT
CB220-224	LATIN PEOPLES
PA2001-2067	LATIN PHILOLOGY
PA6121-6135	LATIN POETRY / *collections*
PA6047-6066	LATIN POETRY / *history*
PA8120-8133	LATIN POETRY, MEDIEVAL AND MODERN / *collections*
PA8050-8065	LATIN POETRY, MEDIEVAL AND MODERN / *history*
PA6138-9	LATIN PROSE LITERATURE / *collections*
PA6081-6097	LATIN PROSE LITERATURE / *history*
PA3265	*LATIN RHETORIC* **SEE** RHETORIC, ANCIENT
QA165	*LATIN SQUARES AND RECTANGLES* **SEE** MAGIC SQUARES
VK565	LATITUDE — TABLES
QB237	LATITUDE VARIATION
QB231-5	LATITUDE
VK565	LATITUDE / *navigation*
TD775-6	*LATRINES* **SEE** PRIVIES
TH6498	*LATRINES* **SEE** WATER-CLOSETS

HE1053-9	LAW, RAILROAD SEE RAILROAD LAW
HE2801-3600	LAW, RAILROAD SEE RAILROAD LAW / other countries
HE2710-2712	LAW, RAILROAD SEE RAILROAD LAW / u.s.
HD9100.7-95	LAW, SUGAR SEE SUGAR LAWS AND LEGISLATION
HB845	LAW, SUMPTUARY SEE SUMPTUARY LAWS
GT527-8	LAW, SUMPTUARY SEE SUMPTUARY LAWS / dress
HD5114	LAW, SUNDAY SEE SUNDAY LEGISLATION / labor
HE6497.S8	LAW, SUNDAY SEE SUNDAY LEGISLATION / mails
HE6239.S8	LAW, SUNDAY SEE SUNDAY LEGISLATION / mails
BV133	LAW, SUNDAY SEE SUNDAY LEGISLATION / religious aspects
HE1825	LAW, SUNDAY SEE SUNDAY LEGISLATION / trains
HD239	LAW, TOWNSITE SEE TOWNSITE LAW
HB521-549	LAW, USURY SEE USURY LAWS / economic theory
HG2052-2069	LAW, USURY SEE USURY LAWS / money lending
GT6230	LAW, WAGER OF SEE WAGER OF LAW
HD1691-8	LAW, WATER SEE WATER — LAWS AND LEGISLATION
PN6231.L4	LAW, WIT AND HUMOR OF SEE LAW — ANECDOTES, FACETIAE, SATIRE, ETC. / wit and humor
PN6268.L4	LAW, WIT AND HUMOR OF SEE LAW — ANECDOTES, FACETIAE, SATIRE, ETC. / anecdotes
Z695.1.L3	LAW-CATALOGING SEE CATALOGING OF LEGAL LITERATURE
BL65.L33	LAW-RELIGIOUS ASPECTS SEE RELIGION AND LAW
Z6451-6466	LAWBOOKS SEE LAW — BIBLIOGRAPHY
GV909	LAWN BOWLS SEE BOWLING ON THE GREEN
GV1017.L	LAWN HOCKEY
GV1017.L48	LAWN TEMPEST (GAME)
GV990-1005	LAWN TENNIS SEE TENNIS
SB433	LAWNS
QE391.L	LAWSONITE
HF5686.P9	LAWYERS — ACCOUNTING
BX1939.L25	LAWYERS (CANON LAW)
JA75	LAWYERS IN POLITICS
PN6231.L4	LAWYERS-ANECDOTES, FACETIAE, SATIRE, ETC. SEE LAW — ANECDOTES, FACETIAE, SATIRE, ETC. / wit and humor
PN6268.L4	LAWYERS-ANECDOTES, FACETIAE, SATIRE, ETC. SEE LAW — ANECDOTES, FACETIAE, SATIRE, ETC. / anecdotes
Z6459	LAW — BIBLIOGRAPHY — — CATALOGS
RM357	LAXATIVES SEE PURGATIVES
BX1759.5.P	LAXISM SEE PROBABILISM
BX2348	LAY APOSTOLATE SEE CATHOLIC ACTION
BX2835	LAY BROTHERS
BV652.1	LAY LEADERSHIP SEE CHRISTIAN LEADERSHIP
BV4235.L3	LAY PREACHING SEE PREACHING, LAY
HD4928.D5	LAY-OFF COMPENSATION SEE WAGES — DISMISSAL WAGE
TT637	LAYETTES
BV873.L3	LAYING ON OF HANDS SEE IMPOSITION OF HANDS / christian sacraments
BM715	LAYING ON OF HANDS SEE IMPOSITION OF HANDS / jewish sacrifices
BP186.38	LAYLAT AL-BARA'AH
BP186.38	LAYLAT NISF AL-SHA'BAN SEE LAYLAT AL-BARA'AH
BV687	LAYMEN SEE LAITY
TS155	LAYOUT, FACTORY SEE FACTORIES — DESIGN AND CONSTRUCTION
TH4511	LAYOUT, FACTORY SEE FACTORIES — DESIGN AND CONSTRUCTION
PN1351-1525	LAYS
PQ1323.L3	LAYS / french
PQ1317	LAYS / french
PN691	LAYS / medieval
PK9151	LAZ LANGUAGE
RC154	LAZARETTOS SEE LEPROSY — HOSPITALS
RA655-758	LAZARETTOS SEE QUARANTINE
BT378.D5	LAZARUS AND DIVES SEE DIVES AND LAZARUS (PARABLE)
PK9151	LAZIAN LANGUAGE SEE LAZ LANGUAGE
BF485	LAZINESS
QC485	LE BON'S RAYS
UF830.L4-5	LE BOULENGE CHRONOGRAPH
D545.L3	LE CATEAU, BATTLE OF, 1914
DC305.5	LE MANS, BATTLE OF, 1871
TP156.L	LEACHING
TN785	LEAD — ELECTROMETALLURGY
TN785	LEAD — METALLURGY
QP913.P3	LEAD — PHYSIOLOGICAL EFFECT
RM666.L3	LEAD — THERAPEUTIC USE
SB951-3	LEAD ARSENATE / insecticides
TN245.A8	LEAD ARSENATE / technology
TH6691	LEAD BURNING
QD181.P3	LEAD COMPOUNDS
HD9539.L38-43	LEAD INDUSTRY AND TRADE
TN450-459	LEAD MINES AND MINING
TN450-459	LEAD ORES
RA1231.L4	LEAD-POISONING
TT265	LEAD-WORK
NK8350	LEAD-WORK / ornamental
QD181.P3	LEAD / chemistry
TL480.L	LEAD-CREEP SEE CREEP OF LEAD
RA1231.L4	LEAD-TOXICOLOGY SEE LEAD-POISONING
BF637.L4	LEADERSHIP / applied psychology
BF723.L4	LEADERSHIP / child psychology
UB210	LEADERSHIP / military science
HM141	LEADERSHIP / sociology
Z695	LEAF CATALOGS SEE CATALOGS, SHEAF
S662.5	LEAF FEEDING SEE FOLIAR FEEDING
SB431	LEAF PLANTS SEE FOLIAGE PLANTS
SB945.L	LEAF-MINERS
S598	LEAF-MOLD
SB945.L	LEAF-ROLLERS
SB741.L45	LEAF-SPOT
HE9739	LEAFLETS SEE LEAFLETS DROPPED FROM AIRCRAFT
Z691	LEAFLETS SEE PAMPHLETS / library science
HE9739	LEAFLETS DROPPED FROM AIRCRAFT
DG678.26	LEAGUE OF CAMBRAI, 1508 SEE CAMBRAI, LEAGUE OF, 1508
JX1975.6	LEAGUE OF NATIONS — SANCTIONS
JX1975	LEAGUE OF NATIONS
D650.T4-651	LEAGUE OF NATIONS-MANDATORY SYSTEM SEE MANDATES / european war questions
JX4021-3	LEAGUE OF NATIONS-MANDATORY SYSTEM SEE MANDATES / international law
JX1975.A49	LEAGUE OF NATIONS-MANDATORY SYSTEM SEE MANDATES / league of nations documents
DD155	LEAGUE OF RHINE CITIES SEE RHINE CITIES, LEAGUE OF, 1254
D397	LEAGUE OF THE THREE EMPERORS, 1881 SEE THREE EMPERORS' LEAGUE, 1881
RC814	LEANNESS
AS	LEARNED INSTITUTIONS AND SOCIETIES
LB1134	LEARNING ABILITY
AZ	LEARNING AND SCHOLARSHIP / etc.
BX961.I5	LEARNING AND SCHOLARSHIP-CATHOLICS SEE CATHOLIC LEARNING AND SCHOLARSHIP
DS113	LEARNING AND SCHOLARSHIP-JEWS SEE JEWISH LEARNING AND SCHOLARSHIP
LB1051	LEARNING, PSYCHOLOGY OF
HV8888-8931	LEASE SYSTEM SEE CONVICT LABOR
D753.2	LEASE-LEND OPERATIONS SEE LEND-LEASE OPERATIONS (1941-1945)
QA871	LEAST ACTION
QA275	LEAST SQUARES
TS1043	LEATHER — MACHINERY
SB315.L4	LEATHER BERGENIA / tannin plants
HD9780	LEATHER INDUSTRY AND TRADE / economics
TS940-1043	LEATHER INDUSTRY AND TRADE / technology
NK6200	LEATHER WORK / art industries
TT290	LEATHER WORK / mechanic trades
QK495.C	LEATHER-FLOWER
TS940-1043	LEATHER
TS1045-7	LEATHER, ARTIFICIAL
NK6200	LEATHER, CORDOVAN SEE LEATHER WORK / art industries
TT290	LEATHER, CORDOVAN SEE LEATHER WORK / mechanic trades
NK6200	LEATHERCRAFT SEE LEATHER WORK / art industries
TT290	LEATHERCRAFT SEE LEATHER WORK / mechanic trades
HD5261	LEAVE WITH PAY SEE VACATIONS, EMPLOYEE
QK649	LEAVES — ANATOMY
QK689	LEAVES — ANATOMY
QK649	LEAVES — MORPHOLOGY
QK649	LEAVES
QK689	LEAVES
S662.5	LEAVES, FEEDING OF SEE FOLIAR FEEDING

QK763	*LEAVES, SHEDDING OF* **SEE** DEFOLIATION
QH245	*LEAVES-PHOTOGRAPHY* **SEE** PHOTOGRAPHY OF LEAVES
SD397.L	LEBBEK TREE
RM666.L4	LECITHIN / *therapeutics*
BX2003	LECTIONARIES / *catholic church*
BX5147.L4	LECTIONARIES / *church of england*
BX8067.L4	LECTIONARIES / *lutheran church*
BX5947	LECTIONARIES / *protestant episcopal church*
LB2393	LECTURE METHOD IN TEACHING
PN4058	LECTURERS
PN4193.L4	LECTURES AND LECTURING
LC6501-6560	LECTURES AND LECTURING / *lyceum and lecture courses*
UD395.L	LEE-ENFIELD RIFLE
E474.61	*LEE'S 1ST NORTHERN INVASION* **SEE** MARYLAND CAMPAIGN, 1862
E475.51-53	*LEE'S 2D NORTHERN INVASION* **SEE** GETTYSBURG CAMPAIGN, 1863
QL391.H6	LEECHES
RM182	LEECHES / *blood-letting*
GN233	LEFT- AND RIGHT-HANDEDNESS / *anthropology*
QP385	LEFT- AND RIGHT-HANDEDNESS / *physiological psychology*
M26.2	*LEFT-HAND PIANO MUSIC* **SEE** PIANO MUSIC (1 HAND)
M26	*LEFT-HAND PIANO MUSIC* **SEE** PIANO MUSIC (1 HAND)
Z43.5	*LEFT-HANDED PENMANSHIP* **SEE** PENMANSHIP, LEFT-HANDED
RD560	LEG — FRACTURE
RC951	LEG — ULCERS
QL950.7	LEG / *comparative anatomy general*
QM165	LEG / *human anatomy muscles*
QL821	LEG / *muscles*
QM117	LEG / *skeleton*
QM549	LEG / *surgical and topographical anatomy*
RD560	*LEG-AMPUTATION* **SEE** AMPUTATIONS OF LEG
PL8380.K5	*LEGA LANGUAGE* **SEE** KILEGA LANGUAGE
HJ5801-5819	*LEGACIES, TAXATION OF* **SEE** INHERITANCE AND TRANSFER TAX
HV680-685	LEGAL AID SOCIETIES
HV680-685	LEGAL AID
PN6231.L4	*LEGAL ANECDOTES* **SEE** LAW — ANECDOTES, FACETIAE, SATIRE, ETC. / *wit and humor*
PN6268.L4	*LEGAL ANECDOTES* **SEE** LAW — ANECDOTES, FACETIAE, SATIRE, ETC. / *anecdotes*
Z6451-6466	*LEGAL BIBLIOGRAPHY* **SEE** LAW — BIBLIOGRAPHY
HV680-685	*LEGAL CHARITIES* **SEE** LEGAL AID SOCIETIES
HV680-685	*LEGAL CHARITIES* **SEE** LEGAL AID
HV8073	*LEGAL CHEMISTRY* **SEE** CHEMISTRY, FORENSIC
RA1057	*LEGAL CHEMISTRY* **SEE** CHEMISTRY, FORENSIC / *medical jurisprudence*
HV8074	LEGAL DOCUMENTS — IDENTIFICATION
GT6230-6280	*LEGAL DRESS* **SEE** JUDGES — COSTUME
HF1243	*LEGAL FORMS* **SEE** FORMS (LAW) / *commercial law u.s.*
HV3167	*LEGAL HOLIDAYS* **SEE** HOLIDAYS / *for shop workers*
GT3930-4995	*LEGAL HOLIDAYS* **SEE** HOLIDAYS / *manners and customs*
JK1761	*LEGAL HOLIDAYS* **SEE** HOLIDAYS / *national u.s.*
PN4305.II7	*LEGAL HOLIDAYS* **SEE** HOLIDAYS / *recitations*
RA1001-1171	*LEGAL MEDICINE* **SEE** MEDICAL JURISPRUDENCE
TR830	*LEGAL PHOTOGRAPHY* **SEE** PHOTOGRAPHY, LEGAL
HV6071	*LEGAL PHOTOGRAPHY* **SEE** PHOTOGRAPHY, LEGAL / *social pathology*
HV8077	*LEGAL PHOTOGRAPHY* **SEE** PHOTOGRAPHY, LEGAL / *social pathology*
HG361-3	LEGAL TENDER
BX1908	LEGATES, PAPAL
JX1621-1894	*LEGATIONS* **SEE** DIPLOMATIC AND CONSULAR SERVICE
QA406	*LEGENDRE'S COEFFICIENTS* **SEE** LEGENDRE'S FUNCTIONS
QA406	*LEGENDRE'S EQUATION* **SEE** LEGENDRE'S FUNCTIONS
QA406	LEGENDRE'S FUNCTIONS
QA406	*LEGENDRE'S POLYNOMIALS* **SEE** LEGENDRE'S FUNCTIONS

PZ	*LEGENDS AND STORIES OF ANIMALS* **SEE** ANIMALS, LEGENDS AND STORIES OF
PN683-7	LEGENDS
N7760	LEGENDS / *iconography*
PZ8.1	LEGENDS / *juvenile*
E59.F6	*LEGENDS, INDIAN* **SEE** INDIANS — LEGENDS
E98.F6	*LEGENDS, INDIAN* **SEE** INDIANS OF NORTH AMERICA — LEGENDS
BP137-7.5	LEGENDS, ISLAMIC
BP137-7.5	*LEGENDS, MUSLIM* **SEE** LEGENDS, ISLAMIC
GV1541-1561	*LEGERDEMAIN* **SEE** CONJURING
GV1541-1561	*LEGERDEMAIN* **SEE** JUGGLERS AND JUGGLING
GN475	*LEGERDEMAIN* **SEE** MAGIC / *ethnology*
BF1585-1623	*LEGERDEMAIN* **SEE** MAGIC / *occult sciences*
SF489.L5	LEGHORNS (POULTRY)
JF525	*LEGISLATION DRAFTING* **SEE** BILL DRAFTING
JN608	*LEGISLATION DRAFTING* **SEE** BILL DRAFTING / *gt. brit.*
JK1106	*LEGISLATION DRAFTING* **SEE** BILL DRAFTING / *u.s.*
JF401-637	LEGISLATION
JF491-7	*LEGISLATION, DIRECT* **SEE** REFERENDUM
BV280	LEGISLATIVE BODIES — CHAPLAINS' PRAYERS
JN2815	LEGISLATIVE BODIES — COMMITTEES / *france*
JN605	LEGISLATIVE BODIES — COMMITTEES / *gt. brit.*
JK1029	LEGISLATIVE BODIES — COMMITTEES / *u.s.*
JK2495	LEGISLATIVE BODIES — COMMITTEES / *u.s.*
JF601-637	LEGISLATIVE BODIES — LOWER CHAMBERS
JF541-567	LEGISLATIVE BODIES — UPPER CHAMBERS
JF501-637	LEGISLATIVE BODIES
JK1091-1128	*LEGISLATIVE BODIES-RULES AND PRACTICE* **SEE** PARLIAMENTARY PRACTICE / *u.s. congress*
JF501-540	*LEGISLATIVE BODIES-RULES AND PRACTICE* **SEE** PARLIAMENTARY PRACTICE
JF441-483	LEGISLATIVE POWER
JF527	LEGISLATIVE REFERENCE BUREAUS
JK1108	LEGISLATIVE REFERENCE BUREAUS / *u.s.*
HJ2050-2052	*LEGISLATIVE, EXECUTIVE, AND JUDICIAL APPROPRIATION BILLS* **SEE** UNITED STATES — APPROPRIATIONS AND EXPENDITURES
HJ10	*LEGISLATIVE, EXECUTIVE, AND JUDICIAL APPROPRIATION BILLS* **SEE** UNITED STATES — APPROPRIATIONS AND EXPENDITURES
HQ998-9	*LEGITIMACY (LAW)* **SEE** ILLEGITIMACY
HB903.I6	*LEGITIMACY (LAW)* **SEE** ILLEGITIMACY / *statistics*
DG657.45	LEGNANO, BATTLE OF, 1176
SB608.L4	LEGUMES — DISEASES AND PESTS
SB203-5	LEGUMES / *horticulture*
QD431	LEGUMIN / *chemistry*
QK495.L52	LEGUMINOSAE
BR355.L5	LEIPZIG DISPUTATION, 1519
D267.L3	LEIPZIG, BATTLE OF, 1631
DC236.5-68	LEIPZIG, BATTLE OF, 1813
RC238	LEISHMAN'S BODIES
RC238	LEISHMANIOSIS
HB831	LEISURE CLASS / *economic theory*
BJ1498	LEISURE
MT90	LEITMOTIV
MT100.W2	LEITMOTIV / *wagner*
DD338	*LEKHS* **SEE** LYGIANS
PL8452	*LELA DIALECT* **SEE** LELE DIALECT
PL8452	LELE DIALECT
PL6621.V3	*LEMING LANGUAGE* **SEE** VALMAN LANGUAGE
QL737.R6	LEMMINGS
SB608.L5	LEMON — DISEASES AND PESTS
TP684.L	LEMON-GRASS OIL
SB370.L4	LEMON
QL737.P9	LEMURS
E99.D2	*LENAPE INDIANS* **SEE** DELAWARE INDIANS
PM1031-4	*LENAPE LANGUAGE* **SEE** DELAWARE LANGUAGE
PM3921	LENCA LANGUAGE
D753.2	LEND-LEASE OPERATIONS (1941-1945)
HG2053-2069	*LENDING* **SEE** LOANS
PL8115	*LENGE LANGUAGE* **SEE** CHOPI LANGUAGE
QC102	LENGTH MEASUREMENT
QC101	*LENGTH, STANDARDS OF* **SEE** STANDARDS OF LENGTH
F2679	LENGUA INDIANS
D764	LENINGRAD — SIEGE, 1941-1944
PL8453	LENJE LANGUAGE

E99.D2	*LENNI LENAPE* **SEE** DELAWARE INDIANS
PM1031-4	*LENNI LENAPE LANGUAGE* **SEE** DELAWARE LANGUAGE
QL949	*LENS, CRYSTALLINE* **SEE** CRYSTALLINE LENS / comparative anatomy
RE401-461	*LENS, CRYSTALLINE* **SEE** CRYSTALLINE LENS / diseases
QM511	*LENS, CRYSTALLINE* **SEE** CRYSTALLINE LENS / human anatomy
QB85-135	LENSES / astronomical instruments
RE961-2	LENSES / ophthalmology
QC385	LENSES / optics
RE977.C6	*LENSES, CONTACT* **SEE** CONTACT LENSES
QC447	*LENSES, MICROWAVE* **SEE** MICROWAVE LENSES / physics
TK6590.M5	*LENSES, MICROWAVE* **SEE** MICROWAVE LENSES / radar
TR270	LENSES, PHOTOGRAPHIC
BV85	LENT — PRAYER-BOOKS AND DEVOTIONS
BX2170.L4	LENT — PRAYER-BOOKS AND DEVOTIONS / catholic
BV85-95	LENT
TX739	LENTEN MENUS
TX837	LENTEN MENUS / with recipes
BV4277	LENTEN SERMONS — OUTLINES
BV4277	LENTEN SERMONS
QK648	LENTICELS
RC394.H4	*LENTICULAR DEGENERATION* **SEE** HEPATOLENTICULAR DEGENERATION
GN495.2	LEOPARD MEN
GN495.2	*LEOPARD SOCIETIES* **SEE** LEOPARD MEN
QL737.C2	LEOPARDS
PL5865	*LEPANTO-IGOROT DIALECT* **SEE** KANKANAY DIALECT
DR516	LEPANTO, BATTLE OF, 1571
PL3801.L4	LEPCHA LANGUAGE
DS485.S5	LEPCHAS
QL541-562	*LEPIDOPTERA DIURNA* **SEE** BUTTERFLIES
QL541-562	*LEPIDOPTERA NOCTURNA* **SEE** MOTHS
QL541-562	LEPIDOPTERA
QE832.L5	LEPIDOPTERA, FOSSIL
RC154	LEPROSY — DIAGNOSIS
RC154	LEPROSY — HOSPITALS
RC154	LEPROSY
QR201.L5	LEPROSY / bacteriology
QL638.A55	*LEPTOCEPHALIDAE* **SEE** EELS
RC124	*LEPTOMENINGITIS* **SEE** MENINGITIS
RC376	*LEPTOMENINGITIS* **SEE** MENINGITIS
SF799	*LEPTOMENINGITIS* **SEE** MENINGITIS / veterinary medicine
QL444.L6	LEPTOSTRACA
PL8452	*LERE DIALECT* **SEE** LELE DIALECT
HQ73	*LESBIAN LOVE* **SEE** LESBIANISM
HQ73	LESBIANISM
PK9201.K8	*LESGHIAN LANGUAGE* **SEE** KURI LANGUAGE
E216	LESLIE'S RETREAT, 1775
BL1480	*LESSER VEHICLE (BUDDHISM)* **SEE** HINAYANA BUDDHISM
PE1481-1497	LETTER-WRITING / english rhetoric
BJ2100-2115	LETTER-WRITING / etiquette
PE1481-1497	*LETTER-WRITING, ENGLISH* **SEE** LETTER-WRITING / english rhetoric
BJ2100-2115	*LETTER-WRITING, ENGLISH* **SEE** LETTER-WRITING / etiquette
NK3600-3640	LETTERING / art industries
T371	LETTERING / mechanical drawing
TT360	LETTERING / signs and show-cards
HG3745	LETTERS OF CREDIT
JX5241	*LETTERS OF MARQUE* **SEE** PRIVATEERING
JX4486	*LETTERS OF MARQUE* **SEE** REPRISALS
JX6608	LETTERS ROGATORY
PN6131-6140	LETTERS / collections
PN4400	LETTERS / history and criticism
BX863	LETTERS, PAPAL
PG8801-8993	*LETTIC LANGUAGE* **SEE** LETTISH LANGUAGE
HD2365	*LETTING OF CONTRACTS* **SEE** CONTRACTS, LETTING OF / competitive system
HD3858-3860	*LETTING OF CONTRACTS* **SEE** CONTRACTS, LETTING OF / public contracts
PG9037	LETTISH DRAMA / collections
PG9010	LETTISH DRAMA / history

PG8801-8993	LETTISH LANGUAGE
PG9000-9198	LETTISH LITERATURE
PN5355.L3	LETTISH NEWSPAPERS
AP95.L4	LETTISH PERIODICALS
PG9034	LETTISH POETRY / collections
PG9009	LETTISH POETRY / history
HV8204	LETTRES DE CACHET
DK511.L15-19	LETTS
GN585.R9	LETTS / anthropology
RM666.L	*LETTUCE OPIUM* **SEE** LACTUCARIUM
SB351.L6	LETTUCE
PL6252.L	LEUANGIUA LANGUAGE
RC643	*LEUCEMIA* **SEE** LEUKEMIA
QP551	LEUCIN
QP95	LEUCOCYTES
RC643	*LEUCOCYTHEMIA* **SEE** LEUKEMIA
RB145	LEUCOCYTOSIS
GN199	*LEUCODERMA* **SEE** ALBINOS AND ALBINISM / anthropology
QL767	*LEUCODERMA* **SEE** ALBINOS AND ALBINISM / zoology
QP801.P7	LEUCOMAINES
GN199	*LEUCOPATHY* **SEE** ALBINOS AND ALBINISM / anthropology
QL767	*LEUCOPATHY* **SEE** ALBINOS AND ALBINISM / zoology
RC640	LEUCOPENIA
RC640	*LEUCOPENIA, MALIGNANT* **SEE** AGRANULOCYTOSIS
RX471	LEUCORRHEA — HOMEOPATHIC TREATMENT
RG190	LEUCORRHEA
DF231.8	LEUCTRA, BATTLE OF, 371 B.C.
PL6252.L	*LEUENEUWA LANGUAGE* **SEE** LEUANGIUA LANGUAGE
RC643	LEUKEMIA
DD412.6.L6	LEUTHEN, BATTLE OF, 1757
DS41-49	LEVANT
TC337	LEVEES / coast protection
TC533	LEVEES / rivers
TA606-610	LEVELING
DA405	LEVELLERS
QE391.L	LEVERRIERITE
BF1385	LEVITATION
QD321	LEVULOSE
HJ4132-3	*LEVY ON CAPITAL* **SEE** CAPITAL LEVY
F592.3-7	LEWIS AND CLARK EXPEDITION
UF620.L5	LEWIS MACHINE-GUN
QD412.A7	LEWISITE (POISON GAS) / chemistry
UG447.5.L	LEWISITE (POISON GAS) / military science
QB723.L6	LEXELL'S COMET
E241.L6	LEXINGTON, BATTLE OF, 1775
E472.25	LEXINGTON, MO., BATTLE OF, 1861
DH192.5	LEYDEN — SIEGE, 1573-1574
QL949	*LEYDIG'S ORGAN* **SEE** EYE, PARIETAL
D774.P	*LEYTE GULF, BATTLE OF, 1944* **SEE** PHILIPPINE SEA, BATTLES OF THE, 1944
PK9201.K8	*LEZGHIAN LANGUAGE* **SEE** KURI LANGUAGE
QE461	LHERZOLITE
PL4251.L5	LI LANGUAGE
CR4480	*LIA FAIL* **SEE** STONE OF SCONE
HG9964.E	*LIABILITY INSURANCE* **SEE** INSURANCE, LIABILITY / employers' liability
JF1621	*LIABILITY OF THE STATE* **SEE** GOVERNMENT LIABILITY
JK-JQ	*LIABILITY OF THE STATE* **SEE** GOVERNMENT LIABILITY
HD7814-7816	*LIABILITY, EMPLOYERS'* **SEE** EMPLOYERS' LIABILITY
DS751	*LIAO DYNASTY* **SEE** CHINA — HISTORY — — LIAO DYNASTY, 907-1125
DS517	LIAO-YANG, BATTLE OF, 1904
QE681-3	*LIAS* **SEE** GEOLOGY, STRATIGRAPHIC — JURASSIC
QE923	*LIAS* **SEE** PALEOBOTANY — JURASSIC
QE733	*LIAS* **SEE** PALEONTOLOGY — JURASSIC
BJ1535.S6	*LIBEL AND SLANDER (ETHICS)* **SEE** SLANDER / ethics
BV4627.S6	*LIBEL AND SLANDER (ETHICS)* **SEE** SLANDER / moral theology
BX2427	*LIBER PROMISSIONUM* **SEE** PROFESSION (IN RELIGIOUS ORDERS, CONGREGATIONS, ETC.)
LC1001-1021	*LIBERAL EDUCATION* **SEE** EDUCATION, HUMANISTIC

JL197.L	LIBERAL PARTY (CANADA)
JN1129.L4-5	LIBERAL PARTY (GT. BRIT.)
JK2391.L78-82	LIBERAL REPUBLICAN PARTY
BR1615-1617	LIBERAL THEOLOGY SEE LIBERALISM (RELIGION) / christianity
BR1615-1617	LIBERALISM (RELIGION) / christianity
HM276	LIBERALISM
DA25	LIBERATE ROLLS
JK-JQ	LIBERTY OF ASSOCIATION SEE FREEDOM OF ASSOCIATION
JC607	LIBERTY OF ASSOCIATION SEE FREEDOM OF ASSOCIATION
BV741	LIBERTY OF CONSCIENCE
HD4903	LIBERTY OF EMPLOYMENT SEE FREE CHOICE OF EMPLOYMENT
HD4903	LIBERTY OF OCCUPATION SEE FREE CHOICE OF EMPLOYMENT
BV741	LIBERTY OF RELIGION SEE RELIGIOUS LIBERTY
BV740	LIBERTY OF SPEECH IN THE CHURCH
JC591	LIBERTY OF SPEECH
Z657-9	LIBERTY OF THE PRESS
BJ1460-1468	LIBERTY OF THE WILL SEE FREE WILL AND DETERMINISM / ethics
BF620-628	LIBERTY OF THE WILL SEE FREE WILL AND DETERMINISM / psychology
JK2391.L	LIBERTY PARTY / u.s.
JC585-599	LIBERTY / political theory
HM271	LIBERTY / sociology
Z677	LIBRARIANS — CERTIFICATION
Z668.5	LIBRARIANS — IN-SERVICE TRAINING
Z682.3	LIBRARIANS — SALARIES, PENSIONS, ETC.
Z673	LIBRARIANS - CONGRESSES SEE LIBRARY CONFERENCES
Z720	LIBRARIANS / biography
Z682	LIBRARIANS / personnel
Z669.8	LIBRARIANS, INTERCHANGE OF
Z672	LIBRARIANS, INTERCHANGE OF / international cooperation
Z720	LIBRARIANS, NEGRO SEE NEGRO LIBRARIANS
Z682	LIBRARIANS, PROFESSIONAL ETHICS FOR
Z668-9	LIBRARIANS, TRAINING OF SEE LIBRARY SCHOOLS AND TRAINING
Z673	LIBRARIANS-CONGRESSES SEE LIBRARY CONFERENCES
Z665-718	LIBRARIANSHIP SEE LIBRARY SCIENCE
Z682.5	LIBRARIES — ANECDOTES, FACETIAE, SATIRE, ETC.
Z686	LIBRARIES — BRANCHES, DELIVERY STATIONS, ETC.
Z678	LIBRARIES — CENTRALIZATION
Z712	LIBRARIES — CIRCULATION, LOANS
Z689	LIBRARIES — GIFTS, LEGACIES
Z720.5	LIBRARIES — HISTORIOGRAPHY
Z721	LIBRARIES — HISTORY
Z711	LIBRARIES — REFERENCE DEPT.
Z703.5	LIBRARIES — SHELF DEPT.
Z688	LIBRARIES — SPECIAL COLLECTIONS
Z682	LIBRARIES — TRUSTEES
Z673	LIBRARIES - CONGRESSES SEE LIBRARY CONFERENCES
Z711.8	LIBRARIES AND FOREIGN POPULATION
Z711.85	LIBRARIES AND LABOR
Z711.9	LIBRARIES AND NEGROES
Z681	LIBRARIES AND PHOTOGRAPHY SEE PHOTOGRAPHY — LIBRARY APPLICATIONS
Z717	LIBRARIES AND PICTURES
Z716.6	LIBRARIES AND PUBLISHING
Z716.7	LIBRARIES AND RADIO
Z711	LIBRARIES AND READERS
Z704	LIBRARIES AND READERS
Z718	LIBRARIES AND SCHOOLS
Z718.7	LIBRARIES AND STUDENTS
Z716.8	LIBRARIES AND TELEVISION
Z711.9	LIBRARIES FOR NEGROES SEE LIBRARIES AND NEGROES
HV1721-1756	LIBRARIES FOR THE BLIND SEE BLIND, LIBRARIES FOR THE
Z675.B6	LIBRARIES FOR THE BLIND SEE BLIND, LIBRARIES FOR THE
Z665-997	LIBRARIES
Z675.A5	LIBRARIES, AERONAUTICAL SEE AERONAUTICAL LIBRARIES

Z675.A8	LIBRARIES, AGRICULTURAL SEE AGRICULTURAL LIBRARIES
Z675.A82	LIBRARIES, ARABIC SEE ARABIC LIBRARIES
Z675.A83	LIBRARIES, ARCHITECTURAL SEE ARCHITECTURAL LIBRARIES
Z675.A85	LIBRARIES, ART SEE ART LIBRARIES
Z686	LIBRARIES, BRANCH SEE LIBRARIES — BRANCHES, DELIVERY STATIONS, ETC.
Z675.W2	LIBRARIES, CAMP SEE EUROPEAN WAR, 1914-1918 — LIBRARIES (IN CAMPS, ETC.)
Z675.W2	LIBRARIES, CAMP SEE WAR LIBRARIES
Z675.C	LIBRARIES, CHEMICAL SEE CHEMICAL LIBRARIES
Z718.1	LIBRARIES, CHILDREN'S
Z675.U5	LIBRARIES, COLLEGE SEE LIBRARIES, UNIVERSITY AND COLLEGE
Z675.C7	LIBRARIES, COMMERCIAL SEE COMMERCIAL LIBRARIES
Z675.C8	LIBRARIES, COUNTY
Z675.D3	LIBRARIES, DENTAL SEE DENTAL LIBRARIES
Z675.D4	LIBRARIES, DEPOSITORY
Z675.E6	LIBRARIES, ENGINEERING SEE ENGINEERING LIBRARIES
Z675.F3	LIBRARIES, FACTORY SEE FACTORY LIBRARIES
Z675.F5	LIBRARIES, FINANCIAL SEE FINANCIAL LIBRARIES
Z675.G7	LIBRARIES, GOVERNMENTAL, ADMINISTRATIVE, ETC.
Z675.J4	LIBRARIES, HEBREW SEE JEWISH LIBRARIES
Z675.S3	LIBRARIES, HIGH SCHOOL SEE SCHOOL LIBRARIES (HIGH SCHOOL)
Z675.H5	LIBRARIES, HISTORICAL SEE HISTORICAL LIBRARIES
Z675.H7	LIBRARIES, HOSPITAL SEE HOSPITAL LIBRARIES
Z1024	LIBRARIES, IMAGINARY SEE IMAGINARY BOOKS AND LIBRARIES
Z675.I6	LIBRARIES, INSTITUTION SEE INSTITUTION LIBRARIES
Z675.I7	LIBRARIES, INSURANCE SEE INSURANCE LIBRARIES
Z675.J4	LIBRARIES, JEWISH SEE JEWISH LIBRARIES
Z675.N4	LIBRARIES, JOURNALISTIC SEE NEWSPAPER OFFICE LIBRARIES
Z675.U5	LIBRARIES, JUNIOR COLLEGE SEE LIBRARIES, UNIVERSITY AND COLLEGE
Z675.L2	LIBRARIES, LAW SEE LAW LIBRARIES
Z675.M4	LIBRARIES, MEDICAL SEE MEDICAL LIBRARIES
Z675.M5	LIBRARIES, MILITARY SEE MILITARY LIBRARIES
Z675.M	LIBRARIES, MONASTIC SEE MONASTIC LIBRARIES
Z675.M9	LIBRARIES, MUNICIPAL REFERENCE SEE MUNICIPAL REFERENCE LIBRARIES
ML136-9	LIBRARIES, MUSIC SEE MUSIC LIBRARIES / catalogs
ML111	LIBRARIES, MUSIC SEE MUSIC LIBRARIES / forming of libraries
Z675.N2	LIBRARIES, NATIONAL
Z675.N3	LIBRARIES, NAVAL
Z711.9	LIBRARIES, NEGROES' SEE LIBRARIES AND NEGROES
Z675.N4	LIBRARIES, NEWSPAPER OFFICE SEE NEWSPAPER OFFICE LIBRARIES
Z675.N8	LIBRARIES, NURSING SCHOOL
Z716.1	LIBRARIES, PACKAGE
Z675.P3	LIBRARIES, PEDAGOGICAL SEE PEDAGOGICAL LIBRARIES
ML111.5	LIBRARIES, PHONORECORD SEE PHONORECORD LIBRARIES
Z675.P	LIBRARIES, POSTAL SEE POSTAL LIBRARIES
7675.P8	LIBRARIES, PRISON SEE PRISON LIBRARIES
Z987-997	LIBRARIES, PRIVATE
Z675.P85	LIBRARIES, PROPRIETARY
Z675.P	LIBRARIES, PUBLIC HEALTH
Z675.Y7	LIBRARIES, RAILROAD Y.M.C.A.
Z675.R	LIBRARIES, REFORMATORY SEE REFORMATORY LIBRARIES
Z1039.R4	LIBRARIES, REFORMATORY SEE REFORMATORY LIBRARIES / books
Z675.R4	LIBRARIES, RENTAL
Z675.C8	LIBRARIES, RURAL SEE RURAL LIBRARIES
Z675.V7	LIBRARIES, RURAL SEE RURAL LIBRARIES
Z675.S3	LIBRARIES, SCHOOL SEE SCHOOL LIBRARIES
Z675.N3	LIBRARIES, SEAMEN'S SEE LIBRARIES, NAVAL
Z675.N3	LIBRARIES, SHIPS' SEE LIBRARIES, NAVAL
Z675.W2	LIBRARIES, SOLDIERS' SEE EUROPEAN WAR, 1914-1918 — LIBRARIES (IN CAMPS, ETC.)
Z675.W2	LIBRARIES, SOLDIERS' SEE WAR LIBRARIES
Z675.A2	LIBRARIES, SPECIAL

Z675.G7	LIBRARIES, STATE **SEE** LIBRARIES, GOVERNMENTAL, ADMINISTRATIVE, ETC.
Z675.S8	LIBRARIES, SUBSCRIPTION
Z675.S9	LIBRARIES, SUNDAY-SCHOOL
Z675.T3	LIBRARIES, TECHNICAL **SEE** TECHNICAL LIBRARIES
Z675.T	LIBRARIES, THEATRICAL
Z702	LIBRARIES, THEFTS FROM **SEE** BOOK THEFTS
Z675.T4	LIBRARIES, THEOLOGICAL **SEE** THEOLOGICAL LIBRARIES
Z732	LIBRARIES, TRAVELING
Z716	LIBRARIES, TRAVELING
Z675.U5	LIBRARIES, UNIVERSITY AND COLLEGE
Z675.W2	LIBRARIES, WAR **SEE** WAR LIBRARIES
Z675.W	LIBRARIES, WORKING-MEN'S
Z675.Y7	LIBRARIES, Y.M.C.A.
Z718.5	LIBRARIES, YOUNG PEOPLE'S
Z683	LIBRARIES-ACCOUNTING **SEE** LIBRARY FINANCE
Z688	LIBRARIES-ACQUISITION OF MATERIAL IN SPECIAL FIELDS **SEE** LIBRARIES — SPECIAL COLLECTIONS
Z678	LIBRARIES-ADMINISTRATION **SEE** LIBRARY ADMINISTRATION
Z665-718	LIBRARIES-ADMINISTRATION **SEE** LIBRARY SCIENCE
Z696-7	LIBRARIES-ARRANGEMENT OF BOOKS ON SHELVES **SEE** CLASSIFICATION — BOOKS
Z696-7	LIBRARIES-ARRANGEMENT OF BOOKS ON SHELVES **SEE** SHELF-LISTING (LIBRARY SCIENCE)
Z682	LIBRARIES-BOARDS **SEE** LIBRARIES — TRUSTEES
Z683	LIBRARIES-BOOKKEEPING **SEE** BOOKKEEPING, LIBRARY
Z710	LIBRARIES-CATALOGS **SEE** LIBRARY CATALOGS
Z714	LIBRARIES-CHARGING SYSTEMS **SEE** CHARGING SYSTEMS (LIBRARIES)
Z718.1	LIBRARIES-CHILDREN'S ROOMS **SEE** LIBRARIES, CHILDREN'S
Z696-7	LIBRARIES-CLASSIFICATION **SEE** CLASSIFICATION — BOOKS
Z673	LIBRARIES-CONGRESSES **SEE** LIBRARY CONFERENCES
Z689	LIBRARIES-DUPLICATE BOOKS **SEE** DUPLICATES IN LIBRARIES
Z673.E	LIBRARIES-EXHIBITIONS **SEE** LIBRARY EXHIBITS
Z711.5	LIBRARIES-FICTION **SEE** FICTION IN LIBRARIES
Z680	LIBRARIES-HEATING AND VENTILATION **SEE** LIBRARY ARCHITECTURE — HEATING AND VENTILATION
Z677	LIBRARIES-LAW AND LEGISLATION **SEE** LIBRARY LEGISLATION
Z680	LIBRARIES-LIGHTING **SEE** LIBRARY ARCHITECTURE — LIGHTING
Z665-997	LIBRARIES-ORGANIZATION **SEE** LIBRARIES
Z678	LIBRARIES-ORGANIZATION **SEE** LIBRARY ADMINISTRATION
Z665-718	LIBRARIES-ORGANIZATION **SEE** LIBRARY SCIENCE
Z711	LIBRARIES-REFERENCE BOOKS **SEE** REFERENCE BOOKS
Z685	LIBRARIES-SHELVING **SEE** SHELVING (FOR BOOKS)
Z673	LIBRARIES-SOCIETIES, ETC. **SEE** LIBRARY ASSOCIATIONS
Z708	LIBRARIES-SUNDAY OPENING **SEE** SUNDAY OPENING OF LIBRARIES
Z684-5	LIBRARIES-SUPPLIES **SEE** LIBRARY FITTINGS AND SUPPLIES
Z688	LIBRARY ACQUISITION OF MATERIAL IN SPECIAL FIELDS **SEE** LIBRARIES — SPECIAL COLLECTIONS
Z678	LIBRARY ADMINISTRATION
Z680	LIBRARY ARCHITECTURE — HEATING AND VENTILATION
Z680	LIBRARY ARCHITECTURE — LIGHTING
Z679	LIBRARY ARCHITECTURE
Z673	LIBRARY ASSOCIATIONS
Z1033.L6	LIBRARY BINDINGS, BOOKS IN **SEE** BIBLIOGRAPHY — LIBRARY EDITIONS
Z682	LIBRARY BOARDS **SEE** LIBRARIES — TRUSTEES
Z683	LIBRARY BOOKKEEPING **SEE** BOOKKEEPING, LIBRARY
Z679	LIBRARY BUILDINGS **SEE** LIBRARY ARCHITECTURE
Z711.3	LIBRARY CATALOGS AND READERS
Z710	LIBRARY CATALOGS
Z695.83	LIBRARY CATALOGS-UNION CATALOGS **SEE** CATALOGS, UNION
Z714	LIBRARY CHARGING SYSTEMS **SEE** CHARGING SYSTEMS (LIBRARIES)

Z696-7	LIBRARY CLASSIFICATION **SEE** CLASSIFICATION — BOOKS
Z716	LIBRARY COMMISSIONS
Z732	LIBRARY COMMISSIONS / *state library commission reports*
Z673	LIBRARY CONFERENCES
Z718	LIBRARY DAY
Z689	LIBRARY DUPLICATES **SEE** DUPLICATES IN LIBRARIES
Z665-718	LIBRARY ECONOMY **SEE** LIBRARY SCIENCE
Z1033.L6	LIBRARY EDITIONS **SEE** BIBLIOGRAPHY — LIBRARY EDITIONS
Z673.E	LIBRARY EXHIBITS
Z716	LIBRARY EXTENSION
Z683	LIBRARY FINANCE
Z684-5	LIBRARY FITTINGS AND SUPPLIES
Z695	LIBRARY HANDWRITING
Z680	LIBRARY HEATING **SEE** LIBRARY ARCHITECTURE — HEATING AND VENTILATION
Z682.5	LIBRARY HUMOR **SEE** LIBRARIES — ANECDOTES, FACETIAE, SATIRE, ETC.
Z677	LIBRARY LAW **SEE** LIBRARY LEGISLATION
Z677	LIBRARY LEGISLATION
Z680	LIBRARY LIGHTING **SEE** LIBRARY ARCHITECTURE — LIGHTING
Z703.5	LIBRARY MOVING
Z696	LIBRARY OF CONGRESS CLASSIFICATION **SEE** CLASSIFICATION, LIBRARY OF CONGRESS
Z712	LIBRARY POST
Z669.7	LIBRARY RESEARCH **SEE** LIBRARY SCIENCE — RESEARCH
Z669.7	LIBRARY RESEARCH **SEE** LIBRARY SCIENCE — RESEARCH
Z731-880	LIBRARY RULES AND REGULATIONS
Z704	LIBRARY RULES AND REGULATIONS
Z668-9	LIBRARY SCHOOLS AND TRAINING
Z1006	LIBRARY SCIENCE — DICTIONARIES
Z670.A2	LIBRARY SCIENCE — EARLY WORKS TO 1800
Z669.7	LIBRARY SCIENCE — RESEARCH
Z673	LIBRARY SCIENCE - CONGRESSES **SEE** LIBRARY CONFERENCES
Z682	LIBRARY SCIENCE AS A PROFESSION
Z665-718	LIBRARY SCIENCE
Z673	LIBRARY SCIENCE-CONGRESSES **SEE** LIBRARY CONFERENCES
Z673	LIBRARY SCIENCE-SOCIETIES, ETC. **SEE** LIBRARY ASSOCIATIONS
Z668-9	LIBRARY SCIENCE-STUDY AND TEACHING **SEE** LIBRARY SCHOOLS AND TRAINING
Z682	LIBRARY SCIENCE-VOCATIONAL GUIDANCE **SEE** LIBRARY SCIENCE AS A PROFESSION
Z711.9	LIBRARY SERVICE TO NEGROES **SEE** LIBRARIES AND NEGROES
Z689	LIBRARY STAMPS
Z711.3	LIBRARY STATISTICS
Z683	LIBRARY STATISTICS
Z672	LIBRARY STUDENTS, INTERCHANGE OF **SEE** LIBRARIANS, INTERCHANGE OF / *international cooperation*
Z669.8	LIBRARY STUDENTS, INTERCHANGE OF **SEE** LIBRARIANS, INTERCHANGE OF
Z684-5	LIBRARY SUPPLIES **SEE** LIBRARY FITTINGS AND SUPPLIES
Z678	LIBRARY SYSTEMS **SEE** LIBRARIES — CENTRALIZATION
Z678	LIBRARY SYSTEMS **SEE** LIBRARIES — CENTRALIZATION
Z682	LIBRARY TRUSTEES **SEE** LIBRARIES — TRUSTEES
Z680	LIBRARY VENTILATION **SEE** LIBRARY ARCHITECTURE — HEATING AND VENTILATION
QB585	LIBRATION OF THE MOON **SEE** MOON — LIBRATION
ML2110	LIBRETTISTS
ML48-49	LIBRETTOS
PJ2369-2399	LIBYAN LANGUAGES **SEE** BERBER LANGUAGES
PJ2340-2349	LIBYAN LANGUAGES **SEE** BERBER LANGUAGES
RA641.L6	LICE AS CARRIERS OF DISEASE
QL503.A6	LICE
HV5084-7	LICENSE SYSTEM
HJ5301-5315	LICENSES / *revenue*
HF1436	LICENSES / *trades*
HJ5791-2	LICENSING OF DOGS **SEE** DOGS — TAXATION

QM548-9	*LIMBS (ANATOMY)* **SEE** EXTREMITIES (ANATOMY) / *human anatomy general*
QM165	*LIMBS (ANATOMY)* **SEE** EXTREMITIES (ANATOMY) / *muscles*
QL831	*LIMBS (ANATOMY)* **SEE** EXTREMITIES (ANATOMY) / *muscles*
QL821	*LIMBS (ANATOMY)* **SEE** EXTREMITIES (ANATOMY) / *skeleton*
QM117	*LIMBS (ANATOMY)* **SEE** EXTREMITIES (ANATOMY) / *skeleton*
RD756	*LIMBS, ARTIFICIAL* **SEE** ARTIFICIAL LIMBS
BT850-860	*LIMBUS* **SEE** LIMBO
RA766.L7	LIME AS A DISINFECTANT
TP886	LIME-KILNS
TA434-5	LIME / *etc.*
S643	LIME / *fertilizers*
TP886	LIME / *technology*
DA945	LIMERICK — SIEGE, 1690
DA946	LIMERICK, TREATY OF, 1691
PN6231.L5	LIMERICKS
TN967	LIMESTONE
JX1974	*LIMITATION OF ARMAMENT* **SEE** DISARMAMENT
HD301-1130	*LIMITATIONS (LAW)* **SEE** REAL PROPERTY / *other countries*
HD251-279	*LIMITATIONS (LAW)* **SEE** REAL PROPERTY / *u. s.*
HD251-279	*LIMITATIONS (LAW)* **SEE** REAL PROPERTY / *u.s.*
J-JQ	*LIMITATIONS, CONSTITUTIONAL* **SEE** CONSTITUTIONAL LAW
HF1253-5	*LIMITATIONS, CONTRACTUAL* **SEE** CONTRACTS / *commercial law*
HD2381-5	*LIMITATIONS, CONTRACTUAL* **SEE** CONTRACTS / *subcontracting*
HG4001-4280	*LIMITED COMPANIES* **SEE** CORPORATIONS / *finance*
HD2709-2930	*LIMITED COMPANIES* **SEE** CORPORATIONS / *theory and policy*
QA300-316	*LIMITS (MATHEMATICS)* **SEE** CALCULUS
QH98	LIMNOLOGY / *biology*
TX360.H3	LIMU / *hawaiian foods*
E99.D2	*LINAPI* **SEE** DELAWARE INDIANS
E457.2	*LINCOLN AS A LAWYER* **SEE** LINCOLN, ABRAHAM, PRES. U.S., 1809-1865 — LAW PRACTICE
E457.2	*LINCOLN AS A LAWYER* **SEE** LINCOLN, ABRAHAM, PRES. U.S., 1809-1865 — LAW PRACTICE
E457.7	LINCOLN DAY
E457.4	LINCOLN-DOUGLAS DEBATES, 1858
E457.32	LINCOLN, ABRAHAM, PRES. U.S., 1809-1865 — CHILDHOOD
E457.2	LINCOLN, ABRAHAM, PRES. U.S., 1809-1865 — LAW PRACTICE
E457.2	LINCOLN, ABRAHAM, PRES. U.S., 1809-1865 — RELATIONS WITH SPANISH AMERICANS
E457.2	LINCOLN, ABRAHAM, PRES. U.S., 1809-1865 — RELATIONS WITH NEGROES
E457	LINCOLN, ABRAHAM, PRES. U.S., 1809-1865
DA227	LINCOLN, BATTLE OF, 1217
E457.7	*LINCOLN'S BIRTHDAY* **SEE** LINCOLN DAY
PM8508	LINCOS (ARTIFICIAL LANGUAGE)
NK3505	LINCRUSTA-WALTON
QP55	*LINDBERGH PUMP* **SEE** PERFUSION PUMP (HEART)
QK495.T5	LINDEN / *botany*
SD397.L6	LINDEN / *sylviculture*
QA608	LINE GEOMETRY
E123	*LINE OF DEMARCATION OF ALEXANDER VI* **SEE** DEMARCATION LINE OF ALEXANDER VI
GV951.2	LINE PLAY (FOOTBALL)
NE	*LINE-ENGRAVING* **SEE** ENGRAVING
QA251	*LINEAR ALGEBRAS* **SEE** ALGEBRAS, LINEAR
QA608	*LINEAR COMPLEXES* **SEE** COMPLEXES
QA372-7	*LINEAR DIFFERENTIAL EQUATIONS* **SEE** DIFFERENTIAL EQUATIONS, LINEAR
QC102	*LINEAR MEASUREMENT* **SEE** LENGTH MEASUREMENT
QA251	*LINEAR OPERATORS* **SEE** ALGEBRAS, LINEAR
NC749-750	*LINEAR PERSPECTIVE* **SEE** PERSPECTIVE
QA515	*LINEAR PERSPECTIVE* **SEE** PERSPECTIVE / *geometry*
T369	*LINEAR PERSPECTIVE* **SEE** PERSPECTIVE / *mechanical drawing*
QA265	LINEAR PROGRAMMING
QA190-201	*LINEAR SUBSTITUTIONS* **SEE** SUBSTITUTIONS, LINEAR
QA402	*LINEAR SYSTEM THEORY* **SEE** SYSTEM ANALYSIS
TS1700-1731	LINEN
HD9930	LINEN / *trade*
PM8509	LING (ARTIFICIAL LANGUAGE)
PL8055	*LINGALA LANGUAGE* **SEE** BANGALA LANGUAGE
BL1245.L5	*LINGAYATISM* **SEE** LINGAYATS
BL1245.L5	LINGAYATS
TT670	LINGERIE
DS644	*LINGGARDJATI AGREEMENT* **SEE** CHERIBON AGREEMENT, 1946
PM8508	*LINGUA COSMICA* **SEE** LINCOS (ARTIFICIAL LANGUAGE)
PM7801-7895	*LINGUA FRANCA* **SEE** LANGUAGES, MIXED
B808.5	*LINGUISTIC ANALYSIS* **SEE** ANALYSIS (PHILOSOPHY)
P375-381	LINGUISTIC GEOGRAPHY
P61-81	LINGUISTIC RESEARCH — HISTORY
P121-5	LINGUISTIC RESEARCH
P1-409	*LINGUISTICS* **SEE** LANGUAGE AND LANGUAGES
P83-85	LINGUISTS
DP635	*LINHAS DE ELVAS, BATTLE OF, 1659* **SEE** ELVAS, LINHAS DE, BATTLE OF, 1659
TL697.T7	LINK TRAINERS
TJ1119	LINK-BELTING
TJ182-3	LINKS AND LINK-MOTION
QL696.P2	LINNETS
NE1330	LINOLEUM BLOCK-PRINTING
TS1779.L5	LINOLEUM
Z120	*LINOTYPE - SOCIETIES, ETC.* **SEE** PRINTING — SOCIETIES, ETC.
Z253	LINOTYPE
Z120	*LINOTYPE-SOCIETIES, ETC.* **SEE** PRINTING — SOCIETIES, ETC.
SB299.F6	*LINSEED* **SEE** FLAXSEED / *culture*
HD9155	*LINSEED* **SEE** FLAXSEED / *trade*
HF5716.F5	*LINSEED* **SEE** FLAXSEED / *trade*
TP682	LINSEED-OIL
PZ10.3	LIONS — LEGENDS AND STORIES / *juvenile*
QL795.L	LIONS — LEGENDS AND STORIES / *zoology*
QL737.C2	LIONS
HV2471-2500	*LIP-READING* **SEE** DEAF — MEANS OF COMMUNICATION
E99.L	LIPAN INDIANS
DB208	LIPAN, BATTLE OF, 1434
QE461	*LIPARITE* **SEE** RHYOLITE
QP601	LIPASE
RB145	LIPEMIA
QP751	*LIPIDES* **SEE** LIPIDS
RC627.L	LIPIDOSIS
QP751	LIPIDS
QP751	*LIPINS* **SEE** LIPIDS
SF293.L	*LIPIZZANER HORSE* **SEE** LIPPIZANER HORSE
QP751	*LIPOIDS* **SEE** LIPIDS
QP601	LIPOLYSIS
BX601	*LIPOVANY* **SEE** PHILIPPOVTSI (RUSSIAN SECT)
SF293.L	LIPPIZANER HORSE
TR525	*LIPPMANN PROCESS* **SEE** COLOR PHOTOGRAPHY — LIPPMANN PROCESS
RD524	LIPS — ABNORMITIES AND DEFORMITIES / *surgery*
RC280.L	LIPS — TUMORS
RD662	LIPS — TUMORS
QL857	LIPS / *comparative anatomy*
QM306	LIPS / *human anatomy*
QD535	*LIQUEFACTION OF GASES* **SEE** GASES — LIQUEFACTION
TP243	LIQUEFIED GASES — TRANSPORTATION
TP243	LIQUEFIED GASES
TP611	LIQUEURS
QD535	LIQUID AIR
HG174	*LIQUID ASSETS* **SEE** LIQUIDITY (ECONOMICS)
Z48	*LIQUID COPYING PROCESSES* **SEE** FLUID COPYING PROCESSES
QD921	LIQUID CRYSTALS
TP343	LIQUID FUELS
TP243	*LIQUID GASES* **SEE** LIQUEFIED GASES
TP245.O9	LIQUID OXYGEN
HD2747	LIQUIDATION
K	LIQUIDATION
HG174	LIQUIDITY (ECONOMICS)
TP156.C	LIQUIDS — CLARIFICATION

TJ930	LIQUIDS — TRANSPORTATION / *pipe-lines*
TF481	LIQUIDS — TRANSPORTATION / *tank-cars*
QC141-159	LIQUIDS
HD3623-4	*LIQUIDS, INFLAMMABLE* **SEE** INFLAMMABLE LIQUIDS / *dangerous industries*
QC175.3	LIQUIDS, KINETIC THEORY OF
QC284	*LIQUIDS-COMPRESSIBILITY* **SEE** COMPRESSIBILITY / *liquids*
QD543	*LIQUIDS-DIFFUSION* **SEE** DIFFUSION / *chemistry*
QC185	*LIQUIDS-DIFFUSION* **SEE** DIFFUSION / *physics*
QC284	*LIQUIDS-EXPANSION* **SEE** EXPANSION OF LIQUIDS
QC189	*LIQUIDS-VISCOSITY* **SEE** VISCOSITY
QL975	*LIQUOR AMNII* **SEE** AMNIOTIC LIQUID / *embryology*
QM611	*LIQUOR AMNII* **SEE** AMNIOTIC LIQUID / *human embryology*
HD9350.8	*LIQUOR DUTIES* **SEE** LIQUOR TRAFFIC — TAXATION
HV5074-5080	LIQUOR LAWS
HV5084-7	*LIQUOR LICENSE SYSTEM* **SEE** LICENSE SYSTEM
HV5001-5720	LIQUOR PROBLEM
HD9350.8	*LIQUOR TAX* **SEE** LIQUOR TRAFFIC — TAXATION
HD9350.8	LIQUOR TRAFFIC — TAXATION
HV5001-5720	LIQUOR TRAFFIC
HD9350-9399	LIQUOR TRAFFIC
SB295.L7	*LIQUORICE* **SEE** LICORICE / *plant culture*
RM666.L5	*LIQUORICE* **SEE** LICORICE / *therapeutics*
TP609	LIQUORS — GAGING AND TESTING
TP609	LIQUORS — TABLES, STANDARDS, ETC.
TP589-618	LIQUORS
TP569-587	*LIQUORS, MALT* **SEE** MALT LIQUORS
TP658	LIQUORS, REFRIGERATION OF
HD9350.8	*LIQUORS-TAXATION* **SEE** LIQUOR TRAFFIC — TAXATION
PL8675	*LISANGO LANGUAGE* **SEE** SHIRA LANGUAGE
PL4001.L6	*LISAW LANGUAGE* **SEE** LISU LANGUAGE
D162.3	LISBON — SIEGE, 1147
DA86.22.D7	LISBON EXPEDITION, 1589 / *drake*
PL8675	*LISIRA LANGUAGE* **SEE** SHIRA LANGUAGE
DG558	LISSA, BATTLE OF, 1866
QC231	LISSAJOUS' CURVES
BF323.L	LISTENING
VK1150-1246	*LISTS OF LIGHTS* **SEE** AIDS TO NAVIGATION — LISTS
PL4001.L6	LISU LANGUAGE
SB379.L8	LITCHI
LC149-160	*LITERACY* **SEE** ILLITERACY
PN6231.B8	*LITERARY ANACHRONISMS* **SEE** ERRORS AND BLUNDERS, LITERARY
PN6231.B8	*LITERARY BLUNDERS* **SEE** ERRORS AND BLUNDERS, LITERARY
PN218	*LITERARY CHARACTERS* **SEE** CHARACTERS AND CHARACTERISTICS IN LITERATURE
BF818-839	*LITERARY CHARACTERS* **SEE** CHARACTERS AND CHARACTERISTICS IN LITERATURE / *psychology*
PN1689	*LITERARY CHARACTERS* **SEE** CHARACTERS AND CHARACTERISTICS IN LITERATURE / *drama*
PN171.P75	*LITERARY COMPETITIONS* **SEE** LITERATURE — COMPETITIONS
BH39-41	*LITERARY CRITICISM* **SEE** CRITICISM / *aesthetics*
PN75-99	*LITERARY CRITICISM* **SEE** CRITICISM / *literary criticism*
PN6231.B8	*LITERARY ERRORS AND BLUNDERS* **SEE** ERRORS AND BLUNDERS, LITERARY
PN154	LITERARY ETHICS
Z690	*LITERARY EXCHANGES* **SEE** EXCHANGES, LITERARY AND SCIENTIFIC
PN165	*LITERARY FEUDS* **SEE** LITERARY QUARRELS
PN171.F6-7	LITERARY FORGERIES AND MYSTIFICATIONS
PN171.F6-7	*LITERARY FRAUDS* **SEE** LITERARY FORGERIES AND MYSTIFICATIONS
PN164	LITERARY LANDMARKS
PN150-171	*LITERARY LIFE* **SEE** LITTERATEURS
Z551-656	*LITERARY PROPERTY* **SEE** COPYRIGHT
PN165	LITERARY QUARRELS
GV1493	LITERARY RECREATIONS
PN4500	*LITERARY SKETCH* **SEE** ESSAY
PN20-30	LITERARY SOCIETIES
PN203	*LITERARY STYLE* **SEE** STYLE, LITERARY
PN58	LITERATURE — ADDRESSES, ESSAYS, LECTURES

PN45	LITERATURE — AESTHETICS
PN169	LITERATURE — ANECDOTES, FACETIAE, SATIRE, ETC.
PN165	LITERATURE — ANECDOTES, FACETIAE, SATIRE, ETC.
Z6511-6525	LITERATURE — BIBLIOGRAPHY
Z6511-6525	LITERATURE — BIO-BIBLIOGRAPHY
Z1010	LITERATURE — BIO-BIBLIOGRAPHY
PN6010-6078	LITERATURE — COLLECTIONS
PN171.P75	LITERATURE — COMPETITIONS
PN41-43	LITERATURE — DICTIONARIES
PN75-99	LITERATURE — HISTORY AND CRITICISM / *criticism*
PN441-595	LITERATURE — HISTORY AND CRITICISM / *history*
PN524-595	LITERATURE — OUTLINES, SYLLABI, ETC.
PN1-9	LITERATURE — PERIODICALS
PN45	LITERATURE — PHILOSOPHY
PN49	LITERATURE — PSYCHOLOGY
PN20-29	LITERATURE — SOCIETIES, ETC.
PN855	LITERATURE — SOCIETIES, ETC. / *comparative literature*
PN44	LITERATURE — STORIES, PLOTS, ETC.
PN59-72	LITERATURE — STUDY AND TEACHING
PN11-19	LITERATURE — YEARBOOKS
N72	*LITERATURE AND ART* **SEE** ART AND LITERATURE / *art*
PR149.A	*LITERATURE AND ART* **SEE** ART AND LITERATURE / *english literature*
PT112	*LITERATURE AND ART* **SEE** ART AND LITERATURE / *german literature*
PN53	*LITERATURE AND ART* **SEE** ART AND LITERATURE / *literature*
PN51	*LITERATURE AND CAPITALISM* **SEE** CAPITALISM AND LITERATURE
PN50	LITERATURE AND HISTORY
PN49	LITERATURE AND MORALS
ML3849	*LITERATURE AND MUSIC* **SEE** MUSIC AND LITERATURE
ML80	*LITERATURE AND MUSIC* **SEE** MUSIC AND LITERATURE
N72	*LITERATURE AND PAINTING* **SEE** ART AND LITERATURE / *art*
PR149.A	*LITERATURE AND PAINTING* **SEE** ART AND LITERATURE / *english literature*
PT112	*LITERATURE AND PAINTING* **SEE** ART AND LITERATURE / *german literature*
PN53	*LITERATURE AND PAINTING* **SEE** ART AND LITERATURE / *literature*
PN55	LITERATURE AND SCIENCE
PR149.S4	LITERATURE AND SCIENCE / *english literature*
N72	*LITERATURE AND SCULPTURE* **SEE** ART AND LITERATURE / *art*
PR149.A	*LITERATURE AND SCULPTURE* **SEE** ART AND LITERATURE / *english literature*
PT112	*LITERATURE AND SCULPTURE* **SEE** ART AND LITERATURE / *german literature*
PN53	*LITERATURE AND SCULPTURE* **SEE** ART AND LITERATURE / *literature*
PN51	LITERATURE AND STATE
PN3448.W3	*LITERATURE AND WAR* **SEE** WAR AND LITERATURE / *fiction*
PN56.W3	*LITERATURE AND WAR* **SEE** WAR AND LITERATURE / *literature*
PN	*LITERATURE AS A PROFESSION* **SEE** AUTHORS / *general*
PN101-249	*LITERATURE AS A PROFESSION* **SEE** AUTHORSHIP
PN4820-4823	*LITERATURE AS A PROFESSION* **SEE** JOURNALISTS
PN4841-5650	*LITERATURE AS A PROFESSION* **SEE** JOURNALISTS
PN5122-3	*LITERATURE AS A PROFESSION* **SEE** JOURNALISTS / *gt. brit.*
PN4871-4	*LITERATURE AS A PROFESSION* **SEE** JOURNALISTS / *u.s.*
PN150-171	*LITERATURE AS A PROFESSION* **SEE** LITTERATEURS
PN500-519	LITERATURE
PN45	LITERATURE
PN611-630	LITERATURE, ANCIENT / *history and criticism*
BS646	*LITERATURE, APOCALYPTIC* **SEE** APOCALYPTIC LITERATURE
BS1705	*LITERATURE, APOCALYPTIC* **SEE** APOCALYPTIC LITERATURE
PA3301-3671	*LITERATURE, CLASSICAL* **SEE** CLASSICAL LITERATURE / *collections*

RC848.A2	LIVER — ABSCESS
RC280.L5	LIVER — CANCER
RC848.C5	LIVER — CIRRHOSIS
RC845-8	LIVER — DISEASES
RC846	LIVER — DISPLACEMENT
QP185	LIVER — GLYCOGENIC FUNCTION
RC184.T6	LIVER — HYDATIDS
RC848.N4	LIVER — NECROSIS
RD546	LIVER — SURGERY
RC201.7.L5	LIVER — SYPHILIS
RC280.L5	LIVER — TUMORS
RC853	LIVER — WOUNDS AND INJURIES
RM800	LIVER EXTRACT
SF968	LIVER-FLUKE / diseases of sheep
QL391.T7	LIVER-FLUKE / zoology
SF968	LIVER-ROT / diseases of sheep
QL867	LIVER / comparative anatomy
QM351	LIVER / human anatomy
QP185	LIVER / physiology
RC846	LIVER, FLOATING SEE LIVER — DISPLACEMENT
RC848.N4	LIVER-ATROPHY SEE LIVER — NECROSIS
RM800	LIVER-EXTRACT SEE LIVER EXTRACT
NK4399.L	LIVERPOOL PORCELAIN
QK551-563	LIVERWORTS
TT626	LIVERY / tailoring
RX333	LIVER — DISEASES — — HOMEOPATHIC TREATMENT
SF	LIVESTOCK SEE DOMESTIC ANIMALS / animal industry
GN426	LIVESTOCK SEE DOMESTIC ANIMALS / ethnology
GT5870-5895	LIVESTOCK SEE DOMESTIC ANIMALS / manners and customs
SF1-121	LIVESTOCK SEE STOCK AND STOCK-BREEDING
TT197.5.L5	LIVING ROOM FURNITURE / cabinet work
NK2117	LIVING ROOM FURNITURE / interior decoration
TS880	LIVING ROOM FURNITURE / manufacture
HD6977-7080	LIVING, COST OF SEE COST AND STANDARD OF LIVING
HD6977-7080	LIVING, STANDARD OF SEE COST AND STANDARD OF LIVING
PH581-9	LIVONIAN LANGUAGE
GN585.R9	LIVONIANS / anthropology
DK511.L3-4	LIVONIANS / history
RS163.L7	LIZARDS — THERAPEUTIC USE
QL666.L2	LIZARDS
QE862.L2	LIZARDS, FOSSIL
BL443.L6	LLAMAS (IN RELIGION, FOLK-LORE, ETC.)
QL737.U5	LLAMAS
SF401.L6	LLAMAS / animal culture
HG8039	LLOYDS ASSOCIATIONS
QL638.C94	LOACHES
VK237	LOAD-LINE
TS159	LOADING AND UNLOADING
HG2121-2156	LOAN ASSOCIATIONS SEE BUILDING AND LOAN ASSOCIATIONS
LB2340	LOAN FUNDS, STUDENT SEE STUDENT LOAN FUNDS
HG9970.C6-89	LOAN INSURANCE SEE INSURANCE, CREDIT
HG2053-2069	LOANS FOR CONSUMPTION SEE LOANS
HG2053-2069	LOANS
HJ8047	LOANS, COMPULSORY SEE FORCED LOANS
HG2052-2069	LOANS, CONSUMER SEE LOANS, PERSONAL
HJ8047	LOANS, FORCED SEE FORCED LOANS
Z713	LOANS, INTER-LIBRARY SEE INTER-LIBRARY LOANS
HG2052-2069	LOANS, PERSONAL
HG2052-2069	LOANS, SMALL SEE LOANS, PERSONAL
QAG85	LOBACHEVSKI GEOMETRY SEE GEOMETRY, HYPERBOLIC
QA685	LOBATSCHEVSKI GEOMETRY SEE GEOMETRY, HYPERBOLIC
JK1118	LOBBYING / congress
JK2498	LOBBYING / u.s. state legislatures
DT553.U7	LOBI (AFRICAN PEOPLE)
QK495.C75	LOBLOLLY-PINE
SD397.P58	LOBLOLLY-PINE / forestry
GN480.1	LOBOLO SEE BRIDE PRICE
SH380	LOBSTER FISHERIES
QL444.D3	LOBSTERS
SH380	LOBSTERS / lobster culture
JS241-285	LOCAL ADMINISTRATION SEE LOCAL GOVERNMENT
JS1701-8429	LOCAL ADMINISTRATION SEE LOCAL GOVERNMENT / other countries

JS408-425	LOCAL ADMINISTRATION SEE LOCAL GOVERNMENT / u.s.
TF670-1124	LOCAL AND LIGHT RAILROADS SEE RAILROADS, LOCAL AND LIGHT
HE3601-4050	LOCAL AND LIGHT RAILROADS SEE RAILROADS, LOCAL AND LIGHT / economics
RD84	LOCAL ANESTHESIA
RD84	LOCAL ANESTHETICS SEE LOCAL ANESTHESIA
BV626	LOCAL CHURCH COUNCILS
PN56.L	LOCAL COLOR IN LITERATURE
HG4726	LOCAL GOVERNMENT BONDS SEE MUNICIPAL BONDS
HG5151-5890	LOCAL GOVERNMENT BONDS SEE MUNICIPAL BONDS / other countries
HG4951-3	LOCAL GOVERNMENT BONDS SEE MUNICIPAL BONDS / u.s.
JS241-285	LOCAL GOVERNMENT
JS1701-8429	LOCAL GOVERNMENT / other countries
JS408-425	LOCAL GOVERNMENT / u.s.
Z695.1.H6	LOCAL HISTORY (CATALOGING) SEE CATALOGING OF LOCAL HISTORY
HV5084-7	LOCAL OPTION
TL726	LOCAL SERVICE AIR LINES SEE AIR LINES, LOCAL SERVICE
QP385	LOCALIZATION OF CEREBRAL FUNCTIONS SEE BRAIN — LOCALIZATION OF FUNCTIONS
QP469	LOCALIZATION OF SOUND SEE SOUND, LOCALIZATION OF
TL696.L3	LOCALIZERS, RUNWAY SEE RUNWAY LOCALIZING BEACONS
HD58	LOCATION IN BUSINESS SEE INDUSTRIES, LOCATION OF
TL725.3.L6	LOCATION OF AIRPORTS SEE AIRPORTS — LOCATION
T56	LOCATION OF FACTORIES SEE FACTORIES — LOCATION
HD58	LOCATION OF INDUSTRIES SEE INDUSTRIES, LOCATION OF
Z255	LOCKING UP (TYPOGRAPHY) SEE PRINTING, PRACTICAL — IMPOSITION, ETC.
RC185	LOCKJAW SEE TETANUS
HD5306-5450	LOCKOUTS SEE STRIKES AND LOCKOUTS
TC761	LOCKS (CANAL) SEE LOCKS (HYDRAULIC ENGINEERING)
TC761	LOCKS (HYDRAULIC ENGINEERING)
TS519-530	LOCKS AND KEYS
TS519-530	LOCKSMITHING SEE LOCKS AND KEYS
SB608.L7	LOCO PLANT INSECTS
SF910.L8	LOCO PLANT
TL215.L65	LOCOMOBILE AUTOMOBILE
TL500-790	LOCOMOTION / aeronautics
GT5220-5280	LOCOMOTION / manners and customs
QP301-311	LOCOMOTION / physiology
RD680	LOCOMOTION, DISORDERED / pathology
QP303	LOCOMOTION, DISORDERED / physiology
TJ642	LOCOMOTIVE BOILERS
TJ656	LOCOMOTIVE SPARKS
TJ680-683	LOCOMOTIVE WORKS
TJ647	LOCOMOTIVES — ASH-PANS
TJ669.B6	LOCOMOTIVES — BOOSTERS
TJ625	LOCOMOTIVES — CATALOGS
TJ635	LOCOMOTIVES — CONSTRUCTION
TJ659	LOCOMOTIVES — CYLINDERS
TJ635	LOCOMOTIVES — DESIGN
TJ604	LOCOMOTIVES — EARLY WORKS TO 1850
TJ650	LOCOMOTIVES — EXHAUST
TJ646	LOCOMOTIVES — FIRE-BOXES
TJ648	LOCOMOTIVES — FUEL CONSUMPTION
TJ607	LOCOMOTIVES — HANDBOOKS, MANUALS, ETC.
TJ668	LOCOMOTIVES — HEADLIGHTS
TJ685	LOCOMOTIVES — INSPECTION
TJ675	LOCOMOTIVES — LUBRICATION
TJ630	LOCOMOTIVES — MODELS
TJ690	LOCOMOTIVES — PERFORMANCE
TJ690	LOCOMOTIVES — TESTING
TJ665	LOCOMOTIVES — VALVE-GEARS
TJ603-695	LOCOMOTIVES
TJ608	LOCOMOTIVES, ARTICULATED
TJ613	LOCOMOTIVES, COMPOUND
RC203.T3	LOCOMOTOR ATAXIA

SF910.L8	*LOCOWEED* **SEE** LOCO PLANT
SB945.L72	LOCUST-BORER
QL508.A2	*LOCUSTIDAE* **SEE** LOCUSTS
SB945.L7	*LOCUSTIDAE* **SEE** LOCUSTS / *economic entomology*
QL508.A2	LOCUSTS
SB945.L7	LOCUSTS / *economic entomology*
QK495.C75	LODGE-POLE PINE
SD397.P585	LODGE-POLE PINE / *forestry*
HD7288	LODGING-HOUSES / *laboring classes*
DS432.L6	LODHAS
DG537	LODI, PEACE OF, 1454
QE697	LOESS
NA8470	LOG CABINS
SD551-7	*LOG SCALING* **SEE** FORESTS AND FORESTRY — MENSURATION
VK211	LOG-BOOKS
QA55-59	LOGARITHMS
PL8458	LOGBARA LANGUAGE
PL8458	*LOGBWARE LANGUAGE* **SEE** LOGBARA LANGUAGE
QL668.C5	LOGGERHEAD TURTLE
SD538-557	*LOGGING* **SEE** LUMBERING
TS800-837	*LOGGING* **SEE** LUMBERING / *manufactures*
BC177	*LOGIC* **SEE** REASONING / *argumentation in logic*
BC	*LOGIC* **SEE** REASONING / *logic*
BT50	*LOGIC AND FAITH* **SEE** FAITH AND REASON
B824.6	*LOGIC AND LANGUAGE* **SEE** LOGICAL POSITIVISM
BC137-8	LOGIC MACHINES
QA9	*LOGIC OF MATHEMATICS* **SEE** MATHEMATICS — PHILOSOPHY
BC	LOGIC
BC25-32	LOGIC, ANCIENT
BC25-26	*LOGIC, BUDDHIST* **SEE** BUDDHIST LOGIC
B162.5	*LOGIC, JAINA* **SEE** JAINA LOGIC
BC25-26	*LOGIC, JAINA* **SEE** JAINA LOGIC / *ancient*
R723	*LOGIC, MEDICAL* **SEE** MEDICAL LOGIC
BC34-35	LOGIC, MEDIEVAL
BC38-39	LOGIC, MODERN
BC177	*LOGIC, SYMBOLIC AND MATHEMATICAL* **SEE** REASONING / *argumentation in logic*
BC	*LOGIC, SYMBOLIC AND MATHEMATICAL* **SEE** REASONING / *logic*
BC131-5	LOGIC, SYMBOLIC AND MATHEMATICAL
BC131-5	*LOGIC, UNIVERSAL* **SEE** LOGIC, SYMBOLIC AND MATHEMATICAL
B808.5	*LOGICAL ANALYSIS* **SEE** ANALYSIS (PHILOSOPHY)
B824.6	*LOGICAL EMPIRICISM* **SEE** LOGICAL POSITIVISM
B824.6	LOGICAL POSITIVISM
U168	LOGISTICS
V179	LOGISTICS, NAVAL
Z253	LOGOGRAPHY
BT210	LOGOS
Z253	*LOGOTYPES* **SEE** LOGOGRAPHY
TP925.L7	LOGWOOD / *dyes and dyeing*
DC309.L7	LOIGNY-POUPRY, BATTLE OF, 1870
B132.L6	LOKAYATA
QL430.2	*LOLIGO* **SEE** SQUIDS
BX4900-4906	LOLLARDS
PL8441	*LOLO (BANTU LANGUAGE)* **SEE** MONGO LANGUAGE
DS731.L6	LOLOS / *china*
PD1350	LOMBARD LANGUAGE
D145	LOMBARDS
DG511-514	LOMBARDS / *italy*
DG657.2	LOMBARDS / *lombardy*
PL8441	*LOMONGO (BANTU LANGUAGE)* **SEE** MONGO LANGUAGE
DA681	LONDON — FIRE, 1666
DA675-689	LONDON — HISTORY
JX1974	LONDON NAVAL TREATY, 1930
JX1974	LONDON NAVAL TREATY, 1936
JX5203 1909	LONDON, DECLARATION OF, 1909
DA47.8	LONDON, TREATY OF, 1604
D283.5	LONDON, TREATY OF, 1718
DH665	LONDON, TREATY OF, 1814
DH665	LONDON, TREATY OF, 1839
D520.I7	LONDON, TREATY OF, 1915
DA683	*LONDON-RIOT, DEC. 2, 1816* **SEE** SPA FIELDS RIOT, 1816 / *london*
DA945	LONDONDERRY, IRE. — SIEGE, 1688-1689
BV4911	LONELINESS
E241.L8	LONG ISLAND, BATTLE OF, 1776

VK560	*LONG RANGE NAVIGATION* **SEE** LORAN
SB608.G6	LONG-HEADED FLOUR-BEETLE
QK495.C75	*LONG-LEAF PINE* **SEE** LONGLEAF PINE
SB397.P59	*LONG-LEAF PINE* **SEE** LONGLEAF PINE / *forestry*
SB379.L	LONGAN
QP85	LONGEVITY / *physiology*
SF199.L6	LONGHORN CATTLE
QB224	LONGITUDE — PRIME MERIDIAN
QB228	LONGITUDE — TABLES
QB225-9	LONGITUDE / *astronomy*
VK565-7	LONGITUDE / *navigation*
TL574.S7	*LONGITUDINAL STABILITY OF AEROPLANES* **SEE** STABILITY OF AEROPLANES, LONGITUDINAL
QK495.C75	LONGLEAF PINE
SB397.P59	LONGLEAF PINE / *forestry*
D145	*LONGOBARDS* **SEE** LOMBARDS
DG511-514	*LONGOBARDS* **SEE** LOMBARDS / *italy*
DG657.2	*LONGOBARDS* **SEE** LOMBARDS / *lombardy*
HD8039.L8-82	LONGSHOREMEN
NK4399.L	LONGTON HALL PORCELAIN
GV1763	*LONGWAYS DANCE* **SEE** COUNTRY-DANCE
DC309.L8	LONGWY, FRANCE — SIEGE, 1871
GV1295.L	LOO (GAME)
NK8440	*LOOKING-GLASSES* **SEE** MIRRORS / *art*
QC385	*LOOKING-GLASSES* **SEE** MIRRORS / *optics*
TP867	*LOOKING-GLASSES* **SEE** MIRRORS / *technology*
E475.97	LOOKOUT MOUNTAIN, BATTLE OF, 1863
TS1493	LOOMS
Z695	*LOOSE-LEAF CATALOGS* **SEE** CATALOGS, SHEAF
QL638.L75	*LOPHIUS* **SEE** ANGLER-FISHES
QL638.L	LOPHOBRANCHII
VK560	LORAN
BS1199.D3	*LORD, DAY OF THE* **SEE** DAY OF JEHOVAH
BM685	*LORD'S DAY* **SEE** SABBATH / *judaism*
BV107-133	*LORD'S DAY* **SEE** SUNDAY
BV232	LORD'S PRAYER — JUVENILE LITERATURE
BV230-233	LORD'S PRAYER
N8054	LORD'S SUPPER — ART
BV823-8	LORD'S SUPPER — PRAYER-BOOKS AND DEVOTIONS
BX2169	LORD'S SUPPER — PRAYER-BOOKS AND DEVOTIONS / *catholic church*
BX5149.C5	LORD'S SUPPER — PRAYER-BOOKS AND DEVOTIONS / *church of england*
BV823-8	LORD'S SUPPER — REAL PRESENCE
BX5149.C5	LORD'S SUPPER — REAL PRESENCE / *church of england*
BX8073	LORD'S SUPPER — REAL PRESENCE / *lutheran*
BV827	LORD'S SUPPER — SERMONS
BX2215	LORD'S SUPPER — SERMONS / *catholic church*
BX1939 16	LORD'S SUPPER (CANON LAW)
PR145	LORD'S SUPPER IN LITERATURE
PR275	LORD'S SUPPER IN LITERATURE
PN49	LORD'S SUPPER IN LITERATURE
BV823-8	LORD'S SUPPER
BX2215	LORD'S SUPPER / *catholic church*
BX5149.C5	LORD'S SUPPER / *church of england*
CJ5407-5415	*LORD'S SUPPER-COMMUNION TOKENS* **SEE** TOKENS, COMMUNION
BX5149.C5	*LORD'S SUPPER-CONSUBSTANTIATION* **SEE** LORD'S SUPPER — REAL PRESENCE / *church of england*
BX8073	*LORD'S SUPPER-CONSUBSTANTIATION* **SEE** LORD'S SUPPER — REAL PRESENCE / *lutheran*
BV823-8	*LORD'S SUPPER-CONSUBSTANTIATION* **SEE** LORD'S SUPPER — REAL PRESENCE
BX2217	*LORD'S SUPPER-FIRST COMMUNION* **SEE** FIRST COMMUNION
BV828	*LORD'S SUPPER-INFANT COMMUNION* **SEE** INFANT COMMUNION
PM6358	LORENZAN LANGUAGE
QL696.P7	*LORIES* **SEE** PARROTS
SF473.P25	*LORIES* **SEE** PARROTS / *care and breeding*
QL737.P9	*LORIS* **SEE** LEMURS
T33	LOST ARTS
BT378.L	LOST COIN (PARABLE)
DS131	LOST TRIBES OF ISRAEL
BF1779.L6	*LOT, CHOICE BY* **SEE** CHOICE BY LOT
HG6105-6270	LOTTERIES
GV1311.L6	LOTTO
BL1442	*LOTUS SECT* **SEE** NICHIREN (SECT)
QK495.L88	LOTUS

TK6565.L6	LOUD-SPEAKERS / radio
TK6565.L6	*LOUDSPEAKERS* **SEE** LOUD-SPEAKERS / radio
GV1511.L8	LOUISA (GAME)
E198	LOUISBURG — SIEGE, 1745
E199	LOUISBURG — SIEGE, 1758
BX4737	LOUISETS
F366-380	LOUISIANA — HISTORY
E333	LOUISIANA PURCHASE / diplomatic history
F366-380	LOUISIANA PURCHASE / louisiana
F351-3	LOUISIANA PURCHASE / mississippi valley
E565	LOUISIANA — HISTORY — — CIVIL WAR
E510	LOUISIANA — HISTORY — — CIVIL WAR
E359.5.L8	LOUISIANA — HISTORY — — WAR OF 1812
F459.L8	LOUISVILLE, KY. — FLOOD, 1937
SF968	LOUPING-ILL
QL503.A6	*LOUSE* **SEE** LICE
BV4639	LOVE (THEOLOGY)
SB201.L	LOVE GRASS
N8220	LOVE IN ART
PN56.L6	LOVE IN LITERATURE
PN6110.L6	LOVE POETRY
PN56.L6	LOVE POETRY
PS595.L6	LOVE POETRY / american literature
PR1184	LOVE POETRY / english literature
HQ801.3-5	LOVE-LETTERS
PS673.L6-7	LOVE-LETTERS / american literature
R1349.L8	LOVE-LETTERS / english literature
PN6140.L7	LOVE-LETTERS / general literature
GR460	LOVE / folk-lore
HQ61	LOVE / love and religion
GT2600-2640	LOVE / manners and customs
BD436	LOVE / philosophy
BF575.L8	LOVE / psychology
GT2620	*LOVE, COURTLY* **SEE** COURTLY LOVE
GT3600	*LOVE, COURTS OF* **SEE** COURTS OF LOVE
DC611.P961	*LOVE, COURTS OF* **SEE** COURTS OF LOVE / provence
HQ759	LOVE, MATERNAL
BT766	*LOVE, PERFECT* **SEE** PERFECTION / theology
B398.L9	LOVE, PLATONIC
SB201.L	*LOVEGRASS* **SEE** LOVE GRASS
E83.72	*LOVEWELL'S FIGHT, 1725* **SEE** PIGWACKET FIGHT, 1725
E83.72	*LOVEWELL'S POND, BATTLE OF* **SEE** PIGWACKET FIGHT, 1725
PT4837-8	LOW GERMAN DRAMA / collections
PT4821	LOW GERMAN DRAMA / history
PF5631-8	LOW GERMAN LANGUAGE — EARLY TO 1500
PF5601-5844	LOW GERMAN LANGUAGE
PF5631-8	*LOW GERMAN LANGUAGE-MIDDLE LOW GERMAN* **SEE** LOW GERMAN LANGUAGE — EARLY TO 1500
PF771-8	*LOW GERMAN LANGUAGE-OLD LOW GERMAN* **SEE** DUTCH LANGUAGE — EARLY TO 1500
PF5631-8	*LOW GERMAN LANGUAGE-OLD LOW GERMAN* **SEE** LOW GERMAN LANGUAGE — EARLY TO 1500
PF3992-4000	*LOW GERMAN LANGUAGE-OLD LOW GERMAN* **SEE** OLD SAXON LANGUAGE
PT4813	LOW GERMAN LITERATURE — EARLY TO 1500
PT4801-4899	LOW GERMAN LITERATURE
PT4813	LOW GERMAN POETRY — EARLY TO 1500
PT4834-6	LOW GERMAN POETRY / collections
PT4817-4820	LOW GERMAN POETRY / history
QD515	*LOW TEMPERATURE CHEMISTRY* **SEE** LOW TEMPERATURES / chemistry
QC278	*LOW TEMPERATURE CHEMISTRY* **SEE** LOW TEMPERATURES / physics
TA407	*LOW TEMPERATURE MATERIALS* **SEE** MATERIALS AT LOW TEMPERATURES
QD515	*LOW TEMPERATURE PHYSICS* **SEE** LOW TEMPERATURES / chemistry
QC278	*LOW TEMPERATURE PHYSICS* **SEE** LOW TEMPERATURES / physics
QC278	LOW TEMPERATURE RESEARCH
TD940-949	*LOW TEMPERATURE SANITARY ENGINEERING* **SEE** SANITARY ENGINEERING, LOW TEMPERATURE
QD515	LOW TEMPERATURES / chemistry
QC278	LOW TEMPERATURES / physics
QE662	*LOWER-SILURIAN PERIOD* **SEE** GEOLOGY, STRATIGRAPHIC — ORDOVICIAN
PM1598	*LOWER UMPQUA LANGUAGE* **SEE** KUITSH LANGUAGE
NK4339.L7	LOWESTOFT PORCELAIN
TP245.O9	*LOX* **SEE** LIQUID OXYGEN
E277	*LOYALISTS, AMERICAN* **SEE** AMERICAN LOYALISTS
BJ1533.L8	LOYALTY. / ethics
JC328	*LOYALTY, POLITICAL* **SEE** ALLEGIANCE
JX4203-4270	*LOYALTY, POLITICAL* **SEE** ALLEGIANCE / nationality
PL8425	*LOYGOB LANGUAGE* **SEE** KWAFI LANGUAGE
PL8425	*LOYKOP LANGUAGE* **SEE** KWAFI LANGUAGE
PL8774	*LU-WUMBU LANGUAGE* **SEE** VILI LANGUAGE
PL6252.L	*LUANGIUA LANGUAGE* **SEE** LEUANGIUA LANGUAGE
PL8815	*LUANGO LANGUAGE* **SEE** YOMBE LANGUAGE
PL6252.L	*LUANIUA LANGUAGE* **SEE** LEUANGIUA LANGUAGE
PL8461	LUBA LANGUAGE
TJ1075-1081	LUBRICATION AND LUBRICANTS
F1655	LUCAYAN INDIANS
F1655	*LUCAYANS* **SEE** LUCAYAN INDIANS
SB205.A4	*LUCERNE (PLANT)* **SEE** ALFALFA
SB945.L	LUCERNE FLEA
DS478	LUCKNOW — SIEGE, 1857
DA535	LUDDITES
DG95	*LUDI SAECULARES* **SEE** SECULAR GAMES / roman antiquities
DG95	*LUDI TARENTINI* **SEE** SECULAR GAMES / roman antiquities
DG95	*LUDI TERENTINI* **SEE** SECULAR GAMES / roman antiquities
BH301.C7	*LUDICROUS, THE* **SEE** COMIC, THE
PN6147-6231	*LUDICROUS, THE* **SEE** WIT AND HUMOR
PL8458	*LUGBARA LANGUAGE* **SEE** LOGBARA LANGUAGE
TS537	LUGER PISTOL
TS2301.L	LUGGAGE
PL8458	*LUGWARE LANGUAGE* **SEE** LOGBARA LANGUAGE
P961.L8	*LUIAN LANGUAGE* **SEE** LUWIAN LANGUAGE
E99.L9	LUISENO INDIANS — RELIGION AND MYTHOLOGY
E99.L9	LUISENO INDIANS
P961.L8	*LUISH LANGUAGE* **SEE** LUWIAN LANGUAGE
F2821	LULE INDIANS
PM6366	LULE LANGUAGE
PL8461	*LULUA LANGUAGE* **SEE** LUBA LANGUAGE
QL821	LUMBAR CURVE / comparative anatomy
QM111	LUMBAR CURVE / human anatomy
TS837	LUMBER — DRYING
TS825	LUMBER — INSPECTION
HE2116.L8	LUMBER — RATE-BOOKS
TS837	*LUMBER DRYING* **SEE** LUMBER — DRYING
HD9750-9769	*LUMBER INDUSTRY AND TRADE* **SEE** LUMBER TRADE
TH4485	LUMBER SHEDS
HF5585.L8	LUMBER TRADE — CREDIT GUIDES
HF5716.L8	LUMBER TRADE — TABLES AND READY-RECKONERS
HD9750-9769	LUMBER TRADE
TH4485	LUMBER-YARDS
TS800-837	LUMBER
TS837	*LUMBER-SEASONING* **SEE** LUMBER — DRYING
HF5686.L	LUMBERING — ACCOUNTING
SD538-557	LUMBERING
TS800-837	LUMBERING / manufactures
SD421	*LUMBERING-FIRES AND FIRE PREVENTION* **SEE** FOREST FIRES — PREVENTION AND CONTROL
M1977.L8	LUMBERMEN — SONGS AND MUSIC
M1978.L8	LUMBERMEN — SONGS AND MUSIC
TS805-6	LUMBERMEN
HD8039.L9	LUMBERMEN / labor
QL391.O4	*LUMBRICUS* **SEE** EARTHWORMS
GN659.K5	*LUMBWAS* **SEE** KIPSIGIS
QC476	*LUMINESCENT SUBSTANCES* **SEE** PHOSPHORS
NE2685	LUMIPRINTS
E99.L95	LUMMI INDIANS
PM1656	LUMMI LANGUAGE
QL638.C9	LUMP-FISH
RC120	*LUMPY JAW* **SEE** ACTINOMYCOSIS / practice of medicine
SF784	*LUMPY JAW* **SEE** ACTINOMYCOSIS / veterinary medicine
HV6133	*LUNACY* **SEE** INSANITY / insanity and crime
HV4977	*LUNACY* **SEE** INSANITY / insanity and degeneration
BF423	*LUNACY* **SEE** INSANITY / insanity and genius
TL480	*LUNAR CARS* **SEE** MOON CARS

PM3981	*MACAHUA LANGUAGE* **SEE** MAZAHUA LANGUAGE
SB191.W5	*MACARONI WHEAT* **SEE** WHEAT
GT5899.W5	*MACARONI WHEAT* **SEE** WHEAT / *manners and customs*
TS2157	MACARONI / *manufacture*
PN1489	MACARONIC LITERATURE / *poetry*
PL5345-8	MACASSAR LANGUAGE
BM695.H3	*MACCABEES, FEAST OF THE* **SEE** HANUKKAH (FEAST OF LIGHTS)
DR701.M13-4	MACEDONIA — HISTORY
P1055	MACEDONIAN LANGUAGE (ANCIENT)
PG1161-4	MACEDONIAN LANGUAGE
PG1164.A2	MACEDONIAN POETRY / *collections*
PG1163.5	MACEDONIAN POETRY / *history*
D651.M3	MACEDONIAN QUESTION / *european war*
DR701.M4	MACEDONIAN QUESTION / *history*
DG251	MACEDONIAN WAR, 1ST, 215-205 B.C.
DG251	MACEDONIAN WAR, 2D, 200-196 B.C.
E184.M	MACEDONIANS IN THE U.S.
DF261.M2	MACEDONIANS / *ancient*
DF233	MACEDONIANS / *ancient*
DR701.M13-4	MACEDONIANS / *modern*
DF261.M2	MACEDONIA — HISTORY — — ANCIENT TO 168 B.C.
DF233-8	MACEDONIA — HISTORY — — ANCIENT TO 168 B.C.
NK7425	MACES, CEREMONIAL
F3430.1.M	*MACHEYENGA INDIANS* **SEE** MACHIGANGA INDIANS
F3430.1.M	MACHIGANGA INDIANS
PM6388	MACHIGANGA LANGUAGE
F3430.1.M	*MACHIGUENGA INDIANS* **SEE** MACHIGANGA INDIANS
HF5679	MACHINE ACCOUNTING
TJ230-235	*MACHINE DESIGN* **SEE** MACHINERY — DESIGN
TS1783	*MACHINE EMBROIDERY* **SEE** EMBROIDERY, MACHINE
HD9705	*MACHINE INDUSTRY* **SEE** MACHINERY — TRADE AND MANUFACTURE
Z51	*MACHINE SHORTHAND* **SEE** STENOTYPY
HD9705	*MACHINE TRADE* **SEE** MACHINERY — TRADE AND MANUFACTURE
P307-310	MACHINE TRANSLATING
U167.5	MACHINE-GUN DRILL AND TACTICS
UF620	MACHINE-GUN DRILL AND TACTICS
UF620	MACHINE-GUNS
VF410	MACHINE-GUNS / *naval*
TJ1165	*MACHINE-SHOP MATHEMATICS* **SEE** SHOP MATHEMATICS
TJ1146	MACHINE-SHOP PRACTICE — ESTIMATES AND COSTS
TJ1148	MACHINE-SHOP PRACTICE — ESTIMATES AND COSTS
TJ1165	MACHINE-SHOP PRACTICE — REPAIRING
TJ1177	MACHINE-SHOP PRACTICE — SAFETY MEASURES
TJ1160-1167	MACHINE-SHOP PRACTICE
HF5686.M2	MACHINE-SHOPS — ACCOUNTING
TJ1125-1150	MACHINE-SHOPS
HD9700	MACHINE-SHOPS / *economics*
TJ1185	MACHINE-TOOLS — DESIGN
TK4058	MACHINE-TOOLS — ELECTRIC DRIVING
TJ1189	MACHINE-TOOLS — NUMERICAL CONTROL
TJ1185	MACHINE-TOOLS — TRADE AND MANUFACTURE / *engineering*
HD9703	MACHINE-TOOLS — TRADE AND MANUFACTURE / *trade*
TJ1180-1313	MACHINE-TOOLS
HD9703	MACHINE-TOOLS / *economics*
TJ1175	MACHINERY — CATALOGS
TJ1160-1175	MACHINERY — CONSTRUCTION
TJ215	MACHINERY — CURIOUS DEVICES
TJ230-235	MACHINERY — DESIGN
TJ144	MACHINERY — EARLY WORKS TO 1800
TJ249	MACHINERY — ERECTING WORK
TJ249	MACHINERY — FOUNDATIONS
TJ148	MACHINERY — INSPECTION
TJ147	MACHINERY — JUVENILE LITERATURE
TJ153	MACHINERY — MAINTENANCE AND REPAIR
TJ248	MACHINERY — MODELS
HD7273	MACHINERY — SAFETY APPLIANCES
TJ1177	MACHINERY — SAFETY APPLIANCES / *machine-shops*
TJ148	MACHINERY — TESTING
HD9705	MACHINERY — TRADE AND MANUFACTURE
TJ173	MACHINERY — WORK DIAGRAMS
CB478	*MACHINERY AND CIVILIZATION* **SEE** TECHNOLOGY AND CIVILIZATION / *history*
HM221	*MACHINERY AND CIVILIZATION* **SEE** TECHNOLOGY AND CIVILIZATION / *sociology*
HD6331	MACHINERY IN INDUSTRY
HG9963.M	*MACHINERY INSURANCE* **SEE** INSURANCE, MACHINERY
TJ	MACHINERY
TJ213-215	MACHINERY, AUTOMATIC
TJ175	MACHINERY, KINEMATICS OF
TJ153	*MACHINERY-BALANCING* **SEE** BALANCING OF MACHINERY
HD9705	*MACHINERY-MANUFACTURE* **SEE** MACHINERY — TRADE AND MANUFACTURE
TJ	*MACHINES* **SEE** MACHINERY
TJ153	*MACHINES, BALANCING OF* **SEE** BALANCING OF MACHINERY
BC137-8	*MACHINES, LOGIC* **SEE** LOGIC MACHINES
HD8039.M2-22	MACHINISTS
TJ1195-1200	MACHINISTS' TOOLS
SH351.M2	MACKEREL FISHERIES
QL638.S35	MACKEREL
QA306	*MACLAURIN'S SERIES (MATHEMATICS)* **SEE** SERIES, TAYLOR'S
F2280.1.M	*MACOUSHI INDIANS* **SEE** MACUSI INDIANS / *british guiana*
TT840	MACRAME
BD493-523	*MACROCOSM AND MICROCOSM* **SEE** MICROCOSM AND MACROCOSM
QL737.M3	*MACROPODIDAE* **SEE** KANGAROOS
PM6393	MACU LANGUAGE
F2280.1.M	*MACUCHY INDIANS* **SEE** MACUSI INDIANS / *british guiana*
QL949	MACULA LUTEA / *comparative anatomy*
QM551	MACULA LUTEA / *human anatomy*
QP479	MACULA LUTEA / *physiology*
BL2590.U5	*MACUMBA (CULTUS)* **SEE** UMBANDA (CULTUS)
F2280.1.M	MACUSI INDIANS / *british guiana*
PM6397	MACUSI LANGUAGE
F2280.1.M	*MACUXI INDIANS* **SEE** MACUSI INDIANS / *british guiana*
QA76.5	*MAD (COMPUTER PROGRAM LANGUAGE)* **SEE** MAD (COMPUTER PROGRAM LANGUAGE)
QA76.5	MAD (COMPUTER PROGRAM LANGUAGE)
PK6393.M	MADAGLASHTI DIALECT
TP925.M2	MADDER
E99.M115	MADEHSI INDIANS
TP559.P8	MADEIRA WINE
DS422.C3	MADIGAS
DS422.C3	*MADIGS* **SEE** MADIGAS
HV6133	*MADNESS* **SEE** INSANITY / *insanity and crime*
HV4977	*MADNESS* **SEE** INSANITY / *insanity and degeneration*
BF423	*MADNESS* **SEE** INSANITY / *insanity and genius*
BT600-680	*MADONNA* **SEE** MARY, VIRGIN
QL377.C7	MADREPORARIA
DC113.5	MADRID, TREATY OF, 1526
DC611.B782	MADRID, TREATY OF, 1526 / *burgundy*
F2684	MADRID, TREATY OF, 1750
PN1493	MADRIGAL
PT581.M3	MADRIGAL / *german literature*
PR1195.M2	MADRIGALS / *english literature*
RC168.M9	*MADURA FOOT* **SEE** MYCETOMA
PL5351-4	MADURESE LANGUAGE
DT934.M2	MAFEKING — SIEGE, 1899-1900
HV6441-6453	MAFIA
PL6279	*MAFOR LANGUAGE* **SEE** NUFOR LANGUAGE
GN671.N5	MAFULUS / *anthropology*
DU740	MAFULUS / *history*
PK1821-4	MAGAHI LANGUAGE
AP	*MAGAZINES* **SEE** PERIODICALS
PN4700-4900	*MAGAZINES* **SEE** PERIODICALS / *etc.*
UF540-545	*MAGAZINES, POWDER* **SEE** POWDER-MAGAZINES
VF380	*MAGAZINES, POWDER* **SEE** POWDER-MAGAZINES / *naval*
DD184	MAGDEBURG — SIEGE, 1550-1551
D267.M2	MAGDEBURG — SIEGE, 1631
QC141	MAGDEBURG EXPERIMENTS
DG554.5.M2	MAGENTA, BATTLE OF, 1859
DA932.4	MAGH RATH, BATTLE OF, 637
N8110	MAGI — ART
PN1880	MAGI — DRAMA
PR643-4	MAGI — DRAMA / *medieval*

PN1761	MAGI — DRAMA / medieval
BT315	MAGI
N8222.M3	MAGIC IN ART
BF1325-1331	*MAGIC MIRRORS* **SEE** MIRRORS, MAGIC
QA165	MAGIC SQUARES
GN475	MAGIC / ethnology
BF1585-1623	MAGIC / occult sciences
BF1591	MAGIC, ASSYRO-BABYLONIAN
BF1591	*MAGIC, CHALDEAN* **SEE** MAGIC, ASSYRO-BABYLONIAN
BF1591	MAGIC, EGYPTIAN
E98.M2	*MAGIC, INDIAN* **SEE** INDIANS OF NORTH AMERICA — MAGIC
BF1591	MAGIC, SEMITIC
BF1597-8	MAGICIANS
PL5911-5914	MAGINDANAU LANGUAGE
JF700-721	*MAGISTRATES* **SEE** JUDGES
JK1507-1599	*MAGISTRATES* **SEE** JUDGES
JN145-7	MAGNA CARTA / constitutional history
DA208	MAGNA CARTA / english history
BV4647.M2	MAGNANIMITY / christianity
BJ1533.M3	MAGNANIMITY / ethics
TP884.M2	MAGNESIA CEMENT
TP889	MAGNESIA / chemical technology
QD181.M4	MAGNESIA / chemistry
TN948.M2	MAGNESITE
QP913.M4	MAGNESIUM — PHYSIOLOGICAL EFFECT
TS560	MAGNESIUM ALLOYS — FOUNDING
TN799.M2	MAGNESIUM ALLOYS / metallurgy
QD181.M4	MAGNESIUM CARBONATE
TS630	MAGNESIUM FOUNDING
QD172.M4	MAGNESIUM GROUP
HD9539.M26	MAGNESIUM INDUSTRY AND TRADE / economics
TN799.M3	MAGNESIUM INDUSTRY AND TRADE / technology
QP913.M4	MAGNESIUM SULPHATE — PHYSIOLOGICAL EFFECT
QD181.M4	MAGNESIUM SULPHATE
QD181.M4	MAGNESIUM / chemistry
TP784.M2	MAGNESIUM / lighting
TN799.M2	MAGNESIUM / metallurgy
TA480.M	*MAGNESIUM-CREEP* **SEE** CREEP OF MAGNESIUM
QC760	*MAGNET WINDING* **SEE** ELECTROMAGNETS
TK2851	MAGNETIC AMPLIFIERS
TK7872.M3	MAGNETIC AMPLIFIERS / electronics
QC809.M25	MAGNETIC FIELDS (COSMIC PHYSICS)
RZ422	MAGNETIC HEALING
QC761	MAGNETIC INDUCTION
QC819	MAGNETIC INSTRUMENTS / terrestrial magnetism
TK453	MAGNETIC MATERIALS / electric engineering
QC761	MAGNETIC MATERIALS / physics
QC761	MAGNETIC MEASUREMENTS
QC818-849	MAGNETIC MEASUREMENTS / terrestrial magnetism
TK7872.M4	MAGNETIC MEMORY (CALCULATING-MACHINES)
VK577	*MAGNETIC NEEDLE* **SEE** COMPASS
QC849	*MAGNETIC NEEDLE* **SEE** COMPASS / deviation
QC830-845	*MAGNETIC OBSERVATIONS* **SEE** MAGNETISM, TERRESTRIAL — OBSERVATIONS
TK6500	*MAGNETIC PHONOGRAPH* **SEE** TELEGRAPHONE
QC849	MAGNETIC RANGES
TK5981	MAGNETIC RECORDERS AND RECORDING
QC544	*MAGNETIC RESONANCE ACCELERATOR* **SEE** CYCLOTRON
TN530	MAGNETIC SEPARATION OF ORES
TK7872.M4	*MAGNETIC STORAGE (CALCULATING-MACHINES)* **SEE** MAGNETIC MEMORY (CALCULATING-MACHINES)
QC835	MAGNETIC STORMS
QC822	*MAGNETIC SURVEY MAPS* **SEE** MAGNETISM, TERRESTRIAL — MAPS
QC761	MAGNETIC TESTING
QC831	*MAGNETIC VARIATIONS, DIURNAL* **SEE** MAGNETISM, TERRESTRIAL — DIURNAL VARIATION
QC828	*MAGNETIC VARIATIONS, SECULAR* **SEE** MAGNETISM, TERRESTRIAL — SECULAR VARIATION
QC751	MAGNETISM — EARLY WORKS TO 1800
QC751-761	MAGNETISM — EXPERIMENTS
RM893-6	MAGNETISM — THERAPEUTIC USE
QC849	MAGNETISM OF AIRCRAFT
QC849	MAGNETISM OF SHIPS
QC751-771	MAGNETISM
BF1111-1156	*MAGNETISM, ANIMAL* **SEE** ANIMAL MAGNETISM / psychical research

RZ430	*MAGNETISM, ANIMAL* **SEE** ANIMAL MAGNETISM / therapeutics
QC831	MAGNETISM, TERRESTRIAL — DIURNAL VARIATION
QC822	MAGNETISM, TERRESTRIAL — MAPS
QC830-845	MAGNETISM, TERRESTRIAL — OBSERVATIONS
QC818	MAGNETISM, TERRESTRIAL — OBSERVATORIES
QC820	MAGNETISM, TERRESTRIAL — OBSERVERS' MANUALS
QC828	MAGNETISM, TERRESTRIAL — SECULAR VARIATION
QC811-849	MAGNETISM, TERRESTRIAL
TK9909	MAGNETO-ELECTRIC MACHINES / amateurs' manuals
QC675	MAGNETO-OPTICS
TK6500	*MAGNETO-PHONOGRAPH* **SEE** TELEGRAPHONE
TL213	MAGNETO / automobiles
TJ787	MAGNETO / oil and gasoline engines
QD591	MAGNETOCHEMISTRY
QC819	MAGNETOMETER
QC761	MAGNETOSTRICTION
RZ422	*MAGNETOTHERAPY* **SEE** MAGNETIC HEALING
RM893-6	*MAGNETOTHERAPY* **SEE** MAGNETISM — THERAPEUTIC USE
TK7872.V3	MAGNETRONS
QC757	MAGNETS
QK495.M24	MAGNOLIA
TL574.M3	MAGNUS EFFECT
QL696.P2	MAGPIES
E356.M	*MAGUAGA, BATTLE OF, 1812* **SEE** MONGUAGON, MICH., BATTLE OF, AUG. 9, 1812
PL5911-5914	*MAGUINDANAO LANGUAGE* **SEE** MAGINDANAU LANGUAGE
HV6441-6453	*MAGUIRES, MOLLY* **SEE** MOLLY MAGUIRES
PH2001-2800	*MAGYAR LANGUAGE* **SEE** HUNGARIAN LANGUAGE
PH3132-3188	*MAGYAR LITERATURE* **SEE** HUNGARIAN LITERATURE / collections
PH3001-3123	*MAGYAR LITERATURE* **SEE** HUNGARIAN LITERATURE / history
DB919	MAGYARS
GV1299.M3	MAH JONG
PL6225	*MAHAGA LANGUAGE* **SEE** BUGOTU LANGUAGE
BL1245.V	*MAHARAJAS (HINDU SECT)* **SEE** VALLABHACHARS
DS422.C3	MAHARS
SH691.M	*MAHASEER* **SEE** MAHSEER / fishing
QL638.C94	*MAHASEER* **SEE** MAHSEER / zoology
BL1483	MAHAYANA BUDDHISM
BP166.93	MAHDI / islam
DT108.3	MAHDI / sudan
BP166.93	MAHDISM
E99.M12	MAHICAN INDIANS
SD397.M2	MAHOGANY / forestry
SB273-8	*MAHORKA* **SEE** TOBACCO / culture
GT3020	*MAHORKA* **SEE** TOBACCO / manners and customs
PJ7111-7114	*MAHRA LANGUAGE* **SEE** MAHRI LANGUAGE
PK2351-2378	*MAHRATTA LANGUAGE* **SEE** MARATHI LANGUAGE
DS432.M2	*MAHRATTAS* **SEE** MARATHAS
PK2351-2378	*MAHRATTI LANGUAGE* **SEE** MARATHI LANGUAGE
PJ7111-7114	MAHRI LANGUAGE
SH691.M	MAHSEER / fishing
QL638.C94	MAHSEER / zoology
SH691.M	*MAHSIR* **SEE** MAHSEER / fishing
QL638.C94	*MAHSIR* **SEE** MAHSEER / zoology
SH691.M	*MAHSUR* **SEE** MAHSEER / fishing
QL638.C94	*MAHSUR* **SEE** MAHSEER / zoology
E99.M18	*MAIDEH INDIANS* **SEE** MAIDU INDIANS
E99.M18	MAIDU INDIANS — RELIGION AND MYTHOLOGY
E99.M18	MAIDU INDIANS
PM1681	MAIDU LANGUAGE
TL685.7	*MAIL PLANES* **SEE** TRANSPORT PLANES
HE6000-7500	*MAIL SERVICE* **SEE** POSTAL SERVICE
UH80-85	*MAIL SERVICE* **SEE** POSTAL SERVICE / military
HE6233	MAIL STEAMERS
HE6477	MAIL STEAMERS / u.s.
VK15-124	*MAIL-BOATS* **SEE** PACKETS / history
TF467	*MAIL-CARS* **SEE** RAILWAY MAIL SERVICE — CARS / construction
HE6475	*MAIL-CARS* **SEE** RAILWAY MAIL SERVICE — CARS / postal service
TJ1398	MAIL-CHUTES
HF5466	MAIL-ORDER BUSINESS
HE9	*MAILING GUIDES* **SEE** SHIPPERS' GUIDES
HE968	*MAILING GUIDES* **SEE** SHIPPERS' GUIDES / marine insurance

HE1009	MAILING GUIDES SEE SHIPPERS' GUIDES / railroads
HE2731-7	MAILING GUIDES SEE SHIPPERS' GUIDES / railroads
HE2801-3600	MAILING GUIDES SEE SHIPPERS' GUIDES / railroads
GN671.N5	MAILU / new guinea
F2230.2.M	MAINA INDIANS SEE MAYNA INDIANS
F16-30	MAINE — HISTORY
E511	MAINE — HISTORY — — CIVIL WAR
E263.M4	MAINE — HISTORY — — REVOLUTION
HF5417	MAINTENANCE OF PRICES SEE PRICE MAINTENANCE
DC220.5	MAINZ — SIEGE, 1793
NK4315.4320	MAIOLICA SEE MAJOLICA
F3094	MAIPO, BATTLE OF, 1818
F3094	MAIPU, BATTLE OF, 1818 SEE MAIPO, BATTLE OF, 1818
PK1811-1819	MAITHILI LANGUAGE
PK1818	MAITHILI LITERATURE
ML3027	MAITRISES
SB608.M2	MAIZE — DISEASES AND PESTS
SB608.M2	MAIZE BILL-BUG
TS1109	MAIZE PAPER SEE PAPER, MAIZE
TP405	MAIZE SUGAR
SB191.M2	MAIZE / culture
HD9049.C8	MAIZE / grain trade
NK4315.4320	MAJOLICA
BV659-685	MAJOR ORDERS SEE CLERGY
JF1051-1075	MAJORITIES / political rights
E99.M19	MAKAH INDIANS
N7760	MAKARA / mythical monsters art
PL8167.F3	MAKE LANGUAGE SEE FAN LANGUAGE
GT2340	MAKE-UP (COSMETICS) SEE COSMETICS / manners and customs
TP983	MAKE-UP (COSMETICS) SEE COSMETICS / manufacture
RA778	MAKE-UP (COSMETICS) SEE COSMETICS / toilet
Z253.5	MAKE-UP (TYPOGRAPHY) SEE PRINTING, PRACTICAL — MAKE-UP
PN2068	MAKE-UP, THEATRICAL
DR27.A8	MAKEDO-RUMANIANS SEE AROMUNES
SB273-8	MAKHORKA SEE TOBACCO / culture
GT3020	MAKHORKA SEE TOBACCO / manners and customs
D767.917	MAKIN, BATTLE OF, 1943
TF593	MAKING UP TRAINS SEE RAILROADS — MAKING UP TRAINS
PL8432.M8	MAKONDE LANGUAGE
PL8483	MAKUA LANGUAGE
F2280.1.M	MAKUCHI INDIANS SEE MACUSI INDIANS / british guiana
PM6397	MAKUCHI LANGUAGE SEE MACUSI LANGUAGE
PL4711-4719	MALABAR LANGUAGE SEE MALAYALAM LANGUAGE
BX1995.M18	MALABAR RITES
RS165.M35	MALABATHRUM
QL401-432	MALACOLOGY SEE MOLLUSKS
QL638.M	MALACOPTERYGII
QL444.M	MALACOSTRACA
PL5371-9	MALAGASY LANGUAGE
PL5378.5	MALAGASY POETRY / history and texts
PL5378.9	MALAGASY POETRY / translations
RC156-166	MALARIA SEE MALARIAL FEVER
QM201.M2	MALARIA SEE MALARIAL FEVER / bacteriology
RM868.5	MALARIA THERAPY SEE MALARIOTHERAPY
SF995	MALARIA, AVIAN SEE MALARIAL FEVER IN BIRDS
RM868.5	MALARIA, THERAPEUTIC SEE MALARIOTHERAPY
RX226.M2	MALARIAL FEVER — HOMEOPATHIC TREATMENT
RA644.M2	MALARIAL FEVER — PREVENTION
RC157	MALARIAL FEVER — TERMINOLOGY
SF995	MALARIAL FEVER IN BIRDS
SF995	MALARIAL FEVER IN POULTRY SEE MALARIAL FEVER IN BIRDS
RM868.5	MALARIAL FEVER THERAPY SEE MALARIOTHERAPY
RC156-166	MALARIAL FEVER
QM201.M2	MALARIAL FEVER / bacteriology
RM868.5	MALARIAL FEVER, THERAPEUTIC SEE MALARIOTHERAPY
RM868.5	MALARIOTHERAPY
PL5052	MALAY ALPHABET SEE JAWI ALPHABET
PL5101-5129	MALAY LANGUAGE
PL5130-5149	MALAY LITERATURE
GN635.M35-4	MALAY RACE / anthropology
GN630.M3	MALAY RACE / anthropology
DS526-689	MALAY RACE / etc. history
PL5021-6571	MALAY-POLYNESIAN LANGUAGES
PL4711-4719	MALAYALAM LANGUAGE
PL5051-9	MALAYAN LANGUAGES
PL5060-5069	MALAYAN LITERATURE
GN630.M3	MALAYS SEE MALAY RACE / anthropology
GN635.M35-4	MALAYS SEE MALAY RACE / anthropology
DS526-689	MALAYS SEE MALAY RACE / etc. history
DS27	MALAZGIRT, BATTLE OF, 1071
E99.M195	MALECITE INDIANS
PM1695	MALECITE LANGUAGE
PL8401-4	MALEMBA LANGUAGE SEE CONGO LANGUAGE
QA557	MALFATTI'S PROBLEM
QM691-9	MALFORMATIONS SEE DEFORMITIES / human anatomy
GN68-69.8	MALFORMATIONS SEE DEFORMITIES / somatic anthropology
PL5371-9	MALGACHE LANGUAGE SEE MALAGASY LANGUAGE
QD305.A2	MALIC ACID
RC640	MALIGNANT LEUCOPENIA SEE AGRANULOCYTOSIS
QE461	MALIGNITE
RA1146	MALINGERING
PL8491	MALINKE LANGUAGE SEE MANDINGO LANGUAGE
E99.M195	MALISEET INDIANS SEE MALECITE INDIANS
PM1695	MALISEET LANGUAGE SEE MALECITE LANGUAGE
RC168.M45	MALLEOIDOSIS SEE MELIOIDOSIS
QL503.M2	MALLOPHAGA SEE BIRD-LICE
QL638.I	MALOCOPTERYGII SEE ISOSPONDYLI
QL494	MALPIGHIAN VESSELS
D283.M	MALPLAQUET, BATTLE OF, 1709
RA1056.5	MALPRACTICE
TP569-587	MALT LIQUORS
RM671.M2	MALT-EXTRACTS
TP587	MALT / chemical technology
RC123.B7	MALTA FEVER SEE UNDULANT FEVER
DG987-994	MALTA / malta
DR505-8	MALTA / turkish history
SF429.M25	MALTESE DOGS
HB861-3	MALTHUSIANISM
QD321	MALTOSE
E473.68	MALVERN HILL, BATTLE OF, 1862
PM3936	MAM LANGUAGE
GN671.N5	MAMBULE SEE MAFULUS / anthropology
DU740	MAMBULE SEE MAFULUS / history
DT96	MAMELUKES
QP246	MAMMAGEN SEE MAMMOGEN
QL739	MAMMALS — ANATOMY
QL708	MAMMALS — CATALOGS AND COLLECTIONS
QL708	MAMMALS — CLASSIFICATION
QL706	MAMMALS — JUVENILE LITERATURE
QL355	MAMMALS — NOMENCLATURE (POPULAR)
QL705	MAMMALS — PICTORIAL WORKS
QL701-739	MAMMALS
QE881-2	MAMMALS, FOSSIL
QL944	MAMMARY GLANDS / comparative anatomy
QM495	MAMMARY GLANDS / human anatomy
QP246	MAMMARY GLANDS / physiology
QP246	MAMMOGEN
QE882.U7	MAMMOTH
GN231	MAN — ATTITUDE AND MOVEMENT
GN60	MAN — CONSTITUTION / anthropology
BF818	MAN — CONSTITUTION / character
BF698	MAN — CONSTITUTION / personality
BF795-811	MAN — CONSTITUTION / temperament
RB150-151	MAN — CONSTITUTION / theories of disease
GF71	MAN — INFLUENCE OF CLIMATE
GN320	MAN — INFLUENCE OF ENVIRONMENT / ethnography
BF353	MAN — INFLUENCE OF ENVIRONMENT / psychology
HM206-8	MAN — INFLUENCE OF ENVIRONMENT / sociology
GF101	MAN — MIGRATIONS / anthropo-geography
GN370	MAN — MIGRATIONS / ethnology
QH361-371	MAN — ORIGIN
BP166.7	MAN (ISLAM)

BT703	MAN (THEOLOGY) — COMPARATIVE STUDIES
BS661	MAN (THEOLOGY) / bible
BT700-745	MAN (THEOLOGY) / doctrinal theology
BL256	MAN (THEOLOGY) / religion
UA17.5	MAN POWER SEE MANPOWER
TN339-340	MAN-ENGINES / mine transportation
TL789.8	MAN-IN-SPACE PROGRAM SEE PROJECT MERCURY
QL696.S6	MAN-OF-WAR BIRDS SEE FRIGATE-BIRDS
GN	MAN / anthropology
QH361-371	MAN / evolution
BD430-435	MAN / philosophy of life
BD450	MAN / philosophy of life
QH361-371	MAN, ANTIQUITY OF SEE MAN — ORIGIN
BS661	MAN, DOCTRINE OF SEE MAN (THEOLOGY) / bible
BT700-745	MAN, DOCTRINE OF SEE MAN (THEOLOGY) / doctrinal theology
BL256	MAN, DOCTRINE OF SEE MAN (THEOLOGY) / religion
GN231	MAN, ERECT POSITION OF SEE MAN — ATTITUDE AND MOVEMENT
GN231	MAN, ERECT POSITION OF SEE POSTURE / anthropology
RA781	MAN, ERECT POSITION OF SEE POSTURE / personal hygiene
GV443	MAN, ERECT POSITION OF SEE POSTURE / physical training
GV341	MAN, ERECT POSITION OF SEE POSTURE / physical training
QP301	MAN, ERECT POSITION OF SEE POSTURE / physiology
LB3427	MAN, ERECT POSITION OF SEE POSTURE / school hygiene
BT710	MAN, FALL OF SEE FALL OF MAN
GN743	MAN, PREHISTORIC — JUVENILE LITERATURE
GN700-875	MAN, PREHISTORIC
GN307-499	MAN, PRIMITIVE
GN290	MAN, WILD SEE WILD MEN
TX357	MAN-FOOD HABITS SEE FOOD HABITS
GT2860	MAN-FOOD HABITS SEE FOOD HABITS
GN471	MANA
F3320.2.M26	MANACICA INDIANS
TS155	MANAGEMENT OF FACTORIES SEE FACTORY MANAGEMENT
HD31-37	MANAGEMENT
HD5650-5659	MANAGEMENT, EMPLOYEES' REPRESENTATION IN SEE EMPLOYEES' REPRESENTATION IN MANAGEMENT
HV40	MANAGEMENT, INSTITUTION SEE INSTITUTION MANAGEMENT / charities
TX147	MANAGEMENT, INSTITUTION SEE INSTITUTION MANAGEMENT / home economics
HF5438-5440	MANAGEMENT, SALES SEE SALES MANAGEMENT
E99.M	MANAHOAC INDIANS
E78.V7	MANAHOAC INDIANS / virginia
F3320.2.M26	MANASICA INDIANS SEE MANACICA INDIANS
E472.18	MANASSAS, BATTLES OF SEE BULL RUN, 1ST BATTLE, 1861
E473.77	MANASSAS, BATTLES OF SEE BULL RUN, 2D BATTLE, 1862
QL737.S6	MANATEES
SF429.M	MANCHESTER TERRIERS
DA690.M4	MANCHESTER, ENG. — PETERLOO MASSACRE, 1819
PL471-9	MANCHU LANGUAGE
PL451-9	MANCHU LANGUAGES SEE TUNGUSIC LANGUAGES
PL480-489	MANCHU LITERATURE
DS754-760	MANCHUS / dynasty
DS781-4	MANCHUS / manchuria
PJ5321-9	MANDAEAN LANGUAGE
BT1405	MANDAEANS
PL8493	MANDAGO LANGUAGE SEE MANDJAK LANGUAGE
B132.M3	MANDALA
E99.M2	MANDAN INDIANS
PM1701	MANDAN LANGUAGE
PL8489	MANDARA LANGUAGE
DT132	MANDARI (AFRICAN PEOPLE)
SB370.T	MANDARIN (FRUIT) SEE TANGERINE
D650.T4-651	MANDATES / european war questions
JX4021-3	MANDATES / international law
JX1975.A49	MANDATES / league of nations documents
D650.T4-651	MANDATES, COLONIAL SEE MANDATES / european war questions

JX4021-3	MANDATES, COLONIAL SEE MANDATES / international law
JX1975.A49	MANDATES, COLONIAL SEE MANDATES / league of nations documents
D650.T4-651	MANDATES, INTERNATIONAL SEE MANDATES / european war questions
JX4021-3	MANDATES, INTERNATIONAL SEE MANDATES / international law
JX1975.A49	MANDATES, INTERNATIONAL SEE MANDATES / league of nations documents
PL8490	MANDE LANGUAGES
PL8491	MANDENGA LANGUAGE SEE MANDINGO LANGUAGE
RK280	MANDIBULAR JOINT SEE TEMPOROMANDIBULAR JOINT
PL8491	MANDINGO LANGUAGE
PL8491	MANDINKA LANGUAGE SEE MANDINGO LANGUAGE
PL8493	MANDJACK LANGUAGE SEE MANDJAK LANGUAGE
PL8493	MANDJAK LANGUAGE
GN652.M3	MANDJAS / anthropology
DT546	MANDJAS / history
M292-3	MANDOLIN AND GUITAR MUSIC
M278-9	MANDOLIN AND HARPSICHORD MUSIC
M278-9	MANDOLIN AND PIANO MUSIC
M278-9	MANDOLIN AND PIANO MUSIC, ARRANGED
M1360	MANDOLIN BAND SEE PLECTRAL ENSEMBLES
M292-3	MANDOLIN MUSIC (2 MANDOLINS)
M130-134	MANDOLIN MUSIC
ML399	MANDOLIN PLAYERS SEE MANDOLINISTS / biography collective
ML419	MANDOLIN PLAYERS SEE MANDOLINISTS / individual
M1037.4.M3	MANDOLIN WITH ORCHESTRA
M1105-6	MANDOLIN WITH STRING ORCHESTRA
ML1015-1018	MANDOLIN / history and construction
ML399	MANDOLINISTS / biography collective
ML419	MANDOLINISTS / individual
M1105-6	MANDOLINS (2) WITH STRING ORCHESTRA
GR790.M3	MANDRAKE / folk-lore
DK759.M3	MANEGRS
U250-255	MANEUVERS, MILITARY SEE MILITARY MANEUVERS
UD460-465	MANEUVERS, MILITARY SEE MILITARY MANEUVERS / infantry
V245	MANEUVERS, NAVAL SEE NAVAL MANEUVERS
PL8593	MANG'ANJA LANGUAGE SEE NYANJA LANGUAGE
PL6463	MANGAIAN LANGUAGE
QD181.M6	MANGANATES
TN799.M3	MANGANESE — METALLURGY
QP913.M6	MANGANESE — PHYSIOLOGICAL EFFECT
TN490.M3	MANGANESE ORES
TN757.M3	MANGANESE STEEL
QD181.M6	MANGANESE / chemistry
TN799.M3	MANGANESE / metallurgy
TN490.M3	MANGANESE / mining
PL6464.M3	MANGAREVA LANGUAGE
GN654	MANGBETUS SEE MONBUTTUS
RC182.S17	MANGE SEE SCABIES
SB211.M27	MANGEL-WURZEL
N8180	MANGER IN CHRISTIAN ART AND TRADITION SEE CRIB IN CHRISTIAN ART AND TRADITION / art
SB379.M2	MANGO
SB211.M27	MANGOLD-WURZEL SEE MANGEL-WURZEL
QK495.M28	MANGROVE
F1434.3.M	MANGUE INDIANS / central america
PM3943	MANGUE LANGUAGE
PL5946	MANGUIAN LANGUAGE SEE MANGYAN LANGUAGE
PL5946	MANGYAN LANGUAGE
DS666.M3	MANGYANS
E99.M	MANHATTAN INDIANS
HV6133	MANIA SEE INSANITY / insanity and crime
HV4977	MANIA SEE INSANITY / insanity and degeneration
BF423	MANIA SEE INSANITY / insanity and genius
RC512-528	MANIA SEE PSYCHOSES
RC516	MANIC-DEPRESSIVE PSYCHOSES
BT1410	MANICHAEISM
RL94	MANICURING
Z48	MANIFOLDING SEE COPYING PROCESSES
QA612	MANIFOLDS, DIFFERENTIABLE SEE DIFFERENTIAL TOPOLOGY
HD6073.M7	MANIKINS (FASHION MODELS) SEE MODELS, FASHION

QM33	*MANIKINS* **SEE** ANATOMY, HUMAN — CHARTS, DIAGRAMS, ETC.	Z695.5	*MANUSCRIPTS-CATALOGING* **SEE** CATALOGING OF MANUSCRIPTS
E717.7	MANILA — SIEGE, 1898	Z6621	*MANUSCRIPTS-CLASSIFICATION* **SEE** CLASSIFICATION — MANUSCRIPTS / *catalogs*
E717.7	MANILA BAY, BATTLE OF, 1898		
TS1784-7	*MANILA ROPE* **SEE** ROPE / *manufacture*	Z697.M	*MANUSCRIPTS-CLASSIFICATION* **SEE** CLASSIFICATION — MANUSCRIPTS
PL8493	*MANJACOS LANGUAGE* **SEE** MANDJAK LANGUAGE		
GN652.M3	*MANJAS* **SEE** MANDJAS / *anthropology*	Z110.C6	*MANUSCRIPTS-COLOPHONS* **SEE** COLOPHONS OF MANUSCRIPTS
DT546	*MANJAS* **SEE** MANDJAS / *history*		
PL471-9	*MANJU LANGUAGE* **SEE** MANCHU LANGUAGE	Z41	*MANUSCRIPTS-FORGERIES* **SEE** FORGERY OF MANUSCRIPTS / *autographs*
BS1245	MANNA / *exodus*		
HD6073.M7	*MANNEQUINS* **SEE** MODELS, FASHION	BX875	*MANUSCRIPTS-FORGERIES* **SEE** FORGERY OF MANUSCRIPTS / *church history*
BJ1533.C9	*MANNERS* **SEE** COURTESY		
BJ1520-1688	*MANNERS* **SEE** COURTESY / *conduct of life*	PN171.F6-7	*MANUSCRIPTS-FORGERIES* **SEE** FORGERY OF MANUSCRIPTS / *literature*
BJ1801-2193	*MANNERS* **SEE** ETIQUETTE		
GT80	MANNERS AND CUSTOMS — PICTORIAL WORKS	PB1801-1847	MANX LANGUAGE
GT	MANNERS AND CUSTOMS	QL696.P6	MANX SHEARWATER
QA73	*MANNHEIM SLIDE-RULE* **SEE** SLIDE-RULE	QB362	*MANY-BODY PROBLEM* **SEE** PROBLEM OF MANY BODIES / *celestial mechanics*
TH5613	*MANNHEIM SLIDE-RULE* **SEE** SLIDE-RULE / *carpentry*		
		QC174.5	*MANY-BODY PROBLEM* **SEE** PROBLEM OF MANY BODIES / *quantum theory*
VK221	*MANNING OF VESSELS* **SEE** SHIPS — MANNING		
QD305.A4	MANNITE	PL6465	MAORI LANGUAGE
UD395.M28	MANNLICHER RIFLE	PL6465.Z7	MAORI LITERATURE
QD321	MANNOSE	PL6465.Z77	MAORI POETRY
U250-255	*MANOEUVERS, MILITARY* **SEE** MILITARY MANEUVERS	GN667.N9	MAORIS / *anthropology*
UD460-465	*MANOEUVERS, MILITARY* **SEE** MILITARY MANEUVERS / *infantry*	DU423	MAORIS / *history*
		GA193	MAP COLLECTIONS
V245	*MANOEUVERS, NAVAL* **SEE** NAVAL MANEUVERS	GA130	MAP DRAWING
QC165	MANOMETER	GA193	*MAP LIBRARIES* **SEE** MAP COLLECTIONS
HC254.3	MANORS	GA150	MAP PRINTING
UA17.5	MANPOWER	UG470	*MAP READING* **SEE** MAPS, MILITARY / *etc.*
GN585.R9	*MANSI* **SEE** VOGULS / *anthropology*	UA985-997	*MAP READING* **SEE** MAPS, MILITARY / *military geography*
DK34.V6	*MANSI* **SEE** VOGULS / *history*		
PH1301-9	*MANSI LANGUAGE* **SEE** VOGUL LANGUAGE	GA110-115	MAP-PROJECTION
HV6499-6535	*MANSLAUGHTER* **SEE** ASSASSINATION	SB239.M3	MAPLE SUGAR
HV6278	*MANSLAUGHTER* **SEE** ASSASSINATION / *political*	SB239.M3	MAPLE SYRUP
		QK495.A17	MAPLE
HV6499-6535	*MANSLAUGHTER* **SEE** HOMICIDE	SD397.M3	MAPLE / *forestry*
HV6499-6542	*MANSLAUGHTER* **SEE** MURDER	QA646	*MAPPING, CONFORMAL* **SEE** CONFORMAL MAPPING
NA3050-3055	MANTELS / *architecture*	QA360	*MAPPING, CONFORMAL* **SEE** CONFORMAL MAPPING
TH2288	MANTELS / *construction*	GA109.8	*MAPS OF RESIDUALS* **SEE** MAPS, STATISTICAL
HV2471-2500	*MANUAL ALPHABETS* **SEE** DEAF — MEANS OF COMMUNICATION	QE33	*MAPS, GEOLOGICAL* **SEE** GEOLOGY — MAPS
		G1033	*MAPS, HISTORICAL* **SEE** GEOGRAPHY, ANCIENT — MAPS
TT168-9	MANUAL TRAINING — METHODS AND MANUALS		
LB1595-9	MANUAL TRAINING / *education*	GA205-213	*MAPS, HISTORICAL* **SEE** GEOGRAPHY, ANCIENT — MAPS
TT161-9	MANUAL TRAINING / *technology*		
TT180-203	*MANUAL TRAINING-WOODWORK* **SEE** WOODWORK (MANUAL TRAINING)	QC878	*MAPS, METEOROLOGICAL* **SEE** METEOROLOGY — CHARTS, DIAGRAMS, ETC.
ML1055.M26	MANUALO	UG470-473	MAPS, MILITARY — SYMBOLS
NA1325	*MANUELINE ARCHITECTURE* **SEE** ARCHITECTURE, MANUELINE	UG470	MAPS, MILITARY / *etc.*
		UA985-997	MAPS, MILITARY / *military geography*
HF5686.M3	MANUFACTURES — COSTS	UG470-473	*MAPS, MILITARY-CONVENTIONAL SIGNS* **SEE** MAPS, MILITARY — SYMBOLS
TS	MANUFACTURES		
HD9720-9739	MANUFACTURES / *economics*	TN273	*MAPS, MINE* **SEE** MINE MAPS
HT1025-1037	*MANUMISSION OF SLAVES* **SEE** SLAVERY — EMANCIPATION	GA150	*MAPS, PRINTING OF* **SEE** MAP PRINTING
		GA109.8	MAPS, STATISTICAL
S631-667	*MANURES* **SEE** FERTILIZERS AND MANURES / *agriculture*	Z695.6	*MAPS-CATALOGING* **SEE** CATALOGING OF MAPS
		Z697.M	*MAPS-CLASSIFICATION* **SEE** CLASSIFICATION — MAPS
TP963	*MANURES* **SEE** FERTILIZERS AND MANURES / *manufacture*		
		GA150	*MAPS-PRINTING* **SEE** MAP PRINTING
HD9483	*MANURES* **SEE** FERTILIZERS AND MANURES / *trade*	F3126	*MAPUCHE INDIANS* **SEE** ARAUCANIAN INDIANS
GN671.A4	MANUS TRIBE / *admiralty islands*	PM5461-9	*MAPUCHE LANGUAGE* **SEE** ARAUCANIAN LANGUAGE
GN671.N5	MANUS TRIBE / *new guinea*	PL5957	MARANAO LANGUAGE
Z6601-6625	MANUSCRIPTS — CATALOGS	PL5957	*MARANAW LANGUAGE* **SEE** MARANAO LANGUAGE
Z113-115	MANUSCRIPTS — FACSIMILES	BM180-190	MARANOS / *judaism*
Z110.R4	MANUSCRIPTS — REPRODUCTION	DS135.P7	MARANOS / *portugal*
Z113-115	MANUSCRIPTS (PAPYRI) — FACSIMILES	DS135.S7	MARANOS / *spain*
Z695.5	*MANUSCRIPTS - CATALOGING* **SEE** CATALOGING OF MANUSCRIPTS	DS485.A86	*MARAS* **SEE** LAKHERS
		E99.M195	*MARASHITE INDIANS* **SEE** MALECITE INDIANS
Z105-115	MANUSCRIPTS	DS473	MARATHA WAR, 1775-1782
Z6601-6625	MANUSCRIPTS	DS475.3	MARATHA WAR, 1803
PJ1809-1921	*MANUSCRIPTS, DEMOTIC (PAPYRI)* **SEE** EGYPTIAN LANGUAGE — PAPYRI, DEMOTIC	DS475.6	MARATHA WAR, 1816-1818
		DS432.M2	MARATHAS
Z41	*MANUSCRIPTS, FORGERY OF* **SEE** FORGERY OF MANUSCRIPTS / *autographs*	PK2414	MARATHI BALLADS AND SONGS / *collections*
		PK2410	MARATHI BALLADS AND SONGS / *history*
BX875	*MANUSCRIPTS, FORGERY OF* **SEE** FORGERY OF MANUSCRIPTS / *church history*	PK2351-2378	MARATHI LANGUAGE
		PK2400-2458	MARATHI LITERATURE
PN171.F6-7	*MANUSCRIPTS, FORGERY OF* **SEE** FORGERY OF MANUSCRIPTS / *literature*	GV1065	MARATHON RUNNING
		DF225.4	MARATHON, BATTLE OF, 490 B.C.
ND2890-3416	*MANUSCRIPTS, ILLUMINATED* **SEE** ILLUMINATION OF BOOKS AND MANUSCRIPTS	BM652	MARBITS TORAH
		TN967	MARBLE

TT345	*MARBLE-STAINING* **SEE** STAINS AND STAINING / *wood-staining*
QL737.C2	MARBLED CAT
GV1213	MARBLES (GAME)
Z271	MARBLING (BOOKBINDING)
TT330	MARBLING / *painting*
QE391.M3	MARCASITE
QK555.M2	MARCHANTIALES
M175.A4	MARCHES (ACCORDION)
M1260	MARCHES (BAND)
M1247	MARCHES (BAND)
M555-9	MARCHES (BASSOON, CLARINET, FLUTE, HORN, OBOE)
M455-9	MARCHES (BASSOON, CLARINET, FLUTE, OBOE)
M248-252	MARCHES (CLARINET AND PIANO)
M240-244	MARCHES (FLUTE AND PIANO)
M60-64	MARCHES (FLUTE)
M276-7	MARCHES (GUITAR AND PIANO)
M115-119	MARCHES (HARP)
M1060	MARCHES (ORCHESTRA)
M1046	MARCHES (ORCHESTRA)
M6-7	MARCHES (ORGAN)
M11-13	MARCHES (ORGAN)
M785	MARCHES (PERCUSSION, 2 TROMBONES, 3 TRUMPETS, TUBA)
M191-5	MARCHES (PIANO (4 HANDS) AND REED-ORGAN)
M28	MARCHES (PIANO)
M920-924	MARCHES (PIANO, BASSOON, CLARINET, FLUTE, OBOE, TRUMPET, VIOLIN, VIOLA, VIOLONCELLO)
M204	MARCHES (PIANO, 4 HANDS)
M200-201	MARCHES (PIANO, 4 HANDS)
M1350	MARCHES (SALON ORCHESTRA)
M268-9	MARCHES (SAXOPHONE AND PIANO)
M1160	MARCHES (STRING ORCHESTRA)
M1145	MARCHES (STRING ORCHESTRA)
M262-3	MARCHES (TROMBONE AND PIANO)
M260-261	MARCHES (TRUMPET AND PIANO)
M85-89	MARCHES (TRUMPET)
M282-3	MARCHES (UKULELE AND PIANO)
M221-3	MARCHES (VIOLIN AND HARPSICHORD)
M217-218	MARCHES (VIOLIN AND HARPSICHORD)
M217-218	MARCHES (VIOLIN AND PIANO)
M221-3	MARCHES (VIOLIN AND PIANO)
M955-7	MARCHES (WIND ENSEMBLE)
M655-9	MARCHES (2 BASSOONS, 2 CLARINETS, 2 HORNS)
M288-9	MARCHES (2 FLUTES)
M385	MARCHES (2 FLUTES, PERCUSSION)
M660-662	MARCHES (2 HORNS, 2 VIOLINS, VIOLA, VIOLONCELLO)
M214-215	MARCHES (2 PIANOS)
M355-9	MARCHES (3 RECORDERS)
M355-7	MARCHES (3 TRUMPETS)
M349-353	MARCHES (3 VIOLINS)
DC234.8	*MARCHFELD, BATTLE OF, JULY 5-6, 1809* **SEE** WAGRAM, BATTLE OF, 1809
DC234.6	*MARCHFELD, BATTLE OF, MAY 21-22, 1809* **SEE** ASPERN, BATTLE OF, 1809
UD310-315	MARCHING
BT1417	*MARCIANITES* **SEE** MESSALIANS
DD78.M3	MARCOMANNI / *germany*
TK5811	*MARCONI SYSTEM OF WIRELESS TELEGRAPHY* **SEE** TELEGRAPH, WIRELESS — MARCONI SYSTEM
E99.M195	*MARECHITE INDIANS* **SEE** MALECITE INDIANS
DC223.7	MARENGO, BATTLE OF, 1800
TP871	MAREZZO MARBLE
QD305.A2	MARGARIC ACID
SF268	*MARGARINE* **SEE** OLEOMARGARINE
HD9441	*MARGARINE* **SEE** OLEOMARGARINE / *trade*
HD201-5	MARGINAL UTILITY
PH801-9	*MARI LANGUAGE* **SEE** CHEREMISSIAN LANGUAGE
CJ2585	MARIA THERESA DOLLAR
BT646	MARIAN YEAR
E99.M195	*MARICHEET INDIANS* **SEE** MALECITE INDIANS
E99.M	MARICOPA INDIANS
PM1711	MARICOPA LANGUAGE
HV5822.M3	MARIHUANA / *social pathology*
PH801-9	*MARII LANGUAGE* **SEE** CHEREMISSIAN LANGUAGE
M284-5	MARIMBA AND PIANO MUSIC
M284-5	MARIMBA AND PIANO MUSIC, ARRANGED
M385	*MARIMBA MUSIC (3 MARIMBAS)* **SEE** TRIOS (3 MARIMBAS)

M175.X6	MARIMBA MUSIC
M1038-9	MARIMBA WITH ORCHESTRA
M1039	MARIMBA WITH ORCHESTRA, ARRANGED — SOLO WITH PIANO
M1038-9	MARIMBA WITH ORCHESTRA, ARRANGED
ML1040	MARIMBA
VK369	MARINAS
TC353-373	MARINAS / *hydraulic engineering*
DU744	MARIND TRIBES / *history*
GN671.N5	MARIND TRIBES / *new guinea*
PL6621.M3	MARINDINESE LANGUAGE
VK1000-1249	*MARINE AIDS* **SEE** AIDS TO NAVIGATION / *lighthouse service*
VK381-397	*MARINE AIDS* **SEE** AIDS TO NAVIGATION / *signaling*
VM	*MARINE ARCHITECTURE* **SEE** NAVAL ARCHITECTURE
VM	*MARINE ARCHITECTURE* **SEE** SHIP-BUILDING
QH91-95	MARINE BIOLOGY / *natural history*
VM741-750	*MARINE BOILERS* **SEE** STEAM-BOILERS, MARINE
TC201	MARINE BORERS
VC370-375	*MARINE COOKERY* **SEE** COOKERY, MARINE
VK224	*MARINE COOKERY* **SEE** COOKERY, MARINE
VE500	MARINE CORPS WIVES
VM951	*MARINE CORROSION* **SEE** SHIPS — CORROSION
GC380-399	*MARINE DEPOSITS* **SEE** MARINE SEDIMENTS
VM770	MARINE DIESEL MOTORS
VK1250-1299	*MARINE DISASTERS* **SEE** SHIPWRECKS / *etc.*
G525-530	*MARINE DISASTERS* **SEE** SHIPWRECKS / *etc.*
JX4436	*MARINE DISASTERS* **SEE** SHIPWRECKS / *international law*
VM325	*MARINE ELECTRONIC EQUIPMENT* **SEE** ELECTRONICS ON BOATS
VM600-989	MARINE ENGINEERING
VM737	MARINE ENGINES — SPECIFICATIONS
VM761	MARINE ENGINES — TESTING
VM731-775	MARINE ENGINES
QL122	MARINE FAUNA — JUVENILE LITERATURE
QL121-138	MARINE FAUNA
QK103	MARINE FLORA
QE39	*MARINE GEOLOGY* **SEE** SUBMARINE GEOLOGY
RA975	*MARINE HOSPITALS* **SEE** HOSPITALS, NAVAL AND MARINE / *marine*
RA980-993	*MARINE HOSPITALS* **SEE** HOSPITALS, NAVAL AND MARINE / *marine*
VG410-450	*MARINE HOSPITALS* **SEE** HOSPITALS, NAVAL AND MARINE / *naval*
VK573-585	*MARINE INSTRUMENTS* **SEE** NAUTICAL INSTRUMENTS
HE961-971	*MARINE INSURANCE* **SEE** INSURANCE, MARINE
QH	MARINE LABORATORIES
JX4408-4449	*MARINE LAW* **SEE** MARITIME LAW / *international law*
JX63	*MARINE LAW* **SEE** MARITIME LAW / *private*
QR106	MARINE MICROBIOLOGY
VM774.3	MARINE NUCLEAR REACTOR PLANTS
TN871.3	*MARINE OIL OPERATIONS* **SEE** OIL WELL DRILLING, SUBMARINE
ND1370	MARINE PAINTING
ND2270	MARINE PAINTING / *water-color*
VM501	MARINE PIPE-FITTING
VM821	MARINE PUMPS
VK369	MARINE RADIO STATIONS
VM925	MARINE RAILWAYS
VM485	MARINE REFRIGERATION
GC380-399	MARINE SEDIMENTS
VK1000-1249	*MARINE SIGNALS* **SEE** AIDS TO NAVIGATION / *lighthouse service*
VK381-397	*MARINE SIGNALS* **SEE** AIDS TO NAVIGATION / *signaling*
VM741-750	*MARINE STEAM-BOILERS* **SEE** STEAM-BOILERS, MARINE
VM470.5	*MARINE STORES* **SEE** SHIP CHANDLERS
VM470.5	*MARINE SUPPLIERS* **SEE** SHIP CHANDLERS
VK591-7	*MARINE SURVEYING* **SEE** HYDROGRAPHIC SURVEYING
VK596-7	*MARINE SURVEYORS* **SEE** SURVEYORS, MARINE
HE561-971	*MARINE TRANSPORTATION* **SEE** SHIPPING
JX4190	*MARINE TRANSPORTATION* **SEE** SHIPPING / *international law*

QL121-138	*MARINE ZOOLOGY* **SEE** MARINE FAUNA
VK577	*MARINER'S COMPASS* **SEE** COMPASS
QC849	*MARINER'S COMPASS* **SEE** COMPASS / *deviation*
HD8039.S4-42	*MARINERS* **SEE** SEAMEN / *labor*
VE	MARINES
DT319	*MARINIDES* **SEE** BENI MARIN DYNASTY
BT645	*MARIOLATRY* **SEE** MARY, VIRGIN — CULTUS
BT610-640	*MARIOLOGY* **SEE** MARY, VIRGIN — THEOLOGY
PN1970-1981	*MARIONETTES* **SEE** PUPPETS AND PUPPET-PLAYS
PT1297	*MARIONETTES* **SEE** PUPPETS AND PUPPET-PLAYS / *german*
E99.Y75	*MARIPOSAN INDIANS* **SEE** YOKUTS INDIANS
PM2681	*MARIPOSAN LANGUAGE* **SEE** YOKUTS LANGUAGE
JX5228	*MARITIME CAPTURE* **SEE** CAPTURE AT SEA
G220-420	*MARITIME DISCOVERIES* **SEE** DISCOVERIES (IN GEOGRAPHY)
G575-890	*MARITIME DISCOVERIES* **SEE** DISCOVERIES (IN GEOGRAPHY) / *polar regions*
G80-99	*MARITIME DISCOVERIES* **SEE** DISCOVERIES (IN GEOGRAPHY)
JX4408-4449	MARITIME LAW / *international law*
JX6311	MARITIME LAW / *private*
HE585-7	MARITIME LAW / *shipping laws*
QC994	*MARITIME METEOROLOGY* **SEE** METEOROLOGY, MARITIME
V13	*MARITIME MUSEUMS* **SEE** NAVAL MUSEUMS
VK591-7	*MARITIME SURVEYING* **SEE** HYDROGRAPHIC SURVEYING
JX5203-5268	*MARITIME WAR* **SEE** WAR, MARITIME (INTERNATIONAL LAW)
JC20-45	MARK / *primitive state*
HC	MARKET SURVEYS / *surveys*
HF5415	MARKET SURVEYS / *technique*
TX356	MARKETING (HOME ECONOMICS)
S571	*MARKETING OF FARM PRODUCE* **SEE** FARM PRODUCE — MARKETING
HD9006	*MARKETING OF FARM PRODUCE* **SEE** FARM PRODUCE — MARKETING / *economics*
HD9000.6	*MARKETING OF FARM PRODUCE* **SEE** FARM PRODUCE — MARKETING / *economics*
SB360	*MARKETING OF FRUIT* **SEE** FRUIT — MARKETING
HF5415	MARKETING
HF5470-5475	MARKETS
LB3051-3063	*MARKING (STUDENTS)* **SEE** GRADING AND MARKING (STUDENTS)
TS2301.M3	MARKING DEVICES
QA273	*MARKOFF PROCESSES* **SEE** MARKOV PROCESSES
QA273	*MARKOV CHAINS* **SEE** MARKOV PROCESSES
QA273	MARKOV PROCESSES
Z237	*MARKS IN PAPER* **SEE** WATER-MARKS / *early printed books*
TS1115	*MARKS IN PAPER* **SEE** WATER-MARKS / *paper manufacture*
HD3625-6	MARKS OF ORIGIN
NK7210	*MARKS ON PLATE* **SEE** HALL-MARKS
N45	*MARKS, ARTISTS'* **SEE** ARTISTS' MARKS
N8380	*MARKS, COLLECTORS'* **SEE** COLLECTORS' MARKS
NE820	*MARKS, ENGRAVERS'* **SEE** ENGRAVERS' MARKS
NK4215	*MARKS, POTTERS'* **SEE** POTTERY — MARKS
Z235-6	*MARKS, PRINTERS'* **SEE** PRINTERS' MARKS
SK37-39	*MARKSMANSHIP* **SEE** SHOOTING / *hunting sports*
GV1151-1181	*MARKSMANSHIP* **SEE** SHOOTING / *sports and games*
S643	MARL / *fertilizers*
QL737.R6	MARMOTS
D545.M3	MARNE, BATTLE OF THE, 1914 — OURCQ
D545.M3	MARNE, BATTLE OF THE, 1914
D545.M35	MARNE, 2D BATTLE OF THE, 1918
BX180-189	MARONITES
BR757	MARPRELATE CONTROVERSY
JX5241	*MARQUE, LETTERS OF* **SEE** PRIVATEERING
JX4486	*MARQUE, LETTERS OF* **SEE** REPRISALS
PL6471	MARQUESAN LANGUAGE
NK9920	MARQUETRY
NK2710	MARQUETRY / *inlaid furniture*
BM180-190	*MARRANOS* **SEE** MARANOS / *judaism*
DS135.P7	*MARRANOS* **SEE** MARANOS / *portugal*
DS135.S7	*MARRANOS* **SEE** MARANOS / *spain*
PN6288.M3	MARRIAGE — ANECDOTES, FACETIAE, SATIRE, ETC. / *epigrams*

HQ1024	MARRIAGE — ANNULMENT (CANON LAW)
HQ822	MARRIAGE — ANNULMENT
HQ1024	MARRIAGE — ANNULMENT / *canon law*
BX2250	MARRIAGE — CATHOLIC CHURCH
BX5149.M2	MARRIAGE — CHURCH OF ENGLAND
HQ1021-4	MARRIAGE — DISPENSATIONS
BX1939.D6	MARRIAGE — DISPENSATIONS / *canon law*
HQ525.M6	MARRIAGE — ISLAM
HQ507	MARRIAGE — JEWS
BX5949.M3	MARRIAGE — PROTESTANT EPISCOPAL CHURCH IN THE U.S.A.
BV837	MARRIAGE — SERMONS
HQ1021-4	MARRIAGE (CANON LAW)
HQ1011-1024	*MARRIAGE -PROHIBITED DEGREES* **SEE** MARRIAGE LAW
JX4231.M3	*MARRIAGE -PROHIBITED DEGREES* **SEE** MARRIAGE LAW / *international law*
JX6428	*MARRIAGE -PROHIBITED DEGREES* **SEE** MARRIAGE LAW / *international law*
CS	*MARRIAGE BONDS* **SEE** MARRIAGE LICENSES
BM713	MARRIAGE CUSTOMS AND RITES — JEWS
GT2660-2800	MARRIAGE CUSTOMS AND RITES
HG9281-7	*MARRIAGE ENDOWMENT INSURANCE* **SEE** INSURANCE, MARRIAGE ENDOWMENT
HQ1011-1024	MARRIAGE LAW
JX6428	MARRIAGE LAW / *international law*
JX4231.M3	MARRIAGE LAW / *international law*
CS	MARRIAGE LICENSES
BT378.M3	MARRIAGE OF THE KING'S SON (PARABLE)
HA38-39	*MARRIAGE REGISTERS* **SEE** REGISTERS OF BIRTHS, ETC.
BV837	*MARRIAGE SERMONS* **SEE** MARRIAGE — SERMONS
HQ745	MARRIAGE SERVICE
BX2250	MARRIAGE SERVICE / *catholic*
BX5149.M2	MARRIAGE SERVICE / *church of england*
BX5949.M3	MARRIAGE SERVICE / *protestant episcopal*
HB881-3700	*MARRIAGE STATISTICS* **SEE** VITAL STATISTICS
HQ1028	MARRIAGE WITH DECEASED WIFE'S SISTER
HQ503-1057	MARRIAGE
GN480	MARRIAGE / *ethnology*
GR465	MARRIAGE / *folk-lore*
HQ803	MARRIAGE, COMPANIONATE
HQ1018.M4	*MARRIAGE, MEDICAL EXAMINATION FOR* **SEE** PREMARITAL EXAMINATIONS
HQ1031	MARRIAGE, MIXED
GT5070	*MARRIAGE, MORGANATIC* **SEE** MARRIAGES OF ROYALTY AND NOBILITY
GT2650	*MARRIAGE, PROMISE OF* **SEE** BETROTHAL
BX5149.M2	*MARRIAGE-ANGLICAN COMMUNION* **SEE** MARRIAGE — CHURCH OF ENGLAND
BX5949.M3	*MARRIAGE-ANGLICAN COMMUNION* **SEE** MARRIAGE — PROTESTANT EPISCOPAL CHURCH IN THE U.S.A.
HQ1026	*MARRIAGE-PROHIBITED DEGREES* **SEE** CONSANGUINITY / *consanguineous marriages*
HV4981	*MARRIAGE-PROHIBITED DEGREES* **SEE** CONSANGUINITY / *degeneration*
HB1113.R38	*MARRIAGE-PROHIBITED DEGREES* **SEE** CONSANGUINITY / *statistics*
HQ1028	*MARRIAGE-PROHIBITED DEGREES* **SEE** MARRIAGE WITH DECEASED WIFE'S SISTER
GT5070	MARRIAGES OF ROYALTY AND NOBILITY
LB3616.M3	MARRIED STUDENTS
RC280.M	MARROW — TUMORS
QM569	MARROW
QB641	MARS (PLANET) — DIAMETERS
QB516	MARS (PLANET) — OPPOSITION, 1849-1850, (1860, 1862, ETC.)
QB775	MARS (PLANET) — SPECTRA
QB376	MARS (PLANET) — TABLES
QB641	MARS (PLANET) / *descriptive astronomy*
QB376	MARS (PLANET) / *theoretical astronomy*
TL799.M3	*MARS (PLANET), FLIGHT TO* **SEE** SPACE FLIGHT TO MARS
DC303.2	*MARS-LA-TOUR, BATTLE OF, 1870* **SEE** VIONVILLE, BATTLE OF, 1870
TN305	*MARSH-GAS* **SEE** FIRE-DAMP
E302.6.M4	*MARSHALL DAY* **SEE** JOHN MARSHALL DAY
PL6255	MARSHALL LANGUAGE
TF590	*MARSHALLING YARDS* **SEE** RAILROADS — YARDS
S621	MARSHES / *agriculture*

TC975	MARSHES / *reclamation*
S621	MARSHES, TIDE / *agriculture*
TC975	MARSHES, TIDE / *reclamation*
E99.M4	*MARSHPEE INDIANS* **SEE** MASHPEE INDIANS
DA417	MARSTON MOOR, BATTLE OF, 1644
QL737.M3	MARSUPIALIA
QE882.M3	MARSUPIALIA, FOSSIL
ML1092	*MARTENOT (MUSICAL INSTRUMENT)* **SEE** ONDES MARTENOT
ML1092	*MARTENOT'S ONDES MUSICALES* **SEE** ONDES MARTENOT
SF405.M	MARTENS / *culture*
QL737.C2	MARTENS / *zoology*
TN731	MARTENSITE
JN261	MARTIAL LAW / *constitutional history gt. brit.*
JX4595	MARTIAL LAW / *international law*
JK343-355	MARTIAL LAW / *u.s.*
E271	*MARTINIQUE, BATTLE OF, 1782* **SEE** DOMINICA, BATTLE OF, 1782
QL396.P2	*MARTINS* **SEE** HOUSE-MARTIN
QL696.P2	*MARTINS* **SEE** PURPLE MARTIN
BR1609	MARTYROLOGIES
BX4660	MARTYROLOGIES / *catholic*
BR1600-1609	MARTYRS — LEGENDS
BX4654-4662	MARTYRS — LEGENDS / *catholic church*
BR1600-1609	MARTYRS
BX2166	MARTYRS — PRAYER-BOOKS AND DEVOTIONS — — ENGLISH, (FRENCH, GERMAN, ETC.)
BF775	MARVELOUS, THE
PK2461-9	*MARWARI LANGUAGE* **SEE** DINGAL LANGUAGE
HX626-795	*MARXISM* **SEE** COMMUNISM
HX1-550	*MARXISM* **SEE** SOCIALISM
BT610	MARY, VIRGIN — ANNUNCIATION
BT650	MARY, VIRGIN — APPARITIONS AND MIRACLES (MODERN)
N8070	MARY, VIRGIN — ART
BT611	MARY, VIRGIN — BIBLICAL TEACHING
BT680	MARY, VIRGIN — CONTROVERSIAL LITERATURE
BT640	MARY, VIRGIN — COREDEMPTION
BT645	MARY, VIRGIN — CULTUS
PN6120.R4	MARY, VIRGIN — DRAMA
BP172	MARY, VIRGIN — ISLAMIC INTERPRETATIONS
BT675	MARY, VIRGIN — LEGENDS
BX2161	MARY, VIRGIN — MAY DEVOTIONS
BT640	MARY, VIRGIN — MEDIATION
BX2160	MARY, VIRGIN — MEDITATIONS
BT609	MARY, VIRGIN — POETRY
BX2160	MARY, VIRGIN — PRAYER-BOOKS AND DEVOTIONS
BT610-640	MARY, VIRGIN — THEOLOGY
BT670.T5	MARY, VIRGIN — TITLES
BT605.5	MARY, VIRGIN — WORDS
BT600-680	MARY, VIRGIN
BT638	MARY, VIRGIN, AND CHRISTIAN UNION
BT608.7	MARY, VIRGIN, AND EDUCATION
BP172	*MARY, VIRGIN, IN ISLAM* **SEE** MARY, VIRGIN — ISLAMIC INTERPRETATIONS
BT645.3	MARY, VIRGIN, IN THE LITURGY
BX2161.5.S	*MARY, VIRGIN-DOLORS* **SEE** SORROWS OF THE BLESSED VIRGIN MARY, DEVOTION TO
N8070	*MARY, VIRGIN-ICONOGRAPHY* **SEE** MARY, VIRGIN — ART
BP172	*MARY, VIRGIN-INTERPRETATIONS, ISLAMIC* **SEE** MARY, VIRGIN — ISLAMIC INTERPRETATIONS
BP172	*MARY, VIRGIN-MUSLIM INTERPRETATIONS* **SEE** MARY, VIRGIN — ISLAMIC INTERPRETATIONS
BT670.T5	*MARY, VIRGIN-NAME* **SEE** MARY, VIRGIN — TITLES
BX2161.5.S	*MARY, VIRGIN-SEVEN SORROWS* **SEE** SORROWS OF THE BLESSED VIRGIN MARY, DEVOTION TO
BX2320-2321	*MARY, VIRGIN-SHRINES* **SEE** SHRINES / *catholic church*
BL580-586	*MARY, VIRGIN-SHRINES* **SEE** SHRINES / *comparative religion*
BT653-660	*MARY, VIRGIN-SHRINES* **SEE** SHRINES / *virgin*
BX2161.5.S	*MARY, VIRGIN-SORROWS* **SEE** SORROWS OF THE BLESSED VIRGIN MARY, DEVOTION TO
BV50.V5	*MARY, VIRGIN-VISITATION* **SEE** VISITATION FESTIVAL
F176-190	MARYLAND — HISTORY
E476.66	MARYLAND CAMPAIGN, JUNE-AUG., 1864
E474.61	MARYLAND CAMPAIGN, 1862
QL696.P2	MARYLAND YELLOWTHROAT
E566	MARYLAND — HISTORY — — CIVIL WAR
E512	MARYLAND — HISTORY — — CIVIL WAR
E263.M3	MARYLAND — HISTORY — — REVOLUTION
E395.5.M2	MARYLAND — HISTORY — — WAR OF 1812
PL8535	*MASA LANGUAGE* **SEE** MUSGU LANGUAGE
PL8501	MASAI LANGUAGE
GN659.M3	MASAI / *anthropology*
DT434.E2	MASAI / *history*
DT429	MASAI / *history*
DT434.E2	MASAI / *kenya*
PL8675	*MASANGO LANGUAGE* **SEE** SHIRA LANGUAGE
PL5281	*MASARETE LANGUAGE* **SEE** BURU LANGUAGE
E99.M3	MASCOUTEN INDIANS
TK7872.M45	MASERS
DT955	MASHONA
E99.M4	MASHPEE INDIANS
PM986-9	*MASKEGON DIALECT* **SEE** CREE LANGUAGE
E99.C9	*MASKOKI INDIANS* **SEE** CREEK INDIANS
PM991	*MASKOKI LANGUAGE* **SEE** CREEK LANGUAGE
PN6120.M3	*MASKS (PLAYS)* **SEE** MASQUES
PN1934	*MASKS (PLAYS)* **SEE** MASQUES
NB1310	MASKS (SCULPTURE)
GT1747	MASKS
HQ79	MASOCHISM
F157.B7	MASON AND DIXON'S LINE
QL568.A6	MASON-BEES
F1376	MASON-SPINDEN EXPEDITION, 1926
TG330	*MASONRY BRIDGES* **SEE** BRIDGES, MASONRY
TH1199-1451	MASONRY / *building*
TA670-683	MASONRY / *engineering*
TH5311-5591	MASONRY / *masonry work*
HS351-929	*MASONS (SECRET ORDER)* **SEE** FREEMASONS
HS551-680	*MASONS (SECRET ORDER)* **SEE** FREEMASONS / *other countries*
HS505-539	*MASONS (SECRET ORDER)* **SEE** FREEMASONS / *u.s.*
TH5401-5421	*MASONS (TRADE)* **SEE** STONE-MASONS / *masonry*
DD338	MASOVIANS
M1523	MASQUES WITH MUSIC — VOCAL SCORES WITH PIANO
M1520-1526	MASQUES WITH MUSIC
PN1934	MASQUES
PN6120.M3	MASQUES
BX1939.M23	MASS (CANON LAW)
QD466	*MASS (CHEMISTRY)* **SEE** ATOMIC MASS / *chemistry*
QC173	*MASS (CHEMISTRY)* **SEE** ATOMIC MASS / *physics*
ML3088	MASS (MUSIC)
QD466	*MASS (NUCLEAR PHYSICS)* **SEE** ATOMIC MASS / *chemistry*
QC173	*MASS (NUCLEAR PHYSICS)* **SEE** ATOMIC MASS / *physics*
RA976	MASS CASUALTIES — MEDICAL RECORDS
RA645.5-7	*MASS CASUALTIES-TREATMENT* **SEE** EMERGENCY MEDICAL SERVICES
HE	*MASS COMMUNICATION* **SEE** COMMUNICATION AND TRAFFIC
GN38	*MASS COMMUNICATION* **SEE** COMMUNICATION AND TRAFFIC / *primitive*
P90	*MASS COMMUNICATION* **SEE** COMMUNICATION
TX946	*MASS FEEDING* **SEE** EMERGENCY MASS FEEDING
HM251-291	*MASS PSYCHOLOGY* **SEE** SOCIAL PSYCHOLOGY
BX2230-2233	MASS / *catholic church*
QC105	*MASS, STANDARDS OF* **SEE** STANDARDS OF MASS
E99.M42	MASSACHUSET INDIANS
PM1736-9	MASSACHUSET LANGUAGE
F61-75	MASSACHUSETTS — HISTORY
E99.M42	*MASSACHUSETTS INDIANS* **SEE** MASSACHUSET INDIANS
E513	MASSACHUSETTS — HISTORY — — CIVIL WAR
E199	MASSACHUSETTS — HISTORY — — FRENCH AND INDIAN WAR, 1755-1763
E198	MASSACHUSETTS — HISTORY — — KING GEORGE'S WAR, 1744-1748
E197	MASSACHUSETTS — HISTORY — — QUEEN ANNE'S WAR, 1702-1713
E263.M4	MASSACHUSETTS — HISTORY — — REVOLUTION
E359.5.M3	MASSACHUSETTS — HISTORY — — WAR OF 1812
BS2545.H	*MASSACRE OF THE INNOCENTS* **SEE** HOLY INNOCENTS, MASSACRE OF THE
RM721	MASSAGE

GN659.M3	*MASSAI* **SEE** MASAI / anthropology
DT429	*MASSAI* **SEE** MASAI / history
DT434.E2	*MASSAI* **SEE** MASAI / history
DT434.E2	*MASSAI* **SEE** MASAI / kenya
BT1417	*MASSALIANS* **SEE** MESSALIANS
E99.I7	*MASSAWOMEKE INDIANS* **SEE** IROQUOIS INDIANS
M33	MASSES — PIANO SCORES
QB814	*MASSES OF STARS* **SEE** STARS — MASSES
M2013-2014	MASSES
M2154.5	MASSES
M2010-2011	MASSES
M14.3	*MASSES, INSTRUMENTAL* **SEE** ORGAN MASSES
M14.3	*MASSES, ORGAN* **SEE** ORGAN MASSES
QB814	*MASSES, STELLAR* **SEE** STARS — MASSES
M2013	MASSES — TO 1800 — — VOCAL SCORES WITH 2 ORGANS
LB2385	MASTER OF ARTS DEGREE
RG491-9	*MASTITIS* **SEE** BREAST — DISEASES
RG861	*MASTITIS* **SEE** BREAST — DISEASES / puerperal state
SF871	*MASTITIS* **SEE** UDDER — DISEASES
QE882.U7	MASTODON
RF235	MASTOID PROCESS — DISEASES
VM531	MASTS AND RIGGING
HQ447	MASTURBATION
DD338	*MASURIANS* **SEE** MASOVIANS
QD181.T35	*MASURIUM* **SEE** TECHNETIUM
PL8723	*MATABELE LANGUAGE* **SEE** TEBELE LANGUAGE
DT958	MATABELE WAR, 1896
F2821	MATACO INDIANS
PM6466	MATACO LANGUAGE
GV1108	*MATADORS* **SEE** BULL-FIGHTERS
F2821	*MATAGUAYA INDIANS* **SEE** MATACO INDIANS
F1779	MATANZAS BAY, CUBA — CAPTURE OF THE SPANISH SILVER-FLEET, 1628
D775.5.M	MATAPAN, BATTLE OF, 1941
NC1885	*MATCH BOX LABELS* **SEE** MATCHBOX LABELS
NC1885	*MATCH COVERS* **SEE** MATCHCOVERS
NC1885	MATCHBOX LABELS
NC1885	MATCHCOVERS
TP310	MATCHES
SB279.M4	MATE (SHRUB)
RS79-88	MATERIA MEDICA — EARLY WORKS TO 1800
RS157	MATERIA MEDICA — EXAMINATIONS, QUESTIONS, ETC.
RS93	MATERIA MEDICA — LABORATORY MANUALS
RS122-3	MATERIA MEDICA — MUSEUMS AND COLLECTIONS
RS153-185	MATERIA MEDICA
RV401-411	MATERIA MEDICA / eclectic
RM121-7	MATERIA MEDICA / materia medica and therapeutics
RS162-3	MATERIA MEDICA, ANIMAL
RK701	MATERIA MEDICA, DENTAL
RS164-5	MATERIA MEDICA, VEGETABLE
B851-4695	MATERIALISM / by country
BD331	MATERIALISM / metaphysics
B825	MATERIALISM / philosophic systems general
HX55	*MATERIALISM, DIALECTICAL* **SEE** DIALECTICAL MATERIALISM / socialism
B809.8	*MATERIALISM, DIALECTICAL* **SEE** DIALECTICAL MATERIALISM / philosophy
BF1378	MATERIALIZATION
TA407	MATERIALS AT LOW TEMPERATURES
HD69.M35	MATERIALS MANAGEMENT
TA403	*MATERIALS, LAMINATED* **SEE** LAMINATED MATERIALS
TK453	*MATERIALS, MAGNETIC* **SEE** MAGNETIC MATERIALS / electric engineering
QC761	*MATERIALS, MAGNETIC* **SEE** MAGNETIC MATERIALS / physics
TA405	*MATERIALS, STRENGTH OF* **SEE** STRENGTH OF MATERIALS
TA410-417	*MATERIALS, STRENGTH OF* **SEE** STRENGTH OF MATERIALS / testing
TA407	*MATERIALS-CREEP* **SEE** CREEP OF MATERIALS
HV697-700	MATERNAL AND INFANT WELFARE
HQ759	*MATERNAL LOVE* **SEE** LOVE, MATERNAL
RG12-16	*MATERNITY HOSPITALS* **SEE** HOSPITALS, GYNECOLOGIC AND OBSTETRIC
HG9291-5	*MATERNITY INSURANCE* **SEE** INSURANCE, MATERNITY
HV697-700	*MATERNITY WELFARE* **SEE** MATERNAL AND INFANT WELFARE
QA497	*MATHEMATICAL DRAWING* **SEE** GEOMETRICAL DRAWING
QA464	*MATHEMATICAL DRAWING* **SEE** GEOMETRICAL DRAWING
T351-377	*MATHEMATICAL DRAWING* **SEE** MECHANICAL DRAWING
QA556.5	*MATHEMATICAL EQUIPOLLENCE* **SEE** EQUIPOLLENCE, MATHEMATICAL
QA41	*MATHEMATICAL FORMULAE* **SEE** MATHEMATICS — FORMULAE
GA	*MATHEMATICAL GEOGRAPHY* **SEE** GEOGRAPHY, MATHEMATICAL
QA71-85	MATHEMATICAL INSTRUMENTS
BC131-5	*MATHEMATICAL LOGIC* **SEE** LOGIC, SYMBOLIC AND MATHEMATICAL
QA11	MATHEMATICAL MODELS
QA41	MATHEMATICAL NOTATION
QC20	MATHEMATICAL PHYSICS
QA95	MATHEMATICAL RECREATIONS
QA276	MATHEMATICAL STATISTICS
Z250.6.M3	*MATHEMATICAL SYMBOLS* **SEE** TYPE AND TYPE-FOUNDING — MATHEMATICAL SYMBOLS
QA28-29	MATHEMATICIANS
Z6651-5	MATHEMATICS — BIO-BIBLIOGRAPHY
QA99	MATHEMATICS — CURIOSA AND MISCELLANY
QA31-35	MATHEMATICS — EARLY WORKS TO 1800
QA41	MATHEMATICS — FORMULAE
QA9	MATHEMATICS — PHILOSOPHY
QA43	MATHEMATICS — PROBLEMS, EXERCISES, ETC.
QA47-59	MATHEMATICS — TABLES, ETC.
QA5	MATHEMATICS — TERMINOLOGY
QA	MATHEMATICS
QA27.A	MATHEMATICS, ARABIC
QA22	MATHEMATICS, BABYLONIAN
QA27.C	MATHEMATICS, CHINESE
QA27.E3	MATHEMATICS, EGYPTIAN
QA22	MATHEMATICS, GREEK
QA27.I4	MATHEMATICS, HINDU
QA27.J3	MATHEMATICS, JAPANESE
QA23	MATHEMATICS, JEWISH
QA9	*MATHEMATICS, LOGIC OF* **SEE** MATHEMATICS — PHILOSOPHY
QA74	*MATHEMATICS-LABORATORIES* **SEE** COMPUTATION LABORATORIES
QA405	MATHIEU FUNCTIONS
BX4160.T4	*MATHURINS* **SEE** TRINITARIANS
PM4193	*MATLALTZINCA LANGUAGE* **SEE** MATLATZINCA LANGUAGE
F1221.M	MATLATZINCA INDIANS
PM4193	MATLATZINCA LANGUAGE
PM3981	*MATLAZAHUA LANGUAGE* **SEE** MAZAHUA LANGUAGE
GN480.4	MATRIARCHY
QA263	MATRICES / mathematics
HV6542	*MATRICIDE* **SEE** PARRICIDE
K	*MATRICIDE* **SEE** PARRICIDE
GN480.4	MATRILINEAL KINSHIP
GN480.4	*MATRILINY* **SEE** MATRILINEAL KINSHIP
HQ503-1057	*MATRIMONY* **SEE** MARRIAGE
GN480	*MATRIMONY* **SEE** MARRIAGE / ethnology
GR465	*MATRIMONY* **SEE** MARRIAGE / folk-lore
QC174.3	MATRIX MECHANICS
PM6466	*MATTACCO LANGUAGE* **SEE** MATACO LANGUAGE
QC173	MATTER — CONSTITUTION
QC171-197	MATTER — PROPERTIES
BD648	*MATTER AND FORM* **SEE** HYLOMORPHISM
BD493-708	MATTER / cosmology
BD331	MATTER / ontology
QC171-197	MATTER / physics
TS1779.M2	MATTING
PM1745.M3	MATTOLE LANGUAGE
TS1850	MATTRESSES
BF710	MATURATION (PSYCHOLOGY)
G690 1918	MAUD EXPEDITION, 1918-1925
F2520.1.M	MAUE INDIANS
F2520.1.M	*MAUES* **SEE** MAUE INDIANS
F2520.1.M	*MAUHE INDIANS* **SEE** MAUE INDIANS
BV94	MAUNDY THURSDAY
NB1800-1885	*MAUSOLEUMS* **SEE** SEPULCHRAL MONUMENTS / sculpture
NA6120-6199	*MAUSOLEUMS* **SEE** TOMBS / architecture

TK7872.A5	*MAVAR (ELECTRONICS)* **SEE** PARAMETRIC AMPLIFIERS
TK7872.A5	*MAVARS* **SEE** PARAMETRIC AMPLIFIERS
PL8432.M8	*MAVIA LANGUAGE* **SEE** MAKONDE LANGUAGE
DS491.M4	MAWKEN / *mergui archipelago*
UF620.M4	MAXIM GUN
TS535	MAXIM SILENCER
QA306	MAXIMA AND MINIMA / *calculus*
QA563	MAXIMA AND MINIMA / *geometry*
PN6299-6308	MAXIMS
HD7791	MAY DAY (LABOR HOLIDAY)
GT4945	MAY DAY
BX2161	*MAY DEVOTIONS* **SEE** MARY, VIRGIN — MAY DEVOTIONS
DS775	MAY FOURTH MOVEMENT
QL513.E7	MAY-FLIES
GT4945	MAY-POLE
B132.M	MAYA (HINDUISM)
F1435.3.C14	*MAYA CALENDAR* **SEE** CALENDAR, MAYA
F1435	*MAYA CHRONOLOGY* **SEE** CHRONOLOGY, MAYA
F1435.M4	*MAYA HYGIENE* **SEE** HYGIENE, MAYA
PM3961-9	MAYA LANGUAGE
PM3968.1	MAYA LITERATURE
F1435.3.R3	*MAYA MYTHOLOGY* **SEE** MAYAS — RELIGION AND MYTHOLOGY
F1435.3.N8	*MAYA NUMERATION* **SEE** NUMERATION, MAYA
PM3961-9	MAYAN LANGUAGES
F1435	MAYAS — ANTIQUITIES / *central america*
F1376	MAYAS — ANTIQUITIES / *yucatan*
F1435.3.R3	MAYAS — RELIGION AND MYTHOLOGY
F1376	MAYAS — WARS
F1435	MAYAS
F1435.3.C14	*MAYAS-CALENDAR* **SEE** CALENDAR, MAYA
F1435.M4	*MAYAS-HYGIENE* **SEE** HYGIENE, MAYA
F1435.3.N8	*MAYAS-NUMERATION* **SEE** NUMERATION, MAYA
QL513.E7	*MAYFLIES* **SEE** MAY-FLIES
F2230.2.M	MAYNA INDIANS
F1221.M	MAYO INDIANS
GN654	MAYOMBE / *anthropology*
DT650	MAYOMBE / *history*
JS143-163	MAYORS
JS3155-3161	MAYORS / *gt. brit.*
JS356-365	MAYORS / *u.s.*
F1221.M	*MAYOS* **SEE** MAYO INDIANS
PM3981	MAZAHUA LANGUAGE
PM3991	MAZATECO LANGUAGE
GV1507.M3	MAZE PUZZLES
BF433.M3	MAZE TESTS
NK4895	*MAZERS (DRINKING BOWLS)* **SEE** DRINKING VESSELS
GV1507.M3	*MAZES* **SEE** MAZE PUZZLES
DD338	*MAZOVIANS* **SEE** MASOVIANS
DD338	*MAZURIANS* **SEE** MASOVIANS
M1060	MAZURKAS (ORCHESTRA)
M1049	MAZURKAS (ORCHESTRA)
M310-314	MAZURKAS (PIANO TRIO)
M32	MAZURKAS (PIANO)
M1145	MAZURKAS (STRING ORCHESTRA)
M1160	MAZURKAS (STRING ORCHESTRA)
M217-218	MAZURKAS (VIOLIN AND PIANO)
M221-3	MAZURKAS (VIOLIN AND PIANO)
TP355	*MAZUT* **SEE** PETROLEUM AS FUEL
TJ619	*MAZUT* **SEE** PETROLEUM AS FUEL / *locomotives*
DT515	*MBA-TIVI* **SEE** TIVI (AFRICAN PEOPLE)
F2520.1.M	MBAYA INDIANS
PM6485	MBAYA LANGUAGE
PL8401-4	*MBOCHI LANGUAGE* **SEE** CONGO LANGUAGE
F2823.M	*MBOCOBI INDIANS* **SEE** MOCOBI INDIANS
BL2465	*MBOETI SECT* **SEE** BWITI SECT
PL8401-4	*MBOMA LANGUAGE* **SEE** CONGO LANGUAGE
DU742	MBOWAMB
BL2465	*MBUETI SECT* **SEE** BWITI SECT
PL8381	*MBUNDU LANGUAGE* **SEE** KIMBUNDU LANGUAGE
UB23	MCCARTHY-ARMY CONTROVERSY, 1954
HF1755	MCKINLEY TARIFF / *discussion*
HJ6085 1890	MCKINLEY TARIFF / *schedules*
E99.M435	MDEWAKANTON INDIANS
SB201.M	MEADOW FESCUE
QL696.P2	MEADOW-LARKS
SB199	MEADOWS
TS2120-2159	MEAL
LB3473-9	*MEALS FOR SCHOOL CHILDREN* **SEE** SCHOOL CHILDREN — FOOD
SB939	MEALY BUGS
SB945.M45	MEALY PLUM APHIS
BF778	MEANING (PSYCHOLOGY)
BF455	MEANING (PSYCHOLOGY) / *thought and language*
RA644.M5	MEASLES — PREVENTION
RC168.M4	MEASLES
Q375	*MEASURE OF UNCERTAINTY (INFORMATION THEORY)* **SEE** UNCERTAINTY (INFORMATION THEORY)
ML174	MEASURED MUSIC
VM880-881	*MEASURED-MILE TRIALS (SHIPS)* **SEE** SHIP TRIALS
GA23	*MEASUREMENT OF AREA* **SEE** AREA MEASUREMENT / *mathematical geography*
QC102	*MEASUREMENT OF DISTANCES* **SEE** DISTANCES — MEASUREMENT / *physics*
TA601	*MEASUREMENT OF DISTANCES* **SEE** DISTANCES — MEASUREMENT / *surveying*
QC102	*MEASUREMENT OF LENGTH* **SEE** LENGTH MEASUREMENT
QC243	*MEASUREMENT OF SOUND* **SEE** SOUND — MEASUREMENT
GB1201-1397	*MEASUREMENT OF STREAMS* **SEE** STREAM MEASUREMENTS / *physical geography*
QC102.5	*MEASUREMENT OF THICKNESS* **SEE** THICKNESS MEASUREMENT
TJ1166	*MEASUREMENT OF THICKNESS* **SEE** THICKNESS MEASUREMENT / *machine shop practice*
LB1131	*MEASUREMENT, MENTAL* **SEE** MENTAL TESTS
BF431	*MEASUREMENT, MENTAL* **SEE** MENTAL TESTS / *psychology*
BF39	*MEASUREMENT, MENTAL* **SEE** PSYCHOMETRICS
BF39	*MEASUREMENT, PSYCHOLOGICAL* **SEE** PSYCHOMETRICS
TL573	*MEASUREMENTS, AERODYNAMIC* **SEE** AERODYNAMIC MEASUREMENTS
TK275-399	*MEASUREMENTS, ELECTRIC* **SEE** ELECTRIC MEASUREMENTS / *electric engineering*
QC535	*MEASUREMENTS, ELECTRIC* **SEE** ELECTRIC MEASUREMENTS / *physics*
QC535	*MEASUREMENTS, ELECTRONIC* **SEE** ELECTRONIC MEASUREMENTS / *physics*
TK7882.M	*MEASUREMENTS, ELECTRONIC* **SEE** ELECTRONIC MEASUREMENTS / *electronics*
QC761	*MEASUREMENTS, MAGNETIC* **SEE** MAGNETIC MEASUREMENTS
QC818-849	*MEASUREMENTS, MAGNETIC* **SEE** MAGNETIC MEASUREMENTS / *terrestrial magnetism*
QC367	*MEASUREMENTS, OPTICAL* **SEE** OPTICAL MEASUREMENTS
QC39	*MEASUREMENTS, PHYSICAL* **SEE** PHYSICAL MEASUREMENTS
QC81-119	*MEASURES* **SEE** WEIGHTS AND MEASURES
RS57	*MEASURES* **SEE** WEIGHTS AND MEASURES / *pharmaceutical*
QA465	*MEASURING* **SEE** MENSURATION / *mathematics*
T50-51	*MEASURING* **SEE** MENSURATION / *technology*
TJ1313	MEASURING INSTRUMENTS / *machine-shop practice*
QC100.5	MEASURING INSTRUMENTS / *physical instruments*
TJ1313	*MEASURING TOOLS* **SEE** MEASURING INSTRUMENTS / *machine-shop practice*
QC100.5	*MEASURING TOOLS* **SEE** MEASURING INSTRUMENTS / *physical instruments*
QC104	MEASURING-PUMPS
TA579-581	MEASURING-TAPES / *surveying*
QR117	MEAT — BACTERIOLOGY
TX599-613	MEAT — PRESERVATION
TS1950-1975	*MEAT CONSUMPTION* **SEE** MEAT INDUSTRY AND TRADE
HD9410-9441	*MEAT CONSUMPTION* **SEE** MEAT INDUSTRY AND TRADE / *economics*
TS1962	MEAT CUTTING
TX389	MEAT EXTRACT
HF5716.M4	MEAT INDUSTRY AND TRADE — TABLES AND READY-RECKONERS
TS1950-1975	MEAT INDUSTRY AND TRADE
HD9410-9441	MEAT INDUSTRY AND TRADE / *economics*
HD9410.9	MEAT INSPECTION / *legislation*
TS1975	MEAT INSPECTION / *practice*

TS1950-1975	MEAT / animal products
TX743-753	MEAT / cookery
TX555-6	MEAT / etc.
TX371-389	MEAT / food supply
TS1962	MEAT-CUTTING SEE MEAT CUTTING
HD9410.9	MEAT-INSPECTION SEE MEAT INSPECTION / legislation
TS1975	MEAT-INSPECTION SEE MEAT INSPECTION / practice
TS1962	MEATCUTTING SEE MEAT CUTTING
TX739	MEATLESS MEALS SEE LENTEN MENUS
TX837	MEATLESS MEALS SEE LENTEN MENUS / with recipes
TX392	MEATLESS MEALS SEE VEGETARIANISM
TX837	MEATLESS MEALS SEE VEGETARIANISM / cookery
RM236	MEATLESS MEALS SEE VEGETARIANISM / therapeutics
PL4001.B3	MECH LANGUAGE SEE BARA LANGUAGE
T-TX	MECHANIC ARTS SEE INDUSTRIAL ARTS
BF433.M4	MECHANICAL ABILITY — TESTING
BF433.M4	MECHANICAL ABILITY TESTS SEE MECHANICAL ABILITY — TESTING
HF5688-9	MECHANICAL ARITHMETIC SEE CALCULATING-MACHINES / bookkeeping
QA75	MECHANICAL ARITHMETIC SEE CALCULATING-MACHINES / mechanical devices
NK4698	MECHANICAL BANKS SEE COIN BANKS
Q327	MECHANICAL BRAINS SEE CONSCIOUS AUTOMATA
QA76	MECHANICAL BRAINS SEE ELECTRONIC CALCULATING-MACHINES
S695	MECHANICAL CORN PICKERS SEE CORN PICKING MACHINERY
TJ335	MECHANICAL DRAFT
T351-377	MECHANICAL DRAWING
T379	MECHANICAL DRAWINGS SEE BLUE-PRINTS / mechanical drawing
T351.5	MECHANICAL DRAWING — STUDY AND TEACHING — — AUDIO-VISUAL AIDS
TJ144	MECHANICAL ENGINEERING — EARLY WORKS TO 1800
TJ151	MECHANICAL ENGINEERING — HANDBOOKS, MANUALS, ETC.
TJ148	MECHANICAL ENGINEERING — LABORATORIES
TA416-417	MECHANICAL ENGINEERING — LABORATORIES
TJ151	MECHANICAL ENGINEERING — TABLES, CALCULATIONS, ETC.
TJ	MECHANICAL ENGINEERING
QC312	MECHANICAL EQUIVALENT OF HEAT SEE HEAT, MECHANICAL EQUIVALENT OF
TA416-417	MECHANICAL LABORATORIES SEE ENGINEERING LABORATORIES
TJ248	MECHANICAL MODELS SEE MACHINERY — MODELS
TJ181-210	MECHANICAL MOVEMENTS
TT300-380	MECHANICAL PAINTING SEE PAINTING, INDUSTRIAL
NC749-750	MECHANICAL PERSPECTIVE SEE PERSPECTIVE
QA515	MECHANICAL PERSPECTIVE SEE PERSPECTIVE / geometry
T369	MECHANICAL PERSPECTIVE SEE PERSPECTIVE / mechanical drawing
TJ345	MECHANICAL STOKERS SEE STOKERS, MECHANICAL
P307-310	MECHANICAL TRANSLATING SEE MACHINE TRANSLATING
QC122-168	MECHANICS / experimental
QA801-935	MECHANICS / theoretical
QA801-935	MECHANICS, ANALYTIC
TA350	MECHANICS, APPLIED
QB351-421	MECHANICS, CELESTIAL
HD8055	MECHANICS' INSTITUTES
HD6519	MECHANICS' INSTITUTES / u.s. local
HD4934.M5-7	MECHANICS' LIENS
TJ1180	MECHANISMS, INTERCHANGEABLE SEE INTERCHANGEABLE MECHANISMS
TJ233	MECHANISMS, INTERCHANGEABLE SEE INTERCHANGEABLE MECHANISMS
HF5679	MECHANIZED ACCOUNTING SEE MACHINE ACCOUNTING
RM719-727	MECHANOTHERAPY
E215.9	MECKLENBURG DECLARATION OF INDEPENDENCE
F1221.C53	MECO INDIANS SEE CHICHIMECA-JONAZ INDIANS
QL601	MECOPTERA

UB435.l	MEDAGLIA D'ORO
UB433	MEDAL OF HONOR
VB333	MEDAL OF HONOR
BX2310.M5	MEDAL OF ST. BENEDICT
CJ5501-6651	MEDALISTS
CJ5501-6651	MEDALLIONS SEE MEDALS
CJ5501-6651	MEDALS
CJ5581-5690	MEDALS, ANCIENT
UB430-435	MEDALS, MILITARY AND NAVAL / military
VB330-335	MEDALS, MILITARY AND NAVAL / naval
CJ5501-6651	MEDALS-COLLECTIONS SEE' MEDALS
CJ5501-6651	MEDALS-PRIVATE COLLECTIONS SEE MEDALS
E99.M435	MEDAWAKANTON INDIANS SEE MDEWAKANTON INDIANS
RC754	MEDIASTINUM — DISEASES
RD667	MEDIASTINUM — TUMORS
QM261	MEDIASTINUM / human anatomy
JX4475	MEDIATION, INTERNATIONAL
BF1718	MEDICAL ASTROLOGY
QR46	MEDICAL BACTERIOLOGY SEE BACTERIOLOGY, MEDICAL
UB368-9.5	MEDICAL CARE OF VETERANS SEE VETERANS — MEDICAL CARE
RC963	MEDICAL CARE, INDUSTRIAL SEE LABOR AND LABORING CLASSES — MEDICAL CARE
HV3000-3003	MEDICAL CHARITIES SEE CHARITIES, MEDICAL
HV687-694	MEDICAL CHARITIES SEE CHARITIES, MEDICAL
RA960-996	MEDICAL CHARITIES SEE CHARITIES, MEDICAL / hospitals
RS402-431	MEDICAL CHEMISTRY SEE CHEMISTRY, MEDICAL AND PHARMACEUTICAL
RA791-954	MEDICAL CLIMATOLOGY SEE CLIMATOLOGY, MEDICAL
R735-832	MEDICAL COLLEGES
R118	MEDICAL COMMUNICATION SEE COMMUNICATION IN MEDICINE
R133	MEDICAL DELUSIONS
R728	MEDICAL ECONOMICS
RA410-415	MEDICAL ECONOMICS
RM869-890	MEDICAL ELECTRICITY SEE ELECTROTHERAPEUTICS
R895	MEDICAL ELECTRONICS
RA639-641	MEDICAL ENTOMOLOGY SEE INSECTS AS CARRIERS OF DISEASE
R724-5	MEDICAL ETHICS
RB37-55	MEDICAL EXAMINATIONS SEE DIAGNOSIS / laboratory methods
RC71-78	MEDICAL EXAMINATIONS SEE DIAGNOSIS / practice of medicine
HG8886-8891	MEDICAL EXAMINATIONS SEE INSURANCE, ACCIDENT — MEDICAL EXAMINATIONS
HG8886-8891	MEDICAL EXAMINATIONS SEE INSURANCE, HEALTH — MEDICAL EXAMINATIONS
HG8886-8891	MEDICAL EXAMINATIONS SEE INSURANCE, LIFE — MEDICAL EXAMINATIONS
RC990-991	MEDICAL EXAMINATIONS SEE PENSIONS, MEDICAL EXAMINATIONS FOR
HQ1018.M4	MEDICAL EXAMINATIONS SEE PREMARITAL EXAMINATIONS
R840	MEDICAL FELLOWSHIPS SEE MEDICINE — SCHOLARSHIPS, FELLOWSHIPS, ETC.
RS125-7	MEDICAL FORMULARIES SEE MEDICINE — FORMULAE, RECEIPTS, PRESCRIPTIONS
RA791-954	MEDICAL GEOGRAPHY
RM719-721	MEDICAL GYMNASTICS SEE GYMNASTICS, MEDICAL
R781	MEDICAL GYMNASTICS SEE GYMNASTICS, MEDICAL
R836	MEDICAL ILLUSTRATION
RA972	MEDICAL INTERNS SEE INTERNS (MEDICINE)
PN4784.M4	MEDICAL JOURNALISM SEE JOURNALISM, MEDICAL
RA1001-1171	MEDICAL JURISPRUDENCE
RA11-405	MEDICAL LAWS AND LEGISLATION
Z675.M4	MEDICAL LIBRARIES
R723	MEDICAL LOGIC
QR63	MEDICAL MICROBIOLOGY — LABORATORY MANUALS
RB43	MEDICAL MICROSCOPY SEE MICROSCOPY, MEDICAL
SF255	MEDICAL MILK COMMISSIONS SEE MILK COMMISSIONS, MEDICAL
RA390-392	MEDICAL MISSIONS SEE MISSIONS, MEDICAL
R722	MEDICAL MISSIONS SEE MISSIONS, MEDICAL
R871-891	MEDICAL MUSEUMS
RC117	MEDICAL MYCOLOGY

R728	MEDICAL OFFICE MANAGEMENT
RA11-405	*MEDICAL PERSONNEL-LEGAL STATUS, LAWS, ETC.* **SEE** MEDICAL LAWS AND LEGISLATION
TR705	*MEDICAL PHOTOGRAPHY* **SEE** PHOTOGRAPHY, MEDICAL
R895	MEDICAL PHYSICS
R	*MEDICAL PROFESSION* **SEE** MEDICINE
GT6330-6370	*MEDICAL PROFESSION* **SEE** PHYSICIANS / *manners and customs*
UH400	*MEDICAL PROFESSION* **SEE** PHYSICIANS / *military*
UH221-324	*MEDICAL PROFESSION* **SEE** PHYSICIANS / *military*
VG100-224	*MEDICAL PROFESSION* **SEE** PHYSICIANS / *naval*
R707	*MEDICAL PROVERBS* **SEE** MEDICINE — QUOTATIONS, MAXIMS, ETC.
RA11-405	*MEDICAL REGISTRATION AND EXAMINATION* **SEE** MEDICAL LAWS AND LEGISLATION
R840	*MEDICAL SCHOLARSHIPS* **SEE** MEDICINE — SCHOLARSHIPS, FELLOWSHIPS, ETC.
R728	MEDICAL SECRETARIES
R10-99	MEDICAL SOCIETIES
RA418	*MEDICAL SOCIOLOGY* **SEE** SOCIAL MEDICINE
R737	*MEDICAL SPECIALIZATION* **SEE** MEDICINE — SPECIALTIES AND SPECIALISTS
RA407-9	MEDICAL STATISTICS / *etc.*
RA11-388	MEDICAL STATISTICS / *reports*
R133	*MEDICAL SUPERSTITIONS* **SEE** MEDICAL DELUSIONS
UH440-445	MEDICAL SUPPLIES / *military*
VG290-295	MEDICAL SUPPLIES / *naval*
RC835	*MEDICAL TELEVISION* **SEE** TELEVISION IN MEDICAL EDUCATION
RC75	*MEDICAL THERMOMETERS* **SEE** ·THERMOMETERS AND THERMOMETRY, MEDICAL
RA791-954	*MEDICAL TOPOGRAPHY* **SEE** MEDICAL GEOGRAPHY
RM822.V2	*MEDICATED BATHS* **SEE** BATHS, MEDICATED
RM647-8	*MEDICATION, ANTISEPTIC* **SEE** ANTISEPTIC MEDICATION
RM163	*MEDICATION, RECTAL* **SEE** RECTUM, MEDICATION BY
PN6231.M4	MEDICINE — ANECDOTES, FACETIAE, SATIRE, ETC.
R705	MEDICINE — ANECDOTES, FACETIAE, SATIRE, ETC.
R126	MEDICINE — APHORISMS
R128.7	MEDICINE — APHORISMS
R153-684	MEDICINE — BIOGRAPHY / *by country*
R134	MEDICINE — BIOGRAPHY / *collected*
R121	MEDICINE — DICTIONARIES
RC58	MEDICINE — EXAMINATIONS, QUESTIONS, ETC.
RS125-7	MEDICINE — FORMULAE, RECEIPTS, PRESCRIPTIONS
R131-684	MEDICINE — HISTORY
R835	MEDICINE — INFORMATION SERVICES
R723	MEDICINE — PHILOSOPHY
RC	MEDICINE — PRACTICE
R707	MEDICINE — QUOTATIONS, MAXIMS, ETC.
R840	MEDICINE — SCHOLARSHIPS, FELLOWSHIPS, ETC.
M1978.M4	MEDICINE — SONGS AND MUSIC
M1977.M4	MEDICINE — SONGS AND MUSIC
R737	MEDICINE — SPECIALTIES AND SPECIALISTS
R735-832	MEDICINE — STUDY AND TEACHING
R123	MEDICINE — TERMINOLOGY
R128.6-7	MEDICINE — 15TH-18TH CENTURIES
N8223	MEDICINE AND ART
BL65.M4	*MEDICINE AND CHRISTIANITY* **SEE** MEDICINE AND RELIGION
RC89	*MEDICINE AND CHRISTIANITY* **SEE** MEDICINE AND RELIGION / *pastoral medicine*
BP166.72	MEDICINE AND ISLAM
BL65.M4	MEDICINE AND RELIGION
RC89	MEDICINE AND RELIGION / *pastoral medicine*
R690	MEDICINE AS A PROFESSION
N8223	*MEDICINE IN ART* **SEE** MEDICINE AND ART
PN56.M	MEDICINE IN LITERATURE
GV1801-1827	MEDICINE SHOWS
GV1017.M5	MEDICINE-BALL
GN477	MEDICINE-MAN / *ethnology*
E98.M4	MEDICINE-MAN / *indians of north america*
R	MEDICINE
R135	MEDICINE, ANCIENT
RC91	*MEDICINE, ATOMIC* **SEE** ATOMIC MEDICINE
R135.5	*MEDICINE, BIBLICAL* **SEE** BIBLE — MEDICINE, HYGIENE, ETC.
RZ422	MEDICINE, BIOCHEMIC
RV1-10	MEDICINE, BOTANIC
RZ414	MEDICINE, CHRONOTHERMAL
RC89	*MEDICINE, CLERICAL* **SEE** PASTORAL MEDICINE
BT732	*MEDICINE, CLERICAL* **SEE** PASTORAL MEDICINE / *theology*
RC31	MEDICINE, CLINICAL — HOSPITAL REPORTS
RB37	MEDICINE, CLINICAL — LABORATORY MANUALS
RC61-69	MEDICINE, CLINICAL
R118	*MEDICINE, COMMUNICATION IN* **SEE** COMMUNICATION IN MEDICINE
RK301-450	*MEDICINE, DENTAL* **SEE** TEETH — DISEASES
RK318-320	*MEDICINE, DENTAL* **SEE** THERAPEUTICS, DENTAL
RZ416	MEDICINE, DOSIMETRIC
RV	MEDICINE, ECLECTIC
RM886	*MEDICINE, ELECTROLYSIS IN* **SEE** ELECTROLYSIS IN MEDICINE
RZ422	*MEDICINE, ELECTROMAGNETISM IN* **SEE** ELECTROMAGNETISM IN MEDICINE
R850-854	MEDICINE, EXPERIMENTAL
RA1001-1171	*MEDICINE, FORENSIC* **SEE** MEDICAL JURISPRUDENCE
RC963-9	MEDICINE, INDUSTRIAL
RA1001-1171	*MEDICINE, LEGAL* **SEE** MEDICAL JURISPRUDENCE
R133	MEDICINE, MAGIC, MYSTIC, AND SPAGIRIC
R128	MEDICINE, MEDIEVAL
RC970-971	MEDICINE, MILITARY / *medical practice*
UH	MEDICINE, MILITARY / *military science*
RC981-6	MEDICINE, NAVAL / *medical practice*
VG	MEDICINE, NAVAL / *naval science*
RC89	*MEDICINE, PASTORAL* **SEE** PASTORAL MEDICINE
BT732	*MEDICINE, PASTORAL* **SEE** PASTORAL MEDICINE / *theology*
RM133	MEDICINE, PHYSIOMEDICAL
RC81-82	MEDICINE, POPULAR
RA421-790	MEDICINE, PREVENTIVE
GN477	MEDICINE, PRIMITIVE
RC49-52	MEDICINE, PSYCHOSOMATIC
RA418	*MEDICINE, SOCIAL* **SEE** SOCIAL MEDICINE
RA	MEDICINE, STATE
RC1000	*MEDICINE, SUBMARINE* **SEE** SUBMARINE MEDICINE
RC960-962	*MEDICINE, TROPICAL* **SEE** TROPICS — DISEASES AND HYGIENE / *tropical medicine*
UH611	*MEDICINE, TROPICAL* **SEE** TROPICS — DISEASES AND HYGIENE / *military hygiene*
VG471	*MEDICINE, TROPICAL* **SEE** TROPICS — DISEASES AND HYGIENE / *naval hygiene*
RA789	*MEDICINE, TROPICAL* **SEE** TROPICS — DISEASES AND HYGIENE / *hygiene*
SF600-998	*MEDICINE, VETERINARY* **SEE** VETERINARY MEDICINE
Z695.1.M48	*MEDICINE-CATALOGING* **SEE** CATALOGING OF MEDICAL LITERATURE
R840	*MEDICINE-FELLOWSHIPS* **SEE** MEDICINE — SCHOLARSHIPS, FELLOWSHIPS, ETC.
RD71-78	*MEDICINE-INSTRUMENTS* **SEE** SURGICAL INSTRUMENTS AND APPARATUS
RA11-405	*MEDICINE-LAWS AND LEGISLATION* **SEE** MEDICAL LAWS AND LEGISLATION
RA418	*MEDICINE-SOCIAL ASPECTS* **SEE** SOCIAL MEDICINE
RA11-405	*MEDICINE-STATE CONTROL* **SEE** MEDICAL LAWS AND LEGISLATION
RC835	*MEDICINE-STUDY AND TEACHING* **SEE** TELEVISION IN MEDICAL EDUCATION
R133	*MEDICINE-SUPERSTITIONS* **SEE** MEDICAL DELUSIONS
RM300	MEDICINES, ANTAGONISM OF
RM671	MEDICINES, PATENT, PROPRIETARY, ETC.
RM	*MEDICINES, PHYSIOLOGICAL EFFECT OF* **SEE** PHARMACOLOGY
QP903-981	*MEDICINES, PHYSIOLOGICAL EFFECT OF* **SEE** PHARMACOLOGY / *experimental*
RS	MEDICINES, SPECIFIC
HF5686.P9	MEDICINE — PRACTICE — — ACCOUNTING
NA350-497	*MEDIEVAL ARCHITECTURE* **SEE** ARCHITECTURE, MEDIEVAL
N5940-6311	*MEDIEVAL ART* **SEE** ART, MEDIEVAL
LA85-98	*MEDIEVAL EDUCATION* **SEE** EDUCATION, MEDIEVAL
D111-203	*MEDIEVAL HISTORY* **SEE** MIDDLE AGES — HISTORY
ML170-190	*MEDIEVAL MUSIC* **SEE** MUSIC — HISTORY AND CRITICISM — — MEDIEVAL
ML170-174	*MEDIEVAL MUSIC* **SEE** MUSIC — THEORY — — MEDIEVAL

BR250-270	*MEDIEVAL SECTS* **SEE** SECTS, MEDIEVAL
BL1478.6	MEDITATION (BUDDHISM)
BV4813	MEDITATION / *christianity*
BL627	MEDITATION / *comparative religion*
BV4800-4870	MEDITATIONS
BX2177-2198	MEDITATIONS / *catholic church*
RC123.B7	*MEDITERRANEAN FEVER* **SEE** UNDULANT FEVER
SB945.M5	MEDITERRANEAN FLOUR-MOTH
SB945.M54	MEDITERRANEAN FRUIT-FLY
GN543	MEDITERRANEAN RACE
CB224	MEDITERRANEAN RACE / *civilization*
BF1281	MEDIUMS
QL933	MEDULLA OBLONGATA / *comparative anatomy*
QM455	MEDULLA OBLONGATA / *human anatomy*
QP377	MEDULLA OBLONGATA / *physiology*
QM569	*MEDULLA OSSIUM* **SEE** MARROW
RC280.C	MEDULLOBLASTOMA
QL375-9	MEDUSAE
QE777-9	MEDUSAE, FOSSIL
TN948.M5	MEERSCHAUM
E99.M69	*MEEWOC INDIANS* **SEE** MIWOK INDIANS
GN791-2	MEGALITHIC MONUMENTS
VK584.S65	*MEGAPHONE* **SEE** SPEAKING-TRUMPET
PL8625	*MEGI LANGUAGE* **SEE** SAGARA LANGUAGE
DT86	MEGIDDO, BATTLE OF, 1479 B.C.
DS422.M5	MEGPUNNA
PJ7111-7114	*MEHRE LANGUAGE* **SEE** MAHRI LANGUAGE
E99.M18	*MEIDOO INDIANS* **SEE** MAIDU INDIANS
NK4380	MEISSEN PORCELAIN
PT245	MEISTERSINGER / *literature*
ML183	MEISTERSINGER / *music*
BX3795.M6	MEKHITARISTS
RC862	MELAENA
RC518	MELANCHOLIA
PL6201-9	MELANESIAN LANGUAGES
RL790	*MELANISM* **SEE** MELANOSIS
GN543	*MELANOCHROIC RACE* **SEE** MEDITERRANEAN RACE
CB224	*MELANOCHROIC RACE* **SEE** MEDITERRANEAN RACE / *civilization*
RC262	MELANOMA
QL767	*MELANOPHORES* **SEE** CHROMATOPHORES
RL790	MELANOSIS
QE461	MELAPHYRE
E99.M195	*MELICETE INDIANS* **SEE** MALECITE INDIANS
TP290.L8	MELINITE
RC168.M45	MELIOIDOSIS
ML975-6	*MELLOPHONE* **SEE** ALTO HORN
ML597	*MELODEON* **SEE** REED-ORGAN
ML2050	MELODRAMA / *history*
PN1910-1919	MELODRAMA / *literature*
ML3861	MELODRAMA / *music aesthetics*
ML3851	MELODY / *aesthetics*
ML440	MELODY / *history*
MT47	MELODY / *instruction*
ML3834	MELODY / *psychology*
ML1090	*MELOGRAPH* **SEE** MUSIC-RECORDERS
SB608.M4	MELON-FLIES
SB608.M4	MELONS — DISEASES AND PESTS
SB339	MELONS
QD518	MELTING POINTS
QM131	*MEMBRANES, SYNOVIAL* **SEE** SYNOVIAL MEMBRANES
RC746	*MEMBRANOUS CROUP* **SEE** CROUP
CT25	*MEMOIRS* **SEE** AUTOBIOGRAPHY
CT	*MEMOIRS* **SEE** BIOGRAPHY
BF380-385	*MEMORIA TECHNICA* **SEE** MNEMONICS / *psychology*
M1629.3.M3	MEMORIAL DAY — SONGS AND MUSIC
E642	MEMORIAL DAY ADDRESSES
E645	MEMORIAL DAY ADDRESSES, CONFEDERATE
E642	MEMORIAL DAY
E645	MEMORIAL DAY, CONFEDERATE
NB1800-1885	*MEMORIAL TABLETS* **SEE** SEPULCHRAL MONUMENTS / *sculpture*
TK7872.M4	*MEMORY DEVICES* **SEE** MAGNETIC MEMORY (CALCULATING-MACHINES)
BF380-385	*MEMORY TRAINING* **SEE** MNEMONICS / *psychology*
TK7872.S7	*MEMORY TUBES* **SEE** STORAGE TUBES
LB1063	MEMORY / *educational*
BF370-385	MEMORY / *psychology*
BF376	MEMORY, DISORDERS OF
RA408.M	MEN — MORTALITY
BJ1855	*MEN'S ETIQUETTE* **SEE** ETIQUETTE FOR MEN / *american*
TT572-630	MEN'S FURNISHING GOODS
QL73	MENAGERIES
PL5415	MENANGKABAU LANGUAGE
DH92.M	MENAPII
BT1405	*MENDAEANS* **SEE** MANDAEANS
PL8511	MENDE LANGUAGE
DT516	MENDE / *sierra leone*
QH421-431	MENDEL'S LAW
HV4480-4630	*MENDICANCY* **SEE** BEGGING
HV6174	*MENDICANCY* **SEE** BEGGING / *pauperism and crime*
BX2820	*MENDICANT ORDERS* **SEE** FRIARS
TT151	*MENDING* **SEE** REPAIRING
E99.I7	*MENGWE INDIANS* **SEE** IROQUOIS INDIANS
SH351.M5	MENHADEN FISHERIES
QL638.C64	MENHADEN
GN790-792	MENHIRS
RF270	MENIERE'S DISEASE
QL835	MENINGEAL ARTERY
QM191	MENINGEAL ARTERY
QL933-7	MENINGES / *comparative anatomy*
QM469	MENINGES / *human anatomy*
RD663	MENINGIOMA
RC124	MENINGITIS
RC376	MENINGITIS
SF799	MENINGITIS / *veterinary medicine*
RC124	MENINGITIS, CEREBROSPINAL
RC124	*MENINGOCOCCIC MENINGITIS* **SEE** MENINGITIS, CEREBROSPINAL
BX8128.C	*MENNONITE COLONIZATION* **SEE** MENNONITES — COLONIZATION
BX8141	*MENNONITE CONVERTS* **SEE** CONVERTS, MENNONITE
TH7458.G7	MENNONITE GRASS-BURNER
BX8128.C	MENNONITES — COLONIZATION
BX8129.A1	MENNONITES — PARTIES AND MOVEMENTS
BX8101-8143	MENNONITES
BX8141	*MENNONITES-CONVERTS* **SEE** CONVERTS, MENNONITE
E99.M44	MENOMINEE INDIANS
PM1761	MENOMINEE LANGUAGE
PM1761	*MENOMONI LANGUAGE* **SEE** MENOMINEE LANGUAGE
BM657.M	MENORAH
RG161-186	MENSTRUATION
QA465	MENSURATION / *mathematics*
T50-51	MENSURATION / *technology*
BF365-7	*MENTAL ASSOCIATION* **SEE** ASSOCIATION OF IDEAS
QP445	*MENTAL CHRONOMETRY* **SEE** TIME PERCEPTION
BF632	*MENTAL CULTURE* **SEE** MENTAL DISCIPLINE / *psychology*
BF173	*MENTAL DEPRESSION* **SEE** DEPRESSION, MENTAL
BF632	MENTAL DISCIPLINE / *psychology*
BF173	*MENTAL DISEASES* **SEE** PSYCHOLOGY, PATHOLOGICAL
RC512-528	*MENTAL DISEASES* **SEE** PSYCHOSES
RC532	*MENTAL EPIDEMICS* **SEE** HYSTERIA, EPIDEMIC
RA788	*MENTAL EXHAUSTION* **SEE** FATIGUE, MENTAL / *mental hygiene*
QP421	*MENTAL EXHAUSTION* **SEE** FATIGUE, MENTAL / *physiology*
RC351	*MENTAL EXHAUSTION* **SEE** FATIGUE, MENTAL / *popular works*
BF481	*MENTAL EXHAUSTION* **SEE** FATIGUE, MENTAL / *psychology*
RA788	*MENTAL FATIGUE* **SEE** FATIGUE, MENTAL / *mental hygiene*
QP421	*MENTAL FATIGUE* **SEE** FATIGUE, MENTAL / *physiology*
RC351	*MENTAL FATIGUE* **SEE** FATIGUE, MENTAL / *popular works*
BF481	*MENTAL FATIGUE* **SEE** FATIGUE, MENTAL / *psychology*
RZ400-406	MENTAL HEALING
RA790	*MENTAL HEALTH* **SEE** MENTAL HYGIENE
RA790	MENTAL HYGIENE

RC455	*MENTAL ILLNESS AND ART* **SEE** ART AND MENTAL ILLNESS / *medicine*
RA1151	*MENTAL ILLNESS AND LAW* **SEE** INSANITY — JURISPRUDENCE
N8237.5	*MENTAL ILLNESS IN ART* **SEE** PSYCHIATRY IN ART
RA788	*MENTAL OVERWORK* **SEE** FATIGUE, MENTAL / *mental hygiene*
QP421	*MENTAL OVERWORK* **SEE** FATIGUE, MENTAL / *physiology*
RC351	*MENTAL OVERWORK* **SEE** FATIGUE, MENTAL / *popular works*
BF481	*MENTAL OVERWORK* **SEE** FATIGUE, MENTAL / *psychology*
B-BJ	*MENTAL PHILOSOPHY* **SEE** PHILOSOPHY
RA790	*MENTAL PHYSIOLOGY AND HYGIENE* **SEE** MENTAL HYGIENE
BV4813	*MENTAL PRAYER* **SEE** MEDITATION / *christianity*
BL627	*MENTAL PRAYER* **SEE** MEDITATION / *comparative religion*
BF1111-1156	MENTAL SUGGESTION
BF431	MENTAL TESTS — TERMINOLOGY
LB1131	MENTAL TESTS
BF431	MENTAL TESTS / *psychology*
BF80	*MENTAL TESTS-APPARATUS AND INSTRUMENTS* **SEE** PSYCHOLOGICAL APPARATUS
LC4601-4700	MENTALLY HANDICAPPED CHILDREN — EDUCATION
RC435-576	MENTALLY ILL — CARE AND TREATMENT
RA1151	*MENTALLY ILL-LEGAL STATUS, LAWS, ETC.* **SEE** INSANITY — JURISPRUDENCE
PL5421	*MENTAVEI LANGUAGE* **SEE** MENTAWI LANGUAGE
PL5421	MENTAWI LANGUAGE
RM666.M	MENTHOL / *therapeutics*
RS165.M	MENTHOL / *vegetable drugs*
QD341.K2	MENTHONE
TX727-8	MENUS
QL737.C2	*MEPHITIS* **SEE** SKUNKS
SF405.S6	*MEPHITIS* **SEE** SKUNKS / *animal culture*
PL6621.M3	*MERAUKESE LANGUAGE* **SEE** MARINDINESE LANGUAGE
NA6210-6280	MERCANTILE BUILDINGS
HF1201-1400	*MERCANTILE LAW* **SEE** COMMERCIAL LAW
VK	*MERCANTILE MARINE* **SEE** MERCHANT MARINE / *navigation*
HE731-953	*MERCANTILE MARINE* **SEE** MERCHANT MARINE / *transportation*
HB91	MERCANTILE SYSTEM
QD305.A4	MERCAPTANS / *chemistry*
QP917.M4	MERCAPTANS / *experimental pharmacology*
BX3800	MERCEDARIANS
TS1515	MERCERIZATION
BX9571	MERCERSBURG THEOLOGY
HF1041-1051	*MERCHANDISE* **SEE** COMMERCIAL PRODUCTS
HF5845-9	*MERCHANDISE, DISPLAY OF* **SEE** DISPLAY OF MERCHANDISE
HF481-491	*MERCHANT COMPANIES* **SEE** COLONIAL COMPANIES
HD6451-6473	*MERCHANT COMPANIES* **SEE** GILDS / *history*
HD2341-6	*MERCHANT COMPANIES* **SEE** GILDS / *modern*
VK221	MERCHANT MARINE — OFFICERS
VK200	MERCHANT MARINE — SAFETY MEASURES
VK381-397	MERCHANT MARINE — SIGNALING
VK	MERCHANT MARINE / *navigation*
HE731-953	MERCHANT MARINE / *transportation*
HE605	*MERCHANT MARINE-ACCOUNTING* **SEE** SHIPPING — ACCOUNTING
VK235-7	*MERCHANT MARINE-CARGO* **SEE** SHIPS — CARGO
JX4408-4449	*MERCHANT MARINE-LAW* **SEE** MARITIME LAW / *international law*
JX63	*MERCHANT MARINE-LAW* **SEE** MARITIME LAW / *private*
HE565-6	*MERCHANT MARINE-LISTS OF VESSELS* **SEE** SHIP REGISTERS
K221	*MERCHANT MARINE-MANNING OF VESSELS* **SEE** SHIPS — MANNING
HE594	*MERCHANT MARINE-RATES* **SEE** SHIPPING — RATES
HE597	*MERCHANT MARINE-RATES* **SEE** SHIPPING — RATES / *by countries*
VG470-475	*MERCHANT MARINE-SANITARY AFFAIRS* **SEE** NAVAL HYGIENE

T325	*MERCHANT MARKS* **SEE** TRADE-MARKS
T221-323	*MERCHANT MARKS* **SEE** TRADE-MARKS / *by country*
HE591	MERCHANT SEAMEN — ACCOMMODATIONS ON SHIPBOARD
BV2660-2678	MERCHANT SEAMEN — MISSIONS AND CHARITIES
HV3025-3163	MERCHANT SEAMEN — MISSIONS AND CHARITIES / *charities*
PN6110.S4	*MERCHANT SEAMEN'S SONGS* **SEE** SAILORS' SONGS / *literature*
M1977.S2	*MERCHANT SEAMEN'S SONGS* **SEE** SAILORS' SONGS / *music*
M1978.S2	*MERCHANT SEAMEN'S SONGS* **SEE** SAILORS' SONGS / *music*
HV3025-3163	*MERCHANT SEAMEN-CHARITIES* **SEE** MERCHANT SEAMEN — MISSIONS AND CHARITIES / *charities*
BV2660-2678	*MERCHANT SEAMEN-CHARITIES* **SEE** MERCHANT SEAMEN — MISSIONS AND CHARITIES
VK235-7	*MERCHANT SHIPS-CARGO* **SEE** SHIPS — CARGO
JX4408-4449	*MERCHANT SHIPS-LAW AND LEGISLATION* **SEE** MARITIME LAW / *international law*
JX63	*MERCHANT SHIPS-LAW AND LEGISLATION* **SEE** MARITIME LAW / *private*
HE565-6	*MERCHANT SHIPS-REGISTERS* **SEE** SHIP REGISTERS
JX4449.N3	*MERCHANT SHIPS-REGISTRY* **SEE** SHIPS — NATIONALITY
VK200	*MERCHANT SHIPS-SAFETY MEASURES* **SEE** MERCHANT MARINE — SAFETY MEASURES
QD181.H6	MERCURIC OXIDE
TN790	MERCURY — METALLURGY
QP913.H6	MERCURY — PHYSIOLOGICAL EFFECT
RM666.M5	MERCURY — THERAPEUTIC USE
RA1231.M5	MERCURY — TOXICOLOGY
QB371	MERCURY (PLANET) — TABLES
QB611	MERCURY (PLANET) / *descriptive astronomy*
QB371	MERCURY (PLANET) / *theoretical astronomy*
QB515	MERCURY (PLANET), TRANSIT OF
TL215.M	MERCURY AUTOMOBILE
QD181.H6	MERCURY COMPOUNDS
QD412.H6	MERCURY COMPOUNDS / *organic*
QD571	*MERCURY DROPPING ELECTRODES* **SEE** ELECTRODES, DROPPING MERCURY
TK4381	*MERCURY ELECTRIC LIGHT* **SEE** ELECTRIC LIGHTING, MERCURY VAPOR
QD181.H6	MERCURY HALOIDS
TN460-469	MERCURY MINES AND MINING
TN460-469	MERCURY ORES
QD181.H6	MERCURY OXYCHLORIDES
TL789.8	*MERCURY PROJECT* **SEE** PROJECT MERCURY
TK2798	MERCURY-ARC RECTIFIERS
QD181.H6	MERCURY / *chemistry*
QD181.H6	MERCURY, SULPHUR COMPOUNDS OF
R726	*MERCY DEATH* **SEE** EUTHANASIA
BV4647.M4	MERCY
BV4647.M4	*MERCY, CORPORAL WORKS OF* **SEE** CORPORAL WORKS OF MERCY
M1264	MERENGUES (BAND) — SCORES
M1248	MERENGUES (BAND) — SCORES
M1264	MERENGUES (BAND)
M1248	MERENGUES (BAND)
M1350	MERENGUES (DANCE ORCHESTRA)
M31	MERENGUES (PIANO)
M310-314	MERENGUES (PIANO, 2 VIOLINS)
QL696.A5	MERGANSERS
QB207	MERIDIAN LINES
QB101	*MERIDIAN-CIRCLE* **SEE** TRANSIT-CIRCLE
QB101	MERIDIAN-MARKS
QB224	*MERIDIAN, PRIME* **SEE** LONGITUDE — PRIME MERIDIAN
PL5379	MERINA DIALECT
DT319	*MERINIDES* **SEE** BENI MARIN DYNASTY
SF373.M5-55	MERINO SHEEP / *flock books*
QK725	MERISTEM
BT773	MERIT (CHRISTIANITY)
BP166.33	MERIT (ISLAM)
BM645.M4	MERIT (JEWISH THEOLOGY)
BT773	*MERIT (THEOLOGY)* **SEE** MERIT (CHRISTIANITY)
BM645.M4	*MERIT OF THE FATHERS* **SEE** MERIT (JEWISH THEOLOGY)
JK681-699	*MERIT SYSTEM* **SEE** CIVIL SERVICE REFORM / *u.s.*
GR910	MERMAIDS

QA331	*MEROMORPHIC FUNCTIONS* **SEE** FUNCTIONS, MEROMORPHIC
N6243	*MEROVINGIAN ART* **SEE** ART, MEROVINGIAN
DC65-69	MEROVINGIANS / *france*
DD128	MEROVINGIANS / *germany*
M175.C3	*MERRY-GO-ROUND MUSIC* **SEE** CALLIOPE MUSIC
QL876-881	*MERY'S GLANDS* **SEE** COWPER'S GLANDS / *comparative anatomy*
QM416-421	*MERY'S GLANDS* **SEE** COWPER'S GLANDS / *human anatomy*
QP265	*MERY'S GLANDS* **SEE** COWPER'S GLANDS / *physiology*
QP257	*MERY'S GLANDS* **SEE** COWPER'S GLANDS / *physiology*
RC840	MERYCISM
QK495.C11	*MESCAL (CACTUS)* **SEE** PEYOTE / *cactus*
RS165.A7	*MESCAL (CACTUS)* **SEE** PEYOTE / *vegetable drugs*
QK495.C11	*MESCAL BUTTONS* **SEE** PEYOTE / *cactus*
RS165.A7	*MESCAL BUTTONS* **SEE** PEYOTE / *vegetable drugs*
TP607.M	MESCAL
PL65.M	*MESCERAK LANGUAGE* **SEE** MISHAR LANGUAGE
RD667	MESENTERY — TUMORS
QL864	MESENTERY / *comparative anatomy*
QM367	MESENTERY / *human anatomy*
PL65.M	*MESHCHERA LANGUAGE* **SEE** MISHAR LANGUAGE
QD341.H9	MESITYLENE
E99.F7	*MESKWAKI INDIANS* **SEE** FOX INDIANS
BF1111-1156	MESMERISM / *hypnotism*
RM917-926	MESMERISM / *therapeutics*
GN775-6	*MESOLITHIC PERIOD* **SEE** STONE AGE
QL872	*MESONEPHROS* **SEE** WOLFFIAN BODY
DS79	MESOPOTAMIA — HISTORY — — INSURRECTION, 1920
QD181.T5	MESOTHORIUM
QL391.M	MESOZOA
QE675-688	*MESOZOIC PERIOD* **SEE** GEOLOGY, STRATIGRAPHIC — MESOZOIC
QE921-4	*MESOZOIC PERIOD* **SEE** PALEOBOTANY — MESOZOIC
QE731-4	*MESOZOIC PERIOD* **SEE** PALEONTOLOGY — MESOZOIC
QD419	MESQUITE
UC700-780	*MESS* **SEE** ARMIES — COMMISSARIAT
BT1417	MESSALIANS
PA2394	MESSAPIAN LANGUAGE
BT235	MESSIAH — PROPHECIES
BT230-240	MESSIAH
BL475	MESSIAH / *comparative religion*
BM615-620	MESSIAH / *judaism*
BM752	*MESSIAHS, FALSE* **SEE** PSEUDO-MESSIAHS
DG828	MESSINA — EARTHQUAKE, 1908
HD6473.S7S4	MESTA
QP801.A	*METABOLIC ANTAGONISTS* **SEE** ANTIMETABOLITES
QH521	METABOLISM / *biology*
QH631	METABOLISM / *cytology*
QP171	METABOLISM / *physiology*
RX331	METABOLISM, DISORDERS OF — HOMEOPATHIC TREATMENT
RB147	METABOLISM, DISORDERS OF / *pathology*
RC803	METABOLISM, DISORDERS OF / *treatment*
TS718	METAL BONDING
TS710	*METAL COLORING* **SEE** METALS — COLORING
TK7882.M4	*METAL DETECTION* **SEE** METAL DETECTORS
TK7882.M4	METAL DETECTORS
NE800	*METAL ENGRAVERS* **SEE** ENGRAVERS / *collective*
NE805	*METAL ENGRAVERS* **SEE** ENGRAVERS / *individual*
NE501-794	*METAL ENGRAVERS* **SEE** ENGRAVERS / *individual*
TS360	METAL FOILS
HD9506-9539	*METAL INDUSTRIES* **SEE** METAL TRADE
HD9743-7	*METAL INDUSTRIES* **SEE** METAL-WORK / *economics*
NK6400-8450	*METAL INDUSTRIES* **SEE** METAL-WORK / *fine arts*
TS200-770	*METAL INDUSTRIES* **SEE** METAL-WORK / *manufactures*
TT205-273	*METAL INDUSTRIES* **SEE** METAL-WORK / *mechanic trades*
TN	*METAL INDUSTRIES* **SEE** MINERAL INDUSTRIES
TS360	*METAL LEAF* **SEE** METAL FOILS
TK7882.M4	*METAL LOCATORS* **SEE** METAL DETECTORS
NE2540-2560	*METAL PLATE PROCESSES-LITHOGRAPHY* **SEE** LITHOGRAPHY — METAL PLATE PROCESSES
TS245	*METAL POWDER PROCESSING* **SEE** POWDER METAL PROCESSES
TH5281	*METAL SCAFFOLDING* **SEE** SCAFFOLDING, METAL
NB1220	METAL SCULPTURE
TS655	METAL SPRAYING
TS213	METAL TRADE — VOCATIONAL GUIDANCE
HD9510-9529	*METAL TRADE* **SEE** IRON INDUSTRY AND TRADE
HD9506-9539	METAL TRADE
QD181.N15	METAL-AMMONIA COMPOUNDS
TS718	*METAL-BONDING TO GLASS* **SEE** GLASS-METAL SEALING
TJ1215-1240	METAL-CUTTING / *machine-tools*
TS718	*METAL-GLASS SEALING* **SEE** GLASS-METAL SEALING
TT206	METAL-SPINNING
TS718	*METAL-TO-GLASS SEALING* **SEE** GLASS-METAL SEALING
NK6400-8450	METAL-WORK — COLLECTORS AND COLLECTING
TT205	METAL-WORK — STUDY AND TEACHING (SECONDARY)
HD9743-7	METAL-WORK / *economics*
NK6400-8450	METAL-WORK / *fine arts*
TS200-770	METAL-WORK / *manufactures*
TT205-273	METAL-WORK / *mechanic trades*
TH1651-5	*METAL-WORK, ARCHITECTURAL* **SEE** ARCHITECTURAL METAL-WORK
TA685	*METAL-WORK, ARCHITECTURAL* **SEE** ARCHITECTURAL METAL-WORK
TT	*METAL-WORK, ART* **SEE** ART METAL-WORK
TS	*METAL-WORK, ART* **SEE** ART METAL-WORK
NK6400-8450	*METAL-WORK, ART* **SEE** ART METAL-WORK
HD7269.M5-52	METAL-WORKERS — DISEASES AND HYGIENE
HD9506-9539	METAL-WORKERS
TJ1180-1338	METAL-WORKING MACHINERY / *machine-tools*
HD9705	METAL-WORKING MACHINERY / *trade*
QC761	*METALLIC ALLOYS* **SEE** ALLOYS / *magnetic induction*
TA490	*METALLIC ALLOYS* **SEE** ALLOYS / *materials of engineering*
TN690	*METALLIC ALLOYS* **SEE** ALLOYS / *metallography*
TS650	*METALLIC ALLOYS* **SEE** ALLOYS / *technology*
TA460	*METALLIC CREEP* **SEE** CREEP OF METALS
TN690	METALLIC FILMS / *metallography*
TP992	METALLIC SOAPS
RM910	*METALLIC TRACTORS* **SEE** TRACTORS, METALLIC / *therapeutics*
TS655	*METALLIZING* **SEE** METAL SPRAYING
TS710	*METALLOCHROMY* **SEE** METALS — COLORING
TN690-693	METALLOGRAPHY
QD133	*METALLURGIC CHEMISTRY* **SEE** CHEMISTRY, METALLURGIC
TN565	METALLURGICAL ANALYSIS / *assaying*
QD133	METALLURGICAL ANALYSIS / *chemistry*
TN570-571	METALLURGICAL LABORATORIES
Z699.5.M4	*METALLURGICAL LITERATURE SEARCHING* **SEE** INFORMATION STORAGE AND RETRIEVAL SYSTEMS — METALLURGY
TN677	METALLURGICAL PLANTS
TN673	METALLURGICAL RESEARCH
TN139-140	METALLURGISTS
TN673	METALLURGY — APPARATUS AND SUPPLIES
TN6	METALLURGY — CATALOGS AND COLLECTIONS
TN669	METALLURGY — LABORATORY MANUALS
TN671	METALLURGY — TABLES, CALCULATIONS, ETC.
TN673	METALLURGY AS A PROFESSION
TN600-799	METALLURGY
RK653	*METALLURGY, DENTAL* **SEE** DENTISTRY — METALLURGY
TN690	*METALLURGY, PHYSICAL* **SEE** PHYSICAL METALLURGY
TN695	*METALLURGY, POWDER* **SEE** POWDER METALLURGY
TN673	*METALLURGY-RESEARCH* **SEE** METALLURGICAL RESEARCH
QD133-7	METALS — ANALYSIS
TS462	METALS — COLD WORKING
TS710	METALS — COLORING
NE2700	METALS — ETCHING
TA460	METALS — FATIGUE

TS213	METALS — FINISHING
QP903-913	METALS — PHYSIOLOGICAL EFFECT
TA467	METALS — PICKLING
HD9506-9539	METALS — PRICES
TA461	METALS — SPECIFICATIONS
TA459-492	METALS — TESTING
RM666	METALS — THERAPEUTIC USE
TA460	METALS — THERMAL PROPERTIES
BL457.M4	METALS (IN RELIGION, FOLK-LORE, ETC.)
RD91.5.M	METALS AS ANTISEPTICS
QP531	METALS IN THE BODY
QD171-2	METALS / chemistry
TN400-490	METALS / mining
TS462	METALS, COLD WORKING OF SEE METALS — COLD WORKING
TN700	METALS, HEAT RESISTANT SEE HEAT RESISTANT ALLOYS
TN758	METALS, NONFERROUS SEE NONFERROUS METALS
TS214	METALS, SCRAP SEE SCRAP METALS
QD24-26.5	METALS, TRANSMUTATION OF SEE ALCHEMY
QD13	METALS, TRANSMUTATION OF SEE ALCHEMY / history
QD461	METALS, TRANSMUTATION OF SEE TRANSMUTATION (CHEMISTRY)
TS718	METALS-BONDING SEE METAL BONDING
TA462	METALS-CORROSION SEE CORROSION AND ANTI-CORROSIVES
TA467	METALS-CORROSION SEE CORROSION AND ANTI-CORROSIVES
TA460	METALS-CREEP SEE CREEP OF METALS
TS250	METALS-DEEP DRAWING SEE DEEP DRAWING (METAL-WORK)
TK7882.M4	METALS-DETECTION SEE METAL DETECTORS
TA460	METALS-EROSION SEE EROSION OF METALS
TS255	METALS-EXTRUSION SEE EXTRUSION (METALS)
TS227	METALS-HARD-FACING SEE HARD-FACING
TS256	METALS-HIGH ENERGY FORMING SEE HIGH ENERGY FORMING
TN690-693	METALS-MICROSCOPIC STRUCTURE SEE METALLOGRAPHY
TS213	METALS-PEENING SEE SHOT PEENING
VM147	METALSMITHS, NAVAL SEE U.S. — METALSMITHS
HD9743-7	METALWORK SEE METAL-WORK / economics
NK6400-8450	METALWORK SEE METAL-WORK / fine arts
TS200-770	METALWORK SEE METAL-WORK / manufactures
TT205-273	METALWORK SEE METAL-WORK / mechanic trades
QA9	METAMATHEMATICS
QE475	METAMORPHIC ROCKS SEE ROCKS, CRYSTALLINE AND METAMORPHIC
BL325.M4	METAMORPHOSIS (IN RELIGION, FOLK-LORE, ETC.)
QL496	METAMORPHOSIS (INSECTS) SEE INSECTS — DEVELOPMENT
QL981	METAMORPHOSIS
PN228.M4	METAPHOR
BD	METAPHYSICS
BF1001-1389	METAPSYCHOLOGY SEE PSYCHICAL RESEARCH
BD331	METAPSYCHOLOGY SEE SPIRITUALISM / metaphysics
B851-4695	METAPSYCHOLOGY SEE SPIRITUALISM / philosophic systems
B841	METAPSYCHOLOGY SEE SPIRITUALISM / philosophic systems
BF1001-1389	METAPSYCHOLOGY SEE SPIRITUALISM / spiritism
QD181.A6	METARGON
HD1478	METAYER SYSTEM
QL45-50	METAZOA
BL525	METEMPSYCHOSIS SEE TRANSMIGRATION / comparative religion
BD426	METEMPSYCHOSIS SEE TRANSMIGRATION / philosophy
QE399	METEORIC GLASS SEE TEKTITE
QB755	METEORITES / astronomy
QE395	METEORITES / mineralogy
QB981	METEORITIC HYPOTHESIS
QC876	METEOROLOGICAL INSTRUMENTS
Z675.M	METEOROLOGICAL LIBRARIES
QC878	METEOROLOGICAL MAPS SEE METEOROLOGY — CHARTS, DIAGRAMS, ETC.
QC983-994	METEOROLOGICAL OBSERVATIONS SEE METEOROLOGY — OBSERVATIONS / reports
QC871-4	METEOROLOGICAL OBSERVATIONS SEE METEOROLOGY — OBSERVATIONS / methods
QC875	METEOROLOGICAL OBSERVATORIES SEE METEOROLOGICAL STATIONS
QC975-6	METEOROLOGICAL OPTICS
QC877	METEOROLOGICAL REPORTS, RADIO SEE WEATHER REPORTING, RADIO
QC869	METEOROLOGICAL RESEARCH
TL798.M4	METEOROLOGICAL SATELLITES
QC875	METEOROLOGICAL STATIONS
QC876	METEOROLOGY — CATALOGS AND COLLECTIONS
QC878	METEOROLOGY — CHARTS, DIAGRAMS, ETC.
QC859	METEOROLOGY — EARLY WORKS TO 1800
QC869	METEOROLOGY — EXAMINATIONS, QUESTIONS, ETC.
QC863	METEOROLOGY — JUVENILE LITERATURE
QC871	METEOROLOGY — OBSERVATION BLANKS
QC871-4	METEOROLOGY — OBSERVATIONS / methods
QC983-994	METEOROLOGY — OBSERVATIONS / reports
QC871	METEOROLOGY — OBSERVERS' MANUALS
QC883	METEOROLOGY — PERIODICITY
QC873	METEOROLOGY — TABLES, ETC.
QC869.5	METEOROLOGY AS A PROFESSION
TL556-8	METEOROLOGY IN AERONAUTICS
TA197	METEOROLOGY IN ENGINEERING SEE ENGINEERING METEOROLOGY
S600	METEOROLOGY, AGRICULTURAL / crops and climate
QC994	METEOROLOGY, MARITIME
QC872	METEOROLOGY-CIPHER AND TELEGRAPH CODES SEE CIPHER AND TELEGRAPH CODES — METEOROLOGY
QC875	METEOROLOGY-OBSERVATORIES SEE METEOROLOGICAL STATIONS
QC869	METEOROLOGY-RESEARCH SEE METEOROLOGICAL RESEARCH
QB85	METEOROSCOPE
QB746	METEORS — AUGUST
QB745	METEORS — NOVEMBER
QB741-755	METEORS
QC91-94	METER (STANDARD OF LENGTH) SEE METRIC SYSTEM / weights and measures
ML3850	METER SEE MUSICAL METER AND RHYTHM / aesthetics
ML437	METER SEE MUSICAL METER AND RHYTHM / history of composition
MT42	METER SEE MUSICAL METER AND RHYTHM / instruction in composition
ML3813	METER SEE MUSICAL METER AND RHYTHM / physics acoustics
MT233	METER SEE MUSICAL METER AND RHYTHM / piano
ML3832	METER SEE MUSICAL METER AND RHYTHM / psychology
PN1031-1055	METER SEE VERSIFICATION
HE6497.M4	METERED MAIL SEE POSTAL SERVICE — METERED MAIL / u.s.
TK301-399	METERS, ELECTRIC SEE ELECTRIC METERS
TC177	METERS, FLOW SEE FLOW METERS
TH7940	METERS, GAS SEE GAS-METERS
TC177	METERS, WATER SEE WATER-METERS / hydraulics
TD499-500	METERS, WATER SEE WATER-METERS / water-supply
SB952	METHALLYL CHLORIDE
QD305.H6	METHANE
RA1242.W8	METHANOL SEE WOOD-ALCOHOL / toxicology
QA275	METHOD OF LEAST SQUARES SEE LEAST SQUARES
LB1049	METHOD OF STUDY SEE STUDY, METHOD OF
LC63	METHOD OF STUDY SEE STUDY, METHOD OF / examinations
BX8201-8495	METHODISM
BX8251-3	METHODIST CHURCH (CANADA)
BX8276-8	METHODIST CHURCH (ENGLAND)
BX8380-8389	METHODIST CHURCH (UNITED STATES)
BX8201-8495	METHODIST CHURCH
BX8346	METHODIST CLASS MEETINGS SEE CLASS MEETINGS, METHODIST
BX8335	METHODIST EPISCOPAL CHURCH — CATECHISMS AND CREEDS

BV415	METHODIST EPISCOPAL CHURCH — HYMNS
M2127	METHODIST EPISCOPAL CHURCH — HYMNS / vocal music
BV2550	METHODIST EPISCOPAL CHURCH — MISSIONS
BX8380-8389	METHODIST EPISCOPAL CHURCH
BX8390-8399	METHODIST EPISCOPAL CHURCH, SOUTH
BX8201-8495	METHODISTS
BX8435-8473	*METHODISTS, COLORED* **SEE** METHODISTS, NEGRO
BX8435-8473	METHODISTS, NEGRO
BD240-241	METHODOLOGY
RA1242.W8	*METHYL ALCOHOL* **SEE** WOOD-ALCOHOL / toxicology
QD305.A8	METHYLAMINES
TP593	*METHYLATED SPIRIT* **SEE** ALCOHOL, DENATURED / technology
HD9399	*METHYLATED SPIRIT* **SEE** ALCOHOL, DENATURED / trade
RA1242.W8	*METHYLATED SPIRIT* **SEE** WOOD-ALCOHOL / toxicology
DF277	METICS
F1063	*METIS REBELLION, 1869-1870* **SEE** RED RIVER REBELLION, 1869-1870
F1060.9	*METIS REBELLION, 1885* **SEE** RIEL REBELLION, 1885
BF840-861	*METOPOSCOPY* **SEE** PHYSIOGNOMY
QA613	*METRIC SPACES* **SEE** DISTANCE GEOMETRY
QC94	METRIC SYSTEM — CONVERSION TABLES
QC93	METRIC SYSTEM — TEXT-BOOKS
QC91-94	METRIC SYSTEM / weights and measures
QA613	*METRIC TOPOLOGY* **SEE** DISTANCE GEOMETRY
QA465	*METROLOGY* **SEE** MENSURATION / mathematics
T50-51	*METROLOGY* **SEE** MENSURATION / technology
QC81-119	*METROLOGY* **SEE** WEIGHTS AND MEASURES
RS57	*METROLOGY* **SEE** WEIGHTS AND MEASURES / pharmaceutical
ML1080	*METROMETER* **SEE** METRONOME
ML1080	METRONOME
DC102.544	METZ — SIEGE, 1444
DC114	METZ — SIEGE, 1552
DC304	METZ — SIEGE, 1870
TR976	*METZOGRAPH* **SEE** MEZZOGRAPH
D756.5.M4	MEUSE, BATTLE OF THE, 1940 — MONTHERME
D756.5.M4	MEUSE, BATTLE OF THE, 1940
E99.M69	*MEWAN INDIANS* **SEE** MIWOK INDIANS
PQ7260	MEXICAN BALLADS AND SONGS / collections
PQ7180	MEXICAN BALLADS AND SONGS / history
SB945.M59	MEXICAN BEAN BEETLE
SB945.C8	*MEXICAN BOLL-WEEVIL* **SEE** BOLL-WEEVIL
F1219.3.C2	*MEXICAN CALENDAR* **SEE** CALENDAR, MEXICAN
SB945.C8	*MEXICAN COTTON-BOLL WEEVIL* **SEE** BOLL-WEEVIL
PQ7264-7270	MEXICAN DRAMA / collections
PQ7183-7195	MEXICAN DRAMA / history
SF805	*MEXICAN FEVER* **SEE** TEXAS FEVER
PQ7275-6	MEXICAN FICTION / collections
PQ7197-7207	MEXICAN FICTION / history
PM4061-9	*MEXICAN LANGUAGE* **SEE** AZTEC LANGUAGE
PQ7231-7293	MEXICAN LITERATURE / collections
PQ7100-7221	MEXICAN LITERATURE / history
PN4961-4979	MEXICAN NEWSPAPERS / history
PQ7279	MEXICAN ORATIONS / collections
PQ7209	MEXICAN ORATIONS / history
PN4961-4980	MEXICAN PERIODICALS / history
PQ7249-7263	MEXICAN POETRY / collections
PQ7161-7181	MEXICAN POETRY / history
PQ7272-7287	MEXICAN PROSE LITERATURE / collections
PQ7197-7221	MEXICAN PROSE LITERATURE / history
E401-415	*MEXICAN WAR, 1845-1848* **SEE** UNITED STATES — HISTORY — — WAR WITH MEXICO, 1845-1848
PN6222.M4	MEXICAN WIT AND HUMOR / collections
PQ7286	MEXICAN WIT AND HUMOR / collections
PQ7215	MEXICAN WIT AND HUMOR / history
E184.M5	MEXICANS IN THE U.S.
F1203-1409	MEXICO — HISTORY
E401-415	*MEXICO-HISTORY-WAR WITH THE U.S., 1845-1848* **SEE** UNITED STATES — HISTORY — — WAR WITH MEXICO, 1845-1848
F1234	MEXICO — FRONTIER TROUBLES — — TO 1910
F786	MEXICO — FRONTIER TROUBLES — — TO 1910 / new southwest
F391	MEXICO — FRONTIER TROUBLES — — TO 1910 / texas
F1234	MEXICO — FRONTIER TROUBLES — — 1910-
F786	MEXICO — FRONTIER TROUBLES — — 1910- / new southwest
F391	MEXICO — FRONTIER TROUBLES — — 1910- / texas
DC309.M4	MEZIERES, FRANCE — SIEGE, 1870-1871
BM657.M4	MEZUZAH
TR976	MEZZOGRAPH
NE1815	MEZZOTINT ENGRAVING
NE1815	MEZZOTINTERS
NE1815	MEZZOTINTS
BP166.57	MI'RAJ
E99.M48	MIAMI INDIANS
PM1781	MIAMI LANGUAGE
F483	MIAMI PURCHASE
PL3311.M5	MIAO LANGUAGE
DS731.M5	MIAO PEOPLE
QE391.M	MIARGYRITE / mineralogy
TN430-439	MIARGYRITE / silver ores
TN933	MICA
GR730.M	MICE (IN RELIGION, FOLK-LORE, ETC.) / folk-lore
BL325.M5	MICE (IN RELIGION, FOLK-LORE, ETC.) / mythology
QL737.R6	MICE
QH581	MICELLAR THEORY
DT515	*MICHI* **SEE** TIVI (AFRICAN PEOPLE)
F561-575	MICHIGAN — HISTORY
QA76.5	*MICHIGAN ALGORITHM DECODER* **SEE** MAD (COMPUTER PROGRAM LANGUAGE)
QA76.8.S4	*MICHIGAN DIGITAL AUTOMATIC COMPUTER* **SEE** SEAC COMPUTER
TK7889.S4	*MICHIGAN DIGITAL AUTOMATIC COMPUTER* **SEE** SEAC COMPUTER / engineering
E514	MICHIGAN — HISTORY — — CIVIL WAR
E359.5.M	MICHIGAN — HISTORY — — WAR OF 1812
PM4296-9	*MICHOACANA LANGUAGE* **SEE** TARASCAN LANGUAGE
PM4296-9	*MICHUACANA LANGUAGE* **SEE** TARASCAN LANGUAGE
E99.M6	*MICKMAK INDIANS* **SEE** MICMAC INDIANS
E99.M6	MICMAC INDIANS
PM1791-4	MICMAC LANGUAGE
QR69	MICRO-ORGANISMS — DRYING
QR	MICRO-ORGANISMS / bacteriology
QH201-277	MICRO-ORGANISMS / microscopy
QR84	MICRO-ORGANISMS, NITROGEN-FIXING
QR113	MICRO-ORGANISMS, NITROGEN-FIXING / root nodules
QR175-351	MICRO-ORGANISMS, PATHOGENIC
QC107	MICROBALANCE
QR75-84	*MICROBES* **SEE** BACTERIA
QR	*MICROBES* **SEE** BACTERIOLOGY
RB214	*MICROBES* **SEE** GERM THEORY OF DISEASE
QR	*MICROBES* **SEE** MICRO-ORGANISMS / bacteriology
QH201-277	*MICROBES* **SEE** MICRO-ORGANISMS / microscopy
QR360	*MICROBES* **SEE** VIRUSES
QR65	MICROBIOLOGY — LABORATORY MANUALS
QR	MICROBIOLOGY
QR53	*MICROBIOLOGY, INDUSTRIAL* **SEE** INDUSTRIAL MICROBIOLOGY
QR106	*MICROBIOLOGY, MARINE* **SEE** MARINE MICROBIOLOGY
QR46	*MICROBIOLOGY, SANITARY* **SEE** SANITARY MICROBIOLOGY
QC291-7	*MICROCALORIMETRY* **SEE** CALORIMETERS AND CALORIMETRY
TR835	*MICROCARDS-READER-PRINTERS* **SEE** READER-PRINTERS (MICROPHOTOGRAPHY)
QM691	MICROCEPHALY
QH543	MICROCLIMATOLOGY / ecology
QC982.7	MICROCLIMATOLOGY / meteorology
BD493-523	MICROCOSM AND MACROCOSM
Z265	*MICROFILM BOOKS* **SEE** BOOKS ON MICROFILM
TR835	*MICROFILMING* **SEE** MICROPHOTOGRAPHY
Z265	*MICROFILMING* **SEE** MICROPHOTOGRAPHY / library science
TR835	*MICROFILMS-READER-PRINTERS* **SEE** READER-PRINTERS (MICROPHOTOGRAPHY)
TR835	*MICROFORM READER-PRINTERS* **SEE** READER-PRINTERS (MICROPHOTOGRAPHY)
QM691	MICROGNATHIA
RD526	MICROGNATHIA / surgery

TN690-693	*MICROGRAPHIC ANALYSIS* **SEE** METALLOGRAPHY
QH201-277	*MICROGRAPHIC ANALYSIS* **SEE** MICROSCOPE AND MICROSCOPY
QC165	*MICROMANOMETER* **SEE** MANOMETER
QC102	MICROMETER
QB113	MICROMETER / *astronomy*
TK7870	*MICROMINIATURIZATION (ELECTRONICS)* **SEE** MINIATURE ELECTRONIC EQUIPMENT
PL6191-5	MICRONESIAN LANGUAGES
QE721	MICROPALEONTOLOGY
TK6478	MICROPHONE
TR835	MICROPHOTOGRAPHY
Z265	MICROPHOTOGRAPHY / *library science*
QC391	MICROPHOTOMETER
QC277	MICROPYROMETER
TR835	*MICROREADER-PRINTERS* **SEE** READER-PRINTERS (MICROPHOTOGRAPHY)
QP121	*MICRORESPIROMETER* **SEE** RESPIROMETER
QH271	MICROSCOPE AND MICROSCOPY — EARLY WORKS TO 1800
QH277	MICROSCOPE AND MICROSCOPY — JUVENILE LITERATURE
QH207	MICROSCOPE AND MICROSCOPY — TECHNIQUE
QH201-277	MICROSCOPE AND MICROSCOPY
TN690-693	*MICROSCOPIC ANALYSIS* **SEE** METALLOGRAPHY
QH201-277	*MICROSCOPIC ANALYSIS* **SEE** MICROSCOPE AND MICROSCOPY
QM550-575	*MICROSCOPIC ANATOMY* **SEE** HISTOLOGY
QR	*MICROSCOPIC ORGANISMS* **SEE** MICRO-ORGANISMS / *bacteriology*
QH201-277	*MICROSCOPIC ORGANISMS* **SEE** MICRO-ORGANISMS / *microscopy*
QH207	*MICROSCOPICAL TECHNIQUE* **SEE** MICROSCOPE AND MICROSCOPY — TECHNIQUE
RB43	MICROSCOPY, MEDICAL
QE539	MICROSEISMS
TK7870	*MICROSTRIP* **SEE** MICROWAVE WIRING
QH207	*MICROTECHNIQUE* **SEE** MICROSCOPE AND MICROSCOPY — TECHNIQUE
QH233	MICROTOME
TK7872.M45	*MICROWAVE AMPLIFICATION BY STIMULATED EMISSION OF RADIATION* **SEE** MASERS
TK7872.A5	*MICROWAVE AMPLIFICATION BY VARIABLE REACTANCE* **SEE** PARAMETRIC AMPLIFIERS
QC447	MICROWAVE LENSES / *physics*
TK6590.M5	MICROWAVE LENSES / *radar*
QC973	*MICROWAVE METEOROLOGY* **SEE** RADIO METEOROLOGY
TK6553	*MICROWAVE RADIO* **SEE** RADIO, SHORT WAVE
TK7870	MICROWAVE WIRING
QA76.8.S4	*MIDAC COMPUTER* **SEE** SEAC COMPUTER
TK7889.S4	*MIDAC COMPUTER* **SEE** SEAC COMPUTER / *engineering*
RA776	MIDDLE AGE / *hygiene*
QP84	MIDDLE AGE / *physiology*
RC967	MIDDLE AGE / *practice of medicine*
D111-203	MIDDLE AGES — HISTORY
D118	MIDDLE AGES — HISTORY, JUVENILE
CB351-5	MIDDLE AGES / *civilization*
HT680-690	MIDDLE CLASSES
PE501-685	*MIDDLE ENGLISH* **SEE** ENGLISH LANGUAGE — MIDDLE ENGLISH (1100-1500)
PR1119-1121	*MIDDLE ENGLISH* **SEE** ENGLISH LITERATURE — MIDDLE ENGLISH (1100-1500) / *collections*
PR251-369	*MIDDLE ENGLISH* **SEE** ENGLISH LITERATURE — MIDDLE ENGLISH (1100-1500) / *history*
PF4043-4350	*MIDDLE HIGH GERMAN LANGUAGE* **SEE** GERMAN LANGUAGE — MIDDLE HIGH GERMAN
PT1375-1479	*MIDDLE HIGH GERMAN LITERATURE* **SEE** GERMAN LITERATURE — MIDDLE HIGH GERMAN / *collections*
PT175-230	*MIDDLE HIGH GERMAN LITERATURE* **SEE** GERMAN LITERATURE — MIDDLE HIGH GERMAN / *history*
P911	*MIDDLE KHOTANESE LANGUAGE* **SEE** KHOTANESE LANGUAGE
F106	MIDDLE STATES — HISTORY
E188	MIDDLE STATES — HISTORY — — COLONIAL PERIOD
E230.5.M6	MIDDLE STATES — HISTORY — — REVOLUTION
BT32	*MIDDLE THINGS* **SEE** ADIAPHORA

QL531-8	*MIDGES* **SEE** DIPTERA
TL236.5	*MIDGET CARS* **SEE** KARTS (MIDGET CARS)
GN681	*MIDGETS* **SEE** DWARFS / *ethnography*
GR555	*MIDGETS* **SEE** DWARFS / *folk-lore*
GN69.3-5	*MIDGETS* **SEE** DWARFS / *somatology*
BM511-518	MIDRASH
V415	MIDSHIPMEN
VB315.G7	MIDSHIPMEN / *gt. brit.*
D774.M5	MIDWAY, BATTLE OF, 1942
BV28	*MIDWEEK SERVICES* **SEE** CHURCH-NIGHT SERVICES
RG	*MIDWIFERY* **SEE** OBSTETRICS
RG950	MIDWIVES
F390	MIER EXPEDITION, 1842
HD5855-6	MIGRANT LABOR
QL698	*MIGRATION OF BIRDS* **SEE** BIRDS — MIGRATION
QL639	*MIGRATION OF FISHES* **SEE** FISHES — MIGRATION
QL496	*MIGRATION OF INSECTS* **SEE** INSECTS — MIGRATION
QD561	*MIGRATION OF IONS* **SEE** IONS — MIGRATION AND VELOCITY
QK101	*MIGRATION OF PLANTS* **SEE** PLANTS — MIGRATION
HB1951-2580	MIGRATION, INTERNAL
GF101	*MIGRATIONS OF MAN* **SEE** MAN — MIGRATIONS / *anthropo-geography*
GN370	*MIGRATIONS OF MAN* **SEE** MAN — MIGRATIONS / *ethnology*
D135-149	MIGRATIONS OF NATIONS
SK351-579	*MIGRATORY BIRDS, PROTECTION OF* **SEE** BIRDS, PROTECTION OF / *game-laws*
QL671	*MIGRATORY BIRDS, PROTECTION OF* **SEE** BIRDS, PROTECTION OF / *etc.*
HD5855-6	*MIGRATORY WORKERS* **SEE** MIGRANT LABOR
F1221.M67	*MIJE INDIANS* **SEE** MIXE INDIANS
PM4011	*MIJE LANGUAGE* **SEE** MIXE LANGUAGE
PL4001.M5	MIKIR LANGUAGE
BR180	*MILAN, EDICT OF* **SEE** EDICT OF MILAN, 313
SB741.M65	MILDEW
VK572	MILE, NAUTICAL
G86	MILE, ROMAN
HE1951-2100	*MILEAGE TICKETS* **SEE** RAILROADS — FARES
TF654	*MILEAGE TICKETS* **SEE** RAILROADS — TICKETS
HE1971	*MILEAGE TICKETS* **SEE** RAILROADS — TICKETS / *economics*
E99.M195	*MILICETE INDIANS* **SEE** MALECITE INDIANS
JX1937-1964	MILITARISM
U21	MILITARISM
UA10	MILITARISM
UB	MILITARY ADMINISTRATION
UG630-670	*MILITARY AERONAUTICS* **SEE** AERONAUTICS, MILITARY
JX5124	*MILITARY AERONAUTICS* **SEE** AERONAUTICS, MILITARY / *international law*
TL685.3	*MILITARY AEROPLANES* **SEE** AEROPLANES, MILITARY
NA490-497	MILITARY ARCHITECTURE / *architecture*
UG460	MILITARY ARCHITECTURE / *military science*
U26	MILITARY ART AND SCIENCE — ABBREVIATIONS
U24-26	MILITARY ART AND SCIENCE — DICTIONARIES
U101	MILITARY ART AND SCIENCE — EARLY WORKS TO 1800
U408.5	MILITARY ART AND SCIENCE — EXAMINATIONS, QUESTIONS, ETC. / *u.s.*
U400-714	MILITARY ART AND SCIENCE — EXAMINATIONS, QUESTIONS, ETC.
U513	MILITARY ART AND SCIENCE — EXAMINATIONS, QUESTIONS, ETC. / *gt. brit.*
U27-43	MILITARY ART AND SCIENCE — HISTORY
U106	MILITARY ART AND SCIENCE — JUVENILE LITERATURE
U130-135	MILITARY ART AND SCIENCE — OFFICERS' HANDBOOKS
U110-115	MILITARY ART AND SCIENCE — SOLDIERS' HANDBOOKS
U26	MILITARY ART AND SCIENCE — TERMINOLOGY
U	MILITARY ART AND SCIENCE
UG680-685	*MILITARY AUTOMOBILES* **SEE** AUTOMOBILES, MILITARY
UG630-670	*MILITARY AVIATION* **SEE** AERONAUTICS, MILITARY
JX5124	*MILITARY AVIATION* **SEE** AERONAUTICS, MILITARY / *international law*
TL609-639	*MILITARY BALLOONS* **SEE** BALLOONS
UC780	MILITARY BASES — WATER-SUPPLY
UH30-35	*MILITARY BICYCLES* **SEE** MILITARY CYCLING

U51-55	MILITARY BIOGRAPHY
UB370-375	*MILITARY BOUNTIES* **SEE** BOUNTIES, MILITARY
UG335	MILITARY BRIDGES
MT735	MILITARY CALLS — HANDBOOKS, MANUALS, ETC.
M1270	MILITARY CALLS
UH40-45	MILITARY CALLS
UC400-405	*MILITARY CAMPS* **SEE** CAMPS (MILITARY)
U180-185	*MILITARY CAMPS* **SEE** CAMPS (MILITARY)
UG365	*MILITARY CAMPS* **SEE** CAMPS (MILITARY) / *camp making*
UB147	*MILITARY CAREER* **SEE** MILITARY SERVICE AS A PROFESSION
U350-365	MILITARY CEREMONIES, HONORS, AND SALUTES
GV1469.M6	MILITARY CHESS
UA940-945	*MILITARY COMMUNICATIONS* **SEE** COMMUNICATIONS, MILITARY
JX5321	*MILITARY CONTRIBUTIONS* **SEE** REQUISITIONS, MILITARY / *international law*
UC15	*MILITARY CONTRIBUTIONS* **SEE** REQUISITIONS, MILITARY / *military science*
UC720-735	*MILITARY COOKERY* **SEE** COOKERY, MILITARY
UC480-485	*MILITARY COSTUME* **SEE** UNIFORMS, MILITARY
U350-365	*MILITARY COURTESY* **SEE** MILITARY CEREMONIES, HONORS, AND SALUTES
UH30-35	MILITARY CYCLING
UG370	*MILITARY DEMOLITION* **SEE** DEMOLITION, MILITARY
UA	MILITARY DEPARTMENTS AND DIVISIONS
UB788	*MILITARY DESERTION* **SEE** DESERTION, MILITARY
UB790-795	MILITARY DISCIPLINE
UB340-355	*MILITARY DRAFT* **SEE** MILITARY SERVICE, COMPULSORY
U400-714	MILITARY EDUCATION
UG	MILITARY ENGINEERING
UG	MILITARY ENGINEERS
UC700-780	*MILITARY EQUIPMENT, SUPPLIES, ETC.* **SEE** ARMIES — COMMISSARIAT
UC460-465	*MILITARY EQUIPMENT, SUPPLIES, ETC.* **SEE** ARMIES — EQUIPMENT
UC260-267	*MILITARY EQUIPMENT, SUPPLIES, ETC.* **SEE** MILITARY SUPPLIES
UC480-485	*MILITARY EQUIPMENT, SUPPLIES, ETC.* **SEE** UNIFORMS, MILITARY
TP268-299	*MILITARY EXPLOSIVES* **SEE** EXPLOSIVES, MILITARY
RC168.M6	*MILITARY FEVER* **SEE** SWEATING-SICKNESS
UG360-390	MILITARY FIELD ENGINEERING
UF860	MILITARY FIREWORKS
UA985-997	MILITARY GEOGRAPHY
UG465	MILITARY GEOLOGY
JV423	MILITARY GOVERNMENT OF DEPENDENCIES
D810.D4	*MILITARY GRAVES* **SEE** SOLDIERS' BODIES, DISPOSITION OF / *world war*
D639.D4	*MILITARY GRAVES* **SEE** SOLDIERS' BODIES, DISPOSITION OF / *european war*
D25.5	MILITARY HISTORY — ANECDOTES
D25	MILITARY HISTORY
U27-43	MILITARY HISTORY / *military science*
U29-35	MILITARY HISTORY, ANCIENT
U37	MILITARY HISTORY, MEDIEVAL
U39-42	MILITARY HISTORY, MODERN
U350-365	*MILITARY HONORS* **SEE** MILITARY CEREMONIES, HONORS, AND SALUTES
UH460-485	*MILITARY HOSPITALS* **SEE** HOSPITALS, MILITARY
UH600-625	MILITARY HYGIENE
UB250-270	MILITARY INTELLIGENCE
UC440	*MILITARY LAUNDRIES* **SEE** LAUNDRIES, MILITARY
UB461-736	MILITARY LAW
Z675.M5	MILITARY LIBRARIES
U1-145	*MILITARY LIFE* **SEE** SOLDIERS
U750-773	*MILITARY LIFE* **SEE** SOLDIERS
U250-255	MILITARY MANEUVERS
UD460-465	MILITARY MANEUVERS / *infantry*
UG470	*MILITARY MAPS* **SEE** MAPS, MILITARY / *etc.*
UA985-997	*MILITARY MAPS* **SEE** MAPS, MILITARY / *military geography*
UB430-435	*MILITARY MEDALS* **SEE** MEDALS, MILITARY AND NAVAL / *military*
VB330-335	*MILITARY MEDALS* **SEE** MEDALS, MILITARY AND NAVAL / *naval*
RC970-971	*MILITARY MEDICINE* **SEE** MEDICINE, MILITARY / *medical practice*
UH	*MILITARY MEDICINE* **SEE** MEDICINE, MILITARY / *military science*
UG490	*MILITARY MINES* **SEE** MINES, MILITARY
UA16	MILITARY MISSIONS
UC340-345	*MILITARY MOTORIZATION* **SEE** MOTORIZATION, MILITARY
U13	MILITARY MUSEUMS
ML1300-1354	MILITARY MUSIC — HISTORY AND CRITICISM
MT735	MILITARY MUSIC — MANUALS, TEXT-BOOKS, ETC.
M1270	MILITARY MUSIC
JX5135.M5	MILITARY NECESSITY
JX5003	MILITARY OCCUPATION
JX4093	MILITARY OCCUPATION
UB280-285	MILITARY PASSES
UB370-375	*MILITARY PENSIONS* **SEE** PENSIONS, MILITARY / *army*
UB400-405	*MILITARY PENSIONS* **SEE** PENSIONS, MILITARY / *army*
VB340-345	*MILITARY PENSIONS* **SEE** PENSIONS, MILITARY / *navy*
VB280-285	*MILITARY PENSIONS* **SEE** PENSIONS, MILITARY / *navy*
E255	*MILITARY PENSIONS* **SEE** PENSIONS, MILITARY / *pension rolls*
UH420-425	*MILITARY PHARMACY* **SEE** PHARMACY, MILITARY
VG270-275	*MILITARY PHARMACY* **SEE** PHARMACY, MILITARY / *naval*
TR785	*MILITARY PHOTOGRAPHY* **SEE** PHOTOGRAPHY, MILITARY
UA11	MILITARY POLICY
UC750-755	*MILITARY POST EXCHANGES* **SEE** POST EXCHANGES
Z675.M6	MILITARY POST LIBRARIES
UA26	MILITARY POSTS / *u.s.*
JX1974	*MILITARY POWER* **SEE** DISARMAMENT
U	*MILITARY POWER* **SEE** MILITARY ART AND SCIENCE
VA37-42	*MILITARY POWER* **SEE** NAVIES
UB800-805	*MILITARY PRISONS* **SEE** PRISONS, MILITARY / *military*
VB890-895	*MILITARY PRISONS* **SEE** PRISONS, MILITARY / *naval*
U21	*MILITARY PSYCHOLOGY* **SEE** PSYCHOLOGY, MILITARY
UG610	*MILITARY RADIO* **SEE** RADIO, MILITARY
UG345	MILITARY RAILROADS
U220	MILITARY RECONNAISSANCE
CR4653	MILITARY RELIGIOUS ORDERS — INSIGNIA
CR4705	MILITARY RELIGIOUS ORDERS — INSIGNIA
CR4701-4775	MILITARY RELIGIOUS ORDERS
JX5321	*MILITARY REQUISITIONS* **SEE** REQUISITIONS, MILITARY / *international law*
UC15	*MILITARY REQUISITIONS* **SEE** REQUISITIONS, MILITARY / *military science*
U390-395	MILITARY RESEARCH
UB390-395	MILITARY RESERVATIONS
UG330	MILITARY ROADS
U350-365	*MILITARY SALUTES* **SEE** MILITARY CEREMONIES, HONORS, AND SALUTES
U400-714	*MILITARY SCHOOLS* **SEE** MILITARY EDUCATION
U	*MILITARY SCIENCE* **SEE** MILITARY ART AND SCIENCE
UB147	MILITARY SERVICE AS A PROFESSION
UB340-355	MILITARY SERVICE, COMPULSORY
UD330-335	*MILITARY SHOOTING* **SEE** SHOOTING, MILITARY
M1270	*MILITARY SIGNALING* **SEE** MILITARY CALLS
UH40-45	*MILITARY SIGNALING* **SEE** MILITARY CALLS
HE9723-9737	*MILITARY SIGNALING* **SEE** SIGNALS AND SIGNALING
UG570-582	*MILITARY SIGNALING* **SEE** SIGNALS AND SIGNALING / *military*
V280-285	*MILITARY SIGNALING* **SEE** SIGNALS AND SIGNALING / *naval*
VK381-397	*MILITARY SIGNALING* **SEE** SIGNALS AND SIGNALING / *navigation*
UH750-769	MILITARY SOCIAL WORK
UB220-225	*MILITARY STAFFS* **SEE** ARMIES — STAFFS
UC590-595	*MILITARY STANDARDS* **SEE** STANDARDS, MILITARY
UA26	*MILITARY STATIONS* **SEE** MILITARY POSTS / *u.s.*
UA19	MILITARY STATISTICS / *theory*
U161-3	*MILITARY STRATEGY* **SEE** STRATEGY / *military*
V160-165	*MILITARY STRATEGY* **SEE** STRATEGY / *naval*
U205	*MILITARY STREAM CROSSING* **SEE** STREAM CROSSING, MILITARY

UC260-267	MILITARY SUPPLIES
RD151-498	*MILITARY SURGERY* **SEE** SURGERY, MILITARY
UC260-265	*MILITARY SURPLUSES* **SEE** SURPLUS MILITARY PROPERTY
UG470	*MILITARY SURVEYING* **SEE** MILITARY TOPOGRAPHY
U26	MILITARY SYMBOLS
U164-7	*MILITARY TACTICS* **SEE** TACTICS
UG590-610	MILITARY TELEGRAPH
UG620	MILITARY TELEPHONE
UG623	MILITARY TELEVISION
U24-26	*MILITARY TERMS* **SEE** MILITARY ART AND SCIENCE — DICTIONARIES
U26	*MILITARY TERMS* **SEE** MILITARY ART AND SCIENCE — TERMINOLOGY
UG470	MILITARY TOPOGRAPHY
U400-714	*MILITARY TRAINING* **SEE** MILITARY EDUCATION
U290-295	MILITARY TRAINING CAMPS
UB340-355	*MILITARY TRAINING, UNIVERSAL* **SEE** MILITARY SERVICE, COMPULSORY
UC270-360	*MILITARY TRANSPORTATION* **SEE** TRANSPORTATION, MILITARY
VC550-555	*MILITARY TRANSPORTATION* **SEE** TRANSPORTATION, MILITARY / *naval*
UH500-505	*MILITARY TRANSPORTATION* **SEE** TRANSPORTATION, MILITARY / *medical service*
UB850-867	*MILITARY TRIBUNALS* **SEE** COURTS-MARTIAL AND COURTS OF INQUIRY / *military*
VB800-815	*MILITARY TRIBUNALS* **SEE** COURTS-MARTIAL AND COURTS OF INQUIRY / *naval*
U815	*MILITARY TROPHIES* **SEE** TROPHIES, MILITARY / *modern arms and armor*
D570.8.T8	*MILITARY TROPHIES* **SEE** TROPHIES, MILITARY / *u.s. in european war*
UC480-485	*MILITARY UNIFORMS* **SEE** UNIFORMS, MILITARY
UH650-655	*MILITARY VETERINARY SERVICE* **SEE** VETERINARY SERVICE, MILITARY
SF251-5	MILK — ANALYSIS AND EXAMINATION
QR121	MILK — BACTERIOLOGY
SF251	MILK — COMPOSITION
SF259	MILK — PASTEURIZATION
SF259	MILK — STERILIZATION
RM233-4	MILK — THERAPEUTIC USE
GR950.M	MILK (IN RELIGION, FOLK-LORE, ETC.) / *folk-lore*
BL730	MILK (IN RELIGION, FOLK-LORE, ETC.) / *greek and roman cults*
SF255	MILK COMMISSIONS, MEDICAL
HD4501.M5	MILK DEPOTS / *economics*
HD9275	*MILK HYGIENE-LAW AND LEGISLATION* **SEE** DAIRY LAWS
HD9000.9	*MILK HYGIENE-LAW AND LEGISLATION* **SEE** DAIRY LAWS
SF255	*MILK INSPECTION* **SEE** DAIRY INSPECTION
TX357	*MILK SUBSTITUTES* **SEE** FOOD SUBSTITUTES
HC286.2	*MILK SUBSTITUTES* **SEE** FOOD SUBSTITUTES / *european war*
QD321	*MILK SUGAR* **SEE** LACTOSE
RM666.L2	*MILK SUGAR* **SEE** LACTOSE / *therapeutics*
SF257-8	MILK SUPPLY
HD9282	MILK TRADE / *economics*
HD9000.9	*MILK TRADE-LAW AND LEGISLATION* **SEE** DAIRY LAWS
HD9275	*MILK TRADE-LAW AND LEGISLATION* **SEE** DAIRY LAWS
SF251-262	MILK
SF259	MILK, CONDENSED
SF259	*MILK, DEHYDRATED* **SEE** MILK, DRIED
SF259	*MILK, DESICCATED* **SEE** MILK, DRIED
SF259	MILK, DRIED
RM234	MILK, FERMENTED
SF259	MILK, HOMOGENIZED
QP246	MILK, HUMAN
SF259	*MILK, PASTEURIZED* **SEE** MILK — PASTEURIZATION
SF259	*MILK, POWDERED* **SEE** MILK, DRIED
SF251-5	*MILK-ADULTERATION* **SEE** MILK — ANALYSIS AND EXAMINATION
SF259	*MILK-HOMOGENIZATION* **SEE** MILK, HOMOGENIZED
HD9275	*MILK-LAW AND LEGISLATION* **SEE** DAIRY LAWS
HD9000.9	*MILK-LAW AND LEGISLATION* **SEE** DAIRY LAWS
HD9282	*MILK-MARKETING* **SEE** MILK TRADE / *economics*

SF247	MILKING MACHINES
SF240	MILKING
QK495.A815	MILKWEED / *botany*
SB618.M5	MILKWEED / *poisonous plants*
QB819	MILKY WAY
E99.M	MILL CREEK INDIANS
E83.858	MILL CREEK INDIANS / *wars*
F72.H3	MILL RIVER DISASTER, 1874
RC794	*MILLAR'S ASTHMA* **SEE** LARYNGISMUS STRIDULUS
PM6511	MILLCAYAC LANGUAGE
TT265	*MILLED LEAD* **SEE** SHEET-LEAD / *lead-work*
NK5430	*MILLEFIORI GLASS* **SEE** GLASS, MILLEFIORI
BT890-891	MILLENNIUM
QL449	*MILLEPEDES* **SEE** MILLEPEDS
QL449	MILLEPEDS
SB608.M	MILLET — DISEASES AND PESTS
SB191.M5	MILLET
QC485	*MILLIKAN RAYS* **SEE** COSMIC RAYS
E475.2	MILLIKEN'S BEND, BATTLE OF, 1863
TT650-665	MILLINERY / *technical works*
HD9999.M5	MILLINERY / *trade*
TN500-535	*MILLING (METALLURGY)* **SEE** ORE-DRESSING
TJ1345	MILLING MACHINERY
HD9056	*MILLING TRADE* **SEE** FLOUR AND FEED TRADE
HF2651.F6	*MILLING TRADE* **SEE** FLOUR AND FEED TRADE / *tariff*
HD2769.M58	*MILLING TRADE* **SEE** FLOUR AND FEED TRADE / *trusts*
TJ1225	MILLING-MACHINES — NUMERICAL CONTROL
TS1225	MILLING-MACHINES — SAFETY MEASURES
TJ1225	MILLING-MACHINES
TJ1225	*MILLING-MACHINES, TAPE-CONTROLLED* **SEE** MILLING-MACHINES — NUMERICAL CONTROL
TJ1225	*MILLING-MACHINES-PUNCHED TAPE CONTROL* **SEE** MILLING-MACHINES — NUMERICAL CONTROL
QL449	*MILLIPEDES* **SEE** MILLEPEDS
TK321	MILLIVOLTMETER
NA6400-6510	*MILLS (BUILDINGS)* **SEE** FACTORIES / *architecture*
TH4511-4541	*MILLS (BUILDINGS)* **SEE** FACTORIES / *building*
HD6270	*MILLS (BUILDINGS)* **SEE** FACTORIES / *junior labor*
HD7406-7510	*MILLS (BUILDINGS)* **SEE** FACTORIES / *model*
HD6974	*MILLS (BUILDINGS)* **SEE** FACTORIES / *social conditions*
HD6068	*MILLS (BUILDINGS)* **SEE** FACTORIES / *women in*
TJ1040-1119	MILLS AND MILL-WORK
HF1755	MILLS BILL / *discussion*
HJ6085-6	MILLS BILL / *schedules*
SB235	MILO / *sorghums*
DG315	*MILVION BRIDGE, BATTLE OF, 312* **SEE** SAXA RUBRA, BATTLE OF, 312
E99.M63	MIMBRENO INDIANS
PN2071.G4	MIME
PA3029	MIME / *classical*
PA6071.M5	MIME / *latin*
Z48	MIMEOGRAPH
QE391.M	MIMETITE
PN1972	*MIMIC THEATER* **SEE** TOY THEATERS
QH546	MIMICRY (BIOLOGY)
QL495.L52	*MIMOSA TREE (ALBIZZIA JULIBRISSIN)* **SEE** SILK TREE
PL3311.M55	MIN-CHIA LANGUAGE
PL8164.Z9	MINA DIALECT
PL5415	*MINANGKABAU LANGUAGE* **SEE** MENANGKABAU LANGUAGE
NA2930	MINARETS
TX389	*MINCE MEAT* **SEE** MINCEMEAT
TX389	MINCEMEAT
BF	*MIND* **SEE** INTELLECT / *psychology*
RA790	MIND AND BODY / *rz400 mental hygiene*
BF150-171	MIND AND BODY / *psychology*
BF1111-1156	*MIND-CURE* **SEE** ANIMAL MAGNETISM / *psychical research*
RZ430	*MIND-CURE* **SEE** ANIMAL MAGNETISM / *therapeutics*
BX6901-6997	*MIND-CURE* **SEE** CHRISTIAN SCIENCE
BT732.5	*MIND-CURE* **SEE** FAITH-CURE
RZ400-401	*MIND-CURE* **SEE** FAITH-CURE / *medical aspects*
RZ400-406	*MIND-CURE* **SEE** MENTAL HEALING
RA790	*MIND-CURE* **SEE** MIND AND BODY / *rz400 mental hygiene*

BF150-171	MIND-CURE SEE MIND AND BODY / psychology
BF1161-1171	MIND-READING
BV4908.5	MIND, PEACE OF SEE PEACE OF MIND
BF637.P3	MIND, PEACE OF SEE PEACE OF MIND / applied psychology
TN311-319	MINE ACCIDENTS
TH4561	MINE BUILDINGS
TN342	MINE CARS SEE MINE RAILROADS — CARS
TN321-5	MINE DRAINAGE
TN272	MINE EXAMINATION
TN313	MINE EXPLOSIONS
TN292	MINE FILLING
TN315	MINE FIRES
TN305-6	MINE GASES
TN331-342	MINE HAULAGE
TN339-340	MINE HOISTING — SAFETY APPLIANCES
TN339-340	MINE HOISTING
TN	MINE INSPECTION
TN307-9	MINE LIGHTING
TN274	MINE MANAGEMENT
TN273	MINE MAPS
UG490	MINE PLANTING SEE MINES, MILITARY
TN325	MINE PUMPS
TN342	MINE RAILROADS — CARS
TN336	MINE RAILROADS
TN297	MINE RESCUE WORK
TN295-309	MINE SANITATION
TN273	MINE SURVEYING
UF563.A77	MINE THROWERS SEE TRENCH MORTARS
TN289	MINE TIMBERING
TN345-7	MINE TOOLS
TN272	MINE VALUATION
TN301-3	MINE VENTILATION
TN318	MINE WATER
TN5	MINERAL INDUSTRIES — CONGRESSES
TN9-10	MINERAL INDUSTRIES — DICTIONARIES
TN12	MINERAL INDUSTRIES — DIRECTORIES
TN144	MINERAL INDUSTRIES — EARLY WORKS TO 1800
TN6	MINERAL INDUSTRIES — EXHIBITIONS
TN15-124	MINERAL INDUSTRIES — HISTORY
TN1-4	MINERAL INDUSTRIES — PERIODICALS
TN1-4	MINERAL INDUSTRIES — SOCIETIES, ETC.
TN15-124	MINERAL INDUSTRIES — STATISTICS
TN13	MINERAL INDUSTRIES — YEARBOOKS
TN	MINERAL INDUSTRIES
HD9506-9585	MINERAL INDUSTRIES / economics
TN273	MINERAL LAND SURVEYING SEE MINE SURVEYING
TN	MINERAL LANDS SEE MINES AND MINERAL RESOURCES
TN215-255	MINERAL LANDS SEE MINING LAW
TP685-692	MINERAL OILS
TP687	MINERAL OILS-RECLAMATION SEE OIL RECLAMATION
TN	MINERAL RESOURCES SEE MINES AND MINERAL RESOURCES
QR105	MINERAL WATER BIOLOGY
QH96	MINERAL WATER BIOLOGY
TN923-9	MINERAL WATERS
RA793-954	MINERAL WATERS / health resorts
RM674-6	MINERAL WATERS / therapeutics
TP625	MINERAL WATERS, ARTIFICIAL
RM676	MINERAL WATERS, ARTIFICIAL / therapeutics
TP695	MINERAL WAX SEE CERESIN
TN857	MINERAL WAX SEE CERESIN
TP695	MINERAL WAX SEE OZOKERITE / chemical technology
TN857	MINERAL WAX SEE OZOKERITE / mineral industries
TH1715	MINERAL WOOL / insulation
QE364	MINERALOGICAL CHEMISTRY
QE386	MINERALOGICAL MUSEUMS
QE361	MINERALOGISTS
QE386-7	MINERALOGY — CATALOGS AND COLLECTIONS
QE388	MINERALOGY — CLASSIFICATION
QE45	MINERALOGY — COLLECTING OF SPECIMENS
QE355	MINERALOGY — DICTIONARIES
QE362	MINERALOGY — EARLY WORKS TO 1800
QE365	MINERALOGY — JUVENILE LITERATURE
QE355	MINERALOGY — NOMENCLATURE
QE351-399	MINERALOGY
QE367-9	MINERALOGY, DETERMINATIVE
QE351-399	MINERALS SEE MINERALOGY
TN	MINERALS SEE MINES AND MINERAL RESOURCES
QK882	MINERALS IN PLANTS SEE PLANTS — ASSIMILATION
GT5960.M5	MINERS — COSTUME
HD7269.M6-61	MINERS — DISEASES AND HYGIENE
PS595.M5	MINERS — SONGS AND MUSIC / american literature
M1977.M5	MINERS — SONGS AND MUSIC / music
ML3780	MINERS — SONGS AND MUSIC / musical history
HD8039.M6-7	MINERS / labor
HD7269.M6-61	MINERS' CONSUMPTION SEE MINERS' PHTHISIS
RE748	MINERS' NYSTAGMUS SEE NYSTAGMUS
HD7269.M6-61	MINERS' PHTHISIS
HD9506-9559	MINES AND MINERAL RESOURCES — GOVERNMENT OWNERSHIP
TN15-124	MINES AND MINERAL RESOURCES — STATISTICS
HJ4169	MINES AND MINERAL RESOURCES — TAXATION
TN	MINES AND MINERAL RESOURCES
TN5	MINES AND MINERAL RESOURCES-CONGRESSES SEE MINERAL INDUSTRIES — CONGRESSES
TN12	MINES AND MINERAL RESOURCES-DIRECTORIES SEE MINERAL INDUSTRIES — DIRECTORIES
HG5071-6	MINES AND MINERAL RESOURCES-DIRECTORIES SEE MINING INDUSTRY AND FINANCE — DIRECTORIES
TN12	MINES AND MINERAL RESOURCES-DIRECTORIES SEE MINING INDUSTRY AND FINANCE — DIRECTORIES
TN165-213	MINES AND MINERAL RESOURCES-EDUCATION SEE MINING SCHOOLS AND EDUCATION
TN6	MINES AND MINERAL RESOURCES-EXHIBITIONS SEE MINERAL INDUSTRIES — EXHIBITIONS
GR900	MINES AND MINERAL RESOURCES-FOLK-LORE SEE FOLK-LORE OF MINES
TN215-255	MINES AND MINERAL RESOURCES-LAW SEE MINING LAW
TN1-4	MINES AND MINERAL RESOURCES-PERIODICALS SEE MINERAL INDUSTRIES — PERIODICALS
HG5071.A1	MINES AND MINERAL RESOURCES-PERIODICALS SEE MINING INDUSTRY AND FINANCE — PERIODICALS / u.s.
HG4811.A3	MINES AND MINERAL RESOURCES-PERIODICALS SEE MINING INDUSTRY AND FINANCE — PERIODICALS
TN1-4	MINES AND MINERAL RESOURCES-SOCIETIES, ETC. SEE MINERAL INDUSTRIES — SOCIETIES, ETC.
TN165-213	MINES AND MINERAL RESOURCES-STUDY AND TEACHING SEE MINING SCHOOLS AND EDUCATION
TN13	MINES AND MINERAL RESOURCES-YEARBOOKS SEE MINERAL INDUSTRIES — YEARBOOKS
HG5071-6	MINES AND MINERAL RESOURCES-YEARBOOKS SEE MINING INDUSTRY AND FINANCE — YEARBOOKS
TN13	MINES AND MINERAL RESOURCES-YEARBOOKS SEE MINING INDUSTRY AND FINANCE — YEARBOOKS
TN	MINES AND MINING SEE MINERAL INDUSTRIES
HD9506-9585	MINES AND MINING SEE MINERAL INDUSTRIES / economics
TN	MINES AND MINING SEE MINES AND MINERAL RESOURCES
TN	MINES AND MINING SEE MINING ENGINEERING
HG4811	MINES AND MINING SEE MINING INDUSTRY AND FINANCE
HG5151-5990	MINES AND MINING SEE MINING INDUSTRY AND FINANCE / other countries
HG5071-6	MINES AND MINING SEE MINING INDUSTRY AND FINANCE / u.s.
GR900	MINES, FOLK-LORE OF SEE FOLK-LORE OF MINES
UG490	MINES, MILITARY
UG490-497	MINES, SUBMARINE
NK4165	MING CH'I / chinese art objects
GT3283	MING CH'I / chinese burial customs
E99.M64	MINGO INDIANS
PK9141	MINGRELIAN LANGUAGE
BM700-720	MINHAGIM SEE JEWS — RITES AND CEREMONIES
GV1570	MINIATURE CAR RACING SEE MODEL CAR RACING
TF857	MINIATURE ELECTRIC RAILROADS SEE ELECTRIC RAILROADS, MINIATURE
TK7870	MINIATURE ELECTRONIC EQUIPMENT
SB419	MINIATURE GARDENS SEE GARDENS, MINIATURE
GV987	MINIATURE GOLF SEE GOLF, MINIATURE
NK492	MINIATURE OBJECTS / art
N7616	MINIATURE PAINTING — REPRODUCTIONS, FACSIMILES, ETC.
ND1330-1337	MINIATURE PAINTING / painting
N7616	MINIATURE PAINTING / portraits

M555-9	MINUETS (BASSOON, CLARINET, FLUTE, HORN, OBOE)
M455-9	MINUETS (BASSOON, CLARINET, FLUTE, OBOE)
M455-9	MINUETS (BASSOON, 2 CLARINETS, FLUTE)
M240-244	MINUETS (FLUTE AND HARPSICHORD)
M125-9	MINUETS (GUITAR)
M32	MINUETS (HARPSICHORD)
M1060	MINUETS (ORCHESTRA)
M1049	MINUETS (ORCHESTRA)
M1049	MINUETS (ORCHESTRA) — TO 1800 — — SCORES (REDUCED) AND PARTS
M6-7	MINUETS (ORGAN)
M11-13	MINUETS (ORGAN)
M310-314	MINUETS (PIANO TRIO)
M32	MINUETS (PIANO)
M204	MINUETS (PIANO, 4 HANDS)
M211	MINUETS (PIANO, 4 HANDS)
M240-244	MINUETS (RECORDER AND PIANO)
M60-64	MINUETS (RECORDER)
M1160	MINUETS (STRING ORCHESTRA)
M1145	MINUETS (STRING ORCHESTRA)
M450-454	MINUETS (STRING QUARTET)
M217-218	MINUETS (VIOLIN AND PIANO)
M221-3	MINUETS (VIOLIN AND PIANO)
M655-9	MINUETS (2 BASSOONS, 2 CLARINETS, 2 HORNS)
M855-9	MINUETS (2 BASSOONS, 2 CLARINETS, 2 HORNS, 2 OBOES)
M455-9	MINUETS (2 CLARINETS, 2 FLUTES)
M214-215	MINUETS (2 PIANOS)
M1360	MINUETS (2 RECORDERS WITH PLECTRAL ENSEMBLE)
M349-353	MINUETS (2 VIOLINS, VIOLONCELLO)
M355-9	MINUETS (3 RECORDERS)
M349-353	MINUETS (3 VIOLINS)
M455-9	MINUETS (4 CLARINETS)
M455-9	MINUETS (4 FLUTES)
E99.M	*MINUSING INDIANS* SEE MINISINK INDIANS
QE694	*MIOCENE PERIOD* SEE GEOLOGY, STRATIGRAPHIC — MIOCENE
QE929	*MIOCENE PERIOD* SEE PALEOBOTANY — MIOCENE
QE739	*MIOCENE PERIOD* SEE PALEONTOLOGY — MIOCENE
HD1289.R9	MIR */ russian*
HD715	MIR */ russian*
PN1761	*MIRACLE-PLAYS* SEE MYSTERIES AND MIRACLE-PLAYS */ history and criticism*
BP166.65	MIRACLES (ISLAM)
BT97	MIRACLES
BS2545.M5	MIRACLES */ new testament*
BS1199.M5	MIRACLES */ old testament*
PC5401-4	MIRANDESE DIALECT
DS485.A86	*MIRI (HILL TRIBE)* SEE MIRIS (HILL TRIBE)
DS485.A86	MIRIS (HILL TRIBE)
NK9955.M5	MIRROR-CASES
BF456.W8	MIRROR-WRITING
TP867	MIRRORS — FRAMES
N8224.M6	MIRRORS IN ART
NK8440	MIRRORS */ art*
QC385	MIRRORS */ optics*
TP867	MIRRORS */ technology*
BF1325-1331	MIRRORS, MAGIC
PL65.M	*MISAR LANGUAGE* SEE MISHAR LANGUAGE
HQ767	*MISCARRIAGE* SEE ABORTION
RA1067	*MISCARRIAGE* SEE ABORTION */ medical jurisprudence*
RG734	*MISCARRIAGE* SEE ABORTION */ obstetrical operations*
RG648	*MISCARRIAGE* SEE ABORTION */ obstetrics*
GN237	MISCEGENATION
E185.62	MISCEGENATION */ negroes in the u.s.*
PL65.M	*MISER LANGUAGE* SEE MISHAR LANGUAGE
NA5075	*MISERERES (SEATS)* SEE CHOIR-STALLS
HB838	MISERS
PL65.M	MISHAR LANGUAGE
DS485.A86	*MISHIMI* SEE MISHMIS
DS485.A86	MISHMIS
PM4036-9	*MISKITO LANGUAGE* SEE MOSQUITO LANGUAGE
HV6691-9	*MISREPRESENTATION (LAW)* SEE FRAUD
BX2015.A55	*MISSALS FOR CHILDREN* SEE CHILDREN'S MISSALS */ catholic*
BX2015	MISSALS
ND3375	MISSALS */ etc.*
RG650	*MISSED LABOR* SEE PREGNANCY, PROTRACTED
QH368	MISSING LINK
BV2063	*MISSIOLOGY* SEE MISSIONS — THEORY

BV2075	*MISSION SERMONS* SEE MISSIONS — SERMONS
BV2063	MISSIONARIES — APPOINTMENT, CALL, AND ELECTION
BV2180	MISSIONARIES — APPOINTMENT, CALL, AND ELECTION */ catholic church*
BV3700-3705	MISSIONARIES */ general biography*
BV3703	MISSIONARIES, WOMEN
BV2180	*MISSIONARIES-VOCATION* SEE MISSIONARIES — APPOINTMENT, CALL, AND ELECTION */ catholic church*
BV2063	*MISSIONARIES-VOCATION* SEE MISSIONARIES — APPOINTMENT, CALL, AND ELECTION
BV2063	*MISSIONARY APOLOGETICS* SEE APOLOGETICS, MISSIONARY
BV2086	MISSIONARY PLAYS
E475.97	MISSIONARY RIDGE, BATTLE OF, 1863
BV2087	MISSIONARY STORIES
S532	MISSIONS — AGRICULTURAL WORK
BV2073	MISSIONS — BIBLICAL TEACHING
BV2630	MISSIONS — EDUCATIONAL WORK
BV3697	MISSIONS — GIPSIES
BV3630.H	MISSIONS — HOTTENTOTS
BV465.M5	MISSIONS — HYMNS
BV2082.I6	MISSIONS — INTERDENOMINATIONAL COOPERATION
BV2637	MISSIONS — LEPERS
BV3423.L	MISSIONS — LISU (TIBETO-BURMAN TRIBE)
BV2075	MISSIONS — SERMONS
BV2063	MISSIONS — THEORY
BV2625	MISSIONS TO MUSLIMS
BV2000-3705	MISSIONS
BV2200	MISSIONS, BRITISH */ catholic*
BV2420	MISSIONS, BRITISH */ protestant*
BL1478.9	*MISSIONS, BUDDHIST* SEE BUDDHA AND BUDDHISM — MISSIONS
BV2000-3705	MISSIONS, FOREIGN
BV2650	MISSIONS, HOME
BV2750-3697	MISSIONS, HOME */ by country*
BV2495-2595	MISSIONS, HOME */ by denomination*
E59.M65	*MISSIONS, INDIAN* SEE INDIANS — MISSIONS
E98.M6	*MISSIONS, INDIAN* SEE INDIANS OF NORTH AMERICA — MISSIONS
F2230-3799	*MISSIONS, INDIAN* SEE INDIANS OF SOUTH AMERICA — MISSIONS
BV2950	*MISSIONS, INNER* SEE INNER MISSIONS */ germany*
BV2000-3705	*MISSIONS, INSTITUTIONAL* SEE INSTITUTIONAL MISSIONS
BP170.3	*MISSIONS, ISLAMIC* SEE ISLAM — MISSIONS
R722	MISSIONS, MEDICAL
RA390-392	MISSIONS, MEDICAL
UA16	*MISSIONS, MILITARY* SEE MILITARY MISSIONS
BP170.3	*MISSIONS, MUSLIM* SEE ISLAM — MISSIONS
UA16	*MISSIONS, NAVAL* SEE MILITARY MISSIONS
BX2375	*MISSIONS, PARISH* SEE PARISH MISSIONS
BX2375	*MISSIONS, PAROCHIAL* SEE PARISH MISSIONS
BX2375	*MISSIONS, POPULAR* SEE PARISH MISSIONS
BV2200	MISSIONS, SCOTTISH */ catholic*
BV2420	MISSIONS, SCOTTISH */ protestant*
HV3025-3163	*MISSIONS, SEAMEN'S* SEE MERCHANT SEAMEN — MISSIONS AND CHARITIES */ charities*
BV2660-2678	*MISSIONS, SEAMEN'S* SEE MERCHANT SEAMEN — MISSIONS AND CHARITIES
E99.M68	MISSISAUGA INDIANS
PM1831	MISSISAUGA LANGUAGE
F336-350	MISSISSIPPI — HISTORY
F351-4	MISSISSIPPI VALLEY — HISTORY
E470.8	MISSISSIPPI VALLEY — HISTORY — — CIVIL WAR
E230.5	MISSISSIPPI VALLEY — HISTORY — — REVOLUTION
QE672	*MISSISSIPPIAN EPOCH* SEE GEOLOGY, STRATIGRAPHIC — MISSISSIPPIAN
QE729	*MISSISSIPPIAN EPOCH* SEE PALEONTOLOGY — MISSISSIPPIAN
E516	MISSISSIPPI — HISTORY — — CIVIL WAR
E568	MISSISSIPPI — HISTORY — — CIVIL WAR
PM4036-9	*MISSKITO LANGUAGE* SEE MOSQUITO LANGUAGE
F461-475	MISSOURI — HISTORY
E373	MISSOURI COMPROMISE
E99.M	MISSOURI INDIANS
E99.M	*MISSOURIA INDIANS* SEE MISSOURI INDIANS
E517	MISSOURI — HISTORY — — CIVIL WAR
E569	MISSOURI — HISTORY — — CIVIL WAR
BX1939.M	MISTAKE (CANON LAW)
PN6231.B8	*MISTAKES* SEE ERRORS AND BLUNDERS, LITERARY

AZ999	*MISTAKES* **SEE** ERRORS, POPULAR
E99.M683	MISTASSIN INDIANS
QA76.8.I5	*MISTIC (COMPUTER)* **SEE** ILLIAC COMPUTER
TK7889.I5	*MISTIC (COMPUTER)* **SEE** ILLIAC COMPUTER / *engineering*
SB615.M51	MISTLETOE FUNGUS
QK495.M6	MISTLETOE / *botany*
GR790.M5	MISTLETOE / *folk-lore*
SB615.M5	MISTLETOE / *pests*
TL686.D4	*MISTRAL (TURBOJET FIGHTER PLANES)* **SEE** VAMPIRE (TURBOJET FIGHTER PLANES)
P951	*MITANI LANGUAGE* **SEE** MITANNIAN LANGUAGE
P951	*MITANI LANGUAGE* **SEE** MITANNIAN LANGUAGE
P951	MITANNIAN LANGUAGE
TH5618	MITER-GAGES
TH5691	MITERING / *carpentry*
QL458.A2	MITES
BL1585	MITHRAISM
QH605	*MITOSIS* **SEE** CELL DIVISION (BIOLOGY)
QH605	*MITOSIS* **SEE** KARYOKINESIS
UF620.M7	MITRAILLEUSES
TH5691	*MITRING* **SEE** MITERING / *carpentry*
SB261.M6	MITSUMATA
GT2170	*MITTENS* **SEE** GLOVES / *costume*
TS2160	*MITTENS* **SEE** GLOVES / *manufacture*
HD9947	*MITTENS* **SEE** GLOVES / *trade*
E99.M69	MIWOK INDIANS
PM1845	MIWOK LANGUAGE
F1221.M67	MIXE INDIANS
PM4011	MIXE LANGUAGE
E99.M693	*MIXED BLOODS (AMERICAN INDIANS)* **SEE** INDIANS OF NORTH AMERICA — MIXED BLOODS
F2230.1.M	*MIXED BLOODS (AMERICAN INDIANS)* **SEE** INDIANS OF SOUTH AMERICA — MIXED BLOODS
BV820	*MIXED COMMUNION* **SEE** CLOSE AND OPEN COMMUNION
QD400-409	*MIXED CYCLOIDS (CHEMISTRY)* **SEE** HETEROCYCLIC COMPOUNDS
PM7801-7895	*MIXED LANGUAGES* **SEE** LANGUAGES, MIXED
HQ1031	*MIXED MARRIAGE* **SEE** MARRIAGE, MIXED
HQ1031	*MIXED RELIGION* **SEE** MARRIAGE, MIXED
TP156.M5	*MIXERS (MACHINERY)* **SEE** MIXING MACHINERY
TP156.M5	MIXING MACHINERY
F1219	MIXTEC INDIANS — WRITING
F1221.M	MIXTEC INDIANS
PM4016	MIXTEC LANGUAGE
F1231	MIXTON WAR, 1541-1542
BM646	*MIZWAHS, SIX HUNDRED AND THIRTEEN* **SEE** COMMANDMENTS, SIX HUNDRED AND THIRTEEN
BF383	MNEMONICS — EARLY WORKS TO 1850
BF380-385	MNEMONICS / *psychology*
PJ4149	MOABITE STONE
E99.M	MOACHE INDIANS
NA660	MOATS / *english castles*
NA490-497	MOATS / *military architecture*
E477.94	MOBILE — SIEGE, 1865
E476.85	MOBILE BAY, BATTLE OF, 1864
TK7882.M6	MOBILE COMMUNICATION SYSTEMS
TL297	*MOBILE HOMES* **SEE** AUTOMOBILES — TRAILERS
HB1951-2580	*MOBILITY* **SEE** MIGRATION, INTERNAL
UA18	*MOBILIZATION, INDUSTRIAL* **SEE** INDUSTRIAL MOBILIZATION
PM6573	*MOBIMA LANGUAGE* **SEE** MOVIMA LANGUAGE
HV6474-6485	MOBS
HM281-3	MOBS / *psychology*
E98.C8	MOCCASINS
F3430.1.M6	MOCHICA INDIANS
QL696.P2	MOCKING-BIRDS
F2823.M	MOCOBI INDIANS
F2823.M	*MOCOVI INDIANS* **SEE** MOCOBI INDIANS
GV1570	*MODEL AUTO RACING* **SEE** MODEL CAR RACING
GV1570	MODEL CAR RACING
TL237	*MODEL CARS* **SEE** AUTOMOBILES — MODELS
TK3226	*MODEL NETWORKS* **SEE** ELECTRIC LINES — MODELS
TK3001	*MODEL NETWORKS* **SEE** ELECTRIC NETWORK ANALYZERS
TK3141	*MODEL NETWORKS* **SEE** ELECTRIC NETWORK ANALYZERS / *alternating current*
TK3111	*MODEL NETWORKS* **SEE** ELECTRIC NETWORK ANALYZERS / *direct current*

TF197	*MODEL RAILROADS* **SEE** RAILROADS — MODELS
LB2153-5	*MODEL SCHOOLS* **SEE** LABORATORY SCHOOLS
TT154	*MODEL-MAKING* **SEE** MODELS AND MODELMAKING
NK9580	*MODELING IN WAX* **SEE** WAX-MODELING
NB1180-1185	MODELING / *sculpture*
QE43	*MODELING, GEOLOGICAL* **SEE** GEOLOGICAL MODELING
TT154	*MODELMAKING* **SEE** MODELS AND MODELMAKING
T324	MODELS (PATENTS)
TT154	MODELS AND MODELMAKING — RADIO CONTROL SYSTEMS
TT154	MODELS AND MODELMAKING
NA2790	*MODELS, ARCHITECTURAL* **SEE** ARCHITECTURAL MODELS
N7434	MODELS, ARTISTS'
QB67	*MODELS, ASTRONOMICAL* **SEE** ASTRONOMICAL MODELS
HD6073.M7	*MODELS, CLOTHING* **SEE** MODELS, FASHION
HD6073.M7	MODELS, FASHION
TC163	*MODELS, HYDRAULIC* **SEE** HYDRAULIC MODELS
TJ248	*MODELS, MECHANICAL* **SEE** MACHINERY — MODELS
NA500-680	*MODERN ARCHITECTURE* **SEE** ARCHITECTURE, MODERN
N6490	*MODERN ART* **SEE** ART, MODERN 20TH CENTURY
N6490-6493	*MODERN ART* **SEE** ART — HISTORY — — 20TH CENTURY
N6490	*MODERN ART* **SEE** MODERNISM (ART)
CB357-425	*MODERN CIVILIZATION* **SEE** CIVILIZATION, MODERN
GV1783	MODERN DANCE
QA473-5	*MODERN GEOMETRY* **SEE** GEOMETRY, MODERN
D204-725	*MODERN HISTORY* **SEE** HISTORY, MODERN
PB1-431	*MODERN LANGUAGES* **SEE** LANGUAGES, MODERN
PN695-779	*MODERN LITERATURE* **SEE** LITERATURE, MODERN
ML197	*MODERN MUSIC* **SEE** MUSIC — HISTORY AND CRITICISM — — 20TH CENTURY
B790-4695	*MODERN PHILOSOPHY* **SEE** PHILOSOPHY, MODERN
BL98	*MODERN RELIGIONS* **SEE** RELIGIONS, MODERN
BX1396	MODERNISM — CATHOLIC CHURCH
BX5126	MODERNISM — CHURCH OF ENGLAND
N6490	MODERNISM (ART)
N6490	*MODERNISM IN ART* **SEE** MODERNISM (ART)
BT78	MODERNISM
N6490	*MODERNIST ART* **SEE** MODERNISM (ART)
BT78	MODERNIST-FUNDAMENTALIST CONTROVERSY
ML3809	*MODES, MUSICAL* **SEE** MUSICAL INTERVALS AND SCALES
E99.M115	*MODESSE INDIANS* **SEE** MADEHSI INDIANS
BJ1533.M8	MODESTY
E99.M7	MODOC INDIANS — RELIGION AND MYTHOLOGY
E83.87	MODOC INDIANS — WARS, 1873
E99.M7	MODOC INDIANS
TH860	*MODULAR BUILDING* **SEE** MODULAR COORDINATION (ARCHITECTURE) / *building*
NA2700	*MODULAR BUILDING* **SEE** MODULAR COORDINATION (ARCHITECTURE) / *drafting*
NA2760	*MODULAR BUILDING* **SEE** MODULAR COORDINATION (ARCHITECTURE) / *design*
NA2760	*MODULAR CONSTRUCTION* **SEE** MODULAR COORDINATION (ARCHITECTURE) / *design*
TH860	*MODULAR CONSTRUCTION* **SEE** MODULAR COORDINATION (ARCHITECTURE) / *building*
NA2700	*MODULAR CONSTRUCTION* **SEE** MODULAR COORDINATION (ARCHITECTURE) / *drafting*
TH860	MODULAR COORDINATION (ARCHITECTURE) / *building*
NA2760	MODULAR COORDINATION (ARCHITECTURE) / *design*
NA2700	MODULAR COORDINATION (ARCHITECTURE) / *drafting*
NA2700	*MODULAR DESIGN* **SEE** MODULAR COORDINATION (ARCHITECTURE) / *drafting*
NA2760	*MODULAR DESIGN* **SEE** MODULAR COORDINATION (ARCHITECTURE) / *design*
TH860	*MODULAR DESIGN* **SEE** MODULAR COORDINATION (ARCHITECTURE) / *building*
QA343	*MODULAR FUNCTIONS* **SEE** FUNCTIONS, MODULAR
MT52	MODULATION (MUSIC) / *music*
E99.M76	MOGOLLON INDIANS
PL8062	*MOGOREB LANGUAGE* **SEE** BARIA LANGUAGE
DS461	MOGUL EMPIRE
F3319	*MOHA INDIANS* **SEE** MOXO INDIANS

DR507	MOHACS, BATTLE OF, 1526
DS38	*MOHAMMEDANS* **SEE** MUSLIMS
E99.Y	*MOHAVE APACHE INDIANS* **SEE** YAVAPAI INDIANS
E99.M77	MOHAVE INDIANS
PM1871	MOHAVE LANGUAGE
E99.M8	MOHAWK INDIANS
PM1881-4	MOHAWK LANGUAGE
E99.M83	MOHEGAN INDIANS
PM1885	MOHEGAN LANGUAGE
E99.M83	*MOHICAN INDIANS* **SEE** MOHEGAN INDIANS
DS432.M	MOHMANDS
DS539.M6	MOI (SOUTHEAST-ASIATIC PEOPLE)
TH9031	*MOISTURE CONTROL IN BUILDINGS* **SEE** DAMPNESS IN BUILDINGS
S594	*MOISTURE OF SOILS* **SEE** SOIL MOISTURE
RA570	*MOISTURE OF SOILS* **SEE** SOIL MOISTURE / *soil moisture and disease*
QC915-929	MOISTURE / *meteorology*
F3319	*MOJA INDIANS* **SEE** MOXO INDIANS
F3319	*MOJO INDIANS* **SEE** MOXO INDIANS
E99.H7	*MOKI INDIANS* **SEE** HOPI INDIANS
PM1351	*MOKI LANGUAGE* **SEE** HOPI LANGUAGE
F2280.1.M	*MOKUSHI INDIANS* **SEE** MACUSI INDIANS / *british guiana*
E99.M84	MOLALA INDIANS
TP413	MOLASSES / *manufacture*
HD9119.M6	MOLASSES / *trade*
QK621	*MOLD (BOTANY)* **SEE** MOLDS (BOTANY)
S598	*MOLD, VEGETABLE* **SEE** HUMUS
S590-599	*MOLD, VEGETABLE* **SEE** SOILS
PC794.M68	MOLDAVIAN BALLADS AND SONGS / *collections*
PC794.M65	MOLDAVIAN BALLADS AND SONGS / *history*
PC794.M6	MOLDAVIAN DIALECT
PC794.M66-69	MOLDAVIAN LITERATURE / *collections*
PC794.M65	MOLDAVIAN LITERATURE / *history*
PC794.M67	MOLDAVIAN POETRY / *collections*
PC794.M65	MOLDAVIAN POETRY / *history*
QE461	MOLDAVITE
NB1180-1185	*MOLDING (CLAY, PLASTER, ETC.)* **SEE** MODELING / *sculpture*
RD118-120.5	*MOLDING (CLAY, PLASTER, ETC.)* **SEE** PROSTHESIS
NB1170-1195	*MOLDING (CLAY, PLASTER, ETC.)* **SEE** SCULPTURE — TECHNIQUE
TP986.5	*MOLDING (PLASTICS)* **SEE** PLASTICS — MOLDING
TS243.5	*MOLDING SAND* **SEE** SAND, FOUNDRY
HF5716.M	MOLDINGS — TABLES AND READY-RECKONERS
NA2960	MOLDINGS / *architecture*
TH2482-3	MOLDINGS / *building exterior*
TH2553	MOLDINGS / *interior*
DR213	*MOLDO-WALLACHIANS* **SEE** RUMANIANS
QK621	MOLDS (BOTANY)
RL793	MOLE (DERMATOLOGY)
BF861.M65	MOLE (DERMATOLOGY) / *physiognomy*
SB945.M7	MOLE-CRICKETS / *insect pests*
QL508.G8	MOLE-CRICKETS / *zoology*
RG591	*MOLE, UTERINE* **SEE** PREGNANCY, MOLAR
QD481	*MOLECULAR ASYMMETRY* **SEE** STEREOCHEMISTRY
QC173	MOLECULAR DYNAMICS
QC183	MOLECULAR DYNAMICS / *capillarity*
QD481	MOLECULAR ROTATION
QD461	MOLECULAR THEORY / *chemistry*
QD545	MOLECULAR WEIGHTS
QC173	MOLECULES
QC179	MOLECULES
QD481	*MOLECULES-INTERNAL ROTATION* **SEE** MOLECULAR ROTATION
E99.M84	*MOLEL INDIANS* **SEE** MOLALA INDIANS
QL737.I5	MOLES (ANIMALS)
BT762	MOLINISM
RS201.03	MOLLIN
QL395-9	MOLLUSCOIDEA
SH365-380	*MOLLUSK FISHERIES* **SEE** SHELLFISH FISHERIES
QL431	MOLLUSKS — ANATOMY
QL406	MOLLUSKS — CATALOGS AND COLLECTIONS
QL406	MOLLUSKS — CLASSIFICATION
QL406.5	MOLLUSKS — COLLECTION AND PRESERVATION
QL406	MOLLUSKS — NOMENCLATURE
QL431	MOLLUSKS — PHYSIOLOGY
QL401-432	MOLLUSKS
QE801-813	MOLLUSKS, FOSSIL
QL401-432	*MOLLUSKS-NOMENCLATURE (POPULAR)* **SEE** SHELLS
QL401-432	*MOLLUSKS-PICTORIAL WORKS* **SEE** SHELLS
HV6441-6453	MOLLY MAGUIRES
BX8530.M6	MOLOKANS
PM6541	MOLUCHE LANGUAGE
QE391.M7	MOLYBDENITE
TN490.M7	MOLYBDENUM ORES
QD181.M7	MOLYBDENUM / *chemistry*
TN799.M7	MOLYBDENUM / *metallurgy*
TN490.M7	MOLYBDENUM / *mining*
TA480.M	*MOLYBDENUM-CREEP* **SEE** CREEP OF MOLYBDENUM
TN799.M	MOLYBDITE
GN654	*MOMBUTTUS* **SEE** MONBUTTUS
QA839	MOMENTS OF INERTIA / *analytic mechanics*
TG265-7	MOMENTS OF INERTIA / *engineering*
TJ901	*MOMENTUM PUMPS* **SEE** JET PUMPS
GV1511	MON (GAME)
DS570.M	MON (SOUTHEAST-ASIATIC PEOPLE)
PL4331-9	MON LANGUAGE
PL4301-9	*MON-ANAM LANGUAGES* **SEE** MON-KHMER LANGUAGES
PL4301-9	MON-KHMER LANGUAGES
E99.M85	MONACAN INDIANS
BL1475.M7	*MONACHISM* **SEE** MONASTICISM AND RELIGIOUS ORDERS / *buddhism*
BX2410-4560	*MONACHISM* **SEE** MONASTICISM AND RELIGIOUS ORDERS / *catholic church*
BX385	*MONACHISM* **SEE** MONASTICISM AND RELIGIOUS ORDERS / *greek church*
BX580-583	*MONACHISM* **SEE** MONASTICISM AND RELIGIOUS ORDERS / *russian church*
BL604.Y5	*MONAD (SYMBOL)* **SEE** YIN YANG SYMBOL
B2599.M8	MONADOLOGY / *leibnitz*
B2599.M8	*MONADS (PHILOSOPHY)* **SEE** MONADOLOGY / *leibnitz*
BT1420	MONARCHIANISM
D107	*MONARCHS* **SEE** KINGS AND RULERS / *biography comprehensive*
JF253	*MONARCHS* **SEE** KINGS AND RULERS / *comparative government*
JC374-408	*MONARCHS* **SEE** KINGS AND RULERS / *political theory*
D399.7	*MONARCHS* **SEE** KINGS AND RULERS / *19th century*
D352.1	*MONARCHS* **SEE** KINGS AND RULERS / *19th century*
D412.7	*MONARCHS* **SEE** KINGS AND RULERS / *20th century*
JL-JQ	MONARCHY / *administration*
JF251-314	MONARCHY / *administration*
JC401-8	MONARCHY / *theory*
JC374-393	MONARCHY / *theory*
QL696.P5	*MONASA* **SEE** NUN-BIRDS
NA4850	MONASTERIES / *architecture*
NA5201-6113	MONASTERIES / *architecture*
BX2460-2749	MONASTERIES / *catholic church*
BX2465	MONASTIC AND RELIGIOUS LIFE — EARLY CHURCH
BX4210	MONASTIC AND RELIGIOUS LIFE OF WOMEN
BX2435	MONASTIC AND RELIGIOUS LIFE
Z675.M	MONASTIC LIBRARIES
BX4210	*MONASTIC LIFE* **SEE** MONASTIC AND RELIGIOUS LIFE OF WOMEN
BX2435	*MONASTIC LIFE* **SEE** MONASTIC AND RELIGIOUS LIFE
BX580-583	*MONASTIC ORDERS* **SEE** MONASTICISM AND RELIGIOUS ORDERS / *russian church*
BL1475.M7	*MONASTIC ORDERS* **SEE** MONASTICISM AND RELIGIOUS ORDERS / *buddhism*
BX385	*MONASTIC ORDERS* **SEE** MONASTICISM AND RELIGIOUS ORDERS / *greek church*
BX2410-4560	*MONASTIC ORDERS* **SEE** MONASTICISM AND RELIGIOUS ORDERS / *catholic church*
BX2427	*MONASTIC PROFESSION* **SEE** PROFESSION (IN RELIGIOUS ORDERS, CONGREGATIONS, ETC.)
BX2380	*MONASTIC VOCATION* **SEE** VOCATION (IN RELIGIOUS ORDERS, CONGREGATIONS, ETC.)
BX2435	MONASTICISM AND RELIGIOUS ORDERS — DISCIPLINE
BX2465	MONASTICISM AND RELIGIOUS ORDERS — EARLY CHURCH
BX2410-2440	MONASTICISM AND RELIGIOUS ORDERS — GOVERNMENT
BX2790	MONASTICISM AND RELIGIOUS ORDERS — HABIT
BX4223	MONASTICISM AND RELIGIOUS ORDERS — HABIT / *sisterhoods*

BX2470	MONASTICISM AND RELIGIOUS ORDERS — MIDDLE AGES	HG381-395	*MONEY, INTERNATIONAL* **SEE** COINAGE, INTERNATIONAL
BX2436-7	MONASTICISM AND RELIGIOUS ORDERS — RULES	HG221	*MONEY, QUANTITY THEORY OF* **SEE** QUANTITY THEORY OF MONEY
BX2427	MONASTICISM AND RELIGIOUS ORDERS (CANON LAW)		
BX385	*MONASTICISM AND RELIGIOUS ORDERS FOR MEN* **SEE** MONASTICISM AND RELIGIOUS ORDERS / greek church	DT650	MONGO (BANTU TRIBE)
		PL8441	MONGO LANGUAGE
		PL401-9	MONGOLIAN LANGUAGE
BX580-583	*MONASTICISM AND RELIGIOUS ORDERS FOR MEN* **SEE** MONASTICISM AND RELIGIOUS ORDERS / russian church	PL401-9	MONGOLIAN LANGUAGES
		PL410-419	MONGOLIAN LITERATURE
		PL416	MONGOLIAN POETRY / collections
BX2410-4560	*MONASTICISM AND RELIGIOUS ORDERS FOR MEN* **SEE** MONASTICISM AND RELIGIOUS ORDERS / catholic church	PL412	MONGOLIAN POETRY / history
		GN548	*MONGOLIANS* **SEE** MONGOLS / ethnography
		DS19-23	*MONGOLIANS* **SEE** MONGOLS / history
BL1475.M7	*MONASTICISM AND RELIGIOUS ORDERS FOR MEN* **SEE** MONASTICISM AND RELIGIOUS ORDERS / buddhism	HQ75- .M7	MONGOLISM / eugenics
		RC571	MONGOLISM / medicine
		GN548	MONGOLS / ethnography
BX4210.5	MONASTICISM AND RELIGIOUS ORDERS FOR WOMEN — EDUCATION	DS19-23	MONGOLS / history
		QL737.C2	MONGOOS
BX4200-4560	MONASTICISM AND RELIGIOUS ORDERS FOR WOMEN	PL4001.A7	*MONGSEN DIALECT* **SEE** AO LANGUAGE
BL1475.M7	*MONASTICISM AND RELIGIOUS ORDERS OF MEN* **SEE** MONASTICISM AND RELIGIOUS ORDERS / buddhism	E356.M	MONGUAGON, MICH., BATTLE OF, AUG. 9, 1812
		PL431.M6	MONGUOR LANGUAGE
BX580-583	*MONASTICISM AND RELIGIOUS ORDERS OF MEN* **SEE** MONASTICISM AND RELIGIOUS ORDERS / russian church	DS731.M	MONGUORS
		B827	MONISM
		B851-4695	MONISM / by country
BX385	*MONASTICISM AND RELIGIOUS ORDERS OF MEN* **SEE** MONASTICISM AND RELIGIOUS ORDERS / greek church	LB1029.M7	MONITORIAL SYSTEM OF EDUCATION
		V860	*MONITORS (WARSHIPS)* **SEE** TURRET SHIPS
BX2410-4560	*MONASTICISM AND RELIGIOUS ORDERS OF MEN* **SEE** MONASTICISM AND RELIGIOUS ORDERS / catholic church	QL795.M7	MONKEYS — LEGENDS AND STORIES
		QL737.P9	MONKEYS
		QE882.P7	MONKEYS / fossil
BL1475.M7	MONASTICISM AND RELIGIOUS ORDERS / buddhism	BL1475.M7	*MONKS* **SEE** MONASTICISM AND RELIGIOUS ORDERS / buddhism
BX2410-4560	MONASTICISM AND RELIGIOUS ORDERS / catholic church		
		BX2410-4560	*MONKS* **SEE** MONASTICISM AND RELIGIOUS ORDERS / catholic church
BX385	MONASTICISM AND RELIGIOUS ORDERS / greek church		
BX580-583	MONASTICISM AND RELIGIOUS ORDERS / russian church	BX385	*MONKS* **SEE** MONASTICISM AND RELIGIOUS ORDERS / greek church
BL1458	MONASTICISM AND RELIGIOUS ORDERS, BUDDHIST — HABIT	BX580-583	*MONKS* **SEE** MONASTICISM AND RELIGIOUS ORDERS / russian church
BP189.2-7	MONASTICISM AND RELIGIOUS ORDERS, ISLAMIC	E241.M7	MONMOUTH, BATTLE OF, 1778
BP189.2-7	*MONASTICISM AND RELIGIOUS ORDERS, MUSLIM* **SEE** MONASTICISM AND RELIGIOUS ORDERS, ISLAMIC	DA448.9	MONMOUTH'S REBELLION, 1685
		E99.M	MONO INDIANS
		PL6256.M7	MONO LANGUAGE
BV4405-6	MONASTICISM AND RELIGIOUS ORDERS, PROTESTANT	E476.66	MONOCACY, BATTLE OF THE, 1864
BX2835	*MONASTICISM AND RELIGIOUS ORDERS-BROTHERS* **SEE** BROTHERS (IN RELIGIOUS ORDERS, CONGREGATIONS, ETC.)	ML3809	MONOCHORD
		QC467	MONOCHROMATOR
		GN353-6	MONOGENISM AND POLYGENISM
BX2835	*MONASTICISM AND RELIGIOUS ORDERS-LAY BROTHERS* **SEE** LAY BROTHERS	NK3640	MONOGRAMS
		NE2710	MONOGRAMS / engraving
BX2840	*MONASTICISM AND RELIGIOUS ORDERS-THIRD ORDERS* **SEE** THIRD ORDERS	NA5201-6113	*MONOLITHIC CHURCHES* **SEE** CAVE CHURCHES
		NA4910	*MONOLITHIC CHURCHES* **SEE** CAVE CHURCHES
BX2435	*MONASTICISM AND RELIGIOUS ORDERS-VOWS* **SEE** VOWS / monasticism	PN1530	MONOLOGUE
		M1625	MONOLOGUES WITH MUSIC (BAND)
BX4211	*MONASTICISM AND RELIGIOUS ORDERS-VOWS* **SEE** VOWS / orders of women	M1625	MONOLOGUES WITH MUSIC (CELESTA, 2 FLUTES, 2 HARPS)
TN948.M7	MONAZITE	M1625	MONOLOGUES WITH MUSIC (CHAMBER MUSIC)
GN654	MONBUTTUS	M1625	MONOLOGUES WITH MUSIC (CHAMBER ORCHESTRA) — SCORES
E199	MONCKTON'S EXPEDITION TO ST. JOHN RIVER, N.B., 1758		
		M1625	MONOLOGUES WITH MUSIC (CHAMBER ORCHESTRA)
PM8629	MONDI LINGUO (ARTIFICIAL LANGUAGE)	M1626	MONOLOGUES WITH MUSIC (CHORUS WITH PIANO)
PM8630	MONDIAL (ARTIFICIAL LANGUAGE)	M1625	MONOLOGUES WITH MUSIC (INSTRUMENTAL ENSEMBLE)
PM8629	*MONDILINGWO (ARTIFICIAL LANGUAGE)* **SEE** MONDI LINGUO (ARTIFICIAL LANGUAGE)		
		M1625	MONOLOGUES WITH MUSIC (ORCHESTRA) — SCORES (REDUCED)
F2520.1.M	*MONDOROCU INDIANS* **SEE** MUNDURUCU INDIANS		
TS650	MONEL METAL / manufacture	M1625	MONOLOGUES WITH MUSIC (ORCHESTRA)
TA490	MONEL METAL / testing	M1625	MONOLOGUES WITH MUSIC (PIANO QUINTET)
HG651-1490	*MONETARY QUESTION* **SEE** CURRENCY QUESTION / other countries	M1626	MONOLOGUES WITH MUSIC (PIANO)
		M1625	MONOLOGUES WITH MUSIC (VIOLIN AND PIANO)
		M1626	MONOLOGUES WITH MUSIC (VOICE, VIOLIN, PIANO)
HG501-538	*MONETARY QUESTION* **SEE** CURRENCY QUESTION / u.s.	M1625-6	MONOLOGUES WITH MUSIC
		PN4305.M6	MONOLOGUES
HG201-1490	*MONETARY QUESTION* **SEE** MONEY	E199	MONONGAHELA, BATTLE OF THE, 1755
GN436.2	*MONETARY QUESTION* **SEE** MONEY / primitive	RB145	*MONONUCLEAR LEUCOCYTOSIS* **SEE** MONONUCLEOSIS
HG203-5	MONEY — CONGRESSES		
HG227	MONEY — LAW / theory	RB145	MONONUCLEOSIS
HG219	MONEY — TABLES, ETC.	QM691	*MONOPHTHALMIA* **SEE** EYE — ABNORMITIES AND DEFORMITIES
HG174	*MONEY RAISING* **SEE** FUND RAISING		
HV40-41	*MONEY RAISING* **SEE** FUND RAISING / charity organization	BT1425	MONOPHYSITES
		HD2709-2930	MONOPOLIES
HE6165-9	*MONEY-ORDERS* **SEE** POSTAL SERVICE — MONEY-ORDERS	HD3853-6	*MONOPOLIES, GOVERNMENT* **SEE** GOVERNMENT MONOPOLIES
HG201-1490	MONEY		
GN436.2	MONEY / primitive	TK6592.M6	MONOPULSE RADAR

TF694	*MONORAIL RAILROADS* **SEE** RAILROADS, SINGLE-RAIL
RC898	*MONORCHIS* **SEE** TESTICLE — ABNORMITIES AND DEFORMITIES
BL221	MONOTHEISM
QL737.M7	MONOTREMATA
QE882.M6	MONOTREMATA / *fossil*
Z253	MONOTYPE
JX1425	MONROE DOCTRINE
DS570.M	*MONS (SOUTHEAST-ASIATIC PEOPLE)* **SEE** MON (SOUTHEAST-ASIATIC PEOPLE)
D542.M7	MONS, BATTLE OF, 1914
PM1961	*MONSEY LANGUAGE* **SEE** MUNSEE LANGUAGE
QC939.M7	MONSOONS
QL991	MONSTERS / *animals*
GR825-830	MONSTERS / *folk-lore*
QM691-9	MONSTERS / *human anatomy*
NK7215	MONSTRANCES
QL991	*MONSTROSITIES* **SEE** MONSTERS / *animals*
GR825-830	*MONSTROSITIES* **SEE** MONSTERS / *folk-lore*
QM691-9	*MONSTROSITIES* **SEE** MONSTERS / *human anatomy*
PM850.C2	*MONTAGNAIS (ATHAPASCAN) LANGUAGE* **SEE** CHIPEWYAN LANGUAGE
E99.M87	MONTAGNAIS INDIANS
PM1921-4	MONTAGNAIS LANGUAGE
DC180	MONTAGNARDS
QE685-8	*MONTANA FORMATION* **SEE** GEOLOGY, STRATIGRAPHIC — CRETACEOUS
QE924	*MONTANA FORMATION* **SEE** PALEOBOTANY — CRETACEOUS
QE734	*MONTANA FORMATION* **SEE** PALEONTOLOGY — CRETACEOUS
QL638.S2	*MONTANA GRAYLING* **SEE** GRAYLING
SH167.G8	*MONTANA GRAYLING* **SEE** GRAYLING / *culture*
BT1435	MONTANISM
BT1435	*MONTANISTS* **SEE** MONTANISM
DG737.2-22	MONTAPERTO, BATTLE OF, 1260 / *florence*
DG975.S5	MONTAPERTO, BATTLE OF, 1260 / *siena*
DC102.527	MONTARGIS, FRANCE — SIEGE, 1427
E99.M	MONTAUK INDIANS
D763.I8	MONTE CASSINO (BENEDICTINE MONASTERY) — SIEGE, 1944
F1232	MONTE DE LAS CRUCES, BATTLE OF, 1810
DR156	*MONTENEGRIN-TURKISH WAR, 1876-1878* **SEE** TURCO-MONTENEGRIN WAR, 1876-1878
E406.M7	MONTEREY, BATTLE OF, 1846
DP635	MONTES CLAROS, BATTLE OF, 1665
LB775.M7-8	MONTESSORI METHOD OF EDUCATION
F2781	MONTEVIDEO — SIEGE, 1814
DC106.3	MONTLHERY, BATTLE OF, 1465
DC309.M8	MONTMEDY, FRANCE — SIEGE, 1870
D462 1936	MONTREUX, SWITZERLAND, TREATY OF, 1936
HG2071-2106	*MONTS-DE-PIETE* **SEE** PAWNBROKING
PL6621.M6	MONUMBO LANGUAGE
NK7800-7899	*MONUMENTAL BRASSES* **SEE** BRASSES / *art objects*
NB1840-1846	*MONUMENTAL BRASSES* **SEE** BRASSES / *sepulchral monuments*
BS620	*MONUMENTAL THEOLOGY* **SEE** BIBLE — ANTIQUITIES
BR130-133	*MONUMENTAL THEOLOGY* **SEE** CHRISTIAN ANTIQUITIES
CC135	MONUMENTS — PRESERVATION
N8850	MONUMENTS — PRESERVATION / *art*
NA9335-9355	MONUMENTS / *municipal art*
NB1330-1885	MONUMENTS / *sculpture*
QH75-77	*MONUMENTS, NATURAL* **SEE** NATURAL MONUMENTS
NB1800-1885	*MONUMENTS, SEPULCHRAL* **SEE** SEPULCHRAL MONUMENTS / *sculpture*
BF1723	MOON — INFLUENCE ON MAN
QB585	MOON — LIBRATION
QB591	MOON — MASS
QB581-595	MOON — OBSERVATIONS
QB397-9	MOON — OBSERVATIONS / *lunar theory*
QB585	MOON — ROTATION
QB591	MOON — SURFACE
QB399	MOON — TABLES / *lunar theory*
VK563-7	MOON — TABLES / *navigation*
QB588	MOON — TEMPERATURE AND RADIATION
TL480	MOON CARS
HV1666-1698	*MOON SYSTEM* **SEE** BLIND — PRINTING AND WRITING SYSTEMS

QB581-595	MOON
TL799.M6	*MOON, FLIGHT TO THE* **SEE** SPACE FLIGHT TO THE MOON
QB391-9	MOON, THEORY OF
TL789-790	*MOON, VOYAGES TO* **SEE** INTERPLANETARY VOYAGES
HV1666-1698	*MOON'S TYPE FOR THE BLIND* **SEE** BLIND — PRINTING AND WRITING SYSTEMS
QB579	*MOON-ECLIPSES* **SEE** ECLIPSES, LUNAR
QC883	*MOON-INFLUENCE ON WEATHER* **SEE** WEATHER, INFLUENCE OF THE MOON ON
QB583	*MOON-PARALLAX* **SEE** PARALLAX — MOON
PM1961	*MOONSEY LANGUAGE* **SEE** MUNSEE LANGUAGE
HJ5021	*MOONSHINING* **SEE** DISTILLING, ILLICIT / *u.s.*
E241.M8	MOORE'S CREEK BRIDGE, N.C., BATTLE OF, 1776
GC41	*MOORED OCEANOGRAPHIC BUOYS* **SEE** OCEANOGRAPHIC BUOYS
NA380-388	*MOORISH ARCHITECTURE* **SEE** ARCHITECTURE, ISLAMIC
N6260-6271	*MOORISH ART* **SEE** ART, ISLAMIC
PK1975-1987	*MOORISH LANGUAGE (INDIA)* **SEE** URDU LANGUAGE
GB621-8	MOORS AND HEATHS
S621	MOORS AND HEATHS / *agriculture*
HD1665-1683	MOORS AND HEATHS / *agriculture*
SK301	MOOSE HUNTING
QL737.U5	MOOSE
DA140	MOOT
E99.M	MOQUELUMNAN INDIANS
HD9909.M	MOQUETTE / *economics*
TS1772-6	MOQUETTE / *textile manufacturers*
E99.H7	*MOQUI INDIANS* **SEE** HOPI INDIANS
QE578	MORAINES
LC251-318	MORAL EDUCATION
LC2751	MORAL EDUCATION / *negro*
BJ	*MORAL PHILOSOPHY* **SEE** ETHICS
BJ10.M6	MORAL REARMAMENT
Z649.M6	*MORAL RIGHTS (COPYRIGHT LAW)* **SEE** COPYRIGHT — MORAL RIGHTS
BJ1190-1278	*MORAL THEOLOGY* **SEE** CHRISTIAN ETHICS
BV4645	*MORAL VIRTUES* **SEE** CARDINAL VIRTUES
U22	MORALE
PN1771	MORALITIES
BJ	*MORALITY* **SEE** ETHICS
PN1771	*MORALITY PLAYS* **SEE** MORALITIES
BJ1545-1695	*MORALS* **SEE** CONDUCT OF LIFE
BJ	*MORALS* **SEE** ETHICS
N70-72	*MORALS AND ART* **SEE** ART AND MORALS
PN49	*MORALS AND LITERATURE* **SEE** LITERATURE AND MORALS
ML3920	*MORALS AND MUSIC* **SEE** MUSIC AND MORALS
DQ104	MORAT, BATTLE OF, 1476
JX5271.M6	MORATORIUM
JX5271.M6	*MORATORY LAW* **SEE** MORATORIUM
BX8556	MORAVIAN CHURCH — PICTURES, ILLUSTRATIONS, ETC.
BX8551-8593	MORAVIAN CHURCH
E99.M9	MORAVIAN INDIANS
BX8570-8578	MORAVIANS — DOCTRINAL AND CONTROVERSIAL WORKS
BV2560	MORAVIANS — MISSIONS
BX8551-8593	MORAVIANS
RB24-57	*MORBID ANATOMY* **SEE** ANATOMY, PATHOLOGICAL
PL8062	*MORDA LANGUAGE* **SEE** BARIA LANGUAGE
TP927	MORDANTS
QE391.M	MORDENITE
PH751-779	*MORDVA LANGUAGE* **SEE** MORDVINIAN LANGUAGE
PH751-779	MORDVINIAN LANGUAGE
PH781-5	MORDVINIAN LITERATURE
BL975.M	MORDVINIANS — RELIGION
QB723.M	MOREHOUSE'S COMET
SF293.M8	MORGAN HORSE
E475.18	MORGAN'S RAID, 1863
GT5070	*MORGANATIC MARRIAGE* **SEE** MARRIAGES OF ROYALTY AND NOBILITY
Z675.N4	*MORGUES (NEWSPAPER LIBRARIES)* **SEE** NEWSPAPER OFFICE LIBRARIES
RA620-621	MORGUES
VM365	MORIARTY SUBMARINE BOAT
DP104	MORISCOS
DB34.S5	MORLAKS / *slavs of austria-hungary*

N7630	MOTHERS IN ART
PN6110.H6	*MOTHERS IN POETRY* **SEE** MOTHERS — POETRY
PN6071.M7	MOTHERS / *literary extracts*
HQ759	MOTHERS / *social sciences*
HV697-700	MOTHERS' PENSIONS
BS575	*MOTHERS-BIBLICAL TEACHING* **SEE** WOMEN IN THE BIBLE
TS1523	MOTHPROOFING
QL541-562	MOTHS
QB507	*MOTION OF THE SOLAR SYSTEM IN SPACE* **SEE** SOLAR SYSTEM — MOTION IN SPACE
PN1992-9	*MOTION PICTURES* **SEE** MOVING-PICTURES
TR845-899	*MOTION PICTURES* **SEE** MOVING-PICTURES / *photography*
RC421	*MOTION SICKNESS* **SEE** SEASICKNESS
RX301.S4	*MOTION SICKNESS* **SEE** SEASICKNESS / *homeopathic treatment*
T60.M65	MOTION STUDY
TR880	*MOTION-PICTURE CAMERAS* **SEE** MOVING-PICTURE CAMERAS
QA801-935	MOTION / *analytic mechanics*
QC122-168	MOTION / *physics*
QH647	*MOTION, COMPENSATORY* **SEE** IRRITABILITY / *cells*
TJ217	*MOTION, PERPETUAL* **SEE** PERPETUAL MOTION
BF683	MOTIVATION (PSYCHOLOGY) / *comparative psychology*
BF199	MOTIVATION (PSYCHOLOGY) / *physiological psychology*
HE5601-5720	MOTOR BUS LINES
TL232	MOTOR BUSES
HE5618.5-5720	*MOTOR CARRIERS* **SEE** TRANSPORTATION, AUTOMOTIVE — LAWS AND REGULATIONS
HD9685-9712	*MOTOR ENGINES* **SEE** MOTORS / *economics*
TJ	*MOTOR ENGINES* **SEE** MOTORS / *technology*
HD9579.G4	MOTOR FUELS — TAXATION / *gasoline*
TP343	MOTOR FUELS
BF295	*MOTOR PSYCHOLOGY* **SEE** MOVEMENT, PSYCHOLOGY OF
TL450	MOTOR SCOOTERS
TL152	*MOTOR VEHICLE DRIVERS* **SEE** AUTOMOBILE DRIVERS
UG680-685	*MOTOR VEHICLES IN WAR* **SEE** AUTOMOBILES, MILITARY
UC340-345	*MOTOR VEHICLES IN WAR* **SEE** MOTORIZATION, MILITARY
UG446.5	*MOTOR VEHICLES IN WAR* **SEE** TANKS (MILITARY SCIENCE)
UC270-360	*MOTOR VEHICLES IN WAR* **SEE** TRANSPORTATION, MILITARY
UH500-505	*MOTOR VEHICLES IN WAR* **SEE** TRANSPORTATION, MILITARY / *medical service*
VC550-555	*MOTOR VEHICLES IN WAR* **SEE** TRANSPORTATION, MILITARY / *naval*
TL	MOTOR VEHICLES
TL229.A	MOTOR VEHICLES, AMPHIBIOUS
V880	MOTOR VEHICLES, AMPHIBIOUS / *naval science*
GV835	MOTOR-BOAT RACING
VM771	MOTOR-BOATS — GASOLINE ENGINES
VM342	MOTOR-BOATS — MODELS
HE585-7	MOTOR-BOATS — SAFETY APPLIANCES
VK200	MOTOR-BOATS — SAFETY MEASURES
VM341-9	MOTOR-BOATS / *naval architecture*
GV835	MOTOR-BOATS / *sports*
TL1-445	*MOTOR-CARS* **SEE** AUTOMOBILES / *history*
HD9710	*MOTOR-CARS* **SEE** AUTOMOBILES / *industry and statistics*
GV1021-1030	*MOTOR-CARS* **SEE** AUTOMOBILES / *sports and amusements*
HE5601-5720	*MOTOR-CARS* **SEE** AUTOMOBILES / *transportation*
TJ619	*MOTOR-CARS* **SEE** RAILROAD MOTOR-CARS / *diesel*
TF975	*MOTOR-CARS* **SEE** RAILROAD MOTOR-CARS / *electric*
TF495	*MOTOR-CARS* **SEE** STEAM MOTOR-CARS / *railroads*
VM315	MOTOR-SHIPS
TL230	MOTOR-TRUCKS
TL296	*MOTOR-TRUCKS, INDUSTRIAL* **SEE** INDUSTRIAL POWER TRUCKS / *manufacture*
TS155	*MOTOR-TRUCKS, INDUSTRIAL* **SEE** INDUSTRIAL POWER TRUCKS / *material handling*
HD9710	*MOTOR-TRUCKS-TAXATION* **SEE** AUTOMOBILES — TAXATION

GV1060	MOTORCYCLE RACING
TL445	MOTORCYCLES — ELECTRIC EQUIPMENT
TL440-445	MOTORCYCLES
GV1059.5	MOTORCYCLING
UC340-345	MOTORIZATION, MILITARY
UC340-345	*MOTORIZED TROOPS* **SEE** MOTORIZATION, MILITARY
TL760	*MOTORLESS FLIGHT* **SEE** GLIDING AND SOARING
GV764-6	*MOTORLESS FLIGHT* **SEE** GLIDING AND SOARING / *sport*
HD9685-9712	MOTORS / *economics*
TJ	MOTORS / *technology*
SB608.C5	MOTTLE-LEAF / *citrus diseases*
PN6309-6318	MOTTOES
CR73-75	MOTTOES / *heraldry*
PL6257	MOTU LANGUAGE
RD118-120.5	*MOULAGE* **SEE** PROSTHESIS
QK621	*MOULD (BOTANY)* **SEE** MOLDS (BOTANY)
S598	*MOULD, VEGETABLE* **SEE** HUMUS
S590-599	*MOULD, VEGETABLE* **SEE** SOILS
TS243.5	*MOULDING SAND* **SEE** SAND, FOUNDRY
NA2960	*MOULDINGS* **SEE** MOLDINGS / *architecture*
TH2482-3	*MOULDINGS* **SEE** MOLDINGS / *building exterior*
TH2553	*MOULDINGS* **SEE** MOLDINGS / *interior*
E241.M9	MOULTRIE, FORT, BATTLE OF, 1776
E73	MOUND-BUILDERS — ART
E73	MOUND-BUILDERS — IMPLEMENTS
E73-74	MOUND-BUILDERS
GN795-6	MOUNDS
DS486.E8	MOUNT EVEREST EXPEDITION, 1921
DS486.E8	MOUNT EVEREST EXPEDITION, 1922
DS486.E8	MOUNT EVEREST EXPEDITION, 1924
DS486.E8	MOUNT EVEREST EXPEDITION, 1938
UF400-445	*MOUNTAIN ARTILLERY* **SEE** ARTILLERY, FIELD AND MOUNTAIN
G505-510	*MOUNTAIN CLIMBING* **SEE** MOUNTAINEERING
QK937	*MOUNTAIN FLORA* **SEE** ALPINE FLORA / *botany*
QK331	*MOUNTAIN FLORA* **SEE** ALPINE FLORA / *botany*
SB421	*MOUNTAIN FLORA* **SEE** ALPINE FLORA / *culture*
UF440-445	MOUNTAIN GUNS
QK495.K3	MOUNTAIN LAUREL / *botany*
QL737.C2	*MOUNTAIN LIONS* **SEE** PUMAS
F826	MOUNTAIN MEADOWS MASSACRE, 1857
TR787	*MOUNTAIN PHOTOGRAPHY* **SEE** PHOTOGRAPHY OF MOUNTAINS
TF680-688	MOUNTAIN RAILROADS / *engineering*
HE4051-4071	MOUNTAIN RAILROADS / *transportation*
TE153	MOUNTAIN ROADS
SK305.M	MOUNTAIN SHEEP / *hunting*
QL737.U5	MOUNTAIN SHEEP / *zoology*
RC103.A4	MOUNTAIN SICKNESS
QK495.C	*MOUNTAIN SPINACH* **SEE** ORACH / *botany*
SB351.O	*MOUNTAIN SPINACH* **SEE** ORACH / *vegetables*
U240	MOUNTAIN WARFARE
QC939.M8	MOUNTAIN WAVE
TL557.A5	MOUNTAIN WAVE / *aeronautics*
F210	MOUNTAIN WHITES (SOUTHERN STATES)
PM1921-4	*MOUNTAINEE LANGUAGE* **SEE** MONTAGNAIS LANGUAGE
E99.M87	*MOUNTAINEER INDIANS* **SEE** MONTAGNAIS INDIANS
G505-510	MOUNTAINEERING
G512.A2	*MOUNTAINEERING-BIOGRAPHY* **SEE** MOUNTAINEERS
G512.A2	MOUNTAINEERS
GR660	MOUNTAINS (IN RELIGION, FOLK-LORE, ETC.) / *folk-lore*
BL447	MOUNTAINS (IN RELIGION, FOLK-LORE, ETC.) / *religion*
N8225.M6	MOUNTAINS IN ART
PN56.M7	MOUNTAINS IN LITERATURE
BS630	MOUNTAINS IN THE BIBLE
GR660	MOUNTAINS / *folk-lore*
GB501-553	MOUNTAINS / *physical geography*
GT3390	MOURNING CUSTOMS
BM712	MOURNING CUSTOMS, JEWISH
QL696.C6	MOURNING DOVES
QL737.R6	*MOUSE* **SEE** MICE
QL737.U5	MOUSE-DEER
SB413.P4	*MOUTAN PEONY* **SEE** TREE PEONY
QR47	MOUTH — BACTERIOLOGY
RC261	MOUTH — CANCER
RC815	MOUTH — DISEASES

RM822.M9	*MUD BATHS* **SEE** BATHS, MOOR AND MUD
TP360	MUD FUEL
HE1781.M8	MUD RUN DISASTER, OCT. 10, 1888
VM463	*MUD-SCOWS* **SEE** SCOWS / *construction*
DP104	*MUDEJARES* **SEE** MORISCOS
PN4165	*MUDRA* **SEE** GESTURE / *public speaking*
TJ789	*MUFFLERS (GAS AND OIL ENGINES)* **SEE** GAS AND OIL ENGINES — MUFFLERS
GT2190	MUFFS / *costume*
GV1299.M	MUGGINS (GAME) / *card games*
GV1467	MUGGINS (GAME) / *dominoes*
DS38	*MUHAMMADANS* **SEE** MUSLIMS
HT851-1445	*MUI TSAI* **SEE** SLAVERY
F2270.2.C4	*MUISCAS* **SEE** CHIBCHA INDIANS
DS517.4	MUKDEN, BATTLE OF, 1905
GN645	MULATTOES / *anthropology*
E185.62	MULATTOES / *u.s.*
SB608.M8	MULBERRY — DISEASES AND PESTS
SB741.M	*MULBERRY BACTERIAL BLIGHT* **SEE** MULBERRY BLIGHT
SB741.M	MULBERRY BLIGHT
SF557	MULBERRY / *culture*
TS1483	*MULES (SPINNING MACHINERY)* **SEE** SPINNING MACHINERY
SF361	*MULES* **SEE** ASSES AND MULES
DQ100	*MULHAUSEN, WAR OF, 1468* **SEE** WALDSHUT, WAR OF, 1468
QL638.M	*MULLETS, GRAY* **SEE** GRAY MULLETS
SH351.G	*MULLETS, GRAY* **SEE** GRAY MULLETS / *fish-culture*
QD181.A4	MULLITE
Z48	MULTIGRAPH
Z48	*MULTILITH* **SEE** MULTIGRAPH
RG696	*MULTIPLE BIRTH* **SEE** BIRTH, MULTIPLE
RC554-574	*MULTIPLE CONSCIOUSNESS* **SEE** PERSONALITY, DISORDERS OF
RC280.M	*MULTIPLE MYELOMA* **SEE** MARROW — TUMORS
Z252.5.M8	MULTIPLE PRINTING
RC377	MULTIPLE SCLEROSIS
QA49	MULTIPLICATION — TABLES
QA115	MULTIPLICATION / *mathematics*
TK7872.E5	*MULTIPLIER PHOTOTUBES* **SEE** PHOTOELECTRIC MULTIPLIERS
TK7872.M8	*MULTIPLIERS (ELECTRONIC CALCULATING-MACHINES)* **SEE** ANALOG MULTIPLIERS
DT62.M7	MUMMIES / *egyptology*
GT4985	MUMMING / *christmas customs*
PR635.F6	MUMMING / *english folk-drama*
RC168.M8	MUMPS
PL4501-9	MUNDA LANGUAGES
PM8637	MUNDAL (ARTIFICIAL LANGUAGE)
PL4559	MUNDARI LANGUAGE
DS432.M8	MUNDAS
F2520.1.M	*MUNDRUCU INDIANS* **SEE** MUNDURUCU INDIANS
F2520.1.M	MUNDURUCU INDIANS
PM6596	MUNDURUCU LANGUAGE
DU397.5	MUNGARAI (AUSTRALIAN TRIBE)
DU397.5	*MUNGARI (AUSTRALIAN TRIBE)* **SEE** MUNGARAI (AUSTRALIAN TRIBE)
PL4001.A7	*MUNGSEN DIALECT* **SEE** AO LANGUAGE
HJ9771-9	*MUNICIPAL ACCOUNTING* **SEE** MUNICIPAL FINANCE — ACCOUNTING
JS	*MUNICIPAL ADMINISTRATION* **SEE** MUNICIPAL GOVERNMENT
JX1248	*MUNICIPAL AND INTERNATIONAL LAW* **SEE** INTERNATIONAL AND MUNICIPAL LAW
JK-JQ	*MUNICIPAL AND INTERNATIONAL LAW* **SEE** INTERNATIONAL AND MUNICIPAL LAW
JS344.A5	*MUNICIPAL ANNEXATION* **SEE** ANNEXATION (MUNICIPAL GOVERNMENT) / *u.s.*
NA9000-9425	*MUNICIPAL ART* **SEE** ART, MUNICIPAL / *aesthetics of cities*
N8700-8850	*MUNICIPAL ART* **SEE** ART, MUNICIPAL / *public art*
HG4726	MUNICIPAL BONDS
HG5151-5890	MUNICIPAL BONDS / *other countries*
HG4951-3	MUNICIPAL BONDS / *u.s.*
JS201-8	MUNICIPAL BUILDINGS
NA4430-4437	MUNICIPAL BUILDINGS / *architecture*
JS	MUNICIPAL CORPORATIONS

TD	MUNICIPAL ENGINEERING
HJ9771-9	MUNICIPAL FINANCE — ACCOUNTING
HJ9000-9697	MUNICIPAL FINANCE
HD2763-8	MUNICIPAL FRANCHISES
JS344.C5	MUNICIPAL GOVERNMENT BY CITY MANAGER / *u.s.*
JS342-3	MUNICIPAL GOVERNMENT BY COMMISSION / *u.s.*
JS	MUNICIPAL GOVERNMENT
JS	*MUNICIPAL GOVERNMENT-LAW AND LEGISLATION* **SEE** MUNICIPAL CORPORATIONS
JS113	MUNICIPAL HOME RULE
JS3131-7	MUNICIPAL HOME RULE / *gt. brit.*
JS348-9	MUNICIPAL HOME RULE / *u.s.*
NA9000-9425	*MUNICIPAL IMPROVEMENTS* **SEE** ART, MUNICIPAL / *aesthetics of cities*
N8700-8850	*MUNICIPAL IMPROVEMENTS* **SEE** ART, MUNICIPAL / *public art*
JS302-3	*MUNICIPAL IMPROVEMENTS* **SEE** CITIES AND TOWNS — CIVIC IMPROVEMENT / *societies u.s.*
JS93-99	*MUNICIPAL IMPROVEMENTS* **SEE** CITIES AND TOWNS — CIVIC IMPROVEMENT
TD1015	*MUNICIPAL LAUNDRIES* **SEE** LAUNDRIES, PUBLIC
JS	*MUNICIPAL LAW (MUNICIPAL CORPORATIONS)* **SEE** MUNICIPAL CORPORATIONS
HD4421-4730	MUNICIPAL OWNERSHIP
Z675.M9	MUNICIPAL REFERENCE LIBRARIES
JS163	MUNICIPAL REPORTS
JS	*MUNICIPAL SERVICES WITHIN CORPORATE LIMITS* **SEE** MUNICIPAL GOVERNMENT
PN2268	*MUNICIPAL THEATER* **SEE** THEATER, MUNICIPAL
LB2329	MUNICIPAL UNIVERSITIES AND COLLEGES
HD2763-8	*MUNICIPAL UTILITIES* **SEE** PUBLIC UTILITIES
HT101-381	*MUNICIPALITIES* **SEE** CITIES AND TOWNS
HV6177	*MUNICIPALITIES* **SEE** CITIES AND TOWNS / *influence on crime*
JS	*MUNICIPALITIES* **SEE** CITIES AND TOWNS / *local government*
JS	*MUNICIPALITIES* **SEE** MUNICIPAL GOVERNMENT
HD7269.M8	MUNITION WORKERS
HD9743	*MUNITIONS TRADE* **SEE** MUNITIONS / *economics*
JX5390	*MUNITIONS TRADE* **SEE** MUNITIONS / *international law*
UF530-537	*MUNITIONS TRADE* **SEE** MUNITIONS / *manufacture*
HD9743	MUNITIONS / *economics*
JX5390	MUNITIONS / *international law*
UF530-537	MUNITIONS / *manufacture*
E99.M93	MUNSEE INDIANS
PM1961	MUNSEE LANGUAGE
PM1961	*MUNSEY LANGUAGE* **SEE** MUNSEE LANGUAGE
DT515	*MUNSHI* **SEE** TIVI (AFRICAN PEOPLE)
DT515	*MUNSI* **SEE** TIVI (AFRICAN PEOPLE)
D269	*MUNSTER, PEACE OF, 1648* **SEE** WESTPHALIA, PEACE OF, 1648
ND2550-2876	MURAL PAINTING AND DECORATION
PK2351-2378	*MURATHEE LANGUAGE* **SEE** MARATHI LANGUAGE
HV6499-6542	MURDER
BM717	*MURDER, RITUAL* **SEE** BLOOD ACCUSATION
DC611.L3	MURET, BATTLE OF, 1213
E474.77	MURFREESBORO, BATTLE OF, 1862-1863
DS432.M	MURIA
TP217.H8	*MURIATIC ACID* **SEE** HYDROCHLORIC ACID / *chemical technology*
QD181.C5	*MURIATIC ACID* **SEE** HYDROCHLORIC ACID / *chemistry*
QL696.A3	MURRES
DQ104	*MURTEN, BATTLE OF, 1476* **SEE** MORAT, BATTLE OF, 1476
DS646.33	MURUTS / *borneo*
BJ1285.5.M8	MUSAR MOVEMENT
BJ1285.5.M8	*MUSARNIKES* **SEE** MUSAR MOVEMENT
QK534-563	MUSCINEAE
QM571	MUSCLE / *histology*
QP321	MUSCLE / *physiology*
QL831	MUSCLES — ABNORMITIES AND DEFORMITIES / *comparative anatomy*
QM151-165	MUSCLES — ABNORMITIES AND DEFORMITIES / *human anatomy*
RC935	MUSCLES — DISEASES
RC925-7	MUSCLES — DISEASES
RD688	MUSCLES — DISEASES

QL831	MUSCLES / *comparative anatomy*
QM151-165	MUSCLES / *human anatomy*
QP301-3	MUSCLES / *movements*
RD688	MUSCLES, HYPERTROPHY OF
E99.C9	*MUSCOGEE INDIANS* **SEE** CREEK INDIANS
PM991	*MUSCOGEE LANGUAGE* **SEE** CREEK LANGUAGE
QE391.M	MUSCOVITE / *mineralogy*
BF285	MUSCULAR SENSE
PL8535	*MUSEKU LANGUAGE* **SEE** MUSGU LANGUAGE
AM151-3	*MUSEOLOGY* **SEE** MUSEUM TECHNIQUES
BL820.M8	MUSES
ML980	*MUSETTE* **SEE** BAGPIPE
AM139	MUSEUM REGISTRATION METHODS
AM151-3	MUSEUM TECHNIQUES
AM127-9	MUSEUMS — FURNITURE, EQUIPMENT, ETC.
AM8	*MUSEUMS FOR CHILDREN* **SEE** CHILDREN'S MUSEUMS
AM	MUSEUMS
AM8	*MUSEUMS, CHILDREN'S* **SEE** CHILDREN'S MUSEUMS
ML136-141	*MUSEUMS, MUSIC* **SEE** MUSIC MUSEUMS / *etc.*
ML462	*MUSEUMS, MUSIC* **SEE** MUSIC MUSEUMS / *instruments*
AM139	*MUSEUMS-ACCESSIONING* **SEE** MUSEUM REGISTRATION METHODS
AM139	*MUSEUMS-REGISTRATION* **SEE** MUSEUM REGISTRATION METHODS
PL8535	MUSGU LANGUAGE
SB353	MUSHROOM CULTURE
SD608.M9	MUSHROOMS — DISEASES AND PESTS
QK617	MUSHROOMS
QK617	MUSHROOMS, EDIBLE
QK617	MUSHROOMS, POISONOUS
SB353	*MUSHROOMS-CULTURE* **SEE** MUSHROOM CULTURE
ML3805-3817	MUSIC — ACOUSTICS AND PHYSICS
ML13-21	MUSIC — ALMANACS, YEARBOOKS, ETC.
MT6	MUSIC — ANALYSIS, APPRECIATION
MT90-150	MUSIC — ANALYTICAL GUIDES
ML65	MUSIC — ANECDOTES, FACETIAE, SATIRE, ETC.
ML111-158	MUSIC — BIBLIOGRAPHY
ML105-7	MUSIC — BIO-BIBLIOGRAPHY / *dictionaries*
ML385-429	MUSIC — BIO-BIBLIOGRAPHY / *history and criticism*
MT15	MUSIC — CHARTS, DIAGRAMS, ETC.
ML161	MUSIC — CHRONOLOGY
ML76	MUSIC — COMPETITIONS
ML100-110	MUSIC — DICTIONARIES
ML156	MUSIC — DISCOGRAPHY
ML63	MUSIC — EDITING
MT9	MUSIC — EXAMINATIONS, QUESTIONS, ETC.
ML141	MUSIC — EXHIBITIONS / *catalogs*
ML462	MUSIC — EXHIBITIONS / *instruments*
ML128	MUSIC — FILM CATALOGS
ML	MUSIC — HISTORIOGRAPHY
ML159-3795	MUSIC — HISTORY AND CRITICISM
MT	MUSIC — INSTRUCTION AND STUDY
ML166	MUSIC — JEWS / *history and criticism*
ML3195	MUSIC — JEWS / *vocal music*
ML3930	MUSIC — JUVENILE LITERATURE
MT6-10	MUSIC — MANUALS, TEXT-BOOKS, ETC.
ML93-98	MUSIC — MANUSCRIPTS
MT82	MUSIC — MEMORIZING
ML3556	MUSIC — NEGROES
ML457	MUSIC — PERFORMANCE
ML1-5	MUSIC — PERIODICALS
ML3785	MUSIC — PERIODICALS / *history*
ML3800-3920	MUSIC — PHILOSOPHY AND AESTHETICS
ML3820-3822	MUSIC — PHYSIOLOGICAL ASPECTS
ML3920	MUSIC — PHYSIOLOGICAL EFFECT
ML3849	MUSIC — POETRY
ML3830-3838	MUSIC — PSYCHOLOGY
ML66	MUSIC — QUOTATIONS, MAXIMS, ETC.
ML25-28	MUSIC — SOCIETIES, ETC.
ML108	MUSIC — TERMINOLOGY
MT7	MUSIC — THEORY, ELEMENTARY
Z653	*MUSIC · COPYRIGHT* **SEE** COPYRIGHT — MUSIC
ML3849	MUSIC AND ARCHITECTURE
ML3840	MUSIC AND COLOR
ML80	MUSIC AND LITERATURE
ML3849	MUSIC AND LITERATURE
ML3920	MUSIC AND MORALS
ML80	*MUSIC AND POETRY* **SEE** MUSIC AND LITERATURE

ML3849	*MUSIC AND POETRY* **SEE** MUSIC AND LITERATURE
ML68	*MUSIC AND RADIO* **SEE** RADIO AND MUSIC
MT150	*MUSIC AND RADIO* **SEE** RADIO AND MUSIC / *analytical guides*
ML196	*MUSIC AND ROMANTICISM* **SEE** ROMANTICISM IN MUSIC
ML3795	MUSIC AND STATE
ML3795	MUSIC AS A PROFESSION
ML1055	MUSIC BOX
ML13-21	MUSIC CALENDARS
ML402	*MUSIC CONDUCTORS* **SEE** CONDUCTORS (MUSIC) / *biography collective*
ML422	*MUSIC CONDUCTORS* **SEE** CONDUCTORS (MUSIC) / *individual*
ML3795	*MUSIC CONSERVATORIES* **SEE** CONSERVATORIES OF MUSIC
ML35-38	MUSIC FESTIVALS
UH40-45	*MUSIC IN ARMIES* **SEE** MUSIC IN THE ARMY / *military science*
ML85	MUSIC IN ART
N8226	MUSIC IN ART
ML3001	MUSIC IN CHURCHES
ML3923	MUSIC IN PHYSICAL EDUCATION
ML3920	MUSIC IN PRISONS
M3195	MUSIC IN SYNAGOGUES
UH40-45	MUSIC IN THE ARMY / *military science*
ML67	MUSIC IN THE HOME
ML63	MUSIC IN UNIVERSITIES AND COLLEGES
MT18	MUSIC IN UNIVERSITIES AND COLLEGES / *instruction*
ML136-9	MUSIC LIBRARIES / *catalogs*
ML111	MUSIC LIBRARIES / *forming of libraries*
ML136-141	MUSIC MUSEUMS / *etc.*
ML462	MUSIC MUSEUMS / *instruments*
ML3840	*MUSIC OF COLORS* **SEE** MUSIC AND COLOR
BD645	*MUSIC OF THE SPHERES* **SEE** HARMONY OF THE SPHERES
ML112	MUSIC PRINTING
ML112	*MUSIC PUBLISHERS* **SEE** MUSIC PRINTING
Z278-550	*MUSIC PUBLISHERS* **SEE** PUBLISHERS AND PUBLISHING
MT85	*MUSIC READING* **SEE** SCORE READING AND PLAYING
MT236	*MUSIC READING* **SEE** SIGHT-READING (MUSIC)
ML3795	*MUSIC SCHOOLS* **SEE** CONSERVATORIES OF MUSIC
ML3795	MUSIC TEACHERS
RC489.M7	MUSIC THERAPY
ML3790	MUSIC TRADE
ML200.5	MUSIC WEEK
PN1960-1969	MUSIC-HALLS (VARIETY-THEATERS, CABARETS, ETC.)
NA6820-6840	MUSIC-HALLS / *architecture*
ML1090	MUSIC-RECORDERS
ML162-9	*MUSIC, ANCIENT* **SEE** MUSIC — HISTORY AND CRITICISM — — ANCIENT
ML162-9	*MUSIC, ANCIENT* **SEE** MUSIC — THEORY — — ANCIENT
MT6	*MUSIC, APPRECIATION OF* **SEE** MUSIC — ANALYSIS, APPRECIATION
ML1500-1554	*MUSIC, CHORAL* **SEE** CHORAL MUSIC / *history general*
ML2900-3275	*MUSIC, CHORAL* **SEE** CHORAL MUSIC / *sacred*
ML2400-2770	*MUSIC, CHORAL* **SEE** CHORAL MUSIC / *secular*
M1997.C5	*MUSIC, COMMUNITY* **SEE** COMMUNITY MUSIC
ML2500-2770	*MUSIC, COMMUNITY* **SEE** COMMUNITY MUSIC / *history and criticism*
MT875	*MUSIC, COMMUNITY* **SEE** COMMUNITY MUSIC / *instruction*
ML1950	*MUSIC, DRAMATIC* **SEE** BALLAD OPERA / *history*
ML3860	*MUSIC, DRAMATIC* **SEE** MUSIC, INCIDENTAL / *aesthetics*
ML2000	*MUSIC, DRAMATIC* **SEE** MUSIC, INCIDENTAL / *history*
ML3858	*MUSIC, DRAMATIC* **SEE** OPERA / *aesthetics*
ML1700-2110	*MUSIC, DRAMATIC* **SEE** OPERA / *history and criticism*
ML1900	*MUSIC, DRAMATIC* **SEE** OPERETTA
ML1950	*MUSIC, DRAMATIC* **SEE** SINGSPIEL
ML1950	*MUSIC, DRAMATIC* **SEE** ZARZUELA
ML3920	*MUSIC, EFFECT OF* **SEE** MUSIC — PHYSIOLOGICAL EFFECT
ML3920	*MUSIC, EFFECT OF* **SEE** MUSIC AND MORALS
RC489.M7	*MUSIC, EFFECT OF* **SEE** MUSIC THERAPY

ML3920	*MUSIC, EFFECT OF* **SEE** MUSIC, INFLUENCE OF
ML3560	*MUSIC, ESKIMO* **SEE** ESKIMOS — MUSIC
ML166	*MUSIC, HEBREW* **SEE** MUSIC — JEWS / *history and criticism*
ML3195	*MUSIC, HEBREW* **SEE** MUSIC — JEWS / *vocal music*
ML430	*MUSIC, IMITATION IN* **SEE** IMITATION (IN MUSIC)
ML197	*MUSIC, IMPRESSIONISM IN* **SEE** IMPRESSIONISM (MUSIC)
ML3575	*MUSIC, INCA* **SEE** INCAS — MUSIC
M1513	MUSIC, INCIDENTAL — PIANO SCORES
M1513	MUSIC, INCIDENTAL — VOCAL SCORES WITH PIANO
ML3860	MUSIC, INCIDENTAL / *aesthetics*
ML2000	MUSIC, INCIDENTAL / *history*
M1518	*MUSIC, INCIDENTAL-VOCAL SCORES WITH PIANO-EXCERPTS* **SEE** MUSIC, INCIDENTAL — EXCERPTS — — VOCAL SCORES WITH PIANO
M1518	MUSIC, INCIDENTAL — EXCERPTS — — VOCAL SCORES WITH PIANO
M1510	MUSIC, INCIDENTAL — TO 1800 — — SCORES
E59.M9	*MUSIC, INDIAN (AMERICAN INDIAN)* **SEE** INDIANS — MUSIC
ML3547	*MUSIC, INDIAN (AMERICAN INDIAN)* **SEE** INDIANS — MUSIC
ML3920	MUSIC, INFLUENCE OF
M5-1459	*MUSIC, INSTRUMENTAL* **SEE** INSTRUMENTAL MUSIC
ML174	*MUSIC, MEASURED* **SEE** MEASURED MUSIC
ML170-190	*MUSIC, MEDIEVAL* **SEE** MUSIC — HISTORY AND CRITICISM — — MEDIEVAL
ML170-174	*MUSIC, MEDIEVAL* **SEE** MUSIC — THEORY — — MEDIEVAL
M1270	*MUSIC, MILITARY* **SEE** MILITARY MUSIC
M1627-1844	*MUSIC, NATIONAL* **SEE** NATIONAL MUSIC
ML162	MUSIC, ORIENTAL / *history and criticism*
ML330-345	MUSIC, ORIENTAL / *history and criticism*
M1795-1825	MUSIC, ORIENTAL / *music*
ML3800	MUSIC, ORIGIN OF
ML3920	*MUSIC, PHYSICAL EFFECT OF* **SEE** MUSIC — PHYSIOLOGICAL EFFECT
RC489.M7	*MUSIC, PHYSICAL EFFECT OF* **SEE** MUSIC THERAPY
ML3920	*MUSIC, PHYSIOLOGICAL EFFECT OF* **SEE** MUSIC — PHYSIOLOGICAL EFFECT
ML63	*MUSIC, PLAGIARISM IN* **SEE** PLAGIARISM IN MUSIC
MT67	MUSIC, POPULAR (SONGS, ETC.) — WRITING AND PUBLISHING
MT67	*MUSIC, POPULAR (SONGS, ETC.)-RECORDING* **SEE** MUSIC, POPULAR (SONGS, ETC.) — WRITING AND PUBLISHING
ML3547	MUSIC, PRIMITIVE
GN465-8	MUSIC, PRIMITIVE / *anthropology*
ML112	*MUSIC, PRINTING OF* **SEE** MUSIC PRINTING
ML3869	*MUSIC, RELIGIOUS* **SEE** CHURCH MUSIC / *aesthetics*
ML178	*MUSIC, RELIGIOUS* **SEE** CHURCH MUSIC / *history*
ML3000-3190	*MUSIC, RELIGIOUS* **SEE** CHURCH MUSIC / *history*
ML3270	*MUSIC, RELIGIOUS* **SEE** CHURCH MUSIC / *history*
MT915	*MUSIC, RELIGIOUS* **SEE** CHURCH MUSIC / *instruction and study*
MT88	*MUSIC, RELIGIOUS* **SEE** CHURCH MUSIC / *instruction and study*
MT860-865	*MUSIC, RELIGIOUS* **SEE** CHURCH MUSIC / *instruction and study*
M2186-7	*MUSIC, RELIGIOUS* **SEE** SYNAGOGUE MUSIC / *services*
M2114.3	*MUSIC, RELIGIOUS* **SEE** SYNAGOGUE MUSIC / *songs*
M2099.5	*MUSIC, RELIGIOUS* **SEE** SYNAGOGUE MUSIC / *special texts*
M2079.5	*MUSIC, RELIGIOUS* **SEE** SYNAGOGUE MUSIC / *special texts*
ML3869	*MUSIC, SACRED* **SEE** CHURCH MUSIC / *aesthetics*
ML3000-3190	*MUSIC, SACRED* **SEE** CHURCH MUSIC / *history*
ML3270	*MUSIC, SACRED* **SEE** CHURCH MUSIC / *history*
ML178	*MUSIC, SACRED* **SEE** CHURCH MUSIC / *history*
MT88	*MUSIC, SACRED* **SEE** CHURCH MUSIC / *instruction and study*
MT860-865	*MUSIC, SACRED* **SEE** CHURCH MUSIC / *instruction and study*
MT915	*MUSIC, SACRED* **SEE** CHURCH MUSIC / *instruction and study*

M2114.3	*MUSIC, SACRED* **SEE** SYNAGOGUE MUSIC / *songs*
M2099.5	*MUSIC, SACRED* **SEE** SYNAGOGUE MUSIC / *special texts*
M2079.5	*MUSIC, SACRED* **SEE** SYNAGOGUE MUSIC / *special texts*
ML1950	*MUSIC, THEATRICAL* **SEE** BALLAD OPERA / *history*
ML3860	*MUSIC, THEATRICAL* **SEE** MUSIC, INCIDENTAL / *aesthetics*
ML2000	*MUSIC, THEATRICAL* **SEE** MUSIC, INCIDENTAL / *history*
ML3858	*MUSIC, THEATRICAL* **SEE** OPERA / *aesthetics*
ML1700-2110	*MUSIC, THEATRICAL* **SEE** OPERA / *history and criticism*
ML1900	*MUSIC, THEATRICAL* **SEE** OPERETTA
ML1950	*MUSIC, THEATRICAL* **SEE** SINGSPIEL
ML1950	*MUSIC, THEATRICAL* **SEE** ZARZUELA
M1495-2199	*MUSIC, VOCAL* **SEE** VOCAL MUSIC
ML166	*MUSIC, YIDDISH* **SEE** MUSIC — JEWS / *history and criticism*
ML3195	*MUSIC, YIDDISH* **SEE** MUSIC — JEWS / *vocal music*
ML3800-3920	*MUSIC-AESTHETICS* **SEE** MUSIC — PHILOSOPHY AND AESTHETICS
ML390	*MUSIC-BIOGRAPHY* **SEE** COMPOSERS / *biography collective*
ML410	*MUSIC-BIOGRAPHY* **SEE** COMPOSERS / *individual*
ML402	*MUSIC-BIOGRAPHY* **SEE** CONDUCTORS (MUSIC) / *biography collective*
ML422	*MUSIC-BIOGRAPHY* **SEE** CONDUCTORS (MUSIC) / *individual*
ML937	*MUSIC-BIOGRAPHY* **SEE** FLUTE-PLAYERS
ML105-7	*MUSIC-BIOGRAPHY* **SEE** MUSIC — BIO-BIBLIOGRAPHY / *dictionaries*
ML385-429	*MUSIC-BIOGRAPHY* **SEE** MUSIC — BIO-BIBLIOGRAPHY / *history and criticism*
ML3795	*MUSIC-BIOGRAPHY* **SEE** MUSIC TEACHERS
ML460-1055	*MUSIC-BIOGRAPHY* **SEE** MUSICAL INSTRUMENTS — MAKERS
HD9999.M8	*MUSIC-BIOGRAPHY* **SEE** MUSICAL INSTRUMENTS — MAKERS
ML385-403	*MUSIC-BIOGRAPHY* **SEE** MUSICIANS
ML396	*MUSIC-BIOGRAPHY* **SEE** ORGANISTS / *biography collective*
ML416	*MUSIC-BIOGRAPHY* **SEE** ORGANISTS / *individual*
ML397	*MUSIC-BIOGRAPHY* **SEE** PIANISTS / *biography collective*
ML417	*MUSIC-BIOGRAPHY* **SEE** PIANISTS / *individual*
ML400	*MUSIC-BIOGRAPHY* **SEE** SINGERS / *biography collective*
ML420	*MUSIC-BIOGRAPHY* **SEE** SINGERS / *individual*
ML111	*MUSIC-CATALOGING* **SEE** CATALOGING OF MUSIC
ML111	*MUSIC-CLASSIFICATION* **SEE** CLASSIFICATION — MUSIC
ML430-455	*MUSIC-COMPOSITION* **SEE** COMPOSITION (MUSIC) / *history*
MT40-67	*MUSIC-COMPOSITION* **SEE** COMPOSITION (MUSIC) / *instruction*
ML3795	*MUSIC-CONSERVATORIES* **SEE** CONSERVATORIES OF MUSIC
Z653	*MUSIC-COPYRIGHT* **SEE** COPYRIGHT — MUSIC
MT7	*MUSIC-ELEMENTARY THEORY* **SEE** MUSIC — THEORY, ELEMENTARY
ML	*MUSIC-HISTORY AND CRITICISM-METHODS* **SEE** MUSIC — HISTORIOGRAPHY
ML3880-3916	*MUSIC-HISTORY AND CRITICISM-METHODS* **SEE** MUSICAL CRITICISM
ML	*MUSIC-HISTORY AND CRITICISM-THEORY, ETC.* **SEE** MUSIC — HISTORIOGRAPHY
ML3880-3916	*MUSIC-HISTORY AND CRITICISM-THEORY, ETC.* **SEE** MUSICAL CRITICISM
ML112	*MUSIC-INCUNABULA* **SEE** INCUNABULA — MUSIC
E59.M9	*MUSIC-INDIANS* **SEE** INDIANS — MUSIC
ML3547	*MUSIC-INDIANS* **SEE** INDIANS — MUSIC
M1990	*MUSIC-KINDERGARTEN* **SEE** KINDERGARTEN — MUSIC
MT920-925	*MUSIC-KINDERGARTEN* **SEE** KINDERGARTEN — MUSIC / *instruction and study*
ML3809	*MUSIC-MODES* **SEE** MUSICAL INTERVALS AND SCALES

ML136-141	*MUSIC-MUSEUMS* **SEE** MUSIC MUSEUMS / *etc.*
ML462	*MUSIC-MUSEUMS* **SEE** MUSIC MUSEUMS / *instruments*
ML431	*MUSIC-NOTATION* **SEE** MUSICAL NOTATION / *history*
MT35	*MUSIC-NOTATION* **SEE** MUSICAL NOTATION / *instruction*
ML432	*MUSIC-NOTATION* **SEE** MUSICAL NOTATION / *reform*
ML156	*MUSIC-PHONOGRAPH RECORDS-BIBLIOGRAPHY* **SEE** MUSIC — DISCOGRAPHY
ML63	*MUSIC-PLAGIARISM* **SEE** PLAGIARISM IN MUSIC
MT35	*MUSIC-PROOF-READING* **SEE** PROOF-READING — MUSIC
MT85	*MUSIC-READING* **SEE** SCORE READING AND PLAYING
MT236	*MUSIC-READING* **SEE** SIGHT-READING (MUSIC)
MT7	*MUSIC-RUDIMENTS* **SEE** MUSIC — THEORY, ELEMENTARY
MT	*MUSIC-STUDY AND TEACHING* **SEE** MUSIC — INSTRUCTION AND STUDY
BV520	*MUSIC-SUNDAY-SCHOOLS* **SEE** SUNDAY-SCHOOLS — HYMNS
RC489.M7	*MUSIC-THERAPEUTIC USE* **SEE** MUSIC THERAPY
ML1-5	*MUSIC-U.S.-PERIODICALS* **SEE** MUSIC — PERIODICALS
ML3785	*MUSIC-U.S.-PERIODICALS* **SEE** MUSIC — PERIODICALS / *history*
ML13-21	*MUSIC-YEARBOOKS* **SEE** MUSIC — ALMANACS, YEARBOOKS, ETC.
ML173	*MUSICA FICTA* **SEE** CHROMATIC ALTERATION (MUSIC)
MT239	MUSICAL ACCOMPANIMENT / *etc.*
MT68	MUSICAL ACCOMPANIMENT / *instruction*
MT190	MUSICAL ACCOMPANIMENT / *organ*
ML1055	*MUSICAL BOX* **SEE** MUSIC BOX
M1985	MUSICAL CARD GAMES
ML25-28	*MUSICAL CLUBS* **SEE** MUSICAL SOCIETIES
M1500-1508	*MUSICAL COMEDIES* **SEE** MUSICAL REVUES, COMEDIES, ETC.
ML430-455	*MUSICAL COMPOSITION* **SEE** COMPOSITION (MUSIC) / *history*
MT40-67	*MUSICAL COMPOSITION* **SEE** COMPOSITION (MUSIC) / *instruction*
ML3880-3916	MUSICAL CRITICISM
M1625-6	*MUSICAL DECLAMATION* **SEE** MONOLOGUES WITH MUSIC
MT872	*MUSICAL DECLAMATION* **SEE** SINGING — DICTION
MT35	MUSICAL DICTATION
MT	*MUSICAL EDUCATION* **SEE** MUSIC — INSTRUCTION AND STUDY
ML1900	*MUSICAL FARCE* **SEE** OPERETTA
ML35-38	*MUSICAL FESTIVALS* **SEE** MUSIC FESTIVALS
ML3925	MUSICAL FICTION
ML448	MUSICAL FORM / *history*
MT58-64	MUSICAL FORM / *instruction*
ML1055	*MUSICAL GLASSES* **SEE** GLASS HARMONICA
MT	*MUSICAL INSTRUCTION* **SEE** MUSIC — INSTRUCTION AND STUDY
ML462	MUSICAL INSTRUMENTS — CATALOGS AND COLLECTIONS
ML155	MUSICAL INSTRUMENTS — CATALOGS, MANUFACTURERS'
ML460	MUSICAL INSTRUMENTS — CONSTRUCTION
ML102	MUSICAL INSTRUMENTS — DICTIONARIES
ML462	MUSICAL INSTRUMENTS — EXHIBITIONS
ML3930	MUSICAL INSTRUMENTS — JUVENILE LITERATURE
ML460-1055	MUSICAL INSTRUMENTS — MAKERS
HD9999.M8	MUSICAL INSTRUMENTS — MAKERS
ML460	MUSICAL INSTRUMENTS — REPAIRING
ML108	MUSICAL INSTRUMENTS — TERMINOLOGY
ML1050-1055	MUSICAL INSTRUMENTS (MECHANICAL) / *history*
MT700	MUSICAL INSTRUMENTS (MECHANICAL) / *instruction*
ML462	MUSICAL INSTRUMENTS / *exhibitions*
ML460-1055	MUSICAL INSTRUMENTS / *history*
HD9999.M8	MUSICAL INSTRUMENTS / *industry*
MT170-805	MUSICAL INSTRUMENTS / *instruction*
ML1092	MUSICAL INSTRUMENTS, ELECTRONIC
GN466-8	MUSICAL INSTRUMENTS, PRIMITIVE / *anthropology*
ML3547	MUSICAL INSTRUMENTS, PRIMITIVE / *music*
ML462	*MUSICAL INSTRUMENTS-COLLECTIONS* **SEE** MUSICAL INSTRUMENTS — CATALOGS AND COLLECTIONS
E59.M9	*MUSICAL INSTRUMENTS-INDIANS* **SEE** INDIANS — MUSIC
ML3547	*MUSICAL INSTRUMENTS-INDIANS* **SEE** INDIANS — MUSIC
ML3790	*MUSICAL INSTRUMENTS-INDUSTRY AND TRADE* **SEE** MUSIC TRADE
MT170	*MUSICAL INSTRUMENTS-INSTRUCTION AND STUDY* **SEE** INSTRUMENTAL MUSIC — INSTRUCTION AND STUDY
ML3809	MUSICAL INTERVALS AND SCALES
ML1040	*MUSICAL JAW BONE* **SEE** JAW BONE, MUSICAL
ML198-370	MUSICAL LANDMARKS
ML3850	MUSICAL METER AND RHYTHM / *aesthetics*
ML437	MUSICAL METER AND RHYTHM / *history of composition*
MT42	MUSICAL METER AND RHYTHM / *instruction in composition*
ML3813	MUSICAL METER AND RHYTHM / *physics acoustics*
MT233	MUSICAL METER AND RHYTHM / *piano*
ML3832	MUSICAL METER AND RHYTHM / *psychology*
ML3809	*MUSICAL MODES* **SEE** MUSICAL INTERVALS AND SCALES
PN1995.7	*MUSICAL MOVING-PICTURES* **SEE** MOVING-PICTURES, MUSICAL
ML431	MUSICAL NOTATION / *history*
MT35	MUSICAL NOTATION / *instruction*
ML432	MUSICAL NOTATION / *reform*
ML3925	*MUSICAL NOVELS* **SEE** MUSICAL FICTION
ML174	*MUSICAL PALEOGRAPHY* **SEE** PALEOGRAPHY, MUSICAL
ML457	*MUSICAL PERFORMANCE* **SEE** MUSIC — PERFORMANCE
ML3807-9	MUSICAL PITCH / *acoustics*
ML3830	MUSICAL PITCH / *psychology*
ML	*MUSICAL RESEARCH* **SEE** MUSICOLOGY
MT955	MUSICAL REVUES, COMEDIES, ETC. — STAGE GUIDES
M1500-1508	MUSICAL REVUES, COMEDIES, ETC.
MT35	MUSICAL SHORTHAND
ML25-28	MUSICAL SOCIETIES
ML3809	MUSICAL TEMPERAMENT
RC489.M7	*MUSICAL THERAPY* **SEE** MUSIC THERAPY
MT42	*MUSICAL TIME* **SEE** TEMPO (MUSIC)
ML3845	*MUSICAL VARIATION* **SEE** VARIATION (MUSIC)
HD9999.M8	*MUSICAL-INSTRUMENT MAKERS* **SEE** MUSICAL INSTRUMENTS — MAKERS
ML460-1055	*MUSICAL-INSTRUMENT MAKERS* **SEE** MUSICAL INSTRUMENTS — MAKERS
ML93-98	MUSICIANS — AUTOGRAPHS
ML87	MUSICIANS — CARICATURES AND CARTOONS
ML410-429	MUSICIANS — CORRESPONDENCE, REMINISCENCES, ETC.
ML3795	MUSICIANS — DISEASES AND HYGIENE
ML63	MUSICIANS — LEGAL STATUS, LAWS, ETC.
ML87-88	MUSICIANS — PORTRAITS
ML3795	MUSICIANS — SALARIES, PENSIONS, ETC.
ML90	MUSICIANS AS AUTHORS
ML80	MUSICIANS IN LITERATURE
ML385-403	MUSICIANS
ML385	MUSICIANS, BLIND
ML82	MUSICIANS, WOMEN
ML65	*MUSICIANS-ANECDOTES, FACETIAE, SATIRE, ETC.* **SEE** MUSIC — ANECDOTES, FACETIAE, SATIRE, ETC.
ML385-429	*MUSICIANS-DICTIONARIES* **SEE** MUSIC — BIO-BIBLIOGRAPHY / *history and criticism*
ML105-7	*MUSICIANS-DICTIONARIES* **SEE** MUSIC — BIO-BIBLIOGRAPHY / *dictionaries*
ML3849	*MUSICIANS-POETRY* **SEE** MUSIC — POETRY
ML140	MUSICIANS — PORTRAITS — — CATALOGS
MT948	MUSICO-CALLISTHENICS / *instruction*
M1993	MUSICO-CALLISTHENICS / *music*
ML	MUSICOLOGY
ML136-158	MUSIC — BIBLIOGRAPHY — — CATALOGS
ML145	MUSIC — BIBLIOGRAPHY — — CATALOGS, PUBLISHERS'
ML135	MUSIC — BIBLIOGRAPHY — — MANUSCRIPTS
ML162-9	MUSIC — HISTORY AND CRITICISM — — ANCIENT
ML170-190	MUSIC — HISTORY AND CRITICISM — — MEDIEVAL
ML194	MUSIC — HISTORY AND CRITICISM — — 17TH CENTURY

ML195	MUSIC — HISTORY AND CRITICISM — — 18TH CENTURY
ML196	MUSIC — HISTORY AND CRITICISM — — 19TH CENTURY
ML197	MUSIC — HISTORY AND CRITICISM — — 20TH CENTURY
ML162-9	MUSIC — THEORY — — ANCIENT
ML170-174	MUSIC — THEORY — — MEDIEVAL
ML193-4	MUSIC — THEORY — — 16TH-17TH CENTURIES
ML195	MUSIC — THEORY — — 18TH CENTURY
QP981.M9	MUSK — PHYSIOLOGICAL EFFECT
QL737.U5	MUSK-DEER
QL737.U5	MUSK-OX
TP983	MUSK / perfumery
RM666.M85	MUSK / therapeutics
SH691.M8	MUSKELLUNGE FISHING
QL638.E7	MUSKELLUNGE / zoology
UD330-335	MUSKETRY SEE SHOOTING, MILITARY
E99.M	MUSKHOGEAN INDIANS
PM1971-4	MUSKHOGEAN LANGUAGES
SB339	MUSKMELON SEE MELONS
E99.C9	MUSKOGEE INDIANS SEE CREEK INDIANS
E99.C9	MUSKOKI INDIANS SEE CREEK INDIANS
PM991	MUSKOKI LANGUAGE SEE CREEK LANGUAGE
PM1971-4	MUSKOKI LANGUAGES SEE MUSKHOGEAN LANGUAGES
QL737.R6	MUSKRATS
E99.F7	MUSKWAKI INDIANS SEE FOX INDIANS
BP166.89	MUSLIM ANGELOLOGY SEE ANGELS (ISLAM)
BP170	MUSLIM APOLOGETICS SEE ISLAM — APOLOGETIC WORKS
NA380-388	MUSLIM ARCHITECTURE SEE ARCHITECTURE, ISLAMIC
N6260-6271	MUSLIM ART SEE ART, ISLAMIC
NK720-725	MUSLIM ART INDUSTRIES AND TRADE SEE ART INDUSTRIES AND TRADE, ISLAMIC
NK6473	MUSLIM ART METAL-WORK SEE ART METAL-WORK, ISLAMIC
BP70-80	MUSLIM BIOGRAPHY SEE ISLAM — BIOGRAPHY
CE59	MUSLIM CALENDAR SEE CALENDAR, ISLAMIC
D199.3	MUSLIM CIVILIZATION SEE CIVILIZATION, ISLAMIC
DS427	MUSLIM CIVILIZATION SEE CIVILIZATION, ISLAMIC / india
BP170.5	MUSLIM CONVERTS FROM CHRISTIANITY
BV2626.3-4	MUSLIM CONVERTS TO CHRISTIANITY SEE CONVERTS FROM ISLAM
BP170.5	MUSLIM CONVERTS
B745.C6	MUSLIM COSMOLOGY SEE COSMOLOGY, ISLAMIC
DS36-40	MUSLIM COUNTRIES SEE ISLAMIC COUNTRIES
NK1270-1275	MUSLIM DECORATION AND ORNAMENT SEE DECORATION AND ORNAMENT, ISLAMIC
BP166.89	MUSLIM DEMONOLOGY SEE DEMONOLOGY, ISLAMIC
BP188.2	MUSLIM DEVOTIONAL LITERATURE SEE ISLAMIC DEVOTIONAL LITERATURE
LC901-915	MUSLIM EDUCATION SEE ISLAM — EDUCATION
BP166.8	MUSLIM ESCHATOLOGY SEE ESCHATOLOGY, ISLAMIC
BJ1291	MUSLIM ETHICS SEE ISLAMIC ETHICS
BP186	MUSLIM FASTS AND FEASTS SEE FASTS AND FEASTS — ISLAM
BP167.5	MUSLIM HERESIES AND HERETICS SEE HERESIES AND HERETICS, ISLAMIC
BP182	MUSLIM HOLY WAR SEE JIHAD
BP184.25	MUSLIM HOMILETICS SEE PREACHING, ISLAMIC
BP183.5	MUSLIM HYMNS SEE ISLAMIC HYMNS
ND2955	MUSLIM ILLUMINATION OF BOOKS AND MANUSCRIPTS SEE ILLUMINATION OF BOOKS AND MANUSCRIPTS, ISLAMIC
CN1153	MUSLIM INSCRIPTIONS SEE INSCRIPTIONS, ISLAMIC
BP137-7.5	MUSLIM LEGENDS SEE LEGENDS, ISLAMIC
BP87-89	MUSLIM LITERATURE SEE ISLAMIC LITERATURE
BP170.3	MUSLIM MISSIONS SEE ISLAM — MISSIONS
BP189.2-7	MUSLIM MONASTICISM AND RELIGIOUS ORDERS SEE MONASTICISM AND RELIGIOUS ORDERS, ISLAMIC
BP189	MUSLIM MYSTICISM SEE MYSTICISM — ISLAM
ND198	MUSLIM PAINTING SEE PAINTING, ISLAMIC
ND198	MUSLIM PAINTINGS SEE PAINTINGS, ISLAMIC
BP184	MUSLIM PASTORAL THEOLOGY SEE PASTORAL THEOLOGY (ISLAM)
B163	MUSLIM PHILOSOPHY SEE PHILOSOPHY, ISLAMIC
B740-753	MUSLIM PHILOSOPHY SEE PHILOSOPHY, ISLAMIC / medieval
NK3880	MUSLIM POTTERY SEE POTTERY, ISLAMIC
BP183.3	MUSLIM PRAYERS SEE ISLAMIC PRAYERS
BP184.25	MUSLIM PREACHING SEE PREACHING, ISLAMIC
HJ233	MUSLIM PUBLIC FINANCE SEE FINANCE, PUBLIC — ISLAMIC COUNTRIES
BP42-48	MUSLIM RELIGIOUS EDUCATION SEE RELIGIOUS EDUCATION, ISLAMIC
BP185	MUSLIM RELIGIOUS FUNCTIONARIES SEE ISLAM — FUNCTIONARIES
BP174	MUSLIM RELIGIOUS PRACTICE SEE ISLAMIC RELIGIOUS PRACTICE
BP189.3-5	MUSLIM SAINTS SEE SAINTS, MUSLIM
BP191-223	MUSLIM SECTS SEE ISLAMIC SECTS
BP183.6	MUSLIM SERMONS SEE ISLAMIC SERMONS
HN40.M6	MUSLIM SOCIOLOGY SEE SOCIOLOGY, ISLAMIC
BP166.7	MUSLIM THEOLOGICAL ANTHROPOLOGY SEE MAN (ISLAM)
BP166	MUSLIM THEOLOGY SEE ISLAMIC THEOLOGY
HQ1170	MUSLIM WOMEN SEE WOMEN, MUSLIM
DS38	MUSLIMS
LC901-915	MUSLIMS-EDUCATION SEE ISLAM — EDUCATION
HQ1170	MUSLIMS-WOMEN SEE WOMEN, MUSLIM
E99.F7	MUSQUAKIE INDIANS SEE FOX INDIANS
SB945.09	MUSSEL SCALE SEE OYSTER-SHELL SCALE
SH373	MUSSELS
SH378	MUSSELS, FRESH-WATER
DQ114	MUSSO, WAR OF, 1531-1532
DQ398	MUSSO, WAR OF, 1531-1532 / basel
DQ498	MUSSO, WAR OF, 1531-1532 / grisons
DS38	MUSSULMEN SEE MUSLIMS
TL685.3	MUSTANG (FIGHTER PLANES)
RM666.M9	MUSTARD — THERAPEUTIC USE
UG447.5.M8	MUSTARD GAS / military science
RA1247.M8	MUSTARD GAS / toxicology
SB307.M	MUSTARD / culture
F3319	MUSU INDIANS SEE MOXO INDIANS
PL8535	MUSUK LANGUAGE SEE MUSGU LANGUAGE
QH406	MUTATION (BIOLOGY) SEE BOTANY — VARIATION
QH361-371	MUTATION (BIOLOGY) SEE EVOLUTION
QE721	MUTATION (BIOLOGY) SEE EVOLUTION / paleontology
B818	MUTATION (BIOLOGY) SEE EVOLUTION / philosophy
QH361-371	MUTATION (BIOLOGY) SEE ORIGIN OF SPECIES
QH401-411	MUTATION (BIOLOGY) SEE VARIATION (BIOLOGY)
Z701	MUTILATION OF BOOKS SEE BOOKS — MUTILATION, DEFACEMENT, ETC.
GN419.2	MUTILATION / ethnology
UB787	MUTINY / military
VB860-867	MUTINY / naval
PM1976-9	MUTSUN LANGUAGE
HS1501-1510	MUTUAL BENEFIT ASSOCIATIONS SEE FRIENDLY SOCIETIES
HG9201-9245	MUTUAL BENEFIT ASSOCIATIONS SEE FRIENDLY SOCIETIES / fraternal insurance
UA12	MUTUAL DEFENSE ASSISTANCE PROGRAM SEE MUTUAL SECURITY PROGRAM, 1951-
HG4530	MUTUAL FUNDS SEE INVESTMENT TRUSTS
HD7287.7	MUTUAL HOUSING SEE HOUSING, COOPERATIVE
QC638	MUTUAL INDUCTANCE
HG8011-9970	MUTUAL INSURANCE SEE INSURANCE
UA12	MUTUAL SECURITY PROGRAM, 1951-
HD2951-3570	MUTUALISM / economics
HM131	MUTUALISM / sociology
F2270.2.C4	MUYSCA INDIANS SEE CHIBCHA INDIANS
PL8535	MUZUK LANGUAGE SEE MUSGU LANGUAGE
PL8538	MWAMBA LANGUAGE
PL8539	MWERA LANGUAGE
QK601	MYCELIUM
RC168.M9	MYCETOMA
QK635	MYCETOZOA SEE MYXOMYCETES
QK604	MYCORHIZA
RL765	MYCOSIS
RE994-7	MYDRIATICS
RC280.M	MYELOMA SEE MARROW — TUMORS
BF285	MYESTHESIA SEE MUSCULAR SENSE
QE475	MYLONITE
QL795.B57	MYNAHS

QL795.B57	*MYNAS* **SEE** MYNAHS
QL831	*MYODYNAMICS* **SEE** MUSCLES / *comparative anatomy*
QM151-165	*MYODYNAMICS* **SEE** MUSCLES / *human anatomy*
QP301-3	*MYODYNAMICS* **SEE** MUSCLES / *movements*
QL831	*MYOLOGY* **SEE** MUSCLES / *comparative anatomy*
QM151-165	*MYOLOGY* **SEE** MUSCLES / *human anatomy*
QP301-3	*MYOLOGY* **SEE** MUSCLES / *movements*
RE938	MYOPIA
RC935	*MYOSITIS* **SEE** MUSCLES — DISEASES
RC925-7	*MYOSITIS* **SEE** MUSCLES — DISEASES
RD688	*MYOSITIS* **SEE** MUSCLES — DISEASES
RD688	MYOTONIA
QL449	MYRIAPODA
QL444.M	MYSTACOCARIDA
PN1761	*MYSTERIES (DRAMATIC)* **SEE** MYSTERIES AND MIRACLE-PLAYS / *history and criticism*
PN1761	MYSTERIES AND MIRACLE-PLAYS / *history and criticism*
BL610	MYSTERIES, RELIGIOUS / *comparative religion*
HS491	MYSTERIES, RELIGIOUS / *freemasonry and ancient mysteries*
PN6120.M9	*MYSTERY PLAYS (MODERN)* **SEE** DETECTIVE AND MYSTERY PLAYS / *collections*
G525-530	*MYSTERY STORIES* **SEE** ADVENTURE AND ADVENTURERS
PZ1-3	*MYSTERY STORIES* **SEE** DETECTIVE AND MYSTERY STORIES / *collections*
PN3448.D4	*MYSTERY STORIES* **SEE** DETECTIVE AND MYSTERY STORIES / *history*
D10	*MYSTERY STORIES* **SEE** HISTORY — CURIOSA AND MISCELLANY
BT769	*MYSTIC UNION* **SEE** MYSTICAL UNION
BV5070-5095	*MYSTICAL THEOLOGY* **SEE** MYSTICISM / *christianity*
BL625	*MYSTICAL THEOLOGY* **SEE** MYSTICISM / *comparative religion*
B728	*MYSTICAL THEOLOGY* **SEE** MYSTICISM / *medieval philosophy*
B828	*MYSTICAL THEOLOGY* **SEE** MYSTICISM / *modern philosophy*
BT769	MYSTICAL UNION
BL625	MYSTICISM — COMPARATIVE STUDIES
BV5075	MYSTICISM — EARLY CHURCH
BL1215.M9	MYSTICISM — HINDUISM
BP189	MYSTICISM — ISLAM
BV5075	MYSTICISM — MIDDLE AGES
BV5083	MYSTICISM — PSYCHOLOGY
PN49	MYSTICISM IN LITERATURE
PR145	MYSTICISM IN LITERATURE / *english literature*
BV5070-5095	MYSTICISM / *christianity*
BL625	MYSTICISM / *comparative religion*
B728	MYSTICISM / *medieval philosophy*
B828	MYSTICISM / *modern philosophy*
GR820-830	*MYTHICAL ANIMALS* **SEE** ANIMALS, MYTHICAL
BL303	MYTHOLOGY — DICTIONARIES
PZ8.1	MYTHOLOGY — JUVENILE LITERATURE
N7760	*MYTHOLOGY IN ART* **SEE** ART AND MYTHOLOGY
PN56.M	MYTHOLOGY IN LITERATURE
PR508.M9	MYTHOLOGY IN LITERATURE / *english literature*
PR149.M	MYTHOLOGY IN LITERATURE / *english literature*
PQ145.1.M9	MYTHOLOGY IN LITERATURE / *french literature*
PT135	MYTHOLOGY IN LITERATURE / *german literature*
BL300-325	MYTHOLOGY / *comparative*
PK3000-3581	*MYTHOLOGY, BRAHMAN* **SEE** VEDAS
BL1115	*MYTHOLOGY, BRAHMAN* **SEE** VEDAS / *hinduism*
BL700-820	MYTHOLOGY, CLASSICAL
BL303	*MYTHOLOGY, CLASSICAL-DICTIONARIES* **SEE** MYTHOLOGY — DICTIONARIES
BL303	*MYTHOLOGY, GREEK-DICTIONARIES* **SEE** MYTHOLOGY — DICTIONARIES
E59.R38	*MYTHOLOGY, INDIAN (AMERICAN INDIAN)* **SEE** INDIANS — RELIGION AND MYTHOLOGY
F1219.3.R38	*MYTHOLOGY, INDIAN (AMERICAN INDIAN)* **SEE** INDIANS OF MEXICO — RELIGION AND MYTHOLOGY
E98.R3	*MYTHOLOGY, INDIAN (AMERICAN INDIAN)* **SEE** INDIANS OF NORTH AMERICA — RELIGION AND MYTHOLOGY
BL2000-2015	MYTHOLOGY, INDIC
F1435.3.R3	*MYTHOLOGY, MAYA* **SEE** MAYAS — RELIGION AND MYTHOLOGY
BL1000-2370	*MYTHOLOGY, NEAR EASTERN* **SEE** MYTHOLOGY, ORIENTAL
BL1000-2370	MYTHOLOGY, ORIENTAL
BL2370.T25	MYTHOLOGY, TAMIL
PK3000-3581	*MYTHOLOGY, VEDIC* **SEE** VEDAS
BL1115	*MYTHOLOGY, VEDIC* **SEE** VEDAS / *hinduism*
BL300-325	*MYTHS* **SEE** MYTHOLOGY / *comparative*
RC657	MYXEDEMA
QK635	*MYXOGASTRES* **SEE** MYXOMYCETES
QK635	MYXOMYCETES
QL391.M9	MYZOSTOMARIA
QC485	N-RAYS
RM862.N2	N-RAYS / *therapeutics*
QA251-263	*N-WAY ALGEBRA* **SEE** ALGEBRA, UNIVERSAL
PL5981	NABALOI DIALECT
PJ5239	*NABATAEAN INSCRIPTIONS* **SEE** INSCRIPTIONS, NABATAEAN
TL681.5	*NACELLES (AEROPLANE)* **SEE** AEROPLANES — NACELLES
E99.D1	*NADOWESSIOUX INDIANS* **SEE** DAKOTA INDIANS
RL793	*NAEVUS* **SEE** MOLE (DERMATOLOGY)
BF861.M65	*NAEVUS* **SEE** MOLE (DERMATOLOGY) / *physiognomy*
QP915.N2	NAFALAN / *physiological effects*
PL3881-4	NAGA LANGUAGES
RC186.T82	*NAGANA* **SEE** TRYPANOSOMIASIS
SF807	*NAGANA* **SEE** TRYPANOSOMIASIS / *veterinary medicine*
DU122.N3	NAGARNOOKS
GN665	NAGARNOOKS / *anthropology*
DS432.N3	NAGAS
GN470	NAGUALISM
PL4585	NAHALI LANGUAGE
F1219	*NAHOAS* **SEE** NAHUAS
F1219	NAHUAS
PM4061-9	*NAHUATL LANGUAGE* **SEE** AZTEC LANGUAGE
PM4070	*NAHUATL LANGUAGE* **SEE** NAHUATL-SPANISH DIALECT
PM4068	*NAHUATL LITERATURE* **SEE** AZTEC LITERATURE
PM4070	NAHUATL-SPANISH DIALECT
F1219	*NAHUATLECAS* **SEE** NAHUAS
HQ784.N3	NAIL-BITING
HD9999.N3-33	*NAILING* **SEE** NAILS AND SPIKES / *economics*
TS440	*NAILING* **SEE** NAILS AND SPIKES / *manufacture*
TA492.N2	*NAILING* **SEE** NAILS AND SPIKES / *testing*
RL94	NAILS (ANATOMY) — CARE AND HYGIENE
RL165	NAILS (ANATOMY) — DISEASES
QL942	NAILS (ANATOMY) / *comparative anatomy*
QM488	NAILS (ANATOMY) / *human anatomy*
HD9999.N3-33	NAILS AND SPIKES / *economics*
TS440	NAILS AND SPIKES / *manufacture*
TA492.N2	NAILS AND SPIKES / *testing*
RD563	NAILS, INGROWING
PK2595-9	*NAIPALI LANGUAGE* **SEE** NEPALI LANGUAGE
PL3801.N4	NAM LANGUAGE
PL8541	NAMA LANGUAGE
CS2300-2389	*NAMES, CHRISTIAN* **SEE** NAMES, PERSONAL
Z1041-1115	*NAMES, FICTITIOUS* **SEE** ANONYMS AND PSEUDONYMS
G104-8	NAMES, GEOGRAPHICAL
E98.N2	*NAMES, GEOGRAPHICAL-INDIAN* **SEE** INDIANS OF NORTH AMERICA — NAMES
E98.N2	*NAMES, INDIAN* **SEE** INDIANS OF NORTH AMERICA — NAMES
Z695.1.P4	NAMES, PERSONAL (CATALOGING)
CS2300-2389	NAMES, PERSONAL
Z695.1.P4	*NAMES, PERSONAL-CATALOGING* **SEE** NAMES, PERSONAL (CATALOGING)
D280.N2	NAMUR — SIEGE, 1692
PL461.G	*NANAI DIALECT* **SEE** GOLDIAN DIALECT
F2688.5	NANAWA, BATTLE OF, 1933
DC106.3	NANCY, BATTLE OF, 1477
PL8544	NANDE LANGUAGE
DS485.O6	*NANGA POROJA* **SEE** BONDOS
PM7171-9	*NANGATU LANGUAGE* **SEE** TUPI LANGUAGE
BR845	*NANTES, EDICT OF* **SEE** EDICT OF NANTES
NK4399.N	NANTGARW PORCELAIN
NK4399.N3	NANTGARW POTTERY
E99.N14	NANTICOKE INDIANS
PM2001	NANTICOKE LANGUAGE

GV835	NAPHTHA-LAUNCHES / boating
VM341	NAPHTHA-LAUNCHES / construction
QP915.N2	NAPHTHA / physiological effects
TP692.4.N3	NAPHTHA / technology
QD391	NAPHTHALENE
TP918.N2	NAPHTHAZARIN / dyes
TC773	NAPIPI EXPEDITION, 1875
DG848.51	NAPLES (KINGDOM) — HISTORY — — REVOLUTION, 1820-1821
DC203	NAPOLEON I, EMPEROR OF THE FRENCH, 1769-1821 — ADDRESSES, SERMONS, ETC.
Z989	NAPOLEON I, EMPEROR OF THE FRENCH, 1769-1821 — BOOKS AND READING
DC212	NAPOLEON I, EMPEROR OF THE FRENCH, 1769-1821 — DEATH AND BURIAL
DC215.5	NAPOLEON I, EMPEROR OF THE FRENCH, 1769-1821 — LITERARY ART
CJ6155.N3-5	NAPOLEON I, EMPEROR OF THE FRENCH, 1769-1821 — MEDALS
DC203.9	NAPOLEON I, EMPEROR OF THE FRENCH, 1769-1821 — MUSEUMS, RELICS, ETC.
DC204	NAPOLEON I, EMPEROR OF THE FRENCH, 1769-1821 — RELATIONS WITH WOMEN
DC197-249	NAPOLEON I, EMPEROR OF THE FRENCH, 1769-1821
DC191-3	NAPOLEON I, EMPEROR OF THE FRENCH, 1769-1821
DC212	NAPOLEON I, EMPEROR OF THE FRENCH, 1769-1821-FUNERAL SEE NAPOLEON I, EMPEROR OF THE FRENCH, 1769-1821 — DEATH AND BURIAL
HF1532	NAPOLEON, CONTINENTAL SYSTEM OF SEE CONTINENTAL SYSTEM OF NAPOLEON
HF1543	NAPOLEON, CONTINENTAL SYSTEM OF SEE CONTINENTAL SYSTEM OF NAPOLEON
DC139-195	NAPOLEONIC WARS SEE FRANCE — HISTORY — — REVOLUTION
DC231-3	NAPOLEONIC WARS SEE PENINSULAR WAR, 1807-1814 / history
DP208	NAPOLEONIC WARS SEE PENINSULAR WAR, 1807-1814 / period in spain
PQ4222.S7	NAPOLITANA SEE STRAMBOTTO / collections
PQ4128.S7	NAPOLITANA SEE STRAMBOTTO / history and criticism
QP915.N2	NAPTHA SEE NAPHTHA / physiological effects
TP692.4.N3	NAPTHA SEE NAPHTHA / technology
SB413.N	NARCISSUS / flower culture
RA974.5	NARCOTIC CLINICS
RC566	NARCOTIC HABIT
HV5800-5840	NARCOTIC HABIT / economics
RA402	NARCOTIC LAWS / public health
HV5800-5840	NARCOTIC LAWS / social pathology
GT3010	NARCOTICS / and customs
RM328	NARCOTICS / therapeutics
GN660.B8	NARON TRIBE / bushmen
E99.N16	NARRAGANSET INDIANS
PM2003	NARRAGANSET LANGUAGE
E99.N16	NARRAGANSETT INDIANS SEE NARRAGANSET INDIANS
PE1425	NARRATION (RHETORIC) / english rhetoric
PN6110.N17	NARRATIVE POETRY / collections
PE1425	NARRATIVE WRITING SEE NARRATION (RHETORIC) / english rhetoric
TL696.D65	NARROW-BAND DME SEE DISTANCE MEASURING EQUIPMENT (AIRCRAFT TO GROUND STATION)
TF675	NARROW-GAGE RAILROADS SEE RAILROADS, NARROW-GAGE
HE3601-4050	NARROW-GAGE RAILROADS SEE RAILROADS, NARROW-GAGE / economics
DL743.N	NARVA, BATTLE OF, 1700
D763.N6	NARVIK, BATTLE OF, 1940
E99.N18	NASCAPEE INDIANS
PM2004.N3	NASCAPEE LANGUAGE
E477.52	NASHVILLE, BATTLE OF, 1864
RC280.N6	NASOPHARYNX — TUMORS
QM505	NASOPHARYNX / human anatomy
BT1405	NASORAEANS SEE MANDAEANS
PM2026.N3	NASQUA LANGUAGE SEE NISKA LANGUAGE
E99.N18	NASQUAPEE INDIANS SEE NASCAPEE INDIANS
SB413.N	NASTURTIUMS / culture
F232.S7	NAT TURNER'S INSURRECTION SEE SOUTHAMPTON INSURRECTION, 1831
GR805	NATAL STONES SEE BIRTH-STONES
E99.N	NATCHESAN INDIANS
E83.716	NATCHEZ INDIANS — WARS, 1716
E99.N2	NATCHEZ INDIANS
PM2004.N4	NATCHEZ LANGUAGE
PL8576.N4	NATH LANGUAGE SEE NUER LANGUAGE
E99.M42	NATICK INDIANS SEE MASSACHUSET INDIANS
PM1736-9	NATICK LANGUAGE SEE MASSACHUSET LANGUAGE
E185.61	NATION OF ISLAM SEE BLACK MUSLIMS / race question
BP221-3	NATION OF ISLAM SEE BLACK MUSLIMS / religion
G850 1901	NATIONAL ANTARCTIC EXPEDITION, 1901-1904
Q115	NATIONAL ANTARCTIC EXPEDITION, 1901-1904
HG651-1490	NATIONAL BANK NOTES / other countries
HG607-9	NATIONAL BANK NOTES / u.s.
HJ8061	NATIONAL BANKRUPTCY SEE STATE BANKRUPTCY
HG2545-2557	NATIONAL BANKS (U.S.)
UB393-4	NATIONAL CEMETERIES — U.S.
E160	NATIONAL CEMETERIES — U.S.
E494	NATIONAL CEMETERIES — U.S.
CB195-7	NATIONAL CHARACTERISTICS
CB203	NATIONAL CHARACTERISTICS / europe
BV633	NATIONAL CHURCHES SEE ESTABLISHED CHURCHES / ecclesiastical aspects
M1627	NATIONAL DANCES SEE FOLK DANCE MUSIC
GV1580-1799	NATIONAL DANCES SEE FOLK DANCING
HJ8003-8897	NATIONAL DEBTS SEE DEBTS, PUBLIC
QK85	NATIONAL FLOWERS
SD426-8	NATIONAL FORESTS SEE FOREST RESERVES
HD6479	NATIONAL GILDS SEE GILD SOCIALISM
HG604-5	NATIONAL GREENBACK PARTY
UA42-43	NATIONAL GUARD (U.S.) SEE UNITED STATES — NATIONAL GUARD
HV3167	NATIONAL HOLIDAYS SEE HOLIDAYS / for shop workers
GT3930-4995	NATIONAL HOLIDAYS SEE HOLIDAYS / manners and customs
JK1761	NATIONAL HOLIDAYS SEE HOLIDAYS / national u.s.
PN4305.H7	NATIONAL HOLIDAYS SEE HOLIDAYS / recitations
CB195-7	NATIONAL IMAGES SEE NATIONAL CHARACTERISTICS
CB203	NATIONAL IMAGES SEE NATIONAL CHARACTERISTICS / europe
HC	NATIONAL INCOME SEE INCOME / national income
HB601	NATIONAL INCOME SEE INCOME / theory
Z675.N2	NATIONAL LIBRARIES SEE LIBRARIES, NATIONAL
SD567-667	NATIONAL MILITARY PARKS SEE NATIONAL PARKS AND RESERVES / other countries
SD426-8	NATIONAL MILITARY PARKS SEE NATIONAL PARKS AND RESERVES / forest reserves u.s.
ML3545	NATIONAL MUSIC — HISTORY AND CRITICISM
ML200.5	NATIONAL MUSIC WEEK SEE MUSIC WEEK
M1627-1844	NATIONAL MUSIC
ML3549-3776	NATIONAL MUSIC, AMERICAN, (ENGLISH, FRENCH, ETC.) — HISTORY AND CRITICISM
SD426-8	NATIONAL PARKS AND RESERVES / forest reserves u.s.
SD567-667	NATIONAL PARKS AND RESERVES / other countries
HD82-85	NATIONAL PLANNING SEE ECONOMIC POLICY
HD	NATIONAL PLANNING SEE ECONOMIC POLICY / by industry
HF1401-2580	NATIONAL PLANNING SEE ECONOMIC POLICY / hc
BF730-738	NATIONAL PSYCHOLOGY SEE ETHNOPSYCHOLOGY
CB195-7	NATIONAL PSYCHOLOGY SEE NATIONAL CHARACTERISTICS
CB203	NATIONAL PSYCHOLOGY SEE NATIONAL CHARACTERISTICS / europe
JK2320	NATIONAL REPUBLICAN PARTY
HC	NATIONAL RESOURCES SEE NATURAL RESOURCES
JX4054	NATIONAL SELF-DETERMINATION SEE SELF-DETERMINATION, NATIONAL
DD253	NATIONAL SOCIALISM / germany
JX4085-4150	NATIONAL TERRITORY SEE TERRITORY, NATIONAL / international law
LC71	NATIONALISM AND EDUCATION
BL65.N3	NATIONALISM AND RELIGION
LC71	NATIONALISM IN EDUCATION SEE NATIONALISM AND EDUCATION
JC311-323	NATIONALISM / political science

JF800-823	*NATIONALITY (CITIZENSHIP)* **SEE** CITIZENSHIP
LC1091	*NATIONALITY (CITIZENSHIP)* **SEE** CITIZENSHIP / education for
JK1751-1788	*NATIONALITY (CITIZENSHIP)* **SEE** CITIZENSHIP / u.s.
JX4449.N3	*NATIONALITY OF SHIPS* **SEE** SHIPS — NATIONALITY
JX4231.D7	*NATIONALITY, DUAL* **SEE** DUAL NATIONALITY
JX4231.O7	*NATIONALITY, OPTION OF* **SEE** OPTION OF NATIONALITY
JX4231.D7	*NATIONALITY, PLURAL* **SEE** DUAL NATIONALITY
HD3840-4420	*NATIONALIZATION* **SEE** GOVERNMENT OWNERSHIP
HD1301-1315	*NATIONALIZATION OF LAND* **SEE** LAND, NATIONALIZATION OF
HE1051-1081	*NATIONALIZATION OF RAILROADS* **SEE** RAILROADS AND STATE
HE2757	*NATIONALIZATION OF RAILROADS* **SEE** RAILROADS AND STATE / u.s.
JX4081	*NATIONS, COMITY OF* **SEE** COMITY OF NATIONS
D135-149	*NATIONS, MIGRATIONS OF* **SEE** MIGRATIONS OF NATIONS
JC365	*NATIONS, SMALL* **SEE** STATES, SMALL
JK2341	*NATIVE AMERICAN PARTY* **SEE** AMERICAN PARTY
JV305-317	NATIVE RACES / colonization
HV3176-7	NATIVE RACES / protection
BT315	*NATIVITY OF CHRIST* **SEE** JESUS CHRIST — NATIVITY
JX4111-4145	*NATURAL BOUNDARIES* **SEE** BOUNDARIES / international law
JC323	*NATURAL BOUNDARIES* **SEE** BOUNDARIES / theory of the state
RG661	*NATURAL CHILDBIRTH* **SEE** CHILDBIRTH — PSYCHOLOGY
TP350	*NATURAL GAS* **SEE** GAS, NATURAL / fuel
HD242.5	*NATURAL GAS* **SEE** GAS, NATURAL / gas lands
TN880	*NATURAL GAS* **SEE** GAS, NATURAL / mineral industries
TN880-883	*NATURAL GAS WELLS* **SEE** GAS WELLS
QH71-72	NATURAL HISTORY — CATALOGS
QH83	NATURAL HISTORY — CLASSIFICATION
QH48	NATURAL HISTORY — JUVENILE LITERATURE
QH53	NATURAL HISTORY — LABORATORY MANUALS
QH83	NATURAL HISTORY — NOMENCLATURE
QH41-48	NATURAL HISTORY — ORGANOGRAPHY
QH81	NATURAL HISTORY — OUTDOOR BOOKS
QH46	NATURAL HISTORY — PICTORIAL WORKS
QH41	NATURAL HISTORY — PRE-LINNEAN WORKS
QH70-71	NATURAL HISTORY — PRIVATE COLLECTIONS
QH61	NATURAL HISTORY — RECORD BLANKS
QH51-53	NATURAL HISTORY — STUDY AND TEACHING
QH60	NATURAL HISTORY — TECHNIQUE
QH83	NATURAL HISTORY — TERMINOLOGY
QH70-71	NATURAL HISTORY MUSEUMS
QH1-7	NATURAL HISTORY SOCIETIES
QH	NATURAL HISTORY
BS660-667	*NATURAL HISTORY, BIBLICAL* **SEE** BIBLE — NATURAL HISTORY
QH41	*NATURAL HISTORY-EARLY WORKS* **SEE** NATURAL HISTORY — PRE-LINNEAN WORKS
QH70-71	*NATURAL HISTORY-MUSEUMS* **SEE** NATURAL HISTORY MUSEUMS
JC571-609	NATURAL LAW
QH75-77	NATURAL MONUMENTS
QC	*NATURAL PHILOSOPHY* **SEE** PHYSICS
BL175-190	*NATURAL RELIGION* **SEE** NATURAL THEOLOGY
HC	NATURAL RESOURCES
JC571-609	*NATURAL RIGHTS* **SEE** NATURAL LAW
BH301.L3	*NATURAL SCENERY* **SEE** LANDSCAPE / aesthetics
QH75	*NATURAL SCENERY* **SEE** LANDSCAPE / natural history
G136-9	*NATURAL SCENERY* **SEE** VIEWS
QH	*NATURAL SCIENCE* **SEE** NATURAL HISTORY
QC	*NATURAL SCIENCE* **SEE** PHYSICS
Q	*NATURAL SCIENCE* **SEE** SCIENCE
QH365-7	NATURAL SELECTION
BL175-190	NATURAL THEOLOGY
ML960-963	*NATURAL TRUMPET* **SEE** TRUMPET / history and construction
GT5020	*NATURAL TRUMPET* **SEE** TRUMPET / manners and customs
N70	NATURALISM IN ART
PN56.R3	NATURALISM IN LITERATURE
B828.2	NATURALISM
BJ1298-1335	*NATURALISTIC ETHICS* **SEE** ETHICS, EVOLUTIONARY
Q145	*NATURALISTS - DIRECTORIES* **SEE** SCIENTISTS — DIRECTORIES
QH26-35	NATURALISTS / biography
Q145	*NATURALISTS-DIRECTORIES* **SEE** SCIENTISTS — DIRECTORIES
JX4216	NATURALIZATION / international law
JF811	NATURALIZATION / theory
JK1800-1836	NATURALIZATION / u.s.
BH301.N3	NATURE (AESTHETICS)
BH301.N3	*NATURE IN ART* **SEE** NATURE (AESTHETICS)
PN48	NATURE IN LITERATURE
PS163	NATURE IN LITERATURE / american literature
PR143	NATURE IN LITERATURE / english literature
PQ145.3	NATURE IN LITERATURE / french literature
PN6071.N3	NATURE IN LITERATURE / general collections
PT139	NATURE IN LITERATURE / german literature
ML3855	*NATURE IN MUSIC* **SEE** PROGRAM MUSIC / aesthetics
ML3300-3354	*NATURE IN MUSIC* **SEE** PROGRAM MUSIC / history
NK1160-1590	*NATURE IN ORNAMENT* **SEE** DECORATION AND ORNAMENT
NK1555	*NATURE IN ORNAMENT* **SEE** DESIGN, DECORATIVE — ANIMAL FORMS
NK1560-1565	*NATURE IN ORNAMENT* **SEE** DESIGN, DECORATIVE — PLANT FORMS
PN1065	NATURE IN POETRY
PS310.N3	NATURE IN POETRY / american literature
PR508.N3	NATURE IN POETRY / english literature
PQ413.N3	NATURE IN POETRY / french literature
PN6110.N2	NATURE IN POETRY / general collections
PT509.N3	NATURE IN POETRY / german literature
BS660-667	NATURE IN THE BIBLE
QH245	NATURE PHOTOGRAPHY
QH53	NATURE STUDY — LABORATORY MANUALS
QH51-53	NATURE STUDY
LB1585	NATURE STUDY / elementary schools
LB1185	NATURE STUDY / kindergarten
LB1532	NATURE STUDY / primary schools
Z259	NATURE-PRINTING AND NATURE-PRINTS
Z259	*NATURE-PRINTS* **SEE** NATURE-PRINTING AND NATURE-PRINTS
BL435-457	NATURE-WORSHIP
R723	NATURE, HEALING POWER OF
JC571-609	*NATURE, LAW OF* **SEE** NATURAL LAW
BD581	*NATURE, PHILOSOPHY OF* **SEE** PHILOSOPHY OF NATURE
BD581	*NATURE-PHILOSOPHY* **SEE** PHILOSOPHY OF NATURE
E99.D1	*NAUDOWESSIE INDIANS* **SEE** DAKOTA INDIANS
RM822.N3	NAUHEIM BATH
E99.N25	NAUSET INDIANS
QB8	NAUTICAL ALMANACS
VK559	NAUTICAL ASTRONOMY — PROBLEMS, EXERCISES, ETC.
VK549-587	NAUTICAL ASTRONOMY
VK573-585	NAUTICAL INSTRUMENTS
VK572	*NAUTICAL MILE* **SEE** MILE, NAUTICAL
V13	*NAUTICAL MUSEUMS* **SEE** NAVAL MUSEUMS
VK591-7	*NAUTICAL SURVEYING* **SEE** HYDROGRAPHIC SURVEYING
V23-24	*NAUTICAL TERMS* **SEE** NAVAL ART AND SCIENCE — TERMINOLOGY
V23-24	*NAUTICAL TERMS* **SEE** NAVAL ART AND SCIENCE — DICTIONARIES
V23-24	*NAUTICAL TERMS* **SEE** NAVAL ART AND SCIENCE — TERMINOLOGY
VK525-9	NAUTICAL TRAINING-SCHOOLS
E99.N3	NAVAHO INDIANS
PM2006-9	NAVAHO LANGUAGE
PM2009	NAVAHO POETRY
E99.N3	*NAVAJO INDIANS* **SEE** NAVAHO INDIANS
PM2006-9	*NAVAJO LANGUAGE* **SEE** NAVAHO LANGUAGE
V	*NAVAL ADMINISTRATION* **SEE** NAVAL ART AND SCIENCE
UG630-670	*NAVAL AERONAUTICS* **SEE** AERONAUTICS, MILITARY
JX5124	*NAVAL AERONAUTICS* **SEE** AERONAUTICS, MILITARY / international law
VM142	NAVAL ARCHITECTURE — EARLY WORKS TO 1800
VM295-6	NAVAL ARCHITECTURE — SPECIFICATIONS

VM151	NAVAL ARCHITECTURE — TABLES, CALCULATIONS, ETC.	UA16	*NAVAL MISSIONS* **SEE** MILITARY MISSIONS
VM	NAVAL ARCHITECTURE	V13	NAVAL MUSEUMS
V23-24	NAVAL ART AND SCIENCE — DICTIONARIES	K	NAVAL OFFENSES
V101	NAVAL ART AND SCIENCE — EARLY WORKS TO 1800	VB850-880	NAVAL OFFENSES
V400-695	NAVAL ART AND SCIENCE — EXAMINATIONS, QUESTIONS, ETC. / *naval education*	VF	*NAVAL ORDNANCE* **SEE** ORDNANCE, NAVAL
VK537	NAVAL ART AND SCIENCE — EXAMINATIONS, QUESTIONS, ETC. / *navigation*	UB400-405	*NAVAL PENSIONS* **SEE** PENSIONS, MILITARY / *army*
V25-55	NAVAL ART AND SCIENCE — HISTORY	UB370-375	*NAVAL PENSIONS* **SEE** PENSIONS, MILITARY / *army*
V109	NAVAL ART AND SCIENCE — JUVENILE LITERATURE	VB280-285	*NAVAL PENSIONS* **SEE** PENSIONS, MILITARY / *navy*
V23-24	NAVAL ART AND SCIENCE — TERMINOLOGY	VB340-345	*NAVAL PENSIONS* **SEE** PENSIONS, MILITARY / *navy*
V	NAVAL ART AND SCIENCE	E255	*NAVAL PENSIONS* **SEE** PENSIONS, MILITARY / *pension rolls*
VK525-9	*NAVAL ART AND SCIENCE-STUDY AND TEACHING* **SEE** NAUTICAL TRAINING-SCHOOLS	NE957	NAVAL PRINTS
V400-695	*NAVAL ART AND SCIENCE-STUDY AND TEACHING* **SEE** NAVAL EDUCATION	UB800-805	*NAVAL PRISONS* **SEE** PRISONS, MILITARY / *military*
VK401-529	*NAVAL ART AND SCIENCE-STUDY AND TEACHING* **SEE** NAVIGATION — STUDY AND TEACHING	VB890-895	*NAVAL PRISONS* **SEE** PRISONS, MILITARY / *naval*
V523-4	*NAVAL ART AND SCIENCE-STUDY AND TEACHING* **SEE** TRAINING-SHIPS / *gt. brit.*	UG610	*NAVAL RADIO* **SEE** RADIO, MILITARY
V435-6	*NAVAL ART AND SCIENCE-STUDY AND TEACHING* **SEE** TRAINING-SHIPS / *u.s.*	V190	NAVAL RECONNAISSANCE
VG600-605	NAVAL ARTIFICERS	VA	NAVAL RESERVES
UF	*NAVAL ARTILLERY* **SEE** ARTILLERY	VA62.5-7	*NAVAL RIVER COMMANDS* **SEE** NAVAL DISTRICTS — U.S.
UG630-670	*NAVAL AVIATION* **SEE** AERONAUTICS, MILITARY	V310	*NAVAL SALUTES* **SEE** NAVAL CEREMONIES, HONORS, AND SALUTES
JX5124	*NAVAL AVIATION* **SEE** AERONAUTICS, MILITARY / *international law*	V400-695	*NAVAL SCHOOLS* **SEE** NAVAL EDUCATION
VG93	*NAVAL AVIATION* **SEE** U.S. — AVIATION	V	*NAVAL SCIENCE* **SEE** NAVAL ART AND SCIENCE
V220-240	*NAVAL BASES* **SEE** NAVY-YARDS AND NAVAL STATIONS	HE9723-9737	*NAVAL SIGNALING* **SEE** SIGNALS AND SIGNALING
VA67-70	*NAVAL BASES* **SEE** NAVY-YARDS AND NAVAL STATIONS / *by country*	UG570-582	*NAVAL SIGNALING* **SEE** SIGNALS AND SIGNALING / *military*
D27	NAVAL BATTLES	V280-285	*NAVAL SIGNALING* **SEE** SIGNALS AND SIGNALING / *naval*
V61-65	NAVAL BIOGRAPHY	VK381-397	*NAVAL SIGNALING* **SEE** SIGNALS AND SIGNALING / *navigation*
D-F	NAVAL BIOGRAPHY / *by country*	V220-240	*NAVAL STATIONS* **SEE** NAVY-YARDS AND NAVAL STATIONS
VM741-750	*NAVAL BOILERS* **SEE** STEAM-BOILERS, MARINE	VA67-70	*NAVAL STATIONS* **SEE** NAVY-YARDS AND NAVAL STATIONS / *by country*
V310	NAVAL CEREMONIES, HONORS, AND SALUTES	TP977-8	NAVAL STORES
UA940-945	*NAVAL COMMUNICATIONS* **SEE** COMMUNICATIONS, MILITARY	V	*NAVAL STRATEGY* **SEE** NAVAL ART AND SCIENCE
VM	*NAVAL CONSTRUCTION* **SEE** NAVAL ARCHITECTURE	U161-3	*NAVAL STRATEGY* **SEE** STRATEGY / *military*
VM	*NAVAL CONSTRUCTION* **SEE** SHIP-BUILDING	V160-165	*NAVAL STRATEGY* **SEE** STRATEGY / *naval*
VK224	*NAVAL COOKERY* **SEE** COOKERY, MARINE	RD151-498	*NAVAL SURGERY* **SEE** SURGERY, NAVAL
VC370-375	*NAVAL COOKERY* **SEE** COOKERY, MARINE	V167-178	NAVAL TACTICS
V310	*NAVAL COURTESY* **SEE** NAVAL CEREMONIES, HONORS, AND SALUTES	VK525-9	*NAVAL TRAINING-SCHOOLS* **SEE** NAUTICAL TRAINING-SCHOOLS
K	*NAVAL CRIMES* **SEE** NAVAL OFFENSES	V523-4	*NAVAL TRAINING-SHIPS* **SEE** TRAINING-SHIPS / *gt. brit.*
VB850-880	*NAVAL CRIMES* **SEE** NAVAL OFFENSES	V435-6	*NAVAL TRAINING-SHIPS* **SEE** TRAINING-SHIPS / *u.s.*
VB870-875	*NAVAL DESERTION* **SEE** DESERTION, NAVAL	V	*NAVAL WARFARE* **SEE** NAVAL ART AND SCIENCE
VA62.5-7	NAVAL DISTRICTS — U.S.	D27	*NAVAL WARFARE* **SEE** NAVAL BATTLES
VA	NAVAL DISTRICTS	V167-178	*NAVAL WARFARE* **SEE** NAVAL TACTICS
V400-695	NAVAL EDUCATION	JX5203 5268	*NAVAL WARFARE* **SEE** WAR, MARITIME (INTERNATIONAL LAW)
VM600-989	*NAVAL ENGINEERING* **SEE** MARINE ENGINEERING	DF810.N3	NAVARINO, BATTLE OF, 1827
VF	NAVAL GUNNERY	DP114.3	NAVAS DE TOLOSA, BATTLE OF, 1212
D27	NAVAL HISTORY	BL2450.N	NAVEL (IN RELIGION, FOLK-LORE, ETC.) / *egyptian religion*
D-F	NAVAL HISTORY / *and battles of particular countries*	VC345	NAVIES — INSIGNIA
D95	NAVAL HISTORY, ANCIENT	VA37-42	NAVIES
V310	*NAVAL HONORS* **SEE** NAVAL CEREMONIES, HONORS, AND SALUTES	VA20-25	NAVIES, COST OF
RA975	*NAVAL HOSPITALS* **SEE** HOSPITALS, NAVAL AND MARINE / *marine*	VA60-750	NAVIES, COST OF / *particular countries*
RA980-993	*NAVAL HOSPITALS* **SEE** HOSPITALS, NAVAL AND MARINE / *marine*	RC981-6	*NAVIES-MEDICAL SERVICE* **SEE** MEDICINE, NAVAL / *medical practice*
VG410-450	*NAVAL HOSPITALS* **SEE** HOSPITALS, NAVAL AND MARINE / *naval*	VG	*NAVIES-MEDICAL SERVICE* **SEE** MEDICINE, NAVAL / *naval science*
VC423	*NAVAL HOUSING* **SEE** U.S. — BARRACKS AND QUARTERS	VK144	NAVIGATION — EARLY WORKS TO 1800
VG470-475	NAVAL HYGIENE	VK559	NAVIGATION — PROBLEMS, EXERCISES, ETC.
UC440	*NAVAL LAUNDRIES* **SEE** LAUNDRIES, MILITARY	VK200	NAVIGATION — SAFETY MEASURES
VB350-785	NAVAL LAW	VK401-529	NAVIGATION — STUDY AND TEACHING
Z675.N3	*NAVAL LIBRARIES* **SEE** LIBRARIES, NAVAL	VK563	NAVIGATION — TABLES
V179	*NAVAL LOGISTICS* **SEE** LOGISTICS, NAVAL	TL586-9	NAVIGATION (AERONAUTICS)
V245	NAVAL MANEUVERS	TL1065	NAVIGATION (ASTRONAUTICS)
UB430-435	*NAVAL MEDALS* **SEE** MEDALS, MILITARY AND NAVAL / *military*	TL1070	*NAVIGATION (ASTRONAUTICS)-CHARTS, DIAGRAMS, ETC.* **SEE** ASTRONAUTICAL CHARTS
VB330-335	*NAVAL MEDALS* **SEE** MEDALS, MILITARY AND NAVAL / *naval*	V23-24	*NAVIGATION - DICTIONARIES* **SEE** NAVAL ART AND SCIENCE — DICTIONARIES
RC981-6	*NAVAL MEDICINE* **SEE** MEDICINE, NAVAL / *medical practice*	HE586-7	*NAVIGATION LAWS* **SEE** INLAND NAVIGATION — LAWS AND REGULATIONS
		JX4408-4449	*NAVIGATION LAWS* **SEE** MARITIME LAW / *international law*
		JX63	*NAVIGATION LAWS* **SEE** MARITIME LAW / *private*

VK397	*NAVIGATION RADIO STATIONS* **SEE** MARINE RADIO STATIONS
VK	NAVIGATION
TL586-9	*NAVIGATION, AERIAL* **SEE** NAVIGATION (AERONAUTICS)
VK560	*NAVIGATION, ELECTRONICS IN* **SEE** ELECTRONICS IN NAVIGATION
TL588.5	*NAVIGATION, INERTIAL (AERONAUTICS)* **SEE** INERTIAL NAVIGATION (AERONAUTICS)
TC601-791	*NAVIGATION, INLAND* **SEE** INLAND NAVIGATION / *engineering*
HE617-720	*NAVIGATION, INLAND* **SEE** INLAND NAVIGATION / *transportation*
GN440	NAVIGATION, PRIMITIVE
VM600-881	*NAVIGATION, STEAM* **SEE** STEAM-NAVIGATION
V23-24	*NAVIGATION-DICTIONARIES* **SEE** NAVAL ART AND SCIENCE — DICTIONARIES
HE586-7	*NAVIGATION-LAW AND LEGISLATION* **SEE** INLAND NAVIGATION — LAWS AND REGULATIONS
JX4408-4449	*NAVIGATION-LAW AND LEGISLATION* **SEE** MARITIME LAW / *international law*
JX63	*NAVIGATION-LAW AND LEGISLATION* **SEE** MARITIME LAW / *private*
G80-99	*NAVIGATORS* **SEE** DISCOVERIES (IN GEOGRAPHY)
G220-420	*NAVIGATORS* **SEE** DISCOVERIES (IN GEOGRAPHY)
G575-890	*NAVIGATORS* **SEE** DISCOVERIES (IN GEOGRAPHY) / *polar regions*
G80-890	*NAVIGATORS* **SEE** EXPLORERS
HD8039.S4-42	*NAVIGATORS* **SEE** SEAMEN / *labor*
HD4801-8942	*NAVVIES* **SEE** LABOR AND LABORING CLASSES
V	*NAVY* **SEE** NAVAL ART AND SCIENCE
VA37-42	*NAVY* **SEE** NAVIES
U43.U	*NAVY DAY* **SEE** ARMED FORCES DAY
F1032	NAVY ISLAND CAMPAIGN, 1837-1838
V735-743	NAVY WIVES
V220-240	NAVY-YARDS AND NAVAL STATIONS
VA67-70	NAVY-YARDS AND NAVAL STATIONS / *by country*
DX289	NAWAR
E99.D1	*NAWDOWISSNEE INDIANS* **SEE** DAKOTA INDIANS
F1221.C	*NAYARIT INDIANS* **SEE** CORA INDIANS
F1220	*NAYARIT INDIANS* **SEE** CORA INDIANS
PM3711	*NAYARITA LANGUAGE* **SEE** CORA LANGUAGE
F1221.C	*NAYERITS* **SEE** CORA INDIANS
F1220	*NAYERITS* **SEE** CORA INDIANS
PL8110.C	*NDAU LANGUAGE* **SEE** CHINDAU LANGUAGE
PL8723	*NDEBELE LANGUAGE* **SEE** TEBELE LANGUAGE
PL8547	NDONGA LANGUAGE
GN75.N3	NEANDERTHAL RACE
RE938	*NEARSIGHTEDNESS* **SEE** MYOPIA
QB851-5	NEBULAE
QB891	NEBULAE / *spectra*
QB981	NEBULAR HYPOTHESIS
JX4079.N4	NECESSITY (INTERNATIONAL LAW)
B187.N4	NECESSITY (PHILOSOPHY) / *greek philosophy*
BD411	NECESSITY (PHILOSOPHY) / *ontology*
BF620-628	NECESSITY (PHILOSOPHY) / *psychology*
E199	NECESSITY, FORT, BATTLE OF, 1754
JX5135.M5	*NECESSITY, MILITARY* **SEE** MILITARY NECESSITY
QM691	NECK — ABNORMITIES AND DEFORMITIES
RD641-2	NECK — ABSCESS
RC936	NECK — DISEASES
RD531	NECK — SURGERY
RD661	NECK — TUMORS
QL504.4	NECK / *comparative anatomy*
QM535	NECK / *human anatomy*
QM155	NECK / *human anatomy*
GT2260	NECKLACES
QE611	NECKS (GEOLOGY)
GT2120	*NECKTIES* **SEE** CRAVATS
GN475	*NECROMANCY* **SEE** MAGIC / *ethnology*
BF1585-1623	*NECROMANCY* **SEE** MAGIC / *occult sciences*
RA1058	*NECROPSY* **SEE** AUTOPSY / *medical jurisprudence*
RB57	*NECROPSY* **SEE** AUTOPSY / *pathology*
RA1058	*NECROSCOPY* **SEE** AUTOPSY / *medical jurisprudence*
RB57	*NECROSCOPY* **SEE** AUTOPSY / *pathology*
QR201.N4	NECROSIS — BACTERIOLOGY
RB133	NECROSIS
SF535	*NECTAR PLANTS* **SEE** HONEY PLANTS
QK657	NECTARIES
RD73.N5	NEEDLE-HOLDERS / *surgery*
HD9999.P6-63	*NEEDLES* **SEE** PINS AND NEEDLES / *economics*
GT2280	*NEEDLES* **SEE** PINS AND NEEDLES / *manners and customs*
TS2301.P5	*NEEDLES* **SEE** PINS AND NEEDLES / *manufacture*
TT715	NEEDLEWORK — IMPLEMENTS AND APPLIANCES
TT753	NEEDLEWORK — PATTERNS
TT708	NEEDLEWORK — STUDY AND TEACHING
TT700-845	NEEDLEWORK
NK8800-9499	NEEDLEWORK / *art needlework*
TR290-310	*NEGATIVES* **SEE** PHOTOGRAPHY — NEGATIVES
JX6288-9	NEGOTIABLE INSTRUMENTS / *international law*
HF1259	NEGOTIABLE INSTRUMENTS / *u.s.*
HJ5901-5919	*NEGOTIABLE INSTRUMENTS-TAXATION* **SEE** TAXATION OF BONDS, SECURITIES, ETC.
BF637.N	NEGOTIATION
JX4473	*NEGOTIATIONS IN INTERNATIONAL DISPUTES* **SEE** DIPLOMATIC NEGOTIATIONS IN INTERNATIONAL DISPUTES
DT16.P8	NEGRILLOS
PL5501-5525	NEGRITO LANGUAGES (PHILIPPINE)
GN664.N3	NEGRITOS / *anthropology*
DS666.N4	NEGRITOS / *philippine islands*
PN2286	NEGRO ACTORS / *u.s.*
E185.82	NEGRO ART / *u.s.*
N6538.N5	NEGRO ART / *u.s.*
N6538.N5	NEGRO ARTISTS / *u.s.*
PS153.N5	NEGRO AUTHORS / *u.s.*
BX6440-6460	*NEGRO BAPTISTS* **SEE** BAPTISTS, NEGRO
BX1407.N4	*NEGRO CATHOLICS* **SEE** CATHOLICS, NEGRO / *u.s.*
E185.89.C3	NEGRO CHILDREN
E185.65	NEGRO CRIMINALS
PN6120.N4	NEGRO DRAMA
PS627.N4	NEGRO DRAMA / *american collections*
PS338.N	NEGRO DRAMA / *history*
PS374.N4	NEGRO FICTION (AMERICAN)
GR350	*NEGRO FOLK-LORE* **SEE** FOLK-LORE, NEGRO / *africa*
GR103	*NEGRO FOLK-LORE* **SEE** FOLK-LORE, NEGRO / *u.s.*
E185.8	NEGRO INVENTORS
E185.82	NEGRO LAWYERS
E185.96	NEGRO LAWYERS / *biography*
Z720	NEGRO LIBRARIANS
BX8060.N5	*NEGRO LUTHERANS* **SEE** LUTHERANS, NEGRO
BX8435-8473	*NEGRO METHODISTS* **SEE** METHODISTS, NEGRO
PN3195	NEGRO MINSTRELS
ML3556	NEGRO MINSTRELS
HB1323.N4	*NEGRO MORTALITY* **SEE** NEGROES — MORTALITY
ML3556	NEGRO MUSICIANS
E185.61	*NEGRO NATIONALISM* **SEE** BLACK MUSLIMS / *race question*
BP221-3	*NEGRO NATIONALISM* **SEE** BLACK MUSLIMS / *religion*
E185.82	NEGRO PHYSICIANS
PS591.N4	NEGRO POETRY (AMERICAN)
GN645.N3	NEGRO RACE / *ethnography*
HT1581-9	NEGRO RACE / *social groups*
ML3556	NEGRO SONGS / *history*
M1670-1671	NEGRO SONGS / *music*
M1670-1671	NEGRO SPIRITUALS
JK1923-9	*NEGRO SUFFRAGE* **SEE** NEGROES — POLITICS AND SUFFRAGE / *suffrage*
JK2275.N4	*NEGRO SUFFRAGE* **SEE** NEGROES — POLITICS AND SUFFRAGE / *politics*
PN6231.N5	NEGRO WIT AND HUMOR
E185.86	*NEGRO WOMEN* **SEE** WOMEN, NEGRO / *u.s.*
PM7871-4	*NEGRO-AMERICAN DIALECTS* **SEE** NEGRO-ENGLISH DIALECTS
PM7836-9	NEGRO-DANISH DIALECT
PM7861-4	NEGRO-DUTCH DIALECT
PM7871-4	NEGRO-ENGLISH DIALECTS
E185.96-97	NEGROES — BIOGRAPHY
HV3181-5	NEGROES — CHARITIES
E185.61	NEGROES — CIVIL RIGHTS
JK1781-3	NEGROES — CIVIL RIGHTS / *citizenship*
JK1921-9	NEGROES — CIVIL RIGHTS / *suffrage*
TT507	NEGROES — CLOTHING AND DRESS
E448	NEGROES — COLONIZATION
GN130.N3	NEGROES — CRANIOLOGY
GV1623	NEGROES — DANCING
E185.5-93	NEGROES — ECONOMIC CONDITIONS

QP368	*NERVOUS SYSTEM, VEGETATIVE* **SEE** NERVOUS SYSTEM, AUTONOMIC / *physiology*
QL939	*NERVOUS SYSTEM, VEGETATIVE* **SEE** NERVOUS SYSTEM, AUTONOMIC / *comparative anatomy*
RC348	NERVOUS SYSTEM — DISEASES — — DIAGNOSIS
RC328	NERVOUS SYSTEM — DISEASES — — DISPENSARIES
RX281-301	NERVOUS SYSTEM — DISEASES — — HOMEOPATHIC TREATMENT
RC328	NERVOUS SYSTEM — DISEASES — — HOSPITALS
E99.N	NESPELIM INDIANS
BX150-159	NESTORIAN CHURCH
BT1440	NESTORIANS
QL675	*NESTS OF BIRDS* **SEE** BIRDS — EGGS AND NESTS
GV887	NETBALL
DH1-207	NETHERLANDS — HISTORY
DH401-811	NETHERLANDS — HISTORY / *belgium*
DJ	NETHERLANDS — HISTORY / *holland*
DH201	NETHERLANDS — HISTORY — — TWELVE YEARS' TRUCE, 1609-1621
E99.N96	*NETLAKAPAMUK INDIANS* **SEE** NTLAKYAPAMUK INDIANS
PM2045	*NETLAKAPAMUK LANGUAGE* **SEE** NTLAKYAPAMUK LANGUAGE
SH344	NETS / *fisheries*
NK6050	NETSUKES
TT840	NETTING / *fancy work*
RL325	*NETTLE-RASH* **SEE** URTICARIA
TK3001	*NETWORK ANALYZERS* **SEE** ELECTRIC NETWORK ANALYZERS
TK3141	*NETWORK ANALYZERS* **SEE** ELECTRIC NETWORK ANALYZERS / *alternating current*
TK3111	*NETWORK ANALYZERS* **SEE** ELECTRIC NETWORK ANALYZERS / *direct current*
TK3226	*NETWORK THEORY* **SEE** ELECTRIC NETWORKS
QA402	*NETWORK THEORY* **SEE** SYSTEM ANALYSIS
TK3226	*NETWORKS, ELECTRIC* **SEE** ELECTRIC NETWORKS .
PL6262	*NEU POMMERN LANGUAGE* **SEE** NEW BRITAIN LANGUAGE
DC309.N3	NEUF-BRISACH, ALSACE — SIEGE, 1870
D545.N4	NEUFCHATEAU, BATTLE OF, 1914
D643.B5-6	NEUILLY-SUR-SEINE, TREATY OF, NOV. 27, 1919 (BULGARIA)
ML174	NEUMES
RX301.N5	NEURALGIA — HOMEOPATHIC TREATMENT
RC412	NEURALGIA
RX301.N5	NEURALGIA, FACIAL — HOMEOPATHIC TREATMENT
RC412	NEURALGIA, FACIAL
RC420	*NEURALGIA, SCIATIC* **SEE** SCIATICA
RC412	NEURALGIA, TRAUMATIC
RC552.N5	NEURASTHENIA
RC416	NEURITIS
RC416	NEURITIS, MULTIPLE
RE731	NEURO-OPHTHALMOLOGY
QM451	NEUROANATOMY
QP356	NEUROCHEMISTRY
QM575	NEUROKERATIN
RA1147	*NEUROLOGY, FORENSIC* **SEE** FORENSIC NEUROLOGY
RA1147	*NEUROLOGY-JURISPRUDENCE* **SEE** FORENSIC NEUROLOGY
QM575	*NEURONS* **SEE** NERVES / *histology*
QP331	*NEURONS* **SEE** NERVES / *physiology*
RC321-429	*NEUROPATHOLOGY* **SEE** NERVOUS SYSTEM — DISEASES
RZ399.N5	NEUROPATHY / *therapeutic system*
QL511-514	NEUROPTERA
RC530-552	NEUROSES
RD593	*NEUROSURGERY* **SEE** NERVOUS SYSTEM — SURGERY
RC201.7.N4	*NEUROSYPHILIS* **SEE** NERVOUS SYSTEM — SYPHILIS
E99.N	NEUTRAL NATION INDIANS
JX5355-5397	*NEUTRALISM* **SEE** NEUTRALITY
JX5355-5397	NEUTRALITY
D295	NEUTRALITY, ARMED / *armed neutrality of 1780*
JX5383	NEUTRALITY, ARMED / *international law*
QC721	*NEUTRON DIFFRACTION* **SEE** NEUTRONS — DIFFRACTION
QC721	NEUTRONS — DIFFRACTION
QH652	NEUTRONS — PHYSIOLOGICAL EFFECT
QC173	NEUTRONS
RL793	*NEVUS* **SEE** MOLE (DERMATOLOGY)
BF861.M65	*NEVUS* **SEE** MOLE (DERMATOLOGY) / *physiognomy*
PL6262	NEW BRITAIN LANGUAGE
PL8276	*NEW CALABAR LANGUAGE* **SEE** IJO LANGUAGE
BX8701-8749	*NEW CHURCH* **SEE** NEW JERUSALEM CHURCH
BR270	*NEW DEVOTION* **SEE** DEVOTIO MODERNA
F1-15	NEW ENGLAND — HISTORY
F10	NEW ENGLAND — HURRICANES, 1954
BX7250	NEW ENGLAND THEOLOGY
B905	*NEW ENGLAND TRANSCENDENTALISM* **SEE** TRANSCENDENTALISM (NEW ENGLAND)
F3	NEW ENGLANDERS / *biography*
E199	NEW ENGLAND — HISTORY — — FRENCH AND INDIAN WAR, 1755-1763
E357-9	NEW ENGLAND — HISTORY — — WAR OF 1812
NK4399.N4	NEW HALL PORCELAIN
F31-45	NEW HAMPSHIRE — HISTORY
E520	NEW HAMPSHIRE — HISTORY — — CIVIL WAR
E198	NEW HAMPSHIRE — HISTORY — — KING GEORGE'S WAR, 1744-1748
E263.N4	NEW HAMPSHIRE — HISTORY — — REVOLUTION
F131-145	NEW JERSEY — HISTORY
E83.79	*NEW JERSEY-HISTORY-EXPEDITION AGAINST THE INDIANS, 1791* **SEE** ST. CLAIR'S CAMPAIGN, 1791
E521	NEW JERSEY — HISTORY — — CIVIL WAR
E263.N5	NEW JERSEY — HISTORY — — REVOLUTION
BV425	NEW JERUSALEM CHURCH — HYMNS
BX8701-8749	NEW JERUSALEM CHURCH
HX696	NEW LANARK ESTABLISHMENT
E476.64	NEW MARKET, BATTLE OF, 1864
F791-805	NEW MEXICO — HISTORY
E571	NEW MEXICO — HISTORY — — CIVIL WAR
E522	NEW MEXICO — HISTORY — — CIVIL WAR
E405.2	NEW MEXICO — HISTORY — — WAR WITH MEXICO, 1845-1848
F379.N5	NEW ORLEANS — HISTORY
E356.N5	NEW ORLEANS, BATTLE OF, 1815
E472.88	NEW ORLEANS, BATTLE OF, 1862
E510	NEW ORLEANS — HISTORY — — CIVIL WAR
F379.N5	NEW ORLEANS — HISTORY — — CIVIL WAR
F27.K3	*NEW PLYMOUTH PURCHASE, MAINE* **SEE** KENNEBEC PATENT
PL6262	*NEW POMERANIA LANGUAGE* **SEE** NEW BRITAIN LANGUAGE
PM2017.N8	NEW RIVER LANGUAGE
PA695-895	*NEW TESTAMENT GREEK* **SEE** GREEK LANGUAGE, BIBLICAL
BF638-645	NEW THOUGHT
P331-361	*NEW WORDS* **SEE** WORDS, NEW / *comparative lexicography*
BV4282	NEW YEAR SERMONS
GT4905	NEW YEAR
BM695.N5	*NEW YEAR, JEWISH* **SEE** ROSH HA-SHANAH
F128	NEW YORK (CITY) — HISTORY
F128.47	NEW YORK (CITY) — STORM, 1888
E230.5-289	NEW YORK (CITY) — HISTORY — — REVOLUTION
E263.N6	NEW YORK (CITY) — HISTORY — — REVOLUTION
E359.5.N6	NEW YORK (CITY) — HISTORY — — WAR OF 1812
F116-130	NEW YORK (STATE) — HISTORY
E523	NEW YORK (STATE) — HISTORY — — CIVIL WAR
E196	NEW YORK (STATE) — HISTORY — — KING WILLIAM'S WAR, 1689-1697
E197	NEW YORK (STATE) — HISTORY — — QUEEN ANNE'S WAR, 1702-1713
E263.N6	NEW YORK (STATE) — HISTORY — — REVOLUTION
E359.5.N6	NEW YORK (STATE) — HISTORY — — WAR OF 1812
E726.N5	NEW YORK (STATE) — HISTORY — — WAR OF 1898
TF430	NEW YORK AIR-BRAKE
HV1666-1698	*NEW YORK POINT SYSTEM* **SEE** BLIND — PRINTING AND WRITING SYSTEMS
PZ1	NEW ZEALAND FICTION / *collections*
PR9635-9	NEW ZEALAND FICTION / *history*
PR9600-9699	NEW ZEALAND LITERATURE
PN5591-5600	NEW ZEALAND NEWSPAPERS / *history*
PR9655-9669	NEW ZEALAND POETRY / *collections*
PR9626-9632	NEW ZEALAND POETRY / *history*
PN6222.N	NEW ZEALAND WIT AND HUMOR / *collections*
PR9642	NEW ZEALAND WIT AND HUMOR / *history*
PL3801.N5	NEWARI LANGUAGE
SF995	NEWCASTLE DISEASE

SF429.N4	NEWFOUNDLAND DOGS
TR820	*NEWS PHOTOGRAPHY* **SEE** PHOTOGRAPHY, JOURNALISTIC
PN4805	NEWS-LETTERS / *early*
PN4784.N5	NEWS-LETTERS / *modern*
HD6247.N5	NEWSBOYS
PN4784.C6	NEWSPAPER AGENTS
HD6247.N5	NEWSPAPER CARRIERS
AG500-551	*NEWSPAPER CLIPPING BUREAUS* **SEE** CLIPPING BUREAUS
Z691	*NEWSPAPER CLIPPINGS* **SEE** CLIPPINGS (BOOKS, NEWSPAPERS, ETC.)
Z697.C6	*NEWSPAPER CLIPPINGS* **SEE** CLIPPINGS (BOOKS, NEWSPAPERS, ETC.)
Z675.N4	NEWSPAPER OFFICE LIBRARIES
PN4784.A5	NEWSPAPERS — ANNIVERSARY EDITIONS
Z6940-6962	NEWSPAPERS — BIBLIOGRAPHY
Z6940-6962	NEWSPAPERS — DIRECTORIES
PN4784.H4	NEWSPAPERS — HEADLINES
NC970	NEWSPAPERS — ILLUSTRATIONS
AI21	NEWSPAPERS — INDEXES
PN4784.L6	NEWSPAPERS — LOCAL EDITIONS
HQ784.N4	NEWSPAPERS AND CHILDREN
HQ784.N4	*NEWSPAPERS AND YOUTH* **SEE** NEWSPAPERS AND CHILDREN
LB1044.9.N4	NEWSPAPERS IN EDUCATION
Z265	NEWSPAPERS ON MICROFILM
AN	NEWSPAPERS
PN4700-4899	NEWSPAPERS / *etc.*
PN98.B7	*NEWSPAPERS-SECTIONS, COLUMNS, ETC.-BOOK SECTION* **SEE** BOOK REVIEWING
PN4784.L6	*NEWSPAPERS-SECTIONS, COLUMNS, ETC.-LOCAL* **SEE** NEWSPAPERS — LOCAL EDITIONS
Z6945	NEWSPAPERS — BIBLIOGRAPHY — — UNION LISTS
PN4784.F5	NEWSPAPERS — SECTIONS, COLUMNS, ETC. — — FINANCE
PN4784.R4	NEWSPAPERS — SECTIONS, COLUMNS, ETC. — — REVIEWS
QC411	*NEWTON'S RINGS* **SEE** INTERFERENCE (LIGHT)
QL668.C2	NEWTS
E83.877	NEZ PERCE INDIANS — WARS, 1877
E99.N5	NEZ PERCE INDIANS
PM2019	NEZ PERCE LANGUAGE
PL8593	*NG'ANGA LANGUAGE* **SEE** NYANJA LANGUAGE
PL8055	*NGALA LANGUAGE* **SEE** BANGALA LANGUAGE
PL8202	*NGANGELA LANGUAGE* **SEE** GANGUELA LANGUAGE
PL8204	*NGBANDI LANGUAGE* **SEE** GBANDI LANGUAGE
PL6240	*NGGELA LANGUAGE* **SEE** FLORIDA LANGUAGE
PL7101.N5	NGGERIKUDI LANGUAGE
DT650.N	NGOMBE (BANTU TRIBE)
GN659.N45	NGONDE (AFRICAN TRIBE)
PL8549	NGONDE LANGUAGE
E356.L9	*NIAGARA FALLS, BATTLE OF, 1814* **SEE** LUNDY'S LANE, BATTLE OF, 1814
E356.L9	*NIAGARA, BATTLE OF, 1814* **SEE** LUNDY'S LANE, BATTLE OF, 1814
DT132	*NIAM-NIAM* **SEE** AZANDE
PM1736-9	*NIANTIC LANGUAGE* **SEE** MASSACHUSET LANGUAGE
PL5433	NIAS LANGUAGE
BR210	NICAEA, COUNCIL OF, 325
F1521-7	NICARAGUA — HISTORY
PQ7516	NICARAGUAN BALLADS AND SONGS / *collections*
PQ7512	NICARAGUAN BALLADS AND SONGS / *history*
PQ7510-7519	NICARAGUAN LITERATURE
PQ7516	NICARAGUAN POETRY / *collections*
PQ7512	NICARAGUAN POETRY / *history*
F1526.3	NICARAGUA — HISTORY — — REVOLUTION, 1909-1910
DC986	NICE — SIEGE, 1543
M2099.L3	*NICENE CREED (MUSIC)* **SEE** CREDO (MUSIC)
M2079.L3	*NICENE CREED (MUSIC)* **SEE** CREDO (MUSIC)
BT999	NICENE CREED
BT1003.C6	*NICENE-CONSTANTINOPOLITAN CREED* **SEE** CONSTANTINOPOLITAN CREED
BL1442	NICHIREN (SECT)
BL1442	*NICHIREN-SHU* **SEE** NICHIREN (SECT)
QP913.N6	NICKEL — PHYSIOLOGICAL EFFECT
TS650	NICKEL ALLOYS / *manufacture*
TA490	NICKEL ALLOYS / *properties*
TN490.N6	NICKEL MINES AND MINING
QD181.N6	NICKEL NITRATE
TN757.N5	NICKEL STEEL / *metallurgy*
TN757.N5	*NICKEL-ALLOY STEEL* **SEE** NICKEL STEEL / *metallurgy*
TS690	NICKEL-PLATING
QD181.N6	NICKEL / *chemistry*
HD9539.N	NICKEL / *economics*
TN799.N6	NICKEL / *metallurgy*
CT108	NICKNAMES / *english*
VM743.N6	*NICLAUSSE BOILER* **SEE** STEAM-BOILERS, MARINE — NICLAUSSE
PL4471	NICOBARESE LANGUAGE
TE253	*NICOLSON PAVEMENTS* **SEE** PAVEMENTS, WOODEN
DR496	*NICOPOLIS, BATTLE OF, 1396* **SEE** NIKOPOLI, BATTLE OF, 1396
RM666.T6	NICOTINE / *therapeutics*
RA1238.N5	NICOTINE / *toxicology*
QL675	*NIDOLOGY* **SEE** BIRDS — EGGS AND NESTS
NK6525	NIELLO
DS759.5	NIEN REBELLION, 1853-1868
DS759.5	*NIENFEI REBELLION* **SEE** NIEN REBELLION, 1853-1868
DH199.N4	NIEUPORT, BATTLE OF, 1600
DT360	NIGER EXPEDITION, 1841-1842
PN1960-1969	*NIGHT CLUBS* **SEE** MUSIC-HALLS (VARIETY-THEATERS, CABARETS, ETC.)
U167	NIGHT FIGHTING (MILITARY SCIENCE)
BP186.38	*NIGHT OF MID-SHA'BAN* **SEE** LAYLAT AL-BARA'AH
BP186.38	*NIGHT OF THE BARA'AH* **SEE** LAYLAT AL-BARA'AH
TR610	*NIGHT PHOTOGRAPHY* **SEE** PHOTOGRAPHY, NIGHT
LC5501-5560	*NIGHT SCHOOLS* **SEE** EVENING AND CONTINUATION SCHOOLS
HV8290	*NIGHT WATCHMEN* **SEE** WATCHMEN
HD5113	NIGHT WORK
QL696.P2	NIGHTINGALES
DT16.P8	*NIGRILLOS* **SEE** NEGRILLOS
PL4585	*NIHALI LANGUAGE* **SEE** NAHALI LANGUAGE
HX914-917	NIHILISM / *russia*
HX914-917	*NIHILISTS* **SEE** NIHILISM / *russia*
D278.5	NIJMEGEN, PEACE OF, 1678-1679
DT429	NIKA (BANTU TRIBE)
DR496	*NIKBOLU, BATTLE OF, 1396* **SEE** NIKOPOLI, BATTLE OF, 1396
PL4471	*NIKOBAR LANGUAGE* **SEE** NICOBARESE LANGUAGE
DR496	NIKOPOLI, BATTLE OF, 1396
DC226.N5	NILE, BATTLE OF THE, 1798
GN659.N5	NILO-HAMITIC TRIBES
DT132	*NILOTES* **SEE** NILOTIC TRIBES
PL8026	NILOTIC LANGUAGES
GN231	*NILOTIC POSITION* **SEE** ONE-LEG RESTING POSITION
DT132	NILOTIC TRIBES
PL4585	*NIMAREE LANGUAGE* **SEE** NAHALI LANGUAGE
N8160	NIMBUS — ART
QA142	NINE (THE NUMBER)
D351-363	NINETEENTH CENTURY
CB415-417	NINETEENTH CENTURY / *civilization*
GV1469.N5	NINETY-NINE (GAME)
E99.N	NIPISSING INDIANS
PM2025	NIPISSING LANGUAGE
E99.N7	NIPMUC INDIANS
E2324	NIQUITAO, BATTLE OF, 1813
BL1475.N5	NIRVANA
PM2026.N3	NISKA LANGUAGE
E99.N74	NISQUALLI INDIANS
PM2026.N5	NISQUALLI LANGUAGE
TP238	*NITER* **SEE** SALTPETER / *manufacture*
QD181.R2	*NITON* **SEE** RADON
QD305.A8	*NITRAMINES* **SEE** NITROAMINES
QD341.A8	*NITRAMINES* **SEE** NITROAMINES
QD181.F4	*NITRATE OF IRON* **SEE** FERRIC NITRATE
TP238	*NITRATE OF POTASH* **SEE** SALTPETER / *manufacture*
QD181.A3	*NITRATE OF SILVER* **SEE** SILVER NITRATE
TN911	*NITRATE OF SODA* **SEE** SALTPETER, CHILE
QP913.N1	NITRATES — PHYSIOLOGICAL EFFECT
TP237-8	NITRATES / *chemical technology*
QD181.N1	NITRATES / *chemistry*
S651	NITRATES / *fertilizers*
TN911	NITRATES / *mineral industries*

M960-962	NONETS (2 HURDY-GURDIES, 2 CLARINETS, 2 HORNS, 2 VIOLAS, VIOLONCELLO)
M960-962	NONETS (3 CLARINETS, CORNET, TROMBONE, TRUMPET, VIOLIN, VIOLA, VIOLONCELLO)
M950-952	*NONETS, STRING* **SEE** STRING NONETS
M955-7	*NONETS, WIND* **SEE** WIND NONETS
TN758	NONFERROUS METALS
BX5087	NONJURORS
DA499	NONJURORS, ENGLISH CATHOLIC / *18th century*
TJ1072	NONMETALLIC BEARINGS
PN6110.N6	NONSENSE-VERSES / *collections*
PN1525	NONSENSE-VERSES / *history*
QE391.N	NONTRONITE
TN948.N	NONTRONITE
TS1781	NONWOVEN FABRICS
ML760	NOORDSCHE BALK
E99.N85	NOOTKA INDIANS
PM2031	NOOTKA LANGUAGE
PL8577	*NOPE LANGUAGE* **SEE** NUPE LANGUAGE
UF620.N8	NORDENFELT MACHINE-GUN
GN549.T4	*NORDIC RACE* **SEE** TEUTONIC RACE
D267.N7	NORDLINGEN, BATTLE OF, 1634
DA87.7	NORE MUTINY, 1797
LB1751-5	*NORMAL INSTITUTES* **SEE** TEACHERS' INSTITUTES
LB1823-2151	*NORMAL INSTITUTES* **SEE** TEACHERS' INSTITUTES
LB1805-2151	*NORMAL SCHOOLS* **SEE** TEACHERS COLLEGES
NA423-9	*NORMAN ARCHITECTURE* **SEE** ARCHITECTURE, NORMAN
SF293.P4	*NORMAN HORSE* **SEE** PERCHERON HORSE
SF199.N	NORMANDY CATTLE
SF193.N8	NORMANDY CATTLE / *herd-books*
D148	NORMANS
PD2485	NORN DIALECT
E78.M4	NORRIDGEWOCK INDIANS
E99.N	NORRIDGEWOCK INDIANS
E78.M4	*NORRIDGWALK INDIANS* **SEE** NORRIDGEWOCK INDIANS
E99.N	*NORRIDGWALK INDIANS* **SEE** NORRIDGEWOCK INDIANS
E78.M4	*NORRIDGWOG INDIANS* **SEE** NORRIDGEWOCK INDIANS
E99.N	*NORRIDGWOG INDIANS* **SEE** NORRIDGEWOCK INDIANS
PD2201-2392	*NORSE LANGUAGES* **SEE** ICELANDIC AND OLD NORSE LANGUAGES
PD1501-5929	*NORSE LANGUAGES* **SEE** SCANDINAVIAN LANGUAGES
PT7101-7211	*NORSE LITERATURE* **SEE** ICELANDIC AND OLD NORSE LITERATURE / *history*
PT7220-7262	*NORSE LITERATURE* **SEE** ICELANDIC AND OLD NORSE LITERATURE / *collections*
PT7090-7099	*NORSE LITERATURE* **SEE** SCANDINAVIAN LITERATURE / *collections*
PT7045-7087	*NORSE LITERATURE* **SEE** SCANDINAVIAN LITERATURE / *history*
DL65	*NORSEMEN* **SEE** NORTHMEN
G108.N8	NORTH (THE WORD)
E77-99	*NORTH AMERICAN INDIANS* **SEE** INDIANS OF NORTH AMERICA
P911	*NORTH ARYAN LANGUAGE* **SEE** KHOTANESE LANGUAGE
F251-265	NORTH CAROLINA — HISTORY
LB3541	NORTH CAROLINA DAY
E573	NORTH CAROLINA — HISTORY — — CIVIL WAR
E524	NORTH CAROLINA — HISTORY — — CIVIL WAR
E263.N8	NORTH CAROLINA — HISTORY — — REVOLUTION
E356.B2	NORTH POINT, BATTLE OF, 1814
G600-700	NORTH POLE
E398	NORTHEAST BOUNDARY OF THE U.S.
G680-690	NORTHEAST PASSAGE
F551	NORTHERN BOUNDARY OF THE U.S.
F597	NORTHERN BOUNDARY OF THE U.S.
BL1483	*NORTHERN BUDDHISM* **SEE** MAHAYANA BUDDHISM
QC971-2	*NORTHERN LIGHTS* **SEE** AURORAS
DL188.5	NORTHERN SEVEN YEARS' WAR, 1563-1570 / *denmark*
BL1483	*NORTHERN VEHICLE* **SEE** MAHAYANA BUDDHISM
DL733-743	NORTHERN WAR, 1700-1721 / *sweden*
DS748.6	*NORTHERN WEI DYNASTY* **SEE** CHINA — HISTORY — — NORTHERN WEI DYNASTY, 386-636

D148	*NORTHMEN IN FRANCE* **SEE** NORMANS
DK70-73	*NORTHMEN IN RUSSIA* **SEE** VARANGIANS / *medieval russia*
DL65	*NORTHMEN IN RUSSIA* **SEE** VARANGIANS / *northmen*
DL65	NORTHMEN
F880	NORTHWEST BOUNDARY OF THE U.S.
F854	NORTHWEST BOUNDARY OF THE U.S.
F851	NORTHWEST COAST OF NORTH AMERICA
E309	*NORTHWEST ORDINANCE* **SEE** ORDINANCE OF 1787
G640-665	NORTHWEST PASSAGE
F1060.9	*NORTHWEST REBELLION, 1885* **SEE** RIEL REBELLION, 1885
F1060	NORTHWEST, CANADIAN
F597	*NORTHWEST, NEW* **SEE** NORTHWESTERN STATES
F476-485	NORTHWEST, OLD — HISTORY
F476-485	NORTHWEST, OLD
E263.N84	NORTHWEST, OLD — HISTORY — — REVOLUTION
E355.2	NORTHWEST, OLD — HISTORY — — WAR OF 1812
E355.4	NORTHWEST, OLD — HISTORY — — WAR OF 1812
F851-2	NORTHWEST, PACIFIC
E458.8	NORTHWESTERN CONSPIRACY, 1864
F597	NORTHWESTERN STATES
DL401-596	NORWAY — HISTORY
SD397.P61	NORWAY PINE
SD397.S77	NORWAY SPRUCE
DL188.5	*NORWAY-HISTORY-NORTHERN SEVEN YEARS' WAR, 1563-1570* **SEE** NORTHERN SEVEN YEARS' WAR, 1563-1570 / *denmark*
DL532	NORWAY — HISTORY — — GERMAN OCCUPATION, 1940-1945
DL525	NORWAY — HISTORY — — SEPARATION FROM SWEDEN, 1905
DL533	NORWAY — HISTORY — — 1945-
PT8690	NORWEGIAN BALLADS AND SONGS / *collections*
PT8486-7	NORWEGIAN BALLADS AND SONGS / *history*
PT9015	NORWEGIAN DRAMA (NYNORSK) — HISTORY AND CRITICISM
PT8699-8718	NORWEGIAN DRAMA / *collections*
PT8500-8534	NORWEGIAN DRAMA / *history*
TT787	*NORWEGIAN DRAWN-WORK* **SEE** HARDANGER NEEDLEWORK
SF429.N	NORWEGIAN ELKHOUNDS
PT8720-8722	NORWEGIAN FICTION / *collections*
PT8555-8567	NORWEGIAN FICTION / *history*
PD2900-2999	*NORWEGIAN LANGUAGE (LANDSMAAL)* **SEE** NORWEGIAN LANGUAGE (NYNORSK)
PD2900-2999	NORWEGIAN LANGUAGE (NYNORSK)
PD2571-2699	NORWEGIAN LANGUAGE
PD2900-2999	*NORWEGIAN LANGUAGE-LANDSMAAL* **SEE** NORWEGIAN LANGUAGE (NYNORSK)
PD2900-2999	*NORWEGIAN LANGUAGE-NYNORSK* **SEE** NORWEGIAN LANGUAGE (NYNORSK)
Z2600	NORWEGIAN LITERATURE — BIO-BIBLIOGRAPHY
PT8615-8733	NORWEGIAN LITERATURE / *collections*
PT8301-8610	NORWEGIAN LITERATURE / *history*
PN5291-9	NORWEGIAN NEWSPAPERS / *history*
PN5291-5300	NORWEGIAN PERIODICALS / *history*
PD2501-2999	NORWEGIAN PHILOLOGY / *language*
PT8301-9155	NORWEGIAN PHILOLOGY / *literature*
PT8675-8695	NORWEGIAN POETRY / *collections*
PT8460-8490	NORWEGIAN POETRY / *history*
PT9131-9150	NORWEGIAN-AMERICAN LITERATURE
PN4885.N59-64	NORWEGIAN-AMERICAN NEWSPAPERS / *history*
PN4885.N59-64	NORWEGIAN-AMERICAN PERIODICALS / *history*
DL401-532	NORWEGIANS / *norway*
BP195.N7	NOSAIRIANS
QL947	NOSE — ANATOMY / *comparative anatomy*
QM505	NOSE — ANATOMY / *human anatomy*
RF341-437	NOSE — DISEASES
RF435	NOSE — LARVAE AND INSECTS
RF51	NOSE — SURGERY
RF451	NOSE — SURGERY / *restoration*
RC312.5.N6	NOSE — TUBERCULOSIS
RC280.N6	NOSE — TUMORS
BF861.N7	NOSE (PHYSIOGNOMY)
QL947	*NOSE* **SEE** FRONTAL SINUS / *comparative anatomy*
QM505	*NOSE* **SEE** FRONTAL SINUS / *human anatomy*
QP458	NOSE / *physiology*
RF421	NOSE, ACCESSORY SINUSES OF / *diseases*

QM505	NOSE, ACCESSORY SINUSES OF / *human anatomy*
RX451	NOSE — DISEASES — — HOMEOPATHIC TREATMENT
RF6	NOSE — DISEASES — — HOSPITALS
RC96	NOSOLOGY
BP195.N7	*NOSSARII* **SEE** NOSAIRIANS
BF575.N6	NOSTALGIA
Z696	*NOTATION (FOR BOOKS IN LIBRARIES)* **SEE** ALPHABETING
Z696-7	*NOTATION (FOR BOOKS IN LIBRARIES)* **SEE** SHELF-LISTING (LIBRARY SCIENCE)
QA41	*NOTATION, MATHEMATICAL* **SEE** MATHEMATICAL NOTATION
ML431	*NOTATION, MUSICAL* **SEE** MUSICAL NOTATION / *history*
MT35	*NOTATION, MUSICAL* **SEE** MUSICAL NOTATION / *instruction*
ML432	*NOTATION, MUSICAL* **SEE** MUSICAL NOTATION / *reform*
GN477.R	NOTCHED RATTLE
LB2395	NOTE-TAKING / *students*
HD7813	*NOTICE OF DISMISSAL* **SEE** EMPLOYEES, DISMISSAL OF
E99.N85	*NOUTKA INDIANS* **SEE** NOOTKA INDIANS
PM2031	*NOUTKA LANGUAGE* **SEE** NOOTKA LANGUAGE
F1036-1039.5	NOVA SCOTIA — HISTORY
E263.N9	NOVA SCOTIA — HISTORY — — 1775-1783
QE391.N	NOVACULITE
QB841	*NOVAE* **SEE** STARS, NEW
QB895	*NOVAE* **SEE** STARS, NEW / *spectra*
DG541	NOVARA — SIEGE, 1495
Q115.N	NOVARA EXPEDITION, 1857-1859
DQ109	NOVARA, BATTLE OF, 1513
DG553.5.N7	NOVARA, BATTLE OF, 1849
PN3451-3503	NOVELISTS
PN3311-3503	*NOVELS* **SEE** FICTION
PN44	*NOVELS* **SEE** PLOTS (DRAMA, NOVEL, ETC.)
PN145	*NOVELS* **SEE** PLOTS (DRAMA, NOVEL, ETC.)
PN1683	*NOVELS* **SEE** PLOTS (DRAMA, NOVEL, ETC.) / *drama*
PN3378	*NOVELS* **SEE** PLOTS (DRAMA, NOVEL, ETC.) / *fiction*
PN3373	*NOVELS* **SEE** PLOTS (DRAMA, NOVEL, ETC.) / *short story*
DL836	*NOVEMBER TREATY, 1855* **SEE** STOCKHOLM, TREATY OF, 1855
BX2170.N7	NOVENAS
PM8685	NOVIAL (ARTIFICIAL LANGUAGE)
RM666.N8	NOVOCAINE — THERAPEUTIC USE
RD86.N8	NOVOCAINE
RK510	NOVOCAINE / *dentistry*
PM8688	NOVOLINGUA
DX289	*NOWAR* **SEE** NAWAR
TH9380	NOZZLES / *fire hose*
TC173	NOZZLES / *hydraulics*
PL8597	*NSIMA LANGUAGE* **SEE** NZIMA LANGUAGE
E99.N96	NTLAKYAPAMUK INDIANS
PM2045	NTLAKYAPAMUK LANGUAGE
PL8568	NTOMBA LANGUAGE
PL8568	*NTUMBA LANGUAGE* **SEE** NTOMBA LANGUAGE
PL8571-5	*NUBA LANGUAGE* **SEE** NUBIAN LANGUAGE
PL8571-5	NUBIAN LANGUAGE
TL708	*NUCLEAR AIRCRAFT ENGINES* **SEE** AEROPLANES — NUCLEAR POWER PLANTS
QC787.C6	NUCLEAR COUNTERS
Z7144.N8	NUCLEAR ENGINEERING — MICROCARD CATALOGS
TK9152	NUCLEAR ENGINEERING — SAFETY MEASURES
TK9001-9401	NUCLEAR ENGINEERING
TK9360	NUCLEAR FUELS
QC791	NUCLEAR FUSION
QE513	*NUCLEAR GEOLOGY* **SEE** NUCLEAR GEOPHYSICS
QE513	NUCLEAR GEOPHYSICS
HD	*NUCLEAR INDUSTRIES* **SEE** ATOMIC ENERGY INDUSTRIES / *economics*
TK9001-9401	*NUCLEAR INDUSTRIES* **SEE** ATOMIC ENERGY INDUSTRIES / *technology*
QC762	NUCLEAR MAGNETISM
QD466	*NUCLEAR MASSES* **SEE** ATOMIC MASS / *chemistry*
QC173	*NUCLEAR MASSES* **SEE** ATOMIC MASS / *physics*
QC794	NUCLEAR MOMENTS
QC784	NUCLEAR PHYSICS — LABORATORY MANUALS
QC778	NUCLEAR PHYSICS — POPULAR WORKS
QC173	NUCLEAR PHYSICS
TL708	*NUCLEAR PROPULSION SYSTEMS (AIRPLANE)* **SEE** AEROPLANES — NUCLEAR POWER PLANTS
TK9230	NUCLEAR PROPULSION
QC783.4	*NUCLEAR REACTOR CALCULATIONS* **SEE** NUCLEAR REACTORS — COMPUTER PROGRAMS
TK9360	*NUCLEAR REACTOR FUEL REPROCESSING* **SEE** REACTOR FUEL REPROCESSING
VM774.3	*NUCLEAR REACTOR PLANTS, MARINE* **SEE** MARINE NUCLEAR REACTOR PLANTS
QC783.4	*NUCLEAR REACTOR PROGRAMS (ELECTRONIC COMPUTERS)* **SEE** NUCLEAR REACTORS — COMPUTER PROGRAMS
HD	*NUCLEAR REACTOR SUPPLY INDUSTRY* **SEE** ATOMIC ENERGY INDUSTRIES / *economics*
TK9001-9401	*NUCLEAR REACTOR SUPPLY INDUSTRY* **SEE** ATOMIC ENERGY INDUSTRIES / *technology*
QC783.4	NUCLEAR REACTORS — COMPUTER PROGRAMS
TK9202	NUCLEAR REACTORS — MATERIALS
QC786	NUCLEAR REACTORS / *physics*
TK9202	NUCLEAR REACTORS / *technology*
QC783.4	*NUCLEAR REACTORS-COMPUTER CODES* **SEE** NUCLEAR REACTORS — COMPUTER PROGRAMS
TK9360	*NUCLEAR REACTORS-FUEL* **SEE** NUCLEAR FUELS
TL783.5	NUCLEAR ROCKETS
QC173	*NUCLEAR SHELL MODELS* **SEE** NUCLEAR SHELL THEORY
QC173	*NUCLEAR SHELL STRUCTURE* **SEE** NUCLEAR SHELL THEORY
QC173	NUCLEAR SHELL THEORY
VM317	*NUCLEAR SHIPS* **SEE** ATOMIC SHIPS
VM451	*NUCLEAR-POWERED ICEBREAKING VESSELS* **SEE** ATOMIC ICEBREAKERS
VM317	*NUCLEAR-POWERED SHIPS* **SEE** ATOMIC SHIPS
TK9230	*NUCLEAR-POWERED VEHICLES* **SEE** NUCLEAR PROPULSION
QC918	*NUCLEATION, ATMOSPHERIC* **SEE** ATMOSPHERIC NUCLEATION
QD341.A2	NUCLEIC ACIDS
QP551	NUCLEIN
QH595	*NUCLEUS (CELLS)* **SEE** CELL NUCLEI
QC173	*NUCLEUS OF THE ATOM* **SEE** NUCLEAR PHYSICS
GV450	*NUDE CULTURE* **SEE** NUDISM
N73	NUDE IN ART / *aesthetics*
TR675	*NUDE PHOTOGRAPHY* **SEE** PHOTOGRAPHY OF THE NUDE
QL430.4	NUDIBRANCHIATA
GV450	NUDISM
GV450	*NUDITY CULTURE* **SEE** NUDISM
BL2480.N7	NUER (AFRICAN TRIBE) — RELIGION
DT132	NUER (AFRICAN TRIBE)
PL8576.N4	NUER LANGUAGE
PL6279	NUFOR LANGUAGE
PL6279	*NUFORIAN LANGUAGE* **SEE** NUFOR LANGUAGE
JX4147	NUISANCES (INTERNATIONAL LAW)
PL6471	NUKAHIVA LANGUAGE
PL6471	*NUKUHIVA LANGUAGE* **SEE** NUKAHIVA LANGUAGE
PM8693	NULA (ARTIFICIAL LANGUAGE)
E384.3	NULLIFICATION
JK310-325	NULLIFICATION / *constitutional history*
BX1939.N	NULLITY (CANON LAW)
HQ822	*NULLITY OF MARRIAGE* **SEE** MARRIAGE — ANNULMENT
HQ1024	*NULLITY OF MARRIAGE* **SEE** MARRIAGE — ANNULMENT / *canon law*
DG252.8	NUMANTINE WAR, 143-133 B.C.
QA9	NUMBER CONCEPT
QA95	*NUMBER GAMES* **SEE** MATHEMATICAL RECREATIONS
GR485	*NUMBER RHYMES* **SEE** COUNTING-OUT RHYMES
QA241-6	*NUMBER STUDY* **SEE** NUMBERS, THEORY OF
BF1623.P9	*NUMBER SYMBOLISM* **SEE** SYMBOLISM OF NUMBERS
QA241-6	*NUMBER THEORY* **SEE** NUMBERS, THEORY OF
Z249	NUMBERING-MACHINES
QA246	*NUMBERS, BERNOULLIAN* **SEE** BERNOULLIAN NUMBERS
QA255	NUMBERS, COMPLEX
QA242	NUMBERS, DIVISIBILITY OF
QA246	*NUMBERS, EULER'S* **SEE** EULER'S NUMBERS

QA247.5	NUMBERS, IRRATIONAL
QA246	NUMBERS, PRIME
Z56.5	*NUMBERS, SHORTHAND* **SEE** SHORTHAND NUMBERS
QA241-6	NUMBERS, THEORY OF
QA247.5	NUMBERS, TRANSCENDENTAL
QA248	NUMBERS, TRANSFINITE
QA21	NUMERALS / *history*
QA40.5	NUMERALS / *juvenile works*
P275	NUMERALS / *language*
QA141	NUMERALS / *systems*
Z696	*NUMERATION OF BOOKS IN LIBRARIES* **SEE** ALPHABETING
Z696-7	*NUMERATION OF BOOKS IN LIBRARIES* **SEE** SHELF-LISTING (LIBRARY SCIENCE)
QA141	NUMERATION
F1435.3.N8	NUMERATION, MAYA
QA74	*NUMERICAL ANALYSIS LABORATORIES* **SEE** COMPUTATION LABORATORIES
QA297	*NUMERICAL ANALYSIS PROGRAMS* **SEE** NUMERICAL CALCULATIONS — COMPUTER PROGRAMS
QA297	NUMERICAL CALCULATIONS — COMPUTER PROGRAMS
QA297	NUMERICAL CALCULATIONS
QA246	NUMERICAL FUNCTIONS
PM8125	*NUMERICAL LANGUAGES* **SEE** CESGES DE DAMIS (ARTIFICIAL LANGUAGE)
Z102	*NUMERICAL LANGUAGES* **SEE** PASIGRAPHY
QA119	*NUMERICAL ROOTS* **SEE** ROOTS, NUMERICAL
QC996	NUMERICAL WEATHER FORECASTING
TJ1225	*NUMERICALLY CONTROLLED MILLING-MACHINES* **SEE** MILLING-MACHINES — NUMERICAL CONTROL
BF1623.P9	*NUMEROLOGY* **SEE** SYMBOLISM OF NUMBERS
PM2019	*NUMIPU LANGUAGE* **SEE** NEZ PERCE LANGUAGE
CJ43-45	NUMISMATIC MUSEUMS
CJ71	NUMISMATICS — ABBREVIATIONS
CJ	NUMISMATICS
CJ201-1397	NUMISMATICS, ANCIENT
CJ1601-1715	NUMISMATICS, MEDIEVAL
QL368.F6	NUMMULITES
SB945.N	NUN MOTH
QL696.P5	NUN-BIRDS
ML760	*NUN'S FIDDLE* **SEE** SEA-TRUMPET / *medieval stringed instrument*
BX1908	*NUNCIATURE CONTROVERSY* **SEE** NUNCIOS, PAPAL
BX1908	NUNCIOS, PAPAL
PL4001.N8	NUNG LANGUAGE
BX4200-4560	*NUNNERIES* **SEE** CONVENTS AND NUNNERIES / *catholic church*
BX4200-4560	*NUNS* **SEE** CONVENTS AND NUNNERIES / *catholic church*
BX4200-4560	*NUNS* **SEE** MONASTICISM AND RELIGIOUS ORDERS FOR WOMEN
PN56.N	*NUNS* **SEE** NUNS IN LITERATURE
PR275	*NUNS* **SEE** NUNS IN LITERATURE / *english literature*
PR151.N	*NUNS* **SEE** NUNS IN LITERATURE / *english literature*
PQ4055.N8	*NUNS* **SEE** NUNS IN LITERATURE / *italian literature*
PN56.N	NUNS IN LITERATURE
PR151.N	NUNS IN LITERATURE / *english literature*
PR275	NUNS IN LITERATURE / *english literature*
PQ4055.N8	NUNS IN LITERATURE / *italian literature*
BX1908	*NUNTIOS, PAPAL* **SEE** NUNCIOS, PAPAL
BL2480.N	NUPE (AFRICAN PEOPLE) — RELIGION
PL8577	NUPE LANGUAGE
SB981-7	NURSERIES (HORTICULTURE) — LAWS AND LEGISLATION
SB	NURSERIES (HORTICULTURE)
HV851-861	*NURSERIES, DAY* **SEE** DAY NURSERIES
PN6110.C4	NURSERY RHYMES
PZ8.3	NURSERY RHYMES
LB1140	NURSERY SCHOOLS
RT25	NURSES AND NURSING — DIRECTORIES
RT55	NURSES AND NURSING — EXAMINATIONS, QUESTIONS, ETC.
RT4-17	NURSES AND NURSING — LEGAL STATUS, LAWS, ETC.
RT71-81	NURSES AND NURSING — STUDY AND TEACHING
RT	NURSES AND NURSING
UH490-495	NURSES AND NURSING / *army*
VG350-355	NURSES AND NURSING / *navy*
RT85	NURSING ETHICS
RT4-17	*NURSING LAW* **SEE** NURSES AND NURSING — LEGAL STATUS, LAWS, ETC.
Z675.N8	*NURSING SCHOOL LIBRARIES* **SEE** LIBRARIES, NURSING SCHOOL
RT71-81	NURSING SCHOOLS
RD99	*NURSING, SURGICAL* **SEE** SURGICAL NURSING
QK495.C997	*NUT GRASS* **SEE** NUTGRASS
QB165	NUTATION / *astronomy*
QK495.C997	NUTGRASS
QL696.P2	NUTHATCHES
E99.N85	*NUTKA INDIANS* **SEE** NOOTKA INDIANS
PM2031	*NUTKA LANGUAGE* **SEE** NOOTKA LANGUAGE
SB307.N	NUTMEG
TX535	NUTRITION — EXHIBITIONS
TX537	NUTRITION — RESEARCH
TX551	NUTRITION — STUDY AND TEACHING
TX535	*NUTRITION EXHIBITS* **SEE** NUTRITION — EXHIBITIONS
TX361.A8	*NUTRITION OF ATHLETES* **SEE** ATHLETES — NUTRITION
RJ206	*NUTRITION OF CHILDREN* **SEE** CHILDREN — NUTRITION
RJ216	*NUTRITION OF CHILDREN* **SEE** INFANTS — NUTRITION
QK867-873	*NUTRITION OF PLANTS* **SEE** PLANTS — NUTRITION
TX537	*NUTRITION RESEARCH* **SEE** NUTRITION — RESEARCH
QP141-185	NUTRITION
SB608.N	NUTS — DISEASES AND PESTS
TJ1330	*NUTS (MACHINERY)* **SEE** BOLTS AND NUTS
SB401	NUTS
PL8727	*NYAI LANGUAGE* **SEE** TETE LANGUAGE
DT132	*NYAM-NYAM* **SEE** AZANDE
PL8828	*NYAM-NYAM LANGUAGE* **SEE** ZANDE LANGUAGE
PL8591	NYAMWESI LANGUAGE
DT443	NYAMWESI
PL8593	*NYANDJA LANGUAGE* **SEE** NYANJA LANGUAGE
DT864	NYANJA (AFRICAN TRIBE)
PL8593	NYANJA LANGUAGE
PL8593	*NYASSA LANGUAGE* **SEE** NYANJA LANGUAGE
B132.N8	NYAYA
DT429	*NYIHA (BANTU TRIBE)* **SEE** NIKA (BANTU TRIBE)
DT429	*NYIKA (BANTU TRIBE)* **SEE** NIKA (BANTU TRIBE)
TT681	*NYLON HOSIERY* **SEE** HOSIERY, NYLON
TS1688	NYLON
PD2900-2999	*NYNORSK* **SEE** NORWEGIAN LANGUAGE (NYNORSK)
PL8595	NYORO LANGUAGE
DL743.N8	NYSTAD, FINLAND, TREATY OF, 1721
RE748	NYSTAGMUS
PL8727	*NYUNGWE LANGUAGE* **SEE** TETE LANGUAGE
PL8597	NZIMA LANGUAGE
E99.M2	O-KEE-PA (RELIGIOUS CEREMONY) / *mandan indians*
F2230.2.08	*OAJANA INDIANS* **SEE** OYANA INDIANS
SB608.0115	OAK — DISEASES AND PESTS
QK495.Q4	OAK
SD397.012	OAK / *forestry*
TS1747.03	OAKUM / *manufacture*
GB611-618	OASES
SB608.02	OAT APHIS
BX1939.02	OATHS (CANON LAW)
HV6326	*OATHS* **SEE** PERJURY
TX393	OATMEAL / *food-supply*
TS2159.0	OATMEAL / *milling*
SB191.02	OATS / *culture*
HD9049.02	OATS / *trade*
PH1251-4	OB UGRIAN LANGUAGES
DT62.02	OBELISKS
E450	OBERLIN-WELLINGTON RESCUE, 1858
RC628	*OBESITY* **SEE** CORPULENCE
LB1519-1520	OBJECT-TEACHING / *primary education*
NK492	*OBJECTS, MINIATURE* **SEE** MINIATURE OBJECTS / *art*
F2846	OBLIGADO, BATTLE OF, 1845
TG329	*OBLIQUE ARCHES* **SEE** ARCHES, OBLIQUE
MT366	OBOE — ORCHESTRA STUDIES
MT365	OBOE — STUDIES AND EXERCISES
M288-9	*OBOE AND BASSOON MUSIC* **SEE** BASSOON AND OBOE MUSIC
M288-9	*OBOE AND CLARINET MUSIC* **SEE** CLARINET AND OBOE MUSIC
M288-9	*OBOE AND ENGLISH HORN MUSIC* **SEE** ENGLISH HORN AND OBOE MUSIC
M288-9	*OBOE AND FLUTE MUSIC* **SEE** FLUTE AND OBOE MUSIC
M296-7	OBOE AND HARP MUSIC

M1105	OBOE AND HARP WITH STRING ORCHESTRA — SCORES AND PARTS
M1105-6	OBOE AND HARP WITH STRING ORCHESTRA
M245-6	OBOE AND HARPSICHORD MUSIC
M1105-6	OBOE AND HARPSICHORD WITH STRING ORCHESTRA
M182-4	OBOE AND ORGAN MUSIC
M298	OBOE AND PERCUSSION MUSIC
M245-6	OBOE AND PIANO MUSIC
M247	OBOE AND PIANO MUSIC, ARRANGED
M288-9	OBOE AND RECORDER MUSIC
M1105-6	OBOE AND RECORDER WITH STRING ORCHESTRA
M290-291	OBOE AND VIOLA MUSIC
M1105-6	OBOE AND VIOLA WITH STRING ORCHESTRA
M290-291	OBOE AND VIOLIN MUSIC
M1040-1041	OBOE AND VIOLIN WITH ORCHESTRA
M1105-6	OBOE AND VIOLIN WITH STRING ORCHESTRA
M65-67	OBOE D'AMORE MUSIC
M1105	OBOE D'AMORE WITH STRING ORCHESTRA — SCORES
M1105-6	OBOE D'AMORE WITH STRING ORCHESTRA
M288-9	OBOE MUSIC (2 OBOES)
M355-7	*OBOE MUSIC (3 OBOES)* **SEE** WIND TRIOS (3 OBOES)
M355-7	*OBOE MUSIC (3 OBOES)* **SEE** WIND TRIOS (3 OBOES)
M65-67	OBOE MUSIC
M1022-3	OBOE WITH CHAMBER ORCHESTRA
M1023	OBOE WITH ORCHESTRA — SOLO WITH PIANO
M1022-3	OBOE WITH ORCHESTRA
M1022-3	OBOE WITH ORCHESTRA, ARRANGED
M1106	OBOE WITH STRING ORCHESTRA — SOLO WITH PIANO
M1105-6	OBOE WITH STRING ORCHESTRA
M1105-6	OBOE WITH STRING ORCHESTRA, ARRANGED — SCORES AND PARTS
M1105-6	OBOE WITH STRING ORCHESTRA, ARRANGED
ML940-943	OBOE */ history and construction*
M1105-6	OBOE, VIOLIN, VIOLONCELLO WITH STRING ORCHESTRA
M1105-6	OBOES (2) AND TRUMPET WITH STRING ORCHESTRA
M1105-6	OBOES (2) WITH STRING ORCHESTRA
HQ471	*OBSCENE LITERATURE* **SEE** LITERATURE, IMMORAL
Z659	*OBSCENE LITERATURE* **SEE** LITERATURE, IMMORAL */ copyright*
PN49	*OBSCENE LITERATURE* **SEE** LITERATURE, IMMORAL */ literature and ethics*
HV6727	*OBSCENE LITERATURE* **SEE** LITERATURE, IMMORAL */ social pathology*
PN1010-1525	*OBSCURITY IN POETRY* **SEE** POETRY
GN486	*OBSEQUIES* **SEE** FUNERAL RITES AND CEREMONIES */ ethnology*
GT3150-3390	*OBSEQUIES* **SEE** FUNERAL RITES AND CEREMONIES */ manners and customs*
QB4	*OBSERVATIONS, ASTRONOMICAL* **SEE** ASTRONOMY — OBSERVATIONS
QC830-845	*OBSERVATIONS, MAGNETIC* **SEE** MAGNETISM, TERRESTRIAL — OBSERVATIONS
QC871-4	*OBSERVATIONS, METEOROLOGICAL* **SEE** METEOROLOGY — OBSERVATIONS */ methods*
QC983-994	*OBSERVATIONS, METEOROLOGICAL* **SEE** METEOROLOGY — OBSERVATIONS */ reports*
QB81-84	OBSERVATORIES */ astronomical*
QC818	OBSERVATORIES */ magnetic*
QC875	OBSERVATORIES */ meteorological*
QE540	OBSERVATORIES */ seismological*
QB81-84	*OBSERVATORIES, ASTRONOMICAL* **SEE** ASTRONOMICAL OBSERVATORIES
QC808	*OBSERVATORIES, GEOPHYSICAL* **SEE** GEOPHYSICAL OBSERVATORIES
QC875	*OBSERVATORIES, METEOROLOGICAL* **SEE** METEOROLOGICAL STATIONS
QB84	OBSERVATORY DOMES
HF5681.D5	*OBSOLESCENCE (ACCOUNTING)* **SEE** DEPRECIATION
UG375	OBSTACLES (MILITARY SCIENCE)
RG732	*OBSTETRIC ANESTHESIA* **SEE** ANESTHESIA IN OBSTETRICS
RG951	OBSTETRICAL NURSING
RG545	OBSTETRICS — APPARATUS AND INSTRUMENTS
RG529	OBSTETRICS — CASES, CLINICAL REPORTS, STATISTICS
RG81-93	OBSTETRICS — EARLY WORKS TO 1800
RG531	OBSTETRICS — EXAMINATIONS, QUESTIONS, ETC.
RG121	OBSTETRICS — POPULAR WORKS
RG525	OBSTETRICS — POPULAR WORKS
RG725-791	OBSTETRICS — SURGERY

RG526	OBSTETRICS — TABLES, ETC.
RG	OBSTETRICS
RG732	*OBSTETRICS, ANESTHETICS IN* **SEE** ANESTHESIA IN OBSTETRICS
RG730	*OBSTETRICS, ANTISEPTICS IN* **SEE** ANTISEPTICS IN OBSTETRICS
RV365	OBSTETRICS, ECLECTIC
RX476	OBSTETRICS, HOMEOPATHIC
SF887	*OBSTETRICS, VETERINARY* **SEE** VETERINARY OBSTETRICS
RG12-16	*OBSTETRICS-HOSPITALS* **SEE** HOSPITALS, GYNECOLOGIC AND OBSTETRIC
UG375	*OBSTRUCTION (MILITARY SCIENCE)* **SEE** OBSTACLES (MILITARY SCIENCE)
MT526	OCARINA — METHODS
M270-271	OCARINA AND PIANO MUSIC
M110.03	OCARINA MUSIC
ML990.03	OCARINA
MT526	*OCARINA-SELF-INSTRUCTION* **SEE** OCARINA — METHODS — — SELF-INSTRUCTION
MT526	OCARINA — METHODS — — SELF-INSTRUCTION
BV4254.2	OCCASIONAL SERMONS
PM8702	OCCIDENTAL (ARTIFICIAL LANGUAGE)
CB245	*OCCIDENTAL CIVILIZATION* **SEE** CIVILIZATION, OCCIDENTAL
PB1-431	*OCCIDENTAL LANGUAGES* **SEE** LANGUAGES, MODERN
QL821	OCCIPITAL BONE
QM105	OCCIPITAL BONE
PC3201-3299	*OCCITANE LANGUAGE* **SEE** PROVENCAL LANGUAGE
QC182	*OCCLUSION OF GASES* **SEE** GASES — OCCLUSION
BF1405-1999	OCCULT SCIENCES
QB175	OCCULTATIONS */ calculation*
BF1405-1999	*OCCULTISM* **SEE** OCCULT SCIENCES
RM735	*OCCUPATION THERAPY* **SEE** OCCUPATIONAL THERAPY
HD4903	*OCCUPATION, FREE CHOICE OF* **SEE** FREE CHOICE OF EMPLOYMENT
JX4093	*OCCUPATION, MILITARY* **SEE** MILITARY OCCUPATION
JX5003	*OCCUPATION, MILITARY* **SEE** MILITARY OCCUPATION
BF431	*OCCUPATIONAL APTITUDE TESTS* **SEE** ABILITY — TESTING
RC552.03	OCCUPATIONAL NEUROSES
JF1057-9	*OCCUPATIONAL REPRESENTATION* **SEE** FUNCTIONAL REPRESENTATION
RM735	OCCUPATIONAL THERAPY AS A PROFESSION
RM735	OCCUPATIONAL THERAPY
HB2581-2790	OCCUPATIONS — CLASSIFICATION */ demography*
HB2581	OCCUPATIONS — TERMINOLOGY
LB1537	*OCCUPATIONS AND BUSY WORK* **SEE** CREATIVE ACTIVITIES AND SEAT WORK
HF5381	OCCUPATIONS */ choice of*
GR890-920	OCCUPATIONS */ folk-lore*
GT5750-6390	OCCUPATIONS */ manners and customs*
HT675-690	OCCUPATIONS */ social classes*
HB2581-2790	OCCUPATIONS */ statistics*
HJ5645-5651	OCCUPATIONS */ taxation*
HD7273	OCCUPATIONS, DANGEROUS — SAFETY APPLIANCES
HD7262	OCCUPATIONS, DANGEROUS
HD3623-4	OCCUPATIONS, DANGEROUS */ legislation*
T54	OCCUPATIONS, DANGEROUS */ technology*
HD7260-7780	*OCCUPATIONS-HYGIENIC ASPECTS* **SEE** INDUSTRIAL HYGIENE
JX5003	*OCCUPIED TERRITORY* **SEE** MILITARY OCCUPATION
JX4093	*OCCUPIED TERRITORY* **SEE** MILITARY OCCUPATION
GR910	*OCEAN (IN RELIGION, FOLK-LORE, ETC.)* **SEE** FOLK-LORE OF THE SEA
GC83	OCEAN BOTTOM
HE7709-7741	*OCEAN CABLES* **SEE** CABLES, SUBMARINE */ economics*
UG607	*OCEAN CABLES* **SEE** CABLES, SUBMARINE */ military art and science*
TK5605-5681	*OCEAN CABLES* **SEE** CABLES, SUBMARINE */ technology*
GC231-296	OCEAN CURRENTS
VM453	*OCEAN DRILLING SHIPS* **SEE** DEEP-SEA DRILLING SHIPS
GC83	*OCEAN FLOOR* **SEE** OCEAN BOTTOM
QH91-95	*OCEAN LIFE* **SEE** MARINE BIOLOGY */ natural history*

HE323-8	*OCEAN ROUTES* **SEE** TRADE ROUTES
GC161-177	OCEAN TEMPERATURE
HE561-971	*OCEAN TRANSPORTATION* **SEE** SHIPPING
JX4190	*OCEAN TRANSPORTATION* **SEE** SHIPPING / international law
G550	OCEAN TRAVEL
G153	OCEAN TRAVEL
RA793	OCEAN TRAVEL / hygiene
GC211	OCEAN WAVES
HE561-971	*OCEAN-ECONOMIC ASPECTS* **SEE** SHIPPING
JX4190	*OCEAN-ECONOMIC ASPECTS* **SEE** SHIPPING / international law
GC57	*OCEAN-RESEARCH* **SEE** OCEANOGRAPHIC RESEARCH
VM453	*OCEANIC DRILLING SHIPS* **SEE** DEEP-SEA DRILLING SHIPS
GC30	OCEANOGRAPHERS
GC41	OCEANOGRAPHIC BUOYS
GC41	OCEANOGRAPHIC INSTRUMENTS
GC57	OCEANOGRAPHIC RESEARCH
GC57	OCEANOGRAPHY — OBSERVERS' MANUALS
GC	OCEANOGRAPHY
GC41	*OCEANOGRAPHY-INSTRUMENTS* **SEE** OCEANOGRAPHIC INSTRUMENTS
GC57	*OCEANOGRAPHY-RESEARCH* **SEE** OCEANOGRAPHIC RESEARCH
GC	*OCEANOLOGY* **SEE** OCEANOGRAPHY
DR548	OCHAKOV, BATTLE OF, 1737
TN948.O2	OCHER
E99.C6	*OCHIPAWA INDIANS* **SEE** CHIPPEWA INDIANS
M880-882	OCTETS (BASSOON, CLARINET, FLUTE, HORN, HARP, VIOLIN, VIOLA, DOUBLE BASS)
M860-862	OCTETS (BASSOON, CLARINET, FLUTE, HORN, OBOE, TROMBONE, TRUMPET, DOUBLE BASS)
M863-4	OCTETS (BASSOON, CLARINET, FLUTE, HORN, TRUMPET, VIOLIN, VIOLONCELLO, DOUBLE BASS), ARRANGED
M860-862	OCTETS (BASSOON, CLARINET, FLUTE, HORN, TRUMPET, VIOLIN, VIOLONCELLO, DOUBLE BASS)
M860-862	OCTETS (BASSOON, CLARINET, FLUTE, HORN, VIOLIN, VIOLA, VIOLONCELLO, DOUBLE BASS)
M860-862	OCTETS (BASSOON, CLARINET, FLUTE, HORN, 2 VIOLINS, VIOLA, VIOLONCELLO)
M860-862	OCTETS (BASSOON, CLARINET, FLUTE, OBOE, VIOLIN, VIOLA, VIOLONCELLO, DOUBLE BASS)
M860-862	OCTETS (BASSOON, CLARINET, FLUTE, OBOE, 2 VIOLINS, VIOLA, VIOLONCELLO)
M860-862	OCTETS (BASSOON, CLARINET, FLUTE, 2 HORNS, VIOLIN, VIOLA, VIOLONCELLO)
M860-862	OCTETS (BASSOON, CLARINET, HORN, OBOE, VIOLIN, VIOLA, VIOLONCELLO, DOUBLE BASS)
M860-862	OCTETS (BASSOON, CLARINET, HORN, OBOE, 2 VIOLINS, VIOLA, VIOLONCELLO)
M860-862	OCTETS (BASSOON, CLARINET, HORN, VIOLIN, 2 VIOLAS, VIOLONCELLO, DOUBLE BASS)
M860-862	OCTETS (BASSOON, CLARINET, HORN, 2 VIOLINS, VIOLA, VIOLONCELLO, DOUBLE BASS)
M885	OCTETS (CELESTA, 2 CLARINETS, FLUTE, MARIMBA, VIOLIN, VIOLONCELLO, DOUBLE BASS)
M860-862	OCTETS (CLARINET, 2 HORNS, VIOLIN, 2 VIOLAS, VIOLONCELLO, DOUBLE BASS)
M860-862	OCTETS (FLUTE, 2 HORNS, 2 OBOES, 2 VIOLINS, VIOLONCELLO)
M820-822	OCTETS (HARPSICHORD, FLUTE, 2 VIOLINS, 2 VIOLAS, 2 VIOLONCELLOS)
M815-817	OCTETS (HARPSICHORD, 7 RECORDERS)
M845-7	OCTETS (PIANO, BASSOON, CLARINET, FLUTE, TRUMPET, PERCUSSION, VIOLIN, VIOLONCELLO)
M820-822	OCTETS (PIANO, FLUTE, HORN, OBOE, VIOLIN, VIOLA, VIOLONCELLO, DOUBLE BASS)
M820-822	OCTETS (PIANO, FLUTE, 2 VIOLINS, 2 VIOLAS, 2 VIOLONCELLOS)
M820-822	OCTETS (PIANO, HORN, 2 VIOLINS, 2 VIOLAS, VIOLONCELLO, DOUBLE BASS)
M845-7	OCTETS (PIANO, PERCUSSION, VIBRAPHONE, 2 VIOLINS, VIOLA, VIOLONCELLO, DOUBLE BASS)
M845-7	OCTETS (PIANO, 2 CLARINETS, FLUTE, TROMBONE, 2 TRUMPETS, PERCUSSION)
M845-7	OCTETS (PIANO, 2 HORNS, TROMBONE, 2 TRUMPETS, PERCUSSION)
M820-822	OCTETS (PIANO, 3 RECORDERS, 2 VIOLINS, VIOLA, VIOLONCELLO)
M815-817	OCTETS (PIANO, 3 TROMBONES, 4 TRUMPETS)
M818-819	OCTETS (PIANO, 3 TROMBONES, 4 TRUMPETS), ARRANGED
M815-817	OCTETS (PIANO, 7 FLUTES)
M885	OCTETS (2 CLARINETS, FLUTE, DRUMS, PERCUSSION, VIOLA, VIOLONCELLO, DOUBLE BASS)
M880-882	OCTETS (2 CLARINETS, HARP, 2 VIOLINS, VIOLA, VIOLONCELLO, DOUBLE BASS)
M880-882	OCTETS (2 CLARINETS, 4 HORNS, HARP, DOUBLE BASS)
M883-4	OCTETS (2 CLARINETS, 4 HORNS, HARP, DOUBLE BASS), ARRANGED
M860-862	OCTETS (2 HORNS, 2 OBOES, 2 VIOLINS, VIOLA, VIOLONCELLO)
M885	OCTETS (2 HORNS, 2 TROMBONES, 2 TRUMPETS, TUBA, PERCUSSION), ARRANGED
M885	OCTETS (2 HORNS, 2 TROMBONES, 2 TRUMPETS, TUBA, PERCUSSION)
M885	OCTETS (3 CLARINETS, HORN, PICCOLO, TRUMPET, KETTLEDRUMS, VIOLIN)
M885	OCTETS (5 TRUMPETS, DRUM, KETTLEDRUMS, PERCUSSION)
M850-852	*OCTETS, STRING* **SEE** STRING OCTETS
M855-7	*OCTETS, WIND* **SEE** WIND OCTETS
QL430.3.O2	OCTOPUS
GN645	*OCTOROONS* **SEE** MULATTOES / anthropology
E185.62	*OCTOROONS* **SEE** MULATTOES / u.s.
HJ9120	OCTROI
RE991-2	*OCULAR THERAPEUTICS* **SEE** THERAPEUTICS, OPHTHALMOLOGICAL
HS1025-6	ODD-FELLOWS, INDEPENDENT ORDER OF — COSTUMES, SUPPLIES, ETC.
HS997	ODD-FELLOWS, INDEPENDENT ORDER OF — FICTION
HS981	ODD-FELLOWS, INDEPENDENT ORDER OF — HANDBOOKS, MANUALS, ETC.
HS987	ODD-FELLOWS, INDEPENDENT ORDER OF — HISTORY
HS1001-1011	ODD-FELLOWS, INDEPENDENT ORDER OF — LAWS, DECISIONS, ETC.
HS951	ODD-FELLOWS, INDEPENDENT ORDER OF — PERIODICALS
HS1019-1021	ODD-FELLOWS, INDEPENDENT ORDER OF — RITUALS
M1905.03	ODD-FELLOWS, INDEPENDENT ORDER OF — SONGS AND MUSIC / music
M1906.03	ODD-FELLOWS, INDEPENDENT ORDER OF — SONGS AND MUSIC / music
HS1015	ODD-FELLOWS, INDEPENDENT ORDER OF — SONGS AND MUSIC
HS993	ODD-FELLOWS, INDEPENDENT ORDER OF — SYMBOLISM
HS951-1179	ODD-FELLOWS, INDEPENDENT ORDER OF
PN6110.04	ODES / collections general
PR1195.03	ODES / english
PR509.03	ODES / english
PN1371	ODES / history general
D764	ODESSA, BATTLE OF, 1941
QL696.P45	*ODONTOGLOSSAE* **SEE** FLAMINGOS
TJ186	ODONTOGRAPH
QL858	*ODONTOGRAPHY* **SEE** TEETH / comparative anatomy
QM311	*ODONTOGRAPHY* **SEE** TEETH / human anatomy
GN209	*ODONTOGRAPHY* **SEE** TEETH / somatology
QL858	*ODONTOLOGY* **SEE** TEETH / comparative anatomy
QM311	*ODONTOLOGY* **SEE** TEETH / human anatomy
GN209	*ODONTOLOGY* **SEE** TEETH / somatology
QP458	ODORS / physiology
BF271	ODORS / psychology
PL8751	*ODSHI LANGUAGE* **SEE** TSHI LANGUAGE
QL508.G8	*OECANTHINAE* **SEE** CRICKETS
QH540-541	*OECOLOGY* **SEE** ECOLOGY
RB144	*OEDEMA* **SEE** EDEMA
RJ268	*OEDEMA* **SEE** EDEMA / infantile
QL861	*OESOPHAGUS* **SEE** ESOPHAGUS / comparative anatomy
QM331	*OESOPHAGUS* **SEE** ESOPHAGUS / human anatomy
QP146	*OESOPHAGUS* **SEE** ESOPHAGUS / physiology
K	*OFFENSES, NAVAL* **SEE** NAVAL OFFENSES
VB850-880	*OFFENSES, NAVAL* **SEE** NAVAL OFFENSES
HF5546-7	*OFFICE ADMINISTRATION* **SEE** OFFICE MANAGEMENT
NA6230-6233	OFFICE BUILDINGS

HF5501	*OFFICE EMPLOYEES* **SEE** CLERKS
HV3165-3173	*OFFICE EMPLOYEES* **SEE** CLERKS / *aid to*
HD8039.M4	*OFFICE EMPLOYEES* **SEE** CLERKS / *mercantile clerks*
HF5548	OFFICE EQUIPMENT AND SUPPLIES
HF5521-5541	OFFICE FURNITURE — CATALOGS
HF5521-5541	OFFICE FURNITURE
HF5548	*OFFICE MACHINES* **SEE** OFFICE EQUIPMENT AND SUPPLIES
HF5546-7	OFFICE MANAGEMENT
BV4379	OFFICE PRACTICE IN CHURCHES
HF5548	*OFFICE SUPPLIES* **SEE** OFFICE EQUIPMENT AND SUPPLIES
JF2081	*OFFICE, NOMINATIONS FOR* **SEE** NOMINATIONS FOR OFFICE / *constitutional history*
JK2053-2096	*OFFICE, NOMINATIONS FOR* **SEE** NOMINATIONS FOR OFFICE / *u.s.*
JK2053-2096	*OFFICE, QUALIFICATIONS FOR* **SEE** NOMINATIONS FOR OFFICE / *u.s.*
JF2081	*OFFICE, QUALIFICATIONS FOR* **SEE** NOMINATIONS FOR OFFICE / *constitutional history*
JF1321-1671	*OFFICE, TENURE OF* **SEE** CIVIL SERVICE
JV443-5	*OFFICE, TENURE OF* **SEE** CIVIL SERVICE / *colonial*
JS148-163	*OFFICE, TENURE OF* **SEE** CIVIL SERVICE / *municipal*
JN-JQ	*OFFICE, TENURE OF* **SEE** CIVIL SERVICE / *other countries*
HD8011-8023	*OFFICE, TENURE OF* **SEE** CIVIL SERVICE / *state labor*
JK631-901	*OFFICE, TENURE OF* **SEE** CIVIL SERVICE / *u.s.*
Z675.G7	*OFFICIAL LIBRARIES* **SEE** LIBRARIES, GOVERNMENTAL, ADMINISTRATIVE, ETC.
JX1995	*OFFICIALS AND EMPLOYEES, INTERNATIONAL* **SEE** INTERNATIONAL OFFICIALS AND EMPLOYEES
GV735	*OFFICIATING, SPORTS* **SEE** SPORTS OFFICIATING
NE2540	OFFSET PRINTING
TN871.3	*OFFSHORE DRILLING (PETROLEUM)* **SEE** OIL WELL DRILLING, SUBMARINE
TN871.3	*OFFSHORE OIL OPERATIONS* **SEE** OIL WELL DRILLING, SUBMARINE
PM2049.03	*OFO LANGUAGE* **SEE** OFOGOULA LANGUAGE
PM2049.03	OFOGOULA LANGUAGE
E99.03	*OGALLALLA INDIANS* **SEE** OGLALA INDIANS
DT429	*OGIEK* **SEE** DOROBO (AFRICAN PEOPLE)
E99.03	OGLALA INDIANS
GR525	*OGRES* **SEE** GHOULS AND OGRES
GR560	*OGRES* **SEE** GHOULS AND OGRES
F486-500	OHIO — HISTORY
F516-520	OHIO VALLEY — HISTORY
E470.4	OHIO VALLEY — HISTORY — — CIVIL WAR
E230.5	OHIO VALLEY — HISTORY — — REVOLUTION
E525	OHIO — HISTORY — — CIVIL WAR
E263.0	OHIO — HISTORY — — REVOLUTION
E359.5.02	OHIO — HISTORY — — WAR OF 1812
E726.03	OHIO — HISTORY — — WAR OF 1898
E409.5.0	OHIO — HISTORY — — WAR WITH MEXICO, 1845-1848
QC607	OHM'S LAW
TP685-692	*OIL* **SEE** MINERAL OILS
TP670-695	*OIL* **SEE** OILS AND FATS
TN860-879	*OIL* **SEE** PETROLEUM / *production*
TP690-692	*OIL* **SEE** PETROLEUM / *refining*
TP671	OIL ANALYSIS
HD3616.U452	OIL BURNER INDUSTRY — LAWS AND REGULATIONS / *u.s. codes*
HD9999.05	OIL BURNER INDUSTRY
TH7466.06	OIL BURNERS / *heating of buildings*
TJ751-805	*OIL ENGINES* **SEE** GAS AND OIL ENGINES
TN871.5	*OIL FIELD EQUIPMENT* **SEE** OIL FIELDS — EQUIPMENT AND SUPPLIES
TN871.5	OIL FIELDS — EQUIPMENT AND SUPPLIES
TN870	OIL FIELDS — PRODUCTION METHODS
TN860-879	OIL FIELDS
TL214.05	*OIL FILTERS, AUTOMOBILE* **SEE** AUTOMOBILES — MOTORS — — OIL FILTERS
TJ843	OIL HYDRAULIC MACHINERY
HF5716.04	OIL INDUSTRIES — TABLES AND READY-RECKONERS
TP670-692	OIL INDUSTRIES
HD9490	OIL INDUSTRIES / *economics*
HD9560.9	OIL INSPECTION / *state reports*
TP691	OIL INSPECTION / *technology*
TN860-879	*OIL LANDS* **SEE** OIL FIELDS
TP684.P	*OIL OF PEPPERMINT* **SEE** PEPPERMINT-OIL
TN860-879	*OIL POOLS* **SEE** OIL FIELDS
TP687	OIL RECLAMATION
TP690	*OIL REFINERIES* **SEE** PETROLEUM REFINERIES
SB298-9	*OIL SEED PLANTS* **SEE** OILSEED PLANTS
TS1669	OIL SILK
TX657.S8	*OIL STOVES* **SEE** STOVES, OIL
TN871.2	*OIL WELL BORING* **SEE** OIL WELL DRILLING
TN871.2	OIL WELL DRILLING — PRICES
TN871.5	OIL WELL DRILLING RIGS
TN871.2	OIL WELL DRILLING
TN871.2	OIL WELL DRILLING, ELECTRIC
TN871.3	OIL WELL DRILLING, SUBMARINE
TN871.35	OIL WELL LOGGING
TN871.35	OIL WELL LOGGING, ELECTRIC
TN871.35	OIL WELL LOGGING, RADIATION
TS1779.05	OIL-CLOTH
TJ1079	*OIL-CUPS* **SEE** OIL-FEEDERS
TJ1079	OIL-FEEDERS
TP355	*OIL-FUEL* **SEE** PETROLEUM AS FUEL
TJ619	*OIL-FUEL* **SEE** PETROLEUM AS FUEL / *locomotives*
ND	*OIL-PAINTING* **SEE** PAINTING
SB299.P3	OIL-PALM
TN871	OIL-SHALES
VM455	*OIL-TANK STEAMERS* **SEE** TANK-VESSELS
TP671	OILS AND FATS — ANALYSIS
TP670-695	OILS AND FATS
QD416	*OILS, ESSENTIAL* **SEE** ESSENCES AND ESSENTIAL OILS / *chemistry*
TP958	*OILS, ESSENTIAL* **SEE** ESSENCES AND ESSENTIAL OILS / *chemical technology*
TK3441.05	*OILS, INSULATING* **SEE** INSULATING OILS
TP670-692	*OILSEED INDUSTRY* **SEE** OIL INDUSTRIES
HD9490	*OILSEED INDUSTRY* **SEE** OIL INDUSTRIES / *economics*
SB298-9	OILSEED PLANTS
TS1669	*OILSILK* **SEE** OIL SILK
RS201.03	OINTMENTS
PL429	*OIRAT LANGUAGE (MONGOLIAN)* **SEE** KALMUCK LANGUAGE
PL45.05	*OIRAT LANGUAGE (TURKIC)* **SEE** OIROT LANGUAGE
PL45.05	OIROT LANGUAGE
PL8751	*OJI LANGUAGE* **SEE** TSHI LANGUAGE
E99.C6	*OJIBWA INDIANS* **SEE** CHIPPEWA INDIANS
PM851-4	*OJIBWA LANGUAGE* **SEE** CHIPPEWA LANGUAGE
PL8276	*OJO LANGUAGE* **SEE** IJO LANGUAGE
E99.0	OKA INDIANS
E99.0	*OKANOGAN INDIANS* **SEE** OKINAGAN INDIANS
QL737.U5	OKAPI
E83.835	OKECHOBEE, BATTLE OF, 1837
E99.0	OKINAGAN INDIANS
PM2066	OKINAGAN LANGUAGE
GV1295.04	OKLAHOMA (GAME)
SB351.0	OKRA
QB723.0	OLBERS' COMET
HV1451-1493	OLD AGE HOMES
N8234	OLD AGE IN ART
HG9426-9446	OLD AGE PENSIONS / *age insurance*
HD7105-6	OLD AGE PENSIONS / *working-men's insurance*
HV1451-1493	OLD AGE / *charities*
BJ1691	OLD AGE / *ethics*
QP86	OLD AGE / *physiology*
RC952-954	*OLD AGE-DISEASES* **SEE** GERIATRICS
PK6101-9	*OLD BACTRIAN LANGUAGE* **SEE** AVESTA LANGUAGE
PG601-698	*OLD BULGARIAN LANGUAGE* **SEE** CHURCH SLAVIC LANGUAGE
BX4751-4793	OLD CATHOLIC CHURCH
BX4751-4793	OLD CATHOLICISM
PG601-698	*OLD CHURCH SLAVIC LANGUAGE* **SEE** CHURCH SLAVIC LANGUAGE
PE101-299	*OLD ENGLISH LANGUAGE* **SEE** ANGLO-SAXON LANGUAGE
PE501-685	*OLD ENGLISH LANGUAGE* **SEE** ENGLISH LANGUAGE — MIDDLE ENGLISH (1100-1500)
PR1490-1508	*OLD ENGLISH LITERATURE* **SEE** ANGLO-SAXON LITERATURE / *collections*
PR171-236	*OLD ENGLISH LITERATURE* **SEE** ANGLO-SAXON LITERATURE / *history*

PR1119-1121	*OLD ENGLISH LITERATURE* **SEE** ENGLISH LITERATURE — MIDDLE ENGLISH (1100-1500) / *collections*
SF429.04	OLD ENGLISH SHEEP-DOGS
PC2801-2896	*OLD FRENCH LANGUAGE* **SEE** FRENCH LANGUAGE — OLD FRENCH
PQ1300-1391	*OLD FRENCH LITERATURE* **SEE** FRENCH LITERATURE — OLD FRENCH / *collections*
PQ151-221	*OLD FRENCH LITERATURE* **SEE** FRENCH LITERATURE — OLD FRENCH / *history*
PQ1300-1391	*OLD FRENCH POETRY* **SEE** FRENCH POETRY — OLD FRENCH / *collections*
PQ151-216	*OLD FRENCH POETRY* **SEE** FRENCH POETRY — OLD FRENCH / *history*
PF3801-3991	*OLD HIGH GERMAN LANGUAGE* **SEE** GERMAN LANGUAGE — OLD HIGH GERMAN
PF3985-3991	*OLD HIGH GERMAN LITERATURE* **SEE** GERMAN LITERATURE — OLD HIGH GERMAN / *collections*
PT183	*OLD HIGH GERMAN LITERATURE* **SEE** GERMAN LITERATURE — OLD HIGH GERMAN / *history*
ML3186	OLD HUNDREDTH (TUNE)
PD2201-2392	*OLD ICELANDIC LANGUAGE* **SEE** ICELANDIC AND OLD NORSE LANGUAGES
PT7220-7262	*OLD ICELANDIC LITERATURE* **SEE** ICELANDIC AND OLD NORSE LITERATURE / *collections*
PT7101-7211	*OLD ICELANDIC LITERATURE* **SEE** ICELANDIC AND OLD NORSE LITERATURE / *history*
PK201-379	*OLD INDIC LANGUAGE* **SEE** VEDIC LANGUAGE
P911	*OLD KHOTANESE LANGUAGE* **SEE** KHOTANESE LANGUAGE
PD2201-2392	*OLD NORSE LANGUAGE* **SEE** ICELANDIC AND OLD NORSE LANGUAGES
PT7220-7262	*OLD NORSE LITERATURE* **SEE** ICELANDIC AND OLD NORSE LITERATURE / *collections*
PT7101-7211	*OLD NORSE LITERATURE* **SEE** ICELANDIC AND OLD NORSE LITERATURE / *history*
PT7170-7174	*OLD NORSE POETRY* **SEE** ICELANDIC AND OLD NORSE POETRY / *history*
PT7230-7252	*OLD NORSE POETRY* **SEE** ICELANDIC AND OLD NORSE POETRY / *collections*
BX8101-8143	*OLD ORDER AMISH* **SEE** MENNONITES
PK6128	OLD PERSIAN INSCRIPTIONS
PK6122	OLD PERSIAN LANGUAGE — WRITING
PK6121-9	OLD PERSIAN LANGUAGE
PG6721-6730	*OLD POLISH LANGUAGE* **SEE** POLISH LANGUAGE — OLD POLISH
PG8201-8	*OLD PRUSSIAN LANGUAGE* **SEE** PRUSSIAN LANGUAGE
QE665	*OLD RED SANDSTONE (GEOLOGY)* **SEE** GEOLOGY, STRATIGRAPHIC — DEVONIAN
PF3992-4000	OLD SAXON LANGUAGE
PG601-698	*OLD SLOVENIAN LANGUAGE* **SEE** CHURCH SLAVIC LANGUAGE
PL31	OLD TURKISH LANGUAGE
PL55.J3	*OLD UZBEK LANGUAGE* **SEE** JAGATAIC LANGUAGE
SF293.04	OLDENBURGER HORSE
D267.06	OLDENDORF, BATTLE OF, 1633
RS201.05	OLEATES
SF268	OLEOMARGARINE
HD9441	OLEOMARGARINE / *trade*
RS201.06	OLEORESINS / *pharmacy*
QL939	OLFACTORY NERVE / *comparative anatomy*
QL947	OLFACTORY NERVE / *comparative anatomy*
QM505	OLFACTORY NERVE / *human anatomy*
QM471	OLFACTORY NERVE / *human anatomy*
QE693	*OLIGOCENE PERIOD* **SEE** GEOLOGY, STRATIGRAPHIC — OLIGOCENE
QE928	*OLIGOCENE PERIOD* **SEE** PALEOBOTANY — OLIGOCENE
QE738	*OLIGOCENE PERIOD* **SEE** PALEONTOLOGY — OLIGOCENE
QL391.04	OLIGOCHAETA
F2532	OLINDA, BRAZIL — CAPTURE, 1630
SB608.04	OLIVE — DISEASES AND PESTS
SB367	OLIVE INDUSTRY AND TRADE / *agriculture*
HD9019.04	OLIVE INDUSTRY AND TRADE / *economics*
TP683	OLIVE-OIL
SB367	OLIVE
QE391.C	*OLIVIN* **SEE** CHRYSOLITE
QE461	OLIVIN-DIABASE
DL725	OLIWA, PEACE OF, 1660
F219	*OLMECAS* **SEE** OLMECS
F219	OLMECS
PH521-9	OLONETSIAN LANGUAGE
DK215.8.06	OLTENITZA, BATTLE OF, 1853
E476.43	OLUSTEE, FLA., BATTLE OF, 1864
GV722	OLYMPIC GAMES — REVIVAL, 1896-
GV841.5	OLYMPIC GAMES (WINTER)
GV23	OLYMPIC GAMES
HD234.05	OMAHA INDIANS — LAND TRANSFERS
E99.04	OMAHA INDIANS
PM2071	OMAHA LANGUAGE
DP105-113	OMAYYADS IN SPAIN
DS234-8	OMAYYADS
GV1295.05	*OMBER (GAME)* **SEE** OMBRE (GAME)
GV1295.05	OMBRE (GAME)
TX745	*OMELETS* **SEE** COOKERY (EGGS)
BF1777	OMENS
QL864	OMENTUM / *comparative anatomy*
QM367	OMENTUM / *human anatomy*
DS234-8	*OMEYYADES* **SEE** OMAYYADS
DS234-8	*OMMIADS* **SEE** OMAYYADS
E423	*OMNIBUS BILL, 1850* **SEE** COMPROMISE OF 1850
HE5601-5720	*OMNIBUS SERVICE* **SEE** MOTOR BUS LINES
HE5601-5720	OMNIBUSES
TL969.0	*OMNIDIRECTIONAL RANGE SYSTEM* **SEE** OMNIRANGE SYSTEM
TL969.0	OMNIRANGE SYSTEM
RJ271	*OMPHALORRHAGIA* **SEE** UMBILICUS — HEMORRHAGE
BL2450.N	*OMPHALOS* **SEE** NAVEL (IN RELIGION, FOLK-LORE, ETC.) / *egyptian religion*
QM543	*OMPHALOS* **SEE** UMBILICUS
F2823.05	ONA INDIANS
PM6691	ONA LANGUAGE
HQ447	*ONANISM* **SEE** MASTURBATION
RC142.5	ONCHOCERCIASIS
RC142.5	*ONCHOCERCOSIS* **SEE** ONCHOCERCIASIS
RC254-282	ONCOLOGY
RD651-678	ONCOLOGY
M298	ONDES MARTENOT AND PERCUSSION MUSIC
M284.05	ONDES MARTENOT AND PIANO MUSIC
M285.05	ONDES MARTENOT AND PIANO MUSIC
M284.05	ONDES MARTENOT AND PIANO MUSIC, ARRANGED
M285.05	ONDES MARTENOT AND PIANO MUSIC, ARRANGED
M175.05	ONDES MARTENOT MUSIC
M1039.4.05	ONDES MARTENOT WITH ORCHESTRA
M1105-6	ONDES MARTENOT WITH STRING ORCHESTRA
ML1092	ONDES MARTENOT
ML1092	*ONDES MUSICALES* **SEE** ONDES MARTENOT
ML1092	*ONDIUM MARTENOT* **SEE** ONDES MARTENOT
Z49.3	*ONE-HAND TYPEWRITING* **SEE** TYPEWRITING, ONE-HAND
GN231	ONE-LEG RESTING POSITION
LB1567	*ONE-ROOM SCHOOLS* **SEE** RURAL SCHOOLS
LB1567	*ONE-TEACHER SCHOOLS* **SEE** RURAL SCHOOLS
HX656.05	ONEIDA COMMUNITY
E99.045	ONEIDA INDIANS
PM2073	ONEIDA LANGUAGE
SB608.05	*ONION PINK-ROOT DISEASE* **SEE** PINK-ROOT DISEASE
SB341	ONION SETS
SB608.05	ONION SMUDGE
SB608.05	ONIONS — DISEASES AND PESTS
RM666.05	ONIONS — THERAPEUTIC USE
SB341	ONIONS
E99.045	*ONNEIOUT INDIANS* **SEE** ONEIDA INDIANS
P137	ONOMATOPOEIA
E99.058	ONONDAGA INDIANS
PM2076	ONONDAGA LANGUAGE
QH491	*ONTOGENESIS* **SEE** ONTOGENY
QH491	ONTOGENY
BT98-101	*ONTOLOGICAL ARGUMENT* **SEE** GOD — PROOF, ONTOLOGICAL
BD300-444	ONTOLOGY
QL448	ONYCHOPHORA
TN967	ONYX MARBLE
CJ3188	*ONZA DE ORO* **SEE** DOUBLOONS
QP91	OOCYTIN
QL965	OOGENESIS

E99.063	OOHENONPA INDIANS
QE471	OOLITE / petrology
QL675	OOLOGY SEE BIRDS — EGGS AND NESTS
TS755.0	OPALS / jewelry
TN997.07	OPALS / mineral resources
QE391.06	OPALS / mineralogy
F1221.06	OPATA INDIANS
Z711	OPEN AND CLOSED SHELVES
HD6488	OPEN AND CLOSED SHOP
BV820	OPEN COMMUNION SEE CLOSE AND OPEN COMMUNION
JX1321	OPEN DOOR POLICY (FAR EAST) SEE EASTERN QUESTION (FAR EAST) / international law
DS515-519	OPEN DOOR POLICY (FAR EAST) SEE EASTERN QUESTION (FAR EAST) / history
LC6501-6560	OPEN FORUM SEE FORUMS (DISCUSSION AND DEBATE)
PN4177-4191	OPEN FORUM SEE FORUMS (DISCUSSION AND DEBATE) / debating
D580	OPEN SEA (MARE LIBERUM) SEE FREEDOM OF THE SEAS / european war
JX4423-5	OPEN SEA (MARE LIBERUM) SEE FREEDOM OF THE SEAS / international law
JX5203-5268	OPEN SEA (MARE LIBERUM) SEE FREEDOM OF THE SEAS / maritime war international law
Z711	OPEN SHELVES IN LIBRARIES SEE OPEN AND CLOSED SHELVES
HD6488	OPEN SHOP SEE OPEN AND CLOSED SHOP
Z711	OPEN STACKS IN LIBRARIES SEE OPEN AND CLOSED SHELVES
RA793	OPEN-AIR INSTITUTIONS / hygiene
AM111	OPEN-AIR MUSEUMS
LB3481-3495	OPEN-AIR SCHOOLS
PN2219.08	OPEN-AIR THEATER SEE THEATER, OPEN-AIR
RA793	OPEN-AIR TREATMENT
TN291	OPEN-CAST MINING SEE STRIP MINING
TN291	OPEN-CUT MINING SEE STRIP MINING
TN740	OPEN-HEARTH FURNACES
TN740-742	OPEN-HEARTH PROCESS
TN291	OPEN-PIT MINING SEE STRIP MINING
E477.33	OPEQUAN CREEK, BATTLE OF, 1864 SEE WINCHESTER, BATTLE OF, SEPT. 19, 1864
ML105-7	OPERA — BIO-BIBLIOGRAPHY
ML102	OPERA — DICTIONARIES
ML3858	OPERA — DRAMATURGY
MT955	OPERA — PRODUCTION AND DIRECTION
MT955	OPERA DIRECTION SEE OPERA — PRODUCTION AND DIRECTION
MT955	OPERA PRODUCTION SEE OPERA — PRODUCTION AND DIRECTION
GT2370	OPERA-GLASSES / manners and customs
NA6820-6845	OPERA-HOUSES SEE THEATERS / architecture
ML3858	OPERA / aesthetics
ML1700-2110	OPERA / history and criticism
ML3858	OPERA, COMIC SEE OPERA / aesthetics
ML1700-2110	OPERA, COMIC SEE OPERA / history and criticism
ML1900	OPERA, COMIC SEE OPERETTA
ML1950	OPERA, COMIC SEE ZARZUELA
MT955	OPERA-DIRECTION SEE OPERA — PRODUCTION AND DIRECTION
ML2110	OPERA-LIBRETTISTS SEE LIBRETTISTS
ML48	OPERA-LIBRETTOS SEE OPERAS — LIBRETTOS
MT100	OPERA-STORIES, PLOTS, ETC. SEE OPERAS — STORIES, PLOTS, ETC.
MT95	OPERA-STORIES, PLOTS, ETC. SEE OPERAS — STORIES, PLOTS, ETC.
MT100	OPERAS
MT95	OPERAS
MT95	OPERAS — ANALYSIS, APPRECIATION
MT100	OPERAS — ANALYSIS, APPRECIATION
ML156.4.046	OPERAS — DISCOGRAPHY
M1505-8	OPERAS — EXCERPTS
ML48	OPERAS — LIBRETTOS
M1500	OPERAS — PARTS (INSTRUMENTAL)
M1500	OPERAS — PARTS
M208	OPERAS — PIANO SCORES (4 HANDS)
M33	OPERAS — PIANO SCORES
ML40	OPERAS — PROGRAMS
M1500	OPERAS — SCORES AND PARTS (INSTRUMENTAL)

M1500	OPERAS — SCORES AND PARTS
M1500	OPERAS — SCORES
MT955	OPERAS — STAGE GUIDES
MT95	OPERAS — STORIES, PLOTS, ETC.
MT100	OPERAS — STORIES, PLOTS, ETC.
ML128.04	OPERAS — THEMATIC CATALOGS
M1503	OPERAS — VOCAL SCORES WITH GUITAR
M1503	OPERAS — VOCAL SCORES WITH PIANO (4 HANDS)
M1503	OPERAS — VOCAL SCORES WITH PIANO AND PARTS (INSTRUMENTAL)
M1503	OPERAS — VOCAL SCORES WITH PIANO
M1503	OPERAS — VOCAL SCORES WITH 2 PIANOS
M1502	OPERAS — VOCAL SCORES
M1505-6	OPERAS - PARTS -- EXCERPTS SEE OPERAS — EXCERPTS — — PARTS
M1505-6	OPERAS - SCORES -- EXCERPTS SEE OPERAS — EXCERPTS — — SCORES
M1508	OPERAS - VOCAL SCORES WITH GUITAR -- EXCERPTS SEE OPERAS — EXCERPTS — — VOCAL SCORES WITH GUITAR
M1507-8	OPERAS - VOCAL SCORES WITH PIANO -- EXCERPTS SEE OPERAS — EXCERPTS — — VOCAL SCORES WITH PIANO
M453-4	OPERAS ARRANGED FOR STRING QUARTETS
M222-3	OPERAS ARRANGED FOR VIOLIN AND PIANO
M1500-1508	OPERAS
M1505-6	OPERAS-PARTS-EXCERPTS SEE OPERAS — EXCERPTS — — PARTS
M1505-6	OPERAS-SCORES-EXCERPTS SEE OPERAS — EXCERPTS — — SCORES
M1508	OPERAS-VOCAL SCORES WITH GUITAR-EXCERPTS SEE OPERAS — EXCERPTS — — VOCAL SCORES WITH GUITAR
M1507-8	OPERAS-VOCAL SCORES WITH PIANO-EXCERPTS SEE OPERAS — EXCERPTS — — VOCAL SCORES WITH PIANO
M1505-6	OPERAS — EXCERPTS — — PARTS
M1505-6	OPERAS — EXCERPTS — — SCORES
M1508	OPERAS — EXCERPTS — — VOCAL SCORES WITH GUITAR
M1507-8	OPERAS — EXCERPTS — — VOCAL SCORES WITH PIANO
M1500	OPERAS — SCORES — — ABRIDGEMENTS
M1500	OPERAS — TO 1800 — — SCORES
M1503	OPERAS — TO 1800 — — VOCAL SCORES WITH PIANO
M1502	OPERAS — TO 1800 — — VOCAL SCORES
M1505	OPERAS — TO 1800 — — EXCERPTS — — — PARTS
M1505	OPERAS — TO 1800 — — EXCERPTS — — — SCORES
M1500	OPERAS — TO 1800 — — SCORES — — — ABRIDGEMENTS
M1503	OPERAS — VOCAL SCORES WITH PIANO — — ABRIDGEMENTS
PN1995.7	OPERATIC MOVING-PICTURES SEE MOVING-PICTURES, MUSICAL
M1509	OPERATIC SCENES
RA975.5.06	OPERATING ROOMS
QA432	OPERATIONAL CALCULUS SEE CALCULUS, OPERATIONAL
QA253	OPERATIONS, CALCULUS OF SEE CALCULUS OF OPERATIONS
RD16	OPERATIONS, SURGICAL — CLASSIFICATION
RD	OPERATIONS, SURGICAL
R705	OPERATIONS, SURGICAL-ANECDOTES, FACETIAE, SATIRE, ETC. SEE MEDICINE — ANECDOTES, FACETIAE, SATIRE, ETC.
PN6231.M4	OPERATIONS, SURGICAL-ANECDOTES, FACETIAE, SATIRE, ETC. SEE MEDICINE — ANECDOTES, FACETIAE, SATIRE, ETC.
RD31.5	OPERATIONS, SURGICAL-PSYCHOLOGICAL ASPECTS SEE SURGERY — PSYCHOLOGICAL ASPECTS
RK501-555	OPERATIVE DENTISTRY SEE DENTISTRY, OPERATIVE
RD32	OPERATIVE SURGERY SEE SURGERY, OPERATIVE
QK623.D6	OPERCULATES SEE DISCOMYCETES
ML1900	OPERETTA
MT95	OPERETTA-STORIES, PLOTS, ETC. SEE OPERAS — STORIES, PLOTS, ETC.
MT100	OPERETTA-STORIES, PLOTS, ETC. SEE OPERAS — STORIES, PLOTS, ETC.

M1500-1508	*OPERETTAS* **SEE** MUSICAL REVUES, COMEDIES, ETC.
M1500-1508	*OPERETTAS* **SEE** OPERAS
M1500-1508	*OPERETTAS* **SEE** ZARZUELAS
ML990.0	OPHICLEIDE
BT1390	OPHITES
QL384.O6	OPHIUROIDEA
RE310-326	*OPHTHALMIA* **SEE** CONJUNCTIVA — DISEASES
RE96	*OPHTHALMIA* **SEE** EYE — INFLAMMATION
RJ296	*OPHTHALMIA NEONATORUM* **SEE** CONJUNCTIVITIS, INFANTILE
RE3	*OPHTHALMIC AND AURAL DISPENSARIES* **SEE** DISPENSARIES, OPHTHALMIC AND AURAL
RE3	*OPHTHALMIC AND AURAL HOSPITALS* **SEE** HOSPITALS, OPHTHALMIC AND AURAL
RF6	*OPHTHALMIC AND AURAL HOSPITALS* **SEE** HOSPITALS, OPHTHALMIC AND AURAL / *nose and throat*
RE88	OPHTHALMIC NURSING
RE	*OPHTHALMOLOGICAL INSTRUMENTS AND APPARATUS* **SEE** EYE, INSTRUMENTS AND APPARATUS FOR
RE991-2	*OPHTHALMOLOGICAL THERAPEUTICS* **SEE** THERAPEUTICS, OPHTHALMOLOGICAL
RE41	OPHTHALMOLOGY — EARLY WORKS TO 1800
RE20	OPHTHALMOLOGY — TERMINOLOGY
RE	OPHTHALMOLOGY
RE82	*OPHTHALMOLOGY, ANESTHETICS IN* **SEE** ANESTHESIA IN OPHTHALMOLOGY
SF891	*OPHTHALMOLOGY, VETERINARY* **SEE** VETERINARY OPHTHALMOLOGY
RE75-79	*OPHTHALMOMETRY* **SEE** EYE — EXAMINATION
RE86	OPHTHALMOSCOPE AND OPHTHALMOSCOPY
GT3010	*OPIATES* **SEE** NARCOTICS / *and customs*
RM328	*OPIATES* **SEE** NARCOTICS / *therapeutics*
HM261	*OPINION, PUBLIC* **SEE** PUBLIC OPINION
QL430.4	OPISTHOBRANCHIATA
QL696.O6	OPISTHOCOMI
QP921.02	OPIUM — PHYSIOLOGICAL EFFECT
RA1242.07	OPIUM — TOXICOLOGY
HV5816	OPIUM HABIT
RC568.O6	OPIUM HABIT
HV5816	OPIUM TRADE
SB295.O6	OPIUM
DP657	OPORTO, PORTUGAL — SIEGE, 1832
QL737.I5	OPOSSUM-SHREW
QL737.M3	OPOSSUMS
QE882.M3	OPOSSUMS, FOSSIL
QP951	*OPOTHERAPY* **SEE** ANIMAL EXTRACTS / *pharmacology*
RM283-298	*OPOTHERAPY* **SEE** ANIMAL EXTRACTS / *therapeutics*
RM283-298	*OPOTHERAPY* **SEE** ORGANOTHERAPY
TS1925	*OPPANOL* **SEE** RUBBER, ARTIFICIAL
BL325.P7	*OPPOSITES (IN RELIGION, FOLK-LORE, ETC.)* **SEE** POLARITY (IN RELIGION, FOLK-LORE, ETC.)
BL325.P7	*OPPOSITION, THEORY OF (RELIGION)* **SEE** POLARITY (IN RELIGION, FOLK-LORE, ETC.)
BC199.06	OPPOSITION, THEORY OF / *logic*
BF455	OPPOSITION, THEORY OF / *psychology*
RM751	OPSONINS AND OPSONIC INDEX
QP381	OPTIC CHIASM
QM455	OPTIC CHIASM
QL937	OPTIC CHIASM
QM455	OPTIC LOBES
QP381	OPTIC LOBES
QL937	OPTIC LOBES
RE701	OPTIC NERVE — DISEASES
RC280.E9	OPTIC NERVE — TUMORS
QL949	OPTIC NERVE
QM511	OPTIC NERVE
QP475	OPTIC NERVE
QP381	OPTIC THALAMUS
QL937	OPTIC THALAMUS
QM455	OPTIC THALAMUS
QD941	*OPTICAL CRYSTALLOGRAPHY* **SEE** CRYSTAL OPTICS
TK7895.06	*OPTICAL DATA PROCESSING EQUIPMENT* **SEE** ELECTRONIC CALCULATING-MACHINES — OPTICAL EQUIPMENT
QC375	*OPTICAL GLASS* **SEE** GLASS, OPTICAL
QP495	OPTICAL ILLUSIONS
RE73	OPTICAL INSTRUMENTS / *examination of eye*

QC371-6	OPTICAL INSTRUMENTS / *optics*
QC367	OPTICAL MEASUREMENTS
QC675	*OPTICAL PHENOMENA, INFLUENCE OF MAGNETISM ON* **SEE** MAGNETO-OPTICS
QD651	OPTICAL ROTATION
HD9999.06	OPTICAL TRADE
RE24-25	OPTICIANS — LEGAL STATUS, LAWS, ETC.
RE940	OPTICIANS
QC366	OPTICS — ATLASES
QC363	OPTICS — CHARTS, DIAGRAMS, ETC.
QC353	OPTICS — EARLY WORKS TO 1800
QC365-7	OPTICS — LABORATORY MANUALS
QC363	OPTICS — PROBLEMS, EXERCISES, ETC.
QC369	OPTICS — TABLES, ETC.
QC353-495	OPTICS
QC447	*OPTICS, ELECTRONIC* **SEE** ELECTRON OPTICS
QC381-9	OPTICS, GEOMETRICAL
QC975-6	*OPTICS, METEOROLOGICAL* **SEE** METEOROLOGICAL OPTICS
TR220	*OPTICS, PHOTOGRAPHIC* **SEE** PHOTOGRAPHIC OPTICS
QC401-495	OPTICS, PHYSICAL
QP474-495	OPTICS, PHYSIOLOGICAL
BJ1477	OPTIMISM / *ethics*
B829	OPTIMISM / *philosophy*
JX4231.07	OPTION OF NATIONALITY
RE961	OPTOMETRY — BUSINESS METHODS
RE959	OPTOMETRY AS A PROFESSION
RE940-986	OPTOMETRY
RE925	OPTOMETRY
QK495.C	ORACH / *botany*
SB351.0	ORACH / *vegetables*
BL613	ORACLES / *comparative religion*
BF1745-1779	ORACLES / *occult sciences*
DF125	ORACLES, GREEK
DU740	*ORAKAIVA* **SEE** BINANDELI (PAPUAN PEOPLE)
GN671.N5	*ORAKAIVA* **SEE** BINANDELI (PAPUAN PEOPLE) / *anthropology*
PN4145	ORAL INTERPRETATION
LB1573.5	ORAL READING
RK305	*ORAL SEPSIS* **SEE** MOUTH — SEPSIS
RD523-7	*ORAL SURGERY* **SEE** MOUTH — SURGERY
QL737.P9	*ORANG-OUTANGS* **SEE** ORANG-UTANS
QL737.P9	ORANG-UTANS
SB608.06	ORANGE — DISEASES AND PESTS
TX558.07	ORANGE JUICE
TP684.07	*ORANGE PEEL OIL* **SEE** ORANGE-OIL
SB608.06	ORANGE THRIPS
TP684.07	ORANGE-OIL
SB370.07	ORANGE
DA950-951	ORANGEMEN / *ireland*
F1058	ORANGEMEN / *ontario*
QL737.P9	*ORANGUTANS* **SEE** ORANG-UTANS
PL4701-4	*ORAON LANGUAGE* **SEE** KURUKH LANGUAGE
PL4704	*ORAON POETRY* **SEE** KURUKH POETRY
DS432.0	ORAONS
PN6121-9	ORATIONS / *collections*
PN4012-4061	ORATIONS / *history and criticism*
BX1939.075	ORATORIES (CANON LAW)
NA4910	ORATORIES
ML3867	ORATORIO / *aesthetics*
ML3201-3251	ORATORIO / *history and criticism*
MT110-115	ORATORIOS — ANALYTICAL GUIDES
M453-4	ORATORIOS ARRANGED FOR STRING QUARTETS
M553-4	ORATORIOS ARRANGED FOR STRING QUINTETS
M2000-2007	ORATORIOS
PN4057	ORATORS / *collective biography*
PN4185	ORATORY — COMPETITIONS / *u.s.*
PN4001-4321	ORATORY
PN4001-4321	ORATORY / *general works*
PA3479-3842	ORATORY, ANCIENT / *collections*
PA6138	ORATORY, ANCIENT / *collections*
PA6144	ORATORY, ANCIENT / *criticism*
PA3561	ORATORY, ANCIENT / *criticism*
PA3038	ORATORY, ANCIENT / *history*
PA3263-4	ORATORY, ANCIENT / *history*
PA6083	ORATORY, ANCIENT / *history*
HX698.0	ORBISTON COMMUNITY
TL796	*ORBITING VEHICLES* **SEE** ARTIFICIAL SATELLITES
TL797	*ORBITING VEHICLES* **SEE** SPACE STATIONS

QB355-7	ORBITS / *theoretical astronomy*
CR4485.07	ORBS
QK495.G74	ORCHARD GRASS / *botany*
SB201.06	ORCHARD GRASS / *culture*
SB354-399	*ORCHARDS* **SEE** FRUIT-CULTURE
ML1200-1251	ORCHESTRA
ML1040	*ORCHESTRAL BELLS* **SEE** GLOCKENSPIEL / *history*
M1000-1049	ORCHESTRAL MUSIC
M1060-1075	ORCHESTRAL MUSIC, ARRANGED
M1420	ORCHESTRAL MUSIC, JUVENILE
MT70	*ORCHESTRATION* **SEE** INSTRUMENTATION AND ORCHESTRATION / *instruction*
ML455	*ORCHESTRATION* **SEE** INSTRUMENTATION AND ORCHESTRATION / *history*
SB409	ORCHID CULTURE
QK495.064	*ORCHIDACEAE* **SEE** ORCHIDS / *botany*
QK495.064	ORCHIDS / *botany*
TP925.L7	ORCHIL
TP925.L7	ORCIN
RS165.C	*ORDEAL BEAN* **SEE** CALABAR BEAN
GN493	ORDEAL / *primitive*
BX4361-4	*ORDER OF ST. CLARE* **SEE** POOR CLARES
CR5511	ORDER OF THE CROWN OF ITALY
HF3505.9	ORDERS IN COUNCIL
CR4501-6305	ORDERS OF KNIGHTHOOD AND CHIVALRY — INSIGNIA
CR4501-6305	ORDERS OF KNIGHTHOOD AND CHIVALRY
CR4701-4731	ORDERS OF KNIGHTHOOD AND CHIVALRY, PAPAL / *military religious orders*
CR5547-5575	ORDERS OF KNIGHTHOOD AND CHIVALRY, PAPAL / *papal states*
BX5178	*ORDERS, ANGLICAN* **SEE** ANGLICAN ORDERS
NA2810-2817	*ORDERS, ARCHITECTURAL* **SEE** ARCHITECTURE — ORDERS
BV659-685	*ORDERS, MAJOR* **SEE** CLERGY
BX385	*ORDERS, MONASTIC* **SEE** MONASTICISM AND RELIGIOUS ORDERS / *greek church*
BX2410-4560	*ORDERS, MONASTIC* **SEE** MONASTICISM AND RELIGIOUS ORDERS / *catholic church*
BL1475.M7	*ORDERS, MONASTIC* **SEE** MONASTICISM AND RELIGIOUS ORDERS / *buddhism*
BX580-583	*ORDERS, MONASTIC* **SEE** MONASTICISM AND RELIGIOUS ORDERS / *russian church*
UB280-285	ORDERS, PREPARATION OF (MILITARY SCIENCE) / *military*
VB255	ORDERS, PREPARATION OF (MILITARY SCIENCE) / *naval*
E309	ORDINANCE OF 1787
BX1939.082	ORDINATION (CANON LAW)
BV676	ORDINATION OF WOMEN
BV4285	ORDINATION SERMONS
BV685	ORDINATION
BV830	ORDINATION / *sacrament*
UF530-537	ORDNANCE — MANUFACTURE
UF526	ORDNANCE RESEARCH
UF890	ORDNANCE TESTING / *military*
VF540	ORDNANCE TESTING / *naval*
UF520-630	ORDNANCE
VF370-375	ORDNANCE, NAVAL — MANUFACTURE
VF	ORDNANCE, NAVAL
UF560-565	ORDNANCE, RAPID-FIRE
PL431.08	ORDOS LANGUAGE
QE662	*ORDOVICIAN FORMATION* **SEE** GEOLOGY, STRATIGRAPHIC — ORDOVICIAN
QE727	*ORDOVICIAN FORMATION* **SEE** PALEONTOLOGY — ORDOVICIAN
VM457	ORE CARRIERS
TN342	*ORE CARS* **SEE** MINE RAILROADS — CARS
VM457	*ORE SHIPS* **SEE** ORE CARRIERS
TN500-535	*ORE TREATMENT* **SEE** ORE-DRESSING
TN263	ORE-DEPOSITS
TN500-535	ORE-DRESSING
DA520.A251812	OREBRO, TREATY OF, 1812
F871-885	OREGON — HISTORY
TA419-420	*OREGON PINE* **SEE** DOUGLAS FIR / *building materials*
SD397.D7	*OREGON PINE* **SEE** DOUGLAS FIR / *forestry*
F880	OREGON QUESTION
F597	OREGON TRAIL / *northwest*
F880	OREGON TRAIL / *oregon*
F592	OREGON TRAIL / *the west*
E526	OREGON — HISTORY — — CIVIL WAR
TN560	ORES — SAMPLING AND ESTIMATION
TN265	ORES
TN530	*ORES, MAGNETIC SEPARATION OF* **SEE** MAGNETIC SEPARATION OF ORES
TN550-580	*ORES-ANALYSIS* **SEE** ASSAYING
HG325-9	*ORES-ANALYSIS* **SEE** ASSAYING / *mints*
TN560	*ORES-ANALYSIS* **SEE** ORES — SAMPLING AND ESTIMATION
ML579	*ORGA-SONIC ORGAN* **SEE** BALDWIN ORGAN
ML550-597	ORGAN — CONSTRUCTION
MT180	ORGAN — INSTRUCTION AND STUDY
MT182	ORGAN — METHODS (JAZZ)
MT182	ORGAN — METHODS
MT189	ORGAN — REGISTRATION
ML552-592	ORGAN — REPAIRING
MT185-191	ORGAN — STUDIES AND EXERCISES
M182-4	*ORGAN AND ENGLISH-HORN MUSIC* **SEE** ENGLISH HORN AND ORGAN MUSIC
MT182-4	*ORGAN AND FLUTE MUSIC* **SEE** FLUTE AND ORGAN MUSIC
M182-4	*ORGAN AND HARP MUSIC* **SEE** HARP AND ORGAN MUSIC
M182-4	*ORGAN AND HARP MUSIC* **SEE** HARP AND ORGAN MUSIC
M182-4	*ORGAN AND HARPSICHORD MUSIC* **SEE** HARPSICHORD AND ORGAN MUSIC
M182-4	*ORGAN AND HARPSICHORD MUSIC* **SEE** HARPSICHORD AND ORGAN MUSIC
M182-4	*ORGAN AND OBOE MUSIC* **SEE** OBOE AND ORGAN MUSIC
M298	*ORGAN AND PERCUSSION MUSIC* **SEE** PERCUSSION AND ORGAN MUSIC
M298	*ORGAN AND PERCUSSION MUSIC* **SEE** PERCUSSION AND ORGAN MUSIC
M182-4	*ORGAN AND PIANO MUSIC* **SEE** PIANO AND ORGAN MUSIC
M182-4	*ORGAN AND TRUMPET MUSIC* **SEE** TRUMPET AND ORGAN MUSIC
M182-6	*ORGAN AND VIOLA D'AMORE MUSIC* **SEE** VIOLA D'AMORE AND ORGAN MUSIC
M182-6	*ORGAN AND VIOLA D'AMORE MUSIC* **SEE** VIOLA D'AMORE AND ORGAN MUSIC
M182-4	*ORGAN AND VIOLA MUSIC* **SEE** VIOLA AND ORGAN MUSIC
M182-4	*ORGAN AND VIOLIN MUSIC* **SEE** VIOLIN AND ORGAN MUSIC
ML647	ORGAN MASS
M14.3	ORGAN MASSES
MT195-7	ORGAN MUSIC — INSTRUCTIVE EDITIONS
MT193	ORGAN MUSIC — TEACHING PIECES
M180-184	ORGAN MUSIC (2 ORGANS)
M6-11	ORGAN MUSIC
M12-13	ORGAN MUSIC, ARRANGED
M1375	ORGAN MUSIC, JUVENILE
ML132.0	*ORGAN MUSIC-GRADED LISTS* **SEE** ORGAN MUSIC — BIBLIOGRAPHY — — GRADED LISTS
ML132.0	ORGAN MUSIC — BIBLIOGRAPHY — — GRADED LISTS
M36.5	*ORGAN REALIZATIONS OF THOROUGH BASS* **SEE** THOROUGH BASS — REALIZATIONS
ML3790	*ORGAN TRADE* **SEE** MUSIC TRADE
M1205	ORGAN WITH BAND
M1105-6	ORGAN WITH CHAMBER ORCHESTRA
M1005-6	ORGAN WITH ORCHESTRA
M1006	ORGAN WITH ORCHESTRA — TO 1800 — — SOLO WITH PIANO
M1105-6	ORGAN WITH STRING ORCHESTRA
M1105	ORGAN WITH STRING ORCHESTRA, ARRANGED — SCORES AND PARTS
M1105-6	ORGAN WITH STRING ORCHESTRA, ARRANGED
ML404	ORGAN-BUILDERS / *biography collective*
ML424	ORGAN-BUILDERS / *individual*
ML595	ORGAN-PIPES
ML1050-1055	*ORGAN-PLAYER* **SEE** PLAYER-ORGAN
MT150	*ORGAN-PLAYER* **SEE** PLAYER-ORGAN / *analytical guides*
MT700	*ORGAN-PLAYER* **SEE** PLAYER-ORGAN / *instruction*
MT59	ORGAN-POINT
ML550-649	ORGAN / *history and criticism*
ML597	*ORGAN, ELECTRONIC* **SEE** ELECTRONIC ORGAN

M1105-6	ORGAN, HARP, KETTLEDRUMS WITH STRING ORCHESTRA
QD248-449	*ORGANIC CHEMISTRY* **SEE** CHEMISTRY, ORGANIC
S598	*ORGANIC MATTER IN SOIL* **SEE** HUMUS
MT35	ORGANINA
ML396	ORGANISTS / *biography collective*
ML416	ORGANISTS / *individual*
GV192-8	*ORGANIZED CAMPS* **SEE** CAMPS
HV6437-9	*ORGANIZED CRIME* **SEE** GANGS
HV6774-7220	*ORGANIZED CRIME* **SEE** GANGS / *by country*
QK641-662	*ORGANOGRAPHY* **SEE** BOTANY — ORGANOGRAPHY
QH41-48	*ORGANOGRAPHY* **SEE** NATURAL HISTORY — ORGANOGRAPHY
QD411-412	ORGANOMETALLIC COMPOUNDS
RM283-298	ORGANOTHERAPY
QP88	ORGANS, CULTURE OF
ML174	ORGANUM / *musical history*
TS650	ORICHALC / *alloys*
TN616	ORICHALC / *ancient metals*
CB251	*ORIENT AND OCCIDENT* **SEE** EAST AND WEST
D175-195	*ORIENT, LATIN* **SEE** LATIN ORIENT
DS56	ORIENTAL ANTIQUITIES / *ancient orient*
N5343-5	ORIENTAL ANTIQUITIES / *art*
DS11	ORIENTAL ANTIQUITIES / *asia*
NA1460-1579	*ORIENTAL ARCHITECTURE* **SEE** ARCHITECTURE, ORIENTAL
N7260	*ORIENTAL ART* **SEE** ART, ORIENTAL
NK6472	*ORIENTAL ART METAL-WORK* **SEE** ART METAL-WORK, ORIENTAL
NK1037	*ORIENTAL ART OBJECTS* **SEE** ART OBJECTS, ORIENTAL
CB253	*ORIENTAL CIVILIZATION* **SEE** CIVILIZATION, ORIENTAL
CJ3430-3890	*ORIENTAL COINS* **SEE** COINS, ORIENTAL
CJ1301-1397	*ORIENTAL COINS* **SEE** COINS, ORIENTAL / *ancient*
PJ371	ORIENTAL DRAMA / *collections*
PJ334	ORIENTAL DRAMA / *history*
PJ431-3	ORIENTAL DRAMA / *translations*
PJ464	ORIENTAL DRAMA / *translations*
NK9272-9285	*ORIENTAL EMBROIDERY* **SEE** EMBROIDERY, ORIENTAL
SB945.063	ORIENTAL FRUIT FLY
SB945.065	ORIENTAL FRUIT MOTH
PJ	ORIENTAL LANGUAGES
PJ347-598	ORIENTAL LITERATURE / *collections*
PJ301-345	ORIENTAL LITERATURE / *history*
Z695.1.07	*ORIENTAL LITERATURE-CATALOGING* **SEE** CATALOGING OF ORIENTAL LITERATURE
ML162	*ORIENTAL MUSIC* **SEE** MUSIC, ORIENTAL / *history and criticism*
ML330-345	*ORIENTAL MUSIC* **SEE** MUSIC, ORIENTAL / *history and criticism*
M1795-1825	*ORIENTAL MUSIC* **SEE** MUSIC, ORIENTAL / *music*
BL1000-2370	*ORIENTAL MYTHOLOGY* **SEE** MYTHOLOGY, ORIENTAL
SB945.065	*ORIENTAL PEACH MOTH* **SEE** ORIENTAL FRUIT MOTH
PJ	ORIENTAL PHILOLOGY
B121	*ORIENTAL PHILOSOPHY* **SEE** PHILOSOPHY, ORIENTAL
PJ356	ORIENTAL POETRY / *collections*
PJ327	ORIENTAL POETRY / *history*
PJ462-3	ORIENTAL POETRY / *translations*
PJ416-418	ORIENTAL POETRY / *translations*
NK4143-4172	*ORIENTAL POTTERY* **SEE** POTTERY, ORIENTAL
NK4543-4572	*ORIENTAL POTTERY* **SEE** POTTERY, ORIENTAL / *porcelain*
NK2808-2810	*ORIENTAL RUGS* **SEE** RUGS, ORIENTAL
RL331	*ORIENTAL SORE* **SEE** DELHI BOIL
NA5960	*ORIENTAL TEMPLES* **SEE** TEMPLES, ORIENTAL
PN6222.07	ORIENTAL WIT AND HUMOR
PJ63	ORIENTALISTS
DS13	ORIENTALS
NA2540	ORIENTATION (ARCHITECTURE)
NA4800	ORIENTATION (ARCHITECTURE) / *churches*
UF850-857	*ORIENTATION (MILITARY SCIENCE)* **SEE** RANGE-FINDING
VF550	*ORIENTATION (MILITARY SCIENCE)* **SEE** RANGE-FINDING / *naval ordnance*
QP443	*ORIENTATION (PSYCHOLOGY)* **SEE** ORIENTATION
BL619.07	ORIENTATION (RELIGION)
LB2397	*ORIENTATION (STUDENTS)* **SEE** STUDENTS / *reminiscences*
LB3602-3635	*ORIENTATION (STUDENTS)* **SEE** STUDENTS / *student life*

LB1705-2285	*ORIENTATION (TEACHERS)* **SEE** TEACHERS, TRAINING OF
QP443	ORIENTATION
TT870	ORIGAMI
QH325	*ORIGIN OF LIFE* **SEE** LIFE — ORIGIN
QH361-371	*ORIGIN OF MAN* **SEE** MAN — ORIGIN
QH361-371	ORIGIN OF SPECIES
HD3625-6	*ORIGIN, MARKS OF* **SEE** MARKS OF ORIGIN
BT720	*ORIGINAL SIN* **SEE** SIN, ORIGINAL
PN45	ORIGINALITY (IN LITERATURE)
BF433.07	ORIGINALITY
QL696.P2	ORIOLES
E233	*ORISKANY CAMPAIGN* **SEE** ST. LEGER'S EXPEDITION, 1777
QE665	*ORISKANY FORMATION* **SEE** GEOLOGY, STRATIGRAPHIC — DEVONIAN
QE918	*ORISKANY FORMATION* **SEE** PALEOBOTANY — DEVONIAN
QE728	*ORISKANY FORMATION* **SEE** PALEONTOLOGY — DEVONIAN
E241.06	ORISKANY, BATTLE OF, 1777
PK2561-9	ORIYA LANGUAGE
DS432.08	ORIYAS
DC305.6	ORLEANS, BATTLE OF, 1870
QL430.5.H3	*ORMERS* **SEE** ABALONES
DS325.07	ORMUS — SIEGE, 1622
NK1160-1590	*ORNAMENT* **SEE** DECORATION AND ORNAMENT
NK3600-3620	*ORNAMENTAL ALPHABETS* **SEE** ALPHABETS / *art*
Z43	*ORNAMENTAL ALPHABETS* **SEE** ALPHABETS / *calligraphy*
P211-213	*ORNAMENTAL ALPHABETS* **SEE** ALPHABETS / *comparative grammar*
TT773	*ORNAMENTAL ALPHABETS* **SEE** ALPHABETS / *fancy work*
T371	*ORNAMENTAL ALPHABETS* **SEE** ALPHABETS / *mechanical drawing*
ND2890-3416	*ORNAMENTAL ALPHABETS* **SEE** ILLUMINATION OF BOOKS AND MANUSCRIPTS
NK3600-3640	*ORNAMENTAL ALPHABETS* **SEE** LETTERING / *art industries*
T371	*ORNAMENTAL ALPHABETS* **SEE** LETTERING / *mechanical drawing*
TT360	*ORNAMENTAL ALPHABETS* **SEE** LETTERING / *signs and show-cards*
NK1160-1590	*ORNAMENTAL DESIGN* **SEE** DESIGN, DECORATIVE
CR29-69	*ORNAMENTAL HERALDRY* **SEE** HERALDRY, ORNAMENTAL
SB403-450	*ORNAMENTAL PLANTS* **SEE** PLANTS, ORNAMENTAL
MT80	*ORNAMENTS (MUSIC)* **SEE** EMBELLISHMENT (MUSIC)
QL671	ORNITHOLOGICAL SOCIETIES
QL26	ORNITHOLOGISTS
QL671-3	ORNITHOLOGY
SB995	*ORNITHOLOGY, ECONOMIC* **SEE** BIRDS, INJURIOUS AND BENEFICIAL
TL717	ORNITHOPTERS
QL737.M7	*ORNITHORHYNCHUS* **SEE** DUCKBILLS
PL461.08	OROCHON DIALECT
GR660	*OROGRAPHY* **SEE** MOUNTAINS / *folk-lore*
GB501-553	*OROGRAPHY* **SEE** MOUNTAINS / *physical geography*
GR660	*OROLOGY* **SEE** MOUNTAINS / *folk-lore*
GB501-553	*OROLOGY* **SEE** MOUNTAINS / *physical geography*
DT390.G2	*OROMONS* **SEE** GALLAS
HV959-1420	*ORPHAN-ASYLUMS* **SEE** ORPHANS AND ORPHAN-ASYLUMS
HV959-1420	ORPHANS AND ORPHAN-ASYLUMS
BL820.B2	*ORPHIC MYSTERIES* **SEE** DIONYSIA
DF123	*ORPHIC MYSTERIES* **SEE** DIONYSIA / *greek antiquities*
PA3203	*ORPHIC MYSTERIES* **SEE** DIONYSIA / *greek drama*
BL820.B2	*ORPHISM* **SEE** DIONYSIA
DF123	*ORPHISM* **SEE** DIONYSIA / *greek antiquities*
PA3203	*ORPHISM* **SEE** DIONYSIA / *greek drama*
SF489.08	ORPINGTONS
QB70	*ORRERIES* **SEE** PLANETARIA
DC233.07	ORTHEZ, BATTLE OF, 1814
TN948.A5	*ORTHITE* **SEE** ALLANITE
TR453	*ORTHOCHROMATIC PHOTOGRAPHY* **SEE** PHOTOGRAPHY, ORTHOCHROMATIC
RK521-528	ORTHODONTIA
RK681-6	*ORTHODONTIC APPLIANCES* **SEE** DENTAL INSTRUMENTS AND APPARATUS

RK521-528	*ORTHODONTICS* **SEE** ORTHODONTIA
BX324	ORTHODOX EASTERN CHURCH — RELATIONS
BX200-750	ORTHODOX EASTERN CHURCH
BX324.3	ORTHODOX EASTERN CHURCH — RELATIONS — — CATHOLIC CHURCH
P221-7	*ORTHOEPY* **SEE** PHONETICS
QA567	*ORTHOGONAL CURVES* **SEE** CURVES, ORTHOGONAL
QA404.5	*ORTHOGONAL FUNCTIONS* **SEE** FUNCTIONS, ORTHOGONAL
GA115	*ORTHOGONAL PROJECTION* **SEE** ORTHOGRAPHIC PROJECTION / *cartography*
QA503	*ORTHOGONAL PROJECTION* **SEE** ORTHOGRAPHIC PROJECTION / *mathematics*
T363	*ORTHOGONAL PROJECTION* **SEE** ORTHOGRAPHIC PROJECTION / *mechanical drawing*
QA404.5	*ORTHOGONAL SERIES* **SEE** SERIES, ORTHOGONAL
QA649	*ORTHOGONAL SURFACES* **SEE** SURFACES, ORTHOGONAL
GA115	ORTHOGRAPHIC PROJECTION / *cartography*
QA503	ORTHOGRAPHIC PROJECTION / *mathematics*
T363	ORTHOGRAPHIC PROJECTION / *mechanical drawing*
Z51	*ORTHOGRAPHIC SHORTHAND* **SEE** STENOTYPY
PE1147-1153	*ORTHOGRAPHY* **SEE** SPELLING REFORM / *english*
RD705	ORTHOPEDIA — HOSPITALS AND INSTITUTIONS
RD701-795	ORTHOPEDIA
RD755-7	ORTHOPEDIC APPARATUS
RD737	ORTHOPEDIC NURSING
RD757.S	ORTHOPEDIC SHOES
RD701-795	*ORTHOPEDIC SURGERY* **SEE** ORTHOPEDIA
QL506-9	ORTHOPTERA
TL717	*ORTHOPTERS* **SEE** ORNITHOPTERS
D569.0	ORTIGARA, BATTLE OF, 1917
PL8276	*ORU LANGUAGE* **SEE** IJO LANGUAGE
PL8598.08	ORUNGU LANGUAGE
QL737.U5	ORYX
E99.08	OSAGE INDIANS — LAND TRANSFERS
HD234.0	OSAGE INDIANS — LAND TRANSFERS
E99.08	OSAGE INDIANS
PM2081	OSAGE LANGUAGE
SD397.08	OSAGE ORANGE
F685	OSAWATOMIE, BATTLE OF, 1856
QA935	OSCILLATIONS
QA930	OSCILLATIONS / *aerodynamics*
QA871	OSCILLATIONS / *dynamics*
QC661	OSCILLATIONS / *electric waves*
QA927	OSCILLATIONS / *hydrodynamics*
TK6565.07	OSCILLATORS, ELECTRIC / *radio*
TK7872.0	OSCILLATORS, VACUUM-TUBE / *electronics*
TK6565.07	OSCILLATORS, VACUUM-TUBE / *radio*
TK381	OSCILLOGRAPH
TK6565.C4	*OSCILLOGRAPH, CATHODE RAY* **SEE** CATHODE RAY OSCILLOGRAPH / *radio*
TK7872	*OSCILLOGRAPH, CATHODE RAY* **SEE** CATHODE RAY OSCILLOGRAPH / *electronics*
GN655.F3	*OSHIBAS* **SEE** FAN (AFRICAN PEOPLE) / *ethnology*
PL8547	*OSHINDONGA LANGUAGE* **SEE** NDONGA LANGUAGE
SD397.082	OSIERS
PL101-199	*OSMANIC LANGUAGE* **SEE** TURKISH LANGUAGE
PL101-199	*OSMANLI LANGUAGE* **SEE** TURKISH LANGUAGE
QD181.07	OSMIUM
QD543	OSMOSIS / *chemistry*
QH615	OSMOSIS / *cytology*
QL696.A2	OSPREYS
DK511.C24	OSSETES
PK6958	OSSETIC FICTION
PK6951-9	OSSETIC LANGUAGE
PK6958.5	OSSETIC LITERATURE / *collections and history*
DH199.08	OSTEND — SIEGE, 1601-1604
RC933	*OSTEOARTHRITIS* **SEE** ARTHRITIS DEFORMANS
RJ482.0	OSTEOCHONDROSIS
RD684	*OSTEOGENESIS IMPERFECTA* **SEE** OSTEOPSATHYROSIS
QL821	*OSTEOLOGY* **SEE** BONES / *animal*
QM101-117	*OSTEOLOGY* **SEE** BONES / *human*
GN70	*OSTEOLOGY* **SEE** SKELETON / *anthropology*
QL821-3	*OSTEOLOGY* **SEE** SKELETON / *comparative anatomy*
QM101-117	*OSTEOLOGY* **SEE** SKELETON / *human anatomy*
RZ336	OSTEOPATHY AS A PROFESSION
RZ301-397	OSTEOPATHY

RD123	*OSTEOPLASTY* **SEE** BONE-GRAFTING
RD684	*OSTEOPLASTY* **SEE** BONES — SURGERY
RD684	OSTEOPOROSIS
RD684	OSTEOPSATHYROSIS
RC931.08	OSTEOSCLEROSIS
RD684	OSTEOTOMY
D137-8	*OSTGOTHS* **SEE** GOTHS / *migrations*
PH1401-1409	OSTIAK LANGUAGE
DK759.K	*OSTIAKS OF THE YENISEI* **SEE** KETS
DK759.08	OSTIAKS
ML448	*OSTINATO* **SEE** GROUND BASS
DK759.08	*OSTJAKS* **SEE** OSTIAKS
QL444.08	OSTRACODA
QE817.08	OSTRACODA, FOSSIL
QL444.08	*OSTRACOPODA* **SEE** OSTRACODA
PJ1675	OSTRAKA / *egyptian*
PA3371	OSTRAKA / *greek*
QL430.7.09	*OSTREA* **SEE** OYSTERS / *zoology*
SF511	OSTRICH FARMS AND FARMING
QL696.S9	OSTRICHES
D137-8	*OSTROGOTHS* **SEE** GOTHS / *migrations*
DK759.08	*OSTYAKS* **SEE** OSTIAKS
E199	OSWEGO, FORT, CAPTURE OF, 1756
F129.07	OSWEGO, FORT, CAPTURE OF, 1756
QL737.P6	*OTARIA* **SEE** SEALS (ANIMALS)
F3722.1.0	*OTAVALA INDIANS* **SEE** OTAVALO INDIANS
F3722.1.0	OTAVALO INDIANS
E99.C6	*OTCHIPWE INDIANS* **SEE** CHIPPEWA INDIANS
PM851-4	*OTCHIPWE LANGUAGE* **SEE** CHIPPEWA LANGUAGE
PL8728	*OTETELA LANGUAGE* **SEE** TETELA LANGUAGE
RF1-320	*OTITIS* **SEE** EAR — DISEASES
DR502.5	OTLUKBELI, BATTLE OF, 1473
E99.087	OTO INDIANS
PM2082.08	OTO LANGUAGE
QP471	*OTOCONIA* **SEE** OTOLITHS / *physiology*
QL948	*OTOCONIA* **SEE** OTOLITHS / *zoology*
QP471	*OTOCONITES* **SEE** OTOLITHS / *physiology*
QL948	*OTOCONITES* **SEE** OTOLITHS / *zoology*
QL696.P2	*OTOCORYS* **SEE** LARKS
QL948	OTOCYSTS
E99.087	*OTOE INDIANS* **SEE** OTO INDIANS
PM2082.08	*OTOE LANGUAGE* **SEE** OTO LANGUAGE
QP471	OTOLITHS / *physiology*
QL948	OTOLITHS / *zoology*
QL948	*OTOLOGY* **SEE** EAR / *comparative anatomy*
QM507	*OTOLOGY* **SEE** EAR / *human anatomy*
QP461-471	*OTOLOGY* **SEE** EAR / *physiology*
PM6703	OTOMACO LANGUAGE
PM6703	*OTOMAQUE LANGUAGE* **SEE** OTOMACO LANGUAGE
F1221.086	OTOMI INDIANS
PM4146-9	OTOMI LANGUAGE
PM4146-9	OTOMIAN LANGUAGES
RF341-437	*OTORHINOLARYNGOLOGY* **SEE** NOSE — DISEASES
RF270	OTOSCLEROSIS
QP471	*OTOSTEA* **SEE** OTOLITHS / *physiology*
QL948	*OTOSTEA* **SEE** OTOLITHS / *zoology*
E99.09	OTTAWA INDIANS
PM2083	OTTAWA LANGUAGE
SH364	OTTER HUNTING
QL737.I5	OTTER-SHREW
DA783.53	OTTERBURN, BATTLE OF, 1388
QL737.C2	OTTERS
QL737.C2	*OTTERS, SEA* **SEE** SEA-OTTERS
SH364	*OTTERS, SEA* **SEE** SEA-OTTERS / *fisheries*
E99.087	*OTTOE INDIANS* **SEE** OTO INDIANS
PM6703	*OTTOMACQUE LANGUAGE* **SEE** OTOMACO LANGUAGE
PM6703	*OTTOMAKU LANGUAGE* **SEE** OTOMACO LANGUAGE
DD136-140.7	*OTTONIAN EMPERORS* **SEE** GERMANY — HISTORY — — SAXON HOUSE, 919-1024
DD136-140.7	*OTTONIAN HOUSE* **SEE** GERMANY — HISTORY — — SAXON HOUSE, 919-1024
F3341.S2	OTUQUIS INDIANS / *bolivia*
PL8263	*OTURKPO DIALECT* **SEE** IDOMA LANGUAGE
SH685	OUANANICHE
F2230.2.08	*OUAYANA INDIANS* **SEE** OYANA INDIANS
PM6714	*OUAYANA LANGUAGE* **SEE** OYANA LANGUAGE
F2380.1.W25	*OUAYEOUE INDIANS* **SEE** WAIWAI INDIANS
PK9201.U3	*OUBYKH LANGUAGE* **SEE** UBYKH LANGUAGE
DA87.5 1778	OUESSANT, BATTLE OF, 1778

F2230.2.W	*OUITOTO INDIANS* **SEE** WITOTO INDIANS
PL8785	*OUOLOF LANGUAGE* **SEE** WOLOF LANGUAGE
D545.M3	*OURCQ, BATTLE OF THE, 1914* **SEE** MARNE, BATTLE OF THE, 1914 — OURCQ
DP570	OURIQUE, BATTLE OF, JULY 25, 1139
F3341.T6	*OUROUS* **SEE** PUQUINA INDIANS / *bolivia*
F2230.2.P	*OUROUS* **SEE** PUQUINA INDIANS / *south america*
LB1047	*OUT-OF-DOORS EDUCATION* **SEE** OUTDOOR EDUCATION
BF1389.A7	*OUT-OF-THE-BODY EXPERIENCES* **SEE** ASTRAL PROJECTION
E99.F7	*OUTAGAMI INDIANS* **SEE** FOX INDIANS
E99.09	*OUTAOUAKS* **SEE** OTTAWA INDIANS
VM348	OUTBOARD MOTOR-BOATS
VM348	*OUTBOARD MOTORBOATS* **SEE** OUTBOARD MOTOR-BOATS
GT6550-6699	OUTCASTS / *manners and customs*
TX823	OUTDOOR COOKERY
LB1047	OUTDOOR EDUCATION
SK601	OUTDOOR LIFE
AM111	*OUTDOOR MUSEUMS* **SEE** OPEN-AIR MUSEUMS
GV182.2	OUTDOOR RECREATION
LB3481-3495	*OUTDOOR SCHOOLS* **SEE** OPEN-AIR SCHOOLS
PN2219.08	*OUTDOOR THEATER* **SEE** THEATER, OPEN-AIR
HD5311	*OUTLAW STRIKES* **SEE** WILDCAT STRIKES
HV6441-6453	OUTLAWS
G129	OUTLINE MAPS — KEYS
GA101-130	OUTLINE MAPS
RA974	*OUTPATIENT SERVICES IN HOSPITALS* **SEE** HOSPITALS — OUTPATIENT SERVICES
U190-195	*OUTPOSTS* **SEE** GUARD DUTY
TK7887.5	*OUTPUT EQUIPMENT (ELECTRONIC COMPUTERS)* **SEE** ELECTRONIC CALCULATING-MACHINES — INPUT-OUTPUT EQUIPMENT
HF5421	*OUTSIDE BROKERS* **SEE** BROKERS
HG4621	*OUTSIDE BROKERS* **SEE** BROKERS / *stockbrokers*
DT709	*OVAHERERO* **SEE** HEREROS
GN657.H	*OVAHERERO* **SEE** HEREROS
PL8417	*OVAMBO LANGUAGE* **SEE** KUANYAMA LANGUAGE
RG441-481	OVARIES — DISEASES
QP261	OVARIES — TRANSPLANTATION
RC280.08	OVARIES — TUMORS
QL881	OVARIES / *comparative anatomy*
QM421	OVARIES / *human anatomy*
QP261	OVARIES / *physiology*
RG481	OVARIOTOMY
TX657.S3-8	*OVENS* **SEE** STOVES / *for cooking*
TH7435-7458	*OVENS* **SEE** STOVES / *for heating*
TS425	*OVENS* **SEE** STOVES / *iron manufactures*
TT595-600	*OVERCOATS* **SEE** COATS
TT530-535	*OVERCOATS* **SEE** COATS
TK3231-3248	*OVERHEAD ELECTRIC LINES* **SEE** ELECTRIC LINES — OVERHEAD
TK3231-3248	*OVERHEAD POWER LINES* **SEE** ELECTRIC LINES — OVERHEAD
F593	OVERLAND JOURNEYS TO THE PACIFIC
LB3431	OVERPRESSURE (EDUCATION)
HD61	OVERPRODUCTION
Z675.G7	*OVERSEAS INFORMATION LIBRARIES* **SEE** INFORMATION LIBRARIES
Z675.G7	*OVERSEAS LIBRARIES* **SEE** INFORMATION LIBRARIES
HD5111	OVERTIME
ML1261	OVERTURE / *history and criticism*
M1204	OVERTURES (BAND)
M1255	OVERTURES (BAND), ARRANGED
M1004	OVERTURES (CHAMBER ORCHESTRA)
M1356	OVERTURES (DANCE ORCHESTRA) — SCORES
M1356	OVERTURES (DANCE ORCHESTRA)
M125-7	OVERTURES (GUITAR)
M985	OVERTURES (INSTRUMENTAL ENSEMBLE)
M25	OVERTURES (PIANO)
M200-201	OVERTURES (PIANO, 4 HANDS)
M204	OVERTURES (PIANO, 4 HANDS)
M1350	OVERTURES (SALON ORCHESTRA)
M1104	OVERTURES (STRING ORCHESTRA)
M1160	OVERTURES (STRING ORCHESTRA), ARRANGED
M175.A4	OVERTURES ARRANGED FOR ACCORDION
M383-4	OVERTURES ARRANGED FOR FLUTE, GUITAR, VIOLA
M383-4	OVERTURES ARRANGED FOR FLUTE, GUITAR, VIOLIN

M276-7	OVERTURES ARRANGED FOR GUITAR AND PIANO
M373-4	OVERTURES ARRANGED FOR GUITAR, VIOLIN, VIOLA
M35	OVERTURES ARRANGED FOR HARPSICHORD
M12-13	OVERTURES ARRANGED FOR ORGAN
M35	OVERTURES ARRANGED FOR PIANO — EXCERPTS
M216	OVERTURES ARRANGED FOR PIANO (2 PIANOS, 8 HANDS)
M209	OVERTURES ARRANGED FOR PIANO (4 HANDS)
M213	OVERTURES ARRANGED FOR PIANO (6 HANDS)
M313-314	OVERTURES ARRANGED FOR PIANO TRIOS
M35	OVERTURES ARRANGED FOR PIANO
M338-9	OVERTURES ARRANGED FOR PIANO, FLUTE, GUITAR
M222-3	OVERTURES ARRANGED FOR VIOLIN AND PIANO
M558-9	OVERTURES ARRANGED FOR WIND QUINTETS
M292-3	OVERTURES ARRANGED FOR 2 GUITARS
M1004	OVERTURES
M1060	OVERTURES, ARRANGED
RA788	*OVERWORK, MENTAL* **SEE** FATIGUE, MENTAL / *mental hygiene*
QP421	*OVERWORK, MENTAL* **SEE** FATIGUE, MENTAL / *physiology*
RC351	*OVERWORK, MENTAL* **SEE** FATIGUE, MENTAL / *popular works*
BF481	*OVERWORK, MENTAL* **SEE** FATIGUE, MENTAL / *psychology*
QL881	OVIDUCT / *comparative anatomy*
QM265	OVIDUCT / *human anatomy*
GN655.08	OVIMBUNDU / *anthropology*
DT611	OVIMBUNDU / *ethnology*
QP261	OVULATION
RG591	OVUM / *diseases*
QM611	OVUM / *human embryology*
QL965	OVUM / *zoology*
QL696.S8	OWLS
QE872.S8	OWLS, FOSSIL
QP197	OX-GALL
QP211	OXALIC ACID — EXCRETION
QP915.08	OXALIC ACID — PHYSIOLOGICAL EFFECT
QP801.08	OXALIC ACID IN THE BODY
QD305.A2	OXALIC ACID
QK495.098	OXALIS
RC918.09	OXALURIA
SF961	OXEN — DISEASES
QL737.U5	OXEN
QE882.U3	OXEN, FOSSIL
BV4915	OXFORD GROUP
BX5094-5100	OXFORD MOVEMENT
QP601	OXIDASES
TD755	*OXIDATION PONDS* **SEE** SEWAGE LAGOONS
QD63.09	OXIDATION / *chemical operations*
QD281.09	OXIDATION / *organic chemistry*
QD501	OXIDATION / *physical chemistry*
QP177	*OXIDATION, BIOLOGICAL* **SEE** OXIDATION, PHYSIOLOGICAL
QP177	OXIDATION, PHYSIOLOGICAL
QD181.01	OXIDES
TS227	OXYACETYLENE WELDING AND CUTTING
HD7269.W	*OXYACETYLENE WELDING AND CUTTING-HYGIENIC ASPECTS* **SEE** WELDING — HYGIENIC ASPECTS
QD305.A6	OXYALDEHYDES
QD341.A6	OXYALDEHYDES
QP921	OXYDIMORPHINE / *physiological effects*
QP913.01	OXYGEN — PHYSIOLOGICAL EFFECT
TL697.08	*OXYGEN EQUIPMENT IN AEROPLANES* **SEE** AEROPLANES — OXYGEN EQUIPMENT
QD181.01	OXYGEN
TP245.09	OXYGEN / *chemical technology*
TP245.09	*OXYGEN, LIQUID* **SEE** LIQUID OXYGEN
QD181.C5	*OXYMURIATIC ACID* **SEE** CHLORINE
QD341.A2	OXYNAPHTHOIC ACID
F2230.2.08	OYANA INDIANS
PM6714	OYANA LANGUAGE
VM311.B8	*OYSTER DREDGERS* **SEE** BUGEYES (BOATS)
VM311.B8	*OYSTER FISHING BOATS* **SEE** BUGEYES (BOATS)
SB211.S	*OYSTER PLANT* **SEE** SALSIFY
SH365-371	OYSTER-CULTURE
SB945.09	OYSTER-SHELL SCALE
SH365-371	OYSTERS — DISEASES AND PESTS
QL430.7.09	OYSTERS / *zoology*
SH365-371	*OYSTERS, PEARL* **SEE** OYSTER-CULTURE

SH375-9	*OYSTERS, PEARL* **SEE** PEARL-FISHERIES
PM8707	OZ (ARTIFICIAL LANGUAGE)
RF431	OZAENA
TP695	OZOKERITE / *chemical technology*
TN857	OZOKERITE / *mineral industries*
QP913.O1	OZONE — PHYSIOLOGICAL EFFECT
RM666.O9	OZONE — THERAPEUTIC USE
QD181.O1	OZONE
TR433	*OZOTYPE* **SEE** PHOTOGRAPHY — PRINTING PROCESSES — — OZOTYPE
TL686.R42	*P-47 (FIGHTER PLANES)* **SEE** THUNDERBOLT (FIGHTER PLANES)
TL686.R42	*P-47 THUNDERBOLT* **SEE** THUNDERBOLT (FIGHTER PLANES)
TL685.3	*P-51 (FIGHTER PLANES)* **SEE** MUSTANG (FIGHTER PLANES)
ML1015-1018	P'I P'A
PM7073	*PACAGUARA DIALECT* **SEE** SIPIBO LANGUAGE
QL933	PACCHIONIAN BODIES / *comparative anatomy*
QM469	PACCHIONIAN BODIES / *human anatomy*
F1233	PACHUCA, BATTLE OF, 1861
QL737.U4-8	PACHYDERMATA
JX4494	*PACIFIC BLOCKADE* **SEE** BLOCKADE, PACIFIC
HE7731	*PACIFIC CABLE* **SEE** CABLES, SUBMARINE — PACIFIC / *economics*
TK5613	*PACIFIC CABLE* **SEE** CABLES, SUBMARINE — PACIFIC / *technology*
E83.84	PACIFIC COAST INDIANS, WARS WITH, 1847-1865
F851-2	*PACIFIC NORTHWEST* **SEE** NORTHWEST, PACIFIC
HE2763	PACIFIC RAILROADS — EARLY PROJECTS
F593	PACIFIC RAILROADS — EXPLORATIONS AND SURVEYS
A-Z	PACIFIC RAILROADS — FINANCE / *individual roads*
HE1062	PACIFIC RAILROADS — FINANCE / *individual roads*
HE2791	PACIFIC RAILROADS — FINANCE / *individual roads*
HE1063-4	PACIFIC RAILROADS — LAND GRANTS
HE2763	PACIFIC RAILROADS
HE2791	PACIFIC RAILROADS / *individual roads*
A-Z	PACIFIC RAILROADS / *individual roads*
HE1062	PACIFIC RAILROADS / *state aid*
DU29	*PACIFIC RELATIONS* **SEE** PAN-PACIFIC RELATIONS
F851	PACIFIC STATES
F591-3	PACIFIC WAGON ROADS
QL939	PACINIAN BODIES / *comparative anatomy*
QM575	PACINIAN BODIES / *histology*
QM471	PACINIAN BODIES / *human anatomy*
UC300-305	PACK TRANSPORTATION / *military*
Z716.1	*PACKAGE LIBRARIES* **SEE** LIBRARIES, PACKAGE
TJ1550	*PACKAGE-WRAPPING MACHINES* **SEE** WRAPPING MACHINES
NA8480	*PACKAGED BUILDINGS* **SEE** BUILDINGS, PREFABRICATED / *architecture*
TH1098	*PACKAGED BUILDINGS* **SEE** BUILDINGS, PREFABRICATED / *building*
TK4359.P2	PACKARD INCANDESCENT LAMP
TP159.P3	PACKED TOWERS
VK15-124	*PACKET-SHIPS* **SEE** PACKETS / *history*
VK15-124	PACKETS / *history*
TJ529	PACKING (MECHANICAL ENGINEERING)
QD466	PACKING FRACTIONS
TS1950-1975	*PACKING INDUSTRY* **SEE** MEAT INDUSTRY AND TRADE
HD9410-9441	*PACKING INDUSTRY* **SEE** MEAT INDUSTRY AND TRADE / *economics*
TS1970-1973	*PACKING INDUSTRY* **SEE** PACKING-HOUSES
HD9410-9429	PACKING-HOUSE PRODUCTS
TS1970-1973	PACKING-HOUSES
HE566.P3	PADDLE STEAMERS
GV1003	PADDLE TENNIS
HE566.P3	*PADDLE-WHEEL STEAMERS* **SEE** PADDLE STEAMERS
VM541	PADDLE-WHEELS
TJ267.B5	*PADDLES (HYDRAULIC MACHINERY)* **SEE** BLADES
HD4871-5	PADRONE SYSTEM
PA3118.P3	PAEAN / *greek literature*
F2270.2.P	*PAES INDIANS* **SEE** PAEZ INDIANS
F2270.2.P	PAEZ INDIANS
CB151	*PAGAN CIVILIZATION* **SEE** CIVILIZATION, PAGAN
M1523	PAGEANTS — VOCAL SCORES WITH ORGAN
M1523	PAGEANTS — VOCAL SCORES WITH PIANO
PN3203-3299	PAGEANTS
GT3980-4099	PAGEANTS / *manners and customs*
Z242.P	PAGINATION
F2891	PAGO LARGO, BATTLE OF, 1839
NA1540-1547	PAGODAS / *chinese*
E99.P2	*PAH-UTE INDIANS* **SEE** PAIUTE INDIANS
PK2591-2610	PAHARI LANGUAGES
PK6141-6181	PAHLAVI LANGUAGE
PK6190-6199	PAHLAVI LITERATURE
GN655.F3	*PAHOUIN* **SEE** FAN (AFRICAN PEOPLE) / *ethnology*
GN655.F3	*PAHUINS* **SEE** FAN (AFRICAN PEOPLE) / *ethnology*
HD5261	*PAID VACATIONS* **SEE** VACATIONS, EMPLOYEE
RC73	PAIN / *diagnostic value*
BJ1409	PAIN / *ethics*
RB112	PAIN / *pathology*
QP401	PAIN / *physiology*
BF515	PAIN / *psychology*
TP937	PAINT — CATALOGS
TP936.5	PAINT — TESTING
SF293.P5	*PAINT HORSE* **SEE** PINTO HORSE
HD9999.P15	PAINT INDUSTRY AND TRADE
TP937.5	PAINT MACHINERY
TT310	PAINT MIXING
HF6201.P35	PAINT SHOPS / *business*
TT300-305	PAINT SHOPS / *technology*
TP937.7	*PAINT THINNERS* **SEE** THINNER (PAINT MIXING)
TT273	*PAINT-SCREEN PROCESS* **SEE** SCREEN PROCESS PRINTING
TP934-7	PAINT / *manufacture*
TP936-7	PAINT, FIREPROOF
NK5300-5410	*PAINTED GLASS* **SEE** GLASS PAINTING AND STAINING
ND30-38	PAINTERS — DICTIONARIES
ND34-38	PAINTERS / *biography*
ND38	*PAINTERS, WOMEN* **SEE** ARTISTS, WOMEN
N43	*PAINTERS, WOMEN* **SEE** ARTISTS, WOMEN
N45	*PAINTERS' MARKS* **SEE** ARTISTS' MARKS
ND1130	PAINTING — EARLY WORKS TO 1800
ND1115-1120	PAINTING — STUDY AND TEACHING
N81-390	PAINTING — STUDY AND TEACHING
ND1259-1286	PAINTING — TECHNIQUE
N72	*PAINTING AND LITERATURE* **SEE** ART AND LITERATURE / *art*
PR149.A	*PAINTING AND LITERATURE* **SEE** ART AND LITERATURE / *english literature*
PT112	*PAINTING AND LITERATURE* **SEE** ART AND LITERATURE / *german literature*
PN53	*PAINTING AND LITERATURE* **SEE** ART AND LITERATURE / *literature*
ND2399	PAINTING BOOKS
ND	PAINTING
ND70-130	PAINTING, ANCIENT
NK	*PAINTING, DECORATIVE* **SEE** ART, DECORATIVE
NK1160-1590	*PAINTING, DECORATIVE* **SEE** DECORATION AND ORNAMENT
ND2550-2876	*PAINTING, DECORATIVE* **SEE** MURAL PAINTING AND DECORATION
ND2370	*PAINTING, FORE-EDGE* **SEE** FORE-EDGE PAINTING
HD7269.P19-2	PAINTING, INDUSTRIAL — SAFETY MEASURES
TT300-380	PAINTING, INDUSTRIAL
ND198	PAINTING, ISLAMIC
TT300-380	*PAINTING, MECHANICAL* **SEE** PAINTING, INDUSTRIAL
ND140-145	PAINTING, MEDIEVAL
ND198	*PAINTING, MUSLIM* **SEE** PAINTING, ISLAMIC
TT323	*PAINTING, PLASTIC* **SEE** TEXTURE PAINTING
BV150-168	*PAINTING, RELIGIOUS* **SEE** CHRISTIAN ART AND SYMBOLISM / *theology*
N7810-8185	*PAINTING, RELIGIOUS* **SEE** CHRISTIAN ART AND SYMBOLISM
ND170	PAINTING, RENAISSANCE
ND615	PAINTING, RENAISSANCE / *italian*
TT323	*PAINTING, TEXTURE* **SEE** TEXTURE PAINTING
N7460-7470	*PAINTING-ANECDOTES, FACETIAE, SATIRE, ETC.* **SEE** ART — ANECDOTES, FACETIAE, SATIRE, ETC.
ND1156	PAINTINGS — CARIACATURES AND CARTOONS
ND40-45	PAINTINGS — CATALOGS
ND1640-1650	PAINTINGS — CONSERVATION AND RESTORATION
N4402-5097	PAINTINGS — EXHIBITIONS
ND1140	PAINTINGS — EXPERTISING
ND46-48	PAINTINGS — PRICES

N5210-5297	PAINTINGS — PRIVATE COLLECTIONS
N6490	*PAINTINGS, ABSTRACT* **SEE** ART, ABSTRACT
ND198	PAINTINGS, ISLAMIC
ND140-145	PAINTINGS, MEDIEVAL
ND198	*PAINTINGS, MUSLIM* **SEE** PAINTINGS, ISLAMIC
N6490	*PAINTINGS, NON-OBJECTIVE* **SEE** ART, ABSTRACT
ND170	PAINTINGS, RENAISSANCE
NE1850-1879	*PAINTINGS-COLOR REPRODUCTIONS* **SEE** COLOR PRINTS
ND1640-1650	*PAINTINGS-PRESERVATION* **SEE** PAINTINGS — CONSERVATION AND RESTORATION
TP934-7	*PAINTS* **SEE** PAINT / *manufacture*
LB1064	*PAIRED ASSOCIATES* **SEE** PAIRED-ASSOCIATION LEARNING
LB1064	PAIRED-ASSOCIATION LEARNING
E99.P2	PAIUTE INDIANS
PM2094	PAIUTE LANGUAGE
DC113.5	*PAIX DES DAMES* **SEE** CAMBRAI, TREATY OF, 1529
SB351.C	*PAK-CHOI* **SEE** CHINESE CABBAGE
PM4158	PAKAWAN LANGUAGES
PK6701-6799	*PAKHTO LANGUAGE* **SEE** PUSHTO LANGUAGE
PK2903-2978	PAKISTAN LITERATURE
PK6701-6799	*PAKKHTO LANGUAGE* **SEE** PUSHTO LANGUAGE
PL6281	PALA LANGUAGE
NA7710-7786	PALACES
NA277	PALACES / *greek*
NA320	PALACES / *roman*
QE391.P3	PALACHEITE
PM2101	PALAIHNIHAN LANGUAGES
PM2101	*PALAIK LANGUAGES* **SEE** PALAIHNIHAN LANGUAGES
RD525	PALATE — SURGERY
RD662	PALATE — TUMORS
GN131	PALATE / *anthropology*
QL857	PALATE / *comparative anatomy*
QM306	PALATE / *human anatomy*
DD801.B5-51	PALATINATES / *bavaria*
JS3063	PALATINATES / *gt. brit.*
F184	PALATINATES / *maryland*
RD525	*PALATORRHAPHY* **SEE** PALATE — SURGERY
PL4411	PALAUNG LANGUAGE
DS560	PALAUNGS
F2230.2.P	*PALENCA INDIANS* **SEE** PALENQUE INDIANS
F2230.2.P	*PALENKE INDIANS* **SEE** PALENQUE INDIANS
F2230.2.P	PALENQUE INDIANS
GN700-875	*PALEOANTHROPOLOGY* **SEE** MAN, PREHISTORIC
PM1-95	*PALEOASIATIC LANGUAGES* **SEE** HYPERBOREAN LANGUAGES
GN673	*PALEOASIATICS* **SEE** ARCTIC RACES
QE916	PALEOBOTANY — CAMBRIAN
QE919	PALEOBOTANY — CARBONIFEROUS
QE908	PALEOBOTANY — CATALOGS AND COLLECTIONS
QE925-931	PALEOBOTANY — CENOZOIC
QE924	PALEOBOTANY — CRETACEOUS
QE918	PALEOBOTANY — DEVONIAN
QE927	PALEOBOTANY — EOCENE
QE915	PALEOBOTANY — HURONIAN
QE923	PALEOBOTANY — JURASSIC
QE921-4	PALEOBOTANY — MESOZOIC
QE929	PALEOBOTANY — MIOCENE
QE903	PALEOBOTANY — NOMENCLATORS
QE928	PALEOBOTANY — OLIGOCENE
QE915-924	PALEOBOTANY — PALEOZOIC
QE919	PALEOBOTANY — PENNSYLVANIAN
QE920	PALEOBOTANY — PERMIAN
QE907	PALEOBOTANY — PICTORIAL WORKS
QE931	PALEOBOTANY — PLEISTOCENE
QE930	PALEOBOTANY — PLIOCENE
QE931	PALEOBOTANY — QUATERNARY
QE922	PALEOBOTANY — RHAETIC
QE917	PALEOBOTANY — SILURIAN
QE926-930	PALEOBOTANY — TERTIARY
QE922	PALEOBOTANY — TRIASSIC
QE901-996	PALEOBOTANY
QE923	*PALEOBOTANY-LIASSIC* **SEE** PALEOBOTANY — JURASSIC
QE916	*PALEOBOTANY-PRIMORDIAL* **SEE** PALEOBOTANY — CAMBRIAN
QE924	*PALEOBOTANY-SENONIAN* **SEE** PALEOBOTANY — CRETACEOUS
QC884	PALEOCLIMATOLOGY
CC	*PALEOETHNOGRAPHY* **SEE** ARCHAEOLOGY
GT	*PALEOETHNOGRAPHY* **SEE** ARCHAEOLOGY / *manners and customs general*
DA-DU	*PALEOETHNOGRAPHY* **SEE** ARCHAEOLOGY / *national antiquities other than american*
E-F	*PALEOETHNOGRAPHY* **SEE** ARCHAEOLOGY / *n indian and other american antiquities*
GN	*PALEOETHNOGRAPHY* **SEE** ARCHAEOLOGY / *prehistoric antiquities*
GN700-875	*PALEOETHNOGRAPHY* **SEE** MAN, PREHISTORIC
QE501	PALEOGEOGRAPHY
Z113-115	PALEOGRAPHY — HANDBOOKS, TREATISES, ETC.
Z105-115	PALEOGRAPHY
ML174	PALEOGRAPHY, MUSICAL
GN775-6	*PALEOLITHIC PERIOD* **SEE** STONE AGE
QE707	PALEONTOLOGISTS
QE726	PALEONTOLOGY — CAMBRIAN
QE729	PALEONTOLOGY — CARBONIFEROUS
QE716	PALEONTOLOGY — CATALOGS AND COLLECTIONS
QE735-741	PALEONTOLOGY — CENOZOIC
QE718	PALEONTOLOGY — COLLECTING OF SPECIMENS
QE734	PALEONTOLOGY — CRETACEOUS
QE728	PALEONTOLOGY — DEVONIAN
QE709-710	PALEONTOLOGY — EARLY WORKS TO 1800
QE737	PALEONTOLOGY — EOCENE
QE733	PALEONTOLOGY — JURASSIC
QE731-4	PALEONTOLOGY — MESOZOIC
QE739	PALEONTOLOGY — MIOCENE
QE729	PALEONTOLOGY — MISSISSIPPIAN
QE739	PALEONTOLOGY — NEOCENE
QE738	PALEONTOLOGY — OLIGOCENE
QE727	PALEONTOLOGY — ORDOVICIAN
QE725-730	PALEONTOLOGY — PALEOZOIC
QE747.P4	PALEONTOLOGY — PENNSYLVANIAN
QE730	PALEONTOLOGY — PERMIAN
QE741	PALEONTOLOGY — PLEISTOCENE
QE740	PALEONTOLOGY — PLIOCENE
QE724-5	PALEONTOLOGY — PRE-CAMBRIAN
QE741	PALEONTOLOGY — QUATERNARY
QE732	PALEONTOLOGY — RHAETIC
QE727	PALEONTOLOGY — SILURIAN
QE736-740	PALEONTOLOGY — TERTIARY
QE732	PALEONTOLOGY — TRIASSIC
QE701-996	PALEONTOLOGY
QE901-996	*PALEONTOLOGY, BOTANICAL* **SEE** PALEOBOTANY
QE701-996	*PALEONTOLOGY, ZOOLOGICAL* **SEE** PALEONTOLOGY
QE727	*PALEONTOLOGY-GOTHLANDIAN* **SEE** PALEONTOLOGY — SILURIAN
QE733	*PALEONTOLOGY-LIASSIC* **SEE** PALEONTOLOGY — JURASSIC
QE727	*PALEONTOLOGY-LOWER SILURIAN* **SEE** PALEONTOLOGY — ORDOVICIAN
QE726	*PALEONTOLOGY-PRIMORDIAL* **SEE** PALEONTOLOGY — CAMBRIAN
QE727	*PALEONTOLOGY-SILURIAN, LOWER* **SEE** PALEONTOLOGY — ORDOVICIAN
R135	PALEOPATHOLOGY
PM1-95	*PALEOSIBERIAN LANGUAGES* **SEE** HYPERBOREAN LANGUAGES
GN673	*PALEOSIBERIANS* **SEE** ARCTIC RACES
QE654-674	*PALEOZOIC PERIOD* **SEE** GEOLOGY, STRATIGRAPHIC — PALEOZOIC
QE915-924	*PALEOZOIC PERIOD* **SEE** PALEOBOTANY — PALEOZOIC
QE725-730	*PALEOZOIC PERIOD* **SEE** PALEONTOLOGY — PALEOZOIC
QE701-996	*PALEOZOOLOGY* **SEE** PALEONTOLOGY
SB945.P	PALES WEEVIL
DS126	PALESTINE — HISTORY — — ARAB RIOTS, 1929
DS126	PALESTINE — HISTORY — — 1917-1948
DS125.5	PALESTINE — HISTORY — — 1917-1948
DS126	PALESTINE — HISTORY — — 1929-1948
BL1480	*PALI BUDDHISM* **SEE** HINAYANA BUDDHISM
PK1001-1095	PALI LANGUAGE
PK4541-4698	PALI LITERATURE / *collections*
PK4501-4535	PALI LITERATURE / *history*
PK1001-1095	PALI PHILOLOGY
PK4525-6	PALI POETRY / *history*
PK4563	PALI POETRY / *modern collections*
QD181.P4	PALLADIUM

DS416-419	PALLAVAS / antiquities
DS451	PALLAVAS / history of india
QK495.P17	PALM TREES SEE PALMS
TP684.P3	PALM-OIL / chemical technology
SB299.P3	PALM-OIL / palm culture
HD9490	PALM-OIL / trade
SB608.P	PALM-WEEVIL
TS913	PALMETTO BRAIDING SEE PALMETTO WEAVING
TS913	PALMETTO WEAVING
SB608.P	PALMETTO-WEEVIL
BF910-918	PALMISTRY — EARLY WORKS TO 1850
BF908-935	PALMISTRY
QD305.A2	PALMITIC ACID
QK495.P17	PALMS
QE891	PALMS, FOSSIL
PJ5229	PALMYRENE LANGUAGE
QL391.P9	PALOLO WORM
SF293.P	PALOMINO HORSE
E99.P	PALOOS INDIANS
RC685.P2	PALPITATION OF THE HEART SEE HEART — PALPITATION
RJ496.P2	PALSY SEE PARALYSIS / children's diseases
RJ301	PALSY SEE PARALYSIS / newborn infants
PK7075	PALULA LANGUAGE SEE PHALURA LANGUAGE
F1221.P	PAME INDIANS
PK6991.P3	PAMIR LANGUAGES
PM6751	PAMPA LANGUAGE
PL5991-4	PAMPANGA LANGUAGE
F2926	PAMPAS
F2230.2.P	PAMPEAN INDIANS
F2823.P	PAMPEAN INDIANS / argentine republic
GV1796.P	PAMPERRUQUE (DANCE)
Z691	PAMPHLETS / library science
GN655.F3	PAMUE SEE FAN (AFRICAN PEOPLE) / ethnology
PL8167.F3	PAMUE LANGUAGE SEE FAN LANGUAGE
E99.P23	PAMUNKEY INDIANS
BL820.P2	PAN (DEITY)
TL521	PAN AMERICAN AVIATION DAY
F1418	PAN AMERICAN DAY
BL1625.P3	PAN-BABYLONISM SEE PANBABYLONISM
DD119	PAN-GERMANISM SEE PANGERMANISM
DR476	PAN-ISLAMISM SEE PANISLAMISM / turkey
D448	PAN-LATINISM SEE PANLATINISM
DU29	PAN-PACIFIC RELATIONS
D377	PAN-SLAVISM SEE PANSLAVISM
D449	PAN-SLAVISM SEE PANSLAVISM
DS17	PAN-TURANIANISM
DS17	PAN-TURKISM SEE PAN-TURANIANISM
ML980	PAN'S PIPES SEE SYRINX (MUSICAL INSTRUMENT)
F1561-1577	PANAMA — HISTORY
F1566	PANAMA EXPEDITION, 1741
TC773	PANAMA EXPEDITION, 1875 / panama canal
F1566	PANAMA EXPEDITION, 1885
PQ7520-7529	PANAMAN LITERATURE
PN4989.P	PANAMAN PERIODICALS
PQ7526	PANAMAN POETRY / collections
PQ7522	PANAMAN POETRY / history
PM8709	PANAMANE (ARTIFICIAL LANGUAGE)
BL1625.P3	PANBABYLONISM
RC857	PANCREAS — DISEASES
QP195	PANCREAS — SECRETIONS
RD546	PANCREAS — SURGERY
QL866	PANCREAS / comparative anatomy
QM353	PANCREAS / human anatomy
RC857	PANCREAS-INFLAMMATION SEE PANCREATITIS
RX336.P2	PANCREAS — DISEASES — — HOMEOPATHIC TREATMENT
QP195	PANCREATIC JUICE SEE PANCREAS — SECRETIONS
RC857	PANCREATITIS
PZ10.3	PANDAS — LEGENDS AND STORIES / juvenile literature
QL795.P	PANDAS — LEGENDS AND STORIES / zoology
QL737.C2	PANDAS
ML980	PANDEAN PIPES SEE SYRINX (MUSICAL INSTRUMENT)
ML1015-1018	PANDUR SEE TAMBURA
TA492.P7	PANELS SEE PLATES (ENGINEERING)
PL6015	PANGASINAN LANGUAGE
QH431	PANGENESIS SEE HEREDITY / biology
HQ753	PANGENESIS SEE HEREDITY / eugenics
RJ91	PANGENESIS SEE HEREDITY / heredity and child culture
HV6121-5	PANGENESIS SEE HEREDITY / heredity and crime
BF418	PANGENESIS SEE HEREDITY / heredity and genius
BF341-6	PANGENESIS SEE HEREDITY / psychology
HM121	PANGENESIS SEE HEREDITY / sociology
QH471-489	PANGENESIS SEE REPRODUCTION
QP251-281	PANGENESIS SEE REPRODUCTION / animals
DD119	PANGERMANISM
GN655.F3	PANGWE SEE FAN (AFRICAN PEOPLE) / ethnology
GV409	PANGYMNASTIKON
E99.P3	PANI INDIANS SEE PAWNEE INDIANS
HB3711-3840	PANICS SEE DEPRESSIONS
DR476	PANISLAMISM / turkey
PK2631-9	PANJABI LANGUAGE
PK2261-2270	PANJABI LANGUAGE, WESTERN SEE LAHNDI LANGUAGE
PK2650-2659	PANJABI LITERATURE
PK2656	PANJABI POETRY / collections
PK2652	PANJABI POETRY / history
D448	PANLATINISM
PM6773	PANO LANGUAGE
PM6773	PANOAN LANGUAGES
F2230.2.P	PANOAN TRIBES
ND2880	PANORAMAS / painting
TR661	PANORAMIC PHOTOGRAPHY SEE PHOTOGRAPHY, PANORAMIC
SB413.P2	PANSIES
D377	PANSLAVISM
D449	PANSLAVISM
BF1561	PANTACLES SEE TALISMANS
GR600	PANTACLES SEE TALISMANS / folk-lore
NC1920	PANTAGRAPH SEE PANTOGRAPH
TT605	PANTALOONS SEE TROUSERS / tailoring
BL220	PANTHEISM / comparative religion
QL737.C2	PANTHERS
LC94.I6	PANTJA WARDHANA
NC1920	PANTOGRAPH
GN464	PANTOMIME / anthropology
PN1985	PANTOMIME / drama
ML3460	PANTOMIME / music
M33	PANTOMIMES WITH MUSIC — PIANO SCORES
M1523	PANTOMIMES WITH MUSIC — VOCAL SCORES WITH PIANO
M1523	PANTOMIMES WITH MUSIC ARRANGED FOR PIANO (2 PIANOS)
M1520-1526	PANTOMIMES WITH MUSIC
M1523	PANTOMIMES WITH MUSIC, SACRED — VOCAL SCORES WITH PIANO
M1520-1526	PANTOMIMES WITH MUSIC, SACRED
PN6120.P3-4	PANTOMIMES
DS17	PANTURANIANISM SEE PAN-TURANIANISM
DS17	PANTURKISM SEE PAN-TURANIANISM
GV1469.P2	PAOLA (GAME)
E241.P2	PAOLI MASSACRE, 1777
DS770-772	PAOTINGFU MASSACRE, 1900
PM4171	PAPABUCO LANGUAGE
BX950-960	PAPACY — HISTORY
BX950-960	PAPACY
DG798-9	PAPACY-HISTORY 1870-1929 SEE ROMAN QUESTION
E99.P25	PAPAGO INDIANS / arizona
PM4176	PAPAGO LANGUAGE
CJ2928.P3	PAPAL COINS SEE COINS, PAPAL
BX1805	PAPAL CONCLAVES SEE POPES — ELECTION
CR5547-5577	PAPAL DECORATIONS OF HONOR SEE DECORATIONS OF HONOR, PAPAL
BX860	PAPAL ENCYCLICALS SEE ENCYCLICALS, PAPAL / collections
UA749.5	PAPAL GUARDS
BX1908	PAPAL LEGATES SEE LEGATES, PAPAL
BX863	PAPAL LETTERS SEE LETTERS, PAPAL
CR5547-5577	PAPAL NOBILITY SEE NOBILITY, PAPAL / etc.
BX1908	PAPAL NUNCIOS SEE NUNCIOS, PAPAL
CR5547-5575	PAPAL ORDERS OF KNIGHTHOOD AND CHIVALRY SEE ORDERS OF KNIGHTHOOD AND CHIVALRY, PAPAL / papal states

BX961.P	*PAPAL PROTECTION* **SEE** PROTECTION, PAPAL
BX1939.R5	*PAPAL RESCRIPTS* **SEE** RESCRIPTS, PAPAL / *canon law*
BX1301	*PAPAL SCHISM* **SEE** SCHISM, THE GREAT WESTERN, 1378-1417
CR4480	*PAPAL TIARA* **SEE** TIARA, PAPAL
GT975	*PAPAL UNIFORMS* **SEE** UNIFORMS, PAPAL
SB379.P2	PAPAW
SB379.P2	*PAPAYA* **SEE** PAPAW
SB608.P	PAPAYA FRUIT-FLY
TS1220	PAPER — SAMPLE BOOKS
HF5716.S6	PAPER — TABLES / *business arithmetic*
Z247	PAPER — TABLES / *printing*
TS1109	PAPER — TESTING
BL619.P3	PAPER (IN RELIGION, FOLK-LORE, ETC.) / *religion*
TX833	PAPER BAG COOKERY
TS1200	PAPER BOX INDUSTRY
TS1200	PAPER BOX MACHINERY
HF5770	*PAPER BOXES* **SEE** CARTONS / *commerce*
TS1200	*PAPER BOXES* **SEE** CARTONS / *manufacture*
HD6247.N5	*PAPER CARRIERS* **SEE** NEWSPAPER CARRIERS
TS1109	PAPER COATINGS
TS1109	PAPER FINISHING
TT870	*PAPER FOLDING* **SEE** PAPER WORK / *decorative handiwork*
LB1542	*PAPER FOLDING* **SEE** PAPER WORK / *elementary education*
TT870	*PAPER FOLDING, JAPANESE* **SEE** ORIGAMI
HF5686.P2	PAPER MAKING AND TRADE — ACCOUNTING
TS1115	PAPER MAKING AND TRADE — TRADE-MARKS
TS1080-1251	PAPER MAKING AND TRADE / *manufacture*
HD9820-9839	PAPER MAKING AND TRADE / *trade*
TS1080-1251	*PAPER MANUFACTURES* **SEE** PAPER PRODUCTS
HG613	PAPER MONEY — HYGIENIC ASPECTS
HG348-353	PAPER MONEY
HG651-1490	PAPER MONEY / *other countries*
HG571-627	PAPER MONEY / *u.s.*
TS1080-1251	PAPER PRODUCTS
TS1260	PAPER RULING
NB1270.P3	PAPER SCULPTURE
TS1544.P	PAPER THREAD
TT870	PAPER WORK / *decorative handiwork*
LB1542	PAPER WORK / *elementary education*
TS1544.P	*PAPER YARN* **SEE** PAPER THREAD
Z1033.P3	*PAPER-BOUND EDITIONS* **SEE** BIBLIOGRAPHY — PAPERBACK EDITIONS
GV1063	*PAPER-CHASING* **SEE** HARE AND HOUNDS / *games*
TT870	*PAPER-CUTTING* **SEE** PAPER WORK / *decorative handiwork*
LB1542	*PAPER-CUTTING* **SEE** PAPER WORK / *elementary education*
TS1109	PAPER-CUTTING MACHINES
Z249	PAPER-CUTTING MACHINES / *printing*
TH8441	PAPER-HANGING
TS1109	PAPER-MAKING MACHINERY
NK5440.P3	*PAPER-WEIGHTS* **SEE** PAPERWEIGHTS
TS1080-1260	PAPER / *manufacture*
Z237	PAPER / *printing*
Z247	PAPER / *printing*
TS1109	PAPER, MAIZE
TS1109	*PAPER, WASTE* **SEE** WASTE PAPER
TS1109	*PAPER-DURABILITY* **SEE** PAPER — TESTING
TS1109	*PAPER-FINISHING* **SEE** PAPER FINISHING
TS1109	*PAPER-PERMANENCE* **SEE** PAPER — TESTING
Z1033.P3	*PAPERBACKS* **SEE** BIBLIOGRAPHY — PAPERBACK EDITIONS
Z1033.P3	*PAPERBOUND EDITIONS* **SEE** BIBLIOGRAPHY — PAPERBACK EDITIONS
NK5440.P3	PAPERWEIGHTS
TS1155	PAPIER-MACHE / *manufacture*
PL6601-6621	PAPUAN LANGUAGES
GN664.P2	PAPUANS / *anthropology*
DU740	PAPUANS / *history*
PJ1501-1921	*PAPYRI, EGYPTIAN* **SEE** EGYPTIAN LANGUAGE — PAPYRI
TS1125	*PAPYRI, EGYPTIAN* **SEE** PAPYRUS (THE PLANT) / *manufactures*
Z112	*PAPYRI, EGYPTIAN* **SEE** PAPYRUS (THE PLANT) / *paleography*

TS1125	PAPYRUS (THE PLANT) / *manufactures*
Z112	PAPYRUS (THE PLANT) / *paleography*
SB401	*PARA NUT* **SEE** BRAZIL NUT
SB291.H	*PARA RUBBER* **SEE** HEVEA
QP47	PARABIOSIS
QL971	PARABLAST
BT373-8	PARABLES
BS680.P3	*PARABLES, BIBLICAL* **SEE** BIBLE — PARABLES
BT373-8	*PARABLES, BIBLICAL* **SEE** JESUS CHRIST — PARABLES
BS680.P3	*PARABLES, CHRISTIAN* **SEE** BIBLE — PARABLES
BT373-8	*PARABLES, CHRISTIAN* **SEE** JESUS CHRIST — PARABLES
BL1215.P3	PARABLES, HINDU
QA559	PARABOLA / *analytical geometry*
QA485	PARABOLA / *plane geometry*
PN228.M4	*PARABOLE* **SEE** METAPHOR
PN227	*PARABOLE* **SEE** SIMILE
PN228.S5	*PARABOLE* **SEE** SIMILE
PN6084.S5	*PARABOLE* **SEE** SIMILE / *collections*
QA561	PARABOLOID
QD431	PARACASEIN / *chemistry*
SF271	PARACASEIN / *dairying*
TL750-755	*PARACHUTE JUMPING* **SEE** PARACHUTING
GV770	*PARACHUTE JUMPING* **SEE** PARACHUTING / *sport*
TL753	*PARACHUTE RIGGING* **SEE** PARACHUTES — RIGGING
UG630-635	PARACHUTE TROOPS
TL753	PARACHUTES — RIGGING
TL750-758	PARACHUTES
TL750-755	PARACHUTING
GV770	PARACHUTING / *sport*
UG630-635	*PARACHUTISTS* **SEE** PARACHUTE TROOPS
BT120-123	*PARACLETE* **SEE** HOLY SPIRIT
RC203.L9	*PARADENOLYMPHITIS* **SEE** LYMPHOGRANULOMA VENEREUM
GT3980-4099	*PARADES* **SEE** PROCESSIONS
BP166.87	PARADISE (ISLAM)
QL696.P2	*PARADISE BIRDS* **SEE** BIRDS OF PARADISE
QL78	*PARADISE-FISH* **SEE** FISH-OF-PARADISE / *aquariums*
BT844-9	PARADISE
PN228.P2	PARADOX / *literature*
BC199.P2	PARADOX / *logic*
PN6361	PARADOXES / *collections*
QD305.H6	PARAFFINS
F2661-2699	PARAGUAY — HISTORY
PQ8250-8259	PARAGUAYAN LITERATURE
PN5076-5080	PARAGUAYAN PERIODICALS
PQ8256	PARAGUAYAN POETRY / *collections*
PQ8252	PARAGUAYAN POETRY / *history*
F2687	PARAGUAYAN WAR, 1865-1870
QL696.P7	*PARAKEET* **SEE** PARROTS
SF473.P25	*PARAKEET* **SEE** PARROTS / *care and breeding*
QB583	PARALLAX — MOON
QB813	PARALLAX — STARS
QB167	PARALLAX — STARS / *correction of observations*
QB508-518	PARALLAX — SUN
QB159	PARALLAX
QA681-5	PARALLELS (GEOMETRY)
QA481	PARALLELS (GEOMETRY)
RJ496.P2	PARALYSIS / *children's diseases*
RJ301	PARALYSIS / *newborn infants*
RC180-181	*PARALYSIS, ANTERIOR SPINAL* **SEE** POLIOMYELITIS
RC388	*PARALYSIS, CEREBRAL* **SEE** CEREBRAL PALSY
RC418	PARALYSIS, FACIAL
RC180-181	*PARALYSIS, INFANTILE* **SEE** POLIOMYELITIS
TK7872.A5	PARAMETRIC AMPLIFIERS
BF376	*PARAMNESIA* **SEE** MEMORY, DISORDERS OF
F2380.1.P	*PARAMONA INDIANS* **SEE** PATAMONA INDIANS / *british guiana*
F2230.2.P	*PARAMONA INDIANS* **SEE** PATAMONA INDIANS / *south america*
F2380.1.P	*PARAMUNI INDIANS* **SEE** PATAMONA INDIANS / *british guiana*
F2230.2.P	*PARAMUNI INDIANS* **SEE** PATAMONA INDIANS / *south america*
SB945.P3	PARANDRA BORER
RC520	PARANOIA
BF1001-1389	*PARAPSYCHOLOGY* **SEE** PSYCHICAL RESEARCH
QL757	PARASITES / *animal*

QK918	PARASITES / *plant*
SF810	PARASITES / *veterinary medicine*
HV33	*PARASITES, SOCIAL* SEE PARASITISM (SOCIAL SCIENCES)
RC226-248	*PARASITES-BLOOD* SEE BLOOD — PARASITES / *parasitic diseases*
QR251	*PARASITES-BLOOD* SEE BLOOD — PARASITES / *pathogenic protozoa*
SB611-615	PARASITIC PLANTS
HV33	PARASITISM (SOCIAL SCIENCES)
QL757	PARASITISM
GT2210	*PARASOLS* SEE UMBRELLAS AND PARASOLS
RC655	PARATHYROID GLANDS — DISEASES
RD599	PARATHYROID GLANDS — SURGERY
QP187	PARATHYROID GLANDS / *physiology*
UG630-635	*PARATROOPS* SEE PARACHUTE TROOPS
SF810.J6	*PARATUBERCULOSIS OF CATTLE* SEE JOHNE'S DISEASE
SF810.J6	*PARATUBERCULOUS ENTERITIS* SEE JOHNE'S DISEASE
RC168.P2	PARATYPHOID FEVER
D581	PARAVANES / *european war*
RD85.P	PARAVERTEBRAL ANESTHESIA
PK2595-9	*PARBATE LANGUAGE* SEE NEPALI LANGUAGE
PK2595-9	*PARBATIYA LANGUAGE* SEE NEPALI LANGUAGE
HE6171-3	PARCELS-POST
HE6471-3	PARCELS-POST / *u.s.*
Z112	PARCHMENT
QL737.C2	*PARDOFELIS MARMORATA* SEE MARBLED CAT
HV8692	PARDON / *penology*
PM6818	PARENTINTIM LANGUAGE
LC225	*PARENTS AND TEACHERS* SEE HOME AND SCHOOL
LC230-235	PARENTS' AND TEACHERS' ASSOCIATIONS
RJ496.P2	*PARESIS* SEE PARALYSIS / *children's diseases*
RJ301	*PARESIS* SEE PARALYSIS / *newborn infants*
TH8120-8137	*PARGETTING* SEE PLASTERING
F2520.1.M	*PARI INDIANS* SEE MUNDURUCU INDIANS
PM6596	*PARI LANGUAGE* SEE MUNDURUCU LANGUAGE
DS432.P25	PARIAHS
QL949	*PARIETAL EYE* SEE EYE, PARIETAL
PM6818	*PARINTINTIN LANGUAGE* SEE PARENTINTIM LANGUAGE
DC701-790	PARIS — HISTORY
DC737	PARIS — RIOT, 1934
DC122.3	PARIS — SIEGE, 1590
DC311-315	PARIS — SIEGE, 1870-1871
SB951	PARIS GREEN
JX1367	PARIS, DECLARATION OF, 1856
S643	*PARIS, PLASTER OF* SEE PLASTER OF PARIS / *fertilizers*
TN946	*PARIS, PLASTER OF* SEE PLASTER OF PARIS / *mineral industries*
TP888	*PARIS, PLASTER OF* SEE PLASTER OF PARIS / *technology*
DC91.3	PARIS, TREATY OF, 1259
D283.5	PARIS, TREATY OF, 1718
D297	PARIS, TREATY OF, 1763
E249	PARIS, TREATY OF, 1778
E249	PARIS, TREATY OF, 1783
E333	PARIS, TREATY OF, 1803
DC238.5	PARIS, TREATY OF, 1814
DC240	PARIS, TREATY OF, 1815
DK215	PARIS, TREATY OF, 1856
E723	PARIS, TREATY OF, 1898
BX5969	PARISH MISSIONS — ANGLICAN COMMUNION / *protestant episcopal*
BX2375	PARISH MISSIONS
BX2375	*PARISH MISSIONS-CATHOLIC CHURCH* SEE PARISH MISSIONS
HA38-39	*PARISH REGISTERS* SEE REGISTERS OF BIRTHS, ETC.
LC427-629	*PARISH SCHOOLS* SEE CHURCH SCHOOLS
BX1939.P	PARISHES (CANON LAW)
BV638.4	*PARISHES, LARGER* SEE LARGER PARISHES
PL4741	PARJI LANGUAGE
SB481	*PARK ADMINISTRATION* SEE PARKS — MANAGEMENT
SB481	*PARK MANAGEMENT* SEE PARKS — MANAGEMENT
TN785	PARKES PROCESS
GV1295.P2	PARKET (GAME)
TL154	*PARKING, AUTOMOBILE* SEE AUTOMOBILE PARKING

LB3253	*PARKING, CAMPUS* SEE CAMPUS PARKING
SB481	PARKS — MANAGEMENT
SB481-5	PARKS
JF331-341	*PARLIAMENTARY GOVERNMENT* SEE CABINET SYSTEM
JK-JQ	*PARLIAMENTARY GOVERNMENT* SEE REPRESENTATIVE GOVERNMENT AND REPRESENTATION / *local*
JF1051-1075	*PARLIAMENTARY GOVERNMENT* SEE REPRESENTATIVE GOVERNMENT AND REPRESENTATION
JF501-540	*PARLIAMENTARY LAW* SEE PARLIAMENTARY PRACTICE
JK1091-1128	*PARLIAMENTARY LAW* SEE PARLIAMENTARY PRACTICE / *u.s. congress*
JF501-540	PARLIAMENTARY PRACTICE
JK1091-1128	PARLIAMENTARY PRACTICE / *u.s. congress*
JF501-637	*PARLIAMENTS* SEE LEGISLATIVE BODIES
GV1017.P2	PARLOR FOOTBALL
TT197.5.L5	*PARLOR FURNITURE* SEE LIVING ROOM FURNITURE / *cabinet work*
NK2117	*PARLOR FURNITURE* SEE LIVING ROOM FURNITURE / *interior decoration*
TS880	*PARLOR FURNITURE* SEE LIVING ROOM FURNITURE / *manufacture*
GV1017.P28	PARLOR TENNIS
PQ437-9	PARNASSIENS
BX2375	*PAROCHIAL MISSIONS* SEE PARISH MISSIONS
LC427-629	*PAROCHIAL SCHOOLS* SEE CHURCH SCHOOLS
PN6110.P3	PARODIES
PN6149.P3	PARODY
HV9278	PAROLE
QL881	PAROOPHOREN / *comparative anatomy*
QM421	PAROOPHOREN / *human anatomy*
QL865	*PAROTID DUCT* SEE PAROTID GLANDS / *comparative anatomy*
QM325	*PAROTID DUCT* SEE PAROTID GLANDS / *human anatomy*
QP191	*PAROTID DUCT* SEE PAROTID GLANDS / *physiology*
RD527.P3	PAROTID GLANDS — EXCISION
RD661	PAROTID GLANDS — TUMORS
QL865	PAROTID GLANDS / *comparative anatomy*
QM325	PAROTID GLANDS / *human anatomy*
QP191	PAROTID GLANDS / *physiology*
RC168.M8	*PAROTITIS* SEE MUMPS
B187.P	PAROUSIA (PHILOSOPHY)
RC280.O8	PAROVARIUM — TUMORS
QL881	PAROVARIUM / *comparative anatomy*
QM421	PAROVARIUM / *human anatomy*
NA2970	PARQUET FLOORS
QL696.P7	*PARRAKEET* SEE PARROTS
SF473.P25	*PARRAKEET* SEE PARROTS / *care and breeding*
K	PARRICIDE
HV6542	PARRICIDE
RC182.P8	*PARROT FEVER* SEE PSITTACOSIS
QL696.P7	PARROTS
SF473.P25	PARROTS / *care and breeding*
DS432.P3	PARSEES / *history*
BL1500-1590	PARSEES / *religion*
PK6141-6181	*PARSI LANGUAGE* SEE PAHLAVI LANGUAGE
DS432.P3	*PARSIS* SEE PARSEES / *history*
BL1500-1590	*PARSIS* SEE PARSEES / *religion*
SB608.P	PARSLEY STALK WEEVIL
SB608.P	PARSNIP LEAF-MINER
SB211.P	PARSNIPS
BV4381	PARSONAGES
LB2844.1	*PART-TIME TEACHERS* SEE TEACHERS, PART-TIME
F2380.1.P	*PARTAMONA INDIANS* SEE PATAMONA INDIANS / *british guiana*
F2230.2.P	*PARTAMONA INDIANS* SEE PATAMONA INDIANS / *south america*
QH487	PARTHENOGENESIS (ANIMALS)
QH487	PARTHENOGENESIS (PLANTS)
PK6185.P3	PARTHIAN LANGUAGE
DG294	PARTHIAN WAR, 113-117
QA374-7	*PARTIAL DIFFERENTIAL EQUATIONS* SEE DIFFERENTIAL EQUATIONS, PARTIAL
QC786	PARTICLE ACCELERATORS

PQ471.P3	PASTOURELLE / french literature
ML2527.P	PASTOURELLE / french music
TX773	PASTRY
SB199	PASTURES / agriculture
HD1635-1641	PASTURES / economics
PM7183	PATAGONIAN LANGUAGE SEE TZONECA LANGUAGE
F2936	PATAGONIANS
F2380.1.P	PATAMONA INDIANS / british guiana
F2230.2.P	PATAMONA INDIANS / south america
DG657.3	PATARIA SEE PATARINES
DG657.3	PATARINES
E99.P	PATAWOMEKE INDIANS SEE POTOMAC INDIANS
NK9100-9199	PATCHWORK
QL821	PATELLA / comparative anatomy
QM117	PATELLA / human anatomy
QP372	PATELLA / reflexes
QK898.P2	PATELLARIC ACID
T215-323	PATENT LAWS AND LEGISLATION
RM671	PATENT MEDICINES SEE MEDICINES, PATENT, PROPRIETARY, ETC.
T324	PATENT MODELS SEE MODELS (PATENTS)
T201-339	PATENTS
T215-323	PATENTS-LAWS AND LEGISLATION SEE PATENT LAWS AND LEGISLATION
DG657.3	PATERINI SEE PATARINES
DS72	PATESIS
QR175-241	PATHOGENIC BACTERIA SEE BACTERIA, PATHOGENIC
QR145	PATHOGENIC FUNGI SEE FUNGI, PATHOGENIC
QR175-351	PATHOGENIC MICRO-ORGANISMS SEE MICRO-ORGANISMS, PATHOGENIC
QR251	PATHOGENIC PROTOZOA SEE PROTOZOA, PATHOGENIC
BF585-593	PATHOGNOMY
RB24-57	PATHOLOGICAL ANATOMY SEE ANATOMY, PATHOLOGICAL
SB599-791	PATHOLOGICAL BOTANY SEE PLANT DISEASES
RS402-431	PATHOLOGICAL CHEMISTRY SEE CHEMISTRY, MEDICAL AND PHARMACEUTICAL
QP501-801	PATHOLOGICAL CHEMISTRY SEE PHYSIOLOGICAL CHEMISTRY
RB24-35	PATHOLOGICAL HISTOLOGY SEE HISTOLOGY, PATHOLOGICAL
RB37	PATHOLOGICAL LABORATORIES / methods
R871-891	PATHOLOGICAL MUSEUMS
RB113	PATHOLOGICAL PHYSIOLOGY SEE PHYSIOLOGY, PATHOLOGICAL
BF173	PATHOLOGICAL PSYCHOLOGY SEE PSYCHOLOGY, PATHOLOGICAL
R153-684	PATHOLOGISTS
RB24	PATHOLOGY — EARLY WORKS TO 1800
RB119	PATHOLOGY — EXAMINATIONS, QUESTIONS, ETC.
RB37	PATHOLOGY — LABORATORY MANUALS
RB	PATHOLOGY
RB25	PATHOLOGY, CELLULAR
RB114	PATHOLOGY, COMPARATIVE
RK301-450	PATHOLOGY, DENTAL SEE TEETH — DISEASES
RB125	PATHOLOGY, EXPERIMENTAL
RA791-954	PATHOLOGY, GEOGRAPHIC SEE MEDICAL GEOGRAPHY
RD57	PATHOLOGY, SURGICAL
SB599-791	PATHOLOGY, VEGETABLE SEE PLANT DISEASES
SF769	PATHOLOGY, VETERINARY SEE VETERINARY PATHOLOGY
GV1261	PATIENCE (GAME) SEE SOLITAIRE (GAME)
BJ1533.P3	PATIENCE
R727.3	PATIENT AND PHYSICIAN SEE PHYSICIAN AND PATIENT
HV688-694	PATIENTS SEE SICK / aid for
NA8375	PATIOS
F2380.1.P	PATOMANA INDIANS SEE PATAMONA INDIANS / british guiana
F2230.2.P	PATOMANA INDIANS SEE PATAMONA INDIANS / south america
PL6281	PATPATAR LANGUAGE SEE PALA LANGUAGE
DG83.3	PATRES (ROME) SEE PATRICIANS (ROME)
PA2350.P	PATRIA (THE WORD) / semantics
BS573	PATRIARCHS (BIBLE)
BX400-440	PATRIARCHS AND PATRIARCHATE
HQ	PATRIARCHY SEE FAMILY
GT2420	PATRIARCHY SEE FAMILY / manners and customs
GN478-486	PATRIARCHY SEE FAMILY / primitive
DG83.3	PATRICIANS (ROME)
HV6542	PATRICIDE SEE PARRICIDE
K	PATRICIDE SEE PARRICIDE
PN1080	PATRIOTIC POETRY
E172.7	PATRIOTIC SOCIETIES — INSIGNIA / u.s.
HS2301-2460	PATRIOTIC SOCIETIES
E202	PATRIOTIC SOCIETIES / american revolution
E172.7	PATRIOTIC SOCIETIES / u.s.
JC329	PATRIOTISM
JK1758-9	PATRIOTISM / u.s.
E231	PATRIOTS' DAY
BR1705	PATRISTICS SEE FATHERS OF THE CHURCH / collective biography
BR60-67	PATRISTICS SEE FATHERS OF THE CHURCH / patrology
U190-195	PATROLS SEE GUARD DUTY
BX4656.5	PATRON SAINTS
N8410	PATRONAGE OF ART SEE ART PATRONAGE
N8750	PATRONAGE OF ART SEE STATE ENCOURAGEMENT OF SCIENCE, LITERATURE, AND ART / art
JC518-519	PATRONAGE OF ART SEE STATE ENCOURAGEMENT OF SCIENCE, LITERATURE, AND ART / political science
Q181	PATRONAGE OF ART SEE STATE ENCOURAGEMENT OF SCIENCE, LITERATURE, AND ART / science
BX1939.P3	PATRONAGE, ECCLESIASTICAL (CANON LAW)
HD1485.P2-55	PATRONS OF HUSBANDRY
TS240	PATTERN-MAKING MACHINERY
TS240	PATTERN-MAKING
TT753-5	PATTERNS FOR EMBROIDERY SEE EMBROIDERY — PATTERNS
TT770-773	PATTERNS FOR EMBROIDERY SEE EMBROIDERY — PATTERNS
TT753	PATTERNS FOR NEEDLEWORK SEE NEEDLEWORK — PATTERNS
E99.P29	PATWIN INDIANS
DR27.P4	PATZINAKS SEE PETCHENEGS
F2520.1.P45	PAUISHANA INDIANS
F2520.1.P45	PAUISIANA SEE PAUISHANA INDIANS
F2520.1.P45	PAUIXANA SEE PAUISHANA INDIANS
BT1445	PAULICIANS
HQ1024	PAULINE PRIVILEGE SEE DIVORCE (CANON LAW)
BX2960.B6	PAULINES SEE BARNABITES
E241.P24	PAULUS HOOK, BATTLE OF, 1779
PL6535	PAUMOTU LANGUAGE SEE TUAMOTUAN LANGUAGE
HV1-527	PAUPERISM SEE POOR / charities
HV4023-4470	PAUPERISM SEE POOR / poor in cities
QL449	PAUROPODA
GV1796.P3	PAVAN
M1248	PAVANS (BAND)
M1264	PAVANS (BAND)
M125-9	PAVANS (GUITAR)
M1048	PAVANS (ORCHESTRA)
M1160	PAVANS (STRING ORCHESTRA)
M1145	PAVANS (STRING ORCHESTRA)
M221-3	PAVANS (VIOLIN AND PIANO)
M217-218	PAVANS (VIOLIN AND PIANO)
TE252	PAVEMENTS — CONTRACTS AND SPECIFICATIONS
TE250-278	PAVEMENTS
TE270-276	PAVEMENTS, ASPHALT
TE270	PAVEMENTS, BITUMINOUS
TE255	PAVEMENTS, BRICK
TE278	PAVEMENTS, CONCRETE
NA3750-3850	PAVEMENTS, MOSAIC
TE253	PAVEMENTS, NICOLSON SEE PAVEMENTS, WOODEN
NA3705	PAVEMENTS, TILE
TE253	PAVEMENTS, WOODEN
DG541	PAVIA, BATTLE OF, 1525
NA8450	PAVILIONS
TE250-278	PAVING SEE PAVEMENTS
F2846	PAVON, BATTLE OF, 1861
HF5686.P23	PAWNBROKING — ACCOUNTING
HG2071-2106	PAWNBROKING
HD234.P3	PAWNEE INDIANS — LAND TRANSFERS
E99.P3	PAWNEE INDIANS — LAND TRANSFERS
E99.P3	PAWNEE INDIANS
PM2137	PAWNEE LANGUAGE
HG2071-2106	PAWNSHOPS SEE PAWNBROKING
SB379.P2	PAWPAW SEE PAPAW
E99.W	PAWTUCKET INDIANS SEE WAMESIT INDIANS

F89.P9	PAWTUXET PURCHASE, RHODE ISLAND
BV196.P3	PAX (OSCULATORY)
F152	*PAXTANG RANGERS* **SEE** PAXTON BOYS
F152	PAXTON BOYS
F1465.2.P	PAYA INDIANS
F2823.P	PAYAGUA INDIANS
F2791.P34	PAYSANDU, URUGUAY (CITY) — SIEGE, 1864-1865
PK6141-6181	*PAZEND* **SEE** PAHLAVI LANGUAGE
SB343	*PEA* **SEE** PEAS
E473.17	PEA RIDGE, BATTLE OF, 1862
SB608.P25	PEA-APHIS
SB608.P25	PEA-LOUSE
SB608.P25	PEA-WEEVIL
BR115.P4	PEACE — BIBLICAL ARGUMENTS / *christianity*
BS2545.P4	PEACE — BIBLICAL ARGUMENTS / *new testament*
M1977.P4	PEACE — SONGS AND MUSIC
M1977.P4	PEACE — SONGS AND MUSIC
BR115.P4	PEACE (THEOLOGY)
JX1965	*PEACE AND WOMEN* **SEE** WOMEN AND PEACE
JX1936.5	PEACE DAY
BV4908.5	PEACE OF MIND
BF637.P3	PEACE OF MIND / *applied psychology*
JX1906-8	PEACE SOCIETIES
JX5181	PEACE TREATIES
JX1901-1991	PEACE / *international law*
BV283.P4	*PEACE, PRAYERS FOR* **SEE** PRAYERS FOR PEACE
SB608.P3	PEACH — DISEASES AND PESTS
SB945.P	PEACH-TREE BORER
SB371	PEACH
E476.7	PEACHTREE CREEK, GA., BATTLE OF, 1864
SF513	*PEACOCKS* **SEE** PEAFOWL
SF513	PEAFOWL
SB351.P3	PEANUTS
SB608.P4	PEAR — DISEASES AND PESTS
SB373	PEAR — STORAGE
PL4351.P4	PEAR LANGUAGE
SB373	PEAR
HD9969.B9	PEARL BUTTON INDUSTRY
HD9678.P	PEARL INDUSTRY AND TRADE
BT378.P	PEARL OF GREAT PRICE (PARABLE)
SH375-9	PEARL-FISHERIES
NK7680	PEARLS / *decoration and ornament*
TS755.P3	PEARLS / *manufacture*
SB373	*PEARS* **SEE** PEAR
G742	PEARY AUXILIARY EXPEDITION OF 1894
G742	PEARY RELIEF EXPEDITION OF 1892
SB343	PEAS
NK	*PEASANT ART* **SEE** ART INDUSTRIES AND TRADE
N9201-9211	*PEASANT ART* **SEE** FOLK ART
NK801-1094	*PEASANT ART* **SEE** FOLK ART
BV4596.P4	PEASANTRY — RELIGIOUS LIFE
GT1850-1875	PEASANTRY / *costumes*
GT5650-5680	PEASANTRY / *customs*
HD1521-1539	PEASANTRY / *economics*
HD1513	PEASANTRY / *peasant proprietors*
GT1850-1875	*PEASANTS* **SEE** PEASANTRY / *costumes*
GT5650-5680	*PEASANTS* **SEE** PEASANTRY / *customs*
HD1521-1539	*PEASANTS* **SEE** PEASANTRY / *economics*
HD1513	*PEASANTS* **SEE** PEASANTRY / *peasant proprietors*
N8235	PEASANTS IN ART
PN56.P	PEASANTS IN LITERATURE
PT747.P4	PEASANTS IN LITERATURE / *german fiction*
PT151.P4	PEASANTS IN LITERATURE / *german literature*
DA235	*PEASANTS' REVOLT, 1381* **SEE** TYLER'S INSURRECTION, 1381
DD174.4	*PEASANTS' WAR, 1493-1517* **SEE** BUNDSCHUH INSURRECTIONS, 1493-1517
DD181-3	PEASANTS' WAR, 1524-1525
DH631	*PEASANTS' WAR, 1798 (BELGIUM)* **SEE** BELGIUM — HISTORY — — PEASANTS' WAR, 1798
S598	PEAT-BOGS / *agriculture*
QK938.M3	PEAT-BOGS / *ecology*
GB621-8	PEAT-BOGS / *physical geography*
HD9559.P4	PEAT / *industry*
TN837-840	PEAT / *production*
TP340	PEAT / *use*
SB608.P45	PECAN CIGAR CASE-BEARER
SB608.P45	PECAN ROSETTE
SB401	PECAN
E83.83	PECATONICA RIVER, BATTLE OF, 1832

QL737.U5	PECCARIES
QE882.U3	PECCARIES, FOSSIL
DR27.P4	*PECHENEQUES* **SEE** PETCHENEGS
Z110.P4	PECIA
QK898.P4	PECTIN / *botany*
TP248.P4	PECTIN / *chemical technology*
TX612.J4	PECTIN / *jelly making*
QP601	PECTINASE
QL430.4	PECTINIBRANCHIATA
QL821	*PECTORAL GIRDLE* **SEE** SHOULDER GIRDLE / *comparative anatomy*
QM101	*PECTORAL GIRDLE* **SEE** SHOULDER GIRDLE / *human anatomy*
Z675.P3	PEDAGOGICAL LIBRARIES
L	*PEDAGOGY* **SEE** EDUCATION
LB	*PEDAGOGY* **SEE** TEACHING
LB1775-1785	*PEDAGOGY* **SEE** TEACHING / *teaching as a profession*
MT59	*PEDAL POINT* **SEE** ORGAN-POINT
BF839.5.P	PEDANTRY / *characterology*
HF5458-9	PEDDLERS AND PEDDLING
RD139	PEDIATRIC ANESTHESIA
RK55.C5	*PEDIATRIC DENTISTRY* **SEE** PEDODONTIA
RJ466	PEDIATRIC GYNECOLOGY
RJ499	*PEDIATRIC PSYCHIATRY* **SEE** CHILD PSYCHIATRY
RJ50	PEDIATRIC RADIOLOGY
RD137	*PEDIATRIC SURGERY* **SEE** CHILDREN — SURGERY
RJ42-43	PEDIATRICIANS — CORRESPONDENCE, REMINISCENCES, ETC.
RJ44	PEDIATRICS — EARLY WORKS TO 1800
RJ80	PEDIATRICS — STUDY AND TEACHING
HD8039.R5	PEDICAB DRIVERS
CS	*PEDIGREES* **SEE** GENEALOGY
JC345	*PEDIGREES* **SEE** HERALDRY / *national theory*
CR	*PEDIGREES* **SEE** HERALDRY / *national*
NA2920	PEDIMENTS
QL458.P3	PEDIPALPI
RK55.C5	PEDODONTIA
QP251	PEDOGENESIS
LB1101-1139	*PEDOLOGY (CHILD STUDY)* **SEE** CHILD STUDY
HQ771-785	*PEDOLOGY (CHILD STUDY)* **SEE** CHILD STUDY / *child in the family*
HQ781-5	*PEDOLOGY (CHILD STUDY)* **SEE** CHILD STUDY / *child life*
BF721	*PEDOLOGY (CHILD STUDY)* **SEE** CHILD STUDY / *child psychology*
GN63	*PEDOLOGY (CHILD STUDY)* **SEE** CHILD STUDY / *somatology*
HQ750-789	*PEDOLOGY (CHILD STUDY)* **SEE** CHILDREN
GV1295.P3	PEDRO (GAME)
TS213	*PEENING* **SEE** SHOT PEENING
HT647	PEERAGE
CS421-3	PEERAGE / *gt. brit.*
QL696.L7	*PEEWITS* **SEE** LAPWINGS
QA76.8.P4	*PEGASUS (COMPUTER)* **SEE** PEGASUS COMPUTER
QA76.8.P4	PEGASUS COMPUTER
QE461	PEGMATITES
PL4331-9	*PEGUAN LANGUAGE* **SEE** MON LANGUAGE
F2823.P	*PEGUENCHE INDIANS* **SEE** PEHUENCHE INDIANS / *argentine republic*
F2230.2.P	*PEGUENCHE INDIANS* **SEE** PEHUENCHE INDIANS / *south american indians*
F2823.P	PEHUENCHE INDIANS / *argentine republic*
F2230.2.P	PEHUENCHE INDIANS / *south american indians*
PM6876	PEHUENCHE LANGUAGE
E99.P58	*PEIGAN INDIANS* **SEE** PIEGAN INDIANS
SF429.P3	*PEKINESE SPANIELS* **SEE** PEKINGESE SPANIELS
DS770-772	PEKING — SIEGE, 1900
SF429.P3	PEKINGESE SPANIELS
BT1450	PELAGIANISM
QL121-138	*PELAGIC FAUNA* **SEE** MARINE FAUNA
QK103	*PELAGIC FLORA* **SEE** MARINE FLORA
SH361-3	*PELAGIC SEALING* **SEE** SEALING
DF635	PELAGONIA, BATTLE OF, 1259
GN549.P3	PELASGI
P1023	PELASGIAN LANGUAGE
QL430.6-7	*PELECYPODA* **SEE** LAMELLIBRANCHIATA
PL5434	PELEW LANGUAGE
QL696.P4	PELICANS
ML970-973	*PELITTONE* **SEE** TUBA

E241.P3	PELL'S POINT, BATTLE OF, 1776
RC299.A	*PELLAGRA SINE PELLAGRA* **SEE** ARIBOFLAVINOSIS
RC625	PELLAGRA
QL381-4	PELMATOZOA
QE781-3	PELMATOZOA, FOSSIL
QK653	PELORIA
GV1017.P4	PELOTA (GAME)
TS967	*PELTS* **SEE** HIDES AND SKINS / *manufactures*
HD9778	*PELTS* **SEE** HIDES AND SKINS / *trade*
RG211	PELVIS — ABNORMITIES AND DEFORMITIES
RG365	PELVIS — ABSCESS
RC946	PELVIS — DISEASES
RG	PELVIS — DISEASES / *gynecology*
RC280.G5	PELVIS — TUMORS
QM115	PELVIS
QE862.P3	PELYCOSAURIA
PM6885	PEMON DIALECTS
RL301	PEMPHIGUS
NC905	*PEN AND INK DRAWING* **SEE** PEN DRAWING
NC905	PEN DRAWING
LB3614	*PEN PALS* **SEE** INTERNATIONAL CORRESPONDENCE / *students*
E99.P4	*PENACOOK INDIANS* **SEE** PENNACOOK INDIANS
JV373	PENAL COLONIES / *colonization*
HV8935-8962	PENAL COLONIES / *penology*
HV8301-9920	*PENAL INSTITUTIONS* **SEE** PRISONS
HV9051-9230	*PENAL INSTITUTIONS* **SEE** REFORMATORIES
HV8748-9	*PENAL INSTITUTIONS* **SEE** WORKHOUSES
HV7231-9920	*PENALTIES (CRIMINAL LAW)* **SEE** PUNISHMENT
GT6710-6715	*PENALTIES (CRIMINAL LAW)* **SEE** PUNISHMENT / *manners and customs*
UB800-815	*PENALTIES (CRIMINAL LAW)* **SEE** PUNISHMENT / *military*
VB890-910	*PENALTIES (CRIMINAL LAW)* **SEE** PUNISHMENT / *naval*
LB3025	*PENALTIES (CRIMINAL LAW)* **SEE** PUNISHMENT / *school*
JX1246	*PENALTIES (INTERNATIONAL LAW)* **SEE** SANCTIONS (INTERNATIONAL LAW)
JX1975.6	*PENALTIES (INTERNATIONAL LAW)* **SEE** SANCTIONS (INTERNATIONAL LAW) / *league of nations*
BX1939.P45	PENANCE (CANON LAW)
BV840	PENANCE
BX2260	PENANCE / *catholic church*
NC890-895	PENCIL DRAWING
GV1493	PENCIL GAMES
HD9999.P3-33	PENCILS / *economics*
TS1268	PENCILS / *manufacture*
E99.K	*PEND D'OREILLE INDIANS* **SEE** KALISPEL INDIANS
PM1431	*PEND D'OREILLE LANGUAGE* **SEE** KALISPEL LANGUAGE
QA862.P4	PENDULUM / *dynamics*
QB331-5	PENDULUM / *geodesy*
QL696.S5	PENGUINS
RS165.P38	PENICILLIN
RM666.P35	PENICILLIN
E356.P4	PENINSULA, BATTLE OF THE, SEPT. 29, 1812
E473.6	PENINSULAR CAMPAIGN, 1862
DC231-3	PENINSULAR WAR, 1807-1814 / *history*
DP208	PENINSULAR WAR, 1807-1814 / *period in spain*
QL878	PENIS / *comparative anatomy*
RC896	PENIS / *diseases*
QM416	PENIS / *human anatomy*
QP257	PENIS / *physiology*
BT800	*PENITENCE* **SEE** REPENTANCE
BX1939.P45	*PENITENTIAL BOOKS* **SEE** PENITENTIALS / *canon law*
BX1939.P45	PENITENTIALS / *canon law*
HV8301-9920	*PENITENTIARIES* **SEE** PRISONS
BX4669	PENITENTS
Z43	PENMANSHIP — COPY-BOOKS
Z43-45	PENMANSHIP
Z43.5	PENMANSHIP, LEFT-HANDED
Z43	PENMANSHIP, VERTICAL
F152	PENN'S TREATY WITH THE INDIANS, 1682
E99.P4	PENNACOOK INDIANS
BV168.F5	*PENNANTS, CHURCH* **SEE** CHURCH PENNANTS / *christian art and symbolism*
QL377.C6	*PENNATULACEA* **SEE** SEA-PENS
E99.P4	*PENNEKOOK INDIANS* **SEE** PENNACOOK INDIANS
ML3653	PENNILLION SINGING

F146-160	PENNSYLVANIA — HISTORY
PF5931-8	PENNSYLVANIA GERMAN DIALECT
E315	*PENNSYLVANIA INSURRECTION OF 1794* **SEE** WHISKEY INSURRECTION, 1794
E475.51-53	*PENNSYLVANIA INVASION, 1863* **SEE** GETTYSBURG CAMPAIGN, 1863
E476.66	*PENNSYLVANIA INVASION, 1864* **SEE** MARYLAND CAMPAIGN, JUNE-AUG., 1864
E315	*PENNSYLVANIA-HISTORY-INSURRECTION OF 1794* **SEE** WHISKEY INSURRECTION, 1794
QE673	*PENNSYLVANIAN EPOCH* **SEE** GEOLOGY, STRATIGRAPHIC — PENNSYLVANIAN
QE919	*PENNSYLVANIAN EPOCH* **SEE** PALEOBOTANY — PENNSYLVANIAN
QE747.P4	*PENNSYLVANIAN EPOCH* **SEE** PALEONTOLOGY — PENNSYLVANIAN
E527	PENNSYLVANIA — HISTORY — — CIVIL WAR
E199	PENNSYLVANIA — HISTORY — — FRENCH AND INDIAN WAR, 1755-1763
E198	PENNSYLVANIA — HISTORY — — KING GEORGE'S WAR, 1744-1748
E263.P4	PENNSYLVANIA — HISTORY — — REVOLUTION
E359.5.P3	PENNSYLVANIA — HISTORY — — WAR OF 1812
NK4698	*PENNY BANKS* **SEE** COIN BANKS
E235	PENOBSCOT EXPEDITION, 1779
E99.P5	PENOBSCOT INDIANS
PM2147	PENOBSCOT LANGUAGE
HV8301-9920	*PENOLOGY* **SEE** PRISONS
HV7231-9920	*PENOLOGY* **SEE** PUNISHMENT
GT6710-6715	*PENOLOGY* **SEE** PUNISHMENT / *manners and customs*
UB800-815	*PENOLOGY* **SEE** PUNISHMENT / *military*
VB890-910	*PENOLOGY* **SEE** PUNISHMENT / *naval*
LB3025	*PENOLOGY* **SEE** PUNISHMENT / *school*
HV9051-9230	*PENOLOGY* **SEE** REFORMATORIES
HD9999.P37-39	PENS / *economics*
TS1262-5	PENS / *manufacture*
F314	PENSACOLA, FLA. — CAPTURE, 1781
JF1671	PENSIONS / *civil service*
HJ7491	PENSIONS / *public fiinance*
LB2842-4	PENSIONS / *teachers*
JF1671	*PENSIONS, CIVIL* **SEE** CIVIL SERVICE PENSIONS
JK791	*PENSIONS, CIVIL* **SEE** CIVIL SERVICE PENSIONS / *u.s.*
BX1950	*PENSIONS, ECCLESIASTICAL* **SEE** CLERGY — SALARIES, PENSIONS, ETC. / *catholic*
BV4380-4382	*PENSIONS, ECCLESIASTICAL* **SEE** CLERGY — SALARIES, PENSIONS, ETC.
RC990-991	PENSIONS, MEDICAL EXAMINATIONS FOR
UB370-375	PENSIONS, MILITARY / *army*
UB400-405	PENSIONS, MILITARY / *army*
VB340-345	PENSIONS, MILITARY / *navy*
VB280-285	PENSIONS, MILITARY / *navy*
E255	PENSIONS, MILITARY / *pension rolls*
UB373	PENSIONS, MILITARY — U.S. — — SPEECHES IN CONGRESS
UB370-375	*PENSIONS, NAVAL* **SEE** PENSIONS, MILITARY / *army*
UB400-405	*PENSIONS, NAVAL* **SEE** PENSIONS, MILITARY / *army*
VB280-285	*PENSIONS, NAVAL* **SEE** PENSIONS, MILITARY / *navy*
VB340-345	*PENSIONS, NAVAL* **SEE** PENSIONS, MILITARY / *navy*
E255	*PENSIONS, NAVAL* **SEE** PENSIONS, MILITARY / *pension rolls*
TJ849	PENSTOCKS
QA567	PENTACARDIOID
BF1561	*PENTACLES* **SEE** TALISMANS
GR600	*PENTACLES* **SEE** TALISMANS / *folk-lore*
QA482	PENTAGON
QL447.P4	PENTASTOMIDA
GV1060.7	PENTATHLON
BV4300.5	PENTECOST — SERMONS
BV60	PENTECOST FESTIVAL / *christian*
BM695.P5	PENTECOST FESTIVAL / *jewish*
BT120-123	PENTECOST
BX8762-8780	PENTECOSTAL CHURCHES
BX8762-8780	*PENTECOSTAL MOVEMENT* **SEE** PENTECOSTAL CHURCHES
QD321	PENTOSES / *organic chemistry*
QP701	PENTOSES / *physiological chemistry*
GV1295.P6	PENUCHLE (GAME)
HD4871-5	PEONAGE
SB413.P4	PEONIES

HG2035-2051	*PEOPLE'S BANKS* **SEE** BANKS AND BANKING, COOPERATIVE
E99.P	PEORIA INDIANS
DD126.5	*PEPIN, DONATION OF* **SEE** DONATION OF PEPIN
TX407.P4	PEPPER (SPICE)
SB307.P4	PEPPER (SPICE) / *culture*
QK495.P48	PEPPER-TREE
SB608.P5	PEPPER-WEEVIL
RM666.M	*PEPPERMINT CAMPHOR* **SEE** MENTHOL / *therapeutics*
RS165.M	*PEPPERMINT CAMPHOR* **SEE** MENTHOL / *vegetable drugs*
TP684.P	PEPPERMINT-OIL
SB295.P4	PEPPERMINT / *culture*
RS165.P4	PEPPERMINT / *pharmacy*
SB608.P5	PEPPERS — DISEASES AND PESTS
SB351.P4	PEPPERS
RM640.P5	PEPSIN
QP551	PEPTONES
RC905	PEPTONURIA
E83.72	*PEQUAUKET FIGHT, 1725* **SEE** PIGWACKET FIGHT, 1725
E99.P	PEQUAWKET INDIANS
E83.7	PEQUAWKET INDIANS / *wars*
E99.S35	*PEQUEA INDIANS* **SEE** SHAWNEE INDIANS
E99.P53	PEQUOT INDIANS
PM1885	*PEQUOT LANGUAGE* **SEE** MOHEGAN LANGUAGE
E83.63	PEQUOT WAR, 1636-1638
TS1580	PERCALE
QA117	PERCENTAGE — TABLES, ETC.
HF5695	PERCENTAGE — TABLES, ETC. / *business*
HF5695	PERCENTAGE
BF311	PERCEPTION
BF323.S	*PERCEPTION, SUBLIMINAL* **SEE** SUBLIMINAL PERCEPTION
SH167.P	PERCH / *fish-culture*
QL638.P4	PERCH / *zoology*
SF293.P4	PERCHERON HORSE
QD63	PERCOLATION
M298	PERCUSSION AND CELESTA MUSIC
M1105-6	PERCUSSION AND CELESTA WITH STRING ORCHESTRA
M298	*PERCUSSION AND HARP MUSIC* **SEE** HARP AND PERCUSSION MUSIC
M298	*PERCUSSION AND OBOE MUSIC* **SEE** OBOE AND PERCUSSION MUSIC
M298	*PERCUSSION AND OBOE MUSIC* **SEE** OBOE AND PERCUSSION MUSIC
M298	*PERCUSSION AND ONDES MARTENOT MUSIC* **SEE** ONDES MARTENOT AND PERCUSSION MUSIC
M298	PERCUSSION AND ORGAN MUSIC
M1105-6	PERCUSSION AND ORGAN WITH STRING ORCHESTRA
M284-5	PERCUSSION AND PIANO MUSIC
M284-5	PERCUSSION AND PIANO MUSIC, ARRANGED
M1105-6	PERCUSSION AND PIANO WITH STRING ORCHESTRA
M298	*PERCUSSION AND TROMBONE MUSIC* **SEE** TROMBONE AND PERCUSSION MUSIC
M298	PERCUSSION AND VIOLA MUSIC
M1105-6	PERCUSSION AND 5 TRUMPETS WITH STRING ORCHESTRA
M146	*PERCUSSION BANDS* **SEE** PERCUSSION MUSIC
MT655	PERCUSSION INSTRUMENTS — METHODS
ML1030-1040	PERCUSSION INSTRUMENTS / *history and criticism*
M146	PERCUSSION MUSIC
M1038-9	PERCUSSION WITH CHAMBER ORCHESTRA
M1039	PERCUSSION WITH ORCHESTRA — SOLO WITH PIANO
M1038-9	PERCUSSION WITH ORCHESTRA
M1105-6	PERCUSSION WITH STRING ORCHESTRA
TS535	*PERCUSSION LOCK* **SEE** FIREARMS — LOCKS
RC76.3	PERCUSSION
SB201.P	PERENNIAL VELDT GRASS
DK508.7	PEREYASLAV, TREATY OF, 1654
BT766	*PERFECT LOVE* **SEE** PERFECTION / *theology*
BL1475.P4	PERFECTION (BUDDHISM)
BT766	PERFECTION / *theology*
BT766	*PERFECTIONISM* **SEE** PERFECTION / *theology*
HX656.05	*PERFECTIONISTS* **SEE** ONEIDA COMMUNITY
T60.R	*PERFORMANCE RATING (OF EMPLOYEES)* **SEE** EMPLOYEES, RATING OF
Z650	*PERFORMING ARTISTS, LEGAL RIGHTS OF* **SEE** COPYRIGHT — ARTISTIC PERFORMANCE
TP983	*PERFUMERY* **SEE** PERFUMES
TP983	PERFUMES
TP983	PERFUMES, SYNTHETIC
QP55	PERFUSION PUMP (HEART)
RC685.P5	PERICARDITIS
QL838	PERICARDIUM / *comparative anatomy*
RC685.P5	PERICARDIUM / *diseases*
QM181	PERICARDIUM / *human anatomy*
BX2003	*PERICOPES* **SEE** LECTIONARIES / *catholic church*
BX5147.L4	*PERICOPES* **SEE** LECTIONARIES / *church of england*
BX8067.L4	*PERICOPES* **SEE** LECTIONARIES / *lutheran church*
BX5947	*PERICOPES* **SEE** LECTIONARIES / *protestant episcopal church*
QE461	PERIDOTITE
TP684.P	PERILLA OIL
RE79.P4	PERIMETRY
QM431	*PERINAEUM* **SEE** PERINEUM
RG713	*PERINEORRHAPHY* **SEE** PERINEUM — SURGERY
RG713	PERINEUM — RUPTURE
RG713	PERINEUM — SURGERY
QM431	PERINEUM
RC422.P	PERINEURIAL CYSTS, SACRAL
RB148	PERIODIC DISEASE
QD467	PERIODIC LAW / *chemistry*
Z6945.A2	PERIODICALS — ABBREVIATIONS OF TITLES
Z6941-6962	PERIODICALS — BIBLIOGRAPHY
Z6947-6962	PERIODICALS — DIRECTORIES
AI	PERIODICALS — INDEXES
Z265	PERIODICALS ON MICROFILM
AP	PERIODICALS
PN4700-4900	PERIODICALS / *etc.*
Z6944.E6	PERIODICALS, EPHEMERAL
PN4835	*PERIODICALS, JUVENILE* **SEE** CHILDREN'S PERIODICALS / *history*
Z6945	*PERIODICALS-UNION LISTS* **SEE** PERIODICALS — BIBLIOGRAPHY — — UNION LISTS
Z6945	PERIODICALS — BIBLIOGRAPHY — — CATALOGS
Z6945	PERIODICALS — BIBLIOGRAPHY — — UNION LISTS
QC883	*PERIODICITY IN METEOROLOGY* **SEE** METEOROLOGY — PERIODICITY
HB3711-3840	PERIODICITY / *business cycles*
QP84	PERIODICITY / *physiology*
Q176	PERIODICITY / *science*
QC912	PERIODOMETER
RK361	PERIODONTIA
RK361	*PERIODONTOLOGY* **SEE** PERIODONTIA
QM569	PERIOSTEUM / *histology*
B522	PERIPATETICS / *greco-roman*
B341	PERIPATETICS / *greek*
RC694	PERIPHERAL VASCULAR DISEASES
VM367.P4	PERISCOPES
QK623.P9	PERISPORIALES
RC867	PERITONEUM — ABSCESS
RC867	PERITONEUM — DISEASES
QL864	PERITONEUM / *comparative anatomy*
QM367	PERITONEUM / *human anatomy*
RC867	PERITONITIS
RD542	*PERITYPHLITIS* **SEE** APPENDICITIS
HV6326	PERJURY
RM910	*PERKINS' TRACTORS* **SEE** TRACTORS, METALLIC / *therapeutics*
QD181.M6	PERMANGANATES
QD181.M6	PERMANGANIC ACID
QC761	PERMEAMETER
QE674	*PERMIAN FORMATION* **SEE** GEOLOGY, STRATIGRAPHIC — PERMIAN
QE920	*PERMIAN FORMATION* **SEE** PALEOBOTANY — PERMIAN
QE730	*PERMIAN FORMATION* **SEE** PALEONTOLOGY — PERMIAN
PH1001-1109	PERMIAN LANGUAGES
QA165	PERMUTATIONS
PH1071-9	PERMYAK DIALECT
TN740	PERNOT STEEL FURNACES
DC309.P4	PERONNE, FRANCE — SIEGE, 1870
QK621.P45	PERONOSPORALES / *botany*
SB608.G7	PERONOSPORALES / *grape pests*
QD181.O1	PEROXIDES
CE91-92	*PERPETUAL ALMANAC* **SEE** CALENDAR, PERPETUAL
CE91-92	*PERPETUAL CALENDAR* **SEE** CALENDAR, PERPETUAL

TJ217	PERPETUAL MOTION
HD9398	PERRY / *economics*
TP588.P	PERRY / *technology*
E474.39	PERRYVILLE, KY., BATTLE OF, 1862
QD193	PERSALTS
BR1600-1608	PERSECUTION / *church history*
BT768	PERSEVERANCE (THEOLOGY)
BF390	PERSEVERATION (PSYCHOLOGY)
PK6128	*PERSIAN CUNEIFORM INSCRIPTIONS* **SEE** OLD PERSIAN INSCRIPTIONS
PK6201-6399	PERSIAN LANGUAGE
PK6141-6181	*PERSIAN LANGUAGE-MIDDLE PERSIAN (PAHLAVI)* **SEE** PAHLAVI LANGUAGE
PK6101-9	*PERSIAN LANGUAGE-OLD PERSIAN (AVESTA)* **SEE** AVESTAN LANGUAGE
PK6121-9	*PERSIAN LANGUAGE-OLD PERSIAN* **SEE** OLD PERSIAN LANGUAGE
PK6141-6181	*PERSIAN LANGUAGE-PAHLAVI* **SEE** PAHLAVI LANGUAGE
PK6401-6599	PERSIAN LITERATURE
PK6111-6119	*PERSIAN LITERATURE-AVESTAN* **SEE** AVESTA / *etc.*
BL1515	*PERSIAN LITERATURE-AVESTAN* **SEE** AVESTA / *zoroastrianism*
PK6190-6199	*PERSIAN LITERATURE-MIDDLE PERSIAN (PAHLAVI)* **SEE** PAHLAVI LITERATURE
PK6128	*PERSIAN LITERATURE-OLD PERSIAN* **SEE** OLD PERSIAN INSCRIPTIONS
PK6190-6199	*PERSIAN LITERATURE-PAHLAVI* **SEE** PAHLAVI LITERATURE
PN5449.P4	PERSIAN NEWSPAPERS / *etc.*
PK6201-6399	PERSIAN PHILOLOGY
PK6433-9	PERSIAN POETRY / *collections*
PK6416-6420	PERSIAN POETRY / *history*
PK6443	PERSIAN PROSE LITERATURE / *collections*
PK6423	PERSIAN PROSE LITERATURE / *history*
SB379.P4	PERSIMMON
B828.5	*PERSON (PHILOSOPHY)* **SEE** PERSONALISM
RA778	*PERSONAL BEAUTY* **SEE** BEAUTY, PERSONAL
BF701-724.8	*PERSONAL DEVELOPMENT* **SEE** GENETIC PSYCHOLOGY
BD331	*PERSONAL DEVELOPMENT* **SEE** PERSONALITY / *ontology*
BF698	*PERSONAL DEVELOPMENT* **SEE** PERSONALITY / *psychology*
HF5386	*PERSONAL DEVELOPMENT* **SEE** SUCCESS / *business*
BJ1611-1618	*PERSONAL DEVELOPMENT* **SEE** SUCCESS / *ethics*
HF5386	*PERSONAL EFFICIENCY* **SEE** SUCCESS / *business*
BJ1611-1618	*PERSONAL EFFICIENCY* **SEE** SUCCESS / *ethics*
QB153	PERSONAL EQUATION / *astronomy*
HG179	*PERSONAL FINANCE* **SEE** FINANCE, PERSONAL
RA771	*PERSONAL HYGIENE* **SEE** HYGIENE / *domestic*
BJ1695	*PERSONAL HYGIENE* **SEE** HYGIENE / *ethical aspects*
RA773-790	*PERSONAL HYGIENE* **SEE** HYGIENE / *personal*
JC585-599	*PERSONAL LIBERTY* **SEE** LIBERTY / *political theory*
HM271	*PERSONAL LIBERTY* **SEE** LIBERTY / *sociology*
E450	PERSONAL LIBERTY LAWS
HG2052-2069	*PERSONAL LOANS* **SEE** LOANS, PERSONAL
CS2300-2389	*PERSONAL NAMES* **SEE** NAMES, PERSONAL
HJ4581-4599	*PERSONAL PROPERTY TAX* **SEE** TAXATION OF PERSONAL PROPERTY
JX6564	PERSONAL PROPERTY / *private international law*
HF1263	PERSONAL PROPERTY / *u.s.*
HJ4581-4599	*PERSONAL PROPERTY-TAXATION* **SEE** TAXATION OF PERSONAL PROPERTY
B828.5	PERSONALISM
BD331	PERSONALITY / *ontology*
BF698	PERSONALITY / *psychology*
RC554-574	PERSONALITY, DISORDERS OF
PN4839	PERSONALS
JX6564	*PERSONALTY* **SEE** PERSONAL PROPERTY / *private international law*
HF1263	*PERSONALTY* **SEE** PERSONAL PROPERTY / *u.s.*
PN56.P	PERSONIFICATION IN LITERATURE
HF5549	*PERSONNEL ADMINISTRATION* **SEE** PERSONNEL MANAGEMENT
T56-58	*PERSONNEL ADMINISTRATION* **SEE** PERSONNEL MANAGEMENT
V880	*PERSONNEL BOATS, NAVAL* **SEE** U.S. — BOATS
T56-58	PERSONNEL MANAGEMENT
HF5549	PERSONNEL MANAGEMENT
LB2846	PERSONNEL RECORDS IN EDUCATION
LC5219	PERSONNEL SERVICE IN ADULT EDUCATION
LB2846	*PERSONNEL SERVICE IN EDUCATION* **SEE** PERSONNEL RECORDS IN EDUCATION
LB1027.5	PERSONNEL SERVICE IN EDUCATION / *application*
LB3046-9	PERSONNEL SERVICE IN EDUCATION / *organization*
LB1731	*PERSONNEL SERVICE IN EDUCATION-STUDY AND TEACHING* **SEE** STUDENT COUNSELORS, TRAINING OF
LB1027.5	PERSONNEL SERVICE IN ELEMENTARY EDUCATION
LB2343	PERSONNEL SERVICE IN HIGHER EDUCATION
LB1567	PERSONNEL SERVICE IN RURAL SCHOOLS
LB1620.5	PERSONNEL SERVICE IN SECONDARY EDUCATION
BX1939.P47	PERSONS (CANON LAW)
JX4000-4081	PERSONS (INTERNATIONAL LAW)
NC749-750	PERSPECTIVE
QA515	PERSPECTIVE / *geometry*
T369	PERSPECTIVE / *mechanical drawing*
QP221	PERSPIRATION
DA783.57	PERTH, BATTLE OF, 1396
QB362	PERTURBATION (ASTRONOMY)
QA871	PERTURBATION (MATHEMATICS)
QC174.5	PERTURBATION (QUANTUM DYNAMICS)
QA871	*PERTURBATION EQUATIONS* **SEE** PERTURBATION (MATHEMATICS)
QA871	*PERTURBATION THEORY* **SEE** PERTURBATION (MATHEMATICS)
QC174.5	*PERTURBATION THEORY, QUANTUM MECHANICAL* **SEE** PERTURBATION (QUANTUM DYNAMICS)
F3401-3619	PERU — HISTORY
F3097	*PERU-HISTORY-WAR WITH CHILE, 1879-1884* **SEE** WAR OF THE PACIFIC, 1879-1884
DG975.P4	PERUGIA — HISTORY — — 1368-1370
TT975	*PERUKES* **SEE** WIGS
GT2310	*PERUKES* **SEE** WIGS / *manners and customs*
QK495.C57	*PERUVIAN BARK* **SEE** CINCHONA / *botany*
SB295.C5	*PERUVIAN BARK* **SEE** CINCHONA / *culture*
RS165.C3	*PERUVIAN BARK* **SEE** CINCHONA / *pharmacy*
RM666.C53	*PERUVIAN BARK* **SEE** CINCHONA / *therapeutics*
PQ8300-8499	PERUVIAN LITERATURE
PN5081-5	PERUVIAN NEWSPAPERS / *history*
PQ8479	PERUVIAN ORATIONS / *collections*
PQ8409	PERUVIAN ORATIONS / *history*
PQ8449-8463	PERUVIAN POETRY / *collections*
PQ8361-8381	PERUVIAN POETRY / *history*
F3405	PERUVIANS / *biography*
HQ71-78	*PERVERSION, SEXUAL* **SEE** SEXUAL PERVERSION
DC224.P3	PESCHIERA — SIEGE, 1801
RG361-3	PESSARIES
PN56.P4	PESSIMISM IN LITERATURE
B829	PESSIMISM
BJ1477	PESSIMISM / *ethics*
B851-4695	PESSIMISM / *philosophy*
RA1270.P4	PESTICIDES — TOXICOLOGY
SB951	PESTICIDES
RA649-653	*PESTILENCES* **SEE** EPIDEMICS
SB599-1100	PESTS / *agriculture*
TX325	PESTS / *domestic economy*
SF411-415	PET SHOPS
DR27.P4	PETCHENEGS
BX1950	PETER'S PENCE
E476.93	PETERSBURG CRATER, BATTLE OF, 1864
E470.2	PETERSBURG, VA. — SIEGE, 1864-1865
E476.93	PETERSBURG, VA. — SIEGE, 1864-1865
JC609	PETITION, RIGHT OF
JL-JQ	PETITION, RIGHT OF / *other countries*
JK1731	PETITION, RIGHT OF / *u.s.*
PQ4537.F7	PETRARCHISM / *french literature*
PQ4546	PETRARCHISM / *petrarch's influence on literature*
PQ4213.A3	PETRARCHISM / *14th century*
QL696.P6	PETRELS
QE721	PETRIFACTION
QE991	PETRIFIED FORESTS
GN799.P4	PETROGLYPHS
QE433.5	PETROGRAPHIC MICROSCOPE

QE420-499	*PETROGRAPHY* **SEE** PETROLOGY
TN879.5	PETROLEUM — PIPE LINES
TP690-692	PETROLEUM — REFINING
TP692.5	PETROLEUM — STORAGE
TP692	PETROLEUM — TABLES, CALCULATIONS, ETC.
TP691	PETROLEUM — TESTING
TP355	PETROLEUM AS FUEL
TJ619	PETROLEUM AS FUEL / *locomotives*
TP692.2	*PETROLEUM CRACKING* **SEE** CRACKING PROCESS / *gasoline*
TJ751-805	*PETROLEUM ENGINES* **SEE** GAS AND OIL ENGINES
HF5686.P3	PETROLEUM INDUSTRY AND TRADE — ACCOUNTING
UA929.95.P4	PETROLEUM INDUSTRY AND TRADE — DEFENSE MEASURES
TN871	PETROLEUM INDUSTRY AND TRADE — FIRES AND FIRE PREVENTION
TN871	PETROLEUM INDUSTRY AND TRADE — SAFETY MEASURES
HD9560-9580	PETROLEUM INDUSTRY AND TRADE
HD9560.9	*PETROLEUM INSPECTION* **SEE** OIL INSPECTION / *state reports*
TP691	*PETROLEUM INSPECTION* **SEE** OIL INSPECTION / *technology*
TN879.5	*PETROLEUM PIPE LINES* **SEE** PETROLEUM — PIPE LINES
TP690.6	PETROLEUM PRODUCTS — ANTISTATIC ADDITIVES
TP690	PETROLEUM REFINERIES
TP690-692	*PETROLEUM REFINING* **SEE** PETROLEUM — REFINING
TN860-879	PETROLEUM / *production*
TP690-692	PETROLEUM / *refining*
TP692.2	*PETROLEUM-CRACKING* **SEE** CRACKING PROCESS / *gasoline*
TN871.5	*PETROLEUM-EQUIPMENT AND SUPPLIES* **SEE** OIL FIELDS — EQUIPMENT AND SUPPLIES
TN871.2	*PETROLEUM-WELL-BORING* **SEE** OIL WELL DRILLING
QE433	PETROLOGY — LABORATORY MANUALS
QE420-499	PETROLOGY
QE425	*PETROLOGY-NOMENCLATURE* **SEE** ROCKS — CLASSIFICATION AND NOMENCLATURE
DK215.8.P	PETROPAVLOVSK-KAMCHATSKIY, BATTLE OF, 1854
SF411-415	PETS / *care and breeding*
SF981-995	PETS / *diseases*
SB351.C	*PETSAI* **SEE** CHINESE CABBAGE
DR27.P4	*PETSCHENEGEN* **SEE** PETCHENEGS
TL215.P	PEUGEOT AUTOMOBILE
PL8181-4	*PEUL LANGUAGE* **SEE** FULAH LANGUAGE
GN652.F9	*PEULHS* **SEE** FULAHS
GA304.Z53	PEUTINGER TABLE
BV763.P4	PEWS AND PEW RIGHTS
NK8400-8419	PEWTER
QK495.C11	PEYOTE / *cactus*
RS165.A7	PEYOTE / *vegetable drugs*
QA381	PFAFF'S PROBLEM
DC236.8.P4	PFALZBURG — SIEGE, 1814
RB145	*PFEIFFER'S DISEASE* **SEE** MONONUCLEOSIS
PL4051-4	*PGHO DIALECT* **SEE** KAREN LANGUAGE
PA4167	PHAEACIANS / *homer*
QL368.R2	PHAEODARIA
QR185	PHAGOCYTOSIS
QL737.M3	*PHALANGERS, FLYING* **SEE** FLYING PHALANGERS
QL458.P5	PHALANGIDA
QL696.L7	PHALAROPES
BL460	PHALLICISM
QL878	*PHALLUS* **SEE** PENIS / *comparative anatomy*
RC896	*PHALLUS* **SEE** PENIS / *diseases*
QM416	*PHALLUS* **SEE** PENIS / *human anatomy*
QP257	*PHALLUS* **SEE** PENIS / *physiology*
PK7075	PHALURA LANGUAGE
DR241	PHANARIOTS
DS422.T5	*PHANSIGARS* **SEE** THUGS / *india*
BF1445-1486	*PHANTOMS* **SEE** APPARITIONS
BF1445-1486	*PHANTOMS* **SEE** GHOSTS
GR580	*PHANTOMS* **SEE** GHOSTS / *folk-lore*
BM175.P4	PHARISEES
RS402-431	*PHARMACEUTICAL CHEMISTRY* **SEE** CHEMISTRY, MEDICAL AND PHARMACEUTICAL
HF6201.D4-6	*PHARMACEUTICAL INDUSTRY* **SEE** DRUG TRADE / *business*
HD9665-9675	*PHARMACEUTICAL INDUSTRY* **SEE** DRUG TRADE / *economics*
RS122	PHARMACEUTICAL RESEARCH
RS	PHARMACISTS
GT6380	PHARMACISTS / *manners and customs*
RS4-17	*PHARMACISTS-LEGAL STATUS, LAWS, ETC.* **SEE** PHARMACY — LAWS AND LEGISLATION
RM	*PHARMACODYNAMICS* **SEE** PHARMACOLOGY
QP903-981	*PHARMACODYNAMICS* **SEE** PHARMACOLOGY / *experimental*
RS160-167	PHARMACOGNOSY
RM	PHARMACOLOGY
QP903-981	PHARMACOLOGY / *experimental*
RS122	*PHARMACOLOGY-RESEARCH* **SEE** PHARMACEUTICAL RESEARCH
RS139-141	PHARMACOPOEIAS
RV421	PHARMACOPOEIAS / *eclectic*
RX675	PHARMACOPOEIAS, HOMEOPATHIC
UH420-425	*PHARMACOPOEIAS, MILITARY* **SEE** PHARMACY, MILITARY
VG270-275	*PHARMACOPOEIAS, MILITARY* **SEE** PHARMACY, MILITARY / *naval*
RS51	PHARMACY — DICTIONARIES
RS78-88	PHARMACY — EARLY WORKS TO 1800
RS98	PHARMACY — EXAMINATIONS, QUESTIONS, ETC.
RS93	PHARMACY — LABORATORY MANUALS
RS4-17	PHARMACY — LAWS AND LEGISLATION
RS55	PHARMACY — NOMENCLATURE
RS101-121	PHARMACY — STUDY AND TEACHING
RS355-6	PHARMACY — SUPPLIES
RS57	PHARMACY — TABLES, CALCULATIONS, ETC.
RS122.5	PHARMACY AS A PROFESSION
RS	PHARMACY
SF915-918	PHARMACY / *veterinary*
RX671-5	PHARMACY, HOMEOPATHIC
UH420-425	PHARMACY, MILITARY
VG270-275	PHARMACY, MILITARY / *naval*
RS122	*PHARMACY-RESEARCH* **SEE** PHARMACEUTICAL RESEARCH
DG266	PHARSALUS, BATTLE OF, 48 B.C.
QM331	PHARYNGEAL BURSA
RF481-497	*PHARYNGEAL PARALYSIS* **SEE** PHARYNX — DISEASES
RC280.P	PHARYNX — CANCER
RF481-497	PHARYNX — DISEASES
RD661	PHARYNX — TUMORS
QL861	PHARYNX / *comparative anatomy*
QM331	PHARYNX / *human anatomy*
QD501	PHASE RULE AND EQUILIBRIUM
QB603	*PHASES OF THE PLANETS* **SEE** PLANETS — PHASES
SK325.P5	*PHEASANT HUNTING* **SEE** PHEASANT SHOOTING
SK325.P5	PHEASANT SHOOTING
SK325.G7	*PHEASANTS (RUFFED GROUSE)* **SEE** RUFFED GROUSE
QL696.G2	*PHEASANTS (RUFFED GROUSE)* **SEE** RUFFED GROUSE
QL696.G2	PHEASANTS
RM666.P	PHENACETIN
QD395	PHENANTHRENE
PJ4171-4197	PHENICIAN LANGUAGE
HF370	PHENICIANS / *commercial history*
DS81-89	PHENICIANS / *history*
QH544	PHENOLOGY
QD441	PHENOLPHTHALEIN / *colored compounds*
QD77	PHENOLPHTHALEIN / *indicators*
QD341.A2	PHENOLPHTHALEIN / *organic chemistry*
QP801.P4	PHENOLS IN THE BODY
QD341.P5	PHENOLS
BD352	PHENOMENALISM
BF204.5	PHENOMENOLOGICAL PSYCHOLOGY
B829.5	PHENOMENOLOGY
RM666.P6	PHESIN / *therapeutics*
M1960.P6	PHI KAPPA PSI — SONGS AND MUSIC
F158	PHILADELPHIA — HISTORY
E527	PHILADELPHIA — HISTORY — — CIVIL WAR
E263.P4	PHILADELPHIA — HISTORY — — REVOLUTION
E233	PHILADELPHIA — HISTORY — — REVOLUTION
E359.5.P3	PHILADELPHIA — HISTORY — — WAR OF 1812
E726.P4	PHILADELPHIA — HISTORY — — WAR OF 1898
HV27-28	PHILANTHROPISTS
HV40-69	*PHILANTHROPY* **SEE** CHARITY ORGANIZATION
Q181	*PHILANTHROPY* **SEE** ENDOWMENT OF RESEARCH

LB2336-7	*PHILANTHROPY* **SEE** ENDOWMENT OF RESEARCH
HV16-25	*PHILANTHROPY* **SEE** ENDOWMENTS / *charities*
LB2336-7	*PHILANTHROPY* **SEE** ENDOWMENTS / *higher education*
HV1-696	*PHILANTHROPY* **SEE** SOCIAL SERVICE
HE6187-6230	*PHILATELY AND PHILATELISTS* **SEE** POSTAGE-STAMPS — COLLECTORS AND COLLECTING
HJ5315	*PHILATELY AND PHILATELISTS* **SEE** REVENUE-STAMPS — COLLECTORS AND COLLECTING
DF807	PHILHELLENISM
E83.866	PHILIP KEARNY, FORT — MASSACRE, 1866
E83.866	PHILIP KEARNY, FORT
PN6121-9	*PHILIPPICS* **SEE** ORATIONS / *collections*
PN4012-4061	*PHILIPPICS* **SEE** ORATIONS / *history and criticism*
M1822-3	PHILIPPINE BALLADS AND SONGS
PS9992.P4	PHILIPPINE DRAMA (ENGLISH)
DS651-689	PHILIPPINE ISLANDS — HISTORY
PL5501-6135	PHILIPPINE LANGUAGES
PR9797.P6	PHILIPPINE LITERATURE (ENGLISH)
PL5531	PHILIPPINE LITERATURE
PL5554-6135	PHILIPPINE LITERATURE
PN5421-9	PHILIPPINE NEWSPAPERS / *history*
DS653	PHILIPPINE ORATIONS / *historical collections*
PN5421-5430	PHILIPPINE PERIODICALS / *history*
PR9797.P	PHILIPPINE POETRY (ENGLISH)
PQ8850-8851	PHILIPPINE POETRY (SPANISH)
D774.P	PHILIPPINE SEA, BATTLES OF THE, 1944
BX601	*PHILIPPONS* **SEE** PHILIPPOVTSI (RUSSIAN SECT)
BX601	PHILIPPOVTSI (RUSSIAN SECT)
DS90	PHILISTINES
P85	PHILOLOGISTS — CORRESPONDENCE, REMINISCENCES, ETC.
P501-769	*PHILOLOGY, ARYAN* **SEE** ARYAN PHILOLOGY
PG4001-4771	*PHILOLOGY, BOHEMIAN* **SEE** CZECH PHILOLOGY
PA1-199	*PHILOLOGY, CLASSICAL* **SEE** CLASSICAL PHILOLOGY
PG4001-4771	*PHILOLOGY, CZECH* **SEE** CZECH PHILOLOGY
PE	*PHILOLOGY, ENGLISH* **SEE** ENGLISH PHILOLOGY
PK101-119	*PHILOLOGY, INDIC* **SEE** INDO-ARYAN PHILOLOGY
PK101-119	*PHILOLOGY, INDO-ARYAN* **SEE** INDO-ARYAN PHILOLOGY
PK1-17	*PHILOLOGY, INDO-IRANIAN* **SEE** INDO-IRANIAN PHILOLOGY
PB1-431	PHILOLOGY, MODERN
PJ	*PHILOLOGY, ORIENTAL* **SEE** ORIENTAL PHILOLOGY
B108-708	PHILOSOPHERS, ANCIENT
B720-785	PHILOSOPHERS, MEDIEVAL
QD24-26.5	*PHILOSOPHERS' EGG* **SEE** ALCHEMY
QD13	*PHILOSOPHERS' EGG* **SEE** ALCHEMY / *history*
QD24-26.5	*PHILOSOPHERS' STONE* **SEE** ALCHEMY
QD13	*PHILOSOPHERS' STONE* **SEE** ALCHEMY / *history*
B808.5	*PHILOSOPHICAL ANALYSIS* **SEE** ANALYSIS (PHILOSOPHY)
BD450	PHILOSOPHICAL ANTHROPOLOGY
P151-295	*PHILOSOPHICAL GRAMMAR* **SEE** GRAMMAR, COMPARATIVE AND GENERAL
BT40	PHILOSOPHICAL THEOLOGY
B51.4-6	PHILOSOPHY — HISTORIOGRAPHY
B69-4695	PHILOSOPHY — HISTORY
BD10-28	PHILOSOPHY — INTRODUCTIONS
B68	PHILOSOPHY — MISCELLANEA
B51.8	PHILOSOPHY — PICTURES, ILLUSTRATIONS, ETC.
B52	PHILOSOPHY — STUDY AND TEACHING
B49-50	PHILOSOPHY — TERMINOLOGY
BC	*PHILOSOPHY* **SEE** LOGIC
Q175	*PHILOSOPHY AND SCIENCE* **SEE** SCIENCE — PHILOSOPHY
PN49	PHILOSOPHY IN LITERATURE
D16.7-9	*PHILOSOPHY OF HISTORY* **SEE** HISTORY — PHILOSOPHY
P101-5	*PHILOSOPHY OF LANGUAGE* **SEE** LANGUAGES — PHILOSOPHY
B65	*PHILOSOPHY OF LAW* **SEE** LAW — PHILOSOPHY
PN45	*PHILOSOPHY OF LITERATURE* **SEE** LITERATURE — PHILOSOPHY
R723	*PHILOSOPHY OF MEDICINE* **SEE** MEDICINE — PHILOSOPHY
BD581	PHILOSOPHY OF NATURE
RC455	*PHILOSOPHY OF PSYCHIATRY* **SEE** PSYCHIATRY — PHILOSOPHY

B-BJ	PHILOSOPHY
B851-945	PHILOSOPHY, AMERICAN
B808.5	*PHILOSOPHY, ANALYTICAL* **SEE** ANALYSIS (PHILOSOPHY)
B108-708	PHILOSOPHY, ANCIENT
B740-753	PHILOSOPHY, ARAB / *medieval*
B740-753	*PHILOSOPHY, ARABIC* **SEE** PHILOSOPHY, ARAB / *medieval*
B163	*PHILOSOPHY, ARABIC* **SEE** PHILOSOPHY, ISLAMIC
B740-753	*PHILOSOPHY, ARABIC* **SEE** PHILOSOPHY, ISLAMIC / *medieval*
B123	PHILOSOPHY, BUDDHIST
B799	PHILOSOPHY, COMPARATIVE
LB2386	*PHILOSOPHY, DOCTOR OF* **SEE** DOCTOR OF PHILOSOPHY DEGREE
BP130-133	*PHILOSOPHY, EAST INDIAN* **SEE** PHILOSOPHY, INDIC
B1815-1818	PHILOSOPHY, FRENCH — 17TH CENTURY
B1911-1925	PHILOSOPHY, FRENCH — 18TH CENTURY
B2185-8	PHILOSOPHY, FRENCH — 19TH CENTURY
B2421-4	PHILOSOPHY, FRENCH — 20TH CENTURY
B108-708	*PHILOSOPHY, GREEK* **SEE** PHILOSOPHY, ANCIENT
BP130-133	PHILOSOPHY, INDIC
B163	PHILOSOPHY, ISLAMIC
B740-753	PHILOSOPHY, ISLAMIC / *medieval*
B162.5	PHILOSOPHY, JAINA
B720-785	PHILOSOPHY, MEDIEVAL
B801	PHILOSOPHY, MODERN — 17TH CENTURY
B802	PHILOSOPHY, MODERN — 18TH CENTURY
B803	PHILOSOPHY, MODERN — 19TH CENTURY
B804	PHILOSOPHY, MODERN — 20TH CENTURY
B790-4695	PHILOSOPHY, MODERN
B770-785	*PHILOSOPHY, MODERN 16TH CENTURY* **SEE** PHILOSOPHY, RENAISSANCE
BJ	*PHILOSOPHY, MORAL* **SEE** ETHICS
B163	*PHILOSOPHY, MUSLIM* **SEE** PHILOSOPHY, ISLAMIC
B740-753	*PHILOSOPHY, MUSLIM* **SEE** PHILOSOPHY, ISLAMIC / *medieval*
QC	*PHILOSOPHY, NATURAL* **SEE** PHYSICS
B121	PHILOSOPHY, ORIENTAL
BR1705	*PHILOSOPHY, PATRISTIC* **SEE** FATHERS OF THE CHURCH / *collective biography*
BR60-67	*PHILOSOPHY, PATRISTIC* **SEE** FATHERS OF THE CHURCH / *patrology*
GN470	PHILOSOPHY, PRIMITIVE
B770-785	PHILOSOPHY, RENAISSANCE
B108-708	*PHILOSOPHY, ROMAN* **SEE** PHILOSOPHY, ANCIENT
BD240-241	*PHILOSOPHY-METHODOLOGY* **SEE** METHODOLOGY
B53	PHILOSOPHY — HISTORY — — METHODOLOGY
RC894	PHIMOSIS
RD590	PHIMOSIS / *surgery*
RC696	PHLEBITIS
RM182	*PHLEBOTOMY* **SEE** BLOODLETTING
QD27	*PHLOGISTON* **SEE** CHEMISTRY — PHLOGISTON
QD14	*PHLOGISTON* **SEE** CHEMISTRY — PHLOGISTON
BF723.F4	*PHOBIAS* **SEE** FEAR / *child study*
BF575.F2	*PHOBIAS* **SEE** FEAR / *psychology*
QL737.C4	*PHOCAENA* **SEE** PORPOISES
QL991	PHOCOMELUS / *teratology*
RC76.3	PHONENDOSCOPE
PE1151	PHONETIC ALPHABET / *english*
P227	PHONETIC ALPHABET / *international*
PE1151	PHONETIC SPELLING / *english*
P221-7	PHONETICS
QC544.P5	PHONIC WHEEL
QP111	*PHONOCARDIOGRAPHY* **SEE** HEART — SOUNDS
TS2301.P3	*PHONODISCS* **SEE** PHONORECORDS / *manufacture*
PN1995.7	*PHONOFILM* **SEE** MOVING-PICTURES, TALKING
LB1044.3	PHONOGRAPH IN EDUCATION
TS2301.P3	*PHONOGRAPH RECORD CHANGERS* **SEE** RECORD CHANGERS
TS2301.P3	*PHONOGRAPH RECORDS* **SEE** PHONORECORDS / *manufacture*
MT150	PHONOGRAPH / *instruction*
TS2301.P3	PHONOGRAPH / *manufacture*
ML1055	PHONOGRAPH / *music history*
Z53-100	*PHONOGRAPHY* **SEE** SHORTHAND
Z54-57	*PHONOGRAPHY* **SEE** SHORTHAND / *english*
QE461	PHONOLITE

P221-7	*PHONOLOGY* **SEE** PHONETICS
TS2301.P3	*PHONORECORD CHANGERS* **SEE** RECORD CHANGERS
ML111.5	PHONORECORD COLLECTING
ML111.5	PHONORECORD LIBRARIES
ML156	PHONORECORDS — CATALOGS
BV2082.A8	PHONORECORDS IN MISSIONARY WORK
TS2301.P3	PHONORECORDS / *manufacture*
Z695.715	*PHONORECORDS-CATALOGING* **SEE** CATALOGING OF PHONORECORDS
Z697.P	*PHONORECORDS-CLASSIFICATION* **SEE** CLASSIFICATION — PHONORECORDS
ML111.5	*PHONORECORDS-COLLECTORS AND COLLECTING* **SEE** PHONORECORD COLLECTING
LB1044.4	PHONOTAPES IN EDUCATION
ML157.3	PHONOTAPES
Z51	*PHONOTYPY* **SEE** STENOTYPY
RE79.P5	PHOROMETER
RE79.P6	PHOROPTOR
TS696	PHOSPHATE COATING
TN913-914	PHOSPHATE INDUSTRY
TP245.P5	PHOSPHATES / *chemical technology*
QD181.P1	PHOSPHATES / *chemistry*
S647	PHOSPHATES / *fertilizers*
TN913-914	PHOSPHATES / *mineral resources*
QP535.P1	PHOSPHATES / *physiological chemistry*
S647	PHOSPHATIC SLAG / *fertilizers*
TS696	*PHOSPHATING* **SEE** PHOSPHATE COATING
QP481	PHOSPHENES
QH641	PHOSPHORESCENCE / *cytology*
QC478	PHOSPHORESCENCE / *optics*
QL639	*PHOSPHORESCENT ORGANS IN FISHES* **SEE** FISHES — ANATOMY
QC478	*PHOSPHORESCENT ORGANS IN FISHES* **SEE** PHOSPHORESCENCE / *optics*
QH641	*PHOSPHORESCENT ORGANS IN FISHES* **SEE** PHOSPHORESCENCE / *cytology*
QP801.P6	PHOSPHORIC ACID IN THE BODY
QD181.P1	PHOSPHORIC ACID / *chemistry*
QP913.P1	PHOSPHORIC ACID / *experimental pharmacology*
TN948.A7	*PHOSPHORITE* **SEE** APATITE / *mineral resources*
QE391.A6	*PHOSPHORITE* **SEE** APATITE / *mineralogy*
QC476	PHOSPHORS
RM666.P7	PHOSPHORUS — THERAPEUTIC USE
RA1231.P5	PHOSPHORUS — TOXICOLOGY
QP535.P1	PHOSPHORUS IN THE BODY
QP535.P1	PHOSPHORUS METABOLISM
TP245.P5	PHOSPHORUS / *chemical technology*
QD181.P1	PHOSPHORUS / *chemistry*
QD535.P1	PHOSPHORUS / *physiological chemistry*
RA1231.P5	*PHOSSY JAW* **SEE** JAWS — NECROSIS / *phosphorus poisoning*
UG476	*PHOTO INTERPRETATION* **SEE** PHOTOGRAPHIC INTERPRETATION (MILITARY SCIENCE)
TR445	*PHOTOAQUATINT* **SEE** PHOTOGRAPHY — PRINTING PROCESSES — — GUM-BICHROMATE
QC715	*PHOTOCELLS* **SEE** PHOTOELECTRIC CELLS
TR500	PHOTOCERAMICS
QD601	PHOTOCHEMISTRY
TR860	PHOTOCHRONOGRAPH
UF840	PHOTOCHRONOGRAPH / *military*
TR825	PHOTOCOPYING PROCESSES
TR825	*PHOTODUPLICATION* **SEE** PHOTOCOPYING PROCESSES
QP671	*PHOTODYN* **SEE** HEMATOPORPHYRIN
TA406	*PHOTOELASTIC METHOD* **SEE** PHOTOELASTICITY
TA406	PHOTOELASTICITY
QC715	PHOTOELECTRIC CELLS
QC611	*PHOTOELECTRIC EFFECT* **SEE** PHOTOELECTRICITY / *electric conductivity*
QC715	*PHOTOELECTRIC EFFECT* **SEE** PHOTOELECTRICITY / *electric discharges*
TK7872.E5	*PHOTOELECTRIC MULTIPLIER TUBES* **SEE** PHOTOELECTRIC MULTIPLIERS
TK7872.E5	PHOTOELECTRIC MULTIPLIERS
QC611	PHOTOELECTRICITY / *electric conductivity*
QC715	PHOTOELECTRICITY / *electric discharges*
QC611	*PHOTOELECTRONS* **SEE** PHOTOELECTRICITY / *electric conductivity*
QC715	*PHOTOELECTRONS* **SEE** PHOTOELECTRICITY / *electric discharges*
TR975	PHOTOENGRAVING — HALFTONE PROCESS
TR970-977	PHOTOENGRAVING
TR990	PHOTOGALVANOGRAPHY
TR995	*PHOTOGLYPTIE* **SEE** WOODBURYTYPE
TR693	PHOTOGRAMMETRY
TA593	PHOTOGRAMMETRY / *surveying*
N4000	PHOTOGRAPH COLLECTIONS
TR139-140	PHOTOGRAPHERS — CORRESPONDENCE, REMINISCENCES, ETC.
TR139	PHOTOGRAPHERS
TR148	*PHOTOGRAPHIC AMUSEMENTS* **SEE** PHOTOGRAPHY, TRICK
TR196-9	*PHOTOGRAPHIC APPARATUS AND SUPPLIES* **SEE** PHOTOGRAPHY — APPARATUS AND SUPPLIES
TR212	PHOTOGRAPHIC CHEMICALS
TR210	PHOTOGRAPHIC CHEMISTRY
TR179	*PHOTOGRAPHIC COMPOSITION* **SEE** COMPOSITION (PHOTOGRAPHY)
TR550-573	*PHOTOGRAPHIC DARKROOMS* **SEE** PHOTOGRAPHY — STUDIOS AND DARK ROOMS
TR925-997	*PHOTOGRAPHIC DUPLICATION* **SEE** PHOTOMECHANICAL PROCESSES
NE2890	*PHOTOGRAPHIC DUPLICATION* **SEE** PHOTOMECHANICAL PROCESSES / *printing of engravings*
UG476	PHOTOGRAPHIC INTERPRETATION (MILITARY SCIENCE)
TR270	*PHOTOGRAPHIC LENSES* **SEE** LENSES, PHOTOGRAPHIC
TR693	*PHOTOGRAPHIC MEASUREMENTS* **SEE** PHOTOGRAMMETRY
TA593	*PHOTOGRAPHIC MEASUREMENTS* **SEE** PHOTOGRAMMETRY / *surveying*
QB121	*PHOTOGRAPHIC MEASUREMENTS OF STARS* **SEE** STARS — PHOTOGRAPHIC MEASUREMENTS
QB815	*PHOTOGRAPHIC MEASUREMENTS OF STARS* **SEE** STARS — PHOTOGRAPHIC MEASUREMENTS
TR220	PHOTOGRAPHIC OPTICS
TR825	*PHOTOGRAPHIC REPRODUCTION PROCESSES* **SEE** PHOTOCOPYING PROCESSES
TT273	*PHOTOGRAPHIC SCREEN PROCESS PRINTING* **SEE** SCREEN PROCESS PRINTING
TR196	PHOTOGRAPHIC SENSITOMETRY
TR196-9	*PHOTOGRAPHIC SUPPLIES* **SEE** PHOTOGRAPHY — APPARATUS AND SUPPLIES
TA593	PHOTOGRAPHIC SURVEYING
TR225	*PHOTOGRAPHIC WASTES* **SEE** PHOTOGRAPHY — WASTES, RECOVERY OF
N4035	PHOTOGRAPHS — CATALOGS / *fine arts*
TR485	PHOTOGRAPHS — COLORING
TR465	PHOTOGRAPHS — CONSERVATION AND RESTORATION
TR340	PHOTOGRAPHS — TRIMMING, MOUNTING, ETC.
Z654	*PHOTOGRAPHS - COPYRIGHT* **SEE** COPYRIGHT — PHOTOGRAPHS
TR495	PHOTOGRAPHS ON CLOTH
TR495	PHOTOGRAPHS ON GLASS
TR495	PHOTOGRAPHS ON PORCELAIN
TR495	*PHOTOGRAPHS ON SILK* **SEE** PHOTOGRAPHS ON CLOTH
Z697.P	*PHOTOGRAPHS-CLASSIFICATION* **SEE** CLASSIFICATION — PHOTOGRAPHS
Z654	*PHOTOGRAPHS-COPYRIGHT* **SEE** COPYRIGHT — PHOTOGRAPHS
TR6	*PHOTOGRAPHS-EXHIBITIONS* **SEE** PHOTOGRAPHY — EXHIBITIONS
TR185	PHOTOGRAPHY — ADDRESSES, ESSAYS, LECTURES
TR196-9	PHOTOGRAPHY — APPARATUS AND SUPPLIES
TR600	PHOTOGRAPHY — ARTIFICIAL LIGHT
TR581	PHOTOGRAPHY — BUSINESS METHODS
TR5	PHOTOGRAPHY — CONGRESSES
TR470	PHOTOGRAPHY — COPYING
TR900-923	PHOTOGRAPHY — COPYING / *industrial*
TR295	PHOTOGRAPHY — DEVELOPING AND DEVELOPERS
TR9	PHOTOGRAPHY — DICTIONARIES
TR144	PHOTOGRAPHY — EARLY WORKS TO 1850
TR475	PHOTOGRAPHY — ENLARGING
TR905	PHOTOGRAPHY — ENLARGING / *industrial*
TR6	PHOTOGRAPHY — EXHIBITIONS
TR591-605	PHOTOGRAPHY — EXPOSURE
TR147	PHOTOGRAPHY — FAILURES
TR283	PHOTOGRAPHY — FILMS

TR151	PHOTOGRAPHY — FORMULAE, TABLES, ETC.
TR146	PHOTOGRAPHY — HANDBOOKS, MANUALS, ETC.
TR15-124	PHOTOGRAPHY — HISTORY
TR620	PHOTOGRAPHY — INTERIORS
TR660	PHOTOGRAPHY — LANDSCAPES
Z681	PHOTOGRAPHY — LIBRARY APPLICATIONS
TR590-620	PHOTOGRAPHY — LIGHTING
TR573	PHOTOGRAPHY — LIGHTING
TR670	PHOTOGRAPHY — MARINES
TR290-310	PHOTOGRAPHY — NEGATIVES
TR1	PHOTOGRAPHY — PERIODICALS
TR281	PHOTOGRAPHY — PLATES
TR680	PHOTOGRAPHY — PORTRAITS
TR575	PHOTOGRAPHY — PORTRAITS
TR285	PHOTOGRAPHY — PRINTING PAPERS
TR330-445	PHOTOGRAPHY — PRINTING PROCESSES
TR920-923	PHOTOGRAPHY — REPRODUCTION OF PLANS, DRAWINGS, ETC.
TR310	PHOTOGRAPHY — RETOUCHING
TR705-710	PHOTOGRAPHY — SCIENTIFIC APPLICATIONS
TR1	PHOTOGRAPHY — SOCIETIES, ETC.
TR550-573	PHOTOGRAPHY — STUDIOS AND DARK ROOMS
TR225	PHOTOGRAPHY — WASTES, RECOVERY OF
TR1	PHOTOGRAPHY — YEARBOOKS
QH245	PHOTOGRAPHY OF ANIMALS
TR630	*PHOTOGRAPHY OF ARCHITECTURE* **SEE** PHOTOGRAPHY, ARCHITECTURAL
QH245	PHOTOGRAPHY OF BIRDS
TR575	PHOTOGRAPHY OF CHILDREN
TR680	PHOTOGRAPHY OF CHILDREN
TR660	PHOTOGRAPHY OF CLOUDS / *artistic photography*
QC923	PHOTOGRAPHY OF CLOUDS / *meteorology*
TR825	*PHOTOGRAPHY OF DOCUMENTS* **SEE** PHOTOCOPYING PROCESSES
QH245	PHOTOGRAPHY OF FISHES
QH245	*PHOTOGRAPHY OF FLOWERS* **SEE** PHOTOGRAPHY OF PLANTS
QH245	PHOTOGRAPHY OF INSECTS
QH245	PHOTOGRAPHY OF LEAVES
Z110.R4	*PHOTOGRAPHY OF MANUSCRIPTS* **SEE** MANUSCRIPTS — REPRODUCTION
TR825	*PHOTOGRAPHY OF MANUSCRIPTS* **SEE** PHOTOCOPYING PROCESSES
TR787	PHOTOGRAPHY OF MOUNTAINS
QH245	*PHOTOGRAPHY OF NATURE* **SEE** NATURE PHOTOGRAPHY
QH245	PHOTOGRAPHY OF PLANTS
TR670	PHOTOGRAPHY OF SHIPS
TR682	PHOTOGRAPHY OF SPORTS
TR705	PHOTOGRAPHY OF THE INVISIBLE
TR675	PHOTOGRAPHY OF THE NUDE
TR960	*PHOTOGRAPHY ON WOOD* **SEE** PHOTOXYLOGRAPHY
TR	PHOTOGRAPHY
TR690	PHOTOGRAPHY, ADVERTISING
TR810	PHOTOGRAPHY, AERIAL
TR630	PHOTOGRAPHY, ARCHITECTURAL
TR650-682	PHOTOGRAPHY, ARTISTIC
TR183	PHOTOGRAPHY, ARTISTIC / *aesthetics*
QB121	*PHOTOGRAPHY, ASTRONOMICAL* **SEE** ASTRONOMICAL PHOTOGRAPHY
UF840	PHOTOGRAPHY, BALLISTIC
QH245	PHOTOGRAPHY, BIOLOGICAL
TR510-525	*PHOTOGRAPHY, COLOR* **SEE** COLOR PHOTOGRAPHY
TR690	PHOTOGRAPHY, COMMERCIAL
TR685	PHOTOGRAPHY, COMPOSITE
TR830	*PHOTOGRAPHY, CRIME* **SEE** PHOTOGRAPHY, LEGAL
HV6071	*PHOTOGRAPHY, CRIME* **SEE** PHOTOGRAPHY, LEGAL / *social pathology*
HV8077	*PHOTOGRAPHY, CRIME* **SEE** PHOTOGRAPHY, LEGAL / *social pathology*
TR605	PHOTOGRAPHY, FLASH-LIGHT
TR830	*PHOTOGRAPHY, FORENSIC* **SEE** PHOTOGRAPHY, LEGAL
HV6071	*PHOTOGRAPHY, FORENSIC* **SEE** PHOTOGRAPHY, LEGAL / *social pathology*
HV8077	*PHOTOGRAPHY, FORENSIC* **SEE** PHOTOGRAPHY, LEGAL / *social pathology*
TR755	PHOTOGRAPHY, INFRA-RED
TR592	PHOTOGRAPHY, INSTANTANEOUS
TR820	PHOTOGRAPHY, JOURNALISTIC
TR830	PHOTOGRAPHY, LEGAL
HV8077	PHOTOGRAPHY, LEGAL / *social pathology*
HV6071	PHOTOGRAPHY, LEGAL / *social pathology*
TR705	PHOTOGRAPHY, MEDICAL
TR785	PHOTOGRAPHY, MILITARY
TR610	PHOTOGRAPHY, NIGHT
TR675	*PHOTOGRAPHY, NUDE* **SEE** PHOTOGRAPHY OF THE NUDE
TR453	PHOTOGRAPHY, ORTHOCHROMATIC
TR661	PHOTOGRAPHY, PANORAMIC
TR650-682	*PHOTOGRAPHY, PICTORIAL* **SEE** PHOTOGRAPHY, ARTISTIC
TR183	*PHOTOGRAPHY, PICTORIAL* **SEE** PHOTOGRAPHY, ARTISTIC / *aesthetics*
TR268	PHOTOGRAPHY, PINHOLE
TR830	*PHOTOGRAPHY, POLICE* **SEE** PHOTOGRAPHY, LEGAL
HV6071	*PHOTOGRAPHY, POLICE* **SEE** PHOTOGRAPHY, LEGAL / *social pathology*
HV8077	*PHOTOGRAPHY, POLICE* **SEE** PHOTOGRAPHY, LEGAL / *social pathology*
TK6600	*PHOTOGRAPHY, RADIO* **SEE** PHOTOTELEGRAPHY
TR780	PHOTOGRAPHY, STEREOSCOPIC
TR800	PHOTOGRAPHY, SUBMARINE
TR650	PHOTOGRAPHY, TABLE-TOP
TR148	PHOTOGRAPHY, TRICK
TR715	PHOTOGRAPHY, TROPICAL
TR650-682	*PHOTOGRAPHY-AESTHETICS* **SEE** PHOTOGRAPHY, ARTISTIC
TR183	*PHOTOGRAPHY-AESTHETICS* **SEE** PHOTOGRAPHY, ARTISTIC / *aesthetics*
TR845-899	*PHOTOGRAPHY-ANIMATED PICTURES* **SEE** CINEMATOGRAPHY
PN1992-9	*PHOTOGRAPHY-ANIMATED PICTURES* **SEE** MOVING-PICTURES
TR845-899	*PHOTOGRAPHY-ANIMATED PICTURES* **SEE** MOVING-PICTURES / *photography*
TR179	*PHOTOGRAPHY-COMPOSITION* **SEE** COMPOSITION (PHOTOGRAPHY)
TR270	*PHOTOGRAPHY-LENSES* **SEE** LENSES, PHOTOGRAPHIC
TR845-899	*PHOTOGRAPHY-MOVING-PICTURES* **SEE** CINEMATOGRAPHY
PN1992-9	*PHOTOGRAPHY-MOVING-PICTURES* **SEE** MOVING-PICTURES
TR845-899	*PHOTOGRAPHY-MOVING-PICTURES* **SEE** MOVING-PICTURES / *photography*
TR285	*PHOTOGRAPHY-PAPERS* **SEE** PHOTOGRAPHY — PRINTING PAPERS
TR415	*PHOTOGRAPHY-PRINTING PROCESSES-BLUE-PRINTING* **SEE** BLUE-PRINTING
TR921	*PHOTOGRAPHY-PRINTING PROCESSES-BLUE-PRINTING* **SEE** BLUE-PRINTING / *industrial reproduction*
TR415	*PHOTOGRAPHY-PRINTING PROCESSES-CYANOTYPE* **SEE** BLUE-PRINTING
TR921	*PHOTOGRAPHY-PRINTING PROCESSES-CYANOTYPE* **SEE** BLUE-PRINTING / *industrial reproduction*
TR415	*PHOTOGRAPHY-PRINTING PROCESSES-FERROPRUSSIATE* **SEE** BLUE-PRINTING
TR921	*PHOTOGRAPHY-PRINTING PROCESSES-FERROPRUSSIATE* **SEE** BLUE-PRINTING / *industrial reproduction*
TR196	*PHOTOGRAPHY-SENSITOMETRY* **SEE** PHOTOGRAPHIC SENSITOMETRY
TR196-9	*PHOTOGRAPHY-SUPPLIES* **SEE** PHOTOGRAPHY — APPARATUS AND SUPPLIES
TR197-8	PHOTOGRAPHY — APPARATUS AND SUPPLIES — — CATALOGS
TR196	PHOTOGRAPHY — APPARATUS AND SUPPLIES — — TESTING
TR573	PHOTOGRAPHY — PORTRAITS — — LIGHTING AND POSING
TR440	PHOTOGRAPHY — PRINTING PROCESSES — — CARBON
TR445	PHOTOGRAPHY — PRINTING PROCESSES — — GUM-BICHROMATE
TR433	PHOTOGRAPHY — PRINTING PROCESSES — — OZOTYPE
TR420	PHOTOGRAPHY — PRINTING PROCESSES — — PLATINOTYPE

TR385-400	PHOTOGRAPHY — PRINTING PROCESSES — — SILVER
TR335	PHOTOGRAPHY — PRINTING PROCESSES — — TONING
TR980	PHOTOGRAVURE
NE2665	PHOTOGRAVURES
NE2615	PHOTOGRAVURES
QB121	PHOTOHELIOGRAPH
TR820	*PHOTOJOURNALISM* **SEE** PHOTOGRAPHY, JOURNALISTIC
TR940-950	PHOTOLITHOGRAPHY
QD601	*PHOTOLYSIS (CHEMISTRY)* **SEE** PHOTOCHEMISTRY
TR925-997	PHOTOMECHANICAL PROCESSES
NE2890	PHOTOMECHANICAL PROCESSES / *printing of engravings*
QC391	PHOTOMETRY
TK4175	PHOTOMETRY / *electric light general*
TP754	PHOTOMETRY / *gas testing*
TK4367	PHOTOMETRY / *incandescent*
QB135	PHOTOMETRY, ASTRONOMICAL
QB815	PHOTOMETRY, ASTRONOMICAL / *stellar magnitudes*
QH251	PHOTOMICROGRAPHY
TK7872.E5	*PHOTOMULTIPLIERS* **SEE** PHOTOELECTRIC MULTIPLIERS
TL783.57	PHOTON ROCKETS
PN1995.7	*PHOTOPHONE* **SEE** MOVING-PICTURES, TALKING
PN1996-7	*PHOTOPLAYS* **SEE** MOVING-PICTURE PLAYS
TR999.P5	PHOTOSCULPTURE
TR470	PHOTOSTAT
QK882	PHOTOSYNTHESIS
TK6600	PHOTOTELEGRAPHY
RM835-844	PHOTOTHERAPY
TA593	*PHOTOTOPOGRAPHY* **SEE** PHOTOGRAPHIC SURVEYING
QH651	PHOTOTROPISM
QK776	PHOTOTROPISM / *botany*
QC715	*PHOTOTUBES* **SEE** PHOTOELECTRIC CELLS
QC715	*PHOTOVOLTAIC CELLS* **SEE** PHOTOELECTRIC CELLS
TR960	PHOTOXYLOGRAPHY
PL4351.K6	*PHOUTENG LANGUAGE* **SEE** KHMU' LANGUAGE
QM471	PHRENIC NERVE
BF866-885	PHRENOLOGY
RZ501	PHRENOLOGY / *phrenology and medicine*
P1057	PHRYGIAN LANGUAGE
QD441	PHTHALEINS
QD341.A2	PHTHALIC ACID
QD441	*PHTHALOCYANINE PIGMENTS* **SEE** PHTHALOCYANINS
QD441	PHTHALOCYANINS
QD341.A2	PHTHALONIC ACID
RC182.P	PHTHEIRIASIS
RC182.P	*PHTHIRIASIS* **SEE** PHTHEIRIASIS
RC306-320	*PHTHISIS* **SEE** TUBERCULOSIS
QR201.T6	*PHTHISIS* **SEE** TUBERCULOSIS / *bacteriology*
RA644.T7	*PHTHISIS* **SEE** TUBERCULOSIS / *public health*
HD7269.M6-61	*PHTHISIS, MINERS'* **SEE** MINERS' PHTHISIS
PM4296-9	*PHURHEMBE LANGUAGE* **SEE** TARASCAN LANGUAGE
QL444.L6	*PHYLLOCARIDA* **SEE** LEPTOSTRACA
QK646	PHYLLOCLADIA
QL444.B8	*PHYLLOPODA* **SEE** BRANCHIOPODA
QK649	PHYLLOTAXIS
SB608.G7	PHYLLOXERA / *grape pests*
QL523.A6	PHYLLOXERA / *zoology*
QK667	PHYLOGENY (BOTANY)
QH371	*PHYLOGENY (ZOOLOGY)* **SEE** PHYLOGENY
QH371	PHYLOGENY
GN51-211	*PHYSICAL ANTHROPOLOGY* **SEE** SOMATOLOGY
GV436	*PHYSICAL CAPACITY* **SEE** PHYSICAL FITNESS — TESTING
QD453-651	*PHYSICAL CHEMISTRY* **SEE** CHEMISTRY, PHYSICAL AND THEORETICAL
RB150-151	*PHYSICAL CONSTITUTION OF MAN* **SEE** MAN — CONSTITUTION / *theories of disease*
BF698	*PHYSICAL CONSTITUTION OF MAN* **SEE** MAN — CONSTITUTION / *personality*
BF818	*PHYSICAL CONSTITUTION OF MAN* **SEE** MAN — CONSTITUTION / *character*
BF795-811	*PHYSICAL CONSTITUTION OF MAN* **SEE** MAN — CONSTITUTION / *temperament*
GN60	*PHYSICAL CONSTITUTION OF MAN* **SEE** MAN — CONSTITUTION / *anthropology*
RM721	*PHYSICAL CULTURE* **SEE** PHYSICAL EDUCATION AND TRAINING / *physical culture and therapeutics*
RA781	*PHYSICAL CULTURE* **SEE** PHYSICAL EDUCATION AND TRAINING / *physical culture and hygiene*
GV201-547	*PHYSICAL CULTURE* **SEE** PHYSICAL EDUCATION AND TRAINING
RC76	PHYSICAL DIAGNOSIS
ML3923	*PHYSICAL EDUCATION AND MUSIC* **SEE** MUSIC IN PHYSICAL EDUCATION
GV346	PHYSICAL EDUCATION AND TRAINING — ADMINISTRATION
GV187	PHYSICAL EDUCATION AND TRAINING — FILM CATALOGS
GV342	PHYSICAL EDUCATION AND TRAINING — PHILOSOPHY
GV344	PHYSICAL EDUCATION AND TRAINING — SAFETY MEASURES
GV363	PHYSICAL EDUCATION AND TRAINING — TEACHER TRAINING
GV201-547	PHYSICAL EDUCATION AND TRAINING
RA781	PHYSICAL EDUCATION AND TRAINING / *physical culture and hygiene*
RM721	PHYSICAL EDUCATION AND TRAINING / *physical culture and therapeutics*
U320-325	PHYSICAL EDUCATION AND TRAINING, MILITARY
GV401	PHYSICAL EDUCATION FACILITIES
GV443	PHYSICAL EDUCATION FOR CHILDREN
HV1767	*PHYSICAL EDUCATION FOR THE BLIND* **SEE** BLIND, PHYSICAL EDUCATION FOR THE
GV439	PHYSICAL EDUCATION FOR WOMEN
TL856	*PHYSICAL EXAMINATION OF ASTRONAUTS* **SEE** ASTRONAUTS — MEDICAL EXAMINATIONS
GV436	PHYSICAL FITNESS — TESTING
GB51	PHYSICAL GEOGRAPHY — EARLY WORKS TO 1800
GB23	PHYSICAL GEOGRAPHY — EXAMINATIONS, QUESTIONS, ETC.
GB25	PHYSICAL GEOGRAPHY — FIELD WORK
GB58	PHYSICAL GEOGRAPHY — JUVENILE LITERATURE
GB23	PHYSICAL GEOGRAPHY — LABORATORY MANUALS
GB	PHYSICAL GEOGRAPHY
GB55-56	PHYSICAL GEOGRAPHY — TEXT-BOOKS — — 1800-1870
GB55-56	PHYSICAL GEOGRAPHY — TEXT-BOOKS — — 1870-1945
TS500	PHYSICAL INSTRUMENTS — TRADE AND MANUFACTURE
QC53	PHYSICAL INSTRUMENTS
QC51	PHYSICAL LABORATORIES
QC39	PHYSICAL MEASUREMENTS
TN690	PHYSICAL METALLURGY
GC	*PHYSICAL OCEANOGRAPHY* **SEE** OCEANOGRAPHY
QC401-495	*PHYSICAL OPTICS* **SEE** OPTICS, PHYSICAL
QD476	*PHYSICAL ORGANIC CHEMISTRY* **SEE** CHEMISTRY, PHYSICAL ORGANIC
RA781	*PHYSICAL TRAINING* **SEE** PHYSICAL EDUCATION AND TRAINING / *physical culture and hygiene*
RM721	*PHYSICAL TRAINING* **SEE** PHYSICAL EDUCATION AND TRAINING / *physical culture and therapeutics*
GV201-547	*PHYSICAL TRAINING* **SEE** PHYSICAL EDUCATION AND TRAINING
B824.6	*PHYSICALISM* **SEE** LOGICAL POSITIVISM
N71.3	*PHYSICALLY HANDICAPPED ARTISTS* **SEE** ARTISTS, PHYSICALLY HANDICAPPED
LC4201-4580	PHYSICALLY HANDICAPPED CHILDREN — EDUCATION
LC4201-4580	PHYSICALLY HANDICAPPED CHILDREN
R727.3	PHYSICIAN AND PATIENT
R134	PHYSICIANS — BIOGRAPHY
R153-684	PHYSICIANS — BIOGRAPHY / *local*
R154-684	PHYSICIANS — CORRESPONDENCE, REMINISCENCES, ETC.
GT6330-6370	PHYSICIANS — COSTUME
N7627-8	PHYSICIANS — PORTRAITS
BV4596.P5	PHYSICIANS — RELIGIOUS LIFE
R707.3	PHYSICIANS AS MUSICIANS
N8223	*PHYSICIANS IN ART* **SEE** MEDICINE AND ART
R707.5	PHYSICIANS IN LITERATURE
GT6330-6370	PHYSICIANS / *manners and customs*
UH400	PHYSICIANS / *military*
UH221-324	PHYSICIANS / *military*
VG100-224	PHYSICIANS / *naval*
RX61-66	PHYSICIANS, HOMEOPATHIC

HF5686.P9	*PHYSICIANS-ACCOUNTING* **SEE** MEDICINE — PRACTICE — — ACCOUNTING
R705	*PHYSICIANS-ANECDOTES, FACETIAE, SATIRE, ETC.* **SEE** MEDICINE — ANECDOTES, FACETIAE, SATIRE, ETC.
PN6231.M4	*PHYSICIANS-ANECDOTES, FACETIAE, SATIRE, ETC.* **SEE** MEDICINE — ANECDOTES, FACETIAE, SATIRE, ETC.
RA11-405	*PHYSICIANS-LEGAL STATUS, LAWS, ETC.* **SEE** MEDICAL LAWS AND LEGISLATION
QC16	PHYSICISTS — CORRESPONDENCE, REMINISCENCES, ETC.
QC15-16	PHYSICISTS
QC17-19	PHYSICS — EARLY WORKS TO 1800
QC32	PHYSICS — EXAMINATIONS, QUESTIONS, ETC.
QC33	PHYSICS — EXPERIMENTS
QC25	PHYSICS — JUVENILE LITERATURE
QC36	PHYSICS — LABORATORY BLANKS
QC35-37	PHYSICS — LABORATORY MANUALS
QC6	PHYSICS — PHILOSOPHY
QC32	PHYSICS — PROBLEMS, EXERCISES, ETC.
QC61	PHYSICS — TABLES, ETC.
QC	PHYSICS
QB461	*PHYSICS, ASTRONOMICAL* **SEE** ASTROPHYSICS
QC173	*PHYSICS, NUCLEAR* **SEE** NUCLEAR PHYSICS
QC806	*PHYSICS, TERRESTRIAL* **SEE** GEOPHYSICS
QE500-501	*PHYSICS, TERRESTRIAL* **SEE** GEOPHYSICS
QC53	*PHYSICS-APPARATUS AND INSTRUMENTS* **SEE** PHYSICAL INSTRUMENTS
HB93	PHYSIOCRATS
BF840-861	PHYSIOGNOMY
QE	*PHYSIOGRAPHY* **SEE** GEOLOGY
GB	*PHYSIOGRAPHY* **SEE** PHYSICAL GEOGRAPHY
GN275	*PHYSIOLOGICAL ACOUSTICS* **SEE** HEARING / anthropology
QP461-9	*PHYSIOLOGICAL ACOUSTICS* **SEE** HEARING / physiology
BF251	*PHYSIOLOGICAL ACOUSTICS* **SEE** HEARING / psychology
ML3805-3817	*PHYSIOLOGICAL ACOUSTICS* **SEE** MUSIC — ACOUSTICS AND PHYSICS
QP55	PHYSIOLOGICAL APPARATUS
RC1075	*PHYSIOLOGICAL ASPECTS OF FLIGHT* **SEE** FLIGHT — PHYSIOLOGICAL ASPECTS
ML3820-3822	*PHYSIOLOGICAL ASPECTS OF MUSIC* **SEE** MUSIC — PHYSIOLOGICAL ASPECTS
QP519	PHYSIOLOGICAL CHEMISTRY — LABORATORY MANUALS
QP501-801	PHYSIOLOGICAL CHEMISTRY
RM666.C2	*PHYSIOLOGICAL EFFECT OF CAFFEIN* **SEE** CAFFEIN — PHYSIOLOGICAL EFFECT / therapeutics
QP921.C3	*PHYSIOLOGICAL EFFECT OF CAFFEIN* **SEE** CAFFEIN — PHYSIOLOGICAL EFFECT
QP913.C1	*PHYSIOLOGICAL EFFECT OF CARBON DIOXIDE* **SEE** CARBON DIOXIDE — PHYSIOLOGICAL EFFECT
RM	*PHYSIOLOGICAL EFFECT OF CHEMICALS* **SEE** PHARMACOLOGY
QP903-981	*PHYSIOLOGICAL EFFECT OF CHEMICALS* **SEE** PHARMACOLOGY / experimental
QP913.H6	*PHYSIOLOGICAL EFFECT OF MERCURY* **SEE** MERCURY — PHYSIOLOGICAL EFFECT
QP51-53	PHYSIOLOGICAL LABORATORIES
QP474-495	*PHYSIOLOGICAL OPTICS* **SEE** OPTICS, PHYSIOLOGICAL
QP177	*PHYSIOLOGICAL OXIDATION* **SEE** OXIDATION, PHYSIOLOGICAL
QP351-499	*PHYSIOLOGICAL PSYCHOLOGY* **SEE** PSYCHOLOGY, PHYSIOLOGICAL
RM695-737	*PHYSIOLOGICAL THERAPEUTICS* **SEE** THERAPEUTICS, PHYSIOLOGICAL
QP25	PHYSIOLOGISTS
QP29	PHYSIOLOGY — EARLY WORKS TO 1800
QP40	PHYSIOLOGY — EXAMINATIONS, QUESTIONS, ETC.
QP37	PHYSIOLOGY — JUVENILE LITERATURE
QP42-44	PHYSIOLOGY — LABORATORY MANUALS
QP	PHYSIOLOGY
QP31-33	PHYSIOLOGY, COMPARATIVE
RB113	PHYSIOLOGY, PATHOLOGICAL
QP55	*PHYSIOLOGY-APPARATUS* **SEE** PHYSIOLOGICAL APPARATUS
RM133	*PHYSIOMEDICALISM* **SEE** MEDICINE, PHYSIOMEDICAL
RB113	*PHYSIOPATHOLOGY* **SEE** PHYSIOLOGY, PATHOLOGICAL
QH	*PHYSIOPHILOSOPHY* **SEE** NATURAL HISTORY
RM695-737	*PHYSIOTHERAPY* **SEE** THERAPEUTICS, PHYSIOLOGICAL
Z259	*PHYSIOTYPY* **SEE** NATURE-PRINTING AND NATURE-PRINTS
QL503.T5	*PHYSOPODA* **SEE** THRIPS
QL638.I	*PHYSOSTOMI* **SEE** ISOSPONDYLI
QK898.P	PHYTIC ACID / botany
QK898.P	PHYTIN / botany
RM666.P	PHYTIN / therapeutics
Z259	*PHYTOGLYPHY* **SEE** NATURE-PRINTING AND NATURE-PRINTS
QK	*PHYTOGRAPHY* **SEE** BOTANY
QK731	*PHYTOHORMONES* **SEE** HORMONES (PLANTS)
QK	*PHYTOLOGY* **SEE** BOTANY
QR351	*PHYTOPATHOGENIC BACTERIA* **SEE** BACTERIA, PHYTOPATHOGENIC
SB599-791	*PHYTOPATHOLOGY* **SEE** PLANT DISEASES
QL596.P5	PHYTOPHAGA
ML397	PIANISTS / biography collective
ML417	PIANISTS / individual
E99.P57	PIANKASHAW INDIANS
MT248	PIANO — CHORD DIAGRAMS
ML652-697	PIANO — CONSTRUCTION
ML102	PIANO — DICTIONARIES
ML650-697	PIANO — HISTORY
MT220-255	PIANO — INSTRUCTION AND STUDY
MT745-758	PIANO — INSTRUCTION AND STUDY / juvenile
MT239	PIANO — METHODS (BOOGIE WOOGIE)
MT239	PIANO — METHODS (JAZZ)
MT222	PIANO — METHODS
ML700-742	PIANO — PERFORMANCE
MT220	PIANO — PRACTICING
MT239	PIANO — STUDIES AND EXERCISES (JAZZ)
MT225-240	PIANO — STUDIES AND EXERCISES
M1011	PIANO (1 HAND) WITH ORCHESTRA — 2-PIANO SCORES
M1010-1011	PIANO (1 HAND) WITH ORCHESTRA
M191-3	PIANO (4 HANDS) AND REED-ORGAN MUSIC
ML990.A4	*PIANO ACCORDION* **SEE** ACCORDION / history and construction
M285.A3	*PIANO AND ACCORDION MUSIC* **SEE** ACCORDION AND PIANO MUSIC
M284.A3	*PIANO AND ACCORDION MUSIC* **SEE** ACCORDION AND PIANO MUSIC
M270-271	*PIANO AND ALTO HORN MUSIC* **SEE** ALTO HORN AND PIANO MUSIC
M282-3	*PIANO AND BALALAIKA MUSIC* **SEE** BALALAIKA AND PIANO MUSIC
M262-3	*PIANO AND BARITONE MUSIC* **SEE** BARITONE AND PIANO MUSIC
M262-3	*PIANO AND BARITONE MUSIC* **SEE** BARITONE AND PIANO MUSIC
M271.B4	*PIANO AND BASSET-HORN MUSIC* **SEE** BASSET-HORN AND PIANO MUSIC
M270.B4	*PIANO AND BASSET-HORN MUSIC* **SEE** BASSET-HORN AND PIANO MUSIC
M253-4	*PIANO AND BASSOON MUSIC* **SEE** BASSOON AND PIANO MUSIC
M282.C5	*PIANO AND CIMBALOM MUSIC* **SEE** CIMBALOM AND PIANO MUSIC
M283.C5	*PIANO AND CIMBALOM MUSIC* **SEE** CIMBALOM AND PIANO MUSIC
M248-250	*PIANO AND CLARINET MUSIC* **SEE** CLARINET AND PIANO MUSIC
M260-261	*PIANO AND CORNET MUSIC* **SEE** CORNET AND PIANO MUSIC
M240-242	*PIANO AND CZAKAN MUSIC* **SEE** CZAKAN AND PIANO MUSIC
M282-3	*PIANO AND DOMRA MUSIC* **SEE** DOMRA AND PIANO MUSIC
M282-3	*PIANO AND DOMRA MUSIC* **SEE** DOMRA AND PIANO MUSIC
M237-8	*PIANO AND DOUBLE-BASS MUSIC* **SEE** DOUBLE-BASS AND PIANO MUSIC
M246.2	*PIANO AND ENGLISH HORN MUSIC* **SEE** ENGLISH HORN AND PIANO MUSIC

M240-242	*PIANO AND FLAGEOLET MUSIC* **SEE** FLAGEOLET AND PIANO MUSIC	M233	*PIANO AND VIOLONCELLO MUSIC* **SEE** VIOLONCELLO AND PIANO MUSIC
M240-242	*PIANO AND FLAGEOLET MUSIC* **SEE** FLAGEOLET AND PIANO MUSIC	M284-5	*PIANO AND XYLOPHONE MUSIC* **SEE** XYLOPHONE AND PIANO MUSIC
M240-242	*PIANO AND FLUTE MUSIC* **SEE** FLUTE AND PIANO MUSIC	M284-5	*PIANO AND XYLOPHONE MUSIC* **SEE** XYLOPHONE AND PIANO MUSIC
M285.G6	*PIANO AND GLASS-HARMONICA MUSIC* **SEE** GLASS-HARMONICA AND PIANO MUSIC	M214	*PIANO DUETS* **SEE** PIANO MUSIC (2 PIANOS)
		M241	*PIANO DUETS* **SEE** PIANO MUSIC (2 PIANOS)
M284.G6	*PIANO AND GLASS-HARMONICA MUSIC* **SEE** GLASS-HARMONICA AND PIANO MUSIC	M200-201	*PIANO DUETS* **SEE** PIANO MUSIC (4 HANDS)
		M204	*PIANO DUETS* **SEE** PIANO MUSIC (4 HANDS)
M276-7	*PIANO AND GUITAR MUSIC* **SEE** GUITAR AND PIANO MUSIC	ML650-697	PIANO MAKERS
		MT145	PIANO MUSIC — ANALYSIS, APPRECIATION
M272-3	*PIANO AND HARP MUSIC* **SEE** HARP AND PIANO MUSIC	MT140	PIANO MUSIC — ANALYSIS, APPRECIATION
		MT140	PIANO MUSIC — ANALYTICAL GUIDES
M214	*PIANO AND HARPSICHORD MUSIC* **SEE** HARPSICHORD AND PIANO MUSIC	MT145	PIANO MUSIC — ANALYTICAL GUIDES
		ML128.P3	PIANO MUSIC — BIBLIOGRAPHY
M255-7	*PIANO AND HORN MUSIC* **SEE** HORN AND PIANO MUSIC	ML700-749	PIANO MUSIC — HISTORY AND CRITICISM
		MT245-7	PIANO MUSIC — INSTRUCTIVE EDITIONS
M278-9	*PIANO AND MANDOLIN MUSIC* **SEE** MANDOLIN AND PIANO MUSIC	MT235	PIANO MUSIC — INTERPRETATION (PHRASING, DYNAMICS, ETC.)
M284-5	*PIANO AND MARIMBA MUSIC* **SEE** MARIMBA AND PIANO MUSIC	ML700	PIANO MUSIC — INTERPRETATION (PHRASING, DYNAMICS, ETC.)
M284-5	*PIANO AND MARIMBA MUSIC* **SEE** MARIMBA AND PIANO MUSIC	M38.3	PIANO MUSIC — SIMPLIFIED EDITIONS
		MT243	PIANO MUSIC — TEACHING PIECES
M284.M6	*PIANO AND MOUTH-ORGAN MUSIC* **SEE** MOUTH-ORGAN AND PIANO MUSIC	MT239	PIANO MUSIC (BOOGIE WOOGIE) — TEACHING PIECES
		M20-32	PIANO MUSIC (BOOGIE WOOGIE)
M285.M6	*PIANO AND MOUTH-ORGAN MUSIC* **SEE** MOUTH-ORGAN AND PIANO MUSIC	M20-32	PIANO MUSIC (JAZZ)
		M38.2	PIANO MUSIC (SOLOVOX REGISTRATION)
M245-6	*PIANO AND OBOE MUSIC* **SEE** OBOE AND PIANO MUSIC	M25.2	PIANO MUSIC (SOLOVOX REGISTRATION)
		M26.2	PIANO MUSIC (1 HAND)
M270-271	*PIANO AND OCARINA MUSIC* **SEE** OCARINA AND PIANO MUSIC	M26	PIANO MUSIC (1 HAND)
		M26	PIANO MUSIC (1 HAND), ARRANGED
M270-271	*PIANO AND OCARINA MUSIC* **SEE** OCARINA AND PIANO MUSIC	M26.2	PIANO MUSIC (1 HAND), ARRANGED
		M20-32	*PIANO MUSIC (2 HANDS)* **SEE** PIANO MUSIC
M284.O5	*PIANO AND ONDES MARTENOT MUSIC* **SEE** ONDES MARTENOT AND PIANO MUSIC	M214	PIANO MUSIC (2 PIANOS)
		M215	PIANO MUSIC (2 PIANOS), ARRANGED
M285.O5	*PIANO AND ONDES MARTENOT MUSIC* **SEE** ONDES MARTENOT AND PIANO MUSIC	M216	PIANO MUSIC (2 PIANOS, 6 HANDS)
		M216	PIANO MUSIC (2 PIANOS, 8 HANDS)
M182-4	PIANO AND ORGAN MUSIC	M216	PIANO MUSIC (2 PIANOS, 8 HANDS), ARRANGED
M186	PIANO AND ORGAN MUSIC, ARRANGED	M205	PIANO MUSIC (3 HANDS)
M284-5	*PIANO AND PERCUSSION MUSIC* **SEE** PERCUSSION AND PIANO MUSIC	M216	PIANO MUSIC (3 PIANOS)
		M216	PIANO MUSIC (3 PIANOS), ARRANGED
M240-242	*PIANO AND PICCOLO MUSIC* **SEE** PICCOLO AND PIANO MUSIC	M204	PIANO MUSIC (4 HANDS)
		M200-201	PIANO MUSIC (4 HANDS)
M240-242	*PIANO AND PICCOLO MUSIC* **SEE** PICCOLO AND PIANO MUSIC	M207-211	PIANO MUSIC (4 HANDS), ARRANGED
		M216	PIANO MUSIC (4 PIANOS)
M240-242	*PIANO AND RECORDER MUSIC* **SEE** RECORDER AND PIANO MUSIC	M216	PIANO MUSIC (4 PIANOS), ARRANGED
		M213	PIANO MUSIC (5 HANDS)
M194-5	PIANO AND REED-ORGAN MUSIC, ARRANGED	M216	PIANO MUSIC (5 PIANOS)
M266-7	*PIANO AND SAXHORN MUSIC* **SEE** SAXHORN AND PIANO MUSIC	M213	PIANO MUSIC (6 HANDS)
		M213	PIANO MUSIC (6 HANDS), ARRANGED
M266-7	*PIANO AND SAXHORN MUSIC* **SEE** SAXHORN AND PIANO MUSIC	M20-32	PIANO MUSIC
		M20-32	*PIANO MUSIC, ARRANGED (JAZZ)* **SEE** PIANO MUSIC (JAZZ)
M268-9	*PIANO AND SAXOPHONE MUSIC* **SEE** SAXOPHONE AND PIANO MUSIC	M32.8-38.5	PIANO MUSIC, ARRANGED
M262-3	*PIANO AND TROMBONE MUSIC* **SEE** TROMBONE AND PIANO MUSIC	MT758	PIANO MUSIC, JUVENILE — TEACHING PIECES
		M1389-1390	PIANO MUSIC, JUVENILE (2 PIANOS)
M260-261	*PIANO AND TRUMPET MUSIC* **SEE** TRUMPET AND PIANO MUSIC	M1389-1390	PIANO MUSIC, JUVENILE (3 HANDS)
		M1389-1390	PIANO MUSIC, JUVENILE (4 HANDS)
M264-5	*PIANO AND TUBA MUSIC* **SEE** TUBA AND PIANO MUSIC	M1389-1390	PIANO MUSIC, JUVENILE (6 HANDS)
		M1378-1380	PIANO MUSIC, JUVENILE
M282-3	*PIANO AND UKULELE MUSIC* **SEE** UKULELE AND PIANO MUSIC	ML132.P	*PIANO MUSIC-GRADED LISTS* **SEE** PIANO MUSIC — BIBLIOGRAPHY — — GRADED LISTS
M284-5	*PIANO AND VIBRAPHONE MUSIC* **SEE** VIBRAPHONE AND PIANO MUSIC	MT758	*PIANO MUSIC-TEACHING PIECES-JUVENILE* **SEE** PIANO MUSIC, JUVENILE — TEACHING PIECES
M284-5	*PIANO AND VIBRAPHONE MUSIC* **SEE** VIBRAPHONE AND PIANO MUSIC	ML128.P3	PIANO MUSIC — BIBLIOGRAPHY — — CATALOGS
		ML132.P	PIANO MUSIC — BIBLIOGRAPHY — — GRADED LISTS
M239	*PIANO AND VIOLA D'AMORE MUSIC* **SEE** VIOLA D'AMORE AND PIANO MUSIC	M38.3	PIANO MUSIC — TO 1800 — — SIMPLIFIED EDITIONS
M239	*PIANO AND VIOLA DA GAMBA MUSIC* **SEE** VIOLA DA GAMBA AND PIANO MUSIC	ML700-742	*PIANO PLAYING* **SEE** PIANO — PERFORMANCE
		MT220	*PIANO PRACTICING* **SEE** PIANO — PRACTICING
M239	*PIANO AND VIOLA DA GAMBA MUSIC* **SEE** VIOLA DA GAMBA AND PIANO MUSIC	ML1165	PIANO QUARTET
		MT140-145	PIANO QUARTETS — ANALYTICAL GUIDES
M224-6	*PIANO AND VIOLA MUSIC* **SEE** VIOLA AND PIANO MUSIC	M216	*PIANO QUARTETS (4 PIANOS)* **SEE** PIANO MUSIC (4 PIANOS)
M217-218	*PIANO AND VIOLIN MUSIC* **SEE** VIOLIN AND PIANO MUSIC	M216	*PIANO QUARTETS (4 PIANOS)* **SEE** PIANO MUSIC (4 PIANOS)
M221	*PIANO AND VIOLIN MUSIC* **SEE** VIOLIN AND PIANO MUSIC	M410-412	PIANO QUARTETS
		M413-414	PIANO QUARTETS, ARRANGED
		MT145	PIANO QUINTETS — ANALYTICAL GUIDES
		MT140	PIANO QUINTETS — ANALYTICAL GUIDES

M216	*PIANO QUINTETS (5 PIANOS)* **SEE** PIANO MUSIC (5 PIANOS)
M216	*PIANO QUINTETS (5 PIANOS)* **SEE** PIANO MUSIC (5 PIANOS)
M510-512	PIANO QUINTETS
M513-514	PIANO QUINTETS, ARRANGED
M36.5	*PIANO REALIZATIONS OF THOROUGH BASS* **SEE** THOROUGH BASS — REALIZATIONS
ML3790	*PIANO TRADE* **SEE** MUSIC TRADE
M1041	PIANO TRIO WITH ORCHESTRA — SOLOS WITH PIANO
M1040-1041	PIANO TRIO WITH ORCHESTRA
M1105-6	PIANO TRIO WITH STRING ORCHESTRA
MT140	PIANO TRIOS — ANALYTICAL GUIDES
MT145	PIANO TRIOS — ANALYTICAL GUIDES
M216	*PIANO TRIOS (3 PIANOS)* **SEE** PIANO MUSIC (3 PIANOS)
M310-312	PIANO TRIOS
M313-314	PIANO TRIOS, ARRANGED
M1415-1417	PIANO TRIOS, JUVENILE
M1205	PIANO WITH BAND — SCORES
M1205	PIANO WITH BAND — 2-PIANO SCORES
M1205	PIANO WITH BAND
M1257	PIANO WITH BAND, ARRANGED — SCORES (REDUCED) AND PARTS
M1257	PIANO WITH BAND, ARRANGED
M1010	PIANO WITH CHAMBER ORCHESTRA — SCORES
M1010-1011	PIANO WITH CHAMBER ORCHESTRA
M1010-1011	PIANO WITH CHAMBER ORCHESTRA, ARRANGED
M1353	PIANO WITH DANCE ORCHESTRA
M1010	PIANO WITH ORCHESTRA — SCORES AND PARTS
M1010	PIANO WITH ORCHESTRA — SCORES
M1011	PIANO WITH ORCHESTRA — 2-PIANO SCORES
M1010-1011	PIANO WITH ORCHESTRA
M1011	PIANO WITH ORCHESTRA, ARRANGED — 2-PIANO SCORES
M1353	PIANO WITH SALON ORCHESTRA
M1105	PIANO WITH STRING ORCHESTRA — SCORES
M1106	PIANO WITH STRING ORCHESTRA — 2-PIANO SCORES
M1105-6	PIANO WITH STRING ORCHESTRA
M1160	PIANO WITH STRING ORCHESTRA, ARRANGED — SCORES AND PARTS
ML1050-1055	*PIANO-PLAYER* **SEE** PLAYER-PIANO
MT150	*PIANO-PLAYER* **SEE** PLAYER-PIANO / analytical guides
MT700	*PIANO-PLAYER* **SEE** PLAYER-PIANO / instruction
ML650-749	PIANO
ML697	*PIANO, ELECTRONIC* **SEE** ELECTRONIC PIANO
M1105-6	PIANO, FLUTE, VIOLIN WITH STRING ORCHESTRA
M1105-6	PIANO, OBOE, TRUMPET, VIOLIN, DOUBLE BASS WITH STRING ORCHESTRA
M1040-1041	PIANO, SAXOPHONE, PERCUSSION, DOUBLE BASS WITH ORCHESTRA
M1041	PIANO, TRUMPET, VIOLA WITH ORCHESTRA — SCORES
M1040-1041	PIANO, TRUMPET, VIOLA WITH ORCHESTRA
M1105	PIANO, 2 VIOLINS WITH STRING ORCHESTRA — SCORES
M1105-6	PIANO, 2 VIOLINS WITH STRING ORCHESTRA
MT248	*PIANO-SELF-INSTRUCTION* **SEE** PIANO — METHODS — — SELF-INSTRUCTION
ML650-749	*PIANOFORTE* **SEE** PIANO
ML1090	*PIANOGRAPH* **SEE** MUSIC-RECORDERS
ML1055	PIANOLA / history
MT700	PIANOLA / instruction and study
MT150	PIANOLA / instruction and study
M1010-1011	PIANOS (2) WITH CHAMBER ORCHESTRA
M1010	PIANOS (2) WITH ORCHESTRA — PARTS
M1010	PIANOS (2) WITH ORCHESTRA — SCORES
M1011	PIANOS (2) WITH ORCHESTRA — 2-PIANO SCORES
M1010-1011	PIANOS (2) WITH ORCHESTRA
M1105-6	PIANOS (2) WITH STRING ORCHESTRA
M1010-1011	PIANOS (3) WITH ORCHESTRA
MT745-758	PIANO — INSTRUCTION AND STUDY — — JUVENILE
MT746	PIANO — METHODS — — JUVENILE
MT248	PIANO — METHODS — — SELF-INSTRUCTION
MT755	PIANO — STUDIES AND EXERCISES — — JUVENILE
BX3865.P5	PIARISTS
D569.P4	PIAVE, 1ST BATTLE OF THE, 1917
D569.P5	PIAVE, 2D BATTLE OF THE, 1918
PN3428-3430	PICARESQUE LITERATURE
PN3428-3430	*PICARESQUE NOVEL* **SEE** PICARESQUE LITERATURE
M240-242	PICCOLO AND PIANO MUSIC
M243-4	PICCOLO AND PIANO MUSIC, ARRANGED
M288-9	PICCOLO MUSIC (2 PICCOLOS)
M60-62	PICCOLO MUSIC
M1105-6	PICCOLO WITH STRING ORCHESTRA
ML935-7	PICCOLO
M1020	PICCOLOS (2) WITH ORCHESTRA — SCORES
M1020-1021	PICCOLOS (2) WITH ORCHESTRA
F3734	PICHINCHA, BATTLE OF, 1822
SH167.P	PICKEREL / fish-culture
QL638.E7	PICKEREL / zoology
U190-195	*PICKET DUTY* **SEE** GUARD DUTY
HD5468	*PICKET DUTY* **SEE** PICKETING
HD5468	PICKETING
TA467	*PICKLING (METALS)* **SEE** METALS — PICKLING
TX599-613	*PICKLING* **SEE** CANNING AND PRESERVING
SB481	PICNIC GROUNDS
GT2955	PICNICKING
QC111	*PICNOMETER* **SEE** PYCNOMETER
RS165.P65	PICROTOXIN / pharmacy
QP981.P5	PICROTOXIN / physiological effects
TR650-682	*PICTORIAL PHOTOGRAPHY* **SEE** PHOTOGRAPHY, ARTISTIC
TR183	*PICTORIAL PHOTOGRAPHY* **SEE** PHOTOGRAPHY, ARTISTIC / aesthetics
DA774	PICTS
BF698	PICTURE ARRANGEMENT TEST
N8020-8037	*PICTURE BIBLES* **SEE** BIBLE — PICTURE BIBLES
BS560	*PICTURE BIBLES* **SEE** BIBLE — PICTURE BIBLES
ND3355	*PICTURE BIBLES* **SEE** BIBLE — PICTURE BIBLES / illuminated manuscripts
N8550-8553	PICTURE FRAMES AND FRAMING
HE6181-5	*PICTURE POST-CARDS* **SEE** POSTAL CARDS
NC1870-1875	*PICTURE POST-CARDS* **SEE** POSTAL CARDS / picture post-cards
NC1800-1850	*PICTURE POSTERS* **SEE** POSTERS
HF5843	*PICTURE POSTERS* **SEE** POSTERS / advertising
GV1507.P47	PICTURE PUZZLES
TK6600	*PICTURE TELEGRAPHY* **SEE** PHOTOTELEGRAPHY
TK6655.P5	*PICTURE TUBES* **SEE** TELEVISION PICTURE TUBES
N400-490	*PICTURE-GALLERIES* **SEE** ART — GALLERIES AND MUSEUMS
E98.P6	PICTURE-WRITING, INDIAN
N4402-5097	PICTURES — CATALOGS / exhibitions
N5210-5297	PICTURES — CATALOGS / private galleries
N405-3990	PICTURES — CATALOGS / public galleries
N8580	PICTURES — COPYING
N8670-8675	PICTURES — PRICES
Z717	*PICTURES IN LIBRARIES* **SEE** LIBRARIES AND PICTURES
N350-375	PICTURES / art study in schools
ND1142-6	PICTURES / popular works
NC1300-1763	*PICTURES, HUMOROUS* **SEE** CARICATURES AND CARTOONS
NC1300-1765	*PICTURES, HUMOROUS* **SEE** WIT AND HUMOR, PICTORIAL
PM7891	*PIDGEON ENGLISH* **SEE** PIDGIN ENGLISH
PM7891	PIDGIN ENGLISH
HD4928.P5	PIECE-WORK / wages
E99.P58	PIEGAN INDIANS
E83.67	PIERCE FIGHT, CENTRAL FALLS, R.I., 1676
TG320	*PIERS (BRIDGE)* **SEE** BRIDGES — FOUNDATIONS AND PIERS
TC357	PIERS
TX773	*PIES* **SEE** PASTRY
N8070	PIETA
BX4980-4983	PIETISM
BX4980-4983	PIETISTS
BV4647.P5	PIETY
QC595	*PIEZO-ELECTRICITY* **SEE** PYRO- AND PIEZO-ELECTRICITY
QC286	PIEZOMETER / gases
QC284	PIEZOMETER / liquids
QL737.U5	*PIG* **SEE** SWINE
SF391-7	*PIG* **SEE** SWINE / animal industries
PE3729.U	PIG LATIN
QL638.H	PIG-FISH
TA474-5	*PIG-IRON* **SEE** CAST-IRON / materials of engineering

TN710	PIG-IRON SEE CAST-IRON / metallurgy
PM7891	PIGEON ENGLISH SEE PIDGIN ENGLISH
E356.P6	PIGEON ROOST MASSACRE, 1812
SB205.P5	PIGEON-PEA
PZ10.3	PIGEONS — LEGENDS AND STORIES / juvenile
QL795.B57	PIGEONS — LEGENDS AND STORIES / zoology
QL696.C6	PIGEONS
SF465-472	PIGEONS / breeding
HE6239.P	PIGEONS / carrier pigeons
UH90	PIGEONS / military communications
E83.72	PIGGWACKET FIGHT, 1725 SEE PIGWACKET FIGHT, 1725
E99.P	PIGGWACKET INDIANS SEE PEQUAWKET INDIANS
E83.7	PIGGWACKET INDIANS SEE PEQUAWKET INDIANS / wars
QL767	PIGMENT CELLS SEE CHROMATOPHORES
QL767	PIGMENTATION SEE COLOR OF ANIMALS
GN197	PIGMENTATION SEE COLOR OF MAN
QP91	PIGMENTS (BLOOD) SEE BLOOD — PIGMENTS
RB145	PIGMENTS (BLOOD) SEE BLOOD — PIGMENTS
TP936-7	PIGMENTS / chemical technology
ND1510	PIGMENTS / painting
QL737.U5	PIGS SEE SWINE
SF391-7	PIGS SEE SWINE / animal industries
E83.72	PIGWACKET FIGHT, 1725
E99.P	PIGWACKET INDIANS SEE PEQUAWKET INDIANS
E83.7	PIGWACKET INDIANS SEE PEQUAWKET INDIANS / wars
QL737.R6	PIKAS
SH691.P6	PIKE FISHING
SH167.P5	PIKE / fish-culture
PM8736	PIKTO
F2823.P5	PILAGA INDIANS
PM6909	PILAGA LANGUAGE
TA780-785	PILE-DRIVING SEE PILING (CIVIL ENGINEERING)
GN785-6	PILE-DWELLINGS SEE LAKE-DWELLERS AND LAKE-DWELLINGS
TA780-785	PILES (CIVIL ENGINEERING) SEE PILING (CIVIL ENGINEERING)
RC865	PILES (DISEASE) SEE HEMORRHOIDS
F68	PILGRIM FATHERS — ADDRESSES, COMMEMORATIONS, ETC.
F68	PILGRIM FATHERS
BX2323	PILGRIMS AND PILGRIMAGES / catholic church
TA780-785	PILING (CIVIL ENGINEERING)
BX4661	PILLAR SAINTS
TH2252-3	PILLARS SEE COLUMNS / building
TA492.C7	PILLARS SEE COLUMNS / testing
BP176	PILLARS OF ISLAM
HV8633	PILLORIES
RS201.P5	PILLS
QP921.P	PILOCARPINE / physiological effect
RM666.P	PILOCARPINE / therapeutics
VK798-995	PILOT GUIDES
E477.16	PILOT KNOB, BATTLE OF, 1864
TL589.5	PILOT, AUTOMATIC SEE AUTOMATIC PILOT (AEROPLANES)
VK1500-1661	PILOTS AND PILOTAGE
GN75.P5	PILTDOWN FORGERY
E99.P6	PIMA INDIANS
PM2171-4	PIMA LANGUAGE
E99.P	PIMAN INDIANS
PM4190	PIMAN LANGUAGES
PM2175	PIMAN LANGUAGES
E99.P6	PIMAS SEE PIMA INDIANS
SD397.O12	PIN OAK
QK495.P	PINANG SEE BETEL NUT / botany
RS165.B	PINANG SEE BETEL NUT / pharmacy
SB295.B	PINANG SEE BETEL NUT / plant culture and horticulture
DS432.P6	PINDAREES
SB608.P65	PINE — DISEASES AND PESTS
SB945.P624	PINE SPITTLE BUG
QK495.P66	PINE / botany
SD397.P55-65	PINE / sylviculture
QL868	PINEAL BODY / comparative anatomy
QM371	PINEAL BODY / human anatomy
QP187	PINEAL BODY / physiology
QL949	PINEAL EYE SEE EYE, PARIETAL
SB375	PINEAPPLE

F1799.I8	PINES, ISLE OF, BATTLE OF, 1596 SEE ISLA DE PINOS, BATTLE OF, 1596
GV1005	PING-PONG SEE TABLE TENNIS
PK2461-9	PINGAL LANGUAGE SEE DINGAL LANGUAGE
TR268	PINHOLE PHOTOGRAPHY SEE PHOTOGRAPHY, PINHOLE
QL391.P	PINITE
SB608.O5	PINK-ROOT DISEASE
SB413.P55	PINKS
QL737.P6	PINNIPEDIA
QE882.C4	PINNIPEDIA, FOSSIL
GV1295.P6	PINOCHLE (GAME) SEE PENUCHLE (GAME)
GV1295.P6	PINOCLE (GAME) SEE PENUCHLE (GAME)
HD9999.P6-63	PINS AND NEEDLES / economics
GT2280	PINS AND NEEDLES / manners and customs
TS2301.P5	PINS AND NEEDLES / manufacture
SF429.P5	PINSCHERS, DOBERMANN SEE DOBERMANN PINSCHERS
RL775	PINTA
TJ1067	PINTLE BEARINGS SEE PIVOT BEARINGS
SF293.P5	PINTO HORSE
SD397.P	PINUS MONTICOLA
E179	PIONEER LIFE SEE FRONTIER AND PIONEER LIFE / u.s.
UG530-535	PIONEER TROOPS ·
JX238.P5-6	PIOUS FUND OF THE CALIFORNIAS
E99.M	PIPATSJE INDIANS SEE MARICOPA INDIANS
TC174	PIPE — HYDRODYNAMICS
TA492.P6	PIPE — TESTING
TS280	PIPE BENDING / metal-work
TH6715	PIPE BENDING / pipe-fitting (general)
TJ421	PIPE FLANGES
TJ933	PIPE LINES — EQUIPMENT AND SUPPLIES
TS280	PIPE MILLS
M455-7	PIPE MUSIC (4 PIPES) SEE WIND QUARTETS (4 PIPES)
M455-7	PIPE MUSIC (4 PIPES) SEE WIND QUARTETS (4 PIPES)
M60-64	PIPE MUSIC
TJ1338-1340	PIPE THREADS SEE SCREW-THREADS
QL638.S9	PIPE-FISH
TH6161-6175	PIPE-FITTING — LAWS AND REGULATIONS
TH6703-6729	PIPE-FITTING / plumbing
VM501	PIPE-FITTING, MARINE SEE MARINE PIPE-FITTING
TP490-495	PIPE-FITTINGS — AMMONIA
TJ418-444	PIPE-FITTINGS — CATALOGS
TJ415-444	PIPE-FITTINGS
ML550-649	PIPE-ORGAN SEE ORGAN / history and criticism
HD9529.P5-53	PIPE / economics
TS280-282	PIPE / metal manufactures
TP885.P5	PIPE, CONCRETE
TS2270	PIPE, TOBACCO SEE TOBACCO-PIPES
QD341.A6	PIPERONAL
TH7683.D8	PIPES, AIR SEE AIR DUCTS
TD491	PIPES, DEPOSITS IN / water-pipes
TS2270	PIPES, TOBACCO SEE TOBACCO-PIPES
QD54.P	PIPETTES / chemical apparatus
M985	PIPHAT MUSIC
ML1251	PIPHAT
PM4191	PIPIL LANGUAGE
QL696.P2	PIPITS
E241.P	PIQUA, BATTLE OF, 1780
E99.S35	PIQUAW INDIANS SEE SHAWNEE INDIANS
NK8590	PIQUE-WORK
GV1295.P7	PIQUET (GAME)
GV1295.A8	PIQUET, AUCTION SEE AUCTION PIQUET
GV1282	PIRATE BRIDGE
G535-7	PIRATES
JX4444.6	PIRATES / international law
PM4193	PIRINDA LANGUAGE SEE MATLATZINCA LANGUAGE
PM5818	PIRO (ARAWAKAN) LANGUAGE SEE CHUNTAQUIRO LANGUAGE
PM2176	PIRO (TANOAN) LANGUAGE
SF968	PIROPLASMOSIS, OVINE
PK7001-7070	PISACHA LANGUAGES
QL614-639	PISCES SEE FISHES
GR745	PISCES SEE FISHES / folk-lore
SH	PISCICULTURE SEE FISH-CULTURE
TH1421	PISE / building construction
SB401	PISTACHIO

GV1175	PISTOL SHOOTING
UD410-415	PISTOLS / army
TS537	PISTOLS / manufacture
VD390	PISTOLS / navy
GV1175	PISTOLS / shooting
TJ915	*PISTON PUMPS* **SEE** RECIPROCATING PUMPS
TJ533	PISTON RINGS
TJ533	PISTONS / steam-engines
SF429.T3	*PIT BULLTERRIERS* **SEE** STAFFORDSHIRE TERRIERS
SF429.T3	*PIT DOGS* **SEE** STAFFORDSHIRE TERRIERS
E99.A15	*PIT RIVER INDIANS* **SEE** ACHOMAWI INDIANS
E99.A875	*PIT RIVER INDIANS* **SEE** ATSUGEWI INDIANS
E99.M115	*PIT RIVER INDIANS* **SEE** MADEHSI INDIANS
GN414	PIT-DWELLERS
QL666.O6	PIT-VIPERS
TN289	PIT-WOOD
SF429.T3	*PITBULL TERRIERS* **SEE** STAFFORDSHIRE TERRIERS
PM7895.P5	PITCAIRNESE LANGUAGE
E99.W15	*PITCH INDIANS* **SEE** WAILAKI INDIANS
QK495.P66	PITCH PINE / botany
SD397.P6113	PITCH PINE / forestry
ML990.P	*PITCH-PIPE* **SEE** PITCHPIPE
TP953	PITCH / coal products
ML3807-9	*PITCH, MUSICAL* **SEE** MUSICAL PITCH / acoustics
ML3830	*PITCH, MUSICAL* **SEE** MUSICAL PITCH / psychology
QE391.U65	*PITCHBLENDE* **SEE** URANINITE
GV871	PITCHING (BASEBALL)
ML990.P	PITCHPIPE
QH368	PITHECANTHROPUS ERECTUS
QD305.A7	*PITROWSKY REACTION* **SEE** BIURET REACTION
E473.54	*PITTSBURG LANDING, BATTLE OF, 1862* **SEE** SHILOH, BATTLE OF, 1862
RC280.P5	PITUITARY BODY — TUMORS
QL868	PITUITARY BODY / comparative anatomy
QM371	PITUITARY BODY / human anatomy
QP187	PITUITARY BODY / physiology
RM800.P6	PITUITARY EXTRACT
GN131	PITUITARY FOSSA / craniology
RM800.P6	*PITUITRIN* **SEE** PITUITARY EXTRACT
RL311	PITYRIASIS RUBRA
E99.P2	*PIUTE INDIANS* **SEE** PAIUTE INDIANS
TJ1067	PIVOT BEARINGS
BM670.P5	PIYYUTIM
BM670.P5	*PIYYUTIM* **SEE** PIYUTIM
G104-8	*PLACE-NAMES* **SEE** NAMES, GEOGRAPHICAL
RG591	PLACENTA — DISEASES
RG701-721	*PLACENTA PREVIA* **SEE** LABOR, COMPLICATED
QL973	PLACENTA / embryology
QM611	PLACENTA / human embryology
RG664	PLACENTA / obstetrics
QP281	PLACENTA / physiology
TN421	*PLACER-MINING* **SEE** HYDRAULIC MINING / gold
F3098	*PLACILLA, BATTLE OF, 1891* **SEE** VALPARAISO, BATTLE OF, 1891
QE852.P5	PLACODERMI
ML63	PLAGIARISM IN MUSIC
PN167-8	PLAGIARISM
QL638.9	PLAGIOSTOMI
QE852.P6	PLAGIOSTOMI / fossil
RA644.P7	PLAGUE — PREVENTION
RC171-9	PLAGUE
SH351.P6	PLAICE / fisheries
QL638.P7	PLAICE / zoology
PL4001.B3	*PLAINS KACHARI LANGUAGE* **SEE** BARA LANGUAGE
GB571-8	PLAINS
BF1343	PLANCHETTE
QA451-485	*PLANE GEOMETRY* **SEE** GEOMETRY, PLANE
QA533	*PLANE TRIGONOMETRY* **SEE** TRIGONOMETRY, PLANE
TA571	PLANE-TABLE
SB608.P	PLANE-TREE — DISEASES AND PESTS
QK495.P	PLANE-TREE / botany
SD397.P8	PLANE-TREE / forestry
QB70	PLANETARIA
QB651	*PLANETOIDS* **SEE** PLANETS, MINOR / descriptive astronomy
QB516	*PLANETOIDS* **SEE** PLANETS, MINOR / observations for solar parallax
QB603	PLANETS — BRIGHTNESS
QB603	PLANETS — DIAMETERS
QB603	PLANETS — FIGURE
QB369	PLANETS — OBSERVATIONS
QB603	PLANETS — PHASES
QB369	PLANETS — TABLES
QB601-701	PLANETS
QB607	PLANETS, INTRAMERCURIAL
QB651	PLANETS, MINOR / descriptive ,astronomy
QB516	PLANETS, MINOR / observations for solar parallax
QB377-8	PLANETS, MINOR / planetary theory
QB361-2	PLANETS, THEORY OF
QB389	PLANETS, ULTRA-NEPTUNIAN / perturbations
QA81	PLANIMETER / mathematics
TA614	PLANIMETER / surveying
TL684.2	PLANING HULLS / aeronautics
VM341-9	PLANING HULLS / naval architecture
TL684.2	*PLANING SURFACES* **SEE** PLANING HULLS / aeronautics
VM341-9	*PLANING SURFACES* **SEE** PLANING HULLS / naval architecture
TJ1205-1210	PLANING-MACHINES
TS850	PLANING-MILLS
QB65	PLANISPHERES
TE245	*PLANK ROADS* **SEE** ROADS, PLANK
QK933-5	PLANKTON / botany ecology
QL143	PLANKTON / fresh-water fauna
QK105	PLANKTON / fresh-water flora
QL123	PLANKTON / marine fauna
QK103	PLANKTON / marine flora
QE767	PLANKTON, FOSSIL
BF433.P6	PLANNING — ABILITY TESTING
NA9000-9284	*PLANNING, CITY* **SEE** CITIES AND TOWNS — PLANNING
HD82-85	*PLANNING, ECONOMIC* **SEE** ECONOMIC POLICY
HD	*PLANNING, ECONOMIC* **SEE** ECONOMIC POLICY / by industry
HF1401-2580	*PLANNING, ECONOMIC* **SEE** ECONOMIC POLICY / hc
HD82-85	*PLANNING, NATIONAL* **SEE** ECONOMIC POLICY
HD	*PLANNING, NATIONAL* **SEE** ECONOMIC POLICY / by industry
HF1401-2580	*PLANNING, NATIONAL* **SEE** ECONOMIC POLICY / hc
NA9000-9284	*PLANNING, REGIONAL* **SEE** REGIONAL PLANNING
HD82-85	*PLANNING, STATE* **SEE** ECONOMIC POLICY
HD	*PLANNING, STATE* **SEE** ECONOMIC POLICY / by industry
HF1401-2580	*PLANNING, STATE* **SEE** ECONOMIC POLICY / hc
NA9000-9284	*PLANNING, STATE* **SEE** REGIONAL PLANNING
NA2700-2780	*PLANS* **SEE** ARCHITECTURAL DRAWING
QA464	*PLANS* **SEE** GEOMETRICAL DRAWING
QA497	*PLANS* **SEE** GEOMETRICAL DRAWING
T351-377	*PLANS* **SEE** MECHANICAL DRAWING
QK641-707	*PLANT ANATOMY* **SEE** BOTANY — ANATOMY
HG4028.C4	*PLANT AND EQUIPMENT INVESTMENTS* **SEE** CAPITAL INVESTMENTS
QK882	*PLANT ASSIMILATION* **SEE** PLANTS — ASSIMILATION
QK725	PLANT CELLS AND TISSUES
QK861-6	*PLANT CHEMISTRY* **SEE** BOTANICAL CHEMISTRY
QK865-6	*PLANT CHEMISTRY* **SEE** PLANTS — CHEMICAL ANALYSIS
QK91-95	*PLANT CLASSIFICATION* **SEE** BOTANY — CLASSIFICATION
TH4511	*PLANT DESIGN* **SEE** FACTORIES — DESIGN AND CONSTRUCTION
TS155	*PLANT DESIGN* **SEE** FACTORIES — DESIGN AND CONSTRUCTION
SB599-791	PLANT DISEASES
QK665	*PLANT EMBRYOLOGY* **SEE** BOTANY — EMBRYOLOGY
QK980	*PLANT EVOLUTION* **SEE** PLANTS — EVOLUTION
NK1560-1565	*PLANT FORMS IN DESIGN* **SEE** DESIGN, DECORATIVE — PLANT FORMS
QK731	*PLANT HORMONES* **SEE** HORMONES (PLANTS)
SB109	PLANT INTRODUCTION
TH4511	*PLANT LAYOUT* **SEE** FACTORIES — DESIGN AND CONSTRUCTION
TS155	*PLANT LAYOUT* **SEE** FACTORIES — DESIGN AND CONSTRUCTION
QK83	PLANT LORE
QK101	*PLANT MIGRATION* **SEE** PLANTS — MIGRATION

PE285.P6	PLANT NAMES, POPULAR — ANGLO-SAXON
QK13	PLANT NAMES, POPULAR
QK11	*PLANT NAMES, SCIENTIFIC* **SEE** BOTANY — NOMENCLATORS
QK96	*PLANT NAMES, SCIENTIFIC* **SEE** BOTANY — NOMENCLATURE
QK867-873	*PLANT NUTRITION* **SEE** PLANTS — NUTRITION
SB599-791	*PLANT PATHOLOGY* **SEE** PLANT DISEASES
SB119-124	PLANT PROPAGATION
SB981-7	PLANT QUARANTINE
QK731	*PLANT REGULATORS* **SEE** GROWTH PROMOTING SUBSTANCES
QK891	*PLANT RESPIRATION* **SEE** PLANTS — RESPIRATION
QK641-707	*PLANT STRUCTURE* **SEE** BOTANY — ANATOMY
QK91-95	*PLANT TAXONOMY* **SEE** BOTANY — CLASSIFICATION
SB123	PLANT-BREEDING
SB945.P64	PLANT-LICE / *insect pests*
QL523.A6	PLANT-LICE / *zoology*
SB111	*PLANTATION CROPS* **SEE** TROPICAL CROPS
ML3556	*PLANTATION SONGS* **SEE** NEGRO SONGS / *history*
M1670-1671	*PLANTATION SONGS* **SEE** NEGRO SONGS / *music*
SD409	*PLANTING* **SEE** AFFORESTATION
SB451-466	*PLANTING* **SEE** GARDENING
SB469-479	*PLANTING* **SEE** LANDSCAPE GARDENING
SB435-7	*PLANTING* **SEE** TREE PLANTING / *city*
SD391	*PLANTING* **SEE** TREE PLANTING / *sylviculture*
QK871	PLANTS — ABSORPTION OF WATER
QK882	PLANTS — ASSIMILATION
QK865-6	PLANTS — CHEMICAL ANALYSIS
QK61	PLANTS — COLLECTION AND PRESERVATION
QK980	PLANTS — EVOLUTION
QK754	PLANTS — HARDINESS
QK871	PLANTS — HYDRATION
QK771-791	PLANTS — IRRITABILITY AND MOVEMENTS
QK881-897	PLANTS — METABOLISM
QK101	PLANTS — MIGRATION
QK867-873	PLANTS — NUTRITION
QK825-7	PLANTS — REPRODUCTION
QK891	PLANTS — RESPIRATION
QK873	PLANTS — TRANSPIRATION
QH84	*PLANTS AND ANIMALS-GEOGRAPHICAL DISTRIBUTION* **SEE** GEOGRAPHICAL DISTRIBUTION OF ANIMALS AND PLANTS
N7680	PLANTS IN ART
NK1560-1565	PLANTS IN ART / *decorative design*
NC805-815	PLANTS IN ART / *drawing*
ND1400	PLANTS IN ART / *painting*
NB1950	PLANTS IN ART / *sculpture*
ND2300-2305	PLANTS IN ART / *water-colors*
QK	PLANTS
GR780-790	PLANTS / *folk-lore*
GT5150	PLANTS / *manners and customs*
SB	PLANTS, CULTIVATED
GT5897-9	PLANTS, CULTIVATED / *manners and customs*
QK98.5	PLANTS, EDIBLE
QK871	*PLANTS, FLUIDS IN* **SEE** PLANTS, MOTION OF FLUIDS IN
QK83	*PLANTS, FOLK-LORE OF* **SEE** PLANT LORE
QE901-996	*PLANTS, FOSSIL* **SEE** PALEOBOTANY
QK875	PLANTS, GASES IN
QK755	PLANTS, HEAT PRODUCTION IN
NA6400-6510	*PLANTS, INDUSTRIAL* **SEE** FACTORIES / *architecture*
TH4511-4541	*PLANTS, INDUSTRIAL* **SEE** FACTORIES / *building*
HD6270	*PLANTS, INDUSTRIAL* **SEE** FACTORIES / *junior labor*
HD7406-7510	*PLANTS, INDUSTRIAL* **SEE** FACTORIES / *model*
HD6974	*PLANTS, INDUSTRIAL* **SEE** FACTORIES / *social conditions*
HD6068	*PLANTS, INDUSTRIAL* **SEE** FACTORIES / *women in*
SB292	PLANTS, INSECTICIDAL
QK871	PLANTS, MOTION OF FLUIDS IN
SB407	PLANTS, ORNAMENTAL — PICTORIAL WORKS
SB403-450	PLANTS, ORNAMENTAL
QH245	*PLANTS, PHOTOGRAPHY OF* **SEE** PHOTOGRAPHY OF PLANTS
SB415	PLANTS, POTTED / *greenhouse plants*
QK86	PLANTS, PROTECTION OF
SB599-999	PLANTS, PROTECTION OF / *diseases and pests*
QK827	PLANTS, SEX IN
QK658-9	PLANTS, SEX IN
SB241-261	*PLANTS, TEXTILE* **SEE** TEXTILE FIBERS / *culture*
TS1540-1549	*PLANTS, TEXTILE* **SEE** TEXTILE FIBERS / *manufacture*
SB107-9	*PLANTS, USEFUL* **SEE** BOTANY, ECONOMIC
QK641-707	*PLANTS-ANATOMY* **SEE** BOTANY — ANATOMY
QK91-95	*PLANTS-CLASSIFICATION* **SEE** BOTANY — CLASSIFICATION
QK899	*PLANTS-COLOR* **SEE** COLOR OF PLANTS
QK664	*PLANTS-DEFORMITIES* **SEE** ABNORMALITIES (PLANTS)
SB599-791	*PLANTS-DISEASES* **SEE** PLANT DISEASES
QK901-976	*PLANTS-ECOLOGY* **SEE** BOTANY — ECOLOGY
QK845	*PLANTS-ELECTROPHYSIOLOGY* **SEE** ELECTROPHYSIOLOGY OF PLANTS
QK665	*PLANTS-EMBRYOLOGY* **SEE** BOTANY — EMBRYOLOGY
QH423	*PLANTS-HYBRIDIZATION* **SEE** HYBRIDIZATION, VEGETABLE
QK641-669	*PLANTS-MORPHOLOGY* **SEE** BOTANY — MORPHOLOGY
QK871	*PLANTS-MOTION OF FLUIDS* **SEE** PLANTS, MOTION OF FLUIDS IN
QK771-791	*PLANTS-MOVEMENTS* **SEE** PLANTS — IRRITABILITY AND MOVEMENTS
QK96	*PLANTS-NOMENCLATURE* **SEE** BOTANY — NOMENCLATURE
QK901-976	*PLANTS-OECOLOGY* **SEE** BOTANY — ECOLOGY
SB599-791	*PLANTS-PATHOLOGY* **SEE** PLANT DISEASES
QK641-707	*PLANTS-STRUCTURE* **SEE** BOTANY — ANATOMY
QK871	*PLANTS-TRANSLOCATION* **SEE** PLANTS, MOTION OF FLUIDS IN
NK6300-6399	PLAQUES, PLAQUETTES
QC711	PLASMA (IONIZED GASES)
QC809.P5	PLASMA (IONIZED GASES) / *cosmic physics*
QC175	PLASMA (IONIZED GASES) / *kinetic theory of gases*
QH325	*PLASMOGENY* **SEE** LIFE — ORIGIN
QH325	*PLASMOGONY* **SEE** LIFE — ORIGIN
TH8139	PLASTER BOARD
NB35	PLASTER CASTS — CATALOGS
NB1190	PLASTER CASTS
RK658	PLASTER CASTS, DENTAL
S643	PLASTER OF PARIS / *fertilizers*
TN946	PLASTER OF PARIS / *mineral industries*
TP888	PLASTER OF PARIS / *technology*
TH8135-7	PLASTER
TH8120-8137	PLASTERING
TP247.7	*PLASTIC ADDITIVES* **SEE** PLASTICIZERS
TJ1073.P6	PLASTIC BEARINGS
TA455.P5	*PLASTIC BUILDING MATERIALS* **SEE** PLASTICS IN BUILDING
HD9661-2	*PLASTIC INDUSTRIES* **SEE** PLASTICS INDUSTRY AND TRADE
TP986	*PLASTIC MATERIALS* **SEE** PLASTICS
TP986.5	*PLASTIC MOLDING* **SEE** PLASTICS — MOLDING
TT323	*PLASTIC PAINTING* **SEE** TEXTURE PAINTING
TP986	*PLASTIC PRODUCTS* **SEE** PLASTICS
NB1270.P5	PLASTIC SCULPTURE
RD118-120.5	*PLASTIC SURGERY* **SEE** SURGERY, PLASTIC
TJ1194	PLASTIC TOOLS
QA931-5	PLASTICITY / *mathematical theory*
QC191	PLASTICITY / *physics*
TP247.7	PLASTICIZERS
TP986.5	PLASTICS — MOLDING
TA455.P5	PLASTICS IN BUILDING
HD9661-2	PLASTICS INDUSTRY AND TRADE
TP986	PLASTICS
TA455.P5	*PLASTICS-CREEP* **SEE** CREEP OF PLASTICS
DF225.7	PLATAEA, BATTLE OF, 479 B.C.
NK7100-7695	PLATE — COLLECTORS AND COLLECTING
TP159.P6	PLATE TOWERS
HG9963.P6	*PLATE-GLASS INSURANCE* **SEE** INSURANCE, PLATE-GLASS
TP860	PLATE-GLASS
TS250	PLATE-METAL WORK
NE2815	PLATE-PRINTING / *engraving*
Z120	PLATE-PRINTING / *etc.*
HG573	PLATE-PRINTING / *paper money*
NK7100-7695	PLATE / *gold and silver*
Z249	PLATEN PRESSES
Z236	PLATEN PRESSWORK

TA492.P7	PLATES (ENGINEERING)
TS555	PLATES, ALUMINUM / manufacture
TA492.P7	PLATES, ALUMINUM / testing
QA935	*PLATES, ELASTIC* SEE ELASTIC PLATES AND SHELLS
TS350	PLATES, IRON AND STEEL
TA492.P7	PLATES, IRON AND STEEL / testing
GT3350	*PLATFORM BURIAL* SEE SCAFFOLD BURIAL
QL391.P7	*PLATHELMINTHES* SEE PLATYHELMINTHES
TS213	PLATING
TR420	*PLATINOTYPE* SEE PHOTOGRAPHY — PRINTING PROCESSES — PLATINOTYPE
QD181.P8	PLATINUM / chemistry
TS770	PLATINUM / manufactures
TN799.P7	PLATINUM / metallurgy
TN490.P7	PLATINUM / mining
B398.L9	*PLATONIC LOVE* SEE LOVE, PLATONIC
B517	*PLATONISM* SEE PLATONISTS
B517	PLATONISTS
B1133.C2	*PLATONISTS, CAMBRIDGE* SEE CAMBRIDGE PLATONISTS
LB2806	PLATOON SCHOOLS
F1787	PLATT AMENDMENT
PF5601-5844	*PLATTDEUTSCH* SEE LOW GERMAN LANGUAGE
E356.P7	PLATTSBURG, BATTLE OF, 1814
QL391.P7	PLATYHELMINTHES
GV421-433	*PLAY CENTERS* SEE PLAYGROUNDS
GV424	PLAY SCHOOLS
RM737	*PLAY THERAPY* SEE RECREATIONAL THERAPY
RJ499	*PLAY THERAPY* SEE RECREATIONAL THERAPY / child psychiatry
RC489.R4	*PLAY THERAPY* SEE RECREATIONAL THERAPY / psychotherapy
PN1692	PLAY WITHIN A PLAY
GV1771	PLAY-PARTY
Z652.D7	*PLAY-RIGHT* SEE COPYRIGHT — DRAMA
BF721	PLAY / child psychology
LB1137	PLAY / educational theory
BF717	PLAY / psychology of play
ML1050-1055	PLAYER-ORGAN
MT150	PLAYER-ORGAN / analytical guides
MT700	PLAYER-ORGAN / instruction
M20-32	PLAYER-PIANO MUSIC
M174	PLAYER-PIANO ROLLS
ML1050-1055	PLAYER-PIANO
MT150	PLAYER-PIANO / analytical guides
MT700	PLAYER-PIANO / instruction
GV881	*PLAYGROUND BALL* SEE SOFTBALL
GV426	PLAYGROUNDS — APPARATUS AND EQUIPMENT
GV421-433	PLAYGROUNDS
GV423	PLAYGROUNDS, SAND
NA6820-6845	*PLAYHOUSES* SEE THEATERS / architecture
GV411-413	*PLAYING FIELDS* SEE ATHLETIC FIELDS
GV1233-1299	*PLAYING-CARDS* SEE CARDS
PN1600-1861	*PLAYS* SEE DRAMA
PN6120.A4-5	*PLAYS FOR CHILDREN* SEE CHILDREN'S PLAYS
PN6120.R4	*PLAYS, BIBLE* SEE BIBLE PLAYS
PN6120.C5	*PLAYS, CHRISTMAS* SEE CHRISTMAS PLAYS
PN3175-3191	*PLAYS, COLLEGE* SEE COLLEGE AND SCHOOL DRAMA / history and criticism
PN3203-5	*PLAYS, COMMUNITY* SEE COMMUNITY PLAYS, ETC.
PN6120.A4-5	*PLAYS, FAIRY* SEE FAIRY PLAYS / juvenile
PT963.C3	*PLAYS, MEDIEVAL* SEE CARNIVAL PLAYS / german literature
PN2159.C	*PLAYS, MEDIEVAL* SEE CHRISTMAS PLAYS, MEDIEVAL
PN1751	*PLAYS, MEDIEVAL* SEE DRAMA, MEDIEVAL
PN1771	*PLAYS, MEDIEVAL* SEE MORALITIES
PN1761	*PLAYS, MEDIEVAL* SEE MYSTERIES AND MIRACLE-PLAYS / history and criticism
PN3203-3299	*PLAYS, MEDIEVAL* SEE PASSION-PLAYS
PN1720-1861	*PLAYWRIGHTS* SEE DRAMATISTS
NA9070	PLAZAS
BJ1480-1486	PLEASURE / ethics
BF515	PLEASURE / psychology
JX4054	PLEBISCITE
JC55.P7	PLEBISCITE / ancient
DG83.3	PLEBS (ROME)
M1360	PLECTRAL ENSEMBLES
ML750-925	*PLECTRAL INSTRUMENTS* SEE STRINGED INSTRUMENTS

QB802	PLEIADES
QE695	*PLEIOCENE PERIOD* SEE GEOLOGY, STRATIGRAPHIC — PLIOCENE
QE930	*PLEIOCENE PERIOD* SEE PALEOBOTANY — PLIOCENE
QE740	*PLEIOCENE PERIOD* SEE PALEONTOLOGY — PLIOCENE
QE696-8	*PLEISTOCENE PERIOD* SEE GEOLOGY, STRATIGRAPHIC — PLEISTOCENE
QE931	*PLEISTOCENE PERIOD* SEE PALEOBOTANY — PLEISTOCENE
QE741	*PLEISTOCENE PERIOD* SEE PALEONTOLOGY — PLEISTOCENE
HD2961	PLENOCRACY
RE92	PLEOPTICS
QE862.P4	PLESIOSAURIA
RB214	PLETHORA (PATHOLOGY)
RC751	PLEURA — DISEASES
RD539	PLEURA — SURGERY
QL849	PLEURA / comparative anatomy
QM261	PLEURA / human anatomy
RC751	PLEURISY
RC751	*PLEURITIS* SEE PLEURISY
DR573.5.P6	PLEVNA — SIEGE, 1877
TP986.P5	PLEXIGLAS
QM471	*PLEXUS, BRACHIAL* SEE BRACHIAL PLEXUS / anatomy
QM455	*PLEXUS, CHOROID* SEE CHOROID PLEXUS
QL937	*PLEXUS, CHOROID* SEE CHOROID PLEXUS
QP368	*PLEXUS, SOLAR* SEE SOLAR PLEXUS
TL940	*PLIANT SPACE STRUCTURES* SEE EXPANDABLE SPACE STRUCTURES
VK237	*PLIMSOLL LINE* SEE LOAD-LINE
NA2875	PLINTHS
QE695	*PLIOCENE PERIOD* SEE GEOLOGY, STRATIGRAPHIC — PLIOCENE
QE930	*PLIOCENE PERIOD* SEE PALEOBOTANY — PLIOCENE
QE740	*PLIOCENE PERIOD* SEE PALEONTOLOGY — PLIOCENE
D766.4	PLOESTI, BATTLES OF, 1943-1944
PN145	PLOTS (DRAMA, NOVEL, ETC.)
PN44	PLOTS (DRAMA, NOVEL, ETC.)
PN1683	PLOTS (DRAMA, NOVEL, ETC.) / drama
PN3378	PLOTS (DRAMA, NOVEL, ETC.) / fiction
PN3373	PLOTS (DRAMA, NOVEL, ETC.) / short story
S683-5	*PLOUGH* SEE PLOWS / agriculture
QL696.L7	PLOVERS
S683	PLOWING
S683-5	PLOWS / agriculture
TK2821	*PLUGS (ELECTRICITY)* SEE ELECTRIC CONTACTORS
SB608.P77	PLUM — DISEASES AND PESTS
SB377	PLUM
QB338	PLUMB-LINE DEFLECTIONS
TN845	*PLUMBAGO* SEE GRAPHITE
TP261.G7	*PLUMBAGO* SEE GRAPHITE / artificial
F1434.2.P6	PLUMBATE WARE / central america
F1219.3.P9	PLUMBATE WARE / mexico
HF5686.P7	PLUMBING — ACCOUNTING
PN6231.P58	PLUMBING — ANECDOTES, FACETIAE, SATIRE, ETC.
TH6255	PLUMBING — CATALOGS
TH6234-5	PLUMBING — ESTIMATES
TH6128	PLUMBING — EXAMINATIONS, QUESTIONS, ETC.
TH6161-6175	PLUMBING — LAWS AND REGULATIONS
TH6681	PLUMBING — REPAIRING
TH6225	PLUMBING — SPECIFICATIONS
TH6241	PLUMBING — TESTING
TH6631-3	PLUMBING — TRAPS
TH6658	PLUMBING — WASTE-PIPES
TK7870	*PLUMBING FOR MICROWAVES* SEE MICROWAVE WIRING
TH6681	*PLUMBING REPAIRS* SEE PLUMBING — REPAIRING
TH6101-6691	PLUMBING
TH6255	*PLUMBING-EQUIPMENT AND SUPPLIES-CATALOGS* SEE PLUMBING — CATALOGS
RA1231.L4	*PLUMBISM* SEE LEAD-POISONING
RG696	*PLURAL BIRTHS* SEE BIRTH, MULTIPLE
JX4231.D7	*PLURAL NATIONALITY* SEE DUAL NATIONALITY
BD394	PLURALISM
QB54	PLURALITY OF WORLDS
TS1680	PLUSH / manufacture
QB701	PLUTO (PLANET)

BX8800-8809	PLYMOUTH BRETHREN
SF489.P7	PLYMOUTH ROCKS (POULTRY)
TS870	PLYWOOD — DRYING
TS870	PLYWOOD
BL290	*PNEUMA* **SEE** SOUL / *comparative religion*
BD426	*PNEUMA* **SEE** SOUL / *pre-existence*
BD428	*PNEUMA* **SEE** SOUL / *soul of animals*
BT740-743	*PNEUMA* **SEE** SOUL / *theology*
TJ950-1030	PNEUMATIC MACHINERY
QC166	*PNEUMATIC PUMP* **SEE** AIR-PUMP / *physics*
TJ955	*PNEUMATIC PUMP* **SEE** AIR-PUMP / *pneumatic machinery*
TJ1005	PNEUMATIC TOOLS
TJ981-1009	*PNEUMATIC TRANSMISSION* **SEE** COMPRESSED AIR / *technology*
TJ1015	*PNEUMATIC TRANSMISSION* **SEE** PNEUMATIC-TUBE TRANSPORTATION
HE7511-7549	*PNEUMATIC TRANSMISSION* **SEE** PNEUMATIC-TUBE TRANSPORTATION / *economics*
TJ1015	PNEUMATIC-TUBE TRANSPORTATION
HE7511-7549	PNEUMATIC-TUBE TRANSPORTATION / *economics*
QC161-8	PNEUMATICS
RM666.G2	*PNEUMATOLOGY (MEDICINE)* **SEE** GASES — THERAPEUTIC USE
QR201.P7	PNEUMOCOCCUS
RC774	*PNEUMOCONIOSIS* **SEE** LUNGS — DUST DISEASES
HD7264	*PNEUMOCONIOSIS* **SEE** LUNGS — DUST DISEASES / *labor*
RC774	*PNEUMOKONIOSIS* **SEE** LUNGS — DUST DISEASES
HD7264	*PNEUMOKONIOSIS* **SEE** LUNGS — DUST DISEASES / *labor*
RM721	*PNEUMOMASSAGE* **SEE** MASSAGE
RA644.P8	PNEUMONIA — PREVENTION
RC771	PNEUMONIA
QR201.P7	PNEUMONIA / *bacteriology*
RC771	*PNEUMONITIS* **SEE** PNEUMONIA
QR201.P7	*PNEUMONITIS* **SEE** PNEUMONIA / *bacteriology*
RM825	PNEUMOPERITONEUM, ARTIFICIAL
RC751	PNEUMOTHORAX
DS539.M6	*PNONG (SOUTHEAST-ASIATIC PEOPLE)* **SEE** MOI (SOUTHEAST-ASIATIC PEOPLE)
GV1017.P7	PO-LO-LO (GAME)
SK36	POACHING
TL215.P67	POBEDA AUTOMOBILE
E99.P	POCASSET INDIANS
ML760	POCHETTE
GV891-9	*POCKET BILLIARDS* **SEE** POOL (GAME)
AG103-191	*POCKET COMPANIONS* **SEE** HANDBOOKS, VADE-MECUMS, ETC.
ML760	*POCKET FIDDLE* **SEE** POCHETTE
QL737.R6	POCKET GOPHERS
QL737.R6	POCKET MICE
PM4201	*POCOMCHI LANGUAGE* **SEE** POKONCHI LANGUAGE
PM4201	*POCONCHI LANGUAGE* **SEE** POKONCHI LANGUAGE
F3430.1.P	POCRA INDIANS
RC291	*PODAGRA* **SEE** GOUT
JS5724.P7	PODESTA
RD563	*PODIATRY* **SEE** CHIROPODY
QL444.D3	PODOPHTHALMIA
RS431.P	PODOPHYLLOTOXIN
S598	*PODSOL* **SEE** PODZOL
S598	PODZOL
PN1059.P7	POETIC LICENSE
PN1040-1059	POETICS
PN1136	POETRY — ADDRESSES, ESSAYS, LECTURES
PN6099-6110	POETRY — COLLECTIONS
PN1040	POETRY — EARLY WORKS TO 1800 / *classical*
PN1041	POETRY — EARLY WORKS TO 1800 / *english*
PN1105-1279	POETRY — HISTORY AND CRITICISM
PN1010	POETRY — PERIODICALS
PN1101	POETRY — STUDY AND TEACHING
ML3849	*POETRY AND MUSIC* **SEE** MUSIC AND LITERATURE
ML80	*POETRY AND MUSIC* **SEE** MUSIC AND LITERATURE
PN55	*POETRY AND SCIENCE* **SEE** LITERATURE AND SCIENCE
PR149.S4	*POETRY AND SCIENCE* **SEE** LITERATURE AND SCIENCE / *english literature*
PZ8.3	*POETRY FOR CHILDREN* **SEE** CHILDREN'S POETRY
PN6110.C4	*POETRY FOR CHILDREN* **SEE** CHILDREN'S POETRY

PZ8.3	*POETRY FOR CHILDREN* **SEE** NURSERY RHYMES
PN6110.C4	*POETRY FOR CHILDREN* **SEE** NURSERY RHYMES
PN6110.P6-7	POETRY OF PLACES
PN1010-1525	POETRY
PN670-691	POETRY, MEDIEVAL / *history*
PJ356	*POETRY, ORIENTAL* **SEE** ORIENTAL POETRY / *collections*
PJ327	*POETRY, ORIENTAL* **SEE** ORIENTAL POETRY / *history*
PJ462-3	*POETRY, ORIENTAL* **SEE** ORIENTAL POETRY / *translations*
PJ416-418	*POETRY, ORIENTAL* **SEE** ORIENTAL POETRY / *translations*
PN1010-1525	*POETRY-PHILOSOPHY* **SEE** POETRY
PN6099-6110	*POETRY-SELECTIONS* **SEE** POETRY — COLLECTIONS
PN1040-1059	*POETRY-TECHNIQUE* **SEE** POETICS
PR505	POETS LAUREATE
PN1105-1279	POETS
PN1064	POETS
PN1097	POETS
PN471-9	POETS, WOMEN
PS147-151	POETS, WOMEN / *american*
PR111-115	POETS, WOMEN / *english*
PL8601	POGORO LANGUAGE
TX360.H3	POI
SB413.P63	POINSETTIAS / *culture*
E83.77	POINT PLEASANT, BATTLE OF, 1774
D766.93	POINT 175, BATTLE OF, 1941
QC307	*POINT, CRITICAL* **SEE** CRITICAL POINT
SF429.P7	POINTERS (DOGS)
G108.C3	*POINTS OF THE COMPASS* **SEE** CARDINAL POINTS
QA248	*POINTS, SETS OF* **SEE** AGGREGATES
UG447	*POISON GAS* **SEE** GASES, ASPHYXIATING AND POISONOUS — WAR USE
RA577	*POISON GAS* **SEE** GASES, ASPHYXIATING AND POISONOUS / *public health*
RA1245-7	*POISON GAS* **SEE** GASES, ASPHYXIATING AND POISONOUS / *toxicology*
SB618.P6	*POISON OAK* **SEE** POISON-IVY
SB618.P	*POISON-ASH* **SEE** POISON-SUMAC
SB618.P	*POISON-DOGWOOD* **SEE** POISON-SUMAC
SB618.P	*POISON-ELDER* **SEE** POISON-SUMAC
SB618.P6	POISON-IVY
SB618.P	POISON-SUMAC
QP941	POISONOUS ANIMALS
QL618.7	POISONOUS FISHES
RA577	*POISONOUS GASES* **SEE** GASES, ASPHYXIATING AND POISONOUS / *public health*
RA1245-7	*POISONOUS GASES* **SEE** GASES, ASPHYXIATING AND POISONOUS / *toxicology*
QK617	*POISONOUS MUSHROOMS* **SEE** MUSHROOMS, POISONOUS
SB617-618	POISONOUS PLANTS
QP941	POISONS — PHYSIOLOGICAL EFFECT
RA1195-1260	POISONS
SB951	*POISONS, ECONOMIC* **SEE** PESTICIDES
RC963.5	*POISONS, INDUSTRIAL* **SEE** INDUSTRIAL TOXICOLOGY
QA405	*POISSON'S EQUATIONS* **SEE** HARMONIC FUNCTIONS
DC99.5.P6	POITIERS, BATTLE OF, 1356
DC71.5	POITIERS, BATTLE OF, 732
E99.W2	*POKANOKET INDIANS* **SEE** WAMPANOAG INDIANS
F3430.1.P	*POKCRA INDIANS* **SEE** POCRA INDIANS
GV1291	POKER-BRIDGE
GV1251-3	POKER
QK495.P	POKEWEED
PM4201	POKOMAM LANGUAGE
PM4201	*POKOMCHI LANGUAGE* **SEE** POKONCHI LANGUAGF
DT429	POKOMO (BANTU TRIBE)
PM4201	POKONCHI LANGUAGE
PG7911-7915	POLABIAN LANGUAGE
PG7911-7915	*POLABISH LANGUAGE* **SEE** POLABIAN LANGUAGE
DK401-440	POLAND — HISTORY
SF393.P7	POLAND-CHINA SWINE / *herd-books*
QA556	*POLAR COORDINATES* **SEE** COORDINATES, POLAR
G850-890	*POLAR EXPEDITIONS* **SEE** ANTARCTIC REGIONS
QK474	*POLAR EXPEDITIONS* **SEE** ANTARCTIC REGIONS / *botany*
QC994.9	*POLAR EXPEDITIONS* **SEE** ANTARCTIC REGIONS / *meteorology*

QC825.9	*POLAR EXPEDITIONS* **SEE** ANTARCTIC REGIONS / *terrestrial magnetism*
QL106	*POLAR EXPEDITIONS* **SEE** ANTARCTIC REGIONS / *zoology*
G600-830	*POLAR EXPEDITIONS* **SEE** ARCTIC REGIONS
QK474	*POLAR EXPEDITIONS* **SEE** ARCTIC REGIONS / *botany*
QC994.8	*POLAR EXPEDITIONS* **SEE** ARCTIC REGIONS / *meteorology*
QH84.1	*POLAR EXPEDITIONS* **SEE** ARCTIC REGIONS / *natural history*
QC825.8	*POLAR EXPEDITIONS* **SEE** ARCTIC REGIONS / *terrestrial magnetism*
QL105	*POLAR EXPEDITIONS* **SEE** ARCTIC REGIONS / *zoology*
G600-700	*POLAR EXPEDITIONS* **SEE** NORTH POLE
Q115	*POLAR EXPEDITIONS* **SEE** SCIENTIFIC EXPEDITIONS
G850-890	*POLAR EXPEDITIONS* **SEE** SOUTH POLE
G599	*POLAR FLIGHTS* **SEE** POLAR REGIONS — AERIAL EXPLORATION
QC971-2	*POLAR LIGHTS* **SEE** AURORAS
G599	POLAR REGIONS — AERIAL EXPLORATION
G575-599	POLAR REGIONS
TD940-949	*POLAR SANITARY ENGINEERING* **SEE** SANITARY ENGINEERING, LOW TEMPERATURE
QC373.P7	*POLARIMETER* **SEE** POLARISCOPE
QC373.P7	*POLARIMETRY* **SEE** POLARISCOPE
QC373.P7	POLARISCOPE
BL325.P7	POLARITY (IN RELIGION, FOLK-LORE, ETC.)
QD571	POLARIZATION (ELECTRICITY) / *electrochemistry*
QC603	POLARIZATION (ELECTRICITY) / *physics*
QC618	POLARIZATION (ELECTRICITY) / *physics*
QC441-5	POLARIZATION (LIGHT)
QC233	POLARIZATION (SOUND)
QH217	*POLARIZATION MICROSCOPE* **SEE** POLARIZING MICROSCOPE
QH217	POLARIZING MICROSCOPE
QD115	POLAROGRAPH AND POLAROGRAPHY
QD115	*POLAROGRAPHIC ANALYSIS* **SEE** POLAROGRAPH AND POLAROGRAPHY
QC176	POLARONS
TK3242-3	*POLE WOOD* **SEE** ELECTRIC LINES — POLES
QB169	POLE-STAR / *practical astronomy*
GV1079-1080	*POLE-VAULTING* **SEE** VAULTING
BT1095-1255	*POLEMICS (THEOLOGY)* **SEE** APOLOGETICS
DK412	POLES
HV7936.C8	POLICE COMMUNICATION SYSTEMS
HV8025	POLICE DOGS
HV7924	POLICE ETHICS
TR830	*POLICE PHOTOGRAPHY* **SEE** PHOTOGRAPHY, LEGAL
HV6071	*POLICE PHOTOGRAPHY* **SEE** PHOTOGRAPHY, LEGAL / *social pathology*
HV8077	*POLICE PHOTOGRAPHY* **SEE** PHOTOGRAPHY, LEGAL / *social pathology*
JK371.P7-8	POLICE POWER / *u.s.*
NA4490-4497	POLICE STATIONS / *architecture*
HV7551-8280	POLICE
JX1981.P7	*POLICE, INTERNATIONAL* **SEE** INTERNATIONAL POLICE
HV8081-9	POLICE, PRIVATE
HV7965-7985	POLICE, RURAL
HV7965-7985	POLICE, STATE
HV7571	POLICE, STATE / *by state*
HV8023	POLICEWOMEN
RC180.2	POLIOMYELITIS — PERSONAL NARRATIVES
RC180-181	POLIOMYELITIS
ML980	*POLISH BAGPIPE* **SEE** DUDA
PG7139	POLISH BALLADS AND SONGS / *collections*
PG7122-9	POLISH BALLADS AND SONGS / *folk-songs*
PG7080	POLISH BALLADS AND SONGS / *history*
PG7142-4	POLISH DRAMA / *collections*
PG7084-7096	POLISH DRAMA / *history*
PG7149-7150	POLISH FICTION / *collections*
PG7098	POLISH FICTION / *history*
PG6721-6730	POLISH LANGUAGE — OLD POLISH
PG6001-6790	POLISH LANGUAGE
PG7134.A2	*POLISH LANGUAGE-OLD POLISH-TEXTS* **SEE** POLISH LITERATURE — OLD POLISH / *collections*
PG7036	*POLISH LANGUAGE-OLD POLISH-TEXTS* **SEE** POLISH LITERATURE — OLD POLISH / *history*

Z2521	POLISH LITERATURE — BIO-BIBLIOGRAPHY
PG7134.A2	POLISH LITERATURE — OLD POLISH / *collections*
PG7036	POLISH LITERATURE — OLD POLISH / *history*
PG7135	POLISH LITERATURE — 19TH CENTURY / *collections*
PG7051	POLISH LITERATURE — 19TH CENTURY / *history*
PG7135	POLISH LITERATURE — 20TH CENTURY / *collections*
PG7051	POLISH LITERATURE — 20TH CENTURY / *history*
PG7132-7446	POLISH LITERATURE / *collections*
PG7001-7130	POLISH LITERATURE / *history*
PG7134.A2	*POLISH LITERATURE-EARLY TO 1500* **SEE** POLISH LITERATURE — OLD POLISH / *collections*
PG7036	*POLISH LITERATURE-EARLY TO 1500* **SEE** POLISH LITERATURE — OLD POLISH / *history*
PN5355.P7	POLISH NEWSPAPERS / *history*
PN4885.P	*POLISH NEWSPAPERS-U.S.* **SEE** POLISH-AMERICAN NEWSPAPERS / *journalism*
PN5355.P7	POLISH PERIODICALS / *history*
PN4885.P	*POLISH PERIODICALS-U.S.* **SEE** POLISH-AMERICAN PERIODICALS / *journalism*
PG6001-6790	POLISH PHILOLOGY
PG7136-7141	POLISH POETRY / *collections*
PG7122-9	POLISH POETRY / *folk-songs*
PG7062-7082	POLISH POETRY / *history*
DK434-440	POLISH QUESTION
DK418	POLISH QUESTION
DK432.5	POLISH SUCCESSION, WAR OF, 1733-1738
PG7155	POLISH WIT AND HUMOR / *collections*
PG7116	POLISH WIT AND HUMOR / *history*
PN4885.P	POLISH-AMERICAN NEWSPAPERS / *journalism*
PN4885.P	POLISH-AMERICAN PERIODICALS / *journalism*
DL712	*POLISH-SWEDISH WAR, 1617-1629* **SEE** SWEDISH-POLISH WAR, 1617-1629
DL725	*POLISH-SWEDISH WAR, 1655-1660* **SEE** SWEDISH-POLISH WAR, 1655-1660
TJ1296	POLISHES / *metal*
TP940	POLISHES / *wood*
TJ1280-1298	*POLISHING* **SEE** GRINDING AND POLISHING
BJ1533.C9	*POLITENESS* **SEE** COURTESY
BJ1520-1688	*POLITENESS* **SEE** COURTESY / *conduct of life*
BJ1801-2193	*POLITENESS* **SEE** ETIQUETTE
JK1991-7	*POLITICAL ASSESSMENTS* **SEE** CAMPAIGN FUNDS / *u.s.*
JF2101	POLITICAL CLUBS
JK2251-6	POLITICAL CONVENTIONS / *u.s.*
HV6254-6321	POLITICAL CRIMES AND OFFENSES
DA950.3	*POLITICAL DISABILITIES (GT. BRIT.)* **SEE** CATHOLIC EMANCIPATION / *act*
BX1492	*POLITICAL DISABILITIES (GT. BRIT.)* **SEE** CATHOLIC EMANCIPATION
BX5200-5207	*POLITICAL DISABILITIES (GT. BRIT.)* **SEE** DISSENTERS, RELIGIOUS — ENGLAND
BR757	*POLITICAL DISABILITIES (GT. BRIT.)* **SEE** TEST ACT, 1673
HB	*POLITICAL ECONOMY* **SEE** ECONOMICS
JK1751-1788	POLITICAL ETHICS / *citizenship*
JA79	POLITICAL ETHICS / *political science and ethics*
HV6254-6321	*POLITICAL OFFENSES* **SEE** POLITICAL CRIMES AND OFFENSES
JF2011-2111	POLITICAL PARTIES
JN1111-1129	POLITICAL PARTIES / *gt. brit.*
JL-JQ	POLITICAL PARTIES / *other countries*
JK2251-2391	POLITICAL PARTIES / *u.s.*
JF2011-2111	*POLITICAL PLATFORMS* **SEE** POLITICAL PARTIES
JN1111-1129	*POLITICAL PLATFORMS* **SEE** POLITICAL PARTIES / *gt. brit.*
JL-JQ	*POLITICAL PLATFORMS* **SEE** POLITICAL PARTIES / *other countries*
JK2251-2391	*POLITICAL PLATFORMS* **SEE** POLITICAL PARTIES / *u.s.*
JX4292.P6	*POLITICAL REFUGEES* **SEE** REFUGEES, POLITICAL / *international law*
JX1975.8	*POLITICAL REFUGEES* **SEE** REFUGEES, POLITICAL / *league of nations*
HV640	*POLITICAL REFUGEES* **SEE** REFUGEES, POLITICAL / *relief*
JA81-84	POLITICAL SCIENCE — HISTORY
JF127	POLITICAL SCIENCE — JUVENILE LITERATURE

JA71	POLITICAL SCIENCE — METHODOLOGY
B65	POLITICAL SCIENCE / *j political science and philosophy*
HM33	POLITICAL SCIENCE / *political science and sociology*
JF2101	*POLITICAL SOCIETIES* **SEE** POLITICAL CLUBS
D108	*POLITICIANS* **SEE** STATESMEN / *general biography*
D399.6	*POLITICIANS* **SEE** STATESMEN / *19th century*
D352.5	*POLITICIANS* **SEE** STATESMEN / *19th century*
D412.6	*POLITICIANS* **SEE** STATESMEN / *20th century*
BR115.P7	*POLITICS AND CHRISTIANITY* **SEE** CHRISTIANITY AND POLITICS
BP173.7	*POLITICS AND ISLAM* **SEE** ISLAM AND POLITICS
JF1321-2111	POLITICS, PRACTICAL
JN-JQ	POLITICS, PRACTICAL / *other countries*
JK1711-2391	POLITICS, PRACTICAL / *u.s.*
BV646-651	*POLITY, ECCLESIASTICAL* **SEE** CHURCH POLITY
M1049	POLKA-MAZURKAS (ORCHESTRA)
M1060	POLKA-MAZURKAS (ORCHESTRA)
M32	POLKA-MAZURKAS (PIANO)
M175.A4	POLKAS (ACCORDION)
M1248	POLKAS (BAND)
M1264	POLKAS (BAND)
M1048	POLKAS (CHAMBER ORCHESTRA) — SCORES
M1048	POLKAS (CHAMBER ORCHESTRA)
M240-244	POLKAS (FLUTE AND PIANO)
M1048	POLKAS (ORCHESTRA)
M1060	POLKAS (ORCHESTRA)
M31	POLKAS (PIANO)
M1160	POLKAS (STRING ORCHESTRA)
M1145	POLKAS (STRING ORCHESTRA)
M450-454	POLKAS (STRING QUARTET)
M217-218	POLKAS (VIOLIN AND PIANO)
M221-3	POLKAS (VIOLIN AND PIANO)
M135-9	POLKAS (ZITHER)
M214-215	POLKAS (2 PIANOS)
HJ4911-4939	POLL-TAX
SF193.A14	*POLLED ABERDEEN CATTLE* **SEE** ABERDEEN-ANGUS CATTLE
SF199.A14	*POLLED ABERDEEN CATTLE* **SEE** ABERDEEN-ANGUS CATTLE
SF193.A14	*POLLED ANGUS CATTLE* **SEE** ABERDEEN-ANGUS CATTLE
SF199.A14	*POLLED ANGUS CATTLE* **SEE** ABERDEEN-ANGUS CATTLE
SF193.D9	POLLED DURHAM CATTLE / *herd-books*
QK658	POLLEN
QK926	*POLLINATION* **SEE** FERTILIZATION OF PLANTS / *pollination*
QK827	*POLLINATION* **SEE** FERTILIZATION OF PLANTS / *sexual reproduction*
JF1001-1191	*POLLS* **SEE** ELECTIONS
JK1951-2246	*POLLS* **SEE** ELECTIONS / *u.s.*
JK2700-9595	*POLLS* **SEE** ELECTIONS / *u.s.*
HM261	*POLLS* **SEE** PUBLIC OPINION POLLS
JF825-1141	*POLLS* **SEE** VOTING
TD420-425	*POLLUTION OF WATER* **SEE** WATER — POLLUTION
GV847	POLO (ON SKATES)
GV1011	POLO
GV1011	POLO, JAPANESE
GV1796.P	POLONAISE / *dancing*
M1362	POLONAISES (ACCORDION ENSEMBLE)
M1249	POLONAISES (BAND) — SCORES AND PARTS
M1266	POLONAISES (BAND) — SCORES AND PARTS
M1266	POLONAISES (BAND)
M1249	POLONAISES (BAND)
M1060	POLONAISES (CHAMBER ORCHESTRA) — SCORES (REDUCED) AND PARTS
M1049	POLONAISES (CHAMBER ORCHESTRA) — SCORES (REDUCED) AND PARTS
M1049	POLONAISES (CHAMBER ORCHESTRA)
M1060	POLONAISES (CHAMBER ORCHESTRA)
M276-7	POLONAISES (GUITAR AND PIANO)
M570-572	POLONAISES (GUITAR, 2 VIOLINS, VIOLA, VIOLONCELLO)
M32	POLONAISES (HARPSICHORD)
M1060	POLONAISES (ORCHESTRA)
M1049	POLONAISES (ORCHESTRA)
M1010-1011	POLONAISES (PIANO WITH ORCHESTRA)
M32	POLONAISES (PIANO)
M217-218	POLONAISES (VIOLIN AND PIANO)
M221-3	POLONAISES (VIOLIN AND PIANO)

M286-7	POLONAISES (VIOLIN AND VIOLONCELLO)
QD181.R1	POLONIUM / *chemistry*
QC721	POLONIUM / *radioactivity*
PL318	*POLOVTSI LANGUAGE* **SEE** KIPCHAK LANGUAGE
DL743.P8	POLTAVA, BATTLE OF, 1709
GN480.6	POLYANDRY / *primitive*
QK495.P95	*POLYANTHUS* **SEE** PRIMROSES / *botany*
SB413.P	*POLYANTHUS* **SEE** PRIMROSES / *culture*
QL391.P9	POLYCHAETA
QE791	POLYCHAETA, FOSSIL
NB93	*POLYCHROME SCULPTURE* **SEE** POLYCHROMY / *sculpture*
NB1275	*POLYCHROME SCULPTURE* **SEE** POLYCHROMY / *sculpture*
NB93	POLYCHROMY / *sculpture*
NB1275	POLYCHROMY / *sculpture*
QL391.P9	POLYCLADIDA
TP986.P	POLYETHYLENE
QP601	*POLYGALACTURONASE* **SEE** PECTINASE
HQ981-996	POLYGAMY
GN480.8	POLYGAMY / *primitive*
GN353-6	*POLYGENISM* **SEE** MONOGENISM AND POLYGENISM
P361	*POLYGLOT DICTIONARIES* **SEE** DICTIONARIES, POLYGLOT
P361	POLYGLOT GLOSSARIES, PHRASE BOOKS, ETC.
PB73	POLYGLOT GLOSSARIES, PHRASE BOOKS, ETC. / *phrase books*
P207	*POLYGLOT GRAMMAR* **SEE** LANGUAGE AND LANGUAGES — GRAMMARS
P351-7	POLYGLOT TEXTS, SELECTIONS, QUOTATIONS, ETC.
QA482	POLYGONS
HV8078	*POLYGRAPH* **SEE** LIE DETECTORS AND DETECTION
QA491	POLYHEDRA
QA611	POLYHEDRA
TP156.P6	*POLYMERIZATION* **SEE** POLYMERS AND POLYMERIZATION / *chemical technology*
QD471	*POLYMERIZATION* **SEE** POLYMERS AND POLYMERIZATION / *chemical structure*
QD281.P	*POLYMERIZATION* **SEE** POLYMERS AND POLYMERIZATION / *organic chemistry*
QD471	POLYMERS AND POLYMERIZATION / *chemical structure*
TP156.P6	POLYMERS AND POLYMERIZATION / *chemical technology*
QD281.P	POLYMERS AND POLYMERIZATION / *organic chemistry*
PL6401-6551	POLYNESIAN LANGUAGES
GN670	POLYNESIANS / *anthropology*
DU510	POLYNESIANS / *history*
RC416	*POLYNEURITIS* **SEE** NEURITIS, MULTIPLE
QA404.5	*POLYNOMIALS, CHEBYSHEV* **SEE** CHEBYSHEV POLYNOMIALS
QA404.5	*POLYNOMIALS, ORTHOGONAL* **SEE** FUNCTIONS, ORTHOGONAL
QD341.A2	*POLYNUCLEOTIDES* **SEE** NUCLEIC ACIDS
TK1161	*POLYPHASE CURRENTS* **SEE** ELECTRIC CURRENTS, ALTERNATING — POLYPHASE
TK2745	*POLYPHASE CURRENTS* **SEE** ELECTRIC MACHINERY — POLYPHASE
QL375-9	*POLYPS* **SEE** COELENTERATA
QE777-9	*POLYPS* **SEE** COELENTERATA / *fossil*
QL396-9	*POLYPS* **SEE** POLYZOA
QD321	POLYSACCHARIDES
BL355	POLYTHEISM
TP986.P	*POLYTHENE* **SEE** POLYETHYLENE
ML3811	*POLYTONALITY* **SEE** TONALITY
QA691	POLYTOPES
QL396-9	POLYZOA
QE798-9	POLYZOA, FOSSIL
SB379.P6	POMEGRANATE / *horticulture*
RS165.P8	POMEGRANATE / *pharmacy*
SB370.G7	*POMELO* **SEE** GRAPEFRUIT
SF429.P8	POMERANIAN DOGS
ML990.P6	POMMER
E99.P65	POMO INDIANS
SB354-399	*POMOLOGY* **SEE** FRUIT-CULTURE
SB354-399	*POMOLOGY* **SEE** FRUIT / *culture*
HD9240-9259	*POMOLOGY* **SEE** FRUIT / *trade*
PL6295	PONAPE LANGUAGE
E99.P7	PONCA INDIANS
QK495.N97	*POND LILIES* **SEE** WATER-LILIES
SB423	*POND LILIES* **SEE** WATER-LILIES / *cultivation*

SB608.P	POND-LILY LEAF-BEETLE
DT764.P6	PONDOS
SH159	*PONDS, FISH* **SEE** FISH PONDS
PL8531	*PONGWE LANGUAGE* **SEE** MPONGWE LANGUAGE
SF315	PONIES
E99.P7	*PONKA INDIANS* **SEE** PONCA INDIANS
QM455	*PONS CEREBELLI* **SEE** PONS VAROLII / *human anatomy*
QM455	PONS VAROLII / *human anatomy*
E83.76	PONTIAC'S CONSPIRACY, 1763-1765
UG335	*PONTON-BRIDGES* **SEE** PONTOON-BRIDGES
UG335	PONTOON-BRIDGES
QL737.C4	*PONTOPORIA* **SEE** DOLPHINS
SF429.P85	POODLES
GV891-9	POOL (GAME)
GV1469.C5	*POOL CHECKER* **SEE** CHECKER POOL
BX4361-4	POOR CLARES
HV85-527	*POOR FARMS* **SEE** ALMSHOUSES
HV61	*POOR FARMS* **SEE** ALMSHOUSES
BX4361-4	*POOR LADIES* **SEE** POOR CLARES
HV75-83	POOR LAWS
BX4900-4906	*POOR PRIESTS* **SEE** LOLLARDS
HV1-527	POOR / *charities*
HV4023-4470	POOR / *poor in cities*
HV61	*POORHOUSES* **SEE** ALMSHOUSES
HV85-527	*POORHOUSES* **SEE** ALMSHOUSES
TX799	POP-CORN / *confectionery*
BX1818	POPES — COURT
BX1805	POPES — ELECTION
CR1115	POPES — HERALDRY
BX1806	POPES — INFALLIBILITY
BX958.F2	POPES — LEGENDS
CJ6205.P7	POPES — MEDALS
BX958.M6	POPES — MONUMENTS
BX958.P6	POPES — PORTRAITS
BX958.R4	POPES — RESIDENCE
BX1810	POPES — TEMPORAL POWER
BX958.T7	POPES — TOMBS
BX958.V7	POPES — VOYAGES AND TRAVELS
BX1805-1810	POPES
BX1001-1378	POPES / *individual popes*
BX1805-1810	*POPES-BIOGRAPHY* **SEE** POPES
BX1001-1378	*POPES-BIOGRAPHY* **SEE** POPES / *individual popes*
BX950-960	*POPES-HISTORY* **SEE** PAPACY — HISTORY
QL596.S3	*POPILLIA JAPONICA* **SEE** JAPANESE BEETLE
SB945.J3	*POPILLIA JAPONICA* **SEE** JAPANESE BEETLE / *insect pests*
DA448	POPISH PLOT, 1678
SB608.P775	POPLAR — DISEASES AND PESTS
F1219-1220	POPOLOCA INDIANS / *indians of mexico*
PM4207	POPOLUCA LANGUAGE (VERA CRUZ)
SB295.P8	POPPY
SB608.P78	POPPY / *diseases and pests*
AZ999	*POPULAR ERRORS* **SEE** ERRORS, POPULAR
BX2375	*POPULAR MISSIONS* **SEE** PARISH MISSIONS
BJ1571-1595	POPULARITY / *ethics*
LB3609	POPULARITY / *student life*
HB881-3700	POPULATION — STATISTICS
HB849-875	POPULATION
JV6205	POPULATION / *population and immigration*
JV6001-9500	*POPULATION, FOREIGN* **SEE** EMIGRATION AND IMMIGRATION
Z711.8	*POPULATION, FOREIGN* **SEE** LIBRARIES AND FOREIGN POPULATION
NK5000-5015	*PORCELAIN ENAMELS* **SEE** ENAMEL AND ENAMELING / *art*
TP812	*PORCELAIN ENAMELS* **SEE** ENAMEL AND ENAMELING / *pottery*
NK4605	*PORCELAIN PAINTING* **SEE** CHINA PAINTING
NK4370-4584	PORCELAIN
TP822	PORCELAIN
NK4399.B7	*PORCELAIN, BOW* **SEE** BOW PORCELAIN
NK4399.B75	*PORCELAIN, BRISTOL* **SEE** BRISTOL PORCELAIN
NK4399.C	*PORCELAIN, CAUGHLEY* **SEE** CAUGHLEY PORCELAIN
NK4399.C5	*PORCELAIN, CHELSEA* **SEE** CHELSEA PORCELAIN
NK4399.C	*PORCELAIN, COALPORT* **SEE** COALPORT PORCELAIN
NK4399.C6	*PORCELAIN, COPENHAGEN* **SEE** COPENHAGEN PORCELAIN
NK4399.D4	*PORCELAIN, DERBY* **SEE** DERBY PORCELAIN
NK4380	*PORCELAIN, DRESDEN* **SEE** DRESDEN PORCELAIN

NK4399.F8	*PORCELAIN, FRANKENTHAL* **SEE** FRANKENTHAL PORCELAIN
NK4399.L	*PORCELAIN, LIVERPOOL* **SEE** LIVERPOOL PORCELAIN
NK4399.L	*PORCELAIN, LONGTON HALL* **SEE** LONGTON HALL PORCELAIN
NK4339.L7	*PORCELAIN, LOWESTOFT* **SEE** LOWESTOFT PORCELAIN
NK4380	*PORCELAIN, MEISSEN* **SEE** MEISSEN PORCELAIN
NK4399.N4	*PORCELAIN, NEW HALL* **SEE** NEW HALL PORCELAIN
NK4399.R6	*PORCELAIN, ROZENBURG* **SEE** ROZENBURG PORCELAIN
NK4390	*PORCELAIN, SEVRES* **SEE** SEVRES PORCELAIN
NK4399.S9	*PORCELAIN, SWANSEA* **SEE** SWANSEA PORCELAIN
NK4395	*PORCELAIN, WORCESTER* **SEE** WORCESTER PORCELAIN
NA4950	PORCHES / *churches*
NA7125	PORCHES / *dwellings*
QL737.R6	PORCUPINES
QL371-4	*PORIFERA* **SEE** SPONGES
SH396	*PORIFERA* **SEE** SPONGES / *fisheries*
QA484	PORISMS
HD9435	PORK INDUSTRY AND TRADE
HD9435	*PORK PACKING* **SEE** PORK INDUSTRY AND TRADE
TS1950-1975	PORK
TX556.P8	PORK / *food values*
HQ471	*PORNOGRAPHY* **SEE** LITERATURE, IMMORAL
Z659	*PORNOGRAPHY* **SEE** LITERATURE, IMMORAL / *copyright*
PN49	*PORNOGRAPHY* **SEE** LITERATURE, IMMORAL / *literature and ethics*
HV6727	*PORNOGRAPHY* **SEE** LITERATURE, IMMORAL / *social pathology*
QP801.P	PORPHYRIN AND PORPHYRIN COMPOUNDS
RC918.P	PORPHYRINURIA
QE461	PORPHYRY
QL737.C4	PORPOISES
QE882.C5	PORPOISES, FOSSIL
TL215.P75	PORSCHE AUTOMOBILE
DS517.3	PORT ARTHUR — SIEGE, 1904-1905
HE951-3	*PORT CHARGES* **SEE** HARBORS — PORT CHARGES
E475.42	PORT HUDSON, LA. — SIEGE, 1863
DP302.B284	PORT MAHON — SIEGE, 1756
HE951-3	*PORT REGULATIONS* **SEE** HARBORS — REGULATIONS
E196	PORT ROYAL (N.S.) EXPEDITION, 1690
E197	PORT ROYAL (N.S.) EXPEDITION, 1710
E472.7	PORT ROYAL (S.C.) EXPEDITION, 1861
TP559.P8	PORT WINE
NA8480	*PORTABLE BUILDINGS* **SEE** BUILDINGS, PORTABLE / *architecture*
TH1098	*PORTABLE BUILDINGS* **SEE** BUILDINGS, PORTABLE / *building*
TN307	*PORTABLE ELECTRIC LAMPS* **SEE** ELECTRIC LAMPS, PORTABLE / *mining*
TJ710	PORTABLE ENGINES
TK6564.P6	PORTABLE RADIOS
TJ710	*PORTABLE STEAM-ENGINES* **SEE** PORTABLE ENGINES
E159	PORTAGES / *u.s.*
NA3010	*PORTALS* **SEE** DOORWAYS
DA890.E2	PORTEOUS RIOTS, 1736
TP578	PORTER
F2275	PORTETE DE TARQUI, BATTLE OF, 1829
TA434-5	PORTLAND CEMENT / *etc.*
TP883	PORTLAND CEMENT / *manufacture*
TA680-683	PORTLAND CEMENT / *use*
DA505-7	PORTO PRAYA, ENGAGEMENT AT, 1781
F864	PORTOLA'S EXPEDITION, 1769-1770
ND1300-1337	PORTRAIT PAINTING
ND2200	PORTRAIT PAINTING / *water-colors*
ND1300-1337	PORTRAIT-PAINTERS
N7621-4	PORTRAITS — CATALOGS
N7622	PORTRAITS — PRIVATE COLLECTIONS
N7575-7649	PORTRAITS
TC203-324	*PORTS* **SEE** HARBORS / *engineering*
JX4138	*PORTS* **SEE** HARBORS / *international law*
HE551-560	*PORTS* **SEE** HARBORS / *transportation*
VK369-369.8	*PORTS OF REFUGE* **SEE** HARBORS OF REFUGE
DS517.7	PORTSMOUTH, TREATY OF, 1905
DP501-900	PORTUGAL — HISTORY
PQ9160	PORTUGUESE BALLADS AND SONGS / *collections*

PQ9080	PORTUGUESE BALLADS AND SONGS / history
PQ9164-9170	PORTUGUESE DRAMA / collections
PQ9083-9095	PORTUGUESE DRAMA / history
PQ9175-6	PORTUGUESE FICTION / collections
PQ9097-9109	PORTUGUESE FICTION / history
PC5360	PORTUGUESE LANGUAGE — EARLY TO 1500
PC5001-5498	PORTUGUESE LANGUAGE
PQ9181	PORTUGUESE LETTERS / collections
PQ9113	PORTUGUESE LETTERS / history
PQ9025.J4	PORTUGUESE LITERATURE — JEWISH AUTHORS
PQ9000-9999	PORTUGUESE LITERATURE
PQ9500-9699	*PORTUGUESE LITERATURE-BRAZIL* **SEE** BRAZILIAN LITERATURE
PN5321-9	PORTUGUESE NEWSPAPERS / history
PN5321-5330	PORTUGUESE PERIODICALS / history
PC5001-5041	PORTUGUESE PHILOLOGY
PQ9149-9163	PORTUGUESE POETRY / collections
PQ9061-9081	PORTUGUESE POETRY / history
PQ9172-9187	PORTUGUESE PROSE LITERATURE / collections
PQ9097-9119	PORTUGUESE PROSE LITERATURE / history
PQ9185	PORTUGUESE WIT AND HUMOR / collections
PQ9117	PORTUGUESE WIT AND HUMOR / history
PN6222.P8	PORTUGUESE WIT AND HUMOR / minor works
QA611	*POSITION ANALYSIS* **SEE** TOPOLOGY / geometry
UF853	POSITION-FINDERS
QC711	*POSITIVE RAYS* **SEE** CANAL RAYS
B831	POSITIVISM
B2200-2249	POSITIVISM / comte
B824.6	*POSITIVISM, LOGICAL* **SEE** LOGICAL POSITIVISM
BJ1365-1385	*POSITIVIST ETHICS* **SEE** ETHICS, POSITIVIST
BS2545.D5	*POSSESSION, DEMONIAC* **SEE** DEMONIAC POSSESSION / new testament
BF1555	*POSSESSION, DEMONIAC* **SEE** DEMONIAC POSSESSION / occult sciences
BC199.P7	POSSIBILITY
UC750-755	POST EXCHANGES
UA929.5-9	*POST-ATTACK REHABILITATION OF INDUSTRY* **SEE** WAR DAMAGE, INDUSTRIAL
HE6181-5	*POST-CARDS* **SEE** POSTAL CARDS
NC1870-1875	*POST-CARDS* **SEE** POSTAL CARDS / picture post-cards
HE6465-9	*POST-CHECK SYSTEM (U.S.)* **SEE** POSTAL SERVICE — U.S. — — POSTAL NOTES
LB2371	*POST-GRADUATE WORK* **SEE** UNIVERSITIES AND COLLEGES — GRADUATE WORK
LB1695	*POST-GRADUATE WORK IN HIGH SCHOOLS* **SEE** HIGH SCHOOLS — POSTGRADUATE WORK
ND1265	POST-IMPRESSIONISM (ART)
RA1058	*POST-MORTEM EXAMINATIONS* **SEE** AUTOPSY / medical jurisprudence
RB57	*POST-MORTEM EXAMINATIONS* **SEE** AUTOPSY / pathology
DA25	*POST-MORTEM INQUISITIONS* **SEE** INQUISITIONES POST MORTEM / english records
CS434-6	*POST-MORTEM INQUISITIONS* **SEE** INQUISITIONES POST MORTEM / english genealogical records
DA670	*POST-MORTEM INQUISITIONS* **SEE** INQUISITIONES POST MORTEM / english counties
RA623.5	POST-MORTEM PLASTIC SURGERY
HE6000-7500	*POST-OFFICE* **SEE** POSTAL SERVICE
UH80-85	*POST-OFFICE* **SEE** POSTAL SERVICE / military
NA4450-4457	*POST-OFFICE BUILDINGS* **SEE** POSTAL SERVICE — BUILDINGS
Z675.P	*POST-OFFICE LIBRARIES* **SEE** POSTAL LIBRARIES
HG1951-6	*POST-OFFICE SAVINGS-BANKS* **SEE** POSTAL SAVINGS-BANKS
RD51	*POST-OPERATIVE CARE* **SEE** POSTOPERATIVE CARE
BV4165	*POST-ORDINATION TRAINING* **SEE** CLERGY — POST-ORDINATION TRAINING
TE15-124	POST-ROADS / engineering
HE353-368	POST-ROADS / transportation
HE6123-6148	*POSTAGE* **SEE** POSTAL SERVICE — RATES
HE6497.M4	*POSTAGE METERS* **SEE** POSTAL SERVICE — METERED MAIL / u.s.
HE6221	POSTAGE-STAMPS — ALBUMS
HE6224-6230	POSTAGE-STAMPS — CATALOGS
HE6187-6230	POSTAGE-STAMPS — COLLECTORS AND COLLECTING
HE6181-5	POSTAGE-STAMPS
HE6181-5	POSTAL CARDS
NC1870-1875	POSTAL CARDS / picture post-cards

TF467	*POSTAL CARS* **SEE** RAILWAY MAIL SERVICE — CARS / construction
HE6475	*POSTAL CARS* **SEE** RAILWAY MAIL SERVICE — CARS / postal service
HG1953.C6	*POSTAL CHECKS* **SEE** POSTAL SERVICE — POSTAL CHECKS
HE6251-6281	POSTAL CONVENTIONS / international and other
HE6307	POSTAL CONVENTIONS / u.s.
HE6081-6099	*POSTAL LAWS AND REGULATIONS* **SEE** POSTAL SERVICE — LAWS AND REGULATIONS
Z675.P	POSTAL LIBRARIES
HG8751-9200	*POSTAL LIFE INSURANCE* **SEE** INSURANCE, LIFE
HE6123-6148	*POSTAL RATES* **SEE** POSTAL SERVICE — RATES
HG1951-6	POSTAL SAVINGS-BANKS
HG1953.C6	*POSTAL SAVINGS-BANKS-CHECKS* **SEE** POSTAL SERVICE — POSTAL CHECKS
NA4450-4457	POSTAL SERVICE — BUILDINGS
HE6078	POSTAL SERVICE — JUVENILE LITERATURE
HE6081-6099	POSTAL SERVICE — LAWS AND REGULATIONS
HE6497.M4	POSTAL SERVICE — METERED MAIL / u.s.
HE6165-9	POSTAL SERVICE — MONEY-ORDERS
HG1953.C6	POSTAL SERVICE — POSTAL CHECKS
HE6123-6148	POSTAL SERVICE — RATES
HE6176	POSTAL SERVICE — REGISTRY SYSTEM
HE6132	POSTAL SERVICE — SECOND-CLASS MATTER
HE6021	POSTAL SERVICE — STATISTICS
HE6300-6499	POSTAL SERVICE — U.S.
HE6000-7500	POSTAL SERVICE
UH80-85	POSTAL SERVICE / military
HG1953.C6	*POSTAL SERVICE-CHECKS* **SEE** POSTAL SERVICE — POSTAL CHECKS
HE6171-3	*POSTAL SERVICE-FOURTH-CLASS MATTER* **SEE** PARCELS-POST
HE6471-3	*POSTAL SERVICE-FOURTH-CLASS MATTER* **SEE** PARCELS-POST / u.s.
HE6171-3	*POSTAL SERVICE-INSURANCE* **SEE** PARCELS-POST
HE6471-3	*POSTAL SERVICE-INSURANCE* **SEE** PARCELS-POST / u.s.
HE6176	*POSTAL SERVICE-INSURANCE* **SEE** POSTAL SERVICE — REGISTRY SYSTEM
HE6171-3	*POSTAL SERVICE-PARCELS-POST* **SEE** PARCELS-POST
HE6471-3	*POSTAL SERVICE-PARCELS-POST* **SEE** PARCELS-POST / u.s.
HE6175	*POSTAL SERVICE-RAILROADS* **SEE** RAILWAY MAIL SERVICE
HE6475	*POSTAL SERVICE-RAILROADS* **SEE** RAILWAY MAIL SERVICE / u.s.
HE6499	*POSTAL SERVICE-U.S.-CLERKS* **SEE** POSTAL SERVICE — U.S. — — EMPLOYEES
HE6148	*POSTAL SERVICE-U.S.-FRANKING PRIVILEGE* **SEE** FRANKING PRIVILEGE
HE6448	*POSTAL SERVICE-U.S.-FRANKING PRIVILEGE* **SEE** FRANKING PRIVILEGE / u.s.
HE6148	*POSTAL SERVICE-U.S.-PENALTY MAIL* **SEE** FRANKING PRIVILEGE
HE6448	*POSTAL SERVICE-U.S.-PENALTY MAIL* **SEE** FRANKING PRIVILEGE / u.s.
HE6455-6	*POSTAL SERVICE-U.S.-RURAL FREE DELIVERY* **SEE** RURAL FREE DELIVERY / u.s.
HE6155	*POSTAL SERVICE-U.S.-RURAL FREE DELIVERY* **SEE** RURAL FREE DELIVERY
HE6323	*POSTAL SERVICE-U.S.-UNMAILABLE MATTER* **SEE** POSTAL SERVICE — U.S. — — LAWS AND REGULATIONS
HE6401-6	POSTAL SERVICE — U.S. — — ACCOUNTING
HE6381-5	POSTAL SERVICE — U.S. — — BIOGRAPHY
NA4451-3	POSTAL SERVICE — U.S. — — BUILDINGS
HE6361-8	POSTAL SERVICE — U.S. — — DIRECTORIES
HE6499	POSTAL SERVICE — U.S. — — EMPLOYEES
HE6411	POSTAL SERVICE — U.S. — — FINANCE
HE6497.F6	POSTAL SERVICE — U.S. — — FOREIGN MAIL
HE6477	POSTAL SERVICE — U.S. — — FOREIGN MAIL / ocean mail
HE6361-8	POSTAL SERVICE — U.S. — — GUIDES
HE6376	POSTAL SERVICE — U.S. — — GUIDES / local
HE6371-6	POSTAL SERVICE — U.S. — — HISTORY
HE6323	POSTAL SERVICE — U.S. — — LAWS AND REGULATIONS
HE6461	POSTAL SERVICE — U.S. — — LETTER-CARRIERS
HE6465-9	POSTAL SERVICE — U.S. — — MONEY-ORDERS

HE6001-9	POSTAL SERVICE — U.S. — — PERIODICALS
HE6465-9	POSTAL SERVICE — U.S. — — POSTAL NOTES
HE6499	POSTAL SERVICE — U.S. — — POSTMASTERS
HE6423-6448	POSTAL SERVICE — U.S. — — RATES
HE6476	POSTAL SERVICE — U.S. — — REGISTRY SYSTEM
HE6432	POSTAL SERVICE — U.S. — — SECOND-CLASS MATTER
HE6001-9	POSTAL SERVICE — U.S. — — SOCIETIES, ETC.
HE6309	POSTAL SERVICE — U.S. — — STATISTICS
HE7601-8630	*POSTAL TELEGRAPH* **SEE** TELEGRAPH / *economics*
TK5105-5865	*POSTAL TELEGRAPH* **SEE** TELEGRAPH / *technology*
HE6181-5	*POSTCARDS* **SEE** POSTAL CARDS
NC1870-1875	*POSTCARDS* **SEE** POSTAL CARDS / *picture post-cards*
NC1800-1850	POSTERS
HF5843	POSTERS / *advertising*
LB2371	*POSTGRADUATE WORK* **SEE** UNIVERSITIES AND COLLEGES — GRADUATE WORK
LB1695	*POSTGRADUATE WORK IN HIGH SCHOOLS* **SEE** HIGH SCHOOLS — POSTGRADUATE WORK
JX5187	POSTLIMINY / *international law*
HE6181-5	POSTMARKS
RD51	POSTOPERATIVE CARE
UA26	*POSTS, MILITARY* **SEE** MILITARY POSTS / *u.s.*
GN231	POSTURE / *anthropology*
RA781	POSTURE / *personal hygiene*
GV341	POSTURE / *physical training*
GV443	POSTURE / *physical training*
QP301	POSTURE / *physiology*
LB3427	POSTURE / *school hygiene*
HD9660.P68-7	POTASH INDUSTRY AND TRADE
TP245.P8	POTASH / *chemical technology*
S645	POTASH / *fertilizers*
TN919	POTASH / *mineral industries*
QP913.K1	POTASSIUM — PHYSIOLOGICAL EFFECT
TX409	*POTASSIUM BITARTRATE* **SEE** CREAM OF TARTAR / *etc.*
RM666.C	*POTASSIUM BITARTRATE* **SEE** CREAM OF TARTAR / *therapeutics*
RM666.B8	POTASSIUM BROMIDE / *therapeutics*
QP913.C5	POTASSIUM CHLORIDE — PHYSIOLOGICAL EFFECT
QD181.K1	POTASSIUM CHLORIDE
QD181.K1	POTASSIUM CYANIDE
RA1231.P	POTASSIUM CYANIDE / *toxicology*
QD181.K1	POTASSIUM DICHROMATE
QP535.K1	POTASSIUM IN THE BODY
HD9660.P68-7	*POTASSIUM INDUSTRY AND TRADE* **SEE** POTASH INDUSTRY AND TRADE
QD181.K1	POTASSIUM IODIDE
TP238	*POTASSIUM NITRATE* **SEE** SALTPETER / *manufacture*
QD181.K1	POTASSIUM PHOSPHATES / *chemistry*
TP245.P8	POTASSIUM SALTS / *chemical technology*
S645	POTASSIUM SALTS / *fertilizers*
TN919	POTASSIUM SALTS / *mineral industries*
QD181.K1	POTASSIUM
TX612.P7	POTATO DRYING
SB608.P8	POTATO LEAFROLL
HD1519	*POTATO PATCHES* **SEE** WORKING-MEN'S GARDENS
TP415	*POTATO STARCH* **SEE** STARCH / *chemical technology*
QD321	*POTATO STARCH* **SEE** STARCH / *organic chemistry*
QK887	*POTATO STARCH* **SEE** STARCH / *plant physiology*
SB608.P8	POTATO WART
SB608.P8	POTATO-BEETLE / *pests*
QL596.C5	POTATO-BEETLE / *zoology*
SB608.P8	*POTATO-BUG* **SEE** POTATO-BEETLE / *pests*
QL596.C5	*POTATO-BUG* **SEE** POTATO-BEETLE / *zoology*
SB608.P8	*POTATO-MOTH* **SEE** POTATO-TUBER MOTH
SB608.P8	POTATO-ROT
SB608.P8	POTATO-SCAB
SB608.P8	*POTATO-STALK WEEVIL* **SEE** POTATO-WEEVIL
SB608.P8	POTATO-TUBER MOTH
SB608.P8	POTATO-WEEVIL
SB608.P8	POTATOES — DISEASES AND PESTS
SB211.P8	POTATOES / *culture*
HD9235.P8	POTATOES / *economics*
SB211.P8	*POTATOES, SEED* **SEE** SEED POTATOES
TX612.P7	*POTATOES-DRYING* **SEE** POTATO DRYING
E99.P8	POTAWATOMI INDIANS

PM2191	POTAWATOMI LANGUAGE
QA374-7	*POTENTIAL FUNCTIONS* **SEE** DIFFERENTIAL EQUATIONS, PARTIAL
QA401-411	*POTENTIAL FUNCTIONS* **SEE** HARMONIC ANALYSIS
QA825	*POTENTIAL FUNCTIONS* **SEE** POTENTIAL, THEORY OF
QA406	*POTENTIAL FUNCTIONS* **SEE** SPHERICAL HARMONICS
QC601-641	*POTENTIAL, ELECTRIC* **SEE** ELECTRIC CURRENTS
QC618	*POTENTIAL, ELECTRIC* **SEE** ELECTROMOTIVE FORCE
QD561	*POTENTIAL, ELECTRIC* **SEE** ELECTROMOTIVE FORCE / *electrolysis*
QC571-595	*POTENTIAL, ELECTRIC* **SEE** ELECTROSTATICS
QA825	*POTENTIAL, ELECTRIC* **SEE** POTENTIAL, THEORY OF
QA825	POTENTIAL, THEORY OF
QC544.P8	POTENTIOMETER
GV1295.P	POTOMAC (GAME)
E99.P	POTOMAC INDIANS
M1268	POTPOURRIS (BAND)
M298	POTPOURRIS (CONCERTINA AND GUITAR)
M296-7	POTPOURRIS (FLUTE AND GUITAR)
M380-384	POTPOURRIS (FLUTE, GUITAR, VIOLA)
M380-384	POTPOURRIS (FLUTE, GUITAR, VIOLIN)
M276-7	POTPOURRIS (GUITAR AND PIANO)
M125-9	POTPOURRIS (GUITAR)
M115-119	POTPOURRIS (HARP)
M1075	POTPOURRIS (ORCHESTRA)
M313-314	POTPOURRIS (PIANO TRIO)
M39	POTPOURRIS (PIANO)
M540-544	POTPOURRIS (PIANO, BASSOON, CLARINET, GUITAR, VIOLIN)
M212	POTPOURRIS (PIANO, 4 HANDS)
M1350	POTPOURRIS (SALON ORCHESTRA)
M1160	POTPOURRIS (STRING ORCHESTRA)
M1012-1013	POTPOURRIS (VIOLIN WITH ORCHESTRA)
M235-6	POTPOURRIS (VIOLONCELLO AND PIANO)
M214-215	POTPOURRIS (2 PIANOS)
PJ1675	*POTSHERDS (OSTRAKA)* **SEE** OSTRAKA / *egyptian*
PA3371	*POTSHERDS (OSTRAKA)* **SEE** OSTRAKA / *greek*
RD533	POTT'S DISEASE / *surgery*
E99.P8	*POTTAWATAMIE INDIANS* **SEE** POTAWATOMI INDIANS
SB415	*POTTED PLANTS* **SEE** PLANTS, POTTED / *greenhouse plants*
HD8039.P8	POTTERS
NK4215	*POTTERS' MARKS* **SEE** POTTERY — MARKS
NK4230	POTTERY — COLLECTORS AND COLLECTING
TP809	POTTERY — FORMULAE, TABLES, ETC.
NK4215	POTTERY — MARKS
NK4230	POTTERY — PRICES
NK3740	POTTERY — PRIVATE COLLECTIONS
NK4235	POTTERY — REPAIRING
HF5716.C	POTTERY — TABLES AND READY-RECKONERS
HG3875.C9	POTTERY — TABLES AND READY-RECKONERS / *exchange*
NK3700-4695	POTTERY / *ceramics*
TP785-825	POTTERY / *chemical technology*
HD9610-9620	POTTERY / *trade*
NK3800-3855	POTTERY, ANCIENT
NK3880	POTTERY, ISLAMIC
NK3880	*POTTERY, MUSLIM* **SEE** POTTERY, ISLAMIC
NK4143-4172	POTTERY, ORIENTAL
NK4543-4572	POTTERY, ORIENTAL / *porcelain*
GN433	*POTTERY, PREHISTORIC* **SEE** POTTERY, PRIMITIVE
GN433	POTTERY, PRIMITIVE
E99.P8	*POTTOWATOMIE INDIANS* **SEE** POTAWATOMI INDIANS
QL737.M3	*POUCHED ANIMALS* **SEE** MARSUPIALIA
PL8181-4	*POUL LANGUAGE* **SEE** FULAH LANGUAGE
SF995	POULTRY — DISEASES
SF494	POULTRY — FEEDING AND FEEDS
S486	*POULTRY APPLIANCES* **SEE** POULTRY HOUSES AND EQUIPMENT
SF487	POULTRY BREEDING
S486	*POULTRY BUILDINGS* **SEE** POULTRY HOUSES AND EQUIPMENT
TX749	*POULTRY COOKERY* **SEE** COOKERY (POULTRY)
S486	*POULTRY COOPS* **SEE** POULTRY HOUSES AND EQUIPMENT
S486	*POULTRY EQUIPMENT* **SEE** POULTRY HOUSES AND EQUIPMENT
SF494	*POULTRY FEEDING* **SEE** POULTRY — FEEDING AND FEEDS

S486	POULTRY HOUSES AND EQUIPMENT
SF494	*POULTRY NUTRITION* **SEE** POULTRY — FEEDING AND FEEDS
SF995	POULTRY PESTS
TX556.P9	POULTRY
TX375	POULTRY
SF481-507	POULTRY
TS1962	POULTRY, DRESSING OF
SF487	*POULTRY-BREEDING* **SEE** POULTRY BREEDING
S486	*POULTRY-EQUIPMENT* **SEE** POULTRY HOUSES AND EQUIPMENT
QL795.B57	*POULTRY-LEGENDS AND STORIES* **SEE** BIRDS — LEGENDS AND STORIES
SF494	*POULTRY-NUTRITION* **SEE** POULTRY — FEEDING AND FEEDS
S486	*POULTRY-SUPPLIES* **SEE** POULTRY HOUSES AND EQUIPMENT
SF56-59	POUNDS / *domestic animals*
PL8605	*POUNOU LANGUAGE* **SEE** PUNU LANGUAGE
HV1-4630	POVERTY
NK9990.P6	POWDER FLASKS
NK9990.P6	*POWDER HORNS* **SEE** POWDER FLASKS
TS245	POWDER METAL PROCESSES
TS245	*POWDER METALLURGY PROCESSES* **SEE** POWDER METAL PROCESSES
TN695	POWDER METALLURGY
UF540-545	POWDER-MAGAZINES
VF380	POWDER-MAGAZINES / *naval*
TP273	*POWDER, SMOKELESS* **SEE** GUNPOWDER, SMOKELESS
SF259	*POWDERED MILK* **SEE** MILK, DRIED
RS201.P8	POWDERS (PHARMACY)
RS201.P8	*POWDERS, MEDICINAL* **SEE** POWDERS (PHARMACY)
RA766.W3	*POWDERS, WASHING* **SEE** WASHING POWDERS / *disinfectants*
TP991	*POWDERS, WASHING* **SEE** WASHING POWDERS / *technology*
SB608.P8	POWDERY SCAB / *potato pests*
TA422-4	*POWELLIZED TIMBER* **SEE** WOOD — PRESERVATION
TJ21-124	POWER (MECHANICS) — STATISTICS
TJ153	POWER (MECHANICS)
BD438	POWER (PHILOSOPHY)
TK3001-3511	*POWER DISTRIBUTION, ELECTRIC* **SEE** ELECTRIC POWER DISTRIBUTION
BJ1469	*POWER OVER LIFE AND DEATH* **SEE** LIFE AND DEATH, POWER OVER
D217	*POWER POLITICS* **SEE** BALANCE OF POWER
JX1318	*POWER POLITICS* **SEE** BALANCE OF POWER / *international law*
TJ1450	POWER PRESSES
TK1001-1831	*POWER PRODUCTION, ELECTRIC* **SEE** ELECTRIC POWER PRODUCTION
TJ1045-1119	POWER TRANSMISSION
S711-713	POWER TRANSMISSION / *agricultural machinery*
TK3201-3261	*POWER TRANSMISSION, ELECTRIC* **SEE** ELECTRIC POWER LINES
TK3001-3511	*POWER TRANSMISSION, ELECTRIC* **SEE** ELECTRIC POWER DISTRIBUTION
TL296	*POWER TRUCKS, INDUSTRIAL* **SEE** INDUSTRIAL POWER TRUCKS / *manufacture*
TS155	*POWER TRUCKS, INDUSTRIAL* **SEE** INDUSTRIAL POWER TRUCKS / *material handling*
VM341-9	*POWER-BOATS* **SEE** MOTOR-BOATS / *naval architecture*
GV835	*POWER-BOATS* **SEE** MOTOR-BOATS / *sports*
TJ164	POWER-PLANTS
TH4581	POWER-PLANTS / *building*
TK1191-1831	POWER-PLANTS / *electric*
TJ395-412	POWER-PLANTS / *steam*
TC147	POWER-PLANTS / *water-power*
TK1191-1831	*POWER-PLANTS, ELECTRIC* **SEE** ELECTRIC POWER-PLANTS
TJ768	*POWER-PLANTS, GAS* **SEE** GAS POWER-PLANTS
TJ395-412	*POWER-PLANTS, STEAM* **SEE** STEAM POWER-PLANTS
D217	*POWER, BALANCE OF* **SEE** BALANCE OF POWER
JX1318	*POWER, BALANCE OF* **SEE** BALANCE OF POWER / *international law*
JF251-314	*POWER, EXECUTIVE* **SEE** EXECUTIVE POWER
JN-JQ	*POWER, EXECUTIVE* **SEE** EXECUTIVE POWER / *other countries*
JK501-901	*POWER, EXECUTIVE* **SEE** EXECUTIVE POWER / *u.s.*
JF700-723	*POWER, JUDICIAL* **SEE** JUDICIAL POWER
JF265	*POWER, JUDICIAL* **SEE** JUDICIAL POWER
JK-JQ	*POWER, JUDICIAL* **SEE** JUDICIAL POWER
JF441-483	*POWER, LEGISLATIVE* **SEE** LEGISLATIVE POWER
BT960-962	*POWERS (THEOLOGY)* **SEE** SPIRITS
JK-JQ	*POWERS, DELEGATION OF* **SEE** DELEGATION OF POWERS
JF225	*POWERS, DELEGATION OF* **SEE** DELEGATION OF POWERS
JF229	*POWERS, SEPARATION OF* **SEE** SEPARATION OF POWERS
JL-JQ	*POWERS, SEPARATION OF* **SEE** SEPARATION OF POWERS / *other countries*
JK305	*POWERS, SEPARATION OF* **SEE** SEPARATION OF POWERS / *u.s.*
E99.P	POWHATAN INDIANS
F1465.2.P	*POYA INDIANS* **SEE** PAYA INDIANS
F1465.2.P	*POYER INDIANS* **SEE** PAYA INDIANS
JN1409-1410	POYNINGS' LAW
DR545	*POZAREVAC, TREATY OF, 1718* **SEE** POZHAREVATS, PEACE OF, 1718
DR545	POZHAREVATS, PEACE OF, 1718
TP881	*POZZOLANAS* **SEE** POZZUOLANAS
TP881	POZZUOLANAS
RT62	PRACTICAL NURSING
JF1321-2111	*PRACTICAL POLITICS* **SEE** POLITICS, PRACTICAL
JN-JQ	*PRACTICAL POLITICS* **SEE** POLITICS, PRACTICAL / *other countries*
JK1711-2391	*PRACTICAL POLITICS* **SEE** POLITICS, PRACTICAL / *u.s.*
LB2157	*PRACTICE TEACHING* **SEE** STUDENT TEACHING
DG83.5.P3	PRAEFECTUS PRAETORIO
DG83.5.P6	*PRAETORS* **SEE** PRETORS / *roman antiquities*
DB69.3	PRAGMATIC SANCTION OF CHARLES VI, 1713
JN1625	PRAGMATIC SANCTION OF CHARLES VI, 1713
B831.5	PRAGMATICS
B832	PRAGMATISM
B945.J23-24	PRAGMATISM / *william james*
DD412.6.P7	PRAGUE, BATTLE OF, 1757
D765.55.P7	PRAGUE, BATTLE OF, 1945
DP657	PRAIA, BATTLE OF, 1829
E474.92	PRAIRIE GROVE, BATTLE OF, 1862
SF510.P7	*PRAIRIE-CHICKENS* **SEE** PRAIRIE-HENS / *culture*
SK325.P7	*PRAIRIE-CHICKENS* **SEE** PRAIRIE-HENS / *hunting*
QL696.G2	*PRAIRIE-CHICKENS* **SEE** PRAIRIE-HENS / *zoology*
QL737.R6	PRAIRIE-DOGS
SF510.P7	PRAIRIE-HENS / *culture*
SK325.P7	PRAIRIE-HENS / *hunting*
QL696.G2	PRAIRIE-HENS / *zoology*
GB571-8	PRAIRIES
QK938.P7	PRAIRIES / *plant ecology*
PK1201-1429	PRAKRIT LANGUAGES
PK5001-5045	PRAKRIT LITERATURE
PK1450-1460	PRAKRIT LITERATURE
PK1201-1429	PRAKRIT PHILOLOGY
QD181.P7	PRASEODYMIUM / *chemistry*
DS451.8	*PRATHIHARAS* **SEE** GURJARA-PRATIHARA DYNASTY
DS451.8	*PRATIHARAS* **SEE** GURJARA-PRATIHARA DYNASTY
BV228	PRAYER — BIBLICAL TEACHING
BV212	PRAYER — JUVENILE LITERATURE
BV225	PRAYER — PSYCHOLOGY
BL1475.P7	PRAYER (HINDUISM)
BP178	PRAYER (ISLAM)
BM669	PRAYER (JUDAISM)
BV287	PRAYER GROUPS
BV245-283	PRAYER-BOOKS
BX	PRAYER-BOOKS / *by denomination*
ND3363-3380	PRAYER-BOOKS / *illuminated*
BV285	PRAYER-MEETINGS
BL1475.W4	*PRAYER-WHEELS* **SEE** WHEELS (IN RELIGION, FOLK-LORE, ETC.)
BV200-227	PRAYER
BV4813	*PRAYER, MENTAL* **SEE** MEDITATION / *christianity*
BL627	*PRAYER, MENTAL* **SEE** MEDITATION / *comparative religion*
BV4870	*PRAYERS FOR CHILDREN* **SEE** CHILDREN — PRAYER-BOOKS AND DEVOTIONS
BV283.P4	PRAYERS FOR PEACE

LC107-120	*PRAYERS IN THE PUBLIC SCHOOLS* **SEE** RELIGION IN THE PUBLIC SCHOOLS
BV228-283	PRAYERS
BL560	PRAYERS / *comparative religion*
PJ3785	*PRAYERS, ASSYRO-BABYLONIAN* **SEE** ASSYRO-BABYLONIAN PRAYERS
BV236	PRAYERS, EARLY CHRISTIAN
BP183.3	*PRAYERS, ISLAMIC* **SEE** ISLAMIC PRAYERS
BP183.3	*PRAYERS, MUSLIM* **SEE** ISLAMIC PRAYERS
BV250-254	*PRAYERS, PASTORAL* **SEE** PASTORAL PRAYERS
BV250-254	*PRAYERS, PULPIT* **SEE** PASTORAL PRAYERS
BV283.G7	*PRAYERS, TABLE* **SEE** GRACE AT MEALS
QE655	*PRE-CAMBRIAN PERIOD* **SEE** GEOLOGY, STRATIGRAPHIC — PRE-CAMBRIAN
QE724-5	*PRE-CAMBRIAN PERIOD* **SEE** PALEONTOLOGY — PRE-CAMBRIAN
E59.C95	*PRE-COLUMBIAN CIVILIZATION* **SEE** INDIANS — CULTURE
HD197	PRE-EMPTION RIGHTS (U.S.)
BD426	PRE-EXISTENCE
BP166.4	*PRE-ISLAMIC PROPHETS* **SEE** PROPHETS, PRE-ISLAMIC
BP137	*PRE-ISLAMIC PROPHETS* **SEE** PROPHETS, PRE-ISLAMIC / *legends*
BP166.4	*PRE-MUHAMMADAN PROPHETS* **SEE** PROPHETS, PRE-ISLAMIC
BP137	*PRE-MUHAMMADAN PROPHETS* **SEE** PROPHETS, PRE-ISLAMIC / *legends*
BR295	*PRE-REFORMATION* **SEE** REFORMATION — EARLY MOVEMENTS
BV4207-8	PREACHING — HISTORY
BX3501-3555	*PREACHING FRIARS* **SEE** DOMINICANS
BX4341-4	*PREACHING FRIARS* **SEE** DOMINICANS / *women*
BV4200-4235	PREACHING
BV4235.E8	PREACHING, EXTEMPORANEOUS
BP184.25	PREACHING, ISLAMIC
BM730	PREACHING, JEWISH
BV4235.L3	PREACHING, LAY
BP184.25	*PREACHING, MUSLIM* **SEE** PREACHING, ISLAMIC
TA683	PRECAST CONCRETE CONSTRUCTION
CR	PRECEDENCE
JX1678-9	PRECEDENCE
JX4081	PRECEDENCE / *diplomatic*
BX1939.P64	PRECEDENCE, ECCLESIASTICAL (CANON LAW)
HF1243	*PRECEDENTS (LAW)* **SEE** FORMS (LAW) / *commercial law u.s.*
BV4720	*PRECEPTS OF THE CHURCH* **SEE** COMMANDMENTS OF THE CHURCH
BM646	*PRECEPTS, SIX HUNDRED AND THIRTEEN* **SEE** COMMANDMENTS, SIX HUNDRED AND THIRTEEN
QB165	PRECESSION
PQ245	PRECIEUSES
BX2159.P7	PRECIOUS BLOOD, DEVOTION TO
BT465	PRECIOUS BLOOD, RELICS OF THE
HG261-313	PRECIOUS METALS / *finance*
TN410-439	PRECIOUS METALS / *mining*
GR805	PRECIOUS STONES / *folk-lore*
TS750-755	PRECIOUS STONES / *manufactures*
QE392-4	PRECIOUS STONES / *mineralogy*
TN980-997	PRECIOUS STONES / *mining*
TP873	PRECIOUS STONES, ARTIFICIAL
TP873	*PRECIOUS STONES, SYNTHETIC* **SEE** PRECIOUS STONES, ARTIFICIAL
PE1477	PRECIS WRITING / *english language*
JN435.P7	PRECIS WRITING / *gt. brit.*
JK717	PRECIS WRITING / *u.s.*
BX9301-9359	*PRECISIANS* **SEE** PURITANS
F67	*PRECISIANS* **SEE** PURITANS / *massachusetts*
F7	*PRECISIANS* **SEE** PURITANS / *new england*
QC39	*PRECISION OF MEASUREMENT* **SEE** PHYSICAL MEASUREMENTS
LC3991-4000	*PRECOCITY* **SEE** GIFTED CHILDREN
BP166.3	PREDESTINATION (ISLAM)
BT810	PREDESTINATION
BX3501-3555	*PREDICADORES* **SEE** DOMINICANS
BX4341-4	*PREDICADORES* **SEE** DOMINICANS / *women*
BD331-346	*PREDICAMENTS (CATEGORIES)* **SEE** CATEGORIES (PHILOSOPHY) / *ontology*
BC172	*PREDICAMENTS (CATEGORIES)* **SEE** CATEGORIES (PHILOSOPHY) / *logic*

LB1131	PREDICTION OF SCHOLASTIC SUCCESS
BF1783-1815	*PREDICTIONS* **SEE** PROPHECIES / *occultism*
TG418	*PREFABRICATED BRIDGES* **SEE** BRIDGES, PREFABRICATED
TH1098	*PREFABRICATED BUILDINGS* **SEE** BUILDINGS, PREFABRICATED / *building*
NA8480	*PREFABRICATED BUILDINGS* **SEE** BUILDINGS, PREFABRICATED / *architecture*
TA683	*PREFABRICATED CONCRETE CONSTRUCTION* **SEE** PRECAST CONCRETE CONSTRUCTION
BX2045.P	PREFACES (LITURGY)
PN171.P7	PREFACES
Z242.P7	PREFACES / *printing*
DG83.5.P3	*PREFECT, PRETORIAN* **SEE** PRAEFECTUS PRAETORIO
BX1910	*PREFECTS APOSTOLIC* **SEE** VICARS APOSTOLIC
GV1291.P8	PREFERENCE (GAME)
JF1071-5	PREFERENTIAL BALLOT
JK2217	PREFERENTIAL BALLOT / *u.s.*
JF1071-5	*PREFERENTIAL VOTING* **SEE** PREFERENTIAL BALLOT
JK2217	*PREFERENTIAL VOTING* **SEE** PREFERENTIAL BALLOT / *u.s.*
RG563	PREGNANCY — SIGNS AND DIAGNOSIS
RG551-591	PREGNANCY
RG586	PREGNANCY, EXTRA-UTERINE
RG591	PREGNANCY, MOLAR
RG650	PREGNANCY, PROTRACTED
CC	*PREHISTORIC ANTIQUITIES* **SEE** ARCHAEOLOGY
GT	*PREHISTORIC ANTIQUITIES* **SEE** ARCHAEOLOGY / *manners and customs general*
DA-DU	*PREHISTORIC ANTIQUITIES* **SEE** ARCHAEOLOGY / *national antiquities other than american*
E-F	*PREHISTORIC ANTIQUITIES* **SEE** ARCHAEOLOGY / *n indian and other american antiquities*
GN	*PREHISTORIC ANTIQUITIES* **SEE** ARCHAEOLOGY / *prehistoric antiquities*
GN700-875	*PREHISTORIC ANTIQUITIES* **SEE** MAN, PREHISTORIC
N5310	*PREHISTORIC ART* **SEE** ART, PRIMITIVE
QE701-996	*PREHISTORIC FAUNA* **SEE** PALEONTOLOGY
GN700-875	*PREHISTORIC MAN* **SEE** MAN, PREHISTORIC
CC	*PREHISTORY* **SEE** ARCHAEOLOGY
GT	*PREHISTORY* **SEE** ARCHAEOLOGY / *manners and customs general*
DA-DU	*PREHISTORY* **SEE** ARCHAEOLOGY / *national antiquities other than american*
E-F	*PREHISTORY* **SEE** ARCHAEOLOGY / *n indian and other american antiquities*
GN	*PREHISTORY* **SEE** ARCHAEOLOGY / *prehistoric antiquities*
GN777-8	*PREHISTORY* **SEE** BRONZE AGE
GN779-780	*PREHISTORY* **SEE** IRON AGE
GN775-6	*PREHISTORY* **SEE** STONE AGE
BF575.P9	PREJUDICES AND ANTIPATHIES
HQ1018.M4	PREMARITAL EXAMINATIONS
RJ250	*PREMATURE INFANTS* **SEE** INFANTS (PREMATURE)
R838	PREMEDICAL EDUCATION
BT890-891	*PREMILLENNIALISM* **SEE** MILLENNIUM
HF6146.P7	PREMIUMS (RETAIL TRADE)
HF2701	*PREMIUMS, EXPORT* **SEE** EXPORT PREMIUMS
Z7840.P9	PREMONSTRATENSIANS — BIO-BIBLIOGRAPHY
BX3901-3955	PREMONSTRATENSIANS
BX4421-4	PREMONSTRATENSIANS / *women*
RG635	PRENATAL INFLUENCES
RJ91	PRENATAL INFLUENCES / *stirpiculture*
P285	*PREPOSITIONS* **SEE** GRAMMAR, COMPARATIVE AND GENERAL — PREPOSITIONS
P285	*PREPOSITIONS* **SEE** GRAMMAR, COMPARATIVE AND GENERAL — PREPOSITIONS
ND467	PRERAPHAELITISM / *painting*
JF305	PREROGATIVE, ROYAL
BV430-431	PRESBYTERIAN CHURCH — HYMNS
BV2570	PRESBYTERIAN CHURCH — MISSIONS
BX8960-8968	PRESBYTERIAN CHURCH IN THE U.S.
LC579-580	PRESBYTERIAN CHURCH IN THE U.S.A. — EDUCATION
BV2570	PRESBYTERIAN CHURCH IN THE U.S.A. — MISSIONS
BX8950-8958	PRESBYTERIAN CHURCH IN THE U.S.A.
BX9052-8	PRESBYTERIAN CHURCH OF ENGLAND
BX8960-8968	*PRESBYTERIAN CHURCH SOUTH* **SEE** PRESBYTERIAN CHURCH IN THE U.S.
BX8901-9225	PRESBYTERIAN CHURCH
BX8901-9225	PRESBYTERIANISM

LB1140	*PRESCHOOL EDUCATION* **SEE** EDUCATION, PRESCHOOL
PN4199-4321	*PRESCHOOL READERS AND SPEAKERS* **SEE** READERS AND SPEAKERS / *recitations*
PE1417	*PRESCHOOL READERS AND SPEAKERS* **SEE** READERS AND SPEAKERS / *rhetoric*
PE1117-1130	*PRESCHOOL READERS AND SPEAKERS* **SEE** READERS AND SPEAKERS / *english*
BX1939.P54	PRESCRIPTION (CANON LAW)
RM139	PRESCRIPTION WRITING
RS125-7	*PRESCRIPTIONS* **SEE** MEDICINE — FORMULAE, RECEIPTS, PRESCRIPTIONS
RM139	*PRESCRIPTIONS* **SEE** PRESCRIPTION WRITING
HG8851-3	*PRESENT-VALUE TABLES* **SEE** INSURANCE, LIFE — RATES AND TABLES
BV50.C3	*PRESENTATION OF JESUS CHRIST, FEAST OF THE* **SEE** CANDLEMAS
BV50.P7	PRESENTATION OF THE BLESSED VIRGIN MARY, FEAST OF THE
GT3050	*PRESENTS* **SEE** GIFTS / *manners and customs*
QL677.7	*PRESERVATION (NATURAL HISTORY)* **SEE** BIRDS — COLLECTION AND PRESERVATION
QL465	*PRESERVATION (NATURAL HISTORY)* **SEE** INSECTS — COLLECTION AND PRESERVATION
QH60	*PRESERVATION (NATURAL HISTORY)* **SEE** NATURAL HISTORY — TECHNIQUE
QK61	*PRESERVATION (NATURAL HISTORY)* **SEE** PLANTS — COLLECTION AND PRESERVATION
QL63	*PRESERVATION (NATURAL HISTORY)* **SEE** TAXIDERMY
QL61-67	*PRESERVATION (NATURAL HISTORY)* **SEE** ZOOLOGICAL SPECIMENS-COLLECTION AND PRESERVATION
N8560	*PRESERVATION OF ART OBJECTS* **SEE** ART OBJECTS — CONSERVATION AND RESTORATION
Z700-701	*PRESERVATION OF BOOKS* **SEE** BOOKS — CONSERVATION AND RESTORATION
NE380	*PRESERVATION OF ENGRAVINGS* **SEE** ENGRAVINGS — CONSERVATION AND RESTORATION
TX599-613	*PRESERVATION OF FOOD* **SEE** FOOD — PRESERVATION
SD	*PRESERVATION OF FORESTS* **SEE** FORESTS AND FORESTRY
HJ3805	*PRESERVATION OF FORESTS* **SEE** FORESTS AND FORESTRY / *income from state forests*
HJ4167	*PRESERVATION OF FORESTS* **SEE** FORESTS AND FORESTRY / *taxation*
HC	*PRESERVATION OF FORESTS* **SEE** NATURAL RESOURCES
TX599-613	*PRESERVATION OF FRUIT* **SEE** CANNING AND PRESERVING
TX609	*PRESERVATION OF FRUIT* **SEE** FRUIT — EVAPORATION
CD931-4279	*PRESERVATION OF HISTORICAL RECORDS* **SEE** ARCHIVES
CD941	*PRESERVATION OF HISTORICAL RECORDS* **SEE** ARCHIVES / *directories*
CD950-965	*PRESERVATION OF HISTORICAL RECORDS* **SEE** ARCHIVES / *handbooks*
QH75-77	*PRESERVATION OF LANDMARKS* **SEE** NATURAL MONUMENTS
N8850	*PRESERVATION OF MONUMENTS* **SEE** MONUMENTS — PRESERVATION / *art*
CC135	*PRESERVATION OF MONUMENTS* **SEE** MONUMENTS — PRESERVATION
QH75-77	*PRESERVATION OF NATURAL SCENERY* **SEE** NATURAL MONUMENTS
ND1640-1650	*PRESERVATION OF PAINTINGS* **SEE** PAINTINGS — CONSERVATION AND RESTORATION
TR465	*PRESERVATION OF PHOTOGRAPHS* **SEE** PHOTOGRAPHS — CONSERVATION AND RESTORATION
NE380	*PRESERVATION OF PRINTS* **SEE** PRINTS — CONSERVATION AND RESTORATION
NB1199	*PRESERVATION OF SCULPTURE* **SEE** SCULPTURE — CONSERVATION AND RESTORATION
TX599-613	*PRESERVATION OF VEGETABLES* **SEE** CANNING AND PRESERVING
TA422-4	*PRESERVATION OF WOOD* **SEE** WOOD — PRESERVATION

TX599-613	*PRESERVING* **SEE** CANNING AND PRESERVING
JF2081	*PRESIDENTIAL PRIMARIES* **SEE** PRIMARIES
JK2071-7	*PRESIDENTIAL PRIMARIES* **SEE** PRIMARIES / *u.s.*
JF285	PRESIDENTS — ELECTION
JK511-609	PRESIDENTS — U.S.
JF255	PRESIDENTS
E176.1	PRESIDENTS — U.S. — — BIOGRAPHY / *collective*
JK1967-8	PRESIDENTS — U.S. — — ELECTION
JK524-9	PRESIDENTS — U.S. — — ELECTION
JK536-540	PRESIDENTS — U.S. — — INAUGURATION / *constitutional history*
F197-9	PRESIDENTS — U.S. — — INAUGURATION / *exercises in washington*
CJ5801-5815	PRESIDENTS — U.S. — — MEDALS
E176.1	PRESIDENTS — U.S. — — PORTRAITS
N7593	PRESIDENTS — U.S. — — PORTRAITS
BR516	PRESIDENTS — U.S. — — RELIGION
JK550	PRESIDENTS — U.S. — — TERM OF OFFICE
Z657-9	*PRESS CENSORSHIP* **SEE** LIBERTY OF THE PRESS
Z691	*PRESS CLIPPINGS* **SEE** CLIPPINGS (BOOKS, NEWSPAPERS, ETC.)
Z697.C6	*PRESS CLIPPINGS* **SEE** CLIPPINGS (BOOKS, NEWSPAPERS, ETC.)
PN4735-4748	PRESS LAW
TJ1450	*PRESS WORK* **SEE** POWER PRESSES
TS250	*PRESS WORKING OF METAL* **SEE** DEEP DRAWING (METAL-WORK)
TS250	*PRESS WORKING OF METAL* **SEE** SHEET-METAL WORK
E357.2-3	*PRESS-GANGS* **SEE** IMPRESSMENT / *war of 1812*
PN4700-5650	PRESS
PN4749	*PRESS-SOCIAL ASPECTS* **SEE** JOURNALISM — SOCIAL ASPECTS
TH1715	*PRESSBOARD* **SEE** WALL BOARD
TP831	PRESSED BRICK
TS837	*PRESSED WOOD* **SEE** WOOD, COMPRESSED
Z231.5.U6	*PRESSES, COLLEGE* **SEE** UNIVERSITY PRESSES
TJ1460	*PRESSES, HYDRAULIC* **SEE** HYDRAULIC PRESSES
TJ1450	*PRESSES, POWER* **SEE** POWER PRESSES
Z249	*PRESSES, PRINTING* **SEE** PRINTING-PRESS
Z131-322	*PRESSES, PRIVATE* **SEE** PRIVATE PRESSES
Z231.5.S4	*PRESSES, SHIP* **SEE** SHIP PRESSES
Z231.5.U6	*PRESSES, UNIVERSITY* **SEE** UNIVERSITY PRESSES
TT583	PRESSING OF GARMENTS
QC165	PRESSURE — MEASUREMENT
TL557.D4	*PRESSURE ALTITUDE COMPUTERS* **SEE** DENSITY ALTITUDE COMPUTERS
TX840.P7	PRESSURE COOKERY
TL574.P7	*PRESSURE DISTRIBUTION (AIRCRAFT)* **SEE** AERODYNAMIC LOAD
TL557.D4	*PRESSURE HEIGHT COMPUTERS* **SEE** DENSITY ALTITUDE COMPUTERS
TL588	PRESSURE PATTERN FLYING
TL697.P7	PRESSURE SUITS
TS283	PRESSURE VESSELS
TJ370-372	PRESSURE-GAGES / *steam-boilers*
QC885-896	*PRESSURE, ATMOSPHERIC* **SEE** ATMOSPHERIC PRESSURE
TK9203.P7	PRESSURIZED WATER REACTORS
TK9203.P7	*PRESSURIZED-WATER POWER REACTORS* **SEE** PRESSURIZED WATER REACTORS
GV1541-1561	*PRESTIDIGITATION* **SEE** CONJURING
GN475	*PRESTIDIGITATION* **SEE** MAGIC / *ethnology*
BF1585-1623	*PRESTIDIGITATION* **SEE** MAGIC / *occult sciences*
HD5367. T4 1853	PRESTON STRIKE, 1853-1854
DA412-415	PRESTON, BATTLE OF, 1648
TA683.9	PRESTRESSED CONCRETE CONSTRUCTION
TA439	PRESTRESSED CONCRETE
TA683.42	*PRESTRESSING REINFORCEMENT* **SEE** TENDONS (PRESTRESSED CONCRETE)
BX1939.P55	PRESUMPTIONS (CANON LAW)
HV6751-6761	*PRETENDERS* **SEE** IMPOSTORS AND IMPOSTURE / *criminal*
DG83.5.P3	*PRETORIAN PREFECT* **SEE** PRAEFECTUS PRAETORIO
DG83.5.P6	PRETORS / *roman antiquities*
TX770	PRETZELS
DC230.E8	PREUSSISCH-EYLAU, BATTLE OF, 1807

HV4701-4959	PREVENTION OF CRUELTY TO ANIMALS **SEE** ANIMALS, TREATMENT OF
TD884	PREVENTION OF SMOKE **SEE** SMOKE PREVENTION
RM739-798	PREVENTIVE INOCULATION **SEE** SERUMTHERAPY
RA401	PREVENTIVE INOCULATION **SEE** SERUMTHERAPY / etc.
RA421-790	PREVENTIVE MEDICINE **SEE** MEDICINE, PREVENTIVE
PT581.P8	PRIAMEL
HB236	PRICE CONTROL **SEE** PRICE REGULATION
HF5415	PRICE CUTTING
HF5415	PRICE DISCRIMINATION
HB236	PRICE FIXING **SEE** PRICE REGULATION
HF5417	PRICE FIXING, RESALE **SEE** PRICE MAINTENANCE
NC1280	PRICE LABELS **SEE** LABELS
HF5417	PRICE MAINTENANCE
HF5415	PRICE POLICY
HB236	PRICE POLICY, GOVERNMENTAL **SEE** PRICE REGULATION
HF5415	PRICE POLICY, INDUSTRIAL **SEE** PRICE POLICY
HB236	PRICE REGULATION
HB236	PRICE STABILIZATION, GOVERNMENTAL **SEE** PRICE REGULATION
HF5417	PRICE STABILIZATION, INDUSTRIAL **SEE** PRICE MAINTENANCE
E477.16	PRICE'S MISSOURI EXPEDITION, 1864
HB221-236	PRICES / economic theory
HG229	PRICES / prices and money
HD6978-7080	PRICES / prices and wages
HF5415	PRICING **SEE** PRICE POLICY
QK650	PRICKLES
SB207.P8	PRICKLY-PEAR / forage crops
SB379.P8	PRICKLY-PEAR / fruits
SB615.P8	PRICKLY-PEAR / pests
BJ1535.P9	PRIDE AND VANITY
PN56.P6	PRIDE IN LITERATURE
DA380	PRIEST'S HOLES **SEE** HIDING-PLACES (SECRET CHAMBERS, ETC.) / england
BV659-660	PRIESTESSES **SEE** PRIESTS
BX1912	PRIESTESSES **SEE** PRIESTS / catholic church
BX5175	PRIESTESSES **SEE** PRIESTS / church of england
BL635	PRIESTESSES **SEE** PRIESTS / comparative religion
BV659-660	PRIESTHOOD **SEE** PRIESTS
BX1912	PRIESTHOOD **SEE** PRIESTS / catholic church
BX5175	PRIESTHOOD **SEE** PRIESTS / church of england
BL635	PRIESTHOOD **SEE** PRIESTS / comparative religion
BX1939.C665	PRIESTS (CANON LAW) **SEE** CLERGY (CANON LAW)
PR120.C	PRIESTS AS AUTHORS **SEE** CLERGYMEN AS AUTHORS
PN171.C	PRIESTS AS AUTHORS **SEE** CLERGYMEN AS AUTHORS
PR120.C	PRIESTS AS WRITERS **SEE** CLERGYMEN AS AUTHORS
PN171.C	PRIESTS AS WRITERS **SEE** CLERGYMEN AS AUTHORS
PR151.C7	PRIESTS IN LITERATURE **SEE** CLERGY IN LITERATURE / english literature
PT151.C7	PRIESTS IN LITERATURE **SEE** CLERGY IN LITERATURE / german literature
BV659-660	PRIESTS
BX1912	PRIESTS / catholic church
BX5175	PRIESTS / church of england
BL635	PRIESTS / comparative religion
BM652	PRIESTS, JEWISH
BL815.P	PRIESTS, ROMAN / religion
DG135	PRIESTS, ROMAN / roman antiquities
DG315	PRIMA PORTA, BATTLE OF, 312 **SEE** SAXA RUBRA, BATTLE OF, 312
JF2081	PRIMARIES
JK2071-7	PRIMARIES / u.s.
QC603-5	PRIMARY BATTERIES **SEE** ELECTRIC BATTERIES
LB1501-1547	PRIMARY EDUCATION **SEE** EDUCATION, PRIMARY
QL737.P9	PRIMATES
QE882.P7	PRIMATES, FOSSIL
QA51	PRIME FACTORS **SEE** FACTOR TABLES
QB224	PRIME MERIDIAN **SEE** LONGITUDE — PRIME MERIDIAN
QA246	PRIME NUMBERS **SEE** NUMBERS, PRIME
ML945-8	PRIMER CLARINET **SEE** CLARINET / history and construction
PE1119	PRIMERS
GN424-6	PRIMITIVE AGRICULTURE **SEE** AGRICULTURE, PRIMITIVE

BR160-240	PRIMITIVE AND EARLY CHURCH **SEE** CHURCH HISTORY — PRIMITIVE AND EARLY CHURCH
N5310	PRIMITIVE ART **SEE** ART, PRIMITIVE
BX6380-6389	PRIMITIVE BAPTISTS
BR160-240	PRIMITIVE CHRISTIANITY **SEE** CHURCH HISTORY — PRIMITIVE AND EARLY CHURCH
PN905-1008	PRIMITIVE LITERATURE **SEE** FOLK LITERATURE
BL430	PRIMITIVE RELIGION **SEE** RELIGION, PRIMITIVE
BL430	PRIMITIVE RELIGION **SEE** RELIGION, PRIMITIVE
GN470-474	PRIMITIVE RELIGION **SEE** RELIGION, PRIMITVE / ethnology
GN470-474	PRIMITIVE RELIGION **SEE** RELIGION,PRIMITIVE / ethnology
ND1267	PRIMITIVISM IN ART
QK495.P95	PRIMROSES / botany
SB413.P	PRIMROSES / culture
D107.5	PRINCES / modern history
D352.1	PRINCES / 19th century
D412.7	PRINCES / 20th century
LC4929-4949	PRINCES, EDUCATION OF **SEE** EDUCATION OF PRINCES
JC393	PRINCES, EDUCATION OF **SEE** EDUCATION OF PRINCES / political theory
DD801.S37	PRINCES, ROBBERY OF THE, 1455
D107.5	PRINCESSES / modern history
D352.3	PRINCESSES / 19th century
D412.8	PRINCESSES / 20th century
E241.P9	PRINCETON, BATTLE OF, 1777
LB2803-2822	PRINCIPALS, SCHOOL **SEE** SCHOOL SUPERINTENDENTS AND PRINCIPALS
NE880-885	PRINT COLLECTORS **SEE** PRINTS — COLLECTORS AND COLLECTING
NE850-855	PRINT MAKING **SEE** PRINTS — TECHNIQUE
NE830-835	PRINT MAKING **SEE** PRINTS — TECHNIQUE
TK7870	PRINTED CIRCUITS / electronics
Z243	PRINTERS — CHARITIES
HD7269.P97	PRINTERS — DISEASES AND HYGIENE
Z119	PRINTERS - PERIODICALS **SEE** PRINTING — PERIODICALS
Z120	PRINTERS - SOCIETIES, ETC. **SEE** PRINTING — SOCIETIES, ETC.
Z231-2	PRINTERS / biography
Z242.I3	PRINTERS' IMPRINTS **SEE** IMPRINTS (IN BOOKS)
Z235-6	PRINTERS' MARKS
Z276	PRINTERS' ORNAMENTS **SEE** BOOK ORNAMENTATION
NK3600-3640	PRINTERS' ORNAMENTS **SEE** INITIALS
ND3335	PRINTERS' ORNAMENTS **SEE** INITIALS / illumination
Z235-6	PRINTERS' ORNAMENTS **SEE** PRINTERS' MARKS
Z256	PRINTERS' ROLLERS **SEE** ROLLERS (PRINTING)
Z119	PRINTERS-PERIODICALS **SEE** PRINTING — PERIODICALS
Z120	PRINTERS-SOCIETIES, ETC. **SEE** PRINTING — SOCIETIES, ETC.
Z116	PRINTING — ANECDOTES, FACETIAE, SATIRE, ETC.
Z242.C2	PRINTING — CANCELS
Z118	PRINTING — DICTIONARIES
Z121	PRINTING — EXHIBITIONS
Z124-242	PRINTING — HISTORY
Z123	PRINTING — JUVENILE LITERATURE
Z119	PRINTING -- PERIODICALS
Z232	PRINTING — POETRY
Z124	PRINTING — POETRY
Z116	PRINTING — POETRY
Z120	PRINTING — SOCIETIES, ETC.
Z250	PRINTING — SPECIMENS
Z695.87	PRINTING - CATALOGS **SEE** CATALOGS — PRINTING
Z127	PRINTING - INVENTION **SEE** PRINTING — HISTORY — — CELEBRATION OF INVENTION
Z126-126.5	PRINTING - INVENTION **SEE** PRINTING — HISTORY — — ORIGIN AND ANTECEDENTS
Z122	PRINTING - STUDY AND TEACHING **SEE** PRINTING, PRACTICAL — STUDY AND TEACHING
Z243	PRINTING AS A TRADE
Z1008	PRINTING CLUBS **SEE** BOOK CLUBS
Z549	PRINTING CLUBS **SEE** BOOK CLUBS
HV1666-1698	PRINTING FOR THE BLIND **SEE** BLIND — PRINTING AND WRITING SYSTEMS

QA273-7	PROBABILITIES
HG8781-2	PROBABILITIES / *life insurance*
BC141	PROBABILITIES / *logic*
BT927	PROBATION AFTER DEATH
HV9278	PROBATION
HV9301-9430	PROBATION
LC148	*PROBATION, ACADEMIC* **SEE** COLLEGE ATTENDANCE
TK7872	*PROBES (CATHODE RAY OSCILLOGRAPH)* **SEE** CATHODE RAY OSCILLOGRAPH / *electronics*
TK6565.C4	*PROBES (CATHODE RAY OSCILLOGRAPH)* **SEE** CATHODE RAY OSCILLOGRAPH / *radio*
QB362	PROBLEM OF MANY BODIES / *celestial mechanics*
QC174.5	PROBLEM OF MANY BODIES / *quantum theory*
QB362	*PROBLEM OF N-BODIES* **SEE** PROBLEM OF MANY BODIES / *celestial mechanics*
QC174.5	*PROBLEM OF N-BODIES* **SEE** PROBLEM OF MANY BODIES / *quantum theory*
QB362	PROBLEM OF THREE BODIES / *planetary theory*
QB401	PROBLEM OF THREE BODIES /·*satellites*
QA466-9	*PROBLEMS, FAMOUS (IN GEOMETRY)* **SEE** GEOMETRY — PROBLEMS, FAMOUS
QL737.U8	PROBOSCIDEA
QE882.U7	PROBOSCIDEA, FOSSIL
RD86.N8	*PROCAINE* **SEE** NOVOCAINE
RK510	*PROCAINE* **SEE** NOVOCAINE / *dentistry*
QA295	PROCESSES, INFINITE
S698	*PROCESSING, AGRICULTURAL* **SEE** AGRICULTURAL PROCESSING
BT114	*PROCESSION (IN THE TRINITY)* **SEE** JESUS CHRIST -- PROCESSION
GT3980-4099	PROCESSIONS
BX1939.P64	PROCESSIONS, ECCLESIASTICAL (CANON LAW)
D5	PROCLAMATIONS
RC864	PROCTOLOGY
BT378.P8	PRODIGAL SON (PARABLE)
HG6046	*PRODUCE EXCHANGES* **SEE** COMMODITY EXCHANGES
HF5686.C5	PRODUCE TRADE — ACCOUNTING
HF5716.P8	PRODUCE TRADE — TABLES AND READY-RECKONERS
HG3875.P8	PRODUCE TRADE — TABLES AND READY-RECKONERS / *exchange tables*
HD9000-9019	PRODUCE TRADE
TJ751-805	*PRODUCER GAS* **SEE** GAS AND OIL ENGINES
TP700-764	*PRODUCER GAS* **SEE** GAS MANUFACTURE AND WORKS
HD4486-4495	*PRODUCER GAS* **SEE** GAS MANUFACTURE AND WORKS / *public ownership*
TP762	*PRODUCER GAS* **SEE** GAS-PRODUCERS
TP751-764	*PRODUCER GAS* **SEE** GAS
TP700	*PRODUCER GAS* **SEE** GAS
TP760	*PRODUCER GAS* **SEE** WATER-GAS
HD	*PRODUCTION* **SEE** INDUSTRY
HC	*PRODUCTION* **SEE** INDUSTRY
HD61	*PRODUCTION* **SEE** OVERPRODUCTION
HB201-5	*PRODUCTION* **SEE** SUPPLY AND DEMAND / *value*
T56	PRODUCTION CONTROL / *technology*
HD2951-3570	*PRODUCTION, COOPERATIVE* **SEE** COOPERATION
HF5431-6	*PRODUCTION, COOPERATIVE* **SEE** COOPERATION / *cooperative business*
QA839	*PRODUCTS OF INERTIA* **SEE** MOMENTS OF INERTIA / *analytic mechanics*
TG265-7	*PRODUCTS OF INERTIA* **SEE** MOMENTS OF INERTIA / *engineering*
RA401	*PRODUCTS, BIOLOGICAL* **SEE** BIOLOGICAL PRODUCTS / *public health*
RM270-282	*PRODUCTS, BIOLOGICAL* **SEE** BIOLOGICAL PRODUCTS / *therapeutics*
TP953	*PRODUCTS, COAL-TAR* **SEE** COAL-TAR PRODUCTS
HF1041-1051	*PRODUCTS, COMMERCIAL* **SEE** COMMERCIAL PRODUCTS
HD9275	*PRODUCTS, DAIRY* **SEE** DAIRY PRODUCTS
TP415	*PRODUCTS, FARINACEOUS* **SEE** STARCH / *chemical technology*
QD321	*PRODUCTS, FARINACEOUS* **SEE** STARCH / *organic chemistry*
QK887	*PRODUCTS, FARINACEOUS* **SEE** STARCH / *plant physiology*
QA295	PRODUCTS, INFINITE
TP995	*PRODUCTS, WASTE* **SEE** WASTE PRODUCTS
BJ1535.P95	*PROFANITY* **SEE** SWEARING
GT3080	*PROFANITY* **SEE** SWEARING / *manners and customs*
BV4627.S9	*PROFANITY* **SEE** SWEARING / *moral theology*
BX2427	PROFESSION (IN RELIGIOUS ORDERS, CONGREGATIONS, ETC.)
UB147	*PROFESSION OF ARMS* **SEE** MILITARY SERVICE AS A PROFESSION
BX1939.P65	PROFESSION OF FAITH (CANON LAW)
BX2427	*PROFESSION, MONASTIC* **SEE** PROFESSION (IN RELIGIOUS ORDERS, CONGREGATIONS, ETC.)
BX2427	*PROFESSION, RELIGIOUS* **SEE** PROFESSION (IN RELIGIOUS ORDERS, CONGREGATIONS, ETC.)
HD2421-9	*PROFESSIONAL ASSOCIATIONS* **SEE** TRADE AND PROFESSIONAL ASSOCIATIONS / *trade associations*
HD6350-6940	*PROFESSIONAL ASSOCIATIONS* **SEE** TRADE AND PROFESSIONAL ASSOCIATIONS / *trade-unions*
GV875.A1	*PROFESSIONAL BASEBALL CLUBS* **SEE** BASEBALL CLUBS
LC1051-1071	PROFESSIONAL EDUCATION
BJ1725	PROFESSIONAL ETHICS
LB2157	*PROFESSIONAL LABORATORY EXPERIENCES (EDUCATION)* **SEE** STUDENT TEACHING
GV733	PROFESSIONALISM IN SPORTS
GT6110-6390	PROFESSIONS / *manners and customs*
HT687	PROFESSIONS / *social groups*
LB1778	*PROFESSORS* **SEE** COLLEGE TEACHERS
TR696	*PROFILE RECORDER, AIRBORNE* **SEE** AIRBORNE PROFILE RECORDER
HF5681.B2	*PROFIT AND LOSS STATEMENTS* **SEE** FINANCIAL STATEMENTS / *balance sheet*
HG4530	*PROFIT-SHARING TRUSTS* **SEE** INVESTMENT TRUSTS
HD2970-3110	PROFIT-SHARING
HB601	PROFIT / *economic theory*
HG9970.B85	*PROFITS INSURANCE* **SEE** INSURANCE, BUSINESS INTERRUPTION
RJ135	*PROGERIA* **SEE** INFANTILISM
GN131	PROGNATHISM
LB1131	*PROGNOSIS OF SCHOLASTIC SUCCESS* **SEE** PREDICTION OF SCHOLASTIC SUCCESS
ML3855	PROGRAM MUSIC / *aesthetics*
ML3300-3354	PROGRAM MUSIC / *history*
HE8697.A8	*PROGRAM RATING, TELEVISION* **SEE** TELEVISION PROGRAMS — RATING
LB1028.5	*PROGRAMED INSTRUCTION* **SEE** PROGRAMMED INSTRUCTION
LB1028.5	PROGRAMMED INSTRUCTION
LB1028.5	*PROGRAMMED LEARNING* **SEE** PROGRAMMED INSTRUCTION
LB1028.5	*PROGRAMMED TEXT-BOOKS* **SEE** PROGRAMMED INSTRUCTION
QA76	PROGRAMMING (ELECTRONIC COMPUTERS)
QA264	PROGRAMMING (MATHEMATICS)
HF5548	PROGRAMMING LANGUAGES (ELECTRONIC COMPUTERS) — BUSINESS
LB2369	*PROGRAMS, ACADEMIC* **SEE** DISSERTATIONS, ACADEMIC / *preparation*
ML25.7	*PROGRAMS, CONCERT* **SEE** CONCERTS — PROGRAMS
ML40-44	*PROGRAMS, CONCERT* **SEE** CONCERTS — PROGRAMS
BV199.D4	*PROGRAMS, CONSECRATION* **SEE** DEDICATION SERVICES
BV199.D4	*PROGRAMS, DEDICATION* **SEE** DEDICATION SERVICES
CB155	PROGRESS / *civilization*
HM101	PROGRESS / *sociology*
GV1249	PROGRESSIVE EUCHRE
RC394.H4	*PROGRESSIVE LENTICULAR DEGENERATION* **SEE** HEPATOLENTICULAR DEGENERATION
JK2386-2390	PROGRESSIVE PARTY (FOUNDED 1912) / *u.s.*
JK2331.P	PROGRESSIVE PARTY (FOUNDED 1948) / *u.s.*
HJ2326-7	*PROGRESSIVE TAXATION* **SEE** TAXATION, PROGRESSIVE
VM880-881	*PROGRESSIVE TRIALS (SHIPS)* **SEE** SHIP TRIALS
BX1939.P67	PROHIBITED BOOKS (CANON LAW)
JK2381-5	PROHIBITION PARTY / *u.s.*
HV5088-5091	PROHIBITION
TL796.5.U6D	*PROJECT DISCOVERER* **SEE** DISCOVERER (ARTIFICIAL SATELLITE)
TL789.8	PROJECT MERCURY
LB1027	PROJECT METHOD IN TEACHING
TL796.5.U6V3	PROJECT VANGUARD

LB1027	*PROJECT-TEACHING* **SEE** PROJECT METHOD IN TEACHING
UF750-770	PROJECTILES / *military*
VF480-500	PROJECTILES / *naval*
UF767	PROJECTILES, AERIAL
UF767	*PROJECTILES, SELF-PROPELLED* **SEE** ROCKETS (ORDNANCE)
QA501-519	PROJECTION / *mathematics*
T363-5	PROJECTION / *mechanical drawing*
QA505	*PROJECTION, ISOMETRIC* **SEE** ISOMETRIC PROJECTION / *mathematics*
T365	*PROJECTION, ISOMETRIC* **SEE** ISOMETRIC PROJECTION / *mechanical drawing*
Q186	*PROJECTION, LANTERN* **SEE** LANTERN PROJECTION
TR890	*PROJECTION, MOVING-PICTURE* **SEE** MOVING-PICTURE PROJECTION
QA503	*PROJECTION, ORTHOGRAPHIC* **SEE** ORTHOGRAPHIC PROJECTION / *mathematics*
GA115	*PROJECTION, ORTHOGRAPHIC* **SEE** ORTHOGRAPHIC PROJECTION / *cartography*
T363	*PROJECTION, ORTHOGRAPHIC* **SEE** ORTHOGRAPHIC PROJECTION / *mechanical drawing*
QA660	*PROJECTIVE DIFFERENTIAL GEOMETRY* **SEE** GEOMETRY, DIFFERENTIAL — PROJECTIVE
QA554	*PROJECTIVE GEOMETRY* **SEE** GEOMETRY, PROJECTIVE
QA471	*PROJECTIVE GEOMETRY* **SEE** GEOMETRY, PROJECTIVE
DR573.5	PROKHOD SHIPCHENSKI, BATTLE OF, 1877
RG361	*PROLAPSUS UTERI* **SEE** UTERUS — DISPLACEMENTS
BT65	*PROLEGOMENA TO DOCTRINAL THEOLOGY* **SEE** THEOLOGY, DOCTRINAL — INTRODUCTIONS
HD4801-4854	PROLETARIAT
QK653	PROLIFICATION / *plant morphology*
PN171.P8	PROLOGUES AND EPILOGUES
PR1195.P7	PROLOGUES AND EPILOGUES / *english literature*
QL561.B6	PROMETHEA MOTH
BJ1500.P7	PROMISES
BX1939.P7	PROMOTERS OF JUSTICE (CANON LAW)
HG4011	PROMOTERS
BX1939.P7	*PROMOTOR JUSTITIAE* **SEE** PROMOTERS OF JUSTICE (CANON LAW)
BC171-3	*PROOF* **SEE** EVIDENCE / *logic*
BF761-8	*PROOF* **SEE** EVIDENCE / *psychology*
MT35	PROOF-READING — MUSIC
Z254	PROOF-READING
BR118	*PROPAEDEUTICS (THEOLOGY)* **SEE** THEOLOGY — METHODOLOGY
JX1674-5	PROPAGANDA / *diplomacy*
D639.P6-7	PROPAGANDA / *european war*
JK1118	PROPAGANDA / *lobbying u.s.*
HM263	PROPAGANDA / *public opinion*
SB119-124	*PROPAGATION OF PLANTS* **SEE** PLANT PROPAGATION
QD305.H6	PROPANE
VM753-7	PROPELLERS
TL705-8	PROPELLERS, AERIAL
M2148.2	PROPERS (MUSIC)
M2148.2	*PROPERS OF THE MASS (MUSIC)* **SEE** PROPERS (MUSIC)
QC171-197	*PROPERTIES OF MATTER* **SEE** MATTER — PROPERTIES
JX5228	*PROPERTY CAPTURED AT SEA* **SEE** CAPTURE AT SEA
HJ4101-4129	PROPERTY TAX
JX4263.P6	*PROPERTY, ALIEN* **SEE** ALIEN PROPERTY
BV775-7	*PROPERTY, CHURCH* **SEE** CHURCH PROPERTY
Z551-656	*PROPERTY, LITERARY* **SEE** COPYRIGHT
JX6564	*PROPERTY, PERSONAL* **SEE** PERSONAL PROPERTY / *private international law*
HF1263	*PROPERTY, PERSONAL* **SEE** PERSONAL PROPERTY / *u.s.*
HD301-1130	*PROPERTY, REAL* **SEE** REAL PROPERTY / *other countries*
HD301-1130	*PROPERTY, REAL* **SEE** REAL PROPERTY / *other countries*
HD251-279	*PROPERTY, REAL* **SEE** REAL PROPERTY / *u.s.*
CS23	*PROPERTY, UNCLAIMED* **SEE** ESTATES, UNCLAIMED
HF5681.V3	*PROPERTY-VALUATION* **SEE** VALUATION / *accounting*
HJ6670	*PROPERTY-VALUATION* **SEE** VALUATION / *customs administration*
TA178	*PROPERTY-VALUATION* **SEE** VALUATION / *engineering*
HD2765	*PROPERTY-VALUATION* **SEE** VALUATION / *public service corporations*
HD1387	*PROPERTY-VALUATION* **SEE** VALUATION / *real estate*
BF1783-1815	PROPHECIES / *occultism*
BS1560	PROPHETS / *bible biography*
BS1505	PROPHETS / *bible biography*
BF1783-1815	PROPHETS / *occultism*
BS1501-1675	PROPHETS / *prophetic books*
BP166.4	PROPHETS, PRE-ISLAMIC
BP137	PROPHETS, PRE-ISLAMIC / *legends*
BP166.4	*PROPHETS, PRE-MUHAMMADAN* **SEE** PROPHETS, PRE-ISLAMIC
BP137	*PROPHETS, PRE-MUHAMMADAN* **SEE** PROPHETS, PRE-ISLAMIC / *legends*
GN66-69	PROPORTION (ANTHROPOMETRY)
NA2760	*PROPORTION (ARCHITECTURE)* **SEE** ARCHITECTURE — COMPOSITION, PROPORTION, ETC.
N76	PROPORTION (ART)
NC745	PROPORTION (ART) / *design*
JF1071-5	PROPORTIONAL REPRESENTATION
HJ2326-7	*PROPORTIONAL TAXATION* **SEE** TAXATION, PROGRESSIVE
BL390	*PROPOSED RELIGIONS* **SEE** RELIGIONS (PROPOSED, UNIVERSAL, ETC.)
Z675.P85	*PROPRIETARY LIBRARIES* **SEE** LIBRARIES, PROPRIETARY
RM671	*PROPRIETARY MEDICINES* **SEE** MEDICINES, PATENT, PROPRIETARY, ETC.
ML3080	*PROSE (LITURGY)* **SEE** SEQUENCES (LITURGY) / *history*
QP801.P67	PROSECRETIN
BM729.P7	PROSELYTES AND PROSELYTING, JEWISH
QL430.4	PROSOBRANCHIATA
QE809.P7	PROSOBRANCHIATA / *fossil*
PN1031-1055	*PROSODY* **SEE** VERSIFICATION
TN269	PROSPECTING — GEOPHYSICAL METHODS
TN270-271	PROSPECTING
RC899	PROSTATE GLAND — DISEASES
RD587	PROSTATE GLAND — SURGERY
QL878	PROSTATE GLAND / *comparative anatomy*
QM416	PROSTATE GLAND / *human anatomy*
QP257	PROSTATE GLAND / *physiology*
RD118-120.5	PROSTHESIS
RD118-120.5	*PROSTHETICS* **SEE** PROSTHESIS
HQ101-440	PROSTITUTION
HF1701-2701	*PROTECTION* **SEE** FREE TRADE AND PROTECTION
QL671	*PROTECTION OF BIRDS* **SEE** BIRDS, PROTECTION OF / *etc.*
SK351-579	*PROTECTION OF BIRDS* **SEE** BIRDS, PROTECTION OF / *game-laws*
HV701-1420	*PROTECTION OF CHILDREN* **SEE** CHILD WELFARE
JX4263.P7-8	*PROTECTION OF CITIZENS ABROAD* **SEE** DIPLOMATIC PROTECTION
SK351-579	*PROTECTION OF GAME* **SEE** GAME PROTECTION
QH75-77	*PROTECTION OF NATURAL MONUMENTS* **SEE** NATURAL MONUMENTS
QK86	*PROTECTION OF PLANTS* **SEE** PLANTS, PROTECTION OF
SB599-999	*PROTECTION OF PLANTS* **SEE** PLANTS, PROTECTION OF / *diseases and pests*
SB599-999	*PROTECTION OF WILD FLOWERS* **SEE** PLANTS, PROTECTION OF / *diseases and pests*
QK86	*PROTECTION OF WILD FLOWERS* **SEE** PLANTS, PROTECTION OF
BX961.P	PROTECTION, PAPAL
TP242	PROTECTIVE ATMOSPHERES
HD7395.C5	*PROTECTIVE CLOTHING* **SEE** CLOTHING, PROTECTIVE
TP935	PROTECTIVE COATINGS
JX4021-3	PROTECTORATES / *international law*
QD431	*PROTEIDS* **SEE** PROTEINS / *chemistry*
QP551	*PROTEIDS* **SEE** PROTEINS / *physiological*
QK899	PROTEIN CRYSTALS **SEE** CRYSTALLOIDS (BOTANY)
RM640.P5	*PROTEINASE, ACID* **SEE** PEPSIN
QP601	*PROTEINASE, ALKALI* **SEE** TRYPSIN
QD431	PROTEINS / *chemistry*
QP551	PROTEINS / *physiological*

QE655	*PROTEROZOIC PERIOD* SEE GEOLOGY, STRATIGRAPHIC — PRE-CAMBRIAN
BX4800-9890	PROTESTANT CHURCHES
BX5966	PROTESTANT EPISCOPAL CHURCH IN THE U.S.A. — BISHOPS
BX5939	PROTESTANT EPISCOPAL CHURCH IN THE U.S.A. — CATECHISMS AND CREEDS
BX5965	PROTESTANT EPISCOPAL CHURCH IN THE U.S.A. — CLERGY
BX5950-5968	PROTESTANT EPISCOPAL CHURCH IN THE U.S.A. — DISCIPLINE
BX5929-5936	PROTESTANT EPISCOPAL CHURCH IN THE U.S.A. — DOCTRINAL AND CONTROVERSIAL WORKS
BX5850-5876	PROTESTANT EPISCOPAL CHURCH IN THE U.S.A. — EDUCATION
LC582-3	PROTESTANT EPISCOPAL CHURCH IN THE U.S.A. — EDUCATION
BX5950-5968	PROTESTANT EPISCOPAL CHURCH IN THE U.S.A. — GOVERNMENT
BV372	PROTESTANT EPISCOPAL CHURCH IN THE U.S.A. — HYMNS
BV2575	PROTESTANT EPISCOPAL CHURCH IN THE U.S.A. — MISSIONS
BX5837	PROTESTANT EPISCOPAL CHURCH IN THE U.S.A. — PASTORAL LETTERS AND CHARGES
BX5937	PROTESTANT EPISCOPAL CHURCH IN THE U.S.A. — SERMONS
BX5943-5	PROTESTANT EPISCOPAL CHURCH IN THE U.S.A. BOOK OF COMMON PRAYER
BX5800-5995	PROTESTANT EPISCOPAL CHURCH IN THE U.S.A.
BX5990-5995	*PROTESTANT EPISCOPAL CHURCH IN THE U.S.A.-CONVERTS* SEE CONVERTS, ANGLICAN / *protestant episcopal church*
BX5197-9	*PROTESTANT EPISCOPAL CHURCH IN THE U.S.A.-CONVERTS* SEE CONVERTS, ANGLICAN / *church of england*
BX5949.M3	*PROTESTANT EPISCOPAL CHURCH IN THE U.S.A.-MARRIAGE* SEE MARRIAGE — PROTESTANT EPISCOPAL CHURCH IN THE U.S.A.
BX5969	*PROTESTANT EPISCOPAL CHURCH IN THE U.S.A.-PARISH MISSIONS* SEE PARISH MISSIONS — ANGLICAN COMMUNION / *protestant episcopal*
NA4821.A	*PROTESTANT EPISCOPAL CHURCHES* SEE CHURCHES, ANGLICAN
BV4405-6	*PROTESTANT MONASTICISM AND RELIGIOUS ORDERS* SEE MONASTICISM AND RELIGIOUS ORDERS, PROTESTANT
D220-234	*PROTESTANT REFORMATION* SEE REFORMATION / *european history*
DD176-189	*PROTESTANT REFORMATION* SEE REFORMATION / *germany*
BR300-420	*PROTESTANT REFORMATION* SEE REFORMATION / *religion*
BX4800-9890	*PROTESTANT SECTS* SEE PROTESTANT CHURCHES
BX4800-4861	PROTESTANTISM
BX4800-9890	PROTESTANTS
QH271-7	*PROTISTA* SEE UNICELLULAR ORGANISMS
QE882.U3	PROTOCERAS
CS460.S4	PROTOCOL-BOOKS / *scottish record society*
QC173	PROTONS
QC711	PROTONS / *electric discharges*
QK505-635	*PROTOPHYTA* SEE CRYPTOGAMS
QH591	PROTOPLASM
QL448	PROTOTRACHEATA
QL366-9	PROTOZOA
QE771-3	PROTOZOA / *fossil*
QR251	PROTOZOA, PATHOGENIC
QA77	PROTRACTORS / *mathematical instruments*
TA611	PROTRACTORS / *survey plotting*
PC3322-3	PROVENCAL BALLADS AND SONGS / *collections*
PC3315-3316	PROVENCAL BALLADS AND SONGS / *history*
PC3395-8	PROVENCAL DRAMA, MODERN / *collections*
PC3386	PROVENCAL DRAMA, MODERN / *history*
PC3201-3299	PROVENCAL LANGUAGE
PC3371-8	PROVENCAL LANGUAGE, MODERN
PC3322-3366	PROVENCAL LITERATURE / *collections*
PC3301-3359	PROVENCAL LITERATURE / *history*
PC3395-3420	PROVENCAL LITERATURE, MODERN / *collections*
PC3381-3391	PROVENCAL LITERATURE, MODERN / *history*
PC3201-3213	PROVENCAL PHILOLOGY
PC3322	PROVENCAL POETRY / *collections*
PC3315-3318	PROVENCAL POETRY / *history*
PC3395-8	PROVENCAL POETRY, MODERN / *collections*
PC3381-2	PROVENCAL POETRY, MODERN / *history*
PC3385	PROVENCAL POETRY, MODERN / *history*
PC3395-8	PROVENCAL PROSE LITERATURE / *modern*
PC3387	PROVENCAL PROSE LITERATURE / *modern*
PC3320	PROVENCAL PROSE LITERATURE / *old*
PC3327	PROVENCAL PROSE LITERATURE / *old*
PN6400-6525	PROVERBS
PN6465.S9	*PROVERBS, GERMAN-SWITZERLAND* SEE PROVERBS, SWISS (GERMAN)
R707	*PROVERBS, MEDICAL* SEE MEDICINE — QUOTATIONS, MAXIMS, ETC.
PN6465.S9	PROVERBS, SWISS (GERMAN)
BT95-96	PROVIDENCE AND GOVERNMENT OF GOD / *government of god*
BT135	PROVIDENCE AND GOVERNMENT OF GOD / *providence*
HG7920-7933	*PROVIDENCE AND THRIFT* SEE SAVING AND THRIFT
BJ1533.E2	*PROVIDENCE AND THRIFT* SEE SAVING AND THRIFT / *ethics*
HG2121-2156	*PROVIDENT LOAN ASSOCIATIONS* SEE BUILDING AND LOAN ASSOCIATIONS
QP801.P	PROVITAMINS
BJ1533.P9	PRUDENCE
SB379.P9	PRUNE
SD407	PRUNING / *forestry*
SB125	PRUNING / *horticulture*
S691-3	PRUNING / *implements*
RL751	PRURITUS
DD301-491	PRUSSIA — HISTORY
DD436-440	*PRUSSIA-HISTORY-AUSTRO-PRUSSIAN WAR, 1866* SEE AUSTRO-PRUSSIAN WAR, 1866
TP936	PRUSSIAN BLUE
PG8201-8	PRUSSIAN LANGUAGE
DD336	PRUSSIANS (SLAVIC TRIBE)
QD181.C15	*PRUSSIC ACID* SEE HYDROCYANIC ACID / *chemistry*
RA766.H8	*PRUSSIC ACID* SEE HYDROCYANIC ACID / *disinfectants*
DR544	PRUTH RIVER, BATTLE OF, 1711
D557.P7	PRZEMYSL — SIEGE, 1915
BV290	PSALMODY
M2079.2.L19	PSALMS (MUSIC) — 19TH PSALM
M2099.2.L19	PSALMS (MUSIC) — 19TH PSALM
RD123	PSEUDARTHROSIS
PN56.C6	*PSEUDO-CLASSICISM* SEE CLASSICISM
QE391.S	*PSEUDO-GALENA* SEE SPHALERITE
BM752	PSEUDO-MESSIAHS
PN603	*PSEUDO-ROMANTICISM* SEE ROMANTICISM
PN750-769	*PSEUDO-ROMANTICISM* SEE ROMANTICISM
RD123	*PSEUDOARTHROSIS* SEE PSEUDARTHROSIS
QD341.A8	PSEUDOCUMIDINE
RD688	*PSEUDOHYPERTROPHY* SEE MUSCLES, HYPERTROPHY OF
RC644	*PSEUDOLEUCEMIA* SEE HODGKIN'S DISEASE
QE399	PSEUDOMORPHS
QL511-514	PSEUDONEUROPTERA
Z1041-1115	*PSEUDONYMS* SEE ANONYMS AND PSEUDONYMS
QA645	*PSEUDOSPHERICAL SURFACES* SEE SURFACES OF CONSTANT CURVATURE
SF810.J6	*PSEUDOTUBERCULAR ENTERITIS* SEE JOHNE'S DISEASE
RC182.P8	PSITTACOSIS
RL321	PSORIASIS
BF636	*PSYCHAGOGY* SEE PSYCHOLOGY, APPLIED
BF67	*PSYCHAGOGY* SEE PSYCHOLOGY, APPLIED
RC435-630	*PSYCHAGOGY* SEE PSYCHOTHERAPY
RC440	PSYCHIATRIC NURSING
HV689	PSYCHIATRIC SOCIAL WORK
RC328	PSYCHIATRISTS — SELECTION AND APPOINTMENT
RC340	PSYCHIATRY — EARLY WORKS TO 1900
RC455	PSYCHIATRY — PHILOSOPHY
RC336	PSYCHIATRY — STUDY AND TEACHING
RC489.A	*PSYCHIATRY AND ART* SEE ART THERAPY
N8237.5	PSYCHIATRY IN ART
RA1151	*PSYCHIATRY, FORENSIC* SEE FORENSIC PSYCHIATRY
RC555	PSYCHIC MASOCHISM

BF1001-1389	PSYCHICAL RESEARCH
PN6231.P78	PSYCHOANALYSIS — ANECDOTES, FACETIAE, SATIRE, ETC.
BF173	PSYCHOANALYSIS
RC500-509	PSYCHOANALYSIS / nervous diseases
RC489	PSYCHODRAMA
P101-5	PSYCHOLINGUISTICS SEE LANGUAGES — PSYCHOLOGY
BF80	PSYCHOLOGICAL APPARATUS
BF39	PSYCHOLOGICAL MEASUREMENT SEE PSYCHOMETRICS
BF204.5	PSYCHOLOGICAL PHENOMENOLOGY SEE PHENOMENOLOGICAL PSYCHOLOGY
BF76.5	PSYCHOLOGICAL RESEARCH
BF39	PSYCHOLOGICAL SCALING SEE PSYCHOMETRICS
BF818-839	PSYCHOLOGICAL TESTS SEE CHARACTER TESTS
LB1131	PSYCHOLOGICAL TESTS SEE MENTAL TESTS
BF431	PSYCHOLOGICAL TESTS SEE MENTAL TESTS / psychology
BF109	PSYCHOLOGISTS
LB3013.6	PSYCHOLOGISTS, SCHOOL SEE SCHOOL PSYCHOLOGISTS
BF110-118	PSYCHOLOGY — EARLY WORKS TO 1850
BF108	PSYCHOLOGY — HISTORY
BF38	PSYCHOLOGY — METHODOLOGY
BC	PSYCHOLOGY SEE LOGIC
BL53	PSYCHOLOGY AND RELIGION SEE PSYCHOLOGY, RELIGIOUS
PN173-9	PSYCHOLOGY AND RHETORIC SEE RHETORIC AND PSYCHOLOGY
BF353	PSYCHOLOGY AND WEATHER SEE WEATHER — MENTAL AND PHYSIOLOGICAL EFFECTS
GT521	PSYCHOLOGY OF CLOTHING SEE CLOTHING AND DRESS — PSYCHOLOGY
BF789.C7	PSYCHOLOGY OF COLOR SEE COLOR — PSYCHOLOGY
BF241	PSYCHOLOGY OF COLOR SEE COLOR — PSYCHOLOGY / psychology of vision
GT521	PSYCHOLOGY OF DRESS SEE CLOTHING AND DRESS — PSYCHOLOGY
P101-5	PSYCHOLOGY OF LANGUAGE SEE LANGUAGES — PSYCHOLOGY
LB1051	PSYCHOLOGY OF LEARNING SEE LEARNING, PSYCHOLOGY OF
BV225	PSYCHOLOGY OF PRAYER SEE PRAYER — PSYCHOLOGY
BF	PSYCHOLOGY
BF173	PSYCHOLOGY, ABNORMAL SEE PSYCHOLOGY, PATHOLOGICAL
BF636	PSYCHOLOGY, APPLIED
BF67	PSYCHOLOGY, APPLIED
BS645	PSYCHOLOGY, BIBLICAL SEE BIBLE — PSYCHOLOGY
BL1475.P7	PSYCHOLOGY, BUDDHIST SEE BUDDHA AND BUDDHISM — PSYCHOLOGY
LB1101-1139	PSYCHOLOGY, CHILD SEE CHILD STUDY
HQ771-785	PSYCHOLOGY, CHILD SEE CHILD STUDY / child in the family
HQ781-5	PSYCHOLOGY, CHILD SEE CHILD STUDY / child life
BF721	PSYCHOLOGY, CHILD SEE CHILD STUDY / child psychology
GN63	PSYCHOLOGY, CHILD SEE CHILD STUDY / somatology
BV4012	PSYCHOLOGY, CLERICAL SEE PASTORAL PSYCHOLOGY
BF660-678	PSYCHOLOGY, COMPARATIVE
HV6080-6113	PSYCHOLOGY, CRIMINAL SEE CRIMINAL PSYCHOLOGY
BF701-724.8	PSYCHOLOGY, DEVELOPMENTAL SEE GENETIC PSYCHOLOGY
LB1051-1091	PSYCHOLOGY, EDUCATIONAL SEE EDUCATIONAL PSYCHOLOGY
BF730-738	PSYCHOLOGY, ETHNIC SEE ETHNOPSYCHOLOGY
QP351-499	PSYCHOLOGY, EXPERIMENTAL SEE PSYCHOLOGY, PHYSIOLOGICAL
BF701-724.8	PSYCHOLOGY, GENETIC SEE GENETIC PSYCHOLOGY
BL1215.P8	PSYCHOLOGY, HINDU SEE HINDUISM — PSYCHOLOGY
BF173	PSYCHOLOGY, MEDICAL SEE PSYCHOLOGY, PATHOLOGICAL
U21	PSYCHOLOGY, MILITARY

BF730-738	PSYCHOLOGY, NATIONAL SEE ETHNOPSYCHOLOGY
CB195-7	PSYCHOLOGY, NATIONAL SEE NATIONAL CHARACTERISTICS
CB203	PSYCHOLOGY, NATIONAL SEE NATIONAL CHARACTERISTICS / europe
BV4012	PSYCHOLOGY, PASTORAL SEE PASTORAL PSYCHOLOGY
BF173	PSYCHOLOGY, PATHOLOGICAL
BF91	PSYCHOLOGY, PATRISTIC
BF204.5	PSYCHOLOGY, PHENOMENOLOGICAL SEE PHENOMENOLOGICAL PSYCHOLOGY
QP351-499	PSYCHOLOGY, PHYSIOLOGICAL
BF67	PSYCHOLOGY, PRACTICAL SEE PSYCHOLOGY, APPLIED
BF636	PSYCHOLOGY, PRACTICAL SEE PSYCHOLOGY, APPLIED
HV6089	PSYCHOLOGY, PRISON SEE PRISON PSYCHOLOGY
BF730-738	PSYCHOLOGY, RACIAL SEE ETHNOPSYCHOLOGY
BL53	PSYCHOLOGY, RELIGIOUS
BF692	PSYCHOLOGY, SEXUAL SEE SEX (PSYCHOLOGY)
HM251-291	PSYCHOLOGY, SOCIAL SEE SOCIAL PSYCHOLOGY
BF203	PSYCHOLOGY, STRUCTURAL SEE GESTALT PSYCHOLOGY
BF39	PSYCHOLOGY-MEASUREMENT SEE PSYCHOMETRICS
BF76.5	PSYCHOLOGY-RESEARCH SEE PSYCHOLOGICAL RESEARCH
BF39	PSYCHOLOGY-SCALING SEE PSYCHOMETRICS
BF39	PSYCHOLOGY-STATISTICS SEE PSYCHOMETRICS
BF39	PSYCHOMETRICS
BF1281-1353	PSYCHOMETRY (OCCULT SCIENCES)
BF39	PSYCHOMETRY (PSYCHOPHYSICS) SEE PSYCHOMETRICS
RC530-552	PSYCHONEUROSES SEE NEUROSES
BF173	PSYCHOPATHOLOGY SEE PSYCHOLOGY, PATHOLOGICAL
BF173	PSYCHOPATHY SEE PSYCHOLOGY, PATHOLOGICAL
QP351-499	PSYCHOPHYSICS SEE PSYCHOLOGY, PHYSIOLOGICAL
RC512-528	PSYCHOSES
RK53	PSYCHOSOMATIC DENTISTRY SEE DENTISTRY — PSYCHOLOGICAL ASPECTS
RC49-52	PSYCHOSOMATIC MEDICINE SEE MEDICINE, PSYCHOSOMATIC
RC52	PSYCHOSOMATIC RESEARCH
RC435-630	PSYCHOTHERAPY
N71.5	PSYCHOTIC ART SEE ART AND MENTAL ILLNESS / art
RC455	PSYCHOTIC ART SEE ART AND MENTAL ILLNESS / medicine
QC915-917	PSYCHROMETERS SEE HYGROMETRY
QL696.G2	PTARMIGANS
QK520-532	PTERIDOPHYTA
QE960-971	PTERIDOPHYTA, FOSSIL
QE961	PTERIDOSPERMAE
QL391.P95	PTEROBRANCHIA
QE862.07	PTERODACTYLS
QL430.4	PTEROPODA
QE809.P8	PTEROPODA / fossil
QE862.07	PTEROSAURIA
RC143	PTOMAINE POISONING
QP801.P7	PTOMAINES
QP84	PUBERTY
HJ9701-9995	PUBLIC ACCOUNTING SEE FINANCE, PUBLIC — ACCOUNTING
HJ9771-9	PUBLIC ACCOUNTING SEE MUNICIPAL FINANCE — ACCOUNTING
HD3850	PUBLIC AUTHORITIES SEE CORPORATIONS, GOVERNMENT
HD4001-4420	PUBLIC AUTHORITIES SEE CORPORATIONS, GOVERNMENT / other countries
HD3881-8	PUBLIC AUTHORITIES SEE CORPORATIONS, GOVERNMENT / u.s.
TH4761	PUBLIC BATHS SEE BATHS, PUBLIC / building
RA605	PUBLIC BATHS SEE BATHS, PUBLIC / public hygiene
TH9445	PUBLIC BUILDINGS — FIRES AND FIRE PREVENTION
NA4170-4510	PUBLIC BUILDINGS / architecture
JN855-9	PUBLIC BUILDINGS / other countries
JK1651	PUBLIC BUILDINGS / state
JK1613-1649	PUBLIC BUILDINGS / u.s. national
NA7020	PUBLIC COMFORT STATIONS / architecture

RA607	PUBLIC COMFORT STATIONS / hygiene
HG4001-4280	PUBLIC CORPORATIONS SEE CORPORATIONS / finance
HD2709-2930	PUBLIC CORPORATIONS SEE CORPORATIONS / theory and policy
JS	PUBLIC CORPORATIONS SEE MUNICIPAL CORPORATIONS
HJ8003-8897	PUBLIC DEBTS SEE DEBTS, PUBLIC
JK1548.P8	PUBLIC DEFENDERS / u.s.
LC6501-6560	PUBLIC FORUMS SEE FORUMS (DISCUSSION AND DEBATE)
PN4177-4191	PUBLIC FORUMS SEE FORUMS (DISCUSSION AND DEBATE) / debating
RA	PUBLIC HEALTH SEE HYGIENE, PUBLIC
RA425	PUBLIC HEALTH SEE HYGIENE, PUBLIC / comprehensive treatises
RA11-388	PUBLIC HEALTH SEE HYGIENE, PUBLIC / general documents
RA440.9	PUBLIC HEALTH AS A PROFESSION
RA5	PUBLIC HEALTH BOARDS SEE HEALTH BOARDS
RA11-388	PUBLIC HEALTH BOARDS SEE HEALTH BOARDS / reports
RA428	PUBLIC HEALTH LABORATORIES
Z675.P	PUBLIC HEALTH LIBRARIES SEE LIBRARIES, PUBLIC HEALTH
RA771	PUBLIC HEALTH, RURAL SEE HYGIENE, RURAL
RA427	PUBLIC HEALTH, RURAL SEE HYGIENE, RURAL
NA7800-7850	PUBLIC HOUSES SEE HOTELS, TAVERNS, ETC. / architecture
GT3770-3899	PUBLIC HOUSES SEE HOTELS, TAVERNS, ETC. / manners and customs
RA	PUBLIC HYGIENE SEE HYGIENE, PUBLIC
RA425	PUBLIC HYGIENE SEE HYGIENE, PUBLIC / comprehensive treatises
RA11-388	PUBLIC HYGIENE SEE HYGIENE, PUBLIC / general documents
HD301-1130	PUBLIC LANDS / other countries
HD216-243	PUBLIC LANDS / u.s.
TD1015	PUBLIC LAUNDRIES SEE LAUNDRIES, PUBLIC
BX1800-1915	PUBLIC LAW (CANON LAW) SEE CATHOLIC CHURCH — GOVERNMENT
Z665-997	PUBLIC LIBRARIES SEE LIBRARIES
HM261	PUBLIC OPINION POLLS
HM261	PUBLIC OPINION RESEARCH SEE PUBLIC OPINION POLLS
HM261	PUBLIC OPINION
HM261	PUBLIC OPINION-RESEARCH SEE PUBLIC OPINION POLLS
K	PUBLIC ORDER SEE PUBLIC POLICY (LAW)
JX6053.P8	PUBLIC ORDER SEE PUBLIC POLICY (LAW)
HD3840-4420	PUBLIC OWNERSHIP SEE GOVERNMENT OWNERSHIP
HD4421-4730	PUBLIC OWNERSHIP SEE MUNICIPAL OWNERSHIP
JN3259	PUBLIC PEACE (LANDFRIEDE) SEE LANDFRIEDE
DD137.5	PUBLIC PEACE (LANDFRIEDE) SEE LANDFRIEDE / german history
DD165.5	PUBLIC PEACE (LANDFRIEDE) SEE LANDFRIEDE / german history
GV421-433	PUBLIC PLAYGROUNDS SEE PLAYGROUNDS
JX6053.P8	PUBLIC POLICY (LAW)
K	PUBLIC POLICY (LAW)
Z232	PUBLIC PRINTING SEE PRINTING, PUBLIC
CD931-4279	PUBLIC RECORDS-PRESERVATION SEE ARCHIVES
CD941	PUBLIC RECORDS-PRESERVATION SEE ARCHIVES / directories
CD950-965	PUBLIC RECORDS-PRESERVATION SEE ARCHIVES / handbooks
HM263	PUBLIC RELATIONS
HM263	PUBLIC RELATIONS-BUSINESS SEE PUBLIC RELATIONS
HM263	PUBLIC RELATIONS-INDUSTRY SEE PUBLIC RELATIONS
VG503	PUBLIC RELATIONS-U.S. NAVY SEE U.S. — PUBLIC RELATIONS
LB2823.5	PUBLIC SCHOOLS — BUSINESS MANAGEMENT
L341-3	PUBLIC SCHOOLS (ENDOWED)-ENGLAND / documents
LA634-5	PUBLIC SCHOOLS (ENDOWED)-ENGLAND / history
LF795	PUBLIC SCHOOLS (ENDOWED)-ENGLAND / individual schools
L-LC	PUBLIC SCHOOLS

LB2830	PUBLIC SCHOOLS-ACCOUNTING SEE SCHOOLS — ACCOUNTING
LB2824-2830	PUBLIC SCHOOLS-FINANCE SEE EDUCATION — FINANCE
LB3401-3495	PUBLIC SCHOOLS-SANITARY AFFAIRS SEE SCHOOL HYGIENE
HG4726	PUBLIC SECURITIES SEE MUNICIPAL BONDS
HG5151-5890	PUBLIC SECURITIES SEE MUNICIPAL BONDS / other countries
HG4951-3	PUBLIC SECURITIES SEE MUNICIPAL BONDS / u.s.
HG4651-5990	PUBLIC SECURITIES SEE SECURITIES
HD2763-8	PUBLIC SERVICE COMMISSIONS
HD2763-8	PUBLIC SERVICE CORPORATIONS SEE PUBLIC UTILITIES
PN4121-4130	PUBLIC SPEAKING
PN4121-4130	PUBLIC SPEAKING-STUDY AND TEACHING SEE PUBLIC SPEAKING
NA9070	PUBLIC SQUARES SEE PLAZAS
HF5686.C7	PUBLIC UTILITIES — ACCOUNTING
TA183	PUBLIC UTILITIES — COST OF CONSTRUCTION
T12	PUBLIC UTILITIES — EQUIPMENT AND SUPPLIES
HD2763	PUBLIC UTILITIES — FINANCE / corporations
HG4011	PUBLIC UTILITIES — FINANCE / finance
HG4961-7	PUBLIC UTILITIES — FINANCE / investments
HD2763	PUBLIC UTILITIES — RATES
HD2753	PUBLIC UTILITIES — TAXATION
HD2765	PUBLIC UTILITIES — VALUATION
HD2763-8	PUBLIC UTILITIES
HD2763-8	PUBLIC UTILITIES-LAW SEE PUBLIC UTILITIES
HD2763-8	PUBLIC UTILITY COMMISSIONS SEE PUBLIC SERVICE COMMISSIONS
TD1015	PUBLIC WASH-HOUSES SEE LAUNDRIES, PUBLIC
HD3840-4420	PUBLIC WORKS / economics
TA21-124	PUBLIC WORKS / national
TD21-124	PUBLIC WORKS / u.s. municipal
BV5-25	PUBLIC WORSHIP
HM263	PUBLICITY
Z278-550	PUBLISHERS AND PUBLISHING
Z242.I3	PUBLISHERS' IMPRINTS SEE IMPRINTS (IN BOOKS)
Z1033.L6	PUBLISHERS' LIBRARY EDITIONS SEE BIBLIOGRAPHY — LIBRARY EDITIONS
Z716.6	PUBLISHING AND LIBRARIES SEE LIBRARIES AND PUBLISHING
Z286	PUBLISHING OF HISTORICAL SOURCES SEE HISTORY — SOURCES — — PUBLISHING
QE391.P	PUCHERITE
TX773	PUDDINGS
TN725	PUDDLING-FURNACES
TN725	PUDDLING
F3095	PUDETO, BATTLE OF, 1826
F1233	PUEBLA, MEXICO (CITY) — SIEGE, 1862
F1233	PUEBLA, MEXICO (CITY) — SIEGE, 1863
E78	PUEBLO INDIANS — ANTIQUITIES
E99.P9	PUEBLO INDIANS — ART
E98.A7	PUEBLO INDIANS — ART
E98.P8	PUEBLO INDIANS — ART
E99.P9	PUEBLO INDIANS — SOCIAL LIFE AND CUSTOMS
E99.P9	PUEBLO INDIANS
E78	PUEBLOS
F2823.P	PUELCHE INDIANS / argentine republic
PM6876	PUENCHE LANGUAGE SEE PEHUENCHE LANGUAGE
RG831	PUERPERAL CONVULSIONS
RG811	PUERPERAL FEVER SEE PUERPERAL SEPTICEMIA
RG811	PUERPERAL SEPTICEMIA
RG801-871	PUERPERAL STATE
PQ7434	PUERTO RICAN BALLADS AND SONGS / collections
PQ7435	PUERTO RICAN BALLADS AND SONGS / collections of folk literature
PQ7430	PUERTO RICAN BALLADS AND SONGS / history
PQ7420-7439	PUERTO RICAN LITERATURE
PQ7434	PUERTO RICAN POETRY / collections
PQ7430	PUERTO RICAN POETRY / history
E184.P9	PUERTO RICANS IN THE U.S.
F1951-1981	PUERTO RICO — HISTORY
HF1896	PUERTO RICO TARIFF BILL OF 1900
E717.3	PUERTO RICO — HISTORY — — WAR OF 1898
QK629.L9	PUFFBALLS
SF429.P9	PUG-DOGS

GV1115-1137	*PUGILISM* **SEE** BOXING
BF723.F5	*PUGNACITY* **SEE** FIGHTING (PSYCHOLOGY) / *child study*
E99.M18	*PUJUNAN INDIANS* **SEE** MAIDU INDIANS
PM1681	*PUJUNAN LANGUAGES* **SEE** MAIDU LANGUAGE
PK6701-6799	*PUKHTU LANGUAGE* **SEE** PUSHTO LANGUAGE
PK6701-6799	*PUKKHTO LANGUAGE* **SEE** PUSHTO LANGUAGE
PK6701-6799	*PUKSHTO LANGUAGE* **SEE** PUSHTO LANGUAGE
GV515	*PULLEY WEIGHTS* **SEE** CHEST WEIGHTS
TJ1103	PULLEYS
TF457	*PULLMAN CARS* **SEE** RAILROADS — PULLMAN CARS
HD5325.	
R12 1894C5	*PULLMAN STRIKE, 1894* **SEE** CHICAGO STRIKE, 1894
SF995	PULLORUM DISEASE
QL835	PULMONARY ARTERY / *comparative anatomy*
QM191	PULMONARY ARTERY / *human anatomy*
RC776.P	PULMONARY EDEMA
RC776.P85	PULMONARY EMBOLISM
RC776	*PULMONARY EMPHYSEMA* **SEE** EMPHYSEMA, PULMONARY
RC306-320	*PULMONARY TUBERCULOSIS* **SEE** TUBERCULOSIS
QR201.T6	*PULMONARY TUBERCULOSIS* **SEE** TUBERCULOSIS / *bacteriology*
RA644.T7	*PULMONARY TUBERCULOSIS* **SEE** TUBERCULOSIS / *public health*
QL430.4	PULMONATA
BV250-254	*PULPIT PRAYERS* **SEE** PASTORAL PRAYERS
NA5065	PULPITS / *architecture*
TS1171-7	*PULPWOOD* **SEE** WOOD-PULP
TP588.P	PULQUE
QP981.P85	PULSATILLA / *physiological effects*
RM666.P9	PULSATILLA / *therapeutics*
QK495.L52	*PULSE FAMILY* **SEE** LEGUMINOSAE
TK6565.O7	*PULSE GENERATORS* **SEE** OSCILLATORS, ELECTRIC / *radio*
TL696.D65	*PULSE MULTIPLEX DME* **SEE** DISTANCE MEASURING EQUIPMENT (AIRCRAFT TO GROUND STATION)
TK6553	*PULSE TIME MODULATION (RADIO)* **SEE** RADIO PULSE TIME MODULATION
QP101	PULSE
RC74	PULSE / *diagnosis*
TP328	*PULVERIZED COAL* **SEE** COAL, PULVERIZED
TJ1345	*PULVERIZERS* **SEE** MILLING MACHINERY
QL737.C2	PUMAS
TJ900-925	PUMPING MACHINERY
TD485-7	PUMPING STATIONS
TD221-324	PUMPING STATIONS / *local*
SB351.P	PUMPKIN
TJ900-925	*PUMPS* **SEE** PUMPING MACHINERY
TJ919	*PUMPS, CENTRIFUGAL* **SEE** CENTRIFUGAL PUMPS
TJ917	*PUMPS, GEAR* **SEE** GEAR PUMPS
PN1970-1979	PUNCH AND JUDY
LB2342	PUNCHED CARD SYSTEMS — EDUCATION / *colleges*
LB2830	PUNCHED CARD SYSTEMS — EDUCATION / *schools*
TT840	PUNCHED WORK
TJ1255-7	PUNCHING MACHINERY
PJ4171-4197	PUNIC LANGUAGE
DG243-4	PUNIC WAR, 1ST, 264-241 B.C.
DG247-9	PUNIC WAR, 2D, 218-201 B.C.
DG242-9	PUNIC WARS / *first and second*
DG252.6	PUNIC WARS / *third*
HV7231-9920	PUNISHMENT
GT6710-6715	PUNISHMENT / *manners and customs*
UB800-815	PUNISHMENT / *military*
VB890-910	PUNISHMENT / *naval*
LB3025	PUNISHMENT / *school*
TH7683.P8	PUNKAS
PN6231.P8	PUNS AND PUNNING
GV951.7	*PUNTING (FOOTBALL)* **SEE** KICKING (FOOTBALL)
PL8605	PUNU LANGUAGE
QL949	PUPIL (EYE) / *comparative anatomy*
QM511	PUPIL (EYE) / *human anatomy*
QP476	PUPIL (EYE) / *physiology*
LB3021	*PUPIL-TEACHER PLANNING* **SEE** SELF-GOVERNMENT (IN EDUCATION) / *student honor*
LB3092-5	*PUPIL-TEACHER PLANNING* **SEE** SELF-GOVERNMENT (IN EDUCATION)

QL537.P8	PUPIPARA
PN1970-1981	*PUPPET-PLAYS* **SEE** PUPPETS AND PUPPET-PLAYS
PT1297	*PUPPET-PLAYS* **SEE** PUPPETS AND PUPPET-PLAYS / *german*
PN1970-1981	PUPPETS AND PUPPET-PLAYS
PT1297	PUPPETS AND PUPPET-PLAYS / *german*
F3341.T6	PUQUINA INDIANS / *bolivia*
F2230.2.P	PUQUINA INDIANS / *south america*
PM6956	PUQUINA LANGUAGE
PK3621	PURANAS
PK2595-9	*PURBUTTI LANGUAGE* **SEE** NEPALI LANGUAGE
HJ5711-5721	*PURCHASE TAX* **SEE** SALES TAX
HG229	PURCHASING POWER
HF5437	PURCHASING
HD9000.9	*PURE FOOD* **SEE** FOOD ADULTERATION AND INSPECTION / *economics*
TX501-595	*PURE FOOD* **SEE** FOOD ADULTERATION AND INSPECTION / *technical works*
HD9000.7-9	*PURE FOOD* **SEE** FOOD LAW AND LEGISLATION
RM357	PURGATIVES
BT840-841	PURGATORY
TP751.1	*PURGING OF GAS-PIPES* **SEE** GAS-PIPES — CLEANING
BV50.C3	*PURIFICATION OF THE BLESSED VIRGIN MARY, FEAST OF THE* **SEE** CANDLEMAS
DT430-477	*PURIFICATION OF WATER* **SEE** WATER — PURIFICATION
F2520.1.I	*PURIGOTOS* **SEE** IPUROCOTO INDIANS / *brazil*
BM695.P8	PURIM (FEAST OF ESTHER)
QP801.P8	PURINES
BX9301-9359	PURITANS
F67	PURITANS / *massachusetts*
F7	PURITANS / *new england*
BP184.4	PURITY, RITUAL (ISLAM)
HQ31	*PURITY, SOCIAL* **SEE** SEXUAL ETHICS
QL696.P2	PURPLE MARTIN
SB205.A4	*PURPLE MEDIC* **SEE** ALFALFA
TP925.P9	PURPLE / *chemical technology*
RC647.P8	PURPURA (PATHOLOGY)
QL596.C5	PURSLANE FLEA-BEETLE
TL685.3	*PURSUIT PLANES* **SEE** FIGHTER PLANES
HJ2287.G7	PURVEYANCE / *gt. brit.*
RB131	*PUS* **SEE** SUPPURATION
GV1017.P9	PUSH-BALL
PG2974	PUSHKIN PRIZES
PK6701-6799	PUSHTO LANGUAGE
PK6701-6799	*PUSHTU LANGUAGE* **SEE** PUSHTO LANGUAGE
PM6838	*PUSTO LANGUAGE* **SEE** PASTO LANGUAGE
QH671	PUTREFACTION
GV979.P8	PUTTING (GOLF)
TP941	PUTTY
E99.P98	PUYALLUP INDIANS
GV1491-1507	PUZZLES
PL4051-4	*PWO DIALECT* **SEE** KAREN LANGUAGE
PL4054.Z9P	PWO KAREN DIALECT
QL447.P2	PYCNOGONIDA
QC111	PYCNOMETER
QL696.P9	PYGOPODES
RJ456.P9	PYLORIC SPASMS / *diseases of children*
RJ456.P9	PYLORUS — DISEASES
QL862	PYLORUS / *comparative anatomy*
QM341	PYLORUS / *human anatomy*
QP601	PYOCYANASE
RK401-410	*PYORRHOEA ALVEOLARIS* **SEE** GUMS — DISEASES
QC99	*PYRAMID INCH* **SEE** PYRAMIDS — CURIOSA AND MISCELLANY
QC99	*PYRAMID METROLOGY* **SEE** PYRAMIDS — CURIOSA AND MISCELLANY
QC99	PYRAMIDS — CURIOSA AND MISCELLANY
DT63	PYRAMIDS
QC912	PYRANOMETER
DC124.45	PYRENEES, PEACE OF THE, 1659
QK623.P9	PYRENOMYCETES
SB951	PYRETHRUM / *insecticides*
TP865	PYREX
RC106	*PYREXIA* **SEE** FEVER
QC912	PYRHELIOMETER
QD401	PYRIDINE
QD401	PYRIMIDINES
TN948.P3	PYRITES / *mineral industries*

QE389.2	PYRITES / *mineralogy*
QC595	PYRO- AND PIEZO-ELECTRICITY
QD341.P5	PYROGALLIC ACID
NK8600-8605	PYROGRAPHY
QD281.P	PYROLYSIS
QC277	PYROMETERS AND PYROMETRY
ML1055	PYROPHONE
RM666.I8	PYROPHOSPHATE OF IRON **SEE** IRON, PHOSPHORIC SALTS OF
TN948.P	PYROPHYLLITE
TP300-301	*PYROTECHNICS* **SEE** FIREWORKS
TP939	PYROXYLIN
QD401	*PYRRHOL* **SEE** PYRROL
QE391.P9	PYRRHOTITE
QP981.P9	PYRROL — PHYSIOLOGICAL EFFECT
QD401	PYRROL
B240-244	PYTHAGORAS AND PYTHAGOREAN SCHOOL
QA460.P8	PYTHAGOREAN PROPOSITION
QE862.P8	PYTHONOMORPHA
QL666.O6	PYTHONS
PK9201.K3	*QABARDIAN LANGUAGE* **SEE** KABARDIAN LANGUAGE
PL55.K	*QARAQALPAQ LANGUAGE* **SEE** KARA-KALPAK LANGUAGE
BP195.K3	*QARMATHIANS* **SEE** KARMATHIANS
BP131.5	*QIRA'AT* **SEE** KORAN — READINGS
PJ2438	*QOMANT LANGUAGE* **SEE** KEMANT LANGUAGE
PM8741	QOSMIANI (ARTIFICIAL LANGUAGE)
SB615.Q3	*QUACK-GRASS* **SEE** QUITCH-GRASS
R730	QUACKS AND QUACKERY
QB105	QUADRANT / *astronomy*
VK583	QUADRANT / *navigation*
QA161	*QUADRATIC EQUATIONS* **SEE** EQUATIONS, QUADRATIC
QA242-4	*QUADRATIC RESIDUES* **SEE** CONGRUENCES AND RESIDUES
QA602	*QUADRATIC TRANSFORMATIONS* **SEE** TRANSFORMATIONS, QUADRATIC
QA626	*QUADRATURE OF CURVES* **SEE** CURVES — RECTIFICATION AND QUADRATURE
QA467	*QUADRATURE OF THE CIRCLE* **SEE** CIRCLE-SQUARING
QA561	QUADRICS
QA201	*QUADRILINEAR FORMS* **SEE** FORMS, QUADRILINEAR
GV1763-7	QUADRILLE (DANCE)
GV1295.O5	QUADRILLE (GAME) / *ombre*
M1060	QUADRILLES (CHAMBER ORCHESTRA) — SCORES
M1048	QUADRILLES (CHAMBER ORCHESTRA) — SCORES
M1048	QUADRILLES (CHAMBER ORCHESTRA)
M1060	QUADRILLES (CHAMBER ORCHESTRA)
M276-7	QUADRILLES (GUITAR AND PIANO)
M1060	QUADRILLES (ORCHESTRA)
M1048	QUADRILLES (ORCHESTRA)
M31	QUADRILLES (PIANO)
M200-201	QUADRILLES (PIANO, 4 HANDS)
M207	QUADRILLES (PIANO, 4 HANDS)
M204	QUADRILLES (PIANO, 4 HANDS)
M217-218	QUADRILLES (VIOLIN AND HARPSICHORD)
M221-3	QUADRILLES (VIOLIN AND HARPSICHORD)
M40-44	QUADRILLES (VIOLIN)
GN645	*QUADROONS* **SEE** MULATTOES / *anthropology*
E185.62	*QUADROONS* **SEE** MULATTOES / *u.s.*
QL737.P9	*QUADRUMANA* **SEE** PRIMATES
D287.5	QUADRUPLE ALLIANCE, 1718
D383	QUADRUPLE ALLIANCE, 1815
NK4895	*QUAICHS* **SEE** DRINKING VESSELS
QL696.G2	QUAILS
SF510.Q2	QUAILS / *breeding*
SK325.Q2	QUAILS / *hunting*
BX7601-7795	*QUAKERS* **SEE** FRIENDS, SOCIETY OF
JF2081	*QUALIFICATIONS FOR OFFICE* **SEE** NOMINATIONS FOR OFFICE / *constitutional history*
JK2053-2096	*QUALIFICATIONS FOR OFFICE* **SEE** NOMINATIONS FOR OFFICE / *u.s.*
QD81-95	*QUALITATIVE ANALYSIS* **SEE** CHEMISTRY, ANALYTIC — QUALITATIVE
TS155	QUALITY CONTROL
QA201	*QUANTICS* **SEE** FORMS (MATHEMATICS)
QA243-4	*QUANTICS* **SEE** FORMS (MATHEMATICS)
QD101-142	*QUANTITATIVE ANALYSIS* **SEE** CHEMISTRY, ANALYTIC — QUANTITATIVE
QA255	*QUANTITIES, IMAGINARY* **SEE** NUMBERS, COMPLEX

TX820	*QUANTITY COOKERY* **SEE** COOKERY FOR INSTITUTIONS, ETC.
TH434-7	*QUANTITY SURVEYING* **SEE** BUILDING — ESTIMATES
HG221	QUANTITY THEORY OF MONEY
QC680	QUANTUM ELECTRODYNAMICS
QC174.45	QUANTUM FIELD THEORY
TK7872.M45	*QUANTUM MECHANICAL AMPLIFIERS* **SEE** MASERS
QC174	*QUANTUM MECHANICS* **SEE** QUANTUM THEORY
QC174.4	QUANTUM STATISTICS
QC174	QUANTUM THEORY
E99.Q2	QUAPAW INDIANS
PJ2439	QUARA LANGUAGE
RA655-758	QUARANTINE
SB981-7	*QUARANTINE, PLANT* **SEE** PLANT QUARANTINE
SF998	QUARANTINE, VETERINARY
SF621-723	QUARANTINE, VETERINARY / *by country*
BV4627.Q	QUARRELING
TN277	QUARRIES AND QUARRYING — SAFETY MEASURES
TN277	QUARRIES AND QUARRYING
HD7269.Q8-82	QUARRIES AND QUARRYING / *labor hygiene*
BV55	*QUARTADECIMANS* **SEE** QUARTODECIMANS
SF293.Q3	QUARTER HORSE
CJ1840	QUARTER-DOLLAR
CJ1835	QUARTER-DOLLAR
GV1141	QUARTER-STAFF
GV951.3	QUARTERBACK (FOOTBALL)
JX5321	*QUARTERING OF SOLDIERS IN PRIVATE HOUSES* **SEE** REQUISITIONS, MILITARY / *international law*
UC15	*QUARTERING OF SOLDIERS IN PRIVATE HOUSES* **SEE** REQUISITIONS, MILITARY / *military science*
UC410	*QUARTERING OF SOLDIERS IN PRIVATE HOUSES* **SEE** SOLDIERS — BILLETING
M480-482	QUARTETS (ACCORDION, CLARINET, GUITAR, DOUBLE BASS)
M483-4	QUARTETS (ACCORDION, CLARINET, GUITAR, DOUBLE BASS), ARRANGED
M460-462	QUARTETS (BASSOON, CLARINET, OBOE, VIOLA)
M460-462	QUARTETS (BASSOON, FLUTE, OBOE, DOUBLE BASS)
M460-462	QUARTETS (BASSOON, HORN, TRUMPET, DOUBLE BASS)
M460-462	QUARTETS (BASSOON, OBOE, VIOLA, VIOLONCELLO)
M460-462	QUARTETS (BASSOON, OBOE, VIOLIN, VIOLA)
M460-462	QUARTETS (BASSOON, OBOE, VIOLIN, VIOLONCELLO)
M460-462	QUARTETS (BASSOON, VIOLIN, VIOLA, VIOLONCELLO)
M485	QUARTETS (CELESTA, SAXOPHONE, HARP, PERCUSSION)
M470-472	QUARTETS (CIMBALOM, VIOLIN, VIOLA, DOUBLE BASS)
M473-4	QUARTETS (CIMBALOM, VIOLIN, VIOLA, DOUBLE BASS), ARRANGED
M480-482	QUARTETS (CLARINET, FLUTE, HARP, VIOLIN)
M460-462	QUARTETS (CLARINET, FLUTE, OBOE, VIOLONCELLO)
M460-462	QUARTETS (CLARINET, FLUTE, TROMBONE, VIOLA)
M460-462	QUARTETS (CLARINET, FLUTE, VIOLIN, VIOLONCELLO)
M480-482	QUARTETS (CLARINET, HARP, VIOLIN, VIOLA)
M480-482	QUARTETS (CLARINET, OBOE, HARP, VIOLA)
M460-462	QUARTETS (CLARINET, VIOLIN, VIOLA, VIOLONCELLO)
M480-482	QUARTETS (CLARINET, 2 GUITARS, VIOLIN)
M460-462	QUARTETS (CLARINET, 2 VIOLINS, VIOLONCELLO)
M485	QUARTETS (CONCRETE MUSIC)
M485	QUARTETS (ENGLISH HORN, HARP, 2 PERCUSSION)
M485	QUARTETS (FLUTE, GLASS HARMONICA, VIOLA, VIOLONCELLO)
M485	QUARTETS (FLUTE, GUITAR, PERCUSSION, VIOLA)
M480-482	QUARTETS (FLUTE, GUITAR, VIOLA, VIOLONCELLO)
M483-4	QUARTETS (FLUTE, GUITAR, VIOLA, VIOLONCELLO), ARRANGED
M485	QUARTETS (FLUTE, HARP, TAMTAM, VIOLONCELLO)
M460-462	QUARTETS (FLUTE, OBOE, VIOLIN, VIOLONCELLO)
M460-462	QUARTETS (FLUTE, VIOLIN, VIOLA, VIOLONCELLO)
M460-462	QUARTETS (FLUTE, 2 VIOLAS, VIOLONCELLO)
M460-462	QUARTETS (FLUTE, 2 VIOLINS, VIOLA)
M460-462	QUARTETS (FLUTE, 2 VIOLINS, VIOLONCELLO)
M470-472	QUARTETS (GUITAR, VIOLIN, VIOLA, VIOLONCELLO)
M473-4	QUARTETS (GUITAR, VIOLIN, VIOLA, VIOLONCELLO), ARRANGED
M470-472	QUARTETS (GUITAR, 2 VIOLINS, VIOLONCELLO)
M470-472	QUARTETS (HARP, 2 VIOLINS, VIOLONCELLO)
M420-422	QUARTETS (HARPSICHORD, BASSOON, FLUTE, VIOLA DA GAMBA)

M420-422	QUARTETS (HARPSICHORD, BASSOON, FLUTE, VIOLIN)
M415-417	QUARTETS (HARPSICHORD, BASSOON, OBOE, RECORDER)
M415-417	QUARTETS (HARPSICHORD, BASSOON, OBOE, TRUMPET)
M420-422	QUARTETS (HARPSICHORD, BASSOON, OBOE, VIOLIN)
M423-4	QUARTETS (HARPSICHORD, BASSOON, OBOE, VIOLIN), ARRANGED
M420-422	QUARTETS (HARPSICHORD, BASSOON, OBOE, VIOLONCELLO)
M415-417	QUARTETS (HARPSICHORD, BASSOON, 2 OBOES)
M420-422	QUARTETS (HARPSICHORD, FLUTE, OBOE, VIOLA)
M420-422	QUARTETS (HARPSICHORD, FLUTE, OBOE, VIOLIN)
M420-422	QUARTETS (HARPSICHORD, FLUTE, OBOE, VIOLONCELLO)
M420-422	QUARTETS (HARPSICHORD, FLUTE, VIOLIN, VIOLA)
M420-422	QUARTETS (HARPSICHORD, FLUTE, VIOLIN, VIOLONCELLO)
M415-417	QUARTETS (HARPSICHORD, FLUTE, 2 RECORDERS)
M420-422	QUARTETS (HARPSICHORD, FLUTE, 2 VIOLINS)
M420-422	QUARTETS (HARPSICHORD, HORN, OBOE, VIOLIN)
M420-422	QUARTETS (HARPSICHORD, OBOE, RECORDER, VIOLIN)
M420-422	QUARTETS (HARPSICHORD, OBOE, VIOLA, VIOLONCELLO)
M420-422	QUARTETS (HARPSICHORD, OBOE, VIOLIN, VIOLA)
M420-422	QUARTETS (HARPSICHORD, RECORDER, VIOLIN, VIOLONCELLO)
M420-422	QUARTETS (HARPSICHORD, RECORDER, 2 VIOLINS)
M420-422	QUARTETS (HARPSICHORD, TRUMPET, 2 VIOLINS)
M410-412	QUARTETS (HARPSICHORD, VIOLIN, VIOLA, VIOLONCELLO)
M412.4	QUARTETS (HARPSICHORD, VIOLIN, 2 VIOLAS)
M410-411	QUARTETS (HARPSICHORD, VIOLIN, 2 VIOLAS)
M420-422	QUARTETS (HARPSICHORD, 2 FLUTES, VIOLONCELLO)
M420-422	QUARTETS (HARPSICHORD, 2 HORNS, VIOLIN)
M415-417	QUARTETS (HARPSICHORD, 2 OBOES, RECORDER)
M415-417	QUARTETS (HARPSICHORD, 2 OBOES, TRUMPET)
M420-422	QUARTETS (HARPSICHORD, 2 OBOES, VIOLONCELLO)
M410-411	QUARTETS (HARPSICHORD, 2 VIOLINS, VIOLA DA GAMBA)
M412.4	QUARTETS (HARPSICHORD, 2 VIOLINS, VIOLA DA GAMBA)
M412.4	QUARTETS (HARPSICHORD, 2 VIOLINS, VIOLA)
M410-411	QUARTETS (HARPSICHORD, 2 VIOLINS, VIOLA)
M412.4	QUARTETS (HARPSICHORD, 2 VIOLINS, VIOLONCELLO)
M410-411	QUARTETS (HARPSICHORD, 2 VIOLINS, VIOLONCELLO)
M412.4	QUARTETS (HARPSICHORD, 2 VIOLINS, VIOLONE)
M415-417	QUARTETS (HARPSICHORD, 3 RECORDERS)
M412.4	QUARTETS (HARPSICHORD, 3 VIOLE DA GAMBA)
M412.2	QUARTETS (HARPSICHORD, 3 VIOLINS)
M410-411	QUARTETS (HARPSICHORD, 3 VIOLINS)
M415-417	QUARTETS (HARPSICHORD, 3 WIND INSTRUMENTS)
M460-462	QUARTETS (HORN, VIOLIN, VIOLA, VIOLONCELLO)
M460-462	QUARTETS (OBOE, VIOLIN, VIOLA, VIOLONCELLO)
M400-402	QUARTETS (ORGAN, BASSOON, 2 VIOLINS)
M400-402	QUARTETS (ORGAN, HORN, TROMBONE, TRUMPET)
M400-402	QUARTETS (ORGAN, VIOLIN, VIOLA, VIOLONCELLO)
M400-402	QUARTETS (ORGAN, 2 FLUTES, VIOLONCELLO)
M400-402	QUARTETS (ORGAN, 2 OBOES, RECORDER)
M400-402	QUARTETS (ORGAN, 2 OBOES, VIOLONCELLO)
M400-402	QUARTETS (ORGAN, 2 VIOLINS, VIOLA DA GAMBA)
M400-402	QUARTETS (ORGAN, 2 VIOLINS, VIOLA)
M400-402	QUARTETS (ORGAN, 2 VIOLINS, VIOLONCELLO)
M400-402	QUARTETS (ORGAN, 3 CORNETS)
M403-4	QUARTETS (ORGAN, 3 CORNETS), ARRANGED
M400-402	QUARTETS (ORGAN, 3 VIOLINS)
M415-417	QUARTETS (PIANO, BASSOON, CLARINET, FLUTE)
M415-417	QUARTETS (PIANO, BASSOON, CLARINET, OBOE)
M418-419	QUARTETS (PIANO, BASSOON, CLARINET, OBOE), ARRANGED
M420-422	QUARTETS (PIANO, BASSOON, CLARINET, VIOLA)
M415-417	QUARTETS (PIANO, BASSOON, FLUTE, OBOE)
M420-422	QUARTETS (PIANO, BASSOON, FLUTE, VIOLIN)
M420-422	QUARTETS (PIANO, BASSOON, FLUTE, VIOLONCELLO)
M420-422	QUARTETS (PIANO, BASSOON, OBOE, VIOLIN)
M420-422	QUARTETS (PIANO, BASSOON, OBOE, VIOLONCELLO)
M415-417	QUARTETS (PIANO, CLARINET, FLUTE, OBOE)
M418-419	QUARTETS (PIANO, CLARINET, FLUTE, OBOE), ARRANGED
M415-417	QUARTETS (PIANO, CLARINET, OBOE, TROMBONE)

M445-7	QUARTETS (PIANO, CLARINET, PERCUSSION, VIOLONCELLO)
M445-7	QUARTETS (PIANO, CLARINET, TRUMPET, PERCUSSION)
M420-422	QUARTETS (PIANO, CLARINET, VIOLIN, VIOLONCELLO)
M440-442	QUARTETS (PIANO, FLUTE, GUITAR, VIOLIN)
M445-7	QUARTETS (PIANO, FLUTE, HARP, GLOCKENSPIEL)
M435-7	QUARTETS (PIANO, FLUTE, OBOE, HARP)
M420-422	QUARTETS (PIANO, FLUTE, OBOE, VIOLIN)
M420-422	QUARTETS (PIANO, FLUTE, OBOE, VIOLONCELLO)
M420-422	QUARTETS (PIANO, FLUTE, VIOLA, VIOLONCELLO)
M420-422	QUARTETS (PIANO, FLUTE, VIOLIN, VIOLA)
M420-422	QUARTETS (PIANO, FLUTE, VIOLIN, VIOLONCELLO)
M423-4	QUARTETS (PIANO, FLUTE, VIOLIN, VIOLONCELLO), ARRANGED
M415-417	QUARTETS (PIANO, FLUTE, 2 RECORDERS)
M420-422	QUARTETS (PIANO, FLUTE, 2 VIOLINS)
M445-7	QUARTETS (PIANO, GUITAR, 2 DRUMS, DOUBLE BASS)
M425-7	QUARTETS (PIANO, GUITAR, 2 MANDOLINS)
M428-9	QUARTETS (PIANO, GUITAR, 2 MANDOLINS), ARRANGED
M420-422	QUARTETS (PIANO, HORN, OBOE, VIOLIN)
M420-422	QUARTETS (PIANO, OBOE, VIOLA, VIOLONCELLO)
M420-422	QUARTETS (PIANO, OBOE, VIOLIN, VIOLA)
M420-422	QUARTETS (PIANO, OBOE, VIOLIN, VIOLONCELLO)
M420-422	QUARTETS (PIANO, RECORDER, VIOLIN, VIOLONCELLO)
M445-7	QUARTETS (PIANO, SAXOPHONE, PERCUSSION, DOUBLE BASS)
M485	QUARTETS (PIANO, SAXOPHONE, TRUMPET, PERCUSSION)
M415-417	QUARTETS (PIANO, TROMBONE, 2 TRUMPETS)
M420-422	QUARTETS (PIANO, TRUMPET, 2 VIOLINS)
M410-412	*QUARTETS (PIANO, VIOLIN, VIOLA, VIOLONCELLO)* **SEE** PIANO QUARTETS
M412.4	QUARTETS (PIANO, VIOLIN, 2 VIOLAS)
M410-411	QUARTETS (PIANO, VIOLIN, 2 VIOLAS)
M420-422	QUARTETS (PIANO, 2 FLUTES, VIOLONCELLO)
M420-422	QUARTETS (PIANO, 2 HORNS, VIOLIN)
M415-417	QUARTETS (PIANO, 2 OBOES, RECORDER)
M415-417	QUARTETS (PIANO, 2 OBOES, TRUMPET)
M420-422	QUARTETS (PIANO, 2 OBOES, VIOLONCELLO)
M445-7	QUARTETS (PIANO, 2 SAXOPHONES, VIBRAPHONE)
M410-411	QUARTETS (PIANO, 2 VIOLINS, DOUBLE BASS)
M412.4	QUARTETS (PIANO, 2 VIOLINS, DOUBLE BASS)
M412.4	QUARTETS (PIANO, 2 VIOLINS, VIOLA)
M410-411	QUARTETS (PIANO, 2 VIOLINS, VIOLONCELLO)
M412.4	QUARTETS (PIANO, 2 VIOLINS, VIOLONCELLO)
M413-414	QUARTETS (PIANO, 2 VIOLINS, VIOLONCELLO), ARRANGED
M415-417	QUARTETS (PIANO, 3 CLARINETS)
M415-417	QUARTETS (PIANO, 3 CORNETS)
M418-419	QUARTETS (PIANO, 3 CORNETS), ARRANGED
M415-417	QUARTETS (PIANO, 3 FLUTES)
M415-417	QUARTETS (PIANO, 3 RECORDERS)
M1413-1417	QUARTETS (PIANO, 3 RECORDERS), JUVENILE
M415-417	QUARTETS (PIANO, 3 TROMBONES)
M415-417	QUARTETS (PIANO, 3 TRUMPETS)
M418-419	QUARTETS (PIANO, 3 TRUMPETS), ARRANGED
M412.4	QUARTETS (PIANO, 3 VIOLE DA GAMBA)
M412.2	QUARTETS (PIANO, 3 VIOLINS)
M410-411	QUARTETS (PIANO, 3 VIOLINS)
M413-414	QUARTETS (PIANO, 3 VIOLINS), ARRANGED
M413-414	QUARTETS (PIANO, 3 VIOLONCELLOS), ARRANGED
M415-417	QUARTETS (PIANO, 3 WIND INSTRUMENTS)
M418-419	QUARTETS (PIANO, 3 WIND INSTRUMENTS), ARRANGED
M460-462	QUARTETS (2 FLUTES, VIOLA, VIOLONCELLO)
M460-462	QUARTETS (2 HORNS, VIOLA, VIOLONCELLO)
M445-7	QUARTETS (2 PIANOS, VIOLIN, VIOLONCELLO)
M448-9	QUARTETS (2 PIANOS, VIOLIN, VIOLONCELLO), ARRANGED
M445-7	QUARTETS (2 PIANOS, 2 VIOLINS)
M470-472	QUARTETS (2 ZITHERS, VIOLIN, VIOLA)
M485	QUARTETS (3 CORNETS, DRUM)
M485	QUARTETS (3 CORNETS, KETTLEDRUMS)
M460-462	QUARTETS (3 RECORDERS, VIOLIN)
M465-7	QUARTETS (4 GUITARS)
M465-7	QUARTETS (4 HARPS)
M410-412	*QUARTETS, PIANO* **SEE** PIANO QUARTETS
M450-452	*QUARTETS, STRING* **SEE** STRING QUARTETS

M455-7	*QUARTETS, WIND* **SEE** WIND QUARTETS
QA565-7	*QUARTIC CURVES* **SEE** CURVES, QUARTIC
QA215	QUARTIC EQUATIONS **SEE** EQUATIONS, QUARTIC
QA573	*QUARTIC SURFACES* **SEE** SURFACES, QUARTIC
BV55	QUARTODECIMANS
QE391.Q2	QUARTZ
QD941	QUARTZ / optical properties
QE475	QUARTZITE
BX1939.D65	*QUASI-DOMICILE (CANON LAW)* **SEE** DOMICILE (CANON LAW)
QK495.Q	QUASSIA / botany
RM666.Q	QUASSIA / therapeutics
RS165.Q	QUASSIA / vegetable drugs
SB951	QUASSIN / insecticides
RM666.Q	QUASSIN / therapeutics
RS165.Q	QUASSIN / vegetable drugs
QE696-9	*QUATERNARY PERIOD* **SEE** GEOLOGY, STRATIGRAPHIC — QUATERNARY
QE931	*QUATERNARY PERIOD* **SEE** PALEOBOTANY — QUATERNARY
QE741	*QUATERNARY PERIOD* **SEE** PALEONTOLOGY — QUATERNARY
QA257	QUATERNIONS
DC240 JUNE16	QUATRE-BRAS, BATTLE OF, 1815
TC357	*QUAYS* **SEE** WHARVES
F1054.5.Q3	QUEBEC (CITY) — HISTORY
E231	QUEBEC (CITY) — SIEGE, 1775-1776
F1051-4	QUEBEC (PROVINCE) — HISTORY
E199	QUEBEC CAMPAIGN, 1759
E196	QUEBEC EXPEDITION, 1690
E197	QUEBEC EXPEDITION, 1711
E231	*QUEBEC EXPEDITION, 1775* **SEE** CANADIAN INVASION, 1775-1776
QK495.Q38	QUEBRACHO / botany
SD397.Q3	QUEBRACHO / forestry
PM4231	*QUECHE LANGUAGE* **SEE** QUICHE LANGUAGE
F2230.2.K4	*QUECHUA INDIANS* **SEE** KECHUA INDIANS
PM6301-9	*QUECHUA LANGUAGE* **SEE** KECHUA LANGUAGE
PM6308	*QUECHUA LITERATURE* **SEE** KECHUA LITERATURE
E197	*QUEEN ANNE'S WAR, 1702-1713* **SEE** UNITED STATES — HISTORY — — QUEEN ANNE'S WAR, 1702-1713
D107.3	QUEENS
D352.3	QUEENS / 19th century
D412.8	QUEENS / 20th century
E356.Q3	QUEENSTON, BATTLE OF, 1812
F1465.2.K5	*QUEKCHI INDIANS* **SEE** KEKCHI INDIANS
PM3913	*QUEKCHI LANGUAGE* **SEE** KEKCHI LANGUAGE
TN731	*QUENCHING OF STEEL* **SEE** STEEL — QUENCHING
F2821	QUERANDI INDIANS
TP925.Q4	QUERCITRON-BARK / dyes
QK495.Q4	*QUERCUS* **SEE** OAK
SD397.O12	*QUERCUS* **SEE** OAK / forestry
F2821	*QUERENDI INDIANS* **SEE** QUERANDI INDIANS
F1221.T	*QUERENE INDIANS* **SEE** TZOTZIL INDIANS
PM4466	*QUERENE LANGUAGE* **SEE** TZOTZIL LANGUAGE
F1233	QUERETARO, MEXICO (CITY) — SIEGE, 1867
AG195-6	*QUESTION BOXES* **SEE** QUESTIONS AND ANSWERS
AG305-313	*QUESTION BOXES* **SEE** QUESTIONS AND ANSWERS
LB1027	QUESTIONING
BV4610-4612	QUESTIONS AND ANSWERS — CHRISTIAN LIFE
BR96	QUESTIONS AND ANSWERS — THEOLOGY
AG195-6	QUESTIONS AND ANSWERS
AG305-313	QUESTIONS AND ANSWERS
BS612	*QUESTIONS AND ANSWERS-BIBLE* **SEE** BIBLE — EXAMINATIONS, QUESTIONS, ETC.
QL696.T7	QUETZALS
DA87.5 1759	QUIBERON BAY, BATTLE OF, 1759
PM4231	QUICHE LANGUAGE
PM4231	QUICHE LITERATURE
F1465	QUICHES / central america
F1219	QUICHES / mexico
F2230.2.K4	*QUICHUA INDIANS* **SEE** KECHUA INDIANS
PM6301-9	*QUICHUA LANGUAGE* **SEE** KECHUA LANGUAGE
PM6308	*QUICHUA LITERATURE* **SEE** KECHUA LITERATURE
SB615.Q3	*QUICK-GRASS* **SEE** QUITCH-GRASS
QD181.H6	*QUICKSILVER* **SEE** MERCURY / chemistry
DC76.3	QUIERZY, CAPITULARY OF, 877
BV5099	QUIETISM
E99.Q	QUILEUTE INDIANS
PM2219	QUILEUTE LANGUAGE
E99.Q	*QUILLAYUTE INDIANS* **SEE** QUILEUTE INDIANS
E99.Q	*QUILLEHUTE INDIANS* **SEE** QUILEUTE INDIANS
NK9100-9199	*QUILTING* **SEE** COVERLETS / art
TT835	*QUILTING* **SEE** COVERLETS / technology
NK9100-9199	*QUILTS* **SEE** COVERLETS / art
TT835	*QUILTS* **SEE** COVERLETS / technology
BL2590.U5	*QUIMBANDA (CULTUS)* **SEE** UMBANDA (CULTUS)
F2269	QUIMBAYA INDIANS
E99.Q6	QUINAIELT INDIANS
E99.Q6	*QUINAULT INDIANS* **SEE** QUINAIELT INDIANS
QD401	QUINAZOLINE
SB379.Q7	QUINCE
QP921.Q3	QUININE — PHYSIOLOGICAL EFFECT
RM666.C53	QUININE — THERAPEUTIC USE
RS165.C3	QUININE
E99.Q7	QUINNIPIAC INDIANS
PM2221	QUINNIPIAC LANGUAGE
SB317.Q	QUINOA
QD281.Q	QUINOIDATION
QD421	QUINOIDINE / chemistry
QP921.Q5	QUINOIDINE / physiological effect
QD401.	QUINOLINE / chemistry
QP921.Q6	QUINOLINE / physiological effect
QD341.K2	QUINONE
M585	QUINTETS (ACCORDION, BASSOON, 2 CLARINETS, TRUMPET)
M585	QUINTETS (ACCORDION, 2 VIOLINS, VIOLA, VIOLONCELLO)
M555-7	QUINTETS (BASSOON, CLARINET, ENGLISH HORN, FLUTE, OBOE)
M560-562	QUINTETS (BASSOON, CLARINET, FLUTE, HORN, VIOLONCELLO)
M575-7	QUINTETS (BASSOON, CLARINET, FLUTE, OBOE, HARP)
M560-562	QUINTETS (BASSOON, CLARINET, HORN, VIOLIN, VIOLA)
M560-562	QUINTETS (BASSOON, CLARINET, OBOE, VIOLIN, DOUBLE BASS)
M560-562	QUINTETS (BASSOON, CLARINET, OBOE, VIOLIN, VIOLONCELLO)
M563-4	QUINTETS (BASSOON, CLARINET, OBOE, VIOLIN, VIOLONCELLO), ARRANGED
M560-562	QUINTETS (BASSOON, CLARINET, VIOLIN, VIOLA, VIOLONCELLO)
M560-562	QUINTETS (BASSOON, FLUTE, HORN, VIOLIN, VIOLA)
M560-562	QUINTETS (BASSOON, OBOE, VIOLIN, VIOLA, DOUBLE BASS)
M560-562	QUINTETS (BASSOON, 2 VIOLINS, VIOLA, VIOLONCELLO)
M520-522	QUINTETS (CELESTA, FLUTE, OBOE, VIOLA, VIOLONCELLO)
M523-4	QUINTETS (CELESTA, FLUTE, OBOE, VIOLA, VIOLONCELLO), ARRANGED
M535-7	QUINTETS (CELESTA, 2 FLUTES, 2 HARPS)
M580-582	QUINTETS (CLARINET, FLUTE, HARP, VIOLA, VIOLONCELLO)
M580-582	QUINTETS (CLARINET, FLUTE, HARP, VIOLIN, VIOLONCELLO)
M560-562	QUINTETS (CLARINET, FLUTE, VIOLIN, VIOLA, VIOLONCELLO)
M560-562	QUINTETS (CLARINET, HORN, TROMBONE, TRUMPET, VIOLA)
M560-562	QUINTETS (CLARINET, OBOE, VIOLIN, VIOLA, DOUBLE BASS)
M560-562	QUINTETS (CLARINET, 2 VIOLAS, 2 VIOLONCELLOS)
M560-562	QUINTETS (CLARINET, 2 VIOLINS, VIOLA, VIOLONCELLO)
M580-582	QUINTETS (FLUTE, GUITAR, VIOLIN, VIOLA, VIOLONCELLO)
M585	QUINTETS (FLUTE, HARP, PERCUSSION, VIOLA, VIOLONCELLO)
M580-582	QUINTETS (FLUTE, HARP, VIOLIN, VIOLA, VIOLONCELLO)
M585	QUINTETS (FLUTE, OBOE, GLASS HARMONICA, VIOLA, VIOLONCELLO)
M560-562	QUINTETS (FLUTE, OBOE, VIOLIN, VIOLA, VIOLONCELLO)
M560-562	QUINTETS (FLUTE, VIOLIN, 2 VIOLAS, VIOLONCELLO)
M563-4	QUINTETS (FLUTE, VIOLIN, 2 VIOLAS, VIOLONCELLO), ARRANGED
M560-562	QUINTETS (FLUTE, 2 VIOLINS, VIOLA, VIOLONCELLO)

M563-4	QUINTETS (FLUTE, 2 VIOLINS, VIOLA, VIOLONCELLO), ARRANGED
M570-572	QUINTETS (GUITAR, 2 VIOLINS, VIOLA, VIOLONCELLO)
M570-572	QUINTETS (HARP, 2 VIOLINS, VIOLA, VIOLONCELLO)
M518-519	QUINTETS (HARPSICHORD, BASSOON, CLARINET, FLUTE, HORN), ARRANGED
M515-517	QUINTETS (HARPSICHORD, BASSOON, CLARINET, FLUTE, HORN)
M515-517	QUINTETS (HARPSICHORD, BASSOON, ENGLISH HORN, 2 OBOES)
M515-517	QUINTETS (HARPSICHORD, BASSOON, FLUTE, HORN, OBOE)
M520-522	QUINTETS (HARPSICHORD, BASSOON, FLUTE, OBOE, VIOLA)
M523-4	QUINTETS (HARPSICHORD, BASSOON, FLUTE, OBOE, VIOLA), ARRANGED
M520-522	QUINTETS (HARPSICHORD, BASSOON, FLUTE, OBOE, VIOLIN)
M523-4	QUINTETS (HARPSICHORD, BASSOON, FLUTE, OBOE, VIOLIN), ARRANGED
M520-522	QUINTETS (HARPSICHORD, FLUTE, OBOE, VIOLIN, VIOLA)
M520-522	QUINTETS (HARPSICHORD, FLUTE, OBOE, VIOLIN, VIOLONCELLO)
M545-7	QUINTETS (HARPSICHORD, FLUTE, PERCUSSION, VIOLA, DOUBLE BASS)
M520-522	QUINTETS (HARPSICHORD, FLUTE, VIOLIN, VIOLA, VIOLONCELLO)
M520-522	QUINTETS (HARPSICHORD, FLUTE, 2 OBOES, VIOLA DA GAMBA)
M520-522	QUINTETS (HARPSICHORD, FLUTE, 2 VIOLINS, VIOLONCELLO)
M515-517	QUINTETS (HARPSICHORD, 2 FLUTES, 2 RECORDERS)
M520-522	QUINTETS (HARPSICHORD, 2 HORNS, 2 VIOLINS)
M515-517	QUINTETS (HARPSICHORD, 2 OBOES, 2 RECORDERS)
M520-522	QUINTETS (HARPSICHORD, 2 RECORDERS, 2 VIOLINS)
M510-512	QUINTETS (HARPSICHORD, 2 VIOLINS, VIOLA, VIOLA DA GAMBA)
M510-512	QUINTETS (HARPSICHORD, 2 VIOLINS, VIOLA, VIOLONCELLO)
M510-512	QUINTETS (HARPSICHORD, 2 VIOLINS, 2 VIOLAS)
M510-512	QUINTETS (HARPSICHORD, 2 VIOLINS, 2 VIOLONCELLOS)
M990	QUINTETS (HARPSICHORD, 2 VIOLS, VIOLA D'AMORE, VIOLA DA GAMBA)
M520-522	QUINTETS (HARPSICHORD, 3 RECORDERS, VIOLA DA GAMBA)
M510-512	QUINTETS (HARPSICHORD, 3 VIOLINS, VIOLA DA GAMBA)
M510-512	QUINTETS (HARPSICHORD, 3 VIOLINS, VIOLONCELLO)
M510-512	QUINTETS (HARPSICHORD, 4 VIOLINS)
M560-562	QUINTETS (HORN, VIOLIN, 2 VIOLAS, VIOLONCELLO)
M560-562	QUINTETS (HORN, 2 VIOLINS, VIOLA, VIOLONCELLO)
M563-4	QUINTETS (HORN, 2 VIOLINS, VIOLA, VIOLONCELLO), ARRANGED
M585	QUINTETS (MOUTH-ORGAN, 2 VIOLINS, VIOLA, VIOLONCELLO)
M560-562	QUINTETS (OBOE, 2 VIOLINS, VIOLA, VIOLONCELLO)
M500-502	QUINTETS (ORGAN, BARITONE, 2 CORNETS, TROMBONE)
M503-4	QUINTETS (ORGAN, BARITONE, 2 CORNETS, TROMBONE), ARRANGED
M500-502	QUINTETS (ORGAN, VIOLIN, 3 VIOLS)
M500-502	QUINTETS (ORGAN, 2 TROMBONES, 2 TRUMPETS)
M503-4	QUINTETS (ORGAN, 2 TROMBONES, 2 TRUMPETS), ARRANGED
M500-502	QUINTETS (ORGAN, 2 VIOLINS, VIOLA, VIOLONCELLO)
M500-502	QUINTETS (ORGAN, 2 VIOLINS, 2 VIOLS)
M515-517	QUINTETS (PIANO, BASSOON, CLARINET, FLUTE, HORN)
M515-517	QUINTETS (PIANO, BASSOON, CLARINET, FLUTE, OBOE)
M515-517	QUINTETS (PIANO, BASSOON, CLARINET, HORN, OBOE)
M518-519	QUINTETS (PIANO, BASSOON, CLARINET, HORN, OBOE), ARRANGED
M515-517	QUINTETS (PIANO, BASSOON, ENGLISH HORN, 2 OBOES)
M515-517	QUINTETS (PIANO, BASSOON, FLUTE, HORN, OBOE)
M518-519	QUINTETS (PIANO, BASSOON, FLUTE, HORN, OBOE), ARRANGED

M520-522	QUINTETS (PIANO, BASSOON, FLUTE, OBOE, VIOLA)
M520-522	QUINTETS (PIANO, BASSOON, FLUTE, OBOE, VIOLIN)
M523-4	QUINTETS (PIANO, BASSOON, OBOE, VIOLIN, VIOLONCELLO), ARRANGED
M535-7	QUINTETS (PIANO, BASSOON, 2 TRUMPETS, HARP)
M520-522	QUINTETS (PIANO, CLARINET, FLUTE, HORN, VIOLA)
M520-522	QUINTETS (PIANO, CLARINET, VIOLIN, VIOLA, VIOLONCELLO)
M523-4	QUINTETS (PIANO, CLARINET, VIOLIN, VIOLA, VIOLONCELLO), ARRANGED
M520-522	QUINTETS (PIANO, CLARINET, 3 VIOLINS)
M520-522	QUINTETS (PIANO, FLUTE, OBOE, VIOLIN, VIOLA)
M520-522	QUINTETS (PIANO, FLUTE, OBOE, VIOLIN, VIOLONCELLO)
M545-7	QUINTETS (PIANO, FLUTE, PERCUSSION, VIOLA, DOUBLE BASS)
M520-522	QUINTETS (PIANO, FLUTE, VIOLIN, VIOLA, VIOLONCELLO)
M520-522	QUINTETS (PIANO, FLUTE, 2 OBOES, VIOLONCELLO)
M520-522	QUINTETS (PIANO, FLUTE, 2 VIOLINS, VIOLONCELLO)
M520-522	QUINTETS (PIANO, OBOE, TRUMPET, VIOLIN, DOUBLE BASS)
M520-522	QUINTETS (PIANO, OBOE, VIOLIN, VIOLA, VIOLONCELLO)
M510-512	QUINTETS (PIANO, VIOLIN, VIOLA, VIOLONCELLO, DOUBLE BASS)
M513-514	QUINTETS (PIANO, VIOLIN, VIOLA, VIOLONCELLO, DOUBLE BASS), ARRANGED
M512.4	QUINTETS (PIANO, VIOLIN, 2 VIOLAS, VIOLONCELLO)
M520-522	QUINTETS (PIANO, 2 CLARINETS, VIOLIN, VIOLONCELLO)
M515-517	QUINTETS (PIANO, 2 FLUTES, 2 RECORDERS)
M520-522	QUINTETS (PIANO, 2 HORNS, 2 VIOLINS)
M515-517	QUINTETS (PIANO, 2 OBOES, 2 RECORDERS)
M520-522	QUINTETS (PIANO, 2 RECORDERS, 2 VIOLINS)
M510-512	*QUINTETS (PIANO, 2 VIOLINS, VIOLA, VIOLONCELLO)* **SEE** PIANO QUINTETS
M510-512	QUINTETS (PIANO, 2 VIOLINS, 2 VIOLAS)
M510-512	QUINTETS (PIANO, 2 VIOLINS, 2 VIOLONCELLOS)
M520-522	QUINTETS (PIANO, 3 FLUTES, VIOLONCELLO)
M510-512	QUINTETS (PIANO, 3 VIOLINS, VIOLONCELLO)
M515-517	QUINTETS (PIANO, 4 CLARINETS)
M518-519	QUINTETS (PIANO, 4 CLARINETS), ARRANGED
M515-517	QUINTETS (PIANO, 4 FLUTES)
M515-517	QUINTETS (PIANO, 4 HORNS)
M515-517	QUINTETS (PIANO, 4 RECORDERS)
M518-519	QUINTETS (PIANO, 4 RECORDERS), ARRANGED
M515-517	QUINTETS (PIANO, 4 TRUMPETS)
M510-512	QUINTETS (PIANO, 4 VIOLINS)
M513-514	QUINTETS (PIANO, 4 VIOLINS), ARRANGED
M515-517	QUINTETS (PIANO, 4 WIND INSTRUMENTS)
M518-519	QUINTETS (PIANO, 4 WIND INSTRUMENTS), ARRANGED
M560-562	QUINTETS (2 CLARINETS, FLUTE, VIOLA, VIOLONCELLO)
M560-564	QUINTETS (2 CLARINETS, VIOLIN, VIOLA, VIOLONCELLO)
M580-582	QUINTETS (2 FLUTES, GUITAR, VIOLA, VIOLONCELLO)
M560-562	QUINTETS (2 FLUTES, 2 VIOLINS, VIOLONCELLO)
M560-562	QUINTETS (2 HORNS, 2 VIOLINS, VIOLONCELLO)
M560-562	QUINTETS (2 RECORDERS, 2 VIOLINS, VIOLONCELLO)
M585	QUINTETS (2 TROMBONES, 2 TRUMPETS, KETTLEDRUMS)
M585	QUINTETS (4 ACCORDIONS, DOUBLE BASS)
M585	QUINTETS (4 ACCORDIONS, DOUBLE BASS), ARRANGED
M585	QUINTETS (4 PIANOS, GLOCKENSPIEL)
M585	QUINTETS (4 PIANOS, GLOCKENSPIEL), ARRANGED
M585	QUINTETS (4 TRUMPETS, KETTLEDRUMS)
M565-7	QUINTETS (5 GUITARS)
M510-512	*QUINTETS, PIANO* **SEE** PIANO QUINTETS
M550-552	*QUINTETS, STRING* **SEE** STRING QUINTETS
M555-7	*QUINTETS, WIND* **SEE** WIND QUINTETS
QA565-7	*QUINTIC CURVES* **SEE** CURVES, QUINTIC
QA215	*QUINTIC EQUATIONS* **SEE** EQUATIONS, QUINTIC
QA573	*QUINTIC SURFACES* **SEE** SURFACES, QUINTIC
GV1295.05	QUINTILLE (GAME) / *ombre*
PL8113	*QUIOCO LANGUAGE* **SEE** CHOKWE LANGUAGE
PM2223	QUIOUCOHANOCK LANGUAGE
F3429.3.Q6	QUIPU
PM2221	*QUIRIPI LANGUAGE* **SEE** QUINNIPIAC LANGUAGE

F1909	QUISQUEYANO INDIANS
SB615.Q3	QUITCH-GRASS
AG305-313	*QUIZ BOOKS* **SEE** QUESTIONS AND ANSWERS
AG195-6	*QUIZ BOOKS* **SEE** QUESTIONS AND ANSWERS
GV1095	QUOITET
GV1095	QUOITS
SK287.Q	QUORN HUNT
HF1401-1650	*QUOTAS, IMPORT* **SEE** IMPORT QUOTAS
Z253	QUOTATION-MARKS / *printing*
PN171.Q6	QUOTATION
PN6080-6095	QUOTATIONS
PN6095.J	QUOTATIONS, JEWISH
PJ7121-4	*QURAWI LANGUAGE* **SEE** SHAURI LANGUAGE
DS219	QURAYSH (ARAB TRIBE)
PJ2439	*QWARA LANGUAGE* **SEE** QUARA LANGUAGE
BM652.5	*RABBINICAL COUNSELING* **SEE** PASTORAL COUNSELING (JUDAISM)
BM652	RABBIS
SF453	RABBIT BREEDING
SF979.R2	RABBITS — DISEASES
SB994.R15	RABBITS — EXTERMINATION
GR730.H	*RABBITS (IN RELIGION, FOLK-LORE, ETC.)* **SEE** HARES (IN RELIGION, FOLK-LORE, ETC.) / *folk-lore*
BL325.H	*RABBITS (IN RELIGION, FOLK-LORE, ETC.)* **SEE** HARES (IN RELIGION, FOLK-LORE, ETC.) / *religion*
QL737.R6	RABBITS
SF451-5	RABBITS / *breeding*
SF979.R2	RABBITS / *diseases*
SF453	*RABBITS-BREEDING* **SEE** RABBIT BREEDING
TH1087	RABITZ CONSTRUCTION
SK341.C6	*RACCOON HUNTING* **SEE** COON HUNTING
QL795.R15	RACCOONS — LEGENDS AND STORIES
QL737.C2	RACCOONS
BF723.R3	RACE AWARENESS / *child study*
HQ750-799	*RACE IMPROVEMENT* **SEE** EUGENICS
HN64	*RACE IMPROVEMENT* **SEE** EUTHENICS
HT1501-1595	RACE PROBLEMS
BF730-738	*RACE PSYCHOLOGY* **SEE** ETHNOPSYCHOLOGY
HT1501-1595	*RACE QUESTION* **SEE** RACE PROBLEMS
GN	RACE / *anthropology*
CB195-281	RACE / *civilization*
BF730-738	RACE / *psychology*
HT1501-1595	RACE / *sociology*
BT734	RACE / *theology*
QD305.A2	*RACEMIC ACID* **SEE** TARTARIC ACID
QD501	RACEMIZATION
GN	*RACES OF MAN* **SEE** ETHNOLOGY
RJ396	*RACHITIS* **SEE** RICKETS
GN237	*RACIAL AMALGAMATION* **SEE** MISCEGENATION
E185.62	*RACIAL AMALGAMATION* **SEE** MISCEGENATION / *negroes in the u.s.*
GN237	*RACIAL CROSSING* **SEE** MISCEGENATION
E185.62	*RACIAL CROSSING* **SEE** MISCEGENATION / *negroes in the u.s.*
TL236	*RACING AUTOMOBILES* **SEE** AUTOMOBILES, RACING
TL236	*RACING CARS* **SEE** AUTOMOBILES, RACING
SF469	*RACING PIGEONS* **SEE** HOMING PIGEONS / *animal culture*
UH90	*RACING PIGEONS* **SEE** HOMING PIGEONS / *military art and science*
GV1018	RACING
TF684	RACK-RAILROADS
GV1002-3	RACKETS (GAME)
GV1002-3	*RACQUETS (GAME)* **SEE** RACKETS (GAME)
QC973.5	RADAR METEOROLOGY
TR696	*RADAR PROFILE RECORDER* **SEE** AIRBORNE PROFILE RECORDER
TK6588	RADAR RECEIVING APPARATUS
TK6575	RADAR
VF530	*RADAR, FIRE CONTROL* **SEE** FIRE CONTROL (NAVAL GUNNERY) — RADAR EQUIPMENT
TK6588	*RADAR-RECEIVERS AND RECEPTION* **SEE** RADAR RECEIVING APPARATUS
RM133.R2	RADEMACHERISM
QL375-9	*RADIATA* **SEE** COELENTERATA
QE777-9	*RADIATA* **SEE** COELENTERATA / *fossil*
QL381-5	*RADIATA* **SEE** ECHINODERMATA
QL396-9	*RADIATA* **SEE** POLYZOA
QH652	*RADIATION BIOLOGY* **SEE** RADIOBIOLOGY
QD601	*RADIATION CHEMISTRY* **SEE** RADIOCHEMISTRY

TN871.35	*RADIATION LOGGING (OIL WELLS)* **SEE** OIL WELL LOGGING, RADIATION
TX611	RADIATION STERILIZATION / *food*
RM845-862	*RADIATION THERAPY* **SEE** RADIOTHERAPY
QC475	RADIATION
QC484	*RADIATION, BLACKBODY* **SEE** BLACKBODY RADIATION
QC483	*RADIATION, ELECTRIC* **SEE** ELECTRIC RADIATION
QB531	*RADIATION, SOLAR* **SEE** SOLAR RADIATION / *astronomy*
QC911	*RADIATION, SOLAR* **SEE** SOLAR RADIATION / *meteorology*
QB817	*RADIATION, STELLAR* **SEE** STARS — RADIATION
SF757.8	*RADIATION-EFFECT ON DOMESTIC ANIMALS* **SEE** DOMESTIC ANIMALS, EFFECT OF RADIATION ON
QC175.2	*RADIATIVE TRANSFER* **SEE** TRANSPORT THEORY
TH7480-7495	RADIATORS
TK4631	RADIATORS / *electric*
TH7547	RADIATORS / *hot water*
TH7597	RADIATORS / *steam*
JN1129.R19-3	RADICAL PARTY (GT. BRIT.)
JN5657.R2	*RADICAL PARTY (ITALY)* **SEE** PARTITO RADICALE (ITALY)
QD471	RADICALS (CHEMISTRY)
QD255	RADICALS (CHEMISTRY)
BF1628.3	RADIESTHESIA
RZ999	RADIESTHESIA / *medicine*
TK9956	RADIO — AMATEURS' MANUALS
TK6565.A6	RADIO — ANTENNAS
TK6560-6565	RADIO — APPARATUS AND SUPPLIES
HD9999.R15	RADIO — APPARATUS AND SUPPLIES / *economics*
TK6545	RADIO — BIOGRAPHY
HE9709-9711	RADIO — CENSORSHIP
TK6561	RADIO — CURRENT SUPPLY
TK6554.5	RADIO — EXAMINATIONS, QUESTIONS, ETC.
TK6563	RADIO — HIGH-FIDELITY SYSTEMS
TK6570.A8	RADIO — INSTALLATION IN AUTOMOBILES
UG446.5	RADIO — INSTALLATION IN TANKS
VK397	RADIO — INSTALLATION ON SHIPS
TK6553	RADIO — INTERFERENCE
HE8666-8670	RADIO — LAWS AND REGULATIONS
TK6553	RADIO — MATERIALS
TK6559	RADIO — PATENTS
HE8677-8688	RADIO — RATES
TK6563	RADIO — RECEIVERS AND RECEPTION
TK6565.R	RADIO — RECTIFIERS
TK6553	RADIO — REPAIRING
TK6552	RADIO — TABLES, CALCULATIONS, ETC.
TK6561	RADIO — TRANSMITTERS AND TRANSMISSION
HF6146.R3	RADIO ADVERTISING
QC544.V3	*RADIO AMPLIFIERS* **SEE** AMPLIFIERS, VACUUM-TUBE
GV880	RADIO AND BASEBALL
Z650	*RADIO AND COPYRIGHT* **SEE** COPYRIGHT — ARTISTIC PERFORMANCE
Z716.7	*RADIO AND LIBRARIES* **SEE** LIBRARIES AND RADIO
ML68	RADIO AND MUSIC
MT150	RADIO AND MUSIC / *analytical guides*
TK6565.A6	*RADIO ANTENNAS* **SEE** RADIO — ANTENNAS
VK397	*RADIO AS AN AID TO NAVIGATION* **SEE** RADIO IN NAVIGATION / *naval science*
QB475	RADIO ASTRONOMY
PN1992	RADIO AUTHORSHIP
TL696.B4	RADIO BEACONS
PN1991.6	RADIO BROADCASTING — MORAL AND RELIGIOUS ASPECTS
TK6570.B7	RADIO BROADCASTING — SOUND EFFECTS
TK6570.B7	RADIO BROADCASTING
HE8666-8670	*RADIO BROADCASTING-LAWS AND REGULATIONS* **SEE** RADIO — LAWS AND REGULATIONS
HF6146.R3	*RADIO COMMERCIALS* **SEE** RADIO ADVERTISING
VK577	RADIO COMPASS
TL696.C7	RADIO COMPASS / *aeronautics*
TL696.D5	RADIO DIRECTION FINDERS / *aeronautics*
TK6565.D5	RADIO DIRECTION FINDERS / *radio*
PN6120.R2	*RADIO DRAMA* **SEE** RADIO PLAYS / *collections*
LB1044.5	*RADIO EDUCATION* **SEE** RADIO IN EDUCATION
TK6600	RADIO FACSIMILE
TK6553	RADIO FREQUENCY MODULATION
TL693-6	RADIO IN AERONAUTICS
LB1044.5	RADIO IN EDUCATION
BV2082.R3	RADIO IN MISSIONARY WORK

VK397	RADIO IN NAVIGATION / naval science
HD9999.	
R15-153	RADIO INDUSTRY AND TRADE
TK6553	*RADIO INTERFERENCE* **SEE** RADIO — INTERFERENCE
PN4820-4823	*RADIO JOURNALISTS* **SEE** JOURNALISTS
PN4841-5650	*RADIO JOURNALISTS* **SEE** JOURNALISTS
PN5122-3	*RADIO JOURNALISTS* **SEE** JOURNALISTS / gt. brit.
PN4871-4	*RADIO JOURNALISTS* **SEE** JOURNALISTS / u.s.
TK6553	*RADIO MATERIALS* **SEE** RADIO — MATERIALS
TK6554	RADIO MEASUREMENTS — LABORATORY MANUALS
TK6553	RADIO MEASUREMENTS
QC973	RADIO METEOROLOGY
M1527.5	RADIO OPERAS — VOCAL SCORES WITH PIANO
M1527.5	RADIO OPERAS
TK6600	*RADIO PHOTOGRAPHY* **SEE** PHOTOTELEGRAPHY
PN1992	RADIO PLAYS — TECHNIQUE
PN6120.R2	RADIO PLAYS / collections
TK6553	RADIO PULSE TIME MODULATION
TK6564.P6	*RADIO RECEIVERS, PORTABLE* **SEE** PORTABLE RADIOS
TK6563	*RADIO RECEPTION* **SEE** RADIO — RECEIVERS AND RECEPTION
TK6554	RADIO RESEARCH
TK6553	*RADIO SERVICING* **SEE** RADIO — REPAIRING
TK6570.B7	*RADIO SOUND EFFECTS* **SEE** RADIO BROADCASTING — SOUND EFFECTS
TK9956	*RADIO STATIONS, AMATEUR* **SEE** AMATEUR RADIO STATIONS
TK6561	*RADIO TRANSMISSION* **SEE** RADIO — TRANSMITTERS AND TRANSMISSION
HE8690-8699	*RADIO VISION* **SEE** TELEVISION
TK6630	*RADIO VISION* **SEE** TELEVISION
QC877	*RADIO WEATHER REPORTING* **SEE** WEATHER REPORTING, RADIO
PN1992	*RADIO WRITING* **SEE** RADIO AUTHORSHIP
HD9999.	
R15-153	*RADIO-APPARATUS INDUSTRY* **SEE** RADIO INDUSTRY AND TRADE
QC876	*RADIO-METEOROGRAPH* **SEE** RADIOSONDES
TK6563	*RADIO-RECEIVING APPARATUS* **SEE** RADIO — RECEIVERS AND RECEPTION
PN1992	*RADIO-SCRIPT WRITING* **SEE** RADIO AUTHORSHIP
PN1992	*RADIO-SCRIPT WRITING* **SEE** RADIO PLAYS — TECHNIQUE
TK6540-6570	RADIO
TK9956	RADIO / amateur construction
UG610	RADIO, MILITARY
UG610	*RADIO, NAVAL* **SEE** RADIO, MILITARY
TK6553	RADIO, SHORT WAVE
TK6565.A6	*RADIO-AERIALS* **SEE** RADIO — ANTENNAS
TK6570.B7	*RADIO-BROADCASTING* **SEE** RADIO BROADCASTING
TK6565.D5	*RADIO-DIRECTION FINDERS* **SEE** RADIO DIRECTION FINDERS / radio
TL696.D5	*RADIO-DIRECTION FINDERS* **SEE** RADIO DIRECTION FINDERS / aeronautics
TK6553	*RADIO-JAMMING* **SEE** RADIO — INTERFERENCE
TK6553	*RADIO-MEASUREMENTS* **SEE** RADIO MEASUREMENTS
TK6553	*RADIO-PULSE TIME MODULATION* **SEE** RADIO PULSE TIME MODULATION
TK6554	*RADIO-RESEARCH* **SEE** RADIO RESEARCH
TK6553	*RADIO-STATIC* **SEE** RADIO — INTERFERENCE
QE508	RADIOACTIVE DATING / geology
QC929.S7	RADIOACTIVE SNOW GAGES
TD812	RADIOACTIVE WASTE DISPOSAL
QC786	RADIOACTIVITY — INSTRUMENTS
TN871.35	*RADIOACTIVITY LOGS* **SEE** OIL WELL LOGGING, RADIATION
QC795	RADIOACTIVITY
TK9400	RADIOACTIVITY / engineering
QH652	RADIOBIOLOGY
QD466.5.C1	*RADIOCARBON* **SEE** CARBON — ISOTOPES
QC798.D3	*RADIOCARBON* **SEE** RADIOCARBON DATING
QE508	*RADIOCARBON* **SEE** RADIOCARBON DATING / geology
QC798.D3	RADIOCARBON DATING
QE508	RADIOCARBON DATING / geology
TP249	RADIOCHEMISTRY — INDUSTRIAL APPLICATIONS
QD601	RADIOCHEMISTRY
RL231	RADIODERMATITIS
RC78	*RADIODIAGNOSIS* **SEE** DIAGNOSIS, RADIOSCOPIC
VK577	*RADIOGONIOMETER* **SEE** RADIO COMPASS

TL696.C7	*RADIOGONIOMETER* **SEE** RADIO COMPASS / aeronautics
RC78	RADIOGRAPHY / medicine
TR750	RADIOGRAPHY / photography
RD36	RADIOGRAPHY / surgery
QC929.S7	*RADIOISOTOPE SNOW GAGES* **SEE** RADIOACTIVE SNOW GAGES
RA1231.R2	RADIOISOTOPES — SAFETY MEASURES
QL368.R2	RADIOLARIA
QE773	RADIOLARIA / fossil
QE773	RADIOLARIA, FOSSIL
SF757.8	*RADIOLOGY, VETERINARY* **SEE** VETERINARY RADIOLOGY
QD601	*RADIOLYSIS* **SEE** RADIOCHEMISTRY
QC176	RADIOMETER
QC338	RADIOMICROMETER
PN1995.7	*RADIOMOVIES* **SEE** MOVING-PICTURES, TALKING
RC78	*RADIOSCOPIC DIAGNOSIS* **SEE** DIAGNOSIS, RADIOSCOPIC
QC876	RADIOSONDES
RM862.5	RADIOTHERAPY — APPARATUS AND SUPPLIES
RM845-862	RADIOTHERAPY
QC721	RADIOTHORIUM
TK6553	RADIO — APPARATUS AND SUPPLIES — — TESTING
SB351.R	RADISHES
QP913.R1	RADIUM — PHYSIOLOGICAL EFFECT
RM859	RADIUM — THERAPEUTIC USE
QD181.R1	RADIUM BROMIDE
QD181.R2	*RADIUM EMANATION* **SEE** RADON
QD181.R1	RADIUM / chemistry
TN948.R3	RADIUM / ores
QC721	RADIUM / physical properties
TP245.R2	RADIUM / technology
RM859	*RADIUMTHERAPY* **SEE** RADIUM — THERAPEUTIC USE
RD101	RADIUS — FRACTURE
QD181.R2	RADON
QL431	RADULA / mollusks
PC901-949	RAETO-ROMANCE LANGUAGE
PC951-986	RAETO-ROMANCE LITERATURE
PC957	RAETO-ROMANCE POETRY / collections
PC951	RAETO-ROMANCE POETRY / history
LB1543	RAFFIA WORK / education
TT875	RAFFIA WORK / handicraft
TS1747.R2	RAFFIA WORK / manufactures
QD321	RAFFINASE
QD321	RAFFINOSE
TH2397	RAFTER GAGES
HD9975	RAG-PICKERS / economics
HD4966.W3	RAG-PICKERS / wages
HD9975	*RAG-PICKING* **SEE** RAGS / rag-picking
LC4051-4100	RAGGED SCHOOLS
HD9975	RAGS / rag-picking
ML3561	*RAGTIME MUSIC* **SEE** JAZZ MUSIC
QK495.A485	RAGWEED / botany
RM769	RAGWEED / hay-fever prevention
SB615.R	RAGWEED / weeds
TF261	*RAIL FASTENINGS* **SEE** RAILROADS — RAILS — — FASTENINGS
TH5675-7	*RAILING* **SEE** HAND-RAILING
HE1779-1795	*RAILROAD ACCIDENTS* **SEE** RAILROADS — ACCIDENTS
TJ619	*RAILROAD AUTOMOBILES* **SEE** RAILROAD MOTOR-CARS / diesel
TF975	*RAILROAD AUTOMOBILES* **SEE** RAILROAD MOTOR-CARS / electric
TF415-430	*RAILROAD BRAKES* **SEE** RAILROADS — BRAKES
TF415-430	*RAILROAD CAR BRAKES* **SEE** RAILROADS — BRAKES
HE1811	RAILROAD CONDUCTORS
TF	*RAILROAD CONSTRUCTION* **SEE** RAILROAD ENGINEERING
TF200-320	*RAILROAD CONSTRUCTION* **SEE** RAILROADS — CONSTRUCTION
HD8039.R315	RAILROAD CONSTRUCTION WORKERS
TF263	*RAILROAD CROSSINGS* **SEE** RAILROADS — CROSSINGS
HE1617-1619	*RAILROAD CROSSINGS* **SEE** RAILROADS — CROSSINGS / economics
TF205	RAILROAD ENGINEERING — TABLES, CALCULATIONS, ETC.
TF	RAILROAD ENGINEERING

TF300-308	RAILROADS — STATIONS
HE1613-1614	RAILROADS — STATIONS / *location*
HE2271-3	RAILROADS — STATISTICS
HE2801-3600	RAILROADS — STATISTICS / *other countries*
HE2713	RAILROADS — STATISTICS / *u.s.*
TF210-217	RAILROADS — SURVEYING
TF266	RAILROADS — SWITCHES
TF635	RAILROADS — SWITCHES / *interlocking*
TF592	RAILROADS — SWITCHING
HE1071-6	RAILROADS — TAXATION
TF627-8	RAILROADS — TELEGRAPH
HE7677.R2	RAILROADS — TELEGRAPH / *codes*
TF627-8	RAILROADS — TELEPHONE
TF9	RAILROADS — TERMINOLOGY
TF654	RAILROADS — TICKETS
HE1971	RAILROADS — TICKETS / *economics*
TF252-6	RAILROADS — TIES
TF256	RAILROADS — TIES, CONCRETE
HE2727	RAILROADS — TIME STANDARDS / *railway guides*
QB223	RAILROADS — TIME STANDARDS / *time systems*
HF5706.R3	RAILROADS — TIME-BOOKS
HE2801-3600	RAILROADS — TIME-TABLES / *other countries*
TF565	RAILROADS — TIME-TABLES / *schedules*
HE2727-9	RAILROADS — TIME-TABLES / *u.s.*
TF350-357	RAILROADS — TOOLS AND IMPLEMENTS
TF240-268	RAILROADS — TRACK
TF248	RAILROADS — TRACKLAYING MACHINERY
HE1821-2591	RAILROADS — TRAFFIC
HE2301-2550	RAILROADS — TRAFFIC / *freight*
HE2561-2591	RAILROADS — TRAFFIC / *passenger*
TF563	RAILROADS — TRAIN DISPATCHING
TF555	RAILROADS — TRAIN LOAD
TF553-4	RAILROADS — TRAIN SPEED
TF557	RAILROADS — TRAINMEN'S MANUALS
TF550-585	RAILROADS — TRAINS
TF276	RAILROADS — TRANSFER-TABLES
TF275	RAILROADS — TURN-TABLES
HE1071-6	RAILROADS — VALUATION
HF5706.R3	RAILROADS — WAGE TABLES
TF290	RAILROADS — WATER-SUPPLY
TF590	RAILROADS — YARDS
HE1051-1081	RAILROADS AND STATE
HE2801-3600	RAILROADS AND STATE / *other countries*
HE2757	RAILROADS AND STATE / *u.s.*
TF	RAILROADS
HE1001-5600	RAILROADS / *economics*
TF692	*RAILROADS, AERIAL* **SEE** RAILROADS, ATMOSPHERIC
TF835	*RAILROADS, AERIAL* **SEE** RAILROADS, CABLE
TF692	RAILROADS, ATMOSPHERIC
TF835	RAILROADS, CABLE — SAFETY APPLIANCES
TF835	RAILROADS, CABLE
TF684	*RAILROADS, COG* **SEE** RACK-RAILROADS
TF838	RAILROADS, COMPRESSED-AIR
TF855-1124	*RAILROADS, ELECTRIC* **SEE** ELECTRIC RAILROADS
HE5351-5600	*RAILROADS, ELECTRIC* **SEE** ELECTRIC RAILROADS / *interurban*
HE4201-5300	*RAILROADS, ELECTRIC* **SEE** ELECTRIC RAILROADS / *street-railroads*
TF840	RAILROADS, ELEVATED
HE4201-5300	RAILROADS, ELEVATED / *economics*
TF835	*RAILROADS, FUNICULAR* **SEE** RAILROADS, CABLE
TF686	RAILROADS, GRAVITY
TF677	RAILROADS, INDUSTRIAL
HE3601-4050	RAILROADS, INDUSTRIAL / *economics*
TF670-1124	RAILROADS, LOCAL AND LIGHT
HE3601-4050	RAILROADS, LOCAL AND LIGHT / *economics*
UG345	*RAILROADS, MILITARY* **SEE** MILITARY RAILROADS
TN336	*RAILROADS, MINE* **SEE** MINE RAILROADS
TF694	*RAILROADS, MONORAIL* **SEE** RAILROADS, SINGLE-RAIL
TF680-688	*RAILROADS, MOUNTAIN* **SEE** MOUNTAIN RAILROADS / *engineering*
HE4051-4071	*RAILROADS, MOUNTAIN* **SEE** MOUNTAIN RAILROADS / *transportation*
TF675	RAILROADS, NARROW-GAGE
HE3601-4050	RAILROADS, NARROW-GAGE / *economics*
HE1051-1081	*RAILROADS, NATIONALIZATION OF* **SEE** RAILROADS AND STATE

TF684	*RAILROADS, RACK* **SEE** RACK-RAILROADS
GV1855	*RAILROADS, SCENIC* **SEE** SCENIC RAILWAYS / *amusement parks*
TC771	*RAILROADS, SHIP* **SEE** SHIP-RAILROADS
TF694	RAILROADS, SINGLE-RAIL
TF701-1124	*RAILROADS, STREET* **SEE** STREET-RAILROADS
HE4201-5300	*RAILROADS, STREET* **SEE** STREET-RAILROADS / *economics*
HE4251	*RAILROADS, STREET* **SEE** STREET-RAILROADS / *taxation*
TF693	RAILROADS, SUSPENDED
TF845-851	*RAILROADS, UNDERGROUND* **SEE** SUBWAYS
TF850-851	*RAILROADS, UNDERGROUND* **SEE** SUBWAYS / *freight*
HE1795	*RAILROADS-ACCIDENTS-CLAIMS* **SEE** RAILROADS — CLAIM DEPARTMENTS
TF420-430	*RAILROADS-AIR-BRAKES* **SEE** AIR-BRAKES
TF638	*RAILROADS-AUTOMATIC SPEED CONTROL* **SEE** RAILROADS — AUTOMATIC TRAIN CONTROL
TF638	*RAILROADS-AUTOMATIC STOP* **SEE** RAILROADS — AUTOMATIC TRAIN CONTROL
HE2242	*RAILROADS-BILLS OF LADING* **SEE** BILLS OF LADING
TF445-453	*RAILROADS-CARS-SANITATION* **SEE** RAILROADS — SANITATION
RA615.1	*RAILROADS-CARS-SANITATION* **SEE** RAILROADS — SANITATION / *public hygiene*
TF639	*RAILROADS-CENTRALIZED TRAFFIC CONTROL* **SEE** RAILROADS — SIGNALING — — CENTRALIZED TRAFFIC CONTROL
HE1811	*RAILROADS-CONDUCTORS* **SEE** RAILROAD CONDUCTORS
TF300-308	*RAILROADS-DEPOTS* **SEE** RAILROADS — STATIONS
HE1613-1614	*RAILROADS-DEPOTS* **SEE** RAILROADS — STATIONS / *location*
HE1071-6	*RAILROADS-DEPRECIATION* **SEE** RAILROADS — VALUATION
TF	*RAILROADS-ENGINEERING* **SEE** RAILROAD ENGINEERING
HE5880-5990	*RAILROADS-EXPRESS SERVICE* **SEE** EXPRESS SERVICE
TF320	*RAILROADS-FERRIES* **SEE** TRAIN FERRIES
GR920.R3	*RAILROADS-FOLK-LORE* **SEE** FOLK-LORE OF RAILROADS
HE1831-2220	*RAILROADS-FREIGHT RATES* **SEE** RAILROADS — RATES
HE2101-2220	*RAILROADS-FREIGHT RATES* **SEE** RAILROADS — RATES / *freight*
HE1951-2100	*RAILROADS-FREIGHT RATES* **SEE** RAILROADS — RATES / *passenger*
HE1051-1081	*RAILROADS-GOVERNMENT OWNERSHIP* **SEE** RAILROADS AND STATE
HE2757	*RAILROADS-GOVERNMENT OWNERSHIP* **SEE** RAILROADS AND STATE / *u.s.*
TF263	*RAILROADS-GRADE CROSSINGS* **SEE** RAILROADS — CROSSINGS
HE1617-1619	*RAILROADS-GRADE CROSSINGS* **SEE** RAILROADS — CROSSINGS / *economics*
HE2801-3600	*RAILROADS-GUIDES* **SEE** RAILROADS — TIME-TABLES / *other countries*
TF565	*RAILROADS-GUIDES* **SEE** RAILROADS — TIME-TABLES / *schedules*
HE2727-9	*RAILROADS-GUIDES* **SEE** RAILROADS — TIME-TABLES / *u.s.*
TF445-453	*RAILROADS-HYGIENE* **SEE** RAILROADS — SANITATION
RA615.1	*RAILROADS-HYGIENE* **SEE** RAILROADS — SANITATION / *public hygiene*
TF262	*RAILROADS-JOINTLESS RAILS* **SEE** RAILROADS — CONTINUOUS RAILS
HE1053-9	*RAILROADS-LAW* **SEE** RAILROAD LAW
HE2801-3600	*RAILROADS-LAW* **SEE** RAILROAD LAW / *other countries*
HE2710-2712	*RAILROADS-LAW* **SEE** RAILROAD LAW / *u.s.*
HE6175	*RAILROADS-MAIL SERVICE* **SEE** RAILWAY MAIL SERVICE
HE6475	*RAILROADS-MAIL SERVICE* **SEE** RAILWAY MAIL SERVICE / *u.s.*
HE2771	*RAILROADS-MERGERS* **SEE** RAILROADS — CONSOLIDATION / *by state*

HE2705	*RAILROADS-MERGERS* **SEE** RAILROADS — CONSOLIDATION / *u.s. documents*
HE1971	*RAILROADS-MILEAGE TICKETS* **SEE** RAILROADS — TICKETS / *economics*
TF654	*RAILROADS-MILEAGE TICKETS* **SEE** RAILROADS — TICKETS
TF501-668	*RAILROADS-OPERATION* **SEE** RAILROADS — MANAGEMENT
HE1621-1730	*RAILROADS-OPERATION* **SEE** RAILROADS — MANAGEMENT / *economics*
HE1951-2100	*RAILROADS-PASSENGER FARES* **SEE** RAILROADS — FARES
TF477	*RAILROADS-REFRIGERATOR-CARS* **SEE** REFRIGERATOR-CARS
HE1051-1081	*RAILROADS-REGULATION* **SEE** RAILROADS AND STATE
HE2757	*RAILROADS-REGULATION* **SEE** RAILROADS AND STATE / *u.s.*
TF262	*RAILROADS-RIBBONRAILS* **SEE** RAILROADS — CONTINUOUS RAILS
TF592	*RAILROADS-SHUNTING* **SEE** RAILROADS — SWITCHING
TD884	*RAILROADS-SMOKE PREVENTION* **SEE** SMOKE PREVENTION
HE2757	*RAILROADS-STATE SUPERVISION* **SEE** RAILROADS AND STATE / *u.s.*
HE1051-1081	*RAILROADS-STATE SUPERVISION* **SEE** RAILROADS AND STATE
TK5241-3	*RAILROADS-TELEGRAPHERS* **SEE** TELEGRAPHERS / *biography*
HD8039.T22-23	*RAILROADS-TELEGRAPHERS* **SEE** TELEGRAPHERS / *labor*
HD6350.T3	*RAILROADS-TELEGRAPHERS* **SEE** TELEGRAPHERS / *trade-union periodicals*
HD6073.T4	*RAILROADS-TELEGRAPHERS* **SEE** TELEGRAPHERS / *women*
TF300-308	*RAILROADS-TERMINALS* **SEE** RAILROADS — STATIONS
HE1613-1614	*RAILROADS-TERMINALS* **SEE** RAILROADS — STATIONS / *location*
TF216-217	*RAILROADS-TURNOUTS* **SEE** RAILROADS — CURVES AND TURNOUTS
HE2771	*RAILROADS-UNIFICATION* **SEE** RAILROADS — CONSOLIDATION / *by state*
HE2757	*RAILROADS-UNIFICATION* **SEE** RAILROADS — CONSOLIDATION / *railroads and state*
HE2705	*RAILROADS-UNIFICATION* **SEE** RAILROADS — CONSOLIDATION / *u.s. documents*
TF290	*RAILROADS-WATER-CRANES* **SEE** WATER-CRANES / *railroads*
TF453	RAILROADS — CARS — — AIR CONDITIONING
TF445-9	RAILROADS — CARS — — HEATING AND VENTILATION
TF445-9	RAILROADS — CARS — — LIGHTING
HD5119.R1	RAILROADS — EMPLOYEES — — HOURS OF SERVICE
BV4596.R3	RAILROADS — EMPLOYEES — — RELIGIOUS LIFE
HE1959-1960	RAILROADS — FARES — — SPECIAL RATES
TF664-6	RAILROADS — FREIGHT — — TABLES, ETC.
TF197	RAILROADS — MODELS — — ELECTRIC EQUIPMENT
TF261	RAILROADS — RAILS — — FASTENINGS
TF630	RAILROADS — SIGNALING — — BLOCK SYSTEM
TF639	RAILROADS — SIGNALING — — CENTRALIZED TRAFFIC CONTROL
TF635	RAILROADS — SIGNALING — — INTERLOCKING SYSTEMS
QL696.G8	RAILS (BIRDS)
TF872	*RAILS (RAILROADS)* **SEE** ELECTRIC RAILROADS — RAILS
TF258-261	*RAILS (RAILROADS)* **SEE** RAILROADS — RAILS
TF262	*RAILS, CONTINUOUS (RAILROADS)* **SEE** RAILROADS — CONTINUOUS RAILS
HE1779-1795	*RAILWAY ACCIDENTS* **SEE** RAILROADS — ACCIDENTS
HE2241	*RAILWAY ACCOUNTING* **SEE** RAILROADS — ACCOUNTS, BOOKKEEPING, ETC.
VM925	*RAILWAY DOCKS* **SEE** MARINE RAILWAYS
TF467	RAILWAY MAIL SERVICE — CARS / *construction*
HE6475	RAILWAY MAIL SERVICE — CARS / *postal service*
HE6175	RAILWAY MAIL SERVICE
HE6475	RAILWAY MAIL SERVICE / *u.s.*
GV1855	*RAILWAYS, SCENIC* **SEE** SCENIC RAILWAYS / *amusement parks*
QC925-9	RAIN AND RAINFALL
QC929.R1	RAIN-MAKING
TD418	RAIN-WATER (WATER-SUPPLY)
GR830.R3	RAINBOW SERPENT
GR830.R3	*RAINBOW SNAKE* **SEE** RAINBOW SERPENT
QC976.R2	RAINBOW
GV1221-9	*RAINY DAY GAMES* **SEE** INDOOR GAMES
E356.R	RAISIN RIVER, BATTLE OF, 1813
SB399	RAISINS
SB608.G7	*RAISINS-DISEASES AND PESTS* **SEE** GRAPES — DISEASES AND PESTS
PK2701-9	RAJASTHANI LANGUAGE
DS432.R3	RAJPUTS
BP183.5	RAMADAN HYMNS
BP183.6	RAMADAN SERMONS
QC454	RAMAN EFFECT
DC309.R2	RAMBERVILLERS, BATTLE OF, 1870
HD9156.R2-4	RAMIE / *economics*
TS1747.R3	RAMIE / *manufactures*
SB259	RAMIE / *plant culture*
TH1421	*RAMMED EARTH* **SEE** PISE / *building construction*
UF765	*RAMPART-GRENADES* **SEE** GRENADES
TJ905	*RAMS, HYDRAULIC* **SEE** HYDRAULIC RAMS
E241.R	RAMSOUR'S MILL, BATTLE OF, 1780
QL668.E2	*RANA* **SEE** FROGS / *zoology*
QK495	RANALES
F3094	RANCAGUA, BATTLE OF, 1814
F596	RANCH LIFE
Q380	RANDOM NOISE THEORY
TK5101	RANDOM NOISE THEORY / *telecommunication*
TL681.C6	*RANGE OF VISION FROM AEROPLANES* **SEE** AEROPLANES — FIELD OF VIEW
UF850-857	RANGE-FINDING
VF550	RANGE-FINDING / *naval ordnance*
SF85	*RANGES (STOCK)* **SEE** STOCK-RANGES
QL737.U5	*RANGIFER* **SEE** CARIBOU
QL737.U5	*RANGIFER* **SEE** REINDEER
SF401.R4	*RANGIFER* **SEE** REINDEER / *breeding*
JX1678-9	*RANK, ORDER OF* **SEE** PRECEDENCE
CR	*RANK, ORDER OF* **SEE** PRECEDENCE
JX4081	*RANK, ORDER OF* **SEE** PRECEDENCE / *diplomatic*
F2823.R2	*RANQUELCHES INDIANS* **SEE** RANQUELES INDIANS
F2823.R2	RANQUELES INDIANS
BX9375.R	RANTERS
QK495	*RANUNCULALES* **SEE** RANALES
D651.I8	RAPALLO, TREATY OF, 1920
D651.I8	RAPALLO, TREATY OF, 1922
PL6498	RAPANUI LANGUAGE
SB608.R	RAPE (PLANT) — DISEASES AND PESTS
SB299.R2	RAPE (PLANT)
TP684.R3	RAPE-OIL
HV6558-6569	RAPE
LB1543	*RAPHIA WORK* **SEE** RAFFIA WORK / *education*
TT875	*RAPHIA WORK* **SEE** RAFFIA WORK / *handicraft*
TS1747.R2	*RAPHIA WORK* **SEE** RAFFIA WORK / *manufactures*
QK923	RAPHIDES
LB1050.5	RAPID READING
UF560-565	*RAPID-FIRE GUNS* **SEE** ORDNANCE, RAPID-FIRE
D763.I82R	RAPIDO RIVER, BATTLE OF THE, 1944
E99.R18	RAPPAHANNOCK INDIANS
PM4291	*RARAMURI LANGUAGE* **SEE** TARAHUMARE LANGUAGE
QL88	RARE ANIMALS
QD172.R2	RARE EARTH METALS
QD172.R2	*RARE EARTHS* **SEE** EARTHS, RARE
PL6499	RAROTONGAN LANGUAGE
DS451	*RASHTRA KUTA* **SEE** RASHTRAKUTAS
DS451	RASHTRAKUTAS
BX601	RASKOLNIKS
SB386.R3	RASPBERRIES
TJ1285-7	*RASPS* **SEE** FILES AND RASPS
D283.5	RASTATT, TREATY OF, 1714
QL737.R6	*RAT* **SEE** RATS
SB994.R2	*RAT* **SEE** RATS / *economic zoology*
QL795.R2	*RAT* **SEE** RATS / *etc.*
VM482	*RAT PROOFING OF SHIPS* **SEE** SHIPS — RATPROOF CONSTRUCTION
SB994.R2	*RAT-CATCHING* **SEE** RATS — EXTERMINATION / *agriculture*

RA641.R2	*RAT-CATCHING* **SEE** RATS — EXTERMINATION / hygiene
VM483	*RAT-CATCHING* **SEE** RATS — EXTERMINATION / ship disinfection
RS165.R3	RATANY / pharmacy
RM666.R3	RATANY / therapeutics
HE1831-2220	*RATE REGULATION* **SEE** RAILROADS — RATES
HE2101-2220	*RATE REGULATION* **SEE** RAILROADS — RATES / freight
HE1951-2100	*RATE REGULATION* **SEE** RAILROADS — RATES / passenger
DS451	*RATHOR DYNASTY* **SEE** RASHTRAKUTAS
JX4171.R3	*RATIFICATION OF TREATIES* **SEE** TREATIES — RATIFICATION
T60.R	*RATING OF EMPLOYEES* **SEE** EMPLOYEES, RATING OF
LB2806	*RATING OF SCHOOL SUPERINTENDENTS AND PRINCIPALS* **SEE** SCHOOL SUPERINTENDENTS AND PRINCIPALS, RATING OF
HF5549.5.J62	*RATING, JOB* **SEE** JOB EVALUATION
QA117	RATIO AND PROPORTION / arithmetic
QA481	RATIO AND PROPORTION / geometry
T60.W65	*RATIO DELAY STUDY* **SEE** WORK SAMPLING
BC177	*RATIOCINATION* **SEE** REASONING / argumentation in logic
BC	*RATIOCINATION* **SEE** REASONING / logic
QA270	*RATIONAL GAMES (MATHEMATICS)* **SEE** GAMES OF STRATEGY (MATHEMATICS)
BT1209-1210	RATIONALISM / apologetics
BD181	RATIONALISM / epistemology
B851-4695	RATIONALISM / local
B833	RATIONALISM / philosophy general
BL2700-2790	RATIONALISM / religion
BL2785-2790	RATIONALISTS
HF5415	RATIONING, CONSUMER
HD3611-3616	*RATIONING, INDUSTRIAL* **SEE** PRIORITIES, INDUSTRIAL
UC700-780	*RATIONS* **SEE** ARMIES — COMMISSARIAT
BR355.R2	RATISBON, COLLOQUY OF, 1541
BR355.R3	RATISBON, COLLOQUY OF, 1546
DD184	RATISBON, DIET OF, 1532
QL696.S9	RATITAE
VM482	*RATPROOFING OF SHIPS* **SEE** SHIPS — RATPROOF CONSTRUCTION
SB994.R2	RATS — EXTERMINATION / agriculture
RA641.R2	RATS — EXTERMINATION / hygiene
VM483	RATS — EXTERMINATION / ship disinfection
RA641.R2	RATS AS CARRIERS OF DISEASE
QL737.R6	RATS
SB994.R2	RATS / economic zoology
QL795.R2	RATS / etc.
SB261.R	RATTAN / agriculture
HD9769.R3	RATTAN / economics
TT200	RATTAN / woodworking
GN467.R	RATTLE / primitive music
GN477.R	*RATTLE, NOTCHED* **SEE** NOTCHED RATTLE
QL666.O6	RATTLESNAKES
DG541	RAVENNA, BATTLE OF, 1512
QL696.P2	RAVENS
TX392	*RAW FOOD* **SEE** FOOD, RAW
HF1041-1051	RAW MATERIALS — CLASSIFICATION
HF1041-1051	RAW MATERIALS
TS1688	RAYON SPINNING
TS1688	RAYON
QL638.9	RAYS (FISHES)
QC721	*RAYS, BECQUEREL* **SEE** BECQUEREL RAYS
QC711	*RAYS, CANAL* **SEE** CANAL RAYS
QC457	*RAYS, INVISIBLE* **SEE** SPECTRUM, INFRA-RED
QC459	*RAYS, INVISIBLE* **SEE** SPECTRUM, ULTRA-VIOLET
QC481	*RAYS, ROENTGEN* **SEE** X-RAYS
RC78	*RAYS, ROENTGEN* **SEE** X-RAYS / medicine
QC459	*RAYS, ULTRA-VIOLET* **SEE** ULTRA-VIOLET RAYS
TT967	RAZORS
DC611.R282	RE EXPEDITION, 1627
UB320-345	*RE-ENLISTMENT* **SEE** RECRUITING AND ENLISTMENT / army
VB260-275	*RE-ENLISTMENT* **SEE** RECRUITING AND ENLISTMENT / navy
QA76.8.R4	*REAC (COMPUTER)* **SEE** REAC COMPUTER
QA76.8.R4	REAC COMPUTER
TK7889.R4	REAC COMPUTER / engineering
TK7872.A5	*REACTANCE AMPLIFIERS* **SEE** PARAMETRIC AMPLIFIERS
QD501	*REACTION RATE (CHEMISTRY)* **SEE** CHEMICAL REACTION, RATE OF
BF317	REACTION-TIME / psychology
QD501	*REACTION, CONDITIONS AND LAWS OF (CHEMISTRY)* **SEE** CHEMICAL REACTION-CONDITIONS AND LAWS
QD73	*REACTIONS, CHEMICAL* **SEE** CHEMICAL REACTIONS
TK9360	REACTOR FUEL REPROCESSING
TK9360	*REACTOR FUELS* **SEE** NUCLEAR FUELS
QC786	*REACTORS (NUCLEAR PHYSICS)* **SEE** NUCLEAR REACTORS / physics
TK9202	*REACTORS (NUCLEAR PHYSICS)* **SEE** NUCLEAR REACTORS / technology
TK2851	*REACTORS, ELECTRIC* **SEE** ELECTRIC REACTORS
TR835	READER-PRINTERS (MICROPHOTOGRAPHY)
Z704	*READERS AND LIBRARIES* **SEE** LIBRARIES AND READERS
Z711	*READERS AND LIBRARIES* **SEE** LIBRARIES AND READERS
Z711.3	*READERS AND LIBRARY CATALOGS* **SEE** LIBRARY CATALOGS AND READERS
PE1117-1130	READERS AND SPEAKERS / english
PN4199-4321	READERS AND SPEAKERS / recitations
PE1417	READERS AND SPEAKERS / rhetoric
PN4199-4321	*READERS AND SPEAKERS, PRESCHOOL* **SEE** READERS AND SPEAKERS / recitations
PE1117-1130	*READERS AND SPEAKERS, PRESCHOOL* **SEE** READERS AND SPEAKERS / english
PE1417	*READERS AND SPEAKERS, PRESCHOOL* **SEE** READERS AND SPEAKERS / rhetoric
LB1132	READINESS FOR SCHOOL
LB1050.5	READING — REMEDIAL TEACHING
LB1573	READING (ELEMENTARY) / elementary schools
LB1525	READING (ELEMENTARY) / primary schools
LB2395	READING (HIGHER EDUCATION)
LB1632	READING (SECONDARY EDUCATION)
LB1573.5	*READING ALOUD* **SEE** ORAL READING
LC6601-6660	*READING CIRCLES* **SEE** GROUP READING
LC6601-6660	*READING GROUPS* **SEE** GROUP READING
Z1003	*READING HABITS* **SEE** BOOKS AND READING
Z1003	*READING INTERESTS* **SEE** BOOKS AND READING
LB1573.5	*READING OUT LOUD* **SEE** ORAL READING
PN83	READING / literature
PN4145	READING / oratory
LB1050	READING / teaching
Z1035	*READING, CHOICE OF* **SEE** BIBLIOGRAPHY — BEST BOOKS
Z1003	*READING, CHOICE OF* **SEE** BOOKS AND READING
LB1050.5	*READING, DEVELOPMENTAL* **SEE** DEVELOPMENTAL READING
PN4145	*READING, INTERPRETATIVE* **SEE** ORAL INTERPRETATION
LB1573.5	*READING, ORAL* **SEE** ORAL READING
BF456.R2	READING, PSYCHOLOGY OF
LB1525	*READING-STUDY AND TEACHING* **SEE** READING (ELEMENTARY) / primary schools
LB1573	*READING-STUDY AND TEACHING* **SEE** READING (ELEMENTARY) / elementary schools
PN83	*READING-STUDY AND TEACHING* **SEE** READING / literature
PN4145	*READING-STUDY AND TEACHING* **SEE** READING / oratory
LB1050	*READING-STUDY AND TEACHING* **SEE** READING / teaching
QA111	READY-RECKONERS / arithmetic
HF5697-5702	READY-RECKONERS / business arithmetic
QD77	*REAGENTS, CHEMICAL* **SEE** CHEMICAL TESTS AND REAGENTS
HD301-1130	*REAL ESTATE* **SEE** REAL PROPERTY / other countries
HD251-279	*REAL ESTATE* **SEE** REAL PROPERTY / u. s.
HD251-279	*REAL ESTATE* **SEE** REAL PROPERTY / u.s.
HF5686.R3	REAL ESTATE BUSINESS — ACCOUNTING
HD1386.5	REAL ESTATE BUSINESS — RECORDS AND CORRESPONDENCE
HD1375-1395	REAL ESTATE BUSINESS
TX955	REAL ESTATE MANAGEMENT

M455-7	*RECORDER MUSIC (4 RECORDERS)* **SEE** WIND QUARTETS (4 RECORDERS)
M455-7	*RECORDER MUSIC (4 RECORDERS)* **SEE** WIND QUARTETS (4 RECORDERS)
M655-7	*RECORDER MUSIC (6 RECORDERS)* **SEE** WIND SEXTETS (6 RECORDERS)
M655-7	*RECORDER MUSIC (6 RECORDERS)* **SEE** WIND SEXTETS (6 RECORDERS)
M60-62	RECORDER MUSIC
M63-64	RECORDER MUSIC, ARRANGED
M1385.R	RECORDER MUSIC, JUVENILE
M1020-1021	RECORDER WITH ORCHESTRA
M1105-6	RECORDER WITH STRING ORCHESTRA
M1020-1021	RECORDERS (2) WITH ORCHESTRA
M1360	RECORDERS (2) WITH PLECTRAL ENSEMBLE
M1105-6	RECORDERS (2) WITH STRING ORCHESTRA
M1105-6	RECORDERS (3) WITH STRING ORCHESTRA
TK393	RECORDING INSTRUMENTS / *electric engineering*
QC53	RECORDING INSTRUMENTS / *physics*
HJ5801-5819	*RECORDING TAX* **SEE** REGISTRATION TAX
HA38-39	*RECORDS OF BIRTHS, ETC.* **SEE** REGISTERS OF BIRTHS, ETC.
HB881-3700	*RECORDS OF BIRTHS, ETC.* **SEE** VITAL STATISTICS
TS2301.P3	*RECORDS, PHONOGRAPH* **SEE** PHONORECORDS / *manufacture*
GV187	RECREATION — FILM CATALOGS
RA605	RECREATION AREAS — HYGIENIC ASPECTS
GV182	RECREATION AREAS
GV14.5	*RECREATION AS A PROFESSION* **SEE** RECREATION LEADERSHIP
GV1231	*RECREATION FOR INVALIDS* **SEE** INVALIDS — RECREATION
GV14.5	RECREATION LEADERSHIP
HD7395.R4	*RECREATION, INDUSTRIAL* **SEE** INDUSTRIAL RECREATION
GV14.5	*RECREATION-STUDY AND TEACHING* **SEE** RECREATION LEADERSHIP
RM737	RECREATIONAL THERAPY
RJ499	RECREATIONAL THERAPY / *child psychiatry*
RC489.R4	RECREATIONAL THERAPY / *psychotherapy*
GV1200-1511	*RECREATIONS* **SEE** GAMES
LB1137	*RECREATIONS* **SEE** GAMES / *educational*
GN454-6	*RECREATIONS* **SEE** GAMES / *ethnology*
GR480-485	*RECREATIONS* **SEE** GAMES / *folk-lore*
LB1177	*RECREATIONS* **SEE** GAMES / *kindergarten*
BF717	*RECREATIONS* **SEE** GAMES / *psychology of play*
LB3031	*RECREATIONS* **SEE** GAMES / *school management*
GV1201	*RECREATIONS* **SEE** HOBBIES
BF721	*RECREATIONS* **SEE** PLAY / *child psychology*
LB1137	*RECREATIONS* **SEE** PLAY / *educational theory*
BF717	*RECREATIONS* **SEE** PLAY / *psychology of play*
LB3015-3031	*RECREATIONS* **SEE** SCHOOLS — EXERCISES AND RECREATIONS
GV	*RECREATIONS* **SEE** SPORTS
GN457	*RECREATIONS* **SEE** SPORTS / *primitive*
GV1485	*RECREATIONS, GEOGRAPHICAL* **SEE** GEOGRAPHICAL RECREATIONS
GV1493	*RECREATIONS, LITERARY* **SEE** LITERARY RECREATIONS
QA95	*RECREATIONS, MATHEMATICAL* **SEE** MATHEMATICAL RECREATIONS
Q164	*RECREATIONS, SCIENTIFIC* **SEE** SCIENTIFIC RECREATIONS
UB320-345	RECRUITING AND ENLISTMENT / *army*
VB260-275	RECRUITING AND ENLISTMENT / *navy*
RM163	*RECTAL MEDICATION* **SEE** RECTUM, MEDICATION BY
TL673.R4	*RECTANGULAR WINGS (AEROPLANES)* **SEE** AEROPLANES — WINGS, RECTANGULAR
QA626	*RECTIFICATION OF CURVES* **SEE** CURVES — RECTIFICATION AND QUADRATURE
QD63.D6	*RECTIFICATION OF SPIRITS* **SEE** DISTILLATION
TP156.D5	*RECTIFICATION OF SPIRITS* **SEE** DISTILLATION
TK2798	*RECTIFIERS (ELECTRIC)* **SEE** ELECTRIC CURRENT RECTIFIERS
TK2798	*RECTIFIERS, ELECTRIC CURRENT* **SEE** ELECTRIC CURRENT RECTIFIERS
BV4381	*RECTORIES (BUILDINGS)* **SEE** PARSONAGES
BV659-685	*RECTORS* **SEE** CLERGY
RC864-6	RECTUM — DISEASES
RD544	RECTUM — SURGERY
RD672	RECTUM — TUMORS
RD677	RECTUM — TUMORS / *dermoid cysts*
QL863	RECTUM / *comparative anatomy*
QM345	RECTUM / *human anatomy*
RM163	RECTUM, MEDICATION BY
QA248.5	RECURSIVE FUNCTIONS
E241.R4	RED BANK, BATTLE OF, 1777
SB608.C8	RED COTTON BUG
HV560-583	RED CROSS
UH535-7	RED CROSS / *army*
D628-630	RED CROSS / *european war*
VG457	RED CROSS / *navy*
QL737.U5	RED DEER
E99.B4	*RED INDIANS OF NEWFOUNDLAND* **SEE** BEOTHUK INDIANS
TP936	RED LEAD
QK495.Q4	RED OAK / *botany*
SD397.O12	RED OAK / *forestry*
SD397.P61	*RED PINE* **SEE** NORWAY PINE
E476.33	RED RIVER EXPEDITION, 1864
F1063	RED RIVER REBELLION, 1869-1870
SD397.S77	RED SPRUCE
SF805	*RED WATER (DISEASE OF CATTLE)* **SEE** TEXAS FEVER
SB945.R	RED-BANDED THRIPS
SB608.R3	RED-GUM (TREE) — DISEASES AND PESTS
SD397.R2	RED-GUM (TREE)
SF199.R4	RED-POLLED CATTLE
SF193.R3	RED-POLLED CATTLE / *herd-books*
SB945.R45	RED-SPIDER
TP910	RED / *dyes*
BM720.R	REDEMPTION OF THE FIRST-BORN
BT775	REDEMPTION
BX4160.T4	*REDEMPTIONISTS* **SEE** TRINITARIANS
BX4020	REDEMPTORISTS
NA9000-9284	*REDEVELOPMENT, URBAN* **SEE** CITIES AND TOWNS — PLANNING
M32	REDOWAS (PIANO)
RC628	*REDUCING (BODY-WEIGHT CONTROL)* **SEE** CORPULENCE
GV509	REDUCING EXERCISES
QD63.R4	REDUCTION, CHEMICAL
QD281.R4	REDUCTION, CHEMICAL / *organic*
QD63.R4	REDUCTION, ELECTROLYTIC
QD281.R4	REDUCTION, ELECTROLYTIC / *organic*
P245	*REDUPLICATION (IN LANGUAGE)* **SEE** GRAMMAR, COMPARATIVE AND GENERAL — REDUPLICATION
P245	*REDUPLICATION (IN LANGUAGE)* **SEE** GRAMMAR, COMPARATIVE AND GENERAL — REDUPLICATION
SF805	*REDWATER (DISEASE OF CATTLE)* **SEE** TEXAS FEVER
SD397.R3	REDWOOD
E99.A8	*REE INDIANS* **SEE** ARIKARA INDIANS
QL692.P2	REED WARBLERS
MT202	REED-ORGAN — METHODS
M191-3	*REED-ORGAN AND PIANO MUSIC (4 HANDS)* **SEE** PIANO (4 HANDS) AND REED-ORGAN MUSIC
M15-17	REED-ORGAN MUSIC
M18-19	REED-ORGAN MUSIC, ARRANGED
M1375	REED-ORGAN MUSIC, JUVENILE
ML597	REED-ORGAN
MT208	*REED-ORGAN-SELF-INSTRUCTION* **SEE** REED-ORGAN — METHODS — — SELF-INSTRUCTION
MT208	REED-ORGAN — METHODS — — SELF-INSTRUCTION
GB461-8	REEFS
TK7889.R4	*REEVES ELECTRONIC ANALOG COMPUTER* **SEE** REAC COMPUTER / *engineering*
QA76.8.R4	*REEVES ELECTRONIC ANALOG COMPUTER* **SEE** REAC COMPUTER
GV735	*REFEREEING (SPORTS)* **SEE** SPORTS OFFICIATING
Z1035	REFERENCE BOOKS — BIBLIOGRAPHY
Z711	REFERENCE BOOKS
JF491-7	REFERENDUM
QB88	*REFLECTING TELESCOPE* **SEE** TELESCOPE, REFLECTING
QC385	REFLECTION (OPTICS) / *geometrical*
QC425	REFLECTION (OPTICS) / *physical*
NC757	REFLECTIONS / *drawing*
QC425	REFLECTOMETER
QP372	*REFLEX ACTION* **SEE** REFLEXES
QP372	REFLEXES
SD409	REFORESTATION

HV6001-9920	*REFORM OF CRIMINALS* **SEE** CRIME AND CRIMINALS
GT6550-6715	*REFORM OF CRIMINALS* **SEE** CRIME AND CRIMINALS / manners and customs
HV9278	*REFORM OF CRIMINALS* **SEE** PROBATION
HV9301-9430	*REFORM OF CRIMINALS* **SEE** PROBATION
HV6049	*REFORM OF CRIMINALS* **SEE** RECIDIVISTS
HV9051-9230	*REFORM OF CRIMINALS* **SEE** REFORMATORIES
HV9051-9230	*REFORM SCHOOLS* **SEE** REFORMATORIES
Z675.R	*REFORM-SCHOOL LIBRARIES* **SEE** REFORMATORY LIBRARIES
Z1039.R4	*REFORM-SCHOOL LIBRARIES* **SEE** REFORMATORY LIBRARIES / books
HN	*REFORM, SOCIAL* **SEE** SOCIAL PROBLEMS
BR315	REFORMATION — BIOGRAPHY
BR307	REFORMATION — CAUSES
BR295	REFORMATION — EARLY MOVEMENTS
BR309	REFORMATION — SERMONS
D220-234	REFORMATION / european history
DD176-189	REFORMATION / germany
BR300-420	REFORMATION / religion
D220-234	*REFORMATION-HISTORY* **SEE** REFORMATION / european history
DD176-189	*REFORMATION-HISTORY* **SEE** REFORMATION / germany
BR300-420	*REFORMATION-HISTORY* **SEE** REFORMATION / religion
HV8738	REFORMATORIES FOR WOMEN
HV9051-9230	REFORMATORIES
Z675.R	REFORMATORY LIBRARIES
Z1039.R4	REFORMATORY LIBRARIES / books
BX9501-9543	REFORMED CHURCH IN AMERICA
BX9551-9593	REFORMED CHURCH IN THE UNITED STATES
BX9401-9595	REFORMED CHURCH
BX9501-9543	*REFORMED DUTCH CHURCH IN AMERICA* **SEE** REFORMED CHURCH IN AMERICA
BX6051-6093	REFORMED EPISCOPAL CHURCH
BX8990-8998	REFORMED PRESBYTERIAN CHURCH IN NORTH AMERICA
BX9501-9543	*REFORMED PROTESTANT DUTCH CHURCH IN NORTH AMERICA* **SEE** REFORMED CHURCH IN AMERICA
QP476	*REFRACTION OF THE EYE* **SEE** EYE — ACCOMMODATION AND REFRACTION / physiology
RE925-939	*REFRACTION OF THE EYE* **SEE** EYE — ACCOMMODATION AND REFRACTION / pathology
QC385	REFRACTION / geometrical
QC425	REFRACTION / physical
QB155-6	REFRACTION, ASTRONOMICAL
QC425	REFRACTION, DOUBLE
QB321	REFRACTION, TERRESTRIAL / geodesy
QC387	REFRACTIVE INDEX
QC387	REFRACTOMETER
TP857-8	*REFRACTORIES* **SEE** REFRACTORY MATERIALS / glass manufactures
TN677	*REFRACTORIES* **SEE** REFRACTORY MATERIALS / metallurgy
TP857-8	REFRACTORY MATERIALS / glass manufactures
TN677	REFRACTORY MATERIALS / metallurgy
TN700	REFRACTORY METALS **SEE** HEAT RESISTANT ALLOYS
PR508.R3	REFRAIN / english poetry
PC2541	REFRAIN / french poetry
TP490-497	REFRIGERATION AND REFRIGERATING MACHINERY
RA766.R3	REFRIGERATION AS A DISINFECTANT
VM485	*REFRIGERATION, MARINE* **SEE** MARINE REFRIGERATION
VM459	REFRIGERATOR SHIPS
TF477	REFRIGERATOR-CARS
TP496-7	REFRIGERATORS
TL711.R4	*REFUELING OF AEROPLANES* **SEE** AEROPLANES — REFUELING
VK369-369.8	*REFUGE HARBORS* **SEE** HARBORS OF REFUGE
HT731	*REFUGEES, COLORED* **SEE** FREEDMEN
E185.2	*REFUGEES, COLORED* **SEE** FREEDMEN / u.s.
E450	*REFUGEES, COLORED* **SEE** SLAVERY IN THE U.S. — FUGITIVE SLAVES
JX4292.P6	REFUGEES, POLITICAL / international law
JX1975.8	REFUGEES, POLITICAL / league of nations
HV640	REFUGEES, POLITICAL / relief
DK273	REFUGEES, RUSSIAN
458.7	REFUGEES, SOUTHERN
TD791-870	REFUSE AND REFUSE DISPOSAL
GV775	REGATTAS
JF314	REGENCY / general theory
QH499	REGENERATION (BIOLOGY)
QK840	REGENERATION (BOTANY)
BT790	REGENERATION (THEOLOGY)
HV6278	REGICIDES
DA419.5	REGICIDES / charles i
BL815.R	REGIFUGIUM
QM531-549	*REGIONAL ANATOMY* **SEE** ANATOMY, SURGICAL AND TOPOGRAPHICAL
RD84	*REGIONAL ANESTHESIA* **SEE** LOCAL ANESTHESIA
NA9000-9284	REGIONAL PLANNING
JX1979	REGIONALISM (INTERNATIONAL ORGANIZATION)
Z242.R	REGISTERS (IN EARLY PRINTED BOOKS)
BX1939.R4	REGISTERS OF BIRTHS, ETC. (CANON LAW)
HA38-39	REGISTERS OF BIRTHS, ETC.
HA38-39	*REGISTERS OF DEATHS* **SEE** REGISTERS OF BIRTHS, ETC.
LB2341	*REGISTRARS, COLLEGE* **SEE** COLLEGE REGISTRARS
MT192	*REGISTRATION (ELECTRONIC ORGAN)* **SEE** ELECTRONIC ORGAN — REGISTRATION
MT189	*REGISTRATION (ORGAN)* **SEE** ORGAN — REGISTRATION
HE6176	*REGISTRATION OF MAIL* **SEE** POSTAL SERVICE — REGISTRY SYSTEM
LB2341	*REGISTRATION OF STUDENTS* **SEE** STUDENT REGISTRATION
HD1188-1208	*REGISTRATION OF TITLE* **SEE** LAND TITLES — REGISTRATION AND TRANSFER
T325	*REGISTRATION OF TRADE-MARKS* **SEE** TRADE-MARKS
T221-323	*REGISTRATION OF TRADE-MARKS* **SEE** TRADE-MARKS / by country
HJ5801-5819	REGISTRATION TAX
JX4449.N3	*REGISTRY OF SHIPS* **SEE** SHIPS — NATIONALITY
HB236	*REGULATION OF PRICES* **SEE** PRICE REGULATION
F731	*REGULATORS (VIGILANTE GROUPS)* **SEE** VIGILANCE COMMITTEES / montana
F865	*REGULATORS (VIGILANTE GROUPS)* **SEE** VIGILANCE COMMITTEES / california
TJ1055	*REGULATORS (MACHINERY)* **SEE** GOVERNORS (MACHINERY)
TK2851	*REGULATORS* **SEE** VOLTAGE REGULATORS
DC302.5	*REICHSHOFEN, BATTLE OF, 1870* **SEE** WORTH, BATTLE OF, 1870
DC139-195	*REIGN OF TERROR* **SEE** FRANCE — HISTORY — — REVOLUTION
BL515	REINCARNATION
BP573.R5	REINCARNATION / theosophy
GN775-6	REINDEER PERIOD
QL737.U5	REINDEER
SF401.R4	REINDEER / breeding
QE882.U3	REINDEER, FOSSIL
TA683	REINFORCED CONCRETE CONSTRUCTION
TH1501	REINFORCED CONCRETE CONSTRUCTION
TA444-5	REINFORCED CONCRETE
HG8059.4	REINSURANCE
HG9669	REINSURANCE / fire
BM695.S	*REJOICING OVER THE LAW, FEAST OF THE* **SEE** SIMHAT TORAH
QP90	REJUVENATION
PK1975-1987	*REKHTA LANGUAGE* **SEE** URDU LANGUAGE
PK1975-1987	*REKHTI LANGUAGE* **SEE** URDU LANGUAGE
RC182.R3	RELAPSING FEVER
B836	RELATIONISM
BD221	*RELATIVISM* **SEE** RELATIVITY / relativity of knowledge
QC174.45	*RELATIVISTIC QUANTUM FIELD THEORY* **SEE** QUANTUM FIELD THEORY
QC6	RELATIVITY (PHYSICS)
BD221	RELATIVITY / relativity of knowledge
QA225	RELAXATION METHODS (MATHEMATICS)
RA790	RELAXATION
HV8887	*RELEASE GRATUITIES, PRISON* **SEE** PRISON RELEASE GRATUITIES
BX1939.R45	RELICS AND RELIQUARIES (CANON LAW)
BX2315	RELICS AND RELIQUARIES / catholic church
BV890	RELICS AND RELIQUARIES / general christian
BX577	RELICS AND RELIQUARIES / russian church
NB1280	RELIEF (SCULPTURE)
HV57	RELIEF STATIONS (FOR THE POOR) / elberfeld system
BL45-46	RELIGION — EXHIBITIONS AND MUSEUMS
BL41	RELIGION — HISTORIOGRAPHY

BL51	RELIGION — PHILOSOPHY
BL41	RELIGION — STUDY AND TEACHING
HX536	*RELIGION AND COMMUNISM* **SEE** COMMUNISM AND RELIGION
BX1396.4	*RELIGION AND COMMUNISM* **SEE** COMMUNISM AND RELIGION / *catholic church*
LC351-629	*RELIGION AND EDUCATION* **SEE** CHURCH AND EDUCATION / *church education*
LA91-131	*RELIGION AND EDUCATION* **SEE** CHURCH AND EDUCATION / *history of education*
LC107-120	*RELIGION AND EDUCATION* **SEE** CHURCH AND EDUCATION / *separation of church and schools*
BL65.G	RELIGION AND GEOGRAPHY
BS657	*RELIGION AND GEOLOGY* **SEE** BIBLE AND GEOLOGY
BS2545.W5	RELIGION AND HUMOR / *new testament*
BX4661	RELIGION AND HUMOR / *saints*
BL65.L33	RELIGION AND LAW
BL65.M4	*RELIGION AND MEDICINE* **SEE** MEDICINE AND RELIGION
RC89	*RELIGION AND MEDICINE* **SEE** MEDICINE AND RELIGION / *pastoral medicine*
BL65.N3	*RELIGION AND NATIONALISM* **SEE** NATIONALISM AND RELIGION
BL53	*RELIGION AND PSYCHOLOGY* **SEE** PSYCHOLOGY, RELIGIOUS
BL239	RELIGION AND SCIENCE — EARLY WORKS TO 1800
BL245	RELIGION AND SCIENCE — HISTORY OF CONTROVERSY
BL240-265	RELIGION AND SCIENCE — 1800-1859
BL240-265	RELIGION AND SCIENCE — 1860-1899
BL240-265	RELIGION AND SCIENCE — 1900-1925
BL239-265	RELIGION AND SCIENCE
HQ61	*RELIGION AND SEX* **SEE** SEX AND RELIGION
HN30-39	*RELIGION AND SOCIAL PROBLEMS* **SEE** CHURCH AND SOCIAL PROBLEMS
HN40.I	*RELIGION AND SOCIAL PROBLEMS* **SEE** ISLAM AND SOCIAL PROBLEMS
HN40.J5	*RELIGION AND SOCIAL PROBLEMS* **SEE** JUDAISM AND SOCIAL PROBLEMS
BL60	*RELIGION AND SOCIAL PROBLEMS* **SEE** RELIGION AND SOCIOLOGY
BL60	*RELIGION AND SOCIETY* **SEE** RELIGION AND SOCIOLOGY
BL60	RELIGION AND SOCIOLOGY
BL65.S8	RELIGION AND STATE
BL65.W2	*RELIGION AND WAR* **SEE** WAR AND RELIGION
BR115.W2	*RELIGION AND WAR* **SEE** WAR AND RELIGION / *christianity*
BV683	*RELIGION AS A PROFESSION* **SEE** CHURCH WORK AS A PROFESSION
BV4012	*RELIGION AS A PROFESSION* **SEE** CLERGY — APPOINTMENT, CALL, AND ELECTION
PN49	RELIGION IN LITERATURE
PS166	RELIGION IN LITERATURE / *american*
PS310.R4	RELIGION IN LITERATURE / *american*
PR145	RELIGION IN LITERATURE / *english*
PR508.R4	RELIGION IN LITERATURE / *english*
LC107-120	RELIGION IN THE PUBLIC SCHOOLS
B831	*RELIGION OF HUMANITY* **SEE** POSITIVISM
B2200-2249	*RELIGION OF HUMANITY* **SEE** POSITIVISM / *comte*
BL390	*RELIGION OF THE FUTURE* **SEE** RELIGIONS (PROPOSED, UNIVERSAL, ETC.)
BL48-50	RELIGION / *science of*
BL1620-1625	*RELIGION, ASSYRO-BABYLONIAN* **SEE** ASSYRO-BABYLONIAN RELIGION
BL74-98	*RELIGION, COMPARATIVE* **SEE** RELIGIONS
HQ1031	*RELIGION, MIXED* **SEE** MARRIAGE, MIXED
BL430	RELIGION, PRIMITIVE
GN470-474	RELIGION, PRIMITIVE / *ethnology*
BL390	*RELIGION, PROPOSED* **SEE** RELIGIONS (PROPOSED, UNIVERSAL, ETC.)
BL390	*RELIGION, UNIVERSAL* **SEE** RELIGIONS (PROPOSED, UNIVERSAL, ETC.)
BL45-46	*RELIGION-MUSEUMS* **SEE** RELIGION — EXHIBITIONS AND MUSEUMS
BL53	*RELIGION-PSYCHOLOGY* **SEE** PSYCHOLOGY, RELIGIOUS
BL72	RELIGIONS — BIOGRAPHY
BL350	RELIGIONS — CLASSIFICATION
BL75	RELIGIONS — EARLY WORKS TO 1800
BL41	RELIGIONS — HISTORIOGRAPHY

BL390	RELIGIONS (PROPOSED, UNIVERSAL, ETC.)
DS94.8.D8	*RELIGIONS* **SEE** DRUSES
BL1695	*RELIGIONS* **SEE** DRUSES
BL74-98	RELIGIONS
BL74-98	*RELIGIONS, COMPARATIVE* **SEE** RELIGIONS
BL98	RELIGIONS, MODERN
BL390	*RELIGIONS, UNIVERSAL* **SEE** RELIGIONS (PROPOSED, UNIVERSAL, ETC.)
BJ1188	*RELIGIONS-ETHICS* **SEE** RELIGIOUS ETHICS
NA4830	*RELIGIOUS ART* **SEE** CATHEDRALS / *architecture*
NA5201-6113	*RELIGIOUS ART* **SEE** CATHEDRALS / *architecture*
N7810-8185	*RELIGIOUS ART* **SEE** CHRISTIAN ART AND SYMBOLISM
BV150-168	*RELIGIOUS ART* **SEE** CHRISTIAN ART AND SYMBOLISM / *theology*
NA4790-6113	*RELIGIOUS ART* **SEE** CHURCH ARCHITECTURE
NB960-1113	*RELIGIOUS ART* **SEE** IDOLS AND IMAGES / *art*
NA4670	*RELIGIOUS ART* **SEE** MOSQUES / *architecture*
NA4600-4641	*RELIGIOUS ART* **SEE** TEMPLES
GR505	*RELIGIOUS ART* **SEE** TEMPLES / *folk-lore*
GT485	*RELIGIOUS ART* **SEE** TEMPLES / *manners and customs*
BD215	*RELIGIOUS BELIEF* **SEE** BELIEF AND DOUBT / *philosophy*
BF773	*RELIGIOUS BELIEF* **SEE** BELIEF AND DOUBT / *psychology*
BV4637	*RELIGIOUS BELIEF* **SEE** FAITH / *moral theology*
BT770-772	*RELIGIOUS BELIEF* **SEE** FAITH / *theology*
BX2835	*RELIGIOUS BROTHERS* **SEE** BROTHERS (IN RELIGIOUS ORDERS, CONGREGATIONS, ETC.)
BX2835	*RELIGIOUS BROTHERS* **SEE** LAY BROTHERS
BM135	RELIGIOUS CAMPS, JEWISH
BV170-199	*RELIGIOUS CEREMONIES* **SEE** RITES AND CEREMONIES / *christian*
BL600-619	*RELIGIOUS CEREMONIES* **SEE** RITES AND CEREMONIES / *comparative religion*
GT	*RELIGIOUS CEREMONIES* **SEE** RITES AND CEREMONIES / *manners and customs*
GN473	*RELIGIOUS CEREMONIES* **SEE** RITES AND CEREMONIES / *primitive religion*
BV765	*RELIGIOUS CORPORATIONS* **SEE** CORPORATIONS, RELIGIOUS
BL74-98	*RELIGIOUS DENOMINATIONS* **SEE** RELIGIONS
BR157	*RELIGIOUS DENOMINATIONS* **SEE** SECTS
PN1880	RELIGIOUS DRAMA — PRESENTATION, ETC. / *literature*
BV1472	RELIGIOUS DRAMA — PRESENTATION, ETC. / *religious education*
PN1880	RELIGIOUS DRAMA
PN6120.R4	RELIGIOUS DRAMA / *collections*
BV1535	RELIGIOUS EDUCATION — AUDIO-VISUAL AIDS
BV1558	RELIGIOUS EDUCATION — CURRICULA / *sunday-schools*
BV1590	RELIGIOUS EDUCATION — HOME TRAINING
BV1471	RELIGIOUS EDUCATION — PSYCHOLOGY
BV1533	RELIGIOUS EDUCATION — TEACHER TRAINING
BV1534-6	RELIGIOUS EDUCATION — TEACHING METHODS
BV1558-1561	RELIGIOUS EDUCATION — TEXT-BOOKS
BV1550	RELIGIOUS EDUCATION OF ADULTS, (CHILDREN, ETC.) / *adults*
BV1474-1590	RELIGIOUS EDUCATION OF ADULTS, (CHILDREN, ETC.) / *children*
BL1418	RELIGIOUS EDUCATION OF CHILDREN, BUDDHIST
BP44-48	RELIGIOUS EDUCATION OF CHILDREN, ISLAMIC
BM103	RELIGIOUS EDUCATION OF CHILDREN, JEWISH
BP44-48	*RELIGIOUS EDUCATION OF CHILDREN, MUSLIM* **SEE** RELIGIOUS EDUCATION OF CHILDREN, ISLAMIC
BV1460-1615	RELIGIOUS EDUCATION
BP42-48	RELIGIOUS EDUCATION, ISLAMIC
BP42-48	*RELIGIOUS EDUCATION, MUSLIM* **SEE** RELIGIOUS EDUCATION, ISLAMIC
BV1558-1561	*RELIGIOUS EDUCATION-TEACHERS' MANUALS* **SEE** RELIGIOUS EDUCATION — TEXT-BOOKS
BJ1188	RELIGIOUS ETHICS
BV30-135	*RELIGIOUS FESTIVALS* **SEE** FASTS AND FEASTS / *christianity*
BV30-135	*RELIGIOUS FESTIVALS* **SEE** FASTS AND FEASTS / *christianity*

CE81	*RELIGIOUS FESTIVALS* **SEE** FASTS AND FEASTS / *church calendar*
CE81	*RELIGIOUS FESTIVALS* **SEE** FASTS AND FEASTS / *church calendar*
BL590	*RELIGIOUS FESTIVALS* **SEE** FASTS AND FEASTS / *comparative religion*
BL590	*RELIGIOUS FESTIVALS* **SEE** FASTS AND FEASTS / *comparative religion*
GT3930-4995	*RELIGIOUS FESTIVALS* **SEE** FASTS AND FEASTS / *manners and customs*
GT3930-4995	*RELIGIOUS FESTIVALS* **SEE** FASTS AND FEASTS / *manners and customs*
BV741	*RELIGIOUS FREEDOM* **SEE** RELIGIOUS LIBERTY
BR	*RELIGIOUS HISTORY* **SEE** CHURCH HISTORY
BT33	*RELIGIOUS INDIFFERENCE* **SEE** INDIFFERENTISM (RELIGION)
PN4888.R4	*RELIGIOUS JOURNALISM* **SEE** JOURNALISM, RELIGIOUS
BV741	RELIGIOUS LIBERTY
BV4500-4595	*RELIGIOUS LIFE (CHRISTIANITY)* **SEE** CHRISTIAN LIFE
BL1228	RELIGIOUS LIFE (HINDUISM)
BP188	RELIGIOUS LIFE (ISLAM)
BM723	*RELIGIOUS LIFE (JUDAISM)* **SEE** JEWISH WAY OF LIFE
BX4210	*RELIGIOUS LIFE* **SEE** MONASTIC AND RELIGIOUS LIFE OF WOMEN
BX2435	*RELIGIOUS LIFE* **SEE** MONASTIC AND RELIGIOUS LIFE
Z7751-7860	RELIGIOUS LITERATURE — BIBLIOGRAPHY
BR45-85	RELIGIOUS LITERATURE / *christian literature collections*
BL29	RELIGIOUS LITERATURE / *comparative literature*
BR117	RELIGIOUS LITERATURE / *history*
PN6084.R3	RELIGIOUS LITERATURE / *quotations*
PN6071.R4	RELIGIOUS LITERATURE / *selections*
ML3869	*RELIGIOUS MUSIC* **SEE** CHURCH MUSIC / *aesthetics*
ML178	*RELIGIOUS MUSIC* **SEE** CHURCH MUSIC / *history*
ML3000-3190	*RELIGIOUS MUSIC* **SEE** CHURCH MUSIC / *history*
ML3270	*RELIGIOUS MUSIC* **SEE** CHURCH MUSIC / *history*
MT88	*RELIGIOUS MUSIC* **SEE** CHURCH MUSIC / *instruction and study*
MT915	*RELIGIOUS MUSIC* **SEE** CHURCH MUSIC / *instruction and study*
MT860-865	*RELIGIOUS MUSIC* **SEE** CHURCH MUSIC / *instruction and study*
M2186-7	*RELIGIOUS MUSIC* **SEE** SYNAGOGUE MUSIC / *services*
M2114.3	*RELIGIOUS MUSIC* **SEE** SYNAGOGUE MUSIC / *songs*
M2079.5	*RELIGIOUS MUSIC* **SEE** SYNAGOGUE MUSIC / *special texts*
M2099.5	*RELIGIOUS MUSIC* **SEE** SYNAGOGUE MUSIC / *special texts*
BL610	*RELIGIOUS MYSTERIES* **SEE** MYSTERIES, RELIGIOUS / *comparative religion*
HS491	*RELIGIOUS MYSTERIES* **SEE** MYSTERIES, RELIGIOUS / *freemasonry and ancient mysteries*
CR4701-4775	*RELIGIOUS ORDERS* **SEE** MILITARY RELIGIOUS ORDERS
BX385	*RELIGIOUS ORDERS* **SEE** MONASTICISM AND RELIGIOUS ORDERS / *greek church*
BX580-583	*RELIGIOUS ORDERS* **SEE** MONASTICISM AND RELIGIOUS ORDERS / *russian church*
BL1475.M7	*RELIGIOUS ORDERS* **SEE** MONASTICISM AND RELIGIOUS ORDERS / *buddhism*
BX2410-4560	*RELIGIOUS ORDERS* **SEE** MONASTICISM AND RELIGIOUS ORDERS / *catholic church*
N7810-8185	*RELIGIOUS PAINTING* **SEE** CHRISTIAN ART AND SYMBOLISM
BV150-168	*RELIGIOUS PAINTING* **SEE** CHRISTIAN ART AND SYMBOLISM / *theology*
PN6110.R4	RELIGIOUS POETRY / *general collections*
BX2427	*RELIGIOUS PROFESSION* **SEE** PROFESSION (IN RELIGIOUS ORDERS, CONGREGATIONS, ETC.)
BL53	*RELIGIOUS PSYCHOLOGY* **SEE** PSYCHOLOGY, RELIGIOUS
BV170-199	*RELIGIOUS RITES* **SEE** RITES AND CEREMONIES / *christian*
BL600-619	*RELIGIOUS RITES* **SEE** RITES AND CEREMONIES / *comparative religion*
GT	*RELIGIOUS RITES* **SEE** RITES AND CEREMONIES / *manners and customs*
BV150-168	*RELIGIOUS SCULPTURE* **SEE** CHRISTIAN ART AND SYMBOLISM / *theology*
N7810-8185	*RELIGIOUS SCULPTURE* **SEE** CHRISTIAN ART AND SYMBOLISM
HV530	*RELIGIOUS SOCIAL WORK* **SEE** CHURCH CHARITIES
BL60	*RELIGIOUS SOCIOLOGY* **SEE** RELIGION AND SOCIOLOGY
BX2438	*RELIGIOUS SUPERIORS* **SEE** SUPERIORS, RELIGIOUS
BV656.3	*RELIGIOUS TELEVISION* **SEE** TELEVISION IN RELIGION
BL96	RELIGIOUS THOUGHT — ANCIENT PERIOD
BL700-805	RELIGIOUS THOUGHT — ANCIENT PERIOD / *classical*
BR250-275	RELIGIOUS THOUGHT — MIDDLE AGES
BL97	RELIGIOUS THOUGHT — MIDDLE AGES
BR280-1500	RELIGIOUS THOUGHT — MODERN PERIOD
BR280-430	RELIGIOUS THOUGHT — 16TH CENTURY
BR440	RELIGIOUS THOUGHT — 17TH CENTURY
BR470	RELIGIOUS THOUGHT — 18TH CENTURY
BR477	RELIGIOUS THOUGHT — 19TH CENTURY
BR479	RELIGIOUS THOUGHT — 20TH CENTURY
BL74-98	RELIGIOUS THOUGHT
BL29	RELIGIOUS THOUGHT
BR140-1500	RELIGIOUS THOUGHT / *christianity*
BV1585	*RELIGIOUS VACATION SCHOOLS* **SEE** VACATION SCHOOLS, RELIGIOUS
BX2380	*RELIGIOUS VOCATION* **SEE** VOCATION (IN RELIGIOUS ORDERS, CONGREGATIONS, ETC.)
DS150.R3-39	RELIGIOUS ZIONISM
BX2315	*RELIQUARIES* **SEE** RELICS AND RELIQUARIES / *catholic church*
BV890	*RELIQUARIES* **SEE** RELICS AND RELIQUARIES / *general christian*
BX577	*RELIQUARIES* **SEE** RELICS AND RELIQUARIES / *russian church*
TX819	*RELISHES* **SEE** COOKERY (RELISHES)
UF740-745	RELOADING-TOOL / *cartridges*
HV9051-9230	*REMAND HOMES* **SEE** REFORMATORIES
QA135	*REMEDIAL ARITHMETIC* **SEE** ARITHMETIC — REMEDIAL TEACHING
LB1050.5	*REMEDIAL READING* **SEE** READING — REMEDIAL TEACHING
BX6195-7	REMONSTRANTS
QL638.E2	REMORA (FISH)
TK6710	*REMOTE FACSIMILE DUPLICATOR* **SEE** FACSIMILE TRANSMISSION
UC600-620	REMOUNT SERVICE
SF757	*REMOVAL OF DEAD ANIMALS* **SEE** DEAD ANIMALS, REMOVAL AND DISPOSAL OF
CB359-369	RENAISSANCE / *history of civilization*
PN715-749	RENAISSANCE / *history of literature*
D127	RENAISSANCE / *medieval history*
CB359-369	*RENAISSANCE-EUROPE* **SEE** RENAISSANCE / *history of civilization*
PN715-749	*RENAISSANCE-EUROPE* **SEE** RENAISSANCE / *history of literature*
D127	*RENAISSANCE-EUROPE* **SEE** RENAISSANCE / *medieval history*
RC902-918	*RENAL DISEASES* **SEE** KIDNEYS — DISEASES
TS1981	RENDERING APPARATUS
HD9441	RENDERING INDUSTRY / *economics*
RA578.R4	RENDERING WORKS / *public health*
TS1980-1981	RENDERING WORKS / *technology*
DT429	RENDILI
QP601	RENNET
HB401	RENT (ECONOMIC THEORY)
HB401	*RENT CHARGE* **SEE** RENT / *economic theory*
HJ4631	*RENT CHARGE* **SEE** RENT / *taxation*
HB401	RENT / *economic theory*
HJ4631	RENT / *taxation*
Z675.R4	*RENTAL LIBRARIES* **SEE** LIBRARIES, RENTAL
JX1987	RENUNCIATION OF WAR TREATY, PARIS, AUG. 27 1928
JX6650.R5	RENVOI
TT151	REPAIRING
HV8688-8691	REPARATION
D648-9	*REPARATIONS (EUROPEAN WAR, 1914-1918)* **SEE** EUROPEAN WAR, 1914-1918 — REPARATIONS
D818-819	*REPARATIONS (WORLD WAR, 1939-1945)* **SEE** WORLD WAR, 1939-1945 — REPARATIONS
JX4231	REPATRIATION

BT800	REPENTANCE
LB2846	*REPORT CARDS* **SEE** PERSONNEL RECORDS IN EDUCATION
LB2846	*REPORT WRITING* **SEE** SCHOOL REPORTS
JK1128	REPORTERS AND REPORTING / *congressional*
PN4781	REPORTERS AND REPORTING / *journalism*
HC1-8	*REPORTS, CONSULAR* **SEE** CONSULAR REPORTS
LB2846	*REPORTS, SCHOOL* **SEE** SCHOOL REPORTS
NK6530	REPOUSSE WORK
JK-JQ	*REPRESENTATION* **SEE** REPRESENTATIVE GOVERNMENT AND REPRESENTATION / *local*
JF1051-1075	*REPRESENTATION* **SEE** REPRESENTATIVE GOVERNMENT AND REPRESENTATION
JF1057-9	*REPRESENTATION, FUNCTIONAL* **SEE** FUNCTIONAL REPRESENTATION
JF1071-5	*REPRESENTATION, PROPORTIONAL* **SEE** PROPORTIONAL REPRESENTATION
JF1051-1075	REPRESENTATIVE GOVERNMENT AND REPRESENTATION
JK-JQ	REPRESENTATIVE GOVERNMENT AND REPRESENTATION / *local*
JX4486	REPRISALS
BF365	REPRODUCTION (PSYCHOLOGY)
BF365	*REPRODUCTION OF IDEAS* **SEE** REPRODUCTION (PSYCHOLOGY)
QH471-489	REPRODUCTION
QP251-281	REPRODUCTION / *animals*
QH475-9	REPRODUCTION, ASEXUAL
QL876-881	*REPRODUCTIVE ORGANS* **SEE** GENERATIVE ORGANS / *comparative anatomy*
QM416-421	*REPRODUCTIVE ORGANS* **SEE** GENERATIVE ORGANS / *human anatomy*
QP251-281	*REPRODUCTIVE ORGANS* **SEE** GENERATIVE ORGANS / *physiology*
QL669	REPTILES — ANATOMY
QL645	REPTILES — CLASSIFICATION
QL666	REPTILES — COLLECTION AND PRESERVATION
QL666	REPTILES — EGGS
QL643	REPTILES — PICTORIAL WORKS
QL641-669	REPTILES
GR740	REPTILES / *folk-lore*
QE861-2	REPTILES, FOSSIL
QL699	*REPTILES-COLOR* **SEE** COLOR OF REPTILES
CE77	*REPUBLICAN CALENDAR* **SEE** CALENDAR, REPUBLICAN
JK2351-9	REPUBLICAN PARTY / *u.s.*
JC421-458	REPUBLICS / *theory*
HJ8064	REPUDIATION
M2010	REQUIEMS — SCORES
M2013	REQUIEMS — VOCAL SCORES WITH ORGAN
M2013	REQUIEMS — VOCAL SCORES WITH PIANO
M2011	REQUIEMS — VOCAL SCORES
M2013	REQUIEMS (EQUAL VOICES) — VOCAL SCORES WITH ORGAN
M2013.5	REQUIEMS (UNISON) — VOCAL SCORES WITH ORGAN
M2013	REQUIEMS (WOMEN'S VOICES) — VOCAL SCORES WITH ORGAN
M2011	*REQUIEMS - VOCAL SCORES -- EXCERPTS* **SEE** REQUIEMS — EXCERPTS — — VOCAL SCORES
M2014	*REQUIEMS - VOCAL SCORES WITH PIANO -- EXCERPTS* **SEE** REQUIEMS — EXCERPTS — — VOCAL SCORES WITH PIANO
M2010-2011	REQUIEMS
M2013-2014	REQUIEMS
M2014	*REQUIEMS-VOCAL SCORES WITH PIANO-EXCERPTS* **SEE** REQUIEMS — EXCERPTS — — VOCAL SCORES WITH PIANO
M2011	*REQUIEMS-VOCAL SCORES-EXCERPTS* **SEE** REQUIEMS — EXCERPTS — — VOCAL SCORES
M2014	REQUIEMS — EXCERPTS — — VOCAL SCORES WITH PIANO
M2011	REQUIEMS — EXCERPTS — — VOCAL SCORES
M33	REQUIEMS — TO 1800 — — PIANO SCORES
M2014	REQUIEMS — TO 1800 — — EXCERPTS — — — VOCAL SCORES WITH PIANO
JX5231-2	*REQUISITIONS (OF NEUTRAL VESSELS AND CARGOES)* **SEE** CONTRABAND OF WAR
JX5245-5266	*REQUISITIONS (OF NEUTRAL VESSELS AND CARGOES)* **SEE** PRIZE LAW
JX5321	REQUISITIONS, MILITARY / *international law*
UC15	REQUISITIONS, MILITARY / *military science*
E476.7	RESACA, BATTLE OF, 1864
HF5417	*RESALE PRICE FIXING* **SEE** PRICE MAINTENANCE
BX1939.R5	RESCRIPTS, PAPAL / *canon law*
SB201.B8	*RESCUE-GRASS* **SEE** BROME-GRASS / *culture*
Q180	RESEARCH — PSYCHOLOGICAL ASPECTS
Q183	*RESEARCH BUILDINGS* **SEE** LABORATORIES
Q183	*RESEARCH BUILDINGS* **SEE** LABORATORIES
Q180	RESEARCH / *science*
T65	RESEARCH / *technology*
Q181	*RESEARCH, ENDOWMENT OF* **SEE** ENDOWMENT OF RESEARCH
LB2336-7	*RESEARCH, ENDOWMENT OF* **SEE** ENDOWMENT OF RESEARCH
T175.5	RESEARCH, INDUSTRIAL — MANAGEMENT
HD20	RESEARCH, INDUSTRIAL / *economics*
T175-8	RESEARCH, INDUSTRIAL / *technology*
U390-395	*RESEARCH, MILITARY* **SEE** MILITARY RESEARCH
ML	*RESEARCH, MUSICAL* **SEE** MUSICOLOGY
BF76.5	*RESEARCH, PSYCHOLOGICAL* **SEE** PSYCHOLOGICAL RESEARCH
RD553	*RESECTIONS* **SEE** EXCISION (SURGERY)
BD236	RESEMBLANCE (PHILOSOPHY)
QH546	*RESEMBLANCE, PROTECTIVE* **SEE** MIMICRY (BIOLOGY)
E78	*RESERVATIONS, INDIAN* **SEE** INDIANS OF NORTH AMERICA — RESERVATIONS
E91-93	*RESERVATIONS, INDIAN* **SEE** INDIANS OF NORTH AMERICA — RESERVATIONS
E99	*RESERVATIONS, INDIAN* **SEE** INDIANS OF NORTH AMERICA — RESERVATIONS
UB390-395	*RESERVATIONS, MILITARY* **SEE** MILITARY RESERVATIONS
UA42	*RESERVE FORCES (U.S.)* **SEE** UNITED STATES — ARMED FORCES — — RESERVES
BX1939.A	*RESERVED CASES (CANON LAW)* **SEE** ABSOLUTION (CANON LAW)
VA	*RESERVES, NAVAL* **SEE** NAVAL RESERVES
TD395	RESERVOIRS
TC167	RESERVOIRS / *hydrostatics*
JX4241	*RESIDENCE (LAW)* **SEE** DOMICILE / *international law*
LB3227	*RESIDENCE HALLS* **SEE** DORMITORIES
NA7100-7786	*RESIDENCES* **SEE** ARCHITECTURE, DOMESTIC
NA7100-7566	*RESIDENCES* **SEE** DWELLINGS / *architecture*
TH148	*RESIDENCES* **SEE** DWELLINGS / *building popular works*
TH8901	*RESIDENCES* **SEE** DWELLINGS / *building maintenance*
TX301-339	*RESIDENCES* **SEE** DWELLINGS / *domestic economy*
HD1341	*RESIDENCES* **SEE** DWELLINGS / *economics*
GR490	*RESIDENCES* **SEE** DWELLINGS / *folk-lore*
GT170-384	*RESIDENCES* **SEE** DWELLINGS / *manners and customs*
NA7100-7573	*RESIDENCES* **SEE** SUBURBAN HOMES / *architecture*
RA972	*RESIDENT PHYSICIANS* **SEE** HOSPITALS — STAFF
GA109.8	*RESIDUALS, MAPS OF* **SEE** MAPS, STATISTICAL
QA242-4	*RESIDUES* **SEE** CONGRUENCES AND RESIDUES
BV4647.R4	RESIGNATION
TP977-8	*RESINS* **SEE** GUMS AND RESINS / *chemical technology*
QD419	*RESINS* **SEE** GUMS AND RESINS / *chemistry*
SB289-291	*RESINS* **SEE** GUMS AND RESINS / *culture*
TP977-8	*RESINS, SYNTHETIC* **SEE** GUMS AND RESINS, SYNTHETIC
TP986	*RESINS, SYNTHETIC* **SEE** GUMS AND RESINS, SYNTHETIC / *plastics*
DD256.3	*RESISTANCE MOVEMENTS (WORLD WAR, 1939-1945)* **SEE** ANTI-NAZI MOVEMENT
TA405	*RESISTANCE OF MATERIALS* **SEE** STRENGTH OF MATERIALS
TA410-417	*RESISTANCE OF MATERIALS* **SEE** STRENGTH OF MATERIALS / *testing*
VM751	*RESISTANCE OF SHIPS* **SEE** SHIP RESISTANCE
JC328	*RESISTANCE TO GOVERNMENT* **SEE** GOVERNMENT, RESISTANCE TO
TK4660	*RESISTANCE WELDING* **SEE** ELECTRIC WELDING
QC638	RESISTANCE-COILS
QC611	*RESISTANCE, ELECTRIC* **SEE** ELECTRIC RESISTANCE

QC241	RESONANCE
QC241	RESONATORS
QC655	*RESONATORS, ELECTRIC* **SEE** ELECTRIC RESONATORS / *electric waves*
TK6565.R43	*RESONATORS, ELECTRIC* **SEE** ELECTRIC RESONATORS / *radio*
QD441	*RESORCINOLPHTHALEIN* **SEE** FLUORESCEIN / *chemistry*
SK601	*RESORTS* **SEE** DUDE RANCHES
RA791-954	*RESORTS* **SEE** HEALTH RESORTS, WATERING-PLACES, ETC.
RA791-954	*RESORTS* **SEE** WINTER RESORTS
NA2800	*RESOUNDING VASES* **SEE** VASES, ACOUSTIC
BJ1533.R4	RESPECT
QP171	RESPIRATION CALORIMETER
QK891	*RESPIRATION OF PLANTS* **SEE** PLANTS — RESPIRATION
QP121	RESPIRATION
RC87	*RESPIRATION, ARTIFICIAL* **SEE** ARTIFICIAL RESPIRATION
HD7275	RESPIRATORS
RC732	*RESPIRATORY OBSTRUCTIONS* **SEE** RESPIRATORY ORGANS — OBSTRUCTIONS
RC705-779	RESPIRATORY ORGANS — DISEASES
RD137	RESPIRATORY ORGANS — FOREIGN BODIES
RC732	RESPIRATORY ORGANS — OBSTRUCTIONS
RD536-9	RESPIRATORY ORGANS — SURGERY
QL845-855	RESPIRATORY ORGANS / *comparative anatomy*
QM251-261	RESPIRATORY ORGANS / *human anatomy*
QP121	RESPIRATORY ORGANS / *physiology*
RX321-6	RESPIRATORY ORGANS — DISEASES — — HOMEOPATHIC TREATMENT
RF365	*RESPIRATORY SCLEROMA* **SEE** RHINOSCLEROMA
QP121	RESPIROMETER
DT62.T6	*RESPONDENTS (EGYPTIAN FUNERARY STATUETTES)* **SEE** USHABTI
JF1621	*RESPONSIBILITY, ADMINISTRATIVE* **SEE** ADMINISTRATIVE RESPONSIBILITY
JF341	*RESPONSIBILITY, MINISTERIAL* **SEE** MINISTERIAL RESPONSIBILITY
BV199.R5	RESPONSIVE WORSHIP
HD5112	REST PERIODS / *labor*
K	REST PERIODS / *law*
BJ1499.R4	REST / *ethics*
RA776	REST / *hygiene*
HD5112-5114	REST / *labor*
RA790	REST / *mental hygiene*
QP301	REST / *physiology*
RM736	REST / *rest cure*
BJ2041	*RESTAURANT ETIQUETTE* **SEE** TABLE ETIQUETTE
HF5686.H75	RESTAURANTS, LUNCH ROOMS, ETC. — ACCOUNTING
NA7855	RESTAURANTS, LUNCH ROOMS, ETC. — DESIGNS AND PLANS
TX945	RESTAURANTS, LUNCH ROOMS, ETC.
BX1939.R52	RESTITUTIO IN INTEGRUM (CANON LAW)
D267.E3	*RESTITUTION, EDICT OF* **SEE** EDICT OF RESTITUTION, 1629
RC88	*RESTORATION FROM DROWNING* **SEE** DROWNING, RESTORATION FROM
N8560	*RESTORATION OF ART OBJECTS* **SEE** ART OBJECTS — CONSERVATION AND RESTORATION
Z700-701	*RESTORATION OF BOOKS* **SEE** BOOKS — CONSERVATION AND RESTORATION
NE380	*RESTORATION OF ENGRAVINGS* **SEE** ENGRAVINGS — CONSERVATION AND RESTORATION
ND1640-1650	*RESTORATION OF PAINTINGS* **SEE** PAINTINGS — CONSERVATION AND RESTORATION
TR465	*RESTORATION OF PHOTOGRAPHS* **SEE** PHOTOGRAPHS — CONSERVATION AND RESTORATION
NE380	*RESTORATION OF PRINTS* **SEE** PRINTS — CONSERVATION AND RESTORATION
NB1199	*RESTORATION OF SCULPTURE* **SEE** SCULPTURE — CONSERVATION AND RESTORATION
ND1640-1650	*RESTORATION OF WATER-COLORS* **SEE** PAINTINGS — CONSERVATION AND RESTORATION
BX9901-9996	RESTORATIONISM / *universalism*
HV4701-4959	*RESTRAINT OF ANIMALS* **SEE** ANIMALS, TREATMENT OF
QA191	*RESULTANTS* **SEE** DETERMINANTS
QA192	*RESULTANTS* **SEE** ELIMINATION

N8050	RESURRECTION — ART
BP166.83	RESURRECTION (ISLAM)
BT480-490	*RESURRECTION OF CHRIST* **SEE** JESUS CHRIST — RESURRECTION
BL503	RESURRECTION / *comparative religion*
BT870-871	RESURRECTION / *theology*
BX4040.R4	RESURRECTIONISTS (RELIGIOUS ORDER)
RC87	RESUSCITATION
HF5801-6191	*RETAIL ADVERTISING* **SEE** ADVERTISING
HJ5711-5721	*RETAIL SALES TAX* **SEE** SALES TAX
HF5429	RETAIL TRADE
HC	*RETAIL TRADING AREAS* **SEE** MARKET SURVEYS / *surveys*
HF5415	*RETAIL TRADING AREAS* **SEE** MARKET SURVEYS / *technique*
TA760-770	RETAINING WALLS
TG325	RETAINING WALLS / *bridges*
HJ6603-7380	*RETALIATION (ECONOMICS)* **SEE** TARIFF / *administration*
HF1761-2580	*RETALIATION (ECONOMICS)* **SEE** TARIFF / *other countries*
HJ6041-6464	*RETALIATION (ECONOMICS)* **SEE** TARIFF / *schedules*
HF1701-2701	*RETALIATION (ECONOMICS)* **SEE** TARIFF / *theory and history*
HF1750-1759	*RETALIATION (ECONOMICS)* **SEE** TARIFF / *u.s.*
QC973	*RETARDATION ES (IONOSPHERE)* **SEE** SPORADIC E (IONOSPHERE)
QC879	*RETARDATION ES (IONOSPHERE)* **SEE** SPORADIC E (IONOSPHERE) / *exploration*
LC4661-4700	*RETARDED CHILDREN* **SEE** SLOW LEARNING CHILDREN
LB1063	*RETENTION (PSYCHOLOGY)* **SEE** MEMORY / *educational*
BF370-385	*RETENTION (PSYCHOLOGY)* **SEE** MEMORY / *psychology*
RE551-661	RETINA — DISEASES
QL949	RETINA / *comparative anatomy*
QM511	RETINA / *human anatomy*
QP479	RETINA / *physiology*
TP684.R7	*RETINOL* **SEE** ROSIN-OIL
RE965	*RETINOSCOPY* **SEE** SKIASCOPY
JF1671	*RETIREMENT PENSIONS* **SEE** CIVIL SERVICE PENSIONS
JK791	*RETIREMENT PENSIONS* **SEE** CIVIL SERVICE PENSIONS / *u.s.*
HG9426-9446	*RETIREMENT PENSIONS* **SEE** OLD AGE PENSIONS / *age insurance*
HD7105-6	*RETIREMENT PENSIONS* **SEE** OLD AGE PENSIONS / *working-men's insurance*
TR310	*RETOUCHING (PHOTOGRAPHY)* **SEE** PHOTOGRAPHY — RETOUCHING
BX1912.5	RETREATS FOR CLERGY
BX2385	RETREATS FOR MEMBERS OF RELIGIOUS ORDERS
BX2435	RETREATS FOR MEMBERS OF RELIGIOUS ORDERS / *men*
BX4214	RETREATS FOR MEMBERS OF RELIGIOUS ORDERS / *women*
BX1912.5	*RETREATS FOR PRIESTS* **SEE** RETREATS FOR CLERGY
BV5068	RETREATS
BX2375	RETREATS / *catholic church*
BL535-547	*RETRIBUTION* **SEE** FUTURE LIFE / *comparative religion*
BT899-904	*RETRIBUTION* **SEE** FUTURE LIFE / *theology*
BT834-8	*RETRIBUTION* **SEE** FUTURE PUNISHMENT
BL1475.H5	*RETRIBUTION* **SEE** HELL / *buddhism*
BL735	*RETRIBUTION* **SEE** HELL / *classical mythology*
BL545	*RETRIBUTION* **SEE** HELL / *comparative religion*
BT834-8	*RETRIBUTION* **SEE** HELL / *theology*
BT840-841	*RETRIBUTION* **SEE** PURGATORY
BT940	*RETRIBUTION* **SEE** REWARD (THEOLOGY)
SF429.R4	RETRIEVERS
BP166.6	REVELATION (ISLAM)
BX8643.R4	REVELATION (MORMONISM)
BS646	REVELATION / *biblical*
BV5091.R4	REVELATION / *mysticism*
BT127	REVELATION / *theology*
BV5091.R4	*REVELATIONS, MODERN* **SEE** PRIVATE REVELATIONS
BV5091.R4	*REVELATIONS, PRIVATE* **SEE** PRIVATE REVELATIONS
BV4627.R4	REVENGE / *theology*

HJ3247	*REVENUE FARMING* **SEE** TAXES, FARMING OF
HJ3251	*REVENUE LAW* **SEE** INTERNAL REVENUE LAW / *u.s.*
HJ3231-3698	*REVENUE LAW* **SEE** TAXATION — LAW
HJ5315	REVENUE-STAMPS — COLLECTORS AND COLLECTING
HJ5315	REVENUE-STAMPS
HJ5321-5515	REVENUE-STAMPS / *by country*
HJ2240-7395	REVENUE
HJ9115-9123	REVENUE / *local*
HJ5001-5231	*REVENUE, INTERNAL* **SEE** INTERNAL REVENUE
TR880	REVERE MOVING-PICTURE CAMERA
GV1469.R5	REVERSI (GAME)
HF5681.R6	REVERSION — ACCOUNTING
JF711	*REVIEW, JUDICIAL* **SEE** JUDICIAL REVIEW
JK1541	*REVIEW, JUDICIAL* **SEE** JUDICIAL REVIEW / *u.s.*
PN98.B7	*REVIEWING (BOOKS)* **SEE** BOOK REVIEWING
PN4784.R4	*REVIEWS* **SEE** NEWSPAPERS — SECTIONS, COLUMNS, ETC. — — REVIEWS
JX4171.R45	*REVISION OF TREATIES* **SEE** TREATIES — REVISION
BV3750-3799	*REVIVAL (RELIGION)* **SEE** EVANGELISTIC WORK
BV3750-3797	*REVIVAL (RELIGION)* **SEE** REVIVALS
BV460	*REVIVAL HYMNS* **SEE** REVIVALS — HYMNS
CB359-369	*REVIVAL OF LETTERS* **SEE** RENAISSANCE / *history of civilization*
PN715-749	*REVIVAL OF LETTERS* **SEE** RENAISSANCE / *history of literature*
D127	*REVIVAL OF LETTERS* **SEE** RENAISSANCE / *medieval history*
BV3797	*REVIVAL SERMONS* **SEE** EVANGELISTIC SERMONS
BR758	*REVIVAL, EVANGELICAL* **SEE** EVANGELICAL REVIVAL / *gt. brit.*
BV3780-3785	*REVIVALISTS* **SEE** EVANGELISTS
BV460	REVIVALS — HYMNS
BV3750-3797	REVIVALS
E201-298	*REVOLUTION, AMERICAN* **SEE** UNITED STATES — HISTORY — — REVOLUTION
DC139-195	*REVOLUTION, FRENCH* **SEE** FRANCE — HISTORY — — REVOLUTION
HM281-3	REVOLUTIONS / *psychology of*
JC491	REVOLUTIONS / *theory*
GV1175	*REVOLVER SHOOTING* **SEE** PISTOL SHOOTING
UD410-415	REVOLVERS / *army*
TS537	REVOLVERS / *manufacture*
VD390	REVOLVERS / *navy*
UF620	*REVOLVING CANNON* **SEE** MACHINE-GUNS
VF410	*REVOLVING CANNON* **SEE** MACHINE-GUNS / *naval*
V860	*REVOLVING CUPOLAS (WARSHIPS)* **SEE** TURRET SHIPS
VF440	*REVOLVING CUPOLAS* **SEE** WARSHIPS — TURRETS
VG90-95	*REVOLVING TURRETS* **SEE** AEROPLANES, MILITARY — TURRETS / *navy*
UG630-635	*REVOLVING TURRETS* **SEE** AEROPLANES, MILITARY — TURRETS / *general and army*
VF440	*REVOLVING TURRETS* **SEE** WARSHIPS — TURRETS
BT940	REWARD (THEOLOGY)
LB3025	REWARDS AND PUNISHMENTS IN EDUCATION
DC303.2	*REZONVILLE, BATTLE OF, AUG. 16, 1870* **SEE** VIONVILLE, BATTLE OF, 1870
DC303.4	*REZONVILLE, BATTLE OF, AUG. 18, 1870* **SEE** GRAVELOTTE, BATTLE OF, 1870
PC901-949	*RHAETO-ROMANIC LANGUAGE* **SEE** RAETO-ROMANCE LANGUAGE
RS165.R3	*RHATANY* **SEE** RATANY / *pharmacy*
RM666.R3	*RHATANY* **SEE** RATANY / *therapeutics*
QD181.R4	RHENIUM
QH505	RHEOLOGY (BIOLOGY)
QC189	RHEOLOGY
TK2851	*RHEOSTATS, ELECTRIC* **SEE** ELECTRIC RHEOSTATS
QP301	RHEOTAXIS / *animals*
QH511	RHEOTAXIS / *biology*
QK776	RHEOTAXIS / *plants*
PN173	RHETORIC — 1500-1800
PE1407	RHETORIC — 1500-1800 / *english*
PE1402	RHETORIC — 1500-1800 / *english*
PN173-9	RHETORIC AND PSYCHOLOGY
PN173-229	RHETORIC
PE1402-1497	RHETORIC / *english*
PA3265	RHETORIC, ANCIENT
PN185	RHETORIC, MEDIEVAL
RC182.R4	RHEUMATIC FEVER
RC933	*RHEUMATIC GOUT* **SEE** ARTHRITIS DEFORMANS

RX261.R4	RHEUMATISM — HOMEOPATHIC TREATMENT
RC927-927.5	RHEUMATISM
RC933	*RHEUMATOID ARTHRITIS* **SEE** ARTHRITIS DEFORMANS
DD155	RHINE CITIES, LEAGUE OF, 1254
DD155	*RHINE LEAGUE* **SEE** RHINE CITIES, LEAGUE OF, 1254
DD199	RHINE, CONFEDERATION OF THE, 1806-1813
SB945.R	RHINOCEROS BEETLE
QL737.U6	RHINOCEROS
QE882.U6	RHINOCEROS / *fossil*
QP458	*RHINOLOGY* **SEE** NOSE / *physiology*
QL737.C5	*RHINOLOPHUS* **SEE** BATS
RF365	RHINOSCLEROMA
QL430.4	RHIPIDOGLOSSA
QK581	RHIZOIDS
QK551	RHIZOIDS
QK535	RHIZOIDS
QK565	RHIZOIDS
QK521	RHIZOIDS
QL368.R4	RHIZOPODA
QD181.C15	*RHODANATES* **SEE** THIOCYANATES
QP913.C15	*RHODANATES* **SEE** THIOCYANATES / *physiology*
QD181.C15	*RHODANIC ACID* **SEE** THIOCYANIC ACID
QP13.C15	*RHODANIC ACID* **SEE** THIOCYANIC ACID / *physiology*
QD181.C15	*RHODANIDES* **SEE** THIOCYANATES
QP913.C15	*RHODANIDES* **SEE** THIOCYANATES / *physiology*
F76-90	RHODE ISLAND — HISTORY
E263.R4	RHODE ISLAND INDEPENDENCE DAY
SF489.R6	RHODE ISLAND REDS
E241.R4	RHODE ISLAND, BATTLE OF, 1778
E528	RHODE ISLAND — HISTORY — — CIVIL WAR
E199	RHODE ISLAND — HISTORY — — FRENCH AND INDIAN WAR, 1755-1763
E198	RHODE ISLAND — HISTORY — — KING GEORGE'S WAR, 1744-1748
E263.R4	RHODE ISLAND — HISTORY — — REVOLUTION
E726.R4	RHODE ISLAND — HISTORY — — WAR OF 1898
DR507	RHODES — SIEGE, 1522
QD181.R5	RHODIUM
SB945.R	RHODODENDRON WHITEFLY
QK495.R47	RHODODENDRON / *botany*
SB413.R47	RHODODENDRON / *plant culture*
QK569.R4	RHODOPHYCEAE
QL949	*RHODOPSIN* **SEE** VISUAL PURPLE
QM511	*RHODOPSIN* **SEE** VISUAL PURPLE
QP479	*RHODOPSIN* **SEE** VISUAL PURPLE / *retinal pigments*
TN948.C95	*RHOETZITE* **SEE** CYANITE
QL541-562	*RHOPALOCERA* **SEE** BUTTERFLIES
SB345	RHUBARB / *culture*
RM666.R5	RHUBARB / *therapeutics*
GV1796.R8	*RHUMBA (DANCE)* **SEE** RUMBA (DANCE)
QL666.R4	RHYNCHOCEPHALIA
QL521-4	*RHYNCHOTA* **SEE** HEMIPTERA
QE461	RHYOLITE
N76	*RHYTHM (ART)* **SEE** PROPORTION (ART)
NC745	*RHYTHM (ART)* **SEE** PROPORTION (ART) / *design*
GV1595	RHYTHM / *dancing*
GV463	RHYTHM / *physical training*
QP465	RHYTHM / *physiology*
QP301	RHYTHM / *physiology*
BF475	RHYTHM / *psychology*
M1993	*RHYTHMIC GAMES* **SEE** GAMES WITH MUSIC
F2687	RIACHUELO, BATTLE OF, 1865
SB945.R	RIBBED-COCOON MAKER / *insect pests*
QL561.T7	RIBBED-COCOON-MAKER / *zoology*
TF262	*RIBBONRAILS* **SEE** RAILROADS — CONTINUOUS RAILS
QP801.V5	RIBOFLAVIN
GN70	RIBS / *anthropology*
QL821	RIBS / *comparative anatomy*
QM113	RIBS / *human anatomy*
QR119	RICE — BACTERIOLOGY
SB608.R5	RICE — DISEASES AND PESTS
TP579	RICE BEER
SB191.R5	RICE BREEDING
SB608.R5	RICE BUG
SB608.R5	RICE MOTH
SB191.R5	RICE RESEARCH
TP579	*RICE-WINE* **SEE** SAKE
SB191.R5	RICE / *culture*
HD9066	RICE / *trade*

SB191.I5	RICE, WILD SEE INDIAN RICE / culture
E98.F7	RICE, WILD SEE INDIAN RICE / indian food
SB191.R5	RICE-RESEARCH SEE RICE RESEARCH
MT59	RICERCARE SEE FUGUE
ML448	RICERCARE SEE FUGUE
BT378.D5	RICH MAN AND LAZARUS (PARABLE) SEE DIVES AND LAZARUS (PARABLE)
HB821	RICHES SEE WEALTH / distribution
HB251	RICHES SEE WEALTH / theory
HB831-8	RICHES SEE WEALTH / use
E470.2	RICHMOND — SIEGE, 1864-1865
E476.27	RICHMOND-RAID, 1864 SEE KILPATRICK-DAHLGREN RAID, 1864
E473.6	RICHMOND-SIEGE, 1862 SEE PENINSULAR CAMPAIGN, 1862
QD431	RICIN / chemistry
QR185	RICIN / immunity
RJ396	RICKETS
DR504	RIDANIA, BATTLE OF, 1517
PN6366-6377	RIDDLES
GR975	RIDDLES / folk literature
PN6366-6377	RIDDLES, ENGLISH SEE RIDDLES
GR975	RIDDLES, ENGLISH SEE RIDDLES / folk literature
F1032	RIDGEWAY, ONT., BATTLE OF, 1866
VF440	RIDGWAY'S REVOLVING BATTERY
BJ1499.R	RIDICULE
BH301.C7	RIDICULOUS, THE SEE COMIC, THE
PN6147-6231	RIDICULOUS, THE SEE WIT AND HUMOR
SF305-7	RIDING SEE COACHING
SF305	RIDING SEE DRIVING
SF309	RIDING SEE HORSEMANSHIP
UE470-475	RIDING SEE HORSEMANSHIP / cavalry
F1063	RIEL REBELLION, 1869-1870 SEE RED RIVER REBELLION, 1869-1870
F1060.9	RIEL REBELLION, 1885
QA689	RIEMANN SPACE SEE SPACES, GENERALIZED
QA333	RIEMANN SURFACES
PJ2377	RIF LANGUAGE
DT328.R5	RIF REVOLT, 1921-1926
UF765	RIFLE GRENADES SEE GRENADES
GV1177	RIFLE PRACTICE
U300-305	RIFLE-RANGES / artillery and rifle-ranges
UD330-335	RIFLE-RANGES / infantry firing
UD390-395	RIFLES / army
SK274	RIFLES / hunting
VD370	RIFLES / navy
DK440.3	RIGA, TREATY OF, 1921
M245-7	RIGAUDONS (OBOE AND PIANO)
M221-3	RIGAUDONS (VIOLIN AND PIANO)
M217-218	RIGAUDONS (VIOLIN AND PIANO)
VM531	RIGGING SEE MASTS AND RIGGING
BJ1410-1418	RIGHT AND WRONG
JC607	RIGHT OF ASSEMBLY SEE ASSEMBLY, RIGHT OF
JK-JQ	RIGHT OF ASSOCIATION SEE FREEDOM OF ASSOCIATION
JC607	RIGHT OF ASSOCIATION SEE FREEDOM OF ASSOCIATION
HV8652-4	RIGHT OF ASYLUM SEE ASYLUM, RIGHT OF
JX4275-4399	RIGHT OF ASYLUM SEE ASYLUM, RIGHT OF
BX1805	RIGHT OF EXCLUSION SEE EXCLUSION, RIGHT OF
JC609	RIGHT OF PETITION SEE PETITION, RIGHT OF
JL-JQ	RIGHT OF PETITION SEE PETITION, RIGHT OF / other countries
JK1731	RIGHT OF PETITION SEE PETITION, RIGHT OF / u.s.
JX5268	RIGHT OF SEARCH SEE SEARCH, RIGHT OF / international law
HD6488	RIGHT TO LABOR (UNION MEMBERSHIP) SEE OPEN AND CLOSED SHOP
HD4903	RIGHT TO LABOR
HD4903	RIGHT TO WORK SEE RIGHT TO LABOR
HD6488	RIGHT TO WORK AND TRADE-UNIONS SEE OPEN AND CLOSED SHOP
GN233	RIGHT- AND LEFT-HANDEDNESS SEE LEFT- AND RIGHT-HANDEDNESS / anthropology
QP385	RIGHT- AND LEFT-HANDEDNESS SEE LEFT- AND RIGHT-HANDEDNESS / physiological psychology
M26	RIGHT-HAND PIANO MUSIC SEE PIANO MUSIC (1 HAND)
M26.2	RIGHT-HAND PIANO MUSIC SEE PIANO MUSIC (1 HAND)

HQ1456-1870	RIGHTS OF WOMEN SEE WOMAN — RIGHTS OF WOMEN / other countries
HQ1423-6	RIGHTS OF WOMEN SEE WOMAN — RIGHTS OF WOMEN / u.s.
JC571-609	RIGHTS, NATURAL SEE NATURAL LAW
QA861-3	RIGID DYNAMICS SEE DYNAMICS, RIGID
QP321	RIGOR MORTIS
QP87	RIGOR MORTIS
TN871.5	RIGS, OIL WELL DRILLING SEE OIL WELL DRILLING RIGS
SF966	RINDERPEST
GV1099	RING HOCKEY
GV1095	RING QUOITS
GV1097	RING-TOSS
GT2270	RINGS — INSCRIPTIONS
QA247	RINGS (ALGEBRA)
GV539	RINGS (GYMNASTICS)
NK7440-7459	RINGS / art
GT2270	RINGS / costume
TS720-770	RINGS / manufacture
RL780	RINGWORM / dermatology
GV852	RINKS SEE SKATING RINKS
D772.G7	RIO DE LA PLATA, BATTLE OF THE, 1939
DC397	RIOM TRIAL, 1942
HV6474-6485	RIOTS
U230	RIOTS / military science
HM281-3	RIOTS / psychology of
HD1691-8	RIPARIAN RIGHTS
SB354-399	RIPENING OF FRUIT SEE FRUIT — RIPENING
GB454.R5	RIPPLE-MARKS
PR8810	RISH DIARIES (ENGLISH) SEE ENGLISH DIARIES — IRISH AUTHORS / history
PR8880	RISH DIARIES (ENGLISH) SEE ENGLISH DIARIES — IRISH AUTHORS / collections
HB615	RISK
HG8055	RISKS (INSURANCE) SEE INSURANCE — WAR RISKS
HG9731.A-Z	RISKS (INSURANCE) SEE INSURANCE, FIRE — RISKS
HG8811.W2	RISKS (INSURANCE) SEE INSURANCE, LIFE — WAR RISKS
HE966	RISKS (INSURANCE) SEE INSURANCE, MARINE — WAR RISKS
UB370-375	RISKS (INSURANCE) SEE INSURANCE, WAR RISK
BV170-199	RITES AND CEREMONIES / christian
BL600-619	RITES AND CEREMONIES / comparative religion
GT	RITES AND CEREMONIES / manners and customs
GN473	RITES AND CEREMONIES / primitive religion
BM700-720	RITES AND CEREMONIES-JEWS SEE JEWS — RITES AND CEREMONIES
BV170-199	RITES OF PASSAGE SEE RITES AND CEREMONIES / christian
BL600-619	RITES OF PASSAGE SEE RITES AND CEREMONIES / comparative religion
GT	RITES OF PASSAGE SEE RITES AND CEREMONIES / manners and customs
GN473	RITES OF PASSAGE SEE RITES AND CEREMONIES / primitive religion
BX1995.M18	RITES, MALABAR SEE MALABAR RITES
CR5109	RITTERKREUZ (GERMANY)
BM717	RITUAL MURDER SEE BLOOD ACCUSATION
BL600	RITUAL
BV181	RITUALISM — CONTROVERSIAL LITERATURE
BV180	RITUALISM
BX5123	RITUALISM / church of england
F1526	RIVAS, BATTLE OF, 1856
U205	RIVER CROSSING, MILITARY SEE STREAM CROSSING, MILITARY
E99.M12	RIVER INDIANS (NEW ENGLAND) SEE MAHICAN INDIANS
E99.M83	RIVER INDIANS (NEW ENGLAND) SEE MOHEGAN INDIANS
E99.S8	RIVER INDIANS (NEW ENGLAND) SEE STOCKBRIDGE INDIANS
TC530-555	RIVERS — REGULATION
QC909	RIVERS — TEMPERATURE
TC404-555	RIVERS / engineering
GR680	RIVERS / folk-lore
GB1201-1397	RIVERS / physical geography
GB1201-1397	RIVERS, FREEZING AND OPENING OF SEE ICE ON RIVERS, LAKES, ETC. T (INDIRECT) / rivers

JX4150	*RIVERS, RIGHT OF NAVIGATION OF* **SEE** INTERNATIONAL RIVERS
TD420-425	*RIVERS-POLLUTION* **SEE** WATER — POLLUTION
TA891	*RIVETING* **SEE** RIVETS AND RIVETING / *riveting*
TJ1310	*RIVETING* **SEE** RIVETS AND RIVETING / *riveting-machines*
TJ1325	*RIVETING* **SEE** RIVETS AND RIVETING / *rivets*
TA891	RIVETS AND RIVETING / *riveting*
TJ1310	RIVETS AND RIVETING / *riveting-machines*
TJ1325	RIVETS AND RIVETING / *rivets*
TL671.5	RIVETS AND RIVETING, AIRCRAFT
PM8751	RO (ARTIFICIAL LANGUAGE)
SH351.R6	ROACH (FISH) / *fisheries*
QL638.C94	ROACH (FISH) / *zoology*
HE5614	*ROAD ACCIDENTS* **SEE** TRAFFIC ACCIDENTS
HF5686.R6	ROAD CONSTRUCTION — ACCOUNTING
HD9717.5.R6	ROAD CONSTRUCTION INDUSTRY
TE175	*ROAD DESIGN* **SEE** ROADS — DESIGN
TE215	ROAD DRAINAGE
GV1024-5	*ROAD GUIDES, AUTOMOBILE* **SEE** AUTOMOBILES — ROAD GUIDES
TE315-424	*ROAD LAW* **SEE** HIGHWAY LAW
TE223	ROAD MACHINERY
TE200-205	ROAD MATERIALS
HE370	*ROAD SIGNS* **SEE** STREET SIGNS
TE170	*ROAD SURVEYING* **SEE** ROADS — SURVEYING
HE5601-5720	*ROAD TRANSPORTATION* **SEE** TRANSPORTATION, AUTOMOTIVE
TE223	*ROAD-BUILDING MACHINERY* **SEE** ROAD MACHINERY
TE223	*ROAD-MAKING MACHINERY* **SEE** ROAD MACHINERY
TE223-7	ROAD-ROLLERS
TE180	ROADS — CONTRACTS AND SPECIFICATIONS
TE175	ROADS — DESIGN
TE144	ROADS — EARLY WORKS TO 1800
TE183	ROADS — ESTIMATES AND COSTS
HE355-368	ROADS — FINANCE / *by country*
TE183	ROADS — FINANCE / *etc.*
TE153	ROADS — FROST DAMAGE
TE220	ROADS — MAINTENANCE AND REPAIR
TE170	ROADS — SURVEYING
TE151	ROADS — TABLES, CALCULATIONS, ETC.
TE	ROADS / *etc.*
HE331-368	ROADS / *transportation*
TE255	ROADS, BRICK
TE278	ROADS, CONCRETE
TE230	ROADS, EARTH
TE191	ROADS, EXPERIMENTAL
TE233	ROADS, GRAVEL
TE245	ROADS, ICE
TE243	ROADS, MACADAMIZED
UG330	*ROADS, MILITARY* **SEE** MILITARY ROADS
TE153	*ROADS, MOUNTAIN* **SEE** MOUNTAIN ROADS
TE221	ROADS, OILED
TE245	ROADS, PLANK
DG28-29	ROADS, ROMAN
TE245	ROADS, SOIL-CEMENT
TE244	ROADS, TARRED
TE315-424	*ROADS-LEGISLATION* **SEE** HIGHWAY LAW
TE153	ROADSIDE IMPROVEMENT
TE153	*ROADSIDE PLANTING* **SEE** ROADSIDE IMPROVEMENT
TE153	*ROADSIDES* **SEE** ROADSIDE IMPROVEMENT
TE228	ROADS — GUARD FENCES — — MODELS
HF5686.R6	ROADS — MAINTENANCE AND REPAIR — — ACCOUNTING
HV6441-6453	*ROBBERS* **SEE** BRIGANDS AND ROBBERS
HG9970.B8	*ROBBERY INSURANCE* **SEE** INSURANCE, BURGLARY
QL696.P2	ROBINS
QL696.P2	*ROBINS, GOLDEN* **SEE** ORIOLES
PN3432	ROBINSONADES
TJ1225	*ROBOT MILLING-MACHINES* **SEE** MILLING-MACHINES — NUMERICAL CONTROL
TL589.5	*ROBOT PILOT* **SEE** AUTOMATIC PILOT (AEROPLANES)
TJ215	*ROBOTS* **SEE** AUTOMATA
ML1055.A8	*ROBOTS* **SEE** AUTOMATA
GR830.R	ROC
HD3328	ROCHDALE SYSTEM
DD412	ROCHEFORT EXPEDITION, 1757
RS167.R	ROCHELLE SALT / *pharmacy*
RM666.R	ROCHELLE SALT / *therapeutics*
GV1796.R	ROCK AND ROLL DANCING
SH351.B3	ROCK BASS
GN799.P4	*ROCK CARVINGS* **SEE** PETROGLYPHS
NA5201-6113	*ROCK CHURCHES* **SEE** CAVE CHURCHES
NA4910	*ROCK CHURCHES* **SEE** CAVE CHURCHES
G513	ROCK CLIMBING
GN799.P4	*ROCK ENGRAVINGS* **SEE** PETROGLYPHS
SB454	ROCK GARDENS
TH1715	*ROCK WOOL* **SEE** MINERAL WOOL / *insulation*
TP636	ROCK-CANDY SYRUP
QE391.Q2	*ROCK-CRYSTAL* **SEE** QUARTZ
QD941	*ROCK-CRYSTAL* **SEE** QUARTZ / *optical properties*
TA745-7	ROCK-DRILLS
TN279-281	ROCK-DRILLS / *use in mines*
QE391.C4	*ROCK-FLINT* **SEE** CHERT
GV1796.R	*ROCK-N-ROLL DANCING* **SEE** ROCK AND ROLL DANCING
TN900-903	ROCK-SALT
NA6120-6199	*ROCK-TOMBS* **SEE** TOMBS / *architecture*
SB454	*ROCKERIES* **SEE** ROCK GARDENS
TL784.C65	ROCKET ENGINES — COOLING
TL790	*ROCKET FLIGHT* **SEE** SPACE FLIGHT
TL784.N65	*ROCKET NOZZLES* **SEE** ROCKETS (AERONAUTICS) — NOZZLES
UF767	*ROCKET ORDNANCE* **SEE** ROCKETS (ORDNANCE)
UF767	*ROCKET PROJECTILES* **SEE** ROCKETS (ORDNANCE)
TL795	*ROCKET SHIPS* **SEE** SPACE SHIPS
VK1479	*ROCKET, LIFE* **SEE** LIFE-ROCKET
TL782.7	ROCKETRY — AMATEURS' MANUALS
TL782.8	ROCKETRY AS A PROFESSION
TL784.E4	*ROCKETRY, ELECTRONICS IN* **SEE** ELECTRONICS IN ROCKETRY
TL782.8	*ROCKETRY-VOCATIONAL GUIDANCE* **SEE** ROCKETRY AS A PROFESSION
TL784.N65	ROCKETS (AERONAUTICS) — NOZZLES
TL782.55	ROCKETS (AERONAUTICS) — PICTORIAL WORKS
TL780-783	ROCKETS (AERONAUTICS)
TL784.S7	*ROCKETS (AERONAUTICS)-STABILITY* **SEE** STABILITY OF ROCKETS
UF767	ROCKETS (ORDNANCE)
TL783.5	*ROCKETS, ATOMIC POWERED* **SEE** NUCLEAR ROCKETS
TL785.8.S6	ROCKETS, SOUNDING
TC543	*ROCKFILL DAMS* **SEE** EARTH DAMS
SH351.B3	*ROCKFISH* **SEE** STRIPED BASS
QE438	ROCKS — ANALYSIS
QE434	ROCKS — ANALYSIS
QE51-55	ROCKS — CATALOGS AND COLLECTIONS
QE425	ROCKS — CLASSIFICATION AND NOMENCLATURE
QE605	ROCKS — CLEAVAGE
QE420-499	ROCKS
GR800	ROCKS / *folk-lore*
QE475	ROCKS, CRYSTALLINE AND METAMORPHIC
QE461	*ROCKS, ERUPTIVE* **SEE** ROCKS, IGNEOUS
QE511	*ROCKS, GASES IN* **SEE** GASES IN ROCKS
QE461	ROCKS, IGNEOUS
QE475	*ROCKS, METAMORPHIC* **SEE** ROCKS, CRYSTALLINE AND METAMORPHIC
QE471	ROCKS, SEDIMENTARY
QE495	ROCKS, SILICEOUS
QE508	*ROCKS-AGE* **SEE** GEOLOGICAL TIME
QE651-699	*ROCKS-AGE* **SEE** GEOLOGY, STRATIGRAPHIC
QL737.U5	ROCKY MOUNTAIN GOAT
SB945.R7	ROCKY MOUNTAIN LOCUST
RC182.R6	ROCKY MOUNTAIN SPOTTED FEVER TICK
RC182.R6	ROCKY MOUNTAIN SPOTTED FEVER
NA590	*ROCOCO ARCHITECTURE* **SEE** ARCHITECTURE, ROCOCO
N6410	*ROCOCO ART* **SEE** ART, ROCOCO
NK1355	*ROCOCO DECORATION AND ORNAMENT* **SEE** DECORATION AND ORNAMENT, ROCOCO
NB193	*ROCOCO SCULPTURE* **SEE** SCULPTURE, ROCOCO
F2230.2.08	*ROCOUYENNE INDIANS* **SEE** OYANA INDIANS
DC123.3	ROCROI, BATTLE OF, 1643
RC280.S5	RODENT ULCER
QL737.R6	RODENTIA
QE882.R6	RODENTIA, FOSSIL
GV1834	RODEOS
E271	*RODNEY'S VICTORY, APRIL 1782* **SEE** DOMINICA, BATTLE OF, 1782
QA935	*RODS* **SEE** ELASTIC RODS AND WIRES

QL737.U5	ROE-DEER
QC481	*ROENTGEN RAYS* **SEE** X-RAYS
RC78	*ROENTGEN RAYS* **SEE** X-RAYS / *medicine*
QC481	*ROENTGENOGRAMS* **SEE** X-RAYS
RC78	*ROENTGENOGRAMS* **SEE** X-RAYS / *medicine*
BV105.R7	ROGATION DAYS
JX6608	*ROGATORY LETTERS* **SEE** LETTERS ROGATORY
F97	ROGERENES
E99.T97	*ROGUE RIVER INDIANS* **SEE** TUTUTNI INDIANS
HV6245-8	ROGUES AND VAGABONDS / *criminals*
CT9980-9981	ROGUES AND VAGABONDS / *etc.*
HV4480-4630	ROGUES AND VAGABONDS / *etc.*
GT6450-6699	ROGUES AND VAGABONDS / *manners and customs*
DS473	ROHILLA WAR, 1774
PD2007.R6	ROK STONE INSCRIPTION
NB1420	ROLAND'S COLUMNS
CD5344	*ROLL SEALS* **SEE** CYLINDER SEALS
TJ1071	ROLLER BEARINGS
GV847	ROLLER POLO
GV847	ROLLER-SKATE HOCKEY
GV851	ROLLER-SKATING
Z256	ROLLERS (PRINTING)
TL574.M6	ROLLING (AERODYNAMICS)
TL574.M6	*ROLLING MOMENTS (AERODYNAMICS)* **SEE** ROLLING (AERODYNAMICS)
TS340	ROLLING-MILL MACHINERY
TS340	ROLLING-MILLS
TJ603-695	*ROLLING-STOCK* **SEE** LOCOMOTIVES
TF371-497	*ROLLING-STOCK* **SEE** RAILROADS — ROLLING-STOCK
TL215.R6	ROLLS-ROYCE AUTOMOBILE
PA1001-1179	*ROMAIC LANGUAGE* **SEE** GREEK LANGUAGE, MODERN
PA5201-5298	*ROMAIC LITERATURE* **SEE** GREEK LITERATURE, MODERN
PA5650-5665	*ROMAIC LITERATURE* **SEE** GREEK LITERATURE, MODERN
DE	*ROMAN ANTIQUITIES* **SEE** CLASSICAL ANTIQUITIES
DF	*ROMAN ANTIQUITIES* **SEE** CLASSICAL ANTIQUITIES / *greece*
DG	*ROMAN ANTIQUITIES* **SEE** CLASSICAL ANTIQUITIES / *rome*
DG28-29	*ROMAN ANTIQUITIES* **SEE** ROADS, ROMAN
NA310-340	*ROMAN ARCHITECTURE* **SEE** ARCHITECTURE, ROMAN
BX801-4715	*ROMAN CATHOLIC CHURCH* **SEE** CATHOLIC CHURCH
TP884.R7	ROMAN CEMENT
CE46	*ROMAN CHRONOLOGY* **SEE** CHRONOLOGY, ROMAN
DG83.5.C7	*ROMAN CONSULS* **SEE** CONSULS, ROMAN
DG123-4	*ROMAN CULTUS* **SEE** CULTUS, ROMAN / *history*
BL800-820	*ROMAN CULTUS* **SEE** CULTUS, ROMAN / *religion*
DG124	*ROMAN EMPEROR WORSHIP* **SEE** EMPEROR WORSHIP, ROMAN
DG270-365	ROMAN EMPERORS
DG124	ROMAN EMPERORS / *cult*
DG124	*ROMAN EMPERORS-CULTUS* **SEE** EMPEROR WORSHIP, ROMAN
PA6101-6139	*ROMAN LITERATURE* **SEE** LATIN LITERATURE / *collections*
PA6001-6098	*ROMAN LITERATURE* **SEE** LATIN LITERATURE / *history*
G86	*ROMAN MILE* **SEE** MILE, ROMAN
B108-708	*ROMAN PHILOSOPHY* **SEE** PHILOSOPHY, ANCIENT
BL815.P	*ROMAN PRIESTS* **SEE** PRIESTS, ROMAN / *religion*
DG135	*ROMAN PRIESTS* **SEE** PRIESTS, ROMAN / *roman antiquities*
DG798-9	ROMAN QUESTION
DG28-29	*ROMAN ROADS* **SEE** ROADS, ROMAN
DC63	ROMAN WALLS — FRANCE
DD53	ROMAN WALLS — GERMANY
DA145-7	ROMAN WALLS — GT. BRIT.
DA777.5-7	ROMAN WALLS — SCOTLAND
PM8753	ROMANAL (ARTIFICIAL LANGUAGE)
PC	ROMANCE LANGUAGES
PC	ROMANCE PHILOLOGY
PN669	ROMANCES — DICTIONARIES / *medieval literature*
PN688-690	ROMANCES — HISTORY AND CRITICISM
PN692-3	ROMANCES — HISTORY AND CRITICISM
PR321-347	ROMANCES / *english*
PR2064-5	ROMANCES / *english*
PQ201-221	ROMANCES / *french*
PQ1411-1545	ROMANCES / *french*

PN688-690	ROMANCES / *medieval*
PN692-3	ROMANCES / *medieval*
PR2064-5	*ROMANCES, FRENCH* **SEE** ROMANCES / *english*
PR321-347	*ROMANCES, FRENCH* **SEE** ROMANCES / *english*
PQ1411-1545	*ROMANCES, FRENCH* **SEE** ROMANCES / *french*
PQ201-221	*ROMANCES, FRENCH* **SEE** ROMANCES / *french*
PN688-690	*ROMANCES, FRENCH* **SEE** ROMANCES / *medieval*
PN692-3	*ROMANCES, FRENCH* **SEE** ROMANCES / *medieval*
NA390-419	*ROMANESQUE ARCHITECTURE* **SEE** ARCHITECTURE, ROMANESQUE
N6280	*ROMANESQUE ART* **SEE** ART, ROMANESQUE
NK1285	*ROMANESQUE DECORATION AND ORNAMENT* **SEE** DECORATION AND ORNAMENT, ROMANESQUE
NB175	*ROMANESQUE SCULPTURE* **SEE** SCULPTURE, ROMANESQUE
PC901-949	*ROMANSH LANGUAGE* **SEE** RAETO-ROMANCE LANGUAGE
N70	ROMANTICISM IN ART
ML196	ROMANTICISM IN MUSIC
PN750-769	ROMANTICISM
PN603	ROMANTICISM
DX161	*ROMANY LANGUAGE* **SEE** GIPSIES — LANGUAGE
DG61-365	ROME — HISTORY
DG803-818	ROME (CITY) — HISTORY
DG812.12	ROME (CITY) — SIEGE, 1527
DG798.5	ROME (CITY) — HISTORY — — REVOLUTION OF 1848-1849
DG812.9	ROME (CITY) — HISTORY — — REVOLUTION OF 1848-1849
E470.3	ROMNEY CAMPAIGN, 1861-1862
DP402.R6	RONCESVALLES, BATTLE OF, 778
DP402.R6	*RONCEVAUX, BATTLE OF, 778* **SEE** RONCESVALLES, BATTLE OF, 778
PN1501	RONDEAUS
ML1165	RONDO / *history*
MT62	RONDO / *instruction*
M1203	RONDOS (BAND)
M455-7	RONDOS (BASSOON, CLARINET, FLUTE, OBOE)
M458-9	RONDOS (BASSOON, CLARINET, FLUTE, OBOE), ARRANGED
M1024	RONDOS (CLARINET WITH CHAMBER ORCHESTRA) — SCORES
M1024-5	RONDOS (CLARINET WITH CHAMBER ORCHESTRA)
M240-242	RONDOS (FLUTE AND PIANO)
M1020-1021	RONDOS (FLUTE WITH ORCHESTRA)
M1020-1021	RONDOS (FLUTE WITH ORCHESTRA), ARRANGED
M1021	RONDOS (FLUTE WITH ORCHESTRA), ARRANGED — TO 1800 — — SOLO WITH PIANO
M1020	RONDOS (FLUTE WITH ORCHESTRA), ARRANGED — TO 1800 — — PARTS
M1105	RONDOS (FLUTE WITH STRING ORCHESTRA) — SCORES
M1105-6	RONDOS (FLUTE WITH STRING ORCHESTRA)
M460-462	RONDOS (FLUTE, 2 VIOLINS, VIOLA)
M463-4	RONDOS (FLUTE, 2 VIOLINS, VIOLA), ARRANGED
M276-7	RONDOS (GUITAR AND PIANO)
M125-7	RONDOS (GUITAR)
M255-7	RONDOS (HORN AND PIANO)
M1028-9	RONDOS (HORN WITH ORCHESTRA)
M1028	RONDOS (HORN WITH ORCHESTRA) — TO 1800 — — SCORES
M1045	RONDOS (ORCHESTRA)
M1060	RONDOS (ORCHESTRA)
M1060	RONDOS (ORCHESTRA), ARRANGED — SCORES
M1060	RONDOS (ORCHESTRA), ARRANGED
M1010-1011	RONDOS (PIANO WITH ORCHESTRA)
M1011	RONDOS (PIANO WITH ORCHESTRA) — TO 1800 — — 2-PIANO SCORES
M25	RONDOS (PIANO)
M200-201	RONDOS (PIANO, 4 HANDS)
M204	RONDOS (PIANO, 4 HANDS)
M207-211	RONDOS (PIANOS, 4 HANDS), ARRANGED
M260-261	RONDOS (TRUMPET AND PIANO)
M1030-1031	RONDOS (TRUMPET WITH ORCHESTRA)
M224-6	RONDOS (VIOLA AND PIANO)
M227-8	RONDOS (VIOLA AND PIANO), ARRANGED
M221	RONDOS (VIOLIN AND PIANO)
M1012-1013	RONDOS (VIOLIN WITH CHAMBER ORCHESTRA)
M1013	RONDOS (VIOLIN WITH CHAMBER ORCHESTRA) — TO 1800 — — SOLO WITH PIANO

M1012-1013	RONDOS (VIOLIN WITH ORCHESTRA)
M1106	RONDOS (VIOLIN WITH STRING ORCHESTRA) — SOLO WITH PIANO
M1105-6	RONDOS (VIOLIN WITH STRING ORCHESTRA)
M229-230	RONDOS (VIOLONCELLO AND PIANO)
M233	RONDOS (VIOLONCELLO AND PIANO)
M1016-1017	RONDOS (VIOLONCELLO WITH ORCHESTRA)
M855-7	RONDOS (2 BASSOONS, 2 CLARINETS, 2 HORNS, 2 OBOES)
M292-3	RONDOS (2 GUITARS)
M755-7	RONDOS (2 HORNS, 2 TROMBONES, 3 TRUMPETS)
M214-215	RONDOS (2 PIANOS)
M215	RONDOS (2 PIANOS), ARRANGED
M216	RONDOS (2 PIANOS, 8 HANDS)
M455-9	RONDOS (4 CLARINETS)
M458-9	RONDOS (4 CLARINETS), ARRANGED
M455-7	RONDOS (4 FLUTES)
M455-7	RONDOS (4 RECORDERS)
PL3801.L4	*RONG LANGUAGE* SEE LEPCHA LANGUAGE
DS485.S5	*RONGS* SEE LEPCHAS
HV6441-6453	*RONIN* SEE OUTLAWS
NA4790-6113	*ROOD-LOFTS* SEE CHURCH ARCHITECTURE
NA5080	*ROOD-LOFTS* SEE SCREENS (CHURCH DECORATION)
TH2495	ROOF CRESTINGS
TH2391-2495	*ROOF-TRUSSES* SEE ROOFS
TG500-507	*ROOF-TRUSSES* SEE TRUSSES / roof-trusses
TG375-380	*ROOF-TRUSSES* SEE TRUSSES / trussed bridges
TH2451	ROOFING PAINT
TH2431-2459	ROOFING
TH2451	ROOFING, CONCRETE
TH2458	ROOFING, COPPER
TH2457	ROOFING, IRON AND STEEL
TH2445	ROOFING, SLATE
TH2455	ROOFING, TIN
TG507	ROOFS — TABLES, CALCULATIONS, ETC. / engineering
TH2398	ROOFS — TABLES, CALCULATIONS, ETC. / rafter tables
TH2391-2495	ROOFS
TH2417	*ROOFS, HANGING* SEE ROOFS, SUSPENSION
TH2416	ROOFS, SHELL
TH2417	ROOFS, SUSPENSION
GV1299.R6	ROOK (GAME)
NA7800-7850	*ROOMING HOUSES* SEE HOTELS, TAVERNS, ETC. / architecture
GT3770-3899	*ROOMING HOUSES* SEE HOTELS, TAVERNS, ETC. / manners and customs
HD7288	*ROOMING HOUSES* SEE LODGING-HOUSES / laboring classes
DC101.5.R8	ROOSEBEKE, BATTLE OF, 1382
SB608.R	ROOT-CROPS — DISEASES AND PESTS
SB209-211	ROOT-CROPS
SB741.R7	ROOT-KNOT
SB741.R75	ROOT-ROT
QK644	ROOT-TUBERCLES
QR113	ROOT-TUBERCLES / bacteriology
QK644	ROOTS (BOTANY) — ANATOMY
QK644	ROOTS (BOTANY) — MORPHOLOGY
QK644	ROOTS (BOTANY)
QK776	ROOTS (BOTANY) / movements
QA212	*ROOTS OF EQUATIONS* SEE EQUATIONS, ROOTS OF
QA119	ROOTS, NUMERICAL
GV498	*ROPE JUMPING* SEE ROPE SKIPPING
GV498	ROPE SKIPPING
HD4966.R6	ROPE-MAKERS / wages
TS1784-7	ROPE / manufacture
BF431	RORSCHACH TEST
NK4122.G6	RORSTRAND POTTERY
BF1623.R7	*ROSAECRUCIANS* SEE ROSICRUCIANS / occult sciences
HS141	*ROSAECRUCIANS* SEE ROSICRUCIANS / secret societies
BX2163	ROSARY — JUVENILE LITERATURE
BX2310.R7	ROSARY
QE391.R7	ROSCOELITE
QK495.R78	*ROSE* SEE ROSES / botany
SB411	*ROSE* SEE ROSES / culture
RC743	*ROSE-COLD* SEE HAY-FEVER
TP684.R	ROSE-GERANIUM OIL
E83.876	ROSEBUD, BATTLE OF THE, 1876
SB201.R6	ROSELLE
BF723.F7	ROSENZWEIG PICTURE-FRUSTRATION TEST
SB608.R8	ROSES — DISEASES AND PESTS
QK495.R78	ROSES / botany
SB411	ROSES / culture
PJ1531.R3-5	ROSETTA STONE INSCRIPTION
BM695.N5	ROSH HA-SHANAH
BF1623.R7	ROSICRUCIAN LANGUAGE
BF1623.R7	ROSICRUCIANS / occult sciences
HS141	ROSICRUCIANS / secret societies
TP977-8	*ROSIN* SEE GUMS AND RESINS / chemical technology
QD419	*ROSIN* SEE GUMS AND RESINS / chemistry
SB289-291	*ROSIN* SEE GUMS AND RESINS / culture
TP684.R7	ROSIN-OIL
DD412.6.R7	ROSSBACH, BATTLE OF, 1757
TS967	ROSSING-MACHINES
BF1623.R7	*ROSY CROSS, ORDER OF THE* SEE ROSICRUCIANS / occult sciences
HS141	*ROSY CROSS, ORDER OF THE* SEE ROSICRUCIANS / secret societies
TK2796	ROTARY CONVERTERS
TP841-2	*ROTARY KILNS* SEE KILNS, ROTARY
TP881	*ROTARY KILNS* SEE KILNS, ROTARY / cement
TJ917	ROTARY PUMPS
TK2699	ROTATING AMPLIFIERS
QC809.F5	*ROTATING DISHPAN* SEE GEOPHYSICS — FLUID MODELS
QB410	ROTATING MASSES OF FLUID / astronomy
QA913	ROTATING MASSES OF FLUID / hydrodynamics
S603	ROTATION OF CROPS
QB633	*ROTATION OF THE EARTH* SEE EARTH — ROTATION
QC441-5	*ROTATION OF THE PLANE OF POLARIZATION* SEE POLARIZATION (LIGHT)
QD481	*ROTATION SPECTRA* SEE MOLECULAR ROTATION
QL391.R8	*ROTATORIA* SEE ROTIFERA
RC182.R8	*ROTELN* SEE RUBELLA
QL391.R8	ROTIFERA
TR470	*ROTOGRAPH* SEE PHOTOSTAT
TJ990	*ROTOR BLADES (COMPRESSORS)* SEE COMPRESSORS — BLADES
VM774	ROTOR SHIPS
QA930	ROTORS
PL5435	*ROTTI LANGUAGE* SEE ROTTINESE LANGUAGE
PL5435	ROTTINESE LANGUAGE
PL6297	ROTUMAN LANGUAGE
F2230.2.O8	*ROUCOUYENNE INDIANS* SEE OYANA INDIANS
PM6714	*ROUCOUYENNE LANGUAGE* SEE OYANA LANGUAGE
GV1311.T7	*ROUGE-ET-NOIR* SEE TRENTE-ET-QUARANTE
GV1309	ROULETTE
QA623	ROULETTES (GEOMETRY)
GV1755	ROUND DANCING
DA920	ROUND TOWERS — IRELAND
GV1017.R6	ROUNDERS
DA410-419	ROUNDHEADS
TF595	*ROUNDHOUSES* SEE RAILROADS — ROUNDHOUSES / administration
TF296	*ROUNDHOUSES* SEE RAILROADS — ROUNDHOUSES / buildings
QL391.N4	ROUNDWORM
TA625	ROUTE SURVEYING
HE323-8	*ROUTES OF TRADE* SEE TRADE ROUTES
G550	*ROUTES OF TRAVEL* SEE OCEAN TRAVEL
G153	*ROUTES OF TRAVEL* SEE OCEAN TRAVEL
RA793	*ROUTES OF TRAVEL* SEE OCEAN TRAVEL / hygiene
G150-153	*ROUTES OF TRAVEL* SEE VOYAGES AND TRAVELS — GUIDE-BOOKS
G150-153	*ROUTES OF TRAVEL* SEE VOYAGES AND TRAVELS — GUIDE-BOOKS
TJ1208	ROUTING-MACHINES
PL6298	ROVIANA LANGUAGE
GV791-809	ROWING
CS27	ROYAL DESCENT, FAMILIES OF
CS586	ROYAL DESCENT, FAMILIES OF / france
CS418	ROYAL DESCENT, FAMILIES OF / gt. brit.
CS55	ROYAL DESCENT, FAMILIES OF / u.s.
D107.7	*ROYAL FAVORITES* SEE FAVORITES, ROYAL
D226.7	ROYAL HOUSES
D352.1	ROYAL HOUSES / 19th century
D412.7	ROYAL HOUSES / 20th century
GV1795	ROYAL MIDDIES (DANCE)
JF305	*ROYAL PREROGATIVE* SEE PREROGATIVE, ROYAL

BX5157	ROYAL SUPREMACY (CHURCH OF ENGLAND)
NK4395	*ROYAL WORCESTER PORCELAIN* **SEE** WORCESTER PORCELAIN
DA400-425	ROYALISTS, 1642-1660
D107	*ROYALTY* **SEE** KINGS AND RULERS / *biography comprehensive*
JF253	*ROYALTY* **SEE** KINGS AND RULERS / *comparative government*
JC374-408	*ROYALTY* **SEE** KINGS AND RULERS / *political theory*
D399.7	*ROYALTY* **SEE** KINGS AND RULERS / *19th century*
D352.1	*ROYALTY* **SEE** KINGS AND RULERS / *19th century*
D412.7	*ROYALTY* **SEE** KINGS AND RULERS / *20th century*
D107.5	*ROYALTY* **SEE** PRINCESSES / *modern history*
D352.3	*ROYALTY* **SEE** PRINCESSES / *19th century*
D412.8	*ROYALTY* **SEE** PRINCESSES / *20th century*
D107.3	*ROYALTY* **SEE** QUEENS
D352.3	*ROYALTY* **SEE** QUEENS / *19th century*
D412.8	*ROYALTY* **SEE** QUEENS / *20th century*
D226.7	*ROYALTY* **SEE** ROYAL HOUSES
D352.1	*ROYALTY* **SEE** ROYAL HOUSES / *19th century*
D412.7	*ROYALTY* **SEE** ROYAL HOUSES / *20th century*
SB201.R6	*ROZELLE* **SEE** ROSELLE
NK4399.R6	ROZENBURG PORCELAIN
PL8608	RUANDA LANGUAGE
TS1892	*RUBBER ARTICLES* **SEE** RUBBER GOODS
TJ1073.R8	RUBBER BEARINGS
TS1910	*RUBBER BOOTS AND SHOES* **SEE** BOOTS AND SHOES, RUBBER
TS1892	RUBBER COATINGS
TS1910	*RUBBER FOOTWEAR* **SEE** BOOTS AND SHOES, RUBBER
TS1892	RUBBER GOODS
HD9161	RUBBER INDUSTRY AND TRADE / *economics*
TS1870-1920	RUBBER INDUSTRY AND TRADE / *technology*
SB289-291	RUBBER PLANTS
TS1892	*RUBBER PRODUCTS* **SEE** RUBBER GOODS
TS1920	RUBBER STAMPS / *manufacture*
TS1912	*RUBBER TIRES* **SEE** TIRES, RUBBER / *manufacture*
TS718	RUBBER TO METAL BONDING
TS718	*RUBBER-METAL BONDING* **SEE** RUBBER TO METAL BONDING
QA611	*RUBBER-SHEET GEOMETRY* **SEE** TOPOLOGY / *geometry*
SB291	RUBBER / *culture*
TS1925	RUBBER, ARTIFICIAL
TS1892	RUBBER, CHLORINATED
TS1925	*RUBBER, SYNTHETIC* **SEE** RUBBER, ARTIFICIAL
TA407	*RUBBING CORROSION* **SEE** FRETTING CORROSION
RC182.R8	RUBELLA
RC182.R8	*RUBEOLA* **SEE** RUBELLA
QD181.R3	RUBIDIUM
QE394.R8	RUBIES
PM6714	*RUCOUYENNE LANGUAGE* **SEE** OYANA LANGUAGE
VM841-5	*RUDDER* **SEE** STEERING-GEAR
QH315	*RUDIMENTARY ORGANS* **SEE** VESTIGIAL ORGANS
BL1225.R8	RUDRA (DEITY) / *hinduism*
QL696.G2	RUFFED GROUSE
SK325.G7	RUFFED GROUSE
HD9937	RUG AND CARPET INDUSTRY
HD9937	*RUG INDUSTRY* **SEE** RUG AND CARPET INDUSTRY
NK2775-2896	*RUG MANUFACTURE* **SEE** RUGS / *art*
TS1777-8	*RUG MANUFACTURE* **SEE** RUGS / *manufacture*
TS1490-1500	*RUG MANUFACTURE* **SEE** WEAVING
GN432	*RUG MANUFACTURE* **SEE** WEAVING / *primitive*
GV1303	RUGBY (DICE GAME)
GV945	RUGBY FOOTBALL
GV945	*RUGGER* **SEE** RUGBY FOOTBALL
NK2790	RUGS — PRIVATE COLLECTIONS
NK2775-2896	RUGS / *art*
TS1777-8	RUGS / *manufacture*
TT850	RUGS, BRAIDED
NK2808-2810	RUGS, ORIENTAL
PL8834	*RUHAYA LANGUAGE* **SEE** ZIBA LANGUAGE
CC	*RUINS* **SEE** ARCHAEOLOGY
GT	*RUINS* **SEE** ARCHAEOLOGY / *manners and customs general*
DA-DU	*RUINS* **SEE** ARCHAEOLOGY / *national antiquities other than american*

GN	*RUINS* **SEE** ARCHAEOLOGY / *prehistoric antiquities*
CC75	*RUINS* **SEE** EXCAVATIONS (ARCHAEOLOGY)
CC165	*RUINS* **SEE** EXCAVATIONS (ARCHAEOLOGY)
PL6318	*RUK LANGUAGE* **SEE** TRUK LANGUAGE
PM6714	*RUKUYENNE LANGUAGE* **SEE** OYANA LANGUAGE
BT88	RULE OF FAITH
HE369-373	*RULE OF THE ROAD (IN TRAFFIC)* **SEE** TRAFFIC REGULATIONS
VK371-8	RULE OF THE ROAD AT SEA
HE586-7	*RULE OF THE ROAD, INLAND* **SEE** INLAND NAVIGATION — LAWS AND REGULATIONS
BL85	*RULE, GOLDEN* **SEE** GOLDEN RULE / *comparative religion*
BV4715	*RULE, GOLDEN* **SEE** GOLDEN RULE / *moral theology*
D107	*RULERS* **SEE** EMPERORS
D107	*RULERS* **SEE** KINGS AND RULERS / *biography comprehensive*
JF253	*RULERS* **SEE** KINGS AND RULERS / *comparative government*
JC374-408	*RULERS* **SEE** KINGS AND RULERS / *political theory*
D399.7	*RULERS* **SEE** KINGS AND RULERS / *19th century*
D352.1	*RULERS* **SEE** KINGS AND RULERS / *19th century*
D412.7	*RULERS* **SEE** KINGS AND RULERS / *20th century*
D107.3	*RULERS* **SEE** QUEENS
D352.3	*RULERS* **SEE** QUEENS / *19th century*
D412.8	*RULERS* **SEE** QUEENS / *20th century*
JF501-540	*RULES OF ORDER* **SEE** PARLIAMENTARY PRACTICE
JK1091-1128	*RULES OF ORDER* **SEE** PARLIAMENTARY PRACTICE / *u.s. congress*
GV731	*RULES OF SPORTS* **SEE** SPORTS — RULES
VK371-8	*RULES OF THE ROAD AT SEA* **SEE** RULE OF THE ROAD AT SEA
HE586-7	*RULES OF THE ROAD, INLAND* **SEE** INLAND NAVIGATION — LAWS AND REGULATIONS
TS1260	*RULING (OF PAPER, ETC.)* **SEE** PAPER RULING
GV1295.C6	*RUM (GAME)* **SEE** COONCAN
GV1295.R8	*RUM (GAME)* **SEE** RUMMY (GAME)
TP607.R9	RUM
PC833-4	RUMANIAN BALLADS AND SONGS / *collections*
PC821	RUMANIAN BALLADS AND SONGS / *folk literature*
PC810	RUMANIAN BALLADS AND SONGS / *history*
PC601-799	RUMANIAN LANGUAGE
PC829-872	RUMANIAN LITERATURE / *collections*
PC800-827	RUMANIAN LITERATURE / *history*
PN5355.R	RUMANIAN PERIODICALS
PC601-872	RUMANIAN PHILOLOGY
PC833-4	RUMANIAN POETRY / *collections*
PC821	RUMANIAN POETRY / *folk literature*
PC810	RUMANIAN POETRY / *history*
PC797	RUMANIAN POETRY / *macedo-rumanian*
DR213	RUMANIANS
DR267	RUMANIA — HISTORY — — 1944-
PC901-949	*RUMANSH LANGUAGE* **SEE** RAETO-ROMANCE LANGUAGE
GV1796.R8	RUMBA (DANCE)
M1248	RUMBAS (BAND)
M1264	RUMBAS (BAND)
M31	RUMBAS (PIANO)
QL737.U5	RUMINANTIA
RC840	*RUMINATION IN MAN* **SEE** MERYCISM
QP151	RUMINATION
GV1295.R8	RUMMY (GAME)
HJ6750-7380	*RUMRUNNING* **SEE** SMUGGLING / *other countries*
HJ6690-6720	*RUMRUNNING* **SEE** SMUGGLING / *u.s.*
PM6301-9	*RUNA-SIMI* **SEE** KECHUA LANGUAGE
PD2013-2014	RUNES
PD2013-2014	*RUNIC ALPHABETS* **SEE** RUNES
PD2014	*RUNIC CALENDARS* **SEE** CALENDARS, RUNIC
GV1061-9	RUNNING
TL696.L3	*RUNWAY LOCALIZERS* **SEE** RUNWAY LOCALIZING BEACONS
TL696.L3	RUNWAY LOCALIZING BEACONS
TL725.3.R8	*RUNWAYS (AERONAUTICS)* **SEE** AIRPORTS — RUNWAYS
RD621-6	*RUPTURE* **SEE** HERNIA
NA7100-7786	*RURAL ARCHITECTURE* **SEE** ARCHITECTURE, DOMESTIC
NA7571-2	*RURAL ARCHITECTURE* **SEE** BUNGALOWS
NA7551-5	*RURAL ARCHITECTURE* **SEE** COTTAGES

BX1939.R8	*RURAL BISHOPS* **SEE** CHOREPISCOPI
BV638.8	RURAL CHURCHES — STORIES
BV638	RURAL CHURCHES
HN	RURAL CONDITIONS
HG2041-2051	*RURAL CREDIT* **SEE** AGRICULTURAL CREDIT / banking
HD1439-1440	*RURAL CREDIT* **SEE** AGRICULTURAL CREDIT / theory
BX1939.R8	RURAL DEANS / canon law
BX1911	RURAL DEANS / catholic church
BX5179	RURAL DEANS / church of england
LC5146-8	*RURAL EDUCATION* **SEE** EDUCATION, RURAL
TK4018	RURAL ELECTRIFICATION
HD9688	RURAL ELECTRIFICATION
HE6155	RURAL FREE DELIVERY
HE6455-6	RURAL FREE DELIVERY / u.s.
LB1567	*RURAL HIGH SCHOOLS* **SEE** RURAL SCHOOLS
RA975	*RURAL HOSPITALS* **SEE** HOSPITALS, RURAL
RA771	*RURAL HYGIENE* **SEE** HYGIENE, RURAL
RA427	*RURAL HYGIENE* **SEE** HYGIENE, RURAL
Z675.V7	RURAL LIBRARIES
Z675.C8	RURAL LIBRARIES
S521	*RURAL LIFE* **SEE** COUNTRY LIFE
GT3470	*RURAL LIFE* **SEE** COUNTRY LIFE / manners and customs
HT401-485	*RURAL LIFE* **SEE** COUNTRY LIFE / social groups
S521	*RURAL LIFE* **SEE** FARM LIFE / popular works
HT421	*RURAL LIFE* **SEE** FARM LIFE / sociology
SK601	*RURAL LIFE* **SEE** OUTDOOR LIFE
GT1850-1875	*RURAL LIFE* **SEE** PEASANTRY / costumes
GT5650-5680	*RURAL LIFE* **SEE** PEASANTRY / customs
HD1521-1539	*RURAL LIFE* **SEE** PEASANTRY / economics
HD1513	*RURAL LIFE* **SEE** PEASANTRY / peasant proprietors
PN1421	*RURAL POETRY* **SEE** PASTORAL POETRY
PN6110.P4	*RURAL POETRY* **SEE** PASTORAL POETRY
HV7965-7985	*RURAL POLICE* **SEE** POLICE, RURAL
RA427	*RURAL PUBLIC HEALTH* **SEE** HYGIENE, RURAL
RA771	*RURAL PUBLIC HEALTH* **SEE** HYGIENE, RURAL
LB1567	RURAL SCHOOLS — CURRICULA
LB1567	RURAL SCHOOLS
TD929	*RURAL SEWERAGE* **SEE** SEWERAGE, RURAL
HT421-455	*RURAL SOCIOLOGY* **SEE** SOCIOLOGY, RURAL
TD927	*RURAL WATER-SUPPLY* **SEE** WATER-SUPPLY, RURAL
GV1017.R9	RUSE (GAME)
TT877	RUSH-WORK
DK	RUSSIA — HISTORY
PG3503	RUSSIA — LITERATURES / collections
PG3500	RUSSIA — LITERATURES / history
U735	*RUSSIA-HISTORY-WAR WITH JAPAN, 1904-1905* **SEE** RUSSO-JAPANESE WAR, 1904-1905 / military observations
V713	*RUSSIA-HISTORY-WAR WITH JAPAN, 1904-1905* **SEE** RUSSO-JAPANESE WAR, 1904-1905 / naval observations
JX1393	*RUSSIA-HISTORY-WAR WITH JAPAN, 1904-1905* **SEE** RUSSO-JAPANESE WAR, 1904-1905 / diplomatic history
DS516-517	*RUSSIA-HISTORY-WAR WITH JAPAN, 1904-1905* **SEE** RUSSO-JAPANESE WAR, 1904-1905
TL796.5.R	*RUSSIAN ARTIFICIAL SATELLITES* **SEE** ARTIFICIAL SATELLITES, RUSSIAN
PG3230-3233	RUSSIAN BALLADS AND SONGS / collections
PG3113	RUSSIAN BALLADS AND SONGS / folk literature
PG3104	RUSSIAN BALLADS AND SONGS / history
PG3041-3056	RUSSIAN BALLADS AND SONGS / history
GV1295.R9	RUSSIAN BANK (GAME)
RM820	*RUSSIAN BATHS* **SEE** BATHS, RUSSIAN
PG3240-3255	RUSSIAN DRAMA / collections
PG3071-3089	RUSSIAN DRAMA / history
PG3293	RUSSIAN ESSAYS / collections
PG3099.E7	RUSSIAN ESSAYS / history
PG3270-3286	RUSSIAN FICTION / collections
PG3095-8	RUSSIAN FICTION / history
PG2120.C6	RUSSIAN LANGUAGE — BUSINESS RUSSIAN
PG2001-2850	RUSSIAN LANGUAGE
PG3292	RUSSIAN LETTERS / collections
PG3099.L4	RUSSIAN LETTERS / history
PG2900-3560	RUSSIAN LITERATURE
PN5271-9	RUSSIAN NEWSPAPERS / history
PN5271-5280	RUSSIAN PERIODICALS / history
PG2001-2069	RUSSIAN PHILOLOGY
PG3231	RUSSIAN POETRY — 17TH CENTURY / collections
PG3046	RUSSIAN POETRY — 17TH CENTURY / history
PG3231	RUSSIAN POETRY — 18TH CENTURY / collections
PG3046	RUSSIAN POETRY — 18TH CENTURY / history
PG3232	RUSSIAN POETRY — 19TH CENTURY / collections
PG3051	RUSSIAN POETRY — 19TH CENTURY / history
PG3233	RUSSIAN POETRY — 20TH CENTURY / collections
PG3056	RUSSIAN POETRY — 20TH CENTURY / history
PG3230-3238	RUSSIAN POETRY / collections
PG3041-3065	RUSSIAN POETRY / history
DK273	*RUSSIAN REFUGEES* **SEE** REFUGEES, RUSSIAN
D847	*RUSSIAN SATELLITES* **SEE** COMMUNIST COUNTRIES
PN6222.R8	RUSSIAN WIT AND HUMOR
SF429.R8	RUSSIAN WOLF-HOUNDS
DK33	RUSSIANS
DK273	RUSSIA — HISTORY — — GERMAN OCCUPATION, 1941-1944
DK265	RUSSIA — HISTORY — — REVOLUTION, 1917-1921 — — — ATROCITIES
DK265.15	RUSSIA — HISTORY — — REVOLUTION, 1917-1921 — — — PICTORIAL WORKS
DK508	*RUSSNIACS* **SEE** UKRAINIANS
D749.5.A	*RUSSO-BRITISH TREATY, 1942* **SEE** ANGLO-RUSSIAN TREATY, 1942
D749.5.A	*RUSSO-ENGLISH TREATY, 1942* **SEE** ANGLO-RUSSIAN TREATY, 1942
DK459.5	RUSSO-FINNISH WAR, 1939-1940
D397	*RUSSO-FRENCH ALLIANCE* **SEE** FRANCO-RUSSIAN ALLIANCE
DS784	RUSSO-JAPANESE BORDER CONFLICTS, 1932-1941
DS517.7	*RUSSO-JAPANESE TREATY, 1905* **SEE** PORTSMOUTH, TREATY OF, 1905
UH306	RUSSO-JAPANESE WAR, 1904-1905 — HOSPITALS, CHARITIES, ETC.
UH306	RUSSO-JAPANESE WAR, 1904-1905 — MEDICAL AND SANITARY AFFAIRS
DS516-517	RUSSO-JAPANESE WAR, 1904-1905
JX1393	RUSSO-JAPANESE WAR, 1904-1905 / diplomatic history
U735	RUSSO-JAPANESE WAR, 1904-1905 / military observations
V713	RUSSO-JAPANESE WAR, 1904-1905 / naval observations
DK889	RUSSO-KHIVAN EXPEDITION, 1873
DL711	RUSSO-SWEDISH WAR, 1608-1617
DK111	RUSSO-SWEDISH WAR, 1608-1617
DL725	RUSSO-SWEDISH WAR, 1656-1658
DL766	RUSSO-SWEDISH WAR, 1788-1790
DL790	RUSSO-SWEDISH WAR, 1808-1809
DR548	RUSSO-TURKISH WAR, 1736-1739
DR553	RUSSO-TURKISH WAR, 1768-1774
DR555.7	RUSSO-TURKISH WAR, 1787-1792
DR561	RUSSO-TURKISH WAR, 1806-1812
DK216	RUSSO-TURKISH WAR, 1828-1829
DR564	RUSSO-TURKISH WAR, 1828-1829
DK214-215	*RUSSO-TURKISH WAR, 1853-1856* **SEE** CRIMEAN WAR, 1853-1856 / russia
DR567	*RUSSO-TURKISH WAR, 1853-1856* **SEE** CRIMEAN WAR, 1853-1856 / turkey
DR573	RUSSO-TURKISH WAR, 1877-1878
TA467	*RUST* **SEE** CORROSION AND ANTI-CORROSIVES
TA462	*RUST* **SEE** CORROSION AND ANTI-CORROSIVES
TT200	RUSTIC WOODWORK
TA467	*RUSTLESS COATINGS* **SEE** CORROSION AND ANTI-CORROSIVES
TA462	*RUSTLESS COATINGS* **SEE** CORROSION AND ANTI-CORROSIVES
QK627	RUSTS (FUNGI)
SB211.R8	RUTABAGA
PG3801-3899	*RUTHENIAN LANGUAGE* **SEE** UKRAINIAN LANGUAGE
PG3900-3998	*RUTHENIAN LITERATURE* **SEE** UKRAINIAN LITERATURE
PG3934	*RUTHENIAN POETRY* **SEE** UKRAINIAN POETRY / collections
PG3926	*RUTHENIAN POETRY* **SEE** UKRAINIAN POETRY / folk literature

PG3917	*RUTHENIAN POETRY* **SEE** UKRAINIAN POETRY / *history*
DK508	*RUTHENIANS* **SEE** UKRAINIANS
QD181.R9	RUTHENIUM
SB608.R9	RYE — DISEASES AND PESTS
SB608.R9	RYE GALL-GNAT
DA448	RYE HOUSE PLOT, 1683
QP921.E6	*RYE SMUT* **SEE** ERGOT / *experimental pharmacology*
RS165.E7	*RYE SMUT* **SEE** ERGOT / *pharmacy*
RM666.E8	*RYE SMUT* **SEE** ERGOT / *therapeutics*
TP605	*RYE WHISKEY* **SEE** WHISKEY
SB191.R9	RYE
HD9049.R8	RYE / *grain trade*
D280.5	RYSWICK, PEACE OF, 1697
PL995	RYUKYU LANGUAGE
PL6301	SAA LANGUAGE
PH701-729	*SAAM LANGUAGE* **SEE** LAPPISH LANGUAGE
BL1690	SABAEANS — RELIGION
E99.S	*SABAGUIS* **SEE** SOBAIPURI INDIANS
BM199.S	*SABBATAEANS* **SEE** SABBATHAIANS
BX9680.S3	SABBATARIANS
BM685	SABBATH / *judaism*
BM199.S	SABBATHAIANS
BM199.S	*SABBATHAISTS* **SEE** SABBATHAIANS
BX9680.S3	*SABBATHARIANS* **SEE** SABBATARIANS
BM199.S	*SABBATIANS* **SEE** SABBATHAIANS
BM720.S2	SABBATICAL YEAR (JUDAISM)
BT1470	SABELLIANISM
U850-856	SABERS
UE420-425	SABERS / *cavalry exercises*
BL1635	*SABIANS* **SEE** HARRANIANS
BT1405	*SABIANS* **SEE** MANDAEANS
E475.4	SABINE PASS, BATTLE OF, 1863
DG225.S2	SABINES
PM7811-7814	SABIR
SF405.S	SABLES
BM501.4	SABORAIM
HV8077	SABOTAGE — EQUIPMENT / *criminal investigation*
UB274	SABOTAGE — EQUIPMENT / *military* ·
HD5473	SABOTAGE
U850-856	*SABRES* **SEE** SABERS
UE420-425	*SABRES* **SEE** SABERS / *cavalry exercises*
E99.S23	*SAC INDIANS* **SEE** SAUK INDIANS
F3722.1.C	*SACCHA INDIANS* **SEE** COLORADO INDIANS (ECUADOR)
TP382	SACCHARIMETER
TP382	*SACCHARIMETRY* **SEE** SUGAR — ANALYSIS AND TESTING
TP248.S3	SACCHARIN / *chemical technology*
QP981.S2	SACCHARIN / *physiological effects*
D90.S3	*SACIANS* **SEE** SAKA
E99.S	*SACO INDIANS* **SEE** SOKOKI INDIANS
RC422.P	*SACRAL NERVE-ROOT CYSTS* **SEE** PERINEURIAL CYSTS, SACRAL
RC422.P	*SACRAL PERINEURIAL CYSTS* **SEE** PERINEURIAL CYSTS, SACRAL
NA5095.S2	SACRAMENT HOUSES
BV823-8	*SACRAMENT OF THE ALTAR* **SEE** LORD'S SUPPER
BX2215	*SACRAMENT OF THE ALTAR* **SEE** LORD'S SUPPER / *catholic church*
BX5149.C5	*SACRAMENT OF THE ALTAR* **SEE** LORD'S SUPPER / *church of england*
BL619.S3	*SACRAMENTAL MEALS* **SEE** SACRED MEALS
BV875-885	*SACRAMENTALIA* **SEE** SACRAMENTALS
BX1939.S23	SACRAMENTALS (CANON LAW)
BV875-885	SACRAMENTALS
BX1939.S25	SACRAMENTS (CANON LAW)
BX2200-2290	SACRAMENTS (LITURGY) / *catholic church*
BV800-873	SACRAMENTS
BX	SACRAMENTS / *by denomination*
N7810-8185	*SACRED ART* **SEE** CHRISTIAN ART AND SYMBOLISM
BV150-168	*SACRED ART* **SEE** CHRISTIAN ART AND SYMBOLISM / *theology*
BL70-71	SACRED BOOKS
M2020-2036	*SACRED CANTATAS* **SEE** CANTATAS, SACRED
M2060	*SACRED CHORUSES* **SEE** CHORUSES, SACRED
M2018	SACRED DUETS WITH CHAMBER ORCHESTRA — SCORES
M2018-2019	SACRED DUETS WITH CHAMBER ORCHESTRA
M2018	SACRED DUETS WITH INSTR. ENSEMBLE

M2018-2019	SACRED DUETS WITH ORCHESTRA
M2018-2019	SACRED DUETS WITH STRING ORCHESTRA
M2018	SACRED DUETS WITH STRING ORCHESTRA — TO 1800 — — SCORES
BX2375	*SACRED EXPEDITIONS* **SEE** PARISH MISSIONS
BL583	SACRED GROVES
BX2157-8	*SACRED HEART OF JESUS, DEVOTION TO* **SEE** SACRED HEART, DEVOTION TO
BX2157	SACRED HEART, DEVOTION TO — PAPAL DOCUMENTS
BX2157-8	SACRED HEART, DEVOTION TO
BV64.S3	SACRED HEART, FEAST OF THE
BL70-71	*SACRED LITERATURES* **SEE** SACRED BOOKS
BL619.S3	SACRED MEALS
M1625-6	SACRED MONOLOGUES WITH MUSIC (CHORUS WITH ORCHESTRA)
M1626	SACRED MONOLOGUES WITH MUSIC (CHORUS WITH ORCHESTRA) — VOCAL SCORES WITH PIANO
GR660	*SACRED MOUNTAINS* **SEE** MOUNTAINS (IN RELIGION, FOLK-LORE, ETC.) / *folk-lore*
BL447	*SACRED MOUNTAINS* **SEE** MOUNTAINS (IN RELIGION, FOLK-LORE, ETC.) / *religion*
ML3869	*SACRED MUSIC* **SEE** CHURCH MUSIC / *aesthetics*
ML3000-3190	*SACRED MUSIC* **SEE** CHURCH MUSIC / *history*
ML3270	*SACRED MUSIC* **SEE** CHURCH MUSIC / *history*
ML178	*SACRED MUSIC* **SEE** CHURCH MUSIC / *history*
MT915	*SACRED MUSIC* **SEE** CHURCH MUSIC / *instruction and study*
MT88	*SACRED MUSIC* **SEE** CHURCH MUSIC / *instruction and study*
MT860-865	*SACRED MUSIC* **SEE** CHURCH MUSIC / *instruction and study*
M2186-7	*SACRED MUSIC* **SEE** SYNAGOGUE MUSIC / *services*
M2114.3	*SACRED MUSIC* **SEE** SYNAGOGUE MUSIC / *songs*
M2079.5	*SACRED MUSIC* **SEE** SYNAGOGUE MUSIC / *special texts*
M2099.5	*SACRED MUSIC* **SEE** SYNAGOGUE MUSIC / *special texts*
BF1623.P9	*SACRED NUMBERS* **SEE** SYMBOLISM OF NUMBERS
M2018-2019	SACRED OCTETS WITH INSTR. ENSEMBLE
M2018	SACRED QUARTETS WITH INSTR. ENSEMBLE
M2062.4	SACRED QUARTETS WITH ORGAN
M2072.4	SACRED QUARTETS WITH ORGAN
M2061.4	SACRED QUARTETS WITH PIANO
M2072.4	SACRED QUARTETS WITH PIANO
M2073.4	SACRED QUARTETS WITH PIANO
M2074.4	SACRED QUARTETS WITH PIANO
M2062.4	SACRED QUARTETS WITH PIANO
M2064.4	SACRED QUARTETS WITH PIANO
M2063.4	SACRED QUARTETS WITH PIANO
M2019	SACRED QUINTETS WITH CHAMBER ORCHESTRA — VOCAL SCORES WITH 2 PIANOS
M2018-2019	SACRED QUINTETS WITH CHAMBER ORCHESTRA
M2018-2019	SACRED QUINTETS WITH INSTR. ENSEMBLE
M2061.5	SACRED QUINTETS WITH 2 PIANOS
M2062.5	SACRED QUINTETS WITH 2 PIANOS
M2072.5	SACRED QUINTETS WITH 2 PIANOS
M2073.5	SACRED QUINTETS WITH 2 PIANOS
M2074.5	SACRED QUINTETS WITH 2 PIANOS
M2064.5	SACRED QUINTETS WITH 2 PIANOS
M2063.5	SACRED QUINTETS WITH 2 PIANOS
M2018-2019	SACRED SEXTETS WITH CHAMBER ORCHESTRA
M2104	SACRED SONGS (HIGH VOICE) WITH CHAMBER ORCHESTRA — VOCAL SCORES WITH PIANO
M2110-2114	SACRED SONGS (HIGH VOICE) WITH HARPSICHORD
M2103.3	SACRED SONGS (HIGH VOICE) WITH INSTR. ENSEMBLE
M2110-2114	SACRED SONGS (HIGH VOICE) WITH ORGAN
M2110-2114	SACRED SONGS (HIGH VOICE) WITH PIANO
M2110-2113	SACRED SONGS (HIGH VOICE) WITH REED-ORGAN
M2104	SACRED SONGS (HIGH VOICE) WITH STRING ORCHESTRA — TO 1800 — — VOCAL SCORES WITH ORGAN
M2103.3	SACRED SONGS (HIGH VOICE) WITH VIOL
M2110-2114	SACRED SONGS (LOW VOICE) WITH HARPSICHORD
M2103.3	SACRED SONGS (LOW VOICE) WITH INSTR. ENSEMBLE
M2110-2114	SACRED SONGS (LOW VOICE) WITH ORGAN
M2110-2114	SACRED SONGS (LOW VOICE) WITH PIANO
M1257	SACRED SONGS (MEDIUM VOICE) WITH BAND
M1205	SACRED SONGS (MEDIUM VOICE) WITH BAND

M2104	SACRED SONGS (MEDIUM VOICE) WITH CHAMBER ORCHESTRA — VOCAL SCORES WITH PIANO
M2110-2114	SACRED SONGS (MEDIUM VOICE) WITH GUITAR
M2110-2114	SACRED SONGS (MEDIUM VOICE) WITH HARPSICHORD
M2103.3	SACRED SONGS (MEDIUM VOICE) WITH INSTR. ENSEMBLE
M2110-2114	SACRED SONGS (MEDIUM VOICE) WITH ORGAN
M2110-2114	SACRED SONGS (MEDIUM VOICE) WITH PIANO
M2110-2113	SACRED SONGS (MEDIUM VOICE) WITH REED-ORGAN
M2112	SACRED SONGS WITH ORGAN
M2110	SACRED SONGS WITH ORGAN
M2112	SACRED SONGS WITH PIANO
M2110	SACRED SONGS WITH PIANO
M2103.3	SACRED SONGS WITH STRING ORCHESTRA
M2104	SACRED SONGS WITH STRING ORCHESTRA
BL450	*SACRED SPRINGS* **SEE** SPRINGS (IN RELIGION, FOLK-LORE, ETC.) / *religion*
GR690	*SACRED SPRINGS* **SEE** SPRINGS (IN RELIGION, FOLK-LORE, ETC.) / *folk-lore*
M2104	SACRED TRIOS WITH CHAMBER ORCHESTRA — VOCAL SCORES WITH PIANO
M2103.3	SACRED TRIOS WITH CHAMBER ORCHESTRA
ML156.4.V4	SACRED VOCAL MUSIC — DISCOGRAPHY
M1999	SACRED VOCAL MUSIC
BS680.S2	SACRIFICE — BIBLICAL TEACHING
BL570	SACRIFICE
BL1215.S2	SACRIFICE / *brahmanism*
DS422.S2	SACRIFICE, HUMAN / *india*
BX1939.S	SACRILEGE (CANON LAW)
BR1620	SACRILEGE / *history*
BV4627.S2	SACRILEGE / *moral theology*
BX1972	SACRISTANS
RD672	SACROCOCCYGEAL REGION — TUMORS
QM111	SACROCOCCYGEAL REGION
RD686	SACROCOXALGIA
RD672	*SACRUM-TUMORS* **SEE** SACROCOCCYGEAL REGION — TUMORS
SF293.A	*SADDLE HORSE, AMERICAN* **SEE** AMERICAN SADDLE HORSE
TS1030-1035	*SADDLE MAKING* **SEE** SADDLERY
TS1030-1035	SADDLERY
TS1030-1035	*SADDLES* **SEE** SADDLERY
BM175.S2	SADDUCEES
HQ79	SADISM
DD439.K7	*SADOWA, BATTLE OF, 1866* **SEE** KONIGGRATZ, BATTLE OF, 1866
JX5151	SAFE-CONDUCTS / *international law*
HG2251-6	SAFE-DEPOSIT BOXES
HG2251-6	SAFE-DEPOSIT COMPANIES
TS420	SAFES / *manufacture*
HD7273	SAFETY APPLIANCES
TL159	*SAFETY BELTS, AUTOMOBILE* **SEE** AUTOMOBILE SEAT BELTS
HD7395.C5	*SAFETY CLOTHING* **SEE** CLOTHING, PROTECTIVE
TP862	*SAFETY GLASS* **SEE** GLASS, SAFETY
TN295	*SAFETY MEASURES* **SEE** COAL MINES AND MINING — SAFETY MEASURES
TK152	*SAFETY MEASURES* **SEE** ELECTRIC ENGINEERING — SAFETY MEASURES
T55	*SAFETY MEASURES* **SEE** INDUSTRIAL SAFETY
VK200	*SAFETY MEASURES* **SEE** NAVIGATION — SAFETY MEASURES
HD7260	SAFETY MUSEUMS
TN307	SAFETY-LAMP
T55	*SAFETY, INDUSTRIAL* **SEE** INDUSTRIAL SAFETY
DS290.S	SAFFARIDS
PL8707	*SAGALLA DIALECT* **SEE** TAITA LANGUAGE
PL8625	SAGARA LANGUAGE
PT7261-2	SAGAS / *collections*
PT7181-7193	SAGAS / *history and criticism*
PT7263-7287	SAGAS / *individual sagas*
SB307.S	SAGE
TP815	*SAGGARS* **SEE** SAGGERS
TP815	SAGGERS
GN131	SAGITTAL CURVE
SB311.S3	SAGO
DG247.12	SAGUNTUM — SIEGE, 219 B.C.
E99.N5	*SAHAPTIN INDIANS* **SEE** NEZ PERCE INDIANS
E99.S	*SAHAPTIN INDIANS* **SEE** SHAHAPTIAN INDIANS
PM2019	*SAHAPTIN LANGUAGES* **SEE** NEZ PERCE LANGUAGE

PM2301	*SAHAPTIN LANGUAGES* **SEE** SHAHAPTIAN LANGUAGES
VM351	SAILBOATS
VM311.B3	SAILING BARGES / *construction*
VM466.B3	SAILING BARGES / *use*
NE965	SAILING CARDS
VM351	*SAILING VESSELS* **SEE** SAILBOATS
VK543	SAILING
GV811	SAILING / *sport*
HD8039.S4-42	*SAILORS* **SEE** SEAMEN / *labor*
G525-550	*SAILORS' LIFE* **SEE** SEAFARING LIFE
PN6110.S4	SAILORS' SONGS / *literature*
M1978.S2	SAILORS' SONGS / *music*
M1977.S2	SAILORS' SONGS / *music*
TL760-769	*SAILPLANES (AERONAUTICS)* **SEE** GLIDERS (AERONAUTICS)
VM532	SAILS
SB207.S	SAINFOIN
D756.5.S	SAINT MALO, FRANCE — SIEGE, 1944
D756.5.S	SAINT NAZAIRE RAID, 1942
D756.5.S2	SAINT-LO, FRANCE — SIEGE, 1944
D756.5.S	SAINT-VALERY-EN-CAUX, BATTLE OF, 1940
E199	SAINTE-FOY, BATTLE OF, 1760
N8080	SAINTS — ART
BV194.C6	SAINTS — COMMEMORATION
BX4654	SAINTS — CORRESPONDENCE, REMINISCENCES, ETC.
BX4650-4662	SAINTS — LEGENDS
BR1710	SAINTS / *biography general*
BX4654-4662	SAINTS / *catholic church*
BL2003	SAINTS, HINDU
BP189.3-5	*SAINTS, ISLAMIC* **SEE** SAINTS, MUSLIM
BX4657	SAINTS, JUVENILE
BP189.3-5	SAINTS, MUSLIM
BX4656.5	*SAINTS, PATRON* **SEE** PATRON SAINTS
BL1170	SAINTS, TAMIL
BX4656	SAINTS, WOMEN / *biography collective*
N8080	*SAINTS-ICONOGRAPHY* **SEE** SAINTS — ART
QL638.G2	*SAITH* **SEE** CODFISH
SH351.C5	*SAITH* **SEE** CODFISH / *fisheries*
BL1245.S5	*SAIVISM* **SEE** SIVAISM
P911	*SAKA LANGUAGE* **SEE** KHOTANESE LANGUAGE
D90.S3	SAKA
D90.S3	*SAKAI (ANCIENT IRANIAN TRIBES)* **SEE** SAKA
PL4391	SAKAI DIALECTS
DS595	SAKAI
TP579	SAKE
DT313	*SAKSIWA* **SEE** SEKSAWA (BERBER TRIBE)
BL1245.S5	*SAKTAS* **SEE** SHAKTISM
BL1245.S5	*SAKTISM* **SEE** SHAKTISM
TX807	SALADS
DC233.S2	SALAMANCA, BATTLE OF, 1812
QL668.C2	SALAMANDERS
DF225.6	SALAMIS, BATTLE OF, 480 B.C.
HF5415	*SALE* **SEE** SALES / *marketing*
E475.35	SALEM CHURCH, BATTLE OF, 1863
D763.I8	SALERNO, BATTLE OF, 1943
HF5438	*SALES CONVENTIONS* **SEE** SALES MEETINGS
HF5730	SALES LETTERS
HF5438-5440	SALES MANAGEMENT
HF5438	SALES MEETINGS
HJ5711-5721	SALES TAX
HF5568	*SALES-FINANCE COMPANIES* **SEE** INSTALMENT PLAN
HF5415	SALES / *marketing*
HJ5711-5721	*SALES-TAXATION* **SEE** SALES TAX
LC495.S	SALESIANS — EDUCATION
BX4040.S2	SALESIANS
HF5438-9	*SALESMANSHIP* **SEE** SALESMEN AND SALESMANSHIP
HF5438-9	SALESMEN AND SALESMANSHIP
HF5441-4	*SALESMEN, TRAVELING* **SEE** COMMERCIAL TRAVELERS
PM7031	*SALIBA LANGUAGE* **SEE** SALIVA LANGUAGE
QP917.S2	SALICYLATES — PHYSIOLOGICAL EFFECT
QD341.A2	SALICYLATES / *chemistry*
RM666.S165	SALICYLATES / *therapeutics*
QP917.S2	SALICYLIC ACID — PHYSIOLOGICAL EFFECT
QD341.A2	SALICYLIC ACID / *chemistry*
RM666.S165	SALICYLIC ACID / *therapeutics*
QL668.E2	*SALIENTIA* **SEE** ANURA
DG135	SALII (PRIESTS OF MARS)
E99.S17	SALINAN INDIANS

PM2251	SALINAN LANGUAGE
RM178	*SALINE INJECTIONS* **SEE** INJECTIONS, SALINE
TN907	SALINES
GC121-7	SALINITY / *sea-water*
RM216.S	SALISBURY TREATMENT
E99.S2	SALISH INDIANS
PM2261-4	SALISH LANGUAGE
PM2264.A2	SALISH POETRY
E99.S21	SALISHAN INDIANS
PM2261-4	SALISHAN LANGUAGES
PM7031	*SALIUA LANGUAGE* **SEE** SALIVA LANGUAGE
PM7031	SALIVA LANGUAGE
QP191	SALIVA
QL865	SALIVARY GLANDS / *comparative anatomy*
QM325	SALIVARY GLANDS / *human anatomy*
QP191	SALIVARY GLANDS / *physiology*
QK495.S16	*SALIX* **SEE** WILLOWS
SD397.W5	*SALIX* **SEE** WILLOWS / *sylviculture*
PM7031	*SALLIBA LANGUAGE* **SEE** SALIVA LANGUAGE
PH521-9	*SALMI DIALECT* **SEE** OLONETSIAN LANGUAGE
SH179.S3	SALMON — DISEASES AND PESTS
SH347-9	SALMON-FISHERIES
SH685	SALMON-FISHING
QL638.S2	SALMON
SH167.S17	SALMON / *culture*
M1350	SALON-ORCHESTRA MUSIC
D211	SALONS
DC33	SALONS / *france*
NA7800-7850	*SALOONS* **SEE** HOTELS, TAVERNS, ETC. / *architecture*
GT3770-3899	*SALOONS* **SEE** HOTELS, TAVERNS, ETC. / *manners and customs*
HV5001-5720	*SALOONS* **SEE** LIQUOR TRAFFIC
HD9350-9399	*SALOONS* **SEE** LIQUOR TRAFFIC
SB211.S	*SALSAFY* **SEE** SALSIFY
SB211.S	SALSIFY
QP913.N2	SALT — PHYSIOLOGICAL EFFECT
HD9213	SALT — TAXATION
RM666.S17	SALT — THERAPEUTIC USE
BL617	*SALT COVENANT* **SEE** COVENANTS (RELIGION)
QP535.N2	SALT IN THE BODY
TN900-909	SALT INDUSTRY AND TRADE / *manufacture*
HD9213	SALT INDUSTRY AND TRADE / *trade*
TN900-909	SALT MINES AND MINING
QD541-9	*SALT SOLUTIONS* **SEE** SOLUTION (CHEMISTRY) / *theory*
SB207.S3	SALT-BUSH
QL561.A8	SALT-MARSH CATERPILLAR
S621	*SALT-MARSHES* **SEE** MARSHES, TIDE / *agriculture*
TC975	*SALT-MARSHES* **SEE** MARSHES, TIDE / *reclamation*
SH457	SALT-WATER FISHING
SF95	SALT / *feeding and feeds*
GT2870	SALT / *manners and customs*
TN900-909	SALT / *mineral industries*
HD9213	SALT / *trade*
M1010	SALTARELLOS (PIANO WITH ORCHESTRA) — SCORES (REDUCED) AND PARTS
M1010-1011	SALTARELLOS (PIANO WITH ORCHESTRA)
QL506-9	SALTATORIA
E99.C6	*SALTEAUX INDIANS* **SEE** CHIPPEWA INDIANS
QP913.K1	SALTPETER — PHYSIOLOGICAL EFFECT
RM666.S18	SALTPETER — THERAPEUTIC USE
TP238	SALTPETER / *manufacture*
TN911	SALTPETER, CHILE
QP912.S	SALTS — PHYSIOLOGICAL EFFECT
SF95	SALTS — PHYSIOLOGICAL EFFECT / *feeding and feeds*
QD189	SALTS
QD191	SALTS, DOUBLE
S590-598	SALTS, SOLUBLE / *soils*
DS451	*SALUNKIS* **SEE** CHALUKYAS
BT755	*SALUS EXTRA ECCLESIAM* **SEE** SALVATION OUTSIDE THE CATHOLIC CHURCH
BT759	*SALUS EXTRA ECCLESIAM* **SEE** SALVATION OUTSIDE THE CHURCH
BX9901-9969	*SALUS EXTRA ECCLESIAM* **SEE** UNIVERSALISM
GT3050	SALUTATIONS
U350-365	*SALUTES, MILITARY* **SEE** MILITARY CEREMONIES, HONORS, AND SALUTES
V310	*SALUTES, NAVAL* **SEE** NAVAL CEREMONIES, HONORS, AND SALUTES
PQ7530-7539	SALVADORIAN LITERATURE
PQ7536	SALVADORIAN POETRY / *collections*
PQ7532	SALVADORIAN POETRY / *history*
HD9975	SALVAGE (WASTE, ETC.)
TP995	SALVAGE (WASTE, ETC.)
VK1491	SALVAGE
JX4436	SALVAGE / *international law*
HE971	SALVAGE / *marine insurance*
RM666.A75	SALVARSAN
BT750	SALVATION — EARLY WORKS TO 1800
BL1215.S	SALVATION (BRAHMANISM)
BT755	*SALVATION (CATHOLIC CHURCH)* **SEE** SALVATION OUTSIDE THE CATHOLIC CHURCH
BT750-759	*SALVATION (CATHOLIC CHURCH)* **SEE** SALVATION
BV2595.S3	SALVATION ARMY — MISSIONS
BX9701-9743	SALVATION ARMY
HV4330-4470	SALVATION ARMY / *etc.*
BT759	*SALVATION OF INFIDELS* **SEE** SALVATION OUTSIDE THE CHURCH
BT759	*SALVATION OF PAGANS* **SEE** SALVATION OUTSIDE THE CHURCH
BT755	SALVATION OUTSIDE THE CATHOLIC CHURCH
BT759	SALVATION OUTSIDE THE CHURCH
BT750-759	SALVATION
RS201.03	*SALVES* **SEE** OINTMENTS
BR817.S3	SALZBURGERS — EMIGRATION, 1731-1735
DB879.S18	SALZBURGERS
PJ5271-9	SAMARITAN LANGUAGE
PJ5279	SAMARITAN LITERATURE
DS129	SAMARITANS
QD181.S2	SAMARIUM
PL6023	SAMARO-LEYTEAN DIALECT
GV1295.S	SAMBA (GAME)
PL8666	*SAMBALA LANGUAGE* **SEE** SHAMBALA LANGUAGE
GN788.B	SAMBAQUIS / *brazil*
PL8666	*SAMBARA LANGUAGE* **SEE** SHAMBALA LANGUAGE
M1264	SAMBAS (BAND) — SCORES AND PARTS
M1248	SAMBAS (BAND) — SCORES AND PARTS
M1248	SAMBAS (BAND)
M1264	SAMBAS (BAND)
PM5817.C4	*SAMBU DIALECT* **SEE** CHOCO LANGUAGE
ML697.A2	SAMBUCA LINCEA
JX238.S25-26	SAMOAN CLAIMS
PL6501	SAMOAN LANGUAGE
PL6501	SAMOAN LITERATURE
DU817	SAMOAN QUESTION
PL15-16	SAMOYEDIC LANGUAGES
SF429.S35	SAMOYEDS (DOGS)
DK34.S2	SAMOYEDS
NK9100-9199	SAMPLERS
QA276.5	SAMPLING (STATISTICS)
TN560	*SAMPLING OF ORES* **SEE** ORES — SAMPLING AND ESTIMATION
F1565.2.C8	*SAN BLAS INDIANS* **SEE** CUNA INDIANS
F869.S3	SAN FRANCISCO — EARTHQUAKE AND FIRE, 1906
F390	SAN JACINTO, BATTLE OF, 1836
SB945.S2	SAN JOSE SCALE
F1232	SAN JUAN DE ULUA, CAPITULATION OF, 1825
E717.1	SAN JUAN HILL, BATTLE OF, 1898
PL8101-4	*SAN LANGUAGES* **SEE** BUSHMAN LANGUAGES
F3097	SAN PABLO, BATTLE OF, 1882
DQ98	*SAN PAOLO, BATTLE OF, 1422* **SEE** ARBEDO, BATTLE OF, 1422
E406.S	SAN PASQUAL, BATTLE OF, 1846
DR573.7	SAN STEFANO, TREATY OF, 1878
RA960-993	SANATORIUMS
RC309	SANATORIUMS / *tuberculosis*
GV1295.P3	SANCHO-PEDRO (GAME)
BT765	SANCTIFICATION
BT767	SANCTIFICATION
JX1246	SANCTIONS (INTERNATIONAL LAW)
JX1975.6	SANCTIONS (INTERNATIONAL LAW) / *league of nations*
JX4275-4399	*SANCTUARY (LAW)* **SEE** ASYLUM, RIGHT OF
HV8652-4	*SANCTUARY (LAW)* **SEE** ASYLUM, RIGHT OF
E83.863	SAND CREEK, BATTLE OF, 1864
GV423	*SAND PLAYGROUNDS* **SEE** PLAYGROUNDS, SAND
NB1270.S3	SAND SCULPTURE
LB1139.C7	SAND TABLES

TC209	SAND-BARS / *harbors and coasts*
TC409	SAND-BARS / *rivers*
TP864	SAND-BLAST / *glass manufacture*
TJ1009	SAND-BLAST / *mechanical engineering*
QL444.D3	SAND-CRABS
GB631-8	SAND-DUNES
TP832.S2	SAND-LIME BRICK
TN939	SAND / *mineral industries*
TS243.5	SAND, FOUNDRY — ADDITIVES
TS243.5	SAND, FOUNDRY
TN939	SAND, GLASS / *mineral industries*
TS243.5	*SAND, MOLDING* **SEE** SAND, FOUNDRY
TN939	*SAND, SILICA* **SEE** SAND, GLASS / *mineral industries*
DT132	*SANDEH* **SEE** AZANDE
BX9747	SANDEMANIANISM
BX9747	*SANDEMANIANS* **SEE** SANDEMANIANISM
QL696.L7	SANDPIPERS
TN957	SANDSTONE
TA492.S25	SANDWICH CONSTRUCTION
TL671.2	SANDWICH CONSTRUCTION / *aeroplanes*
TX818	SANDWICHES
PL6025	SANGIR LANGUAGE
PK6996.Z4	*SANGLICI DIALECT* **SEE** ZEBAKI DIALECT
RA960-993	*SANITARIUMS* **SEE** SANATORIUMS
RC309	*SANITARIUMS* **SEE** SANATORIUMS / *tuberculosis*
RA	*SANITARY AFFAIRS* **SEE** HYGIENE, PUBLIC
RA425	*SANITARY AFFAIRS* **SEE** HYGIENE, PUBLIC / *comprehensive treatises*
RA11-388	*SANITARY AFFAIRS* **SEE** HYGIENE, PUBLIC / *general documents*
QR46	*SANITARY BACTERIOLOGY* **SEE** SANITARY MICROBIOLOGY
TX149	SANITARY CHEMISTRY / *home economics*
TD940-949	*SANITARY ENGINEERING IN FROZEN GROUND* **SEE** SANITARY ENGINEERING, LOW TEMPERATURE
TD940-949	*SANITARY ENGINEERING IN PERMAFROST* **SEE** SANITARY ENGINEERING, LOW TEMPERATURE
TD	SANITARY ENGINEERING
TD940-949	SANITARY ENGINEERING, LOW TEMPERATURE
TD795	*SANITARY FILLS* **SEE** SANITARY LANDFILLS
TD795	SANITARY LANDFILLS
QR46	SANITARY MICROBIOLOGY
TH7700-7975	*SANITATION, HOUSEHOLD* **SEE** LIGHTING
GT440-445	*SANITATION, HOUSEHOLD* **SEE** LIGHTING / *manners and customs*
TH6021-7696	SANITATION, HOUSEHOLD / *building*
TD905-935	SANITATION, HOUSEHOLD / *sanitary engineering*
PK3811	SANKHYA / *philology*
B132.S3	SANKHYA / *philosophy*
DQ99	SANKT JAKOB AN DER BIRS, BATTLE OF, 1444
SB261.S	SANN / *fiber plants*
E99.S215	SANPOIL INDIANS
E99.S217	SANS ARC INDIANS
DC158.8	SANSCULOTTES
PK2931-3	SANSKRIT DRAMA
PK4131	SANSKRIT DRAMA / *dramaturgy*
PK4471-4489	SANSKRIT DRAMA / *translations*
PK401-969	SANSKRIT LANGUAGE
PK2901-4485	SANSKRIT LITERATURE
PK401-418	SANSKRIT PHILOLOGY
PK2971-5	SANSKRIT POETRY / *collections*
PK2916-2929	SANSKRIT POETRY / *history*
PK4471-4485	SANSKRIT POETRY / *post-vedic*
PK3601-3741	SANSKRIT POETRY / *post-vedic*
PK2977-8	SANSKRIT POETRY / *translations*
F869.S45	SANTA BARBARA, CALIF. — EARTHQUAKE, 1925
GT4985	SANTA CLAUS
DA86.8 1657	SANTA CRUZ DE TENERIFE, BATTLE OF, 1657
F2325	SANTA INES, BATTLE OF, 1859
DS432.S	*SANTAL (BENGAL TRIBE)* **SEE** SANTALS
DS485.B49	SANTAL REBELLION, 1855-1856
PL4563	SANTALI LANGUAGE
DS432.S	SANTALS
PM1021-4	SANTEE DIALECT
E99.S22	SANTEE INDIANS
BL2530.S2	SANTERIA (CULTUS)
E717.1	SANTIAGO CAMPAIGN, 1898
F1779	SANTIAGO EXPEDITION, 1741
F1779	SANTIAGO EXPEDITION, 1747
E727	SANTIAGO, BATTLE OF, 1898
JX238.S3-4	SANTO DOMINGO CLAIMS
QD341.A2	SANTONIC ACID / *chemistry*
QP917.S3	SANTONIC ACID / *physiological effect*
QD341.A2	SANTONIN / *chemistry*
QP917.S3	SANTONIN / *physiological effect*
RM666.S	SANTONIN / *therapeutics*
F2631	SAO PAULO, BRAZIL (STATE) — HISTORY — — REVOLUTION, 1932
E99.S225	SAONE INDIANS
SB741.S	SAP-ROT
SK871	SAP
QD325	SAPONINS
QE389.62	SAPONITE
TN948.S	SAPONITE
TS755.S3	SAPPHIRES / *jewelry*
QE394.S3	SAPPHIRES / *mineralogy*
QE391.S	SAPPHIRINE
UG510-515	SAPPING
TN800	SAPROPELITES
QK918	SAPROPHYTISM
PL5571	*SAPTANG LANGUAGE* **SEE** BATAN LANGUAGE
M240-244	SARABANDS (FLUTE AND HARPSICHORD)
M240-244	SARABANDS (FLUTE AND PIANO)
M1010-1011	SARABANDS (HARPSICHORD WITH ORCHESTRA)
M1045	SARABANDS (ORCHESTRA)
M1060	SARABANDS (ORCHESTRA)
M1145	SARABANDS (STRING ORCHESTRA)
M239	SARABANDS (VIOLA D'AMORE AND PIANO)
NA380-388	*SARACENIC ARCHITECTURE* **SEE** ARCHITECTURE, ISLAMIC
N6260-6271	*SARACENIC ART* **SEE** ART, ISLAMIC
PN56.S	SARACENS IN LITERATURE
DS234-8	SARACENS
DC233.S3	SARAGOSSA — SIEGE, 1808-1809
DS432.S	SARAKS
F2726	SARANDI, BATTLE OF, 1825
M298	SARANGI AND TABLA MUSIC
ML927.S4	SARANGI
E241.S2	SARATOGA CAMPAIGN, 1777
E241.S2	*SARATOGA, BATTLE OF, 1777* **SEE** SARATOGA CAMPAIGN, 1777
DS432.S	*SARAWAKS* **SEE** SARAKS
BH301.I7	*SARCASM* **SEE** IRONY / *aesthetics*
PN1680	*SARCASM* **SEE** IRONY / *drama*
QR82.S3	SARCINA
QH591	*SARCODE* **SEE** PROTOPLASM
RM133	SARCOGNOMY
RD651-678	*SARCOMA* **SEE** TUMORS
RC254-272	*SARCOMA* **SEE** TUMORS
NB1810	SARCOPHAGI / *sculpture*
GV1796.S3	SARDANA / *dance*
SH351.S3	SARDINE FISHERIES
GT2350	*SAREES* **SEE** SARIS
GT2350	*SARI* **SEE** SARIS
GT2350	SARIS
DK34.S3	SARMATIANS
RS165.S	SARSAPARILLA / *pharmacy*
RM666.S2	SARSAPARILLA / *therapeutics*
E99.S	SARSI INDIANS
PM2275	SARSI LANGUAGE
PL5439	*SASAK LANGUAGE* **SEE** SASSAK LANGUAGE
TH2272	SASHES / *window fittings*
F1060.9	*SASKATCHEWAN REBELLION, 1885* **SEE** RIEL REBELLION, 1885
PL5439	SASSAK LANGUAGE
DS286	*SASSANIANS* **SEE** SASSANIDS
DS286	SASSANIDS
PM2305	*SASTEAN LANGUAGES* **SEE** SHASTAN LANGUAGES
BL480	*SATAN* **SEE** DEVIL / *comparative religion*
BF1546-1561	*SATAN* **SEE** DEVIL / *demonology*
BT980-981	*SATAN* **SEE** DEVIL / *theology*
BL480	SATANISM / *comparative religion*
BF1546-1550	SATANISM / *occult sciences*
TL796	*SATELLITE VEHICLES* **SEE** ARTIFICIAL SATELLITES
TL797	*SATELLITE VEHICLES* **SEE** SPACE STATIONS
QB401-7	SATELLITES
TL796	*SATELLITES, ARTIFICIAL* **SEE** ARTIFICIAL SATELLITES
SB945.S	SATIN MOTH
TS1640-1673	SATIN / *silk manufacture*

PN6231.S2	SATIRE / collections
PN6149.S2	SATIRE / history
QB671	SATURN (PLANET) — PHASES
QB405	SATURN (PLANET) — RING SYSTEM
QB384	SATURN (PLANET) — TABLES
QB671	SATURN (PLANET) / descriptive astronomy
QB384	SATURN (PLANET) / theoretical astronomy
PA2337.S2	SATURNIAN VERSE
PA3160	*SATYRIC DRAMA, GREEK* **SEE** GREEK DRAMA (SATYR PLAY)
PA3464	*SATYRIC DRAMA, GREEK* **SEE** GREEK DRAMA (SATYR PLAY)
TX819	SAUCES
TX612.S45	SAUERKRAUT
E99.S23	SAUK INDIANS
E99.C6	*SAULTEAUX INDIANS* **SEE** CHIPPEWA INDIANS
E99.C	*SAURA INDIANS* **SEE** CHERAW INDIANS
QL668.C2	*SAUROBATRACHIA* **SEE** URODELA
QE862.D5	SAUROPODA
TS1962	SAUSAGES
TS1970-1971	SAUSAGES / packing-house industries
E99.C6	*SAUTEUX INDIANS* **SEE** CHIPPEWA INDIANS
PM851-4	*SAUTEUX LANGUAGE* **SEE** CHIPPEWA LANGUAGE
GN307-499	*SAVAGES* **SEE** MAN, PRIMITIVE
E241.S26	SAVANNAH — SIEGE, 1779
E477.41	SAVANNAH — SIEGE, 1864
PL4587	SAVARA LANGUAGE
GV1115-1137	*SAVATE* **SEE** BOXING
HG7920-7933	SAVING AND THRIFT
BJ1533.E2	SAVING AND THRIFT / ethics
HG2121-2156	*SAVINGS AND LOAN ASSOCIATIONS* **SEE** BUILDING AND LOAN ASSOCIATIONS
HG1662	*SAVINGS INSURANCE* **SEE** INSURANCE, DEPOSIT
HG1881-1966	SAVINGS-BANKS
HG1951-6	*SAVINGS-BANKS, POSTAL* **SEE** POSTAL SAVINGS-BANKS
HG1961-6	*SAVINGS-BANKS, SCHOOL* **SEE** SCHOOL SAVINGS-BANKS
D774.S318	SAVO ISLAND, BATTLE OF, 1942
DA125.S	SAVOYARDS IN ENGLAND
DC611. S361-372	SAVOYARDS
TJ1235	SAW-FILING / machine-tools
TS851	SAW-FILING / woodworking
QK495.C997	SAW-GRASS
QK495.P17	SAW-PALMETTO
TP996.W6	*SAWDUST* **SEE** WOOD WASTE
QL568.T3	SAWFLIES
QK945.S3	SAWFLIES / agricultural pests
TS850	SAWMILLS
TJ1233-5	SAWS / machine-tools
TS851	SAWS / woodworking
DG315	SAXA RUBRA, BATTLE OF, 312
M266-7	SAXHORN AND PIANO MUSIC
DD136-140.7	*SAXON EMPERORS* **SEE** GERMANY — HISTORY — — SAXON HOUSE, 919-1024
DD136-140.7	*SAXON HOUSE* **SEE** GERMANY — HISTORY — — SAXON HOUSE, 919-1024
DD78.S3	SAXONS / germanic races and tribes
DA150-155	SAXONS / saxons in england
DD801.S2	SAXONS / saxony
DD801.S3-59	SAXONY — HISTORY
DD136-140.7	*SAXONY, HOUSE OF* **SEE** GERMANY — HISTORY — — SAXON HOUSE, 919-1024
MT502	SAXOPHONE — METHODS (JAZZ)
M268-9	SAXOPHONE AND PIANO MUSIC (JAZZ)
M268-9	SAXOPHONE AND PIANO MUSIC
M268-9	*SAXOPHONE AND PIANO MUSIC, ARRANGED (JAZZ)* **SEE** SAXOPHONE AND PIANO MUSIC (JAZZ)
M268-9	SAXOPHONE AND PIANO MUSIC, ARRANGED
M1040-1041	SAXOPHONE AND PIANO WITH ORCHESTRA
M288-9	SAXOPHONE MUSIC (2 SAXOPHONES)
M355-7	*SAXOPHONE MUSIC (3 SAXOPHONES)* **SEE** WIND TRIOS (3 SAXOPHONES)
M355-7	*SAXOPHONE MUSIC (3 SAXOPHONES)* **SEE** WIND TRIOS (3 SAXOPHONES)
M455-7	*SAXOPHONE MUSIC (4 SAXOPHONES)* **SEE** WIND QUARTETS (4 SAXOPHONES)
M455-7	*SAXOPHONE MUSIC (4 SAXOPHONES)* **SEE** WIND QUARTETS (4 SAXOPHONES)

M105-7	SAXOPHONE MUSIC
M108-9	SAXOPHONE MUSIC, ARRANGED
M1035	SAXOPHONE WITH CHAMBER ORCHESTRA — SOLO WITH PIANO
M1034-5	SAXOPHONE WITH CHAMBER ORCHESTRA
M1353	SAXOPHONE WITH DANCE ORCHESTRA
M1035	SAXOPHONE WITH ORCHESTRA — SOLO WITH PIANO
M1034-5	SAXOPHONE WITH ORCHESTRA
M1105-6	SAXOPHONE WITH STRING ORCHESTRA
ML975	SAXOPHONE
PL16.K3	*SAYAN-SAMOYEDIC LANGUAGE* **SEE** KAMASSIN LANGUAGE
PN6269-6278	*SAYINGS* **SEE** APHORISMS AND APOTHEGMS
PN6299-6308	*SAYINGS* **SEE** APHORISMS AND APOTHEGMS
PN6328.C5	*SAYINGS* **SEE** CHILDREN — ANECDOTES AND SAYINGS
PN6279-6288	*SAYINGS* **SEE** EPIGRAMS
PN1441	*SAYINGS* **SEE** EPIGRAMS / poetry
PN6299-6308	*SAYINGS* **SEE** MAXIMS
PN6400-6525	*SAYINGS* **SEE** PROVERBS
PN6080-6095	*SAYINGS* **SEE** QUOTATIONS
PN6259-6268	*SAYINGS* **SEE** TABLE-TALK
ML1015-1018	SAZ
SF970	SCAB DISEASE IN SHEEP
RC182.S17	SCABIES
GT3350	SCAFFOLD BURIAL
TH5281	SCAFFOLDING
TH5281	SCAFFOLDING, METAL
RD131	*SCALDS* **SEE** BURNS AND SCALDS
RC87	*SCALDS* **SEE** BURNS AND SCALDS / popular medicine
PT7244-6	SCALDS AND SCALDIC POETRY / collections
PT7172	SCALDS AND SCALDIC POETRY / history
QL523.C7	SCALE-INSECTS
SB939	SCALE-INSECTS / economic entomology
QK650	SCALES (BOTANY)
QL639	SCALES (FISHES)
ML3809	*SCALES (MUSIC)* **SEE** MUSICAL INTERVALS AND SCALES
N8239.S6	SCALES (WEIGHING INSTRUMENTS) IN ART
QC107	SCALES (WEIGHING INSTRUMENTS)
TS410	SCALES (WEIGHING INSTRUMENTS) / manufacture
BF39	*SCALING, PSYCHOLOGICAL* **SEE** PSYCHOMETRICS
QL430.7.P3	SCALLOPS
SH373	SCALLOPS / fisheries
RL151-9	SCALP — DISEASES
HE1971	*SCALPING OF RAILROAD TICKETS* **SEE** TICKET BROKERAGE
E98.W2	SCALPING / indian warfare
PT7093	SCANDINAVIAN BALLADS AND SONGS / collections
PT7088-9	SCANDINAVIAN BALLADS AND SONGS / folk literature
PT7080	SCANDINAVIAN BALLADS AND SONGS / history
CE61.G3	*SCANDINAVIAN CALENDAR* **SEE** CALENDAR, GERMANIC
PT7095	SCANDINAVIAN FICTION / collections
PT7083	SCANDINAVIAN FICTION / history
PD1501-5929	SCANDINAVIAN LANGUAGES
PT7090-7099	SCANDINAVIAN LITERATURE / collections
PT7045-7087	SCANDINAVIAN LITERATURE / history
PD1501-1541	SCANDINAVIAN PHILOLOGY
PT7093	SCANDINAVIAN POETRY / collections
PT7080	SCANDINAVIAN POETRY / history
PN4885.S2	SCANDINAVIAN-AMERICAN NEWSPAPERS / etc.
DL57	SCANDINAVIANISM
DL41	SCANDINAVIANS
QD181.S4	SCANDIUM
QL430.8	SCAPHOPODA
QE813	SCAPHOPODA, FOSSIL
QL821	SCAPULA / comparative anatomy
QM101	SCAPULA / human anatomy
QL821	*SCAPULAR ARCH* **SEE** SHOULDER GIRDLE / comparative anatomy
QM101	*SCAPULAR ARCH* **SEE** SHOULDER GIRDLE / human anatomy
BX2310.S3	SCAPULARS
QL596.S3	SCARABAEIDAE
NK5561	SCARABS / art
DT62.S3	SCARABS / egyptology
RA664.S2	SCARLATINA — PREVENTION

RC182.S17	SCARLATINA — PREVENTION
RC182.S2	SCARLATINA
RX226.S2	SCARLATINA / *homeopathic treatment*
RM782.S2	SCARLATINA / *serumtherapy*
RC182.S2	*SCARLET FEVER* **SEE** SCARLATINA
RX226.S2	*SCARLET FEVER* **SEE** SCARLATINA / *homeopathic treatment*
RM782.S2	*SCARLET FEVER* **SEE** SCARLATINA / *serumtherapy*
RL621	*SCARS* **SEE** CICATRICES
GV1257	*SCAT (GAME)* **SEE** SKAT (GAME)
HJ3464.S	SCAT (TAX)
E78.C7	SCATICOOK INDIANS (CONN.)
E78.N7	SCATICOOK INDIANS (N.Y.)
GT99	SCATOLOGY
PN1996-7	*SCENARIOS* **SEE** MOVING-PICTURE PLAYS
PN145	*SCENARIOS* **SEE** PLOTS (DRAMA, NOVEL, ETC.)
PN44	*SCENARIOS* **SEE** PLOTS (DRAMA, NOVEL, ETC.)
PN1683	*SCENARIOS* **SEE** PLOTS (DRAMA, NOVEL, ETC.) / *drama*
PN3378	*SCENARIOS* **SEE** PLOTS (DRAMA, NOVEL, ETC.) / *fiction*
PN3373	*SCENARIOS* **SEE** PLOTS (DRAMA, NOVEL, ETC.) / *short story*
ND2885	SCENE PAINTING
PN1995	*SCENERY (STAGE)* **SEE** MOVING-PICTURES — SETTING AND SCENERY
PN2091.S8	*SCENERY (STAGE)* **SEE** THEATERS — STAGE-SETTING AND SCENERY
BH301.L3	*SCENERY* **SEE** LANDSCAPE / *aesthetics*
QH75	*SCENERY* **SEE** LANDSCAPE / *natural history*
G136-9	*SCENERY* **SEE** VIEWS
GV1855	SCENIC RAILWAYS / *amusement parks*
DS422.C3	*SCHEDULED CASTES (INDIA)* **SEE** UNTOUCHABLES
QE391.S3	SCHEELITE
ML760	*SCHEITHOLT* **SEE** NOORDSCHE BALK
F129.S5	SCHENECTADY, N.Y. — DESTRUCTION, 1690
PM7073	*SCHIPIBO DIALECT* **SEE** SIPIBO LANGUAGE
BX303	SCHISM — EASTERN AND WESTERN CHURCH
BX1301	SCHISM, THE GREAT WESTERN, 1378-1417
BX303	*SCHISM-GREEK AND LATIN CHURCH* **SEE** SCHISM — EASTERN AND WESTERN CHURCH
BX303	*SCHISM-LATIN AND GREEK CHURCH* **SEE** SCHISM — EASTERN AND WESTERN CHURCH
QE605	SCHISTOSITY
RC122.B5	SCHISTOSOMIASIS
QE475	SCHISTS
RC514	SCHIZOPHRENIA
QL444.S3	SCHIZOPODA
GV1017.S2	SCHLAGBALL
DD491.S68	SCHLESWIG-HOLSTEIN QUESTION
DL217-223	SCHLESWIG-HOLSTEIN WAR, 1848-1850
DL236-9	SCHLESWIG-HOLSTEIN WAR, 1864
QC373.S3	SCHLIEREN APPARATUS
DL743.S3	SCHLÜSSELBERG, RUSSIA — SIEGE, 1702 / *northern war*
DK136	SCHLÜSSELBERG, RUSSIA — SIEGE, 1702 / *russian history*
DD184	SCHMALKALDIC LEAGUE, 1530-1547
DD184	SCHMALKALDIC WAR, 1546-1547
F2501.1.S	*SCHOKLENG INDIANS* **SEE** SHOKLENG INDIANS / *indians of brazil*
CT	SCHOLARS / *biography*
PA83-85	SCHOLARS / *classical scholars*
AZ	*SCHOLARSHIP* **SEE** LEARNING AND SCHOLARSHIP / *etc.*
LB2338-9	SCHOLARSHIPS / *college and university*
LB2848-9	SCHOLARSHIPS / *school*
LB1131	*SCHOLASTIC SUCCESS, PREDICTION OF* **SEE** PREDICTION OF SCHOLASTIC SUCCESS
B839	SCHOLASTICISM / *general and modern*
B851-4695	SCHOLASTICISM / *local*
B734	SCHOLASTICISM / *medieval*
BD125	SCHOLASTICISM / *scholastic metaphysics*
DC234.9	*SCHONBRUNN, TREATY OF, 1809* **SEE** VIENNA, TREATY OF, 1809
GV1017.S3	SCHOOL (GAME)
LB3407	SCHOOL ACCIDENTS
LB2830	*SCHOOL ACCOUNTING* **SEE** SCHOOLS — ACCOUNTING

LB3011-3095	*SCHOOL ADMINISTRATION* **SEE** SCHOOL MANAGEMENT AND ORGANIZATION / *management and discipline*
LB2801-2997	*SCHOOL ADMINISTRATION* **SEE** SCHOOL MANAGEMENT AND ORGANIZATION / *organization and supervision*
LB2803-2822	*SCHOOL ADMINISTRATORS* **SEE** SCHOOL SUPERINTENDENTS AND PRINCIPALS
LC142-5	*SCHOOL AGE (ENTRANCE AGE)* **SEE** SCHOOL ATTENDANCE / *limitation*
LB3081	*SCHOOL AGE (ENTRANCE AGE)* **SEE** SCHOOL ATTENDANCE / *truancy*
LB1133	SCHOOL AGE (ENTRANCE AGE)
LC215	*SCHOOL AND COMMUNITY* **SEE** COMMUNITY AND SCHOOL
LC225	*SCHOOL AND HOME* **SEE** HOME AND SCHOOL
LB3621	*SCHOOL ANNUALS* **SEE** SCHOOL YEARBOOKS
LB3205-3295	*SCHOOL ARCHITECTURE* **SEE** SCHOOL-HOUSES
LB3221	*SCHOOL ARCHITECTURE* **SEE** SCHOOL-HOUSES / *plans*
LB3015-3031	*SCHOOL ASSEMBLY* **SEE** SCHOOLS — EXERCISES AND RECREATIONS
LC146	SCHOOL ATTENDANCE — HIGH SCHOOL
LC142·5	SCHOOL ATTENDANCE / *limitation*
LB3081	SCHOOL ATTENDANCE / *truancy*
LC148	*SCHOOL ATTENDANCE-COLLEGE* **SEE** COLLEGE ATTENDANCE
TH4761	*SCHOOL BATHS* **SEE** BATHS, PUBLIC / *building*
RA605	*SCHOOL BATHS* **SEE** BATHS, PUBLIC / *public hygiene*
LB2831	SCHOOL BOARDS
LB2824-2830	SCHOOL BONDS / *education*
HG4951-3	SCHOOL BONDS / *investments u.s.*
LB3205-3295	*SCHOOL BUILDINGS* **SEE** SCHOOL-HOUSES
LB3221	*SCHOOL BUILDINGS* **SEE** SCHOOL-HOUSES / *plans*
LB2823.5	*SCHOOL BUSINESS MANAGEMENT* **SEE** PUBLIC SCHOOLS — BUSINESS MANAGEMENT
GV197.S3	SCHOOL CAMPS
LC142-5	*SCHOOL CENSUS* **SEE** SCHOOL ATTENDANCE / *limitation*
LB3081	*SCHOOL CENSUS* **SEE** SCHOOL ATTENDANCE / *truancy*
LC130	SCHOOL CENSUS
LB2861	*SCHOOL CENTRALIZATION* **SEE** SCHOOLS — CENTRALIZATION / *rural*
LB3473-9	SCHOOL CHILDREN — FOOD
LB2864	SCHOOL CHILDREN — TRANSPORTATION
LB2846	*SCHOOL CHILDREN-PERSONNEL RECORDS* **SEE** PERSONNEL RECORDS IN EDUCATION
LB3081	*SCHOOL CHILDREN-TRANSPORTATION* **SEE** SCHOOL ATTENDANCE / *truancy*
LC142-5	*SCHOOL CHILDREN-TRANSPORTATION* **SEE** SCHOOL ATTENDANCE / *limitation*
LB3093-5	SCHOOL CITY, STATE, ETC.
LB3602	*SCHOOL CLUBS* **SEE** STUDENTS' SOCIETIES
LB3630	SCHOOL COLORS
LB3068-9	SCHOOL CONTESTS
LB3051-3063	SCHOOL CREDITS — OUTSIDE WORK / *etc.*
LB1048	SCHOOL CREDITS — OUTSIDE WORK / *home study*
MT733	*SCHOOL DANCE BAND* **SEE** DANCE ORCHESTRA
ML1200	*SCHOOL DANCE BAND* **SEE** DANCE ORCHESTRA
LB3257	SCHOOL DECORATION
LB3011-3095	SCHOOL DISCIPLINE
LB2830	*SCHOOL DISTRICTS-ACCOUNTING* **SEE** SCHOOLS — ACCOUNTING
PN3175-3191	*SCHOOL DRAMA* **SEE** COLLEGE AND SCHOOL DRAMA / *history and criticism*
LC142-8	*SCHOOL DROPOUTS* **SEE** DROPOUTS
HV16-25	*SCHOOL ENDOWMENTS* **SEE** ENDOWMENTS / *charities*
LB2336-7	*SCHOOL ENDOWMENTS* **SEE** ENDOWMENTS / *higher education*
LB2823	*SCHOOL EVALUATION* **SEE** EDUCATIONAL SURVEYS
LB1047	SCHOOL EXCURSIONS
LB2846	*SCHOOL FILING SYSTEMS* **SEE** SCHOOLS — RECORDS AND CORRESPONDENCE
LB2824-2830	*SCHOOL FINANCE* **SEE** EDUCATION — FINANCE
TH9445.S3	*SCHOOL FIRES* **SEE** SCHOOLS — FIRES AND FIRE PREVENTION / *prevention*
L-LC	*SCHOOL FUNDS* **SEE** PUBLIC SCHOOLS
LB2827	*SCHOOL FUNDS* **SEE** SCHOOL LANDS

LB3261-3281	*SCHOOL FURNITURE* **SEE** SCHOOLS — FURNITURE, EQUIPMENT, ETC.
SB55-56	SCHOOL GARDENS
LB3251	SCHOOL GROUNDS
LB3401-3495	SCHOOL HYGIENE
LB3011-3095	*SCHOOL INSPECTION* **SEE** SCHOOL MANAGEMENT AND ORGANIZATION / *management and discipline*
LB2801-2997	*SCHOOL INSPECTION* **SEE** SCHOOL MANAGEMENT AND ORGANIZATION / *organization and supervision*
PN4825-4830	*SCHOOL JOURNALISM* **SEE** COLLEGE AND SCHOOL JOURNALISM / *amateur journalism*
LB3621	*SCHOOL JOURNALISM* **SEE** COLLEGE AND SCHOOL JOURNALISM
LB2827	SCHOOL LANDS
LB2503-2797	*SCHOOL LAW* **SEE** EDUCATIONAL LAW AND LEGISLATION
Z675.S3	SCHOOL LIBRARIES (HIGH SCHOOL)
Z675.S3	SCHOOL LIBRARIES
LB2397	*SCHOOL LIFE* **SEE** STUDENTS / *reminiscences*
LB3602-3635	*SCHOOL LIFE* **SEE** STUDENTS / *student life*
LB3243	*SCHOOL LIGHTING* **SEE** SCHOOL-HOUSES — LIGHTING
LB3473-9	*SCHOOL LUNCHES* **SEE** SCHOOL CHILDREN — FOOD
LC142-5	*SCHOOL MANAGEMENT AND ORGANIZATION* **SEE** SCHOOL ATTENDANCE / *limitation*
LB3081	*SCHOOL MANAGEMENT AND ORGANIZATION* **SEE** SCHOOL ATTENDANCE / *truancy*
LB3011-3095	SCHOOL MANAGEMENT AND ORGANIZATION / *management and discipline*
LB2801-2997	SCHOOL MANAGEMENT AND ORGANIZATION / *organization and supervision*
LB3407	SCHOOL NURSES
LB3011-3095	*SCHOOL ORGANIZATION* **SEE** SCHOOL MANAGEMENT AND ORGANIZATION / *management and discipline*
LB2801-2997	*SCHOOL ORGANIZATION* **SEE** SCHOOL MANAGEMENT AND ORGANIZATION / *organization and supervision*
LB2831.5	SCHOOL PERSONNEL MANAGEMENT
LB3407	SCHOOL PHYSICIANS
GV421-433	*SCHOOL PLAYGROUNDS* **SEE** PLAYGROUNDS
PN6120.A4-5	*SCHOOL PLAYS* **SEE** CHILDREN'S PLAYS
PN3175-3191	*SCHOOL PLAYS* **SEE** COLLEGE AND SCHOOL DRAMA / *history and criticism*
LB2803-2822	*SCHOOL PRINCIPALS* **SEE** SCHOOL SUPERINTENDENTS AND PRINCIPALS
LB3013.6	SCHOOL PSYCHOLOGISTS
LB2846	SCHOOL PUBLICITY
LB3033	*SCHOOL RECESSES* **SEE** RECESSES
LB2846	*SCHOOL RECORDS* **SEE** SCHOOLS — RECORDS AND CORRESPONDENCE
LB2846	*SCHOOL REPORTS* **SEE** PERSONNEL RECORDS IN EDUCATION
LB2846	SCHOOL REPORTS
LB3093-5	*SCHOOL REPUBLIC* **SEE** SCHOOL CITY, STATE, ETC.
HG1961-6	SCHOOL SAVINGS-BANKS
LB2844.4	SCHOOL SECRETARIES
LB3220	SCHOOL SITES
LB3013	SCHOOL SIZE
M1994	SCHOOL SONG-BOOKS
M1994	SCHOOL SONG-BOOKS, CATHOLIC
LB3093-5	*SCHOOL STATE* **SEE** SCHOOL CITY, STATE, ETC.
LB1738.5	SCHOOL SUPERINTENDENTS AND PRINCIPALS — IN-SERVICE TRAINING
LB2803-2822	SCHOOL SUPERINTENDENTS AND PRINCIPALS
LB2806	SCHOOL SUPERINTENDENTS AND PRINCIPALS, RATING OF
LB2805-2822	SCHOOL SUPERINTENDENTS AND PRINCIPALS, TRAINING OF
LB2801-2822	SCHOOL SUPERVISION
LB2813	SCHOOL SUPERVISION, COUNTY
LB2822.5	SCHOOL SUPERVISION, ELEMENTARY
LB1567	SCHOOL SUPERVISION, RURAL
LB2822	SCHOOL SUPERVISION, SECONDARY
LB3261-3281	*SCHOOL SUPPLIES* **SEE** SCHOOLS — FURNITURE, EQUIPMENT, ETC.
LB2823	*SCHOOL SURVEYS* **SEE** EDUCATIONAL SURVEYS
LB2824-2830	*SCHOOL TAXES* **SEE** EDUCATION — FINANCE
LB	*SCHOOL TEACHING* **SEE** TEACHING
LB1775-1785	*SCHOOL TEACHING* **SEE** TEACHING / *teaching as a profession*
LB2864	*SCHOOL TRANSPORTATION* **SEE** SCHOOL CHILDREN — TRANSPORTATION
LB2831	*SCHOOL TRUSTEES* **SEE** SCHOOL BOARDS
LB3249	SCHOOL VANDALISM
PS591.S3	SCHOOL VERSE / *american literature*
PR1178.S3	SCHOOL VERSE / *english literature*
LB2844.2	*SCHOOL VOLUNTEERS* **SEE** VOLUNTEER WORKERS IN EDUCATION
LB3034	SCHOOL YEAR
LB3621	SCHOOL YEARBOOKS
LT	*SCHOOL-BOOKS* **SEE** TEXT-BOOKS
LB2851-3	*SCHOOL-BOOKS* **SEE** TEXT-BOOKS
LB3045	*SCHOOL-BOOKS* **SEE** TEXT-BOOKS
LB3241-4	SCHOOL-HOUSES — HEATING AND VENTILATION
LB3243	SCHOOL-HOUSES — LIGHTING
LB3205-3295	SCHOOL-HOUSES
LB3221	SCHOOL-HOUSES / *plans*
TH9445.S3	*SCHOOL-HOUSES-FIRES AND FIRE PREVENTION* **SEE** SCHOOLS — FIRES AND FIRE PREVENTION / *prevention*
M1420	*SCHOOL-ORCHESTRA MUSIC* **SEE** BAND MUSIC, JUVENILE
M1420	*SCHOOL-ORCHESTRA MUSIC* **SEE** ORCHESTRAL MUSIC, JUVENILE
V523-4	*SCHOOL-SHIPS* **SEE** TRAINING-SHIPS / *gt. brit.*
V435-6	*SCHOOL-SHIPS* **SEE** TRAINING-SHIPS / *u.s.*
LB3205-3295	*SCHOOLHOUSES* **SEE** SCHOOL-HOUSES
LB3221	*SCHOOLHOUSES* **SEE** SCHOOL-HOUSES / *plans*
LB2830	SCHOOLS — ACCOUNTING
LB2861	SCHOOLS — CENTRALIZATION / *rural*
LB3015-3031	SCHOOLS — EXERCISES AND RECREATIONS
TH9445.S3	SCHOOLS — FIRES AND FIRE PREVENTION / *prevention*
LB3261-3281	SCHOOLS — FURNITURE, EQUIPMENT, ETC.
LB3630	SCHOOLS — INSIGNIA
BV283.S3	SCHOOLS — PRAYERS
LB2846	SCHOOLS — RECORDS AND CORRESPONDENCE
Z718	*SCHOOLS AND LIBRARIES* **SEE** LIBRARIES AND SCHOOLS
PN56.E	*SCHOOLS IN LITERATURE* **SEE** EDUCATION IN LITERATURE
PN3448.S4	*SCHOOLS IN LITERATURE* **SEE** EDUCATION IN LITERATURE / *schools in fiction*
PS169.S4	*SCHOOLS IN LITERATURE* **SEE** EDUCATION IN LITERATURE / *schools in american literature*
RT71-81	*SCHOOLS OF NURSING* **SEE** NURSING SCHOOLS
L	SCHOOLS
HF1101-1181	*SCHOOLS, COMMERCIAL* **SEE** BUSINESS EDUCATION
LB2153-5	*SCHOOLS, DEMONSTRATION* **SEE** LABORATORY SCHOOLS
LC427-629	*SCHOOLS, DENOMINATIONAL* **SEE** CHURCH SCHOOLS
BM125	SCHOOLS, JEWISH — EXERCISES AND RECREATIONS
LB2153-5	*SCHOOLS, LABORATORY* **SEE** LABORATORY SCHOOLS
U400-714	*SCHOOLS, MILITARY* **SEE** MILITARY EDUCATION
LB2153-5	*SCHOOLS, MODEL* **SEE** LABORATORY SCHOOLS
LC427-629	*SCHOOLS, PAROCHIAL* **SEE** CHURCH SCHOOLS
LB1567	*SCHOOLS, RURAL* **SEE** RURAL SCHOOLS
LB3013	*SCHOOLS, SIZE OF* **SEE** SCHOOL SIZE
LB2342	*SCHOOLS-ACCOUNTING* **SEE** PUNCHED CARD SYSTEMS — EDUCATION / *colleges*
LB2830	*SCHOOLS-ACCOUNTING* **SEE** PUNCHED CARD SYSTEMS — EDUCATION / *schools*
LB3068-9	*SCHOOLS-COMPETITIONS* **SEE** SCHOOL CONTESTS
LB2361-5	*SCHOOLS-CURRICULA* **SEE** EDUCATION — CURRICULA / *colleges and universities*
LB1570-1571	*SCHOOLS-CURRICULA* **SEE** EDUCATION — CURRICULA / *elementary schools*
LB1628-9	*SCHOOLS-CURRICULA* **SEE** EDUCATION — CURRICULA / *secondary schools*
LB2361-5	*SCHOOLS-CURRICULA* **SEE** UNIVERSITIES AND COLLEGES — CURRICULA
LB2861	*SCHOOLS-DECENTRALIZATION* **SEE** SCHOOLS — CENTRALIZATION / *rural*
LB3257	*SCHOOLS-DECORATION* **SEE** SCHOOL DECORATION
LB3261-3281	*SCHOOLS-EQUIPMENT AND SUPPLIES* **SEE** SCHOOLS — FURNITURE, EQUIPMENT, ETC.
LB2824-2830	*SCHOOLS-FINANCE* **SEE** EDUCATION — FINANCE

LB3011-3095	*SCHOOLS-INSPECTION* **SEE** SCHOOL MANAGEMENT AND ORGANIZATION / *management and discipline*
LB2801-2997	*SCHOOLS-INSPECTION* **SEE** SCHOOL MANAGEMENT AND ORGANIZATION / *organization and supervision*
LB2503-2797	*SCHOOLS-LAW AND LEGISLATION* **SEE** EDUCATIONAL LAW AND LEGISLATION
LB3220	*SCHOOLS-LOCATION* **SEE** SCHOOL SITES
LB2801-2997	*SCHOOLS-MANAGEMENT AND ORGANIZATION* **SEE** SCHOOL MANAGEMENT AND ORGANIZATION / *organization and supervision*
LB3011-3095	*SCHOOLS-MANAGEMENT AND ORGANIZATION* **SEE** SCHOOL MANAGEMENT AND ORGANIZATION / *management and discipline*
LB3015-3031	*SCHOOLS-OPENING EXERCISES* **SEE** SCHOOLS — EXERCISES AND RECREATIONS
LB2831.5	*SCHOOLS-PERSONNEL MANAGEMENT* **SEE** SCHOOL PERSONNEL MANAGEMENT
LB2830	*SCHOOLS-RECORDS AND CORRESPONDENCE* **SEE** PUNCHED CARD SYSTEMS — EDUCATION / *schools*
LB2342	*SCHOOLS-RECORDS AND CORRESPONDENCE* **SEE** PUNCHED CARD SYSTEMS — EDUCATION / *colleges*
LB2846	*SCHOOLS-RECORDS AND CORRESPONDENCE* **SEE** SCHOOL REPORTS
LB3015-3031	*SCHOOLS-RECREATIONS* **SEE** SCHOOLS — EXERCISES AND RECREATIONS
LB3401-3495	*SCHOOLS-SANITARY AFFAIRS* **SEE** SCHOOL HYGIENE
LB	*SCHOOLTEACHING* **SEE** TEACHING
LB1775-1785	*SCHOOLTEACHING* **SEE** TEACHING / *teaching as a profession*
DJ136	SCHOONEVELD, BATTLE OF, 1673
M31	SCHOTTISCHES (PIANO)
QB723.S	SCHWASSMANN-WACHMANN'S COMET (II)
BX9749	*SCHWENCKFELDERS* **SEE** SCHWENKFELDERS
BX9749	SCHWENKFELDER CHURCH
F160.S2	SCHWENKFELDERS IN PENNSYLVANIA
BX9749	SCHWENKFELDERS
QL939	SCIATIC NERVE / *comparative anatomy*
QM471	SCIATIC NERVE / *human anatomy*
RX301.S	SCIATICA — HOMEOPATHIC TREATMENT
RC420	SCIATICA
Q167	SCIENCE — ANECDOTES, FACETIAE, SATIRE, ETC.
Z7404	SCIENCE — BIO-BIBLIOGRAPHY
Q151-7	SCIENCE — EARLY WORKS TO 1800
Q182	SCIENCE — EXAMINATIONS, QUESTIONS, ETC.
Q125-7	SCIENCE — HISTORY
Q163	SCIENCE — JUVENILE LITERATURE
Q161	SCIENCE — LABORATORY MANUALS
Q175	SCIENCE — METHODOLOGY
B1151-1197	SCIENCE — METHODOLOGY / *bacon*
BD240-241	SCIENCE — METHODOLOGY / *metaphysics*
Q179	SCIENCE — NOMENCLATURE
Q175	SCIENCE — PHILOSOPHY
Q182	SCIENCE — PROBLEMS, EXERCISES, ETC.
Q181	SCIENCE — STUDY AND TEACHING
Q179	SCIENCE — TERMINOLOGY
Q124.5	SCIENCE — TRANSLATING SERVICES
Q124.5	SCIENCE — TRANSLATING
Q180	*SCIENCE - RESEARCH* **SEE** RESEARCH / *science*
T65	*SCIENCE - RESEARCH* **SEE** RESEARCH / *technology*
BL1435.S35	*SCIENCE AND BUDDHISM* **SEE** BUDDHISM AND SCIENCE
CB151	SCIENCE AND CIVILIZATION
CB151	*SCIENCE AND HISTORY* **SEE** SCIENCE AND CIVILIZATION
BP190.5.S	*SCIENCE AND ISLAM* **SEE** ISLAM AND SCIENCE
PN55	*SCIENCE AND LITERATURE* **SEE** LITERATURE AND SCIENCE
PR149.S4	*SCIENCE AND LITERATURE* **SEE** LITERATURE AND SCIENCE / *english literature*
PN55	*SCIENCE AND POETRY* **SEE** LITERATURE AND SCIENCE
PR149.S4	*SCIENCE AND POETRY* **SEE** LITERATURE AND SCIENCE / *english literature*
BL239-265	*SCIENCE AND RELIGION* **SEE** RELIGION AND SCIENCE
QB500	*SCIENCE AND SPACE* **SEE** SPACE SCIENCES
Q125-7	SCIENCE AND STATE / *history*
BS650-667	*SCIENCE AND THE BIBLE* **SEE** BIBLE AND SCIENCE
AZ361	SCIENCE AND THE HUMANITIES
Q147	SCIENCE AS A PROFESSION
Q181	SCIENCE CLUBS
Q223	*SCIENCE COMMUNICATION* **SEE** COMMUNICATION IN SCIENCE
Q225	*SCIENCE IN THE MASS MEDIA* **SEE** SCIENCE NEWS
Q223	*SCIENCE INFORMATION* **SEE** COMMUNICATION IN SCIENCE
QH70-71	*SCIENCE MUSEUMS* **SEE** NATURAL HISTORY MUSEUMS
Q225	SCIENCE NEWS
Z286	SCIENCE PUBLISHING
Q167	*SCIENCE STORIES* **SEE** SCIENCE — ANECDOTES, FACETIAE, SATIRE, ETC.
Q167	*SCIENCE STORIES* **SEE** SCIENCE — ANECDOTES, FACETIAE, SATIRE, ETC.
Q124.5	*SCIENCE TRANSLATING* **SEE** SCIENCE — TRANSLATING
Q	SCIENCE
Q125	SCIENCE, ANCIENT
T-TX	*SCIENCE, APPLIED* **SEE** TECHNOLOGY
Q223	*SCIENCE, COMMUNICATION IN* **SEE** COMMUNICATION IN SCIENCE
BM729.J4	*SCIENCE, JEWISH* **SEE** JEWISH SCIENCE
Q153	SCIENCE, MEDIEVAL / *early works*
Q125-7	SCIENCE, MEDIEVAL / *history*
BJ	*SCIENCE, MORAL* **SEE** ETHICS
B65	*SCIENCE, POLITICAL* **SEE** POLITICAL SCIENCE / *j political science and philosophy*
HM33	*SCIENCE, POLITICAL* **SEE** POLITICAL SCIENCE / *political science and sociology*
Q125	*SCIENCE, PRIMITIVE* **SEE** SCIENCE, ANCIENT
HM-HV	*SCIENCE, SOCIAL* **SEE** SOCIOLOGY
BL60	*SCIENCE, SOCIAL* **SEE** SOCIOLOGY / *religion and sociology*
JX1251	*SCIENCE, SOCIAL* **SEE** SOCIOLOGY / *sociology and international law*
B63	*SCIENCE, SOCIAL* **SEE** SOCIOLOGY / *sociology and philosophy*
HM26	*SCIENCE, SOCIAL* **SEE** SOCIOLOGY / *sociology and philosophy*
JA76	*SCIENCE, SOCIAL* **SEE** SOCIOLOGY / *sociology and political science*
HM33	*SCIENCE, SOCIAL* **SEE** SOCIOLOGY / *sociology and political science*
BF57	*SCIENCE, SOCIAL* **SEE** SOCIOLOGY / *sociology and psychology*
HM27	*SCIENCE, SOCIAL* **SEE** SOCIOLOGY / *sociology and psychology*
Q181	*SCIENCE, STATE ENCOURAGEMENT OF* **SEE** STATE ENCOURAGEMENT OF SCIENCE, LITERATURE, AND ART / *science*
JC518-519	*SCIENCE, STATE ENCOURAGEMENT OF* **SEE** STATE ENCOURAGEMENT OF SCIENCE, LITERATURE, AND ART / *political science*
N8750	*SCIENCE, STATE ENCOURAGEMENT OF* **SEE** STATE ENCOURAGEMENT OF SCIENCE, LITERATURE, AND ART / *art*
Q177	*SCIENCE-CLASSIFICATION* **SEE** CLASSIFICATION OF SCIENCES
BD240-241	*SCIENCE-CLASSIFICATION* **SEE** CLASSIFICATION OF SCIENCES / *methodology*
BC	*SCIENCE-METHODOLOGY* **SEE** LOGIC
Q225	*SCIENCE-POPULARIZATION* **SEE** SCIENCE NEWS
Z286	*SCIENCE-PUBLISHING* **SEE** SCIENCE PUBLISHING
Q177	*SCIENCES, CLASSIFICATION OF* **SEE** CLASSIFICATION OF SCIENCES
BD240-241	*SCIENCES, CLASSIFICATION OF* **SEE** CLASSIFICATION OF SCIENCES / *methodology*
BF1405-1999	*SCIENCES, OCCULT* **SEE** OCCULT SCIENCES
H	*SCIENCES, SOCIAL* **SEE** SOCIAL SCIENCES
Q184-5	SCIENTIFIC APPARATUS AND INSTRUMENTS
AS	*SCIENTIFIC ASSOCIATIONS* **SEE** SCIENTIFIC SOCIETIES / *academies and learned societies*
Q183	SCIENTIFIC BUREAUS
Q223	*SCIENTIFIC COMMUNICATIONS* **SEE** COMMUNICATION IN SCIENCE
Q181	*SCIENTIFIC EDUCATION* **SEE** SCIENCE — STUDY AND TEACHING
Z690	*SCIENTIFIC EXCHANGES* **SEE** EXCHANGES, LITERARY AND SCIENTIFIC

Q116	SCIENTIFIC EXPEDITIONS — EQUIPMENT AND SUPPLIES
Q115	SCIENTIFIC EXPEDITIONS
AS	*SCIENTIFIC INSTITUTIONS* **SEE** SCIENTIFIC SOCIETIES / *academies and learned societies*
Q184-5	*SCIENTIFIC INSTRUMENTS* **SEE** SCIENTIFIC APPARATUS AND INSTRUMENTS
PN4888.S	*SCIENTIFIC JOURNALISM* **SEE** JOURNALISM, SCIENTIFIC
Z699.5.S3	*SCIENTIFIC LITERATURE SEARCHING* **SEE** INFORMATION STORAGE AND RETRIEVAL SYSTEMS — SCIENCE
T215-323	*SCIENTIFIC PROPERTY* **SEE** PATENT LAWS AND LEGISLATION
Q164	SCIENTIFIC RECREATIONS
AS	SCIENTIFIC SOCIETIES / *academies and learned societies*
Q124.5	*SCIENTIFIC TRANSLATING* **SEE** SCIENCE — TRANSLATING
Q115	*SCIENTIFIC VOYAGES* **SEE** SCIENTIFIC EXPEDITIONS
Q145	SCIENTISTS — DIRECTORIES
Z7404	*SCIENTISTS - BIO-BIBLIOGRAPHY* **SEE** SCIENCE — BIO-BIBLIOGRAPHY
Q141-3	SCIENTISTS / *biography*
Z7404	*SCIENTISTS-BIO-BIBLIOGRAPHY* **SEE** SCIENCE — BIO-BIBLIOGRAPHY
QL666.L2	*SCINKS* **SEE** SKINKS
QC787.C6	SCINTILLATION COUNTERS
QC373.S7	*SCINTILLATION SPECTROMETER* **SEE** SCINTILLATION SPECTROMETRY
QC373.S7	SCINTILLATION SPECTROMETRY
QC787.C6	*SCINTILLATORS* **SEE** SCINTILLATION COUNTERS
QL377.C7	*SCLERACTINIA* **SEE** MADREPORARIA
RL451	SCLERODERMA
RF365	*SCLEROMA RESPIRATORIUM* **SEE** RHINOSCLEROMA
RC377	*SCLEROSIS, MULTIPLE* **SEE** MULTIPLE SCLEROSIS
RD768	*SCOLIOSIS* **SEE** SPINE — ABNORMITIES AND DEFORMITIES
BX3865.P5	*SCOLOPIANS* **SEE** PIARISTS
CR4480	*SCONE, STONE OF* **SEE** STONE OF SCONE
GV1299.S4	SCOOP (GAME)
TL450	*SCOOTERS, MOTOR* **SEE** MOTOR SCOOTERS
GV1295.S	SCOPA
QD421	SCOPOLAMINE / *chemistry*
QP921.S4	SCOPOLAMINE / *physiology*
GV1295.S	*SCOPONE* **SEE** SCOPA
MT85	SCORE READING AND PLAYING
GV735	*SCORING (SPORTS)* **SEE** SPORTS OFFICIATING
QL458.S4	SCORPIONS
SF429.D4	*SCOTCH DEER-HOUNDS* **SEE** DEER-HOUNDS
SD397.S	SCOTCH PINE
TP605	*SCOTCH WHISKY* **SEE** WHISKEY
DA927	SCOTCH-IRISH
DA774	SCOTCH
DA750-890	SCOTLAND — HISTORY
DA814.3	*SCOTLAND-HISTORY-JACOBITE REBELLION, 1715* **SEE** JACOBITE REBELLION, 1715
DA814.5	*SCOTLAND-HISTORY-JACOBITE REBELLION, 1745-1746* **SEE** JACOBITE REBELLION, 1745-1746
DA774	*SCOTS* **SEE** SCOTCH
PR1181	SCOTTISH BALLADS AND SONGS / *collections*
PR8580	SCOTTISH BALLADS AND SONGS / *history*
JC20-45	*SCOTTISH CLANS* **SEE** CLANS AND CLAN SYSTEM
GN492	*SCOTTISH CLANS* **SEE** CLANS AND CLAN SYSTEM / *ethnology*
PR8610	*SCOTTISH DIARIES (ENGLISH)* **SEE** ENGLISH DIARIES — SCOTTISH AUTHORS / *history*
PR8680	*SCOTTISH DIARIES (ENGLISH)* **SEE** ENGLISH DIARIES — SCOTTISH AUTHORS / *collections*
PR8664-8670	SCOTTISH DRAMA / *collections*
PR8583-8595	SCOTTISH DRAMA / *history*
PR8675-6	SCOTTISH FICTION / *collections*
PR8597-8607	SCOTTISH FICTION / *history*
PR8640-8641	SCOTTISH LITERATURE — EARLY TO 1700 / *collections*
PR8544-7	SCOTTISH LITERATURE — EARLY TO 1700 / *history*
PR8641	SCOTTISH LITERATURE — 18TH CENTURY / *collections*
PR8547	SCOTTISH LITERATURE — 18TH CENTURY / *history*

PR8550	SCOTTISH LITERATURE — 19TH CENTURY / *history*
PR8644	SCOTTISH LITERATURE — 20TH CENTURY / *collections*
PR8553	SCOTTISH LITERATURE — 20TH CENTURY / *history*
PR8631-8644	SCOTTISH LITERATURE / *collections*
PR8510-8553	SCOTTISH LITERATURE / *history*
BV2200	*SCOTTISH MISSIONS* **SEE** MISSIONS, SCOTTISH / *catholic*
BV2420	*SCOTTISH MISSIONS* **SEE** MISSIONS, SCOTTISH / *protestant*
Q115	SCOTTISH NATIONAL ANTARCTIC EXPEDITION, 1902-1904 / *scientific results*
G850 1902	SCOTTISH NATIONAL ANTARCTIC EXPEDITION, 1902-1904
PN5131-9	SCOTTISH NEWSPAPERS / *history*
PN5131-5140	SCOTTISH PERIODICALS / *history*
PR8655-6	SCOTTISH POETRY — EARLY TO 1700 / *collections*
PR8567	SCOTTISH POETRY — EARLY TO 1700 / *history*
PR8538	SCOTTISH POETRY — EARLY TO 1700 / *history*
PR8657	SCOTTISH POETRY — 19TH CENTURY / *collections*
PR8569	SCOTTISH POETRY — 19TH CENTURY / *history*
PR8658	SCOTTISH POETRY — 20TH CENTURY / *collections*
PR8571	SCOTTISH POETRY — 20TH CENTURY / *history*
PR8649-8661	SCOTTISH POETRY / *collections*
PR8561-8581	SCOTTISH POETRY / *history*
PR8672-8687	SCOTTISH PROSE LITERATURE / *collections*
PR8597-8607	SCOTTISH PROSE LITERATURE / *history*
DA880.H76	*SCOTTISH TARTANS* **SEE** TARTANS
SF429.S4	SCOTTISH TERRIERS
PN6178.S4	SCOTTISH WIT AND HUMOR
TP987.S3	SCOURING COMPOUNDS
GV959	*SCOUTING, FOOTBALL* **SEE** FOOTBALL SCOUTING
U220	SCOUTS AND SCOUTING / *military*
V190	SCOUTS AND SCOUTING / *naval*
HE585-7	SCOWS — SAFETY APPLIANCES
VM463	SCOWS / *construction*
GV1507.S3	SCRABBLE (GAME)
HD9510-9529	SCRAP METAL INDUSTRY
TS214	SCRAP METALS
NC915.S4	*SCRAPER BOARD DRAWING* **SEE** SCRATCHBOARD DRAWING
NC915.S4	SCRATCHBOARD DRAWING
TH2278	SCREEN DOORS
TT273	SCREEN PROCESS PRINTING
NA5080	SCREENS (CHURCH DECORATION)
TN515	SCREENS (MINING)
NK2910	SCREENS / *art*
VM753-7	*SCREW PROPELLERS* **SEE** PROPELLERS
SF810.S	*SCREW WORM* **SEE** SCREWWORM / *agriculture*
QL537.M7	*SCREW WORM* **SEE** SCREWWORM / *zoology*
TJ1222	SCREW-CUTTING MACHINES
TJ1338-1340	SCREW-THREADS
TJ1340	SCREW-THREADS, STANDARD
TJ1338-1340	SCREWS
QA841	SCREWS, THEORY OF
SF810.S	SCREWWORM / *agriculture*
QL537.M7	SCREWWORM / *zoology*
BM659.S3	SCRIBES, JEWISH
UB370-375	*SCRIP* **SEE** BOUNTIES, MILITARY
HG651-1490	*SCRIP* **SEE** CURRENCY QUESTION / *other countries*
HG501-538	*SCRIP* **SEE** CURRENCY QUESTION / *u.s.*
HD1337	*SCRIP* **SEE** HOMESTEAD LAW / *homestead and exemption*
HD197-205	*SCRIP* **SEE** HOMESTEAD LAW / *land law*
HG4651-5990	*SCRIP* **SEE** SECURITIES
RC429	*SCRIVENERS' PALSY* **SEE** WRITERS' CRAMP
RC311.1	SCROFULA
NK1580	SCROLLS (DECORATIVE DESIGN)
NK9930	*SCROLLWORK* **SEE** FRETWORK
QL878	SCROTUM / *comparative anatomy*
RC897	SCROTUM / *diseases*
QM416	SCROTUM / *human anatomy*
RC186.T83	*SCRUB TYPHUS* **SEE** TSUTSUGAMUSHI DISEASE
QK495.P17	*SCRUB-PALMETTO* **SEE** SAW-PALMETTO
SD397.P615	SCRUB-PINE

BX1759.5.S4	SCRUPLES
BX1759.5.S4	*SCRUPULOSITY* **SEE** SCRUPLES
GV791-809	*SCULLING* **SEE** ROWING
QL638.C8	SCULPIN
NB1115	SCULPTORS
NB35	SCULPTURE — CATALOGS
NB1199	SCULPTURE — CONSERVATION AND RESTORATION
NB15-17	SCULPTURE — EXHIBITIONS
NB30	SCULPTURE — PRIVATE COLLECTIONS
NB1170-1195	SCULPTURE — TECHNIQUE
Z654	*SCULPTURE - COPYRIGHT* **SEE** COPYRIGHT — SCULPTURE
N72	*SCULPTURE AND LITERATURE* **SEE** ART AND LITERATURE / *art*
PR149.A	*SCULPTURE AND LITERATURE* **SEE** ART AND LITERATURE / *english literature*
PT112	*SCULPTURE AND LITERATURE* **SEE** ART AND LITERATURE / *german literature*
PN53	*SCULPTURE AND LITERATURE* **SEE** ART AND LITERATURE / *literature*
NB	SCULPTURE
NB69-169	SCULPTURE, ANCIENT
NB193	SCULPTURE, BAROQUE
NB69	SCULPTURE, CHRYSELEPHANTINE
.NB180	SCULPTURE, GOTHIC
NB170-180	SCULPTURE, MEDIEVAL
NB62	SCULPTURE, PRIMITIVE
GN462	SCULPTURE, PRIMITIVE / *ethnology*
BV150-168	*SCULPTURE, RELIGIOUS* **SEE** CHRISTIAN ART AND SYMBOLISM / *theology*
N7810-8185	*SCULPTURE, RELIGIOUS* **SEE** CHRISTIAN ART AND SYMBOLISM
NB190	SCULPTURE, RENAISSANCE
NB615	SCULPTURE, RENAISSANCE / *italian*
NB193	SCULPTURE, ROCOCO
NB175	SCULPTURE, ROMANESQUE
NB1275	*SCULPTURE-COLOR* **SEE** POLYCHROMY / *sculpture*
NB93	*SCULPTURE-COLOR* **SEE** POLYCHROMY / *sculpture*
Z654	*SCULPTURE-COPYRIGHT* **SEE** COPYRIGHT — SCULPTURE
NB1199	*SCULPTURE-RESTORATION* **SEE** SCULPTURE — CONSERVATION AND RESTORATION
RC626	SCURVY
RJ399.S3	SCURVY, INFANTILE
JC116.S4	SCUTAGE
DR46.7	SCUTARI, ALBANIA — SIEGE, 1912-1913
QL377.S4	SCYPHOMEDUSAE
S695-7	SCYTHES / *implements*
HD9486	SCYTHES / *trade*
PL1-9	*SCYTHIAN LANGUAGES* **SEE** ALTAIC LANGUAGES
PL1-489	*SCYTHIAN LANGUAGES* **SEE** URAL-ALTAIC LANGUAGES
DK33-34	SCYTHIANS
GN549.S3	SCYTHIANS / *anthropology*
RA794	SEA AIR / *medical climatology*
SH457	*SEA ANGLING* **SEE** SALT-WATER FISHING
QL121-138	*SEA ANIMALS* **SEE** MARINE FAUNA
QL638.S48	SEA BASS
RM819	*SEA BATHS* **SEE** BATHS, SEA
SH457	*SEA FISHING* **SEE** SALT-WATER FISHING
TX385-7	SEA FOOD
TX747	SEA FOOD / *cookery*
TX753	SEA FOOD / *cookery*
GB2401-2598	SEA ICE DRIFT
GB2401-2598	*SEA ICE-DRIFT* **SEE** SEA ICE DRIFT
JX4408-4449	*SEA LAWS* **SEE** MARITIME LAW / *international law*
JX63	*SEA LAWS* **SEE** MARITIME LAW / *private*
G525-550	*SEA LIFE* **SEE** SEAFARING LIFE
HD8039.S4-42	*SEA LIFE* **SEE** SEAMEN / *labor*
TC761	*SEA LOCKS* **SEE** LOCKS (HYDRAULIC ENGINEERING)
TL684	*SEA PLANES* **SEE** SEAPLANES
PN6110.S4	SEA POETRY / *collections*
PR508.S4	SEA POETRY / *english literature*
PN6427.S5	SEA PROVERBS / *english*
QK495.C	*SEA PURSLANE* **SEE** ORACH / *botany*
SB351.O	*SEA PURSLANE* **SEE** ORACH / *vegetables*
HE323-8	*SEA ROUTES* **SEE** TRADE ROUTES
QL89	SEA SERPENT
SB460	*SEA SIDE GARDENING* **SEE** SEASIDE GARDENING
M1977.S2	SEA SONGS / *collections*
ML3780	SEA SONGS / *history and criticism*
PN6110.S4	SEA SONGS / *poetry*
GC75-78	*SEA SOUNDINGS* **SEE** DEEP-SEA SOUNDING
VK584.S6	*SEA SOUNDINGS* **SEE** SOUNDING AND SOUNDINGS / *navigation*
GS69-78	*SEA SOUNDINGS* **SEE** SOUNDING AND SOUNDINGS / *oceanography*
QL613	*SEA SQUIRTS* **SEE** TUNICATA
PZ7	SEA STORIES / *juvenile*
PR830.S4	SEA STORIES / *sea in english fiction*
G550	*SEA TRAVEL* **SEE** OCEAN TRAVEL
G153	*SEA TRAVEL* **SEE** OCEAN TRAVEL
RA793	*SEA TRAVEL* **SEE** OCEAN TRAVEL / *hygiene*
VM880-881	*SEA TRIALS (SHIPS)* **SEE** SHIP TRIALS
GC211	*SEA WAVES* **SEE** OCEAN WAVES
QL377.C7	SEA-ANEMONES
QL384.H7	*SEA-CUCUMBERS* **SEE** HOLOTHURIANS
QL430.5.H3	*SEA-EARS* **SEE** ABALONES
SH	*SEA-FISHERIES* **SEE** FISHERIES
QL638.S9	SEA-HORSE
QL737.P6	*SEA-LIONS* **SEE** SEALS (ANIMALS)
QL737.C2	SEA-OTTERS
SH364	SEA-OTTERS / *fisheries*
QL377.C6	SEA-PENS
GB451-460	*SEA-SHORE* **SEE** SEASHORE
RC421	*SEA-SICKNESS* **SEE** SEASICKNESS
RX301.S4	*SEA-SICKNESS* **SEE** SEASICKNESS / *homeopathic treatment*
QL447.P2	*SEA-SPIDERS* **SEE** PYCNOGONIDA
QL384.A8	*SEA-STARS* **SEE** STARFISHES
ML760	SEA-TRUMPET / *medieval stringed instrument*
QL384.E2	SEA-URCHINS
QE783.E2	SEA-URCHINS, FOSSIL
TC335	SEA-WALLS
QR106	SEA-WATER — BACTERIOLOGY
GC111	SEA-WATER — COMPOSITION
RM819	SEA-WATER — PHYSIOLOGICAL EFFECT
RM819	SEA-WATER — THERAPEUTIC USE
GC101-181	SEA-WATER
VM505	SEA-WATER, DISTILLATION OF
GC161-177	*SEA-WATER-TEMPERATURE* **SEE** DEEP-SEA TEMPERATURE
GC161-177	*SEA-WATER-TEMPERATURE* **SEE** OCEAN TEMPERATURE
JX4408-4449	*SEA, DOMINION OF THE* **SEE** MARITIME LAW / *international law*
JX63	*SEA, DOMINION OF THE* **SEE** MARITIME LAW / *private*
GR910	*SEA, FOLK-LORE OF THE* **SEE** FOLK-LORE OF THE SEA
D580	*SEA, FREEDOM OF THE* **SEE** FREEDOM OF THE SEAS / *european war*
JX4423-5	*SEA, FREEDOM OF THE* **SEE** FREEDOM OF THE SEAS / *international law*
JX5203-5268	*SEA, FREEDOM OF THE* **SEE** FREEDOM OF THE SEAS / *maritime war international law*
QA76.8.S4	*SEAC (COMPUTER)* **SEE** SEAC COMPUTER
TK7889.S4	*SEAC (COMPUTER)* **SEE** SEAC COMPUTER / *engineering*
QA76.8.S4	SEAC COMPUTER
TK7889.S4	SEAC COMPUTER / *engineering*
UF450-455	*SEACOAST ARTILLERY* **SEE** ARTILLERY, COAST
UG410-448	*SEACOAST DEFENSES* **SEE** COAST DEFENSES
TL725.7	*SEADROMES* **SEE** AIRPORTS, FLOATING
G525-550	SEAFARING LIFE
TX385-7	*SEAFOOD* **SEE** SEA FOOD
TX753	*SEAFOOD* **SEE** SEA FOOD / *cookery*
TX747	*SEAFOOD* **SEE** SEA FOOD / *cookery*
TP988	SEALING-WAX
SH361-3	SEALING
QL737.P6	SEALS (ANIMALS)
NC1280	SEALS (CHRISTMAS, ETC.) — COLLECTORS AND COLLECTING
NC1280	SEALS (CHRISTMAS, ETC.)
CD5001-6471	SEALS (NUMISMATICS)
JC345-7	SEALS (NUMISMATICS) / *national*
SF429.S45	SEALYHAM TERRIERS
VK541-7	SEAMANSHIP

BV463	SEAMEN — HYMNS
HD8039.S4-42	SEAMEN / *labor*
Z675.N3	*SEAMEN'S LIBRARIES* **SEE** LIBRARIES, NAVAL
BV2660-2678	*SEAMEN'S MISSIONS* **SEE** MERCHANT SEAMEN — MISSIONS AND CHARITIES
HV3025-3163	*SEAMEN'S MISSIONS* **SEE** MERCHANT SEAMEN — MISSIONS AND CHARITIES / *charities*
PN6110.S4	*SEAMEN'S SONGS* **SEE** SAILORS' SONGS / *literature*
M1977.S2	*SEAMEN'S SONGS* **SEE** SAILORS' SONGS / *music*
M1978.S2	*SEAMEN'S SONGS* **SEE** SAILORS' SONGS / *music*
UB356-9	*SEAMEN-CIVIL EMPLOYMENT* **SEE** VETERANS — EMPLOYMENT
U715-717	*SEAMEN-EDUCATION, NON-MILITARY* **SEE** SOLDIERS — EDUCATION, NON-MILITARY
JK1876-8	*SEAMEN-SUFFRAGE* **SEE** SOLDIERS — SUFFRAGE / *u.s.*
TL725.6	SEAPLANE BASES
TL684	SEAPLANES
TL554	*SEAPLANES-POETRY* **SEE** AERONAUTICS — POETRY
TL553.8	SEARCH AND RESCUE OPERATIONS / *aeronautics*
TK4399.S4	SEARCH-LIGHTS
UG626-9	SEARCH-LIGHTS / *military*
VM493	SEARCH-LIGHTS / *naval*
JX5268	SEARCH, RIGHT OF / *international law*
D580	*SEAS, FREEDOM OF THE* **SEE** FREEDOM OF THE SEAS / *european war*
JX4423-5	*SEAS, FREEDOM OF THE* **SEE** FREEDOM OF THE SEAS / *international law*
JX5203-5268	*SEAS, FREEDOM OF THE* **SEE** FREEDOM OF THE SEAS / *maritime war international law*
GB451-460	SEASHORE
RC421	SEASICKNESS
RX301.S4	SEASICKNESS / *homeopathic treatment*
SB460	SEASIDE GARDENING
QB631	SEASONS / *astronomical geography*
GR930	SEASONS / *folk-lore*
TL159	*SEAT BELTS, AUTOMOBILE* **SEE** AUTOMOBILE SEAT BELTS
LB1537	*SEAT WORK* **SEE** CREATIVE ACTIVITIES AND SEAT WORK
TL685.5.S4	*SEATS, AEROPLANE* **SEE** AEROPLANES — SEATS
RL131	SEBACEOUS GLANDS — DISEASES
QL943	SEBACEOUS GLANDS / *comparative anatomy*
QM491	SEBACEOUS GLANDS / *human anatomy*
DP615	SEBASTIANISM
JK310-331	SECESSION / *constitutionality*
E458-9	SECESSION / *u.s. civil war*
PL8651	SECHUANA LANGUAGE
PL8651	*SECHWANA LANGUAGE* **SEE** SECHUANA LANGUAGE
PL8651	*SECOANA LANGUAGE* **SEE** SECHUANA LANGUAGE
BT885	SECOND ADVENT
BX6101-6193	*SECOND ADVENTISTS* **SEE** ADVENTISTS
BF1325	SECOND SIGHT / *clairvoyance*
QA76.8.S4	*SECOND STANDARDS EASTERN AUTOMATIC COMPUTER* **SEE** SEAC COMPUTER
TK7889.S4	*SECOND STANDARDS EASTERN AUTOMATIC COMPUTER* **SEE** SEAC COMPUTER / *engineering*
HE6132	*SECOND-CLASS MATTER* **SEE** POSTAL SERVICE — SECOND-CLASS MATTER
HE6432	*SECOND-CLASS MATTER* **SEE** POSTAL SERVICE — U.S. — — SECOND-CLASS MATTER
QC605	*SECONDARY BATTERIES* **SEE** STORAGE BATTERIES
TL272	*SECONDARY BATTERIES* **SEE** STORAGE BATTERIES / *automobile*
TK2891	*SECONDARY BATTERIES* **SEE** STORAGE BATTERIES / *central stations*
TK5378	*SECONDARY BATTERIES* **SEE** STORAGE BATTERIES / *telegraph*
TK6278	*SECONDARY BATTERIES* **SEE** STORAGE BATTERIES / *telephone*
HD5461	*SECONDARY BOYCOTTS* **SEE** BOYCOTT
LB1603-1694	*SECONDARY EDUCATION* **SEE** EDUCATION, SECONDARY
LA410	*SECONDARY EDUCATION* **SEE** EDUCATION, SECONDARY / *other countries*
BF323.S4	SECONDARY FUNCTION (PSYCHOLOGY)
TS214	*SECONDARY METALS* **SEE** SCRAP METALS
LB1603-1694	*SECONDARY SCHOOLS* **SEE** EDUCATION, SECONDARY
LA410	*SECONDARY SCHOOLS* **SEE** EDUCATION, SECONDARY / *other countries*
LA222	*SECONDARY SCHOOLS* **SEE** EDUCATION, SECONDARY / *u.s.*
LB1603-1694	*SECONDARY SCHOOLS* **SEE** HIGH SCHOOLS
LC47-57	*SECONDARY SCHOOLS* **SEE** PRIVATE SCHOOLS
L-LC	*SECONDARY SCHOOLS* **SEE** PUBLIC SCHOOLS
DA380	*SECRET CHAMBERS* **SEE** HIDING-PLACES (SECRET CHAMBERS, ETC.) / *england*
HV7961	SECRET SERVICE
HS155-8	SECRET SOCIETIES — RITUALS
HS155	SECRET SOCIETIES — RITUALS, CIPHER
HS614	SECRET SOCIETIES AND CATHOLIC CHURCH
HS	SECRET SOCIETIES
GN495.2	SECRET SOCIETIES / *primitive*
Z103-4	*SECRET WRITING* **SEE** CRYPTOGRAPHY
JK610-616	*SECRETARIES OF STATE* **SEE** CABINET OFFICERS / *u.s.*
QP801.S	SECRETIN
QP190-246	SECRETION / *physiology*
JK310-331	SECTIONALISM (U.S.) / *constitutional history*
E468	SECTIONALISM (U.S.) / *history*
E169.1	SECTIONALISM (U.S.) / *national characteristics*
BR157	SECTS
BL1480	*SECTS, BUDDHIST* **SEE** BUDDHIST SECTS
BL1245.A1	*SECTS, HINDU* **SEE** HINDU SECTS
BP191-223	*SECTS, ISLAMIC* **SEE** ISLAMIC SECTS
BM175	*SECTS, JEWISH* **SEE** JEWISH SECTS
BR250-270	SECTS, MEDIEVAL
BP191-223	*SECTS, MUSLIM* **SEE** ISLAMIC SECTS
BX4800-9890	*SECTS, PROTESTANT* **SEE** PROTESTANT CHURCHES
PL8651	*SECUANA LANGUAGE* **SEE** SECHUANA LANGUAGE
M1530-1546	*SECULAR CANTATAS* **SEE** CANTATAS, SECULAR
M1547	*SECULAR CHORUSES* **SEE** CHORUSES, SECULAR
DG95	SECULAR GAMES / *roman antiquities*
BX818	SECULAR INSTITUTES
QC828	*SECULAR VARIATION (TERRESTRIAL MAGNETISM)* **SEE** MAGNETISM, TERRESTRIAL — SECULAR VARIATION
BL2700-2790	SECULARISM
HG4551-4595	*SECURITIES EXCHANGE* **SEE** STOCK-EXCHANGE
HG4651-5990	SECURITIES
HJ5901-5919	*SECURITIES-TAXATION* **SEE** TAXATION OF BONDS, SECURITIES, ETC.
UB249	*SECURITY MEASURES (MILITARY INFORMATION)* **SEE** INDUSTRY — SECURITY MEASURES
UB249	*SECURITY MEASURES, INDUSTRIAL* **SEE** INDUSTRY — SECURITY MEASURES
JX1901-1995	SECURITY, INTERNATIONAL
PL8651	*SECWANA LANGUAGE* **SEE** SECHUANA LANGUAGE
DC306-7	SEDAN CAMPAIGN, 1870
GT5280	SEDAN-CHAIRS
DS539.S4	SEDANGS / *french indochina*
RM325	SEDATIVES
QE471	*SEDIMENTARY ROCKS* **SEE** ROCKS, SEDIMENTARY
QD117	SEDIMENTATION ANALYSIS
QE581	SEDIMENTATION AND DEPOSITION
GC380-399	*SEDIMENTS, MARINE* **SEE** MARINE SEDIMENTS
E327-8	*SEDITION LAW, 1798* **SEE** ALIEN AND SEDITION LAWS, 1798
HV6285	SEDITION / *u.s.*
HV6584-9	SEDUCTION
BX950-960	*SEE, HOLY* **SEE** PAPACY
BX1805-1810	*SEE, HOLY* **SEE** POPES
BX1001-1378	*SEE, HOLY* **SEE** POPES / *individual popes*
SB114	SEED ADULTERATION AND INSPECTION
SB117	*SEED DISINFECTION* **SEE** SEEDS — DISINFECTION
S21.Z2-8	SEED DISTRIBUTION / *congressional committee hearings*
S21.S2	SEED DISTRIBUTION / *dept. of agriculture publications*
SB114-117	SEED INDUSTRY AND TRADE / *agriculture*
HD9019.S	SEED INDUSTRY AND TRADE / *economics*
SB211.P8	SEED POTATOES
SB114-117	*SEED PRODUCTION* **SEE** SEED INDUSTRY AND TRADE / *agriculture*

HD9019.S	*SEED PRODUCTION* **SEE** SEED INDUSTRY AND TRADE / *economics*
SB114-117	*SEED TRADE* **SEE** SEED INDUSTRY AND TRADE / *agriculture*
HD9019.S	*SEED TRADE* **SEE** SEED INDUSTRY AND TRADE / *economics*
S687-9	*SEEDING MACHINERY* **SEE** DRILL (AGRICULTURAL IMPLEMENT)
QK661	SEEDS — ANATOMY
SB115	SEEDS — CATALOGS
QK73	SEEDS — CATALOGS / *seed lists of individual botanic gardens*
SB117	SEEDS — DISINFECTION
QK929	SEEDS — DISSEMINATION
QK661	SEEDS — MORPHOLOGY
QK661	SEEDS / *botany*
SB114-117	SEEDS / *plant culture*
QE995	SEEDS, FOSSIL
SB117	*SEEDS-FUMIGATION* **SEE** SEEDS — DISINFECTION
QK740	*SEEDS-GERMINATION* **SEE** GERMINATION
SB114	*SEEDS-INSPECTION* **SEE** SEED ADULTERATION AND INSPECTION
BX9750.S	SEEKERS (SECT)
DS135.A-Z	*SEFARDIC JEWS* **SEE** SEPHARDIM
LB3062	SEGREGATION IN EDUCATION
PQ7001.A6	*SEGUIRIYA GITANA* **SEE** CANTE HONDO
ML3712	*SEGUIRIYA GITANA* **SEE** CANTE HONDO
D545.S35	SEICHEPREY, BATTLE OF, 1918
GC217	SEICHES
QC595	*SEIGNETTE-ELECTRICITY* **SEE** FERROELECTRICITY
TN269	SEISMIC PROSPECTING
QE541	*SEISMOGRAPH* **SEE** SEISMOMETERS
QE531-541	*SEISMOGRAPHY* **SEE** SEISMOLOGY
QE541	*SEISMOGRAPHY* **SEE** SEISMOMETRY
QE532	SEISMOLOGY — OBSERVATIONS
QE540	SEISMOLOGY — OBSERVATORIES
QE531-541	SEISMOLOGY
QE541	SEISMOMETERS
QE541	SEISMOMETRY
QE532	*SEISMOMETRY-OBSERVATIONS* **SEE** SEISMOLOGY — OBSERVATIONS
PL8598.O8	*SEKIANI LANGUAGE* **SEE** ORUNGU LANGUAGE
DT313	SEKSAWA (BERBER TRIBE)
QL638.9	SELACHII
QE852.P6	SELACHII, FOSSIL
QL737.U5	*SELADANG* **SEE** BUFFALOES
QH365-7	*SELECTION, NATURAL* **SEE** NATURAL SELECTION
QC437	*SELECTIVE ABSORPTION* **SEE** ABSORPTION OF LIGHT
QC437	*SELECTIVE ABSORPTION* **SEE** ABSORPTION SPECTRA
UB340-355	*SELECTIVE SERVICE* **SEE** MILITARY SERVICE, COMPULSORY
QD181.S5	SELENIC ACID
QC603	SELENIUM CELLS
QD181.S5	SELENIUM COMPOUNDS
QD412.S6	SELENIUM COMPOUNDS
QD181.S5	SELENIUM
QB581-595	*SELENOLOGY* **SEE** MOON
DC309.S3	SELESTAT, ALSACE — SIEGE, 1870
DS96	SELEUCIDS
CJ1141-3	SELEUCIDS / *numismatics*
CJ699-701	SELEUCIDS / *numismatics*
CD5369	SELEUCIDS / *seals*
CD5377	SELEUCIDS / *seals*
CD5348	SELEUCIDS / *seals*
BJ1533.S27	*SELF-ASSURANCE* **SEE** SELF-RELIANCE
BJ1533.S27	*SELF-CONFIDENCE* **SEE** SELF-RELIANCE
BF575.S5	SELF-CONSCIOUSNESS
BJ1520-1595	SELF-CONTROL / *ethics*
BF638-645	SELF-CONTROL / *new thought*
LC25-31	SELF-CULTURE
JX4071-4077	SELF-DEFENSE (INTERNATIONAL LAW)
GV1111	SELF-DEFENSE
HV6543-8	*SELF-DESTRUCTION* **SEE** SUICIDE
RA1136	*SELF-DESTRUCTION* **SEE** SUICIDE / *medical jurisprudence*
JX4054	SELF-DETERMINATION, NATIONAL
BX2377	*SELF-EXAMINATION* **SEE** CONSCIENCE, EXAMINATION OF
LB3092-5	SELF-GOVERNMENT (IN EDUCATION)
LB3021	SELF-GOVERNMENT (IN EDUCATION) / *student honor*
JC421-458	*SELF-GOVERNMENT* **SEE** DEMOCRACY
JF1051-1075	*SELF-GOVERNMENT* **SEE** REPRESENTATIVE GOVERNMENT AND REPRESENTATION
JK-JQ	*SELF-GOVERNMENT* **SEE** REPRESENTATIVE GOVERNMENT AND REPRESENTATION / *local*
QC638	SELF-INDUCTANCE
HF1133	*SELF-INSTRUCTION* **SEE** CORRESPONDENCE SCHOOLS AND COURSES / *business schools*
LC5901-6101	*SELF-INSTRUCTION* **SEE** CORRESPONDENCE SCHOOLS AND COURSES
HF1116	*SELF-INSTRUCTION* **SEE** CORRESPONDENCE SCHOOLS AND COURSES / *business schools*
T172	*SELF-INSTRUCTION* **SEE** CORRESPONDENCE SCHOOLS AND COURSES / *technology*
LC25-31	*SELF-INSTRUCTION* **SEE** SELF-CULTURE
MT893	*SELF-INSTRUCTION* **SEE** SINGING — METHODS — — SELF-INSTRUCTION
BJ1474	SELF-INTEREST / *ethics*
PA3015.K6	SELF-KNOWLEDGE IN LITERATURE / *classics*
BJ1520-1595	*SELF-MASTERY* **SEE** SELF-CONTROL / *ethics*
BF638-645	*SELF-MASTERY* **SEE** SELF-CONTROL / *new thought*
RC602	SELF-MUTILATION / *insanity*
RA1146	SELF-MUTILATION / *medical jurisprudence*
BF789.S4	SELF-MUTILATION / *psychology*
Q325	*SELF-OPTIMIZING SYSTEMS* **SEE** SELF-ORGANIZING SYSTEMS
Q325	SELF-ORGANIZING SYSTEMS
BV4509.5	*SELF-REALIZATION (RELIGION)* **SEE** IDENTIFICATION (RELIGION)
BJ1533.S27	SELF-RELIANCE
BJ1533.S3	SELF-RESPECT
BJ1533.S4	SELF-SACRIFICE
HD82-85	*SELF-SUFFICIENCY, ECONOMIC* **SEE** AUTARCHY
BF311	SELF / *consciousness*
BF697	SELF / *individuality*
BF173	SELF / *pathological psychology*
TR263.S	SELFIX CAMERA
DS27	SELJUKS
DG79	*SELLA (ROMAN ANTIQUITIES)* **SEE** CHAIRS (SELLA)
GN131	*SELLA TURCICA* **SEE** PITUITARY FOSSA / *craniology*
RA866.S5	SELTERS WATER
RA866.S5	*SELTZER WATER* **SEE** SELTERS WATER
PL4391	SEMANG DIALECTS
DS595	SEMANG RACE / *malay peninsula*
P325	SEMANTICS
B820	*SEMANTICS, GENERAL* **SEE** GENERAL SEMANTICS
P325	*SEMASIOLOGY* **SEE** SEMANTICS
RC69	*SEMEIOLOGY* **SEE** SEMIOLOGY
MT35	*SEMEIOMELODION* **SEE** SEMIOMELODION
QP255	SEMEN
BT1460	SEMI-PELAGIANISM
GR805	*SEMI-PRECIOUS STONES* **SEE** PRECIOUS STONES / *folk-lore*
TS750-755	*SEMI-PRECIOUS STONES* **SEE** PRECIOUS STONES / *manufactures*
QE392-4	*SEMI-PRECIOUS STONES* **SEE** PRECIOUS STONES / *mineralogy*
TN980-997	*SEMI-PRECIOUS STONES* **SEE** PRECIOUS STONES / *mining*
QL948	SEMICIRCULAR CANALS / *comparative anatomy*
QM507	SEMICIRCULAR CANALS / *human anatomy*
QP471	SEMICIRCULAR CANALS / *physiology*
RC898	SEMINAL VESICLES — DISEASES
QP257	SEMINAL VESICLES
QM416	SEMINAL VESICLES
QL878	SEMINAL VESICLES
BX2170.S4	SEMINARIANS — PRAYER-BOOKS AND DEVOTIONS / *catholic*
BX903	SEMINARIANS / *catholic*
BV4019-4160	*SEMINARIES, THEOLOGICAL* **SEE** THEOLOGICAL SEMINARIES
E99.S28	SEMINOLE INDIANS
HD234.S4	SEMINOLE INDIANS / *land transfers*
PM2291	SEMINOLE LANGUAGE
E83.817	SEMINOLE WAR, 1ST, 1817-1818
E83.835	SEMINOLE WAR, 2D, 1835-1842
E83.855	SEMINOLE WAR, 3D, 1855-1858
RC69	SEMIOLOGY
MT35	SEMIOMELODION

BL1600-1710	SEMITES — RELIGION
GN547	SEMITES
GR97	SEMITES / folk-lore
CB241	*SEMITIC CIVILIZATION* **SEE** CIVILIZATION, SEMITIC
PJ3001-9278	SEMITIC LANGUAGES
PJ3097	SEMITIC LITERATURE
BF1591	*SEMITIC MAGIC* **SEE** MAGIC, SEMITIC
PJ3001-9278	SEMITIC PHILOLOGY
PJ991-5	*SEMITO-HAMITIC LANGUAGES* **SEE** HAMITO-SEMITIC LANGUAGES
TX395	SEMOLINA
DQ96	SEMPACH, BATTLE OF, 1386
PL8655	SENA LANGUAGE
QE391.S	SENARMONTITE
HD234.S	SENECA INDIANS — LAND TRANSFERS
E99.S3	SENECA INDIANS
PM2296	SENECA LANGUAGE
D278.S4	SENEFFE, BATTLE OF, 1674
HV1451-1493	*SENESCENCE* **SEE** OLD AGE / charities
BJ1691	*SENESCENCE* **SEE** OLD AGE / ethics
QP86	*SENESCENCE* **SEE** OLD AGE / physiology
PJ2391	*SENHADJA LANGUAGE* **SEE** ZENAGA LANGUAGE
HV1451-1493	*SENIOR CITIZENS* **SEE** AGED
LB3621	*SENIOR YEARBOOKS* **SEE** SCHOOL YEARBOOKS
HF5549	SENIORITY, EMPLOYEE
PL8655	*SENNA LANGUAGE* **SEE** SENA LANGUAGE
RS165.S4	SENNA / pharmacy
RM666.S	SENNA / therapeutics
DS595	*SENOI* **SEE** SAKAI
DT551.42	*SENOUFO (AFRICAN PEOPLE)* **SEE** SENUFO (AFRICAN PEOPLE)
PL768	SENRYU
QP431-499	*SENSATION* **SEE** SENSES AND SENSATION / physiology
BF231-299	*SENSATION* **SEE** SENSES AND SENSATION / psychology
PN4784.S4	SENSATIONALISM IN NEWSPAPERS
QL945-9	SENSE-ORGANS / comparative anatomy
QM501-511	SENSE-ORGANS / human anatomy
QP431-499	SENSE-ORGANS / physiology and psychology
GN201	SENSE-ORGANS / somatology
QP431-499	SENSES AND SENSATION / physiology
BF231-299	SENSES AND SENSATION / psychology
TR196	*SENSITOMETRY, PHOTOGRAPHIC* **SEE** PHOTOGRAPHIC SENSITOMETRY
HV8715	*SENTENCE, INDETERMINATE* **SEE** INDETERMINATE SENTENCE
U190-195	*SENTINELS* **SEE** GUARD DUTY
DT551.42	SENUFO (AFRICAN PEOPLE)
HQ1024	SEPARATION (CANON LAW)
QD466	*SEPARATION OF ISOTOPES* **SEE** ISOTOPE SEPARATION
TK9350	*SEPARATION OF ISOTOPES* **SEE** ISOTOPE SEPARATION / engineering
JF229	SEPARATION OF POWERS
JL-JQ	SEPARATION OF POWERS / other countries
JK305	SEPARATION OF POWERS / u.s.
F68	SEPARATISTS / new england
SF247	SEPARATORS (MACHINES) / dairy machinery
TN515	SEPARATORS (MACHINES) / mining
TJ1540	SEPARATORS (MACHINES) / screening
SF247	*SEPARATORS, CREAM* **SEE** CREAM-SEPARATORS
TP156.E5	*SEPARATORS, ELECTROSTATIC* **SEE** ELECTROSTATIC SEPARATORS
SF247	*SEPARATORS, WHEY* **SEE** WHEY-SEPARATORS
DS135.A-Z	*SEPHARDIC JEWS* **SEE** SEPHARDIM
DS135.A-Z	SEPHARDIM
ND2460	*SEPIA DRAWING* **SEE** SEPIA PAINTING
ND2460	SEPIA PAINTING
ND2460	SEPIA PAINTINGS
TN948.M5	*SEPIOLITE* **SEE** MEERSCHAUM
M755-7	SEPTETS (BASSOON, CLARINET, ENGLISH HORN, FLUTE, HORN, OBOE, SAXOPHONE)
M780-782	SEPTETS (BASSOON, CLARINET, FLUTE, HORN, OBOE, HARP, VIOLA)
M760-762	SEPTETS (BASSOON, CLARINET, FLUTE, HORN, OBOE, VIOLIN, VIOLONCELLO)
M760-762	SEPTETS (BASSOON, CLARINET, FLUTE, HORN, OBOE, VIOLA, VIOLONCELLO)

M760-762	SEPTETS (BASSOON, CLARINET, FLUTE, VIOLIN, VIOLA, VIOLONCELLO, DOUBLE BASS)
M760-762	SEPTETS (BASSOON, CLARINET, HORN, VIOLIN, VIOLA, VIOLONCELLO, DOUBLE BASS)
M785	SEPTETS (CLARINET, FLUTE, HARP, VIBRAPHONE, VIOLIN, VIOLA, VIOLONCELLO)
M780-784	SEPTETS (CLARINET, FLUTE, HARP, 2 VIOLINS, VIOLA, VIOLONCELLO)
M780-782	SEPTETS (CLARINET, FLUTE, HORN, HARP, VIOLIN, VIOLA, VIOLONCELLO)
M760-762	SEPTETS (CLARINET, FLUTE, HORN, VIOLIN, VIOLA, VIOLONCELLO, DOUBLE BASS)
M760-762	SEPTETS (CLARINET, FLUTE, OBOE, 2 VIOLINS, VIOLA, VIOLONCELLO)
M785	SEPTETS (CLARINET, FLUTE, TRUMPET, KETTLEDRUMS, PERCUSSION, DOUBLE BASS)
M760-762	SEPTETS (CLARINET, OBOE, 4 VIOLINS, VIOLONCELLO)
M760-762	SEPTETS (FLUTE, 2 HORNS, 2 VIOLINS, VIOLA, DOUBLE BASS)
M745-7	SEPTETS (HARPSICHORD, BASSOON, CLARINET, TROMBONE, PERCUSSION, VIOLIN, VIOLONCELLO)
M720-722	SEPTETS (HARPSICHORD, BASSOON, FLUTE, OBOE, VIOLIN, VIOLA, VIOLONCELLO)
M720-722	SEPTETS (HARPSICHORD, FLUTE, OBOE, 2 VIOLINS, VIOLONCELLO, DOUBLE BASS)
M720-722	SEPTETS (HARPSICHORD, FLUTE, OBOE, 2 VIOLINS, VIOLA, VIOLONCELLO)
M620-622	SEPTETS (HARPSICHORD, 2 FLUTES, VIOLIN, 2 VIOLAS, VIOLONCELLO)
M720-722	SEPTETS (HARPSICHORD, 2 FLUTES, 2 OBOES, 2 VIOLINS)
M720-722	SEPTETS (HARPSICHORD, 2 HORNS, 2 OBOES, 2 VIOLINS)
M720-722	SEPTETS (HARPSICHORD, 2 OBOES, 2 RECORDERS, 2 VIOLINS)
M720-722	SEPTETS (HARPSICHORD, 3 OBOES, 3 VIOLINS)
M710-712	SEPTETS (HARPSICHORD, 4 VIOLINS, VIOLA, VIOLONCELLO)
M700-702	SEPTETS (ORGAN, 2 TROMBONES, 3 TRUMPETS, PERCUSSION)
M720-722	SEPTETS (PIANO, BASSOON, CLARINET, HORN, VIOLIN, VIOLA, VIOLONCELLO)
M720-722	SEPTETS (PIANO, BASSOON, CLARINET, HORN, 2 VIOLINS, VIOLA)
M720-722	SEPTETS (PIANO, BASSOON, CLARINET, OBOE, TRUMPET, 2 VIOLINS)
M720-722	SEPTETS (PIANO, BASSOON, FLUTE, OBOE, VIOLIN, VIOLA, VIOLONCELLO)
M720-722	SEPTETS (PIANO, FLUTE, HORN, OBOE, VIOLA, VIOLONCELLO, DOUBLE BASS)
M720-722	SEPTETS (PIANO, FLUTE, HORN, TROMBONE, TRUMPET, VIOLA, VIOLONCELLO)
M720-722	SEPTETS (PIANO, FLUTE, OBOE, 2 VIOLINS, VIOLONCELLO, DOUBLE BASS)
M730-732	SEPTETS (PIANO, HARP, 2 VIOLINS, VIOLA, VIOLONCELLO, DOUBLE BASS)
M620-622	SEPTETS (PIANO, 2 FLUTES, VIOLIN, 2 VIOLAS, VIOLONCELLO)
M720-722	SEPTETS (PIANO, 2 FLUTES, 2 OBOES, 2 VIOLINS)
M720-722	SEPTETS (PIANO, 2 HORNS, 2 OBOES, 2 VIOLINS)
M720-722	SEPTETS (PIANO, 2 OBOES, 2 RECORDERS, 2 VIOLINS)
M720-722	SEPTETS (PIANO, 3 CLARINETS, VIOLIN, VIOLA, VIOLONCELLO)
M720-722	SEPTETS (PIANO, 3 OBOES, 3 VIOLINS)
M785	SEPTETS (PIANO, 3 TROMBONES, TUBA, PERCUSSION)
M710-712	SEPTETS (PIANO, 4 VIOLINS, VIOLA, VIOLONCELLO)
M785	SEPTETS (2 CLARINETS, FLUTE, PERCUSSION, VIOLIN, VIOLA, VIOLONCELLO)
M780-782	SEPTETS (2 CLARINETS, GUITAR, MANDOLIN, VIOLIN, VIOLA, VIOLONCELLO)
M785	SEPTETS (2 CLARINETS, TROMBONE, 3 TRUMPETS, KETTLEDRUMS), ARRANGED
M785	SEPTETS (2 CLARINETS, TROMBONE, 3 TRUMPETS, KETTLEDRUMS)
M760-762	SEPTETS (2 FLUTES, TRUMPET, 2 VIOLINS, VIOLA, VIOLONCELLO)
M760-762	SEPTETS (2 FLUTES, 2 VIOLAS, 2 VIOLONCELLOS, DOUBLE BASS)
M760-762	SEPTETS (2 HORNS, OBOE, 2 VIOLINS, VIOLA, VIOLONCELLO)

M785	SEPTETS (3 TROMBONES, 2 TRUMPETS, TUBA, KETTLEDRUMS)
M760-762	SEPTETS (4 HORNS, VIOLIN, VIOLA, VIOLONCELLO)
M750-752	*SEPTETS, STRING* **SEE** STRING SEPTETS
M755-7	*SEPTETS, WIND* **SEE** WIND SEPTETS
TD778	SEPTIC TANKS
RM798.S	SEPTICEMIA — PREVENTIVE INOCULATION
RC182.S4	SEPTICEMIA / *infectious diseases*
SF802	SEPTICEMIA / *veterinary medicine*
RG811	*SEPTICEMIA, PUERPERAL* **SEE** PUERPERAL SEPTICEMIA
DS109.4	*SEPULCHER, HOLY* **SEE** HOLY SEPULCHER
NA6120-6199	*SEPULCHERS* **SEE** TOMBS / *architecture*
NK7800-7899	*SEPULCHRAL BRASSES* **SEE** BRASSES / *art objects*
NB1840-1846	*SEPULCHRAL BRASSES* **SEE** BRASSES / *sepulchral monuments*
NB1800-1885	SEPULCHRAL MONUMENTS / *sculpture*
NK3700-4657	*SEPULCHRAL URNS* **SEE** URNS / *ceramics*
DG264	SEQUANI (GALLIC TRIBE) / *gallic war*
ML3080	SEQUENCES (LITURGY) / *history*
SB945.S	SEQUOIA PITCH MOTH
QK495.S5	SEQUOIA / *botany*
SD397.S4	SEQUOIA / *forestry*
DS432.S	*SERAKS* **SEE** SARAKS
BL477	*SERAPHIM* **SEE** ANGELS / *comparative religion*
BT965-8	*SERAPHIM* **SEE** ANGELS / *theology*
DS432.S	*SERAWAKS* **SEE** SARAKS
PG1450-1466	SERBIAN BALLADS AND SONGS / *folk literature*
PG601-698	*SERBIAN CHURCH SLAVIC LANGUAGE* **SEE** CHURCH SLAVIC LANGUAGE
PG1415	SERBIAN DRAMA / *collections*
PG1411	SERBIAN DRAMA / *history*
PG1416	SERBIAN FICTION / *collections*
PG1412	SERBIAN FICTION / *history*
PG1224-1399	*SERBIAN LANGUAGE* **SEE** SERBO-CROATIAN LANGUAGE
PG1500-1596	SERBIAN LITERATURE
PG1400-1469	SERBIAN LITERATURE / *serbo-croatian*
PG1414	SERBIAN POETRY / *collections*
PG1464	SERBIAN POETRY / *folk literature*
PG1410	SERBIAN POETRY / *history*
DR354	*SERBIAN-BULGARIAN WAR, 1885* **SEE** SERBO-BULGARIAN WAR, 1885
DR353	*SERBIAN-TURKISH WAR, 1876* **SEE** SERBO-TURKISH WAR, 1876
DR343	SERBIA — HISTORY — — INSURRECTION, 1804-1813
DR354	SERBO-BULGARIAN WAR, 1885
PG1224-1399	SERBO-CROATIAN LANGUAGE
DB33-34	*SERBO-CROATIANS* **SEE** CROATS / *austria*
DB361-379	*SERBO-CROATIANS* **SEE** CROATS / *croatia*
DR364-7	*SERBO-CROATIANS* **SEE** CROATS / *yugoslavia*
DR312-314	*SERBO-CROATIANS* **SEE** SERBS
GN585.S5	*SERBO-CROATIANS* **SEE** SERBS / *anthropology*
DR353	SERBO-TURKISH WAR, 1876
DR312-314	SERBS
GN585.S5	SERBS / *anthropology*
DT549	SERERS
HT751-815	SERFDOM
F1221.S43	SERI INDIANS
PM4251	SERI LANGUAGE
AP	*SERIALS* **SEE** PERIODICALS
PN4700-4900	*SERIALS* **SEE** PERIODICALS / *etc.*
SF541-559	*SERICICULTURE* **SEE** SERICULTURE
QP551	SERICIN
SF541-559	SERICULTURE
QA295	SERIES
QA295	SERIES, DIRICHLET'S
QA295	SERIES, DIVERGENT
QA404	*SERIES, FOURIER* **SEE** FOURIER SERIES
QA295	SERIES, INFINITE
QA306	SERIES, LAGRANGE'S
QA306	*SERIES, MACLAURIN'S* **SEE** SERIES, TAYLOR'S
QA404.5	SERIES, ORTHOGONAL
QA306	SERIES, TAYLOR'S
QA404	*SERIES, TRIGONOMETRIC* **SEE** FOURIER SERIES
NE1843-4	SERIGRAPHY / *art*
GV1796.S4	SERIMPI (DANCE)
BT380	SERMON ON THE MOUNT
BV4307.S7	SERMON STORIES
BV4223	SERMONS — OUTLINES

BV4307.S7	*SERMONS IN STORY FORM* **SEE** SERMON STORIES
BV4240-4316	SERMONS
BX	SERMONS / *by denomination*
BP183.6	*SERMONS, ARABIC, (INDONESIAN, TURKISH, ETC.)-ISLAMIC AUTHORS* **SEE** ISLAMIC SERMONS, ARABIC, (INDONESIAN, TURKISH, ETC.)
BP183.6	*SERMONS, ARABIC, (INDONESIAN, TURKISH, ETC.)-MUSLIM AUTHORS* **SEE** ISLAMIC SERMONS, ARABIC, (INDONESIAN, TURKISH, ETC.)
BR60-63	SERMONS, EARLY CHRISTIAN
BP183.6	*SERMONS, ISLAMIC* **SEE** ISLAMIC SERMONS
BM732	SERMONS, JEWISH — OUTLINES
BP183.6	*SERMONS, MUSLIM* **SEE** ISLAMIC SERMONS
BM695.P3	*SERMONS, PASSOVER* **SEE** PASSOVER SERMONS
BV3797	*SERMONS, REVIVAL* **SEE** EVANGELISTIC SERMONS
BV4224-4230	*SERMONS-ILLUSTRATIONS* **SEE** HOMILETICAL ILLUSTRATIONS
RM739-798	*SEROTHERAPY* **SEE** SERUMTHERAPY
RA401	*SEROTHERAPY* **SEE** SERUMTHERAPY / *etc.*
ML980	SERPENT (MUSICAL INSTRUMENT) / *history*
BL441	SERPENT-WORSHIP
GR830.R3	*SERPENT, RAINBOW* **SEE** RAINBOW SERPENT
SB945.S	SERPENTINE LEAF-MINER
QE391.S47	SERPENTINE / *mineralogy*
QE475	SERPENTINE / *petrology*
SB205.S	SERRADELLA
E99.S31	SERRANO INDIANS
RB146	SERUM DIAGNOSIS
RM739-798	SERUMTHERAPY
RA401	SERUMTHERAPY / *etc.*
HJ5797	SERVANTS — TAXATION
TX331-3	SERVANTS / *home economics*
HD8039.D5-52	SERVANTS / *labor*
HD4871-5	*SERVANTS, INDENTURED* **SEE** INDENTURED SERVANTS
HD4875.U5	*SERVANTS, INDENTURED* **SEE** INDENTURED SERVANTS / *u.s.*
BX1972	*SERVERS* **SEE** ALTAR BOYS / *catholic church*
DR312-314	*SERVIANS* **SEE** SERBS
GN585.S5	*SERVIANS* **SEE** SERBS / *anthropology*
HD2763	SERVICE AT COST (PUBLIC UTILITIES)
NA6598	*SERVICE BUILDINGS, EMPLOYEES'* **SEE** EMPLOYEES' BUILDINGS AND FACILITIES
T60.R	*SERVICE RATING* **SEE** EMPLOYEES, RATING OF
TL153	*SERVICE STATIONS, AUTOMOBILE* **SEE** AUTOMOBILES — SERVICE STATIONS
UB340-355	*SERVICE, COMPULSORY MILITARY* **SEE** MILITARY SERVICE, COMPULSORY
HD4871-5	SERVICE, COMPULSORY NON-MILITARY
HD4905.5	SERVICE, COMPULSORY NON-MILITARY / *in wartime*
U1-145	*SERVICEMEN, MILITARY* **SEE** SOLDIERS
U750-773	*SERVICEMEN, MILITARY* **SEE** SOLDIERS
BV199.D4	*SERVICES, CONSECRATION* **SEE** DEDICATION SERVICES
BV199.D4	*SERVICES, DEDICATION* **SEE** DEDICATION SERVICES
BX4040.S5	SERVITES
HD4871-5	*SERVITUDE* **SEE** PEONAGE
HT751-815	*SERVITUDE* **SEE** SERFDOM
HT851-1445	*SERVITUDE* **SEE** SLAVERY
HD1523	*SERVITUDE* **SEE** VILLEINAGE
HD4871-5	*SERVITUDE FOR DEBT* **SEE** PEONAGE
JX4068.S5	SERVITUDES (INTERNATIONAL LAW)
TE315-424	*SERVITUDES* **SEE** HIGHWAY LAW
JX4068.S5	SERVITUDES / *international law*
TJ857	*SERVOMECHANISMS, HYDRAULIC* **SEE** HYDRAULIC SERVOMECHANISMS
QA76.8.S5	*SESM (COMPUTER)* **SEE** SESM COMPUTER
TK7889.S	*SESM (COMPUTER)* **SEE** SESM COMPUTER / *technology*
QA76.8.S5	SESM COMPUTER
TK7889.S	SESM COMPUTER / *technology*
PQ4128.C6	SESTINAS / *history*
PQ4222.C6	SESTINAS / *italian poetry collections*
PL8689	*SESUTO LANGUAGE* **SEE** SOTHO LANGUAGE
QA248	*SETS (MATHEMATICS)* **SEE** AGGREGATES
SF429.S5	SETTERS (DOGS)
PN1995	*SETTING (STAGE)* **SEE** MOVING-PICTURES — SETTING AND SCENERY
PN2091.S8	*SETTING (STAGE)* **SEE** THEATERS — STAGE-SETTING AND SCENERY

HV4175-4320	*SETTLEMENTS, SOCIAL* **SEE** SOCIAL SETTLEMENTS
DK215.7	SEVASTOPOL — SIEGE, 1854-1855
D764	SEVASTOPOL — SIEGE, 1942
BF1623.P9	SEVEN (THE NUMBER) / *symbolism*
BV4626-7	*SEVEN CAPITAL SINS* **SEE** DEADLY SINS
E473.68	SEVEN DAYS' BATTLES, 1862
BV4626-7	*SEVEN DEADLY SINS* **SEE** DEADLY SINS
BX2161.5.S	*SEVEN DOLORS OF MARY, DEVOTION TO* **SEE** SORROWS OF THE BLESSED VIRGIN MARY, DEVOTION TO
BT455-6	*SEVEN LAST WORDS* **SEE** JESUS CHRIST — SEVEN LAST WORDS
LA85-98	*SEVEN LIBERAL ARTS* **SEE** EDUCATION, MEDIEVAL
F1063	SEVEN OAKS, MANITOBA, BATTLE OF, 1816
E473.65	*SEVEN PINES, BATTLE OF, 1862* **SEE** FAIR OAKS, BATTLE OF, 1862
F2684	SEVEN REDUCTIONS, WAR OF THE, 1754-1756
BX2161.5.S	*SEVEN SORROWS OF THE BLESSED VIRGIN MARY, DEVOTION TO* **SEE** SORROWS OF THE BLESSED VIRGIN MARY, DEVOTION TO
DD436-440	*SEVEN WEEKS' WAR* **SEE** AUSTRO-PRUSSIAN WAR, 1866
N5333	SEVEN WONDERS OF THE WORLD
DD411.5	SEVEN YEARS' WAR, 1756-1763 — ECONOMIC ASPECTS
DD409-412	SEVEN YEARS' WAR, 1756-1763
D242-7	SEVENTEENTH CENTURY
CB353.7	SEVENTH CENTURY
BX6151-5	SEVENTH-DAY ADVENTISTS
BX6390-6399	SEVENTH-DAY BAPTISTS
HD4928.D5	*SEVERANCE PAY* **SEE** WAGES — DISMISSAL WAGE
HJ4169	*SEVERANCE TAX* **SEE** MINES AND MINERAL RESOURCES — TAXATION
D287.8	SEVILLE, TREATY OF, 1729
NK4390	SEVRES PORCELAIN
D651.T9	SEVRES, TREATY OF, 1920
DR589	SEVRES, TREATY OF, 1920 / *turkish history*
TD735	SEWAGE — ANALYSIS
TD745-757	SEWAGE — PURIFICATION
TD741-780	SEWAGE DISPOSAL
RA567	SEWAGE DISPOSAL / *public health*
TD760	SEWAGE IRRIGATION
TD755	SEWAGE LAGOONS
TD760	*SEWAGE-FARMS* **SEE** SEWAGE IRRIGATION
TP360	SEWAGE-SLUDGE FUEL
TD730-735	SEWAGE
S657	SEWAGE / *fertilizer*
E99.S32	SEWEE INDIANS
TD678-688	SEWER DESIGN
TD913	SEWER-GAS
TP839	SEWER-PIPE
HD9600.S3	SEWER-PIPE / *industry*
TD653	SEWERAGE — CONTRACTS AND SPECIFICATIONS
TD511-780	SEWERAGE
TD929	SEWERAGE, RURAL
TD511-780	*SEWERS* **SEE** SEWERAGE
TD682	SEWERS, CONCRETE
TT712	SEWING — JUVENILE LITERATURE
TT708	SEWING SCHOOLS
TJ1501-1519	SEWING-MACHINES
TT700-715	SEWING
QP251	SEX — CAUSE AND DETERMINATION
HB1741-1950	SEX — STATISTICS
HB903.S5	SEX — STATISTICS / *birth rate*
HB1323.S5	SEX — STATISTICS / *death rate*
QH481-5	SEX (BIOLOGY)
BF692	SEX (PSYCHOLOGY)
HQ61	SEX AND RELIGION
HQ12-18	SEX CUSTOMS
HQ56	*SEX EDUCATION* **SEE** SEX INSTRUCTION
N8217.E6	SEX IN ART / *erotica*
PN56.S5	SEX IN LITERATURE
PR149.S5	SEX IN LITERATURE / *english literature*
PN1994-5.5	*SEX IN MOVING-PICTURES* **SEE** MOVING-PICTURES — MORAL AND RELIGIOUS ASPECTS
QK827	*SEX IN PLANTS* **SEE** PLANTS, SEX IN
QK658-9	*SEX IN PLANTS* **SEE** PLANTS, SEX IN
BS680.S5	SEX IN THE BIBLE
HQ56	SEX INSTRUCTION

QM416-421	*SEX ORGANS* **SEE** GENERATIVE ORGANS / *human anatomy*
QP251-281	*SEX ORGANS* **SEE** GENERATIVE ORGANS / *physiology*
HQ71-78	*SEX PERVERSION* **SEE** SEXUAL PERVERSION
HQ21	SEX RESEARCH
QP251	SEX RESEARCH / *physiology*
BL460	*SEX WORSHIP* **SEE** PHALLICISM
HQ21	*SEX-RESEARCH* **SEE** SEX RESEARCH
QP251	*SEX-RESEARCH* **SEE** SEX RESEARCH / *physiology*
VK583	SEXTANT
M685	SEXTETS (ACCORDION, CLARINET, 2 VIOLINS, VIOLA, DOUBLE BASS)
M675-7	SEXTETS (BASSOON, CLARINET, FLUTE, HORN, OBOE, HARP)
M660-662	SEXTETS (BASSOON, CLARINET, FLUTE, HORN, OBOE, VIOLIN)
M660-662	SEXTETS (BASSOON, CLARINET, FLUTE, TRUMPET, VIOLIN, VIOLONCELLO)
M660-662	SEXTETS (BASSOON, HORN, OBOE, VIOLIN, VIOLA, DOUBLE BASS)
M685	SEXTETS (BELLS, XYLOPHONE, STRING QUARTET)
M635	SEXTETS (CELESTA, FLUTE, OBOE, SAXOPHONE, GUITAR, HARP)
M683-4	SEXTETS (CLARINET, FLUTE, HARP, VIOLIN, VIOLA, VIOLONCELLO), ARRANGED
M680-682	SEXTETS (CLARINET, FLUTE, HARP, VIOLIN, VIOLA, VIOLONCELLO)
M685	SEXTETS (CLARINET, FLUTE, HORN, HARP, PERCUSSION)
M680-682	SEXTETS (CLARINET, FLUTE, OBOE, HARP, VIOLA, VIOLONCELLO)
M680-682	SEXTETS (CLARINET, FLUTE, 2 GUITARS, VIOLIN, VIOLONCELLO)
M660-662	SEXTETS (CLARINET, FLUTE, 2 VIOLINS, VIOLA, VIOLONCELLO)
M680-682	SEXTETS (CLARINET, HARP, 2 VIOLINS, VIOLA, VIOLONCELLO)
M660-662	SEXTETS (CLARINET, HORN, 2 VIOLINS, VIOLA, VIOLONCELLO)
M660-662	SEXTETS (CLARINET, HORN, 3 VIOLINS, VIOLA)
M660-662	SEXTETS (CLARINET, OBOE, 2 VIOLINS, VIOLA, VIOLONCELLO)
M680-682	SEXTETS (FLUTE, GUITAR, HARP, VIOLIN, VIOLA, VIOLONCELLO)
M680-682	SEXTETS (FLUTE, HARP, 2 VIOLINS, VIOLA, VIOLONCELLO)
M660-662	SEXTETS (FLUTE, HORN, 2 VIOLINS, VIOLA, VIOLONCELLO)
M685	SEXTETS (FLUTE, OBOE, HARP, PERCUSSION, VIOLIN, VIOLA)
M660-662	SEXTETS (FLUTE, 2 HORNS, VIOLIN, VIOLA, VIOLONCELLO)
M660-662	SEXTETS (FLUTE, 2 VIOLINS, VIOLA, VIOLONCELLO, DOUBLE BASS)
M685	SEXTETS (GLOCKENSPIEL, MARIMBA, PERCUSSION)
M620-622	SEXTETS (HARPSICHORD, CLARINET, FLUTE, OBOE, VIOLIN, VIOLONCELLO
M620-622	SEXTETS (HARPSICHORD, FLUTE, OBOE, VIOLIN, VIOLA, VIOLONCELLO)
M620-622	SEXTETS (HARPSICHORD, FLUTE, RECORDER, 2 VIOLINS, VIOLA)
M620-622	SEXTETS (HARPSICHORD, RECORDER, 2 VIOLINS, VIOLA, VIOLONCELLO)
M620-622	SEXTETS (HARPSICHORD, TRUMPET, 2 VIOLINS, VIOLA, DOUBLE BASS)
M620-622	SEXTETS (HARPSICHORD, 2 HORNS, OBOE, VIOLIN, VIOLONCELLO)
M610-612	SEXTETS (HARPSICHORD, 2 VIOLINS, 2 VIOLAS, VIOLONCELLO)
M610-612	SEXTETS (HARPSICHORD, 3 VIOLINS, VIOLA, VIOLONCELLO)
M660-662	SEXTETS (HORN, 2 VIOLINS, VIOLA, 2 VIOLONCELLOS)
M670-672	SEXTETS (LUTE, 2 VIOLINS, VIOLA, 2 VIOLONCELLOS)
M600-602	SEXTETS (ORGAN, PERCUSSION, 2 TROMBONES, 2 TRUMPETS)
M600-602	SEXTETS (ORGAN, 2 HORNS, TROMBONE, 2 TRUMPETS)

M620-622	SEXTETS (PIANO (4 HANDS), CLARINET, VIOLIN, VIOLA, VIOLONCELLO)
M618-619	SEXTETS (PIANO, BASSOON, CLARINET, FLUTE, HORN, OBOE), ARRANGED
M615-617	SEXTETS (PIANO, BASSOON, CLARINET, FLUTE, HORN, OBOE)
M615-617	SEXTETS (PIANO, BASSOON, CLARINET, FLUTE, OBOE, TRUMPET)
M635	SEXTETS (PIANO, BASSOON, CLARINET, PERCUSSION, VIOLIN)
M635	SEXTETS (PIANO, CLARINET, FLUTE, PERCUSSION, VIOLIN, VIOLONCELLO)
M620-622	SEXTETS (PIANO, CLARINET, HORN, VIOLIN, VIOLA, VIOLONCELLO)
M685	SEXTETS (PIANO, CLARINET, PERCUSSION)
M620-622	SEXTETS (PIANO, CLARINET, VIOLIN, VIOLA, VIOLONCELLO, DOUBLE BASS)
M620-622	SEXTETS (PIANO, CLARINET, 2 VIOLINS, VIOLA, VIOLONCELLO)
M623-4	SEXTETS (PIANO, CLARINET, 2 VIOLINS, VIOLA, VIOLONCELLO), ARRANGED
M635	SEXTETS (PIANO, FLUTE, KETTLEDRUMS, PERCUSSION, VIBRAPHONE, XYLOPHONE)
M630-632	SEXTETS (PIANO, FLUTE, OBOE, HARP, VIOLIN, VIOLA)
M620-622	SEXTETS (PIANO, FLUTE, OBOE, VIOLIN, VIOLA, VIOLONCELLO)
M620-622	SEXTETS (PIANO, FLUTE, RECORDER, 2 VIOLINS, VIOLA)
M635	SEXTETS (PIANO, FLUTE, TUBA, VIBRAPHONE, VIOLIN, VIOLONCELLO)
M620-622	SEXTETS (PIANO, FLUTE, 2 VIOLINS, VIOLA, VIOLONCELLO)
M620-622	SEXTETS (PIANO, TRUMPET, 2 VIOLINS, VIOLA, DOUBLE BASS)
M635	SEXTETS (PIANO, 2 HORNS, TROMBONE, TRUMPET, PERCUSSION)
M635	SEXTETS (PIANO, 2 SAXOPHONES, TROMBONE, TRUMPET, DRUMS)
M613-614	SEXTETS (PIANO, 2 VIOLINS, VIOLA, VIOLONCELLO, DOUBLE BASS), ARRANGED
M610-612	SEXTETS (PIANO, 2 VIOLINS, VIOLA, VIOLONCELLO, DOUBLE BASS)
M610-612	SEXTETS (PIANO, 2 VIOLINS, 2 VIOLAS, VIOLONCELLO)
M610-612	SEXTETS (PIANO, 3 VIOLINS, VIOLA, VIOLONCELLO)
M613-614	SEXTETS (PIANO, 3 VIOLINS, VIOLONCELLO, DOUBLE BASS), ARRANGED
M635	SEXTETS (PIANO, 4 TRUMPETS, PERCUSSION)
M655-7	SEXTETS (2 CLARINETS, 2 HORNS, TROMBONE, TRUMPET)
M658-9	SEXTETS (2 CLARINETS, 2 HORNS, TROMBONE, TRUMPET), ARRANGED
M660-662	SEXTETS (2 HORNS, 2 VIOLINS, VIOLA, VIOLONCELLO)
M660-662	SEXTETS (2 RECORDERS, 2 VIOLINS, VIOLA, VIOLONCELLO)
M663-4	SEXTETS (2 RECORDERS, 2 VIOLINS, VIOLA, VIOLONCELLO), ARRANGED
M680-682	SEXTETS (3 TROMBONES, TRUMPET, GUITAR, DOUBLE BASS)
M650-652	*SEXTETS, STRING* **SEE** STRING SEXTETS
M655-7	*SEXTETS, WIND* **SEE** WIND SEXTETS
QA215	*SEXTIC EQUATIONS* **SEE** EQUATIONS, SEXTIC
QA573	*SEXTIC SURFACES* **SEE** SURFACES, SEXTIC
HQ31	SEXUAL ETHICS
HQ31-58	*SEXUAL HYGIENE* **SEE** HYGIENE, SEXUAL
RC881	*SEXUAL HYGIENE* **SEE** HYGIENE, SEXUAL / men
RG121	*SEXUAL HYGIENE* **SEE** HYGIENE, SEXUAL / women
RG103	SEXUAL INSTINCT / gynecology
QP251	SEXUAL INSTINCT / physiology
HQ19-23	SEXUAL INSTINCT / social sciences
QL876-881	*SEXUAL ORGANS* **SEE** GENERATIVE ORGANS / comparative anatomy
QM416-421	*SEXUAL ORGANS* **SEE** GENERATIVE ORGANS / human anatomy
QP251-281	*SEXUAL ORGANS* **SEE** GENERATIVE ORGANS / physiology
HQ71-78	SEXUAL PERVERSION
BF692	*SEXUAL PSYCHOLOGY* **SEE** SEX (PSYCHOLOGY)
PL4054.Z9S	*SGAU KAREN DIALECT* **SEE** SGAW KAREN DIALECT
PL4054.Z9S	SGAW KAREN DIALECT
BP186.38	*SHAB-I BARAT* **SEE** LAYLAT AL-BARA'AH

BP195.3	SHABAK
BM199.S	*SHABBATHAIANS* **SEE** SABBATHAIANS
BM199.S	*SHABBETHAIANS* **SEE** SABBATHAIANS
BM695.S5	*SHABU'OTH* **SEE** SHAVU'OTH (FEAST OF WEEKS)
QL638.C64	SHAD
SH167.S5	SHAD / culture
SH351.S5	SHAD / fisheries
NC755	SHADES AND SHADOWS / drawing
QA519	SHADES AND SHADOWS / geometry
PN1979.S5	SHADOW PANTOMIMES AND PLAYS / texts
PN6120.S5	SHADOW PANTOMIMES AND PLAYS / texts
GV1218.S5	SHADOW-PICTURES
RE965	*SHADOW-TEST* **SEE** SKIASCOPY
NC755	*SHADOWS* **SEE** SHADES AND SHADOWS / drawing
QA519	*SHADOWS* **SEE** SHADES AND SHADOWS / geometry
TN283	SHAFT SINKING / mining
TJ1057	SHAFTING
E99.S	SHAHAPTIAN INDIANS
PM2301	SHAHAPTIAN LANGUAGES
D90.S3	*SHAKA* **SEE** SAKA
BV2595.S5	SHAKERS — MISSIONS
BX9751-9793	SHAKERS
PR2877-9	SHAKESPEARE, WILLIAM, 1564-1616 — ADAPTATIONS
PR2959	SHAKESPEARE, WILLIAM, 1564-1616 — ALLUSIONS
PR2923	SHAKESPEARE, WILLIAM, 1564-1616 — ANNIVERSARIES, ETC.
PR2965-2979	SHAKESPEARE, WILLIAM, 1564-1616 — APPRECIATION
PR2937-2961	SHAKESPEARE, WILLIAM, 1564-1616 — AUTHORSHIP
PR2949	SHAKESPEARE, WILLIAM, 1564-1616 — AUTOGRAPHS
PR2949	SHAKESPEARE, WILLIAM, 1564-1616 — AUTOGRAPHS, SPURIOUS
Z8811-8813	SHAKESPEARE, WILLIAM, 1564-1616 — BIBLIOGRAPHY
PR2894-2920	SHAKESPEARE, WILLIAM, 1564-1616 — BIOGRAPHY
PR2770-2771	SHAKESPEARE, WILLIAM, 1564-1616 — BIRTHDAY BOOKS
PR2770-2771	SHAKESPEARE, WILLIAM, 1564-1616 — CALENDARS, ETC.
PR2989	SHAKESPEARE, WILLIAM, 1564-1616 — CHARACTERS
PR2961	SHAKESPEARE, WILLIAM, 1564-1616 — CHRONOLOGY OF THE PLAYS
PR2981	SHAKESPEARE, WILLIAM, 1564-1616 — COMEDIES
PR2892	SHAKESPEARE, WILLIAM, 1564-1616 — CONCORDANCES
PR2957-8	SHAKESPEARE, WILLIAM, 1564-1616 — CONTEMPORARIES
PR2911-2913	SHAKESPEARE, WILLIAM, 1564-1616 — CONTEMPORARIES
PR2910	SHAKESPEARE, WILLIAM, 1564-1616 — CONTEMPORARY ENGLAND
PR2965-2979	SHAKESPEARE, WILLIAM, 1564-1616 — CRITICISM AND INTERPRETATION
PR3070-3071	SHAKESPEARE, WILLIAM, 1564-1616 — CRITICISM, TEXTUAL
PR2900	SHAKESPEARE, WILLIAM, 1564-1616 — CURIOSA AND MISCELLANY
PR2929	SHAKESPEARE, WILLIAM, 1564-1616 — DEATH MASK
PR2892	SHAKESPEARE, WILLIAM, 1564-1616 — DICTIONARIES, INDEXES, ETC.
PR3091-9	SHAKESPEARE, WILLIAM, 1564-1616 — DRAMATURGY
PR2995-7	SHAKESPEARE, WILLIAM, 1564-1616 — DRAMATURGY
PR2965-2972	SHAKESPEARE, WILLIAM, 1564-1616 — EDITORS
PR3004	SHAKESPEARE, WILLIAM, 1564-1616 — FOLK-LORE, MYTHOLOGY
PR3009	SHAKESPEARE, WILLIAM, 1564-1616 — FOLK-LORE, MYTHOLOGY
PR2949-2951	SHAKESPEARE, WILLIAM, 1564-1616 — FORGERIES
PR2911-2913	SHAKESPEARE, WILLIAM, 1564-1616 — FRIENDS AND ASSOCIATES
PR2916	SHAKESPEARE, WILLIAM, 1564-1616 — GRAVE
PR2895-8	SHAKESPEARE, WILLIAM, 1564-1616 — HANDBOOKS, MANUALS, ETC.
PR2982	SHAKESPEARE, WILLIAM, 1564-1616 — HISTORIES
PR2915-2920	SHAKESPEARE, WILLIAM, 1564-1616 — HOMES AND HAUNTS
PR2994	SHAKESPEARE, WILLIAM, 1564-1616 — HUMOR
PR2883	SHAKESPEARE, WILLIAM, 1564-1616 — ILLUSTRATIONS

PR2965-2971	SHAKESPEARE, WILLIAM, 1564-1616 — INFLUENCE
PR2952-5	SHAKESPEARE, WILLIAM, 1564-1616 — KNOWLEDGE AND LEARNING / *literature*
PR3000	SHAKESPEARE, WILLIAM, 1564-1616 — KNOWLEDGE AND LEARNING
PR2903	SHAKESPEARE, WILLIAM, 1564-1616 — KNOWLEDGE AND LEARNING / *education*
PR3072	SHAKESPEARE, WILLIAM, 1564-1616 — LANGUAGE
PR2930	SHAKESPEARE, WILLIAM, 1564-1616 — MONUMENTS, ETC.
PR2931-3	SHAKESPEARE, WILLIAM, 1564-1616 — MUSEUMS, RELICS, ETC.
PR3034	SHAKESPEARE, WILLIAM, 1564-1616 — MUSIC / *etc.*
ML80.S5	SHAKESPEARE, WILLIAM, 1564-1616 — MUSIC / *history*
PR2901	SHAKESPEARE, WILLIAM, 1564-1616 — NAME
PR3039-3044	SHAKESPEARE, WILLIAM, 1564-1616 — NATURAL HISTORY
PR2923	SHAKESPEARE, WILLIAM, 1564-1616 — PAGEANTS
PR2877-9	SHAKESPEARE, WILLIAM, 1564-1616 — PARODIES, TRAVESTIES, ETC.
PR3069.P3	SHAKESPEARE, WILLIAM, 1564-1616 — PATRIOTISM
PR2986	SHAKESPEARE, WILLIAM, 1564-1616 — PHILOSOPHY
PR3001	SHAKESPEARE, WILLIAM, 1564-1616 — PHILOSOPHY
PR2997.P6	SHAKESPEARE, WILLIAM, 1564-1616 — PLOTS
PR3017	SHAKESPEARE, WILLIAM, 1564-1616 — POLITICAL AND SOCIAL VIEWS
PR3024	SHAKESPEARE, WILLIAM, 1564-1616 — POLITICAL AND SOCIAL VIEWS
PR2928-9	SHAKESPEARE, WILLIAM, 1564-1616 — PORTRAITS, ETC.
PR3087	SHAKESPEARE, WILLIAM, 1564-1616 — PROSE
PR2892	SHAKESPEARE, WILLIAM, 1564-1616 — QUOTATIONS
PR3007	SHAKESPEARE, WILLIAM, 1564-1616 — RELIGION AND ETHICS
PR3011-3012	SHAKESPEARE, WILLIAM, 1564-1616 — RELIGION AND ETHICS
PR2885-9	SHAKESPEARE, WILLIAM, 1564-1616 — SOCIETIES, PERIODICALS, ETC.
PR2952-5	SHAKESPEARE, WILLIAM, 1564-1616 — SOURCES
PR3091-3112	SHAKESPEARE, WILLIAM, 1564-1616 — STAGE HISTORY
PR2987	SHAKESPEARE, WILLIAM, 1564-1616 — STUDY
PR3072-3088	SHAKESPEARE, WILLIAM, 1564-1616 — STYLE
PR3004	SHAKESPEARE, WILLIAM, 1564-1616 — SUPERNATURAL ELEMENT
PR2995-7	SHAKESPEARE, WILLIAM, 1564-1616 — TECHNIQUE
PR2983	SHAKESPEARE, WILLIAM, 1564-1616 — TRAGEDIES
PR2881	SHAKESPEARE, WILLIAM, 1564-1616 — TRANSLATIONS
PR2881	SHAKESPEARE, WILLIAM, 1564-1616 — TRANSLATORS
PR3085	SHAKESPEARE, WILLIAM, 1564-1616 — VERSIFICATION
PR2908	SHAKESPEARE, WILLIAM, 1564-1616 — WILL
PR2750-3112	SHAKESPEARE, WILLIAM, 1564-1616
PR2941-6	SHAKESPEARE, WILLIAM, 1564-1616 — AUTHORSHIP — — BACONIAN THEORY
PR2947.B	SHAKESPEARE, WILLIAM, 1564-1616 — AUTHORSHIP — — BURTON THEORY
PR2937	SHAKESPEARE, WILLIAM, 1564-1616 — AUTHORSHIP — — COLLABORATION
PR2947.O9	SHAKESPEARE, WILLIAM, 1564-1616 — AUTHORSHIP — — OXFORD THEORY
Z8811-8813	SHAKESPEARE, WILLIAM, 1564-1616 — BIBLIOGRAPHY — — QUARTOS
Z8811-8813	SHAKESPEARE, WILLIAM, 1564-1616 — BIBLIOGRAPHY — — FOLIOS
PR2901	SHAKESPEARE, WILLIAM, 1564-1616 — BIOGRAPHY — — ANCESTRY
PR2894-2900	SHAKESPEARE, WILLIAM, 1564-1616 — BIOGRAPHY — — CHARACTER
PR2908	SHAKESPEARE, WILLIAM, 1564-1616 — BIOGRAPHY — — LAST YEARS
PR2907	SHAKESPEARE, WILLIAM, 1564-1616 — BIOGRAPHY — — LONDON LIFE
PR2905	SHAKESPEARE, WILLIAM, 1564-1616 — BIOGRAPHY — — MARRIAGE
PR2893	SHAKESPEARE, WILLIAM, 1564-1616 — BIOGRAPHY — — SOURCES
PR2903	SHAKESPEARE, WILLIAM, 1564-1616 — BIOGRAPHY — — YOUTH
PR2992.C4	SHAKESPEARE, WILLIAM, 1564-1616 — CHARACTERS — — CHILDREN
PR3026	SHAKESPEARE, WILLIAM, 1564-1616 — CHARACTERS — — CRIMINALS
PR3004	SHAKESPEARE, WILLIAM, 1564-1616 — CHARACTERS — — FAIRIES
PR2992.F3	SHAKESPEARE, WILLIAM, 1564-1616 — CHARACTERS — — FATHERS
PR3009	SHAKESPEARE, WILLIAM, 1564-1616 — CHARACTERS — — FAIRIES
PR2992.F6	SHAKESPEARE, WILLIAM, 1564-1616 — CHARACTERS — — FOOLS
PR3004	SHAKESPEARE, WILLIAM, 1564-1616 — CHARACTERS — — GHOSTS
PR2992.I	SHAKESPEARE, WILLIAM, 1564-1616 — CHARACTERS — — IRISH
PR2992.J	SHAKESPEARE, WILLIAM, 1564-1616 — CHARACTERS — — JEWS
PR3065	SHAKESPEARE, WILLIAM, 1564-1616 — CHARACTERS — — MADMEN
PR2992.R	SHAKESPEARE, WILLIAM, 1564-1616 — CHARACTERS — — ROGUES AND VAGABONDS
PR2992.V	SHAKESPEARE, WILLIAM, 1564-1616 — CHARACTERS — — VILLAINS
PR2992.W4	SHAKESPEARE, WILLIAM, 1564-1616 — CHARACTERS — — WELSHMEN
PR2991	SHAKESPEARE, WILLIAM, 1564-1616 — CHARACTERS — — WOMEN
PR2951	SHAKESPEARE, WILLIAM, 1564-1616 — FORGERIES — — COLLIER
PR2950	SHAKESPEARE, WILLIAM, 1564-1616 — FORGERIES — — IRELAND
PR3069.A6	SHAKESPEARE, WILLIAM, 1564-1616 — KNOWLEDGE — — ARCHERY
PR3034	SHAKESPEARE, WILLIAM, 1564-1616 — KNOWLEDGE — — ART
PR3012	SHAKESPEARE, WILLIAM, 1564-1616 — KNOWLEDGE — — BIBLE
PR3037	SHAKESPEARE, WILLIAM, 1564-1616 — KNOWLEDGE — — CLASSICAL LITERATURE
PR3069.C6	SHAKESPEARE, WILLIAM, 1564-1616 — KNOWLEDGE — — COSTUME
PR3021	SHAKESPEARE, WILLIAM, 1564-1616 — KNOWLEDGE — — ECONOMICS
PR3067	SHAKESPEARE, WILLIAM, 1564-1616 — KNOWLEDGE — — GAMES
PR3014	SHAKESPEARE, WILLIAM, 1564-1616 — KNOWLEDGE — — GEOGRAPHY
PR3069.H4	SHAKESPEARE, WILLIAM, 1564-1616 — KNOWLEDGE — — HERALDRY
PR3014	SHAKESPEARE, WILLIAM, 1564-1616 — KNOWLEDGE — — HISTORY
PR3065	SHAKESPEARE, WILLIAM, 1564-1616 — KNOWLEDGE — — INSANITY
PR3069.I	SHAKESPEARE, WILLIAM, 1564-1616 — KNOWLEDGE — — ITALY
PR3028	SHAKESPEARE, WILLIAM, 1564-1616 — KNOWLEDGE — — LAW
PR3062	SHAKESPEARE, WILLIAM, 1564-1616 — KNOWLEDGE — — MEDICINE
PR3069.N3	SHAKESPEARE, WILLIAM, 1564-1616 — KNOWLEDGE — — NAVAL ART AND SCIENCE
PR3069.P7	SHAKESPEARE, WILLIAM, 1564-1616 — KNOWLEDGE — — PRECIOUS STONES
PR3036	SHAKESPEARE, WILLIAM, 1564-1616 — KNOWLEDGE — — PRINTING
PR3047-3059	SHAKESPEARE, WILLIAM, 1564-1616 — KNOWLEDGE — — SCIENCE
PR3067	SHAKESPEARE, WILLIAM, 1564-1616 — KNOWLEDGE — — SPORTS
PR3088	SHAKESPEARE, WILLIAM, 1564-1616 — LANGUAGE — — DIALECTS
PR2892	SHAKESPEARE, WILLIAM, 1564-1616 — LANGUAGE — — GLOSSARIES, ETC.
PR3075-3081	SHAKESPEARE, WILLIAM, 1564-1616 — LANGUAGE — — GRAMMAR
PR3081	SHAKESPEARE, WILLIAM, 1564-1616 — LANGUAGE — — PRONUNCIATION

PR3081	SHAKESPEARE, WILLIAM, 1564-1616 — LANGUAGE — — PUNCTUATION
PR3099	SHAKESPEARE, WILLIAM, 1564-1616 — STAGE HISTORY — — 1800-
PR3097	SHAKESPEARE, WILLIAM, 1564-1616 — STAGE HISTORY — — 1625-1800
PR3095	SHAKESPEARE, WILLIAM, 1564-1616 — STAGE HISTORY — — TO 1625
PR2895	SHAKESPEARE, WILLIAM, 1564-1616 — STUDY — — OUTLINES, SYLLABI, ETC.
PR2987	SHAKESPEARE, WILLIAM, 1564-1616 — STUDY — — OUTLINES, SYLLABI, ETC.
BL1245.S5	SHAKTISM
QE471	SHALE
BJ1535.S8	*SHALLOWNESS* **SEE** SUPERFICIALITY
SF473.S6	SHAMA / cage-birds
QL696.P2	SHAMA / ornithology
BL2370.S5	SHAMANISM
PL8666	SHAMBALA LANGUAGE
BF575.S45	SHAME
PL4251.S6	SHAN LANGUAGE
DS796.S2	SHANGHAI — RIOT, MAY 30, 1925
HD8039.S4-42	SHANGHAIING
Q375	*SHANNON'S MEASURE OF UNCERTAINTY* **SEE** UNCERTAINTY (INFORMATION THEORY)
DS560	SHANS
PN6110.S4	*SHANTIES* **SEE** SAILORS' SONGS / literature
M1977.S2	*SHANTIES* **SEE** SAILORS' SONGS / music
M1978.S2	*SHANTIES* **SEE** SAILORS' SONGS / music
ML3780	*SHANTIES* **SEE** WORK-SONGS
M1977.L3	*SHANTIES* **SEE** WORK-SONGS
TJ1208	SHAPERS
TJ1208	*SHAPING-MACHINES* **SEE** SHAPERS
HD1478	SHARE-CROPPING
HD1478	*SHARECROPPING* **SEE** SHARE-CROPPING
HG4661	*SHARES OF STOCK* **SEE** STOCKS
HG4751-5990	*SHARES OF STOCK* **SEE** STOCKS / special or local
BP174	SHARIA (ISLAMIC RELIGIOUS PRACTICE)
QL638.9	SHARKS
QE852.P6	SHARKS, FOSSIL
PM2305	SHASTA LANGUAGE
PM2305	*SHASTA-ACHOMAWI LANGUAGES* **SEE** SHASTAN LANGUAGES
E99.S332	SHASTAN INDIANS
PM2305	SHASTAN LANGUAGES
TP862	*SHATTER-PROOF GLASS* **SEE** GLASS, SAFETY
PJ7121-4	SHAURI LANGUAGE
TT967	*SHAVERS, ELECTRIC* **SEE** ELECTRIC SHAVERS
NK4695.S	SHAVING MUGS
TS2301.B8	SHAVING-BRUSHES / manufacture
HD9999.B84-86	SHAVING-BRUSHES / trade
BM695.S5	SHAVU'OTH (FEAST OF WEEKS)
E99.S35	*SHAWANESE INDIANS* **SEE** SHAWNEE INDIANS
PM2311	*SHAWANESE LANGUAGE* **SEE** SHAWNEE LANGUAGE
E99.S35	*SHAWANOE INDIANS* **SEE** SHAWNEE INDIANS
NK8900-8999	SHAWLS / art
TS1781	SHAWLS / technology
HD234.S5	SHAWNEE INDIANS — LAND TRANSFERS
E83.775	SHAWNEE INDIANS — WARS, 1775-1783
E99.S35	SHAWNEE INDIANS
PM2311	SHAWNEE LANGUAGE
PJ7121-4	*SHAWRI LANGUAGE* **SEE** SHAURI LANGUAGE
F69	SHAYS' REBELLION, 1786-1787
Z695	*SHEAF CATALOGS* **SEE** CATALOGS, SHEAF
TJ1240	SHEARS (MACHINE TOOLS)
QK763	*SHEDDING OF FRUIT* **SEE** ABSCISSION (BOTANY)
QK763	*SHEDDING OF LEAVES* **SEE** DEFOLIATION
SF968-970	SHEEP — DISEASES
SF373	SHEEP — FLOCK-BOOKS
QL795.S	SHEEP — LEGENDS AND STORIES
PZ10.3	SHEEP — LEGENDS AND STORIES / juvenile literature
SF371	SHEEP BREEDERS' SOCIETIES
SF593.T5	*SHEEP KED* **SEE** SHEEP-TICK
SF918.D5	SHEEP-DIP
SF379	SHEEP-SHEARING
SF593.T5	SHEEP-TICK
QL737.U5	SHEEP
SF371-9	SHEEP / animal industries
TS360	SHEET-IRON
TT265	SHEET-LEAD / lead-work

TS250	SHEET-METAL WORK — PATTERN-MAKING
TS250	SHEET-METAL WORK
TS360	SHEET-METAL / iron and steel
TS250	SHEET-METAL / metal-work
TA460	SHEET-METAL / testing
TA785	SHEET-PILING
TS360	SHEET-STEEL
NK7250	SHEFFIELD PLATE
PL8598.O8	*SHEKIANI LANGUAGE* **SEE** ORUNGU LANGUAGE
Z703.5	*SHELF DEPARTMENT (LIBRARY SCIENCE)* **SEE** LIBRARIES — SHELF DEPT
Z696-7	SHELF-LISTING (LIBRARY SCIENCE)
QC173	*SHELL MODELS (NUCLEAR PHYSICS)* **SEE** NUCLEAR SHELL THEORY
TS233	*SHELL MOLD CASTING* **SEE** SHELL MOLDING (FOUNDING)
TS233	SHELL MOLDING (FOUNDING)
GN436.2	SHELL MONEY / ethnology
HG235	SHELL MONEY / finance
SF473.B	*SHELL PARAKEET* **SEE** BUDGERIGARS
TH2416	*SHELL ROOFS* **SEE** ROOFS, SHELL
GN787-8	*SHELL-HEAPS* **SEE** KITCHEN-MIDDENS
TP938	SHELLAC
GR910	SHELLBACKS
NK8643	SHELLCRAFT
SH171-9	SHELLFISH — DISEASES AND PESTS
SH365-380	SHELLFISH FISHERIES
TX753	SHELLFISH / cookery
RA602.S6	SHELLFISH / public health
TX387	SHELLFISH / shellfish as food
QL401-445	SHELLFISH / zoology
QL406	SHELLS — CATALOGS AND COLLECTIONS
UF750-770	*SHELLS (PROJECTILES)* **SEE** PROJECTILES / military
VF480-500	*SHELLS (PROJECTILES)* **SEE** PROJECTILES / naval
N8243.S4	SHELLS IN ART
QL401-432	SHELLS
QA935	*SHELLS, ELASTIC* **SEE** ELASTIC PLATES AND SHELLS
PM9001	SHELTA
SF429.S	*SHELTIE (DOG)* **SEE** SHETLAND SHEEP-DOGS
Z685	SHELVING (FOR BOOKS)
E477.33	SHENANDOAH VALLEY CAMPAIGN, AUG.-NOV., 1864
E473.7	SHENANDOAH VALLEY CAMPAIGN, MAR.-SEPT., 1862
E476.6	SHENANDOAH VALLEY CAMPAIGN, MAY-AUG., 1864
E477.65	SHENANDOAH VALLEY CAMPAIGN, 1865
DS485.A86	*SHENDUS* **SEE** LAKHERS
M1050-1053	SHENG (MUSICAL INSTRUMENT)
BL1475.H5	*SHEOL* **SEE** HELL / buddhism
BL735	*SHEOL* **SEE** HELL / classical mythology
BL545	*SHEOL* **SEE** HELL / comparative religion
BT834-8	*SHEOL* **SEE** HELL / theology
SF429.S6	SHEPHERD DOGS
DT86	*SHEPHERD KINGS* **SEE** HYKSOS
PL8093	*SHERBRO LANGUAGE* **SEE** BULLOM LANGUAGE
DT516	SHERBRO
DA814.3	SHERIFFMUIR, BATTLE OF, 1715
DS39	*SHERIFFS (DESCENDANTS OF MOHAMMED)* **SEE** SHERIFS
HV7979	SHERIFFS
DS39	SHERIFS
HG529	SHERMAN SILVER LAW, 1890
E476.69	SHERMAN'S MARCH TO THE SEA
TP559.S8	SHERRY
E99.C7	*SHETIMASHA INDIANS* **SEE** CHITIMACHA INDIANS
SF315	SHETLAND PONIES
SF429.S	SHETLAND SHEEP-DOGS
BM695.S5	*SHEVUOTH* **SEE** SHAVU'OTH (FEAST OF WEEKS)
BP193	*SHIAHS* **SEE** SHIITES
CR91-93	*SHIELDS (HERALDRY)* **SEE** ESCUTCHEONS
U805-813	SHIELDS / ancient and medieval
GN499.S5	SHIELDS / ethnology
CR91-93	SHIELDS / heraldry
BL1695	*SHIITES* **SEE** DRUSES
DS94.8.D8	*SHIITES* **SEE** DRUSES
BP193	SHIITES
PL8115	*SHILENGE LANGUAGE* **SEE** CHOPI LANGUAGE
PJ2379	SHILHA LANGUAGE
PL8671	SHILLUK LANGUAGE
GN652.S5	SHILLUKS / anthropology
DT132	SHILLUKS / sudan

E473.54	SHILOH, BATTLE OF, 1862
BL1442.S5	SHIN (SECT)
QL821	*SHINBONE* **SEE** TIBIA / *comparative anatomy*
QM117	*SHINBONE* **SEE** TIBIA / *human anatomy*
PL8723	*SHINDEBELE LANGUAGE* **SEE** TEBELE LANGUAGE
RC147.H6	*SHINGLES (DISEASE)* **SEE** HERPES ZOSTER
BL1442.S55	SHINGON (SECT)
E99.S38	SHINNECOCK INDIANS
BL2211.S4	SHINTO SHRINES
BL2220	SHINTO
GT3380	SHIP BURIAL
VM470.5	SHIP CHANDLERS
HE596	*SHIP CHARTERING* **SEE** CHARTER-PARTIES / *water transport*
VM299.5-7	*SHIP CONSTRUCTION SUBSIDIES* **SEE** SHIP-BUILDING SUBSIDIES
HE589-591	*SHIP INSPECTION* **SEE** SHIPS — INSPECTION
VM761	SHIP MODELS — TESTING
BV168.S5	SHIP MODELS (CHURCH DECORATION)
VM298	SHIP MODELS
VM6	SHIP MODELS / *etc.*
VM299.5-7	*SHIP MORTGAGE INSURANCE* **SEE** INSURANCE, SHIP MORTGAGE
VM470.5	*SHIP OUTFITTERS* **SEE** SHIP CHANDLERS
VK1500-1661	*SHIP PILOTS* **SEE** PILOTS AND PILOTAGE
Z231.5.S4	SHIP PRESSES
Z231.5.S4	*SHIP PRINTING PRESSES* **SEE** SHIP PRESSES
VM751-7	SHIP PROPULSION
VM774.3	*SHIP PROPULSION, ATOMIC* **SEE** MARINE NUCLEAR REACTOR PLANTS
VM773	SHIP PROPULSION, ELECTRIC
VK397	*SHIP RADIO STATIONS* **SEE** MARINE RADIO STATIONS
VM482	*SHIP RATPROOFING* **SEE** SHIPS — RATPROOF CONSTRUCTION
HE565-6	SHIP REGISTERS
VM751	SHIP RESISTANCE
HE740-743	*SHIP SUBSIDIES* **SEE** SHIPPING BOUNTIES AND SUBSIDIES
VM470.5	*SHIP SUPPLIERS* **SEE** SHIP CHANDLERS
VM880-881	SHIP TRIALS
QA913	*SHIP WAKES* **SEE** WAKES (FLUID DYNAMICS)
HF5686.S5	SHIP-BUILDING — ACCOUNTING
VM295-6	SHIP-BUILDING — CONTRACTS AND SPECIFICATIONS
VM300	SHIP-BUILDING — COSTS
VM142	SHIP-BUILDING — EARLY WORKS TO 1800
VM300	SHIP-BUILDING — PRODUCTION STANDARDS
VM781-861	SHIP-BUILDING — SUPPLIES
VM299.5-7	*SHIP-BUILDING BOUNTIES* **SEE** SHIP-BUILDING SUBSIDIES
VM299.5-7	*SHIP-BUILDING COST DIFFERENTIAL SUBSIDIES* **SEE** SHIP-BUILDING SUBSIDIES
VM299.5-7	SHIP-BUILDING SUBSIDIES
VM	SHIP-BUILDING
DA397-8	SHIP-MONEY / *english history*
HJ2612	SHIP-MONEY / *finance*
TC771	SHIP-RAILROADS
QL430.7.T4	SHIP-WORMS
TC201	SHIP-WORMS / *hydraulic engineering*
QE812.T	SHIP-WORMS, FOSSIL
VM	*SHIPBUILDING* **SEE** SHIP-BUILDING
PM7073	*SHIPIBO DIALECT* **SEE** SIPIBO LANGUAGE
HF5761-5780	SHIPMENT OF GOODS
HE9	SHIPPERS' GUIDES
HE968	SHIPPERS' GUIDES / *marine insurance*
HE2731-7	SHIPPERS' GUIDES / *railroads*
HE2801-3600	SHIPPERS' GUIDES / *railroads*
HE1009	SHIPPERS' GUIDES / *railroads*
HE605	SHIPPING — ACCOUNTING
HE603-5	SHIPPING — FINANCE
HE594	SHIPPING — RATES
HE597	SHIPPING — RATES / *by countries*
HE563	SHIPPING — STATISTICS / *water transport*
HE745-940	*SHIPPING AGREEMENTS* **SEE** SHIPPING CONFERENCES
HE740-743	SHIPPING BOUNTIES AND SUBSIDIES
HE745-940	*SHIPPING COMBINES* **SEE** SHIPPING CONFERENCES
HE745-940	SHIPPING CONFERENCES
SF967.H	*SHIPPING FEVER OF CATTLE* **SEE** HEMORRHAGIC SEPTICEMIA OF CATTLE
HE745-940	*SHIPPING TRUSTS* **SEE** SHIPPING CONFERENCES
HE561-971	SHIPPING
JX4190	SHIPPING / *international law*
JX4408-4449	*SHIPPING-LAW* **SEE** MARITIME LAW / *international law*
JX63	*SHIPPING-LAW* **SEE** MARITIME LAW / *private*
HE565-6	*SHIPPING-REGISTERS* **SEE** SHIP REGISTERS
NK5010-5015	*SHIPPO* **SEE** CLOISONNE
VK235-7	SHIPS — CARGO
VM951	SHIPS — CORROSION
VM483	SHIPS — DISINFECTION
VM781-861	SHIPS — EQUIPMENT AND SUPPLIES
VK1250-1294	SHIPS — FIRES AND FIRE PREVENTION
VM481	SHIPS — HEATING AND VENTILATION
HE589-591	SHIPS — INSPECTION
VM150	SHIPS — JUVENILE LITERATURE
VM147	SHIPS — LAUNCHING
VM491-3	SHIPS — LIGHTING
VK221	SHIPS — MANNING
VM155	SHIPS — MEASUREMENT
JX4449.N3	SHIPS — NATIONALITY
VM961	SHIPS — PAINTING
VM482	SHIPS — RATPROOF CONSTRUCTION
VM481	SHIPS — SANITATION
VM503-5	SHIPS — WATER-SUPPLY
VM147	SHIPS — WELDING
VM307	SHIPS IN ART
VK	SHIPS / *navigation*
GN440.1	SHIPS / *primitive*
VM	SHIPS / *ship-building*
VM148	SHIPS, CONCRETE
VM471-9	*SHIPS, ELECTRICITY ON* **SEE** ELECTRICITY ON SHIPS
VM146-7	SHIPS, IRON AND STEEL
QC849	*SHIPS, MAGNETISM OF* **SEE** MAGNETISM OF SHIPS
JX4449.N3	*SHIPS, NATIONALITY OF* **SEE** SHIPS — NATIONALITY
JX5231-2	*SHIPS, REQUISITION OF* **SEE** CONTRABAND OF WAR
JX5245-5266	*SHIPS, REQUISITION OF* **SEE** PRIZE LAW
JX5203-5268	*SHIPS, REQUISITION OF* **SEE** WAR, MARITIME (INTERNATIONAL LAW)
VM880-881	*SHIPS, TRIALS OF* **SEE** SHIP TRIALS
Z675.N3	*SHIPS' LIBRARIES* **SEE** LIBRARIES, NAVAL
VM815	SHIPS' LIGHTS
VM159	*SHIPS' STABILITY* **SEE** STABILITY OF SHIPS
VM485	*SHIPS-COLD STORAGE* **SEE** COLD STORAGE ON SHIPBOARD
VM157	*SHIPS-DISPLACEMENT* **SEE** DISPLACEMENT (SHIPS)
VM308	*SHIPS-FIGUREHEADS* **SEE** FIGUREHEADS OF SHIPS
VM531	*SHIPS-MASTS AND RIGGING* **SEE** MASTS AND RIGGING
VK221	*SHIPS-OFFICERS* **SEE** MERCHANT MARINE — OFFICERS
VM501	*SHIPS-PIPE-FITTING* **SEE** MARINE PIPE-FITTING
VK397	*SHIPS-RADIO* **SEE** RADIO — INSTALLATION ON SHIPS
VK397	*SHIPS-RADIO* **SEE** RADIO IN NAVIGATION / *naval science*
HE565-6	*SHIPS-REGISTERS* **SEE** SHIP REGISTERS
JX4449.N3	*SHIPS-REGISTRY* **SEE** SHIPS — NATIONALITY
VM295-6	*SHIPS-SPECIFICATIONS* **SEE** SHIP-BUILDING — CONTRACTS AND SPECIFICATIONS
VM481	*SHIPS-VENTILATION* **SEE** SHIPS — HEATING AND VENTILATION
VK1250-1299	SHIPWRECKS / *etc.*
G525-530	SHIPWRECKS / *etc.*
JX4436	SHIPWRECKS / *international law*
VM12-124	SHIPYARDS
PL8675	SHIRA LANGUAGE
SF293.S	SHIRE HORSE
PJ2379	*SHLU LANGUAGE* **SEE** SHILHA LANGUAGE
PL4051-4	*SHO DIALECT* **SEE** KAREN LANGUAGE
TL567.S4	SHOCK TUBES / *equipment*
TL574.S4	SHOCK WAVES / *aeronautics*
QA927	SHOCK WAVES / *fluid dynamics*
QA930	SHOCK WAVES / *mathematical aerodynamics*
HD9787	*SHOE INDUSTRY AND TRADE* **SEE** BOOTS AND SHOES — TRADE AND MANUFACTURE
TS989-1025	*SHOE INDUSTRY AND TRADE* **SEE** BOOTS AND SHOES — TRADE AND MANUFACTURE
TS1005	SHOE MACHINERY
HD9787	SHOE MACHINERY / *economics*
TS1023	*SHOE REPAIRING* **SEE** BOOTS AND SHOES — REPAIRING

TP670	SHOE-POLISH
TS1020	SHOE-POLISH / shoe manufacture
QL696.A7	SHOEBILL
HD8039.B7-72	SHOEMAKERS / labor
GT2130	SHOES SEE BOOTS AND SHOES / manners and customs
ML990.S	SHOFAR SEE SHOPHAR
GV1458.C5	SHOGI (GAME) SEE CHINESE CHESS
F2501.1.S	SHOKLENG INDIANS / indians of brazil
DT955	SHONA SEE MASHONA
PL8681	SHONA LANGUAGE
GV1167-1172	SHOOTING CONTESTS
QB741-755	SHOOTING-STARS SEE METEORS
SK37-39	SHOOTING / hunting sports
GV1151-1181	SHOOTING / sports and games
UD330-335	SHOOTING, MILITARY
HD5650-5660	SHOP COMMITTEES SEE WORKS COUNCILS
HD5650-5660	SHOP COUNCILS SEE WORKS COUNCILS
NA6225	SHOP FRONTS / architecture
TS155	SHOP MANAGEMENT SEE FACTORY MANAGEMENT
TJ1165	SHOP MATHEMATICS
TJ1160-1167	SHOP PRACTICE SEE MACHINE-SHOP PRACTICE
M110.S5	SHOPHAR-CALLS
ML990.S	SHOPHAR
TX335	SHOPPERS' GUIDES SEE CONSUMER EDUCATION
TX335	SHOPPERS' GUIDES SEE SHOPPING
NA6218	SHOPPING CENTERS
TX335	SHOPPING
TS155	SHOPS SEE WORKSHOPS / factory management
PL45.S4	SHOR LANGUAGE
TC330-345	SHORE EROSION SEE COAST CHANGES / hydraulic engineering
GB451-460	SHORE EROSION SEE COAST CHANGES / physical geography
SB460	SHORE GARDENING SEE SEASIDE GARDENING
Z675.N3	SHORE LIBRARIES SEE LIBRARIES, NAVAL
TC330-339	SHORE PROTECTION
GB451-460	SHORE-LINES / physical geography
PL45.S4	SHORIAN LANGUAGE SEE SHOR LANGUAGE
TH5281	SHORING AND UNDERPINNING
JF1091-1177	SHORT BALLOT SEE BALLOT
JK2215-2217	SHORT BALLOT SEE BALLOT / u.s.
TK3226	SHORT CIRCUITS
PZ1	SHORT STORIES / collections
PN3373-5	SHORT STORIES-HISTORY AND CRITICISM SEE SHORT STORY
PR829	SHORT STORIES-HISTORY AND CRITICISM SEE SHORT STORY / english literature
PS374.S5	SHORT STORIES-HISTORY AND CRITICISM SEE SHORT STORY / american literature
PN3373-5	SHORT STORY
PS374.S5	SHORT STORY / american literature
PR829	SHORT STORY / english literature
TK6553	SHORT WAVE RADIO SEE RADIO, SHORT WAVE
GV1287	SHORT WHIST
SF199.S56	SHORT-HORN CATTLE SEE SHORTHORN CATTLE
SF193.S5	SHORT-HORN CATTLE SEE SHORTHORN CATTLE / herd-books
RE938	SHORT-SIGHTEDNESS SEE MYOPIA
Z57	SHORTHAND — TEXTS
Z56.5	SHORTHAND NUMBERS
Z56	SHORTHAND REPORTING
Z53	SHORTHAND REPORTING
Z53-100	SHORTHAND
Z54-57	SHORTHAND / english
Z53-100	SHORTHAND, ENGLISH SEE SHORTHAND
Z54-57	SHORTHAND, ENGLISH SEE SHORTHAND / english
SF199.S56	SHORTHORN CATTLE
SF193.S5	SHORTHORN CATTLE / herd-books
SD397.P617	SHORTLEAF PINE
PL45.S4	SHORTSIAN LANGUAGE SEE SHOR LANGUAGE
RE938	SHORTSIGHTEDNESS SEE MYOPIA
PL45.S4	SHORTZY LANGUAGE SEE SHOR LANGUAGE
E99.S39	SHOSHONEAN INDIANS
PM2321	SHOSHONEAN LANGUAGES
E83.863	SHOSHONI INDIANS — WARS, 1863-1865
E99.S4	SHOSHONI INDIANS
HD234.S	SHOSHONI INDIANS / land transfers
PM2321	SHOSHONI LANGUAGE
E99.S39	SHOSHONIAN INDIANS SEE SHOSHONEAN INDIANS

TS213	SHOT BLASTING SEE SHOT PEENING
TS213	SHOT PEENING
GV1093	SHOT PUTTING SEE WEIGHT THROWING
SK274	SHOT-GUNS / hunting
TS535	SHOT-GUNS / manufacture
RD664	SHOULDER — TUMORS
QL821	SHOULDER BLADE SEE SCAPULA / comparative anatomy
QM101	SHOULDER BLADE SEE SCAPULA / human anatomy
QL821	SHOULDER GIRDLE / comparative anatomy
QM101	SHOULDER GIRDLE / human anatomy
RD686	SHOULDER JOINT — ANKYLOSIS
RD557	SHOULDER JOINT — DISLOCATION
RD687.S	SHOULDER JOINT — RUPTURE
QL950.3	SHOULDER / comparative anatomy
QM541	SHOULDER / human anatomy
RD557	SHOULDER-DISLOCATION SEE SHOULDER JOINT — DISLOCATION
GV1099	SHOVEL-BOARD SEE SHUFFLEBOARD
HF5851	SHOW CARDS SEE ADVERTISING CARDS
TT360	SHOW CARDS SEE ADVERTISING CARDS / card and sign writing
GV1472.5	SHOW-MEN SEE ENTERTAINERS
HF5845-9	SHOW-WINDOWS
TH6492	SHOWER-BATHS
QL737.I5	SHREWS
QE882.I5	SHREWS, FOSSIL
QL696.P2	SHRIKES
SH380	SHRIMP FISHERIES
QL444.D3	SHRIMPS
SH380	SHRIMPS / fishery
BX2320-2321	SHRINES / catholic church
BL580-586	SHRINES / comparative religion
BT653-660	SHRINES / virgin
SF373.S56	SHROPSHIRE SHEEP / flock-books
BT587.S4	SHROUD, HOLY SEE HOLY SHROUD
QK475-494	SHRUBS / botany
SB435-7	SHRUBS / culture
PL3891-4	SHU LANGUAGES SEE CHIN LANGUAGES
DS422.C3	SHUDRAS SEE UNTOUCHABLES
GV1099	SHUFFLEBOARD
PK6996.S5	SHUGHNI DIALECT
PL8041	SHULI LANGUAGE SEE ACOLI LANGUAGE
TF592	SHUNTING (RAILROADS) SEE RAILROADS — SWITCHING
E99.S45	SHUSWAP INDIANS
PM2325	SHUSWAP LANGUAGE
HD7269.T38-4	SHUTTLES, THREADING OF / labor hygiene
PL381-4	SHUVAK LANGUAGE SEE CHUVASHIAN LANGUAGE
PL3801.S5	SI-HIA LANGUAGE
PL8115	SI-TSWA LANGUAGE SEE CHOPI LANGUAGE
E99.S5	SIA INDIANS
SF449	SIAMESE CAT
SB608.G6	SIAMESE GRAIN-BEETLE
PL4151-4199	SIAMESE LANGUAGE
PL4200-4229	SIAMESE LITERATURE
QM691	SIAMESE TWINS
SF429.5	SIBERIAN HUSKIES
Q115.S	SIBOGA EXPEDITION
F1769	SIBONEY INDIANS SEE CIBONEY INDIANS
BF1745-1773	SIBYLS
DA87.5 1744	SICIE, CAPE, BATTLE OF, 1744 SEE TOULON, BATTLE OF, 1744
PQ4094-9	SICILIAN POETRY SEE ITALIAN POETRY — EARLY TO 1400
DG867.3	SICILIAN VESPERS, 1282
M240-244	SICILIANAS (FLUTE AND PIANO)
M31	SICILIANAS (PIANO)
M410-411	SICILIANAS (PIANO, 2 VIOLINS, VIOLONCELLO)
M412.4	SICILIANAS (PIANO, 2 VIOLINS, VIOLONCELLO)
M413-414	SICILIANAS (PIANO, 2 VIOLINS, VIOLONCELLO)
M217-218	SICILIANAS (VIOLIN AND PIANO)
M221-3	SICILIANAS (VIOLIN AND PIANO)
DG861-875	SICILY — HISTORY
DG55	SICILY — HISTORY — — TO 800
HD5115.5	SICK LEAVE
HV688-694	SICK / aid for
S695	SICKLES
HG9383-9399	SICKNESS INSURANCE SEE INSURANCE, HEALTH

PJ2491-2515	SIDAMA LANGUAGE
DT380	SIDAMAS
PJ2491-2515	*SIDAMO LANGUAGE* **SEE** SIDAMA LANGUAGE
ML1035	*SIDE DRUM* **SEE** DRUM
GN467.D8	*SIDE DRUM* **SEE** DRUM / *primitive*
GV1851-5	*SIDE SHOWS* **SEE** AMUSEMENT PARKS
GV1835	*SIDE SHOWS* **SEE** AMUSEMENT PARKS
HE566.P3	*SIDE-WHEELERS* **SEE** PADDLE STEAMERS
QB801-903	*SIDEREAL SYSTEM* **SEE** STARS
GR625	*SIDEREAL SYSTEM* **SEE** STARS / *folk-lore*
QE391.S	SIDERITE
NE	*SIDEROGRAPHY* **SEE** ENGRAVING
QB97	*SIDEROSTAT* **SEE** COELOSTAT
GV1851-5	*SIDESHOWS* **SEE** AMUSEMENT PARKS
GV1835	*SIDESHOWS* **SEE** AMUSEMENT PARKS
TH7799	SIDEWALK-LIGHTS
TE280-295	SIDEWALKS
JF1800	*SIEGE, STATE OF* **SEE** STATE OF SIEGE / *martial law*
JX5117	SIEGES / *international law*
TN740	*SIEMENS-MARTIN FURNACE* **SEE** OPEN-HEARTH FURNACES
DT551.42	*SIENA (AFRICAN PEOPLE)* **SEE** SENUFO (AFRICAN PEOPLE)
PM4207	*SIERRA POPOLUCA LANGUAGE (VERA CRUZ)* **SEE** POPOLUCA LANGUAGE (VERA CRUZ)
DD184.7	SIEVERSHAUSEN, BATTLE OF, 1553
TS275	SIEVES
TA681	SIEVES / *cement*
TN515	SIEVES / *ores*
MT236	SIGHT-READING (MUSIC)
RE51	*SIGHT-SAVING* **SEE** EYE — CARE AND HYGIENE
MT870	SIGHT-SINGING / *instruction*
TS535	*SIGHTS FOR FIREARMS* **SEE** FIREARMS — SIGHTS
UF854	*SIGHTS FOR FIREARMS* **SEE** FIREARMS — SIGHTS / *artillery*
UD390	*SIGHTS FOR FIREARMS* **SEE** FIREARMS — SIGHTS / *military rifles*
UF855	*SIGHTS, TELESCOPIC* **SEE** TELESCOPIC SIGHTS / *artillery*
CD5001-6471	*SIGILLOGRAPHY* **SEE** SEALS (NUMISMATICS)
JC345-7	*SIGILLOGRAPHY* **SEE** SEALS (NUMISMATICS) / *national*
P135	SIGN LANGUAGE
E98.S5	SIGN LANGUAGE / *american indians*
HV2474	SIGN LANGUAGE / *deaf*
BV197.S5	*SIGN OF THE CROSS* **SEE** CROSS, SIGN OF THE
BX2048.S5	*SIGN OF THE CROSS* **SEE** CROSS, SIGN OF THE / *catholic church*
TT360	SIGN PAINTING
TK7872.S7	*SIGNAL STORAGE TUBES* **SEE** STORAGE TUBES
HE9723-9737	SIGNALS AND SIGNALING
UG570-582	SIGNALS AND SIGNALING / *military*
V280-285	SIGNALS AND SIGNALING / *naval*
VK381-397	SIGNALS AND SIGNALING / *navigation*
TL152	SIGNALS AND SIGNALING, AUTOMOBILE / *motoring*
HE5615	SIGNALS AND SIGNALING, AUTOMOBILE / *regulations*
HE369-370	SIGNALS AND SIGNALING, AUTOMOBILE / *street signs*
VK388	SIGNALS AND SIGNALING, SUBMARINE
R133	SIGNATURES (MEDICINE)
Z242.S6	SIGNATURES (PRINTING)
Z41-42	SIGNATURES (WRITING)
CD5001-6471	*SIGNETS* **SEE** SEALS (NUMISMATICS)
JC345-7	*SIGNETS* **SEE** SEALS (NUMISMATICS) / *national*
TK4399.S6	*SIGNS (ADVERTISING)* **SEE** ELECTRIC SIGNS
BF1777	*SIGNS (OMENS)* **SEE** OMENS
HE370	*SIGNS, STREET* **SEE** STREET SIGNS
E99.S53	SIHASAPA INDIANS
PL3801.S5	*SIHIA LANGUAGE* **SEE** SI-HIA LANGUAGE
DS477.1	SIKH WAR, 1845-1846
DS477.63	SIKH WAR, 1848-1849
BL2017.2-4	SIKHISM — SACRED BOOKS
BL2017-2018	SIKHISM
DS432.S5	SIKHS / *ethnography*
DS485.P3	SIKHS / *punjab*
BL2020.S5	SIKHS / *religious sect*
BL2017-2018	*SIKHS-RELIGION* **SEE** SIKHISM
DS477.8	SIKKIM EXPEDITION, 1861
DS479.7	SIKKIM EXPEDITION, 1888
E99.S54	SIKSIKA INDIANS
PM2341-4	SIKSIKA LANGUAGE
SB195	*SILAGE* **SEE** ENSILAGE
BJ1499.S5	SILENCE / *ethics*
PL8115	*SILENGE LANGUAGE* **SEE** CHOPI LANGUAGE
DD491.S4-55	SILESIA — HISTORY
DD406-7	SILESIAN WAR, 1ST, 1740-1742
DD406-7	SILESIAN WAR, 2D, 1744-1745
DD409-412	*SILESIAN WAR, 3D, 1756-1763* **SEE** SEVEN YEARS' WAR, 1756-1763
DD491.S53	SILESIA — HISTORY — — PARTITION, 1919-1922 / *upper silesia*
NC910	SILHOUETTES / *drawing*
TN939	*SILICA SAND* **SEE** SAND, GLASS / *mineral industries*
TP245.S5	SILICA / *chemical technology*
QD181.S6	SILICA / *chemistry*
TN948.S6	SILICA / *mineral resources*
QD181.S6	SILICATES / *chemistry*
QE389.62	SILICATES / *mineralogy*
QE495	*SILICEOUS ROCKS* **SEE** ROCKS, SILICEOUS
QD181.S6	SILICIC ACID
QD181.S6	SILICIDES
QD181.S6	*SILICIUM* **SEE** SILICON
QD181.S6	*SILICOALUMINATES* **SEE** ALUMINUM SILICATES
TN757.F4	*SILICON-IRON* **SEE** FERROSILICON
TA479.S5	*SILICON-IRON ALLOYS* **SEE** IRON-SILICON ALLOYS
QD181.S6	SILICON
RC774	*SILICOSIS* **SEE** LUNGS — DUST DISEASES
HD7264	*SILICOSIS* **SEE** LUNGS — DUST DISEASES / *labor*
DK215.8.S6	SILISTRIA — SIEGE, 1854
TS1669	SILK — TESTING
SF541-559	*SILK CULTURE* **SEE** SERICULTURE
TP901	*SILK DYEING* **SEE** DYES AND DYEING — SILK
QP551	*SILK GELATIN* **SEE** SERICIN
TT681	*SILK HOSIERY* **SEE** HOSIERY, SILK
TS1643	SILK MANUFACTURE AND TRADE — DIRECTORIES
TS1640-1688	SILK MANUFACTURE AND TRADE / *manufacture*
HF2651.S6	SILK MANUFACTURE AND TRADE / *tariff*
HD9910-9929	SILK MANUFACTURE AND TRADE / *trade*
TT273	*SILK SCREEN PRINTING* **SEE** SCREEN PROCESS PRINTING
NE1843-4	*SILK SCREEN PRINTING* **SEE** SERIGRAPHY / *art*
TT273	*SILK SCREEN PROCESS* **SEE** SCREEN PROCESS PRINTING
NE1843-4	*SILK SCREEN PROCESS* **SEE** SERIGRAPHY / *art*
QL495.L52	SILK TREE
TP901	SILK-PRINTING
NK8900-8999	SILK / *art industries*
TS1640-1688	SILK / *manufacture*
SF541-559	SILK / *silk culture*
TS1546	SILK / *textile fibers*
TS1688	*SILK, ARTIFICIAL* **SEE** RAYON
TS1669	*SILK, OILED* **SEE** OIL SILK
SF555	SILKWORMS — DISEASES
SF541-599	SILKWORMS
QE391.S	SILLIMANITE
QE611	SILLS (GEOLOGY)
TC175	SILT / *hydraulics*
TD395	SILT / *reservoirs*
QE581	SILT / *sedimentation*
TC175	*SILTING* **SEE** SILT / *hydraulics*
TD395	*SILTING* **SEE** SILT / *reservoirs*
QE581	*SILTING* **SEE** SILT / *sedimentation*
QE661-3	*SILURIAN PERIOD* **SEE** GEOLOGY, STRATIGRAPHIC — SILURIAN
QE917	*SILURIAN PERIOD* **SEE** PALEOBOTANY — SILURIAN
QE727	*SILURIAN PERIOD* **SEE** PALEONTOLOGY — SILURIAN
QE662	*SILURIAN PERIOD, LOWER* **SEE** GEOLOGY, STRATIGRAPHIC — ORDOVICIAN
QE727	*SILURIAN PERIOD, LOWER* **SEE** PALEONTOLOGY — ORDOVICIAN
QD181.A3	SILVER — ANALYSIS
TN580.S5	SILVER — ASSAYING
TN768-770	SILVER — ELECTROMETALLURGY
TN693.S5	SILVER — METALLOGRAPHY
TN760-770	SILVER — METALLURGY
TN762	SILVER — MILLING
QP913.A3	SILVER — PHYSIOLOGICAL EFFECT
HD9747	SILVER — STANDARDS OF FINENESS
SF405.F8	SILVER FOX / *animal culture*

HD9536	SILVER MINES AND MINING / economics
TN430-439	SILVER MINES AND MINING / mineral industries
RM666.S	SILVER NITRATE — THERAPEUTIC USE
QD181.A3	SILVER NITRATE
TN430-439	SILVER ORES
NK7240	SILVER PLATE SEE SILVER-PLATED WARE / art industries
HG532-4	SILVER QUESTION — SPEECHES IN CONGRESS
HG527-538	SILVER QUESTION
QD181.A3	SILVER SALTS
QD181.A3	SILVER SULPHIDE
NK7240	SILVER-PLATED WARE / art industries
TS680	SILVER-PLATING
QD181.A3	SILVER / chemistry
HG301-311	SILVER / finance
TN430-439	SILVER / mineral resources
TS715	SILVERING
QL638.A8	SILVERSIDES
HF5686.S55	SILVERSMITHING — ACCOUNTING
NK7100-7235	SILVERSMITHING / art industries
TS730-735	SILVERSMITHING / manufactures
M14.8	SILVERTONE ORGAN MUSIC SEE ELECTRONIC ORGAN MUSIC (SILVERTONE REGISTRATION)
M14.85	SILVERTONE ORGAN MUSIC SEE ELECTRONIC ORGAN MUSIC (SILVERTONE REGISTRATION)
ML597	SILVERTONE ORGAN
MT192	SILVERTONE ORGAN — METHODS — — SELF-INSTRUCTION
BM695.S	SIMCHAS TORAH SEE SIMHAT TORAH
PL5439.3	SIMEULUE LANGUAGE
BM695.S	SIMHAT TORAH
BD236	SIMILARITY SEE RESEMBLANCE (PHILOSOPHY)
PN227	SIMILE
PN228.S5	SIMILE
PN6084.S5	SIMILE / collections
TA177	SIMILITUDE IN ENGINEERING SEE ENGINEERING MODELS
PM5818	SIMIRENCHI LANGUAGE SEE CHUNTAQUIRO LANGUAGE
LB1131	SIMON-BINET TEST SEE BINET-SIMON TEST
BX1939.S4	SIMONY (CANON LAW)
BV779	SIMONY
BJ1496	SIMPLICITY
PE1147-1153	SIMPLIFIED SPELLING SEE SPELLING REFORM / english
V252	SIMULATED TRAINING DEVICES SEE SYNTHETIC TRAINING DEVICES
QA195	SIMULTANEOUS EQUATIONS SEE EQUATIONS, SIMULTANEOUS
TK6592.M6	SIMULTANEOUS-LOBING TECHNIQUES SEE MONOPULSE RADAR
BM630	SIN — JEWISH INTERPRETATIONS
BP166.75	SIN (ISLAM)
BT721	SIN AGAINST THE HOLY SPIRIT SEE SIN, UNPARDONABLE
BT715-721	SIN / doctrinal theology
BV4625	SIN / moral theology
BT795	SIN, FORGIVENESS OF SEE FORGIVENESS OF SIN
BV4625	SIN, MORTAL
BT720	SIN, ORIGINAL
BT721	SIN, UNPARDONABLE
BV4625.6	SIN, VENIAL
PM4498.X3	SINCA LANGUAGE SEE XINCA LANGUAGE
PL8723	SINDEBELE LANGUAGE SEE TEBELE LANGUAGE
PK2781-2790	SINDHI LANGUAGE
ML400	SINGERS / biography collective
ML420	SINGERS / individual
DS489.2	SINGHALESE SEE SINHALESE
MT872	SINGING — DICTION
ML1460	SINGING — HISTORY AND CRITICISM
MT823	SINGING — HISTORY AND CRITICISM
MT820-821	SINGING — INSTRUCTION AND STUDY
MT855	SINGING — INSTRUCTION AND STUDY
MT853	SINGING — INSTRUCTION AND STUDY
MT878	SINGING — INSTRUCTION AND STUDY
MT892	SINGING — INTERPRETATION (PHRASING, DYNAMICS, ETC.)
MT825-850	SINGING — METHODS
MT882	SINGING — METHODS
ML1-5	SINGING — PERIODICALS
MT870	SINGING — STUDIES AND EXERCISES
MT885	SINGING — STUDIES AND EXERCISES
ML25-28	SINGING SOCIETIES SEE CHORAL SOCIETIES
MT88	SINGING SOCIETIES SEE CHORAL SOCIETIES
MT855	SINGING
MT853	SINGING
ML3877	SINGING
MT820-821	SINGING
MT875	SINGING, CHORAL SEE CHORAL SINGING
M1997.C5	SINGING, COMMUNITY SEE COMMUNITY MUSIC
ML2500-2770	SINGING, COMMUNITY SEE COMMUNITY MUSIC / history and criticism
MT875	SINGING, COMMUNITY SEE COMMUNITY MUSIC / instruction
MT892	SINGING-EXPRESSION SEE SINGING — INTERPRETATION (PHRASING, DYNAMICS, ETC.)
MT893	SINGING-SELF-INSTRUCTION SEE SINGING — METHODS — — SELF-INSTRUCTION
MT900	SINGING — METHODS — — JUVENILE
MT893	SINGING — METHODS — — SELF-INSTRUCTION
TL588	SINGLE HEADING FLYING SEE PRESSURE PATTERN FLYING
BX2350.9	SINGLE PEOPLE — RELIGIOUS LIFE / catholic
HD1311-1313	SINGLE TAX
HQ800	SINGLE WOMEN
TF694	SINGLE-RAIL RAILROADS SEE RAILROADS, SINGLE-RAIL
GV1141	SINGLE-STICK
PL4001.K3	SINGPHO LANGUAGE SEE KACHIN LANGUAGE
DS485.B85	SINGPHOS SEE KACHIN TRIBES / burma
ML1950	SINGSPIEL
PK2850-2888	SINHALESE FICTION
PK2801-2845	SINHALESE LANGUAGE
PK2850-2888	SINHALESE LITERATURE
PK2856	SINHALESE POETRY / collections
PK2852	SINHALESE POETRY / history
DS489.2	SINHALESE
HJ8052	SINKING-FUNDS
HG1634	SINKING-FUNDS / tables
E99.S	SINKYONE INDIANS
DA960-962	SINN FEIN
DS549	SINO-FRENCH WAR, 1884-1885 SEE CHINESE-FRENCH WAR, 1884-1885
DS480.85	SINO-INDIAN BORDER DISPUTE, 1957-
DS765-7	SINO-JAPANESE WAR, 1894-1895 SEE CHINESE-JAPANESE WAR, 1894-1895
PL3521-9	SINO-TIBETAN LANGUAGES SEE INDOCHINESE LANGUAGES
PL1001-1095	SINOLOGY SEE CHINESE STUDIES (SINOLOGY)
DK215.8.S7	SINOP, BATTLE OF, 1853
BV4625-7	SINS
BV4626-7	SINS, CAPITAL SEE DEADLY SINS
BV4626-7	SINS, DEADLY SEE DEADLY SINS
TS245	SINTERED METAL PROCESS SEE POWDER METAL PROCESSES
RF421	SINUS CAVERNOSUS SEE CAVERNOUS SINUS / diseases
QM505	SINUS CAVERNOSUS SEE CAVERNOUS SINUS / human anatomy
RF421	SINUS PARANASALIS SEE NOSE, ACCESSORY SINUSES OF / diseases
QM505	SINUS PARANASALIS SEE NOSE, ACCESSORY SINUSES OF / human anatomy
QM505	SINUS SPHENOIDALIS SEE SPHENOID SINUS / human anatomy
RF421	SINUS SPHENOIDALIS SEE SPHENOID SINUS / medicine
QL947	SINUS, FRONTAL SEE FRONTAL SINUS / comparative anatomy
QM505	SINUS, FRONTAL SEE FRONTAL SINUS / human anatomy
PJ2361	SIOUAH LANGUAGE SEE SIWA LANGUAGE
E99.S6	SIOUAN INDIANS
PM2351	SIOUAN LANGUAGES
E99.S225	SIOUNE INDIANS SEE SAONE INDIANS
E99.D1	SIOUX INDIANS SEE DAKOTA INDIANS
PM1021-4	SIOUX LANGUAGE SEE DAKOTA LANGUAGE
QL521-4	SIPHONATA SEE HEMIPTERA
QL377.H9	SIPHONOPHORA
PM7073	SIPIBO LANGUAGE

QE391.S	SIPYLITE
QL737.S6	SIRENIA
QE882.S6	SIRENIA / fossil
BL820.S5	SIRENS (MYTHOLOGY)
PH1051-9	SIRIANIAN LANGUAGE SEE SYRYENIAN LANGUAGE
DK34.S9	SIRIANIANS SEE SYRYENIANS
F3320.2.S5	SIRIONE INDIANS SEE SIRIONO INDIANS
F3320.2.S5	SIRIONO INDIANS
PM7074	SIRIONO LANGUAGE
SD397.L	SIRIS TREE SEE LEBBEK TREE
QB805.S5	SIRIUS
SB261.S4	SISAL SEE SISAL HEMP / culture
TS1747.S5	SISAL SEE SISAL HEMP / manufacture
HD9156.S6-8	SISAL SEE SISAL HEMP / trade
SB261.S4	SISAL HEMP / culture
TS1747.S5	SISAL HEMP / manufacture
HD9156.S6-8	SISAL HEMP / trade
PL6308	SISSANO LANGUAGE
E99.S62	SISSETON INDIANS
BX4200-4560	SISTERHOODS / catholic church
BX5183	SISTERHOODS / church of england
BX5185	SISTERHOODS / church of england
BX4452-4470	SISTERS OF CHARITY
BX4470	SISTERS OF CHARITY, IRISH
BX4361-4	SISTERS OF ST. CLARE SEE POOR CLARES
ML1040	SISTRUM
M142.S5	SITAR MUSIC
SD397.S77	SITKA SPRUCE
TT197.5.L5	SITTING ROOM FURNITURE SEE LIVING ROOM FURNITURE / cabinet work
NK2117	SITTING ROOM FURNITURE SEE LIVING ROOM FURNITURE / interior decoration
TS880	SITTING ROOM FURNITURE SEE LIVING ROOM FURNITURE / manufacture
PJ2361	SIUA LANGUAGE SEE SIWA LANGUAGE
PM2357	SIUSLAW LANGUAGE
PJ2361	SIUWAH LANGUAGE SEE SIWA LANGUAGE
BL1245.S5	SIVAISM
BL1245.S5	SIVISM SEE SIVAISM
PJ2361	SIWA LANGUAGE
E99.S	SIWANOY INDIANS
E99.S21	SIWASH INDIANS SEE SALISHAN INDIANS
PJ2361	SIWI LANGUAGE SEE SIWA LANGUAGE
BM646	SIX HUNDRED AND THIRTEEN COMMANDMENTS SEE COMMANDMENTS, SIX HUNDRED AND THIRTEEN
E99.I7	SIX NATIONS SEE IROQUOIS INDIANS
GV953	SIX-MAN FOOTBALL
CB367-401	SIXTEENTH CENTURY / civilization
D220-234	SIXTEENTH CENTURY / history
PL137	SIYAKAT ALPHABET SEE SIYAQAT ALPHABET
PL137	SIYAQAT ALPHABET
PL4001.S	SIYIN LANGUAGE
LB3013	SIZE OF SCHOOL SEE SCHOOL SIZE
TS1488	SIZING (TEXTILE)
DA122.J8	SKAGERRAK, BATTLE OF, 1916 SEE JUTLAND, BATTLE OF, 1916 / english history
D582.J8	SKAGERRAK, BATTLE OF, 1916 SEE JUTLAND, BATTLE OF, 1916
E99.K85	SKALZI INDIANS SEE KUTENAI INDIANS
GV1257	SKAT (GAME)
HJ3464.S	SKAT (TAX) SEE SCAT (TAX)
GV850	SKATERS
QL638.9	SKATES (FISHES)
TS2301.S5	SKATES / manufacture
HD9999.S56	SKATES / trade
GV849	SKATING — COMPETITIONS
GV852	SKATING RINKS
GV849	SKATING
GV850	SKATING-BIOGRAPHY SEE SKATERS
GV854	SKEES AND SKEE-RUNNING SEE SKIS AND SKIING
GV1181	SKEET SEE TRAP-SHOOTING
GN70	SKELETON / anthropology
QL821-3	SKELETON / comparative anatomy
QM101-117	SKELETON / human anatomy
B837	SKEPTICISM SEE SKEPTICISM
BD201	SKEPTICISM SEE SKEPTICISM / epistemology
B851-4695	SKEPTICISM SEE SKEPTICISM / local
BL2700-2790	SKEPTICISM SEE SKEPTICISM / rationalism
B779	SKEPTICISM SEE SKEPTICISM / renaissance philosophy

B837	SKEPTICISM
BD201	SKEPTICISM / epistemology
B851-4695	SKEPTICISM / local
BL2700-2790	SKEPTICISM / rationalism
B779	SKEPTICISM / renaissance philosophy
B525	SKEPTICS (GREEK PHILOSOPHY)
PN4500	SKETCH, LITERARY SEE ESSAY
NC	SKETCHING SEE DRAWING
UD470	SKI TROOPS
RC78	SKIAGRAPHY SEE RADIOGRAPHY / medicine
TR750	SKIAGRAPHY SEE RADIOGRAPHY / photography
RD36	SKIAGRAPHY SEE RADIOGRAPHY / surgery
RE965	SKIASCOPY
GV1295.S5	SKICKET (GAME)
GV854	SKIING SEE SKIS AND SKIING
GV840.S5	SKIING ON WATER SEE WATER SKIING
RC280.S5	SKIN — CANCER
RL87	SKIN — CARE AND HYGIENE
RL	SKIN — DISEASES
QR155	SKIN — MICRO-ORGANISMS
RC280.S5	SKIN — TUMORS
TL574.F7	SKIN DRAG SEE SKIN FRICTION (AERODYNAMICS)
TL574.F7	SKIN FRICTION (AERODYNAMICS)
VM981-9	SKIN-DIVING SEE DIVING, SUBMARINE
TC183	SKIN-DIVING SEE DIVING, SUBMARINE / submarine construction
RD121	SKIN-GRAFTING
GN191-9	SKIN / anthropology
QL941	SKIN / comparative anatomy
QM481-4	SKIN / human anatomy
GN197	SKIN, COLOR OF SEE COLOR OF MAN
GN192	SKIN-PAPILLARY RIDGES SEE FINGERPRINTS / anthropology
HV6074	SKIN-PAPILLARY RIDGES SEE FINGERPRINTS / criminology
QL666.L2	SKINKS
TS967	SKINS SEE HIDES AND SKINS / manufactures
HD9778	SKINS SEE HIDES AND SKINS / trade
RX561-581	SKIN — DISEASES — — HOMEOPATHIC TREATMENT
VM331	SKIPJACKS
GV498	SKIPPING ROPE SEE ROPE SKIPPING
U210	SKIRMISHING
TT540	SKIRTS / dressmaking
M1978.S727	SKIS AND SKIING — SONGS AND MUSIC
M1977.S727	SKIS AND SKIING — SONGS AND MUSIC
GV854	SKIS AND SKIING
E99.S63	SKITSWISH INDIANS
E99.H2	SKITTAGETAN INDIANS SEE HAIDA INDIANS
PM1271-4	SKITTAGETAN LANGUAGES SEE HAIDA LANGUAGE
BX9798.S47	SKOPTSI
BX9798.S47	SKOPTZI SEE SKOPTSI
GN131	SKULL — ABNORMITIES AND DEFORMITIES / craniology
QM691	SKULL — ABNORMITIES AND DEFORMITIES / human anatomy
GN477.6	SKULL — ARTIFICIAL DEFORMITIES / anthropology
RD529	SKULL — FRACTURE
RD529	SKULL — WOUNDS AND INJURIES
GN71-131	SKULL / anthropology
QL821-3	SKULL / comparative anatomy
QM105	SKULL / human anatomy
GN131	SKULL, SUTURES OF SEE CRANIAL SUTURES / anthropology
QL821	SKULL, SUTURES OF SEE CRANIAL SUTURES / comparative anatomy
QM105	SKULL, SUTURES OF SEE CRANIAL SUTURES / human anatomy
QL638.C8	SKULPIN SEE SCULPIN
QL737.C2	SKUNKS
SF405.S6	SKUNKS / animal culture
PM2381.S6	SKWAMISH LANGUAGE SEE SQUAWMISH LANGUAGE
GR620	SKY (IN RELIGION, FOLK-LORE, ETC.) SEE FOLK-LORE OF THE SKY
QC976.C6	SKY, COLOR OF
GR620	SKY, FOLK-LORE OF THE SEE FOLK-LORE OF THE SKY
TH2486-7	SKYLIGHTS
TL722.5	SKYWRITING
DT844.3	SLACHTERS NEK REBELLION, 1815

TT605	*SLACKS* **SEE** TROUSERS / *tailoring*
TA434-5	SLAG CEMENT / *engineering materials*
TP884.S	SLAG CEMENT / *manufacture*
TH1715	*SLAG WOOL* **SEE** MINERAL WOOL / *insulation*
TP832.S5	SLAG / *bricks*
TN707	SLAG / *iron and steel*
TN799.M3	SLAG / *manganese*
TN673	SLAG / *metallurgy*
BJ1535.S6	SLANDER / *ethics*
BV4627.S6	SLANDER / *moral theology*
P409	SLANG
PE3701-3729	SLANG / *english*
PC3721-3761	SLANG / *french*
TH2445	*SLATE ROOFING* **SEE** ROOFING, SLATE
TN958	SLATE
TS1960-1967	SLAUGHTERING AND SLAUGHTER-HOUSES / *butchering*
HD9410.9	SLAUGHTERING AND SLAUGHTER-HOUSES / *inspection*
RA578.A6	SLAUGHTERING AND SLAUGHTER-HOUSES / *public health*
E99.S65	SLAVE INDIANS
HD4861-5	SLAVE LABOR
PM2365	SLAVE LANGUAGE
HT975-1445	SLAVE-TRADE
JX4447	SLAVE-TRADE / *international law*
E446	SLAVE-TRADE / *u.s.*
E442	SLAVE-TRADE / *u.s.*
HT1025-1037	SLAVERY — EMANCIPATION
E449	SLAVERY — JUSTIFICATION
HT910-921	SLAVERY AND THE CHURCH
HT915	SLAVERY IN THE BIBLE
E446	SLAVERY IN THE U.S. — ANTI-SLAVERY MOVEMENTS
E449	SLAVERY IN THE U.S. — ANTI-SLAVERY MOVEMENTS
E449	SLAVERY IN THE U.S. — CONDITION OF SLAVES
E443	SLAVERY IN THE U.S. — CONDITION OF SLAVES
E449	SLAVERY IN THE U.S. — CONTROVERSIAL LITERATURE
E446	SLAVERY IN THE U.S. — CONTROVERSIAL LITERATURE
E453	SLAVERY IN THE U.S. — EMANCIPATION
E415.7-450	SLAVERY IN THE U.S. — EXTENSION TO THE TERRITORIES
E450	SLAVERY IN THE U.S. — FUGITIVE SLAVES
E441-9	SLAVERY IN THE U.S. — HISTORY
E447	SLAVERY IN THE U.S. — INSURRECTIONS, ETC.
E450	SLAVERY IN THE U.S. — KIDNAPPING
E441-453	SLAVERY IN THE U.S. — LAW
E450	SLAVERY IN THE U.S. — LEGAL STATUS OF SLAVES IN FREE STATES
E415.6-453	SLAVERY IN THE U.S. — SPEECHES IN CONGRESS
E338-440	SLAVERY IN THE U.S. / *political aspects*
E441-453	SLAVERY IN THE U.S. / *slavery and anti-slavery movement*
E448	*SLAVERY IN THE U.S.-COLONIZATION* **SEE** NEGROES — COLONIZATION
E188	SLAVERY IN THE U.S. — HISTORY — — COLONIAL PERIOD
E441-6	SLAVERY IN THE U.S. — HISTORY — — COLONIAL PERIOD
HT851-1445	SLAVERY
E453	*SLAVES, EMANCIPATION OF* **SEE** EMANCIPATION PROCLAMATION
HT1025-1037	*SLAVES, EMANCIPATION OF* **SEE** SLAVERY — EMANCIPATION
E453	*SLAVES, EMANCIPATION OF* **SEE** SLAVERY IN THE U.S. — EMANCIPATION
PM2365	*SLAVEY LANGUAGE* **SEE** SLAVE LANGUAGE
PM2365	*SLAVI LANGUAGE* **SEE** SLAVE LANGUAGE
PG1-9198	SLAVIC LANGUAGES
PG500-9198	SLAVIC LITERATURE
PG1-41	SLAVIC PHILOLOGY
PG521	SLAVIC POETRY / *collections*
PG510	SLAVIC POETRY / *history*
PG552	SLAVIC POETRY / *translations*
DR25	*SLAVIC RACE* **SEE** SLAVS / *eastern europe*
GN549.S6	*SLAVIC RACE* **SEE** SLAVS / *ethnography*
D147	*SLAVIC RACE* **SEE** SLAVS / *migrations*
DK33	*SLAVIC RACE* **SEE** SLAVS / *russia*
D377	*SLAVIC RACE* **SEE** SLAVS / *19th century*
D449	*SLAVIC RACE* **SEE** SLAVS / *20th century*
DR25	SLAVS / *eastern europe*
GN549.S6	SLAVS / *ethnography*
D147	SLAVS / *migrations*
DK33	SLAVS / *russia*
D377	SLAVS / *19th century*
D449	SLAVS / *20th century*
SF428.7	*SLED DOGS* **SEE** SLEDGE DOGS
GV855	*SLEDDING* **SEE** COASTING
SF428.7	SLEDGE DOGS
GT5220-5280	*SLEDGES* **SEE** SLEIGHS AND SLEDGES / *manners and customs*
TS2301.S	*SLEDGES* **SEE** SLEIGHS AND SLEDGES / *manufacture*
BF1068-1071	*SLEEP-WALKING* **SEE** SOMNAMBULISM
RA786	SLEEP / *hygiene*
QP425	SLEEP / *physiology*
BF1068-1073	SLEEP / *psychology*
TF459	*SLEEPING-CARS* **SEE** RAILROADS — SLEEPING-CARS
RC246	SLEEPING-SICKNESS
RC548	*SLEEPLESSNESS* **SEE** INSOMNIA
GV857.S6	SLEIGHING
GT5220-5280	SLEIGHS AND SLEDGES / *manners and customs*
TS2301.S	SLEIGHS AND SLEDGES / *manufacture*
GV1541-1561	*SLEIGHT OF HAND* **SEE** CONJURING
GV1541-1561	*SLEIGHT OF HAND* **SEE** JUGGLERS AND JUGGLING
GN475	*SLEIGHT OF HAND* **SEE** MAGIC / *ethnology*
BF1585-1623	*SLEIGHT OF HAND* **SEE** MAGIC / *occult sciences*
QA73	SLIDE-RULE
TH5613	SLIDE-RULE / *carpentry*
TJ545	SLIDE-VALVES
ND1595	*SLIDES, LANTERN* **SEE** LANTERN SLIDES / *painting*
TR730	*SLIDES, LANTERN* **SEE** LANTERN SLIDES / *photography*
QA73	*SLIDING-RULE* **SEE** SLIDE-RULE
TH5613	*SLIDING-RULE* **SEE** SLIDE-RULE / *carpentry*
QL638.1	*SLIME EEL* **SEE** HAGFISH
QK635	*SLIME FUNGI* **SEE** MYXOMYCETES
QK635	*SLIME-MOLD* **SEE** MYXOMYCETES
QL668.C2	SLIMY SALAMANDER
GN498.S	SLINGS
TT198	SLIP COVERS
TT198	*SLIPCOVERS* **SEE** SLIP COVERS
TJ1560	*SLOT MACHINES* **SEE** VENDING MACHINES
BF485	*SLOTH* **SEE** LAZINESS
QL737.E2	SLOTHS
QE882.E2	SLOTHS, FOSSIL
PG5415	SLOVAK BALLADS AND SONGS / *collections*
PG5413	SLOVAK BALLADS AND SONGS / *history*
PG5201-5399	SLOVAK LANGUAGE
PG5400-5546	SLOVAK LITERATURE
PG5425	SLOVAK POETRY / *collections*
PG5415	SLOVAK POETRY / *folk literature*
PG5408	SLOVAK POETRY / *history*
PG5546	SLOVAK POETRY / *translations*
PG5429	SLOVAK PROSE LITERATURE / *collections*
PG5410	SLOVAK PROSE LITERATURE / *history*
PN6222.S5	SLOVAK WIT AND HUMOR / *collections*
PG5412	SLOVAK WIT AND HUMOR / *history*
DB34.S5	SLOVAKS / *austria-hungary*
DB215	SLOVAKS / *czechoslovak republic*
DB919	SLOVAKS / *hungary*
DB34.S6	SLOVENES / *austria-hungary*
DR364-7	SLOVENES / *yugoslavia*
PG601-698	*SLOVENIAN LANGUAGE (OLD)* **SEE** CHURCH SLAVIC LANGUAGE
PG1801-1899	SLOVENIAN LANGUAGE
PG1900-1962	SLOVENIAN LITERATURE
PG1914	SLOVENIAN POETRY / *collections*
PG1900-1901	SLOVENIAN POETRY / *history*
PG1961-2	SLOVENIAN POETRY / *translations*
PG1916	SLOVENIAN PROSE LITERATURE / *collections*
PG1901	SLOVENIAN PROSE LITERATURE / *history*
DD491.P748	SLOVINCI
LC4661-4700	*SLOW LEARNERS* **SEE** SLOW LEARNING CHILDREN
LC4661-4700	SLOW LEARNING CHILDREN
Z1039.S5	SLOW LEARNING CHILDREN, BOOKS FOR / *bibliography*
TT187-8	SLOYD

QP91	*SLUDGED BLOOD* **SEE** BLOOD — AGGLUTINATION / *physiology*
QL568.T3	SLUG-WORMS
CJ4801-5415	*SLUGS* **SEE** TOKENS / *numismatics*
HG651-1490	*SLUGS* **SEE** TOKENS / *other countries*
HG629	*SLUGS* **SEE** TOKENS / *u.s.*
TC553	SLUICE GATES
TC553	SLUICES
NA9000-9284	*SLUM CLEARANCE* **SEE** CITIES AND TOWNS — PLANNING
HD7286-7390	*SLUM CLEARANCE* **SEE** HOUSING
DD184	*SMALKALDIC WAR, 1546-1547* **SEE** SCHMALKALDIC WAR, 1546-1547
TS535-7	*SMALL ARMS* **SEE** FIREARMS / *manufacture*
V	*SMALL ARMS* **SEE** FIREARMS / *u naval science*
VM325	*SMALL BOAT ELECTRONICS* **SEE** ELECTRONICS ON BOATS
GV826.5-832	*SMALL BOAT RACING* **SEE** YACHT RACING
HF5601-5689	*SMALL BUSINESS-ACCOUNTING* **SEE** ACCOUNTING
LB2327	SMALL COLLEGES
JC365	*SMALL COUNTRIES* **SEE** STATES, SMALL
HG2052-2069	*SMALL LOANS* **SEE** LOANS, PERSONAL
JC365	*SMALL NATIONS* **SEE** STATES, SMALL
JC365	*SMALL STATES* **SEE** STATES, SMALL
RC183	SMALLPOX — HOSPITALS
RA644.S6	SMALLPOX — PREVENTION
SF809.S	SMALLPOX IN ANIMALS
RC183	SMALLPOX
RC183	SMALLPOX, INOCULATION OF
QP458	SMELL / *physiology*
BF271	SMELL / *psychology*
RA577.S5	SMELTING — HYGIENIC ASPECTS
TN677	SMELTING FURNACES
TN607-799	SMELTING
QL638.A8	SMELTS / *atherinidae*
SH351.S7	SMELTS / *fisheries*
QL638.O	SMELTS / *osmeridae true smelts*
TT840	SMOCKING
RA576	SMOG / *air pollution*
TD884	SMOG / *sanitary and municipal engineering*
TD884	SMOKE — PHYSIOLOGICAL EFFECT
UG447.7	*SMOKE (MILITARY SCIENCE)* **SEE** SMOKE SCREENS
TD884	*SMOKE ABATEMENT* **SEE** SMOKE PREVENTION
TD884	SMOKE PREVENTION
UG447.7	SMOKE SCREENS
TH2281	*SMOKE-PIPES* **SEE** FLUES
RA576	SMOKE / *air pollution*
QC929.S6	SMOKE / *atmosphere*
SB745	SMOKE / *effect on plants*
TP273	*SMOKELESS POWDER* **SEE** GUNPOWDER, SMOKELESS
TH2281-4	*SMOKESTACKS* **SEE** CHIMNEYS
NA3040	*SMOKESTACKS* **SEE** CHIMNEYS / *architecture*
TH4591	*SMOKESTACKS* **SEE** CHIMNEYS / *power-plants*
GT3020	SMOKING / *manners and customs*
HV5725-5770	SMOKING / *tobacco habit*
SB945.C88	SMOKY CRANE-FLY
PK2901-4485	*SMRTI LITERATURE* **SEE** SANSKRIT LITERATURE
HJ6750-7380	SMUGGLING / *other countries*
HJ6690-6720	SMUGGLING / *u.s.*
QK628	*SMUT FUNGI* **SEE** SMUTS
QK628	SMUTS
QL430.4	SNAILS
QE808-9	*SNAILS, FOSSIL* **SEE** GASTEROPODA, FOSSIL
E216	SNAKE DEVICES (AMERICAN COLONIES)
E99.S4	*SNAKE INDIANS* **SEE** SHOSHONI INDIANS
HD234.S	*SNAKE INDIANS* **SEE** SHOSHONI INDIANS / *land transfers*
QP235	*SNAKE POISONS* **SEE** VENOM / *secretion*
E99.H7	SNAKE-DANCE / *hopi indians*
BL441	*SNAKE-WORSHIP* **SEE** SERPENT-WORSHIP
QL666.06	SNAKES
HD9999.F3-33	*SNAP FASTENINGS* **SEE** FASTENINGS / *trade*
TR592	*SNAPSHOTS* **SEE** PHOTOGRAPHY, INSTANTANEOUS
ML1035	*SNARE DRUM* **SEE** DRUM
GN467.D8	*SNARE DRUM* **SEE** DRUM / *primitive*
QK495.C74	SNEEZEWEED / *botany*
SB618.S7	SNEEZEWEED / *weeds*
SK329.S6	*SNIPE HUNTING* **SEE** SNIPE SHOOTING
SK329.S6	SNIPE SHOOTING
QL696.L7	SNIPES
PM2371	SNOHOMISH LANGUAGE
GV900.S6	SNOOKER
QL696.P2	SNOW BUNTINGS
QC929.S7	SNOW CRYSTALS
QC929.S7	*SNOW FLAKES* **SEE** SNOW CRYSTALS
QC929.S7	*SNOW GAGES, RADIOACTIVE* **SEE** RADIOACTIVE SNOW GAGES
SB741.F9	SNOW MOLD
TF542	SNOW REMOVAL / *railroads*
TD868	SNOW REMOVAL / *streets*
GB2405	SNOW-LINE
QC929.S7	SNOW / *meteorology*
GB2401-2597	SNOW / *physical geography*
TF542	*SNOW-REMOVAL* **SEE** SNOW REMOVAL / *railroads*
TD868	*SNOW-REMOVAL* **SEE** SNOW REMOVAL / *streets*
QL696.P2	*SNOWFLAKES (BIRDS)* **SEE** SNOW BUNTINGS
QC929.S7	*SNOWFLAKES* **SEE** SNOW CRYSTALS
GV853	SNOWSHOES AND SNOWSHOEING
NK9507	*SNUFF BOTTLES* **SEE** SNUFF BOXES AND BOTTLES
NK9507	SNUFF BOXES AND BOTTLES
GT3030	SNUFF
GV1029.7	SOAP BOX DERBIES
NB1270.S6	*SOAP CARVING* **SEE** SOAP SCULPTURE
NB1270.S6	SOAP SCULPTURE
HD9999.S7-9	SOAP TRADE
QC183	SOAP-BUBBLES / *surface tension*
TP990-991	SOAP
TP992	*SOAPS, METALLIC* **SEE** METALLIC SOAPS
TN948.T2	SOAPSTONE / *mineral resources*
QE475	SOAPSTONE / *petrology*
TL760	*SOARING (AERONAUTICS)* **SEE** GLIDING AND SOARING
GV764-6	*SOARING (AERONAUTICS)* **SEE** GLIDING AND SOARING / *sport*
TL760	*SOARING FLIGHT* **SEE** GLIDING AND SOARING
GV764-6	*SOARING FLIGHT* **SEE** GLIDING AND SOARING / *sport*
E99.S	SOBAIPURI INDIANS
E99.S	*SOBAYPURI INDIANS* **SEE** SOBAIPURI INDIANS
PL5439.5	SOBOJO LANGUAGE
DS477.1	SOBRAON, BATTLE OF, 1846
CT108	*SOBRIQUETS* **SEE** NICKNAMES / *english*
GV943	SOCCER COACHING
GV943	SOCCER
HM101	SOCIAL CHANGE
JA81-84	*SOCIAL COMPACT* **SEE** SOCIAL CONTRACT / *history*
JC179.R7-9	*SOCIAL COMPACT* **SEE** SOCIAL CONTRACT / *rousseau*
JC336	*SOCIAL COMPACT* **SEE** SOCIAL CONTRACT / *theory*
JA81-84	SOCIAL CONTRACT / *history*
JC179.R7-9	SOCIAL CONTRACT / *rousseau*
JC336	SOCIAL CONTRACT / *theory*
HG355-9	SOCIAL CREDIT
E59.S	*SOCIAL CUSTOMS* **SEE** INDIANS — SOCIAL LIFE AND CUSTOMS
DS112-113	*SOCIAL CUSTOMS* **SEE** JEWS — SOCIAL LIFE AND CUSTOMS
GT	*SOCIAL CUSTOMS* **SEE** MANNERS AND CUSTOMS
GV1751	*SOCIAL DANCING* **SEE** BALLROOM DANCING
HX1-550	*SOCIAL DEMOCRACY* **SEE** SOCIALISM
JC575-8	*SOCIAL EQUALITY* **SEE** EQUALITY / *political science*
HM146	*SOCIAL EQUALITY* **SEE** EQUALITY / *sociology*
HM216	SOCIAL ETHICS
HM131	SOCIAL GROUPS
RA771	*SOCIAL HYGIENE* **SEE** HYGIENE / *domestic*
BJ1695	*SOCIAL HYGIENE* **SEE** HYGIENE / *ethical aspects*
RA773-790	*SOCIAL HYGIENE* **SEE** HYGIENE / *personal*
RA	*SOCIAL HYGIENE* **SEE** HYGIENE, PUBLIC
RA425	*SOCIAL HYGIENE* **SEE** HYGIENE, PUBLIC / *comprehensive treatises*
RA11-388	*SOCIAL HYGIENE* **SEE** HYGIENE, PUBLIC / *general documents*
HQ31-58	*SOCIAL HYGIENE* **SEE** HYGIENE, SEXUAL
RC881	*SOCIAL HYGIENE* **SEE** HYGIENE, SEXUAL / *men*
RG121	*SOCIAL HYGIENE* **SEE** HYGIENE, SEXUAL / *women*
HQ101-440	*SOCIAL HYGIENE* **SEE** PROSTITUTION

RC200-203	*SOCIAL HYGIENE* **SEE** VENEREAL DISEASES
HD7090-7250	*SOCIAL INSURANCE* **SEE** INSURANCE, SOCIAL
HM291	SOCIAL INTERACTION
RA418	SOCIAL MEDICINE
HV33	*SOCIAL PARASITES* **SEE** PARASITISM (SOCIAL SCIENCES)
HN40.I	*SOCIAL PROBLEMS AND ISLAM* **SEE** ISLAM AND SOCIAL PROBLEMS
HN40.J5	*SOCIAL PROBLEMS AND JUDAISM* **SEE** JUDAISM AND SOCIAL PROBLEMS
HN30-39	*SOCIAL PROBLEMS AND THE CHURCH* **SEE** CHURCH AND SOCIAL PROBLEMS
LC71-245	*SOCIAL PROBLEMS IN EDUCATION* **SEE** EDUCATIONAL SOCIOLOGY
PN51	SOCIAL PROBLEMS IN LITERATURE
HN	SOCIAL PROBLEMS
CB155	*SOCIAL PROGRESS* **SEE** PROGRESS / civilization
HM101	*SOCIAL PROGRESS* **SEE** PROGRESS / sociology
HM251-291	SOCIAL PSYCHOLOGY
HV43	*SOCIAL PSYCHOTECHNICS* **SEE** INTERVIEWING / charities
BF761-8	*SOCIAL PSYCHOTECHNICS* **SEE** INTERVIEWING / evidence
BF67	*SOCIAL PSYCHOTECHNICS* **SEE** PSYCHOLOGY, APPLIED
BF636	*SOCIAL PSYCHOTECHNICS* **SEE** PSYCHOLOGY, APPLIED
HQ31	*SOCIAL PURITY* **SEE** SEXUAL ETHICS
HN	*SOCIAL REFORM* **SEE** SOCIAL PROBLEMS
H	*SOCIAL SCIENCE* **SEE** SOCIAL SCIENCES
HM-HV	*SOCIAL SCIENCE* **SEE** SOCIOLOGY
BL60	*SOCIAL SCIENCE* **SEE** SOCIOLOGY / religion and sociology
JX1251	*SOCIAL SCIENCE* **SEE** SOCIOLOGY / sociology and international law
HM26	*SOCIAL SCIENCE* **SEE** SOCIOLOGY / sociology and philosophy
B63	*SOCIAL SCIENCE* **SEE** SOCIOLOGY / sociology and philosophy
HM33	*SOCIAL SCIENCE* **SEE** SOCIOLOGY / sociology and political science
JA76	*SOCIAL SCIENCE* **SEE** SOCIOLOGY / sociology and political science
HM27	*SOCIAL SCIENCE* **SEE** SOCIOLOGY / sociology and psychology
BF57	*SOCIAL SCIENCE* **SEE** SOCIOLOGY / sociology and psychology
Z675.S6	SOCIAL SCIENCE LIBRARIES
Z7161-6	SOCIAL SCIENCES — BIBLIOGRAPHY
H51-53	SOCIAL SCIENCES — HISTORY
H95	SOCIAL SCIENCES — JUVENILE LITERATURE
H61	SOCIAL SCIENCES — METHODOLOGY
H61	SOCIAL SCIENCES — TERMINOLOGY
H	SOCIAL SCIENCES
HD7090-7250	*SOCIAL SECURITY* **SEE** INSURANCE, SOCIAL
UH750-769	*SOCIAL SERVICE AND MILITARY MOBILIZATION* **SEE** MILITARY SOCIAL WORK
HV1-696	SOCIAL SERVICE
UH750-769	*SOCIAL SERVICE, MILITARY* **SEE** MILITARY SOCIAL WORK
HV689	*SOCIAL SERVICE, PSYCHIATRIC* **SEE** PSYCHIATRIC SOCIAL WORK
HV4175-4320	SOCIAL SETTLEMENTS
H	*SOCIAL STUDIES* **SEE** SOCIAL SCIENCES
HN29	SOCIAL SURVEYS
HN	*SOCIAL WELFARE* **SEE** SOCIAL PROBLEMS
HV1-696	*SOCIAL WELFARE* **SEE** SOCIAL SERVICE
HV1-696	*SOCIAL WORK* **SEE** SOCIAL SERVICE
M1664.S67	SOCIALISM — SONGS AND MUSIC
HX536	SOCIALISM AND CATHOLIC CHURCH
HX526	SOCIALISM AND EDUCATION
HX550.I8	SOCIALISM AND ISLAM
HX536	SOCIALISM AND RELIGION
HX545	*SOCIALISM AND WAR* **SEE** WAR AND SOCIALISM
HX546	*SOCIALISM AND WOMEN* **SEE** WOMEN AND SOCIALISM
HX1-550	SOCIALISM
HX51-54	SOCIALISM, CHRISTIAN
BJ1388	SOCIALIST ETHICS

HX89	SOCIALIST LABOR PARTY / u.s.
HX89	SOCIALIST PARTY (U.S.)
HX23	SOCIALISTS / collected biography
HD3840-4420	*SOCIALIZATION OF INDUSTRY* **SEE** GOVERNMENT OWNERSHIP
HD1301-1315	*SOCIALIZATION OF LAND* **SEE** LAND, NATIONALIZATION OF
HV3000-3003	*SOCIALIZED MEDICINE* **SEE** CHARITIES, MEDICAL
HV687-694	*SOCIALIZED MEDICINE* **SEE** CHARITIES, MEDICAL
RA960-996	*SOCIALIZED MEDICINE* **SEE** CHARITIES, MEDICAL / hospitals
HG9383-9399	*SOCIALIZED MEDICINE* **SEE** INSURANCE, HEALTH
HD7101-2	*SOCIALIZED MEDICINE* **SEE** INSURANCE, HEALTH / industrial
RA	*SOCIALIZED MEDICINE* **SEE** MEDICINE, STATE
LC4051-4100	SOCIALLY HANDICAPPED CHILDREN — EDUCATION
HS25-35	SOCIETIES — HISTORY, ORGANIZATION, ETC.
AS	SOCIETIES / academies and learned societies
HS	SOCIETIES / etc.
HS1501-1510	*SOCIETIES, BENEFIT* **SEE** FRIENDLY SOCIETIES
HG9201-9245	*SOCIETIES, BENEFIT* **SEE** FRIENDLY SOCIETIES / fraternal insurance
HV1-4959	*SOCIETIES, BENEVOLENT* **SEE** CHARITABLE SOCIETIES
GV1299.S6	SOCIETY (GAME)
N72	*SOCIETY AND ART* **SEE** ART AND SOCIETY
N72	*SOCIETY AND ART* **SEE** ART AND SOCIETY
LC71-245	*SOCIETY AND EDUCATION* **SEE** EDUCATIONAL SOCIOLOGY
BL60	*SOCIETY AND RELIGION* **SEE** RELIGION AND SOCIOLOGY
HS159-160	SOCIETY EMBLEMS
TS761	SOCIETY EMBLEMS / jewelry
BX3701-3755	*SOCIETY OF JESUS* **SEE** JESUITS
BX4371-4	*SOCIETY OF JESUS* **SEE** JESUITS / women
Z695.8	*SOCIETY PUBLICATIONS (CATALOGING)* **SEE** CATALOGING OF SOCIETY PUBLICATIONS
PN1451	SOCIETY VERSE
PN6110.V4	SOCIETY VERSE
PS593.V4	SOCIETY VERSE / american
PR1195.V3	SOCIETY VERSE / english
GN400-499	SOCIETY, PRIMITIVE
BT1480	SOCINIANISM
LC203	*SOCIO-ECONOMIC STATUS OF STUDENTS* **SEE** STUDENTS' SOCIO-ECONOMIC STATUS
HM19-22	SOCIOLOGISTS
HM19-22	SOCIOLOGY — HISTORY
HM24	SOCIOLOGY — METHODOLOGY
N72	*SOCIOLOGY AND ART* **SEE** ART AND SOCIETY
N72	*SOCIOLOGY AND ART* **SEE** ART AND SOCIETY
BL60	*SOCIOLOGY AND RELIGION* **SEE** RELIGION AND SOCIOLOGY
BD175	*SOCIOLOGY OF KNOWLEDGE* **SEE** KNOWLEDGE, SOCIOLOGY OF
HM-HV	SOCIOLOGY
BL60	SOCIOLOGY / religion and sociology
JX1251	SOCIOLOGY / sociology and international law
HM26	SOCIOLOGY / sociology and philosophy
B63	SOCIOLOGY / sociology and philosophy
HM33	SOCIOLOGY / sociology and political science
JA76	SOCIOLOGY / sociology and political science
HM27	SOCIOLOGY / sociology and psychology
BF57	SOCIOLOGY / sociology and psychology
BS670	SOCIOLOGY, BIBLICAL
BR163-5	SOCIOLOGY, CHRISTIAN — EARLY CHURCH
HC41	SOCIOLOGY, CHRISTIAN — MIDDLE AGES
BR275.S	SOCIOLOGY, CHRISTIAN — MIDDLE AGES
BT738	SOCIOLOGY, CHRISTIAN
BT738	*SOCIOLOGY, CHRISTIAN-MODERN PERIOD* **SEE** SOCIOLOGY, CHRISTIAN
LC71-245	*SOCIOLOGY, EDUCATIONAL* **SEE** EDUCATIONAL SOCIOLOGY
HM104	*SOCIOLOGY, HISTORICAL* **SEE** HISTORICAL SOCIOLOGY
HD6971-4	*SOCIOLOGY, INDUSTRIAL* **SEE** INDUSTRIAL SOCIOLOGY
HN40.M6	SOCIOLOGY, ISLAMIC
HN40.J5	SOCIOLOGY, JEWISH
HN40.M6	*SOCIOLOGY, MUSLIM* **SEE** SOCIOLOGY, ISLAMIC

HT421-455	SOCIOLOGY, RURAL
HM253	SOCIOMETRY
TK2821	*SOCKETS, ELECTRIC* **SEE** ELECTRIC CONTACTORS
LB1027	*SOCRATIC METHOD* **SEE** QUESTIONING
TP245.S7	SODA INDUSTRY
TN911	*SODA NITER* **SEE** SALTPETER, CHILE
TP628-636	*SODA WATER* **SEE** CARBONATED BEVERAGES
BX808-9	*SODALITIES* **SEE** CONFRATERNITIES / *catholic church*
QD181.N2	SODAMIDE
QP913.N2	SODIUM — PHYSIOLOGICAL EFFECT
QD181.N2	SODIUM ACETATE
QD181.N2	SODIUM BENZOATE
QP917.S7	SODIUM BENZOATE / *physiology*
SF95	*SODIUM CHLORIDE* **SEE** SALT / *feeding and feeds*
GT2870	*SODIUM CHLORIDE* **SEE** SALT / *manners and customs*
TN900-909	*SODIUM CHLORIDE* **SEE** SALT / *mineral industries*
HD9213	*SODIUM CHLORIDE* **SEE** SALT / *trade*
TK9203.S6	SODIUM GRAPHITE REACTORS
TK9203.S6	*SODIUM REACTORS* **SEE** SODIUM GRAPHITE REACTORS
TK4381	*SODIUM-VAPOR LIGHT* **SEE** ELECTRIC LIGHTING, SODIUM VAPOR
QD181.N2	SODIUM
TP245.S7	SODIUM / *technology*
PL8110.C	*SOFALA LANGUAGE* **SEE** CHINDAU LANGUAGE
BP189	*SOFISM* **SEE** SUFISM
TP628-636	*SOFT DRINKS* **SEE** CARBONATED BEVERAGES
GV881	SOFTBALL
P921	SOGDIAN LANGUAGE
S594	SOIL ABSORPTION
S593.5	SOIL ACIDITY
QR111-113	*SOIL BACTERIOLOGY* **SEE** SOILS — BACTERIOLOGY
S591	*SOIL CLASSIFICATION* **SEE** SOILS — CLASSIFICATION
S623	SOIL CONSERVATION
S603	*SOIL CULTIVATION* **SEE** TILLAGE
TA710	*SOIL ENGINEERING* **SEE** SOIL MECHANICS
QE571-597	*SOIL EROSION* **SEE** EROSION
S598	SOIL EXHAUSTION
TA713	SOIL FREEZING
S652	SOIL INOCULATION
TA710	SOIL MECHANICS
QR111	SOIL MICRO-ORGANISMS
QR111	*SOIL MICROBIOLOGY* **SEE** SOIL MICRO-ORGANISMS
S594	SOIL MOISTURE
RA570	SOIL MOISTURE / *soil moisture and disease*
S598	*SOIL ORGANIC MATTER* **SEE** HUMUS
S593	SOIL OXIDATION
S594	SOIL PERCOLATION
RA571	SOIL POLLUTION
S594.5	SOIL TEMPERATURE
S591	*SOIL TYPES* **SEE** SOILS — CLASSIFICATION
S623	SOIL-BINDING
TE245	*SOIL-CEMENT ROADS* **SEE** ROADS, SOIL-CEMENT
S591	SOIL-SURVEYS
S599	SOIL-SURVEYS / *local*
S593	SOILS — ANALYSIS
QR111-113	SOILS — BACTERIOLOGY
S591	SOILS — CLASSIFICATION
TA710	*SOILS (ENGINEERING)* **SEE** SOIL MECHANICS
S590-599	SOILS
TA710	*SOILS-MECHANICS* **SEE** SOIL MECHANICS
S598	*SOILS-ORGANIC MATTER* **SEE** HUMUS
TP684.S6	*SOJA-BEAN OIL* **SEE** SOY-BEAN OIL
DK759.S7	*SOJOTES* **SEE** SOYOTES
E99.S	SOKOKI INDIANS
PJ7131-4	SOKOTRI LANGUAGE
MT30	*SOL-FA SYSTEM* **SEE** TONIC SOL-FA / *instruction*
QK495.S7	*SOLANUM DULCAMARA* **SEE** BITTERSWEET
DS451	*SOLANKIS* **SEE** CHALUKYAS
TL796.6.S	*SOLAR ARTIFICIAL SATELLITES* **SEE** ARTIFICIAL SATELLITES — SUN
QB105	SOLAR COMPASS
QB529	*SOLAR CORONA* **SEE** SUN — CORONA
QB541-551	*SOLAR ECLIPSES* **SEE** ECLIPSES, SOLAR
TJ810	SOLAR ENERGY
TJ810	SOLAR ENGINES
TH7145	SOLAR FURNACES
TH7644	*SOLAR HEAT* **SEE** SOLAR HEATING

QB531	*SOLAR HEAT* **SEE** SUN — TEMPERATURE
TH7644	SOLAR HEATING
QB507	*SOLAR MOTION* **SEE** SOLAR SYSTEM — MOTION IN SPACE
QB508-518	*SOLAR PARALLAX* **SEE** PARALLAX — SUN
QB521-539	*SOLAR PHYSICS* **SEE** SUN
GR625	*SOLAR PHYSICS* **SEE** SUN / *folk-lore*
QP368	SOLAR PLEXUS
TJ810	*SOLAR POWER* **SEE** SOLAR ENERGY
QB528	*SOLAR PROMINENCES* **SEE** SUN — PROMINENCES
QB531	SOLAR RADIATION / *astronomy*
QC911	SOLAR RADIATION / *meteorology*
QC455	*SOLAR SPECTRUM* **SEE** SPECTRUM, SOLAR / *physics*
QB551	*SOLAR SPECTRUM* **SEE** SPECTRUM, SOLAR / *solar eclipses*
QB502	SOLAR SYSTEM — CURIOSA AND MISCELLANY
QB507	SOLAR SYSTEM — MOTION IN SPACE
QB501-518	SOLAR SYSTEM
QB7-9	*SOLAR SYSTEM-EPHEMERIDES* **SEE** EPHEMERIDES
TT267	SOLDER AND SOLDERING
TH6297	SOLDER AND SOLDERING / *plumbing*
UC410	SOLDIERS — BILLETING
UB770	SOLDIERS — CIVIL STATUS
U715-717	SOLDIERS — EDUCATION, NON-MILITARY
BV463	SOLDIERS — HYMNS
BP188.3.S6	SOLDIERS — RELIGIOUS LIFE (ISLAM)
JK1876-8	SOLDIERS — SUFFRAGE / *u.s.*
N8260	SOLDIERS IN ART
G539	SOLDIERS OF FORTUNE
U750-773	SOLDIERS
U1-145	SOLDIERS
UB360-366	*SOLDIERS, INVALID* **SEE** VETERANS, DISABLED
D639.D4	SOLDIERS' BODIES, DISPOSITION OF / *european war*
D810.D4	SOLDIERS' BODIES, DISPOSITION OF / *world war*
D810.D4	*SOLDIERS' GRAVES* **SEE** SOLDIERS' BODIES, DISPOSITION OF / *world war*
D639.D4	*SOLDIERS' GRAVES* **SEE** SOLDIERS' BODIES, DISPOSITION OF / *european war*
U110-115	*SOLDIERS' HANDBOOKS* **SEE** MILITARY ART AND SCIENCE — SOLDIERS' HANDBOOKS
UB380-385	SOLDIERS' HOMES
Z675.W2	*SOLDIERS' LIBRARIES* **SEE** EUROPEAN WAR, 1914-1918 — LIBRARIES (IN CAMPS, ETC.)
Z675.W2	*SOLDIERS' LIBRARIES* **SEE** WAR LIBRARIES
U750-773	*SOLDIERS' LIFE* **SEE** SOLDIERS
U1-145	*SOLDIERS' LIFE* **SEE** SOLDIERS
NA9325-9355	SOLDIERS' MONUMENTS
UB356-9	*SOLDIERS-CIVIL EMPLOYMENT* **SEE** VETERANS — EMPLOYMENT
UH600-625	*SOLDIERS-HYGIENE* **SEE** MILITARY HYGIENE
UB400-405	*SOLDIERS-PENSIONS* **SEE** PENSIONS, MILITARY / *army*
UB370-375	*SOLDIERS-PENSIONS* **SEE** PENSIONS, MILITARY / *army*
VB280-285	*SOLDIERS-PENSIONS* **SEE** PENSIONS, MILITARY / *navy*
VB340-345	*SOLDIERS-PENSIONS* **SEE** PENSIONS, MILITARY / *navy*
E255	*SOLDIERS-PENSIONS* **SEE** PENSIONS, MILITARY / *pension rolls*
UC480-485	*SOLDIERS-UNIFORMS* **SEE** UNIFORMS, MILITARY
D278.S7	SOLEBAY, BATTLE OF, 1672
BX9081	SOLEMN LEAGUE AND COVENANT
QL430.1	SOLENOGASTRES
QC761	SOLENOIDS
QL638.S7	SOLES
SH351.S	SOLES / *fisheries*
MT870	*SOLFEGGIO* **SEE** SIGHT-SINGING / *instruction*
DG554.5.S7	SOLFERINO, BATTLE OF, 1859
PJ2379	*SOLHA LANGUAGE* **SEE** SHILHA LANGUAGE
DD124	SOLICINIUM, BATTLE OF, 368
QC378	SOLID FILM — OPTICAL PROPERTIES
TK9203.S65	SOLID FUEL REACTORS
QA457	*SOLID GEOMETRY* **SEE** GEOMETRY, SOLID
QA491	*SOLID GEOMETRY* **SEE** GEOMETRY, SOLID
QD541	*SOLID SOLUTIONS* **SEE** SOLUTIONS, SOLID
HM126	SOLIDARITY
QC303	SOLIDIFICATION
QC191	SOLIDS / *elastic properties*

QC282	SOLIDS / expansion
QC295	SOLIDS / specific heats
QC321-3	SOLIDS / thermal conductivity
QE571	SOLIFLUCTION
QE872.C7	SOLITAIRE (BIRD)
GV1261	SOLITAIRE (GAME)
BJ1499.S6	SOLITUDE
MT44	SOLMIZATION
GV1289	SOLO WHIST
GV1295.S6	SOLO-SIXTY (GAME)
QK495.P783	SOLOMON'S SEAL / botany
QD543	SOLUBILITY
QP601	SOLUBLE FERMENTS SEE ENZYMES
TP869	SOLUBLE GLASS
S590-598	SOLUBLE SALTS SEE SALTS, SOLUBLE / soils
QD541-9	SOLUTION (CHEMISTRY) / theory
QC310	SOLUTION, HEAT OF SEE HEAT OF SOLUTION
RS201.S6	SOLUTIONS (PHARMACY)
QD541	SOLUTIONS, SOLID
QD548	SOLUTIONS, SUPERSATURATED
TP247.5	SOLVENTS
BL1215.S6	SOMA / hinduism
PJ2531-9	SOMALI LANGUAGE
PJ2533.5-2534	SOMALI LITERATURE
PJ2533-4	SOMALI POETRY
DT401-420	SOMALIS
DT401-420	SOMALS SEE SOMALIS
GN51-211	SOMATOLOGY
D545.S7	SOMME, BATTLE OF THE, 1916
D545.S75	SOMME, 2D BATTLE OF THE, 1918
BF1068-1071	SOMNAMBULISM
BT232	SON OF MAN
PM8795	SONA (ARTIFICIAL LANGUAGE)
VK388	SONAR
VK560	SONAR / navigation
ML745	SONATA (PIANO)
ML895	SONATA (VIOLIN)
MT62	SONATA / composition
ML1156	SONATA / history
M270-271	SONATAS (ALTO HORN AND PIANO)
M282-3	SONATAS (BALALAIKA AND PIANO)
M1203	SONATAS (BAND) SEE SYMPHONIES (BAND)
M288-9	SONATAS (BASSOON AND FLUTE)
M253-4	SONATAS (BASSOON AND HARPSICHORD)
M253-4	SONATAS (BASSOON AND PIANO)
M290-291	SONATAS (BASSOON AND VIOLONCELLO)
M75-77	SONATAS (BASSOON)
M172	SONATAS (CARILLON)
M288-9	SONATAS (CLARINET AND FLUTE
M248-250	SONATAS (CLARINET AND PIANO)
M251-2	SONATAS (CLARINET AND PIANO), ARRANGED
M290-291	SONATAS (CLARINET AND VIOLONCELLO)
M70-72	SONATAS (CLARINET)
M260-261	SONATAS (CORNET AND PIANO)
M237-8	SONATAS (DOUBLE BASS AND PIANO)
M237-8	SONATAS (DOUBLE BASS AND PIANO), ARRANGED
M246.2	SONATAS (ENGLISH HORN AND PIANO)
M296-7	SONATAS (FLUTE AND GUITAR)
M296-7	SONATAS (FLUTE AND HARP)
M241-2	SONATAS (FLUTE AND HARPSICHORD)
M243-4	SONATAS (FLUTE AND HARPSICHORD), ARRANGED
M182-4	SONATAS (FLUTE AND ORGAN)
M185-6	SONATAS (FLUTE AND ORGAN), ARRANGED
M240-242	SONATAS (FLUTE AND PIANO)
M243-4	SONATAS (FLUTE AND PIANO), ARRANGED
M290-291	SONATAS (FLUTE AND VIOLA)
M60-62	SONATAS (FLUTE)
M276-7	SONATAS (GUITAR AND PIANO)
M125-7	SONATAS (GUITAR)
M128-9	SONATAS (GUITAR), ARRANGED
M272-3	SONATAS (HARP AND PIANO)
M115-117	SONATAS (HARP)
M118-119	SONATAS (HARP), ARRANGED
M224-6	SONATAS (HARPSICHORD AND VIOLA) SEE SONATAS (VIOLA AND HARPSICHORD)
M23	SONATAS (HARPSICHORD)
M255-7	SONATAS (HORN AND PIANO)
M284-5	SONATAS (KETTLEDRUMS AND PIANO)
M140-141	SONATAS (LUTE)
M278-9	SONATAS (MANDOLIN AND PIANO)
M270-271	SONATAS (MOUTH-ORGAN AND PIANO)
M270-271	SONATAS (MOUTH-ORGAN AND PIANO), ARRANGED
M110.M7	SONATAS (MOUTH-ORGAN)
M110.M7	SONATAS (MOUTH-ORGAN), ARRANGED
M245-6	SONATAS (OBOE AND HARPSICHORD)
M245-6	SONATAS (OBOE AND PIANO)
M247	SONATAS (OBOE AND PIANO), ARRANGED
M65-67	SONATAS (OBOE)
M8	SONATAS (ORGAN)
M12-13	SONATAS (ORGAN), ARRANGED
M23	SONATAS (PIANO)
M205	SONATAS (PIANO, 3 HANDS)
M202	SONATAS (PIANO, 4 HANDS)
M207	SONATAS (PIANO, 4 HANDS), ARRANGED
M211	SONATAS (PIANO, 4 HANDS), ARRANGED
M296-7	SONATAS (RECORDER AND GUITAR)
M296-7	SONATAS (RECORDER AND GUITAR), ARRANGED
M240-242	SONATAS (RECORDER AND HARPSICHORD)
M243-4	SONATAS (RECORDER AND HARPSICHORD), ARRANGED
M240-242	SONATAS (RECORDER AND PIANO)
M243-4	SONATAS (RECORDER AND PIANO), ARRANGED
M268-9	SONATAS (SAXOPHONE AND PIANO)
M262-3	SONATAS (TROMBONE AND PIANO)
M262-3	SONATAS (TROMBONE AND PIANO), ARRANGED
M182-4	SONATAS (TRUMPET AND ORGAN)
M260-261	SONATAS (TRUMPET AND PIANO)
M264-5	SONATAS (TUBA AND PIANO)
M224-6	SONATAS (VIOLA AND HARPSICHORD)
M224-6	SONATAS (VIOLA AND PIANO)
M227-8	SONATAS (VIOLA AND PIANO), ARRANGED
M286-7	SONATAS (VIOLA AND VIOLONCELLO)
M286-7	SONATAS (VIOLA D'AMORE AND DOUBLE BASS)
M239	SONATAS (VIOLA D'AMORE AND HARPSICHORD)
M239	SONATAS (VIOLA D'AMORE AND PIANO)
M239	SONATAS (VIOLA DA GAMBA AND HARPSICHORD)
M239	SONATAS (VIOLA DA GAMBA AND HARPSICHORD), ARRANGED
M239	SONATAS (VIOLA POMPOSA AND HARPSICHORD)
M45-47	SONATAS (VIOLA)
M294-5	SONATAS (VIOLIN AND GUITAR)
M294-5	SONATAS (VIOLIN AND GUITAR), ARRANGED
M294-5	SONATAS (VIOLIN AND HARP)
M294-5	SONATAS (VIOLIN AND HARP), ARRANGED
M219	SONATAS (VIOLIN AND HARPSICHORD)
M219	SONATAS (VIOLIN AND PIANO)
M223	SONATAS (VIOLIN AND PIANO), ARRANGED
M286-7	SONATAS (VIOLIN AND VIOLA DA GAMBA)
M286-7	SONATAS (VIOLIN AND VIOLA)
M286-7	SONATAS (VIOLIN AND VIOLONCELLO)
M286-7	SONATAS (VIOLIN AND VIOLONCELLO), ARRANGED
M42	SONATAS (VIOLIN)
M231	SONATAS (VIOLONCELLO AND HARPSICHORD)
M235-6	SONATAS (VIOLONCELLO AND HARPSICHORD), ARRANGED
M231	SONATAS (VIOLONCELLO AND PIANO)
M235-6	SONATAS (VIOLONCELLO AND PIANO), ARRANGED
M50-52	SONATAS (VIOLONCELLO)
M135-7	SONATAS (ZITHER)
M288-9	SONATAS (2 BASSOONS)
M288-9	SONATAS (2 CLARINETS)
M288-9	SONATAS (2 CLARINETS), ARRANGED
M288-9	SONATAS (2 FLUTES)
M214	SONATAS (2 HARPSICHORDS)
M288-9	SONATAS (2 HORNS)
M288-9	SONATAS (2 OBOES)
M214	SONATAS (2 PIANOS)
M215	SONATAS (2 PIANOS), ARRANGED
M288-9	SONATAS (2 RECORDERS)
M288-9	SONATAS (2 RECORDERS), ARRANGED
M286-7	SONATAS (2 VIOLE DA GAMBA)
M286-7	SONATAS (2 VIOLINS)
M286-7	SONATAS (2 VIOLONCELLOS)
M286-7	SONATAS (2 VIOLONCELLOS), ARRANGED
PL8685	SONAY LANGUAGE SEE SONGHAI LANGUAGE
ML1040	SONG BELLS SEE XYLOPHONE
M2113.4	SONG CYCLES
M1621.4	SONG CYCLES
ML935-6	SONG FLUTE SEE RECORDER (MUSICAL INSTRUMENT)
M1977.C5	SONG-BOOKS (MEN'S VOICES)

M1977.C5	SONG-BOOKS (WOMEN'S VOICES)
M1977.C5	SONG-BOOKS
M1977.C5	*SONG-BOOKS, AMERICAN* **SEE** SONG-BOOKS
M1977.C5	*SONG-BOOKS, ENGLISH* **SEE** SONG-BOOKS
BV520	*SONG-BOOKS, SUNDAY-SCHOOL* **SEE** SUNDAY-SCHOOLS — HYMNS
QL696.P2	SONG-SPARROWS
DT551	*SONGAY* **SEE** SONGHAI
PL8685	SONGHAI LANGUAGE
DT551	SONGHAI
ML3875	SONGS — HISTORY AND CRITICISM / aesthetics
ML2500-2862	SONGS — HISTORY AND CRITICISM / history
ML128.S3	SONGS — INDEXES
M1624.7	SONGS (HIGH VOICE) WITH CLARINET
M1623.8	SONGS (HIGH VOICE) WITH CLARINET
M1624.7	SONGS (HIGH VOICE) WITH FLUTE
M1623.8	SONGS (HIGH VOICE) WITH FLUTE
M1623	SONGS (HIGH VOICE) WITH GUITAR
M1624	SONGS (HIGH VOICE) WITH GUITAR
M1623.4	SONGS (HIGH VOICE) WITH HARP
M1624.4	SONGS (HIGH VOICE) WITH HARP
M1619-1621	SONGS (HIGH VOICE) WITH HARPSICHORD
M1623.5	SONGS (HIGH VOICE) WITH LUTE
M1624.7	SONGS (HIGH VOICE) WITH OBOE
M1623.8	SONGS (HIGH VOICE) WITH OBOE
M1619-1621	SONGS (HIGH VOICE) WITH ORGAN
M1619-1621	SONGS (HIGH VOICE) WITH PIANO
M1619-1621	SONGS (HIGH VOICE) WITH PIANO, 4 HANDS
M1624.8	SONGS (HIGH VOICE) WITH VIOL
M1623.8	SONGS (HIGH VOICE) WITH VIOL
M1624.8	SONGS (HIGH VOICE) WITH VIOLONCELLO
M1623.8	SONGS (HIGH VOICE) WITH VIOLONCELLO
M1619-1621	SONGS (HIGH VOICE) WITH 2 PIANOS
M1619-1621	SONGS (LOW VOICE) WITH HARPSICHORD
M1619-1621	SONGS (LOW VOICE) WITH PIANO
M1613.3	SONGS (LOW VOICE) WITH STRING ORCHESTRA — SCORES AND PARTS (INSTRUMENTAL)
M1614	SONGS (LOW VOICE) WITH STRING ORCHESTRA — VOCAL SCORES WITH PIANO
M1624	SONGS (MEDIUM VOICE) WITH BANJO
M1623	SONGS (MEDIUM VOICE) WITH BANJO
M1624.7	SONGS (MEDIUM VOICE) WITH FLUTE
M1623.8	SONGS (MEDIUM VOICE) WITH FLUTE
M1624	SONGS (MEDIUM VOICE) WITH GUITAR
M1623	SONGS (MEDIUM VOICE) WITH GUITAR
M1624.4	SONGS (MEDIUM VOICE) WITH HARP
M1623.4	SONGS (MEDIUM VOICE) WITH HARP
M1619-1621	SONGS (MEDIUM VOICE) WITH HARPSICHORD
M1623.5	SONGS (MEDIUM VOICE) WITH LUTE
M1624.5	SONGS (MEDIUM VOICE) WITH LUTE
M1619-1621	SONGS (MEDIUM VOICE) WITH PIANO
M1623.8	SONGS (MEDIUM VOICE) WITH VIOLIN
M1624.8	SONGS (MEDIUM VOICE) WITH VIOLIN
M1624.8	SONGS WITH ACCORDION
M1623.8	SONGS WITH ACCORDION
M1611	SONGS WITH CHAMBER ORCHESTRA — SCORES AND PARTS
M1613	SONGS WITH CHAMBER ORCHESTRA — SCORES AND PARTS
M1624.8	SONGS WITH CONCERTINA
M1623.8	SONGS WITH CONCERTINA
M1624.8	SONGS WITH DULCIMER
M1623.8	SONGS WITH DULCIMER
M1623	SONGS WITH GUITAR
M1624	SONGS WITH GUITAR
M1624	SONGS WITH HARP-LUTE GUITAR
M1623	SONGS WITH HARP-LUTE GUITAR
M1619-1621	SONGS WITH HARPSICHORD
M1624	SONGS WITH KOBZA
M1623	SONGS WITH KOBZA
M1623.5	SONGS WITH LUTE
M1624.5	SONGS WITH LUTE
M1619-1621	SONGS WITH PIANO
M1619-1621	SONGS WITH REED-ORGAN
M1623.8	SONGS WITH VIOLA DA GAMBA
M1624.8	SONGS WITH VIOLA DA GAMBA
M1624.8	SONGS WITH VIOLONCELLO
M1623.8	SONGS WITH VIOLONCELLO
M1810-1811	SONGS, ISRAELI
ML3556	*SONGS, NEGRO* **SEE** NEGRO SONGS / history

M1670-1671	*SONGS, NEGRO* **SEE** NEGRO SONGS / music
M1810-1811	SONGS, PALESTINIAN
M1621.2	SONGS, UNACCOMPANIED
TA365	*SONIC ENGINEERING* **SEE** ACOUSTICAL ENGINEERING
VK584	*SONIC SOUNDING* **SEE** ECHO SOUNDING / navigation
GC78.E	*SONIC SOUNDING* **SEE** ECHO SOUNDING / oceanography
TA365	*SONICS* **SEE** ACOUSTICAL ENGINEERING
PN1514	SONNET
PN6110.S6	SONNETS / collections
PM2175	*SONORAN LANGUAGES* **SEE** PIMAN LANGUAGES
PM4190	*SONORAN LANGUAGES* **SEE** PIMAN LANGUAGES
DT551	*SONRAI* **SEE** SONGHAI
PL4563	*SONTHAL LANGUAGE* **SEE** SANTALI LANGUAGE
DS432.S	*SONTHALS* **SEE** SANTALS
PL6041-4	*SOOLOO LANGUAGE* **SEE** SULU LANGUAGE
TH2285	SOOT / removal
BL613	*SOOTHSAYING* **SEE** DIVINATION / comparative religion
BF1745-1779	*SOOTHSAYING* **SEE** DIVINATION / occult sciences
BC175	*SOPHISTRY (LOGIC)* **SEE** FALLACIES (LOGIC)
B288	SOPHISTS (GREEK PHILOSOPHY)
QD421.C	*SOPHORINE* **SEE** CYTISINE / chemistry
QP921.C	*SOPHORINE* **SEE** CYTISINE / physiological effect
GT3010	*SOPORIFICS* **SEE** NARCOTICS / and customs
RM328	*SOPORIFICS* **SEE** NARCOTICS / therapeutics
PJ7131-4	*SOQOTRI LANGUAGE* **SEE** SOKOTRI LANGUAGE
PL4587	*SORA LANGUAGE* **SEE** SAVARA LANGUAGE
PG5631-5659	*SORBIC LANGUAGE* **SEE** WENDIC LANGUAGE
DD78.W4	*SORBS* **SEE** WENDS / germany
DD491.L348	*SORBS* **SEE** WENDS / lusatia
DD38	*SORBS* **SEE** WENDS / prussia
DD801.S348	*SORBS* **SEE** WENDS / saxony
GN475	*SORCERY* **SEE** MAGIC / ethnology
BF1585-1623	*SORCERY* **SEE** MAGIC / occult sciences
BF1563-1584	*SORCERY* **SEE** WITCHCRAFT
GR530	*SORCERY* **SEE** WITCHCRAFT / folk-lore
RF1-81	*SORE THROAT* **SEE** THROAT — DISEASES
RC182.S3	*SORE THROAT* **SEE** THROAT — DISEASES
RF460-535	*SORE THROAT* **SEE** THROAT — DISEASES
SB608.S6	SORGHUM — DISEASES AND PESTS
TP405	SORGHUM SUGAR
TP405	SORGHUM SYRUP
SB608.S6	SORGHUM-MIDGE
SB235	SORGHUM
TP405	SORGHUM / chemical technology
SB235	*SORGO* **SEE** SORGHUM
TP405	*SORGO* **SEE** SORGHUM / chemical technology
QA75	*SOROBAN* **SEE** ABACUS
LJ	*SORORITIES, GREEK LETTER* **SEE** GREEK LETTER SOCIETIES
M1960	*SORORITY SONGS* **SEE** FRATERNITY SONGS
QC182	*SORPTION OF GASES* **SEE** GASES — ABSORPTION AND ADSORPTION
NK9930	*SORRENTO WORK* **SEE** FRETWORK
BJ1480-1487	*SORROW* **SEE** JOY AND SORROW
BX2161.5.S	*SORROWS OF OUR LADY, DEVOTION TO* **SEE** SORROWS OF THE BLESSED VIRGIN MARY, DEVOTION TO
BX2161.5.S	SORROWS OF THE BLESSED VIRGIN MARY, DEVOTION TO
PL8695	*SOSO LANGUAGE* **SEE** SUSU LANGUAGE
PL8689	SOTHO LANGUAGE
CJ2676	SOU MARQUE
CT108	*SOUBRIQUETS* **SEE** NICKNAMES / english
TX773	SOUFFLES
BP166.73	SOUL (ISLAM)
N8180	SOUL IN ART
BL290	SOUL / comparative religion
BD426	SOUL / pre-existence
BD428	SOUL / soul of animals
BT740-743	SOUL / theology
DF747.S8	*SOULIOTES* **SEE** SULIOTES
QC227	SOUND — APPARATUS
QC222	SOUND — EARLY WORKS TO 1800
QC243	SOUND — MEASUREMENT
QC233	SOUND — SPEED
QC233	*SOUND ABSORPTION* **SEE** ABSORPTION OF SOUND

HE386.S7	SOUND DUTIES / *oresund*
TK6570.B7	*SOUND EFFECTS (RADIO)* **SEE** RADIO BROADCASTING — SOUND EFFECTS
PN2091.S6	*SOUND EFFECTS IN THEATERS* **SEE** THEATERS — SOUND EFFECTS
TA365	*SOUND ENGINEERING* **SEE** ACOUSTICAL ENGINEERING
TH1725	*SOUND INSULATION* **SEE** SOUNDPROOFING
PN1995.7	*SOUND MOTION PICTURES* **SEE** MOVING-PICTURES, TALKING
VK388	*SOUND NAVIGATION AND RANGING* **SEE** SONAR
VK560	*SOUND NAVIGATION AND RANGING* **SEE** SONAR / *navigation*
PN1995.7	*SOUND PICTURES* **SEE** MOVING-PICTURES, TALKING
QL765	SOUND PRODUCTION BY ANIMALS
ML157.3	*SOUND RECORDING TAPES* **SEE** PHONOTAPES
QC235	SOUND-WAVES — DAMPING
QC243	SOUND-WAVES — DAMPING
QC243	SOUND-WAVES
TA365	*SOUND-WAVES-INDUSTRIAL APPLICATIONS* **SEE** ACOUSTICAL ENGINEERING
QC220-246	SOUND
DL192	SOUND, BATTLE OF THE, 1658
QP469	SOUND, LOCALIZATION OF
QC233	*SOUND-ABSORPTION* **SEE** ABSORPTION OF SOUND
TH1725	*SOUND-INSULATION* **SEE** SOUNDPROOFING
QC233	*SOUND-VELOCITY* **SEE** SOUND — SPEED
VK584.S6	SOUNDING AND SOUNDINGS / *navigation*
GS69-78	SOUNDING AND SOUNDINGS / *oceanography*
TL631	*SOUNDING BALLOONS* **SEE** BALLOONS, SOUNDING
TL785.8.S6	*SOUNDING ROCKETS* **SEE** ROCKETS, SOUNDING
TH1725	SOUNDPROOFING
TL210	*SOUPED-UP MOTORS* **SEE** AUTOMOBILES, RACING — MOTORS
TX757	SOUPS
ML970-973	*SOUSAPHONE* **SEE** TUBA
SF967.A	*SOUTH AFRICAN GALL SICKNESS* **SEE** ANAPLASMOSIS
PT6500-6590	*SOUTH AFRICAN LITERATURE (AFRIKAANS)* **SEE** AFRIKAANS LITERATURE
PN5450	SOUTH AFRICAN NEWSPAPERS
PT6545	*SOUTH AFRICAN POETRY (AFRIKAANS)* **SEE** AFRIKAANS POETRY / *folk literature*
PT6560	*SOUTH AFRICAN POETRY (AFRIKAANS)* **SEE** AFRIKAANS POETRY / *collections*
PT6515	*SOUTH AFRICAN POETRY (AFRIKAANS)* **SEE** AFRIKAANS POETRY / *history*
PR9855-9869	SOUTH AFRICAN POETRY (ENGLISH)
PT6525	*SOUTH AFRICAN PROSE LITERATURE (AFRIKAANS)* **SEE** AFRIKAANS PROSE LITERATURE / *history*
PT6570	*SOUTH AFRICAN PROSE LITERATURE (AFRIKAANS)* **SEE** AFRIKAANS PROSE LITERATURE / *collections*
PR9878-9892	SOUTH AFRICAN PROSE LITERATURE (ENGLISH)
DT935	SOUTH AFRICAN WAR, 1899-1902 — ATROCITIES
DT930-939	SOUTH AFRICAN WAR, 1899-1902
F2201-2239	SOUTH AMERICA — HISTORY
F266-280	SOUTH CAROLINA — HISTORY
E529	SOUTH CAROLINA — HISTORY — — CIVIL WAR
E471.1	SOUTH CAROLINA — HISTORY — — CIVIL WAR
E577	SOUTH CAROLINA — HISTORY — — CIVIL WAR
E197	SOUTH CAROLINA — HISTORY — — QUEEN ANNE'S WAR, 1702-1713
E263.S7	SOUTH CAROLINA — HISTORY — — REVOLUTION
E474.61	SOUTH MOUNTAIN, BATTLE OF, 1862
G850-890	SOUTH POLE
PL16.K3	*SOUTH SAMOYEDIC LANGUAGE* **SEE** KAMASSIN LANGUAGE
PL5456	*SOUTH TORADJA LANGUAGE* **SEE** TAE' LANGUAGE
F232.S7	SOUTHAMPTON INSURRECTION, 1831
SF373.S7	SOUTHDOWN SHEEP / *flock books*
SB608.B4	SOUTHERN BEET WEB-WORM
F213	SOUTHERN BOUNDARY OF THE U.S.
BL1480	*SOUTHERN BUDDHISM* **SEE** HINAYANA BUDDHISM
SF805	*SOUTHERN CATTLE FEVER* **SEE** TEXAS FEVER
E458.7	*SOUTHERN REFUGEES* **SEE** REFUGEES, SOUTHERN
F206-220	SOUTHERN STATES — HISTORY
E487-8	*SOUTHERN STATES-HISTORY-CIVIL WAR* **SEE** CONFEDERATE STATES OF AMERICA — HISTORY

E230.5	SOUTHERN STATES — HISTORY — — REVOLUTION
E355.1	SOUTHERN STATES — HISTORY — — WAR OF 1812
E213	SOUTHERN STATES — HISTORY — — 1775-1865
F216	SOUTHERN STATES — HISTORY — — 1865-1877
BL1480	*SOUTHERN VEHICLE (BUDDHISM)* **SEE** HINAYANA BUDDHISM
F786	SOUTHWEST, NEW
E470.9	SOUTHWEST, NEW — HISTORY — — CIVIL WAR
F396	SOUTHWEST, OLD
E470.8	SOUTHWEST, OLD — HISTORY — — CIVIL WAR
E470.9	SOUTHWEST, OLD — HISTORY — — CIVIL WAR
E470.45	SOUTHWEST, OLD — HISTORY — — CIVIL WAR
E230.5	SOUTHWEST, OLD — HISTORY — — REVOLUTION
SB945.S	SOUTHWESTERN CORN BORER
D278.S7	*SOUTHWOLD, BATTLE OF, 1672* **SEE** SOLEBAY, BATTLE OF, 1672
D107	*SOVEREIGNS* **SEE** EMPERORS
D107	*SOVEREIGNS* **SEE** KINGS AND RULERS / *biography comprehensive*
JF253	*SOVEREIGNS* **SEE** KINGS AND RULERS / *comparative government*
JC374-408	*SOVEREIGNS* **SEE** KINGS AND RULERS / *political theory*
D352.1	*SOVEREIGNS* **SEE** KINGS AND RULERS / *19th century*
D399.7	*SOVEREIGNS* **SEE** KINGS AND RULERS / *19th century*
D412.7	*SOVEREIGNS* **SEE** KINGS AND RULERS / *20th century*
JL-JQ	*SOVEREIGNS* **SEE** MONARCHY / *administration*
JF251-314	*SOVEREIGNS* **SEE** MONARCHY / *administration*
JC374-393	*SOVEREIGNS* **SEE** MONARCHY / *theory*
JC401-8	*SOVEREIGNS* **SEE** MONARCHY / *theory*
D107.3	*SOVEREIGNS* **SEE** QUEENS
D352.3	*SOVEREIGNS* **SEE** QUEENS / *19th century*
D412.8	*SOVEREIGNS* **SEE** QUEENS / *20th century*
DG270-365	*SOVEREIGNS* **SEE** ROMAN EMPERORS
DG124	*SOVEREIGNS* **SEE** ROMAN EMPERORS / *cult*
JX4041-4068	SOVEREIGNTY / *international law*
JC327	SOVEREIGNTY / *theory*
TL796.5.R	*SOVIET ARTIFICIAL SATELLITES* **SEE** ARTIFICIAL SATELLITES, RUSSIAN
D847	*SOVIET BLOC* **SEE** COMMUNIST COUNTRIES
PG3503	*SOVIET LITERATURE* **SEE** RUSSIA — LITERATURES / *collections*
PG3500	*SOVIET LITERATURE* **SEE** RUSSIA — LITERATURES / *history*
DK459.5	*SOVIET-FINNISH WAR, 1939-1940* **SEE** RUSSO-FINNISH WAR, 1939-1940
DK265-272	SOVIETS
S687-9	SOWING
TP684.S6	SOY-BEAN OIL
SB205.S7	SOY-BEAN
TP684.S6	*SOYA-BEAN OIL* **SEE** SOY-BEAN OIL
DK759.S7	*SOYONS* **SEE** SOYOTES
PL45.S6	SOYOT LANGUAGE
DK759.S7	SOYOTES
DA683	SPA FIELDS RIOT, 1816 / *london*
BD621-638	SPACE AND TIME / *metaphysics*
BF467-475	SPACE AND TIME / *psychology*
TL797	*SPACE CARS* **SEE** SPACE STATIONS
TL793	SPACE FLIGHT — JUVENILE LITERATURE
TL799.M3	SPACE FLIGHT TO MARS
TL799.M6	SPACE FLIGHT TO THE MOON
TL790	SPACE FLIGHT
TG260	*SPACE FRAMES* **SEE** STRUCTURAL FRAMES
QA171.5	*SPACE LATTICE (MATHEMATICS)* **SEE** LATTICE THEORY
QD911-915	*SPACE LATTICE (MATHEMATICS)* **SEE** LATTICE THEORY / *crystallography*
QA699	*SPACE OF MORE THAN THREE DIMENSIONS* **SEE** FOURTH DIMENSION
QA691	*SPACE OF MORE THAN THREE DIMENSIONS* **SEE** HYPERSPACE
BD621-638	*SPACE OF MORE THAN THREE DIMENSIONS* **SEE** SPACE AND TIME / *metaphysics*
BF467-475	*SPACE OF MORE THAN THREE DIMENSIONS* **SEE** SPACE AND TIME / *psychology*

QB500	SPACE SCIENCES
TL795	SPACE SHIPS
TL797	SPACE STATIONS
TL697.P7	*SPACE SUITS* **SEE** PRESSURE SUITS
TL4030	*SPACE TRACKING* **SEE** SPACE VEHICLES — TRACKING
TL1075	SPACE TRAJECTORIES
TL789-790	*SPACE TRAVEL* **SEE** INTERPLANETARY VOYAGES
TL790	*SPACE TRAVEL* **SEE** SPACE FLIGHT
TL4030	*SPACE VEHICLE TRACKING* **SEE** SPACE VEHICLES — TRACKING
TL900	SPACE VEHICLES — SOLAR ENGINES
TL900	SPACE VEHICLES — THERMODYNAMICS
TL4030	SPACE VEHICLES — TRACKING
TL1075	*SPACE VEHICLES-TRAJECTORIES* **SEE** SPACE TRAJECTORIES
QP443	SPACE-PERCEPTION
QP491	SPACE-PERCEPTION / *visual*
QA689	SPACES, GENERALIZED
TS2157	*SPAGHETTI* **SEE** MACARONI / *manufacture*
DP1-402	SPAIN — HISTORY
PN56.S	SPAIN IN LITERATURE
E714-735	*SPAIN-HISTORY-WAR OF 1898* **SEE** UNITED STATES — HISTORY — — WAR OF 1898
DP270	SPAIN — HISTORY — — 1939-
DP269	SPAIN — HISTORY — — CIVIL WAR, 1936-1939 — — — ART AND THE WAR
DP269	SPAIN — HISTORY — — CIVIL WAR, 1936-1939 — — — HUMOR, CARICATURES, ETC.
DP48-53	SPANIARDS
SF429.S7	SPANIELS
PC4813	*SPANIOL LANGUAGE* **SEE** LADINO LANGUAGE
NA1301-1313	*SPANISH ARCHITECTURE* **SEE** ARCHITECTURE, SPANISH
DA360	*SPANISH ARMADA* **SEE** ARMADA, 1588
ML980	*SPANISH BAGPIPE* **SEE** GAITA
PQ6210	SPANISH BALLADS AND SONGS / *collections*
PQ6195-6205	SPANISH BALLADS AND SONGS / *collections*
PQ6089-6091	SPANISH BALLADS AND SONGS / *history*
SB317.S	SPANISH BROOM
CE61.S	*SPANISH CHRONOLOGY* **SEE** CHRONOLOGY, SPANISH
CB226	*SPANISH CIVILIZATION* **SEE** CIVILIZATION, HISPANIC
PQ6233	SPANISH DRAMA (COMEDY) / *collections*
PQ6120	SPANISH DRAMA (COMEDY) / *history*
PQ6217-6241	SPANISH DRAMA / *collections*
PQ6099-6129	SPANISH DRAMA / *history*
CE61.S7	SPANISH ERA (CHRONOLOGY)
PQ6250	SPANISH ESSAYS / *collections*
PQ6150	SPANISH ESSAYS / *history*
PQ6239.E6	SPANISH FARCES / *collections*
PQ6127.E6	SPANISH FARCES / *history*
SF805	*SPANISH FEVER* **SEE** TEXAS FEVER
PQ6251-7	SPANISH FICTION / *collections*
PQ6138-6147	SPANISH FICTION / *history*
F314	SPANISH FLORIDA CLAIMS
E83.817	SPANISH FLORIDA CLAIMS / *1st seminole war*
ML1015-1018	*SPANISH GUITAR* **SEE** GUITAR
PC4120.C6	SPANISH LANGUAGE — BUSINESS SPANISH
PC4715	SPANISH LANGUAGE — OLD SPANISH
PC4001-4977	SPANISH LANGUAGE
Z2681-2709	SPANISH LITERATURE — BIBLIOGRAPHY
PQ6056	SPANISH LITERATURE — JEWISH AUTHORS
PQ6001-8929	SPANISH LITERATURE
PQ9463-8	*SPANISH LITERATURE-GALICIA* **SEE** GALLEGAN LITERATURE / *collections*
PQ9450-9462	*SPANISH LITERATURE-GALICIA* **SEE** GALLEGAN LITERATURE / *history*
F2161-2175	SPANISH MAIN
PN5311-5319	SPANISH NEWSPAPERS / *history*
PQ6258	SPANISH ORATIONS / *collections*
PQ6148	SPANISH ORATIONS / *history*
PN5311-5320	SPANISH PERIODICALS / *history*
PC4001-4071	SPANISH PHILOLOGY
PQ6175-6215	SPANISH POETRY / *collections*
PQ6076-6098	SPANISH POETRY / *history*
PQ6267-9	SPANISH POETRY / *translations*
GV1469.C5	*SPANISH POOL* **SEE** CHECKER POOL
PQ6247-6264	SPANISH PROSE LITERATURE / *collections*
PQ6131-6153	SPANISH PROSE LITERATURE / *history*
D281-3	SPANISH SUCCESSION, WAR OF, 1701-1714
DP196	SPANISH SUCCESSION, WAR OF, 1701-1714 / *period in spain*
SB205.A4	*SPANISH TREFOIL* **SEE** ALFALFA
PQ6263	SPANISH WIT AND HUMOR / *collections*
PQ6152	SPANISH WIT AND HUMOR / *history*
PN6213-6215	SPANISH WIT AND HUMOR / *minor works*
NC1630-1639	SPANISH WIT AND HUMOR, PICTORIAL
PQ7084	SPANISH-AMERICAN BALLADS AND SONGS / *collections*
PQ7082.P7	SPANISH-AMERICAN BALLADS AND SONGS / *history*
PQ7085	SPANISH-AMERICAN FICTION / *collections*
PQ7082	SPANISH-AMERICAN FICTION / *history*
Z1601-1939	SPANISH-AMERICAN LITERATURE — BIBLIOGRAPHY
PQ7081-8560	SPANISH-AMERICAN LITERATURE
PN4960	SPANISH-AMERICAN NEWSPAPERS
Z6953.5.S	SPANISH-AMERICAN NEWSPAPERS / *bibliography u.s.*
Z6954	SPANISH-AMERICAN NEWSPAPERS / *other countries*
PN4960	SPANISH-AMERICAN PERIODICALS
Z6954.5.S	SPANISH-AMERICAN PERIODICALS / *bibliography u.s.*
Z6954	SPANISH-AMERICAN PERIODICALS / *other countries*
PQ7084	SPANISH-AMERICAN POETRY / *collections*
PQ7082.P7	SPANISH-AMERICAN POETRY / *history*
PQ7085	SPANISH-AMERICAN PROSE LITERATURE
E714-735	*SPANISH-AMERICAN WAR, 1898* **SEE** UNITED STATES — HISTORY — — WAR OF 1898
PN6213-6215	SPANISH-AMERICAN WIT AND HUMOR
F1409	SPANISH-AMERICANS
PQ6056	*SPANISH-ARABIC POETRY* **SEE** MOZARABIC POETRY
DC124.45	*SPANISH-FRENCH WAR, 1635-1659* **SEE** FRANCO-SPANISH WAR, 1635-1659
D275-6	*SPANISH-FRENCH WAR, 1667-1668* **SEE** DEVOLUTION, WAR OF, 1667-1668
DT324	SPANISH-MOROCCAN WAR, 1859-1860
DP220	SPANISH-MOROCCAN WAR, 1859-1860 / *period in spain*
TJ1201.W8	*SPANNERS* **SEE** WRENCHES
TJ787	SPARK-PLUGS
QC703	*SPARK, ELECTRIC* **SEE** ELECTRIC SPARK
GV1115-1137	*SPARRING* **SEE** BOXING
QL696.A2	*SPARROW-HAWKS* **SEE** HAWKS
QL696.P2	SPARROWS
QP921.S7	SPARTEINE / *physiological effect*
RM666.S	SPARTEINE / *therapeutics*
RA791-954	*SPAS* **SEE** HEALTH RESORTS, WATERING-PLACES, ETC.
RC431.S7	*SPASMOPHILIA* **SEE** SPASMS
RC431.S7	SPASMS
SF959.S6	SPAVIN
SF889	SPAYING
PN4305.C4	*SPEAKERS (RECITATION BOOKS)* **SEE** CHORAL RECITATIONS
PN4199-4321	*SPEAKERS (RECITATION BOOKS)* **SEE** READERS AND SPEAKERS / *recitations*
PE1117-1130	*SPEAKERS (RECITATION BOOKS)* **SEE** READERS AND SPEAKERS / *english*
PE1417	*SPEAKERS (RECITATION BOOKS)* **SEE** READERS AND SPEAKERS / *rhetoric*
PN4058	*SPEAKERS* **SEE** LECTURERS
PN4057	*SPEAKERS* **SEE** ORATORS / *collective biography*
PN4181-4191	*SPEAKING* **SEE** DEBATES AND DEBATING
PN4071-4197	*SPEAKING* **SEE** ELOCUTION
PN4193.L4	*SPEAKING* **SEE** LECTURES AND LECTURING
LC6501-6560	*SPEAKING* **SEE** LECTURES AND LECTURING / *lyceum and lecture courses*
PN4001-4321	*SPEAKING* **SEE** ORATORY / *general works*
BV4200-4235	*SPEAKING* **SEE** PREACHING
PN173-229	*SPEAKING* **SEE** RHETORIC
PE1402-1497	*SPEAKING* **SEE** RHETORIC / *english*
QP306	*SPEAKING* **SEE** VOICE / *physiology*
QL765	*SPEAKING* **SEE** VOICE / *sound production in animals*
PN4193.C5	*SPEAKING CHOIRS* **SEE** CHORAL SPEAKING
BL54	*SPEAKING WITH TONGUES* **SEE** GLOSSOLALIA
TS2301.P3	*SPEAKING-MACHINES* **SEE** TALKING-MACHINES
VK584.S65	SPEAKING-TRUMPET
SH459	SPEAR FISHING
QL638.H	SPEAR-FISH
GN498.T5	*SPEAR-THROWERS* **SEE** THROWING-STICKS

RC74	SPHYGMOGRAPH
RC74	SPHYGMOMANOMETER
TX587-8	SPICES / *adulteration*
SB305-7	SPICES / *culture*
TX406-7	SPICES / *home economics*
GT2870	SPICES / *manners and customs*
HD9210	SPICES / *trade*
DC302.7	SPICHEREN, BATTLE OF, 1870
GV1511.S7	SPIDER (GAME)
QL737.P9	SPIDER MONKEYS
QL459	SPIDER WEBS
QL451-9	SPIDERS
GR755	SPIDERS / *folk-lore*
TN757.S7	SPIEGEL-IRON
JX5121	SPIES / *international law*
UB270	SPIES / *military*
VB250	SPIES / *naval*
QD305.A8	SPIGELINE
SB945.S65	SPIKE-HORNED LEAF-MINER
QK495.S75	SPIKENARD
HD9999.N3-33	*SPIKES* **SEE** NAILS AND SPIKES / *economics*
TS440	*SPIKES* **SEE** NAILS AND SPIKES / *manufacture*
TA492.N2	*SPIKES* **SEE** NAILS AND SPIKES / *testing*
TC555	SPILLWAYS
RC406.S6	SPINA BIFIDA
TX612.S6	SPINACH / *canning*
SB351.S7	SPINACH / *culture*
RZ399.S6	SPINAL ADJUSTMENT
RD85.S7	SPINAL ANESTHESIA
QL821	*SPINAL COLUMN* **SEE** SPINE / *comparative anatomy*
QM111	*SPINAL COLUMN* **SEE** SPINE / *human anatomy*
RC400-406	SPINAL CORD — DISEASES
QP374	SPINAL CORD — LOCALIZATION OF FUNCTIONS
RD594.3	SPINAL CORD — SURGERY
RC280.S	SPINAL CORD — TUMORS
RD673	SPINAL CORD — TUMORS
RD594.3	SPINAL CORD — WOUNDS AND INJURIES
QL933-7	SPINAL CORD / *comparative anatomy*
QM465	SPINAL CORD / *human anatomy*
QP371-5	SPINAL CORD / *physiology*
RD690	SPINAL IRRITATION
RZ399.S7	*SPINAL THERAPY* **SEE** SPONDYLOTHERAPY
QK495.E	SPINDLE-TREE
RS165.E	SPINDLE-TREE / *vegetable drugs*
DS419	SPINDLE-WHORLS / *buddhist antiquities*
TJ1167	SPINDLES (MACHINE-TOOLS)
RD768	SPINE — ABNORMITIES AND DEFORMITIES
RD533	SPINE — WOUNDS AND INJURIES
QL821	SPINE / *comparative anatomy*
QM111	SPINE / *human anatomy*
RD768	*SPINE-CURVATURE* **SEE** SPINE — ABNORMITIES AND DEFORMITIES
QE391.S	SPINEL / *mineralogy*
QK923	SPINES (BOTANY) / *ecology*
QK650	SPINES (BOTANY) / *morphology*
QL385	SPINES (ZOOLOGY)
ML650-697	*SPINET* **SEE** HARPSICHORD / *history and construction*
TS1483	SPINNING MACHINERY
QA862.T7	*SPINNING-TOP* **SEE** TOP / *dynamics*
TS1484	SPINNING-WHEEL
TS1480-1487	SPINNING
GN432	SPINNING / *primitive*
TT206	*SPINNING, METAL* **SEE** METAL-SPINNING
QA433	SPINOR ANALYSIS
QA433	*SPINOR CALCULUS* **SEE** SPINOR ANALYSIS
QA433	*SPINORS, THEORY OF* **SEE** SPINOR ANALYSIS
HQ800	*SPINSTERS* **SEE** SINGLE WOMEN
TJ192	*SPIRAL GEARING* **SEE** GEARING, SPIRAL
TJ901	*SPIRAL PUMP* **SEE** ARCHIMEDEAN SCREW
QA567	SPIRALS / *geometry*
NA2930	SPIRES / *architecture*
BR355.S7	SPIRES, DIET OF, 1529
RC112	SPIRILLOSIS
Z48	*SPIRIT DUPLICATING* **SEE** FLUID COPYING PROCESSES
E83.857	SPIRIT LAKE, IOWA — MASSACRE, 1857
TA606-610	*SPIRIT LEVELING* **SEE** LEVELING
TP517	*SPIRIT-METER* **SEE** ALCOHOLOMETER
BT120-123	*SPIRIT, HOLY* **SEE** HOLY SPIRIT
BD331	*SPIRITISM* **SEE** SPIRITUALISM / *metaphysics*
B851-4695	*SPIRITISM* **SEE** SPIRITUALISM / *philosophic systems*
B841	*SPIRITISM* **SEE** SPIRITUALISM / *philosophic systems*
BF1001-1389	*SPIRITISM* **SEE** SPIRITUALISM / *spiritism*
BP166.89	SPIRITS (ISLAM)
BT960-962	SPIRITS
TP589-618	*SPIRITS, ALCOHOLIC* **SEE** LIQUORS
BV5083	*SPIRITS, DISCERNMENT OF* **SEE** DISCERNMENT OF SPIRITS
BV5053	SPIRITUAL DIRECTION
BX2350.7	SPIRITUAL DIRECTION / *catholic*
BX2348	SPIRITUAL DIRECTION / *monastic*
BX382.5	SPIRITUAL DIRECTION / *orthodox eastern*
BT769	*SPIRITUAL GIFTS* **SEE** GIFTS, SPIRITUAL
BT732.5	*SPIRITUAL HEALING* **SEE** FAITH-CURE
RZ400-401	*SPIRITUAL HEALING* **SEE** FAITH-CURE / *medical aspects*
BV4485-4596	SPIRITUAL LIFE
BX2349-2373	SPIRITUAL LIFE / *catholic*
BV4490-4510	*SPIRITUAL-MINDEDNESS* **SEE** SPIRITUALITY
BD331	SPIRITUALISM / *metaphysics*
B841	SPIRITUALISM / *philosophic systems*
B851-4695	SPIRITUALISM / *philosophic systems*
BF1001-1389	SPIRITUALISM / *spiritism*
BV4490-4510	SPIRITUALITY
M1670-1671	*SPIRITUALS, NEGRO* **SEE** NEGRO SPIRITUALS
TP589-618	*SPIRITUOUS LIQUORS* **SEE** LIQUORS
RC184.S5	SPIROCHAETOSIS
QR251	SPIROCHAETOSIS / *pathogenic protozoa*
RC778	*SPIROCHAETOSIS, BRONCHOPULMONARY* **SEE** BRONCHOPULMONARY SPIROCHAETOSIS
RC184.S5	*SPIROCHETOSIS* **SEE** SPIROCHAETOSIS
QR251	*SPIROCHETOSIS* **SEE** SPIROCHAETOSIS / *pathogenic protozoa*
DA87.7 1797	SPITHEAD MUTINY, 1797
QL939	*SPLANCHNIC NERVES* **SEE** NERVES, SPLANCHNIC
QM471	*SPLANCHNIC NERVES* **SEE** NERVES, SPLANCHNIC
QC159	SPLASHES
RC645	SPLEEN — DISEASES
RC184.T6	SPLEEN — HYDATIDS
RC280.S	SPLEEN — TUMORS
QL868	SPLEEN / *comparative anatomy*
QM371	SPLEEN / *human anatomy*
QP187	SPLEEN / *physiology*
SF805	*SPLENETIC FEVER IN CATTLE* **SEE** TEXAS FEVER
VM533	*SPLICING* **SEE** KNOTS AND SPLICES
RD113	SPLINTS (SURGERY)
QE394.S	SPODUMENE / *gems*
QE391.S	SPODUMENE / *minerals*
JK681-699	*SPOILS SYSTEM* **SEE** CIVIL SERVICE REFORM / *u.s.*
JF1081	*SPOILS SYSTEM* **SEE** CORRUPTION (IN POLITICS)
JK-JQ	*SPOILS SYSTEM* **SEE** CORRUPTION (IN POLITICS) / *by country*
JS	*SPOILS SYSTEM* **SEE** CORRUPTION (IN POLITICS) / *etc.*
E99.S68	SPOKAN INDIANS
E99.S68	*SPOKANE INDIANS* **SEE** SPOKAN INDIANS
PM8821-3	SPOKIL (ARTIFICIAL LANGUAGE)
RZ399.S7	SPONDYLOTHERAPY
QL374	SPONGES — ANATOMY
QL371-4	SPONGES
SH396	SPONGES / *fisheries*
QE775	SPONGES, FOSSIL
BX1939.S65	SPONSORS (CANON LAW)
TN817	*SPONTANEOUS COMBUSTION* **SEE** COMBUSTION, SPONTANEOUS / *coal storage*
TH9198	*SPONTANEOUS COMBUSTION* **SEE** COMBUSTION, SPONTANEOUS / *fire prevention*
TN313-315	*SPONTANEOUS COMBUSTION* **SEE** COMBUSTION, SPONTANEOUS / *mine accidents*
QH325	SPONTANEOUS GENERATION
RA1171	*SPONTANEOUS HUMAN COMBUSTION* **SEE** COMBUSTION, SPONTANEOUS HUMAN
QL696.A7	SPOONBILLS
PN6231.S	SPOONERISMS
NK7235	SPOONS / *art industries*
GT2950	SPOONS / *manners and customs*
QC973	SPORADIC E (IONOSPHERE)
QC879	SPORADIC E (IONOSPHERE) / *exploration*
QK662	SPORANGIUM
RC184.S6	SPOROTRICHOSIS

QL368.G8	SPOROZOA
QL368.M8	SPOROZOA
QL368.C7	SPOROZOA
SH401-691	*SPORT FISHING* **SEE** FISHING
SF428.5	*SPORTING DOGS* **SEE** HUNTING DOGS
GV747	SPORTING GOODS — CATALOGS
GV743-7	SPORTING GOODS
PN4784.S6	*SPORTING JOURNALISM* **SEE** SPORTS JOURNALISM
NE960	SPORTING PRINTS
GV731	*SPORTING RULES* **SEE** SPORTS — RULES
RD131	SPORTS — ACCIDENTS AND INJURIES
GV713	SPORTS — ORGANIZATION AND ADMINISTRATION
GV706	SPORTS — PHILOSOPHY
GV195	SPORTS — PICTORIAL WORKS
PN6110.S65	SPORTS — POETRY
GV731	SPORTS — RULES
M1977.S7	SPORTS — SONGS AND MUSIC
GV563	*SPORTS CLUBS* **SEE** ATHLETIC CLUBS
GV708	SPORTS FOR INDIVIDUALS
HV1767	*SPORTS FOR THE BLIND* **SEE** BLIND, PHYSICAL EDUCATION FOR THE
GV709	SPORTS FOR WOMEN
N8250	SPORTS IN ART
PN4784.S6	SPORTS JOURNALISM
GV735	SPORTS OFFICIATING
TR682	*SPORTS PHOTOGRAPHY* **SEE** PHOTOGRAPHY OF SPORTS
GV715	*SPORTS SPECTATORS* **SEE** SPECTATOR CONTROL
GV713	*SPORTS TOURNAMENTS* **SEE** SPORTS — ORGANIZATION AND ADMINISTRATION
GV	SPORTS
GN457	SPORTS / *primitive*
RD131	*SPORTS, INJURIES FROM* **SEE** SPORTS — ACCIDENTS AND INJURIES
GV710	*SPORTS, INTRAMURAL* **SEE** INTRAMURAL SPORTS
TR682	*SPORTS, PHOTOGRAPHY OF* **SEE** PHOTOGRAPHY OF SPORTS
TR682	*SPORTS-PHOTOGRAPHY* **SEE** PHOTOGRAPHY OF SPORTS
QD98	*SPOT ANALYSIS* **SEE** SPOT TESTS (CHEMISTRY)
QD98	*SPOT REACTIONS* **SEE** SPOT TESTS (CHEMISTRY)
QD98	SPOT TESTS (CHEMISTRY)
TK4660	*SPOT WELDING* **SEE** ELECTRIC WELDING
E476.52	SPOTSYLVANIA, BATTLE OF, 1864
RC182.R6	*SPOTTED FEVER OF THE ROCKY MOUNTAINS* **SEE** ROCKY MOUNTAIN SPOTTED FEVER
RC182.R6	*SPOTTED FEVER TICK* **SEE** ROCKY MOUNTAIN SPOTTED FEVER TICK
S662.5	*SPRAY APPLICATION OF LIQUID FERTILIZERS* **SEE** FOLIAR FEEDING
SB953	SPRAYING
RC815	*SPREW* **SEE** THRUSH (MOUTH DISEASE)
RJ463	*SPREW* **SEE** THRUSH (MOUTH DISEASE) / *children*
SB945.G7	*SPRING GRAIN-APHIS* **SEE** GRAIN-LOUSE
QL523.A6	*SPRING GRAIN-APHIS* **SEE** GRAIN-LOUSE / *zoology*
E477.52	SPRING HILL, TENN., BATTLE OF, 1864
QH81	SPRING / *natural history*
E241.S	SPRINGFIELD, N.J., BATTLE OF, 1780
GR690	SPRINGS (IN RELIGION, FOLK-LORE, ETC.) / *folk-lore*
BL450	SPRINGS (IN RELIGION, FOLK-LORE, ETC.) / *religion*
TJ210	SPRINGS (MECHANISM)
GB1001-1197	SPRINGS
GR690	SPRINGS / *folk-lore*
QL503.C6	SPRINGTAIL
TH9336	*SPRINKLING SYSTEMS* **SEE** FIRE SPRINKLERS
GV1069	SPRINTING
SB608.S8	SPRUCE BARK-BEETLE
SB608.S8	SPRUCE BUD-WORM
SD397.S77	SPRUCE
TJ189	*SPUR GEARING* **SEE** GEARING, SPUR
QP921.E6	*SPURRED RYE* **SEE** ERGOT / *experimental pharmacology*
RS165.E7	*SPURRED RYE* **SEE** ERGOT / *pharmacy*
RM666.E8	*SPURRED RYE* **SEE** ERGOT / *therapeutics*
GT5888	SPURS
TL796.5.R	*SPUTNIKS* **SEE** ARTIFICIAL SATELLITES, RUSSIAN
RB51	SPUTUM / *pathology*
QL696.C6	*SQUABS* **SEE** PIGEONS

SF465-472	*SQUABS* **SEE** PIGEONS / *breeding*
HE6239.P	*SQUABS* **SEE** PIGEONS / *carrier pigeons*
UH90	*SQUABS* **SEE** PIGEONS / *military communications*
E99.S7	*SQUAMISH INDIANS* **SEE** SQUAWMISH INDIANS
TH5619	*SQUARE (INSTRUMENT)* **SEE** CARPENTERS' SQUARE
GV1763	SQUARE DANCING
TT840	*SQUARE KNOTTING* **SEE** MACRAME
QA119	SQUARE ROOT
QA49	SQUARE ROOT / *tables*
QA482	SQUARE / *geometry*
QA275	*SQUARES, LEAST* **SEE** LEAST SQUARES
QA165	*SQUARES, MAGIC* **SEE** MAGIC SQUARES
NA9070	*SQUARES, PUBLIC* **SEE** PLAZAS
QA49	SQUARES, TABLES OF
QA467	*SQUARING OF THE CIRCLE* **SEE** CIRCLE-SQUARING
GV1006	SQUASH (GAME)
GV1002-3	SQUASH RACKETS (GAME)
QL523.C	SQUASH-BUGS
SB608.S	SQUASH-BUGS / *pests*
SB347	SQUASH / *culture*
E415.7	SQUATTER SOVEREIGNTY / *american politics*
JK318	SQUATTER SOVEREIGNTY / *constitutional history u.s.*
E99.S7	SQUAWMISH INDIANS
PM2381.S6	SQUAWMISH LANGUAGE
QL638.S34	*SQUETEAGUE* **SEE** WEAKFISH
SH351.B3	*SQUIDHOUND* **SEE** STRIPED BASS
QL430.2	SQUIDS
RE771	*SQUINTING* **SEE** STRABISMUS
QL795.S7	SQUIRRELS — LEGENDS AND STORIES
QL737.R6	SQUIRRELS
QL737.R6	*SQUIRRELS, GROUND* **SEE** GROUND-SQUIRRELS
DS432.S	*SRAWAKS* **SEE** SARAKS
PL4351.S6	SRE LANGUAGE
E470.95	ST. ALBANS CONFEDERATE RAID, 1864
F314	ST. AUGUSTINE EXPEDITION, 1740
F314	ST. AUGUSTINE EXPEDITION, 1743
BX2901-2955	*ST. AUGUSTINE, ORDER OF* **SEE** AUGUSTINIANS
BX4265-8	*ST. AUGUSTINE, ORDER OF* **SEE** AUGUSTINIANS / *women*
DC118	ST. BARTHOLOMEW'S DAY, MASSACRE OF, 1572
BX3001-3055	*ST. BENEDICT, ORDER OF* **SEE** BENEDICTINES
BX4275-8	*ST. BENEDICT, ORDER OF* **SEE** BENEDICTINES / *women*
SF429.S3	ST. BERNARD DOGS
GT4995.S	ST. CECILIA'S DAY
E83.79	ST. CLAIR'S CAMPAIGN, 1791
GT4995.S	ST. DAVID'S DAY
LB3567.G7	ST. DAVID'S DAY / *school festivals gt. brit.*
BX3501-3555	*ST. DOMINIC, ORDER OF* **SEE** DOMINICANS
BX4341-4	*ST. DOMINIC, ORDER OF* **SEE** DOMINICANS / *women*
BX3601-3655	*ST. FRANCIS, ORDER OF* **SEE** FRANCISCANS
BX4361-4	*ST. FRANCIS, ORDER OF* **SEE** FRANCISCANS / *women*
D643.A8-9	ST. GERMAIN, TREATY OF, SEPT. 10, 1919 (AUSTRIA)
D651.C9	ST. GERMAIN, TREATY OF, SEPT. 10, 1919 (CZECHOSLOVAK REPUBLIC)
D651.J9	ST. GERMAIN, TREATY OF, SEPT. 10, 1919 (SERBIA)
DB63 1664	ST. GOTTHARD, HUNGARY, BATTLE OF, 1664
BV70.J	*ST. JOHN THE BAPTIST'S DAY* **SEE** JOHN THE BAPTIST'S DAY
BT1405	*ST. JOHN'S CHRISTIANS* **SEE** MANDAEANS
E233	ST. LEGER'S EXPEDITION, 1777
F474.S2	ST. LOUIS — HISTORY
E517	ST. LOUIS — HISTORY — — CIVIL WAR
D545.S313	ST. MIHIEL, BATTLE OF, 1918
GT4995.S3	ST. PATRICK'S DAY
DP302.B284	*ST. PHILIP'S FORT-SIEGE, 1756* **SEE** PORT MAHON — SIEGE, 1756
DC303.4	*ST. PRIVAT, BATTLE OF, 1870* **SEE** GRAVELOTTE, BATTLE OF, 1870
DP179	ST. QUENTIN, BATTLE OF, 1557
E99.S	ST. REGIS INDIANS
E78.N7	ST. REGIS INDIANS / *new york*
DA87.5 1797	ST. VINCENT (CAPE), BATTLE OF, 1797
RC389	*ST. VITUS'S DANCE* **SEE** CHOREA
TL574.S7	STABILITY OF AEROPLANES
TL547.S7	STABILITY OF AEROPLANES, LATERAL
TL574.S7	STABILITY OF AEROPLANES, LONGITUDINAL
TL716	STABILITY OF HELICOPTERS
TL784.S7	STABILITY OF ROCKETS
VM159	STABILITY OF SHIPS

QA871	STABILITY / *stability of systems*
HB3730	*STABILIZATION, ECONOMIC* **SEE** ECONOMIC STABILIZATION
NA8340	STABLES / *architecture*
SF91-92	STABLES / *fittings*
RA582	STABLES / *stables and public health*
Z711	*STACK ACCESS IN LIBRARIES* **SEE** OPEN AND CLOSED SHELVES
Z685	*STACKS (FOR BOOKS)* **SEE** SHELVING (FOR BOOKS)
SB186	STACKS (HAY, GRAIN, ETC.)
QC102	*STADE (STANDARD OF LENGTH)* **SEE** STADIUM (STANDARD OF LENGTH)
HF2109.H2	STADE TOLLS / *hanover*
TA588	STADIA MEASUREMENTS
TA588	STADIA TABLES
NA6860	STADIA / *architecture*
QC102	STADIUM (STANDARD OF LENGTH)
BV168.S7	STAFF, PASTORAL
SF429.T3	*STAFFORDSHIRE BULLTERRIERS* **SEE** STAFFORDSHIRE TERRIERS
NK4087.S6	STAFFORDSHIRE POTTERY
SF429.T3	STAFFORDSHIRE TERRIERS
GT2220	STAFFS (STICKS, CANES, ETC.)
UB220-225	*STAFFS, MILITARY* **SEE** ARMIES — STAFFS
SF429.D4	*STAG-HOUNDS* **SEE** DEER-HOUNDS
PN2205-2217	*STAGE* **SEE** ACTORS
PN2205-2217	*STAGE* **SEE** ACTRESSES
PN1600-1861	*STAGE* **SEE** DRAMA
PN2000-3299	*STAGE* **SEE** THEATER
NA6820-6845	*STAGE CONSTRUCTION* **SEE** THEATERS — CONSTRUCTION
MT955	*STAGE GUIDES* **SEE** MUSICAL REVUES, COMEDIES, ETC. — STAGE GUIDES
MT955	*STAGE GUIDES* **SEE** OPERAS — STAGE GUIDES
PN2091.S8	*STAGE GUIDES* **SEE** THEATERS — STAGE-SETTING AND SCENERY
PN2091.E4	STAGE LIGHTING
PN2091.M6	*STAGE MODELS* **SEE** THEATERS — MODELS
PN1995	*STAGE SCENERY* **SEE** MOVING-PICTURES — SETTING AND SCENERY
PN2091.S8	*STAGE SCENERY* **SEE** THEATERS — STAGE-SETTING AND SCENERY
Z652.D7	*STAGE-RIGHT* **SEE** COPYRIGHT — DRAMA
PN1995	*STAGE-SETTING* **SEE** MOVING-PICTURES — SETTING AND SCENERY
PN2091.S8	*STAGE-SETTING* **SEE** THEATERS — STAGE-SETTING AND SCENERY
SF305-7	*STAGECOACH LINES* **SEE** COACHING
SF305-7	*STAGECOACHES* **SEE** COACHING
SB618.S8	STAGGER-GRASS
SF967.G7	*STAGGERS, GRASS* **SEE** GRASS TETANY
TH5281	*STAGING (CONSTRUCTION)* **SEE** SCAFFOLDING
PN1995	*STAGING* **SEE** MOVING-PICTURES — SETTING AND SCENERY
PN2091.S8	*STAGING* **SEE** THEATERS — STAGE-SETTING AND SCENERY
NK5300-5410	*STAINED GLASS* **SEE** GLASS PAINTING AND STAINING
TA479.S	*STAINLESS STEEL* **SEE** STEEL, STAINLESS
QH237	STAINS AND STAINING (MICROSCOPY)
TT345	STAINS AND STAINING / *wood-staining*
TH5667-5680	STAIR BUILDING
NA3060	STAIRCASES / *architecture*
TH5667-5680	STAIRCASES / *building*
D764	STALINGRAD, BATTLE OF, 1942-1943
NA5075	*STALLS, CHOIR* **SEE** CHOIR-STALLS
PM2381.S8	STALO LANGUAGE
DA195.8	STAMFORD BRIDGE, BATTLE OF, 1066
RC424	STAMMERING
E215.2	STAMP ACT, 1765
HJ5315	*STAMP COLLECTING AND STAMP COLLECTORS* **SEE** REVENUE-STAMPS — COLLECTORS AND COLLECTING
HJ5301-5515	*STAMP TAX* **SEE** STAMP-DUTIES
HJ5321-5374	*STAMP TAX* **SEE** STAMP-DUTIES / *u.s.*
HE6221	*STAMP-ALBUMS* **SEE** POSTAGE-STAMPS — ALBUMS
HE6187-6230	*STAMP-COLLECTING AND STAMP-COLLECTORS* **SEE** POSTAGE-STAMPS — COLLECTORS AND COLLECTING
Z661	STAMP-DUTIES — NEWSPAPERS
HJ5301-5515	STAMP-DUTIES
HJ5321-5374	STAMP-DUTIES / *u.s.*

HE6181-5	*STAMPS, POSTAGE* **SEE** POSTAGE-STAMPS
HJ5315	*STAMPS, REVENUE* **SEE** REVENUE-STAMPS
HJ5321-5515	*STAMPS, REVENUE* **SEE** REVENUE-STAMPS / *by country*
TS1920	*STAMPS, RUBBER* **SEE** RUBBER STAMPS / *manufacture*
HJ5315	*STAMPS, TELEGRAPH* **SEE** TELEGRAPH STAMPS
HJ5375-5515	*STAMPS, TELEGRAPH* **SEE** TELEGRAPH STAMPS / *other countries*
HJ5321.Z7	*STAMPS, TELEGRAPH* **SEE** TELEGRAPH STAMPS / *u.s.*
TD489	STAND-PIPES
TL557.A8	STANDARD ATMOSPHERE / *aeronautics*
QC603	STANDARD CELLS
HD6977-7080	*STANDARD OF LIVING* **SEE** COST AND STANDARD OF LIVING
HG201-1490	*STANDARD OF VALUE* **SEE** MONEY
GN436.2	*STANDARD OF VALUE* **SEE** MONEY / *primitive*
HB201-5	*STANDARD OF VALUE* **SEE** VALUE / *economic theory*
HG223	*STANDARD OF VALUE* **SEE** VALUE / *standard of value*
QB223	*STANDARD TIME* **SEE** TIME — SYSTEMS AND STANDARDS
HD62	STANDARDIZATION / *economics*
T59	STANDARDIZATION / *engineering management*
TA368	STANDARDIZATION / *engineering materials*
QC100	STANDARDIZATION / *weights and measures*
QA76.8.S4	*STANDARDS EASTERN AUTOMATIC COMPUTER* **SEE** SEAC COMPUTER
TK7889.S4	*STANDARDS EASTERN AUTOMATIC COMPUTER* **SEE** SEAC COMPUTER / *engineering*
QC101	STANDARDS OF LENGTH
QC105	STANDARDS OF MASS
QA76.8.S8	*STANDARDS WESTERN AUTOMATIC COMPUTER* **SEE** SWAC COMPUTER
TK7889.S8	*STANDARDS WESTERN AUTOMATIC COMPUTER* **SEE** SWAC COMPUTER / *engineering*
QC537	*STANDARDS, ELECTRIC* **SEE** ELECTRIC STANDARDS
TA368	STANDARDS, ENGINEERING
UC590-595	STANDARDS, MILITARY
U104	STANDING ARMY
GN231	*STANDING ON ONE FOOT* **SEE** ONE-LEG RESTING POSITION
TN470-479	*STANNARIES* **SEE** TIN MINES AND MINING
E241.S7	STANWIX, FORT, N.Y. — SIEGE, 1777
E99.I7	STANWIX, FORT, TREATY OF, 1768 / *iroquois indians*
E99.I7	STANWIX, FORT, TREATY OF, 1784 / *iroquois indians*
RC116.S8	STAPHYLOCOCCAL DISEASE
RC116.S8	*STAPHYLOCOCCAL INFECTION* **SEE** STAPHYLOCOCCAL DISEASE
QR82.S7	STAPHYLOCOCCUS
RD525	*STAPHYLORRHAPHY* **SEE** PALATE — SURGERY
HF401.S8	STAPLE SYSTEM / *medieval*
TJ1320	STAPLES AND STAPLING MACHINES
QB6	*STAR CATALOGS* **SEE** STARS — CATALOGS
QB851-3	*STAR CLUSTERS* **SEE** STARS — CLUSTERS
HE6491	STAR ROUTES
QL638.U7	STAR-GAZERS
QK495.P66	*STAR-PINE* **SEE** CLUSTER-PINE / *botany*
SD397.P	*STAR-PINE* **SEE** CLUSTER-PINE / *forestry*
TP415	STARCH INDUSTRY
TP415	STARCH / *chemical technology*
QD321	STARCH / *organic chemistry*
QK887	STARCH / *plant physiology*
QL384.A8	STARFISHES
QE783.A7	STARFISHES, FOSSIL
QC467	STARK EFFECT
QL696.P2	STARLINGS
QB65	STARS — ATLASES
QB801	STARS — ATMOSPHERES
QB6	STARS — CATALOGS
QB881	STARS — CLASSIFICATION
QB851-3	STARS — CLUSTERS
QB816	STARS — COLOR
QB829	STARS — COLOR
QB875	STARS — CONSTITUTION
QB903	STARS — DENSITY / *double stars*
QB819	STARS — DISTRIBUTION
QB7-9	STARS — EPHEMERIDES
QB815	STARS — MAGNITUDES
QB814	STARS — MASSES

QB901	STARS — MOTION IN LINE OF SIGHT
QB802	STARS — NAMES
QB6	STARS — OBSERVATIONS
QB815	STARS — PHOTOGRAPHIC MEASUREMENTS
QB121	STARS — PHOTOGRAPHIC MEASUREMENTS
QB811	STARS — PROPER MOTION
QB817	STARS — RADIATION
QB871-903	STARS — SPECTRA
QB817	STARS — TEMPERATURE
GR625	STARS (IN RELIGION, FOLK-LORE, ETC.)
QB801-903	STARS
GR625	STARS / folk-lore
QB821-9	*STARS, BINARY* **SEE** STARS, DOUBLE
QB903	*STARS, BINARY* **SEE** STARS, DOUBLE / spectra
QB421	*STARS, BINARY* **SEE** STARS, DOUBLE / theory
QB821-3	STARS, DOUBLE — ORBITS
QB821-9	STARS, DOUBLE
QB903	STARS, DOUBLE / spectra
QB421	STARS, DOUBLE / theory
QB814	*STARS, DOUBLE-MASSES* **SEE** STARS — MASSES
QB741-755	*STARS, FALLING* **SEE** METEORS
QB841	STARS, NEW
QB895	STARS, NEW / spectra
QB835-7	STARS, VARIABLE
QB895	STARS, VARIABLE / spectra
QB815	*STARS-ABSOLUTE MAGNITUDE* **SEE** STARS — MAGNITUDES
QB813	*STARS-DISTANCE* **SEE** PARALLAX — STARS
QB167	*STARS-DISTANCE* **SEE** PARALLAX — STARS / correction of observations
QB851-3	*STARS-GROUPS* **SEE** STARS — CLUSTERS
QB813	*STARS-PARALLAX* **SEE** PARALLAX — STARS
QB167	*STARS-PARALLAX* **SEE** PARALLAX — STARS / correction of observations
QB901	*STARS-RADIAL VELOCITY* **SEE** STARS — MOTION IN LINE OF SIGHT
RA1116	STARVATION / medical jurisprudence
HE9915-9925	*STATE AND AERONAUTICS* **SEE** AERONAUTICS AND STATE
N8700-8850	*STATE AND ART* **SEE** ART AND STATE
BV629-631	*STATE AND CHURCH* **SEE** CHURCH AND STATE / general
JC510-514	*STATE AND CHURCH* **SEE** CHURCH AND STATE / political theory
LC71-188	*STATE AND EDUCATION* **SEE** EDUCATION AND STATE
SD561-668	*STATE AND FORESTRY* **SEE** FOREST POLICY
LC171-182	*STATE AND HIGHER EDUCATION* **SEE** HIGHER EDUCATION AND STATE
HD3611-3790	*STATE AND INDUSTRY* **SEE** INDUSTRY AND STATE
HG8111-8117	*STATE AND INSURANCE* **SEE** INSURANCE — STATE SUPERVISION
HD7090-7250	*STATE AND INSURANCE* **SEE** INSURANCE, SOCIAL
BP173.6	*STATE AND ISLAM* **SEE** ISLAM AND STATE
BM538.S7	*STATE AND JUDAISM* **SEE** JUDAISM AND STATE
PN51	*STATE AND LITERATURE* **SEE** LITERATURE AND STATE ן
ML3795	*STATE AND MUSIC* **SEE** MUSIC AND STATE
HE1051-1081	*STATE AND RAILROADS* **SEE** RAILROADS AND STATE
HE2757	*STATE AND RAILROADS* **SEE** RAILROADS AND STATE / u.s.
BL65.S8	*STATE AND RELIGION* **SEE** RELIGION AND STATE
Q125-7	*STATE AND SCIENCE* **SEE** SCIENCE AND STATE / history
HJ8061	STATE BANKRUPTCY
QL699	STATE BIRDS
HG4946-8	STATE BONDS / u.s.
BV633	*STATE CHURCHES* **SEE** ESTABLISHED CHURCHES / ecclesiastical aspects
JK2413-2428	*STATE CONSTITUTIONS* **SEE** CONSTITUTIONS, STATE
JK18-19	*STATE CONSTITUTIONS* **SEE** CONSTITUTIONS, STATE
LB2809	STATE DEPARTMENTS OF EDUCATION
Q181	STATE ENCOURAGEMENT OF SCIENCE, LITERATURE, AND ART / science
N8750	STATE ENCOURAGEMENT OF SCIENCE, LITERATURE, AND ART / art
JC518-519	STATE ENCOURAGEMENT OF SCIENCE, LITERATURE, AND ART / political science
S567	STATE FARMS — ACCOUNTING
QK85	STATE FLOWERS
JK2408-9595	STATE GOVERNMENTS / u.s.

JK-JQ	*STATE LIABILITY* **SEE** GOVERNMENT LIABILITY
JF1621	*STATE LIABILITY* **SEE** GOVERNMENT LIABILITY
Z675.G7	*STATE LIBRARIES* **SEE** LIBRARIES, GOVERNMENTAL, ADMINISTRATIVE, ETC.
Z716	*STATE LIBRARY COMMISSIONS* **SEE** LIBRARY COMMISSIONS
Z732	*STATE LIBRARY COMMISSIONS* **SEE** LIBRARY COMMISSIONS / state library commission reports
RA	*STATE MEDICINE* **SEE** MEDICINE, STATE
HD3853-6	*STATE MONOPOLIES* **SEE** GOVERNMENT MONOPOLIES
JF1800	STATE OF SIEGE / martial law
HD3840-4420	*STATE OWNERSHIP* **SEE** GOVERNMENT OWNERSHIP
HE1051-1081	*STATE OWNERSHIP OF RAILROADS* **SEE** RAILROADS AND STATE
HE2757	*STATE OWNERSHIP OF RAILROADS* **SEE** RAILROADS AND STATE / u.s.
HD82-85	*STATE PLANNING* **SEE** ECONOMIC POLICY
HD	*STATE PLANNING* **SEE** ECONOMIC POLICY / by industry
HF1401-2580	*STATE PLANNING* **SEE** ECONOMIC POLICY / hc
NA9000-9284	*STATE PLANNING* **SEE** REGIONAL PLANNING
HV7965-7985	*STATE POLICE* **SEE** POLICE, STATE
HV7571	*STATE POLICE* **SEE** POLICE, STATE / by state
BV633	*STATE RELIGION* **SEE** ESTABLISHED CHURCHES / ecclesiastical aspects
JK-JQ	*STATE RESPONSIBILITY* **SEE** GOVERNMENT LIABILITY
JF1621	*STATE RESPONSIBILITY* **SEE** GOVERNMENT LIABILITY
JK310-325	STATE RIGHTS
LB2809	*STATE SCHOOL SYSTEMS* **SEE** STATE DEPARTMENTS OF EDUCATION
M1657-8	STATE SONGS
JX4053	STATE SUCCESSION
HJ2391-2442	*STATE TAXATION* **SEE** TAXATION, STATE
HJ2385	*STATE TAXATION* **SEE** TAXATION, STATE
LB2329.5	STATE UNIVERSITIES AND COLLEGES
HD3611-3616	*STATE, CORPORATE* **SEE** CORPORATE STATE / economic history
JC481	*STATE, CORPORATE* **SEE** CORPORATE STATE / fascism
D-F	*STATE, HEADS OF* **SEE** HEADS OF STATE
JF251	*STATE, HEADS OF* **SEE** HEADS OF STATE
JC	STATE, THE
JA81-84	*STATE, THE-HISTORY OF THEORIES* **SEE** POLITICAL SCIENCE — HISTORY
JK2408-9595	STATEHOOD (AMERICAN POLITICS)
JX4231.S8	STATELESSNESS
GV1485	STATES (GAME)
JX4053	*STATES, CREATION OF* **SEE** STATE SUCCESSION
HX806-811	*STATES, IDEAL* **SEE** UTOPIAS
LC2601-5	STATES, NEW — EDUCATION
JC365	STATES, SMALL
JX4053	*STATES, SUCCESSION OF* **SEE** STATE SUCCESSION
JK310-325	*STATES' RIGHTS* **SEE** STATE RIGHTS
D108	STATESMEN / general biography
D399.6	STATESMEN / 19th century
D352.5	STATESMEN / 19th century
D412.6	STATESMEN / 20th century
QC573	*STATIC ELECTRICITY* **SEE** ELECTRIC MACHINES
QC571-595	*STATIC ELECTRICITY* **SEE** ELECTROSTATICS
TK2799	*STATIC FREQUENCY CHANGERS* **SEE** FREQUENCY MULTIPLIERS
QA821-835	STATICS
VK584.S7	STATION-POINTER / navigation
TJ268-740	*STATIONARY ENGINEERING* **SEE** STEAM ENGINEERING
HD9820-9839	STATIONERY TRADE
HF5716.S6	STATIONERY TRADE / tables
TS1228-1268	STATIONERY / manufacture
BX2040	STATIONS OF THE CROSS
UA26	*STATIONS, MILITARY* **SEE** MILITARY POSTS / u.s.
TF300-308	*STATIONS, RAILROAD* **SEE** RAILROADS — STATIONS
HE1613-1614	*STATIONS, RAILROAD* **SEE** RAILROADS — STATIONS / location
TK6211-6281	*STATIONS, TELEPHONE* **SEE** TELEPHONE STATIONS
QB149	STATISTICAL ASTRONOMY
HA48	*STATISTICAL DIAGRAMS* **SEE** STATISTICS — CHARTS, TABLES, ETC.
HA31	*STATISTICAL DIAGRAMS* **SEE** STATISTICS — GRAPHIC METHODS

QA276	*STATISTICAL INFERENCE* **SEE** MATHEMATICAL STATISTICS
QA273-7	*STATISTICAL INFERENCE* **SEE** PROBABILITIES
HG8781-2	*STATISTICAL INFERENCE* **SEE** PROBABILITIES / *life insurance*
BC141	*STATISTICAL INFERENCE* **SEE** PROBABILITIES / *logic*
GA109.8	*STATISTICAL MAPS* **SEE** MAPS, STATISTICAL
QC175	STATISTICAL MECHANICS
QC311.5	STATISTICAL THERMODYNAMICS
HA48	STATISTICS — CHARTS, TABLES, ETC.
HA31	STATISTICS — GRAPHIC METHODS
QA276.5	*STATISTICS OF SAMPLING* **SEE** SAMPLING (STATISTICS)
HA	STATISTICS
QA276	*STATISTICS, MATHEMATICAL* **SEE** MATHEMATICAL STATISTICS
TJ990	*STATOR BLADES (COMPRESSORS)* **SEE** COMPRESSORS — BLADES
NB	STATUES
NK7900-7999	*STATUETTES* **SEE** BRONZES / *art*
TS570	*STATUETTES* **SEE** BRONZES / *technology*
NB960-1113	*STATUETTES* **SEE** IDOLS AND IMAGES / *art*
NK5800-5998	*STATUETTES* **SEE** IVORIES / *art industries*
TS1050	*STATUETTES* **SEE** IVORIES / *manufacture*
NK5750	*STATUETTES* **SEE** JADE / *art industries*
QE391.J2	*STATUETTES* **SEE** JADE / *mineralogy*
NK4165	*STATUETTES* **SEE** MING CH'I / *chinese art objects*
GT3283	*STATUETTES* **SEE** MING CH'I / *chinese burial customs*
NB145-159	*STATUETTES* **SEE** TERRA-COTTAS / *statuettes*
NB157	*STATUETTES* **SEE** TERRA-COTTAS / *tanagra figurines*
DT62.T6	*STATUETTES* **SEE** USHABTI
JN1409-1410	*STATUTE OF DROGHEDA* **SEE** POYNINGS' LAW
TS890	STAVES AND STAVE TRADE / *manufacture*
TJ270	STEAM — TABLES, CALCULATIONS, ETC.
TJ393	STEAM ACCUMULATORS
RA766.S8	STEAM AS A DISINFECTANT
TL200	*STEAM AUTOMOBILES* **SEE** AUTOMOBILES, STEAM
TJ280.A6	STEAM ENGINEERING — EXAMINATIONS, QUESTIONS, ETC.
TJ268-740	STEAM ENGINEERING
TJ271	STEAM FLOW
TT990	*STEAM LAUNDRY* **SEE** LAUNDRY, STEAM
TF495	STEAM MOTOR-CARS / *railroads*
TJ403	STEAM POWER-PLANTS — BINARY VAPOR SYSTEMS
TJ395-412	STEAM POWER-PLANTS
TJ412	STEAM POWER-PLANTS — ACCESSORIES — — CATALOGS
TE223-7	*STEAM ROAD-ROLLERS* **SEE** ROAD-ROLLERS
TL230	*STEAM ROAD-WAGONS* **SEE** MOTOR-TRUCKS
TJ299-301	STEAM-BOILER EXPLOSIONS
TJ298-308	STEAM-BOILER INSPECTION
TJ328	STEAM-BOILERS — AIR PREHEATING
TJ296	STEAM-BOILERS — CATALOGS
TJ290	STEAM-BOILERS — DESIGN
TJ284	STEAM-BOILERS — EARLY WORKS TO 1850
TJ297	STEAM-BOILERS — EFFICIENCIES
TJ390-392	STEAM-BOILERS — INCRUSTATIONS
TJ350-357	STEAM-BOILERS — SAFETY APPLIANCES
TJ356	STEAM-BOILERS — SAFETY-PLUGS
TJ281-393	STEAM-BOILERS
VM743.N6	STEAM-BOILERS, MARINE — NICLAUSSE
VM741-750	STEAM-BOILERS, MARINE .
TJ314-315	STEAM-BOILERS, WATER-TUBE
TJ298-308	*STEAM-BOILERS-INSPECTION* **SEE** STEAM-BOILER INSPECTION
TJ705	STEAM-CARRIAGES
TJ478	*STEAM-ENGINE INDICATORS* **SEE** INDICATORS FOR STEAM-ENGINES
TJ515-551	STEAM-ENGINES — CONSTRUCTION
TJ529	STEAM-ENGINES — CYLINDER PACKING
TJ527-9	STEAM-ENGINES — CYLINDERS
TJ515-551	STEAM-ENGINES — DESIGN
TJ464	STEAM-ENGINES — EARLY WORKS TO 1850
TJ475	STEAM-ENGINES — EFFICIENCIES
TJ471	STEAM-ENGINES — HANDBOOKS, MANUALS, ETC.
TJ480	STEAM-ENGINES — MODELS
TJ539	STEAM-ENGINES — SHAFTS
TJ475	STEAM-ENGINES — TESTING
TJ547-8	STEAM-ENGINES — VALVE-GEARS
TJ461-740	STEAM-ENGINES
TJ497-9	STEAM-ENGINES, COMPOUND
TJ507	STEAM-ENGINES, CURIOUS AND UNUSUAL
VM731-775	*STEAM-ENGINES, MARINE* **SEE** MARINE ENGINES
TJ710	*STEAM-ENGINES, PORTABLE* **SEE** PORTABLE ENGINES
TH6703-6729	*STEAM-FITTING* **SEE** PIPE-FITTING / *plumbing*
TJ415-444	*STEAM-FITTING* **SEE** STEAM-PIPES
TH7595	STEAM-HEATING — AIR-VALVES
TH7591	STEAM-HEATING — REGULATORS
TH7561-7599	STEAM-HEATING
TH7570-7578	STEAM-HEATING, LOW PRESSURE
TJ387	*STEAM-INJECTORS* **SEE** INJECTORS / *steam-boilers*
TJ531	STEAM-JACKETS
TJ271	STEAM-METERS
VM600-881	STEAM-NAVIGATION
TJ427	STEAM-PIPE COVERINGS
TJ415-444	STEAM-PIPES
TJ900-925	*STEAM-PUMPS* **SEE** PUMPING MACHINERY
TJ441	STEAM-SEPARATORS
TA735-7	STEAM-SHOVELS
TJ438	STEAM-TRAPS
TJ267.5.D5	STEAM-TURBINE DISKS
TJ737	STEAM-TURBINES — MODELS
TJ735-740	STEAM-TURBINES
TJ267.5.D5	*STEAM-TURBINES-DISKS* **SEE** STEAM-TURBINE DISKS
HE9323-9337	STEAM-WHISTLES / *signaling*
TJ268-272	STEAM
TJ279	STEAM, HIGH-PRESSURE
TJ272	STEAM, SUPERHEATED
VK1250-1257	STEAMBOAT DISASTERS
HE945	STEAMBOAT LINES
VM781-861	STEAMBOATS — FITTINGS
VM298	STEAMBOATS — MODELS
HE599-601	STEAMBOATS — PASSENGER ACCOMMODATION
VM	STEAMBOATS / *construction*
VK	STEAMBOATS / *navigation*
VM451	*STEAMBOATS, ICE-BREAKING* **SEE** ICE-BREAKING VESSELS
HE589-591	*STEAMBOATS-INSPECTION* **SEE** SHIPS — INSPECTION
HE565-6	*STEAMBOATS-REGISTERS* **SEE** SHIP REGISTERS
VM739	*STEAMBOATS-VIBRATION* **SEE** VIBRATION (MARINE ENGINEERING)
HE945	*STEAMSHIP LINES* **SEE** STEAMBOAT LINES
VM	*STEAMSHIPS* **SEE** STEAMBOATS / *construction*
VK	*STEAMSHIPS* **SEE** STEAMBOATS / *navigation*
QP195	STEAPSIN
QD305.A2	STEARATES
QD305.A2	STEARIC ACID
QD305.A2	STEARIN / *chemistry*
TP670	STEARIN / *oils and fats*
TX608.S8	STEARIN / *preservatives*
TN948.T2	*STEATITE* **SEE** TALC / *mineral industries*
QE391.T	*STEATITE* **SEE** TALC / *mineralogy*
QE475	*STEATITE* **SEE** TALC / *petrology*
E477.61	STEDMAN, FORT, BATTLE OF, 1865
QD133	STEEL — ANALYSIS
TN706	STEEL — ELECTROMETALLURGY
TA473	STEEL — FATIGUE
TN693.I7	STEEL — METALLOGRAPHY
TN703-757	STEEL — METALLURGY
HD9514	STEEL — PRICES / *u.s.*
TN731	STEEL — QUENCHING
TA472	STEEL — SPECIFICATIONS
TA466	STEEL — SPECIFICATIONS / *iron and steel*
TA464-479	STEEL — TESTING / *iron and steel*
TA478-9	STEEL ALLOYS / *etc.*
TN693.I7	STEEL ALLOYS / *metallography*
TN756-7	STEEL ALLOYS / *metallurgy*
TA684-5	*STEEL AND IRON BUILDING* **SEE** BUILDING, IRON AND STEEL / *engineering*
TH1610-1621	*STEEL AND IRON BUILDING* **SEE** BUILDING, IRON AND STEEL / *building*
TH1610-1625	*STEEL AND IRON COLUMNS* **SEE** COLUMNS, IRON AND STEEL / *building*
TA492.C7	*STEEL AND IRON COLUMNS* **SEE** COLUMNS, IRON AND STEEL / *testing*

TS350	*STEEL AND IRON PLATES* **SEE** PLATES, IRON AND STEEL
TA492.P7	*STEEL AND IRON PLATES* **SEE** PLATES, IRON AND STEEL / *testing*
VM146-7	*STEEL AND IRON SHIPS* **SEE** SHIPS, IRON AND STEEL
TS320	STEEL BARS
TS320	STEEL CASTINGS
TG416	*STEEL DECK BRIDGES* **SEE** BRIDGES, STEEL PLATE DECK
TS320	STEEL FORGINGS
HF5716.S7	STEEL INDUSTRY AND TRADE — TABLES AND READY-RECKONERS
HD9510-9529	*STEEL INDUSTRY AND TRADE* **SEE** IRON INDUSTRY AND TRADE
HD9510-9529	STEEL INDUSTRY AND TRADE
TA579-581	*STEEL MEASURING-TAPES* **SEE** MEASURING-TAPES / *surveying*
TG416	*STEEL PLATE DECK BRIDGES* **SEE** BRIDGES, STEEL PLATE DECK
TA434-5	STEEL PORTLAND CEMENT / *engineering materials*
TP884.S	STEEL PORTLAND CEMENT / *manufacture*
TH2457	*STEEL ROOFING* **SEE** ROOFING, IRON AND STEEL
TH5619	*STEEL SQUARE* **SEE** CARPENTERS' SQUARE
TS320	*STEEL WORK* **SEE** STEELWORK
TP885.P5	*STEEL-CONCRETE PIPE* **SEE** PIPE, CONCRETE
NE	*STEEL-ENGRAVING* **SEE** ENGRAVING
TS300-360	STEEL-WORKS
TN755	STEEL-WORKS / *metallurgy*
TS300-445	STEEL / *manufacture*
TL699.S8	*STEEL, AIRCRAFT* **SEE** AIRCRAFT STEEL
TA472	STEEL, AUTOMOBILE
TS660	STEEL, GALVANIZED
TA473	STEEL, GALVANIZED / *testing*
TA479.S	STEEL, STAINLESS
TA685	STEEL, STRUCTURAL — TABLES, CALCULATIONS, ETC.
TA472-3	STEEL, STRUCTURAL — TESTING
TA684-5	STEEL, STRUCTURAL / *engineering*
TS350	STEEL, STRUCTURAL / *manufacture*
TS320	STEELWORK
QC107	STEELYARDS
T54	STEEPLE-JACKS
SF359	STEEPLECHASING
NA2930	*STEEPLES* **SEE** SPIRES / *architecture*
HE599-601	*STEERAGE ACCOMMODATION* **SEE** STEAMBOATS — PASSENGER ACCOMMODATION
VM841-5	STEERING-GEAR
Z103-4	*STEGANOGRAPHY* **SEE** CRYPTOGRAPHY
QL696.S6	STEGANOPODES
QE868.S8	STEGOCEPHALI
QL737.U5	*STEINBOCK* **SEE** BOUQUETIN / *zoology*
DT62.S8	STELE (ARCHAEOLOGY)
QK686	STELE (BOTANY)
QK646	STELE (BOTANY)
QB801	*STELLAR ATMOSPHERES* **SEE** STARS — ATMOSPHERES
QB814	*STELLAR MASSES* **SEE** STARS — MASSES
QB813	*STELLAR PARALLAX* **SEE** PARALLAX — STARS
QB167	*STELLAR PARALLAX* **SEE** PARALLAX — STARS / *correction of observations*
QB149	*STELLAR STATISTICS* **SEE** STATISTICAL ASTRONOMY
TS650	STELLITE / *manufacture*
TA490	STELLITE / *testing*
UF620.S8	*STEN GUN* **SEE** STEN MACHINE CARBINE
UF620.S8	STEN MACHINE CARBINE
TT273	*STENCIL PRINTING* **SEE** SCREEN PROCESS PRINTING
NE1843-4	*STENCIL PRINTING* **SEE** SERIGRAPHY / *art*
NK8650	STENCIL WORK / *art*
TT270	STENCILS AND STENCIL CUTTING
HF5547	STENOGRAPHERS / *business manuals*
Z56	STENOGRAPHERS / *shorthand*
Z53	STENOGRAPHERS / *shorthand*
Z53-100	*STENOGRAPHY* **SEE** SHORTHAND
Z54-57	*STENOGRAPHY* **SEE** SHORTHAND / *english*
Z51	STENOTYPY
QL865	*STENSON'S DUCT* **SEE** PAROTID GLANDS / *comparative anatomy*
QM325	*STENSON'S DUCT* **SEE** PAROTID GLANDS / *human anatomy*
QP191	*STENSON'S DUCT* **SEE** PAROTID GLANDS / *physiology*
TJ1067	*STEP BEARINGS* **SEE** PIVOT BEARINGS
QE391.S	STEPHANITE
E356.S7	STEPHENSON, FORT, OHIO, DEFENSE OF, 1813
GB571-8	STEPPES
QD481	STEREOCHEMISTRY
QA465	*STEREOMETRY* **SEE** MENSURATION / *mathematics*
T50-51	*STEREOMETRY* **SEE** MENSURATION / *technology*
TK7882.S7	STEREOPHONIC SOUND SYSTEMS
TR693	*STEREOPHOTOGRAMMETRY* **SEE** PHOTOGRAMMETRY
TA593	*STEREOPHOTOGRAMMETRY* **SEE** PHOTOGRAMMETRY / *surveying*
TR780	*STEREOPHOTOGRAPHY* **SEE** PHOTOGRAPHY, STEREOSCOPIC
GA109	STEREOPLANIGRAPH
QC373.S8	STEREOSCOPE
TR780	*STEREOSCOPIC PHOTOGRAPHY* **SEE** PHOTOGRAPHY, STEREOSCOPIC
TR199	STEREOSCOPIC VIEWS / *catalogs*
TA672	STEREOTOMY
Z252	STEREOTYPING
SF881	STERILITY IN ANIMALS
QK827	STERILITY IN PLANTS
RG201	STERILITY / *female*
RC889	STERILITY / *male*
HB875	*STERILIZATION (BIRTH CONTROL)* **SEE** CONCEPTION — PREVENTION / *neo-malthusianism*
RG136	*STERILIZATION (BIRTH CONTROL)* **SEE** CONCEPTION — PREVENTION
HQ763-6	*STERILIZATION (BIRTH CONTROL)* **SEE** CONCEPTION — PREVENTION / *limitation of offspring*
HV4989	STERILIZATION OF CRIMINALS AND DEFECTIVES
QR69	STERILIZATION / *bacteriology*
TX611	STERILIZATION / *home economics*
HE566.P3	*STERN-WHEELERS* **SEE** PADDLE STEAMERS
QM691	STERNUM — ABNORMITIES AND DEFORMITIES
QL821	STERNUM / *comparative anatomy*
QM113	STERNUM / *human anatomy*
HD8039.L8-82	*STEVEDORES* **SEE** LONGSHOREMEN
VK235	*STEVEDORING* **SEE** CARGO HANDLING
BT378.U5	*STEWARD, UNJUST (PARABLE)* **SEE** UNJUST STEWARD (PARABLE)
TX921	STEWARDS / *manuals*
BV772	STEWARDSHIP, CHRISTIAN
QD181.S3	*STIBIUM* **SEE** ANTIMONY / *chemistry*
TN799.A6	*STIBIUM* **SEE** ANTIMONY / *metallurgy*
TN490.A6	*STIBIUM* **SEE** ANTIMONY / *mining*
Z110.S8	STICHOMETRY
PA3136	STICHOMYTHIA / *classical literature*
PA3031	STICHOMYTHIA / *classical literature*
QE391.S8	STICHTITE
GV1141	STICK FIGHTING
GT2220	*STICKS* **SEE** STAFFS (STICKS, CANES, ETC.)
PL4341-4	STIENG LANGUAGE
BV5091.S7	STIGMATIZATION
PQ4094-9	*STILE NUOVO (ITALIAN POETRY)* **SEE** ITALIAN POETRY — EARLY TO 1400
RG631	STILL-BIRTH
ND1390-1400	STILL-LIFE PAINTING
ND2290-2305	STILL-LIFE PAINTING / *water-color*
E99.S	STILLAQUAMISH INDIANS
E241.S2	*STILLWATER, BATTLE OF, 1777* **SEE** SARATOGA CAMPAIGN, 1777
QE391.S	STILPNOMELANE
GV1085	STILTS
RM332	STIMULANTS / *therapeutics*
QL568.M	STINGLESS BEES
NE1795	STIPPLE ENGRAVERS
NE1795	STIPPLE ENGRAVING
NE1795	STIPPLE ENGRAVINGS
NE1795	*STIPPLING* **SEE** STIPPLE ENGRAVING
QK649	STIPULES (BOTANY)
TP156.M5	*STIRRERS (MACHINERY)* **SEE** MIXING MACHINERY
SF1-121	STOCK AND STOCK-BREEDING
SF757.8	*STOCK AND STOCK-BREEDING-RADIATION EFFECTS* **SEE** DOMESTIC ANIMALS, EFFECT OF RADIATION ON
HF5421	*STOCK BROKERS* **SEE** BROKERS
HG4621	*STOCK BROKERS* **SEE** BROKERS / *stockbrokers*
HD2709-2930	STOCK COMPANIES / *corporations*

HG4001-4480	STOCK COMPANIES / *finance*
HF5681.S8	*STOCK CONTROL* **SEE** INVENTORIES
HF5495	*STOCK CONTROL* **SEE** STORES OR STOCK-ROOM KEEPING
TS160	*STOCK CONTROL* **SEE** STORES OR STOCK-ROOM KEEPING / *factory*
HG4001-4280	*STOCK CORPORATIONS* **SEE** CORPORATIONS / *finance*
HD2709-2930	*STOCK CORPORATIONS* **SEE** CORPORATIONS / *theory and policy*
HF5681.S8	*STOCK IN TRADE* **SEE** INVENTORIES
SF998	STOCK INSPECTION
SF621-723	STOCK INSPECTION / *by country*
HG4551-4595	*STOCK MARKET* **SEE** STOCK-EXCHANGE
PN6231.S73	STOCK OWNERSHIP — ANECDOTES, FACETIAE, SATIRE, ETC.
HD2970-3110	*STOCK OWNERSHIP FOR EMPLOYEES* **SEE** EMPLOYEE OWNERSHIP / *profit-sharing*
HD2781.S7	*STOCK OWNERSHIP FOR EMPLOYEES* **SEE** EMPLOYEE OWNERSHIP / *stockholders*
HG4555-6	STOCK-EXCHANGE — LAW
HG4551-4595	STOCK-EXCHANGE
HF5686.B65	*STOCK-EXCHANGE-ACCOUNTING* **SEE** BROKERS — ACCOUNTING
SF115-121	STOCK-JUDGING
SF85	STOCK-RANGES
HF5495	*STOCK-ROOM KEEPING* **SEE** STORES OR STOCK-ROOM KEEPING
TS160	*STOCK-ROOM KEEPING* **SEE** STORES OR STOCK-ROOM KEEPING / *factory*
HF5681.S8	*STOCK-TAKING* **SEE** INVENTORIES
SF967.H	*STOCK-YARDS FEVER* **SEE** HEMORRHAGIC SEPTICEMIA OF CATTLE
SF967.H	*STOCK-YARDS PNEUMONIA* **SEE** HEMORRHAGIC SEPTICEMIA OF CATTLE
TS1970-1971	STOCK-YARDS
HD9410-9441	STOCK-YARDS / *economics*
SF1-121	*STOCKBREEDING* **SEE** STOCK AND STOCK-BREEDING
E99.S8	STOCKBRIDGE INDIANS
HF5421	*STOCKBROKERS* **SEE** BROKERS
HG4621	*STOCKBROKERS* **SEE** BROKERS / *stockbrokers*
DL699-700	STOCKHOLM — MASSACRE, 1520
DL836	STOCKHOLM, TREATY OF, 1855
SH	*STOCKING OF STREAMS, ETC.* **SEE** FISH-CULTURE
TT679-695	*STOCKINGS* **SEE** HOSIERY / *manufacture*
HG4537	STOCKS — TABLES, ETC.
HG4661	STOCKS
HG4751-5990	STOCKS / *special or local*
HJ5901-5919	*STOCKS-TAXATION* **SEE** TAXATION OF BONDS, SECURITIES, ETC.
HD2781	*STOCKS-VALUATION* **SEE** CORPORATIONS — VALUATION / *u.s.*
CN350	STOICHEDON INSCRIPTIONS
QD42	*STOICHIOMETRY* **SEE** CHEMISTRY — PROBLEMS, EXERCISES, ETC.
QD453-651	*STOICHIOMETRY* **SEE** CHEMISTRY, PHYSICAL AND THEORETICAL
B528	STOICS
TJ345	STOKERS, MECHANICAL
DL708	STOLBOVO, TREATY OF, 1617
RC840.A	STOMACH — ABSCESS
RC280.S8	STOMACH — CANCER
RC831	STOMACH — CATARRH
RC816-840	STOMACH — DISEASES
RC804	STOMACH — SECRETIONS / *diagnosis*
QP193	STOMACH — SECRETIONS / *physiology*
RD540.5	STOMACH — SURGERY
RC201.7.S	STOMACH — SYPHILIS
RC280.S8	STOMACH — TUMORS
RC822	STOMACH — ULCERS
RC819	STOMACH-PUMP
QL862	STOMACH / *comparative anatomy*
QM341	STOMACH / *human anatomy*
QP151	STOMACH / *physiology*
RC803-5	STOMACH — DISEASES — — DIAGNOSIS
RX332	STOMACH — DISEASES — — HOMEOPATHIC TREATMENT
QK689	STOMATA
QK649	STOMATA
QK873	STOMATA / *transpiration*

SF910.S7	STOMATITIS IN ANIMALS
RC815	STOMATITIS
RJ460	STOMATITIS / *children*
RC815	*STOMATOLOGY* **SEE** MOUTH — DISEASES
QL857	*STOMATOLOGY* **SEE** MOUTH / *comparative anatomy*
QM306	*STOMATOLOGY* **SEE** MOUTH / *human anatomy*
RK301-450	*STOMATOLOGY* **SEE** TEETH — DISEASES
QL858	*STOMATOLOGY* **SEE** TEETH / *comparative anatomy*
QM311	*STOMATOLOGY* **SEE** TEETH / *human anatomy*
GN209	*STOMATOLOGY* **SEE** TEETH / *somatology*
QL444.S8	STOMATOPODA
GN775-6	STONE AGE
TN510	STONE AND ORE BREAKERS / *mining engineering*
TE239	STONE AND ORE BREAKERS / *road material*
E241.S	STONE ARABIA, BATTLE OF, 1780
TG330	*STONE BRIDGES* **SEE** BRIDGES, STONE
TH1201	*STONE BUILDING* **SEE** BUILDING, STONE
GN790-792	*STONE CIRCLES* **SEE** CROMLECHS
TH1201	*STONE CONSTRUCTION* **SEE** BUILDING, STONE
NA7170	STONE HOUSES / *architecture*
TH1201	STONE HOUSES / *building*
GN446.1	STONE IMPLEMENTS / *primitive*
CR4480	*STONE OF DESTINY* **SEE** STONE OF SCONE
CR4480	STONE OF SCONE
E474.77	*STONE RIVER, BATTLE OF, 1862-1863* **SEE** MURFREESBORO, BATTLE OF, 1862-1863
NB	*STONE-CARVING* **SEE** SCULPTURE
TH5401-5421	*STONE-CARVING* **SEE** STONE-CUTTING
HF5716.S8	STONE-CUTTING — TABLES, CALCULATIONS, ETC.
TH5401-5421	STONE-CUTTING
QL513.P4	STONE-FLIES
TH5401-5421	STONE-MASONS / *masonry*
TA426-8	STONE / *construction material*
TN950-973	STONE / *mineral resources*
TP871	STONE, ARTIFICIAL
TN950-973	*STONE, BUILDING* **SEE** BUILDING STONES
TA426-8	*STONE, BUILDING* **SEE** BUILDING STONES
TP871	STONE, CAST
TE235-9	STONE, CRUSHED / *road material*
QD24-26.5	*STONE, PHILOSOPHERS'* **SEE** ALCHEMY
QD13	*STONE, PHILOSOPHERS'* **SEE** ALCHEMY / *history*
E475.38	STONEMAN'S RAID, 1863
E477.9	STONEMAN'S RAID, 1865
GR805	*STONES, PRECIOUS* **SEE** PRECIOUS STONES / *folk-lore*
TS750-755	*STONES, PRECIOUS* **SEE** PRECIOUS STONES / *manufactures*
QE392-4	*STONES, PRECIOUS* **SEE** PRECIOUS STONES / *mineralogy*
TN980-997	*STONES, PRECIOUS* **SEE** PRECIOUS STONES / *mining*
NK3700-4695	*STONEWARE* **SEE** POTTERY / *ceramics*
TP785-825	*STONEWARE* **SEE** POTTERY / *chemical technology*
HD9610-9620	*STONEWARE* **SEE** POTTERY / *trade*
NA3310-3950	*STONEWORK, DECORATIVE* **SEE** DECORATION AND ORNAMENT, ARCHITECTURAL
NB	*STONEWORK, DECORATIVE* **SEE** SCULPTURE
E356.S8	STONINGTON, CONN. — BOMBARDMENT, 1814
QL377.C7	*STONY CORALS* **SEE** MADREPORARIA
GV1017.S8	STOOL-BALL
TN287	STOPING (MINING)
TP493	*STORAGE* **SEE** COLD STORAGE
NA6340	*STORAGE* **SEE** WAREHOUSES / *architecture*
HF5484-9	*STORAGE* **SEE** WAREHOUSES / *commerce*
HF5484-5495	STORAGE AND MOVING TRADE / *storage*
HE5601-5999	STORAGE AND MOVING TRADE / *transportation*
QC605	STORAGE BATTERIES — ADDITIVES
QC605	STORAGE BATTERIES
TL272	STORAGE BATTERIES / *automobile*
TK2891	STORAGE BATTERIES / *central stations*
TK5378	STORAGE BATTERIES / *telegraph*
TK6278	STORAGE BATTERIES / *telephone*
TK7872.M4	*STORAGE ELEMENTS (CALCULATING-MACHINES)* **SEE** MAGNETIC MEMORY (CALCULATING-MACHINES)
TK7872.S7	STORAGE TUBES
NA6340	*STORAGE WAREHOUSES* **SEE** WAREHOUSES / *architecture*
HF5484-9	*STORAGE WAREHOUSES* **SEE** WAREHOUSES / *commerce*

NA6210-6280	*STORE BUILDINGS* **SEE** MERCANTILE BUILDINGS
HF5761-5780	*STORE DELIVERY SERVICES* **SEE** DELIVERY OF GOODS
HF5521	STORE FIXTURES
SB129	*STORED PRODUCTS* **SEE** FARM PRODUCE — STORAGE
HD9000.9	*STORED PRODUCTS* **SEE** FARM PRODUCE — STORAGE / *economics*
HF5495	STORES OR STOCK-ROOM KEEPING
TS160	STORES OR STOCK-ROOM KEEPING / *factory*
HF5468	*STORES, CHAIN* **SEE** CHAIN STORES
HF5461-5	*STORES, DEPARTMENT* **SEE** DEPARTMENT STORES
HD7515	*STORES, DEPARTMENT* **SEE** DEPARTMENT STORES / *employees*
HJ5669.D3	*STORES, DEPARTMENT* **SEE** DEPARTMENT STORES / *taxation*
TH9445.S	STORES, RETAIL — FIRES AND FIRE PREVENTION
PN6259-6268	*STORIES* **SEE** ANECDOTES / *collections*
D10	*STORIES* **SEE** ANECDOTES / *historical*
BS546-559	*STORIES* **SEE** BIBLE STORIES
PZ5-90	*STORIES* **SEE** CHILDREN'S STORIES / *collections*
BV4515	*STORIES* **SEE** CHRISTIAN LIFE — STORIES
PN6071.C6	*STORIES* **SEE** CHRISTMAS STORIES
PZ1-7	*STORIES* **SEE** COLLEGE STORIES
PZ1-3	*STORIES* **SEE** DETECTIVE AND MYSTERY STORIES / *collections*
PN3448.D4	*STORIES* **SEE** DETECTIVE AND MYSTERY STORIES / *history*
BV4224	*STORIES* **SEE** EXEMPLA
PN980-994	*STORIES* **SEE** FABLES
PZ8.2	*STORIES* **SEE** FABLES
PZ14.2	*STORIES* **SEE** FABLES
PN3311-3503	*STORIES* **SEE** FICTION
PZ1-3	*STORIES* **SEE** GHOST STORIES / *fiction in english*
PN3435	*STORIES* **SEE** GHOST STORIES / *history and criticism*
BF1445-1486	*STORIES* **SEE** GHOST STORIES / *occult sciences*
BV4224-4230	*STORIES* **SEE** HOMILETICAL ILLUSTRATIONS
BM723	*STORIES* **SEE** JEWISH WAY OF LIFE — STORIES
BP130.58	*STORIES* **SEE** KORAN STORIES
PN683-7	*STORIES* **SEE** LEGENDS
N7760	*STORIES* **SEE** LEGENDS / *iconography*
PZ8.1	*STORIES* **SEE** LEGENDS / *juvenile*
BV2087	*STORIES* **SEE** MISSIONARY STORIES
BT373-8	*STORIES* **SEE** PARABLES
PR321-347	*STORIES* **SEE** ROMANCES / *english*
PR2064-5	*STORIES* **SEE** ROMANCES / *english*
PQ201-221	*STORIES* **SEE** ROMANCES / *french*
PQ1411-1545	*STORIES* **SEE** ROMANCES / *french*
PN688-690	*STORIES* **SEE** ROMANCES / *medieval*
PN692-3	*STORIES* **SEE** ROMANCES / *medieval*
BV638.8	*STORIES* **SEE** RURAL CHURCHES — STORIES
PZ7	*STORIES* **SEE** SEA STORIES / *juvenile*
PR830.S4	*STORIES* **SEE** SEA STORIES / *sea in english fiction*
BV4307.S7	*STORIES* **SEE** SERMON STORIES
PZ1	*STORIES* **SEE** SHORT STORIES / *collections*
QL696.A7	STORKS
GC225-6	*STORM FLOODS* **SEE** STORM SURGES
HG9968.H2-5	*STORM INSURANCE* **SEE** INSURANCE, HAIL
HG9968.T5-7	*STORM INSURANCE* **SEE** INSURANCE, TORNADO
QC877	*STORM SIGNALS* **SEE** WEATHER SIGNALS
GC225-6	STORM SURGES
GC225-6	*STORM TIDES* **SEE** STORM SURGES
GC225-6	*STORM WAVES* **SEE** STORM SURGES
QC941-959	STORMS
QC835	*STORMS, MAGNETIC* **SEE** MAGNETIC STORMS
LB1042	STORY-TELLING / *education*
Z718.3	STORY-TELLING / *in libraries*
PN4193.I5	STORY-TELLING / *public speaking*
PN3373-5	*STORY, SHORT* **SEE** SHORT STORY
PS374.S5	*STORY, SHORT* **SEE** SHORT STORY / *american literature*
PR829	*STORY, SHORT* **SEE** SHORT STORY / *english literature*
HD9999.S9	STOVE INDUSTRY AND TRADE / *economics*
TS425	STOVE INDUSTRY AND TRADE / *manufacture*
TX657.S3-8	STOVES / *for cooking*
TH7435-7458	STOVES / *for heating*
TS425	STOVES / *iron manufactures*
NK4670	STOVES, EARTHENWARE / *art*
TX827	STOVES, ELECTRIC / *for cooking*
TK4631	STOVES, ELECTRIC / *for heating*
TX657.S5	STOVES, ELECTRIC / *home economics*
TX657.S6	STOVES, GAS / *for cooking*
TH7454-7	STOVES, GAS / *for heating*
TX657.S7	STOVES, GASOLINE
TX657.S8	STOVES, OIL
VK235	STOWAGE
JV6268-6271	STOWAWAYS / *immigration*
RE771	STRABISMUS
TA405.5	*STRAINS AND STRESSES* **SEE** THERMAL STRESSES
TH845-891	STRAINS AND STRESSES / *architectural engineering*
TG265-7	STRAINS AND STRESSES / *bridge and roof engineering*
QA931-5	STRAINS AND STRESSES / *elasticity*
JX4141	STRAITS / *international law*
D267.S8	STRALSUND — SIEGE, 1628
PQ4222.S7	STRAMBOTTO / *collections*
PQ4128.S7	STRAMBOTTO / *history and criticism*
SF959.S8	STRANGLES
DC308	STRASSBURG — SIEGE, 1870
DF277	STRATEGI, ATHENIAN
U161-3	STRATEGY / *military*
V160-165	STRATEGY / *naval*
QA270	*STRATEGY, GAMES OF (MATHEMATICS)* **SEE** GAMES OF STRATEGY (MATHEMATICS)
QE651-699	*STRATIGRAPHIC GEOLOGY* **SEE** GEOLOGY, STRATIGRAPHIC
QC879	*STRATOPAUSE* **SEE** STRATOSPHERE
QC879	STRATOSPHERE
ML1040	*STRAW FIDDLE* **SEE** XYLOPHONE
TS1747	STRAW INDUSTRIES
HM261	*STRAW VOTES* **SEE** PUBLIC OPINION POLLS
TS1747	STRAW / *manufactures*
TS1109	STRAW / *paper making*
SB385	STRAWBERRIES
SB205.S	STRAWBERRY CLOVER
SB608.S85	STRAWBERRY ROOT-WORM
SB205.S	*STRAWBERRY TREFOIL* **SEE** STRAWBERRY CLOVER
SB608.S85	STRAWBERRY-WEEVIL
SH351.B3	*STREAKED BASS* **SEE** STRIPED BASS
U205	STREAM CROSSING, MILITARY
GB1201-1397	STREAM MEASUREMENTS / *physical geography*
TD420-425	*STREAM POLLUTION* **SEE** WATER — POLLUTION
QA930	*STREAMLINING* **SEE** AERODYNAMICS
TL570-574	*STREAMLINING* **SEE** AERODYNAMICS
TD813-870	STREET CLEANING
GT3450	*STREET CRIES* **SEE** CRIES
BF204.S7	STREET GESTALT COMPLETION TEST
TF935	*STREET RAILWAY MOTORS* **SEE** ELECTRIC RAILWAY MOTORS
HE370	STREET SIGNS
GT3450	*STREET SONGS* **SEE** CRIES
SB436	*STREET TREES* **SEE** TREES IN CITIES
TF920-949	*STREET-CARS* **SEE** ELECTRIC RAILROADS — CARS
TP741	STREET-LIGHTING
TK4188	STREET-LIGHTING / *electric*
HE4351	STREET-RAILROADS — ACCOUNTING
HE4391	STREET-RAILROADS — ADJUSTMENT OF CLAIMS
TF705	STREET-RAILROADS — CONSTRUCTION
TF863-912	STREET-RAILROADS — CONSTRUCTION / *electric*
TF962	STREET-RAILROADS — COST OF OPERATION
TF216-217	STREET-RAILROADS — CURVES AND TURNOUTS
HE4311	STREET-RAILROADS — EMPLOYEES
HE4341	STREET-RAILROADS — FARES
HE4351	STREET-RAILROADS — FINANCE
TF707	STREET-RAILROADS — LOCATION
TF947	STREET-RAILROADS — SAFETY APPLIANCES
HE4347	STREET-RAILROADS — TRANSFERS
TF701-1124	STREET-RAILROADS / *economics*
HE4201-5300	STREET-RAILROADS / *economics*
HE4251	STREET-RAILROADS / *taxation*
HE1779-1795	*STREET-RAILROADS-ACCIDENTS* **SEE** RAILROADS — ACCIDENTS
TF920-949	*STREET-RAILROADS-CARS* **SEE** ELECTRIC RAILROADS — CARS
TF970	*STREET-RAILROADS-FREIGHT* **SEE** ELECTRIC RAILROADS — FREIGHT
HE369-373	*STREET-TRAFFIC REGULATIONS* **SEE** TRAFFIC REGULATIONS
TE183	STREETS — ESTIMATES AND COSTS
TE315-424	*STREETS* **SEE** HIGHWAY LAW

QD911-915	*STRUCTURAL ANALYSIS (MATHEMATICS)* **SEE** LATTICE THEORY / *crystallography*
QA171.5	*STRUCTURAL ANALYSIS (MATHEMATICS)* **SEE** LATTICE THEORY
QK641-707	*STRUCTURAL BOTANY* **SEE** BOTANY — ANATOMY
T355	STRUCTURAL DRAWING
TA684-5	*STRUCTURAL ENGINEERING* **SEE** BUILDING, IRON AND STEEL / *engineering*
TH1610-1621	*STRUCTURAL ENGINEERING* **SEE** BUILDING, IRON AND STEEL / *building*
TH845-891	*STRUCTURAL ENGINEERING* **SEE** STRAINS AND STRESSES / *architectural engineering*
TG265-7	*STRUCTURAL ENGINEERING* **SEE** STRAINS AND STRESSES / *bridge and roof engineering*
QA931-5	*STRUCTURAL ENGINEERING* **SEE** STRAINS AND STRESSES / *elasticity*
TA405	*STRUCTURAL ENGINEERING* **SEE** STRENGTH OF MATERIALS
TA410-417	*STRUCTURAL ENGINEERING* **SEE** STRENGTH OF MATERIALS / *testing*
TG260	*STRUCTURAL ENGINEERING* **SEE** STRUCTURES, THEORY OF
TG260	STRUCTURAL FRAMES
QE601-611	*STRUCTURAL GEOLOGY* **SEE** GEOLOGY, STRUCTURAL
TA684-5	*STRUCTURAL IRON* **SEE** IRON, STRUCTURAL / *engineering*
TS350	*STRUCTURAL IRON* **SEE** IRON, STRUCTURAL / *manufacture*
TA401-492	*STRUCTURAL MATERIALS* **SEE** BUILDING MATERIALS
TA492.P7	*STRUCTURAL PLATES* **SEE** PLATES (ENGINEERING)
BF203	*STRUCTURAL PSYCHOLOGY* **SEE** GESTALT PSYCHOLOGY
TA684-5	*STRUCTURAL STEEL* **SEE** STEEL, STRUCTURAL / *engineering*
TS350	*STRUCTURAL STEEL* **SEE** STEEL, STRUCTURAL / *manufacture*
BF202	*STRUCTURE PSYCHOLOGY* **SEE** WHOLE AND PARTS (PSYCHOLOGY)
TG260	STRUCTURES, THEORY OF — PROBLEMS, EXERCISES, ETC.
TG260	STRUCTURES, THEORY OF
TA684	*STRUCTURES, WELDED STEEL* **SEE** WELDED STEEL STRUCTURES
BD437	STRUGGLE
TG265	STRUTS (ENGINEERING)
QP921.S8	STRYCHNINE — PHYSIOLOGICAL EFFECT
RM666.S8	STRYCHNINE / *therapeutics*
RA1238.S8	STRYCHNINE / *toxicology*
NA7160	STUCCO / *domestic architecture*
SF423	*STUD-BOOKS* **SEE** DOGS — STUD-BOOKS
SF293	*STUD-BOOKS* **SEE** HORSES — STUD-BOOKS
HD9434	*STUD-FARMS* **SEE** HORSE BREEDING
SF277-318	*STUD-FARMS* **SEE** HORSE BREEDING
LB3605	STUDENT ACTIVITIES
LC1567	*STUDENT ADVISERS* **SEE** DEANS (IN SCHOOLS) / *education of women*
LB2341	*STUDENT ADVISERS* **SEE** DEANS (IN SCHOOLS) / *higher education*
LB3602	*STUDENT CLUBS* **SEE** STUDENTS' SOCIETIES
LB3612	STUDENT COOPERATIVES
LB3021	*STUDENT COUNCILS* **SEE** SELF-GOVERNMENT (IN EDUCATION) / *student honor*
LB3092-5	*STUDENT COUNCILS* **SEE** SELF-GOVERNMENT (IN EDUCATION)
LB1731	STUDENT COUNSELORS, TRAINING OF
LB3611	STUDENT EMPLOYMENT
LB3609	STUDENT ETHICS
BJ1857.S75	*STUDENT ETIQUETTE* / *american*
LB2342	*STUDENT EXPENDITURES* **SEE** COLLEGE COSTS
LB1027.5	*STUDENT GUIDANCE* **SEE** PERSONNEL SERVICE IN EDUCATION / *application*
LB3046-9	*STUDENT GUIDANCE* **SEE** PERSONNEL SERVICE IN EDUCATION / *organization*
LB3621	*STUDENT JOURNALISM* **SEE** COLLEGE AND SCHOOL JOURNALISM
PN4825-4830	*STUDENT JOURNALISM* **SEE** COLLEGE AND SCHOOL JOURNALISM / *amateur journalism*
LB2397	*STUDENT LIFE AND CUSTOMS* **SEE** STUDENTS / *reminiscences*

LB3602-3635	*STUDENT LIFE AND CUSTOMS* **SEE** STUDENTS / *student life*
LB2340	STUDENT LOAN FUNDS
LB3616.M3	*STUDENT MARRIAGES* **SEE** MARRIED STUDENTS
HN19	*STUDENT MOVEMENT* **SEE** YOUTH MOVEMENT
LB2341	STUDENT REGISTRATION
LB3021	*STUDENT SELF-GOVERNMENT* **SEE** SELF-GOVERNMENT (IN EDUCATION) / *student honor*
LB3092-5	*STUDENT SELF-GOVERNMENT* **SEE** SELF-GOVERNMENT (IN EDUCATION)
LB3604	*STUDENT SLANG* **SEE** STUDENTS — LANGUAGE (NEW WORDS, SLANG, ETC.)
LB3602	*STUDENT SOCIETIES* **SEE** STUDENTS' SOCIETIES
LB2157	STUDENT TEACHING
LC6681	STUDENT TRAVEL
LB3640	STUDENT UNIONS
LB1033	*STUDENT-TEACHER RELATIONSHIPS* **SEE** TEACHER-STUDENT RELATIONSHIPS
LB3604	STUDENTS — LANGUAGE (NEW WORDS, SLANG, ETC.)
Z718.7	*STUDENTS AND LIBRARIES* **SEE** LIBRARIES AND STUDENTS
N8251.S4	STUDENTS IN ART
LB2397	STUDENTS / *reminiscences*
LB3602-3635	STUDENTS / *student life*
LB2376	STUDENTS, INTERCHANGE OF
LB3613.J4	STUDENTS, JEWISH
LB3064	STUDENTS, TRANSFER OF
LB2359	STUDENTS, TRANSFER OF / *higher education*
U290-295	*STUDENTS' MILITARY TRAINING CAMPS* **SEE** MILITARY TRAINING CAMPS
LB3602	STUDENTS' SOCIETIES
LC203	STUDENTS' SOCIO-ECONOMIC STATUS
M1940-1973	STUDENTS' SONGS / *music*
PN6110.C7	STUDENTS' SONGS / *poetry*
LB3611	*STUDENTS-EMPLOYMENT* **SEE** STUDENT EMPLOYMENT
LB3609	*STUDENTS-ETHICS* **SEE** STUDENT ETHICS
LB3051-3063	*STUDENTS-GRADING AND MARKING* **SEE** GRADING AND MARKING (STUDENTS)
LB2846	*STUDENTS-PERSONNEL RECORDS* **SEE** PERSONNEL RECORDS IN EDUCATION
LB3046-9	*STUDENTS-PERSONNEL WORK* **SEE** PERSONNEL SERVICE IN EDUCATION / *organization*
LB1027.5	*STUDENTS-PERSONNEL WORK* **SEE** PERSONNEL SERVICE IN EDUCATION / *application*
LB3602	*STUDENTS-SOCIETIES, ETC.* **SEE** STUDENTS' SOCIETIES
LB1029.C	*STUDY-WORK PLAN* **SEE** EDUCATION, COOPERATIVE
LB2361-5	*STUDY, COURSES OF* **SEE** EDUCATION — CURRICULA / *colleges and universities*
LB1570-1571	*STUDY, COURSES OF* **SEE** EDUCATION — CURRICULA / *elementary schools*
LB1628-9	*STUDY, COURSES OF* **SEE** EDUCATION — CURRICULA / *secondary schools*
LB1049	STUDY, METHOD OF
LC63	STUDY, METHOD OF / *examinations*
BX9798.S8	STUNDISTS
TL711.S8	STUNT FLYING
DS416-419	*STUPAS* **SEE** TOPES (MONUMENTS) / *antiquities*
NA6001	*STUPAS* **SEE** TOPES (MONUMENTS) / *architecture*
BF435-7	*STUPIDITY* **SEE** INEFFICIENCY, INTELLECTUAL
QL638.5	STURGEONS
RC424	*STUTTERING* **SEE** STAMMERING
Z253	*STYLE (PRACTICAL PRINTING)* **SEE** PRINTING, PRACTICAL — STYLE MANUALS
GT500-2370	*STYLE IN DRESS* **SEE** COSTUME / *manners and customs*
TT500-645	*STYLE IN DRESS* **SEE** FASHION
GT500-2370	*STYLE IN DRESS* **SEE** FASHION
HD6073.M7	*STYLE MANIKINS* **SEE** MODELS, FASHION
Z253	*STYLE MANUALS (PRINTING)* **SEE** PRINTING, PRACTICAL — STYLE MANUALS
TT502	*STYLE SHOWS* **SEE** FASHION SHOWS
PN203	STYLE, LITERARY
BX4661	*STYLITES* **SEE** PILLAR SAINTS
QE495	STYLOLITES
RD33.3	*STYPTICS* **SEE** HEMOSTATICS
QD341.A4	STYROLENE ALCOHOL

PL8701-4	*SUAHELI LANGUAGE* **SEE** SWAHILI LANGUAGE
PL6035	*SUBANO LANGUAGE* **SEE** SUBANUN LANGUAGE
DS666.S8	*SUBANOS* **SEE** SUBANUNS
GN671.P5	*SUBANOS* **SEE** SUBANUNS / *anthropology*
PL6035	SUBANUN LANGUAGE
DS666.S8	SUBANUNS
GN671.P5	SUBANUNS / *anthropology*
TN871.3	*SUBAQUEOUS WELL-BORING (PETROLEUM)* **SEE** OIL WELL DRILLING, SUBMARINE
DS59.S	*SUBARAEANS* **SEE** SUBARIANS
P951	*SUBARIAN LANGUAGE* **SEE** MITANNIAN LANGUAGE
P951	*SUBARIAN LANGUAGE* **SEE** MITANNIAN LANGUAGE
DS59.S	SUBARIANS
BF323.S	*SUBCEPTION* **SEE** SUBLIMINAL PERCEPTION
BF1001-1389	SUBCONSCIOUSNESS
BF1211-1218	SUBCONSCIOUSNESS / *multiple consciousness*
BF315	SUBCONSCIOUSNESS / *unconscious mind*
PR2923	*SUBDIVISION CENTENNIAL CELEBRATIONS, ETC.* **SEE** SHAKESPEARE, WILLIAM, 1564-1616 — ANNIVERSARIES, ETC.
E312.25	*SUBDIVISION FAREWELL AS COMMANDER-IN-CHIEF OF THE ARMY* **SEE** WASHINGTON, GEORGE, PRES. U.S., 1732-1799 — RESIGNATION OF MILITARY COMMISSION
PR2949	*SUBDIVISION HANDWRITING* **SEE** SHAKESPEARE, WILLIAM, 1564-1616 — AUTOGRAPHS
ML80.S5	*SUBDIVISION KNOWLEDGE-MUSIC* **SEE** SHAKESPEARE, WILLIAM, 1564-1616 — MUSIC / *history*
PR3034	*SUBDIVISION KNOWLEDGE-MUSIC* **SEE** SHAKESPEARE, WILLIAM, 1564-1616 — MUSIC / *etc.*
TD1015	*SUBDIVISION PUBLIC LAUNDRIES UNDER NAMES OF CITIES, E.G. LONDON-PUBLIC LAUNDRIES* **SEE** LAUNDRIES, PUBLIC
PR2911-2913	*SUBDIVISION RELATIONS WITH CONTEMPORARIES* **SEE** SHAKESPEARE, WILLIAM, 1564-1616 — FRIENDS AND ASSOCIATES
DC203.9	*SUBDIVISION RELICS* **SEE** NAPOLEON I, EMPEROR OF THE FRENCH, 1769-1821 — MUSEUMS, RELICS, ETC.
PR3091-9	*SUBDIVISION STAGE-SETTING AND SCENERY* **SEE** SHAKESPEARE, WILLIAM, 1564-1616 — DRAMATURGY
PR2995-7	*SUBDIVISION STAGE-SETTING AND SCENERY* **SEE** SHAKESPEARE, WILLIAM, 1564-1616 — DRAMATURGY
DC204	*SUBDIVISION WOMEN* **SEE** NAPOLEON I, EMPEROR OF THE FRENCH, 1769-1821 — RELATIONS WITH WOMEN
PR3007	*SUBDIVISIONS ETHICAL IDEAS* **SEE** SHAKESPEARE, WILLIAM, 1564-1616 — RELIGION AND ETHICS
PR3011-3012	*SUBDIVISIONS ETHICAL IDEAS* **SEE** SHAKESPEARE, WILLIAM, 1564-1616 — RELIGION AND ETHICS
QA405	*SUBHARMONIC FUNCTIONS* **SEE** HARMONIC FUNCTIONS
Z695	*SUBJECT CATALOGS* **SEE** CATALOGS, SUBJECT
Z695	SUBJECT HEADINGS
Z695	*SUBJECT HEADINGS, ENGLISH* **SEE** SUBJECT HEADINGS
BF687.S	SUBLIMATION
BH301.S8	SUBLIME, THE
BF323.S	SUBLIMINAL PERCEPTION
QL865	*SUBMANDIBULAR GLAND* **SEE** SALIVARY GLANDS / *comparative anatomy*
QM325	*SUBMANDIBULAR GLAND* **SEE** SALIVARY GLANDS / *human anatomy*
QP191	*SUBMANDIBULAR GLAND* **SEE** SALIVARY GLANDS / *physiology*
TC191-2	*SUBMARINE BLASTING* **SEE** BLASTING, SUBMARINE
VM365	SUBMARINE BOATS — SAFETY APPLIANCES
V858-9	SUBMARINE BOATS / *by country*
VM365	SUBMARINE BOATS / *construction*
V210	SUBMARINE BOATS / *use in war*
HE7709-7741	*SUBMARINE CABLES* **SEE** CABLES, SUBMARINE / *economics*
UG607	*SUBMARINE CABLES* **SEE** CABLES, SUBMARINE / *military art and science*
TK5605-5681	*SUBMARINE CABLES* **SEE** CABLES, SUBMARINE / *technology*
D590	SUBMARINE CHASERS / *european war*
VM981-9	*SUBMARINE DIVING* **SEE** DIVING, SUBMARINE
TC183	*SUBMARINE DIVING* **SEE** DIVING, SUBMARINE / *submarine construction*
TC193	*SUBMARINE DRILLING* **SEE** UNDERWATER DRILLING
QE39	SUBMARINE GEOLOGY
RC1000	SUBMARINE MEDICINE
UG490-497	*SUBMARINE MINES* **SEE** MINES, SUBMARINE
TR800	*SUBMARINE PHOTOGRAPHY* **SEE** PHOTOGRAPHY, SUBMARINE
VK388	*SUBMARINE SIGNALING* **SEE** SIGNALS AND SIGNALING, SUBMARINE
HE7709-7741	*SUBMARINE TELEGRAPH* **SEE** CABLES, SUBMARINE / *economics*
UG607	*SUBMARINE TELEGRAPH* **SEE** CABLES, SUBMARINE / *military art and science*
TK5605-5681	*SUBMARINE TELEGRAPH* **SEE** CABLES, SUBMARINE / *technology*
GC83	SUBMARINE TOPOGRAPHY
V210	SUBMARINE WARFARE
VM965	*SUBMARINE WELDING AND CUTTING* **SEE** UNDERWATER WELDING AND CUTTING
QL865	*SUBMAXILLARY GLAND* **SEE** SALIVARY GLANDS / *comparative anatomy*
QM325	*SUBMAXILLARY GLAND* **SEE** SALIVARY GLANDS / *human anatomy*
QP191	*SUBMAXILLARY GLAND* **SEE** SALIVARY GLANDS / *physiology*
GB481-8	*SUBMERGED FORESTS* **SEE** FORESTS, SUBMERGED
TK7870	*SUBMINIATURE ELECTRONIC EQUIPMENT* **SEE** MINIATURE ELECTRONIC EQUIPMENT
TK7870	*SUBMINIATURIZATION (ELECTRONICS)* **SEE** MINIATURE ELECTRONIC EQUIPMENT
HF5456.B7	*SUBSCRIPTION BOOK TRADE* **SEE** BOOKSELLERS AND BOOKSELLING — COLPORTAGE, SUBSCRIPTION TRADE, ETC.
Z675.S8	*SUBSCRIPTION LIBRARIES* **SEE** LIBRARIES, SUBSCRIPTION
GB481-8	SUBSIDENCES (EARTH MOVEMENTS)
TN319	SUBSIDENCES (EARTH MOVEMENTS) / *mining*
TH1094	*SUBSIDENCES AND BUILDING* **SEE** EARTH MOVEMENTS AND BUILDING
VM299.5-7	*SUBSIDIES, SHIP-BUILDING* **SEE** SHIP-BUILDING SUBSIDIES
UC260-267	*SUBSISTENCE STORES* **SEE** MILITARY SUPPLIES
TN215-255	*SUBSOIL RIGHTS* **SEE** MINING LAW
QA930	*SUBSONIC AERODYNAMICS* **SEE** AERODYNAMICS
TL570-574	*SUBSONIC AERODYNAMICS* **SEE** AERODYNAMICS
BD331	SUBSTANCE (PHILOSOPHY)
TK1751	*SUBSTATIONS, ELECTRIC* **SEE** ELECTRIC SUBSTATIONS
LB2844.1.S8	SUBSTITUTE TEACHERS
TX357	*SUBSTITUTES FOR FOOD* **SEE** FOOD SUBSTITUTES
HC286.2	*SUBSTITUTES FOR FOOD* **SEE** FOOD SUBSTITUTES / *european war*
TX357	*SUBSTITUTES FOR FOOD* **SEE** FOOD, ARTIFICIAL
RM258-261	*SUBSTITUTES FOR FOOD* **SEE** FOOD, ARTIFICIAL / *diet*
QA171	*SUBSTITUTIONS* **SEE** GROUPS, THEORY OF
QA190-201	SUBSTITUTIONS, LINEAR
TA712	*SUBTERRANEAN CONSTRUCTION* **SEE** UNDERGROUND CONSTRUCTION
DA380	*SUBTERRANEAN PASSAGES* **SEE** HIDING-PLACES (SECRET CHAMBERS, ETC.) / *england*
GB1001-1197	*SUBTERRANEAN WATER* **SEE** WATER, UNDERGROUND
QA115	SUBTRACTION
HG2535-9	*SUBTREASURY BILL, 1840* **SEE** INDEPENDENT TREASURY / *u.s.*
HG2535-9	*SUBTREASURY SYSTEM* **SEE** INDEPENDENT TREASURY / *u.s.*
SB359	*SUBTROPICAL FRUIT* **SEE** TROPICAL FRUIT
BV637.7	SUBURBAN CHURCHES
BX1407.S8	SUBURBAN CHURCHES / *catholic*
NA7100-7573	SUBURBAN HOMES / *architecture*
HT351	SUBURBAN LIFE
TF845-851	SUBWAYS
TF850-851	SUBWAYS / *freight*
HF5386	SUCCESS / *business*
BJ1611-1618	SUCCESS / *ethics*
JX4053	*SUCCESSION OF STATES* **SEE** STATE SUCCESSION
HJ5801-5819	*SUCCESSION TAXES* **SEE** INHERITANCE AND TRANSFER TAX
JF285	*SUCCESSION TO THE CROWN* **SEE** KINGS AND RULERS — SUCCESSION

JN351-7	*SUCCESSION TO THE CROWN* **SEE** KINGS AND RULERS — SUCCESSION
BV665	*SUCCESSION, APOSTOLIC* **SEE** APOSTOLIC SUCCESSION
HB715	*SUCCESSION, INTESTATE* **SEE** INHERITANCE AND SUCCESSION / *economics*
QD305.A2	SUCCINIC ACID
BM695.S	*SUCCOS* **SEE** SUKKOTH
BM695.S	*SUCCOTH (FEAST OF TABERNACLES)* **SEE** SUKKOTH
SB438	SUCCULENT PLANTS
SB438	*SUCCULENTS* **SEE** SUCCULENT PLANTS
TN871.5	SUCKER RODS / *petroleum well pumps*
TJ915	SUCKER RODS / *suction pumps*
SB201.S8	SUDAN GRASS
RC168.M6	*SUDOR ANGLICUS* **SEE** SWEATING-SICKNESS
DD78.S8	*SUEBI* **SEE** SUEVI
DD78.S8	SUEVI
BV4900-4908	SUFFERING / *christian life*
BF789.S8	SUFFERING / *psychology*
BF515	SUFFERING / *psychology*
BD530-595	SUFFICIENT REASON
RJ256	*SUFFOCATION* **SEE** ASPHYXIA / *diseases of newly born*
RC87-88	*SUFFOCATION* **SEE** ASPHYXIA / *first aid*
RA1071	*SUFFOCATION* **SEE** ASPHYXIA / *legal medicine*
SF293.S8	SUFFOLK HORSE
JF825-1191	SUFFRAGE
JC75.S8	SUFFRAGE / *ancient greece*
JC85.S8	SUFFRAGE / *ancient rome*
JS393	SUFFRAGE / *municipal js215 u.s.*
JS1700	SUFFRAGE / *other countries*
JK1846-1936	SUFFRAGE / *u.s.*
BP189	SUFISM
TP382	SUGAR — ANALYSIS AND TESTING
QD321	SUGAR — INVERSION / *chemistry*
TP375-414	SUGAR — MANUFACTURE AND REFINING
QP923	SUGAR — PHYSIOLOGICAL EFFECT
HD9104	SUGAR — STATISTICS
HD9100.4	SUGAR — STATISTICS
HD9100.8	SUGAR — TAXATION
HD9100.7-95	*SUGAR BOUNTIES* **SEE** SUGAR LAWS AND LEGISLATION
HD9100-9119	*SUGAR BOUNTIES* **SEE** SUGAR TRADE
SB215-239	SUGAR GROWING
QP701	SUGAR IN THE BODY
HD9100.7-95	SUGAR LAWS AND LEGISLATION
TP407	SUGAR MACHINERY
QD321	*SUGAR OF MILK* **SEE** LACTOSE
RM666.L2	*SUGAR OF MILK* **SEE** LACTOSE / *therapeutics*
QK496.P66	SUGAR PINE
SD397.P63	SUGAR PINE / *forestry*
TP382	*SUGAR TESTING* **SEE** SUGAR — ANALYSIS AND TESTING
HF5716.S9	SUGAR TRADE — TABLES AND READY-RECKONERS
HD9100-9119	SUGAR TRADE
HD9100.7-95	*SUGAR TRADE-LAW AND LEGISLATION* **SEE** SUGAR LAWS AND LEGISLATION
HD9100.8	*SUGAR TRADE-TAXATION* **SEE** SUGAR — TAXATION
SB329	*SUGAR-BEET* **SEE** BEETS AND BEET SUGAR / *culture*
SB219-221	*SUGAR-BEET* **SEE** BEETS AND BEET SUGAR / *culture*
HD9100-9119	*SUGAR-BEET* **SEE** BEETS AND BEET SUGAR / *industry*
TP390-391	*SUGAR-BEET* **SEE** BEETS AND BEET SUGAR / *technology*
SB608.S9	SUGAR-CANE — DISEASES AND PESTS
SB945.S	SUGAR-CANE MEALY BUG
SB228-231	SUGAR-CANE
SB235	*SUGAR-CANE, CHINESE* **SEE** SORGHUM
TP405	*SUGAR-CANE, CHINESE* **SEE** SORGHUM / *chemical technology*
QK495.A17	SUGAR-MAPLE
SD397.M3	SUGAR-MAPLE / *forestry*
TP375-414	*SUGAR-REFINING* **SEE** SUGAR — MANUFACTURE AND REFINING
SB215-239	SUGAR / *agriculture*
QD321	SUGAR / *chemistry*
TX560.S9	SUGAR / *food values*
TP375-414	SUGAR / *manufacture*

HD9100-9119	SUGAR / *trade*
QD321	*SUGAR-HYDROLYSIS* **SEE** SUGAR — INVERSION / *chemistry*
HD9100.7-95	*SUGAR-LAW AND LEGISLATION* **SEE** SUGAR LAWS AND LEGISLATION
QD321	SUGARS / *organic chemistry*
QP923	SUGARS / *physiological effect*
TP378	SUGAR — MANUFACTURE AND REFINING — — ELECTROLYSIS
BF1111-1156	*SUGGESTION, MENTAL* **SEE** MENTAL SUGGESTION
RC490-499	*SUGGESTIVE THERAPEUTICS* **SEE** THERAPEUTICS, SUGGESTIVE
HB1323.S8	SUICIDE — STATISTICS
HV6543-8	SUICIDE
RA1136	SUICIDE / *medical jurisprudence*
ML1158	SUITE (MUSIC) / *chamber music*
ML1258	SUITE (MUSIC) / *orchestral music*
M175.A4	SUITES (ACCORDION)
M585	SUITES (ACCORDION, BASSOON, 2 CLARINETS, TRUMPET)
M282-3	SUITES (BALALAIKA AND PIANO)
M1203	SUITES (BAND)
M1254	SUITES (BAND), ARRANGED
M288-9	SUITES (BARITONE AND CORNET)
M655-7	SUITES (BARITONE, CORNET, HORN, TROMBONE, TRUMPET, TUBA)
M655-7	SUITES (BARITONE, HORN, TROMBONE, 2 TRUMPETS, TUBA)
M355-7	SUITES (BARITONE, 2 CORNETS)
M358-9	SUITES (BARITONE, 2 CORNETS), ARRANGED
M658-9	SUITES (BARITONE, 2 CORNETS, HORN, TROMBONE, TUBA), ARRANGED
M655-7	SUITES (BARITONE, 2 CORNETS, HORN, TROMBONE, TUBA)
M349-351	SUITES (BARYTON, VIOLA, VIOLONCELLO)
M288-9	SUITES (BASSOON AND FLUTE)
M253-4	SUITES (BASSOON AND PIANO)
M1027	SUITES (BASSOON WITH ORCHESTRA) — SOLO WITH PIANO
M1026-7	SUITES (BASSOON WITH ORCHESTRA)
M75-77	SUITES (BASSOON)
M355-7	SUITES (BASSOON, CLARINET, FLUTE)
M555-7	SUITES (BASSOON, CLARINET, FLUTE, HORN, OBOE)
M558-9	SUITES (BASSOON, CLARINET, FLUTE, HORN, OBOE), ARRANGED
M675-7	SUITES (BASSOON, CLARINET, FLUTE, HORN, OBOE, HARP)
M960-962	SUITES (BASSOON, CLARINET, FLUTE, HORN, OBOE, VIOLIN, VIOLA, VIOLONCELLO, DOUBLE BASS)
M455-7	SUITES (BASSOON, CLARINET, FLUTE, OBOE)
M555-7	SUITES (BASSOON, CLARINET, FLUTE, OBOE, TRUMPET)
M960-962	SUITES (BASSOON, CLARINET, FLUTE, OBOE, TRUMPET, VIOLIN, VIOLA, VIOLONCELLO, DOUBLE BASS)
M960-962	SUITES (BASSOON, CLARINET, FLUTE, OBOE, 2 VIOLINS, VIOLA, VIOLONCELLO, DOUBLE BASS)
M355-7	SUITES (BASSOON, CLARINET, HORN)
M358-9	SUITES (BASSOON, CLARINET, HORN), ARRANGED
M455-7	SUITES (BASSOON, CLARINET, HORN, OBOE)
M1105	SUITES (BASSOON, CLARINET, OBOE WITH STRING ORCHESTRA) — SCORES
M1105-6	SUITES (BASSOON, CLARINET, OBOE WITH STRING ORCHESTRA), ARRANGED
M1106	SUITES (BASSOON, CLARINET, OBOE WITH STRING ORCHESTRA), ARRANGED — SOLOS WITH PIANO
M1105-6	SUITES (BASSOON, CLARINET, OBOE WITH STRING ORCHESTRA)
M355-7	SUITES (BASSOON, CLARINET, OBOE)
M985	SUITES (BASSOON, CLARINET, OBOE, PERCUSSION, 2 VIOLINS, VIOLA, VIOLONCELLO, DOUBLE BASS)
M560-562	SUITES (BASSOON, CLARINET, VIOLIN, VIOLA, VIOLONCELLO)
M560-562	SUITES (BASSOON, FLUTE, HORN, VIOLIN, VIOLA)
M355-7	SUITES (BASSOON, FLUTE, OBOE)
M560-562	SUITES (BASSOON, OBOE, VIOLIN, VIOLA, DOUBLE BASS)
M355-7	SUITES (BASSOON, 2 CLARINETS)
M655-7	SUITES (BASSOON, 2 CLARINETS, FLUTE, HORN, OBOE)
M555-7	SUITES (BASSOON, 2 CLARINETS, 2 HORNS)
M555-7	SUITES (BASSOON, 2 CLARINETS, 2 OBOES)

M555-7	SUITES (BASSOON, 2 HORNS, 2 OBOES)
M655-7	SUITES (BASSOON, 3 CLARINETS, 2 FLUTES)
M1003	SUITES (CHAMBER ORCHESTRA)
M1060	SUITES (CHAMBER ORCHESTRA), ARRANGED
M1040-1041	SUITES (CLARINET AND FLUTE WITH CHAMBER ORCHESTRA)
M1040	SUITES (CLARINET AND FLUTE WITH CHAMBER ORCHESTRA) — SCORES
M1105	SUITES (CLARINET AND FLUTE WITH STRING ORCHESTRA) — SCORES
M1105-6	SUITES (CLARINET AND FLUTE WITH STRING ORCHESTRA)
M288-9	SUITES (CLARINET AND FLUTE)
M288-9	SUITES (CLARINET AND OBOE)
M248-250	SUITES (CLARINET AND PIANO)
M251-2	SUITES (CLARINET AND PIANO), ARRANGED
M290-291	SUITES (CLARINET AND VIOLIN)
M1025	SUITES (CLARINET WITH ORCHESTRA) — SOLO WITH PIANO
M1024-5	SUITES (CLARINET WITH ORCHESTRA)
M70-72	SUITES (CLARINET)
M73-74	SUITES (CLARINET), ARRANGED
M1105	SUITES (CLARINET, ENGLISH HORN, FLUTE, OBOE WITH STRING ORCHESTRA) — SCORES
M1105-6	SUITES (CLARINET, ENGLISH HORN, FLUTE, OBOE WITH STRING ORCHESTRA)
M375-7	SUITES (CLARINET, FLUTE, HARP)
M580-582	SUITES (CLARINET, FLUTE, HARP, VIOLIN, VIOLONCELLO)
M355-7	SUITES (CLARINET, FLUTE, OBOE)
M680-682	SUITES (CLARINET, FLUTE, OBOE, HARP, VIOLA, VIOLONCELLO)
M1105-6	SUITES (CLARINET, FLUTE, TRUMPET WITH STRING ORCHESTRA)
M1105	SUITES (CLARINET, FLUTE, TRUMPET WITH STRING ORCHESTRA) — SCORES
M785	SUITES (CLARINET, FLUTE, TRUMPET, KETTLEDRUMS, PERCUSSION, DOUBLE BASS)
M360-362	SUITES (CLARINET, OBOE, VIOLA)
M560-562	SUITES (CLARINET, 2 VIOLINS, VIOLA, VIOLONCELLO)
M260-261	SUITES (CORNET AND PIANO)
M855-7	SUITES (CORNET, 2 HORNS, 2 TROMBONES, 2 TRUMPETS, TUBA)
M1356	SUITES (DANCE ORCHESTRA)
M1018	SUITES (DOUBLE BASS WITH ORCHESTRA) — SOLO WITH PIANO
M1018	SUITES (DOUBLE BASS WITH ORCHESTRA)
M55-57	SUITES (DOUBLE BASS)
M58-59	SUITES (DOUBLE BASS), ARRANGED
M296-7	SUITES (FLUTE AND GUITAR)
M240-242	SUITES (FLUTE AND HARPSICHORD)
M240-242	SUITES (FLUTE AND PIANO)
M243-4	SUITES (FLUTE AND PIANO), ARRANGED
M1106	SUITES (FLUTE AND VIOLIN WITH STRING ORCHESTRA) — SOLOS WITH PIANO
M1105-6	SUITES (FLUTE AND VIOLIN WITH STRING ORCHESTRA)
M1020-1021	SUITES (FLUTE WITH ORCHESTRA)
M1105-6	SUITES (FLUTE WITH STRING ORCHESTRA)
M1106	SUITES (FLUTE WITH STRING ORCHESTRA), ARRANGED — SOLO WITH PIANO
M1105-6	SUITES (FLUTE WITH STRING ORCHESTRA), ARRANGED
M60-62	SUITES (FLUTE)
M380-382	SUITES (FLUTE, GUITAR, VIOLA)
M380-382	SUITES (FLUTE, GUITAR, VIOLA)
M380-382	SUITES (FLUTE, HARP, VIOLA)
M580-582	SUITES (FLUTE, HARP, VIOLIN, VIOLA, VIOLONCELLO)
M380-382	SUITES (FLUTE, LYRE-GUITAR, VIOLIN)
M560-562	SUITES (FLUTE, OBOE, VIOLIN, VIOLA, VIOLONCELLO)
M460-462	SUITES (FLUTE, VIOLIN, VIOLA, VIOLONCELLO)
M360-364	SUITES (FLUTE, VIOLIN, VIOLONCELLO)
M360-362	SUITES (FLUTE, 2 VIOLINS)
M460-462	SUITES (FLUTE, 2 VIOLINS, VIOLA)
M660-662	SUITES (FLUTE, 2 VIOLINS, VIOLA, VIOLONCELLO, DOUBLE BASS)
M663-4	SUITES (FLUTE, 2 VIOLINS, VIOLA, VIOLONCELLO, DOUBLE BASS), ARRANGED
M276-7	SUITES (GUITAR AND PIANO)
M1037.4.G8	SUITES (GUITAR WITH CHAMBER ORCHESTRA) — SOLO WITH PIANO
M1037.4.G8	SUITES (GUITAR WITH CHAMBER ORCHESTRA)
M1037.4.G8	SUITES (GUITAR WITH ORCHESTRA) — SOLO WITH PIANO
M1037.4.G8	SUITES (GUITAR WITH ORCHESTRA)
M125-7	SUITES (GUITAR)
M128-9	SUITES (GUITAR), ARRANGED
M370-372	SUITES (GUITAR, VIOLIN, VIOLA)
M1036-7	SUITES (HARP WITH CHAMBER ORCHESTRA)
M1036-7	SUITES (HARP WITH ORCHESTRA)
M115-117	SUITES (HARP)
M142.H2	SUITES (HARP-LUTE GUITAR)
M24	SUITES (HARPSICHORD)
M415-417	SUITES (HARPSICHORD, BASSOON, CLARINET, OBOE)
M418-419	SUITES (HARPSICHORD, BASSOON, CLARINET, OBOE), ARRANGED
M745-7	SUITES (HARPSICHORD, BASSOON, CLARINET, TROMBONE, PERCUSSION, VIOLIN, VIOLONCELLO)
M515-517	SUITES (HARPSICHORD, BASSOON, ENGLISH HORN, 2 OBOES)
M415-417	SUITES (HARPSICHORD, BASSOON, OBOE, TRUMPET)
M1105-6	SUITES (HARPSICHORD, FLUTE, HARP WITH STRING ORCHESTRA)
M1105	SUITES (HARPSICHORD, FLUTE, HARP WITH STRING ORCHESTRA) — SCORES
M720-722	SUITES (HARPSICHORD, FLUTE, OBOE, 2 VIOLINS, VIOLA, VIOLONCELLO)
M720-722	SUITES (HARPSICHORD, FLUTE, OBOE, 2 VIOLINS, VIOLONCELLO, DOUBLE BASS)
M320-322	SUITES (HARPSICHORD, FLUTE, VIOLA)
M323-4	SUITES (HARPSICHORD, FLUTE, VIOLA), ARRANGED
M320-322	SUITES (HARPSICHORD, FLUTE, VIOLIN)
M420-422	SUITES (HARPSICHORD, FLUTE, VIOLIN, VIOLONCELLO)
M420-422	SUITES (HARPSICHORD, RECORDER, VIOLIN, VIOLONCELLO)
M310-312	SUITES (HARPSICHORD, VIOLIN, VIOLA DA GAMBA)
M310-312	SUITES (HARPSICHORD, VIOLIN, VIOLONCELLO)
M315-317	SUITES (HARPSICHORD, 2 FLUTES)
M720-722	SUITES (HARPSICHORD, 2 HORNS, 2 OBOES, 2 VIOLINS)
M520-522	SUITES (HARPSICHORD, 2 HORNS, 2 VIOLINS)
M315-317	SUITES (HARPSICHORD, 2 RECORDERS)
M310-311	SUITES (HARPSICHORD, 2 VIOLAS)
M312.4	SUITES (HARPSICHORD, 2 VIOLAS)
M313-314	SUITES (HARPSICHORD, 2 VIOLAS), ARRANGED
M310-311	SUITES (HARPSICHORD, 2 VIOLE D'AMORE)
M312.4	SUITES (HARPSICHORD, 2 VIOLE D'AMORE)
M313-314	SUITES (HARPSICHORD, 2 VIOLE D'AMORE), ARRANGED
M312.4	SUITES (HARPSICHORD, 2 VIOLINS)
M310-311	SUITES (HARPSICHORD, 2 VIOLINS)
M412.4	SUITES (HARPSICHORD, 2 VIOLINS, VIOLA DA GAMBA)
M412.4	SUITES (HARPSICHORD, 2 VIOLINS, VIOLA)
M410-411	SUITES (HARPSICHORD, 2 VIOLINS, VIOLA)
M412.4	SUITES (HARPSICHORD, 2 VIOLINS, VIOLONCELLO)
M410-411	SUITES (HARPSICHORD, 2 VIOLINS, VIOLONCELLO)
M510-512	SUITES (HARPSICHORD, 2 VIOLINS, 2 VIOLAS)
M990	SUITES (HARPSICHORD, 2 VIOLS)
M312.4	SUITES (HARPSICHORD, 2 VIOLS)
M310-311	SUITES (HARPSICHORD, 2 VIOLS)
M415-417	SUITES (HARPSICHORD, 3 RECORDERS)
M255-7	SUITES (HORN AND PIANO)
M83-84	SUITES (HORN), ARRANGED
M455-7	SUITES (HORN, TROMBONE, 2 TRUMPETS)
M555-7	SUITES (HORN, TROMBONE, 2 TRUMPETS, TUBA)
M555-7	SUITES (HORN, 2 TROMBONES, 2 TRUMPETS)
M900-985	SUITES (INSTRUMENTAL ENSEMBLE)
M140-141	SUITES (LUTE)
M1039.4.M2	SUITES (MARIMBA WITH ORCHESTRA) — SOLO WITH PIANO
M1039.4.M2	SUITES (MARIMBA WITH ORCHESTRA)
M284.M6	SUITES (MOUTH-ORGAN AND PIANO)
M285.M6	SUITES (MOUTH-ORGAN AND PIANO)
M585	SUITES (MOUTH-ORGAN, 2 VIOLINS, VIOLA, VIOLONCELLO)
M245-6	SUITES (OBOE AND PIANO)
M247	SUITES (OBOE AND PIANO), ARRANGED
M1105	SUITES (OBOE WITH STRING ORCHESTRA) — SCORES
M1105-6	SUITES (OBOE WITH STRING ORCHESTRA)
M360-362	SUITES (OBOE, VIOLA, VIOLONCELLO)
M560-562	SUITES (OBOE, 2 VIOLINS, VIOLA, VIOLONCELLO)
M1003	SUITES (ORCHESTRA)

M1060	SUITES (ORCHESTRA), ARRANGED
M1003	*SUITES (ORCHESTRA)-SCORES (REDUCED) AND PARTS-EXCERPTS* **SEE** SUITES (ORCHESTRA) — EXCERPTS — — SCORES (REDUCED) AND PARTS
M1003	*SUITES (ORCHESTRA)-SCORES-EXCERPTS* **SEE** SUITES (ORCHESTRA) — EXCERPTS — — SCORES
M1003	SUITES (ORCHESTRA) — EXCERPTS — — SCORES (REDUCED) AND PARTS
M1003	SUITES (ORCHESTRA) — EXCERPTS — — SCORES
M9	SUITES (ORGAN)
M12-13	SUITES (ORGAN), ARRANGED
M300-302	SUITES (ORGAN, VIOLIN, VIOLA)
M400-402	SUITES (ORGAN, 2 VIOLINS, VIOLONCELLO)
M585	SUITES (PIANO (4 HANDS), CYMBALS, DRUM, TAMBOURINE, TRIANGLE)
M182-4	SUITES (PIANO AND ORGAN)
M185-6	SUITES (PIANO AND ORGAN), ARRANGED
M410-412	SUITES (PIANO QUARTET)
M510-512	SUITES (PIANO QUINTET)
M310-312	SUITES (PIANO TRIO)
M1010	SUITES (PIANO WITH CHAMBER ORCHESTRA) — SCORES
M1010-1011	SUITES (PIANO WITH CHAMBER ORCHESTRA)
M1011	SUITES (PIANO WITH ORCHESTRA) — 2-PIANO SCORES
M1010-1011	SUITES (PIANO WITH ORCHESTRA)
M1105-6	SUITES (PIANO WITH STRING ORCHESTRA)
M1160	SUITES (PIANO WITH STRING ORCHESTRA), ARRANGED
M24	SUITES (PIANO)
M24	SUITES (PIANO), ARRANGED
M615-617	SUITES (PIANO, BASSOON, CLARINET, FLUTE, HORN, OBOE)
M515-517	SUITES (PIANO, BASSOON, CLARINET, FLUTE, OBOE)
M415-417	SUITES (PIANO, BASSOON, CLARINET, OBOE)
M515-517	SUITES (PIANO, BASSOON, ENGLISH HORN, 2 OBOES)
M315-317	SUITES (PIANO, BASSOON, OBOE)
M915-917	SUITES (PIANO, BASSOON, 2 CLARINETS, ENGLISH HORN, FLUTE, HORN, OBOE, TRUMPET)
M315-317	SUITES (PIANO, CLARINET, FLUTE)
M455-7	SUITES (PIANO, CLARINET, TRUMPET, PERCUSSION)
M320-322	SUITES (PIANO, CLARINET, VIOLIN)
M323-4	SUITES (PIANO, CLARINET, VIOLIN), ARRANGED
M315-317	SUITES (PIANO, FLUTE, OBOE)
M320-322	SUITES (PIANO, FLUTE, VIOLIN)
M420-422	SUITES (PIANO, FLUTE, VIOLIN, VIOLONCELLO)
M420-422	SUITES (PIANO, OBOE, VIOLIN, VIOLONCELLO)
M340-342	SUITES (PIANO, PERCUSSION, VIOLIN)
M315-317	SUITES (PIANO, TROMBONE, TRUMPET)
M315-317	SUITES (PIANO, 2 FLUTES)
M720-722	SUITES (PIANO, 2 HORNS, 2 OBOES, 2 VIOLINS)
M520-522	SUITES (PIANO, 2 HORNS, 2 VIOLINS)
M310-311	SUITES (PIANO, 2 VIOLE D'AMORE)
M312.4	SUITES (PIANO, 2 VIOLE D'AMORE)
M310-311	SUITES (PIANO, 2 VIOLINS)
M312.4	SUITES (PIANO, 2 VIOLINS)
M313-314	SUITES (PIANO, 2 VIOLINS), ARRANGED
M510-512	SUITES (PIANO, 2 VIOLINS, VIOLA, VIOLONCELLO)
M412.4	SUITES (PIANO, 2 VIOLINS, VIOLONCELLO)
M413-414	SUITES (PIANO, 2 VIOLINS, VIOLONCELLO), ARRANGED
M720-722	SUITES (PIANO, 3 CLARINETS, VIOLIN, VIOLA, VIOLONCELLO)
M412.2	SUITES (PIANO, 3 VIOLINS)
M203	SUITES (PIANO, 4 HANDS)
M211	SUITES (PIANO, 4 HANDS), ARRANGED
M1360	SUITES (PLECTRAL ENSEMBLE)
M296-7	SUITES (RECORDER AND GUITAR)
M296-7	SUITES (RECORDER AND GUITAR), ARRANGED
M240-242	SUITES (RECORDER AND HARPSICHORD)
M240-242	SUITES (RECORDER AND PIANO)
M243-4	SUITES (RECORDER AND PIANO), ARRANGED
M1105-6	SUITES (RECORDER WITH STRING ORCHESTRA)
M360-362	SUITES (RECORDER, VIOLIN, VIOLA)
M1350	SUITES (SALON ORCHESTRA)
M268-9	SUITES (SAXOPHONE AND PIANO)
M1035	SUITES (SAXOPHONE WITH ORCHESTRA) — SOLO WITH PIANO
M1034-5	SUITES (SAXOPHONE WITH ORCHESTRA)
M950-952	SUITES (STRING ENSEMBLE)
M1103	SUITES (STRING ORCHESTRA)
M1160	SUITES (STRING ORCHESTRA), ARRANGED
M450-452	SUITES (STRING QUARTET)

M453-4	SUITES (STRING QUARTET), ARRANGED
M349-351	SUITES (STRING TRIO)
M352-3	SUITES (STRING TRIO), ARRANGED
M1105	SUITES (TROMBONE AND KETTLEDRUMS WITH STRING ORCHESTRA) — SCORES
M1105-6	SUITES (TROMBONE AND KETTLEDRUMS WITH STRING ORCHESTRA)
M262-3	SUITES (TROMBONE AND PIANO)
M1031	SUITES (TRUMPET WITH ORCHESTRA) — SOLO WITH PIANO
M1030-1031	SUITES (TRUMPET WITH ORCHESTRA)
M1105-6	SUITES (TRUMPET WITH STRING ORCHESTRA)
M1105	SUITES (TRUMPET WITH STRING ORCHESTRA), ARRANGED — SCORES
M1105-6	SUITES (TRUMPET WITH STRING ORCHESTRA), ARRANGED
M264-5	SUITES (TUBA AND PIANO)
M224-6	SUITES (VIOLA AND HARPSICHORD)
M227-8	SUITES (VIOLA AND HARPSICHORD), ARRANGED
M224-6	SUITES (VIOLA AND PIANO)
M227-8	SUITES (VIOLA AND PIANO), ARRANGED
M286-7	SUITES (VIOLA AND VIOLONCELLO)
M1015	SUITES (VIOLA WITH CHAMBER ORCHESTRA) — SOLO WITH PIANO
M1014-1015	SUITES (VIOLA WITH CHAMBER ORCHESTRA)
M1015	SUITES (VIOLA WITH ORCHESTRA) — SOLO WITH PIANO
M1014-1015	SUITES (VIOLA WITH ORCHESTRA)
M1014	SUITES (VIOLA WITH ORCHESTRA), ARRANGED — SCORES
M1014-1015	SUITES (VIOLA WITH ORCHESTRA), ARRANGED
M1105-6	SUITES (VIOLA WITH STRING ORCHESTRA)
M1106	SUITES (VIOLA WITH STRING ORCHESTRA), ARRANGED — SOLO WITH PIANO
M1105-6	SUITES (VIOLA WITH STRING ORCHESTRA), ARRANGED
M1106	SUITES (VIOLA WITH STRING ORCHESTRA) — TO 1800 — — SOLO WITH PIANO
M45-47	SUITES (VIOLA)
M48-49	SUITES (VIOLA), ARRANGED
M294-5	SUITES (VIOLIN AND GUITAR)
M294-5	SUITES (VIOLIN AND HARP)
M220	SUITES (VIOLIN AND HARPSICHORD)
M1040-1041	SUITES (VIOLIN AND PIANO WITH CHAMBER ORCHESTRA)
M1041	SUITES (VIOLIN AND PIANO WITH ORCHESTRA) — SOLOS WITH PIANO
M1040-1041	SUITES (VIOLIN AND PIANO WITH ORCHESTRA)
M220	SUITES (VIOLIN AND PIANO)
M222-3	SUITES (VIOLIN AND PIANO), ARRANGED
M1105-6	SUITES (VIOLIN AND VIOLA WITH STRING ORCHESTRA)
M286-7	SUITES (VIOLIN AND VIOLA)
M286-7	SUITES (VIOLIN AND VIOLONCELLO)
M1012	SUITES (VIOLIN WITH CHAMBER ORCHESTRA) — SCORES
M1012-1013	SUITES (VIOLIN WITH CHAMBER ORCHESTRA)
M1012-1013	SUITES (VIOLIN WITH CHAMBER ORCHESTRA), ARRANGED
M1013	SUITES (VIOLIN WITH ORCHESTRA) — SOLO WITH PIANO
M1012-1013	SUITES (VIOLIN WITH ORCHESTRA)
M1060-1061	SUITES (VIOLIN WITH ORCHESTRA), ARRANGED
M1105	SUITES (VIOLIN WITH STRING ORCHESTRA) — SCORES
M1105-6	SUITES (VIOLIN WITH STRING ORCHESTRA)
M40-42	SUITES (VIOLIN)
M349-351	SUITES (VIOLIN, VIOLA, DOUBLE BASS)
M349-351	SUITES (VIOLIN, VIOLONCELLO, DOUBLE BASS)
M294-5	SUITES (VIOLONCELLO AND GUITAR)
M294-5	SUITES (VIOLONCELLO AND HARP)
M232	SUITES (VIOLONCELLO AND PIANO)
M235-6	SUITES (VIOLONCELLO AND PIANO), ARRANGED
M1017	SUITES (VIOLONCELLO WITH CHAMBER ORCHESTRA) — SOLO WITH PIANO
M1016-1017	SUITES (VIOLONCELLO WITH CHAMBER ORCHESTRA)
M1016-1017	SUITES (VIOLONCELLO WITH CHAMBER ORCHESTRA), ARRANGED
M1016-1017	SUITES (VIOLONCELLO WITH ORCHESTRA)
M1105-6	SUITES (VIOLONCELLO WITH STRING ORCHESTRA) — TO 1800
M1105-6	SUITES (VIOLONCELLO WITH STRING ORCHESTRA)

M50-52	SUITES (VIOLONCELLO)
M53-54	SUITES (VIOLONCELLO), ARRANGED
M955-7	SUITES (WIND ENSEMBLE)
M955-7	SUITES (2 BASSOONS, 2 CLARINETS, FLUTE, 2 HORNS, 2 OBOES)
M855-7	SUITES (2 BASSOONS, 2 CLARINETS, 2 FLUTES, 2 OBOES)
M655-7	SUITES (2 BASSOONS, 2 CLARINETS, 2 HORNS)
M855-7	SUITES (2 BASSOONS, 2 CLARINETS, 2 HORNS, 2 OBOES)
M655-7	SUITES (2 BASSOONS, 2 HORNS, 2 OBOES)
M885	SUITES (2 CLARINETS, FLUTE, DRUMS, PERCUSSION, VIOLA, VIOLONCELLO, DOUBLE BASS)
M560-564	SUITES (2 CLARINETS, VIOLIN, VIOLA, VIOLONCELLO)
M455-7	SUITES (2 CLARINETS, 2 HORNS)
M960-962	SUITES (2 CLARINETS, 2 HORNS, 2 VIOLINS, 2 VIOLAS, VIOLONCELLO)
M555-7	SUITES (2 CORNETS, 3 TRUMPETS)
M558-9	SUITES (2 CORNETS, 3 TRUMPETS), ARRANGED
M1105	SUITES (2 FLUTES WITH STRING ORCHESTRA) — SCORES
M1105-6	SUITES (2 FLUTES WITH STRING ORCHESTRA)
M1106	SUITES (2 FLUTES WITH STRING ORCHESTRA), ARRANGED — SOLO WITH PIANO
M1105-6	SUITES (2 FLUTES WITH STRING ORCHESTRA), ARRANGED
M288-9	SUITES (2 FLUTES)
M375-7	SUITES (2 FLUTES, GUITAR)
M760-762	SUITES (2 FLUTES, TRUMPET, 2 VIOLINS, VIOLA, VIOLONCELLO)
M292-3	SUITES (2 GUITARS)
M1105	SUITES (2 HARPS WITH STRING ORCHESTRA) — SCORES
M1105-6	SUITES (2 HARPS WITH STRING ORCHESTRA)
M292-3	SUITES (2 HARPS) — EXCERPTS
M292-3	SUITES (2 HARPS)
M214	SUITES (2 HARPSICHORDS)
M215	SUITES (2 HARPSICHORDS), ARRANGED
M760-762	SUITES (2 HORNS, OBOE, 2 VIOLINS, VIOLA, VIOLONCELLO)
M860-862	SUITES (2 HORNS, 2 OBOES, 2 VIOLINS, VIOLA, VIOLONCELLO)
M960-962	SUITES (2 HORNS, 2 OBOES, 2 VIOLINS, 2 VIOLAS, VIOLONCELLO)
M660-662	SUITES (2 HORNS, 2 VIOLINS, VIOLA, VIOLONCELLO)
M1010-1011	SUITES (2 PIANOS WITH ORCHESTRA)
M1105	SUITES (2 PIANOS WITH STRING ORCHESTRA) — SCORES
M1105-6	SUITES (2 PIANOS WITH STRING ORCHESTRA)
M214	SUITES (2 PIANOS)
M215	SUITES (2 PIANOS), ARRANGED
M288-9	SUITES (2 RECORDERS)
M375-7	SUITES (2 RECORDERS, GUITAR)
M455-7	SUITES (2 TROMBONES, 2 TRUMPETS)
M286-7	SUITES (2 VIOLINS)
M349-351	SUITES (2 VIOLINS, VIOLA)
M550-552	SUITES (2 VIOLINS, VIOLA, VIOLONCELLO, DOUBLE BASS)
M553-4	SUITES (2 VIOLINS, VIOLA, VIOLONCELLO, DOUBLE BASS), ARRANGED
M349-351	SUITES (2 VIOLINS, VIOLONCELLO)
M352-3	SUITES (2 VIOLINS, VIOLONCELLO), ARRANGED
M550-552	SUITES (2 VIOLINS, 2 VIOLAS, VIOLONCELLO)
M650-652	SUITES (2 VIOLINS, 2 VIOLAS, VIOLONCELLO, DOUBLE BASS)
M660-662	SUITES (2 VIOLINS, 2 VIOLAS, 2 VIOLONCELLOS)
M286-7	SUITES (2 VIOLONCELLOS)
M286-7	SUITES (2 VIOLONCELLOS), ARRANGED
M355-7	SUITES (3 CLARINETS)
M960-962	SUITES (3 CLARINETS, CORNET, TROMBONE, TRUMPET, VIOLIN, VIOLA, VIOLONCELLO)
M555-7	SUITES (3 CLARINETS, 2 FLUTES)
M355-7	SUITES (3 FLUTES)
M355-7	SUITES (3 RECORDERS)
M358-9	SUITES (3 RECORDERS), ARRANGED
M460-462	SUITES (3 RECORDERS, VIOLIN)
M355-7	SUITES (3 TROMBONES)
M358-9	SUITES (3 TROMBONES), ARRANGED
M785	SUITES (3 TROMBONES, 2 TRUMPETS, TUBA, KETTLEDRUMS)

M885	SUITES (3 TROMBONES, 3 TRUMPETS, TUBA, KETTLEDRUMS)
M355-7	SUITES (3 TRUMPETS)
M349-351	SUITES (3 VIOLINS)
M352-3	SUITES (3 VIOLINS), ARRANGED
M452.4	SUITES (3 VIOLINS, VIOLONCELLO)
M450-451	SUITES (3 VIOLINS, VIOLONCELLO)
M349-351	SUITES (3 VIOLS)
M455-7	SUITES (4 BASSOONS)
M455-7	SUITES (4 CLARINETS)
M458-9	SUITES (4 CLARINETS), ARRANGED — EXCERPTS
M458-9	SUITES (4 CLARINETS), ARRANGED
M455-7	SUITES (4 FLUTES)
M465-7	SUITES (4 GUITARS)
M455-7	SUITES (4 HORNS)
M760-762	SUITES (4 HORNS, VIOLIN, VIOLA, VIOLONCELLO)
M216	SUITES (4 PIANOS)
M455-7	SUITES (4 PIPES)
M455-7	SUITES (4 RECORDERS)
M455-7	SUITES (4 SAXOPHONES)
M455-7	SUITES (4 TROMBONES)
M458-9	SUITES (4 TROMBONES), ARRANGED
M755-7	SUITES (4 TROMBONES, 3 TRUMPETS)
M758-9	SUITES (4 TROMBONES, 3 TRUMPETS), ARRANGED
M455-7	SUITES (4 TRUMPETS)
M585	SUITES (4 TRUMPETS, KETTLEDRUMS)
M450-451	SUITES (4 VIOLONCELLOS)
M452.4	SUITES (4 VIOLONCELLOS)
M453-4	SUITES (4 VIOLONCELLOS), ARRANGED
M465-7	SUITES (4 ZITHERS)
M565-7	SUITES (5 GUITARS)
BM695.S	SUKKOTH
BM695.S	*SUKOS* **SEE** SUKKOTH
DT429	SUKS
GN652.S8	SUKS / *anthropology*
DF747.S8	SULIOTES
TN281	SULLIVAN DIAMOND DRILL
E235	SULLIVAN'S INDIAN CAMPAIGN, 1779
E241.M9	*SULLIVAN'S ISLAND, BATTLE OF* **SEE** MOULTRIE, FORT, BATTLE OF, 1776
QP913.S1	SULPHATES — PHYSIOLOGICAL EFFECT
QD181.S1	SULPHATES / *inorganic*
QE389.66	SULPHATES / *mineralogy*
TN673	SULPHIDES — METALLURGY
QD181.S1	SULPHIDES / *inorganic*
QE389.2	SULPHIDES / *mineralogy*
QD341.A2	SULPHINIC ACIDS
TP327	SULPHITE PITCH / *coal briquets*
QP913.S1	SULPHITES — PHYSIOLOGICAL EFFECT
RM666.S9	SULPHITES — THERAPEUTIC USE
QD181.S1	SULPHITES
QD181.C15	*SULPHOCYANATES* **SEE** THIOCYANATES
QP913.C15	*SULPHOCYANATES* **SEE** THIOCYANATES / *physiology*
QD181.C15	*SULPHOCYANIC ACID* **SEE** THIOCYANIC ACID
QP13.C15	*SULPHOCYANIC ACID* **SEE** THIOCYANIC ACID / *physiology*
QD181.C15	*SULPHOCYANIDES* **SEE** THIOCYANATES
QP913.C15	*SULPHOCYANIDES* **SEE** THIOCYANATES / *physiology*
TP675	SULPHONATED OILS
QD341.A2	SULPHONCHLORIDES
QD341.A2	SULPHONES
QD341.A2	SULPHONFLUORESCEIN
QD341.A2	SULPHONIC ACIDS
QD305.S8	SULPHONIUM COMPOUNDS
QD341.S8	SULPHONIUM COMPOUNDS
RM666.S9	SULPHUR — THERAPEUTIC USE
QR84	SULPHUR BACTERIA
QD181.S1	SULPHUR DIOXIDE
RA766.S9	SULPHUR DIOXIDE / *disinfectants*
QP535.S1	SULPHUR IN THE BODY
TN890	SULPHUR MINES AND MINING
HD9585.S7	SULPHUR MINES AND MINING
RA793-954	SULPHUR-SPRINGS / *medical geography*
RM674	SULPHUR-SPRINGS / *mineral waters*
QD181.S1	SULPHUR
TP245.S9	SULPHURATION
QD181.S1	*SULPHURETED HYDROGEN* **SEE** HYDROGEN SULPHIDE

HD9660.S78	SULPHURIC ACID INDUSTRY / economics
TP215	SULPHURIC ACID INDUSTRY / technology
QD181.S1	SULPHURIC ACID
TP215	SULPHURIC ACID / manufacture
QD181.S1	SULPHUROUS ACID
TX572.S9	SULPHUROUS ACID / food preservatives
BX4060	SULPICIANS
D107	*SULTANS* **SEE** KINGS AND RULERS / biography comprehensive
JF253	*SULTANS* **SEE** KINGS AND RULERS / comparative government
JC374-408	*SULTANS* **SEE** KINGS AND RULERS / political theory
D399.7	*SULTANS* **SEE** KINGS AND RULERS / 19th century
D352.1	*SULTANS* **SEE** KINGS AND RULERS / 19th century
D412.7	*SULTANS* **SEE** KINGS AND RULERS / 20th century
PL6041-4	SULU LANGUAGE
PM8840	SUMA (ARTIFICIAL LANGUAGE)
SB315.S9	SUMAC / field crops
TS985	SUMAC / tanning materials
SB315.S9	*SUMACH* **SEE** SUMAC / field crops
TS985	*SUMACH* **SEE** SUMAC / tanning materials
PJ4051-4075	*SUMERIAN CUNEIFORM INSCRIPTIONS* **SEE** CUNEIFORM INSCRIPTIONS, SUMERIAN
PJ4001-4041	SUMERIAN LANGUAGE
PJ4051-4083	SUMERIAN LITERATURE
PJ4001-4041	SUMERIAN PHILOLOGY
PJ3191-3225	*SUMERIAN SYLLABARIES* **SEE** CUNEIFORM WRITING
DS72	SUMERIANS
BV4714	SUMMARY OF THE LAW (THEOLOGY)
BX1939.S	SUMMARY PROCEEDINGS (CANON LAW)
GV192-8	*SUMMER CAMPS* **SEE** CAMPS
RC811	SUMMER DISEASES
TH4835	SUMMER HOMES
LC5701-5760	SUMMER SCHOOLS
QH81	SUMMER / outdoor books
B737	SUMMISTS
VK569	SUMNER'S METHOD
GV1197	SUMO
HB845	SUMPTUARY LAWS
GT527-8	SUMPTUARY LAWS / dress
F1434.3.S	SUMU INDIANS / central america
QB529	SUN — CORONA
QB528	SUN — DIAMETERS
QB525	SUN — FACULAE
QB551	SUN — FLOCCULI
QB528	SUN — PROMINENCES
QB216	SUN — RISING AND SETTING
QB523	SUN — ROTATION
QB551	SUN — ROTATION / spectrographic observations
QB374	SUN — TABLES
QB531	SUN — TEMPERATURE
QB105	*SUN COMPASS* **SEE** SOLAR COMPASS
TH4970	*SUN DECKS (ARCHITECTURE)* **SEE** DECKS (ARCHITECTURE, DOMESTIC)
N8251.S6	SUN IN ART
RM843	SUN-BATHS
E98.D2	SUN-DANCE / american indians
QB215	SUN-DIALS
QB525	SUN-SPOTS
QC883	SUN-SPOTS / meteorological phenomena
QC836	SUN-SPOTS / terrestrial magnetism
BL438	SUN-WORSHIP
QB521-539	SUN
GR625	SUN / folk-lore
TL796.6.S	*SUN-ARTIFICIAL SATELLITES* **SEE** ARTIFICIAL SATELLITES — SUN
QB508-518	*SUN-PARALLAX* **SEE** PARALLAX — SUN
QB531	*SUN-RADIATION* **SEE** SOLAR RADIATION / astronomy
QC911	*SUN-RADIATION* **SEE** SOLAR RADIATION / meteorology
QC455	*SUN-SPECTRUM* **SEE** SPECTRUM, SOLAR / physics
QB551	*SUN-SPECTRUM* **SEE** SPECTRUM, SOLAR / solar eclipses
QL696.P2	SUNBIRDS
PL5451-4	SUNDANESE LANGUAGE
PL5454	SUNDANESE LITERATURE
HD5114	SUNDAY LEGISLATION / labor
HE6239.S8	SUNDAY LEGISLATION / mails
HE6497.S8	SUNDAY LEGISLATION / mails
BV133	SUNDAY LEGISLATION / religious aspects
HE1825	SUNDAY LEGISLATION / trains
D766.93	*SUNDAY OF THE DEAD, BATTLE OF, 1941* **SEE** POINT 175, BATTLE OF, 1941
Z708	SUNDAY OPENING OF LIBRARIES
NA4890	SUNDAY-SCHOOL BUILDINGS
Z675.S9	*SUNDAY-SCHOOL LIBRARIES* **SEE** LIBRARIES, SUNDAY-SCHOOL
Z1003	SUNDAY-SCHOOL LITERATURE / choice of books
PN4231	SUNDAY-SCHOOL LITERATURE / recitations
BV4560-4579	SUNDAY-SCHOOL LITERATURE / religious books for children
BV1531	SUNDAY-SCHOOL SUPERINTENDENTS
BV520	SUNDAY-SCHOOLS — HYMNS
BV1521.5	SUNDAY-SCHOOLS — JUVENILE LITERATURE
BV1527	SUNDAY-SCHOOLS — RECORDS
BV1500-1578	SUNDAY-SCHOOLS
NA4890	*SUNDAY-SCHOOLS-BUILDINGS* **SEE** SUNDAY-SCHOOL BUILDINGS
Z675.S9	*SUNDAY-SCHOOLS-LIBRARIES* **SEE** LIBRARIES, SUNDAY-SCHOOL
BV520	*SUNDAY-SCHOOLS-MUSIC* **SEE** SUNDAY-SCHOOLS — HYMNS
BV107-133	SUNDAY
HJ2050-2052	*SUNDRY CIVIL APPROPRIATION BILLS* **SEE** UNITED STATES — APPROPRIATIONS AND EXPENDITURES
HJ10	*SUNDRY CIVIL APPROPRIATION BILLS* **SEE** UNITED STATES — APPROPRIATIONS AND EXPENDITURES
QL638.C3	SUNFISHES / fresh-water fishes
E99.D1	SUNFLOWER DANCE / dakota indians
QK495.H5	SUNFLOWERS / botany
SB299.S9	SUNFLOWERS / culture
SB261.S	*SUNN* **SEE** SANN / fiber plants
BP175.S8	*SUNNIS* **SEE** SUNNITES
BP175.S8	SUNNITES
QB216	*SUNRISE AND SUNSET* **SEE** SUN — RISING AND SETTING
QC976.C6	SUNSET PHENOMENA
QC912	SUNSHINE-RECORDER
QC911-912	SUNSHINE
QB525	*SUNSPOTS* **SEE** SUN-SPOTS
QC883	*SUNSPOTS* **SEE** SUN-SPOTS / meteorological phenomena
QC836	*SUNSPOTS* **SEE** SUN-SPOTS / terrestrial magnetism
E99.H3	*SUPAI INDIANS* **SEE** HAVASUPAI INDIANS
TJ787	SUPERCHARGERS
QC611	SUPERCONDUCTIVITY
QC303	SUPERCOOLING
Z993.A	SUPEREXLIBRIS
BJ1535.S8	SUPERFICIALITY
TJ272	*SUPERHEATED STEAM* **SEE** STEAM, SUPERHEATED
TJ272	SUPERHEATERS
TX339	*SUPERINTENDENTS OF BUILDINGS AND GROUNDS* **SEE** JANITORS
LB2803-2822	*SUPERINTENDENTS OF SCHOOLS* **SEE** SCHOOL SUPERINTENDENTS AND PRINCIPALS
LC3991-4000	*SUPERIOR CHILDREN* **SEE** GIFTED CHILDREN
BX2438	SUPERIORS, RELIGIOUS
PN56.S8	SUPERNATURAL IN LITERATURE
PN1995.9.S8	SUPERNATURAL IN MOVING-PICTURES
BL100	SUPERNATURAL / comparative religion
GR500-510	SUPERNATURAL / folk-lore
BF1001-1999	SUPERNATURAL / occult sciences
TP245.P5	*SUPERPHOSPHATES* **SEE** PHOSPHATES / chemical technology
QD181.P1	*SUPERPHOSPHATES* **SEE** PHOSPHATES / chemistry
S647	*SUPERPHOSPHATES* **SEE** PHOSPHATES / fertilizers
TN913-914	*SUPERPHOSPHATES* **SEE** PHOSPHATES / mineral resources
QP535.P1	*SUPERPHOSPHATES* **SEE** PHOSPHATES / physiological chemistry
BH301.S75	*SUPERREALISM* **SEE** SURREALISM / aesthetics
ND1265	*SUPERREALISM* **SEE** SURREALISM / painting
QD548	*SUPERSATURATED SOLUTIONS* **SEE** SOLUTIONS, SUPERSATURATED
TL551.5	*SUPERSONIC AERONAUTICS* **SEE** HIGH-SPEED AERONAUTICS

TL685.7	*SUPERSONIC AIRLINERS* **SEE** SUPERSONIC TRANSPORT PLANES
TJ267.5.C6	SUPERSONIC COMPRESSORS
TL709.5.I5	*SUPERSONIC INLETS (JET PLANES)* **SEE** AEROPLANES — RAMJET ENGINES — — AIR INTAKES
TL709.5.I5	*SUPERSONIC INLETS (JET PLANES)* **SEE** AEROPLANES — TURBOJET ENGINES — — AIR INTAKES
TJ267.5.N6	SUPERSONIC NOZZLES
TA406.5	*SUPERSONIC TESTING* **SEE** ULTRASONIC TESTING
RM951	*SUPERSONIC THERAPY* **SEE** ULTRASONIC WAVES — THERAPEUTIC USE
TL685.7	SUPERSONIC TRANSPORT PLANES
QC244	*SUPERSONIC WAVES* **SEE** ULTRASONIC WAVES / acoustics
QC244	*SUPERSONICS* **SEE** ULTRASONICS / acoustics
BF1001-1999	SUPERSTITION / occult sciences
AZ999	SUPERSTITION / popular delusions
BL490	SUPERSTITION / religion
LB1047.5	SUPERVISED STUDY
LB2801-2822	*SUPERVISION OF SCHOOLS* **SEE** SCHOOL SUPERVISION
HF5549	*SUPERVISORS, INDUSTRIAL* **SEE** FOREMEN / business management
T56	*SUPERVISORS, INDUSTRIAL* **SEE** FOREMEN / technology
TS155	*SUPERVISORS, INDUSTRIAL* **SEE** FOREMEN / technology
HF5035.C3	*SUPPLIES, ECCLESIASTICAL* **SEE** CHURCH SUPPLIES
TS2301.C5	*SUPPLIES, ECCLESIASTICAL* **SEE** CHURCH SUPPLIES
UH440-445	*SUPPLIES, MEDICAL* **SEE** MEDICAL SUPPLIES / military
VG290-295	*SUPPLIES, MEDICAL* **SEE** MEDICAL SUPPLIES / naval
UC260-267	*SUPPLIES, MILITARY* **SEE** MILITARY SUPPLIES
HB201-5	SUPPLY AND DEMAND / value
BC183	*SUPPOSITION* **SEE** HYPOTHESIS / logic
RB131	SUPPURATION
Z993.A	*SUPRALIBROS* **SEE** SUPEREXLIBRIS
BX5157	*SUPREMACY OF THE KING* **SEE** ROYAL SUPREMACY (CHURCH OF ENGLAND)
BX5157	*SUPREMACY, ROYAL* **SEE** ROYAL SUPREMACY (CHURCH OF ENGLAND)
E99.S	SUQUAMISH INDIANS
DS432.S	*SURAWAKS* **SEE** SARAKS
HG9970.S4-8	*SURETY AND FIDELITY INSURANCE* **SEE** INSURANCE, SURETY AND FIDELITY / economics
K	*SURETY AND FIDELITY INSURANCE* **SEE** INSURANCE, SURETY AND FIDELITY / law
HG9970.S4-8	*SURETY BONDS* **SEE** INSURANCE, SURETY AND FIDELITY / economics
K	*SURETY BONDS* **SEE** INSURANCE, SURETY AND FIDELITY / law
HG9970.S4-8	*SURETY COMPANIES* **SEE** INSURANCE, SURETY AND FIDELITY / economics
K	*SURETY COMPANIES* **SEE** INSURANCE, SURETY AND FIDELITY / law
GC211	*SURF* **SEE** OCEAN WAVES
SH457	*SURF FISHING* **SEE** SALT-WATER FISHING
GV840.S8	SURF RIDING
VK1473	*SURF-BOATS* **SEE** LIFE-BOATS
QL638.E5	SURF-FISHES
QD506	SURFACE CHEMISTRY
QD506	*SURFACE PHENOMENA* **SEE** SURFACE CHEMISTRY
QC183	SURFACE TENSION
QA636	SURFACES — AREAS AND VOLUMES
QD506	*SURFACES (CHEMISTRY)* **SEE** SURFACE CHEMISTRY
TA407	SURFACES (TECHNOLOGY)
QA645	SURFACES OF CONSTANT CURVATURE
QA571-3	SURFACES / analytic geometry
QA641-9	SURFACES / differential geometry
QA631-8	SURFACES / infinitesimal geometry
QA646	*SURFACES, CONFORMAL REPRESENTATION OF* **SEE** SURFACES, REPRESENTATION OF
QA561	*SURFACES, CONIC* **SEE** QUADRICS
QA573	SURFACES, CUBIC
QA643	*SURFACES, CURVES ON* **SEE** CURVES ON SURFACES
QA648	SURFACES, DEFORMATION OF
QA645	*SURFACES, ENNEPER* **SEE** SURFACES OF CONSTANT CURVATURE
QC176	*SURFACES, FERMI* **SEE** FERMI SURFACES

QA835	*SURFACES, FLEXIBLE (STATICS)* **SEE** EQUILIBRIUM OF FLEXIBLE SURFACES
QA649	SURFACES, ISOTHERMIC
QA644	SURFACES, MINIMAL
QA649	SURFACES, ORTHOGONAL
QA645	*SURFACES, PSEUDOSPHERICAL* **SEE** SURFACES OF CONSTANT CURVATURE
QA561	*SURFACES, QUADRIC* **SEE** QUADRICS
QA573	SURFACES, QUARTIC
QA573	SURFACES, QUINTIC
QA646	SURFACES, REPRESENTATION OF
QA333	*SURFACES, RIEMANN* **SEE** RIEMANN SURFACES
QA573	SURFACES, SEXTIC
GV840.S8	*SURFBOARD RIDING* **SEE** SURF RIDING
TK3226	*SURGE (ELECTRICITY)* **SEE** TRANSIENTS (ELECTRICITY)
R134-684	SURGEONS
UH400	SURGEONS / military
UH221-324	SURGEONS / military
VG260-265	SURGEONS / naval
RD19-27	SURGEONS / surgery history
RA11-405	*SURGEONS-LEGAL STATUS, LAWS, ETC.* **SEE** MEDICAL LAWS AND LEGISLATION
RD34	SURGERY — CASES, CLINICAL REPORTS, STATISTICS
RD30	SURGERY — EARLY WORKS TO 1800
RD37	SURGERY — EXAMINATIONS, QUESTIONS, ETC.
RD31.5	SURGERY — PSYCHOLOGICAL ASPECTS
RD	SURGERY
RD91-96	SURGERY, ASEPTIC AND ANTISEPTIC
RD118-120.5	*SURGERY, COSMETIC* **SEE** SURGERY, PLASTIC
RK501-555	*SURGERY, DENTAL* **SEE** DENTISTRY, OPERATIVE
RV301-311	SURGERY, ECLECTIC
RD61	SURGERY, EXPERIMENTAL
RX366-376	SURGERY, HOMEOPATHIC
RD151-498	SURGERY, MILITARY
RD111-125	SURGERY, MINOR
RD151-498	SURGERY, NAVAL
RD41	SURGERY, OPERATIVE — ATLASES
RD32	SURGERY, OPERATIVE
RD523-7	*SURGERY, ORAL* **SEE** MOUTH — SURGERY
RD701-795	*SURGERY, ORTHOPEDIC* **SEE** ORTHOPEDIA
RD137	*SURGERY, PEDIATRIC* **SEE** CHILDREN — SURGERY
RD118-120.5	SURGERY, PLASTIC
RA623.5	*SURGERY, PLASTIC-POST-MORTEM* **SEE** POST-MORTEM PLASTIC SURGERY
GN477.5-7	SURGERY, PRIMITIVE
SF911-913	*SURGERY, VETERINARY* **SEE** VETERINARY SURGERY
RD35	*SURGERY-DIAGNOSIS* **SEE** DIAGNOSIS, SURGICAL
RD71-78	*SURGERY-INSTRUMENTS* **SEE** SURGICAL INSTRUMENTS AND APPARATUS
QM531-549	*SURGICAL ANATOMY* **SEE** ANATOMY, SURGICAL AND TOPOGRAPHICAL
RD35	*SURGICAL DIAGNOSIS* **SEE** DIAGNOSIS, SURGICAL
RD113	*SURGICAL DRESSINGS* **SEE** BANDAGES AND BANDAGING
RD113	*SURGICAL DRESSINGS* **SEE** SPLINTS (SURGERY)
RD71-78	SURGICAL INSTRUMENTS AND APPARATUS
RD99	SURGICAL NURSING
RD	*SURGICAL OPERATIONS* **SEE** OPERATIONS, SURGICAL
RD57	*SURGICAL PATHOLOGY* **SEE** PATHOLOGY, SURGICAL
RD51	*SURGICAL THERAPEUTICS* **SEE** THERAPEUTICS, SURGICAL
D774.P	*SURIGAO STRAIT, BATTLE OF, 1944* **SEE** PHILIPPINE SEA, BATTLES OF THE, 1944
CS2300-2389	*SURNAMES* **SEE** NAMES, PERSONAL
UC260-265	*SURPLUS GOVERNMENT PROPERTY* **SEE** SURPLUS MILITARY PROPERTY
UC260-265	SURPLUS MILITARY PROPERTY
BF575.S8	SURPRISE
RC186.T82	*SURRA* **SEE** TRYPANOSOMIASIS
SF807	*SURRA* **SEE** TRYPANOSOMIASIS / veterinary medicine
BH301.S75	SURREALISM / aesthetics
ND1265	SURREALISM / painting
TA544	SURVEYING — EARLY WORKS TO 1800
TA537	SURVEYING — EXAMINATIONS, QUESTIONS, ETC.
TA562-581	SURVEYING — INSTRUMENTS
TA622	SURVEYING — PUBLIC LANDS
TA552	SURVEYING — TABLES, ETC.
TA562-581	*SURVEYING INSTRUMENTS* **SEE** SURVEYING — INSTRUMENTS

TA501-625	SURVEYING
VK591-7	*SURVEYING, MARINE* **SEE** HYDROGRAPHIC SURVEYING
UG470	*SURVEYING, MILITARY* **SEE** MILITARY TOPOGRAPHY
TA563	SURVEYOR'S COMPASS
TA515-531	SURVEYORS
VK596-7	SURVEYORS, MARINE
TA579	SURVEYORS' CHAINS
TA575	*SURVEYORS' TRANSIT* **SEE** TRANSIT, SURVEYORS'
TA611	SURVEYS — PLOTTING
GA51-87	SURVEYS
QB296	SURVEYS / *by country*
QB301-325	SURVEYS / *geodetic surveying*
QE61-350	SURVEYS / *geological*
QH101-199	SURVEYS / *natural history*
HD301-1130	*SURVEYS, CADASTRAL* **SEE** REAL PROPERTY / *other countries*
HD301-1130	*SURVEYS, CATASTRAL* **SEE** REAL PROPERTY / *other countries*
LB2823	*SURVEYS, EDUCATIONAL* **SEE** EDUCATIONAL SURVEYS
HN29	*SURVEYS, SOCIAL* **SEE** SOCIAL SURVEYS
HE369-373	*SURVEYS, TRAFFIC* **SEE** TRAFFIC SURVEYS
TL553.7	SURVIVAL (AFTER AEROPLANE ACCIDENTS, SHIPWRECKS, ETC.) / *aeronautics*
HD7105-6	*SURVIVORS' BENEFITS (OLD AGE PENSIONS)* **SEE** OLD AGE PENSIONS / *working-men's insurance*
HG9426-9446	*SURVIVORS' BENEFITS (OLD AGE PENSIONS)* **SEE** OLD AGE PENSIONS / *age insurance*
SK305.W5	*SUS SCROFA* **SEE** WILD BOAR / *hunting*
P943	*SUSIAN LANGUAGE* **SEE** ELAMITE LANGUAGE
QL737.R6	*SUSLIKS* **SEE** GROUND-SQUIRRELS
PL8695	*SUSOO LANGUAGE* **SEE** SUSU LANGUAGE
TF693	*SUSPENDED RAILROADS* **SEE** RAILROADS, SUSPENDED
HV9278	*SUSPENDED SENTENCE* **SEE** PROBATION
HV9301-9430	*SUSPENDED SENTENCE* **SEE** PROBATION
TG400	*SUSPENSION BRIDGES* **SEE** BRIDGES, SUSPENSION
TH2417	*SUSPENSION ROOFS* **SEE** ROOFS, SUSPENSION
F157.W9	SUSQUEHANNA CLAIM
E99.S9	SUSQUEHANNA INDIANS
E99.S9	*SUSQUEHANNOCK INDIANS* **SEE** SUSQUEHANNA INDIANS
PL8695	SUSU LANGUAGE
PL8689	*SUTO LANGUAGE* **SEE** SOTHO LANGUAGE
GT3370	SUTTEE
PL8689	*SUTU LANGUAGE* **SEE** SOTHO LANGUAGE
RD73.S8	SUTURES
GN131	*SUTURES, CRANIAL* **SEE** CRANIAL SUTURES / *anthropology*
QL821	*SUTURES, CRANIAL* **SEE** CRANIAL SUTURES / *comparative anatomy*
QM105	*SUTURES, CRANIAL* **SEE** CRANIAL SUTURES / *human anatomy*
DK34.S8	*SVANES* **SEE** SVANETIANS
DK34.S8	SVANETIANS
DK34.S8	*SVANS* **SEE** SVANETIANS
BL604.S8	*SVASTIKA* **SEE** SWASTIKA
NK1177	*SVASTIKA* **SEE** SWASTIKA / *art*
DL192	*SVECO-DANISH WARS, 1657-1660* **SEE** DANO-SWEDISH WARS, 1657-1660
TK6553	*SW RADIO* **SEE** RADIO, SHORT WAVE
DD801.W976	SWABIAN LEAGUE, 1488-1533
DQ106-7	SWABIAN WAR, 1499
QA76.8.S8	*SWAC (COMPUTER)* **SEE** SWAC COMPUTER
TK7889.S8	*SWAC (COMPUTER)* **SEE** SWAC COMPUTER / *engineering*
QA76.8.S8	SWAC COMPUTER
TK7889.S8	SWAC COMPUTER / *engineering*
PL8701-4	SWAHILI LANGUAGE
PL8704.A-Z5	SWAHILI LITERATURE
QP311	*SWALLOWING* **SEE** DEGLUTITION
QL696.P2	SWALLOWS
QL696.C9	*SWALLOWS, CHIMNEY* **SEE** SWIFTS
SB618.P	*SWAMP-DOGWOOD* **SEE** POISON-SUMAC
SB618.P	*SWAMP-SUMAC* **SEE** POISON-SUMAC
DA670.F33	*SWAMPS* **SEE** FENS / *england*
S621	*SWAMPS* **SEE** MARSHES / *agriculture*
TC975	*SWAMPS* **SEE** MARSHES / *reclamation*
GB621-8	*SWAMPS* **SEE** MOORS AND HEATHS

S621	*SWAMPS* **SEE** MOORS AND HEATHS / *agriculture*
HD1665-1683	*SWAMPS* **SEE** MOORS AND HEATHS / *agriculture*
GR735	SWAN (IN RELIGION, FOLK-LORE, ETC.) / *folk-lore*
PN687.S8	SWAN (IN RELIGION, FOLK-LORE, ETC.) / *medieval legends*
BL325.S	SWAN (IN RELIGION, FOLK-LORE, ETC.) / *mythology*
GR75.S8	SWAN-MAIDENS
DK34.S8	*SWANETIANS* **SEE** SVANETIANS
QL696.A5	SWANS
NK4399.S9	SWANSEA PORCELAIN
NK4399.S9	SWANSEA POTTERY
DT971	*SWASI* **SEE** SWAZI (AFRICAN TRIBE)
BL604.S8	SWASTIKA
NK1177	SWASTIKA / *art*
DT971	SWAZI (AFRICAN TRIBE)
PL8705	SWAZI LANGUAGE
PL8538	*SWCIRI LANGUAGE* **SEE** MWAMBA LANGUAGE
BJ1535.P95	SWEARING
GT3080	SWEARING / *manners and customs*
BV4627.S9	SWEARING / *moral theology*
QP221	*SWEAT* **SEE** PERSPIRATION
RL141	SWEAT GLANDS — DISEASES
TT825	SWEATERS
HD2337-9	SWEATING SYSTEM
RC168.M6	SWEATING-SICKNESS
DL601-991	SWEDEN — HISTORY
DL190	*SWEDEN-HISTORY-DANO-SWEDISH WARS, 1643-1660* **SEE** DANO-SWEDISH WAR, 1643-1645
DL192	*SWEDEN-HISTORY-DANO-SWEDISH WARS, 1643-1660* **SEE** DANO-SWEDISH WARS, 1657-1660
DL188.5	*SWEDEN-HISTORY-NORTHERN SEVEN YEARS' WAR, 1563-1570* **SEE** NORTHERN SEVEN YEARS' WAR, 1563-1570 / *denmark*
BX8701-8749	*SWEDENBORGIANISM* **SEE** NEW JERUSALEM CHURCH
DL631-9	SWEDES
PT9595	SWEDISH BALLADS AND SONGS / *collections*
PT9401	SWEDISH BALLADS AND SONGS / *history*
PT9618	SWEDISH DRAMA (COMEDY) / *collections*
PT9441	SWEDISH DRAMA (COMEDY) / *history*
PT9605-9625	SWEDISH DRAMA / *collections*
PT9415-9449	SWEDISH DRAMA / *history*
PT9635	SWEDISH ESSAYS / *collections*
PT9497	SWEDISH ESSAYS / *history*
PT9627-9630	SWEDISH FICTION / *collections*
PT9480-9492	SWEDISH FICTION / *history*
GV467	SWEDISH GYMNASTICS
RM721	SWEDISH GYMNASTICS / *therapeutics*
PD5771-8	SWEDISH LANGUAGE — OLD SWEDISH
PD5001-5929	SWEDISH LANGUAGE
PT9550-9555	SWEDISH LITERATURE / *collections*
PT9201-9370	SWEDISH LITERATURE / *history*
PN5301-5310	SWEDISH PERIODICALS / *history*
PT9582	SWEDISH POETRY — OLD SWEDISH / *collections*
PT9580-9599	SWEDISH POETRY / *collections*
PT9375-9405	SWEDISH POETRY / *history*
PT9626-9639	SWEDISH PROSE LITERATURE / *collections*
PT9460-9499	SWEDISH PROSE LITERATURE / *history*
SB211.R8	*SWEDISH TURNIP* **SEE** RUTABAGA
GV1291.P8	*SWEDISH WHIST* **SEE** PREFERENCE (GAME)
PT9636	SWEDISH WIT AND HUMOR / *collections*
PT9498	SWEDISH WIT AND HUMOR / *history*
PT9980-9994	SWEDISH-AMERICAN LITERATURE
PN4885.S79-84	SWEDISH-AMERICAN NEWSPAPERS
PN4885.S79-84	SWEDISH-AMERICAN PERIODICALS
PT9991	SWEDISH-AMERICAN POETRY / *collections*
PT9986	SWEDISH-AMERICAN POETRY / *history*
DL192	*SWEDISH-DANISH WARS, 1657-1660* **SEE** DANO-SWEDISH WARS, 1657-1660
DL192	SWEDISH-DUTCH WAR, 1658-1659
DL712	SWEDISH-POLISH WAR, 1617-1629
DL725	SWEDISH-POLISH WAR, 1655-1660
VK594	*SWEEPS (HYDROGRAPHY)* **SEE** DRAGS (HYDROGRAPHY)
SB205.S9	SWEET CLOVER
SB191.M2	*SWEET CORN* **SEE** MAIZE / *culture*
HD9049.C8	*SWEET CORN* **SEE** MAIZE / *grain trade*
SB413.S9	SWEET PEAS

SB608.S95	SWEET PEAS / pests
SB351.P4	*SWEET PEPPERS* **SEE** PEPPERS
SB608.S98	SWEET POTATOES — DISEASES AND PESTS
SB211.S9	SWEET POTATOES
SD397.S78	SWEET-GUM
GC211	*SWELL* **SEE** OCEAN WAVES
QL696.C9	SWIFTS
QL855	*SWIM BLADDER* **SEE** AIR-BLADDER (IN FISHES)
QL855	*SWIMBLADDER* **SEE** AIR-BLADDER (IN FISHES)
TH4763	SWIMMING POOLS
RA606	SWIMMING POOLS / public health
QL855	*SWIMMING-BLADDER* **SEE** AIR-BLADDER (IN FISHES)
GV837	SWIMMING / aquatic sports
HV6691-9	SWINDLERS AND SWINDLING
SF971-7	SWINE — DISEASES
SF393	SWINE — HERD-BOOKS
SF392	SWINE BREEDERS — DIRECTORIES
SF392	*SWINE BREEDERS' DIRECTORIES* **SEE** SWINE BREEDERS — DIRECTORIES
SF391	SWINE BREEDERS' SOCIETIES
SF973	*SWINE FEVER* **SEE** HOG CHOLERA
QL391.N4	SWINE KIDNEY WORM / zoology
SF977	SWINE PLAGUE
QL737.U5	SWINE
SF391-7	SWINE / animal industries
QE882.U3	SWINE, FOSSIL
GV979.S9	SWING (GOLF)
GV1796.J	*SWING DANCING* **SEE** JITTERBUG DANCING
ML3561	*SWING MUSIC* **SEE** JAZZ MUSIC
GV1771	*SWINGING PLAYS* **SEE** PLAY-PARTY
PT3874	*SWISS BALLADS AND SONGS (GERMAN)* **SEE** GERMAN BALLADS AND SONGS — SWISS AUTHORS / collections
PT3870	*SWISS BALLADS AND SONGS (GERMAN)* **SEE** GERMAN BALLADS AND SONGS — SWISS AUTHORS / history
DQ3	SWISS LETTERS / collections
PQ3888.G	SWISS LITERATURE (FRENCH) — GENEVA
PQ3870-3888	SWISS LITERATURE (FRENCH)
PT3860-3872	*SWISS LITERATURE (GERMAN)* **SEE** GERMAN LITERATURE — SWISS AUTHORS / history
PT3873-6	*SWISS LITERATURE (GERMAN)* **SEE** GERMAN LITERATURE — SWISS AUTHORS / collections
D25.5	SWISS MERCENARIES
PN5331-9	SWISS NEWSPAPERS / history
PN5331-5340	SWISS PERIODICALS / history
PT3874	SWISS POETRY (GERMAN) / collections
PT3870	SWISS POETRY (GERMAN) / history
PT3876.W5	SWISS WIT AND HUMOR / german
PN6222.S	SWISS WIT AND HUMOR / minor collections
DQ36-48	SWISS
TK6391-7	*SWITCHBOARDS, TELEPHONE* **SEE** TELEPHONE SWITCHBOARDS
TK2821-2846	*SWITCHES, ELECTRIC* **SEE** ELECTRIC SWITCHGEAR
TF266	*SWITCHES, RAILROAD* **SEE** RAILROADS — SWITCHES
TF635	*SWITCHES, RAILROAD* **SEE** RAILROADS — SWITCHES / interlocking
TF592	*SWITCHING (RAILROADS)* **SEE** RAILROADS — SWITCHING
TF590	*SWITCHING YARDS* **SEE** RAILROADS — YARDS
HD8039.R4	SWITCHMEN / labor
HD6350.R4	SWITCHMEN / trade-union periodicals
DQ	SWITZERLAND — HISTORY
GV1796.S9	SWORD-DANCE
SH351.S8	SWORDFISH
U860	SWORDPLAY
U850-872	SWORDS
NK6700-6799	SWORDS / art
UE420-425	SWORDS / cavalry
UD420-425	SWORDS / infantry
U860	*SWORDSMANSHIP* **SEE** SWORDPLAY
QK495.P72	SYCAMORE
SD397.S8	SYCAMORE / forestry
DT551.42	*SYENA (AFRICAN PEOPLE)* **SEE** SENUFO (AFRICAN PEOPLE)
QE475	SYENITE
PJ3191-3225	*SYLLABARIES, ASSYRO-BABYLONIAN* **SEE** CUNEIFORM WRITING
PJ3191-3225	*SYLLABARIES, SUMERIAN* **SEE** CUNEIFORM WRITING

P236	*SYLLABLE* **SEE** GRAMMAR, COMPARATIVE AND GENERAL — SYLLABLE
BC185	*SYLLOGISM* / logic
QD341.A2	*SYLVIC ACID* **SEE** ABIETIC ACID
SD	*SYLVICULTURE* **SEE** FORESTS AND FORESTRY
HJ3805	*SYLVICULTURE* **SEE** FORESTS AND FORESTRY / income from state forests
HJ4167	*SYLVICULTURE* **SEE** FORESTS AND FORESTRY / taxation
QH548	SYMBIOSIS / biology
QK918	SYMBIOSIS / botany
BC131-5	*SYMBOLIC AND MATHEMATICAL LOGIC* **SEE** LOGIC, SYMBOLIC AND MATHEMATICAL
ND1286	*SYMBOLIC COLORS* **SEE** SYMBOLISM OF COLORS
PM8508	*SYMBOLIC LANGUAGE* **SEE** LINCOS (ARTIFICIAL LANGUAGE)
QA76.5	*SYMBOLIC LANGUAGE* **SEE** MAD (COMPUTER PROGRAM LANGUAGE)
BF1623.P9	*SYMBOLIC NUMBERS* **SEE** SYMBOLISM OF NUMBERS
BX	*SYMBOLICS* **SEE** CREEDS / by denomination
BT990-999	*SYMBOLICS* **SEE** CREEDS / general
BF723.S	SYMBOLISM (PSYCHOLOGY) / child study
BF458	SYMBOLISM (PSYCHOLOGY) / psychology
N7740	SYMBOLISM IN ART
PN56.S9	SYMBOLISM IN LITERATURE
ML3838	SYMBOLISM IN MUSIC
BF723.S	*SYMBOLISM IN PSYCHOLOGY* **SEE** SYMBOLISM (PSYCHOLOGY) / child study
BF458	*SYMBOLISM IN PSYCHOLOGY* **SEE** SYMBOLISM (PSYCHOLOGY) / psychology
ND1286	SYMBOLISM OF COLORS
QK84	SYMBOLISM OF FLOWERS
BF1623.P9	SYMBOLISM OF NUMBERS
BV150-165	SYMBOLISM / christian
CB475	SYMBOLISM / civilization
BL600-620	SYMBOLISM / comparative religion
BF1623.S9	SYMBOLISM / occult sciences
BF458	SYMBOLISM / psychology
QA212	SYMMETRIC FUNCTIONS
MT50	SYMMETRICAL INVERSION (MUSIC)
N76	*SYMMETRY (ART)* **SEE** PROPORTION (ART)
NC745	*SYMMETRY (ART)* **SEE** PROPORTION (ART) / design
Q175	SYMMETRY (BIOLOGY)
N76	SYMMETRY / art
NC745	SYMMETRY / design
QM471	*SYMPATHETIC NERVOUS SYSTEM* **SEE** NERVOUS SYSTEM, SYMPATHETIC / human anatomy
QL939	*SYMPATHETIC NERVOUS SYSTEM* **SEE** NERVOUS SYSTEM, SYMPATHETIC / comparative anatomy
QP368	*SYMPATHETIC NERVOUS SYSTEM* **SEE** NERVOUS SYSTEM, SYMPATHETIC / physiology
HD5309	*SYMPATHETIC STRIKES AND LOCKOUTS* **SEE** STRIKES AND LOCKOUTS, SYMPATHETIC
R133	SYMPATHY (PHYSIOLOGY)
R128.7	SYMPATHY (PHYSIOLOGY) / 17th and 18th century medicine
BJ1533.S9	SYMPATHY
ML1270.S9	SYMPHONIC POEM
M1203	SYMPHONIC POEMS (BAND)
M1254	SYMPHONIC POEMS (BAND), ARRANGED
M1002	SYMPHONIC POEMS (CHAMBER ORCHESTRA) — SCORES
M1002	SYMPHONIC POEMS (CHAMBER ORCHESTRA)
M9	SYMPHONIC POEMS (ORGAN)
M1102	SYMPHONIC POEMS (STRING ORCHESTRA) — SCORES
M1102	SYMPHONIC POEMS (STRING ORCHESTRA)
M215	SYMPHONIC POEMS ARRANGED FOR PIANO (2 PIANOS)
M216	SYMPHONIC POEMS ARRANGED FOR PIANO (2 PIANOS, 8 HANDS)
M209	SYMPHONIC POEMS ARRANGED FOR PIANO (4 HANDS)
M35	SYMPHONIC POEMS ARRANGED FOR PIANO
M235-6	SYMPHONIC POEMS ARRANGED FOR VIOLONCELLO AND PIANO
M1002	SYMPHONIC POEMS
MT130	SYMPHONIES — ANALYSIS, APPRECIATION
MT125	SYMPHONIES — ANALYSIS, APPRECIATION
MT130	SYMPHONIES — ANALYTICAL GUIDES
MT125	SYMPHONIES — ANALYTICAL GUIDES
ML156.4.S	SYMPHONIES — DISCOGRAPHY

MT130	SYMPHONIES — THEMATIC CATALOGS
MT125	SYMPHONIES — THEMATIC CATALOGS
M1203	SYMPHONIES (BAND) — EXCERPTS
M1203	SYMPHONIES (BAND)
M1254	SYMPHONIES (BAND), ARRANGED
M1203	*SYMPHONIES (BAND)-SCORES (REDUCED) AND PARTS-EXCERPTS* **SEE** SYMPHONIES (BAND) — EXCERPTS — — SCORES (REDUCED) AND PARTS
M1203	SYMPHONIES (BAND) — EXCERPTS — — SCORES (REDUCED) AND PARTS
M1001	SYMPHONIES (CHAMBER ORCHESTRA)
M1106	SYMPHONIES (ORGAN WITH ORCHESTRA) — SOLO WITH PIANO
M1105-6	SYMPHONIES (ORGAN WITH ORCHESTRA)
M1101	SYMPHONIES (STRING ORCHESTRA)
M1160	SYMPHONIES (STRING ORCHESTRA), ARRANGED
M1016	SYMPHONIES (VIOLONCELLO WITH ORCHESTRA) — SCORES
M1016-1017	SYMPHONIES (VIOLONCELLO WITH ORCHESTRA)
M955-7	SYMPHONIES - (WIND ENSEMBLE)
M1001	*SYMPHONIES - VOCAL SCORES WITH PIANO -- EXCERPTS* **SEE** SYMPHONIES — EXCERPTS — — VOCAL SCORES WITH PIANO
M563-4	SYMPHONIES ARRANGED FOR FLUTE, 2 VIOLINS, VIOLA, VIOLONCELLO
M215	SYMPHONIES ARRANGED FOR PIANO (2 PIANOS)
M216	SYMPHONIES ARRANGED FOR PIANO (2 PIANOS, 8 HANDS)
M209	SYMPHONIES ARRANGED FOR PIANO (4 HANDS)
M314	SYMPHONIES ARRANGED FOR PIANO TRIOS
M35	SYMPHONIES ARRANGED FOR PIANO
M423-4	SYMPHONIES ARRANGED FOR PIANO, FLUTE, VIOLIN, VIOLONCELLO
M553-4	SYMPHONIES ARRANGED FOR STRING QUINTETS
M222-3	SYMPHONIES ARRANGED FOR VIOLIN AND PIANO
M235-6	SYMPHONIES ARRANGED FOR VIOLONCELLO AND PIANO
M352-3	SYMPHONIES ARRANGED FOR 2 VIOLINS, VIOLONCELLO
M1001	SYMPHONIES
M1001	*SYMPHONIES-VOCAL SCORES WITH PIANO-EXCERPTS* **SEE** SYMPHONIES — EXCERPTS — — VOCAL SCORES WITH PIANO
M1001	SYMPHONIES — EXCERPTS — — VOCAL SCORES WITH PIANO
ML1255	SYMPHONY
RG791	SYMPHYSEOTOMY
PA3031	SYMPOSIUM (CLASSICAL LITERATURE)
SF787	*SYMPTOMATIC ANTHRAX* **SEE** ANTHRAX, SYMPTOMATIC / *veterinary medicine*
RB37-55	*SYMPTOMS* **SEE** DIAGNOSIS / *laboratory methods*
RC71-78	*SYMPTOMS* **SEE** DIAGNOSIS / *practice of medicine*
RC69	*SYMPTOMS* **SEE** SEMIOLOGY
NA4690	SYNAGOGUE ARCHITECTURE
BM744.6	SYNAGOGUE DEDICATION SERMONS
ML166	SYNAGOGUE MUSIC — HISTORY AND CRITICISM
ML3195	SYNAGOGUE MUSIC — HISTORY AND CRITICISM
M2186-7	SYNAGOGUE MUSIC / *services*
M2114.3	SYNAGOGUE MUSIC / *songs*
M2099.5	SYNAGOGUE MUSIC / *special texts*
M2079.5	SYNAGOGUE MUSIC / *special texts*
BM653	SYNAGOGUES — ORGANIZATION AND ADMINISTRATION
BM653	SYNAGOGUES
NA4690	SYNAGOGUES / *architecture*
TK2796	*SYNCHRONOUS CONVERTERS* **SEE** ROTARY CONVERTERS
TK2787	*SYNCHRONOUS MOTORS* **SEE** ELECTRIC MOTORS, SYNCHRONOUS
QC787.S9	SYNCHROTRON
BR127	*SYNCRETISM (CHRISTIANITY)* **SEE** CHRISTIANITY AND OTHER RELIGIONS / *general*
BX8020	*SYNCRETISM (LUTHERAN CHURCH)* **SEE** SYNCRETISTIC CONTROVERSY / *lutheranism*
BX8020	SYNCRETISTIC CONTROVERSY / *lutheranism*
HD6477	SYNDICALISM
DS111.2	SYNEDRION
BF495-9	SYNESTHESIA
BV710	*SYNODS* **SEE** COUNCILS AND SYNODS / *general*
QM131	SYNOVIAL MEMBRANES
RC280.S	*SYNOVIALOMA* **SEE** SYNOVIOMA
RC280.S	SYNOVIOMA
P291-5	*SYNTAX* **SEE** GRAMMAR, COMPARATIVE AND GENERAL — SYNTAX
QD262	*SYNTHETIC CHEMISTRY* **SEE** CHEMISTRY, ORGANIC — SYNTHESIS
Q327	*SYNTHETIC CONSCIOUSNESS* **SEE** CONSCIOUS AUTOMATA
TP873.5.D5	*SYNTHETIC DIAMONDS* **SEE** DIAMONDS, ARTIFICIAL
TS1688	SYNTHETIC FABRICS
TP983	*SYNTHETIC PERFUMES* **SEE** PERFUMES, SYNTHETIC
TP873	*SYNTHETIC PRECIOUS STONES* **SEE** PRECIOUS STONES, ARTIFICIAL
TP986	SYNTHETIC PRODUCTS / *plastics*
TP977-8	*SYNTHETIC RESINS* **SEE** GUMS AND RESINS, SYNTHETIC
TP986	*SYNTHETIC RESINS* **SEE** GUMS AND RESINS, SYNTHETIC / *plastics*
TS1925	*SYNTHETIC RUBBER* **SEE** RUBBER, ARTIFICIAL
V252	SYNTHETIC TRAINING DEVICES
PJ2361	*SYOUAH LANGUAGE* **SEE** SIWA LANGUAGE
RC201.2	SYPHILIS — DIAGNOSIS
RX226.S8	SYPHILIS — HOMEOPATHIC TREATMENT
RC200.6.I	SYPHILIS — INOCULATION
RA1141	SYPHILIS — JURISPRUDENCE
RC201.5-67	SYPHILIS — PREVENTION / *by country*
RA644.V4	SYPHILIS — PREVENTION / *public health*
RC201	SYPHILIS
RC201	SYPHILIS, CONGENITAL, HEREDITARY, AND INFANTILE
RC201.2	SYPHILIS — DIAGNOSIS — — WASSERMANN REACTION
PJ5701-5809	SYRIAC LANGUAGE
PJ5401-5494	SYRIAC LANGUAGE
PJ5801-9	SYRIAC LANGUAGE, MODERN
PJ5241-9	SYRIAC LANGUAGE, PALESTINIAN / *christian*
PJ5251-9	SYRIAC LANGUAGE, PALESTINIAN / *jewish*
PJ5601-5695	SYRIAC LITERATURE
PJ5617	SYRIAC POETRY / *collections*
PJ5604	SYRIAC POETRY / *history*
BX170-179	SYRIAN CHURCH
DS93-94	SYRIANS
RD73.S9	SYRINGES
QD341.A2	SYRINGIC ACID
RC385	SYRINGOMYELIA
ML980	SYRINX (MUSICAL INSTRUMENT)
QL697	SYRINX (OF BIRDS)
PH1051-9	*SYRJENIAN LANGUAGE* **SEE** SYRYENIAN LANGUAGE
DK34.S9	*SYRJENIANS* **SEE** SYRYENIANS
TP413	SYRUPS
RS201.S8	SYRUPS / *pharmacy*
PH1051-9	SYRYENIAN LANGUAGE
PH1071-9	*SYRYENIAN LANGUAGE-DIALECTS-PERMYAK* **SEE** PERMYAK DIALECT
PH1058.5-1059	SYRYENIAN LITERATURE / *collections*
PH1058	SYRYENIAN LITERATURE / *history*
DK34.S9	SYRYENIANS
QA402	SYSTEM ANALYSIS
TA168	*SYSTEM ENGINEERING* **SEE** SYSTEMS ENGINEERING
QA402	*SYSTEM THEORY* **SEE** SYSTEM ANALYSIS
Q375	*SYSTEM UNCERTAINTY* **SEE** UNCERTAINTY (INFORMATION THEORY)
QA402	*SYSTEMS ANALYSIS* **SEE** SYSTEM ANALYSIS
TA168	SYSTEMS ENGINEERING
QA402	*SYSTEMS, THEORY OF* **SEE** SYSTEM ANALYSIS
DS731.M	*T'U-JEN* **SEE** MONGUORS
DS759	*T'AI P'ING REBELLION* **SEE** TAIPING REBELLION, 1850-1864
DS748.6	*T'O PA DYNASTY* **SEE** CHINA — HISTORY — — NORTHERN WEI DYNASTY, 386-636
DS754-760	*TA CH'ING DYNASTY* **SEE** MANCHUS / *dynasty*
DS781-4	*TA CH'ING DYNASTY* **SEE** MANCHUS / *manchuria*
PF861-884	*TAAL* **SEE** AFRIKAANS LANGUAGE
ML1040	*TABALA* **SEE** TABLA
PK9201.T	TABASARAN LANGUAGE
PK9201.T	*TABASSARAN LANGUAGE* **SEE** TABASARAN LANGUAGE
TA681	TABBY (CONCRETE)
E99.T114	TABEGUACHE INDIANS
BM695.S	*TABERNACLES, FEAST OF* **SEE** SUKKOTH

RC203.T3	*TABES DORSALIS* **SEE** LOCOMOTOR ATAXIA
M298	*TABLA AND SARANGI MUSIC* **SEE** SARANGI AND TABLA MUSIC
M298	*TABLA AND SARANGI MUSIC* **SEE** SARANGI AND TABLA MUSIC
ML1040	TABLA
ML431	TABLATURE (MUSICAL NOTATION) / *history*
MT35	TABLATURE (MUSICAL NOTATION) / *instruction*
MT538	TABLATURE (MUSICAL NOTATION) / *wind instruments*
TX645-840	*TABLE* **SEE** COOKERY
BV283.G7	*TABLE BLESSINGS* **SEE** GRACE AT MEALS
TX871-9	*TABLE DECORATION* **SEE** TABLE SETTING AND DECORATION
BJ2041	TABLE ETIQUETTE
BV283.G7	*TABLE PRAYERS* **SEE** GRACE AT MEALS
TX871-9	TABLE SETTING AND DECORATION
GV1005	TABLE TENNIS
NK8900-8999	TABLE-CLOTHS / *art*
TS1580	TABLE-CLOTHS / *textile manufactures*
BF1375	TABLE-MOVING (SPIRITUALISM)
BF1375	*TABLE-RAPPING* **SEE** TABLE-MOVING (SPIRITUALISM)
PN6259-6268	TABLE-TALK
BF1375	*TABLE-TIPPING* **SEE** TABLE-MOVING (SPIRITUALISM)
TR650	*TABLE-TOP PHOTOGRAPHY* **SEE** PHOTOGRAPHY, TABLE-TOP
TX871-9	TABLE
PN6120.T3	TABLEAUX
PN4305.T3	TABLEAUX / *recitations*
HA48	*TABLES (SYSTEMATIC LISTS)* **SEE** STATISTICS — CHARTS, TABLES, ETC.
TL551	*TABLES OF DISTANCES* **SEE** DISTANCES — TABLES, ETC. / *aeronautics*
GV1024-5	*TABLES OF DISTANCES* **SEE** DISTANCES — TABLES, ETC. / *automobiling*
G109-110	*TABLES OF DISTANCES* **SEE** DISTANCES — TABLES, ETC. / *geography*
VF550	*TABLES OF DISTANCES* **SEE** DISTANCES — TABLES, ETC. / *naval ordnance*
VK799	*TABLES OF DISTANCES* **SEE** DISTANCES — TABLES, ETC. / *navigation*
UF857	*TABLES OF DISTANCES* **SEE** DISTANCES — TABLES, ETC. / *ordnance*
QC895	*TABLES OF HEIGHTS* **SEE** ALTITUDES — MEASUREMENT / *meteorology*
TA606-9	*TABLES OF HEIGHTS* **SEE** ALTITUDES — MEASUREMENT / *surveying*
TT197.5.T3	TABLES / *cabinet work*
TS880	TABLES / *manufacture*
QA111	*TABLES, COMPUTING* **SEE** READY-RECKONERS / *arithmetic*
HF5697-5702	*TABLES, COMPUTING* **SEE** READY-RECKONERS / *business arithmetic*
HG1626-1638	*TABLES, INTEREST* **SEE** INTEREST AND USURY — TABLES, ETC.
QB399	*TABLES, LUNAR* **SEE** MOON — TABLES / *lunar theory*
VK563-7	*TABLES, LUNAR* **SEE** MOON — TABLES / *navigation*
QA49	*TABLES, MATHEMATICAL* **SEE** DIVISION — TABLES
QA51	*TABLES, MATHEMATICAL* **SEE** FACTOR TABLES
QA55-59	*TABLES, MATHEMATICAL* **SEE** LOGARITHMS
QA47-59	*TABLES, MATHEMATICAL* **SEE** MATHEMATICS — TABLES, ETC.
QA49	*TABLES, MATHEMATICAL* **SEE** MULTIPLICATION — TABLES
QA111	*TABLES, MATHEMATICAL* **SEE** READY-RECKONERS / *arithmetic*
HF5697-5702	*TABLES, MATHEMATICAL* **SEE** READY-RECKONERS / *business arithmetic*
QA49	*TABLES, MATHEMATICAL* **SEE** SQUARES, TABLES OF
QA55	*TABLES, MATHEMATICAL* **SEE** TRIGONOMETRY — TABLES, ETC.
TT848	*TABLET WEAVING* **SEE** CARD WEAVING
TR650	*TABLETOP PHOTOGRAPHY* **SEE** PHOTOGRAPHY, TABLE-TOP
RS201.T2	TABLETS (MEDICINE)
CN397.H4	*TABLETS, HERACLEAN* **SEE** HERACLEAN TABLETS
NB1800-1885	*TABLETS, MEMORIAL* **SEE** SEPULCHRAL MONUMENTS / *sculpture*
PJ3885-7	*TABLETS, TELL-EL-AMARNA* **SEE** TELL-EL-AMARNA TABLETS

GN494	TABOO
M1035	*TABOR* **SEE** TAMBOURIN
HA31	TABULATING MACHINES / *statistical*
Z50.7	TABULATION TYPEWRITING
Z50.7	*TABULATION TYPING* **SEE** TABULATION TYPEWRITING
TL696.T3	TACAN
PM7088	TACANAN LANGUAGE
TA579	*TACHEOMETER (SURVEYING INSTRUMENT)* **SEE** TACHYMETER
TL589.7.T3	TACHOMETER / *aeronautical instruments*
Z53-100	*TACHYGRAPHY* **SEE** SHORTHAND
Z54-57	*TACHYGRAPHY* **SEE** SHORTHAND / *english*
TA579	TACHYMETER
VM531	*TACKLING* **SEE** MASTS AND RIGGING
TS440-445	TACKS
F3097.3	TACNA-ARICA QUESTION
TL696.T3	*TACTICAL AIR NAVIGATION* **SEE** TACAN
U312 E	TACTICS — PROBLEMS, EXERCISES, ETC.
U164-7	TACTICS
E99.T17	*TACULLI INDIANS* **SEE** TAKULLI INDIANS
PM2411	*TACULLI LANGUAGE* **SEE** TAKULLI LANGUAGE
PK6971-9	*TADJIK LANGUAGE* **SEE** TAJIK LANGUAGE
QL668.E2	*TADPOLES* **SEE** FROGS / *zoology*
QL668.E2	*TADPOLES* **SEE** TOADS
PK6971-9	*TADZHIK LANGUAGE* **SEE** TAJIK LANGUAGE
PL5456	TAE' LANGUAGE
E99.T115	*TAENCA INDIANS* **SEE** TAENSA INDIANS
QL391.C4	TAENIA
E99.T115	TAENSA INDIANS
PM2391	TAENSA LANGUAGE
E99.T115	*TAENSO INDIANS* **SEE** TAENSA INDIANS
E99.T115	*TAENZA INDIANS* **SEE** TAENSA INDIANS
DS759	*TAEPING REBELLION* **SEE** TAIPING REBELLION, 1850-1864
PL6048	TAGABILI LANGUAGE
PL6058	TAGALOG DRAMA
PL6051-9	TAGALOG LANGUAGE
PL6058	TAGALOG LITERATURE
PL6060	TAGALOG LITERATURE / *history*
PL6058	TAGALOG POETRY
DS666.T2	TAGALOGS
DS666.T2	*TAGALS* **SEE** TAGALOGS
DS666.T3	TAGBANUAS
GN671.P5	TAGBANUAS / *anthropology*
PL6515	TAHITIAN LANGUAGE
E99.T17	*TAHKALI INDIANS* **SEE** TAKULLI INDIANS
PM2411	*TAHKALI LANGUAGE* **SEE** TAKULLI LANGUAGE
E99.T12	TAHLTAN INDIANS
E99.T	*TAHWAHCARRO INDIANS* **SEE** TAWAKONI INDIANS
PL4151-4199	*TAI LANGUAGE* **SEE** SIAMESE LANGUAGE
PL4111-4251	TAI LANGUAGES
DS560	TAI RACE
QL950.6	TAIL
GN651	TAILED MEN / *central africa*
QL696.P2	TAILOR-BIRDS
TT570-630	*TAILORESSES* **SEE** TAILORS
GT5960.T2	*TAILORESSES* **SEE** TAILORS / *manners and customs*
UC510	*TAILORESSES* **SEE** TAILORS / *military*
TT585	TAILORING — TABLES, CALCULATIONS, ETC.
TT500-565	TAILORING (WOMEN'S)
TT570-630	TAILORING
TT570-630	TAILORS
GT5960.T2	TAILORS / *manners and customs*
UC510	TAILORS / *military*
D775.5.M	*TAINARON, CAPE, BATTLE OF, 1941* **SEE** MATAPAN, BATTLE OF, 1941
F1619.2.T3	TAINO INDIANS
PM7093	TAINO LANGUAGE
DS759	TAIPING REBELLION, 1850-1864
F2270.2.T	TAIRONA INDIANS
DT429	TAITA (BANTU TRIBE)
PL8707	TAITA LANGUAGE
DK855.4	*TAJAKS* **SEE** TAJIKS
DK861.P2	*TAJAKS* **SEE** TAJIKS / *pamir*
PK6978.5	TAJIK DRAMA
PK6971-9	TAJIK LANGUAGE
PK6978	TAJIK LITERATURE
DK855.4	TAJIKS
DK861.P2	TAJIKS / *pamir*
SB741.O7	TAKE-ALL DISEASE

E99.T15	TAKELMA INDIANS
PM2401	TAKELMA LANGUAGE
E99.T15	*TAKILMAN INDIANS* **SEE** TAKELMA INDIANS
DS771	TAKU FORTS, CHINA — BOMBARDMENT, 1900
PM2496	*TAKUDH LANGUAGE* **SEE** TUKKUTHKUTCHIN LANGUAGE
E99.T17	TAKULLI INDIANS
PM2411	TAKULLI LANGUAGE
PL4331-9	*TALAING LANGUAGE* **SEE** MON LANGUAGE
F1545	TALAMANCA INDIANS
PM4288	TALAMANCA LANGUAGE
BL2480.T3	TALANSI (AFRICAN TRIBE) — RELIGION
NK4340.T3	TALAVERA POTTERY
QP481	TALBOT'S LAW (OPTICS)
QC391	TALBOT'S LAW (OPTICS) / *photometry*
TR395	*TALBOTYPE* **SEE** CALOTYPE
TN948.T2	TALC / *mineral industries*
QE391.T	TALC / *mineralogy*
QE475	TALC / *petrology*
LC3991-4000	*TALENTED CHILDREN* **SEE** GIFTED CHILDREN
CJ2715	TALER
BF1561	TALISMANS
GR600	TALISMANS / *folk-lore*
TL696.L33	*TALK-DOWN SYSTEM* **SEE** GROUND CONTROLLED APPROACH
PN1995.7	*TALKIES* **SEE** MOVING-PICTURES, TALKING
BJ2120-2128	*TALKING* **SEE** CONVERSATION
PN6259-6268	*TALKING* **SEE** TABLE-TALK
HV1731	TALKING BOOK MACHINES / *libraries for the blind*
HV1701	TALKING BOOK MACHINES / *libraries for the blind*
Z5347	TALKING BOOKS
PN1995.7	*TALKING MOVIES* **SEE** MOVING-PICTURES, TALKING
PN1995.7	*TALKING PICTURES* **SEE** MOVING-PICTURES, TALKING
TS2301.P3	TALKING-MACHINES
BM503.9	TALMUD — CRITICISM, TEXTUAL
BM500-509	TALMUD
BM503.9	*TALMUD-TEXTUAL CRITICISM* **SEE** TALMUD — CRITICISM, TEXTUAL
PK6996.T3	TALYSH LANGUAGE
PJ2381-2	*TAMACHEK LANGUAGE* **SEE** TAMASHEK LANGUAGE
F2319	TAMANAC INDIANS
QL737.E2	*TAMANOIR* **SEE** ANT BEAR
PJ2381-2	TAMASHEK LANGUAGE
MT647	TAMBI — METHODS
ML1015-1018	TAMBI
PL8753	*TAMBOKA LANGUAGE* **SEE** TUMBUKA LANGUAGE
M1035	*TAMBOUR DE BASQUE* **SEE** TAMBOURIN
M1035	*TAMBOUR THE PROVENCE* **SEE** TAMBOURIN
ML1015-1018	*TAMBOURA* **SEE** TAMBURA
M298	*TAMBOURIN AND GALOUBET MUSIC* **SEE** GALOUBET AND TAMBOURIN MUSIC
M298	*TAMBOURIN AND GALOUBET MUSIC* **SEE** GALOUBET AND TAMBOURIN MUSIC
M1035	TAMBOURIN
MT720	TAMBOURINE — INSTRUCTION AND STUDY
ML1035	TAMBOURINE
MT642	TAMBURA — METHODS
ML1015-1018	TAMBURA
PL4751-9	TAMIL LANGUAGE
PL4758	TAMIL LITERATURE
BL2370.T25	*TAMIL MYTHOLOGY* **SEE** MYTHOLOGY, TAMIL
PL4758	TAMIL POETRY
BL1170	*TAMIL SAINTS* **SEE** SAINTS, TAMIL
DS432.T3	TAMILS
F390	TAMPICO EXPEDITION, 1835
MT720	TAMTAM
ML1040	TAMTAM
SF393.T3	TAMWORTH SWINE
SB945.T	TAN-BARK BEETLE
E99.T	TANAI INDIANS
BM177	*TANAIM* **SEE** TANNAIM
E99.T	*TANAINA INDIANS* **SEE** TANAI INDIANS
BM177	*TANAITES* **SEE** TANNAIM
DT469.M264	TANALAS
ML1015-1018	*TANBUR* **SEE** TAMBURA
QA385	*TANGENTIAL TRANSFORMATIONS* **SEE** CONTACT TRANSFORMATIONS
SB370.T	TANGERINE
QE537	TANGO — EARTHQUAKE, 1927

GV1796.T3	TANGO (DANCE)
M175.A4	TANGOS (ACCORDION)
M1248	TANGOS (BAND) — SCORES AND PARTS
M1264	TANGOS (BAND) — SCORES AND PARTS
M1248	TANGOS (BAND)
M1264	TANGOS (BAND)
M1048	TANGOS (ORCHESTRA) — SCORES
M31	TANGOS (PIANO)
M415-417	TANGOS (PIANO, 3 RECORDERS)
M221-3	TANGOS (VIOLIN AND PIANO)
M217-218	TANGOS (VIOLIN AND PIANO)
PL3801.S5	*TANGUT LANGUAGE* **SEE** SI-HIA LANGUAGE
TF481	TANK-CARS
VM455	TANK-VESSELS
UG446.5	TANKS (MILITARY SCIENCE)
UG446.5	*TANKS (MILITARY SCIENCE)-RADIO* **SEE** RADIO — INSTALLATION IN TANKS
TA360	TANKS / *engineering*
HF5716.L5	TANKS / *gaging*
TF290	TANKS / *railroad*
TF271	TANKS / *track tanks*
BM177	TANNAIM
CR4765	TANNENBERG, BATTLE OF, 1410 / *teutonic knights*
D552.T3	TANNENBERG, BATTLE OF, 1914
QK898.T2	*TANNIC ACID* **SEE** TANNINS / *botany*
QD327	*TANNIC ACID* **SEE** TANNINS / *chemistry*
SB313	*TANNIC ACID* **SEE** TANNINS / *tannin plants*
TS985	*TANNIC ACID* **SEE** TANNINS / *tanning*
RM666.T15	*TANNIC ACID* **SEE** TANNINS / *therapeutics*
SB211.Y	*TANNIER* **SEE** YAUTIA / *food plants*
N8251.T3	TANNING IN ART
TS940-985	TANNING
QK898.T2	TANNINS / *botany*
QD327	TANNINS / *chemistry*
SB313	TANNINS / *tannin plants*
TS985	TANNINS / *tanning*
RM666.T15	TANNINS / *therapeutics*
PL45.S6	*TANNU-TUVA LANGUAGE* **SEE** SOYOT LANGUAGE
E99.T	TANOAN INDIANS
PM2413	TANOAN LANGUAGES
TK4359.T	TANTALUM LAMP
QD181.T2	TANTALUM
BL1495.T3	*TANTRIC BUDDHISM* **SEE** TANTRISM, BUDDHIST
BL1495.T3	TANTRISM, BUDDHIST
BL1900-1940	TAOISM
E99.T2	TAOS INDIANS — LEGENDS
E99.T2	TAOS INDIANS
BL1900-1940	*TAOUISM* **SEE** TAOISM
GV1794	TAP DANCING
GN432	TAPA / *primitive fabrics*
PM2223	*TAPAHANOCK LANGUAGE* **SEE** QUIOUCOHANOCK LANGUAGE
ML157.3	*TAPE RECORDINGS (SOUND REPRODUCTIONS)* **SEE** PHONOTAPES
TJ1189	*TAPE-CONTROLLED MACHINE-TOOLS* **SEE** MACHINE-TOOLS — NUMERICAL CONTROL
TJ1225	*TAPE-CONTROLLED MILLING-MACHINES* **SEE** MILLING-MACHINES — NUMERICAL CONTROL
ML157.3	*TAPES* **SEE** PHONOTAPES
NK2999	TAPESTRY — CATALOGS
NK2980	TAPESTRY — EXHIBITIONS
NK2990	TAPESTRY — PRIVATE COLLECTIONS
NK2975-3096	TAPESTRY / *art*
TS1780	TAPESTRY / *manufacture*
QL391.C4	TAPEWORMS
RC184.T5-6	TAPEWORMS / *parasitic diseases*
QL737.U6	TAPIRS
TJ1335	TAPS AND DIES
F2520.1.T	TAPUYA INDIANS
PM7108	TAPUYAN LANGUAGES
M1015-1018	TAR (MUSICAL INSTRUMENT)
M282.T3	TAR AND PIANO MUSIC, ARRANGED
M283.T3	TAR AND PIANO MUSIC, ARRANGED
M142.T3	TAR MUSIC
TP953	TAR
E99.T3	TARAHUMARE INDIANS
PM4291	TARAHUMARE LANGUAGE
DS793.E2	*TARANCHI* **SEE** UIGURS
GV1796.T	TARANTELLA
ML3920	TARANTELLA / *effects of music*

M355-9	TARANTELLAS (CLARINET, FLUTE, OBOE)
M1045	TARANTELLAS (ORCHESTRA)
M1060	TARANTELLAS (ORCHESTRA)
M1011	TARANTELLAS (PIANO WITH ORCHESTRA) — 2-PIANO SCORES
M1010-1011	TARANTELLAS (PIANO WITH ORCHESTRA)
M25	TARANTELLAS (PIANO)
M204	TARANTELLAS (PIANO, 4 HANDS)
M294-5	TARANTELLAS (VIOLIN AND GUITAR)
M221-3	TARANTELLAS (VIOLIN AND PIANO)
M217-218	TARANTELLAS (VIOLIN AND PIANO)
M40-44	TARANTELLAS (VIOLIN)
M214-215	TARANTELLAS (2 PIANOS)
GV1796.T	*TARANTULA DANCE* **SEE** TARANTELLA
ML3920	*TARANTULA DANCE* **SEE** TARANTELLA / *effects of music*
PL4001.T35	TARAON LANGUAGE
F1221.T	*TARASCAN INDIANS* **SEE** TARASCO INDIANS
F1219	*TARASCAN INDIANS* **SEE** TARASCO INDIANS / *mexican antiquities*
PM4296-9	TARASCAN LANGUAGE
F1221.T	TARASCO INDIANS
F1219	TARASCO INDIANS / *mexican antiquities*
F1219.3.C2	*TARASCO INDIANS-CALENDAR* **SEE** CALENDAR, TARASCAN
D767.917	TARAWA, BATTLE OF, 1943
SB291.K	*TARAXACUM KOK-SAGHYZ* **SEE** KOK-SAGHYZ / *culture*
GN775.5.T3	TARDENOISIAN CULTURE
QL447.T2	TARDIGRADA
SB205.V58	*TARE (PLANT)* **SEE** VETCH
U300-305	*TARGET RANGES* **SEE** BOMBING AND GUNNERY RANGES
U300-305	*TARGET RANGES* **SEE** RIFLE-RANGES / *artillery and rifle-ranges*
UD330-335	*TARGET RANGES* **SEE** RIFLE-RANGES / *infantry firing*
UF340-345	TARGET-PRACTICE / *artillery*
UD330-335	TARGET-PRACTICE / *infantry*
VF310-315	TARGET-PRACTICE / *naval*
HJ6041-6464	TARIFF — LAW
HJ6041-6464	*TARIFF LISTS* **SEE** TARIFF — LAW
HJ6603-7380	*TARIFF ON RAW MATERIALS* **SEE** TARIFF / *administration*
HF1761-2580	*TARIFF ON RAW MATERIALS* **SEE** TARIFF / *other countries*
HJ6041-6464	*TARIFF ON RAW MATERIALS* **SEE** TARIFF / *schedules*
HF1701-2701	*TARIFF ON RAW MATERIALS* **SEE** TARIFF / *theory and history*
HF1750-1759	*TARIFF ON RAW MATERIALS* **SEE** TARIFF / *u.s.*
N8770	TARIFF ON WORKS OF ART
HF1715-1718	*TARIFF REBATES* **SEE** DRAWBACKS
HJ6041-6464	*TARIFF SCHEDULES* **SEE** TARIFF — LAW
HF1713	*TARIFF UNIONS* **SEE** CUSTOMS UNIONS
HJ6603-7380	TARIFF / *administration*
HF1761-2580	TARIFF / *other countries*
HJ6041-6464	TARIFF / *schedules*
HF1701-2701	TARIFF / *theory and history*
HF1750-1759	TARIFF / *u.s.*
HJ9120	*TARIFF, INTERNAL* **SEE** OCTROI
GV1295.T	*TARO (GAME)* **SEE** TAROT (GAME)
GN671.N5	TARO CULT / *new guinea*
SB211.T2	TARO
GV1295.T	*TAROC (GAME)* **SEE** TAROT (GAME)
GV1295.T	TAROT (GAME)
BF1879.T2	TAROT / *fortune-telling*
QL638.E4	TARPON
SH691.T2	TARPON / *fisheries*
F2275	*TARQUI, BATTLE OF, 1829* **SEE** PORTETE DE TARQUI, BATTLE OF, 1829
E99.A13	*TARRATINE INDIANS* **SEE** ABNAKI INDIANS
DA880.H76	TARTANS
RM666.T2	TARTAR EMETIC
PL21-384	*TARTAR LANGUAGES* **SEE** TURKO-TATARIC LANGUAGES
QD305.A2	TARTARIC ACID
DS25	*TARTARS* **SEE** TATARS
DK459.4	TARTU, TREATY OF, 1920 (FINLAND)
BM646	*TARYAG MIZWOT* **SEE** COMMANDMENTS, SIX HUNDRED AND THIRTEEN

ML760	*TASCHENGEIGE* **SEE** POCHETTE
PL7001-9	TASMANIAN LANGUAGES
PQ4656.A2	TASSO-ARIOSTO CONTROVERSY, 1584-1590
N61-79	*TASTE (AESTHETICS)* **SEE** AESTHETICS / *art*
BH	*TASTE (AESTHETICS)* **SEE** AESTHETICS / *philosophy*
QP456	TASTE / *physiology*
BF261	TASTE / *psychology*
BF436.A6	*TAT* **SEE** THEMATIC APPERCEPTION TEST
PL65.T3	TATAR LANGUAGE (VOLGA REGION)
PL65.T3	TATAR LITERATURE
DK511.C7	TATARS IN THE CRIMEA
DS25	TATARS
QC183	TATE'S LAWS
TT840	TATTING
GN419.3	TATTOOING / *ethnology*
SB291.T	TAU-SAGHYZ
SB291.T	*TAU-SAGYZ* **SEE** TAU-SAGHYZ
F2319.2.T3	*TAULIPANG INDIANS* **SEE** TAUREPAN INDIANS
F2319.2.T3	TAUREPAN INDIANS
PM7113	TAUREPAN LANGUAGE
QP801.T	TAURIN
QD471	TAUTOMERISM
PL8715	*TAVEITA LANGUAGE* **SEE** TAVETA LANGUAGE
NA7800-7850	*TAVERNS* **SEE** HOTELS, TAVERNS, ETC. / *architecture*
GT3770-3899	*TAVERNS* **SEE** HOTELS, TAVERNS, ETC. / *manners and customs*
PL8715	TAVETA LANGUAGE
E99.T	TAWAKONI INDIANS
HJ2348.5	*TAX DELINQUENCY* **SEE** TAX EVASION
HJ4653.E75	*TAX DELINQUENCY* **SEE** TAX EVASION / *k income tax*
HJ2348.5	TAX EVASION
HJ4653.E75	TAX EVASION / *k income tax*
HJ2336-7	*TAX EXEMPTION* **SEE** TAXATION, EXEMPTION FROM
HJ3247	*TAX FARMING* **SEE** TAXES, FARMING OF
HJ3231-3698	*TAX LAW* **SEE** TAXATION — LAW
HJ2348.5	*TAX-DODGING* **SEE** TAX EVASION
HJ4653.E75	*TAX-DODGING* **SEE** TAX EVASION / *k income tax*
HJ5801-5819	*TAXABLE TRANSFERS* **SEE** INHERITANCE AND TRANSFER TAX
HJ3231-3698	TAXATION — LAW
HJ9991-5	TAXATION — RATES AND TABLES / *public accounting*
HJ5797	*TAXATION OF ADMISSIONS* **SEE** AMUSEMENTS — TAXATION
HJ5711-5721	TAXATION OF ARTICLES OF CONSUMPTION
HD9100.8	*TAXATION OF BEET SUGAR* **SEE** SUGAR — TAXATION
HJ5901-5919	TAXATION OF BONDS, SECURITIES, ETC.
HJ4639	*TAXATION OF CAPITAL GAINS* **SEE** CAPITAL GAINS TAX / *general*
HJ4653.C3	*TAXATION OF CAPITAL GAINS* **SEE** CAPITAL GAINS TAX / *u.s.*
HJ5711-5721	*TAXATION OF CONSUMER GOODS* **SEE** TAXATION OF ARTICLES OF CONSUMPTION
HJ4631	*TAXATION OF EXCESS PROFITS* **SEE** EXCESS PROFITS TAX
HJ4653.E8	*TAXATION OF EXCESS PROFITS* **SEE** EXCESS PROFITS TAX / *u.s.*
HD2753	*TAXATION OF FRANCHISES* **SEE** CORPORATIONS — TAXATION
HJ2612	*TAXATION OF HEARTHS* **SEE** HEARTH-MONEY / *english tax*
HJ4621-4831	*TAXATION OF INCOME* **SEE** INCOME TAX
HJ4651-5	*TAXATION OF INCOME* **SEE** INCOME TAX / *u.s.*
HJ5801-5819	*TAXATION OF LEGACIES* **SEE** INHERITANCE AND TRANSFER TAX
HD9350.8	*TAXATION OF LIQUORS* **SEE** LIQUOR TRAFFIC — TAXATION
HJ5771-5797	*TAXATION OF LUXURIES* **SEE** LUXURIES — TAXATION
HJ4581-4599	TAXATION OF PERSONAL PROPERTY
HJ4101-4129	*TAXATION OF PROPERTY* **SEE** PROPERTY TAX
HJ5711-5721	*TAXATION OF SALES* **SEE** SALES TAX
HJ5901-5919	*TAXATION OF SECURITIES* **SEE** TAXATION OF BONDS, SECURITIES, ETC.
HJ5901-5919	*TAXATION OF STOCKS* **SEE** TAXATION OF BONDS, SECURITIES, ETC.
HJ5905	TAXATION OF U.S. BONDS
HJ5711-5721	*TAXATION OF USE* **SEE** USE TAX
HJ2240-7395	TAXATION
HJ2341-3	TAXATION, DOUBLE

HJ2348.5	TAXATION, EVASION OF SEE TAX EVASION
HJ4653.E75	TAXATION, EVASION OF SEE TAX EVASION / k income tax
HJ2336-7	TAXATION, EXEMPTION FROM
HJ2240-7395	TAXATION, INCIDENCE OF SEE TAXATION
HJ2326-7	TAXATION, PROGRESSIVE
HJ2391-2442	TAXATION, STATE
HJ2385	TAXATION, STATE
HJ2348.5	TAXATION-EVASION SEE TAX EVASION
HJ4653.E75	TAXATION-EVASION SEE TAX EVASION / k income tax
HJ2348.5	TAXATION-LAW-CRIMINAL PROVISIONS SEE TAX EVASION
HJ4653.E75	TAXATION-LAW-CRIMINAL PROVISIONS SEE TAX EVASION / k income tax
HJ9991-5	TAXATION-U.S.-RATES AND TABLES SEE TAXATION — RATES AND TABLES / public accounting
HJ2240-7395	TAXES SEE TAXATION
HJ3247	TAXES, FARMING OF
LB2824-2830	TAXES, SCHOOL SEE EDUCATION — FINANCE
HJ9123.V5	TAXES, VISITORS' SEE VISITORS' TAXES
PN6231.T23	TAXICABS — ANECDOTES, FACETIAE, SATIRE, ETC.
HE5601-5720	TAXICABS
QL63	TAXIDERMY
QB723.T	TAYLOR'S COMET
QA306	TAYLOR'S SERIES (MATHEMATICS) SEE SERIES, TAYLOR'S
DS560	TCHAMES SEE CHAMS
QA404.5	TCHEBYCHEFF'S POLYNOMIALS SEE CHEBYSHEV POLYNOMIALS
DK34.C5	TCHEREMISSES SEE CHEREMISSES
PH801-9	TCHEREMISSIAN LANGUAGE SEE CHEREMISSIAN LANGUAGE
PK9201.C3	TCHETCHEN LANGUAGE SEE CHECHEN LANGUAGE
PM41-44	TCHUKTCHI LANGUAGE SEE CHUKCHI LANGUAGE
PL381-4	TCHUVAK LANGUAGE SEE CHUVASHIAN LANGUAGE
PL381-4	TCHUVASHIAN LANGUAGE SEE CHUVASHIAN LANGUAGE
SB608.T3	TEA — DISEASES AND PESTS
RM251	TEA — PHYSIOLOGICAL EFFECT
HF5716.T25	TEA — TABLES, ETC.
HD9198	TEA — TAXATION
GT2910	TEA CEREMONY, JAPANESE SEE JAPANESE TEA CEREMONY
TP650	TEA MACHINERY
TX945	TEA ROOMS SEE RESTAURANTS, LUNCH ROOMS, ETC.
E215.7	TEA TAX (AMERICAN COLONIES)
HD9198	TEA TRADE
HD9195	TEA TRADE
TX585	TEA / adulteration
SB271	TEA / culture
TP650	TEA / technology
RM251	TEA / therapeutics
HF1133	TEACH YOURSELF COURSES SEE CORRESPONDENCE SCHOOLS AND COURSES / business schools
HF1116	TEACH YOURSELF COURSES SEE CORRESPONDENCE SCHOOLS AND COURSES / business schools
LC5901-6101	TEACH YOURSELF COURSES SEE CORRESPONDENCE SCHOOLS AND COURSES
T172	TEACH YOURSELF COURSES SEE CORRESPONDENCE SCHOOLS AND COURSES / technology
LC25-31	TEACH YOURSELF COURSES SEE SELF-CULTURE
MT893	TEACH YOURSELF COURSES SEE SINGING — METHODS — — SELF-INSTRUCTION
LB2835	TEACHER PLACEMENT SEE TEACHERS — SELECTION AND APPOINTMENT
LB2835	TEACHER SELECTION SEE TEACHERS — SELECTION AND APPOINTMENT
LB3021	TEACHER-PUPIL PLANNING SEE SELF-GOVERNMENT (IN EDUCATION) / student honor
LB3092-5	TEACHER-PUPIL PLANNING SEE SELF-GOVERNMENT (IN EDUCATION)
LB3013	TEACHER-PUPIL RATIO SEE CLASS SIZE
LB1033	TEACHER-PUPIL RELATIONSHIPS SEE TEACHER-STUDENT RELATIONSHIPS
LB1033	TEACHER-STUDENT RELATIONSHIPS
LB1771	TEACHERS — CERTIFICATION
LB1731	TEACHERS — IN-SERVICE TRAINING
LB2843.L4	TEACHERS — LEAVES OF ABSENCE

BX2373.T4	TEACHERS — MEDITATIONS / catholic
LB2842-4	TEACHERS — SALARIES, PENSIONS, ETC.
LB2334-5	TEACHERS — SALARIES, PENSIONS, ETC. / higher education
LB2835	TEACHERS — SELECTION AND APPOINTMENT
LB2367	TEACHERS - EXAMINATIONS SEE EXAMINATIONS / college
C1070-1071	TEACHERS - EXAMINATIONS SEE EXAMINATIONS / professional courses
LB3051-3060	TEACHERS - EXAMINATIONS SEE EXAMINATIONS / school
LC225	TEACHERS AND PARENTS SEE HOME AND SCHOOL
LB1805-2151	TEACHERS COLLEGES
LB1781-5	TEACHERS IN LITERATURE
LA2301-2397	TEACHERS / biography
LB1771	TEACHERS, CERTIFICATION OF SEE TEACHERS — CERTIFICATION
LB2283-5	TEACHERS, INTERCHANGE OF
LB2844.1	TEACHERS, PART-TIME
LB1779	TEACHERS, PROFESSIONAL ETHICS FOR
LB1705-2285	TEACHERS, TRAINING OF
LC43	TEACHERS, VISITING SEE VISITING TEACHERS / home teachers
LB3013.5	TEACHERS, VISITING SEE VISITING TEACHERS / school social workers
LB2844.2	TEACHERS, VOLUNTEER SEE VOLUNTEER WORKERS IN EDUCATION
LB2837	TEACHERS, WOMEN SEE WOMEN AS TEACHERS
LB2844.1.A	TEACHERS' ASSISTANTS
LB1823-2151	TEACHERS' INSTITUTES
LB1751-5	TEACHERS' INSTITUTES
LB2842-4	TEACHERS' PENSIONS SEE TEACHERS — SALARIES, PENSIONS, ETC.
LB2334-5	TEACHERS' PENSIONS SEE TEACHERS — SALARIES, PENSIONS, ETC. / higher education
L10-97	TEACHERS' UNIONS SEE EDUCATIONAL ASSOCIATIONS
LB1782	TEACHERS' WIVES
LB1743	TEACHERS' WORKSHOPS
LB2835	TEACHERS-APPOINTMENT SEE TEACHERS — SELECTION AND APPOINTMENT
LB2334-5	TEACHERS-PENSIONS SEE TEACHERS — SALARIES, PENSIONS, ETC. / higher education
LB2842-4	TEACHERS-PENSIONS SEE TEACHERS — SALARIES, PENSIONS, ETC.
LB2831.5	TEACHERS-PERSONNEL MANAGEMENT SEE SCHOOL PERSONNEL MANAGEMENT
LB1775-9	TEACHING AS A PROFESSION
LB1779	TEACHING ETHICS SEE TEACHERS, PROFESSIONAL ETHICS FOR
LB2157	TEACHING LABORATORIES SEE STUDENT TEACHING
LB1029.A85	TEACHING MACHINES
LB	TEACHING
LB1775-1785	TEACHING / teaching as a profession
LB1029.D4	TEACHING, DEPARTMENTAL SYSTEM OF
LB2332	TEACHING, FREEDOM OF
LB1775-9	TEACHING-VOCATIONAL GUIDANCE SEE TEACHING AS A PROFESSION
BS2415-2417	TEACHINGS OF JESUS SEE JESUS CHRIST — TEACHINGS
SD397.T	TEAK / forestry
HD9769.T4	TEAK / trade
QL696.A5	TEALS, BLUE-WINGED SEE BLUE-WINGED TEALS
QL949	TEAR SACS SEE LACRIMAL ORGANS / comparative anatomy
QM511	TEAR SACS SEE LACRIMAL ORGANS / human anatomy
QP231	TEAR SACS SEE LACRIMAL ORGANS / physiology
TX945	TEAROOMS SEE RESTAURANTS, LUNCH ROOMS, ETC.
PL8723	TEBELE LANGUAGE
QD181.T35	TECHNETIUM
TP	TECHNICAL CHEMISTRY SEE CHEMISTRY, TECHNICAL
T9-10	TECHNICAL DICTIONARIES SEE TECHNOLOGY — DICTIONARIES
T351-377	TECHNICAL DRAWING SEE MECHANICAL DRAWING
T65	TECHNICAL EDUCATION — CURRICULA
T61-173	TECHNICAL EDUCATION

LC1081	TECHNICAL EDUCATION / theory
LC1041-7	TECHNICAL EDUCATION / vocational education
T61-173	*TECHNICAL INSTITUTES* **SEE** TECHNICAL EDUCATION
LC1081	*TECHNICAL INSTITUTES* **SEE** TECHNICAL EDUCATION / theory
LC1041-7	*TECHNICAL INSTITUTES* **SEE** TECHNICAL EDUCATION / vocational education
T1-4	*TECHNICAL INSTITUTES* **SEE** TECHNICAL SOCIETIES
PN4784.T3	*TECHNICAL JOURNALISM* **SEE** JOURNALISM, TECHNICAL
Z675.T3	TECHNICAL LIBRARIES
T61-173	*TECHNICAL SCHOOLS* **SEE** TECHNICAL EDUCATION
LC1081	*TECHNICAL SCHOOLS* **SEE** TECHNICAL EDUCATION / theory
LC1041-7	*TECHNICAL SCHOOLS* **SEE** TECHNICAL EDUCATION / vocational education
T1-4	TECHNICAL SOCIETIES
T9-10	*TECHNICAL TERMS* **SEE** TECHNOLOGY — DICTIONARIES
T9-10	*TECHNICAL TERMS* **SEE** TECHNOLOGY — TERMINOLOGY
T11	*TECHNICAL VOCABULARY* **SEE** TECHNOLOGY — LANGUAGE
TA158	TECHNICIANS IN INDUSTRY
MT258	TECHNICON
HB87	TECHNOCRACY
T179-183	*TECHNOLOGICAL MUSEUMS* **SEE** INDUSTRIAL MUSEUMS
T1-4	*TECHNOLOGICAL SOCIETIES* **SEE** TECHNICAL SOCIETIES
HD6331	*TECHNOLOGICAL UNEMPLOYMENT* **SEE** UNEMPLOYMENT, TECHNOLOGICAL
Z7911-7916	TECHNOLOGY — BIBLIOGRAPHY
T9-10	TECHNOLOGY — DICTIONARIES
T44	TECHNOLOGY — EARLY WORKS TO 1800
T48	TECHNOLOGY — JUVENILE LITERATURE
T11	TECHNOLOGY — LANGUAGE
T14	TECHNOLOGY — PHILOSOPHY
T9-10	TECHNOLOGY — TERMINOLOGY
T11.5	TECHNOLOGY — TRANSLATING SERVICES
CB478	TECHNOLOGY AND CIVILIZATION / history
HM221	TECHNOLOGY AND CIVILIZATION / sociology
T-TX	TECHNOLOGY
GN429-434	*TECHNOLOGY, PRIMITIVE* **SEE** INDUSTRIES, PRIMITIVE
Z695.1.S3	*TECHNOLOGY-CATALOGING* **SEE** CATALOGING OF TECHNICAL LITERATURE
T391-999	*TECHNOLOGY-EXHIBITIONS* **SEE** EXHIBITIONS
T179-183	*TECHNOLOGY-MUSEUMS* **SEE** INDUSTRIAL MUSEUMS
F1219	TECO INDIANS
F1219	*TECPANECAS* **SEE** TEPANECAS
SD397.T	*TECTONA GRANDIS* **SEE** TEAK / forestry
HD9769.T4	*TECTONA GRANDIS* **SEE** TEAK / trade
QE601-611	*TECTONICS (GEOLOGY)* **SEE** GEOLOGY, STRUCTURAL
GV1469.T	TEEKO (GAME)
HQ35	*TEEN-AGE* **SEE** ADOLESCENCE
LB1135	*TEEN-AGE* **SEE** ADOLESCENCE / child study
RJ550	*TEEN-AGE* **SEE** ADOLESCENCE / diseases
GN63	*TEEN-AGE* **SEE** ADOLESCENCE / somatology
HQ796-9	*TEEN-AGERS* **SEE** YOUTH
E98.D9	*TEEPEES* **SEE** INDIANS OF NORTH AMERICA — DWELLINGS
SF199.S56	*TEESWATER CATTLE* **SEE** SHORTHORN CATTLE
SF193.S5	*TEESWATER CATTLE* **SEE** SHORTHORN CATTLE / herd-books
RK521-8	TEETH — ABNORMITIES AND DEFORMITIES
RK61	TEETH — CARE AND HYGIENE
RK301-450	TEETH — DISEASES
RK531	TEETH — EXTRACTION
GN419.2	TEETH — MUTILATION
RK309	TEETH — RADIOGRAPHY
GR489	TEETH (IN RELIGION, FOLK-LORE, ETC.) / folk-lore
BL325.T	TEETH (IN RELIGION, FOLK-LORE, ETC.) / religion
QL858	TEETH / comparative anatomy
QM311	TEETH / human anatomy
GN209	TEETH / somatology
QR47	*TEETH-BACTERIOLOGY* **SEE** MOUTH — BACTERIOLOGY
RK285	*TEETHING* **SEE** DENTITION / children

G700 1872	TEGETTHOFF EXPEDITION, 1872-1874
F1221.O6	*TEGUIMA INDIANS* **SEE** OPATA INDIANS
F2936	*TEHUELCHE INDIANS* **SEE** TZONECA INDIANS / patagonia
PM7183	*TEHUELCHE LANGUAGE* **SEE** TZONECA LANGUAGE
DT429	*TEITA (BANTU TRIBE)* **SEE** TAITA (BANTU TRIBE)
PL8707	*TEITA LANGUAGE* **SEE** TAITA LANGUAGE
PL8725	TEKE LANGUAGE
DK854-861	*TEKKE-TURKOMANS* **SEE** TURKOMANS
DT313	TEKNA
DT515	*TEKROURIENS* **SEE** TOUCOULEURS
QE399	TEKTITE
TK453	TELECOMMUNICATION — MATERIALS
TK6710	*TELEFAX* **SEE** FACSIMILE TRANSMISSION
QH431	TELEGONY
HE7601-8630	*TELEGRAMS* **SEE** TELEGRAPH / economics
TK5105-5865	*TELEGRAMS* **SEE** TELEGRAPH / technology
TK5509	TELEGRAPH — ALPHABETS
TK5264	TELEGRAPH — AMATEURS' MANUALS
TK9941-6	TELEGRAPH — AMATEURS' MANUALS / construction
TK5501	TELEGRAPH — APPARATUS AND SUPPLIES / instruments
TK5541-7	TELEGRAPH — AUTOMATIC SYSTEMS
TK5371	TELEGRAPH — CURRENT SUPPLY
TK5531	TELEGRAPH — DUPLEX SYSTEM
TK5266	TELEGRAPH — HANDBOOKS, MANUALS, ETC.
TK5445	TELEGRAPH — HANDBOOKS, MANUALS, ETC. / wiremen's manuals
HE7611-7616	TELEGRAPH — LAWS AND REGULATIONS
HE7703	TELEGRAPH — LAWS AND REGULATIONS / international
HE7801-8630	TELEGRAPH — LAWS AND REGULATIONS / other countries
HE7761-5	TELEGRAPH — LAWS AND REGULATIONS / u.s.
TK5295	TELEGRAPH — MATERIALS / catalogs
TK5385	TELEGRAPH — MATERIALS / testing
TK5538	TELEGRAPH — MULTIPLEX SYSTEMS
TK5263	TELEGRAPH — OPERATORS' MANUALS
TK5547	TELEGRAPH — PERFORATING SYSTEM
TK5543	TELEGRAPH — PRINTING SYSTEM
TK5535	TELEGRAPH — QUADRUPLEX SYSTEM
HE7681-7691	TELEGRAPH — RATES
HE7801-8650	TELEGRAPH — RATES / other countries
HE7787	TELEGRAPH — RATES / u.s.
TK5266	TELEGRAPH — TABLES, CALCULATIONS, ETC.
TK5385	TELEGRAPH — TESTING
TK5481	TELEGRAPH CABLES
HE7669-7679	*TELEGRAPH CODES* **SEE** CIPHER AND TELEGRAPH CODES
HE7676-7	*TELEGRAPH CODES* **SEE** CIPHER AND TELEGRAPH CODES / commercial codes
HE7678	*TELEGRAPH CODES* **SEE** CIPHER AND TELEGRAPH CODES / foreign languages
TK5301-5481	TELEGRAPH LINES
HJ5315	TELEGRAPH STAMPS
HJ5375-5515	TELEGRAPH STAMPS / other countries
HJ5321.Z7	TELEGRAPH STAMPS / u.s.
TK5381	TELEGRAPH STATIONS — MANAGEMENT / technical
TK5481	TELEGRAPH WIRE
HE7601-8630	TELEGRAPH / economics
TK5105-5865	TELEGRAPH / technology
UG590-610	*TELEGRAPH, MILITARY* **SEE** MILITARY TELEGRAPH
HE7709-7741	*TELEGRAPH, SUBMARINE* **SEE** CABLES, SUBMARINE / economics
UG607	*TELEGRAPH, SUBMARINE* **SEE** CABLES, SUBMARINE / military art and science
TK5605-5681	*TELEGRAPH, SUBMARINE* **SEE** CABLES, SUBMARINE / technology
TK5811	TELEGRAPH, WIRELESS — ARTOM SYSTEM
VK397	TELEGRAPH, WIRELESS — INSTALLATION ON SHIPS
HE8666-8670	TELEGRAPH, WIRELESS — LAWS AND REGULATIONS
TK5811	TELEGRAPH, WIRELESS — MARCONI SYSTEM
TK5700-5865	TELEGRAPH, WIRELESS
HE8660-8688	TELEGRAPH, WIRELESS / economics
VK397	TELEGRAPH, WIRELESS / marine signaling
UG610	TELEGRAPH, WIRELESS / military
VG76-78	TELEGRAPH, WIRELESS / naval

HE7669-7679	*TELEGRAPH-CODES* **SEE** CIPHER AND TELEGRAPH CODES
HE7676-7	*TELEGRAPH-CODES* **SEE** CIPHER AND TELEGRAPH CODES / *commercial codes*
HE7678	*TELEGRAPH-CODES* **SEE** CIPHER AND TELEGRAPH CODES / *foreign languages*
TK6600	*TELEGRAPH-PICTURE TRANSMISSION* **SEE** PHOTOTELEGRAPHY
TK5241-3	TELEGRAPHERS / *biography*
HD8039.T22-23	TELEGRAPHERS / *labor*
HD6350.T3	TELEGRAPHERS / *trade-union periodicals*
HD6073.T4	TELEGRAPHERS / *women*
RC429	TELEGRAPHERS' CRAMP
TK6500	TELEGRAPHONE
TK5295	TELEGRAPH — APPARATUS AND SUPPLIES — — CATALOGS
PL4771-9	*TELEGU LANGUAGE* **SEE** TELUGU LANGUAGE
TK399	TELEMETER
UF850.T4	TELEMETER / *range finders*
BT98-101	*TELEOLOGICAL ARGUMENT* **SEE** GOD — PROOF, TELEOLOGICAL
BD530-595	TELEOLOGY
QL638	TELEOSTEI
QE852.T2	TELEOSTEI / *fossil*
BF1161-1171	*TELEPATHY* **SEE** THOUGHT-TRANSFERENCE
HE8785	TELEPHONE — ACCOUNTING
TK9951	TELEPHONE — AMATEURS' MANUALS
TK1681	TELEPHONE — CONTRACTS AND SPECIFICATIONS
TK6271-8	TELEPHONE — CURRENT SUPPLY
TK6011	TELEPHONE — DIRECTORIES
TK6421	TELEPHONE — ECCARD SYSTEM
TK6167	TELEPHONE — HANDBOOKS, MANUALS, ETC.
TK6345	TELEPHONE — HANDBOOKS, MANUALS, ETC. / *wiremen's manuals*
TK6421	TELEPHONE — HOPKINS SYSTEM
HE8745-8	TELEPHONE — LAWS AND REGULATIONS
HE8749	TELEPHONE — LAWS AND REGULATIONS / *international*
TK6163	TELEPHONE — OPERATORS' MANUALS
TK6201-6285	TELEPHONE — POWER-PLANTS
HE8777-9	TELEPHONE — RATES
HE8851-9700	TELEPHONE — RATES / *other countries*
HE8825	TELEPHONE — RATES / *u.s.*
TK6285	TELEPHONE — TESTING
HE8783	TELEPHONE — VALUATION
TK6381	TELEPHONE CABLES
BJ2193	TELEPHONE ETIQUETTE
TK6211-6281	*TELEPHONE EXCHANGES* **SEE** TELEPHONE STATIONS
TK6301-6397	TELEPHONE LINES — CONSTRUCTION
TK6181	TELEPHONE LINES — SPECIFICATIONS
TK6201-6285	TELEPHONE LINES
TK6281	TELEPHONE STATIONS — MANAGEMENT / *technical*
TK6211-6281	TELEPHONE STATIONS
TK6391-7	TELEPHONE SWITCHBOARDS
TK6381	TELEPHONE WIRE
HE8701-9700	TELEPHONE / *economics*
TK6005-6575	TELEPHONE / *technology*
TK6397	TELEPHONE, AUTOMATIC
UG620	*TELEPHONE, MILITARY* **SEE** MILITARY TELEPHONE
TK6560-6565	TELEPHONE, WIRELESS — APPARATUS AND SUPPLIES
HE8666-8670	TELEPHONE, WIRELESS — LAWS AND REGULATIONS
TK6555	TELEPHONE, WIRELESS — STATIONS
TK6540-6570	TELEPHONE, WIRELESS
TK9956	TELEPHONE, WIRELESS / *amateurs' manuals*
TK6301-6397	*TELEPHONE-CONSTRUCTION* **SEE** TELEPHONE LINES — CONSTRUCTION
TK6195	TELEPHONE — APPARATUS AND SUPPLIES — — CATALOGS
BJ2193	*TELEPHONING* **SEE** TELEPHONE ETIQUETTE
TK6500	*TELEPHONOGRAPH* **SEE** TELEGRAPHONE
TR770	TELEPHOTOGRAPHY
BF1628.3	*TELERADIESTHESIA* **SEE** RADIESTHESIA
RZ999	*TELERADIESTHESIA* **SEE** RADIESTHESIA / *medicine*
QB88	TELESCOPE — JUVENILE LITERATURE
QB88	TELESCOPE / *astronomy*
UF845	TELESCOPE / *military science*
QB88	TELESCOPE, REFLECTING

UF845	*TELESCOPE, REFRACTING* **SEE** TELESCOPE / *military science*
QB101	TELESCOPE, ZENITH
UF855	TELESCOPIC SIGHTS / *artillery*
TL694.T4	TELETYPE IN AERONAUTICS
TK9960	TELEVISION — AMATEURS' MANUALS
TK6655.A6	TELEVISION — ANTENNAS
TK6641	TELEVISION — LABORATORY MANUALS
PN1992.75	TELEVISION — PRODUCTION AND DIRECTION
TK6653	TELEVISION — RECEIVERS AND RECEPTION
TK6655.U6	TELEVISION — ULTRAHIGH FREQUENCY APPARATUS AND SUPPLIES
GV880	TELEVISION AND BASEBALL
GV1779	*TELEVISION AND DANCING* **SEE** DANCING IN MOVING-PICTURES, TELEVISION, ETC.
TL798.M4	*TELEVISION AND INFRARED OBSERVATION SATELLITE* **SEE** TIROS (METEOROLOGICAL SATELLITE)
Z716.8	*TELEVISION AND LIBRARIES* **SEE** LIBRARIES AND TELEVISION
TK6655.A6	*TELEVISION ANTENNAS* **SEE** TELEVISION — ANTENNAS
PN1992.57	TELEVISION BROADCASTING — JUVENILE LITERATURE
PN1992.6	TELEVISION BROADCASTING — MORAL AND RELIGIOUS ASPECTS
PN1992.8.F5	TELEVISION BROADCASTING OF FILMS
HE8697.A8	*TELEVISION BROADCASTING-AUDIENCE REACTION* **SEE** TELEVISION PROGRAMS — RATING
PN1992.8.F5	*TELEVISION BROADCASTING-FILMS* **SEE** TELEVISION BROADCASTING OF FILMS
PN1992.8.F5	*TELEVISION BROADCASTING-MOVING-PICTURES* **SEE** TELEVISION BROADCASTING OF FILMS
HE8697.A8	*TELEVISION BROADCASTING-PROGRAM RATING* **SEE** TELEVISION PROGRAMS — RATING
TR882	TELEVISION CAMERAS
PN1992.75	*TELEVISION DIRECTION* **SEE** TELEVISION — PRODUCTION AND DIRECTION
TK6720	*TELEVISION FACSIMILE* **SEE** ULTRAFAX
RC835	*TELEVISION IN EDUCATION* **SEE** TELEVISION IN MEDICAL EDUCATION
LB1044.7	TELEVISION IN EDUCATION
LB1044.7	*TELEVISION IN EDUCATION-U.S.* **SEE** TELEVISION IN EDUCATION
RA440.5	TELEVISION IN HEALTH EDUCATION
RC835	TELEVISION IN MEDICAL EDUCATION
U104	TELEVISION IN MILITARY EDUCATION
BV656.3	TELEVISION IN RELIGION
HD9999.T37	TELEVISION INDUSTRY
TR882	*TELEVISION PICK-UP TUBES* **SEE** IMAGE ICONOSCOPE
TK6655.P5	TELEVISION PICTURE TUBES
PN1992.75	*TELEVISION PRODUCTION* **SEE** TELEVISION — PRODUCTION AND DIRECTION
HE8697.A8	*TELEVISION PROGRAM RATING* **SEE** TELEVISION PROGRAMS — RATING
HE8697.A8	TELEVISION PROGRAMS — RATING
PN6072	TELEVISION SCRIPTS
TK6630	TELEVISION
HE8690-8699	TELEVISION
TK6680	*TELEVISION, CLOSED-CIRCUIT* **SEE** CLOSED-CIRCUIT TELEVISION
TK6670	*TELEVISION, COLOR* **SEE** COLOR TELEVISION
UG623	*TELEVISION, MILITARY* **SEE** MILITARY TELEVISION
TK6655.A6	*TELEVISION-AERIALS* **SEE** TELEVISION — ANTENNAS
PN1992.75	*TELEVISION-DIRECTION* **SEE** TELEVISION — PRODUCTION AND DIRECTION
TK6655.P5	*TELEVISION-PICTURE TUBES* **SEE** TELEVISION PICTURE TUBES
PN2091.E4	*TELEVISION-STAGE LIGHTING* **SEE** STAGE LIGHTING
TK6655	TELEVISION — RECEIVERS AND RECEPTION — — TESTING
PL4771-9	*TELINGA LANGUAGE* **SEE** TELUGU LANGUAGE
DS432.T4	*TELINGAS* **SEE** TELUGUS
PJ3885-7	TELL-EL-AMARNA TABLETS
GV1511.T2	TELL-TALE (GAME)
QD181.T4	TELLURATES
QD181.T4	TELLURIC ACID
QD181.T4	TELLURIDES
QD181.T4	TELLURITES
QD181.T4	TELLURIUM
PL4771-9	*TELOOGOO LANGUAGE* **SEE** TELUGU LANGUAGE

PL4771-9	TELUGU LANGUAGE
PL4780	TELUGU LITERATURE
DS432.T4	TELUGUS
DS595	*TEMIAR* **SEE** SAKAI
PL8735	*TEMNE LANGUAGE* **SEE** TIMNE LANGUAGE
QB723.T3	TEMPEL'S COMET (I)
BF575.A5	TEMPER
ND2470	TEMPERA PAINTING
BF795-811	TEMPERAMENT / *psychology*
RB150-151	TEMPERAMENT / *temperament and disease*
ML3809	*TEMPERAMENT, MUSICAL* **SEE** MUSICAL TEMPERAMENT
HV5068-5072	TEMPERANCE — ANECDOTES, FACETIAE, SATIRE, ETC.
HV5182-3	TEMPERANCE — BIBLICAL ARGUMENTS
HV5069	TEMPERANCE — DRAMA
HV5069-5071	TEMPERANCE — EXERCISES, RECITATIONS, ETC.
HV5068	TEMPERANCE — FICTION
HV5070	TEMPERANCE — POETRY
M2198-9	TEMPERANCE — SONGS AND MUSIC
HV5182-3	*TEMPERANCE IN THE BIBLE* **SEE** TEMPERANCE — BIBLICAL ARGUMENTS
HV5006	TEMPERANCE SOCIETIES / *international*
HV5301-5720	TEMPERANCE SOCIETIES / *other countries*
HV5297-8	TEMPERANCE SOCIETIES / *u.s.*
HV5291-2	TEMPERANCE SOCIETIES / *u.s.*
HV5001-5720	TEMPERANCE
HV5074-5080	*TEMPERANCE-LAW* **SEE** LIQUOR LAWS
TA405.5	*TEMPERATURE* **SEE** THERMAL STRESSES
RC75	*TEMPERATURE CURVE* **SEE** BODY TEMPERATURE / *diagnosis*
QP135	*TEMPERATURE CURVE* **SEE** BODY TEMPERATURE / *physiology*
QP451	TEMPERATURE SENSE
QC271	TEMPERATURE
RC75	*TEMPERATURE, ANIMAL AND HUMAN* **SEE** BODY TEMPERATURE / *diagnosis*
QP135	*TEMPERATURE, ANIMAL AND HUMAN* **SEE** BODY TEMPERATURE / *physiology*
QD515	*TEMPERATURES, LOW* **SEE** LOW TEMPERATURES / *chemistry*
QC278	*TEMPERATURES, LOW* **SEE** LOW TEMPERATURES / *physics*
TS320	TEMPERING / *steel*
CR4735-4755	TEMPLARS
NA4600-4641	TEMPLES
GR505	TEMPLES / *folk-lore*
GT485	TEMPLES / *manners and customs*
NA5960	TEMPLES, BUDDHIST
NA300	TEMPLES, ETRUSCAN
NA281-5	TEMPLES, GREEK
NA275	TEMPLES, GREEK
BL1227	TEMPLES, HINDU
NA5960	TEMPLES, ORIENTAL
MT42	TEMPO (MUSIC)
RD661	TEMPORAL BONE — TUMORS
QM105	TEMPORAL BONE / *human anatomy*
RK280	TEMPOROMANDIBULAR JOINT
RK280	*TEMPOROMAXILLARY JOINT* **SEE** TEMPOROMANDIBULAR JOINT
BT725	TEMPTATION / *theology*
BV4655-4710	*TEN COMMANDMENTS* **SEE** COMMANDMENTS, TEN / *moral theology*
BS1281-5	*TEN COMMANDMENTS* **SEE** COMMANDMENTS, TEN / *texts*
DS131	*TEN LOST TRIBES OF ISRAEL* **SEE** LOST TRIBES OF ISRAEL
BT378.T4	TEN VIRGINS (PARABLE)
E99.I5	*TEN'A INDIANS* **SEE** INGALIK INDIANS
PM1373	*TEN'A LANGUAGE* **SEE** INGALIK LANGUAGE
DA995	TENANT LEAGUE, 1850-1854 / *ireland*
SH391.T	TENCH / *fishing*
QL638.C94	TENCH / *zoology*
QM141	TENDON OF ACHILLES
RD688	TENDONS — INJURIES AND RUPTURES
TA683.42	TENDONS (PRESTRESSED CONCRETE)
QM141	TENDONS
RD688	TENDONS / *diseases*
QK773	TENDRILS
NA7880	TENEMENT-HOUSES / *architecture*
HD7286-7390	TENEMENT-HOUSES / *economics*

PJ2371	*TENERIFFAN LANGUAGE* **SEE** GUANCHE LANGUAGE
F1221.C56	*TENEZ INDIANS* **SEE** CHINANTEC INDIANS
F431-445	TENNESSEE — HISTORY
E88.813	TENNESSEE MILITIAMEN, EXECUTION OF, 1815
SF293.T	TENNESSEE WALKING HORSE
E579	TENNESSEE — HISTORY — — CIVIL WAR
E531	TENNESSEE — HISTORY — — CIVIL WAR
DC166.O62	TENNIS COURT OATH, JUNE 20, 1789
GV1004	TENNIS COURTS
GV990-1005	TENNIS
ML760	TENOR VIOLIN
GV901-9	*TENPINS* **SEE** BOWLING
BL2222.T4	TENRI (SECT)
BL2222.T4	*TENRIKYO* **SEE** TENRI (SECT)
E99.T115	*TENSA INDIANS* **SEE** TAENSA INDIANS
E99.T115	*TENSAGINI INDIANS* **SEE** TAENSA INDIANS
E99.T115	*TENSAU INDIANS* **SEE** TAENSA INDIANS
E99.T115	*TENSAW INDIANS* **SEE** TAENSA INDIANS
QA433	*TENSOR ANALYSIS* **SEE** CALCULUS OF TENSORS
QP461	TENSOR TYMPANI MUSCLE
QM507	TENSOR TYMPANI MUSCLE
UC580-585	TENT DRILL
SB945.T36	TENT-CATERPILLARS
UC570-575	TENTS / *army*
TS1860	TENTS / *manufacture*
HD101-1395	*TENURE OF LAND* **SEE** LAND TENURE
JF1321-1671	*TENURE OF OFFICE* **SEE** CIVIL SERVICE
JV443-5	*TENURE OF OFFICE* **SEE** CIVIL SERVICE / *colonial*
JS148-163	*TENURE OF OFFICE* **SEE** CIVIL SERVICE / *municipal*
JN-JQ	*TENURE OF OFFICE* **SEE** CIVIL SERVICE / *other countries*
HD8011-8023	*TENURE OF OFFICE* **SEE** CIVIL SERVICE / *state labor*
JK631-901	*TENURE OF OFFICE* **SEE** CIVIL SERVICE / *u.s.*
JK550	*TENURE OF OFFICE* **SEE** PRESIDENTS — U.S. — — TERM OF OFFICE
F1219	TEPANECAS
E98.D9	*TEPEES* **SEE** INDIANS OF NORTH AMERICA — DWELLINGS
F1221.T39	TEPEHUA INDIANS
F1231	TEPEHUANE INDIANS — INSURRECTION, 1616
F1221.T	TEPEHUANE INDIANS / *mexico*
F2319.2.T	TEQUE INDIANS
PM3651	*TEQUISTLATECA LANGUAGE* **SEE** CHONTAL LANGUAGE
QL991	*TERATOLOGY* **SEE** ABNORMALITIES (ANIMALS)
QK664	*TERATOLOGY* **SEE** ABNORMALITIES (PLANTS)
QM691-9	*TERATOLOGY* **SEE** DEFORMITIES / *human anatomy*
GN68-69.8	*TERATOLOGY* **SEE** DEFORMITIES / *somatic anthropology*
QL991	*TERATOLOGY* **SEE** MONSTERS / *animals*
GR825-830	*TERATOLOGY* **SEE** MONSTERS / *folk-lore*
QM691-9	*TERATOLOGY* **SEE** MONSTERS / *human anatomy*
TP977-8	*TEREBINTHINA* **SEE** TURPENTINE / *chemical technology*
RM666.T9	*TEREBINTHINA* **SEE** TURPENTINE / *therapeutics*
SD547	*TEREBINTHINA* **SEE** TURPENTINE / *turpentine orcharding*
F2230.2.T	TERENO INDIANS
UC70-75	*TERMINAL-LEAVE PAY FOR ENLISTED PERSONNEL* **SEE** U.S. — PAY, ALLOWANCES, ETC.
VC50-65	*TERMINAL-LEAVE PAY FOR ENLISTED PERSONNEL* **SEE** U.S. — PAY, ALLOWANCES, ETC.
TF300-308	*TERMINALS, RAILROAD* **SEE** RAILROADS — STATIONS
HE1613-1614	*TERMINALS, RAILROAD* **SEE** RAILROADS — STATIONS / *location*
QL513.T3	TERMITES
QL696.L3	TERNS
QD416	TERPENES
NA3700	TERRA-COTTA / *architectural decoration*
TH1077-1083	TERRA-COTTA / *building*
NK4267	TERRA-COTTA / *ceramic art*
TA432-3	TERRA-COTTA / *etc.*
HD9607	TERRA-COTTA / *industry*
TP835	TERRA-COTTA / *technology*
NB145-159	TERRA-COTTAS / *statuettes*
NB157	TERRA-COTTAS / *tanagra figurines*
F1545	TERRABA INDIANS / *costa rica*
PM4371	TERRABA LANGUAGE

TH4970	TERRACES (ARCHITECTURE) **SEE** DECKS (ARCHITECTURE, DOMESTIC)
QL666.C5	TERRAPINS **SEE** TURTLES
NA3850.T	TERRAZZO
GN785-6	TERREMARE
G3170	TERRESTRIAL GLOBES **SEE** GLOBES
QC811-849	TERRESTRIAL MAGNETISM **SEE** MAGNETISM, TERRESTRIAL
VK	TERRESTRIAL NAVIGATION, ASTRONAUTICS IN **SEE** ASTRONAUTICS IN NAVIGATION
QC806	TERRESTRIAL PHYSICS **SEE** GEOPHYSICS
QE500-501	TERRESTRIAL PHYSICS **SEE** GEOPHYSICS
QB321	TERRESTRIAL REFRACTION **SEE** REFRACTION, TERRESTRIAL / geodesy
SF429.T3	TERRIERS
JX4122-4141	TERRITORIAL WATERS
JX4068.I6	TERRITORIES, INTERNATIONAL **SEE** INTERNATIONALIZED TERRITORIES
JX4088	TERRITORY, ACQUISITION OF **SEE** ACQUISITION OF TERRITORY
JX4085-4150	TERRITORY, NATIONAL / international law
DC139-195	TERROR, REIGN OF **SEE** FRANCE — HISTORY — — REVOLUTION
JX6731.T4	TERRORISM
JX1981.T45	TERRORISM / league of nations
BX2840	TERTIARIES **SEE** THIRD ORDERS
QE691-5	TERTIARY PERIOD **SEE** GEOLOGY, STRATIGRAPHIC — TERTIARY
QE926-930	TERTIARY PERIOD **SEE** PALEOBOTANY — TERTIARY
QE736-740	TERTIARY PERIOD **SEE** PALEONTOLOGY — TERTIARY
BM720.T5	TERUMAH
PL8726	TESO LANGUAGE
BR757	TEST ACT, 1673
E277	TEST ACT, 1777 / loyalists in the revolution
F153	TEST ACT, 1777 / pennsylvania history
TD410-412	TEST BORING **SEE** BORING / etc.
TN281	TEST BORING **SEE** BORING / mining
TN281	TEST BORING **SEE** BORING / mining
QD77	TEST-PAPERS, CHEMICAL **SEE** INDICATORS AND TEST-PAPERS / analytic chemistry
QL401-432	TESTACEA **SEE** MOLLUSKS
RC898	TESTICLE — ABNORMITIES AND DEFORMITIES
QL878	TESTICLE / comparative anatomy
QM416	TESTICLE / human anatomy
QP255	TESTICLE / physiology
TA416-417	TESTING LABORATORIES
UF890	TESTING OF ORDNANCE **SEE** ORDNANCE TESTING / military
VF540	TESTING OF ORDNANCE **SEE** ORDNANCE TESTING / naval
TA413	TESTING-MACHINES
TA401-492	TESTING / materials
QC100-111	TESTING / standards
LB3051	TESTS AND MEASUREMENTS IN EDUCATION **SEE** EDUCATIONAL TESTS AND MEASUREMENTS
BF818-839	TESTS, CHARACTER **SEE** CHARACTER TESTS
LB1131	TESTS, MENTAL **SEE** MENTAL TESTS
BF431	TESTS, MENTAL **SEE** MENTAL TESTS / psychology
RC185	TETANUS ANTITOXIN
RC185	TETANUS
RC632.T4	TETANY
SF967.G7	TETANY, GRASS **SEE** GRASS TETANY
PL8727	TETE LANGUAGE
PL8728	TETELA LANGUAGE
E99.T33	TETES DE BOULE INDIANS
GV1017.T	TETHER-BALL
E99.T34	TETON INDIANS
QL430.2	TETRABRANCHIATA
QE806	TETRABRANCHIATA, FOSSIL
QD181.C5	TETRACHLORIDES
QA561	TETRAHEDRA / analytic geometry
QA491	TETRAHEDRA / solid geometry
QL391.C4	TETRARHYNCHIDEA
PL8727	TETTE LANGUAGE **SEE** TETE LANGUAGE
F1221.C56	TEUTECAS INDIANS **SEE** CHINANTEC INDIANS
DD123	TEUTOBURGER WALD, BATTLE OF, 9 A.D.
CB213-214	TEUTONIC CIVILIZATION **SEE** CIVILIZATION, GERMANIC
CR4759-4775	TEUTONIC KNIGHTS / chivalry
DD491.O46-558	TEUTONIC KNIGHTS / history
PD-PF	TEUTONIC LANGUAGES **SEE** GERMANIC LANGUAGES
CR4759-4775	TEUTONIC ORDER **SEE** TEUTONIC KNIGHTS / chivalry
DD491.O46-558	TEUTONIC ORDER **SEE** TEUTONIC KNIGHTS / history
GN549.T4	TEUTONIC RACE
PM8861-3	TEUTONISH
E99.T35	TEWA INDIANS
PM2431	TEWA LANGUAGE
F390	TEXAN MIER EXPEDITION, 1842 **SEE** MIER EXPEDITION, 1842
F390	TEXAN SANTA FE EXPEDITION, 1841
F381-395	TEXAS — HISTORY
SF805	TEXAS FEVER
E580	TEXAS — HISTORY — — CIVIL WAR
E532	TEXAS — HISTORY — — CIVIL WAR
F1221.T	TEXCOCAN INDIANS **SEE** TEZCUCAN INDIANS
D278.T4	TEXEL, BATTLE OF THE, 1673
LB2851-3	TEXT-BOOKS
LT	TEXT-BOOKS
LB3045	TEXT-BOOKS
TX1449	TEXTILE CHEMISTRY
TS1475	TEXTILE DESIGN
NK8800-8999	TEXTILE DESIGN / art industries
TS1781	TEXTILE FABRICS **SEE** NONWOVEN FABRICS
NK8800-8999	TEXTILE FABRICS **SEE** TEXTILE INDUSTRY AND FABRICS / art industries
TS1300-1781	TEXTILE FABRICS **SEE** TEXTILE INDUSTRY AND FABRICS / manufacture
HD9850-9869	TEXTILE FABRICS **SEE** TEXTILE INDUSTRY AND FABRICS / trade
TH4521	TEXTILE FACTORIES / building
SB241-261	TEXTILE FIBERS / culture
TS1540-1549	TEXTILE FIBERS / manufacture
TS1545	TEXTILE FIBERS, ANIMAL **SEE** ANIMAL FIBERS
TS1510	TEXTILE FINISHING
HF5585.T	TEXTILE INDUSTRY AND FABRICS — CREDIT GUIDES
NK8803	TEXTILE INDUSTRY AND FABRICS — PRIVATE COLLECTIONS
TS1450	TEXTILE INDUSTRY AND FABRICS — STANDARDS
TS1449	TEXTILE INDUSTRY AND FABRICS — TESTING
NK8800-8999	TEXTILE INDUSTRY AND FABRICS / art industries
TS1300-1781	TEXTILE INDUSTRY AND FABRICS / manufacture
HD9850-9869	TEXTILE INDUSTRY AND FABRICS / trade
TX1449	TEXTILE INDUSTRY AND FABRICS-CHEMISTRY **SEE** TEXTILE CHEMISTRY
TS1525	TEXTILE MACHINERY
NK9505	TEXTILE PAINTING
SB241-261	TEXTILE PLANTS **SEE** TEXTILE FIBERS / culture
TS1540-1549	TEXTILE PLANTS **SEE** TEXTILE FIBERS / manufacture
TP930-931	TEXTILE PRINTING
TS1471-3	TEXTILE SCHOOLS
NK8800-8999	TEXTILES **SEE** TEXTILE INDUSTRY AND FABRICS / art industries
TS1300-1781	TEXTILES **SEE** TEXTILE INDUSTRY AND FABRICS / manufacture
HD9850-9869	TEXTILES **SEE** TEXTILE INDUSTRY AND FABRICS / trade
P351-7	TEXTS, POLYGLOT **SEE** POLYGLOT TEXTS, SELECTIONS, QUOTATIONS, ETC.
PA47	TEXTUAL CRITICISM **SEE** CRITICISM, TEXTUAL
P47	TEXTUAL CRITICISM **SEE** CRITICISM, TEXTUAL
TT323	TEXTURE PAINTING
F1221.T	TEZCUCAN INDIANS
PL4001.T4	THADO LANGUAGE
DS485.B85	THADOS
PL4151-4199	THAI LANGUAGE **SEE** SIAMESE LANGUAGE
PL4111-4251	THAI LANGUAGES **SEE** TAI LANGUAGES
DS560	THAI RACE **SEE** TAI RACE
DS585	THAI-INDOCHINESE CONFLICT, 1940-1941
DS585	THAILAND-INDOCHINA CONFLICT, 1940-1941 **SEE** THAI-INDOCHINESE CONFLICT, 1940-1941
QL368.F6	THALAMOPHORA **SEE** FORAMINIFERA
QP381	THALAMUS **SEE** OPTIC THALAMUS
QL937	THALAMUS **SEE** OPTIC THALAMUS
QM455	THALAMUS **SEE** OPTIC THALAMUS
GC	THALASSOGRAPHY **SEE** OCEANOGRAPHY
CJ2715	THALER **SEE** TALER

QD181.T7	THALLIUM
E356.T3	THAMES, BATTLE OF, 1813
SB951	THANITE / insecticides
BJ1533.G8	*THANKFULNESS* **SEE** GRATITUDE / ethics
BV4647.G8	*THANKFULNESS* **SEE** GRATITUDE / theology
E178.6	THANKSGIVING DAY ADDRESSES / american history
E649	THANKSGIVING DAY ADDRESSES / american history
BV4305	THANKSGIVING DAY ADDRESSES / etc. sermons
GT4975	THANKSGIVING DAY
BV75	THANKSGIVING DAY / religion
QE391.T	THAUMASITE
TH6685	THAWING / plumbing
BT378.T3	*THE POUNDS (PARABLE)* **SEE** THE TALENTS (PARABLE)
BT378.S7	THE SOWER (PARABLE)
BT378.T3	THE TALENTS (PARABLE)
N8253	THE THINKER IN ART
F591-6	THE WEST — HISTORY
E470.9	THE WEST — HISTORY — — CIVIL WAR
HF5686.T	THEATER — ACCOUNTING
PN2093-5	THEATER — ANECDOTES, FACETIAE, SATIRE, ETC.
PN2091.A7	THEATER — APPLAUSE, DEMONSTRATIONS, ETC.
PN2042-5	THEATER — CENSORSHIP
PN3035	THEATER — JEWS
PN2042-5	THEATER — LAWS AND REGULATIONS
PN2267	THEATER — LITTLE THEATER MOVEMENT / u.s.
PN2047-2051	THEATER — MORAL AND RELIGIOUS ASPECTS
PN1620	THEATER — MUSEUMS AND COLLECTIONS
PN2111	THEATER — PICTORIAL WORKS
PN2074	THEATER AS A PROFESSION
PN1707	*THEATER CRITICISM* **SEE** DRAMATIC CRITICISM
N8252	THEATER IN ART
Z675.T	*THEATER LIBRARIES* **SEE** LIBRARIES, THEATRICAL
PN2091.M6	*THEATER MODELS* **SEE** THEATERS — MODELS
PN2000-3299	THEATER
PN3035	*THEATER, HEBREW* **SEE** THEATER — JEWS
PN2071.I5	*THEATER, IMPROMPTU* **SEE** IMPROVISATION (ACTING)
PN2268	THEATER, MUNICIPAL
PN2219.O8	THEATER, OPEN-AIR
PN1972	*THEATER, TOY* **SEE** TOY THEATERS
PN3035	*THEATER, YIDDISH* **SEE** THEATER — JEWS
GT500-2370	*THEATER-COSTUME* **SEE** COSTUME / manners and customs
PN2091.M6	*THEATER-MODELS* **SEE** THEATERS — MODELS
PN2091.E4	*THEATER-STAGE LIGHTING* **SEE** STAGE LIGHTING
PN2074	*THEATER-VOCATIONAL GUIDANCE* **SEE** THEATER AS A PROFESSION
PN2091.A	THEATERS — ACCIDENTS
NA6820-6845	THEATERS — CONSTRUCTION
NA6820-6845	THEATERS — DECORATION
TH9445.T3-4	THEATERS — FIRES AND FIRE PREVENTION
PN2042-5	THEATERS — LAWS AND REGULATIONS
TH7975.T	THEATERS — LIGHTING
TK4399.T6	THEATERS — LIGHTING / electric
PN2091.M6	THEATERS — MODELS
TH9445.T3-4	THEATERS — SAFETY MEASURES / fires
TH7684.T3	THEATERS — SANITATION / ventilation
PN2091.S6	THEATERS — SOUND EFFECTS
PN2091.S8	THEATERS — STAGE-SETTING AND SCENERY
NA6820-6845	THEATERS / architecture
GV1521	THEATERS, MINIATURE
PN1993-9	*THEATERS, MOVING-PICTURE* **SEE** MOVING-PICTURE THEATERS
NA6845	*THEATERS, MOVING-PICTURE* **SEE** MOVING-PICTURE THEATERS / architecture
NA6820-6845	*THEATERS-ARCHITECTURE* **SEE** THEATERS — CONSTRUCTION
NA6820-6845	*THEATERS-ARCHITECTURE* **SEE** THEATERS — DECORATION
NA6820-6845	*THEATERS-DESIGNS AND PLANS* **SEE** THEATERS — CONSTRUCTION
GT500-2370	*THEATRICAL COSTUME* **SEE** COSTUME / manners and customs
Z675.T	*THEATRICAL LIBRARIES* **SEE** LIBRARIES, THEATRICAL
PN2068	*THEATRICAL MAKE-UP* **SEE** MAKE-UP, THEATRICAL
ML1950	*THEATRICAL MUSIC* **SEE** BALLAD OPERA / history
ML3860	*THEATRICAL MUSIC* **SEE** MUSIC, INCIDENTAL / aesthetics
ML3858	*THEATRICAL MUSIC* **SEE** OPERA / aesthetics
ML1700-2110	*THEATRICAL MUSIC* **SEE** OPERA / history and criticism
ML1900	*THEATRICAL MUSIC* **SEE** OPERETTA
ML1950	*THEATRICAL MUSIC* **SEE** SINGSPIEL
ML1950	*THEATRICAL MUSIC* **SEE** ZARZUELA
PN2091.S8	*THEATRICAL SCENERY* **SEE** THEATERS — STAGE-SETTING AND SCENERY
PN1972	*THEATRICAL SHEETS* **SEE** TOY THEATERS
PN3151-3191	*THEATRICALS, AMATEUR* **SEE** AMATEUR THEATRICALS
PN3175-3191	*THEATRICALS, COLLEGE* **SEE** COLLEGE AND SCHOOL DRAMA / history and criticism
PL3801.K3	*THEBORSKAD LANGUAGE* **SEE** KANAURI LANGUAGE
QL430.4	THECOSOMATA
HV6646-6665	*THEFT* **SEE** THIEVES
HG9970.B8	*THEFT INSURANCE* **SEE** INSURANCE, BURGLARY
QD421	THEINE / chemistry
RM666.T	THEINE / therapeutics
BL200	THEISM
BT98-101	THEISM / doctrinal theology
BD555	THEISM / teleology
BF436.A6	THEMATIC APPERCEPTION TEST
ML128.V7	*THEMATIC CATALOGS (MUSIC)* **SEE** VOCAL MUSIC — THEMATIC CATALOGS
JC20-89	THEOCRACY / political science
BT160	THEODICY
TA575	THEODOLITES
BS661	*THEOLOGICAL ANTHROPOLOGY* **SEE** MAN (THEOLOGY) / bible
BT700-745	*THEOLOGICAL ANTHROPOLOGY* **SEE** MAN (THEOLOGY) / doctrinal theology
BL256	*THEOLOGICAL ANTHROPOLOGY* **SEE** MAN (THEOLOGY) / religion
BV1460-1615	*THEOLOGICAL EDUCATION* **SEE** RELIGIOUS EDUCATION
BV4019-4160	*THEOLOGICAL EDUCATION* **SEE** THEOLOGY — STUDY AND TEACHING
Z675.T4	THEOLOGICAL LIBRARIES
BV4316.T5	THEOLOGICAL SEMINARIES — SERMONS
BX1939.S45	THEOLOGICAL SEMINARIES (CANON LAW)
BV4019-4160	THEOLOGICAL SEMINARIES
BX903	*THEOLOGICAL STUDENTS* **SEE** SEMINARIANS / catholic
BV4635	THEOLOGICAL VIRTUES
Z7751-7855	THEOLOGY — BIBLIOGRAPHY
BR118	THEOLOGY — METHODOLOGY
BV4019-4160	THEOLOGY — STUDY AND TEACHING
BR96.5	THEOLOGY — TERMINOLOGY
BR-BX	THEOLOGY
BL625	*THEOLOGY, ASCETICAL* **SEE** ASCETICISM
BV5021-5068	*THEOLOGY, ASCETICAL* **SEE** ASCETICISM / christian
BJ1491	*THEOLOGY, ASCETICAL* **SEE** ASCETICISM / ethics
BS543	*THEOLOGY, BIBLICAL* **SEE** BIBLE — THEOLOGY
BT155	*THEOLOGY, COVENANT* **SEE** COVENANTS (THEOLOGY)
BT78	*THEOLOGY, CRISIS* **SEE** DIALECTICAL THEOLOGY
BV4800-4870	*THEOLOGY, DEVOTIONAL* **SEE** DEVOTIONAL EXERCISES
BX	*THEOLOGY, DEVOTIONAL* **SEE** DEVOTIONAL EXERCISES / by denomination
BV4800-4895	*THEOLOGY, DEVOTIONAL* **SEE** DEVOTIONAL LITERATURE
BX2177-2198	*THEOLOGY, DEVOTIONAL* **SEE** DEVOTIONAL LITERATURE / catholic church
BV4800-4870	*THEOLOGY, DEVOTIONAL* **SEE** MEDITATIONS
BX2177-2198	*THEOLOGY, DEVOTIONAL* **SEE** MEDITATIONS / catholic church
BV228-283	*THEOLOGY, DEVOTIONAL* **SEE** PRAYERS
BL560	*THEOLOGY, DEVOTIONAL* **SEE** PRAYERS / comparative religion
BT157	*THEOLOGY, DISPENSATIONAL* **SEE** DISPENSATIONALISM
BT20-30	THEOLOGY, DOCTRINAL — HISTORY
BT65	THEOLOGY, DOCTRINAL — INTRODUCTIONS
BT77	THEOLOGY, DOCTRINAL — POPULAR WORKS
BT65	*THEOLOGY, DOCTRINAL-PROLEGOMENA* **SEE** THEOLOGY, DOCTRINAL — INTRODUCTIONS
BV590-640	*THEOLOGY, ECCLESIASTICAL* **SEE** CHURCH

BJ1190-1278	THEOLOGY, ETHICAL **SEE** CHRISTIAN ETHICS
BT155	THEOLOGY, FEDERAL **SEE** COVENANTS (THEOLOGY)
BT1095-1255	THEOLOGY, FUNDAMENTAL **SEE** APOLOGETICS
BP166	THEOLOGY, ISLAMIC **SEE** ISLAMIC THEOLOGY
BM600	THEOLOGY, JEWISH **SEE** JEWISH THEOLOGY
BJ1190-1278	THEOLOGY, MORAL **SEE** CHRISTIAN ETHICS
BP166	THEOLOGY, MUSLIM **SEE** ISLAMIC THEOLOGY
BV5070-5095	THEOLOGY, MYSTICAL **SEE** MYSTICISM / christianity
BL625	THEOLOGY, MYSTICAL **SEE** MYSTICISM / comparative religion
B728	THEOLOGY, MYSTICAL **SEE** MYSTICISM / medieval philosophy
B828	THEOLOGY, MYSTICAL **SEE** MYSTICISM / modern philosophy
BL175-190	THEOLOGY, NATURAL **SEE** NATURAL THEOLOGY
BX7250	THEOLOGY, NEW ENGLAND **SEE** NEW ENGLAND THEOLOGY
BV4000-4396	THEOLOGY, PASTORAL **SEE** PASTORAL THEOLOGY
BT40	THEOLOGY, PHILOSOPHICAL **SEE** PHILOSOPHICAL THEOLOGY
BP174	THEOLOGY, PRACTICAL (ISLAM) **SEE** ISLAMIC RELIGIOUS PRACTICE
BV1-4	THEOLOGY, PRACTICAL
B839	THEOLOGY, SCHOLASTIC **SEE** SCHOLASTICISM / general and modern
B851-4695	THEOLOGY, SCHOLASTIC **SEE** SCHOLASTICISM / local
B734	THEOLOGY, SCHOLASTIC **SEE** SCHOLASTICISM / medieval
BD125	THEOLOGY, SCHOLASTIC **SEE** SCHOLASTICISM / scholastic metaphysics
BR100	THEOLOGY-PHILOSOPHY **SEE** CHRISTIANITY — PHILOSOPHY
BR118	THEOLOGY-PROPAEDEUTICS **SEE** THEOLOGY — METHODOLOGY
BR96	THEOLOGY-QUESTIONS AND ANSWERS **SEE** QUESTIONS AND ANSWERS — THEOLOGY
BT128	THEOPHANIES / christian theology
QD453-651	THEORETICAL CHEMISTRY **SEE** CHEMISTRY, PHYSICAL AND THEORETICAL
QA211-218	THEORY OF EQUATIONS **SEE** EQUATIONS, THEORY OF
QA275	THEORY OF ERRORS **SEE** ERRORS, THEORY OF
QA269	THEORY OF GAMES **SEE** GAME THEORY
QA171	THEORY OF GROUPS **SEE** GROUPS, THEORY OF
B398.I3	THEORY OF IDEAS **SEE** IDEA (PHILOSOPHY) / plato
QB361-2	THEORY OF PLANETS **SEE** PLANETS, THEORY OF
TG260	THEORY OF STRUCTURES **SEE** STRUCTURES, THEORY OF
BP527	THEOSOPHY — TERMINOLOGY
BP500-585	THEOSOPHY
BM175.T	THERAPEUTAE
RM103	THERAPEUTICS — COMPLICATIONS AND SEQUELAE
RM84	THERAPEUTICS — EARLY WORKS TO 1800
RM81	THERAPEUTICS — EARLY WORKS TO 1800
RM126	THERAPEUTICS — EXAMINATIONS, QUESTIONS, ETC.
RM	THERAPEUTICS
RZ422	THERAPEUTICS, BIOCHEMIC **SEE** MEDICINE, BIOCHEMIC
RK318-320	THERAPEUTICS, DENTAL
RM111	THERAPEUTICS, EXPERIMENTAL
RE991-2	THERAPEUTICS, OCULAR **SEE** THERAPEUTICS, OPHTHALMOLOGICAL
RE991-2	THERAPEUTICS, OPHTHALMOLOGICAL
RM695-737	THERAPEUTICS, PHYSIOLOGICAL
RC490-499	THERAPEUTICS, SUGGESTIVE
RD51	THERAPEUTICS, SURGICAL
RM287	THERAPY, CELLULAR **SEE** CELLULAR THERAPY
BL1480	THERAVADA BUDDHISM **SEE** HINAYANA BUDDHISM
QC321-3	THERMAL DIFFUSIVITY
QC251-338	THERMAL EQUILIBRIUM **SEE** HEAT
QC311-319	THERMAL EQUILIBRIUM **SEE** THERMODYNAMICS
TJ265	THERMAL EQUILIBRIUM **SEE** THERMODYNAMICS / mechanical engineering
TP492.5	THERMAL EQUILIBRIUM **SEE** THERMODYNAMICS / refrigeration
QC281-6	THERMAL EXPANSION **SEE** EXPANSION (HEAT)
TH1715	THERMAL INSULATION **SEE** INSULATION (HEAT)
TK7872.T4	THERMAL RESISTORS **SEE** THERMISTORS

TA405.5	THERMAL STRESSES
QC320-338	THERMAL TRANSFER **SEE** HEAT — TRANSMISSION
QE528	THERMAL WATERS **SEE** GEYSERS
GB1001-1197	THERMAL WATERS **SEE** SPRINGS
GR690	THERMAL WATERS **SEE** SPRINGS / folk-lore
TA405.5	THERMAL-EXPANSION STRESSES **SEE** THERMAL STRESSES
TK7872.T4	THERMISTORS
QD511-536	THERMOCHEMISTRY
QC274	THERMOCOUPLES
QC311-319	THERMODYNAMICS
TJ265	THERMODYNAMICS / mechanical engineering
TP492.5	THERMODYNAMICS / refrigeration
QA933	THERMOELASTICITY
QC621	THERMOELECTRICITY
QC761	THERMOMAGNETISM
QC271-8	THERMOMETERS AND THERMOMETRY
RC75	THERMOMETERS AND THERMOMETRY, MEDICAL
RC75	THERMOMETERS, CLINICAL **SEE** THERMOMETERS AND THERMOMETRY, MEDICAL
QR84	THERMOPHILIC BACTERIA **SEE** BACTERIA, THERMOPHILIC
QC338	THERMOPILES
DF225.5	THERMOPYLAE, BATTLE OF, 480 B.C.
TH7466.5	THERMOSTAT / central heating
QD54.T4	THERMOSTAT / chemistry
RM865-8	THERMOTHERAPY
RJ456.G	THESAURIMOSIS GLYCOGENICA **SEE** GLYCOGENOSIS
LB2369	THESES **SEE** DISSERTATIONS, ACADEMIC / preparation
LB2369	THESIS WRITING **SEE** DISSERTATIONS, ACADEMIC / preparation
QA345	THETA FUNCTIONS **SEE** FUNCTIONS, THETA
QC102.5	THICKNESS MEASUREMENT
TJ1166	THICKNESS MEASUREMENT / machine-shop practice
HV6646-6665	THIEVES
RD101	THIGH-FRACTURE **SEE** FEMUR — FRACTURE
PM2451	THIMAGOA LANGUAGE **SEE** TIMUCUA LANGUAGE
BF455	THINKING **SEE** THOUGHT AND THINKING / thought and language
TP937.7	THINNER (PAINT MIXING)
SD396.5	THINNING OF FORESTS **SEE** FOREST THINNING
QD181.C15	THIOCYANATES
QP913.C15	THIOCYANATES / physiology
QD181.C15	THIOCYANIC ACID
QP13.C15	THIOCYANIC ACID / physiology
QD181.C15	THIOCYANIDES **SEE** THIOCYANATES
QP913.C15	THIOCYANIDES **SEE** THIOCYANATES / physiology
TS1925	THIOKOL **SEE** RUBBER, ARTIFICIAL
QD305.A2	THIOLACTIC ACID
QD403	THIOPHENE
BX2840	THIRD ORDERS
JK550	THIRD TERM, PRESIDENTIAL **SEE** PRESIDENTS — U.S. — — TERM OF OFFICE
TF890	THIRD-RAIL RAILROADS **SEE** ELECTRIC RAILROADS — THIRD RAIL
QP141	THIRST
GR933	THIRTEEN (THE NUMBER) / folk-lore
CB355	THIRTEENTH CENTURY / civilization
DF231.3	THIRTY TYRANTS
D261	THIRTY YEARS' WAR, 1618-1648 — ECONOMIC ASPECTS
D251-271	THIRTY YEARS' WAR, 1618-1648
SB615.T4	THISTLE
E99.T6	THLINKET INDIANS **SEE** TLINGIT INDIANS
E99.T6	THLINKITHEN INDIANS **SEE** TLINGIT INDIANS
PL4251.T	THO LANGUAGE
TN736-8	THOMAS PROCESS **SEE** BESSEMER PROCESS
GV1511.T4	THOMAS' BASEBALL GAME
B839	THOMISM (MODERN PHILOSOPHY) **SEE** NEO-SCHOLASTICISM
E99.N96	THOMPSON INDIANS **SEE** NTLAKYAPAMUK INDIANS
PM2045	THOMPSON LANGUAGE **SEE** NTLAKYAPAMUK LANGUAGE
E99.N96	THOMPSON RIVER INDIANS **SEE** NTLAKYAPAMUK INDIANS
QC621	THOMSON EFFECT
RV1-10	THOMSONIANISM **SEE** MEDICINE, BOTANIC
GN657.T5	THONGA TRIBE

HE1971	*TICKETS, RAILROAD* **SEE** RAILROADS — TICKETS / *economics*
QL458.A2	TICKS
E199	TICONDEROGA, BATTLE NEAR, 1757
E199	TICONDEROGA, BATTLE OF, 1758
E241.T5	TICONDEROGA, N.Y. — CAPTURE, 1775
GC231-296	*TIDAL CURRENTS* **SEE** OCEAN CURRENTS
GC301-376	*TIDAL CURRENTS* **SEE** TIDES
QB414-419	*TIDAL CURRENTS* **SEE** TIDES / *astronomy*
S621	*TIDAL MARSHES* **SEE** MARSHES, TIDE / *agriculture*
TC975	*TIDAL MARSHES* **SEE** MARSHES, TIDE / *reclamation*
TC147	TIDAL POWER
GC306	TIDE-GAGES
S621	*TIDE-MARSHES* **SEE** MARSHES, TIDE / *agriculture*
TC975	*TIDE-MARSHES* **SEE** MARSHES, TIDE / *reclamation*
GC306	TIDE-PREDICTORS
SD397.S77	*TIDELAND SPRUCE* **SEE** SITKA SPRUCE
VK601-794	TIDES — TABLES
GC301-376	TIDES
QB414-419	TIDES / *astronomy*
TC147	*TIDES-UTILIZATION* **SEE** TIDAL POWER
S621	*TIDEWATER MARSHES* **SEE** MARSHES, TIDE / *agriculture*
TC975	*TIDEWATER MARSHES* **SEE** MARSHES, TIDE / *reclamation*
PL5461	TIDONG DIALECTS
DS762	TIENTSIN MASSACRE, 1870
GT2120	*TIES (NECKWEAR)* **SEE** CRAVATS
TF252-6	*TIES, RAILROAD* **SEE** RAILROADS — TIES
SK305.T5	TIGER HUNTING
QL737.C2	TIGERS
PJ9131	TIGRE LANGUAGE
PJ9111	TIGRINA BALLADS AND SONGS
E99.T52	TIGUA INDIANS
PM2441	TIGUA LANGUAGE
DU850	TIKOPIANS / *solomon islands*
TH1083	TILE CONSTRUCTION
TH8531	TILE LAYING
NA3705	*TILE PAVEMENTS* **SEE** PAVEMENTS, TILE
NK4670	*TILE STOVES* **SEE** STOVES, EARTHENWARE / *art*
QL638.L	TILE-FISH
NA3705	TILES / *architecture*
NA2980-2985	TILES / *architecture*
NK4670-4675	TILES / *art industries*
TH8521-8542	TILES / *building*
TP837-9	TILES / *technology*
TH2448	TILES, ROOFING
S603	TILLAGE
QE471	TILLITE
DC230.T5	TILSIT, TREATY OF, 1807
TA683	*TILT-UP CONCRETE CONSTRUCTION* **SEE** PRECAST CONCRETE CONSTRUCTION
PM2451	*TIMAGOA LANGUAGE* **SEE** TIMUCUA LANGUAGE
SD551-7	*TIMBER CRUISING* **SEE** FORESTS AND FORESTRY — MENSURATION
SD551-7	*TIMBER CRUISING* **SEE** FORESTS AND FORESTRY — VALUATION
HG9970.F	*TIMBER INSURANCE* **SEE** INSURANCE, FOREST
SD561-668	*TIMBER LAWS AND LEGISLATION* **SEE** FORESTRY LAW AND LEGISLATION
QK477	TIMBER-LINE
SD430-557	TIMBER / *forestry*
TA419-424	TIMBER / *materials of construction*
SD551-7	*TIMBER-MENSURATION* **SEE** FORESTS AND FORESTRY — MENSURATION
TA422-4	*TIMBER-PRESERVATION* **SEE** WOOD — PRESERVATION
TA419-420	*TIMBER-TESTING* **SEE** WOOD — TESTING / *engineering*
SD433	*TIMBER-TESTING* **SEE** WOOD — TESTING / *forestry*
TN289	*TIMBERING OF MINES* **SEE** MINE TIMBERING
QB211	TIME — CONVERSION TABLES
QB223	TIME — SYSTEMS AND STANDARDS
BX1939.T5	TIME (CANON LAW)
BF467-475	*TIME AND SPACE* **SEE** SPACE AND TIME / *psychology*
QB213	TIME MEASUREMENTS
TS542	TIME MEASUREMENTS / *clocks and watches*
QP445	TIME PERCEPTION
T60.T5	TIME STUDY
QB221	*TIME-BALLS* **SEE** TIME-SIGNALS
QA276	TIME-SERIES ANALYSIS
QB221	TIME-SIGNALS
HE2801-3600	*TIME-TABLES, RAILROAD* **SEE** RAILROADS — TIME-TABLES / *other countries*
TF565	*TIME-TABLES, RAILROAD* **SEE** RAILROADS — TIME-TABLES / *schedules*
HE2727-9	*TIME-TABLES, RAILROAD* **SEE** RAILROADS — TIME-TABLES / *u.s.*
QB209-224	TIME
BF467-475	TIME / *psychology*
BD638	TIME / *speculative philosophy*
QP445	*TIME, COGNITION OF* **SEE** TIME PERCEPTION
QB217	TIME, EQUATION OF
QE508	*TIME, GEOLOGICAL* **SEE** GEOLOGICAL TIME
MT42	*TIME, MUSICAL* **SEE** TEMPO (MUSIC)
BF317	*TIME, REACTION* **SEE** REACTION-TIME / *psychology*
TJ214.T5	*TIMERS, AUTOMATIC* **SEE** AUTOMATIC TIMERS
BF575.T5	TIMIDITY
TJ214.T5	*TIMING DEVICES* **SEE** AUTOMATIC TIMERS
E99.T	TIMISKAMING INDIANS
PL8735	TIMNE LANGUAGE
PL5465	TIMORESE LANGUAGE
SB741.T5	TIMOTHY RUST
SB608.T6	TIMOTHY STEM-BORER
SB201.T5	TIMOTHY-GRASS
SF99	TIMOTHY-GRASS / *value as feed*
ML1035	*TIMPANI* **SEE** KETTLEDRUM / *history*
PM2451	*TIMUACA LANGUAGE* **SEE** TIMUCUA LANGUAGE
PM2451	TIMUCUA LANGUAGE
PM2451	TIMUCUAN LANGUAGES
PM2451	*TIMUQUAN LANGUAGES* **SEE** TIMUCUAN LANGUAGES
TN793	TIN — METALLURGY
QD181.S7	TIN COMPOUNDS
QD412.S7	TIN COMPOUNDS / *organic*
HD9539.T5-6	TIN INDUSTRY
HD9539.T6	TIN MINERS / *economics*
TN470-479	TIN MINES AND MINING
QD187.S7	TIN ORES — ANALYSIS
TN470-479	TIN ORES
HF5716.T4	TIN PLATE — TABLES AND READY-RECKONERS / *economics*
TS597	TIN PLATE — TABLES AND READY-RECKONERS / *manufacture*
TS590-599	TIN PLATE
QD181.S7	TIN / *chemistry*
TS590-619	TIN / *manufactures*
QL696.T4	TINAMIFORMES
QL696.T4	*TINAMOMORPHAE* **SEE** TINAMIFORMES
HD9999.D8-9	*TINCTORIAL SUBSTANCES* **SEE** DYES AND DYEING / *economics*
TP897-929	*TINCTORIAL SUBSTANCES* **SEE** DYES AND DYEING / *technology*
DT443	TINDIGA (AFRICAN PEOPLE)
GN671.P5	TINGUIANES / *anthropology*
DS666.T5	TINGUIANES / *philippine islands*
HD8039.T6-62	TINKERS
E99.T56	TINNE INDIANS
PM2453	TINNE LANGUAGES
TS660	TINNING
TS590-599	*TINPLATE* **SEE** TIN PLATE
NK7695	TINSEL
TS600	TINSMITHING
T357	TINTING / *mechanical drawing*
TR375	TINTYPE
TS619	TINWARE
NK492	*TINY OBJECTS* **SEE** MINIATURE OBJECTS / *art*
E98.D9	*TIPIS* **SEE** INDIANS OF NORTH AMERICA — DWELLINGS
E83.81	TIPPECANOE, BATTLE OF, 1811
HD5102-4	TIPPING

TS1912	TIRES, RUBBER / *manufacture*
TJ640	TIRES, STEEL / *locomotives*
PK1811-1819	*TIRHUTIA LANGUAGE* **SEE** MAITHILI LANGUAGE
BX4080.T	TIRONENSIANS
Z81	TIRONIAN NOTES
TL798.M4	*TIROS (METEOROLOGICAL SATELLITE)* **SEE** TIROS (METEOROLOGICAL SATELLITE)
TL798.M4	TIROS (METEOROLOGICAL SATELLITE)
PM4371	*TIRRIBI LANGUAGE* **SEE** TERRABA LANGUAGE
F1545	*TIRUB INDIANS* **SEE** TERRABA INDIANS / *costa rica*
PL6101-4	TIRURAI LANGUAGE
GN671.P5	TIRURAI TRIBE / *anthropology*
DS666.T6	TIRURAI TRIBE / *philippine islands*
QM551-575	TISSUES / *histology*
QP88	TISSUES / *physiology*
QK641-707	*TISSUES, VEGETABLE* **SEE** BOTANY — ANATOMY
QK725	*TISSUES, VEGETABLE* **SEE** PLANT CELLS AND TISSUES
QE391.T	TITANITE
TN799.T5	TITANIUM — HYDROGEN CONTENT
TA480.T54	TITANIUM ALLOYS — TESTING
QD181.T6	TITANIUM COMPOUNDS
TN799.T	TITANIUM ORES
TN757.T5	TITANIUM STEEL
QD181.T6	TITANIUM
TN799.T5	*TITANIUM, HYDROGEN IN* **SEE** TITANIUM — HYDROGEN CONTENT
TA480.T	*TITANIUM-CREEP* **SEE** CREEP OF TITANIUM
BL820.T6	TITANS (MYTHOLOGY)
DA950.4	TITHE WAR, 1829-1838
HJ2281-7	TITHES
BV771	TITHES / *church finance*
BX5165	TITHES / *church of england*
HG9970.T4-68	*TITLE GUARANTY* **SEE** INSURANCE, TITLE
HG9970.T4-68	*TITLE INSURANCE* **SEE** INSURANCE, TITLE
Z242.T6	TITLE-PAGE
TR899	*TITLES (MOVING-PICTURES)* **SEE** MOVING-PICTURES — TITLING
CR3499-4420	*TITLES OF ADDRESS* **SEE** FORMS OF ADDRESS
CR3499-4420	*TITLES OF ADDRESS* **SEE** TITLES OF HONOR AND NOBILITY
LB2381-2391	*TITLES OF DEGREE* **SEE** DEGREES, ACADEMIC
CR3499-4420	TITLES OF HONOR AND NOBILITY
HD1181-1211	*TITLES, LAND* **SEE** LAND TITLES
QL696.P2	TITMICE
QD111	*TITRATION* **SEE** VOLUMETRIC ANALYSIS
QD115	*TITRATION, CONDUCTOMETRIC* **SEE** CONDUCTOMETRIC ANALYSIS
DT515	*TIV* **SEE** TIVI (AFRICAN PEOPLE)
DT515	TIVI (AFRICAN PEOPLE)
PL8738	TIVI LANGUAGE
E99.T52	*TIWA INDIANS* **SEE** TIGUA INDIANS
PM2441	*TIWA LANGUAGE* **SEE** TIGUA LANGUAGE
DT515	*TIWI* **SEE** TIVI (AFRICAN PEOPLE)
PL5295	*TJAMORO LANGUAGE* **SEE** CHAMORRO LANGUAGE
E99.T58	TLAKLUIT INDIANS
E99.C83	*TLAOQUATSH INDIANS* **SEE** CLAYOQUOT INDIANS
F1221.T	TLASCALAN INDIANS
PM4383	TLASCALTECA LANGUAGE
E99.T6	TLINGIT INDIANS
PM2455	TLINGIT LANGUAGE
QL638.B3	TOAD-FISH
QL668.E2	TOADS
QK617	*TOADSTOOLS* **SEE** MUSHROOMS
PN6340-6348	TOASTS
F2823.T7	TOBA INDIANS
PM7146	TOBA LANGUAGE (INDIAN)
PL5471	TOBA LANGUAGE (MALAYAN)
DS748.6	*TOBA TATARS* **SEE** CHINA — HISTORY — — NORTHERN WEI DYNASTY, 386-636
SB275	TOBACCO — ANALYSIS AND CHEMISTRY
SB608.T7	TOBACCO — DISEASES AND PESTS
QP981.T6	TOBACCO — PHYSIOLOGICAL EFFECT
RC567	TOBACCO — PHYSIOLOGICAL EFFECT / *nervous diseases*
RM666.T6	TOBACCO — PHYSIOLOGICAL EFFECT / *therapeutics*
HV5732-3	TOBACCO — PHYSIOLOGICAL EFFECT / *tobacco habit*
GT3020	TOBACCO — POETRY
HD9130.8	TOBACCO — TAXATION

RM666.T6	TOBACCO — THERAPEUTIC USE
SB608.T	TOBACCO BLUE MOLD
NK9507	*TOBACCO BOXES* **SEE** TOBACCO JARS AND BOXES / *art*
TS2249	TOBACCO CURING
SB608.T	*TOBACCO DOWNY MILDEW* **SEE** TOBACCO BLUE MOLD
HV5725-5770	TOBACCO HABIT
RC567	TOBACCO HABIT / *medicine*
NK9507	TOBACCO JARS AND BOXES / *art*
HF5585.T6	TOBACCO MANUFACTURE AND TRADE — CREDIT GUIDES
HF5716.T5	TOBACCO MANUFACTURE AND TRADE — TABLES AND READY-RECKONERS
TS2220-2283	TOBACCO MANUFACTURE AND TRADE / *manufacture*
HD9130-9149	TOBACCO MANUFACTURE AND TRADE / *trade*
HD9130.8	*TOBACCO MANUFACTURE AND TRADE-TAXATION* **SEE** TOBACCO — TAXATION
SB945.T	TOBACCO MOTH
TS2270	TOBACCO-PIPES
SB273-8	TOBACCO / *culture*
GT3020	TOBACCO / *manners and customs*
SB275	*TOBACCO-CHEMISTRY* **SEE** TOBACCO — ANALYSIS AND CHEMISTRY
TS2249	*TOBACCO-CURING* **SEE** TOBACCO CURING
HD9130-9149	*TOBACCO-MANUFACTURE AND TRADE* **SEE** TOBACCO MANUFACTURE AND TRADE / *trade*
TS2220-2283	*TOBACCO-MANUFACTURE AND TRADE* **SEE** TOBACCO MANUFACTURE AND TRADE / *manufacture*
TS2220-2283	*TOBACCO-MARKETING* **SEE** TOBACCO MANUFACTURE AND TRADE / *manufacture*
HD9130-9149	*TOBACCO-MARKETING* **SEE** TOBACCO MANUFACTURE AND TRADE / *trade*
D278.T6	TOBAGO, BATTLE OF, 1677
F2116	TOBAGO, BATTLE OF, 1677 / *tobago history*
PL5481	TOBELORESE LANGUAGE
E99.G15	*TOBIKHAR INDIANS* **SEE** GABRIELENO INDIANS
PM1201	*TOBIKHAR LANGUAGE* **SEE** GABRIELENO LANGUAGE
GV855	TOBOGGANING
BV1280.T6	TOC H
ML448	TOCCATA / *musical form*
ML647	TOCCATA / *organ music*
P911.T	*TOCHARISH LANGUAGE* **SEE** TOKHARIAN LANGUAGE
PL4785	TODA LANGUAGE
DS432.T6	TODAS
RD563	TOES — ABNORMITIES AND DEFORMITIES
QM549	TOES
E83.813	*TOHOPEKA, BATTLE OF, 1814* **SEE** HORSE SHOE, BATTLE OF THE, 1814
HD9999.T6-63	TOILET PREPARATIONS
RA778	TOILET / *hygiene for women*
TH6498	*TOILETS* **SEE** WATER-CLOSETS
PM3601	*TOJOLABAL LANGUAGE* **SEE** CHANABAL LANGUAGE
CJ4801-5415	TOKENS / *numismatics*
HG651-1490	TOKENS / *other countries*
HG629	TOKENS / *u.s.*
CJ5407-5415	TOKENS, COMMUNION
P911.T	TOKHARIAN LANGUAGE
DT515	*TOKOROR* **SEE** TOUCOULEURS
TA368	TOLERANCE (ENGINEERING)
BR1610	TOLERATION
HE197	TOLLS
TG15-123	TOLLS / *bridges*
HE341-368	TOLLS / *roads*
HE384-520	TOLLS / *waterways*
DP114.3	*TOLOSA, BATTLE OF, 1212* **SEE** NAVAS DE TOLOSA, BATTLE OF, 1212
E99.T7	TOLOWA INDIANS
F1219	TOLTECS
RA1242.T	TOLUENE — TOXICOLOGY
QD341.H9	TOLUENE
QD341.A2	TOLUIC ACID
QD341.H9	*TOLUOL* **SEE** TOLUENE
TX612.T7	TOMATO CATCHUP
SB945.T	TOMATO PINWORM
SB349	TOMATOES
SB608.T75	TOMATOES / *diseases and pests*
PL8568	*TOMBA LANGUAGE* **SEE** NTOMBA LANGUAGE
NA6120-6199	TOMBS / *architecture*

NB1800-1885	*TOMBSTONES* **SEE** SEPULCHRAL MONUMENTS / *sculpture*
BF698	*TOMKINS-HORN PICTURE ARRANGEMENT TEST* **SEE** PICTURE ARRANGEMENT TEST
PM2451	*TOMOCO LANGUAGE* **SEE** TIMUCUA LANGUAGE
ML1747	TONADILLA
ML3811	TONALITY
ML3082	TONARIUS
ML171-4	TONARIUS / *history*
MT935	TONE-WORD SYSTEM
MT801	TONETTE — METHODS
PL8739	*TONGA LANGUAGE (GITONGA)* **SEE** TONGA LANGUAGE (INHAMBANE)
PL8739	TONGA LANGUAGE (INHAMBANE)
PL8740	TONGA LANGUAGE (NYASA)
PL8741	*TONGA LANGUAGE (RHODESIA)* **SEE** TONGA LANGUAGE (ZAMBESI)
PL6531	TONGA LANGUAGE (TONGA ISLANDS)
PL8741	TONGA LANGUAGE (ZAMBESI)
GN657.T5	*TONGA TRIBE* **SEE** THONGA TRIBE
QL946	TONGUE / *comparative anatomy*
QM503	TONGUE / *human anatomy*
RC815	TONGUE, HYPERTROPHY OF
RD523	TONGUE, HYPERTROPHY OF / *surgery*
RC73.5	TONGUE, SEMIOLOGY OF
RX635	TONGUE, SEMIOLOGY OF / *homeopathy*
P101	*TONGUES, CONFUSION OF* **SEE** CONFUSION OF TONGUES
BL54	*TONGUES, GIFT OF* **SEE** GLOSSOLALIA
PL6531	*TONGUESE LANGUAGE* **SEE** TONGA LANGUAGE (TONGA ISLANDS)
MT30	TONIC SOL-FA / *instruction*
F2823.T8	*TONICOTE INDIANS* **SEE** TONOCOTE INDIANS
PM7151	*TONICOTE LANGUAGE* **SEE** TONOCOTE LANGUAGE
SB307.T6	TONKA BEAN
E99.T	TONKAWA INDIANS
PM2481	TONKAWA LANGUAGE
HE738	TONNAGE — TABLES, ETC. / *freight measurements*
VM153	TONNAGE — TABLES, ETC. / *measurement of ships*
HE565	TONNAGE / *shipping*
F2823.T8	TONOCOTE INDIANS
PM7151	TONOCOTE LANGUAGE
PM7151	*TONOKOTE LANGUAGE* **SEE** TONOCOTE LANGUAGE
SB307.T6	*TONQUA BEAN* **SEE** TONKA BEAN
SB307.T6	*TONQUIN BEAN* **SEE** TONKA BEAN
QR171	TONSILS — BACTERIOLOGY
RF481-499	TONSILS — DISEASES
QM331	TONSILS / *human anatomy*
QP146	TONSILS / *physiology*
RX326.T6	TONSILS — DISEASES — — HOMEOPATHIC TREATMENT
BX1927	TONSURE / *catholic church*
PL5484	TONTEMBOAN LANGUAGE
HG8817	*TONTINE POLICIES* **SEE** INSURANCE, LIFE — TONTINE POLICIES
E99.T98	*TOO-AN-HOOCH INDIANS* **SEE** TWANA INDIANS
TJ1150	*TOOL CRIBS* **SEE** TOOLS — STORAGE
TS320	TOOL-STEEL
TJ1190	TOOLS — CATALOGS
TJ1200	TOOLS — CATALOGS / *hand tools*
TJ1150	TOOLS — STORAGE
TJ1180-1313	TOOLS
GN446-7	TOOLS / *ethnology*
TJ1195-1201	TOOLS / *hand tools*
S676	*TOOLS, AGRICULTURAL* **SEE** AGRICULTURAL IMPLEMENTS
RK301-450	*TOOTHACHE* **SEE** TEETH — DISEASES
QA862.T7	TOP / *dynamics*
QE394.T	TOPAZ / *gems*
QE391.T6	TOPAZ / *minerals*
RD594	*TOPECTOMY* **SEE** BRAIN — SURGERY
DS416-419	TOPES (MONUMENTS) / *antiquities*
NA6001	TOPES (MONUMENTS) / *architecture*
SB463	TOPIARY WORK
M1670-1671	TOPICAL SONGS (NEGRO)
SB211.J	*TOPINAMBUR* **SEE** JERUSALEM ARTICHOKE
QM531-549	*TOPOGRAPHICAL ANATOMY* **SEE** ANATOMY, SURGICAL AND TOPOGRAPHICAL
TA616	TOPOGRAPHICAL DRAWING
TA590	TOPOGRAPHICAL SURVEYING

G104-8	*TOPOGRAPHICAL TERMS* **SEE** GEOGRAPHY — TERMINOLOGY
RA791-954	*TOPOGRAPHY, MEDICAL* **SEE** MEDICAL GEOGRAPHY
UG470	*TOPOGRAPHY, MILITARY* **SEE** MILITARY TOPOGRAPHY
GC83	*TOPOGRAPHY, SUBMARINE* **SEE** SUBMARINE TOPOGRAPHY
QA611.5	TOPOLOGICAL DYNAMICS
QA611	TOPOLOGY / *geometry*
GN635.C	TORADJAS
GN635.C	*TORAJAS* **SEE** TORADJAS
TN827	TORBANITE
E123	TORDESILLAS, TREATY OF, 1494
DD412.6.T6	TORGAU, BATTLE OF, 1760
DS19	*TORGODS* **SEE** TORGOTS
DS793.M7	*TORGODS* **SEE** TORGOTS / *mongolia*
DS19	TORGOTS
DS793.M7	TORGOTS / *mongolia*
DS19	*TORGUTS* **SEE** TORGOTS
DS793.M7	*TORGUTS* **SEE** TORGOTS / *mongolia*
E277	*TORIES, AMERICAN* **SEE** AMERICAN LOYALISTS
JN1129.T7	TORIES, ENGLISH
HG9968.T5-7	*TORNADO INSURANCE* **SEE** INSURANCE, TORNADO
QC955	TORNADOES
DT429	*TOROBO* **SEE** DOROBO (AFRICAN PEOPLE)
DT515	*TORODO* **SEE** TOUCOULEURS
QA411	TOROIDAL HARMONICS
V840	TORPEDO-BOAT DESTROYERS
V830-838	TORPEDO-BOATS
V850-855	TORPEDOES
TJ1201.W8	TORQUE WRENCHES
HD1208	TORRENS SYSTEM
SK333.T	TORRENT DUCKS / *agriculture*
QL696.A5	TORRENT DUCKS / *zoology*
F1234	TORREON, BATTLE OF, 1914
QK495.P66	TORREY PINE
QC107	TORSION BALANCE
QA935	TORSION / *analytic mechanics*
QC191	TORSION / *physics*
HD7814-7816	*TORT LIABILITY OF EMPLOYERS* **SEE** EMPLOYERS' LIABILITY
RA1056.5	*TORT LIABILITY OF PHYSICIANS* **SEE** MALPRACTICE
JF1621	*TORT LIABILITY OF THE GOVERNMENT* **SEE** GOVERNMENT LIABILITY
JK-JQ	*TORT LIABILITY OF THE GOVERNMENT* **SEE** GOVERNMENT LIABILITY
JF1621	*TORT LIABILITY OF THE STATE* **SEE** GOVERNMENT LIABILITY
JK-JQ	*TORT LIABILITY OF THE STATE* **SEE** GOVERNMENT LIABILITY
DC233.T7	TORTOSA — SIEGE, 1810-1811
BM535	TORTOSA DISPUTATION, 1413-1414
HV8593-9	TORTURE / *judicial*
RC186.T7	TORULOSIS
BR858.T	*TORUN, MASSACRE OF* **SEE** TORUN, POLAND — RIOT, 1724
BR858.T	TORUN, POLAND — RIOT, 1724
PK7045.T6	*TORWALAK DIALECT* **SEE** TORWALI DIALECT
PK7045.T6	TORWALI DIALECT
JN1129.T7	*TORY PARTY (ENGLAND)* **SEE** TORIES, ENGLISH
HV5001-5720	*TOTAL ABSTINENCE* **SEE** TEMPERANCE
BJ1392	TOTALITARIAN ETHICS
JC481	*TOTALITARIAN STATE* **SEE** TOTALITARIANISM
BF758	TOTALITARIANISM — PSYCHOLOGY
JC481	TOTALITARIANISM
BD396	*TOTALITY (PHILOSOPHY)* **SEE** WHOLE AND PARTS (PHILOSOPHY)
GN491	TOTEMISM
GN491	TOTEMS
D766.93	*TOTENSONNTAG BATTLE, 1941* **SEE** POINT 175, BATTLE OF, 1941
PM4426	TOTONAC LANGUAGE
F1219	*TOTONACAS* **SEE** TOTONACOS
F1219	TOTONACOS
DT346.T7	*TOUAREGS* **SEE** TUAREGS
PL8121.D5	*TOUBOU LANGUAGE* **SEE** DAZA LANGUAGE
QL696.R3	TOUCANS
GV952	TOUCH FOOTBALL
QP451	TOUCH / *physiology*
BF275	TOUCH / *psychology*

DT515	TOUCOULEURS
D283.T7	TOULON — SIEGE, 1707
DC222.T7	TOULON — SIEGE, 1793
DA87.5 1744	TOULON, BATTLE OF, 1744
DC222	TOURCOING, BATTLE OF, 1794 / *france*
DA87.5 1794	TOURCOING, BATTLE OF, 1794 / *gt. brit.*
G155	*TOURISM* SEE TOURIST TRADE
TX901-941	TOURIST CAMPS, HOSTELS, ETC.
G155	TOURIST TRADE
G155	*TOURIST TRAFFIC* SEE TOURIST TRADE
G155	*TOURISTS* SEE TOURIST TRADE
QE391.T7	TOURMALINE
CR4553-7	TOURNAMENTS / *heraldry*
GV1191	TOURNAMENTS / *sports*
G420-440	*TOURS AROUND THE WORLD* SEE VOYAGES AROUND THE WORLD
DC71.5	*TOURS, BATTLE OF, 732* SEE POITIERS, BATTLE OF, 732
E99.T	*TOWAKARRO INDIANS* SEE TAWAKONI INDIANS
VM464	*TOWBOATS* SEE TUGBOATS
TS1580	TOWELS
GT3350	*TOWERS OF SILENCE* SEE DOKHMAS
NA2930	TOWERS / *architecture*
TP159.P3	*TOWERS, PACKED* SEE PACKED TOWERS
TP159.P6	*TOWERS, PLATE* SEE PLATE TOWERS
QL696.P2	TOWHEES
TC767-9	TOWING / *canals*
LC237	*TOWN AND GOWN* SEE COMMUNITY AND COLLEGE
BV637	*TOWN CHURCHES* SEE CITY CHURCHES
HT151-3	*TOWN LIFE* SEE CITY AND TOWN LIFE
HT361	*TOWN LIFE* SEE CITY AND TOWN LIFE
JS241-285	*TOWN MEETING* SEE LOCAL GOVERNMENT
JS1701-8429	*TOWN MEETING* SEE LOCAL GOVERNMENT / *other countries*
JS408-425	*TOWN MEETING* SEE LOCAL GOVERNMENT / *u.s.*
NA9000-9284	*TOWN PLANNING* SEE CITIES AND TOWNS — PLANNING
HT101-381	*TOWNS* SEE CITIES AND TOWNS
HV6177	*TOWNS* SEE CITIES AND TOWNS / *influence on crime*
JS	*TOWNS* SEE CITIES AND TOWNS / *local government*
JS241-285	*TOWNSHIP GOVERNMENT* SEE LOCAL GOVERNMENT
JS1701-8429	*TOWNSHIP GOVERNMENT* SEE LOCAL GOVERNMENT / *other countries*
JS408-425	*TOWNSHIP GOVERNMENT* SEE LOCAL GOVERNMENT / *u.s.*
HD239	TOWNSITE LAW
QP551	*TOXALBUMINS* SEE ALBUMIN
RA1240	TOXALBUMINS
RA401	TOXINS AND ANTITOXINS / *etc.*
QP941	TOXINS AND ANTITOXINS / *experimental pharmacology*
QP631	TOXINS AND ANTITOXINS / *physiological chemistry*
TL237	*TOY AUTOMOBILES* SEE AUTOMOBILES — MODELS
HD9999.T68-7	TOY INDUSTRY
PN1972	TOY THEATERS
TS2301.T7	TOYS / *manufacture*
GN799.T7	TOYS / *prehistoric*
GN454-6	TOYS / *primitive*
Q164	TOYS / *scientific*
QH531	TRACERS (BIOLOGY)
RF510-535	TRACHEA — DISEASES
RF514	TRACHEA — EXPLORATION
RF476	TRACHEA — EXPLORATION
RF516-517	TRACHEA — SURGERY
QL854	TRACHEA / *comparative anatomy*
QM257	TRACHEA / *human anatomy*
QL847	TRACHEAE IN ARTHROPODA
QL451-9	TRACHEATA
RX456	TRACHEA — DISEASES — — HOMEOPATHIC TREATMENT
RF516-517	*TRACHEOTOMY* SEE TRACHEA — SURGERY
QE461	TRACHYTE
T375-7	TRACING-CLOTH
GV1060.8	TRACK-ATHLETICS FOR WOMEN
GV561-751	TRACK-ATHLETICS
GV1061-1099	TRACK-ATHLETICS / *special*
TL4030	*TRACKING* SEE SPACE VEHICLES — TRACKING
SK282	TRACKING AND TRAILING / *hunting*
SK601	TRACKING AND TRAILING / *woodcraft*
TF248	*TRACKLAYING MACHINERY (RAILROADS)* SEE RAILROADS — TRACKLAYING MACHINERY
TL232	*TRACKLESS TROLLEYS* SEE TROLLEY BUSES
QE845	*TRACKS, FOSSIL* SEE FOOTPRINTS, FOSSIL
TF240-268	*TRACKS, RAILROAD* SEE RAILROADS — TRACK
QE845	*TRACKWAYS, FOSSIL* SEE FOOTPRINTS, FOSSIL
BV2374-5	TRACT SOCIETIES
BX5094-5100	*TRACTARIANISM* SEE OXFORD MOVEMENT
TL233	TRACTION-ENGINES / *gasoline tractors*
UC340-345	TRACTION-ENGINES / *military*
TJ700	TRACTION-ENGINES / *steam-engines*
TL153.5	TRACTORS — LUBRICATION
TL237	TRACTORS — MODELS
RM910	TRACTORS, METALLIC / *therapeutics*
BV4510	TRACTS
GV1299.T7	TRADE (GAME)
HF5001-6201	*TRADE* SEE BUSINESS
HF	*TRADE* SEE COMMERCE
GT6010-6050	*TRADE* SEE COMMERCE / *commercial customs*
GN436-440	*TRADE* SEE COMMERCE / *primitive*
HF1721-1733	*TRADE AGREEMENTS (COMMERCE)* SEE COMMERCIAL TREATIES
HD2421-9	TRADE AND PROFESSIONAL ASSOCIATIONS / *trade associations*
HD6350-6940	TRADE AND PROFESSIONAL ASSOCIATIONS / *trade-unions*
HF1401-1650	*TRADE BARRIERS* SEE COMMERCIAL POLICY
HV544	*TRADE FAIRS* SEE FAIRS / *charity fairs*
GT4580-4699	*TRADE FAIRS* SEE FAIRS / *manners and customs*
HF5470-5475	*TRADE FAIRS* SEE FAIRS / *markets*
HF5481	*TRADE FAIRS* SEE FAIRS / *street fairs*
PN4784.C7	*TRADE JOURNALISM* SEE JOURNALISM, COMMERCIAL
T325	*TRADE NAMES* SEE TRADE-MARKS
T221-323	*TRADE NAMES* SEE TRADE-MARKS / *by country*
HE323-8	TRADE ROUTES
T325	TRADE-MARKS (INTERNATIONAL LAW)
T325	TRADE-MARKS
T221-323	TRADE-MARKS / *by country*
HD6488	*TRADE-UNIONS AND RIGHT TO WORK* SEE OPEN AND CLOSED SHOP
HD6350-6940	TRADE-UNIONS
QC939.T7	TRADE-WINDS
HF1014	*TRADE, BALANCE OF* SEE BALANCE OF TRADE
HF294	*TRADE, BOARDS OF* SEE BOARDS OF TRADE
HF295-343	*TRADE, BOARDS OF* SEE BOARDS OF TRADE / *etc.*
HD9715	*TRADES* SEE BUILDING TRADES / *economics*
TH	*TRADES* SEE BUILDING TRADES / *technology*
T-TX	*TRADES* SEE INDUSTRIAL ARTS
HF5381	*TRADES* SEE OCCUPATIONS / *choice of*
GR890-920	*TRADES* SEE OCCUPATIONS / *folk-lore*
GT5750-6390	*TRADES* SEE OCCUPATIONS / *manners and customs*
HT675-690	*TRADES* SEE OCCUPATIONS / *social classes*
HB2581-2790	*TRADES* SEE OCCUPATIONS / *statistics*
HJ5645-5651	*TRADES* SEE OCCUPATIONS / *taxation*
TD897-9	*TRADES-WASTE* SEE FACTORY AND TRADE WASTE
TP995	*TRADES-WASTE* SEE WASTE PRODUCTS
HD4889	*TRADES, INITIATIONS INTO* SEE INITIATIONS (INTO TRADES, SOCIETIES, ETC.) / *labor*
HF5851	*TRADESMEN'S CARDS* SEE ADVERTISING CARDS
TT360	*TRADESMEN'S CARDS* SEE ADVERTISING CARDS / *card and sign writing*
E98.C7	*TRADING POSTS (NORTH AMERICAN INDIAN)* SEE INDIANS OF NORTH AMERICA — TRADING POSTS
JX5270-5271	TRADING WITH THE ENEMY
HF5436	TRADING-STAMPS
BP135	*TRADITION (ISLAM)* SEE HADITH
BT90	TRADITION (THEOLOGY) — EARLY CHURCH
BT90	TRADITION (THEOLOGY)
GR	*TRADITIONS* SEE FOLK-LORE
PN683-7	*TRADITIONS* SEE LEGENDS
N7760	*TRADITIONS* SEE LEGENDS / *iconography*
PZ8.1	*TRADITIONS* SEE LEGENDS / *juvenile*
BF1001-1999	*TRADITIONS* SEE SUPERSTITION / *occult sciences*
AZ999	*TRADITIONS* SEE SUPERSTITION / *popular delusions*
BL490	*TRADITIONS* SEE SUPERSTITION / *religion*
DA88.5 1805	TRAFALGAR (CAPE), BATTLE OF, 1805
HE	*TRAFFIC* SEE COMMUNICATION AND TRAFFIC
GN38	*TRAFFIC* SEE COMMUNICATION AND TRAFFIC / *primitive*
HE5614	TRAFFIC ACCIDENTS
HE369-373	*TRAFFIC CENSUS* SEE TRAFFIC SURVEYS

HE369-373	*TRAFFIC CONTROL* **SEE** TRAFFIC REGULATIONS
HF5761-5780	*TRAFFIC MANAGEMENT, INDUSTRIAL* **SEE** SHIPMENT OF GOODS
HE369-373	TRAFFIC REGULATIONS
TE228	TRAFFIC SIGNS AND SIGNALS — MAINTENANCE AND REPAIR
HE369-373	TRAFFIC SURVEYS
ML63	TRAGEDY IN MUSIC
PN6111-6120	TRAGEDY / collections
PN1890-1899	TRAGEDY / history and criticism
BH301.T7	TRAGIC, THE / aesthetics
PN1675	TRAGIC, THE / drama
E98.T7	*TRAILS, INDIAN* **SEE** INDIAN TRAILS
TF563	*TRAIN DISPATCHING* **SEE** RAILROADS — TRAIN DISPATCHING
TF320	TRAIN FERRIES
TF555	*TRAIN LOAD* **SEE** RAILROADS — TRAIN LOAD
TF553-4	*TRAIN SPEED* **SEE** RAILROADS — TRAIN SPEED
GV1282.9.G5	*TRAIN-BRIDGE* **SEE** GHOULIE
RT	*TRAINED NURSES* **SEE** NURSES AND NURSING
UH490-495	*TRAINED NURSES* **SEE** NURSES AND NURSING / army
VG350-355	*TRAINED NURSES* **SEE** NURSES AND NURSING / navy
V252	*TRAINERS, SYNTHETIC* **SEE** SYNTHETIC TRAINING DEVICES
U290-295	*TRAINING CAMPS, MILITARY* **SEE** MILITARY TRAINING CAMPS
LB1805-2151	*TRAINING COLLEGES FOR TEACHERS* **SEE** TEACHERS COLLEGES
V252	*TRAINING DEVICES, SYNTHETIC* **SEE** SYNTHETIC TRAINING DEVICES
GV1829-1831	*TRAINING OF ANIMALS* **SEE** ANIMALS, TRAINING OF
HQ769-780	*TRAINING OF CHILDREN* **SEE** CHILDREN — MANAGEMENT
HF5549.5.T7	*TRAINING OF EMPLOYEES* **SEE** EMPLOYEES, TRAINING OF
T58	*TRAINING OF EMPLOYEES* **SEE** EMPLOYEES, TRAINING OF
LB1731	*TRAINING OF STUDENT COUNSELORS* **SEE** STUDENT COUNSELORS, TRAINING OF
BF380-385	*TRAINING OF THE MEMORY* **SEE** MNEMONICS / psychology
RT71-81	*TRAINING SCHOOLS FOR NURSES* **SEE** NURSING SCHOOLS
HF5549.5.T7	*TRAINING WITHIN INDUSTRY* **SEE** EMPLOYEES, TRAINING OF
T58	*TRAINING WITHIN INDUSTRY* **SEE** EMPLOYEES, TRAINING OF
V523-4	TRAINING-SHIPS / gt. brit.
V435-6	TRAINING-SHIPS / u.s.
LB1595-9	*TRAINING, MANUAL* **SEE** MANUAL TRAINING / education
TT161-9	*TRAINING, MANUAL* **SEE** MANUAL TRAINING / technology
RA781	*TRAINING, PHYSICAL* **SEE** PHYSICAL EDUCATION AND TRAINING / physical culture and hygiene
GV201-547	*TRAINING, PHYSICAL* **SEE** PHYSICAL EDUCATION AND TRAINING
RM721	*TRAINING, PHYSICAL* **SEE** PHYSICAL EDUCATION AND TRAINING / physical culture and therapeutics
TF557	*TRAINMEN'S MANUALS* **SEE** RAILROADS — TRAINMEN'S MANUALS
UG345	*TRAINS, ARMORED* **SEE** ARMORED TRAINS
TL235	*TRAINS, AUTOMOBILE* **SEE** AUTOMOBILE TRAINS
TF550-585	*TRAINS, RAILROAD* **SEE** RAILROADS — TRAINS
TL1075	*TRAJECTORIES, SPACE* **SEE** SPACE TRAJECTORIES
G504	*TRAMPING* **SEE** HIKING
HV4480-4630	TRAMPS
TF701-1124	*TRAMWAYS* **SEE** STREET-RAILROADS
HE4201-5300	*TRAMWAYS* **SEE** STREET-RAILROADS / economics
HE4251	*TRAMWAYS* **SEE** STREET-RAILROADS / taxation
BV5090-5091	TRANCE / religion
BF1321-1353	TRANCE / spiritualism
GV1469.T7	TRANGLE CHECKERS
GV1469.T7	TRANGLE CHESS
TL721	*TRANSATLANTIC FLIGHTS* **SEE** AERONAUTICS — FLIGHTS
QA628	*TRANSCENDENTAL CURVES* **SEE** CURVES, TRANSCENDENTAL
QA247.5	*TRANSCENDENTAL NUMBERS* **SEE** NUMBERS, TRANSCENDENTAL
B905	TRANSCENDENTALISM (NEW ENGLAND)
B823	TRANSCENDENTALISM
B851-4695	TRANSCENDENTALISM / local
F593	*TRANSCONTINENTAL JOURNEYS (U.S.)* **SEE** OVERLAND JOURNEYS TO THE PACIFIC
P226	*TRANSCRIPTION (TRANSLITERATION)* **SEE** TRANSLITERATION
TK2851	*TRANSDUCTORS* **SEE** MAGNETIC AMPLIFIERS
TK7872.M3	*TRANSDUCTORS* **SEE** MAGNETIC AMPLIFIERS / electronics
Z649.T7	*TRANSFER OF COPYRIGHT* **SEE** COPYRIGHT — TRANSFER
LB1059	*TRANSFER OF LEARNING* **SEE** TRANSFER OF TRAINING
LB3064	*TRANSFER OF STUDENTS* **SEE** STUDENTS, TRANSFER OF
LB2359	*TRANSFER OF STUDENTS* **SEE** STUDENTS, TRANSFER OF / higher education
LB1059	TRANSFER OF TRAINING
HJ5801-5819	*TRANSFER TAX* **SEE** INHERITANCE AND TRANSFER TAX
NK4607	TRANSFER-PRINTING / pottery
TF276	*TRANSFER-TABLES* **SEE** RAILROADS — TRANSFER-TABLES
BF175	TRANSFERENCE (PSYCHOLOGY)
BT410	*TRANSFIGURATION OF CHRIST* **SEE** JESUS CHRIST — TRANSFIGURATION
QA248	*TRANSFINITE NUMBERS* **SEE** NUMBERS, TRANSFINITE
QA248	*TRANSFINITE ORDINALS* **SEE** NUMBERS, TRANSFINITE
BL325.M4	*TRANSFORMATION (IN RELIGION, FOLK-LORE, ETC.)* **SEE** METAMORPHOSIS (IN RELIGION, FOLK-LORE, ETC.)
QA646	*TRANSFORMATION, CONFORMAL* **SEE** CONFORMAL MAPPING
QA360	*TRANSFORMATION, CONFORMAL* **SEE** CONFORMAL MAPPING
QA432	*TRANSFORMATION, LAPLACE* **SEE** LAPLACE TRANSFORMATION
QA601-8	TRANSFORMATIONS (MATHEMATICS)
QA385	*TRANSFORMATIONS, CONTACT* **SEE** CONTACT TRANSFORMATIONS
QA385	TRANSFORMATIONS, INFINITESIMAL
QA602	TRANSFORMATIONS, QUADRATIC
QA385	*TRANSFORMATIONS, TANGENTIAL* **SEE** CONTACT TRANSFORMATIONS
TK3441.O5	*TRANSFORMER OIL* **SEE** INSULATING-OILS
TK2551	*TRANSFORMERS, ELECTRIC* **SEE** ELECTRIC TRANSFORMERS
RM171	*TRANSFUSION OF BLOOD* **SEE** BLOOD — TRANSFUSION
HD5855-6	*TRANSIENT LABOR* **SEE** MIGRANT LABOR
TK3226	TRANSIENTS (ELECTRICITY)
TK7872.T73	TRANSISTOR CIRCUITS
TK7872.T73	*TRANSISTORS, JUNCTION* **SEE** JUNCTION TRANSISTORS
QB101	TRANSIT-CIRCLE
QB101-5	TRANSIT-INSTRUMENTS
TA575	TRANSIT, SURVEYORS'
TF216-217	*TRANSITION CURVE* **SEE** CURVES IN ENGINEERING / railroads
TE153	*TRANSITION CURVE* **SEE** CURVES IN ENGINEERING / roads
TF216-217	*TRANSITION CURVE* **SEE** RAILROADS — CURVES AND TURNOUTS
QB175	TRANSITS / calculation
BT827	TRANSLATION TO HEAVEN
PN6010	TRANSLATIONS
P226	TRANSLITERATION
QK871	*TRANSLOCATION (BOTANY)* **SEE** PLANTS, MOTION OF FLUIDS IN
BL525	TRANSMIGRATION / comparative religion
BD426	TRANSMIGRATION / philosophy
QC320-338	*TRANSMISSION OF HEAT* **SEE** HEAT — TRANSMISSION
TJ1045-1119	*TRANSMISSION, POWER* **SEE** POWER TRANSMISSION
S711-713	*TRANSMISSION, POWER* **SEE** POWER TRANSMISSION / agricultural machinery

TK6561	TRANSMITTING SETS, RADIO SEE RADIO — TRANSMITTERS AND TRANSMISSION
QD461	TRANSMUTATION (CHEMISTRY)
BL325.M4	TRANSMUTATION (IN RELIGION, FOLK-LORE, ETC.) SEE METAMORPHOSIS (IN RELIGION, FOLK-LORE, ETC.)
QL89	TRANSMUTATION OF ANIMALS
QD461	TRANSMUTATION OF ELEMENTS SEE TRANSMUTATION (CHEMISTRY)
QD24-26.5	TRANSMUTATION OF METALS SEE ALCHEMY
QD13	TRANSMUTATION OF METALS SEE ALCHEMY / history
QD461	TRANSMUTATION OF METALS SEE TRANSMUTATION (CHEMISTRY)
TR720-730	TRANSPARENCIES / photography
ND1573	TRANSPARENCIES / transparency painting
QC185	TRANSPIRATION (PHYSICS)
QK873	TRANSPIRATION OF PLANTS SEE PLANTS — TRANSPIRATION
QP89	TRANSPLANTATION OF ORGANS, TISSUES, ETC.
QC175.2	TRANSPORT PHENOMENA SEE TRANSPORT THEORY
TL685.7	TRANSPORT PLANES
QC175.2	TRANSPORT THEORY
HD8039.T	TRANSPORT WORKERS
HD5321-5450	TRANSPORT WORKERS / strikes
HE194-5	TRANSPORTATION — LAWS AND REGULATIONS
HE1831-2220	TRANSPORTATION — RATES / railroads
HE593-601	TRANSPORTATION — RATES / waterways
TA1160	TRANSPORTATION — VOCATIONAL GUIDANCE / engineering
HG9903	TRANSPORTATION INSURANCE SEE INSURANCE, INLAND MARINE
HE961-971	TRANSPORTATION INSURANCE SEE INSURANCE, MARINE
JV373	TRANSPORTATION OF CRIMINALS SEE PENAL COLONIES / colonization
HV8935-8962	TRANSPORTATION OF CRIMINALS SEE PENAL COLONIES / penology
LB2864	TRANSPORTATION OF SCHOOL CHILDREN SEE SCHOOL CHILDREN — TRANSPORTATION
HE	TRANSPORTATION
HE5618.5-5720	TRANSPORTATION, AUTOMOTIVE — LAWS AND REGULATIONS
HE5601-5720	TRANSPORTATION, AUTOMOTIVE
UC270-360	TRANSPORTATION, MILITARY
UH500-505	TRANSPORTATION, MILITARY / medical service
VC550-555	TRANSPORTATION, MILITARY / naval
GN439-440	TRANSPORTATION, PRIMITIVE
HE2301-2500	TRANSPORTATION-FREIGHT SEE FREIGHT AND FREIGHTAGE / railroads
HE593-7	TRANSPORTATION-FREIGHT SEE FREIGHT AND FREIGHTAGE / shipping
HE968	TRANSPORTATION-HANDBOOKS, MANUALS, ETC. SEE SHIPPERS' GUIDES / marine insurance
HE2731-7	TRANSPORTATION-HANDBOOKS, MANUALS, ETC. SEE SHIPPERS' GUIDES / railroads
HE2801-3600	TRANSPORTATION-HANDBOOKS, MANUALS, ETC. SEE SHIPPERS' GUIDES / railroads
HE9	TRANSPORTATION-HANDBOOKS, MANUALS, ETC. SEE SHIPPERS' GUIDES
HE1009	TRANSPORTATION-HANDBOOKS, MANUALS, ETC. SEE SHIPPERS' GUIDES / railroads
TE315-424	TRANSPORTATION-LAWS AND REGULATIONS SEE HIGHWAY LAW
TG435	TRANSPORTER-BRIDGES
UC325	TRANSPORTS
MT68	TRANSPOSITION (MUSIC)
BX2220	TRANSUBSTANTIATION / catholic church
DT911-944	TRANSVAAL — HISTORY
QK495.C	TRANSVAAL DAISY SEE GERBERA / botany
SB413.G	TRANSVAAL DAISY SEE GERBERA / floriculture
DT930-939	TRANSVAAL WAR, 1899-1902 SEE SOUTH AFRICAN WAR, 1899-1902
QL458.C8	TRAP-DOOR SPIDERS
GV1181	TRAP-SHOOTING
QM131	TRAPEZIUM (ANATOMY)
SK283	TRAPPING
BX4101-4155	TRAPPISTS
TH6631-3	TRAPS (PLUMBING) SEE PLUMBING — TRAPS

DT283	TRARA (ALGERIAN TRIBE)
TD791-870	TRASH SEE REFUSE AND REFUSE DISPOSAL
RC106	TRAUMATIC FEVER
DD439.T7	TRAUTENAU, BATTLE OF, 1866
M110.T	TRAUTONIUM MUSIC
M1039.4.T	TRAUTONIUM WITH ORCHESTRA
ML1092	TRAUTONIUM
PN6231.T7	TRAVEL — ANECDOTES, FACETIAE, SATIRE, ETC.
G150.A2	TRAVEL — EARLY WORKS TO 1800
G469	TRAVEL — JUVENILE LITERATURE
G153	TRAVEL - COSTS SEE TRAVEL COSTS
G105-153	TRAVEL - GUIDE BOOKS SEE VOYAGES AND TRAVELS — GUIDE-BOOKS
LC6681	TRAVEL AND EDUCATION SEE STUDENT TRAVEL
G149-890	TRAVEL BOOKS SEE VOYAGES AND TRAVELS
G420-440	TRAVEL BOOKS SEE VOYAGES AROUND THE WORLD
G153	TRAVEL COSTS
G153	TRAVEL EXPENSE SEE TRAVEL COSTS
G153	TRAVEL EXPENSE SEE TRAVEL COSTS
G155.A1	TRAVEL RESEARCH
G149-157	TRAVEL
GT5220-5280	TRAVEL / manners and customs
GT5230	TRAVEL, ANCIENT
GT5240	TRAVEL, MEDIEVAL
G153	TRAVEL-COSTS SEE TRAVEL COSTS
G150-153	TRAVEL-GUIDE-BOOKS SEE VOYAGES AND TRAVELS — GUIDE-BOOKS
G155.A1	TRAVEL-RESEARCH SEE TRAVEL RESEARCH
G200-306	TRAVELERS
CT3203	TRAVELERS / women
HF5441-4	TRAVELERS, COMMERCIAL SEE COMMERCIAL TRAVELERS
GV1206	TRAVELERS, GAMES FOR SEE GAMES FOR TRAVELERS
HV696.T7	TRAVELERS' AID SOCIETIES
LC6691	TRAVELING EDUCATIONAL EXHIBITS SEE EDUCATIONAL EXHIBITS, TRAVELING
Z732	TRAVELING LIBRARIES SEE LIBRARIES, TRAVELING
Z716	TRAVELING LIBRARIES SEE LIBRARIES, TRAVELING
HF5441-4	TRAVELING SALESMEN SEE COMMERCIAL TRAVELERS
TK7872.T75	TRAVELING-WAVE TUBES
F593	TRAVELS SEE OVERLAND JOURNEYS TO THE PACIFIC
Q115	TRAVELS SEE SCIENTIFIC EXPEDITIONS
G149-890	TRAVELS SEE VOYAGES AND TRAVELS
G420-440	TRAVELS SEE VOYAGES AROUND THE WORLD
G560	TRAVELS, IMAGINARY SEE VOYAGES, IMAGINARY
TA552	TRAVERSE-TABLES / surveying
TA585	TRAVERSES (SURVEYING)
QB325	TRAVERSES (SURVEYING)
PN6110.P3	TRAVESTIES SEE PARODIES
PN6149.B8	TRAVESTY SEE BURLESQUE (LITERATURE)
PN6149.P3	TRAVESTY SEE PARODY
SH331	TRAWLS AND TRAWLING
SH255	TRAWLS AND TRAWLING / gt. brit.
SH221	TRAWLS AND TRAWLING / u.s.
SB419	TRAY GARDENS SEE GARDENS, MINIATURE
HV8775	TREADMILL / punishment
HV6275	TREASON
JC328	TREASON / political theory
HG2535-9	TREASURY, INDEPENDENT SEE INDEPENDENT TREASURY / u.s.
JX4171.I6	TREATIES — INTERPRETATION AND CONSTRUCTION
JX4171.R3	TREATIES — RATIFICATION
JX4171.R45	TREATIES — REVISION
JX4171.T5	TREATIES — TERMINATION
JX4005	TREATIES OF ALLIANCE SEE ALLIANCES
JX4171.G8	TREATIES OF GUARANTY SEE GUARANTY, TREATIES OF
JX5181	TREATIES OF PEACE SEE PEACE TREATIES
JX4161-4171	TREATIES
JX1985-9	TREATIES / arbitration
JX351-1195	TREATIES / collections
JX120-191	TREATIES / collections
JX235-6	TREATIES / collections
HF1721-1733	TREATIES / commercial
HE6281	TREATIES / postal
JX4171.R45	TREATIES, REVISION OF SEE TREATIES — REVISION

DD901.H27	*TREATY OF GOTTORF, MAY 27, 1768* **SEE** GOTTORF, TREATY OF, MAY 27, 1768 / *hamburg*
E408	*TREATY OF GUADALUPE HIDALGO, 1848* **SEE** GUADALUPE HIDALGO, TREATY OF, 1848
D287.7	*TREATY OF HANOVER, 1725* **SEE** HANOVER, TREATY OF, 1725
D651.I8	*TREATY OF RAPALLO, 1920* **SEE** RAPALLO, TREATY OF, 1920
D651.I8	*TREATY OF RAPALLO, 1922* **SEE** RAPALLO, TREATY OF, 1922
D283.5	*TREATY OF RASTATT, 1714* **SEE** RASTATT, TREATY OF, 1714
D287.8	*TREATY OF SEVILLE, 1729* **SEE** SEVILLE, TREATY OF, 1729
D651.T9	*TREATY OF SEVRES, 1920* **SEE** SEVRES, TREATY OF, 1920
DR589	*TREATY OF SEVRES, 1920* **SEE** SEVRES, TREATY OF, 1920 / *turkish history*
D283.5	*TREATY OF THE HAGUE, 1717* **SEE** HAGUE, TREATY OF, 1717
DC101.5.T	*TREATY OF TROYES, 1420* **SEE** TROYES, TREATY OF, 1420
JX1974	*TREATY ON THE LIMITATION OF NAVAL ARMAMENT, LONDON, 1930* **SEE** LONDON NAVAL TREATY, 1930
JX4171.R3	*TREATY RATIFICATION* **SEE** TREATIES — RATIFICATION
JX4171.R45	*TREATY REVISION* **SEE** TREATIES — REVISION
DG247.24	TREBIA, BATTLE OF THE, 218 B.C.
HV8626	*TREBUCHET (PUNISHMENT)* **SEE** CUCKING STOOL
SB435	TREE BREEDING
SD399.5	TREE BREEDING
SB413.P4	TREE PEONY
SB435-7	TREE PLANTING / *city*
SD391	TREE PLANTING / *sylviculture*
SB239.M3	*TREE TAPPING* **SEE** MAPLE SUGAR
QC883	*TREE-RING ANALYSIS* **SEE** DENDROCHRONOLOGY
QC883	*TREE-RING HYDROLOGY* **SEE** DENDROCHRONOLOGY
BL444	TREE-WORSHIP
SB761-791	TREES — DISEASES AND PESTS
SB608	TREES — DISEASES AND PESTS
SB436	TREES IN CITIES
PN56.T8	TREES IN LITERATURE
PN6110.T75	TREES IN LITERATURE / *poetry*
PN56.T8	*TREES IN POETRY* **SEE** TREES IN LITERATURE
PN6110.T75	*TREES IN POETRY* **SEE** TREES IN LITERATURE / *poetry*
QK475-494	TREES / *botany*
GR785	TREES / *folk-lore*
GT5150	TREES / *manners and customs*
SB435-7	TREES / *ornamental*
SD391-535	TREES / *sylviculture*
GR785	*TREES, FOLK-LORE OF* **SEE** FOLK-LORE OF TREES
QE991	TREES, FOSSIL
SD399.5	*TREES-BREEDING* **SEE** TREE BREEDING
SB435	*TREES-BREEDING* **SEE** TREE BREEDING
TA421	*TREES-CHEMISTRY* **SEE** WOOD — CHEMISTRY
SB435-7	*TREES-PLANTING* **SEE** TREE PLANTING / *city*
SD391	*TREES-PLANTING* **SEE** TREE PLANTING / *sylviculture*
QL391.T7	TREMATODA
QK629.T7	TREMELLALES
ML3817	*TREMOLO* **SEE** VIBRATO
MT271	*TREMOLO* **SEE** VIBRATO / *violin*
MT882	*TREMOLO* **SEE** VIBRATO / *voice*
RC186.T8	TRENCH FEVER
UF563.A77	*TRENCH GUNS* **SEE** TRENCH MORTARS
PC3747.S7	*TRENCH LANGUAGE (EUROPEAN WAR)* **SEE** EUROPEAN WAR, 1914-1918 — LANGUAGE (NEW WORDS, SLANG, ETC.)
D523	*TRENCH LANGUAGE (EUROPEAN WAR)* **SEE** EUROPEAN WAR, 1914-1918 — LANGUAGE (NEW WORDS, SLANG, ETC.)
PE3727.S7	*TRENCH LANGUAGE (EUROPEAN WAR)* **SEE** EUROPEAN WAR, 1914-1918 — LANGUAGE (NEW WORDS, SLANG, ETC.)
U24-26	*TRENCH LANGUAGE (EUROPEAN WAR)* **SEE** MILITARY ART AND SCIENCE — DICTIONARIES
U26	*TRENCH LANGUAGE (EUROPEAN WAR)* **SEE** MILITARY ART AND SCIENCE — TERMINOLOGY
UF563.A77	TRENCH MORTARS

UG403	*TRENCH WARFARE* **SEE** INTRENCHMENTS / *field fortification*
UG446	*TRENCH WARFARE* **SEE** INTRENCHMENTS / *trenches and trench warfare*
E469	TRENT AFFAIR, NOV. 8, 1861
JX1414	TRENT AFFAIR, NOV. 8, 1861 / *international law*
BX830 1545	TRENT, COUNCIL OF, 1545-1563
GV1311.T7	TRENTE-ET-QUARANTE
E241.T7	TRENTON, BATTLE OF, 1776
SH399.T8	TREPANG / *fisheries*
QL384.H7	TREPANG / *zoology*
RD529	*TREPANNING* **SEE** TREPHINING
GN477.7	*TREPANNING* **SEE** TREPHINING / *primitive*
RD529	TREPHINING
GN477.7	TREPHINING / *primitive*
GV1295.T7	TRESETTE (GAME)
GV1295.O5	*TRESILLO (GAME)* **SEE** OMBRE (GAME)
TG365-370	TRESTLES
PB1607	TRIADS (LITERATURE) / *gaelic*
PB1333	TRIADS (LITERATURE) / *irish*
BL474	*TRIADS (RELIGION)* **SEE** TRINITIES
CR4565	*TRIAL BY BATTLE* **SEE** WAGER OF BATTLE
JF723	*TRIAL BY JURY* **SEE** JURY
JN923	*TRIAL BY JURY* **SEE** JURY / *england*
JK1736	*TRIAL BY JURY* **SEE** JURY / *u.s.*
GN493	*TRIAL BY ORDEAL* **SEE** ORDEAL / *primitive*
JF723	*TRIAL BY PEERS* **SEE** JURY
JN923	*TRIAL BY PEERS* **SEE** JURY / *england*
JK1736	*TRIAL BY PEERS* **SEE** JURY / *u.s.*
BX1939.T65	TRIAL PRACTICE (CANON LAW)
GT6715	*TRIALS OF ANIMALS* **SEE** ANIMALS, PROSECUTION AND PUNISHMENT OF
VM880-881	*TRIALS OF VESSELS* **SEE** SHIP TRIALS
BL604.T7	TRIANGLE (IN RELIGION, FOLK-LORE, ETC.)
GV1282.9.T7	*TRIANGLE BRIDGE* **SEE** THREE-HANDED BRIDGE
QA557	TRIANGLE / *analytic geometry*
QA482	TRIANGLE / *plane geometry*
TL673.T7	*TRIANGULAR WINGS (AEROPLANE)* **SEE** AEROPLANES — WINGS, TRIANGULAR
TL673.T7	*TRIANGULAR WINGS (AEROPLANES)* **SEE** AEROPLANES — WINGS, TRIANGULAR
QB311-321	TRIANGULATION
TA583	TRIANGULATION / *engineering*
D643.H8 1920	TRIANON, TREATY OF, JUNE 4, 1920 (HUNGARY)
QE676-9	*TRIASSIC PERIOD* **SEE** GEOLOGY, STRATIGRAPHIC — TRIASSIC
QE922	*TRIASSIC PERIOD* **SEE** PALEOBOTANY — TRIASSIC
QE732	*TRIASSIC PERIOD* **SEE** PALEONTOLOGY — TRIASSIC
JC20-29	TRIBES AND TRIBAL SYSTEM
RD86.A9	*TRIBROMOETHANOL* **SEE** AVERTIN / *anesthetics*
QD981.A9	*TRIBROMOETHANOL* **SEE** AVERTIN / *experimental pharmacy*
JC85.T7	TRIBUNUS PLEBIS
RC186.T815	TRICHINA AND TRICHINOSIS
RC186.T815	*TRICHINOSIS* **SEE** TRICHINA AND TRICHINOSIS
QK650	TRICHOMES
QL516-519	*TRICHOPTERA* **SEE** CADDIS-FLIES
TR148	*TRICK PHOTOGRAPHY* **SEE** PHOTOGRAPHY, TRICK
GV1541-1561	TRICKS
GV1041-1059	*TRICYCLES* **SEE** BICYCLES AND TRICYCLES / *sports and amusements*
TL400-445	*TRICYCLES* **SEE** BICYCLES AND TRICYCLES / *technology*
HD9999.B4-43	*TRICYCLES* **SEE** BICYCLES AND TRICYCLES / *trade*
QM471	TRIGEMINAL NERVE
QP366	TRIGEMINAL NERVE
QL939	TRIGEMINAL NERVE
TK7872.T	TRIGGER CIRCUITS
QA404	*TRIGONOMETRIC SERIES* **SEE** FOURIER SERIES
QA55	TRIGONOMETRICAL FUNCTIONS / *tables*
QA342	TRIGONOMETRICAL FUNCTIONS / *theory of functions*
QA531-8	TRIGONOMETRICAL FUNCTIONS / *trigonometry*
QA31-35	TRIGONOMETRY — EARLY WORKS TO 1800
QA537	TRIGONOMETRY — PROBLEMS, EXERCISES, ETC.
QA55	TRIGONOMETRY — TABLES, ETC.
QA531-8	TRIGONOMETRY
QA533	TRIGONOMETRY, PLANE
QA535	TRIGONOMETRY, SPHERICAL
BL1245.S5	*TRIKA (HINDU PHILOSOPHY)* **SEE** SIVAISM

GV1511.T8	TRILBY (GAME)
QE821	TRILOBITES
VK235	TRIM (OF SHIPS)
BX4160.T4	TRINITARIANS
BL474	TRINITIES
TP285	*TRINITRIN* **SEE** NITROGLYCERIN
N8045	TRINITY — ART
BT110-115	TRINITY
BT114	*TRINITY-PROCESSION* **SEE** JESUS CHRIST — PROCESSION
GV1282.9.T7	*TRIO BRIDGE* **SEE** THREE-HANDED BRIDGE
M312.4	TRIO-SONATAS
M314	TRIO-SONATAS, ARRANGED
M385	TRIOS (ACCORDION, VIOLIN, VIOLONCELLO)
M365-7	TRIOS (BALALAIKA, GUITAR, MANDOLIN)
M360-362	TRIOS (BASSOON, CLARINET, VIOLIN)
M360-362	TRIOS (BASSOON, CLARINET, VIOLONCELLO)
M363-4	TRIOS (BASSOON, CLARINET, VIOLONCELLO), ARRANGED
M375-7	TRIOS (BASSOON, FLUTE, HARP)
M360-362	TRIOS (BASSOON, FLUTE, VIOLA)
M360-362	TRIOS (BASSOON, FLUTE, VIOLIN)
M360-362	TRIOS (BASSOON, HORN, VIOLIN)
M360-362	TRIOS (BASSOON, OBOE, VIOLA)
M385	TRIOS (BASSOON, TRUMPET, PERCUSSION)
M320-322	TRIOS (CELESTA, FLUTE, VIOLONCELLO)
M375-7	TRIOS (CLARINET, FLUTE, HARP)
M360-362	TRIOS (CLARINET, FLUTE, VIOLA)
M380-382	TRIOS (CLARINET, GUITAR, VIOLA)
M380-382	TRIOS (CLARINET, HARP, VIOLIN)
M360-362	TRIOS (CLARINET, OBOE, VIOLA)
M360-362	TRIOS (CLARINET, VIOLA, VIOLONCELLO)
M360-362	TRIOS (CLARINET, VIOLIN, VIOLONCELLO)
M385	TRIOS (ENGLISH HORN, HARP, KETTLEDRUMS)
M385	TRIOS (ENGLISH HORN, HARP, KETTLEDRUMS), ARRANGED
M380-382	TRIOS (FLUTE, GUITAR, VIOLA)
M383-4	TRIOS (FLUTE, GUITAR, VIOLA), ARRANGED
M380-382	TRIOS (FLUTE, GUITAR, VIOLIN)
M383-4	TRIOS (FLUTE, GUITAR, VIOLIN), ARRANGED
M380-382	TRIOS (FLUTE, HARP, VIOLA D'AMORE)
M380-382	TRIOS (FLUTE, HARP, VIOLA)
M380-382	TRIOS (FLUTE, HARP, VIOLONCELLO)
M375-7	TRIOS (FLUTE, HORN, HARP)
M385	TRIOS (FLUTE, KETTLEDRUMS, VIOLIN)
M380-382	TRIOS (FLUTE, LYRE-GUITAR, VIOLIN)
M385	TRIOS (FLUTE, OBOE D'AMORE, PERCUSSION)
M360-362	TRIOS (FLUTE, OBOE D'AMORE, VIOLA D'AMORE)
M360-362	TRIOS (FLUTE, OBOE, VIOLA)
M360-362	TRIOS (FLUTE, VIOLA, VIOLONCELLO)
M360-362	TRIOS (FLUTE, VIOLIN, VIOLA)
M360-362	TRIOS (FLUTE, VIOLIN, VIOLONCELLO)
M363-4	TRIOS (FLUTE, VIOLIN, VIOLONCELLO), ARRANGED
M360-362	TRIOS (FLUTE, 2 VIOLINS)
M370-372	TRIOS (GUITAR, VIOLA, VIOLONCELLO)
M370-372	TRIOS (GUITAR, VIOLIN, VIOLA)
M373-4	TRIOS (GUITAR, VIOLIN, VIOLA), ARRANGED
M370-372	TRIOS (GUITAR, VIOLIN, VIOLONCELLO)
M373-4	TRIOS (GUITAR, VIOLIN, VIOLONCELLO), ARRANGED
M365-7	TRIOS (GUITAR, 2 MANDOLINS)
M368-9	TRIOS (GUITAR, 2 MANDOLINS), ARRANGED
M373-4	TRIOS (GUITAR, 2 VIOLINS), ARRANGED
M340-342	TRIOS (HARP, HARPSICHORD, PIANO)
M370-372	TRIOS (HARP, VIOLIN, VIOLONCELLO)
M315-317	TRIOS (HARPSICHORD, BASSOON, CLARINET)
M340-342	TRIOS (HARPSICHORD, ENGLISH HORN, KETTLEDRUMS)
M335-7	TRIOS (HARPSICHORD, FLUTE, HARP)
M315-317	TRIOS (HARPSICHORD, FLUTE, OBOE D'AMORE)
M315-317	TRIOS (HARPSICHORD, FLUTE, OBOE)
M315-317	TRIOS (HARPSICHORD, FLUTE, RECORDER)
M315-317	TRIOS (HARPSICHORD, FLUTE, VIOLA D'AMORE)
M320-322	TRIOS (HARPSICHORD, FLUTE, VIOLA DA GAMBA)
M320-322	TRIOS (HARPSICHORD, FLUTE, VIOLA)
M320-322	TRIOS (HARPSICHORD, FLUTE, VIOLIN)
M320-322	TRIOS (HARPSICHORD, FLUTE, VIOLONCELLO)
M315-317	TRIOS (HARPSICHORD, OBOE, RECORDER)
M320-322	TRIOS (HARPSICHORD, OBOE, VIOLA DA GAMBA)
M320-322	TRIOS (HARPSICHORD, OBOE, VIOLIN)
M320-322	TRIOS (HARPSICHORD, RECORDER, VIOLA DA GAMBA)

M312.4	TRIOS (HARPSICHORD, VIOLA, VIOLONCELLO)
M310-311	TRIOS (HARPSICHORD, VIOLA, VIOLONCELLO)
M310-312	TRIOS (HARPSICHORD, VIOLIN, VIOLA DA GAMBA)
M310-311	TRIOS (HARPSICHORD, VIOLIN, VIOLA)
M312.4	TRIOS (HARPSICHORD, VIOLIN, VIOLA)
M310-312	TRIOS (HARPSICHORD, VIOLIN, VIOLONCELLO)
M313-314	TRIOS (HARPSICHORD, VIOLIN, VIOLONCELLO), ARRANGED
M315-317	TRIOS (HARPSICHORD, 2 FLUTES)
M315-317	TRIOS (HARPSICHORD, 2 OBOES)
M315-317	TRIOS (HARPSICHORD, 2 RECORDERS)
M310-311	TRIOS (HARPSICHORD, 2 VIOLAS)
M312.4	TRIOS (HARPSICHORD, 2 VIOLAS)
M310-312	TRIOS (HARPSICHORD, 2 VIOLE DA GAMBA)
M310-311	TRIOS (HARPSICHORD, 2 VIOLINS)
M312.4	TRIOS (HARPSICHORD, 2 VIOLINS)
M313-314	TRIOS (HARPSICHORD, 2 VIOLINS), ARRANGED
M312.4	TRIOS (HARPSICHORD, 2 VIOLONCELLOS)
M310-311	TRIOS (HARPSICHORD, 2 VIOLONCELLOS)
M312.4	TRIOS (HARPSICHORD, 2 VIOLS)
M990	TRIOS (HARPSICHORD, 2 VIOLS)
M310-311	TRIOS (HARPSICHORD, 2 VIOLS)
M360-362	TRIOS (HORN, VIOLIN, VIOLONCELLO)
M370-372	TRIOS (LUTE, VIOLIN, VIOLONCELLO)
M373-4	TRIOS (LUTE, VIOLIN, VIOLONCELLO), ARRANGED
M360-362	TRIOS (OBOE, VIOLA, VIOLONCELLO)
M360-362	TRIOS (OBOE, VIOLIN, VIOLA)
M360-362	TRIOS (OBOE, VIOLIN, VIOLONCELLO)
M300-302	TRIOS (ORGAN, FLUTE, VIOLONCELLO)
M385	TRIOS (ORGAN, HARP, KETTLEDRUMS)
M300-302	TRIOS (ORGAN, HARP, VIOLIN)
M300-302	TRIOS (ORGAN, VIOLIN, VIOLA DA GAMBA)
M300-302	TRIOS (ORGAN, VIOLIN, VIOLA)
M300-302	TRIOS (ORGAN, VIOLIN, VIOLONCELLO)
M300-302	TRIOS (ORGAN, 2 TRUMPETS)
M303-4	TRIOS (ORGAN, 2 TRUMPETS), ARRANGED
M300-302	TRIOS (ORGAN, 2 VIOLINS)
M385	TRIOS (PIANO, ACCORDION, VIOLIN)
M315-317	TRIOS (PIANO, BASSOON, CLARINET)
M318-319	TRIOS (PIANO, BASSOON, CLARINET), ARRANGED
M315-317	TRIOS (PIANO, BASSOON, OBOE)
M318-319	TRIOS (PIANO, BASSOON, OBOE), ARRANGED
M318-319	TRIOS (PIANO, BASSOON, TRUMPET), ARRANGED
M320-322	TRIOS (PIANO, BASSOON, VIOLONCELLO)
M315-317	TRIOS (PIANO, CLARINET, DOUBLE BASS)
M315-317	TRIOS (PIANO, CLARINET, FLUTE)
M340-342	TRIOS (PIANO, CLARINET, GLOCKENSPIEL)
M340-342	TRIOS (PIANO, CLARINET, PERCUSSION)
M315-317	TRIOS (PIANO, CLARINET, TROMBONE)
M315-317	TRIOS (PIANO, CLARINET, TRUMPET)
M320-322	TRIOS (PIANO, CLARINET, VIOLA)
M320-322	TRIOS (PIANO, CLARINET, VIOLIN)
M323-4	TRIOS (PIANO, CLARINET, VIOLIN), ARRANGED
M320-322	TRIOS (PIANO, CLARINET, VIOLONCELLO)
M323-4	TRIOS (PIANO, CLARINET, VIOLONCELLO), ARRANGED
M315-317	TRIOS (PIANO, ENGLISH HORN, FLUTE)
M318-319	TRIOS (PIANO, ENGLISH HORN, FLUTE), ARRANGED
M315-317	TRIOS (PIANO, ENGLISH HORN, TRUMPET)
M318-319	TRIOS (PIANO, ENGLISH HORN, TRUMPET), ARRANGED
M335-7	TRIOS (PIANO, FLUTE, GUITAR)
M338-9	TRIOS (PIANO, FLUTE, GUITAR), ARRANGED
M335-7	TRIOS (PIANO, FLUTE, HARP)
M338-9	TRIOS (PIANO, FLUTE, HARP), ARRANGED
M320-322	TRIOS (PIANO, FLUTE, HORN)
M323-4	TRIOS (PIANO, FLUTE, HORN), ARRANGED
M315-317	TRIOS (PIANO, FLUTE, OBOE)
M318-319	TRIOS (PIANO, FLUTE, OBOE), ARRANGED
M315-317	TRIOS (PIANO, FLUTE, RECORDER)
M320-322	TRIOS (PIANO, FLUTE, VIOLA D'AMORE)
M323-4	TRIOS (PIANO, FLUTE, VIOLA D'AMORE), ARRANGED
M320-322	TRIOS (PIANO, FLUTE, VIOLA)
M323-4	TRIOS (PIANO, FLUTE, VIOLA), ARRANGED
M320-322	TRIOS (PIANO, FLUTE, VIOLIN)
M323-4	TRIOS (PIANO, FLUTE, VIOLIN), ARRANGED
M320-322	TRIOS (PIANO, FLUTE, VIOLONCELLO)
M323-4	TRIOS (PIANO, FLUTE, VIOLONCELLO), ARRANGED
M335-7	TRIOS (PIANO, HORN, HARP)
M320-322	TRIOS (PIANO, HORN, VIOLIN)
M320-322	TRIOS (PIANO, HORN, VIOLONCELLO)
M385	TRIOS (PIANO, KETTLEDRUMS, PERCUSSION)

M315-317	TRIOS (PIANO, OBOE, RECORDER)
M320-322	TRIOS (PIANO, OBOE, VIOLA)
M320-322	TRIOS (PIANO, OBOE, VIOLIN)
M320-322	TRIOS (PIANO, OBOE, VIOLONCELLO)
M385	TRIOS (PIANO, ONDES MARTENOT, PERCUSSION)
M385	TRIOS (PIANO, PERCUSSION, DOUBLE BASS)
M340-342	TRIOS (PIANO, PERCUSSION, VIOLA)
M340-342	TRIOS (PIANO, PERCUSSION, VIOLIN)
M320-322	TRIOS (PIANO, RECORDER, VIOLA DA GAMBA)
M323-4	TRIOS (PIANO, RECORDER, VIOLA DA GAMBA), ARRANGED
M320-322	TRIOS (PIANO, RECORDER, VIOLIN)
M323-4	TRIOS (PIANO, RECORDER, VIOLIN), ARRANGED
M315-317	TRIOS (PIANO, SAXOPHONE, TRUMPET)
M320-322	TRIOS (PIANO, SAXOPHONE, VIOLA D'AMORE)
M315-317	TRIOS (PIANO, TROMBONE, TRUMPET)
M318-319	TRIOS (PIANO, TROMBONE, TRUMPET), ARRANGED
M385	TRIOS (PIANO, TRUMPET, DRUM)
M385	TRIOS (PIANO, TRUMPET, DRUM), ARRANGED
M335-7	TRIOS (PIANO, TRUMPET, GUITAR)
M320-322	TRIOS (PIANO, TRUMPET, VIOLA)
M312.4	TRIOS (PIANO, VIOLA, VIOLONCELLO)
M310-311	TRIOS (PIANO, VIOLIN, VIOLONCELLO)
M310-311	TRIOS (PIANO, VIOLIN, VIOLA)
M312.4	TRIOS (PIANO, VIOLIN, VIOLA)
M313-314	TRIOS (PIANO, VIOLIN, VIOLA), ARRANGED
M310-312	*TRIOS (PIANO, VIOLIN, VIOLONCELLO)* **SEE** PIANO TRIOS
M315-317	TRIOS (PIANO, 2 CLARINETS)
M318-319	TRIOS (PIANO, 2 CLARINETS), ARRANGED
M315-317	TRIOS (PIANO, 2 FLUTES)
M318-319	TRIOS (PIANO, 2 FLUTES), ARRANGED
M315-317	TRIOS (PIANO, 2 HORNS)
M318-319	TRIOS (PIANO, 2 HORNS), ARRANGED
M315-317	TRIOS (PIANO, 2 OBOES)
M315-317	TRIOS (PIANO, 2 RECORDERS)
M318-319	TRIOS (PIANO, 2 RECORDERS), ARRANGED
M1413-1417	TRIOS (PIANO, 2 RECORDERS), JUVENILE
M315-317	TRIOS (PIANO, 2 TRUMPETS)
M318-319	TRIOS (PIANO, 2 TRUMPETS), ARRANGED
M310-311	TRIOS (PIANO, 2 VIOLE D'AMORE)
M312.4	TRIOS (PIANO, 2 VIOLE D'AMORE)
M310-312	TRIOS (PIANO, 2 VIOLE DA GAMBA)
M310-311	TRIOS (PIANO, 2 VIOLINS)
M312.4	TRIOS (PIANO, 2 VIOLINS)
M313-314	TRIOS (PIANO, 2 VIOLINS), ARRANGED
M310-311	TRIOS (PIANO, 2 VIOLONCELLOS)
M312.4	TRIOS (PIANO, 2 VIOLONCELLOS)
M313-314	TRIOS (PIANO, 2 VIOLONCELLOS), ARRANGED
M990	TRIOS (PIANO, 2 VIOLS)
M310-311	TRIOS (PIANO, 2 VIOLS)
M315-317	TRIOS (PIANO, 2 WIND INSTRUMENTS)
M318-319	TRIOS (PIANO, 2 WIND INSTRUMENTS), ARRANGED
M340-342	TRIOS (PIANO, 2 XYLOPHONES)
M343-4	TRIOS (PIANO, 2 XYLOPHONES), ARRANGED
M380-382	TRIOS (RECORDER, LUTE, VIOL)
M360-362	TRIOS (RECORDER, VIOLIN, VIOLA)
M385	TRIOS (2 FLUTES, GLOCKENSPIEL)
M375-7	TRIOS (2 FLUTES, GUITAR)
M378-9	TRIOS (2 FLUTES, GUITAR), ARRANGED
M385	TRIOS (2 FLUTES, MARIMBA)
M360-362	TRIOS (2 FLUTES, VIOLA D'AMORE)
M360-362	TRIOS (2 FLUTES, VIOLA)
M363-4	TRIOS (2 FLUTES, VIOLA), ARRANGED
M360-362	TRIOS (2 FLUTES, VIOLONCELLO)
M305-7	TRIOS (2 HARPS, REED-ORGAN)
M308-9	TRIOS (2 HARPS, REED-ORGAN), ARRANGED
M385	TRIOS (2 OBOES, PERCUSSION)
M375-7	TRIOS (2 RECORDERS, GUITAR)
M375-7	TRIOS (2 RECORDERS, LUTE)
M360-362	TRIOS (2 RECORDERS, VIOLIN)
M365-7	TRIOS (3 GUITARS)
M385	TRIOS (3 MARIMBAS)
M385	TRIOS (3 MARIMBAS), ARRANGED
M310-312	*TRIOS, PIANO* **SEE** PIANO TRIOS
M349-351	*TRIOS, STRING* **SEE** STRING TRIOS
M355-7	*TRIOS, WIND* **SEE** WIND TRIOS
RC186.T82	*TRIPANOSOMIASIS* **SEE** TRYPANOSOMIASIS
SF807	*TRIPANOSOMIASIS* **SEE** TRYPANOSOMIASIS / veterinary medicine

QE391.T	TRIPHYLITE
F2687	*TRIPLE ALLIANCE, WAR OF THE, 1865-1870* **SEE** PARAGUAYAN WAR, 1865-1870
D273.5	TRIPLE ALLIANCE, 1668
D287	TRIPLE ALLIANCE, 1717
D511	TRIPLE ALLIANCE, 1882
D397	TRIPLE ALLIANCE, 1882
D443	TRIPLE ALLIANCE, 1882
D443	TRIPLE ENTENTE, 1907
D511	TRIPLE ENTENTE, 1907
QA311	*TRIPLE INTEGRALS* **SEE** INTEGRALS, MULTIPLE
GN265.M8	TRIPLETS
GV1291.T8	TRIPLICATE WHIST
E335	*TRIPOLINE WAR* **SEE** UNITED STATES — HISTORY — — TRIPOLITAN WAR, 1801-1805
G420-440	*TRIPS AROUND THE WORLD* **SEE** VOYAGES AROUND THE WORLD
VM16	TRIREMES
QA468	TRISECTION OF ANGLE
CR67	TRISKELE / heraldry
NK1177	TRISKELE / primitive art
RC185	*TRISMUS* **SEE** TETANUS
TL215.T	TRIUMPH AUTOMOBILE
N8254	TRIUMPH / art
DG89	TRIUMPH / roman antiquities
NA9360-9380	*TRIUMPHAL ARCHES* **SEE** ARCHES, TRIUMPHAL
GV1796.T	TRIUNFO (DANCE)
NK9990.T7	TRIVETS
PL6252.K5	*TROBRIAND LANGUAGE* **SEE** KIRIWINIAN LANGUAGE
QA623	*TROCHOIDS* **SEE** CYCLOIDS
QA623	*TROCHOIDS* **SEE** EPICYCLOIDS AND HYPOCYCLOIDS
TK7872.V3	TROCHOTRONS
GN783-4	TROGLODYTES
DF221.T8	TROJANS
TL232	TROLLEY BUSES
TF885	*TROLLEY-WHEELS* **SEE** ELECTRIC RAILROADS — TROLLEY-WHEELS
GR555	TROLLS
ML760	*TROMBA MARINA* **SEE** SEA-TRUMPET / medieval stringed instrument
QL458.A2	*TROMBICULINAE* **SEE** CHIGGERS (MITES)
MT466	TROMBONE — ORCHESTRA STUDIES
MT465	TROMBONE — STUDIES AND EXERCISES
M1105-6	TROMBONE AND KETTLEDRUMS WITH STRING ORCHESTRA
M298	TROMBONE AND PERCUSSION MUSIC
M262-3	TROMBONE AND PIANO MUSIC (JAZZ)
M262-3	TROMBONE AND PIANO MUSIC
M262-3	*TROMBONE AND PIANO MUSIC, ARRANGED (JAZZ)* **SEE** TROMBONE AND PIANO MUSIC (JAZZ)
M262-3	TROMBONE AND PIANO MUSIC, ARRANGED
M288-9	TROMBONE AND TRUMPET MUSIC
M1205	TROMBONE AND TRUMPET WITH BAND — SCORES
M1205-6	TROMBONE AND TRUMPET WITH BAND
M1105-6	TROMBONE AND TRUMPET WITH STRING ORCHESTRA
M288-9	TROMBONE MUSIC (2 TROMBONES)
M355-7	*TROMBONE MUSIC (3 TROMBONES)* **SEE** WIND TRIOS (3 TROMBONES)
M355-7	*TROMBONE MUSIC (3 TROMBONES)* **SEE** WIND TRIOS (3 TROMBONES)
M455-7	*TROMBONE MUSIC (4 TROMBONES)* **SEE** WIND QUARTETS (4 TROMBONES)
M455-7	*TROMBONE MUSIC (4 TROMBONES)* **SEE** WIND QUARTETS (4 TROMBONES)
M855-7	*TROMBONE MUSIC (8 TROMBONES)* **SEE** WIND OCTETS (8 TROMBONES)
M855-7	*TROMBONE MUSIC (8 TROMBONES)* **SEE** WIND OCTETS (8 TROMBONES)
M90-92	TROMBONE MUSIC
M1205	TROMBONE WITH BAND
M1257	TROMBONE WITH BAND, ARRANGED
M1033	TROMBONE WITH ORCHESTRA — SOLO WITH PIANO
M1032-3	TROMBONE WITH ORCHESTRA
M1105-6	TROMBONE WITH STRING ORCHESTRA
ML965-8	TROMBONE
MT468	*TROMBONE-SELF-INSTRUCTION* **SEE** TROMBONE — METHODS — — SELF-INSTRUCTION
M1205	TROMBONES (4) WITH BAND
MT468	TROMBONE — METHODS — — SELF-INSTRUCTION
UC410	*TROOPS, BILLETING OF* **SEE** SOLDIERS — BILLETING

TG375-380	TRUSSES / trussed bridges
HG4301-4480	TRUST COMPANIES
HG4301-4480	*TRUST DEPARTMENTS IN BANKS* **SEE** TRUST COMPANIES
BV4637	TRUST IN GOD
HG4485-4497	*TRUSTEES* **SEE** TRUSTS AND TRUSTEES
LB2341	*TRUSTEES, COLLEGE* **SEE** COLLEGE TRUSTEES
HF5686.T8	TRUSTS AND TRUSTEES — ACCOUNTING
HG4485-4497	TRUSTS AND TRUSTEES
HD2750-2752	TRUSTS, INDUSTRIAL — LAW
HD2777-2781	TRUSTS, INDUSTRIAL — LAW / u.s.
HD2795	TRUSTS, INDUSTRIAL — SPEECHES IN CONGRESS
HD2709-2930	TRUSTS, INDUSTRIAL
HD2801-2930	TRUSTS, INDUSTRIAL / other countries
HD2771-2798	TRUSTS, INDUSTRIAL / u.s.
BC171	TRUTH-FUNCTIONS
BT50	TRUTH / doctrinal theology
BC171	TRUTH / logic
BD150-171	TRUTH / metaphysics
BJ1420-1428	TRUTHFULNESS AND FALSEHOOD / ethics
QH237	TRYPAN BLUE / stains
QL391.C4	*TRYPANORHYNCHA* **SEE** TETRARHYNCHIDEA
RC186.T82	TRYPANOSOMIASIS
SF807	TRYPANOSOMIASIS / veterinary medicine
RM666.T	TRYPARSAMIDE
QP601	*TRYPSASE* **SEE** TRYPSIN
QP601	TRYPSIN
PL2967.T9	*TS'EU* **SEE** TZ'U
PA1153.T8	TSACONIAN DIALECT
F3722.1.C	*TSATCHELA INDIANS* **SEE** COLORADO INDIANS (ECUADOR)
E99.T77	TSATTINE INDIANS
PM2493	TSATTINE LANGUAGE
PL55.J3	*TSCHAGATAJ LANGUAGE* **SEE** JAGATAIC LANGUAGE
PL8110.C3	*TSCHAGGA LANGUAGE* **SEE** CHAGA LANGUAGE
DR504	*TSCHALDIRAN, BATTLE OF, 1514* **SEE** CALDERAN, BATTLE OF, 1514
PK9201.C	*TSCHAMALAL LANGUAGE* **SEE** CHAMALAL LANGUAGE
DS485.B85	*TSCHINGPOS* **SEE** KACHIN TRIBES / burma
PL2967.T9	*TSE* **SEE** TZ'U
RC186.T82	TSETSE-FLIES / tsetse-flies and disease
SF807	TSETSE-FLIES / veterinary medicine
PL8751	TSHI LANGUAGE
PL8461	*TSHILUBA LANGUAGE* **SEE** LUBA LANGUAGE
PL8771	*TSHIVENDA LANGUAGE* **SEE** VENDA LANGUAGE
E99.T78	TSILKOTIN INDIANS
E99.T8	TSIMSHIAN INDIANS
PM831	TSIMSHIAN LANGUAGE
PM5814.C3	*TSINTSAYSUYU DIALECT* **SEE** CHINCHASUYU DIALECT
F2936	*TSONECA INDIANS* **SEE** TZONECA INDIANS / patagonia
PM7183	*TSONECA LANGUAGE* **SEE** TZONECA LANGUAGE
GN657.T5	*TSONGA TRIBE* **SEE** THONGA TRIBE
PK9201.T8	TSOVA-TUSH LANGUAGE
DS517.5	TSUSHIMA, BATTLE OF, 1905
RC186.T83	TSUTSUGAMUSHI DISEASE
DT797	TSWANA (BANTU TRIBE)
PL8651	*TSWANA LANGUAGE* **SEE** SECHUANA LANGUAGE
PL8751	*TSWI LANGUAGE* **SEE** TSHI LANGUAGE
PL6535	*TUAMOTU LANGUAGE* **SEE** TUAMOTUAN LANGUAGE
PL6535	TUAMOTUAN LANGUAGE
PJ2381-2	*TUAREG LANGUAGE* **SEE** TAMASHEK LANGUAGE
DT346.T7	TUAREGS
DT346.T7	*TUARIKS* **SEE** TUAREGS
MT486	TUBA — ORCHESTRA STUDIES
MT485	TUBA — STUDIES AND EXERCISES
M264-5	TUBA AND PIANO MUSIC
M264-5	TUBA AND PIANO MUSIC, ARRANGED
M95-97	TUBA MUSIC
M1205	TUBA WITH BAND
M1257	TUBA WITH BAND, ARRANGED — SCORES (REDUCED) AND PARTS
M1257	TUBA WITH BAND, ARRANGED
M1034-5	TUBA WITH ORCHESTRA
ML970-973	TUBA
E99.T83	*TUBATULABAL INDIANS* **SEE** TUBATULABAL INDIANS
E99.T83	TUBATULABAL INDIANS
PM2495.T7	TUBATULABAL LANGUAGE

TS280	TUBE BENDING / metal-work
RM796	TUBERCULIN
RC311.2	TUBERCULOSIS — DIAGNOSIS
RC307	TUBERCULOSIS — EXHIBITIONS
RX226.T8	TUBERCULOSIS — HOMEOPATHIC TREATMENT
RC309	TUBERCULOSIS — HOSPITALS AND SANATORIUMS
RA644.T7	TUBERCULOSIS — PREVENTION
RC311.3.S4	TUBERCULOSIS — PREVENTIVE INOCULATION
RC311.1	TUBERCULOSIS — TRANSMISSION
QR201.T6	TUBERCULOSIS — TRANSMISSION / bacteriology
SF808	TUBERCULOSIS IN ANIMALS
SF995	TUBERCULOSIS IN POULTRY
RC311.8	TUBERCULOSIS NURSING
RC311.4	TUBERCULOSIS RESEARCH
RC306-320	TUBERCULOSIS
QR201.T6	TUBERCULOSIS / bacteriology
RA644.T7	TUBERCULOSIS / public health
RC311.1	TUBERCULOSIS, CONGENITAL, HEREDITARY, AND INFANTILE
RC311.1	*TUBERCULOSIS, CONTAGIOUSNESS OF* **SEE** TUBERCULOSIS — TRANSMISSION
QR201.T6	*TUBERCULOSIS, CONTAGIOUSNESS OF* **SEE** TUBERCULOSIS — TRANSMISSION / bacteriology
RC311.4	*TUBERCULOSIS-RESEARCH* **SEE** TUBERCULOSIS RESEARCH
QK646	TUBERS
TS280-282	TUBES / metal-working
TA492.T8	TUBES / testing
QL696.P6	TUBINARES
PL8121.D5	*TUBU LANGUAGE* **SEE** DAZA LANGUAGE
TG390	*TUBULAR BRIDGES* **SEE** BRIDGES, TUBULAR
TH5281	*TUBULAR SCAFFOLDING* **SEE** SCAFFOLDING, METAL
PM7164	TUCANO LANGUAGE
DU850	*TUCOPIANS* **SEE** TIKOPIANS / solomon islands
F2845	TUCUMAN, BATTLE OF, 1812
PL4785	*TUDA LANGUAGE* **SEE** TODA LANGUAGE
DS432.T6	*TUDAS* **SEE** TODAS
PM7183	*TUELCHE LANGUAGE* **SEE** TZONECA LANGUAGE
QE461	*TUFF* **SEE** VOLCANIC ASH, TUFF, ETC.
VM464	TUGBOATS
PL6621.M3	*TUGERI LANGUAGE* **SEE** MARINDINESE LANGUAGE
LB2342	*TUITION* **SEE** COLLEGE COSTS
LB2824-2830	*TUITION* **SEE** EDUCATION — FINANCE
LB2342	*TUITION* **SEE** UNIVERSITIES AND COLLEGES — FINANCE
E99.T	TUKKUTHKUTCHIN INDIANS
PM2496	TUKKUTHKUTCHIN LANGUAGE
E99.T85	TUKUARIKA INDIANS
PM2496	*TUKUDH LANGUAGE* **SEE** TUKKUTHKUTCHIN LANGUAGE
DT515	*TUKULOR* **SEE** TOUCOULEURS
GV1511.T9	TULA-LOO (GAME)
GV1511.T	TULA-PINS (GAME)
D764	TULA, RUSSIA — SIEGE, 1941
E99.T87	TULALIP INDIANS
GV1511.T	TULAQUETTE (GAME)
RC186.T85	TULAREMIA
F1565.2.C8	*TULE INDIANS* **SEE** CUNA INDIANS
SB425	TULIP MANIA, 17TH CENTURY
QK495.T9	TULIPS / botany
SB608.T85	TULIPS / diseases and pests
SB425	TULIPS / horticulture
NK9400-9499	*TULLE EMBROIDERY* **SEE** LACE AND LACE MAKING / fine arts
TS1782	*TULLE EMBROIDERY* **SEE** LACE AND LACE MAKING / manufacture
TT800-805	*TULLE EMBROIDERY* **SEE** LACE AND LACE MAKING / needlework
HD9933	*TULLE EMBROIDERY* **SEE** LACE AND LACE MAKING / trade
PL4791-4	TULU LANGUAGE
GV545	TUMBLING
HV8626	*TUMBREL (PUNISHMENT)* **SEE** CUCKING STOOL
PL8753	TUMBUKA LANGUAGE
PL6319	TUMLEO LANGUAGE
RX376	TUMORS — HOMEOPATHIC TREATMENT
RC254-272	TUMORS
RD651-678	TUMORS

GN795-6	*TUMULI* **SEE** MOUNDS		PL21-384	*TURCO-TATARIC LANGUAGES* **SEE** TURKO-TATARIC LANGUAGES
QL638.T	TUNA FISH		DK854-861	*TURCOMANS* **SEE** TURKOMANS
SH351.T8	TUNA FISH / *fisheries*		CC710	*TURF FIGURES* **SEE** HILL FIGURES
GB571-8	TUNDRAS		P911.T	*TURFANISH LANGUAGE* **SEE** TOKHARIAN LANGUAGE
SB299.T8	TUNG TREE		QK725	TURGOR / *plant cells*
SB299.T8	*TUNG-OIL TREE* **SEE** TUNG TREE		D283.T3	TURIN — SIEGE, 1706
TP684.T8	TUNG-OIL		PL31	*TURK LANGUAGE (OLD TURKISH)* **SEE** OLD TURKISH LANGUAGE
QD181.W1	TUNGSTATES			
TN757.T9	TUNGSTEN ALLOYS / *steel*		PL21-384	*TURK LANGUAGES* **SEE** TURKO-TATARIC LANGUAGES
TA479.T8	TUNGSTEN ALLOYS / *steel testing*		DT429	TURKANA (AFRICAN TRIBE)
TK4359.T9	TUNGSTEN LAMP		DR401-741	TURKEY — HISTORY
TN490.T9	TUNGSTEN ORES		SF995	TURKEYS — DISEASES
TN757.T9	TUNGSTEN STEEL		QL696.G2	TURKEYS
QD181.W1	TUNGSTEN		SF507	TURKEYS / *breeding*
TP245.T9	TUNGSTEN / *chemical technology*		DT429	*TURKHANA* **SEE** TURKANA (AFRICAN TRIBE)
TN799.T9	TUNGSTEN / *metallurgy*		PL21-384	*TURKI LANGUAGES* **SEE** TURKO-TATARIC LANGUAGES
TN490.T9	TUNGSTEN / *mining*			
QD181.W1	TUNGSTIC ACID		RM821	*TURKISH BATHS* **SEE** BATHS, TURKISH
PL451-9	TUNGUS LANGUAGE		PL237-8	TURKISH DRAMA / *collections*
DK759.T9	TUNGUSES		PL221	TURKISH DRAMA / *history*
PL451-9	TUNGUSIC LANGUAGES		PL101-199	TURKISH LANGUAGE
PM2498	TUNICA LANGUAGE		PL107	TURKISH LANGUAGE — HISTORY — — GUNES THEORY
QL613	TUNICATA			
QC235	TUNING-FORKS		PL201-298	TURKISH LITERATURE
ML3809	TUNING / *history*		PN5355	TURKISH NEWSPAPERS / *history*
MT165	TUNING / *instruction*		PN5355	TURKISH PERIODICALS / *history*
BX7801-7843	*TUNKERS* **SEE** CHURCH OF THE BRETHREN		PL101-199	TURKISH PHILOLOGY
TA800-820	TUNNELING		PL217-220	TURKISH POETRY
UG340	TUNNELING / *military*		PL234-6	TURKISH POETRY
TN285	TUNNELING / *mining*		PL244	TURKISH WIT AND HUMOR / *collections*
TF230-232	TUNNELING / *railroad*		PL227	TURKISH WIT AND HUMOR / *history*
TF236	TUNNELS — LIGHTING		DS17	*TURKISM* **SEE** PAN-TURANIANISM
TF235	TUNNELS — VENTILATION		PL331-4	*TURKMAN LANGUAGE* **SEE** TURKOMAN LANGUAGE
TA800-820	TUNNELS		PL21-384	TURKO-TATARIC LANGUAGES
UG340	TUNNELS / *military*		PL333-4	TURKOMAN FICTION
TN285	TUNNELS / *mining*		PL331-4	TURKOMAN LANGUAGE
TF230-232	TUNNELS / *railroad*		PL333-4	TURKOMAN LITERATURE
QL638.T	*TUNNY* **SEE** TUNA FISH		DK854-861	TURKOMANS
SH351.T8	*TUNNY* **SEE** TUNA FISH / *fisheries*		DS26-27	TURKS
E99.T	TUNXIS INDIANS		DR434	TURKS
PM7178.5	TUPI DRAMA		F232.S7	*TURNER'S NEGRO INSURRECTION, 1831* **SEE** SOUTHAMPTON INSURRECTION, 1831
F2230.2.T84	TUPI INDIANS			
PM7171-9	TUPI LANGUAGE		TT201-3	TURNING
PM7178	TUPI POETRY		TT207	TURNING / *metal*
F2520.1.T94	TUPINAMBA INDIANS		SB608.T	TURNIPS — DISEASES AND PESTS
PL1-489	*TURANIAN LANGUAGES* **SEE** URAL-ALTAIC LANGUAGES		SB211.T8	TURNIPS
			TF216-217	*TURNOUTS, RAILROAD* **SEE** RAILROADS — CURVES AND TURNOUTS
DS17	*TURANIANS* **SEE** URAL-ALTAIC TRIBES			
QD325	TURANOSE		HF5549	*TURNOVER OF LABOR* **SEE** LABOR TURNOVER
GV1796.T	TURAS (DANCE)		HJ5711-5721	*TURNOVER TAX* **SEE** SALES TAX
QL391.T9	TURBELLARIA		QP917.T9	TURPENTINE — PHYSIOLOGICAL EFFECT
TL685.7	*TURBINE-POWERED TRANSPORTS* **SEE** JET TRANSPORTS		HD9769.T9	TURPENTINE INDUSTRY AND TRADE
			TP977-8	TURPENTINE / *chemical technology*
TJ267-267.5	TURBINES		RM666.T9	TURPENTINE / *therapeutics*
TJ966-9	TURBOBLOWERS		SD547	TURPENTINE / *turpentine orcharding*
TJ787	*TURBOCHARGERS* **SEE** SUPERCHARGERS		QE394.T8	TURQUOISE
TL685.7	*TURBOJET TRANSPORTS* **SEE** JET TRANSPORTS		V860	TURRET SHIPS
TL685.7	*TURBOLINERS* **SEE** JET TRANSPORTS		NA2930	TURRETS / *architecture*
TJ267	TURBOMACHINES — AERODYNAMICS		V860	TURRETS / *war-vessels*
TJ267-267.5	TURBOMACHINES		QL666.C5	TURTLES
TJ267.I6	*TURBOMACHINES-IMPELLERS* **SEE** IMPELLERS		QE862.C5	TURTLES, FOSSIL
TJ267.I6	*TURBOMACHINES-ROTORS* **SEE** IMPELLERS		E99.H7	*TUSAYAN INDIANS* **SEE** HOPI INDIANS
QL638.P7	TURBOT		HD234.T	TUSCARORA INDIANS — LAND TRANSFERS
SH167.T9	TURBOT / *fisheries*		E83.71	TUSCARORA INDIANS — WARS, 1711-1713
DR46	*TURCO-BALKAN WAR, 1912-1913* **SEE** BALKAN PENINSULA — HISTORY — WAR OF 1912-1913		E99.T9	TUSCARORA INDIANS
			PM41-44	*TUSKI LANGUAGE* **SEE** CHUKCHI LANGUAGE
DS97.5	TURCO-EGYPTIAN CONFLICT, 1831-1840		QL858	TUSKS
DF827	*TURCO-GREEK WAR, 1897* **SEE** GRECO-TURKISH WAR, 1897		PL8113	*TUTCHOKUE LANGUAGE* **SEE** CHOKWE LANGUAGE
			E99.T96	TUTELO INDIANS
DR575	*TURCO-GREEK WAR, 1897* **SEE** GRECO-TURKISH WAR, 1897 / *period in turkey*		PM2507	TUTELO LANGUAGE
			PM8861-3	*TUTONISH* **SEE** TEUTONISH
DT234	TURCO-ITALIAN WAR, 1911-1912 — AERIAL OPERATIONS		LB1029.A85	*TUTORIAL MACHINES* **SEE** TEACHING MACHINES
			LC41	*TUTORIAL METHOD IN EDUCATION* **SEE** TUTORS AND TUTORING
UH319.T	TURCO-ITALIAN WAR, 1911-1912 — MEDICAL AND SANITARY AFFAIRS / *tripoli*			
			LC41	TUTORS AND TUTORING
DT234	TURCO-ITALIAN WAR, 1911-1912 / *tripoli*		DT443	*TUTSI* **SEE** BATUTSI
DR586	TURCO-ITALIAN WAR, 1911-1912 / *turkey*		QB723.T8	TUTTLE'S COMET
DR156	TURCO-MONTENEGRIN WAR, 1876-1878		E99.T97	TUTUTNI INDIANS
DR353	*TURCO-SERBIAN WAR, 1876* **SEE** SERBO-TURKISH WAR, 1876		PL45.S6	*TUVA LANGUAGE* **SEE** SOYOT LANGUAGE

F2687	TUYUTY, BATTLE OF, 1866 / *paraguay*
E99.T98	TWANA INDIANS
CB353	TWELFTH CENTURY / *civilization*
D201.7-8	TWELFTH CENTURY / *history*
BV50.E7	*TWELFTH DAY* **SEE** EPIPHANY
BV50.E7	*TWELFTH NIGHT* **SEE** EPIPHANY
BP193	*TWELVERS* **SEE** SHIITES
CB160	TWENTIETH CENTURY — FORECASTS
HN389	TWENTIETH CENTURY — FORECASTS / *england*
HN64	TWENTIETH CENTURY — FORECASTS / *social reform general*
CB425	TWENTIETH CENTURY / *civilization*
D401-725	TWENTIETH CENTURY / *history*
GV1473	TWENTY QUESTIONS (GAME)'
GV1295.B	*TWENTY-ONE (GAME)* **SEE** BLACKJACK (GAME)
PL8751	*TWI LANGUAGE* **SEE** TSHI LANGUAGE
SB945.T	TWIG-PRUNERS
E99.M48	*TWIGHTWEES* **SEE** MIAMI INDIANS
QB155	TWILIGHT / *astronomy*
QC976.T9	TWILIGHT / *meteorological optics*
Z252.5.M8	*TWIN PRINTING* **SEE** MULTIPLE PRINTING
TS1795	TWINE
GN265.M8	TWINS / *anthropology*
QL971	TWINS / *embryology*
GV1796.T	TWIST (DANCE)
TJ1263	TWIST DRILLS
M1105-6	*TWO FLUTES AND GLOCKENSPIEL WITH STRING ORCHESTRA* **SEE** FLUTES (2), GLOCKENSPIEL WITH STRING ORCHESTRA
M1020-1021	*TWO FLUTES WITH CHAMBER ORCHESTRA* **SEE** FLUTES (2) WITH CHAMBER ORCHESTRA
M1020-1021	*TWO FLUTES WITH ORCHESTRA* **SEE** FLUTES (2) WITH ORCHESTRA
M1105-6	*TWO FLUTES WITH STRING ORCHESTRA* **SEE** FLUTES (2) WITH STRING ORCHESTRA
M1105-6	*TWO FLUTES, HARPSICHORD WITH STRING ORCHESTRA* **SEE** HARPSICHORD, 2 FLUTES WITH STRING ORCHESTRA
M1105-6	*TWO FLUTES, MARIMBA WITH STRING ORCHESTRA* **SEE** FLUTES (2), MARIMBA WITH STRING ORCHESTRA
M1037.4.G8	*TWO GUITARS WITH CHAMBER ORCHESTRA* **SEE** GUITARS (2) WITH CHAMBER ORCHESTRA
M1010-1011	*TWO HARPSICHORDS WITH ORCHESTRA* **SEE** HARPSICHORDS (2) WITH ORCHESTRA
M1105-6	*TWO HARPSICHORDS WITH STRING ORCHESTRA* **SEE** HARPSICHORDS (2) WITH STRING ORCHESTRA
M1028-9	*TWO HORNS WITH ORCHESTRA* **SEE** HORNS (2) WITH ORCHESTRA
E99.063	*TWO KETTLE INDIANS* **SEE** OOHENONPA INDIANS
M1105-6	*TWO OBOES AND TRUMPET WITH STRING ORCHESTRA* **SEE** OBOES (2) AND TRUMPET WITH STRING ORCHESTRA
M1010-1011	*TWO PIANOS WITH ORCHESTRA* **SEE** PIANOS (2) WITH ORCHESTRA
M1020-1021	*TWO RECORDERS WITH ORCHESTRA* **SEE** RECORDERS (2) WITH ORCHESTRA
M1105-6	*TWO RECORDERS WITH STRING ORCHESTRA* **SEE** RECORDERS (2) WITH STRING ORCHESTRA
M1012-1013	*TWO VIOLINS WITH ORCHESTRA* **SEE** VIOLINS (2) WITH ORCHESTRA
M1105-6	*TWO VIOLINS WITH STRING ORCHESTRA* **SEE** VIOLINS (2) WITH STRING ORCHESTRA
M1105-6	*TWO VIOLINS, PIANO WITH STRING ORCHESTRA* **SEE** PIANO, 2 VIOLINS WITH STRING ORCHESTRA
M1040-1041	*TWO VIOLINS, VIOLA WITH ORCHESTRA* **SEE** VIOLINS (2), VIOLA WITH ORCHESTRA
M1016-1017	*TWO VIOLONCELLOS WITH ORCHESTRA* **SEE** VIOLONCELLOS (2) WITH ORCHESTRA
DA235	TYLER'S INSURRECTION, 1381
QK725	TYLOSES / *vegetable cells*
QL948	TYMPANAL ORGAN
ML1035	*TYMPANI* **SEE** KETTLEDRUM / *history*
QL948	TYMPANIC MEMBRANE / *comparative anatomy*
QM507	TYMPANIC MEMBRANE / *human anatomy*
QP461	TYMPANIC MEMBRANE / *physiology*
Z250.6.M3	TYPE AND TYPE-FOUNDING — MATHEMATICAL SYMBOLS
Z250-251	TYPE AND TYPE-FOUNDING
ML112	*TYPE AND TYPE-FOUNDING-MUSIC-TYPE* **SEE** MUSIC PRINTING
Z250	*TYPE SPECIMENS (PRINTING)* **SEE** PRINTING — SPECIMENS
Z253	TYPE-SETTING MACHINES
Z49-50	*TYPE-WRITERS* **SEE** TYPEWRITERS
HD9999.T8-83	*TYPE-WRITERS* **SEE** TYPEWRITERS / *trade*
BS478	*TYPES, BIBLICAL* **SEE** TYPOLOGY (THEOLOGY) / *bible*
BT225	*TYPES, BIBLICAL* **SEE** TYPOLOGY (THEOLOGY) / *jesus christ*
Z51	*TYPEWRITER SHORTHAND* **SEE** STENOTYPY
HV1701	*TYPEWRITERS FOR THE BLIND* **SEE** BLIND, APPARATUS FOR THE
Z49-50	TYPEWRITERS
HD9999.T8-83	TYPEWRITERS / *trade*
HV8075	TYPEWRITING — IDENTIFICATION
Z49-50	TYPEWRITING
Z49.3	TYPEWRITING, ONE-HAND
Z48	*TYPEWRITING-COPYING PROCESSES* **SEE** COPYING PROCESSES
RX226.T8	TYPHOID FEVER — HOMEOPATHIC TREATMENT
RA644.T8	TYPHOID FEVER — PREVENTION
RC187-197	TYPHOID FEVER
QR201.T9	TYPHOID FEVER / *bacteriology*
RA644.T8	TYPHOID FEVER / *public health measures*
QR201.T9	TYPHOID FEVER — DIAGNOSIS — — AGGLUTINATION REACTION
QR189.T	TYPHOID VACCINE
QC948	TYPHOONS
RC199	TYPHUS FEVER
QR201.T95	TYPHUS FEVER / *bacteriology*
GA150	TYPO-AUTOGRAPHY / *cartography*
Z235-6	*TYPOGRAPHICAL DEVICES* **SEE** PRINTERS' MARKS
Z120	*TYPOGRAPHICAL SOCIETIES* **SEE** PRINTING — SOCIETIES, ETC.
Z120	*TYPOGRAPHICAL SOCIETIES* **SEE** PRINTING — SOCIETIES, ETC.
Z116-265	*TYPOGRAPHY* **SEE** PRINTING
TR999.T8	TYPOGRAVURES
BS478	TYPOLOGY (THEOLOGY) / *bible*
BT225	TYPOLOGY (THEOLOGY) / *jesus christ*
JC375-392	*TYRANNY* **SEE** DESPOTISM
JC495	*TYRANTS* **SEE** DICTATORS
DB770.5	TYROLESE
DB778	TYROL — HISTORY — — UPRISING OF 1809
DA937.3	TYRONE'S REBELLION, 1597-1603
BX4080.T	*TYRONENSIANS* **SEE** TIRONENSIANS
QD341.A2	TYROSINE
PL2967.T9	TZ'U
PM4461	*TZEL-TAL LANGUAGE* **SEE** TZELTAL LANGUAGE
PM4461	*TZELDAL LANGUAGE* **SEE** TZELTAL LANGUAGE
F1435.3.C14	*TZELTAL CALENDAR* **SEE** CALENDAR, TZELTAL
F1435.3.C14	*TZELTAL INDIANS-CALENDAR* **SEE** CALENDAR, TZELTAL
PM4461	TZELTAL LANGUAGE
PM4461	*TZENDAL LANGUAGE* **SEE** TZELTAL LANGUAGE
PM4461	*TZENTAL LANGUAGE* **SEE** TZELTAL LANGUAGE
F2936	TZONECA INDIANS / *patagonia*
PM7183	TZONECA LANGUAGE
F1221.T	TZOTZIL INDIANS
PM4466	TZOTZIL LANGUAGE
PM4471	TZUTUHIL LANGUAGE
VC503	U.S. — ACCOUNTING*
D769.346	U.S. — AIRBORNE TROOPS
UH503	U.S. — AMBULANCES
JK168-170	U.S. — AMENDMENTS
JK165-6	U.S. — ANNIVERSARIES
VB313-314	U.S. — APPOINTMENTS AND RETIREMENTS
UB412-413	U.S. — APPOINTMENTS AND RETIREMENTS
V435	U.S. — APPRENTICES
VA53	U.S. — APPROPRIATIONS AND EXPENDITURES
UA24.A7	U.S. — APPROPRIATIONS AND EXPENDITURES
VG93	U.S. — AVIATION BOATSWAIN'S MATES
VG93	U.S. — AVIATION
U43	U.S. — BANDMASTERS
VC423	U.S. — BARRACKS AND QUARTERS
UC403	U.S. — BARRACKS AND QUARTERS
E181	U.S. — BIOGRAPHY
E467	U.S. — BIOGRAPHY / *civil war*
D570-570.9	U.S. — BIOGRAPHY / *european war*
E403	U.S. — BIOGRAPHY / *mexican war*

*Inadequacy of Library of Congress format design produced incorrect listing of headings beginning U.S. and United States.

JK2551-9	*U.S.-COLONIES* **SEE** UNITED STATES — TERRITORIES AND POSSESSIONS / *government*
F970	*U.S.-COLONIES* **SEE** UNITED STATES — TERRITORIES AND POSSESSIONS
HF105	*U.S.-COMMERCE-STATISTICS* **SEE** UNITED STATES — COMMERCE / *serial documents*
HF3001-3163	*U.S.-COMMERCE-STATISTICS* **SEE** UNITED STATES — COMMERCE
JX1705-6	*U.S.-CONSULAR SERVICE* **SEE** UNITED STATES — DIPLOMATIC AND CONSULAR SERVICE
JK771-781	*U.S.-DEPARTMENTAL SALARIES* **SEE** UNITED STATES — OFFICIALS AND EMPLOYEES — — SALARIES, ALLOWANCES, ETC.
JK	*U.S.-EMPLOYEES* **SEE** UNITED STATES — OFFICIALS AND EMPLOYEES
HE6497.F6	*U.S.-FOREIGN MAIL* **SEE** POSTAL SERVICE — U.S. — — FOREIGN MAIL
HE6477	*U.S.-FOREIGN MAIL* **SEE** POSTAL SERVICE — U.S. — FOREIGN MAIL / *ocean mail*
JK	*U.S.-GOVERNMENT* **SEE** UNITED STATES — POLITICS AND GOVERNMENT
NA4205-8	*U.S.-GOVERNMENT BUILDINGS* **SEE** UNITED STATES — PUBLIC BUILDINGS / *architecture*
JK1613-1641	*U.S.-GOVERNMENT BUILDINGS* **SEE** UNITED STATES — PUBLIC BUILDINGS / *government*
NA4411-4510	*U.S.-GOVERNMENT BUILDINGS* **SEE** UNITED STATES — PUBLIC BUILDINGS / *architecture*
JK	*U.S.-GOVERNMENT EMPLOYEES* **SEE** UNITED STATES — OFFICIALS AND EMPLOYEES
E178.4	*U.S.-HISTORY, COMIC, SATIRICAL, ETC.* **SEE** UNITED STATES — HISTORY — — HUMOR, CARICATURES, ETC.
HC101-9	*U.S.-HISTORY, ECONOMIC* **SEE** UNITED STATES — ECONOMIC CONDITIONS
JK	*U.S.-HISTORY, POLITICAL* **SEE** UNITED STATES — POLITICS AND GOVERNMENT
E83.83	*U.S.-HISTORY-BLACK HAWK WAR, 1832* **SEE** BLACK HAWK WAR, 1832
E334	*U.S.-HISTORY-BURR CONSPIRACY, 1805-1807* **SEE** BURR CONSPIRACY, 1805-1807
E647	*U.S.-HISTORY-CIVIL WAR-CARTOONS* **SEE** UNITED STATES — HISTORY — — CIVIL WAR — — — HUMOR, CARICATURES, ETC.
E609	*U.S.-HISTORY-CIVIL WAR-CORRESPONDENTS* **SEE** UNITED STATES — HISTORY — — CIVIL WAR — — — JOURNALISTS
NA9325-9355	*U.S.-HISTORY-CIVIL WAR-MONUMENTS* **SEE** SOLDIERS' MONUMENTS
E491	*U.S.-HISTORY-CIVIL WAR-RAILROADS* **SEE** UNITED STATES — HISTORY — — CIVIL WAR — — — TRANSPORTATION
E548	*U.S.-HISTORY-CIVIL WAR-REGISTERS, LISTS, ETC.-CONFEDERATE STATES* **SEE** CONFEDERATE STATES OF AMERICA. — REGISTERS
E468.7	*U.S.-HISTORY-CIVIL WAR-VIEWS* **SEE** UNITED STATES — HISTORY — — CIVIL WAR — — — PICTORIAL WORKS
D501-680	*U.S.-HISTORY-EUROPEAN WAR, 1914-1918* **SEE** EUROPEAN WAR, 1914-1918
E83.67	*U.S.-HISTORY-KING PHILIP'S WAR, 1675-1676* **SEE** KING PHILIP'S WAR, 1675-1676
N7634	*U.S.-HISTORY-PORTRAITS* **SEE** UNITED STATES — BIOGRAPHY — — PORTRAITS / *women*
NE260	*U.S.-HISTORY-PORTRAITS* **SEE** UNITED STATES — BIOGRAPHY — — PORTRAITS / *catalogs of engravings*
N7593	*U.S.-HISTORY-PORTRAITS* **SEE** UNITED STATES — BIOGRAPHY — — PORTRAITS
HJ247	*U.S.-HISTORY-REVOLUTION-COMMERCE* **SEE** UNITED STATES — HISTORY — — REVOLUTION — — — FINANCE, COMMERCE, CONFISCATIONS, ETC.
HJ247	*U.S.-HISTORY-REVOLUTION-ECONOMIC ASPECTS* **SEE** UNITED STATES — HISTORY — — REVOLUTION — — — FINANCE, COMMERCE, CONFISCATIONS, ETC.
M1631	*U.S.-HISTORY-REVOLUTION-MUSIC* **SEE** UNITED STATES — HISTORY — — REVOLUTION — — — SONGS AND MUSIC / *music*
E209	*U.S.-HISTORY-REVOLUTION-VIEWS* **SEE** UNITED STATES — HISTORY — — REVOLUTION — — — PICTORIAL WORKS
E315	*U.S.-HISTORY-WHISKEY INSURRECTION, 1794* **SEE** WHISKEY INSURRECTION, 1794
JV6403-7127	*U.S.-IMMIGRATION* **SEE** UNITED STATES — EMIGRATION AND IMMIGRATION
HC101-9	*U.S.-INDUSTRIES-STATISTICS* **SEE** UNITED STATES — INDUSTRIES
HE6300-6499	*U.S.-MAIL* **SEE** POSTAL SERVICE — U.S.
E160	*U.S.-NATIONAL CEMETERIES* **SEE** NATIONAL CEMETERIES — U.S.
E494	*U.S.-NATIONAL CEMETERIES* **SEE** NATIONAL CEMETERIES — U.S.
UB393-4	*U.S.-NATIONAL CEMETERIES* **SEE** NATIONAL CEMETERIES — U.S.
VA62.5-7	*U.S.-NAVAL DISTRICTS AND RIVER COMMANDS* **SEE** NAVAL DISTRICTS — U.S.
F970	*U.S.-NONCONTIGUOUS POSSESSIONS* **SEE** UNITED STATES — INSULAR POSSESSIONS
JK2551-9	*U.S.-NONCONTIGUOUS POSSESSIONS* **SEE** UNITED STATES — TERRITORIES AND POSSESSIONS / *government*
F970	*U.S.-NONCONTIGUOUS POSSESSIONS* **SEE** UNITED STATES — TERRITORIES AND POSSESSIONS
JV500-599	*U.S.-NONCONTIGUOUS POSSESSIONS* **SEE** UNITED STATES — TERRITORIES AND POSSESSIONS / *government*
UA42-43	*U.S.-ORGANIZED MILITIA, 1903-1916* **SEE** UNITED STATES — NATIONAL GUARD
F970	*U.S.-OUTLYING POSSESSIONS* **SEE** UNITED STATES — INSULAR POSSESSIONS
JK2551-9	*U.S.-OUTLYING POSSESSIONS* **SEE** UNITED STATES — TERRITORIES AND POSSESSIONS / *government*
JV500-599	*U.S.-OUTLYING POSSESSIONS* **SEE** UNITED STATES — TERRITORIES AND POSSESSIONS / *government*
F970	*U.S.-OUTLYING POSSESSIONS* **SEE** UNITED STATES — TERRITORIES AND POSSESSIONS
HE6300-6499	*U.S.-POSTAL SERVICE* **SEE** POSTAL SERVICE — U.S.
JK511-609	*U.S.-PRESIDENTS* **SEE** PRESIDENTS — U.S.
Z232.U	*U.S.-PUBLIC DOCUMENTS* **SEE** UNITED STATES — GOVERNMENT PUBLICATIONS / *printing*
Z1223	*U.S.-PUBLIC DOCUMENTS* **SEE** UNITED STATES — GOVERNMENT PUBLICATIONS / *bibliography*
JK1661-7	*U.S.-PUBLIC PROPERTY* **SEE** UNITED STATES — GOVERNMENT PROPERTY
JX235-6	*U.S.-TREATIES* **SEE** UNITED STATES — FOREIGN RELATIONS — — TREATIES / *texts*
JK570-573	*U.S.-TREATIES* **SEE** UNITED STATES — FOREIGN RELATIONS — — TREATIES
UB343	*U.S. ARMY-ENLISTMENT* **SEE** U.S. — RECRUITING, ENLISTMENT, ETC.
UB323	*U.S. ARMY-ENLISTMENT* **SEE** U.S. — RECRUITING, ENLISTMENT, ETC.
M1629-1630	*U.S. ARMY-MUSIC* **SEE** U.S. — SONGS AND MUSIC
UC273	*U.S. ARMY-PACK TRANSPORTATION* **SEE** U.S. — TRANSPORTATION
UB412-413	*U.S. ARMY-RETIREMENTS* **SEE** U.S. — APPOINTMENTS AND RETIREMENTS
U113	*U.S. ARMY-SOLDIERS' HANDBOOKS* **SEE** U.S. — HANDBOOKS, MANUALS, ETC.
VB258	*U.S. NAVY-BILLET DESCRIPTIONS* **SEE** U.S. — JOB DESCRIPTIONS
VG953	*U.S. NAVY-BOATSWAIN'S MATES* **SEE** U.S. — BOATSWAINS
VB258	*U.S. NAVY-DUTY SPECIFICATIONS* **SEE** U.S. — JOB DESCRIPTIONS
VB263	*U.S. NAVY-ENLISTMENT* **SEE** U.S. — RECRUITING, ENLISTMENT, ETC.
VC263	*U.S. NAVY-EQUIPMENT, SUPPLIES, ETC.* **SEE** U.S. — SUPPLIES AND STORES
M1629-1630	*U.S. NAVY-MUSIC* **SEE** U.S. — SONGS AND MUSIC
VA62.5-7	*U.S. NAVY-NAVAL DISTRICTS AND RIVER COMMANDS* **SEE** NAVAL DISTRICTS — U.S.
VB313-314	*U.S. NAVY-RETIREMENTS* **SEE** U.S. — APPOINTMENTS AND RETIREMENTS
HE6499	*U.S. POST OFFICE DEPT.-OFFICIALS AND EMPLOYEES* **SEE** POSTAL SERVICE — U.S. — — EMPLOYEES
E492.5	U.S. — HISTORY — — CIVIL WAR
UF533	U.S. — ORDNANCE AND ORDNANCE STORES — — INSPECTION
F2520.1.U3	*UABOHY INDIANS* **SEE** UABOI INDIANS
F2520.1.U3	UABOI INDIANS
PM7185	UAIUAI LANGUAGE
PM6714	*UAYANA LANGUAGE* **SEE** OYANA LANGUAGE

PK9201.U3	UBYKH LANGUAGE
F3430.1.C	*UCAYALE INDIANS* **SEE** COCAMA INDIANS / *peru*
PM5823	*UCAYALE LANGUAGE* **SEE** COCAMA LANGUAGE
E99.Y9	*UCHEAN INDIANS* **SEE** YUCHI INDIANS
E99.Y9	*UCHEE INDIANS* **SEE** YUCHI INDIANS
HD1160	UDAL SYSTEM
DA880.O6	UDAL SYSTEM / *orkney islands*
DA880.S5	UDAL SYSTEM / *shetland islands*
QR303	UDDER — BACTERIOLOGY
QR171	UDDER — BACTERIOLOGY
SF871	UDDER — DISEASES
QL944	UDDER
DK759.U	*UDE* **SEE** UDEKHE
PL461.U4	*UDE LANGUAGE* **SEE** UDEKHE LANGUAGE
PK9201.U4	*UDE LANGUAGE* **SEE** UDI LANGUAGE
PL461.U4	UDEKHE LANGUAGE
DK759.U	UDEKHE
PK9201.U4	UDI LANGUAGE
PK9201.U4	*UDIC LANGUAGE* **SEE** UDI LANGUAGE
GN585.R9	*UDMURT* **SEE** VOTIAKS / *anthropology*
DK34.V7	*UDMURT* **SEE** VOTIAKS / *history*
PH1101-9	*UDMURT LANGUAGE* **SEE** VOTIAK LANGUAGE
SB351.U	UDO / *vegetables*
PL8276	*UDZO LANGUAGE* **SEE** IJO LANGUAGE
PL6551	UEA LANGUAGE
E99.E7	UGALAKMIUT INDIANS / *eskimos*
PM89	UGALAKMIUT LANGUAGE
PJ4150	UGARITIC LANGUAGE
BH301.U5	UGLINESS
TK6655.U6	*UHF* **SEE** TELEVISION — ULTRAHIGH FREQUENCY APPARATUS AND SUPPLIES
TK6553	*UHF RADIO* **SEE** RADIO, SHORT WAVE
TK6655.U6	*UHF TELEVISION* **SEE** TELEVISION — ULTRAHIGH FREQUENCY APPARATUS AND SUPPLIES
PL49	*UIGHUR LANGUAGE* **SEE** UIGUR LANGUAGE
PL49	UIGUR LANGUAGE
PL49	UIGUR PHILOLOGY
DS793.E2	UIGURS
E99.U8	UINTA INDIANS
QE391.G	*UINTAITE* **SEE** GILSONITE
F2230.2.W	*UITOTO INDIANS* **SEE** WITOTO INDIANS
PG3934	UKRAINIAN BALLADS AND SONGS / *collections*
PG3917	UKRAINIAN BALLADS AND SONGS / *history*
PG3937	UKRAINIAN DRAMA / *collections*
PG3921	UKRAINIAN DRAMA / *history*
PG3801-3899	UKRAINIAN LANGUAGE
PG3900-3998	UKRAINIAN LITERATURE IN FOREIGN COUNTRIES
PG3900-3998	UKRAINIAN LITERATURE
PG3934	UKRAINIAN POETRY / *collections*
PG3926	UKRAINIAN POETRY / *folk literature*
PG3917	UKRAINIAN POETRY / *history*
DK508	UKRAINIANS
MT645	UKULELE — METHODS
M282-3	UKULELE AND PIANO MUSIC
M1360	*UKULELE BAND* **SEE** PLECTRAL ENSEMBLES
M142.U5	UKULELE MUSIC
ML1015-1018	UKULELE
MT645	*UKULELE-SELF-INSTRUCTION* **SEE** UKULELE — METHODS — — SELF-INSTRUCTION
MT645	UKULELE — METHODS — — SELF-INSTRUCTION
PL6321	ULAWA LANGUAGE
RD631	ULCERS
PL6338	*ULEAI LANGUAGE* **SEE** WOLEAI LANGUAGE
QD421	*ULEXINE* **SEE** CYTISINE / *chemistry*
QP921.C	*ULEXINE* **SEE** CYTISINE / *physiological effect*
DC227.5.U6	ULM — CAPITULATION, 1805
D267.U6	ULM, TRUCE OF, 1647
F219	*ULMECAS* **SEE** OLMECS
QB389	*ULTRA-NEPTUNIAN PLANETS* **SEE** PLANETS, ULTRA-NEPTUNIAN / *perturbations*
QC459	ULTRA-VIOLET RAYS
QC459	*ULTRA-VIOLET SPECTRUM* **SEE** SPECTRUM, ULTRA-VIOLET
QD54.C4	*ULTRACENTRIFUGES* **SEE** CENTRIFUGES / *chemistry*
TK6720	ULTRAFAX
TK6553	*ULTRAHIGH FREQUENCY RADIO* **SEE** RADIO, SHORT WAVE

QC276	*ULTRAHIGH TEMPERATURES* **SEE** HIGH TEMPERATURES
TP936	*ULTRAMARINE BLUE* **SEE** ULTRAMARINE / *pigments*
TP936	ULTRAMARINE / *pigments*
BX1805-1810	ULTRAMONTANISM
TA406.5	ULTRASONIC TESTING
RM951	*ULTRASONIC THERAPY* **SEE** ULTRASONIC WAVES — THERAPEUTIC USE
RM951	ULTRASONIC WAVES — THERAPEUTIC USE
QC244	ULTRASONIC WAVES / *acoustics*
QC244	ULTRASONICS / *acoustics*
E99.U4	UMATILLA INDIANS
DS234-8	*UMAYYADS* **SEE** OMAYYADS
BL2590.U5	UMBANDA (CULTUS)
QM543	*UMBILICAL CORD* **SEE** UMBILICUS
RJ271	UMBILICUS — HEMORRHAGE
QM543	UMBILICUS
GT2210	UMBRELLAS AND PARASOLS
PL8755	UMBUNDU LANGUAGE
F2520.1.U	UMOTINA INDIANS
GV876	*UMPIRES (BASEBALL)* **SEE** BASEBALL — UMPIRING
GV735	*UMPIRING (SPORTS)* **SEE** SPORTS OFFICIATING
PM1598	*UMPQUA (LOWER) LANGUAGE* **SEE** KUITSH LANGUAGE
E99.U45	UMPQUA INDIANS
F2520.1.U	*UMUTINA INDIANS* **SEE** UMOTINA INDIANS
DU122.W	*UNAMBAL (AUSTRALIAN TRIBE)* **SEE** WUNAMBAL (AUSTRALIAN TRIBE)
B837	*UNBELIEF* **SEE** SKEPTICISM
BD201	*UNBELIEF* **SEE** SKEPTICISM / *epistemology*
B851-4695	*UNBELIEF* **SEE** SKEPTICISM / *local*
BL2700-2790	*UNBELIEF* **SEE** SKEPTICISM / *rationalism*
B779	*UNBELIEF* **SEE** SKEPTICISM / *renaissance philosophy*
Q375	UNCERTAINTY (INFORMATION THEORY)
RC199.95	*UNCINARIA* **SEE** HOOKWORMS
RC199.95	*UNCINARIASIS* **SEE** HOOKWORM DISEASE
CS23	*UNCLAIMED ESTATES* **SEE** ESTATES, UNCLAIMED
CS23	*UNCLAIMED PROPERTY* **SEE** ESTATES, UNCLAIMED
GV1299.U5	UNCLE SAM (GAME)
E179	UNCLE SAM (NICKNAME)
BF1001-1389	*UNCONSCIOUSNESS* **SEE** SUBCONSCIOUSNESS
BF1211-1218	*UNCONSCIOUSNESS* **SEE** SUBCONSCIOUSNESS / *multiple consciousness*
BF315	*UNCONSCIOUSNESS* **SEE** SUBCONSCIOUSNESS / *unconscious mind*
TX392	*UNCOOKED FOOD* **SEE** FOOD, RAW
BX2203	UNCTION / *catholic sacraments*
BV4337	UNCTION / *pastoral theology*
BV875	UNCTION / *sacramentals*
BV800	UNCTION / *sacraments*
BV860	UNCTION / *unction of the sick*
BX2290	UNCTION, EXTREME **SEE** EXTREME UNCTION
BC199.D4	*UNDEFINABILITY* **SEE** DEFINITION (LOGIC)
BV636	*UNDENOMINATIONAL CHURCHES* **SEE** COMMUNITY CHURCHES
RA779	*UNDERCLOTHING* **SEE** UNDERWEAR / *hygiene*
TT670-678	*UNDERCLOTHING* **SEE** UNDERWEAR / *manufacture*
HD9969.U5-6	*UNDERCLOTHING* **SEE** UNDERWEAR / *trade*
HG4517	UNDERDEVELOPED AREAS — FINANCE
TA712	UNDERGROUND CONSTRUCTION
TH4518	UNDERGROUND FACTORIES / *construction*
TP759	*UNDERGROUND GASIFICATION OF COAL* **SEE** COAL GASIFICATION, UNDERGROUND
TK3251-3261	*UNDERGROUND LINES (TROLLEYS)* **SEE** ELECTRIC LINES — UNDERGROUND
DD256.3	*UNDERGROUND MOVEMENTS (WORLD WAR, 1939-1945)* **SEE** ANTI-NAZI MOVEMENT
E450	UNDERGROUND RAILROAD
TF845-851	*UNDERGROUND RAILROADS* **SEE** SUBWAYS
TF850-851	*UNDERGROUND RAILROADS* **SEE** SUBWAYS / *freight*
GB1001-1197	*UNDERGROUND WATER* **SEE** WATER, UNDERGROUND
TH5281	*UNDERPINNING* **SEE** SHORING AND UNDERPINNING
BF325	*UNDERSTANDING* **SEE** COMPREHENSION
RA622.A7	UNDERTAKERS AND UNDERTAKING — DIRECTORIES
RA622-3	UNDERTAKERS AND UNDERTAKING
TS2301.U5	UNDERTAKERS AND UNDERTAKING / *supplies*
QC225	UNDERWATER ACOUSTICS

VM965	UNDERWATER CUTTING **SEE** UNDERWATER WELDING AND CUTTING
TN871.3	UNDERWATER DRILLING (PETROLEUM) **SEE** OIL WELL DRILLING, SUBMARINE
TC193	UNDERWATER DRILLING
VM981-9	UNDERWATER EXPLORATION **SEE** DIVING, SUBMARINE
TC183	UNDERWATER EXPLORATION **SEE** DIVING, SUBMARINE / submarine construction
TR800	UNDERWATER PHOTOGRAPHY **SEE** PHOTOGRAPHY, SUBMARINE
RC1015	UNDERWATER PHYSIOLOGY
QC225	UNDERWATER SOUND **SEE** UNDERWATER ACOUSTICS
VM965	UNDERWATER WELDING AND CUTTING
RA779	UNDERWEAR / hygiene
TT670-678	UNDERWEAR / manufacture
HD9969.U5-6	UNDERWEAR / trade
HG8011-9970	UNDERWRITING **SEE** INSURANCE
HG4651-5990	UNDERWRITING **SEE** SECURITIES
HJ4653.U46	UNDISTRIBUTED PROFITS TAX / u.s.
RC123.B7	UNDULANT FEVER
SF473.B	UNDULATED PARAKEET **SEE** BUDGERIGARS
QA927	UNDULATORY THEORY **SEE** WAVE-MOTION, THEORY OF
HD1315	UNEARNED INCREMENT
HD5701-5851	UNEMPLOYED
HD5701-5851	UNEMPLOYMENT **SEE** LABOR SUPPLY
HD5701-5851	UNEMPLOYMENT **SEE** UNEMPLOYED
HD7095-6	UNEMPLOYMENT COMPENSATION **SEE** INSURANCE, UNEMPLOYMENT
HD7095-6	UNEMPLOYMENT INSURANCE **SEE** INSURANCE, UNEMPLOYMENT
HD6331	UNEMPLOYMENT, TECHNOLOGICAL
HD3625-6	UNFAIR COMPETITION **SEE** COMPETITION, UNFAIR
HD3625-6	UNFAIR TRADE PRACTICES **SEE** COMPETITION, UNFAIR
Z1033.U6	UNFINISHED BOOKS
TX392	UNFIRED FOOD **SEE** FOOD, RAW
LB3061	UNGRADED SCHOOLS **SEE** ABILITY GROUPING IN EDUCATION
LB3051-3063	UNGRADED SCHOOLS **SEE** GRADING AND MARKING (STUDENTS)
QL737.U4-8	UNGULATA
QE882.U2-8	UNGULATA, FOSSIL
JF501-637	UNICAMERAL LEGISLATURES **SEE** LEGISLATIVE BODIES
QH271-7	UNICELLULAR ORGANISMS
GR830.U6	UNICORNS
U260	UNIFIED COMMANDS (MILITARY SCIENCE) **SEE** UNIFIED OPERATIONS (MILITARY SCIENCE)
QC6.5	UNIFIED FIELD THEORIES
QC6.5	UNIFIED FIELD THEORY, EINSTEIN **SEE** UNIFIED FIELD THEORIES
Z678	UNIFIED LIBRARIES **SEE** LIBRARIES — CENTRALIZATION
Z678	UNIFIED LIBRARIES **SEE** LIBRARIES — CENTRALIZATION
U260	UNIFIED OPERATIONS (MILITARY SCIENCE)
TT625	UNIFORMS / catalogs and price-lists
HV8007	UNIFORMS, CIVIL / police
UC480-485	UNIFORMS, MILITARY
UC480-485	UNIFORMS, NAVAL **SEE** UNIFORMS, MILITARY
GT975	UNIFORMS, PAPAL
BT769	UNIO MYSTICA **SEE** MYSTICAL UNION
Z695.83	UNION CATALOGS **SEE** CATALOGS, UNION
BV636	UNION CHURCHES **SEE** COMMUNITY CHURCHES
HD6489	UNION LABEL
Z6945	UNION LISTS OF PERIODICALS **SEE** PERIODICALS — BIBLIOGRAPHY — — UNION LISTS
HD6490.U5	UNION SECURITY
HD6488	UNION SHOP **SEE** OPEN AND CLOSED SHOP
BT769	UNION WITH CHRIST **SEE** MYSTICAL UNION
BT205	UNION, HYPOSTATIC **SEE** HYPOSTATIC UNION
BT769	UNION, MYSTICAL **SEE** MYSTICAL UNION
QL430.7.U6	UNIONIDAE
QE812.U6	UNIONIDAE / fossil
JN1129.C7	UNIONIST PARTY (GT. BRIT.) **SEE** CONSERVATIVE PARTY (GT. BRIT.)
LB3640	UNIONS, STUDENT **SEE** STUDENT UNIONS
HD6350-6940	UNIONS, TRADE **SEE** TRADE-UNIONS
PN4193.C5	UNISON SPEAKING **SEE** CHŌRAL SPEAKING
HG4530	UNIT TRUSTS **SEE** INVESTMENT TRUSTS
BX9856	UNITARIAN CHURCHES — CHARITIES
BX9801-9869	UNITARIAN CHURCHES
BX9801-9869	UNITARIANISM
BX8551-8593	UNITAS FRATRUM **SEE** MORAVIANS
BX6370-6379	UNITED AMERICAN FREEWILL BAPTISTS
BX8551-8593	UNITED BRETHREN **SEE** MORAVIANS
BX9875-6	UNITED BRETHREN IN CHRIST
BX9881-3	UNITED CHURCH OF CANADA
BV636	UNITED CHURCHES **SEE** COMMUNITY CHURCHES
E277	UNITED EMPIRE LOYALISTS
F1058	UNITED EMPIRE LOYALISTS / ontario
BX8048	UNITED LUTHERAN CHURCH IN AMERICA
JX1977.S3	UNITED NATIONS — SANCTIONS
M1627	UNITED NATIONS — SONGS AND MUSIC
M1627.15	UNITED NATIONS — SONGS AND MUSIC
JX1977.4	UNITED NATIONS AND NON-MEMBER NATIONS
NA4184.2	UNITED NATIONS EDUCATIONAL, SCIENTIFIC AND CULTURAL ORGANIZATION — BUILDINGS
M1627	UNITED NATIONS-MUSIC **SEE** UNITED NATIONS — SONGS AND MUSIC
M1627.15	UNITED NATIONS-MUSIC **SEE** UNITED NATIONS — SONGS AND MUSIC
BX8980-8988	UNITED PRESBYTERIAN CHURCH OF NORTH AMERICA
GB494-6	UNITED STATES — ALTITUDES*
QB296.U	UNITED STATES — ALTITUDES / geodesy
E51-74	UNITED STATES — ANTIQUITIES
HJ10	UNITED STATES — APPROPRIATIONS AND EXPENDITURES
HJ2050-2052	UNITED STATES — APPROPRIATIONS AND EXPENDITURES
E159	UNITED STATES — AREA
Z1224	UNITED STATES — BIO-BIBLIOGRAPHY
E176	UNITED STATES — BIOGRAPHY
E179.5	UNITED STATES — BOUNDARIES
JK1606	UNITED STATES — CAPITAL
Z7554.U	UNITED STATES — CENSUS / bibliography
HA37.U2-7	UNITED STATES — CENSUS / organization
HA201	UNITED STATES — CENSUS / publications by date
BR513-569	UNITED STATES — CHURCH HISTORY
E169.1	UNITED STATES — CIVILIZATION
E162-8	UNITED STATES — CIVILIZATION / early periods
HJ8931-8941	UNITED STATES — CLAIMS
JX238	UNITED STATES — CLAIMS / international
QC983-4	UNITED STATES — CLIMATE
UG410-412	UNITED STATES — COAST DEFENSES
E713	UNITED STATES — COLONIAL QUESTION
HF3001-3163	UNITED STATES — COMMERCE
HF105	UNITED STATES — COMMERCE / serial documents
HF1455-6	UNITED STATES — COMMERCIAL POLICY
HF1731-2	UNITED STATES — COMMERCIAL TREATIES
JK	UNITED STATES — CONSTITUTIONAL HISTORY
JK	UNITED STATES — CONSTITUTIONAL LAW
UA23	UNITED STATES — DEFENSES
E162-9	UNITED STATES — DESCRIPTION AND TRAVEL
JX1705-6	UNITED STATES — DIPLOMATIC AND CONSULAR SERVICE
E154.5-9	UNITED STATES — DIRECTORIES
E159	UNITED STATES — DISTANCES, ETC.
HC101-9	UNITED STATES — ECONOMIC CONDITIONS
HC101-9	UNITED STATES — ECONOMIC POLICY
JV6403-7127	UNITED STATES — EMIGRATION AND IMMIGRATION
JK631-821	UNITED STATES — EXECUTIVE DEPARTMENTS
E184	UNITED STATES — FOREIGN POPULATION
JX1405-1428	UNITED STATES — FOREIGN RELATIONS
CS42-71	UNITED STATES — GENEALOGY
JK1661-7	UNITED STATES — GOVERNMENT PROPERTY
Z7164.L8	UNITED STATES — GOVERNMENT PUBLICATIONS (COUNTIES)
Z7164.L8	UNITED STATES — GOVERNMENT PUBLICATIONS (MUNICIPAL GOVERNMENTS)
Z1223.5	UNITED STATES — GOVERNMENT PUBLICATIONS (STATE GOVERNMENTS)
Z1223	UNITED STATES — GOVERNMENT PUBLICATIONS / bibliography
Z232.U	UNITED STATES — GOVERNMENT PUBLICATIONS / printing
VA61-65	UNITED STATES — GOVERNMENT VESSELS

*Inadequacy of Library of Congress format design produced incorrect listing of headings beginning U.S. and United States.

E159	UNITED STATES — HISTORIC HOUSES, ETC.
E179.5	UNITED STATES — HISTORICAL GEOGRAPHY
E178	UNITED STATES — HISTORY
E178.3	UNITED STATES — HISTORY, JUVENILE
E180	UNITED STATES — HISTORY, LOCAL
F1-970	UNITED STATES — HISTORY, LOCAL
E181	UNITED STATES — HISTORY, MILITARY
E182	UNITED STATES — HISTORY, NAVAL
HC101-9	UNITED STATES — INDUSTRIES
F970	UNITED STATES — INSULAR POSSESSIONS
E169.1	UNITED STATES — INTELLECTUAL LIFE
E162-8	UNITED STATES — INTELLECTUAL LIFE / early periods
P377	UNITED STATES — LANGUAGES
AS21-36	UNITED STATES — LEARNED INSTITUTIONS AND SOCIETIES
HD9721-9	UNITED STATES — MANUFACTURES
UA42	UNITED STATES — MILITIA
HN57-64	UNITED STATES — MORAL CONDITIONS / social history
E179	UNITED STATES — NAME
UA42-43	UNITED STATES — NATIONAL GUARD
VA80	UNITED STATES — NAVAL MILITIA
D619	UNITED STATES — NEUTRALITY / european war before entrance of the u.s.
JX1416	UNITED STATES — NEUTRALITY / international law
HB2595	UNITED STATES — OCCUPATIONS
JK	UNITED STATES — OFFICIALS AND EMPLOYEES
JK	UNITED STATES — POLITICS AND GOVERNMENT
HB915-3505	UNITED STATES — POPULATION / demography
HA195-209	UNITED STATES — POPULATION / statistics
NA4205-8	UNITED STATES — PUBLIC BUILDINGS / architecture
NA4411-4510	UNITED STATES — PUBLIC BUILDINGS / architecture
JK1613-1641	UNITED STATES — PUBLIC BUILDINGS / government
HD216-243	UNITED STATES — PUBLIC LANDS
TA23	UNITED STATES — PUBLIC WORKS
E185.61	UNITED STATES — RACE QUESTION / negroes
E184	UNITED STATES — RACE QUESTION / other racial elements
JK5-7	UNITED STATES — REGISTERS
BR513-569	UNITED STATES — RELIGION
Q183	UNITED STATES — SCIENTIFIC BUREAUS
Q127.U6	UNITED STATES — SCIENTIFIC BUREAUS / history
CD5610	UNITED STATES — SEAL
HN51-85	UNITED STATES — SOCIAL CONDITIONS
E161	UNITED STATES — SOCIAL LIFE AND CUSTOMS
HA195-219	UNITED STATES — STATISTICS
RA445	UNITED STATES — STATISTICS, MEDICAL
HB915-3505	UNITED STATES — STATISTICS, VITAL / demography
HA195-209	UNITED STATES — STATISTICS, VITAL / statistics
GA59	UNITED STATES — SURVEYS
F592-4	UNITED STATES — SURVEYS / the west
E179.5	UNITED STATES — TERRITORIAL EXPANSION
F970	UNITED STATES — TERRITORIES AND POSSESSIONS
JK2551-9	UNITED STATES — TERRITORIES AND POSSESSIONS / government
JV500-599	UNITED STATES — TERRITORIES AND POSSESSIONS / government
Q115.W6-8	UNITED STATES EXPLORING EXPEDITION, 1838-1842
DS809	UNITED STATES NAVAL EXPEDITION TO JAPAN, 1852-1854
UC703	UNITED STATES — ARMED FORCES — — COMMISSARIAT
UH83	UNITED STATES — ARMED FORCES — — POSTAL SERVICE
UC260-267	UNITED STATES — ARMED FORCES — — PROCUREMENT
E181	UNITED STATES — ARMED FORCES — — REGISTERS OF DEAD
UA42	UNITED STATES — ARMED FORCES — — RESERVES
U328.U	UNITED STATES — ARMED FORCES — — SPORTS
UB408	UNITED STATES — ARMED FORCES — — WARRANT OFFICERS
UA45	UNITED STATES — ARMED FORCES — — WOMEN'S RESERVES
N7593	UNITED STATES — BIOGRAPHY — — PORTRAITS

NE260	UNITED STATES — BIOGRAPHY — — PORTRAITS / catalogs of engravings
N7634	UNITED STATES — BIOGRAPHY — — PORTRAITS / women
E398	UNITED STATES — BOUNDARIES — — CANADA
F880	UNITED STATES — BOUNDARIES — — CANADA
F912.B7	UNITED STATES — BOUNDARIES — — CANADA
F551	UNITED STATES — BOUNDARIES — — CANADA
F854	UNITED STATES — BOUNDARIES — — CANADA
F786	UNITED STATES — BOUNDARIES — — MEXICO
BR520	UNITED STATES — CHURCH HISTORY — — COLONIAL PERIOD
E713	UNITED STATES — COLONIAL QUESTION — — SPEECHES IN CONGRESS
HF3065-3150	UNITED STATES — COMMERCE — — AFRICA, (BELGIUM, CHINA, ETC.)
HF3021-3031	UNITED STATES — COMMERCE — — HISTORY
E158	UNITED STATES — DESCRIPTION AND TRAVEL — — GUIDE-BOOKS
E162-9	UNITED STATES — DESCRIPTION AND TRAVEL — — VIEWS
JX1706	UNITED STATES — DIPLOMATIC AND CONSULAR SERVICE — — APPROPRIATIONS AND EXPENDITURES
JX1706	UNITED STATES — DIPLOMATIC AND CONSULAR SERVICE — — BUILDINGS
HC106.3-4	UNITED STATES — ECONOMIC CONDITIONS — — 1918-1945
HC106.5	UNITED STATES — ECONOMIC CONDITIONS — — 1945-
JV6485	UNITED STATES — EMIGRATION AND IMMIGRATION — — MEDICAL INSPECTION
JK1671-9	UNITED STATES — EXECUTIVE DEPARTMENTS — — EQUIPMENT AND SUPPLIES
CD3030-3041	UNITED STATES — EXECUTIVE DEPARTMENTS — — RECORDS AND CORRESPONDENCE
E173	UNITED STATES — FOREIGN RELATIONS — — SPEECHES IN CONGRESS / collections
JK570-573	UNITED STATES — FOREIGN RELATIONS — — TREATIES
JX235-6	UNITED STATES — FOREIGN RELATIONS — — TREATIES / texts
VM623	UNITED STATES — GOVERNMENT VESSELS — — INSPECTION / marine engineering
E178.6	UNITED STATES — HISTORY — — ADDRESSES, ESSAYS, LECTURES
E178.3	UNITED STATES — HISTORY — — ANECDOTES
E174.5	UNITED STATES — HISTORY — — CHRONOLOGY
E456-655	UNITED STATES — HISTORY — — CIVIL WAR
E186-199	UNITED STATES — HISTORY — — COLONIAL PERIOD
E303	UNITED STATES — HISTORY — — CONFEDERATION, 1783-1789
E310	UNITED STATES — HISTORY — — CONSTITUTIONAL PERIOD, 1789-1809
E174	UNITED STATES — HISTORY — — DICTIONARIES
E179	UNITED STATES — HISTORY — — DRAMA
E178.25	UNITED STATES — HISTORY — — EXAMINATIONS, QUESTIONS, ETC.
E199	UNITED STATES — HISTORY — — FRENCH AND INDIAN WAR, 1755-1763
E175	UNITED STATES — HISTORY — — HISTORIOGRAPHY
E178.4	UNITED STATES — HISTORY — — HUMOR, CARICATURES, ETC.
E198	UNITED STATES — HISTORY — — KING GEORGE'S WAR, 1744-1748
E196	UNITED STATES — HISTORY — — KING WILLIAM'S WAR, 1689-1697
E178.2	UNITED STATES — HISTORY — — OUTLINES, SYLLABI, ETC.
E201-2	UNITED STATES — HISTORY — — PERIODICALS
E171	UNITED STATES — HISTORY — — PERIODICALS
E175.9	UNITED STATES — HISTORY — — PHILOSOPHY
E178.5	UNITED STATES — HISTORY — — PICTORIAL WORKS
E178.9	UNITED STATES — HISTORY — — POETRY
E197	UNITED STATES — HISTORY — — QUEEN ANNE'S WAR, 1702-1713
E201-298	UNITED STATES — HISTORY — — REVOLUTION
E172	UNITED STATES — HISTORY — — SOCIETIES, ETC.
E173	UNITED STATES — HISTORY — — SOURCES
E175.8	UNITED STATES — HISTORY — — STUDY AND TEACHING

E335	UNITED STATES — HISTORY — — TRIPOLITAN WAR, 1801-1805	E540.I3	UNITED STATES — HISTORY — — CIVIL WAR — — — INDIAN TROOPS
E351-364	UNITED STATES — HISTORY — — WAR OF 1812	E540.I6	UNITED STATES — HISTORY — — CIVIL WAR — — — IRISH TROOPS
E714-735	UNITED STATES — HISTORY — — WAR OF 1898		
E365	UNITED STATES — HISTORY — — WAR WITH ALGERIA, 1815	E540.J	UNITED STATES — HISTORY — — CIVIL WAR — — — JEWISH TROOPS
E323	UNITED STATES — HISTORY — — WAR WITH FRANCE, 1798-1800	E609	UNITED STATES — HISTORY — — CIVIL WAR — — — JOURNALISTS
E401-415	UNITED STATES — HISTORY — — WAR WITH MEXICO, 1845-1848	E621-5	UNITED STATES — HISTORY — — CIVIL WAR — — — MEDICAL AND SANITARY AFFAIRS
E301	UNITED STATES — HISTORY — — 1783-1865	E491	UNITED STATES — HISTORY — — CIVIL WAR — — — MEDICAL AND SANITARY AFFAIRS
E338	UNITED STATES — HISTORY — — 1815-1861		
E671-680	UNITED STATES — HISTORY — — 1849-1877	E631	UNITED STATES — HISTORY — — CIVIL WAR — — — MEDICAL AND SANITARY AFFAIRS
E415.7	UNITED STATES — HISTORY — — 1849-1877		
E661	UNITED STATES — HISTORY — — 1865-	E646	UNITED STATES — HISTORY — — CIVIL WAR — — — MUSEUMS
E661	UNITED STATES — HISTORY — — 1865-1898		
E712	UNITED STATES — HISTORY — — 1898-	E591-600	UNITED STATES — HISTORY — — CIVIL WAR — — — NAVAL OPERATIONS
E784	UNITED STATES — HISTORY — — 1919-1933		
E740	UNITED STATES — HISTORY — — 20TH CENTURY	E540.N3	UNITED STATES — HISTORY — — CIVIL WAR — — — NEGRO TROOPS
E181	UNITED STATES — HISTORY, MILITARY — — ANECDOTES	E585.N3	UNITED STATES — HISTORY — — CIVIL WAR — — — NEGRO TROOPS
E182	UNITED STATES — HISTORY, NAVAL — — ANECDOTES	E540.N3	UNITED STATES — HISTORY — — CIVIL WAR — — — NEGROES
E458-458.5	UNITED STATES — HISTORY — — CIVIL WAR — — — ADDRESSES, SERMONS, ETC. / contemporary	E459	UNITED STATES — HISTORY — — CIVIL WAR — — — PEACE
E649-650	UNITED STATES — HISTORY — — CIVIL WAR — — — ADDRESSES, SERMONS, ETC. / later	E482	UNITED STATES — HISTORY — — CIVIL WAR — — — PERIODICALS / confederate
E492.7	UNITED STATES — HISTORY — — CIVIL WAR — — — AERIAL OPERATIONS / federal	E461	UNITED STATES — HISTORY — — CIVIL WAR — — — PERIODICALS
E546.7	UNITED STATES — HISTORY — — CIVIL WAR — — — AERIAL OPERATIONS / confederate	E611-612	UNITED STATES — HISTORY — — CIVIL WAR — — — PERSONAL NARRATIVES
E468.8	UNITED STATES — HISTORY — — CIVIL WAR — — — ALMANACS	E464	UNITED STATES — HISTORY — — CIVIL WAR — — — PERSONAL NARRATIVES
E655	UNITED STATES — HISTORY — — CIVIL WAR — — — ANECDOTES	E591	UNITED STATES — HISTORY — — CIVIL WAR — — — PERSONAL NARRATIVES
E467-467.1	UNITED STATES — HISTORY — — CIVIL WAR — — — BIOGRAPHY	E601	UNITED STATES — HISTORY — — CIVIL WAR — — — PERSONAL NARRATIVES
E600	UNITED STATES — HISTORY — — CIVIL WAR — — — BLOCKADE	E468.7	UNITED STATES — HISTORY — — CIVIL WAR — — — PICTORIAL WORKS
E470-478	UNITED STATES — HISTORY — — CIVIL WAR — — — CAMPAIGNS AND BATTLES	E647	UNITED STATES — HISTORY — — CIVIL WAR — — — POETRY
E458-9	UNITED STATES — HISTORY — — CIVIL WAR — — — CAUSES	PS261	UNITED STATES — HISTORY — — CIVIL WAR — — — POETRY / history and criticism
E551-582	UNITED STATES — HISTORY — — CIVIL WAR — — — CAVALRY OPERATIONS / confederate	E611-616	UNITED STATES — HISTORY — — CIVIL WAR — — — PRISONERS AND PRISONS
E546.5	UNITED STATES — HISTORY — — CIVIL WAR — — — CAVALRY OPERATIONS / confederate	E611-616	UNITED STATES — HISTORY — — CIVIL WAR — — — PRISONERS, EXCHANGE OF
E492.5	UNITED STATES — HISTORY — — CIVIL WAR — — — CAVALRY OPERATIONS / federal	E468.9	UNITED STATES — HISTORY — — CIVIL WAR — — — PROPAGANDA
E495-537	UNITED STATES — HISTORY — — CIVIL WAR — — — CAVALRY OPERATIONS / federal	E545-7	UNITED STATES — HISTORY — — CIVIL WAR — — — REGIMENTAL HISTORIES
E468.3	UNITED STATES — HISTORY — — CIVIL WAR — — — CHRONOLOGY	E495-537	UNITED STATES — HISTORY — — CIVIL WAR — — — REGIMENTAL HISTORIES
E480	UNITED STATES — HISTORY — — CIVIL WAR — — — CLAIMS	E491-3	UNITED STATES — HISTORY — — CIVIL WAR — — — REGIMENTAL HISTORIES
E483	UNITED STATES — HISTORY — — CIVIL WAR — — — CONFEDERATE STATES	E551-582	UNITED STATES — HISTORY — — CIVIL WAR — — — REGIMENTAL HISTORIES
E647	UNITED STATES — HISTORY — — CIVIL WAR — — — DRAMA	E494	UNITED STATES — HISTORY — — CIVIL WAR — — — REGISTERS OF DEAD
HC105.6	UNITED STATES — HISTORY — — CIVIL WAR — — — ECONOMICS ASPECTS	E548	UNITED STATES — HISTORY — — CIVIL WAR — — — REGISTERS, LISTS, ETC.
PZ3-7	UNITED STATES — HISTORY — — CIVIL WAR — — — FICTION	E494	UNITED STATES — HISTORY — — CIVIL WAR — — — REGISTERS, LISTS, ETC.
E648	UNITED STATES — HISTORY — — CIVIL WAR — — — FICTION	E635	UNITED STATES — HISTORY — — CIVIL WAR — — — RELIGIOUS ASPECTS / etc.
HJ251-2	UNITED STATES — HISTORY — — CIVIL WAR — — — FINANCE, COMMERCE, CONFISCATIONS, ETC.	E540	UNITED STATES — HISTORY — — CIVIL WAR — — — RELIGIOUS ASPECTS / churches and the war
E480	UNITED STATES — HISTORY — — CIVIL WAR — — — FINANCE, COMMERCE, CONFISCATIONS, ETC.	E540.S	UNITED STATES — HISTORY — — CIVIL WAR — — — SCOTCH TROOPS
E469.8	UNITED STATES — HISTORY — — CIVIL WAR — — — FOREIGN PUBLIC OPINION	E457.6	UNITED STATES — HISTORY — — CIVIL WAR — — — SCOTCH TROOPS / monuments
E540.G3	UNITED STATES — HISTORY — — CIVIL WAR — — — GERMAN TROOPS	E608	UNITED STATES — HISTORY — — CIVIL WAR — — — SCOUTS AND SCOUTING
E470.45	UNITED STATES — HISTORY — — CIVIL WAR — — — GUERRILLAS	E462-3	UNITED STATES — HISTORY — — CIVIL WAR — — — SOCIETIES, ETC.
E621-635	UNITED STATES — HISTORY — — CIVIL WAR — — — HOSPITALS, CHARITIES, ETC.	E464	UNITED STATES — HISTORY — — CIVIL WAR — — — SOURCES
E647	UNITED STATES — HISTORY — — CIVIL WAR — — — HUMOR, CARICATURES, ETC.	E484	UNITED STATES — HISTORY — — CIVIL WAR — — — SOURCES
E540.H6	UNITED STATES — HISTORY — — CIVIL WAR — — — HUNGARIAN PARTICIPATION		

LB2342	UNIVERSITIES AND COLLEGES — ACCOUNTING
LB2341	UNIVERSITIES AND COLLEGES — ADMINISTRATION
LB2411	UNIVERSITIES AND COLLEGES — ALUMNI
NA6600-6603	UNIVERSITIES AND COLLEGES — BUILDINGS
BV26	UNIVERSITIES AND COLLEGES — CHAPEL EXERCISES
LB2361-5	UNIVERSITIES AND COLLEGES — CURRICULA
LB2351-2360	UNIVERSITIES AND COLLEGES — ENTRANCE REQUIREMENTS
LB2353	UNIVERSITIES AND COLLEGES — EXAMINATIONS / entrance
LB2367	UNIVERSITIES AND COLLEGES — EXAMINATIONS / term
LB2342	UNIVERSITIES AND COLLEGES — FINANCE
LB2371	UNIVERSITIES AND COLLEGES — GRADUATE WORK
LB2364	UNIVERSITIES AND COLLEGES — HONORS COURSES
LB3630	UNIVERSITIES AND COLLEGES — INSIGNIA
BV283.C7	UNIVERSITIES AND COLLEGES — PRAYERS
LC391	UNIVERSITIES AND COLLEGES — RELIGION / religious instruction
BV1170	UNIVERSITIES AND COLLEGES — RELIGION / y.m.c.a.
BV4310	UNIVERSITIES AND COLLEGES — SERMONS
LC184-8	UNIVERSITIES AND COLLEGES — TAXATION
LB2300-2411	UNIVERSITIES AND COLLEGES
LD-LG	UNIVERSITIES AND COLLEGES / individual institutions
LA410-2270	UNIVERSITIES AND COLLEGES / other countries
LA225-8	UNIVERSITIES AND COLLEGES / u.s.
LB2830	*UNIVERSITIES AND COLLEGES-ACCOUNTING* **SEE** PUNCHED CARD SYSTEMS — EDUCATION / schools
LB2342	*UNIVERSITIES AND COLLEGES-ACCOUNTING* **SEE** PUNCHED CARD SYSTEMS — EDUCATION / colleges
LB2331.5	*UNIVERSITIES AND COLLEGES-COOPERATION* **SEE** UNIVERSITY COOPERATION
LB3261-3281	*UNIVERSITIES AND COLLEGES-FURNITURE, EQUIPMENT, ETC.* **SEE** SCHOOLS — FURNITURE, EQUIPMENT, ETC.
LB3220	*UNIVERSITIES AND COLLEGES-LOCATION* **SEE** SCHOOL SITES
LB2350.5	*UNIVERSITIES AND COLLEGES-SELECTION* **SEE** COLLEGE, CHOICE OF
LB1778	*UNIVERSITIES AND COLLEGES-TEACHERS* **SEE** COLLEGE TEACHERS
LB2341	*UNIVERSITIES AND COLLEGES-TRUSTEES* **SEE** COLLEGE TRUSTEES
LC237	*UNIVERSITY AND COMMUNITY* **SEE** COMMUNITY AND COLLEGE
LC148	*UNIVERSITY ATTENDANCE* **SEE** COLLEGE ATTENDANCE
LB2331.5	UNIVERSITY COOPERATION
LB2381-2391	*UNIVERSITY DEGREES* **SEE** DEGREES, ACADEMIC
PN3175-3191	*UNIVERSITY DRAMA* **SEE** COLLEGE AND SCHOOL DRAMA / history and criticism
LC6201-6401	UNIVERSITY EXTENSION
LC6301-6401	UNIVERSITY EXTENSION / individual institutions
LC6254-6260	UNIVERSITY EXTENSION / other countries
LC6251-3	UNIVERSITY EXTENSION / u.s.
Z675.U5	*UNIVERSITY LIBRARIES* **SEE** LIBRARIES, UNIVERSITY AND COLLEGE
Z231.5.U6	UNIVERSITY PRESSES
BV4310	*UNIVERSITY SERMONS* **SEE** UNIVERSITIES AND COLLEGES — SERMONS
HV4175-4320	*UNIVERSITY SETTLEMENTS* **SEE** SOCIAL SETTLEMENTS
LB3220	*UNIVERSITY SITES* **SEE** SCHOOL SITES
LB1778	*UNIVERSITY TEACHERS* **SEE** COLLEGE TEACHERS
LB2331	*UNIVERSITY TEACHING* **SEE** COLLEGE TEACHING
LB2341	*UNIVERSITY TRUSTEES* **SEE** COLLEGE TRUSTEES
BT378.U4	UNJUST JUDGE (PARABLE)
BT378.U5	UNJUST STEWARD (PARABLE)
TS159	*UNLOADING* **SEE** LOADING AND UNLOADING
GC41	*UNMANNED FLOATING INSTRUMENT PLATFORMS* **SEE** OCEANOGRAPHIC BUOYS
HQ800	*UNMARRIED WOMEN* **SEE** SINGLE WOMEN
BT721	*UNPARDONABLE SIN* **SEE** SIN, UNPARDONABLE
DS422.C3	UNTOUCHABLES
BJ1420-1428	*UNTRUTHFULNESS* **SEE** TRUTHFULNESS AND FALSEHOOD / ethics
BL1120	UPANISHADS / brahmanism
PK3501-3581	UPANISHADS / vedic literature
QK100	UPAS
HD9999.U6-63	UPHOLSTERY TRADE / industry
HD4966.U7-72	UPHOLSTERY TRADE / labor
TT198	UPHOLSTERY TRADE / technology
NK3175-3296	UPHOLSTERY / art industries
TT198	UPHOLSTERY / mechanic trades
JF541-567	*UPPER CHAMBERS* **SEE** LEGISLATIVE BODIES — UPPER CHAMBERS
PM6714	*UPURUI LANGUAGE* **SEE** OYANA LANGUAGE
RC915	*URAEMIA* **SEE** UREMIA
PL1-489	URAL-ALTAIC LANGUAGES
DS17	URAL-ALTAIC TRIBES
PH	*URALIAN LANGUAGES* **SEE** FINNO-UGRIAN LANGUAGES
PM1-95	*URALIAN LANGUAGES* **SEE** HYPERBOREAN LANGUAGES
PL15-16	*URALIAN LANGUAGES* **SEE** SAMOYEDIC LANGUAGES
QE391.U65	URANINITE
TP245.U7	URANIUM — ISOTOPES / chemical technology
QD464.5.U	URANIUM — ISOTOPES / chemistry
TN799.U7	URANIUM — METALLURGY
QP913.U7	URANIUM — PHYSIOLOGICAL EFFECT
TP245.U7	*URANIUM ISOTOPES* **SEE** URANIUM — ISOTOPES / chemical technology
QD464.5.U	*URANIUM ISOTOPES* **SEE** URANIUM — ISOTOPES / chemistry
TN490.U7	URANIUM MINES AND MINING
TN490.U7	URANIUM ORES
TN757.U7	URANIUM STEEL
QD181.U7	URANIUM
QB387	URANUS (PLANET) — TABLES
QB681	URANUS (PLANET) / descriptive astronomy
QB387	URANUS (PLANET) / theoretical astronomy
DS432.O	*URAONS* **SEE** ORAONS
P959	*URARTAEAN LANGUAGE* **SEE** VANNIC LANGUAGE
P959	*URARTIC LANGUAGE* **SEE** VANNIC LANGUAGE
QP601	*URASE* **SEE** UREASE
QD401	URAZOLES
BV637	*URBAN CHURCHES* **SEE** CITY CHURCHES
BV637.5	*URBAN CLERGY* **SEE** CITY CLERGY
NA9000-9284	*URBAN DEVELOPMENT* **SEE** CITIES AND TOWNS — PLANNING
LC5101-5143	*URBAN EDUCATION* **SEE** EDUCATION, URBAN
HT361	*URBAN LIFE* **SEE** CITY AND TOWN LIFE
HT151-3	*URBAN LIFE* **SEE** CITY AND TOWN LIFE
BV637.5	*URBAN MINISTRY* **SEE** CITY CLERGY
HT101-381	*URBANISM* **SEE** CITIES AND TOWNS
HV6177	*URBANISM* **SEE** CITIES AND TOWNS / influence on crime
JS	*URBANISM* **SEE** CITIES AND TOWNS / local government
BV637	*URBANIZATION-RELIGIOUS ASPECTS* **SEE** CITY CHURCHES
PK1975-1987	URDU LANGUAGE
PK2030-58	URDU LITERATURE
QD315	UREA DERIVATIVES
QD315	UREA / chemistry
QP801.U7	UREA / physiological chemistry
QP601	UREASE
QK627	*UREDINALES* **SEE** RUSTS (FUNGI)
QK627	*UREDINEAE* **SEE** RUSTS (FUNGI)
RC915	UREMIA
RC900-901	URETERS — DISEASES
QL872	URETERS / comparative anatomy
QM408	URETERS / human anatomy
QD305.A2	URETHANES
RC892	URETHRA — DISEASES
RC892	URETHRA — STRICTURE
RD583	URETHRA — SURGERY
QL872	URETHRA / comparative anatomy
QM413	URETHRA / human anatomy
RD583	URETHROTOMY
QL696.A3	*URIA* **SEE** MURRES
PL45.S6	*URIANKHAI LANGUAGE* **SEE** SOYOT LANGUAGE
RM216-219	URIC ACID / diet
RC918.L7	URIC ACID / lithemia
RB147	URIC ACID / pathology
QP801.U7	URIC ACID / physiological chemistry
RB53	*URINALYSIS* **SEE** URINE — ANALYSIS AND PATHOLOGY

SF773	*URINALYSIS* **SEE** URINE — ANALYSIS AND PATHOLOGY / *veterinary medicine*
RC921.V4	*URINARY CALCULI* **SEE** CALCULI, URINARY
RD581	*URINARY CALCULI* **SEE** CALCULI, URINARY
RC900-923	URINARY ORGANS — DISEASES
RC901	URINARY ORGANS — RADIOGRAPHY
RD571-583	URINARY ORGANS — SURGERY
QL872	URINARY ORGANS / *comparative anatomy*
QM401-413	URINARY ORGANS / *human anatomy*
RD581	*URINARY ORGANS-CALCULI* **SEE** CALCULI, URINARY
RC921.V4	*URINARY ORGANS-CALCULI* **SEE** CALCULI, URINARY
RC901	*URINARY ORGANS-X-RAY EXAMINATION* **SEE** URINARY ORGANS — RADIOGRAPHY
RX351-6	URINARY ORGANS — DISEASES — — HOMEOPATHIC TREATMENT
QP211	*URINATION* **SEE** URINE — SECRETION
RB53	URINE — ANALYSIS AND PATHOLOGY
SF773	URINE — ANALYSIS AND PATHOLOGY / *veterinary medicine*
QR171	URINE — BACTERIOLOGY
QP211	URINE — FERMENTATION AND FERMENTS
RC918.U5	URINE — INCONTINENCE
RC918.U7	URINE — RETENTION
QP211	URINE — SECRETION
RC918.U8	URINE — SUPPRESSION
BL619.06	URINE DANCE
E99.Z9	URINE DANCE / *zuni indians*
QP211	URINE
PK2561-9	*URIYA LANGUAGE* **SEE** ORIYA LANGUAGE
DS432.08	*URIYAS* **SEE** ORIYAS
GT3335	URN BURIAL
NK3700-4657	URNS / *ceramics*
NK3845	URNS, ETRUSCAN / *ceramics*
NB110	URNS, ETRUSCAN / *sculpture*
QP211	UROBILIN
QL613	*UROCHORDATA* **SEE** TUNICATA
QL668.C2	URODELA
QP211	*UROFERRIC ACID* **SEE** UROFERRINIC ACID
QP211	UROFERRINIC ACID
RC901	*UROLOGIC ROENTGENOLOGY* **SEE** URINARY ORGANS — RADIOGRAPHY
RC874.7	UROLOGICAL NURSING
QL697	UROPYGIAL GLAND
BX4541-4	URSULINES
RL325	URTICARIA
F3341.T6	*URU INDIANS* **SEE** PUQUINA INDIANS / *bolivia*
F2230.2.P	*URU INDIANS* **SEE** PUQUINA INDIANS / *south america*
PM6714	*URUCUIANA LANGUAGE* **SEE** OYANA LANGUAGE
F2701-2799	URUGUAY — HISTORY
PQ8517	URUGUAYAN DRAMA / *collections*
PQ8513	URUGUAYAN DRAMA / *history*
PQ8510-8519	URUGUAYAN LITERATURE
PN5091-5	URUGUAYAN NEWSPAPERS / *history*
PN5091-5	URUGUAYAN PERIODICALS / *history*
PQ8516	URUGUAYAN POETRY / *collections*
PQ8512	URUGUAYAN POETRY / *history*
DS315	URUMIAH — MASSACRE, 1915 / *iran*
PL8595	*URUNYORO LANGUAGE* **SEE** NYORO LANGUAGE
BJ1801-2193	*USAGES* **SEE** ETIQUETTE
GT	*USAGES* **SEE** MANNERS AND CUSTOMS
QK495.G4	*USAMBARA VIOLETS* **SEE** AFRICAN VIOLETS / *botany*
SB413.A4	*USAMBARA VIOLETS* **SEE** AFRICAN VIOLETS / *culture*
DK878	*USBEGS* **SEE** UZBEGS / *bokhara*
DK855.4	*USBEGS* **SEE** UZBEGS / *russian turkestan*
DK861.U8	*USBEGS* **SEE** UZBEGS / *uzbekistan*
DB34.U	*USCOCKS* **SEE** USKOKS
HG9970.B85	*USE AND OCCUPANCY INSURANCE* **SEE** INSURANCE, BUSINESS INTERRUPTION
HJ5711-5721	USE TAX
HD9710	USED CAR TRADE
TL154	USED CARS
T-TX	*USEFUL ARTS* **SEE** INDUSTRIAL ARTS
T-TX	*USEFUL ARTS* **SEE** TECHNOLOGY
DT62.T6	USHABTI
DB34.U	USKOKS
TK7888	USM-1 COMPUTER
QA76.4	USM-1 COMPUTER
PM4478	USPANTECA LANGUAGE

HG1621-3	*USURY* **SEE** INTEREST AND USURY / *banking practice*
HB521-539	*USURY* **SEE** INTEREST AND USURY / *theory of interest*
HB521-549	USURY LAWS / *economic theory*
HG2052-2069	USURY LAWS / *money lending*
E99.U8	*UTA INDIANS* **SEE** UTE INDIANS
E99.U8	UTE INDIANS
PM2515	UTE LANGUAGE
GN446-7	*UTENSILS* **SEE** IMPLEMENTS, UTENSILS, ETC. / *primitive*
QM421	UTERUS — BLOOD-VESSELS / *human anatomy*
RC280.U8	UTERUS — CANCER
RG301-391	UTERUS — DISEASES
RG361	UTERUS — DISPLACEMENTS
RG361	UTERUS — RUPTURE
RG104	UTERUS — SURGERY
RG391	UTERUS — SURGERY / *excision*
RC280.U8	UTERUS — TUMORS
QL881	UTERUS / *comparative anatomy*
QM421	UTERUS / *human anatomy*
QP265	UTERUS / *physiology*
RG519-520	UTERUS, PREGNANT
RG711	*UTERUS-HEMORRHAGE* **SEE** HEMORRHAGE, UTERINE / *labor*
RG573	*UTERUS-HEMORRHAGE* **SEE** HEMORRHAGE, UTERINE / *pregnancy*
RG821	*UTERUS-HEMORRHAGE* **SEE** HEMORRHAGE, UTERINE / *puerperal state*
BX1939.I5	*UTI POSSIDETIS (CIVIL LAW)* **SEE** INTERDICT (CANON LAW)
B843	UTILITARIANISM
B851-4695	UTILITARIANISM / *local*
V880	*UTILITY BOATS, NAVAL* **SEE** U.S. — BOATS
HD201-5	*UTILITY, FINAL* **SEE** MARGINAL UTILITY
HD201-5	*UTILITY, MARGINAL* **SEE** MARGINAL UTILITY
TP995	*UTILIZATION OF WASTE* **SEE** WASTE PRODUCTS
PM4231	*UTLATECA LANGUAGE* **SEE** QUICHE LANGUAGE
E99.U85	UTO-AZTECAN INDIANS
PM4479	UTO-AZTECAN LANGUAGES
PM2517	UTO-AZTECAN LANGUAGES
HX806-811	UTOPIAS
D283.5	UTRECHT, TREATY OF, 1713
D283.5	UTRECHT, TREATY OF, 1714
DH195	UTRECHT, UNION OF, 1579
JN5737	UTRECHT, UNION OF, 1579 / *constitutional history*
RS165.U9	UVA-URSI / *pharmacy*
RM666.U9	UVA-URSI / *therapeutics*
QM306	UVULA
PL8758	UWANA LANGUAGE
PL55.U8	*UZBEG LANGUAGE* **SEE** UZBEK LANGUAGE
DK878	UZBEGS / *bokhara*
DK855.4	UZBEGS / *russian turkestan*
DK861.U8	UZBEGS / *uzbekistan*
PL55.J3	*UZBEK LANGUAGE (OLD)* **SEE** JAGATAIC LANGUAGE
PL55.U8	UZBEK LANGUAGE
PL55.U8	UZBEK PHILOLOGY
BL604.V2	*V FOR VICTORY* **SEE** V SYMBOL
BL604.V2	V SYMBOL
HD1519	*VACANT-LOT CULTIVATION* **SEE** WORKING-MEN'S GARDENS
BV1585	*VACATION BIBLE SCHOOLS* **SEE** VACATION SCHOOLS, RELIGIOUS
BV1585	*VACATION CHURCH SCHOOLS* **SEE** VACATION SCHOOLS, RELIGIOUS
TH4835	*VACATION HOUSES* **SEE** SUMMER HOMES
LC5701-5760	VACATION SCHOOLS
BV1585	VACATION SCHOOLS, RELIGIOUS
HD5261	*VACATIONS WITH PAY* **SEE** VACATIONS, EMPLOYEE
LB3041	VACATIONS / *school*
HD5261	VACATIONS, EMPLOYEE
RM276	*VACCINA* **SEE** VACCINIA
RM276	*VACCINE LYMPH* **SEE** VACCINIA
RM281	VACCINES
QR189	VACCINES
RM276	VACCINIA
TH7692-8	VACUUM CLEANING
TJ940	*VACUUM IN INDUSTRY* **SEE** VACUUM TECHNOLOGY
TS695	*VACUUM METALLIZING* **SEE** VAPOR-PLATING
QC107	VACUUM MICROBALANCE
TJ940	VACUUM TECHNOLOGY

QC166	VACUUM-GAGES
TJ955	VACUUM-PUMPS
QC544.V3	*VACUUM-TUBE AMPLIFIERS* **SEE** AMPLIFIERS, VACUUM-TUBE
TK7872.O	*VACUUM-TUBE OSCILLATORS* **SEE** OSCILLATORS, VACUUM-TUBE / *electronics*
TK6565.O7	*VACUUM-TUBE OSCILLATORS* **SEE** OSCILLATORS, VACUUM-TUBE / *radio*
QC544.V3	VACUUM-TUBES / *electric apparatus*
TK7872.V3	VACUUM-TUBES / *electronics*
QC476	VACUUM-TUBES / *radiation*
TK6565.V3	VACUUM-TUBES / *radio*
TK5865	VACUUM-TUBES / *wireless telegraph*
QC166	VACUUM
TJ940	*VACUUM-INDUSTRIAL APPLICATIONS* **SEE** VACUUM TECHNOLOGY
AG103-191	*VADE-MECUMS, ETC.* **SEE** HANDBOOKS, VADE-MECUMS, ETC.
HV4480-4630	*VAGABONDAGE* **SEE** VAGRANCY
K	*VAGABONDAGE* **SEE** VAGRANCY
HV6245-8	*VAGABONDS* **SEE** ROGUES AND VAGABONDS / *criminals*
CT9980-9981	*VAGABONDS* **SEE** ROGUES AND VAGABONDS / *etc.*
HV4480-4630	*VAGABONDS* **SEE** ROGUES AND VAGABONDS / *etc.*
GT6450-6699	*VAGABONDS* **SEE** ROGUES AND VAGABONDS / *manners and customs*
HV4480-4630	*VAGABONDS* **SEE** TRAMPS
PA8065.S8	*VAGANTES* **SEE** GOLIARDS / *latin verse*
PA8065.S8	*VAGI SCHOLARES* **SEE** GOLIARDS / *latin verse*
RG268-272	VAGINA — DISEASES
QL881	VAGINA / *comparative anatomy*
QM421	VAGINA / *human anatomy*
HV4480-4630	VAGRANCY
K	VAGRANCY
HV4480-4630	*VAGRANTS* **SEE** TRAMPS
DT630.5.V2	*VAI (AFRICAN TRIBE)* **SEE** VEI (AFRICAN TRIBE)
B132.V2	VAISESIKA
BL1245.V3	VAISHNAVISM
DU590	VAITUPUANS
E241.V14	VALCOUR ISLAND, BATTLE OF, 1776
BX4872-4883	*VALDENSES* **SEE** WALDENSES
Q115	VALDIVIA EXPEDITION
GN654	*VALEGAS* **SEE** WAREGAS / *anthropology*
DT650	*VALEGAS* **SEE** WAREGAS / *history*
QD469	VALENCE (THEORETICAL CHEMISTRY)
D278.V	VALENCIENNES, FRANCE — SIEGE, 1677 / *dutch wars*
DC127.6	VALENCIENNES, FRANCE — SIEGE, 1677 / *french military history*
DC222.V15	VALENCIENNES, FRANCE — SIEGE, 1793
QD469	*VALENCY* **SEE** VALENCE (THEORETICAL CHEMISTRY)
BT1490	VALENTINIANS
BL1245.V	VALLABHACHARS
GB561-8	VALLEYS
BX4180.V3	VALLOMBROSANS
BX4180.V3	*VALLOMBROSIANS* **SEE** VALLOMBROSANS
PL6621.V3	VALMAN LANGUAGE
DC222.V2	VALMY, BATTLE OF, 1792
F3098	VALPARAISO, BATTLE OF, 1891
HD1393	*VALUATION OF LAND* **SEE** FARMS — VALUATION
HD2765	*VALUATION OF PUBLIC UTILITIES* **SEE** PUBLIC UTILITIES — VALUATION
HF5681.V3	VALUATION / *accounting*
HG4028.V3	VALUATION / *corporation finance*
HJ6670	VALUATION / *customs administration*
TA178	VALUATION / *engineering*
HD2765	VALUATION / *public service corporations*
HD1387	VALUATION / *real estate*
HB201-5	VALUE / *economic theory*
HG223	VALUE / *standard of value*
BD232	*VALUES* **SEE** WORTH / *metaphysics*
BD430-435	*VALUES* **SEE** WORTH / *philosophy of life*
BF778	*VALUES* **SEE** WORTH / *psychology*
ML960-963	*VALVE TRUMPET* **SEE** TRUMPET / *history and construction*
GT5020	*VALVE TRUMPET* **SEE** TRUMPET / *manners and customs*
TJ548.C8	*VALVE-GEARS* **SEE** CORLISS VALVE-GEAR
TJ665	*VALVE-GEARS* **SEE** LOCOMOTIVES — VALVE-GEARS
TJ547-8	*VALVE-GEARS* **SEE** STEAM-ENGINES — VALVE-GEARS
TJ665	*VALVE-GEARS* **SEE** WALSCHAERT VALVE-GEAR

TJ432	VALVES — CATALOGS / *steam-valves*
TJ430-433	VALVES / *steam-valves*
TK2798	*VALVES, ELECTRIC* **SEE** ELECTRIC CURRENT RECTIFIERS
RC685.V2	*VALVULAR DISEASES* **SEE** HEART — VALVES — — DISEASES
TL686.D4	VAMPIRE (TURBOJET FIGHTER PLANES)
QL737.C5	VAMPIRE BATS
GR830	VAMPIRES / *folk-lore*
BF1556	VAMPIRES / *occult sciences*
QB723.V	VAN BIESBROECK'S COMET
GV1295.B	*VAN JOHN (GAME)* **SEE** BLACKJACK (GAME)
QD181.V2	VANADATES
TN799.V	VANADIUM — METALLURGY
TN757.V3	VANADIUM STEEL
QD181.V2	VANADIUM
PD1270	VANDAL LANGUAGE
D139	VANDALS
DT171	VANDALS / *northern africa*
PL8110.C	*VANDAU LANGUAGE* **SEE** CHINDAU LANGUAGE
TJ267.B5	*VANES (MECHANICAL ENGINEERING)* **SEE** BLADES
NK9585	VANES
TL796.5.U6V3	*VANGUARD PROJECT* **SEE** PROJECT VANGUARD
SB307.V2	VANILLA
QD341.A6	VANILLIN
QL88	*VANISHING ANIMALS* **SEE** RARE ANIMALS
BJ1535.P9	*VANITY* **SEE** PRIDE AND VANITY
P959	*VANNIC INSCRIPTIONS* **SEE** CUNEIFORM INSCRIPTIONS, VANNIC
P959	VANNIC LANGUAGE
E99.V	*VANTA KUTCHIN INDIANS* **SEE** VUNTAKUTCHIN INDIANS
TP363	*VAPOR CONDENSERS* **SEE** CONDENSERS (VAPORS AND GASES)
TS213	VAPOR DEGREASING
QD533	VAPOR DENSITY
TS695	*VAPOR DEPOSITION* **SEE** VAPOR-PLATING
QC304	VAPOR PRESSURE
QC309	VAPOR PRESSURE / *solids*
TL557.C7	*VAPOR TRAILS* **SEE** CONDENSATION TRAILS
RM822.V2	*VAPOR-BATHS* **SEE** BATHS, VAPOR
TS695	*VAPOR-PHASE DEPOSITION* **SEE** VAPOR-PLATING
TS695	VAPOR-PLATING
QC304	VAPORIZATION, HEATS OF
QC161-8	VAPORS / *physics*
QC304	VAPORS / *saturated*
F596	*VAQUEROS* **SEE** COWBOYS
TL969.O	*VAR* **SEE** OMNIRANGE SYSTEM
DK70-73	VARANGIANS / *medieval russia*
DL65	VARANGIANS / *northmen*
TK7872.A5	*VARIABLE PARAMETER AMPLIFIERS* **SEE** PARAMETRIC AMPLIFIERS
QB835-7	*VARIABLE STARS* **SEE** STARS, VARIABLE
QB895	*VARIABLE STARS* **SEE** STARS, VARIABLE / *spectra*
QH401-411	VARIATION (BIOLOGY)
ML3845	VARIATION (MUSIC)
QB237	*VARIATION OF LATITUDE* **SEE** LATITUDE VARIATION
VK577	*VARIATION OF THE COMPASS* **SEE** COMPASS
QC849	*VARIATION OF THE COMPASS* **SEE** COMPASS / *deviation*
M145	VARIATIONS (BAGPIPE)
M1203	VARIATIONS (BAND)
M1254	VARIATIONS (BAND), ARRANGED — SCORES AND PARTS
M1254	VARIATIONS (BAND), ARRANGED
M555-7	VARIATIONS (BASSOON, CLARINET, FLUTE, HORN, OBOE)
M655-7	VARIATIONS (BASSOON, CLARINET, FLUTE, HORN, OBOE, TRUMPET)
M960-962	VARIATIONS (BASSOON, CLARINET, FLUTE, HORN, 2 VIOLINS, VIOLA, VIOLONCELLO, DOUBLE BASS)
M860-862	VARIATIONS (BASSOON, CLARINET, FLUTE, HORN, 2 VIOLINS, VIOLA, VIOLONCELLO)
M1040	VARIATIONS (BASSOON, CLARINET, FLUTE, OBOE WITH CHAMBER ORCHESTRA) — SCORES
M1040-1041	VARIATIONS (BASSOON, CLARINET, FLUTE, OBOE WITH CHAMBER ORCHESTRA)
M455-7	VARIATIONS (BASSOON, CLARINET, FLUTE, OBOE)
M458-9	VARIATIONS (BASSOON, CLARINET, FLUTE, OBOE), ARRANGED

RJ406.C4	*VARICELLA* **SEE** CHICKEN-POX
RC898	VARICOCELE
RC695	*VARICOSE VEINS* **SEE** VARIX
QH406	VARIEGATION
HF5461-5	VARIETY STORES
PN1960-1969	*VARIETY-THEATERS* **SEE** MUSIC-HALLS (VARIETY-THEATERS, CABARETS, ETC.)
PN6120.V3	*VARIETY-THEATERS* **SEE** VAUDEVILLE / collections
PN1960-1969	*VARIETY-THEATERS* **SEE** VAUDEVILLE / history and criticism
PN2219.V3	*VARIETY-THEATERS* **SEE** VAUDEVILLE / theaters
RC183	*VARIOLA* **SEE** SMALLPOX
RC183	*VARIOLOID* **SEE** SMALLPOX
QE391.V	VARISCITE
RC695	VARIX
DS432.W	*VARLIS* **SEE** WARLIS
DR498	VARNA, BATTLE OF, 1444
TP938	VARNISH AND VARNISHING — CATALOGS
TP938	VARNISH AND VARNISHING / varnish
TT340	VARNISH AND VARNISHING / varnishing
TP934-7	*VARNISH PAINTS* **SEE** PAINT / manufacture
TP938	*VARNISH PAINTS* **SEE** VARNISH AND VARNISHING / varnish
TT340	*VARNISH PAINTS* **SEE** VARNISH AND VARNISHING / varnishing
TC175	*VARVE* **SEE** SILT / hydraulics
TD395	*VARVE* **SEE** SILT / reservoirs
QE581	*VARVE* **SEE** SILT / sedimentation
QK520-532	*VASCULAR CRYPTOGAMS* **SEE** PTERIDOPHYTA
RC691-700	*VASCULAR DISEASES* **SEE** BLOOD-VESSELS — DISEASES
RC666-701	*VASCULAR DISEASES* **SEE** CARDIOVASCULAR SYSTEM — DISEASES
RC694	*VASCULAR DISEASES* **SEE** PERIPHERAL VASCULAR DISEASES
QK	*VASCULAR PLANTS* **SEE** BOTANY
QL835	*VASCULAR SYSTEM* **SEE** BLOOD-VESSELS / comparative anatomy
QM191	*VASCULAR SYSTEM* **SEE** BLOOD-VESSELS / human anatomy
QL835-841	*VASCULAR SYSTEM* **SEE** CARDIOVASCULAR SYSTEM / comparative anatomy
QM178-197	*VASCULAR SYSTEM* **SEE** CARDIOVASCULAR SYSTEM / human anatomy
NK4620-4659	VASE-PAINTING
QP90	VASECTOMY / rejuvenation
QP255	VASECTOMY / reproduction
RD571	VASECTOMY / surgery
NK4624	VASES — PRIVATE COLLECTIONS
NK4620-4657	VASES / ceramics
NK7220	VASES / gold
NK4623-4	VASES / museums collections
NK7230	VASES / silver
NA2800	VASES, ACOUSTIC
QP111	*VASOMOTOR NERVOUS SYSTEM* **SEE** NERVOUS SYSTEM, VASOMOTOR / physiology
GN549.B3	*VASQUES* **SEE** BASQUES / ethnology
DC611.B31-322	*VASQUES* **SEE** BASQUES / french history
DP302.B46	*VASQUES* **SEE** BASQUES / spanish history
PL6231	*VATE LANGUAGE* **SEE** EFATE LANGUAGE
BX830 1869	VATICAN COUNCIL, 1869-1870
PH561-9	*VATJAN LANGUAGE* **SEE** VOTISH LANGUAGE
DK34.V	*VATJANS* **SEE** VOTES (PEOPLE)
DC114.3	VAUCELLES, TRUCE OF, 1556
PN6120.V3	VAUDEVILLE / collections
PN1960-1969	VAUDEVILLE / history and criticism
PN2219.V3	VAUDEVILLE / theaters
BX4872-4883	*VAUDOIS* **SEE** WALDENSES
PC3147.V3	VAUDOIS DIALECT
PC3147.V3	VAUDOIS POETRY
GV517	VAULTING-HORSE
GV1079-1080	VAULTING
NA6120-6199	*VAULTS (SEPULCHRAL)* **SEE** TOMBS / architecture
NA2880	VAULTS / architecture
TH2150-2160	VAULTS / building
TA357	VAULTS / engineering mechanics
PL3801.V2	VAYU DIALECT
TX556.V	VEAL / food value
TS1975	VEAL / meat inspection
QA261	VECTOR ANALYSIS
RC683.5.E5	VECTORCARDIOGRAPHY
B132.V3	VEDANTA
DS425	VEDAS — GEOGRAPHY
PK3000-3581	VEDAS
BL1115	VEDAS / hinduism
DS489.2	VEDDAHS
V880	VEDETTE BOATS
DS423-5	*VEDIC CIVILIZATION* **SEE** CIVILIZATION, HINDU
BL1216-1225	*VEDIC GODS* **SEE** GODS, VEDIC
PK201-379	VEDIC LANGUAGE
PK3000-3581	VEDIC LITERATURE / collections
PK2911	VEDIC LITERATURE / history
QK641-707	*VEGETABLE ANATOMY* **SEE** BOTANY — ANATOMY
QK665	*VEGETABLE EMBRYOLOGY* **SEE** BOTANY — EMBRYOLOGY
SB320-353	VEGETABLE GARDENING
QK641-707	*VEGETABLE HISTOLOGY* **SEE** BOTANY — ANATOMY
QH423	*VEGETABLE HYBRIDIZATION* **SEE** HYBRIDIZATION, VEGETABLE
SB317.I	*VEGETABLE IVORY* **SEE** IVORY-NUT / vegetable ivory
TX391	VEGETABLE JUICES
QK	*VEGETABLE KINGDOM* **SEE** BOTANY
QK	*VEGETABLE KINGDOM* **SEE** PLANTS
GR780-790	*VEGETABLE KINGDOM* **SEE** PLANTS / folk-lore
GT5150	*VEGETABLE KINGDOM* **SEE** PLANTS / manners and customs
S598	*VEGETABLE MOLD* **SEE** HUMUS
S590-599	*VEGETABLE MOLD* **SEE** SOILS
QD416	*VEGETABLE OILS* **SEE** ESSENCES AND ESSENTIAL OILS / chemistry
TP958	*VEGETABLE OILS* **SEE** ESSENCES AND ESSENTIAL OILS / chemical technology
TP670-692	*VEGETABLE OILS* **SEE** OIL INDUSTRIES
HD9490	*VEGETABLE OILS* **SEE** OIL INDUSTRIES / economics
TP670-695	*VEGETABLE OILS* **SEE** OILS AND FATS
SB211.S	*VEGETABLE OYSTER* **SEE** SALSIFY
SB599-791	*VEGETABLE PATHOLOGY* **SEE** PLANT DISEASES
SB621-999	VEGETABLES — DISEASES AND PESTS
SB608.T81	VEGETABLES — DISEASES AND PESTS / truck crops
SB320-353	VEGETABLES
HD9220-9235	VEGETABLES / trade
SB127	*VEGETABLES, FORCING OF* **SEE** FORCING (PLANTS)
TP493.5	VEGETABLES, FROZEN
TX392	VEGETARIANISM
TX837	VEGETARIANISM / cookery
RM236	VEGETARIANISM / therapeutics
QM471	*VEGETATIVE NERVOUS SYSTEM* **SEE** NERVOUS SYSTEM, AUTONOMIC / human anatomy
QL939	*VEGETATIVE NERVOUS SYSTEM* **SEE** NERVOUS SYSTEM, AUTONOMIC / comparative anatomy
QP368	*VEGETATIVE NERVOUS SYSTEM* **SEE** NERVOUS SYSTEM, AUTONOMIC / physiology
PC890	VEGLIOTE DIALECT
HJ5780.V4	VEHICLES — TAXATION
GT5280	VEHICLES / manners and customs
TK7882.M6	*VEHICLES-COMMUNICATION SYSTEMS* **SEE** MOBILE COMMUNICATION SYSTEMS
TK7882.M6	*VEHICULAR COMMUNICATION SYSTEMS* **SEE** MOBILE COMMUNICATION SYSTEMS
JN3269	*VEHMGERICHTE* **SEE** FEHMIC COURTS
DT630.5.V2	VEI (AFRICAN TRIBE)
PL8761	VEI LANGUAGE
GT2350	VEILS
RC695-7	VEINS — DISEASES
RD33	VEINS — LIGATURE
QL835	VEINS / comparative anatomy
QM191	VEINS / human anatomy
RC695	*VEINS, VARICOSE* **SEE** VARIX
PM7241	*VEJOSO LANGUAGE* **SEE** VEJOZ LANGUAGE
PM7241	VEJOZ LANGUAGE
DS451	*VELALAS* **SEE** VELLALAS
DS451	*VELIR* **SEE** VELLALAS
DS451	VELLALAS
D293.5.V4	VELLETRI, BATTLE OF, 1744
DG553.5.V4	VELLETRI, BATTLE OF, 1849
Z112	*VELLUM* **SEE** PARCHMENT
Z112	*VELLUM* **SEE** PARCHMENT

Z1030	VELLUM PRINTED BOOKS
GV1041-1059	*VELOCIPEDES* **SEE** BICYCLES AND TRICYCLES / sports and amusements
TL400-445	*VELOCIPEDES* **SEE** BICYCLES AND TRICYCLES / technology
HD9999.B4-43	*VELOCIPEDES* **SEE** BICYCLES AND TRICYCLES / trade
QD501	*VELOCITY OF CHEMICAL REACTION* **SEE** CHEMICAL REACTION, RATE OF
QC407	*VELOCITY OF LIGHT* **SEE** LIGHT — SPEED
QC233	*VELOCITY OF SOUND* **SEE** SOUND — SPEED
DS451	*VELS* **SEE** VELLALAS
PM8937	VELTLANG (ARTIFICIAL LANGUAGE)
SB205.V	VELVET-BEAN
TS1675	VELVET
QL835	VENA CAVA / comparative anatomy
QM191	VENA CAVA / human anatomy
PL8771	VENDA LANGUAGE
DC218	VENDEAN WAR, 1793-1800
HV6441-6453	VENDETTA
GN495	VENDETTA / primitive
TJ1560	VENDING MACHINES
HF5476	*VENDUES* **SEE** AUCTIONS
D147	VENEDI
TS870	VENEERS AND VENEERING
BX2310.C7	*VENERATION OF THE CROSS* **SEE** CROSSES — CULTUS
RV286.V4	VENEREAL DISEASES — ECLECTIC TREATMENT
RX226.V4	VENEREAL DISEASES — HOMEOPATHIC TREATMENT
RC201-3	VENEREAL DISEASES — HOSPITALS
HQ101-440	VENEREAL DISEASES — PREVENTION / prostitution
RA644.V4	VENEREAL DISEASES — PREVENTION / public health
RC200-203	VENEREAL DISEASES
RM182	*VENESECTION* **SEE** BLOODLETTING
D147	*VENETI* **SEE** VENEDI
TS2301.W5	*VENETIAN BLINDS* **SEE** WINDOW-SHADES
PA2395	VENETIC LANGUAGE
F2301-2349	VENEZUELA — HISTORY
PQ8545	VENEZUELAN BALLADS AND SONGS
PQ8546	VENEZUELAN FICTION / collections
PQ8542	VENEZUELAN FICTION / history
PQ8530-8549	VENEZUELAN LITERATURE
PN5102	VENEZUELAN NEWSPAPERS / history
PN5102	VENEZUELAN PERIODICALS / history
PQ8544	VENEZUELAN POETRY / collections
PQ8540	VENEZUELAN POETRY / history
BV4627.R4	*VENGEANCE* **SEE** REVENGE / theology
BV4625.6	*VENIAL SIN* **SEE** SIN, VENIAL
DG670-679	VENICE — HISTORY
QP941	VENOM — PHYSIOLOGICAL EFFECT
RM666.V35	VENOM — THERAPEUTIC USE
QP235	VENOM / secretion
TH7081-4	VENTILATION — LAWS AND REGULATIONS
TH7647-7685	VENTILATION
TH7683.D8	*VENTILATION-DUCTS* **SEE** AIR DUCTS
GV1557	VENTRILOQUISM
QB621	VENUS (PLANET) — DIAMETERS
QB775	VENUS (PLANET) — SPECTRA
QB372	VENUS (PLANET) — TABLES
QB621	VENUS (PLANET) / descriptive astronomy
QB372	VENUS (PLANET) / theoretical astronomy
QB509-513	VENUS (PLANET), TRANSIT OF
DK34.V	VEPS
DK34.V	*VEPSE* **SEE** VEPS
PH541-9	*VEPSIAN LANGUAGE* **SEE** VEPSISH LANGUAGE
DK34.V	*VEPSIANS* **SEE** VEPS
PH541-9	VEPSISH LANGUAGE
D1815.V3	VER SACRUM
F1234	VERA CRUZ, MEXICO (CITY) — HISTORY — — AMERICAN OCCUPATION, 1914
F1232	VERA CRUZ, MEXICO (CITY) — HISTORY — — FRENCH INVASION, 1838-1839
E406.V4	VERA CRUZ, MEXICO (CITY) — HISTORY — — SURRENDER, 1847
QP921.V5	VERATRINE / pharmacology
RM666.V4	VERATRINE / therapeutics
P281	*VERB* **SEE** GRAMMAR, COMPARATIVE AND GENERAL — VERB
P259	*VERB* **SEE** GRAMMAR, COMPARATIVE AND GENERAL — VERB
BF455	VERBAL BEHAVIOR
SB608.V	VERBENA BUD-MOTH
D545.V25	VERDUN, BATTLE OF, 1914
D545.V3	VERDUN, BATTLE OF, 1916
D756.5.V3	VERDUN, BATTLE OF, 1940
DC309.V4	VERDUN, FRANCE — SIEGE, 1870
DC75	VERDUN, TREATY OF, 843
QL386-394	*VERMES* **SEE** WORMS
TS2157	*VERMICELLI* **SEE** MACARONI / manufacture
QL863	*VERMIFORM APPENDIX* **SEE** APPENDIX (ANATOMY) / comparative anatomy
QM345	*VERMIFORM APPENDIX* **SEE** APPENDIX (ANATOMY) / human anatomy
RM635	*VERMIFUGES* **SEE** ANTHELMINTICS
TX325	*VERMIN* **SEE** HOUSEHOLD PESTS
SB599-1100	*VERMIN* **SEE** PESTS / agriculture
TX325	*VERMIN* **SEE** PESTS / domestic economy
F46-60	VERMONT — HISTORY
E533	VERMONT — HISTORY — — CIVIL WAR
E263.V5	VERMONT — HISTORY — — REVOLUTION
E359.5.V3	VERMONT — HISTORY — — WAR OF 1812
TJ1166	VERNIERS / machine-shop practice
QA77	VERNIERS / mathematics
DG572	VERONA TRIAL, 1943-1944
PN6110.V4	*VERS DE SOCIETE* **SEE** SOCIETY VERSE
PN1451	*VERS DE SOCIETE* **SEE** SOCIETY VERSE
PS593.V4	*VERS DE SOCIETE* **SEE** SOCIETY VERSE / american
PR1195.V3	*VERS DE SOCIETE* **SEE** SOCIETY VERSE / english
PN1059.F	*VERS LIBRE* **SEE** FREE VERSE
D643.A2-7	VERSAILLES, TREATY OF, JUNE 28, 1919 (GERMANY)
D295	VERSAILLES, TREATY OF, 1783
PN1031-1055	VERSIFICATION
RG741	VERSION (OBSTETRICS)
QL821	VERTEBRAE / comparative anatomy
QM111	VERTEBRAE / human anatomy
QL821	VERTEBRAE, CERVICAL
QM111	VERTEBRAE, CERVICAL
QL821	*VERTEBRAL COLUMN* **SEE** SPINE / comparative anatomy
QM111	*VERTEBRAL COLUMN* **SEE** SPINE / human anatomy
QL801-950	VERTEBRATES — ANATOMY
QL605-739	VERTEBRATES
QL841-899	VERTEBRATES, FOSSIL
QB103	VERTICAL CIRCLE
Z43	*VERTICAL PENMANSHIP* **SEE** PENMANSHIP, VERTICAL
M2151	VESPERALS (MUSIC)
DG867.3	*VESPERS, SICILIAN, 1282* **SEE** SICILIAN VESPERS, 1282
QL737.C5	*VESPERTILIO* **SEE** BATS
VK	*VESSELS (SHIPS)* **SEE** SHIPS / navigation
GN440.1	*VESSELS (SHIPS)* **SEE** SHIPS / primitive
VM	*VESSELS (SHIPS)* **SEE** SHIPS / ship-building
GN446-7	*VESSELS (UTENSILS)* **SEE** IMPLEMENTS, UTENSILS, ETC. / primitive
V799-800	*VESSELS, ARMORED* **SEE** ARMORED VESSELS
DG123	VESTALS / roman antiquities
BL815.V4	VESTALS / roman religion
QL948	*VESTIBULAR APPARATUS* **SEE** LABYRINTH (EAR) / comparative anatomy
QM507	*VESTIBULAR APPARATUS* **SEE** LABYRINTH (EAR) / human anatomy
QP461	*VESTIBULAR APPARATUS* **SEE** LABYRINTH (EAR) / physiology
HF5549.5.T7	*VESTIBULE SCHOOLS* **SEE** EMPLOYEES, TRAINING OF
T58	*VESTIBULE SCHOOLS* **SEE** EMPLOYEES, TRAINING OF
QH315	VESTIGIAL ORGANS
BV167	*VESTMENTS* **SEE** CHURCH VESTMENTS
BX1925	*VESTMENTS* **SEE** CHURCH VESTMENTS / catholic church
BX5180	*VESTMENTS* **SEE** CHURCH VESTMENTS / church of england
BX2790	*VESTMENTS* **SEE** CHURCH VESTMENTS / monastic
TT615	VESTS / tailoring
QE391.V55	VESUVIANITE
QE523.V5	VESUVIUS, ERUPTION OF, 1906
SB945.V45	VETCH BRUCHID
SB945.V45	*VETCH WEEVIL* **SEE** VETCH BRUCHID
SB205.V58	VETCH
UB356-9	VETERANS — EDUCATION

UB356-9	VETERANS — EMPLOYMENT
UB368-9.5	VETERANS — MEDICAL CARE
UB356-9	VETERANS / *military science*
UB360-366	VETERANS, DISABLED
UB400-405	*VETERANS' BENEFITS* **SEE** PENSIONS, MILITARY / *army*
UB370-375	*VETERANS' BENEFITS* **SEE** PENSIONS, MILITARY / *army*
VB280-285	*VETERANS' BENEFITS* **SEE** PENSIONS, MILITARY / *navy*
VB340-345	*VETERANS' BENEFITS* **SEE** PENSIONS, MILITARY / *navy*
E255	*VETERANS' BENEFITS* **SEE** PENSIONS, MILITARY / *pension rolls*
UB356-9	*VETERANS' BENEFITS* **SEE** VETERANS — EDUCATION
UB356-9	*VETERANS' BENEFITS* **SEE** VETERANS — EMPLOYMENT
UB368-9.5	*VETERANS' BENEFITS* **SEE** VETERANS — MEDICAL CARE
UB380-385	*VETERANS' HOMES* **SEE** SOLDIERS' HOMES
UH460-485	*VETERANS' HOSPITALS* **SEE** HOSPITALS, MILITARY
UB370-375	*VETERANS' PENSIONS* **SEE** PENSIONS, MILITARY / *army*
UB400-405	*VETERANS' PENSIONS* **SEE** PENSIONS, MILITARY / *army*
VB340-345	*VETERANS' PENSIONS* **SEE** PENSIONS, MILITARY / *navy*
VB280-285	*VETERANS' PENSIONS* **SEE** PENSIONS, MILITARY / *navy*
E255	*VETERANS' PENSIONS* **SEE** PENSIONS, MILITARY / *pension rolls*
UB356-9	*VETERANS' RIGHTS* **SEE** VETERANS — EDUCATION
UB356-9	*VETERANS' RIGHTS* **SEE** VETERANS — EMPLOYMENT
UB368-9.5	*VETERANS' RIGHTS* **SEE** VETERANS — MEDICAL CARE
SF612-613	VETERINARIANS — CORRESPONDENCE, REMINISCENCES, ETC.
SF600-780	VETERINARIANS
SF761-7	VETERINARY ANATOMY
QR49	VETERINARY BACTERIOLOGY
SF775-9	VETERINARY COLLEGES
SF867	VETERINARY DENTISTRY
SF901	VETERINARY DERMATOLOGY
SF771-4	*VETERINARY DIAGNOSIS* **SEE** VETERINARY MEDICINE — DIAGNOSIS
SF761	VETERINARY EMBRYOLOGY
SF761	VETERINARY HISTOLOGY
SF757	VETERINARY HYGIENE
SF913	VETERINARY INSTRUMENTS AND APPARATUS
SF780	VETERINARY JURISPRUDENCE
SF915-919	VETERINARY MATERIA MEDICA AND PHARMACY
SF771-4	VETERINARY MEDICINE — DIAGNOSIS
SF743	VETERINARY MEDICINE — EARLY WORKS TO 1800
SF779.5	VETERINARY MEDICINE AS A PROFESSION
SF600-998	VETERINARY MEDICINE
SF780	*VETERINARY MEDICINE, FORENSIC* **SEE** VETERINARY JURISPRUDENCE
SF746	VETERINARY MEDICINE, HOMEOPATHIC
SF887	VETERINARY OBSTETRICS
SF891	VETERINARY OPHTHALMOLOGY
SF769	VETERINARY PATHOLOGY
SF998	*VETERINARY QUARANTINE* **SEE** QUARANTINE, VETERINARY
SF621-723	*VETERINARY QUARANTINE* **SEE** QUARANTINE, VETERINARY / *by country*
SF757.8	VETERINARY RADIOLOGY
UH650-655	VETERINARY SERVICE, MILITARY
SF600-780	*VETERINARY SURGEONS* **SEE** VETERINARIANS
SF911-913	VETERINARY SURGERY
JF261	VETO
JK2454	VETO / *state*
JK586	VETO / *u.s. federal*
TF280-284	VIADUCTS / *railroad*
DL743.V	VIBORG, BATTLE OF, 1710
M284-5	VIBRAPHONE AND PIANO MUSIC (JAZZ)
M284-5	VIBRAPHONE AND PIANO MUSIC
M284-5	*VIBRAPHONE AND PIANO MUSIC, ARRANGED (JAZZ)* **SEE** VIBRAPHONE AND PIANO MUSIC (JAZZ)
M175.X6	VIBRAPHONE MUSIC
ML1040	VIBRAPHONE
TA255	VIBRATION — TABLES, ETC.
TG350	VIBRATION — TABLES, ETC. / *girders*
TL574.V5	VIBRATION (AERONAUTICS)
VM739	VIBRATION (MARINE ENGINEERING)
RM721	VIBRATION (THERAPEUTICS)
QA935	VIBRATION / *analytic mechanics*
QC241	VIBRATION / *etc.*
QC235	VIBRATION / *plates*
QC231	VIBRATION / *sound*
ML3817	VIBRATO
MT271	VIBRATO / *violin*
MT882	VIBRATO / *voice*
ML755	VIBRATOR (FOR BOWED INSTRUMENTS)
TK6565.T7	VIBRATOR TRANSFORMERS
BV4381	*VICARAGES (BUILDINGS)* **SEE** PARSONAGES
BX1910	VICARS APOSTOLIC
BX1939.V52	VICARS CAPITULAR / *canon law*
BX1910	VICARS-GENERAL
BX1939.V5	VICARS-GENERAL / *canon law*
BJ1534-5	VICE / *ethics*
BV4625-7	VICE / *moral theology*
JV431-8	VICEROYALTY / *colonial*
BJ1534-5	VICES / *conduct of life*
BV4625-7	VICES / *moral theology*
UF620.V4	VICKERS MACHINE-GUN
E475.27	VICKSBURG, MISS. — SIEGE, 1863
PL5581-4	*VICOL LANGUAGE* **SEE** BIKOL LANGUAGE
CR4885	VICTORIA CROSS
SF393.V6	VICTORIA SWINE
TK6655.V5	*VIDEO RECORDING* **SEE** VIDEO TAPE RECORDERS AND RECORDING
TK6655.V5	VIDEO TAPE RECORDERS AND RECORDING
TK6655.V5	*VIDEO TAPE RECORDING* **SEE** VIDEO TAPE RECORDERS AND RECORDING
TK6655.V5	*VIDEOTAPE RECORDERS AND RECORDING* **SEE** VIDEO TAPE RECORDERS AND RECORDING
ML760	*VIELLE* **SEE** VIOL / *history and construction*
DR536	VIENNA — SIEGE, 1683
GV1295.V	VIENNA (GAME)
DK432.7	VIENNA, TREATY OF, 1738
DC234.9	VIENNA, TREATY OF, 1809
DB855	VIENNA — HISTORY — — 1918-
BX830 1311	VIENNE, COUNCIL OF, 1311-1312
B824.6	*VIENNESE CIRCLE* **SEE** LOGICAL POSITIVISM
PL4371-9	VIETNAMESE LANGUAGE
G136-9	VIEWS
F865	VIGILANCE COMMITTEES / *california*
F731	VIGILANCE COMMITTEES / *montana*
Z1023	VIGNETTES / *bibliography*
NC960	VIGNETTES / *illustration*
D283.V5	VIGO, BATTLE OF, 1702
ML1010	VIHUELA
V46	VIKING SHIPS
DL65	VIKINGS
DK70-73	*VIKINGS, EAST* **SEE** VARANGIANS / *medieval russia*
DL65	*VIKINGS, EAST* **SEE** VARANGIANS / *northmen*
F2823.V	VILELA INDIANS
PL8774	VILI LANGUAGE
DG554.5.V	VILLAFRANCA, PEACE OF, 1859
BV638	*VILLAGE CHURCHES* **SEE** RURAL CHURCHES
JC31-46	VILLAGE COMMUNITIES / *primitive*
HT431	*VILLAGE GOVERNMENT* **SEE** VILLAGES
HT431	VILLAGES
HD1523	*VILLAINAGE* **SEE** VILLEINAGE
NA7100-7786	*VILLAS* **SEE** ARCHITECTURE, DOMESTIC
NA7100-7573	*VILLAS* **SEE** SUBURBAN HOMES / *architecture*
HD1523	VILLEINAGE
DC309.A5	*VILLERS-BRETONNEUX, BATTLE OF, 1870* **SEE** AMIENS, BATTLE OF, 1870
ML338	VINA / *music of india*
ML1015	VINA / *musical instruments*
RM666.V6	VINEGAR — THERAPEUTIC USE
TP445	VINEGAR / *vinegar-making*
QK773	*VINES* **SEE** CLIMBING PLANTS / *botany*
SB427	*VINES* **SEE** CLIMBING PLANTS / *culture*
QK495.V84	*VINEYARDS* **SEE** GRAPES / *botany*
SB387-399	*VINEYARDS* **SEE** GRAPES / *culture*
HD9259.G68-7	*VINEYARDS* **SEE** GRAPES / *trade*
SB387-399	*VINEYARDS* **SEE** VITICULTURE

GV1295.B	*VINGT ET UN (GAME)* **SEE** BLACKJACK (GAME)
SB387-399	*VINICULTURE* **SEE** VITICULTURE
RD96.V	VIOFORM
M349-351	*VIOL MUSIC (3 VIOLS)* **SEE** STRING TRIOS (3 VIOLS)
M452.4	*VIOL MUSIC (4 VIOLS)* **SEE** STRING QUARTETS (4 VIOLS)
M450-451	*VIOL MUSIC (4 VIOLS)* **SEE** STRING QUARTETS (4 VIOLS)
M550-552	*VIOL MUSIC (5 VIOLS)* **SEE** STRING QUINTETS (5 VIOLS)
M990	*VIOL MUSIC (5 VIOLS)* **SEE** STRING QUINTETS (5 VIOLS)
M59	VIOL MUSIC
ML760	VIOL / history and construction
MT286	VIOLA — ORCHESTRA STUDIES
MT285	VIOLA — STUDIES AND EXERCISES
M290-291	*VIOLA AND FLUTE MUSIC* **SEE** FLUTE AND VIOLA MUSIC
M294-5	VIOLA AND GUITAR MUSIC
M294-5	VIOLA AND GUITAR MUSIC, ARRANGED
M294-5	*VIOLA AND HARP MUSIC* **SEE** HARP AND VIOLA MUSIC
M294-5	*VIOLA AND HARP MUSIC* **SEE** HARP AND VIOLA MUSIC
M224-6	VIOLA AND HARPSICHORD MUSIC
M290-291	*VIOLA AND OBOE MUSIC* **SEE** OBOE AND VIOLA MUSIC
M182-4	VIOLA AND ORGAN MUSIC
M185-6	VIOLA AND ORGAN MUSIC, ARRANGED
M298	*VIOLA AND PERCUSSION MUSIC* **SEE** PERCUSSION AND VIOLA MUSIC
M224-6	VIOLA AND PIANO MUSIC
M227-8	VIOLA AND PIANO MUSIC, ARRANGED
M1393-5	VIOLA AND PIANO MUSIC, JUVENILE
M1205-6	VIOLA AND PIANO WITH BAND
M1040-1041	VIOLA AND PIANO WITH ORCHESTRA
M286-7	*VIOLA AND VIOLIN MUSIC* **SEE** VIOLIN AND VIOLA MUSIC
M286-7	VIOLA AND VIOLONCELLO MUSIC
ML760	*VIOLA BASTARDA* **SEE** LYRA VIOL
M286-7	VIOLA D'AMORE AND DOUBLE-BASS MUSIC
M290-291	*VIOLA D'AMORE AND FLUTE MUSIC* **SEE** FLUTE AND VIOLA D'AMORE MUSIC
M294-5	VIOLA D'AMORE AND GUITAR MUSIC
M239	VIOLA D'AMORE AND HARPSICHORD MUSIC
M294-5	VIOLA D'AMORE AND LUTE MUSIC
M1105-6	VIOLA D'AMORE AND LUTE WITH STRING ORCHESTRA
M182-6	VIOLA D'AMORE AND ORGAN MUSIC
M239	VIOLA D'AMORE AND PIANO MUSIC
M239	VIOLA D'AMORE AND PIANO MUSIC, ARRANGED
M286-7	VIOLA D'AMORE AND VIOLA DA GAMBA MUSIC
M59	VIOLA D'AMORE MUSIC
M1019	VIOLA D'AMORE WITH CHAMBER ORCHESTRA
M1019	VIOLA D'AMORE WITH ORCHESTRA
M1105-6	VIOLA D'AMORE WITH STRING ORCHESTRA
M1105	VIOLA D'AMORE WITH STRING ORCHESTRA, ARRANGED — SCORES
M1105-6	VIOLA D'AMORE WITH STRING ORCHESTRA, ARRANGED
ML760	VIOLA D'AMORE / history and criticism
M239	VIOLA DA GAMBA AND HARPSICHORD MUSIC
M239	VIOLA DA GAMBA AND PIANO MUSIC
M290-291	*VIOLA DA GAMBA AND RECORDER MUSIC* **SEE** RECORDER AND VIOLA DA GAMBA MUSIC
M286-7	*VIOLA DA GAMBA AND VIOLA D'AMORE MUSIC* **SEE** VIOLA D'AMORE AND VIOLA DA GAMBA MUSIC
M286-7	*VIOLA DA GAMBA AND VIOLA D'AMORE MUSIC* **SEE** VIOLA D'AMORE AND VIOLA DA GAMBA MUSIC
M286-7	*VIOLA DA GAMBA AND VIOLIN MUSIC* **SEE** VIOLIN AND VIOLA DA GAMBA MUSIC
M286-7	VIOLA DA GAMBA MUSIC (2 VIOLE DA GAMBA)
M59	VIOLA DA GAMBA MUSIC
M1019	VIOLA DA GAMBA WITH ORCHESTRA
M1105-6	VIOLA DA GAMBA WITH STRING ORCHESTRA
ML760	VIOLA DA GAMBA
ML760	*VIOLA DI BORDONE* **SEE** BARYTON
M286-7	VIOLA MUSIC (2 VIOLAS)
M45-47	VIOLA MUSIC
M48-49	VIOLA MUSIC, ARRANGED
ML760	*VIOLA PAREDON* **SEE** BARYTON

ML418	*VIOLA PLAYERS* **SEE** VIOLINISTS, VIOLONCELLISTS, ETC. / individual
M239	VIOLA POMPOSA AND HARPSICHORD MUSIC
M59	VIOLA POMPOSA MUSIC
M1205-6	VIOLA WITH BAND
M1015	VIOLA WITH CHAMBER ORCHESTRA — SOLO WITH PIANO
M1014-1015	VIOLA WITH CHAMBER ORCHESTRA
M1015	VIOLA WITH ORCHESTRA — SOLO WITH PIANO
M1014-1015	VIOLA WITH ORCHESTRA
M1105	VIOLA WITH STRING ORCHESTRA — SCORES
M1105-6	VIOLA WITH STRING ORCHESTRA
M1105-6	VIOLA WITH STRING ORCHESTRA, ARRANGED
ML900-905	VIOLA
M175.V5	VIOLANO-VIRTUOSO MUSIC
ML1055	VIOLANO-VIRTUOSO
SB608.V8	VIOLETS — DISEASES AND PESTS
SB413.V8	VIOLETS
MT260-279	VIOLIN — INSTRUCTION AND STUDY
ML845	VIOLIN — LABELS
MT262	VIOLIN — METHODS (JAZZ)
MT262	VIOLIN — METHODS
MT266	VIOLIN — ORCHESTRA STUDIES
ML64	VIOLIN — POETRY
ML802	VIOLIN — REPAIRING
MT265	VIOLIN — STUDIES AND EXERCISES (JAZZ)
MT267-271	VIOLIN — STUDIES AND EXERCISES
MT265	VIOLIN — STUDIES AND EXERCISES
M290-291	*VIOLIN AND BASSOON MUSIC* **SEE** BASSOON AND VIOLIN MUSIC
M290-291	*VIOLIN AND BASSOON MUSIC* **SEE** BASSOON AND VIOLIN MUSIC
M290-291	*VIOLIN AND CLARINET MUSIC* **SEE** CLARINET AND VIOLIN MUSIC
M290	*VIOLIN AND FLAGEOLET MUSIC* **SEE** FLAGEOLET AND VIOLIN MUSIC
M290	*VIOLIN AND FLAGEOLET MUSIC* **SEE** FLAGEOLET AND VIOLIN MUSIC
M290-291	*VIOLIN AND FLUTE MUSIC* **SEE** FLUTE AND VIOLIN MUSIC
M294-5	VIOLIN AND GUITAR MUSIC
M294-5	VIOLIN AND GUITAR MUSIC, ARRANGED
M294-5	VIOLIN AND HARP MUSIC
M1040-1041	VIOLIN AND HARP WITH ORCHESTRA
M221	VIOLIN AND HARPSICHORD MUSIC
M217-218	VIOLIN AND HARPSICHORD MUSIC
M1040-1041	VIOLIN AND HARPSICHORD WITH ORCHESTRA
M1105-6	VIOLIN AND HARPSICHORD WITH STRING ORCHESTRA
M290-291	*VIOLIN AND OBOE MUSIC* **SEE** OBOE AND VIOLIN MUSIC
M182-4	VIOLIN AND ORGAN MUSIC
M185-6	VIOLIN AND ORGAN MUSIC, ARRANGED
M217-218	VIOLIN AND PIANO MUSIC (JAZZ)
M221-3	VIOLIN AND PIANO MUSIC (JAZZ)
M221	VIOLIN AND PIANO MUSIC
M217-218	VIOLIN AND PIANO MUSIC
M217-218	*VIOLIN AND PIANO MUSIC, ARRANGED (JAZZ)* **SEE** VIOLIN AND PIANO MUSIC (JAZZ)
M221-3	*VIOLIN AND PIANO MUSIC, ARRANGED (JAZZ)* **SEE** VIOLIN AND PIANO MUSIC (JAZZ)
M222-3	VIOLIN AND PIANO MUSIC, ARRANGED
M1393-5	VIOLIN AND PIANO MUSIC, JUVENILE
M1040-1041	VIOLIN AND PIANO WITH CHAMBER ORCHESTRA
M1040-1041	VIOLIN AND PIANO WITH ORCHESTRA
M1105-6	VIOLIN AND PIANO WITH STRING ORCHESTRA
M290-291	*VIOLIN AND RECORDER MUSIC* **SEE** RECORDER AND VIOLIN MUSIC
M286-7	VIOLIN AND VIOLA DA GAMBA MUSIC
M286-7	VIOLIN AND VIOLA MUSIC
M286-7	VIOLIN AND VIOLA MUSIC, ARRANGED
M1040-1041	VIOLIN AND VIOLA WITH CHAMBER ORCHESTRA
M1040-1041	VIOLIN AND VIOLA WITH ORCHESTRA
M1105-6	VIOLIN AND VIOLA WITH STRING ORCHESTRA
M286-7	VIOLIN AND VIOLONCELLO MUSIC
M1410	VIOLIN AND VIOLONCELLO MUSIC, JUVENILE
M985	VIOLIN AND VIOLONCELLO WITH INSTR. ENSEMBLE
M1040-1041	VIOLIN AND VIOLONCELLO WITH ORCHESTRA
M1105-6	VIOLIN AND VIOLONCELLO WITH STRING ORCHESTRA
M286-7	*VIOLIN DUETS* **SEE** VIOLIN MUSIC (2 VIOLINS)
ML404	VIOLIN MAKERS / biography collective

BV4625-7	VIRTUES / *moral theology*
BV4645	*VIRTUES, CARDINAL* **SEE** CARDINAL VIRTUES
BV4645	*VIRTUES, MORAL* **SEE** CARDINAL VIRTUES
BV4635	*VIRTUES, THEOLOGICAL* **SEE** THEOLOGICAL VIRTUES
ML3853	VIRTUOSITY IN MUSIC / *interpretation*
SB736	VIRUS DISEASES OF PLANTS
QR360	VIRUSES
JX4251-3	*VISAS* **SEE** PASSPORTS / *international law*
PL5621-9	*VISAYAN LANGUAGE* **SEE** BISAYA LANGUAGE
DS666.B	*VISAYAS (PHILIPPINE TRIBE)* **SEE** BISAYAS (PHILIPPINE TRIBE)
QL991	VISCERA — ABNORMITIES AND DEFORMITIES / *comparative anatomy*
QM691	VISCERA — ABNORMITIES AND DEFORMITIES / *human anatomy*
RC941	VISCERA — DISEASES
QL801-950	VISCERA / *comparative anatomy*
QM21-81	VISCERA / *human anatomy*
QC189	*VISCOMETER* **SEE** VISCOSIMETER
TS1688	*VISCOSE RAYON* **SEE** RAYON
TS1688	*VISCOSE SILK* **SEE** RAYON
QC189	VISCOSIMETER
QC189	VISCOSITY
TL557.V5	*VISIBILITY CONDITIONS AT AIRPORTS* **SEE** AIRPORTS — VISIBILITY
HV2471-2500	*VISIBLE SPEECH* **SEE** DEAF — MEANS OF COMMUNICATION
N6242	*VISIGOTHIC ART* **SEE** ART, VISIGOTHIC
DP96	VISIGOTHS IN SPAIN
D137	VISIGOTHS
RE58	VISION RESEARCH
RE75-79	*VISION SCREENING* **SEE** EYE — EXAMINATION
RE58	*VISION-RESEARCH* **SEE** VISION RESEARCH
BT580	VISIONS / *christology*
BV5091.V6	VISIONS / *mysticism*
BF1100-1108	VISIONS / *occult sciences*
BT650-660	VISIONS / *virgin*
JX5268	*VISIT AND SEARCH* **SEE** SEARCH, RIGHT OF / *international law*
BV50.V5	VISITATION FESTIVAL
BV50.V5	*VISITATION OF THE BLESSED VIRGIN MARY, FEAST OF THE* **SEE** VISITATION FESTIVAL
BV4320	VISITATIONS (CHURCH WORK)
BX1939.V55	VISITATIONS, ECCLESIASTICAL (CANON LAW)
CS410-497	VISITATIONS, HERALDIC
BV4320	*VISITATIONS, PASTORAL* **SEE** VISITATIONS (CHURCH WORK)
LC43	VISITING TEACHERS / *home teachers*
LB3013.5	VISITING TEACHERS / *school social workers*
BJ2081-8	VISITING-CARDS / *etiquette*
HJ9123.V5	VISITORS' TAXES
TS1688	*VISTRA* **SEE** RAYON
LB1043.5	VISUAL EDUCATION
LB1043.5	*VISUAL INSTRUCTION* **SEE** VISUAL EDUCATION
QM511	VISUAL PURPLE
QL949	VISUAL PURPLE
QP479	VISUAL PURPLE / *retinal pigments*
TL557.V5	*VISUAL RANGE AT AIRPORTS* **SEE** AIRPORTS — VISIBILITY
TL969.0	*VISUAL-AURAL RANGE* **SEE** OMNIRANGE SYSTEM
QH341	VITAL FORCE
HA38-39	*VITAL RECORDS* **SEE** REGISTERS OF BIRTHS, ETC.
HB881-3700	VITAL STATISTICS
QH331	VITALISM
QH331	VITALITY / *biology*
RA445	VITALITY / *public health u.s.*
QP801.V5	*VITAMIN B 2* **SEE** RIBOFLAVIN
QP801.V5	*VITAMIN G* **SEE** RIBOFLAVIN
QP801.V5	VITAMIN METABOLISM
TX553.V5	VITAMINS / *nutrition*
QP801.V5	VITAMINS / *physiology*
QK898.V5	VITAMINS / *plant physiology*
PN1995.7	*VITAPHONE* **SEE** MOVING-PICTURES, TALKING
QP551	VITELLOSE
PL6235	*VITI LANGUAGE* **SEE** FIJIAN LANGUAGE
SB387-399	VITICULTURE
RE501	VITREOUS HUMOR — DISEASES
QL949	VITREOUS HUMOR / *comparative anatomy*
QM511	VITREOUS HUMOR / *human anatomy*
D569.V5	VITTORIO VENETO, BATTLE OF, 1918

DL710	VITTSJO, BATTLE OF, 1612
PR1111.I65	*VITUPERATION* **SEE** INVECTIVE / *english literature*
QL78	VIVARIUMS
QP45	VIVISECTION
HV4905-4959	VIVISECTION / *antivivisection*
GN549.B3	*VIZCAYANS* **SEE** BASQUES / *ethnology*
DC611.B31-322	*VIZCAYANS* **SEE** BASQUES / *french history*
DP302.B46	*VIZCAYANS* **SEE** BASQUES / *spanish history*
DR27.A8	*VLACHS* **SEE** AROMUNES
P305	VOCABULARY / *philology*
M1497	*VOCAL CADENZAS* **SEE** VOCAL MUSIC — CADENZAS
MT820-821	*VOCAL CULTURE* **SEE** SINGING
MT855	*VOCAL CULTURE* **SEE** SINGING
MT853	*VOCAL CULTURE* **SEE** SINGING
ML3877	*VOCAL CULTURE* **SEE** SINGING
PN4162	*VOCAL CULTURE* **SEE** VOICE CULTURE
M1529	VOCAL DUETS WITH STRING ORCHESTRA — VOCAL SCORES WITH PIANO
M1528-9	VOCAL DUETS WITH STRING ORCHESTRA
ML128.V7	VOCAL MUSIC — BIBLIOGRAPHY
M1497	VOCAL MUSIC — CADENZAS
ML156.4.V7	VOCAL MUSIC — DISCOGRAPHY
ML1400-3270	VOCAL MUSIC — HISTORY AND CRITICISM
ML128.V7	VOCAL MUSIC — THEMATIC CATALOGS
M1495-2199	VOCAL MUSIC
M1999	*VOCAL MUSIC, SACRED* **SEE** SACRED VOCAL MUSIC
ML132.V7	*VOCAL MUSIC-GRADED LISTS* **SEE** VOCAL MUSIC — BIBLIOGRAPHY — — GRADED LISTS
ML132.V7	VOCAL MUSIC — BIBLIOGRAPHY — — GRADED LISTS
ML156.4.V7	VOCAL MUSIC — TO 1800 — — DISCOGRAPHY
M1528-9	VOCAL OCTETS WITH ORCHESTRA
M1529	VOCAL QUARTETS WITH CHAMBER ORCHESTRA — VOCAL SCORES WITH PIANO
M1528-9	VOCAL QUARTETS WITH CHAMBER ORCHESTRA
M1353	VOCAL QUARTETS WITH DANCE ORCHESTRA
M1529	VOCAL QUARTETS WITH ORCHESTRA — VOCAL SCORES WITH PIANO
M1528-9	VOCAL QUARTETS WITH ORCHESTRA
M1529	VOCAL SEXTETS WITH ORCHESTRA — VOCAL SCORES WITH PIANO
M1528-9	VOCAL SEXTETS WITH ORCHESTRA
M1529	VOCAL TRIOS WITH INSTR. ENSEMBLE
M1528	VOCAL TRIOS WITH ORCHESTRA — SCORES
M1528-9	VOCAL TRIOS WITH ORCHESTRA
ML597	*VOCALION* **SEE** REED-ORGAN
ML1055.A3	*VOCALION, AEOLIAN* **SEE** AEOLIAN-VOCALION
M1613.3	VOCALISES (HIGH VOICE) WITH CHAMBER ORCHESTRA — SCORES
M1613.3	VOCALISES (HIGH VOICE) WITH CHAMBER ORCHESTRA
MT885	VOCALISES (HIGH VOICE) WITH HARPSICHORD
M1613	VOCALISES (HIGH VOICE) WITH ORCHESTRA
M1617	VOCALISES (HIGH VOICE) WITH ORCHESTRA
M1613.3	VOCALISES (MEDIUM VOICE) WITH CHAMBER ORCHESTRA — SCORES
M1613.3	VOCALISES (MEDIUM VOICE) WITH CHAMBER ORCHESTRA
M1614	VOCALISES (MEDIUM VOICE) WITH CHAMBER ORCHESTRA
MT885	VOCALISES (MEDIUM VOICE) WITH PIANO
M1497	VOCALISES (MEDIUM VOICE), UNACCOMPANIED
M1613.3	VOCALISES WITH INSTR. ENSEMBLE
MT885	VOCALISES WITH PIANO
ML400	*VOCALISTS* **SEE** SINGERS / *biography collective*
ML420	*VOCALISTS* **SEE** SINGERS / *individual*
BX2380	VOCATION (IN RELIGIOUS ORDERS, CONGREGATIONS, ETC.)
BV4740	VOCATION, ECCLESIASTICAL
BX2380	VOCATION, ECCLESIASTICAL / *catholic church*
BV4011.4	VOCATION, ECCLESIASTICAL / *pastoral theology*
BX2380	*VOCATION, MONASTIC* **SEE** VOCATION (IN RELIGIOUS ORDERS, CONGREGATIONS, ETC.)
BX2380	*VOCATION, RELIGIOUS* **SEE** VOCATION (IN RELIGIOUS ORDERS, CONGREGATIONS, ETC.)
LC1043	VOCATIONAL EDUCATION — CURRICULA
LC1041-7	VOCATIONAL EDUCATION
HF5381.5	VOCATIONAL INTERESTS
JF1057-9	*VOCATIONAL REPRESENTATION* **SEE** FUNCTIONAL REPRESENTATION
BX2380	*VOCATIONS, ECCLESIASTICAL* **SEE** VOCATION, ECCLESIASTICAL / *catholic church*

HD9999.C3-34	WAGONS / *trade*	M115-119	WALTZES (HARP)
DC234.8	WAGRAM, BATTLE OF, 1809	M1049	WALTZES (ORCHESTRA)
QL696.P2	WAGTAILS	M1060	WALTZES (ORCHESTRA)
BP195.W2	*WAHABEES* **SEE** WAHHABIS	M310-314	WALTZES (PIANO (4 HANDS), VIOLIN, VIOLONCELLO)
BP195.W2	*WAHABIS* **SEE** WAHHABIS	M1010	WALTZES (PIANO WITH ORCHESTRA) — SCORES
BP195.W2	*WAHABITES* **SEE** WAHHABIS	M1010-1011	WALTZES (PIANO WITH ORCHESTRA)
DT443	WAHEHE	M32	WALTZES (PIANO)
PL6265.Z9W	WAHGI DIALECT	M310-314	WALTZES (PIANO, VIOLIN, VIOLA)
BP195.W2	WAHHABIS	M410-414	WALTZES (PIANO, 2 VIOLINS, VIOLONCELLO)
E99.W	*WAHPACOOTA INDIANS* **SEE** WAHPEKUTE INDIANS	M415-419	WALTZES (PIANO, 3 CORNETS)
E99.D1	*WAHPAKOOTA SIOUX INDIANS* **SEE** DAKOTA INDIANS	M207	WALTZES (PIANO, 4 HANDS)
E99.W	WAHPEKUTE INDIANS	M200-201	WALTZES (PIANO, 4 HANDS)
E99.W	WAHPETON INDIANS	M209	WALTZES (PIANO, 4 HANDS)
E99.M2	*WAHTANI INDIANS* **SEE** MANDAN INDIANS	M204	WALTZES (PIANO, 4 HANDS)
E99.W15	WAILAKI INDIANS	M1350	WALTZES (SALON ORCHESTRA) — SCORES AND PARTS
DU420	WAITANGI, TREATY OF, 1840	M1350	WALTZES (SALON ORCHESTRA)
TX925	WAITERS / *manuals*	M1160	WALTZES (STRING ORCHESTRA)
TX925	*WAITRESSES* **SEE** WAITERS / *manuals*	M1145	WALTZES (STRING ORCHESTRA)
ML286	WAITS / *music in england*	M450-454	WALTZES (STRING QUARTET)
F2380.1.W25	WAIWAI INDIANS	M262-3	WALTZES (TROMBONE AND PIANO)
F2380.1.W25	*WAIWE INDIANS* **SEE** WAIWAI INDIANS	M260-261	WALTZES (TRUMPET AND PIANO)
GN659.W2	*WAJAGGA* **SEE** WACHAGA / *ethnology*	M1205	WALTZES (TRUMPET WITH BAND) — SCORES AND PARTS
DT449.K4	*WAJAGGA* **SEE** WACHAGA / *kilimanjaro region*	M1205-6	WALTZES (TRUMPET WITH BAND)
E99.W	WAKASHAN INDIANS	M264-5	WALTZES (TUBA AND PIANO)
PM2531	WAKASHAN LANGUAGES	M294-5	WALTZES (VIOLA AND GUITAR)
RC548	*WAKEFULNESS* **SEE** INSOMNIA	M224-8	WALTZES (VIOLA AND PIANO)
TL574.W3	WAKES (AERODYNAMICS)	M217-218	WALTZES (VIOLIN AND PIANO)
QA913	WAKES (FLUID DYNAMICS)	M221-3	WALTZES (VIOLIN AND PIANO)
GN667.Q8	WAKKA TRIBE / *anthropology*	M229-236	WALTZES (VIOLONCELLO AND PIANO)
DU274	WAKKA TRIBE / *history*	M135-9	WALTZES (ZITHER)
GN659.N45	*WAKONDE* **SEE** NGONDE (AFRICAN TRIBE)	M292-3	WALTZES (2 GUITARS)
DU122.W	WALBIRI TRIBE	M214-215	WALTZES (2 PIANOS)
SF199.W2	WALDECKER CATTLE	M286-7	WALTZES (2 VIOLINS)
QD651	WALDEN INVERSION	M385	WALTZES (3 MARIMBAS)
BX4872-4883	WALDENSES	M355-9	WALTZES (3 MOUTH-ORGANS)
DQ100	WALDSHUT, WAR OF, 1468	M550-554	WALTZES (3 VIOLINS, VIOLA, DOUBLE BASS)
GN654	*WALEGAS* **SEE** WAREGAS / *anthropology*	QL737.R6	*WALTZING MICE* **SEE** DANCING MICE
DT650	*WALEGAS* **SEE** WAREGAS / *history*	PL318	*WALWEN LANGUAGE* **SEE** KIPCHAK LANGUAGE
DA700-745	WALES — HISTORY	E99.W	WAMESIT INDIANS
GV1071	WALKING (SPORTS)	E78.M4	WAMPANOAG INDIANS — MISSIONS
GT2220	*WALKING-STICKS* **SEE** STAFFS (STICKS, CANES, ETC.)	E99.W2	WAMPANOAG INDIANS
TH1715	WALL BOARD	E98.C8	WAMPUM BELTS
ND2550-2876	*WALL DECORATION* **SEE** MURAL PAINTING AND DECORATION	E98.C8	WAMPUM / *costume*
		E98.M7	WAMPUM / *money*
HG4571-5	WALL STREET	PL8538	*WANDA LANGUAGE* **SEE** MWAMBA LANGUAGE
ND2550-2876	*WALL-PAINTING* **SEE** MURAL PAINTING AND DECORATION	PL8489	*WANDALA LANGUAGE* **SEE** MANDARA LANGUAGE
		GR75.W3	WANDERING JEW / *folk-lore*
NK3375-3496	WALL-PAPER	PN687.W3	WANDERING JEW / *medieval literature*
E99.W18	WALLA WALLA INDIANS	DT429	*WANDOROBO* **SEE** DOROBO (AFRICAN PEOPLE)
DR27.A8	*WALLACHIANS* **SEE** AROMUNES	PL8779	WANGA LANGUAGE
TH1715	*WALLBOARD* **SEE** WALL BOARD	DT429	*WANIKA* **SEE** NIKA (BANTU TRIBE)
E241.B4	*WALLOOMSAC, N.Y., BATTLE OF, 1777* **SEE** BENNINGTON, BATTLE OF, 1777	F3430.1.H	*WANKA INDIANS* **SEE** HUANCA INDIANS
		GN659.N45	*WANKONDE* **SEE** NGONDE (AFRICAN TRIBE)
PC3041-8	WALLOON DIALECT	DT429	*WANYIKA* **SEE** NIKA (BANTU TRIBE)
PC3048	WALLOON LITERATURE	DT429	*WAPOKOMO* **SEE** POKOMO (BANTU TRIBE)
PC3048	WALLOON POETRY	E83.655	WAPPINGER INDIANS — WARS, 1655-1660
PN6222.B4	WALLOON WIT AND HUMOR	E99.W	WAPPINGER INDIANS
DH492.W3	WALLOONS	E99.W35	WAPPO INDIANS
NA2940	WALLS / *architecture*	PM2547	WAPPO LANGUAGE
TH2201-2251	WALLS / *building*	D25.5	WAR — CASUALTIES (STATISTICS, ETC.) / *military history*
PL6621.V3	*WALMAN LANGUAGE* **SEE** VALMAN LANGUAGE		
SB608.W3	WALNUT SPAN-WORM	UH215	WAR — CASUALTIES (STATISTICS, ETC.) / *military medical service*
SB608.W3	WALNUT-BLIGHT		
SB401	WALNUT	HB195	WAR — ECONOMIC ASPECTS
E99.W185	WALPAPI INDIANS	JX5144	WAR — PROTECTION OF CIVILIANS
QL737.P6	WALRUSES	UH201-551	WAR — RELIEF OF SICK AND WOUNDED / *medical and sanitary service*
TJ665	WALSCHAERT VALVE-GEAR		
GV1761	WALTZ	JX4505-5326	WAR (INTERNATIONAL LAW)
M1362	WALTZES (ACCORDION ENSEMBLE)	BL65.W2	*WAR AND CHRISTIANITY* **SEE** WAR AND RELIGION
M175.A4	WALTZES (ACCORDION)	BR115.W2	*WAR AND CHRISTIANITY* **SEE** WAR AND RELIGION / *christianity*
M282-3	WALTZES (BALALAIKA AND PIANO)		
M1266	WALTZES (BAND)	CB481	WAR AND CIVILIZATION
M1249	WALTZES (BAND)	HV6189	WAR AND CRIME
M1060	WALTZES (CHAMBER ORCHESTRA)	JF256	WAR AND EMERGENCY POWERS
M1049	WALTZES (CHAMBER ORCHESTRA)	JK339	WAR AND EMERGENCY POWERS / *u.s. government*
M240-244	WALTZES (FLUTE AND PIANO)	JK560	WAR AND EMERGENCY POWERS / *u.s. president*
M380-384	WALTZES (FLUTE, GUITAR, VIOLIN)	HB195	*WAR AND INDUSTRY* **SEE** WAR — ECONOMIC ASPECTS
M276-7	WALTZES (GUITAR AND PIANO)		
M125-9	WALTZES (GUITAR)	PN3448.W3	WAR AND LITERATURE / *fiction*
M370-374	WALTZES (GUITAR, 2 VIOLINS)		

PN56.W3	WAR AND LITERATURE / *literature*
BR195.W3	WAR AND RELIGION — EARLY CHURCH
BL65.W2	WAR AND RELIGION
BR115.W2	WAR AND RELIGION / *christianity*
HX545	WAR AND SOCIALISM
BL65.W2	*WAR AND THE CHURCH* **SEE** WAR AND RELIGION
BR115.W2	*WAR AND THE CHURCH* **SEE** WAR AND RELIGION / *christianity*
HJ8903-8963	*WAR CLAIMS* **SEE** CLAIMS
JX238	*WAR CLAIMS* **SEE** CLAIMS / *international law*
PN4823	WAR CORRESPONDENTS
D625-6	WAR CRIMES / *european war*
UB360-366	*WAR CRIPPLES* **SEE** VETERANS, DISABLED
UA929.5-9	*WAR DAMAGE CONTROL IN INDUSTRY* **SEE** WAR DAMAGE, INDUSTRIAL
UA929.5-9	WAR DAMAGE, INDUSTRIAL
HJ135	WAR FINANCE
U310	WAR GAMES
V250	WAR GAMES / *naval*
UG465	*WAR GEOLOGY* **SEE** MILITARY GEOLOGY
HG8055	*WAR INSURANCE* **SEE** INSURANCE — WAR RISKS
HG8811.W2	*WAR INSURANCE* **SEE** INSURANCE, LIFE — WAR RISKS
HE966	*WAR INSURANCE* **SEE** INSURANCE, MARINE — WAR RISKS
UB370-375	*WAR INSURANCE* **SEE** INSURANCE, WAR RISK
D635	*WAR LEGISLATION (1914-1918)* **SEE** EUROPEAN WAR, 1914-1918 — LAW AND LEGISLATION
D505	*WAR LEGISLATION (1914-1918)* **SEE** EUROPEAN WAR, 1914-1918 — LAW AND LEGISLATION
Z675.W2	WAR LIBRARIES
GA205-213	*WAR MAPS* **SEE** GEOGRAPHY, ANCIENT — MAPS
G1033	*WAR MAPS* **SEE** GEOGRAPHY, ANCIENT — MAPS
UC260-265	*WAR MATERIAL, SURPLUS* **SEE** SURPLUS MILITARY PROPERTY
NA9325	WAR MEMORIALS
U13	*WAR MUSEUMS* **SEE** MILITARY MUSEUMS
RC550	WAR NEUROSES
D275-6	*WAR OF DEVOLUTION, 1667-1668* **SEE** DEVOLUTION, WAR OF, 1667-1668
DQ100	*WAR OF MULHAUSEN, 1468* **SEE** WALDSHUT, WAR OF, 1468
E456-655	*WAR OF SECESSION (U.S.)* **SEE** UNITED STATES — HISTORY — — CIVIL WAR
E201-298	*WAR OF THE AMERICAN REVOLUTION* **SEE** UNITED STATES — HISTORY — — REVOLUTION
D291-4	*WAR OF THE AUSTRIAN SUCCESSION, 1740-1748* **SEE** AUSTRIAN SUCCESSION, WAR OF, 1740-1748
DB72	*WAR OF THE AUSTRIAN SUCCESSION, 1740-1748* **SEE** AUSTRIAN SUCCESSION, WAR OF, 1740-1748 / *austria*
DD801.B376	*WAR OF THE BAVARIAN SUCCESSION, 1778-1779* **SEE** BAVARIAN SUCCESSION, WAR OF, 1778-1779
F3097	WAR OF THE PACIFIC, 1879-1884
F2684	*WAR OF THE SEVEN REDUCTIONS, 1754-1756* **SEE** SEVEN REDUCTIONS, WAR OF THE, 1754-1756
DP196	*WAR OF THE SPANISH SUCCESSION, 1701-1714* **SEE** SPANISH SUCCESSION, WAR OF, 1701-1714 / *period in spain*
D281-3	*WAR OF THE SPANISH SUCCESSION, 1701-1714* **SEE** SPANISH SUCCESSION, WAR OF, 1701-1714
F2687	*WAR OF THE TRIPLE ALLIANCE, 1865-1870* **SEE** PARAGUAYAN WAR, 1865-1870
DQ100	*WAR OF WALDSHUT, 1468* **SEE** WALDSHUT, WAR OF, 1468
E351-364	*WAR OF 1812* **SEE** UNITED STATES — HISTORY — — WAR OF 1812
E351-364	*WAR OF 1812* **SEE** UNITED STATES — HISTORY — — WAR OF 1812
D501-680	*WAR OF 1914* **SEE** EUROPEAN WAR, 1914 1918
UB400-405	*WAR PENSIONS* **SEE** PENSIONS, MILITARY / *army*
UB370-375	*WAR PENSIONS* **SEE** PENSIONS, MILITARY / *army*
VB280-285	*WAR PENSIONS* **SEE** PENSIONS, MILITARY / *navy*
VB340-345	*WAR PENSIONS* **SEE** PENSIONS, MILITARY / *navy*
E255	*WAR PENSIONS* **SEE** PENSIONS, MILITARY / *pension rolls*
PS595.H5	WAR POETRY / *american literature*
E647	WAR POETRY / *civil war*
PN6110.H3	WAR POETRY / *collections*
PR1195.H5	WAR POETRY / *english literature*

D526	WAR POETRY / *european war*
JF256	*WAR POWERS* **SEE** WAR AND EMERGENCY POWERS
JK339	*WAR POWERS* **SEE** WAR AND EMERGENCY POWERS / *u.s. government*
JK560	*WAR POWERS* **SEE** WAR AND EMERGENCY POWERS / *u.s. president*
HJ4631	*WAR PROFITS TAX* **SEE** EXCESS PROFITS TAX
HJ4653.E8	*WAR PROFITS TAX* **SEE** EXCESS PROFITS TAX / *u.s.*
D639.P6-7	*WAR PROPAGANDA* **SEE** EUROPEAN WAR, 1914-1918 — PROPAGANDA
D619.3	*WAR PROPAGANDA* **SEE** EUROPEAN WAR, 1914-1918 — PROPAGANDA
D810.P6-7	*WAR PROPAGANDA* **SEE** WORLD WAR, 1939-1945 — PROPAGANDA
UB370-375	*WAR RISK INSURANCE* **SEE** INSURANCE, WAR RISK
HG8055	*WAR RISKS (INSURANCE)* **SEE** INSURANCE — WAR RISKS
HG8811.W2	*WAR RISKS (INSURANCE)* **SEE** INSURANCE, LIFE — WAR RISKS
HE966	*WAR RISKS (INSURANCE)* **SEE** INSURANCE, MARINE — WAR RISKS
UB370-375	*WAR RISKS (INSURANCE)* **SEE** INSURANCE, WAR RISK
UC260-265	*WAR SURPLUSES* **SEE** `SURPLUS MILITARY PROPERTY
D637-9	*WAR WORK* **SEE** EUROPEAN WAR, 1914-1918 — WAR WORK
D637-9	*WAR WORKS* **SEE** EUROPEAN WAR, 1914-1918 — WAR WORKS
RD156	WAR WOUNDS
GV1469.W3	WAR-CHESS (GAME)
CR79	*WAR-CRIES* **SEE** BATTLE-CRIES / *heraldry*
V750-980	*WAR-SHIPS* **SEE** WARSHIPS / *construction*
VA	*WAR-SHIPS* **SEE** WARSHIPS / *naval organization*
GN497-9	WAR / *v primitive*
UB461-736	*WAR, ARTICLES OF* **SEE** MILITARY LAW
UA17	WAR, COST OF
JX4552-4564	WAR, DECLARATION OF
JF256	WAR, DECLARATION OF / *constitutional law*
JX5203-5268	WAR, MARITIME (INTERNATIONAL LAW)
V	*WAR, MARITIME* **SEE** NAVAL ART AND SCIENCE
D27	*WAR, MARITIME* **SEE** NAVAL BATTLES
V167-178	*WAR, MARITIME* **SEE** NAVAL TACTICS
JX5141	*WAR, PRISONERS OF* **SEE** PRISONERS OF WAR / *international law*
UH100	*WAR, USE OF DOGS IN* **SEE** DOGS, WAR USE OF
HV6189	*WAR-MORAL ASPECTS* **SEE** WAR AND CRIME
BL65.W2	*WAR-MORAL ASPECTS* **SEE** WAR AND RELIGION
BR115.W2	*WAR-MORAL ASPECTS* **SEE** WAR AND RELIGION / *christianity*
PS595.H5	*WAR-POETRY* **SEE** WAR POETRY / *american literature*
E647	*WAR-POETRY* **SEE** WAR POETRY / *civil war*
PN6110.H3	*WAR-POETRY* **SEE** WAR POETRY / *collections*
PR1195.H5	*WAR-POETRY* **SEE** WAR POETRY / *english literature*
D526	*WAR-POETRY* **SEE** WAR POETRY / *european war*
F2420	*WARAO INDIANS* **SEE** WARRAU INDIANS
QK495.W	WARATAHS / *botany*
NK1560	WARATAHS / *decorative design*
F2420	*WARAU INDIANS* **SEE** WARRAU INDIANS
QL537.O3	WARBLE-FLIES
SF967.W3	WARBLE-FLIES / *cattle pests*
SF473.B	*WARBLING GRASS PARAKEET* **SEE** BUDGERIGARS
LB775.G22	WARDHA SCHEME OF EDUCATION
SB417	WARDIAN CASES
GN654	WAREGAS / *anthropology*
DT650	WAREGAS / *history*
TH9445.W2	WAREHOUSES — FIRES AND FIRE PREVENTION
NA6340	WAREHOUSES / *architecture*
HF5484-9	WAREHOUSES / *commerce*
E98.W2	*WARFARE, INDIAN* **SEE** INDIAN WARFARE
U240	*WARFARE, INDIAN* **SEE** INDIAN WARFARE
V210	*WARFARE, SUBMARINE* **SEE** SUBMARINE WARFARE
QA165	*WARING'S PROBLEM* **SEE** PARTITIONS (MATHEMATICS)
DS432.W	WARLIS
TH7601-7635	*WARM-AIR HEATING* **SEE** HOT-AIR HEATING
GV461-547	*WARM-UP* **SEE** EXERCISE
RA781	*WARM-UP* **SEE** EXERCISE / *hygiene*
QP301	*WARM-UP* **SEE** EXERCISE / *physiology*
RM721	*WARM-UP* **SEE** EXERCISE / *therapeutics*
TS1490-1500	*WARPING* **SEE** WEAVING
GN432	*WARPING* **SEE** WEAVING / *primitive*

HG2041-2051	*WARRANTS, AGRICULTURAL* **SEE** AGRICULTURAL CREDIT / *banking*
HD1439-1440	*WARRANTS, AGRICULTURAL* **SEE** AGRICULTURAL CREDIT / *theory*
F2420	WARRAU INDIANS
D25	*WARS* **SEE** MILITARY HISTORY
U27-43	*WARS* **SEE** MILITARY HISTORY / *military science*
D27	*WARS* **SEE** NAVAL HISTORY
D-F	*WARS* **SEE** NAVAL HISTORY / *and battles of particular countries*
GN497-9	*WARS* **SEE** WAR / *v primitive*
U313	*WARS AND BATTLES, IMAGINARY* **SEE** IMAGINARY WARS AND BATTLES
JX1964	*WARS AND BATTLES, IMAGINARY* **SEE** IMAGINARY WARS AND BATTLES / *peace literature*
UA	*WARS AND BATTLES, IMAGINARY* **SEE** IMAGINARY WARS AND BATTLES / *military situation in special countries*
D445	*WARS AND BATTLES, IMAGINARY* **SEE** IMAGINARY WARS AND BATTLES / *world politics*
V253	*WARS AND BATTLES, IMAGINARY* **SEE** IMAGINARY WARS AND BATTLES / *naval*
E83.72	*WARS WITH THE EASTERN INDIANS, 1722-1726* **SEE** EASTERN INDIANS, WARS WITH, 1722-1726
D765.2.W3	WARSAW — SIEGE, 1939
D765.2.W3	*WARSAW UPRISING, 1944* **SEE** WARSAW — HISTORY — — UPRISING OF 1944
D765.2.W3	*WARSAW-HISTORY-SIEGE, 1939* **SEE** WARSAW — SIEGE, 1939
DK651.W2	WARSAW — HISTORY — — REVOLUTION OF 1794
D765.2.W3	WARSAW — HISTORY — — UPRISING OF 1944
V805	WARSHIPS — MATERIALS
VF440	WARSHIPS — TURRETS
V750-980	WARSHIPS / *construction*
VA	WARSHIPS / *naval organization*
V810	*WARSHIPS-DAMAGE CONTROL* **SEE** DAMAGE CONTROL (WARSHIPS)
V810	*WARSHIPS-EMERGENCY REPAIR* **SEE** DAMAGE CONTROL (WARSHIPS)
BF698.W36	WARTEGG TEST
BF698	WARTEGG-BIEDMA TEST
BF698.W36	*WARTEGG-ZEICHENTEST* **SEE** WARTEGG TEST
DT443	*WARUNDI* **SEE** BARUNDI
SB307.W	WASABI
E99.W	WASCO INDIANS
ND2460	*WASH DRAWING* **SEE** BRUSH DRAWING
TD1015	*WASH-HOUSES, PUBLIC* **SEE** LAUNDRIES, PUBLIC
TT980-999	*WASHING* **SEE** LAUNDRY
BV873.F7	*WASHING OF FEET* **SEE** FOOT WASHING (RITE)
RA766.W3	WASHING POWDERS / *disinfectants*
TP991	WASHING POWDERS / *technology*
RA766.W3	*WASHING SOLUTIONS* **SEE** WASHING POWDERS / *disinfectants*
TP991	*WASHING SOLUTIONS* **SEE** WASHING POWDERS / *technology*
TT997-9	WASHING-MACHINES
E312.17	*WASHINGTON AS A FREEMASON* **SEE** WASHINGTON, GEORGE, PRES. U.S., 1732-1799 — FREEMASONRY
F191-205	WASHINGTON, D.C. — HISTORY
E356.W3	WASHINGTON, D.C. — HISTORY — — CAPTURE BY THE BRITISH, 1814
E501	WASHINGTON, D.C. — HISTORY — — CIVIL WAR
E241.W3	WASHINGTON, FORT, CAPTURE OF, 1776
E312.17	WASHINGTON, GEORGE, PRES. U.S., 1732-1799 — FREEMASONRY
E312.25	WASHINGTON, GEORGE, PRES. U.S., 1732-1799 — RESIGNATION OF MILITARY COMMISSION
E312	WASHINGTON, GEORGE, PRES. U.S., 1732-1799
E474.55	WASHINGTON, N.C. — SIEGE, 1863
F314	WASHINGTON, TREATY OF, 1819
E398	WASHINGTON, TREATY OF, 1842
JX235	WASHINGTON, TREATY OF, 1871
E312.6	WASHINGTON'S BIRTHDAY
E312.23	WASHINGTON'S EXPEDITION TO THE OHIO, 1ST, 1753-1754
E312.8	WASHINGTON'S EXPEDITION TO THE OHIO, 1ST, 1753-1754
E312.8	WASHINGTON'S EXPEDITION TO THE OHIO, 2D, 1754
E312.23	WASHINGTON'S EXPEDITION TO THE OHIO, 2D, 1754
E99.W38	WASHO INDIANS
PM2551	WASHO LANGUAGE
E99.W38	*WASHOAN INDIANS* **SEE** WASHO INDIANS
PM2551	*WASHOAN LANGUAGE* **SEE** WASHO LANGUAGE
QL568.V5	WASPS
RC201.2	*WASSERMANN REACTION* **SEE** SYPHILIS — DIAGNOSIS — — WASSERMANN REACTION
HD62.5	WASTE (ECONOMICS)
HC106.3	WASTE (ECONOMICS) / *u.s.*
TP319	WASTE HEAT
HD1665-1671	WASTE LANDS
TS1109	WASTE PAPER
TP995	WASTE PRODUCTS
HD9975	*WASTE RECLAMATION* **SEE** SALVAGE (WASTE, ETC.)
TP995	*WASTE RECLAMATION* **SEE** SALVAGE (WASTE, ETC.)
TD755	*WASTE STABILIZATION LAGOONS* **SEE** SEWAGE LAGOONS
TJ780	WASTE-HEAT ENGINES
TH6658	*WASTE-PIPES* **SEE** PLUMBING — WASTE-PIPES
TD897-9	*WASTE, DISPOSAL OF* **SEE** FACTORY AND TRADE WASTE
TD791-870	*WASTE, DISPOSAL OF* **SEE** REFUSE AND REFUSE DISPOSAL
TD741-780	*WASTE, DISPOSAL OF* **SEE** SEWAGE DISPOSAL
RA567	*WASTE, DISPOSAL OF* **SEE** SEWAGE DISPOSAL / *public health*
TS1109	*WASTE, DISPOSAL OF* **SEE** WASTE PAPER
TP995	*WASTE, DISPOSAL OF* **SEE** WASTE PRODUCTS
TS1109	*WASTEPAPER* **SEE** WASTE PAPER
DA235	*WAT TYLER'S INSURRECTION, 1381* **SEE** TYLER'S INSURRECTION, 1381
NK7486-7497	*WATCH MAKERS* **SEE** CLOCK AND WATCH MAKERS / *art*
TS542-3	*WATCH MAKERS* **SEE** CLOCK AND WATCH MAKERS / *technology*
HD9999.C6	*WATCH MAKING* **SEE** CLOCK AND WATCH MAKING / *economics*
TS540-549	*WATCH MAKING* **SEE** CLOCK AND WATCH MAKING / *technology*
TS547	*WATCH REPAIRING* **SEE** CLOCKS AND WATCHES — REPAIRING AND ADJUSTING
SF428.8	*WATCH-DOGS* **SEE** WATCHDOGS
SF428.8	WATCHDOGS
NK7480-7499	*WATCHES* **SEE** CLOCKS AND WATCHES / *art*
HD9999.C6	*WATCHES* **SEE** CLOCKS AND WATCHES / *economics*
TS540-549	*WATCHES* **SEE** CLOCKS AND WATCHES / *technology*
HV8290	WATCHMEN
TD458	WATER — AERATION
QD142	WATER — ANALYSIS
TD380-387	WATER — ANALYSIS / *sanitary analysis*
QR105	WATER — BACTERIOLOGY
QD181.H1	WATER — COMPOSITION
TD481-491	WATER — DISTRIBUTION
TP259	WATER — ELECTROLYSIS
HD1691-8	WATER — LAWS AND LEGISLATION
QP913.H1	WATER — PHYSIOLOGICAL EFFECT
TD420-425	WATER — POLLUTION
DT430-477	WATER — PURIFICATION
TP263	WATER — SOFTENING
TT998	WATER — SOFTENING / *laundry work*
TD495-7	WATER — WASTE
QL447.T2	*WATER BEARS* **SEE** TARDIGRADA
GV775	*WATER CARNIVALS* **SEE** REGATTAS
VM357	WATER CYCLES
SB423	WATER GARDENS
TC553	*WATER GATES* **SEE** SLUICE GATES
TP869	*WATER GLASS* **SEE** SOLUBLE GLASS
TC174	WATER HAMMER
TN318	*WATER IN MINES* **SEE** MINE WATER
QP535.H1	WATER IN THE BODY
QP88	WATER IN THE BODY / *physiology of the tissues*
QD951	*WATER OF CRYSTALLIZATION* **SEE** CRYSTALLIZATION, WATER OF
RC391	*WATER ON THE BRAIN* **SEE** HYDROCEPHALUS
ML553	*WATER ORGAN* **SEE** HYDRAULIC ORGAN
SB423	*WATER PLANTS* **SEE** AQUATIC PLANTS
TD420-425	*WATER POLLUTION* **SEE** WATER — POLLUTION
DT430-477	*WATER PURIFICATION* **SEE** WATER — PURIFICATION

TJ901	*WATER SCREW* **SEE** ARCHIMEDEAN SCREW
GV840.S5	WATER SKIING
TP263	*WATER SOFTENING* **SEE** WATER — SOFTENING
TT998	*WATER SOFTENING* **SEE** WATER — SOFTENING / *laundry work*
GV771-840	*WATER SPORTS* **SEE** AQUATIC SPORTS
TA360	*WATER TANKS* **SEE** TANKS / *engineering*
HF5716.L5	*WATER TANKS* **SEE** TANKS / *gaging*
TF290	*WATER TANKS* **SEE** TANKS / *railroad*
TF271	*WATER TANKS* **SEE** TANKS / *track tanks*
HE561-971	*WATER TRANSPORTATION* **SEE** SHIPPING
JX4190	*WATER TRANSPORTATION* **SEE** SHIPPING / *international law*
TJ870-875	*WATER TURBINES* **SEE** HYDRAULIC TURBINES
BF1628	*WATER WITCHING* **SEE** DIVINING-ROD
QD142	*WATER-ANALYSIS* **SEE** WATER — ANALYSIS
TD380-387	*WATER-ANALYSIS* **SEE** WATER — ANALYSIS / *sanitary analysis*
QL671-698	WATER-BIRDS
SK351-579	WATER-BIRDS / *game preservation*
SK331-3	WATER-BIRDS / *hunting*
QL671	*WATER-BIRDS, PROTECTION OF* **SEE** BIRDS, PROTECTION OF / *etc.*
SK351-579	*WATER-BIRDS, PROTECTION OF* **SEE** BIRDS, PROTECTION OF / *game-laws*
TH6498	WATER-CLOSETS
ND2125	WATER-COLOR PAINTING — EARLY WORKS TO 1800
ND2133-7	WATER-COLOR PAINTING — TECHNIQUE
ND1700-2399	WATER-COLOR PAINTING
ND1725	WATER-COLORS — PRIVATE COLLECTIONS
ND1700-2399	WATER-COLORS
ND1640-1650	*WATER-COLORS-CONSERVATION AND RESTORATION* **SEE** PAINTINGS — CONSERVATION AND RESTORATION
TK9203.P7	*WATER-COOLED REACTORS* **SEE** PRESSURIZED WATER REACTORS
TF290	WATER-CRANES / *railroads*
SB608.W32	WATER-CRESS LEAF-BEETLE
SB608.W32	WATER-CRESS SOWBUG
SB351.W3	WATER-CRESS / *culture*
RM801-822	*WATER-CURE* **SEE** HYDROTHERAPY
QL444.C6	*WATER-FLEAS* **SEE** CLADOCERA
QL531-8	*WATER-FLIES* **SEE** FLIES
QL671-698	*WATER-FOWL* **SEE** WATER-BIRDS
SK351-579	*WATER-FOWL* **SEE** WATER-BIRDS / *game preservation*
SK331-3	*WATER-FOWL* **SEE** WATER-BIRDS / *hunting*
TP760	WATER-GAS
SB615.W3	WATER-HYACINTH
TC173	WATER-JET
QK495.N97	WATER-LILIES
SB423	WATER-LILIES / *cultivation*
TD491	*WATER-MAINS* **SEE** WATER-PIPES
Z237	WATER-MARKS / *early printed books*
TS1115	WATER-MARKS / *paper manufacture*
TC177	WATER-METERS / *hydraulics*
TD499-500	WATER-METERS / *water-supply*
TD491	WATER-PIPES
GV839	WATER-POLO
TK1081	WATER-POWER ELECTRIC PLANTS
TK1421-1524	WATER-POWER ELECTRIC PLANTS / *by plant*
TC415-524	WATER-POWER / *by place*
TC147	WATER-POWER / *hydraulic engineering*
TJ840-890	WATER-POWER / *machinery*
HD1691-8	*WATER-POWER-LAW AND LEGISLATION* **SEE** WATER — LAWS AND LEGISLATION
TJ890	WATER-PRESSURE ENGINES
HD1691-8	WATER-RIGHTS
QL451-2	WATER-SPIDERS
TC404-555	WATER-STORAGE / *hydraulic engineering*
TD201-500	WATER-STORAGE / *water-supply*
HF5686.W3	WATER-SUPPLY — ACCOUNTING
TD360	WATER-SUPPLY — RATES
TD221-324	WATER-SUPPLY — RATES / *local*
TD353	WATER-SUPPLY ENGINEERING — APPARATUS AND SUPPLIES
TD351	WATER-SUPPLY ENGINEERING — TABLES, CALCULATIONS, ETC.
TC404-555	WATER-SUPPLY ENGINEERING
TD201-500	WATER-SUPPLY ENGINEERING / *municipal*
TD201-500	WATER-SUPPLY / *municipal*
GB651-1997	WATER-SUPPLY / *physical geography*
GN443	WATER-SUPPLY / *primitive*
SD425	WATER-SUPPLY / *water-supply and forests*
UC780	*WATER-SUPPLY, MILITARY* **SEE** MILITARY BASES — WATER-SUPPLY
TD927	WATER-SUPPLY, RURAL
HD1691-8	*WATER-SUPPLY-LAW AND LEGISLATION* **SEE** WATER — LAWS AND LEGISLATION
TH9332-4	WATER-TOWERS / *fire extinction*
TD489	WATER-TOWERS / *water-supply*
TJ314-315	*WATER-TUBE BOILERS* **SEE** STEAM-BOILERS, WATER-TUBE
TJ860-866	WATER-WHEELS
QD181.H1	WATER / *chemistry*
HD1691-8	WATER / *conservation*
QC920	WATER / *meteorology*
GB651-2397	WATER / *physical geography*
TP262-3	WATER / *water in industry*
TD201-500	WATER / *water-supply*
BX2307.3	*WATER, BAPTISMAL* **SEE** BAPTISMAL WATER / *catholic church*
BX2307	*WATER, BLESSED* **SEE** HOLY WATER / *catholic church*
BV885	*WATER, BLESSED* **SEE** HOLY WATER / *practical theology*
QD181.H1	WATER, DISTILLED
VM505	WATER, DISTILLED / *sea-water*
QD181.H1	*WATER, HEAVY* **SEE** DEUTERIUM OXIDE
BX2307	*WATER, HOLY* **SEE** HOLY WATER / *catholic church*
BV885	*WATER, HOLY* **SEE** HOLY WATER / *practical theology*
GB1001-1197	*WATER, SUBTERRANEAN* **SEE** WATER, UNDERGROUND
GB1001-1197	WATER, UNDERGROUND
TD468	*WATER-CHLORINATION* **SEE** WATER — PURIFICATION — — CHLORINATION
TC160-179	*WATER-FLOW* **SEE** HYDRAULICS
TD461	*WATER-OZONIZATION* **SEE** WATER — PURIFICATION — — OZONIZATION
RM801-822	*WATER-THERAPEUTIC USE* **SEE** HYDROTHERAPY
GB1401-1597	WATERFALLS
QL671-698	*WATERFOWL* **SEE** WATER-BIRDS
SK351-579	*WATERFOWL* **SEE** WATER-BIRDS / *game preservation*
SK331-3	*WATERFOWL* **SEE** WATER-BIRDS / *hunting*
RA791-954	*WATERING-PLACES* **SEE** HEALTH RESORTS, WATERING-PLACES, ETC.
DC241-4	WATERLOO, BATTLE OF, 1815
Z237	*WATERMARKS* **SEE** WATER-MARKS / *early printed books*
TS1115	*WATERMARKS* **SEE** WATER-MARKS / *paper manufacture*
TS1520	WATERPROOFING OF FABRICS
TH9031	WATERPROOFING / *building*
TA901	WATERPROOFING / *engineering*
TN923-9	*WATERS, MINERAL* **SEE** MINERAL WATERS
RA793-954	*WATERS, MINERAL* **SEE** MINERAL WATERS / *health resorts*
RM674-6	*WATERS, MINERAL* **SEE** MINERAL WATERS / *therapeutics*
GB906	WATERSHEDS
SD425	WATERSHEDS / *forestry*
QC957	WATERSPOUTS
HE381-560	WATERWAYS / *transportation*
TC623.4-624	*WATERWAYS, INTRACOASTAL* **SEE** INTRACOASTAL WATERWAYS / *u.s.*
TD201-500	*WATERWORKS* **SEE** WATER-SUPPLY / *municipal*
GB651-1997	*WATERWORKS* **SEE** WATER-SUPPLY / *physical geography*
GN443	*WATERWORKS* **SEE** WATER-SUPPLY / *primitive*
SD425	*WATERWORKS* **SEE** WATER-SUPPLY / *water-supply and forests*
TD468	WATER — PURIFICATION — — CHLORINATION
TD461	WATER — PURIFICATION — — OZONIZATION
DT443	*WATINDEGA (AFRICAN PEOPLE)* **SEE** TINDIGA (AFRICAN PEOPLE)
PM2082.O8	*WATOTO LANGUAGE* **SEE** OTO LANGUAGE
TK351	WATT-HOUR METER
SD397.W3	WATTLE (TREE)
TK341	WATTMETER
DT443	*WATUSSI* **SEE** BATUTSI
QC661	*WAVE FILTERS, ELECTRIC* **SEE** ELECTRIC FILTERS

TK6565.F5	WAVE FILTERS, ELECTRIC SEE ELECTRIC FILTERS / radio
QC661	WAVE GUIDES
QC174.2	WAVE MECHANICS
QC453	WAVE-LENGTH TABLES SEE SPECTRUM ANALYSIS — TABLES, ETC.
QA927	WAVE-MOTION, THEORY OF
QE391.W	WAVELLITE
GC211-222	WAVES
QC157	WAVES / physics
VK547	WAVES, CALMING OF
QA927	WAVES, GRAVITY SEE GRAVITY WAVES / mathematics
QC244	WAVES, ULTRASONIC SEE ULTRASONIC WAVES / acoustics
E99.W	WAWENOCK INDIANS
PM2555	WAWENOCK LANGUAGE
TP670-695	WAX SEE WAXES / oils
NK9580	WAX FIGURES
TT894	WAX FLOWERS
SB447	WAX FLOWERS / reproduction of flowers
SB299.W3	WAX PALMS / plant culture
NK9580	WAX PORTRAITS SEE WAX-MODELING
NK9580	WAX-MODELING
ND2480	WAX-PAINTING SEE ENCAUSTIC PAINTING
SB299.W3	WAX-PALM OF BRAZIL
TN857	WAX, MINERAL SEE CERESIN
TP695	WAX, MINERAL SEE CERESIN
TP695	WAX, MINERAL SEE OZOKERITE / chemical technology
TN857	WAX, MINERAL SEE OZOKERITE / mineral industries
TP670-695	WAXES / oils
QL561.P9	WAXMOTH SEE BEE-MOTH
QL696.P2	WAXWINGS
GV1836	WAXWORKS
BM723	WAY OF LIFE, JEWISH SEE JEWISH WAY OF LIFE
BX2040	WAY OF THE CROSS SEE STATIONS OF THE CROSS
PM7185	WAYAWAI LANGUAGE SEE UAIUAI LANGUAGE
PM7185	WAYEWE LANGUAGE SEE UAIUAI LANGUAGE
GT6450-6490	WAYFARING LIFE / manners and customs
E83.794	WAYNE'S CAMPAIGN, 1794
E99.W	WEA INDIANS
QL638.S34	WEAKFISH
QE924	WEALDEN FLORA SEE PALEOBOTANY — CRETACEOUS
QE734	WEALDEN FOSSILS SEE PALEONTOLOGY — CRETACEOUS
HB821	WEALTH / distribution
HB251	WEALTH / theory
HB831-8	WEALTH / use
HB821	WEALTH, DISTRIBUTION OF SEE WEALTH / distribution
HB251	WEALTH, DISTRIBUTION OF SEE WEALTH / theory
HB831-8	WEALTH, DISTRIBUTION OF SEE WEALTH / use
HB835	WEALTH, ETHICS OF
RJ216	WEANING OF INFANTS SEE INFANTS — WEANING
U800-825	WEAPONS SEE ARMS AND ARMOR
NK6600-6699	WEAPONS SEE ARMS AND ARMOR / art
HD9743	WEAPONS SEE ARMS AND ARMOR / industry
TS535-7	WEAPONS SEE FIREARMS / manufacture
V	WEAPONS SEE FIREARMS / u naval science
V990-993	WEAPONS SYSTEMS — PRODUCTION CONTROL
TA407	WEAR OXIDATION SEE FRETTING CORROSION
LB3431	WEARINESS SEE FATIGUE / educational hygiene
LB1075	WEARINESS SEE FATIGUE / educational psychology
QP321	WEARINESS SEE FATIGUE / muscle
BF481	WEARINESS SEE FATIGUE / psychology
QL737.C2	WEASELS
BF353	WEATHER — MENTAL AND PHYSIOLOGICAL EFFECTS
QC877	WEATHER BROADCASTING
QC928	WEATHER CONTROL
QC995	WEATHER FORECASTING
QC928	WEATHER MODIFICATION SEE WEATHER CONTROL
QC877	WEATHER REPORTING, RADIO
QC877	WEATHER REPORTS, RADIO SEE WEATHER BROADCASTING
TL798.M4	WEATHER SATELLITES SEE METEOROLOGICAL SATELLITES
QC877	WEATHER SIGNALS
QC875	WEATHER TELEGRAPHY
QC998	WEATHER-LORE
QC851-999	WEATHER
QC982-993	WEATHER / reports
QC883	WEATHER, INFLUENCE OF THE MOON ON
BF353	WEATHER-PHYSIOLOGICAL EFFECT SEE WEATHER — MENTAL AND PHYSIOLOGICAL EFFECTS
NK9585	WEATHERCOCKS SEE VANES
TN817	WEATHERING OF COAL SEE COAL-WEATHERING
QL696.P2	WEAVER-BIRDS
HD8039.W3	WEAVERS / labor
TS1490	WEAVING — TABLES AND READY-RECKONERS
LB1543	WEAVING (MANUAL TRAINING) / primary schools
TS1490-1500	WEAVING
GN432	WEAVING / primitive
GV1511.W3	WEB (GAME)
BF237	WEBER-FECHNER LAW SEE FECHNER'S LAW / psychology
QP435	WEBER-FECHNER LAW SEE WEBER'S LAW
QP435	WEBER'S LAW
QE391.W	WEBERITE
DS489.2	WEDDAHS SEE VEDDAHS
BJ2051-2065	WEDDING ETIQUETTE
BT378.M3	WEDDING GARMENT (PARABLE) SEE MARRIAGE OF THE KING'S SON (PARABLE)
TR575	WEDDING PHOTOGRAPHY
PR1195.E6	WEDDING PUBLICATIONS SEE EPITHALAMIA / english
PM8963	WEDE (ARTIFICIAL LANGUAGE)
QA935	WEDGES / analytical mechanics
QC131	WEDGES / physics
NK4335	WEDGWOOD WARE
SB611-618	WEED CONTROL
SB611-618	WEED ERADICATION SEE WEED CONTROL
Z689	WEEDING (BOOKS) SEE BOOK SELECTION
Z1035.A1	WEEDING (BOOKS) SEE BOOK SELECTION
SB611-615	WEEDS
SB611-618	WEEDS-CONTROL SEE WEED CONTROL
SB611-618	WEEDS-ERADICATION SEE WEED CONTROL
BV1580-1583	WEEK-DAY CHURCH SCHOOLS
BV28	WEEK-NIGHT SERVICES SEE CHURCH-NIGHT SERVICES
CE85	WEEK
HD5114	WEEKLY REST-DAY
E99.W	WEEMINUCHE INDIANS SEE WIMINUCHE INDIANS
HQ748.C	WEEPING SEE CRYING
QL638.T4	WEEVERS
QL571-597	WEEVILS SEE BEETLES
GV1469.G7	WEI CHI (GAME) SEE GO (GAME)
DS748.6	WEI DYNASTY, NORTHERN SEE CHINA — HISTORY — — NORTHERN WEI DYNASTY, 386-636
GV1469.G7	WEI-KI (GAME) SEE GO (GAME)
QC107	WEIGHING-MACHINES
RC628	WEIGHT CONTROL (PHYSIOLOGY) SEE CORPULENCE
GN63	WEIGHT IN INFANCY SEE INFANTS — WEIGHT
GV511	WEIGHT LIFTING
GV509	WEIGHT REDUCING EXERCISES SEE REDUCING EXERCISES
GV1093	WEIGHT THROWING
HF5711-5716	WEIGHTS AND MEASURES — TABLES, ETC.
QC81-119	WEIGHTS AND MEASURES
RS57	WEIGHTS AND MEASURES / pharmaceutical
QC84	WEIGHTS AND MEASURES, ANCIENT
RC184.S5	WEIL'S DISEASE
SF429.W33	WEIMARANERS (DOGS)
DD901.W	WEINSBERG — SIEGE, 1140
PN56.W	WEINSBERG — SIEGE, 1140 / literature
TC555	WEIRS
TC175	WEIRS / hydraulics
DC302.3	WEISSENBURG, BATTLE OF, 1870
D267.W4	WEISSER BERG, BATTLE OF, 1620
TA684	WELDED STEEL STRUCTURES
HD7269.W	WELDING — HYGIENIC ASPECTS
TS227	WELDING / machine
TT211	WELDING / manual
NA6598	WELFARE BUILDINGS IN INDUSTRY SEE EMPLOYEES' BUILDINGS AND FACILITIES
HV40-41	WELFARE FEDERATIONS SEE FEDERATIONS, FINANCIAL (SOCIAL SERVICE)

HV97	*WELFARE FEDERATIONS* **SEE** FEDERATIONS, FINANCIAL (SOCIAL SERVICE) / *national*
HD7260-7780	*WELFARE INSTITUTIONS FOR LABORERS* **SEE** WELFARE WORK IN INDUSTRY
HD7260-7780	WELFARE WORK IN INDUSTRY
TD410-412	*WELL-BORING* **SEE** BORING / *etc.*
TD410-412	*WELL-BORING* **SEE** BORING / *etc.*
TN281	*WELL-BORING* **SEE** BORING / *mining*
TD407	WELLS — STANDARDS
TD405-414	WELLS
GR690	WELLS / *folk-lore*
GR690	*WELLS, HOLY* **SEE** HOLY WELLS
PB2281	WELSH BALLADS AND SONGS / *collections*
PB2248	WELSH BALLADS AND SONGS / *collections*
PB2289	WELSH BALLADS AND SONGS / *collections*
PB2311	WELSH BALLADS AND SONGS / *folk literature*
PB2227-2231	WELSH BALLADS AND SONGS / *history*
SF429.W	WELSH CORGIS
PB2283	WELSH DRAMA / *collections*
PB2234	WELSH DRAMA / *history*
E99.W5	WELSH INDIANS
PB2101-2199	WELSH LANGUAGE
PB2206-2499	WELSH LITERATURE
PN5127.W	WELSH PERIODICALS / *gt. brit.*
PN4885.W	WELSH PERIODICALS / *u.s.*
PB2101-2199	WELSH PHILOLOGY
PR8926-8932	*WELSH POETRY (ENGLISH)* **SEE** ENGLISH POETRY — WELSH AUTHORS / *history*
PR8955-8969	*WELSH POETRY (ENGLISH)* **SEE** ENGLISH POETRY — WELSH AUTHORS / *collections*
PB2289	WELSH POETRY / *collections*
PB2281	WELSH POETRY / *collections*
PB2248	WELSH POETRY / *collections*
PB2227-2231	WELSH POETRY / *history*
TX825	WELSH RABBIT
TX759	WELSH RABBIT
DA700-730	WELSH
PL8771	*WENDA LANGUAGE* **SEE** VENDA LANGUAGE
PG5675	WENDIC BALLADS AND SONGS / *collections*
PG5669	WENDIC BALLADS AND SONGS / *history*
PG1801-1899	*WENDIC DIALECT (SLOVENIAN)* **SEE** SLOVENIAN LANGUAGE
PG5631-5659	WENDIC LANGUAGE
PG5661-5698	WENDIC LITERATURE
DD78.W4	WENDS / *germany*
DD491.L348	WENDS / *lusatia*
DD38	WENDS / *prussia*
DD801.S348	WENDS / *saxony*
E99.W54	WENROHRONON INDIANS
PL7501.B8	WERCHIKWAR DIALECT
PL7501.B8	*WERCIKWAR DIALECT* **SEE** WERCHIKWAR DIALECT
GN495.2	*WERELEOPARDS* **SEE** LEOPARD MEN
GR830.W4	*WEREWOLVES* **SEE** WERWOLVES
GN495.2	*WERLEOPARDS* **SEE** LEOPARD MEN
PL7501.B8	*WERSHIKWAR DIALECT* **SEE** WERCHIKWAR DIALECT
GR830.W4	WERWOLVES
E184.W5	WESORTS
CB251	*WEST AND EAST* **SEE** EAST AND WEST
PK8001-8454	*WEST ARMENIAN LANGUAGE* **SEE** ARMENIAN LANGUAGE
D137	*WEST GOTHS* **SEE** VISIGOTHS
SF429.W4	WEST HIGHLAND WHITE TERRIERS
F1601-1623	WEST INDIES — HISTORY
E263.W5	WEST INDIES — HISTORY — — 1775-1783
F236-260	WEST VIRGINIA — HISTORY
E472.17	WEST VIRGINIA CAMPAIGN, 1861
E536	WEST VIRGINIA — HISTORY — — CIVIL WAR
E582	WEST VIRGINIA — HISTORY — — CIVIL WAR / *confederate*
TJ717	WEST'S ENGINE
CB245	*WESTERN CIVILIZATION* **SEE** CIVILIZATION, OCCIDENTAL
E315	*WESTERN INSURRECTION, 1794* **SEE** WHISKEY INSURRECTION, 1794
PB1-431	*WESTERN LANGUAGES* **SEE** LANGUAGES, MODERN
SB608.P65	WESTERN RED-ROT
BX1301	*WESTERN SCHISM* **SEE** SCHISM, THE GREAT WESTERN, 1378-1417
SD397.P	*WESTERN WHITE PINE* **SEE** PINUS MONTICOLA
SD397.P75	*WESTERN YELLOW PINE* **SEE** YELLOW PINE

TF425	WESTINGHOUSE AIR-BRAKE
BX8905.W4	WESTMINSTER GUILDS
DJ181-2	WESTMINSTER, ENG., TREATY OF, 1654
D269	WESTPHALIA, PEACE OF, 1648
E477.16	WESTPORT, MO., BATTLE OF, 1864
RJ216	WET-NURSES
QC310	*WETTING, HEAT OF* **SEE** HEAT OF WETTING
E99.W	*WEWEENOCK INDIANS* **SEE** WAWENOCK INDIANS
QA689	*WEYL SPACE* **SEE** SPACES, GENERALIZED
QL638.9	WHALE-SHARK
SH385	WHALEBONE
QL737.C4	WHALES
QE882.C5	WHALES, FOSSIL
SH381	WHALING — LAWS AND REGULATIONS
SH381	*WHALING LAWS AND REGULATIONS* **SEE** WHALING — LAWS AND REGULATIONS
SH381-7	WHALING
G545	WHALING / *voyages*
TC357	WHARVES
SB608.W5	WHEAT — DISEASES AND PESTS
SB190	WHEAT — STORAGE
TP684.W	WHEAT GERM OIL / *chemical technology*
TP684.W	*WHEAT OIL* **SEE** WHEAT GERM OIL / *chemical technology*
TX357	*WHEAT SUBSTITUTES* **SEE** FOOD CONSERVATION
HF5716.G7	WHEAT TRADE — TABLES AND READY-RECKONERS
HD9049.W4	WHEAT TRADE
SB191.W5	WHEAT
GT5899.W5	WHEAT / *manners and customs*
E475.87	WHEELER AND RODDEY'S RAID, 1863
BL1475.W4	WHEELS (IN RELIGION, FOLK-LORE, ETC.)
TJ181.5	WHEELS / *mechanical movements*
TF383	WHEELS / *railway car construction*
SF247	WHEY-SEPARATORS
SF259	WHEY
JN1129.W6-65	WHIG PARTY (GT. BRIT.)
JK2326-2335	WHIG PARTY
SF429.W5	WHIPPETS
HV8609	*WHIPPING* **SEE** CORPORAL PUNISHMENT / *penology*
LB3025	*WHIPPING* **SEE** CORPORAL PUNISHMENT / *schools*
HV8613-8621	*WHIPPING* **SEE** FLAGELLANTS AND FLAGELLATION
GC239	WHIRLPOOLS / *ocean currents*
QC159	WHIRLPOOLS / *physics*
HJ5021	WHISKEY FRAUDS
E315	WHISKEY INSURRECTION, 1794
TP605	WHISKEY
TP605	*WHISKY* **SEE** WHISKEY
GV1271-1291	WHIST
QL737.R6	*WHISTLERS (WOODCHUCKS)* **SEE** MARMOTS
HE9323-9337	*WHISTLES (STEAM)* **SEE** STEAM-WHISTLES / *signaling*
MT705	WHISTLING
QL513.T3	*WHITE ANTS* **SEE** TERMITES
SD397.A6	WHITE ASH
QP95	*WHITE BLOOD CELLS* **SEE** LEUCOCYTES
HF5501	*WHITE COLLAR WORKERS* **SEE** CLERKS
HV3165-3173	*WHITE COLLAR WORKERS* **SEE** CLERKS / *aid to*
HD8039.M4	*WHITE COLLAR WORKERS* **SEE** CLERKS / *mercantile clerks*
SF995	*WHITE DIARRHEA* **SEE** PULLORUM DISEASE
SD397.E	WHITE ELM / *forestry*
BV2300.W5	WHITE FATHERS
BX3201-3255	*WHITE FRIARS* **SEE** CARMELITES
BX4321-4	*WHITE FRIARS* **SEE** CARMELITES / *women*
TP936	WHITE LEAD
RA1231.L4	WHITE LEAD / *lead-poisoning*
D267.W4	*WHITE MOUNTAIN, BATTLE OF, 1620* **SEE** WEISSER BERG, BATTLE OF, 1620
E477.67	WHITE OAK ROAD, VA., BATTLE OF, 1865
QK495.Q4	WHITE OAK / *botany*
SD397.O12	WHITE OAK / *forestry*
SD397.P65	WHITE PINE
E241.W5	WHITE PLAINS, BATTLE OF, 1776
PG2831-6	WHITE RUSSIAN LANGUAGE
PG2835	WHITE RUSSIAN LITERATURE
DK507	WHITE RUSSIANS
QL737.C4	WHITE WHALE
QL568.V5	WHITE-FACED HORNET
SB495.W	WHITE-FRINGED BEETLES

HQ101-440	*WHITE-SLAVE TRAFFIC* **SEE** PROSTITUTION
SF997	WHITE-TAILED DEER — DISEASES
SF510.P7	*WHITEBELLY* **SEE** PRAIRIE-HENS / *culture*
SK325.P7	*WHITEBELLY* **SEE** PRAIRIE-HENS / *hunting*
QL696.G2	*WHITEBELLY* **SEE** PRAIRIE-HENS / *zoology*
HV6535.G8	WHITECHAPEL MURDERS, 1888
QL638.S2	WHITEFISHES
V855.W5	WHITEHEAD TORPEDOES
TP245.C3	*WHITING* **SEE** CHALK / *chemical technology*
HD9999.C36	*WHITING* **SEE** CHALK / *economics*
QH471	*WHITING* **SEE** CHALK / *geology*
TN948.C5	*WHITING* **SEE** CHALK / *mineral resources*
BV60	*WHITSUNDAY* **SEE** PENTECOST FESTIVAL / *christian*
BM695.P5	*WHITSUNDAY* **SEE** PENTECOST FESTIVAL / *jewish*
BV60	*WHITSUNTIDE* **SEE** PENTECOST FESTIVAL / *christian*
BM695.P5	*WHITSUNTIDE* **SEE** PENTECOST FESTIVAL / *jewish*
NK9700-9799	*WHITTLING* **SEE** WOOD-CARVING
BD396	WHOLE AND PARTS (PHILOSOPHY)
BF202	WHOLE AND PARTS (PSYCHOLOGY)
BD396	*WHOLENESS (PHILOSOPHY)* **SEE** WHOLE AND PARTS (PHILOSOPHY)
BF202	*WHOLENESS (PSYCHOLOGY)* **SEE** WHOLE AND PARTS (PSYCHOLOGY)
HF5341-5353	WHOLESALE TRADE
RX226.W6	WHOOPING-COUGH — HOMEOPATHIC TREATMENT
RC204	WHOOPING-COUGH
E99.W6	WICHITA INDIANS
HD234.W5	WICHITA INDIANS / *land transfers*
GV1017.W6	WICKET-POLO
GV1017.W5	WICKET
BX4900-4906	*WICLIFITES* **SEE** LOLLARDS
QR201.T9	*WIDAL'S REACTION* **SEE** TYPHOID FEVER — DIAGNOSIS — — AGGLUTINATION REACTION
TR855	WIDE-SCREEN PROCESSES (CINEMATOGRAPHY)
BV4596.W	WIDOWS — RELIGIOUS LIFE
HV697-700	WIDOWS / *pensions*
HV697-700	*WIDOWS' PENSIONS* **SEE** MOTHERS' PENSIONS
HV697-700	*WIDOWS-PENSIONS* **SEE** MOTHERS' PENSIONS
B824.6	*WIENER KREIS* **SEE** LOGICAL POSITIVISM
HV6626	WIFE BEATING
TT975	WIGS
GT2310	WIGS / *manners and customs*
E98.D9	*WIGWAMS* **SEE** INDIANS OF NORTH AMERICA — DWELLINGS
SK305.W5	WILD BOAR / *hunting*
SB439	WILD FLOWER GARDENING
QK86	*WILD FLOWERS, PROTECTION OF* **SEE** PLANTS, PROTECTION OF
SB599-999	*WILD FLOWERS, PROTECTION OF* **SEE** PLANTS, PROTECTION OF / *diseases and pests*
GN290	WILD MEN
SB191.I5	*WILD RICE* **SEE** INDIAN RICE / *culture*
E98.F7	*WILD RICE* **SEE** INDIAN RICE / *indian food*
SK	*WILD-FOWL* **SEE** GAME AND GAME-BIRDS / *hunting*
QL696.G2	*WILD-FOWL* **SEE** GAME AND GAME-BIRDS / *ornithology*
QL671-698	*WILD-FOWL* **SEE** WATER-BIRDS
SK351-579	*WILD-FOWL* **SEE** WATER-BIRDS / *game preservation*
SK331-3	*WILD-FOWL* **SEE** WATER-BIRDS / *hunting*
HD5311	WILDCAT STRIKES
E476.52	WILDERNESS, BATTLE OF THE, 1864
SK311-333	*WILDFOWLING* **SEE** FOWLING
RA1270.P4	*WILDLIFE, EFFECT OF PESTICIDES ON* **SEE** PESTICIDES — TOXICOLOGY
QB723.W	WILK'S COMET
Q115.W6-8	*WILKES EXPLORING EXPEDITION* **SEE** UNITED STATES EXPLORING EXPEDITION, 1838-1842
BF818-839	*WILL-TEMPERAMENT TESTS* **SEE** CHARACTER TESTS
LB1071	WILL / *educational*
BJ1460-1468	WILL / *ethics*
BF608-635	WILL / *psychology*
E199	WILLIAM HENRY, FORT, CAPTURE OF, 1757
E473.63	WILLIAMSBURG, BATTLE OF, 1862
SB608.W65	WILLOWS — DISEASES AND PESTS
QK495.S16	WILLOWS
SD397.W5	WILLOWS / *sylviculture*
BX1939.W5	WILLS (CANON LAW)
BJ1286.W59-6	WILLS, ETHICAL

E416	WILMOT PROVISO, 1846
E477.96	WILSON'S CAVALRY RAID, 1865
E472.23	WILSON'S CREEK, BATTLE OF, 1861
RC394.H4	*WILSON'S DISEASE* **SEE** HEPATOLENTICULAR DEGENERATION
E99.W	WIMINUCHE INDIANS
E473.72	*WINCHESTER, BATTLE OF, MAR. 23, 1862* **SEE** KERNSTOWN, BATTLE OF, 1862
E477.33	WINCHESTER, BATTLE OF, SEPT. 19, 1864
QC931-940	*WIND* **SEE** WINDS
M955-7	WIND ENSEMBLES
M958-9	WIND ENSEMBLES, ARRANGED
ML930	WIND INSTRUMENTS — CONSTRUCTION
MT339	WIND INSTRUMENTS — INSTRUCTION AND STUDY
ML404	WIND INSTRUMENTS — MAKERS / *biography collective*
ML424	WIND INSTRUMENTS — MAKERS / *individual*
MT339	WIND INSTRUMENTS — METHODS (JAZZ)
MT339	WIND INSTRUMENTS — METHODS
ML930	WIND INSTRUMENTS — REPAIRING
MT339	WIND INSTRUMENTS — STUDIES AND EXERCISES (JAZZ)
MT339	WIND INSTRUMENTS / STUDIES AND EXERCISES
ML930-980	WIND INSTRUMENTS / *history and construction*
M955-7	WIND NONETS (EUPHONIUM, 2 HORNS, 2 TROMBONES, 3 TRUMPETS, TUBA)
M958-9	WIND NONETS (EUPHONIUM, 2 HORNS, 2 TROMBONES, 3 TRUMPETS, TUBA), ARRANGED
M955-7	WIND NONETS (2 BASSOONS, 2 CLARINETS, FLUTE, 2 HORNS, OBOE, TRUMPET)
M955-7	WIND NONETS (2 BASSOONS, 2 CLARINETS, FLUTE, 2 HORNS, 2 OBOES)
M955-7	WIND NONETS (2 HORNS, 3 TROMBONES, 3 TRUMPETS, TUBA)
M955-7	WIND NONETS (3 BASSOONS, 2 CLARINETS, 2 HORNS, 2 OBOES)
M958-9	WIND NONETS (3 BASSOONS, 2 CLARINETS, 2 HORNS, 2 OBOES), ARRANGED
M955-7	WIND NONETS (3 HORNS, 3 TROMBONES, 3 TRUMPETS)
M955-7	WIND NONETS
M855-7	WIND OCTETS (BASSOON, 3 CLARINETS, FLUTE, 2 HORNS, OBOE)
M855-7	WIND OCTETS (CORNET, 2 HORNS, 2 TROMBONES, 2 TRUMPETS, TUBA)
M855-7	WIND OCTETS (EUPHONIUM, 2 HORNS, 3 TROMBONES, 2 TRUMPETS)
M855-7	WIND OCTETS (2 BARITONES, 2 CORNETS, 2 HORNS, 2 TROMBONES)
M855-7	WIND OCTETS (2 BARITONES, 4 CORNETS, 2 HORNS)
M855-7	WIND OCTETS (2 BASSOONS, CLARINET, FLUTE, 2 TROMBONES, 2 TRUMPETS)
M855-7	WIND OCTETS (2 BASSOONS, 2 CLARINETS, ENGLISH HORN, FLUTE, HORN, OBOE)
M858-9	WIND OCTETS (2 BASSOONS, 2 CLARINETS, FLUTE, 2 HORNS, OBOE), ARRANGED
M855-7	WIND OCTETS (2 BASSOONS, 2 CLARINETS, FLUTE, 2 HORNS, OBOE)
M855-7	WIND OCTETS (2 BASSOONS, 2 CLARINETS, 2 FLUTES, 2 OBOES)
M855-7	WIND OCTETS (2 BASSOONS, 2 CLARINETS, 2 HORNS, 2 OBOES)
M855-7	WIND OCTETS (2 BASSOONS, 2 ENGLISH HORNS, 2 HORNS, 2 OBOES)
M858-9	WIND OCTETS (2 BASSOONS, 2 ENGLISH HORNS, 2 HORNS, 2 OBOES), ARRANGED
M858-9	WIND OCTETS (2 CORNETS, 2 HORNS, 3 TROMBONES, TUBA), ARRANGED
M855-7	WIND OCTETS (2 HORNS, 2 TROMBONES, 4 TRUMPETS)
M855-7	WIND OCTETS (3 HORNS, 2 TROMBONES, 3 TRUMPETS)
M858-9	WIND OCTETS (3 HORNS, 2 TROMBONES, 3 TRUMPETS), ARRANGED
M855-7	WIND OCTETS (3 TROMBONES, 4 TRUMPETS, TUBA)
M855-7	WIND OCTETS (4 TROMBONES, 4 TRUMPETS)
M858-9	WIND OCTETS (4 TROMBONES, 4 TRUMPETS), ARRANGED
M855-7	WIND OCTETS (8 CLARINETS)
M855-7	WIND OCTETS (8 RECORDERS)
M858-9	WIND OCTETS (8 RECORDERS), ARRANGED

M855-7	WIND OCTETS (8 TROMBONES)
M858-9	WIND OCTETS (8 TROMBONES), ARRANGED
M855-7	WIND OCTETS
M455-7	WIND QUARTETS (BARITONE, CORNET, HORN, TROMBONE)
M458-9	WIND QUARTETS (BARITONE, CORNET, HORN, TROMBONE), ARRANGED
M455-7	WIND QUARTETS (BARITONE, TROMBONE, 2 TRUMPETS)
M455-7	WIND QUARTETS (BARITONE, 2 CORNETS, HORN)
M458-9	WIND QUARTETS (BARITONE, 2 CORNETS, HORN), ARRANGED
M455-7	WIND QUARTETS (BARITONE, 2 CORNETS, TROMBONE)
M458-9	WIND QUARTETS (BARITONE, 2 CORNETS, TROMBONE), ARRANGED
M455-7	WIND QUARTETS (BASSOON, CLARINET, FLUTE, HORN)
M458-9	WIND QUARTETS (BASSOON, CLARINET, FLUTE, HORN), ARRANGED
M455-7	WIND QUARTETS (BASSOON, CLARINET, FLUTE, OBOE)
M458-9	WIND QUARTETS (BASSOON, CLARINET, FLUTE, OBOE), ARRANGED
M455-7	WIND QUARTETS (BASSOON, CLARINET, FLUTE, TRUMPET)
M455-7	WIND QUARTETS (BASSOON, CLARINET, HORN, OBOE)
M458-9	WIND QUARTETS (BASSOON, CLARINET, HORN, OBOE), ARRANGED
M455-7	WIND QUARTETS (BASSOON, CLARINET, OBOE, PICCOLO)
M458-9	WIND QUARTETS (BASSOON, CLARINET, OBOE, PICCOLO), ARRANGED
M455-7	WIND QUARTETS (BASSOON, CLARINET, OBOE, TRUMPET)
M455-7	WIND QUARTETS (BASSOON, FLUTE, HORN, OBOE)
M455-7	WIND QUARTETS (BASSOON, 2 CLARINETS, FLUTE)
M455-7	WIND QUARTETS (BASSOON, 2 CLARINETS, OBOE)
M455-7	WIND QUARTETS (BASSOON, 2 CLARINETS, SAXOPHONE)
M458-9	WIND QUARTETS (BASSOON, 2 CLARINETS, SAXOPHONE), ARRANGED
M455-7	WIND QUARTETS (CLARINET, ENGLISH HORN, FLUTE, OBOE)
M455-7	WIND QUARTETS (CORNET, HORN, 2 TROMBONES)
M455-7	WIND QUARTETS (CORNET, 3 TROMBONES)
M455-7	WIND QUARTETS (HORN, TROMBONE, TRUMPET, TUBA)
M455-7	WIND QUARTETS (HORN, TROMBONE, 2 TRUMPETS)
M455-7	WIND QUARTETS (HORN, 2 TROMBONES, TRUMPET)
M455-7	WIND QUARTETS (2 CLARINETS, FLUTE, OBOE)
M455-7	WIND QUARTETS (2 CLARINETS, 2 FLUTES)
M455-7	WIND QUARTETS (2 CLARINETS, 2 HORNS)
M455-7	WIND QUARTETS (2 CORNETS, EUPHONIUM, HORN)
M458-9	WIND QUARTETS (2 CORNETS, EUPHONIUM, HORN), ARRANGED
M455-7	WIND QUARTETS (2 CORNETS, HORN, TROMBONE)
M455-7	WIND QUARTETS (2 TROMBONES, 2 TRUMPETS)
M458-9	WIND QUARTETS (2 TROMBONES, 2 TRUMPETS), ARRANGED
M455-7	WIND QUARTETS (3 TROMBONES, TRUMPET)
M458-9	WIND QUARTETS (3 TROMBONES, TRUMPET), ARRANGED
M455-7	WIND QUARTETS (3 TROMBONES, TUBA)
M458-9	WIND QUARTETS (3 TROMBONES, TUBA), ARRANGED
M455-7	WIND QUARTETS (4 BASSOONS)
M455-7	WIND QUARTETS (4 CLARINETS)
M458-9	WIND QUARTETS (4 CLARINETS), ARRANGED
M455-7	WIND QUARTETS (4 CORNETS)
M458-9	WIND QUARTETS (4 CORNETS), ARRANGED
M455-7	WIND QUARTETS (4 FLUTES)
M458-9	WIND QUARTETS (4 FLUTES), ARRANGED
M1205	WIND QUARTETS (4 HORNS) WITH BAND
M455-7	WIND QUARTETS (4 HORNS)
M455-7	WIND QUARTETS (4 PIPES)
M455-7	WIND QUARTETS (4 RECORDERS)
M458-9	WIND QUARTETS (4 RECORDERS), ARRANGED
M455-7	WIND QUARTETS (4 SAXOPHONES)
M458-9	WIND QUARTETS (4 SAXOPHONES), ARRANGED
M455-7	WIND QUARTETS (4 TROMBONES)
M458-9	WIND QUARTETS (4 TROMBONES), ARRANGED
M455-7	WIND QUARTETS (4 TRUMPETS)
M458-9	WIND QUARTETS (4 TRUMPETS), ARRANGED
M455-7	WIND QUARTETS
M458-9	WIND QUARTETS, ARRANGED
M555-7	WIND QUINTETS (ALTO HORN, BARITONE, 2 CORNETS, TUBA)
M555-7	WIND QUINTETS (BARITONE, CORNET, HORN, TROMBONE, TUBA)
M558-9	WIND QUINTETS (BARITONE, CORNET, HORN, TROMBONE, TUBA), ARRANGED
M555-7	WIND QUINTETS (BARITONE, CORNET, HORN, TRUMPET, TUBA)
M558-9	WIND QUINTETS (BARITONE, HORN, TROMBONE, 2 TRUMPETS), ARRANGED
M555-7	WIND QUINTETS (BARITONE, HORN, TROMBONE, 2 TRUMPETS)
M555-7	WIND QUINTETS (BARITONE, 2 CORNETS, HORN, TROMBONE)
M558-9	WIND QUINTETS (BARITONE, 2 CORNETS, HORN, TROMBONE), ARRANGED
M555-7	WIND QUINTETS (BARITONE, 2 CORNETS, HORN, TUBA)
M558-9	WIND QUINTETS (BARITONE, 2 CORNETS, HORN, TUBA), ARRANGED
M558-9	WIND QUINTETS (BARITONE, 2 CORNETS, TROMBONE, TUBA), ARRANGED
M555-7	WIND QUINTETS (BARITONE, 2 CORNETS, TROMBONE, TUBA)
M555-7	WIND QUINTETS (BASSOON, CLARINET, ENGLISH HORN, FLUTE, OBOE)
M555-7	WIND QUINTETS (BASSOON, CLARINET, FLUTE, HORN, OBOE)
M558-9	WIND QUINTETS (BASSOON, CLARINET, FLUTE, HORN, OBOE), ARRANGED
M555-7	WIND QUINTETS (BASSOON, CLARINET, FLUTE, OBOE, TROMBONE)
M555-7	WIND QUINTETS (BASSOON, CLARINET, 2 HORNS, OBOE)
M557-9	WIND QUINTETS (BASSOON, 2 CLARINETS, FLUTE, HORN)
M555-7	WIND QUINTETS (BASSOON, 2 CLARINETS, FLUTE, OBOE)
M555-7	WIND QUINTETS (BASSOON, 2 CLARINETS, 2 HORNS)
M555-7	WIND QUINTETS (BASSOON, 2 CLARINETS, 2 OBOES)
M555-7	WIND QUINTETS (BASSOON, 2 FLUTES, 2 HORNS)
M555-7	WIND QUINTETS (BASSOON, 2 HORNS, 2 OBOES)
M555-7	WIND QUINTETS (BASSOON, 3 HORNS, OBOE)
M555-7	WIND QUINTETS (BASSOON, 4 CLARINETS)
M558-9	WIND QUINTETS (BASSOON, 4 CLARINETS), ARRANGED
M555-7	WIND QUINTETS (EUPHONIUM, HORN, TROMBONE, 2 TRUMPETS)
M555-7	WIND QUINTETS (HORN, TROMBONE, 2 TRUMPETS, TUBA)
M558-9	WIND QUINTETS (HORN, TROMBONE, 2 TRUMPETS, TUBA), ARRANGED
M555-7	WIND QUINTETS (HORN, 2 TROMBONES, 2 TRUMPETS)
M555-7	WIND QUINTETS (2 BARITONES, TROMBONE, 2 TRUMPETS)
M558-9	WIND QUINTETS (2 BARITONES, TROMBONE, 2 TRUMPETS), ARRANGED
M555-7	WIND QUINTETS (2 BASSOONS, 2 OBOES, TRUMPET)
M555-7	WIND QUINTETS (2 CORNETS, HORN, TROMBONE, TUBA)
M555-7	WIND QUINTETS (2 CORNETS, 3 TRUMPETS)
M555-7	WIND QUINTETS (2 HORNS, TROMBONE, 2 TRUMPETS)
M555-7	WIND QUINTETS (2 HORNS, 3 TROMBONES)
M558-9	WIND QUINTETS (2 HORNS, 3 TROMBONES), ARRANGED
M555-7	WIND QUINTETS (3 CLARINETS, 2 FLUTES)
M555-7	WIND QUINTETS (3 TROMBONES, 2 TRUMPETS)
M555-7	WIND QUINTETS (4 CLARINETS, SAXOPHONE)
M555-7	WIND QUINTETS (4 SAXOPHONES, TRUMPET)
M555-7	WIND QUINTETS (4 TROMBONES, TUBA)
M558-9	WIND QUINTETS (4 TROMBONES, TUBA), ARRANGED
M555-7	WIND QUINTETS (5 FLUTES)
M555-7	WIND QUINTETS (5 RECORDERS)
M555-7	WIND QUINTETS
M558-9	WIND QUINTETS, ARRANGED
M755-7	WIND SEPTETS (BARITONE, 2 CORNETS, 2 HORNS, TROMBONE, TUBA)
M758-9	WIND SEPTETS (BARITONE, 2 CORNETS, 2 HORNS, TROMBONE, TUBA), ARRANGED

M758-9	WIND SEPTETS (BARITONE, 2 HORNS, TROMBONE, 2 TRUMPETS, TUBA), ARRANGED
M758-9	WIND SEPTETS (BARITONE, 3 CORNETS, HORN, 2 TROMBONES), ARRANGED
M755-7	WIND SEPTETS (BARITONE, 3 CORNETS, HORN, 2 TROMBONES)
M755-7	WIND SEPTETS (BASSOON, 2 CLARINETS, FLUTE, HORN, OBOE, TRUMPET)
M755-7	WIND SEPTETS (BASSOON, 2 CLARINETS, 2 HORNS, 2 OBOES)
M755-7	WIND SEPTETS (BASSOON, 4 CLARINETS, FLUTE, OBOE)
M758-9	WIND SEPTETS (BASSOON, 4 CLARINETS, FLUTE, OBOE), ARRANGED
M755-7	WIND SEPTETS (2 BASSOONS, 2 CLARINETS, FLUTE, HORN, OBOE)
M755-7	WIND SEPTETS (2 HORNS, 2 TROMBONES, 2 TRUMPETS, TUBA)
M755-7	WIND SEPTETS (2 HORNS, 2 TROMBONES, 3 TRUMPETS)
M755-7	WIND SEPTETS (3 TROMBONES, 3 TRUMPETS, TUBA)
M755-7	WIND SEPTETS (3 TROMBONES, 4 TRUMPETS)
M755-7	WIND SEPTETS (4 TROMBONES, 3 TRUMPETS)
M755-7	WIND SEPTETS
M655-7	WIND SEXTETS (BARITONE, CORNET, HORN, TROMBONE, TRUMPET, TUBA)
M655-7	WIND SEXTETS (BARITONE, HORN, TROMBONE, 2 TRUMPETS, TUBA)
M658-9	WIND SEXTETS (BARITONE, HORN, TROMBONE, 2 TRUMPETS, TUBA), ARRANGED
M658-9	WIND SEXTETS (BARITONE, 2 CORNETS, HORN, TROMBONE, TUBA), ARRANGED
M655-7	WIND SEXTETS (BARITONE, 2 CORNETS, HORN, TROMBONE, TUBA)
M655-7	WIND SEXTETS (BASSOON, CLARINET, FLUTE, HORN, OBOE, TRUMPET)
M658-9	WIND SEXTETS (BASSOON, 2 CLARINETS, ENGLISH HORN, FLUTE, OBOE), ARRANGED
M655-7	WIND SEXTETS (BASSOON, 2 CLARINETS, FLUTE, HORN, OBOE)
M658-9	WIND SEXTETS (BASSOON, 2 CLARINETS, FLUTE, HORN, OBOE), ARRANGED
M655-7	WIND SEXTETS (BASSOON, 3 CLARINETS, FLUTE, OBOE)
M658-9	WIND SEXTETS (BASSOON, 3 CLARINETS, FLUTE, OBOE), ARRANGED
M655-7	WIND SEXTETS (BASSOON, 3 CLARINETS, 2 FLUTES)
M655-7	WIND SEXTETS (HORN, 2 TROMBONES, 2 TRUMPETS, TUBA)
M658-9	WIND SEXTETS (HORN, 2 TROMBONES, 2 TRUMPETS, TUBA), ARRANGED
M655-7	WIND SEXTETS (HORN, 3 TROMBONES, 2 TRUMPETS)
M655-7	WIND SEXTETS (2 BASSOONS, 2 CLARINETS, 2 HORNS)
M655-7	WIND SEXTETS (2 BASSOONS, 2 HORNS, 2 OBOES)
M655-7	WIND SEXTETS (2 CORNETS, HORN, 2 TROMBONES, TUBA)
M655-7	WIND SEXTETS (2 HORNS, TROMBONE, 2 TRUMPETS, TUBA)
M658-9	WIND SEXTETS (2 HORNS, TROMBONE, 2 TRUMPETS, TUBA), ARRANGED
M655-7	WIND SEXTETS (3 TROMBONES, 3 TRUMPETS)
M655-7	WIND SEXTETS (4 TROMBONES, 2 TRUMPETS)
M655-7	WIND SEXTETS (6 CLARINETS)
M655-7	WIND SEXTETS (6 HORNS)
M655-7	WIND SEXTETS (6 RECORDERS)
M658-9	WIND SEXTETS (6 RECORDERS), ARRANGED
M655-7	WIND SEXTETS (6 TRUMPETS)
M655-7	WIND SEXTETS
GC225-6	*WIND TIDES* **SEE** STORM SURGES
M355-7	WIND TRIOS (BARITONE, 2 CORNETS)
M355-7	WIND TRIOS (BASSOON, CLARINET, FLUTE)
M355-7	WIND TRIOS (BASSOON, CLARINET, HORN)
M355-7	WIND TRIOS (BASSOON, CLARINET, OBOE)
M358-9	WIND TRIOS (BASSOON, CLARINET, OBOE), ARRANGED
M355-7	WIND TRIOS (BASSOON, CLARINET, TRUMPET)
M355-7	WIND TRIOS (BASSOON, FLUTE, OBOE)
M358-9	WIND TRIOS (BASSOON, FLUTE, OBOE), ARRANGED
M355-7	WIND TRIOS (BASSOON, OBOE, TRUMPET)
M355-7	WIND TRIOS (BASSOON, 2 CLARINETS)

M355-7	WIND TRIOS (BASSOON, 2 OBOES)
M355-7	WIND TRIOS (CLARINET, FLUTE, OBOE)
M355-7	WIND TRIOS (CLARINET, FLUTE, TRUMPET)
M355-7	WIND TRIOS (CLARINET, OBOE, PICCOLO)
M355-7	WIND TRIOS (CLARINET, TROMBONE, TRUMPET)
M355-7	WIND TRIOS (CLARINET, 2 FLUTES)
M355-7	WIND TRIOS (ENGLISH HORN, 2 OBOES)
M355-7	WIND TRIOS (FLUTE, OBOE, TRUMPET)
M355-7	WIND TRIOS (HORN, TROMBONE, TRUMPET)
M358-9	WIND TRIOS (HORN, TROMBONE, TRUMPET), ARRANGED
M355-7	WIND TRIOS (TROMBONE, 2 TRUMPETS)
M355-7	WIND TRIOS (2 CLARINETS, HORN)
M355-7	WIND TRIOS (2 OBOES, TRUMPET)
M355-7	WIND TRIOS (3 CLARINETS)
M358-9	WIND TRIOS (3 CLARINETS), ARRANGED
M355-7	WIND TRIOS (3 FLUTES)
M358-9	WIND TRIOS (3 FLUTES), ARRANGED
M1205	WIND TRIOS (3 HORNS) WITH BAND
M355-7	WIND TRIOS (3 HORNS)
M358-9	WIND TRIOS (3 HORNS), ARRANGED
M355-7	WIND TRIOS (3 MOUTH-ORGANS)
M355-7	WIND TRIOS (3 OBOES)
M355-7	WIND TRIOS (3 RECORDERS)
M358-9	WIND TRIOS (3 RECORDERS), ARRANGED
M355-7	WIND TRIOS (3 SAXOPHONES)
M355-7	WIND TRIOS (3 TROMBONES)
M355-7	WIND TRIOS (3 TRUMPETS)
M355-7	WIND TRIOS
TL567.W5	WIND TUNNELS
TG303	WIND-PRESSURE / bridge building
TA497	WIND-PRESSURE / engineering
TH891	WIND-PRESSURE / wind-pressure and building
PG1801-1899	*WINDIC DIALECT (SLOVENIAN)* **SEE** SLOVENIAN LANGUAGE
HD2747	*WINDING UP OF COMPANIES* **SEE** LIQUIDATION
K	*WINDING UP OF COMPANIES* **SEE** LIQUIDATION
VM811	WINDLASSES
N8216.W5	WINDMILLS IN ART
TJ823-7	WINDMILLS
HF5845-9	*WINDOW DRESSING* **SEE** SHOW-WINDOWS
TH2273	WINDOW GUARDS
TH2276	*WINDOW SHUTTERS* **SEE** BLINDS
SB419	WINDOW-GARDENING
TS2301.W5	WINDOW-SHADES
HJ2608	WINDOWS — TAXATION / gt. brit.
NA3000-3020	WINDOWS / architecture
TH2261-2276	WINDOWS / building
NK5300-5410	*WINDOWS, STAINED GLASS* **SEE** GLASS PAINTING AND STAINING
QL854	*WINDPIPE* **SEE** TRACHEA / comparative anatomy
QM257	*WINDPIPE* **SEE** TRACHEA / human anatomy
GR635	WINDS (IN RELIGION, FOLK-LORE, ETC.)
QC931-940	WINDS
TL275	*WINDSHIELDS (AUTOMOBILE)* **SEE** AUTOMOBILES — WINDOWS AND WINDSHIELDS
M1977.W54	WINE — SONGS AND MUSIC
M1978.W54	WINE — SONGS AND MUSIC
RM256	WINE — THERAPEUTIC USE
TP548	WINE AND WINE MAKING — ANALYSIS
TP548	WINE AND WINE MAKING — FILTRATION
TP546-559	WINE AND WINE MAKING
HD9370-9389	WINE AND WINE MAKING / industry
N8262	WINE IN ART
PN6237	WINE IN LITERATURE
TL672-3	*WINGS (AEROPLANES)* **SEE** AEROPLANES — WINGS
TL675	*WINGS (AEROPLANES)* **SEE** AEROPLANES — WINGS
QL697-8	WINGS / birds
QL494-5	WINGS / insects
QP301	WINGS / physiology
E99.W7	WINNEBAGO INDIANS
PM2591	WINNEBAGO LANGUAGE
SH685	*WINNINISH* **SEE** OUANANICHE
S699	*WINNOWING-MACHINES* **SEE** FANNING-MILLS
F1038	WINSLOW'S EXPEDITION FOR THE EXPULSION OF THE ACADIANS, 1755
GV841.5	*WINTER OLYMPICS* **SEE** OLYMPIC GAMES (WINTER)
RA791-954	WINTER RESORTS
GV841-857	WINTER SPORTS

U167.5.W5	WINTER WARFARE
QC981	WINTER / *climatology*
RA776	WINTER / *hygiene*
QH81	WINTER / *natural history*
E99.W79	WINTUN INDIANS
TK6570.B7	WIRE BROADCASTING
TS273	*WIRE CLOTH* **SEE** WIRE NETTING
VK594	*WIRE DRAGS (HYDROGRAPHY)* **SEE** DRAGS (HYDROGRAPHY)
UG407	*WIRE ENTANGLEMENTS* **SEE** WIRE OBSTACLES / *military engineering*
QC703	*WIRE EXPLOSIONS, ELECTRIC* **SEE** EXPLODING WIRE PHENOMENA
TS273	*WIRE FABRIC* **SEE** WIRE NETTING
TS273	*WIRE MESH* **SEE** WIRE NETTING
TS273	WIRE NETTING
UG407	WIRE OBSTACLES / *military engineering*
TK6600	*WIRE PHOTOS* **SEE** PHOTOTELEGRAPHY
TS1787	WIRE ROPE
TA492.W8	WIRE ROPE / *testing*
TH2276-8	WIRE SCREENS
VK594	*WIRE SWEEPS (HYDROGRAPHY)* **SEE** DRAGS (HYDROGRAPHY)
TJ1385	WIRE-ROPE TRANSPORTATION
TS270	WIRE / *manufacture*
TA492.W7	WIRE / *testing*
TK5700-5865	*WIRELESS TELEGRAPH* **SEE** TELEGRAPH, WIRELESS
HE8660-8688	*WIRELESS TELEGRAPH* **SEE** TELEGRAPH, WIRELESS / *economics*
VK397	*WIRELESS TELEGRAPH* **SEE** TELEGRAPH, WIRELESS / *marine signaling*
UG610	*WIRELESS TELEGRAPH* **SEE** TELEGRAPH, WIRELESS / *military*
VG76-78	*WIRELESS TELEGRAPH* **SEE** TELEGRAPH, WIRELESS / *naval*
TK6540-6570	*WIRELESS TELEPHONE* **SEE** TELEPHONE, WIRELESS
TK9956	*WIRELESS TELEPHONE* **SEE** TELEPHONE, WIRELESS / *amateurs' manuals*
TK6600	*WIREPHOTOS* **SEE** PHOTOTELEGRAPHY
SB945.W65	WIREWORMS
TK4255	*WIRING, ELECTRIC* **SEE** ELECTRIC LIGHTING — WIRING
TF880-900	*WIRING, ELECTRIC* **SEE** ELECTRIC RAILROADS — WIRES AND WIRING
TK3201-3285	*WIRING, ELECTRIC* **SEE** ELECTRIC WIRING
F576-590	WISCONSIN — HISTORY
E537	WISCONSIN — HISTORY — — CIVIL WAR
PN6149.P5	WIT AND HUMOR — PHILOSOPHY
PN6147-6231	WIT AND HUMOR
PN694.W	WIT AND HUMOR, MEDIEVAL
PN6154	WIT AND HUMOR, MEDIEVAL / *greek and latin*
NC1300-1765	WIT AND HUMOR, PICTORIAL
RS165.H2	WITCH-HAZEL / *pharmacy*
RM666.H	WITCH-HAZEL / *therapeutics*
BF1563-1584	WITCHCRAFT
GR530	WITCHCRAFT / *folk-lore*
BV4520	WITNESS BEARING (CHRISTIANITY)
BX1939.W57	WITNESSES (CANON LAW)
F2230.2.W	WITOTO INDIANS
PM7254	WITOTO LANGUAGE
DL710	*WITTSJO, BATTLE OF, 1612* **SEE** VITTSJO, BATTLE OF, 1612
D267.W6	WITTSTOCK, BATTLE OF, 1636
E99.W8	WIYAT INDIANS
PM2605	WIYAT LANGUAGE
SB287.W8	WOAD
PM7185	*WOAGWAI LANGUAGE* **SEE** UAIUAI LANGUAGE
DJ401.L662	*WOERINGEN, BATTLE OF, 1288* **SEE** WORRINGEN, BATTLE OF, 1288
PH1301-9	*WOGUL LANGUAGE* **SEE** VOGUL LANGUAGE
PL6338	WOLEAI LANGUAGE
GN290	WOLF CHILDREN
E98.R2	*WOLF DANCE* **SEE** WOLF RITUAL
E98.R2	WOLF RITUAL
QL638.B6	WOLF-FISH
SK305.W6	WOLF-HUNTING
QB723.W	WOLF'S COMET
RC685.W6	WOLFF-PARKINSON-WHITE SYNDROME
QL872	WOLFFIAN BODY
QE391.W	WOLFRAMITE GROUP

TN490.T9	WOLFRAMITE
QD181.W1	*WOLFRAMIUM* **SEE** TUNGSTEN
TP245.T9	*WOLFRAMIUM* **SEE** TUNGSTEN / *chemical technology*
TN799.T9	*WOLFRAMIUM* **SEE** TUNGSTEN / *metallurgy*
TN490.T9	*WOLFRAMIUM* **SEE** TUNGSTEN / *mining*
PL5490	WOLIO LANGUAGE
E99.W185	*WOLL-PAH-PE INDIANS* **SEE** WALPAPI INDIANS
PL8785	WOLOF LANGUAGE
QL737.C2	WOLVES
GN	WOMAN — ANATOMY AND PHYSIOLOGY / *anthropology*
RG121	WOMAN — ANATOMY AND PHYSIOLOGY / *health and hygiene*
CT3203	WOMAN — ANECDOTES, FACETIAE, SATIRE, ETC. / *biography*
PN6084.W6	WOMAN — ANECDOTES, FACETIAE, SATIRE, ETC. / *english*
PN6231.W6	WOMAN — ANECDOTES, FACETIAE, SATIRE, ETC. / *wit and humor*
Z7963.B6	WOMAN — BIO-BIBLIOGRAPHY
CT3200-3830	WOMAN — BIOGRAPHY
HQ1123	WOMAN — BIOGRAPHY / *feminism*
HQ1455-1870	WOMAN — BIOGRAPHY / *other countries*
HQ1412-1413	WOMAN — BIOGRAPHY / *reformers u.s.*
RG	WOMAN — DISEASES
HD6050-6220	WOMAN — EMPLOYMENT
RG121	WOMAN — HEALTH AND HYGIENE
RA778	WOMAN — HEALTH AND HYGIENE / *hygiene*
HQ1121-1172	WOMAN — HISTORY AND CONDITION OF WOMEN
HQ1239-1380	WOMAN — LEGAL STATUS, LAWS, ETC.
PN6288.W6	WOMAN — QUOTATIONS, MAXIMS, ETC. / *epigrams*
PN6089.W6	WOMAN — QUOTATIONS, MAXIMS, ETC. / *french*
PN6308.W6	WOMAN — QUOTATIONS, MAXIMS, ETC. / *maxims*
PN6110.W6	WOMAN — QUOTATIONS, MAXIMS, ETC. / *poetry*
PN6084.W6	WOMAN — QUOTATIONS, MAXIMS, ETC. / *quotations english*
BV4527	WOMAN — RELIGIOUS LIFE
BX2353	WOMAN — RELIGIOUS LIFE / *catholic church*
HQ1456-1870	WOMAN — RIGHTS OF WOMEN / *other countries*
HQ1423-6	WOMAN — RIGHTS OF WOMEN / *u.s.*
HQ1871-2030	WOMAN — SOCIETIES AND CLUBS
JF847-855	WOMAN — SUFFRAGE
JN2954	WOMAN — SUFFRAGE / *france*
JN3825	WOMAN — SUFFRAGE / *germany*
JN976-985	WOMAN — SUFFRAGE / *gt. brit.*
JN4648	WOMAN — SUFFRAGE / *prussia*
JK1880-1911	WOMAN — SUFFRAGE / *u.s.*
GN	WOMAN / *anthropology*
GT1720	WOMAN / *costumes*
GT2520-2540	WOMAN / *customs*
GR470	WOMAN / *folk-lore*
GN481	WOMAN / *primitive society*
HQ1101-2030	WOMAN / *sociology*
BS575	*WOMAN-BIBLICAL TEACHING* **SEE** WOMEN IN THE BIBLE
HQ1871-2030	*WOMAN-CLUBS* **SEE** WOMAN — SOCIETIES AND CLUBS
HV6046	*WOMAN-CRIME* **SEE** DELINQUENT WOMEN
GT500-2370	*WOMAN-DRESS* **SEE** COSTUME / *manners and customs*
LC1401-2571	*WOMAN-EDUCATION* **SEE** EDUCATION OF WOMEN
HQ1456-1870	*WOMAN-EMANCIPATION* **SEE** WOMAN — RIGHTS OF WOMEN / *other countries*
HQ1423-6	*WOMAN-EMANCIPATION* **SEE** WOMAN — RIGHTS OF WOMEN / *u.s.*
JF847-855	*WOMAN-ENFRANCHISEMENT* **SEE** WOMAN — SUFFRAGE
JN2954	*WOMAN-ENFRANCHISEMENT* **SEE** WOMAN — SUFFRAGE / *france*
JN3825	*WOMAN-ENFRANCHISEMENT* **SEE** WOMAN — SUFFRAGE / *germany*
JN976-985	*WOMAN-ENFRANCHISEMENT* **SEE** WOMAN — SUFFRAGE / *gt. brit.*
JN4648	*WOMAN-ENFRANCHISEMENT* **SEE** WOMAN — SUFFRAGE / *prussia*
JK1880-1911	*WOMAN-ENFRANCHISEMENT* **SEE** WOMAN — SUFFRAGE / *u.s.*
GR470	*WOMAN-FOLK-LORE* **SEE** FOLK-LORE OF WOMAN
RG12-16	*WOMAN-HOSPITALS* **SEE** HOSPITALS, GYNECOLOGIC AND OBSTETRIC

HD5106-5250	*WOMAN-HOURS OF LABOR* **SEE** HOURS OF LABOR
HF5381	*WOMAN-OCCUPATIONS* **SEE** OCCUPATIONS / *choice of*
GR890-920	*WOMAN-OCCUPATIONS* **SEE** OCCUPATIONS / *folk-lore*
GT5750-6390	*WOMAN-OCCUPATIONS* **SEE** OCCUPATIONS / *manners and customs*
HT675-690	*WOMAN-OCCUPATIONS* **SEE** OCCUPATIONS / *social classes*
HB2581-2790	*WOMAN-OCCUPATIONS* **SEE** OCCUPATIONS / *statistics*
HJ5645-5651	*WOMAN-OCCUPATIONS* **SEE** OCCUPATIONS / *taxation*
GT6110-6390	*WOMAN-OCCUPATIONS* **SEE** PROFESSIONS / *manners and customs*
HT687	*WOMAN-OCCUPATIONS* **SEE** PROFESSIONS / *social groups*
HD6050-6220	*WOMAN-OCCUPATIONS* **SEE** WOMAN — EMPLOYMENT
GV439	*WOMAN-PHYSICAL EDUCATION* **SEE** PHYSICAL EDUCATION FOR WOMEN
N7633-9	*WOMAN-PORTRAITS* **SEE** WOMEN — PORTRAITS
GV709	*WOMAN-SPORTS* **SEE** SPORTS FOR WOMEN
RG107	WOMAN — DISEASES — — DIAGNOSIS
RV361-3	WOMAN — DISEASES — — ECLECTIC TREATMENT
RG127	WOMAN — DISEASES — — ELECTROTHERAPEUTICS
RX460-473	WOMAN — DISEASES — — HOMEOPATHIC TREATMENT
HQ1143	WOMAN — HISTORY AND CONDITION OF WOMEN — — MIDDLE AGES
HQ1148	WOMAN — HISTORY AND CONDITION OF WOMEN — — RENAISSANCE
QL881	*WOMB* **SEE** UTERUS / *comparative anatomy*
QM421	*WOMB* **SEE** UTERUS / *human anatomy*
QP265	*WOMB* **SEE** UTERUS / *physiology*
N7633-9	WOMEN — PORTRAITS
JX1965	WOMEN AND PEACE
BL458	WOMEN AND RELIGION / *religion*
HQ1393	WOMEN AND RELIGION / *sociology*
HX546	WOMEN AND SOCIALISM
ND38	*WOMEN ARTISTS* **SEE** ARTISTS, WOMEN
N43	*WOMEN ARTISTS* **SEE** ARTISTS, WOMEN
PN2205-2217	*WOMEN AS ACTORS* **SEE** ACTRESSES
TL539-540	*WOMEN AS AIR PILOTS* **SEE** WOMEN IN AERONAUTICS
TL553	*WOMEN AS AIR PILOTS* **SEE** WOMEN IN AERONAUTICS
NA1997	WOMEN AS ARCHITECTS
N43	WOMEN AS ARTISTS / *collective biography*
PN471-9	WOMEN AS AUTHORS
HG1616	WOMEN AS BANKERS
Z989	WOMEN AS BOOK COLLECTORS
ML82	WOMEN AS COMPOSERS
HV6046	*WOMEN AS CRIMINALS* **SEE** DELINQUENT WOMEN
RK60	WOMEN AS DENTISTS
TA157	WOMEN AS ENGINEERS
HQ1397	WOMEN AS INVENTORS
PN4784.W7	WOMEN AS JOURNALISTS
Z682	WOMEN AS LIBRARIANS
QA21-28	WOMEN AS MATHEMATICIANS / *history*
QA11	WOMEN AS MATHEMATICIANS / *vocational guidance*
BV676	WOMEN AS MINISTERS
BV2610	WOMEN AS MISSIONARIES
ML82	WOMEN AS MUSICIANS
B105.W6	WOMEN AS PHILOSOPHERS
PN1091	WOMEN AS POETS
HV8023	*WOMEN AS POLICE OFFICERS* **SEE** POLICEWOMEN
Z244.5	WOMEN AS PRINTERS
Q130	WOMEN AS SCIENTISTS
HQ1397	WOMEN AS SCIENTISTS
CT3203	WOMEN AS SOLDIERS
HA46	WOMEN AS STATISTICIANS
LB2837	WOMEN AS TEACHERS
PN471-9	*WOMEN AUTHORS* **SEE** AUTHORS, WOMEN
PS147-151	*WOMEN AUTHORS* **SEE** AUTHORS, WOMEN / *american*
PR111-115	*WOMEN AUTHORS* **SEE** AUTHORS, WOMEN / *english*
PQ149	*WOMEN AUTHORS* **SEE** AUTHORS, WOMEN / *french*
HV6046	*WOMEN DELINQUENTS* **SEE** DELINQUENT WOMEN

TL539-540	WOMEN IN AERONAUTICS
TL553	WOMEN IN AERONAUTICS
N7630-7639	WOMEN IN ART
HV541	WOMEN IN CHARITABLE WORK
BV639.W7	WOMEN IN CHRISTIANITY
BV4415	WOMEN IN CHURCH WORK
LB2837	*WOMEN IN EDUCATION* **SEE** WOMEN AS TEACHERS
GR470	*WOMEN IN FOLK-LORE* **SEE** FOLK-LORE OF WOMAN
BL2015.W5	WOMEN IN HINDUISM
HD6050-6220	*WOMEN IN INDUSTRY* **SEE** WOMAN — EMPLOYMENT
BP173.4	WOMEN IN ISLAM
BM729.W6	WOMEN IN JUDAISM
HQ1386	WOMEN IN LITERATURE
PN56.W6	WOMEN IN LITERATURE
BV2610	WOMEN IN MISSIONARY WORK
PN6110.W6	WOMEN IN POETRY
HQ1236	WOMEN IN POLITICS
HQ1402-1870	WOMEN IN PUBLIC LIFE
HQ1236	WOMEN IN PUBLIC LIFE
BL458	WOMEN IN RELIGION
BS575	WOMEN IN THE BIBLE
BP134.W6	WOMEN IN THE KORAN
BM509.W7	WOMEN IN THE TALMUD
HD6350-6940	*WOMEN IN TRADE-UNIONS* **SEE** TRADE-UNIONS
QA21-28	*WOMEN MATHEMATICIANS* **SEE** WOMEN AS MATHEMATICIANS / *history*
QA11	*WOMEN MATHEMATICIANS* **SEE** WOMEN AS MATHEMATICIANS / *vocational guidance*
HV6046	*WOMEN OFFENDERS* **SEE** DELINQUENT WOMEN
HA46	*WOMEN STATISTICIANS* **SEE** WOMEN AS STATISTICIANS
HV6046	*WOMEN, DELINQUENT* **SEE** DELINQUENT WOMEN
HQ1172	*WOMEN, HEBREW* **SEE** WOMEN, JEWISH
HQ1170	*WOMEN, ISLAMIC* **SEE** WOMEN, MUSLIM
HQ1172	WOMEN, JEWISH
HQ1170	WOMEN, MUSLIM
E185.86	WOMEN, NEGRO / *u.s.*
BV676	*WOMEN, ORDINATION OF* **SEE** ORDINATION OF WOMEN
HQ1871-2030	*WOMEN'S CLUBS* **SEE** WOMAN — SOCIETIES AND CLUBS
BJ1856	*WOMEN'S ETIQUETTE* **SEE** ETIQUETTE FOR WOMEN / *american*
HD6076	WOMEN'S EXCHANGES
HQ1946	WOMEN'S INSTITUTES / *england*
HV8738	*WOMEN'S PRISONS* **SEE** REFORMATORIES FOR WOMEN
HV8738	*WOMEN'S REFORMATORIES* **SEE** REFORMATORIES FOR WOMEN
TT670	*WOMEN'S UNDERWEAR* **SEE** LINGERIE
GT500-2350	*WOMEN-DRESS* **SEE** CLOTHING AND DRESS
TT507	*WOMEN-DRESS* **SEE** CLOTHING AND DRESS / *design*
TX340	*WOMEN-DRESS* **SEE** CLOTHING AND DRESS / *domestic economy*
GN418-419	*WOMEN-DRESS* **SEE** CLOTHING AND DRESS / *ethnology*
RA779	*WOMEN-DRESS* **SEE** CLOTHING AND DRESS / *hygiene*
BV4844	WOMEN — PRAYER-BOOKS AND DEVOTIONS — — ENGLISH, (FRENCH, GERMAN, ETC.)
AG240-243	WONDERS
TA421	WOOD — CHEMISTRY
QR160	WOOD — MICROBIOLOGY
TA419-422	WOOD — MOISTURE
TA422-4	WOOD — PRESERVATION
HD9750.4	WOOD — PRICES
HD9754	WOOD — PRICES
HF5716.L8	WOOD — TABLES AND READY-RECKONERS
TA419-420	WOOD — TESTING / *engineering*
SD433	WOOD — TESTING / *forestry*
TP324	WOOD AS FUEL
TS852	WOOD BENDING
TP997	WOOD DISTILLATION
TT325-340	WOOD FINISHING
SD543	WOOD FLOUR
E83.86	WOOD LAKE, BATTLE OF, 1862
BL820.D	*WOOD NYMPHS* **SEE** DRYADS
TP996.W6	WOOD WASTE
RA1242.W8	WOOD-ALCOHOL / *toxicology*
NK8600-8605	*WOOD-BURNING* **SEE** PYROGRAPHY

NK9700-9799	WOOD-CARVING
NE1000-1325	*WOOD-CUTTING (ENGRAVING)* **SEE** WOOD-ENGRAVING
SK333.D8	WOOD-DUCK / *hunting*
QL696.A5	WOOD-DUCK / *zoology*
NE1200-1217	WOOD-ENGRAVERS
NE1225	WOOD-ENGRAVING — TECHNIQUE
NE1220	WOOD-ENGRAVING — TECHNIQUE
NE1000-1325	WOOD-ENGRAVING
NE2830	WOOD-ENGRAVINGS — PRINTING
NE1000-1325	WOOD-ENGRAVINGS
NE1850-1879	*WOOD-ENGRAVINGS, COLORED* **SEE** COLOR PRINTS
SD373-381	WOOD-LOTS
TP684.W6	WOOD-OIL
TS1171-7	WOOD-PULP INDUSTRY
TS1171-7	WOOD-PULP
QL737.R6	WOOD-RATS
TT345	*WOOD-STAINING* **SEE** STAINS AND STAINING / *wood-staining*
TP997	WOOD-TAR
TT201-3	*WOOD-TURNING* **SEE** TURNING
TT207	*WOOD-TURNING* **SEE** TURNING / *metal*
ML930-980	*WOOD-WIND INSTRUMENTS* **SEE** WIND INSTRUMENTS / *history and construction*
TA419-424	WOOD / *properties and testing*
QK647	WOOD / *structural botany*
SD431-536	WOOD / *wood supply*
TS837	WOOD, COMPRESSED
TA419-422	*WOOD, EFFECT OF MOISTURE ON* **SEE** WOOD — MOISTURE
QE991	*WOOD, FOSSIL* **SEE** TREES, FOSSIL
SD543	*WOOD, PULVERIZED* **SEE** WOOD FLOUR
TA421	*WOOD-ANALYSIS* **SEE** WOOD — CHEMISTRY
QR160	*WOOD-BACTERIOLOGY* **SEE** WOOD — MICROBIOLOGY
TA420	*WOOD-CREEP* **SEE** CREEP OF WOOD
TP997	*WOOD-DISTILLATION* **SEE** WOOD DISTILLATION
TS837	*WOOD-DRYING* **SEE** LUMBER — DRYING
TT345	*WOOD-STAINING* **SEE** STAINS AND STAINING / *wood-staining*
TR995	WOODBURYTYPE
SK341.W	WOODCHUCK HUNTING
QL737.R6	*WOODCHUCKS* **SEE** MARMOTS
QL696.L7	WOODCOCK
SK325.W7	WOODCOCK / *hunting*
NE1000-1325	*WOODCUTS* **SEE** WOOD-ENGRAVINGS
NE1000-1325	*WOODCUTTING (ENGRAVING)* **SEE** WOOD-ENGRAVING
TJ1073.W6	WOODEN BEARINGS
TG375	*WOODEN BRIDGES* **SEE** BRIDGES, WOODEN
TG365	*WOODEN BRIDGES* **SEE** BRIDGES, WOODEN
TH2252-3	*WOODEN COLUMNS* **SEE** COLUMNS, WOODEN
QL696.P5	WOODPECKERS
TS853	WOODWORK — CATALOGS
TH1155	WOODWORK — CATALOGS / *architectural*
HF5716.L8	WOODWORK — TABLES, CALCULATIONS, ETC.
TT180-203	WOODWORK (MANUAL TRAINING)
NA3900	WOODWORK / *architectural decoration*
NK9600-9955	WOODWORK / *industrial art*
TS840-905	WOODWORK / *manufactures*
TT180-203	WOODWORK / *mechanic trades and handicrafts*
HD9750-9769	WOODWORK / *wood-using industries*
HD7825.W6	WOODWORKERS / *legislation*
HD4966.W7	WOODWORKERS / *wages*
HD7269.W8	WOODWORKING MACHINERY — SAFETY APPLIANCES / *labor*
TS850	WOODWORKING MACHINERY — SAFETY APPLIANCES / *manufactures*
TS850-853	WOODWORKING MACHINERY
TS1547	WOOL — TESTING
TP899	*WOOL DYEING* **SEE** DYES AND DYEING — WOOL
TS1627	*WOOL SPINNING* **SEE** WOOLEN AND WORSTED SPINNING
HF5686.T4	WOOL TRADE AND INDUSTRY — ACCOUNTING
HD9890-9909	WOOL TRADE AND INDUSTRY
TP676	*WOOL WAX* **SEE** WOOL-FAT
TS1628	WOOL-CARDING
TS1628	WOOL-COMBING
TP676	WOOL-FAT
SF371-9	WOOL / *sheep raising*
TS1547	WOOL / *textile fibers*
TS1635	WOOL, ARTIFICIAL
TS1630	WOOLEN AND WORSTED MANUFACTURE — SAFETY MEASURES
TS1631	WOOLEN AND WORSTED MANUFACTURE — TABLES, CALCULATIONS, ETC.
TS1600-1631	WOOLEN AND WORSTED MANUFACTURE
TS1627	WOOLEN AND WORSTED SPINNING
SB608.O6	WOOLLY WHITE FLY / *orange pests*
NK4395	WORCESTER PORCELAIN
DA425	WORCESTER, BATTLE OF, 1651
P245	*WORD FORMATION* **SEE** GRAMMAR, COMPARATIVE AND GENERAL — WORD FORMATION
GV1507.W8	WORD GAMES
PB213	*WORD ORDER* **SEE** LANGUAGES, MODERN — WORD ORDER
P331-361	*WORDS, COINAGE OF* **SEE** WORDS, NEW / *comparative lexicography*
P331-361	WORDS, NEW / *comparative lexicography*
P305	*WORDS, STOCK OF* **SEE** VOCABULARY / *philology*
BF481	WORK — PSYCHOLOGICAL ASPECTS
BT738.5	WORK (THEOLOGY)
N8219.L	*WORK AND WORKERS IN ART* **SEE** LABOR AND LABORING CLASSES IN ART
VM388	WORK BOATS
HD7290	*WORK CAMPS* **SEE** LABOR CAMPS
HD4881-5	*WORK EXPERIENCE* **SEE** APPRENTICES
Z122.5	*WORK EXPERIENCE* **SEE** APPRENTICES / *printers' apprentices*
LB1029.C	*WORK EXPERIENCE* **SEE** EDUCATION, COOPERATIVE
LC1041-7	*WORK EXPERIENCE* **SEE** VOCATIONAL EDUCATION
T60.W6	WORK MEASUREMENT
T60.W65	WORK SAMPLING
HD5306-5450	*WORK STOPPAGES* **SEE** STRIKES AND LOCKOUTS
ML3780	WORK-SONGS
M1977.L3	WORK-SONGS
LB1029.C	*WORK-STUDY PLAN* **SEE** EDUCATION, COOPERATIVE
BJ1498	WORK / *ethics*
BF481	WORK / *psychology*
HD4903	*WORK, RIGHT TO* **SEE** RIGHT TO LABOR
RM735	*WORK, THERAPEUTIC EFFECT OF* **SEE** OCCUPATIONAL THERAPY
T60.W6	*WORK-MEASUREMENT* **SEE** WORK MEASUREMENT
VM388	*WORKBOATS* **SEE** WORK BOATS
HD4801-8942	*WORKERS* **SEE** LABOR AND LABORING CLASSES
HV85-527	*WORKHOUSES (POORHOUSES)* **SEE** ALMSHOUSES
HV61	*WORKHOUSES (POORHOUSES)* **SEE** ALMSHOUSES
HV8748-9	WORKHOUSES
TS320	*WORKING OF STEEL* **SEE** STEELWORK
HD4801-8942	*WORKING-CLASSES* **SEE** LABOR AND LABORING CLASSES
HD5106-5250	*WORKING-DAY* **SEE** HOURS OF LABOR
HD6228-6250	*WORKING-GIRLS* **SEE** CHILDREN — EMPLOYMENT
HD6050-6220	*WORKING-GIRLS* **SEE** WOMAN — EMPLOYMENT
HD6451-6473	*WORKING-MEN'S ASSOCIATIONS* **SEE** GILDS / *history*
HD2341-6	*WORKING-MEN'S ASSOCIATIONS* **SEE** GILDS / *modern*
HD6350-6940	*WORKING-MEN'S ASSOCIATIONS* **SEE** TRADE-UNIONS
HD1519	WORKING-MEN'S GARDENS
Z675.W	*WORKING-MEN'S LIBRARIES* **SEE** LIBRARIES, WORKING-MEN'S
TX945	*WORKING-MEN'S LUNCH ROOMS* **SEE** RESTAURANTS, LUNCH ROOMS, ETC.
HD6050-6220	*WORKING-WOMEN* **SEE** WOMAN — EMPLOYMENT
HD4801-8942	*WORKINGMEN* **SEE** LABOR AND LABORING CLASSES
HD5650-5660	*WORKS COMMITTEES* **SEE** WORKS COUNCILS
HD5650-5660	WORKS COUNCILS
BV4647.M4	*WORKS OF MERCY, CORPORAL* **SEE** CORPORAL WORKS OF MERCY
HD5650-5660	*WORKSHOP COMMITTEES* **SEE** WORKS COUNCILS
HD5650-5660	*WORKSHOP COUNCILS* **SEE** WORKS COUNCILS
T49	WORKSHOP RECEIPTS
TH7684.F2	WORKSHOPS — HEATING AND VENTILATION
TH7392.F	WORKSHOPS — HEATING AND VENTILATION
LC6501-6560	*WORKSHOPS (GROUP DISCUSSION)* **SEE** FORUMS (DISCUSSION AND DEBATE)
PN4177-4191	*WORKSHOPS (GROUP DISCUSSION)* **SEE** FORUMS (DISCUSSION AND DEBATE) / *debating*
TS155	WORKSHOPS / *factory management*

D639.D4	WORLD WAR, 1939-1945-SOLDIERS' BODIES, DISPOSITION OF **SEE** SOLDIERS' BODIES, DISPOSITION OF / european war
D810.D4	WORLD WAR, 1939-1945-SOLDIERS' BODIES, DISPOSITION OF **SEE** SOLDIERS' BODIES, DISPOSITION OF / world war
D780	WORLD WAR, 1939-1945-SUBMARINE OPERATIONS **SEE** WORLD WAR, 1939-1945 — NAVAL OPERATIONS — — SUBMARINE
D810.C	WORLD WAR, 1939-1945-TELECOMMUNICATIONS **SEE** WORLD WAR, 1939-1945 — COMMUNICATIONS
DD256.3	WORLD WAR, 1939-1945-UNDERGROUND MOVEMENTS-GERMANY **SEE** ANTI-NAZI MOVEMENT
D747	WORLD WAR, 1939-1945 — BATTLE-FIELDS — — GUIDE-BOOKS
D763.5	WORLD WAR, 1939-1945 — CAMPAIGNS — — ARCTIC REGIONS
D764	WORLD WAR, 1939-1945 — CAMPAIGNS — — DNIEPER RIVER
D767.99.N4	WORLD WAR, 1939-1945 — CAMPAIGNS — — NEW BRITAIN (ISLAND)
D756-763	WORLD WAR, 1939-1945 — CAMPAIGNS — — WESTERN
D780	WORLD WAR, 1939-1945 — NAVAL OPERATIONS — — SUBMARINE
D769.8.A	WORLD WAR, 1939-1945 — WAR WORK — — AMERICAN LEGION
D810.B7	WORLD WAR, 1939-1945 — WAR WORK — — BOY SCOUTS
D810.M	WORLD WAR, 1939-1945 — WAR WORK — — METHODIST CHURCH
D810.S15	WORLD WAR, 1939-1945 — WAR WORK — — SALVATION ARMY
D810.Y7	WORLD WAR, 1939-1945 — WAR WORK — — Y.M.C.A.
D810.Y	WORLD WAR, 1939-1945 — WAR WORK — — Y.W.C.A.
BT875-6	WORLD, END OF THE **SEE** END OF THE WORLD
T391-999	WORLD'S FAIRS **SEE** EXHIBITIONS
QB54	WORLDS, PLURALITY OF **SEE** PLURALITY OF WORLDS
TJ200	WORM-GEAR **SEE** GEARING, WORM
QL393	WORMS — ANATOMY
QL386-394	WORMS
BR353	WORMS, DIET OF, 1521
QE791	WORMS, FOSSIL
RM666.C38	WORMSEED-OIL **SEE** CHENOPODIUM OIL
RS165.C35	WORMSEED-OIL **SEE** CHENOPODIUM OIL
SB317.W	WORMWOOD
DU122.W6	WORORA TRIBE
DJ401.L662	WORRINGEN, BATTLE OF, 1288
BF575.W8	WORRY / psychology
BP184.2	WORSHIP (ISLAM)
BV1522	WORSHIP (RELIGIOUS EDUCATION)
BV1522	WORSHIP PROGRAMS FOR YOUTH **SEE** WORSHIP (RELIGIOUS EDUCATION)
BV5-525	WORSHIP / christian
BL550-620	WORSHIP / comparative religion
GN470-474	WORSHIP / primitive
BL465	WORSHIP, EMPEROR **SEE** EMPEROR WORSHIP
TS1600-1631	WORSTED
TP587	WORT
BD232	WORTH / metaphysics
BD430-435	WORTH / philosophy of life
BF778	WORTH / psychology
DC302.5	WORTH, BATTLE OF, 1870
GN585.R9	WOTIAKS **SEE** VOTIAKS / anthropology
DK34.V7	WOTIAKS **SEE** VOTIAKS / history
UH201-551	WOUNDED IN BATTLE **SEE** WAR — RELIEF OF SICK AND WOUNDED / medical and sanitary service
E83.89	WOUNDED KNEE CREEK, BATTLE OF, 1890
E99.D1	WOUNDED KNEE CREEK, BATTLE OF, 1890 / dakota indians
RC86-88	WOUNDED, FIRST AID TO **SEE** FIRST AID IN ILLNESS AND INJURY
RC87	WOUNDS / first aid
RA1121	WOUNDS / medical jurisprudence
RD58	WOUNDS / reparative processes
RD93-96.6	WOUNDS / surgery
F2380.1.W25	WOYAMANA INDIANS **SEE** WAIWAI INDIANS
PM7185	WOYAWAI LANGUAGE **SEE** UAIUAI LANGUAGE

TJ1550	WRAPPING MACHINES
TT870	WRAPPING OF GIFTS **SEE** GIFT WRAPPING
G525-530	WRECKS **SEE** SHIPWRECKS / etc.
VK1250-1299	WRECKS **SEE** SHIPWRECKS / etc.
JX4436	WRECKS **SEE** SHIPWRECKS / international law
HE1779-1795	WRECKS, RAILROAD **SEE** RAILROADS — ACCIDENTS
TJ1201.W8	WRENCHES
QL696.P2	WRENS
GV1195	WRESTLING
QL825	WRIST / comparative anatomy
QM131	WRIST / human anatomy
PN	WRITERS **SEE** AUTHORS / general
RC429	WRITERS' CRAMP
HV8074-6	WRITING — IDENTIFICATION
Z45	WRITING — MATERIALS AND INSTRUMENTS
HV1701	WRITING — MATERIALS AND INSTRUMENTS / for the blind
PN101-249	WRITING (AUTHORSHIP) **SEE** AUTHORSHIP
BF1779.W7	WRITING (IN RELIGION, FOLK-LORE, ETC.)
PN101-249	WRITING AS A PROFESSION **SEE** AUTHORSHIP
N8265	WRITING IN ART
PE1481-1497	WRITING OF LETTERS **SEE** LETTER-WRITING / english rhetoric
BJ2100-2115	WRITING OF LETTERS **SEE** LETTER-WRITING / etiquette
Z40-115	WRITING
PJ1623-6	WRITING, ARABIC
BF1779.W7	WRITING, FOLK-LORE OF **SEE** WRITING (IN RELIGION, FOLK-LORE, ETC.)
PD1117	WRITING, GOTHIC
Z104.5	WRITING, INVISIBLE
Z43	WRITING, ITALIC
PL5162	WRITING, JAVANESE
Z48	WRITING-COPYING PROCESSES **SEE** COPYING PROCESSES
E215.1	WRITS OF ASSISTANCE / revolutionary war
BJ1410-1418	WRONG AND RIGHT **SEE** RIGHT AND WRONG
TA469-470	WROUGHT-IRON / etc.
TS300-360	WROUGHT-IRON / manufacture
TN693.I7	WROUGHT-IRON / metallography
TN720-725	WROUGHT-IRON / metallurgy
TA684-5	WROUGHT-IRON / structural engineering
DU122.W	WUNAMBAL (AUSTRALIAN TRIBE)
E99.H9	WYANDOT INDIANS **SEE** HURON INDIANS
SF489.W9	WYANDOTTES
BX4900-4906	WYCLIFITES **SEE** LOLLARDS
F157.W9	WYOMING MASSACRE, 1763
E241.W9	WYOMING MASSACRE, 1778
BF698.W36	WZT **SEE** WARTEGG TEST
QC373.X2	X-RAY MICROSCOPE
QC373.X2	X-RAY MICROSCOPY **SEE** X-RAY MICROSCOPE
RC78	X-RAY PHOTOGRAPHY **SEE** RADIOGRAPHY / medicine
TR750	X-RAY PHOTOGRAPHY **SEE** RADIOGRAPHY / photography
RD36	X-RAY PHOTOGRAPHY **SEE** RADIOGRAPHY / surgery
QC482	X-RAY SCATTERING **SEE** X-RAYS — SCATTERING
RC78.5	X-RAYS — APPARATUS AND SUPPLIES / medical diagnosis
QC481	X-RAYS — APPARATUS AND SUPPLIES / physics
QC482	X-RAYS — DIFFRACTION
QC482	X-RAYS — SCATTERING
RK309	X-RAYS IN DENTISTRY **SEE** TEETH — RADIOGRAPHY
QC481	X-RAYS
RC78	X-RAYS / medicine
QD401	XANTHINE
QE391.V55	XANTHITE **SEE** VESUVIANITE
QD405	XANTHONE
F2520.1.C5	XAVANTE INDIANS **SEE** CHAVANTE INDIANS
BX4190.X3	XAVERIAN BROTHERS
QD181.X1	XENON
QK922	XEROPHYTES
PL8321-4	XHOSA LANGUAGE **SEE** KAFIR LANGUAGE (BANTU)
F1505.2.X	XICAQUE INDIANS
PL8115	XILENGE LANGUAGE **SEE** CHOPI LANGUAGE
F1434.3.X4	XINCA INDIANS
PM4498.X3	XINCA LANGUAGE
QL447.X7	XIPHOSURA
F3722.1.J5	XIVARO INDIANS **SEE** JIVARO INDIANS

F1465.2.L2	*XOQUINOE INDIANS* **SEE** LACANDON INDIANS / *guatemala*
F1221.L2	*XOQUINOE INDIANS* **SEE** LACANDON INDIANS / *mexico*
PL8321-4	*XOSA LANGUAGE* **SEE** KAFIR LANGUAGE (BANTU)
RD86.X	XYLOCAINE
Z240-241	*XYLOGRAPHY* **SEE** BLOCK-BOOKS
NE1000-1325	*XYLOGRAPHY* **SEE** WOOD-ENGRAVING
M284-5	XYLOPHONE AND PIANO MUSIC (JAZZ)
M284-5	XYLOPHONE AND PIANO MUSIC
M284-5	*XYLOPHCNE AND PIANO MUSIC, ARRANGED (JAZZ)* **SEE** XYLOPHONE AND PIANO MUSIC (JAZZ)
M284.X9	XYLOPHONE AND PIANO MUSIC, ARRANGED
M285.X9	XYLOPHONE AND PIANO MUSIC, ARRANGED
M175.X6	XYLOPHONE MUSIC
M1385.X9	XYLOPHONE MUSIC, JUVENILE
ML1040	XYLOPHONE
PL6251	*YABIN LANGUAGE* **SEE** JABIM LANGUAGE
VK369	*YACHT BASINS* **SEE** MARINAS
TC353-373	*YACHT BASINS* **SEE** MARINAS / *hydraulic engineering*
GV826	YACHT FLAGS
GV826.5-832	YACHT RACING
VM331	YACHT-BUILDING
VM332	YACHTS AND YACHTING — MODELS
VK200	YACHTS AND YACHTING — SAFETY MEASURES
GV813-833	YACHTS AND YACHTING
PL55.J3	*YAGATAI LANGUAGE* **SEE** JAGATAIC LANGUAGE
PK6996.Y2	YAGHNOBI DIALECT
PK6996.Y2	*YAGNOBI DIALECT* **SEE** YAGHNOBI DIALECT
F3430.1.Y3	YAGUA INDIANS
PM7266	YAHGAN LANGUAGE
F3430.1.Y3	*YAHUA INDIANS* **SEE** YAGUA INDIANS
E99.Y	YAHUSKIN INDIANS
BS1199.D3	*YAHVEH, DAY OF* **SEE** DAY OF JEHOVAH
PL8605	*YAKA LANGUAGE* **SEE** PUNU LANGUAGE
F2270.2.Y3	YAKALAMARURE INDIANS
E99.Y2	*YAKAMA INDIANS* **SEE** YAKIMA INDIANS
PM2611	*YAKAMA LANGUAGE* **SEE** YAKIMA LANGUAGE
E99.Y2	YAKIMA INDIANS
PM2611	YAKIMA LANGUAGE
PL361-4	YAKUT LANGUAGE
PL364.A2	YAKUT POETRY / *collections*
PL363.5	YAKUT POETRY / *history*
DK771.Y2	YAKUTS
SF541-599	*YAMA-MAI* **SEE** SILKWORMS
E99.C9	*YAMACRAW INDIANS* **SEE** CREEK INDIANS
E99.Y	YAMASSEE INDIANS
PL6120	YAMI LANGUAGE
E99.Y	YAMPA INDIANS
SB211.Y3	YAMS
E99.Y23	YANA INDIANS
PM2641	YANA LANGUAGE
F3447	YANACOCHA, BATTLE OF, 1835
DS432.Y	YANADIS
GV1469.Y2	YANK (GAME)
NE965	*YANKEE CLIPPER CARDS* **SEE** SAILING CARDS
SF429.T3	*YANKEE TERRIERS* **SEE** STAFFORDSHIRE TERRIERS
PM1021-4	YANKTON DIALECT
E99.Y25	YANKTON INDIANS
PM1021-4	*YANKTONAI DIALECT* **SEE** YANKTON DIALECT
E99.Y26	YANKTONAI INDIANS
DT429	YAO (AFRICAN TRIBE)
PL8801-4	YAO LANGUAGE
PL6341	YAP LANGUAGE
F1346	YAQUI INDIANS — WARS, 1896-1900 / *mexico*
E99.Y3	YAQUI INDIANS
PM4526	YAQUI LANGUAGE
PL8821-4	*YARIBA LANGUAGE* **SEE** YORUBA LANGUAGE
PL55.Y3	YARKAND LANGUAGE
TS1581	YARN — TABLES, CALCULATIONS, ETC. / *cotton*
TS1631	YARN — TABLES, CALCULATIONS, ETC. / *wool*
TS1550-1581	YARN / *cotton*
TS1600-1631	YARN / *wool*
SB211.Y	YAUTIA / *food plants*
E99.Y	YAVAPAI INDIANS
TL574.M6	YAWING (AERODYNAMICS)
TL574.M6	*YAWING MOMENTS (AERODYNAMICS)* **SEE** YAWING (AERODYNAMICS)
RC205	YAWS
PL4001.L6	*YAWYIN LANGUAGE* **SEE** LISU LANGUAGE
PK6996.Y4	YAZGHULAMI LANGUAGE
BV30	*YEAR, CHURCH* **SEE** CHURCH YEAR
BX961.H6	*YEAR, HOLY* **SEE** HOLY YEAR
BX961.H6	*YEAR, JUBILEE* **SEE** HOLY YEAR
BT646	*YEAR, MARIAN* **SEE** MARIAN YEAR
AY	YEARBOOKS
TP580-581	YEAST / *brewing*
TP460	YEAST / *compressed*
QR151	YEAST / *micro-organisms*
DT518.Y	YEBU (AFRICAN PEOPLE)
PL8811	YEBU LANGUAGE
QK495.C57	*YELLOW BARK* **SEE** CINCHONA / *botany*
SB295.C5	*YELLOW BARK* **SEE** CINCHONA / *culture*
RS165.C3	*YELLOW BARK* **SEE** CINCHONA / *pharmacy*
RM666.C53	*YELLOW BARK* **SEE** CINCHONA / *therapeutics*
RX226.Y4	YELLOW FEVER — HOMEOPATHIC TREATMENT
RA644.Y4	YELLOW FEVER — PREVENTION
RC206-216	YELLOW FEVER
RA644.Y4	YELLOW FEVER / *public health measures*
RA655-758	YELLOW FEVER / *quarantine*
E99.A28	*YELLOW KNIVES (INDIANS)* **SEE** AHTENA INDIANS
RC848.N4	*YELLOW LIVER ATROPHY* **SEE** LIVER — NECROSIS
DS519	YELLOW PERIL
SD397.P75	YELLOW PINE
QK495.Q4	*YELLOW-BARK OAK* **SEE** BLACK OAK / *botany*
SD397.012	*YELLOW-BARK OAK* **SEE** BLACK OAK / *forestry*
SB945.Y	YELLOW-BEAR CATERPILLAR
SB608.C55	YELLOW-CLOVER APHIS
SB608	YELLOW-DWARF DISEASE
SB945.Y	YELLOW-NECKED FLEA-BEETLE
QC495.Y	YELLOW / *color*
TP918.Y	YELLOW / *dyes*
DG135	YELLOW / *roman antiquities*
QL696.P2	*YELLOWTHROAT, MARYLAND* **SEE** MARYLAND YELLOWTHROAT
LB3635	*YELLS* **SEE** CHEERS / *school life*
G690 1875	YENISEI EXPEDITION, 1875
G690 1876	YENISEI EXPEDITION, 1876
DK759.K	*YENISEY-OSTYAKS* **SEE** KETS
D639.W7	*YEOMANETTES* **SEE** YEOMEN (F)
D639.W7	YEOMEN (F)
SB279.M4	*YERBA-MATE* **SEE** MATE (SHRUB)
QK495.T	YEW / *botany*
SD397.Y	YEW / *forestry*
BL1595	YEZIDIS
PL3311.Y	YI LANGUAGE
PJ5127	YIDDISH DRAMA / *collections*
PJ5123	YIDDISH DRAMA / *history*
PJ5191-2	YIDDISH DRAMA / *translations*
PJ5111-5119	YIDDISH LANGUAGE
PJ5128	YIDDISH LETTERS / *collections*
PJ5124	YIDDISH LETTERS / *history*
PJ5120-5192	YIDDISH LITERATURE
PN4885.Y5	YIDDISH NEWSPAPERS / *u.s.*
PJ5126	YIDDISH POETRY / *collections*
PJ5122	YIDDISH POETRY / *history*
PN3035	*YIDDISH THEATER* **SEE** THEATER — JEWS
BL604.Y5	YIN YANG SYMBOL
F3320.2.C	*YOFUAHA INDIANS* **SEE** CHOROTI INDIANS
PM5817.C7	*YOFUAHA LANGUAGE* **SEE** CHOROTI LANGUAGE
B132.Y6	YOGA
SF275.Y	*YOGHURT* **SEE** YOGURT
SF275.Y	YOGURT
SF275.Y	*YOHOURT* **SEE** YOGURT
TS903	YOKES
E99.Y75	YOKUTS INDIANS
PM2681	YOKUTS LANGUAGE
PL8134	*YOLA LANGUAGE* **SEE** DIOLA LANGUAGE
PL8785	*YOLOF LANGUAGE* **SEE** WOLOF LANGUAGE
BM695.A8	*YOM HA-KIPPURIM* **SEE** YOM KIPPUR
BM675.A8	*YOM HA-KIPPURIM* **SEE** YOM KIPPUR / *liturgical forms*
BM695.A8	YOM KIPPUR
BM675.A8	YOM KIPPUR / *liturgical forms*
PL8815	YOMBE LANGUAGE
E241.Y6	YORKTOWN, VA. — SIEGE, 1781
E473.61	YORKTOWN, VA. — SIEGE, 1862
PL8821-4	YORUBA LANGUAGE
DT513	YORUBAS
D465	*YOUGOSLAVS* **SEE** YUGOSLAVS

F1221.C56	*ZINANTEC INDIANS* **SEE** CHINANTEC INDIANS
PM3630	*ZINANTEC LANGUAGE* **SEE** CHINANTEC LANGUAGE
TN796	ZINC — ELECTROMETALLURGY
TN796	ZINC — METALLURGY
QP913.Z6	ZINC — PHYSIOLOGICAL EFFECT
TS640	ZINC ALLOYS / *manufacture*
TN796	ZINC ALLOYS / *metallurgy*
QE391.S	*ZINC BLENDE* **SEE** SPHALERITE
HD9539.Z6	ZINC INDUSTRY AND TRADE
TN480-489	ZINC MINES AND MINING
TN480-489	ZINC ORES
QD181.Z6	ZINC
TA480.Z6	ZINC / *etc.*
TS640	ZINC / *manufacture*
NE2550	ZINCOGRAPHY
DR27.A8	*ZINZARS* **SEE** AROMUNES
DS149	ZIONISM
DS150.G4-6	*ZIONISM, GENERAL* **SEE** GENERAL ZIONISM
DS149	*ZIONIST MOVEMENT* **SEE** ZIONISM
QE391.Z7	ZIRCON
QD181.Z7	ZIRCONIUM
PH1051-9	*ZIRIAN LANGUAGE* **SEE** SYRYENIAN LANGUAGE
DK34.S9	*ZIRIANIANS* **SEE** SYRYENIANS
M292-3	ZITHER MUSIC (2 ZITHERS)
M135-7	ZITHER MUSIC
M138-9	ZITHER MUSIC, ARRANGED
ML1015-1018	ZITHER
QL377.C7	ZOANTHARIA
QB803	ZODIAC
QB802	ZODIAC / *constellations*
QB15-26	ZODIAC / *history of astronomy*
QB761	ZODIACAL LIGHT
QE391.Z8	ZOISITE
TP156.Z6	*ZONE LEVELING* **SEE** ZONE MELTING / *chemical engineering*
TN686.5.Z6	*ZONE LEVELING* **SEE** ZONE MELTING / *metallurgy*
TP156.Z6	ZONE MELTING / *chemical engineering* .
TN686.5.Z6	ZONE MELTING / *metallurgy*
TP156.Z6	*ZONE REFINING* **SEE** ZONE MELTING / *chemical engineering*
TN686.5.Z6	*ZONE REFINING* **SEE** ZONE MELTING / *metallurgy*
S439	*ZONES, CROP* **SEE** CROP ZONES
QH84	*ZONES, LIFE* **SEE** LIFE ZONES
GV1299.Z8	ZOO (GAME)
BL439-443	*ZOOLATRY* **SEE** ANIMAL-WORSHIP
QL76-77	ZOOLOGICAL GARDENS
QL71	ZOOLOGICAL MUSEUMS
GR820-830	*ZOOLOGICAL MYTHOLOGY* **SEE** ANIMAL LORE
QL89	*ZOOLOGICAL MYTHOLOGY* **SEE** ANIMAL LORE
QL791-5	*ZOOLOGICAL MYTHOLOGY* **SEE** ANIMALS, LEGENDS AND STORIES OF
PZ	*ZOOLOGICAL MYTHOLOGY* **SEE** ANIMALS, LEGENDS AND STORIES OF
GR820-830	*ZOOLOGICAL MYTHOLOGY* **SEE** ANIMALS, MYTHICAL
QL76-77	*ZOOLOGICAL PARKS* **SEE** ZOOLOGICAL GARDENS
QL61-67	ZOOLOGICAL SPECIMENS-COLLECTION AND PRESERVATION
QL26-31	ZOOLOGISTS / *biography*
QL35	ZOOLOGISTS / *directories*
QL351-2	ZOOLOGY — CLASSIFICATION
QL750-775	ZOOLOGY — ECOLOGY
QL49	ZOOLOGY — JUVENILE LITERATURE
QL53	ZOOLOGY — LABORATORY MANUALS
QL354	ZOOLOGY — NOMENCLATORS
QL355	ZOOLOGY — NOMENCLATURE (POPULAR)
QL353-5	ZOOLOGY — NOMENCLATURE
QL46	ZOOLOGY — PICTORIAL WORKS
QL41	ZOOLOGY — PRE-LINNEAN WORKS
QL10	ZOOLOGY — TERMINOLOGY
QH408	ZOOLOGY — VARIATION
BS660-667	*ZOOLOGY OF THE BIBLE* **SEE** BIBLE — NATURAL HISTORY
QL	ZOOLOGY
SB801-999	ZOOLOGY, ECONOMIC
QL99	ZOOLOGY, MEDICAL
QL951-973	*ZOOLOGY-EMBRYOLOGY* **SEE** EMBRYOLOGY
QL801-950	*ZOOLOGY-MORPHOLOGY* **SEE** ANATOMY, COMPARATIVE

QL799	*ZOOLOGY-MORPHOLOGY* **SEE** MORPHOLOGY (ANIMALS)
QL71	*ZOOLOGY-MUSEUMS* **SEE** ZOOLOGICAL MUSEUMS
QL375-9	*ZOOPHYTA* **SEE** COELENTERATA
QE777-9	*ZOOPHYTA* **SEE** COELENTERATA / *fossil*
QL381-5	*ZOOPHYTA* **SEE** ECHINODERMATA
QL396-9	*ZOOPHYTA* **SEE** POLYZOA
QL371-4	*ZOOPHYTA* **SEE** SPONGES
SH396	*ZOOPHYTA* **SEE** SPONGES / *fisheries*
DX289	*ZOOT* **SEE** NAWAR
QL801-950	*ZOOTOMY* **SEE** ANATOMY, COMPARATIVE
F1221.Z6	ZOQUE INDIANS
PM4556	ZOQUE LANGUAGE
BL1500-1590	ZOROASTRIANISM
F1221.T	*ZOTZIL INDIANS* **SEE** TZOTZIL INDIANS
PM4466	*ZOTZIL LANGUAGE* **SEE** TZOTZIL LANGUAGE
PL8844.A2	ZULU BALLADS AND SONGS
PL8841-4	ZULU LANGUAGE
DT777	ZULU REBELLION, 1906
DT777	ZULU WAR, 1879
DT878.Z9	ZULUS
PL4001.A7	*ZUNGI DIALECT* **SEE** AO LANGUAGE
E99.Z9	ZUNI INDIANS
DX289	*ZUTT* **SEE** NAWAR
PM4471	*ZUTUHIL LANGUAGE* **SEE** TZUTUHIL LANGUAGE
BX9995.Z8	ZWIJNDRECHTSCHE NIEUWLICHTERS
PL4001.A7	*ZWINGI DIALECT* **SEE** AO LANGUAGE
QH581	ZYGOTES
QP601	ZYMASE
DK34.S9	*ZYRIANS* **SEE** SYRYENIANS
PH1051-9	*ZYRJENIAN LANGUAGE* **SEE** SYRYENIAN LANGUAGE
DC222.Z8	ZÜRICH, BATTLE OF, SEPT.25-26, 1799
S533	4-H CLUBS

EXPLANATORY NOTES

1. Volume 2 is an alphabetic index to Volume 1 of *The Classified List of Library of Congress Subject Headings.*

2. All the main headings with classification numbers, including those with subdivisions are listed. All the **SEE** references to main headings are listed in alphabetic order, to the right of the classification number.

3. Main headings are in Roman capital letters; subdivisions include a dash; **SEE** references are in capital italics.

4. The classification numbers are shown at the left of the list of headings.

5. A main heading may have several classification numbers. When the areas are identified by the Library of Congress, these are shown in lower case italics following a slash mark (/).

6. No attempt has been made to correct certain peculiarities of the Library of Congress list, so that not all the headings are included in this index—only those with suggested classification numbers are listed.

7. At the top of each page, the alphabetic range contained on that page is indicated; for example, Acids—Administration.

8. Each entry contains Classification number, space, heading or **SEE** reference, subdivision, if any, and then slash mark and area of classification.